REFERENCE ENCYCLOPEDIA OF AI COMPANIES – 2020

Reference Encyclopedia of AI Companies – 2020

Volume 2 - World Companies

AI Reference Publishers

Printed Version

Library of Congress Control Number: 2021936497
ISSN 2692-2649 (Print)
Reference Encyclopedia of AI Companies - 2020 – 2 Volumes ISBN-13: **978-1-952823-00-8 (Set)**
Reference Encyclopedia of AI Companies - 2020 Volume 1 - US Companies ISBN-13: **978-1-952823-01-5**
Reference Encyclopedia of AI Companies - 2020 Volume 2 - World Companies ISBN-13: **978-1-952823-02-2**

Web Version

ISSN 2692-2657 (Online)

To subscribe to the web version, visit:
www.reference-encyclopedia-ai.net

AI Reference Publishers
31915 Rancho California Rd. Suite 200-349
Temecula, California 92591 USA
Phone: (951) 414-5450
sales@ai-reference-publishers.com

For more product information, visit:
www.ai-reference-publishers.com

TABLE OF CONTENTS

Introduction

In 2020, Artificial Intelligence (AI) and its related technologies are developing at a dramatic pace, and this has resulted in the formation of over 15,000 AI companies as of December 2020. Large technology companies (IBM, Microsoft, Google, Amazon etc.) are expanding and offering platforms/services to assist AI Companies with development and deployment of services/solutions for a wide range of industries.

The ***Reference Encyclopedia of AI Companies*** is the most comprehensive resource for detailed information on more than 15,000 AI companies worldwide that develop and/or utilize AI.

The Reference Encyclopedia of AI Companies Web Version (Website) and two Printed Volumes track the latest changes in the status of AI companies, their key personnel (including Human Resources), their solutions/services, and the industries they serve. Our editors work directly with over 15,000 AI companies worldwide to update their company profiles on a regular basis. In addition, our editors record new companies as they are formed and revise the status of companies as they are acquired, merged, or have terminated developing AI. Each company profile offers a wealth of valuable data, and collectively it provides the broadest spectrum of information available on AI companies.

The Reference Encyclopedia of AI Companies Web Version and Printed Volumes

As of December 2020, there is no "permanent" long-term electronic storage media that would be considered as archival. Printed books offer the only long-term version of any reference source, and we are publishing a printed edition to serve this archival purpose. The paper used in the printed edition is on Archival Paper.

Archival Paper is an especially permanent, durable acid-free paper. Archival Paper is meant to be used for publications of legal, historical, or significant value, commonly referred to as "300-year paper". In the USA, such paper must also be approved in accordance with the ANSI standards. The international standard for "permanent" paper is ISO 9706 and for "archival" paper, the standard is ISO 11108.

The **Printed Volumes** contain the core data in each company's profile, including the company's status in 2020.

Company Name
Description
Website
Phone
Email
City/State/Zip/Country
Year Established
Status
Industries

The **Web Version** contains the core data plus the company's **Key Personnel** & their **Contact Information**:

CEO
Founder
CTO
AI Engineers
Sales/Marketing
Human Resources

AI Reference Publishers Department Information:

General: Questions, concerns, comments may be sent:
editor@ai-reference-publishers.com

Sales: sales@ai-reference-publishers.com

Editor: To have your company listed contact: amy@reference-encyclopedia-ai.com

Amy Hydock
Managing Editor
Reference Encyclopedia of AI Companies

Guide to Use

Arrangement

Volume 1 consists of profiles for AI companies in the United States arranged alphabetically by

1. **state,**
2. **city,**
3. **company name.**

Volume 2 contains profiles for AI companies in the balance of the world arranged alphabetically by

1. **country,**
2. **state,**
3. **city,**
4. **company name.**

How to Use

1. **Geographical Search:** To look up AI companies by location, choose the correct volume:

    United States Companies – Volume 1: *Search by:* **State, City, Company Name**

    World Companies – Volume 2: *Search by:* **Country, State, City, Company Name**

2. **Company Name Search:** To look up a specific AI company by name, use the **Company Name Index** at the back of Volume 1. Locate the **Company Name** alphabetically and identify the Volume:

    Vol. 1 – U.S. *Then locate by* **State & City**

    Vol. 2 – World *Then locate by* **Country, State & City**

3. **Web Version Search:** In addition to Company Name and Geographical searches, the Web Version allows searches by:

    Keyword
    Industry
    Services/Solutions
    Company Personnel by Name

Sample Profile

Company Name: Pareto Group

Company Name: Pareto Group
Description: Pareto Group automates pay-per-click campaigns through artificial intelligence.
Website: http://pareto.io
Phone: 55 (21) 3228-0063 **Email:** comercial@paretogroup.com.br
City: Rio De Janeiro **State:** RJ **PC:** **Country:** Brazil
Year Established: 2016 **Status 2020:** Active
Industries: Artificial Intelligence for:, Digital Marketing

AI Services/Solutions Guide

The **Services and Solutions** identified in the **Reference Encyclopedia of AI Companies** were compiled from *The Cambridge Handbook of Artificial Intelligence,* edited by Frankish, K., & Ramsey, W. [2014] published by Cambridge University Press. (ISBN 978-0-521-87142-6) The editors also chose to expand and refine the list of services/solutions based on those offered by AI Companies.

Artificial Intelligence
Aftermarket Services
Analytics
Application Program Interfaces (APIs)
Application Services
Augmented Reality
Automation
Backup and Archive
Big Data and Analytics
Blockchain
Business Applications
Business Intelligence
Business Process and Operations
Business Process as a Service (BPaaS)
Business Resiliency Services
Business Software as a Service Apps (SaaS Apps)
Business Strategy and Design
Cloud
Cognitive
Collaboration Solutions
Collections (Debt)
Compliance
Compute
Computer Vision
Containers
Content
Cyber Security
Data Lakes
Data Management
Databases
Development and Operations (DevOps)
Development and Test
Digital Marketing
Digital Media
Digital Workplace Services

Industries Guide

The **Industries** identified in the ***Reference Encyclopedia of AI Companies*** were selected from the North American Industry Classification System (NAICS) and slightly modified to accommodate the industries that are utilizing artificial intelligence and related technology applications.

Administrative and Support Services
Aerospace and Defense
Agriculture
Arts-Entertainment-Recreation
Automotive
Autonomous Vehicles
Banking and Financial Markets-Services
Beauty
Biotechnology
Construction
Customer Relationship Management (CRM)
E-Commerce
Education
Energy and Utilities
Event Management
Fashion
Food and Beverage
Gaming
Government
Healthcare
High Tech
Hospitality
Human Resources
Insurance
Law-Legal Services
Life Sciences
Management of Companies
Manufacturing-Agricultural-Animal
Manufacturing-Electronic
Manufacturing-General
Manufacturing-Machinery
Manufacturing-Medical Equipment-Supplies
Manufacturing-Miscellaneous
Manufacturing-Nonmetallic Mineral
Manufacturing-Office-Household Furniture
Manufacturing-Petroleum-Coal-Chemicals-Plastics-Rubber

Manufacturing-Primary-Fabricated Metal
Manufacturing-Transportation Equipment
Manufacturing-Wood-Paper-Printing
Media-Communications
Metals and Mining
Oil and Gas
Peer to Peer
Personal-Religious-Civic-Private Household Services
Pharmaceuticals
Politics
Professional Services
Real Estate
Rental and Leasing (except Real Estate)
Repair Services
Retail and Consumer Products
Social Assistance-Non-Profits
Social Media
Social-Environmental-Physical-Engineering Sciences
Telecommunications
Transportation and Logistics
Travel and Transportation
Waste Management and Remediation Services
Wholesale Trade
Wineries

Major Artificial Intelligence Companies

These companies offer a variety of services and may have many offices in the US and the World.

Company Name: Alibaba
Description: Alibaba Group Holding Limited operates as a holding company. The Company provides internet infrastructure, electronic commerce, online financial, and internet content services through its subsidiaries. Alibaba Group Holding offers its products and services worldwide.
Website: https://alibaba.com
Phone: 86-571-8502-2088 **Email:**
Headquarters Address: 699 Wang Shang Road
City: Hangzhou **State:** Binjiang District **Zip:** 310052 **Country:** China
Year Established: 1999 **Status:** Active

Company Name: Amazon
Description: Amazon is an e-commerce website for consumers, sellers, and content creators.
Website: https://www.amazon.com/
Phone: (206) 266-1000 **Email:** primary@amazon.com
Headquarters Address: 410 Terry Ave
City: N. Seattle **State:** WA **Zip:** 98109 **Country:** United States
Year Established: 1994 **Status:** Active

Company Name: Apple
Description: Apple is a multinational corporation that designs, manufactures, and markets consumer electronics, personal computers, and software.
Website: https://www.apple.com/
Phone: (408) 996-1010 **Email:**
Headquarters Address: One Apple Park Way
City: Cupertino **State:** CA **Zip:** 95104 **Country:** United States
Year Established: 1976 **Status:** Active

Company Name: AT&T
Description: AT&T Inc. is a communication holding company. The Company, through its subsidiaries and affiliates, provides local and long-distance phone service, wireless and data communications, Internet access and messaging, IP-based and satellite television, security services, telecommunications equipment, and directory advertising and publishing.
Website: https://www.att.com
Phone: (210) 821-4105 **Email:**
Headquarters Address: 208 S. Akard St
City: Dallas **State:** TX **Zip:** 75202 **Country:** United States
Year Established: **Status:** Active

Company Name: Clarifai
Description: Clarifai provides advanced image recognition systems for customers to detect near-duplicates and visual searches.
Website: https://www.clarifai.com/
Phone: **Email:** info@clarifai.com
Headquarters Address: 137 Varick Street
City: New York **State:** NY **Zip:** 10013 **Country:** United States
Year Established: 2013 **Status:** Active

Company Name: Deepmind
Description: Google DeepMind develops learning algorithms that use data or raw experience to better themselves.
Website: https://deepmind.com/
Phone: **Email:** contact@deepmind.com
Headquarters Address: 5 New Street Square
City: London **State:** **Zip:** EC4A 3TW **Country:** United Kingdom
Year Established: 2010 **Status:** Active

Company Name: Facebook
Description: Facebook is an online social networking service that enables its users to connect with friends and family.
Website: https://www.facebook.com/
Phone: **Email:**
Headquarters Address: 1601 Willow Road
City: Menlo Park **State:** CA **Zip:** 94025 **Country:** United States
Year Established: 2004 **Status:** Active

Company Name: Google
Description: Google is a multinational corporation that specializes in Internet-related services and products.
Website: https://www.google.com/
Phone: (650) 253-0000 **Email:** google@google.com
Headquarters Address: 1600 Amphitheatre Parkway
City: Mountain View **State:** CA **Zip:** 94043 **Country:** United States
Year Established: 2002 **Status:** Active

Company Name: HP Hewlett-Packard
Description: HP is a manufacturer and seller of personal computers, printers, computer hardware, and business solutions.
Website: https://www.hp.com/
Phone: (650) 857-1501 **Email:**
Headquarters Address: 1501 Page Mill Road
City: Palo Alto **State:** CA **Zip:** 94304 **Country:** United States
Year Established: 1939 **Status:** Active

Company Name: IBM
Description: IBM is an IT technology and consulting firm providing computer hardware, software, infrastructure, and hosting services.
Website: https://www.ibm.com/
Phone: (914) 499-1900 **Email:** ews@us.ibm.com
Headquarters Address: 1 New Orchard Road
City: Armonk **State:** NY **Zip:** 10504 **Country:** United States
Year Established: 1911 **Status:** Active

Company Name: Intel
Description: Intel designs, manufactures, and sells integrated digital technology platforms worldwide.
Website: https://www.intel.com/
Phone: (408) 765-8080 **Email:**
Headquarters Address: 2200 Mission College Blvd
City: Santa Clara **State:** CA **Zip:** 95054 **Country:** United States
Year Established: 1989 **Status:** Active

Company Name: Microsoft
Description: Microsoft is a software corporation that develops, manufactures, licenses, supports, and sells a range of software products and services.
Website: https://www.microsoft.com/
Phone: (800) 441-0158 **Email:** mdcc@microsoft.com
Headquarters Address: 1 Microsoft Way
City: Redmond **State:** WA **Zip:** 98052 **Country:** United States
Year Established: 1993 **Status:** Active

Company Name: NVIDIA
Description: NVIDIA is a computing platform company, innovating at the intersection of graphics, HPC, and AI.
Website: https://www.nvidia.com/
Phone: (408) 848-6200 **Email:** info@nvidia.com
Headquarters Address: 2701 San Tomas Expressway
City: Santa Clara **State:** CA **Zip:** 95050 **Country:** United States
Year Established: 1993 **Status:** Active

Company Name: Salesforce
Description: Salesforce is a global cloud computing company that develops CRM solutions and provides business software on a subscription basis.
Website: https://www.salesforce.com/
Phone: (800) 667-6389 **Email:**
Headquarters Address: 415 Mission Street 3rd Floor
City: San Francisco **State:** CA **Zip:** 94105 **Country:** United States
Year Established: 1999 **Status:** Active

Company Name: Samsung
Description: Samsung Electronics is a South Korean multinational electronics company.
Website: https://www.samsung.com/
Phone: 82-31-200-1114 **Email:**
Headquarters Address: 129 Samseong-ro Yeongtong-gu Gyeonggi-do Suwon-Shi Korea
Zip: 16677 **Country:** Republic of Korea (South)
Year Established: 1969 **Status:** Active

Company Name: Tencent
Description: Tencent is an internet service portal offering value-added internet, mobile, telecom, and online advertising services.
Website: https://www.tencent.com/
Phone: 86 75 5860 13388 **Email:** gc@tencent.com
Headquarters Address: Tencent Binhai Building, No 33 Haitian Second Road, Nanshan Shenzhen
Zip: 518054 **Country:** China
Year Established: 1998 **Status:** Active

Company Name: Twilio
Description: Twilio is a cloud communication company that enables users to use standard web languages to build voice, VoIP, and SMS apps via a web API.
Website: www.twilio.com
Phone: (415) 227-9968 **Email:** help@twilio.com
Headquarters Address: 645 Harrison Street 3rd Floor
City: San Francisco **State:** CA **Zip:** 94107 **Country:** United States
Year Established: 2008 **Status:** Active

Company Name: Twitter
Description: Twitter is a social networking platform that allows its users to send and read micro-blogs of up to 280-characters known as tweets.
Website: https://www.twilio.com/
Phone: (415) 222-9670 **Email:** press@twitter.com
Headquarters Address: 1355 Market Street Suite 900
City: San Francisco **State:** CA **Zip:** 94103 **Country:** United States
Year Established: 2007 **Status:** Active

Company Name: Yahoo
Description: Yahoo operates an online web portal intended to provide the latest news on finance, lifestyle, movies, celebrity, travel, and more.
Website: https://www.yahoo.com/
Phone: (408) 349-3300 **Email:**
Headquarters Address: 701 First Ave.
City: Sunnyvale **State:** CA **Zip:** 94089 **Country:** United States
Year Established: 1994 **Status:** Active

Volume 2 - World Companies

Argentina - Zimbabwe

Company Name: DataHipsters
Description: Streaming Recommender Systems and Machine Learning
Website: http://datahipsters.com
Phone: **Email:** 36395@reference-encyclopedia-ai.net
City: Buenos Aires **State:** CABA **PC:** **Country:** Argentina
Year Established: 2014 **Status 2020:** Active
Industries: Artificial Intelligence for:, ~ Education (13), Machine Learning

Company Name: Dondeloveo
Description: Movies and Series Universal Search Engine for Latin America, Brazil and Spa: India
Website: http://dondeloveo.com
Phone: 1(305)7046455 **Email:** info@dondeloveo.com
City: Buenos Aires **State:** CABA **PC:** **Country:** Argentina
Year Established: 2017 **Status 2020:** Active
Industries: Analytics for:, Business Intelligence for:, Content for:, ~ Media-Communications (41), Databases for:, ~ Arts-Entertainment-Recreation (4), Predictive Analytics for:, Predictive Analytics for:, Web for:, ~ Arts-Entertainment-Recreation (4)

Company Name: Dymaxion Labs
Description: Dymaxion Labs is building a business intelligence platform for the physical world.
Website: http://www.dymaxionlabs.com
Phone: **Email:** hola@dymaxionlabs.com
City: Buenos Aires **State:** CABA **PC:** **Country:** Argentina
Year Established: 2018 **Status 2020:** Active
Industries: Artificial Intelligence for:, Computer Vision for:, Application Services for:, Internet of Things (IoT) for:, Machine Learning

Company Name: Emi Labs
Description: AI recruitment platform (Y Combinator W19 batch).
Website: http://www.emilabs.ai/
Phone: **Email:** info@holaemi.com
City: Buenos Aires **State:** CABA **PC:** **Country:** Argentina
Year Established: 2017 **Status 2020:** Active
Industries: Artificial Intelligence

Company Name: Evenance
Description: We use machine learning to learn and recommend to each athlete their perfect competition event. Every single time.
Website: http://www.evenance.com
Phone: **Email:** leopoldo crunchbase@evenance.com
City: Buenos Aires **State:** DF **PC:** **Country:** Argentina
Year Established: 2019 **Status 2020:** Active
Industries: ~ Event Management (15), ~ Event Management (15), ~ Event Management (15), ~ Healthcare (20), ~ Arts-Entertainment-Recreation (4), ~ Arts-Entertainment-Recreation (4)

Company Name: Fichap
Description: SaaS, Mobile App - Smart system for tracking employees' working hours and location (integrated face recognition and geolocation).
Website: http://fichap.com/
Phone: **Email:** info@fichap.com
City: Buenos Aires **State:** CABA **PC:** **Country:** Argentina
Year Established: 2018 **Status 2020:** Active
Industries: Application Services for:, IT Managed Services for:, Application Services

Company Name: HR360
Description: Saas, Engagement Surveys in real time
Website:
Phone: (1347) 274-8807 **Email:** david@faerman.us
City: Buenos Aires **State:** CABA **PC:** **Country:** Argentina
Year Established: 2019 **Status 2020:** Active
Industries: Analytics for:, Artificial Intelligence for:, IT Managed Services for:, Machine Learning for:, Compute for:, Business Software as a Service Apps (SaaS Apps)

Company Name: Iaar
Description: Iaar is a community of artificial intelligence.
Website: http://www.iaar.site/
Phone: **Email:** 36732@reference-encyclopedia-ai.net
City: Buenos Aires **State:** CABA **PC:** **Country:** Argentina
Year Established: 2016 **Status 2020:** Active
Industries: Artificial Intelligence

Company Name: MisPichos.com
Description: Data driven pet parents solutions ecosystem. Software for hire custom pet products/service, frictionless
Website: http://mispichos.com
Phone: 54 11 5171-4343 **Email:** ventas@mispichos.com
City: Buenos Aires **State:** CABA **PC:** **Country:** Argentina
Year Established: 2016 **Status 2020:** Active
Industries:

Company Name: NYDRO
Description: NYDRO provides fast-deployable and resilient grids based on optical fiber links and smart meters with embedded machine learning.
Website: http://nydro.energy
Phone: **Email:** hi@nydro.energy
City: Buenos Aires **State:** CABA **PC:** **Country:** Argentina
Year Established: **Status 2020:** Active
Industries: Artificial Intelligence for:, Blockchain for:, IT Managed Services for:, ~ Energy and Utilities (14), ~ Professional Services (48)

Company Name: Pinggers
Description: Pinggers is a personalized daily deal aggregator website that learns users' preferences and delivers relevant deals for them.
Website: http://www.pinggers.com
Phone: **Email:** info@pinggers.com
City: Buenos Aires **State:** CABA **PC:** **Country:** Argentina
Year Established: 2010 **Status 2020:** Closed
Industries: Artificial Intelligence for:, ~ E-Commerce (12), E-Commerce

Company Name: Spect: Romania
Description: Spectro is a location intelligence platform that uses sensors to digitize commercial spaces.
Website: http://www.spect.ro/
Phone: **Email:** info@spect.: Romania
City: Buenos Aires **State:** CABA **PC:** **Country:** Argentina
Year Established: 2015 **Status 2020:** Active
Industries:

Company Name: Wearly
Description: When your dresser meets AI
Website: http://Wearly.wtf
Phone: **Email:** founders@wearly.wtf
City: Buenos Aires **State:** CABA **PC:** **Country:** Argentina
Year Established: 2020 **Status 2020:** Active
Industries: Artificial Intelligence for:, ~ Fashion (16), Machine Learning for:, ~ Social-Environmental-Physical-Engineering Sciences (55)

Company Name: Worcket
Description: Job Search App based on Artificial Inteligence, Videos and a unique UX
Website: http://www.worcket.com
Phone: 54911 50058515 **Email:** contact@worcket.com
City: Buenos Aires **State:** CABA **PC:** **Country:** Argentina
Year Established: 2016 **Status 2020:** Active
Industries: Application Services for:, Artificial Intelligence for:, IT Managed Services for:, Machine Learning

Company Name: Inipop
Description: Innovation Hub based in Buenos Aires. We make Hard Tech
Website: http://www.inipop.com
Phone: 54 11 5368 0540 **Email:** info@inipop.com

City: San Isidro **State:** Buenos Aires Province **PC:** **Country:** Argentina
Year Established: 2013 **Status 2020:** Active
Industries: Artificial Intelligence for:, IT Managed Services for:, Web for:, Internet of Things (IoT)

Company Name: Essent: ITALY
Description: Data Science for Startu: Palestine
Website: http://www.essentit.com
Phone: **Email:** hello@essentit.com
City: Resistencia **State:** Chaco Province **PC:** **Country:** Argentina
Year Established: 2016 **Status 2020:** Active
Industries: Big Data and Analytics for:, Data Management for:, Data Management for:, Machine Learning

Company Name: Pick It 4 Me
Description: A Smart Recommender for Retail Industry
Website: http://pickit4.me
Phone: **Email:** agustin@pickit4.me
City: Resistencia **State:** Chaco Province **PC:** **Country:** Argentina
Year Established: **Status 2020:** Active
Industries: Artificial Intelligence for:, E-Commerce for:, Machine Learning for:, ~ Retail and Consumer Products (52)

Company Name: Aivo
Description: Aivo develops customer services solutions with Artificial Intelligence
Website: http://www.aivo.co/
Phone: (415) 849-2288 **Email:** sales@aivo.co
City: Córdoba **State:** Cordoba **PC:** **Country:** Argentina
Year Established: 2012 **Status 2020:** Active
Industries: Artificial Intelligence for:, Business Applications for:, ~ Customer Relationship Management (11), Machine Learning for:, Natural Language Processing for:, Business Software as a Service Apps (SaaS Apps)

Company Name: Nubimetrics
Description: BigData and Business Intelligence vendors for MercadoLibre.
Website: http://www.nubimetrics.com
Phone: 54 11 5352 0038 **Email:** 37081@reference-encyclopedia-ai.net
City: Jujuy **State:** Jujuy **PC:** **Country:** Argentina
Year Established: 2013 **Status 2020:** Active
Industries: Big Data and Analytics for:, Business Intelligence for:, ~ Customer Relationship Management (11), E-Commerce for:, IT Managed Services for:, Web for:, Predictive Analytics

Company Name: FamilyGuard
Description: FamilyGuard is a mobile application based on artificial intelligence that connects family members around latinoamerica market.
Website: http://www.familyguard.net
Phone: **Email:** info@familyguard.net
City: Mendoza **State:** Mendoza Province **PC:** **Country:** Argentina
Year Established: 2015 **Status 2020:** Active
Industries: Artificial Intelligence for:, Big Data and Analytics for:, Internet of Things (IoT) for:, Application Services for:, Security

Company Name: blastrip
Description: The Future of Logistics
Website: http://www.blastrip.com
Phone: **Email:** info@blastrip.com
City: Rosario **State:** Santa Fe Province **PC:** **Country:** Argentina
Year Established: 2017 **Status 2020:** Active
Industries: ~ Telecommunications (56), Predictive Analytics

Company Name: Gbot
Description: Gbot is an autonomous robot that controls weeds without using agrochemicals. We also collect data in fields and generate precision maps.
Website: http://gbot.ag/en/home-2/
Phone: **Email:** juani@gbot.ag
City: Rosario **State:** Santa Fe Province **PC:** **Country:** Argentina
Year Established: 2019 **Status 2020:** Active
Industries: ~ Agriculture (3), ~ Agriculture (3), Artificial Intelligence for:, Robotics

Company Name: Menubot
Description: Food ordering and table reservation assistant
Website: http://www.menubot.com
Phone: **Email:** hello@menubot.com
City: Santa Fe **State:** Santa Fe Province **PC:** **Country:** Argentina
Year Established: 2014 **Status 2020:** Active
Industries:

Armenia

Company Name: Recoloring App
Description: Recoloring creates new category of fantasy art, in which drawing interacts with photography.
Website: http://apps.apple.com/app/id1487955509
Phone: 37494401034 **Email:** recoloringapp@gmail.com
City: Sevan **State:** Gegharkunik Province **PC:** **Country:** **Armenia**
Year Established: 2019 **Status 2020:** Active
Industries: Artificial Intelligence for:, Application Services

Company Name: cognaize
Description: Serial entrepreneur.
Website: http://cognaize.com/
Phone: 1 (650) 417 3930 **Email:** info@cognaize.com
City: Yerevan **State:** ER **PC:** **Country:** Armenia
Year Established: **Status 2020:** Active
Industries: Artificial Intelligence for:, ~ Banking and Financial Markets-Services (7), Automation for:, ~ Banking and Financial Markets-Services (373), Business Applications for:, Data Management for:, ~ Banking and Financial Markets-Services (1715), Machine Learning for:,

Company Name: Escape Reality
Description: Fuse your surrounding into the game
Website: http://uescapereality.wordpress.com/
Phone: **Email:** gorgrigoryangor@gmail.com
City: Yerevan **State:** ER **PC:** **Country:** Armenia
Year Established: **Status 2020:** Active
Industries: Artificial Intelligence for:, Machine Learning for:, Application Services for:, ~ Arts-Entertainment-Recreation (4)

Company Name: Photrix App
Description: Deep Learning Based IOS Photo Editor.
Website:
Phone: 37494401034 **Email:** 37165@reference-encyclopedia-ai.net
City: Yerevan **State:** Yerevan **PC:** **Country:** Armenia
Year Established: 2017 **Status 2020:** Active
Industries: ~ Media-Communications (41)

Company Name: SmartClick
Description: SmartClick is a full-service software provider delivering artificial intelligence and machine learning solutions for Enterprises.
Website: http://smartclick.ai
Phone: 37495088188 **Email:** info@smartclick.ai
City: Yerevan **State:** Yerevan **PC:** **Country:** Armenia
Year Established: 2018 **Status 2020:** Active
Industries: Artificial Intelligence for:, Business Intelligence for:, Facial Recognition for:, Image Recognition for:, Machine Learning for:, Predictive Analytics for:

Company Name: Softhenge
Description: Software Engineering
Website: http://www.softhenge.com/
Phone: 374 10 51 43 29 **Email:** info@softhenge.com
City: Yerevan **State:** Yerevan **PC:** **Country:** Armenia
Year Established: 2016 **Status 2020:** Active
Industries: Artificial Intelligence for:, Blockchain for:, Computer Vision for:, Application Services for:, Embedded for:, Embedded for:, IT Managed Services for:, Machine Learning for:, Machine Learning

Australia

Company Name: Hummingbird AI PTY Ltd.
Description: Hummingbird AI is a personal assistant chatbot powered by artificial intelligence.
Website: http://hummingbird.ai/
Phone: **Email:** hello@hummingbird.ai
City: **State:** **PC:** **Country:** Australia
Year Established: **Status 2020:** Active
Industries: Artificial Intelligence

Company Name: iRecruit Australia PTY LTD
Description: Our mission is to transform the recruitment process into an effective, efficient, and enjoyable experience for both talent and employers.
Website: http://www.irecruit.com.au
Phone: **Email:** hello@irecruit.com.au
City: **State:** **PC:** **Country:** Australia
Year Established: **Status 2020:** Active
Industries: Artificial Intelligence for:, Big Data and Analytics for:, Machine Learning for:, Predictive Analytics for:, ~ Human Resources (24)

Company Name: Penten
Description: Penten helps the digital transformation of defence & government - creating, building & operating new cyber tech for the modern workforce.
Website: http://www.penten.com/
Phone: 61 2 6171 1111 **Email:** info@penten.com
City: Canberra **State:** ACT **PC:** **Country:** Australia
Year Established: 2014 **Status 2020:** Active
Industries: ~ Government (19), IT Managed Services for:, Cyber Security for:, Security

Company Name: Wotsay
Description: Wotsay is an artificial intelligence tourism application.
Website: http://partners.wotsay.com/
Phone: **Email:** 37686@reference-encyclopedia-ai.net
City: Canberra **State:** ACT **PC:** **Country:** Australia
Year Established: 2018 **Status 2020:** Active
Industries: Artificial Intelligence for:, ~ Travel and Transportation (58)

Company Name: Agerr
Description: Agerris is a field robotics and AI start-up based on technology created at the Australian Centre for Field Robotics.
Website: https://agerris.com/
Phone: **Email:** enquiries@agerris.com
City: Chippendale **State:** NSW **PC:** **Country:** Australia
Year Established: 2019 **Status 2020:** Active
Industries: ~ Agriculture (3), Artificial Intelligence for:, ~ Agriculture (3), Machine Learning for:, Robotics

Company Name: Sajari
Description: Sajari is a cloud-based, instant search platform for websites and e-commerce. Flexible and adaptable, Sajari drives business performance.
Website: http://www.sajari.com
Phone: **Email:** hello@sajari.com
City: Chippendale **State:** NSW **PC:** **Country:** Australia
Year Established: 2017 **Status 2020:** Active
Industries: Artificial Intelligence

Company Name: Peard
Description: Mobile Dating App
Website: http://www.getpeard.com.au
Phone: 1466657675 **Email:** corbin@getpeard.com.au
City: Cronulla **State:** NSW **PC:** **Country:** Australia
Year Established: **Status 2020:** Active
Industries:

Company Name: Realm Australia
Description: Realm Australia is dedicated to supporting real estate professionals at all stages of their career.
Website: http://propertyrealm.com.au/
Phone: 1300 21 92 99 **Email:** info@propertyrealm.com.au
City: Erina **State:** NSW **PC:** **Country:** Australia
Year Established: **Status 2020:** Active
Industries:

Company Name: Call Journey
Description:
Website: http://calljourney.com
Phone: (760) 221-8907 **Email:** 12475@reference-encyclopedia-ai.net
City: Granville **State:** NSW **Zip:** 2142 **Country**: Australia
Year Established: **Status 2020:** Active
Industries:

Company Name: EzzyBills
Description: EzzyBills, the first invoice processing system that uses Deep Learning.
Website: http://www.ezzybills.com
Phone: 02 8003 3097 **Email:** support@ezzydoc.com
City: Kingscliff **State:** NSW **PC:** **Country:** Australia
Year Established: 2014 **Status 2020:** Active
Industries: Artificial Intelligence for:, Big Data and Analytics

Company Name: FactNexus
Description: FactNexus is a software services provider that offers smart technologies to up bring the healthcare sector.
Website: http://factnexus.com
Phone: **Email:** info@factnexus.com
City: Newcastle **State:** NSW **PC:** **Country:** Australia
Year Established: 2010 **Status 2020:** Active
Industries: Application Program Interfaces (APIs) for:, Natural Language Processing for:, Content for:, Web

Company Name: Restack
Description: The full-stack platform for connected devices.
Website: http://restack.io/
Phone: **Email:** 37293@reference-encyclopedia-ai.net
City: Newcastle **State:** NSW **PC:** **Country:** Australia
Year Established: 2014 **Status 2020:** Closed
Industries: Application Services for:, Artificial Intelligence

Company Name: Agate
Description: Agate is the world most comprehensive decentralized blockchain platform for instant payment without volatility risk.
Website: http://www.agatechain.org
Phone: **Email:** hello@agatechain.org
City: North Sydney **State:** NSW **PC:** **Country:** Australia
Year Established: **Status 2020:** Active
Industries: Artificial Intelligence for:, Blockchain for:, ~ Banking and Financial Markets-Services (7), ~ Banking and Financial Markets-Services (7), ~ Banking and Financial Markets-Services (7), ~ Banking and Financial Markets-Services (7)

Company Name: Dream LOT
Description: AI Property Service Platform
Website: http://www.dreamlot.com
Phone: 61 499 568 568 **Email:** service@dreamlot.com
City: North Sydney **State:** NSW **PC:** **Country:** Australia
Year Established: 2017 **Status 2020:** Active
Industries: Artificial Intelligence for:, ~ Customer Relationship Management (11), IT Managed Services for:, Machine Learning for:, Enterprise Application Services for:, ~ Real Estate (49), ~ Real Estate (49), ~ Real Estate (49)

Company Name: Fivecast
Description: Fivecast is an Australian technology start-up that uses artificial intelligence to trawl the internet to assess potential business.
Website: http://fivecast.com/
Phone: **Email:** info@fivecast.com
City: North Sydney **State:** NSW **PC:** **Country:** Australia
Year Established: 2017 **Status 2020:** Active
Industries: Artificial Intelligence for:, Security

Company Name: Quixxi
Description: Quixxi
Website: http://quixxisecurity.com/
Phone: **Email:** info@quixxi.com
City: North Sydney **State:** NSW **PC:** **Country:** Australia
Year Established: 2013 **Status 2020:** Active
Industries: Artificial Intelligence for:, Blockchain for:, Application Program Interfaces (APIs) for:, Application Services for:, ~ Banking and Financial Markets-Services (7), IT Managed Services for:, Application Services

Company Name: MPT AgTech
Description: MPT AgTech are building a new generation of smart farming equipment for large scale cropping.
Website:
Phone: **Email:** 4416@reference-encyclopedia-ai.net
City: Orange **State:** NSW **PC:** **Country:** Australia
Year Established: **Status 2020:** Active
Industries: ~ Agriculture (3), ~ Agriculture (3), Artificial Intelligence for:, ~ Banking and Financial Markets-Services (7), Robotics

Company Name: Metigy
Description: Metigy uses AI and deep learning to deliver real time insights and actions that radically enhance reach and converison
Website: http://metigy.com/
Phone: 61 280 724 101 **Email:** contact@metigy.com
City: Pyrmont **State:** NSW **PC:** **Country:** Australia
Year Established: **Status 2020:** Active
Industries: ~ Media-Communications (41), Artificial Intelligence for:, ~ Media-Communications (41), ~ Social Media (54)

Company Name: Muzaara
Description: Muzaara, adopts a SaaS model to offer a platform that can generate ads to networks such as Facebook & Google.
Website: http://www.muzaara.com/
Phone: **Email:** hello@muzaara.com
City: Surry Hills **State:** NSW **PC:** **Country:** Australia
Year Established: 2016 **Status 2020:** Active
Industries: Big Data and Analytics for:, Internet of Things (IoT) for:, Machine Learning for:, Business Software as a Service Apps (SaaS Apps)

Company Name: Roamz
Description: Roamz is a location-based application that informs users about the happenings in their cities.
Website: http://www.roamz.com
Phone: 61 2 9288 4479 **Email:** info@roamz.com
City: Surry Hills **State:** NSW **PC:** **Country:** Australia
Year Established: 2013 **Status 2020:** Closed
Industries: Machine Learning for:, Business Intelligence for:, ~ Social Assistance-Non-Profits (53)

Company Name: a Star
Description: A Star Infomation Analytics
Website:
Phone: 61435770557 **Email:** jqadan@gmail.com
City: Sydney **State:** NSW **PC:** **Country:** Australia
Year Established: 2017 **Status 2020:** Active
Industries: Data Management for:, IT Managed Services for:, Machine Learning for:, Computer Vision

Company Name: AerVision Technologies
Description: AerVision Technologies is a Biometrics and Artificial Intelligence solutions.
Website: http://www.aervision.com/
Phone: **Email:** sales@aervision.com
City: Sydney **State:** NSW **PC:** **Country:** Australia
Year Established: 2013 **Status 2020:** Active
Industries:

Company Name: AI Lawracle
Description: AI Lawracle offers an application which automates legal services using artificial intelligence and unique algorithms.
Website:
Phone: **Email:** 35989@reference-encyclopedia-ai.net
City: Sydney **State:** NSW **PC:** **Country:** Australia
Year Established: 2017 **Status 2020:** Active
Industries: Application Services for:, Artificial Intelligence

Company Name: Akin
Description: a·kin's is the responsible co-evolution of humanity and artificial intelligence.
Website: https://www.akin.com/
Phone: **Email:** 36027@reference-encyclopedia-ai.net
City: Sydney **State:** NSW **PC:** **Country:** Australia
Year Established: 2018 **Status 2020:** Active
Industries: Artificial Intelligence for:, Machine Learning

Company Name: AppSunder PTY. LTD.
Description: We use technology to solve human problems
Website: http://appsunder.com
Phone: **Email:** sales@appsunder.com
City: Sydney **State:** NSW **PC:** **Country:** Australia
Year Established: 2015 **Status 2020:** Active
Industries: Artificial Intelligence for:, ~ Healthcare (20), IT Managed Services

Company Name: Auraya Systems
Description: A world leader in voice biometrics technology empowering people and organisations to interact and engage with convenience and security.
Website: http://aurayasystems.com/
Phone: 1800 940 894 **Email:** info@aurayasystems.com
City: Sydney **State:** NSW **PC:** **Country:** Australia
Year Established: 2010 **Status 2020:** Active
Industries: Artificial Intelligence for:, ~ Biotechnology (9), Cyber Security for:, Identity for:, IT Managed Services for:, Security

Company Name: Averoft
Description: Work on technologies such as Big Data, BI, Data Analytics, Cloud Computing, Artificial Intelligence and Robotics.
Website: http://www.averoft.com
Phone: **Email:** contact@averoft.com
City: Sydney **State:** NSW **PC:** **Country:** Australia
Year Established: **Status 2020:** Active
Industries: Analytics for:, Application Services for:, Artificial Intelligence for:, Big Data and Analytics for:, Business Intelligence for:, Cloud for:, Databases for:, Data Management for:, Enterprise Application Services for:, Enterprise Application Services for:, IT Manage

Company Name: Bravi
Description: Bravi is mobile app for couples powered by Artificial Intelligence
Website: http://www.bravi.life
Phone: **Email:** hello@bravi.life
City: Sydney **State:** NSW **PC:** **Country:** Australia
Year Established: **Status 2020:** Active
Industries: Artificial Intelligence for:, Application Services for:, ~ Healthcare (20)

Company Name: BR: India
Description: BRiN is the world's first artificially intelligent business advisor & she's able to provide support to millions of clients simultaneously.
Website: http://brin.ai
Phone: (415) 231-2829 **Email:** ceo@brin.ai
City: Sydney **State:** NSW **PC:** **Country:** Australia
Year Established: 2015 **Status 2020:** Active
Industries: Artificial Intelligence

Company Name: Compo
Description: Shortlyster is an intelligent hiring optimisation platform.
Website: http://compono.com
Phone: 1300 716 004 **Email:** info@shortlyster.com
City: Sydney **State:** NSW **PC:** **Country:** Australia
Year Established: 2017 **Status 2020:** Active
Industries: Artificial Intelligence for:, IT Managed Services for:, IT Managed Services for:, Web

Company Name: Contexti
Description: Contexti is a specialist data and analytics company that delivers actionable insights with automation, machine learning and AI solutions.
Website: http://www.contexti.com
Phone: 61-2-8294-2161 **Email:** 36330@reference-encyclopedia-ai.net
City: Sydney **State:** NSW **PC:** **Country:** Australia
Year Established: 2012 **Status 2020:** Active
Industries: Artificial Intelligence for:, IT Managed Services for:, Machine Learning

Company Name: Cozitrip
Description: AI & tech powered online B2B platform for Chinese travel agents
Website: http://cozitrip.com
Phone: (6130) 050-3377 **Email:** contact@cozitrip.com
City: Sydney **State:** NSW **PC:** **Country:** Australia
Year Established: 2015 **Status 2020:** Active
Industries: Artificial Intelligence for:, Web for:, ~ Travel and Transportation (58)

Company Name: Cubewi
Description:
Website: www.cubewise.com
Phone: 857-208-7267 **Email:** rricafranca@cubewise.com
City: Sydney **State:** NSW **Zip:** 2065 **Country**: Australia
Year Established: **Status 2020:** Active
Industries:

Company Name: Cubewi
Description:
Website: http://www.cubewise.com
Phone: 91 9820043309 **Email:** tushar.banode@dhdigital.co.: India
City: Sydney **State:** NSW **Zip:** 2065 **Country**: Australia
Year Established: **Status 2020:** Active
Industries:

Company Name: Curious Thing
Description: Conversational AI, SaaS, Talent Acquisition Software
Website: http://www.curiousthing.io
Phone: **Email:** hello@curiousthing.io
City: Sydney **State:** NSW **PC:** **Country:** Australia
Year Established: 2018 **Status 2020:** Active
Industries: Artificial Intelligence for:, ~ Customer Relationship Management (11), IT Managed Services for:, Business Software as a Service Apps (SaaS Apps)

Company Name: Daisee
Description: Artificial Intelligence Software
Website: www.daisee.com
Phone: **Email:** info@daisee.com
City: Sydney **State:** NSW **PC:** **Country:** Australia
Year Established: **Status 2020:** Active
Industries:

Company Name: Discidium
Description: Technology challenging every existing economic models
Website: http://www.discidiumtech.com
Phone: **Email:** info@discidium.tech
City: Sydney **State:** NSW **PC:** **Country:** Australia
Year Established: **Status 2020:** Active
Industries: Artificial Intelligence for:, Blockchain for:, Machine Learning

Company Name: Doclink
Description: Human and Artificial Intelligence against Cancer
Website: http://www.doclink.io
Phone: (6144) 700-2784 **Email:** info@doclink.io
City: Sydney **State:** NSW **PC:** **Country:** Australia
Year Established: 2017 **Status 2020:** Active
Industries: Artificial Intelligence for:, ~ Healthcare (20)

Company Name: Driven
Description: Driven is a virtual coach in your pocket. We use narrative design & AI to help businesses improve the wellbeing of their people.
Website: http://hellodriven.com/
Phone: **Email:** info@hellodriven.com
City: Sydney **State:** NSW **PC:** **Country:** Australia
Year Established: 2017 **Status 2020:** Active
Industries: Application Services for:, Artificial Intelligence for:, ~ Education (13), ~ Healthcare (20), ~ Healthcare (20), ~ Healthcare (20), IT Managed Services for:, ~ Healthcare (20), ~ Healthcare (20), ~ Healthcare (20)

Company Name: DroneLancer
Description: DroneLancer is powering the future of commerce with their autonomous drone technology
Website: http://www.dronelancer.com
Phone: 800 555 5555 **Email:** support@dronelancer.com
City: Sydney **State:** NSW **PC:** **Country:** Australia
Year Established: **Status 2020:** Active
Industries: Artificial Intelligence for:, ~ Transportation and Logistics (57), Application Services for:, Robotics for:, ~ Professional Services (48)

Company Name: EORA 3D
Description: EORA 3D is changing the way point cloud data is extracted, used and analysed from 3D models captured of physical reality.
Website: http://www.eora3d.com
Phone: **Email:** hello@eora3d.com
City: Sydney **State:** NSW **PC:** **Country:** Australia
Year Established: 2015 **Status 2020:** Active
Industries: Augmented Reality for:, Computer Vision for:, Machine Learning for:, Virtual Reality (VR) for:, Virtual Reality (VR) for:

Company Name: Fincast
Description: Fincast has built a 2nd generation automated wealth management platform, with 'adaptive technology that learns'
Website: http://www.fincast.com.au
Phone: 61292932875 **Email:** info@fincast.com.au
City: Sydney **State:** NSW **PC:** **Country:** Australia
Year Established: **Status 2020:** Active
Industries: Artificial Intelligence for:, ~ Banking and Financial Markets-Services (7), Machine Learning for:, Mobile for:, ~ Banking and Financial Markets-Services (7)

Company Name: Flobox
Description: Flobox uses machine learning algorithm to help businesses make smarter online advertising decision.
Website: http://www.flobox.io
Phone: **Email:** 36582@reference-encyclopedia-ai.net
City: Sydney **State:** NSW **PC:** **Country:** Australia
Year Established: 2016 **Status 2020:** Active
Industries: Machine Learning

Company Name: FluroSat
Description: FluroSat offers crop health monitoring and analytics services.
Website: http://www.flurosat.com/
Phone: (043)100-3688 **Email:** hello@flurosat.com
City: Sydney **State:** NSW **PC:** **Country:** Australia
Year Established: 2016 **Status 2020:** Active
Industries: ~ Agriculture (3), Analytics for:, ~ Agriculture (3), Machine Learning

Company Name: GeoInteractive
Description: AI Platform and Inspection Drones that are automating sewer inspections
Website: http://www.geointeractive.co
Phone: 415 619 1415 **Email:** info@geointeractive.co
City: Sydney **State:** NSW **PC:** **Country:** Australia
Year Established: **Status 2020:** Active
Industries: Artificial Intelligence for:, Big Data and Analytics for:, Machine Learning for:, ~ Professional Services (48), ~ Waste Management and Remediation Services (59)

Company Name: GiFang
Description: where investors find tokens backed by international real estate assets
Website: http://www.gifang.com
Phone: 61390088167 **Email:** office@gifang.com
City: Sydney **State:** NSW **PC:** **Country:** Australia
Year Established: **Status 2020:** Active
Industries: Artificial Intelligence for:, Big Data and Analytics for:, Blockchain for:, ~ Real Estate (49), ~ Banking and Financial Markets-Services (7), ~ Real Estate (49), ~ Real Estate (49), ~ Real Estate (49)

Company Name: HIVERY
Description: Data Has A Better Idea. At HIVERY we build prescriptive analytics tools to solve individual business problems in ways that humans cannot.
Website: http://www.hivery.com
Phone: 61028218210 **Email:** hello@hivery.com
City: Sydney **State:** NSW **PC:** **Country:** Australia
Year Established: **Status 2020:** Active
Industries: Analytics for:, Artificial Intelligence for:, Machine Learning

Company Name: HomeOn
Description: An independent estimate of what your home might be worth in today's Australian real estate market, powered by AI.
Website: http://homeon.com.au/
Phone: **Email:** partner@homeon.com.au
City: Sydney **State:** NSW **PC:** **Country:** Australia
Year Established: 2018 **Status 2020:** Active
Industries: Artificial Intelligence for:, Machine Learning

Company Name: Hyper Anna
Description: Hyper Anna is an AI powered data analyst - Siri for analytics.
Website: http://www.hyperanna.com
Phone: **Email:** nat@hyperanna.com
City: Sydney **State:** NSW **PC:** **Country:** Australia
Year Established: **Status 2020:** Active
Industries: Analytics for:, Artificial Intelligence for:, ~ Banking and Financial Markets-Services (7), ~ Banking and Financial Markets-Services (7), ~ Professional Services (48)

Company Name: Hyperflow
Description: Intelligent workflow tools for video teams.
Website: http://www.hyperflow.tv
Phone: **Email:** 36727@reference-encyclopedia-ai.net
City: Sydney **State:** NSW **PC:** **Country:** Australia
Year Established: 2017 **Status 2020:** Active
Industries:

Company Name: Intersective
Description: Intersective develops technology and provides services to help educators deliver better experiential learning.
Website: http://www.intersective.com/
Phone: **Email:** connect@intersective.com
City: Sydney **State:** NSW **PC:** **Country:** Australia
Year Established: **Status 2020:** Active
Industries: Analytics for:, Artificial Intelligence for:, ~ Education (13), ~ Education (13), Machine Learning

Company Name: IXUP
Description: IXUP is innovative data collaboration platform.
Website: http://www.ixup.com/
Phone: 61 (0)2 8206 8888 **Email:** contact@ixup.com
City: Sydney **State:** NSW **PC:** **Country:** Australia
Year Established: 2011 **Status 2020:** Active
Industries: Analytics for:, Artificial Intelligence for:, Cloud for:, Collaboration Solutions for:, Cyber Security for:, Data Management for:, Enterprise Application Services for:, IT Managed Services for:, IT Managed Services for:, Web

Company Name: Lakeba Group Pty Ltd
Description: Lakeba is a privately held international technology innovation group.
Website: http://www.lakeba.com
Phone: 1300 656 705 **Email:** info@lakeba.com
City: Sydney **State:** NSW **PC:** **Country:** Australia
Year Established: 2013 **Status 2020:** Active
Industries: Artificial Intelligence for:, Blockchain for:, ~ Banking and Financial Markets-Services (7), IT Managed Services for:, Internet of Things (IoT) for:, Security

Company Name: League of Schola: Serbia
Description: Research Talent Discovery. Attract, recruit and retain the world's best high-potential researche: Serbia
Website: http://leagueofscholars.com
Phone: **Email:** paul@leagueofscholars.com
City: Sydney **State:** NSW **PC:** **Country:** Australia
Year Established: **Status 2020:** Active
Industries: Artificial Intelligence for:, ~ Education (13), ~ Human Resources (24), ~ Administrative and Support Services (1), Predictive Analytics

Company Name: LENS Immersive
Description: LENS Immersive develops deep core tech - focused on Artificial Intelligence accelerating streaming delivery of 4K, VR, and AR.
Website: http://lens-immersive.com/
Phone: 315-308-0101 **Email:** travis@lens-immersive.com
City: Sydney **State:** NSW **PC:** **Country:** Australia

Year Established: **Status 2020:** Active
Industries: Artificial Intelligence for:, Augmented Reality for:, Machine Learning for:, ~ Professional Services (48), ~ Media-Communications (41), ~ Media-Communications (41)

Company Name: LexX Technologies
Description: LexX Technologies is an intelligent platform that uses NLP and machine learning for maintenance of complex industrial assets and equipment
Website: http://https//www.lexxtechnologies.com/
Phone: **Email:** hello@lexxtechnologies.com
City: Sydney **State:** NSW **PC:** **Country:** Australia
Year Established: 2013 **Status 2020:** Active
Industries: Artificial Intelligence for:, ~ Banking and Financial Markets-Services (7), Cloud for:, Enterprise Application Services for:, IT Managed Services for:, Machine Learning for:, Natural Language Processing for:, Content for:, Content

Company Name: LockinFuel
Description: LockinFuel is a fuel app that uses advanced artificial intelligence to forecast future fuel prices in the coming days.
Website: http://lockinfuel.com/
Phone: **Email:** info@lockinfuel.com
City: Sydney **State:** NSW **PC:** **Country:** Australia
Year Established: 2018 **Status 2020:** Active
Industries: Application Services for:, Artificial Intelligence

Company Name: Longtail UX Pty Ltd
Description: User Experience and Search Marketing Automation
Website: http://longtailux.com
Phone: 61291815724 **Email:** info@longtailux.com.au
City: Sydney **State:** NSW **PC:** **Country:** Australia
Year Established: **Status 2020:** Active
Industries: Artificial Intelligence for:, Content for:, Content for:, ~ Media-Communications (41), Digital Marketing for:, Content for:, ~ Professional Services (48)

Company Name: Lumaway
Description: Lumaway is an AI powered skills tracking software. Provides businesses with workforce insights, and enables career pathing for employe: Spain
Website: http://www.lumaway.com
Phone: **Email:** info@statuszero.io
City: Sydney **State:** NSW **PC:** **Country:** Australia
Year Established: 2018 **Status 2020:** Active
Industries:

Company Name: Medius Heal:Thailand
Description: An AI health assistant trained by doctors & built by computer data scientists to self-triage the patients to the right level of care.
Website: http://mediushealth.org/
Phone: **Email:** hi@mediushealth.org
City: Sydney **State:** NSW **PC:** **Country:** Australia
Year Established: **Status 2020:** Active
Industries: Artificial Intelligence for:, ~ Healthcare (20), ~ Professional Services (48)

Company Name: MFR Dating
Description: Bringing Artificial Intelligence to Dating
Website: http://mfrdating.com/
Phone: 61 452 140 711 **Email:** hanisa@mfrdating.com
City: Sydney **State:** NSW **PC:** **Country:** Australia
Year Established: 2019 **Status 2020:** Active
Industries: Artificial Intelligence for:, Machine Learning for:, Application Services

Company Name: Muru Music
Description: An AI music startup based in Sydney. Creator of the AI Music Brain that listens to all digital music and connects it to the right audience
Website: http://murumusic.com/
Phone: 61484 606 822 **Email:** nicc@murumusic.com
City: Sydney **State:** NSW **PC:** **Country:** Australia
Year Established: **Status 2020:** Active
Industries: Artificial Intelligence for:, Business Applications for:, Big Data and Analytics for:, Application Services for:, ~ Arts-Entertainment-Recreation (4)

Company Name: NightCafe
Description: AI Art Generator App
Website: http://creator.nightcafe.studio
Phone: **Email:** nightcafestudio@gmail.com
City: Sydney **State:** NSW **PC:** **Country:** Australia
Year Established: 2019 **Status 2020:** Active
Industries: ~ Arts-Entertainment-Recreation (4), Artificial Intelligence for:, E-Commerce

Company Name: Nitrobots Pty Ltd
Description: Conversational AI platform
Website: http://bit.ly/2vsBSzs
Phone: (6141) 315-4784 **Email:** mark.halstead@icumulus.com.au
City: Sydney **State:** NSW **PC:** **Country:** Australia
Year Established: 2018 **Status 2020:** Active
Industries:

Company Name: Nod
Description: Nod is a natural language artificial intelligence platform that generates documents for experts in real-time.
Website: http://nod.money/
Phone: **Email:** support@nod.money
City: Sydney **State:** NSW **PC:** **Country:** Australia
Year Established: **Status 2020:** Active
Industries: Artificial Intelligence for:, Knowledge Management for:, ~ Banking and Financial Markets-Services (7), Application Services for:, Natural Language Processing for:, Finance and Accounting

Company Name: Objective Leader
Description: Leadership Development, Simplified
Website: http://www.objectiveleader.com
Phone: **Email:** jack@objectiveleader.com
City: Sydney **State:** NSW **PC:** **Country:** Australia
Year Established: 2019 **Status 2020:** Active
Industries:

Company Name: OCR Labs
Description: OCR Labs provides multi platform development tools for OCR and Face Matching of Identity Documents, Credit Cards and more globally
Website: http://ocrlabs.com
Phone: **Email:** hello@ocrlabs.com
City: Sydney **State:** NSW **PC:** **Country:** Australia
Year Established: 2014 **Status 2020:** Active
Industries: Artificial Intelligence for:, Identity for:, IT Managed Services for:, Mobile

Company Name: Oovvuu
Description: Oovvuu manages an artificial intelligence platform that matches ad-funded videos with articles anywhere in the world almost instantaneously.
Website: http://oovvuu.com/
Phone: 6 431 478009 **Email:** ricky@oovvuu.com
City: Sydney **State:** NSW **PC:** **Country:** Australia
Year Established: 2014 **Status 2020:** Active
Industries: Artificial Intelligence for:, Digital Media for:, Web for:, ~ Arts-Entertainment-Recreation (4)

Company Name: PainChek
Description: PainChek is a App for Intelligent Pain Assessment
Website: http://www.painchek.com/
Phone: 1800 098 809 **Email:** info@painchek.com
City: Sydney **State:** NSW **PC:** **Country:** Australia

Year Established: 2016 **Status 2020:** Active
Industries: Application Services for:, Artificial Intelligence for:, ~ Healthcare (20)

Company Name: Particular Audience
Description: Connecting The World To Relevant Information, Effortlessly & Contextually
Website: http://www.particularaudience.com
Phone: **Email:** info@particularaudience.com
City: Sydney **State:** NSW **PC:** **Country:** Australia
Year Established: 2017 **Status 2020:** Active
Industries: Artificial Intelligence for:, Big Data and Analytics for:, E-Commerce for:, Web for:, Machine Learning

Company Name: Presentation AI
Description: Presentation.ai uses machine learning to analyse your presentation and provide feedback to help you to understand how you can improve.
Website: http://www.presentation.ai
Phone: **Email:** 37204@reference-encyclopedia-ai.net
City: Sydney **State:** NSW **PC:** **Country:** Australia
Year Established: 2017 **Status 2020:** Active
Industries: Analytics for:, Artificial Intelligence for:, ~ Education (13), ~ Education (13)

Company Name: ProYourWay
Description: ProYourWay is next generation TaaS platform that allow companies to engage independent experts, hire pre-formed teams or build bespoke teams
Website: http://www.proyourway.com/
Phone: 61450401542 **Email:** services@proyourway.com
City: Sydney **State:** NSW **PC:** **Country:** Australia
Year Established: **Status 2020:** Active
Industries: Finance and Accounting for:, ~ Media-Communications (41), Artificial Intelligence for:, Big Data and Analytics for:, ~ Banking and Financial Markets-Services (7), IT Managed Services for:, ~ Media-Communications (41)

Company Name: Rawfor
Description: Machine learning for Construction and Facilities Management
Website: http://www.rawfor.com
Phone: **Email:** info@rawfor.com
City: Sydney **State:** NSW **PC:** **Country:** Australia
Year Established: 2018 **Status 2020:** Active
Industries: Artificial Intelligence for:, ~ Construction (10), Data Management for:, Machine Learning for:, Business Software as a Service Apps (SaaS Apps) for:, ~ Construction (10)

Company Name: Red Marker - AI powered compliance
Description: Red Marker's cloud-based SaaS platform automatically analyses digital content for probabilistic compliance risk using AI, ML and NLP
Website: http://www.redmarker.ai
Phone: 61 2 9908 0200 **Email:** sales@redmarker.com.ai
City: Sydney **State:** NSW **PC:** **Country:** Australia
Year Established: 2013 **Status 2020:** Active
Industries: Artificial Intelligence for:, Compliance for:, ~ Education (13), IT Managed Services for:, Web for:, Machine Learning for:, Business Software as a Service Apps (SaaS Apps) for:, Business Software as a Service Apps (SaaS Apps)

Company Name: Reejig
Description: Reejig is a recruitment software startup.
Website: http://reejig.com/
Phone: **Email:** Samantha.lidbetter@reejig.com
City: Sydney **State:** NSW **PC:** **Country:** Australia
Year Established: 2019 **Status 2020:** Active
Industries: Artificial Intelligence for:, Business Software as a Service Apps (SaaS Apps)

Company Name: Retro Analytics
Description: Retro is a self-service web & mobile analytics platform that uses a unique approach to user analytics.
Website: http://retroanalytics.io
Phone: **Email:** hello@retroanalytics.io
City: Sydney **State:** NSW **PC:** **Country:** Australia
Year Established: **Status 2020:** Active
Industries: Analytics for:, Artificial Intelligence for:, IT Managed Services

Company Name: Rich Data Corporation
Description: RDC provides Data and AI powered Situational Lending leveraging an integrated scoring and decisioning Credit Risk platform
Website: http://www.richdataco.com
Phone: **Email:** info@richdataco.com
City: Sydney **State:** NSW **PC:** **Country:** Australia
Year Established: 2015 **Status 2020:** Active
Industries: Analytics for:, Artificial Intelligence for:, ~ Banking and Financial Markets-Services (7), ~ Banking and Financial Markets-Services (7), Machine Learning

Company Name: Seneca
Description: Seneca is your smart personal library.
Website: http://www.seneca.one
Phone: **Email:** black@2x.png
City: Sydney **State:** NSW **PC:** **Country:** Australia
Year Established: **Status 2020:** Active
Industries:

Company Name: Shop You
Description: Shop You is simplifying shopping and saving you time by matching you with brands that suit your style, preferences and body shape.
Website: http://www.shopyou.com.au/
Phone: 428208969 **Email:** u@shopyou.com.au
City: Sydney **State:** NSW **PC:** **Country:** Australia
Year Established: **Status 2020:** Active
Industries: Artificial Intelligence for:, E-Commerce for:, ~ Fashion (16), Machine Learning for:, Mobile for:, Application Services for:, ~ Media-Communications (41), Predictive Analytics for:, ~ Retail and Consumer Products (52)

Company Name: SimpleBrains
Description: SimpleBrains is an online marketplace that connects Australian businesses with the top brains in Data Science, Analytics, and AI space.
Website: http://simplebrains.com.au
Phone: **Email:** support@simplebrains.com.au
City: Sydney **State:** NSW **PC:** **Country:** Australia
Year Established: **Status 2020:** Active
Industries: Analytics for:, Artificial Intelligence for:, Big Data and Analytics

Company Name: SoapBox.ai
Description: SoapBox is developing the first Intelligent Customer Service Platform leveraging leading edge ML and NLP.
Website: http://www.soapbox.ai
Phone: **Email:** info@soapbox.ai
City: Sydney **State:** NSW **PC:** **Country:** Australia
Year Established: 2016 **Status 2020:** Active
Industries: ~ Customer Relationship Management (11), Natural Language Processing

Company Name: SpaceConnect
Description: SpaceConnect offers office space utilization, meeting room booking, desk booking, and collaboration using Bluetooth ibeacon sensors.
Website: http://www.spaceconnect.co
Phone: **Email:** thefuture@spaceconnect.net.au
City: Sydney **State:** NSW **PC:** **Country:** Australia
Year Established: 2015 **Status 2020:** Active
Industries: Business Intelligence for:, ~ Real Estate (49), Application Services for:, Compute

Company Name: Stratejos
Description: Digital assistant for software and IT teams
Website: http://stratejos.ai/
Phone: **Email:** hello@stratejos.ai
City: Sydney **State:** NSW **PC:** **Country:** Australia
Year Established: **Status 2020:** Active
Industries: Application Services for:, Artificial Intelligence for:, IT Managed Services for:, ~ Professional Services (48)

Company Name: Tiliter
Description: We teach checkouts to recognise products without barcod: Spain
Website: http://www.tiliter.com/
Phone: **Email:** sales@tiliter.com
City: Sydney **State:** NSW **PC:** **Country:** Australia
Year Established: **Status 2020:** Active
Industries: Artificial Intelligence for:, Machine Learning for:, ~ Retail and Consumer Products (52), ~ Retail and Consumer Products (52)

Company Name: Trig: Greece
Description: Triggr is a SaaS platform that is automating prospecting for B2B sales teams
Website: http://www.triggr.ai/
Phone: 61 451 291 646 **Email:** hello@triggr.ai
City: Sydney **State:** NSW **PC:** **Country:** Australia
Year Established: 2017 **Status 2020:** Active
Industries: Artificial Intelligence for:, Databases for:, IT Managed Services for:, Business Software as a Service Apps (SaaS Apps)

Company Name: TytoAI
Description: TytoAI is an artificial intelligence product and consulting company that explores the new world of A.I. software and services.
Website: http://tyto.ai/
Phone: **Email:** 37583@reference-encyclopedia-ai.net
City: Sydney **State:** NSW **PC:** **Country:** Australia
Year Established: 2018 **Status 2020:** Active
Industries: Application Services for:, Artificial Intelligence

Company Name: Umbra AI
Description: Simulations, Artificial Intelligence, Data Search Engine, Question and Answer, Whole Earth Modelling
Website: http://daniel3112.typeform.com/to/K84Qu0
Phone: **Email:** danielhanchen@gmail.com
City: Sydney **State:** NSW **PC:** **Country:** Australia
Year Established: **Status 2020:** Active
Industries: Artificial Intelligence for:, IT Managed Services for:, Machine Learning for:, Natural Language Processing for:, ~ Professional Services (48)

Company Name: Unleash live
Description: Unleash live is a secure cloud platform which uses AI on live video streams from a number of sources including cameras, drones, sat and IoT.
Website: http://unleashlive.com
Phone: **Email:** getstarted@unleashlive.com
City: Sydney **State:** NSW **PC:** **Country:** Australia
Year Established: 2016 **Status 2020:** Active
Industries: Artificial Intelligence for:, ~ Telecommunications (56), Enterprise Application Services for:, ~ Media-Communications (41)

Company Name: Upwi
Description: Startup Discovery & Collaboration Platform
Website: http://www.upwise.io/
Phone: **Email:** info@upwise.io
City: Sydney **State:** NSW **PC:** **Country:** Australia
Year Established: **Status 2020:** Active
Industries: Artificial Intelligence for:, IT Managed Services for:, Web

Company Name: VAPAR
Description: Software development firm using artificial intelligence to drive operational efficiencies for water utilities and councils
Website: http://www.vapar.co
Phone: (61) 450 893 868 **Email:** info@vapar.co
City: Sydney **State:** NSW **PC:** **Country:** Australia
Year Established: 2018 **Status 2020:** Active
Industries: Artificial Intelligence for:, IT Managed Services for:, Machine Learning for:, Robotics

Company Name: VizRefra
Description: VizRefra is a platform for reading text in 3D that enables users to navigate through a stream of textual data.
Website: http://vizrefra.com
Phone: 04-35770557 **Email:** info@vizrefra.com
City: Sydney **State:** NSW **PC:** **Country:** Australia
Year Established: 2019 **Status 2020:** Active
Industries: IT Managed Services for:, IT Managed Services for:, Natural Language Processing for:, Data Management

Company Name: WEJUGO
Description: WEJUGO is a global adventure hub platform.
Website: http://wejugo.co
Phone: **Email:** support@keenthemes.com
City: Sydney **State:** NSW **PC:** **Country:** Australia
Year Established: 2014 **Status 2020:** Active
Industries:

Company Name: Zova
Description: Zova gives you a smarter way to get and stay fit.
Website: http://www.zova.com
Phone: 61421973399 **Email:** info@zova.com
City: Sydney **State:** NSW **PC:** **Country:** Australia
Year Established: **Status 2020:** Active
Industries: Artificial Intelligence for:, ~ Healthcare (20), Mobile for:, ~ Healthcare (20)

Company Name: Zuper
Description: Zuper is a financial technology company helping people to understand the power of their money and put it to work to make an impact.
Website: http://zuper.com.au
Phone: **Email:** zuper@zuper.com.au
City: Sydney **State:** NSW **PC:** **Country:** Australia
Year Established: **Status 2020:** Active
Industries: Artificial Intelligence for:, Blockchain for:, ~ Banking and Financial Markets-Services (7), ~ Banking and Financial Markets-Services (7), Finance and Accounting

Company Name: Lifebox
Description: Record your life. Automatically.
Website: http://lifeboxapp.com
Phone: **Email:** feedback@lifeboxapp.com
City: Wollongong **State:** NSW **PC:** **Country:** Australia
Year Established: 2012 **Status 2020:** Active
Industries: Artificial Intelligence for:, Mobile

Company Name: Pending.AI
Description: Developing AI solutions to empower scientists in the pharmaceutical industry to design, make, and test new drugs to treat diseases.
Website: http://pending.ai
Phone: **Email:** mark@pending.ai
City: Wollongong **State:** NSW **PC:** **Country:** Australia
Year Established: 2018 **Status 2020:** Active
Industries: Artificial Intelligence for:, ~ Healthcare (20)

Company Name: Age of Robots magazine & platform
Description: Age of Robots magazine reports on the technology of the Second Machine Age and its impact on our society and psychology.
Website: https://www.ageofrobots.net/
Phone: **Email:** matt@neuroroboticsmag.com
City: Brisbane **State:** QLD **PC:** **Country:** Australia

Year Established: 2017 **Status 2020:** Active
Industries: Artificial Intelligence for:, ~ Media-Communications (41), ~ Healthcare (20), Robotics

Company Name: bothhello
Description: Chatbot design and development
Website: http://bothello.io/
Phone: **Email:** email@bothello.io
City: Brisbane **State:** QLD **PC:** **Country:** Australia
Year Established: **Status 2020:** Active
Industries: Artificial Intelligence for:, Machine Learning for:, Natural Language Processing for:, Development and Test

Company Name: Bridj
Description: BRIDJ is an intelligent public transport service powered by a demand responsive technology platform.
Website: http://www.bridj.com/
Phone: 02 8118 7261 **Email:** connect@bridj.com
City: Brisbane **State:** QLD **PC:** **Country:** Australia
Year Established: 2014 **Status 2020:** Active
Industries: Big Data and Analytics for:, Machine Learning for:, ~ Social Media (54)

Company Name: Cloud Ctrl
Description: Leading cloud billing management platform that accurately predicts and optimizes virtual resource usage and spend across public clouds.
Website: http://www.cloudctrl.com.au
Phone: **Email:** faith.rees@cloudctrl.com.au
City: Brisbane **State:** QLD **PC:** **Country:** Australia
Year Established: 2015 **Status 2020:** Active
Industries: Artificial Intelligence for:, IT Managed Services for:, Business Software as a Service Apps (SaaS Apps)

Company Name: CloudBNE
Description: We are a AI, Creative and Augmented Reality startup based in Brisbane, Australia making an impact globally
Website: http://www.cloudbne.com.au
Phone: **Email:** hello@cloudbne.com.au
City: Brisbane **State:** QLD **PC:** **Country:** Australia
Year Established: 2015 **Status 2020:** Active
Industries: Artificial Intelligence

Company Name: Codafication
Description: Insurtech - PaaS & SaaS innovating value chain and solving data complexity.
Website: http://www.codafication.com
Phone: 1300 265 736 **Email:** hello@codafication.com
City: Brisbane **State:** QLD **PC:** **Country:** Australia
Year Established: **Status 2020:** Active
Industries: Analytics for:, Artificial Intelligence for:, ~ Banking and Financial Markets-Services (7), Cloud for:, Data Management for:, ~ Insurance (25), ~ Insurance (25), Machine Learning for:, ~ Media-Communications (41)

Company Name: Endeavour Programme
Description: Enterprise and B2B SaaS artificial intelligence platform which prevents time and cost overrun of projects of all types.
Website: http://www.endeavourprogramme.com/
Phone: 61 411 494294 **Email:** davidporter@endeavourprogramme.com
City: Brisbane **State:** QLD **PC:** **Country:** Australia
Year Established: 2018 **Status 2020:** Active
Industries: Artificial Intelligence for:, ~ Construction (10), ~ Banking and Financial Markets-Services (7), IT Managed Services

Company Name: Engag3d
Description: An AI augmented 'Marketing-as-a-Service' platform that generates and delivers emotive messaging using 'smart' automation.
Website: http://www.engag3d.com
Phone: 61433135587 **Email:** roop@engag3d.com
City: Brisbane **State:** QLD **PC:** **Country:** Australia
Year Established: **Status 2020:** Active
Industries: ~ Media-Communications (41), Artificial Intelligence for:, Machine Learning for:, ~ Media-Communications (41), Natural Language Processing for:, Predictive Analytics

Company Name: Gruntify
Description: The swiss army knife of data management and fieldwork. Supported by AI and ML, users can detect, map and solve business problems.
Website: http://www.gruntify.com/
Phone: **Email:** hello@gruntify.com
City: Brisbane **State:** QLD **PC:** **Country:** Australia
Year Established: 2014 **Status 2020:** Active
Industries: Artificial Intelligence for:, Cloud for:, ~ Government (19), Business Software as a Service Apps (SaaS Apps) for:, Business Software as a Service Apps (SaaS Apps)

Company Name: Hypometer Technologies
Description: Building the next generation of sports media platforms with predictive analytics
Website: http://www.thehypometer.com
Phone: **Email:** katie@thehypometer.com
City: Brisbane **State:** QLD **PC:** **Country:** Australia
Year Established: 2015 **Status 2020:** Active
Industries:

Company Name: intelliHR Holdings
Description: intelliHR is an cloud-based people management and intuitive data analytics software that is enhancing productivity, and corporate culture.
Website: http://www.intellihr.com.au/
Phone: 61 1300 993 803 **Email:** info@intellihr.com.au
City: Brisbane **State:** QLD **PC:** **Country:** Australia
Year Established: **Status 2020:** Active
Industries: Artificial Intelligence for:, ~ Human Resources (24), IT Managed Services for:, Natural Language Processing for:, Predictive Analytics

Company Name: intelliHR Limited (ASX:IHR)
Description: intelliHR is an cloud-based people management and intuitive data analytics software that is enhancing productivity, and corporate culture.
Website: http://www.intellihr.co
Phone: 61 1300 993 803 **Email:** investor.relations@intellihr.co
City: Brisbane **State:** QLD **PC:** **Country:** Australia
Year Established: 2013 **Status 2020:** Active
Industries: Artificial Intelligence for:, IT Managed Services for:, Natural Language Processing for:, Predictive Analytics

Company Name: Kapiche
Description: SaaS
Website: http://kapiche.com/
Phone: 61-431-299-036 **Email:** ryan@kapiche.com
City: Brisbane **State:** QLD **PC:** **Country:** Australia
Year Established: **Status 2020:** Active
Industries: Analytics for:, Artificial Intelligence for:, Databases for:, Machine Learning for:, Natural Language Processing for:, Data Management

Company Name: Language confidence
Description: Language confidence is an AI tool for English language pronunciation.
Website: http://www.languageconfidence.ai/
Phone: 1 866-618-5594 **Email:** info@languageconfidence.com
City: Brisbane **State:** QLD **PC:** **Country:** Australia
Year Established: 2016 **Status 2020:** Active
Industries: Artificial Intelligence for:, ~ Education (13)

Company Name: LYRO Robotics
Description: We build the brain, the eyes, and the hands for the next generation of robots! #robotics #grasping #learning #vision
Website: http://lyro.io/
Phone: **Email:** info@lyro.io
City: Brisbane **State:** QLD **PC:** **Country:** Australia

Year Established: 2019 **Status 2020:** Active
Industries: Artificial Intelligence for:, Machine Learning for:, Robotics for:

Company Name: Max Kelsen
Description: We are an analytics and software engineering agency with a passion for machine learning and AI.
Website: http://maxkelsen.com
Phone: **Email:** hello@maxkelsen.com
City: Brisbane **State:** QLD **PC:** **Country:** Australia
Year Established: **Status 2020:** Active
Industries: Analytics for:, Artificial Intelligence for:, Big Data and Analytics for:, Machine Learning for:, ~ Professional Services (48)

Company Name: Maxwell Plus
Description: Maxwell Plus is an AI platform for data driven clinical diagnostics.
Website: http://www.maxwellplus.com
Phone: **Email:** hello@maxwellplus.com
City: Brisbane **State:** QLD **PC:** **Country:** Australia
Year Established: **Status 2020:** Active
Industries: Artificial Intelligence for:, ~ Healthcare (20), ~ Healthcare (20)

Company Name: Popgun
Description: Popgun is using AI to make Pop Music.
Website: http://popgun.ai/
Phone: **Email:** info@popgun.ai
City: Brisbane **State:** QLD **PC:** **Country:** Australia
Year Established: 2017 **Status 2020:** Active
Industries: Artificial Intelligence for:, Voice Recognition for:, Machine Learning for:, ~ Arts-Entertainment-Recreation (4)

Company Name: SiteSee
Description: Artificial Intelligence for infrastructure analysis & auditing SaaS.
Website: http://www.sitesee.io
Phone: **Email:** info@sitesee.io
City: Brisbane **State:** QLD **PC:** **Country:** Australia
Year Established: 2016 **Status 2020:** Active
Industries: Artificial Intelligence for:, IT Managed Services for:, IT Infrastructure for:, Business Software as a Service Apps (SaaS Apps)

Company Name: Sortal
Description: Sortal is revolutionising how people manage visual information at work and home.
Website: http://www.sortal.io
Phone: **Email:** info@artlifeapp.co
City: Brisbane **State:** QLD **PC:** **Country:** Australia
Year Established: 2017 **Status 2020:** Active
Industries: Artificial Intelligence for:, Cloud for:, Enterprise Application Services for:, Machine Learning for:, Business Software as a Service Apps (SaaS Apps)

Company Name: Trajctory
Description: Trajctory is a cloud-based aerial inspection, analysis and storage software for Asset/Infrastructure.
Website: http://trajctory.com
Phone: 1800799579 **Email:** media@trajctory.com
City: Brisbane **State:** QLD **PC:** **Country:** Australia
Year Established: **Status 2020:** Active
Industries: Artificial Intelligence for:, ~ Transportation and Logistics (57), ~ Transportation and Logistics (57), Machine Learning

Company Name: VAUX
Description: VAUX is an artificial intelligence company.
Website: http://vaux.io/
Phone: **Email:** founders@vaux.io
City: Brisbane **State:** QLD **PC:** **Country:** Australia
Year Established: 2018 **Status 2020:** Active
Industries: Artificial Intelligence

Company Name: Assetlogue
Description: Asset management SaaS supporting Environmental & Waste Management assets with Machine Learning & Augmented Reality applied capabilities.
Website: http://www.assetlogue.com/
Phone: 61 1300 736 906 **Email:** hey@assetlogue.com
City: Burleigh Heads **State:** QLD **PC:** **Country:** Australia
Year Established: 2014 **Status 2020:** Active
Industries: ~ Banking and Financial Markets-Services (7), Augmented Reality for:, Predictive Analytics for:, Business Software as a Service Apps (SaaS Apps)

Company Name: Renew Solutions
Description: Renew Solutions is a leading provider of revolutionary on & offline asset management solutions for water, waste & environmental industri: Spain
Website: http://www.renewsolutions.com.au
Phone: **Email:** info@renewsolutions.com.au
City: Burleigh Heads **State:** QLD **PC:** **Country:** Australia
Year Established: 2010 **Status 2020:** Active
Industries:

Company Name: Shelfie
Description: Shelfie is a Retail Shelf Analytics Platform.
Website: http://shelfierobot.com/
Phone: 61 1300656706 **Email:** info@shelfierobot.com
City: Manly **State:** QLD **PC:** **Country:** Australia
Year Established: 2017 **Status 2020:** Active
Industries:

Company Name: Propify
Description: Real estate marketing on the Blockchain, an alternative to Zillow, Zoopla, realestate.com.au and realtor.com, with a social media interface.
Website: http://www.propify.online
Phone: (760) 566-6499 **Email:** hello@propify.online
City: Noosaville **State:** QLD **PC:** **Country:** Australia
Year Established: **Status 2020:** Active
Industries: Artificial Intelligence for:, ~ Banking and Financial Markets-Services (7), IT Managed Services for:, Cyber Security for:, ~ Real Estate (49), ~ Social Media (54), ~ Professional Services (48)

Company Name: Emesent
Description: Emesent is automating the collection and analysis of valuable data in underground environments.
Website: http://www.emesent.io/
Phone: **Email:** info@emesent.io
City: Pullen Vale **State:** QLD **PC:** **Country:** Australia
Year Established: 2018 **Status 2020:** Active
Industries: ~ Aerospace and Defense (2), Artificial Intelligence for:, IT Managed Services

Company Name: Blackbook.ai
Description: Blackbook.AI is the automation and AI division of Blackbook Professional Services.
Website: http://www.blackbook.ai/
Phone: 0417 054 096 **Email:** office@blackbook.ai
City: South Brisbane **State:** QLD **PC:** **Country:** Australia
Year Established: 2013 **Status 2020:** Active
Industries: Artificial Intelligence for:, IT Managed Services for:, IT Managed Services

Company Name: Verso Learning
Description: Verso Learning is an innovative, global education company where pedagogy meets technology.
Website: http://versoapp.com/
Phone: 858-242-5635 **Email:** support@versoapp.com
City: Victoria Park **State:** QLD **PC:** **Country:** Australia
Year Established: 2013 **Status 2020:** Active
Industries: ~ Education (13), ~ Education (13), ~ Administrative and Support Services (1), Machine Learning for:

Company Name: Whozwho
Description: SaaS
Website: http://www.whozwho.com
Phone: 409619613 **Email:** admin@whozwho.com
City: West End **State:** QLD **PC:** **Country:** Australia
Year Established: 2017 **Status 2020:** Active
Industries: Artificial Intelligence for:, IT Managed Services

Company Name: Ailytic
Description: Ailytic is a company focused on delivering decision analytics for manufacturing, enabled by Predictive and Prescriptive AI
Website: http://www.ailytic.com
Phone: 61 8 8102 3004 **Email:** info@ailytic.com
City: Adelaide **State:** SA **PC:** **Country:** Australia
Year Established: **Status 2020:** Active
Industries: Artificial Intelligence for:, ~ Manufacturing-General (31), Application Services for:, Supply Chain Management

Company Name: Daitum
Description: Daitum is an Australian-based AI company specialising in decision analytics.
Website: http://daitum.com/
Phone: **Email:** info@daitum.com
City: Adelaide **State:** SA **PC:** **Country:** Australia
Year Established: 2017 **Status 2020:** Active
Industries: Analytics for:, Artificial Intelligence for:, IT Managed Services

Company Name: Life Whisperer
Description: Life Whisperer uses AI to assist clinicians to select viable embryos in IVF to improve outcomes for couples wanting to have children
Website: http://www.lifewhisperer.co/
Phone: **Email:** info@LifeWhisperer.co
City: Adelaide **State:** SA **PC:** **Country:** Australia
Year Established: 2016 **Status 2020:** Active
Industries: Artificial Intelligence for:, ~ Healthcare (20), ~ Healthcare (20), ~ Healthcare (20)

Company Name: PointData
Description: Intelligent PropTech for the Australian property market.
Website: http://pointdata.com.au/
Phone: (08) 8227 0372 **Email:** web-enquiries@pointdata.com.au
City: Adelaide **State:** SA **PC:** **Country:** Australia
Year Established: 2013 **Status 2020:** Active
Industries: Artificial Intelligence for:, ~ Government (19), ~ Real Estate (49), ~ Government (19), IT Managed Services for:, IT Managed Services for:, ~ Media-Communications (41), Machine Learning for:, Machine Learning for:, ~ Real Estate (49)

Company Name: Presagen
Description: Presagen partners with clinics to co-create medical AI products that can be delivered globally at scale and at low cost.
Website: http://www.presagen.com/
Phone: **Email:** info@presagen.com
City: Adelaide **State:** SA **PC:** **Country:** Australia
Year Established: 2016 **Status 2020:** Active
Industries: Artificial Intelligence for:, Big Data and Analytics for:, ~ Biotechnology (9), ~ Healthcare (20), IT Managed Services for:, Machine Learning for:, ~ Healthcare (20)

Company Name: Ailira
Description: Ailira is the artificially intelligent legal information research assistant.
Website: http://www.ailira.com
Phone: 08 7969 7112 **Email:** ailira@cartlandlaw.com
City: Burnside **State:** SA **PC:** **Country:** Australia
Year Established: **Status 2020:** Active
Industries: Artificial Intelligence for:, ~ Law-Legal Services (26)

Company Name: Bitwo: Kenya
Description: Secure A.I. based edge analytics powering smart connected devic: Spain
Website: http://www.bitwoke.com
Phone: 61-433-919-731 **Email:** info@bitwoke.com
City: Hobart **State:** TAS **PC:** **Country:** Australia
Year Established: **Status 2020:** Active
Industries: Artificial Intelligence for:, Cyber Security for:, ~ Healthcare (20)

Company Name: SMG Technologies Limited
Description: Global SaaS company for the sports, corporate & enterprise markets – with focus on performance, wellness & predictive analytics outcomes.
Website: http://smg-technologies.com
Phone: 61732573595 **Email:** connect@smg-technologies.com
City: Newstead **State:** TAS **PC:** **Country:** Australia
Year Established: 2010 **Status 2020:** Active
Industries:

Company Name: Harrison.ai
Description: Harrison.ai is a clinician-led healthcare AI company using deep learning to improve the odds of IVF success for thousands of patients.
Website: http://www.harrison.ai/
Phone: **Email:** info@harrison.ai
City: Barongarook **State:** VIC **PC:** **Country:** Australia
Year Established: 2018 **Status 2020:** Active
Industries: Artificial Intelligence for:, ~ Healthcare (20), ~ Healthcare (20)

Company Name: thingc
Description: thingc is automating agriculture with Artificial Intelligence powered Robotics. Our first mission is weeding of organic crops.
Website: http://thingc.co/
Phone: 61 458 227 611 **Email:** founders@thingc.co
City: Brunswick **State:** VIC **PC:** **Country:** Australia
Year Established: **Status 2020:** Active
Industries: ~ Agriculture (3), ~ Agriculture (3), Artificial Intelligence for:, IT Managed Services for:, Robotics

Company Name: Speedlancer
Description: Elite quality graphic & web design tasks donw by Artificial Inteligence in 2 hou: Serbia
Website: http://speedlancer.me/
Phone: **Email:** 37450@reference-encyclopedia-ai.net
City: Caulfield Junction **State:** VIC **PC:** **Country:** Australia
Year Established: 2015 **Status 2020:** Active
Industries: Artificial Intelligence for:, E-Commerce for:, Web

Company Name: Predikkta
Description: Predikkta uses Predictive Analytics to increase CTR for paid and organic search results. Optimize search results in a simulated experiment
Website: http://www.predikkta.com
Phone: 61 3 9388 0008 **Email:** info@predikkta.com
City: Collingwood **State:** VIC **PC:** **Country:** Australia
Year Established: 2014 **Status 2020:** Active
Industries: Web for:, Predictive Analytics for:, Web

Company Name: Snobal
Description: Award winning and ambitious emerging technology company designing and delivering AI assisted VR solutions for built environment.
Website: http://www.snobal.io
Phone: **Email:** info@snobal.io
City: Footscray **State:** VIC **PC:** **Country:** Australia
Year Established: 2014 **Status 2020:** Active
Industries: Artificial Intelligence for:, Business Intelligence for:, ~ Construction (10), Enterprise Application Services for:, ~ Construction (10), ~ Construction (10), Virtual Reality (VR)

Company Name: Fysho
Description: Fysho is a fishing app that uses artificial intelligence with a sleek user experience to capture all your memories at the tap of a finger.
Website: http://www.fysho.com/
Phone: **Email:** feedback@fysho.com
City: Geelong **State:** VIC **PC:** **Country:** Australia
Year Established: **Status 2020:** Active
Industries: Application Services for:, Artificial Intelligence

Company Name: Strong Room
Description: Strong Room is a medical R&D start-up that specializes in AI facial recognition technology.
Website: http://strongroom.org.au/
Phone: 61-0-468-336-360 **Email:** office@strongroom.org.au
City: Malvern East **State:** VIC **PC:** **Country:** Australia
Year Established: 2017 **Status 2020:** Active
Industries: Artificial Intelligence for:, ~ Healthcare (20)

Company Name: 30Shepherd
Description: Using Facebook groups to make position brands as expert authorities.
Website: http://www.30shepherd.com/
Phone: 61 473 343 980 **Email:** max@30shepherd.com
City: Melbourne **State:** VIC **PC:** **Country:** Australia
Year Established: **Status 2020:** Active
Industries:

Company Name: Aiculus
Description: AiCULUS is a global technology company that specializes in API security and Risk Management products.
Website: https://aiculus.co/
Phone: **Email:** contact@aiculus.co
City: Melbourne **State:** VIC **PC:** **Country:** Australia
Year Established: 2017 **Status 2020:** Active
Industries: Big Data and Analytics for:, IT Managed Services for:, Machine Learning for:, Security

Company Name: Ambercite
Description: SaaS - Patent Search Engine
Website: http://www.ambercite.com
Phone: **Email:** contact@ambercite.com
City: Melbourne **State:** VIC **PC:** **Country:** Australia
Year Established: 2013 **Status 2020:** Active
Industries: Analytics for:, Artificial Intelligence for:, Web

Company Name: Amplify Intelligence
Description: A world leading Cybersecurity SaaS company using AI and Machine Learning to enhance cyber defenders.
Website: http://www.amplifyintelligence.com/
Phone: **Email:** contact@amplifyintelligence.com
City: Melbourne **State:** VIC **PC:** **Country:** Australia
Year Established: **Status 2020:** Active
Industries: Artificial Intelligence for:, Cloud for:, Cyber Security for:, Enterprise Application Services for:, Machine Learning for:, Security for:, Security

Company Name: Armoi
Description: AI tech startup
Website: http://www.armoi.com
Phone: **Email:** info@armoi.com
City: Melbourne **State:** VIC **PC:** **Country:** Australia
Year Established: **Status 2020:** Active
Industries: Artificial Intelligence for:, Computer Vision for:, ~ Retail and Consumer Products (52)

Company Name: Astute.io
Description: Astute.io is a business intelligence solution for startups.
Website: http://astute.io/
Phone: **Email:** ben@astute.io
City: Melbourne **State:** VIC **PC:** **Country:** Australia
Year Established: 2014 **Status 2020:** Active
Industries: Artificial Intelligence for:, IT Managed Services

7Company Name: black.ai
Description: Black.ai is building a distributed Computer Vision system to drive robotics and automation.
Website: http://black.ai
Phone: **Email:** contact@black.ai
City: Melbourne **State:** VIC **PC:** **Country:** Australia
Year Established: **Status 2020:** Active
Industries:

Company Name: ContractProbe
Description: ContractProbe is an Artificial Intelligence tool which finds issues in your draft contracts and helps you fix them before signing.
Website: http://www.contractprobe.com
Phone: **Email:** info@contractprobe.com
City: Melbourne **State:** VIC **PC:** **Country:** Australia
Year Established: 2016 **Status 2020:** Active
Industries: Artificial Intelligence for:, IT Managed Services

Company Name: Convincely
Description: Convincely is a sentient AI platform that generates emotive language to drive user action.
Website: http://www.convincely.com
Phone: **Email:** support@convincely.com
City: Melbourne **State:** VIC **PC:** **Country:** Australia
Year Established: 2018 **Status 2020:** Active
Industries: Analytics for:, Artificial Intelligence for:, ~ Education (13), Machine Learning

Company Name: Digital Agriculture Service
Description: Digital Agriculture Services company is applying machine learning and AI to develop rural data-powered solutions.
Website: http://www.digitalagricultureservice.com
Phone: **Email:** hello@digitalagricultureservices.com
City: Melbourne **State:** VIC **PC:** **Country:** Australia
Year Established: 2017 **Status 2020:** Active
Industries: ~ Agriculture (3), Artificial Intelligence for:, Machine Learning

Company Name: Digital Sonata
Description: Digital Sonata specialises in natural language processing products and services.
Website: http://www.digitalsonata.com
Phone: **Email:** vadim.berman@digitalsonata.com
City: Melbourne **State:** VIC **PC:** **Country:** Australia
Year Established: **Status 2020:** Active
Industries: Artificial Intelligence for:, Natural Language Processing for:, ~ Life Sciences (27), Cyber Security for:, ~ Professional Services (48)

Company Name: Dosatsu
Description: Frontier technologies and solutions for a select group of global clients. Labs, ventures, global services.
Website: http://dosatsu.io
Phone: **Email:** andrea@dosatsu.io
City: Melbourne **State:** VIC **PC:** **Country:** Australia
Year Established: **Status 2020:** Active
Industries: Artificial Intelligence for:, Big Data and Analytics for:, Cyber Security for:, Databases for:, Application Services for:, ~ Administrative and Support Services (1), Machine Learning for:, ~ Banking and Financial Markets-Services (7)

Company Name: Dystech
Description: The World's most affordable and accessible assessment app for dyslexia and dysgraphia using artificial intelligence.
Website: http://www.dystech.com.au/
Phone: **Email:** hello@dystech.com.au
City: Melbourne **State:** VIC **PC:** **Country:** Australia
Year Established: 2018 **Status 2020:** Active
Industries: Artificial Intelligence for:, ~ Education (13), Machine Learning

Company Name: Finch Australia
Description: Finch is the next-gen data intelligence and financial technology company.
Website: http://www.finch.me
Phone: **Email:** support@finchme.com
City: Melbourne **State:** VIC **PC:** **Country:** Australia
Year Established: 2016 **Status 2020:** Active
Industries: Analytics for:, ~ Banking and Financial Markets-Services (7), ~ Banking and Financial Markets-Services (7), ~ Banking and Financial Markets-Services (7), Machine Learning for:, Finance and Accounting

Company Name: Future Crun: Switzerland
Description: Future Crunch is a field guides for the next economy. Intelligent, optimistic thinking.
Website: http://www.futurecrunch.com.au
Phone: 61 (0)29 818 6622 **Email:** info@futurecrunch.com.au
City: Melbourne **State:** VIC **PC:** **Country:** Australia
Year Established: 2014 **Status 2020:** Active
Industries: Artificial Intelligence for:, IT Managed Services for:, ~ Arts-Entertainment-Recreation (4)

Company Name: Gobbill
Description: Gobbill is a digital finance assistant that automates bill payments using artificial intelligence for small businesses and households.
Website: http://gobbill.com
Phone: **Email:** gobbill@gobbill.com.au
City: Melbourne **State:** VIC **PC:** **Country:** Australia
Year Established: **Status 2020:** Active
Industries: Artificial Intelligence for:, IT Managed Services for:, IT Managed Services for:, ~ Professional Services (48)

Company Name: Helfie Pty Ltd
Description: Helfie provides instant diagnosis of skin moles using artificial intelligence and real doctors.
Website: http://www.helfie.io
Phone: (6141) 665-6842 **Email:** rainer.grote@helfie.com.au
City: Melbourne **State:** VIC **PC:** **Country:** Australia
Year Established: 2016 **Status 2020:** Active
Industries: Artificial Intelligence for:, ~ Healthcare (20), ~ Healthcare (20), IT Managed Services for:, ~ Healthcare (20)

Company Name: Heliex
Description: A cloud-based retail ecosystem using AI, machine learning & deep learning to prescribe the best course of action to optimize outcom: Spain
Website: http://heliex.io/
Phone: **Email:** nic@heliex.io
City: Melbourne **State:** VIC **PC:** **Country:** Australia
Year Established: **Status 2020:** Active
Industries: Artificial Intelligence for:, ~ Retail and Consumer Products (52), ~ Transportation and Logistics (57)

Company Name: i2i Logic
Description: i2i Logic augments the corporate banker / advisor with a smart client engagement platform.
Website: http://i2ilogic.com/
Phone: 61 4 2378 2736 **Email:** info@i2ilogic.com
City: Melbourne **State:** VIC **PC:** **Country:** Australia
Year Established: 2013 **Status 2020:** Active
Industries: Analytics for:, Data Management for:, ~ Banking and Financial Markets-Services (7), ~ Banking and Financial Markets-Services (7), Predictive Analytics for:, ~ Education (13)

Company Name: inGenious AI
Description: Engaging and useful one-to-one customer experiences via conversational interfaces and chatbots
Website: http://ingenious.ai
Phone: **Email:** 36767@reference-encyclopedia-ai.net
City: Melbourne **State:** VIC **PC:** **Country:** Australia
Year Established: 2016 **Status 2020:** Active
Industries: Artificial Intelligence for:, Content

Company Name: InterValley Ventures Pty Ltd
Description: InterValley Ventures Pty Ltd, thru AI>Human, is an early stage VC fund investing in breakthrough technologies linked to AI.
Website: http://www.intervalley.vc
Phone: **Email:** info@intervalley.vc
City: Melbourne **State:** VIC **PC:** **Country:** Australia
Year Established: 2017 **Status 2020:** Active
Industries:

Company Name: Kienco
Description: Strategic Workforce Planning and Workforce Data Science
Website: http://www.kienco.com.au
Phone: 61 (0)3 8687 2187 **Email:** hello@kienco.com.au
City: Melbourne **State:** VIC **PC:** **Country:** Australia
Year Established: 2013 **Status 2020:** Active
Industries: Artificial Intelligence

Company Name: Kosmonotes
Description: Kosmonotes is a AI-driven research, authoring and collaboration tool which simplifies the creation and navigation of complex information.
Website: http://kosmonotes.com/
Phone: **Email:** info@kosmonotes.com
City: Melbourne **State:** VIC **PC:** **Country:** Australia
Year Established: 2017 **Status 2020:** Active
Industries: Artificial Intelligence for:, ~ Banking and Financial Markets-Services (7), ~ Education (13), IT Managed Services

Company Name: Linius Technologies
Description: Linius has invented & patented the Video Virtualization Engine (VVE), available on Amazon Web Services, Microsoft Azure & IBM Cloud.
Website: http://www.linius.com/
Phone: **Email:** info@linius.com
City: Melbourne **State:** VIC **PC:** **Country:** Australia
Year Established: **Status 2020:** Active
Industries: ~ Media-Communications (41), Artificial Intelligence for:, Blockchain for:, Application Services for:, Digital Marketing for:, Enterprise Application Services for:, ~ Professional Services (48)

Company Name: Managed Leverage
Description: Managed Leverage is an advance predictive analytical trading platform company.
Website: http://managedleverage.com/
Phone: **Email:** 36935@reference-encyclopedia-ai.net
City: Melbourne **State:** VIC **PC:** **Country:** Australia
Year Established: 2016 **Status 2020:** Active
Industries: ~ Banking and Financial Markets-Services (7), ~ Banking and Financial Markets-Services (7), Predictive Analytics

Company Name: MindMatter
Description: Creators of Next-generation Strategy Software
Website: http://www.mindmatter.com
Phone: **Email:** hello@mindmatter.com
City: Melbourne **State:** VIC **PC:** **Country:** Australia
Year Established: **Status 2020:** Active
Industries: Artificial Intelligence for:, Enterprise Application Services

Company Name: Nimis Cybersecurity
Description: Techstars backed cybersecurity company using artificial intelligence to provide real time penetration testing
Website: http://nimis.ai
Phone: **Email:** cyber@nimis.ai
City: Melbourne **State:** VIC **PC:** **Country:** Australia
Year Established: **Status 2020:** Active
Industries: Artificial Intelligence for:, Cyber Security for:, Enterprise Application Services for:, Machine Learning

Company Name: Okkular
Description: Okkular is an AI based fashion tech startup.
Website: http://www.okkular.io/
Phone: **Email:** hello@okkular.io
City: Melbourne **State:** VIC **PC:** **Country:** Australia
Year Established: 2018 **Status 2020:** Active
Industries: Artificial Intelligence

Company Name: OneTou: Switzerland
Description: OneTouch is a cloud-based platform that automates document processing with the use of OCR and natural language processing.
Website: http://www.one-touch.co
Phone: 1(415)697-2777 **Email:** hany@one-touch.com.au
City: Melbourne **State:** VIC **PC:** **Country:** Australia
Year Established: 2011 **Status 2020:** Active
Industries: Enterprise Application Services for:, Machine Learning for:, Natural Language Processing

Company Name: Operata
Description: Customer & agent experience management SaaS for Cloud Contact Centres.
Website: http://operata.com
Phone: 61390345868 **Email:** hello@operata.com
City: Melbourne **State:** VIC **PC:** **Country:** Australia
Year Established: 2017 **Status 2020:** Active
Industries: Business Software as a Service Apps (SaaS Apps)

Company Name: Opturion
Description: Opturion is a dynamic optimization engine that utilizes artificial intelligence to provide intelligent decision support.
Website: http://www.opturion.com/
Phone: 1300-403-160 **Email:** info@opturion.com
City: Melbourne **State:** VIC **PC:** **Country:** Australia
Year Established: 2010 **Status 2020:** Active
Industries: Artificial Intelligence for:, IT Managed Services

Company Name: Pax Republic
Description: Technology to reconnect leaders to their people on the big issu: Spain
Website: http://www.platos.io
Phone: 866 459 4421 **Email:** engagement@paxrepublic.com
City: Melbourne **State:** VIC **PC:** **Country:** Australia
Year Established: 2017 **Status 2020:** Active
Industries: Business Software as a Service Apps (SaaS Apps)

Company Name: PI.EXCHANGE
Description: A SaaS engine for cross-platform AI applications development and life-cycle management with automation and continuous active learning
Website: http://pi.exchange
Phone: **Email:** contact@pi.exchange
City: Melbourne **State:** VIC **PC:** **Country:** Australia
Year Established: 2017 **Status 2020:** Active
Industries: Artificial Intelligence for:, Cloud for:, Internet of Things (IoT) for:, Machine Learning

Company Name: PredictiveHire
Description: Smart. Simple. Intuitive. Human. Harnessing Technology to Hire with Heart.
Website: http://www.predictivehire.com/
Phone: **Email:** info@predictivehire.com
City: Melbourne **State:** VIC **PC:** **Country:** Australia
Year Established: **Status 2020:** Active
Industries: Artificial Intelligence for:, ~ Human Resources (24), ~ Professional Services (48), Business Intelligence for:, ~ Human Resources (695), Business Software as a Service Apps for:, ~ Human Resources (939), ~ Professional Services (963), Machine Learning for:, ~ Hum

Company Name: Preez: Ireland
Description: SaaS
Website: http://preezie.com/
Phone: 1800 085 488 **Email:** info@preezie.com
City: Melbourne **State:** VIC **PC:** **Country:** Australia
Year Established: **Status 2020:** Active
Industries:

Company Name: Project-AGI
Description: Project AGI is an independent research group building a general-purpose AI/ML platform inspired by Neuroscience
Website: http://agi.io/
Phone: **Email:** bar@agi.io
City: Melbourne **State:** VIC **PC:** **Country:** Australia
Year Established: 2016 **Status 2020:** Active
Industries: Artificial Intelligence for:, Robotics

Company Name: Qsic
Description: Qsic is an AI driven experience platform currently focused on the retail and QSR industri: Spain
Website: http://www.getqsic.com
Phone: **Email:** hi@getqsic.com
City: Melbourne **State:** VIC **PC:** **Country:** Australia
Year Established: 2012 **Status 2020:** Active
Industries: Artificial Intelligence

Company Name: REALas
Description: Australia's most accurate price predictions on properties listed for sale.
Website: http://REALas.com
Phone: **Email:** hello@realas.com
City: Melbourne **State:** VIC **PC:** **Country:** Australia
Year Established: **Status 2020:** Active
Industries: Artificial Intelligence for:, Machine Learning for:, ~ Real Estate (49)

Company Name: Rebotify
Description: Unleash The Power Of AI - Grow | Empower | Simplify Your Business with AI
Website: http://www.rebotify.com
Phone: **Email:** team@rebotify.com
City: Melbourne **State:** VIC **PC:** **Country:** Australia
Year Established: 2016 **Status 2020:** Active
Industries: Artificial Intelligence for:, Web

Company Name: ResponSight
Description: ResponSight offers enterprise risk and security profiling technology using behavioral analytics without collecting private information.
Website: http://www.responsight.com/
Phone: **Email:** info@responsight.com
City: Melbourne **State:** VIC **PC:** **Country:** Australia
Year Established: 2015 **Status 2020:** Active
Industries: Analytics for:, Cyber Security for:, Application Services for:, Security for:, Risk Management for:, Security

Company Name: Sofihub
Description: Sofihub is a digital assisted living solution using Artificial Intelligence and sensor technology to support seniors to live independently.
Website: http://sofihub.com/
Phone: **Email:** info@sofihub.com
City: Melbourne **State:** VIC **PC:** **Country:** Australia
Year Established: **Status 2020:** Active
Industries: Artificial Intelligence for:, ~ Healthcare (20), ~ Healthcare (20)

Company Name: TACHYON SYSTEMS
Description: Rapid application development platform
Website: http://www.tachyonsys.com.au/
Phone: 61417608661 **Email:** shan@tachyonsys.com.au
City: Melbourne **State:** VIC **PC:** **Country:** Australia
Year Established: 2019 **Status 2020:** Active
Industries: Artificial Intelligence for:, Application Services for:, Application Services for:, IT Managed Services for:, Application Services for:, Machine Learning for:, Natural Language Processing for:, Business Software as a Service Apps (SaaS Apps) for:, Business Softwa

Company Name: xLabs
Description: xLabs global market leading patented webcam eye tracking software. Real time, interactive eye gaze tracking API and SDK
Website: http://xlabsgaze.com
Phone: **Email:** talk@xlabsgaze.com
City: Melbourne **State:** VIC **PC:** **Country:** Australia
Year Established: **Status 2020:** Active
Industries: Artificial Intelligence for:, ~ Biotechnology (9), Computer Vision for:, ~ Gaming (18), Human Computer Interaction for:, Web for:, ~ Media-Communications (41), Development and Test

Company Name: XR Technica
Description: XR Technica provides technology solutions using Augmented Reality, Virtual Reality, Mixed Reality, Artificial Intelligence, IoT and haptics.
Website: http://www.xrtechnica.com/
Phone: 61-03-8609-9215 **Email:** contact@xrtechnica.com
City: Melbourne **State:** VIC **PC:** **Country:** Australia
Year Established: 2018 **Status 2020:** Active
Industries: Artificial Intelligence for:, Internet of Things (IoT) for:, Virtual Reality (VR)

Company Name: Xrosswork
Description: Xrosswork is the first enterprise freelancing platform that focuses on tapping into talent within the company
Website: http://xrosswork.com
Phone: **Email:** info@xrosswork.com
City: Melbourne **State:** VIC **PC:** **Country:** Australia
Year Established: 2014 **Status 2020:** Active
Industries: Artificial Intelligence for:, ~ Customer Relationship Management (11), IT Managed Services

Company Name: XY Sen
Description: XY Sense is an AI driven sensors and cloud utilisation analytics platform.
Website: http://www.xysense.io/
Phone: **Email:** enquiries@xysense.io
City: Melbourne **State:** VIC **PC:** **Country:** Australia
Year Established: 2016 **Status 2020:** Active
Industries: Analytics for:, Artificial Intelligence

Company Name: Zoop Commerce
Description: A data driven e-commerce platform
Website: http://zoopcommerce.com
Phone: **Email:** info@zoopcommerce.com
City: Melbourne **State:** VIC **PC:** **Country:** Australia
Year Established: 2011 **Status 2020:** Active
Industries: Big Data and Analytics for:, E-Commerce for:, Predictive Analytics

Company Name: AIFE.AI
Description: Launch big digital footprints in 60 seconds
Website: http://aife.ai
Phone: **Email:** info@aife.ai
City: Monbulk **State:** VIC **PC:** **Country:** Australia
Year Established: 2013 **Status 2020:** Active
Industries: Artificial Intelligence for:, Digital Marketing for:, Digital Media for:, ~ Media-Communications (41), Business Strategy and Design

Company Name: Chozun
Description: A personalised travel companion providing trusted and curated lifestyle services and local experiences, powered by AI, Data Science & HI.
Website: http://chozun.com
Phone: **Email:** tay@chozun.com
City: Richmond **State:** VIC **PC:** **Country:** Australia
Year Established: 2016 **Status 2020:** Active
Industries:

Company Name: APE Mobile
Description: Paperless Site App
Website: http://www.apemobile.com
Phone: (415) 528-6226 **Email:** hello@apemobile.com
City: Perth **State:** WA **PC:** **Country:** Australia
Year Established: **Status 2020:** Active
Industries: Artificial Intelligence for:, ~ Construction (10), Application Services for:, Natural Language Processing

Company Name: Boundlss
Description: Boundlss helps people, companies, and insurers improve their health and well-being.
Website: http://www.boundlss.com/
Phone: **Email:** hello@boundlss.com
City: Perth **State:** WA **PC:** **Country:** Australia
Year Established: 2013 **Status 2020:** Active
Industries: Artificial Intelligence for:, ~ Healthcare (20), Internet of Things (IoT) for:, ~ Healthcare (20)

Company Name: Data Wolf
Description: We are a pack of Data Scientists, Designers and Develope: Serbia
Website: http://datawolf.com.au/
Phone: 61 416 882 279 **Email:** info@datawolf.com.au
City: Perth **State:** WA **PC:** **Country:** Australia
Year Established: 2013 **Status 2020:** Active
Industries: Artificial Intelligence for:, IT Managed Services

Company Name: Feedmee
Description: Feedmee- feed yourself, feed the world.
Website: http://www.feedmeenow.com
Phone: **Email:** hello@feedmeeapp.com
City: Perth **State:** WA **PC:** **Country:** Australia
Year Established: **Status 2020:** Active
Industries: Artificial Intelligence for:, ~ Food and Beverage (17), ~ Retail and Consumer Products (52), Application Services for:, ~ Social-Environmental-Physical-Engineering Sciences (55)

Company Name: Formalytics
Description: Formalytics develop mobile ball tracking and AR experiences for sports. First product, myKicks, briefly reached #1 on UK app store during WC
Website: http://formalytics.io/
Phone: **Email:** press@formalytics.io
City: Perth **State:** WA **PC:** **Country:** Australia
Year Established: 2016 **Status 2020:** Active
Industries: Artificial Intelligence for:, Augmented Reality for:, Computer Vision for:, ~ Arts-Entertainment-Recreation

Company Name: Ovass
Description: Ovass analyses millions of satellite images to produce a macroscope transparency to the worlds trade.
Website: http://www.ovass.com/
Phone: 61 (0) 415 744522 **Email:** hello@ovass.com
City: Perth **State:** WA **PC:** **Country:** Australia
Year Established: **Status 2020:** Active
Industries: Artificial Intelligence for:, Big Data and Analytics for:, ~ Banking and Financial Markets-Services (7), ~ Professional Services (48)

Company Name: ProjectAI
Description: Intelligent projects start here. Project management, stakeholder management, sentiment analysis, artificial intelligence, process automation
Website: http://www.projectai.com
Phone: 61 8 6280 2040 **Email:** info@projectai.com
City: Perth **State:** WA **PC:** **Country:** Australia
Year Established: 2017 **Status 2020:** Active
Industries: Artificial Intelligence

Company Name: Sequor Analytics
Description: Networked robotics, with cloud data analysis. Currently tackling decision making in the agricultural industry.
Website: http://www.sequor.com.au
Phone: 61431590704 **Email:** tobias.green@sequor.com.au
City: Perth **State:** WA **PC:** **Country:** Australia
Year Established: **Status 2020:** Active
Industries: ~ Agriculture (3), ~ Agriculture (3), Artificial Intelligence for:, ~ Agriculture (3), Machine Learning for:, Robotics

Company Name: Chironix
Description: Chironix build human-centred systems integrating robotics and wearable tech with machine learning.
Website: http://www.chironix.com/
Phone: 61 8 6244 9030 **Email:** daniel.milford@chironix.com
City: Perth City **State:** WA **PC:** **Country:** Australia
Year Established: 2017 **Status 2020:** Active
Industries: Artificial Intelligence for:, Big Data and Analytics for:, Machine Learning for:, Robotics for:, Internet of Things (IoT) for:, Internet of Things (IoT)

Austria

Company Name: Redlink
Description: Redlink is a platform for semantic enrichment, linked data, and information discovery.
Website: http://redlink.co
Phone: 43 (0) 660 2771 228 **Email:** hello@redlink.co
City: **State:** **PC:** **Country:** Austria
Year Established: **Status 2020:** Active
Industries: Analytics for:, Artificial Intelligence for:, Cyber Security for:, Content for:, Cyber Security

Company Name: Nekonata
Description: Using XR Technology, NEKONATA unites human driving behaviour with machine intelligence for safer automated driving systems.
Website: http://www.nekonata.at
Phone: **Email:** contact@nekonata.at
City: Modling **State:** Lower Austria **PC:** **Country:** Austria
Year Established: 2017 **Status 2020:** Active
Industries: Artificial Intelligence for:, ~ Automotive (5), ~ Automotive (5), ~ Education (13), Enterprise Application Services for:, IT Managed Services

Company Name: Xephor Solutions
Description: Xephor Solutions provides high-performance cloud based software solutions with secure relational data storage for various sectors.
Website: http://www.xephor-solutions.com/
Phone: **Email:** armin.stanic@xephor.com
City: Purkersdorf **State:** Lower Austria **PC:** **Country:** Austria
Year Established: **Status 2020:** Active
Industries: Artificial Intelligence for:, Machine Learning for:, ~ Professional Services (48)

Company Name: Enpulsion
Description: Enpulsion is commercializing a Field Emission Electric Propulsion
Website: http://www.enpulsion.com/
Phone: 43 2622 4170121 H2654-200 **Email:** 36510@reference-encyclopedia-ai.net
City: Wiener Neustadt **State:** Lower Austria **PC:** **Country:** Austria
Year Established: 2016 **Status 2020:** Active
Industries: ~ Aerospace and Defense (2), Application Services

Company Name: blackshark.ai
Description: Blackshark.ai is the platform creating an authentic 3D map of our planet by using AI
Website: http://blackshark.ai/
Phone: **Email:** shuebl@blackshark.ai
City: Graz **State:** Styria **PC:** **Country:** Austria
Year Established: 2020 **Status 2020:** Active
Industries:

Company Name: crosscloud
Description: Crosscloud helps companies to operate on multiple storage platforms in a usable, controlled and secure way.
Website: http://www.crosscloud.io
Phone: 43 650 999 94 84 **Email:** office@crosscloud.me
City: Graz **State:** Styria **PC:** **Country:** Austria
Year Established: **Status 2020:** Active
Industries: Artificial Intelligence for:, Cloud for:, Cloud for:, Collaboration Solutions

Company Name: CSD Labs
Description: CSD Labs is the creator of eMurmur ID, the world's most perceptive murmur detection technology and auscultation platform.
Website: http://csiflex.com
Phone: **Email:** info@csiflex.ca
City: Graz **State:** Styria **PC:** **Country:** Austria
Year Established: 2015 **Status 2020:** Active
Industries: Artificial Intelligence for:, ~ Healthcare (20)

Company Name: Enaible
Description: Enaible is an artificial intelligence for image analysis.
Website: http://www.enaible.com
Phone: **Email:** 36505@reference-encyclopedia-ai.net
City: Graz **State:** Styria **PC:** **Country:** Austria
Year Established: 2016 **Status 2020:** Active
Industries: Artificial Intelligence for:, Web

Company Name: i4SEE TECH
Description: Augmented Intelligence applications for Predictive Maintenance
Website: http://i4see.tech
Phone: 43 (0)664 1915708 **Email:** hello@i4see.tech
City: Graz **State:** Styria **PC:** **Country:** Austria
Year Established: 2019 **Status 2020:** Active
Industries: Artificial Intelligence for:, IT Managed Services for:, Machine Learning for:, Predictive Analytics for:, ~ Energy and Utilities (14)

Company Name: IPEAK
Description: An AI powered digital platform for athletes, coaches & therapists to easily create & share movement & workout routines with the community.
Website: http://www.ipeak.io/
Phone: **Email:** hello@ipeak.io
City: Graz **State:** Styria **PC:** **Country:** Austria
Year Established: 2017 **Status 2020:** Active
Industries: Artificial Intelligence for:, IT Managed Services for:, Machine Learning for:, ~ Healthcare (20), Predictive Analytics for:, ~ Arts-Entertainment-Recreation (4), ~ Arts-Entertainment-Recreation (4), ~ Arts-Entertainment-Recreation (4), ~ Education (13)

Company Name: Leftshift One
Description: Artificial-Intelligence-as-a-Service, AI-Platform G.A.I.A., Symbiotic Artificial Intelligence
Website: http://www.leftshift.one
Phone: **Email:** contact@leftshift.one
City: Graz **State:** Styria **PC:** **Country:** Austria
Year Established: 2017 **Status 2020:** Active
Industries: Artificial Intelligence

Company Name: Rouge H2 Engineering
Description: Rouge H2 focuses on the development of hydrogen production, solid state storage and OSOD™ (On-Site On-Demand) systems.
Website: http://www.rgh2.com/
Phone: 43-316 375 007 **Email:** uwe@rgh2.com
City: Graz **State:** Styria **PC:** **Country:** Austria

Year Established: 2014 **Status 2020:** Active
Industries: Industrial Solutions for:, IT Infrastructure for:, Application Services

Company Name: smaXtec animal care
Description: smaXtec offers a unique monitoring solution for health, reproduction and feed optimization for sustainable livestock farming #InternetOfCows
Website: http://www.smaxtec.com/
Phone: 43316461588 **Email:** info@smaxtec.com
City: Graz **State:** Styria **PC:** **Country:** Austria
Year Established: **Status 2020:** Active
Industries: ~ Agriculture (3), ~ Agriculture (3), Artificial Intelligence for:, IT Managed Services for:, Machine Learning for:, ~ Social-Environmental-Physical-Engineering Sciences (55)

Company Name: SteadySen
Description: SteadySense is an innovative start-up that aims to set new standards in medical data collection.
Website: http://www.steadysense.at/
Phone: 43 660 88 50 100 **Email:** office@steadysense.at
City: Graz **State:** Styria **PC:** **Country:** Austria
Year Established: 2016 **Status 2020:** Active
Industries: Artificial Intelligence for:, ~ Healthcare (20), ~ Healthcare (20), ~ Healthcare (20), ~ Healthcare (20), ~ Healthcare (20), Internet of Things (IoT) for:, Internet of Things (IoT)

Company Name: Monkee
Description: Monkee combines behavioral design, gamification and machine learning to help people to improve their financial health and save more money.
Website: http://www.monkee.rocks
Phone: **Email:** info@monkee.rocks
City: Innsbruck **State:** Tyrol **PC:** **Country:** Austria
Year Established: 2018 **Status 2020:** Active
Industries: ~ Banking and Financial Markets-Services (7), ~ Banking and Financial Markets-Services (7), Machine Learning for:, Application Services for:, Finance and Accounting

Company Name: Onl: Isle of Man
Description: Automated Customer Communication via Chatbots, Intelligent Personal Assistants and Social Media!
Website: http://www.onlim.com
Phone: 43 676 4470978 **Email:** office@onlim.com
City: Innsbruck **State:** Tyrol **PC:** **Country:** Austria
Year Established: **Status 2020:** Active
Industries: Artificial Intelligence for:, IT Managed Services for:, ~ Media-Communications (41), ~ Social Media (54)

Company Name: Swarm Analytics
Description: Swarm Analytics simplifies complex analytics from multiples input sources with a cloud-solution.
Website: http://swarm-analytics.com
Phone: 43 664 4678233 **Email:** info@swarm-analytics.com
City: Wattens **State:** Tyrol **PC:** **Country:** Austria
Year Established: **Status 2020:** Active
Industries: Analytics for:, Artificial Intelligence for:, Big Data and Analytics for:, Machine Learning

Company Name: BALLDESIGNER
Description: BALLDESIGNER is an AI-Design configurator for sportballs.
Website: http://www.ball.design
Phone: (4372) 486-1836 **Email:** office@balldesigner.com
City: Gallspach **State:** Upper Austria **PC:** **Country:** Austria
Year Established: 2017 **Status 2020:** Active
Industries: Artificial Intelligence for:, Robotics for:, ~ Arts-Entertainment-Recreation (4), ~ Arts-Entertainment-Recreation (4)

Company Name: FRUX
Description: FRUX is an artificial intelligence platform for predictive b2b leadgeneration.
Website: http://www.frux.io/index.html
Phone: 43.732.207230 **Email:** office@frux.io
City: Leonding **State:** Upper Austria **PC:** **Country:** Austria
Year Established: **Status 2020:** Active
Industries:

Company Name: 10hoch10 GmbH
Description: Big Data Agency
Website: http://www.10hoch10.com/
Phone: **Email:** office@10hoch10.com
City: Linz **State:** Upper Austria **PC:** **Country:** Austria
Year Established: **Status 2020:** Active
Industries: Artificial Intelligence for:, Big Data and Analytics for:, Databases for:, ~ Professional Services (48), Data Management

Company Name: Butleroy
Description: Butleroy improves your work-life balance by managing your schedule. Its artificial intelligence finds time for the priorities in your life.
Website: http://butleroy.com
Phone: **Email:** support@butleroy.com
City: Linz **State:** Upper Austria **PC:** **Country:** Austria
Year Established: 2017 **Status 2020:** Active
Industries: Artificial Intelligence for:, Big Data and Analytics for:, Internet of Things (IoT) for:, Machine Learning for:, Application Services

Company Name: Fretello
Description: Fretello creates AI-powered apps that teach you musical instruments.
Website: http://fretello.com
Phone: **Email:** office@fretello.com
City: Linz **State:** Upper Austria **PC:** **Country:** Austria
Year Established: **Status 2020:** Active
Industries: Artificial Intelligence for:, Application Services for:, ~ Education (13)

Company Name: Newsadoo
Description: Newsadoo personalizes news with artificial intelligence.
Website: http://www.newsadoo.com/en
Phone: **Email:** office@newsadoo.com
City: Linz **State:** Upper Austria **PC:** **Country:** Austria
Year Established: 2017 **Status 2020:** Active
Industries: Artificial Intelligence for:, Web for:, Internet of Things (IoT)

Company Name: ROBART GmbH
Description: It's focused on developing autonomous mobile robots based upon its AICU.
Website: robart.cc
Phone: **Email:** office@robart.cc
City: Linz **State:** Upper Austria **PC:** **Country:** Austria
Year Established: **Status 2020:** Active
Industries: Artificial Intelligence for:, Robotics for:, ~ Construction (10)

Company Name: Roomle GmbH
Description: Plan, furnish and buy based on your rooms, your style and your budget.
Website: roomle.com
Phone: **Email:** albert.ortig@roomle.com
City: Linz **State:** Upper Austria **PC:** **Country:** Austria
Year Established: **Status 2020:** Active
Industries: ~ Media-Communications (41), ~ Professional Services (48), Artificial Intelligence for:, Augmented Reality for:, E-Commerce for:, ~ Professional Services (48), ~ Real Estate (49)

Company Name: Abacus.ac
Description: Abacus.ac is a self-learning, artificial intelligence system that automates the activities of accounting service providers.
Website: http://www.abacus.ac/
Phone: **Email:** patrick.sagmeister@abacus.ac
City: Vienna **State:** Vienna **PC:** **Country:** Austria
Year Established: **Status 2020:** Active
Industries: Artificial Intelligence

Company Name: Adverity
Description: Adverity enables users of its platform to easily connect and work with their entire media, marketing, and e-commerce ecosystems.
Website: https://www.adverity.com/
Phone: 43-1-8903155 **Email:** office@adverity.com
City: Vienna **State:** Vienna **PC:** **Country:** Austria
Year Established: 2015 **Status 2020:** Active
Industries: Analytics for:, Artificial Intelligence for:, Big Data and Analytics for:, Business Intelligence for:, Data Management for:, Data Management for:, E-Commerce for:, Business Software as a Service Apps (SaaS Apps) for:, Business Software as a Service Apps (SaaS App

Company Name: Ares Genetics GmbH
Description: Ares Genetics develops Artificial Intelligence informed DNA-Sequencing Tests to revolutionize Infectious Disease and Drug Resistance Testing
Website: http://www.ares-genetics.com
Phone: **Email:** contact@ares-genetics.com
City: Vienna **State:** Vienna **PC:** **Country:** Austria
Year Established: 2017 **Status 2020:** Active
Industries: Analytics for:, Artificial Intelligence for:, ~ Biotechnology (9), ~ Healthcare (20)

Company Name: Break Stuff Market
Description: We are an AI-driven marketplace app for sports cards.
Website: http://tradingcards.ai
Phone: **Email:** office@breakstuff.market
City: Vienna **State:** Vienna **PC:** **Country:** Austria
Year Established: **Status 2020:** Active
Industries: Artificial Intelligence for:, ~ E-Commerce (12), ~ Retail and Consumer Products (52), E-Commerce for:, ~ Retail and Consumer Products (2248), Machine Learning for:, ~ Retail and Consumer Products (3407)

Company Name: Calero Technologies
Description: Calero is a decentralized platform that implements leading edge Artificial intelligence and blockchain to improve.
Website: http://calero.io/
Phone: **Email:** 36223@reference-encyclopedia-ai.net
City: Vienna **State:** Vienna **PC:** **Country:** Austria
Year Established: 2017 **Status 2020:** Active
Industries: Artificial Intelligence for:, Blockchain

Company Name: contextflow
Description: See beyond a single case. contextflow uses AI imaging technology to support radiologists during their daily clinical routine.
Website: http://contextflow.com/
Phone: 43 699 1902 5131 **Email:** office@contextflow.com
City: Vienna **State:** Vienna **PC:** **Country:** Austria
Year Established: 2016 **Status 2020:** Active
Industries: Artificial Intelligence for:, Big Data and Analytics for:, ~ Healthcare (20), ~ Healthcare (20), Machine Learning for:, ~ Healthcare (20)

Company Name: Cortical.io
Description: Cortical.io delivers AI-based solutions that relieve your employees of the burden of reviewing large amounts of documents or sifting through masses of text messages.
Website: https://www.cortical.io
Phone: **Email:** info@cortical.io
City: Vienna **State:** Vienna **Zip:** 1070 **Country**: Austria
Year Established: **Status 2020:** Active
Industries: Analytics for:, Artificial Intelligence for:, Big Data and Analytics for:, Business Applications for:, ~ Automotive (615), ~ Banking and Financial Markets-Services (617), ~ Biotechnology (619), ~ Construction (620), ~ Customer Relationship Management (621), ~ E-Co

Company Name: Cozyo
Description: COZYO is a novel furniture e-commerce recommendation engine, which generates automatic interior design proposals within seconds.
Website: http://www.cozyo.io
Phone: 43 664 75075143 **Email:** mail@cozyo.io
City: Vienna **State:** Vienna **PC:** **Country:** Austria
Year Established: 2017 **Status 2020:** Active
Industries:

Company Name: DataScience Service GmbH
Description: Data Science Service is a Professional Automated Property Valuation.
Website: http://www.datascience-service.at/
Phone: **Email:** office@datascience-service.at
City: Vienna **State:** Vienna **PC:** **Country:** Austria
Year Established: 2016 **Status 2020:** Active
Industries: Artificial Intelligence for:, IT Managed Services

Company Name: Delta 4
Description: Uses AI for drug repurposing.
Website: http://delta4.ai/
Phone: **Email:** office@delta4.ai
City: Vienna **State:** Vienna **PC:** **Country:** Austria
Year Established: 2018 **Status 2020:** Active
Industries: Artificial Intelligence for:, ~ Biotechnology (9)

Company Name: Digital Cla: Isle of Man
Description: Insuretech - automating claim recovery for insuranc: Spain
Website: http://www.digitalclaim.de
Phone: **Email:** karl@digitalclaim.de
City: Vienna **State:** Vienna **PC:** **Country:** Austria
Year Established: 2017 **Status 2020:** Active
Industries: ~ Banking and Financial Markets-Services (7), ~ Banking and Financial Markets-Services (7), IT Managed Services for:, Machine Learning

Company Name: EDAQS
Description: Solving the world's problems with the magic of Electronic and Digital Automated Quantification Systems.
Website: http://www.edaqs.com
Phone: **Email:** press@edaqs.com
City: Vienna **State:** Vienna **PC:** **Country:** Austria
Year Established: **Status 2020:** Active
Industries: Artificial Intelligence for:, Big Data and Analytics for:, Business Applications for:, ~ Media-Communications (41)

Company Name: emotion3D
Description: Camera-Based In-Cabin Analys
Website: http://www.emotion3d.ai
Phone: 43-1-293 32 63 **Email:** office@emotion3d.ai
City: Vienna **State:** Vienna **PC:** **Country:** Austria
Year Established: 2010 **Status 2020:** Active
Industries: Artificial Intelligence for:, ~ Automotive (5), Computer Vision for:, Human Computer Interaction for:, Machine Learning

Company Name: EnliteAI
Description: Saas, Artifical Intelligence, Competitive Intelligence
Website: http://www.enlite.ai
Phone: **Email:** office@enlite.ai
City: Vienna **State:** Vienna **PC:** **Country:** Austria
Year Established: **Status 2020:** Active
Industries: Artificial Intelligence for:, IT Managed Services

Company Name: Frameless
Description: Intelligent High-Quality Mixed Reality Environments
Website: http://www.frameless.me/
Phone: **Email:** info@frameless.me
City: Vienna **State:** Vienna **PC:** **Country:** Austria
Year Established: 2018 **Status 2020:** Active
Industries: Artificial Intelligence for:, Augmented Reality for:, Mobile for:, Virtual Reality (VR)

Company Name: Healcloud
Description: Europe's leading healthcare big data enabler | real world evidence | clinical trials | patient management
Website: http://www.healcloud.com
Phone: **Email:** 36677@reference-encyclopedia-ai.net
City: Vienna **State:** Vienna **PC:** **Country:** Austria
Year Established: 2015 **Status 2020:** Active
Industries: Artificial Intelligence for:, Big Data and Analytics for:, ~ Healthcare (20), ~ Healthcare (20)

Company Name: hiMoment
Description: Your digital happiness gu: Russia
Website: http://himoment.com
Phone: **Email:** hi@himoment.com
City: Vienna **State:** Vienna **PC:** **Country:** Austria
Year Established: 2016 **Status 2020:** Active
Industries: Artificial Intelligence for:, Application Services for:, ~ Education (13), ~ Healthcare (20), ~ Healthcare (20)

Company Name: HPW Quant4Market
Description: Big Data Predictive Analysis and Deep Learning
Website: http://www.quant4market.com/
Phone: **Email:** 36712@reference-encyclopedia-ai.net
City: Vienna **State:** Vienna **PC:** **Country:** Austria
Year Established: 2015 **Status 2020:** Active
Industries: Analytics for:, Artificial Intelligence for:, Big Data and Analytics for:, ~ Education (13)

Company Name: IFDAQ
Description: The IFDAQ is a powerful AI-system that provides infinite insight into the real market & benchmark values of the fashion and luxury industry.
Website: http://www.ifdaq.com
Phone: **Email:** staging@ifdaq.com
City: Vienna **State:** Vienna **PC:** **Country:** Austria
Year Established: **Status 2020:** Active
Industries: Analytics for:, Artificial Intelligence for:, Big Data and Analytics for:, Business Intelligence for:, ~ Fashion (16), IT Managed Services for:, Application Services for:, Machine Learning for:, ~ Media-Communications (41), ~ Banking and Financial Markets-Service

Company Name: ImageBiopsy Lab
Description: ImageBiopsy Lab is deploying AI-based software solutions for the early detection and diagnosis of various bone & joint diseases.
Website: http://imagebiopsylab.ai/
Phone: (43) 905-1206 **Email:** mail@imagebiopsy.com
City: Vienna **State:** Vienna **PC:** **Country:** Austria
Year Established: 2016 **Status 2020:** Active
Industries: Artificial Intelligence for:, ~ Healthcare (20), ~ Healthcare (20), Image Recognition for:, Machine Learning for:, ~ Healthcare (20)

Company Name: JetClass
Description: JetClass is a tech-startup with the vision to merge business and commercial aviation and bring private jets to the masses.
Website: http://www.jetclass.com
Phone: 43 1 25 300 25 25 **Email:** info@jetclass.com
City: Vienna **State:** Vienna **PC:** **Country:** Austria
Year Established: **Status 2020:** Active
Industries: Artificial Intelligence for:, ~ Travel and Transportation (58), Web for:, ~ Travel and Transportation (58)

Company Name: Knoyd
Description: Customized data science solutions for businesses of any size. Future is Data.
Website: http://www.knoyd.com
Phone: **Email:** lukas@knoyd.com
City: Vienna **State:** Vienna **PC:** **Country:** Austria
Year Established: **Status 2020:** Active
Industries:

Company Name: MARS - Modeling Agencies Rating System
Description: Establishing the idea of ratings in the world of modeling, MARS is an automated and intelligent rating system to evaluate a model-agency.
Website: http://www.mars.: Isle of Man
Phone: **Email:** contact@mars.: Isle of Man
City: Vienna **State:** Vienna **PC:** **Country:** Austria
Year Established: 2014 **Status 2020:** Active
Industries: Artificial Intelligence for:, ~ Arts-Entertainment-Recreation (4), ~ Social Assistance-Non-Profits (53), ~ Social Assistance-Non-Profits (53)

Company Name: Medicus AI
Description: Medicus AI designs and develops an artificial intelligence (AI) based platform that converts health data.
Website: http://medicus.ai
Phone: 43 720 90 23 90 **Email:** hello@medicus.ai
City: Vienna **State:** Vienna **PC:** **Country:** Austria
Year Established: 2015 **Status 2020:** Active
Industries: Analytics for:, Artificial Intelligence for:, ~ Healthcare (20), Application Services for:, ~ Healthcare (20), Predictive Analytics

Company Name: Metriox
Description: Digital Transformation and telematics in Public Transport! We offer solutions for all kind of vehicles (multimodal)
Website: http://www.metriox.com
Phone: **Email:** contact@metriox.com
City: Vienna **State:** Vienna **PC:** **Country:** Austria
Year Established: 2018 **Status 2020:** Active
Industries: Big Data and Analytics for:, ~ Telecommunications (56), ~ Energy and Utilities (14), IT Managed Services for:, Internet of Things (IoT) for:, Predictive Analytics for:, ~ Transportation and Logistics (57)

Company Name: Mostly AI
Description: Mostly AI is an IT company enabling privacy-preserving big data applications in the digital age.
Website: http://mostly.ai/
Phone: **Email:** hello@mostly.ai
City: Vienna **State:** Vienna **PC:** **Country:** Austria
Year Established: 2017 **Status 2020:** Active
Industries: Artificial Intelligence for:, Big Data and Analytics for:, IT Managed Services for:, Machine Learning for:, Predictive Analytics for:, Cyber Security

Company Name: ONDEWO
Description: AI-based technology to enable good natural conversations
Website: http://www.ondewo.com
Phone: **Email:** social@ondewo.com
City: Vienna **State:** Vienna **PC:** **Country:** Austria
Year Established: **Status 2020:** Active
Industries: Artificial Intelligence

Company Name: Ordito
Description: Machine Learning based Prediction System for the retail sector to forecast demand - SaaS - save foodwaste!
Website: http://www.ordito.at
Phone: **Email:** contact@ordito.at
City: Vienna **State:** Vienna **PC:** **Country:** Austria
Year Established: 2020 **Status 2020:** Active
Industries: Artificial Intelligence for:, Machine Learning for:, Predictive Analytics for:, Business Software as a Service Apps (SaaS Apps) for:, Supply Chain Management

Company Name: Prewave
Description: Prewave and stems from five years of advanced machine learning research.
Website: http://www.prewave.ai/
Phone: **Email:** info@prewave.ai
City: Vienna **State:** Vienna **PC:** **Country:** Austria
Year Established: 2017 **Status 2020:** Active
Industries: Artificial Intelligence for:, IT Managed Services

Company Name: Remove.bg
Description: Remove.bg removes backgrounds from photos. Automatically.
Website: http://www.remove.bg/
Phone: **Email:** team@remove.bg
City: Vienna **State:** Vienna **PC:** **Country:** Austria
Year Established: **Status 2020:** Active
Industries: Artificial Intelligence for:, Web for:, ~ Professional Services (48)

Company Name: Riskine
Description: riskine is a fintech startup
Website: http://www.riskine.com
Phone: **Email:** office@riskine.com
City: Vienna **State:** Vienna **PC:** **Country:** Austria
Year Established: 2016 **Status 2020:** Active
Industries: Artificial Intelligence for:, ~ Banking and Financial Markets-Services (7)

Company Name: Sheepblue
Description: Sheepblue is a software company based in Vienna, Austria.
Website: http://sheepblue.com/
Phone: **Email:** info@sheepblue.com
City: Vienna **State:** Vienna **PC:** **Country:** Austria
Year Established: **Status 2020:** Active
Industries: Artificial Intelligence for:, Machine Learning for:, ~ Professional Services (48)

Company Name: tailorpost
Description: machine learning company for news
Website: http://www.tailorpost.com
Phone: **Email:** hello@tailorpost.com
City: Vienna **State:** Vienna **PC:** **Country:** Austria
Year Established: **Status 2020:** Active
Industries: Artificial Intelligence for:, Big Data and Analytics for:, IT Managed Services for:, Web for:, Machine Learning for:, Mobile for:, Natural Language Processing for:, ~ Media-Communications (41), Data Management

Company Name: The MoonVision
Description: The MoonVision is an efficient visual object recognition plattform for your business.
Website: http://moonvision.io/
Phone: 4318901287 **Email:** office@moonvision.io
City: Vienna **State:** Vienna **PC:** **Country:** Austria
Year Established: 2017 **Status 2020:** Active
Industries: Artificial Intelligence for:, IT Managed Services for:, IT Managed Services

Company Name: The MoonVision GmbH
Description: Transfering Expert Know How to AI - using Visual Object Recognition
Website: http://moonvision.io/
Phone: 4318901287 **Email:** office@moonvision.io
City: Vienna **State:** Vienna **PC:** **Country:** Austria
Year Established: **Status 2020:** Active
Industries: Artificial Intelligence for:, IT Managed Services for:, IT Managed Services for:, ~ Professional Services (48)

Company Name: Toby
Description: Toby comes from To-Buy and makes sure you have everything you need.
Website: http://tobyapp.com/
Phone: **Email:** danny@tobyapp.com
City: Vienna **State:** Vienna **PC:** **Country:** Austria
Year Established: 2016 **Status 2020:** Active
Industries:

Company Name: ToolSense
Description: Connecting the way OEMs do business.
Website: http://www.toolsense.io
Phone: **Email:** office@toolsense.io
City: Vienna **State:** Vienna **PC:** **Country:** Austria
Year Established: 2017 **Status 2020:** Active
Industries: Analytics for:, Artificial Intelligence for:, Cloud for:, ~ Construction (10), IT Managed Services for:, Internet of Things (IoT) for:, Machine Learning

Company Name: twingz
Description: twingz delivers predictive analytics based on anomaly detection out of energy meterdata feeds & provides damage prevention services on top.
Website: http://www.twingz.com
Phone: 43 (0) 660 937 6379 **Email:** wws@twingz.com
City: Vienna **State:** Vienna **PC:** **Country:** Austria
Year Established: **Status 2020:** Active
Industries: Artificial Intelligence for:, Business Applications for:, ~ Energy and Utilities (14), ~ Energy and Utilities (14), ~ Insurance (25), Machine Learning for:, Predictive Analytics

Company Name: weffect (a brand of STRATACT)
Description: weffect: the AI-driven way to empower all workers to contribute fully to the company's bottom line!
Website: http://weffect.app
Phone: 43 1 375 05 050 **Email:** office@stratact.org
City: Vienna **State:** Vienna **PC:** **Country:** Austria
Year Established: 2013 **Status 2020:** Active
Industries: Application Services for:, Artificial Intelligence for:, ~ Education (13), Internet of Things (IoT) for:, Machine Learning for:, Application Services for:, Business Software as a Service Apps (SaaS Apps)

Company Name: weXelerate GmbH
Description: Europe's biggest and smartest startup&innovation hub
Website: http://wexelerate.com/apply_now/
Phone: **Email:** office@wexelerate.com
City: Vienna **State:** Vienna **PC:** **Country:** Austria
Year Established: **Status 2020:** Active
Industries: Artificial Intelligence for:, ~ Banking and Financial Markets-Services (7), Big Data and Analytics for:, Blockchain for:, ~ Media-Communications (41), Cyber Security for:, ~ Transportation and Logistics (57), Digital Media for:, ~ Energy and Utilities (14), ~ Ener

Company Name: XUND
Description: XUND is an AI-powered mobile health assistant designed to navigate patients along their health journey
Website: http://xund.ai
Phone: **Email:** hello@xund.ai
City: Vienna **State:** Vienna **PC:** **Country:** Austria
Year Established: **Status 2020:** Active
Industries: Application Services for:, Artificial Intelligence for:, ~ Healthcare (20), ~ Healthcare (20), ~ Healthcare (20)

Azerbaijan

Company Name: BNB DYNAMICS
Description: BNB DYNAMICS is specialize in the commercial use of robots, where our ultimate goal is to take human living conditions.
Website: http://bnbdynamics.az/
Phone: **Email:** info@bnbdynamics.az
City: Baku **State:** Baki **PC:** **Country:** Azerbaijan
Year Established: **Status 2020:** Active
Industries: Artificial Intelligence for:, Machine Learning for:, Robotics

Bangladesh

Company Name: AdsCollect
Description: Ad search engine. Creates index of ads published on newspaper.
Website: https://www.adscollect.com/
Phone: **Email:** info@adscollect.com
City: Dhaka **State:** Dhaka Division **PC:** **Country:** Bangladesh
Year Established: 2016 **Status 2020:** Active
Industries: Computer Vision for:, Machine Learning for:, Natural Language Processing

Company Name: aiXai
Description: Synthetic data production marketplace and a social hub for AI driven startups seeking customized and labelled data.
Website: http://www.getaixai.com
Phone: **Email:** contact@aixai.ema: Israel
City: Dhaka **State:** Dhaka Division **PC:** **Country:** Bangladesh
Year Established: **Status 2020:** Active
Industries: Artificial Intelligence

Company Name: ALICE Labs PTE Ltd.
Description: ALICE is a omni-channel conversational AI platform to enhance customer experience and generate actionable insights.
Website: http://getalice.ai/
Phone: 880-1749-945055 **Email:** info@getalice.ai
City: Dhaka **State:** Dhaka Division **PC:** **Country:** Bangladesh
Year Established: **Status 2020:** Active
Industries: Analytics for:, Artificial Intelligence for:, IT Managed Services for:, Machine Learning for:, Natural Language Processing for:, ~ Social Media (54)

Company Name: cWork Microjob Limited
Description: cWork is mobile app based microjob platform.
Website: http://cworkmicrojob.com/
Phone: **Email:** mustafa@cworkmicrojob.com
City: Dhaka **State:** Dhaka Division **PC:** **Country:** Bangladesh
Year Established: **Status 2020:** Active
Industries: Artificial Intelligence for:, IT Managed Services for:, Web for:, Application Services

Company Name: Gaze
Description: Artificial intelligence that can generate actionable insights and analytics from images and video feeds
Website: http://gaze.ai/
Phone: **Email:** hello@gaze.ai
City: Dhaka **State:** Dhaka Division **PC:** **Country:** Bangladesh
Year Established: 2018 **Status 2020:** Active
Industries: Artificial Intelligence

Company Name: Intelligent Machin: Spain
Description: AI and analytics as service
Website: http://intelligentmachin.: Spain
Phone: 880 1713-384435 **Email:** now@intelligentmachin.: Spain
City: Dhaka **State:** Dhaka Division **PC:** **Country:** Bangladesh
Year Established: 2018 **Status 2020:** Active
Industries:

Company Name: Lantas Technologies, Inc
Description: Developer of Yello, a mobile application which allows fast and easy Contacts Sharing and Collaboration. Making Contacts Social!
Website:
Phone: **Email:** 36878@reference-encyclopedia-ai.net
City: Dhaka **State:** Dhaka Division **PC:** **Country:** Bangladesh
Year Established: 2015 **Status 2020:** Closed
Industries: Machine Learning

Company Name: Maya
Description: Maya is an anonymous messaging platform connecting users to expert advice on physical and mental health using AI and NLP.
Website: http://maya.com.bd
Phone: **Email:** noreply@maya.com.bd
City: Dhaka **State:** Dhaka Division **PC:** **Country:** Bangladesh
Year Established: 2011 **Status 2020:** Active
Industries: ~ Healthcare (20), IT Managed Services for:, Natural Language Processing

Company Name: SIGMIND
Description: The very first A.I. research group and engineering solution provider in Bangladesh, SIGMIND Group consists of three individual companies.
Website: http://www.sigmindai.net
Phone: **Email:** abushuvom@sigmindai.net
City: Dhaka **State:** Dhaka Division **PC:** **Country:** Bangladesh
Year Established: **Status 2020:** Active
Industries: Artificial Intelligence for:, Machine Learning for:, Application Services

Company Name: Socian Ltd
Description: AI based Security Intelligence Company specializing in Speech, Visual, Textual & Cyber Analysis on Digital & Social Media in 81 languag: Spain
Website: http://socian.ai
Phone: **Email:** tanvir@socian.ai
City: Dhaka **State:** Dhaka Division **PC:** **Country:** Bangladesh
Year Established: **Status 2020:** Active
Industries: Artificial Intelligence for:, Cyber Security for:, Cyber Security for:, Security for:, Security

Company Name: Tiger Digital
Description: One of the leading chatbot developer companies around the world. Expert in Conversational UX. AI pioneer in Bangladesh.
Website: http://www.tigerdigital.xyz/
Phone: **Email:** hello@tigerdigital.xyz
City: Dhaka **State:** Dhaka Division **PC:** **Country:** Bangladesh
Year Established: **Status 2020:** Active
Industries: Artificial Intelligence for:, Digital Marketing for:, Machine Learning

Belarus

Company Name: AIMatter
Description: Neural network-based AI platform and SDK to detect and process images quickly on mobile devic: Spain
Website: https://www.aimatter.com/
Phone: 375 44 514 35 56 **Email:** 36013@reference-encyclopedia-ai.net
City: Minsk **State:** Minsk Region **PC:** **Country:** Belarus
Year Established: 2016 **Status 2020:** Active
Industries: Artificial Intelligence for:, Computer Vision

Company Name: Banuba
Description: Banuba is a developer of augmented reality enabled mobile applications and technologies.
Website: http://banuba.com/
Phone: 375 29 320-60-00 **Email:** info@banuba.com
City: Minsk **State:** Minsk Region **PC:** **Country:** Belarus
Year Established: 2016 **Status 2020:** Active
Industries: Artificial Intelligence for:, Augmented Reality for:, IT Managed Services for:, Machine Learning

Company Name: BotCube
Description: BotCube designs and builds chatbots enhanced with artificial intelligence for multiple platforms.
Website: http://botcube.co/
Phone: 375 25 750-80-71 **Email:** hello@botcube.co
City: Minsk **State:** Minsk Region **PC:** **Country:** Belarus

Year Established: 2016 **Status 2020:** Active
Industries: Artificial Intelligence for:, IT Managed Services for:, Web

Company Name: Cybergizer
Description: Cybergizer is a software development and hardware prototyping company.
Website: http://cybergizer.com
Phone: 375 (29) 89 89 497 **Email:** hello@cybergizer.com
City: Minsk **State:** Minsk Region **PC:** **Country:** Belarus
Year Established: 2016 **Status 2020:** Active
Industries: Artificial Intelligence for:, IT Managed Services for:, Machine Learning for:, Web

Company Name: DashBouquet Developement
Description: Dashbouquet is reliable partner aligned to deliver solutions. JavaScript, Computer Vision and Data Science.
Website: http://dashbouquet.com/
Phone: 1 484 423 4474 **Email:** contact@dashbouquet.com
City: Minsk **State:** Minsk Region **PC:** **Country:** Belarus
Year Established: 2014 **Status 2020:** Active
Industries: Artificial Intelligence for:, Computer Vision for:, IT Managed Services for:, Application Services for:, Web

Company Name: DATASPECTRUM
Description: DATASPECTRUM is a software development company specializing in data science.
Website: http://www.dataspectrum.io/
Phone: 1 (302) 7244798 **Email:** info@dataspectrum.io
City: Minsk **State:** Minsk Region **PC:** **Country:** Belarus
Year Established: 2016 **Status 2020:** Active
Industries: Artificial Intelligence for:, Big Data and Analytics for:, Machine Learning

Company Name: GiniMachine
Description: Fighting bad loans with AI
Website: http://ginimachine.com/
Phone: (1347) 632-8900 **Email:** invite@ginimachine.com
City: Minsk **State:** Minsk Region **PC:** **Country:** Belarus
Year Established: 2016 **Status 2020:** Active
Industries: Artificial Intelligence for:, Business Applications for:, ~ Banking and Financial Markets-Services (7), Machine Learning for:, Risk Management for:, Risk Management

Company Name: Innovative Future Technologies
Description: Focuses on AI-driven RPA technologies that are directed at business processes automation and data capturing.
Website: http://infuturetech.com/
Phone: **Email:** sales@infuturetech.com
City: Minsk **State:** Minsk Region **PC:** **Country:** Belarus
Year Established: **Status 2020:** Active
Industries: Artificial Intelligence for:, IT Managed Services for:, Machine Learning for:, ~ Professional Services (48)

Company Name: MakeML
Description: Train Neural Network with ea
Website: http://makeml.app
Phone: **Email:** info@makeml.app
City: Minsk **State:** Minsk Region **PC:** **Country:** Belarus
Year Established: 2019 **Status 2020:** Active
Industries:

Company Name: OneSoil
Description: Disruptive AI-powered Platform for Every Farmer on Ear:Thailand
Website: http://onesoil.ai
Phone: **Email:** hello@onesoil.ai
City: Minsk **State:** Minsk Region **PC:** **Country:** Belarus
Year Established: **Status 2020:** Active
Industries: ~ Agriculture (3), Artificial Intelligence for:, Computer Vision for:, ~ Agriculture (3), Machine Learning

Company Name: Pythia
Description: Pythia is a customer support automation platform
Website: http://pythia.cc
Phone: **Email:** hello@pythia.cc
City: Minsk **State:** Minsk Region **PC:** **Country:** Belarus
Year Established: 2018 **Status 2020:** Active
Industries: Artificial Intelligence for:, IT Managed Services for:, Web for:, Machine Learning for:, IT Managed Services

Company Name: Singulart
Description: Singulart provides machine learning software development.
Website: http://singulart.tech
Phone: 1 (415) 980-9632 **Email:** contact@singulart.tech
City: Minsk **State:** Minsk Region **PC:** **Country:** Belarus
Year Established: 2017 **Status 2020:** Active
Industries: Machine Learning

Company Name: VOCHI
Description: Computer Vision, Mobile App, Video
Website: http://vochi.com
Phone: **Email:** hello@vochi.ai
City: Minsk **State:** Minsk Region **PC:** **Country:** Belarus
Year Established: 2019 **Status 2020:** Active
Industries: Artificial Intelligence

Company Name: Wandle
Description: Smart assistant for management of your calls and notification messages on a smartphone.
Website: http://wandle.io
Phone: **Email:** alexey.ceo@wandle.io
City: Minsk **State:** Minsk Region **PC:** **Country:** Belarus
Year Established: 2015 **Status 2020:** Active
Industries: Artificial Intelligence for:, IT Managed Services for:, Mobile for:, Application Services

Company Name: WANNABY
Description: Our latest product is Wanna Kicks, first-ever shoes AR Try-On
Website: http://wanna.by/
Phone: **Email:** hi@wanna.by
City: Minsk **State:** Minsk Region **PC:** **Country:** Belarus
Year Established: **Status 2020:** Active
Industries: Artificial Intelligence for:, Augmented Reality for:, E-Commerce

Belgium

Company Name: Zensor
Description: Predictive maintenance for installations and assets - Making the life of production installations safer, longer and more efficient
Website: http://www.zensor.be
Phone: **Email:** info@zensor.be
City: Brussel **State:** Brussels **PC:** **Country:** Belgium
Year Established: 2013 **Status 2020:** Active
Industries: Internet of Things (IoT) for:, Predictive Analytics for:, ~ Energy and Utilities (14)

Company Name: AiVidens
Description: Predictive Cash & Risk Management
Website: http://www.aividens.com
Phone: **Email:** ebeauvois@aividens.com
City: Brussels **State:** Brussels **PC:** **Country:** Belgium
Year Established: **Status 2020:** Active
Industries: Artificial Intelligence for:, IT Managed Services for:, Risk Management for:, ~ Professional Services (48)

Company Name: BruBotics
Description: Brussels Human Robotics Research Center of the Vrije Universiteit Brussel (VUB) located in Brussels, Belgium.
Website: http://www.brubotics.eu
Phone: 0032(0)2 629 2808 **Email:** info@brubotics.eu
City: Brussels **State:** Brussels **PC:** **Country:** Belgium

Year Established: 2015 **Status 2020:** Active
Industries: Artificial Intelligence for:, Augmented Reality for:, ~ Healthcare (20), ~ Healthcare (20), Robotics for:, ~ Education (13), Virtual Reality (VR)

Company Name: FAQBOT
Description: Advanced customer support technology that transform your companies's FAQs page into a conversational agent
Website: http://www.faqbot.co/
Phone: **Email:** hey@faqbot.co
City: Brussels **State:** Brussels **PC:** **Country:** Belgium
Year Established: 2017 **Status 2020:** Active
Industries: Artificial Intelligence for:, IT Managed Services for:, IT Managed Services

Company Name: Fyn.ai
Description: Fyn.ai is an invoice parsing tool that makes it easy for you to extract information from invoices.
Website: http://www.fyn.ai/
Phone: **Email:** 36604@reference-encyclopedia-ai.net
City: Brussels **State:** Brussels **PC:** **Country:** Belgium
Year Established: 2016 **Status 2020:** Active
Industries: Finance and Accounting for:, Artificial Intelligence for:, ~ Banking and Financial Markets-Services (7), IT Managed Services

Company Name: Gabi SmartCare
Description: Gabi SmartCare improves children's lives thanks to outpatient predictive monitoring tool
Website: http://www.gabismartcare.com
Phone: **Email:** info@gabismartcare.com
City: Brussels **State:** Brussels **PC:** **Country:** Belgium
Year Established: 2017 **Status 2020:** Active
Industries: ~ Healthcare (20), Predictive Analytics

Company Name: Innovation Sprint Sprl
Description: eClinical platform, SaaS, Real World Data, AI
Website: http://innovationsprint.eu/
Phone: **Email:** info@innovationsprint.eu
City: Brussels **State:** Brussels **PC:** **Country:** Belgium
Year Established: 2016 **Status 2020:** Active
Industries: Artificial Intelligence for:, ~ Customer Relationship Management (11), ~ Healthcare (20), IT Managed Services for:, Robotics

Company Name: Instaon
Description: AI-based ad platform that fully automates the creation & management of Google Ads for SMBs
Website: http://instaon.io/
Phone: **Email:** contact@instaon.io
City: Brussels **State:** Brussels **PC:** **Country:** Belgium
Year Established: **Status 2020:** Active
Industries:

Company Name: Jetpack.AI
Description: Jetpack.AI builds on data science and software development capabilities to embed analytics into the day-to-day of operations.
Website: http://jetpack.ai
Phone: **Email:** info@jetpack.ai
City: Brussels **State:** Brussels **PC:** **Country:** Belgium
Year Established: 2017 **Status 2020:** Active
Industries: Analytics for:, Artificial Intelligence for:, Big Data and Analytics for:, Data Management for:, Predictive Analytics

Company Name: Kantify
Description: We create tailored AI-based applications for our customers to help them gain a competitive advantage.
Website: http://www.kantify.com/
Phone: (3248) 491-4217 **Email:** hello@kantify.com
City: Brussels **State:** Brussels **PC:** **Country:** Belgium
Year Established: 2015 **Status 2020:** Active
Industries: Natural Language Processing for:, Predictive Analytics

Company Name: Look Live Media
Description: Look is a NewsTech Startup active in the citizen journalism space.
Website: http://look-app.net
Phone: **Email:** hello@look-app.net
City: Brussels **State:** Brussels **PC:** **Country:** Belgium
Year Established: **Status 2020:** Active
Industries: Application Services for:, Artificial Intelligence for:, ~ Arts-Entertainment-Recreation (4), Mobile for:, ~ Media-Communications (41)

Company Name: Neologic Vision
Description: Video Analytics, Online Video Edition software, Computer Vision
Website: http://www.neologicvision.com
Phone: 32 486 086 705 **Email:** contact@neologicvision.com
City: Brussels **State:** Brussels **Zip:** 1040 **Country**: Belgium
Year Established: **Status 2020:** Active
Industries: Artificial Intelligence for:, Big Data and Analytics for:, Machine Learning for:, ~ Media-Communications (41)

Company Name: Nodalview
Description: Nodalview combines smartphone technology, AI and cloud computing to produce high-quality visuals for real estate properti: Spain
Website: http://www.nodalview.com
Phone: 32 2 585 32 10 **Email:** info@nodalview.com
City: Brussels **State:** Brussels **PC:** **Country:** Belgium
Year Established: 2016 **Status 2020:** Active
Industries: Application Services for:, Artificial Intelligence for:, Web for:, Business Software as a Service Apps (SaaS Apps) for:, Virtual Reality (VR) for:, Virtual Reality (VR)

Company Name: radix.ai
Description: Accelerating Machine Learning
Website: http://radix.ai
Phone: **Email:** hello@radix.ai
City: Brussels **State:** Brussels **PC:** **Country:** Belgium
Year Established: **Status 2020:** Active
Industries: Artificial Intelligence for:, Machine Learning for:, ~ Professional Services (48)

Company Name: Sagacify
Description: We harness the power of BigData technologies and cutting-edge SoftwareDevelopment to build smart, human-centered, data-driven solutions.
Website: http://sagacify.com
Phone: 32 496 96 12 18 **Email:** info@sagacify.com
City: Brussels **State:** Brussels **PC:** **Country:** Belgium
Year Established: 2012 **Status 2020:** Active
Industries: Big Data and Analytics for:, Business Intelligence for:, Cloud for:, Cloud for:, Web for:, Machine Learning for:, Mobile

Company Name: Sensifai
Description: Sensifai offers World's most comprehensive video tagging technology.
Website: http://www.sensifai.com
Phone: 32-484-901582 **Email:** sales.support@sensifai.com
City: Brussels **State:** Brussels **PC:** **Country:** Belgium
Year Established: **Status 2020:** Active
Industries: Artificial Intelligence for:, Enterprise Application Services for:, Image Recognition for:, Speech Recognition for:, ~ Media-Communications (41), Computer Vision

Company Name: Shungham
Description: Shungham is a a provider of systematic regulatory and legislative intelligence about European Union issues.
Website: http://www.shungham.com/
Phone: 32 477 435 456 **Email:** info@shungham.com
City: Brussels **State:** Brussels **PC:** **Country:** Belgium
Year Established: 2010 **Status 2020:** Active
Industries: Data Management for:, Predictive Analytics

Company Name: Swan Insights
Description: Swan Insights is a Big Data company providing new-generation Business Information solutions.
Website: http://swaninsights.com
Phone: 203 769 7723 **Email:** 37492@reference-encyclopedia-ai.net
City: Brussels **State:** Brussels **PC:** **Country:** Belgium
Year Established: 2013 **Status 2020:** Active
Industries: Big Data and Analytics for:, Business Applications for:, ~ E-Commerce (12), Predictive Analytics

Company Name: Treedy's
Description: Treedy's is a Belgian 3D body scanning technology provider with ties to leading machine learning researchers and companies.
Website: http://www.treedys.com
Phone: 32 (0) 2 781 03 03 **Email:** stephan@treedys.com
City: Brussels **State:** Brussels **PC:** **Country:** Belgium
Year Established: 2016 **Status 2020:** Active
Industries: Artificial Intelligence for:, IT Managed Services

Company Name: Vadis Technologies
Description: Vadis Technologies is a European regtech company specialized Big Data Analytics.
Website: http://www.vadis.com/
Phone: 32 2 7619270 **Email:** jean-francois.heering@vadis.com
City: Brussels **State:** Brussels **PC:** **Country:** Belgium
Year Established: 2018 **Status 2020:** Active
Industries: Data Management for:, Databases for:, Data Management for:, Predictive Analytics

Company Name: Yagram Heal:Thailand
Description: Yagram is a mHealth solution lining up therapeutic guidelines with data analytics to improve birth outcomes and to empower mums-to-be.
Website: http://yagram.com/
Phone: **Email:** hello@yagram.com
City: Brussels **State:** Brussels **PC:** **Country:** Belgium
Year Established: 2014 **Status 2020:** Active
Industries: Artificial Intelligence for:, ~ Customer Relationship Management (11), ~ Healthcare (20), IT Managed Services for:, ~ Healthcare (20)

Company Name: Geckomatics
Description: Geckomatics builds AI in the cloud that enables businesses and governments to create and update their own geographical information
Website: http://geckomatics.com/
Phone: **Email:** 36610@reference-encyclopedia-ai.net
City: Antwerp **State:** Flanders **PC:** **Country:** Belgium
Year Established: 2013 **Status 2020:** Active
Industries:

Company Name: REstore
Description: REstore is an award-winning energy technology company leading the delivery of advanced automated Demand Respone
Website: http://www.restore.energy/
Phone: 32 3 320 80 39 **Email:** liene.donckers@restore.energy
City: Antwerp **State:** Flanders **PC:** **Country:** Belgium
Year Established: **Status 2020:** Active
Industries: Artificial Intelligence for:, ~ Energy and Utilities (14), ~ Energy and Utilities (14), ~ Energy and Utilities (14), ~ Energy and Utilities (14), ~ Energy and Utilities (14)

Company Name: Salesflare
Description: Simply powerful CRM that automates your data to build better relationships and make more sales.
Website: http://www.salesflare.com
Phone: 32 499 21 77 82 **Email:** jeroen@salesflare.com
City: Antwerp **State:** Flanders **PC:** **Country:** Belgium
Year Established: **Status 2020:** Active
Industries: Artificial Intelligence for:, ~ Media-Communications (41), Automation for:, ~ Social Media (54)

Company Name: ScriptBook
Description: Artificial intelligent screenplay-analysis and box office forecasts
Website: http://www.scriptbook.io
Phone: **Email:** support@scriptbook.io
City: Antwerp **State:** Flanders **PC:** **Country:** Belgium
Year Established: **Status 2020:** Active
Industries: Artificial Intelligence for:, Machine Learning for:, Natural Language Processing

Company Name: Taglayer
Description: Easy-to-use Personalisation software
Website: http://taglayer.com
Phone: **Email:** willem@taglayer.com
City: Antwerp **State:** Flanders **PC:** **Country:** Belgium
Year Established: **Status 2020:** Active
Industries: Analytics for:, Artificial Intelligence for:, Big Data and Analytics for:, Content for:, Machine Learning for:, ~ Media-Communications (41), ~ Media-Communications (41), ~ Professional Services (48)

Company Name: theMatchBox
Description: Search & Matching Solutions NLP, Machine Learning, Language Analyzers, Ontologi: Spain
Website: http://www.thematchbox.be
Phone: 32474914314 **Email:** contact@thematchbox.be
City: Antwerp **State:** Flanders **PC:** **Country:** Belgium
Year Established: 2015 **Status 2020:** Active
Industries: IT Managed Services for:, ~ Education (13), Machine Learning for:, Natural Language Processing for:, Content

Company Name: Chatlayer
Description: Chatlayer is a platform to build high performing chatbots.
Website: http://www.chatlayer.ai/
Phone: 32 3 500 87 09 **Email:** info@chatlayer.ai
City: Antwerpen **State:** Flanders **PC:** **Country:** Belgium
Year Established: 2016 **Status 2020:** Active
Industries: Analytics for:, Artificial Intelligence for:, Web

Company Name: DataStories International
Description: DataStories delivers data-driven solutions to help clients improve their businesses.
Website: http://datastories.com
Phone: (321)480-0414 **Email:** info@datastories.com
City: Antwerpen **State:** Flanders **PC:** **Country:** Belgium
Year Established: **Status 2020:** Active
Industries: Analytics for:, Artificial Intelligence for:, Predictive Analytics

Company Name: Hello Contento - Smart social marketing software for business: Spain
Description: Contento supports the online growth of small businesses and busy entrepreneurs through A.I. powered social media marketing software
Website: http://www.hellocontento.com
Phone: **Email:** ludwig@hellocontento.com
City: Antwerpen **State:** Flanders **PC:** **Country:** Belgium
Year Established: **Status 2020:** Active
Industries: Artificial Intelligence for:, Digital Marketing for:, ~ Media-Communications (41)

Company Name: Sentiance
Description: Sentiance is a data science company turning IOT sensor data into rich insights about people's behavior and real-time context.
Website: http://www.sentiance.com
Phone: **Email:** info@sentiance.com
City: Antwerpen **State:** Flanders **PC:** **Country:** Belgium
Year Established: **Status 2020:** Active
Industries: Artificial Intelligence for:, Machine Learning for:, Predictive Analytics

Company Name: WeGroup
Description: WeGroup is a digital peer-to-peer (P2P) InsurTech company.
Website: wegroup.be/en-home
Phone: **Email:** hello@wegroup.be
City: Bruges **State:** Flanders **PC:** **Country:** Belgium
Year Established: **Status 2020:** Active
Industries: Artificial Intelligence for:, ~ Banking and Financial Markets-Services (7), Natural Language Processing for:, Network

Company Name: Cloudalize
Description: GPU Desktop-as-a-Service Platform delivers virtual cloud desktops for 3D collaboration, CAD or software distribution in a partner model
Website: http://www.cloudalize.com/
Phone: **Email:** info@cloudalize.com
City: Gent **State:** Flanders **PC:** **Country:** Belgium
Year Established: **Status 2020:** Active
Industries: Artificial Intelligence for:, Cloud for:, Enterprise Application Services for:, ~ Manufacturing-Electronic (30), Enterprise Application Services for:, ~ Administrative and Support Services (1)

Company Name: waylay
Description: Waylay is an orchestration and automation platform for the enterprise IOT, connecting devices, and enterprise IT systems.
Website: http://www.waylay.io
Phone: 32 475 283 861 **Email:** info@waylay.io
City: Gent **State:** Flanders **PC:** **Country:** Belgium
Year Established: **Status 2020:** Active
Industries: Artificial Intelligence for:, IT Managed Services for:, ~ Professional Services (48)

Company Name: YAZZOOM
Description: Yazzoom leverages its expertise in advanced data analytics and industrial process control to improve company processes.
Website: http://www.yazzoom.com/
Phone: 32486801043 **Email:** info@yazzoom.com
City: Gent **State:** Flanders **PC:** **Country:** Belgium
Year Established: 2011 **Status 2020:** Active
Industries: Artificial Intelligence for:, Cyber Security for:, Databases for:, Automation for:, IT Managed Services for:, Machine Learning for:, Predictive Analytics for:, Security for:, Security

Company Name: Contento - Smart digital marketing software for small business: Spain
Description: Contento supports the growth of small businesses through A.I. powered digital marketing software
Website: http://www.contento.us
Phone: 4158598321 **Email:** ludwig@contento.us
City: Ghent **State:** Flanders **PC:** **Country:** Belgium
Year Established: **Status 2020:** Active
Industries:

Company Name: MailMine
Description: MailMine - AI that understands the mailbox
Website: http://www.mailmine.io
Phone: (347) 960-6507 **Email:** hello@mailmine.io
City: Ghent **State:** Flanders **PC:** **Country:** Belgium
Year Established: 2017 **Status 2020:** Active
Industries: Artificial Intelligence for:, Automation

Company Name: ML6
Description: ML6 is a machine learning experts that empower businesses with artificial intelligence.
Website: http://ml6.eu/
Phone: **Email:** info@ml6.eu
City: Ghent **State:** Flanders **PC:** **Country:** Belgium
Year Established: 2017 **Status 2020:** Active
Industries: Artificial Intelligence for:, Machine Learning

Company Name: uman.ai
Description: The power of knowledge, for you and your team
Website: http://uman.ai
Phone: **Email:** info@uman.ai
City: Ghent **State:** Flanders **PC:** **Country:** Belgium
Year Established: 2019 **Status 2020:** Active
Industries: Artificial Intelligence

Company Name: Waylay NV
Description:
Website: https://www.waylay.io/
Phone: 32 9 311 55 66 **Email:** Miruna@waylay.io
City: Ghent **State:** Flanders **PC:** **Country:** Belgium
Year Established: **Status 2020:** Active
Industries:

Company Name: WebMonks
Description: Bring state-of-the-art Computer Vision Research to your Development
Website: http://webmonks.vision
Phone: **Email:** hello@webmonks.vision
City: Hasselt **State:** Flanders **PC:** **Country:** Belgium
Year Established: **Status 2020:** Active
Industries: Artificial Intelligence for:, Computer Vision for:, Image Recognition for:, Computer Vision

Company Name: Neuroteg AI
Description: AI for neurodegenerative diseases like Alzheimer's disease, Parkinson and TBI
Website: http://www.neuroteg.com/
Phone: **Email:** uy@neuroteg.com
City: Houthalen **State:** Flanders **PC:** **Country:** Belgium
Year Established: 2016 **Status 2020:** Active
Industries: Artificial Intelligence for:, ~ Healthcare (20)

Company Name: is it a plane
Description: Is it a plane provides solutions to accelerate the adoption of drones.
Website: http://www.isitaplane.com
Phone: **Email:** stefaan@isitaplane.com
City: Kortrijk **State:** Flanders **PC:** **Country:** Belgium
Year Established: **Status 2020:** Active
Industries: Artificial Intelligence for:, ~ Transportation and Logistics (57), ~ Transportation and Logistics (57), Automation for:, Machine Learning for:, ~ Professional Services (48)

Company Name: Amethix Technologies
Description: At Amethix we use machine learning and AI to augment human capital and empower organisations
Website: http://amethix.com
Phone: 32478998936 **Email:** hello@amethix.com
City: Leuven **State:** Flanders **PC:** **Country:** Belgium
Year Established: 2017 **Status 2020:** Active
Industries: Artificial Intelligence for:, ~ Education (13)

Company Name: ArtiQ
Description: ArtiQ developed AI-based software to help doctors save time & improve interpretation of lung function tests & diagnosis of lung diseas: Spain
Website: http://www.artiq.eu/
Phone: **Email:** info@artiq.eu
City: Leuven **State:** Flanders **PC:** **Country:** Belgium
Year Established: 2019 **Status 2020:** Active
Industries: Artificial Intelligence for:, ~ Healthcare (20), IT Managed Services

Company Name: Craftwor: Kazakhstan
Description: Craftworkz uses innovative technologies such as artificial intelligence, augmented reality, chatbots, IoT... to build software prototypes.
Website: http://www.craftworkz.co
Phone: (3249) 844-5061 **Email:** info@craftworkz.be
City: Leuven **State:** Flanders **PC:** **Country:** Belgium

Year Established: 2016 **Status 2020:** Active
Industries: Artificial Intelligence for:, IT Managed Services for:, Robotics

Company Name: dataroots
Description: Bent on delivering best-in-class AI solutions
Website: http://dataroots.io
Phone: (3247) 172-3122 **Email:** bart@dataroots.io
City: Leuven **State:** Flanders **PC:** **Country:** Belgium
Year Established: 2016 **Status 2020:** Active
Industries: Analytics for:, Artificial Intelligence for:, IT Managed Services

Company Name: Intermodalics
Description: From software to robots. Intermodalics develops software for robotic applications world-wide.
Website: http://www.intermodalics.eu/
Phone: 31-7478 **Email:** info@intermodalics.eu
City: Leuven **State:** Flanders **PC:** **Country:** Belgium
Year Established: 2010 **Status 2020:** Active
Industries: Artificial Intelligence for:, IT Managed Services for:, IT Managed Services for:, Robotics

Company Name: Macty
Description: Macty is an AI company that enables the latest technology in computer vision and natural language processing.
Website: http://macty.eu/
Phone: **Email:** info@macty.eu
City: Leuven **State:** Flanders **PC:** **Country:** Belgium
Year Established: 2017 **Status 2020:** Active
Industries: Artificial Intelligence for:, Computer Vision for:, IT Managed Services for:, Natural Language Processing

Company Name: Oppia Performance
Description: Hardware independent AI streaming solution for sport and events, End2End solution including OTT, Apps and Media Services. Data Analytics
Website: http://oppia.tv
Phone: 001 714 728 4055 **Email:** info@oppiaperformance.com
City: Leuven **State:** Flanders **PC:** **Country:** Belgium
Year Established: 2015 **Status 2020:** Active
Industries:

Company Name: Pick-it
Description: Pick-it gives eyes to robots. It offers plug and play smart automation products for any robot.
Website: http://www.pickit3d.com
Phone: 32 468 20 27 26 **Email:** info@pickit3d.com
City: Leuven **State:** Flanders **PC:** **Country:** Belgium
Year Established: **Status 2020:** Active
Industries: Artificial Intelligence for:, Computer Vision for:, Robotics

Company Name: Seven Sensing Software BV
Description: Spectral sensing, computer vision, machine learning, Embedded software
Website: http://www.7sensingsoftware.com
Phone: 32468507161 **Email:** sales@7sensingsoftware.com
City: Leuven **State:** Flanders **PC:** **Country:** Belgium
Year Established: 2017 **Status 2020:** Active
Industries: Artificial Intelligence for:, Computer Vision for:, Embedded for:, Facial Recognition for:, IT Managed Services for:, Machine Learning for:, Robotics for:, Robotics

Company Name: Seven Sensing Software NV
Description: Embedded software, face recognition, face authentication, computer vision, machine learning, Spectral sensing, 3D fitting
Website: http://www.7sensingsoftware.com
Phone: 32468507161 **Email:** sales@7sensingsoftware.com
City: Leuven **State:** Flanders **PC:** **Country:** Belgium
Year Established: **Status 2020:** Active
Industries: Artificial Intelligence for:, Computer Vision for:, Embedded for:, Facial Recognition for:, IT Managed Services for:, Machine Learning for:, Robotics for:, ~ Manufacturing-Electronic (30), ~ Professional Services (48)

Company Name: Sitemark
Description: AI-Powered Aerial Data Platform
Website: http://www.sitemark.com/
Phone: **Email:** 37403@reference-encyclopedia-ai.net
City: Leuven **State:** Flanders **PC:** **Country:** Belgium
Year Established: 2016 **Status 2020:** Active
Industries: ~ Aerospace and Defense (2), Artificial Intelligence

Company Name: Twipe Mobile Solutions
Description: Twipe Mobile Solutions enables publishers to engage more readers on mobile platforms.
Website: http://www.twipemobile.com
Phone: 32 (0)16 23 53 94 **Email:** danny.lein@twipemobile.com
City: Leuven **State:** Flanders **PC:** **Country:** Belgium
Year Established: 2011 **Status 2020:** Active
Industries: Digital Media for:, Predictive Analytics for:, Business Software as a Service Apps (SaaS Apps)

Company Name: iReachm
Description: iReachm has chosen reachability as its core business.
Website: http://ireachm.com
Phone: (322)588-0339 **Email:** mail@ireachm.com
City: Mechelen **State:** Flanders **PC:** **Country:** Belgium
Year Established: 2013 **Status 2020:** Active
Industries: Application Services for:, Application Services

Company Name: Accurat
Description: We offer location intelligence solutions to better understand the offline behaviour of app users for publishers and retailers.
Website: http://accurat.ai
Phone: 32486139162 **Email:** bart@accurat.ai
City: Merelbeke **State:** Flanders **PC:** **Country:** Belgium
Year Established: **Status 2020:** Active
Industries: Artificial Intelligence for:, Machine Learning for:, ~ Media-Communications (41), ~ Media-Communications (41), ~ Retail and Consumer Products (52)

Company Name: Infinity Mobile
Description: E-commerce platform to facilitate mobile order & pay. Combined with our AI customer support solution beating all conversion rates!
Website: http://infinity-mobile.io
Phone: **Email:** info@infinity-mobile.io
City: Nevele **State:** Flanders **PC:** **Country:** Belgium
Year Established: 2016 **Status 2020:** Active
Industries: Artificial Intelligence for:, E-Commerce for:, ~ Event Management (15), Mobile

Company Name: Complidata
Description: Regtech, Fintech, AI, Anti Money Laundering, AML, Financial Crime, Compliance
Website: http://www.complidata.io
Phone: **Email:** matthias@complidata.io
City: Tervuren **State:** Flanders **PC:** **Country:** Belgium
Year Established: **Status 2020:** Active
Industries: Artificial Intelligence for:, Compliance for:, ~ Banking and Financial Markets-Services (7), ~ Banking and Financial Markets-Services (7), IT Managed Services

Company Name: EngineerX
Description: Engineer recruiting company
Website: http://www.EngineerX.com
Phone: **Email:** Byron@EngineerX.com
City: Zaventem **State:** Flanders **PC:** **Country:** Belgium
Year Established: **Status 2020:** Active
Industries: Artificial Intelligence for:, ~ Human Resources (24)

Company Name: Musimap
Description: Musimap emulates the complex emotional interaction that humans have with music.
Website: http://www.musimap.net/
Phone: **Email:** info@musimap.com
City: Liege **State:** Wallonia **PC:** **Country:** Belgium
Year Established: **Status 2020:** Active
Industries: ~ Media-Communications (41), Artificial Intelligence for:, Business Applications for:, ~ Arts-Entertainment-Recreation (4)

Company Name: Piximate
Description: Piximate empowers businesses by delivering tailor-made computer vision AI boosting productivity while saving costs.
Website: http://www.piximate.net
Phone: **Email:** 37174@reference-encyclopedia-ai.net
City: Louvain-la-neuve **State:** Wallonia **PC:** **Country:** Belgium
Year Established: 2016 **Status 2020:** Active
Industries: Artificial Intelligence for:, Web for:, Internet of Things (IoT)

Company Name: Swingu: Russia
Description: Swinguru brings wireless and sensor-less body motion data and analytics to players.
Website: http://www.swinguru.com/
Phone: 32 10 84 01 33 **Email:** info@swinguru.com
City: Louvain-la-neuve **State:** Wallonia **PC:** **Country:** Belgium
Year Established: **Status 2020:** Active
Industries: Artificial Intelligence for:, ~ Arts-Entertainment-Recreation (4)

Company Name: Features Analytics
Description: Has developed eyeDES AI powered Complete Transaction Surveillance Solutions for detecting Market Abuse in FX and Equities, AML and Fraud.
Website: http://www.features-analytics.com
Phone: **Email:** info@features-analytics.com
City: Nivelles **State:** Wallonia **PC:** **Country:** Belgium
Year Established: **Status 2020:** Active
Industries:

Belize

Company Name: Etta Epidermis
Description: Skin and STD/STI Diagnostic Mobile App (AI/AR)
Website: http://www.etta.io
Phone: 630-607-9373 **Email:** hello@etta.io
City: Chicago **State:** Belize **PC:** **Country:** Belize
Year Established: 2017 **Status 2020:** Active
Industries: Artificial Intelligence for:, ~ Healthcare (20), Machine Learning for:, Mobile

Bosnia and Herzegovina

Company Name: Kumi
Description: SaaS
Website:
Phone: **Email:** 4932@reference-encyclopedia-ai.net
City: Cochabamba **State:** Cochabamba Department **PC:** **Country:** BO
Year Established: **Status 2020:** Active
Industries: Analytics for:, Artificial Intelligence for:, Machine Learning

Company Name: Koola
Description: Koola is a predictive maintenance platform utilizing AI and machine learning that connects car dealerships and OEM's with its clients.
Website: http://www.koola.io
Phone: (3876) 118-0923 **Email:** sergio@getkoola.com
City: Sarajevo **State:** Federation of Bosnia and Herzegovina **PC:** **Country:** Bosnia and Herzegovina
Year Established: 2015 **Status 2020:** Active
Industries: Artificial Intelligence for:, ~ Automotive (5), Big Data and Analytics for:, ~ Customer Relationship Management (11), Machine Learning for:, Predictive Analytics for:, Compute

Company Name: Qorio
Description: Singing Assistant AI
Website: http://www.qorio.com
Phone: **Email:** info@qorio.com
City: Banja Luka **State:** Republika Srpska **PC:** **Country:** Bosnia and Herzegovina
Year Established: 2014 **Status 2020:** Active
Industries: Artificial Intelligence for:, ~ Education (13)

Brazil

Company Name: Intelivix
Description: Intelivix develops smart solutions that help legal departments deal with and analyze data.
Website: http://intelivix.com/
Phone: 55 81 3097-3038 **Email:** contato@intelivix.com
City: Recife **State:** BA **PC:** **Country:** Brazil
Year Established: 2015 **Status 2020:** Active
Industries: Artificial Intelligence for:, Databases for:, IT Managed Services

Company Name: PickCells
Description: PickCells uses computer vision and artificial intelligence to automate microscopy examinations.
Website: http://www.pickcells.bio/
Phone: 55 81 9 9764 8605 **Email:** hello@pickcells.bio
City: Recife **State:** BA **PC:** **Country:** Brazil
Year Established: 2014 **Status 2020:** Active
Industries: Artificial Intelligence for:, Computer Vision for:, ~ Healthcare (20), ~ Healthcare (20), Machine Learning

Company Name: Scriber
Description: The Natural Language Processing API tailored for healthcare enterprise.
Website: http://www.scriberapi.com/
Phone: 727-631-4878 **Email:** scriberapi@gmail.com
City: Recife **State:** BA **PC:** **Country:** Brazil
Year Established: 2018 **Status 2020:** Active
Industries: ~ Healthcare (20), Machine Learning for:, Natural Language Processing

Company Name: SET - Construcao Virtual
Description: SET - Construção Virtual is a construction company that develops projects for real estate development and hospitality.
Website: http://www.setconstrucaovirtual.com.br
Phone: 55 (81) 9.7114-1234 **Email:** contato@setconstrucaovirtual.com.br
City: Recife **State:** BA **PC:** **Country:** Brazil
Year Established: 2014 **Status 2020:** Active
Industries: Application Services for:, ~ Construction (10), Virtual Reality (VR)

Company Name: Chatbot Maker
Description: Chatbot Maker helps companies get more customers by automatically capturing leads using a chatbot.
Website: http://chatbotmaker.io/
Phone: (85) 9.9994.7015 **Email:** contato@chatbotmaker.io
City: Fortaleza **State:** MS **PC:** **Country:** Brazil
Year Established: 2016 **Status 2020:** Active
Industries: Artificial Intelligence for:, IT Managed Services for:, Business Software as a Service Apps (SaaS Apps)

Company Name: Delfos
Description: Delfos provides Artificial Intelligence for the Energy Industry in order to predict failures.
Website: http://delfosim.com
Phone: 55 85 3267 2660 **Email:** contato@delfosim.com
City: Fortaleza **State:** MS **PC:** **Country:** Brazil

Year Established: 2016 **Status 2020:** Active
Industries: Artificial Intelligence for:, Databases for:, Machine Learning for:, ~ Energy and Utilities (14)

Company Name: agryo
Description: The agryo company is a Data Driven Blockchain Peer-to-Peer and Marketplace Lending platform which connects farmers to lenders.
Website: http://agryo.com
Phone: **Email:** agryo@agryo.com
City: Brasilandia **State:** DF **PC:** **Country:** Brazil
Year Established: **Status 2020:** Active
Industries: ~ Agriculture (3), Artificial Intelligence for:, Big Data and Analytics for:, ~ Banking and Financial Markets-Services (7), Network

Company Name: Cxclick
Description: Cxclick is a company dedicated to the management of Brazilian business reputation.
Website: http://cxclick.com.br
Phone: **Email:** 36367@reference-encyclopedia-ai.net
City: Campinas **State:** GO **PC:** **Country:** Brazil
Year Established: 2016 **Status 2020:** Active
Industries: Artificial Intelligence for:, Big Data and Analytics for:, Web

Company Name: Evolt Energia e Automacao
Description: Evolt Energia e Automacao develops technology-based innovation for industry, especially through solutions in energy and automation.
Website: http://www.evoltenergia.com/
Phone: 85 30674601 **Email:** evolt@evoltenergia.com.br
City: Fortaleza **State:** MS **PC:** **Country:** Brazil
Year Established: 2016 **Status 2020:** Active
Industries: Databases for:, ~ Energy and Utilities (14), Automation for:, Application Services for:, Internet of Things (IoT)

Company Name: Datastorm
Description: Datastorm focuses on Big Data solutions, providing services and products that helps companies.
Website: http://datastorm.com.br/
Phone: (313) 025-3845 **Email:** suporte@datastorm.com.br
City: **State:** AC **PC:** **Country:** Brazil
Year Established: 2014 **Status 2020:** Active
Industries:

Company Name: MI4U
Description: MI4U is focused on transforming health data into applied intelligence to health.
Website: http://www.mi4u.com.br/
Phone: **Email:** contato@mi4u.com.br
City: Ribeirao Preto **State:** MG **PC:** **Country:** Brazil
Year Established: 2015 **Status 2020:** Active
Industries: Artificial Intelligence for:, Big Data and Analytics for:, ~ Healthcare (20)

Company Name: Cloud Clinic
Description: Cloud Clinic is a clinical management system that enables clinics and offices to assist the process of care.
Website:
Phone: 55 13 3229-1962 **Email:** 36292@reference-encyclopedia-ai.net
City: Santos **State:** MG **PC:** **Country:** Brazil
Year Established: 2014 **Status 2020:** Closed
Industries: Application Services

Company Name: Brisa Robotica
Description: Robotics, Autonomous Systems and Machine Intelligence solutions
Website: http://brisa.tech
Phone: **Email:** thiago@brisa.tech
City: Santo Agostinho **State:** PE **PC:** **Country:** Brazil
Year Established: **Status 2020:** Active
Industries: Artificial Intelligence for:, IT Managed Services for:, Machine Learning for:, Robotics

Company Name: Zaitt
Description: Zaitt seeks to deliver a simplification of the user's purchasing process.
Website: http://www.zaitt.com.br/
Phone: **Email:** contato@zaitt.com.br
City: Vitória **State:** PI **PC:** **Country:** Brazil
Year Established: 2016 **Status 2020:** Active
Industries: IT Managed Services for:, Application Services for:, Web

Company Name: Tobyto
Description: Tobyto is a brown bear cub robot, designed to keep people company and help with everyday tasks.
Website: http://www.tobyto.net
Phone: **Email:** tobyto@tobyto.net
City: Rio **State:** RJ **PC:** **Country:** Brazil
Year Established: 2016 **Status 2020:** Active
Industries: Artificial Intelligence for:, Robotics

Company Name: Estudologia
Description: Estudologia is an E-learning platform that combines big data and artificial intelligence.
Website: http://estudologia.com.br/
Phone: **Email:** ola@estudologia.com.br
City: Brasilia **State:** RN **PC:** **Country:** Brazil
Year Established: 2017 **Status 2020:** Active
Industries: Artificial Intelligence for:, ~ Education (13), ~ Education (13), ~ Education (13)

Company Name: Legal Labs
Description: Legal Labs is a startup that specializes in artificial intelligence applied to the law.
Website: http://legalabs.com.br/
Phone: **Email:** contato@legalabs.com.br
City: Brasilia **State:** RN **PC:** **Country:** Brazil
Year Established: 2016 **Status 2020:** Active
Industries: Artificial Intelligence for:, Databases for:, Machine Learning for:, Natural Language Processing

Company Name: Nimbus TI
Description: Nimbus TI builds web and mobile applications powered by cloud computing and artificial intelligence technologies.
Website: http://www.nimbusti.com/
Phone: **Email:** contato@nimbusti.com
City: Brasilia **State:** RN **PC:** **Country:** Brazil
Year Established: 2014 **Status 2020:** Active
Industries: Artificial Intelligence for:, Cloud for:, IT Managed Services for:, Web

Company Name: Pulpo
Description: Pulpo is a knowledge management solution company that assist in the optimization and creation of the knowledge flow for companies.
Website: http://pulpo.work
Phone: 55 (54) 99979-2257 **Email:** welcome@pulpo.work
City: Erechim **State:** Rio Grande do Sul **PC:** **Country:** Brazil
Year Established: 2016 **Status 2020:** Active
Industries: IT Managed Services for:, Machine Learning for:, Business Software as a Service Apps (SaaS Apps)

Company Name: MontaAI
Description: MontaAI develops artificial intelligence solutions.
Website:
Phone: **Email:** 37015@reference-encyclopedia-ai.net
City: Gravatai **State:** RS **PC:** **Country:** Brazil
Year Established: 2015 **Status 2020:** Active
Industries: Artificial Intelligence for:, Business Applications for:, E-Commerce for:, IT Managed Services

Company Name: BringUp
Description: BringUp is a machine learning platform for franchise training and retail qualification.
Website: http://www.bringupapp.com.br/
Phone: 55 51 3781 0548 **Email:** contato@bringupapp.com.br
City: Novo Hamburgo **State:** RS **PC:** **Country:** Brazil
Year Established: 2011 **Status 2020:** Active
Industries: ~ Retail and Consumer Products (52), Machine Learning for:, ~ Education (13)

Company Name: ODM
Description: ODM is a management consulting company that develops systems and offers consultancy for companies and industries.
Website: http://odmcentral.com/
Phone: 55 (16) 99710 - 5329 **Email:** contato@odmcentral.com
City: São Carlos **State:** RO **PC:** **Country:** Brazil
Year Established: 2017 **Status 2020:** Active
Industries:

Company Name: Sigalei
Description: Sigalei uses legislative data, technology, and legal knowledge and government relations to develop technology.
Website: http://sigalei.com.br/
Phone: 55 16 3419-7018 **Email:** contato@sigalei.com.br
City: São Carlos **State:** RO **PC:** **Country:** Brazil
Year Established: 2016 **Status 2020:** Active
Industries: Artificial Intelligence for:, ~ Government (19), ~ Government (19)

Company Name: Contratools
Description: Contratools reduces real estate contract recessions in the approval of funding through artificial intelligence and big data.
Website: http://www.contratools.com.br/
Phone: **Email:** 36331@reference-encyclopedia-ai.net
City: Palhoca **State:** SC **PC:** **Country:** Brazil
Year Established: 2017 **Status 2020:** Active
Industries:

Company Name: Ontrack Software
Description: Ontrack Software maximizes retention and expansion of the customer base for B2B businesses .
Website: http://userontrack.com/
Phone: **Email:** 37108@reference-encyclopedia-ai.net
City: Palhoça **State:** SC **PC:** **Country:** Brazil
Year Established: 2017 **Status 2020:** Closed
Industries: Artificial Intelligence for:, Business Applications for:, Big Data and Analytics for:, Business Software as a Service Apps (SaaS Apps)

Company Name: Maply Tecnologia
Description: Maply offers a cloud based platform to capture, process and analyze commercial drone data.
Website: http://maply.io/
Phone: 55 11 2122-4062 **Email:** alexandre@maply.io
City: Barueri **State:** SP **PC:** **Country:** Brazil
Year Established: 2016 **Status 2020:** Active
Industries: ~ Customer Relationship Management (11), IT Managed Services for:, Application Services

Company Name: ViaObjects
Description: Custom software service
Website: http://www.viaobjects.com
Phone: **Email:** hello@viaobjects.com
City: Bento Gonçalves **State:** SP **PC:** **Country:** Brazil
Year Established: 2013 **Status 2020:** Active
Industries: Artificial Intelligence for:, Natural Language Processing

Company Name: Agrointeli
Description: Agrointeli is a digital agriculture company that helps farmers make decisions based on real numbers of their crops in a sustainable way.
Website: http://agrointeli.com.br/
Phone: **Email:** contato@agrointeli.com.br
City: Campo Grande **State:** SP **PC:** **Country:** Brazil
Year Established: 2017 **Status 2020:** Active
Industries: ~ Agriculture (3), ~ Agriculture (3), Artificial Intelligence for:, Machine Learning

Company Name: Zeenflow
Description: Zeenflow is an IT company that offers real-time team analysis platform.
Website: http://www.zeenflow.com/
Phone: **Email:** equipe@zeenflow.com
City: Campo Grande **State:** SP **PC:** **Country:** Brazil
Year Established: 2017 **Status 2020:** Active
Industries: Analytics for:, Artificial Intelligence for:, IT Managed Services

Company Name: EEMovel
Description: EEMovel provides real time information, investment analysis, insights, and market reports.
Website: http://www.eemovel.com.br
Phone: (5) 544-5859 **Email:** contato@eemovel.com.br
City: Cascavel **State:** SP **PC:** **Country:** Brazil
Year Established: 2014 **Status 2020:** Active
Industries: Artificial Intelligence for:, Big Data and Analytics for:, Business Applications for:, Compute

Company Name: Gupy
Description: Gupy is a recruitment technology companies that offers online platform for companies looking for efficiency and accuracy when hiring talent.
Website: http://gupy.io
Phone: **Email:** mariana@gupy.com.br
City: Cerqueira Cesar **State:** SP **PC:** **Country:** Brazil
Year Established: 2015 **Status 2020:** Active
Industries: Analytics for:, Web for:, Machine Learning

Company Name: SEV Soluco: Spain
Description: SEV Soluções offers to the market the chatbot Meebo, a robot that interacts with the customer and sells in an automated way on Facebook.
Website: http://sevsolucoes.com/
Phone: 14 981973358 **Email:** contato@sevsolucoes.com
City: Marília **State:** SP **PC:** **Country:** Brazil
Year Established: 2017 **Status 2020:** Active
Industries: Artificial Intelligence for:, E-Commerce for:, IT Managed Services for:, Machine Learning

Company Name: DrFarm
Description: DrFarm monitors the weather conditions in a farm through data collected by capsules with sensors.
Website: http://drfarm.com.br/
Phone: **Email:** 36456@reference-encyclopedia-ai.net
City: Salvador **State:** SP **PC:** **Country:** Brazil
Year Established: 2016 **Status 2020:** Active
Industries: ~ Agriculture (3), ~ Agriculture (3), ~ Agriculture (3), Machine Learning

Company Name: Hand Ta: Sri Lanka
Description: Hand Talk is a mobile translator for smartphones and tablets which converts in real time content in port.
Website: http://www.handtalk.me
Phone: **Email:** assessoria@handtalk.com.br
City: Maceio **State:** AL **PC:** **Country:** Brazil
Year Established: 2012 **Status 2020:** Active
Industries: Application Services for:, ~ Education (13), Natural Language Processing

Company Name: Ilhasoft
Description: Ilhasoft is a Brazilian company that specializes in chatbots and AI development in optimizing services that has a social impact.
Website: http://ilhasoft.com.br/
Phone: **Email:** contato@ilhasoft.com.br
City: Maceio **State:** AL **PC:** **Country:** Brazil
Year Established: 2012 **Status 2020:** Active
Industries: Artificial Intelligence for:, Business Applications for:, ~ Customer Relationship Management (11), Natural Language Processing for:, Business Software as a Service Apps (SaaS Apps)

Company Name: Keep Smiling
Description: KeepSmiling monitors the brushing of children through educational games using techniques of artificial intelligence and fun.
Website:
Phone: **Email:** 36848@reference-encyclopedia-ai.net
City: Manaus **State:** AM **PC:** **Country:** Brazil
Year Established: 2017 **Status 2020:** Active
Industries: Artificial Intelligence for:, Business Applications for:, Business Applications for:, ~ Arts-Entertainment-Recreation (4), ~ Education (13)

Company Name: Bitcast - Inteligencia em Hardware
Description: Bitcast - Inteligencia em Hardware specializes in embedded systems engineering focusing on micro-controlled electronic development.
Website: http://www.bitcast.com.br/
Phone: 55 (27) 3029-0845 **Email:** administrativo@bitcast.com.br
City: Victoria **State:** ES **PC:** **Country:** Brazil
Year Established: 2011 **Status 2020:** Active
Industries: Embedded for:, Automation for:, Application Services

Company Name: A3Data
Description: A3Data is a company focused on intelligence that can be extracted from data.
Website: http://www.a3data.com.br/
Phone: **Email:** 35930@reference-encyclopedia-ai.net
City: Belo Horizonte **State:** MG **PC:** **Country:** Brazil
Year Established: 2012 **Status 2020:** Active
Industries:

Company Name: Aiplates Technologies
Description: Aiplates Technologies can turn any conventional surveillance camera into a vehicle recognition identification camera.
Website: http://www.aiplates.com.br/
Phone: **Email:** contato@aiplates.com.br
City: Belo Horizonte **State:** MG **PC:** **Country:** Brazil
Year Established: 2017 **Status 2020:** Active
Industries: Artificial Intelligence for:, Business Applications for:, Big Data and Analytics for:, Security

Company Name: Cogitant
Description: Cogitant brings advanced artificial intelligence techniques to small and medium businesses.
Website: http://cogitant.ai/
Phone: **Email:** contato@cogitant.ai
City: Belo Horizonte **State:** MG **PC:** **Country:** Brazil
Year Established: **Status 2020:** Active
Industries: Artificial Intelligence for:, IT Managed Services

Company Name: Coodesh
Description: Assess tech skills with real-world tasks
Website: http://coodesh.com
Phone: **Email:** contact@coodesh.com
City: Belo Horizonte **State:** MG **PC:** **Country:** Brazil
Year Established: 2018 **Status 2020:** Active
Industries: ~ Education (13), IT Managed Services for:, Machine Learning

Company Name: Grupo Cortex
Description: Grupo Cortex provides innovative solutions in Blockchain, Crypto, Ai & Deep Learning.
Website: http://www.grupocortex.com.br
Phone: **Email:** 36653@reference-encyclopedia-ai.net
City: Belo Horizonte **State:** MG **PC:** **Country:** Brazil
Year Established: 2011 **Status 2020:** Active
Industries: Artificial Intelligence for:, Business Applications for:, Big Data and Analytics for:, Blockchain

Company Name: Hop Digital
Description: Hop is a startup that applies artificial intelligence solutions in the digital transformation of business.
Website: http://www.hop.digital/
Phone: 55 (31) 2551-3535 **Email:** contato@hop.digital
City: Belo Horizonte **State:** MG **PC:** **Country:** Brazil
Year Established: 2017 **Status 2020:** Active
Industries: Artificial Intelligence for:, Business Applications for:, Digital Marketing for:, Machine Learning for:, Natural Language Processing

Company Name: Kapputo
Description: Business Intelligence tool that makes the decision-process in the real estate market easier.
Website: http://www.kapputo.com
Phone: **Email:** contato@kapputo.com
City: Belo Horizonte **State:** MG **PC:** **Country:** Brazil
Year Established: 2016 **Status 2020:** Active
Industries: Big Data and Analytics for:, Machine Learning

Company Name: Kunumi
Description: A Brazilian company that develops A.I with responsibility, enabling the wide distribution of knowledge, prosperity, and well-being.
Website: http://kunumi.com
Phone: (5) 530-8028 **Email:** social@kunumi.com
City: Belo Horizonte **State:** MG **PC:** **Country:** Brazil
Year Established: 2016 **Status 2020:** Active
Industries: Artificial Intelligence for:, Machine Learning

Company Name: Netbee
Description: Netbee develops and supplies solutions in the ITS market for improving safety, urban mobility, and vehicle performance.
Website: http://www.netbeetech.com.br/
Phone: **Email:** netbee@netbeetech.com.br
City: Belo Horizonte **State:** MG **PC:** **Country:** Brazil
Year Established: 2010 **Status 2020:** Active
Industries: Databases for:, IT Managed Services for:, Application Services for:, Internet of Things (IoT)

Company Name: Radar do Futu: Romania
Description: Radar do Futuro generates analytics on how economic, technological, social, cultural changes impact the entrepreneurial community.
Website: http://radardofuturo.com.br/
Phone: **Email:** 37254@reference-encyclopedia-ai.net
City: Belo Horizonte **State:** MG **PC:** **Country:** Brazil
Year Established: 2011 **Status 2020:** Active
Industries: Analytics for:, Application Services for:, Web for:, Data Management

Company Name: ROBOS.: Isle of Man
Description: ROBOS.im focused in delivering products that solve Natural Processing Language (NLP) and Machine Learning (ML) issues.
Website: http://www.robos.im/
Phone: **Email:** info@robos.com.: Turkey
City: Belo Horizonte **State:** MG **PC:** **Country:** Brazil
Year Established: 2016 **Status 2020:** Active
Industries: Artificial Intelligence for:, Digital Marketing for:, IT Managed Services for:, Machine Learning for:, Natural Language Processing

Company Name: SVATech
Description: SVATech offers a programmable smart vision system for security and operations.
Website: http://site.svatech.com.br
Phone: 55 (31) 3243-5590 **Email:** contato@svatech.com.br
City: Belo Horizonte **State:** MG **PC:** **Country:** Brazil
Year Established: 2015 **Status 2020:** Active
Industries: Analytics for:, Artificial Intelligence for:, IT Managed Services for:, Compute for:, Cyber Security

Company Name: Vende AI
Description: Vende AI is an online platform for people interested in reselling products over the internet.
Website: http://vendeai.com.br/
Phone: 55 31 99432-1100 **Email:** 37614@reference-encyclopedia-ai.net
City: Belo Horizonte **State:** MG **PC:** **Country:** Brazil
Year Established: 2017 **Status 2020:** Active
Industries: Artificial Intelligence for:, E-Commerce for:, Web

Company Name: WorldSen
Description: WorldSense is an adtech startup chartered to change the way publishers and advertisers connect around content.
Website: http://www.worldsense.com/
Phone: **Email:** 37683@reference-encyclopedia-ai.net
City: Belo Horizonte **State:** MG **PC:** **Country:** Brazil
Year Established: 2015 **Status 2020:** Active
Industries: Artificial Intelligence for:, Web

Company Name: Gamefic
Description: Gamefic is a gamification company and our solution is the only one in the world to apply the B2B and B2C methodology .
Website: http://www.gamefic.me
Phone: **Email:** contato@gamefic.com.br
City: Uberlandia **State:** MG **PC:** **Country:** Brazil
Year Established: 2016 **Status 2020:** Active
Industries:

Company Name: Mobez
Description: Mobez is a startup in the field of smart cities, which creates solutions for urban mobility, based on computer vision.
Website: http://mobez.com.br/
Phone: 55 34 98804-7961 **Email:** contato@mobez.com.br
City: Uberlandia **State:** MG **PC:** **Country:** Brazil
Year Established: 2016 **Status 2020:** Active
Industries: Artificial Intelligence for:, Big Data and Analytics for:, Image Recognition

Company Name: Recrutei
Description: Recrutei offers to HR a platform similar to an ATS but with artificial intelligence to help companies hire the candidates.
Website: http://www.recrutei.com.br
Phone: (34) 99171-1549 **Email:** contato@recrutei.com.br
City: Uberlandia **State:** MG **PC:** **Country:** Brazil
Year Established: **Status 2020:** Active
Industries: Artificial Intelligence for:, IT Managed Services for:, Machine Learning

Company Name: Sensix
Description: Sensix is an imagery-enabled agritech that uses machine learning to analyse crop performance through the web-based platform Fieldscan.
Website: http://sensix.com.br/
Phone: **Email:** contato@sensix.com.br
City: Uberlandia **State:** MG **PC:** **Country:** Brazil
Year Established: 2015 **Status 2020:** Active
Industries: ~ Agriculture (3), ~ Agriculture (3), Artificial Intelligence for:, IT Managed Services for:, Machine Learning

Company Name: Portal do Arquiteto
Description: Portal do Arquiteto uses artificial intelligence to create digital architecture.
Website: http://portaldoarquiteto.com.br/
Phone: **Email:** 37191@reference-encyclopedia-ai.net
City: João Pessoa **State:** PB **PC:** **Country:** Brazil
Year Established: 2017 **Status 2020:** Active
Industries: Artificial Intelligence for:, Digital Media for:, Machine Learning

Company Name: 4VANTS
Description: Artificial intelligence company that identifies and analyzes assets in images.
Website: http://www.4vants.com.br/
Phone: **Email:** michel@4vants.com.br
City: Curitiba **State:** PR **PC:** **Country:** Brazil
Year Established: 2016 **Status 2020:** Active
Industries: Artificial Intelligence for:, Application Services for:, Machine Learning

Company Name: EI Tools
Description: EI Tools offers a solution for the development of human skills associated with emotional intelligence.
Website: http://www.eitools.com.br/
Phone: **Email:** 36485@reference-encyclopedia-ai.net
City: Curitiba **State:** PR **PC:** **Country:** Brazil
Year Established: 2017 **Status 2020:** Active
Industries: Artificial Intelligence for:, Machine Learning

Company Name: FOHAT
Description: Energy Intelligence company with innovative solutions for the energy sector.
Website: http://www.fohat.co
Phone: 55 41 9239-0123 **Email:** energy@fohat.co
City: Curitiba **State:** PR **PC:** **Country:** Brazil
Year Established: 2017 **Status 2020:** Active
Industries: Blockchain for:, ~ Energy and Utilities (14), ~ Energy and Utilities (14), Application Services for:, ~ Energy and Utilities (14)

Company Name: Hariken
Description: Hariken allows this data to be used in the main activation tools.
Website: http://www.hariken.co/
Phone: **Email:** 36670@reference-encyclopedia-ai.net
City: Curitiba **State:** PR **PC:** **Country:** Brazil
Year Established: 2015 **Status 2020:** Active
Industries: Big Data and Analytics for:, Databases for:, Data Management for:, Data Management for:, Predictive Analytics

Company Name: HumanRobotics
Description: Robot As a Service. We rent our robots.
Website: http://www.humanrobotics.io
Phone: **Email:** olivier@humanrobotics.io
City: Curitiba **State:** PR **PC:** **Country:** Brazil
Year Established: **Status 2020:** Active
Industries: Artificial Intelligence for:, ~ Manufacturing-Electronic (30), ~ Human Resources (24), Robotics

Company Name: Leads2b
Description: Leads2b is a technology solutions company that specializes in the generation of Leads in the B2B market.
Website: http://leads2b.com
Phone: (41) 3336-4949 **Email:** contato@leads2b.com
City: Curitiba **State:** PR **PC:** **Country:** Brazil
Year Established: 2014 **Status 2020:** Active
Industries: Artificial Intelligence for:, Big Data and Analytics for:, Business Software as a Service Apps (SaaS Apps)

Company Name: Neurologic AI
Description: Predict analytics algorithm that identify users with high probability of buying, only by behavior browsing in the site.
Website: http://neurologic.com.br
Phone: 554195875 **Email:** contato@neurologic.com.br
City: Curitiba **State:** PR **PC:** **Country:** Brazil

Year Established: 2015 **Status 2020:** Active
Industries: Artificial Intelligence for:, E-Commerce for:, Machine Learning for:, Predictive Analytics

Company Name: Robô Laura
Description: Robô Laura is a company specialized in the development of systems equipped with cognitive computing and artificial intelligence.
Website: http://www.lauranetworks.com/
Phone: 55 41 99142-2111 **Email:** contato@laura-br.com
City: Curitiba **State:** PR **PC:** **Country:** Brazil
Year Established: 2016 **Status 2020:** Active
Industries: Artificial Intelligence for:, IT Managed Services

Company Name: SM4RT Digital
Description: SM4RT Digital empowers its customers to the 4.0 world through solutions in IoT, Industry 4.0, Artificial Intelligence and Big Data.
Website: http://sm4rt.com.br/
Phone: (41) 3155-9559 **Email:** contato@sm4rt.com.br
City: Curitiba **State:** PR **PC:** **Country:** Brazil
Year Established: 2014 **Status 2020:** Active
Industries: Artificial Intelligence for:, IT Managed Services for:, Internet of Things (IoT)

Company Name: UBIV
Description: UBIVIS offers a complete solution to optimize its industrial operation via IoT System for data collection exchange and cognitive analysis.
Website: http://www.ubivis.io/
Phone: **Email:** contato@ubivis.io
City: Curitiba **State:** PR **PC:** **Country:** Brazil
Year Established: 2014 **Status 2020:** Active
Industries:

Company Name: FarmGO
Description: FarmGO helps make field operations more efficient by using exponential technologies.
Website: http://www.farmgo.com.br/
Phone: **Email:** ricardo.matiello@farmgo.com.br
City: Maringa **State:** PR **PC:** **Country:** Brazil
Year Established: 2017 **Status 2020:** Active
Industries: ~ Agriculture (3), ~ Agriculture (3), Artificial Intelligence for:, Internet of Things (IoT) for:, Business Software as a Service Apps (SaaS Apps)

Company Name: Aentropico
Description: Aentropico offers a predictive analytics platform that allows businesses to get predictive insights into their daily business activities.
Website:
Phone: **Email:** 35964@reference-encyclopedia-ai.net
City: Rio De Janeiro **State:** RJ **PC:** **Country:** Brazil
Year Established: **Status 2020:** Closed
Industries: Analytics for:, Big Data and Analytics for:, Business Intelligence for:, Predictive Analytics

Company Name: AIO Educação
Description: Learning made easy with artificial intelligence working to create individualized journeys for each student.
Website: https://aioeducacao.com.br/
Phone: **Email:** patricia@garagem.com
City: Rio De Janeiro **State:** RJ **PC:** **Country:** Brazil
Year Established: 2020 **Status 2020:** Active
Industries: Artificial Intelligence for:, ~ Education (13)

Company Name: Aliger a Empresa de Inteligência das Coisas
Description: Aliger is a digital curator, developer, manufacturer and systems integrator working in the IoT segment.
Website: https://www.aliger.com.br/
Phone: 55 21 2135-2343 **Email:** contato@aliger.com.br
City: Rio De Janeiro **State:** RJ **PC:** **Country:** Brazil
Year Established: 2011 **Status 2020:** Active
Industries: Artificial Intelligence for:, Business Applications for:, IT Managed Services for:, IT Managed Services for:, ~ Customer Relationship Management (11)

Company Name: Bilo
Description: Bilo is an intelligent platform for the management and complete operation of events.
Website: http://getbilo.com/
Phone: **Email:** contato@getbilo.com
City: Rio De Janeiro **State:** RJ **PC:** **Country:** Brazil
Year Established: 2016 **Status 2020:** Active
Industries: Artificial Intelligence for:, IT Managed Services

Company Name: BlogIA
Description: BlogIA is an AI system that searches for news on the best international sites, translates texts and publishes on the website.
Website: http://blogia.com.br/
Phone: **Email:** 36177@reference-encyclopedia-ai.net
City: Rio De Janeiro **State:** RJ **PC:** **Country:** Brazil
Year Established: 2014 **Status 2020:** Active
Industries: Artificial Intelligence for:, ~ Social Assistance-Non-Profits (53)

Company Name: CyberLabs
Description: CyberLabs is a deep-tech company based in Rio de Janeiro, Brazil. CyberLabs deploys MLaaS and computer vision solutions to firms in LatAm.
Website: http://www.cyberlabs.ai
Phone: **Email:** contact@cyberlabs.ai
City: Rio De Janeiro **State:** RJ **PC:** **Country:** Brazil
Year Established: 2017 **Status 2020:** Active
Industries: Artificial Intelligence for:, Computer Vision for:, Internet of Things (IoT) for:, Machine Learning for:, Predictive Analytics for:, Robotics

Company Name: GreenAnt
Description: Machine Learning enabled SaaS energy management system.
Website: http://www.greenant.com.br
Phone: 55 21 98495-3043 **Email:** contato@greenant.com.br
City: Rio De Janeiro **State:** RJ **PC:** **Country:** Brazil
Year Established: 2015 **Status 2020:** Active
Industries: Analytics for:, Artificial Intelligence for:, ~ Energy and Utilities (14), ~ Energy and Utilities (14), ~ Energy and Utilities (14), Internet of Things (IoT) for:, Business Software as a Service Apps (SaaS Apps)

Company Name: Milestone Digital
Description: Milestone Digital, a product design and development firm, leverages the power of artificial intelligence to generate code automatically.
Website: http://www.milestone.digital/
Phone: **Email:** 36977@reference-encyclopedia-ai.net
City: Rio De Janeiro **State:** RJ **PC:** **Country:** Brazil
Year Established: 2016 **Status 2020:** Active
Industries: Artificial Intelligence

Company Name: MIXVIP
Description: We want to do what BITCOIN could not, making our cryptocurrency have usability on a daily basis and not used only as an investment.
Website: http://mixvip.io
Phone: **Email:** mixvip@mixvip.io
City: Rio De Janeiro **State:** RJ **PC:** **Country:** Brazil
Year Established: 2018 **Status 2020:** Active
Industries: Artificial Intelligence for:, Blockchain for:, ~ Banking and Financial Markets-Services (7), ~ Social Assistance-Non-Profits (53)

Company Name: Nativoo
Description: Nativoo is a startup offering an artificial intelligence platform for travelers to decide on what to do and where to go.
Website: http://www.nativoo.com
Phone: **Email:** 37041@reference-encyclopedia-ai.net
City: Rio De Janeiro **State:** RJ **PC:** **Country:** Brazil
Year Established: 2012 **Status 2020:** Active
Industries: Artificial Intelligence for:, ~ Travel and Transportation (58)

Company Name: Pareto Group
Description: Pareto Group automates pay-per-click campaigns through artificial intelligence.
Website: http://pareto.io
Phone: 55 (21) 3228-0063 **Email:** comercial@paretogroup.com.br
City: Rio De Janeiro **State:** RJ **PC:** **Country:** Brazil
Year Established: 2016 **Status 2020:** Active
Industries: Artificial Intelligence for:, Digital Marketing

Company Name: Responde Ai
Description: Responde Ai is an online platform that helps college students optimize studies and have better test scores.
Website: http://www.respondeai.com.br/
Phone: 55 21 99769-1981 **Email:** faleai@respondeai.com.br
City: Rio De Janeiro **State:** RJ **PC:** **Country:** Brazil
Year Established: 2013 **Status 2020:** Active
Industries: Artificial Intelligence for:, ~ Education (13), ~ Education (13), Web

Company Name: BCOG
Description: BCOG is a company that focuses on expert systems and artificial intelligence consulting.
Website: http://www.bcog.net.br
Phone: 55 21 97479-2826 **Email:** joel@bcog.net.br
City: Tijuca **State:** RJ **PC:** **Country:** Brazil
Year Established: 2016 **Status 2020:** Active
Industries:

Company Name: BeAnalytic
Description: Company specialized in solving problem through data analytics. We have solutions for productivity and sales increase, and costs reduction.
Website: http://www.beanalytic.com.br/
Phone: **Email:** contato@beanalytic.com.br
City: Natal **State:** RN **PC:** **Country:** Brazil
Year Established: 2018 **Status 2020:** Active
Industries: Analytics for:, Big Data and Analytics for:, Business Intelligence for:, Predictive Analytics

Company Name: WBIO
Description: WBIO offers low cost technological solutions for hospitals and clinical analysis laboratories.
Website: http://www.wbio.co/
Phone: **Email:** contato@wbio.co
City: Campo Bom **State:** RS **PC:** **Country:** Brazil
Year Established: 2016 **Status 2020:** Active
Industries: Artificial Intelligence for:, Big Data and Analytics for:, ~ Biotechnology (9), Blockchain for:, ~ Healthcare (20), ~ Healthcare (20)

Company Name: Predi: South Africa
Description: Prediza is a startup that helps people through the prediction and identification of events in the cloud.
Website: http://prediza.io
Phone: 55 (54) 3218-2034 **Email:** 37199@reference-encyclopedia-ai.net
City: Caxias Do Sul **State:** RS **PC:** **Country:** Brazil
Year Established: 2018 **Status 2020:** Active
Industries: ~ Agriculture (3), IT Managed Services for:, Predictive Analytics for:, Compute

Company Name: Omine
Description: Omine is a technology company that develops systems and applications and helps with company tasks, productivity, and efficiency.
Website: http://www.ominesoftware.com.br/
Phone: 55 51 3933-7619 **Email:** contato@ominesoftware.com.br
City: Gravataí **State:** RS **PC:** **Country:** Brazil
Year Established: 2016 **Status 2020:** Active
Industries: Application Services for:, IT Managed Services for:, Application Services for:, Application Services

Company Name: Demander - Gestao Comercial
Description: Demander is a system that can be used by outside vendors and business representatives for ordering on smartphones and tablets.
Website: http://site.demanderweb.com.br/
Phone: **Email:** contato@retta.com.br
City: Lajeado **State:** RS **PC:** **Country:** Brazil
Year Established: 2013 **Status 2020:** Active
Industries: Application Services for:, Management Information Systems

Company Name: A00s Software Inteligente
Description: A00s comes prepared for communication with an artificial intelligence system.
Website: http://a00s.com/
Phone: (54) 3242 7901 **Email:** suporte@a00s.com
City: Nova Prata **State:** RS **PC:** **Country:** Brazil
Year Established: 2016 **Status 2020:** Active
Industries: Artificial Intelligence for:, Business Applications for:, IT Managed Services for:, Web for:, Management Information Systems

Company Name: Elysios
Description: Elysios is an AgriTech company that offers agricultural intelligence solutions for crop control, sensing, and automation.
Website: http://elysios.com.br
Phone: (55 51) 99745-7607 **Email:** contact@elysios.com.br
City: Porto Alegre **State:** RS **PC:** **Country:** Brazil
Year Established: 2017 **Status 2020:** Active
Industries: ~ Agriculture (3), ~ Agriculture (3), Artificial Intelligence for:, Internet of Things (IoT)

Company Name: Evo2Gether
Description: Evo2Gether offers services to bring your company the experience of artifical intelligence.
Website: http://www.evo2g.co/
Phone: 55 51 98906-6006 **Email:** hello@evo2g.co
City: Porto Alegre **State:** RS **PC:** **Country:** Brazil
Year Established: **Status 2020:** Active
Industries: Artificial Intelligence for:, Business Applications for:, Business Applications for:, ~ Customer Relationship Management (11)

Company Name: GreenTech & Projects
Description: GreenTech & Projects works with project management and installing systems in homes and small businesses.
Website: http://www.greentep.com
Phone: (51) 3225-4300 **Email:** contato@greentep.com
City: Porto Alegre **State:** RS **PC:** **Country:** Brazil
Year Established: 2018 **Status 2020:** Active
Industries: ~ Energy and Utilities (14)

Company Name: James Tip
Description: James Tip focuses in the stock and dimensions to avoid ruptures and excess using artificial intelligence.
Website: http://www.jamestip.com/
Phone: 55 51 991029289 **Email:** 36820@reference-encyclopedia-ai.net
City: Porto Alegre **State:** RS **PC:** **Country:** Brazil

Year Established: 2017 **Status 2020:** Active
Industries: Artificial Intelligence for:, Business Intelligence for:, ~ Banking and Financial Markets-Services (7), ~ Banking and Financial Markets-Services (7)

Company Name: Meerkat Computer Vision
Description: Meerkat is a tech startup focused on advancing computer vision and image analysis for process automation.
Website: http://www.meerkat.com.br/
Phone: **Email:** contato@meerkat.com.br
City: Porto Alegre **State:** RS **PC:** **Country:** Brazil
Year Established: 2015 **Status 2020:** Active
Industries: Artificial Intelligence for:, Business Applications for:, Image Recognition for:, Machine Learning

Company Name: Planejei
Description: Planejei analyzes clients' finances and deliver financial tips directly to mobile devices through a robot.
Website:
Phone: **Email:** 37175@reference-encyclopedia-ai.net
City: Porto Alegre **State:** RS **PC:** **Country:** Brazil
Year Established: 2018 **Status 2020:** Closed
Industries: Artificial Intelligence for:, ~ Banking and Financial Markets-Services (7), ~ Banking and Financial Markets-Services (7), Mobile for:, Application Services

Company Name: Shoptutor
Description: Shoptutor is a virtual shopping assistant, so everyone can find the model of a product.
Website: http://www.shoptutor.com.br
Phone: **Email:** hello@shoptutor.com.br
City: Porto Alegre **State:** RS **PC:** **Country:** Brazil
Year Established: 2015 **Status 2020:** Active
Industries: Artificial Intelligence for:, E-Commerce for:, ~ Fashion (16)

Company Name: Ubots
Description: Ubots is a Brazilian company that specializes in the construction of chatbots through its own platform, based on artificial intelligence.
Website: http://ubots.com.br/
Phone: (51) 984 031 196 **Email:** contact@ubots.com.br
City: Porto Alegre **State:** RS **PC:** **Country:** Brazil
Year Established: 2016 **Status 2020:** Active
Industries:

Company Name: Anota AI
Description: Anota AI develops artificial intelligence solutions for restaurants.
Website: http://anota.ai/
Phone: 53981639995 **Email:** contato@anota-ai.com
City: Rio Grande Do Sul **State:** RS **PC:** **Country:** Brazil
Year Established: **Status 2020:** Active
Industries: Artificial Intelligence for:, Business Applications for:, Business Applications for:, Machine Learning

Company Name: MeekaLabs
Description: MeekaLabs specializes in creating Artificial Intelligence products and services to serve its customer and optimize processes.
Website: http://meekalabs.com/
Phone: **Email:** contato@meekalabs.com
City: Sao Leopoldo **State:** RS **PC:** **Country:** Brazil
Year Established: 2017 **Status 2020:** Active
Industries: Artificial Intelligence for:, Business Intelligence

Company Name: Saipos
Description: Saipos is a POS system that changes the way restaurant owners run their businesses.
Website: http://saipos.com/
Phone: **Email:** saipos@saipos.com
City: São Leopoldo **State:** RS **PC:** **Country:** Brazil
Year Established: 2017 **Status 2020:** Active
Industries: Artificial Intelligence for:, ~ Banking and Financial Markets-Services (7), IT Managed Services for:, Machine Learning for:, ~ Retail and Consumer Products (52)

Company Name: Connect Total
Description: Connect Total specializes in market intelligence for technology-based companies.
Website: http://www.connecttotal.com/
Phone: 55 51 999471-4000 **Email:** CONTATO@CONNECTTOTAL.COM
City: Viamao **State:** RS **PC:** **Country:** Brazil
Year Established: 2018 **Status 2020:** Active
Industries: IT Managed Services for:, Application Services for:, Web

Company Name: Leoa
Description: Leoa is an artificial intelligence that helps you claim your income tax
Website:
Phone: **Email:** 4956@reference-encyclopedia-ai.net
City: Balneario De Camboriu+AL1367 **State:** SC **PC:** **Country:** Brazil
Year Established: **Status 2020:** Active
Industries: Artificial Intelligence

Company Name: Ezok
Description: Ezok automates bureaucratic and repetitive work using virtual robots with Artificial Intelligence.
Website: http://ezok.ai/
Phone: 55 47 99252-3737 **Email:** contato@ezok.ai
City: Blumenau **State:** SC **PC:** **Country:** Brazil
Year Established: 2012 **Status 2020:** Active
Industries: Artificial Intelligence for:, IT Managed Services for:, IT Managed Services

Company Name: Aquarela Advanced Analytics
Description: Aquarela is a startup specialized in Big Data and Data Analytics tools.
Website: http://aquare.la/
Phone: 55 48 3304-1137 **Email:** falecom@aquare.la
City: Florianópolis **State:** SC **PC:** **Country:** Brazil
Year Established: 2012 **Status 2020:** Active
Industries: Analytics for:, Big Data and Analytics for:, Databases for:, Data Management for:, IT Managed Services for:, Machine Learning for:, Predictive Analytics

Company Name: Datarisk.io
Description: DataRisk is an online predictive modeling platform focused on credit, collection, and fraud serving mainly financial institutions.
Website: http://datarisk.io
Phone: 55 11 98231-8764 **Email:** contato@datarisk.io
City: Florianópolis **State:** SC **PC:** **Country:** Brazil
Year Established: 2015 **Status 2020:** Active
Industries: Security for:, IT Managed Services for:, IT Managed Services for:, Machine Learning for:, Predictive Analytics for:, Business Software as a Service Apps (SaaS Apps)

Company Name: DriveOn
Description: DriveOn empowers drivers with strategic information about their mobility and drives them to driving perfection.
Website: http://www.driveonauto.com
Phone: **Email:** marcio.pessoa@driveonauto.com
City: Florianópolis **State:** SC **PC:** **Country:** Brazil
Year Established: 2017 **Status 2020:** Active
Industries: Artificial Intelligence for:, Business Applications for:, Business Applications

Company Name: Graphics for Decision
Description: Graphics for Decision operates in the Big Data segment.
Website: http://www.g4decision.com.br/
Phone: **Email:** contato@deepen.com.br
City: Florianópolis **State:** SC **PC:** **Country:** Brazil

Year Established: 2016 **Status 2020:** Active
Industries: Artificial Intelligence

Company Name: Kee: Palestine
Description: Keeps is an EdTech company that focuses on bringing to the corporate education market disruptive and high impact business solutions.
Website: http://keeps.com.br/
Phone: **Email:** contato@keeps.com.br
City: Florianópolis **State:** SC **PC:** **Country:** Brazil
Year Established: 2015 **Status 2020:** Active
Industries: Artificial Intelligence for:, ~ Education (13), ~ Education (13)

Company Name: O2Obots
Description: O2Obots develops an artificial intelligence platform that helps insurers and brokers in selling insurance.
Website: http://o2obots.com
Phone: 55 11 3042.5374 **Email:** leonardo.rochadel@o2obots.com
City: Florianópolis **State:** SC **PC:** **Country:** Brazil
Year Established: 2017 **Status 2020:** Active
Industries: Artificial Intelligence for:, IT Managed Services

Company Name: Openimob
Description: Openimoba is a technology company that, through Machine Learning, searches all real estate offers.
Website: http://openimob.com
Phone: **Email:** 37110@reference-encyclopedia-ai.net
City: Florianópolis **State:** SC **PC:** **Country:** Brazil
Year Established: 2017 **Status 2020:** Active
Industries: IT Managed Services for:, Machine Learning

Company Name: Ptolomeu
Description: Ptolomeu is a solution that broadcasts access to intelligent automation of tasks on digital documents.
Website: http://ptolomeu.io/
Phone: **Email:** contato@ptolomeu.io
City: Florianópolis **State:** SC **PC:** **Country:** Brazil
Year Established: **Status 2020:** Active
Industries:

Company Name: Reviewr | Customer Review Intelligence
Description: SaaS - Online Reviews Management Plattform and Big Data company focus on online reputation data for companies.
Website: http://www.reviewr.me/
Phone: 55 48 3030 1212 **Email:** reviewr@reviewr.me
City: Florianópolis **State:** SC **PC:** **Country:** Brazil
Year Established: 2016 **Status 2020:** Active
Industries: Big Data and Analytics for:, IT Managed Services for:, IT Managed Services for:, Application Services for:, Business Intelligence for:, Business Software as a Service Apps (SaaS Apps)

Company Name: SAJ ADV
Description: SAJ ADV is a legal software with artificial intelligence that assists in the management of deadlines and processes of law firm.
Website: http://www.sajadv.com.br/
Phone: 55 48 3298 9030 **Email:** contato@sajadv.com.br
City: Florianópolis **State:** SC **PC:** **Country:** Brazil
Year Established: 2013 **Status 2020:** Active
Industries: Artificial Intelligence for:, IT Managed Services for:, IT Managed Services

Company Name: UpPoints
Description: UP POINTS, a high-tech company, delivers analysis solutions of products and campaign behavior by employing artificial neural networks.
Website: http://uppoints.com/en/en_index.html
Phone: (55)-48-88308484 **Email:** uppoints@uppoints.com
City: Florianópolis **State:** SC **PC:** **Country:** Brazil
Year Established: 2012 **Status 2020:** Active
Industries: Analytics for:, Artificial Intelligence for:, Business Applications for:, Big Data and Analytics for:, Cloud for:, Predictive Analytics

Company Name: Yonface Tecnologia
Description: Yonface Tecnologia artificial intelligence and big data analytics broadening business insight and performance..
Website: http://yonface.com.br/
Phone: 55 42 98808-5551 **Email:** contato@yonface.com.br
City: Florianópolis **State:** SC **PC:** **Country:** Brazil
Year Established: 2016 **Status 2020:** Active
Industries: Artificial Intelligence for:, Big Data and Analytics for:, IT Managed Services

Company Name: ZeroDistrato
Description: ZeroDistrato employs predictive and preventive machine-learning algorithms in combating cancellation of real estate purchase contracts.
Website: http://www.zerodistrato.com/
Phone: 55 47 9 9626 0990 **Email:** contato@zerodistrato.com
City: Florianópolis **State:** SC **PC:** **Country:** Brazil
Year Established: 2017 **Status 2020:** Active
Industries: ~ Construction (10), IT Managed Services for:, Machine Learning for:, Predictive Analytics

Company Name: Agrize
Description: Agrize makes solutions for air monitoring, intelligence, and control of agricultural crops.
Website: https://agrize.co/
Phone: 55 47 3455-3183 **Email:** contato@agrize.com.br
City: Joinville **State:** SC **PC:** **Country:** Brazil
Year Established: 2016 **Status 2020:** Active
Industries: ~ Agriculture (3), ~ Agriculture (3), Artificial Intelligence

Company Name: Camerite
Description: Camerite is an online video surveillance platform that has artificial intelligence without infrastructure costs.
Website: http://camerite.com
Phone: 0800 600 1781 **Email:** contato@camerite.com
City: Joinville **State:** SC **PC:** **Country:** Brazil
Year Established: 2012 **Status 2020:** Active
Industries: Artificial Intelligence for:, Cloud for:, Web for:, Security

Company Name: ProJur
Description: ProJuris offers online legal software and chatbot with artificial intelligence.
Website: http://www.projuris.com.br/
Phone: 0800-608-0056 **Email:** 37217@reference-encyclopedia-ai.net
City: Joinville **State:** SC **PC:** **Country:** Brazil
Year Established: 2010 **Status 2020:** Active
Industries: Artificial Intelligence for:, Business Software as a Service Apps (SaaS Apps)

Company Name: Treasy
Description: Treasy is an online solution provider for planning and controlling with a fine cost-benefit ratio in the market.
Website: http://www.treasy.com.br/
Phone: 55 47 3431-7322 **Email:** contato@treasy.com.br
City: Joinville **State:** SC **PC:** **Country:** Brazil
Year Established: 2014 **Status 2020:** Active
Industries: Enterprise Application Services for:, ~ Banking and Financial Markets-Services (7), Predictive Analytics

Company Name: UpFlux
Description: UpFlux helps Organizations to Improve the Process Efficiency and Quality using Artificial Intelligence and Process Mining.
Website: http://upflux.net/
Phone: 55 47 99609 1191 **Email:** comercial@upflux.net
City: Joinville **State:** SC **PC:** **Country:** Brazil

Year Established: **Status 2020:** Active
Industries: Analytics for:, Artificial Intelligence for:, IT Managed Services for:, IT Managed Services for:, ~ Professional Services (48)

Company Name: TNH Heal:Thailand
Description: TNH Health creates AI-powered chatbots to help healthcare organizations engage and monitor large patient populations.
Website: http://tnh.heal:Thailand
Phone: 55 (11) 3807-8737 **Email:** contato@ta-na-hora.com
City: Rio Negrinho **State:** SC **PC:** **Country:** Brazil
Year Established: 2013 **Status 2020:** Active
Industries: Artificial Intelligence for:, ~ Healthcare (20), ~ Healthcare (20)

Company Name: BirdView
Description: BirdView develops and applies positive technologies to agribusiness in order to meet the needs of both producers and industry.
Website: http://www.birdview.com.br/
Phone: **Email:** 36161@reference-encyclopedia-ai.net
City: Botucatu **State:** SP **PC:** **Country:** Brazil
Year Established: 2014 **Status 2020:** Active
Industries: ~ Agriculture (3), ~ Agriculture (3), Machine Learning

Company Name: Kognita
Description: Kognita is a conversational commerce platform. Selling has just become much easier! ;)
Website: http://www.kognita.ai
Phone: 11 3042-3282 **Email:** contact@kognita.ai
City: Brasil **State:** SP **PC:** **Country:** Brazil
Year Established: 2017 **Status 2020:** Active
Industries: Artificial Intelligence for:, Business Software as a Service Apps (SaaS Apps) for:, Automation

Company Name: HOOBOX Robotics
Description: Face Recognition and Robotics
Website: http://www.hoo-box.com
Phone: (628) 228-1864 **Email:** team@hoo-box.com
City: Campina **State:** SP **PC:** **Country:** Brazil
Year Established: 2016 **Status 2020:** Active
Industries:

Company Name: NeuralMind
Description: NeuralMind is a Brazilian startup that specializes in product development using advanced artificial intelligence techniques.
Website: http://neuralmind.ai/
Phone: 55 19 3256-1300 **Email:** contato@neuralmind.ai
City: Campina **State:** SP **PC:** **Country:** Brazil
Year Established: 2017 **Status 2020:** Active
Industries: Artificial Intelligence for:, IT Managed Services for:, Machine Learning

Company Name: I3FOCUS SOLUTIONS IN GEOPROCESSING SYSTEMS
Description: I3focus is a company that specializes in developing and providing solutions in geographic systems.
Website: http://www.i3focus.com.br
Phone: 55 988576321 **Email:** agenciai3focus@gmail.com
City: Lorena **State:** SP **PC:** **Country:** Brazil
Year Established: 2014 **Status 2020:** Active
Industries: Internet of Things (IoT) for:, Application Services

Company Name: SensorVision
Description: SensorVision is a computer vision company with artificial intelligence applied to solutions in agriculture.
Website: http://www.sensorvision.com.br
Phone: 55-19- 33074912 **Email:** contact@sensorvision.com.br
City: Paulinia **State:** SP **PC:** **Country:** Brazil
Year Established: **Status 2020:** Active
Industries: ~ Agriculture (3), ~ Agriculture (3), Artificial Intelligence for:, Computer Vision for:, IT Managed Services

Company Name: Dr. Sintomas
Description: Dr. Sintomas is a platform for symptom analysis developed based on artificial intelligence and machine learning technologies.
Website: http://drsintomas.com.br/en
Phone: (11) 2924-7286 **Email:** contato@drsintomas.com.br
City: Pinheiros **State:** SP **PC:** **Country:** Brazil
Year Established: 2016 **Status 2020:** Active
Industries: Artificial Intelligence for:, ~ Healthcare (20), ~ Healthcare (20), Machine Learning

Company Name: Neomove
Description: Neomove is a Brazilian startup.
Website: http://www.neomove.com.br/
Phone: (1197) 518-1125 **Email:** contato@neomove.com.br
City: Pinheiros **State:** SP **PC:** **Country:** Brazil
Year Established: 2015 **Status 2020:** Active
Industries: Business Applications for:, Digital Media for:, Application Services

Company Name: Smartbreeder
Description: Smartbreeder is a digital agronomic intelligence company that promotes sustainable agriculture.
Website: http://www.smartbreeder.com.br
Phone: (19) 3423-9508 **Email:** contato@smartbreeder.com.br
City: Piracicaba **State:** SP **PC:** **Country:** Brazil
Year Established: 2010 **Status 2020:** Active
Industries: ~ Agriculture (3), ~ Agriculture (3), Artificial Intelligence for:, ~ Agriculture (3), Predictive Analytics for:, ~ Social-Environmental-Physical-Engineering Sciences (55)

Company Name: Arquivei
Description: Arquivei provides a database of legal documents issued in Brazil.
Website: http://arquivei.com.br/
Phone: 55 16 3509 5555 **Email:** mkt@arquivei.com.br
City: São Carlos Do Pinhal **State:** SP **PC:** **Country:** Brazil
Year Established: 2013 **Status 2020:** Active
Industries: IT Managed Services for:, IT Managed Services for:, Application Services for:, Business Software as a Service Apps (SaaS Apps)

Company Name: WDG Automation
Description: WDG Automation designs and develops robotic process automation (RPA), intelligent virtual agents (IVA) and artificial intelligence software.
Website: http://www.wdgautomation.com
Phone: 678-436-1689 **Email:** robson.felix@wdgautomation.com
City: São José do Rio Prêto **State:** SP **PC:** **Country:** Brazil
Year Established: 2014 **Status 2020:** Active
Industries: Artificial Intelligence for:, Enterprise Application Services for:, IT Managed Services

Company Name: Allgoo
Description: Allgoo is a digital solution company for Retailers, Banks, Financial Institutions, and Financial Sector Companies.
Website: http://allgoo.com.br/
Phone: 55 12 3945-1366 **Email:** contato@allgoo.com.br
City: São José Dos Campos **State:** SP **PC:** **Country:** Brazil
Year Established: 2014 **Status 2020:** Active
Industries: Artificial Intelligence for:, ~ Banking and Financial Markets-Services (7), Robotics

Company Name: Autaza Tecnologia
Description: Autaza Tecnologia specializes in computer vision and artificial intelligence for quality inspection in industrial products.
Website: http://www.autaza.com
Phone: 55 12 3876-7757 **Email:** contato@autaza.com
City: São José Dos Campos **State:** SP **PC:** **Country:** Brazil

Year Established: 2016 **Status 2020:** Active
Industries: Artificial Intelligence for:, Computer Vision for:, ~ Manufacturing-General (31), IT Managed Services for:, Business Process and Operations

Company Name: Treevia - Forest Technologies
Description: Treevia is literally connecting forests around the world into the internet to ensure more sustainable use of natural resources.
Website: http://treevia.com.br/
Phone: 55 12 3921-2319 **Email:** contato@treevia.com.br
City: São José Dos Campos **State:** SP **PC:** **Country:** Brazil
Year Established: 2016 **Status 2020:** Active
Industries: ~ Agriculture (3), ~ Agriculture (3), Artificial Intelligence for:, ~ Agriculture (3), ~ Energy and Utilities (14), Internet of Things (IoT) for:, Internet of Things (IoT) for:, Predictive Analytics

Company Name: AI-Investimentos.com
Description: start-up that uses artificial intelligence to analyze and decide asset investments in stocks.
Website: http://ai-investimentos.com
Phone: **Email:** info@ai-investimentos.com
City: Sao Paulo **State:** SP **PC:** **Country:** Brazil
Year Established: **Status 2020:** Active
Industries: Artificial Intelligence

Company Name: Autom: Nigeria
Description: Automni develops products and solutions for industrial automation.
Website: http://www.automni.com.br
Phone: **Email:** contato@automni.com.br
City: Sao Paulo **State:** SP **PC:** **Country:** Brazil
Year Established: 2014 **Status 2020:** Active
Industries: Artificial Intelligence for:, ~ Automotive (5), Automation

Company Name: AxonData Tecnologia Analitica
Description: AXONDATA is an INTEL Center of Excellence in Artificial Intelligence.
Website: http://axondata.com.br/
Phone: 55 11 2766 7707 **Email:** contato@axondata.com.br
City: Sao Paulo **State:** SP **PC:** **Country:** Brazil
Year Established: 2016 **Status 2020:** Active
Industries:

Company Name: BotDaddy
Description: BotDaddy is an artificial intelligence company that delivers customer services technology to digital business and content creators.
Website: http://bot-daddy.com/
Phone: **Email:** 36191@reference-encyclopedia-ai.net
City: Sao Paulo **State:** SP **PC:** **Country:** Brazil
Year Established: 2017 **Status 2020:** Active
Industries: Artificial Intelligence for:, Machine Learning

Company Name: Bunee.io
Description: Bunee.io is a recruitment platform that employs the power of artificial intelligence to find the best developers.
Website: http://bunee.io/
Phone: **Email:** 36218@reference-encyclopedia-ai.net
City: Sao Paulo **State:** SP **PC:** **Country:** Brazil
Year Established: 2016 **Status 2020:** Active
Industries: Artificial Intelligence

Company Name: Castti
Description: Castti is a technology company that aims to transform slow and repetitive processes into agile and efficient processes.
Website: http://www.castti.com.br/
Phone: **Email:** contato@castti.com.br
City: Sao Paulo **State:** SP **PC:** **Country:** Brazil
Year Established: 2014 **Status 2020:** Active
Industries:

Company Name: CityTech
Description: CityTech is a technology company that emerged from a global research on the development of smart cities.
Website: http://citytech.ai/en/
Phone: **Email:** hi@citytech.ai
City: Sao Paulo **State:** SP **PC:** **Country:** Brazil
Year Established: 2017 **Status 2020:** Active
Industries: Artificial Intelligence for:, IT Managed Services for:, IT Managed Services for:, Machine Learning for:, ~ Construction (10), ~ Construction (10)

Company Name: CLAV
Description: CLAV promote ideas, sustainable connections between brands, artists, the public and partners.
Website: http://www.clav.com.br/
Phone: (55) 11 972 283 078 **Email:** contato@clav.com.br
City: Sao Paulo **State:** SP **PC:** **Country:** Brazil
Year Established: **Status 2020:** Active
Industries: Artificial Intelligence for:, Application Services for:, ~ Arts-Entertainment-Recreation (4)

Company **Name:** Cognitivo.ai
Description: In order to turn Big Data and AI accessible to every company, we help them transform their business problems into data solutions.
Website: http://www.cognitivo.ai
Phone: 55 11 96996-5658 **Email:** contato@cognitivo.ai
City: Sao Paulo **State:** SP **PC:** **Country:** Brazil
Year Established: 2016 **Status 2020:** Active
Industries: Artificial Intelligence for:, IT Managed Services

Company Name: ConnectData
Description: ConnectData aims to increase the productivity and efficiency of the construction industry through predictive analytics.
Website: http://www.connectdata.net/
Phone: 55 (11) 94072-9982 **Email:** gabriel.borges@connectdata.net
City: Sao Paulo **State:** SP **PC:** **Country:** Brazil
Year Established: 2016 **Status 2020:** Active
Industries: IT Managed Services for:, IT Managed Services for:, Predictive Analytics

Company Name: CosmoBots
Description: CosmoBots is a self-service ChatBot platform with focus in AI and automated customer service.
Website: http://cosmobots.io
Phone: **Email:** support@cosmobots.io
City: Sao Paulo **State:** SP **PC:** **Country:** Brazil
Year Established: 2017 **Status 2020:** Active
Industries: Artificial Intelligence for:, IT Managed Services for:, Internet of Things (IoT)

Company Name: Data Goal
Description: Data Goal is a technology for field data collection.
Website:
Phone: **Email:** 36383@reference-encyclopedia-ai.net
City: Sao Paulo **State:** SP **PC:** **Country:** Brazil
Year Established: 2018 **Status 2020:** Active
Industries: Learning and Marketing Communications Services (MarComm) for:, Databases for:, IT Managed Services for:, Predictive Analytics

Company Name: Datus
Description: Datus is a company that makes business processes smarter.
Website: http://datus.com.br
Phone: 5511 2669.1598 **Email:** contato@datus.com.br
City: Sao Paulo **State:** SP **PC:** **Country:** Brazil
Year Established: 2011 **Status 2020:** Active
Industries: Analytics for:, Artificial Intelligence for:, Machine Learning

Company Name: Decoded Trends
Description: Decoded Trends is a market intelligence platform engineered to help fashion merchandisers make data-driven assortment decisions
Website: http://www.decodedtrends.com
Phone: **Email:** contato@decodedtrends.com
City: Sao Paulo **State:** SP **PC:** **Country:** Brazil
Year Established: 2019 **Status 2020:** Active
Industries: Analytics for:, Artificial Intelligence for:, Big Data and Analytics for:, ~ Fashion (16)

Company Name: Digesto
Description: Digesto uses computational tools to improve the practice of law in Brazil
Website: http://www.digesto.com.br/servicos
Phone: 55 (11) 2626-0532 **Email:** digesto@digesto.com.br
City: Sao Paulo **State:** SP **PC:** **Country:** Brazil
Year Established: 2013 **Status 2020:** Active
Industries: Artificial Intelligence for:, Data Management for:, Databases for:, Data Management

Company Name: Dom Rock
Description: Dom Rock is a provider of cloud-based analysis solutions designed and built to be a unified business data integrity environment.
Website: http://www.domrock.ai/
Phone: 55 11 4688-1335 **Email:** contact@domrock.ai
City: Sao Paulo **State:** SP **PC:** **Country:** Brazil
Year Established: 2013 **Status 2020:** Active
Industries: Databases for:, IT Managed Services for:, Predictive Analytics

Company Name: eConciliador
Description: Fully automated online negotiation platform that leverages Big Data, Machine Learning and Artificial Intelligence.
Website: http://www.econciliador.com.br/
Phone: **Email:** 36472@reference-encyclopedia-ai.net
City: Sao Paulo **State:** SP **PC:** **Country:** Brazil
Year Established: 2013 **Status 2020:** Active
Industries:

Company Name: EhloReport
Description: EhloReport provides an analysis and protection tool for online use of a company's most valuable asset, its brand.
Website: http://www.ehloreport.com/
Phone: **Email:** 36484@reference-encyclopedia-ai.net
City: Sao Paulo **State:** SP **PC:** **Country:** Brazil
Year Established: 2018 **Status 2020:** Active
Industries: Analytics for:, IT Managed Services for:, Predictive Analytics

Company Name: Fanclic
Description: Mobile app and content distribution platform
Website: http://www.fanclic.com
Phone: **Email:** contact@fanclic.com
City: Sao Paulo **State:** SP **PC:** **Country:** Brazil
Year Established: **Status 2020:** Active
Industries:

Company Name: Fhinck
Description: Fhinck is a technology startup focusing on increasing productivity and process efficiency for businesses.
Website: http://www.fhinck.com/
Phone: 55 11 3198-3685 **Email:** fale.conosco@fhinck.com
City: Sao Paulo **State:** SP **PC:** **Country:** Brazil
Year Established: 2014 **Status 2020:** Active
Industries: Application Services for:, IT Managed Services for:, Application Program Interfaces (APIs) for:, Compute

Company Name: Fred
Description: Fred is a chatbot platform for micro-applications and micro-services that allows users to integrate chatbot technology with their platforms.
Website: http://fredbots.com
Phone: **Email:** contato@fredbots.com
City: Sao Paulo **State:** SP **PC:** **Country:** Brazil
Year Established: 2016 **Status 2020:** Active
Industries: Artificial Intelligence for:, E-Commerce

Company Name: Getbots
Description: GetBots creates and enables chatbots for easy conversation.
Website: http://getbots.com.br/
Phone: **Email:** hi@getbots.com.br
City: Sao Paulo **State:** SP **PC:** **Country:** Brazil
Year Established: 2017 **Status 2020:** Active
Industries: Artificial Intelligence

Company Name: GlucoGear
Description: GlucoGear, the artificial intelligence to personalize Diabetes treatment.
Website: http://www.glucogear.io
Phone: **Email:** contact@glucogear.io
City: Sao Paulo **State:** SP **PC:** **Country:** Brazil
Year Established: 2015 **Status 2020:** Active
Industries: Artificial Intelligence for:, ~ Healthcare (20), ~ Healthcare (20), Machine Learning for:, ~ Healthcare (20), ~ Healthcare (20)

Company Name: HupData
Description: HupData is a startup company that provides solutions for machine learning, demanding data integration, and big data analytics.
Website: http://hupdata.com/br
Phone: 55 11 3407-2440 **Email:** contato@hupdata.com
City: Sao Paulo **State:** SP **PC:** **Country:** Brazil
Year Established: 2016 **Status 2020:** Active
Industries: Analytics for:, Big Data and Analytics for:, Data Management for:, Databases for:, IT Managed Services for:, Machine Learning

Company Name: ICX Labs
Description: ICX Labs creates products that enhance business processes in retail through IoT solutions, artificial intelligence and analytics.
Website: http://www.icxlabs.com/
Phone: (11) 94320-5626 **Email:** info@icxlabs.com
City: Sao Paulo **State:** SP **PC:** **Country:** Brazil
Year Established: 2017 **Status 2020:** Active
Industries: Analytics for:, Artificial Intelligence for:, Big Data and Analytics for:, Internet of Things (IoT)

Company Name: Iopeople
Description: Iopeople develops conversational A.I. solutions which can provide human-like interactions with end-users.
Website: http://www.iopeople.com.br/
Phone: (11)2339-7150 **Email:** info@iopeople.com.br
City: Sao Paulo **State:** SP **PC:** **Country:** Brazil
Year Established: 2016 **Status 2020:** Active
Industries: Artificial Intelligence for:, IT Managed Services for:, Machine Learning for:, Natural Language Processing

Company Name: iSPORTiSTiCS
Description: We train algorithms to interpret sporting events like a human would.
Website: http://www.isportistics.com/
Phone: **Email:** info@isportistics.com
City: Sao Paulo **State:** SP **PC:** **Country:** Brazil
Year Established: 2017 **Status 2020:** Active
Industries: Computer Vision for:, Machine Learning for:, Predictive Analytics for:, ~ Arts-Entertainment-Recreation (4)

Company Name: JoyCar
Description: JoyCar develops an artificial intelligence platform for carpool services.
Website: http://joycar.com.br/
Phone: **Email:** suporte@joycar.com.br
City: Sao Paulo **State:** SP **PC:** **Country:** Brazil
Year Established: 2012 **Status 2020:** Active
Industries:

Company Name: Kakau
Description: Kakau is a digital insurance platform that uses Artificial Intelligence technology.
Website: http://www.kakau.co
Phone: **Email:** 30927@reference-encyclopedia-ai.net
City: Sao Paulo **State:** SP **PC:** **Country:** Brazil
Year Established: 2016 **Status 2020:** Active
Industries: Artificial Intelligence for:, ~ Banking and Financial Markets-Services (7), IT Managed Services for:, Internet of Things (IoT)

Company Name: Kzas.AI
Description: Kzas is a platform that matches real buyers with real properties with assistance of conversational AI simplifying from the search to notary.
Website: http://www.kzas.ai
Phone: **Email:** roberto@kzas.ai
City: Sao Paulo **State:** SP **PC:** **Country:** Brazil
Year Established: 2019 **Status 2020:** Active
Industries: Artificial Intelligence for:, Web for:, Machine Learning

Company Name: Levee
Description: Levee develops solutions to help large enterprises remove bottlenecks in productivity and efficiency.
Website: http://levee.com.br/
Phone: 55 (11) 4118.0535 **Email:** levee@levee.com.br
City: Sao Paulo **State:** SP **PC:** **Country:** Brazil
Year Established: 2016 **Status 2020:** Active
Industries:

Company Name: LEXAI
Description: Contract Review Platform
Website: http://www.lexai.legal/
Phone: **Email:** virginia@appriori.com.br
City: Sao Paulo **State:** SP **PC:** **Country:** Brazil
Year Established: 2018 **Status 2020:** Active
Industries: Artificial Intelligence

Company Name: Manual Blockchain
Description: Manual Blockchain is a company of education for innovation and transforming technologies, whose objective is the technological inclusion.
Website: http://www.manualblockchain.com.br/
Phone: 55 11 94182-3054 **Email:** contato@manualblockchain.com.br
City: Sao Paulo **State:** SP **PC:** **Country:** Brazil
Year Established: 2017 **Status 2020:** Active
Industries: Artificial Intelligence for:, Big Data and Analytics for:, Blockchain for:, Cloud for:, Internet of Things (IoT) for:, Machine Learning

Company Name: MAR ventur: Spain
Description: We are a venture capital firm dedicated to turning meaningful projects into incredible endeavors.
Website: http://www.mar.ventur: Spain
Phone: **Email:** bewater@mar.ventur: Spain
City: Sao Paulo **State:** SP **PC:** **Country:** Brazil
Year Established: 2007 **Status 2020:** Active
Industries: Artificial Intelligence for:, ~ Banking and Financial Markets-Services (7), ~ Banking and Financial Markets-Services (7), ~ Banking and Financial Markets-Services (7)

Company Name: Milenio Bus
Description: Milenio Bus integrates a hardware, application, and software capable of knowing the stocking in buses, in real time.
Website: http://mileniobus.com.br/
Phone: **Email:** contato@mileniobus.com.br
City: Sao Paulo **State:** SP **PC:** **Country:** Brazil
Year Established: 2017 **Status 2020:** Active
Industries: Artificial Intelligence for:, Computer Vision for:, Internet of Things (IoT) for:, ~ Transportation and Logistics (57)

Company Name: Moco
Description: Moco is a facial recognition system with artificial intelligence that delivers valuable data extracted from IP cameras.
Website: http://moco.technology/
Phone: **Email:** 37000@reference-encyclopedia-ai.net
City: Sao Paulo **State:** SP **PC:** **Country:** Brazil
Year Established: 2018 **Status 2020:** Active
Industries: Artificial Intelligence for:, Facial Recognition for:, IT Managed Services

Company Name: Motop
Description: App for bikers who want to find the best products and the best services with the best price!
Website: http://www.motop.com.br
Phone: **Email:** contato@motop.com.br
City: Sao Paulo **State:** SP **PC:** **Country:** Brazil
Year Established: **Status 2020:** Active
Industries:

Company Name: Murabei Data Science
Description: Murabei is a data science startup that develops machine learning models based on large volumes of information.
Website: http://www.murabei.com
Phone: 55 11 4949 9599 **Email:** contact@murabei.com
City: Sao Paulo **State:** SP **PC:** **Country:** Brazil
Year Established: 2013 **Status 2020:** Active
Industries:

Company Name: Nama Software
Description: Nama is redefining search engines, transforming it into a request based conversational interface.
Website: http://www.nama.ai
Phone: **Email:** hi@nama.ai
City: Sao Paulo **State:** SP **PC:** **Country:** Brazil
Year Established: 2014 **Status 2020:** Active
Industries: Artificial Intelligence for:, IT Managed Services for:, Web for:, Machine Learning

Company Name: Nexus Edge
Description: Nexus Edge provides its customers with unique data to empower intelligence and strategic business processes.
Website: http://www.nexusedge.com.br
Phone: **Email:** contato@nexusedge.com.br
City: Sao Paulo **State:** SP **PC:** **Country:** Brazil
Year Established: 2013 **Status 2020:** Active
Industries: Predictive Analytics for:, ~ Social Assistance-Non-Profits (53)

Company Name: Pay4Bra: India
Description: Pay4Brain is a technological innovation laboratory specializing in the development of voice bots, integrations, and chatbots.
Website: http://www.pay4brain.com
Phone: **Email:** felipe@pay4brain.com
City: Sao Paulo **State:** SP **PC:** **Country:** Brazil
Year Established: **Status 2020:** Active
Industries: Artificial Intelligence for:, Big Data and Analytics for:, ~ Biotechnology (9), IT Managed Services for:, IT Managed Services for:, ~ Professional Services (48)

Company Name: Planner.bot
Description: Life and Financial Planning A.I. Chatbot
Website: http://planner.bot
Phone: **Email:** humano@planner.bot
City: Sao Paulo **State:** SP **PC:** **Country:** Brazil

Year Established: **Status 2020:** Active
Industries: Artificial Intelligence for:, ~ Banking and Financial Markets-Services (7), ~ Insurance (25), Finance and Accounting

Company Name: 55PBX Cloud Contact Center
Description: 55pbx is a virtual PBX with AI, Dialer, Secured IVR and more
Website: http://www.55pbx.com
Phone: **Email:** quero@55pbx.com.br
City: São Paulo **State:** SP **PC:** **Country:** Brazil
Year Established: 2016 **Status 2020:** Active
Industries: Artificial Intelligence for:, E-Commerce for:, IT Managed Services for:, Web

Company Name: Accera
Description: Accera offers a complete solutions for industry collaborations with distribution channels.
Website: http://www.accerapharma.com/
Phone: (303) 999-3700 **Email:** info@accerapharma.com
City: São Paulo **State:** SP **PC:** **Country:** Brazil
Year Established: 2001 **Status 2020:** Active
Industries: Business Intelligence for:, IT Managed Services for:, IT Managed Services for:, Predictive Analytics

Company Name: Agiliza.Aí
Description: Agiliza.Aí develops an artificial intelligence platform for drivers and event producers.
Website: http://agiliza.com/
Phone: **Email:** 35974@reference-encyclopedia-ai.net
City: São Paulo **State:** SP **PC:** **Country:** Brazil
Year Established: **Status 2020:** Active
Industries:

Company Name: AgriConnected
Description: AgriConnected is a startup bringing innovation and technology to transform the Brazilian agribusiness.
Website: http://www.agriconnected.com/
Phone: **Email:** contato@agriconnected.com
City: São Paulo **State:** SP **PC:** **Country:** Brazil
Year Established: 2017 **Status 2020:** Active
Industries: ~ Agriculture (3), ~ Agriculture (3), IT Managed Services for:, Web for:, Internet of Things (IoT) for:, Internet of Things (IoT) for:, Machine Learning

Company Name: Nuper
Description: Nuper is an application that serves as a personal shopping assistant to its users.
Website:
Phone: **Email:** ola@meumordomo.online
City: São Paulo **State:** SP **PC:** **Country:** Brazil
Year Established: 2016 **Status 2020:** Active
Industries: Artificial Intelligence for:, E-Commerce for:, ~ Fashion (16)

Company Name: NutriSoft Brazil
Description: NutriSoft Brazil provides of software platform for nutrition.
Website: http://nutrisoft.com.br/
Phone: **Email:** brazil@nutrisoft.com.br
City: São Paulo **State:** SP **PC:** **Country:** Brazil
Year Established: 2013 **Status 2020:** Active
Industries: Artificial Intelligence for:, Business Applications for:, ~ Healthcare (20), ~ Healthcare (20), ~ Healthcare (20), ~ Healthcare (20)

Company Name: Nuveo Technologies Ltda
Description: Nuveo Technologies Ltda boosts partners competitiveness by applying the latest technology tools through artificial intelligence.
Website: http://www.nuveo.ai
Phone: 55 (11) 4780-9328 **Email:** contato@nuveo.ai
City: São Paulo **State:** SP **PC:** **Country:** Brazil
Year Established: 2016 **Status 2020:** Active
Industries: IT Managed Services for:, Natural Language Processing

Company Name: Omni-Eletronica
Description: Omni-Eletrônica is a developer of products and solutions in Internet of Things.
Website: http://www.omni-electronica.com.br/index.php/en/
Phone: **Email:** contato@omni-electronica.com.br
City: São Paulo **State:** SP **PC:** **Country:** Brazil
Year Established: 2016 **Status 2020:** Active
Industries: Artificial Intelligence for:, Internet of Things (IoT)

Company Name: Pin People
Description: Pin People is the 1st Employee Experience (EX) management platform in Brazil.
Website: http://www.pinpeople.com.br
Phone: 55 11 2385-6397 **Email:** contato@pinpeople.com.br
City: São Paulo **State:** SP **PC:** **Country:** Brazil
Year Established: 2014 **Status 2020:** Active
Industries: Big Data and Analytics for:, ~ Education (13), Predictive Analytics for:, ~ Education (13)

Company Name: PromoContent
Description: PromoContent changes how using artificial intelligence and machine learning to add data to content creation changes the market.
Website: http://promocontent.io
Phone: **Email:** contato@promocontent.io
City: São Paulo **State:** SP **PC:** **Country:** Brazil
Year Established: 2014 **Status 2020:** Active
Industries: Artificial Intelligence for:, Content

Company Name: Propz
Description: Propz improves retailers' direct relationship with consume: Serbia
Website: http://www.propz.com.br
Phone: **Email:** info@propz.com.br
City: São Paulo **State:** SP **PC:** **Country:** Brazil
Year Established: 2012 **Status 2020:** Active
Industries: Big Data and Analytics for:, ~ Retail and Consumer Products (52), Machine Learning for:, Predictive Analytics

Company Name: Quicko
Description: Maas, Mobile App, Navigation App, Big Data, Artificial Intelligence, Mobility
Website: http://www.quicko.com.br
Phone: **Email:** falecom@quicko.com.br
City: São Paulo **State:** SP **PC:** **Country:** Brazil
Year Established: 2018 **Status 2020:** Active
Industries:

Company Name: Receiv
Description: CRM Inteligente para gerenciar e recuperar recebíveis | Smart CRM to manage and receive receivabl: Spain
Website: http://www.receiv.: Italy
Phone: (11) 3090-6102 **Email:** contato@receiv.: Italy
City: São Paulo **State:** SP **PC:** **Country:** Brazil
Year Established: 2014 **Status 2020:** Active
Industries: Business Intelligence for:, ~ Banking and Financial Markets-Services (7), IT Managed Services for:, Machine Learning

Company Name: Ressarce
Description: Ressarce is an artificial intelligence platform that analyzes invoices.
Website: http://www.ressarce.com/br/
Phone: **Email:** marcelo@ressarce.com
City: São Paulo **State:** SP **PC:** **Country:** Brazil
Year Established: 2017 **Status 2020:** Active
Industries: Artificial Intelligence for:, ~ Banking and Financial Markets-Services (7), IT Managed Services

Company Name: ROBBIoT IoT Solutions
Description: ROBBIoT is an IoT startup focused on workers protection in hazardous environment using industrial wearable, cloud computing and analytics.
Website: http://www.robbiot.com
Phone: 1(407)639-9572 **Email:** contact@robbiot.com
City: São Paulo **State:** SP **PC:** **Country:** Brazil
Year Established: 2015 **Status 2020:** Active
Industries: Artificial Intelligence for:, Industrial Solutions for:, Internet of Things (IoT) for:, Risk Management

Company Name: SciCrop
Description: SciCrop is a smart farming and big data analytics platform for agriculture.
Website: http://scicrop.com/
Phone: **Email:** info@scicrop.com
City: São Paulo **State:** SP **PC:** **Country:** Brazil
Year Established: 2014 **Status 2020:** Active
Industries: ~ Agriculture (3), Analytics for:, Artificial Intelligence for:, Big Data and Analytics for:, ~ Agriculture (3), Web for:, Internet of Things (IoT) for:, Machine Learning for:, Machine Learning

Company Name: Scoutfy
Description: Scoutfy is an engineering and sports science company.
Website: http://www.scoutfy.com
Phone: **Email:** brandao@scoutfy.com
City: São Paulo **State:** SP **PC:** **Country:** Brazil
Year Established: 2014 **Status 2020:** Active
Industries:

Company Name: Seed Digital
Description: Seed Digital uses an intelligent platform to help companies analyze consumer behavior.
Website: http://www.seeddigital.com.br/
Phone: 55 11 2344.9100 **Email:** seed@seeddigital.com.br
City: São Paulo **State:** SP **PC:** **Country:** Brazil
Year Established: 2015 **Status 2020:** Active
Industries: Analytics for:, IT Managed Services for:, Application Services for:, Web

Company Name: Shelfpix
Description: Shelfpix is a retail performance provider startup company using Artificial Intelligence.
Website: http://www.shelfpix.com.br/en/home-eng/
Phone: 55 11 94300-4001 **Email:** comercial@shelfpix.com.br
City: São Paulo **State:** SP **PC:** **Country:** Brazil
Year Established: 2014 **Status 2020:** Active
Industries: E-Commerce for:, ~ Retail and Consumer Products (52), IT Managed Services for:, IT Managed Services for:, Machine Learning for:, Machine Learning

Company Name: ShopBack
Description: ShopBack is a behavioral email re-marketing platform focused on identifying and converting visitors for their websites.
Website: http://www.shopback.co
Phone: **Email:** 37380@reference-encyclopedia-ai.net
City: São Paulo **State:** SP **PC:** **Country:** Brazil
Year Established: 2013 **Status 2020:** Active
Industries: Analytics for:, Big Data and Analytics for:, ~ Customer Relationship Management (11), E-Commerce for:, IT Managed Services for:, Predictive Analytics for:, Web for:, Web for:, Web

Company Name: Silver Shark Solutions
Description: Silver Shark Solutions assists in the availability, extraction, and visualization of information to improve the decision process.
Website: http://silversharksolutions.com.br/
Phone: **Email:** 37392@reference-encyclopedia-ai.net
City: São Paulo **State:** SP **PC:** **Country:** Brazil
Year Established: **Status 2020:** Active
Industries: Analytics for:, Artificial Intelligence for:, IT Managed Services for:, IT Managed Services

Company Name: Smart Projects Consultoria e Participacoes Eireli
Description: Consultants and Investments in FMCG, Mobile, Digital projects.
Website:
Phone: **Email:** miguel.caeiro@smartprojects.net.br
City: São Paulo **State:** SP **PC:** **Country:** Brazil
Year Established: 2015 **Status 2020:** Active
Industries: Analytics for:, IT Managed Services for:, Web

Company Name: smarters
Description: Smarters is an online application that offers artificial intelligence available real-time on any device.
Website: http://smarte.rs/
Phone: **Email:** hello@smarte.: Serbia
City: São Paulo **State:** SP **PC:** **Country:** Brazil
Year Established: 2013 **Status 2020:** Active
Industries: Artificial Intelligence for:, Big Data and Analytics for:, Web

Company Name: Speedio
Description: SpeedIO is a startup that applies big data to sales.
Website: http://speedio.com.br/
Phone: 55 31 98922-4442 **Email:** atendimento@speedio.com.br
City: São Paulo **State:** SP **PC:** **Country:** Brazil
Year Established: 2014 **Status 2020:** Active
Industries: Business Applications for:, Big Data and Analytics for:, Web for:, Machine Learning

Company Name: SpumeNews
Description: SpumeNews is a smartphone application that utilizes artificial intelligence to enable users to understand news quickly.
Website: http://spumenews.com
Phone: **Email:** 37461@reference-encyclopedia-ai.net
City: São Paulo **State:** SP **PC:** **Country:** Brazil
Year Established: 2014 **Status 2020:** Active
Industries: Artificial Intelligence for:, Big Data and Analytics for:, ~ Administrative and Support Services (1)

Company Name: Stilingue
Description: Stilingue is an AI platform for the management of brands in real time, based on consumers' opinions on digital channels.
Website: http://stilingue.com.br/
Phone: **Email:** contato@stilingue.com.br
City: São Paulo **State:** SP **PC:** **Country:** Brazil
Year Established: 2014 **Status 2020:** Active
Industries: Artificial Intelligence

Company Name: TEVEC
Description: Tevec is an optimizes supply chain logistics with predictive machine learning algorithms, by reducing stockout issues, delays and losses.
Website: http://www.tevec.com.br/
Phone: 55 11 3093-2040 **Email:** contato@tevec.com.br
City: São Paulo **State:** SP **PC:** **Country:** Brazil
Year Established: 2013 **Status 2020:** Active
Industries: Artificial Intelligence for:, IT Managed Services for:, ~ Telecommunications (56), Machine Learning for:, Supply Chain Management

Company Name: Trage
Description: Trage is a fintech company that makes use of technology to spread the culture of investments in digital currencies.
Website: http://trage.com.br/
Phone: **Email:** 37553@reference-encyclopedia-ai.net
City: São Paulo **State:** SP **PC:** **Country:** Brazil

Year Established: 2017 **Status 2020:** Active
Industries: Artificial Intelligence for:, ~ Banking and Financial Markets-Services (7), ~ Banking and Financial Markets-Services (7)

Company Name: Virtual Vision
Description: We use Artificial Intelligence to build the future industrial internet and technologies.
Website: http://www.virtualvision.ai
Phone: **Email:** 37630@reference-encyclopedia-ai.net
City: São Paulo **State:** SP **PC:** **Country:** Brazil
Year Established: 2018 **Status 2020:** Active
Industries: Analytics for:, Artificial Intelligence for:, Big Data and Analytics for:, IT Managed Services

Company Name: we.CoLab
Description: We help companies and startups to solve problems using Data Science
Website: http://www.wecolab.com.br
Phone: 55 11 2339-7150 **Email:** contato@wecolab.com.br
City: São Paulo **State:** SP **PC:** **Country:** Brazil
Year Established: 2016 **Status 2020:** Active
Industries: Analytics for:, Data Management for:, IT Managed Services for:, Machine Learning for:, Machine Learning

Company Name: Yurah
Description: Just access our website, tell us what and where you want to learn. And that's it, you'll get content in your free moments on your WhatsApp.
Website: http://www.yurah.com.br
Phone: 55 11 99822 1987 **Email:** oi@yurah.com.br
City: São Paulo **State:** SP **PC:** **Country:** Brazil
Year Established: 2017 **Status 2020:** Active
Industries:

Company Name: Zetta Health Analytics
Description: Health Analytics and Artificial Intelligence for Brazilian healthcare market
Website: http://www.zetta.heal:Thailand
Phone: **Email:** rodrigo@zetta.heal:Thailand
City: São Paulo **State:** SP **PC:** **Country:** Brazil
Year Established: 2019 **Status 2020:** Active
Industries: Artificial Intelligence for:, ~ Healthcare (20), Machine Learning

Company Name: J!Quant
Description: J!Quant develops enterprise software based on artificial intelligence algorithms and optimization with the aim of cutting company costs.
Website: http://www.jquant.com.br/
Phone: **Email:** contato@jquant.com.br
City: Sorocaba **State:** SP **PC:** **Country:** Brazil
Year Established: 2013 **Status 2020:** Active
Industries: Artificial Intelligence for:, IT Managed Services

Company Name: W3M Labs
Description: W3M Labs provides platforms for Marketing inside and outside Social Media with powerful tools based on Artificial Intelligence
Website: http://www.w3mlabs.com.br
Phone: 55 15 3031-5039 **Email:** contato@w3mweb.com.br
City: Sorocaba **State:** SP **PC:** **Country:** Brazil
Year Established: 2011 **Status 2020:** Active
Industries: Analytics for:, Artificial Intelligence for:, Machine Learning for:, Predictive Analytics for:, ~ Social Assistance-Non-Profits (53), ~ Social Assistance-Non-Profits (53)

Company Name: SpecLab
Description: SpecLab is a soil fertility analysis solution that spun out of Brazilian agriculture lab IBRA.
Website: http://www.speclab.com.br/
Phone: **Email:** contato@speclab.com.br
City: Sumaré **State:** SP **PC:** **Country:** Brazil
Year Established: 2017 **Status 2020:** Active
Industries: ~ Agriculture (3), Analytics for:, Artificial Intelligence for:, ~ Biotechnology (9), ~ Agriculture (3), IT Managed Services

Bulgaria

Company Name: Trigonon
Description: Trigonon utilizes smart data and machine learning to deliver personalized shopping experiences.
Website: http://trigonongroup.com
Phone: 359 (0) 745 90289 **Email:** 37567@reference-encyclopedia-ai.net
City: Petrich **State:** Blagoevgrad Province **PC:** **Country:** Bulgaria
Year Established: 2015 **Status 2020:** Active
Industries: Artificial Intelligence for:, E-Commerce for:, Machine Learning for:, ~ Retail and Consumer Products (52)

Company Name: A4Everyone
Description: A4Everyone offers affordable analytical solutions that improve small and medium businesses efficiency.
Website: http://www.a4everyone.com
Phone: 35924411243 **Email:** branimir.nikolov@a4everyone.com
City: Sofia **State:** Sofia City Province **PC:** **Country:** Bulgaria
Year Established: **Status 2020:** Active
Industries: Analytics for:, Artificial Intelligence for:, IT Managed Services

Company Name: BAIHUI AI
Description: Advanced algorithms and emerging AI Technologies
Website: http://docs.google.com/forms/d/e/1FAIpQLSe34bekuCCn9ex...
Phone: **Email:** baihui.ai@protonmail.com
City: Sofia **State:** Sofia City Province **PC:** **Country:** Bulgaria
Year Established: 2019 **Status 2020:** Active
Industries: Machine Learning

Company Name: Damocles Analytics
Description: AI Driven Political Insights Platform
Website: http://damoclesanalytics.com
Phone: **Email:** info@damoclesanalytics.com
City: Sofia **State:** Sofia City Province **PC:** **Country:** Bulgaria
Year Established: **Status 2020:** Active
Industries: Artificial Intelligence for:, Big Data and Analytics for:, ~ Government (19), Databases for:, Data Management for:, ~ Politics (47), Predictive Analytics

Company Name: DigiMark - Digital Innovations Development
Description: Digimark is an international full-cycle app development company, specialized in cloud based cross platform apps, tailored digital solutions
Website: http://www.digimark.co
Phone: **Email:** contact@digimark.co
City: Sofia **State:** Sofia City Province **PC:** **Country:** Bulgaria
Year Established: **Status 2020:** Active
Industries: Artificial Intelligence for:, Augmented Reality for:, Digital Media for:, Enterprise Application Services for:, Application Services for:, ~ Gaming (18), Business Process and Operations for:, ~ Professional Services (48), Development and Test for:, Cyber Security

Company Name: Gaida.ai
Description: Gaida.ai is a care of all your digital enquiries (leads) across their full journey all the way until deal.
Website: http://gaida.ai
Phone: (359) 888 111 845 **Email:** office@gaida.ai
City: Sofia **State:** Sofia City Province **PC:** **Country:** Bulgaria
Year Established: **Status 2020:** Active
Industries: Artificial Intelligence for:, IT Managed Services for:, IT Managed Services for:, ~ E-Commerce (12)

Company Name: Humans in the Loop
Description: Humans in the Loop provides continuous ML model improvement, from dataset collection and annotation to model verification and monitoring.
Website: http://humansintheloop.org/
Phone: 359 884 068 821 **Email:** hello@humansintheloop.org
City: Sofia **State:** Sofia City Province **PC:** **Country:** Bulgaria
Year Established: 2017 **Status 2020:** Active
Industries: Artificial Intelligence for:, Machine Learning for:, Business Process and Operations

Company Name: Imagga
Description: Imagga is an Image Recognition PaaS providing Image Tagging APIs for developers & businesses to build scalable, image intensive cloud ap: Palestine
Website: http://www.imagga.com
Phone: 359 899 001 887 **Email:** sales@imagga.com
City: Sofia **State:** Sofia City Province **PC:** **Country:** Bulgaria
Year Established: **Status 2020:** Active
Industries: Artificial Intelligence for:, Big Data and Analytics for:, Image Recognition for:, Machine Learning for:, ~ Media-Communications (41), Computer Vision

Company Name: Immaga Technologies Ltd
Description:
Website: http://www.imagga.com
Phone: 35-989-900-1887 **Email:** 12234@reference-encyclopedia-ai.net
City: Sofia **State:** Sofia City Province **Zip:** 1407 **Country**: Bulgaria
Year Established: **Status 2020:** Active
Industries:

Company Name: Micar Innovation (Micar21)
Description: Micar21 is a biotechnology company provide Drug Discovery FASTER - using in silico and Artificial Intelligence
Website: http://micar21.com
Phone: **Email:** info@micar21.com
City: Sofia **State:** Sofia City Province **PC:** **Country:** Bulgaria
Year Established: 2016 **Status 2020:** Active
Industries:

Company Name: Neural Brothers
Description: Neural Brothers develop software for web and mobile applications based on artificial intelligence techniques.
Website: http://neuralbrothers.com
Phone: 359 2 8475565 **Email:** office@neuralbrothers.com
City: Sofia **State:** Sofia City Province **PC:** **Country:** Bulgaria
Year Established: **Status 2020:** Active
Industries: Artificial Intelligence for:, ~ Professional Services (48)

Company Name: SafeConnect
Description: SafeConnect helps online travel agencies, airlines, and insurance companies enter the world of virtual interlining.
Website: http://www.safeconnect.pl/
Phone: 359 886 835 950 **Email:** contact@safeconnect.: Poland
City: Sofia **State:** Sofia City Province **PC:** **Country:** Bulgaria
Year Established: 2017 **Status 2020:** Active
Industries: Big Data and Analytics for:, IT Managed Services for:, Predictive Analytics for:, ~ Travel and Transportation (58)

Company Name: Tavan
Description: Tavan is a Weather-based individualized clothing recommendations for runners and cyclists.
Website: http://tavan.app/
Phone: **Email:** admin@tavan.app
City: Sofia **State:** Sofia City Province **PC:** **Country:** Bulgaria
Year Established: 2019 **Status 2020:** Active
Industries: ~ Healthcare (20), Machine Learning for:, Application Services for:, ~ Arts-Entertainment-Recreation (4)

Company Name: Transmetrics
Description: Transmetrics provides cargo companies with data cleansing, demand forecasting and network optimization based on AI and predictive analytics.
Website: http://transmetrics.eu
Phone: 359 2 865 0064 **Email:** info@transmetrics.eu
City: Sofia **State:** Sofia City Province **PC:** **Country:** Bulgaria
Year Established: **Status 2020:** Active
Industries: Analytics for:, Artificial Intelligence for:, Business Applications for:, Big Data and Analytics for:, Business Intelligence for:, ~ Transportation and Logistics (57), Machine Learning for:, Predictive Analytics for:, ~ Transportation and Logistics (57), ~ Transpo

Company Name: Ubitrack
Description: Ubitrack is a one-stop-shop for football performance data. We extract the data with our proprietary optical tracking system.
Website: http://ubitrack.eu/
Phone: **Email:** tashev@ubitrack.eu
City: Sofia **State:** Sofia City Province **PC:** **Country:** Bulgaria
Year Established: 2019 **Status 2020:** Active
Industries: Artificial Intelligence for:, Big Data and Analytics for:, Computer Vision for:, Machine Learning for:, ~ Arts-Entertainment-Recreation (4)

Cameroon

Company Name: cornertech
Description: Cornertech.co is an expanding online categories of all companies around the world.
Website: http://cornertech.co
Phone: 85516822809 **Email:** cornertechnology2016@gmail.com
City: **State:** **PC:** **Country:** Cambodia
Year Established: **Status 2020:** Active
Industries: Artificial Intelligence for:, Big Data and Analytics for:, Business Intelligence for:, Cloud for:, Cyber Security

Company Name: Interndada
Description: Web App/ mobile App to enable university students to apply for internships online , either locally or internationally
Website: http://interndada.com
Phone: 23777104421 **Email:** originalinnovation2018@gmail.com
City: Yaounde **State:** Centre **PC:** **Country:** Cameroon
Year Established: **Status 2020:** Active
Industries: Artificial Intelligence for:, ~ Education (13), ~ Education (13), Machine Learning

Company Name: kentnix
Description: Saas Iot Company
Website: http://www.kentnix.com
Phone: **Email:** infos@kentnix.com
City: Yaounde **State:** Centre **PC:** **Country:** Cameroon
Year Established: 2016 **Status 2020:** Active
Industries: Artificial Intelligence for:, Big Data and Analytics for:, Internet of Things (IoT)

Company Name: OASIS Africa Innovation
Description: The Decentralized Digital Innovation Hub For African Blockchain and AI Startu: Palestine
Website: http://oasis.cm
Phone: **Email:** info@oasis.cm
City: Yaounde **State:** Centre **PC:** **Country:** Cameroon
Year Established: 2016 **Status 2020:** Active
Industries: Artificial Intelligence for:, IT Managed Services

Company Name: VIRGOTECH
Description: Technology and : ITALY
Website: http://virgotech.cm
Phone: **Email:** lateh.larry@gmail.com
City: Yaounde **State:** Centre **PC:** **Country:** Cameroon

Year Established: 2017 **Status 2020:** Active
Industries: Artificial Intelligence for:, Big Data and Analytics for:, IT Managed Services for:, Internet of Things (IoT)

Company Name: adelrick
Description: adelrick is a manufacturer and developer of mobile application to communicate with smartphone and computer.
Website: http://www.adelrick.com/
Phone: 237 97 47 20 00 **Email:** adel.rick@adelrick.com
City: Douala **State:** Littoral **PC:** **Country:** Cameroon
Year Established: 2011 **Status 2020:** Active
Industries: Artificial Intelligence

Canada

Company Name: Aaa Cnc Machining Service
Description: Aaa Cnc Machining Services is an oil and gas machine learning company located in Calgary.
Website: https://www.aaacncmachining.com/
Phone: **Email:** aaa.cnc.machining@gmail.com
City: Calgary **State:** AB **PC:** **Country:** Canada
Year Established: 2010 **Status 2020:** Active
Industries: Machine Learning

Company Name: Acuspire
Description: Acuspire is an AI-powered job search and recruiting platform. We connect employers with qualified jobseekers within seconds.
Website: https://acuspire.ai/
Phone: **Email:** hello@acuspire.ai
City: Calgary **State:** AB **PC:** **Country:** Canada
Year Established: 2016 **Status 2020:** Active
Industries: Artificial Intelligence for:, IT Managed Services for:, Web

Company Name: Ambyint
Description: Ambyint company bringing a new level of intelligence to the oil and gas industry.
Website: http://ambyint.com/
Phone: (800) 205-1311 **Email:** hello@ambyint.com
City: Calgary **State:** AB **PC:** **Country:** Canada
Year Established: 2015 **Status 2020:** Active
Industries:

Company Name: Atheria.io
Description: Enterprise Software
Website: http://atheria.io
Phone: 4039939426 **Email:** hello@atheria.io
City: Calgary **State:** AB **PC:** **Country:** Canada
Year Established: **Status 2020:** Active
Industries: Artificial Intelligence for:, IT Managed Services for:, ~ Professional Services (48)

Company Name: Aware360
Description: Aware360 is a leading the People IoT movement with solutions which helps hundreds of businesses become more efficient.
Website: http://aware360.com
Phone: 1(877)352-8522 **Email:** info@aware360.com
City: Calgary **State:** AB **PC:** **Country:** Canada
Year Established: 2015 **Status 2020:** Active
Industries: IT Managed Services for:, IT Managed Services for:, Internet of Things (IoT) for:, Machine Learning

Company Name: BoxOfDocs
Description: BoxOfDocs is an Artificial Intelligence enabled SaaS product that provides an industry-specific document library those who conduct research.
Website: http://boxofdocs.info/
Phone: 403-966-7200 **Email:** derrick@boxofdocs.info
City: Calgary **State:** AB **PC:** **Country:** Canada
Year Established: 2017 **Status 2020:** Active
Industries: Artificial Intelligence for:, ~ Government (19), IT Managed Services for:, Machine Learning for:, Business Software as a Service Apps (SaaS Apps)

Company Name: Building Bloc
Description: AI Incubator
Website: http://www.bbloc.ca
Phone: 403 617 4624 **Email:** info@bbloc.ca
City: Calgary **State:** AB **PC:** **Country:** Canada
Year Established: 2015 **Status 2020:** Active
Industries: Artificial Intelligence

Company Name: Chata
Description: Delivering conversational data experiences through the dynamic translation of Natural Language (NL) to database query languages.
Website: http://chata.ai/
Phone: **Email:** info@chata.ai
City: Calgary **State:** AB **PC:** **Country:** Canada
Year Established: 2016 **Status 2020:** Active
Industries: Artificial Intelligence for:, IT Managed Services for:, Machine Learning for:, Business Software as a Service Apps (SaaS Apps)

Company Name: Crux OCM
Description: Crux OCM utilizes AI and real-time optimization to enable autonomous operation of major oil and gas assets.
Website: http://cruxocm.com/
Phone: (1403) 923-2322 **Email:** vicki@cruxocm.com
City: Calgary **State:** AB **PC:** **Country:** Canada
Year Established: 2017 **Status 2020:** Active
Industries: Artificial Intelligence for:, ~ Energy and Utilities (14), ~ Energy and Utilities (14), Machine Learning

Company Name: E.O.I Technologies Inc.
Description: Smart Hardware, SaaS
Website: http://eoktechnologies.com
Phone: (480) 452-0880 **Email:** info@eoktechnologies.com
City: Calgary **State:** AB **PC:** **Country:** Canada
Year Established: **Status 2020:** Active
Industries: ~ Food and Beverage (17), Predictive Analytics

Company Name: Envio Systems
Description: Envio Systems develops cloud-based building technologies for existing commercial buildings.
Website: http://www.enviosystems.com/
Phone: 604 417 7223 **Email:** contact@enviosystems.com
City: Calgary **State:** AB **PC:** **Country:** Canada
Year Established: 2013 **Status 2020:** Active
Industries: Cloud for:, ~ Energy and Utilities (14), ~ Energy and Utilities (14), ~ Energy and Utilities (14), IT Managed Services for:, Predictive Analytics for:, Business Software as a Service Apps (SaaS Apps) for:, Business Software as a Service Apps (SaaS Apps) for:, ~ C

Company Name: EZ-Robot
Description: EZ-Robot is an edtech solution that supports teaching and inspires learning.
Website: http://www.ez-robot.com/
Phone: (888)346-4333 **Email:** customersupport@ez-robot.com
City: Calgary **State:** AB **PC:** **Country:** Canada
Year Established: 2011 **Status 2020:** Active
Industries: Artificial Intelligence for:, ~ Personal-Religious-Civic (45), ~ Education (13), ~ Administrative and Support Services (1), Internet of Things (IoT) for:, Application Services for:, Application Services

Company Name: Hone Virtual Education Ltd.
Description: Combining psychology and technology to improve user medical cue recognition in high-risk, high-stress environments.
Website: http://www.honeve.com
Phone: 403-680-1524 **Email:** alex@honeve.com
City: Calgary **State:** AB **PC:** **Country:** Canada

Year Established: **Status 2020:** Active
Industries: Artificial Intelligence for:, Augmented Reality for:, ~ Education (13), Machine Learning for:, ~ Education (13)

Company Name: Imaginea Ai
Description: AI Company
Website: http://imaginea.ai/
Phone: 844-462-4446 **Email:** info@imaginea.ai
City: Calgary **State:** AB **PC:** **Country:** Canada
Year Established: 2017 **Status 2020:** Active
Industries: Artificial Intelligence

Company Name: Menome Technologies
Description: Menome Technologies provides SaaS knowledge management tool that gives customers a 360 degree view of their data.
Website: http://menome.com
Phone: 587-891-5075 **Email:** communications@menome.com
City: Calgary **State:** AB **PC:** **Country:** Canada
Year Established: 2016 **Status 2020:** Active
Industries: Artificial Intelligence for:, Big Data and Analytics for:, IT Managed Services for:, Business Software as a Service Apps (SaaS Apps)

Company Name: Osprey Informatics
Description: Osprey Informatics provides a computer vision platform that transforms images and video into actionable enterprise intelligence.
Website: http://osperity.com/
Phone: 1(844) 590-0824 **Email:** info@ospreyinformatics.com
City: Calgary **State:** AB **PC:** **Country:** Canada
Year Established: 2012 **Status 2020:** Active
Industries: Artificial Intelligence for:, Computer Vision for:, Automation for:, IT Managed Services for:, Machine Learning

Company Name: PawsAdm: India
Description: PawsAdmin is a powerful and easy to use pet software that manages end to end business needs from daily operations to AI marketing.
Website: http://www.pawsadmin.com
Phone: **Email:** hello@pawsadmin.com
City: Calgary **State:** AB **PC:** **Country:** Canada
Year Established: 2016 **Status 2020:** Active
Industries:

Company Name: Physio4D
Description: Physio4D is a vision-based physical therapy startup that provides a vision-based upfront assessment tool.
Website: http://www.physio4d.com
Phone: (403) 998-9607 **Email:** info@physio4d.com
City: Calgary **State:** AB **PC:** **Country:** Canada
Year Established: 2015 **Status 2020:** Active
Industries: Artificial Intelligence for:, Computer Vision for:, ~ Healthcare (20), ~ Healthcare (20), ~ Healthcare (20), ~ Healthcare (20)

Company Name: Sawback Technologies
Description: Sawback Technologies is a remote-sensing company that specializes in UAVs, and sensors.
Website: http://www.sawbacktech.ca
Phone: 844-210-2950 **Email:** neil@sawbacktech.ca
City: Calgary **State:** AB **PC:** **Country:** Canada
Year Established: **Status 2020:** Active
Industries: Artificial Intelligence for:, IT Managed Services for:, ~ Transportation and Logistics (57), ~ Professional Services (48)

Company Name: Sidekick.co
Description: Sidekick.co is the best way to discover, research and source software solutions and services around the world.
Website: http://sidekick.co
Phone: 1-403-860-3741 **Email:** doug.mackay@sidekick.co
City: Calgary **State:** AB **PC:** **Country:** Canada
Year Established: 2016 **Status 2020:** Active
Industries: Artificial Intelligence for:, ~ E-Commerce (12), Content for:, ~ Social Assistance-Non-Profits (53)

Company Name: Symend
Description: Symend transforms consumer experience of debt resolution for telcos, banks, and utilities.
Website: http://www.symend.com/
Phone: (855)579-6363 **Email:** info@symend.com
City: Calgary **State:** AB **PC:** **Country:** Canada
Year Established: 2016 **Status 2020:** Active
Industries: ~ Administrative and Support Services (1), ~ Banking and Financial Markets-Services (7), Predictive Analytics

Company Name: Unsist
Description: Unsist is a predictive analytics company creating technology for the oil & gas industry that never stops.
Website: http://www.unsist.com
Phone: (587)-288-6685 **Email:** hello@unsist.com
City: Calgary **State:** AB **PC:** **Country:** Canada
Year Established: 2017 **Status 2020:** Active
Industries: Artificial Intelligence for:, ~ Energy and Utilities (14), Machine Learning

Company Name: VOR Research & Development
Description: AI-enabled IoT & IIoT application company.
Website: http://vorrd.com
Phone: **Email:** info@vorrd.com
City: Calgary **State:** AB **PC:** **Country:** Canada
Year Established: 2018 **Status 2020:** Active
Industries: Artificial Intelligence for:, Cyber Security for:, IT Managed Services for:, Internet of Things (IoT) for:, Predictive Analytics

Company Name: White Whale Analytics
Description: White Whale Analytics have built Deep Sea, an end-to-end AI insight engine with simulative, predictive and diagnostic capabilities.
Website: http://whitewhaleanalytics.com
Phone: **Email:** williams@whitewhaleanalytics.com
City: Calgary **State:** AB **PC:** **Country:** Canada
Year Established: 2015 **Status 2020:** Active
Industries: Artificial Intelligence for:, Big Data and Analytics

Company Name: AltaML
Description: Machine Learning. Applied.
Website: http://www.altaml.com/
Phone: 1 780-702-1416 **Email:** hello@altaml.com
City: Edmonton **State:** AB **PC:** **Country:** Canada
Year Established: **Status 2020:** Active
Industries: Artificial Intelligence for:, Application Services for:, Machine Learning for:, Natural Language Processing for:, ~ Professional Services (48)

Company Name: Gabbi.Ai
Description: Gabbi.Ai is an AI platform revolutionizing how agents build relationships with their clients.
Website: http://www.gabbi.ai/
Phone: **Email:** 36605@reference-encyclopedia-ai.net
City: Edmonton **State:** AB **PC:** **Country:** Canada
Year Established: 2017 **Status 2020:** Active
Industries: Artificial Intelligence

Company Name: Granify
Description: Granify employs big data and machine learning technologies to enable online retailers to enhance their sales via a SaaS-based solution.
Website: http://granify.com
Phone: 1(888) 340-8429 **Email:** hello@granify.com
City: Edmonton **State:** AB **PC:** **Country:** Canada
Year Established: 2011 **Status 2020:** Active
Industries: Analytics for:, Big Data and Analytics for:, E-Commerce for:, Machine Learning for:, Business Software as a Service Apps (SaaS Apps)

Company Name: HonestDoor
Description: HonestDoor's tech uses big data, machine learning, and predictive analytics.
Website: http://honestdoor.com/
Phone: **Email:** info@honestdoor.com
City: Edmonton **State:** AB **PC:** **Country:** Canada
Year Established: 2018 **Status 2020:** Active
Industries: Big Data and Analytics for:, IT Managed Services for:, Machine Learning for:, Predictive Analytics

Company Name: Nanoprecise Sci Corp
Description: An AI & IoT company that is revolutionizing the field of predictive maintenance
Website: http://www.nanoprecisesc.com
Phone: **Email:** svedula@nanoprecisesc.com
City: Edmonton **State:** AB **PC:** **Country:** Canada
Year Established: 2017 **Status 2020:** Active
Industries: Artificial Intelligence for:, Automation for:, IT Managed Services for:, Internet of Things (IoT) for:, Predictive Analytics

Company Name: SAM
Description: SAM turns unstructured social media into actionable insight and awareness.
Website: http://www.samdesk.io/
Phone: 1(800) 275-4144 **Email:** admin@samdesk.io
City: Edmonton **State:** AB **PC:** **Country:** Canada
Year Established: 2013 **Status 2020:** Active
Industries: Artificial Intelligence for:, Enterprise Application Services for:, Machine Learning for:, Security for:, ~ Social Assistance-Non-Profits (53)

Company Name: Tensorgra: Philippin: Spain
Description: Tensorgraph offers Enzo Expert, an AI-powered conversational platform that can help businesses interact with customers on a personal level.
Website: http://tensorgraph.io/
Phone: **Email:** cmail@tensorgraph.io
City: Edmonton **State:** AB **PC:** **Country:** Canada
Year Established: 2018 **Status 2020:** Active
Industries:

Company Name: Testfire Labs
Description: Testfire Labs is a software and consulting services company building products that take advantage of the latest developments in A.I.
Website: http://www.testfirelabs.com/
Phone: 1 780-809-0888 **Email:** support@testfirelabs.com
City: Edmonton **State:** AB **PC:** **Country:** Canada
Year Established: 2017 **Status 2020:** Active
Industries: Artificial Intelligence for:, Application Services for:, Machine Learning for:, Business Process and Operations for:, Natural Language Processing

Company Name: Trust Science
Description: Trust Science is a provider of AI-powered alternative credit scoring solutions.
Website: http://www.trustscience.com
Phone: 1 (587) 393-6619 **Email:** info@trustscience.com
City: Edmonton **State:** AB **PC:** **Country:** Canada
Year Established: 2014 **Status 2020:** Active
Industries: Analytics for:, Artificial Intelligence for:, IT Managed Services for:, IT Managed Services for:, Machine Learning

Company Name: ZanQ
Description: ZanQ is a social mentorship platform targeted for founders.
Website: http://zanq.co
Phone: **Email:** ptang@zanq.co
City: Edmonton **State:** AB **PC:** **Country:** Canada
Year Established: 2016 **Status 2020:** Active
Industries: Natural Language Processing for:, ~ Social Assistance-Non-Profits (53)

Company Name: The Latium Group of Compani: Spain
Description: Industrial IoT, SaaS, Edge Computing, Artificial Intelligence
Website: http://www.thelatiumgroup.com/
Phone: 7809551088 **Email:** info@thelatiumgroup.com
City: Nisku **State:** AB **PC:** **Country:** Canada
Year Established: 2019 **Status 2020:** Active
Industries: Artificial Intelligence for:, IT Managed Services for:, ~ Telecommunications (56), Machine Learning for:, Business Software as a Service Apps (SaaS Apps)

Company Name: SafeContact
Description: SafeContact is solving the Hospital Acquired Infection (HAI) epidemic plaguing its global healthcare facilities.
Website: http://safecontact.com/
Phone: **Email:** info@safecontact.com
City: Saint Albert **State:** AB **PC:** **Country:** Canada
Year Established: 2017 **Status 2020:** Active
Industries: Artificial Intelligence for:, ~ Healthcare (20), ~ Healthcare (20), Internet of Things (IoT)

Company Name: Eio Diagnostics
Description: EIO Diagnostics is a farming company that focuses on developing agricultural tools to diagnose udder diseases in dairy animals.
Website: http://eiodiagnostics.com
Phone: 206-565-8405 **Email:** 36486@reference-encyclopedia-ai.net
City: Duncan **State:** BC **PC:** **Country:** Canada
Year Established: 2017 **Status 2020:** Active
Industries: ~ Agriculture (3), ~ Agriculture (3), ~ Healthcare (20), Machine Learning

Company Name: Strawhou
Description: We blend financial resources, creative, strategy and machine learning to launch and scale billion dollar consumer brands
Website: http://www.strawhouse.com
Phone: (778)699-2161 **Email:** hello@strawhouse.com
City: Kelowna **State:** BC **PC:** **Country:** Canada
Year Established: 2013 **Status 2020:** Active
Industries: Digital Marketing for:, ~ Banking and Financial Markets-Services (7), Web for:, Machine Learning for:, ~ Banking and Financial Markets-Services (7)

Company Name: Two Hat Security
Description: Two Hat is the world-leader in filtering of high-risk content.
Website: http://www.twohat.com
Phone: (855)407-0889 **Email:** hello@twohat.com
City: Kelowna **State:** BC **PC:** **Country:** Canada
Year Established: 2012 **Status 2020:** Active
Industries: Analytics for:, Big Data and Analytics for:, ~ Personal-Religious-Civic (45), Application Services for:, Machine Learning for:, Natural Language Processing for:, Business Software as a Service Apps (SaaS Apps) for:, Security for:, Security for:, Cyber Security for

Company Name: Juicey Turf
Description: SaaS
Website: http://juiceyturf.com
Phone: **Email:** info@juiceyturf.com
City: New Westminster **State:** BC **PC:** **Country:** Canada
Year Established: 2019 **Status 2020:** Active
Industries: Artificial Intelligence for:, Big Data and Analytics for:, Machine Learning for:, Predictive Analytics for:, Business Software as a Service Apps (SaaS Apps) for:, Automation for:, Automation

Company Name: ProToGo
Description: Creating an innovative service and platform in the Construction Industry which makes Construction more efficient, reliable, and transparent.
Website: http://protogo.co/
Phone: 604-347-6191 **Email:** sangev@protogo.co
City: North Vancouver **State:** BC **PC:** **Country:** Canada

Year Established: 2016 **Status 2020:** Active
Industries: Artificial Intelligence for:, ~ Construction (10), Machine Learning for:, Predictive Analytics

Company Name: sparkgeo
Description: a geospatial consultancy
Website: http://www.sparkgeo.com
Phone: (250)981-6946 **Email:** hi@sparkgeo.com
City: Prince George **State:** BC **PC:** **Country:** Canada
Year Established: 2010 **Status 2020:** Active
Industries: Web

Company Name: Disrupted Logic
Description: Big Data and Artificial Intelligence for Interactive Media Experienc: Spain
Website: http://www.disruptedlogic.com
Phone: (604)800-0721 **Email:** info@disruptedlogic.com
City: Surrey **State:** BC **PC:** **Country:** Canada
Year Established: 2012 **Status 2020:** Active
Industries: Artificial Intelligence for:, Big Data and Analytics for:, ~ Media-Communications (41)

Company Name: Eleos Robotics
Description: Eleos Robotics invented the RoboWeeder an artificially intelligent weeding killing robot.
Website: http://eleosrobotics.com
Phone: **Email:** info@eleosrobotics.com
City: Surrey **State:** BC **PC:** **Country:** Canada
Year Established: 2016 **Status 2020:** Active
Industries: ~ Agriculture (3), Artificial Intelligence for:, ~ Energy and Utilities (14), ~ Social-Environmental-Physical-Engineering Sciences (55)

Company Name: GenerationsE Software Solutions, Inc.
Description: AI, Deep Learning, Medical Imaging Analytic Solutions
Website: http://www.GenerationsE.com
Phone: **Email:** info@generationse.com
City: Surrey **State:** BC **PC:** **Country:** Canada
Year Established: 2014 **Status 2020:** Active
Industries:

Company Name: Techofinity Inc.
Description: An Intelligent Database Systems Company
Website: http://www.techofinity.com
Phone: (604) 440-8001 **Email:** contact@techofinity.com
City: Surrey **State:** BC **PC:** **Country:** Canada
Year Established: 2014 **Status 2020:** Active
Industries: Artificial Intelligence for:, IT Managed Services for:, Web

Company Name: UrbanLogiq
Description: UrbanLogiq provides a data analytics platform that makes city planning faster, cheaper, and more accurate.
Website: http://www.urbanlogiq.com
Phone: **Email:** info@urbanlogiq.com
City: Surrey **State:** BC **PC:** **Country:** Canada
Year Established: 2016 **Status 2020:** Active
Industries: ~ Government (19), Machine Learning

Company Name: AbCellera Biologics
Description: AbCellera Biologics offers development of antibody therapeutics to improve patient outcomes.
Website: https://www.abcellera.com/
Phone: (604) 559-9005 **Email:** 35933@reference-encyclopedia-ai.net
City: Vancouver **State:** BC **PC:** **Country:** Canada
Year Established: 2012 **Status 2020:** Active
Industries: Artificial Intelligence for:, ~ Biotechnology (9), ~ Healthcare (20), ~ Healthcare (20)

Company Name: AddBrain Inc
Description: AddBrain Inc. is devoted to making brain healthcare space intelligent, data driven and available to everyone.
Website: http://addbrain.ca
Phone: 650-690-8956 **Email:** dorian.aur@addbrain.ca
City: Vancouver **State:** BC **PC:** **Country:** Canada
Year Established: **Status 2020:** Active
Industries: Artificial Intelligence for:, ~ Healthcare (20), IT Managed Services for:, ~ Professional Services (48)

Company Name: Advize
Description: Advize is AI powered text analytics software that analyzes voice of customer data from multiple channels.
Website:
Phone: **Email:** 35960@reference-encyclopedia-ai.net
City: Vancouver **State:** BC **PC:** **Country:** Canada
Year Established: 2018 **Status 2020:** Closed
Industries: Artificial Intelligence for:, Data Management

Company Name: Answer Intelligence
Description: Answer Intelligence is a consultancy that provides product design strategy, technical roadmaps, marketing, web applications, etc.
Website: http://answerintelligence.com
Phone: 1 917-540-9727 **Email:** hi@answerintelligence.com
City: Vancouver **State:** BC **PC:** **Country:** Canada
Year Established: 2015 **Status 2020:** Active
Industries: Machine Learning

Company Name: AntEater
Description: Team Intelligence Software for Google GSuite & Slack
Website: http://www.anteateranalytics.com/
Phone: 1 604-764 0899 **Email:** contact@anteateranalytics.com
City: Vancouver **State:** BC **PC:** **Country:** Canada
Year Established: **Status 2020:** Active
Industries: Artificial Intelligence for:, IT Managed Services for:, ~ Professional Services (48)

Company Name: Aplic.io
Description: Aplic is a connecting global education ecosystem, powered by block chain and AI technologies.
Website: http://www.e1ectr0n.com
Phone: 503-350-4125 **Email:** robert.toppel@e1ectr0n.com
City: Vancouver **State:** BC **PC:** **Country:** Canada
Year Established: **Status 2020:** Active
Industries: Artificial Intelligence for:, Blockchain for:, ~ Education (13)

Company Name: Archetec Business Solutions
Description: Archetec Business Solutions is an expert on the business side of technology.
Website: http://archetec.com
Phone: **Email:** 36080@reference-encyclopedia-ai.net
City: Vancouver **State:** BC **PC:** **Country:** Canada
Year Established: 2018 **Status 2020:** Active
Industries:

Company Name: Ascent Systems Technologies
Description: Private R&D and integrated solutions provider in the area of clean energy, using adaptive control, machine learning and intelligent network.
Website: http://www.ascentsystemstechnologies.com
Phone: 604-761-4020 **Email:** ascent@ascentsystems.ca
City: Vancouver **State:** BC **PC:** **Country:** Canada
Year Established: 2012 **Status 2020:** Active
Industries: Artificial Intelligence for:, ~ Energy and Utilities (14), IT Managed Services for:, ~ Energy and Utilities (14)

Company Name: Bio Conscious
Description: Health analytics
Website: http://www.bioconscious.tech
Phone: **Email:** info@bioconscious.tech
City: Vancouver **State:** BC **PC:** **Country:** Canada

Year Established: 2015 **Status 2020:** Active
Industries: ~ Healthcare (20), Machine Learning

Company Name: BLUEPRIME Analytics Inc
Description: Data Analytics as a Service, leveraging IoT, Blockchain and AI technologies to power end-to-end smart data solutions
Website: http://www.blueprime.com
Phone: 1 855-782-6882 **Email:** info@blueprime.com
City: Vancouver **State:** BC **PC:** **Country:** Canada
Year Established: 2012 **Status 2020:** Active
Industries: Analytics for:, Artificial Intelligence for:, Blockchain for:, IT Managed Services

Company Name: Bureau Labs Inc.
Description: Bureau is the on-demand personal assistant service for busy professionals
Website: http://bureau.co
Phone: **Email:** 36219@reference-encyclopedia-ai.net
City: Vancouver **State:** BC **PC:** **Country:** Canada
Year Established: 2015 **Status 2020:** Active
Industries: Artificial Intelligence for:, Internet of Things (IoT)

Company Name: Carbon Trainer
Description: fitness, hardware, consumer, saas, ai
Website: http://www.carbontrainer.com
Phone: **Email:** hello@carbontrainer.com
City: Vancouver **State:** BC **PC:** **Country:** Canada
Year Established: 2019 **Status 2020:** Active
Industries:

Company Name: CareCru
Description: CareCru is the creator of Donna, A virtual dental practice assistant, powered by AI, that grows and manages dental practices.
Website: http://carecru.com/
Phone: (888) 870-0077 **Email:** hello@carecru.com
City: Vancouver **State:** BC **PC:** **Country:** Canada
Year Established: 2016 **Status 2020:** Active
Industries: Artificial Intelligence

Company Name: Compression.ai
Description: Media Compression Web Service
Website: http://compression.ai/
Phone: **Email:** hello@compression.ai
City: Vancouver **State:** BC **PC:** **Country:** Canada
Year Established: 2018 **Status 2020:** Active
Industries: Machine Learning

Company Name: CoPilot AI
Description: CoPilot AI is a SaaS company that uses A.I. and rich social data to connect businesses with customers in a whole new way.
Website: http://copilotai.com
Phone: 347-343-8671 **Email:** sales@copilotadvisor.com
City: Vancouver **State:** BC **PC:** **Country:** Canada
Year Established: 2016 **Status 2020:** Active
Industries: Artificial Intelligence for:, Business Software as a Service Apps (SaaS Apps) for:, ~ Social Assistance-Non-Profits (53)

Company Name: CUBIC MOV: IRELAND
Description: CUBIC MOVIE is a Hologram Streaming Platform.
Website: http://cubicmovie.com
Phone: **Email:** info@cubicmovie.com
City: Vancouver **State:** BC **PC:** **Country:** Canada
Year Established: **Status 2020:** Active
Industries: Artificial Intelligence for:, Augmented Reality

Company Name: delecta Technologies Inc.
Description: AI as a Service/Fintech
Website: http://delecta.co/
Phone: **Email:** info@delecta.co
City: Vancouver **State:** BC **PC:** **Country:** Canada
Year Established: 2017 **Status 2020:** Active
Industries: Artificial Intelligence for:, ~ Banking and Financial Markets-Services (7), Machine Learning

Company Name: Demizine Technology
Description: Our mission is to make decentralized energy and water available to everyone, everywhere.
Website: http://www.demizinetechnology.com
Phone: **Email:** jonathan@demizinetechnology.com
City: Vancouver **State:** BC **PC:** **Country:** Canada
Year Established: 2017 **Status 2020:** Active
Industries: Artificial Intelligence for:, ~ Energy and Utilities (14), ~ Waste Management and Remediation Services (59)

Company Name: DG1 Group Holdings - EcommEarth Ltd
Description: SaaS big-data and digital landscape management for any type of SME
Website: http://www.dg1.com
Phone: (1604) 670-7533 **Email:** info@ecommearth.com
City: Vancouver **State:** BC **PC:** **Country:** Canada
Year Established: 2016 **Status 2020:** Active
Industries: Artificial Intelligence for:, Big Data and Analytics for:, E-Commerce for:, Business Software as a Service Apps (SaaS Apps)

Company Name: Downtown.AI
Description: Downtown.AI uses machine learning and big location data to analyze and predict human movements in cities.
Website: http://www.downtown.ai/
Phone: **Email:** contact@downtown.ai
City: Vancouver **State:** BC **PC:** **Country:** Canada
Year Established: 2017 **Status 2020:** Active
Industries: Artificial Intelligence for:, Machine Learning

Company Name: Emtelligent Software Ltd.
Description: SaaS Clinical NLP Solutions
Website: http://www.emtelligent.com
Phone: 1-877-463-6835 **Email:** info@emtelligent.ai
City: Vancouver **State:** BC **PC:** **Country:** Canada
Year Established: 2016 **Status 2020:** Active
Industries: Artificial Intelligence for:, ~ Healthcare (20), IT Managed Services for:, ~ Healthcare (20)

Company Name: EquitySoft Investments
Description: Canada's only private wealth management entity specialized in machine-learning sentiment-scoring trading algorithms.
Website: http://equitysoftvaluations.com
Phone: **Email:** ir@equitysoftvaluations.com
City: Vancouver **State:** BC **PC:** **Country:** Canada
Year Established: 2013 **Status 2020:** Active
Industries: Artificial Intelligence for:, ~ Banking and Financial Markets-Services (7), Machine Learning

Company Name: Finn AI
Description: Finn AI provides AI-powered conversational banking technology for personal banking and finance.
Website: http://finn.ai
Phone: 1(604) 256-8005 **Email:** info@finn.ai
City: Vancouver **State:** BC **PC:** **Country:** Canada
Year Established: 2014 **Status 2020:** Active
Industries: Finance and Accounting for:, Application Services for:, Artificial Intelligence for:, ~ Banking and Financial Markets-Services (7), ~ Banking and Financial Markets-Services (7), ~ Banking and Financial Markets-Services (7), Mobile for:, ~ Social Assistance-Non-P

Company Name: Fire Out
Description: Fire Out automates fire extinguisher with AI, for smarter and quicker detection and reaction to fire.
Website: http://www.fireout.io
Phone: (604)600-2341 **Email:** erliktbauckman@gmail.com
City: Vancouver **State:** BC **PC:** **Country:** Canada

Year Established: 2017 **Status 2020:** Active
Industries: Artificial Intelligence

Company Name: FIRMOGRAM
Description: FIRMOGRAM is an AI-driven Business to Business (B2B) marketplace and sales intelligence platform.
Website: http://www.firmogram.com
Phone: 1(855)782-6882 **Email:** info@firmogram.com
City: Vancouver **State:** BC **PC:** **Country:** Canada
Year Established: 2014 **Status 2020:** Active
Industries: Artificial Intelligence for:, Business Intelligence

Company Name: FTSY
Description: FTSY ('footsy') is an A.I. platform that matches people to consumer goods where fit and comfort matter.
Website: http://www.ftsy.ai/
Phone: **Email:** capital@ftsy.co
City: Vancouver **State:** BC **PC:** **Country:** Canada
Year Established: 2015 **Status 2020:** Active
Industries:

Company Name: Gitalytics
Description: Gitalytics is an analytics platform that helps engineering teams visualize workflow data from all of their projects in one place.
Website: http://www.gitalytics.com
Phone: **Email:** jin@gitalytics.com
City: Vancouver **State:** BC **PC:** **Country:** Canada
Year Established: 2017 **Status 2020:** Active
Industries: Analytics for:, Big Data and Analytics for:, Data Management for:, Predictive Analytics

Company Name: Growlyn
Description: Your Marketing on Auto-Pilot.
Website: http://growlyn.com
Phone: 1-855-476-9596 **Email:** support@growlyn.com
City: Vancouver **State:** BC **PC:** **Country:** Canada
Year Established: **Status 2020:** Active
Industries: Artificial Intelligence for:, Content for:, Digital Marketing for:, Machine Learning for:, ~ Media-Communications (41), ~ Media-Communications (41)

Company Name: Illusen
Description: Machine Vision Without Compromi
Website: http://illusense.com/
Phone: **Email:** info@illusense.com
City: Vancouver **State:** BC **PC:** **Country:** Canada
Year Established: 2013 **Status 2020:** Active
Industries: Artificial Intelligence for:, Machine Learning

Company Name: Internuncio Technologies Inc.
Description: A Crowdsourcing Control Center, Built for Develope: Serbia
Website: http://www.hitblocks.ai/
Phone: **Email:** 36799@reference-encyclopedia-ai.net
City: Vancouver **State:** BC **PC:** **Country:** Canada
Year Established: 2015 **Status 2020:** Active
Industries: Artificial Intelligence for:, Computer Vision for:, Application Program Interfaces (APIs) for:, Enterprise Application Services for:, Machine Learning for:, Natural Language Processing

Company Name: Istuary Innovation Group
Description: Cultivate innovation and launch businesses in fast-growing markets
Website: http://www.istuary.com/
Phone: **Email:** info@memcpu.com
City: Vancouver **State:** BC **PC:** **Country:** Canada
Year Established: 2012 **Status 2020:** Active
Industries: Artificial Intelligence for:, Virtual Reality (VR)

Company Name: Knomos Knowledge Management
Description: Knomos is an enhanced knowledge management platform for corporate legal departments leveraging data visualization and deep machine learning.
Website: http://knomos.law/
Phone: (604) 563 0478 **Email:** info@knomos.ca
City: Vancouver **State:** BC **PC:** **Country:** Canada
Year Established: 2014 **Status 2020:** Active
Industries: Data Management for:, Application Program Interfaces (APIs) for:, Machine Learning

Company Name: LearningBran: Switzerland
Description: LearningBranch provides tools to assess spoken and written soft skills for the workplace.
Website: http://www.learningbranch.com/
Phone: 604 377 4149 **Email:** info@learningbranch.com
City: Vancouver **State:** BC **PC:** **Country:** Canada
Year Established: 2018 **Status 2020:** Active
Industries: Mobile for:, Natural Language Processing

Company Name: LifeBooster inc.
Description: A predictive injury risk platform for the enterprise health and safety market that identifies risk, and prevents workplace injuries.
Website: http://lifebooster.ca
Phone: 1 (604) 379-2990 **Email:** info@lifebooster.ca
City: Vancouver **State:** BC **PC:** **Country:** Canada
Year Established: 2012 **Status 2020:** Active
Industries: Big Data and Analytics for:, ~ Healthcare (20), Predictive Analytics for:, Internet of Things (IoT)

Company Name: LivNao Technologies
Description: SaaS
Website: http://livnao.com
Phone: **Email:** info@livnao.com
City: Vancouver **State:** BC **PC:** **Country:** Canada
Year Established: 2018 **Status 2020:** Active
Industries: ~ Healthcare (20), ~ Healthcare (20), Machine Learning

Company Name: Logo.com
Description: Logo.com is a Graphic Design and Branding platform.
Website:
Phone: **Email:** 4955@reference-encyclopedia-ai.net
City: Vancouver **State:** BC **PC:** **Country:** Canada
Year Established: **Status 2020:** Active
Industries: Artificial Intelligence for:, E-Commerce for:, ~ Professional Services (48), ~ Media-Communications (41), ~ Media-Communications (41)

Company Name: M0THER.AI INTELLIGENCE INC.
Description: AI Consulting Agency
Website: http://www.m0ther.ai
Phone: **Email:** 36922@reference-encyclopedia-ai.net
City: Vancouver **State:** BC **PC:** **Country:** Canada
Year Established: 2017 **Status 2020:** Active
Industries: Artificial Intelligence

Company Name: Machine Halo
Description: Smart City Innovation, Internet of Things, Artificial Intelligence, Computer Vision
Website: http://machinehalo.com/
Phone: **Email:** 36924@reference-encyclopedia-ai.net
City: Vancouver **State:** BC **PC:** **Country:** Canada
Year Established: 2015 **Status 2020:** Active
Industries: Artificial Intelligence for:, Computer Vision for:, IT Infrastructure for:, Internet of Things (IoT) for:, ~ Construction (10)

Company Name: MashUp Machine
Description: We're using machine learning to teach computers animated storytelling, allowing content to adapt to the viewer.
Website: http://www.mashupmachine.io
Phone: **Email:** chris@mashupmachine.io
City: Vancouver **State:** BC **PC:** **Country:** Canada
Year Established: 2015 **Status 2020:** Active
Industries: Artificial Intelligence for:, ~ Education (13), Machine Learning

Company Name: Metafor Software
Description: Anomaly detection for IT operations analytics and security intelligence
Website: http://metaforsoftware.com
Phone: 1 415-848-8400 **Email:** info@metaforsoftware.com
City: Vancouver **State:** BC **PC:** **Country:** Canada
Year Established: 2010 **Status 2020:** Active
Industries:

Company Name: Minerva Intelligence Inc.
Description: Knowledge Engineering, Artificial intelligence, SaaS, Semantics, Ontology, Taxonomy, INSPIRE, Explainable AI
Website: http://minervaintelligence.com
Phone: 604-620-1051 **Email:** info@minervaintelligence.com
City: Vancouver **State:** BC **PC:** **Country:** Canada
Year Established: 2017 **Status 2020:** Active
Industries: Artificial Intelligence for:, IT Managed Services for:, Web for:, Business Software as a Service Apps (SaaS Apps)

Company Name: Mintent
Description: Mintent is defining a collaborative content management software framework to get customers from strategy through execution with ease.
Website: http://www.getmintent.com/
Phone: 1 (855) 248-7377 **Email:** info@getmintent.com
City: Vancouver **State:** BC **PC:** **Country:** Canada
Year Established: 2012 **Status 2020:** Active
Industries: Artificial Intelligence for:, Big Data and Analytics for:, Content for:, IT Managed Services

Company Name: Nextwave Software
Description: Nextwave Software employs advanced graph database research and visualization methods to develop and deploy knowledge graph technologies.
Website: http://www.nxtwv.com
Phone: 1 (415) 800-4942 **Email:** sales@nxtwv.com
City: Vancouver **State:** BC **PC:** **Country:** Canada
Year Established: 2012 **Status 2020:** Active
Industries: Artificial Intelligence for:, Enterprise Application Services

Company Name: Olive
Description: AI technology / business consulting
Website: http://www.olive.app
Phone: **Email:** 4670@reference-encyclopedia-ai.net
City: Vancouver **State:** BC **PC:** **Country:** Canada
Year Established: **Status 2020:** Active
Industries: Artificial Intelligence for:, IT Managed Services for:, Machine Learning for:, ~ Administrative and Support Services (1)

Company Name: Orangedox
Description: Orangedox is a company that will help track the analytics of documents.
Website: http://orangedox.com
Phone: **Email:** contact@orangedox.com
City: Vancouver **State:** BC **PC:** **Country:** Canada
Year Established: 2013 **Status 2020:** Active
Industries: Analytics for:, Application Services for:, Predictive Analytics

Company Name: Pathful
Description: Pathful shows B2B marketers the business impact of their content marketing.
Website: http://www.pathful.com
Phone: 1 (866) 662-0786 **Email:** info@pathful.com
City: Vancouver **State:** BC **PC:** **Country:** Canada
Year Established: 2012 **Status 2020:** Active
Industries: Content for:, Application Services for:, Mobile for:, Predictive Analytics

Company Name: piALGO Technologies
Description: piALGO offers solutions to capital markets using adaptive algorithms with machine-learning technologies for analyzing big data.
Website: http://www.pi-algo.com
Phone: **Email:** info@pi-ALGO.com
City: Vancouver **State:** BC **PC:** **Country:** Canada
Year Established: 2013 **Status 2020:** Closed
Industries: Analytics for:, Artificial Intelligence for:, Big Data and Analytics for:, Databases for:, ~ Banking and Financial Markets-Services (7), ~ Banking and Financial Markets-Services (7), Machine Learning

Company Name: Plasmatic Technologies Inc.
Description: Empowering service providers and their customers to benefit from the Connected Home through whole-home insights and mobile experiences.
Website: http://www.plasmatic.ai
Phone: (604)265-6002 **Email:** hello@plasmatic.ai
City: Vancouver **State:** BC **PC:** **Country:** Canada
Year Established: 2016 **Status 2020:** Active
Industries: Artificial Intelligence for:, Internet of Things (IoT) for:, Machine Learning

Company Name: Productlift
Description: Productlift is an applied analytics platform that turns trial & freemium account user behavior data into actionable sales insights.
Website: http://www.productlift.io
Phone: **Email:** info@productlift.io
City: Vancouver **State:** BC **PC:** **Country:** Canada
Year Established: 2019 **Status 2020:** Active
Industries: Business Intelligence for:, Machine Learning for:, Predictive Analytics for:, Business Process and Operations for:, Business Software as a Service Apps (SaaS Apps) for:, Automation

Company Name: Produvia
Description: Produvia offers an on-demand platform for hiring artificial intelligence (AI) developers.
Website: http://produvia.com/
Phone: **Email:** hello@produvia.com
City: Vancouver **State:** BC **PC:** **Country:** Canada
Year Established: 2013 **Status 2020:** Active
Industries: Artificial Intelligence for:, Computer Vision for:, IT Managed Services for:, Machine Learning for:, Natural Language Processing

Company Name: Q Blocks
Description: Q Blocks is a computing company that builds affordable supercomputers.
Website: http://www.qblocks.cloud/
Phone: **Email:** support@qblocks.cloud
City: Vancouver **State:** BC **PC:** **Country:** Canada
Year Established: 2019 **Status 2020:** Active
Industries: Artificial Intelligence for:, Machine Learning

Company Name: QT-Data Inc.
Description: QT-Data specializes in capitalizing enterprise data by combining state-of-the-art of ML/AI algorithms, Blockchain /DLT, software solutions.
Website:
Phone: **Email:** info@qntdata.com
City: Vancouver **State:** BC **PC:** **Country:** Canada
Year Established: 2017 **Status 2020:** Active
Industries: Artificial Intelligence for:, IT Managed Services

Company Name: Sanctuary AI
Description: Sanctuary AI is an artificial general intelligence company.
Website: https://www.sanctuary.ai/
Phone: **Email:** 37337@reference-encyclopedia-ai.net
City: Vancouver **State:** BC **PC:** **Country:** Canada

Year Established: 2018 **Status 2020:** Active
Industries: Artificial Intelligence for:, Machine Learning

Company Name: Scanbo
Description: Democratizing Access To Medical Diagnostics
Website: http://www.scanbo.com
Phone: 1 604 200 0752 **Email:** info@scanbo.com
City: Vancouver **State:** BC **PC:** **Country:** Canada
Year Established: 2018 **Status 2020:** Active
Industries:

Company Name: ScopeMedia
Description: ScopeMedia built an advanced video and image recognition artificial intelligence platform for image data visualization and applications
Website: http://www.scopemedia.com
Phone: (604)559-6513 **Email:** contact@scopemedia.com
City: Vancouver **State:** BC **PC:** **Country:** Canada
Year Established: 2013 **Status 2020:** Active
Industries: Analytics for:, Artificial Intelligence for:, Computer Vision for:, Image Recognition for:, Machine Learning for:, Computer Vision

Company Name: Semantile
Description: Semantic Relevance Engine
Website: http://www.semantile.com/
Phone: **Email:** info@semantile.com
City: Vancouver **State:** BC **PC:** **Country:** Canada
Year Established: 2015 **Status 2020:** Active
Industries: Analytics for:, Artificial Intelligence for:, Big Data and Analytics for:, Web

Company Name: SHADE.ai
Description: SHADE.ai uses AI technology to transform how insurers inform, advise and build lasting relationships with today's digital-first consumers.
Website: http://www.shadeai.ai/
Phone: **Email:** info@shadeai.ai
City: Vancouver **State:** BC **PC:** **Country:** Canada
Year Established: 2017 **Status 2020:** Active
Industries: Artificial Intelligence for:, ~ Banking and Financial Markets-Services (7), Enterprise Application Services for:, Mobile for:, Business Software as a Service Apps (SaaS Apps)

Company Name: SkyHive
Description: Skills-based AI technology for workforce reskilling and upskilling.
Website: http://www.skyhive.io
Phone: **Email:** hello@skyhive.io
City: Vancouver **State:** BC **PC:** **Country:** Canada
Year Established: 2017 **Status 2020:** Active
Industries: Artificial Intelligence for:, ~ Education (13), Enterprise Application Services for:, Machine Learning for:, Natural Language Processing for:, Business Software as a Service Apps (SaaS Apps) for:, Business Software as a Service Apps (SaaS Apps) for:, ~ Education

Company Name: Spliqs Intelligent Media
Description: Spliqs is an application that enables users to create music.
Website: http://www.spliqs.com
Phone: 778-899-5254 **Email:** info@spliqs.com
City: Vancouver **State:** BC **PC:** **Country:** Canada
Year Established: 2016 **Status 2020:** Active
Industries: Application Services for:, Artificial Intelligence for:, ~ Arts-Entertainment-Recreation (4)

Company Name: Steamsharp Technology
Description: Steamsharp is a sports analytics company that provides an automated API for all-play oddsmaking data.
Website: http://steamsharp.com/
Phone: 16047151879 **Email:** bernie@steamsharp.com
City: Vancouver **State:** BC **PC:** **Country:** Canada
Year Established: 2011 **Status 2020:** Active
Industries: Analytics for:, Big Data and Analytics for:, Enterprise Application Services for:, Machine Learning for:, ~ Arts-Entertainment-Recreation (4)

Company Name: Sw: United Arab Emirates
Description: SaaS platform combining Anonymity, AI and collective intelligence to help organizations reveal valuable ideas & make better decisions.
Website: http://swae.io
Phone: **Email:** info@swae.io
City: Vancouver **State:** BC **PC:** **Country:** Canada
Year Established: **Status 2020:** Active
Industries: Artificial Intelligence for:, ~ Professional Services (48), Business Software as a Service Apps (SaaS Apps)

Company Name: Talentful.ai
Description: Talentful leverages AI to help tech companies acquire great developer leads, quickly.
Website: http://www.talentful.ai
Phone: **Email:** support@talentful.ai
City: Vancouver **State:** BC **PC:** **Country:** Canada
Year Established: 2015 **Status 2020:** Active
Industries: Artificial Intelligence for:, Databases

Company Name: Thena
Description: Thena exists so entrepreneurs can fulfill their dreams in business.
Website:
Phone: **Email:** 4817@reference-encyclopedia-ai.net
City: Vancouver **State:** BC **PC:** **Country:** Canada
Year Established: **Status 2020:** Active
Industries: Artificial Intelligence for:, Business Intelligence for:, IT Managed Services for:, ~ Professional Services (48)

Company Name: ThinkCX
Description: Social Intelligence for Call Cente: Serbia
Website: http://www.thinkcx.com
Phone: 1(866)575-6549 **Email:** info@thinkcx.com
City: Vancouver **State:** BC **PC:** **Country:** Canada
Year Established: 2012 **Status 2020:** Active
Industries: Analytics for:, Artificial Intelligence

Company Name: UCW Labs Ltd.
Description: Services in the IoT prototyping, embedded systems programming, custom hardware design, IoT integration, and custom software development.
Website: http://ucwlabs.com
Phone: (604)368-6157 **Email:** info@ucwlabs.com
City: Vancouver **State:** BC **PC:** **Country:** Canada
Year Established: 2017 **Status 2020:** Active
Industries: Analytics for:, Artificial Intelligence for:, Big Data and Analytics for:, Cloud for:, Cloud for:, Cloud for:, Cloud for:, Application Services for:, Application Services for:, Embedded for:, Embedded for:, Enterprise Application Services for:, Internet of Things (Io

Company Name: Vancouver Computer Vision Ltd.
Description: AI, Machine Vision, Robotics
Website: http://www.vcvision.ca/
Phone: **Email:** info@vcvision.ca
City: Vancouver **State:** BC **PC:** **Country:** Canada
Year Established: 2016 **Status 2020:** Active
Industries: Artificial Intelligence for:, Big Data and Analytics for:, Robotics

Company Name: Variational AI
Description: AI for small molecule discovery
Website: http://variational.ai
Phone: 6047617199 **Email:** handol@variational.ai
City: Vancouver **State:** BC **PC:** **Country:** Canada
Year Established: 2019 **Status 2020:** Active
Industries: Artificial Intelligence for:, ~ Biotechnology (9)

Company Name: Viewpoint AI
Description: Viewpoint is an AI powered decision software company that combines the best of human and machine intelligence amplifying human skill levels.
Website:
Phone: **Email:** 4478@reference-encyclopedia-ai.net
City: Vancouver **State:** BC **PC:** **Country:** Canada
Year Established: **Status 2020:** Active
Industries:

Company Name: WAVO Closed
Description: WAVO aims to disrupt the entire healthcare industry by helping patients who desire affordable treatment.
Website: http://app.wavo.health/
Phone: **Email:** hello@wavo.heal:Thailand
City: Vancouver **State:** BC **PC:** **Country:** Canada
Year Established: 2018 **Status 2020:** Closed
Industries: Artificial Intelligence for:, ~ Healthcare (20), ~ Healthcare (20), ~ Healthcare (20), ~ Healthcare (20), IT Managed Services for:, Machine Learning for:, ~ Healthcare (20), ~ Healthcare (20), Predictive Analytics

Company Name: Xtract AI
Description: We design, build and deploy advanced AI and deep learning technology.
Website: http://www.xtract.ai/
Phone: **Email:** info@xtract.ai
City: Vancouver **State:** BC **PC:** **Country:** Canada
Year Established: 2016 **Status 2020:** Active
Industries: Artificial Intelligence for:, Machine Learning

Company Name: Yactraq Online
Description: Yactraq provides market leading business intelligence on audio & video media with custom solutions built on our patent pending platform.
Website: http://www.yactraq.com
Phone: 6043416217 **Email:** info@yactraq.com
City: Vancouver **State:** BC **PC:** **Country:** Canada
Year Established: 2010 **Status 2020:** Active
Industries: Business Intelligence for:, Natural Language Processing for:, Speech Recognition

Company Name: Ziva Dynamics
Description: Ziva Dynamics is a software company that specializes in character creation and human simulation.
Website: http://zivadynamics.com/
Phone: 1 855-285-2351 **Email:** humans@zivadynamics.com
City: Vancouver **State:** BC **PC:** **Country:** Canada
Year Established: 2015 **Status 2020:** Active
Industries: ~ Arts-Entertainment-Recreation (4)

Company Name: Conscious Thought Revolution
Description: Quantifying consciousness through analytics
Website: http://ctr.com
Phone: **Email:** 36325@reference-encyclopedia-ai.net
City: Victoria **State:** BC **PC:** **Country:** Canada
Year Established: 2015 **Status 2020:** Active
Industries: Analytics for:, Artificial Intelligence

Company Name: Echosec Systems Ltd.
Description: Echosec Systems provides organizations with the ability to detect critical online data faster, for threat intelligence and risk management.
Website: http://echosec.net
Phone: (844) 324-6732 **Email:** info@echosec.net
City: Victoria **State:** BC **PC:** **Country:** Canada
Year Established: 2013 **Status 2020:** Active
Industries: Analytics for:, Artificial Intelligence for:, Business Intelligence for:, Cyber Security for:, Identity for:, Machine Learning for:, Cyber Security for:, Cyber Security for:, Predictive Analytics for:, Security

Company Name: SimpleReport
Description: SimpleReport is a safety reporting and analytics tool for companies that make OHS their priority.
Website: http://www.simplereport.ca
Phone: 5874370111 **Email:** info@simplereport.ca
City: Victoria **State:** BC **PC:** **Country:** Canada
Year Established: 2018 **Status 2020:** Active
Industries: Analytics for:, Artificial Intelligence for:, Data Management for:, Machine Learning for:, Predictive Analytics for:, Business Software as a Service Apps (SaaS Apps)

Company Name: Zag.ai
Description: SaaS marketing intelligence for content strategy & SEO.
Website: http://zag.ai
Phone: 7787196060 **Email:** hello@zag.ai
City: Victoria **State:** BC **PC:** **Country:** Canada
Year Established: 2016 **Status 2020:** Active
Industries: Analytics for:, Artificial Intelligence for:, Big Data and Analytics for:, ~ Customer Relationship Management (11)

Company Name: MicroTraffic
Description: Road Safety Video Analytics - Data as a Service - GovTech
Website: http://www.microtraffic.com/
Phone: 204-996-9550 **Email:** craig.milligan@microtraffic.com
City: Winnipeg **State:** MB **PC:** **Country:** Canada
Year Established: **Status 2020:** Active
Industries: Artificial Intelligence for:, ~ Automotive (5), Computer Vision for:, ~ Government (19), Machine Learning for:, Predictive Analytics for:, ~ Government (19), ~ Transportation and Logistics (57)

Company Name: Sightline Innovation
Description: Sightline is the company behind MLaaS (Machine Learning as a Service), bringing ML capabilities to a variety of industries.
Website: http://www.sightlineinnovation.com
Phone: (416) 628-7095 **Email:** info@sightlineinnovation.com
City: Winnipeg **State:** MB **PC:** **Country:** Canada
Year Established: 2012 **Status 2020:** Active
Industries: Artificial Intelligence for:, Machine Learning

Company Name: TaiV
Description: HaaS
Website: http://www.taiv.tv
Phone: 204-330-4546 **Email:** hello@taiv.tv
City: Winnipeg **State:** MB **PC:** **Country:** Canada
Year Established: **Status 2020:** Active
Industries: Artificial Intelligence for:, Digital Marketing for:, ~ Media-Communications (41), ~ Manufacturing-Electronic (30), ~ Professional Services (48)

Company Name: Apprento
Description: Apprento, a provider of artificial intelligence and natural language processing technology solutions.
Website: http://www.apprento.com/
Phone: **Email:** info@apprento.io
City: Fredericton **State:** NB **PC:** **Country:** Canada
Year Established: 2012 **Status 2020:** Active
Industries: Artificial Intelligence for:, IT Managed Services for:, ~ Education (13)

Company Name: Eigen Innovations
Description: Eigen's Intellexon platform is an industrial vision system that is different.
Website: http://www.eigen.io/
Phone: 506-458-7770 **Email:** info@eigeninnovations.com
City: Fredericton **State:** NB **PC:** **Country:** Canada
Year Established: 2012 **Status 2020:** Active
Industries: Artificial Intelligence for:, Industrial Solutions for:, Automation for:, Internet of Things (IoT)

Company Name: Eyesover
Description: Eyesover is a platform collecting public opinion and providing clients with actionable data intended for their industry or sector.
Website: http://www.eyesover.com/
Phone: 506-478-7141 **Email:** info@eyesover.com
City: Fredericton **State:** NB **PC:** **Country:** Canada
Year Established: 2015 **Status 2020:** Active
Industries:

Company Name: SomaDetect
Description: SomaDetect provides dairy farmers with the information they need to produce the best possible milk.
Website: http://www.somadetect.com
Phone: 716-579-1951 **Email:** info@somadetect.com
City: Fredericton **State:** NB **PC:** **Country:** Canada
Year Established: 2016 **Status 2020:** Active
Industries: ~ Agriculture (3), Analytics for:, Artificial Intelligence for:, Internet of Things (IoT) for:, Machine Learning

Company Name: EhEye
Description: EhEye understands the importance of effective security.
Website: http://www.eheye.com/
Phone: **Email:** solutions@eheye.com
City: Saint John **State:** NB **PC:** **Country:** Canada
Year Established: 2016 **Status 2020:** Active
Industries: Artificial Intelligence for:, ~ Government (19), Security

Company Name: Creatros Technologies Inc
Description: Developing the worlds first internal support plugin for technology companies.
Website: http://www.creatros.ca/
Phone: 709-725-2292 **Email:** hr@creatros.ca
City: St. John's **State:** NL **PC:** **Country:** Canada
Year Established: **Status 2020:** Active
Industries: Artificial Intelligence for:, IT Managed Services for:, Application Services for:, Machine Learning for:, ~ Professional Services (48), IT Managed Services

Company Name: Sentinel Alert
Description: Sentinel Alert's worker safety solution helps industrial companies reduce worker accidents and achieve safer productivity.
Website: http://sentinelalert.co/
Phone: 1(709)685-5524 **Email:** info@sentinelalert.co
City: St. John's **State:** NL **PC:** **Country:** Canada
Year Established: 2014 **Status 2020:** Active
Industries: Predictive Analytics for:, Internet of Things (IoT)

Company Name: Hanatech
Description: Hanatech's OneSmartView platform utilizes IoT, AI, and data analytics to help companies increase revenues and improve efficiencies.
Website: http://hanatech.ca/
Phone: **Email:** 36665@reference-encyclopedia-ai.net
City: Bedford **State:** NS **PC:** **Country:** Canada
Year Established: 2013 **Status 2020:** Active
Industries: ~ Agriculture (3), Analytics for:, Artificial Intelligence for:, ~ Energy and Utilities (14), IT Managed Services for:, Internet of Things (IoT) for:, ~ Construction (10)

Company Name: LIVELENZ
Description: Restaurant Performance Improvement
Website: http://www.livelenz.com
Phone: 902-692-1208 **Email:** info@livelenz.com
City: Bedford **State:** NS **PC:** **Country:** Canada
Year Established: 2010 **Status 2020:** Active
Industries: Predictive Analytics for:, Compute for:, ~ Food and Beverage (17), Business Software as a Service Apps (SaaS Apps) for:, Business Software as a Service Apps (SaaS Apps)

Company Name: KARV Data Consulting Ltd.
Description: AI Startup Company
Website: http://karvit.ca
Phone: 9022220945 **Email:** info@karvit.ca
City: Dartmouth **State:** NS **PC:** **Country:** Canada
Year Established: **Status 2020:** Active
Industries: Artificial Intelligence for:, IT Managed Services for:, Machine Learning for:, Robotics

Company Name: Analyze Re
Description: Analyze Re is a software company developing portfolio risk management and pricing systems for the reinsurance industry.
Website: http://www.analyzere.com
Phone: 19028808998 **Email:** info@analyzere.com
City: Halifax **State:** NS **PC:** **Country:** Canada
Year Established: 2013 **Status 2020:** Active
Industries: Analytics for:, Big Data and Analytics for:, Enterprise Application Services for:, ~ Banking and Financial Markets-Services (7), ~ Banking and Financial Markets-Services (7), Predictive Analytics

Company Name: B-Line
Description: Helping green building owners measure tenant mobility patterns
Website: http://www.bline.io
Phone: (416) 305-7858 **Email:** aaron@bline.io
City: Halifax **State:** NS **PC:** **Country:** Canada
Year Established: 2016 **Status 2020:** Active
Industries: Analytics for:, Big Data and Analytics for:, Enterprise Application Services for:, ~ Construction (10), Predictive Analytics for:, Business Software as a Service Apps (SaaS Apps)

Company Name: Densitas
Description: Our vision is to move the needle in breast cancer screening through precision breast health technologies.
Website: http://densitas.health/
Phone: 1(902)405-4610 **Email:** INFO@DENSITAS.CA
City: Halifax **State:** NS **PC:** **Country:** Canada
Year Established: 2011 **Status 2020:** Active
Industries: Artificial Intelligence for:, Big Data and Analytics for:, ~ Healthcare (20)

Company Name: Harbr Inc.
Description: Harbr is a construction data company.
Website: http://www.harbr.com
Phone: **Email:** team@harbr.com
City: Halifax **State:** NS **PC:** **Country:** Canada
Year Established: 2016 **Status 2020:** Active
Industries: ~ Construction (10), IT Managed Services for:, Predictive Analytics for:, ~ Real Estate (49)

Company Name: Invisible Agents
Description: Invisible Agents is developing technology to improve fundraising for non-profits and churches through machine learning.
Website: http://invisible-agents.com/
Phone: **Email:** info@invisible-agents.com
City: Halifax **State:** NS **PC:** **Country:** Canada
Year Established: 2018 **Status 2020:** Active
Industries: Machine Learning

Company Name: LegendBots
Description: LegendBots is a next generation entertainment platform.
Website: http://legendbots.bravenewworld.io
Phone: **Email:** 36888@reference-encyclopedia-ai.net
City: Halifax **State:** NS **PC:** **Country:** Canada
Year Established: 2017 **Status 2020:** Active
Industries: Artificial Intelligence for:, Robotics

Company Name: ReelData AI
Description: ReelData AI provides artificially intelligent monitoring for finned fish aquaculture.
Website: http://www.reeldata.ai/
Phone: **Email:** info@reeldata.ai
City: Halifax **State:** NS **PC:** **Country:** Canada
Year Established: 2019 **Status 2020:** Active
Industries:

Company Name: RovBOT
Description: RovBOT is a tool to help international students with their Canadian visa process.
Website: http://www.rovbot.ca/
Phone: 1 (902) 579 7993 **Email:** info@rovbot.ca
City: Halifax **State:** NS **PC:** **Country:** Canada
Year Established: 2017 **Status 2020:** Active
Industries: Artificial Intelligence

Company Name: TopLog
Description: TopLog is a tech platform that provides system administrators with log data for analysis.
Website: http://toplog.io/
Phone: 902.401.3292 **Email:** ozge@toplog.ca
City: Halifax **State:** NS **PC:** **Country:** Canada
Year Established: 2013 **Status 2020:** Active
Industries: Machine Learning

Company Name: Intransigen: Sweden
Description: AI powered real-time marketing and analytics.
Website: http://intransigense.com
Phone: **Email:** inquiries@intransigense.com
City: Barrie **State:** ON **PC:** **Country:** Canada
Year Established: 2015 **Status 2020:** Active
Industries: Artificial Intelligence for:, Digital Marketing

Company Name: Acquired Insights Inc.
Description: AI/ML, Artificial Intelligence, Machine Learning, Predictive Analytics, Workforce Optimization
Website: http://www.aiinc.cloud
Phone: 1-800-627-4151 **Email:** info@AIinc.Cloud
City: Burlington **State:** ON **PC:** **Country:** Canada
Year Established: **Status 2020:** Active
Industries: Artificial Intelligence for:, Machine Learning

Company Name: CSQ Research:
Description: CSQ Research is a Robotics and Government Policy Think-tank researching Automation and Sustainable Societi: Spain
Website: http://csq1.org
Phone: **Email:** info@worthwhileinc.com
City: Burlington **State:** ON **PC:** **Country:** Canada
Year Established: 2014 **Status 2020:** Active
Industries: Artificial Intelligence for:, ~ Automotive (5), ~ Construction (10), ~ Government (19), Automation for:, ~ Metals and Mining (42), Robotics

Company Name: Just Sales Jobs
Description: Just Sales Jobs sources and places Top Sales Talent from Toronto to Kitchener/Waterloo and Cities in between.
Website: http://justsalesjobs.ca
Phone: 905-674-5982 **Email:** toptalent@justsalesjobs.ca
City: Burlington **State:** ON **PC:** **Country:** Canada
Year Established: 2018 **Status 2020:** Active
Industries: Artificial Intelligence

Company Name: Mirsee Robotics
Description: Mirsee develops advanced robotics platforms and deep learning-based embedded vision systems.
Website: http://mirsee.com
Phone: 1-855-472-3309 **Email:** 36990@reference-encyclopedia-ai.net
City: Cambridge **State:** ON **PC:** **Country:** Canada
Year Established: 2017 **Status 2020:** Active
Industries: Artificial Intelligence for:, Computer Vision for:, Embedded for:, Machine Learning for:, Robotics

Company Name: Adapsyn Bioscience
Description: Adapsyn is developing a bioinformatics platform devoted to discovering previously unidentified natural product drug candidates.
Website: http://adapsyn.com/
Phone: **Email:** info@adapsyn.com
City: Hamilton **State:** ON **PC:** **Country:** Canada
Year Established: 2016 **Status 2020:** Active
Industries: Artificial Intelligence for:, ~ Biotechnology (9), ~ Biotechnology (9), Machine Learning

Company Name: NeuralSeg
Description: Medical Image Analys
Website: http://www.neuralseg.com
Phone: (905) 510-4489 **Email:** anthony@neuralseg.com
City: Hamilton **State:** ON **PC:** **Country:** Canada
Year Established: 2017 **Status 2020:** Active
Industries: Cloud for:, Computer Vision for:, Machine Learning for:, ~ Healthcare (20)

Company Name: Azoig Corp.
Description: Enabling Artificial Intelligence and Machine Learning to reduce your ever increasing information security threat landscape.
Website: http://azoig.com
Phone: 289-841-8191 **Email:** sales@azoig.com
City: Keswick **State:** ON **PC:** **Country:** Canada
Year Established: 2018 **Status 2020:** Active
Industries: Artificial Intelligence for:, Cloud for:, Cyber Security for:, Identity for:, IT Managed Services for:, Machine Learning for:, Security for:, Cyber Security for:, Cyber Security

Company Name: StrategicDB Corporation
Description: StrategicDB focuses on data to drive your Marketing and Sales!
Website: http://www.strategicdb.com
Phone: 877-332-4923 **Email:** Hello@strategicdb.com
City: King City **State:** ON **PC:** **Country:** Canada
Year Established: 2015 **Status 2020:** Active
Industries: Analytics for:, Databases for:, Data Management for:, Predictive Analytics

Company Name: 1001 Squared Artificial Intelligence
Description: 1001 Squared Artificial Intelligence
Website: http://www.1001squared.com/
Phone: 1 343-333-2078 **Email:** info@1001squared.com
City: Kingston **State:** ON **PC:** **Country:** Canada
Year Established: **Status 2020:** Active
Industries: Artificial Intelligence for:, Machine Learning

Company Name: MESH AI
Description: MESH AI is the socially intelligent staff scheduling saas for healthcare.
Website: http://meshai.io/
Phone: 1 (613) 900-6141 **Email:** info@meshai.io
City: Kingston **State:** ON **PC:** **Country:** Canada
Year Established: 2018 **Status 2020:** Active
Industries: Artificial Intelligence for:, IT Managed Services for:, Business Software as a Service Apps (SaaS Apps) for:, Application Services

Company Name: Accumine
Description: Accumine is the leader in Digital Manufacturing.
Website: https://accuminetech.com/
Phone: (888) 474-1224 **Email:** support@accuminetech.com
City: Kitchener **State:** ON **PC:** **Country:** Canada
Year Established: 2015 **Status 2020:** Active
Industries:

Company Name: Acerta Analytics
Description: Acerta is a software company that delivers machine learning technology to the manufacturing and automotive industries.
Website: http://acerta.ca/
Phone: (519) 341-6080 **Email:** info@acerta.ca
City: Kitchener **State:** ON **PC:** **Country:** Canada
Year Established: 2017 **Status 2020:** Active
Industries: Artificial Intelligence for:, ~ Automotive (5), Machine Learning

Company Name: Avidbots
Description: Avidbots builds indoor autonomous robotics systems to solve business problems in real world environments.
Website: http://www.avidbots.com/
Phone: **Email:** 36123@reference-encyclopedia-ai.net
City: Kitchener **State:** ON **PC:** **Country:** Canada
Year Established: 2014 **Status 2020:** Active
Industries: Artificial Intelligence for:, Computer Vision for:, Robotics

Company Name: Beagle
Description: Beagle is taught to read based on what you want, and gives you the information you need to know.
Website: http://www.beagle.ai
Phone: **Email:** info@beagle.ai
City: Kitchener **State:** ON **PC:** **Country:** Canada
Year Established: **Status 2020:** Active
Industries: Artificial Intelligence for:, Collaboration Solutions for:, Compliance for:, IT Managed Services for:, Machine Learning for:, Natural Language Processing

Company Name: CampusMate Inc
Description: CampusMate is an AI-powered course-based messaging app for all educational and social engagement needs.
Website: http://campusmate.co/
Phone: (226)755-3032 **Email:** info@campusmate.co
City: Kitchener **State:** ON **PC:** **Country:** Canada
Year Established: 2017 **Status 2020:** Active
Industries: Application Services for:, Artificial Intelligence for:, ~ Education (13)

Company Name: Caspy
Description: Caspy is an AI Powered Chrome Extension. It mutes Inbox noise to help you stay on top of your important emails.
Website: http://caspy.com
Phone: (519) 721-3984 **Email:** info@caspy.com
City: Kitchener **State:** ON **PC:** **Country:** Canada
Year Established: 2016 **Status 2020:** Active
Industries: Artificial Intelligence for:, IT Managed Services for:, Web

Company Name: Curiato Inc.
Description: Provides caregivers and patients a holistic, end-to-end, management system.
Website: http://www.curiato.com/
Phone: **Email:** info@curiato.com
City: Kitchener **State:** ON **PC:** **Country:** Canada
Year Established: 2015 **Status 2020:** Active
Industries: Artificial Intelligence for:, ~ Healthcare (20), IT Managed Services for:, Internet of Things (IoT)

Company Name: EMAG: India
Description: Where AI meets Water
Website: http://emagin.ca/
Phone: **Email:** contact@emagin.ca
City: Kitchener **State:** ON **PC:** **Country:** Canada
Year Established: **Status 2020:** Active
Industries: Artificial Intelligence for:, Predictive Analytics for:, ~ Waste Management and Remediation Services (59)

Company Name: Fid: Spain
Description: Social media predictive analytics
Website: http://myfides.co
Phone: **Email:** kimbe@fidessocial.com
City: Kitchener **State:** ON **PC:** **Country:** Canada
Year Established: 2013 **Status 2020:** Active
Industries: Analytics for:, Predictive Analytics for:, ~ Social Assistance-Non-Profits (53)

Company Name: Haachy
Description: The smart way to bring your lost pets home faster
Website: http://www.haachy.ca/
Phone: 519-729-7013 **Email:** hjayaraman@manakn.ca
City: Kitchener **State:** ON **PC:** **Country:** Canada
Year Established: **Status 2020:** Active
Industries: Artificial Intelligence for:, ~ Retail and Consumer Products (52)

Company Name: Landmine Boys
Description: The Landmine Boys is building an autonomous machine to defuse landmines safely.
Website: http://deminerobotics.com
Phone: 519-729-3885 **Email:** richard@deminerobotics.com
City: Kitchener **State:** ON **PC:** **Country:** Canada
Year Established: 2016 **Status 2020:** Active
Industries: Artificial Intelligence for:, Machine Learning for:, Robotics

Company Name: LoyaltyMatch Inc.
Description: Our AI platform uses machine learning to discover and predict a venue's best customers. A focus on the live music and entertainment sectors.
Website: http://www.loyaltymatch.com
Phone: (866) 356-7187 **Email:** support@loyaltymatch.com
City: Kitchener **State:** ON **PC:** **Country:** Canada
Year Established: 2010 **Status 2020:** Active
Industries: Artificial Intelligence for:, Cloud for:, ~ Retail and Consumer Products (52), Predictive Analytics for:, Business Software as a Service Apps (SaaS Apps)

Company Name: Meya.ai
Description: Meya.ai is a platform to build, train and deploy bots.
Website: http://meya.ai/
Phone: (888) 907-7680 **Email:** bots@meya.ai
City: Kitchener **State:** ON **PC:** **Country:** Canada
Year Established: **Status 2020:** Active
Industries: Artificial Intelligence for:, Web for:, ~ Telecommunications (56)

Company Name: Motion Gestur: Spain
Description: A Canadian machine learning startup specializing in gesture recognition software.
Website: http://motiongestures.com/
Phone: **Email:** info@motiongestures.com
City: Kitchener **State:** ON **PC:** **Country:** Canada
Year Established: 2017 **Status 2020:** Active
Industries:

Company Name: Plex.ai
Description: Plex.ai is an insurance start-up working on using artificial intelligence to re-engineer the way insurance and risk management is done.
Website: http://plex.ai/
Phone: **Email:** hello@plex.ai
City: Kitchener **State:** ON **PC:** **Country:** Canada
Year Established: **Status 2020:** Active
Industries:

Company Name: Primal
Description: Bringing content that matters to you.
Website: http://www.primal.com
Phone: **Email:** info@primal.com
City: Kitchener **State:** ON **PC:** **Country:** Canada

Year Established: **Status 2020:** Active
Industries: Artificial Intelligence for:, ~ Professional Services (48)

Company Name: ProNavigator
Description: ProNavigator provides a leading conversational AI platform to reinvent customer service and drive growth in the insurance industry.
Website: http://pronavigator.ai
Phone: 1-855-906-5323 **Email:** contact@pronavigator.io
City: Kitchener **State:** ON **PC:** **Country:** Canada
Year Established: 2016 **Status 2020:** Active
Industries: Machine Learning for:, Natural Language Processing

Company Name: Rave Inc.
Description: Rave is a new way to watch videos, listen to music, and hang out with friends.
Website: http://rave.io
Phone: **Email:** contact@rave.io
City: Kitchener **State:** ON **PC:** **Country:** Canada
Year Established: **Status 2020:** Active
Industries: Application Services for:, Artificial Intelligence for:, Machine Learning for:, ~ Arts-Entertainment-Recreation (4), ~ Social Media (54)

Company Name: SolverGen
Description: SaaS for genomics data analys
Website: http://www.solvergen.com
Phone: **Email:** email@email.com
City: Kitchener **State:** ON **PC:** **Country:** Canada
Year Established: 2019 **Status 2020:** Active
Industries: Artificial Intelligence for:, ~ Education (13), IT Managed Services

Company Name: Tabnex
Description: Tabnex offers an AI-powered recruitment enablement solution to enhance and modernize recruitment systems.
Website: http://tabnex.com
Phone: **Email:** 37504@reference-encyclopedia-ai.net
City: Kitchener **State:** ON **PC:** **Country:** Canada
Year Established: 2016 **Status 2020:** Active
Industries: Artificial Intelligence for:, Web

Company Name: Wriber
Description: Wriber, a Canadian company, develops content creation software to help companies and PR agencies create marketing content more effectively.
Website: http://wriber.com
Phone: **Email:** info@wriber.com
City: Kitchener **State:** ON **PC:** **Country:** Canada
Year Established: **Status 2020:** Active
Industries: Application Services for:, Artificial Intelligence for:, ~ Professional Services (48)

Company Name: Densyfy Inc.
Description: Densyfy eliminates all filler, repeat and unimportant video utilizing AI
Website: http://www.densyfy.com
Phone: **Email:** info@densyfy.com
City: London **State:** ON **PC:** **Country:** Canada
Year Established: **Status 2020:** Active
Industries: Artificial Intelligence for:, Machine Learning for:, ~ Arts-Entertainment-Recreation (4), ~ Media-Communications (41)

Company Name: Packet39
Description: Packet39 designs custom Virtual Reality systems for the industrial, automotive and aerospace industries.
Website: http://Packet39.com
Phone: 5199026191 **Email:** 37136@reference-encyclopedia-ai.net
City: London **State:** ON **PC:** **Country:** Canada
Year Established: 2015 **Status 2020:** Active
Industries:

Company Name: Alive Mobile
Description: Mobile App Developer
Website: http://www.voice-translator.net/
Phone: **Email:** support@alivemob.com
City: Markham **State:** ON **PC:** **Country:** Canada
Year Established: 2018 **Status 2020:** Active
Industries: Application Services for:, Natural Language Processing

Company Name: Densify
Description:
Website: www.densify.com
Phone: 905.731.0090 **Email:** tkeller@walkerlimited.com
City: Markham **State:** ON **Zip:** L6G 0E7 **Country**: Canada
Year Established: **Status 2020:** Active
Industries:

Company Name: inField Solutions Inc.
Description: Enhance how you work
Website: http://www.infieldclipboard.com
Phone: 1-833-inField (463-4353) **Email:** info@infieldclipboard.com
City: Markham **State:** ON **PC:** **Country:** Canada
Year Established: **Status 2020:** Active
Industries: Artificial Intelligence for:, Big Data and Analytics for:, Enterprise Application Services for:, Application Services for:, ~ Professional Services (48)

Company Name: Mary AgroTechnologies
Description: Grow what you want, when you want, where you want.
Website: http://mary.ag
Phone: **Email:** hi@mary.ag
City: Markham **State:** ON **PC:** **Country:** Canada
Year Established: 2017 **Status 2020:** Active
Industries: ~ Agriculture (3), Artificial Intelligence for:, ~ Agriculture (3), ~ Agriculture (3), Internet of Things (IoT)

Company Name: TimeSaved
Description: We build apps for staffing agencies so they can leverage tech to better capitalize on the shifting economy.
Website: http://gettimesaved.com
Phone: 1(833)GET-TIME **Email:** support@timesaved.ca
City: Markham **State:** ON **PC:** **Country:** Canada
Year Established: **Status 2020:** Active
Industries: Artificial Intelligence for:, Enterprise Application Services for:, Machine Learning for:, ~ Human Resources (24), ~ Human Resources (24)

Company Name: 1Kosmos - BlockID
Description: BlockID by OneKosmos enables authentication of decentralized verified digital identities on the blockchain using biometrics.
Website: http://onekosmos.com
Phone: 647-293-3236 **Email:** info@1kosmos.com
City: Mississauga **State:** ON **PC:** **Country:** Canada
Year Established: **Status 2020:** Active
Industries:

Company Name: Algo8.ai
Description: Empowering businesses through AI
Website: http://algo8.ai/
Phone: 9986713707 **Email:** tanushri.dixit@adgo8.ai
City: Mississauga **State:** ON **PC:** **Country:** Canada
Year Established: 2015 **Status 2020:** Active
Industries: Artificial Intelligence

Company Name: Altedata Systems
Description: Artificial Intelligence Consultancy Company
Website: https://altedatasystems.com/
Phone: (647) 394-3384 **Email:** altedatasystems@gmail.com
City: Mississauga **State:** ON **PC:** **Country:** Canada
Year Established: 2020 **Status 2020:** Active
Industries: Artificial Intelligence

Company Name: Autonomous System Certification Labs Inc.
Description: Assure and Insure (AI/As) systems such as self-driving cars, robots and machines. We are Human Assurance Technology!
Website: http://ascltech.com/about.html
Phone: 416-320-5770 **Email:** mraffi@ascl.tech
City: Mississauga **State:** ON **PC:** **Country:** Canada
Year Established: **Status 2020:** Active
Industries: Artificial Intelligence for:, ~ Automotive (5), Robotics

Company Name: Conscia
Description: Conscia is a SaaS company that provides AI-powered content enrichment and discovery solutions.
Website: http://www.conscia.co
Phone: 1 (877) 500-6544 **Email:** info@conscia.ai
City: Mississauga **State:** ON **PC:** **Country:** Canada
Year Established: 2016 **Status 2020:** Active
Industries: Artificial Intelligence for:, Business Software as a Service Apps (SaaS Apps)

Company Name: Jagged Networks
Description: Location Analytics Platform
Website:
Phone: **Email:** wayne@jaggednetworks.com
City: Mississauga **State:** ON **PC:** **Country:** Canada
Year Established: **Status 2020:** Active
Industries: Analytics for:, Artificial Intelligence for:, Predictive Analytics

Company Name: Nytec
Description:
Website: www.nytec.com
Phone: **Email:** garys@nytec.com
City: Mississauga **State:** ON **Zip:** L4V 1R5 **Country**: Canada
Year Established: **Status 2020:** Active
Industries:

Company Name: Piik Insights
Description: Piik uses data analytics and artificial intelligence to provide actionable insights and integrate actions within organizations' workflows.
Website: http://www.piikinsights.com
Phone: (416) 454-5630 **Email:** info@massivedynamic.com
City: Mississauga **State:** ON **PC:** **Country:** Canada
Year Established: 2016 **Status 2020:** Active
Industries: Artificial Intelligence for:, Big Data and Analytics

Company Name: Rebalance Technology
Description: Canadian Business Intelligence Agency ~ eXploring solutions, for the forward thinking!
Website: http://www.rebalance.tech
Phone: 2898151276 **Email:** info@rebalance.tech
City: Mississauga **State:** ON **PC:** **Country:** Canada
Year Established: 2014 **Status 2020:** Active
Industries: Business Intelligence for:, Data Management for:, Predictive Analytics

Company Name: Savormetrics
Description: Savormetrics makes sensors and air cleaning systems to reduce food spoilage.
Website: http://savormetrics.com/
Phone: 1.800.409.8144 **Email:** 37340@reference-encyclopedia-ai.net
City: Mississauga **State:** ON **PC:** **Country:** Canada
Year Established: 2017 **Status 2020:** Active
Industries: ~ Agriculture (3), Artificial Intelligence for:, ~ Food and Beverage (17)

Company Name: Luci.AI Inc.
Description: An AI company innovates by lubricating the world in motion.
Website: http://luci.ai/
Phone: **Email:** info@luci.ai
City: North York **State:** ON **PC:** **Country:** Canada
Year Established: 2019 **Status 2020:** Active
Industries: Artificial Intelligence for:, Robotics

Company Name: BubbleGlass Real Estate Market Forecasting - A Worthwhile PLC Company
Description: BubbleGlass best-in-class A.I. Analytics in Real Estate. For sustainable Investment, Marketing & Government Policy
Website:
Phone: **Email:** 36213@reference-encyclopedia-ai.net
City: Oakville **State:** ON **PC:** **Country:** Canada
Year Established: 2017 **Status 2020:** Active
Industries: Artificial Intelligence for:, ~ Government (19), ~ Real Estate (49)

Company Name: Hexagon Technology
Description: Services in the areas of Deep Learning, AI, design, improvement, test & validation and safety certification
Website: http://www.hexagontechinc.com
Phone: **Email:** info@hexagontechinc.com
City: Oakville **State:** ON **PC:** **Country:** Canada
Year Established: 2012 **Status 2020:** Active
Industries: Machine Learning for:, ~ Government (19), Business Process and Operations

Company Name: 360pi Corp.
Description: 360pi derives profitable insights from product and pricing big data to help leading omnichannel retailers and brands compete and win.
Website: http://www.360pi.com
Phone: (613) 562-2525 **Email:** info@360pi.com
City: Ottawa **State:** ON **PC:** **Country:** Canada
Year Established: **Status 2020:** Active
Industries: Artificial Intelligence for:, ~ Retail and Consumer Products (52), Cyber Security for:, ~ Retail and Consumer Products (52), ~ Professional Services (48)

Company Name: Advanced Symbolics
Description: A market research firm that uses AI to analyze social media to monitor brand health while predicting trends and consumer behavior
Website: https://www.advancedsymbolics.com/
Phone: (613) 620-3386 **Email:** info@advancedsymbolics.com
City: Ottawa **State:** ON **PC:** **Country:** Canada
Year Established: 2015 **Status 2020:** Active
Industries:

Company Name: Aina Software
Description: AINA software is a software research & development company focused on AI solutions in both B2C & B2B arenas.
Website: https://www.aina.ai/about
Phone: (613) 982-0777 **Email:** info@aina.ai
City: Ottawa **State:** ON **PC:** **Country:** Canada
Year Established: 2019 **Status 2020:** Active
Industries: Artificial Intelligence for:, Business Applications for:, Business Applications for:, Human Computer Interaction for:, Predictive Analytics

Company Name: Arvizio
Description: mixed reality (AR & MR) tech to enhance your business & enable you to tackle challenging problems via shared experience.
Website: http://www.arvizio.io
Phone: **Email:** info@arvizio.io
City: Ottawa **State:** ON **PC:** **Country:** Canada
Year Established: 2016 **Status 2020:** Active
Industries: Artificial Intelligence for:, IT Managed Services for:, IT Managed Services

Company Name: BluWave-ai
Description: SaaS-based grid energy optimization platform for more sustainable, reliable, & affordable energy decisions.
Website: http://www.bluwave-ai.com/
Phone: 613-882-1544 **Email:** info@bluwave-ai.com
City: Ottawa **State:** ON **PC:** **Country:** Canada

Year Established: 2017 **Status 2020:** Active
Industries: Artificial Intelligence for:, ~ Energy and Utilities (14), ~ Telecommunications (56), IT Managed Services for:, Machine Learning for:, ~ Metals and Mining (42), ~ Energy and Utilities (14), Business Software as a Service Apps (SaaS Apps) for:, Business Software a

Company Name: Contextere
Description: Contextere is an industrial software company focused on human performance and developing the 21st century industrial workforce.
Website: http://contextere.com/
Phone: **Email:** info@contextere.com
City: Ottawa **State:** ON **PC:** **Country:** Canada
Year Established: **Status 2020:** Active
Industries: Artificial Intelligence for:, Augmented Reality for:, Enterprise Application Services for:, Machine Learning

Company Name: eMurmur
Description: EMurmur is a digital health company that creates apps that specializes in detecting, analyzing, and classifying heart murmurs.
Website: http://emurmur.com/
Phone: 1 617 701 7451 **Email:** office@emurmur.com
City: Ottawa **State:** ON **PC:** **Country:** Canada
Year Established: 2015 **Status 2020:** Active
Industries: Artificial Intelligence for:, ~ Healthcare (20), Machine Learning

Company Name: Gc Strategies
Description: Gc Strategies is a artificial intelligence company located in Ottawa.
Website: http://www.gcstrategies.ca
Phone: **Email:** kristian@gcstrategies.ca
City: Ottawa **State:** ON **PC:** **Country:** Canada
Year Established: 2015 **Status 2020:** Active
Industries: Artificial Intelligence for:, IT Managed Services for:, IT Managed Services

Company Name: Gnow: Italy
Description: Digital Media Monitoring & Analys
Website: http://www.gnowit.com
Phone: 855-561-4447 **Email:** hello@gnowit.com
City: Ottawa **State:** ON **PC:** **Country:** Canada
Year Established: 2011 **Status 2020:** Active
Industries: Artificial Intelligence for:, ~ Healthcare (20)

Company Name: Interset
Description: Interset is an AI & machine learning platform that accurately detects insider threats in days instead of months
Website: http://interset.ai
Phone: (844)241-2163 **Email:** sales@interset.com
City: Ottawa **State:** ON **PC:** **Country:** Canada
Year Established: **Status 2020:** Active
Industries: Analytics for:, Artificial Intelligence for:, Big Data and Analytics for:, Cyber Security for:, Machine Learning for:, Predictive Analytics

Company Name: Kaptur
Description: Image analytics and computer vision technology
Website: http://kaptur.tech
Phone: **Email:** 36842@reference-encyclopedia-ai.net
City: Ottawa **State:** ON **PC:** **Country:** Canada
Year Established: 2017 **Status 2020:** Closed
Industries: Internet of Things (IoT)

Company Name: Mema: Iran
Description: Extended Mind Application
Website: http://memair.com
Phone: **Email:** greg@memair.com
City: Ottawa **State:** ON **PC:** **Country:** Canada
Year Established: 2016 **Status 2020:** Active
Industries: Artificial Intelligence for:, Data Management

Company Name: MindBridge AI
Description: MindBridge AI. is a Entreprise FinTech company based in Canada
Website: http://www.mindbridge.ai
Phone: 613-667-1236 **Email:** info@mindbridge.ai
City: Ottawa **State:** ON **PC:** **Country:** Canada
Year Established: 2016 **Status 2020:** Active
Industries: Analytics for:, Artificial Intelligence for:, Business Intelligence

Company Name: Mission Control Space Services Inc.
Description: Space Exploration & Robotics: Spacecraft Operations, Onboard Autonomy, Artificial Intelligence
Website: http://missioncontrolspaceservices.com
Phone: **Email:** info@missioncontrolspaceservices.com
City: Ottawa **State:** ON **PC:** **Country:** Canada
Year Established: 2015 **Status 2020:** Active
Industries: ~ Aerospace and Defense (2), Artificial Intelligence for:, Machine Learning for:, Robotics

Company Name: Paphus Solutions
Description: Paphus Solutions Inc. is a Canadian corporation that specializes in intelligence automation products and services.
Website: http://paphussolutions.com/
Phone: 613-421-0445 **Email:** king@paphussolutions.com
City: Ottawa **State:** ON **PC:** **Country:** Canada
Year Established: **Status 2020:** Active
Industries: Artificial Intelligence for:, ~ Automotive (5), ~ Professional Services (48)

Company Name: Periculum Labs Inc
Description: Artificial Intelligence
Website: http://periculumlabs.com
Phone: 1-613-447-8233 **Email:** henry.jaffe@periculumlabs.com
City: Ottawa **State:** ON **PC:** **Country:** Canada
Year Established: 2016 **Status 2020:** Active
Industries:

Company Name: Raven Telemetry
Description: A leading artificial intelligence company.
Website: http://raven.ai/
Phone: 1.888.637.4443 **Email:** info@raventelemetry.com
City: Ottawa **State:** ON **PC:** **Country:** Canada
Year Established: 2013 **Status 2020:** Active
Industries: Artificial Intelligence for:, Industrial Solutions for:, Automation

Company Name: reDock
Description: reDock uses AI to extract meaning from content in order to accelerate and automate the content creation process.
Website: http://www.redock.com/
Phone: **Email:** info@redock.com
City: Ottawa **State:** ON **PC:** **Country:** Canada
Year Established: **Status 2020:** Active
Industries: Artificial Intelligence for:, ~ Professional Services (48)

Company Name: Sensor Cortek
Description: Creating embedded AI solutions for the vehicle of the future.
Website: http://www.sensorcortek.ai
Phone: **Email:** info@sensorcortek.ai
City: Ottawa **State:** ON **PC:** **Country:** Canada
Year Established: **Status 2020:** Active
Industries: Artificial Intelligence for:, ~ Automotive (5), ~ Automotive (5), Computer Vision for:, Application Services for:, Machine Learning for:, ~ Manufacturing-Electronic (30), ~ Construction (10), ~ Professional Services (48)

Company Name: Smats Traffic Solutions
Description: Smats Traffic Solutions is a technology company pioneering use of Machine Learning & Artificial Intelligence company.
Website: http://www.smatstraffic.com/
Phone: 1 (888) 441-5666 **Email:** info@smats.ca
City: Ottawa **State:** ON **PC:** **Country:** Canada
Year Established: 2015 **Status 2020:** Active
Industries: Artificial Intelligence for:, IT Managed Services

Company Name: Stallion AI
Description: Artificial Intelligence Solutions & Service
Website: http://stallion.ai
Phone: 971 44270774 **Email:** hello@stallion.ai
City: Ottawa **State:** ON **PC:** **Country:** Canada
Year Established: 2016 **Status 2020:** Active
Industries: Artificial Intelligence for:, Machine Learning for:, Natural Language Processing

Company Name: Tilia Labs
Description: AI-Driven Software for Planning and Imposition
Website: http://www.tilialabs.com
Phone: **Email:** info@tilialabs.com
City: Ottawa **State:** ON **PC:** **Country:** Canada
Year Established: 2012 **Status 2020:** Active
Industries: Artificial Intelligence for:, IT Managed Services for:, ~ Transportation and Logistics (57), ~ Media-Communications (41)

Company Name: Zighra
Description: Decentralized AI powered continuous authentication and fraud detection
Website: http://www.zighra.com
Phone: **Email:** info@zighra.com
City: Ottawa **State:** ON **PC:** **Country:** Canada
Year Established: **Status 2020:** Active
Industries: Artificial Intelligence for:, ~ Biotechnology (9), Enterprise Application Services for:, Identity for:, Machine Learning for:, Mobile

Company Name: Corporate IQ Solutions Inc.
Description: An unpredictable workforce puts business continuity is at risk. Are YOU capturing corporate memory?
Website: http://www.ciq.cloud
Phone: 1(805)354-5828 **Email:** investorrelations@ciq.cloud
City: Perth **State:** ON **PC:** **Country:** Canada
Year Established: **Status 2020:** Active
Industries: Artificial Intelligence for:, ~ Banking and Financial Markets-Services (7), ~ Banking and Financial Markets-Services (7), ~ Healthcare (20), ~ Insurance (25), Machine Learning for:, ~ Telecommunications (56)

Company Name: Kavtek
Description: Kavtek is a technology company specializing in augmented reality, connecting real estate professionals and their clients on one platform.
Website: http://www.kavtek.com
Phone: 705-812-2322 **Email:** info@kavtek.com
City: Peterborough **State:** ON **PC:** **Country:** Canada
Year Established: **Status 2020:** Active
Industries: Artificial Intelligence for:, Augmented Reality for:, ~ Real Estate (49), ~ Professional Services (48)

Company Name: rel8ed.to
Description: A Niagara-based data analytics company.
Website: http://www.rel8ed.to/
Phone: 905.321.0466 **Email:** info@rel8ed.to
City: Saint Catharines **State:** ON **PC:** **Country:** Canada
Year Established: **Status 2020:** Active
Industries: Analytics for:, Artificial Intelligence for:, Big Data and Analytics for:, IT Managed Services

Company Name: Skritswap
Description: skritswap has AI technology that enables anyone to understand anything regardless of complexity.
Website: http://skritswap.com/
Phone: **Email:** info@skritswap.com
City: Sault Sainte Marie **State:** ON **PC:** **Country:** Canada
Year Established: 2015 **Status 2020:** Active
Industries: Artificial Intelligence for:, IT Managed Services for:, IT Managed Services

Company Name: 8 Billion Acts of Innovation - Investment Firm
Description: 8 Billion Acts of Innovations is an investment firm that invests $45 million in various artificial intelligence and blockchain compani: Spain
Website: https://8billionactsofinnovation.com/
Phone: 1 416-6297924 **Email:** taimour@8billionactsofinnovation.com
City: Toronto **State:** ON **PC:** **Country:** Canada
Year Established: 2016 **Status 2020:** Active
Industries: Artificial Intelligence for:, Blockchain for:, Business Intelligence for:, IT Managed Services for:, ~ Banking and Financial Markets-Services (7)

Company Name: Account HQ
Description: Re-booting CRM by putting the focus on end users using the latest in tech, game design theory, consumer UX & AI Machine Learning.
Website: http://www.accounthq.com
Phone: **Email:** info@accounthq.com
City: Toronto **State:** ON **PC:** **Country:** Canada
Year Established: **Status 2020:** Active
Industries: Artificial Intelligence for:, Business Applications for:, Enterprise Application Services

Company Name: achu heal:Thailand
Description: achu is a predictive health platform that tracks vital patterns to warn you of impending future illness: Spain
Website: https://www.achuhealth.com/
Phone: (647) 404-0529 **Email:** mike@achu.ca
City: Toronto **State:** ON **PC:** **Country:** Canada
Year Established: 2016 **Status 2020:** Active
Industries:

Company Name: ACTO
Description: The Commercialization Cloud for Life Scienc: Spain
Website: https://acto.com/
Phone: (844) 277-2286 **Email:** marketing@actoapp.com
City: Toronto **State:** ON **PC:** **Country:** Canada
Year Established: 2014 **Status 2020:** Active
Industries: Artificial Intelligence for:, Business Intelligence for:, ~ Healthcare (20), Machine Learning for:, Predictive Analytics for:, ~ Education (13)

Company Name: Ada
Description: Ada is a computer software company that features a chatbot-based platform that helps enterprise businesses to automate customer experience.
Website: https://ada.support/
Phone: (877) 242-8232 **Email:** hello@ada.support
City: Toronto **State:** ON **PC:** **Country:** Canada
Year Established: 2014 **Status 2020:** Active
Industries: Artificial Intelligence for:, IT Managed Services for:, Application Services for:, Machine Learning

Company Name: Ada Support
Description: We make automating and scaling your customer support simple. With chatbots powered by AI, you can provide instant support to your customers.
Website: http://ada.support
Phone: **Email:** hello@ada.support
City: Toronto **State:** ON **PC:** **Country:** Canada
Year Established: **Status 2020:** Active
Industries: Artificial Intelligence for:, Machine Learning for:, ~ Professional Services (48)

Company Name: AdaptCore Heal:Thailand
Description: We are passionate about applying the latest technological innovations in AI and data management toward revolutionizing healthcare IT.
Website: http://www.adaptcore.com
Phone: 1 (416) 901-3498 **Email:** hello@adaptcore.com
City: Toronto **State:** ON **PC:** **Country:** Canada
Year Established: **Status 2020:** Active
Industries: Artificial Intelligence for:, Data Management for:, ~ Healthcare (20), IT Managed Services

Company Name: AdChat.ai
Description: It's like a chatbot and a display ad got together and had a baby.
Website: https://adchat.ai/
Phone: (416) 803-8205 **Email:** tim@adchat.ai
City: Toronto **State:** ON **PC:** **Country:** Canada
Year Established: 2016 **Status 2020:** Active
Industries: Artificial Intelligence for:, Digital Marketing for:, Digital Media for:, Machine Learning for:, Natural Language Processing

Company Name: AdeptMind
Description: AdeptMind is an AI company that innovates in e-commerce search using active learning and deep learning.
Website: http://adeptmind.ai/
Phone: (415) 684-9566 **Email:** info@adeptmind.ai
City: Toronto **State:** ON **PC:** **Country:** Canada
Year Established: **Status 2020:** Active
Industries: Artificial Intelligence for:, E-Commerce for:, Machine Learning for:, Cyber Security

Company Name: ADV: India
Description: The ADVIN Care system is a connected, portable and intelligent health care system embedded with artificial intelligence.
Website: http:// www.advin.ca
Phone: 1(647)781-4085 **Email:** Ahad@advin.ca
City: Toronto **State:** ON **PC:** **Country:** Canada
Year Established: **Status 2020:** Active
Industries: Artificial Intelligence for:, ~ Healthcare (20), ~ Healthcare (20)

Company Name: AedoAI Inc.
Description: A Productivity Software Platform for Elite Trade Contracto: Serbia
Website: http://www.aedo.ai
Phone: **Email:** marketing@aedo.ai
City: Toronto **State:** ON **PC:** **Country:** Canada
Year Established: **Status 2020:** Active
Industries: Artificial Intelligence for:, ~ Construction (10), IT Managed Services for:, Machine Learning for:, ~ Professional Services (48)

Company Name: AHA Platform Inc
Description: The missing IaaS platform for educators, athletic coaches and military generals.
Website:
Phone: **Email:** admin@ahainc.ca
City: Toronto **State:** ON **PC:** **Country:** Canada
Year Established: 2019 **Status 2020:** Active
Industries: ~ Education (13), ~ Education (13), Cloud for:, Natural Language Processing

Company Name: AiHello
Description: AiHello enables cross border ecommerce and helps business scale up their sales via sales forecasting and their 3pl warehouse network
Website: https://www.aihello.com/
Phone: (415) 625-9110 **Email:** info@aihello.com
City: Toronto **State:** ON **PC:** **Country:** Canada
Year Established: 2017 **Status 2020:** Active
Industries: E-Commerce for:, ~ Telecommunications (56), Machine Learning for:, Supply Chain Management for:, ~ Transportation and Logistics (57)

Company Name: aiKismet
Description: A service that provides labeling services for machine learning data sets.
Website: https://aikismet.com/
Phone: **Email:** 36007@reference-encyclopedia-ai.net
City: Toronto **State:** ON **PC:** **Country:** Canada
Year Established: 2018 **Status 2020:** Active
Industries: Machine Learning

Company Name: Alexsei
Description: Alexsei's advanced artificial intelligence platform delivers affordable and high-quality answers to legal questions in memo format.
Website: https://www.alexsei.com/
Phone: 4067708541 **Email:** mark@alexsei.com
City: Toronto **State:** ON **PC:** **Country:** Canada
Year Established: 2017 **Status 2020:** Active
Industries: Artificial Intelligence for:, IT Managed Services

Company Name: Alitheia Technologies Inc.
Description: AI for Real Estate brokerag: Spain
Website: http://www.alitheiatech.com/
Phone: **Email:** info@thealitheia.com
City: Toronto **State:** ON **PC:** **Country:** Canada
Year Established: 2017 **Status 2020:** Active
Industries:

Company Name: Allegory Insurance
Description: Allegory is building the future of insurance to help good drivers to save money and prevent accidents by using AI and machine vision.
Website: https://allegoryinsurance.com/
Phone: **Email:** info@allegoryinsurance.com
City: Toronto **State:** ON **PC:** **Country:** Canada
Year Established: 2019 **Status 2020:** Active
Industries:

Company Name: AlphaBlock
Description: AlphaBlock is the essence of everything linked with data predictability,
Website: http://alphablock.org/
Phone: **Email:** contact@alphablock.org
City: Toronto **State:** ON **PC:** **Country:** Canada
Year Established: 2017 **Status 2020:** Active
Industries: Artificial Intelligence

Company Name: Altis Labs
Description: Altis Labs is a clinical information company transforming cancer care.
Website: https://altislabs.com/
Phone: **Email:** info@altislabs.com
City: Toronto **State:** ON **PC:** **Country:** Canada
Year Established: 2019 **Status 2020:** Active
Industries: Artificial Intelligence for:, ~ Biotechnology (9), ~ Biotechnology (9), ~ Healthcare (20), Cloud for:, ~ Healthcare (20), ~ Healthcare (20), ~ Healthcare (20), Machine Learning

Company Name: Altius Analytics Labs
Description: Altius Analytics Labs is a health tech startup helping workplaces prevent expensive musculoskeletal injuri: Spain
Website: http://www.altiusanalyticslabs.com/
Phone: 226 505 1834 **Email:** ben@altiusanalyticslabs.com
City: Toronto **State:** ON **PC:** **Country:** Canada
Year Established: **Status 2020:** Active
Industries: Artificial Intelligence for:, Big Data and Analytics for:, Computer Vision for:, ~ Healthcare (20), Industrial Solutions for:, ~ Insurance (25), Machine Learning

Company Name: Ametros Learning
Description: Ametros develops and markets intelligent, adaptive, and experiential digital learning tools.
Website: http://ametroslearning.com/
Phone: **Email:** info@ametroslearning.com
City: Toronto **State:** ON **PC:** **Country:** Canada

Year Established: 2016 **Status 2020:** Active
Industries: Artificial Intelligence for:, ~ Education (13)

Company Name: Ample Labs
Description: Tech nonprofit to empower individuals facing homelessness through technology.
Website: http://www.amplelabs.co
Phone: **Email:** general@amplelabs.co
City: Toronto **State:** ON **PC:** **Country:** Canada
Year Established: 2018 **Status 2020:** Active
Industries: IT Managed Services for:, Natural Language Processing

Company Name: Analytics 4 Life
Description: Pioneering digital health using artificial intelligence to develop a completely new form of medical imaging for coronary artery disea: Sweden
Website: http://analytics4life.com/
Phone: **Email:** info@analytics4life.com
City: Toronto **State:** ON **PC:** **Country:** Canada
Year Established: **Status 2020:** Active
Industries: Analytics for:, Artificial Intelligence for:, ~ Healthcare (20), Machine Learning for:, ~ Manufacturing-Medical Equipment-Supplies (33)

Company Name: Answers Engine
Description: Developer Friendly Platform for Web Scraping, Data Processing, and Generating Insights from Web Data
Website: http://answersengine.com
Phone: **Email:** parama@answersengine.com
City: Toronto **State:** ON **PC:** **Country:** Canada
Year Established: 2017 **Status 2020:** Active
Industries: Analytics for:, Big Data and Analytics for:, ~ Customer Relationship Management (11), IT Managed Services for:, Web for:, Machine Learning

Company Name: Apollen Inc.
Description: Apollen is a data driven organisation utilising predictive analytics to provide accurate recommendations in naturopathic medicine.
Website: http://www.apollen.com/
Phone: **Email:** info@apollen.com
City: Toronto **State:** ON **PC:** **Country:** Canada
Year Established: 2017 **Status 2020:** Active
Industries: Artificial Intelligence for:, ~ Healthcare (20)

Company Name: Assister.ai
Description: The Artificial Programming Pa: Iran
Website: http://assister.ai/
Phone: **Email:** assister.ai@gmail.com
City: Toronto **State:** ON **PC:** **Country:** Canada
Year Established: **Status 2020:** Active
Industries: Artificial Intelligence for:, Application Services for:, Application Services for:, Machine Learning for:, Natural Language Processing

Company Name: Astrum.ai
Description: Machine learning as a service
Website: http://www.astrum.ai
Phone: **Email:** hello@astrum.ai
City: Toronto **State:** ON **PC:** **Country:** Canada
Year Established: 2020 **Status 2020:** Active
Industries: Artificial Intelligence for:, Databases for:, Machine Learning

Company Name: Athena
Description: Athena is on a mission to build a universal platform of autonomous collaborative robots.
Website: http://www.athenaisystems.com/
Phone: **Email:** info@athenaisystems.com
City: Toronto **State:** ON **PC:** **Country:** Canada
Year Established: 2017 **Status 2020:** Active
Industries: Artificial Intelligence for:, Machine Learning for:, Robotics

Company Name: Atomic Rea: Switzerland
Description: Atomic Reach is a content optimization platform built to help marketers create high quality content.
Website: http://www.atomicreach.com
Phone: 647.799.1025 **Email:** bradleysilver@atomicreach.com
City: Toronto **State:** ON **PC:** **Country:** Canada
Year Established: **Status 2020:** Active
Industries: Artificial Intelligence for:, Content for:, Machine Learning

Company Name: Atomic X
Description: Atomic X is an experiential artificial intelligence (AI) firm and consulting business.
Website: http://www.atomicx.ai/
Phone: 416-556-2077 **Email:** dan@atomicx.ai
City: Toronto **State:** ON **PC:** **Country:** Canada
Year Established: 2017 **Status 2020:** Active
Industries: IT Managed Services

Company Name: Authintic
Description: Authintic provides analytics and technology solutions, helping retailers drive sales revenue using social data.
Website: http://www.authintic.com
Phone: **Email:** andrew@authintic.com
City: Toronto **State:** ON **PC:** **Country:** Canada
Year Established: 2012 **Status 2020:** Active
Industries:

Company Name: Auxility
Description: We are a fast, agile and cost conscious software development agency. Every project we treat as our own to build the best product for you.
Website: http://auxility.ca
Phone: (1559) 921-9595 **Email:** say@hi.auxility.ca
City: Toronto **State:** ON **PC:** **Country:** Canada
Year Established: 2016 **Status 2020:** Active
Industries: Artificial Intelligence for:, IT Managed Services for:, Application Services

Company Name: Avanteo Consulting
Description: Digital Health Innovation and Strategy
Website: http://www.avanteoconsulting.com
Phone: (647)834-2139 **Email:** kailesh@avanteoconsulting.com
City: Toronto **State:** ON **PC:** **Country:** Canada
Year Established: **Status 2020:** Active
Industries: Artificial Intelligence for:, ~ Biotechnology (9), ~ Healthcare (20), ~ Administrative and Support Services (1), ~ Healthcare (20)

Company Name: Baby Doppler
Description: Mom and Baby - Maternity & Medical Health Products and Service
Website: http://www.babydoppler.com
Phone: 800-590-2767 **Email:** info@babydoppler.com
City: Toronto **State:** ON **PC:** **Country:** Canada
Year Established: **Status 2020:** Active
Industries: Artificial Intelligence for:, Big Data and Analytics for:, ~ Manufacturing-Electronic (30), Machine Learning for:, ~ Manufacturing-Medical Equipment-Supplies (33), Application Services for:, ~ Professional Services (48)

Company Name: BenchSci
Description: BenchSci is a reagent intelligence platform that transforms published data into experiment-specific recommendations.
Website: http://www.benchsci.com/
Phone: **Email:** simon@benchsci.com
City: Toronto **State:** ON **PC:** **Country:** Canada
Year Established: **Status 2020:** Active
Industries: Artificial Intelligence for:, ~ Biotechnology (9), ~ Life Sciences (27), Machine Learning for:, ~ Pharmaceuticals (46)

Company Name: BioIntelDoc Inc.
Description: BioIntelDoc Inc. leads the future of digital bio-intelligence with technologies including quantum computing, AI/ ML, and XR interfaces!
Website: http://nurenyx.ai/
Phone: **Email:** innovations@nurenyx.ai
City: Toronto **State:** ON **PC:** **Country:** Canada
Year Established: 2019 **Status 2020:** Active
Industries: Artificial Intelligence for:, Big Data and Analytics for:, ~ Customer Relationship Management (11), IT Managed Services

Company Name: Blanc Labs
Description: Blanc Labs is an entrepreneurial organization that builds the next generation of digital solutions for the enterpri: Sweden
Website: http://blanclabs.com
Phone: 1(164)799-45465 **Email:** info@blanclabs.com
City: Toronto **State:** ON **PC:** **Country:** Canada
Year Established: **Status 2020:** Active
Industries: Artificial Intelligence for:, Big Data and Analytics for:, ~ Banking and Financial Markets-Services (7), ~ Banking and Financial Markets-Services (7), IT Managed Services for:, ~ Administrative and Support Services (1), ~ Management of Companies (28), Mobile for

Company Name: Blue J Legal
Description: Blue J Legal is a machine learning and artificial intelligence that delivers absolute clarity to the law.
Website: http://www.bluejlegal.com/
Phone: **Email:** info@bluejlegal.com
City: Toronto **State:** ON **PC:** **Country:** Canada
Year Established: 2015 **Status 2020:** Active
Industries: Artificial Intelligence for:, Machine Learning

Company Name: BOHR
Description: BOHR (Bohr Technology Inc.) develops quantum machine learning software and algorithms for solving complex optimization problems
Website: http://www.bohr.technology
Phone: **Email:** office@bohr.technology
City: Toronto **State:** ON **PC:** **Country:** Canada
Year Established: **Status 2020:** Active
Industries: Artificial Intelligence for:, IT Managed Services for:, Machine Learning for:, ~ Professional Services (48)

Company Name: Boosted.ai
Description: Machine Learning Platform for Investment Manage: Serbia
Website: http://boosted.ai
Phone: **Email:** contact@boosted.ai
City: Toronto **State:** ON **PC:** **Country:** Canada
Year Established: 2017 **Status 2020:** Active
Industries: Artificial Intelligence for:, ~ Banking and Financial Markets-Services (7), Machine Learning for:, ~ Banking and Financial Markets-Services (7)

Company Name: Borealis AI
Description: Borealis AI is an RBC Institute for Research.
Website: https://package.ai/
Phone: **Email:** mi.research@borealisai.com
City: Toronto **State:** ON **PC:** **Country:** Canada
Year Established: 2016 **Status 2020:** Active
Industries: Artificial Intelligence

Company Name: Boss Insights
Description: ACCELERATING LENDING FROM MONTHS TO MINUT: SPAIN
Website: http://bossinsights.com
Phone: 1-844-579-2777 **Email:** info@bossinsights.com
City: Toronto **State:** ON **PC:** **Country:** Canada
Year Established: 2017 **Status 2020:** Active
Industries: Artificial Intelligence for:, ~ Banking and Financial Markets-Services (7), Big Data and Analytics for:, ~ Banking and Financial Markets-Services (7), ~ Banking and Financial Markets-Services (7), ~ Banking and Financial Markets-Services (7), Cloud for:, ~ Banki

Company Name: BrainStation
Description: BrainStation is a global leader in digital skills training. We empower businesses and brands to succeed in the digital age.
Website: http://www.brainstation.io
Phone: 1 (800) 903-5159 **Email:** contact@brainstation.io
City: Toronto **State:** ON **PC:** **Country:** Canada
Year Established: **Status 2020:** Active
Industries: Analytics for:, Artificial Intelligence for:, Digital Marketing for:, ~ Education (13), ~ Education (13), Human Computer Interaction for:, Mobile for:, Business Process and Operations for:, ~ Professional Services (48), Development and Test for:, Cyber Security for

Company Name: bridge7 Oncology
Description: Bridge7 uses AI to scale clinical expertise digitally to improve the efficiency, consistency and quality of delivering cancer care.
Website: http://www.bridge7.ai
Phone: **Email:** info@bridge7.ai
City: Toronto **State:** ON **PC:** **Country:** Canada
Year Established: 2017 **Status 2020:** Active
Industries: Artificial Intelligence for:, ~ Healthcare (20)

Company Name: C3 Insight Group
Description: C3 is a consulting firm with advanced analytics expertise in big data, machine learning and artificial intelligence.
Website: http://c3-inc.com
Phone: 888.651.3332 **Email:** 36222@reference-encyclopedia-ai.net
City: Toronto **State:** ON **PC:** **Country:** Canada
Year Established: 2014 **Status 2020:** Active
Industries:

Company Name: CakeAI
Description: The Next Evolution in Machine Learning, A.I. and Robotics
Website: http://www.cake-ai.com
Phone: **Email:** info@cake-ai.com
City: Toronto **State:** ON **PC:** **Country:** Canada
Year Established: 2020 **Status 2020:** Active
Industries: Artificial Intelligence for:, Machine Learning for:, Robotics

Company Name: Candor.ai
Description: Candor.ai is an artificial intelligence-driven platform that helps users in their real estate and home buying journey.
Website: http://candor.ai/
Phone: **Email:** 36227@reference-encyclopedia-ai.net
City: Toronto **State:** ON **PC:** **Country:** Canada
Year Established: 2018 **Status 2020:** Active
Industries: Artificial Intelligence for:, ~ Real Estate (49), Internet of Things (IoT)

Company Name: Canvass Analytics
Description: Canvass Analytics is an AI-based predictive analytics platform designed for the Industrial Internet of Things.
Website: http://canvass.io
Phone: **Email:** info@canvass.io
City: Toronto **State:** ON **PC:** **Country:** Canada
Year Established: **Status 2020:** Active
Industries: Artificial Intelligence for:, Automation for:, ~ Manufacturing-General (31), Predictive Analytics

Company Name: Chatk: Italy
Description: Chatkit is an AI Conversational Marketing chatbot platform that helps brands create and nurture lasting customer relationships.
Website: http://chatkit.com/
Phone: **Email:** hello@chatkit.com
City: Toronto **State:** ON **PC:** **Country:** Canada

Year Established: 2016 **Status 2020:** Active
Industries: Artificial Intelligence for:, Content for:, ~ Social Assistance-Non-Profits (53)

Company Name: Chisel.ai
Description: Chisel.ai use Natural Language Processing and Artificial Intelligence to help you work smart with documents.
Website: http://chisel.ai
Phone: **Email:** contact@chisel.ai
City: Toronto **State:** ON **PC:** **Country:** Canada
Year Established: 2015 **Status 2020:** Active
Industries: Artificial Intelligence for:, IT Managed Services for:, Machine Learning

Company Name: CIX - Canadian Innovation Exchange
Description: Accelerating the development of the ground-breaking technologies, products and services propelling the Canadian economy into the future.
Website: http://www.cixsummit.com
Phone: 416-408-2300 **Email:** swhite@brunico.com
City: Toronto **State:** ON **PC:** **Country:** Canada
Year Established: **Status 2020:** Active
Industries: Artificial Intelligence for:, ~ Banking and Financial Markets-Services (7), IT Managed Services for:, IT Managed Services for:, ~ Banking and Financial Markets-Services (7)

Company Name: Clearfit Analytics
Description: Clearfit Analytics leverages science and big data to help leaders make better people decisions.
Website: http://www.clearfitanalytics.com
Phone: (416)540-4327 **Email:** jamie@clearfit.com
City: Toronto **State:** ON **PC:** **Country:** Canada
Year Established: 2016 **Status 2020:** Active
Industries: Business Applications for:, Enterprise Application Services for:, IT Managed Services for:, Predictive Analytics

Company Name: Click Less Do More
Description: Multi-channel actionable e-presence for small service businesses via platform that powers market-tailored all-in-one cloud services.
Website: http://clicklessdomore.com
Phone: **Email:** maxkarlin@clicklessdomore.com
City: Toronto **State:** ON **PC:** **Country:** Canada
Year Established: **Status 2020:** Active
Industries: Artificial Intelligence for:, E-Commerce for:, E-Commerce for:, Cyber Security for:, Application Services for:, Cyber Security for:, Cyber Security for:, Cyber Security for:, Cyber Security

Company Name: Clik.ai
Description: Clik.ai is a AI Powered Automated Underwriting Platform for Commercial Real Estate Brokers and Lenders.
Website: http://clik.ai/
Phone: 1-647 389 6552 **Email:** info@clik.ai
City: Toronto **State:** ON **PC:** **Country:** Canada
Year Established: 2017 **Status 2020:** Active
Industries: Artificial Intelligence

Company Name: Cluep
Description: Cluep is a mobile ad platform that targets people based on what they are sharing, how they are feeling and where they have been.
Website: http://cluep.com/
Phone: **Email:** hello@cluep.com
City: Toronto **State:** ON **PC:** **Country:** Canada
Year Established: **Status 2020:** Active
Industries: ~ Media-Communications (41), ~ Media-Communications (41), Artificial Intelligence for:, Computer Vision for:, Mobile for:, ~ Media-Communications (41), ~ Social Media (54), ~ Social Media (54), Data Management

Company Name: CONDOLYTICS
Description: Condolytics is a SaaS product that provides condominium buildings with measurable metrics that deliver smart building insights.
Website: http://www.condolytics.ca
Phone: **Email:** Hello@condolytics.ca
City: Toronto **State:** ON **PC:** **Country:** Canada
Year Established: 2018 **Status 2020:** Active
Industries: Analytics for:, Big Data and Analytics for:, Predictive Analytics for:, ~ Administrative and Support Services (1), Business Software as a Service Apps (SaaS Apps) for:, ~ Construction (10)

Company Name: Consensus
Description: Consensus is a decentralized artificial intelligence network for collective governance
Website: http://consensus.ai
Phone: **Email:** 36326@reference-encyclopedia-ai.net
City: Toronto **State:** ON **PC:** **Country:** Canada
Year Established: 2016 **Status 2020:** Active
Industries: Artificial Intelligence for:, Big Data and Analytics for:, Blockchain for:, IT Managed Services for:, Web for:, Machine Learning

Company Name: Consilium Crypto
Description: Consilium Crypto offers an institutional-grade data and analytics for the digital asset markets.
Website: http://consiliumcrypto.ai/
Phone: **Email:** info@consiliumcrypto.ai
City: Toronto **State:** ON **PC:** **Country:** Canada
Year Established: 2017 **Status 2020:** Active
Industries: Analytics for:, Artificial Intelligence for:, Blockchain for:, IT Managed Services for:, IT Managed Services

Company Name: coSquare Inc.
Description: First fully integrated commercial leasing platform.
Website: http://www.cosquare.ca/
Phone: **Email:** info@cosquare.ca
City: Toronto **State:** ON **PC:** **Country:** Canada
Year Established: **Status 2020:** Active
Industries:

Company Name: Crowdmark
Description: Crowdmark is a grading & analytics platform powered by AI to streamline assessment, increase productivity & provide personalized learning.
Website: http://crowdmark.com
Phone: 416-978-3645 **Email:** info@crowdmark.com
City: Toronto **State:** ON **PC:** **Country:** Canada
Year Established: 2012 **Status 2020:** Active
Industries: Artificial Intelligence for:, Big Data and Analytics for:, ~ Education (13)

Company Name: CryptoNumerics
Description: Use data to gain insights while protecting people's privacy
Website:
Phone: **Email:** 4414@reference-encyclopedia-ai.net
City: Toronto **State:** ON **PC:** **Country:** Canada
Year Established: **Status 2020:** Active
Industries: Analytics for:, Artificial Intelligence for:, IT Managed Services for:, Machine Learning for:, Cyber Security for:, ~ Professional Services (48)

Company Name: Culturalite
Description: Culturalite is a platform curating the world's cultural information on a daily basis.
Website: http://www.culturalitemedia.com
Phone: 1 (416) 588-6789 **Email:** info@culturalitemedia.com
City: Toronto **State:** ON **PC:** **Country:** Canada
Year Established: **Status 2020:** Active
Industries: Artificial Intelligence for:, Databases for:, Data Management for:, ~ Media-Communications (41), ~ Media-Communications (41)

Company Name: Curv
Description: Curv is a platform of AI-powered tools for building and tracking athletic talent.
Website: http://www.curv.ai/
Phone: (647) 331-0949 **Email:** shea@curv.ai
City: Toronto **State:** ON **PC:** **Country:** Canada
Year Established: 2017 **Status 2020:** Active
Industries: Artificial Intelligence for:, Machine Learning

Company Name: Cyclica
Description: Enhancing drug discovery by harnessing big data and predictive analytics; cloud-based, AI-assisted drug discovery
Website: http://www.cyclicarx.com
Phone: 1 (416) 304-9202 **Email:** natasha.puri@cyclicarx.com
City: Toronto **State:** ON **Zip:** 90013 **Country**: Canada
Year Established: **Status 2020:** Active
Industries: Artificial Intelligence for:, Big Data and Analytics for:, ~ Biotechnology (9), ~ Pharmaceuticals (46)

Company Name: Dash Intelligence, Inc
Description: Dash is an Artificial Intelligence and Robotics company based in downtown Toronto, working on the first ever singular AI system.
Website: http://dashintelligence.com
Phone: 1(647) 571 1912 **Email:** team@dashintelligence.com
City: Toronto **State:** ON **PC:** **Country:** Canada
Year Established: 2018 **Status 2020:** Active
Industries: Artificial Intelligence for:, ~ Education (13)

Company Name: Dashflows Inc.
Description: Dashboards, Artificial Intelligence and Data Analytics, CyberSecurity
Website: http://www.dashflows.com
Phone: **Email:** info@dashflows.com
City: Toronto **State:** ON **PC:** **Country:** Canada
Year Established: 2010 **Status 2020:** Active
Industries: Analytics for:, Artificial Intelligence for:, IT Managed Services for:, Machine Learning for:, Security for:, Security

Company Name: Datachili Inc.
Description: Using machine learning to improve data quality.
Website: http://www.datachili.com
Phone: **Email:** 36391@reference-encyclopedia-ai.net
City: Toronto **State:** ON **PC:** **Country:** Canada
Year Established: 2016 **Status 2020:** Active
Industries: Artificial Intelligence for:, IT Managed Services

Company Name: datacracy.io
Description: The first global sustainability intelligence ecosystem that is aimed at enabling enterprises and governments around the world to reach SDGs.
Website: http://datacracy.io/
Phone: **Email:** info@datacracy.io
City: Toronto **State:** ON **PC:** **Country:** Canada
Year Established: 2016 **Status 2020:** Active
Industries: Big Data and Analytics for:, Business Intelligence for:, Collaboration Solutions for:, Databases for:, Data Management for:, Internet of Things (IoT) for:, Machine Learning for:, ~ Social-Environmental-Physical-Engineering Sciences (55), ~ Social-Environmental-: Philippin: Spain

Company Name: Datadex
Description: Datadex is an intelligent data augmentation platform for advanced data science and AI.
Website: http://datadex.net/
Phone: **Email:** info@datadex.net
City: Toronto **State:** ON **PC:** **Country:** Canada
Year Established: 2017 **Status 2020:** Active
Industries: Artificial Intelligence

Company Name: Dataspine
Description: Dataspine provides the fastest & simplest way to build, deploy & manage AI applications, at scale, on any infrastructure
Website: http://www.dataspine.io
Phone: 437-989-8983 **Email:** contact@dataspine.io
City: Toronto **State:** ON **PC:** **Country:** Canada
Year Established: 2017 **Status 2020:** Active
Industries: Artificial Intelligence for:, Application Services for:, Machine Learning

Company Name: Deep Genomics
Description: Deep Genomics is using artificial intelligence to build a new universe of life-saving genetic therapies.
Website: http://www.deepgenomics.com/
Phone: **Email:** contact@deepgenomics.com
City: Toronto **State:** ON **PC:** **Country:** Canada
Year Established: **Status 2020:** Active
Industries: Artificial Intelligence for:, ~ Biotechnology (9), ~ Healthcare (20), ~ Healthcare (20)

Company Name: deepPiXEL Inc.
Description: deepPiXEL develops AI software for businesses to automate and augment their customer engagement to reduce cost and delight customers.
Website: http://www.deeppixel.ai
Phone: 866-341-5575 **Email:** gamarakone@deeppixel.ai
City: Toronto **State:** ON **PC:** **Country:** Canada
Year Established: 2015 **Status 2020:** Active
Industries: Artificial Intelligence for:, ~ Customer Relationship Management (11), Natural Language Processing for:, ~ Customer Relationship Management (11)

Company Name: Delphia
Description: Delphia builds artificially intelligent surveys that help people make complex, important decisions.
Website: http://delphia.com
Phone: **Email:** hello@delphia.com
City: Toronto **State:** ON **PC:** **Country:** Canada
Year Established: **Status 2020:** Active
Industries:

Company Name: Dentem
Description: Dentem is a platform that allows dental practices to be more reliable and flexible to attain business growth.
Website: http://www.dentem.co
Phone: **Email:** info@dentem.co
City: Toronto **State:** ON **PC:** **Country:** Canada
Year Established: **Status 2020:** Active
Industries: Artificial Intelligence for:, ~ Healthcare (20), ~ Healthcare (20), Web for:, Machine Learning for:, ~ Healthcare (20)

Company Name: Denti.AI
Description: Denti.AI is a cloud platform improving quality & productivity in dentistry with automated analysis of dental imag: Spain
Website: http://www.denti.ai
Phone: **Email:** ir@denti.ai
City: Toronto **State:** ON **PC:** **Country:** Canada
Year Established: 2017 **Status 2020:** Active
Industries: Artificial Intelligence for:, ~ Healthcare (20), Image Recognition for:, Machine Learning for:, ~ Healthcare (20)

Company Name: Des: Saudi Arabia
Description: Dessa collaborates with enterprise teams to blueprint, build and deploy customized AI systems that reinvent what's possible for business.
Website: http://www.dessa.com/
Phone: **Email:** contact@dessa.com
City: Toronto **State:** ON **PC:** **Country:** Canada
Year Established: **Status 2020:** Active
Industries: Artificial Intelligence for:, Machine Learning for:, ~ Professional Services (48)

Company Name: Destin AI
Description: Destin is the Artificial Intelligence powered integrated solution for immigration to Canada.
Website: http://www.destin.ai
Phone: **Email:** hello@destin.ai
City: Toronto **State:** ON **PC:** **Country:** Canada
Year Established: **Status 2020:** Active
Industries: Artificial Intelligence for:, IT Managed Services for:, ~ Law-Legal Services (26)

Company Name: Diligen
Description: Diligen manages and streamlines legal due diligence and contract reviews using AI and collaborative project management.
Website: http://www.diligen.com
Phone: 1 (800) 939-0889 **Email:** help@diligen.com
City: Toronto **State:** ON **PC:** **Country:** Canada
Year Established: 2015 **Status 2020:** Active
Industries: **Company Name:** DirectedAI
Description: DirectedAI is a utilizes various artificial intelligence technologies platform.
Website: http://www.directedai.com/
Phone: **Email:** 36440@reference-encyclopedia-ai.net
City: Toronto **State:** ON **PC:** **Country:** Canada
Year Established: 2014 **Status 2020:** Active
Industries: Artificial Intelligence for:, IT Managed Services for:, Machine Learning

Company Name: Discovery Loft Inc.
Description: Discovery Loft accelerates the ideas that will transform everyone's automotive and mobility experience.
Website: http://discoveryloft.com/
Phone: 1-888-229-8552 **Email:** steve.southin@discoveryloft.com
City: Toronto **State:** ON **PC:** **Country:** Canada
Year Established: 2017 **Status 2020:** Active
Industries: Application Services for:, Artificial Intelligence for:, Internet of Things (IoT) for:, ~ Telecommunications (56)

Company Name: Diversio
Description: Diversio is a single platform to help you attract, develop and retain diverse talent, diversity, inclusion.
Website: http://www.diversio.com
Phone: **Email:** 36444@reference-encyclopedia-ai.net
City: Toronto **State:** ON **PC:** **Country:** Canada
Year Established: 2018 **Status 2020:** Active
Industries: Artificial Intelligence for:, IT Managed Services

Company Name: DNNResearch:
Description: DNNresearch develops voice and image recognition solutions.
Website: http://www.dnnresearch.com/
Phone: **Email:** 36446@reference-encyclopedia-ai.net
City: Toronto **State:** ON **PC:** **Country:** Canada
Year Established: 2012 **Status 2020:** Active
Industries: Artificial Intelligence for:, Image Recognition for:, Machine Learning

Company Name: Drizti
Description: Drizti delivers a cloud High Performance Computing (HPC) solution as easy to use as a PC.
Website: http://www.drizti.com
Phone: **Email:** 36458@reference-encyclopedia-ai.net
City: Toronto **State:** ON **PC:** **Country:** Canada
Year Established: 2017 **Status 2020:** Active
Industries: Cloud for:, Cloud for:, Cloud for:, Enterprise Application Services for:, IT Managed Services

Company Name: Drona
Description: Social Learning Platform for better, richer, inclusive learning experience
Website: http://drona.ca
Phone: 6472691831 **Email:** shashank-n@outlook.com
City: Toronto **State:** ON **PC:** **Country:** Canada
Year Established: **Status 2020:** Active
Industries: Artificial Intelligence for:, ~ Education (13), ~ Media-Communications (41), ~ Professional Services (48)

Company Name: EAIGLE
Description: Cleantech, Water, Energy, Artificial Intelligence, Machine Learning, SaaS
Website: http://eaigle.com/
Phone: 1(866) 832 6350 **Email:** contact@eaigle.com
City: Toronto **State:** ON **PC:** **Country:** Canada
Year Established: 2018 **Status 2020:** Active
Industries: Artificial Intelligence for:, Business Software as a Service Apps (SaaS Apps)

Company Name: Ecopia.AI
Description: Digitizing the world using AI
Website: http://www.ecopia.ai
Phone: (519)342-0193 **Email:** info@ecopiatech.com
City: Toronto **State:** ON **PC:** **Country:** Canada
Year Established: 2013 **Status 2020:** Active
Industries: Artificial Intelligence for:, Internet of Things (IoT) for:, Image Recognition for:, IT Managed Services for:, Machine Learning

Company Name: Eddy Travels
Description: AI-powered travel assistant that simplifies the trip planning experience for millennials
Website: http://www.eddytravels.com/
Phone: **Email:** info@eddytravels.com
City: Toronto **State:** ON **PC:** **Country:** Canada
Year Established: 2018 **Status 2020:** Active
Industries:

Company Name: Eduro AI
Description: SaaS
Website: http://www.eduro.ai
Phone: 6472920280 **Email:** hello@eduro.ai
City: Toronto **State:** ON **PC:** **Country:** Canada
Year Established: **Status 2020:** Active
Industries: Artificial Intelligence for:, Automation for:, IT Managed Services for:, Web for:, Machine Learning for:, ~ Manufacturing-Miscellaneous (34), Predictive Analytics for:, ~ Professional Services (48)

Company Name: Electric Brain Software Corporation
Description: Electric Brain Software Corporation is a machine learning company located in Toronto.
Website: http://www.electricbrain.io
Phone: **Email:** 36487@reference-encyclopedia-ai.net
City: Toronto **State:** ON **PC:** **Country:** Canada
Year Established: 2016 **Status 2020:** Active
Industries: Artificial Intelligence for:, Databases for:, Machine Learning

Company Name: Electronica Ai
Description: Electronica Ai is a machine learning analytics company located in Toronto.
Website: http://www.electai.ca
Phone: **Email:** 36488@reference-encyclopedia-ai.net
City: Toronto **State:** ON **PC:** **Country:** Canada
Year Established: 2013 **Status 2020:** Active
Industries: Analytics for:, Machine Learning

Company Name: Empty Cubicle
Description: Empty Cubicle is the world's first VERIFIED hiring platform.
Website: http://www.emptycubicle.com/
Phone: 844-837-4395 **Email:** info@emptycubicle.com
City: Toronto **State:** ON **PC:** **Country:** Canada
Year Established: **Status 2020:** Active
Industries: Artificial Intelligence for:, Machine Learning for:, ~ Human Resources (24), ~ Customer Relationship Management (11), ~ Human Resources (24)

Company Name: Engagement Logic
Description: Customer Usage Intelligence for B2B SaaS vendors. We use predictive analytics to help lower churn & grow revenue from existing customers.
Website: http://www.engagementlogic.com
Phone: **Email:** 36509@reference-encyclopedia-ai.net
City: Toronto **State:** ON **PC:** **Country:** Canada
Year Established: 2015 **Status 2020:** Active
Industries: Enterprise Application Services for:, Machine Learning for:, Predictive Analytics for:, Business Software as a Service Apps (SaaS Apps)

Company Name: ENGAIZ
Description: AI-Driven SaaS platform for Effective Third-Party Governance & Risk Management
Website: http://www.engaiz.com
Phone: **Email:** info@ENGAIZ.com
City: Toronto **State:** ON **PC:** **Country:** Canada
Year Established: 2019 **Status 2020:** Active
Industries: Analytics for:, Artificial Intelligence for:, ~ Customer Relationship Management (11), IT Managed Services for:, Machine Learning for:, Business Software as a Service Apps (SaaS Apps)

Company Name: Eon Media Corp.
Description: We build next-generation tech solutions for media companies that are easy to integrate, save customers 60-70% on backend costs and improve end-user viewing experience
Website: https://eonmedia.ai
Phone: 4169074174 **Email:** info@eonmedia.ai
City: Toronto **State:** ON **Zip:** M5H1A1 **Country**: Canada
Year Established: **Status 2020:** Active
Industries: Artificial Intelligence for:, ~ Media-Communications (41), ~ Telecommunications (56), Blockchain for:, IT Managed Services for:, Machine Learning for:, ~ Media-Communications (3396), ~ Telecommunications (3411), Technology Consulting for:, ~ Media-Communications (

Company Name: Essen
Description: Read news smarter and 10x faster.
Website: http://essen.ai/
Phone: **Email:** hi@essen.ai
City: Toronto **State:** ON **PC:** **Country:** Canada
Year Established: **Status 2020:** Active
Industries: Artificial Intelligence for:, Machine Learning for:, Application Services for:, Natural Language Processing for:, Cyber Security

Company Name: Fetch Bioscienc: Spain
Description: Engineering the next generation of proteins using machine learning
Website: http://www.fetch.bio
Phone: **Email:** 36561@reference-encyclopedia-ai.net
City: Toronto **State:** ON **PC:** **Country:** Canada
Year Established: 2019 **Status 2020:** Active
Industries: Artificial Intelligence for:, ~ Biotechnology (9)

Company Name: Finatechal
Description: Finatechal is a financial research company providing AI based predictive analytics, detailed investor portfolio info and analysis.
Website: http://www.finatechal.com
Phone: **Email:** 36563@reference-encyclopedia-ai.net
City: Toronto **State:** ON **PC:** **Country:** Canada
Year Established: 2016 **Status 2020:** Active
Industries: Artificial Intelligence for:, Big Data and Analytics for:, ~ Banking and Financial Markets-Services (7)

Company Name: Firebird
Description: Firebird is a quantum machine intelligence company, building machine learning software for the most advanced computers on the planet.
Website:
Phone: **Email:** 36570@reference-encyclopedia-ai.net
City: Toronto **State:** ON **PC:** **Country:** Canada
Year Established: 2015 **Status 2020:** Active
Industries: Artificial Intelligence for:, Business Intelligence for:, IT Managed Services for:, Machine Learning for:, ~ Education (13)

Company Name: FITFI Inc.
Description: AI powered fitness platform
Website: http://www.fitfi.ai
Phone: **Email:** info@fitfi.ai
City: Toronto **State:** ON **PC:** **Country:** Canada
Year Established: **Status 2020:** Active
Industries: Artificial Intelligence for:, IT Managed Services

Company Name: FleetO: Palestine
Description: Freight marketplace
Website: http://fleetops.ai
Phone: 6476809876 **Email:** hello@fleetrover.com
City: Toronto **State:** ON **PC:** **Country:** Canada
Year Established: **Status 2020:** Active
Industries: Analytics for:, Artificial Intelligence for:, Big Data and Analytics for:, ~ Transportation and Logistics (57)

Company Name: Flybits
Description: Flybits creates value for customers by enabling micro-personalized experiences, powered by contextual intelligence.
Website: http://flybits.com
Phone: 1-844-359-2487 **Email:** info@flybits.com
City: Toronto **State:** ON **PC:** **Country:** Canada
Year Established: 2013 **Status 2020:** Active
Industries:

Company Name: Flybits, Inc.
Description: Flybits creates value for customers by enabling micro-personalized experiences, powered by contextual intelligence.
Website: http://flybits.com
Phone: 1-844-359-2487 **Email:** info@flybits.com
City: Toronto **State:** ON **PC:** **Country:** Canada
Year Established: **Status 2020:** Active
Industries: Analytics for:, Artificial Intelligence for:, Application Services for:, Enterprise Application Services for:, Machine Learning for:, Mobile for:, Predictive Analytics

Company Name: Fortay Inc
Description:
Website: http://www.fortay.co
Phone: **Email:** hello@fortay.co
City: Toronto **State:** ON **Zip:** M5G 1L7 **Country**: Canada
Year Established: **Status 2020:** Active
Industries: Analytics for:, Artificial Intelligence for:, Enterprise Application Services for:, ~ Human Resources (24), ~ Human Resources (24)

Company Name: Fortuna.ai
Description: AI platform automating business development
Website: http://www.fortuna.ai/
Phone: **Email:** hello@fortuna.ai
City: Toronto **State:** ON **PC:** **Country:** Canada
Year Established: **Status 2020:** Active
Industries: Artificial Intelligence for:, IT Managed Services for:, Automation for:, ~ Professional Services (48)

Company Name: Goldspot Discoveries Inc.
Description: Goldspot Discoveries is revolutionizing the mineral exploration business.
Website: http://www.goldspot.ca/
Phone: **Email:** denis@goldspot.ca
City: Toronto **State:** ON **PC:** **Country:** Canada
Year Established: **Status 2020:** Active
Industries: Artificial Intelligence for:, Machine Learning for:, ~ Management of Companies (28)

Company Name: Gradient Ascent AI
Description: Our mission is to empower businesses with Artificial Intelligence
Website: http://www.gradient-ascent.com/
Phone: **Email:** contact@gradient-ascent.com
City: Toronto **State:** ON **PC:** **Country:** Canada
Year Established: **Status 2020:** Active
Industries: Artificial Intelligence for:, Machine Learning

Company Name: Granata Decision Systems
Description: Granata's prescriptive analytics technology helps organizations and individuals make decisions in the optimal way.
Website:
Phone: **Email:** 36641@reference-encyclopedia-ai.net
City: Toronto **State:** ON **PC:** **Country:** Canada
Year Established: 2012 **Status 2020:** Active
Industries: Artificial Intelligence for:, Machine Learning

Company Name: GraphEQ
Description: GraphEQ is an Artificial Intelligence engine built to give computers the power of Human Empathy.
Website: http://grapheq.com/
Phone: **Email:** 36642@reference-encyclopedia-ai.net
City: Toronto **State:** ON **PC:** **Country:** Canada
Year Established: 2016 **Status 2020:** Active
Industries: Artificial Intelligence

Company Name: GrowthGenius
Description: GrowthGenius is your AI-assisted sales development team.
Website: http://www.growthgenius.com
Phone: (778) 889-3825 **Email:** traction@growthgenius.com
City: Toronto **State:** ON **PC:** **Country:** Canada
Year Established: 2016 **Status 2020:** Active
Industries: Artificial Intelligence for:, Business Applications for:, Web

Company Name: Happiify
Description: Happiify is a technology Company providing users with instant matching of health and happy living products, services and information needs.
Website: http://www.happiify.me/
Phone: **Email:** 4456@reference-encyclopedia-ai.net
City: Toronto **State:** ON **PC:** **Country:** Canada
Year Established: **Status 2020:** Active
Industries: Artificial Intelligence for:, IT Managed Services for:, Mobile for:, Application Services

Company Name: Hatchways
Description: Hatchways is a platform focused on making career transitions easier. Focused on web developers.
Website: http://hatchways.io
Phone: **Email:** hello@hatchways.io
City: Toronto **State:** ON **PC:** **Country:** Canada
Year Established: 2018 **Status 2020:** Active
Industries: Artificial Intelligence for:, ~ Education (13)

Company Name: Hello Ir
Description: Hello Iris provides psychometric profiles to help people build better relationships, starting with themselves.
Website: http://helloiris.io
Phone: **Email:** 36682@reference-encyclopedia-ai.net
City: Toronto **State:** ON **PC:** **Country:** Canada
Year Established: 2019 **Status 2020:** Active
Industries: Artificial Intelligence for:, ~ Healthcare (20)

Company Name: Hopeful Inc.
Description: Hopeful Inc. is a company that helps nonprofits drive donations, reduce operating costs, and make better decisions using data.
Website: http://www.hopefulinc.me/
Phone: 647-624-4362 **Email:** ajivov@hopefulinc.me
City: Toronto **State:** ON **PC:** **Country:** Canada
Year Established: 2019 **Status 2020:** Active
Industries: Analytics for:, Artificial Intelligence for:, Big Data and Analytics for:, Machine Learning for:, ~ Retail and Consumer Products (52), Predictive Analytics

Company Name: Hubdoc
Description: Your key financial docs in one place. Automatically.
Website: http://hubdoc.com
Phone: (800)577-2842 **Email:** support@hubdoc.com
City: Toronto **State:** ON **PC:** **Country:** Canada
Year Established: 2011 **Status 2020:** Active
Industries: Finance and Accounting for:, Artificial Intelligence for:, Data Management for:, IT Managed Services for:, Business Software as a Service Apps (SaaS Apps)

Company Name: Hungry Belly
Description: Using Predictive analytics, we learn what you like and recommend you the best local restaurants based on your personal food profile.
Website: http://hungrybelly.me
Phone: **Email:** 36723@reference-encyclopedia-ai.net
City: Toronto **State:** ON **PC:** **Country:** Canada
Year Established: 2014 **Status 2020:** Active
Industries:

Company Name: Ideal
Description: Ideal provides talent intelligence for high-volume hiring. Ideal uses AI to centralize rich candidate data and screen candidates.
Website: http://www.ideal.com
Phone: 1(800)693-1076 **Email:** kaylakozan@gmail.com
City: Toronto **State:** ON **PC:** **Country:** Canada
Year Established: 2013 **Status 2020:** Active
Industries: Artificial Intelligence for:, Business Software as a Service Apps (SaaS Apps)

Company Name: Ikanuki
Description: AI Software Platform to manage Data Bottleneck, root-cause and user feedback - Application for Vehicle and Drone Management
Website: http://www.ikanuki.ca
Phone: (416) 450-4528 **Email:** cedriccanu@ikanuki.ca
City: Toronto **State:** ON **PC:** **Country:** Canada
Year Established: 2016 **Status 2020:** Active
Industries: Artificial Intelligence for:, ~ Automotive (5), ~ Telecommunications (56), Machine Learning

Company Name: iNAGO
Description: iNAGO is the leading company providing intelligent conversational assistants with artificial intelligence and natural language.
Website: http://www.inago.com/
Phone: 416-343-0032 **Email:** marketingna@inago.com
City: Toronto **State:** ON **PC:** **Country:** Canada
Year Established: **Status 2020:** Active
Industries: Artificial Intelligence

Company Name: Integrate.ai
Description: Integrate.ai is an applied AI enterprise software company.
Website: http://www.integrate.ai
Phone: **Email:** info@integrate.ai
City: Toronto **State:** ON **PC:** **Country:** Canada
Year Established: **Status 2020:** Active
Industries: Artificial Intelligence for:, Data Management for:, Enterprise Application Services for:, Machine Learning for:, ~ Telecommunications (56), Natural Language Processing for:, ~ Healthcare (20)

Company Name: Intellizence
Description: Intellizence is an AI startup that discovers insights from external unstructured data sources.
Website: http://www.intellizence.com
Phone: **Email:** info@intellizence.com
City: Toronto **State:** ON **PC:** **Country:** Canada

Year Established: 2016 **Status 2020:** Active
Industries: Artificial Intelligence

Company Name: Invision AI
Description: Invision AI software enables mainstream processors to run accurate real-time object detection, classification and tracking.
Website: http://invision.ai/
Phone: **Email:** hello@invision.ai
City: Toronto **State:** ON **PC:** **Country:** Canada
Year Established: 2017 **Status 2020:** Active
Industries: Artificial Intelligence for:, ~ Automotive (5), Computer Vision for:, Enterprise Application Services for:, Facial Recognition for:, Internet of Things (IoT) for:, Machine Learning

Company Name: Iota Security
Description: Iota Security prevents cybercrime on connected devic: Spain
Website: http://www.iotasecurity.com/
Phone: 647-785-8773 **Email:** info@iotasecurity.com
City: Toronto **State:** ON **PC:** **Country:** Canada
Year Established: **Status 2020:** Active
Industries: Artificial Intelligence for:, Cyber Security for:, ~ Banking and Financial Markets-Services (7), ~ Banking and Financial Markets-Services (7), Machine Learning

Company Name: JADE Healthcare Group Inc.
Description: Intelligent Cloud Computed Health Monitoring
Website: http://www.jadehealthcaregroup.com
Phone: **Email:** info@jhcgi.com
City: Toronto **State:** ON **PC:** **Country:** Canada
Year Established: **Status 2020:** Active
Industries: Artificial Intelligence for:, Big Data and Analytics for:, ~ Healthcare (20), ~ Healthcare (20), ~ Healthcare (20), IT Managed Services for:, ~ Manufacturing-Medical Equipment-Supplies (33)

Company Name: Jan
Description: AI Management
Website: http://www.Janis.ai
Phone: **Email:** support@janis.ai
City: Toronto **State:** ON **PC:** **Country:** Canada
Year Established: **Status 2020:** Active
Industries: Artificial Intelligence for:, ~ Telecommunications (56)

Company Name: Jibestream
Description: Jibestream is a premier indoor navigation platform accessing real-time data to help navigate complex venues.
Website:
http://www.jibestream.com?utm_source=TechCrunch&utm_me...
Phone: (855)502-9455 **Email:** marketing@jibestream.com
City: Toronto **State:** ON **PC:** **Country:** Canada
Year Established: **Status 2020:** Active
Industries: Artificial Intelligence for:, IT Managed Services for:, ~ Transportation and Logistics (57), Compute for:, ~ Professional Services (48)

Company Name: JOEZOO
Description: 'Next generation' classwork assessment app that uses AI to automate student improvement while saving 80% of teacher time.
Website: http://getjoezoo.com/
Phone: **Email:** contact@joezooapp.com
City: Toronto **State:** ON **PC:** **Country:** Canada
Year Established: 2014 **Status 2020:** Active
Industries: Artificial Intelligence for:, ~ Education (13), ~ Education (13), ~ Education (13), Machine Learning for:, ~ Education (13), ~ Education (13)

Company Name: JUCY
Description: Data science platform and service
Website: http://jucyai.com
Phone: **Email:** hello@jucyai.com
City: Toronto **State:** ON **PC:** **Country:** Canada
Year Established: 2019 **Status 2020:** Active
Industries: Artificial Intelligence

Company Name: Kardian Autonomous Health Monitoring
Description: Kardian is a start-up with 6 years of R&D in advanced machine-learning algorithm utilizing Impulse Radio UWB RADAR technology.
Website: http://www.kardian.io
Phone: **Email:** sam@kardian.io
City: Toronto **State:** ON **PC:** **Country:** Canada
Year Established: **Status 2020:** Active
Industries: Analytics for:, Artificial Intelligence for:, ~ Healthcare (20), Machine Learning

Company Name: Karen HR
Description: Karen HR is an AI company with a recruiting software tool for human resources workers.
Website: http://karen.ai/
Phone: **Email:** 36844@reference-encyclopedia-ai.net
City: Toronto **State:** ON **PC:** **Country:** Canada
Year Established: 2016 **Status 2020:** Active
Industries:

Company Name: Kaspian Innovations
Description: Kaspian Innovations offers Augmented Reality application development, Mobile Application, Artificial Intelligent Solutions services.
Website: http://www.kaspian.ca/
Phone: **Email:** info@kaspian.ca
City: Toronto **State:** ON **PC:** **Country:** Canada
Year Established: 2012 **Status 2020:** Active
Industries: Artificial Intelligence for:, Augmented Reality for:, Application Services

Company Name: Kira Systems
Description: Kira Systems is a machine learning software that identifies, extracts, and analyzes text in contracts and other documents.
Website: http://kirasystems.com/
Phone: 1(888) 710-3454 **Email:** info@kirasystems.com
City: Toronto **State:** ON **PC:** **Country:** Canada
Year Established: 2010 **Status 2020:** Active
Industries: Analytics for:, Artificial Intelligence for:, IT Managed Services for:, Machine Learning for:, Data Management

Company Name: KitchenMate
Description: KitchenMate leverages robotics and AI to provide delicious, freshly prepared meals at great prices.
Website: http://www.kitchenmate.com
Phone: 800-998-4129 **Email:** info@kitchenmate.com
City: Toronto **State:** ON **PC:** **Country:** Canada
Year Established: 2015 **Status 2020:** Active
Industries: Artificial Intelligence for:, ~ Food and Beverage (17), Internet of Things (IoT)

Company Name: Kiwi.ai
Description: Kiwi is the world leader in motion recognition technology.
Website: http://www.kiwi.ai
Phone: **Email:** info@kiwi.ai
City: Toronto **State:** ON **PC:** **Country:** Canada
Year Established: **Status 2020:** Active
Industries: Artificial Intelligence for:, IT Managed Services for:, Machine Learning for:, ~ Professional Services (48)

Company Name: Knockri
Description: A.I. Video Recruiting
Website: http://www.knockri.com
Phone: **Email:** info@knockri.com
City: Toronto **State:** ON **PC:** **Country:** Canada
Year Established: **Status 2020:** Active
Industries: Artificial Intelligence for:, Computer Vision for:, ~ Human Resources (24), Natural Language Processing for:, Predictive Analytics

Company Name: Knowtions Research
Description: Knowtions combines machine learning and expert communities to solve multilingual data challenges in social listening, patient experience
Website: http://www.knowtions.com/
Phone: **Email:** hello@knowtions.com
City: Toronto **State:** ON **PC:** **Country:** Canada
Year Established: 2013 **Status 2020:** Active
Industries: Artificial Intelligence for:, Enterprise Application Services for:, Machine Learning for:, Natural Language Processing

Company Name: Ladon Labs
Description: Ladon Labs offers a handheld barcode scanner which uses machine learning to identify produce items without the need for barcodes.
Website: http://ladonlabs.com/
Phone: **Email:** founders@phashtag.com
City: Toronto **State:** ON **PC:** **Country:** Canada
Year Established: **Status 2020:** Active
Industries: Artificial Intelligence for:, Machine Learning

Company Name: La: Kenya
Description: Building smart financial tools for the world.
Website: http://lake.finance/
Phone: **Email:** hello@lake.finance
City: Toronto **State:** ON **PC:** **Country:** Canada
Year Established: **Status 2020:** Active
Industries: Artificial Intelligence for:, Blockchain for:, ~ Banking and Financial Markets-Services (7), ~ Banking and Financial Markets-Services (7)

Company Name: Layer 6 AI
Description: Layer 6 enables enterprise clients to deploy the advanced Deep Learning solutions to accelerate their business through better use of data.
Website: http://layer6.ai/
Phone: **Email:** info@layer6.ai
City: Toronto **State:** ON **PC:** **Country:** Canada
Year Established: 2016 **Status 2020:** Active
Industries: Artificial Intelligence for:, ~ Banking and Financial Markets-Services (7), IT Managed Services for:, IT Managed Services

Company Name: Lemeister
Description: Sports Analytics, Algorithms, IoT Wearables & Broadcasting Rights
Website: http://www.lemeister.com
Phone: **Email:** info@lemeister.com
City: Toronto **State:** ON **PC:** **Country:** Canada
Year Established: 2016 **Status 2020:** Active
Industries: Analytics for:, Internet of Things (IoT) for:, Predictive Analytics for:, ~ Arts-Entertainment-Recreation (4), Internet of Things (IoT)

Company Name: Likalo, LLC
Description: Embedded catalog and analytics solutions
Website: http://likalo.com
Phone: **Email:** info@likalo.com
City: Toronto **State:** ON **PC:** **Country:** Canada
Year Established: 2016 **Status 2020:** Active
Industries: Analytics for:, IT Managed Services for:, Machine Learning

Company Name: Little Robot Friends
Description: They are Cute, programmable robots for learning code electronics.
Website: http://littlerobotfriends.com/
Phone: **Email:** hello@littlerobotfriends.com
City: Toronto **State:** ON **PC:** **Country:** Canada
Year Established: 2016 **Status 2020:** Active
Industries: Artificial Intelligence for:, ~ Education (13), Machine Learning for:, Robotics

Company Name: Looka
Description: Looka is an artificial intelligence and machine learning company located in Toronto.
Website: http://logojoy.com
Phone: (888) 966-0917 **Email:** support@looka.com
City: Toronto **State:** ON **PC:** **Country:** Canada
Year Established: 2016 **Status 2020:** Active
Industries: Application Services for:, Artificial Intelligence for:, Machine Learning for:, ~ Media-Communications (41)

Company Name: Magemi Mining Inc.
Description: data analytics solutions for the mining industry
Website: http://www.magemi.com
Phone: **Email:** georgi@magemi.com
City: Toronto **State:** ON **PC:** **Country:** Canada
Year Established: 2017 **Status 2020:** Active
Industries:

Company Name: Massively.ai
Description: SaaS platform enabling publishers, agencies and brands to build and deploy automated and live conversations inside any digital ad unit.
Website: http://massively.ai/
Phone: (416) 703 2124 **Email:** info@massively.ai
City: Toronto **State:** ON **PC:** **Country:** Canada
Year Established: 2014 **Status 2020:** Active
Industries: Application Services for:, Artificial Intelligence for:, IT Managed Services for:, Business Software as a Service Apps (SaaS Apps)

Company Name: MatchFuel
Description: MatchFuel provides personalized game recommendations on Android by using GameOracle AI technology.
Website: http://www.matchfuel.com
Phone: 19059626069 **Email:** faisal@matchfuel.com
City: Toronto **State:** ON **PC:** **Country:** Canada
Year Established: **Status 2020:** Active
Industries: Artificial Intelligence for:, Mobile for:, ~ Professional Services (48)

Company Name: MBExperts, Inc.
Description: Biomedical Engineering
Website: http://www.mbexperts.co
Phone: 734-679-7187 **Email:** info@mbexperts.co
City: Toronto **State:** ON **PC:** **Country:** Canada
Year Established: **Status 2020:** Active
Industries: Artificial Intelligence for:, ~ Biotechnology (9), IT Managed Services for:, ~ Manufacturing-Electronic (30), ~ Manufacturing-Miscellaneous (34), ~ Professional Services (48)

Company Name: MeetScribe
Description: Smart AI Meeting Assistant
Website: http://meetscribe.io/
Phone: 647-230-1993 **Email:** contact@meetscribe.io
City: Toronto **State:** ON **PC:** **Country:** Canada
Year Established: **Status 2020:** Active
Industries: Artificial Intelligence for:, IT Managed Services

Company Name: Men: Turkey
Description: Mentr helps career switchers reskill for their next job.
Website: http://www.mentr.ai
Phone: **Email:** info@mentr.ai
City: Toronto **State:** ON **PC:** **Country:** Canada
Year Established: **Status 2020:** Active
Industries: Artificial Intelligence for:, ~ Education (13), ~ Education (13), Web for:, Machine Learning for:, ~ Human Resources (24), ~ Social Media (54)

Company **Name:** Meta
Description: Meta is an intelligent system that can read, understand, and reason over scientific and technical literature.
Website: http://meta.org
Phone: **Email:** hello@meta.com
City: Toronto **State:** ON **PC:** **Country:** Canada
Year Established: **Status 2020:** Active

Industries: Analytics for:, Artificial Intelligence for:, Big Data and Analytics for:, ~ Healthcare (20), Machine Learning for:, Predictive Analytics

Company Name: mettleAI
Description: Leveraging ML/AI to predict substance abuse relapse before it happens.
Website: http://mettleai.com
Phone: **Email:** hello@mettleai.com
City: Toronto **State:** ON **PC:** **Country:** Canada
Year Established: 2018 **Status 2020:** Active
Industries: Artificial Intelligence for:, ~ Healthcare (20), ~ Healthcare (20), ~ Healthcare (20), ~ Healthcare (20)

Company Name: Migrations.ml Inc.
Description: Migrations.ml is a cloud-based technology solution that generates credit risk analytics for public debt using big data and machine learning
Website: http://migrations.ml
Phone: (647) 239-0101 **Email:** info@migrations.ml
City: Toronto **State:** ON **PC:** **Country:** Canada
Year Established: 2019 **Status 2020:** Active
Industries: IT Managed Services for:, Machine Learning for:, Risk Management

Company Name: MIMOSA Diagnostics
Description: MIMOSA Diagnostics is an connected care platform which allows physicians to remotely monitor and triage patients with diabetic foot ulcers.
Website: http://mimosadiagnostics.com/
Phone: 844-646-6721 **Email:** info@mimosadiagnostics.com
City: Toronto **State:** ON **PC:** **Country:** Canada
Year Established: 2016 **Status 2020:** Active
Industries: Artificial Intelligence for:, ~ Biotechnology (9), ~ Healthcare (20), ~ Healthcare (20), ~ Healthcare (20), Mobile

Company Name: Mindful Lens
Description: Intelligent Retail Analytics
Website: http://mindfullens.co
Phone: **Email:** 36979@reference-encyclopedia-ai.net
City: Toronto **State:** ON **PC:** **Country:** Canada
Year Established: 2017 **Status 2020:** Active
Industries: Artificial Intelligence for:, E-Commerce

Company Name: Ml gap
Description: Ml Gap is to empower organizations using machine learning tools
Website: http://www.mlgap.com
Phone: 1 647 383 9633 **Email:** info@mlgap.com
City: Toronto **State:** ON **PC:** **Country:** Canada
Year Established: 2018 **Status 2020:** Active
Industries: ~ Banking and Financial Markets-Services (7), Machine Learning

Company Name: Morphio
Description: The World's First Advanced Marketing Security Software.
Website: http://www.morphio.ai
Phone: (647) 367-2457 **Email:** hello@morphio.ai
City: Toronto **State:** ON **PC:** **Country:** Canada
Year Established: 2015 **Status 2020:** Active
Industries: Analytics for:, Artificial Intelligence for:, Business Intelligence for:, Digital Marketing for:, Machine Learning for:, Security for:, Security

Company Name: Morrow -
Description: AI for planning your day
Website:
Phone: **Email:** 37020@reference-encyclopedia-ai.net
City: Toronto **State:** ON **PC:** **Country:** Canada
Year Established: 2015 **Status 2020:** Closed
Industries: Artificial Intelligence

Company Name: Mutuo Health Solutions
Description: SaaS
Website: http://mutuohealth.com
Phone: 647-951-2510 **Email:** info@mutuohealth.com
City: Toronto **State:** ON **PC:** **Country:** Canada
Year Established: 2018 **Status 2020:** Active
Industries:

Company Name: Naborly
Description: Intelligent credit reporting and scores.
Website: http://naborly.com
Phone: (844)622-6759 **Email:** contact@naborly.com
City: Toronto **State:** ON **PC:** **Country:** Canada
Year Established: **Status 2020:** Active
Industries: Artificial Intelligence for:, Big Data and Analytics for:, ~ Banking and Financial Markets-Services (7), ~ Banking and Financial Markets-Services (7), ~ Real Estate (49)

Company Name: Naudix
Description: We're reimagining the hiring and recruitment experience
Website: http://www.naudix.com
Phone: (1647) 629-7417 **Email:** stephen.beh@naudix.com
City: Toronto **State:** ON **PC:** **Country:** Canada
Year Established: 2017 **Status 2020:** Active
Industries: Artificial Intelligence for:, IT Managed Services

Company Name: Neatware
Description: ISV for Video, Mobile, AI, Cloud Technologies and Software Innovation
Website: www.neatware.com
Phone: **Email:** channel@neatware.com
City: Toronto **State:** ON **PC:** **Country:** Canada
Year Established: **Status 2020:** Active
Industries: Artificial Intelligence for:, Cloud for:, Mobile for:, ~ Media-Communications (41)

Company Name: NetraMark
Description: Combines proprietary QML/ML algorithms with cross-domain expertise to bring ML commercialization into reality
Website: http://netramark.com
Phone: **Email:** 37049@reference-encyclopedia-ai.net
City: Toronto **State:** ON **PC:** **Country:** Canada
Year Established: 2015 **Status 2020:** Active
Industries: Artificial Intelligence

Company Name: Neuromorph Inc.
Description: Quantum machine learning and neural rehabilitation for PTSD survivo: Serbia
Website: http://neuromorph-inc.business.site
Phone: (443) 515-1353 **Email:** cartik.sharma@utoronto.ca
City: Toronto **State:** ON **PC:** **Country:** Canada
Year Established: **Status 2020:** Active
Industries: Artificial Intelligence for:, ~ Education (13), ~ Healthcare (20), ~ Healthcare (20), ~ Professional Services (48)

Company Name: NextAI
Description: NextAI is a global innovation hub for artificial intelligence related venture creation and technology commercialization.
Website: http://www.nextai.com/
Phone: **Email:** info@nextai.com
City: Toronto **State:** ON **PC:** **Country:** Canada
Year Established: 2016 **Status 2020:** Active
Industries: Artificial Intelligence for:, IT Managed Services for:, Machine Learning for:, ~ Retail and Consumer Products (52), ~ Education (13)

Company Name: nmod: Spain
Description: nmodes offers AI solutions that personalize and scale the sales process of consumers.
Website: http://nmodes.com
Phone: 1(855) 552-5035 **Email:** 30925@reference-encyclopedia-ai.net
City: Toronto **State:** ON **PC:** **Country:** Canada

Year Established: 2010 **Status 2020:** Active
Industries: Artificial Intelligence for:, IT Managed Services

Company Name: NorthLabs
Description: North Labs is an R&D firm focused on pattern recognition and machine learning for urban planning, real estate, finance, and consumer retail.
Website: http://northlabs.ca/
Phone: **Email:** contact@northlabs.ca
City: Toronto **State:** ON **PC:** **Country:** Canada
Year Established: 2014 **Status 2020:** Closed
Industries: Machine Learning

Company Name: Nostrato Corporation
Description: Nostrato provides AI-assisted customer support and customer relationship management (CRM) to automate your business
Website: http://nostrato.com
Phone: **Email:** 37073@reference-encyclopedia-ai.net
City: Toronto **State:** ON **PC:** **Country:** Canada
Year Established: 2017 **Status 2020:** Active
Industries: Analytics for:, Artificial Intelligence for:, IT Managed Services

Company Name: NURL
Description: NURL develops proprietary AI models to improve efficiency, safety, and financial returns for smart cities, telecom, mobility, and security.
Website: http://nurl-ai.com
Phone: **Email:** shauna@nurl-ai.com
City: Toronto **State:** ON **PC:** **Country:** Canada
Year Established: 2019 **Status 2020:** Active
Industries: Artificial Intelligence for:, Machine Learning for:, Security for:, ~ Construction (10)

Company Name: Nytilus
Description: Nytilus is developing a novel computational imaging technology for augmented reality.
Website: http://nytilus.com/
Phone: **Email:** debanga@nytilus.com
City: Toronto **State:** ON **PC:** **Country:** Canada
Year Established: **Status 2020:** Active
Industries: Artificial Intelligence for:, IT Managed Services for:, ~ Professional Services (48), Robotics

Company Name: OptimiseLab
Description: Artificial intelligence married with musicianship creates recipe for hit music
Website: http://www.optimiselab.com/
Phone: **Email:** founder@optimiselab.com
City: Toronto **State:** ON **PC:** **Country:** Canada
Year Established: **Status 2020:** Active
Industries: Artificial Intelligence for:, ~ Arts-Entertainment-Recreation (4)

Company Name: Peersight
Description: Peersight helps job seekers get to know their colleagues before they accept an offer.
Website: http://www.peersight.com
Phone: 778-998-1153 **Email:** mike@peersight.com
City: Toronto **State:** ON **PC:** **Country:** Canada
Year Established: **Status 2020:** Active
Industries:

Company Name: perchbox
Description: Intelligent, could based learning strategies.
Website: http://perchbox.com
Phone: **Email:** info@perchbox.com
City: Toronto **State:** ON **PC:** **Country:** Canada
Year Established: 2015 **Status 2020:** Active
Industries:

Company Name: Phaseshift Technologies
Description: We discover new Bulk Metallic Glasses using Artificial Intelligence and Quantum Computing.
Website: http://www.thephaseshift.com
Phone: **Email:** fazal@thephaseshift.com
City: Toronto **State:** ON **PC:** **Country:** Canada
Year Established: 2019 **Status 2020:** Active
Industries: Artificial Intelligence for:, IT Managed Services for:, Machine Learning for:, ~ Education (13)

Company Name: Phenomic AI
Description: Develops computer vision tools for a faster and more accurate analysis of microscopy data.
Website: http://phenomic.ai/
Phone: **Email:** info@phenomic.ai
City: Toronto **State:** ON **PC:** **Country:** Canada
Year Established: **Status 2020:** Active
Industries: Artificial Intelligence for:, IT Managed Services for:, ~ Professional Services (48)

Company Name: PigeonLine
Description: We want you to stop wasting time building reports, so we built a platform that automates report building while respecting your data privacy.
Website: http://www.pigeonline.io
Phone: **Email:** hello@pigeonline.io
City: Toronto **State:** ON **PC:** **Country:** Canada
Year Established: 2017 **Status 2020:** Active
Industries: Artificial Intelligence for:, Machine Learning for:, Natural Language Processing for:, Predictive Analytics

Company Name: Pitstop
Description: PitStop is a platform that aggregates data and uses machine learning to perform predictive maintenance for vehicles.
Website: www.pitstopconnect.com
Phone: **Email:** info@pitstopconnect.com
City: Toronto **State:** ON **PC:** **Country:** Canada
Year Established: **Status 2020:** Active
Industries: Analytics for:, Artificial Intelligence for:, ~ Automotive (5), Big Data and Analytics

Company Name: Pixedate
Description: Pixedate is a social networking app that sets you up on spontaneous blind dates or meetups.
Website: http://www.pixedate.com/
Phone: **Email:** contact@pixedate.com
City: Toronto **State:** ON **PC:** **Country:** Canada
Year Established: 2017 **Status 2020:** Active
Industries: Predictive Analytics

Company Name: Plumlytics Social
Description: Social Media Marketing suite with the Power of Artificial Intelligence.
Website: http://www.plumlytics.com
Phone: **Email:** contact@plumlytics.com
City: Toronto **State:** ON **PC:** **Country:** Canada
Year Established: 2016 **Status 2020:** Active
Industries: Analytics for:, Artificial Intelligence for:, Web for:, Business Software as a Service Apps (SaaS Apps)

Company Name: PressureNet
Description: Pressurenet.io is company of cunsatency firm for the many way to resion to way to find this way.
Website: http://www.pressurenet.io
Phone: **Email:** android@thesunshine.co
City: Toronto **State:** ON **PC:** **Country:** Canada
Year Established: **Status 2020:** Active
Industries: Artificial Intelligence for:, ~ Energy and Utilities (14), Predictive Analytics

Company Name: Private AI
Description: Empowering privacy-preserving software development.
Website: http://www.private-ai.ca
Phone: **Email:** info@private-ai.ca
City: Toronto **State:** ON **PC:** **Country:** Canada
Year Established: 2017 **Status 2020:** Active
Industries: Artificial Intelligence for:, Cloud for:, Cloud for:, Cyber Security for:, Machine Learning for:, Natural Language Processing for:, Security

Company Name: Pure Strategy
Description: Pure Strategy provides the solution by analyzing the language data from interviews, call centres, sales systems.
Website: http://purestrategy.ai/
Phone: **Email:** info@purestrategyinc.com
City: Toronto **State:** ON **PC:** **Country:** Canada
Year Established: 2015 **Status 2020:** Active
Industries: Artificial Intelligence for:, ~ Customer Relationship Management (11), IT Managed Services

Company Name: Qassurance AI
Description: AI for customer support ticket automation and insights that help close the feedback loop between product and support teams
Website: http://qassurance.ai
Phone: **Email:** hello@qassurance.ai
City: Toronto **State:** ON **PC:** **Country:** Canada
Year Established: **Status 2020:** Active
Industries: Artificial Intelligence for:, Enterprise Application Services for:, Machine Learning for:, Application Services

Company Name: Qindom Inc.
Description: Premier Quantum Intelligence (QI) solution and application provider. At Qindom, we introduce you to the world of Quantum Intelligence!
Website: http://qindom.com/
Phone: 4164935098 **Email:** info@qindom.com
City: Toronto **State:** ON **PC:** **Country:** Canada
Year Established: 2018 **Status 2020:** Active
Industries: Artificial Intelligence for:, IT Managed Services for:, Machine Learning for:, ~ Education (13)

Company Name: Quantigo AI
Description: Quantigo AI is a provider of high-quality training data for computer vision models.
Website: http://www.quantigo.ai
Phone: 647-241-1299 **Email:** info@quantigo.ai
City: Toronto **State:** ON **PC:** **Country:** Canada
Year Established: 2018 **Status 2020:** Active
Industries: Artificial Intelligence for:, IT Managed Services

Company Name: QuantumSen: Sweden
Description: QuantumSense is an artificial intelligence company that provides a top semantic search engine that works on the sentence level.
Website: http://quantumsense.ai/
Phone: 41783106884 **Email:** contact@quantumsense.ai
City: Toronto **State:** ON **PC:** **Country:** Canada
Year Established: **Status 2020:** Active
Industries: Analytics for:, Artificial Intelligence for:, Big Data and Analytics for:, ~ Banking and Financial Markets-Services (7), ~ Insurance (25), Machine Learning for:, ~ Banking and Financial Markets-Services (7), Cyber Security

Company Name: Radium
Description: Radium is an IaaS company, providing High Performance Cloud computing to enable the development and deployment of Ai and Machine Learning
Website: http://radium.cloud
Phone: **Email:** Info@radium.cloud
City: Toronto **State:** ON **PC:** **Country:** Canada
Year Established: 2019 **Status 2020:** Active
Industries:

Company Name: Receptiviti
Description: The human understanding platform that enables organizations to make smarter people decisions using real-time psychological insights.
Website: http://receptiviti.com
Phone: **Email:** hello@receptiviti.com
City: Toronto **State:** ON **PC:** **Country:** Canada
Year Established: 2014 **Status 2020:** Active
Industries: Analytics for:, Artificial Intelligence for:, Machine Learning for:, Natural Language Processing for:, ~ Healthcare (20), Risk Management

Company Name: Rival.ai
Description: Rival-ai is an Esports company that provides industry standard scouting reports for teams & the betting community through the use of AI
Website: http://www.rival.ai
Phone: 416-333-4225 **Email:** james@rival.ai
City: Toronto **State:** ON **PC:** **Country:** Canada
Year Established: **Status 2020:** Active
Industries: Artificial Intelligence for:, ~ Arts-Entertainment-Recreation (4)

Company Name: RNDflo
Description: RNDflo is a blockchain-first startup that is focused on building robust DLT infrastructure to grow the Web 3.0 stack.
Website: http://www.rndflo.com
Phone: **Email:** 37303@reference-encyclopedia-ai.net
City: Toronto **State:** ON **PC:** **Country:** Canada
Year Established: 2016 **Status 2020:** Active
Industries: Artificial Intelligence for:, Big Data and Analytics for:, Enterprise Application Services for:, Business Software as a Service Apps (SaaS Apps)

Company Name: Rubikloud
Description: Rubikloud uses AI to deliver intelligent decision automation to enterprise retailers through its cloud-native platform.
Website: http://www.rubikloud.ai
Phone: **Email:** marketing@rubikloud.com
City: Toronto **State:** ON **PC:** **Country:** Canada
Year Established: **Status 2020:** Active
Industries: Artificial Intelligence for:, Big Data and Analytics for:, Cloud for:, ~ Retail and Consumer Products (52), ~ Retail and Consumer Products (52)

Company Name: Safe Lagoon
Description: Safe Lagoon's app and cloud AI engine provide a safer smartphone experience for children and peace of mind for their parents
Website: http://safelagoon.com
Phone: 416-964-9300 **Email:** info@safelagoon.com
City: Toronto **State:** ON **PC:** **Country:** Canada
Year Established: **Status 2020:** Active
Industries: Artificial Intelligence for:, Machine Learning for:, Application Services for:, ~ Education (13)

Company Name: SalesChoice
Description: SalesChoice is an AI SaaS-based predictive and prescriptive analytics company that increases the performance of business-to-business sales.
Website: http://www.saleschoice.com
Phone: (647)477-6254 **Email:** cindy@saleschoice.com
City: Toronto **State:** ON **PC:** **Country:** Canada
Year Established: **Status 2020:** Active
Industries: Artificial Intelligence for:, Business Intelligence for:, Machine Learning for:, Predictive Analytics for:, ~ Media-Communications (41), ~ Professional Services (48)

Company Name: Senso.ai
Description: Senso is a cloud-based AI platform which enables financial service providers to manage and grow their consumer credit portfolios.
Website: http://www.senso.ai
Phone: **Email:** hello@senso.ai
City: Toronto **State:** ON **PC:** **Country:** Canada

Year Established: 2016 **Status 2020:** Active
Industries: Artificial Intelligence for:, Big Data and Analytics for:, Machine Learning

Company Name: SharpestMinds
Description: SharpestMinds is a network of STEM students with proven machine learning skills.
Website: http://www.sharpestminds.com
Phone: **Email:** contact@sharpestminds.com
City: Toronto **State:** ON **PC:** **Country:** Canada
Year Established: **Status 2020:** Active
Industries: Artificial Intelligence for:, ~ Education (13), Machine Learning

Company Name: Sitata
Description: Sitata keeps you safe when you travel with real-time health & safety information & by connecting you to someone you trust if you need help.
Website: http://www.sitata.com/
Phone: (877) 571-1089 **Email:** 37402@reference-encyclopedia-ai.net
City: Toronto **State:** ON **PC:** **Country:** Canada
Year Established: 2012 **Status 2020:** Active
Industries: Machine Learning for:, ~ Government (19), Risk Management

Company Name: Solid State AI
Description: Solid State AI is building a SaaS platform for process and equipment engineers in complex manufacturing industries.
Website: http://www.solidstate.ai/
Phone: 416-988-7923 **Email:** info@solidstate.ai
City: Toronto **State:** ON **PC:** **Country:** Canada
Year Established: 2017 **Status 2020:** Active
Industries: Artificial Intelligence for:, Business Software as a Service Apps (SaaS Apps)

Company Name: Sortspo: Kenya
Description: SortSpoke helps businesses turn their documents into data automatically.
Website: http://www.sortspoke.com
Phone: **Email:** sales@sortspoke.com
City: Toronto **State:** ON **PC:** **Country:** Canada
Year Established: **Status 2020:** Active
Industries: Artificial Intelligence for:, Machine Learning for:, ~ Professional Services (48)

Company Name: Spxtrm AI
Description: Spxtrm AI is an Autonomous Visual Intelligence Systems for Improving Elder Care Quality & Safety
Website: http://spxtrm.ai
Phone: **Email:** info@spxtrm.com
City: Toronto **State:** ON **PC:** **Country:** Canada
Year Established: 2017 **Status 2020:** Active
Industries: Artificial Intelligence for:, Big Data and Analytics for:, ~ Healthcare (20)

Company Name: Statflo
Description: Driving more revenue and stronger relationships in reta: Israel
Website: http://www.statflo.com
Phone: 1 (844) 782-8356 **Email:** hello@statflo.com
City: Toronto **State:** ON **PC:** **Country:** Canada
Year Established: **Status 2020:** Active
Industries: Artificial Intelligence for:, Big Data and Analytics for:, Enterprise Application Services for:, Machine Learning for:, ~ Retail and Consumer Products (52), ~ Media-Communications (41), ~ Telecommunications (56)

Company Name: StoreForce
Description: StoreForce provides Specialty Retailers with an integrated, flexible SaaS Solution that helps maximize the return on labor investment.
Website: http://www.storeforcesolutions.com
Phone: (416) 642-7438 **Email:** getintouch@storeforcesolutions.com
City: Toronto **State:** ON **PC:** **Country:** Canada
Year Established: 2010 **Status 2020:** Active
Industries:

Company Name: StreamWorx.AI
Description: StreamWorx.AI provides continuous intelligence on streams for businesses.
Website: http://streamworx.ai/
Phone: **Email:** info@streamworx.ai
City: Toronto **State:** ON **PC:** **Country:** Canada
Year Established: 2016 **Status 2020:** Active
Industries: Artificial Intelligence for:, Business Intelligence for:, IT Managed Services

Company Name: Stuck AI
Description: Hyperlocal D-OOH Advertising powered by Artificial Intelligence
Website: http://www.stuck.ai/
Phone: **Email:** naga@stuck.ai
City: Toronto **State:** ON **PC:** **Country:** Canada
Year Established: 2018 **Status 2020:** Active
Industries: Artificial Intelligence for:, ~ Media-Communications (41)

Company Name: Success.ai
Description: Success.ai is the conversational intelligence platform for the enterpri: Sweden
Website: http://success.ai
Phone: 647-998-3660 **Email:** kattan.shoukri@success.ai
City: Toronto **State:** ON **PC:** **Country:** Canada
Year Established: 2016 **Status 2020:** Active
Industries: Artificial Intelligence for:, IT Managed Services

Company Name: Suede Lane
Description: Suede Lane is redefining how we discover and buy original design.
Website: http://suedelane.com
Phone: **Email:** 37476@reference-encyclopedia-ai.net
City: Toronto **State:** ON **PC:** **Country:** Canada
Year Established: 2011 **Status 2020:** Active
Industries: ~ Arts-Entertainment-Recreation (4), Artificial Intelligence for:, E-Commerce for:, ~ Fashion (16)

Company Name: SuiteSpot Technology
Description: SaaS, Real Estate, AI, Turnover
Website: http://www.suitespottechnology.com
Phone: 647-797-1997 **Email:** hello@suitespottechnology.com
City: Toronto **State:** ON **PC:** **Country:** Canada
Year Established: **Status 2020:** Active
Industries: Artificial Intelligence for:, Cloud for:, ~ Real Estate (49), Application Services for:, ~ Real Estate (49)

Company Name: TasteGuru
Description: TasteGuru is a taste-based AI discovery software for retailers, brands and consumers.
Website: http://tasteguru.ai/
Phone: 647-823-8869 **Email:** taste@tasteguru.ai
City: Toronto **State:** ON **PC:** **Country:** Canada
Year Established: 2018 **Status 2020:** Active
Industries: Artificial Intelligence

Company Name: tealbook
Description: Peer driven supplier intelligence, discovery and identification; increasing scale and speed of procurement teams.
Website: http://tealbook.com
Phone: 866-620-6640 **Email:** rachel@tealbook.com
City: Toronto **State:** ON **PC:** **Country:** Canada

Year Established: **Status 2020:** Active
Industries: Artificial Intelligence for:, Business Intelligence for:, Collaboration Solutions for:, Databases for:, Machine Learning for:, ~ Administrative and Support Services (1), Supply Chain Management

Company Name: Teamsly
Description: SaaS platform
Website: http://www.teamsly.co
Phone: **Email:** michael@teams.ly
City: Toronto **State:** ON **PC:** **Country:** Canada
Year Established: **Status 2020:** Active
Industries:

Company Name: TellSpec
Description: Real time nondestructive solution for food testing, food-safety, food-authenticity and food-traceability
Website: http://tellspec.com/
Phone: 4807037359 **Email:** isabel@tellspec.com
City: Toronto **State:** ON **PC:** **Country:** Canada
Year Established: **Status 2020:** Active
Industries: Artificial Intelligence for:, Big Data and Analytics for:, Blockchain

Company Name: Tenstorrent
Description: Tenstorrent is building a new processor engineered to power machine learning and smart hardware.
Website: http://tenstorrent.com/
Phone: **Email:** info@tenstorrent.com
City: Toronto **State:** ON **PC:** **Country:** Canada
Year Established: **Status 2020:** Active
Industries: Artificial Intelligence for:, ~ Manufacturing-Electronic (30), Machine Learning for:, ~ Manufacturing-Miscellaneous (34), ~ Manufacturing-Electronic (30)

Company Name: ThinkSquare
Description: Intelligent career matching and optimized job search for young professionals.
Website: http://www.thinksquare.io
Phone: **Email:** hello@thinksquare.io
City: Toronto **State:** ON **PC:** **Country:** Canada
Year Established: **Status 2020:** Active
Industries: Artificial Intelligence

Company Name: This Century Software
Description: Inventor of new 100% unsupervised deep generative model that learns to create complex variations on imag: Spain
Website: http://thiscenturysoftware.com
Phone: **Email:** Contact@ThisCenturySoftware.com
City: Toronto **State:** ON **PC:** **Country:** Canada
Year Established: **Status 2020:** Active
Industries: Artificial Intelligence for:, Machine Learning for:, ~ Professional Services (48)

Company Name: thynq3D
Description: thynq3D is a Canada-based creative agency that develops mixed reality products for the enterprise.
Website: http://thynq3d.com/
Phone: **Email:** innovations@thynq3d.com
City: Toronto **State:** ON **PC:** **Country:** Canada
Year Established: **Status 2020:** Active
Industries: Artificial Intelligence for:, Augmented Reality for:, ~ Media-Communications (41), Enterprise Application Services for:, ~ Professional Services (48)

Company Name: TimeHero Inc.
Description: Plan daily tasks & projects automatically. Visualize risk and see the future with real-time forecasting powered by artificial intelligence.
Website: http://www.timehero.com
Phone: 18885644376 **Email:** bernie@timehero.com
City: Toronto **State:** ON **PC:** **Country:** Canada
Year Established: 2015 **Status 2020:** Active
Industries:

Company Name: TMT Analysts (To Market Technologies)
Description: To Market Technologies was formed to help enterprises deploy disruptive technology such as VR, AR & AI in a meaningful & profitable manner.
Website:
Phone: 416-725-2821 **Email:** info@TMTanalysts.com
City: Toronto **State:** ON **PC:** **Country:** Canada
Year Established: 2017 **Status 2020:** Active
Industries: Artificial Intelligence for:, Big Data and Analytics for:, IT Managed Services for:, Machine Learning

Company Name: Toronto Machine Learning Series (TMLS)
Description: A community of over 5, 000 practitioners, researchers, entrepreneurs and executives focusing on advanced ML research and business cases.
Website: http://www.torontomachinelearning.com
Phone: **Email:** info@torontomachinelearning.com
City: Toronto **State:** ON **PC:** **Country:** Canada
Year Established: 2017 **Status 2020:** Active
Industries: Analytics for:, Artificial Intelligence for:, Big Data and Analytics for:, Machine Learning

Company Name: Towards Data Science
Description: Data Science is a platform for thousands of people to exchange ideas and to expand our understanding of data science.
Website: http://www.towardsdatascience.com
Phone: **Email:** 37549@reference-encyclopedia-ai.net
City: Toronto **State:** ON **PC:** **Country:** Canada
Year Established: 2016 **Status 2020:** Active
Industries: Artificial Intelligence for:, ~ Personal-Religious-Civic (45), Machine Learning

Company Name: Triage
Description: Triage is an app using AI to instantly screen skin disorders using a smartphone.
Website: http://www.triage.com/
Phone: **Email:** 37565@reference-encyclopedia-ai.net
City: Toronto **State:** ON **PC:** **Country:** Canada
Year Established: 2015 **Status 2020:** Active
Industries: Application Services for:, Artificial Intelligence for:, ~ Healthcare (20), Application Services

Company Name: TritonWear
Description: TritonWear develops sports wearable system that helps swimmers track their performance and improve their training.
Website: http://www.tritonwear.com/
Phone: 800-249-0104 **Email:** info@tritonwear.com
City: Toronto **State:** ON **PC:** **Country:** Canada
Year Established: 2014 **Status 2020:** Active
Industries: Artificial Intelligence for:, ~ Arts-Entertainment-Recreation (4)

Company **Name:** TRYON Technology
Description: We use artificial intelligence to create new E-Commerce tool that can change the way people buy jewelry online.
Website: http://tryon.technology
Phone: 1 416 606 0163 **Email:** info@tryon.technology
City: Toronto **State:** ON **PC:** **Country:** Canada
Year Established: **Status 2020:** Active
Industries: Artificial Intelligence for:, Augmented Reality for:, E-Commerce

Company Name: Turnout
Description: Turnout is making every social gathering more personalized and interactive with machine learning.
Website: http://www.hypelabs.org
Phone: **Email:** info@hypelabs.org
City: Toronto **State:** ON **PC:** **Country:** Canada
Year Established: **Status 2020:** Active
Industries: Artificial Intelligence for:, Augmented Reality for:, Machine Learning

Company Name: Tuzzle
Description: SaaS business that predicts top performers with AI and developmental psychology and solves the talent sourcing problem.
Website:
Phone: **Email:** josh@tuzzle.ai
City: Toronto **State:** ON **PC:** **Country:** Canada
Year Established: 2019 **Status 2020:** Active
Industries: Artificial Intelligence for:, Enterprise Application Services for:, IT Managed Services for:, Business Software as a Service Apps (SaaS Apps)

Company Name: Unified Computer Intelligence Corporation
Description: Unified Computer Intelligence Corporation is a tools and services for rapidly prototyping and adding voice interaction to hardware devices.
Website: http://ucic.io
Phone: (855) 908-0706 **Email:** info@theubi.com
City: Toronto **State:** ON **PC:** **Country:** Canada
Year Established: 2012 **Status 2020:** Active
Industries: Human Computer Interaction for:, IT Managed Services for:, Internet of Things (IoT) for:, ~ Banking and Financial Markets-Services (7), Natural Language Processing

Company Name: Untether AI
Description: Ultra-efficient AI inference processor for edge devices.
Website: http://untether.ai
Phone: 647-772-2479 **Email:** us@untether.ai
City: Toronto **State:** ON **PC:** **Country:** Canada
Year Established: 2017 **Status 2020:** Active
Industries: Artificial Intelligence for:, ~ Energy and Utilities (14), ~ Energy and Utilities (14)

Company Name: Usful
Description: Be useful, change the world.
Website: http://usful.co
Phone: **Email:** clint@usful.co
City: Toronto **State:** ON **PC:** **Country:** Canada
Year Established: **Status 2020:** Active
Industries: Artificial Intelligence for:, ~ Energy and Utilities (14)

Company Name: Validere
Description: Validere builds software and hardware solutions that improve visibility and trust in oil testing.
Website: http://validere.com/
Phone: (647)938-6435 **Email:** admin@validere.com
City: Toronto **State:** ON **PC:** **Country:** Canada
Year Established: 2014 **Status 2020:** Active
Industries: Artificial Intelligence for:, ~ Energy and Utilities (14), Internet of Things (IoT)

Company Name: Vantage
Description: Vantage tracks the heartbeat of your store and delivers plain English advice you can act on with one click. We make success excitingly easy.
Website: http://gotvantage.com/
Phone: 1 646-513-4749 **Email:** support@gotvantage.com
City: Toronto **State:** ON **PC:** **Country:** Canada
Year Established: 2013 **Status 2020:** Active
Industries: Analytics for:, Predictive Analytics

Company Name: Vector Institute
Description: Vector Institute focuses on the transformative field of artificial intelligence, excelling in machine and deep learning.
Website: http://vectorinstitute.ai/
Phone: **Email:** info@vectorinstitute.ai
City: Toronto **State:** ON **PC:** **Country:** Canada
Year Established: 2017 **Status 2020:** Active
Industries:

Company Name: Verve.ai
Description: Verve.ai opertes as an augmented intelligence data platform.
Website: http://verve.ai/
Phone: 800.821.1365 **Email:** hello@verve.ai
City: Toronto **State:** ON **PC:** **Country:** Canada
Year Established: 2016 **Status 2020:** Active
Industries: Artificial Intelligence

Company Name: VetSuccess
Description: VetSuccess, a company that specializes in data analytics and machine learning.
Website: http://vetsuccess.com/
Phone: **Email:** support@vetsuccess.com
City: Toronto **State:** ON **PC:** **Country:** Canada
Year Established: 2011 **Status 2020:** Active
Industries: Artificial Intelligence for:, ~ Life Sciences (27)

Company Name: VtiSystems
Description: sensor fusion platform
Website: http://www.vtisystems.com
Phone: 4166287095 x 2115 **Email:** mmavinkurve@vtisystems.com
City: Toronto **State:** ON **PC:** **Country:** Canada
Year Established: 2012 **Status 2020:** Closed
Industries: Machine Learning

Company Name: VTREND: SOUTH AFRICA
Description: Social Shopping - Personalized
Website: http://www.vtrendza.com
Phone: 416 702 4312 **Email:** info@vtrendza.com
City: Toronto **State:** ON **PC:** **Country:** Canada
Year Established: **Status 2020:** Active
Industries: Artificial Intelligence for:, E-Commerce for:, ~ Social Media (54), ~ Retail and Consumer Products (52)

Company Name: WatrHub
Description: WatrHub is a Digital Intelligence company that delivers custom insights into your best sales opportunities in U.S. municipal water markets.
Website: www.watrhub.com
Phone: **Email:** info@watrhub.com
City: Toronto **State:** ON **PC:** **Country:** Canada
Year Established: **Status 2020:** Active
Industries: Analytics for:, Artificial Intelligence for:, Big Data and Analytics for:, ~ Waste Management and Remediation Services (59)

Company **Name:** Wherego
Description: Wherego helps Chinese tourists discover and enjoy Canada as a Chinese-friendly destination.
Website: http://wewherego.com
Phone: **Email:** contact@wewherego.com
City: Toronto **State:** ON **PC:** **Country:** Canada
Year Established: **Status 2020:** Active
Industries: Artificial Intelligence for:, IT Managed Services for:, ~ Travel and Transportation (58)

Company Name: Whirlsca:
Description: Whirlscape high-tech startup with roots in human-computer interaction (HCI) and advanced machine learning/computational linguistics.
Website: http://whirlscape.com/
Phone: **Email:** 37668@reference-encyclopedia-ai.net
City: Toronto **State:** ON **PC:** **Country:** Canada
Year Established: 2012 **Status 2020:** Active
Industries: Artificial Intelligence for:, IT Managed Services for:, Machine Learning

Company Name: Winterlight Labs
Description: Winterlight builds technology that can quickly and accurately detect signs of cognitive impairment from a sample of speech.
Website: http://www.winterlightlabs.com/
Phone: **Email:** 37676@reference-encyclopedia-ai.net
City: Toronto **State:** ON **PC:** **Country:** Canada
Year Established: 2015 **Status 2020:** Active
Industries: Artificial Intelligence for:, IT Managed Services for:, Machine Learning for:, Business Intelligence for:, Speech Recognition

Company Name: Wirkn
Description: End to End Mobile, Video and AI Solution for Recruiting and Connnecting your WorkPlace
Website: http://www.wirkn.com
Phone: (416) 999-3195 **Email:** todd@wirkn.com
City: Toronto **State:** ON **PC:** **Country:** Canada
Year Established: 2014 **Status 2020:** Active
Industries: Artificial Intelligence for:, Mobile

Company Name: Wisely
Description: Wisely provides fundraising enablement software that accelerates nonprofit fundraising, helped by artificial intelligence.
Website: http://fundraisewisely.com/
Phone: **Email:** hello@fundraisewisely.com
City: Toronto **State:** ON **PC:** **Country:** Canada
Year Established: 2017 **Status 2020:** Active
Industries: Artificial Intelligence

Company Name: Wondeur Ai
Description: Wondeur is data-driven, unbiased and powered by art historians.
Website: http://wondeur.ai
Phone: **Email:** contact@wondeur.ai
City: Toronto **State:** ON **PC:** **Country:** Canada
Year Established: **Status 2020:** Active
Industries: Artificial Intelligence for:, Machine Learning

Company Name: Worthwhile Industries Campus: Spain
Description: We build self-sufficient, sustainable automated communities that build high-quality low-cost export wealth while we sleep.
Website: http://WorthwhileInc.com
Phone: 416-915-3193 **Email:** info@worthwhileinc.com
City: Toronto **State:** ON **PC:** **Country:** Canada
Year Established: **Status 2020:** Active
Industries: Artificial Intelligence for:, ~ Construction (10), ~ Transportation and Logistics (57), ~ Transportation and Logistics (57), E-Commerce for:, ~ Transportation and Logistics (57), ~ Food and Beverage (17), ~ Transportation and Logistics (57), ~ Manufacturing-Machi

Company Name: Wysdom
Description: They provide one place to listen and understand the customer.
Website: http://wysdom.ai/
Phone: 647 559 9190 **Email:** marketing@wysdom.ai
City: Toronto **State:** ON **PC:** **Country:** Canada
Year Established: **Status 2020:** Active
Industries: Artificial Intelligence for:, ~ Education (13)

Company Name: Wysdom.AI
Description: Conversational AI as a Service
Website: http://wysdom.ai/
Phone: 647 559 9190 **Email:** marketing@wysdom.ai
City: Toronto **State:** ON **PC:** **Country:** Canada
Year Established: 2012 **Status 2020:** Active
Industries:

Company Name: Xanadu
Description: Quantum Computing
Website: http://www.xanadu.ai
Phone: **Email:** hello@xanadu.ai
City: Toronto **State:** ON **PC:** **Country:** Canada
Year Established: **Status 2020:** Active
Industries: Artificial Intelligence for:, Big Data and Analytics for:, ~ Manufacturing-Electronic (30), ~ Professional Services (48)

Company Name: Xesto
Description: A machine learning platform making gesture recognition and AI application development easy, quick and increasingly more precise.
Website: http://xesto.io
Phone: **Email:** 37695@reference-encyclopedia-ai.net
City: Toronto **State:** ON **PC:** **Country:** Canada
Year Established: 2016 **Status 2020:** Active
Industries: Artificial Intelligence for:, Augmented Reality for:, Computer Vision for:, Machine Learning for:, Virtual Reality (VR)

Company Name: XR Ignite
Description: XR Ignite is a community hub and virtual accelerator for startups, studios, and developers to connect with corporate customers.
Website: http://xrignite.com/
Phone: **Email:** info@xrignite.com
City: Toronto **State:** ON **PC:** **Country:** Canada
Year Established: 2019 **Status 2020:** Active
Industries: Augmented Reality for:, Machine Learning for:, Automation for:, Virtual Reality (VR)

Company Name: zeroone.ai
Description: We make AI-driven financial products on the decentralized ecosystem.
Website: http://www.zeroone.ai
Phone: **Email:** zeroone.ai@zeroone.ai
City: Toronto **State:** ON **PC:** **Country:** Canada
Year Established: **Status 2020:** Active
Industries: Artificial Intelligence for:, ~ Banking and Financial Markets-Services (7), ~ Banking and Financial Markets-Services (7)

Company Name: Zoom.ai
Description: Automated Assistant for Your Workday
Website: http://zoom.ai
Phone: **Email:** hello@zoom.ai
City: Toronto **State:** ON **PC:** **Country:** Canada
Year Established: **Status 2020:** Active
Industries: Artificial Intelligence for:, Application Services

Company Name: 99robotics Inc.
Description: Robotics Software Development
Website: https://99robotics.com/
Phone: **Email:** noobaca2@gmail.com
City: Waterloo **State:** ON **PC:** **Country:** Canada
Year Established: 2018 **Status 2020:** Active
Industries: Artificial Intelligence

Company Name: Applied Brain Research Inc.
Description: ABR makes Nengo, the world's most advanced neuromoprhic compiler, runtime and libraries for the emerging space of low-power neuromorphic computing.
Website: http://www.appliedbrainresearch.com
Phone: 4165058973 **Email:** peter.suma@appliedbrainresearch.com
City: Waterloo **State:** ON **Zip:** N2L3G5 **Country**: Canada
Year Established: **Status 2020:** Active
Industries: Artificial Intelligence for:, ~ Aerospace and Defense (2), ~ Automotive (5), ~ Autonomous Vehicles (6), ~ Life Sciences (27), ~ Manufacturing-Electronic (30), ~ Manufacturing-General (31), ~ Manufacturing-Machinery (32), Automation for:, ~ Aerospace and Defense (3

Company Name: Ark Paradigm
Description: Ark Paradigm is regulatory intelligence service for those who need to report financial material free of errors and omissions.
Website: http://www.arkparadigm.com/
Phone: **Email:** murraylove@arkparadigm.com
City: Waterloo **State:** ON **PC:** **Country:** Canada
Year Established: **Status 2020:** Active
Industries: Analytics for:, Artificial Intelligence for:, ~ Banking and Financial Markets-Services (7)

Company Name: Betterwor:Thailand
Description: Betterworth is a cognitive AI platform for the financial services industry
Website: http://www.betterworth.com
Phone: 416-410-0360 **Email:** info@betterworth.com
City: Waterloo **State:** ON **PC:** **Country:** Canada
Year Established: 2018 **Status 2020:** Active
Industries: Artificial Intelligence for:, ~ Banking and Financial Markets-Services (7)

Company Name: Blue Lion Labs
Description: Blue Lion Labs is made up of a dedicated team of experienced experts in Artificial Intelligence and Water Quality.
Website:
Phone: **Email:** 36179@reference-encyclopedia-ai.net
City: Waterloo **State:** ON **PC:** **Country:** Canada
Year Established: 2009 **Status 2020:** Active
Industries: Artificial Intelligence for:, Business Process and Operations for:, ~ Waste Management and Remediation Services (59)

Company Name: Brink Bionics
Description: Brink Bionics is developing bionic arms with machine learning that integrate with the human body.
Website: http://www.brinkbionics.com/
Phone: **Email:** 36210@reference-encyclopedia-ai.net
City: Waterloo **State:** ON **PC:** **Country:** Canada
Year Established: 2018 **Status 2020:** Active
Industries: Artificial Intelligence for:, ~ Education (13), ~ Healthcare (20)

Company Name: Chillwall AI
Description: Disruptive New Desire Prediction AI. Deep Learning Personality AI Concierge predicting your customers desires and interests.
Website: http://www.chillwall.ai/
Phone: **Email:** hello@chillwall.ai
City: Waterloo **State:** ON **PC:** **Country:** Canada
Year Established: 2015 **Status 2020:** Active
Industries: Artificial Intelligence for:, Enterprise Application Services for:, Natural Language Processing for:, Predictive Analytics for:, Business Software as a Service Apps (SaaS Apps) for:, Business Software as a Service Apps (SaaS Apps) for:, Web for:, ~ Travel and : Turkey

Company Name: ClearVoxel
Description: ClearVoxel is creating a human-in-the-loop platform so that radiologists may diagnose patients more quickly and accurately using AI.
Website: http://clearvoxel.com/
Phone: 1 02263503595 **Email:** hello@clearvoxel.com
City: Waterloo **State:** ON **PC:** **Country:** Canada
Year Established: **Status 2020:** Active
Industries: Artificial Intelligence for:, ~ Healthcare (20), ~ Healthcare (20), Machine Learning for:, ~ Healthcare (20), ~ Manufacturing-Medical Equipment-Supplies (33)

Company Name: DarwinAI
Description: DarwinAI's Generative Synthesis 'AI building AI' technology enables optimized and explainable deep learning.
Website: http://darwinai.ca/
Phone: **Email:** 36379@reference-encyclopedia-ai.net
City: Waterloo **State:** ON **PC:** **Country:** Canada
Year Established: 2017 **Status 2020:** Active
Industries:

Company Name: DeepSubconscious.ai Inc.
Description: We are dedicated to solving high performance at scale and AI for humankind.
Website: http://www.deepsubconscious.com
Phone: 226 606 8613 **Email:** info@deepsubconscious.com
City: Waterloo **State:** ON **PC:** **Country:** Canada
Year Established: 2015 **Status 2020:** Active
Industries: Artificial Intelligence

Company Name: GainX
Description: Advanced Analytics to Help Executives Manage Complex Change
Website: http://www.gainx.com
Phone: 44 7403 773577 **Email:** nofear@gainx.com
City: Waterloo **State:** ON **PC:** **Country:** Canada
Year Established: 2012 **Status 2020:** Active
Industries: Analytics for:, Big Data and Analytics for:, Business Intelligence for:, Data Management for:, Enterprise Application Services for:, Predictive Analytics

Company Name: Gnowi: Sweden
Description: Predictive Real Estate analytics & Insights | Big Data | Saas | ML | AI | Predictive Analytics | Fintech
Website: http://gnowise.com
Phone: (226)666-2566 **Email:** info@gnowise.com
City: Waterloo **State:** ON **PC:** **Country:** Canada
Year Established: 2016 **Status 2020:** Active
Industries: Predictive Analytics

Company Name: Guard Ex
Description: Guard Ex provides a portable device which uses artificial intelligence & one's physiological indicators to detect real-time impairment.
Website: http://www.guard-ex.net/
Phone: **Email:** info@guard-ex.net
City: Waterloo **State:** ON **PC:** **Country:** Canada
Year Established: 2017 **Status 2020:** Active
Industries: Artificial Intelligence for:, ~ Government (19), Machine Learning

Company Name: Hound Alert
Description: We create AI enabled security solutions. Our current product is a remote outdoor security solution that minimizes false alarms.
Website:
Phone: **Email:** 36708@reference-encyclopedia-ai.net
City: Waterloo **State:** ON **PC:** **Country:** Canada
Year Established: 2018 **Status 2020:** Active
Industries: Artificial Intelligence for:, Machine Learning for:, Security

Company Name: Kiite
Description: AI for Sales Enablement
Website: http://kiite.ai
Phone: 1-800-499-2659 **Email:** info@kiite.ai
City: Waterloo **State:** ON **PC:** **Country:** Canada
Year Established: **Status 2020:** Active
Industries: Artificial Intelligence for:, ~ Media-Communications (41), Automation

Company Name: Maluuba
Description: Maluuba conducts research and develops state-of-the-art deep learning algorithms to teach literacy to machines.
Website: http://www.maluuba.com
Phone: (416)849-566 **Email:** contact@maluuba.com
City: Waterloo **State:** ON **PC:** **Country:** Canada
Year Established: **Status 2020:** Active
Industries: Artificial Intelligence for:, Machine Learning for:, Natural Language Processing for:, Speech Recognition

Company Name: Navi
Description: Navi builds innovative AI-powered content analysis and content curation products for the media industry.
Website: http://usenavi.com
Phone: **Email:** hello@usenavi.com
City: Waterloo **State:** ON **PC:** **Country:** Canada
Year Established: **Status 2020:** Active
Industries: Artificial Intelligence for:, Machine Learning for:, Mobile

Company Name: NURO CORP.
Description: NURO is a Waterloo scale-up specializing in Neuroscience and Neurotechnology. NURO is the manufacturer of NUOS, the Neural Operating System.
Website: www.nuro.ca
Phone: **Email:** hello@nuro.ca
City: Waterloo **State:** ON **PC:** **Country:** Canada
Year Established: **Status 2020:** Active
Industries: Artificial Intelligence for:, ~ Biotechnology (9), Human Computer Interaction for:, Machine Learning for:, ~ Healthcare (20), ~ Life Sciences (27)

Company Name: Plum.io
Description: Plum combines AI and Industrial/Organizational Psychology to help companies hire, grow, and retain top talent.
Website: http://plum.io/
Phone: (855) 552-7326 **Email:** hello@plum.io
City: Waterloo **State:** ON **PC:** **Country:** Canada
Year Established: 2012 **Status 2020:** Active
Industries: Artificial Intelligence for:, Enterprise Application Services for:, Business Software as a Service Apps (SaaS Apps)

Company Name: Snapsort
Description: Snapsort offers an online platform that enables its users to find and compare cameras by its features.
Website: http://snapsort.com
Phone: 519 594 0036 **Email:** team@snapsort.com
City: Waterloo **State:** ON **PC:** **Country:** Canada
Year Established: **Status 2020:** Active
Industries: Artificial Intelligence for:, ~ Automotive (5), E-Commerce

Company Name: Springdel
Description: Data-Centric Mobile Device Management Platform Based on Federated Learning & Artificial Intelligence
Website: http://www.springdel.com
Phone: 1 844 636 6339 **Email:** hello@springdel.com
City: Waterloo **State:** ON **PC:** **Country:** Canada
Year Established: 2018 **Status 2020:** Active
Industries: Analytics for:, Artificial Intelligence for:, Big Data and Analytics for:, Cyber Security for:, Enterprise Application Services for:, IT Managed Services for:, Application Services for:, Machine Learning for:, Machine Learning

Company Name: Syngli
Description: Syngli is an educational technology startup that develops an online platform for teaching and learning efficiency.
Website: http://syngli.com/
Phone: **Email:** talk@syngli.com
City: Waterloo **State:** ON **PC:** **Country:** Canada
Year Established: 2014 **Status 2020:** Active
Industries: Big Data and Analytics for:, ~ Education (13), ~ Education (13), Natural Language Processing for:, Speech Recognition for:, ~ Education (13), ~ Education (13)

Company Name: Terrene
Description: Terrene is an AI engine that helps power your business.
Website: http://terrene.co
Phone: **Email:** info@terrene.co
City: Waterloo **State:** ON **PC:** **Country:** Canada
Year Established: **Status 2020:** Activc
Industries:

Company Name: YOURIKA
Description: YOURIKA is a conversational AI SaaS platfrom for learning
Website: http://www.yourika.ai
Phone: **Email:** info@yourika.ai
City: Waterloo **State:** ON **PC:** **Country:** Canada
Year Established: 2016 **Status 2020:** Active
Industries: Artificial Intelligence for:, ~ Education (13), ~ Education (13), Enterprise Application Services for:, Business Software as a Service Apps (SaaS Apps)

Company Name: Omnirobotic
Description: Autonomous industrial robots for High Mix, Low Volume manufacturers. Robots who can see, plan and execute.
Website: http://www.omnirobotic.com/
Phone: 4502326428 **Email:** sales@omnirobotic.com
City: Laval **State:** QC **PC:** **Country:** Canada
Year Established: 2016 **Status 2020:** Active
Industries: Artificial Intelligence for:, Computer Vision for:, ~ Manufacturing-General (31), Robotics

Company Name: FLATLAY
Description: FLATLAY is the visual storytelling marketplace for creators.
Website: www.flat-lay.com
Phone: **Email:** support@theflatlay.com
City: Levis **State:** QC **PC:** **Country:** Canada
Year Established: **Status 2020:** Active
Industries: ~ E-Commerce (12), Artificial Intelligence for:, Blockchain for:, ~ Media-Communications (41), E-Commerce for:, Image Recognition for:, Machine Learning for:, Application Services for:, ~ Social Media (115)

Company Name: Heatmine
Description:
Website: https://www.heatmine.com
Phone: **Email:** heatmine@heatmine.com
City: Levis **State:** QC **Zip:** G7A 4X6 **Country**: Canada
Year Established: **Status 2020:** Active
Industries:

Company Name: AIR (AI Redefined)
Description: AI Redefined is a software company dedicated to building a brighter, smarter future by improving the synergy between people and AI.
Website: https://www.ai-r.com/
Phone: **Email:** contact@ai-r.com
City: Montreal **State:** QC **PC:** **Country:** Canada
Year Established: 2017 **Status 2020:** Active
Industries: **Company Name:** allai
Description: app store of AI micro-services for the Canadian Insurance Industry want to be able to offer a quote by a pic of a car we have an AI for that
Website: http://www.allai.ca
Phone: **Email:** info@allai.ca
City: Montreal **State:** QC **PC:** **Country:** Canada
Year Established: **Status 2020:** Active
Industries: Artificial Intelligence for:, ~ Banking and Financial Markets-Services (7), ~ Insurance (25), ~ Insurance (25)

Company Name: Automat
Description:
Website: http://www.automat.ai
Phone: **Email:** info@automat.ai
City: Montreal **State:** QC **Zip:** H2X 2T6 **Country**: Canada
Year Established: **Status 2020:** Active
Industries: Artificial Intelligence for:, Human Computer Interaction for:, ~ Telecommunications (56)

Company Name: BioMindR
Description: A complete system to provide personalized bio-feedback enabled by new non-invasive and highly accurate wearable sensors.
Website: http://www.biomindr.com
Phone: **Email:** info@biomindr.com
City: Montreal **State:** QC **PC:** **Country:** Canada
Year Established: 2016 **Status 2020:** Active
Industries: Machine Learning

Company Name: Botler AI
Description: Botler AI uses the power of Artificial Intelligence to fight sexual misconduct, one incident at a time.
Website: http://botler.ai/
Phone: **Email:** support@botler.ai
City: Montreal **State:** QC **PC:** **Country:** Canada
Year Established: **Status 2020:** Active
Industries: Artificial Intelligence for:, IT Managed Services for:, Machine Learning for:, ~ Professional Services (48)

Company Name: Broid
Description: Broid enables bots & softwares to reach users on 20 messaging channels, including an interactive live chat with a single API integration
Website: http://www.broid.ai
Phone: **Email:** hello@broid.ai
City: Montreal **State:** QC **PC:** **Country:** Canada
Year Established: 2017 **Status 2020:** Active
Industries: Artificial Intelligence for:, Application Program Interfaces (APIs) for:, Application Services for:, Natural Language Processing for:, Application Services

Company Name: Brossard App Design
Description: Brossard App Design, designs, builds and develops very successful mobile and web applications for start-ups and enterprises.
Website: http://www.brossarddesign.com/
Phone: 1.514.970.8998 **Email:** direction@brossarddesign.com
City: Montreal **State:** QC **PC:** **Country:** Canada
Year Established: 2013 **Status 2020:** Active
Industries: Artificial Intelligence for:, Application Services for:, Web

Company Name: C2: ROMANIA
Description: Privacy-aware video analytics using proprietary edge-cloud AI for Physical Retail, Mall, Smart City and Enterprise Market.
Website: http://c2ro.com
Phone: (438) 380-5445 **Email:** Info@c2ro.com
City: Montreal **State:** QC **PC:** **Country:** Canada
Year Established: 2016 **Status 2020:** Active
Industries: Artificial Intelligence for:, Big Data and Analytics for:, Business Intelligence for:, Cloud for:, Computer Vision for:, Business Software as a Service Apps (SaaS Apps)

Company Name: Civalgo
Description: Predicts costs, delays & resources with artificial intelligence in the construction industry.
Website: http://civalgo.com/
Phone: 438-871-5287 **Email:** info@civalgo.com
City: Montreal **State:** QC **PC:** **Country:** Canada
Year Established: 2017 **Status 2020:** Active
Industries: Artificial Intelligence for:, ~ Construction (10), Enterprise Application Services for:, Business Software as a Service Apps (SaaS Apps)

Company Name: CONTXTFUL Technologies
Description: CONTXTFUL provide attention, viewability and business intelligence on the environment context of any digital audience.
Website: http://www.contxtful.com
Phone: 1-514-360-8714 **Email:** contact@contxtful.com
City: Montreal **State:** QC **PC:** **Country:** Canada
Year Established: 2017 **Status 2020:** Active
Industries:

Company Name: Crypto.Quebec
Description: computer security, geopolitics, privacy, information technology and intelligence.
Website:
Phone: **Email:** luc@crypto.quebec
City: Montreal **State:** QC **PC:** **Country:** Canada
Year Established: 2015 **Status 2020:** Active
Industries: Cyber Security for:, Application Services for:, Cyber Security

Company Name: Dataperformers
Description: Dataperformers is a world-class AI company focused on delivering operational AI solutions.
Website: http://dataperformers.com/
Phone: 514-907-0014 **Email:** contact@dataperformers.com
City: Montreal **State:** QC **PC:** **Country:** Canada
Year Established: 2017 **Status 2020:** Active
Industries: ~ Aerospace and Defense (2), Artificial Intelligence for:, Machine Learning for:, ~ Social-Environmental-Physical-Engineering Sciences (55), Natural Language Processing

Company Name: Deeplite
Description: Deeplite provides intelligent optimization software to make Deep Neural Networks faster, smaller and energy--efficient.
Website: http://www.deeplite.ai
Phone: **Email:** info@deeplite.ai
City: Montreal **State:** QC **PC:** **Country:** Canada
Year Established: **Status 2020:** Active
Industries: Artificial Intelligence for:, Computer Vision for:, Embedded for:, IT Managed Services for:, Machine Learning

Company Name: Delve Labs
Description: Autonomous, collaborative Artificial Intelligence-driven, continuous vulnerability assessment software.
Website: http://www.delve-labs.com
Phone: 844 353-3583 **Email:** info@delvelabs.ca
City: Montreal **State:** QC **PC:** **Country:** Canada
Year Established: 2014 **Status 2020:** Active
Industries: Artificial Intelligence for:, Collaboration Solutions

Company Name: Delve Security
Description: Delve Security develops and provides a complete, automated, AI-Driven vulnerability management solution.
Website: http://delvesecurity.com/
Phone: **Email:** info@delvesecurity.com
City: Montreal **State:** QC **PC:** **Country:** Canada
Year Established: 2014 **Status 2020:** Active
Industries: Artificial Intelligence for:, Automation for:, Application Services for:, Security

Company Name: Edutelly
Description: EduTelly - Education Platform for Leaders of New Age. We teach Blockchain, Data Science, Big Data Artificial Intelligence, Machine Learning
Website: http://www.edutelly.com
Phone: **Email:** x@edutelly.com
City: Montreal **State:** QC **PC:** **Country:** Canada
Year Established: 2017 **Status 2020:** Active
Industries: Artificial Intelligence for:, ~ Arts-Entertainment-Recreation (4), ~ Education (13), IT Managed Services for:, ~ Media-Communications (41)

Company Name: Element AI
Description: Element AI is an artificial intelligence company that gives organizations unparalleled access to cutting-edge technology.
Website: http://www.elementai.com/
Phone: 1 (514) 379-3568 **Email:** hello@elementai.com
City: Montreal **State:** QC **PC:** **Country:** Canada
Year Established: 2016 **Status 2020:** Active
Industries: Natural Language Processing

Company Name: EMANSO Technologies
Description: AI based educational mobile applications and R&D consulting services.
Website: http://emanso.io
Phone: 1 438 868 6732 **Email:** info@emanso.io
City: Montreal **State:** QC **PC:** **Country:** Canada
Year Established: 2018 **Status 2020:** Active
Industries: Artificial Intelligence for:, ~ Education (13)

Company Name: EniAI
Description: #MLsec
Website: http://www.eniai.com
Phone: **Email:** info@eniai.com
City: Montreal **State:** QC **PC:** **Country:** Canada
Year Established: 2019 **Status 2020:** Active
Industries: Cloud for:, Cyber Security for:, Machine Learning for:, Security

Company Name: Enkidoo AI
Description: Enkidoo is a Montreal-based company specializing in artificial intelligence for businesses using cloud computing applications.
Website: http://www.enkidoo.ai
Phone: 1 844-365-4366 **Email:** info@enkidoo.ai
City: Montreal **State:** QC **PC:** **Country:** Canada
Year Established: 2015 **Status 2020:** Active
Industries: Artificial Intelligence for:, IT Managed Services

Company Name: EruditeAI
Description: Augmenting Collective Intelligence
Website: http://www.erudite.ai
Phone: **Email:** info@erudite.ai
City: Montreal **State:** QC **PC:** **Country:** Canada
Year Established: 2013 **Status 2020:** Active
Industries: Artificial Intelligence for:, ~ Education (13), Application Program Interfaces (APIs) for:, Machine Learning for:, Natural Language Processing for:, Compute for:, Content for:, ~ Education (13)

Company Name: Evovest
Description: AI powered asset manager
Website: http://evovest.com/
Phone: **Email:** info@evovest.com
City: Montreal **State:** QC **PC:** **Country:** Canada
Year Established: 2017 **Status 2020:** Active
Industries: Artificial Intelligence for:, ~ Banking and Financial Markets-Services (7), Machine Learning

Company Name: Exagens
Description: Autonomous AI digital banking assistant with proven results increasing engagement, conversion rates & retention while lowering support costs
Website: http://www.exagens.com/
Phone: 438-387-4107 xt. 203 **Email:** exagens@exagens.com
City: Montreal **State:** QC **PC:** **Country:** Canada
Year Established: 2014 **Status 2020:** Active
Industries: Artificial Intelligence for:, ~ Banking and Financial Markets-Services (7), Application Services for:, Machine Learning for:, Predictive Analytics

Company Name: Faimdata
Description: Leading computer vision AI platform for location-based operators in retail, food service, hospitality, and finance.
Website: http://www.faimdata.com/
Phone: **Email:** info@faimdata.com
City: Montreal **State:** QC **PC:** **Country:** Canada
Year Established: 2017 **Status 2020:** Active
Industries:

Company Name: FlexPay
Description: FlexPay is an AI-driven decline salvage platform that uses machine learning to recover declined transactions.
Website: http://flexpay.io/
Phone: 1-800-273-4689 **Email:** info@flexpay.io
City: Montreal **State:** QC **PC:** **Country:** Canada
Year Established: 2017 **Status 2020:** Active
Industries: Artificial Intelligence for:, Machine Learning for:, IT Managed Services

Company Name: Flod
Description: Flod develops a surveillance device based on a proprietary AI technology.
Website: http://flod.ai/
Phone: **Email:** contact@flod.ai
City: Montreal **State:** QC **PC:** **Country:** Canada
Year Established: 2015 **Status 2020:** Active
Industries: Artificial Intelligence for:, Internet of Things (IoT)

Company Name: Fluent.ai
Description: Speech understanding and intent recognition that learns from speech, behavior and context, for embedded voice user Interfaces
Website: http://fluent.ai/
Phone: **Email:** contact@fluent.ai
City: Montreal **State:** QC **PC:** **Country:** Canada
Year Established: 2015 **Status 2020:** Active
Industries: Artificial Intelligence for:, Automation for:, Internet of Things (IoT) for:, Speech Recognition

Company Name: fuzzy.ai
Description: Easy machine learning for develope: Serbia
Website: http://fuzzy.ai
Phone: 1 (888) 602-9675 **Email:** support@fuzzy.ai
City: Montreal **State:** QC **PC:** **Country:** Canada
Year Established: 2014 **Status 2020:** Closed
Industries: Artificial Intelligence for:, Application Program Interfaces (APIs) for:, Machine Learning

Company Name: Gazelle.ai
Description: Gazelle.ai is the first application designed to use AI and big data to consistently identify companies poised for growth and expansion.
Website: http://gazelle.ai
Phone: 514-448-7777 **Email:** simon@gazelle.ai
City: Montreal **State:** QC **PC:** **Country:** Canada
Year Established: **Status 2020:** Active
Industries: Artificial Intelligence for:, Machine Learning

Company Name: HAXIO
Description: Empowering manufacturing companies with easy-to-deploy AI-based vision systems
Website: http://www.haxio.co
Phone: (450) 530-5218 **Email:** info@haxio.co
City: Montreal **State:** QC **PC:** **Country:** Canada
Year Established: 2018 **Status 2020:** Active
Industries: Artificial Intelligence for:, Computer Vision for:, Automation for:, Internet of Things (IoT) for:, Business Software as a Service Apps (SaaS Apps)

Company Name: Heyday
Description: Heyday is an AI-powered chat platform for e-commerce
Website: http://heyday.ai/
Phone: 1 514.267.5984 **Email:** humans@heyday.ai
City: Montreal **State:** QC **PC:** **Country:** Canada
Year Established: 2017 **Status 2020:** Active
Industries: Artificial Intelligence for:, E-Commerce

Company Name: HumanFirst
Description: HumanFirst is an AI-powered product that helps human chat agents type less, and reply faster. It's the opposite of chatbots.
Website: http://www.humanfirst.ai
Phone: 1 514 700-0276 **Email:** greg@humanfirst.ai
City: Montreal **State:** QC **PC:** **Country:** Canada
Year Established: **Status 2020:** Active
Industries: Artificial Intelligence

Company Name: Imagia
Description: Imagia is the indispensable AI healthcare partner for pharma, medical devices and clinical providers.
Website: http://www.imagia.com/
Phone: (438)800-0487 **Email:** info@imagia.com
City: Montreal **State:** QC **PC:** **Country:** Canada
Year Established: 2015 **Status 2020:** Active
Industries: Analytics for:, Artificial Intelligence for:, ~ Healthcare (20), ~ Healthcare (20)

Company Name: Intellogo Inc.
Description: Big Data for publishing industry: matching authors, publishers and readers with the right content.
Website: http://intellogo.com/
Phone: **Email:** 36794@reference-encyclopedia-ai.net
City: Montreal **State:** QC **PC:** **Country:** Canada
Year Established: 2014 **Status 2020:** Active
Industries: Artificial Intelligence for:, Big Data and Analytics for:, Content for:, Enterprise Application Services for:, Machine Learning for:, Natural Language Processing for:, Data Management for:, Data Management

Company Name: InVivo Ai
Description: InVivo AI is using artificial intelligence to streamline the development of new medications
Website: http://invivoai.com
Phone: **Email:** hello@invivoai.com
City: Montreal **State:** QC **PC:** **Country:** Canada
Year Established: 2018 **Status 2020:** Active
Industries: Artificial Intelligence for:, ~ Healthcare (20)

Company Name: IVADO Labs
Description: IVADO Labs is an AI-powered start-up.
Website: http://ivadolabs.com
Phone: **Email:** 36813@reference-encyclopedia-ai.net
City: Montreal **State:** QC **PC:** **Country:** Canada
Year Established: 2018 **Status 2020:** Active
Industries: Artificial Intelligence

Company Name: Jasper -
Description: Jasper is an AI-powered bot who recruits enginee: Serbia
Website:
Phone: **Email:** 36823@reference-encyclopedia-ai.net
City: Montreal **State:** QC **PC:** **Country:** Canada
Year Established: 2015 **Status 2020:** Closed
Industries: Artificial Intelligence for:, Machine Learning for:, Natural Language Processing

Company Name: KAIRA
Description: Kaira, is a Financial Wellness App that will help people achieve a better financial life by understanding their psychological profile
Website: http://kaira.ai/
Phone: 5147703033 **Email:** eric.macnicoll@kaira.ai
City: Montreal **State:** QC **PC:** **Country:** Canada
Year Established: **Status 2020:** Active
Industries:

Company Name: Keatext
Description: Keatext synthesizes large volumes of unstructured feedback data from multiple channels to produce one comprehensive custom dashboard.
Website: http://www.keatext.ai/en/
Phone: 1(514)312-2601 **Email:** info@keatext.ai
City: Montreal **State:** QC **PC:** **Country:** Canada
Year Established: 2015 **Status 2020:** Active
Industries: Analytics for:, IT Managed Services for:, Natural Language Processing for:, Data Management for:, Data Management

Company Name: Korbit.ai
Description: To enhance the efficiency of data science and ML training for business, Korbit uses AI tutoring system to teach corporate workers through personalized learning paths.
Website: https://korbit.ai/for-business
Phone: 4389333207 **Email:** ansona@korbit.ai
City: Montreal **State:** QC **Zip:** H2T 2A3 **Country**: Canada
Year Established: **Status 2020:** Active
Industries: Artificial Intelligence for:, ~ Education (13), Big Data and Analytics for:, ~ Human Resources (512), IT Managed Services for:, Machine Learning for:, Natural Language Processing

Company Name: LANDR
Description: The world's #1 machine-learning audio production platform, offering audio creators a suite of tools to support the lifecycle of creation
Website: http://www.landr.com
Phone: 514-840-9700 **Email:** contact@landr.com
City: Montreal **State:** QC **PC:** **Country:** Canada
Year Established: 2012 **Status 2020:** Active
Industries: Big Data and Analytics for:, Machine Learning for:, ~ Arts-Entertainment-Recreation (4)

Company Name: Letmeta
Description: We Help Businesses Automate Their Processes & Generate More Revenue Using Conversational Marketing
Website: http://letmetalk.ai
Phone: **Email:** info@letmetalk.ai
City: Montreal **State:** QC **PC:** **Country:** Canada
Year Established: 2019 **Status 2020:** Active
Industries: Artificial Intelligence for:, ~ Customer Relationship Management (11), Human Computer Interaction

Company Name: Local Logic
Description: Local Logic is an information company that empowers thoughtful decision making by providing insight into locations.
Website: http://www.locallogic.co/
Phone: (888)501-6208 **Email:** info@locallogic.co
City: Montreal **State:** QC **PC:** **Country:** Canada
Year Established: 2014 **Status 2020:** Active
Industries: Big Data and Analytics for:, ~ Real Estate (49), IT Managed Services for:, IT Managed Services for:, Predictive Analytics for:, ~ Real Estate (49)

Company **Name:** Lyrebird
Description: Lyrebird offers a new generation of speech synthesis technologies for developers.
Website: http://lyrebird.ai/
Phone: **Email:** contact@lyrebird.ai
City: Montreal **State:** QC **PC:** **Country:** Canada
Year Established: 2017 **Status 2020:** Active
Industries: Artificial Intelligence for:, Voice Recognition for:, Application Program Interfaces (APIs)

Company Name: Magicplan
Description: Magicplan is a combination of Augmented Reality and Artificial Intelligence enables on-site data acquisition, categorization and processing
Website: http://www.magicplan.app/
Phone: **Email:** support@magicplan.app
City: Montreal **State:** QC **PC:** **Country:** Canada
Year Established: 2010 **Status 2020:** Active
Industries: Artificial Intelligence for:, Augmented Reality for:, ~ Home (22), Internet of Things (IoT)

Company Name: Metalogique
Description: Metalogique is an artificial intelligence company located in Montreal.
Website: http://www.metalogique.com
Phone: **Email:** info@metalogique.com
City: Montreal **State:** QC **PC:** **Country:** Canada
Year Established: 2010 **Status 2020:** Active
Industries: Artificial Intelligence for:, IT Managed Services

Company Name: mind.me
Description: mind.me is an app which helps people who suffer from depression, diagnose, manage and predict their disorder.
Website: http://www.mind.me
Phone: (514) 342-0633 **Email:** funds@mind.me
City: Montreal **State:** QC **PC:** **Country:** Canada
Year Established: 2017 **Status 2020:** Active
Industries: Artificial Intelligence for:, ~ Healthcare (20), IT Managed Services for:, Internet of Things (IoT) for:, Mobile

Company Name: ML (MLplus)
Description: ML provides machine learning and deep learning solutions to businesses and organizations.
Website:
Phone: **Email:** 36995@reference-encyclopedia-ai.net
City: Montreal **State:** QC **PC:** **Country:** Canada
Year Established: 2016 **Status 2020:** Active
Industries: Artificial Intelligence for:, ~ Education (13), IT Managed Services for:, Machine Learning

Company Name: Mlplus
Description: Mlplus is a artificial intelligence consulting company.
Website: http://www.ml.plus
Phone: **Email:** 36996@reference-encyclopedia-ai.net
City: Montreal **State:** QC **PC:** **Country:** Canada
Year Established: 2016 **Status 2020:** Active
Industries:

Company Name: mnubo
Description: mnubo is an IoT company that provides data analytics solutions.
Website: http://www.mnubo.com
Phone: (514) 313-1400 **Email:** info@mnubo.com
City: Montreal **State:** QC **PC:** **Country:** Canada
Year Established: 2012 **Status 2020:** Active
Industries: Analytics for:, Big Data and Analytics for:, Internet of Things (IoT) for:, Machine Learning for:, Predictive Analytics

Company Name: Montreal AI Ethics Institute
Description: Montreal AI Ethics Institute is researching in the ethical, safe and inclusive development of AI.
Website: http://montrealethics.ai
Phone: **Email:** 37016@reference-encyclopedia-ai.net
City: Montreal **State:** QC **PC:** **Country:** Canada
Year Established: 2018 **Status 2020:** Active
Industries: Artificial Intelligence for:, ~ Government (19)

Company Name: Moov AI
Description: Consulting service
Website: http://moov.ai
Phone: 514-458-2069 **Email:** info@moov.ai
City: Montreal **State:** QC **PC:** **Country:** Canada
Year Established: 2018 **Status 2020:** Active
Industries:

Company Name: Motorleaf
Description: Greenhouse automation technology using artificial intelligence
Website: http://www.motorleaf.com
Phone: **Email:** info@motorleaf.com
City: Montreal **State:** QC **PC:** **Country:** Canada
Year Established: 2015 **Status 2020:** Active
Industries: ~ Agriculture (3), ~ Agriculture (3), Artificial Intelligence for:, Big Data and Analytics for:, ~ Agriculture (3), Automation for:, Machine Learning

Company Name: My Intelligent Machines
Description: Platform as a service helping biologists analyze genomic data.
Website: http://www.mims.ai/
Phone: **Email:** info@mims.ai
City: Montreal **State:** QC **PC:** **Country:** Canada
Year Established: 2016 **Status 2020:** Active
Industries: Artificial Intelligence for:, ~ Biotechnology (9), ~ Biotechnology (9), ~ Healthcare (20), ~ Customer Relationship Management (11), ~ Healthcare (20), IT Managed Services

Company Name: Nebula AI
Description: Decentralized AI Computing, AI Cloud
Website: http://nebula-ai.com
Phone: **Email:** contact@nebula-ai.com
City: Montreal **State:** QC **PC:** **Country:** Canada
Year Established: **Status 2020:** Active
Industries: Artificial Intelligence for:, Blockchain for:, IT Managed Services for:, ~ Professional Services (48)

Company Name: nGUVU
Description: nGUVU uses machine learning and gamification to make work experience better for contact center agents and reduces employee turnover.
Website: http://www.nguvu.com
Phone: (514)907-5988 **Email:** info@nguvu.com
City: Montreal **State:** QC **PC:** **Country:** Canada
Year Established: 2014 **Status 2020:** Active
Industries: Machine Learning for:, Business Software as a Service Apps (SaaS Apps)

Company Name: Perceiv Research, Inc.
Description: Transforming biopharma through intelligent patient selection
Website: https://perceiv.ai
Phone: **Email:** info@perceiv.ai
City: Montreal **State:** QC **PC:** **Country:** Canada
Year Established: **Status 2020:** Active
Industries: Analytics for:, Artificial Intelligence for:, ~ Healthcare (20), ~ Pharmaceuticals (46), Machine Learning for:, Predictive Analytics

Company Name: Redlive
Description: Our vision is to put technology at the service of academic acto: Serbia
Website: http://redlive.co/
Phone: **Email:** redlive314@gmail.com
City: Montreal **State:** QC **PC:** **Country:** Canada
Year Established: **Status 2020:** Active
Industries: Artificial Intelligence for:, ~ Education (13), IT Managed Services

Company Name: Semeon Analytics
Description: Semeon is a text analytics platform specializing in VOC data.
Website: http://www.semeon.com
Phone: 514-439-6400 **Email:** info@semeon.com
City: Montreal **State:** QC **PC:** **Country:** Canada
Year Established: 2013 **Status 2020:** Active
Industries: Business Intelligence for:, Predictive Analytics for:, Data Management

Company Name: Sia
Description:
Website: http://www.sia.ai
Phone: (617) 684-2600 **Email:** info@SmartBear.com
City: Montreal **State:** QC **Zip:** H3B 4W5 **Country**: Canada
Year Established: **Status 2020:** Active
Industries: Big Data and Analytics

Company Name: Silverbolt
Description: Silverbolt is an information technology company that offers AI-based technologies it specializes in 24/7 cyber detection.
Website: http://www.silverbolt.ai
Phone: **Email:** info@silverbolt.ai.
City: Montreal **State:** QC **PC:** **Country:** Canada
Year Established: 2017 **Status 2020:** Active
Industries: Artificial Intelligence for:, Business Applications for:, IT Managed Services for:, IT Managed Services

Company Name: SpotEv
Description: ..
Website: http://www.spotev.com
Phone: 1 (855) 531-0123 **Email:** info@spotev.com
City: Montreal **State:** QC **PC:** **Country:** Canada
Year Established: 2016 **Status 2020:** Active
Industries: Artificial Intelligence for:, Machine Learning for:, Natural Language Processing for:, Business Software as a Service Apps (SaaS Apps) for:, ~ Travel and Transportation (58)

Company Name: SweetData.io
Description: SweetData.io is a data marketplace allowing to search, buy, sell and download datasets aimed for machine learning and big data purposes.
Website: http://sweetdata.io
Phone: **Email:** hello@sweetdata.io
City: Montreal **State:** QC **PC:** **Country:** Canada
Year Established: 2020 **Status 2020:** Active
Industries: Big Data and Analytics for:, Data Management for:, Data Management for:, Data Management for:, Application Program Interfaces (APIs) for:, Application Services for:, Machine Learning for:, ~ Social Assistance-Non-Profits (53), ~ Social Assistance-Non-Profits (53)

Company Name: Tylio
Description: The affordable solution to increase brand visibility
Website: http://www.tylio.com
Phone: (514)773-0907 **Email:** info@tyl.io
City: Montreal **State:** QC **PC:** **Country:** Canada
Year Established: 2015 **Status 2020:** Active
Industries: Artificial Intelligence for:, Content for:, Web for:, Web

Company Name: Valital
Description: Valital validates talent data using AI to help companies make faster and more comfortable hiring decisions.
Website: http://www.valital.com
Phone: 514-825-4934 **Email:** contact@valital.com
City: Montreal **State:** QC **PC:** **Country:** Canada
Year Established: **Status 2020:** Active
Industries: Artificial Intelligence for:, Enterprise Application Services for:, IT Managed Services

Company Name: Workali
Description: Use A.I to accelerate the recruitment process so both employer and employee can be directly productive.
Website: http://workali.com
Phone: **Email:** info@workali.com
City: Montreal **State:** QC **PC:** **Country:** Canada
Year Established: **Status 2020:** Active
Industries:

Company Name: wrnch
Description: wrnchAI is a software platform to digitize human motion and behaviour from standard video.
Website: http://www.wrnch.AI
Phone: **Email:** paul.kruszewski@wrnch.AI
City: Montreal **State:** QC **PC:** **Country:** Canada
Year Established: 2014 **Status 2020:** Active
Industries: Artificial Intelligence for:, Augmented Reality for:, Computer Vision for:, Image Recognition

Company Name: AI.DA 2.0
Description: Artificial Intelligence, SaaS, Automated Marketing Technology,
Website: https://www.aida2.ca/
Phone: (514) 945-6708 **Email:** info@jsusolutions.com
City: Montréal **State:** QC **PC:** **Country:** Canada
Year Established: 2016 **Status 2020:** Active
Industries: Artificial Intelligence for:, Machine Learning for:, Predictive Analytics for:, Business Software as a Service Apps (SaaS Apps)

Company Name: Aifred Heal:Thailand
Description: Aifred Health is a Montreal-based startup using artificial intelligence to enhance treatment response in mental health.
Website: https://aifredhealth.com/
Phone: **Email:** info@aifredheal:Thailand
City: Montréal **State:** QC **PC:** **Country:** Canada
Year Established: 2017 **Status 2020:** Active
Industries: Artificial Intelligence for:, ~ Healthcare (20)

Company Name: Akitig
Description: We Grow Food On Trees. The Solution Is Delicious.
Website: https://www.akitig.com/
Phone: **Email:** info@akitig.com
City: Montréal **State:** QC **PC:** **Country:** Canada
Year Established: 2015 **Status 2020:** Active
Industries: ~ Agriculture (3), Artificial Intelligence for:, ~ Agriculture (3), ~ Food and Beverage (17), Robotics for:, ~ Social-Environmental-Physical-Engineering Sciences (55)

Company Name: Algolux
Description: Algolux is a Canada-based company building machine-learning software that optimizes imaging and computer vision systems.
Website: http://algolux.com/
Phone: (877) 424-9107 **Email:** info@algolux.com
City: Montréal **State:** QC **PC:** **Country:** Canada
Year Established: 2014 **Status 2020:** Active
Industries: Artificial Intelligence for:, Computer Vision for:, Machine Learning

Company Name: Audible Reality
Description: Audible Reality connects the world with unique, personalized and shared sound experiences through proprietary AI-driven 3D audio technology.
Website: http://www.audiblereality.com/
Phone: **Email:** info@audiblereality.com
City: Montréal **State:** QC **PC:** **Country:** Canada
Year Established: 2015 **Status 2020:** Active
Industries: Artificial Intelligence for:, Voice Recognition for:, ~ Arts-Entertainment-Recreation (4), ~ Arts-Entertainment-Recreation (4)

Company Name: North Scientific
Description: AI powered DevOps SaaS that instantly designs custom architectures for businesses based on their needs.
Website: http://www.northscientific.com
Phone: 4384963373 **Email:** info@northscientific.com
City: Montréal **State:** QC **PC:** **Country:** Canada
Year Established: 2016 **Status 2020:** Active
Industries: Artificial Intelligence for:, Cloud for:, Machine Learning for:, Enterprise Application Services for:, Business Software as a Service Apps (SaaS Apps)

Company Name: Perfiqt.com
Description: Perfiqt is AI that uses gamification to simplify finance to help people make smarter life decisions.
Website: http://www.perfiqt.com/
Phone: **Email:** 37157@reference-encyclopedia-ai.net
City: Montréal **State:** QC **PC:** **Country:** Canada
Year Established: 2016 **Status 2020:** Active
Industries: Artificial Intelligence for:, ~ Banking and Financial Markets-Services (7), ~ Banking and Financial Markets-Services (7), ~ Banking and Financial Markets-Services (7), Finance and Accounting

Company Name: Propulse Analytics
Description: Propulse analyzes the desires and intent of each consumer and provides the timeliest and accurate product choice available.
Website: http://propulseanalytics.com
Phone: **Email:** info@propulseanalytics.com
City: Montréal **State:** QC **PC:** **Country:** Canada

Year Established: 2015 **Status 2020:** Active
Industries: Natural Language Processing

Company Name: ProximityHCI
Description: THE Interaction REVOLUTION driven by A.I. We offer a software-only tool kit to enable HCI via machine-learning.
Website: http://www.proximityhci.com
Phone: **Email:** info@proximityhci.com
City: Montréal **State:** QC **PC:** **Country:** Canada
Year Established: 2017 **Status 2020:** Active
Industries: Machine Learning

Company Name: Quantolio
Description: We build AI-powered software for financial institutions
Website: http://quantolio.com/
Phone: **Email:** info@quantolio.com
City: Montréal **State:** QC **PC:** **Country:** Canada
Year Established: 2017 **Status 2020:** Active
Industries: Artificial Intelligence for:, ~ Banking and Financial Markets-Services (7), IT Managed Services for:, Machine Learning for:, Natural Language Processing

Company Name: Remedium
Description: Remedium is capitalizing on recent breakthrough developments in Artificial Intelligence.
Website: http://www.remediumai.com
Phone: **Email:** info@remediumai.com
City: Montréal **State:** QC **PC:** **Country:** Canada
Year Established: 2017 **Status 2020:** Active
Industries: Artificial Intelligence for:, ~ Biotechnology (9)

Company Name: Say Allo
Description: Say Allo is an intelligent dating app that guides singles to compatibility.
Website: http://www.justsayallo.com
Phone: **Email:** allo@justsayallo.com
City: Montréal **State:** QC **PC:** **Country:** Canada
Year Established: 2017 **Status 2020:** Active
Industries: Application Services for:, Artificial Intelligence for:, Machine Learning for:, Application Services for:, ~ Social Assistance-Non-Profits (53), ~ Social Assistance-Non-Profits (53)

Company Name: SenseAI
Description: AI and IIoT platform to optimize industrial operations.
Website: http://www.senseai.com/
Phone: 855-205-7324 **Email:** info@senseai.com
City: Montréal **State:** QC **PC:** **Country:** Canada
Year Established: 2016 **Status 2020:** Active
Industries:

Company Name: Skullscan
Description: Skullscan uses its own proprietary, AI-driven technology to reconstruct 3D models of humans from a single photo of their face.
Website: http://www.skullscan.com/
Phone: **Email:** hello@skullscan.com
City: Montréal **State:** QC **PC:** **Country:** Canada
Year Established: 2016 **Status 2020:** Active
Industries: Artificial Intelligence for:, Augmented Reality for:, Virtual Reality (VR)

Company Name: Stradigi AI
Description: Stradigi AI provides AI-powered solutions intended to bring innovation in AI technologies.
Website: http://www.stradigi.ai/
Phone: 514-395-9018 **Email:** info@stradigi.ai
City: Montréal **State:** QC **PC:** **Country:** Canada
Year Established: 2014 **Status 2020:** Active
Industries: Artificial Intelligence for:, IT Managed Services for:, Machine Learning

Company Name: Stratuscent
Description: Stratuscent is a start-up from Montreal, Canada that is developing an electronic nose platform.
Website: http://www.stratuscent.com
Phone: 833-247-3673 **Email:** info@stratuscent.com
City: Montréal **State:** QC **PC:** **Country:** Canada
Year Established: 2014 **Status 2020:** Active
Industries: Artificial Intelligence for:, Cloud for:, Internet of Things (IoT)

Company Name: truba.news
Description: The Personalized News Aggregator that cares about you
Website: http://truba.news
Phone: 514-992-2056 **Email:** info@truba.news
City: Montréal **State:** QC **PC:** **Country:** Canada
Year Established: 2017 **Status 2020:** Active
Industries: Artificial Intelligence for:, ~ Event Management (15), IT Managed Services

Company Name: Ubico
Description: AI-Powered Lead Engagement
Website: http://www.ubico.io/
Phone: **Email:** 37585@reference-encyclopedia-ai.net
City: Montréal **State:** QC **PC:** **Country:** Canada
Year Established: 2018 **Status 2020:** Active
Industries: Machine Learning for:, Automation

Company Name: UNRYO
Description: Industry's First Hybrid Multi-Cloud Monitoring Platform
Website: http://www.unryo.com
Phone: 1 (514) 900-1068 **Email:** info@unryo.com
City: Montréal **State:** QC **PC:** **Country:** Canada
Year Established: 2017 **Status 2020:** Active
Industries: Cloud for:, Enterprise Application Services for:, IT Managed Services for:, Predictive Analytics for:, Business Software as a Service Apps (SaaS Apps)

Company Name: Valital Technologies
Description: Real-time analysis of candidates' online behavior and automated confirmation of their work experience.
Website: http://www.valital.com
Phone: 1-866-973-8393 **Email:** contact@valital.com
City: Montréal **State:** QC **PC:** **Country:** Canada
Year Established: 2018 **Status 2020:** Active
Industries: Artificial Intelligence for:, Enterprise Application Services for:, IT Managed Services

Company Name: Vlyy AI Inc.
Description: Snap & Shop. Our AI takes care of the rest. Personalized fashion recommendations based on color, style and design.
Website: http://cocomint.io
Phone: **Email:** quaintanceai@gmail.com
City: Montréal **State:** QC **PC:** **Country:** Canada
Year Established: 2017 **Status 2020:** Active
Industries: Artificial Intelligence for:, E-Commerce for:, ~ Fashion (16)

Company Name: Voxedia
Description: Voxedia is helping content platforms to increase the user time spent by developing a content recommendation tool based on user's feelings
Website: http://voxedia.com
Phone: **Email:** info@voxedia.com
City: Montréal **State:** QC **PC:** **Country:** Canada
Year Established: 2015 **Status 2020:** Active
Industries: Artificial Intelligence for:, Big Data and Analytics for:, Computer Vision for:, Business Software as a Service Apps (SaaS Apps)

Company Name: Wastack
Description: Automating Landfill Operations
Website: http://www.wastack.com/
Phone: 1 438-405-6787 **Email:** julien@wastack.com
City: Montréal **State:** QC **PC:** **Country:** Canada
Year Established: 2016 **Status 2020:** Active
Industries: Artificial Intelligence for:, Machine Learning for:, ~ Waste Management and Remediation Services (59)

Company Name: We3, Meet People Inc
Description: Smart Tinder for Friends, privately matching 3 at a time.
Website: http://www.we3app.com
Phone: **Email:** support@we3app.com
City: Montréal **State:** QC **PC:** **Country:** Canada
Year Established: 2017 **Status 2020:** Active
Industries: Application Services for:, Artificial Intelligence for:, Application Services

Company Name: Zetane Systems Inc.
Description: SaaS software company producing products for the development of artificial intelligence & the processing of data used in training algorithms
Website: http://www.zetane.com
Phone: **Email:** info@zetane.com
City: Montréal **State:** QC **PC:** **Country:** Canada
Year Established: 2016 **Status 2020:** Active
Industries: Analytics for:, Artificial Intelligence for:, Big Data and Analytics for:, Data Management for:, IT Managed Services for:, Machine Learning for:, Natural Language Processing for:, Predictive Analytics for:, Predictive Analytics for:, Business Software as a Service

Company Name: Alworx
Description: Alworx is provides artificial intelligence solutions to increase productivity in the industrial, defense and aerospace sectors.
Website: http://aiworx.com/
Phone: (418) 653-8192 **Email:** info@aiworx.com
City: Quebec **State:** QC **PC:** **Country:** Canada
Year Established: 2011 **Status 2020:** Active
Industries: ~ Aerospace and Defense (2), Artificial Intelligence for:, Industrial Solutions

Company Name: Extend AI
Description: Understand, describe and optimize the physical world with our Spacetime AI system
Website: http://extend.ai
Phone: **Email:** hello@extend.ai
City: Quebec **State:** QC **PC:** **Country:** Canada
Year Established: 2018 **Status 2020:** Active
Industries:

Company Name: Neuraxio
Description: Deep Learning, Consulting
Website: http://www.neuraxio.com/
Phone: 4182627912 **Email:** info@neuraxio.com
City: Quebec **State:** QC **PC:** **Country:** Canada
Year Established: **Status 2020:** Active
Industries: Artificial Intelligence for:, Machine Learning for:, Natural Language Processing for:, Predictive Analytics

Company Name: OVA
Description: OVA is a B2B business that uses a virtual and augmented reality platform to create skill-building experiences.
Website: http://ova.ai/
Phone: 1(866)385-8687 **Email:** info@ova.ai
City: Quebec **State:** QC **PC:** **Country:** Canada
Year Established: 2014 **Status 2020:** Active
Industries: Artificial Intelligence for:, Augmented Reality for:, Machine Learning for:, Virtual Reality (VR)

Company Name: Umaneo
Description: Umaneo is a Quebec startup whose mission is to revolutionize the process of responding to public tenders through artificial intelligence.
Website: http://www.umaneo.com
Phone: 1418 999-3740 **Email:** Hello@umaneo.com
City: Quebec **State:** QC **PC:** **Country:** Canada
Year Established: 2016 **Status 2020:** Active
Industries: Artificial Intelligence for:, IT Managed Services for:, Application Program Interfaces (APIs) for:, Natural Language Processing for:, Business Software as a Service Apps (SaaS Apps) for:, Automation

Company Name: Waste Robotics
Description: Waste Robotics designs and delivers intelligent recycling robots to replace human pickers in recycling centres.
Website: http://wasterobotic.com/
Phone: 514-567-5239 **Email:** info@wasterobotic.com
City: Quebec **State:** QC **PC:** **Country:** Canada
Year Established: 2016 **Status 2020:** Active
Industries: Artificial Intelligence for:, Automation for:, ~ Social-Environmental-Physical-Engineering Sciences (55), Robotics for:, ~ Waste Management and Remediation Services (59)

Company Name: XpertSea
Description: Our AI-driven data management platform offers real-time insights making aquaculture more efficient and sustainable.
Website: http://xpertsea.com/
Phone: 1(581)981-9811 **Email:** info@xpertsea.com
City: Quebec **State:** QC **PC:** **Country:** Canada
Year Established: 2011 **Status 2020:** Active
Industries: ~ Agriculture (3), Artificial Intelligence for:, IT Managed Services for:, IT Managed Services for:, Machine Learning for:, Business Software as a Service Apps (SaaS Apps)

Company Name: Zilia
Description: Medical Device
Website: http://ziliahealth.com
Phone: 1-833-501-6996 **Email:** info@ziliahealth.com
City: Quebec **State:** QC **PC:** **Country:** Canada
Year Established: 2012 **Status 2020:** Active
Industries: Artificial Intelligence for:, ~ Healthcare (20)

Company Name: Experco: India
Description: Expercoin intends to build one of the world's largest decentralized networks of marketplaces called Republics.
Website: http://www.expercoin.com/
Phone: **Email:** 36535@reference-encyclopedia-ai.net
City: Grand Cayman **State:** Midland **PC:** **Country:** Cayman Islands
Year Established: 2018 **Status 2020:** Active
Industries: Artificial Intelligence for:, Blockchain for:, Web

Cayman Islands

Company Name: Tobius Group
Description: Advisory and Support for decentralized AI-based Predictive technologies and applications
Website: http://tobius.group
Phone: **Email:** hello@sentigraph.io
City: Grand Cayman **State:** Midland **PC:** **Country:** Cayman Islands
Year Established: **Status 2020:** Active
Industries: Artificial Intelligence for:, Big Data and Analytics for:, IT Managed Services for:, Machine Learning for:, ~ Professional Services (48)

Company Name: TokenAI
Description: On-demand crypto market and portfolio analysis platform driven by Artificial Intelligence (AI).
Website: http://TokenAI.io
Phone: **Email:** seth@tokenai.io
City: Grand Cayman **State:** Midland **PC:** **Country:** Cayman Islands

Year Established: 2017 **Status 2020:** Active
Industries: Artificial Intelligence for:, Blockchain for:, ~ Banking and Financial Markets-Services (7)

Chile

Company Name: XV Robotics -
Description: XV Robotics is to solve complex problems by developing robots with simple interfaces, with an innovative and scientific approach.
Website:
Phone: 56 9 9701 5632 **Email:** 37705@reference-encyclopedia-ai.net
City: Arica **State:** Arica y Parinacota **PC:** **Country:** Chile
Year Established: 2017 **Status 2020:** Closed
Industries: Artificial Intelligence for:, Automation for:, Robotics

Company Name: barQode
Description: Artificial Intelligence for Reta: Israel
Website: http://www.barqode.com/
Phone: **Email:** hello@barQode.com
City: Las Condes **State:** Santiago Metropolitan Region **PC:**
Country: Chile
Year Established: 2017 **Status 2020:** Active
Industries: Artificial Intelligence for:, Machine Learning

Company Name: NuLight
Description: NuLight develops IvY, an artificial intelligence lighting ecosystem that operates as a triple-impact ecosystem for lighting.
Website: http://www.nulight.cl/es_CL/
Phone: 56977965404 **Email:** contact@nulight.cl
City: Las Condes **State:** Santiago Metropolitan Region **PC:**
Country: Chile
Year Established: 2017 **Status 2020:** Active
Industries:

Company Name: AI Merchant
Description: Merchant efficiency software
Website: http://www.aimerchant.com/
Phone: **Email:** 35991@reference-encyclopedia-ai.net
City: Santiago **State:** Santiago Metropolitan Region **PC:**
Country: Chile
Year Established: 2010 **Status 2020:** Active
Industries: Artificial Intelligence for:, E-Commerce

Company Name: Altum Lab
Description: SaaS platforms to optimize inventory through intelligent blending
Website: http://www.altumlab.cl/
Phone: 56995070170 **Email:** info@altumlab.ci
City: Santiago **State:** Santiago Metropolitan Region **PC:**
Country: Chile
Year Established: 2017 **Status 2020:** Active
Industries:

Company Name: Arara
Description: Arara is the leading player in Wifi Analytics & Indoor Location Service
Website: http://www.arara.ai
Phone: 56222441177 **Email:** manu@arara.ai
City: Santiago **State:** Santiago Metropolitan Region **PC:**
Country: Chile
Year Established: 2015 **Status 2020:** Active
Industries: Artificial Intelligence for:, IT Managed Services for:, Machine Learning

Company Name: Awesome Jobs
Description: Awesome Jobs operates as a startup jobs portal.
Website: http://www.awesome.jobs
Phone: **Email:** 36126@reference-encyclopedia-ai.net
City: Santiago **State:** Santiago Metropolitan Region **PC:**
Country: Chile
Year Established: 2017 **Status 2020:** Active
Industries: Artificial Intelligence for:, Web

Company Name: BDataLabs -
Description: Open Big Data Analytics Platform focused on provided Big Data Analytics technologies available to small and medium compani: Spain
Website:
Phone: (123) 678-8674 **Email:** 36137@reference-encyclopedia-ai.net
City: Santiago **State:** Santiago Metropolitan Region **PC:**
Country: Chile
Year Established: 2016 **Status 2020:** Active
Industries: Big Data and Analytics for:, Machine Learning for:, Enterprise Application Services

Company Name: BioPub-WriteWi: Sweden
Description: The Next-Generation Artificial Intelligence Writing Platform for Students
Website: http://writewise.cl
Phone: **Email:** av@biopub.cl
City: Santiago **State:** Santiago Metropolitan Region **PC:**
Country: Chile
Year Established: 2015 **Status 2020:** Active
Industries: Artificial Intelligence for:, ~ Education (13), ~ Education (13), IT Managed Services for:, Machine Learning for:, Natural Language Processing for:, Data Management for:, Data Management

Company Name: Birdi
Description: Birdi is an app to buy and sell safer, much more comfortable and easier to use than existing solutions
Website: http://www.birdi.cl
Phone: **Email:** mauro@birdi.cl
City: Santiago **State:** Santiago Metropolitan Region **PC:**
Country: Chile
Year Established: 2016 **Status 2020:** Active
Industries: E-Commerce for:, ~ Transportation and Logistics (57), Machine Learning

Company Name: Cellter
Description: Cellter is developing Artificiall Intelligence solutions to speeding-up the search of life saving diagnostics, medicines and therapies.
Website: http://www.cellter.cl/
Phone: (5695) 600-0100 **Email:** info@cellter.cl
City: Santiago **State:** Santiago Metropolitan Region **PC:**
Country: Chile
Year Established: 2016 **Status 2020:** Active
Industries: Artificial Intelligence for:, ~ Biotechnology (9), ~ Healthcare (20)

Company Name: Classroomate
Description: Edtech
Website: http://www.classroomate.com
Phone: 56991384977 **Email:** ebobenrieth@classroomate.com
City: Santiago **State:** Santiago Metropolitan Region **PC:**
Country: Chile
Year Established: **Status 2020:** Active
Industries: Artificial Intelligence for:, ~ Education (13), ~ Education (13), ~ Education (13), IT Managed Services for:, Application Services for:, Machine Learning for:, ~ Life Sciences (27), ~ Education (13), ~ Education (13)

Company Name: Colektia
Description: Colektia is a digital platform that helps financial institutions create new digital collections models, based on artificial intelligence.
Website: http://colektia.com/
Phone: **Email:** hello@colektia.com
City: Santiago **State:** Santiago Metropolitan Region **PC:**
Country: Chile

Year Established: 2018 **Status 2020:** Active
Industries: Artificial Intelligence for:, ~ Banking and Financial Markets-Services (7), ~ Banking and Financial Markets-Services (7)

Company Name: Forcast
Description: Machine Learning, Software, Engineering, Systems, Data Science, Tech Transfer
Website: http://www.forcast.cl/
Phone: **Email:** contacto@forcast.cl
City: Santiago **State:** Santiago Metropolitan Region **PC:**
Country: Chile
Year Established: 2013 **Status 2020:** Active
Industries: Machine Learning

Company Name: Guara
Description: Guara is Natural Language Processing API that localizes products to fit in the Latin American market.
Website: http://www.guara.ai
Phone: **Email:** guara.devs@gmail.com
City: Santiago **State:** Santiago Metropolitan Region **PC:**
Country: Chile
Year Established: 2017 **Status 2020:** Active
Industries: Artificial Intelligence for:, E-Commerce for:, Natural Language Processing

Company Name: inCursu
Description: inCursu focuses on analyzing user behavior on web platforms SaaS B2B to measure userengagement and predict churn using machine learn.
Website: http://www.incursu.com
Phone: **Email:** contact@incursu.com
City: Santiago **State:** Santiago Metropolitan Region **PC:**
Country: Chile
Year Established: **Status 2020:** Active
Industries: Artificial Intelligence for:, IT Managed Services for:, Web for:, Machine Learning for:, ~ Professional Services (48)

Company Name: Intelligens
Description: Intelligens.ai, a provider of conversational AI for sales and marketing focused on the Latin American market.
Website: http://intelligens.ai/isa/index_en.html
Phone: **Email:** 36786@reference-encyclopedia-ai.net
City: Santiago **State:** Santiago Metropolitan Region **PC:**
Country: Chile
Year Established: 2016 **Status 2020:** Active
Industries:

Company Name: Kappo
Description: SaaS platform that helps smart cities increase the urban bicycle usage worldwide
Website: http://www.kappo.bi: Kenya
Phone: **Email:** ivan.paez@kpoapp.com
City: Santiago **State:** Santiago Metropolitan Region **PC:**
Country: Chile
Year Established: 2014 **Status 2020:** Active
Industries: Application Services for:, Big Data and Analytics for:, Predictive Analytics for:, ~ Construction (10), ~ Healthcare (20)

Company Name: MED360
Description: MED360 is SaaS that optimizes booking management for healthcare with the use of AI
Website: http://www.med360.cl
Phone: 562 2 8873700 **Email:** ifernandez@option.cl
City: Santiago **State:** Santiago Metropolitan Region **PC:**
Country: Chile
Year Established: 2017 **Status 2020:** Active
Industries:

Company Name: Odd Industries
Description: Odd builds computer vision platforms to transform offline processes into online data using artificial intelligence.
Website: http://odd.co
Phone: **Email:** hello@odd.co
City: Santiago **State:** Santiago Metropolitan Region **PC:**
Country: Chile
Year Established: 2018 **Status 2020:** Active
Industries: Artificial Intelligence for:, Computer Vision for:, ~ Construction (10), Industrial Solutions for:, Machine Learning for:, Business Software as a Service Apps (SaaS Apps)

Company Name: PEGASI International
Description: We manage Healthcare information smartly, creating Business Intelligence with Big Data mining and Machine Learning
Website: http://www.pegasi.io
Phone: 56941545301 **Email:** info@pegasi.io
City: Santiago **State:** Santiago Metropolitan Region **PC:**
Country: Chile
Year Established: 2019 **Status 2020:** Active
Industries: Artificial Intelligence for:, Big Data and Analytics for:, Enterprise Application Services for:, ~ Healthcare (20), IT Managed Services for:, Machine Learning

Company Name: PleIQ Smart Toys
Description: PleIQ creates smart educational toys using AR and AI to stimulate the multiple intelligences on preschoolers.
Website: http://www.pleiq.com
Phone: 56967516278 **Email:** hola@pleiq.com
City: Santiago **State:** Santiago Metropolitan Region **PC:**
Country: Chile
Year Established: 2016 **Status 2020:** Active
Industries: Artificial Intelligence for:, Augmented Reality for:, ~ Education (13)

Company Name: Pyvana
Description: BI & Analytics software as a service
Website: http://www.pyvana.com
Phone: 56999983614 **Email:** andresvergarah@gmail.com
City: Santiago **State:** Santiago Metropolitan Region **PC:**
Country: Chile
Year Established: **Status 2020:** Active
Industries:

Company Name: Rocketbot
Description: Cloud solution (Saas) for the development of Robotic Process Automation.
Website: http://www.rocketbot.cl
Phone: 56972518446 **Email:** rafael@rocketbot.cl
City: Santiago **State:** Santiago Metropolitan Region **PC:**
Country: Chile
Year Established: **Status 2020:** Active
Industries: Artificial Intelligence for:, Machine Learning for:, Natural Language Processing for:, Robotics

Company Name: Smart Mining
Description: . SmartMining is an information technology company applied to the mining world, which brings intelligence to mining processes to increases in productivity.
Website: http://www.smartmining.biz
Phone: 56964461240 **Email:** daniel.baquedano.alvarez@gmail.com
City: Santiago **State:** Santiago Metropolitan Region **Zip:** 7500000 **Country**: Chile
Year Established: **Status 2020:** Active
Industries: Application Program Interfaces (APIs) for:, Artificial Intelligence for:, ~ Manufacturing-Electronic (30), ~ Metals and Mining (42), Big Data and Analytics for:, Business Software as a Service Apps (SaaS Apps) for:, IT Managed Services for:, Machine Learning for

Company Name: StrongSteam
Description: StrongSteam is an app store of artificial intelligence and data mining APIs to pull information out of images, video, and audio.
Website: http://strongsteam.com
Phone: **Email:** info@strongsteam.com
City: Santiago **State:** Santiago Metropolitan Region **PC:**
Country: Chile
Year Established: 2011 **Status 2020:** Active
Industries: Application Services for:, Artificial Intelligence for:, Voice Recognition for:, Databases

Company Name: Teamcore Solutions
Description: Teamcore captures the value from retail sales, inventory and instore data and generates Potential Sales opportunities through AI and tasks
Website: http://www.teamcore.net
Phone: 56228402146 **Email:** contact@teamcore.net
City: Santiago **State:** Santiago Metropolitan Region **PC:**
Country: Chile
Year Established: 2015 **Status 2020:** Active
Industries: Artificial Intelligence for:, IT Managed Services for:, ~ Telecommunications (56), Machine Learning for:, Supply Chain Management for:, Supply Chain Management

Company Name: Tesseracto
Description: Artificial Inteligence for Mining and Health Industri: Spain
Website: http://www.tesseracto.com/
Phone: 56994196209 **Email:** jordaj.zuleta@tesseracto.com
City: Santiago **State:** Santiago Metropolitan Region **PC:**
Country: Chile
Year Established: 2018 **Status 2020:** Active
Industries: Artificial Intelligence for:, Machine Learning for:, ~ Metals and Mining (42)

Company Name: The Not Company
Description: NotCo is combining AI with food-science to craft cutting-edge plant-based foods.
Website: http://www.notco.com/
Phone: 569 6425 6336 **Email:** whynot@thenotcompany.com
City: Santiago **State:** Santiago Metropolitan Region **PC:**
Country: Chile
Year Established: 2015 **Status 2020:** Active
Industries: Artificial Intelligence for:, ~ Food and Beverage (17)

Company Name: Trend Group America
Description: Optimizing real estate sales with smart data.
Website: http://www.trendgroupamerica.com
Phone: 562 2233 4658 **Email:** hello@trendgroupamerica.com
City: Santiago **State:** Santiago Metropolitan Region **PC:**
Country: Chile
Year Established: 2010 **Status 2020:** Active
Industries: Artificial Intelligence for:, ~ Customer Relationship Management (11), Databases for:, Machine Learning for:, ~ Real Estate (49), Business Software as a Service Apps (SaaS Apps)

Company Name: Udeet
Description: Help travel companies increase their revenue providing them qualified leads using AI.
Website: http://www.blosgo.com
Phone: **Email:** tatiana@blosgo.com
City: Santiago **State:** Santiago Metropolitan Region **PC:**
Country: Chile
Year Established: 2019 **Status 2020:** Active
Industries: Artificial Intelligence for:, Databases for:, Application Program Interfaces (APIs) for:, Machine Learning

Company Name: UsabilityChefs
Description: Plataforma de evaluación y testing para sitios web usables. UsabilityChefs acompaña los profesionales en experiencia del usuario (UX) y
Website: http://usabilitychefs.com
Phone: **Email:** usabilitychefs@gmail.com
City: Santiago **State:** Santiago Metropolitan Region **PC:**
Country: Chile
Year Established: 2013 **Status 2020:** Closed
Industries: Artificial Intelligence for:, Web

Company Name: Veronica Core
Description: Video Efficient Recognition Of Named Identities and Content Analysis.
Website: http://www.veronicacore.com/Home.aspx
Phone: 993105150 **Email:** contacto@veronicacore.com
City: Santiago **State:** Santiago Metropolitan Region **PC:**
Country: Chile
Year Established: 2012 **Status 2020:** Active
Industries:

Company Name: Webdox
Description: CLMs, SaaS
Website: http://www.webdox.cl/
Phone: **Email:** jmjimenez@webdox.cl
City: Santiago **State:** Santiago Metropolitan Region **PC:**
Country: Chile
Year Established: 2012 **Status 2020:** Active
Industries: Cloud for:, Collaboration Solutions for:, Enterprise Application Services for:, IT Managed Services for:, Natural Language Processing for:, ~ Administrative and Support Services (1), Business Software as a Service Apps (SaaS Apps)

Company Name: WriteBetter
Description: Writing assistant integrated into word editors. It works in Word, Google docs, Overleaf, etc.
Website: http://writebetter.io/
Phone: **Email:** hello@writebetter.io
City: Santiago **State:** Santiago Metropolitan Region **PC:**
Country: Chile
Year Established: 2018 **Status 2020:** Active
Industries: Application Services for:, Natural Language Processing

Company Name: Z Data Lab
Description: Powered by AI, Z Data Lab helps companies discover new significant growth opportunities, accelerate revenue and boost their margins
Website: http://www.pricemaker.io
Phone: **Email:** nicolas@zdatalab.com
City: Santiago **State:** Santiago Metropolitan Region **PC:**
Country: Chile
Year Established: 2016 **Status 2020:** Active
Industries: Analytics for:, Artificial Intelligence for:, Data Management for:, Machine Learning for:, Predictive Analytics

Company Name: ZimpleMa:Thailand
Description: Math Learning Educational Platform powered by AI.
Website: http://zimplemath.com/
Phone: 562-22438410 **Email:** info@zimplemath.com
City: Santiago **State:** Santiago Metropolitan Region **PC:**
Country: Chile
Year Established: 2018 **Status 2020:** Active
Industries: Artificial Intelligence for:, ~ Education (13), IT Managed Services

China

Company Name: Zhongke Haoy: India
Description: Zhongke Haoyin is a Voiceprint AI Solution Provider.
Website:
Phone: **Email:** 4460@reference-encyclopedia-ai.net
City: Hefei **State:** Anhui **PC:** **Country:** China

Year Established: **Status 2020:** Active
Industries: Artificial Intelligence for:, Robotics

Company Name: 12 Sigma Technologies
Description: 12 Sigma Technologies is a software company focused on bringing artificial intelligence solutions to medical diagnosis.
Website: http://www.12sigma.cn/en
Phone: **Email:** contact@12sigma.ai
City: Beijing **State:** Beijing **PC:** **Country:** China
Year Established: 2015 **Status 2020:** Active
Industries:

Company Name: 4Paradigm
Description: 4Paradigm is an AI technology that helps enterprises to improve work efficiency, reduce risks and achieve greater commercial values.
Website: https://www.4paradigm.com/
Phone: 010-82780800 **Email:** contact@4paradigm.com
City: Beijing **State:** Beijing **PC:** **Country:** China
Year Established: 2014 **Status 2020:** Active
Industries: Artificial Intelligence for:, IT Managed Services

Company Name: 51VR
Description: 51VR is a leading VR/AR company headquartered in China. Founded in early 2015.
Website: http://www.51hitech.com/
Phone: 400-816-5151 **Email:** 51service@51hitech.com
City: Beijing **State:** Beijing **PC:** **Country:** China
Year Established: **Status 2020:** Active
Industries: Artificial Intelligence for:, Augmented Reality for:, ~ Automotive (5), ~ Real Estate (49)

Company Name: Abbots Technology
Description: Abbots Technology is committed to using AI technology in the SaaS mode for the various industries to provide BI service
Website:
Phone: 1082428720 **Email:** jbzheng@abcft.com
City: Beijing **State:** Beijing **PC:** **Country:** China
Year Established: **Status 2020:** Active
Industries: Artificial Intelligence for:, Cloud

Company Name: ABC Fintech
Description: ABC Fintech provides AI-driven cloud services for financial professionals.
Website: http://www.abcfintech.com/
Phone: **Email:** pr@abcft.com
City: Beijing **State:** Beijing **PC:** **Country:** China
Year Established: **Status 2020:** Active
Industries: Artificial Intelligence for:, Enterprise Application Services for:, ~ Banking and Financial Markets-Services (7), ~ Banking and Financial Markets-Services (7), Machine Learning

Company Name: Addx.ai
Description: Addx.ai is a smart home operating system developer dedicated to building an AIOT intelligent platform.
Website: https://www.addx.ai/
Phone: **Email:** info@addx.ai
City: Beijing **State:** Beijing **PC:** **Country:** China
Year Established: 2018 **Status 2020:** Active
Industries: Web

Company Name: AI Star
Description: AI Star is an AI video face changing service platform.
Website:
Phone: **Email:** 35995@reference-encyclopedia-ai.net
City: Beijing **State:** Beijing **PC:** **Country:** China
Year Established: 2018 **Status 2020:** Active
Industries: Artificial Intelligence for:, Robotics

Company Name: Aibee
Description: Aibee is an artificial intelligence solution developer company.
Website: http://aibee.com
Phone: 86 (10) 6060 9699 **Email:** contact@aibee.com
City: Beijing **State:** Beijing **PC:** **Country:** China
Year Established: **Status 2020:** Active
Industries: Artificial Intelligence for:, IT Managed Services for:, Robotics

Company Name: AIQI Technology
Description: AIQI Technology specialized in research and development in the field of artificial intelligent and robotic technology.
Website: http://www.iqi-inc.com/?lang=en
Phone: **Email:** iqi@iqi-inc.com
City: Beijing **State:** Beijing **PC:** **Country:** China
Year Established: 2013 **Status 2020:** Active
Industries:

Company Name: Airdoc
Description: Airdoc is an medical care solutions provider based in China that uses artificial intelligence.
Website:
Phone: **Email:** 36019@reference-encyclopedia-ai.net
City: Beijing **State:** Beijing **PC:** **Country:** China
Year Established: 2015 **Status 2020:** Closed
Industries: Artificial Intelligence for:, ~ Healthcare (20), Machine Learning for:, ~ Healthcare (20)

Company Name: Ai-Robotics
Description: AI-ROBOTICS (AI-ROBOTICS) is a leading provider of R & D, production, sales and service integration of soft and hardware products in China.
Website: http://www.ai-robotics.cn/
Phone: **Email:** airobot@ai-robot.tech
City: Beijing **State:** Beijing **PC:** **Country:** China
Year Established: 2016 **Status 2020:** Active
Industries: Artificial Intelligence for:, Industrial Solutions for:, Robotics

Company Name: Aqrose Technology
Description: Aqrose Technology is a China-based company that applies machine vision and machine learning technology into industrial automation.
Website: http://aqrose.com/
Phone: **Email:** contact@aqrose.com
City: Beijing **State:** Beijing **PC:** **Country:** China
Year Established: **Status 2020:** Active
Industries: Artificial Intelligence for:, Industrial Solutions for:, Automation for:, Machine Learning for:, Robotics

Company Name: AutoAI
Description: AutoAI is an intelligent networked system developer and operator for a new generation of self-driving cars.
Website: http://www.autoai.com
Phone: 400-661-6677 **Email:** Marketing@autoai.com
City: Beijing **State:** Beijing **PC:** **Country:** China
Year Established: **Status 2020:** Active
Industries: Analytics for:, Artificial Intelligence for:, ~ Automotive (5)

Company Name: Bailian.AI
Description: Bailian.AI is an artificial intelligence company
Website: http://www.bailian-ai.com/
Phone: **Email:** market@bailian.ai
City: Beijing **State:** Beijing **PC:** **Country:** China
Year Established: 2018 **Status 2020:** Active
Industries: Artificial Intelligence for:, Robotics

Company Name: Bankorus
Description: Bankorus is the first AI-powered, crypto-wealth management platform, and security token marketplace built on the blockchain.
Website: http://www.bankorus.com

Phone: **Email:** support@micaiapp.com
City: Beijing **State:** Beijing **PC:** **Country:** China
Year Established: **Status 2020:** Active
Industries: Artificial Intelligence for:, Blockchain for:, ~ Banking and Financial Markets-Services (7), ~ Banking and Financial Markets-Services (7), ~ Banking and Financial Markets-Services (7), Finance and Accounting

Company Name: Bayelearn Intelligent Technology
Description: Bayelearn Intelligent is a high-tech enterprise specializing in the development of intelligent software technology.
Website: http://www.bayelearn.com/
Phone: **Email:** 010-68881682
City: Beijing **State:** Beijing **PC:** **Country:** China
Year Established: **Status 2020:** Active
Industries: Artificial Intelligence for:, ~ Professional Services (48)

Company Name: BeagleData
Description: Beijing Based Enterprise services Company.
Website: http://www.beagledata.com/
Phone: **Email:** websales@beagledata.com
City: Beijing **State:** Beijing **PC:** **Country:** China
Year Established: 2010 **Status 2020:** Active
Industries: Artificial Intelligence

Company Name: Bell.ai
Description: Bell.ai is an education training institution based in China.
Website: http://bell.ai/
Phone: 400-609-0919 **Email:** customerservice@bell.ai
City: Beijing **State:** Beijing **PC:** **Country:** China
Year Established: 2011 **Status 2020:** Active
Industries: Artificial Intelligence for:, ~ Education (13), ~ Education (13)

Company Name: Bishen
Description: Bishen is an AI-assisted writing app.
Website: http://www.bishen.ink/
Phone: 010-62136858 **Email:** support@onepen.ink
City: Beijing **State:** Beijing **PC:** **Country:** China
Year Established: 2018 **Status 2020:** Active
Industries: Application Services for:, Artificial Intelligence

Company Name: Bishi Technology
Description: Bishi Technology is committed to building the world's leading AI operation and maintenance engine.
Website:
Phone: **Email:** 36162@reference-encyclopedia-ai.net
City: Beijing **State:** Beijing **PC:** **Country:** China
Year Established: 2016 **Status 2020:** Active
Industries:

Company Name: BIT All Technology
Description: BAT Anti-UAV System is a low-altitude protection system that features integrated detection technology using sound, light and electricity.
Website: http://www.bitalltech.com/
Phone: **Email:** hr@bitalltech.com
City: Beijing **State:** Beijing **PC:** **Country:** China
Year Established: **Status 2020:** Active
Industries: Artificial Intelligence for:, Cloud for:, Security

Company Name: BooCax
Description: BooCax is a mobile robot positioning and navigation technology firm.
Website: http://www.boocax.com/
Phone: 86 10 6410 1228 **Email:** 36185@reference-encyclopedia-ai.net
City: Beijing **State:** Beijing **PC:** **Country:** China
Year Established: 2014 **Status 2020:** Active
Industries: Application Services for:, ~ Social-Environmental-Physical-Engineering Sciences (55), Robotics

Company Name: Cambricon Technologies
Description: Cambricon Technologies builds core processor chips for intelligent cloud servers, intelligent terminals, and intelligent robots.
Website: http://www.cambricon.com
Phone: 010 83030003 **Email:** hr@cambricon.com
City: Beijing **State:** Beijing **PC:** **Country:** China
Year Established: **Status 2020:** Active
Industries:

Company Name: C-Exoskeleton Robot
Description: C-Exoskeleton Robot is a soft robotic exoskeleton system developer.
Website:
Phone: **Email:** 36251@reference-encyclopedia-ai.net
City: Beijing **State:** Beijing **PC:** **Country:** China
Year Established: 2017 **Status 2020:** Active
Industries: Artificial Intelligence for:, Robotics

Company Name: Changmugu Medical
Description: Changmugu Medicalis an artificial intelligence (AI)-powered healthcare start-up
Website: http://117hah.hk2.htmlsz.com/
Phone: **Email:** Contact@changmugu.com
City: Beijing **State:** Beijing **PC:** **Country:** China
Year Established: 2017 **Status 2020:** Active
Industries: Artificial Intelligence for:, ~ Healthcare (20)

Company Name: China Weather Network
Description: China Weather Network is the in-depth application of new technologies such as cloud computing, Internet of Things, mobile internet
Website: http://www.weatherdt.com/
Phone: 010-68408994 **Email:** weatherdt@weather.com.cn
City: Beijing **State:** Beijing **PC:** **Country:** China
Year Established: 2017 **Status 2020:** Active
Industries: Application Services for:, Web

Company Name: Cloud: India
Description: CloudIn is an international technology company that provides IaaS- and PaaS-based cloud services.
Website: http://www.cloudin.cn/
Phone: **Email:** info@cloudin.cn
City: Beijing **State:** Beijing **PC:** **Country:** China
Year Established: **Status 2020:** Active
Industries: Artificial Intelligence for:, Big Data and Analytics for:, Cloud for:, Cloud for:, ~ Professional Services (48)

Company Name: CloudWalk Technology
Description: CloudWalk independent intellectual property rights core algorithm, is the face of national standards for the drafting and formulation.
Website: http://www.cloudwalk.cn/
Phone: 400-151-5992 **Email:** business@cloudwalk.cn
City: Beijing **State:** Beijing **PC:** **Country:** China
Year Established: **Status 2020:** Active
Industries: Artificial Intelligence for:, IT Managed Services for:, Machine Learning

Company Name: Clustar
Description: Beijing based Robotics company.
Website: http://www.clustar.ai/
Phone: 010 - 68005320 **Email:** contact@clustar.ai
City: Beijing **State:** Beijing **PC:** **Country:** China
Year Established: **Status 2020:** Active
Industries: Artificial Intelligence for:, Cloud for:, Robotics

Company Name: Comper
Description: Comper is an independent designer and manufacturer of smart healthcare devices.
Website: http://comperhealth.myshopify.com/
Phone: 400 900 1020 **Email:** service@comper.com
City: Beijing **State:** BJ **PC:** **Country:** China

Year Established: 2014 **Status 2020:** Active
Industries: Artificial Intelligence for:, ~ Healthcare (20)

Company Name: CurveRobot
Description: CurveRobot is anAI & Robotics company.
Website: http://curverobot.cn/
Phone: **Email:** hr@curverobot.com
City: Beijing **State:** Beijing **PC:** **Country:** China
Year Established: 2018 **Status 2020:** Active
Industries: Artificial Intelligence for:, Robotics

Company Name: DarwinML
Description: DarwinML is an artificial intelligence application model automation design platform.
Website: http://iqubic.net/
Phone: **Email:** Contact@iqubic.net
City: Beijing **State:** Beijing **PC:** **Country:** China
Year Established: 2017 **Status 2020:** Active
Industries: Artificial Intelligence

Company Name: Databaker
Description: Databaker is a AI data service provider, focusing on speech synthesis, speech recognition, image recognition data services.
Website: http://www.data-baker.com/
Phone: 010-58092466 **Email:** 36386@reference-encyclopedia-ai.net
City: Beijing **State:** Beijing **PC:** **Country:** China
Year Established: 2016 **Status 2020:** Active
Industries: Artificial Intelligence for:, Robotics

Company Name: DataO: JORDAN
Description: DataOJO is a new data intelligence company
Website: http://www.dataojo.com/
Phone: **Email:** Bd@dataojo.com
City: Beijing **State:** BJ **PC:** **Country:** China
Year Established: 2017 **Status 2020:** Active
Industries: Artificial Intelligence for:, Robotics

Company Name: Deep Glint
Description: Deep Glint is a computer vision startup providing 3D image analysis and pattern recognition technologies for mission-critical applications.
Website: http://www.deepglint.com
Phone: 010-62950616 **Email:** hr@deepglint.com
City: Beijing **State:** BJ **PC:** **Country:** China
Year Established: 2012 **Status 2020:** Active
Industries: Analytics for:, Application Services for:, Artificial Intelligence for:, Computer Vision for:, Machine Learning

Company Name: DEEP Informatics
Description: DEEP Informatics is a smart AI medical treatment and imaging company.
Website: http://www.deepinformatics.com.cn/
Phone: **Email:** 36409@reference-encyclopedia-ai.net
City: Beijing **State:** Beijing **PC:** **Country:** China
Year Established: 2017 **Status 2020:** Active
Industries: Artificial Intelligence for:, ~ Biotechnology (9), ~ Healthcare (20), ~ Healthcare (20)

Company Name: Deepcare
Description: DeepCare is a technology company that uses artificial intelligence for diagnosis of medical imaging.
Website: http://www.deepcare.com
Phone: 010-62662866 **Email:** business@deepcare.com
City: Beijing **State:** Beijing **PC:** **Country:** China
Year Established: 2016 **Status 2020:** Active
Industries:

Company Name: Deepleaper
Description: Deepleaper is a business semantics processing engine developer based in China.
Website: http://www.deepleaper.com/
Phone: 86 10 8438 4272 **Email:** 36419@reference-encyclopedia-ai.net
City: Beijing **State:** Beijing **PC:** **Country:** China
Year Established: 2016 **Status 2020:** Active
Industries: Artificial Intelligence for:, Content for:, Web

Company Name: Deepoly
Description: Deepoly consists of the top FPGA software and hardware development team and AI expert group in China.
Website: http://www.deepoly.com/
Phone: (010) 62578668 **Email:** Sales@deepoly.com
City: Beijing **State:** Beijing **PC:** **Country:** China
Year Established: 2016 **Status 2020:** Active
Industries: Artificial Intelligence for:, IT Managed Services

Company Name: Deepwi: Sweden
Description: Deepwise is an artificial intelligence technology-based clinical imaging services provider.
Website: http://www.deepwise.com/
Phone: 010-82888090 **Email:** contact@deepwise.com
City: Beijing **State:** Beijing **PC:** **Country:** China
Year Established: 2017 **Status 2020:** Active
Industries: Artificial Intelligence for:, ~ Healthcare (20)

Company Name: eBra: India
Description: eBrain is an artificial intelligence application developer.
Website:
Phone: **Email:** 36468@reference-encyclopedia-ai.net
City: Beijing **State:** Beijing **PC:** **Country:** China
Year Established: 2017 **Status 2020:** Active
Industries: Artificial Intelligence for:, Robotics

Company Name: Evolver
Description: Evolver is an AI & Robotics company.
Website: http://www.efrobot.com
Phone: 400-008-9869 **Email:** weixin@ren001.com
City: Beijing **State:** BJ **PC:** **Country:** China
Year Established: 2015 **Status 2020:** Active
Industries: Artificial Intelligence for:, Robotics

Company Name: Founder.AI
Description: Founder.AI is an AI recruitment product developer.
Website: http://founder.ai/
Phone: **Email:** hr@founder.ai
City: Beijing **State:** BJ **PC:** **Country:** China
Year Established: 2017 **Status 2020:** Active
Industries: Artificial Intelligence

Company Name: HealAI
Description: Beijing Based Healthcare Start Up
Website: http://www.healai.com/
Phone: **Email:** support@healai.com
City: Beijing **State:** Beijing **PC:** **Country:** China
Year Established: 2016 **Status 2020:** Active
Industries: Artificial Intelligence for:, ~ Healthcare (20)

Company Name: Health Ho:
Description: Health Hope is an AI powered medical technology firm offering health care technology empowerment for smart families.
Website: http://www.jiankangyouyi.com
Phone: 010-64735987 **Email:** hr@jiankangyouyi.com
City: Beijing **State:** BJ **PC:** **Country:** China
Year Established: 2014 **Status 2020:** Active
Industries: Artificial Intelligence for:, ~ Healthcare (20), Application Services

Company Name: HoloMatic
Description: HoloMatic is a autonomous driving technology start-up .
Website: http://www.holomatic.cn/
Phone: **Email:** contact@holomatic.com
City: Beijing **State:** Beijing **PC:** **Country:** China
Year Established: 2017 **Status 2020:** Active
Industries: Artificial Intelligence for:, ~ Automotive (5), ~ Automotive (5), IT Managed Services

Company Name: Horizon Robotics
Description: Horizon Robotics develops artificial intelligence chips for robots.
Website: http://www.horizon.ai/
Phone: 1 6692303151 **Email:** bd@horizon.ai
City: Beijing **State:** BJ **PC:** **Country:** China
Year Established: 2015 **Status 2020:** Active
Industries: Artificial Intelligence for:, Robotics

Company Name: Huarui Xinzhi
Description: Huarui Xinzhi is an AI technology service provider
Website: http://huarui.ai/
Phone: **Email:** 36715@reference-encyclopedia-ai.net
City: Beijing **State:** Beijing **PC:** **Country:** China
Year Established: 2017 **Status 2020:** Active
Industries: Artificial Intelligence for:, IT Managed Services

Company Name: Hui Nao Yun
Description: Hui Nao Yun is an AI medical company.
Website:
Phone: **Email:** 36719@reference-encyclopedia-ai.net
City: Beijing **State:** Beijing **PC:** **Country:** China
Year Established: 2018 **Status 2020:** Active
Industries: Artificial Intelligence for:, ~ Healthcare (20)

Company Name: Hui'an Jinke (Ahi Fintech)
Description: Hui'an Jinke (Ahi Fintech) is a company that specializes in using artificial intelligence technology
Website: http://www.ahi-fintech.com/
Phone: 86-10-82886672 **Email:** info@fintec.ai
City: Beijing **State:** Beijing **PC:** **Country:** China
Year Established: 2017 **Status 2020:** Active
Industries: Artificial Intelligence for:, IT Managed Services for:, IT Managed Services

Company Name: Huimei Healthcare
Description: Dr.White is an AI & Robotics company.
Website: http://www.huiyidabai.com/
Phone: **Email:** 36454@reference-encyclopedia-ai.net
City: Beijing **State:** Beijing **PC:** **Country:** China
Year Established: 2017 **Status 2020:** Active
Industries:

Company Name: Huiyi Hui Ying
Description: Huiyi Hui Ying is an international cloud computing & AI tech that has created a digital medical imaging and tumor radiotherapy platform.
Website: http://www.huiyihuiying.com/idoctor/html/
Phone: 400-890-9020 **Email:** service@huiyihuiying.com
City: Beijing **State:** Beijing **PC:** **Country:** China
Year Established: **Status 2020:** Active
Industries: Artificial Intelligence for:, Big Data and Analytics for:, Cloud for:, ~ Healthcare (20), ~ Healthcare (20), ~ Manufacturing-Medical Equipment-Supplies (33)

Company Name: Huiyi Huiying
Description: Huiyi Huiying is an international cloud computing & AI tech that has created a digital medical imaging and tumor radiotherapy platform.
Website: http://www.huiyihuiying.com/
Phone: 400-890-9020 **Email:** service@huiyihuiying.com
City: Beijing **State:** BJ **PC:** **Country:** China
Year Established: 2015 **Status 2020:** Active
Industries: Artificial Intelligence for:, Big Data and Analytics for:, Cloud for:, ~ Healthcare (20), ~ Healthcare (20), ~ Healthcare (20)

Company Name: Hujing Tiaoyue
Description: Hujing Tiaoyue is an AI sales marketing solution provider.
Website: http://www.aihujing.com/
Phone: **Email:** louhaichao@aihujing.com
City: Beijing **State:** Beijing **PC:** **Country:** China
Year Established: 2017 **Status 2020:** Active
Industries: Artificial Intelligence for:, Robotics

Company Name: HUMAN
Description: An Artificial Intelligence & Robotics Company based in Beijing, China.
Website: http://www.ishuman.co/
Phone: **Email:** hello@ishuman.co
City: Beijing **State:** Beijing **PC:** **Country:** China
Year Established: **Status 2020:** Active
Industries: Artificial Intelligence for:, Robotics

Company Name: Humanplus
Description: computer visionï¼Œartificial intelligence
Website: http://www.humanplus.ai
Phone: 86-18201062758 **Email:** lijiaxuan@humanplus.ai
City: Beijing **State:** Beijing **PC:** **Country:** China
Year Established: **Status 2020:** Active
Industries: Artificial Intelligence for:, Computer Vision

Company Name: HyperAI Cloud
Description: HyperAI Cloud is a high-tech enterprise specializing in the research and development
Website: http://hyperai.net
Phone: (1861) 116-7921 **Email:** sales@hyperai.net
City: Beijing **State:** Beijing **PC:** **Country:** China
Year Established: 2018 **Status 2020:** Active
Industries: Artificial Intelligence for:, Cloud

Company Name: ICE Tech Science & Technology
Description: ICE Tech Science & Technology is a Ai company , Which focuses on the development of AI algorithms and chips.
Website: http://www.icetech-bj.com/
Phone: **Email:** grace.wang@icetech-ai.com
City: Beijing **State:** Beijing **PC:** **Country:** China
Year Established: 2012 **Status 2020:** Active
Industries: Artificial Intelligence

Company Name: Infervision
Description: Infervision is an AI high-tech company that uses deep learning technology and computer vision to help diagnose cancers.
Website: http://www.infervision.com/
Phone: **Email:** contact@infervision.com
City: Beijing **State:** Beijing **PC:** **Country:** China
Year Established: 2015 **Status 2020:** Active
Industries: Artificial Intelligence for:, ~ Healthcare (20), Machine Learning for:, ~ Healthcare (20)

Company Name: Infimind
Description: Infimind is a Clothing-focused AI startup.
Website: http://infimind.com/
Phone: 010-86460660 **Email:** wubin@infimind.com
City: Beijing **State:** Beijing **PC:** **Country:** China
Year Established: 2017 **Status 2020:** Active
Industries: Artificial Intelligence for:, ~ Fashion (16)

Company Name: Jiabao Kangle
Description: Jiabao Kangle is a pediatric clinic franchise operator.
Website: http://www.jiabaokangle.com/
Phone: 0851-85552489 **Email:** contactus@jiabaokangle.com
City: Beijing **State:** Beijing **PC:** **Country:** China
Year Established: 2016 **Status 2020:** Active
Industries: Artificial Intelligence for:, ~ Healthcare (20)

Company Name: Jingji
Description: Jingji is a semi-open and high-end talent platform.
Website:
Phone: **Email:** 36827@reference-encyclopedia-ai.net
City: Beijing **State:** BJ **PC:** **Country:** China
Year Established: 2018 **Status 2020:** Active
Industries: Artificial Intelligence

Company Name: Jingle Magic (Beijing) Technology
Description: Jingle Magic is mainly involved in the development of VR, AR and AI based educational equipment and software.
Website:
Phone: **Email:** 36828@reference-encyclopedia-ai.net
City: Beijing **State:** BJ **PC:** **Country:** China
Year Established: 2016 **Status 2020:** Active
Industries: Artificial Intelligence for:, Augmented Reality for:, Virtual Reality (VR)

Company Name: Jiqi Zhix: India
Description: Jiqi Zhixin is a technology media platform focusing on artificial intelligence, robots, and neurocognitive science.
Website: http://www.jiqizhixin.com/
Phone: 86 010-57150141 **Email:** contact@jiqizhixin.com
City: Beijing **State:** Beijing **PC:** **Country:** China
Year Established: **Status 2020:** Active
Industries: Artificial Intelligence for:, Application Services for:, IT Managed Services

Company Name: Juefx
Description: Juefx is a Developer of AI technology that focuses on building an autonomous driving decision data platform.
Website: http://www.juefx.com/
Phone: **Email:** support@julyedu.com
City: Beijing **State:** Beijing **PC:** **Country:** China
Year Established: 2018 **Status 2020:** Active
Industries:

Company Name: Julyedu.com
Description: Julyedu.com is the leading artificial intelligence education platform
Website: http://www.julyedu.com/
Phone: **Email:** contact@juefx.com
City: Beijing **State:** Beijing **PC:** **Country:** China
Year Established: 2015 **Status 2020:** Active
Industries: Artificial Intelligence for:, ~ Education (13), ~ Education (13)

Company Name: Kuaile Zhihui
Description: Kuaile Zhihui is an artificial intelligence start-up develops educational robots for children.
Website:
Phone: **Email:** 36869@reference-encyclopedia-ai.net
City: Beijing **State:** Beijing **PC:** **Country:** China
Year Established: 2015 **Status 2020:** Active
Industries: Artificial Intelligence for:, ~ Education (13), Robotics

Company Name: Laiye
Description: Laiye is an interactive platform that offers consumers and enterprises with intelligent assistant products.
Website: http://www.laiye.com/
Phone: 400-0018-136 **Email:** business@uibot.com.cn
City: Beijing **State:** Beijing **PC:** **Country:** China
Year Established: 2015 **Status 2020:** Active
Industries: Application Services for:, Mobile for:, Application Services for:, ~ Banking and Financial Markets-Services (7), Natural Language Processing for:, Natural Language Processing

Company Name: Light Theto
Description: Reinlight is a diffraction optical solutions provider.
Website: http://reinlight.cc/
Phone: 0573-89380238 **Email:** 36896@reference-encyclopedia-ai.net
City: Beijing **State:** Beijing **PC:** **Country:** China
Year Established: 2016 **Status 2020:** Active
Industries: ~ Automotive (5), IT Managed Services for:, Application Services for:, Security

Company Name: Ling
Description: Ling Technology was established during September 2016 as a global AI technology company targeting the AI Internet era.
Website: http://intl.ling.ai/
Phone: **Email:** ling@ling.ai
City: Beijing **State:** Beijing **PC:** **Country:** China
Year Established: 2016 **Status 2020:** Active
Industries: Artificial Intelligence for:, IT Managed Services for:, Web for:, Machine Learning for:, Robotics

Company Name: Linkool Labs
Description: Innovation from China
Website: http://linkool.biz
Phone: 86 10 6267 0450 **Email:** inquiries@linkool.biz
City: Beijing **State:** Beijing **PC:** **Country:** China
Year Established: **Status 2020:** Active
Industries: Artificial Intelligence for:, ~ Arts-Entertainment-Recreation (4)

Company Name: Longmao Data
Description: Longmao Data specializes in offering data services intended for artificial intelligence platforms.
Website: http://www.longmaosoft.com
Phone: **Email:** dengyuchun@longmasosoft.com
City: Beijing **State:** Beijing **PC:** **Country:** China
Year Established: 2014 **Status 2020:** Active
Industries: Artificial Intelligence for:, Big Data and Analytics for:, Databases

Company Name: Lunzi Technology
Description: Lunzi Technology is a AI & Robotics company.
Website:
Phone: **Email:** 36921@reference-encyclopedia-ai.net
City: Beijing **State:** Beijing **PC:** **Country:** China
Year Established: 2015 **Status 2020:** Active
Industries: Artificial Intelligence for:, Robotics

Company Name: Machinely
Description: Machinely is revolutionizing the way in which goat farmers communicate and educate their herds through machine learning.
Website: http://www.machinely.info
Phone: **Email:** info@machinely.info
City: Beijing **State:** Beijing **PC:** **Country:** China
Year Established: 2016 **Status 2020:** Active
Industries: ~ Agriculture (3), ~ Agriculture (3), Machine Learning

Company Name: Maimeng Group
Description: Maimeng Group is an artificial intelligence technology company focusing on intelligent marketing in the education and insurance industry.
Website: http://www.maimenggroup.com/
Phone: **Email:** Contact@maimenggroup.com
City: Beijing **State:** Beijing **PC:** **Country:** China
Year Established: **Status 2020:** Active
Industries: Artificial Intelligence

Company Name: Mcfly
Description: Mcfly is an AI big data company with international technology background, Internet genes.
Website: http://www.mcfly.com.cn/
Phone: 010-53959868 **Email:** BD@mcfly.com.cn
City: Beijing **State:** BJ **PC:** **Country:** China
Year Established: 2016 **Status 2020:** Active
Industries: Artificial Intelligence for:, Big Data and Analytics for:, Web

Company Name: Mech-Mind
Description: Mech-Mind is dedicated to giving intelligence to industrial robots.
Website: http://www.mech-mind.net/
Phone: **Email:** info@mech-mind.net
City: Beijing **State:** Beijing **PC:** **Country:** China
Year Established: 2016 **Status 2020:** Active
Industries: Artificial Intelligence for:, Robotics

Company Name: MEGVII
Description: Megvii builds AI Engine, a core fundamental technology powering various AI application.
Website: http://www.megvii.com/
Phone: 400-6700-866 **Email:** media@megvii.com
City: Beijing **State:** Beijing **PC:** **Country:** China
Year Established: 2011 **Status 2020:** Active
Industries: Artificial Intelligence for:, Facial Recognition for:, Image Recognition for:, Mobile for:, Robotics

Company Name: Megvii Technology
Description: Megvii Technology operates a face detection, recognition, and analysis platform for Websites, mobile applications, and smart televisions.
Website: http://www.megvii.com/
Phone: 400-910-1616 **Email:** media@megvii.com
City: Beijing **State:** Beijing **PC:** **Country:** China
Year Established: **Status 2020:** Active
Industries:

Company Name: Meilin
Description: Meilin is a high-tech enterprise focusing on artificial intelligence, Internet of Things technology.
Website: http://www.meilin.cc/
Phone: 010-52890311 **Email:** 36961@reference-encyclopedia-ai.net
City: Beijing **State:** Beijing **PC:** **Country:** China
Year Established: 2011 **Status 2020:** Active
Industries: ~ Agriculture (3), Artificial Intelligence for:, Big Data and Analytics for:, Internet of Things (IoT)

Company Name: Meme (Allgeng.com)
Description: Allgeng.com is an artificial intelligence writing tool service provider.
Website: http://allgeng.com/
Phone: **Email:** join@allgeng.com
City: Beijing **State:** Beijing **PC:** **Country:** China
Year Established: **Status 2020:** Active
Industries: Artificial Intelligence for:, Robotics

Company Name: MicroBT
Description: MicroBT is a technology company that specializes in block chain and artificial intelligence.
Website: http://www.microbt.com
Phone: 86 755-26640921 **Email:** Support@microbt.com
City: Beijing **State:** Beijing **PC:** **Country:** China
Year Established: 2016 **Status 2020:** Active
Industries: Artificial Intelligence for:, Blockchain

Company Name: MiningLamp
Description: MiningLamp helps clients to build their own knowledge graphs and apply AI to their business, and finally transform data into insights.
Website: http://www.mininglamp.com/
Phone: (108) 492-3389 **Email:** 36982@reference-encyclopedia-ai.net
City: Beijing **State:** BJ **PC:** **Country:** China
Year Established: 2014 **Status 2020:** Active
Industries: Artificial Intelligence for:, Big Data and Analytics for:, Machine Learning

Company Name: Mintegral International Limited
Description: A leading mobile advertising platform in APAC.
Website: http://www.mintegral.com
Phone: **Email:** 36984@reference-encyclopedia-ai.net
City: Beijing **State:** Beijing **PC:** **Country:** China
Year Established: 2016 **Status 2020:** Active
Industries: Analytics for:, Artificial Intelligence for:, Big Data and Analytics for:, Mobile for:, Application Services

Company Name: Mioji Travel
Description: Mioji provides a smart approach to personalise your travel experience.
Website: http://www.mioji.com
Phone: (1840) 145-7783 **Email:** marketing@mioji.com
City: Beijing **State:** Beijing **PC:** **Country:** China
Year Established: 2014 **Status 2020:** Active
Industries: Artificial Intelligence for:, ~ Travel and Transportation (58)

Company Name: MixT
Description: MixTMTis revolutionize sports through artificial intelligence platform, commercializes multimedia sports content across digital platforms.
Website: http://www.mixtmt.com
Phone: 086-18612186110 **Email:** chen_dongyu@newautogroup.cn
City: Beijing **State:** Beijing **PC:** **Country:** China
Year Established: 2016 **Status 2020:** Active
Industries: Artificial Intelligence for:, Big Data and Analytics for:, Computer Vision for:, Enterprise Application Services for:, Machine Learning

Company Name: Mobvoi
Description: Mobvoi develops technologies in Chinese language speech recognition, natural language processing, and vertical mobile search.
Website: http://www.chumenwenwen.com/en/site/index.html
Phone: 86 10 5617 7000 **Email:** business@mobvoi.com
City: Beijing **State:** Beijing **PC:** **Country:** China
Year Established: **Status 2020:** Active
Industries: Analytics for:, Artificial Intelligence for:, Web for:, Mobile for:, Natural Language Processing

Company Name: Momenta
Description: Momenta is an autonomous driving startup operating out of Beijing.
Website: http://www.momenta.ai
Phone: 010 82526609 **Email:** contact@momenta.ai
City: Beijing **State:** Beijing **PC:** **Country:** China
Year Established: **Status 2020:** Active
Industries: Artificial Intelligence for:, ~ Automotive (5), ~ Automotive (5), Computer Vision for:, IT Managed Services for:, IT Managed Services for:, ~ Professional Services (48), ~ Professional Services (48), ~ Transportation and Logistics (57)

Company Name: Moran Cognitive Technology
Description: Founded in May 2016, located in 768 Creative Industrial Zone, Haidian, Beijing, China
Website: http://mor.ai/
Phone: **Email:** info@imoran.net
City: Beijing **State:** Beijing **PC:** **Country:** China
Year Established: 2016 **Status 2020:** Active
Industries: Artificial Intelligence for:, Human Computer Interaction for:, Internet of Things (IoT) for:, Natural Language Processing for:, Speech Recognition

Company Name: New Tranx Information Technology
Description: New Tranx Information Technology is a Chinese artificial intelligence-powered translation company.
Website: http://www.newtranx.com/
Phone: **Email:** support@newtranx.com
City: Beijing **State:** Beijing **PC:** **Country:** China
Year Established: 2014 **Status 2020:** Active
Industries: Artificial Intelligence for:, IT Managed Services for:, IT Managed Services

Company Name: NEXTClass.ai
Description: NEXTClass.ai is a high-tech company in the field of Internet technology.
Website:
Phone: **Email:** 37061@reference-encyclopedia-ai.net
City: Beijing **State:** Beijing **PC:** **Country:** China
Year Established: 2018 **Status 2020:** Active
Industries: Artificial Intelligence for:, ~ Education (13), ~ Education (13)

Company Name: Nuohui Heal:Thailand
Description: New Horizon Health researches and develops technology for early-stage cancer screening.
Website: http://www.newhorizonbio.com/
Phone: 0571-81107210 **Email:** info@nhbio.com.cn
City: Beijing **State:** Beijing **PC:** **Country:** China
Year Established: 2013 **Status 2020:** Active
Industries: Artificial Intelligence for:, Big Data and Analytics for:, ~ Healthcare (20), ~ Healthcare (20)

Company Name: OrionStar
Description: OrionStar develops artificial intelligence based robots and voice interactive operating system.
Website: http://www.ainirobot.com/
Phone: 400 610 7777 **Email:** robot_rental@cmcm.com
City: Beijing **State:** Beijing **PC:** **Country:** China
Year Established: 2016 **Status 2020:** Active
Industries:

Company Name: Paipaizhuan
Description: Paipaizhuan provides an image identification technology company.
Website: http://www.ppznet.com
Phone: 010-62029910 **Email:** business_service@ppznet.com
City: Beijing **State:** Beijing **PC:** **Country:** China
Year Established: 2015 **Status 2020:** Active
Industries: Artificial Intelligence for:, Image Recognition

Company Name: Panda Technology
Description: China's leading FinTech startup Panda Technology is an AI-based credit management &lead-gen platform that serves users in China and SE Asia.
Website: http://www.panda-fintech.com
Phone: **Email:** panda@panda-fintech.com
City: Beijing **State:** Beijing **PC:** **Country:** China
Year Established: 2017 **Status 2020:** Active
Industries: ~ Banking and Financial Markets-Services (7), ~ E-Commerce (12), Machine Learning for:, Finance and Accounting

Company Name: PENSE: SPAIN
Description: PENSEES is an AI-driven security technology firm.
Website: http://pensees-ai.com/
Phone: 010-67751150 **Email:** business@pensees.ai
City: Beijing **State:** Beijing **PC:** **Country:** China
Year Established: **Status 2020:** Active
Industries: Artificial Intelligence for:, Computer Vision

Company Name: Perfant Technology
Description: Develops imaging and video technologies for artificial intelligence, machine vision, 3-D reconstruction and virtual reality.
Website: http://www.perfant.com/en/index.html
Phone: 1(151)010-90302 **Email:** HR@perfant.com
City: Beijing **State:** Beijing **PC:** **Country:** China
Year Established: **Status 2020:** Active
Industries: Artificial Intelligence

Company Name: Play Secret
Description: Play Secret is the most advanced life field in China
Website: http://www.happyhuo.com/
Phone: **Email:** 37179@reference-encyclopedia-ai.net
City: Beijing **State:** Beijing **PC:** **Country:** China
Year Established: 2015 **Status 2020:** Active
Industries: Artificial Intelligence for:, Machine Learning

Company Name: Pulse language (Maizhiyu)
Description: Pulse language is an Internet Chinese medicine intelligent equipment company
Website: http://www.maizhiyu.com/
Phone: **Email:** hr@maizhiyu.com
City: Beijing **State:** Beijing **PC:** **Country:** China
Year Established: 2018 **Status 2020:** Active
Industries: Web for:, Natural Language Processing

Company Name: QfeelTech
Description: QfeelTech is a Beijing-based artificial intelligence company focusing on machine vision.
Website: http://www.qfeeltech.com/
Phone: 010-56228576 **Email:** service@qfeeltech.com
City: Beijing **State:** BJ **PC:** **Country:** China
Year Established: 2014 **Status 2020:** Active
Industries: Artificial Intelligence for:, IT Managed Services

Company Name: Qingwei Intelligent Technology
Description: Qingwei Intelligent Technology is a Chinese artificial intelligence (AI) chip maker
Website:
Phone: **Email:** 4468@reference-encyclopedia-ai.net
City: Beijing **State:** Beijing **PC:** **Country:** China
Year Established: **Status 2020:** Active
Industries: Artificial Intelligence for:, Robotics

Company Name: Raven Tech
Description: Raven Tech is building the next generation OS.
Website: http://www.raventech.com/
Phone: 14088022707 **Email:** support@raventech.com
City: Beijing **State:** Beijing **PC:** **Country:** China
Year Established: **Status 2020:** Active
Industries: Artificial Intelligence for:, Big Data and Analytics for:, Mobile

Company Name: RealAI
Description: RealAI is an artificial intelligence technology company.
Website: http://realai.ai
Phone: **Email:** hr@realai.ai
City: Beijing **State:** Beijing **PC:** **Country:** China
Year Established: 2018 **Status 2020:** Active
Industries: Artificial Intelligence for:, Robotics

Company Name: Remebot
Description: Remebot is an AI & Robotics company.
Website: http://www.remebot.com.cn/
Phone: **Email:** info@remebot.com.cn
City: Beijing **State:** Beijing **PC:** **Country:** China
Year Established: 2010 **Status 2020:** Active
Industries: Artificial Intelligence for:, Robotics

Company Name: Rich AI
Description: Rich AI is an artificial intelligence startup company
Website: http://www.richinfoai.com/home
Phone: **Email:** 37300@reference-encyclopedia-ai.net
City: Beijing **State:** Beijing **PC:** **Country:** China
Year Established: 2017 **Status 2020:** Active
Industries: Artificial Intelligence

Company Name: ROOBO
Description: Roobo is a hardware and AI company that offers pre-orders of Domgy via crowdfunding sites in China.
Website: http://www.roobo.com
Phone: 010-85141111 **Email:** tellme@roobo.com
City: Beijing **State:** Beijing **PC:** **Country:** China
Year Established: 2014 **Status 2020:** Active
Industries: Artificial Intelligence for:, Internet of Things (IoT) for:, Robotics for:, Virtual Reality (VR)

Company Name: Roome
Description: ROOME brings home automation technology to your life and makes your home more convenient and comfortable.
Website: http://en.myroome.com/
Phone: 400-178-2155 **Email:** marketing@heyhomi.com
City: Beijing **State:** Beijing **PC:** **Country:** China
Year Established: 2015 **Status 2020:** Active
Industries:

Company Name: Rulebit Technology
Description: Rulebit Technology is an AI & Robotics company.
Website: http://www.rulebittech.com/
Phone: 400-628-8863 **Email:** Marketing@rulebittech.com
City: Beijing **State:** Beijing **PC:** **Country:** China
Year Established: 2015 **Status 2020:** Active
Industries: Artificial Intelligence for:, Machine Learning for:, Robotics

Company Name: SandStar
Description: SandStar develops checkout-free convenience store technologies.
Website: http://www.sandstar.com/
Phone: 400-660-9898 **Email:** business@sandstar.com
City: Beijing **State:** BJ **PC:** **Country:** China
Year Established: 2016 **Status 2020:** Active
Industries: Artificial Intelligence for:, Computer Vision for:, IT Managed Services for:, Machine Learning

Company Name: Seehome
Description: Seehome is an artificial intelligence home design platform
Website: http://seehome.cn/
Phone: 010-88865268 **Email:** Hi@3plus.ltd
City: Beijing **State:** Beijing **PC:** **Country:** China
Year Established: **Status 2020:** Active
Industries: Artificial Intelligence for:, ~ Home (22)

Company Name: Seengene
Description: Seengene is an augmented reality company developing software, hardware such as AR glasses.
Website: http://xiijan.com/
Phone: 010-57171177 **Email:** BD@seengene.com
City: Beijing **State:** BJ **PC:** **Country:** China
Year Established: 2016 **Status 2020:** Active
Industries: Artificial Intelligence for:, Augmented Reality

Company Name: SeetaTech
Description: SeetaTech is a machine vision company based in Beijing.
Website: http://www.seetatech.com/
Phone: **Email:** hr@seetatech.com
City: Beijing **State:** BJ **PC:** **Country:** China
Year Established: 2016 **Status 2020:** Active
Industries: Business Intelligence for:, IT Managed Services for:, Machine Learning

Company Name: SenseTime
Description: SenseTime is an artificial intelligence company that focuses on innovative computer vision and deep learning technologies.
Website: http://www.sensetime.com/
Phone: 1052725279 **Email:** media@sensetime.com
City: Beijing **State:** Beijing **PC:** **Country:** China
Year Established: **Status 2020:** Active
Industries: Artificial Intelligence for:, Computer Vision for:, Facial Recognition for:, Image Recognition for:, ~ Professional Services (48)

Company Name: Sensingtech
Description: A hi-tech innovative company dedicating to artificial intelligence, integrates development, production and sale in business.
Website: http://www.sensingtech.com.cn/
Phone: (86) 010-82356641 **Email:** bd@sensingtech.com.cn
City: Beijing **State:** Beijing **PC:** **Country:** China
Year Established: **Status 2020:** Active
Industries: Artificial Intelligence for:, Facial Recognition for:, Robotics

Company Name: Shenzhen Rui Medical (Deep Core)
Description: Shenzhen Rui Medica is an artificial intelligence technology-based clinical imaging services provider.
Website: http://www.deepwise.com/
Phone: 010-82888090 **Email:** contact@deepwise.com
City: Beijing **State:** Beijing **PC:** **Country:** China
Year Established: **Status 2020:** Active
Industries: Artificial Intelligence for:, ~ Healthcare (20)

Company Name: Shukun Technology
Description: Shukun Technology is a Chinese healthcare company that develops diagnostics systems for chronic diseases.
Website: http://www.shukun.net
Phone: **Email:** media@shukun.net
City: Beijing **State:** Beijing **PC:** **Country:** China
Year Established: 2017 **Status 2020:** Active
Industries: Artificial Intelligence for:, ~ Healthcare (20), ~ Healthcare (20), ~ Healthcare (20)

Company Name: SIGAI
Description: SIGAI is an artificial intelligence development platform.
Website: http://www.sigai.cn/
Phone: **Email:** 37388@reference-encyclopedia-ai.net
City: Beijing **State:** Beijing **PC:** **Country:** China
Year Established: 2018 **Status 2020:** Active
Industries: Artificial Intelligence for:, Robotics

Company Name: Singsound
Description: Singsound is an artificial intelligence EdTech company, focusing on speech recognition and natural language processing technologies.
Website: http://www.singsound.com/
Phone: **Email:** 37401@reference-encyclopedia-ai.net
City: Beijing **State:** Beijing **PC:** **Country:** China
Year Established: 2016 **Status 2020:** Active
Industries: Artificial Intelligence for:, ~ Education (13), ~ Education (13)

Company Name: Smart Data China
Description: Smart Data is a machine vision technology firm.
Website: http://www.bmi-tech.cn/
Phone: 010-56254029 **Email:** sales@bmi-tech.cn
City: Beijing **State:** Beijing **PC:** **Country:** China
Year Established: 2012 **Status 2020:** Active
Industries: Artificial Intelligence for:, Robotics

Company Name: Soft Robot Tech
Description: Soft Robot Tech is an Industrial automation flexible gripping robot service provider
Website: http://www.softrobottech.com/
Phone: 010-86467770 **Email:** srt@softrobottech.com
City: Beijing **State:** Beijing **PC:** **Country:** China
Year Established: 2016 **Status 2020:** Active
Industries: Artificial Intelligence for:, Robotics

Company Name: SoundAI
Description: SoundAI is an innovation company that specializes in acoustics frontier technology and artificial intelligence interaction.
Website: http://www.soundai.com/
Phone: 86-10-82135881 **Email:** bd@soundai.com
City: Beijing **State:** BJ **PC:** **Country:** China
Year Established: 2016 **Status 2020:** Active
Industries:

Company Name: Surfing Technology
Description: Surfing Technology AI company who provides autonomous driving training data.
Website: http://www.surfing.ai/
Phone: **Email:** contact@surfingtech.cn
City: Beijing **State:** BJ **PC:** **Country:** China

Year Established: 2017 **Status 2020:** Active
Industries: Artificial Intelligence for:, Big Data and Analytics for:, IT Managed Services for:, Robotics

Company Name: Terminus Technologies
Description: Terminus Technologies is a city-level AI IoT platform operator in China.
Website: http://www.terminusgroup.com/
Phone: 400 6899 638 **Email:** contact@tslsmart.com
City: Beijing **State:** Beijing **PC:** **Country:** China
Year Established: 2015 **Status 2020:** Active
Industries: Artificial Intelligence for:, IT Managed Services for:, Internet of Things (IoT)

Company Name: Tricorn
Description: An Artificial Intelligence startup focused on developing a conversational platform that enables people to interact with various smart device
Website: http://trio.ai/en
Phone: **Email:** info@trio.ai
City: Beijing **State:** Beijing **PC:** **Country:** China
Year Established: **Status 2020:** Active
Industries: Artificial Intelligence for:, Machine Learning for:, ~ Professional Services (48)

Company Name: Tryye Technology
Description: Tryye Technology is a developer of artificial intelligence and robot education products.
Website: http://www.tryyetechnology.com/
Phone: **Email:** support@qiyuchina.com
City: Beijing **State:** Beijing **PC:** **Country:** China
Year Established: 2018 **Status 2020:** Active
Industries: Artificial Intelligence for:, Robotics

Company Name: uCRobotics Technology
Description: uCRobotics Technology is a Hi-tech company which is focus on the technology develop and product promotion in 3D printing solution.
Website: http://www.ucrobotics.com.cn/
Phone: 400-8080-613 **Email:** info@ucrobotics.com
City: Beijing **State:** Beijing **PC:** **Country:** China
Year Established: **Status 2020:** Active
Industries: Artificial Intelligence for:, Robotics

Company Name: Unisound
Description: Beijing Yunzhisheng Information Technology is a mobile internet startup focused on intelligent voice and speech processing technologies.
Website: http://www.unisound.com/
Phone: 010-62369899 **Email:** chenfen@unisound.com
City: Beijing **State:** BJ **PC:** **Country:** China
Year Established: 2012 **Status 2020:** Active
Industries: Cloud for:, Natural Language Processing for:, Speech Recognition

Company Name: Universal Mofly
Description: Universal Mofly is an AI digital visual effect and image operator.
Website:
Phone: **Email:** 37594@reference-encyclopedia-ai.net
City: Beijing **State:** Beijing **PC:** **Country:** China
Year Established: 2017 **Status 2020:** Active
Industries: Artificial Intelligence

Company Name: Ver: Saudi Arabia
Description: Versa is a Chinese-based company that offers an artificial intelligence-based video and photo editing app.
Website: http://www.versa-ai.com/
Phone: **Email:** contact@versa-ai.com
City: Beijing **State:** Beijing **PC:** **Country:** China
Year Established: **Status 2020:** Active
Industries: Application Services for:, Artificial Intelligence for:, ~ Media-Communications (41)

Company Name: Vincross
Description: Vincross is a consumer robotics company.
Website: http://www.vincross.com/
Phone: **Email:** hello@vincross.com
City: Beijing **State:** Beijing **PC:** **Country:** China
Year Established: **Status 2020:** Active
Industries: Artificial Intelligence for:, ~ Manufacturing-Electronic (30), Robotics

Company Name: VIPCODE
Description: Beijing based Education company.
Website: https://www.vipcode.com
Phone: **Email:** hello@vipcode.com
City: Beijing **State:** Beijing **PC:** **Country:** China
Year Established: 2017 **Status 2020:** Active
Industries: Artificial Intelligence for:, ~ Education (13), ~ Education (13)

Company Name: W&R (Wisdom Reputation)
Description: W&R (Wisdom Reputation) is a Healthcare company.
Website: http://www.bjzzdx.com/
Phone: **Email:** zzdx@bjzzdx.com
City: Beijing **State:** Beijing **PC:** **Country:** China
Year Established: 2014 **Status 2020:** Active
Industries: Artificial Intelligence for:, ~ Healthcare (20), IT Managed Services

Company Name: WATRIX.AI
Description: WATRIX.AI is an artificial intelligence company focusing on computer vision and video big data analysis.
Website: http://www.watrix.ai/
Phone: **Email:** Partnership@watrix.ai
City: Beijing **State:** Beijing **PC:** **Country:** China
Year Established: 2016 **Status 2020:** Active
Industries: Artificial Intelligence for:, Robotics

Company Name: Wormhole
Description: Downloads the first voice assistant
Website: http://www.uzoo.cn/
Phone: **Email:** 37685@reference-encyclopedia-ai.net
City: Beijing **State:** Beijing **PC:** **Country:** China
Year Established: 2011 **Status 2020:** Active
Industries: Application Services for:, Machine Learning

Company Name: XuanYi Tech
Description: XuanYi Techis an AI emotional analysis and computing technology firm.
Website: http://www.xuanyiai.com/
Phone: **Email:** mmp@xuanyiai.com
City: Beijing **State:** Beijing **PC:** **Country:** China
Year Established: 2018 **Status 2020:** Active
Industries:

Company Name: Yawlih
Description: Scaling big data across healthcare
Website: http://www.yawlih.com.cn/
Phone: **Email:** info@Yawlih.cn
City: Beijing **State:** Beijing **PC:** **Country:** China
Year Established: **Status 2020:** Active
Industries: Artificial Intelligence for:, Big Data and Analytics for:, Enterprise Application Services for:, ~ Healthcare (20), ~ Healthcare (20)

Company Name: Yizhun Intelligent
Description: Yizhun Intelligentis an AI & Robotics company.
Website: http://www.yizhun-ai.com/
Phone: 010-86393784 **Email:** chenchong.lv@yizhun-ai.com
City: Beijing **State:** BJ **PC:** **Country:** China
Year Established: 2017 **Status 2020:** Active
Industries: Artificial Intelligence for:, Robotics

Company Name: Yobbom QiSheng Technology
Description: Yobbom QiSheng Technology is an intelligent acoustics enterprise.
Website: http://www.yobbom.com/
Phone: 400-000-5688 **Email:** service@yobbom.com
City: Beijing **State:** Beijing **PC:** **Country:** China
Year Established: **Status 2020:** Active
Industries: Artificial Intelligence

Company Name: Yongqianbao
Description: Yongqianbao is an AI-based financial service APP that provides small amount, short term loans to underbanked population in China.
Website: http://smartfinancegroup.com
Phone: **Email:** media@daixiaomi.com
City: Beijing **State:** Beijing **PC:** **Country:** China
Year Established: 2013 **Status 2020:** Active
Industries: Artificial Intelligence for:, ~ Banking and Financial Markets-Services (7), ~ Banking and Financial Markets-Services (7), Web

Company Name: Yuanshan AI
Description: Yuanshan AI is an Industrial intelligent platform provider
Website: http://www.yuanshan-ai.com/
Phone: **Email:** 37723@reference-encyclopedia-ai.net
City: Beijing **State:** Beijing **PC:** **Country:** China
Year Established: 2018 **Status 2020:** Active
Industries: Artificial Intelligence for:, Robotics

Company Name: Zero Zero Robotics
Description: Zero Zero Robotics is working to develop an innovative new device called the Hover Camera.
Website: http://GetHover.com/
Phone: **Email:** partnerships@gethover.com
City: Beijing **State:** Beijing **PC:** **Country:** China
Year Established: **Status 2020:** Active
Industries: Artificial Intelligence for:, ~ Transportation and Logistics (57), Robotics

Company Name: Zhuge.com
Description: Zhuge.com is a Chinese property search engine company that provides users with real estate information search services in their cities.
Website: http://bj.zhuge.com/
Phone: 010-59142318 **Email:** kefu@zhuge.com
City: Beijing **State:** BJ **PC:** **Country:** China
Year Established: 2015 **Status 2020:** Active
Industries: Artificial Intelligence for:, ~ Insurance (25), ~ Real Estate (49), Web

Company Name: Zhugefang
Description: Zhugefang is the leading domestic real estate big data and real estate artificial intelligence startup company.
Website: http://bj.zhugefang.com/
Phone: 400-810-5188 **Email:** kefu@zhugefang.com
City: Beijing **State:** Beijing **PC:** **Country:** China
Year Established: **Status 2020:** Active
Industries: Artificial Intelligence for:, Big Data and Analytics for:, ~ Real Estate (49)

Company Name: ZingFront
Description: ZingFront Software is an AI technology company that has built AD Creative Cloud and 3D-Creative Cloud.
Website: http://www.zingfront.com
Phone: **Email:** hello@zingfront.com
City: Beijing **State:** Beijing **PC:** **Country:** China
Year Established: 2015 **Status 2020:** Active
Industries: Artificial Intelligence for:, Cloud for:, Business Software as a Service Apps (SaaS Apps) for:, Virtual Reality (VR)

Company Name: Zionchina
Description: Focus on Precision Diabetes Management through innovation in IT and AI technology.
Website: http://www.zionchina.com
Phone: **Email:** contact@zionchina.com
City: Beijing **State:** BJ **PC:** **Country:** China
Year Established: 2013 **Status 2020:** Active
Industries: Artificial Intelligence for:, ~ Healthcare (20), IT Managed Services for:, Machine Learning

Company Name: Ztelic
Description: Ztelic is focused on social-network data and develops a social platform for big data analytics.
Website: http://ztelic.com
Phone: **Email:** info@ztelic.com
City: Beijing **State:** Beijing **PC:** **Country:** China
Year Established: 2012 **Status 2020:** Active
Industries: Databases for:, Enterprise Application Services for:, Natural Language Processing

Company Name: AbitAI
Description: AbitAI is a shopping guide solution provider based in China.
Website: http://www.abitai.com/
Phone: **Email:** Media@abitai.com
City: Haidian **State:** Beijing **PC:** **Country:** China
Year Established: **Status 2020:** Active
Industries: Artificial Intelligence for:, E-Commerce for:, ~ Retail and Consumer Products (52)

Company Name: AInnovation
Description: AInnovation is an artificial intelligence (AI) business solutions provider.
Website: http://www.ainnovation.com/tech/en
Phone: **Email:** 4424@reference-encyclopedia-ai.net
City: Haidian **State:** Beijing **PC:** **Country:** China
Year Established: **Status 2020:** Active
Industries: Artificial Intelligence for:, Business Applications for:, Machine Learning

Company Name: Beijing Ewaybot Technology LLC
Description: Beijing Ewaybot LLC is a startup robotics company, building high performance teen-size semi-humanoid mobile robot.
Website: http://www.ewaybot.cn/index_en
Phone: **Email:** info@ewaybot.com
City: Haidian **State:** Beijing **PC:** **Country:** China
Year Established: **Status 2020:** Active
Industries:

Company Name: ELITE Technology
Description: ELITE Technology is a domestic industrial robot company
Website: http://www.elibot.cn/
Phone: (400) 189-9358 **Email:** market@elibot.cn
City: Haidian **State:** BJ **PC:** **Country:** China
Year Established: 2016 **Status 2020:** Active
Industries: Artificial Intelligence for:, Robotics

Company Name: Etoury
Description: Etoury is an artificial intelligence navigation technology and industry solution provider.
Website: http://www.etoury.com
Phone: 025 - 66043489 **Email:** kefu@etoury.com
City: Haidian **State:** Beijing **PC:** **Country:** China
Year Established: 2016 **Status 2020:** Active
Industries: Artificial Intelligence

Company Name: Fosafer
Description: Fosafer is a high-tech innovative enterprise, focusing on artificial intelligence - biometric field, and machine learning algorithm.
Website: http://www.fosafer.com/
Phone: 1088111888 **Email:** BD@fosafer.com
City: Haidian **State:** Beijing **PC:** **Country:** China

Year Established: **Status 2020:** Active
Industries: Artificial Intelligence for:, ~ Biotechnology (9)

Company Name: Huimei Technology
Description: Huimei Technology is an artificial intelligence (AI)-powered medical solutions provider.
Website: http://www.huimei.net/
Phone: **Email:** info@huimeicap.com
City: Haidian **State:** Beijing **PC:** **Country:** China
Year Established: 2015 **Status 2020:** Active
Industries: Artificial Intelligence for:, ~ Healthcare (20)

Company Name: iDeepWi: Sweden
Description: iDeepWise is an AI company that specializes in brain-based artificial intelligence and deep learning core technology.
Website: http://www.ideepwise.ai/
Phone: 010 - 62981512 **Email:** bd@ideepwise.ai
City: Haidian **State:** BJ **PC:** **Country:** China
Year Established: 2015 **Status 2020:** Active
Industries: Artificial Intelligence for:, Machine Learning

Company Name: i-Kingtec
Description: i-Kingtec is an industrial UAV developer.
Website: http://ikingtec.com/
Phone: **Email:** 36742@reference-encyclopedia-ai.net
City: Haidian **State:** Beijing **PC:** **Country:** China
Year Established: 2017 **Status 2020:** Active
Industries: Artificial Intelligence for:, Robotics

Company Name: InnoTree
Description: InnoTree is China's artificial intelligence equity investment and financing data service platform.
Website: http://www.innotree.cn/
Phone: 010-53342595 **Email:** service@innotree.cn
City: Haidian **State:** BJ **PC:** **Country:** China
Year Established: 2014 **Status 2020:** Active
Industries: Artificial Intelligence for:, Big Data and Analytics for:, ~ Banking and Financial Markets-Services (7)

Company Name: Magic Data Tech
Description: Magic Data Tech is a leading domestic artificial intelligence big data resource service company.
Website: http://www.magicdatatech.com
Phone: **Email:** business@magicdatatech.com
City: Haidian **State:** Beijing **PC:** **Country:** China
Year Established: 2016 **Status 2020:** Active
Industries: Analytics for:, Artificial Intelligence for:, Big Data and Analytics for:, IT Managed Services

Company Name: Moka
Description: Moka is a SaaS software that helps companies optimize their recruiting services and find the right talent for their business.
Website: http://mokahr.com/
Phone: **Email:** marketing@mokahr.com
City: Haidian **State:** BJ **PC:** **Country:** China
Year Established: 2015 **Status 2020:** Active
Industries: Artificial Intelligence for:, IT Managed Services for:, Web for:, Business Software as a Service Apps (SaaS Apps) for:, Business Software as a Service Apps (SaaS Apps)

Company Name: Recurrent.ai
Description: Recurrent.ai is a Chinese company that provides AI-enabled corporate services to improve sales efficiency.
Website: http://www.rcrai.com
Phone: 010-56271640 **Email:** market@rcrai.com
City: Haidian **State:** BJ **PC:** **Country:** China
Year Established: 2017 **Status 2020:** Active
Industries: Artificial Intelligence for:, Business Software as a Service Apps (SaaS Apps)

Company Name: Shannon.ai
Description: Shannon.ai is an artificial intelligence company.
Website: http://shannon.ai/
Phone: 86 (010) 6256 9982 **Email:** contact@shannonai.com
City: Haidian **State:** Beijing **PC:** **Country:** China
Year Established: **Status 2020:** Active
Industries: Artificial Intelligence for:, Machine Learning

Company Name: Sobot
Description: Sobot Let every business customer service brings to enjoy change WisdomThe perfect fusion of robotics, artificial, work orders.
Website: http://www.sobot.com/
Phone: 400-869-0981 **Email:** marketing@sobot.com
City: Haidian **State:** Beijing **PC:** **Country:** China
Year Established: 2014 **Status 2020:** Active
Industries: Artificial Intelligence for:, ~ Customer Relationship Management (11), IT Managed Services for:, Robotics

Company Name: StoneWi: Sweden
Description: StoneWise is committed to establishing the world's leading intelligent drug discovery platform.
Website: http://www.stonewise.cn
Phone: **Email:** bd@stonewise.cn
City: Haidian **State:** BJ **PC:** **Country:** China
Year Established: 2018 **Status 2020:** Active
Industries: Artificial Intelligence for:, ~ Biotechnology (9), Web

Company Name: Turing Robot
Description: Turing Robot is the best AI Robot company in China.
Website: http://www.turingapi.com/
Phone: 010-58349447 **Email:** turing@uzoo.cn
City: Haidian **State:** Beijing **PC:** **Country:** China
Year Established: 2010 **Status 2020:** Active
Industries:

Company Name: WITINMEM
Description: WITINMEM is a low power AI chips and system solutions based on processing-in-memory technology in NOR Flash memory.
Website: http://witin.net/
Phone: **Email:** shaodi.wang@witin.net
City: Haidian **State:** Beijing **PC:** **Country:** China
Year Established: 2017 **Status 2020:** Active
Industries: Artificial Intelligence for:, IT Managed Services

Company Name: Yi
Description: Yi is a Chinese artificial intelligence start-up developing machine vision technology for content marketing.
Website: http://www.yijia.ai/
Phone: 400-108-3066 **Email:** hr@dress-plus.com
City: Haidian **State:** Beijing **PC:** **Country:** China
Year Established: **Status 2020:** Active
Industries: Artificial Intelligence for:, Computer Vision for:, Machine Learning for:, Robotics

Company Name: ZhenRobotics
Description: ZhenRobotics develops package delivery robots.
Website: http://www.zhenrobot.com/
Phone: **Email:** met.li@zhenrobot.com
City: Haidian **State:** Beijing **PC:** **Country:** China
Year Established: 2016 **Status 2020:** Active
Industries: Artificial Intelligence for:, Robotics

Company Name: Zhongke Fanyu Technology
Description: Zhongke Fanyu Technology is a cross-lingual information retrieval service provider.
Website: http://www.anylangtech.com/
Phone: **Email:** hr@anylangtech.com
City: Haidian **State:** BJ **PC:** **Country:** China
Year Established: 2018 **Status 2020:** Active
Industries: Artificial Intelligence

Company Name: Deep Intelligent Phar: Morocco
Description: Deep Intelligent Pharma is a Beijing based Healthcare company.
Website: http://deepintepharma.com/
Phone: 010-86225158 **Email:** 36410@reference-encyclopedia-ai.net
City: Wangjing **State:** BJ **PC:** **Country:** China
Year Established: 2017 **Status 2020:** Active
Industries: Artificial Intelligence for:, ~ Biotechnology (9), ~ Healthcare (20)

Company **Name:** Kaiyi Technology
Description: Kaiyi Technology provides advanced driver-assistance systems algorithms for vehicles.
Website: http://www.adasplus.com/
Phone: 010-57276424 **Email:** jennypang@adasplus.com
City: Wangjing **State:** Beijing **PC:** **Country:** China
Year Established: 2016 **Status 2020:** Active
Industries: Artificial Intelligence for:, ~ Automotive (5), IT Managed Services for:, Machine Learning

Company Name: Imperial Vision Technology
Description: Imperial Vision Technology is an AI & Robotics company.
Website: http://www.imperial-vision.com/en/
Phone: **Email:** bd@imperial-vision.com
City: Foochow **State:** FJ **PC:** **Country:** China
Year Established: 2016 **Status 2020:** Active
Industries: Artificial Intelligence for:, Robotics

Company Name: Datadeta
Description: Datadeta is a global enterprise and contact recommendation platform, we dedicate to helping you find your next business partner.
Website: http://www.datadeta.com/
Phone: **Email:** support@datadeta.cm
City: Xiamen **State:** Fujian **PC:** **Country:** China
Year Established: 2016 **Status 2020:** Active
Industries: Artificial Intelligence for:, Big Data and Analytics for:, Business Intelligence for:, Data Management for:, IT Managed Services for:, Web

Company Name: DataExa
Description: DataExa is a full-stack artificial intelligence empowerment platform.
Website: http://www.dataexa.com/
Phone: **Email:** hr@dataexa.com
City: Xiamen **State:** FJ **PC:** **Country:** China
Year Established: 2014 **Status 2020:** Active
Industries: Artificial Intelligence

Company Name: Reconova Technologies
Description: Reconova is a leading artificial intelligence company in China.
Website: http://www.reconova.com/en/
Phone: 86 592-5939517 **Email:** sales@reconova.com
City: Xiamen **State:** Fujian **PC:** **Country:** China
Year Established: 2012 **Status 2020:** Active
Industries: Artificial Intelligence for:, IT Managed Services

Company Name: Sucheon
Description: Sucheon is a AI-driven machine fault diagnostic equipment developer.
Website: http://www.sucheon.com/
Phone: 0592-5222938 **Email:** Info@sucheon.com
City: Xiamen **State:** Fujian **PC:** **Country:** China
Year Established: 2016 **Status 2020:** Active
Industries: Artificial Intelligence for:, Robotics

Company Name: Zfusion Tech
Description: Zfusion Tech provides an end-to-end solution to determine the services needed by customers efficiently.
Website: http://www.zfusion.cn/
Phone: **Email:** contact@zfusion.cn
City: Xiamen **State:** Fujian **PC:** **Country:** China
Year Established: 2017 **Status 2020:** Active
Industries: ~ Media-Communications (41), Machine Learning

Company Name: Zhijiu Robot
Description: Zhijiu Robot is an industrial robot and service robot maker.
Website: http://www.agv8.com/
Phone: 5925854599 **Email:** zj@zj-r.com
City: Xiamen **State:** Fujian **PC:** **Country:** China
Year Established: 2013 **Status 2020:** Active
Industries: Artificial Intelligence for:, Robotics

Company Name: VIPionee: Serbia
Description: VIPioneers is a Driverless Technology Developer
Website: http://www.vipioneers.com/
Phone: 010-62699622 **Email:** fei.jiang@waytous.com
City: Qingdao **State:** Fujian Sheng **PC:** **Country:** China
Year Established: 2014 **Status 2020:** Active
Industries:

Company Name: Zhiyuanhui
Description: Zhiyuanhui is a provider of intelligent intelligence solutions for artificial intelligence.
Website:
Phone: **Email:** 37737@reference-encyclopedia-ai.net
City: Sichuan **State:** GS **PC:** **Country:** China
Year Established: 2010 **Status 2020:** Active
Industries: Artificial Intelligence

Company Name: KUBO
Description: KUBO is an AI & Robotics company.
Website:
Phone: **Email:** 36871@reference-encyclopedia-ai.net
City: Dongguan **State:** HE **PC:** **Country:** China
Year Established: 2016 **Status 2020:** Active
Industries: Artificial Intelligence for:, Robotics

Company Name: HelloWorld Robotics
Description: Last Mile Delivery Robot
Website: http://www.helloworldrobotics.xyz/
Phone: **Email:** kennedywai@helloworldrobotics.xyz
City: Dongguang **State:** Guangdong Province **PC:** **Country:** China
Year Established: **Status 2020:** Active
Industries: Artificial Intelligence for:, ~ Manufacturing-Electronic (30), IT Managed Services for:, Machine Learning for:, Robotics

Company Name: CloudsPlus
Description: CloudsPlus is a core technology driven by cloud computing, artificial intelligence, and the Internet of Things.
Website: http://www.cloudsplus.com.cn/
Phone: 020-66778777 **Email:** zhangping@cloudsplus.com.cn
City: Guangzhou **State:** Guangdong Province **PC:** **Country:** China
Year Established: 2013 **Status 2020:** Active
Industries:

Company Name: DMAI
Description: DMAI is committed to building a new generation of artificial intelligence operating system
Website: http://www.dm-ai.cn/
Phone: 020-39275688 **Email:** contact@dm-ai.cn
City: Guangzhou **State:** Guangdong Province **PC:** **Country:** China
Year Established: 2018 **Status 2020:** Active
Industries: Artificial Intelligence

Company Name: EcooSteam
Description: EcooSteam is an AI property management platform developer.
Website:
Phone: **Email:** 36473@reference-encyclopedia-ai.net
City: Guangzhou **State:** Guangdong Province **PC:** **Country:** China
Year Established: 2017 **Status 2020:** Active

Industries: Artificial Intelligence

Company Name: F5 Future Store
Description: F5 Future Store is a convenience store that uses a combination of machine automation and artificial algorithms instead of labor.
Website: http://www.f5-futurestore.com/
Phone: **Email:** bd@f5store.cn
City: Guangzhou **State:** GD **PC:** **Country:** China
Year Established: 2014 **Status 2020:** Active
Industries: Artificial Intelligence for:, Machine Learning

Company Name: Fulmz AI
Description: Fulmz AI is a pharmaceutical technology developer
Website: http://www.fulmz.com/
Phone: 020-29067016 **Email:** 36600@reference-encyclopedia-ai.net
City: Guangzhou **State:** Guangdong Province **PC:** **Country:** China
Year Established: 2015 **Status 2020:** Active
Industries: Artificial Intelligence for:, ~ Healthcare (20)

Company Name: GumpCome
Description: A Company which conduct research, manufacture of smart vending machines with orientation of artificial intelligence innovation.
Website: http://www.gumpcome.com/en/
Phone: (400)873-7770 **Email:** 36657@reference-encyclopedia-ai.net
City: Guangzhou **State:** Guangdong Province **PC:** **Country:** China
Year Established: 2015 **Status 2020:** Active
Industries: Artificial Intelligence for:, Machine Learning

Company Name: Homerun Smart
Description: Homerun Smart is an independent research and development enterprise dedicated to artificial intelligence.
Website: http://www.homerunsmart.com/
Phone: 020-26227677 **Email:** Info@homerunsmart.com
City: Guangzhou **State:** Guangdong Province **PC:** **Country:** China
Year Established: 2015 **Status 2020:** Active
Industries: Artificial Intelligence

Company Name: Jim Koala
Description: Jim Koala is a health service robot manufacturer.
Website: http://www.jimkoala.cn/
Phone: 020-39213826 **Email:** jimkoala@163.com
City: Guangzhou **State:** Guangdong Province **PC:** **Country:** China
Year Established: **Status 2020:** Active
Industries: Artificial Intelligence for:, ~ Manufacturing-Miscellaneous (34), Robotics

Company Name: Kuaizi Technology
Description: Kuaizi Tech is World's leading and China's first AI Creative Platform
Website: http://kuaizi.co
Phone: **Email:** 36870@reference-encyclopedia-ai.net
City: Guangzhou **State:** GD **PC:** **Country:** China
Year Established: 2013 **Status 2020:** Active
Industries: Artificial Intelligence

Company Name: Tianxiang Aviation Technology
Description: Tianxiang Aviation Technology is a AI & Robotics company.
Website: http://www.txauav.com/
Phone: 4008 922 876 **Email:** Sales@txauav.com
City: Guangzhou **State:** GD **PC:** **Country:** China
Year Established: 2010 **Status 2020:** Active
Industries: Artificial Intelligence for:, Robotics

Company Name: TUNGEE
Description: TUNGEE is a leading intelligent sales service provider in China.
Website: http://www.tungee.com
Phone: 020-31136465 **Email:** service@tungee.com
City: Guangzhou **State:** Guangdong Province **PC:** **Country:** China
Year Established: 2016 **Status 2020:** Active
Industries:

Company Name: Tuputech
Description: Tuputech provides image recognition services with state-of-the-art AI algorithms and computer vision technology.
Website: http://us.tuputech.com/
Phone: 020-29898058 **Email:** bd@tuputech.com
City: Guangzhou **State:** Guangdong Province **PC:** **Country:** China
Year Established: **Status 2020:** Active
Industries: Artificial Intelligence for:, Image Recognition for:, IT Managed Services for:, Web

Company Name: UFO.AI
Description: UFO.AI is an Enterprise services company.
Website: http://www.ufo-ai.com/
Phone: 029-81131150 **Email:** market@ufo-ai.com
City: Guangzhou **State:** GD **PC:** **Country:** China
Year Established: 2017 **Status 2020:** Active
Industries: Artificial Intelligence

Company Name: WeRide.ai
Description: WeRide.ai is a mobility company powered by AI technology and Robotics.
Website: http://www.weride.ai/
Phone: **Email:** contactus@weride.ai
City: Guangzhou **State:** Guangdong Province **PC:** **Country:** China
Year Established: 2017 **Status 2020:** Active
Industries:

Company Name: 0glass
Description: Open industrial AR application era .
Website: www.0glass.cn/
Phone: **Email:** marketing@0glass.cn
City: Shenzhen **State:** Guangdong Province **PC:** **Country:** China
Year Established: **Status 2020:** Active
Industries: Application Services for:, Artificial Intelligence for:, Human Computer Interaction for:, ~ Telecommunications (56), ~ Professional Services (48)

Company Name: AI Motion Sports
Description: AI Motion Sports is a youth sports education and management platform.
Website: https://www.aimotinsports.com/
Phone: 852 91341938 **Email:** info@aimotionsports.com
City: Shenzhen **State:** Guangdong Province **PC:** **Country:** China
Year Established: 2018 **Status 2020:** Active
Industries: Artificial Intelligence for:, ~ Arts-Entertainment-Recreation (4)

Company **Name:** Aiator
Description: Aiator is an artificial intelligence product and technology solutions company
Website: http://www.aiator.com/
Phone: 0755-86523053 **Email:** info@aiator.com
City: Shenzhen **State:** Guangdong Province **PC:** **Country:** China
Year Established: 2010 **Status 2020:** Active
Industries: Artificial Intelligence for:, ~ Biotechnology (9), IT Managed Services

Company Name: Aicrobo
Description: Aicrobo is the industry's leading robotic autonomous mobile solutions and robotics application products supplier.
Website: http://www.aicrobo.com
Phone: 0755-86576525 **Email:** support@aicrobo.com
City: Shenzhen **State:** Guangdong Province **PC:** **Country:** China
Year Established: **Status 2020:** Active
Industries: Artificial Intelligence for:, Robotics

Company Name: AiDriving
Description: AiDriving develops intelligent and advanced sensor based anti-collision smart devices.
Website: http://www.aidriving.com/
Phone: 0755-26600406 **Email:** Sales@aidriving.com
City: Shenzhen **State:** Guangdong Province **PC:** **Country:** China
Year Established: 2013 **Status 2020:** Active
Industries: Artificial Intelligence for:, ~ Automotive (5)

Company Name: Allgmented Vision
Description: Allgmented Vision Focus on AR smart glasses products, with hardware and algorithms as the core, and build solutions for the industry.
Website: http://www.allgmented.com/
Phone: 86-13651635343 **Email:** gaofei@allgmented.com
City: Shenzhen **State:** Guangdong Province **PC:** **Country:** China
Year Established: **Status 2020:** Active
Industries: Artificial Intelligence for:, Augmented Reality

Company Name: AMBER AI
Description: DIGITAL ASSET TRADING
Website: http://www.amberaigroup.com
Phone: **Email:** contact@amberaigroup.com
City: Shenzhen **State:** Guangdong Province **PC:** **Country:** China
Year Established: **Status 2020:** Active
Industries: Artificial Intelligence for:, ~ Banking and Financial Markets-Services (7), Machine Learning

Company Name: Andespace
Description: Andespace is a provider of artificial intelligence and big data applications and services for the underground space
Website: http://www.andespace.com/
Phone: 0755-23610689 **Email:** ande_market@andespace.com
City: Shenzhen **State:** Guangdong Province **PC:** **Country:** China
Year Established: 2018 **Status 2020:** Active
Industries: Artificial Intelligence

Company Name: Bello China
Description: Bello is an AI-based automated recruitment system developer
Website: http://www.belloai.com/
Phone: (0755) 8657 6905 **Email:** bz@belloai.com
City: Shenzhen **State:** Guangdong Province **PC:** **Country:** China
Year Established: 2016 **Status 2020:** Active
Industries: Artificial Intelligence

Company Name: Bominwell Robotics
Description: Shenzhen Bominwell Robotics is a artificial & robotics company.
Website: http://www.bominwell.com/
Phone: 0755-25889479 **Email:** info@bominwell.com
City: Shenzhen **State:** Guangdong Province **PC:** **Country:** China
Year Established: 2014 **Status 2020:** Active
Industries: Artificial Intelligence for:, Robotics

Company Name: Chewrobot
Description: Chewrobot is an artificial intelligence & robotic company.
Website: http://www.chewrobot.com/
Phone: (86)755-86968772 **Email:** contact@qiwu.ai
City: Shenzhen **State:** Guangdong Province **PC:** **Country:** China
Year Established: **Status 2020:** Active
Industries:

Company Name: DeepVision Innovation Technology
Description: DeepVision is a fast deep learning and visual identification technology company.
Website: http://www.deepvai.com
Phone: **Email:** hr@deepvai.com
City: Shenzhen **State:** GD **PC:** **Country:** China
Year Established: 2016 **Status 2020:** Active
Industries: Artificial Intelligence for:, Computer Vision

Company Name: Dobot
Description: Dobot is a leading robotic arm solutions provider.
Website: www.dobot.cc/
Phone: **Email:** sales@dobot.cc
City: Shenzhen **State:** Guangdong Province **PC:** **Country:** China
Year Established: **Status 2020:** Active
Industries: Artificial Intelligence for:, ~ Manufacturing-Electronic (30), Industrial Solutions for:, Robotics

Company Name: Dorabot
Description: Dorabot is a venture-backed AI and robotics company focused on developing logistics solutions.
Website: http://www.dorabot.com/
Phone: **Email:** info@dorabot.com
City: Shenzhen **State:** Guangdong Province **PC:** **Country:** China
Year Established: **Status 2020:** Active
Industries: Artificial Intelligence for:, ~ Transportation and Logistics (57), Machine Learning for:, Robotics for:, ~ Customer Relationship Management (11), ~ Transportation and Logistics (57)

Company Name: Ekang99.com
Description: Ekang99.com is an AI community-based healthcare products platform
Website: http://www.ekang99.com/
Phone: **Email:** service@ekang99.com
City: Shenzhen **State:** Guangdong Province **PC:** **Country:** China
Year Established: 2016 **Status 2020:** Active
Industries: Artificial Intelligence for:, ~ Healthcare (20)

Company Name: FATS.AI
Description: FATS.AI is a revolutional turn-key solution for Android device assembly line testing and analytics.
Website: http://fats.ai/
Phone: **Email:** nik@fats.ai
City: Shenzhen **State:** GD **PC:** **Country:** China
Year Established: 2018 **Status 2020:** Active
Industries: Analytics for:, Application Services for:, Artificial Intelligence for:, IT Managed Services

Company Name: Fortsense
Description: Fortsense is an AI-aware chip designer, focusing on core component design, outsourcing semiconductor supply chain foundry.
Website: http://www.fortsense.com
Phone: **Email:** public@fortsense.com
City: Shenzhen **State:** Guangdong Province **PC:** **Country:** China
Year Established: 2017 **Status 2020:** Active
Industries: Artificial Intelligence

Company Name: GJS Robot
Description: GJS Robot is an AI & Robotics company.
Website: http://www.gjs.so/
Phone: (400) 100-2624 **Email:** support@gjs.so
City: Shenzhen **State:** Guangdong Province **PC:** **Country:** China
Year Established: 2015 **Status 2020:** Active
Industries: Artificial Intelligence for:, Robotics

Company Name: Gold-Wood
Description: Gold-Wood is an intelligent learning platform.
Website: http://gaomuxuexi.com/
Phone: **Email:** hcxy@gaomuxuexi.com
City: Shenzhen **State:** Guangdong Province **PC:** **Country:** China
Year Established: 2015 **Status 2020:** Active
Industries: Business Intelligence for:, Machine Learning

Company Name: Gowild
Description: Gowild is a group of artificial intelligence as the core and the constant pursuit of black technology products.
Website: http://www.gowild.cn
Phone: 400-823-9139 **Email:** 36637@reference-encyclopedia-ai.net
City: Shenzhen **State:** Guangdong Province **PC:** **Country:** China
Year Established: 2013 **Status 2020:** Active
Industries: Artificial Intelligence for:, Robotics

Company Name: GuaTeng Technology
Description: GuaTeng Technology is a Professional Software Service Provider of IVD Instrument Internet Based Management SaaS Platform.
Website: http://www.guatengtech.com/
Phone: **Email:** 36655@reference-encyclopedia-ai.net
City: Shenzhen **State:** Guangdong Province **PC:** **Country:** China
Year Established: 2015 **Status 2020:** Active
Industries: Artificial Intelligence for:, ~ Healthcare (20)

Company Name: Haylion Technologies
Description: Urban Mobility Platform Provider
Website: http://www.haylion.cn/index_e.jsp
Phone: **Email:** contactus@haylion.cn
City: Shenzhen **State:** Guangdong Province **PC:** **Country:** China
Year Established: 2016 **Status 2020:** Active
Industries: Artificial Intelligence for:, IT Managed Services

Company Name: Huafu Information
Description: Huafu Information is committed to research and application development in the fields of artificial intelligence, big data and IT software.
Website: http://www.hfepay.com/
Phone: 400-7722-337 **Email:** bussiness@hfepay.com
City: Shenzhen **State:** GD **PC:** **Country:** China
Year Established: 2015 **Status 2020:** Active
Industries: Artificial Intelligence

Company Name: HUAZHI I:
Description: Intelligent manufacturing solutions provider .
Website: http://www.ehz.cn/
Phone: 0755-82270266 **Email:** 36716@reference-encyclopedia-ai.net
City: Shenzhen **State:** GD **PC:** **Country:** China
Year Established: 2015 **Status 2020:** Active
Industries: Application Services

Company Name: Huiyu Education
Description: Huiyu Education is an AI & Robotics company.
Website:
Phone: **Email:** 36720@reference-encyclopedia-ai.net
City: Shenzhen **State:** GD **PC:** **Country:** China
Year Established: 2016 **Status 2020:** Active
Industries:

Company Name: iCarbonX
Description: iCarbonX is a China-based artificial intelligence platform for health data company.
Website: http://www.icarbonx.com/
Phone: 75533605888 **Email:** hr@icarbonx.com
City: Shenzhen **State:** Guangdong Province **PC:** **Country:** China
Year Established: **Status 2020:** Active
Industries: Artificial Intelligence for:, ~ Biotechnology (9), ~ Healthcare (20)

Company Name: iCarbonX
Description:
Website: https://www.icarbonx.com/en/
Phone: 86 755 3360 5888 **Email:** press@h2o.ai
City: Shenzhen **State:** Guangdong Province **PC:** **Country:** China
Year Established: **Status 2020:** Active
Industries:

Company Name: Imsight
Description: Imsight Medical develops artificial intelligence assisted medical imaging analysis tools.
Website: http://www.imsightmed.com
Phone: 0755-22675803 **Email:** business@imsightmed.com
City: Shenzhen **State:** Guangdong Province **PC:** **Country:** China
Year Established: 2016 **Status 2020:** Active
Industries: Artificial Intelligence for:, ~ Healthcare (20)

Company Name: ioranges Automation
Description: ioranges Automation is an AI & Robotics Company.
Website: http://www.ioranges.cn/
Phone: 0755-23011582/9582 **Email:** info@ioranges.cn
City: Shenzhen **State:** Guangdong Province **PC:** **Country:** China
Year Established: **Status 2020:** Active
Industries: Artificial Intelligence for:, Robotics

Company Name: iP: India
Description: iPIN is a collective intelligence system providing all kinds of highly personalized information, especially for career development.
Website: http://www.ipin.com
Phone: 86-13715251722 **Email:** contact@ipin.com
City: Shenzhen **State:** Guangdong Province **PC:** **Country:** China
Year Established: 2013 **Status 2020:** Active
Industries: Artificial Intelligence for:, IT Managed Services for:, Web for:, Machine Learning

Company Name: Kewei Robot
Description: Kewei Robot is a security robot developer.
Website: http://www.keweitai.com/
Phone: **Email:** sales@keweitai.com
City: Shenzhen **State:** Guangdong Province **PC:** **Country:** China
Year Established: 2018 **Status 2020:** Active
Industries: Artificial Intelligence for:, Robotics for:, Security

Company Name: Kuang-Chi Science
Description: Kuang-Chi Science is a China-based high-tech company that provides users with experiences, products, and solutions.
Website: http://www.kuangchiscience.com/
Phone: **Email:** service@kuang-chi.com
City: Shenzhen **State:** Guangdong Province **PC:** **Country:** China
Year Established: **Status 2020:** Active
Industries: ~ Aerospace and Defense (2), Artificial Intelligence for:, ~ Personal-Religious-Civic (45)

Company Name: Langogo AI
Description: Langogo is an AI company that provides customer-oriented language product and service.
Website: http://www.langogo.ai/
Phone: **Email:** marketing@langogo.ai
City: Shenzhen **State:** Guangdong Province **PC:** **Country:** China
Year Established: 2018 **Status 2020:** Active
Industries: Artificial Intelligence for:, ~ Education (13), Machine Learning for:, Application Services for:, Natural Language Processing

Company Name: Leengstar Technology
Description: Leengstar Technology is an oilfield multiphase flow metering equipment developer.
Website:
Phone: 0755-22670940 **Email:** 36885@reference-encyclopedia-ai.net
City: Shenzhen **State:** Guangdong Province **PC:** **Country:** China
Year Established: 2014 **Status 2020:** Closed
Industries: Artificial Intelligence for:, ~ Education (13), ~ Energy and Utilities (14), ~ Energy and Utilities (14)

Company Name: Lezhi Robot
Description: Lezhi Robot is an AI & Robotics company.
Website: http://www.lzrobot.com/
Phone: **Email:** 36893@reference-encyclopedia-ai.net
City: Shenzhen **State:** Guangdong Province **PC:** **Country:** China
Year Established: 2013 **Status 2020:** Active
Industries: Artificial Intelligence for:, Robotics

Company Name: Linsation Intelligent Technology Limited
Description: Audio/Voice Interaction Soluiton
Website: http://www.lin-sation.com
Phone: **Email:** service@lin-sation.com
City: Shenzhen **State:** Guangdong Province **PC:** **Country:** China
Year Established: 2017 **Status 2020:** Active
Industries: Artificial Intelligence for:, IT Managed Services

Company Name: Loyoo
Description: Luyou Technology is a high-tech company that specializes in machine learning and computer vision-related hardware and software development.
Website: http://www.ilooyo.com
Phone: **Email:** 36918@reference-encyclopedia-ai.net
City: Shenzhen **State:** Guangdong Province **PC:** **Country:** China
Year Established: 2015 **Status 2020:** Active
Industries: Computer Vision for:, Machine Learning

Company Name: Mall Parking
Description: Mall Parking is a smart parking service provider.
Website: http://www.mallparking.cn
Phone: 0755-86962150 **Email:** hr@mallparking.cn
City: Shenzhen **State:** GD **PC:** **Country:** China
Year Established: 2014 **Status 2020:** Active
Industries: IT Managed Services for:, Application Services for:, ~ Travel and Transportation (58)

Company Name: Malong Technologies
Description: Malong Technologies is an award-winning AI startup that produces ProductAI; high accuracy product recognition platform and service
Website: http://www.malong.com
Phone: **Email:** hr@malongtech.cn
City: Shenzhen **State:** Guangdong Province **PC:** **Country:** China
Year Established: **Status 2020:** Active
Industries:

Company Name: Mingpianxia
Description: Mingpianxia is an artificial intelligence business card with its own shopping mall
Website: http://www.mingpianxia.cn/
Phone: **Email:** 36981@reference-encyclopedia-ai.net
City: Shenzhen **State:** Guangdong Province **PC:** **Country:** China
Year Established: 2016 **Status 2020:** Active
Industries: Artificial Intelligence for:, Web for:, Mobile

Company Name: MOZI
Description: MOZI builts a suite of AI tools for scientists to use on their discovery of next generation therapeutics.
Website: http://mozi.ai/
Phone: **Email:** 37025@reference-encyclopedia-ai.net
City: Shenzhen **State:** Guangdong Province **PC:** **Country:** China
Year Established: 2016 **Status 2020:** Active
Industries: Artificial Intelligence for:, ~ Biotechnology (9), ~ Healthcare (20), ~ Healthcare (20)

Company Name: nTheta
Description: nTheta is China's 1st cross-border operations-enabled growth builder that lands & grows overseas tech startups' business in the new China.
Website: http://www.ntheta.com
Phone: **Email:** admin@ntheta.com
City: Shenzhen **State:** Guangdong Province **PC:** **Country:** China
Year Established: **Status 2020:** Active
Industries: ~ Aerospace and Defense (2), Artificial Intelligence for:, Big Data and Analytics for:, Blockchain for:, Cloud for:, Computer Vision for:, Enterprise Application Services for:, ~ Banking and Financial Markets-Services (7), ~ Administrative and Support Services (1

Company Name: Odivee Digital
Description: AI-powered content marketing platform. We want to help businesses to CROSS-BORDER marketing with a simple, quick, and affordable solution
Website: http://odivee.com
Phone: 86 13713930853 **Email:** marketing@odivee.com
City: Shenzhen **State:** GD **PC:** **Country:** China
Year Established: 2019 **Status 2020:** Active
Industries: Artificial Intelligence

Company Name: ONES.AI
Description: ONES.AI is a technology company that provides enterprise-level R&D management solutions.
Website: http://ones.ai/
Phone: 400-188-1518 **Email:** support@ones.ai
City: Shenzhen **State:** GD **PC:** **Country:** China
Year Established: 2015 **Status 2020:** Active
Industries: IT Managed Services

Company Name: Orbbec
Description: The Orbbec mission is to create intelligent technologies for every human, everywhere through 3D image sensors and smart cameras.
Website: http://www.orbbec3d.com/
Phone: **Email:** info@orbbec3d.com
City: Shenzhen **State:** Guangdong Province **PC:** **Country:** China
Year Established: **Status 2020:** Active
Industries: Artificial Intelligence for:, IT Managed Services for:, Robotics

Company Name: Particle Accelerator Limited
Description: Hong Kong-based tech startup investor and accelerator
Website: http://www.particlex.com
Phone: **Email:** hello@particlex.com
City: Shenzhen **State:** Guangdong Province **PC:** **Country:** China

Year Established: 2017 **Status 2020:** Active
Industries: Big Data and Analytics for:, Blockchain for:, ~ Arts-Entertainment-Recreation (4), ~ Banking and Financial Markets-Services (7), ~ Energy and Utilities (14), Application Services for:, Internet of Things (IoT) for:, ~ Construction (10), ~ Construction (10)

Company Name: PuduTech
Description: PuduTech is an AI & Robotics Company.
Website: http://www.pudutech.com/en/
Phone: **Email:** global_sales@pudutech.com
City: Shenzhen **State:** Guangdong Province **PC:** **Country:** China
Year Established: 2016 **Status 2020:** Active
Industries: Artificial Intelligence for:, Robotics

Company Name: Reexen Technology
Description: Reexen specializes in cutting-edge research and development of high-end neural network processor for sensor-end applications.
Website: http://www.reexen.ch/
Phone: **Email:** info@reexen.com
City: Shenzhen **State:** Guangdong Province **PC:** **Country:** China
Year Established: 2018 **Status 2020:** Active
Industries: Artificial Intelligence for:, Big Data and Analytics for:, IT Managed Services

Company Name: Ringle.AI
Description: Ringle.AI is a Artificial Intellignece & Robotics based company.
Website: http://ringleai.com/
Phone: 0755-86662451 **Email:** info@ringleai.com
City: Shenzhen **State:** Guangdong Province **PC:** **Country:** China
Year Established: **Status 2020:** Active
Industries: Artificial Intelligence for:, Robotics

Company Name: Riseye
Description: Machine vision technology company based in Shenzhen.
Website: http://www.riseye.ai/
Phone: **Email:** RISEYE@RISEYE.AI
City: Shenzhen **State:** Guangdong Province **PC:** **Country:** China
Year Established: 2017 **Status 2020:** Active
Industries: Machine Learning

Company Name: Roadstar.ai
Description: Roadstar.ai empowers cars and trucks with artificial intelligence, so as to make transportation safer, more enjoyable, more efficient.
Website: http://roadstar.ai
Phone: **Email:** info@roadstar.ai
City: Shenzhen **State:** Guangdong Province **PC:** **Country:** China
Year Established: 2017 **Status 2020:** Active
Industries: Artificial Intelligence for:, ~ Automotive (5), Internet of Things (IoT) for:, Machine Learning for:, Robotics

Company Name: Ruixin Smart Medical
Description: Ruixin Smart Medical develops real-time monitoring equipment for the detection of cardiovascular and cerebrovascular diseases.
Website:
Phone: **Email:** 37321@reference-encyclopedia-ai.net
City: Shenzhen **State:** Guangdong Province **PC:** **Country:** China
Year Established: 2017 **Status 2020:** Active
Industries: Artificial Intelligence for:, ~ Healthcare (20), ~ Healthcare (20)

Company Name: Semacare
Description: Semacare mainly provides products for heart AI real-time care
Website: http://www.semacare.com/
Phone: 61 3 9421 6331 **Email:** info@semacare.com
City: Shenzhen **State:** Guangdong Province **PC:** **Country:** China
Year Established: 2014 **Status 2020:** Active
Industries:

Company Name: Shenzhen Gowild Robotics
Description: A Shenzhen AI and personal robot startup.
Website:
Phone: **Email:** 37376@reference-encyclopedia-ai.net
City: Shenzhen **State:** Guangdong Province **PC:** **Country:** China
Year Established: 2013 **Status 2020:** Active
Industries: Artificial Intelligence for:, Robotics

Company Name: SpeakIn
Description: Speakin is a voiceprint recognition and identity security solutions AI company.
Website: http://www.speakin.mobi/
Phone: 0755-36915323 **Email:** pr@speakin.mobi
City: Shenzhen **State:** Guangdong Province **PC:** **Country:** China
Year Established: 2015 **Status 2020:** Active
Industries: Artificial Intelligence for:, Voice Recognition for:, Cyber Security for:, Web for:, Robotics

Company Name: Sunvato
Description: Shenzhen Sunvato Robot System Co., Ltd. specializes in the research, development and service of intelligent sorting technology.
Website: http://www.sunvato.com/
Phone: 0755 23737353 **Email:** sales@sunvato.com
City: Shenzhen **State:** Guangdong Province **PC:** **Country:** China
Year Established: 2016 **Status 2020:** Active
Industries: Artificial Intelligence for:, Robotics

Company Name: SuperNode
Description: Super Node LLC.
Website: http://www.supernode.cn/
Phone: **Email:** contact@supernode.cn
City: Shenzhen **State:** Guangdong Province **PC:** **Country:** China
Year Established: 2016 **Status 2020:** Active
Industries: Artificial Intelligence for:, Augmented Reality for:, Big Data and Analytics for:, IT Managed Services for:, Virtual Reality (VR)

Company Name: Symphergy Corp
Description: Symphergy Corp is an artificial intelligence high-tech enterprise.
Website: http://www.symphergy.cn/
Phone: 86 (731) 2250 0390 **Email:** Sale@symphergy.cn
City: Shenzhen **State:** Guangdong Province **PC:** **Country:** China
Year Established: 2017 **Status 2020:** Active
Industries: Artificial Intelligence for:, ~ Manufacturing-General (31)

Company **Name:** Syrius Robotics
Description: Syrius Robotics is an AI & Roboticscompany.
Website: http://www.syriusrobotics.com/
Phone: 86-755-8656-1344 **Email:** sales@syriusrobotics.com
City: Shenzhen **State:** Guangdong Province **PC:** **Country:** China
Year Established: 2018 **Status 2020:** Active
Industries: Artificial Intelligence for:, Robotics

Company Name: Taobotics
Description: Taobotics offers educational and enterprise robotic products and solutions. .
Website: http://taobotics.com/
Phone: **Email:** 30935@reference-encyclopedia-ai.net
City: Shenzhen **State:** Guangdong Province **PC:** **Country:** China
Year Established: 2018 **Status 2020:** Active
Industries: Artificial Intelligence for:, Machine Learning

Company Name: Tencent
Description:
Website: https://www.tencent.com/en-us
Phone: 86 83765566 **Email:** 27333@reference-encyclopedia-ai.net
City: Shenzhen **State:** Guangdong Province **PC:** **Country:** China
Year Established: **Status 2020:** Active
Industries:

Company Name: Timekettle
Description: Timekettle is committed to building a global brand of AI translator so immersive that it disappears into the experience.
Website: http://www.timekettle.co
Phone: **Email:** kazaf.ye@timekettke.co
City: Shenzhen **State:** Guangdong Province **PC:** **Country:** China
Year Established: 2016 **Status 2020:** Active
Industries: Artificial Intelligence for:, ~ Education (13), Machine Learning for:, Internet of Things (IoT)

Company Name: UBTech Robotics
Description: UBTech Robotics is as an artificial intelligence and humanoid robotic company.
Website: http://www.ubtrobot.com/
Phone: 800-276-6137 **Email:** support@ubtrobot.com
City: Shenzhen **State:** Guangdong Province **PC:** **Country:** China
Year Established: 2012 **Status 2020:** Active
Industries: Artificial Intelligence for:, Machine Learning for:, Business Intelligence for:, Robotics

Company Name: Ufactory
Description: UFACTORY is a tech start-up that had created the world's first desktop robotic arm, the uArm.
Website: http://www.ufactory.cc/
Phone: **Email:** support@ufactory.cc
City: Shenzhen **State:** GD **PC:** **Country:** China
Year Established: 2013 **Status 2020:** Active
Industries: Artificial Intelligence for:, ~ Personal-Religious-Civic (45), Robotics

Company Name: VisualDeep
Description: VisualDeep is a high-tech enterprise specializing in the field of artificial intelligence mobile video recognition.
Website: http://www.visualdeep.com/
Phone: 0755-33028888 **Email:** marketing@visualdeep.com
City: Shenzhen **State:** Guangdong Province **PC:** **Country:** China
Year Established: 2015 **Status 2020:** Active
Industries: Artificial Intelligence

Company Name: VoiceAI
Description: VoiceAI is the industry's leading provider of voiceprint recognition and intelligent voice solutions.
Website: http://www.voiceaitech.com/
Phone: 13603009853 **Email:** info@voiceaitech.com
City: Shenzhen **State:** Guangdong Province **PC:** **Country:** China
Year Established: 2016 **Status 2020:** Active
Industries: Artificial Intelligence for:, IT Managed Services for:, Robotics

Company Name: Webot
Description: Webot is an artificial intelligence company focused on deep learning and breakthroughs in knowledge mapping technology.
Website: http://www.webot.ai/
Phone: 0755-33379887 **Email:** contact@webot.ai
City: Shenzhen **State:** Guangdong Province **PC:** **Country:** China
Year Established: 2016 **Status 2020:** Active
Industries:

Company Name: Whalehouse Technology
Description: Whalehouse Technology is a Shenzhen-based automated warehouse solutions provider.
Website: http://www.jc.house/index-en.html
Phone: **Email:** 37664@reference-encyclopedia-ai.net
City: Shenzhen **State:** Guangdong Province **PC:** **Country:** China
Year Established: 2014 **Status 2020:** Active
Industries: IT Managed Services for:, Application Services for:, ~ Telecommunications (56), ~ Transportation and Logistics (57)

Company Name: Xbiome
Description: Xbiome is an Intestinal Microbial AI Pharmaceutical Company.
Website: http://xbiome.cn/
Phone: 0755-86530994 **Email:** contact@Xbiome.cn
City: Shenzhen **State:** Guangdong Province **PC:** **Country:** China
Year Established: 2017 **Status 2020:** Active
Industries: Artificial Intelligence for:, ~ Biotechnology (9), ~ Healthcare (20)

Company Name: Xuanyu Tech
Description: Xuanyu Tech is a AI & Robotics start up Based in Shenzhen.
Website: http://www.xuanyutech.net/
Phone: **Email:** 37704@reference-encyclopedia-ai.net
City: Shenzhen **State:** Guangdong Province **PC:** **Country:** China
Year Established: 2017 **Status 2020:** Active
Industries: Artificial Intelligence for:, Robotics

Company Name: Youjie Zhix: India
Description: Youjie Zhixin is a Voice interactive service provider.
Website: http://eliteai.com.cn/
Phone: 86-0755-26690366 **Email:** Lxingzuo@eliteai.com.cn
City: Shenzhen **State:** Guangdong Province **PC:** **Country:** China
Year Established: **Status 2020:** Active
Industries: Artificial Intelligence

Company Name: YouSayIDo
Description: YouSayIDo is a AI & Robotics company.
Website:
Phone: **Email:** 37720@reference-encyclopedia-ai.net
City: Shenzhen **State:** Guangdong Province **PC:** **Country:** China
Year Established: 2017 **Status 2020:** Active
Industries: Artificial Intelligence for:, Robotics

Company Name: YZ Robot
Description: Shenzhen YZ Technology specializes in the research and development of artificial intelligence(AI) products.
Website: http://www.yzrobot.cn/en
Phone: **Email:** 37729@reference-encyclopedia-ai.net
City: Shenzhen **State:** GD **PC:** **Country:** China
Year Established: 2014 **Status 2020:** Active
Industries: Artificial Intelligence for:, IT Managed Services for:, Robotics

Company Name: Zhifubao
Description: Zhifubao is an AI intelligent repayment terminal.
Website:
Phone: **Email:** 37736@reference-encyclopedia-ai.net
City: Shenzhen **State:** Guangdong Province **PC:** **Country:** China
Year Established: 2019 **Status 2020:** Active
Industries: Artificial Intelligence for:, ~ Banking and Financial Markets-Services (7), ~ Banking and Financial Markets-Services (7)

Company Name: Zhiyi Tech
Description: AI, Machine Learning, Cloud-based Platform
Website: http://www.zhiyi.ai
Phone: **Email:** info@zhiyi.ai
City: Shenzhen **State:** Guangdong Province **PC:** **Country:** China
Year Established: **Status 2020:** Active
Industries: Artificial Intelligence

Company Name: Zhuiyi Technology
Description: Zhuiyi Technology is an artificial intelligence start-up that develops AI platform.
Website: http://www.zhuiyi.ai
Phone: 186-8066-8856 **Email:** pr@wezhuiyi.com
City: Shenzhen **State:** Guangdong Province **PC:** **Country:** China
Year Established: 2016 **Status 2020:** Active
Industries: Artificial Intelligence for:, Machine Learning

Company Name: Intelligent Automation
Description: Intelligent Automation was founded in 2006 in Zhuhai.
Website: http://i-a-i.com
Phone: (301) 294-5200 **Email:** contact@i-a-i.com
City: Zhuhai **State:** Guangdong Province **PC:** **Country:** China
Year Established: **Status 2020:** Active
Industries: Artificial Intelligence for:, Automation for:, Application Services

Company Name: 4DAGE
Description: 4DAGE specializes in applied Artificial Intelligence for machine/computer vision and 3D reconstruction solutions.
Website: http://www.4dage.com/en/#/
Phone: **Email:** zhengkuan@4dage.com
City: Zhuhai **State:** GD **PC:** **Country:** China
Year Established: 2014 **Status 2020:** Active
Industries: Artificial Intelligence for:, Cloud for:, Computer Vision for:, Machine Learning

Company Name: Xiaoxiao Robot
Description: Xiaoxiao Robot is anAI & Robotics company.
Website:
Phone: **Email:** 37696@reference-encyclopedia-ai.net
City: Chongqing **State:** Heilongjiang Sheng **PC:** **Country:** China
Year Established: 2017 **Status 2020:** Active
Industries: Artificial Intelligence for:, Robotics

Company Name: Fast Car Wash
Description: Fast Car Wash is an intelligent automatic car washing machine that offers standardized cleaning process.
Website: http://www.chexijie.com/
Phone: **Email:** 36554@reference-encyclopedia-ai.net
City: Henan **State:** Henan **PC:** **Country:** China
Year Established: 2016 **Status 2020:** Active
Industries: Application Services for:, ~ Automotive (5), Application Services for:, ~ Customer Relationship Management (11)

Company Name: Coherent AI
Description: Coherent AI is a Machine vision and artificial intelligence technologies of the future.
Website: http://www.coherent.ai
Phone: **Email:** 36309@reference-encyclopedia-ai.net
City: Wuhan **State:** Hubei **PC:** **Country:** China
Year Established: 2017 **Status 2020:** Active
Industries:

Company Name: Henghai Ocean
Description: Henghai Ocean is a AI & Robotics Start up Based in Wuhan.
Website:
Phone: **Email:** 36685@reference-encyclopedia-ai.net
City: Wuhan **State:** Hubei **PC:** **Country:** China
Year Established: 2016 **Status 2020:** Active
Industries: Artificial Intelligence for:, Robotics

Company Name: In-Driving
Description: In-Driving is a AI & Robotics Start Up Based in Wuhan.
Website:
Phone: **Email:** 36755@reference-encyclopedia-ai.net
City: Wuhan **State:** Hubei **PC:** **Country:** China
Year Established: 2015 **Status 2020:** Active
Industries: Artificial Intelligence for:, Application Services for:, Robotics

Company Name: JIMU Intelligent
Description: an autonomous driving technology provider
Website: http://www.jmadas.com
Phone: 86-027-87003313 **Email:** service@jmadas.com
City: Wuhan **State:** HB **PC:** **Country:** China
Year Established: 2011 **Status 2020:** Active
Industries: Artificial Intelligence for:, Computer Vision for:, IT Managed Services

Company Name: Jingdouyun Wireless Technology
Description: Jingdouyun Wireless Technology is a AI & Robotics Start up Based in Wuhan.
Website:
Phone: **Email:** 36826@reference-encyclopedia-ai.net
City: Wuhan **State:** Hubei **PC:** **Country:** China
Year Established: 2012 **Status 2020:** Active
Industries: Artificial Intelligence for:, IT Managed Services for:, Robotics

Company Name: Simshine
Description: Simshine is an artificial intelligence (AI) start-up focused on embedded computer vision technology.
Website: http://www.simshine.cn/
Phone: 027-8775-6910 **Email:** info@simshine.cn
City: Wuhan **State:** Hubei **PC:** **Country:** China
Year Established: 2017 **Status 2020:** Active
Industries: Artificial Intelligence for:, Computer Vision

Company Name: Chishine Optoelectronics
Description: Chishine Optoelectronics is a 3D digital and intelligent hardware developer.
Website: http://en.chishine3d.com/
Phone: **Email:** 36271@reference-encyclopedia-ai.net
City: Xian **State:** Hunan **PC:** **Country:** China
Year Established: 2014 **Status 2020:** Active
Industries: Artificial Intelligence

Company Name: Midai
Description: Midai is an AI-based tax service platform.
Website:
Phone: **Email:** 36974@reference-encyclopedia-ai.net
City: Xian **State:** Hunan **PC:** **Country:** China
Year Established: 2018 **Status 2020:** Active
Industries: Artificial Intelligence for:, ~ Banking and Financial Markets-Services (7)

Company Name: Muniu Box
Description: Muniu Box is a financial and tax accounting solution provider.
Website: http://www.muniubox.com/
Phone: **Email:** webkefu@muniubox.com
City: Xian **State:** Hunan **PC:** **Country:** China

Year Established: 2016 **Status 2020:** Active
Industries: Artificial Intelligence for:, ~ Banking and Financial Markets-Services (7), IT Managed Services

Company Name: Hengkai Intelligent Technology
Description: Hengkai Intelligent Technology is an Automated equipment and intelligent robot developer
Website: http://www.hk-zn.com/
Phone: 0731-84078166 **Email:** Service@hk-zn.com
City: Changsha **State:** Jiangsu **PC:** **Country:** China
Year Established: 2016 **Status 2020:** Active
Industries: Artificial Intelligence for:, Robotics

Company Name: Tidu Information Technology
Description: AI Cloud computing company
Website: http://tiduyun.com/
Phone: **Email:** hr@tiduyun.com
City: Changsha **State:** Jiangsu **PC:** **Country:** China
Year Established: 2016 **Status 2020:** Active
Industries: Artificial Intelligence for:, ~ Customer Relationship Management (11), IT Managed Services

Company Name: AllRide.ai
Description: AllRide.ai is an AI & Robotic company.
Website: http://allride.ai/
Phone: **Email:** 36044@reference-encyclopedia-ai.net
City: Nanjing **State:** Jiangsu **PC:** **Country:** China
Year Established: 2018 **Status 2020:** Active
Industries: Artificial Intelligence for:, Robotics

Company Name: Iluvatar CoreX
Description: Iluvatar CoreX is a developer of high-performance computing solutions including System-on-a-Chip (SoC) chipset and its software platform.
Website: http://www.iluvatar.a: Israel
Phone: 025-52600691 **Email:** 36745@reference-encyclopedia-ai.net
City: Nanjing **State:** Jiangsu **PC:** **Country:** China
Year Established: 2015 **Status 2020:** Active
Industries: Artificial Intelligence for:, Cloud for:, IT Managed Services for:, IT Managed Services

Company Name: Silexon
Description: Silexon is an AI-based pharmaceutical research and development service provider.
Website: http://www.silexon.tech/
Phone: **Email:** Contact@silexon.tech
City: Nanjing **State:** Jiangsu **PC:** **Country:** China
Year Established: 2018 **Status 2020:** Active
Industries: Artificial Intelligence for:, Machine Learning

Company Name: Silicon Intelligence
Description: Silicon Intelligence focuses on AI applications.
Website: http://www.guiji.ai/
Phone: 18520099699 **Email:** Guijixs@guiji.ai
City: Nanjing **State:** Jiangsu **PC:** **Country:** China
Year Established: 2017 **Status 2020:** Active
Industries:

Company Name: Weiyun AI
Description: Weiyun AI combines medical health and artificial intelligence that manufactures clinical dental products.
Website:
Phone: **Email:** 37660@reference-encyclopedia-ai.net
City: Nanjing **State:** Jiangsu **PC:** **Country:** China
Year Established: 2018 **Status 2020:** Active
Industries: Artificial Intelligence for:, ~ Healthcare (20), Robotics

Company Name: Xinktech
Description: Nanjing Based AI & Robotics Start Up
Website: http://www.xinktech.com
Phone: **Email:** 37700@reference-encyclopedia-ai.net
City: Nanjing **State:** Jiangsu **PC:** **Country:** China

Year Established: 2016 **Status 2020:** Active
Industries: Artificial Intelligence for:, IT Managed Services for:, Robotics

Company Name: Allgsight
Description: Allgsight is an AR smart glasses developer.
Website: http://www.allgsight.com/
Phone: 0512-6815-1486 **Email:** gaofei@allgmented.com
City: Suzhou **State:** Jiangsu **PC:** **Country:** China
Year Established: 2018 **Status 2020:** Active
Industries: Artificial Intelligence for:, ~ Healthcare (20), IT Managed Services

Company Name: C5 Face Recognition Cloud Platform
Description: C5 Face Recognition Cloud Platform is a project for the Suzhou Youth Community and Parks.
Website:
Phone: **Email:** 4511@reference-encyclopedia-ai.net
City: Suzhou **State:** Jiangsu **PC:** **Country:** China
Year Established: **Status 2020:** Active
Industries: Artificial Intelligence for:, Robotics

Company Name: CalmCar Vision System
Description: CalmCar enables deep learning based embedded system for complex road data recognition and localization.
Website: http://www.calmcar.com/
Phone: 86 (22) 2377 8482 **Email:** contact@calmcar.com
City: Suzhou **State:** Jiangsu **PC:** **Country:** China
Year Established: 2016 **Status 2020:** Active
Industries: ~ Automotive (5), Computer Vision for:, Machine Learning

Company Name: Conscience
Description: AI, Big Data, Machine Learning Algorithms, Cosmetics, Skincare, E-commerce
Website: http://www.conscienceai.co/
Phone: **Email:** 36324@reference-encyclopedia-ai.net
City: Suzhou **State:** Jiangsu **PC:** **Country:** China
Year Established: 2017 **Status 2020:** Active
Industries: Artificial Intelligence for:, ~ Beauty (8), Big Data and Analytics for:, ~ Beauty (8), E-Commerce for:, Machine Learning

Company Name: eduBot.cn
Description: eduBot.cn is a AI & Robotics company.
Website: http://edubot.cn/
Phone: **Email:** 36478@reference-encyclopedia-ai.net
City: Suzhou **State:** Jiangsu **PC:** **Country:** China
Year Established: 2015 **Status 2020:** Active
Industries: Artificial Intelligence for:, Robotics

Company Name: iMotion.ai
Description: iMotion.ai is a AI & Robotics company.
Website: http://imotion.ai/
Phone: **Email:** 36748@reference-encyclopedia-ai.net
City: Suzhou **State:** Jiangsu **PC:** **Country:** China
Year Established: 2016 **Status 2020:** Active
Industries: Artificial Intelligence for:, Robotics

Company Name: Kaven: Iran
Description: Kavenir is an AI & Robotics company.
Website:
Phone: **Email:** 36846@reference-encyclopedia-ai.net
City: Suzhou **State:** Jiangsu **PC:** **Country:** China
Year Established: 2015 **Status 2020:** Active
Industries: Artificial Intelligence for:, Robotics

Company Name: Niumengmeng
Description: Niumengmeng is a beef cattle AI aquaculture service provider .
Website:
Phone: **Email:** 37068@reference-encyclopedia-ai.net
City: Suzhou **State:** Jiangsu **PC:** **Country:** China

Year Established: 2019 **Status 2020:** Active
Industries: ~ Agriculture (3), ~ Agriculture (3), Artificial Intelligence for:, ~ Agriculture (3)

Company Name: Yinengtong
Description: Yinengtong is an intelligent voice system developer.
Website: http://kalamodo.com/
Phone: **Email:** 37713@reference-encyclopedia-ai.net
City: Suzhou **State:** Jiangsu **PC:** **Country:** China
Year Established: 2015 **Status 2020:** Active
Industries: Artificial Intelligence for:, Robotics

Company Name: Youxiu
Description: The Worlds First Intelligent Recommendation Engine for the Beautycare Industry
Website: http://www.youshowtech.com/
Phone: **Email:** joe@youshowtech.com
City: Suzhou **State:** Jiangsu **PC:** **Country:** China
Year Established: 2018 **Status 2020:** Active
Industries: ~ Healthcare (20), Machine Learning for:, Robotics

Company Name: Fclassroom
Description: Fclassroom is an artificial intelligence-powered education firm.
Website: http://www.fclassroom.com/
Phone: **Email:** fclassroom@bytedance.com
City: Wuxi Shi **State:** Jiangsu **PC:** **Country:** China
Year Established: 2014 **Status 2020:** Active
Industries: Artificial Intelligence for:, ~ Education (13), ~ Education (13)

Company Name: MYNT AI
Description: MYNT AI is a Silicon Valley AI startup that creates superhuman eyes for robots and cars.
Website: http://www.myntai.com
Phone: 669-264-6763 **Email:** support-en@myntai.com
City: Wuxi Shi **State:** Jiangsu **PC:** **Country:** China
Year Established: 2014 **Status 2020:** Active
Industries:

Company Name: Adenovo
Description: Adenovo is apply an artificial intelligence (AI) to help financial institutions to do the risk management.
Website: http://www.adenovo.com/
Phone: **Email:** service@adenovo.com
City: Taiwan **State:** JS **PC:** **Country:** China
Year Established: 2015 **Status 2020:** Active
Industries: Artificial Intelligence for:, IT Managed Services

Company Name: mit.Jobs
Description: Mit.Jobs can be seen as a huge union, connecting employees, job seekers, and all those who care about the value of work;.
Website: http://mit.jobs/
Phone: **Email:** service@mit.jobs
City: Taiwan **State:** Jiangsu Sheng **PC:** **Country:** China
Year Established: **Status 2020:** Active
Industries: Artificial Intelligence for:, Blockchain for:, ~ Human Resources (24), IT Managed Services for:, ~ Human Resources (24), ~ Social Media (54)

Company Name: Yihang.ai
Description: Yihang.ai manufactures autonomous driving systems.
Website: http://yihang.ai/
Phone: **Email:** contact@yihang.ai
City: Changchun **State:** Jilin **PC:** **Country:** China
Year Established: 2015 **Status 2020:** Active
Industries: Artificial Intelligence for:, ~ Automotive (5), ~ Aerospace and Defense (2)

Company Name: Kehigh Acade: Malaysia
Description: Kehigh Academy offers Primary English teaching products.
Website: http://www.kehigh.com/
Phone: **Email:** business@kehigh.com
City: Guangdong **State:** JL **PC:** **Country:** China
Year Established: 2016 **Status 2020:** Active
Industries: Artificial Intelligence for:, ~ Education (13), ~ Education (13), ~ Education (13)

Company Name: botBrain.ai
Description: Enterprise service company providing software solutions for content aggregation based in China.
Website: http://botbrain.ai/
Phone: 400-616-9216 **Email:** contact@botBrain.ai
City: Chaoyang **State:** Liaoning **PC:** **Country:** China
Year Established: **Status 2020:** Active
Industries: Artificial Intelligence for:, Application Services for:, ~ Professional Services (48)

Company **Name:** Polaris Education Technology
Description: Polaris Education Technology is an educational technology enterprise specializing in the field of "AI education.
Website: http://www.51polestar.com/
Phone: 4001-010-202 **Email:** Beijixing@51polestar.com
City: Chaoyang **State:** Liaoning **PC:** **Country:** China
Year Established: 2015 **Status 2020:** Active
Industries: Artificial Intelligence for:, ~ Education (13)

Company Name: Yunwen Technology
Description: Yunwen Technology is an AI company developing customer service robot.
Website:
Phone: **Email:** 37725@reference-encyclopedia-ai.net
City: Shenyang **State:** LN **PC:** **Country:** China
Year Established: 2019 **Status 2020:** Active
Industries: Artificial Intelligence for:, ~ Customer Relationship Management (11)

Company Name: AIDOC
Description: AIDOC is the pioneer in the field of distributed intelligent medical treatment and the world's first project to mine with life data...
Website: http://www.aidoc.me/
Phone: **Email:** 36005@reference-encyclopedia-ai.net
City: Tianyi **State:** Liaoning Sheng **PC:** **Country:** China
Year Established: 2015 **Status 2020:** Active
Industries: Artificial Intelligence for:, Big Data and Analytics for:, ~ Healthcare (20)

Company Name: STEERING AI
Description: STEERING AI is researching early warning system of fatigue driving.
Website: http://www.steering.ai
Phone: **Email:** info@steering.ai
City: Dongcheng **State:** Shaanxi **PC:** **Country:** China
Year Established: 2017 **Status 2020:** Active
Industries: Artificial Intelligence for:, Learning and Marketing Communications Services (MarComm)

Company Name: Jrobot
Description: Jrobot is a AI & Robotics company.
Website: http://www.jcrobots.com/
Phone: **Email:** jcrobot@163.com
City: Taian **State:** Shandong **PC:** **Country:** China
Year Established: 2014 **Status 2020:** Active
Industries: Artificial Intelligence for:, Robotics

Company Name: Rikai Labs
Description: Rikai Labs engages and educates WeChat users by blending chatbots powered by Artificial Intelligence with live people.
Website: http://rikai.co
Phone: **Email:** info@rikai.co
City: Jingan **State:** Shanghai **PC:** **Country:** China

Year Established: 2015 **Status 2020:** Active
Industries: Artificial Intelligence for:, ~ Education (13), ~ Social Assistance-Non-Profits (53)

Company Name: Clobotics
Description: Clobotics provides intelligent computer vision solutions for the retail and wind power sectors.
Website: http://www.clobotics.com/
Phone: **Email:** info@clobotics.com
City: Minghang **State:** Shanghai **PC:** **Country:** China
Year Established: 2016 **Status 2020:** Active
Industries: Analytics for:, Artificial Intelligence for:, Computer Vision for:, IT Managed Services for:, Machine Learning

Company Name: DeepBra: India
Description: DeepBrain is an artificial intelligence products company.
Website: http://www.deepbrain.ai
Phone: **Email:** tony@deepbrain.ai
City: Minhang **State:** Shanghai **PC:** **Country:** China
Year Established: 2012 **Status 2020:** Active
Industries: Artificial Intelligence for:, Robotics

Company Name: AccutarBio
Description: AccutarBio employs artificial intelligence to revolutionize drug discovery.
Website: https://www.accutarbio.com/
Phone: **Email:** Media@accutarbio.com
City: Shanghai **State:** Shanghai **PC:** **Country:** China
Year Established: 2015 **Status 2020:** Active
Industries:

Company Name: AEXELE.
Description: Digital
Website: http://www.aexele.com/en/
Phone: (86) 18516000303 **Email:** hello@aexele.com
City: Shanghai **State:** Shanghai **Zip:** 200060 **Country**: China
Year Established: **Status 2020:** Active
Industries: Analytics for:, Application Program Interfaces for:, Data Management for:, Development and Operations for:, ~ Media-Communications (1871), ~ Social Media (1884), Digital Marketing for:, ~ Media-Communications (1993), ~ Social Media (2006), Digital Media for:, ~ M

Company Name: AI Prime
Description: AI Prime is a life sciences company focused on developing oncology therapeutics targeting the growth and proliferation of cancer cells.
Website: http://ai-prime.ai/
Phone: 86 21 6841 3396 **Email:** contactus@ai-prime.ai
City: Shanghai **State:** Shanghai **PC:** **Country:** China
Year Established: 2017 **Status 2020:** Active
Industries: Artificial Intelligence

Company Name: AIWAYS
Description: AIWAYS is a manufacturer of smart electric car, based in Shanghai.
Website: https://www.ai-ways.com/
Phone: **Email:** bd@ai-ways.com
City: Shanghai **State:** SH **PC:** **Country:** China
Year Established: 2017 **Status 2020:** Active
Industries: Artificial Intelligence for:, ~ Automotive (5), ~ Automotive (5)

Company Name: APEX Technologies
Description: APEX Technologies is a customer data technology and AI company .
Website: http://www.chinapex.com
Phone: 400-820-8022 **Email:** info@chinapex.com
City: Shanghai **State:** Shanghai **PC:** **Country:** China
Year Established: 2012 **Status 2020:** Active
Industries: Artificial Intelligence for:, Enterprise Application Services

Company Name: ATN.io
Description: Artificial Intelligence API marketplace where developers, suppliers and buyers access & develop A.I. in a trusted collaborative environment
Website: http://atn.io
Phone: **Email:** contact@atn.io
City: Shanghai **State:** Shanghai **PC:** **Country:** China
Year Established: **Status 2020:** Active
Industries: Artificial Intelligence for:, Blockchain

Company Name: Buyint
Description: Buyint is a FinTech startup located in Shanghai, China. We provide capital matchmaking, cooperation, and deal making services.
Website: http://www.aiguanxi.ai/
Phone: **Email:** info@buyint.com
City: Shanghai **State:** Shanghai **PC:** **Country:** China
Year Established: 2015 **Status 2020:** Active
Industries: Artificial Intelligence for:, ~ Banking and Financial Markets-Services (7)

Company Name: ByteDance
Description: ByteDance is an internet technology company that enables to discover a world of creative content platforms.
Website: http://bytedance.com
Phone: **Email:** globalmedia@bytedance.com
City: Shanghai **State:** SH **PC:** **Country:** China
Year Established: 2012 **Status 2020:** Active
Industries: Artificial Intelligence for:, Content for:, Databases for:, Web for:, Machine Learning

Company Name: China Rapid Finance
Description: China Rapid Finance is an online consumer lending marketplace serving online users and China's emerging middle class.
Website: http://www.ChinaRapidFinance.com
Phone: 646 308 1635 **Email:** crf@crfchina.com
City: Shanghai **State:** Shanghai **PC:** **Country:** China
Year Established: **Status 2020:** Active
Industries: Artificial Intelligence for:, Big Data and Analytics for:, ~ Banking and Financial Markets-Services (7)

Company Name: Coffee Exchange
Description: Coffee Exchange is a global marketplace that connects roasters directly to coffee farmers.
Website: http://www.coffee.exchange
Phone: **Email:** hello@coffee.exchange
City: Shanghai **State:** Shanghai **PC:** **Country:** China
Year Established: 2018 **Status 2020:** Active
Industries: ~ Agriculture (3), Artificial Intelligence for:, Business Applications for:, ~ Agriculture (3), E-Commerce

Company Name: Coolpo
Description: Omnidirectional sensing
Website: http://www.coolpolens.com/CoolpoPANA/index.html
Phone: **Email:** matthew@coolpolens.com
City: Shanghai **State:** Shanghai **PC:** **Country:** China
Year Established: 2016 **Status 2020:** Active
Industries: Artificial Intelligence

Company Name: Cosmo: Sweden
Description: Cosmose AI understands, predicts and influences how 1 billion people shop offline.
Website: http://cosmose.co
Phone: **Email:** business@cosmose.co
City: Shanghai **State:** Shanghai **PC:** **Country:** China
Year Established: 2015 **Status 2020:** Active
Industries: Analytics for:, Artificial Intelligence for:, Big Data and Analytics for:, ~ Media-Communications (41), ~ Media-Communications (41)

Company Name: Cowarobot
Description: Cowarobot is to bring people the future travel experience by using robotics, self-driving technology and other intelligent solutions.
Website: http://en.cowarobot.com/en
Phone: 2159883721 **Email:** channel@cowarobot.com
City: Shanghai **State:** Shanghai **PC:** **Country:** China
Year Established: **Status 2020:** Active
Industries: Artificial Intelligence for:, IT Managed Services for:, Robotics

Company Name: Cubee Technology
Description: Cubee Technology is a global commercial develop service provider in multi-sports fields based on artificial intelligence and big data.
Website: http://en.cubee.com
Phone: 021-61849686 **Email:** bd@cubee.com
City: Shanghai **State:** SH **PC:** **Country:** China
Year Established: 2012 **Status 2020:** Active
Industries: ~ Arts-Entertainment-Recreation (4)

Company Name: Cyclone Robotics
Description: Cyclone Robotics is Providing enterprises with digital labor with artificial intelligence
Website: http://www.cyclone-robotics.com/
Phone: 400-800-8560 **Email:** Sales@cyclone-robotics.com
City: Shanghai **State:** Shanghai **PC:** **Country:** China
Year Established: 2015 **Status 2020:** Active
Industries:

Company Name: DataYes
Description: DataYes is China's leading edge financial technology company that offers a world-class and revolutionary global financial services platform.
Website: http://www.datayes.com/en
Phone: 1(408)645-6751 **Email:** info@datayes.com
City: Shanghai **State:** Shanghai **PC:** **Country:** China
Year Established: **Status 2020:** Active
Industries: Artificial Intelligence for:, Big Data and Analytics for:, Cloud for:, ~ Banking and Financial Markets-Services (7), ~ Banking and Financial Markets-Services (7), Machine Learning

Company Name: Deep AR
Description: Making things expressible
Website: http://www.deepar.io
Phone: **Email:** hello@deepar.io
City: Shanghai **State:** Shanghai **PC:** **Country:** China
Year Established: 2015 **Status 2020:** Active
Industries:

Company Name: DeepBlue Technology
Description: DeepBlue Technology (Shanghai) Co. Ltd creates smart retail systems using computer vision, AI, and analytics.
Website: http://www.deepblueai.com/
Phone: 400-117-7928 **Email:** market@deepblueai.com
City: Shanghai **State:** SH **PC:** **Country:** China
Year Established: 2014 **Status 2020:** Active
Industries: Artificial Intelligence for:, Computer Vision for:, IT Managed Services for:, Machine Learning

Company Name: Driva - AI Dash Cam Driving Assistant
Description: Mobile app that accurately locates the front cars and traffic lights based on AI computer vision technology.
Website: http://www.driva.ai/
Phone: **Email:** 36457@reference-encyclopedia-ai.net
City: Shanghai **State:** Shanghai **PC:** **Country:** China
Year Established: 2017 **Status 2020:** Active
Industries: Artificial Intelligence for:, IT Managed Services

Company Name: Encootech
Description: Encootech is a Digital Consulting and Digital Robot Solution Provider
Website: http://www.encootech.com
Phone: 400-639-2198 **Email:** Contact@encootech.com
City: Shanghai **State:** Shanghai **PC:** **Country:** China
Year Established: **Status 2020:** Active
Industries: Artificial Intelligence for:, Robotics

Company Name: Enflame
Description: Enflame is an artificial intelligence start-up developing cloud-based deep learning chips for AI training platforms.
Website: http://www.enflame-tech.com
Phone: **Email:** 30922@reference-encyclopedia-ai.net
City: Shanghai **State:** Shanghai **PC:** **Country:** China
Year Established: 2018 **Status 2020:** Active
Industries: Artificial Intelligence for:, ~ Education (13)

Company Name: Fantai AI
Description: Fantai AI is a Smart Hardware company.
Website: http://www.fantaiai.com/
Phone: **Email:** bd@aifantai.com
City: Shanghai **State:** Shanghai **PC:** **Country:** China
Year Established: 2018 **Status 2020:** Active
Industries:

Company Name: Foyoung Drone
Description: Foyoung Drone is an AI & Robotics company.
Website:
Phone: **Email:** 36592@reference-encyclopedia-ai.net
City: Shanghai **State:** Shanghai **PC:** **Country:** China
Year Established: 2017 **Status 2020:** Active
Industries: Artificial Intelligence for:, Robotics

Company Name: Gantu AI
Description: Gantu AI is a computer vision technology and product developer.
Website: http://www.gantuai.com/
Phone: 152-2113-1405 **Email:** Hello@GantuAI.com
City: Shanghai **State:** Shanghai **PC:** **Country:** China
Year Established: 2018 **Status 2020:** Active
Industries: Artificial Intelligence for:, Robotics

Company Name: Gaussian Robot
Description: Shanghai Based AI & Robotics Start Up.
Website: http://www.gs-robot.com/
Phone: **Email:** info@gs-robot.com
City: Shanghai **State:** Shanghai **PC:** **Country:** China
Year Established: 2013 **Status 2020:** Active
Industries: Artificial Intelligence for:, Robotics

Company Name: Genius
Description: Genius is an artificial intelligence education platform.
Website: http://www.ubgenius.cn/
Phone: 150 8493 2113 **Email:** genius@changeducation.cn
City: Shanghai **State:** Shanghai **PC:** **Country:** China
Year Established: 2017 **Status 2020:** Active
Industries: Artificial Intelligence for:, ~ Education (13), ~ Education (13)

Company Name: Graviti
Description: Graviti is an artificial intelligence data service platform dedicated to growing into a one-stop AI data service platform for storing.
Website: http://www.graviti.cn/
Phone: **Email:** 36644@reference-encyclopedia-ai.net
City: Shanghai **State:** Shanghai **PC:** **Country:** China
Year Established: 2019 **Status 2020:** Active
Industries: Artificial Intelligence

Company Name: GRisk
Description: GRisk is an analytics and early warning platform for global macro risk.
Website: http://www.grisk.net
Phone: **Email:** team@grisk.cn
City: Shanghai **State:** Shanghai **PC:** **Country:** China

Year Established: 2018 **Status 2020:** Active
Industries: Big Data and Analytics for:, ~ Banking and Financial Markets-Services (7), IT Managed Services for:, Machine Learning for:, Business Software as a Service Apps (SaaS Apps)

Company Name: Gritworld
Description: Push the boundaries of realtime graphics and computer vision.
Website: http://www.gritworld.com/
Phone: **Email:** contact@gritworld.com
City: Shanghai **State:** Shanghai **PC:** **Country:** China
Year Established: 2015 **Status 2020:** Active
Industries:

Company Name: Haishen Technology
Description: Haishen Technology is an Image commodity search platform based on deep learning
Website: http://www.haishentech.com/
Phone: 021-61316906 **Email:** Info@oceandark.com
City: Shanghai **State:** Shanghai **PC:** **Country:** China
Year Established: 2016 **Status 2020:** Active
Industries: E-Commerce for:, Machine Learning

Company Name: Hi-in
Description: Hi-in is an AI-powered platform that helps Chinese students studying abroad find the job they want at leading companies back in China .
Website: http://www.hi-in.com
Phone: **Email:** 36691@reference-encyclopedia-ai.net
City: Shanghai **State:** Shanghai **PC:** **Country:** China
Year Established: 2016 **Status 2020:** Active
Industries: Machine Learning

Company Name: IceKred: Italy
Description: IceKredit is a risk management platform based on big data and artificial intelligence.
Website: http://www.icekredit.com/
Phone: **Email:** info@icekredit.com
City: Shanghai **State:** Shanghai **PC:** **Country:** China
Year Established: **Status 2020:** Active
Industries: Artificial Intelligence for:, Big Data and Analytics for:, ~ Banking and Financial Markets-Services (7), Machine Learning

Company Name: IRISIAN
Description: IRISIAN is one of the few companies in the world to master the core algorithm of independent.
Website: http://www.irisian.com
Phone: 86 021-65568086 **Email:** service@irisian.com
City: Shanghai **State:** SH **PC:** **Country:** China
Year Established: 2011 **Status 2020:** Active
Industries: Artificial Intelligence for:, Robotics

Company Name: Kankan Smart
Description: Kankan Smart is an AI & Robotics company.
Website:
Phone: **Email:** 36840@reference-encyclopedia-ai.net
City: Shanghai **State:** Shanghai **PC:** **Country:** China
Year Established: 2013 **Status 2020:** Closed
Industries: Artificial Intelligence for:, Robotics

Company Name: Leapstack
Description: Leapstack is an insurtech company that specializes in big data artificial intelligence technology, serving the healthcare industry.
Website: http://www.leapstack.cn/
Phone: **Email:** contact@leapstack.cn
City: Shanghai **State:** Shanghai **PC:** **Country:** China
Year Established: 2016 **Status 2020:** Active
Industries: Artificial Intelligence for:, Big Data and Analytics for:, ~ Banking and Financial Markets-Services (7)

Company Name: Lieluobo
Description: Lieluobo is a Shanghai-based headhunting and recruitment platform.
Website: http://www.lieluobo.com/
Phone: **Email:** higgs@lieluobo.com
City: Shanghai **State:** Shanghai **PC:** **Country:** China
Year Established: 2017 **Status 2020:** Active
Industries: Artificial Intelligence for:, Security

Company Name: Lingniaoyun (DTbird)
Description: Lingniaoyun is a Hybrid cloud intelligent management platform.
Website: http://www.dtbird.cn/
Phone: **Email:** vivian@dtbird.cn
City: Shanghai **State:** Shanghai **PC:** **Country:** China
Year Established: 2017 **Status 2020:** Active
Industries: Artificial Intelligence

Company Name: Lingzhi Technology
Description: Lingzhi Technology is a service robot maker.
Website:
Phone: **Email:** 36901@reference-encyclopedia-ai.net
City: Shanghai **State:** Shanghai **PC:** **Country:** China
Year Established: 2016 **Status 2020:** Active
Industries: Artificial Intelligence for:, Robotics

Company Name: Liulishuo
Description: Liulishuo is an AI-driven educational technology company that helps users to learn English more efficiently and communicate with the world.
Website: http://www.liulishuo.com/
Phone: 400-688-9999 **Email:** bd@liulishuo.com
City: Shanghai **State:** SH **PC:** **Country:** China
Year Established: 2012 **Status 2020:** Active
Industries: Application Services for:, Artificial Intelligence for:, ~ Education (13), ~ Education (13)

Company Name: MetroDataTech
Description: MetroDataTech is a bigdata service provider for real estate developers through data mining and reconstruction.
Website: http://www.metrodata.cn/
Phone: **Email:** support@metrodata.cn
City: Shanghai **State:** Shanghai **PC:** **Country:** China
Year Established: 2015 **Status 2020:** Active
Industries: Artificial Intelligence for:, Big Data and Analytics for:, Databases

Company Name: mltrons
Description: mltrons enables organizations to leverage & build advanced machine learning algorithms without ever writing a single line of code.
Website: http://mltrons.com/
Phone: 86 19921512944 **Email:** contact@mltrons.com
City: Shanghai **State:** Shanghai **PC:** **Country:** China
Year Established: 2019 **Status 2020:** Active
Industries: Artificial Intelligence for:, Machine Learning for:, Predictive Analytics

Company Name: MobTech
Description: MobTech is the world's leading integrated intelligent technology enterprise.
Website: http://www.mob.com/
Phone: **Email:** marketing@mob.com
City: Shanghai **State:** Shanghai **PC:** **Country:** China
Year Established: 2012 **Status 2020:** Active
Industries: Artificial Intelligence for:, IT Managed Services

Company Name: MoSeeker
Description: MoSeeker is an AI based social recruitment tool that provides recruiting technology solutions for talent acquisition teams.
Website: http://www.moseeker.com
Phone: 86 (400) 101-8049 **Email:** Userask@moseeker.net
City: Shanghai **State:** Shanghai **PC:** **Country:** China

Year Established: 2014 **Status 2020:** Active
Industries:

Company Name: Motovis
Description: Motovis is a Chinese autonomous driving technology firm.
Website: http://www.motovis.cn/
Phone: **Email:** hr@motovis.com
City: Shanghai **State:** SH **PC:** **Country:** China
Year Established: 2015 **Status 2020:** Active
Industries: Artificial Intelligence for:, ~ Automotive (5), ~ Automotive (5)

Company Name: MrS.ai
Description: MrS.ai is a leading Conversational AI platform for corporations in consumer and professional services.
Website: http://www.mrs.ai
Phone: **Email:** mrs@mrs.ai
City: Shanghai **State:** Shanghai **PC:** **Country:** China
Year Established: 2015 **Status 2020:** Active
Industries: Artificial Intelligence for:, IT Managed Services

Company Name: NextVPU
Description: NextVPU offers embedded AI solutions for most of the smart devices and applications.
Website: http://nextvpu.com/
Phone: 86 21 5077 3678 **Email:** pr@nextvpu.com
City: Shanghai **State:** Shanghai **PC:** **Country:** China
Year Established: 2016 **Status 2020:** Active
Industries: Artificial Intelligence

Company Name: OCheng
Description: OCheng
Website: http://ocheng.me
Phone: 400-784-3286 **Email:** service@4chen.cn
City: Shanghai **State:** Shanghai **PC:** **Country:** China
Year Established: 2015 **Status 2020:** Active
Industries:

Company Name: OpenAILab
Description: OpenAILab provides artificial intelligence solutions.
Website: http://www.openailab.com/
Phone: 021-80181176 **Email:** contact@openailab.com
City: Shanghai **State:** Shanghai **PC:** **Country:** China
Year Established: 2016 **Status 2020:** Active
Industries: Artificial Intelligence for:, IT Managed Services for:, Application Services for:, Machine Learning

Company Name: ORIGITECH
Description: ORIGITECH is an AI technologies and enabling manufacturing company.
Website: http://origi-tech.com/
Phone: **Email:** hr@origi-tech.com
City: Shanghai **State:** SH **PC:** **Country:** China
Year Established: 2017 **Status 2020:** Active
Industries: Artificial Intelligence for:, Machine Learning for:, Robotics

Company Name: OYMotion Technologies, Inc
Description: OYMotion develops bio-metric sensors, machine-learning based algorithm for processing bionic signals and gesture control based on EMG.
Website: http://www.oymotion.com
Phone: **Email:** info@oymotion.com
City: Shanghai **State:** Shanghai **PC:** **Country:** China
Year Established: 2015 **Status 2020:** Active
Industries: ~ Biotechnology (9), Machine Learning

Company Name: Perspicace Intelligence Technology
Description: Perspicace Intelligence Technology is an AI & Robotics company.
Website: http://www.perspicace-china.com/
Phone: 400 6006 006 **Email:** Service@perspicace-china.com
City: Shanghai **State:** Shanghai **PC:** **Country:** China
Year Established: 2016 **Status 2020:** Active
Industries: Artificial Intelligence for:, Robotics

Company Name: Pinlan
Description: Pinlan is a Chinese AI scene marketing service provider.
Website: http://www.pinlandata.com/
Phone: 400-700-8700 **Email:** Info@pinlandata.com
City: Shanghai **State:** Shanghai **PC:** **Country:** China
Year Established: 2018 **Status 2020:** Active
Industries: Artificial Intelligence

Company Name: Polaris Technology Inc.
Description: It provides biomedical stakeholders with cloud services of computational visualization and analysis to heterogeneous biomedical data.
Website: http://elongevity.: Italy
Phone: 18696104490 **Email:** makehust@gmail.com
City: Shanghai **State:** Shanghai **PC:** **Country:** China
Year Established: 2018 **Status 2020:** Active
Industries: Artificial Intelligence for:, IT Managed Services

Company Name: PowerShare
Description: The leading provider of AI for EV Charging and Battery Lifecycle and Energy Storage System
Website: http://www.powershare.com.cn
Phone: **Email:** info@powershare.com.cn
City: Shanghai **State:** Shanghai **PC:** **Country:** China
Year Established: 2015 **Status 2020:** Active
Industries: Artificial Intelligence for:, ~ Energy and Utilities (14), ~ Telecommunications (56), IT Managed Services for:, ~ Energy and Utilities (14), ~ Energy and Utilities (14), ~ Construction (10)

Company Name: Puying Intelligence
Description: Puying Intelligence is an AI-driven insurance service provider.
Website: http://puying.ai/
Phone: **Email:** BD@puying.ai
City: Shanghai **State:** SH **PC:** **Country:** China
Year Established: 2017 **Status 2020:** Active
Industries: Artificial Intelligence for:, ~ Banking and Financial Markets-Services (7), ~ Banking and Financial Markets-Services (7)

Company Name: ReadSen: Sweden
Description: Embedded computer vision solutions for human-computer interaction
Website: http://www.readsense.ai/
Phone: **Email:** business@readsense.cn
City: Shanghai **State:** Shanghai **PC:** **Country:** China
Year Established: 2015 **Status 2020:** Active
Industries: Artificial Intelligence for:, Computer Vision for:, Human Computer Interaction

Company Name: Re-Hub
Description: Retail Tech Hub
Website: http://rehub.tech/
Phone: **Email:** hello@rehub.tech
City: Shanghai **State:** Shanghai **PC:** **Country:** China
Year Established: **Status 2020:** Active
Industries:

Company Name: SANPEI VENTURES
Description: Fueling start-ups growth in China
Website: http://www.sanpeiventures.com
Phone: **Email:** nihao@sanpeiventures.com
City: Shanghai **State:** Shanghai **PC:** **Country:** China
Year Established: 2015 **Status 2020:** Active
Industries: Artificial Intelligence for:, ~ Banking and Financial Markets-Services (7), ~ Administrative and Support Services (1), ~ Banking and Financial Markets-Services (7)

Company Name: Shanghai AI Innovation
Description: Shanghai AI Innovation (SAII) develops artificial intelligence software for the e-commerce industry.
Website:
Phone: **Email:** liuweiinnovation3@gmail.com
City: Shanghai **State:** Shanghai **PC:** **Country:** China
Year Established: 2019 **Status 2020:** Active
Industries: Artificial Intelligence for:, E-Commerce

Company Name: SkinRun
Description: China's Leading Beauty AI Hardware Developer
Website: http://www.skinrun.me/
Phone: **Email:** rex@skinrun.me
City: Shanghai **State:** Shanghai **PC:** **Country:** China
Year Established: 2011 **Status 2020:** Active
Industries: Artificial Intelligence for:, ~ Beauty (8), Machine Learning

Company Name: Soul
Description: SOUL is a social network that uses AI to help users find their soul mates.
Website: http://www.soulapp.cn
Phone: (021)2613 5824 **Email:** soul@soulapp.cn
City: Shanghai **State:** Shanghai **PC:** **Country:** China
Year Established: 2016 **Status 2020:** Active
Industries: Application Services for:, Artificial Intelligence for:, Web for:, ~ Social Assistance-Non-Profits (53)

Company Name: Superhuman Studios
Description: Venture studio offering advisory, venture capital, and investment strategy to high impact early stage companies.
Website: http://www.superhumn.co
Phone: **Email:** info@thegrand.global
City: Shanghai **State:** Shanghai **PC:** **Country:** China
Year Established: 2017 **Status 2020:** Active
Industries: Artificial Intelligence for:, ~ Banking and Financial Markets-Services (7), ~ Personal-Religious-Civic (45), ~ Banking and Financial Markets-Services (7)

Company **Name:** Supremind
Description: Supremind is a Chinese AI-based video big data analysis company.
Website: http://www.supremind.com/
Phone: **Email:** 37485@reference-encyclopedia-ai.net
City: Shanghai **State:** Shanghai **PC:** **Country:** China
Year Established: 2019 **Status 2020:** Active
Industries:

Company Name: ThinkForce
Description: ThinkForce is a Shanghai-based artificial intelligence chip maker.
Website: http://www.think-force.com/
Phone: 021-6143 9123 **Email:** info@think-force.com
City: Shanghai **State:** Shanghai **PC:** **Country:** China
Year Established: 2017 **Status 2020:** Active
Industries: Artificial Intelligence for:, IT Managed Services

Company Name: Tianrang
Description: Tianrang is a Chinese artificial intelligence startup.
Website: http://www.tianrang.com
Phone: **Email:** media@tianrang-inc.com
City: Shanghai **State:** Shanghai **PC:** **Country:** China
Year Established: **Status 2020:** Active
Industries: Artificial Intelligence for:, Cloud for:, IT Managed Services

Company Name: Tigerobo
Description: Tigerobo is an artificial intelligence technology driven technology company.
Website: http://www.tigerobo.com
Phone: 021-63888086 **Email:** Contact@tigerobo.com
City: Shanghai **State:** Shanghai **PC:** **Country:** China
Year Established: **Status 2020:** Active
Industries: Artificial Intelligence for:, Robotics

Company Name: Timesilicon
Description: Timesilicon is a professional AI edge computing chip and solution provider.
Website: http://www.timesilicon.com/
Phone: (86)15601949965 **Email:** da.zhu@timingsilicon.com
City: Shanghai **State:** Shanghai **PC:** **Country:** China
Year Established: 2016 **Status 2020:** Active
Industries: Artificial Intelligence

Company Name: ULS Robotics
Description: ULS Robotics is a robot technology company based on an exoskeleton technology platform.
Website: http://www.ulsrobotics.com/
Phone: **Email:** info@ulsrobotics.com
City: Shanghai **State:** Shanghai **PC:** **Country:** China
Year Established: 2018 **Status 2020:** Active
Industries: Artificial Intelligence for:, IT Managed Services for:, Robotics

Company Name: Value Simplex
Description: Value Simplex provides big data, machine learning, and management services for the financial industry.
Website: http://valuesimplex.com/
Phone: **Email:** hr@entropyreduce.com
City: Shanghai **State:** SH **PC:** **Country:** China
Year Established: 2017 **Status 2020:** Active
Industries: Big Data and Analytics for:, IT Managed Services for:, Machine Learning

Company Name: VideoPlusPlus
Description: AI Video Entertainment
Website: http://www.videopls.com
Phone: 400-808-9578 **Email:** support@videopls.com
City: Shanghai **State:** Shanghai **PC:** **Country:** China
Year Established: **Status 2020:** Active
Industries: ~ Media-Communications (41), Artificial Intelligence for:, ~ Media-Communications (41)

Company Name: Westwell Lab
Description: A Shanghai-based AI chipmaker.
Website: http://www.westwell-lab.com/
Phone: **Email:** hello@westwell-lab.com
City: Shanghai **State:** Shanghai **PC:** **Country:** China
Year Established: 2015 **Status 2020:** Active
Industries:

Company Name: WhalesBot
Description: WhalesBot is a Robotics and programming education service provider
Website: http://www.whalesbot.com/
Phone: 8621-33585660 **Email:** sales@whalesbot.com
City: Shanghai **State:** Shanghai **PC:** **Country:** China
Year Established: **Status 2020:** Active
Industries: Artificial Intelligence for:, Robotics

Company Name: Wision A.I.
Description: Build Computer Aided Diagnosis (CAD) algorithms and systems in clinical imaging, to improve diagnostic accuracy and effectiveness.
Website: http://www.wision.com
Phone: **Email:** ai@wision.com
City: Shanghai **State:** Shanghai **PC:** **Country:** China
Year Established: 2016 **Status 2020:** Active
Industries: Artificial Intelligence for:, ~ Healthcare (20)

Company Name: Xiaochi Robot
Description: Xiaochi Robot is a customer service robot developer.
Website: http://home.xiaochiai.com/
Phone: 199 2134 9453 **Email:** xiaochi@xiaochiai.com
City: Shanghai **State:** Shanghai **PC:** **Country:** China
Year Established: 2016 **Status 2020:** Active
Industries: Artificial Intelligence for:, Robotics

Company Name: Xmov
Description: Xmov is an AI company focusing on computer vision and computer graphics.
Website: http://xmov.ai/
Phone: **Email:** 37701@reference-encyclopedia-ai.net
City: Shanghai **State:** SH **PC:** **Country:** China
Year Established: 2017 **Status 2020:** Active
Industries: Artificial Intelligence for:, Computer Vision for:, Robotics

Company Name: Y.H. Capital
Description: Y.H. Capital is an investment company that focuses on capturing business models or innovative technologies.
Website: http://www.brillcapital.com
Phone: **Email:** Service@brillcapital.com
City: Shanghai **State:** Shanghai **PC:** **Country:** China
Year Established: 2017 **Status 2020:** Active
Industries: Artificial Intelligence for:, Web for:, Mobile

Company Name: YesGo
Description: YesGo is an unmanned convenience store brand.
Website: http://www.cnnrgroup.com/
Phone: (21) 400-0999-779 **Email:** info@cnnrgroup.com
City: Shanghai **State:** Shanghai **PC:** **Country:** China
Year Established: 2012 **Status 2020:** Active
Industries: Artificial Intelligence for:, ~ Arts-Entertainment-Recreation (4)
Company Name: Yitu Technology
Description: YITU Technology integrates state-of-the-art AI technologies with industrial applications to build a safer, faster and healthier world.
Website: http://www.yitutech.com/en/
Phone: **Email:** marketing@YITU-inc.com
City: Shanghai **State:** Shanghai **PC:** **Country:** China
Year Established: **Status 2020:** Active
Industries: Application Services for:, Artificial Intelligence for:, ~ Banking and Financial Markets-Services (7), ~ Healthcare (20)

Company Name: Yixue Education Inc.
Description:
Website: http://www.squirrelai.us/
Phone: (086) 400-000-9900 **Email:** office@classba.com
City: Shanghai **State:** Shanghai **PC:** **Country:** China
Year Established: **Status 2020:** Active
Industries:

Company Name: Yunna Technology (Cloudpick)
Description: Yunna Technology is a high-tech enterprise specializing in the development of computer vision and artificial intelligence applications.
Website: http://cloudpick.me/
Phone: **Email:** 37724@reference-encyclopedia-ai.net
City: Shanghai **State:** SH **PC:** **Country:** China
Year Established: 2017 **Status 2020:** Active
Industries: Artificial Intelligence for:, Computer Vision for:, Robotics

Company Name: Zebra Zhixing
Description: Zebra Zhixing is a vehicle intelligent service provider.
Website: http://www.hellobanma.com/
Phone: 400-821-8811 **Email:** enquiry@hellobanma.com
City: Xuhui **State:** Shanghai **PC:** **Country:** China
Year Established: **Status 2020:** Active
Industries: Artificial Intelligence for:, ~ Automotive (5)

Company Name: HiScene
Description: HiScene focuses on researching and developing core technologies and products for augmented reality.
Website: http://www.hiscene.com
Phone: (263)842-074 **Email:** business@hiscene.com
City: Pudong **State:** Shanghai Shi **PC:** **Country:** China
Year Established: **Status 2020:** Active
Industries: Artificial Intelligence for:, Augmented Reality for:, IT Managed Services for:, Data Management

Company Name: Chejin 360
Description: Chejin 360 is a financial service provider that connects car dealers with banks.
Website: http://www.chejin360.com
Phone: **Email:** 36264@reference-encyclopedia-ai.net
City: Chengdu **State:** Sichuan **PC:** **Country:** China
Year Established: 2017 **Status 2020:** Active
Industries: Artificial Intelligence for:, ~ Banking and Financial Markets-Services (7), Business Software as a Service Apps (SaaS Apps)

Company Name: Fiture
Description: Fiture is a smart household fitness equipment brand.
Website: http://www.fiture.com/
Phone: **Email:** 36576@reference-encyclopedia-ai.net
City: Chengdu **State:** Sichuan **PC:** **Country:** China
Year Established: 2019 **Status 2020:** Active
Industries: Artificial Intelligence for:, ~ Healthcare (20), Robotics for:, ~ Arts-Entertainment-Recreation (4)

Company Name: Kaola Youran
Description: Kaola Youran is a Chengdu Based AI & Robotics Start Up.
Website: http://www.kaolayouran.cn/
Phone: 028-8750 1620 **Email:** koala@yourangroup.com
City: Chengdu **State:** Sichuan **PC:** **Country:** China
Year Established: **Status 2020:** Active
Industries:

Company Name: Knowledge Vision
Description: Knowledge Vision is an AI & Robotics company.
Website: http://www.knowledge-vision.com/
Phone: **Email:** contact@knowledge-vision.com
City: Chengdu **State:** Sichuan **PC:** **Country:** China
Year Established: 2016 **Status 2020:** Active
Industries: Artificial Intelligence for:, Robotics

Company Name: Ruiyan Technology
Description: Ruiyan Technology is an Artificial intelligence video identification service provider
Website: http://www.ruiyanai.com/
Phone: **Email:** mkt@ruiyanai.com
City: Chengdu **State:** Sichuan **PC:** **Country:** China
Year Established: 2016 **Status 2020:** Active
Industries: Artificial Intelligence

Company Name: TerraQuanta
Description: TerraQuanta is a data platform based in China.
Website: http://www.terraquanta.io/
Phone: 028-87033310 **Email:** contact@terraquanta.io
City: Chengdu **State:** Sichuan **PC:** **Country:** China
Year Established: 2017 **Status 2020:** Active
Industries: Artificial Intelligence for:, Machine Learning

Company Name: Topplus
Description: Topplus is a AI startup that providing software/hardware vision solutions for 3D camera and industries.
Website: http://www.topplusvision.com/
Phone: 86.28.83227667 **Email:** sales@topplusvision.com
City: Chengdu **State:** Sichuan **PC:** **Country:** China
Year Established: 2015 **Status 2020:** Active
Industries: Artificial Intelligence

Company Name: Xiaoduo
Description: Xiaoduo is an intelligent customer service robot developer.
Website: http://www.xiaoduoai.com/
Phone: 400-028-8810 **Email:** customer@xiaoduotech.com
City: Chengdu **State:** Sichuan **PC:** **Country:** China
Year Established: 2014 **Status 2020:** Active
Industries: Artificial Intelligence for:, ~ Customer Relationship Management (11), Robotics

Company Name: NingBo Marvoto Intelligent Technology Co., Ltd

Description: Marvoto focuses on hand-held 3D ultrasound application, in terms of artificial intelligence and smart algorithms
Website: http://www.marvoto.com
Phone: **Email:** wwang@marvoto.com
City: Cixi **State:** ZJ **PC:** **Country:** China
Year Established: 2015 **Status 2020:** Active
Industries: Artificial Intelligence for:, ~ Healthcare (20)

Company Name: 1KMXC
Description: 1KMXC is a high-tech research and development company for artificial intelligence robot solutions.
Website: https://www.1kmxc.com/
Phone: **Email:** 35917@reference-encyclopedia-ai.net
City: Hangzhou **State:** Zhejiang **PC:** **Country:** China
Year Established: 2013 **Status 2020:** Active
Industries: Artificial Intelligence for:, Robotics for:, ~ Customer Relationship Management (11)

Company Name: Baiying Technology
Description: Baiying Technology is a Big data and artificial intelligence technology service provide: Serbia
Website: http://www.byai.com/
Phone: 400-0235-100 **Email:** 36133@reference-encyclopedia-ai.net
City: Hangzhou **State:** Zhejiang **PC:** **Country:** China
Year Established: 2016 **Status 2020:** Active
Industries: Artificial Intelligence for:, IT Managed Services

Company Name: ccvui.com
Description: ccvui.com is an AI chip design company.
Website: http://www.ccvui.com/
Phone: **Email:** tang.jian@vuichip.com
City: Hangzhou **State:** Zhejiang **PC:** **Country:** China
Year Established: 2018 **Status 2020:** Active
Industries: Artificial Intelligence for:, Robotics

Company Name: Changing Study
Description: Changing Study is an AI & Roboticscompany.
Website:
Phone: **Email:** 36256@reference-encyclopedia-ai.net
City: Hangzhou **State:** Zhejiang **PC:** **Country:** China
Year Established: 2015 **Status 2020:** Active
Industries: Artificial Intelligence for:, Robotics

Company Name: City Cloud Technology (CCI)
Description: City Cloud Technology is an AI-based smart city internet operator.
Website:
Phone: **Email:** 36282@reference-encyclopedia-ai.net
City: Hangzhou **State:** Zhejiang **PC:** **Country:** China
Year Established: 2012 **Status 2020:** Active
Industries: Artificial Intelligence

Company Name: Deepdraw
Description: Deepdraw is an artificial intelligence visual and data service provider.
Website: http://www.deepdraw.cn/
Phone: 400-0220-620 **Email:** Market@deepdraw.cn
City: Hangzhou **State:** ZJ **PC:** **Country:** China
Year Established: 2015 **Status 2020:** Active
Industries: Artificial Intelligence for:, ~ Fashion (16), IT Managed Services for:, Web

Company Name: DongXiaoBang
Description: DongXiaoBang is an intelligent circulation service provider
Website: http://www.dongdikuai.com/
Phone: **Email:** 36451@reference-encyclopedia-ai.net
City: Hangzhou **State:** Zhejiang **PC:** **Country:** China
Year Established: 2017 **Status 2020:** Active
Industries: Artificial Intelligence

Company Name: EasyXR Advanced Technology
Description: EasyXR Advanced Tech is an augmented reality and artificial intelligence start up for augmented reality developers.
Website: http://www.ezxr.com
Phone: (86) 571-89852191 **Email:** grp.bd@ezxr.com
City: Hangzhou **State:** Zhejiang **PC:** **Country:** China
Year Established: 2018 **Status 2020:** Active
Industries:

Company Name: Eigen
Description: Eigen is applying the latest AI technologies to variety of business domains, making AI the center of thegravity in industrial evolutions.
Website: http://www.eigentech.ai
Phone: 0571-81061991 **Email:** hr@aidigger.com
City: Hangzhou **State:** Zhejiang **PC:** **Country:** China
Year Established: 2016 **Status 2020:** Active
Industries: Artificial Intelligence for:, Industrial Solutions for:, Machine Learning

Company Name: Enjoyor
Description: Enjoyor is a Ch K3741inese provider of urban intelligent turnkey solutions.
Website: http://www.enjoyor.net/
Phone: **Email:** service@enjoyor.net
City: Hangzhou **State:** Zhejiang **PC:** **Country:** China
Year Established: **Status 2020:** Active
Industries: ~ Professional Services (48), Artificial Intelligence for:, Enterprise Application Services

Company Name: FABU.ai
Description: FABU is an AI company devoted to proprietary technology of ADAS and Autonomous Driving.
Website: http://www.fabu.ai/en
Phone: 408-475-2556 **Email:** angela.suen@fabu.ai
City: Hangzhou **State:** Zhejiang **PC:** **Country:** China
Year Established: **Status 2020:** Active
Industries: ~ Manufacturing-Electronic (30), Artificial Intelligence for:, ~ Automotive (5), ~ Automotive (5), ~ Transportation and Logistics (57), ~ Manufacturing-Electronic (30)

Company Name: Fullink
Description: Fullink Tech is an intelligent risk control and operation service provider
Website: http://www.fullink.tech/
Phone: 0571-88610375 **Email:** bd@fulintechfin.com
City: Hangzhou **State:** ZJ **PC:** **Country:** China
Year Established: 2017 **Status 2020:** Active
Industries: Artificial Intelligence for:, ~ Banking and Financial Markets-Services (7), IT Managed Services for:, Web

Company Name: GalaxyEye
Description: GalaxyEye is a AI & Robotics based Company.
Website: http://galaxyeye-tech.com/
Phone: **Email:** business@galaxyeye-tech.com
City: Hangzhou **State:** Zhejiang **PC:** **Country:** China
Year Established: 2015 **Status 2020:** Active
Industries: Artificial Intelligence for:, Robotics

Company Name: Genius Pros
Description: Genius Pros is a world's leading provider of 3D ToF sensor systems, solutions, and data ultimately used for artificial intelligence.
Website: http://www.genius-pros.com
Phone: **Email:** business@genius-pros.com
City: Hangzhou **State:** Zhejiang **PC:** **Country:** China
Year Established: **Status 2020:** Active
Industries: Artificial Intelligence

Company Name: Guochen Robot
Description: Hangzhou Guochen Robot Technology is a company dedicated to robot application research and industrial development.
Website: http://www.zjrob.com/
Phone: 0571-5675 7600 **Email:** services@zjrob.com
City: Hangzhou **State:** Zhejiang **PC:** **Country:** China
Year Established: 2015 **Status 2020:** Active
Industries: Artificial Intelligence for:, Application Services for:, Robotics

Company Name: Intelligent Learning
Description: Intelligent Learning is an Artificial Intelligence & Robotics Company.
Website: http://www.91jzx.cn/
Phone: **Email:** 36789@reference-encyclopedia-ai.net
City: Hangzhou **State:** Zhejiang **PC:** **Country:** China
Year Established: 2018 **Status 2020:** Active
Industries: Artificial Intelligence for:, ~ Education (13), Robotics

Company Name: Joinhealth Technology
Description: Joinhealth Technology is a Healthcare company.
Website: http://www.lanniuh.com/
Phone: **Email:** business@joinhealth.cn
City: Hangzhou **State:** ZJ **PC:** **Country:** China
Year Established: 2015 **Status 2020:** Active
Industries: Artificial Intelligence for:, ~ Healthcare (20), ~ Healthcare (20), ~ Healthcare (20)

Company Name: Leaper Technology
Description: Leaper Technology is a AI & Robotics company.
Website: http://www.hzleaper.com/
Phone: **Email:** beyond.guo@hzleaper.com
City: Hangzhou **State:** Zhejiang **PC:** **Country:** China
Year Established: 2012 **Status 2020:** Active
Industries: Artificial Intelligence for:, Robotics

Company Name: ListenRobot
Description: ListenRobot is an AI Outbound Robot Company.
Website: http://www.listenrobot.com/
Phone: 400-119-9800 **Email:** requirements@lsrobot.vip
City: Hangzhou **State:** Zhejiang **PC:** **Country:** China
Year Established: 2016 **Status 2020:** Active
Industries: Artificial Intelligence for:, Machine Learning for:, Robotics

Company Name: Mairui Robot
Description: Mairui Robot is an Intelligent robot solutions and service provide: Serbia
Website: http://www.mrrobotics.com/
Phone: (1806) 986-0603 **Email:** Sales@mrrobotics.com
City: Hangzhou **State:** Zhejiang **PC:** **Country:** China
Year Established: 2017 **Status 2020:** Active
Industries: Artificial Intelligence for:, Robotics

Company Name: Moredian
Description: Moredian is a recognition technology provider, combining artificial intelligence technology with industry applications.
Website: http://www.moredian.com/index.html
Phone: 400-033-7675 **Email:** market@moredian.com
City: Hangzhou **State:** ZJ **PC:** **Country:** China
Year Established: 2016 **Status 2020:** Active
Industries: Artificial Intelligence for:, Facial Recognition for:, IT Managed Services

Company Name: Myaidoctor
Description: Myaidoctor is an AI virtual doctor assistant application.
Website: http://www.myaidoctor.com/
Phone: **Email:** info@myaidoctor.com
City: Hangzhou **State:** Zhejiang **PC:** **Country:** China
Year Established: 2014 **Status 2020:** Active
Industries:

Company Name: Resthour Technology
Description: Resthour Technology is an AI & Robotics company.
Website: http://www.resthour.net/
Phone: 0571-8866 7577 **Email:** business@resthour.net
City: Hangzhou **State:** Zhejiang **PC:** **Country:** China
Year Established: 2017 **Status 2020:** Active
Industries: Artificial Intelligence for:, Robotics

Company Name: Rokid
Description: Rokid is an innovative technology company specializing in robotics research and AI development.
Website: http://www.rokid.com/en
Phone: (400)113-0099 **Email:** info@rokid.ai
City: Hangzhou **State:** Zhejiang **PC:** **Country:** China
Year Established: **Status 2020:** Active
Industries: Artificial Intelligence for:, Augmented Reality for:, ~ Manufacturing-Electronic (30), Human Computer Interaction for:, Robotics

Company Name: Santa Medical Technology
Description: Santa Medical Technology is an AI surgical robot developer.
Website: http://www.hzstyl.com/
Phone: 86 - 571--89719087 **Email:** stly@santan-md.com
City: Hangzhou **State:** Zhejiang **PC:** **Country:** China
Year Established: 2011 **Status 2020:** Active
Industries: Artificial Intelligence for:, ~ Healthcare (20), Robotics

Company Name: Shentong Wan: Morocco
Description: Shentong Wanma is a big data artificial intelligence company
Website:
Phone: **Email:** 4493@reference-encyclopedia-ai.net
City: Hangzhou **State:** Zhejiang **PC:** **Country:** China
Year Established: **Status 2020:** Active
Industries: Artificial Intelligence for:, Big Data and Analytics

Company Name: TaoData
Description: A Professional AI Start Up Of Machine Learning.
Website: http://www.taodatarobot.com/homepage.html
Phone: 0571-89703310 **Email:** Contact@taodatarobot.com
City: Hangzhou **State:** Zhejiang **PC:** **Country:** China
Year Established: 2016 **Status 2020:** Active
Industries: Artificial Intelligence for:, Databases for:, Digital Marketing for:, IT Managed Services for:, IT Managed Services for:, Machine Learning

Company Name: Tuya
Description: Tuya is an IOT solutions provider that helps manufacturers develop their app and bring their product to market and at competitive prices.
Website: http://www.tuya.com/
Phone: 86 (571) 56038587 **Email:** sales@tuya.com
City: Hangzhou **State:** Zhejiang **PC:** **Country:** China
Year Established: 2014 **Status 2020:** Active
Industries: Application Services for:, Artificial Intelligence for:, Enterprise Application Services for:, Web for:, Internet of Things (IoT) for:, Web

Company Name: UGO
Description: UGO is an AI & Robotics company.
Website:
Phone: **Email:** 37588@reference-encyclopedia-ai.net
City: Hangzhou **State:** Zhejiang **PC:** **Country:** China
Year Established: 2017 **Status 2020:** Active
Industries: Artificial Intelligence for:, Robotics

Company Name: Uni-Ubi
Description: Uni-Ubiis a AI & Robotics Start Up based in Hangzhou.
Website: http://www.uni-ubi.com/
Phone: **Email:** pr@uni-ubi.com
City: Hangzhou **State:** Zhejiang **PC:** **Country:** China

Year Established: 2014 **Status 2020:** Active
Industries: Artificial Intelligence for:, Robotics

Company Name: Utarn Technology
Description: Utarn Technology is a spiking neural network technology company.
Website:
Phone: **Email:** 37607@reference-encyclopedia-ai.net
City: Hangzhou **State:** Zhejiang **PC:** **Country:** China
Year Established: 2019 **Status 2020:** Active
Industries: Artificial Intelligence for:, Robotics

Company Name: Xiaoyu Robot
Description: Xiaoyu Robot is an AI & Robotics company.
Website: http://www.xiaoyu168.com/
Phone: **Email:** marketing@xiaoyu168.com
City: Hangzhou **State:** Zhejiang **PC:** **Country:** China
Year Established: 2018 **Status 2020:** Active
Industries: Artificial Intelligence for:, Robotics

Company Name: Xigua City
Description: Xigua City is an online computer programming education platform for children.
Website: http://www.xiguacity.cn/
Phone: **Email:** 37697@reference-encyclopedia-ai.net
City: Hangzhou **State:** ZJ **PC:** **Country:** China
Year Established: 2013 **Status 2020:** Active
Industries: Artificial Intelligence for:, ~ Education (13), Web for:, ~ Education (13)

Company Name: Yiwi: Sweden
Description: Yiwise is a research and development artificial intelligence company.
Website: http://www.yiwise.com/
Phone: 4009260706 **Email:** Business@yiwise.com
City: Hangzhou **State:** Zhejiang **PC:** **Country:** China
Year Established: 2017 **Status 2020:** Active
Industries: Artificial Intelligence for:, Robotics

Company Name: YizhiIntelligent
Description: Yizhi Intelligent Technology is a Company which designs and develops an artificial intelligence.
Website:
Phone: **Email:** 37715@reference-encyclopedia-ai.net
City: Hangzhou **State:** Zhejiang **PC:** **Country:** China
Year Established: 2017 **Status 2020:** Active
Industries: Artificial Intelligence for:, Robotics

Company Name: Yunxi Technology
Description: Yunxi Technology is an enterprise digital service provider.
Website: http://www.dtyunxi.com/
Phone: 020-82517615 **Email:** 37726@reference-encyclopedia-ai.net
City: Hangzhou **State:** ZJ **PC:** **Country:** China
Year Established: 2016 **Status 2020:** Active
Industries:

Company Name: Yuyi Technology
Description: Yuyi Technology is a AI & Robotics start up based in Hangzhou
Website: http://www.kismet-emotions.com/
Phone: **Email:** 37728@reference-encyclopedia-ai.net
City: Hangzhou **State:** Zhejiang **PC:** **Country:** China
Year Established: 2016 **Status 2020:** Active
Industries: Artificial Intelligence for:, Robotics

Company Name: Zen Video(Zhiying)
Description: Zen Video is a Artificial intelligence & robotics based company.
Website: http://zenvideo.cn/
Phone: 0571-56014066 **Email:** 37732@reference-encyclopedia-ai.net
City: Hangzhou **State:** Zhejiang **PC:** **Country:** China
Year Established: 2016 **Status 2020:** Active
Industries: Artificial Intelligence for:, Robotics

Company Name: Ortron
Description: Ortron is a Chinese semantic analysis technology firm.
Website: http://www.ortron.cn/
Phone: **Email:** 37127@reference-encyclopedia-ai.net
City: Jiaxing **State:** Zhejiang **PC:** **Country:** China
Year Established: 2013 **Status 2020:** Active
Industries: Artificial Intelligence for:, Robotics

Company Name: I DO park
Description: I DO park is an AI and blockchain technology-driven social networking platform.
Website:
Phone: **Email:** 36729@reference-encyclopedia-ai.net
City: Shaoxing **State:** Zhejiang **PC:** **Country:** China
Year Established: 2019 **Status 2020:** Active
Industries: Artificial Intelligence for:, Blockchain

Company Name: Alibabi
Description:
Website: https://alibaba.com
Phone: 86-571-8502-2077 **Email:** 27286@reference-encyclopedia-ai.net
City: Yu Hang District **State:** Zhejiang **Zip:** 311121 **Country**: China
Year Established: **Status 2020:** Active
Industries:

Company Name: Eeasy Tech
Description: Eeasy Tech is a high-tech company that provides advanced and complete solutions for industrial control
Website: http://www.eeasytech.com/
Phone: 0756-6918851 **Email:** Hr@eeasytech.com
City: Tangjiabang **State:** ZJ **PC:** **Country:** China
Year Established: 2016 **Status 2020:** Active
Industries: Artificial Intelligence

Columbia

Company Name: B2Chat
Description: The most intuitive and powerful means for businesses to connect with their custome: Serbia
Website: http://www.b2chat.io/en/
Phone: 57 312 2575612 **Email:** pedro@b2chat.io
City: Medellin **State:** Antioquia **PC:** **Country:** Colombia
Year Established: 2017 **Status 2020:** Active
Industries: Artificial Intelligence for:, ~ Customer Relationship Management (11), IT Managed Services

Company Name: Geniusly
Description: Big Data Analytics as a Service for Transportation and Logistics SMB's in Emerging Markets
Website: http://geniusly.com/
Phone: **Email:** hi@barista-v.com
City: Medellin **State:** Antioquia **PC:** **Country:** Colombia
Year Established: 2013 **Status 2020:** Active
Industries: Analytics for:, Big Data and Analytics for:, Predictive Analytics

Company Name: INpla: South Africa
Description: INplaza is a blockchain technology company that focuses on international trade.
Website: http://inplaza.co
Phone: **Email:** info@inplaza.co
City: Medellin **State:** Antioquia **PC:** **Country:** Colombia
Year Established: 2016 **Status 2020:** Active
Industries: Artificial Intelligence for:, Business Applications for:, Blockchain for:, ~ Banking and Financial Markets-Services (7), E-Commerce for:, ~ Telecommunications (56), Machine Learning for:, Finance and Accounting for:, Finance and Accounting

Company Name: MOONBLOCK
Description: MOONBLOCK develops all the professional tools you need to trade in the CRYPTO market, in one single platform.
Website: http://moonblock.ai
Phone: **Email:** hello@moonblock.ai
City: Medellin **State:** ANT **PC:** **Country:** Colombia
Year Established: **Status 2020:** Active
Industries: Artificial Intelligence for:, Blockchain for:, ~ Banking and Financial Markets-Services (7), ~ Banking and Financial Markets-Services (7), ~ Banking and Financial Markets-Services (7), IT Managed Services for:, Machine Learning for:, ~ Professional Services (48)

Company Name: Ressolve
Description: Artificial intelligence focused in Speech/text analytics and NLP/N: Luxembourg
Website: http://www.ressolve.ai
Phone: 3202642290 **Email:** hdiaz@ressolve.ai
City: Medellin **State:** Antioquia **PC:** **Country:** Colombia
Year Established: 2019 **Status 2020:** Active
Industries: Artificial Intelligence for:, IT Managed Services for:, Machine Learning for:, Speech Recognition for:, Data Management

Company Name: Vozy
Description: Vozy is a voice communication platform helping businesses and customers to engage in productive conversations.
Website: http://www.vozy.co
Phone: 305 590-8534 **Email:** info@vozy.co
City: Medellin **State:** Antioquia **PC:** **Country:** Colombia
Year Established: 2016 **Status 2020:** Active
Industries: Artificial Intelligence for:, Enterprise Application Services for:, Business Software as a Service Apps (SaaS Apps) for:, Speech Recognition for:, Internet of Things (IoT)

Company Name: Bleenco
Description: Bleenco offers an AI software for detecting hazardous driver behavior and improving driving experience in the wild.
Website: http://bleenco.com/
Phone: **Email:** hello@bleenco.com
City: Bavaria **State:** Cundinamarca **PC:** **Country:** Colombia
Year Established: 2017 **Status 2020:** Active
Industries: Artificial Intelligence for:, ~ Automotive (5)

Company Name: CollectPay
Description: Es una plataforma web especializada en la gestin inteligente de cuentas por cobrar de pequeas y medianas empresas.
Website: http://www.collectpay.co
Phone: 57 311 2127944 **Email:** marketing@collectpay.co
City: Bogota **State:** Bogota **PC:** **Country:** Colombia
Year Established: 2017 **Status 2020:** Active
Industries:

Company Name: Elemento Alpha
Description: Elemento Alpha is a FinTech company powered by AI & ML, providing Asset Managers quantitative advisory products for portfolio construction.
Website: http://elementoalpha.com/
Phone: 57 350 343 0405 **Email:** srocha@elementoalpha.com
City: Bogota **State:** Bogota **PC:** **Country:** Colombia
Year Established: 2019 **Status 2020:** Active
Industries: Artificial Intelligence for:, ~ Banking and Financial Markets-Services (7), Machine Learning for:, Business Software as a Service Apps (SaaS Apps) for:, ~ Banking and Financial Markets-Services (7)

Company Name: Empresas Inteligentes
Description: Big Data and Artificial Intelligence Ap: Palestine
Website: http://empresasinteligentes.com
Phone: (571) 742-0175 **Email:** info@empresasinteligentes.com
City: Bogota **State:** Bogota **PC:** **Country:** Colombia
Year Established: 2013 **Status 2020:** Active
Industries: Artificial Intelligence for:, ~ Banking and Financial Markets-Services (7), Big Data and Analytics for:, Machine Learning

Company Name: Feelenials
Description: Feelenials develops an emotion analytics that helps to track and improve the moods of companies.
Website: http://feelenials.com/
Phone: **Email:** hello@feelenials.com
City: Bogota **State:** Bogota **PC:** **Country:** Colombia
Year Established: 2019 **Status 2020:** Active
Industries: Analytics for:, Artificial Intelligence for:, Facial Recognition

Company Name: Grupo Bernier
Description: Grupo Bernier is a Colombian company focused on consulting in information technologies. Artificial Intelligence & Quantum Computing
Website: http://www.berniergroup.com/
Phone: **Email:** jean.bernier@berniergroup.com
City: Bogota **State:** Bogota **PC:** **Country:** Colombia
Year Established: 2014 **Status 2020:** Active
Industries: Artificial Intelligence for:, IT Managed Services for:, ~ Education (13)

Company Name: Intelligent Trading Machin: Spain
Description: Intelligent Trading Machines is a B2B SaaS Platform, providing Systematic Investment Solutions leveraged on AI & ML.
Website: http://www.itrmachines.com/
Phone: 57 350 3430405 **Email:** sebastian.rocha@itrmachines.com
City: Bogota **State:** Bogota **PC:** **Country:** Colombia
Year Established: 2016 **Status 2020:** Active
Industries: Artificial Intelligence for:, ~ Banking and Financial Markets-Services (7), Machine Learning for:, Risk Management for:, Business Software as a Service Apps (SaaS Apps) for:, ~ Banking and Financial Markets-Services (7)

Company **Name:** MENTe Labs
Description: Company specializing in human behavior analysis using algorithms and artificial intelligence to profile people.
Website: http://www.mentelabs.com/
Phone: **Email:** mauricio@coleoptera.co
City: Bogota **State:** Bogota **PC:** **Country:** Colombia
Year Established: 2017 **Status 2020:** Active
Industries: Analytics for:, Artificial Intelligence for:, Big Data and Analytics for:, Business Intelligence for:, Machine Learning

Company Name: MO Tecnologias
Description: MO Tecnologias is an innovative Fintech that aims at revolutionizing the credit scoring industry and promoting financial inclusion
Website: http://www.motecnologias.com
Phone: **Email:** info@motecnologias.com
City: Bogota **State:** Bogota **PC:** **Country:** Colombia
Year Established: 2016 **Status 2020:** Active
Industries: Artificial Intelligence for:, ~ Banking and Financial Markets-Services (7), IT Managed Services for:, ~ Banking and Financial Markets-Services (7), ~ Banking and Financial Markets-Services (7), ~ Banking and Financial Markets-Services (7)

Company Name: Spin Quantum
Description: Spin Quantum Tech, is an adaptative cybersecurity collection of quantum algorithms that solves the next cybersecurity trends and wave.
Website: http://www.spinqtech.com
Phone: **Email:** jean.bernier@spinqtech.com
City: Bogota **State:** Bogota **PC:** **Country:** Colombia
Year Established: 2018 **Status 2020:** Active
Industries: Artificial Intelligence for:, Cyber Security

Company Name: Transport Systems
Description: Transport Systems is a company focused on building tech for Smart Cities. It also has a "Software Factory" working for different sectors.
Website: http://www.transportsystems.co
Phone: 5717460355 **Email:** info@transportsystems.co
City: Bogota **State:** Bogota **PC:** **Country:** Colombia
Year Established: 2011 **Status 2020:** Active
Industries: Enterprise Application Services for:, ~ Banking and Financial Markets-Services (7), Application Services for:, ~ Banking and Financial Markets-Services (7), ~ Construction (10), ~ Construction (10)

Company Name: VincuVentas
Description: Using data-driven matching to revolutionize recruitment in Latin America.
Website: http://vincuventas.com/
Phone: (031)508-8448 **Email:** trabajos@vincuventas.com
City: Bogota **State:** Bogota **PC:** **Country:** Colombia
Year Established: 2014 **Status 2020:** Active
Industries: Analytics for:, Artificial Intelligence for:, IT Managed Services

Company Name: Work.r
Description: Work.r is a machine learning company that builds easy to adopt ML solutions that propel revenue growth and improve customer experienc: Spain
Website: http://www.workr.com.co
Phone: 57 3204498465 **Email:** laureano.diaz@workr.com.co
City: Bogota **State:** Bogota **PC:** **Country:** Colombia
Year Established: 2018 **Status 2020:** Active
Industries: Artificial Intelligence for:, Machine Learning

Company Name: Xper: Tanzania
Description: Making compensation transparent for everyone, using AI algorythms to improve users carree: Serbia
Website: http://www.xpertz.co
Phone: 311 592 0548 **Email:** data@xpertz.co
City: Bogota **State:** Bogota **PC:** **Country:** Colombia
Year Established: **Status 2020:** Active
Industries: Artificial Intelligence for:, Big Data and Analytics for:, Databases for:, ~ Human Resources (24), Machine Learning for:, ~ Media-Communications (41)

Company Name: Focus Data
Description: Marketing Analytics
Website:
Phone: 57 3217463632 **Email:** focusdata.comercial@gmail.com
City: Pereira **State:** Risaralda **PC:** **Country:** Colombia
Year Established: 2019 **Status 2020:** Active
Industries: Artificial Intelligence

Congo

Company Name: Itot Africa
Description: itotafrica is an organization focused on research in open data , artificial intelligence and the Internet of Things in DRCongo context.
Website: http://www.itotafrica.com
Phone: **Email:** contact@itotafrica.com
City: Lubumbashi **State:** Katanga **PC:** **Country:** Congo
Year Established: 2017 **Status 2020:** Active
Industries:

Company Name: Upsail
Description: A data platform to leverage your strength, Better business with analytics.
Website: http://www.upsail.co/
Phone: 32483517537 **Email:** info@upsailgroup.com
City: Kinshasa **State:** Kinshasa **PC:** **Country:** Congo
Year Established: 2015 **Status 2020:** Active
Industries: Analytics for:, IT Managed Services for:, Machine Learning

Costa Rica

Company Name: Newton Board
Description: APIs, bot, NLP & AI
Website: http://botsnlp.github.io/newtonboard/
Phone: 506 8715 0485 **Email:** leandrocg@consultant.com
City: San Jose **State:** San José Province **PC:** **Country:** Costa Rica
Year Established: 2016 **Status 2020:** Active
Industries: Artificial Intelligence for:, IT Managed Services for:, Natural Language Processing for:, Speech Recognition

Croatia

Company Name: DenCity
Description: DenCity is an AI and Blockchain enabled powered virtual platform where people can come and become the ideal version of themselves.
Website: http://dencity.life/
Phone: **Email:** contact@dencity.life
City: Zagreb **State:** Grad Zagreb **PC:** **Country:** Croatia
Year Established: **Status 2020:** Active
Industries: Artificial Intelligence for:, Blockchain

Company Name: Gideon Brothe: Serbia
Description: Gideon Brothers solves industrial problems with AI-powered autonomous robots.
Website: http://www.gideonbros.net
Phone: **Email:** robo@gideonbros.net
City: Zagreb **State:** Grad Zagreb **PC:** **Country:** Croatia
Year Established: **Status 2020:** Active
Industries: Artificial Intelligence for:, ~ Automotive (5), Machine Learning for:, Robotics

Company Name: Orange & Green
Description: The Innovation Company in primary preventive healthcare
Website: http://orange-green-lifestyle.com/
Phone: 38598343408 **Email:** info@orange-green-lifestyle.com
City: Zagreb **State:** Grad Zagreb **PC:** **Country:** Croatia
Year Established: **Status 2020:** Active
Industries: Application Services for:, Artificial Intelligence for:, Business Applications for:, Business Applications for:, ~ Healthcare (20), ~ Healthcare (20), ~ Pharmaceuticals (46), Robotics for:, ~ Arts-Entertainment-Recreation (4), ~ Healthcare (20)

Company **Name:** Piculjan Technologies
Description: Artificial Intelligence Research & Development and Consulting
Website: http://www.piculjantechnologies.ai
Phone: **Email:** contact@piculjantechnologies.ai
City: Zagreb **State:** Grad Zagreb **PC:** **Country:** Croatia
Year Established: 2019 **Status 2020:** Active
Industries: Artificial Intelligence

Company Name: Robotiq.ai
Description: Creating a platform for software robots (Robotic Process Automation)
Website: http://robotiq.ai
Phone: **Email:** info@robotiq.ai
City: Zagreb **State:** Grad Zagreb **PC:** **Country:** Croatia
Year Established: 2018 **Status 2020:** Active
Industries: Artificial Intelligence for:, Business Applications for:, Cloud for:, Enterprise Application Services for:, Machine Learning

Company Name: TIS Objecktni informacijski sustavi d.o.o.
Description:
Website: http://www.tis.hr
Phone: 41 41 766 71 31 **Email:** 12776@reference-encyclopedia-ai.net
City: Zagreb **State:** **PC:** **Country:** Croatia
Year Established: **Status 2020:** Active
Industries:

Cyprus

Company Name: SENPAI Technologies
Description: Consulting and R&D
Website: http://www.Senpai.tech/
Phone: **Email:** info@Senpai.
City: Limasol **State:** Limassol **PC:** **Country:** Cyprus
Year Established: 2015 **Status 2020:** Active
Industries: Big Data and Analytics for:, Cyber Security for:, Data Management for:, IT Managed Services for:, Predictive Analytics

Company Name: L2P LIMITED
Description: International e-learning e-sports company
Website: http://l2p.game
Phone: **Email:** info@l2p.game
City: Limassol **State:** Limassol **PC:** **Country:** Cyprus
Year Established: **Status 2020:** Active
Industries: Artificial Intelligence for:, ~ Education (13), ~ Arts-Entertainment-Recreation (4), Machine Learning for:, ~ Media-Communications (41), ~ Gaming (18)

Company Name: Prediti
Description: A decision making tool, which analyses consumer's purchase behavior, while providing to them, the capability for real time recommendations.
Website: http://www.prediti.com/
Phone: 35799576424 **Email:** info@prediti.com
City: Limassol **State:** Limassol **PC:** **Country:** Cyprus
Year Established: 2015 **Status 2020:** Active
Industries: ~ Retail and Consumer Products (52), Predictive Analytics

Company Name: Soffos
Description: AI-Powered TutorBot. Hyper-personalized teaching delivery. Democratizing and Personalizing Learning.
Website: http://soffos.ai/
Phone: **Email:** ai@fountech.ai
City: Yermasoyia **State:** Limassol **PC:** **Country:** Cyprus
Year Established: 2018 **Status 2020:** Active
Industries: Artificial Intelligence for:, ~ Education (13), ~ Education (13)

Company Name: Regtify
Description:
Website: http://regtify.com
Phone: **Email:** info@regtify.com
City: **State:** Nicosia **PC:** **Country:** Cyprus
Year Established: **Status 2020:** Active
Industries: Artificial Intelligence for:, ~ Banking and Financial Markets-Services (7), Compliance for:, Finance and Accounting for:, ~ Banking and Financial Markets-Services (2447), Risk Management

Company Name: FraudScore
Description: FraudScore is a high-precision and feature-rich fraud-fighting platform that uses machine learning.
Website: http://fraudscore.ai/
Phone: **Email:** sales@fraudscore.mobi
City: Nicosia **State:** Nicosia **PC:** **Country:** Cyprus
Year Established: 2016 **Status 2020:** Active
Industries:

Company Name: Mangosoft
Description: We bring your vision to life with world class ap: Palestine
Website: http://mangosoft.tech/
Phone: **Email:** contact@mangosoft.te:
City: Nicosia **State:** Nicosia **PC:** **Country:** Cyprus
Year Established: 2012 **Status 2020:** Active
Industries: Artificial Intelligence for:, ~ Banking and Financial Markets-Services (7), ~ Arts-Entertainment-Recreation (4), ~ Arts-Entertainment-Recreation (4)

Company Name: power games
Description: gaming
Website: http://notreadyyet.com
Phone: **Email:** 37193@reference-encyclopedia-ai.net
City: Nicosia **State:** Nicosia **PC:** **Country:** Cyprus
Year Established: 2012 **Status 2020:** Active
Industries: Machine Learning for:, Mobile

Company Name: Stickeroid AI
Description: Stickeroid is a cloud platform for Stickers based on neural networks that translates text to sticker for most any situation of conversation.
Website: http://stickeroid.com
Phone: **Email:** team@stickeroid.com
City: Nicosia **State:** Nicosia **PC:** **Country:** Cyprus
Year Established: **Status 2020:** Active
Industries: Artificial Intelligence for:, Cloud for:, Application Services for:, Enterprise Application Services for:, Web for:, Machine Learning for:, Enterprise Application Services for:, Cyber Security

Company Name: Teastock
Description: We are using machine learning and Big Data to bring you the most accurate stock movement information algorithm.
Website: http://teastock.io
Phone: **Email:** info@teastock.io
City: Nicosia **State:** Nicosia **PC:** **Country:** Cyprus
Year Established: 2015 **Status 2020:** Active
Industries: Big Data and Analytics for:, ~ Banking and Financial Markets-Services (7), Machine Learning

Company Name: PHOEBE Research and Innovation
Description: Intelligent Monitoring Solutions for Industrial Systems
Website: http://www.phoebeinnovations.com
Phone: **Email:** management@phoebeinnovations.com
City: Strovolos **State:** Nicosia **PC:** **Country:** Cyprus
Year Established: 2016 **Status 2020:** Active
Industries: Artificial Intelligence for:, IT Managed Services for:, Web

Czechia

Company Name: Recombee
Description: Saas
Website: http://www.recombee.com/
Phone: **Email:** business@recombee.com
City: Nove Mesto **State:** Hradec Králové Region **PC:** **Country:** Czechia
Year Established: 2015 **Status 2020:** Active
Industries: Analytics for:, Artificial Intelligence for:, ~ Customer Relationship Management (11), IT Managed Services for:, Web

Company Name: 24 Vision System
Description: Artificial Intelligence in E2E visual quality control
Website: http://www.24vs.io/
Phone: 777869755 **Email:** m.cvicek@24vs.io
City: Frýdek-místek **State:** Moravian-Silesian Region **PC:** **Country:** Czechia
Year Established: 2019 **Status 2020:** Active
Industries: Artificial Intelligence

Company Name: ApuTime
Description: ApuTime is a web-based application for Project Management that you will love. Key parameters are Emotions, Visualization and Game
Website: http://www.aputime.com
Phone: 1 (775) 553-5305 **Email:** info@aputime.com
City: Moravska Ostrava **State:** Moravskoslezský kraj **PC:**
Country: Czechia
Year Established: **Status 2020:** Active
Industries: Artificial Intelligence for:, ~ Media-Communications (41), Business Process and Operations for:, Application Services for:, ~ Professional Services (48), Cyber Security

Company Name: SentiSquare
Description: SentiSquare is an online service for digital marketing managers who deal with high traffic and noise in social media
Website: http://www.sentisquare.com/
Phone: 420 724 059 754 **Email:** info@sentisquare.com
City: Pilsen **State:** Plzeň Region **PC:** **Country:** Czechia
Year Established: 2014 **Status 2020:** Active
Industries: Analytics for:, Natural Language Processing for:, ~ Social Assistance-Non-Profits (53)

Company Name: 2Realistic.com
Description: Rapid application development in field of AR/VR
Website: http://www.2realistic.com/
Phone: **Email:** info@2realistic.com
City: Prague **State:** Prague **PC:** **Country:** Czechia
Year Established: 2017 **Status 2020:** Active
Industries: Artificial Intelligence for:, Big Data and Analytics for:, Virtual Reality (VR)

Company Name: A.I.racer
Description: Artificial Intelligence Platform providing F1 like experience to any driver interested in improving own racing skills.
Website:
Phone: **Email:** honza@flexer.cz
City: Prague **State:** Prague **PC:** **Country:** Czechia
Year Established: 2019 **Status 2020:** Active
Industries: Artificial Intelligence

Company Name: adELA
Description: AdTech startup providing online publishers, websites and blogs with ultimate ad market
Website: https://adela.digital/
Phone: **Email:** web@adela.digital
City: Prague **State:** Prague **PC:** **Country:** Czechia
Year Established: 2018 **Status 2020:** Active
Industries: Digital Marketing for:, IT Managed Services for:, Web for:, Predictive Analytics for:, Finance and Accounting

Company Name: asheep
Description: I'm young conversational chatbot. You can teach me stuff just by talking. I learn your business, APIs & existing infrastructure.
Website: http://www.asheep.ai
Phone: **Email:** info@asheep.ai
City: Prague **State:** Prague **PC:** **Country:** Czechia
Year Established: **Status 2020:** Active
Industries: Artificial Intelligence

Company Name: Bohemian AI
Description: Custom AI Solutions for Visionary Compani: Spain
Website: http://bohemian.ai
Phone: 1 (650) 600-1536 **Email:** lukas@bohemian.ai
City: Prague **State:** Prague **PC:** **Country:** Czechia
Year Established: 2017 **Status 2020:** Active
Industries:

Company Name: Boxtrap Security
Description: Cyber Security, AI, Machine Learning
Website: http://boxtrapsecurity.net/
Phone: **Email:** boxtrap@boxtrap.net
City: Prague **State:** Prague **PC:** **Country:** Czechia
Year Established: 2014 **Status 2020:** Active
Industries: Artificial Intelligence for:, Cloud for:, ~ Customer Relationship Management (11), Cyber Security for:, Security for:, Security

Company Name: CLEO Finance
Description: Ultimate Trading Tool. Write trading algorithms in plain English, connect and analyze your trading or crypto account and much more!
Website: http://cleo.one
Phone: **Email:** info@cleo.one
City: Prague **State:** Prague **PC:** **Country:** Czechia
Year Established: **Status 2020:** Active
Industries: Artificial Intelligence for:, ~ Banking and Financial Markets-Services (7), ~ Banking and Financial Markets-Services (7), ~ Banking and Financial Markets-Services (7), Finance and Accounting

Company Name: Cognitive Security
Description: Cognitive Security provides network security solutions for enterprises and small- to medium-sized business markets.
Website: http://www.cognitivesecurity.cz
Phone: **Email:** info@cognitive-security.com
City: Prague **State:** Prague **PC:** **Country:** Czechia
Year Established: **Status 2020:** Active
Industries: Artificial Intelligence for:, Security

Company Name: datasapiens
Description: We empower companies to make better business decisions through understanding their data.
Website: http://www.datasapiens.co.uk/
Phone: **Email:** michal@datasapiens.co.uk
City: Prague **State:** Prague **PC:** **Country:** Czechia
Year Established: 2014 **Status 2020:** Active
Industries: Analytics for:, Big Data and Analytics for:, Business Intelligence for:, ~ Customer Relationship Management (11), IT Managed Services for:, IT Managed Services for:, ~ Retail and Consumer Products (52), Machine Learning for:, Machine Learning

Company Name: Decissio
Description: Decissio is enhance your investor gut feeling with data.
Website: http://decissio.com
Phone: 420 777 019 241 **Email:** info@decissio.com
City: Prague **State:** Prague **PC:** **Country:** Czechia
Year Established: **Status 2020:** Active
Industries: Artificial Intelligence for:, Databases

Company Name: Deepnote
Description: Deepnote is a collaboration platform for data scientists.
Website: http://www.deepnote.com/
Phone: **Email:** 4540@reference-encyclopedia-ai.net
City: Prague **State:** Prague **PC:** **Country:** Czechia
Year Established: **Status 2020:** Active
Industries: Analytics for:, Artificial Intelligence for:, Big Data and Analytics for:, Cloud for:, Machine Learning for:, Enterprise Application Services

Company Name: Farfalia
Description: Farfalia is a first-class automated personal consultant to the ecommerce managers.
Website: http://www.farfalia.com
Phone: 420 608 353 358 **Email:** my@farfalia.com
City: Prague **State:** Prague **PC:** **Country:** Czechia
Year Established: 2013 **Status 2020:** Active
Industries: Analytics for:, Big Data and Analytics for:, Business Intelligence for:, E-Commerce for:, Predictive Analytics

Company Name: GoodAI
Description: GoodAI is a general artificial intelligence research and development company.
Website: http://www.goodai.com/
Phone: **Email:** info@goodai.com
City: Prague **State:** Prague **PC:** **Country:** Czechia
Year Established: **Status 2020:** Active
Industries: Artificial Intelligence for:, Machine Learning for:, ~ Professional Services (48)

Company Name: GoodVision
Description: Mining events from camera recordings through artificial intelligence
Website: http://www.goodvisionlive.com
Phone: **Email:** info@goodvisionlive.com
City: Prague **State:** Prague **PC:** **Country:** Czechia
Year Established: **Status 2020:** Active
Industries: Analytics for:, Artificial Intelligence for:, Big Data and Analytics for:, Cloud for:, Computer Vision for:, Data Management for:, ~ Retail and Consumer Products (52), ~ Professional Services (48)

Company Name: KAICORE
Description: Your personal Artificial Intelligence
Website: http://kaicore.net
Phone: 420 774 344 377 **Email:** contact@kaicore.net
City: Prague **State:** Prague **PC:** **Country:** Czechia
Year Established: 2012 **Status 2020:** Active
Industries: Artificial Intelligence

Company Name: Memento
Description: We build AI-driven solutions that empower users by putting them in control of their digital identities.
Website: http://www.zivter.com
Phone: **Email:** contact@zivter.com
City: Prague **State:** Prague **PC:** **Country:** Czechia
Year Established: 2018 **Status 2020:** Active
Industries: Artificial Intelligence for:, Blockchain for:, ~ Healthcare (20)

Company Name: Oddin.gg
Description: Gaming, Betting, AI, Machine learning, Analytics
Website: http://oddin.gg
Phone: **Email:** info@oddin.gg
City: Prague **State:** Prague **PC:** **Country:** Czechia
Year Established: 2018 **Status 2020:** Active
Industries: Artificial Intelligence

Company Name: Samba.ai
Description: Great customer experiences are built with Samba's artificial intelligence and automation capabilities.
Website: http://samba.ai
Phone: 420 731 193 149 **Email:** info@samba.ai
City: Prague **State:** Prague **PC:** **Country:** Czechia
Year Established: 2011 **Status 2020:** Active
Industries: Artificial Intelligence for:, E-Commerce

Company Name: Smart Record
Description: Disruptive platform offering complex recording & transcription services, fusing AI and human talent to deliver top-notch quality outputs.
Website: http://smartrecordapp.com/
Phone: **Email:** hello@smartrecordapp.com
City: Prague **State:** Prague **PC:** **Country:** Czechia
Year Established: **Status 2020:** Active
Industries:

Company Name: Stadyum
Description: Smart CRM system for sports club management and refreshment delivery to seat.
Website: http://stadyumcrm.com
Phone: 420 731 453 763 **Email:** info@stadyum.cz
City: Prague **State:** Prague **PC:** **Country:** Czechia
Year Established: **Status 2020:** Active
Industries: ~ Media-Communications (41), ~ Media-Communications (41), Analytics for:, Application Services for:, Artificial Intelligence for:, Business Applications for:, Business Applications for:, Big Data and Analytics for:, Business Applications for:, Business Intelligenc

Company Name: Teachable Machines™
Description: Amazingly accurate predictive modeling for product and marketing teams. The future is now.
Website: http://teachablemachines.com
Phone: 1 (512) 516-1739 **Email:** alexander.popov@teachablemachines.com
City: Prague **State:** Prague **PC:** **Country:** Czechia
Year Established: 2017 **Status 2020:** Active
Industries: Artificial Intelligence

Company Name: Time is Ltd.
Description: Time is Ltd. offers software based on machine learning to truly analyze inter-company time productivity.
Website: http://www.timeisltd.com/
Phone: **Email:** 37542@reference-encyclopedia-ai.net
City: Prague **State:** Prague **PC:** **Country:** Czechia
Year Established: 2017 **Status 2020:** Active
Industries: Artificial Intelligence for:, ~ Customer Relationship Management (11), IT Managed Services for:, Machine Learning for:, Robotics for:, Business Software as a Service Apps (SaaS Apps)

Company Name: Wikidi.cz
Description: Wikidi is a web development company creating intelligent technology solutions that are robust, flexible and accessible.
Website: http://wikidi.cz
Phone: **Email:** info@wikidi.cz
City: Prague **State:** Prague **PC:** **Country:** Czechia
Year Established: **Status 2020:** Active
Industries: Artificial Intelligence for:, Databases for:, Application Services for:, Machine Learning for:, ~ Professional Services (48), Cyber Security

Company Name: IP Fabric
Description: IP Fabric develops Automated Network Assurance Platform, uncovering risks and threats before they occur by simulating global networks.
Website: http://www.ipfabric.io/
Phone: **Email:** sales@ipfabric.io
City: Prague-vinohrady **State:** Prague **PC:** **Country:** Czechia
Year Established: 2015 **Status 2020:** Active
Industries: Big Data and Analytics for:, Cloud for:, IT Infrastructure for:, Security for:, Predictive Analytics

Company Name: Incomaker
Description: Incomaker is an AI-based marketing optimization system that turns data into income.
Website: http://www.incomaker.com
Phone: **Email:** info@incomaker.com
City: Praha **State:** Prague **PC:** **Country:** Czechia
Year Established: **Status 2020:** Active
Industries: Artificial Intelligence for:, Big Data and Analytics for:, Data Management for:, ~ Media-Communications (41), ~ Media-Communications (41), ~ Professional Services (48)

Company Name: Modgen
Description: Modgen provides its commercial customers with artificial intelligence and data analysis solutions to assist in their decision making.
Website: http://modgen.net/
Phone: (420) 724-9196 **Email:** info@modgen.net
City: Praha **State:** Prague **PC:** **Country:** Czechia
Year Established: 2012 **Status 2020:** Active
Industries: Artificial Intelligence for:, Databases

Company Name: Trivi
Description: Trivi is a Prague-based AI company providing complete financial services for small and medium businesses.
Website: http://www.trivi.com/
Phone: 800 80 60 40 **Email:** hello@trivi.com
City: Praha **State:** Prague **PC:** **Country:** Czechia
Year Established: 2015 **Status 2020:** Active
Industries: Artificial Intelligence for:, ~ Banking and Financial Markets-Services (7), Machine Learning

Company Name: Mailcheap (Cyberlabs s.r.o. & Cyberlabs, Inc.)
Description: Enterprise email solutions with machine learning spam classifiers at affordable pric: Spain
Website: https://www.mailcheap.co/
Phone: **Email:** pavin@mailcheap.co
City: Praha 1 **State:** Prague **Zip:** 110 00 **Country**: Czechia
Year Established: **Status 2020:** Active
Industries: Application Program Interfaces (APIs) for:, Artificial Intelligence for:, ~ Media-Communications (41), Business Software as a Service Apps (SaaS Apps) for:, Cyber Security for:, Machine Learning

Company Name: eParkomat
Description: eParkomat is a platform that provides real-time parking information using AI to analyze Big Data of cellular networks of mobile operato: Serbia
Website: http://www.eparkomat.com/
Phone: **Email:** info@eparkomat.com
City: Smichov **State:** Prague **PC:** **Country:** Czechia
Year Established: 2016 **Status 2020:** Active
Industries: Artificial Intelligence for:, ~ Automotive (5), ~ Travel and Transportation (58)

Company Name: Fragments
Description: Decentralized micro-task platform where people can earn cryptocurrency on their smartphones by completing simple tasks.
Website: http://fragments.network/
Phone: **Email:** hello@fragments.network
City: Brno **State:** South Moravian Region **PC:** **Country:** Czechia
Year Established: **Status 2020:** Active
Industries: Artificial Intelligence for:, Blockchain for:, ~ Banking and Financial Markets-Services (7), Machine Learning for:, Collaboration Solutions

Company Name: GreyCortex
Description: A solutions for advanced network security and performance monitoring for enterprise, government and other critical infrastructure.
Website: http://www.greycortex.com/
Phone: 420 511 205 216 **Email:** petr.chmelar@greycortex.com
City: Brno **State:** South Moravian Region **PC:** **Country:** Czechia
Year Established: **Status 2020:** Active
Industries: Artificial Intelligence for:, IT Managed Services for:, ~ Government (19), IT Infrastructure for:, Security

Company Name: SANEZOO
Description: We make industrial robots faster and smarter by empowering them with 3D machine vision and AI.
Website: http://sanezoo.com
Phone: 420 721966366 **Email:** lubosb@sanezoo.com
City: Brno **State:** South Moravian Region **PC:** **Country:** Czechia
Year Established: 2017 **Status 2020:** Active
Industries: ~ Automotive (5), Computer Vision for:, ~ Manufacturing-General (31), Machine Learning for:, Robotics

Company Name: Ximilar
Description: Computer vision platform for Image Recognition, Visual Search and Machine Learning
Website: http://www.ximilar.com/
Phone: **Email:** sales@ximilar.com
City: Brno **State:** South Moravian Region **PC:** **Country:** Czechia
Year Established: 2016 **Status 2020:** Active
Industries:

Company Name: Iterait
Description: Experts in AI development for edge (IoT) devic: Spain
Website: http://www.iterait.com
Phone: **Email:** vividi@iterait.com
City: Karlin **State:** Středočeský kraj **PC:** **Country:** Czechia
Year Established: 2018 **Status 2020:** Active
Industries: Artificial Intelligence

Denmark

Company Name: PRECURE
Description: Smart wearables that help reduce the risk of work-related strain injuries by providing a cloud-based real time body activity analys
Website: http://www.precure.dk/
Phone: 0045 5355 8217 **Email:** mail@precure.dk
City: Allinge **State:** Hovedstaden **PC:** **Country:** Denmark
Year Established: 2016 **Status 2020:** Active
Industries: Artificial Intelligence for:, ~ Healthcare (20)

Company Name: 2021.AI
Description: 2021.AI develops and delivers Grace, a next generation AI platform, which supports the entire data science workflow, and AI model Governance
Website: https://www.2021.ai/
Phone: 459391 2021 **Email:** mmu@2021.ai
City: Copenhagen **State:** Hovedstaden **PC:** **Country:** Denmark
Year Established: 2016 **Status 2020:** Active
Industries: Artificial Intelligence for:, Big Data and Analytics for:, Enterprise Application Services for:, IT Managed Services for:, Machine Learning

Company Name: 3Dintegrated
Description: Healthcare, Medical Devices, 3D sensors, Augmented Reality
Website: http://3dintegrated.com/
Phone: **Email:** info@3dintegrated.com
City: Copenhagen **State:** Hovedstaden **PC:** **Country:** Denmark
Year Established: 2013 **Status 2020:** Active
Industries: Artificial Intelligence for:, ~ Customer Relationship Management (11), ~ Healthcare (20), IT Managed Services for:, ~ Healthcare (20)

Company Name: Archii
Description: Archii is an AI powered document assistant that automatically identifies and sorts your company'™s most important documents.
Website: http://archii.ai
Phone: 4540407000 **Email:** hello@archii.ai
City: Copenhagen **State:** Hovedstaden **PC:** **Country:** Denmark
Year Established: **Status 2020:** Active
Industries: Artificial Intelligence for:, Data Management for:, ~ Media-Communications (41), Machine Learning for:, Natural Language Processing

Company Name: Blackwood Seven
Description: Blackwood Seven is a digital marketing firm focusing on predictive analytics for businesses.
Website: http://blackwoodseven.com
Phone: (455)366-0777 **Email:** info@blackwoodseven.com
City: Copenhagen **State:** Hovedstaden **PC:** **Country:** Denmark
Year Established: **Status 2020:** Active

Industries: Artificial Intelligence for:, Machine Learning for:, ~ Media-Communications (41), Predictive Analytics

Company Name: bmetric
Description: Intelligent Channel Management technologies: For increased sales, optimised conversions, and enhanced CX--online and in contact centre.
Website: http://bmetric.com
Phone: 45 78 79 22 22 **Email:** hello@bmetric.com
City: Copenhagen **State:** Hovedstaden **PC:** **Country:** Denmark
Year Established: 2012 **Status 2020:** Active
Industries: Analytics for:, Business Intelligence for:, ~ Customer Relationship Management (11), Digital Marketing for:, IT Managed Services for:, Machine Learning for:, Business Software as a Service Apps (SaaS Apps) for:, Business Software as a Service Apps (SaaS Apps) fo

Company Name: BotSupply
Description: AI & Bots agency | Conversational Experience Platform | Proprietary AI
Website: http://botsupply.ai
Phone: 45 2646 9997 **Email:** yourfriends@botsupply.ai
City: Copenhagen **State:** Hovedstaden **PC:** **Country:** Denmark
Year Established: **Status 2020:** Active
Industries: Artificial Intelligence for:, ~ Telecommunications (56)

Company Name: BotXO
Description: Working with bots, Machine Learning and A.I. to build the software for the conversational era.
Website: http://www.botxo.co
Phone: 45 26 71 58 45 **Email:** hello@botxo.co
City: Copenhagen **State:** Hovedstaden **PC:** **Country:** Denmark
Year Established: 2016 **Status 2020:** Active
Industries: Artificial Intelligence for:, Machine Learning

Company Name: CanopyLAB
Description: CanopyLAB enables adaptive learning experiences online based on algorithms and soon AI.
Website: http://canopylab.com/
Phone: 4526176613 **Email:** info@canopylab.com
City: Copenhagen **State:** Hovedstaden **PC:** **Country:** Denmark
Year Established: **Status 2020:** Active
Industries: Artificial Intelligence for:, ~ Education (13), ~ Education (13), ~ Gaming (18), ~ Education (13), Machine Learning for:, ~ Education (13)

Company Name: Cobi: Romania
Description: Cobiro is an Artificial Intelligence for Google Ads and Google Shopping.
Website: http://cobiro.com
Phone: **Email:** info@cobiro.com
City: Copenhagen **State:** Hovedstaden **PC:** **Country:** Denmark
Year Established: 2016 **Status 2020:** Active
Industries: Artificial Intelligence for:, Digital Marketing

Company Name: Comparo.dk
Description: Comparo.dk is an online service that helps its users find the cheapest car and travel insurance packages.
Website: http://www.comparo.dk
Phone: 45 71 70 01 00 **Email:** info@comparo.dk
City: Copenhagen **State:** Hovedstaden **PC:** **Country:** Denmark
Year Established: **Status 2020:** Active
Industries: Artificial Intelligence for:, ~ Automotive (5), ~ Banking and Financial Markets-Services (7), ~ Insurance (25), ~ Insurance (25)

Company Name: Corti
Description: The artificial intelligence platform for medical triaging, that reduces errors and increases the accuracy of humans to save more lives.
Website: http://www.corti.ai/
Phone: **Email:** hello@corti.ai
City: Copenhagen **State:** Hovedstaden **PC:** **Country:** Denmark
Year Established: **Status 2020:** Active
Industries: Artificial Intelligence for:, IT Managed Services for:, Machine Learning for:, ~ Professional Services (48), Speech Recognition

Company Name: cVation
Description: Delivering product, consulting, architecture, tools, methodology, and outsourced development on Microsoft Azure Technology with DevO: Palestine
Website: http://www.cvation.com
Phone: **Email:** info@cvation.com
City: Copenhagen **State:** Hovedstaden **PC:** **Country:** Denmark
Year Established: 2014 **Status 2020:** Active
Industries:

Company Name: Defudger
Description: Media manipulation detection with AI and blockcha: India
Website: http://defudger.com
Phone: **Email:** 36425@reference-encyclopedia-ai.net
City: Copenhagen **State:** Hovedstaden **PC:** **Country:** Denmark
Year Established: 2019 **Status 2020:** Active
Industries: Artificial Intelligence for:, Blockchain for:, Digital Media for:, IT Managed Services for:, Machine Learning

Company Name: Dixa
Description: Dixa is conversational customer engagement software that connects brands with customers through real-time communication
Website: http://dixa.com
Phone: (1888) 910-7555 **Email:** hello@dixa.com
City: Copenhagen **State:** Hovedstaden **PC:** **Country:** Denmark
Year Established: 2015 **Status 2020:** Active
Industries: Artificial Intelligence for:, ~ Customer Relationship Management (11), Enterprise Application Services for:, Business Software as a Service Apps (SaaS Apps)

Company Name: Dreamdata.io
Description: Data driven decisions for B2B companies. Adjust your channels and touchpoints to drive optimal growth for your business.
Website: http://dreamdata.io
Phone: **Email:** friends@dreamdata.io
City: Copenhagen **State:** Hovedstaden **PC:** **Country:** Denmark
Year Established: 2018 **Status 2020:** Active
Industries: Analytics for:, Business Applications for:, Cloud for:, Data Management for:, Data Management for:, Predictive Analytics

Company Name: Easysize
Description: Easysize delivers actionable insights into consumer fashion choices.
Website: http://www.easysize.me
Phone: **Email:** info@easysize.me
City: Copenhagen **State:** Hovedstaden **PC:** **Country:** Denmark
Year Established: **Status 2020:** Active
Industries: Artificial Intelligence for:, Big Data and Analytics for:, E-Commerce for:, ~ Fashion (16), ~ Retail and Consumer Products (52)

Company Name: Forecast
Description: Forecast is an intelligent project automation platform for improving your company's financial & operational performance
Website: http://www.forecast.app
Phone: (45) 61779722 **Email:** info@forecast.app
City: Copenhagen **State:** Hovedstaden **PC:** **Country:** Denmark
Year Established: 2016 **Status 2020:** Active
Industries: Artificial Intelligence for:, Application Services for:, Machine Learning for:, Natural Language Processing for:, Application Services for:, Business Software as a Service Apps (SaaS Apps) for:, Application Services

Company Name: GetSupremacy
Description: The worlds first AI trainer and coach in Esports that learn the training habits, skill level and create the perfect training schedule.

Website: http://www.getsupremacy.com
Phone: **Email:** hello@getsupremacy.com
City: Copenhagen **State:** Hovedstaden **PC:** **Country:** Denmark
Year Established: **Status 2020:** Active
Industries: Artificial Intelligence for:, ~ Arts-Entertainment-Recreation (4), ~ Arts-Entertainment-Recreation (4)

Company Name: Grain: Italy
Description: Agtech platform that enables farmers to easily track and create overview of inventory - increasing productivity and liquidity.
Website: http://grainit.net
Phone: **Email:** sebastian@grainit.net
City: Copenhagen **State:** Hovedstaden **PC:** **Country:** Denmark
Year Established: 2016 **Status 2020:** Active
Industries: ~ Agriculture (3), ~ Agriculture (3), Big Data and Analytics for:, ~ Agriculture (3), Machine Learning for:, Business Software as a Service Apps (SaaS Apps)

Company Name: Grazper
Description: Grazper creates the first truly real-time and embedded 3D analytics AI solution.
Website: http://grazper.com/
Phone: 45 42 42 43 42 **Email:** info@grazper.com
City: Copenhagen **State:** Hovedstaden **PC:** **Country:** Denmark
Year Established: 2013 **Status 2020:** Active
Industries: Analytics for:, Artificial Intelligence

Company Name: Hafnium Labs
Description: Accurately predicting chemistry to speed up development of new drugs, materials, and process: Spain
Website: http://hafniumlabs.com
Phone: **Email:** contact@hafniumlabs.com
City: Copenhagen **State:** Hovedstaden **PC:** **Country:** Denmark
Year Established: **Status 2020:** Active
Industries: Artificial Intelligence for:, ~ Biotechnology (9), ~ Manufacturing-Petroleum-Coal-Chemicals-Plastics-Rubber (37), Cloud for:, ~ Energy and Utilities (14), ~ Pharmaceuticals (46), ~ Professional Services (48)

Company Name: Headhunterportal.com
Description: Headhunterportal uses machine learning and AI to connect relevant candidates to matching headhunters.
Website: http://headhunterportal.com
Phone: (457) 174-1113 **Email:** info@headhunterportal.com
City: Copenhagen **State:** Hovedstaden **PC:** **Country:** Denmark
Year Established: 2016 **Status 2020:** Active
Industries: Artificial Intelligence for:, ~ Education (13)

Company Name: Hedia
Description: Hedia is a personal diabetes-assistant, based on artificial intelligence.
Website: http://www.hedia.co
Phone: 45 71 74 16 63 **Email:** hello@hedia.co
City: Copenhagen **State:** Hovedstaden **PC:** **Country:** Denmark
Year Established: 2016 **Status 2020:** Active
Industries: Artificial Intelligence for:, ~ Healthcare (20), ~ Healthcare (20)

Company Name: Hedia diabetes assistant
Description: Hedia has been developed as a tool that will make everyday life easier for people suffering from type 1 and 2 diabetes.
Website: http://www.hedia.dk
Phone: **Email:** hello@hedia.dk
City: Copenhagen **State:** Hovedstaden **PC:** **Country:** Denmark
Year Established: **Status 2020:** Active
Industries: Artificial Intelligence for:, ~ Healthcare (20), ~ Life Sciences (27), ~ Healthcare (20)

Company Name: Jatana
Description: Bringing Deep Learning at the fingertip of every customer support team.
Website: http://www.jatana.ai
Phone: **Email:** francesco@jatana.ai
City: Copenhagen **State:** Hovedstaden **PC:** **Country:** Denmark
Year Established: **Status 2020:** Active
Industries: Artificial Intelligence

Company Name: JourneyXP
Description: Experience orchestration platform that empowers teams to build data-driven journeys without coding a single line.
Website: http://www.journeyxp.com/
Phone: 45 20202020 **Email:** invest@journeyxp.com
City: Copenhagen **State:** Hovedstaden **PC:** **Country:** Denmark
Year Established: **Status 2020:** Active
Industries:

Company Name: Leapcraft
Description: Leapcraft orchestrates healthy and efficient urban habitat - with sensor fusion, cloud computing and good design.
Website: http://www.leapcraft.com
Phone: 45 29107468 **Email:** info@leapcraft.dk
City: Copenhagen **State:** Hovedstaden **PC:** **Country:** Denmark
Year Established: 2013 **Status 2020:** Active
Industries: Artificial Intelligence for:, ~ Construction (10), ~ Construction (10)

Company Name: Lokalist
Description: We are developing an AI that can determine the value of an item on your local secondhand market
Website: http://www.lokalist.dk
Phone: 45 91113247 **Email:** tegan@lokalist.dk
City: Copenhagen **State:** Hovedstaden **PC:** **Country:** Denmark
Year Established: **Status 2020:** Active
Industries: Artificial Intelligence for:, Big Data and Analytics for:, ~ Banking and Financial Markets-Services (7), ~ Retail and Consumer Products (52)

Company Name: Nordic Eye Venture Capital
Description: Nordic Eye is a Danish venture capital firm based in Copenhagen, Denmark.
Website: http://nordiceye.com/
Phone: **Email:** info@nordiceye.com
City: Copenhagen **State:** Hovedstaden **PC:** **Country:** Denmark
Year Established: **Status 2020:** Active
Industries: Artificial Intelligence for:, ~ Banking and Financial Markets-Services (7), ~ Retail and Consumer Products (52), Blockchain for:, Cyber Security for:, Robotics

Company Name: Ontame io
Description: Ontame is a recruitment analytics and planning platform, enables HR to measure and optimize talent attraction efforts in real-time
Website: http://ontame.io/
Phone: 4531661663 **Email:** hello@ontame.io
City: Copenhagen **State:** Hovedstaden **PC:** **Country:** Denmark
Year Established: 2015 **Status 2020:** Active
Industries: Analytics for:, Data Management for:, Data Management for:, Predictive Analytics

Company Name: Openledger A: Palestine
Description:
Website: https://openledger.info/
Phone: 45 3 699 0607 **Email:** alex.timoshenko@openledger.info
City: Copenhagen **State:** Hovedstaden **PC:** **Country:** Denmark
Year Established: **Status 2020:** Active
Industries: **Company Name:** Plant Jammer
Description: We empower plantbased home cooking, by bringing machine learning to your kitchen. Our app is a chef in your pocket!
Website: http://www.plantjammer.com
Phone: **Email:** info@plantjammer.com
City: Copenhagen **State:** Hovedstaden **PC:** **Country:** Denmark
Year Established: 2016 **Status 2020:** Active

Industries: Application Services for:, ~ Food and Beverage (17), Machine Learning

Company Name: Portcha: India
Description: Using technology to solve the hardest operational problems in shipping.
Website: http://www.portchain.com
Phone: 45 3010 6904 **Email:** contact@portchain.com
City: Copenhagen **State:** Hovedstaden **PC:** **Country:** Denmark
Year Established: 2017 **Status 2020:** Active
Industries: Artificial Intelligence for:, Business Applications for:, Enterprise Application Services for:, Machine Learning for:, Business Software as a Service Apps (SaaS Apps) for:, ~ Transportation and Logistics (57)

Company Name: Relink
Description: Our machine learning technology matches applicants to jobs and jobs to applicants
Website: http://www.relinklabs.com
Phone: 47 48 40 29 49 **Email:** contactus@relinklabs.com
City: Copenhagen **State:** Hovedstaden **PC:** **Country:** Denmark
Year Established: 2013 **Status 2020:** Active
Industries: Artificial Intelligence for:, Machine Learning for:, Business Software as a Service Apps (SaaS Apps)

Company Name: Reveal
Description: Reveal uses advanced mathematical models to provide insight about the job market.
Website: http://revealhub.com/
Phone: **Email:** 37295@reference-encyclopedia-ai.net
City: Copenhagen **State:** Hovedstaden **PC:** **Country:** Denmark
Year Established: 2015 **Status 2020:** Closed
Industries: Machine Learning

Company Name: Roger.ai
Description: Roger.ai is a bill pay and accounts payable automation for SMBs and accountants.
Website: http://www.roger.ai
Phone: **Email:** support@roger.ai
City: Copenhagen **State:** Hovedstaden **PC:** **Country:** Denmark
Year Established: **Status 2020:** Active
Industries: Artificial Intelligence for:, ~ Banking and Financial Markets-Services (7), ~ Banking and Financial Markets-Services (7), ~ Banking and Financial Markets-Services (7), Machine Learning for:, ~ Banking and Financial Markets-Services (7), ~ Banking and Financial

Company Name: Rokoko
Description: Rokoko is making human motion data universally accessible
Website: http://rokoko.com
Phone: **Email:** hi@rokoko.com
City: Copenhagen **State:** Hovedstaden **PC:** **Country:** Denmark
Year Established: **Status 2020:** Active
Industries: Artificial Intelligence for:, IT Managed Services for:, Content for:, ~ Healthcare (20), ~ Arts-Entertainment-Recreation (4), ~ Professional Services (48), ~ Arts-Entertainment-Recreation (4), ~ Education (13)

Company Name: Sensor Six
Description: Measuring human activity around us
Website: http://www.sensorsix.com
Phone: 45 28 55 87 99 **Email:** al@sensorsix.com
City: Copenhagen **State:** Hovedstaden **PC:** **Country:** Denmark
Year Established: 2012 **Status 2020:** Active
Industries: Artificial Intelligence for:, Computer Vision for:, Machine Learning

Company Name: Simplyture
Description: Simplyture aims to reduce the complexity of commercial parking though innovation and artificial intelligence.
Website: http://www.simplyture.com
Phone: (452)241-9113 **Email:** info@simplyture.com
City: Copenhagen **State:** Hovedstaden **PC:** **Country:** Denmark
Year Established: **Status 2020:** Active
Industries: Artificial Intelligence for:, IT Managed Services for:, IT Managed Services for:, ~ Travel and Transportation (58)

Company Name: Spektral
Description: Spektral is a visual effects company that applies machine learning to image and video editing.
Website: http://spektral.com/
Phone: (452) 070-3400 **Email:** info@spektral.com
City: Copenhagen **State:** Hovedstaden **PC:** **Country:** Denmark
Year Established: **Status 2020:** Active
Industries:

Company Name: Storyflow
Description: Powering effective content at scale.
Website: http://storyflow.ai
Phone: 4520767710 **Email:** hello@storyflow.ai
City: Copenhagen **State:** Hovedstaden **PC:** **Country:** Denmark
Year Established: 2019 **Status 2020:** Active
Industries: Artificial Intelligence for:, IT Managed Services for:, Web

Company Name: SupWiz
Description: AI and Machine Learning platform for Customer Service and Service
Website: http://www.supwiz.com
Phone: **Email:** contact@supwiz.com
City: Copenhagen **State:** Hovedstaden **PC:** **Country:** Denmark
Year Established: **Status 2020:** Active
Industries: Artificial Intelligence for:, Machine Learning

Company Name: The European Federation of Robotics
Description: Promote research, development and inventions in the entire field of robotics, industrial robots.
Website: http://www.robofed.eu
Phone: (455)067-2163 **Email:** info@robofed.eu
City: Copenhagen **State:** Hovedstaden **PC:** **Country:** Denmark
Year Established: 2011 **Status 2020:** Active
Industries:

Company Name: Tomorrow
Description: Tomorrow builds tech products empowering people and organisations to understand and reduce their carbon footprint
Website: http://www.tmrow.com
Phone: **Email:** hello@tmrow.com
City: Copenhagen **State:** Hovedstaden **PC:** **Country:** Denmark
Year Established: 2016 **Status 2020:** Active
Industries: Artificial Intelligence for:, Data Management for:, ~ Social-Environmental-Physical-Engineering Sciences (55)

Company Name: Uizard Technologies
Description: Uizard is a computer software company developing AI tools to transform user interface images into code for building apps and websites.
Website: http://uizard.io
Phone: **Email:** info@uizard.io
City: Copenhagen **State:** Hovedstaden **PC:** **Country:** Denmark
Year Established: 2017 **Status 2020:** Active
Industries: Artificial Intelligence for:, Machine Learning for:, Application Services for:, Development and Test for:, Web for:, Web

Company Name: Valuer
Description: Valuer is a digital bridge between entrepreneurs and established businesses.
Website: http://valuer.ai/
Phone: **Email:** info@valuer.ai
City: Copenhagen **State:** Hovedstaden **PC:** **Country:** Denmark
Year Established: 2017 **Status 2020:** Active
Industries: Artificial Intelligence for:, Enterprise Application Services for:, Machine Learning

Company Name: WasteHe: Romania
Description: Greener, Cleaner and Smarter Waste Collection Worldwide
Website: http://www.wastehero.io/
Phone: **Email:** info@wastehero.io
City: Copenhagen **State:** Hovedstaden **PC:** **Country:** Denmark
Year Established: 2017 **Status 2020:** Active
Industries: ~ Telecommunications (56), IT Managed Services for:, ~ Telecommunications (56), Machine Learning for:, ~ Waste Management and Remediation Services (59)

Company Name: Whis: Puerto Rico
Description: Voice guidance and on-demand expertise for frontline worke: Serbia
Website: http://www.whispr.ai/
Phone: **Email:** hello@whispr.ai
City: Copenhagen **State:** Hovedstaden **PC:** **Country:** Denmark
Year Established: **Status 2020:** Active
Industries: Artificial Intelligence for:, Natural Language Processing for:, Speech Recognition

Company Name: Wind Power LAB
Description: Automated wind turbine blade defect detection and assessment through AI
Website: http://windpowerlab.com/
Phone: **Email:** mbk@windpowerlab.com
City: Copenhagen **State:** Hovedstaden **PC:** **Country:** Denmark
Year Established: 2016 **Status 2020:** Active
Industries:

Company Name: ZEV: ITALY
Description: ZEVIT specializes in advanced predictive analytics and digitalization of field services.
Website: http://www.zevit.net
Phone: 45 51 60 38 80 **Email:** info@zevit.net
City: Copenhagen **State:** Hovedstaden **PC:** **Country:** Denmark
Year Established: 2017 **Status 2020:** Active
Industries: ~ Banking and Financial Markets-Services (7), IT Managed Services for:, Predictive Analytics

Company Name: Digital Recognition Limited
Description:
Website: http://www.digital-recognition.com
Phone: 453-693-4610 **Email:** 12215@reference-encyclopedia-ai.net
City: Copenhagen S **State:** Hovedstaden **Zip:** 2300 **Country**: Denmark
Year Established: **Status 2020:** Active
Industries: ~ Retail and Consumer Products (52), ~ Manufacturing-Miscellaneous (34)

Company Name: Spenderlog
Description: Spenderlog is a fintech that uses AI to help you keep track of your spending
Website: http://spenderlog.dk
Phone: **Email:** maria@spenderlog.dk
City: Hillerød **State:** Hovedstaden **PC:** **Country:** Denmark
Year Established: 2017 **Status 2020:** Active
Industries: Artificial Intelligence for:, ~ Banking and Financial Markets-Services (7), Machine Learning for:, ~ Healthcare (20)

Company Name: Delta
Description:
Website: http://madebydelta.com
Phone: 45 72 19 42 51 **Email:** GJ@delta.dk
City: Hørsholm **State:** **Zip:** 2970 **Country**: Denmark
Year Established: **Status 2020:** Active
Industries:

Company Name: Abzu
Description: SaaS, Artificial Intelligence
Website: https://abzu.ai/
Phone: 4529298524 **Email:** info@abzu.ai
City: Kongens Lyngby **State:** Hovedstaden **PC:** **Country:** Denmark
Year Established: 2018 **Status 2020:** Active
Industries:

Company Name: Canecto
Description: Advanced web analytic tool delivering insights and recommendations, based on user behaviour.
Website: http://canecto.com
Phone: 71 92 60 00 **Email:** support@canecto.com
City: Kongens Lyngby **State:** Hovedstaden **PC:** **Country:** Denmark
Year Established: 2017 **Status 2020:** Active
Industries:

Company Name: Shade
Description: SHADE is a Danish tech startup that has set out to revolutionize artificial lighting.
Website: http://www.kickstartshade.com
Phone: (452)218-0885 **Email:** info@shade.one
City: Kongens Lyngby **State:** Hovedstaden **PC:** **Country:** Denmark
Year Established: **Status 2020:** Active
Industries: Artificial Intelligence for:, ~ Professional Services (48)

Company Name: Chatbot Interactive
Description: Innovating online communications through AI and machine learning
Website: http://www.chatbotinteractive.com
Phone: **Email:** 36259@reference-encyclopedia-ai.net
City: Aarhus **State:** Midtjylland **PC:** **Country:** Denmark
Year Established: 2017 **Status 2020:** Active
Industries: Artificial Intelligence for:, ~ Education (13), Web

Company Name: Eachthing
Description: The tool of the conscious consumer
Website: http://www.eachthing.com
Phone: **Email:** hi@eachthing.com
City: Aarhus **State:** Midtjylland **PC:** **Country:** Denmark
Year Established: **Status 2020:** Active
Industries: Artificial Intelligence for:, Augmented Reality for:, Machine Learning

Company Name: Leicht and Thruesen
Description: L&T specializes in consultancy & intelligent software solutions by engaging in new research into algorithms & technology in AI & big data.
Website: http://www.ltaps.dk
Phone: 45 28704664 **Email:** contact@leicht-thruesen.com
City: Aarhus **State:** Midtjylland **PC:** **Country:** Denmark
Year Established: 2012 **Status 2020:** Active
Industries: Artificial Intelligence for:, Big Data and Analytics

Company Name: Raptor Services A/S
Description: Raptor is a complete personalization solution, SaaS. Our recommendation engine collect, learn and recognize each individual on a 1:1 scale
Website: http://www.raptorsmartadvisor.com
Phone: 45 20 26 65 94 **Email:** sales@raptorsmartadvisor.com
City: Aarhus **State:** Midtjylland **PC:** **Country:** Denmark
Year Established: **Status 2020:** Active
Industries: Artificial Intelligence for:, Big Data and Analytics for:, Databases for:, Machine Learning for:, ~ Media-Communications (41)

Company Name: Unsilo
Description: UNSILO is an online service offering tools that help researchers and IP professionals search patents and academic papers.
Website: http://unsilo.com
Phone: 45 24 63 04 58 **Email:** tmrl@unsilo.com
City: Aarhus **State:** Midtjylland **PC:** **Country:** Denmark
Year Established: **Status 2020:** Active
Industries: Artificial Intelligence for:, Natural Language Processing for:, Cyber Security

Company Name: Suntherm
Description: Suntherm develops the world's first SmartGrid prepared heating system with built-in heat storage.
Website: http://www.suntherm.dk/
Phone: 97 566 166 **Email:** info@suntherm.dk
City: Højslev **State:** Midtjylland **PC:** **Country:** Denmark
Year Established: 2014 **Status 2020:** Active
Industries: ~ Manufacturing-General (31), Application Services

Company Name: RS Software
Description: RS Software offers automatic administration and management of book-keeping with the help of book-keeping robots.
Website: http://rssoftware.dk/
Phone: 45 29 90 35 97 **Email:** info@codexit.dk
City: Risskov **State:** Midtjylland **PC:** **Country:** Denmark
Year Established: 2011 **Status 2020:** Active
Industries: Finance and Accounting for:, Artificial Intelligence

Company Name: Dezide
Description: Dezide is a developer of software for decision support and guided troubleshooting operations.
Website: http://www.dezide.com
Phone: 0045 96557370 **Email:** info@dezide.com
City: Aalborg **State:** Nordjylland **PC:** **Country:** Denmark
Year Established: **Status 2020:** Active
Industries: Artificial Intelligence for:, ~ Healthcare (20), ~ Professional Services (48)

Company Name: Patiro · Patient Recruitment
Description: Tech startup for data-driven patient recruitment in Europe, USA and Canada. Pay only per randomized patient.
Website: http://www.patiro.com
Phone: 45 71992214 **Email:** hello@patiro.com
City: Aalborg **State:** Nordjylland **PC:** **Country:** Denmark
Year Established: 2014 **Status 2020:** Active
Industries: Artificial Intelligence

Company Name: LangCorr
Description: LangCorr is a Scandinavian corporation that develops language assessment and correction tools.
Website: http://langcorr.com/
Phone: (452) 334-3021 **Email:** info@langcorr.com
City: Fredericia **State:** Syddanmark **PC:** **Country:** Denmark
Year Established: 2013 **Status 2020:** Active
Industries: Natural Language Processing

Company Name: Blue Ocean Robotics
Description: Denmark-based robotis company with a mission to bridge academic-based research to businesses. Focus is on commercializing robotics R&D.
Website: http://www.blue-ocean-robotics.com
Phone: 45 8182 4674 **Email:** info@blue-ocean-robotics.com
City: Odense **State:** Syddanmark **PC:** **Country:** Denmark
Year Established: 2013 **Status 2020:** Active
Industries: Artificial Intelligence for:, Automation for:, Robotics

Company Name: CP Robotics
Description: CP Robotics is an emerging robot software company, currently based in Odense Robotics StartUp Hub.
Website: http://cprobotics.dk/
Phone: 45 2117 2752 **Email:** jobs@cprobotics.dk
City: Odense **State:** Syddanmark **PC:** **Country:** Denmark
Year Established: 2015 **Status 2020:** Active
Industries:

Company Name: Tachodata
Description: Optidata uses camera solutions to optimize and digitalize business processes in parallel specialists in intelligent software systems.
Website: http://www.tachodata.dk
Phone: 45 70222330 **Email:** salg@tachodata.dk
City: Odense **State:** Syddanmark **PC:** **Country:** Denmark
Year Established: 2012 **Status 2020:** Active
Industries: IT Managed Services for:, Application Services

Company Name: Tendo
Description: Tendo is a slim glove-like exoskeleton with build in sensor technology which adds strength to the finger movement.
Website: http://www.tendoforpeople.se/
Phone: (46) 073-3310414 **Email:** info@tendoforpeople.: Sweden
City: Odense **State:** Syddanmark **PC:** **Country:** Denmark
Year Established: 2016 **Status 2020:** Active
Industries: Artificial Intelligence for:, Robotics

Company Name: Smooth Robotics
Description: Smooth Robotics developed a system that allows robots to no longer be programmed.
Website: http://smooth-robotics.dk/
Phone: 45 41 27 37 12 **Email:** info@smooth-robotics.com
City: Svendborg **State:** Syddanmark **PC:** **Country:** Denmark
Year Established: 2016 **Status 2020:** Active
Industries: Artificial Intelligence for:, Automation for:, Robotics

Company Name: MarketingPlatform
Description: MarketingPlatform is an advanced marketing automation platform that serves large companies with SMS, email and intelligent marketing.
Website: http://marketingplatform.com/da/
Phone: 45 72444444 **Email:** info@marketingplatform.com
City: Vejen **State:** Syddanmark **PC:** **Country:** Denmark
Year Established: 2011 **Status 2020:** Active
Industries: Artificial Intelligence

Company Name: Vertikal AI
Description: AI for Predictive Maintenance
Website: http://vertikal-ai.com
Phone: 45 52 887 999 **Email:** info@vertikal-ai.com
City: Vejle **State:** Syddanmark **PC:** **Country:** Denmark
Year Established: 2018 **Status 2020:** Active
Industries: Artificial Intelligence for:, Enterprise Application Services for:, Business Software as a Service Apps (SaaS Apps)

Dominican Republic

Company Name: Aqualux International
Description: We set out to create SaaS products that would transform the way organizations use their data using Artificial Intelligence.
Website: http://www.aqualux.co/
Phone: **Email:** info@aqualux.co
City: Santo Domingo De Guzmán **State:** Distrito Nacional **PC:**
Country: Dominican Republic
Year Established: 2014 **Status 2020:** Active
Industries: Artificial Intelligence for:, Business Software as a Service Apps (SaaS Apps) for:, Internet of Things (IoT)

Company Name: Melvin - AI Personal Shopper
Description: Melvin is an artificial intelligence personal shopper to assist the growth of micro, small and medium-sized enterprises.
Website: http://melvin.ai
Phone: 1829-419-9464 **Email:** team@blipevolution.com
City: Punta Cana **State:** AL **PC:** **Country:** Dominican Republic
Year Established: **Status 2020:** Active
Industries: Artificial Intelligence for:, Big Data and Analytics for:, Machine Learning

Ecuador

Company Name: Mujeres WOW
Description: A fintech start-up that uses AI technology for alternative credit scoring, targeting female entrepreneurs.
Website: http://www.wowmujeres.com/
Phone: **Email:** info@wowmujeres.com
City: Guayaquil **State:** Guayas **PC:** **Country:** Ecuador

Year Established: 2019 **Status 2020:** Active
Industries: Artificial Intelligence for:, ~ Banking and Financial Markets-Services (7), IT Managed Services for:, ~ Banking and Financial Markets-Services (7)

Company Name: Himiko Tech
Description: Mobile App
Website:
Phone: **Email:** 4943@reference-encyclopedia-ai.net
City: Quito **State:** P **PC:** **Country:** Ecuador
Year Established: **Status 2020:** Active
Industries: Artificial Intelligence for:, ~ Transportation and Logistics (57), Application Services

Company Name: Mensajea
Description: Mensajea is an AI-powered chatbot builder that integrates financial institutions and e-commerce platforms.
Website: http://www.mensajea.net
Phone: **Email:** info@mensajea.net
City: Quito **State:** Pichincha **PC:** **Country:** Ecuador
Year Established: 2017 **Status 2020:** Active
Industries: Artificial Intelligence for:, E-Commerce for:, ~ Banking and Financial Markets-Services (7)

Company Name: Werpx
Description: AI Supply Chain Management Solution .
Website: http://werpx.com
Phone: **Email:** yakout@werpx.com
City: Alexandria **State:** Alexandria Governorate **PC:** **Country:** Egypt
Year Established: 2017 **Status 2020:** Active
Industries: Artificial Intelligence for:, ~ Retail and Consumer Products (52), Predictive Analytics for:, Supply Chain Management

Company Name: Autotell
Description: Autotell is a platform to communicate with your car, on road analytics, detecting faults, instant driver advice with AI personal assistant
Website: http://autotell.ai
Phone: 20-100-6851107 **Email:** a.essam@autotell.ai
City: Cairo **State:** Cairo Governorate **PC:** **Country:** Egypt
Year Established: **Status 2020:** Active
Industries: Artificial Intelligence for:, ~ Automotive (5)

Company Name: BotCommander
Description: AI, Chatbots
Website: http://botcommander.io/
Phone: **Email:** info@botcommander.io
City: Cairo **State:** Cairo Governorate **PC:** **Country:** Egypt
Year Established: **Status 2020:** Active
Industries: Artificial Intelligence for:, E-Commerce for:, IT Managed Services for:, Web for:, Robotics for:, ~ Professional Services (48)

Company Name: Botme
Description: Botme is a standalone platform for building chatbots for businesses and managing the whole business process: Spain
Website: http://www.botme.com/
Phone: **Email:** info@botme.com
City: Cairo **State:** Cairo Governorate **PC:** **Country:** Egypt
Year Established: **Status 2020:** Active
Industries:

Company Name: Chefaa
Description: Mobile app helping patients order/schedule & refill medicine in a GPS-enabled 3-step user journey
Website: http://www.chefaa.com
Phone: 2 01003363656 **Email:** info@chefaa.com
City: Cairo **State:** Cairo Governorate **PC:** **Country:** Egypt
Year Established: 2017 **Status 2020:** Active
Industries: Artificial Intelligence for:, Big Data and Analytics for:, E-Commerce for:, ~ Healthcare (20), IT Managed Services for:, Machine Learning for:, Application Services for:, Application Services

Company Name: CubeZy
Description: AI Engine that helps learners to acquire new skill or certificate
Website: http://www.cubezy.net
Phone: 002 01228870990 **Email:** youssef.medhat@cubezy.net
City: Cairo **State:** Cairo Governorate **PC:** **Country:** Egypt
Year Established: 2016 **Status 2020:** Active
Industries: Artificial Intelligence for:, Big Data and Analytics for:, ~ Education (13)

Company Name: DevisionX
Description: DevisionX is coming from using Deep learning in X of machine Vision solutions in X fields of industries.
Website: http://devisionx.com
Phone: **Email:** info@devisionx.com
City: Cairo **State:** Cairo Governorate **PC:** **Country:** Egypt
Year Established: 2016 **Status 2020:** Active
Industries: Artificial Intelligence for:, IT Managed Services for:, Machine Learning

Company Name: Etqan-Tech
Description: IT Consulting Company and Oracle Gold Partner specialized in Business Intelligence and Artificial Intelligence
Website: http://www.etqan-tech.com
Phone: **Email:** info@etqan-tech.com
City: Cairo **State:** Cairo Governorate **PC:** **Country:** Egypt
Year Established: 2010 **Status 2020:** Active
Industries:

Company Name: HireHunt
Description: HireHunt helps employers and recruiters hire faster with a powerful toolset of recruitment technologies powered by AI.
Website: http://www.hirehunt.com
Phone: **Email:** admin@hirehunt.com
City: Cairo **State:** Cairo Governorate **PC:** **Country:** Egypt
Year Established: 2015 **Status 2020:** Active
Industries: Artificial Intelligence

Company Name: INSITE OOH Media Platform
Description: Online/Mobile app
Website: http://insiteooh.com
Phone: **Email:** hi@insiteooh.com
City: Cairo **State:** Cairo Governorate **PC:** **Country:** Egypt
Year Established: 2017 **Status 2020:** Active
Industries: Business Intelligence for:, Content for:, IT Managed Services for:, Application Services for:, Web for:, ~ Arts-Entertainment-Recreation (4), ~ Arts-Entertainment-Recreation (4), ~ Media-Communications (41)

Company Name: Intixel
Description: AI-powered Solutions for Diagnostic Imaging
Website: http://www.intixel.com
Phone: **Email:** contact@intixel.com
City: Cairo **State:** Cairo Governorate **PC:** **Country:** Egypt
Year Established: 2018 **Status 2020:** Active
Industries: Artificial Intelligence for:, ~ Healthcare (20)

Company Name: MedBold
Description: MedBold is a fast AI based Medical Search Engine, helps Arabic users to know the accurate information about health-cases, diseases ..ect
Website: http://medbold.com/
Phone: **Email:** husam@medbold.com
City: Cairo **State:** Cairo Governorate **PC:** **Country:** Egypt
Year Established: 2018 **Status 2020:** Active
Industries: Artificial Intelligence for:, ~ Healthcare (20), ~ Healthcare (20), ~ Healthcare (20), ~ Healthcare (20), Web for:, Content for:, Computer Vision for:, Computer Vision

Company Name: Mintrics
Description: A Social Video Analytics & Intelligence Platform that empowers publishers to double their viewership by making data driven decisions
Website: http://mintrics.com
Phone: **Email:** info@mintrics.com
City: Cairo **State:** Cairo Governorate **PC:** **Country:** Egypt
Year Established: 2016 **Status 2020:** Active
Industries: Analytics for:, Artificial Intelligence for:, Big Data and Analytics for:, Machine Learning

Company Name: Roz: Morocco
Description: Rozma is an on-line marketplace connecting small to medium scale local farmers to retailers and restaurants directly.
Website:
Phone: **Email:** sherif.hosny@schaduf.com
City: Cairo **State:** Cairo Governorate **PC:** **Country:** Egypt
Year Established: **Status 2020:** Active
Industries:

Company Name: TMento: Serbia
Description: Global company, with solid foot steps on 2 major countries: USA & Egypt. Our products: SHIXY–The Robot, FaceGraph–Facial-Recognition Auth.
Website: http://TMentors.com
Phone: **Email:** Ahmed.Ramy@TMentors.com
City: Cairo **State:** Cairo Governorate **PC:** **Country:** Egypt
Year Established: 2010 **Status 2020:** Active
Industries: Artificial Intelligence for:, Image Recognition for:, Robotics

Company Name: WideBot
Description: The First Arabic-Focused Bot Builder Platform.
Website: http://widebot.net/
Phone: **Email:** nabil@widebot.net
City: Cairo **State:** Cairo Governorate **PC:** **Country:** Egypt
Year Established: 2016 **Status 2020:** Active
Industries: Artificial Intelligence for:, Big Data and Analytics for:, Machine Learning for:, Natural Language Processing

Company Name: MerQ
Description: Artificial Intelligence
Website: http://merq.ai
Phone: **Email:** talk@merq.ai
City: Ismailia **State:** Ismailia Governorate **PC:** **Country:** Egypt
Year Established: **Status 2020:** Active
Industries: Artificial Intelligence

El Salvador

Company Name: SPOT
Description: SPOT is an artificial intelligence company that focuses on innovative computer vision and deep learning technologies.
Website: http://spotcloud.io/
Phone: **Email:** 37458@reference-encyclopedia-ai.net
City: San Salvador **State:** San Salvador Department **PC:**
Country: El Salvador
Year Established: **Status 2020:** Active
Industries:

Company Name: TreeCloud Technologies
Description: We develop Technological Solutions for Companies and Governments with Artificial Intelligence and Big Data Analys
Website: http://treecloud.co
Phone: 503 2268-6416 **Email:** info@tree-cloud.com
City: San Salvador **State:** San Salvador Department **PC:**
Country: El Salvador
Year Established: 2018 **Status 2020:** Active
Industries: Artificial Intelligence for:, Big Data and Analytics for:, Machine Learning

Estonia

Company Name: Xift
Description: Artificial Intelligence, Cyber Security, Embedded Systems
Website: http://xift.ai
Phone: 34609557351 **Email:** info@xift.ai
City: Kuusalu **State:** Harju County **PC:** **Country:** Estonia
Year Established: **Status 2020:** Active
Industries: Artificial Intelligence for:, Cyber Security for:, Embedded for:, IT Managed Services for:, ~ Professional Services (48)

Company Name: LEXIT Technologies OU
Description: LEXIT is an all-in-one marketplace for entrepreneurs and M&A professionals offering deal sourcing, negotiations, and data room services.
Website: http://www.lexit.com
Phone: **Email:** contact@lexit.com
City: Tallin **State:** Harju County **PC:** **Country:** Estonia
Year Established: 2016 **Status 2020:** Active
Industries: Artificial Intelligence for:, Blockchain for:, ~ Banking and Financial Markets-Services (7), IT Managed Services for:, Web for:, Internet of Things (IoT)

Company Name: Quantastica
Description: Software tools and solutions for quantum computing
Website: http://quantastica.com
Phone: **Email:** info@quantastica.com
City: Tallin **State:** Harju County **PC:** **Country:** Estonia
Year Established: **Status 2020:** Active
Industries: Artificial Intelligence for:, IT Managed Services for:, ~ Education (13), ~ Professional Services (48)

Company Name: AdHive
Description: Adhive.tv is an AI and community powered platform for native video advertising for video influencers.
Website: http://adhive.tv
Phone: 372 880-13-82 **Email:** ak@adhive.com
City: Tallinn **State:** Harju County **PC:** **Country:** Estonia
Year Established: **Status 2020:** Active
Industries: ~ Media-Communications (41), Artificial Intelligence for:, Blockchain for:, ~ Media-Communications (41), Digital Marketing for:, ~ Media-Communications (41), ~ Media-Communications (41), ~ Social Media (54)

Company **Name:** AgroGNOME
Description: AgriTech, Yield Prediction, Farm Management Suggestions
Website: https://www.agrognome.eu/
Phone: **Email:** info@agrognome.eu
City: Tallinn **State:** Harju County **PC:** **Country:** Estonia
Year Established: 2018 **Status 2020:** Active
Industries: ~ Agriculture (3), ~ Agriculture (3), Internet of Things (IoT) for:, Machine Learning

Company Name: AiBB
Description: Ai Assistant for crypto currency
Website: http://www.aibb.io
Phone: 6475048533 **Email:** ai@aibb.io
City: Tallinn **State:** Harju County **PC:** **Country:** Estonia
Year Established: **Status 2020:** Active
Industries: Artificial Intelligence for:, Blockchain for:, ~ Banking and Financial Markets-Services (7), Machine Learning

Company Name: Alpha AR
Description: Alpha AR helps to create lifelike 3D model from single shot 2D image in seconds
Website: https://alphaar.io/
Phone: 37256637621 **Email:** info@alphaar.io
City: Tallinn **State:** Harju County **PC:** **Country:** Estonia

Year Established: 2018 **Status 2020:** Active
Industries: Artificial Intelligence for:, Augmented Reality for:, E-Commerce

Company Name: AlphaBlu: Spain
Description: AI-based Virtual Assistants and Live Chat seamlessly integrated into one coherent solution to improve your customer service.
Website: http://www.alphablues.com
Phone: 372 5884 1694 **Email:** hello@alphablues.com
City: Tallinn **State:** Harju County **PC:** **Country:** Estonia
Year Established: **Status 2020:** Active
Industries: Artificial Intelligence for:, Machine Learning for:, Data Management

Company Name: AUTOM8
Description: Autom8 builds the Next Generation - Adaptive Security tools powered by deep learning.
Website: http://www.autom8.ai
Phone: 372 58387090 **Email:** pinar@autom8now.com
City: Tallinn **State:** Harju County **PC:** **Country:** Estonia
Year Established: 2019 **Status 2020:** Active
Industries: IT Managed Services for:, Machine Learning

Company Name: BaseTracK
Description: All-weather vehicle automation that already brings profits for business
Website: http://www.basetrack.net/
Phone: **Email:** join@basetrack.net
City: Tallinn **State:** Harju County **PC:** **Country:** Estonia
Year Established: 2018 **Status 2020:** Active
Industries: Artificial Intelligence for:, ~ Automotive (5), ~ Automotive (5)

Company Name: BeED
Description: Beed is an AI-based education platform.
Website: http://beed.world
Phone: 60 3 77316068 **Email:** rr@beed.world
City: Tallinn **State:** Harju County **PC:** **Country:** Estonia
Year Established: **Status 2020:** Active
Industries: Artificial Intelligence for:, ~ Education (13)

Company Name: Crypto Brokers OÃœ
Description: Crypto Brokers is developing a virtual assistant to provide a faster, safer and more convenient way to trade cryptocurrencies.
Website: http://telexai.com
Phone: **Email:** info@telexai.com
City: Tallinn **State:** Harju County **PC:** **Country:** Estonia
Year Established: **Status 2020:** Active
Industries: Artificial Intelligence for:, Blockchain for:, ~ Banking and Financial Markets-Services (7), ~ Banking and Financial Markets-Services (7), ~ Professional Services (48)

Company Name: cyex
Description: We develop an AI based tool that generates personalized cybersecurity exercises with special focus on cyber threat specifics of the client.
Website:
Phone: **Email:** hello@cyex.io
City: Tallinn **State:** Harju County **PC:** **Country:** Estonia
Year Established: 2018 **Status 2020:** Active
Industries:

Company Name: Envisioning
Description: Emerging technology Research:
Website: http://envisioning.technology/
Phone: **Email:** hello@envisioning.io
City: Tallinn **State:** Harju County **PC:** **Country:** Estonia
Year Established: 2011 **Status 2020:** Active
Industries: Artificial Intelligence for:, IT Managed Services for:, Machine Learning

Company Name: FanSifter
Description: FanSifter is a machine learning-powered fan data analytics and performance marketing platform for live events.
Website: http://fansifter.com/
Phone: (372) 502-7350 **Email:** hello@fansifter.com
City: Tallinn **State:** Harju County **PC:** **Country:** Estonia
Year Established: 2019 **Status 2020:** Active
Industries: Analytics for:, ~ Event Management (15), ~ Event Management (15), Machine Learning for:, ~ Arts-Entertainment-Recreation (4), ~ Arts-Entertainment-Recreation (4), ~ Arts-Entertainment-Recreation (4)

Company Name: FeelingStream
Description: Analyzes customer messages, be emails or feedback comments. Reacting to customer opinion improves closing new sales and avoids them leaving.
Website: http://feelingstream.com/
Phone: **Email:** terje@feelingstream.com
City: Tallinn **State:** Harju County **PC:** **Country:** Estonia
Year Established: 2015 **Status 2020:** Active
Industries: Artificial Intelligence for:, Data Management

Company Name: Fenorri
Description: The world's smartest enterprise social network, zero coding instant apps and AI platform
Website: http://www.fenorri.com
Phone: **Email:** info@fenorri.com
City: Tallinn **State:** Harju County **PC:** **Country:** Estonia
Year Established: 2014 **Status 2020:** Active
Industries: Artificial Intelligence for:, IT Managed Services for:, ~ Social Assistance-Non-Profits (53)

Company Name: Gettranslation
Description: Gettranslation is a global, people-powered translation platform enabling everyone to read and publish across languages with one click.
Website: http://gettranslation.eu
Phone: (372) 880-4540 **Email:** hello@gettranslation.eu
City: Tallinn **State:** Harju County **PC:** **Country:** Estonia
Year Established: 2017 **Status 2020:** Active
Industries: ~ Education (13), Natural Language Processing

Company Name: HealthCode AI
Description: HealthCode AI is offering physicians support in day to day patient management by using Artificial Intelligence to pre-evaluate patients
Website: http://www.healthcodeai.com
Phone: **Email:** info@healthcodeai.com
City: Tallinn **State:** Harju County **PC:** **Country:** Estonia
Year Established: **Status 2020:** Active
Industries: Artificial Intelligence for:, ~ Healthcare (20), Machine Learning for:, ~ Healthcare (20)

Company Name: Hepta Airborne
Description: Autonomous airborne data collection and analysis for utilities, replacing six engineers with one
Website: http://airborne.hepta.ee
Phone: 3725179698 **Email:** info@hepta.ee
City: Tallinn **State:** Harju County **PC:** **Country:** Estonia
Year Established: **Status 2020:** Active
Industries: Analytics for:, Artificial Intelligence for:, ~ Automotive (5), Big Data and Analytics for:, ~ Energy and Utilities (14), ~ Transportation and Logistics (57), ~ Energy and Utilities (14), Predictive Analytics for:, ~ Professional Services (48), ~ Professional Serv

Company Name: HUGO.legal
Description: HUGO.legal is the first sharing economy based legal platform using A.I to match people with the best lawyer for their case.
Website: http://hugo.legal
Phone: 372 687 1223 **Email:** hugo@hugo.egal
City: Tallinn **State:** Harju County **PC:** **Country:** Estonia

Year Established: 2015 **Status 2020:** Active
Industries: Artificial Intelligence

Company Name: Lalafo
Description: Lalafo is a C2C marketplace powered by artificial intelligence.
Website: http://lalafo.com/
Phone: **Email:** info@lalafo.com
City: Tallinn **State:** Harju County **PC:** **Country:** Estonia
Year Established: 2015 **Status 2020:** Active
Industries: Application Services

Company Name: Lingvist
Description: Lingvist is language learning software based on mathematical optimization and statistical analysis.
Website: http://lingvist.com
Phone: **Email:** hello@lingvist.io
City: Tallinn **State:** Harju County **PC:** **Country:** Estonia
Year Established: **Status 2020:** Active
Industries: Artificial Intelligence for:, Big Data and Analytics for:, ~ Education (13), ~ Education (13)

Company Name: Logistify AI
Description: Logistify AI is an AI platform for warehousing businesses.
Website: http://www.logistify.ai/
Phone: 680-011-3267 **Email:** support@logistify.ai
City: Tallinn **State:** Harju County **PC:** **Country:** Estonia
Year Established: 2019 **Status 2020:** Active
Industries: Artificial Intelligence for:, ~ Transportation and Logistics (57)

Company Name: Medicy
Description: Platform for healthcare ecosystem
Website: http://medicy.com
Phone: **Email:** info@medicy.com
City: Tallinn **State:** Harju County **PC:** **Country:** Estonia
Year Established: 2016 **Status 2020:** Active
Industries: Artificial Intelligence for:, ~ Healthcare (20), Machine Learning for:, ~ Healthcare (20), Mobile for:, ~ Banking and Financial Markets-Services (7)

Company Name: Nimi
Description: An AI that names your business for success
Website: http://nimi.ai
Phone: **Email:** hello@nimi.io
City: Tallinn **State:** Harju County **PC:** **Country:** Estonia
Year Established: **Status 2020:** Active
Industries: Artificial Intelligence

Company Name: OSA Hybrid Platform
Description: OSA HP is a provider of AI-based proactive scalable service for the FMCG sector.
Website: http://osahp.com
Phone: 7074008910 **Email:** company@osahp.com
City: Tallinn **State:** Harju County **PC:** **Country:** Estonia
Year Established: **Status 2020:** Active
Industries:

Company Name: Persius
Description: Talent Promotion , Art Adviser , talent Adviser
Website: http://persius.: India
Phone: 37254560015 **Email:** contact@persius.: India
City: Tallinn **State:** Harju County **PC:** **Country:** Estonia
Year Established: 2019 **Status 2020:** Active
Industries: Artificial Intelligence for:, Blockchain for:, IT Managed Services for:, Machine Learning

Company Name: Robotex
Description: Robotex is a global robotics education network, focusing on robotics (incl. AI & Drones) education and startup training.
Website: http://robotex.international/
Phone: 37256218861 **Email:** info@robotex.ee
City: Tallinn **State:** Harju County **PC:** **Country:** Estonia
Year Established: **Status 2020:** Active
Industries: Artificial Intelligence for:, Content for:, ~ Education (13), ~ Transportation and Logistics (57), ~ Education (13), ~ Education (13), ~ Event Management (15), ~ Event Management (15), ~ Administrative and Support Services (1), Machine Learning for:, Robotics for:,

Company Name: RocketScience.ai
Description: AI Consulting Company
Website: http://rocketscience.ai
Phone: **Email:** mkr@rocketscience.ai
City: Tallinn **State:** Harju County **PC:** **Country:** Estonia
Year Established: 2014 **Status 2020:** Active
Industries: Artificial Intelligence for:, Big Data and Analytics for:, Machine Learning

Company Name: Samplify.io
Description: AI knowledge curation tool for professionals
Website: http://samplify.io
Phone: **Email:** sam@1x.png
City: Tallinn **State:** Harju County **PC:** **Country:** Estonia
Year Established: 2017 **Status 2020:** Active
Industries: Artificial Intelligence for:, IT Managed Services for:, Web

Company Name: School OS
Description: School OS is an AI-based education platform.
Website: http://schoolos.eu
Phone: 372 602 7353 **Email:** contact@bamboogroup.eu
City: Tallinn **State:** Harju County **PC:** **Country:** Estonia
Year Established: 2016 **Status 2020:** Active
Industries: Artificial Intelligence for:, ~ Education (13)

Company **Name:** Scoriff
Description: Scoriff protects businesses against credit losses and late payments
Website: http://scoriff.com
Phone: 37255685297 **Email:** peep.kungas@scoriff.com
City: Tallinn **State:** Harju County **PC:** **Country:** Estonia
Year Established: 2018 **Status 2020:** Active
Industries: Artificial Intelligence for:, ~ Banking and Financial Markets-Services (7), ~ Banking and Financial Markets-Services (7), Machine Learning for:, Web

Company Name: Skuuper
Description: Translations booster, SaaS, CAT tool, crowdsourcing, TM marketplace
Website: http://www.skuuper.com/
Phone: (372) 501-7756 **Email:** raul@skuuper.com
City: Tallinn **State:** Harju County **PC:** **Country:** Estonia
Year Established: **Status 2020:** Active
Industries: Artificial Intelligence for:, ~ Professional Services (48)

Company Name: Styleshark
Description: Mobile shopping app that helps users find new clothing items that match their unique style and favorite items
Website: http://www.styleshark.eu
Phone: **Email:** styleshark@styleshark.eu
City: Tallinn **State:** Harju County **PC:** **Country:** Estonia
Year Established: **Status 2020:** Active
Industries: Artificial Intelligence for:, E-Commerce for:, ~ Retail and Consumer Products (52)

Company Name: Teamsco:
Description: A.I. driven talent analytics platform for executive search professionals
Website: http://teamscope.io
Phone: 372 53 302 919 **Email:** alo@teamscope.io
City: Tallinn **State:** Harju County **PC:** **Country:** Estonia
Year Established: 2015 **Status 2020:** Active
Industries: Analytics for:, Artificial Intelligence for:, Big Data and Analytics

Company Name: TRAPMINE
Description: Next-Generation Threat Prevention
Website: http://www.trapmine.com
Phone: 3726682437 **Email:** info@trapmine.com
City: Tallinn **State:** Harju County **PC:** **Country:** Estonia
Year Established: 2016 **Status 2020:** Active
Industries: Cyber Security for:, Machine Learning for:, Security for:, Security

Company Name: Triggmine
Description: AI-powered email marketing for e-commerce
Website: http://www.triggmine.com/en/
Phone: 372 880 12 09 **Email:** ms@triggmine.com
City: Tallinn **State:** Harju County **PC:** **Country:** Estonia
Year Established: 2015 **Status 2020:** Active
Industries: Artificial Intelligence for:, E-Commerce for:, Business Software as a Service Apps (SaaS Apps)

Company Name: Viveo Heal:Thailand
Description: Artificial Intelligence, HealthTech, InsureTech
Website: http://www.viveohealth.com
Phone: 3725011089 **Email:** raul@viveohealth.com
City: Tallinn **State:** Harju County **PC:** **Country:** Estonia
Year Established: 2017 **Status 2020:** Active
Industries: Artificial Intelligence for:, ~ Healthcare (20)

Company Name: Yanu
Description: Fully autonomous A.I. and robot empowered bartending unit. It serves drinks, handles payments, identifies and communicates with clients.
Website: http://yanu.ai
Phone: 3725107723 **Email:** alan@yanu.ai
City: Tallinn **State:** Harju County **PC:** **Country:** Estonia
Year Established: 2016 **Status 2020:** Active
Industries: Artificial Intelligence for:, ~ Banking and Financial Markets-Services (7), ~ Food and Beverage (17), ~ Arts-Entertainment-Recreation (4), Robotics

Company Name: Zuflo
Description: Zuflo coin is trading & financing platform on blockchain.
Website:
Phone: **Email:** 37745@reference-encyclopedia-ai.net
City: Tallinn **State:** Harju County **PC:** **Country:** Estonia
Year Established: 2017 **Status 2020:** Closed
Industries:

Company Name: Hala
Description: AI Platform for business with the decentralized knowledge base on the blockcha: India
Website: http://hala.ai
Phone: **Email:** rudchuk@hala.ai
City: Harju **State:** Hiiu County **PC:** **Country:** Estonia
Year Established: **Status 2020:** Active
Industries: Artificial Intelligence for:, Blockchain for:, Machine Learning

Ethiopia

Company Name: iCog Labs
Description: iCog Labs is a research and development company, collaborating with international AI research groups and serving customers around the world.
Website: http://icog-labs.com/
Phone: 251 93 792 7047 **Email:** 36734@reference-encyclopedia-ai.net
City: Addis Ababa **State:** Addis Ababa **PC:** **Country:** Ethiopia
Year Established: 2012 **Status 2020:** Active
Industries: Artificial Intelligence

Company Name: Valam
Description: Valamis is designed for multi-generation training, with the ability to identify skill gaps before they affect your business.
Website: http://www.valamis.com
Phone: 358 13 748335 **Email:** hello@valamis.com
City: Joensuu **State:** Eastern Finland **PC:** **Country:** **Finland**nland
Year Established: **Status 2020:** Active
Industries: Artificial Intelligence for:, ~ Education (13), ~ Education (13), Enterprise Application Services

Company Name: Rocsole
Description: Rocsole enable challenging conditions process monitoring with IOT and AI for the industry
Website: http://www.rocsole.com
Phone: 358 5032 82648 **Email:** info@rocsole.com
City: Kuopio **State:** Eastern Finland **PC:** **Country: Finland**
Year Established: 2012 **Status 2020:** Active
Industries: ArtiFinlandcial Intelligence for:, ~ Energy and Utilities (14), ~ Energy and Utilities (14), Predictive Analytics

Company Name: AISpotter
Description: Better video analysis - tell better stories. AISpotter automatically analysis any video with fast video analysis service based on AI.
Website: http://www.aispotter.com/
Phone: **Email:** anri@aispotter.com
City: Oulu **State:** Oulu **PC:** **Country:** FINLAND
Year Established: 2018 **Status 2020:** Active
Industries: Analytics for:, Data Management for:, ~ Media-Communications (41), ~ Arts-Entertainment-Recreation (4), Predictive Analytics for:, ~ Media-Communications (41)

Company **Name:** Augumenta
Description: Augumenta is a software company that turning wearable devices into powerful tools for enterprises.
Website: http://augumenta.com
Phone: **Email:** sales@augumenta.com
City: Oulu **State:** Oulu **PC:** **Country:** FINLAND
Year Established: **Status 2020:** Active
Industries: ArtiFinlandcial Intelligence for:, Augmented Reality for:, Computer Vision for:, ~ Manufacturing-Electronic (30), Human Computer Interaction for:, ~ Professional Services (48)

Company Name: Cerenion
Description: Cerenion is a medical company working on a technology that monitors the brain function of intensive care patients.
Website: http://cerenion.com
Phone: 358 40 5773 706 **Email:** info@cerenion.com
City: Oulu **State:** Oulu **PC:** **Country:** FINLAND
Year Established: 2017 **Status 2020:** Active
Industries: ArtiFinlandcial Intelligence for:, ~ Healthcare (20), ~ Healthcare (20), Machine Learning

Company Name: CubiCa: Saudi Arabia
Description: The most scalable way to acquire property interior data. Enabling any space to be indexed, searched, sorted, and understood.
Website: http://cubi.casa/video
Phone: **Email:** harri@cubicasa.com
City: Oulu **State:** Oulu **PC:** **Country:** FINLAND
Year Established: **Status 2020:** Active
Industries: ArtiFinlandcial Intelligence for:, Big Data and Analytics for:, Cloud for:, Enterprise Application Services for:, Web for:, ~ Real Estate (49), ~ Professional Services (48), ~ Media-Communications (41)

Company Name: Onni Care Closed
Description: When you become a parent, you're Fillled with joy and fear & doubt for the unknown. We help you share the former and banish the latter.
Website: http://www.onnicare.com/
Phone: **Email:** 37107@reference-encyclopedia-ai.net
City: Oulu **State:** Oulu **PC:** **Country:** FINLAND
Year Established: 2012 **Status 2020:** Active
Industries: Artifcial Intelligence for:, Business Applications for:, Internet of Things (IoT) for:, Mobile for:, Mobile

Company Name: Smartifik
Description: Smartifik is a software company, which focuses on natural language processing and artificial intelligence technologies.
Website: http://smartifik.com/
Phone: **Email:** info@smartifik.fi
City: Oulu **State:** Oulu **PC:** **Country:** Finland
Year Established: **Status 2020:** Active
Industries: Artificial Intelligence for:, E-Commerce for:, Natural Language Processing

Company Name: Valos: Saudi Arabia
Description: Valossa created an AI-powered video intelligence and recognition platform
Website: www.valossa.com
Phone: **Email:** info@valossa.com
City: Oulu **State:** Oulu **PC:** **Country:** Finland
Year Established: **Status 2020:** Active
Industries: Artificial Intelligence for:, Computer Vision for:, Content for:, Digital Media for:, Facial Recognition for:, Image Recognition for:, IT Managed Services for:, IT Managed Services for:, Machine Learning for:, Natural Language Processing for:, Cyber Security for:, C

Company Name: Caidio
Description: Caidio provides AI-based software for improving the quality and productivity of concrete construction.
Website: http://www.caidio.io
Phone: 358-400-726060 **Email:** aku.wilenius@caidio.io
City: Espoo **State:** Southern Finland **PC:** **Country:** Finland
Year Established: **Status 2020:** Active
Industries: Artificial Intelligence for:, ~ Construction (10), ~ Construction (10)

Company Name: CollectiveCrun: Switzerland
Description: CollectiveCrunch is a leader in AI for the forestry industry. We bring a step-change to prediction of wood inventories.
Website: http://www.collectivecrunch.com/
Phone: **Email:** info@collectivecrunch.com
City: Espoo **State:** Southern Finland **PC:** **Country:** Finland
Year Established: 2016 **Status 2020:** Active
Industries: Analytics for:, Artificial Intelligence for:, ~ Energy and Utilities (14), ~ Agriculture (3), ~ Manufacturing-General (31), ~ Energy and Utilities (14)

Company Name: Flexound Systems
Description: Flexound Systems is a young growth-hungry Finnish start-up company whose mission is to create magic sound & feel experiences.
Website: http://flexound.com/
Phone: **Email:** info@flexound.com
City: Espoo **State:** Southern Finland **PC:** **Country:** Finland
Year Established: **Status 2020:** Active
Industries:

Company Name: Forethink
Description: SaaS for eCommerce, offering UX Design solution and AI-based Personalization.
Website: http://www.forethink.net/
Phone: **Email:** contact@forethink.net
City: Espoo **State:** Southern Finland **PC:** **Country:** Finland
Year Established: 2018 **Status 2020:** Active
Industries: E-Commerce for:, Machine Learning for:, Development and Test

Company Name: Hoxhunt
Description: World leading Security Engagement Platform
Website: http://www.hoxhunt.com/
Phone: **Email:** contact@hoxhunt.com
City: Espoo **State:** Southern Finland **PC:** **Country:** Finland
Year Established: 2016 **Status 2020:** Active
Industries: Security

Company Name: InnoSchool
Description: InnoSchool is a captures the opportunity of advanced technology and AI for a New Renaissance of Learning.
Website: http://www.innoschool.fi/
Phone: **Email:** support@innoschool.fi
City: Espoo **State:** Southern Finland **PC:** **Country:** Finland
Year Established: 2011 **Status 2020:** Active
Industries: Artificial Intelligence for:, ~ Education (13), IT Managed Services

Company Name: Kollageeni.com
Description: Kollageeni.com on kollageeniin erikoistunut verkkokauppa
Website: http://www.kollageeni.com
Phone: **Email:** kollageenicom@gmail.com
City: Espoo **State:** Southern Finland **PC:** **Country:** Finland
Year Established: **Status 2020:** Active
Industries:

Company Name: Ladimo
Description: Ladimo develops machine vision applications for different industry needs.
Website: http://www.ladimo.fi/
Phone: **Email:** info@ladimo.fi
City: Espoo **State:** Southern Finland **PC:** **Country:** Finland
Year Established: 2015 **Status 2020:** Active
Industries: Computer Vision for:, Automation for:, Machine Learning

Company Name: Lifetime Group
Description: Lifetime Group is an IT consulting and software product development company that designs, develops and deploys solutions based on AI/ML/DL.
Website: http://lifetime.fi
Phone: 358 400 319 010 **Email:** risto.anton@lifetime.fi
City: Espoo **State:** Southern Finland **PC:** **Country:** Finland
Year Established: 2018 **Status 2020:** Active
Industries: ~ Banking and Financial Markets-Services (7), Application Services for:, Application Services for:, Predictive Analytics

Company Name: Sensible4
Description: Sensible4 is an autonomous driving software company that develops self-driving vehicles for all-year round use.
Website: http://www.sensible4.fi/
Phone: 358 400 516778 **Email:** info@sensible4.fi
City: Espoo **State:** Southern Finland **PC:** **Country:** Finland
Year Established: 2017 **Status 2020:** Active
Industries: Artificial Intelligence for:, ~ Automotive (5), ~ Automotive (5)

Company Name: AdGold Inc
Description: Online advertising enhanced with artificial intelligence
Website: http://www.adgold.fi/
Phone: 358 44 5005004 **Email:** vili.lilja@adgold.fi
City: Helsinki **State:** Southern Finland **PC:** **Country:** Finland
Year Established: 2015 **Status 2020:** Active
Industries: Artificial Intelligence for:, ~ Customer Relationship Management (11), Web for:, Machine Learning

Company Name: AdLaun: Switzerland
Description: The Easiest Way To Start a Video Advertising Campaign™
Website: http://www.adlaunch.com/
Phone: **Email:** support@adlaunch.com
City: Helsinki **State:** Southern Finland **PC:** **Country:** Finland

Year Established: 2015 **Status 2020:** Active
Industries: Artificial Intelligence for:, Machine Learning

Company Name: Advisus
Description: SaaS tool helping advertisers to do their jobs better.
Website: http://advisus.io/
Phone: **Email:** hello@advisus.io
City: Helsinki **State:** Southern Finland **PC:** **Country:** Finland
Year Established: 2017 **Status 2020:** Active
Industries: Analytics for:, Machine Learning for:, Business Software as a Service Apps (SaaS Apps)

Company Name: AI Strategy Company
Description: AI Strategy Company is an artificial intelligence and machine learning company.
Website: https://www.aistrategycompany.com/
Phone: **Email:** 35996@reference-encyclopedia-ai.net
City: Helsinki **State:** Southern Finland **PC:** **Country:** Finland
Year Established: 2018 **Status 2020:** Active
Industries: Artificial Intelligence for:, Machine Learning

Company Name: Aiforia
Description: Aiforia's mission is to provide global access to AI-powered image analysis for medical and healthcare professionals.
Website: https://www.aiforia.com/about-us/
Phone: **Email:** contact@aiforia.com
City: Helsinki **State:** Southern Finland **PC:** **Country:** Finland
Year Established: 2013 **Status 2020:** Active
Industries: Artificial Intelligence for:, ~ Education (13), ~ Healthcare (20), IT Managed Services for:, Machine Learning for:, ~ Healthcare (20)

Company Name: aito.ai
Description: Aito is a predictive database that uses existing relational datasets for predictions and recommendations.
Website: https://aito.ai/
Phone: **Email:** hello@aito.ai
City: Helsinki **State:** Southern Finland **PC:** **Country:** Finland
Year Established: 2018 **Status 2020:** Active
Industries: Artificial Intelligence for:, Databases for:, Machine Learning for:, Enterprise Application Services for:, Business Software as a Service Apps (SaaS Apps)

Company Name: Artific Intelligence
Description: Artific helps companies explore the power of AI to benefit people and society.
Website: http://artific.ai
Phone: **Email:** info@artific.ai
City: Helsinki **State:** Southern Finland **PC:** **Country:** Finland
Year Established: 2017 **Status 2020:** Active
Industries:

Company Name: Asenno
Description: Asenno is building service robots of future
Website: http://asenno.com
Phone: **Email:** info@asenno.com
City: Helsinki **State:** Southern Finland **PC:** **Country:** Finland
Year Established: 2018 **Status 2020:** Active
Industries: Artificial Intelligence for:, ~ Automotive (5), Computer Vision for:, Internet of Things (IoT) for:, Machine Learning for:, Robotics for:, ~ Customer Relationship Management (11)

Company Name: Avansera
Description: Avansera delivers real-time predictive analytics and targeted digital marketing solutions for fast-moving consumer goods (FMCG) companies.
Website: http://www.avansera.com
Phone: **Email:** contact@avansera.com
City: Helsinki **State:** Southern Finland **PC:** **Country:** Finland
Year Established: 2013 **Status 2020:** Active
Industries: Analytics for:, Predictive Analytics

Company Name: Axinoss
Description: AI-powered algorithmic trading and risk taking strategi: Spain
Website: http://www.axinoss.com/
Phone: **Email:** research@axinoss.com
City: Helsinki **State:** Southern Finland **PC:** **Country:** Finland
Year Established: 2019 **Status 2020:** Active
Industries: Artificial Intelligence for:, ~ Banking and Financial Markets-Services (7), Machine Learning

Company Name: Basemark
Description: Rocksolid Engine by Basemark is the leading real-time engine for applications ranging from machine vision to automotive HMIs, AR and VR
Website: http://www.basemark.com
Phone: **Email:** sales@basemark.com
City: Helsinki **State:** Southern Finland **PC:** **Country:** Finland
Year Established: 2015 **Status 2020:** Active
Industries: ~ Aerospace and Defense (2), Artificial Intelligence for:, Augmented Reality for:, ~ Automotive (5), Computer Vision for:, Application Services for:, Application Services for:, Machine Learning for:, ~ Healthcare (20), ~ Government (19), Virtual Reality (VR)

Company Name: callstats.io
Description: callstats.io offers analytics and optimization services for real-time communication products using WebRTC.
Website: http://www.callstats.io
Phone: **Email:** growth@callstats.io
City: Helsinki **State:** Southern Finland **PC:** **Country:** Finland
Year Established: 2014 **Status 2020:** Active
Industries: Analytics for:, Enterprise Application Services for:, Predictive Analytics for:, Compute for:, Business Software as a Service Apps (SaaS Apps)

Company Name: CHAOS
Description: CHAOS is an urban forecasting company for creating livable cities.
Website: http://www.chaosarchitects.com
Phone: **Email:** hello@chaosarchitects.com
City: Helsinki **State:** Southern Finland **PC:** **Country:** Finland
Year Established: 2017 **Status 2020:** Active
Industries: Artificial Intelligence for:, ~ Customer Relationship Management (11), ~ Construction (10)

Company Name: Dain Studios
Description: Helps companies to fully leveraging the potential of Digital, AI, and Insights. Rolling out an AI platform for the travel industry
Website: http://www.dainstudios.com
Phone: **Email:** dirk.hofmann@dainstudios.com
City: Helsinki **State:** Southern Finland **PC:** **Country:** Finland
Year Established: **Status 2020:** Active
Industries: Artificial Intelligence for:, Big Data and Analytics for:, Databases

Company Name: DIGITAIKA
Description: Automated video production with AI
Website: http://www.digitaika.com
Phone: **Email:** 36434@reference-encyclopedia-ai.net
City: Helsinki **State:** Southern Finland **PC:** **Country:** Finland
Year Established: 2017 **Status 2020:** Active
Industries: Artificial Intelligence for:, Business Applications

Company Name: Doctual
Description: Doctual is an AI based platform for legal documents, contracts, delegation and signing for startups and small scale enterprises.
Website: http://www.doctual.com
Phone: **Email:** info@doctual.com
City: Helsinki **State:** Southern Finland **PC:** **Country:** Finland
Year Established: 2017 **Status 2020:** Active
Industries:

Company Name: Edudata.io
Description: EDUDATA.IO connects, transforms and makes sense of educational organizations' own data.
Website: http://www.edudata.io/
Phone: **Email:** info@edudata.io
City: Helsinki **State:** Southern Finland **PC:** **Country:** Finland
Year Established: 2019 **Status 2020:** Active
Industries: Analytics for:, ~ Education (13), ~ Education (13), IT Managed Services for:, Predictive Analytics

Company Name: Elias Robot
Description: Elias Robot is the first language learning app for humanoid robots
Website: http://www.eliasrobot.com/
Phone: 358 45 78754645 **Email:** info@eliasrobot.com
City: Helsinki **State:** Southern Finland **PC:** **Country:** Finland
Year Established: 2017 **Status 2020:** Active
Industries: Artificial Intelligence for:, ~ Education (13), ~ Education (13), ~ Education (13), ~ Education (13), Robotics

Company Name: Eqela
Description: Automation solutions and intelligent processes for software development and maintenance
Website: http://www.eqela.com
Phone: 358 44 240 8784 **Email:** contact@eqela.com
City: Helsinki **State:** Southern Finland **PC:** **Country:** Finland
Year Established: **Status 2020:** Active
Industries: Artificial Intelligence for:, Application Services for:, Enterprise Application Services for:, Application Services for:, ~ Professional Services (48), ~ Professional Services (48)

Company Name: Fleetonomy.ai
Description: Providing AI-based solutions to plan, manage and optimize smart mobility services and autonomous vehicles.
Website: http://www.fleetonomy.ai/
Phone: **Email:** markus.kantonen@fleetonomy.ai
City: Helsinki **State:** Southern Finland **PC:** **Country:** Finland
Year Established: 2016 **Status 2020:** Active
Industries: Artificial Intelligence for:, ~ Automotive (5), ~ Telecommunications (56), IT Managed Services for:, ~ Construction (10)

Company Name: Fourkind
Description: Fourkind is The Hands-on Advisory Company.
Website: http://fourkind.com/
Phone: **Email:** contact@fourkind.com
City: Helsinki **State:** Southern Finland **PC:** **Country:** Finland
Year Established: 2017 **Status 2020:** Active
Industries:

Company Name: Front AI
Description: Front AI is an Conversational AI and 2nd Generation Services Bot company
Website: http://front.ai/
Phone: **Email:** info@front.ai
City: Helsinki **State:** Southern Finland **PC:** **Country:** Finland
Year Established: 2019 **Status 2020:** Active
Industries: Artificial Intelligence for:, ~ Customer Relationship Management (11), Natural Language Processing

Company Name: F-Secure
Description: Since 1988, F-Secure has driven innovations in cyber security, defending tens of thousands of companies and millions of people.
Website: http://www.f-secure.com
Phone: 358 9 25200700 **Email:** helsinki@f-secure.com
City: Helsinki **State:** Southern Finland **PC:** **Country:** Finland
Year Established: **Status 2020:** Active
Industries: Artificial Intelligence for:, Cyber Security for:, Security

Company Name: GetJenny
Description: GetJenny is a conversational AI for customer Service.
Website: http://www.getjenny.com/
Phone: **Email:** jenny@getjenny.com
City: Helsinki **State:** Southern Finland **PC:** **Country:** Finland
Year Established: 2016 **Status 2020:** Active
Industries: Artificial Intelligence for:, IT Managed Services

Company Name: Inscripta
Description: PROFESSIONAL DICTATION MADE EASY
Website: http://inscripta.io/
Phone: **Email:** 36771@reference-encyclopedia-ai.net
City: Helsinki **State:** Southern Finland **PC:** **Country:** Finland
Year Established: 2015 **Status 2020:** Active
Industries: ~ Healthcare (20), Web for:, Machine Learning for:, Speech Recognition

Company Name: Intelligence Reta: Israel
Description: Intelligence Retail is the leading provider of AI solutions for Retail.
Website: http://intrtl.com/
Phone: 7 (499) 550-34-63 **Email:** info@intrtl.com
City: Helsinki **State:** Southern Finland **PC:** **Country:** Finland
Year Established: 2016 **Status 2020:** Active
Industries: Artificial Intelligence for:, Big Data and Analytics for:, Computer Vision for:, Image Recognition for:, IT Managed Services

Company Name: IPRally
Description: IPRally serves patent business by providing the first AI that thinks like a patent professional.
Website: http://www.iprally.com
Phone: **Email:** contact@iprally.com
City: Helsinki **State:** Southern Finland **PC:** **Country:** Finland
Year Established: 2018 **Status 2020:** Active
Industries: Artificial Intelligence for:, IT Managed Services

Company Name: Jenny
Description: Jenny is an open source conversational engine that automates conversations in any language.
Website: http://www.getjenny.com/
Phone: **Email:** jenny@getjenny.com
City: Helsinki **State:** Southern Finland **PC:** **Country:** Finland
Year Established: **Status 2020:** Active
Industries: Artificial Intelligence

Company Name: Klevu, Inc.
Description:
Website: http://www.klevu.com
Phone: 358 9 2514 4301 **Email:** nilay.oza@klevu.com
City: Helsinki **State:** **PC:** **Country:** Finland
Year Established: **Status 2020:** Active
Industries: E-Commerce for:, Web

Company Name: Kodit.io
Description: Kodit.io is an AI-powered residential real estate data platform.
Website: http://www.kodit.io/en
Phone: **Email:** hello@kodit.io
City: Helsinki **State:** Southern Finland **PC:** **Country:** Finland
Year Established: **Status 2020:** Active
Industries: Artificial Intelligence for:, ~ Real Estate (49)

Company Name: kontoor
Description: Kontoor reads all news and while monitoring markets learns to think like a trader combining human intuition with machine intelligence.
Website: http://kontoor.com
Phone: **Email:** 36860@reference-encyclopedia-ai.net
City: Helsinki **State:** Southern Finland **PC:** **Country:** Finland
Year Established: 2014 **Status 2020:** Active
Industries: Big Data and Analytics for:, ~ Banking and Financial Markets-Services (7), Machine Learning for:, Predictive Analytics

Company Name: LeanHeat
Description: Leanheat is the smartest solution for energy efficient building management.
Website: http://leanheat.com/
Phone: **Email:** info.leanheat@danfoss.com
City: Helsinki **State:** Southern Finland **PC:** **Country:** Finland
Year Established: 2011 **Status 2020:** Active
Industries: Artificial Intelligence for:, Internet of Things (IoT)

Company Name: Lokal House
Description: LokalHouse offers a real estate meta search engine and predictive analysis solution.
Website:
Phone: **Email:** 36912@reference-encyclopedia-ai.net
City: Helsinki **State:** Southern Finland **PC:** **Country: Finland**
Year Established: 2013 **Status 2020:** Closed
Industries: Big Data and Analytics for:, Predictive Analytics for:, Web

Company Name: Lumoa
Description: Save time and money with Lumoa´s online service. We help companies to identify and solve customer problems faster, cheaper and easier.
Website: http://lumoa.me
Phone: 358 504860598 **Email:** support@lumoa.me
City: Helsinki **State:** Southern Finland **PC:** **Country:** Finland
Year Established: **Status 2020:** Active
Industries: Analytics for:, Artificial Intelligence for:, Machine Learning for:, ~ Professional Services (48), Data Management

Company Name: Malls of Globe
Description: Malls of Globe Oy is a Finnish start-up offering Smart Retail - Platform as a Service for Malls, brand, & store worldwide.
Website: http://www.mallsofglobe.com/
Phone: **Email:** info@mallsofglobe.com
City: Helsinki **State:** Southern Finland **PC:** **Country:** Finland
Year Established: 2018 **Status 2020:** Active
Industries:

Company Name: Meeshkan
Description: Meeshkan is a network where you can train and test Machine Learning models in a massively parallel way on distributed nodes.
Website: http://meeshkan.com
Phone: **Email:** your.friends@meeshkan.com
City: Helsinki **State:** Southern Finland **PC:** **Country: Finland**
Year Established: **Status 2020:** Active
Industries: Analytics for:, Artificial Intelligence for:, ~ Education (13), Machine Learning for:, ~ Professional Services (48)

Company Name: MOPRIM LTD.
Description: MOPRIM - AI Platform for Mobility Analys
Website: http://www.moprim.com
Phone: **Email:** info@moprim.com
City: Helsinki **State:** Southern Finland **PC:** **Country: Finland**
Year Established: 2015 **Status 2020:** Active
Industries: Analytics for:, Artificial Intelligence for:, IT Managed Services for:, ~ Construction (10)

Company Name: MVision AI
Description: MVision AI is on a mission to bring AI into Radiotherapy and Radiology imaging. Our deep learning based organ contouring tool saves time
Website: http://www.mvision.ai
Phone: 358 (0) 40 5489 229 **Email:** info@mvision.ai
City: Helsinki **State:** Southern Finland **PC:** **Country: Finland**
Year Established: **Status 2020:** Active
Industries: Artificial Intelligence for:, ~ Healthcare (20), Machine Learning for:, ~ Healthcare (20)

Company Name: Natify Inc.
Description: Natify is a DMP for B2B enterprises with complex sales process.
Website: http://www.natify.io/
Phone: **Email:** ville@natify.io
City: Helsinki **State:** Southern Finland **PC:** **Country: Finland**
Year Established: **Status 2020:** Active
Industries: ~ Media-Communications (41), ~ Media-Communications (41), Artificial Intelligence for:, Business Applications for:, Big Data and Analytics for:, Enterprise Application Services for:, Machine Learning for:, ~ Media-Communications (41)

Company Name: Neuroflux
Description: Smart water solution for analyzing and visualizing water network. Detect leaks in sewage system with machine learning before they happen.
Website: http://www.rpalabs.com
Phone: 650-204-0128 **Email:** automate@rpalabs.com
City: Helsinki **State:** Southern Finland **PC:** **Country: Finland**
Year Established: **Status 2020:** Active
Industries: Artificial Intelligence for:, IT Managed Services for:, Web for:, ~ Professional Services (48)

Company **Name:** Neyra
Description: AI Sales & Marketing Analytic Tool
Website: http://neyra.ai
Phone: 1 619 780 4012 **Email:** alex@kira.ooo
City: Helsinki **State:** Southern Finland **PC:** **Country: Finland**
Year Established: 2019 **Status 2020:** Active
Industries: Artificial Intelligence

Company Name: Rating VC
Description: Big data platform for startup analytics
Website:
Phone: **Email:** 37262@reference-encyclopedia-ai.net
City: Helsinki **State:** Southern Finland **PC:** **Country: Finland**
Year Established: 2014 **Status 2020:** Closed
Industries: Analytics for:, Big Data and Analytics for:, Predictive Analytics for:, Business Software as a Service Apps (SaaS Apps) for:, ~ Banking and Financial Markets-Services (7)

Company Name: School Day
Description: AI-enhanced School Wellbeing Solution for K12 Education
Website: http://www.schoolday.fi/en
Phone: **Email:** info@schoolday.fi
City: Helsinki **State:** Southern Finland **PC:** **Country: Finland**
Year Established: 2017 **Status 2020:** Active
Industries: Analytics for:, Artificial Intelligence for:, ~ Education (13)

Company Name: Selko Technologies Oy
Description: Selko develops deep learning technologies for the automation of text analysis processes in engineering.
Website: http://selko.io
Phone: 358 (0) 40 829 3300 **Email:** info@selko.io
City: Helsinki **State:** Southern Finland **PC:** **Country: Finland**
Year Established: 2017 **Status 2020:** Active
Industries: Artificial Intelligence for:, IT Managed Services for:, Web

Company Name: Someturva
Description: Someturva offers free legal help for users of social media and other online platforms.
Website: http://www.someturva.fi/
Phone: **Email:** info@someturva.fi
City: Helsinki **State:** Southern Finland **PC:** **Country: Finland**
Year Established: 2017 **Status 2020:** Active
Industries: Artificial Intelligence for:, ~ Social Assistance-Non-Profits (53)

Company Name: SoSho
Description: Sosho is an AI powered virtual assistant
Website: http://www.sosho.co
Phone: **Email:** 37439@reference-encyclopedia-ai.net
City: Helsinki **State:** Southern Finland **PC:** **Country: Finland**
Year Established: 2014 **Status 2020:** Active
Industries: Artificial Intelligence for:, Big Data and Analytics for:, ~ Fashion (16), ~ E-Commerce (12), Machine Learning

Company Name: Superest
Description: AI infused online platform where users can automate their cold calling and know who is interested to buy and who is not
Website: http://www.superest.fi
Phone: 505140448 **Email:** office@superest.ai
City: Helsinki **State:** Southern Finland **PC:** **Country: Finland**
Year Established: 2019 **Status 2020:** Active
Industries: Artificial Intelligence for:, E-Commerce

Company Name: Teqmine
Description: Teqmine Analytics Oy is a Finnish Artificial Intelligence startup.
Website: http://teqmine.com/
Phone: **Email:** info@teqmine.com
City: Helsinki **State:** Southern Finland **PC:** **Country: Finland**
Year Established: 2013 **Status 2020:** Active
Industries: Artificial Intelligence for:, IT Managed Services for:, Web

Company Name: Terramonitor
Description: Terramonitor gives the power to analyze, build and organize geographical information into actionable insights.
Website: http://www.terramonitor.com/
Phone: 358 41 501 0732 **Email:** sales@terramonitor.com
City: Helsinki **State:** Southern Finland **PC:** **Country: Finland**
Year Established: **Status 2020:** Active
Industries:

Company Name: The Curious AI Company
Description: Curious AI is a deep tech startup. Building on decades of research, we build future AI components capable of e.g. autonomy and exploration.
Website: http://www.thecuriousaicompany.com/
Phone: **Email:** info@cai.fi
City: Helsinki **State:** Southern Finland **PC:** **Country: Finland**
Year Established: **Status 2020:** Active
Industries: Artificial Intelligence for:, Machine Learning

Company Name: Top Data Science
Description: Data analytics and computer vision solutions powered by AI.
Website: http://topdatascience.com
Phone: 358 40 589 4400 **Email:** oguzhan.gencoglu@topdatascience.com
City: Helsinki **State:** Southern Finland **PC:** **Country: Finland**
Year Established: **Status 2020:** Active
Industries: Analytics for:, Artificial Intelligence for:, Big Data and Analytics for:, ~ Healthcare (20), Image Recognition for:, Automation for:, Machine Learning

Company Name: ultimate.ai
Description: Customer Service AI: ultimate.ai gives customer service agents the AI tools they need to provide faster, smarter responses.
Website: http://www.ultimate.ai
Phone: **Email:** contact@ultimate.ai
City: Helsinki **State:** Southern Finland **PC:** **Country: Finland**
Year Established: **Status 2020:** Active
Industries: Artificial Intelligence

Company Name: Underhood
Description: Online reputation analyses of compani: Spain
Website: http://underhood.co/
Phone: **Email:** underhood@hoodiedude.com
City: Helsinki **State:** Southern Finland **PC:** **Country: Finland**
Year Established: **Status 2020:** Active
Industries: Artificial Intelligence for:, Business Applications for:, Business Intelligence for:, Web

Company Name: Upseller
Description: Upseller is an outsourced Sales Service lets you convert passive visitors to your webpages into active customers.
Website: http://www.upseller.fi/miksi-upseller/
Phone: 358 40 715 5343 **Email:** 37598@reference-encyclopedia-ai.net
City: Helsinki **State:** Southern Finland **PC:** **Country: Finland**
Year Established: 2014 **Status 2020:** Active
Industries: Artificial Intelligence

Company Name: Usetrace
Description: Usetrace develops test automation solutions for web applications.
Website: http://usetrace.com
Phone: 415 320 9987 **Email:** contact@usetrace.com
City: Helsinki **State:** Southern Finland **PC:** **Country: Finland**
Year Established: **Status 2020:** Active
Industries: Artificial Intelligence for:, Cloud for:, Web for:, ~ Professional Services (48)

Company Name: Vainu
Description: Sales intelligence, prospecting and account insights platform with a database of 108 million companies enriched with open data.
Website: http://www.vainu.com
Phone: (646)859-9334 **Email:** mikko@vainu.io
City: Helsinki **State:** Southern Finland **PC:** **Country: Finland**
Year Established: 2013 **Status 2020:** Active
Industries: Big Data and Analytics for:, Business Intelligence for:, Data Management for:, Databases for:, ~ E-Commerce (12), Predictive Analytics for:, Automation for:, Automation

Company Name: Voimada
Description: AI PaaS transforming blogging and creative writing.
Website: http://www.voimada.com
Phone: **Email:** o.j@enpsegroup.com
City: Helsinki **State:** Southern Finland **PC:** **Country: Finland**
Year Established: **Status 2020:** Active
Industries: Artificial Intelligence for:, Digital Media

Company Name: WebMicrosco:
Description: WebMicroscope is designed to handle large, gigapixel size, digitized whole slide images of scanned tissues and biopsies.
Website: http://www.webmicroscope.com/
Phone: **Email:** contact@webmicroscope.com
City: Helsinki **State:** Southern Finland **PC:** **Country: Finland**
Year Established: **Status 2020:** Active
Industries: Artificial Intelligence for:, IT Managed Services for:, ~ Healthcare (20), ~ Professional Services (48)

Company Name: Witrafi
Description: We want to make parking a positive experience and a sustainable activity.
Website: http://www.witrafi.com
Phone: **Email:** info@witrafi.com
City: Helsinki **State:** Southern Finland **PC:** **Country: Finland**
Year Established: 2014 **Status 2020:** Active
Industries: Big Data and Analytics for:, Application Services for:, ~ Banking and Financial Markets-Services (7), ~ Travel and Transportation (58), Predictive Analytics

Company Name: ZenRobotics
Description: ZenRobotics is a Finnish high-tech company specializing in robotic recycling technologies and products.
Website: http://www.zenrobotics.com
Phone: **Email:** info@zenrobotics.com
City: Helsinki **State:** Southern Finland **PC:** **Country: Finland**

Year Established: **Status 2020:** Active
Industries: Artificial Intelligence for:, ~ Manufacturing-Miscellaneous (34), ~ Social-Environmental-Physical-Engineering Sciences (55), Robotics

Company Name: Zyfra
Description: Zyfra is an international company developing products on the basis of the Industrial Internet of Things and Artificial Intelligence.
Website: http://www.zyfra.com/en/
Phone: 358 (4) 0 547-92-29 **Email:** hello@zyfra.ai
City: Helsinki **State:** Southern Finland **PC:** **Country: Finland**
Year Established: 2017 **Status 2020:** Active
Industries: Artificial Intelligence for:, IT Managed Services for:, Internet of Things (IoT)

Company Name: TalentAdore
Description: Enabling 100% personalized feedback to each job candidate, powered by AI.
Website: http://talentadore.com/
Phone: **Email:** info@talentadore.com
City: Kerava **State:** Southern Finland **PC:** **Country: Finland**
Year Established: 2014 **Status 2020:** Active
Industries: Artificial Intelligence for:, Big Data and Analytics for:, Enterprise Application Services

Company Name: OVObots
Description: AI Robots Oy designs, manufactures and sells social assistant robots, software, services and related intangible rights.
Website: http://www.ovobots.com
Phone: 358 40-501-8637 **Email:** info@ovobots.com
City: Lohja **State:** Southern Finland **PC:** **Country: Finland**
Year Established: 2016 **Status 2020:** Active
Industries:

Company Name: CAP Data Technologies
Description: CAP Data Technologies spots anomalies automatically without fingerprints in large volumes of data using machine learning algorithms.
Website: http://www.capdatatechnologies.com
Phone: **Email:** info@capdatatechnologies.com
City: Jyvaskyla **State:** Western Finland **PC:** **Country: Finland**
Year Established: **Status 2020:** Active
Industries: Analytics for:, Artificial Intelligence for:, Big Data and Analytics for:, Databases for:, Machine Learning

Company Name: Aiwo Digital
Description: Aiwo implements productive machine learning solutions
Website: http://www.aiwo.ai/
Phone: **Email:** atso.vesterinen@aiwo.ai
City: Jyväskylä **State:** Western Finland **PC:** **Country: Finland**
Year Established: 2018 **Status 2020:** Active
Industries: Artificial Intelligence for:, Data Management for:, IT Managed Services

Company Name: On-Time
Description: Helping companies to improve customer communications and relationships using calling robots.
Website: http://ontime.fi/en/
Phone: **Email:** hello@ontime.fi
City: Jyväskylä **State:** Western Finland **PC:** **Country: Finland**
Year Established: 2013 **Status 2020:** Active
Industries: Artificial Intelligence for:, IT Managed Services for:, Web for:, Robotics

Company Name: Headai
Description: General Semantic AI to enable explainable and transparent decision-making.
Website: http://www.headai.com/
Phone: **Email:** 36675@reference-encyclopedia-ai.net
City: Pori **State:** Western Finland **PC:** **Country: Finland**
Year Established: 2015 **Status 2020:** Active
Industries: Artificial Intelligence for:, Natural Language Processing

Company Name: FabricAI
Description: FabricAI - Automates accounting with artificial intelligence. Remove manual labour and speed up the accounting process by 10x.
Website: http://fabricai.fi/
Phone: 358 505219152 **Email:** moro@fabricai.fi
City: Tampere **State:** Western Finland **PC:** **Country: Finland**
Year Established: 2018 **Status 2020:** Active
Industries: Artificial Intelligence for:, ~ Banking and Financial Markets-Services (7), IT Managed Services

Company Name: Lumoin
Description: Lumoin Community removes construction yard communication and coordination problems.
Website: http://lumoin.com/
Phone: 358 40 737 0396 **Email:** contact@lumoin.com
City: Tampere **State:** Western Finland **PC:** **Country: Finland**
Year Established: 2017 **Status 2020:** Active
Industries: Artificial Intelligence

Company Name: NeonSpark
Description: Information Technology
Website: http://www.neonspark.fi
Phone: **Email:** nader.hariri@neonspark.fi
City: Tampere **State:** Western Finland **PC:** **Country: Finland**
Year Established: **Status 2020:** Active
Industries: Artificial Intelligence for:, Big Data and Analytics for:, Blockchain for:, Databases for:, Data Management for:, Machine Learning

Company Name: Neuro Event Labs
Description: SaaS. Helping doctors by assisting to diagnose epilepsy through video monitoring with the help of machine intelligence
Website: http://www.neuroeventlabs.com
Phone: **Email:** kaapo.annala@neuroeventlabs.com
City: Tampere **State:** Western Finland **PC:** **Country: Finland**
Year Established: 2015 **Status 2020:** Active
Industries: Analytics for:, Artificial Intelligence for:, ~ Healthcare (20), IT Managed Services for:, ~ Healthcare (20)

Company Name: Vau Company
Description: VAU Company is revolutionizing graphics and video content creation with automation and artificial intelligence
Website: http://vau.company/
Phone: 358 (0)40 765 8908 **Email:** juuso.kaari@vau.company
City: Tampere **State:** Western Finland **PC:** **Country: Finland**
Year Established: 2015 **Status 2020:** Active
Industries: ~ Arts-Entertainment-Recreation (4), Artificial Intelligence

Company Name: Wiview
Description: Witview helps consumers make better purchasing decisions by gathering "What the Internet Thinks' of products being purchased online.
Website: http://witview.io/
Phone: **Email:** contact@witview.io
City: Tampere **State:** Western Finland **PC:** **Country: Finland**
Year Established: 2018 **Status 2020:** Active
Industries: Artificial Intelligence for:, E-Commerce for:, Web

Company Name: Beemray
Description: Beemray is the API and analytics for human context data. Anonymously. In real-time.
Website: http://www.beemray.com/
Phone: **Email:** sales@beemray.com
City: Turku **State:** Western Finland **PC:** **Country: Finland**
Year Established: 2015 **Status 2020:** Active
Industries: Artificial Intelligence for:, Business Intelligence for:, Predictive Analytics for:, Predictive Analytics

Company Name: Empirica Finland
Description: Empirica Finland provides blockchain, artificial intelligence and IoT solutions.
Website: http://www.empirica.fi/
Phone: **Email:** hello@empirica.fi
City: Turku **State:** Western Finland **PC:** **Country: Finland**
Year Established: 2015 **Status 2020:** Active
Industries: Artificial Intelligence for:, Blockchain for:, Computer Vision for:, Internet of Things (IoT) for:, Machine Learning for:, Supply Chain Management

Company Name: Etsimo Healthcare
Description: The Digital Health Assistant
Website: http://www.etsimo.com
Phone: 358 50 532 4809 **Email:** tuomas.yla-kauttu@etsimo.com
City: Turku **State:** Western Finland **PC:** **Country: Finland**
Year Established: 2016 **Status 2020:** Active
Industries: Artificial Intelligence for:, ~ Healthcare (20), ~ Healthcare (20), Machine Learning for:, ~ Healthcare (20)

Company Name: Silo.AI
Description: Artificial Intelligence as a Service
Website: https://silo.ai
Phone: 358 40 359 1299 **Email:** info@silo.ai
City: Turku **State:** Western Finland **PC:** **Country: Finland**
Year Established: **Status 2020:** Active
Industries:

Company Name: Tidy Technologies
Description: Data analysis and insights automation
Website: http://www.causalytics.ai
Phone: **Email:** hello@causalytics.ai
City: Turku **State:** Western Finland **PC:** **Country: Finland**
Year Established: 2014 **Status 2020:** Active
Industries: Analytics for:, Artificial Intelligence for:, Digital Marketing for:, Web for:, Machine Learning

Company Name: Valohai
Description: A SaaS machine learning platform that automates training and deployment infrastructure. ðŸ¦ˆ
Website: http://valohai.com
Phone: **Email:** info@valohai.com
City: Turku **State:** Western Finland **PC:** **Country: Finland**
Year Established: **Status 2020:** Active
Industries: Artificial Intelligence for:, Enterprise Application Services for:, Machine Learning for:, ~ Professional Services (48)

France

Company Name: Volta Medical
Description: Volta.Medical is an innovative start-up with headquarters in Marseille (France).
Website: http://www.volta-medical.com/
Phone: **Email:** anton.vorobev@volta-medical.com
City: Marseille **State:** Provence-Alpes-Cote d'Azur **PC:** **Country: France**
Year Established: 2016 **Status 2020:** Active
Industries: Artificial Intelligence for:, ~ Healthcare (20)

Company Name: Homepul: Sweden
Description: HomePulse delivers real time analytics for profitable smart energy services.
Website: http://www.homepulse.fr
Phone: **Email:** info@gethomekey.com
City: Aix **State:** Auvergne-Rhône-Alpes **PC:** **Country: France**
Year Established: 2011 **Status 2020:** Active
Industries: Cloud for:, ~ Energy and Utilities (14), ~ Energy and Utilities (14), Internet of Things (IoT) for:, Machine Learning for:, Enterprise Application Services

Company Name: Opla
Description: A virtual assistant that allows you to create and manage your website by a natural conversation on your favorite messenger app.
Website: http://opla.ai
Phone: 33612209931 **Email:** marie@opla.ai
City: Clermont-ferrand **State:** Auvergne-Rhône-Alpes **PC:** **Country: Franceance**
Year Established: **Status 2020:** Active
Industries: Artificial Intelligence for:, Business Applications for:, IT Managed Services for:, Web for:, ~ Telecommunications (56), Natural Language Processing for:, Robotics for:, ~ Professional Services (48)

Company **Name:** WattSense
Description: The Building API
Website: http://wattsense.com/
Phone: 33 4 28 29 83 49 **Email:** contact@wattsense.com
City: Dardilly **State:** Auvergne-Rhône-Alpes **PC:** **Country: Franceance**
Year Established: **Status 2020:** Active
Industries: Artificial Intelligence for:, Big Data and Analytics for:, Cloud for:, ~ Energy and Utilities (14), Enterprise Application Services for:, ~ Construction (10)

Company Name: GreenWaves Technologies
Description: GreenWaves Technologies develops and distributes IoT-based products.
Website: http://greenwaves-technologies.com/
Phone: 33 970 96 21 44 **Email:** 36647@reference-encyclopedia-ai.net
City: Grenoble **State:** Auvergne-Rhône-Alpes **PC:** **Country: France**
Year Established: 2014 **Status 2020:** Active
Industries: Artificial Intelligence for:, Machine Learning

Company Name: Pixyl
Description: AI-Powered Brain Image Analysis for Enhanced Patient Care
Website: http://pixylmedical.com/
Phone: **Email:** contact@pixyl.io
City: La Tronche **State:** Auvergne-Rhône-Alpes **PC:** **Country: France**
Year Established: 2015 **Status 2020:** Active
Industries: Artificial Intelligence for:, ~ Healthcare (20)

Company Name: ELISE Technologies
Description: ELISE provides a powerful solution to help advertisers increase and measure the impact of their outdoor campaigns.
Website: http://elise.tech
Phone: **Email:** hello@elise.tech
City: Limonest **State:** Auvergne-Rhône-Alpes **PC:** **Country: France**
Year Established: **Status 2020:** Active
Industries: ~ Media-Communications (41), Artificial Intelligence for:, Big Data and Analytics for:, ~ Media-Communications (41), ~ Social Media (54)

Company Name: 365talents
Description: 365talents is the artificial intelligence SaaS solution for HR recommendations.
Website: https://www.365talents.com/
Phone: 33 1 88 32 75 49 **Email:** hello@365talents.com
City: Lyon **State:** Auvergne-Rhône-Alpes **PC:** **Country: France**
Year Established: 2015 **Status 2020:** Active
Industries: Artificial Intelligence for:, Management Information Systems for:, Business Software as a Service Apps (SaaS Apps)

Company Name: Cosmo Tech
Description: Cosmo Tech is a global technology company that helps the C-suite make optimal business decisions.
Website: http://cosmotech.com/
Phone: 33 4 37 66 67 65 **Email:** 36340@reference-encyclopedia-ai.net
City: Lyon **State:** Auvergne-Rhône-Alpes **PC:** **Country: France**
Year Established: 2010 **Status 2020:** Active
Industries: Analytics for:, ~ Banking and Financial Markets-Services (7), Business Applications for:, Predictive Analytics

Company Name: holi
Description: Artificial intelligence for sleep disorder diagnosis and treatment follow up
Website: http://www.holi.io
Phone: 33952700575 **Email:** contact@holi.io
City: Lyon **State:** Auvergne-Rhône-Alpes **PC:** **Country: France**
Year Established: **Status 2020:** Active
Industries: Artificial Intelligence for:, ~ Manufacturing-Electronic (30), ~ Healthcare (20), ~ Healthcare (20)

Company Name: Hooma
Description: Hoomano enhances interaction and user experience on machines, devices, social robots, smart displays, car user interfaces and more
Website: http://hoomano.com/
Phone: 33 825 95 08 00 **Email:** contact@hoomano.com
City: Lyon **State:** Auvergne-Rhône-Alpes **PC:** **Country: France**
Year Established: 2014 **Status 2020:** Active
Industries: Artificial Intelligence for:, IT Managed Services for:, Robotics

Company Name: MailClark
Description: MailClark is a tech company specializing in email groups, team inboxes, help desks, and more.
Website: http://mailclark.ai/email-to-slack
Phone: **Email:** support@mailclark.ai
City: Lyon **State:** Auvergne-Rhône-Alpes **PC:** **Country: France**
Year Established: **Status 2020:** Active
Industries:

Company Name: Miuros
Description: Miuros is a cloud-based platform, transparently integrated into your everyday tools.
Website: http://www.miuros.com
Phone: **Email:** info@miuros.com
City: Lyon **State:** Auvergne-Rhône-Alpes **PC:** **Country: France**
Year Established: 2016 **Status 2020:** Active
Industries: Business Software as a Service Apps (SaaS Apps)

Company Name: mojo
Description: We are creating the future of fertility care using AI and robotics, offering everyone access to reliable and affordable treatment.
Website: http://www.mojofertility.co
Phone: **Email:** hello@mojofertility.co
City: Lyon **State:** Auvergne-Rhône-Alpes **PC:** **Country: France**
Year Established: 2017 **Status 2020:** Active
Industries: Artificial Intelligence for:, ~ Healthcare (20), ~ Healthcare (20), Machine Learning

Company Name: Mojo Fertility
Description: Mojo Fertility is the diagnostic platform that uses computer vision and AI to help fertility clinics reduce their 75% failure rate.
Website: http://www.mojo-fertility.com
Phone: **Email:** hello@get-mojo.com
City: Lyon **State:** Auvergne-Rhône-Alpes **PC:** **Country: France**
Year Established: **Status 2020:** Active
Industries: Artificial Intelligence for:, ~ Healthcare (20), ~ Healthcare (20), Machine Learning

Company Name: novadiscovery
Description: Health technology company specialized in in silico biomedical simulation
Website: http://www.novadiscovery.com
Phone: 33463600506 **Email:** julie@novadiscovery.com
City: Lyon **State:** Auvergne-Rhône-Alpes **PC:** **Country: France**
Year Established: 2010 **Status 2020:** Active
Industries: Artificial Intelligence for:, ~ Biotechnology (9), ~ Customer Relationship Management (11), ~ Healthcare (20), IT Managed Services for:, ~ Healthcare (20)

Company Name: ProovStation
Description: New Standard of Automated Vehicle Inspection
Website: http://www.proovstation.com/
Phone: 33670300100 **Email:** a.komyza@proovstation.com
City: Lyon **State:** Auvergne-Rhône-Alpes **PC:** **Country: France**
Year Established: **Status 2020:** Active
Industries: Artificial Intelligence for:, ~ Automotive (5), Blockchain for:, Cloud for:, ~ Transportation and Logistics (57), Machine Learning

Company Name: Ubiant
Description: Ubiant created technology solutions to make buildings and smart objects.
Website: http://www.ubiant.com/
Phone: 33 4 78 18 44 16 **Email:** 37584@reference-encyclopedia-ai.net
City: Lyon **State:** Auvergne-Rhône-Alpes **PC:** **Country: France**
Year Established: 2011 **Status 2020:** Active
Industries: Artificial Intelligence for:, ~ Energy and Utilities (14), Internet of Things (IoT) for:, ~ Energy and Utilities (14), ~ Construction (10)

Company Name: VeriCampus
Description: VeriCampus helps students successfully navigate their way through school by utilizing AI-Powered Smart Messaging
Website: http://vericampus.com/
Phone: 33769696521 **Email:** hello@vericampus.com
City: Lyon **State:** Auvergne-Rhône-Alpes **PC:** **Country: France**
Year Established: **Status 2020:** Active
Industries: Artificial Intelligence for:, ~ Education (13), Web for:, Machine Learning for:, ~ Telecommunications (56), Application Services

Company Name: DocProcess
Description: DocProcess is a cloud finance and accounting automation solution based on RPA and eInvoicing. Designed for enterprises, SSCs and BPOs.
Website: http://doc-process.com/
Phone: 1-888-246-7679 **Email:** hello@doc-process.com
City: Meylan **State:** Auvergne-Rhône-Alpes **PC:** **Country: France**
Year Established: **Status 2020:** Active
Industries: Artificial Intelligence for:, Blockchain for:, Cloud for:, IT Managed Services for:, Machine Learning for:, Robotics

Company Name: Smart Me Up
Description: Smart Me Up is a face recognition technology platform.
Website: http://www.smartmeup.org/
Phone: 33 (0) 4 56 85 00 21 **Email:** CONTACT@SMARTMEUP.IO
City: Meylan **State:** Auvergne-Rhône-Alpes **PC:** **Country: France**
Year Established: **Status 2020:** Active
Industries: Artificial Intelligence for:, Embedded for:, Machine Learning for:, ~ Media-Communications (41)

Company Name: Streamdata.io
Description: Streamdata.io turns APIs into real-time experiences.
Website: http://www.streamdata.io/
Phone: **Email:** community@streamdata.io
City: Meylan **State:** Auvergne-Rhône-Alpes **PC:** **Country: France**

Year Established: **Status 2020:** Active
Industries: Artificial Intelligence for:, Cloud for:, Machine Learning for:, Mobile for:, Compute for:, ~ Professional Services (48)

Company Name: Sentryo
Description: Sentryo develops and provides cybersecurity and situation awareness solutions to industrial networks and the internet of things.
Website: http://www.sentryo.net
Phone: 33 9 70 46 96 94 **Email:** contact@sentryo.net
City: Villeurbanne **State:** Auvergne-Rhône-Alpes **PC:** **Country: France**
Year Established: 2014 **Status 2020:** Active
Industries: IT Managed Services for:, Internet of Things (IoT) for:, Security for:, IT Managed Services for:, IT Managed Services

Company Name: Imeon Energy
Description: Imeon Energy specializes in distribution of hybrid solar inverters incorporating artificial intelligence to produce solar electricity.
Website: http://www.imeon-energy.com
Phone: 33 184175115 **Email:** contact@imeon-energy.com
City: Brest **State:** Brittany **PC:** **Country: France**
Year Established: 2013 **Status 2020:** Active
Industries: Artificial Intelligence for:, ~ Energy and Utilities (14)

Company Name: NEXT-MOB
Description: NEXT-MOB provides a next-generation mobility services AI Platform and smart apps required to operate autonomous vehicle fleets.
Website: http://next-mob.com
Phone: **Email:** contact@next-mob.com
City: Bruz **State:** Brittany **PC:** **Country: France**
Year Established: **Status 2020:** Active
Industries: Artificial Intelligence for:, ~ Automotive (5), ~ Transportation and Logistics (57), Mobile for:, Application Services

Company Name: Logpic: South Korea
Description: Business Process Intelligence to map, explore and monitor business processses as its really occur.
Website: http://www.logpickr.com
Phone: 33677863938 **Email:** estelle.prie@logpickr.com
City: Cesson-Sevigne Bretagne **State:** Brittany **PC:** **Country: France**
Year Established: **Status 2020:** Active
Industries:

Company Name: PredicSis
Description: PredicSis.ai is a self-serve predictive analytics platform which helps assists its users in optimizing sales through actionable insights.
Website: http://predicsis.ai
Phone: 33257630005 **Email:** info@predicsis.ai
City: Lannion **State:** Brittany **PC:** **Country: France**
Year Established: **Status 2020:** Active
Industries: Analytics for:, Artificial Intelligence for:, Big Data and Analytics

Company Name: askblu.ai (by Happy Blue Fish)
Description: AI-SaaS Difficulty Balancing solution to Improve Player retention in Mobile Gam: Spain
Website: http://www.askblu.ai
Phone: **Email:** info@askblu.ai
City: Rennes **State:** Brittany **PC:** **Country: France**
Year Established: 2017 **Status 2020:** Active
Industries: Artificial Intelligence for:, IT Managed Services for:, Machine Learning for:, Business Software as a Service Apps (SaaS Apps) for:, ~ Arts-Entertainment-Recreation (4)

Company Name: CogniMap
Description: CogniMap uses artificial intelligence to find the operational knowledge.
Website: http://www.cognimap.eu/
Phone: **Email:** contact@cognimap.eu
City: Rennes **State:** Brittany **PC:** **Country: France**

Year Established: **Status 2020:** Active
Industries: Artificial Intelligence for:, Big Data and Analytics

Company Name: Dilepix
Description: Deep Learning Vision Control Systems startup addressing Precision Agriculture markets
Website: http://dilepix.com/
Phone: 33 7 61 16 76 70 **Email:** contact@dilepix.com
City: Rennes **State:** Brittany **PC:** **Country: France**
Year Established: 2018 **Status 2020:** Active
Industries: Artificial Intelligence for:, Computer Vision for:, ~ Agriculture (3), Application Services

Company Name: DriveTrust
Description: DriveTrust is an AI-powered dash cam with short range V2X and LTE communication capabilities.
Website: http://drivetrust.eu
Phone: 49 176 817 819 83 **Email:** info@drivetrust.eu
City: Rennes **State:** Brittany **PC:** **Country: France**
Year Established: 2017 **Status 2020:** Active
Industries: Artificial Intelligence for:, ~ Automotive (5), IT Managed Services for:, Machine Learning

Company Name: MAbSilico
Description: Deeptech driven solutions for antibody development based on Artificial Intelligence and machine learning
Website: http://www.mabsilico.com
Phone: **Email:** contact@mabsilico.com
City: Nouzilly **State:** Centre-Val de Loire **PC:** **Country: France**
Year Established: 2017 **Status 2020:** Active
Industries: Artificial Intelligence for:, ~ Biotechnology (9), ~ Healthcare (20), Machine Learning

Company Name: Janasen: Sweden
Description: Janasense reinvents the way to offer older people well being at home, with serenity for caregiver.
Website: http://www.janasense.com/en
Phone: 33664665619 **Email:** contact@janasense.com
City: Orleans **State:** Centre-Val de Loire **PC:** **Country: France**
Year Established: **Status 2020:** Active
Industries: Application Services for:, Artificial Intelligence for:, Cloud for:, ~ Healthcare (20), ~ Healthcare (20)

Company Name: SESA: Myanmar
Description: SESAMm is an innovative FinTech company specializing in Big Data and Artificial Intelligence for Asset Management.
Website: www.sesamm.com/
Phone: **Email:** contact@sesamm.com
City: Metz **State:** Grand Est **PC:** **Country: France**
Year Established: **Status 2020:** Active
Industries: Analytics for:, Artificial Intelligence for:, Big Data and Analytics for:, ~ Banking and Financial Markets-Services (7), Data Management for:, ~ Banking and Financial Markets-Services (7), ~ Banking and Financial Markets-Services (7), ~ Banking and Financial Mar

Company Name: Tresorio
Description: The Fog Computing platform based on a distributed network of Green Nod: Spain
Website: http://tresorio.com/
Phone: 33971000371 **Email:** contact@tresorio.com
City: Metz **State:** Grand Est **PC:** **Country: France**
Year Established: **Status 2020:** Active
Industries: Artificial Intelligence for:, Cloud for:, Cloud for:, Databases for:, ~ Energy and Utilities (14), Machine Learning for:, ~ Construction (10), ~ Construction (10)

Company Name: Aquil: United Arab Emirates
Description: Aquilae provides video analytics solution based on AI.
Website: http://i-aquilae.com/
Phone: 03 75 23 81 94 **Email:** contact@aquilae.Tech
City: Rosières-près-troyes **State:** Grand Est **PC:** **Country: France**

Year Established: 2017 **Status 2020:** Active
Industries: Analytics for:, Artificial Intelligence

Company Name: Holodia SAS
Description: Holodia provides virtual reality solutions for fitness, sports, and health.
Website: http://www.holodia.com
Phone: **Email:** contact@holodia.com
City: Strasbourg **State:** Grand Est **PC:** **Country: France**
Year Established: **Status 2020:** Active
Industries: Artificial Intelligence for:, ~ Healthcare (20), ~ Healthcare (20), ~ Professional Services (48)

Company Name: Brainwave
Description: Brainwave is a French independent software company.
Website: http://www.brainwave.fr
Phone: 33184190410 **Email:** contact@brainwaveGRC.com
City: Asnieres-sur-Seine **State:** Hauts-de-France **PC:** **Country: France**
Year Established: **Status 2020:** Active
Industries: Artificial Intelligence for:, Application Services for:, Enterprise Application Services for:, Predictive Analytics for:, ~ Customer Relationship Management (11)

Company Name: Everysens
Description: Everysens is a supply chain optimization platform intended for asset-intensive industries.
Website: http://www.everysens.com
Phone: 33 3 66 72 57 04 **Email:** vd@everysens.com
City: Lille **State:** Hauts-de-France **PC:** **Country: France**
Year Established: **Status 2020:** Active
Industries: Artificial Intelligence for:, Big Data and Analytics for:, ~ Transportation and Logistics (57), Supply Chain Management

Company Name: Jooxter
Description: Jooxter provides real time services to create peaceful and productive work environment.
Website: http://www.jooxter.com/
Phone: 33 3 66 72 48 26 **Email:** contact@jooxter.com
City: Lille **State:** Hauts-de-France **PC:** **Country: France**
Year Established: 2014 **Status 2020:** Active
Industries:

Company Name: Nuukik
Description: Nuukik is a Omnichannel Personalized Recommandation Engine We use artificial intelligence and smart algorithms that enable retailers to
Website: http://www.nuukik.com
Phone: 33 3 66 72 29 00 **Email:** contact@nuukik.com
City: Lille **State:** Hauts-de-France **PC:** **Country: France**
Year Established: 2013 **Status 2020:** Active
Industries: IT Managed Services for:, Robotics

Company Name: Sparo Social
Description: Easy-to-use social media management and analytics platform to help brands and agencies increase fan engagement and measure performances.
Website: http://www.sparosocial.com
Phone: 33 9 67 45 92 55 **Email:** hello@sparosocial.com
City: Lille **State:** Hauts-de-France **PC:** **Country: France**
Year Established: **Status 2020:** Active
Industries: ~ Media-Communications (41), Analytics for:, Artificial Intelligence for:, ~ Social Media (54), ~ Social Media (54), ~ Social Media (54), ~ Professional Services (48), ~ Social Media (54)

Company Name: Vekia
Description:
Website: www.vekia.fr/
Phone: **Email:** contact@vekia.fr
City: Lille **State:** Hauts-de-France **PC:** **Country: France**
Year Established: **Status 2020:** Active
Industries: Artificial Intelligence

Company Name: Taskiness
Description: The first intelligent note-based productivity tool. The World's First Natural Language Processing To-Do List.
Website: http://www.taskiness.com
Phone: **Email:** contact@taskiness.com
City: Roubaix **State:** Hauts-de-France **PC:** **Country: France**
Year Established: 2017 **Status 2020:** Active
Industries: Artificial Intelligence for:, Big Data and Analytics for:, IT Managed Services for:, Web for:, Mobile for:, Mobile for:, Business Software as a Service Apps (SaaS Apps)

Company Name: Yala
Description: Yala is a friendly Slack bot that makes use of machine learning to understand users and their audience.
Website: http://yala.yalabot.com/
Phone: **Email:** yalas@yalabot.com
City: Slack **State:** Hauts-de-France **PC:** **Country: France**
Year Established: **Status 2020:** Active
Industries: Artificial Intelligence for:, ~ Education (13), IT Managed Services for:, Machine Learning for:, ~ Telecommunications (56)

Company **Name:** qsays
Description: startup
Website: http://qsays.com
Phone: 33617521862 **Email:** lucian.vidrascu@qsays.com
City: Paris **State:** Ile-de-France **PC:** **Country: France**
Year Established: **Status 2020:** Active
Industries: Artificial Intelligence

Company Name: CARMAT
Description: CARMAT is a medtech company, offering biocompatible, auto-regulated total artificial hearts as close as possible to the human heart.
Website: http://www.carmatsa.com/index.php
Phone: 33139456450 **Email:** contact@carmatsas.com
City: Velizy-villacoublay **State:** Ile-de-France **PC:** **Country: France**
Year Established: **Status 2020:** Active
Industries: Artificial Intelligence for:, ~ Healthcare (20), IT Managed Services

Company Name: BRICKS
Description: Bricks is an agile project management app for architecture. It allows to collaborate efficiently to design architecture projects.
Website: http://www.bricksapp.io
Phone: 1234567890 **Email:** hello@openbricks.io
City: Aubervilliers **State:** IDF **PC:** **Country: France**
Year Established: **Status 2020:** Active
Industries: ~ Professional Services (48), Artificial Intelligence

Company Name: Sidetrade
Description: Sidetrade is the most compelling A.I Customer Platform. We empower Sales, Marketing & Finace teams to Grow Revenues and Accelerate Cash
Website: http://www.sidetrade.com
Phone: 33146841400 **Email:** info@sidetrade.com
City: Billancourt **State:** IDF **PC:** **Country: France**
Year Established: **Status 2020:** Active
Industries: Artificial Intelligence for:, Predictive Analytics for:, ~ Professional Services (48)

Company Name: Konverso
Description: Konverso is a IT & Communication - Media company.
Website: http://www.konverso.ai/
Phone: 33 (0)1 41 10 83 **Email:** contact@konverso.ai
City: Boulogne-billancourt **State:** IDF **PC:** **Country: France**
Year Established: 2017 **Status 2020:** Active
Industries: IT Managed Services for:, Machine Learning

Company Name: Leakmited
Description: Leakmited is a company locate water leaking pipes using AI and Satellite Images.
Website: http://leakmited.com/
Phone: 678178569 **Email:** 4721@reference-encyclopedia-ai.net
City: Carrieres-sur-seine **State:** IDF **PC:** **Country: France**
Year Established: **Status 2020:** Active
Industries: Artificial Intelligence for:, ~ Telecommunications (56)

Company Name: COPYRIGHT
Description: COPYRIGHT is a French digital company focused in development of Artificial intelligence machine.
Website: http://copyright.international
Phone: **Email:** dk@copyright.international
City: Champlan **State:** IDF **PC:** **Country: France**
Year Established: **Status 2020:** Active
Industries: Analytics for:, Artificial Intelligence for:, ~ Media-Communications (41), Machine Learning for:, ~ Arts-Entertainment-Recreation (4)

Company Name: EXA3D
Description: The new AI-powered 3D modeling platform
Website: http://exa3d.fr
Phone: 33 1 85 08 89 82 **Email:** contact@exa3d.fr
City: Clichy **State:** IDF **PC:** **Country: France**
Year Established: 2015 **Status 2020:** Active
Industries: Artificial Intelligence

Company Name: Visiblee
Description: Visiblee is a generation automation solution to boost B2B website conversion.
Website: http://www.visiblee.io/
Phone: 33 1 57 64 05 85 **Email:** contact@visiblee.io
City: Courbevoie **State:** IDF **PC:** **Country: France**
Year Established: 2014 **Status 2020:** Active
Industries:

Company Name: AiiNTENSE
Description: e-health, Artificial Intelligence
Website: http://www.aiintense.eu
Phone: 33 685074647 **Email:** contact@aiintense.eu
City: Evry **State:** IDF **PC:** **Country: France**
Year Established: **Status 2020:** Active
Industries: Artificial Intelligence for:, ~ Healthcare (20), ~ Healthcare (20)

Company Name: Ubeeko
Description: We do HFactory: Big Data virtualization platform for Hadoop and Spark.
Website: http://ubeeko.com
Phone: 33 160 713 598 **Email:** contact@ubeeko.com
City: Evry **State:** IDF **PC:** **Country: France**
Year Established: **Status 2020:** Active
Industries: Analytics for:, Artificial Intelligence for:, Big Data and Analytics for:, Enterprise Application Services for:, Automation for:, Predictive Analytics

Company Name: DataValor
Description: Your Artificial Intelligence, Our Mission - DeepNeuroEvolution solutions for compani: Spain
Website: http://www.datavaloris.com
Phone: 33619015214 **Email:** claire@datavaloris.com
City: Fontenay-sous-bois **State:** IDF **PC:** **Country: France**
Year Established: **Status 2020:** Active
Industries: Artificial Intelligence for:, Big Data and Analytics for:, Data Management for:, Databases

Company Name: Silex Cognitive Sourcing
Description: Silex is the first cognitive sourcing platfrom based on AI technologies.
Website: http://www.silex-france.com
Phone: 33 1 84 23 29 08 **Email:** contact@silex-france.com
City: Gentilly **State:** IDF **PC:** **Country: France**
Year Established: 2014 **Status 2020:** Active
Industries: Artificial Intelligence for:, Big Data and Analytics for:, IT Managed Services for:, Web for:, Business Software as a Service Apps (SaaS Apps)

Company Name: Oxibox
Description: Cyber-resilience, Cybersecurity, SaaS, BaaS, backup, D: SERBIA
Website: http://www.oxibox.fr
Phone: 33130544579 **Email:** 37134@reference-encyclopedia-ai.net
City: Guyancourt **State:** IDF **PC:** **Country: France**
Year Established: 2014 **Status 2020:** Active
Industries: Artificial Intelligence for:, Cyber Security for:, IT Managed Services for:, Business Software as a Service Apps (SaaS Apps)

Company Name: Sogeti
Description: Digital Transformation
Website: http://www.sogeti.com
Phone: 512 340 2200 **Email:** crc@suse.com
City: Issy-les-Moulineaux **State:** IDF **Zip:** 92136 **Country: France**
Year Established: **Status 2020:** Active
Industries:

Company Name: Wemaik
Description: XPaas, IT, Artificial intelligence, Software
Website: http://www.wemaik.com
Phone: **Email:** hello@wemaik.com
City: Issy-les-moulineaux **State:** IDF **PC:** **Country: France**
Year Established: 2014 **Status 2020:** Active
Industries: Application Services for:, Artificial Intelligence for:, IT Managed Services for:, Web

Company Name: Datapole
Description: DATAPOLE is a young innovative company that develops and offers solutions of analysis, forecasting, resource planning and optimization.
Website: http://www.datapole.com/
Phone: (3397) 044-6672 **Email:** contact@datapole.com
City: La Plaine-saint-denis **State:** IDF **PC:** **Country: France**
Year Established: 2010 **Status 2020:** Active
Industries:

Company Name: Scortex
Description: Harnessing the power of deep learning, we provide a end-to-end smart inspection solution for quality control in the manufacturing space.
Website: http://scortex.io/
Phone: **Email:** contact@scortex.io
City: Le Plessis-robinson **State:** IDF **PC:** **Country: France**
Year Established: **Status 2020:** Active
Industries: Artificial Intelligence for:, Computer Vision for:, ~ Manufacturing-Electronic (30), Automation for:, Machine Learning for:, ~ Manufacturing-Miscellaneous (34), Business Process and Operations for:, ~ Professional Services (48)

Company Name: Raisup
Description: The AI-powered Startup Selection engine.
Website: http://raisup.com/
Phone: **Email:** 37259@reference-encyclopedia-ai.net
City: Le Vésinet **State:** IDF **PC:** **Country: France**
Year Established: 2013 **Status 2020:** Active
Industries: Internet of Things (IoT) for:, Application Services

Company Name: B2CLOUD
Description: Cloud Computing value chain expertises based on supervised machine learning (AI)
Website: http://www.btocloud.eu
Phone: 33 1 80 88 62 28 **Email:** connect@btocloud.fr
City: Levallois-perret **State:** IDF **PC:** **Country: France**

Year Established: 2013 **Status 2020:** Active
Industries: Artificial Intelligence for:, Cloud for:, IT Managed Services for:, Machine Learning

Company Name: Cleed
Description: Personal shopping assistant
Website: http://www.cleed.com
Phone: 33147817310 **Email:** contact@cleed.com
City: Levallois-perret **State:** IDF **PC:** **Country: France**
Year Established: **Status 2020:** Active
Industries: Artificial Intelligence for:, ~ Fashion (16)

Company Name: ETAON
Description: ETAONIS provides machine learning based APIs for business and real-world problem solving enhanced with real-time web data acquisition
Website: http://www.etaonis.com
Phone: 33 6 81 87 32 16 **Email:** contact@etaonis.com
City: Levallois-perret **State:** IDF **PC:** **Country: France**
Year Established: 2015 **Status 2020:** Active
Industries: Analytics for:, Artificial Intelligence for:, Big Data and Analytics for:, IT Managed Services

Company Name: Salest: Isle of Man
Description: Sales AI Assistant for sales in Microsoft Teams and connected to Salesforce
Website: http://www.salestim.com
Phone: **Email:** 37332@reference-encyclopedia-ai.net
City: Levallois-perret **State:** IDF **PC:** **Country: France**
Year Established: 2018 **Status 2020:** Active
Industries:

Company Name: Bertin IT
Description: Bertin IT is an expert provider of advanced software solutions for cyber-security, cyber intelligence, strategic intelligence
Website: http://www.bertin-it.com/
Phone: **Email:** 36147@reference-encyclopedia-ai.net
City: Montigny-le-bretonneux **State:** IDF **PC:** **Country: France**
Year Established: 2014 **Status 2020:** Active
Industries: Artificial Intelligence for:, Cyber Security for:, Security

Company Name: Lingua Custodia
Description: Lingua Custodia is a machine translation company.
Website: http://www.linguacustodia.finance/en/homepage/
Phone: 33 1 80 82 59 70 **Email:** contact@linguacustodia.com
City: Montigny-le-bretonneux **State:** IDF **PC:** **Country: France**
Year Established: 2011 **Status 2020:** Active
Industries: Machine Learning

Company Name: Parkoview
Description: Parkoview is a designs, manufactures and maintains parking sensors based on Artificial Intelligence image recognition
Website: http://www.parkoview.com/
Phone: 33 (0) 6 84 10 47 16 **Email:** contact@parkoview.com
City: Montreuil **State:** IDF **PC:** **Country: France**
Year Established: 2017 **Status 2020:** Active
Industries: Artificial Intelligence

Company Name: Case Law Analytics
Description: Case Law Analytics allows legal professionals to quantify and visualize their judicial risks.
Website: http://caselawanalytics.com
Phone: 689765196 **Email:** jacques.levy.vehel@caselawanalytics.com
City: Nantes **State:** IDF **PC:** **Country: France**
Year Established: **Status 2020:** Active
Industries: Artificial Intelligence for:, ~ Law-Legal Services (26), ~ Telecommunications (56), Big Data and Analytics for:, ~ Law-Legal Services (514), IT Managed Services for:, Machine Learning for:, ~ Law-Legal Services (3381), Natural Language Processing for:, ~ Law-Legal

Company Name: Bee The Move
Description: Organize differently, Organize efficiently
Website: http://bee-the-move.com
Phone: (3363) 299-3917 **Email:** contact@bee-the-move.com
City: Neuilly-sur-seine **State:** IDF **PC:** **Country: France**
Year Established: 2016 **Status 2020:** Active
Industries: Business Intelligence for:, Collaboration Solutions for:, Learning and Marketing Communications Services (MarComm) for:, Predictive Analytics for:, Application Services

Company Name: CareOS
Description: CareOS, the digital center of self-care, is a platform that works naturally into your care, beauty and health rituals.
Website: http://care-os.com/
Phone: **Email:** contact@care-os.com
City: Neuilly-sur-seine **State:** IDF **PC:** **Country: France**
Year Established: 2018 **Status 2020:** Active
Industries: Internet of Things (IoT) for:, ~ Retail and Consumer Products (52), Security

Company Name: Cenova
Description: Cenova is a fast-growing consulting and data firm
Website: http://www.cenova.fr/
Phone: 01 80 88 75 80 **Email:** contact@cenova.fr
City: Neuilly-sur-seine **State:** IDF **PC:** **Country: France**
Year Established: 2016 **Status 2020:** Active
Industries: Databases for:, Data Management for:, IT Managed Services for:, Natural Language Processing for:, Predictive Analytics

Company Name: Datakeen
Description: Datakeen makes data science accessible to everyone.
Website: http://www.datakeen.co
Phone: **Email:** contact@datakeen.co
City: Neuilly-sur-seine **State:** IDF **PC:** **Country: France**
Year Established: **Status 2020:** Active
Industries: Artificial Intelligence for:, ~ Professional Services (48)

Company Name: DATATEGY
Description: Mobility Solutions
Website: http://www.datategy.net
Phone: (3365) 914-3303 **Email:** contact@datategy.net
City: Neuilly-sur-seine **State:** IDF **PC:** **Country: France**
Year Established: 2016 **Status 2020:** Active
Industries: Artificial Intelligence for:, ~ Automotive (5), Big Data and Analytics for:, IT Managed Services

Company Name: Myriad Data
Description: Myriad Data is a French startup that specializes in textmining, language interpretation, and machine and deep learning technologies.
Website: http://myriad-data.com/
Phone: 33 (0) 1 85 73 59 51 **Email:** contact@myriad-data.com
City: Neuilly-sur-seine **State:** IDF **PC:** **Country: France**
Year Established: 2016 **Status 2020:** Active
Industries: Artificial Intelligence for:, Big Data and Analytics for:, IT Managed Services for:, Machine Learning

Company Name: vFeed, Inc
Description: Vulnerability and Threat Intelligence Database Provider
Website: http://vfeed.io
Phone: **Email:** support@vfeed.io
City: Newark **State:** IDF **PC:** **Country: France**
Year Established: **Status 2020:** Active
Industries: Artificial Intelligence for:, Cyber Security for:, Application Services for:, Machine Learning for:, Security for:, Risk Management for:, Security for:, ~ Professional Services (48)

Company Name: Anamne: Sweden
Description: Anamnese is a medical artificial intelligence that questions the patient through a web interface or a chatbot.
Website: http://anamnese.me
Phone: **Email:** 36058@reference-encyclopedia-ai.net
City: Palaiseau **State:** IDF **PC:** **Country: France**
Year Established: 2017 **Status 2020:** Active
Industries: Artificial Intelligence for:, ~ Healthcare (20), ~ Healthcare (20)

Company Name: Arkangel
Description: The next generation solution for security and threat intelligence
Website:
Phone: **Email:** hello@arkangel.io
City: Palaiseau **State:** IDF **PC:** **Country: France**
Year Established: **Status 2020:** Active
Industries: Artificial Intelligence for:, Cyber Security for:, IT Managed Services for:, ~ Professional Services (48)

Company Name: IoTify
Description: End-to-end IIoT solutions to enable predictive maintenance and asset tracking thanks to smart sensorsand AI-based analytics.
Website: http://www.iotify.me
Phone: **Email:** hello@iotify.me
City: Palaiseau **State:** IDF **PC:** **Country: France**
Year Established: 2018 **Status 2020:** Active
Industries:

Company Name: Jeeliz
Description: We run deep learning neural networks inside the web browser using webgl. We do real-time face detection and tracking, glasses VTO, webAR.
Website: http://jeeliz.com
Phone: (1609) 250-8795 **Email:** contact@jeeliz.com
City: Palaiseau **State:** IDF **PC:** **Country: France**
Year Established: 2016 **Status 2020:** Closed
Industries: Augmented Reality for:, Computer Vision for:, Machine Learning for:, Web

Company Name: Justice.cool
Description: Justice.cool is the first AI driven Mediation Platform
Website: http://www.justice.cool
Phone: (3366) 245-1364 **Email:** drosne@justice.cool
City: Pantin **State:** IDF **PC:** **Country: France**
Year Established: 2019 **Status 2020:** Active
Industries: Artificial Intelligence for:, ~ Banking and Financial Markets-Services (7)

Company Name: A.I.Mergence
Description: Company specialised in Artificial Intelligence and Autonomous Robotics
Website: http://www.ai-mergence.com/
Phone: 33 (0)7 68 16 36 92 **Email:** contact@ai-mergence.com
City: Paris **State:** IDF **PC:** **Country: France**
Year Established: 2015 **Status 2020:** Active
Industries: Robotics

Company Name: AI Commons Foundation
Description: The Artificial Intelligence Commons
Website: http://www.aicommons.com/
Phone: **Email:** info@aicommons.com
City: Paris **State:** IDF **PC:** **Country: France**
Year Established: 2017 **Status 2020:** Active
Industries: Artificial Intelligence for:, ~ Education (13), Machine Learning for:, ~ Retail and Consumer Products (52)

Company Name: aimi
Description: AI software designed to help restaurant owners manage inventory and reduce food waste.
Website: http://www.gaderlamy.wixsite.com/aimi
Phone: **Email:** mohamedalidaoudi@gmail.com
City: Paris **State:** IDF **PC:** **Country: France**
Year Established: **Status 2020:** Active
Industries: **Company Name:** Air360
Description: Understand who is your web & mobile audience and what drives growth. Analytics reinvented to be useful, actionable and simple.
Website: http://www.air360.io/
Phone: **Email:** hello@air360.io
City: Paris **State:** IDF **PC:** **Country: France**
Year Established: 2016 **Status 2020:** Active
Industries: Analytics for:, Application Services for:, IT Managed Services

Company Name: AiZimov
Description: AiZimov proposes Artificial Intelligence autonomous outbound services that allow businesses to transform the way that they engage.
Website: http://www.aizimov.com
Phone: **Email:** info@aizimov.com
City: Paris **State:** IDF **PC:** **Country: France**
Year Established: **Status 2020:** Active
Industries: Artificial Intelligence for:, Enterprise Application Services for:, Automation

Company Name: AKHEROS
Description: Akheros develops unsupervised machine learning net-appliances that anticipates, detects and prevents dangerous incongruous behavio: Serbia
Website: http://akheros.com/about/
Phone: **Email:** ceo@akheros.com
City: Paris **State:** IDF **PC:** **Country: France**
Year Established: 2012 **Status 2020:** Active
Industries: Artificial Intelligence for:, Machine Learning

Company Name: Allo-Media
Description: Allo-Media is a platform that allows marketing optimization of phone calls using call tracking.
Website: http://www.allo-media.net/
Phone: 33 1 70 82 78 95 **Email:** contact@allo-media.fr
City: Paris **State:** IDF **PC:** **Country: France**
Year Established: **Status 2020:** Active
Industries: ~ Media-Communications (41), ~ Media-Communications (41), Artificial Intelligence for:, ~ E-Commerce (12), ~ Media-Communications (41), Speech Recognition

Company Name: Allphins
Description: Allphins delivers the only AI-native risk management solution built specifically for the energy insurance industry.
Website: https://www.allphins.com/
Phone: **Email:** contact@allphins.com
City: Paris **State:** IDF **PC:** **Country: France**
Year Established: 2018 **Status 2020:** Active
Industries: Artificial Intelligence for:, ~ Energy and Utilities (14), Machine Learning for:, Business Software as a Service Apps (SaaS Apps)

Company Name: Altaroad
Description: ALTAROAD offers a real-time analysis of data allowing to measure the footprint or the weight of a specific vehicle.
Website:
Phone: **Email:** 36049@reference-encyclopedia-ai.net
City: Paris **State:** IDF **PC:** **Country: France**
Year Established: 2017 **Status 2020:** Active
Industries: Artificial Intelligence for:, ~ Automotive (5), ~ Telecommunications (56)

Company Name: Angus.ai
Description: Angus.ai is an hosted video monitoring API that delivers automatic notifications when something interesting happens.
Website: http://www.angus.ai
Phone: **Email:** contact@angus.ai
City: Paris **State:** IDF **PC:** **Country: France**
Year Established: **Status 2020:** Active
Industries: Artificial Intelligence for:, Robotics

Company Name: Another Bra: India
Description: Another Brain is an artificial intelligence startup that develops AI in a way far beyond deep learning.
Website: http://anotherbrain.ai
Phone: 33187819928 **Email:** contact@anotherbrain.ai
City: Paris **State:** IDF **PC:** **Country: France**
Year Established: 2017 **Status 2020:** Active
Industries: Machine Learning for:, Robotics

Company Name: Antescofo
Description: Antescofo empowers mobile devices with musical AI.
Website: http://www.antescofo.com
Phone: **Email:** 36068@reference-encyclopedia-ai.net
City: Paris **State:** IDF **PC:** **Country: France**
Year Established: 2016 **Status 2020:** Active
Industries:

Company Name: AntVoice
Description: Our mission is to help e-merchants, media companies and brands to offer a personalized user experience on each touch points.
Website: http://www.antvoice.com
Phone: **Email:** contact@antvoice.com
City: Paris **State:** IDF **PC:** **Country: France**
Year Established: **Status 2020:** Active
Industries: ~ Media-Communications (41), Artificial Intelligence for:, Digital Marketing for:, Digital Media for:, E-Commerce for:, ~ Professional Services (48)

Company Name: Apricity
Description: Apricity is the UK's trusted companion for personalised fertility treatment.
Website: http://www.apricity.life/
Phone: 44 (0) 115 824 3928 **Email:** contact@apricity.life
City: Paris **State:** IDF **PC:** **Country: France**
Year Established: 2016 **Status 2020:** Active
Industries: Artificial Intelligence for:, ~ Healthcare (20)

Company Name: Artur': India
Description: Artur'In is an AI-based platform to help real-estate professionals deploy an advanced digital marketing solution.
Website: http://www.arturin.com/
Phone: **Email:** 36090@reference-encyclopedia-ai.net
City: Paris **State:** IDF **PC:** **Country: France**
Year Established: 2016 **Status 2020:** Active
Industries: Artificial Intelligence

Company Name: asgard.ai
Description: Asgard is a market intelligence company that helps businesses to track any market or company's activity.
Website: http://www.asgard.ai
Phone: **Email:** 36094@reference-encyclopedia-ai.net
City: Paris **State:** IDF **PC:** **Country: France**
Year Established: 2016 **Status 2020:** Active
Industries: Artificial Intelligence for:, IT Managed Services

Company Name: AskHub
Description: Actionable insights to enhance the capacities and ROI of conversational agents (chatbots and voicebots)
Website: http://www.askhub.io
Phone: 33 1 45 81 76 41 **Email:** contact@askhub.io
City: Paris **State:** IDF **PC:** **Country: France**
Year Established: **Status 2020:** Active
Industries: Artificial Intelligence for:, Machine Learning for:, Natural Language Processing

Company Name: askR.ai
Description: askR.ai the first AI-based data assistant which instantly answers your business questions by processing your data, with no skills needed.
Website: http://fr.askr.ai
Phone: **Email:** hello@askr.ai
City: Paris **State:** IDF **PC:** **Country: France**
Year Established: 2016 **Status 2020:** Active
Industries: Analytics for:, Artificial Intelligence for:, Big Data and Analytics for:, Collaboration Solutions

Company Name: ASPerti: Sweden
Description: Tech firm providing IA, Big Data and Cybersecurity services powered by unique cognitive skills of Atypical experts (Aspergers, Gifted)
Website: http://www.aspertise.net/index_en.html
Phone: (514) 812-8196 **Email:** contact@aspertise.net
City: Paris **State:** IDF **PC:** **Country: France**
Year Established: **Status 2020:** Active
Industries: Artificial Intelligence for:, Big Data and Analytics for:, Cyber Security

Company Name: Axel
Description: Axel is an AI-powered virtual assistant makes your onboardings simple and successful.
Website: http://www.axel.org
Phone: **Email:** info@axel.org
City: Paris **State:** IDF **PC:** **Country: France**
Year Established: 2012 **Status 2020:** Active
Industries: Artificial Intelligence for:, Internet of Things (IoT)

Company Name: Axionable
Description: Axionable provides bigdate and AI services.
Website: http://www.axionable.com
Phone: 33 1 84 16 01 41 **Email:** contact@axionable.com
City: Paris **State:** IDF **PC:** **Country: France**
Year Established: 2016 **Status 2020:** Active
Industries: Artificial Intelligence for:, IT Managed Services for:, IT Managed Services

Company Name: Ayomi
Description: Ayomi is the first Artificial Intelligence to automatically fund any business.
Website: http://ayomi.fr/
Phone: 33(0)1 83 95 45 04 **Email:** plateforme@ayomi.fr
City: Paris **State:** IDF **PC:** **Country: France**
Year Established: **Status 2020:** Active
Industries: Artificial Intelligence for:, ~ Banking and Financial Markets-Services (7), ~ Professional Services (48)

Company Name: AZmed
Description: AZmed offers innovative solutions to optimize healthcare specialists' workflow by using AI.
Website: http://www.azmed.co/
Phone: **Email:** contact@azmed.co
City: Paris **State:** IDF **PC:** **Country: France**
Year Established: 2018 **Status 2020:** Active
Industries: Artificial Intelligence for:, ~ Customer Relationship Management (11), ~ Healthcare (20), IT Managed Services for:, Machine Learning for:, ~ Healthcare (20)

Company Name: Babyprogress
Description: MRI, AI, and finite elements with GPU accelerated simulation for childbirth biomechanical risks assessment.
Website: http://www.babyprogress.fr
Phone: (3366) 114-3924 **Email:** olivier.ami@babyprogress.fr
City: Paris **State:** IDF **PC:** **Country: France**
Year Established: 2014 **Status 2020:** Active
Industries: Artificial Intelligence

Company Name: Batvoice
Description: Leverage the power of speech analytics to quickly spot trends and obstacles in the Customer Journey
Website: http://www.batvoice.com/
Phone: **Email:** contact@batvoice.com
City: Paris **State:** IDF **PC:** **Country: France**
Year Established: 2015 **Status 2020:** Active
Industries:

Company Name: bepleez
Description: Bepleez is an e-commerce platform that connects vendors and buyers together to buy and sell goods.
Website: http://www.bepleez.com
Phone: 33(0)614604626 **Email:** sebastien@bepleez.com
City: Paris **State:** IDF **PC:** **Country: France**
Year Established: **Status 2020:** Active
Industries:

Company Name: BlaBlaCar
Description: BlaBlaCar is a long distance carpooling platform that connects drivers with empty seats and passengers to share travel costs.
Website: http://www.blablacar.com
Phone: **Email:** team-legal@blablacar.com
City: Paris **State:** IDF **PC:** **Country: France**
Year Established: **Status 2020:** Active
Industries: Artificial Intelligence for:, Collaboration Solutions for:, Web for:, Network for:, ~ Social Media (54), ~ Transportation and Logistics (57), ~ Travel and Transportation (58)

Company Name: Bon de Visite
Description: Creates and develops algorithms and analytics based digital information in the space of urbanism
Website: http://bondevisite.fr/
Phone: **Email:** 36183@reference-encyclopedia-ai.net
City: Paris **State:** IDF **PC:** **Country: France**
Year Established: 2015 **Status 2020:** Active
Industries: Analytics for:, Artificial Intelligence

Company Name: Botfuel
Description: Fueling the next generation of chat bots
Website: botfuel.io
Phone: **Email:** hi@botfuel.io
City: Paris **State:** IDF **PC:** **Country: France**
Year Established: **Status 2020:** Active
Industries: Artificial Intelligence for:, ~ Telecommunications (56)

Company Name: Botmind
Description: SaaS platform that helps companies to deliver a better customer experience combining human and artificial intelligence.
Website: http://www.botmind.io
Phone: **Email:** hello@botmind.io
City: Paris **State:** IDF **PC:** **Country: France**
Year Established: **Status 2020:** Active
Industries: Artificial Intelligence for:, ~ E-Commerce (12), Machine Learning for:, ~ Professional Services (48)

Company Name: BOTNATION AI
Description: BOTNATION AI is a bot building platform for engaging voice and text-based conversational apps.
Website:
Phone: 33 9 74 59 58 72 **Email:** contact@botnation.ai
City: Paris **State:** IDF **PC:** **Country: France**
Year Established: 2016 **Status 2020:** Active
Industries: Artificial Intelligence for:, IT Managed Services for:, IT Managed Services

Company Name: Brainattic
Description: We empower e-commerce with AI Deep Learning Recommendation Engine.
Website: http://www.brainattic.io
Phone: (3365) 287-2193 **Email:** david@brainattic.io
City: Paris **State:** IDF **PC:** **Country: France**
Year Established: 2017 **Status 2020:** Active
Industries: Artificial Intelligence for:, E-Commerce for:, ~ Education (13), Machine Learning

Company Name: BRAINCITI: SPAIN
Description: Making Cities & Businesses Smarter With Human-Supportive Artificial Intelligence.
Website: http://www.braincities.co
Phone: **Email:** hello@braincities.co
City: Paris **State:** IDF **PC:** **Country: France**
Year Established: **Status 2020:** Active
Industries: Analytics for:, Artificial Intelligence for:, Databases for:, Machine Learning for:, Predictive Analytics

Company Name: Brennus Analytics
Description: Brennus is an AI-powered pricing solution for B2B companies.
Website: http://brennus-analytics.com
Phone: 33 9 70 09 10 09 **Email:** contact@brennus-analytics.com
City: Paris **State:** IDF **PC:** **Country: France**
Year Established: 2015 **Status 2020:** Active
Industries: Artificial Intelligence for:, Business Applications for:, Big Data and Analytics for:, Business Intelligence for:, Enterprise Application Services

Company Name: CallDesk
Description: CallDesk is a customer service start up.
Website: http://www.calldesk.ai/index.html
Phone: (819)861-436 **Email:** contact@calldesk.ai
City: Paris **State:** IDF **PC:** **Country: France**
Year Established: **Status 2020:** Active
Industries: Artificial Intelligence for:, IT Managed Services

Company Name: Cardabel
Description: Cardabel provides a new management of risks and frauds in capital markets activities leveraging unsupervised machine learning research.
Website: http://cardabel.com
Phone: 646 250 0030 **Email:** sales@cardabel.com
City: Paris **State:** IDF **PC:** **Country: France**
Year Established: 2015 **Status 2020:** Active
Industries: Artificial Intelligence for:, ~ Education (13), Security for:, Machine Learning

Company Name: CardioLogs
Description: CardioLogs is a medical technology startup that uses AI to cloud technology to help detect heart conditions.
Website: http://www.cardiologs.com/
Phone: 33 1 42 61 32 16 **Email:** contact@cardiologs.com
City: Paris **State:** IDF **PC:** **Country: France**
Year Established: 2014 **Status 2020:** Active
Industries: Artificial Intelligence for:, Big Data and Analytics for:, ~ Healthcare (20), ~ Healthcare (20), Machine Learning

Company Name: Citodi
Description: Citodi is an artificial intelligence solution for routing optimization that takes into consideration all variables of a delivery.
Website: http://www.citodi.com
Phone: 33185762029 **Email:** contact@citodi.fr
City: Paris **State:** IDF **PC:** **Country: France**
Year Established: **Status 2020:** Active
Industries: Artificial Intelligence for:, Big Data and Analytics for:, ~ Transportation and Logistics (57), ~ Transportation and Logistics (57), ~ Transportation and Logistics (57), Compute for:, ~ Transportation and Logistics (57)

Company Name: Clustaar
Description: Clustaar is a chatbot platform dedicated to customer support automation for all businesses and apps.
Website: http://clustaar.com/
Phone: 33 6 51 42 79 05 **Email:** contact@clustaar.com
City: Paris **State:** IDF **PC:** **Country: France**
Year Established: 2013 **Status 2020:** Active
Industries: ~ Customer Relationship Management (11), Machine Learning for:, Natural Language Processing for:, Business Software as a Service Apps (SaaS Apps)

Company Name: Clustree
Description: Clustree offers an artificial intelligence solution that makes career management accessible to all employees.
Website: http://www.clustree.com/en/
Phone: **Email:** hello@clustree.com
City: Paris **State:** IDF **PC:** **Country: France**

Year Established: 2014 **Status 2020:** Active
Industries:

Company Name: Cobbai
Description: Eradicate Non Quality with AI
Website: https://cobbai.com/
Phone: **Email:** 36297@reference-encyclopedia-ai.net
City: Paris **State:** IDF **PC:** **Country: France**
Year Established: **Status 2020:** Active
Industries: Analytics for:, Artificial Intelligence

Company Name: Collective Thinking
Description: Collective Thinking is specialized in the analysis of large amounts of qualitative data.
Website: http://www.collective-thinking.com
Phone: (3378) 116-2840 **Email:** contact@collective-thinking.com
City: Paris **State:** IDF **PC:** **Country: France**
Year Established: 2013 **Status 2020:** Active
Industries: Analytics for:, Artificial Intelligence for:, Machine Learning

Company Name: ContentSquare
Description: ContentSquare is a specialist for optimizing Web and mobile sites.
Website: http://www.contentsquare.com/
Phone: 33183758800 **Email:** contact@content-square.fr
City: Paris **State:** IDF **PC:** **Country: France**
Year Established: **Status 2020:** Active
Industries: Artificial Intelligence for:, E-Commerce for:, Web for:, Cyber Security

Company Name: craft ai
Description: Craft Ai provides AI-as-a-service for Mobile, Web and IoT. craft ai enables developers to bring awareness and learning to their apps.
Website: http://craft.ai
Phone: 33155431320 **Email:** contact@craft.ai
City: Paris **State:** IDF **PC:** **Country: France**
Year Established: **Status 2020:** Active
Industries: Artificial Intelligence for:, Enterprise Application Services for:, Machine Learning for:, ~ Professional Services (48)

Company Name: Cupido
Description: Askcupido provides an AI-based profile analyzing API for dating apps to increase user retention and engagement.
Website: http://askcupido.com
Phone: **Email:** 36360@reference-encyclopedia-ai.net
City: Paris **State:** IDF **PC:** **Country: France**
Year Established: 2019 **Status 2020:** Active
Industries: Artificial Intelligence for:, Business Applications for:, Business Applications for:, Computer Vision for:, Web for:, Machine Learning

Company Name: CybelAngel
Description: CybelAngel is a cybersecurity startup watching over the precious data of some of the world's biggest companies.
Website: http://www.cybelangel.com
Phone: **Email:** contact@cybelangel.com
City: Paris **State:** IDF **PC:** **Country: France**
Year Established: **Status 2020:** Active
Industries: Artificial Intelligence for:, Cyber Security for:, Machine Learning for:, Compute for:, Security

Company Name: Cyclope.ai
Description: Cyclope is an innovative high-tech company specialized in artificial intelligence applied to video analysis and image processing.
Website: http://cyclope.ai/en/home.html
Phone: **Email:** 36371@reference-encyclopedia-ai.net
City: Paris **State:** IDF **PC:** **Country: France**
Year Established: 2017 **Status 2020:** Active
Industries: Artificial Intelligence for:, IT Managed Services for:, IT Managed Services

Company Name: DATA2B
Description: New player in the Big Data and Data Science World, Data2B revolutionizes the way how the world works with data by offering data products.
Website: http://www.data2b.net
Phone: **Email:** 36385@reference-encyclopedia-ai.net
City: Paris **State:** IDF **PC:** **Country: France**
Year Established: 2015 **Status 2020:** Active
Industries: Analytics for:, Artificial Intelligence for:, Big Data and Analytics for:, IT Managed Services

Company Name: DataHawk Technologies
Description: DataHawk is a SaaS analytics tool that helps the 2M Amazon marketplace sellers grow by leveraging unique data insights.
Website: http://datahawk.co
Phone: **Email:** contact@datahawk.co
City: Paris **State:** IDF **PC:** **Country: France**
Year Established: 2017 **Status 2020:** Active
Industries: Analytics for:, E-Commerce for:, Predictive Analytics for:, Business Software as a Service Apps (SaaS Apps)

Company Name: DatakaLab
Description: The Braintech startup that uses neuroscientific tools and AI algorithms to quantify users emotions and improve customer behavior
Website: http://www.datakalab.com
Phone: 33 6 25 52 49 21 **Email:** hello@datakalab.com
City: Paris **State:** IDF **PC:** **Country: France**
Year Established: 2017 **Status 2020:** Active
Industries: Artificial Intelligence

Company Name: Datap
Description: Datap is a Chrome extension that uses advanced AI to turn any website into structured data.
Website: http://datap.io/
Phone: **Email:** contact@datap.io
City: Paris **State:** IDF **PC:** **Country: France**
Year Established: **Status 2020:** Active
Industries: Artificial Intelligence for:, Cyber Security

Company Name: DATASA: MOROCCO
Description: DATASAMA is a Machine Learning platform.
Website: http://www.datasama.com/
Phone: 33 6 27 48 44 31 **Email:** contact@datasama.com
City: Paris **State:** IDF **PC:** **Country: France**
Year Established: 2014 **Status 2020:** Active
Industries: Analytics

Company Name: Datavey: Spain
Description: Dataveyes is a professional who focuses on human data interactions and help people understand, operate and communicate their data.
Website: http://dataveyes.com
Phone: **Email:** contact@dataveyes.com
City: Paris **State:** IDF **PC:** **Country: France**
Year Established: 2010 **Status 2020:** Active
Industries: Artificial Intelligence for:, IT Managed Services for:, Internet of Things (IoT)

Company Name: DCODE.AI -
Description: HelloEarnest is the first AI based Virtual Travel Manager with focus on Business Travels.
Website:
Phone: **Email:** 36404@reference-encyclopedia-ai.net
City: Paris **State:** IDF **PC:** **Country: France**
Year Established: 2018 **Status 2020:** Active
Industries:

Company Name: DECONSEIL
Description: Energy broker by AI in France
Website: http://deconseil.com
Phone: (97) 236-4539 **Email:** contact@deconseil.com
City: Paris **State:** IDF **PC:** **Country: France**

Year Established: 2019 **Status 2020:** Active
Industries: Artificial Intelligence for:, ~ Energy and Utilities (14), IT Managed Services

Company Name: Deepomatic
Description: Visual Automation Platform. Deepomatic enables companies to set up Vision-based solutions to augment workers and customers.
Website: http://www.deepomatic.com
Phone: **Email:** hey@deepomatic.com
City: Paris **State:** IDF **Zip:** 73003 **Country: France**
Year Established: **Status 2020:** Active
Industries: Artificial Intelligence for:, Computer Vision for:, ~ Energy and Utilities (1417), ~ Healthcare (1423), ~ Manufacturing-Electronic (1433), ~ Manufacturing-General (1434), ~ Manufacturing-Machinery (1435), ~ Telecommunications (1459), ~ Transportation and Logistic

Company Name: DeepOR
Description: The 1st Smart Assistant in the Hospital Operating Room
Website: http://deepor.ai
Phone: 33.7.55.75.14.42 **Email:** contact@deepor.ai
City: Paris **State:** IDF **PC:** **Country: France**
Year Established: **Status 2020:** Active
Industries: Artificial Intelligence for:, ~ Healthcare (20)

Company Name: Deepsight
Description: Deepsight provides a SaaS predictive planning solution for retail stor: Spain
Website: http://deepsight.io
Phone: **Email:** brice@deepsight.io
City: Paris **State:** IDF **PC:** **Country: France**
Year Established: 2016 **Status 2020:** Active
Industries: Artificial Intelligence for:, Predictive Analytics for:, ~ Food and Beverage (17), ~ Social Assistance-Non-Profits (53)

Company Name: Dental Monitoring
Description: DENTAL MONITORING is the world's first web and mobile application designed for self-monitoring dental treatment.
Website: http://dental-monitoring.com
Phone: 33(0)186950101 **Email:** contact@dental-monitoring.com
City: Paris **State:** IDF **PC:** **Country: France**
Year Established: 2013 **Status 2020:** Active
Industries: Artificial Intelligence for:, ~ Healthcare (20), Machine Learning

Company Name: Doctrine
Description: Doctrine builds a legal research and analytics software for legal professionals.
Website: http://www.doctrine.fr
Phone: 33 1 86 95 42 09 **Email:** contact@doctrine.fr
City: Paris **State:** IDF **PC:** **Country: France**
Year Established: **Status 2020:** Active
Industries: Analytics for:, Artificial Intelligence for:, ~ Law-Legal Services (26)

Company Name: Domoscio
Description: Domoscio is a French start-up specialized in Big Data for learning.
Website: http://www.domoscio.com/
Phone: **Email:** contact@domoscio.com
City: Paris **State:** IDF **PC:** **Country: France**
Year Established: 2013 **Status 2020:** Active
Industries: Artificial Intelligence for:, ~ Education (13), IT Managed Services for:, ~ Education (13)

Company Name: Dotsify
Description: AI & Neuroscience
Website: http://www.dotsify.com
Phone: **Email:** contact@dotsify.com
City: Paris **State:** IDF **PC:** **Country: France**
Year Established: 2018 **Status 2020:** Active
Industries: Artificial Intelligence

Company Name: DreamQuark
Description: DreamQuark helps banks, insurance companies, and asset management firms for all their artificial intelligence needs.
Website: http://www.dreamquark.com
Phone: **Email:** contact@dreamquark.com
City: Paris **State:** IDF **PC:** **Country: France**
Year Established: **Status 2020:** Active
Industries: Artificial Intelligence for:, ~ Banking and Financial Markets-Services (7), ~ Banking and Financial Markets-Services (7), ~ Insurance (25)

Company Name: DreamUp Vision
Description: DreamUp Vision is building an innovative analysis technics which uses machine learning engines to perform retinal diseases screening
Website: http://dreamupvision.com/
Phone: **Email:** contact@dreamupvision.com
City: Paris **State:** IDF **PC:** **Country: France**
Year Established: **Status 2020:** Active
Industries: Artificial Intelligence for:, Big Data and Analytics for:, ~ Healthcare (20), ~ Healthcare (20), ~ Manufacturing-Medical Equipment-Supplies (33)

Company Name: DRUST
Description: DRUST is an automotive intelligence platform that powers connected and driver-oriented services, from any data source.
Website: http://drust.com
Phone: **Email:** contact@drust.io
City: Paris **State:** IDF **PC:** **Country: France**
Year Established: **Status 2020:** Active
Industries: Artificial Intelligence for:, ~ Automotive (5), Big Data and Analytics for:, ~ Professional Services (48)

Company Name: Eiffo Analytics
Description: Eiffo Analytics develops SaaS to implement AI in businesses.
Website: http://www.eiffo-analytics.com/
Phone: **Email:** contact@eiffo-analytics.com
City: Paris **State:** IDF **PC:** **Country: France**
Year Established: 2019 **Status 2020:** Active
Industries: Artificial Intelligence for:, Business Software as a Service Apps (SaaS Apps)

Company Name: EliteWay
Description: EliteWay helps runners of all levels improve through training plans generated by Artificial Intelligence.
Website: http://elite-way.com/en
Phone: **Email:** 36491@reference-encyclopedia-ai.net
City: Paris **State:** IDF **PC:** **Country: France**
Year Established: 2017 **Status 2020:** Active
Industries: Artificial Intelligence

Company Name: Elum
Description: Elum bring artificial intelligence to renewable energy systems to reduce electricity costs.
Website: http://elum-energy.com/
Phone: 33 6 87 99 61 88 **Email:** contact@elum-energy.com
City: Paris **State:** IDF **PC:** **Country: France**
Year Established: 2015 **Status 2020:** Active
Industries:

Company Name: ESA Business Applications
Description: Your business powered by Space
Website: http://business.esa.int
Phone: **Email:** business@esa.int
City: Paris **State:** IDF **PC:** **Country: France**
Year Established: **Status 2020:** Active
Industries: ~ Agriculture (3), Artificial Intelligence for:, Cyber Security for:, ~ Government (19), ~ Healthcare (20), ~ Insurance (25)

Company Name: Euler Hermes Digital Agency
Description: Euler Hermes Digital Agency is a reinvents trade finance and support long term growth with disruptive innovations.
Website: http://www.ehda.co/
Phone: 33 1 84 11 32 30 **Email:** 36523@reference-encyclopedia-ai.net
City: Paris **State:** IDF **PC:** **Country: France**
Year Established: 2015 **Status 2020:** Active
Industries: Artificial Intelligence for:, ~ Banking and Financial Markets-Services (7), ~ Banking and Financial Markets-Services (7), Machine Learning

Company Name: Evergig
Description: Concerts' massively multi-pov videos
Website: http://www.evergig.com
Phone: 33 6 60 67 77 97 **Email:** contact@evergig.com
City: Paris **State:** IDF **PC:** **Country: France**
Year Established: **Status 2020:** Active
Industries: Artificial Intelligence for:, ~ Arts-Entertainment-Recreation (4), ~ Media-Communications (41)

Company Name: Expenli -
Description: Expenli is developing an expert marketplace for legal, medical, automotive
Website:
Phone: **Email:** 36534@reference-encyclopedia-ai.net
City: Paris **State:** IDF **PC:** **Country: France**
Year Established: 2013 **Status 2020:** Active
Industries: Natural Language Processing

Company Name: FASTE | The Smart Luxury Marketplace
Description: The first marketplace of high-end services and products designed to become the one-stop solution for travel and lifestyle markets.
Website: http://www.faste.com
Phone: 33781688738 **Email:** concierge@faste.com
City: Paris **State:** IDF **PC:** **Country: France**
Year Established: **Status 2020:** Active
Industries: Artificial Intelligence for:, Business Applications for:, Business Applications for:, ~ Hospitality (23), ~ Travel and Transportation (58), ~ Travel and Transportation (58)

Company **Name:** Favizone
Description: Favizone is a SaaS solution to automate conversational commerce and customer service through multilingual and multichannel virtual assistant
Website: http://www.favizone.com
Phone: 33 1 82 88 67 97 **Email:** contact@favizone.com
City: Paris **State:** IDF **PC:** **Country: France**
Year Established: 2016 **Status 2020:** Active
Industries: Application Services for:, Artificial Intelligence for:, E-Commerce for:, IT Managed Services for:, Mobile for:, Business Software as a Service Apps (SaaS Apps)

Company Name: FiftyFor
Description: B2B rating platform of African compani: Spain
Website: http://www.fiftyfor.com/
Phone: 33 1 84 17 20 66 **Email:** contact@fiftyfor.com
City: Paris **State:** IDF **PC:** **Country: France**
Year Established: 2011 **Status 2020:** Active
Industries: Business Applications for:, ~ Banking and Financial Markets-Services (7), ~ Banking and Financial Markets-Services (7), Predictive Analytics

Company Name: Fivve
Description: Employees Smart Mobility Assistant
Website: http://www.fivve.io
Phone: **Email:** thibault@sparkhorizon.com
City: Paris **State:** IDF **PC:** **Country: France**
Year Established: 2018 **Status 2020:** Active
Industries: Artificial Intelligence for:, IT Managed Services

Company Name: Flowlity
Description: Flowlity is the first Cogntive Supply Chain Network, using AI to optimize stock levels, reduce shortages and avoid lost sales.
Website: http://www.flowlity.com
Phone: **Email:** jbc@flowlity.com
City: Paris **State:** IDF **PC:** **Country: France**
Year Established: **Status 2020:** Active
Industries: Artificial Intelligence for:, Machine Learning for:, Supply Chain Management

Company Name: Foxintelligence
Description: Foxintelligence is the first company in Europe to provide market data based on online transactions. We are a privacy by design company.
Website: http://foxintelligence.fr/
Phone: (33) 06.20.94.64.24 **Email:** edouard@misterfox.co
City: Paris **State:** IDF **PC:** **Country: France**
Year Established: **Status 2020:** Active
Industries: Artificial Intelligence for:, Big Data and Analytics for:, Business Intelligence for:, ~ Media-Communications (41)

Company Name: Fred de la compta
Description: Fred is a collaborative platform that dematerializes the entire administrative life of your company.
Website: http://www.freddelacompta.com/
Phone: (018)283-0837 **Email:** bonjour@freddelacompta.com
City: Paris **State:** IDF **PC:** **Country: France**
Year Established: **Status 2020:** Active
Industries: Artificial Intelligence for:, ~ Social Media (54), ~ Social Media (54), ~ Professional Services (48)

Company Name: futurescore.io
Description: Steer your future offer : futurescore.io combines client survey with AI to measure and localize the match between your ideas and the demand
Website: http://www.futurescore.io
Phone: 33140079511 **Email:** contact@futurescore.io
City: Paris **State:** IDF **PC:** **Country: France**
Year Established: **Status 2020:** Active
Industries: Artificial Intelligence for:, Databases for:, Digital Marketing for:, Machine Learning for:, ~ Media-Communications (41), ~ Professional Services (48), ~ Retail and Consumer Products (52)

Company Name: Geekste: Serbia
Description: Transforming ideas into applications
Website: http://geeksters.co
Phone: **Email:** hello@geeksters.co
City: Paris **State:** IDF **PC:** **Country: France**
Year Established: 2013 **Status 2020:** Active
Industries: Artificial Intelligence for:, Web for:, Application Services for:, Web

Company Name: GEO4CAST
Description: an artificial intelligence platform for collecting, analysing and providing real time advanced location service
Website: http://www.geo4cast.ai
Phone: **Email:** antoine.couret@geo4cast.ai
City: Paris **State:** IDF **PC:** **Country: France**
Year Established: 2012 **Status 2020:** Active
Industries:

Company Name: Georges.tech
Description: Georges.tech offers an end-to-end and advanced AI-powered accounting software for freelancers and professionals.
Website: http://www.georges.tech/
Phone: (3377) 606-0918 **Email:** contact@georges.Tech
City: Paris **State:** IDF **PC:** **Country: France**
Year Established: 2016 **Status 2020:** Active
Industries: Finance and Accounting for:, Artificial Intelligence for:, ~ Banking and Financial Markets-Services (7)

Company Name: Gleamer
Description: Gleamer develops an AI-powered software to enhance radiologists productivity.
Website: http://www.gleamer.ai/
Phone: **Email:** contact@gleamer.ai
City: Paris **State:** IDF **PC:** **Country: France**
Year Established: 2017 **Status 2020:** Active
Industries: Artificial Intelligence

Company Name: Golem.ai
Description: Golem.ai is a natural language interpretation technology for developers.
Website: http://golem.ai/
Phone: **Email:** contact@golem.ai
City: Paris **State:** IDF **PC:** **Country: France**
Year Established: 2016 **Status 2020:** Active
Industries:

Company Name: Good Tech Lab
Description: Impact, Research, Data, DeepTech
Website: http://goodtechlab.io
Phone: **Email:** hello@goodtechlab.io
City: Paris **State:** IDF **PC:** **Country: France**
Year Established: 2017 **Status 2020:** Active
Industries: Analytics for:, Artificial Intelligence for:, ~ Banking and Financial Markets-Services (7), IT Managed Services

Company Name: GrAI Matter Labs
Description: GrAI Matter Labs, a pioneer of ultra-low power neuromorphic computing.
Website: http://www.graimatterlabs.ai/
Phone: **Email:** 36639@reference-encyclopedia-ai.net
City: Paris **State:** IDF **PC:** **Country: France**
Year Established: 2016 **Status 2020:** Active
Industries: Company Name: Hadrian Advisors
Description: Hadrian Advisors is a research facility offering machine learning and data-mining technologies company located in Paris.
Website: http://hadrian-advisors.com
Phone: 33-1-82-83-75-40 **Email:** contact@hadrian-advisors.com
City: Paris **State:** IDF **PC:** **Country: France**
Year Established: 2014 **Status 2020:** Active
Industries: Analytics for:, Databases for:, Machine Learning

Company Name: HandsCart
Description: HandsCart is a machine learning marketplace.
Website: http://handscart.com/
Phone: 33-755757571 **Email:** support@handscart.com
City: Paris **State:** IDF **PC:** **Country: France**
Year Established: 2015 **Status 2020:** Active
Industries: Machine Learning

Company Name: Heex Technologies
Description: Heex Technologies offers a smart data management software improving access to relevant data for autonomous driving.
Website: http://heex.io
Phone: **Email:** contact@heex.io
City: Paris **State:** IDF **PC:** **Country: France**
Year Established: 2019 **Status 2020:** Active
Industries: Artificial Intelligence for:, ~ Automotive (5), Blockchain for:, Machine Learning for:, Robotics

Company Name: Heuri
Description: Big Data Analytics and Machine Learning
Website: http://www.heuritech.com
Phone: 33620546180 **Email:** info@heuritech.com
City: Paris **State:** IDF **PC:** **Country: France**
Year Established: **Status 2020:** Active
Industries: Artificial Intelligence for:, ~ Fashion (16), Image Recognition for:, IT Managed Services for:, IT Managed Services for:, Data Management

Company Name: Homeys
Description: Energy efficiency in buildings | IoT & AI
Website: http://www.homeys.io
Phone: 33 1 45 81 72 03 **Email:** contact@homeys.io
City: Paris **State:** IDF **PC:** **Country: France**
Year Established: **Status 2020:** Active
Industries: Artificial Intelligence for:, Big Data and Analytics for:, ~ Energy and Utilities (14), ~ Energy and Utilities (14), Machine Learning

Company Name: HostnFly
Description: HostnFly is a B2C start-up that develops machine-learning algorithms to optimize revenue on platforms like Airbnb.
Website: http://www.hostnfly.com
Phone: 33 (0) 1 86 76 12 82 **Email:** contact@hostnfly.com
City: Paris **State:** IDF **PC:** **Country: France**
Year Established: 2016 **Status 2020:** Active
Industries: Web for:, Machine Learning for:, ~ Customer Relationship Management (11)

Company Name: Hub France IA
Description: Hub France IA is an organization to develop a French initiative in the fields of AI.
Website: http://www.hub-franceia.fr/
Phone: **Email:** melanie.arnould@hub-franceia.fr
City: Paris **State:** IDF **PC:** **Country: France**
Year Established: 2017 **Status 2020:** Active
Industries: Artificial Intelligence for:, Machine Learning

Company Name: Hubstai: Serbia
Description: Hubstairs is a AI/3D visual merchandising platform empowering Homeware Retailers, Realtors, Medias to create scalable dynamic visual content
Website: http://www.hubstairs.com
Phone: **Email:** contact@hubstairs.com
City: Paris **State:** IDF **PC:** **Country: France**
Year Established: 2016 **Status 2020:** Active
Industries: Artificial Intelligence for:, Content for:, Content for:, Web for:, Web for:, Computer Vision

Company Name: Hyperlex
Description: Hyperlex is the #1 intelligent contract management platform that helps you organize and annotate your legal documents
Website: http://www.hyperlex.ai
Phone: **Email:** contact@hyperlex.fr
City: Paris **State:** IDF **PC:** **Country: France**
Year Established: **Status 2020:** Active
Industries:

Company Name: Hyphen
Description: Automating B2C Conversations with AI
Website: http://hyphen.ai
Phone: (078)084-4831 **Email:** info@hyphen.ai
City: Paris **State:** IDF **PC:** **Country: France**
Year Established: **Status 2020:** Active
Industries: Artificial Intelligence for:, Machine Learning

Company Name: Ideo Parfumeurs
Description: Perfume creation brand ready to wear and Artificial Intelligence based bespoke perfume creations
Website: http://www.ideoparfumeurs.com
Phone: **Email:** contact@ideoparfums.com
City: Paris **State:** IDF **PC:** **Country: France**
Year Established: 2018 **Status 2020:** Active
Industries: Artificial Intelligence for:, E-Commerce

Company Name: Ideta
Description: Ideta is a solution of conversational intelligence and process automation.
Website: http://meet-ideta.com/
Phone: **Email:** contact@meet-ideta.com
City: Paris **State:** IDF **PC:** **Country: France**

Year Established: 2017 **Status 2020:** Active
Industries: Artificial Intelligence for:, IT Managed Services for:, Machine Learning for:, Robotics

Company Name: IKO System
Description: IKO System is an outbound prospecting & email engagement platform for B2B sales & marketing professionals.
Website: http://www.iko-system.com
Phone: **Email:** nico@iko-system.com
City: Paris **State:** IDF **PC:** **Country: France**
Year Established: 2010 **Status 2020:** Active
Industries: ~ E-Commerce (12), Predictive Analytics for:, Automation

Company Name: Iktos
Description: Artificial Intelligence for new drug design
Website: http://www.iktos.ai
Phone: **Email:** adam.skiredj@iktos.com
City: Paris **State:** IDF **PC:** **Country: France**
Year Established: **Status 2020:** Active
Industries: Artificial Intelligence for:, ~ Manufacturing-Petroleum-Coal-Chemicals-Plastics-Rubber (37), ~ Pharmaceuticals (46)

Company **Name:** Impala
Description: Blending Data & Human Sciences to help you find your career pa:Thailand
Website: http://impala.in/
Phone: **Email:** contact@impala.: India
City: Paris **State:** IDF **PC:** **Country: France**
Year Established: **Status 2020:** Active
Industries: Artificial Intelligence

Company Name: Inato
Description: Inato is a platform designed for clinical trials that can unlock research site potential.
Website: http://inato.com
Phone: **Email:** contact@inato.com
City: Paris **State:** IDF **PC:** **Country: France**
Year Established: 2016 **Status 2020:** Active
Industries: Artificial Intelligence for:, ~ Healthcare (20), Machine Learning

Company Name: Incepto Medical
Description: Incepto Medical is a Medical imaging solution based on artificial intelligence
Website: http://incepto-medical.com/
Phone: **Email:** 36752@reference-encyclopedia-ai.net
City: Paris **State:** IDF **PC:** **Country: France**
Year Established: 2018 **Status 2020:** Active
Industries: Artificial Intelligence for:, ~ Healthcare (20), IT Managed Services for:, IT Managed Services for:, ~ Healthcare (20)

Company Name: Indexi: Morocco
Description: Indexima is creating momentum for Data Driven companies aiming for Zero Time to Data.
Website: http://indexima.com/
Phone: (3361) 232-1946 **Email:** 36754@reference-encyclopedia-ai.net
City: Paris **State:** IDF **PC:** **Country: France**
Year Established: 2016 **Status 2020:** Active
Industries:

Company Name: Influans
Description: Influans powers the ultimate personalization of marketing through a next-generation, cloud platform.
Website: http://www.influans.com/
Phone: **Email:** contact@influans.com
City: Paris **State:** IDF **PC:** **Country: France**
Year Established: 2014 **Status 2020:** Active
Industries: Big Data and Analytics for:, Machine Learning

Company Name: Insiliance
Description: AI for CNS drug (re)positioning and treatment optimization
Website: http://www.insiliance.com
Phone: **Email:** 36777@reference-encyclopedia-ai.net
City: Paris **State:** IDF **PC:** **Country: France**
Year Established: 2019 **Status 2020:** Active
Industries: Artificial Intelligence for:, ~ Biotechnology (9)

Company Name: InU: Sweden
Description: Software editor founded in 2015, offering a SaaS application that delivers IoT based connected services for factori: Spain
Website: http://inuse.eu
Phone: **Email:** contact@inuse.eu
City: Paris **State:** IDF **PC:** **Country: France**
Year Established: 2015 **Status 2020:** Active
Industries: Artificial Intelligence for:, Big Data and Analytics for:, Internet of Things (IoT) for:, Business Software as a Service Apps (SaaS Apps)

Company Name: Inven
Description: Invenis Helps Data Driven Businesses Taking Better Business Decisions Powered by Big Data and Artificial Intelligence
Website: http://www.invenis.co
Phone: 337 71 67 70 91 **Email:** hello@invenis.co
City: Paris **State:** IDF **PC:** **Country: France**
Year Established: 2015 **Status 2020:** Active
Industries: Artificial Intelligence for:, Big Data and Analytics

Company Name: IPwe
Description: IPwe is patent market that combines the information and tools to identify, research, understand and transact in patents.
Website: http://ipwe.com
Phone: **Email:** Info@ipwe.com
City: Paris **State:** IDF **PC:** **Country: France**
Year Established: 2017 **Status 2020:** Active
Industries:

Company Name: iziwork
Description: temporary work marketplace
Website:
Phone: **Email:** 4409@reference-encyclopedia-ai.net
City: Paris **State:** IDF **PC:** **Country: France**
Year Established: **Status 2020:** Active
Industries: Artificial Intelligence for:, Big Data and Analytics for:, ~ Human Resources (24), IT Managed Services for:, Application Services for:, ~ Human Resources (24)

Company Name: Jam
Description: Jam is a creator of SMS texting response service based on artificial intelligence.
Website: http://hellojam.fr
Phone: 33659130083 **Email:** team@hellojam.fr
City: Paris **State:** IDF **PC:** **Country: France**
Year Established: **Status 2020:** Active
Industries: Artificial Intelligence for:, ~ Education (13), ~ Telecommunications (56)

Company Name: Jellynote
Description: Jellynote is an EdTech startup offering an innovative way to learn music through its proprietary AI-technology
Website: http://www.jellynote.com
Phone: **Email:** contact@jellynote.com
City: Paris **State:** IDF **PC:** **Country: France**
Year Established: **Status 2020:** Active
Industries: Artificial Intelligence for:, ~ Education (13), ~ Arts-Entertainment-Recreation (4)

Company Name: Jola
Description: Risk analytics and brokerage platform
Website: http://www.jolasolutions.com
Phone: **Email:** info@jolasolutions.com
City: Paris **State:** IDF **PC:** **Country: France**

Year Established: 2018 **Status 2020:** Active
Industries: Machine Learning

Company Name: Julie Desk
Description: Julie Desk is a virtual assistant that uses artificial intelligence to schedule meetings and appointments of a user.
Website: http://www.juliedesk.com/
Phone: 1(415)712-0083 **Email:** contact@juliedesk.com
City: Paris **State:** IDF **PC: Country: France**
Year Established: Status 2020: Active
Industries: Artificial Intelligence for:, ~ Media-Communications (41), Application Services

Company Name: Jus Mundi
Description: The Search Engine for International Law
Website: http://jusmundi.com/en/
Phone: 33 6 40 73 11 93 **Email:** jr.demaistre@jusmundi.com
City: Paris **State:** IDF **PC: Country: France**
Year Established: Status 2020: Active
Industries: Artificial Intelligence for:, Web for:, ~ Law-Legal Services (26), ~ Law-Legal Services (26), Machine Learning for:, ~ Professional Services (48)

Company Name: Karos
Description: Karos transform available car seats into public transport networks, leveraging AI and mobile technologies.
Website: http://www.karos.fr/
Phone: Email: contact@karos.fr
City: Paris **State:** IDF **PC: Country: France**
Year Established: Status 2020: Active
Industries: Artificial Intelligence for:, Machine Learning for:, Application Services for:, ~ Social Media (54)

Company Name: Kayrros
Description: Kayrros is an advanced data analytics company that helps global energy market participants make better investment decisions.
Website: http://www.kayrros.com/
Phone: Email: contact@kayrros.com
City: Paris **State:** IDF **PC: Country: France**
Year Established: Status 2020: Active
Industries: Analytics for:, Artificial Intelligence for:, Big Data and Analytics for:, Business Intelligence for:, ~ Energy and Utilities (14), ~ Banking and Financial Markets-Services (7), ~ Transportation and Logistics (57), Image Recognition for:, IT Managed Services

Company Name: Keen Eye Technologies
Description: Keen Eye Technologies is a health tech company.
Website: http://www.keeneye.tech/
Phone: 01 53 46 27 01 **Email:** contact@keeneye.tech
City: Paris **State:** IDF **PC: Country: France**
Year Established: 2015 **Status 2020:** Active
Industries: Artificial Intelligence for:, ~ Biotechnology (9), ~ Healthcare (20)

Company Name: Khresterion
Description: Khresterion is the editor of a reasoning engine based on exclusive algorithms of artificial intelligence.
Website: http://khresterion.com/
Phone: Email: contact@khresterion.com
City: Paris **State:** IDF **PC: Country: France**
Year Established: Status 2020: Active
Industries: Artificial Intelligence for:, ~ Professional Services (48)

Company Name: Kiwisoft
Description: Kiwisoft is a Machine Learning consulting firm.
Website: http://www.kiwisoft.fr
Phone: Email: contact@kiwisoft.fr
City: Paris **State:** IDF **PC: Country: France**
Year Established: 2013 **Status 2020:** Active
Industries: Machine Learning

Company Name: LabSen: Sweden
Description: LabSense develops artificial intelligence solutions (NLG; NLU) to ease communication.
Website: http://www.lab-sense.com/
Phone: 33 9 67 29 69 44 **Email:** contact@lab-sense.com
City: Paris **State:** IDF **PC: Country: France**
Year Established: 2011 **Status 2020:** Active
Industries: Artificial Intelligence for:, Web for:, ~ Metals and Mining (42)

Company Name: Lawgarithm
Description: Lawgarithm is an innovative company that offers software that uses artificial intelligence to address contracts.
Website: http://www.lawgarithm.net/
Phone: 837 758 556 **Email:** 36882@reference-encyclopedia-ai.net
City: Paris **State:** IDF **PC: Country: France**
Year Established: 2017 **Status 2020:** Active
Industries: Artificial Intelligence for:, Big Data and Analytics for:, IT Managed Services for:, Machine Learning

Company Name: LEELOO
Description: LEELOO improves foreign language conversational skills with industry and domain-specific chatbots.
Website:
Phone: Email: 36884@reference-encyclopedia-ai.net
City: Paris **State:** IDF **PC: Country: France**
Year Established: 2018 **Status 2020:** Active
Industries:

Company Name: LETTRIA
Description: LETTRIA is one of the most advanced Natural Language Processing players in the French-speaking market.
Website: http://lettria.com
Phone: Email: hello@lettria.com
City: Paris **State:** IDF **PC: Country: France**
Year Established: Status 2020: Active
Industries: Artificial Intelligence for:, ~ Education (13), ~ Professional Services (48)

Company Name: LightOn
Description: LightOn conceives and builds Optical Processing Units for Artificial Intelligence.
Website: http://www.lighton.io
Phone: Email: contact@lighton.io
City: Paris **State:** IDF **PC: Country: France**
Year Established: Status 2020: Active
Industries: Artificial Intelligence for:, ~ Manufacturing-Electronic (30)

Company Name: Lili.ai
Description: Artificial Intelligence applied to Project Management
Website: http://www.lili.ai
Phone: Email: human@lili.ai
City: Paris **State:** IDF **PC: Country: France**
Year Established: 2016 **Status 2020:** Active
Industries:

Company Name: Linkfluence
Description: Linkfluence, a social media intelligence company, analyzes conversations on social networks to create business opportunities for brands.
Website: http://linkfluence.com
Phone: 33 1 80 40 08 00 **Email:** contact@linkfluence.com
City: Paris **State:** IDF **PC: Country: France**
Year Established: Status 2020: Active
Industries: Analytics for:, Artificial Intelligence for:, ~ Media-Communications (41), Web for:, ~ Social Media (54), ~ Social Media (54), ~ Social Media (54), ~ Social Media (54)

Company Name: Lore Ai
Description: Lore's core system Salient automates document analysis, information extraction and knowledge management using Artificial Intelligence.
Website: http://www.lore.ai/
Phone: **Email:** info@lore.ai
City: Paris **State:** IDF **PC:** **Country: France**
Year Established: 2013 **Status 2020:** Active
Industries: Artificial Intelligence for:, IT Managed Services for:, Web

Company Name: Luko
Description: Luko is an insurance company that provides a device that focuses on home security and reduces electricity bills.
Website: http://www.getluko.com
Phone: 33 1 76 35 08 23 **Email:** hello@getluko.com
City: Paris **State:** IDF **PC:** **Country: France**
Year Established: 2016 **Status 2020:** Active
Industries: Artificial Intelligence

Company Name: Luxurynsight
Description: Luxurynsight smart data platform and data services provide luxury insights to leading luxury brands.
Website: http://www.luxurynsight.com/
Phone: 33 1 73 77 43 09 **Email:** support@luxurysight.com
City: Paris **State:** IDF **PC:** **Country: France**
Year Established: 2010 **Status 2020:** Active
Industries: Analytics for:, Artificial Intelligence for:, Databases for:, IT Managed Services

Company Name: MAJ
Description: SAS
Website: http://mosaicapp.io
Phone: (0033) 624219827 **Email:** anna@mosaicapp.io
City: Paris **State:** IDF **PC:** **Country: France**
Year Established: 2017 **Status 2020:** Active
Industries: Artificial Intelligence for:, Application Services

Company Name: Mee: Romania
Description: Meero is an AI company providing enhanced photography services.
Website: http://www.meero.com
Phone: (3317) 631-0052 **Email:** marketing@meero.com
City: Paris **State:** IDF **PC:** **Country: France**
Year Established: 2016 **Status 2020:** Active
Industries: Artificial Intelligence for:, Computer Vision for:, Machine Learning

Company Name: METRON
Description: METRON is a foundation stone using artificial intelligence based on Energy Data and ontologies.
Website: http://www.metronlab.com/
Phone: 33 (0)1 40 28 65 65 **Email:** info@metronlab.com
City: Paris **State:** IDF **PC:** **Country: France**
Year Established: 2013 **Status 2020:** Active
Industries: Artificial Intelligence for:, IT Managed Services

Company Name: mewo.io
Description: SaaS, Music, Artificial Intelligence
Website: http://mewo.io/
Phone: 33 1 82 83 75 80 **Email:** hello@mewo.io
City: Paris **State:** IDF **PC:** **Country: France**
Year Established: 2016 **Status 2020:** Active
Industries: Artificial Intelligence for:, E-Commerce for:, Web for:, ~ Arts-Entertainment-Recreation (4), Business Software as a Service Apps (SaaS Apps) for:, ~ Social Assistance-Non-Profits (53)

Company Name: Mindee
Description: Mindee transforms documents into usable data.
Website: http://mindee.co
Phone: 33 (0) 1 72 60 50 92 **Email:** contact@mindee.co
City: Paris **State:** IDF **PC:** **Country: France**
Year Established: 2018 **Status 2020:** Active
Industries: Analytics for:, Artificial Intelligence for:, IT Managed Services

Company Name: MindLytiX
Description: MindLytiX is a marketing and advertising data platform
Website: http://www.mindlytix.com/
Phone: 33 9 72 57 39 17 **Email:** contact@mindlytix.com
City: Paris **State:** IDF **PC:** **Country: France**
Year Established: **Status 2020:** Active
Industries: ~ Media-Communications (41), Artificial Intelligence for:, ~ Media-Communications (41)

Company Name: Mindsay
Description: Mindsay helps companies provide one-to-one care at scale with automated customer marketing.
Website: http://www.mindsay.com
Phone: **Email:** contact@mindsay.com
City: Paris **State:** IDF **PC:** **Country: France**
Year Established: 2016 **Status 2020:** Active
Industries:

Company Name: Mindsay
Description: Mindsay enables companies to provide 1-to-1 customer care at scale through Conversational AI.
Website: https://www.mindsay.com/
Phone: **Email:** bonnie.bailly@mindsay.com
City: Paris **State:** IDF **PC:** **Country: France**
Year Established: **Status 2020:** Active
Industries: Artificial Intelligence for:, ~ Banking and Financial Markets-Services (7), ~ E-Commerce (12), ~ Energy and Utilities (14), ~ Hospitality (23), ~ Insurance (25), ~ Telecommunications (56), ~ Transportation and Logistics (57), ~ Travel and Transportation (58), Auto

Company Name: Mirakl
Description:
Website: www.mirakl.com
Phone: 33 1 72 31 62 00 **Email:** info@mirakl.com
City: Paris **State:** IDF **Zip:** 75008 **Country: France**
Year Established: **Status 2020:** Active
Industries:

Company Name: monart
Description: Monart the innovative international art community & marketplace
Website: http://www.translatefx.com
Phone: **Email:** info@translatefx.com
City: Paris **State:** IDF **PC:** **Country: France**
Year Established: **Status 2020:** Active
Industries: ~ Arts-Entertainment-Recreation (4), Artificial Intelligence for:, Blockchain for:, ~ Banking and Financial Markets-Services (7)

Company Name: Monk.ai
Description: We create trust wherever an item changes hands by providing automated & objective condition reports showing every change.
Website: http://www.monk.ai
Phone: **Email:** 37013@reference-encyclopedia-ai.net
City: Paris **State:** IDF **PC:** **Country: France**
Year Established: 2019 **Status 2020:** Active
Industries: Artificial Intelligence for:, Computer Vision

Company Name: Moodstocks
Description: Moodstocks provides an API and ready-to-use cross-platform SDK for developers to integrate scanning.
Website: http://www.moodstocks.com
Phone: 33147704751 **Email:** contact@moodstocks.com
City: Paris **State:** IDF **PC:** **Country: France**
Year Established: **Status 2020:** Active
Industries: Artificial Intelligence for:, ~ Manufacturing-Electronic (30), Image Recognition for:, Machine Learning for:, Mobile for:, ~ Media-Communications (41), Compute for:, Computer Vision

Company Name: Mooves
Description: Mooves is a mobile cloud platform that offers sports clubs the ability to fully automate private & small group training for their custome: Serbia
Website: http://www.sportsmooves.com/en/
Phone: **Email:** contact@sportsmooves.com
City: Paris **State:** IDF **PC:** **Country: France**
Year Established: **Status 2020:** Active
Industries: Artificial Intelligence for:, Application Services for:, ~ Arts-Entertainment-Recreation (4), ~ Healthcare (20)

Company Name: Most: Romania
Description: AI and robotics for the recycling industry
Website: http://www.mostro.com
Phone: **Email:** contact@mostro.com
City: Paris **State:** IDF **PC:** **Country: France**
Year Established: 2018 **Status 2020:** Active
Industries: Artificial Intelligence for:, ~ Social-Environmental-Physical-Engineering Sciences (55), Robotics

Company Name: MyTraffic
Description: Location hunter for commercial real estate
Website: http://www.mytraffic.fr
Phone: **Email:** support@mytraffic.fr
City: Paris **State:** IDF **PC:** **Country: France**
Year Established: 2015 **Status 2020:** Active
Industries:

Company Name: Nabla
Description: Empowering people and businesses with machine intelligence
Website: http://www.nabla.com/
Phone: **Email:** 4537@reference-encyclopedia-ai.net
City: Paris **State:** IDF **PC:** **Country: France**
Year Established: **Status 2020:** Active
Industries: Artificial Intelligence

Company Name: NCODE.ai
Description: Digital Agency & AI
Website: http://www.ncode.ai/
Phone: **Email:** 37043@reference-encyclopedia-ai.net
City: Paris **State:** IDF **PC:** **Country: France**
Year Established: 2018 **Status 2020:** Active
Industries: Artificial Intelligence for:, Development and Test for:, Web for:, Web for:, Web

Company Name: Nexterite
Description: Nexterite provides crowdsourced and semantics transportation and business intelligence information solutions.
Website: http://www.nexterite.com/
Phone: **Email:** sales@nexterite.com
City: Paris **State:** IDF **PC:** **Country: France**
Year Established: **Status 2020:** Active
Industries: Artificial Intelligence for:, Business Intelligence for:, Databases for:, ~ Transportation and Logistics (57)

Company Name: niland
Description: Niland is a music technology company that provides music search & discovery engines based on Deep Learning & Machine Listening algorithms
Website: http://www.niland.io
Phone: **Email:** contac@niland.io
City: Paris **State:** IDF **PC:** **Country: France**
Year Established: **Status 2020:** Active
Industries: Artificial Intelligence for:, ~ Arts-Entertainment-Recreation (4), Cyber Security

Company Name: Novasecur
Description: Novasecur is an artificial intelligence decision-making software company that specializes in risk and fraud management.
Website: http://www.novasecur.com/
Phone: 33 170983405 **Email:** contact@novasecur.com
City: Paris **State:** IDF **PC:** **Country: France**
Year Established: 2010 **Status 2020:** Active
Industries: Artificial Intelligence for:, Risk Management

Company Name: Onogone
Description: Onogone is an AI software company that helps international clients automate and save time by doing math and writing code they own.
Website: http://www.onogone.com/
Phone: 33 1 42 40 13 80 **Email:** team@onogone.com
City: Paris **State:** IDF **PC:** **Country: France**
Year Established: 2016 **Status 2020:** Active
Industries:

Company Name: Open Mind Neurotechnologies
Description: VR biometrics AI-based assessments, behavioral & emotional neurotrainings for corporates - Future of jobs
Website: http://lab.omind.me/en/
Phone: 33188320123 **Email:** hello@omind.me
City: Paris **State:** IDF **PC:** **Country: France**
Year Established: 2016 **Status 2020:** Active
Industries: Artificial Intelligence for:, ~ Biotechnology (9), Machine Learning for:, ~ Education (13), Data Management for:, Virtual Reality (VR) for:, Virtual Reality (VR)

Company Name: Otherwise
Description: Otherwise is France's first collaborative (peer-to-peer) insurance broker.
Website: http://otherwise.fr/
Phone: 33975181300 **Email:** contact@otherwise.fr
City: Paris **State:** IDF **PC:** **Country: France**
Year Established: 2016 **Status 2020:** Active
Industries: Machine Learning for:, Network

Company Name: Outsight
Description: Outsight develops a revolutionary kind of sensor, a 3D Semantic Camera that brings Full Situation Awareness to Smart Machines and Cities.
Website: http://www.outsight.tech/
Phone: **Email:** 37130@reference-encyclopedia-ai.net
City: Paris **State:** IDF **PC:** **Country: France**
Year Established: 2019 **Status 2020:** Active
Industries: Artificial Intelligence for:, Robotics for:, ~ Customer Relationship Management (11)

Company Name: PacketAi
Description: PacketAI uses AI to automate IT Operations.
Website: http://www.packetai.co/
Phone: **Email:** hardik@packetai.co
City: Paris **State:** IDF **PC:** **Country: France**
Year Established: **Status 2020:** Active
Industries: Artificial Intelligence for:, IT Managed Services

Company Name: Padam
Description: Padam offers AI & mobile powered SaaS solutions for on-demand transit.
Website: https://padam-mobility.com/
Phone: **Email:** contact@padam.io
City: Paris **State:** IDF **Zip:** 75010 **Country: France**
Year Established: **Status 2020:** Active
Industries: Artificial Intelligence for:, ~ Automotive (5), ~ Transportation and Logistics (57), Business Applications for:, Enterprise Application Services for:, Mobile

Company Name: Pandascore
Description: PandaScore is an e-sport data and odds provider.
Website: http://www.pandascore.co
Phone: **Email:** flavien@pandascore.co
City: Paris **State:** IDF **PC:** **Country: France**
Year Established: 2015 **Status 2020:** Active
Industries: Artificial Intelligence for:, ~ Arts-Entertainment-Recreation (4), ~ Arts-Entertainment-Recreation (4)

Company Name: Paris Machine Learning Applications meetup
Description: The Paris Machine Learning meetup provides an avenue for Data Science and Machine Learning professionals to meet monthly in the Paris area.
Website: https://www.meetup.com/
Phone: **Email:** 37141@reference-encyclopedia-ai.net
City: Paris **State:** IDF **PC:** **Country: France**
Year Established: 2013 **Status 2020:** Active
Industries: Analytics for:, ~ Education (13)

Company Name: Pinpo
Description: Pinpo is a lead qualification as service solution for medium and large B2C compani: Spain
Website: http://www.pinpo.fr
Phone: **Email:** contact@pinpo.fr
City: Paris **State:** IDF **PC:** **Country: France**
Year Established: 2015 **Status 2020:** Active
Industries: Artificial Intelligence for:, Machine Learning for:, Business Software as a Service Apps (SaaS Apps)

Company Name: Plume Labs
Description: Plume Labs develops an app for personalized alerts and a personal air quality tracker.
Website: http://plumelabs.com
Phone: 33631865941 **Email:** team@plumelabs.com
City: Paris **State:** IDF **PC:** **Country: France**
Year Established: **Status 2020:** Active
Industries: Application Services for:, Artificial Intelligence for:, ~ Manufacturing-Electronic (30)

Company Name: Pocket Result
Description: Pocket Result solutions were designed on the basis of your needs.
Website: http://www.pocketresult.com/
Phone: **Email:** contact@pocketresult.com
City: Paris **State:** IDF **PC:** **Country: France**
Year Established: 2013 **Status 2020:** Active
Industries: Artificial Intelligence for:, Big Data and Analytics for:, Business Intelligence for:, Data Management for:, IT Managed Services for:, IT Managed Services for:, Machine Learning

Company Name: Ponicode
Description: Create, modify and visualise your Javascript unit tests in just a few clicks on our straightforward AI-powered interface.
Website: http://ponicode.com
Phone: **Email:** ping@ponicode.com
City: Paris **State:** IDF **PC:** **Country: France**
Year Established: 2019 **Status 2020:** Active
Industries: Artificial Intelligence for:, Application Services for:, Application Services

Company Name: Predictice
Description: Predictice provides real time, concrete, and strategic predictive analysis to law professionals.
Website: http://www.predictice.com/
Phone: 1 84 60 02 21 **Email:** contact@predictice.com
City: Paris **State:** IDF **PC:** **Country: France**
Year Established: 2015 **Status 2020:** Active
Industries: Analytics for:, Predictive Analytics for:, Compute

Company Name: PredictiveDB
Description: confidential data analysis in a click
Website: http://predictivedb.com
Phone: **Email:** contact@predictivedb.com
City: Paris **State:** IDF **PC:** **Country: France**
Year Established: 2010 **Status 2020:** Closed
Industries: Databases for:, Machine Learning for:, Business Software as a Service Apps (SaaS Apps) for:, Web

Company Name: Predilex
Description: Predilex develops an artificial intelligence-based solution for bodily injury claims
Website: http://predilex.io/
Phone: **Email:** contact@predilex.io
City: Paris **State:** IDF **PC:** **Country: France**
Year Established: **Status 2020:** Active
Industries:

Company Name: Pretto
Description: Pretto is making mortgages simple thanks to artificial intelligence and product design.
Website: http://www.pretto.fr/
Phone: **Email:** hello@pretto.fr
City: Paris **State:** IDF **PC:** **Country: France**
Year Established: 2016 **Status 2020:** Active
Industries: Artificial Intelligence for:, Web

Company Name: Prevision.io
Description: Prevision.io provides an automatic predictive analytics platform to immediately build and deploy predictive models (on-premises or cloud)
Website: http://www.prevision.io
Phone: **Email:** prevision@prevision.io
City: Paris **State:** IDF **PC:** **Country: France**
Year Established: **Status 2020:** Active
Industries: Artificial Intelligence for:, IT Managed Services

Company Name: Pricemoov
Description: Pricemoov is an AI-powered price management platform.
Website: http://www.pricemoov.com/
Phone: **Email:** contact@pricemoov.com
City: Paris **State:** IDF **PC:** **Country: France**
Year Established: **Status 2020:** Active
Industries: Artificial Intelligence for:, Big Data and Analytics for:, Machine Learning

Company Name: Prophesee
Description: Prophesee provides bio-inspired computer vision solutions for autonomous navigation and connected objects.
Website: http://www.prophesee.ai/
Phone: 33 (0) 1 85 73 27 33 **Email:** info@chronocam.com
City: Paris **State:** IDF **PC:** **Country: France**
Year Established: **Status 2020:** Active
Industries: Artificial Intelligence for:, ~ Automotive (5), ~ Automotive (5), ~ Transportation and Logistics (57), Robotics for:, ~ Manufacturing-Electronic (30)

Company Name: QantEv
Description: QantEv optimizes provider networks for health insurers.
Website: http://www.qantev.com/
Phone: **Email:** contact@qantev.com
City: Paris **State:** IDF **PC:** **Country: France**
Year Established: **Status 2020:** Active
Industries: Analytics for:, Artificial Intelligence

Company Name: Qopius
Description: Qopius digitizes shelves to help retailers measure shelf performance, increase productivity and reduce out-of-stock scenarios.
Website: http://www.qopius.com/
Phone: 33658620164 **Email:** contact@qopius.com
City: Paris **State:** IDF **PC:** **Country: France**
Year Established: 2015 **Status 2020:** Active
Industries: Artificial Intelligence for:, Computer Vision for:, ~ Retail and Consumer Products (52), Image Recognition for:, Internet of Things (IoT) for:, Robotics

Company Name: qsays.com
Description: Machine learning and augmented intelligence for business solutions.
Website: http://qsays.com
Phone: 33617521862 **Email:** lucian.vidrascu@qsays.com
City: Paris **State:** IDF **PC:** **Country: France**
Year Established: 2017 **Status 2020:** Active
Industries: Artificial Intelligence for:, Business Intelligence

Company Name: QuantCube Technology
Description: QuantCube Technology is a Fintech startup specialized in real-time Big Data analytics for Finance and Economy.
Website: http://www.q3-technology.com/
Phone: 33 1 43 58 48 46 **Email:** info@q3-technology.com
City: Paris **State:** IDF **PC:** **Country: France**
Year Established: 2013 **Status 2020:** Active
Industries: Analytics for:, Artificial Intelligence for:, ~ Banking and Financial Markets-Services (7), ~ Banking and Financial Markets-Services (7), IT Managed Services

Company Name: Quantmetry
Description: Quantmetry help our clients to manage Data Science and Big Data across various business functions such as Marketing, Sales, Finance.
Website: http://www.quantmetry.com/
Phone: **Email:** contact@quantmetry.com
City: Paris **State:** IDF **PC:** **Country: France**
Year Established: 2010 **Status 2020:** Active
Industries: Machine Learning

Company Name: Realytics
Description: Realytics is a real-time TV ads analytics platform for online brands.
Website: http://www.realytics.io
Phone: 33185092112 **Email:** contact@realytics.io
City: Paris **State:** IDF **PC:** **Country: France**
Year Established: 2013 **Status 2020:** Active
Industries: Analytics for:, Artificial Intelligence for:, Machine Learning for:, Compute for:, ~ Arts-Entertainment-Recreation (4)

Company Name: Recast.AI
Description: Automate conversation with AI
Website: http://recast.ai
Phone: **Email:** hello@recast.ai
City: Paris **State:** IDF **PC:** **Country: France**
Year Established: **Status 2020:** Active
Industries: Artificial Intelligence for:, Collaboration Solutions for:, Natural Language Processing

Company Name: reciTAL
Description: ReciTAL is an AI company specializing in natural language processing, providing automatic email processing and documents querying solutions.
Website: http://recital.ai/en/
Phone: **Email:** contact@recital.ai
City: Paris **State:** IDF **PC:** **Country: France**
Year Established: 2017 **Status 2020:** Active
Industries: Artificial Intelligence for:, Automation for:, Enterprise Application Services for:, Machine Learning for:, Natural Language Processing

Company Name: Reelevant
Description: Reelevant is an internet marketing service in Paris.
Website: http://www.reelevant.com
Phone: **Email:** team@reelevant.com
City: Paris **State:** IDF **PC:** **Country: France**
Year Established: 2016 **Status 2020:** Active
Industries: Artificial Intelligence for:, Business Software as a Service Apps (SaaS Apps)

Company Name: Regaind
Description: Regaind gives meaning to photos and help businesses and developers deal with massive flows of images by using AI to analyze and sort them.
Website: http://regaind.io/
Phone: **Email:** hello@regaind.io
City: Paris **State:** IDF **PC:** **Country: France**
Year Established: 2015 **Status 2020:** Active
Industries:

Company Name: Riminder
Description: Riminder operates as an AI assistant that automates talent assessment by leveraging state of the art deep learning technology.
Website: http://riminder.net
Phone: **Email:** contact@riminder.net
City: Paris **State:** IDF **PC:** **Country: France**
Year Established: **Status 2020:** Active
Industries: Artificial Intelligence for:, ~ Human Resources (24), ~ Human Resources (24)

Company Name: Robby
Description: Robby is Your Smart Calendar Powered by an AI Assistant
Website: http://www.robby.ai
Phone: **Email:** contact@robby.ai
City: Paris **State:** IDF **PC:** **Country: France**
Year Established: 2016 **Status 2020:** Active
Industries: Application Services for:, Artificial Intelligence for:, ~ Event Management (15), Mobile for:, Application Services for:, Web for:, ~ Social Assistance-Non-Profits (53)

Company Name: Robolution Capital
Description: Robolution Capital is the first private equity fund dedicated to service robotics in the world.
Website: http://www.robolutioncapital.com/
Phone: 33175442250 **Email:** info@robolutioncapital.com
City: Paris **State:** IDF **PC:** **Country: France**
Year Established: **Status 2020:** Active
Industries: Artificial Intelligence for:, ~ Banking and Financial Markets-Services (7), Robotics for:, ~ Banking and Financial Markets-Services (7)

Company Name: RTCX
Description: Using AI to provide real-time social media monitoring, sentiment analysis and engagement metrics for varied use cas: Spain
Website: http://rtcx.io
Phone: **Email:** info@rtcx.io
City: Paris **State:** IDF **PC:** **Country: France**
Year Established: **Status 2020:** Active
Industries: Artificial Intelligence for:, ~ Media-Communications (41), ~ Arts-Entertainment-Recreation (4), ~ Social Media (54)

Company Name: Sancare
Description: Sancare has designed a software to help coding hospital stays, able to predict diagnoses from the Computerized Patient Record.
Website: http://www.sancare.fr/
Phone: **Email:** 37336@reference-encyclopedia-ai.net
City: Paris **State:** IDF **PC:** **Country: France**
Year Established: 2016 **Status 2020:** Active
Industries: Artificial Intelligence for:, IT Managed Services

Company Name: scrudlabs
Description: saas
Website:
Phone: **Email:** 37351@reference-encyclopedia-ai.net
City: Paris **State:** IDF **PC:** **Country: France**
Year Established: 2017 **Status 2020:** Active
Industries: Artificial Intelligence for:, Blockchain

Company Name: Selectionnist
Description: An image recognition technology with the aim to connect print readers with the world's largest brands through an application or a chatbot
Website: http://business.selectionnist.com
Phone: **Email:** contact@selectionnist.com
City: Paris **State:** IDF **PC:** **Country: France**
Year Established: **Status 2020:** Active
Industries: ~ Media-Communications (41), Artificial Intelligence for:, ~ Beauty (8), Computer Vision for:, ~ Fashion (16), Image Recognition for:, Mobile

Company Name: Sensewav: Spain
Description: Predictive Analytics for Utilities, Gas, Water, and Industrial Assets
Website: http://sensewaves.io
Phone: **Email:** contact@sensewaves.io
City: Paris **State:** IDF **PC:** **Country: France**
Year Established: **Status 2020:** Active
Industries: Analytics for:, Artificial Intelligence for:, Big Data and Analytics for:, ~ Energy and Utilities (14), ~ Energy and Utilities (14), Automation for:, Machine Learning for:, Predictive Analytics for:, ~ Construction (10)

Company Name: Serenytics
Description: Serenytics offers a cloud-based all-in-one data platform (data pipeline - dataviz - python scheduler - AWS Redshift embedded).
Website: http://www.serenytics.com
Phone: 33 1 76 44 00 48 **Email:** contact@serenytics.com
City: Paris **State:** IDF **PC:** **Country: France**
Year Established: 2014 **Status 2020:** Active
Industries: Analytics for:, Business Intelligence for:, Cloud for:, IT Managed Services for:, Machine Learning for:, Business Software as a Service Apps (SaaS Apps)

Company Name: Shift Technology
Description: Shift Technology leverages the best of data science to automatically detect networks of fraudsters in insurance.
Website: http://www.shift-technology.com
Phone: 33172605058 **Email:** contact@shift-technology.com
City: Paris **State:** IDF **PC:** **Country: France**
Year Established: **Status 2020:** Active
Industries: Artificial Intelligence for:, Big Data and Analytics for:, IT Managed Services for:, ~ Insurance (25)

Company Name: SHORTOU: SWITZERLAND
Description: ShorTouch finds the strongest path of connection to any person/key-word you want to reach, by analyzing social info and emails.
Website: http://www.shortouch.com
Phone: **Email:** 37384@reference-encyclopedia-ai.net
City: Paris **State:** IDF **PC:** **Country: France**
Year Established: 2015 **Status 2020:** Active
Industries: Analytics for:, Predictive Analytics for:, Data Management

Company Name: Sicara
Description: Sicara provides advanced AI systems for B2B
Website: http://www.sicara.com/
Phone: **Email:** contact@sicara.com
City: Paris **State:** IDF **PC:** **Country: France**
Year Established: 2016 **Status 2020:** Active
Industries: Artificial Intelligence

Company Name: Sineq: Ukraine
Description: Sinequa Provides a Cognitive Search & Analytics Platform for Fortune Global 2000 Companies and Government Agenci: Spain
Website: www.sinequa.com
Phone: **Email:** info@sinequa.com
City: Paris **State:** IDF **PC:** **Country: France**
Year Established: **Status 2020:** Active
Industries: Artificial Intelligence for:, Big Data and Analytics for:, Enterprise Application Services for:, Machine Learning for:, Natural Language Processing for:, Cyber Security for:, ~ Professional Services (48), Data Management

Company Name: Singlespot
Description: Singlespot is a startup specializing in the collection, processing and analysis of anonymous geolocated data for retailers.
Website: http://www.singlespot.com/
Phone: 33 6 24 08 29 81 **Email:** contact@singlespot.com
City: Paris **State:** IDF **PC:** **Country: France**
Year Established: 2015 **Status 2020:** Active
Industries:

Company Name: SkillCorner
Description: SkillCorner is a computer vision startup who uses artificial intelligence and deep learning to broadcast live football match visualization.
Website: http://skillcorner.com/
Phone: **Email:** contact@skillcorner.com
City: Paris **State:** IDF **PC:** **Country: France**
Year Established: 2016 **Status 2020:** Active
Industries: Artificial Intelligence for:, ~ Arts-Entertainment-Recreation (4)

Company Name: Smartly.ai
Description: Smartly.ai is a all in one platform for your voice and chat bots projects.
Website: http://smartly.ai
Phone: 33665015357 **Email:** hello@smartly.ai
City: Paris **State:** IDF **PC:** **Country: France**
Year Established: **Status 2020:** Active
Industries: Artificial Intelligence for:, Enterprise Application Services for:, Robotics

Company Name: SoftBank Robotics
Description:
Website: http://www.softbankrobotics.com
Phone: 3317-737-1752 **Email:** pr@softbank.co.: Japan
City: Paris **State:** IDF **Zip:** 94111 **Country: France**
Year Established: **Status 2020:** Active
Industries: ~ Banking and Financial Markets-Services (7), Web for:, Mobile for:, ~ Telecommunications (56)

Company Name: Sommelier du Parfum
Description: AI for perfume recommendation
Website: http://sommelierduparfum.com
Phone: **Email:** hello@sommelierduparfum.com
City: Paris **State:** IDF **PC:** **Country: France**
Year Established: 2017 **Status 2020:** Active
Industries: Artificial Intelligence

Company Name: SPooN
Description: Builds artificial creatures whose intelligence is locally & collectively shaped to foster human relationships through natural interactions.
Website: http://spoon.ai
Phone: 33 (0)1 53 35 51 41 **Email:** contact@spoon.ai
City: Paris **State:** IDF **PC:** **Country: France**
Year Established: 2016 **Status 2020:** Active
Industries: Artificial Intelligence for:, Robotics

Company Name: Stacktical
Description: A Decentralized Service Level Management Platform on the Blockcha: India
Website: http://stacktical.com
Phone: **Email:** contact@stacktical.com
City: Paris **State:** IDF **PC:** **Country: France**
Year Established: 2017 **Status 2020:** Active
Industries: Application Services for:, Blockchain for:, Cloud for:, IT Managed Services for:, Predictive Analytics for:, Business Software as a Service Apps (SaaS Apps)

Company Name: STATS4TRADE
Description: Unlock the Power of Machine-Learning for Investo: Serbia
Website: http://www.stats4trade.com
Phone: **Email:** contact@stats4trade.com
City: Paris **State:** IDF **PC:** **Country: France**
Year Established: 2016 **Status 2020:** Active
Industries: Artificial Intelligence for:, ~ Banking and Financial Markets-Services (7), IT Managed Services

Company Name: Storelift
Description: Storelift is building a micro retailer by designing a new store format that is fully autonomous and deployed where people work and live
Website: http://www.storelift.co
Phone: 33618985156 **Email:** info@storelift.co
City: Paris **State:** IDF **PC:** **Country: France**
Year Established: 2018 **Status 2020:** Active
Industries: Artificial Intelligence for:, Computer Vision for:, Machine Learning

Company Name: Storyzy
Description: Storyzy is an ad tech company that offers a solution for brands to exclude their ads from fake news and inappropriate context.
Website: http://storyzy.com
Phone: **Email:** marketing@storyzy.com
City: Paris **State:** IDF **PC:** **Country: France**
Year Established: 2012 **Status 2020:** Active
Industries: ~ Media-Communications (41), Machine Learning for:, Natural Language Processing for:, Web for:, Web for:, Content

Company Name: Suricog
Description: SuriCog is building a unique expertise at the intersection of optoelectronics, neurosciences, algorithms.
Website: http://suricog.fr
Phone: **Email:** 37487@reference-encyclopedia-ai.net
City: Paris **State:** IDF **PC:** **Country: France**
Year Established: 2013 **Status 2020:** Active
Industries: Artificial Intelligence for:, IT Managed Services for:, Web for:, Machine Learning for:, ~ Social Assistance-Non-Profits (53)

Company Name: Swapcard
Description: Swapcard is an event app & matchmaking platform powered by artificial intelligence.
Website: http://www.swapcard.com
Phone: 33 (0) 1 83 89 72 88 **Email:** hello@swapcard.com
City: Paris **State:** IDF **PC:** **Country: France**
Year Established: 2013 **Status 2020:** Active
Industries: Application Services for:, Artificial Intelligence for:, Enterprise Application Services for:, ~ Event Management (15), IT Managed Services

Company Name: Syllabs
Description: Natural Language Generation
Website: http://www.syllabs.com
Phone: **Email:** hello@syllabs.com
City: Paris **State:** IDF **PC:** **Country: France**
Year Established: **Status 2020:** Active
Industries: Artificial Intelligence for:, Cyber Security for:, ~ Professional Services (48)

Company Name: Symaps.io
Description: Symaps.io is the AI application that finds the best location for business based on profitability.
Website: http://www.symaps.io
Phone: 33 (0) 9 54 99 29 65 **Email:** contact@symaps.io
City: Paris **State:** IDF **PC:** **Country: France**
Year Established: 2016 **Status 2020:** Active
Industries: Analytics for:, Artificial Intelligence for:, Machine Learning for:, Business Software as a Service Apps (SaaS Apps)

Company Name: Target2Sell
Description: Target2Sell is a provider of a Saas-based predictive marketing tool designed to offer a personalized recommendation engine.
Website: http://www.target2sell.com/en/
Phone: 33 1 44 54 94 55 **Email:** contact@target2sell.com
City: Paris **State:** IDF **PC:** **Country: France**
Year Established: 2012 **Status 2020:** Active
Industries:

Company Name: TasteHit
Description: TasteHit is the data-driven UX platform for online shops.
Website: http://tastehit.com
Phone: **Email:** contact@tastehit.com
City: Paris **State:** IDF **PC:** **Country: France**
Year Established: 2013 **Status 2020:** Active
Industries: Big Data and Analytics for:, E-Commerce for:, E-Commerce for:, Machine Learning for:, Business Software as a Service Apps (SaaS Apps)

Company Name: TeamBrain
Description: TeamBrain is develops an artificial intelligence based knowledge platform.
Website: http://teambrain.fr/
Phone: 33 1 30 66 32 37 **Email:** contact@teambrain.fr
City: Paris **State:** IDF **PC:** **Country: France**
Year Established: 2013 **Status 2020:** Active
Industries: Artificial Intelligence

Company Name: The Chatbot Factory
Description: The Chatbot Factory is a technology startup specializing in the design, development & artificial intelligence algorithms.
Website: http://www.thechatbotfactory.com
Phone: 33665939667 **Email:** thomas@thechatbotfactory.com
City: Paris **State:** IDF **PC:** **Country: France**
Year Established: 2016 **Status 2020:** Active
Industries: Artificial Intelligence for:, Cyber Security

Company Name: The Data Strategy
Description: AI for Digital Transformation
Website: http://www.thedatastrategy.com
Phone: 33 9 84 36 81 82 **Email:** hello@thedatastrategy.com
City: Paris **State:** IDF **PC:** **Country: France**
Year Established: 2015 **Status 2020:** Active
Industries: Analytics for:, Artificial Intelligence for:, IT Managed Services for:, Web

Company Name: The H.o.l.o.g.ram
Description: Mobile App
Website:
Phone: 781073478 **Email:** bkly@protonmail.com
City: Paris **State:** IDF **PC:** **Country: France**
Year Established: **Status 2020:** Active
Industries: Artificial Intelligence for:, Application Services

Company Name: TheGreenData
Description: TheGreenData provides cutting edge management tools for the agriculture and food supply chain, powered by data and AI analytics.
Website: http://www.thegreendata.com/
Phone: **Email:** 37529@reference-encyclopedia-ai.net
City: Paris **State:** IDF **PC:** **Country: France**
Year Established: 2015 **Status 2020:** Active
Industries: ~ Agriculture (3), Artificial Intelligence for:, Big Data and Analytics

Company Name: Tinyclu: Spain
Description: Tinyclues is an AI-driven campaign marketing solution provider that helps B2C marketers drive revenue and engagement from their customers.
Website: http://www.tinyclues.com
Phone: 33175506726 **Email:** contact@tinyclues.com
City: Paris **State:** IDF **PC:** **Country: France**

Year Established: **Status 2020:** Active
Industries: Analytics for:, Artificial Intelligence for:, Big Data and Analytics

Company Name: Tokendata
Description: Crypto asset for everyone
Website: http://tokendata.ai/
Phone: **Email:** hello@tokendata.ai
City: Paris **State:** IDF **PC:** **Country: France**
Year Established: **Status 2020:** Active
Industries: Artificial Intelligence for:, Cloud for:, ~ Banking and Financial Markets-Services (7), Databases for:, ~ Banking and Financial Markets-Services (7), Machine Learning

Company Name: TrackAd Group
Description: Digital performances for Marketing professionals
Website: http://www.trackad.ai
Phone: **Email:** contact@trackad.ai
City: Paris **State:** IDF **PC:** **Country: France**
Year Established: 2014 **Status 2020:** Active
Industries: Digital Marketing for:, E-Commerce for:, Predictive Analytics

Company Name: Trade Quorum
Description: Trade Quorum streamlines and secures international trade execution by providing a decentralised platform.
Website: http://www.tradequorum.com/
Phone: **Email:** info@tradequorum.com
City: Paris **State:** IDF **PC:** **Country: France**
Year Established: **Status 2020:** Active
Industries: Artificial Intelligence for:, ~ Banking and Financial Markets-Services (7), ~ Banking and Financial Markets-Services (7), IT Managed Services for:, ~ Banking and Financial Markets-Services (7)

Company Name: U Change
Description: U Change's innovative, open and scalable methodologies accelerate the digital transformation of your organization.
Website: http://www.uchange.co/en/
Phone: 33 1 82 83 92 30 **Email:** contact@uchange.co
City: Paris **State:** IDF **PC:** **Country: France**
Year Established: 2015 **Status 2020:** Active
Industries: Artificial Intelligence

Company Name: UntieNots
Description: SaaS solution for AI based Targeted Loyalty in Reta: Israel
Website: http://www.untienots.com
Phone: 33609861069 **Email:** zyed@untienots.com
City: Paris **State:** IDF **PC:** **Country: France**
Year Established: 2015 **Status 2020:** Active
Industries: Artificial Intelligence for:, IT Managed Services

Company Name: UrbanHello
Description: UrbanHello designs, manufactures and distributes connected objects powered by AI to improve family lives and strengthen family bonds
Website: http://www.urbanhello.com
Phone: **Email:** contact@urbanhello.com
City: Paris **State:** IDF **PC:** **Country: France**
Year Established: 2012 **Status 2020:** Active
Industries: Artificial Intelligence

Company Name: Veesion
Description: Real-time gesture recognition algorithm to automatically detect shoplifting behaviors.
Website: http://veesion.io/
Phone: **Email:** contact@veesion.io
City: Paris **State:** IDF **PC:** **Country: France**
Year Established: 2018 **Status 2020:** Active
Industries:

Company Name: Veygo
Description: Veygo Digital Experience Intelligence Platform makes premium multiscreen video services simple and profitable
Website: http://www.veygo.co
Phone: **Email:** 37621@reference-encyclopedia-ai.net
City: Paris **State:** IDF **PC:** **Country: France**
Year Established: 2012 **Status 2020:** Active
Industries: ~ Media-Communications (41), Application Services

Company Name: VITAnLINK
Description: VITAnLINK is the highway bringing start-ups in e-health MedTech & Diagnostics from their proof of concept to pre-commercialization faster
Website: http://www.vitanlink.com
Phone: **Email:** infos@vitanlink.com
City: Paris **State:** IDF **PC:** **Country: France**
Year Established: 2013 **Status 2020:** Active
Industries: Artificial Intelligence for:, ~ Healthcare (20), ~ Healthcare (20), ~ Healthcare (20)

Company Name: Viz: Iran
Description: Vizir.co is a SaaS product helping corporates automate their processes with chatbots.
Website: http://vizir.co/entreprise/
Phone: **Email:** hello@vizir.co
City: Paris **State:** IDF **PC:** **Country: France**
Year Established: 2014 **Status 2020:** Active
Industries: Enterprise Application Services for:, Web for:, Machine Learning for:, Business Software as a Service Apps (SaaS Apps)

Company Name: VR SQUAD
Description: The XR Company. VR SQUAD builds a SaaS training platform in VR & AR (X LEARN) powered by AI for smart recommandations.
Website: http://www.vrsquad.co
Phone: 33662370431 **Email:** fdv@vrsquad.co
City: Paris **State:** IDF **PC:** **Country: France**
Year Established: 2017 **Status 2020:** Active
Industries: Artificial Intelligence for:, Augmented Reality for:, ~ Education (13), ~ Education (13), Enterprise Application Services for:, Enterprise Application Services for:, Business Software as a Service Apps (SaaS Apps) for:, Business Software as a Service Apps (SaaS

Company Name: Wakeo
Description: Wakeo provides a Saas platform to bring real time visibility on B2B transport flows.
Website: http://wakeo.co
Phone: 33642436707 **Email:** hello@wakeo.co
City: Paris **State:** IDF **PC:** **Country: France**
Year Established: 2016 **Status 2020:** Active
Industries: ~ Transportation and Logistics (57), Internet of Things (IoT) for:, ~ Telecommunications (56), Machine Learning for:, Business Software as a Service Apps (SaaS Apps) for:, ~ Transportation and Logistics (57), Supply Chain Management

Company Name: Walnut Algorithms
Description: Artificial Intelligence for Investment Management
Website: http://www.walnutalgorithms.com
Phone: **Email:** contact@walnut-algo.com
City: Paris **State:** IDF **PC:** **Country: France**
Year Established: **Status 2020:** Active
Industries: Artificial Intelligence for:, ~ Banking and Financial Markets-Services (7), ~ Banking and Financial Markets-Services (7), ~ Banking and Financial Markets-Services (7), Machine Learning for:, ~ Banking and Financial Markets-Services (7)

Company Name: Whoz
Description: Whoz AI reveals your workforce skills and finds positions, assignments, and trainings that suit them best.
Website: http://www.whoz.com
Phone: **Email:** contact@whoz.com
City: Paris **State:** IDF **PC:** **Country: France**

Year Established: 2016 **Status 2020:** Active
Industries: Artificial Intelligence for:, Machine Learning for:, Business Software as a Service Apps (SaaS Apps)

Company Name: Widilo
Description: Coupons AI = Widilo. Available on iOS, Android and Messenger
Website: http://www.widilo.com
Phone: **Email:** partners@widilo.com
City: Paris **State:** IDF **PC:** **Country: France**
Year Established: 2016 **Status 2020:** Active
Industries: Artificial Intelligence

Company Name: Winglet
Description: Building AI driven next generation's Air Pricing Engine for Airlin: Spain
Website: http://www.winglet.io/
Phone: **Email:** info@winglet.io
City: Paris **State:** IDF **PC:** **Country: France**
Year Established: 2018 **Status 2020:** Active
Industries: Artificial Intelligence for:, Business Software as a Service Apps (SaaS Apps)

Company Name: Wirk
Description: Wirk offers you the best of artificial intelligence and collective intelligence to automate and outsource your low value-added tasks.
Website: http://www.wirk.io/
Phone: **Email:** 37677@reference-encyclopedia-ai.net
City: Paris **State:** IDF **PC:** **Country: France**
Year Established: 2014 **Status 2020:** Active
Industries: Artificial Intelligence for:, IT Managed Services

Company Name: Wiseb: Isle of Man
Description: Wisebim is an Artificial Intelligence for BIM automatic generation of 3D models of buildings from 2D plans.
Website: http://wisebim.fr/
Phone: **Email:** contact@wisebim.fr
City: Paris **State:** IDF **PC:** **Country: France**
Year Established: 2017 **Status 2020:** Active
Industries: Artificial Intelligence

Company Name: xLearn
Description: xLearn is a SaaS solution for skills management and knowledge sharing
Website: http://xlearn.fr
Phone: **Email:** contact@xlearn.fr
City: Paris **State:** IDF **PC:** **Country: France**
Year Established: **Status 2020:** Active
Industries: Artificial Intelligence for:, ~ Education (13), ~ Human Resources (24)

Company Name: Yokai
Description: Life-like synthetic photography
Website: http://yokai.ai
Phone: **Email:** olivier@yokai.ai
City: Paris **State:** IDF **PC:** **Country: France**
Year Established: 2019 **Status 2020:** Active
Industries: Artificial Intelligence for:, Big Data and Analytics for:, ~ Biotechnology (9), ~ Education (13)

Company Name: Ysance
Description: Ysance is the provider of a people-based marketing platform, the emerging leader in Europe in marketing solutions for retailers.
Website: http://www.ysance.com/en
Phone: 763092763 **Email:** jonathan.pitcher@ysance.com
City: Paris **State:** IDF **PC:** **Country: France**
Year Established: **Status 2020:** Active
Industries:

Company Name: Yseop
Description: Global Leader in Natural Language Generation: transforming data into reports and expertise, in multiple languages & in real time.
Website: http://yseop.com
Phone: 33 4 78 47 07 49 **Email:** contact-us@yseop.com
City: Paris **State:** IDF **PC:** **Country: France**
Year Established: **Status 2020:** Active
Industries: Artificial Intelligence for:, Databases for:, Compute

Company Name: Zelros
Description: AI for Augmented Insure: Serbia
Website: http://www.zelros.com/
Phone: **Email:** leonardo.deschaseaux@zelros.com
City: Paris **State:** IDF **PC:** **Country: France**
Year Established: **Status 2020:** Active
Industries: Artificial Intelligence for:, ~ Insurance (25), Machine Learning

Company Name: Zirrk
Description: Zirrk is an intelligent curation engine that helps you find what you seek without searching
Website:
Phone: **Email:** 37739@reference-encyclopedia-ai.net
City: Paris **State:** IDF **PC:** **Country: France**
Year Established: 2010 **Status 2020:** Closed
Industries: Artificial Intelligence for:, Content

Company Name: SysTechMar
Description: Systems Integrator
Website: http://www.systechmar.com
Phone: 0033-638-201-288 **Email:** contact@systechmar.com
City: Pontoise **State:** IDF **PC:** **Country: France**
Year Established: 2016 **Status 2020:** Active
Industries: Embedded for:, IT Managed Services for:, Application Services for:, ~ Construction (10), ~ Construction (10)

Company Name: ArchiWine
Description: ArchiWine is an Artificial Intelligence Wine Expert dedicated to wine trade.
Website: http://www.archi-bot.com/
Phone: **Email:** xavier@archi-bot.com
City: Puteaux **State:** IDF **PC:** **Country: France**
Year Established: 2017 **Status 2020:** Active
Industries: Artificial Intelligence for:, ~ Food and Beverage (17)

Company **Name:** Izifret
Description: Izifret is a digital freight platform allowing matching between shippers and carriers with AI
Website: http://izifret.com
Phone: 33 179 739 191 **Email:** contact@izifret.com
City: Saint-denis **State:** IDF **PC:** **Country: France**
Year Established: 2017 **Status 2020:** Active
Industries: Artificial Intelligence for:, ~ Transportation and Logistics (57), IT Managed Services for:, ~ Telecommunications (56), Supply Chain Management

Company Name: KEOLIO
Description: KEOLIO is an innovative digital agency using AI, data et UX to improve conversion rat: Spain
Website: http://www.keolio.com
Phone: 33 (0)9 51 08 35 22 **Email:** keolio@keolio.com
City: Saint-maur-des-fossés **State:** IDF **PC:** **Country: France**
Year Established: 2012 **Status 2020:** Active
Industries: Artificial Intelligence for:, Big Data and Analytics for:, Web

Company Name: Zyl
Description: Zyl is a smart photo assistant that manages your photos on iPhone and Android, with a privacy-by-design approach.
Website: http://zyl.ai
Phone: **Email:** contact@zyl.ai
City: Saint-maur-des-fossés **State:** IDF **PC:** **Country: France**

Year Established: **Status 2020:** Active
Industries: Application Services for:, Artificial Intelligence for:, Mobile for:, ~ Media-Communications (41)

Company Name: XXII GROUP
Description: Innovation & deep tech company, in love with virtual, augmented and mixed reality, artificial intelligence and neurosciences.
Website: http://www.xxiigroup.com
Phone: **Email:** hello@xxii.fr
City: Suresnes **State:** IDF **PC:** **Country: France**
Year Established: **Status 2020:** Active
Industries: Artificial Intelligence for:, Augmented Reality for:, Computer Vision for:, Content for:, Human Computer Interaction for:, Machine Learning for:, Natural Language Processing for:, ~ Life Sciences (27), ~ Retail and Consumer Products (52), Security for:, ~ Professio

Company Name: Dquant
Description: Artificial intelligence for financial market predictions
Website: http://www.dquant.ai
Phone: **Email:** contact@dquant.ai
City: Versailles **State:** IDF **PC:** **Country: France**
Year Established: **Status 2020:** Active
Industries: Artificial Intelligence for:, ~ Banking and Financial Markets-Services (7), ~ Banking and Financial Markets-Services (7), ~ Banking and Financial Markets-Services (7), ~ Banking and Financial Markets-Services (7), IT Managed Services for:, Machine Learning

Company Name: QuantsUnited
Description: Artificial intelligence for financial markets
Website: http://www.quantsunited.com
Phone: **Email:** contact@quantsunited.com
City: Versailles **State:** IDF **PC:** **Country: France**
Year Established: 2019 **Status 2020:** Active
Industries: Artificial Intelligence for:, ~ Banking and Financial Markets-Services (7), ~ Banking and Financial Markets-Services (7), ~ Banking and Financial Markets-Services (7), ~ Banking and Financial Markets-Services (7), IT Managed Services for:, Machine Learning

Company Name: AfterData
Description: AfterData is a startup that specializes in predictive marketing.
Website: https://www.afterdata.fr/index-en.php
Phone: 09 83 56 65 50 **Email:** 35970@reference-encyclopedia-ai.net
City: Villejuif **State:** IDF **PC:** **Country: France**
Year Established: 2016 **Status 2020:** Active
Industries: Artificial Intelligence for:, Big Data and Analytics for:, IT Managed Services for:, Internet of Things (IoT) for:, Machine Learning

Company Name: HiBrainy
Description: Create your own smart assistant who recognizes your language, your voice and your face by HiBrainy AI services.
Website: http://hibrainy.com/
Phone: **Email:** 36690@reference-encyclopedia-ai.net
City: Villejuif **State:** IDF **PC:** **Country: France**
Year Established: 2015 **Status 2020:** Active
Industries: Artificial Intelligence for:, IT Managed Services

Company Name: AlgoDeep
Description: The Next-Generation Platform for Enterprise AI
Website: https://www.algodeep.ai/
Phone: **Email:** 36033@reference-encyclopedia-ai.net
City: Vincennes **State:** IDF **PC:** **Country: France**
Year Established: 2017 **Status 2020:** Active
Industries:

Company Name: Uavia
Description: Uavia enables industries to connect autonomous drones and robots to the cloud and deploy mobile robots at scale in a smart and secure way.
Website: http://www.uavia.eu
Phone: **Email:** contact@uavia.eu
City: Vitry-sur-seine **State:** IDF **PC:** **Country: France**
Year Established: 2015 **Status 2020:** Active
Industries: Artificial Intelligence for:, Cloud for:, Cloud for:, ~ Telecommunications (56), Enterprise Application Services for:, Application Services for:, Machine Learning for:, Compute for:, Compute for:, Predictive Analytics

Company Name: Saagie
Description: Saagie is an end-to-end data platform to extract and refine your data, to build and run AI-based applications, .
Website: www.saagie.com/
Phone: **Email:** contact@saagie.com
City: Petit-quevilly **State:** Normandy **PC:** **Country: France**
Year Established: **Status 2020:** Active
Industries: Artificial Intelligence for:, Big Data and Analytics for:, Enterprise Application Services for:, ~ Banking and Financial Markets-Services (7), IT Managed Services for:, Enterprise Application Services

Company Name: omicX
Description: omicX created OMICtools® harnessing the exponentially growing collective intelligence in bioinformatics to exploit biological big data.
Website: http://omictools.com
Phone: 33 2 79 02 75 22 **Email:** administrative@omictools.com
City: Rouen **State:** Normandy **PC:** **Country: France**
Year Established: **Status 2020:** Active
Industries: Artificial Intelligence for:, ~ Biotechnology (9), ~ Biotechnology (9), Cloud for:, ~ Life Sciences (27), Machine Learning

Company Name: bzii: Italy
Description: Physical and digital data captation platform to increase notoriety and develop physical traffic inside physical stores.
Website: http://www.bziiitbooster.com/
Phone: **Email:** bc@bziiiit.com
City: Begles **State:** Nouvelle-Aquitaine **PC:** **Country: France**
Year Established: **Status 2020:** Active
Industries: Artificial Intelligence for:, Digital Marketing

Company Name: Kipers Industri: Spain
Description: Customized predictive maintenance solutions: real time monitoring and failure prognostics of your in-service equipment.
Website: https://www.kipers-industries.com/
Phone: **Email:** contact@kipers-industries.com
City: Begles **State:** Nouvelle-Aquitaine **PC:** **Country: France**
Year Established: 2017 **Status 2020:** Active
Industries: IT Managed Services for:, Predictive Analytics

Company Name: Qucit
Description: Qucit is for Quantified Cities, improves well being in cities using Artificial Intelligence.
Website: http://www.qucit.com/
Phone: (33) 6 89 46 61 61 **Email:** contact@qucit.com
City: Bègles **State:** Nouvelle-Aquitaine **PC:** **Country: France**
Year Established: 2014 **Status 2020:** Active
Industries: Artificial Intelligence for:, ~ Telecommunications (56)

Company Name: Crowdmap
Description: Crowdmap supports brands on creating 5 stars innovation based on omnichannel voice of customers feedback.
Website: http://www.crowdmap.io
Phone: **Email:** ben@crowdmap.io
City: Bordeaux **State:** Nouvelle-Aquitaine **PC:** **Country: France**

Year Established: **Status 2020:** Active
Industries: Artificial Intelligence for:, Business Applications for:, ~ Banking and Financial Markets-Services (7), ~ Retail and Consumer Products (52), Data Management

Company Name: DESKi
Description: Spreading Medical Experti: Sweden
Website: http://deski.io
Phone: **Email:** contact@deski.io
City: Bordeaux **State:** Nouvelle-Aquitaine **PC:** **Country: France**
Year Established: 2016 **Status 2020:** Active
Industries: Artificial Intelligence for:, ~ Healthcare (20), Machine Learning

Company Name: FieldBox.ai
Description: FieldBox.ai helps industries dramatically improve operational efficiency by deploying artificial intelligence in the heart of factories.
Website: http://www.fieldbox.ai
Phone: 33 (0) 98 128 7172 **Email:** enquiry@fieldbox.ai
City: Bordeaux **State:** Nouvelle-Aquitaine **PC:** **Country: France**
Year Established: 2011 **Status 2020:** Active
Industries: IT Managed Services

Company Name: Keyclic
Description: Keyclic Promote collective intelligence to help you optimize your costs, your risk control and satisfaction of your users and employees.
Website: http://keyclic.com/
Phone: 33 5 33 48 36 10 **Email:** hello@keyclic.com
City: Bordeaux **State:** Nouvelle-Aquitaine **PC:** **Country: France**
Year Established: 2014 **Status 2020:** Active
Industries: Artificial Intelligence for:, IT Managed Services for:, Web for:, Machine Learning

Company Name: KNOCK
Description: KNOCK is an ai-based housing research solution. Answer our questions, we'll do everything else.
Website: http://knock-knock.io
Phone: 33(0)777887910 **Email:** contact@knock-knock.io
City: Bordeaux **State:** Nouvelle-Aquitaine **PC:** **Country: France**
Year Established: 2017 **Status 2020:** Active
Industries: Artificial Intelligence

Company Name: Millesime.ai
Description: At Millesime.ai we develop Machine Learning algorithms to predict fine wine pric: Spain
Website: http://www.millesime.ai
Phone: **Email:** contact@millesime.ai
City: Bordeaux **State:** Nouvelle-Aquitaine **PC:** **Country: France**
Year Established: **Status 2020:** Active
Industries: Artificial Intelligence for:, Machine Learning for:, Predictive Analytics

Company Name: Nova-box
Description: Web and video games development company, R&D lab specialized in A.I., mobile plateforms and Ergonomics.
Website: http://www.nova-box.com
Phone: 33.(0).970.446.232 **Email:** contact@nova-box.com
City: Bordeaux **State:** Nouvelle-Aquitaine **PC:** **Country: France**
Year Established: **Status 2020:** Active
Industries: Artificial Intelligence for:, Mobile for:, ~ Education (13), Cyber Security

Company Name: PAPIs.io
Description: Independent community events dedicated to real-world Machine Learning
Website: http://www.papis.io/
Phone: **Email:** 37139@reference-encyclopedia-ai.net
City: Bordeaux **State:** Nouvelle-Aquitaine **PC:** **Country: France**
Year Established: 2014 **Status 2020:** Active
Industries:

Company Name: PayLead
Description: Paylead uses transaction data to get to know the customer better and to recommend personalized cashback offers based on purchasing behavior.
Website: http://www.paylead.fr/
Phone: **Email:** contact@paylead.fr
City: Bordeaux **State:** Nouvelle-Aquitaine **PC:** **Country: France**
Year Established: **Status 2020:** Active
Industries: Artificial Intelligence for:, Finance and Accounting for:, ~ Retail and Consumer Products (52), ~ Banking and Financial Markets-Services (7)

Company Name: Pollen Robotics
Description: Robotic product development made simple
Website: http://pollen-robotics.com/
Phone: **Email:** contact@pollen-robotics.com
City: Bordeaux **State:** Nouvelle-Aquitaine **PC:** **Country: France**
Year Established: **Status 2020:** Active
Industries: Artificial Intelligence for:, Application Services for:, ~ Professional Services (48), Robotics

Company Name: Synapse Medicine
Description: Synapse Medicine provides the most advanced AI solutions for #Healthcare and drugs prescriptions.
Website: http://synapse-medicine.com/
Phone: **Email:** contact@synapse-medicine.com
City: Bordeaux **State:** Nouvelle-Aquitaine **PC:** **Country: France**
Year Established: 2017 **Status 2020:** Active
Industries: Artificial Intelligence for:, ~ Healthcare (20), ~ Healthcare (20)

Company Name: Ubiquity.ai
Description: Ubiquity.ai is a Real Time Prescriptive Modeling Platform.
Website: http://ubiquity.ai
Phone: **Email:** webcontact@ubiquity.ai
City: Bordeaux **State:** Nouvelle-Aquitaine **PC:** **Country: France**
Year Established: 2016 **Status 2020:** Active
Industries: Analytics for:, Artificial Intelligence for:, IT Managed Services for:, IT Managed Services for:, Web

Company Name: Wiidii
Description: Wiidii was created in 2014 from the meeting of artificial intelligence and personal assistance.
Website: http://www.wiidii.com
Phone: 05 56 23 44 95 **Email:** contact@wiidii.com
City: Bordeaux **State:** Nouvelle-Aquitaine **PC:** **Country: France**
Year Established: 2014 **Status 2020:** Active
Industries: Artificial Intelligence for:, IT Managed Services

Company Name: Keypup
Description: SaaS, Software Development, Artificial Intelligence, Machine Learning
Website: http://keypup.io
Phone: **Email:** contact@keypup.io
City: La Rochelle **State:** Nouvelle-Aquitaine **PC:** **Country: France**
Year Established: 2019 **Status 2020:** Active
Industries: Artificial Intelligence for:, IT Managed Services for:, Web for:, Business Software as a Service Apps (SaaS Apps)

Company Name: SpikeNet Technologies
Description: A vision artificial technology based on human visual system
Website: http://www.spikenet-technology.com/en/pages/Home-Page.php
Phone: **Email:** contact@spikenet-technology.com
City: Balma **State:** Occitanie **PC:** **Country: France**
Year Established: **Status 2020:** Active
Industries: Analytics for:, Artificial Intelligence for:, ~ Professional Services (48)

Company Name: Alphanosos S.A.S.
Description: Alphanosos S.A.S.is a genuine Artificial Intelligence based methodology,
Website: http://www.alphanosos.com/
Phone: 33 982 216 506 **Email:** contact@alphanosos.com
City: Goulier **State:** Occitanie **PC:** **Country: France**
Year Established: 2014 **Status 2020:** Active
Industries: Artificial Intelligence for:, ~ Biotechnology (9)

Company Name: FUSYON
Description: Stay calm & focus on your customers by automating your maintenance & support. Satisfaction first ! We provide a SaaS solution for you !
Website: http://fusyon.io/
Phone: 33 4 66 45 33 14 **Email:** communication@fusyon.fr
City: Mende **State:** Occitanie **PC:** **Country: France**
Year Established: 2015 **Status 2020:** Active
Industries: Artificial Intelligence for:, IT Managed Services for:, IT Managed Services

Company Name: jollyclick
Description: jollyclick is a dating site for projects and talents
Website: http://www.jollyclick.com/
Phone: 33624542467 **Email:** hello@jollyclick.com
City: Mende **State:** Occitanie **PC:** **Country: France**
Year Established: **Status 2020:** Active
Industries: ~ Media-Communications (41), ~ Media-Communications (41), Artificial Intelligence for:, Big Data and Analytics for:, ~ Human Resources (24)

Company Name: Aive
Description: Creative AI for video creation and distribution automation
Website: https://www.aive.com/
Phone: **Email:** job@aive.com
City: Montpellier **State:** Occitanie **PC:** **Country: France**
Year Established: 2019 **Status 2020:** Active
Industries: Artificial Intelligence for:, IT Managed Services

Company Name: Daneel
Description: SASU
Website: https://daneel.io
Phone: 21018025295 **Email:** mohammed@daneel.io
City: Montpellier **State:** Occitanie **PC:** **Country: France**
Year Established: **Status 2020:** Active
Industries: Artificial Intelligence for:, Blockchain for:, ~ Banking and Financial Markets-Services (7), Machine Learning

Company Name: Tellmeplus
Description: We leverage Artificial Intelligence & Meta Active Machine Learning to automatically produce & deploy the best predictive models.
Website: www.tellmeplus.com
Phone: **Email:** smcdonagh@tellmeplus.com
City: Montpellier **State:** Occitanie **PC:** **Country: France**
Year Established: **Status 2020:** Active
Industries: Artificial Intelligence for:, Big Data and Analytics for:, Embedded for:, Automation

Company Name: Tharios
Description: Curate, Produce and Enrich textual content using artificial intelligence!
Website: http://www.tharios.com
Phone: **Email:** info@tharios.com
City: Montpellier **State:** Occitanie **PC:** **Country: France**
Year Established: **Status 2020:** Active
Industries:

Company Name: Wezr
Description: Wezr is disrupting $500b weather dependent B2B market, delivering hyperlocal real time forecast through AI/deep learning technology
Website:
Phone: **Email:** 37663@reference-encyclopedia-ai.net
City: Montpellier **State:** Occitanie **PC:** **Country: France**
Year Established: 2013 **Status 2020:** - Closed
Industries: Artificial Intelligence

Company Name: Delair
Description: Delair enables enterprises to digitize and analyze their assets to extract powerful business insights.
Website: http://www.delair.ae: Romania
Phone: 33 5 82 95 44 06 **Email:** contact@delair.ae: Romania
City: Toulouse **State:** Occitanie **PC:** **Country: France**
Year Established: 2011 **Status 2020:** Active
Industries: Artificial Intelligence for:, IT Managed Services for:, Machine Learning for:, Robotics

Company Name: DEXS: TURKEY
Description: DEXSTR enables a translational vision of the Life Science research activities offering researchers.
Website: http://www.dexstr.io/
Phone: 33981777336 **Email:** contact@dexstr.io
City: Toulouse **State:** Occitanie **PC:** **Country: France**
Year Established: **Status 2020:** Active
Industries: Artificial Intelligence for:, ~ Biotechnology (9), ~ Life Sciences (27), Content

Company Name: EarthCube
Description: Earthcube's mission is to increase satellite and airborne imagery accessibility thanks to the latest artificial intelligence developments.
Website: http://www.earthcube.eu/
Phone: **Email:** contact@earthcube.eu
City: Toulouse **State:** Occitanie **PC:** **Country: France**
Year Established: 2016 **Status 2020:** Active
Industries: ~ Aerospace and Defense (2), Artificial Intelligence for:, Computer Vision for:, IT Managed Services for:, ~ Telecommunications (56)

Company Name: FlightWatching
Description: FlightWatching offers flight monitoring services based on ACARS aviation data for commercial aircrafts in many countries.
Website: http://www.flightwatching.com
Phone: **Email:** beaujard@flightwatching.com
City: Toulouse **State:** Occitanie **PC:** **Country: France**
Year Established: **Status 2020:** Active
Industries: ~ Aerospace and Defense (2), Artificial Intelligence for:, Data Management for:, Predictive Analytics for:, ~ Professional Services (48)

Company **Name:** Gogowego
Description: Gogowego is a Software Company. It's building Proximity, the first platform for building, interconnecting and optimizing Virtual Assistants
Website: http://www.gogowego.com/
Phone: 33626885707 **Email:** hello@gogowego.com
City: Toulouse **State:** Occitanie **PC:** **Country: France**
Year Established: **Status 2020:** Active
Industries: Artificial Intelligence for:, Enterprise Application Services

Company Name: Hubware
Description: Hubware is a developer of a professional assistance platform intended to improve customer services.
Website: http://hubwa.re
Phone: **Email:** contact@hubwa.re
City: Toulouse **State:** Occitanie **PC:** **Country: France**
Year Established: 2016 **Status 2020:** Active
Industries: Artificial Intelligence for:, ~ Customer Relationship Management (11), IT Managed Services for:, Web

Company Name: Kaduceo
Description: Healthcare data and process analysts, predictive medicine, patient journey modeling
Website: http://www.kaduceo.com
Phone: **Email:** contact@kaduceo.com
City: Toulouse **State:** Occitanie **PC:** **Country: France**

Year Established: 2014 **Status 2020:** Active
Industries: Artificial Intelligence for:, ~ Healthcare (20), IT Managed Services for:, ~ Healthcare (20)

Company Name: Netwave
Description: Netwave is needed in France as the leading player in the market customized solutions in Real Time with 5 of the top 10 commercial sites.
Website: http://www.netwave.eu
Phone: (014) 067-9934 **Email:** contact@netwave.eu
City: Toulouse **State:** Occitanie **PC:** **Country: France**
Year Established: **Status 2020:** Active
Industries: ~ Media-Communications (41), Analytics for:, Artificial Intelligence for:, Big Data and Analytics for:, E-Commerce for:, Web for:, ~ Media-Communications (41), Predictive Analytics for:, ~ Retail and Consumer Products (52)

Company Name: vinginee: Serbia
Description: Digitizing wineries to get the best wine from every vine.
Website: http://www.vingineers.com
Phone: **Email:** contact@vingineers.com
City: Toulouse **State:** Occitanie **PC:** **Country: France**
Year Established: 2016 **Status 2020:** Active
Industries: ~ Aerospace and Defense (2), ~ Agriculture (3), Artificial Intelligence for:, Image Recognition for:, Predictive Analytics

Company Name: Naonext
Description: Naonext designs and develops innovative human-machine interfaces for digital arts.
Website: http://www.crystall-ball.com
Phone: 33 2 52 10 44 99 **Email:** 37039@reference-encyclopedia-ai.net
City: Coueron **State:** Pays de la Loire **PC:** **Country: France**
Year Established: 2012 **Status 2020:** Active
Industries: Machine Learning

Company Name: 42 Factory
Description: The network of environmental sensors which measures the air quality, street by street, with real-time data feedback in HD mapping.
Website: http://atmotrack.fr/en/index
Phone: 33240486939 **Email:** atmotrack@42 factory.com
City: Nantes **State:** Pays de la Loire **PC:** **Country: France**
Year Established: 2015 **Status 2020:** Active
Industries: Analytics for:, Machine Learning

Company Name: Dictanova
Description: Dictanova has developed a text analytics and sentiment analysis cloud based platform, for customer feedback analysis purpose.
Website: http://www.dictanova.com/
Phone: 33285524236 **Email:** contact@dictanova.com
City: Nantes **State:** Pays de la Loire **PC:** **Country: France**
Year Established: **Status 2020:** Active
Industries: Artificial Intelligence for:, ~ Media-Communications (41), Natural Language Processing for:, ~ Professional Services (48), Data Management

Company Name: E-cobot
Description: E-cobot is specialized in cobotics and artificial intelligence solution.
Website: http://www.e-cobot.com
Phone: 33 2 52 20 09 78 **Email:** Contact@e-cobot.com
City: Nantes **State:** Pays de la Loire **PC:** **Country: France**
Year Established: 2016 **Status 2020:** Active
Industries:

Company Name: Ween
Description: Predict real-time flows of people to adapt the behavior of all their environments
Website: www.ween.ai
Phone: **Email:** hello@ween.fr
City: Aix-en-provence **State:** Provence-Alpes-Cote d'Azur **PC:** **Country: France**
Year Established: **Status 2020:** Active
Industries: Artificial Intelligence for:, ~ Automotive (5), ~ Energy and Utilities (14)

Company Name: ProHacktive
Description: Mitigate Cyber risks to prevent attacks. Plug and Play solution to detect connected devices vulnerabilities on your network
Website: http://prohacktive.io
Phone: **Email:** team@prohacktive.io
City: Gap **State:** Provence-Alpes-Cote d'Azur **PC:** **Country: France**
Year Established: **Status 2020:** Active
Industries: Artificial Intelligence for:, Cyber Security for:, ~ Professional Services (48)

Company Name: MILANAMOS
Description: Milanamos is a big data mining company that specializes in big data analytics for the travel industry.
Website: http://www.milanamos.com
Phone: **Email:** christophe.ritter@milanamos.com
City: Les Issambres **State:** Provence-Alpes-Cote d'Azur **Zip:** 83380 **Country: France**
Year Established: **Status 2020:** Active
Industries: Analytics for:, Artificial Intelligence for:, ~ Aerospace and Defense (2), ~ Travel and Transportation (58), Big Data and Analytics for:, Databases for:, Enterprise Application Services

Company Name: PocketConfidant AI
Description: Self-coaching with AI. Real-time conversations that facilitate awareness, reflection and learning.
Website: http://pocketconfidant.com/
Phone: **Email:** hello@pocketconfidant.com
City: Nice **State:** Provence-Alpes-Cote d'Azur **PC:** **Country: France**
Year Established: 2016 **Status 2020:** Active
Industries: Artificial Intelligence for:, ~ Education (13), ~ Education (13), ~ Healthcare (20), ~ Healthcare (20)

Company Name: SynchroNext
Description: SynchroNext is a start up working on the research, development and production of algorithms based on the physics of information.
Website: http://www.synchronext.com
Phone: 33497201204 **Email:** contact@synchronext.com
City: Nice **State:** Provence-Alpes-Cote d'Azur **PC:** **Country: France**
Year Established: **Status 2020:** Active
Industries: Company Name: Bots as a Service
Description: We are an international BaaS venture, Bots as a Service. Specialising in Mixed Reality (chat)bot iterations relying on NLP & ML-based AI.
Website: http://www.botsasaservice.eu
Phone: **Email:** tania@botsasaservice.eu
City: Saint-jean-cap-ferrat **State:** Provence-Alpes-Cote d'Azur **PC:** **Country: France**
Year Established: **Status 2020:** Active
Industries: ~ Media-Communications (41), Artificial Intelligence for:, Machine Learning for:, Natural Language Processing for:, ~ Media-Communications (41)

Company Name: Cartesiam
Description: Cartesiam is a artificial intelligence company that adds value to objects by making them smart, intuitive, and self-contained.
Website: http://cartesiam.ai/
Phone: 04 93 01 02 03 **Email:** contact@cartesiam.com
City: Toulon **State:** Provence-Alpes-Cote d'Azur **PC:** **Country:** France
Year Established: 2016 **Status 2020:** Active
Industries: Analytics for:, Artificial Intelligence for:, ~ Energy and Utilities (14)

Company Name: LILLUP
Description: LILLUP is focused on Lifelong Learning and Human Capital Management, a digital workspace as solution to manage the performance.
Website: http://www.lillup.com/
Phone: 33650346244 **Email:** ampersand@lillup.com
City: Valbonne **State:** Provence-Alpes-Cote d'Azur **PC:** **Country: France**
Year Established: **Status 2020:** Active
Industries: Artificial Intelligence for:, ~ Education (13)

Company Name: Therapixel
Description: Therapixel is a software company specialized in artificial intelligence for medical image analytics.
Website: http://www.therapixel.com/
Phone: 33972552039 **Email:** contact@therapixel.com
City: Valbonne **State:** Provence-Alpes-Cote d'Azur **PC:** **Country: France**
Year Established: 2013 **Status 2020:** Active
Industries: Artificial Intelligence for:, ~ Healthcare (20)

Company Name: Vigiglobe
Description: Real-time Social Media Analytics for all!
Website: http://www.vigiglobe.com
Phone: 32 (0) 473 33 41 04 **Email:** vigiglobe@vigiglobe.com
City: Valbonne **State:** Provence-Alpes-Cote d'Azur **PC:** **Country: France**
Year Established: 2011 **Status 2020:** Active
Industries: Application Services for:, Big Data and Analytics for:, Databases for:, Machine Learning for:, Web for:, ~ Social Assistance-Non-Profits (53), ~ Social Assistance-Non-Profits (53)

Georgia

Company Name: GFAIVE
Description: Machine Learning Demand Forecasting For Fashion Reta: Israel
Website: http://www.gfaive.com/
Phone: 995 322 88 5006 **Email:** contact@gfaive.com
City: Tbilisi **State:** Tbilisi **PC:** **Country:** Georgia
Year Established: 2018 **Status 2020:** Active
Industries: Natural Language Processing for:, Predictive Analytics

Company Name: Kepler Technogoli: Spain
Description: AI & Robotics Ecosystem Powered By Blockcha: India
Website: http://keplertek.io/
Phone: **Email:** support@keplertek.org
City: Tbilisi **State:** Tbilisi **PC:** **Country:** Georgia
Year Established: **Status 2020:** Active
Industries: Artificial Intelligence for:, Robotics

Company Name: MaxinAI
Description: MaxinAI offers consulting services to clients focusing on AI, machine learning, big data analysis, and distributed computing.
Website: http://maxinai.com
Phone: **Email:** info@maxinai.com
City: Tbilisi **State:** Tbilisi **PC:** **Country:** Georgia
Year Established: 2017 **Status 2020:** Active
Industries: Artificial Intelligence

Germany

Company Name: collectAI
Description: collectAI provides AI-based collection services to help its clients manage account receivables.
Website: http://www.collect.ai/
Phone: **Email:** info@collect.ai
City: **State:** **PC:** **Country:** Germany
Year Established: **Status 2020:** Active
Industries:

Company Name: 5Analytics GmbH
Description: A software platform for the deployment/integration of Artificial Intelligence (R & Python) into Enterprise IT Systems.
Website: http://5analytics.com
Phone: 49-07024-9772780 **Email:** info@5analytics.com
City: **State:** BW **PC:** **Country:** Germany
Year Established: **Status 2020:** Active
Industries: Analytics for:, Artificial Intelligence for:, Business Applications for:, Big Data and Analytics for:, Business Intelligence for:, Enterprise Application Services for:, Machine Learning for:, Predictive Analytics for:, ~ Professional Services (48)

Company Name: Ciocene
Description: Ciocene is an independent IT-Solutions provider with a strong focus on AI applications.
Website: http://ciocene.com
Phone: 49 711 96882482 **Email:** info@ciocene.com
City: Baden **State:** BW **PC:** **Country:** Germany
Year Established: 2018 **Status 2020:** Active
Industries: Application Services for:, Artificial Intelligence for:, IT Managed Services

Company Name: HS INNOVATION
Description: Design of new business models and use cases based on artificial intelligence. Holding for management of intellectual property.
Website:
Phone: **Email:** 36713@reference-encyclopedia-ai.net
City: Baden-baden **State:** BW **PC:** **Country:** Germany
Year Established: 2014 **Status 2020:** Active
Industries: Robotics

Company Name: IndeeWork
Description: IndeeWork provides software backed by artificial intelligence and helps companies optimize and automate their field service scheduling.
Website: http://indeework.com/
Phone: **Email:** hello@indeework.com
City: Freiberg Am Neckar **State:** BW **PC:** **Country:** Germany
Year Established: 2016 **Status 2020:** Active
Industries: Artificial Intelligence for:, Machine Learning for:, Business Software as a Service Apps (SaaS Apps)

Company Name: Extheria
Description: Extheria create a trusted digital reflexion by combining technologies like IOT, printed electronics, and artificial intelligence.
Website: http://www.extheria.com/
Phone: **Email:** Contact@extheria.com
City: Freiburg **State:** BW **PC:** **Country:** Germany
Year Established: 2019 **Status 2020:** Active
Industries: Artificial Intelligence for:, IT Managed Services for:, Supply Chain Management
Company Name: Sundance
Description: Sundance provides embedded signal processing solutions.
Website: www.sundance.com
Phone: **Email:** sales@sundance.com
City: Freiburg **State:** BW **Zip:** 79098 **Country:** Germany
Year Established: **Status 2020:** Active

Industries: Artificial Intelligence

Company Name: Heronius
Description: Intelligente Vernetzung von Maschinen, Anlagen, Robotern - SaaS, Cloud, Automation, Digitalisierung, Software-Entwicklung - Industrie 4.0
Website: http://www.heronius.de
Phone: 49 7161 3540748 **Email:** kontakt@heronius.de
City: Goppingen **State:** BW **PC:** **Country:** Germany
Year Established: **Status 2020:** Active
Industries: Artificial Intelligence for:, Cloud for:, Automation for:, Machine Learning for:, ~ Manufacturing-Machinery (32), Robotics for:, ~ Professional Services (48)

Company Name: niiio finance group AG
Description: Software Company B2B Robo Advisor, API-Interfaces, AI-Development, Onboarding-App-Development
Website: http://niiio.finance/
Phone: **Email:** info@dser.de
City: Gorlitz **State:** BW **PC:** **Country:** Germany
Year Established: 2016 **Status 2020:** Active
Industries: Artificial Intelligence for:, Machine Learning for:, Application Services for:, ~ Banking and Financial Markets-Services (7)

Company Name: Brand a Trend GmbH
Description: Brand a Trend GmbH is a privately funded start up and a leader in cloud based text analytics.
Website: http://www.brandatrend.com
Phone: 49 6221 7260 0 **Email:** mail@brandatrend.com
City: Heidelberg **State:** BW **PC:** **Country:** Germany
Year Established: **Status 2020:** Active
Industries: Analytics for:, Artificial Intelligence for:, ~ Education (13), ~ Media-Communications (41), Data Management

Company Name: Getsafe
Description: Getsafe offers a platform of innovative, data-driven insurance products that users can subscribe to on demand.
Website: http://www.hellogetsafe.com
Phone: 0049-6221-3579990 **Email:** support@hellogetsafe.com
City: Heidelberg **State:** BW **PC:** **Country:** Germany
Year Established: **Status 2020:** Active
Industries: Artificial Intelligence for:, ~ Insurance (25), ~ Insurance (25), ~ Insurance (25), ~ Insurance (25), ~ Insurance (25), ~ Insurance (25)

Company Name: ambioassist
Description: ambio assist offers worldwide coverage with exact geoposition and voice connection.
Website: http://www.ambioassist.com/
Phone: **Email:** info@ambioassist.com
City: Karlsruhe **State:** BW **PC:** **Country:** Germany
Year Established: **Status 2020:** Active
Industries: Artificial Intelligence

Company Name: Blue Yonder
Description: A Germany-based provider of big data analytics and predictive applications
Website: http://www.blue-yonder.com/
Phone: **Email:** info@blue-yonder.com
City: Karlsruhe **State:** BW **PC:** **Country:** Germany
Year Established: **Status 2020:** Active
Industries: Analytics for:, Artificial Intelligence for:, Big Data and Analytics for:, Predictive Analytics

Company Name: Calpa
Description: Calpano offers a concept-map style modeling tool - DenkWerkZeug.com
Website: http://www.calpano.com
Phone: **Email:** service@calpano.com
City: Karlsruhe **State:** BW **PC:** **Country:** Germany
Year Established: **Status 2020:** Active
Industries: Artificial Intelligence for:, Data Management for:, Application Services for:, Content

Company Name: Neohelden
Description: Neo is a digital assistant powered by AI.
Website: http://neohelden.com
Phone: 49 (0) 721 461 39 887 **Email:** hello@neohelden.com
City: Karlsruhe **State:** BW **PC:** **Country:** Germany
Year Established: **Status 2020:** Active
Industries:

Company Name: Qymatix Solutions GmbH
Description: Predictive Sales Analytics for B2B
Website: http://qymatix.de/en
Phone: 49 721 86016373 **Email:** lucas.pedretti@qymatix.com
City: Karlsruhe **State:** BW **PC:** **Country:** Germany
Year Established: **Status 2020:** Active
Industries: Artificial Intelligence for:, Enterprise Application Services for:, Machine Learning for:, Predictive Analytics for:, Automation

Company Name: retest
Description: retest is a software startup that uses the revolutionary testing paradigm Difference Testing and AI to create innovative testing solutions.
Website: http://retest.de/
Phone: 49 721 72380106 **Email:** info@retest.de
City: Karlsruhe **State:** BW **PC:** **Country:** Germany
Year Established: 2017 **Status 2020:** Active
Industries: Artificial Intelligence for:, IT Managed Services

Company Name: thingsTHINKING
Description: thingsTHINKING develops a platform designed to understand and processes human language.
Website: http://thingsthinking.net
Phone: 49 721 96493138 **Email:** info@thingsTHINKING.net
City: Karlsruhe **State:** BW **PC:** **Country:** Germany
Year Established: 2016 **Status 2020:** Active
Industries: Artificial Intelligence for:, IT Managed Services for:, IT Managed Services for:, Web

Company Name: understand.ai
Description: understand.ai provides the training and validation data to make autonomous driving safe and reliable.
Website: http://understand.ai
Phone: **Email:** info@understand.ai
City: Karlsruhe **State:** BW **PC:** **Country:** Germany
Year Established: **Status 2020:** Active
Industries: Artificial Intelligence for:, ~ Automotive (5), ~ Automotive (5)

Company Name: Zana
Description: Zana is an intelligent assistant that responds to health questions and empower people to get and stay healthy.
Website: http://www.zana.com
Phone: **Email:** info@zana.com
City: Karlsruhe **State:** BW **PC:** **Country:** Germany
Year Established: 2017 **Status 2020:** Active
Industries: Artificial Intelligence for:, ~ Healthcare (20), ~ Healthcare (20), ~ Healthcare (20), ~ Healthcare (20)

Company Name: www.taniapeitzker.expert consultant, author & educator
Description: I freelance as an Applied AI consultant for the private and public sectors. CogX, CX & voice tech. Author, educator & digital marketer.
Website: http://taniapeitzker.expert
Phone: **Email:** tania.peitzker@protonmail.com
City: Konstanz **State:** BW **PC:** **Country:** Germany
Year Established: 2020 **Status 2020:** Active
Industries: Artificial Intelligence for:, Digital Marketing for:, E-Commerce for:, Enterprise Application Services for:, IT Managed Services for:, IT Managed Services for:, Cyber Security

Company Name: VESTUR
Description: Mobile App
Website: http://www.vestur.de/
Phone: 07152 90659928 **Email:** info@vestur.de
City: Leonberg **State:** BW **PC:** **Country:** Germany
Year Established: 2015 **Status 2020:** Active
Industries: Application Services for:, IT Managed Services for:, Predictive Analytics

Company Name: CYANITE
Description: AI for the music industry, SaaS
Website: http://cyanite.ai/
Phone: **Email:** markus@cyanite.ai
City: Mannheim **State:** BW **PC:** **Country:** Germany
Year Established: 2016 **Status 2020:** Active
Industries: Analytics for:, Artificial Intelligence for:, Business Applications for:, Big Data and Analytics for:, Data Management for:, Machine Learning for:, ~ Arts-Entertainment-Recreation (4)

Company Name: MotionsCloud
Description: Mobile & artificial intelligence claims solutions for non-life insure: Serbia
Website: motionscloud.com
Phone: **Email:** team@motionscloud.com
City: Mannheim **State:** BW **PC:** **Country:** Germany
Year Established: **Status 2020:** Active
Industries: Artificial Intelligence for:, Mobile

Company Name: V-INDUSTRY
Description: Industrial Manufacturing, Marketplace, Sharing Econo: Malaysia
Website: http://v-industry.com/
Phone: 49 711 25269355 **Email:** info@v-industry.com
City: Ostfildern **State:** BW **PC:** **Country:** Germany
Year Established: 2018 **Status 2020:** Active
Industries: IT Managed Services for:, Machine Learning

Company Name: Varomo : UGANDA
Description: Modular, autonomous low-cost transportation robots
Website: http://varomo.de/
Phone: **Email:** t.link@varomo.de
City: Pforzheim **State:** BW **PC:** **Country:** Germany
Year Established: 2017 **Status 2020:** Active
Industries: Artificial Intelligence for:, ~ Automotive (5), ~ Healthcare (20), ~ Healthcare (20), Robotics

Company Name: 5Analytics
Description: 5Analytics is an AI software company that helps companies integrate Artificial Intelligence into business processes.
Website: http://5analytics.com
Phone: 07024-9772780 **Email:** info@5analytics.com
City: Stuttgart **State:** BW **PC:** **Country:** Germany
Year Established: 2016 **Status 2020:** Active
Industries: Analytics for:, Artificial Intelligence for:, Machine Learning for:, Predictive Analytics

Company Name: AX Semantics
Description: AX Semantics is a content creation software based on data for e-commerce and publishing customers.
Website: http://www.ax-semantics.com
Phone: **Email:** info@ax-semantics.com
City: Stuttgart **State:** BW **PC:** **Country:** Germany
Year Established: **Status 2020:** Active
Industries: Artificial Intelligence for:, Content for:, ~ Media-Communications (41), E-Commerce for:, ~ Media-Communications (41), ~ Professional Services (48)

Company Name: Blickshift
Description: Blickshift provides innovative software solutions for the efficient analysis of eye movements.
Website: http://www.blickshift.com/
Phone: 49 711 184 245 26 **Email:** info@blickshift.com
City: Stuttgart **State:** BW **PC:** **Country:** Germany
Year Established: 2016 **Status 2020:** Active
Industries:

Company Name: CassandHRa GmbH
Description: SaaS
Website: http://www.cassandhra.com/
Phone: **Email:** contact@cassandhra.com
City: Stuttgart **State:** BW **PC:** **Country:** Germany
Year Established: 2018 **Status 2020:** Active
Industries: Artificial Intelligence for:, IT Managed Services for:, Business Software as a Service Apps (SaaS Apps)

Company Name: glazy GmbH
Description: The virtual assistant for your business
Website: http://www.glazy.ai
Phone: 49 (0) 711 - 40046270 **Email:** info@glazy.io
City: Stuttgart **State:** BW **PC:** **Country:** Germany
Year Established: 2016 **Status 2020:** Active
Industries: Application Services for:, Artificial Intelligence for:, Business Intelligence for:, Enterprise Application Services

Company Name: Mojin Robotics
Description: Mojin Robotics develops an assistant robot for humans called Care-O-bot 4.
Website: http://www.mojin-robotics.de/
Phone: 49 711 21950970 **Email:** info@mojin-robotics.de
City: Stuttgart **State:** BW **PC:** **Country:** Germany
Year Established: 2015 **Status 2020:** Active
Industries: Artificial Intelligence for:, ~ Healthcare (20), Machine Learning for:, Robotics

Company Name: Swarm Logistics
Description: We organize the world's flow of goods. A Decentralized Autonomous Logistics Organization (DALO) - run by machines & based on blockcha: India
Website: http://www.swarmlogistics.net
Phone: **Email:** info@swarmlogistics.net
City: Stuttgart **State:** BW **PC:** **Country:** Germany
Year Established: **Status 2020:** Active
Industries: Artificial Intelligence for:, Blockchain for:, ~ Transportation and Logistics (57), ~ Transportation and Logistics (57), ~ Professional Services (48)

Company Name: Layer7 AI
Description: Layer7 AI is an IT company that helps clients identify, implement, and maintain customized AI solutions.
Website: http://www.layer7.ai/
Phone: 49 - 159 - 01479 983 **Email:** info@layer7.ai
City: Tubingen **State:** BW **PC:** **Country:** Germany
Year Established: 2018 **Status 2020:** Active
Industries: Machine Learning

Company Name: Meshcapade
Description: SaaS
Website: http://www.meshcapade.com
Phone: **Email:** info@meshcapade.com
City: Tubingen **State:** BW **PC:** **Country:** Germany
Year Established: 2018 **Status 2020:** Active
Industries: ~ Arts-Entertainment-Recreation (4), Computer Vision for:, Machine Learning for:, Business Software as a Service Apps (SaaS Apps)

Company Name: beeBlum
Description: SaaS
Website: http://www.beeblum.com
Phone: **Email:** info@beeblum.com
City: Wiesloch **State:** BW **PC:** **Country:** Germany
Year Established: 2020 **Status 2020:** Active
Industries: Application Services for:, Collaboration Solutions for:, Application Services for:, Business Software as a Service Apps (SaaS Apps)

Company Name: Liquid Newsroom (LNR)
Description: We decode your market DNA
Website: http://www.liquidnewsroom.com/
Phone: **Email:** steffen.konrath@liquidnewsroom.com
City: Bad Reichenhall **State:** BY **PC:** **Country:** Germany
Year Established: 2012 **Status 2020:** Active
Industries: Artificial Intelligence for:, Business Applications for:, Business Intelligence for:, ~ Social Assistance-Non-Profits (53)

Company Name: EDUCATION4SIGHT
Description: Education4sight is an education analytics company.
Website: http://education4sight.com/
Phone: 49 91 31 69 13 25 **Email:** contact@education4sight.com
City: Erlangen **State:** BY **PC:** **Country:** Germany
Year Established: 2014 **Status 2020:** Active
Industries: Analytics for:, ~ Education (13), ~ Education (13), Machine Learning

Company Name: appliedAI Initiative at UnternehmerTUM
Description: AI, International, Applied AI, Industrial, Deep Learning
Website: http://www.appliedai.de
Phone: **Email:** 36075@reference-encyclopedia-ai.net
City: Garching Bei München **State:** BY **PC:** **Country:** Germany
Year Established: 2018 **Status 2020:** Active
Industries: Artificial Intelligence for:, Big Data and Analytics for:, ~ Education (13), Machine Learning

Company Name: Ariadne Ma: Palestine
Description: Ariadne Maps is a high technology company that provides detailed customer analytics with its cutting edge artificial intelligence approach.
Website: http://ariadnemaps.com/
Phone: 49 (0) 1744079675 **Email:** contact@ariadnemaps.com
City: Garching Bei München **State:** BY **PC:** **Country:** Germany
Year Established: 2019 **Status 2020:** Active
Industries: Artificial Intelligence for:, Internet of Things (IoT)

Company Name: Vemcon
Description: Vemcon is a rethinks machine control.
Website: http://www.vemcon.de/
Phone: 49 89 21541 100 **Email:** info@vemcon.de
City: Garching Bei München **State:** BY **PC:** **Country:** Germany
Year Established: 2012 **Status 2020:** Active
Industries: Robotics

Company Name: Cube Robot X
Description: haleez.com is working on Brand Design & Communications
Website: http://www.haleez.com
Phone: **Email:** kubilayhalis@haleez.com
City: Gersthofen **State:** BY **PC:** **Country:** Germany
Year Established: **Status 2020:** Active
Industries: Artificial Intelligence for:, ~ Media-Communications (41), Digital Media for:, E-Commerce for:, ~ Media-Communications (41), Robotics

Company Name: Agile Robots
Description: Agile Robots is an artificial intelligence robot maker.
Website: http://www.agile-robots.com/
Phone: 49 8105 3980 - 101 **Email:** welcome@agile-robots.com
City: Gilching **State:** BY **PC:** **Country:** Germany
Year Established: 2018 **Status 2020:** Active
Industries:

Company Name: audEERING
Description: audEERING GmbH is a leading company in the area of intelligent audio analysis.
Website: http://audeering.com/
Phone: 49 8105 7756150 **Email:** info@audeering.com
City: Gilching **State:** BY **PC:** **Country:** Germany
Year Established: 2012 **Status 2020:** Active
Industries: Analytics for:, Artificial Intelligence for:, IT Managed Services for:, Machine Learning

Company Name: Cuciniale
Description: Cuciniale GmbH, a Lindau, Germany-based company develops and markets intelligent cooking assistance systems for the consumer goods market.
Website: http://www.cuciniale.com
Phone: 49 8283 9110410 **Email:** holger.henke@cuciniale.com
City: Lindau **State:** BY **PC:** **Country:** Germany
Year Established: 2012 **Status 2020:** Active
Industries: Application Services for:, ~ Food and Beverage (17), Application Services for:, Internet of Things (IoT)

Company Name: BetterTaxi (BetterTec GmbH)
Description: The meta-booking platform for taxis and airport transfers.
Website: http://www.bettertaxi.com
Phone: 49 030 220137330 **Email:** service@bettertaxi.de
City: Munchen **State:** BY **PC:** **Country:** Germany
Year Established: 2012 **Status 2020:** Active
Industries: Business Applications for:, Machine Learning for:, ~ Social Media (54)

Company Name: Crashtest Security
Description: Crashtest Security provides AI powered security.
Website: http://crashtest-security.com/
Phone: 49 (0) 89 215 41 665 **Email:** info@crashtest-security.com
City: Munchen **State:** BY **PC:** **Country:** Germany
Year Established: 2017 **Status 2020:** Active
Industries: Security

Company Name: Dynamic Components
Description: Dynamic Components digitizes elevators by retrofitting hardware & software in order to enable condition monitoring & predictive maintenance.
Website:
Phone: **Email:** 36463@reference-encyclopedia-ai.net
City: Munchen **State:** BY **PC:** **Country:** Germany
Year Established: 2016 **Status 2020:** - Closed
Industries: Big Data and Analytics for:, Internet of Things (IoT) for:, Predictive Analytics

Company Name: Free Machines
Description: Free Machines is developing a SaaS solution based on Deep Reinforcement Learning.
Website: http://free-machines.com/
Phone: **Email:** 36595@reference-encyclopedia-ai.net
City: Munchen **State:** BY **PC:** **Country:** Germany
Year Established: 2017 **Status 2020:** Active
Industries: Artificial Intelligence for:, IT Managed Services for:, Machine Learning for:, Business Software as a Service Apps (SaaS Apps)

Company Name: navel robotics
Description: navel robotics creates social robots with a liveliness known from pets or characters in 3D animation movies.
Website: http://www.navelrobotics.com/
Phone: **Email:** claude.toussaint@navelrobotics.com
City: Munchen **State:** BY **PC:** **Country:** Germany
Year Established: 2017 **Status 2020:** Active
Industries: Artificial Intelligence for:, Robotics

Company Name: Presize.ai
Description: By combining the latest breakthroughs in Computer Vision and Deep Learning, presize.ai develops the most accurate body scanning software
Website: http://www.presize.ai/
Phone: **Email:** info@presize.ai
City: Munchen **State:** BY **PC:** **Country:** Germany

Year Established: **Status 2020:** Active
Industries: Artificial Intelligence for:, Computer Vision for:, E-Commerce for:, Machine Learning for:, ~ Retail and Consumer Products (52), ~ Professional Services (48)

Company Name: Scylla
Description: Scylla develops a real-time human behavior detection system.
Website: http://scylla.ai/
Phone: 49 170 8930472 **Email:** solutions@develandoo.com
City: Munchen **State:** BY **PC:** **Country:** Germany
Year Established: **Status 2020:** Active
Industries: Artificial Intelligence for:, Cyber Security for:, Security for:, Application Services for:, Security

Company Name: StudySmarter
Description: StudySmarter is an intelligent learning platform for digitizing the written exam preparation for students.
Website: http://www.studysmarter.de/en/
Phone: **Email:** hello@studysmarter.de
City: München **State:** BY **PC:** **Country:** Germany
Year Established: 2017 **Status 2020:** Active
Industries: Artificial Intelligence for:, ~ Education (13), Machine Learning

Company Name: travelloc
Description: The AI travel guide
Website: http://www.travelloc.com
Phone: **Email:** support@qiyuchina.co
City: München **State:** BY **PC:** **Country:** Germany
Year Established: 2018 **Status 2020:** Active
Industries: Artificial Intelligence

Company Name: 4tiitoo
Description: 4tiitoo is a leading company in eye tracking interaction that makes digital workplaces more productive, attractive and secure.
Website: http://www.4tiitoo.com
Phone: (415) 627-0970 **Email:** contact@4tiitoo.com
City: Munich **State:** BY **PC:** **Country:** Germany
Year Established: 2013 **Status 2020:** Active
Industries: Augmented Reality for:, Computer Vision for:, Enterprise Application Services for:, Human Computer Interaction for:, Mobile for:, Predictive Analytics for:, Speech Recognition

Company Name: agrilution
Description: agrilution offers smart gardening solutions for you to grow organic, fresh & clean greens at home all year round.
Website: http://www.agrilution.com
Phone: **Email:** info@agrilution.com
City: Munich **State:** BY **PC:** **Country:** Germany
Year Established: **Status 2020:** Active
Industries: ~ Agriculture (3), ~ Agriculture (3), Artificial Intelligence for:, ~ Agriculture (3), ~ Agriculture (3), ~ Healthcare (20)

Company Name: AI Bots as a Service/AI BaaS™ - "we integrate your cognitive interfaces"© Key Brand: Cogx Avatars™
Description: CogX Avatars™ are MR (chat)bots, NLP & ML-type AI. "Motion detection & hand tracking with botified voice installations / touch free CogX"™
Website: http://www.ai-baas.com/
Phone: 49 (0)15167756699 **Email:** tania.peitzker@ai-baas.com
City: Munich **State:** BY **PC:** **Country:** Germany
Year Established: 2020 **Status 2020:** Active
Industries:

Company Name: ankhlabs GmbH
Description: AI, Blockchain and Bigdata combined at our Application BeANKH
Website: http://ankhlabs.io
Phone: 49 (0)89 590 814 62 **Email:** ico@ankhlabs.com
City: Munich **State:** BY **PC:** **Country:** Germany
Year Established: **Status 2020:** Active
Industries: Artificial Intelligence for:, Big Data and Analytics for:, Blockchain

Company Name: Apostera
Description: Automotive software product company
Website: http://apostera.com
Phone: 49 89 90170720 **Email:** info@apostera.com
City: Munich **State:** BY **PC:** **Country:** Germany
Year Established: **Status 2020:** Active
Industries: Artificial Intelligence for:, Augmented Reality for:, ~ Automotive (5), Computer Vision for:, ~ Manufacturing-Electronic (30), ~ Telecommunications (56)

Company Name: blik
Description: blik provides process optimisation in real-time with live data in logistics. blik connects smart industry sensors to a Big Data backend.
Website: http://www.blik.io
Phone: **Email:** info@blik.io
City: Munich **State:** BY **PC:** **Country:** Germany
Year Established: 2017 **Status 2020:** Active
Industries: Internet of Things (IoT) for:, ~ Telecommunications (56), Predictive Analytics for:, Compute for:, ~ Customer Relationship Management (11), Supply Chain Management

Company Name: Build38
Description: Build38 is a global provider of mobile application protection solutions: in-app shielding, in-app monitoring and AI based in-app reaction.
Website: http://www.build38.com
Phone: **Email:** servus@build38.com
City: Munich **State:** BY **PC:** **Country:** Germany
Year Established: 2018 **Status 2020:** Active
Industries: Artificial Intelligence for:, Cyber Security for:, IT Managed Services for:, Mobile for:, Application Services for:, ~ Banking and Financial Markets-Services (7), Security

Company Name: Celon
Description: Celonis designs an intelligent big data technology that analyze and visualizes every process in a company.
Website: http://www.celonis.com/
Phone: **Email:** info@celonis.de
City: Munich **State:** BY **PC:** **Country:** Germany
Year Established: **Status 2020:** Active
Industries: Analytics for:, Artificial Intelligence for:, Computer Vision for:, Data Management for:, Databases for:, ~ Professional Services (48)

Company **Name:** Checkout Technologies
Description: http://www.checkoutfree.: Italy
Website: http://www.checkoutfree.: Italy
Phone: **Email:** jegor@checkoutfree.: Italy
City: Munich **State:** BY **PC:** **Country:** Germany
Year Established: **Status 2020:** Active
Industries: Artificial Intelligence for:, Computer Vision for:, ~ Retail and Consumer Products (52)

Company Name: combyne
Description: Dress on your Phone.
Website: http://www.combyne.com
Phone: **Email:** contact@combyne.com
City: Munich **State:** BY **PC:** **Country:** Germany
Year Established: **Status 2020:** Active
Industries: Application Services for:, Artificial Intelligence for:, Business Intelligence for:, E-Commerce for:, ~ Fashion (16), Mobile

Company Name: Conten
Description: The global AI-driven trading place for journalistic content
Website: http://www.contenno.com
Phone: 49-89-45099340 **Email:** contact@contenno.com
City: Munich **State:** BY **PC:** **Country:** Germany

Year Established: **Status 2020:** Active
Industries:

Company Name: craftguide
Description: craftguide is the platform delivering virtual assistant for machine-related tasks that works across mobile and VR systems.
Website: http://craftguide.com
Phone: 49 (0)89/ 70 95 70 60 **Email:** info@craftguide.com
City: Munich **State:** BY **PC:** **Country:** Germany
Year Established: 2018 **Status 2020:** Active
Industries: Application Services for:, Artificial Intelligence for:, Augmented Reality for:, ~ Education (13), ~ Education (13), IT Managed Services for:, Application Services for:, Virtual Reality (VR)

Company Name: Curiosity
Description: Unlocking the knowledge in unstructured documents
Website: http://curiosity.ai/
Phone: **Email:** hello@curiosity.ai
City: Munich **State:** BY **PC:** **Country:** Germany
Year Established: **Status 2020:** Active
Industries: Artificial Intelligence for:, Enterprise Application Services for:, Machine Learning for:, Natural Language Processing

Company Name: Delicious Data
Description: Demand forecasts for catering businesses to optimize procurement and increase sustainability - We are hiring!
Website: http://www.delicious-data.com
Phone: **Email:** info@delicious-data.com
City: Munich **State:** BY **PC:** **Country:** Germany
Year Established: 2017 **Status 2020:** Active
Industries: Analytics for:, Artificial Intelligence for:, ~ Food and Beverage (17)

Company Name: e-bot7
Description: e-bot7 develops and integrates artificial intelligence for your customer service.
Website: http://www.e-bot7.com
Phone: 1234567890 **Email:** info@e-bot7.com
City: Munich **State:** BY **PC:** **Country:** Germany
Year Established: **Status 2020:** Active
Industries: Artificial Intelligence for:, ~ Telecommunications (56)

Company Name: eCozy
Description: Your frictionless smart heating experience.
Website: http://www.ecozy.de
Phone: 49 89 18932570 **Email:** andre@ecozy.de
City: Munich **State:** BY **PC:** **Country:** Germany
Year Established: 2013 **Status 2020:** Active
Industries: ~ Energy and Utilities (14), Application Services for:, Internet of Things (IoT) for:, ~ Construction (10)

Company Name: eev: Ireland
Description: your guide to a sustainable life
Website: http://www.eevie.io/
Phone: **Email:** info@eevie.io
City: Munich **State:** BY **PC:** **Country:** Germany
Year Established: 2017 **Status 2020:** Active
Industries:

Company Name: Evercot.ai
Description: Artificial Intelligence in Health Care and Mobility.
Website: http://evercot.ai
Phone: **Email:** info@evercot.ai
City: Munich **State:** BY **PC:** **Country:** Germany
Year Established: 2017 **Status 2020:** Active
Industries: Artificial Intelligence for:, ~ Healthcare (20)

Company Name: ExB Mobility GmbH
Description: ExB Mobility is the Artificial Intelligence player of choice to make intermodal mobility in an autonomous driving era possible.
Website: http://www.exb-mobility.com/
Phone: **Email:** contact@exb.de
City: Munich **State:** BY **PC:** **Country:** Germany
Year Established: **Status 2020:** Active
Industries: Artificial Intelligence for:, Machine Learning for:, Natural Language Processing

Company Name: Fineway
Description: We're building an A.I. to decode your travel DNA. The purpose? To magically deliver perfectly tailored travel experiences.
Website: http://www.fineway.ai
Phone: 49 89 124 146 093 **Email:** hello@fineway.de
City: Munich **State:** BY **PC:** **Country:** Germany
Year Established: **Status 2020:** Active
Industries: Artificial Intelligence for:, ~ Travel and Transportation (58)

Company Name: Franka Emika
Description: Franka Emika is a design and develop cutting edge robotic hardware and software.
Website: http://www.franka.de
Phone: 49 89 2006069 20 **Email:** info@franka.de
City: Munich **State:** BY **PC:** **Country:** Germany
Year Established: 2016 **Status 2020:** Active
Industries: Artificial Intelligence for:, Industrial Solutions for:, ~ Social-Environmental-Physical-Engineering Sciences (55), Robotics

Company Name: Freeelio
Description: Freeelio develop a decentralized digital intelligence that learns to make electricity usage more productive.
Website: http://sites.google.com/view/freeelio-de/
Phone: **Email:** news@freeel.io
City: Munich **State:** BY **PC:** **Country:** Germany
Year Established: **Status 2020:** Active
Industries: Artificial Intelligence for:, Blockchain for:, ~ Energy and Utilities (14)

Company Name: Gini
Description: Gini provides a SaaS solution for extracting content from documents.
Website: http://www.gini.net
Phone: 49 89 21 55 60 06 **Email:** hello@gini.net
City: Munich **State:** BY **PC:** **Country:** Germany
Year Established: **Status 2020:** Active
Industries: Artificial Intelligence for:, Data Management for:, Web for:, Machine Learning for:, Content for:, ~ Social Media (54)

Company Name: HiveNet
Description: HiveNet is developing a distributed cloud computing network, enabling computer owners to securely rent out their idle computing power
Website: http://www.hivenet.cloud/
Phone: **Email:** info@hivenet.cloud
City: Munich **State:** BY **PC:** **Country:** Germany
Year Established: 2018 **Status 2020:** Active
Industries: Artificial Intelligence for:, Blockchain for:, Cloud for:, IT Managed Services

Company Name: iATROS
Description: Artificial Intelligence (AI), Cardiology, E-Health, Internet of Things (IoT), Machine Learning, Healthcare
Website: http://www.i-atros.com
Phone: 49 89 237 888 07 **Email:** contact@i-atros.com
City: Munich **State:** BY **PC:** **Country:** Germany
Year Established: 2019 **Status 2020:** Active
Industries: Artificial Intelligence for:, ~ Healthcare (20), ~ Healthcare (20), Machine Learning

Company Name: ImmoPresenter 3D
Description: ImmoPresenter3D is a business model innovation & solution that relies on innovation technologies and will radically change real estate sal: Spain
Website: http://immopresenter3d.com/
Phone: 49 (0)89 21536948-0 **Email:** herrmann@immopresenter3d.com
City: Munich **State:** BY **PC:** **Country:** Germany
Year Established: 2019 **Status 2020:** Active
Industries: Artificial Intelligence for:, Cloud for:, IT Managed Services for:, Virtual Reality (VR)

Company Name: INNOSPOT
Description: INNOSPOT is a technology company specializing in scouting startups around the world using artificial intelligence.
Website: http://innospot.de/
Phone: 49 89 5187 5374 **Email:** contact@innospot.de
City: Munich **State:** BY **PC:** **Country:** Germany
Year Established: **Status 2020:** Active
Industries: Artificial Intelligence for:, IT Managed Services

Company Name: KAITE by DeepEy: Spain
Description: KAITE is the world´s first fully autonomous cargo drone - we are currently looking for an investor
Website: http://www.kaite.co
Phone: 49 1636 397475 **Email:** sergs@deepeyes.co
City: Munich **State:** BY **PC:** **Country:** Germany
Year Established: **Status 2020:** Active
Industries: ~ Travel and Transportation (58), Artificial Intelligence for:, ~ Automotive (5), ~ Transportation and Logistics (57), ~ Transportation and Logistics (57), ~ Transportation and Logistics (57)

Company Name: KONUX
Description: KONUX is a Munich-based IIoT company that integrates smart sensor systems and artificial intelligence to maximize asset performance.
Website: http://www.konux.com
Phone: **Email:** info@konux.de
City: Munich **State:** BY **PC:** **Country:** Germany
Year Established: **Status 2020:** Active
Industries: Artificial Intelligence for:, Machine Learning for:, Predictive Analytics

Company Name: Luminovo
Description: Luminovo is building the leading electronics engineering operating system for OEMs and EMS.
Website: http://www.luminovo.ai
Phone: **Email:** hello@luminovo.ai
City: Munich **State:** BY **PC:** **Country:** Germany
Year Established: 2017 **Status 2020:** Active
Industries: Artificial Intelligence for:, Machine Learning for:, Natural Language Processing

Company Name: Luminovo.ai
Description: Luminovo is a deep learning solutions and tooling company, founded by a team of AI experts from Stanford.
Website: http://www.luminovo.ai
Phone: **Email:** hello@luminovo.ai
City: Munich **State:** BY **PC:** **Country:** Germany
Year Established: **Status 2020:** Active
Industries:

Company Name: medicalmotion
Description: medicalmotion empowers people to live their highest level of health and enables health professionals to provide effective and better care.
Website: http://www.medicalmotion.de/
Phone: **Email:** contact@medicalmotion.de
City: Munich **State:** BY **PC:** **Country:** Germany
Year Established: 2017 **Status 2020:** Active
Industries: Application Services for:, Artificial Intelligence for:, ~ Healthcare (20), ~ Healthcare (20), ~ Healthcare (20)

Company Name: PAVE Group
Description: PropTech, ConstructionTech, Construction, Buildings, Infrastructure, SaaS, Deep Learning, AI, Machine Learning, Business process automation
Website: http://www.pavegroup.de/
Phone: 49 (89) 21540420 **Email:** info@pavegroup.de
City: Munich **State:** BY **PC:** **Country:** Germany
Year Established: **Status 2020:** Active
Industries: Artificial Intelligence for:, Cloud for:, ~ Construction (10), IT Infrastructure for:, Machine Learning for:, ~ Real Estate (49)

Company Name: PerfectPattern GmbH
Description: Mathematical optimization and scheduling of highly complex industrial processes based on Artificial Intelligence and Prescriptive Analytics
Website: http://www.perfectpattern.de
Phone: 49895880181 **Email:** aa@perfectpattern.de
City: Munich **State:** BY **PC:** **Country:** Germany
Year Established: **Status 2020:** Active
Industries: Artificial Intelligence for:, ~ Manufacturing-General (31), Predictive Analytics for:, ~ Media-Communications (41)

Company Name: Picsure
Description: Picsure provides a global AI-platform with tailored AI solutions in object recognition and fraud detection for the insurance industry.
Website: http://www.picsure.ai
Phone: **Email:** mail@snapsure.ai
City: Munich **State:** BY **PC:** **Country:** Germany
Year Established: **Status 2020:** Active
Industries: Artificial Intelligence for:, Image Recognition for:, IT Managed Services for:, ~ Professional Services (48)

Company Name: Predictive Works.
Description: Self-Serve Augmented Intelligence for Everyone
Website: http://www.predictiveworks.eu
Phone: 0049-171-3336957 **Email:** david@predictiveworks.eu
City: Munich **State:** BY **PC:** **Country:** Germany
Year Established: **Status 2020:** Active
Industries: Artificial Intelligence for:, IT Managed Services for:, Machine Learning for:, ~ Professional Services (48)

Company **Name:** Retorio
Description: Video analytics artificial Intelligence that analyses human communication behavior
Website: http://www.retorio.com
Phone: **Email:** contact@retorio.com
City: Munich **State:** BY **PC:** **Country:** Germany
Year Established: **Status 2020:** Active
Industries: Artificial Intelligence for:, ~ Education (13), ~ Education (13), Human Computer Interaction for:, ~ Human Resources (24), Machine Learning for:, ~ Media-Communications (41)

Company Name: robominds GmbH
Description: making robots smart.
Website: http://www.robominds.de
Phone: 49 89 38989093 **Email:** info@robominds.de
City: Munich **State:** BY **PC:** **Country:** Germany
Year Established: 2016 **Status 2020:** Active
Industries: Artificial Intelligence for:, Computer Vision for:, Automation for:, ~ Telecommunications (56), Robotics

Company Name: sensation.io
Description: An omnichannel feedback software company helping organizations start making better decisions.
Website: http://sensation.io
Phone: **Email:** paul@sensation.io
City: Munich **State:** BY **PC:** **Country:** Germany
Year Established: 2014 **Status 2020:** Active
Industries: Analytics for:, Big Data and Analytics for:, ~ Customer Relationship Management (11), Data Management for:, Enterprise Application Services for:, Machine Learning for:, Business

Software as a Service Apps (SaaS Apps) for:, Business Software as a Service Apps (: Saudi Arabia

Company Name: SIGRA Technologies
Description: SIGRA Technologies is platform for automotive control units (ECU), Wireless Power, Deep learning and Neural Networks for autonomous driving
Website: http://www.sigratech.de/
Phone: **Email:** info@sigratech.de
City: Munich **State:** BY **PC:** **Country:** Germany
Year Established: 2015 **Status 2020:** Active
Industries: Artificial Intelligence for:, ~ Automotive (5), ~ Automotive (5), Internet of Things (IoT)

Company Name: Smart Reporting
Description: Smart Reporting offers a digital health solution for structured medical reporting.
Website: http://www.smart-radiology.com
Phone: 49-89-215540-210 **Email:** info@smart-radiology.com
City: Munich **State:** BY **PC:** **Country:** Germany
Year Established: **Status 2020:** Active
Industries: Artificial Intelligence for:, ~ Healthcare (20), ~ Healthcare (20), ~ Healthcare (20)

Company Name: Smartlane
Description: Smartlane Transport Intelligence is a cloud-based software for the continuous automation and optimization of transport processes.
Website: http://smartlane.de/en/
Phone: **Email:** info@smartlane.de
City: Munich **State:** BY **PC:** **Country:** Germany
Year Established: 2015 **Status 2020:** Active
Industries: Predictive Analytics

Company Name: SMP - Intelligent Scents
Description: We aim to make people happier by having personalized fragrance at the right time, wherever they need : Italy
Website: http://www.smp.ai
Phone: **Email:** info@smp.ai
City: Munich **State:** BY **PC:** **Country:** Germany
Year Established: 2018 **Status 2020:** Active
Industries: Artificial Intelligence for:, IT Managed Services

Company Name: Social Sweethearts
Description: Make people smile
Website: http://www.socialsweethearts.de
Phone: **Email:** hr@socialsweethearts.de
City: Munich **State:** BY **PC:** **Country:** Germany
Year Established: 2011 **Status 2020:** Active
Industries: Content for:, Machine Learning for:, ~ Social Assistance-Non-Profits (53), Web

Company Name: Sunday League
Description: AI powered training algorithm and social network for football (soccer) people
Website: http://sundayleague.app
Phone: **Email:** 37480@reference-encyclopedia-ai.net
City: Munich **State:** BY **PC:** **Country:** Germany
Year Established: 2020 **Status 2020:** Closed
Industries:

Company Name: TerraLoupe
Description: TerraLoupe empowers autonomous mobility by providing machine learning generated virtual 3D twins of the environment for simulation/ HD maps.
Website: http://www.terraloupe.com/
Phone: **Email:** info@terraloupe.com
City: Munich **State:** BY **PC:** **Country:** Germany
Year Established: 2015 **Status 2020:** Active
Industries: Artificial Intelligence for:, ~ Automotive (5), ~ Automotive (5), Big Data and Analytics for:, Computer Vision for:, Internet of Things (IoT) for:, Machine Learning for:, Machine Learning

Company Name: UX3D
Description: UX3D designs and develops graphics processing unit (GPU) software and middleware.
Website: http://www.ux3d.io/
Phone: 49 (0)89 215 44-258-0 **Email:** info@ux3d.io
City: Munich **State:** BY **PC:** **Country:** Germany
Year Established: **Status 2020:** Active
Industries: ~ Aerospace and Defense (2), Artificial Intelligence for:, ~ Automotive (5), Computer Vision for:, Industrial Solutions for:, Compute

Company Name: Yon: Spain
Description: Yones offers a news application with machine learning technologies that personalizes content based on the user's interests.
Website: http://www.yones.net
Phone: 15123253873 **Email:** mfs@yones.net
City: Munich **State:** BY **PC:** **Country:** Germany
Year Established: 2013 **Status 2020:** Active
Industries: Machine Learning

Company Name: Roboyo
Description: Roboyo is a global leading automation pure-play consulting company .
Website: http://www.roboyo.de/
Phone: 49 911 4771610 **Email:** info@roboyo.de
City: Nürnberg **State:** BY **PC:** **Country:** Germany
Year Established: 2016 **Status 2020:** Active
Industries: Artificial Intelligence for:, IT Managed Services for:, IT Managed Services

Company Name: Smart City System
Description: Smart City System uses information technology to streamline parking management.
Website: http://smart-city-system.com/en/
Phone: **Email:** info@smart-city-system.com
City: Nürnberg **State:** BY **PC:** **Country:** Germany
Year Established: 2017 **Status 2020:** Active
Industries: Enterprise Application Services for:, Enterprise Application Services for:, IT Managed Services for:, Application Services for:, ~ Travel and Transportation (58)

Company Name: zauberware
Description: zauberware offers digital solutions such as software development, digital strategy, web development, apps, AI, data science and analytics.
Website: http://www.zauberware.com/en/
Phone: 49 8051 988 69 46 **Email:** hello@zauberware.com
City: Prien Am Chiemsee **State:** BY **PC:** **Country:** Germany
Year Established: 2012 **Status 2020:** Active
Industries: Artificial Intelligence for:, Web

Company Name: Deep Data Analytics
Description: A.I. for unstructured data
Website: http://deep-data-analytics.com
Phone: 498151 9193 883 **Email:** hello@deep-data-analytics.com
City: Starnberg **State:** BY **PC:** **Country:** Germany
Year Established: **Status 2020:** Active
Industries: Artificial Intelligence

Company Name: Perinno Labs
Description: Augmented reality and artificial intelligence based collaboration platform for remote support & sales and marketing.
Website: http://perinno.com/
Phone: **Email:** contact@perinno.com
City: Taufkirchen **State:** BY **PC:** **Country:** Germany
Year Established: **Status 2020:** Active
Industries: Artificial Intelligence for:, IT Managed Services for:, Machine Learning for:, Robotics

Company Name: StratWorX
Description: StratWorX is the AI-based and talent-centric platform for strategic workforce management.
Website: http://cm.stratworx.de
Phone: 09187-979753 **Email:** info@stratworx.de
City: Winkelhaid **State:** BY **PC:** **Country:** Germany
Year Established: 2017 **Status 2020:** Active
Industries: Artificial Intelligence for:, Blockchain for:, IT Managed Services

Company Name: BOTfriends
Description: BOTfriends is a provider of custom chatbot solutions and vendor of a conversational middleware platform for enterprise customers.
Website: http://botfriends.de/
Phone: **Email:** info@botfriends.de
City: Wurzburg **State:** BY **PC:** **Country:** Germany
Year Established: 2017 **Status 2020:** Active
Industries: Artificial Intelligence for:, Collaboration Solutions for:, Enterprise Application Services for:, Machine Learning for:, Natural Language Processing for:, Enterprise Application Services for:, Business Software as a Service Apps (SaaS Apps) for:, Business Softwa

Company Name: Pyoneer.io
Description: AI-powered SaaS that analyzes customer feedback and makes it actionable to develop the right products.
Website: http://pyoneer.io/
Phone: **Email:** info@pyoneer.io
City: Wurzburg **State:** BY **PC:** **Country:** Germany
Year Established: **Status 2020:** Active
Industries: Artificial Intelligence for:, Business Process and Operations

Company Name: Xplain Data GmbH
Description: Xplain Data develop innovations in the context of big data and artificial intelligence.
Website: http://www.xplain-data.com/
Phone: **Email:** info@xplain-data.com
City: Zorneding **State:** BY **PC:** **Country:** Germany
Year Established: 2015 **Status 2020:** Active
Industries: Artificial Intelligence for:, Big Data and Analytics for:, IT Managed Services

Company Name: Qlaym
Description: Qlaym is a methods from artificial intelligence and machine learning .
Website: http://qlaym.com/
Phone: 49 211 8828000 **Email:** info@qlaym.com
City: Wilhelm **State:** BY **PC:** **Country:** Germany
Year Established: 2011 **Status 2020:** Active
Industries: Machine Learning

Company Name: 12K Research
Description: A tech-driven research company. We combine smart algorithms with a deep understanding of the tech landscape to help companies stay ahead.
Website:
Phone: **Email:** 35912@reference-encyclopedia-ai.net
City: Berlin **State:** Berlin **PC:** **Country:** Germany
Year Established: 2015 **Status 2020:** - Closed
Industries:

Company Name: 12traits
Description: 12traits is the missing piece to understanding human behavior in digital environments.
Website:
Phone: **Email:** 35913@reference-encyclopedia-ai.net
City: Berlin **State:** BE **PC:** **Country:** Germany
Year Established: 2018 **Status 2020:** Closed
Industries: IT Managed Services for:, Machine Learning for:, ~ Healthcare (20)

Company Name: 1SDK
Description: 1SDK Inc. is a SaaS-based platform for Mobile Attribution Analytics & User Engagement
Website: http://www.1sdk.com/
Phone: **Email:** team@1sdk.com
City: Berlin **State:** Berlin **PC:** **Country:** Germany
Year Established: 2013 **Status 2020:** Active
Industries: Analytics for:, Mobile for:, ~ Media-Communications (41), Predictive Analytics for:, Business Software as a Service Apps (SaaS Apps)

Company Name: 2txt - natural language generation GmbH
Description: SaaS, Natural Language Generation, E-Commerce, Product descriptions, SEO, AI, Machine Learning
Website: https://2txt.de/
Phone: 49 30 65831120 **Email:** hello@2txt.de
City: Berlin **State:** Berlin **PC:** **Country:** Germany
Year Established: 2013 **Status 2020:** Active
Industries: Artificial Intelligence for:, Big Data and Analytics for:, E-Commerce for:, Business Software as a Service Apps (SaaS Apps)

Company Name: 42reports
Description: 42reports offers an online platform for businesses to analyze their performance and make data-driven decisions.
Website: http://42reports.com
Phone: **Email:** info@42reports.com
City: Berlin **State:** Berlin **PC:** **Country:** Germany
Year Established: **Status 2020:** Active
Industries: Analytics for:, Artificial Intelligence

Company Name: 7Fields
Description: Integrated AI-enabled Development & Coaching Platform , SaaS, Mobile App
Website: https://www.7fields.io/
Phone: 49 30 43400294 **Email:** guido.fiolka@7fields.io
City: Berlin **State:** Berlin **PC:** **Country:** Germany
Year Established: 2018 **Status 2020:** Active
Industries: Artificial Intelligence for:, ~ Education (13), ~ Education (13), IT Managed Services for:, Machine Learning for:, Business Software as a Service Apps (SaaS Apps)

Company Name: Aaron.ai
Description: Aaron.ai understands customer requests in natural language and handles them as desired.
Website: http://aaron.ai/
Phone: **Email:** hi@aaron.ai
City: Berlin **State:** Berlin **PC:** **Country:** Germany
Year Established: **Status 2020:** Active
Industries: Artificial Intelligence

Company Name: Ad Rockt
Description: Making The Most Advance AI Driven DSP
Website:
Phone: **Email:** 35948@reference-encyclopedia-ai.net
City: Berlin **State:** Berlin **PC:** **Country:** Germany
Year Established: 2016 **Status 2020:** Active
Industries: Analytics for:, Artificial Intelligence

Company Name: Ada Heal:Thailand
Description: Ada Health offers a new approach to personalized health, supported by sophisticated artificial intelligence technology.
Website: http://www.ada.com
Phone: **Email:** hello@ada.com
City: Berlin **State:** Berlin **PC:** **Country:** Germany
Year Established: **Status 2020:** Active
Industries: Application Services for:, Artificial Intelligence for:, ~ Healthcare (20), ~ Healthcare (20), ~ Healthcare (20)

Company Name: ai4medicine
Description: ai4medicine AI-based platform for personalized prevention and treatment of stroke.
Website: http://www.ai4medicine.com/
Phone: **Email:** mail@ai4medicine.com
City: Berlin **State:** Berlin **PC:** **Country:** Germany

Year Established: 2018 **Status 2020:** Active
Industries: Artificial Intelligence for:, ~ Healthcare (20), ~ Healthcare (20)

Company Name: AiRelo
Description: World's First City Registration Assistant
Website: http://AiRelo.Me
Phone: 49 30 56795499 **Email:** contact@airelo.me
City: Berlin **State:** Berlin **PC:** **Country:** Germany
Year Established: **Status 2020:** Active
Industries: Artificial Intelligence

Company Name: AiServe Technologies
Description: Computer Vision Assisted Software stack
Website: http://www.aiserve.co
Phone: **Email:** hello@aiserve.co
City: Berlin **State:** Berlin **PC:** **Country:** Germany
Year Established: **Status 2020:** Active
Industries: Artificial Intelligence for:, Business Applications for:, Computer Vision for:, ~ Healthcare (20), ~ Transportation and Logistics (57)

Company Name: AiSight
Description: Automating machine diagnostics for manufacturing
Website: https://aisight.de/
Phone: 49 (0) 30 40363399 **Email:** info@aisight.de
City: Berlin **State:** Berlin **PC:** **Country:** Germany
Year Established: 2018 **Status 2020:** Active
Industries: Artificial Intelligence for:, Machine Learning

Company Name: Aitokaiku
Description: Aitokaiku creates apps for iOS and Android that use sensors to transform the users's activities and environment into personalized music.
Website: http://www.aitokaiku.com
Phone: **Email:** info@aitokaiku.com
City: Berlin **State:** Berlin **PC:** **Country:** Germany
Year Established: **Status 2020:** Active
Industries: Artificial Intelligence for:, Augmented Reality for:, Application Services

Company Name: Aladdin Blockchain Technologies
Description: Aladdin is an early-stage software company seeking to use big data, blockchain, AI and machine-learning technologies.
Website: https://aladdinid.com/
Phone: 49 30 700 140 449 **Email:** info@aladdinid.com
City: Berlin **State:** Berlin **PC:** **Country:** Germany
Year Established: 2017 **Status 2020:** Active
Industries:

Company Name: alcemy
Description: alcemy is a integration service provider.
Website: https://alcemy.tech/
Phone: 49 30 20848677 **Email:** info@alcemy.tech
City: Berlin **State:** Berlin **PC:** **Country:** Germany
Year Established: 2018 **Status 2020:** Active
Industries: Data Management for:, Machine Learning

Company Name: Aleph Search
Description: AI for e-commerce with focus on fashion
Website: https://www.alephsearch.com/
Phone: **Email:** contact@alephsearch.com
City: Berlin **State:** Berlin **PC:** **Country:** Germany
Year Established: 2019 **Status 2020:** Active
Industries: Artificial Intelligence for:, E-Commerce

Company Name: apo.ai
Description: App Review Autoresponder: We reply to your app store reviews to improve your app rating, maximize organic downloads and increase retention.
Website: http://apo.ai
Phone: **Email:** team@apo.ai
City: Berlin **State:** Berlin **PC:** **Country:** Germany
Year Established: **Status 2020:** Active
Industries: Application Services for:, Application Services for:, Artificial Intelligence for:, Machine Learning for:, Natural Language Processing

Company Name: Arcona
Description: Arcona is an adaptive music platform.
Website: http://arcona.ai/
Phone: **Email:** 36081@reference-encyclopedia-ai.net
City: Berlin **State:** Berlin **PC:** **Country:** Germany
Year Established: 2019 **Status 2020:** Active
Industries: ~ Arts-Entertainment-Recreation (4)

Company Name: ascribe
Description: Take control over your digital intellectual property. ascribe helps you share your digital creations with the world.
Website: http://www.ascribe.io
Phone: **Email:** info@ascribe.io
City: Berlin **State:** Berlin **PC:** **Country:** Germany
Year Established: **Status 2020:** Active
Industries: ~ Arts-Entertainment-Recreation (4), Artificial Intelligence for:, Big Data and Analytics for:, ~ Banking and Financial Markets-Services (7), ~ Banking and Financial Markets-Services (7), ~ Media-Communications (41), Web for:, Machine Learning

Company Name: AskBy.ai
Description: The NLP Company - Understanding Natural Language.
Website: http://www.askby.ai/
Phone: **Email:** info@askby.ai
City: Berlin **State:** Berlin **PC:** **Country:** Germany
Year Established: **Status 2020:** Active
Industries: Analytics for:, Artificial Intelligence for:, Business Intelligence for:, Machine Learning for:, Natural Language Processing for:, Content for:, Data Management

Company Name: AtomLeap
Description: AtomLeap uses machine learning and big data to help organizations make better decisions.
Website: http://atomleap.com
Phone: **Email:** contact@atomleap.com
City: Berlin **State:** Berlin **PC:** **Country:** Germany
Year Established: 2015 **Status 2020:** Active
Industries: Analytics for:, Artificial Intelligence for:, Big Data and Analytics for:, Business Intelligence for:, IT Managed Services for:, Machine Learning for:, Natural Language Processing for:, Business Software as a Service Apps (SaaS Apps) for:, Business Software as a Service

Company Name: Attaching: ITALY
Description: Accelerating the transition of companies to the (public) cloud.
Website: http://www.attachingit.com
Phone: **Email:** info@attachingit.com
City: Berlin **State:** Berlin **PC:** **Country:** Germany
Year Established: **Status 2020:** Active
Industries: Artificial Intelligence for:, Cloud for:, Enterprise Application Services for:, ~ Professional Services (48)

Company Name: AUCTA
Description: AR based training and instructions via Head-Mounted Displays. An Augmented Reality industry SaaS platform.
Website: http://aucta.io
Phone: **Email:** 36112@reference-encyclopedia-ai.net
City: Berlin **State:** Berlin **PC:** **Country:** Germany
Year Established: 2019 **Status 2020:** Active
Industries: Artificial Intelligence for:, IT Managed Services

Company Name: Audatic
Description: Audatic builds systems to intelligently modify the sound in real-time using state of the art deep learning technology and unique datasets.
Website: http://audatic.ai/
Phone: **Email:** info@audatic.ai
City: Berlin **State:** Berlin **PC:** **Country:** Germany
Year Established: 2018 **Status 2020:** Active
Industries: Artificial Intelligence for:, Machine Learning

Company Name: AUPEO!
Description: AUPEO! provides personalized audio streams for internet-capable hardware devices and offers radio stations that recommend songs.
Website: http://aupeo.com
Phone: 16462565207 **Email:** hello@aupeo.com
City: Berlin **State:** Berlin **PC:** **Country:** Germany
Year Established: **Status 2020:** Active
Industries: Artificial Intelligence for:, Voice Recognition for:, ~ Automotive (5), ~ Manufacturing-Electronic (30), Mobile for:, ~ Arts-Entertainment-Recreation (4), ~ Media-Communications (41), ~ Professional Services (48), ~ Media-Communications (41)

Company Name: Automotive Artificial Intelligence
Description: Automotive Artificial Intelligence offers a real-world simulation for autonomous driving to test with.
Website: http://automotive-ai.com/
Phone: **Email:** 36117@reference-encyclopedia-ai.net
City: Berlin **State:** Berlin **PC:** **Country:** Germany
Year Established: 2017 **Status 2020:** Active
Industries: Artificial Intelligence for:, ~ Automotive (5)

Company Name: Autumn AI
Description: Autumn AI makes machine learning and artificial intelligence accessible for developers and companies. Developed Leaf
Website: http://autumnai.com
Phone: **Email:** support@autumnai.com
City: Berlin **State:** Berlin **PC:** **Country:** Germany
Year Established: **Status 2020:** Active
Industries: Artificial Intelligence for:, Machine Learning for:, Application Services

Company Name: AVA
Description: AVA provides personal safety solution to keeps track on whether you and your loved ones are safe.
Website: http://ava.info/
Phone: **Email:** info@blockpeek.com
City: Berlin **State:** Berlin **PC:** **Country:** Germany
Year Established: **Status 2020:** Active
Industries:

Company Name: Axiom AI
Description: Axiom AI is an AI browser assistant that lets you automate business processes, and share them with others on a process app-store.
Website: http://axiom.ai
Phone: **Email:** ai@axiom.ai
City: Berlin **State:** Berlin **PC:** **Country:** Germany
Year Established: 2018 **Status 2020:** Active
Industries: Artificial Intelligence for:, Business Intelligence for:, Machine Learning

Company Name: Baumeister AI
Description: Developing deep-learning based computer vision applications to re-engineer the way humans interact with machines.
Website: http://www.baumeister-ai.com
Phone: **Email:** contact@baumeister-ai.com
City: Berlin **State:** Berlin **PC:** **Country:** Germany
Year Established: 2019 **Status 2020:** Active
Industries: Artificial Intelligence for:, Computer Vision for:, Machine Learning

Company Name: BEAD Technology
Description: BEAD creates digital models of buildings by using real-time data and AI.
Website: http://www.enbead.com
Phone: 1 650 600 9072 **Email:** soner@enbead.com
City: Berlin **State:** Berlin **PC:** **Country:** Germany
Year Established: 2014 **Status 2020:** Active
Industries: Artificial Intelligence for:, Internet of Things (IoT) for:, ~ Construction (10)

Company Name: BETAFASHION
Description: SaaS, B2B, Fashion, predictive analytics, automation
Website: http://beta.fashion
Phone: **Email:** sr@beta.fashion
City: Berlin **State:** Berlin **PC:** **Country:** Germany
Year Established: 2018 **Status 2020:** Active
Industries: E-Commerce for:, ~ Fashion (16), Predictive Analytics for:, Business Software as a Service Apps (SaaS Apps) for:, Automation

Company Name: biotx.ai
Description: Biotx.ai delivers next-generation biomarkers as a basis for decision support in precision medicine.
Website: http://www.biotx.ai
Phone: **Email:** info@biotx.ai
City: Berlin **State:** Berlin **PC:** **Country:** Germany
Year Established: 2017 **Status 2020:** Active
Industries: Artificial Intelligence for:, ~ Biotechnology (9)

Company **Name:** Bliq
Description: Real-time intelligence for urban street mobility
Website: http://bliq.ai/
Phone: **Email:** hello@bliq.ai
City: Berlin **State:** Berlin **PC:** **Country:** Germany
Year Established: 2017 **Status 2020:** Active
Industries: Artificial Intelligence for:, IT Managed Services

Company Name: botconnect
Description: Enable service/sales reps to sell in every interaction wit AI. Collaboration of teams and AI for the enterprise.
Website: http://botconnect.ai
Phone: **Email:** contact@botconnect.io
City: Berlin **State:** Berlin **PC:** **Country:** Germany
Year Established: **Status 2020:** Active
Industries: Artificial Intelligence for:, Business Applications for:, Enterprise Application Services for:, Machine Learning for:, Cloud

Company Name: Brighter AI Technologies
Description: Brighter AI, offering visual reconstruction - based on state of the art deep learning.
Website: www.brighter.ai/
Phone: **Email:** hello@brighter.ai
City: Berlin **State:** Berlin **PC:** **Country:** Germany
Year Established: **Status 2020:** Active
Industries: Artificial Intelligence for:, IT Managed Services for:, Machine Learning

Company Name: Bubblehunt
Description: Statistics & analytics on Youtube vloggers.
Website: http://bubblehunt.com
Phone: **Email:** hello@bubblehunt.com
City: Berlin **State:** Berlin **PC:** **Country:** Germany
Year Established: 2016 **Status 2020:** Active
Industries: Analytics for:, Big Data and Analytics for:, Collaboration Solutions for:, IT Managed Services for:, Predictive Analytics for:, ~ Social Assistance-Non-Profits (53), ~ Social Assistance-Non-Profits (53)

Company Name: CAND
Description: CANDIS is the intelligent platform for automated accounting.
Website: http://candis.io
Phone: 030 346 556 10-0 **Email:** info@candis.io
City: Berlin **State:** Berlin **PC:** **Country:** Germany

Year Established: 2015 **Status 2020:** Active
Industries: Finance and Accounting for:, Artificial Intelligence for:, Business Software as a Service Apps (SaaS Apps)

Company Name: Cangler
Description: Cangler automates and democratises enterprise data analytics, making it simple, easy, and accessible for everyone.
Website: http://www.getcangler.com/
Phone: **Email:** hello@getcangler.com
City: Berlin **State:** Berlin **PC:** **Country:** Germany
Year Established: 2019 **Status 2020:** Active
Industries: Analytics for:, Artificial Intelligence for:, Big Data and Analytics for:, Business Intelligence for:, Cloud for:, Data Management for:, Enterprise Application Services for:, Business Software as a Service Apps (SaaS Apps) for:, Business Software as a Service App

Company Name: Cangler Analytics
Description: Cangler automates and democratises enterprise data analytics, making it simple, easy, and accessible for everyone.
Website: http://www.getcangler.com/
Phone: **Email:** info@cangleranalytics.com
City: Berlin **State:** Berlin **PC:** **Country:** Germany
Year Established: **Status 2020:** Active
Industries: Analytics for:, Artificial Intelligence for:, Big Data and Analytics for:, Business Intelligence for:, Cloud for:, Data Management for:, Enterprise Application Services for:, ~ Professional Services (48)

Company Name: Cartwat: Switzerland
Description: AI for retail stores focusing on loss prevention
Website: http://www.cartwatch.de
Phone: 49 173 4923084 **Email:** info@cartwatch.de
City: Berlin **State:** Berlin **PC:** **Country:** Germany
Year Established: **Status 2020:** Active
Industries: Artificial Intelligence for:, Machine Learning for:, ~ Retail and Consumer Products (52), ~ Retail and Consumer Products (52)

Company Name: Caspar Heal:Thailand
Description: Democratizing rehabilitation experti: Sweden
Website: http://www.caspar-health.com/en
Phone: **Email:** info@caspar-health.com
City: Berlin **State:** Berlin **PC:** **Country:** Germany
Year Established: **Status 2020:** Active
Industries:

Company Name: Caspian
Description: Caspian is a company that develops technological platforms targeted at the Commercial & Civil UAV (Unmanned Aerial Vehicle) market.
Website: http://caspian.io/
Phone: **Email:** info@caspian.io
City: Berlin **State:** Berlin **PC:** **Country:** Germany
Year Established: **Status 2020:** Active
Industries: Artificial Intelligence for:, Computer Vision for:, ~ Transportation and Logistics (57), ~ Government (19), Robotics for:, ~ Transportation and Logistics (57)

Company Name: chatShopper
Description: AI-powered conversational fashion engine
Website: http://www.chatshopper.com/
Phone: **Email:** hello@chatshopper.com
City: Berlin **State:** Berlin **PC:** **Country:** Germany
Year Established: **Status 2020:** Active
Industries: Artificial Intelligence for:, E-Commerce for:, Natural Language Processing for:, Business Intelligence for:, Content for:, ~ Retail and Consumer Products (52)

Company Name: CleanAI
Description: Computer Vision, Machine Learning, AI, Artificial Intelligence, IoT, Mobility Service
Website: http://www.cleanai.co
Phone: **Email:** hello@cleanai.co
City: Berlin **State:** Berlin **PC:** **Country:** Germany
Year Established: **Status 2020:** Active
Industries: Artificial Intelligence for:, ~ Automotive (5), IT Managed Services for:, IT Managed Services

Company Name: CogniScent
Description: CogniScent is a provider of AI-guided early detection of neurodegenerative diseases.
Website: http://www.cogniscent.io/
Phone: **Email:** 4633@reference-encyclopedia-ai.net
City: Berlin **State:** Berlin **PC:** **Country:** Germany
Year Established: **Status 2020:** Active
Industries: Artificial Intelligence for:, ~ Healthcare (20)

Company Name: colabel
Description: colabel enables companies to build custom deep learning solutions in no time without code
Website: http://colabel.com
Phone: **Email:** hello@colabel.com
City: Berlin **State:** Berlin **PC:** **Country:** Germany
Year Established: 2018 **Status 2020:** Active
Industries: Artificial Intelligence for:, Computer Vision for:, Machine Learning for:, Natural Language Processing

Company Name: collbet
Description: "First AI-powered chatbot for gamblers" collaboration via Facebook Messenger or Telegram
Website: http://www.collbet.com
Phone: **Email:** info@collbet.com
City: Berlin **State:** Berlin **PC:** **Country:** Germany
Year Established: **Status 2020:** Active
Industries: Application Services for:, Artificial Intelligence for:, IT Managed Services for:, ~ Telecommunications (56)

Company Name: Comodule
Description: Comodule is a universal data monitoring and visualisation platform for light electric vehicles.
Website: http://comodule.com/
Phone: 372 5552 4266 **Email:** info@comodule.com
City: Berlin **State:** Berlin **PC:** **Country:** Germany
Year Established: 2012 **Status 2020:** Active
Industries: Analytics for:, ~ Automotive (5), ~ Automotive (5), Predictive Analytics

Company Name: compaio
Description: Compaio will be the most customer centric financial advisor. We provide a single interface to the world of finance.
Website: http://www.compaio.com/
Phone: **Email:** hello@compaio.de
City: Berlin **State:** Berlin **PC:** **Country:** Germany
Year Established: **Status 2020:** Active
Industries: Artificial Intelligence for:, ~ Banking and Financial Markets-Services (7), ~ Banking and Financial Markets-Services (7), ~ Insurance (25), Application Services for:, Cyber Security

Company Name: Concierge
Description: Concierge lets guests chat and transact from the comfort of their own devices with their favorite hotels.
Website: http://www.youthere.ai
Phone: **Email:** founders@youthere.ai
City: Berlin **State:** Berlin **PC:** **Country:** Germany
Year Established: **Status 2020:** Active
Industries: Artificial Intelligence for:, IT Managed Services for:, ~ Telecommunications (56)

Company Name: conductiv.ai
Description: conductiv.ai combines machine learning with physics-based simulation to maximize production yield for precision manufacturing.
Website: http://www.conductiv.ai
Phone: **Email:** contact@conductiv.ai
City: Berlin **State:** Berlin **PC:** **Country:** Germany
Year Established: 2019 **Status 2020:** Active
Industries: Artificial Intelligence for:, Automation for:, ~ Manufacturing-General (31), Machine Learning

Company Name: CoPlannery
Description: The digital solution for mass customization in real estate development
Website: http://www.coplannery.com/
Phone: 49 (0)30 590083313 **Email:** info@coplannery.com
City: Berlin **State:** Berlin **PC:** **Country:** Germany
Year Established: **Status 2020:** Active
Industries: ~ Professional Services (48), Artificial Intelligence for:, ~ Real Estate (49)

Company Name: Coya
Description: Coya offers scalable protection at the point of need with an AI risk guardian and simple, transparent, and personalized insurance cover.
Website: http://www.coya.com
Phone: 49 (0) 30 588 49400 **Email:** hello@coya.com
City: Berlin **State:** Berlin **PC:** **Country:** Germany
Year Established: 2016 **Status 2020:** Active
Industries: Artificial Intelligence for:, Web

Company Name: creative.ai
Description: Artificial Intelligence for Creative Industri: Spain
Website: http://creative.ai/
Phone: **Email:** team@creative.ai
City: Berlin **State:** Berlin **PC:** **Country:** Germany
Year Established: **Status 2020:** Active
Industries: Artificial Intelligence for:, ~ Professional Services (48), Machine Learning

Company Name: D3M Labs
Description: Creating and monetizing amazing AI and Big Data products through strategic vision, ecosystem development, execution and scalability
Website: http://www.d3mlabs.de/
Phone: **Email:** elizabeth.press@d3mlabs.de
City: Berlin **State:** Berlin **PC:** **Country:** Germany
Year Established: 2015 **Status 2020:** Active
Industries:

Company Name: Deckard A.I.
Description: Predicts the future of your software projects-
Website: http://deckard.ai
Phone: **Email:** hello@deckard.ai
City: Berlin **State:** Berlin **PC:** **Country:** Germany
Year Established: **Status 2020:** Active
Industries: Artificial Intelligence for:, Application Services for:, Natural Language Processing

Company Name: Deckard
Description: Deckard is an AI engine that learns about the structure and performance of a software development team.
Website: http://deckard.ai
Phone: **Email:** hello@deckard.ai
City: Berlin **State:** Berlin **PC:** **Country:** Germany
Year Established: 2016 **Status 2020:** Closed
Industries: Artificial Intelligence for:, Application Services for:, Machine Learning for:, Natural Language Processing

Company Name: DeepSp: India
Description: DeepSpin is a company developing an artificial intelligence-powered MRI imaging machine.
Website: http://www.deepspin.io/
Phone: **Email:** contact@deepspin.io
City: Berlin **State:** Berlin **PC:** **Country:** Germany
Year Established: 2019 **Status 2020:** Active
Industries: Artificial Intelligence for:, ~ Healthcare (20)

Company Name: DialogShift
Description: DialogShift provides conversational AI solutions for travel & hospitality.
Website: http://www.dialogshift.com/en
Phone: **Email:** hello@dialogshift.com
City: Berlin **State:** Berlin **PC:** **Country:** Germany
Year Established: **Status 2020:** Active
Industries: Artificial Intelligence for:, IT Managed Services for:, ~ Telecommunications (56)

Company Name: DOJO Madness
Description: DOJO Madness builds tools and services that help players and fans to understand and master their favorite esports games.
Website: http://www.dojomadness.com
Phone: **Email:** contact@dojomadness.com
City: Berlin **State:** Berlin **PC:** **Country:** Germany
Year Established: **Status 2020:** Active
Industries: Analytics for:, Artificial Intelligence for:, ~ Arts-Entertainment-Recreation (4), Machine Learning for:, ~ Arts-Entertainment-Recreation (4)

Company **Name:** Dronesperhour GmbH
Description: We unleash the potential of a new era
Website: http://www.dronesperhour.com
Phone: **Email:** contact@dronesperhour.com
City: Berlin **State:** Berlin **PC:** **Country:** Germany
Year Established: 2016 **Status 2020:** Active
Industries: ~ Agriculture (3), Artificial Intelligence for:, ~ Education (13), ~ Media-Communications (41)

Company Name: EntroPi
Description: EntroPi is a Germany-based app development company that offers its users with Gait mobile app.
Website: http://entropi.io
Phone: **Email:** 36513@reference-encyclopedia-ai.net
City: Berlin **State:** Berlin **PC:** **Country:** Germany
Year Established: 2015 **Status 2020:** Active
Industries: IT Managed Services for:, Application Services for:, Predictive Analytics

Company Name: Explosion AI
Description: Explosion AI is a digital studio specialising in Artificial Intelligence and Natural Language Processing.
Website: http://explosion.ai
Phone: **Email:** contact@explosion.ai
City: Berlin **State:** Berlin **PC:** **Country:** Germany
Year Established: **Status 2020:** Active
Industries: Artificial Intelligence for:, Application Services for:, Machine Learning for:, Natural Language Processing

Company Name: EyeEm
Description: EyeEm is a photography company building computer vision technology to connect its creative community to leading brands and agencies.
Website: http://www.eyeem.com
Phone: (855) 551-8855 **Email:** press@eyeem.com
City: Berlin **State:** Berlin **PC:** **Country:** Germany
Year Established: **Status 2020:** Active
Industries: Artificial Intelligence for:, ~ Media-Communications (41), Computer Vision

Company Name: Faer
Description: Discover fair and sustainable fashion you love
Website: http://www.wearefaer.com
Phone: **Email:** hello@wearefaer.com
City: Berlin **State:** Berlin **PC:** **Country:** Germany
Year Established: **Status 2020:** Active
Industries: Artificial Intelligence for:, E-Commerce for:, ~ Fashion (16)

Company Name: FeedbackPanda
Description: SaaS for Online Teache: Serbia
Website: http://www.feedbackpanda.com/
Phone: 49 176 80597326 **Email:** dani@feedbackpanda.com
City: Berlin **State:** Berlin **PC:** **Country:** Germany
Year Established: 2017 **Status 2020:** Active
Industries: ~ Education (13), ~ Education (13), ~ Education (13), ~ Education (13), Machine Learning for:, Business Software as a Service Apps (SaaS Apps)

Company Name: Feingold Technologies -
Description: Feingold Technologies develops applications that analyze and understand human mindsets.
Website:
Phone: **Email:** 36558@reference-encyclopedia-ai.net
City: Berlin **State:** Berlin **PC:** **Country:** Germany
Year Established: 2010 **Status 2020:** Active
Industries: Artificial Intelligence for:, ~ Biotechnology (9), ~ Healthcare (20), IT Managed Services for:, Application Services

Company Name: Fliplingo
Description: Automate your translation on Twitter.
Website: http://www.fliplingo.com
Phone: (140) 438-9245 **Email:** matt@fliplingo.com
City: Berlin **State:** Berlin **PC:** **Country:** Germany
Year Established: 2013 **Status 2020:** Active
Industries: Natural Language Processing for:, ~ Social Assistance-Non-Profits (53)

Company Name: Flowletics
Description: Flowletics is a training app for mental and emotional fitness that helps ambitious people experience more flow and productivity
Website: http://www.flowletics.com
Phone: **Email:** david.jacob@flowletics.com
City: Berlin **State:** Berlin **PC:** **Country:** Germany
Year Established: **Status 2020:** Active
Industries:

Company Name: Fresh Energy
Description: Fresh Energy is a digital electricity provider that is eco-friendly, low-cost, data-driven and based on machine learning algorithms.
Website: http://www.getfresh.energy
Phone: 49 (0) 800 7244536 **Email:** service@getfresh.energy
City: Berlin **State:** Berlin **PC:** **Country:** Germany
Year Established: 2017 **Status 2020:** Active
Industries: ~ Energy and Utilities (14), ~ Energy and Utilities (14), ~ Energy and Utilities (14), Machine Learning

Company Name: German Autolabs
Description: German Autolabs is a Berlin based technology company, focussing on the future of the car. Making every car smarter and safer.
Website: http://germanautolabs.com
Phone: **Email:** mail@germanautolabs.com
City: Berlin **State:** Berlin **PC:** **Country:** Germany
Year Established: **Status 2020:** Active
Industries: Artificial Intelligence for:, ~ Automotive (5), ~ Transportation and Logistics (57)

Company Name: Gestalt Robotics
Description: Gestalt Robotics is a software and solution provider working at the interface of classic industrial automation and artificial intelligence.
Website: http://www.gestalt-robotics.com
Phone: 49 30 61651560 **Email:** info@gestalt-robotics.com
City: Berlin **State:** Berlin **PC:** **Country:** Germany
Year Established: 2016 **Status 2020:** Active
Industries: Artificial Intelligence for:, Augmented Reality for:, Computer Vision for:, Human Computer Interaction for:, Machine Learning for:, Robotics

Company Name: GESTALT Robotics GmbH
Description: GESTALT Robotics is a robotics innovation hub and solution provider with focus on cognition, interaction and perception.
Website: http://www.gestalt-robotics.com
Phone: 49 30 61651560 **Email:** info@gestalt-robotics.com
City: Berlin **State:** Berlin **PC:** **Country:** Germany
Year Established: **Status 2020:** Active
Industries: Artificial Intelligence for:, Augmented Reality for:, Computer Vision for:, Human Computer Interaction for:, Machine Learning for:, Robotics

Company Name: Giance Technologies
Description: GIANCE empowers enterprises to utilize the value of worldwide data and knowledge in real-time.
Website: http://www.giance.ai
Phone: **Email:** Team@Giance.ai
City: Berlin **State:** Berlin **PC:** **Country:** Germany
Year Established: **Status 2020:** Active
Industries: Artificial Intelligence for:, Big Data and Analytics for:, Enterprise Application Services for:, IT Managed Services for:, Machine Learning for:, Natural Language Processing

Company Name: goedle.io
Description: Goedle.io provides algorithms to track and help increase customer spending.
Website: http://goedle.io/
Phone: **Email:** info@goedle.io
City: Berlin **State:** Berlin **PC:** **Country:** Germany
Year Established: **Status 2020:** Active
Industries: Artificial Intelligence for:, Machine Learning for:, ~ Media-Communications (41), Predictive Analytics

Company Name: Greendeck
Description: Greendeck helps fashion brands and retailers with competitive intelligence to make better pricing and promotion decisions.
Website: http://www.greendeck.co
Phone: **Email:** contact@greendeck.co
City: Berlin **State:** Berlin **PC:** **Country:** Germany
Year Established: **Status 2020:** Active
Industries: Artificial Intelligence for:, Machine Learning for:, ~ Retail and Consumer Products (52)

Company Name: Groop
Description: Groop is the smart nightlife planner to find concert & party suggestions.
Website: http://www.groop.co
Phone: **Email:** info@groop.co
City: Berlin **State:** Berlin **PC:** **Country:** Germany
Year Established: **Status 2020:** Active
Industries: Artificial Intelligence for:, Mobile for:, ~ Event Management (15), ~ Hospitality (23)

Company Name: gust.network
Description: gust.network is the candidate data infrastructure for HR tech.
Website: http://gust.network
Phone: **Email:** 4588@reference-encyclopedia-ai.net
City: Berlin **State:** Berlin **PC:** **Country:** Germany
Year Established: **Status 2020:** Active
Industries: Artificial Intelligence for:, Blockchain for:, ~ Human Resources (24), IT Managed Services

Company Name: Hallid.ai AI Gaming
Description: Building Fridai, the A.I. powered virtual gaming assistant - the future of personalized, voice activated gaming companion.
Website: http://hellofridai.com/
Phone: 36303982489 **Email:** mark@hallidai.com
City: Berlin **State:** Berlin **Zip:** 10969 **Country:** Germany
Year Established: **Status 2020:** Active
Industries: Analytics for:, ~ Gaming (140), Artificial Intelligence for:, ~ Arts-Entertainment-Recreation (4), ~ Gaming (18), Big Data and Analytics for:, ~ Gaming (506), Business Applications for:, ~ Gaming (628), Data Management for:, ~ Gaming (1726), Integration for:, ~ Gam: India

Company Name: Hallidai AI Gaming
Description: We at Hallidai are building Fridai, the voice assistant for gamers.
Website: http://hellofridai.com/
Phone: 00 36 30 398 2489 **Email:** isaac@hallidai.com
City: Berlin **State:** Berlin **PC:** **Country:** Germany

Year Established: 2018 **Status 2020:** Active
Industries: Artificial Intelligence for:, ~ Arts-Entertainment-Recreation (4)

Company Name: Hasty.ai
Description: Hasty is an image annotation tool that uses AI to speed up the process of annotation.
Website: http://hasty.ai
Phone: **Email:** herbert@hasty.ai
City: Berlin **State:** Berlin **PC:** **Country:** Germany
Year Established: **Status 2020:** Active
Industries: Artificial Intelligence for:, Computer Vision for:, Machine Learning

Company Name: Heuro Labs
Description: Building an intelligent, modularised and scalable platform incorporating AI and Machine Learning.
Website: http://www.heurolabs.com
Phone: **Email:** martin@heurolabs.com
City: Berlin **State:** Berlin **PC:** **Country:** Germany
Year Established: **Status 2020:** Active
Industries: Artificial Intelligence for:, Machine Learning

Company Name: HeyJobs
Description: HeyJobs is a talent platform matching the world's talent to opportunities.
Website: http://hire.heyjobs.co/en-us/
Phone: 49 30 516958550 **Email:** info@heyjobs.co
City: Berlin **State:** Berlin **PC:** **Country:** Germany
Year Established: 2016 **Status 2020:** Active
Industries:

Company Name: High Mobility
Description: Digital Developer Tools for the Automotive Industry
Website: http://www.high-mobility.com
Phone: **Email:** founders@high-mobility.com
City: Berlin **State:** Berlin **PC:** **Country:** Germany
Year Established: **Status 2020:** Active
Industries: Artificial Intelligence for:, ~ Automotive (5), Application Services for:, Mobile for:, ~ Professional Services (48)

Company Name: hyScore
Description: As B2B SaaS, we understand content by using AI and Machine Learning algorithms to analyze any kind of digital content e.g. Text/Web, Audio, .
Website: http://hyscore.io
Phone: **Email:** contact@hyscore.io
City: Berlin **State:** Berlin **PC:** **Country:** Germany
Year Established: 2017 **Status 2020:** Active
Industries: Artificial Intelligence for:, Databases for:, Enterprise Application Services for:, Business Software as a Service Apps (SaaS Apps) for:, Web for:, Content for:, Speech Recognition for:, Data Management

Company Name: i2x
Description: i2x leverages the power of AI to transform the human voice into actionable insights at the speed of a face-to-face conversation.
Website: http://i2x.ai/
Phone: 49 1590 4414263 **Email:** legal@i2x.ai
City: Berlin **State:** Berlin **PC:** **Country:** Germany
Year Established: 2017 **Status 2020:** Active
Industries: Artificial Intelligence for:, IT Managed Services for:, Web for:, Machine Learning

Company Name: iCityGuide
Description: Buyer flow marketplace based on city navigator for tourists, AI routes generator, GPS navigation, voice guidance and augmented reality
Website: http://www.icityguide.online/
Phone: **Email:** info@icityguide.online
City: Berlin **State:** Berlin **PC:** **Country:** Germany
Year Established: **Status 2020:** Active
Industries: ~ Media-Communications (41), Artificial Intelligence for:, Augmented Reality for:, ~ Travel and Transportation (58)

Company Name: IconPeak
Description: IconPeak is a fully managed performance marketing service helping agencies, brands, and app developers scale their user acquisition.
Website: http://www.iconpeak.com
Phone: **Email:** contact@iconpeak.com
City: Berlin **State:** BE **PC:** **Country:** Germany
Year Established: 2013 **Status 2020:** Active
Industries: Application Services for:, Big Data and Analytics for:, Machine Learning for:, Mobile for:, ~ Media-Communications (41)

Company **Name:** idalab
Description: We help our clients achieve breakthrough progress with Artificial Intelligence
Website: http://idalab.de/
Phone: **Email:** vahik.soghom@idalab.de
City: Berlin **State:** Berlin **PC:** **Country:** Germany
Year Established: 2016 **Status 2020:** Active
Industries: Machine Learning

Company Name: Implisen: Sweden
Description: Implisense provides a platform for B2B Sales Automation based on external company information
Website: http://www.implisense.com/en
Phone: **Email:** hello@implisense.com
City: Berlin **State:** Berlin **PC:** **Country:** Germany
Year Established: **Status 2020:** Active
Industries: Analytics for:, Artificial Intelligence for:, Business Applications for:, Big Data and Analytics for:, Databases for:, ~ Media-Communications (41), ~ Media-Communications (41), Predictive Analytics for:, Automation

Company Name: Industrial Analytics IA GmbH
Description: Co-Founder
Website: https://industrial-analytics.io
Phone: **Email:** robert.strube@industrial-analytics.io
City: Berlin **State:** Berlin **Zip:** 10999 **Country:** Germany
Year Established: **Status 2020:** Active
Industries:

Company Name: Infosys Innovation Fabrik
Description: Ai & digital Innovation Lab. Co-working space & incubator for Ai & analytics startu: Palestine
Website:
Phone: **Email:** 36766@reference-encyclopedia-ai.net
City: Berlin **State:** Berlin **PC:** **Country:** Germany
Year Established: 2016 **Status 2020:** Active
Industries: Artificial Intelligence for:, IT Managed Services for:, Web

Company Name: INHUBBER
Description: CLM (Contract Lifecycle Management) solution on the blockchain, SaaS, B2B
Website: http://inhubber.com/
Phone: 49 176 420 429 33 **Email:** info@inhubber.com
City: Berlin **State:** Berlin **PC:** **Country:** Germany
Year Established: **Status 2020:** Active
Industries: Analytics for:, Artificial Intelligence for:, Business Applications for:, Blockchain for:, IT Managed Services

Company Name: Inspirient
Description: Inspirient simplifies data analysis by automatically searching for insights in your business data.
Website: https://www.inspirient.com
Phone: **Email:** contact@inspirient.com
City: Berlin **State:** Berlin **Zip:** 14195 **Country:** Germany
Year Established: **Status 2020:** Active
Industries: Artificial Intelligence for:, ~ Administrative and Support Services (1), ~ Aerospace and Defense (2), ~ Agriculture (3), ~ Arts-Entertainment-Recreation (4), ~ Automotive (5), ~ Banking

and Financial Markets-Services (7), ~ Beauty (8), ~ Biotechnology (9), ~ Const

Company Name: Inspora
Description: The digital shopping assistant for fashion brands & retaile: Serbia
Website: http://www.inspora.com/business
Phone: **Email:** hey@inspora.com
City: Berlin **State:** Berlin **PC:** **Country:** Germany
Year Established: 2017 **Status 2020:** Active
Industries: Artificial Intelligence for:, E-Commerce for:, ~ Fashion (16), Internet of Things (IoT)

Company Name: IPlytics
Description: IPlytics develops a market intelligence tool to analyze technology trends and market competition
Website: http://www.iplytics.com
Phone: 49 (0) 30 5557 4282 **Email:** info@iplytics.com
City: Berlin **State:** Berlin **PC:** **Country:** Germany
Year Established: 2012 **Status 2020:** Active
Industries: Analytics for:, Artificial Intelligence for:, IT Managed Services for:, Data Management

Company Name: Janus Genomics
Description: Janus Genomics is a company that builds AI tools for sharing of biomedical data while preserving data privacy.
Website: http://www.janus-genomics.com/
Phone: **Email:** 36821@reference-encyclopedia-ai.net
City: Berlin **State:** Berlin **PC:** **Country:** Germany
Year Established: 2018 **Status 2020:** Active
Industries:

Company Name: JobBot.me
Description: JobBot is an AI powered HR bot pioneer. He helps humans to find new jobs and helps companies to hire talents all around the world.
Website: http://www.jobbot.me
Phone: **Email:** jobs@jobbot.me
City: Berlin **State:** Berlin **PC:** **Country:** Germany
Year Established: **Status 2020:** Active
Industries: Artificial Intelligence for:, ~ Human Resources (24)

Company Name: Joblift
Description: Joblift is a job search platform providing candidates with the most intuitive and frictionless experience during the recruiting process.
Website: http://joblift.de/
Phone: **Email:** info@joblift.co.uk
City: Berlin **State:** Berlin **PC:** **Country:** Germany
Year Established: 2015 **Status 2020:** Active
Industries: Artificial Intelligence for:, Web

Company Name: jobpal
Description: jobpal build custom chatbots that facilitate the engagement between companies and candidates.
Website: http://jobpal.ai
Phone: **Email:** contact@jobpal.ai
City: Berlin **State:** Berlin **PC:** **Country:** Germany
Year Established: 2016 **Status 2020:** Active
Industries: Artificial Intelligence for:, IT Managed Services for:, Mobile for:, Natural Language Processing

Company Name: Jobspotting
Description: Jobspotting is a recommendations engine that suggests relevant jobs to users based on their skills and experience.
Website: http://jobspotting.com
Phone: 49 30809 35087 **Email:** hello@jobspotting.com
City: Berlin **State:** Berlin **PC:** **Country:** Germany
Year Established: **Status 2020:** Active
Industries: Artificial Intelligence for:, ~ Human Resources (24), Cyber Security

Company Name: Justsnap
Description: Justsnap is cloud-based promotion campaign management tool for businesses.
Website: http://www.justsnap.co
Phone: **Email:** info@justsnap.de
City: Berlin **State:** Berlin **PC:** **Country:** Germany
Year Established: 2015 **Status 2020:** Active
Industries: Databases for:, IT Managed Services for:, Predictive Analytics

Company Name: Kelsen
Description: Kelsen is a learning algorithm that computes answers to legal questions in real time by combining big data and machine learning.
Website:
Phone: **Email:** services@ask-kelsen.com
City: Berlin **State:** Berlin **PC:** **Country:** Germany
Year Established: 2014 **Status 2020:** Active
Industries: Big Data and Analytics for:, Databases for:, Machine Learning for:, Compute

Company Name: Ken: Jordan
Description: All-in-one effortless HR software. For engaged individuals.
Website: http://www.kenjo.io
Phone: **Email:** marketing@kenjo.io
City: Berlin **State:** Berlin **PC:** **Country:** Germany
Year Established: 2019 **Status 2020:** Active
Industries: Predictive Analytics

Company Name: KERSPI GmbH
Description: Be what you wribe. wribe is the social network where crowd based writing is the heart of the story.
Website: http://www.wribe.: India
Phone: **Email:** hello@wribe.: India
City: Berlin **State:** Berlin **PC:** **Country:** Germany
Year Established: **Status 2020:** Active
Industries: Artificial Intelligence

Company Name: KIProtect
Description: Building the security layer for data science and AI
Website: http://kiprotect.com
Phone: **Email:** info@kiprotect.com
City: Berlin **State:** Berlin **PC:** **Country:** Germany
Year Established: 2018 **Status 2020:** Active
Industries: Artificial Intelligence for:, Big Data and Analytics for:, Cyber Security for:, Machine Learning for:, Cyber Security for:, Security

Company Name: Konetik
Description: Konetik helps companies to integrate electric vehicles with their automated AI driven vehicle and charging advisor.
Website: http://www.konetik.com
Phone: 49 162 254 8583 **Email:** info@konetik.de
City: Berlin **State:** Berlin **PC:** **Country:** Germany
Year Established: 2014 **Status 2020:** Active
Industries: Artificial Intelligence for:, ~ Automotive (5), Internet of Things (IoT)

Company Name: Lableb
Description: Arabic Search & NLP Technology
Website: http://lableb.com
Phone: **Email:** ahlan@lableb.com
City: Berlin **State:** Berlin **PC:** **Country:** Germany
Year Established: **Status 2020:** Active
Industries: Artificial Intelligence for:, IT Managed Services for:, Natural Language Processing

Company Name: LabTw: India
Description: Voice and AI-powered digital lab assistant
Website: http://www.labtwin.com/
Phone: **Email:** 34243@reference-encyclopedia-ai.net
City: Berlin **State:** BE **PC:** **Country:** Germany

Year Established: 2018 **Status 2020:** Active
Industries: Artificial Intelligence for:, ~ Biotechnology (9)

Company Name: Lateral
Description: Empowering developers with the latest advancements in machine learning
Website: http://lateral.io/
Phone: 49 30 91442665 **Email:** hello@lateral.io
City: Berlin **State:** Berlin **PC:** **Country:** Germany
Year Established: **Status 2020:** Active
Industries: Artificial Intelligence for:, Content for:, Machine Learning

Company Name: lengoo
Description: lengoo is the future of translation. A full-service technology platform for customer-specific machine translation using Neural networks.
Website: http://www.lengoo.com
Phone: 49 721 7880 8533 **Email:** info@lengoo.de
City: Berlin **State:** Berlin **PC:** **Country:** Germany
Year Established: 2014 **Status 2020:** Active
Industries:

Company Name: LexaTexer
Description: LexaTexer is next generation software for predictive analytics.
Website: http://www.lexatexer.com
Phone: 49 30 60 98 98 060 **Email:** contact@lexatexer.com
City: Berlin **State:** Berlin **PC:** **Country:** Germany
Year Established: 2017 **Status 2020:** Active
Industries: Predictive Analytics

Company Name: LightTag
Description: LightTag is a new startup that has developed a platform designed to assist data scientists in creating training data for their AI systems.
Website: http://lighttag.io
Phone: **Email:** 36898@reference-encyclopedia-ai.net
City: Berlin **State:** Berlin **PC:** **Country:** Germany
Year Established: 2018 **Status 2020:** Active
Industries: Artificial Intelligence for:, Application Services for:, Application Services for:, IT Managed Services

Company Name: Lunar Ventur: Spain
Description: Lunar Ventures is a deep-tech, seed-stage venture fund with a team of 3 deep-tech expert partners in Berlin.
Website: http://lunarventures.eu/
Phone: **Email:** hello@lunarventures.eu
City: Berlin **State:** Berlin **PC:** **Country:** Germany
Year Established: 2017 **Status 2020:** Active
Industries: Artificial Intelligence for:, Blockchain for:, Cloud for:, Computer Vision for:, Cyber Security for:, ~ Banking and Financial Markets-Services (7), ~ Banking and Financial Markets-Services (7), IT Managed Services

Company Name: MADANA
Description: MADANA is securely bridging the gap between data and insights through the use of #PrivTech
Website: http://www.madana.io
Phone: **Email:** info@madana.io
City: Berlin **State:** Berlin **PC:** **Country:** Germany
Year Established: 2017 **Status 2020:** Active
Industries: Analytics for:, Big Data and Analytics for:, Blockchain for:, ~ Banking and Financial Markets-Services (7), IT Managed Services for:, IT Managed Services for:, Predictive Analytics

Company Name: Makers' Den
Description: Makers' Den is a software company that offers apps services, visualization and machine learning with custom solutions.
Website: http://makersden.io
Phone: **Email:** hello@makersden.io
City: Berlin **State:** Berlin **PC:** **Country:** Germany
Year Established: 2017 **Status 2020:** Active
Industries: Application Services for:, Machine Learning

Company Name: MAPEGY
Description: The most comprehensive data-driven technology intelligence platform & source.
Website: http://www.mapegy.com
Phone: 49 30 43022120 **Email:** contact@mapegy.com
City: Berlin **State:** Berlin **PC:** **Country:** Germany
Year Established: 2012 **Status 2020:** Active
Industries: Artificial Intelligence for:, Business Applications for:, Business Intelligence for:, Databases for:, Data Management for:, ~ Administrative and Support Services (1), Machine Learning for:, Natural Language Processing for:, Natural Language Processing for:, Predic

Company Name: mapegy GmbH
Description: Data-driven intelligence which helps identify the opportunities & threats of tomorrow'™s technology innovations
Website: http://www.mapegy.com
Phone: 49 30 43022120 **Email:** contact@mapegy.com
City: Berlin **State:** Berlin **PC:** **Country:** Germany
Year Established: **Status 2020:** Active
Industries: Analytics for:, Artificial Intelligence for:, Business Applications for:, Business Intelligence for:, Databases for:, Data Management for:, IT Managed Services for:, IT Managed Services for:, Application Services for:, Machine Learning for:, Natural Language Proc: Spain

Company Name: MatchX
Description: MatchX manufacturers superior LPWAN AI hardware and software, delivering comprehensive IoT Edge AI Solutions.
Website: http://www.matchx.io
Phone: 49 (0)3081457740 **Email:** awesome@matchx.io
City: Berlin **State:** Berlin **PC:** **Country:** Germany
Year Established: 2016 **Status 2020:** Active
Industries: Artificial Intelligence for:, IT Managed Services for:, IT Managed Services

Company Name: MediaMetrics
Description: MediaMetrics is a provider of an intelligent media monitoring solution.
Website:
Phone: 49 30 60 98 57 500 **Email:** 36953@reference-encyclopedia-ai.net
City: Berlin **State:** Berlin **PC:** **Country:** Germany
Year Established: 2011 **Status 2020:** Active
Industries: Application Services for:, ~ Arts-Entertainment-Recreation (4), Business Software as a Service Apps (SaaS Apps)

Company Name: MedMee
Description: Digitizing the healthcare industry and reducing medical & medication errors to a minimal via incorporation of Augmented Intelligence & Cloud
Website: http://medmee.co
Phone: **Email:** contact@medmee.co
City: Berlin **State:** Berlin **PC:** **Country:** Germany
Year Established: **Status 2020:** Active
Industries: Artificial Intelligence for:, ~ Healthcare (20), ~ Healthcare (20), ~ Healthcare (20), Machine Learning for:, ~ Healthcare (20), ~ Healthcare (20)

Company Name: Melodrive Inc.
Description: AI Music solution for adaptive music in interactive media.
Website: http://melodrive.com
Phone: **Email:** info@melodrive.com
City: Berlin **State:** Berlin **PC:** **Country:** Germany
Year Established: 2017 **Status 2020:** Active
Industries: Artificial Intelligence for:, ~ Arts-Entertainment-Recreation (4)

Company Name: Merantix
Description: Merantix is a pioneering platform for commercializing AI in industry.
Website: http://merantix.com
Phone: **Email:** team@merantix.com
City: Berlin **State:** Berlin **PC:** **Country:** Germany
Year Established: **Status 2020:** Active
Industries: Artificial Intelligence for:, Computer Vision for:, Machine Learning

Company Name: micropsi industri: Spain
Description: micropsi industries provides high-end machine learning solutions for robotics and process control.
Website: http://www.micropsi-industries.com/
Phone: **Email:** contact@micropsi-industries.com
City: Berlin **State:** Berlin **PC:** **Country:** Germany
Year Established: **Status 2020:** Active
Industries: Artificial Intelligence for:, ~ Manufacturing-General (31), Machine Learning for:, Robotics

Company Name: MIGHT
Description: IRL
Website: http://might.do
Phone: **Email:** hello@might.do
City: Berlin **State:** Berlin **PC:** **Country:** Germany
Year Established: **Status 2020:** Active
Industries:

Company Name: MindMatch
Description: MindMatch connects with your recruiting software, enabling you to find the ideal candidates by data enrichment and artificial intelligence.
Website: http://mindmatch.ai/
Phone: **Email:** hello@mindmatcha.ai
City: Berlin **State:** Berlin **PC:** **Country:** Germany
Year Established: 2017 **Status 2020:** Active
Industries: Artificial Intelligence

Company Name: Moalla Ventures
Description: Micro investment in early stage startup companies with a focus on fin-tech, data science and AI
Website:
Phone: **Email:** office@amoalla.com
City: Berlin **State:** Berlin **PC:** **Country:** Germany
Year Established: 2015 **Status 2020:** Active
Industries: Artificial Intelligence for:, IT Managed Services

Company Name: MoBerri: Spain
Description: MoBerries is a fast growing network connecting companies and professionals.
Website: www.moberries.com/
Phone: **Email:** community@moberries.com
City: Berlin **State:** Berlin **PC:** **Country:** Germany
Year Established: **Status 2020:** Active
Industries: Artificial Intelligence for:, ~ Human Resources (24), ~ Human Resources (24)

Company Name: MoneyCoa: Switzerland
Description: MoneyCoach is an AI-powered financial empowerment app that helps you get out of debt faster by tracking your budgets and expenses.
Website: http://moneycoach-app.com
Phone: 49 30 92147594 **Email:** info@moneycoach-app.com
City: Berlin **State:** Berlin **PC:** **Country:** Germany
Year Established: 2016 **Status 2020:** Active
Industries: Application Services for:, Artificial Intelligence for:, ~ Banking and Financial Markets-Services (7), ~ Banking and Financial Markets-Services (7), IT Managed Services

Company Name: MonitorFish
Description: MonitorFish is a multicultural team of innovation-driven experts offering cognitive capabilities of Artificial Intelligence in fish farming.
Website: http://www.monitorfish.com
Phone: **Email:** info@monitorfish.com
City: Berlin **State:** Berlin **PC:** **Country:** Germany
Year Established: 2017 **Status 2020:** Active
Industries: Artificial Intelligence

Company Name: MOTOR AI
Description: Motor AI developed an autonomous driving system based on cognitive neuroscience and groundbreaking German research.
Website: http://motor-ai.com/
Phone: **Email:** info@motor-ai.com
City: Berlin **State:** Berlin **PC:** **Country:** Germany
Year Established: 2017 **Status 2020:** Active
Industries: Artificial Intelligence for:, ~ Automotive (5)

Company Name: Ms. AI
Description: Ms. AI is a artificial intelligence company.
Website: http://www.nemesventures.com/
Phone: **Email:** office@nemesventures.com
City: Berlin **State:** Berlin **PC:** **Country:** Germany
Year Established: 2018 **Status 2020:** Active
Industries: Artificial Intelligence

Company Name: MVP Factory
Description: MVP Factory enables companies of all sizes to build and scale technology.
Website: http://mvpfactory.co/
Phone: **Email:** contact@mvpfactory.co
City: Berlin **State:** Berlin **PC:** **Country:** Germany
Year Established: 2017 **Status 2020:** Active
Industries: Artificial Intelligence

Company Name: Myos
Description: Rethinking working capital | Myos helps merchants of all kind grow to scale, fully digital, flexible and without personal guarante: Spain
Website: http://myos.co
Phone: 49 (30) 220 136 42-0 **Email:** invest@myos.co
City: Berlin **State:** Berlin **PC:** **Country:** Germany
Year Established: 2018 **Status 2020:** Active
Industries: Big Data and Analytics for:, E-Commerce for:, ~ Banking and Financial Markets-Services (7), Machine Learning

Company Name: neurocat
Description: AI-Safety Berl: India
Website: http://www.neurocat.ai/
Phone: **Email:** miau@neurocat.ai
City: Berlin **State:** **PC:** **Country:** Germany
Year Established: **Status 2020:** Active
Industries: Artificial Intelligence for:, ~ Administrative and Support Services (1), ~ Aerospace and Defense (2), ~ Agriculture (3), ~ Arts-Entertainment-Recreation (4), ~ Automotive (5), ~ Autonomous Vehicles (6), ~ Banking and Financial Markets-Services (7), ~ Beauty (8), ~

Company Name: Nostos Genomics
Description: AI-driven deciphering of genetic diseas: Spain
Website: http://nostos-genomics.com/
Phone: **Email:** team@nostos-genomics.com
City: Berlin **State:** Berlin **PC:** **Country:** Germany
Year Established: 2018 **Status 2020:** Active
Industries: Artificial Intelligence for:, ~ Biotechnology (9), Machine Learning

Company Name: omni:us
Description: omni:us delivers structured data from highly variable documents to streamline insurance back end processes.
Website: omnius.com/
Phone: **Email:** berlin@omnius.com
City: Berlin **State:** Berlin **PC:** **Country:** Germany

Year Established: **Status 2020:** Active
Industries:

Company Name: Onwrks
Description: Onwrks is a Berlin-based software startup, specializing in digital tools for wind turbine data management.
Website: http://onwrks.com/
Phone: **Email:** info@onwrks.com
City: Berlin **State:** Berlin **PC:** **Country:** Germany
Year Established: 2016 **Status 2020:** Active
Industries: Big Data and Analytics for:, IT Managed Services for:, Machine Learning for:, Robotics

Company Name: outsmart.ai -
Description: Business process automation based on RPA robots called AI Workers that learn through human-AI teamwork
Website:
Phone: **Email:** 37131@reference-encyclopedia-ai.net
City: Berlin **State:** Berlin **PC:** **Country:** Germany
Year Established: 2019 **Status 2020:** Closed
Industries:

Company Name: parlamind
Description: parlamind offers artificial intelligence solutions that analyzes, routes, and autonomously answers incoming customer communication.
Website: http://parlamind.com
Phone: **Email:** info@parlamind.com
City: Berlin **State:** Berlin **PC:** **Country:** Germany
Year Established: **Status 2020:** Active
Industries: Artificial Intelligence for:, Web for:, ~ Professional Services (48)

Company Name: Phantasma Labs
Description: Phantasma Labs is helping self-driving cars understand humans better.
Website: http://phantasma.global/
Phone: **Email:** 37161@reference-encyclopedia-ai.net
City: Berlin **State:** Berlin **PC:** **Country:** Germany
Year Established: 2018 **Status 2020:** Active
Industries: Artificial Intelligence for:, ~ Automotive (5), ~ Automotive (5)

Company Name: Pharmary
Description: instant delivery, connecting pharmacies, developing digital prescriptions and analysing these meta-information
Website: http://www.pharmary.de
Phone: 030 7676 3233 **Email:** info@pharmary.de
City: Berlin **State:** Berlin **PC:** **Country:** Germany
Year Established: 2017 **Status 2020:** Active
Industries: ~ Healthcare (20), IT Infrastructure for:, Predictive Analytics

Company Name: Pivii Technologies
Description: Pivii Technologies is an AI powered digital assistant that analyzes visual content posted on Instagram in one easy-to-use web-app.
Website: http://pivii.co/
Phone: **Email:** 37173@reference-encyclopedia-ai.net
City: Berlin **State:** Berlin **PC:** **Country:** Germany
Year Established: 2016 **Status 2020:** Active
Industries: Artificial Intelligence for:, Big Data and Analytics for:, Computer Vision for:, IT Managed Services for:, IT Managed Services for:, Machine Learning

Company Name: Plantix
Description: Biggest digital agro-ecosystem around small holder farming, including an AI powered crop doctor, disease alerts and the right remedies.
Website: http://plantix.net/
Phone: 49 176 43537145 **Email:** contact@peat.ai
City: Berlin **State:** Berlin **PC:** **Country:** Germany
Year Established: 2015 **Status 2020:** Active
Industries: ~ Agriculture (3), Application Services for:, Artificial Intelligence for:, Image Recognition

Company Name: Polyaxon
Description: An open source platform for reproducible machine learning at scale.
Website: http://polyaxon.com
Phone: **Email:** contact@polyaxon.com
City: Berlin **State:** Berlin **PC:** **Country:** Germany
Year Established: 2018 **Status 2020:** Active
Industries: Artificial Intelligence for:, Cloud for:, IT Infrastructure for:, Machine Learning for:, Enterprise Application Services

Company Name: PO:
Description: POPE is a free service that helps users find what they will love in the jungle of digital choice.
Website:
Phone: **Email:** 37190@reference-encyclopedia-ai.net
City: Berlin **State:** Berlin **PC:** **Country:** Germany
Year Established: 2011 **Status 2020:** Active
Industries: Big Data and Analytics for:, Machine Learning for:, ~ Media-Communications (41), Web

Company Name: Porsche Digital Lab
Description: Porsche Digital Lab provides a platform for collaborating with technology companies, startups and the scientific community.
Website: http://newsroom.porsche.de/digital
Phone: **Email:** astrid.boettinger@porsche.de
City: Berlin **State:** Berlin **PC:** **Country:** Germany
Year Established: 2016 **Status 2020:** Active
Industries: Artificial Intelligence for:, ~ Automotive (5), Blockchain for:, Internet of Things (IoT)

Company Name: POSpul: Sweden
Description: Leading crowd based Shopper Insights Intelligence company, enabling leading industry segments better market their products and services.
Website: http://www.pospulse.com
Phone: **Email:** service@pospulse.com
City: Berlin **State:** Berlin **PC:** **Country:** Germany
Year Established: **Status 2020:** Active
Industries: Artificial Intelligence for:, ~ Retail and Consumer Products (52), Compute for:, ~ Retail and Consumer Products (52)

Company Name: Practix Innovative Workout
Description: Practix enables gyms to give personalized service to their customers.
Website: http://practix-workout.com
Phone: **Email:** info@practix-workout.com
City: Berlin **State:** Berlin **PC:** **Country:** Germany
Year Established: **Status 2020:** Active
Industries: Artificial Intelligence for:, ~ Healthcare (20), Machine Learning

Company Name: Produc: Tanzania
Description: Productz is an encyclopedia of products that gets all the valuable pieces of information by using machine learning and crawling the web.
Website: http://productz.com
Phone: **Email:** hello@productz.com
City: Berlin **State:** Berlin **PC:** **Country:** Germany
Year Established: 2016 **Status 2020:** Active
Industries: Business Applications for:, Business Applications for:, Big Data and Analytics for:, Data Management for:, IT Managed Services for:, Machine Learning

Company Name: Proximity.ai -
Description: Proximity.ai blurs the line between the physical and digital world using advanced proximity sensing technology.
Website:
Phone: **Email:** 37219@reference-encyclopedia-ai.net
City: Berlin **State:** Berlin **PC:** **Country:** Germany
Year Established: 2016 **Status 2020:** Closed
Industries: Artificial Intelligence for:, IT Managed Services

Company Name: Qreuz
Description: Qreuz helps entrepreneurs to grow their digital business. Smart business intelligence for e-commerce.
Website: http://qreuz.com
Phone: **Email:** hello@qreuz.com
City: Berlin **State:** Berlin **PC:** **Country:** Germany
Year Established: **Status 2020:** Active
Industries: Analytics for:, ~ E-Commerce (134), Application Program Interfaces for:, ~ E-Commerce (195), ~ Media-Communications (224), ~ Social Media (237), Artificial Intelligence for:, ~ E-Commerce (12), ~ Media-Communications (41), ~ Social Media (54), Automation for:, ~ E-

Company Name: Qubit Ventur: Spain
Description: AI driven ventures builder
Website: http://www.qubitventures.com
Phone: **Email:** info@qubitventures.com
City: Berlin **State:** Berlin **PC:** **Country:** Germany
Year Established: **Status 2020:** Active
Industries:

Company Name: re2you
Description: re2you operates a cloud-based browser technology platform that enables data movement across all devices.
Website: http://www.re2you.com
Phone: 49 30 209 93951 **Email:** gk@re2you.com
City: Berlin **State:** Berlin **PC:** **Country:** Germany
Year Established: 2010 **Status 2020:** Active
Industries:

Company Name: RealRate
Description: Insurance Ratings based on Artificial Intelligence
Website: http://www.realrate.de
Phone: 49 160 957 90 844 **Email:** holger.bartel@realrate.de
City: Berlin **State:** Berlin **PC:** **Country:** Germany
Year Established: 2018 **Status 2020:** Active
Industries: Artificial Intelligence for:, ~ Banking and Financial Markets-Services (7), ~ Banking and Financial Markets-Services (7)

Company Name: RealSyn:Thailand
Description: Fully custom synthetic annotated image data for machine learning
Website: http://www.realsynth.de/
Phone: (929)330-9783 **Email:** founders@realsynth.de
City: Berlin **State:** Berlin **PC:** **Country:** Germany
Year Established: **Status 2020:** Active
Industries: Artificial Intelligence for:, Computer Vision for:, Automation for:, Machine Learning

Company Name: realxdata
Description: realxdata aims to offer data driven, analytic solutions for commercial real estate and make it more approachable for our customers.
Website: http://www.realxdata.com
Phone: 49 30 54909757 **Email:** info@realxdata.com
City: Berlin **State:** Berlin **PC:** **Country:** Germany
Year Established: 2016 **Status 2020:** Active
Industries: Big Data and Analytics for:, ~ Real Estate (49), Machine Learning

Company Name: Recotap
Description: AI-driven Personalization and Customer Experience Platform for Markete: Serbia
Website: http://www.recotap.com
Phone: 91 8951700280 **Email:** contact@recotap.com
City: Berlin **State:** Berlin **PC:** **Country:** Germany
Year Established: **Status 2020:** Active
Industries: Artificial Intelligence for:, Machine Learning for:, ~ Media-Communications (41), ~ Media-Communications (41)

Company **Name:** RecTag
Description: Podcast Discovery Platform
Website: http://www.rectag.eu
Phone: **Email:** team@rect.ag
City: Berlin **State:** Berlin **PC:** **Country:** Germany
Year Established: 2019 **Status 2020:** Active
Industries: Voice Recognition for:, Content for:, Web for:, Natural Language Processing for:, ~ Media-Communications (41), Speech Recognition

Company Name: ResearchCue
Description: ResearchCue answers many business questions on any topic or company, using NLP and deep learning techniques on web aggregated data
Website: http://www.researchcue.com
Phone: 49 178 6902429 **Email:** premraj@researchcue.com
City: Berlin **State:** Berlin **PC:** **Country:** Germany
Year Established: 2018 **Status 2020:** Active
Industries: Artificial Intelligence for:, Business Applications for:, Big Data and Analytics for:, Business Intelligence for:, IT Managed Services for:, Business Software as a Service Apps (SaaS Apps) for:, Data Management for:, Data Management

Company Name: Retresco GmbH
Description: Retresco is a leader in automated content, natural language generation and artificial intelligence.
Website: http://www.retresco.de/
Phone: **Email:** contakt@retresco.com
City: Berlin **State:** Berlin **PC:** **Country:** Germany
Year Established: **Status 2020:** Active
Industries: Artificial Intelligence for:, Automation for:, IT Managed Services for:, Natural Language Processing for:, ~ Media-Communications (41)

Company Name: RiseML
Description: RiseML creates software to help machine learning teams scale their deep learning infrastructure.
Website: http://riseml.com
Phone: **Email:** contact@riseml.com
City: Berlin **State:** Berlin **PC:** **Country:** Germany
Year Established: 2019 **Status 2020:** Closed
Industries: Artificial Intelligence for:, Web for:, Machine Learning

Company Name: Roq.ad
Description:
Website: https://www.roq.ad/
Phone: **Email:** marketing@roq.ad
City: Berlin **State:** Berlin **Zip:** 10969 **Country:** Germany
Year Established: **Status 2020:** Active
Industries:

Company Name: Sciencemap
Description: Sciencemap is an accelerate R&D by empowering researchers in their daily routine of reviewing scientific papers.
Website:
Phone: **Email:** 37347@reference-encyclopedia-ai.net
City: Berlin **State:** Berlin **PC:** **Country:** Germany
Year Established: 2017 **Status 2020:** Closed
Industries: Artificial Intelligence for:, ~ Education (13), IT Managed Services for:, Application Program Interfaces (APIs)

Company Name: Scoutbee
Description: Scoutbee is an artificial intelligence platform for procurement & supply chain experts.
Website: http://scoutbee.com
Phone: (1) 202-549-3672 **Email:** marketing@scoutbee.com
City: Berlin **State:** Berlin **PC:** **Country:** Germany
Year Established: 2015 **Status 2020:** Active
Industries: Analytics for:, Artificial Intelligence for:, Business Applications for:, Big Data and Analytics for:, IT Managed Services for:, ~ Telecommunications (56), Machine Learning

Company Name: Seatris.ai
Description: Seatris.ai is a reservation and revenue management assistant that supports restaurant teams to sell every seat they have available.
Website: http://www.seatris.ai
Phone: 49 30 81 45 40 400 **Email:** office@seatris.com
City: Berlin **State:** Berlin **PC:** **Country:** Germany

Year Established: 2018 **Status 2020:** Active
Industries: Artificial Intelligence for:, ~ Customer Relationship Management (11), Data Management for:, ~ Food and Beverage (17), Machine Learning for:, ~ Travel and Transportation (58), ~ Travel and Transportation (58), Business Software as a Service Apps (SaaS Apps)

Company Name: Sensefinity
Description: Sensefinity is working on social machines, which provides Internet of Things for the Masses harnessing the Power of the Blockchain.
Website: http://www.sensefinity.com
Phone: **Email:** info@sensefinity.com
City: Berlin **State:** Berlin **PC:** **Country:** Germany
Year Established: 2013 **Status 2020:** Active
Industries:

Company Name: Signal Cruncher
Description: Development of software solutions for integrated real-time data analysis for use as OEM software (Embedded Machine Learning).
Website: http://signal-cruncher.com/
Phone: **Email:** info@signal-cruncher.com
City: Berlin **State:** Berlin **PC:** **Country:** Germany
Year Established: 2016 **Status 2020:** Active
Industries: Artificial Intelligence for:, Big Data and Analytics for:, Databases for:, Automation for:, Internet of Things (IoT) for:, Machine Learning for:, Predictive Analytics for:, ~ Construction (10)

Company Name: Signal Cruncher GmbH
Description: Development of software solutions for integrated real-time data analysis for use as OEM software.
Website: http://signal-cruncher.com/
Phone: **Email:** info@signal-cruncher.com
City: Berlin **State:** Berlin **PC:** **Country:** Germany
Year Established: **Status 2020:** Active
Industries: Artificial Intelligence for:, Big Data and Analytics for:, Databases for:, ~ Energy and Utilities (14), Automation for:, Machine Learning for:, Predictive Analytics

Company Name: Signatrix
Description: Signatrix uses artificial intelligence to protect cash points and customer behavior, enabling retail stores to protect themselves.
Website: http://www.signatrix.com
Phone: 49 (0) 30 403670851 **Email:** info@signatrix.com
City: Berlin **State:** BE **PC:** **Country:** Germany
Year Established: 2017 **Status 2020:** Active
Industries: Artificial Intelligence for:, Computer Vision for:, Machine Learning for:, Security

Company Name: Simby
Description: Artificial intelligence that will make you a super he: Romania
Website: http://simby.com
Phone: **Email:** hello@simby.com
City: Berlin **State:** Berlin **PC:** **Country:** Germany
Year Established: **Status 2020:** Active
Industries: Artificial Intelligence

Company Name: Simplaex
Description: Simplaex is the company behind the world's most advanced artificial intelligence-powered user targeting technology.
Website: http://www.simplaex.com/
Phone: 49 30 922512772 **Email:** info@simplaex.com
City: Berlin **State:** Berlin **PC:** **Country:** Germany
Year Established: 2015 **Status 2020:** Active
Industries: Artificial Intelligence for:, Big Data and Analytics for:, Data Management for:, Digital Marketing for:, Machine Learning for:, Machine Learning

Company Name: Sizolution
Description: Sizolution is an AI based SaaS for fashion ecommerce.
Website: http://www.sizolution.com
Phone: **Email:** welcome@sizolution.com
City: Berlin **State:** Berlin **PC:** **Country:** Germany
Year Established: 2015 **Status 2020:** Active
Industries: Artificial Intelligence for:, E-Commerce for:, ~ Fashion (16), Business Software as a Service Apps (SaaS Apps)

Company Name: SmartCloudFarming
Description: AgTech, Agriculture, DeepTech, Remote Sensing, Data Analytics, Soil Analytics
Website: http://www.smartcloudfarming.com
Phone: **Email:** info@smartcloudfarming.com
City: Berlin **State:** Berlin **PC:** **Country:** Germany
Year Established: 2019 **Status 2020:** Active
Industries: ~ Agriculture (3), ~ Agriculture (3), Artificial Intelligence for:, Big Data and Analytics for:, Machine Learning for:, ~ Construction (10)

Company Name: SNAZZ
Description: The green and fair AI-based fashion platform for the sustainable fashion industry.
Website: http://www.snazz.app
Phone: **Email:** info@snazzapp.de
City: Berlin **State:** Berlin **PC:** **Country:** Germany
Year Established: 2019 **Status 2020:** Active
Industries: Application Services for:, Artificial Intelligence for:, Big Data and Analytics for:, IT Managed Services for:, ~ Social Assistance-Non-Profits (53), ~ Social Assistance-Non-Profits (53)

Company Name: SO1.ai - Segment of One
Description: SO1 brings artificial intelligence to grocery retail and allows retailers to create personalized offers to their customers.
Website: http://www.so1.ai
Phone: 49 30 6098 548 10 **Email:** info@so1.ai
City: Berlin **State:** Berlin **PC:** **Country:** Germany
Year Established: **Status 2020:** Active
Industries: Artificial Intelligence for:, ~ Retail and Consumer Products (52), Machine Learning for:, ~ Media-Communications (41), ~ Retail and Consumer Products (52), ~ Retail and Consumer Products (52), ~ Retail and Consumer Products (52)

Company Name: Solvemate
Description: Solvemate is a machine learning platform for automating customer support.
Website: http://www.solvemate.com
Phone: **Email:** y.vasileiou@solvemate.com
City: Berlin **State:** Berlin **PC:** **Country:** Germany
Year Established: **Status 2020:** Active
Industries: Artificial Intelligence for:, ~ Telecommunications (56), ~ Professional Services (48)

Company Name: SOTA SOLUTIONS GmbH
Description: Software which creates itself and increases profit - this is the successful concept of SOTA SOLUTIONS
Website: http://sota-solutions.de/
Phone: 49 30 63925990 **Email:** info@sota-solutions.de
City: Berlin **State:** Berlin **PC:** **Country:** Germany
Year Established: **Status 2020:** Active
Industries: Artificial Intelligence for:, Machine Learning for:, ~ Professional Services (48)

Company Name: SPREAD
Description: We create digital product perception like no machine understood before – less artificial, more intelligent!
Website: http://www.spread.ai
Phone: **Email:** info@spread.ai
City: Berlin **State:** Berlin **PC:** **Country:** Germany
Year Established: 2019 **Status 2020:** Active
Industries: Artificial Intelligence for:, Application Services for:, ~ Social-Environmental-Physical-Engineering Sciences (55), Business Process and Operations

Company Name: Storeness
Description: Artificial Intelligence Applied To Business Problems
Website: http://storeness.de
Phone: **Email:** 37470@reference-encyclopedia-ai.net
City: Berlin **State:** Berlin **PC:** **Country:** Germany
Year Established: 2014 **Status 2020:** Active
Industries: Artificial Intelligence for:, Machine Learning

Company Name: Super Izzy AI
Description: Super Izzy AI is a femtech chatbot that offers personalized health advice for women, based on data collection and contextual understanding.
Website: http://www.superizzy.ai
Phone: **Email:** hajnalka@superizzy.ai
City: Berlin **State:** Berlin **PC:** **Country:** Germany
Year Established: 2016 **Status 2020:** Active
Industries:

Company Name: SwitchUp.de
Description: Assistant that automatically optimises all of your subscriptions
Website: http://www.switchup.de/
Phone: **Email:** 37496@reference-encyclopedia-ai.net
City: Berlin **State:** Berlin **PC:** **Country:** Germany
Year Established: 2014 **Status 2020:** Active
Industries: Artificial Intelligence

Company Name: synergist.io
Description: Create, negotiate and sign contracts without redlines or email.
Website: http://synergist.io
Phone: **Email:** info@synergist.io
City: Berlin **State:** Berlin **PC:** **Country:** Germany
Year Established: **Status 2020:** Active
Industries: Artificial Intelligence for:, IT Managed Services for:, ~ Law-Legal Services (26), ~ Professional Services (48)

Company Name: The SaaS Co.
Description: Artificial intelligence for sales & customer care
Website: http://thesaas.co/
Phone: **Email:** info@thesaascompany.de
City: Berlin **State:** Berlin **PC:** **Country:** Germany
Year Established: **Status 2020:** Active
Industries: Artificial Intelligence for:, Business Applications for:, ~ Media-Communications (41)

Company Name: TheMinuteApp
Description: HR, App, AI, SaaS, Staffing, Voice
Website: http://www.theminuteapp.com
Phone: 555174-1920 **Email:** hubert.moik@theminuteapp.com
City: Berlin **State:** Berlin **PC:** **Country:** Germany
Year Established: **Status 2020:** Active
Industries: Artificial Intelligence for:, ~ Human Resources (24), ~ Human Resources (24)

Company Name: Tracks
Description: German tech company Tracks pioneers the road freight industry's transformation towards greater efficiency and ecological sustainability.
Website: http://tracksfortrucks.com/
Phone: 49 152 26318286 **Email:** contact@tracksfortrucks.com
City: Berlin **State:** Berlin **PC:** **Country:** Germany
Year Established: 2018 **Status 2020:** Active
Industries: Artificial Intelligence for:, ~ Automotive (5), IT Managed Services

Company Name: tribeapp
Description: The perfect eyewear look and fit: realistic try-on and precise eye measurements with a mobile app
Website: http://www.tribeapp.com
Phone: **Email:** info@tribeapp.com
City: Berlin **State:** Berlin **PC:** **Country:** Germany
Year Established: 2018 **Status 2020:** Active
Industries: Artificial Intelligence for:, Augmented Reality for:, Business Applications for:, Machine Learning

Company Name: TunedIn
Description: TunedIn is a social media startup building an app to improve the way users discover, connect, and participate with television content.
Website: http://www.tunedin.de
Phone: 49 30 609 377 88 **Email:** info@tunedin.de
City: Berlin **State:** Berlin **PC:** **Country:** Germany
Year Established: 2010 **Status 2020:** Closed
Industries: Content for:, Machine Learning for:, ~ Social Assistance-Non-Profits (53)

Company Name: Twenty Billion Neurons
Description: Twenty Billion Neurons builds advanced machine learning systems that understand video.
Website: http://20bn.com
Phone: **Email:** info@twentybn.com
City: Berlin **State:** Berlin **PC:** **Country:** Germany
Year Established: **Status 2020:** Active
Industries: Artificial Intelligence for:, Embedded for:, Enterprise Application Services for:, Industrial Solutions for:, Machine Learning

Company Name: Twyla
Description: AI Chatbots for Customer Service
Website: http://twylahelps.com
Phone: **Email:** hello@twylahelps.com
City: Berlin **State:** Berlin **PC:** **Country:** Germany
Year Established: **Status 2020:** Active
Industries: Artificial Intelligence for:, Machine Learning for:, Natural Language Processing for:, IT Managed Services

Company Name: Ubermetrics
Description: Ubermetrics is a content intelligence platform for Marketing & PR experts.
Website: http://www.ubermetrics-technologies.com/
Phone: 49 (0) 30 57702130 **Email:** hello@ubermetrics.com
City: Berlin **State:** Berlin **PC:** **Country:** Germany
Year Established: 2011 **Status 2020:** Active
Industries: Analytics for:, Artificial Intelligence for:, Content

Company Name: urban ENERGY GmbH
Description: Urban ENERGY specializes in eMobility in urban areas, taking energy management with IoT and data analytics to a new level.
Website: http://urbanenergy.de/de/
Phone: **Email:** 4687@reference-encyclopedia-ai.net
City: Berlin **State:** Berlin **PC:** **Country:** Germany
Year Established: **Status 2020:** Active
Industries: Artificial Intelligence for:, ~ Transportation and Logistics (57)

Company Name: Verne
Description: Verne's a group of people passionate about solving technological mazes.
Website: http://www.verne-ai.com
Phone: 49 30 346 496 764 **Email:** info@verne-ai.com
City: Berlin **State:** Berlin **PC:** **Country:** Germany
Year Established: **Status 2020:** Active
Industries: Artificial Intelligence for:, IT Managed Services

Company Name: Versus
Description: Versus is a global data-driven comparison platform for over 90 categories, from consumer electronics to countries.
Website: http://versus.com
Phone: **Email:** office@urge.io
City: Berlin **State:** Berlin **PC:** **Country:** Germany
Year Established: **Status 2020:** Active
Industries: Artificial Intelligence for:, ~ Manufacturing-Electronic (30), ~ Professional Services (48), ~ Retail and Consumer Products (52), E-Commerce for:, ~ E-Commerce (2208), ~ Gaming (2214), ~ High Tech (2217)

Company Name: voiXen GmbH
Description: speech technology using AI/ML to improve customer service and sal: Spain
Website: http://www.voixen.ai
Phone: **Email:** info@voixen.com
City: Berlin **State:** Berlin **PC:** **Country:** Germany
Year Established: 2014 **Status 2020:** Active
Industries:

Company Name: Voyc.ai
Description: The Customer Discovery Company
Website: http://www.voyc.ai/
Phone: **Email:** hello@voyc.ai
City: Berlin **State:** Berlin **PC:** **Country:** Germany
Year Established: **Status 2020:** Active
Industries: Analytics for:, Artificial Intelligence for:, IT Managed Services

Company Name: WARD
Description: WARD is a fantasy sport game, where fans can watch their favourite eSports matches and predict what will happen in real time.
Website: http://ward.world
Phone: **Email:** hello@ward.world
City: Berlin **State:** Berlin **PC:** **Country:** Germany
Year Established: 2017 **Status 2020:** Closed
Industries: ~ Arts-Entertainment-Recreation (4), Predictive Analytics for:, Compute

Company Name: wefox Group
Description: wefox: Platform that connects insurances to brokers that consult their customers completely digital; ONE: Fully digital insurance company
Website: http://www.wefoxgroup.com
Phone: **Email:** service@wefox.: Switzerland
City: Berlin **State:** Berlin **PC:** **Country:** Germany
Year Established: **Status 2020:** Active
Industries: Artificial Intelligence for:, ~ Banking and Financial Markets-Services (7), ~ Insurance (25), ~ Insurance (25)

Company Name: We: Palestine
Description: Weps is a chatbot website builder for microbusiness owners.
Website: http://getweps.com
Phone: 37258443876 **Email:** juhan@getweps.com
City: Berlin **State:** Berlin **PC:** **Country:** Germany
Year Established: **Status 2020:** Active
Industries: Artificial Intelligence for:, Human Computer Interaction for:, Cyber Security for:, Cyber Security

Company Name: whoelse.ai
Description: Make AIs talk to each other! We develop a simplified language as a shared namespace between conversational AIs.
Website: http://whoelse.ai
Phone: 49 30 - 939 109 57 **Email:** hello@whoelse.ai
City: Berlin **State:** Berlin **PC:** **Country:** Germany
Year Established: 2018 **Status 2020:** Active
Industries: Artificial Intelligence

Company Name: Wizart API
Description: Artificial Intelligence Based Photo Editing
Website: http://wizart.io/
Phone: **Email:** 37680@reference-encyclopedia-ai.net
City: Berlin **State:** Berlin **PC:** **Country:** Germany
Year Established: 2016 **Status 2020:** Active
Industries: Artificial Intelligence for:, Application Services for:, ~ Media-Communications (41)

Company Name: WUNDER
Description: Real-Time Cognitive AI for trustful customer engagement
Website: http://www.wunder.ai
Phone: **Email:** office@wunder.ai
City: Berlin **State:** Berlin **PC:** **Country:** Germany
Year Established: **Status 2020:** Active
Industries: Artificial Intelligence for:, Big Data and Analytics for:, Web for:, Machine Learning for:, ~ Media-Communications (41), ~ Healthcare (20)

Company Name: XA: India
Description: XAIN builds the technology to scale your AI training.
Website: http://www.xain.io
Phone: **Email:** info@xain.io
City: Berlin **State:** Berlin **PC:** **Country:** Germany
Year Established: 2017 **Status 2020:** Active
Industries: Artificial Intelligence for:, Cyber Security for:, IT Infrastructure for:, Machine Learning for:, Cyber Security

Company Name: Xbird
Description: Xbird is a medical artificial intelligence company focused on prevention of curable diseases through mobile data.
Website: http://www.xbird.io/
Phone: 49 030 54905335 **Email:** info@xbird.io
City: Berlin **State:** BE **PC:** **Country:** Germany
Year Established: 2015 **Status 2020:** Active
Industries: Analytics for:, Artificial Intelligence for:, Databases for:, ~ Healthcare (20), ~ Healthcare (20), Internet of Things (IoT)

Company Name: Yolife
Description: Yolife is a mobile app that coaches people how to live longer in good heal:Thailand
Website: http://yolife.io/
Phone: 49 1578 4299318 **Email:** hello@yolife.io
City: Berlin **State:** Berlin **PC:** **Country:** Germany
Year Established: 2019 **Status 2020:** Active
Industries: Artificial Intelligence for:, ~ Healthcare (20), ~ Healthcare (20)

Company Name: Zeitgold
Description: Zeitgold is a Berlin-based AI company providing a complete solution for financial administration of small businesses.
Website: http://www.zeitgold.com/
Phone: **Email:** info@zeitgold.com
City: Berlin **State:** Berlin **PC:** **Country:** Germany
Year Established: **Status 2020:** Active
Industries: Artificial Intelligence for:, ~ Banking and Financial Markets-Services (7)

Company Name: ZyseMe
Description: ZyseMe is a technology platform that empowers fashion brands to produce and sell fully personalized clothing at scale.
Website: http://www.zyse.me/
Phone: 49-151-18617032 **Email:** hello@zyse.me
City: Berlin **State:** Berlin **PC:** **Country:** Germany
Year Established: **Status 2020:** Active
Industries: Artificial Intelligence for:, E-Commerce for:, ~ Fashion (16), Automation for:, Machine Learning for:, ~ Manufacturing-Miscellaneous (34), ~ Retail and Consumer Products (52), Supply Chain Management for:, ~ Social-Environmental-Physical-Engineering Sciences (55)

Company Name: Industrial Analytics IA GmbH
Description: AI-IoT for industrial processes and turbomachinery.
Website: http://www.industrial-analytics.io
Phone: 30629388111 **Email:** info@industrial-analytics.io
City: Berlin - Kreuzberg **State:** Berlin **Zip:** 10999 **Country:** Germany
Year Established: **Status 2020:** Active
Industries: Analytics for:, ~ Aerospace and Defense (124), ~ Agriculture (125), ~ Biotechnology (131), ~ Energy and Utilities (136), ~ Food and Beverage (139), ~ Manufacturing-Petroleum-Coal-Chemicals-Plastics-Rubber (159), ~ Manufacturing-Primary-Fabricated Metal (160), ~ M

Company Name: Wikifriend
Description: Our conversational chatbots talk for your brand
Website: http://www.wikifriend.net/
Phone: **Email:** info@wikifriend.net
City: Charlottenburg **State:** Berlin **PC:** **Country:** Germany
Year Established: **Status 2020:** Active
Industries:

Company Name: Job Pal
Description: We build 100% customised chat bots for companies that automate candidate engagement, pre-screening and interview logistics.
Website: http://jobpal.ai
Phone: **Email:** contact@jobpal.ai
City: Kreuzberg **State:** Berlin **PC:** **Country:** Germany
Year Established: **Status 2020:** Active
Industries: Artificial Intelligence for:, ~ Human Resources (24), IT Managed Services for:, Mobile for:, Natural Language Processing for:, ~ Human Resources (24)

Company Name: Heili
Description: AI-ASSISTED SITE RELIABILITY AI-ASSISTED SITE RELIABILITY AI-ASSISTED SITE RELIABILITY
Website: http://www.heilihq.com/
Phone: 972 72-245-6104 **Email:** info@heilihq.com
City: Belin **State:** Brandenburg **PC:** **Country:** Germany
Year Established: **Status 2020:** Active
Industries: Artificial Intelligence for:, Cloud

Company Name: Cinuru Research:
Description: Data analytics for the movie industry, offering AI-powered digital loyalty systems to cinemas and data-driven online campaigns to studios.
Website: http://www.cinuru.com
Phone: **Email:** contact@cinuru.com
City: Potsdam **State:** BB **PC:** **Country:** Germany
Year Established: 2017 **Status 2020:** Active
Industries: Analytics for:, Artificial Intelligence

Company Name: Kweak.ly
Description: Kweak.ly is a artificial intelligence messaging platform that converts texts into visual GIFs.
Website: http://kweak.ly/
Phone: 49 (0) 331 70 48 43 29 **Email:** connect@kweak.ly
City: Potsdam **State:** BB **PC:** **Country:** Germany
Year Established: 2015 **Status 2020:** Active
Industries: Artificial Intelligence for:, Augmented Reality for:, Mobile

Company Name: Letos
Description: Letos is a Machine Learning algorithm, allowing for prediction of human behavioral reactions as they occur within different scenarios
Website: http://letos.me/
Phone: **Email:** info@letos.me
City: Potsdam **State:** BB **PC:** **Country:** Germany
Year Established: **Status 2020:** Active
Industries: Artificial Intelligence for:, Machine Learning

Company Name: nxtbase
Description: nxtBase technologies has focused serving a global industrial segment with solutions for efficient processes using AI powered Assited Reality
Website: http://nxtbase.io/
Phone: **Email:** jjk@nxtbase.de
City: Potsdam **State:** BB **PC:** **Country:** Germany
Year Established: 2016 **Status 2020:** Active
Industries: Artificial Intelligence for:, Augmented Reality for:, Business Process and Operations

Company Name: Seerene
Description: Seerene is a code people management platform.
Website: http://www.seerene.com
Phone: **Email:** mail@seerene.com
City: Potsdam **State:** BB **PC:** **Country:** Germany
Year Established: **Status 2020:** Active
Industries: Analytics for:, Artificial Intelligence for:, Big Data and Analytics for:, Business Intelligence for:, Data Management for:, Enterprise Application Services for:, Predictive Analytics for:, ~ Professional Services (48)

Company Name: Statisti: Palestine
Description: Data analytics service.
Website: http://www.statistips.com
Phone: 33124364901 **Email:** info@statistips.com
City: Potsdam **State:** BB **PC:** **Country:** Germany
Year Established: **Status 2020:** Active
Industries: Analytics for:, Artificial Intelligence for:, Big Data and Analytics for:, Databases for:, Data Management for:, Predictive Analytics for:, ~ Arts-Entertainment-Recreation (4)

Company Name: stenon
Description: stenon is a laboratory independent real-time soil analyst that offers solutions for agriculture.
Website: http://www.stenon.io
Phone: 49 (0) 151 23936887 **Email:** info@stenon.io
City: Potsdam **State:** BB **PC:** **Country:** Germany
Year Established: **Status 2020:** Active
Industries: ~ Agriculture (3), ~ Agriculture (3), Artificial Intelligence for:, ~ Manufacturing-Electronic (30), ~ Professional Services (48)

Company Name: Oculyze
Description: The Oculyze computer vision cloud platform combines methodical patern recognition with AI to offer quantitative real-time image analysis.
Website: http://www.oculyze.de/
Phone: **Email:** info@oculyze.de
City: Wildau **State:** BB **PC:** **Country:** Germany
Year Established: 2016 **Status 2020:** Active
Industries: Artificial Intelligence for:, ~ Biotechnology (9), Computer Vision for:, ~ Food and Beverage (17), ~ Healthcare (20), Image Recognition for:, Machine Learning for:, ~ Food and Beverage (17), ~ Food and Beverage (17)

Company Name: Blackout Technologies
Description: Blackout Technologies offer an easy-to-use low-code Digital Assistant platform.
Website: http://blackout.ai/
Phone: **Email:** hi@blackout.ai
City: Bremen **State:** HB **PC:** **Country:** Germany
Year Established: 2017 **Status 2020:** Active
Industries: Artificial Intelligence for:, Machine Learning for:, Robotics

Company Name: PlanBlue
Description: PlanBlue utilities a new seafloor monitoring technology that's changing the way they map and assess the health of seafloor areas.
Website: http://www.planblue.com/
Phone: 49 421 2208120 **Email:** info@planblue.com
City: Bremen **State:** HB **PC:** **Country:** Germany
Year Established: 2017 **Status 2020:** Active
Industries: Artificial Intelligence for:, Machine Learning

Company Name: Valispace
Description: Valispace is a browser-based software that enables engineers to collaboratively develop satellites, rockets, and other complex hardware.
Website: http://www.valispace.com
Phone: **Email:** contact-us@valispace.com
City: Bremen **State:** HB **PC:** **Country:** Germany
Year Established: 2016 **Status 2020:** Active
Industries: Enterprise Application Services for:, Application Services for:, ~ Social-Environmental-Physical-Engineering Sciences (55), Business Software as a Service Apps (SaaS Apps)

Company Name: WearHeal:Thailand
Description: WearHealth is the AI-driven platform that learns from Health Experts and data from Wearables to empower personal health assistance.
Website: http://www.wearhealth.com/
Phone: **Email:** hello@wearhealth.com
City: Bremen **State:** HB **PC:** **Country:** Germany
Year Established: 2011 **Status 2020:** Active
Industries:

Company Name: Absolute Software GmbH
Description: Absolute Software GmbH is a software development company that develops tailored software solutions to its clients.
Website: http://www.absolute.de
Phone: (403) 496-1810 **Email:** info@absolute.de
City: Hamburg **State:** HH **PC:** **Country:** Germany
Year Established: **Status 2020:** Active
Industries: Analytics for:, Artificial Intelligence for:, Big Data and Analytics for:, Databases for:, IT Managed Services for:, ~ Professional Services (48)

Company Name: Adtriba
Description: AI-powered marketing decisions to optimize your marketing performance
Website: http://www.adtriba.com/
Phone: **Email:** contact@adtriba.com
City: Hamburg **State:** HH **PC:** **Country:** Germany
Year Established: **Status 2020:** Active
Industries: Analytics for:, Artificial Intelligence for:, Business Applications for:, Big Data and Analytics for:, Machine Learning

Company Name: aiconix.ai
Description: aiconix offers an established AI-driven platform with automatic access to high precision metadata that generates new value to the classical CMS and DAM offerings.
Website: https://aiconix.ai/language/en/
Phone: **Email:** office@aiconix.ai
City: Hamburg **State:** HH **PC:** **Country:** Germany
Year Established: **Status 2020:** Active
Industries:

Company Name: Akanoo
Description: Akanoo connects visitors of online-shops with tailor-made incentives to boost shop revenues.
Website: http://www.akanoo.com/
Phone: 49 40 609 462 3 40 **Email:** hi@akanoo.com
City: Hamburg **State:** HH **PC:** **Country:** Germany
Year Established: 2013 **Status 2020:** Active
Industries: Analytics for:, Business Applications for:, Big Data and Analytics for:, E-Commerce for:, Predictive Analytics for:, Business Software as a Service Apps (SaaS Apps)

Company Name: Attention Insight
Description: Attention Insight is an artificial intelligence platform for consumer visual engagement monitoring.
Website: http://www.attentioninsight.ai/
Phone: 37062281384 **Email:** Hi@attentioninsight.ai
City: Hamburg **State:** HH **PC:** **Country:** Germany
Year Established: **Status 2020:** Active
Industries: Artificial Intelligence

Company Name: BIPortal
Description: Business Intelligence SaaS and on-premise software.
Website: http://bi-portal.com
Phone: 49 40-507-1948-1 **Email:** luedtke@bi-portal.com
City: Hamburg **State:** HH **PC:** **Country:** Germany
Year Established: 2012 **Status 2020:** Active
Industries: Artificial Intelligence for:, IT Managed Services for:, Machine Learning for:, Business Software as a Service Apps (SaaS Apps)

Company Name: Cargonexx
Description: First digital freight forwarder in Europe using AI to improve utilization of trucks. Long-Haul Trucking, Logistic, Transportation, AI.
Website: http://www.cargonexx.de
Phone: 49 178 3866521 **Email:** rdl@cargonexx.de
City: Hamburg **State:** HH **PC:** **Country:** Germany
Year Established: 2016 **Status 2020:** Active
Industries: Artificial Intelligence for:, ~ Telecommunications (56)

Company Name: Cauliflower
Description: SaaS Comment Classification: Cauliflower uses AI to deliver deep and intuitive insights from text. No manual training required.
Website: http://cauliflower.ai/
Phone: 49 40 696 388 611 **Email:** hello@cauliflower.ai
City: Hamburg **State:** HH **PC:** **Country:** Germany
Year Established: 2019 **Status 2020:** Active
Industries: Artificial Intelligence for:, IT Managed Services for:, Natural Language Processing for:, Business Software as a Service Apps (SaaS Apps) for:, Data Management

Company Name: CellmatiQ
Description: CellmatiQ is creates artificial intelligence products that benefit patients and medical professionals alike.
Website: http://cellmatiq.com/
Phone: **Email:** contact@cellmatiq.com
City: Hamburg **State:** HH **PC:** **Country:** Germany
Year Established: **Status 2020:** Active
Industries: Artificial Intelligence for:, ~ Healthcare (20), ~ Professional Services (48)

Company Name: Deepk: Italy
Description: First native, real-time, offline-first app to support the full machine learning experiment life cycle with deep learning debugger.
Website: http://deepkit.ai/
Phone: **Email:** info@deepkit.ai
City: Hamburg **State:** HH **PC:** **Country:** Germany
Year Established: 2018 **Status 2020:** Active
Industries: Artificial Intelligence for:, Machine Learning

Company Name: DeepK
Description: Deep Learning Kit for training infrastructure, management and analytical interfaces.
Website: http://deepkit.ai/
Phone: **Email:** info@deepkit.ai
City: Hamburg **State:** HH **PC:** **Country:** Germany
Year Established: **Status 2020:** Active
Industries: Artificial Intelligence for:, Machine Learning

Company Name: Evertracker
Description: Evertracker enables manufacturers and producers to gain full control over supply chains and logistics through prediction and automation.
Website: http://www.evertracker.com
Phone: **Email:** info@evertracker.com
City: Hamburg **State:** HH **PC:** **Country:** Germany
Year Established: **Status 2020:** Active
Industries: Artificial Intelligence for:, Big Data and Analytics for:, Automation for:, Web for:, ~ Transportation and Logistics (57), ~ Professional Services (48), Supply Chain Management

Company Name: Exponenta
Description: AI co-writer that helps create content your audience is going to share.
Website: http://exponenta.io
Phone: **Email:** dm@exponenta.io
City: Hamburg **State:** HH **PC:** **Country:** Germany
Year Established: 2017 **Status 2020:** Active
Industries: Artificial Intelligence for:, IT Managed Services for:, IT Managed Services

Company Name: GitMate
Description: GitMate is a ML based ticket manager for Jira and GitHub.
Website: http://gitmate.io/
Phone: **Email:** info@gitmate.io
City: Hamburg **State:** HH **PC:** **Country:** Germany
Year Established: 2017 **Status 2020:** Active
Industries:

Company Name: GNOD
Description: GNOD is a self-learning system that enables users to discover and discuss new music, books, products, art, and movies.
Website: http://www.gnod.com
Phone: **Email:** marek@gibney.de
City: Hamburg **State:** HH **PC:** **Country:** Germany
Year Established: **Status 2020:** Active
Industries: Artificial Intelligence

Company Name: Gpredictive GmbH
Description: Every marketer can optimize all the touchpoints in their customer journey through our DIY A.I.
Website: http://www.gpredictive.com
Phone: **Email:** info@gpredictive.com
City: Hamburg **State:** HH **PC:** **Country:** Germany
Year Established: **Status 2020:** Active
Industries: ~ Media-Communications (41), Artificial Intelligence for:, E-Commerce for:, Machine Learning for:, Predictive Analytics

Company Name: Heldenkombinat Technologies
Description: Heldenkombinat Technologies builds AI systems that accelerate productivity and discover new strategies.
Website: http://www.heldenkombinat.com/
Phone: 49 40 20 91 52 55 **Email:** commander@heldenkombinat.com
City: Hamburg **State:** HH **PC:** **Country:** Germany
Year Established: 2018 **Status 2020:** Active
Industries: Artificial Intelligence for:, Machine Learning

Company Name: Kreditech Holding
Description: Kreditech uses machine-learning technologies to provide access to better credit for the underbanked
Website: http://www.kreditech.com
Phone: **Email:** info@kreditech.com
City: Hamburg **State:** HH **PC:** **Country:** Germany
Year Established: **Status 2020:** Active
Industries: Artificial Intelligence for:, ~ Banking and Financial Markets-Services (7), Big Data and Analytics for:, ~ Banking and Financial Markets-Services (7), ~ Banking and Financial Markets-Services (7), ~ Banking and Financial Markets-Services (7), ~ Banking and Fina

Company Name: Mesaic
Description: Mesaic empowers companies with automation & AI to build great relationships with customers, leveraging conversational channels.
Website: http://www.mesaic.co
Phone: 49 40 28863690 **Email:** hello@mesaic.co
City: Hamburg **State:** HH **PC:** **Country:** Germany
Year Established: 2016 **Status 2020:** Active
Industries: Enterprise Application Services for:, Business Software as a Service Apps (SaaS Apps)

Company Name: MinuteHero
Description: MinuteHero is a smart, AI-based virtual assistant that automatically creates meeting minutes.
Website: http://www.minutehero.net
Phone: **Email:** 36986@reference-encyclopedia-ai.net
City: Hamburg **State:** HH **PC:** **Country:** Germany
Year Established: 2017 **Status 2020:** Active
Industries: Artificial Intelligence

Company Name: NATIX
Description: low cost and privacy-preserving Edge Computer Vision solutions for smart citi: Spain
Website: http://natix.io/en
Phone: **Email:** hello@natix.io
City: Hamburg **State:** HH **PC:** **Country:** Germany
Year Established: 2020 **Status 2020:** Active
Industries: Artificial Intelligence for:, Computer Vision for:, IT Infrastructure for:, Internet of Things (IoT) for:, ~ Construction (10)

Company Name: PANDA
Description: PANDA uses a self-developed open source software framework to address the specific problems of industrial data.
Website: http://panda.technology/
Phone: 49 (0) 40 808 104 120 **Email:** info@panda.technology
City: Hamburg **State:** HH **PC:** **Country:** Germany
Year Established: 2018 **Status 2020:** Active
Industries: Artificial Intelligence

Company Name: Qroda
Description: Providing AI solutions to business: Spain
Website: http://www.qroda.com/
Phone: **Email:** info@qroda.com
City: Hamburg **State:** HH **PC:** **Country:** Germany
Year Established: 2020 **Status 2020:** Active
Industries: Artificial Intelligence for:, Machine Learning

Company Name: Risk Ident
Description: Risk Ident offers anti-fraud solutions for global companies within the e-commerce and financial sectors.
Website: http://riskident.com
Phone: 49 40 609452590 **Email:** contact@riskident.com
City: Hamburg **State:** HH **PC:** **Country:** Germany
Year Established: **Status 2020:** Active
Industries: Artificial Intelligence for:, Security for:, Machine Learning for:, Security

Company Name: Ron Elba
Description: Dry Rum without sugar or other artificial aromas.
Website: http://ronelba.com/
Phone: **Email:** 37312@reference-encyclopedia-ai.net
City: Hamburg **State:** HH **PC:** **Country:** Germany
Year Established: 2016 **Status 2020:** Active
Industries: Artificial Intelligence for:, ~ Food and Beverage (17)

Company Name: Savicon
Description: Savicon platform links departments, HR and purchasing with artificial intelligence and anchors the processes around the staffing.
Website: http://www.savicon.de/
Phone: 040-181 189 39 **Email:** info@mysite.com
City: Hamburg **State:** HH **PC:** **Country:** Germany
Year Established: 2018 **Status 2020:** Active
Industries:

Company Name: Skyposium
Description: Skyposiums revolutionary technology, Wormhole, is capable of transferring data at maximum bandwidth efficiency and therefore faster!
Website: http://www.skyposium.com
Phone: **Email:** 37410@reference-encyclopedia-ai.net
City: Hamburg **State:** HH **PC:** **Country:** Germany
Year Established: 2015 **Status 2020:** Active
Industries: Analytics for:, Artificial Intelligence for:, Cloud for:, ~ Customer Relationship Management (11), IT Managed Services

Company Name: Space and Lemon
Description: Space and Lemon is an INNOVATION LAB, in start-up mode. Two activities: 1/ digital TRENDS scouting 2/ CHATBOT and AI projects.
Website: http://www.spaceandlemon.com/
Phone: **Email:** laurent.burdin@spaceandlemon.com
City: Hamburg **State:** HH **PC:** **Country:** Germany

Year Established: 2016 **Status 2020:** Active
Industries:

Company Name: StudioPass
Description: Your Fitness, Reinvented - AI driven Management Software for Fitness Studios and Mobile Booking App
Website: http://www.studiopass.de
Phone: **Email:** info@studiopass.de
City: Hamburg **State:** HH **PC:** **Country:** Germany
Year Established: **Status 2020:** Active
Industries: Artificial Intelligence for:, Application Services for:, ~ Professional Services (48)

Company Name: Timecake
Description: Your intelligent calendar. Our approach is to combine attractive design and planning tools with an artificial intelligence in one calendar.
Website: http://www.timecake.me
Phone: **Email:** team@timecake.me
City: Hamburg **State:** HH **PC:** **Country:** Germany
Year Established: 2017 **Status 2020:** Active
Industries: Application Services for:, Artificial Intelligence for:, Digital Marketing for:, ~ Social Assistance-Non-Profits (53), ~ Social Assistance-Non-Profits (53)

Company Name: upta: India
Description: AI-driven Marketing Technology Platform for SME
Website: http://www.uptain.de/
Phone: 49 40 696 39 10 30 **Email:** info@uptain.de
City: Hamburg **State:** HH **PC:** **Country:** Germany
Year Established: 2016 **Status 2020:** Active
Industries: Artificial Intelligence for:, Web for:, Machine Learning for:, Business Software as a Service Apps (SaaS Apps) for:, ~ Retail and Consumer Products (52)

Company Name: verlingo
Description: German AI-Startup - The digital recruiting solution build on AI to hire best talents - fast, intelligent and easy
Website: http://www.verlingo.de
Phone: **Email:** info@verlingo.de
City: Hamburg **State:** HH **PC:** **Country:** Germany
Year Established: 2017 **Status 2020:** Active
Industries: Artificial Intelligence for:, IT Managed Services

Company Name: vilisto GmbH
Description: vilisto: The AI Solution to Europe's Office Energy Consumption Problem
Website: http://www.vilisto.de
Phone: 49 (0)40 / 76629 - 2541 **Email:** info@vilisto.de
City: Hamburg **State:** HH **PC:** **Country:** Germany
Year Established: **Status 2020:** Active
Industries: Artificial Intelligence for:, ~ Real Estate (49), ~ Energy and Utilities (14), ~ Energy and Utilities (14), ~ Real Estate (49), ~ Manufacturing-Electronic (30), ~ Construction (10), ~ Professional Services (48)

Company **Name:** Visualino UG (haftungsbeschränkt)
Description: Visualino is an HR tech company based in Hamburg.
Website: http://www.stafff.io
Phone: **Email:** 37635@reference-encyclopedia-ai.net
City: Hamburg **State:** HH **PC:** **Country:** Germany
Year Established: 2017 **Status 2020:** Active
Industries: Natural Language Processing for:, Business Software as a Service Apps (SaaS Apps)

Company Name: YOBO
Description: YOBO is an intelligent hyperlocal app providing visual photo- and emoji-based local recommendations.
Website: http://yobo-app.com/
Phone: **Email:** info@yobo-app.com
City: Hamburg **State:** HH **PC:** **Country:** Germany
Year Established: 2017 **Status 2020:** Active
Industries: Application Services for:, Artificial Intelligence

Company Name: YOBO App
Description: YOBO is an intelligent hyperlocal app providing visual photo- and emoji-based local recommendations.
Website: http://yobo-app.com/
Phone: **Email:** info@yobo-app.com
City: Hamburg **State:** HH **PC:** **Country:** Germany
Year Established: **Status 2020:** Active
Industries: Artificial Intelligence

Company Name: 3sp: India
Description: Tech & design company. Germany's fastest growing digital agency (BVDW 2016) and one of the top 20 creative agencies (PAGE 2017).
Website: http://www.3spin.com
Phone: **Email:** new-business@3spin.de
City: Darmstadt **State:** HE **PC:** **Country:** Germany
Year Established: **Status 2020:** Active
Industries: Artificial Intelligence for:, ~ Healthcare (20), Augmented Reality for:, ~ Media-Communications (41), ~ Administrative and Support Services (1), Application Services

Company Name: intelligent views
Description: Smart data engine based on Semantic graph database software
Website: http://www.i-views.com
Phone: **Email:** contact@i-views.com
City: Darmstadt **State:** HE **PC:** **Country:** Germany
Year Established: **Status 2020:** Active
Industries: Artificial Intelligence for:, Big Data and Analytics for:, Content

Company Name: TripleCheck
Description: The x-ray for software.
Website: http://triplecheck.tech
Phone: 49 162 327 2929 **Email:** contact@triplecheck.tech
City: Darmstadt **State:** HE **PC:** **Country:** Germany
Year Established: **Status 2020:** Active
Industries: Artificial Intelligence

Company Name: Quantitec
Description: Indoor Navigaton, Positioning and Wearable Sensor-Systems
Website: http://quantitec.de/
Phone: 49 6192 47011170 **Email:** info@quantitec.de
City: Hofheim **State:** HE **PC:** **Country:** Germany
Year Established: **Status 2020:** Active
Industries: Artificial Intelligence for:, ~ Transportation and Logistics (57)

Company Name: vencortex
Description: Hybrid Intelligence Platform for Smart Decisions
Website: http://www.vencortex.com
Phone: **Email:** dominik.dellermann@vencortex.com
City: Kassel **State:** HE **PC:** **Country:** Germany
Year Established: **Status 2020:** Active
Industries: Artificial Intelligence for:, ~ Banking and Financial Markets-Services (7), Application Services for:, Machine Learning for:, Enterprise Application Services

Company Name: Compredict
Description: Compredict's software predicts failures, enables lightweight design and accelerates the development process for automotive components.
Website: http://compredict.de/
Phone: 49 (0)6151 3844614 **Email:** contact@compredict.de
City: Darmstadt **State:** HE **PC:** **Country:** Germany
Year Established: 2016 **Status 2020:** Active
Industries:

Company Name: L-One Systems
Description: We develop intelligent NLP systems, web and mobile ap: Palestine
Website: http://www.l-one.de
Phone: 0049-6151-4920450 **Email:** info@l-one.de
City: Darmstadt **State:** HE **PC:** **Country:** Germany

Year Established: 2012 **Status 2020:** Active
Industries: Artificial Intelligence for:, ~ Healthcare (20), Cloud for:, Cloud for:, Cloud for:, ~ Home (22), Machine Learning for:, Application Services for:, Application Services for:, Natural Language Processing

Company Name: Spacenus
Description: Spacenus offers AI platforms that use smartphone cameras and satellite imagery for agriculture.
Website: http://spacenus.com/
Phone: 49 (0) 6151 6290960 **Email:** info@spacenus.com
City: Darmstadt **State:** HE **PC:** **Country:** Germany
Year Established: 2015 **Status 2020:** Active
Industries: ~ Agriculture (3), Artificial Intelligence for:, ~ Agriculture (3)

Company Name: Growth Channel
Description: SaaS for personalised marketing planning
Website: http://growthchannel.io
Phone: **Email:** hello@growthchannel.org
City: Dreieich **State:** HE **PC:** **Country:** Germany
Year Established: 2017 **Status 2020:** Active
Industries: Artificial Intelligence for:, Big Data and Analytics

Company Name: MountLytics
Description: MountLytics is a travelTech startup based in Leipzig and Eschborn.
Website: http://www.mountlytics.com
Phone: 49 (0) 69 153 22 72 60 **Email:** info@mountlytics.com
City: Eschborn **State:** HE **PC:** **Country:** Germany
Year Established: 2015 **Status 2020:** Active
Industries: Artificial Intelligence for:, ~ Customer Relationship Management (11), IT Managed Services for:, ~ Travel and Transportation (58)

Company Name: racksnet
Description: SaaS, Software Defined Networking; Network Automation (multi-vendor)
Website: http://racksnet.com
Phone: **Email:** ir@racksnet.com
City: Eschborn **State:** HE **PC:** **Country:** Germany
Year Established: 2017 **Status 2020:** Active
Industries: Artificial Intelligence for:, IT Managed Services for:, Web for:, Business Software as a Service Apps (SaaS Apps)

Company Name: Acellere
Description: Acellere aims to industrialize software development services and changing the end user experience.
Website: http://www.acellere.com
Phone: 49 69 244333198 **Email:** mona.szyperski@acellere.com
City: Frankfurt **State:** HE **PC:** **Country:** Germany
Year Established: **Status 2020:** Active
Industries: Artificial Intelligence for:, Business Intelligence for:, IT Managed Services for:, ~ Professional Services (48)

Company Name: AISO: MOROCCO
Description: AISOMA is a manufacturer AI consulting in the areas of artificial intelligence and big data analytics.
Website: http://www.aisoma.de/
Phone: 49 69 257375160 **Email:** info@aisoma.de
City: Frankfurt **State:** HE **PC:** **Country:** Germany
Year Established: 2017 **Status 2020:** Active
Industries: Artificial Intelligence for:, Machine Learning

Company Name: AISOMA AG
Description: Technology consulting, data science, predictive analytics, data visualization, applications based on machine learning and AI
Website: http://www.aisoma.de
Phone: 49 69 257375-160 **Email:** info@aisoma.de
City: Frankfurt **State:** HE **PC:** **Country:** Germany
Year Established: **Status 2020:** Active
Industries: Artificial Intelligence for:, Big Data and Analytics for:, Databases for:, Data Management for:, Natural Language Processing for:, Predictive Analytics for:, ~ Professional Services (48)

Company Name: Aivy
Description: Aivy predicts proactively the customers environment and recommends situation- and user-related products.
Website: http://aivy.io
Phone: **Email:** hello@aivy.io
City: Frankfurt **State:** HE **PC:** **Country:** Germany
Year Established: **Status 2020:** Active
Industries:

Company Name: bd4travel
Description: Bd4travel provides IT solutions to assist firms in targeting and segmenting their customer base.
Website: http://www.bd4travel.com
Phone: **Email:** info@bd4travel.com
City: Frankfurt **State:** HE **PC:** **Country:** Germany
Year Established: **Status 2020:** Active
Industries: Artificial Intelligence for:, ~ Retail and Consumer Products (52), ~ Travel and Transportation (58)

Company Name: Embold Technologies GmbH
Description: Acellere aims to industrialize software development services and changing the end user experience.
Website: http://www.embold.io
Phone: **Email:** info@embold.io
City: Frankfurt **State:** HE **PC:** **Country:** Germany
Year Established: **Status 2020:** Active
Industries: Artificial Intelligence for:, Business Intelligence for:, IT Managed Services for:, ~ Professional Services (48)

Company Name: feelyt
Description: Movie Search Engine - recommendations based on the user's occasion, mood & the desired movie atmosphere
Website: http://www.feel.yt
Phone: **Email:** hello@feel.yt
City: Frankfurt **State:** HE **PC:** **Country:** Germany
Year Established: 2014 **Status 2020:** Active
Industries: Business Applications for:, ~ Arts-Entertainment-Recreation (4), ~ Arts-Entertainment-Recreation (4), Predictive Analytics for:, Web

Company Name: Finanzgu: Russia
Description: Finanzguru is an AI based financial assistant.
Website: http://www.finanzguru.de
Phone: **Email:** dein@finanzguru.de
City: Frankfurt **State:** HE **PC:** **Country:** Germany
Year Established: 2015 **Status 2020:** Active
Industries: Artificial Intelligence for:, ~ Healthcare (20), ~ Banking and Financial Markets-Services (7), ~ Banking and Financial Markets-Services (7), Machine Learning

Company Name: Finanzguru by dwins GmbH
Description: AI based financial assistant
Website: http://www.finanzguru.de
Phone: **Email:** dein@finanzguru.de
City: Frankfurt **State:** HE **PC:** **Country:** Germany
Year Established: **Status 2020:** Active
Industries:

Company Name: inga.
Description: inga. automates active sourcing in social media with chatbots and artificial intelligence.
Website: http://www.inga.one
Phone: 49 69 348 71 92-0 **Email:** hello@inga.one
City: Frankfurt **State:** HE **PC:** **Country:** Germany
Year Established: 2017 **Status 2020:** Active
Industries: Artificial Intelligence for:, ~ Social Assistance-Non-Profits (53)

Company Name: Innoplexus
Description: Innoplexus is a technology and product development company focussed on solving challenges in life sciences and pharmaceuticals.
Website: http://www.innoplexus.com
Phone: **Email:** info@innoplexus.com
City: Frankfurt **State:** HE **PC:** **Country:** Germany
Year Established: **Status 2020:** Active
Industries: Artificial Intelligence for:, ~ Banking and Financial Markets-Services (7), IT Managed Services for:, ~ Life Sciences (27), Machine Learning for:, ~ Pharmaceuticals (46)

Company Name: Record Evolution
Description: Record Evolution offer end-to-end consulting expertise in data science & IT-Architecture.
Website: http://www.record-evolution.de
Phone: 49 176 2195 9797 **Email:** marko.petzold@record-evolution.de
City: Frankfurt **State:** HE **PC:** **Country:** Germany
Year Established: 2015 **Status 2020:** Active
Industries: Analytics for:, Big Data and Analytics for:, Business Intelligence for:, Cloud for:, Data Management for:, Machine Learning

Company Name: Robots Go Mental
Description: We make deep learning learn from small amounts of data. We offer pre-trained AI agents and a platform for training such agents at scale.
Website: http://robotsgomental.com/
Phone: **Email:** davor@robotsgomental.com
City: Frankfurt **State:** HE **PC:** **Country:** Germany
Year Established: 2016 **Status 2020:** Active
Industries: Artificial Intelligence for:, Cloud

Company Name: savedroid
Description: savedroid exists to bring personal piggy bank savings into the modern world.
Website: http://www.savedroid.com
Phone: **Email:** hallo@savedroid.de
City: Frankfurt **State:** HE **PC:** **Country:** Germany
Year Established: 2015 **Status 2020:** Active
Industries: Artificial Intelligence for:, ~ Banking and Financial Markets-Services (7), ~ Banking and Financial Markets-Services (7), ~ Banking and Financial Markets-Services (7), Application Services

Company Name: Spotixx
Description: Spotixx is an AI-based fraud detection and prevention company.
Website: http://spotixx.com/
Phone: **Email:** info@spotixx.com
City: Frankfurt **State:** HE **PC:** **Country:** Germany
Year Established: 2019 **Status 2020:** Active
Industries: Artificial Intelligence for:, Security for:, Machine Learning

Company Name: Valdon Mesh GmbH
Description: Consulting Boutique for Quant Finance and Data Science
Website: http://valdon.de
Phone: **Email:** contact@valdon.de
City: Frankfurt **State:** HE **PC:** **Country:** Germany
Year Established: 2015 **Status 2020:** Active
Industries: Analytics for:, ~ Banking and Financial Markets-Services (7), Predictive Analytics for:, Predictive Analytics for:, Risk Management

Company Name: INTRANAV
Description: INTRANAV is an industrial IoT platform to build RTLS based applications for supply chain visbility, optimization & navigation.
Website: http://intranav.com
Phone: 49 (0) 6192 470111-7 **Email:** info@intranav.com
City: Hofheim **State:** HE **PC:** **Country:** Germany
Year Established: 2014 **Status 2020:** Active
Industries: Artificial Intelligence for:, Internet of Things (IoT) for:, IT Managed Services

Company Name: Enercast
Description: Enercast is an online service that enables to create and manage performance forecasts for wind and solar energy.
Website: http://enercast.de
Phone: **Email:** info@enercast.de
City: Kassel **State:** HE **PC:** **Country:** Germany
Year Established: 2011 **Status 2020:** Active
Industries: Artificial Intelligence for:, ~ Energy and Utilities (14), ~ Energy and Utilities (14), ~ Energy and Utilities (14), ~ Energy and Utilities (14)

Company Name: Proboter Robotics
Description: Experts in the fields of Cloud Robotics, Machine Learning, Robot Design and home of the smart robots.
Website: http://proboter.com/index.php/en/proboter-home/
Phone: **Email:** contact@proboter.com
City: Waldbrunn **State:** HE **PC:** **Country:** Germany
Year Established: 2015 **Status 2020:** Active
Industries: Industrial Solutions for:, Machine Learning for:, Robotics

Company Name: BrainPlug GmbH & Co. KG
Description: Digitalisation of Security with AI
Website: http://www.brainplug.de/
Phone: **Email:** contact@brainplug.de
City: Braunschweig **State:** NDS **PC:** **Country:** Germany
Year Established: 2018 **Status 2020:** Closed
Industries: Artificial Intelligence for:, Security

Company Name: Healthcare X.0 - HealthAssist
Description: Cognitive Computing - Healthcare - Software - Digitisation has revolutionised medicine and the healthcare sector -
Website: http://www.healthcare-xnull.com
Phone: **Email:** info@health-assist.com
City: Hameln **State:** NDS **PC:** **Country:** Germany
Year Established: **Status 2020:** Active
Industries: Artificial Intelligence for:, ~ Healthcare (20), ~ Healthcare (20), ~ Professional Services (48)

Company Name: HorseAnalytics
Description: HorseAnalytics empowers horse enthusiasts to monitor and improve health and training of horses by applying reliable technologies.
Website: http://www.horseanalytics.de/
Phone: **Email:** info@horse-analytics.de
City: Hanover **State:** NDS **PC:** **Country:** Germany
Year Established: **Status 2020:** Active
Industries: Artificial Intelligence for:, ~ Manufacturing-Electronic (30), ~ Arts-Entertainment-Recreation (4)

Company Name: Nerd Factory
Description: Recruting IT- Profeessionals for StartUps; optimize processes with machine learning / Big Data
Website: http://nerdfactory.org
Phone: 49 (0) 1759963789 **Email:** info@nerdfactory.org
City: Hanover **State:** NDS **PC:** **Country:** Germany
Year Established: 2016 **Status 2020:** Active
Industries:

Company Name: SYNAOS
Description: SYNAOS leverages AI and cloud technologies to orchestrate the factory and warehouse of the future.
Website: http://synaos.com/
Phone: **Email:** info@synaos.com
City: Hanover **State:** NDS **PC:** **Country:** Germany
Year Established: **Status 2020:** Active
Industries: Artificial Intelligence for:, Cloud for:, ~ Transportation and Logistics (57), ~ Professional Services (48)

Company Name: Racler Productions UG (haftungsbeschränkt)
Description: Software Developer
Website: http://racler.productions
Phone: **Email:** info@racler.productions
City: Melle **State:** NDS **PC:** **Country:** Germany
Year Established: 2017 **Status 2020:** Active
Industries: E-Commerce for:, Machine Learning

Company Name: Brille24
Description: Brille24 is a worldwide innovator in the optical industry - from e-commerce to AI- and tech-driven solution in the eyewear market #eyetech
Website: http://www.brille24.de
Phone: **Email:** marketing@brille24.de
City: Oldenburg **State:** NDS **PC:** **Country:** Germany
Year Established: **Status 2020:** Active
Industries: Artificial Intelligence for:, E-Commerce for:, ~ Healthcare (20), Machine Learning for:, ~ Retail and Consumer Products (52)

Company Name: OmniBot
Description: The OmniBot Conversational AI Platforms enables Enterprises to add Voice- and Chat interfaces to nearly any Software and Hardware
Website: http://omnibot.ai/
Phone: **Email:** info@omnibot.ai
City: Oldenburg **State:** MV **PC:** **Country:** Germany
Year Established: **Status 2020:** Active
Industries: Artificial Intelligence for:, IT Managed Services for:, Natural Language Processing for:, ~ Professional Services (48), Speech Recognition for:, Compute

Company Name: bitsta: Serbia
Description: R&D facility of HoloBuilder: The fastest solution for teams to capture & share 360 degree virtual job walks of construction sites or buildings.
Website: http://www.bitstars.com/
Phone: 49 241 97908049 **Email:** info@bitstars.com
City: Aachen **State:** NRW **PC:** **Country:** Germany
Year Established: 2014 **Status 2020:** Active
Industries: Artificial Intelligence for:, IT Managed Services

Company Name: Gridhound
Description: Affordable AI-based State Estimation for Distribution Grids
Website: http://www.gridhound.de
Phone: 49 241 927876940 **Email:** info@gridhound.de
City: Aachen **State:** NRW **PC:** **Country:** Germany
Year Established: 2015 **Status 2020:** Active
Industries: Artificial Intelligence for:, ~ Banking and Financial Markets-Services (7), ~ Energy and Utilities (14), ~ Energy and Utilities (14), ~ Energy and Utilities (14), ~ Energy and Utilities (14)

Company Name: nevisQ
Description: nevisQ develops a technology platform that supports nurses in their work and residents/patients in their everyday lives in health faciliti: Spain
Website: http://www.nevisq.com
Phone: 49 241 927884010 **Email:** breuer@nevisq.com
City: Aachen **State:** NRW **PC:** **Country:** Germany
Year Established: **Status 2020:** Active
Industries: Artificial Intelligence for:, ~ Manufacturing-Electronic (30), ~ Healthcare (20), Machine Learning for:, ~ Professional Services (48)

Company Name: PRECIRE Technologies GmbH
Description: PRECIRE decodes written speech to provide psychological and communicational insights.
Website: http://www.precire.com
Phone: **Email:** info@precire.com
City: Aachen **State:** NRW **PC:** **Country:** Germany
Year Established: 2012 **Status 2020:** Active
Industries: Application Program Interfaces (APIs) for:, Predictive Analytics for:, Data Management

Company Name: SONAH GmbH
Description: SONAH developed a flexible embedded vision sensor that we install at building or streetlights to solve urban problems.
Website: http://www.sonah.tech
Phone: **Email:** contact@sonah.tech
City: Aachen **State:** NRW **PC:** **Country:** Germany
Year Established: 2016 **Status 2020:** Active
Industries: Application Services for:, Artificial Intelligence for:, Computer Vision for:, Embedded for:, IT Managed Services for:, Web for:, Machine Learning for:, ~ Travel and Transportation (58), ~ Travel and Transportation (58), ~ Construction (10)

Company Name: Taxy.io
Description: Taxy.io is develops a software for the automation of tax consulting and research.
Website: http://www.taxy.io/
Phone: **Email:** info@taxy.io
City: Aachen **State:** NRW **PC:** **Country:** Germany
Year Established: 2018 **Status 2020:** Active
Industries: Artificial Intelligence

Company Name: Mercury.ai
Description: Conversational AI to build multilingual natural language agents and chatbots with dynamic data driven dialogue.
Website: http://www.mercury.ai
Phone: **Email:** 36965@reference-encyclopedia-ai.net
City: Bielefeld **State:** NRW **PC:** **Country:** Germany
Year Established: 2016 **Status 2020:** Active
Industries: Artificial Intelligence for:, ~ Customer Relationship Management (11), Human Computer Interaction for:, Machine Learning for:, Natural Language Processing for:, Business Software as a Service Apps (SaaS Apps)

Company Name: Semalytix
Description: Semalytix focusses on Dark Data Understanding. Turning unstructured into structured data.
Website: http://www.semalytix.de
Phone: 49 (0) 521 914 561 27 **Email:** info@semalytix.de
City: Bielefeld **State:** NRW **PC:** **Country:** Germany
Year Established: **Status 2020:** Active
Industries: Analytics for:, Artificial Intelligence for:, Big Data and Analytics for:, Business Intelligence for:, Machine Learning for:, Predictive Analytics

Company Name: Compensation2Go
Description: Compensation2Go is a legal-tech company utilizing technology to enforce flight compensation claims within the European Union.
Website: http://compensation2go.com/
Phone: 49 (0) 234 414 707 50 **Email:** support@compensation2go.com
City: Bochum **State:** NRW **PC:** **Country:** Germany
Year Established: 2016 **Status 2020:** Active
Industries: Big Data and Analytics for:, IT Managed Services for:, Predictive Analytics

Company Name: TraceMedics Data Science
Description: AI-Backed Process Automation for Global Healthcare Workflows
Website: http://tracemedics.com
Phone: **Email:** insights@tracemedics.com
City: Bochum **State:** NRW **PC:** **Country:** Germany
Year Established: **Status 2020:** Active
Industries:

Company Name: sweetbits GbR
Description: apps & more
Website: http://sweetbits.de/
Phone: 49 160 1529500 **Email:** info@sweetbits.de
City: Bonn **State:** NRW **PC:** **Country:** Germany
Year Established: 2011 **Status 2020:** Active
Industries: Application Services for:, Web

Company Name: voicesphere
Description: voice control app
Website: http://voice-sphere.com
Phone: 49 175 827 1550 **Email:** contact@voice-sphere.com
City: Bonn **State:** NRW **PC:** **Country:** Germany
Year Established: 2013 **Status 2020:** Active
Industries: Voice Recognition for:, ~ Education (13), Natural Language Processing for:, Web for:, Web

Company Name: Augmentation Industri: Spain
Description: Augmentation Industries (AI) provides mobile assisted driving, a patent-pending technology that connects cars to the internet.
Website:
Phone: **Email:** amr@mad.ai
City: Cologne **State:** NRW **PC:** **Country:** Germany
Year Established: **Status 2020:** Active
Industries: Artificial Intelligence for:, ~ Automotive (5), Mobile

Company Name: e-navik GmbH
Description: e-navik GmbH invests in early stage startups or startup funds focussed on AI, Deep Tech, SaaS, PaaS and Blockchain technologies.
Website: http://www.e-navik.com
Phone: **Email:** ebag@e-navik.com
City: Cologne **State:** NRW **PC:** **Country:** Germany
Year Established: 2011 **Status 2020:** Active
Industries: Artificial Intelligence for:, IT Managed Services for:, ~ Banking and Financial Markets-Services (7)

Company Name: fedger
Description: fedger provides Smart Data to grow your Business. Our state-of-the-art Intelligence APIs make high quality Data accessible for Everyone.
Website: http://fedger.io
Phone: 49 221 **Email:** discover@fedger.io
City: Cologne **State:** NRW **PC:** **Country:** Germany
Year Established: **Status 2020:** Active
Industries: Analytics for:, Artificial Intelligence for:, Big Data and Analytics for:, Business Intelligence

Company Name: hijob
Description: Career Management for Generation Alexa. Our AI matching engine finds jobs that really fit, based on your skills.
Website: http://www.hijob.me
Phone: 0049 151 12173924 **Email:** hi@hijob.me
City: Cologne **State:** NRW **PC:** **Country:** Germany
Year Established: 2015 **Status 2020:** Active
Industries: Artificial Intelligence for:, IT Managed Services for:, Web for:, Machine Learning

Company Name: Insurers.ai
Description: insurers.ai is offering AI services and developing custom AI solutions.
Website: http://insurers.ai
Phone: **Email:** info@insurers.ai
City: Cologne **State:** NRW **PC:** **Country:** Germany
Year Established: **Status 2020:** Active
Industries: Artificial Intelligence for:, IT Managed Services for:, ~ Insurance (25)

Company Name: Internet of Voice
Description: Experts, Consulting, Software and Products for intelligent Digital Voice Assistents
Website: http://internet-of-voice.de
Phone: 0049-15776083553 **Email:** info@internet-of-voice.de
City: Cologne **State:** NRW **PC:** **Country:** Germany
Year Established: **Status 2020:** Active
Industries: Artificial Intelligence for:, ~ Arts-Entertainment-Recreation (4), Digital Marketing for:, Digital Media for:, Human Computer Interaction for:, Web for:, ~ Professional Services (48), Speech Recognition for:, Cyber Security

Company Name: Puttmee by Kausoft GmbH
Description: Puttmee accelerates the transition to golf enjoyment with an Artificial Intelligence platform designed to simplify golf deep learning.
Website: http://puttmee.com
Phone: (49) 171 9927 272 **Email:** info@puttmee.com
City: Cologne **State:** NRW **PC:** **Country:** Germany
Year Established: **Status 2020:** Active
Industries: Artificial Intelligence for:, IT Managed Services

Company Name: Tunnelware
Description: Tunnelware is a VaaS (Virtuality as a Service) for tunnel construction industry.
Website: http://www.digitaltwin.technology
Phone: **Email:** r.tomar@tunnelware.io
City: Cologne **State:** NRW **PC:** **Country:** Germany
Year Established: 2018 **Status 2020:** Active
Industries: Augmented Reality for:, ~ Construction (10), Data Management for:, Predictive Analytics for:, Virtual Reality (VR)

Company Name: UNBIND
Description: Enabling POS-data monetization
Website: http://unbind.io/impressum
Phone: **Email:** 37589@reference-encyclopedia-ai.net
City: Cologne **State:** NRW **PC:** **Country:** Germany
Year Established: 2018 **Status 2020:** Active
Industries: Analytics for:, Data Management for:, Machine Learning for:, ~ Retail and Consumer Products (52)

Company Name: Asure
Description: Rethink insurance! Open decentralized autonomous insurance platform, powered by blockchain innovation.
Website: http://www.asure.io
Phone: **Email:** info@asure.io
City: Dortmund **State:** NRW **PC:** **Country:** Germany
Year Established: **Status 2020:** Active
Industries: Artificial Intelligence for:, Big Data and Analytics for:, Blockchain for:, Application Services for:, ~ Education (13), Blockchain for:, ~ Government (19), IT Managed Services for:, ~ Administrative and Support Services (1), ~ Insurance (25), ~ Insurance (25), Ma: Switzerland

Company Name: aifora
Description: aifora offers powerful SaaS solutions for more accurate and targeted pricing, promotions and merchandise flow for brands and retailers.
Website: http://www.aifora.com/
Phone: 49 (0)211 233 950 90 **Email:** info@aifora.com
City: Duesseldorf **State:** NRW **PC:** **Country:** Germany
Year Established: **Status 2020:** Active
Industries: Analytics for:, ~ Retail and Consumer Products (174), Artificial Intelligence for:, ~ Retail and Consumer Products (52), Big Data and Analytics for:, Business Applications for:, Machine Learning for:, ~ Retail and Consumer Products (3407), Predictive Analytics fo

Company Name: DABBEL - Automation Intelligence GmbH
Description: The AI Digital twin of your building energy manager that saves up to 40% of the HVAC energy consumption and CO_2 emissions
Website: https://www.dabbel.eu
Phone: 49 171 289 55 58 **Email:** info@dabbel.eu
City: Duesseldorf **State:** NRW **PC:** **Country:** Germany
Year Established: **Status 2020:** Active
Industries:

Company Name: HEUREMO
Description: Providing 100% automation of transport management. Focus on a holistic optimization increase the revenue of 20% for freight forwarders.
Website: http://www.heuremo.de/
Phone: **Email:** info@heuremo.de
City: Duisburg **State:** NRW **PC:** **Country:** Germany

Year Established: 2018 **Status 2020:** Active
Industries: Artificial Intelligence for:, ~ Telecommunications (56), Business Software as a Service Apps (SaaS Apps) for:, Supply Chain Management

Company Name: mifitto GmbH
Description: mifitto GmbH is a Germany-based company that provides an iOS app to measure the size for shoes and apparel in e-commerce websites.
Website: http://mifitto.com
Phone: 49 203 8784480 **Email:** contact@mifitto.com
City: Duisburg **State:** NRW **PC:** **Country:** Germany
Year Established: 2011 **Status 2020:** Active
Industries: E-Commerce for:, ~ Fashion (16), ~ Retail and Consumer Products (52), Predictive Analytics for:, ~ Retail and Consumer Products (52)

Company Name: Network Insight
Description: Next Generation Social Intelligence B2B SaaS Platform
Website: http://network-insight.com
Phone: **Email:** info@network-insight.com
City: Dus+AL1682seldorf **State:** NRW **PC:** **Country:** Germany
Year Established: **Status 2020:** Active
Industries: Analytics for:, Artificial Intelligence for:, Machine Learning for:, ~ Social Media (54), ~ Social Media (54), ~ Social Media (54), Data Management

Company Name: 149 Technologies
Description: 149 Technology builds a next-generation calendar platform, connecting events to helpful and relevant information, services, places or apps.
Website: http://www.149tech.com
Phone: **Email:** dirk@149tech.com
City: Dusseldorf **State:** NRW **PC:** **Country:** Germany
Year Established: **Status 2020:** Active
Industries: Artificial Intelligence for:, Mobile for:, Natural Language Processing for:, Application Services

Company Name: Kauz
Description: Kauz answers the questions of your customers around the clock.
Website: http://kauz.net/
Phone: 21130049622 **Email:** thomas-ruedel@kauz.net
City: Dusseldorf **State:** NRW **PC:** **Country:** Germany
Year Established: **Status 2020:** Active
Industries: Artificial Intelligence

Company Name: Mybuilderpal
Description: Construction technology developers and deep learning engineers.
Website: http://www.mybuilderpal.co.uk
Phone: **Email:** Big-O-notation@mybuilderpal.co.uk
City: Dusseldorf **State:** NRW **PC:** **Country:** Germany
Year Established: **Status 2020:** Active
Industries: Artificial Intelligence for:, Big Data and Analytics for:, ~ Social Assistance-Non-Profits (53), Robotics for:, ~ Construction (10)

Company Name: PAREQ
Description: PAREQ identify predictive biomarkers through analyzing the systematics of a disease.
Website: http://pareq.com
Phone: 41 (44)7319400 **Email:** info@pareq.com
City: Dusseldorf **State:** NRW **PC:** **Country:** Germany
Year Established: **Status 2020:** Active
Industries: Artificial Intelligence for:, ~ Biotechnology (9), ~ Healthcare (20)

Company Name: talpasolutions
Description: talpasolutions offers a predictive analytics SaaS platform that delivers unparalleled added value for the heavy industries.
Website: http://www.talpasolutions.com
Phone: **Email:** info@talpa-solutions.com
City: Essen **State:** NRW **PC:** **Country:** Germany
Year Established: 2016 **Status 2020:** Active
Industries: Artificial Intelligence for:, IT Managed Services for:, Machine Learning for:, Business Software as a Service Apps (SaaS Apps)

Company Name: Cognotekt
Description: Cognotekt optimises business processes with the help of artificial intelligence.
Website: http://www.cognotekt.com/en/
Phone: 49221-643065-10 **Email:** info@cognotekt.com
City: Koln **State:** NRW **PC:** **Country:** Germany
Year Established: **Status 2020:** Active
Industries: Artificial Intelligence for:, IT Managed Services for:, IT Managed Services for:, ~ Insurance (25)

Company Name: Hivemind Technologies AG
Description: Machine-Learning enabled Data Analytics
Website: http://www.hivemindtechnologies.com/
Phone: **Email:** info@hivemindtechnologies.com
City: Koln **State:** NRW **PC:** **Country:** Germany
Year Established: 2014 **Status 2020:** Active
Industries: Artificial Intelligence

Company Name: FoodTracks
Description: FoodTracks is a software solution that tracks and predicts selling trends for businesses in the food industry.
Website: http://www.foodtracks.de/en
Phone: 0251 / 203 191 70 **Email:** info@foodtracks.de
City: Münster **State:** NRW **PC:** **Country:** Germany
Year Established: 2016 **Status 2020:** Active
Industries: Business Intelligence for:, ~ Food and Beverage (17), IT Managed Services for:, Predictive Analytics

Company Name: pimentaGROUP
Description: Tech Startup fueling great IT-Consultors by powerful tools and newest technologies to deliver bespoke solutions.
Website: http://pimentagroup.de/
Phone: 49 251 7484 9741 **Email:** info@pimentagroup.de
City: Münster **State:** NRW **PC:** **Country:** Germany
Year Established: 2014 **Status 2020:** Active
Industries: IT Managed Services for:, Web for:, IT Managed Services for:, Web for:, Web

Company Name: Xamla
Description: Xamla is an internal Start-Up of PROVISIO GmbH, Germany, focussing on adaptive robotics using AI processes.
Website: http://xamla.com/en/
Phone: **Email:** 37692@reference-encyclopedia-ai.net
City: Münster **State:** NRW **PC:** **Country:** Germany
Year Established: 2014 **Status 2020:** Active
Industries: Artificial Intelligence for:, IT Managed Services for:, IT Managed Services for:, Machine Learning for:, Robotics

Company Name: Robiotic
Description:
Website: http://www.robiotic.biz
Phone: 49 5251-6939090 **Email:** info@robiotic.biz
City: Paderborn **State:** NRW **Zip:** 33106 **Country:** Germany
Year Established: **Status 2020:** Active
Industries:

Company Name: Docunite GMBH
Description: Docunite is a asset management platform for efficient data management and real-time transactions Company.
Website: http://docunite.com/
Phone: 49 202 29789120 **Email:** 36449@reference-encyclopedia-ai.net
City: Wuppertal **State:** NRW **PC:** **Country:** Germany

Year Established: 2017 **Status 2020:** Active
Industries: Artificial Intelligence for:, IT Managed Services

Company Name: Digital Transformation Hub GmbH
Description: DT:HUB is the eco system for digital innovation, entrepreneurship and growth.
Website: http://www.dthub.de/en/
Phone: 49 (0)631 343 591 0 **Email:** info@dthub.de
City: Kaiserslautern **State:** RP **PC:** **Country:** Germany
Year Established: **Status 2020:** Active
Industries: Artificial Intelligence for:, ~ Administrative and Support Services (1)

Company Name: Citunius GmbH
Description: Citunius is a software company providing professional chatbots to the mid-market and public sector.
Website: http://www.citunius.de/
Phone: 49 6131 8921846 **Email:** support@citunius.de
City: Mainz **State:** RP **PC:** **Country:** Germany
Year Established: 2016 **Status 2020:** Active
Industries: Artificial Intelligence for:, Business Intelligence for:, Enterprise Application Services for:, IT Managed Services

Company Name: DATAlove: Serbia
Description: DATAlovers provides a platform for collection, analysis, and use of data for new business opportunities.
Website: http://www.datalovers.com
Phone: 49 6131 327008-0 **Email:** info@datalovers.com
City: Mainz **State:** RP **PC:** **Country:** Germany
Year Established: 2015 **Status 2020:** Active
Industries: Analytics for:, Business Applications for:, Predictive Analytics for:, Business Software as a Service Apps (SaaS Apps)

Company Name: DATAlovers AG
Description: B2B discover and predictive analytics for further grow:Thailand
Website: http://www.datalovers.com
Phone: **Email:** info@datalovers.com
City: Mainz **State:** RP **PC:** **Country:** Germany
Year Established: **Status 2020:** Active
Industries: Analytics for:, Artificial Intelligence for:, Business Applications for:, Predictive Analytics

Company Name: allymatch
Description: allymatch is an AI based B2B matchmaking platform.
Website: http://www.allymatch.com/
Phone: 49 6241 935213 **Email:** contact@allymatch.com
City: Worms **State:** RP **PC:** **Country:** Germany
Year Established: **Status 2020:** Active
Industries: Artificial Intelligence

Company Name: Ambiver: Sweden
Description: Ambiverse extracts machine-understandable knowledge from big text data.
Website: http://www.ambiverse.com
Phone: 49 681 9325-5099 **Email:** hello@ambiverse.com
City: Saarbrucken **State:** SL **PC:** **Country:** Germany
Year Established: **Status 2020:** Active
Industries: Artificial Intelligence for:, Natural Language Processing for:, Cyber Security for:, Data Management

Company Name: Pxio
Description: Pxio develops software infrastructure to form a single display surface.
Website: http://www.pxio.de
Phone: **Email:** contact@pxio.de
City: Saarbrucken **State:** SL **PC:** **Country:** Germany
Year Established: 2016 **Status 2020:** Active
Industries: Artificial Intelligence for:, Collaboration Solutions for:, Data Management for:, ~ Media-Communications (41)

Company Name: Sematell GmbH
Description: Sematell is a leading provider of intelligent response management solutions based on AI for use in contact centers.
Website: http://www.sematell.com
Phone: 49681857670 **Email:** info@sematell.com
City: Saarbrucken **State:** SL **PC:** **Country:** Germany
Year Established: **Status 2020:** Active
Industries: Artificial Intelligence

Company Name: White_C
Description: white_c is a spin-off company of the German Research Center for Artificial Intelligence.
Website: http://www.white-c.com
Phone: **Email:** info@white-c.com
City: Saarbrucken **State:** SL **PC:** **Country:** Germany
Year Established: 2011 **Status 2020:** Active
Industries: Artificial Intelligence for:, ~ Automotive (5), IT Managed Services

Company Name: 3dvisionlabs GmbH
Description: 3dvisionlabs is a Germany-based depth camera startup, emerging with a novel extreme-wide angle vision technology called HemiStereo.
Website: http://3dvisionlabs.com/
Phone: **Email:** info@3dvisionlabs.com
City: Chemnitz **State:** SN **PC:** **Country:** Germany
Year Established: **Status 2020:** Active
Industries: Artificial Intelligence for:, IT Managed Services for:, ~ Manufacturing-Electronic (30)

Company Name: Morpheus Space
Description: Morpheus Space is disrupting the NewSpace industry by introducing Agile Constellations, a fusion between cutting edge propulsion and AI.
Website: http://www.morpheus-space.com
Phone: **Email:** contact@morpheus-space.com
City: Dresden **State:** SN **PC:** **Country:** Germany
Year Established: **Status 2020:** Active
Industries: ~ Aerospace and Defense (2), Artificial Intelligence for:, ~ Manufacturing-Electronic (30), ~ Manufacturing-Miscellaneous (34), ~ Telecommunications (56), ~ Professional Services (48)

Company Name: Sachcontrol
Description: Sachcontrol GmbH has become within a few years the market leader in the field of cost estimate and audit in Germany.
Website: http://www.sachcontrol.de
Phone: 49(0)351 89 66 47 - 0 **Email:** dresden@sachcontrol.de
City: Dresden **State:** SN **PC:** **Country:** Germany
Year Established: **Status 2020:** Active
Industries: Artificial Intelligence for:, IT Managed Services for:, ~ Insurance (25)

Company Name: SupraTix GmbH
Description: cloud solution startup, spin-off TUDresden | Produkte und Services: mobileLearning IoT AI VR AR SeriousGames bigdata analytics hrtech
Website: http://supratix.com
Phone: **Email:** info@supratix.com
City: Dresden **State:** SN **PC:** **Country:** Germany
Year Established: **Status 2020:** Active
Industries:

Company Name: Wandelbots
Description: Wandelbots develops a wearable sensor-laden suit that enables user to demonstrate actions for a robot to replicate.
Website: http://www.wandelbots.com
Phone: **Email:** contact@wandelbots.com
City: Dresden **State:** SN **PC:** **Country:** Germany
Year Established: 2017 **Status 2020:** Active
Industries: Human Computer Interaction for:, Automation for:, Machine Learning for:, Robotics for:, Internet of Things (IoT)

Company Name: AiServe
Description: AiServe develops pedestrian navigation technologies to make walking safe and accessible to everyone.
Website: http://www.aiserve.co/
Phone: 49 341 92881167 **Email:** hello@aiserve.co
City: Leipzig **State:** SN **PC:** **Country:** Germany
Year Established: 2017 **Status 2020:** Active
Industries: Artificial Intelligence for:, Business Applications for:, Computer Vision

Company Name: diafyt
Description: MedTech
Website: http://www.diafyt.com
Phone: 415-243-6454 **Email:** Thomas@diafyt.com
City: Leipzig **State:** SN **PC:** **Country:** Germany
Year Established: **Status 2020:** Active
Industries: Artificial Intelligence for:, ~ Healthcare (20), ~ Healthcare (20), ~ Manufacturing-Medical Equipment-Supplies (33), Application Services

Company Name: diafyt MedTech
Description: insulin dosage calculation for people with diabet: Spain
Website: http://diafyt-eu.jimdosite.com
Phone: **Email:** Thomas@diafyt.com
City: Leipzig **State:** SN **PC:** **Country:** Germany
Year Established: 2016 **Status 2020:** Active
Industries: Artificial Intelligence for:, ~ Healthcare (20), ~ Healthcare (20), Application Services for:, Internet of Things (IoT)

Company Name: DOCYET
Description: DOCYET is an early-stage startup looking to help travelers around the world in accessing medical treatment.
Website: http://www.docyet.com
Phone: **Email:** info@docyet.com
City: Leipzig **State:** SN **PC:** **Country:** Germany
Year Established: 2016 **Status 2020:** Active
Industries: Artificial Intelligence for:, ~ Healthcare (20)

Company **Name:** immo.ai GmbH
Description: we-do.ai is a dynamic startup committed to seeing artificial intelligence.
Website: http://www.we-do.ai/
Phone: **Email:** 36747@reference-encyclopedia-ai.net
City: Leipzig **State:** SN **PC:** **Country:** Germany
Year Established: 2018 **Status 2020:** Active
Industries: Artificial Intelligence for:, IT Managed Services

Company Name: KENDAXA Group
Description: KENDAXA is a fast-growing partner for the digitisation & automation of corporate processes - we help you take part in the digital evolution.
Website: http://kendaxa.com
Phone: 49 (0)341 523 808 00 **Email:** contact@kendaxa.com
City: Leipzig **State:** SN **PC:** **Country:** Germany
Year Established: **Status 2020:** Active
Industries: Analytics for:, Artificial Intelligence for:, Big Data and Analytics for:, Business Intelligence for:, Cloud for:, Databases for:, Data Management for:, Enterprise Application Services for:, Machine Learning for:, ~ Media-Communications (41), Enterprise Application

Company Name: Raylytic
Description: Raylytic develops the only fully integrated platform for automated medical image analysis and clinical data extraction.
Website: http://www.raylytic.com/
Phone: 49 (711) 787-4162 **Email:** info@raylytic.com
City: Leipzig **State:** SN **PC:** **Country:** Germany
Year Established: **Status 2020:** Active
Industries: Artificial Intelligence for:, Big Data and Analytics for:, ~ Healthcare (20), Image Recognition for:, ~ Manufacturing-Medical Equipment-Supplies (33)

Company Name: Sensa:
Description: Sensape revolutionize the way you approach customers with artificial intelligence and augmented reality.
Website: http://sensape.com/en/
Phone: **Email:** hallo@sensape.com
City: Leipzig **State:** SN **PC:** **Country:** Germany
Year Established: 2015 **Status 2020:** Active
Industries: Artificial Intelligence

Company Name: SIS Software GmbH
Description: SIS Software a pioneer in the field of visitor stream analysis and targeted communication on the market.
Website: http://www.sis-software.de/
Phone: **Email:** info@sis-software.de
City: Leipzig **State:** SN **PC:** **Country:** Germany
Year Established: 2012 **Status 2020:** Active
Industries: Artificial Intelligence for:, IT Managed Services for:, Machine Learning

Company Name: Indalyz Monitoring & Prognostics
Description: Indalyz Monitoring & Prognostics is a software company offering a proven predictive maintenance software solution.
Website: http://www.imprognostics.com/
Phone: 49 345 1314 2770 **Email:** info@imprognostics.com
City: Halle **State:** SA **PC:** **Country:** Germany
Year Established: 2015 **Status 2020:** Active
Industries: Predictive Analytics

Company Name: Brainalyzed
Description: Enterprise AI platform that makes artificial swarm intelligence accessible for everyone.
Website: http://www.brainalyzed.com/
Phone: 49 174 2093049 **Email:** info@brainalyzed.com
City: Bad Bramstedt **State:** SH **PC:** **Country:** Germany
Year Established: 2017 **Status 2020:** Active
Industries: Artificial Intelligence for:, ~ Banking and Financial Markets-Services (7), ~ Banking and Financial Markets-Services (7), IT Managed Services

Company Name: Bareways
Description: Automotive Startup
Website: http://www.bareways.com
Phone: **Email:** info@bareways.com
City: Lubeck **State:** SH **PC:** **Country:** Germany
Year Established: 2019 **Status 2020:** Active
Industries: Application Services for:, Artificial Intelligence for:, ~ Automotive (5), IT Managed Services

Company Name: gestigon
Description: gestigon develops body tracking and gesture recognition software for body, hand, and finger gestures.
Website: http://www.gestigon.com
Phone: **Email:** info@gestigon.com
City: Lubeck **State:** SH **PC:** **Country:** Germany
Year Established: **Status 2020:** Active
Industries:

Company Name: ScaleHub AG
Description: Managed Service, CrowdSourcing Services for Data Entry & Data Labeling
Website: http://www.scalehub.com
Phone: 1 239 841 3455 **Email:** contact@scalehub.com
City: Norderstedt **State:** SH **PC:** **Country:** Germany
Year Established: 2015 **Status 2020:** Active
Industries: Artificial Intelligence for:, ~ Automotive (5), Cloud for:, Computer Vision for:, Databases for:, Image Recognition for:, IT Managed Services for:, Natural Language Processing for:, Natural Language Processing for:, Business Process and Operations

Company Name: ifesca
Description: ifesca is an AI-Company that enables optimal decision making for energy companies.
Website: http://www.ifesca.de/
Phone: 49 3677 7613240 **Email:** info@ifesca.de
City: Ilmenau **State:** TH **PC:** **Country:** Germany
Year Established: 2016 **Status 2020:** Active
Industries: Artificial Intelligence for:, ~ Energy and Utilities (14), ~ Energy and Utilities (14), ~ Energy and Utilities (14), IT Managed Services for:, IT Managed Services for:, Internet of Things (IoT)

Company Name: Enginsight
Description: Autonomously acting SaaS and on premise solution that monitors entire IT landscapes and finds security-relevant events.
Website: http://enginsight.com
Phone: 49 (0)3641 2714966 **Email:** hello@enginsight.com
City: Jena **State:** TH **PC:** **Country:** Germany
Year Established: **Status 2020:** Active
Industries: Artificial Intelligence for:, Cyber Security for:, IT Infrastructure for:, IT Managed Services for:, Predictive Analytics for:, ~ Professional Services (48)

Company Name: epicinsights
Description: epicinsights analyzes data from e-commerce systems, websites or digital campaigns and creates maximum content-relevance for every user.
Website: http://epic-insights.com/
Phone: 49 3641 316 99 76 **Email:** info@epic-insights.com
City: Jena **State:** TH **PC:** **Country:** Germany
Year Established: **Status 2020:** Active
Industries: Artificial Intelligence for:, Big Data and Analytics for:, Databases for:, Machine Learning for:, ~ Media-Communications (41), Predictive Analytics

Ghana

Company Name: COLDS
Description: IoT, Data collection, Artificial Intelligence (AI), Proximity and Location based solutions.
Website: http://coldsis.com
Phone: **Email:** sayhi@coldsis.com
City: Accra **State:** Greater Accra Region **PC:** **Country:** GHANA
Year Established: 2010 **Status 2020:** Active
Industries: Analytics for:, Artificial Intelligence for:, IT Managed Services

Company Name: QualiTrace
Description: Traceability and Anti-counterfeiting Solutions
Website: http://qualitracegh.com/
Phone: 233 241572361 **Email:** knelson@qualitracegh.com
City: Accra **State:** Greater Accra Region **PC:** **Country:** GHANA
Year Established: **Status 2020:** Active
Industries: ~ Agriculture (3), ~ Agriculture (3), Artificial Intelligence for:, IT Managed Services

Company Name: Triva
Description: Triva is a robo-financial services platform that helps people to achieve their dreams by providing access to tailored financial products.
Website: http://hitriva.com
Phone: 248666859 **Email:** hello@hitriva.com
City: Accra **State:** Greater Accra Region **PC:** **Country:** GHANA
Year Established: 2017 **Status 2020:** Active
Industries: Artificial Intelligence for:, ~ Banking and Financial Markets-Services (7), ~ Banking and Financial Markets-Services (7), ~ Banking and Financial Markets-Services (7), Finance and Accounting for:, Predictive Analytics

Gibraltar

Company Name: Amon
Description: The every-day Crypto debit card powered by AI and multi-currency crypto wallet
Website: http://www.amon.tech
Phone: **Email:** hello@amon.tech
City: Gibraltar **State:** Gibraltar **PC:** **Country:** GIBRALTAR
Year Established: **Status 2020:** Active
Industries: Artificial Intelligence for:, ~ Banking and Financial Markets-Services (7), ~ Banking and Financial Markets-Services (7)

Company Name: Sporta
Description: Sporta is a self-learning that is able to make data-driven predictions for MMA competitors.
Website: http://sporta.io
Phone: **Email:** support@sporta.io
City: Gibraltar **State:** Gibraltar **PC:** **Country:** GIBRALTAR
Year Established: 2017 **Status 2020:** Active
Industries: Artificial Intelligence for:, Predictive Analytics for:, ~ Arts-Entertainment-Recreation (4)

Greece

Company Name: NOOW
Description: Media Made Smart
Website: http://www.noowit.com
Phone: 30 6979376322 **Email:** team@noowit.com
City: **State:** **PC:** **Country:** GREECE
Year Established: **Status 2020:** Active
Industries: Artificial Intelligence for:, ~ Media-Communications (41), ~ Media-Communications (41), ~ Media-Communications (41)

Company Name: accusonus
Description: Accusonus is a high technology start-up focused on innovation in digital audio technologies.
Website: http://accusonus.com/
Phone: **Email:** info@accusonus.com
City: Patras **State:** Akhaia **PC:** **Country:** GREECE
Year Established: **Status 2020:** Active
Industries: Artificial Intelligence for:, Voice Recognition for:, ~ Arts-Entertainment-Recreation (4)

Company Name: Think Silicon
Description: Think Silicon offers a range of Graphics (GPUs) and Display Processors for the IoT, wearable and broader display devices markets.
Website: http://www.think-silicon.com/index.php
Phone: 30 2610 911543 **Email:** info@think-silicon.com
City: Patras **State:** Akhaia **PC:** **Country:** GREECE
Year Established: **Status 2020:** Active
Industries: Artificial Intelligence for:, Computer Vision for:, Machine Learning for:, ~ Manufacturing-Electronic (30)

Company Name: Augmenta
Description: Automated Precision Application of farm inputs in real-time, boosting yield, enhancing quality & reducing input spend using deep learning.
Website: http://www.augmenta.ag
Phone: 30 698 2941 519 **Email:** george@augmenta.ag
City: Athens **State:** Attiki **PC:** **Country:** GREECE
Year Established: 2016 **Status 2020:** Active
Industries: ~ Agriculture (3), ~ Agriculture (3), Artificial Intelligence for:, Computer Vision for:, Embedded for:, ~ Agriculture (3), Image Recognition for:, Image Recognition for:, Machine Learning

Company Name: BCASH
Description: Fintech, Cryptocurrency, Blockchain, Bitcoin, ATM, Software, Hardware, Artificial Intelligence
Website: http://bcash.eu
Phone: **Email:** info@bcash.eu
City: Athens **State:** Attiki **PC:** **Country:** GREECE

Year Established: 2017 **Status 2020:** Active
Industries:

Company Name: BibeCoffee
Description: BibeCoffee is an IoT real-time monitoring solution company.
Website: http://bibecoffee.com/
Phone: **Email:** info@bibecoffee.com
City: Athens **State:** Attiki **PC:** **Country:** GREECE
Year Established: 2018 **Status 2020:** Active
Industries: Big Data and Analytics for:, ~ Agriculture (3), Internet of Things (IoT) for:, Machine Learning

Company Name: ChainProof
Description: Proof of evidence authentication based on Computer Vision Algorithms and blockchain technologies.
Website:
Phone: **Email:** 36254@reference-encyclopedia-ai.net
City: Athens **State:** Attiki **PC:** **Country:** GREECE
Year Established: 2017 **Status 2020:** Active
Industries: Artificial Intelligence for:, Big Data and Analytics for:, Blockchain for:, IT Managed Services

Company Name: Crypteia Networks
Description: Responsive security based on threat intelligence & analytics
Website: http://www.crypteianetworks.com
Phone: 30 211 80 00 680 **Email:** info@crypteianetworks.com
City: Athens **State:** Attiki **PC:** **Country:** GREECE
Year Established: 2011 **Status 2020:** Active
Industries: Cyber Security for:, IT Managed Services for:, Security for:, Predictive Analytics for:, Security

Company Name: E-MAIL: Italy
Description: Earn money by sharing your site content
Website: http://www.e-mailit.com
Phone: **Email:** nikitas.georgopoulos@e-mailit.com
City: Athens **State:** Attiki **PC:** **Country:** GREECE
Year Established: **Status 2020:** Active
Industries: ~ Media-Communications (41), Analytics for:, Artificial Intelligence for:, Big Data and Analytics for:, Application Services for:, Data Management for:, ~ Social Media (54)

Company Name: FightHoax
Description: FightHoax empowers news analysis and data journalism with Artificial Intelligence and Big Data.
Website: http://FightHoax.com
Phone: 2130994050 **Email:** support@fighthoax.com
City: Athens **State:** Attiki **PC:** **Country:** GREECE
Year Established: **Status 2020:** Active
Industries: Artificial Intelligence for:, ~ Arts-Entertainment-Recreation (4), Natural Language Processing for:, ~ Media-Communications (41)

Company **Name:** InAccel
Description: InAccel provides high performance accelerators for Machine Learning & Analytics applications based on novel FPGA engines as IP blocks
Website: http://www.inaccel.com/
Phone: (1) 408 260 5724 **Email:** chris@inaccel.com
City: Athens **State:** Attiki **PC:** **Country:** GREECE
Year Established: 2018 **Status 2020:** Active
Industries: Cloud for:, Machine Learning

Company Name: Intoolab
Description: Intoolab is a platform for teams (University teams, R&Ds, student teams) that work in projects, connected with institutions and businesses.
Website: http://www.intoolab.com
Phone: **Email:** info@iyouthlab.com
City: Athens **State:** Attiki **PC:** **Country:** GREECE
Year Established: **Status 2020:** Active
Industries: Artificial Intelligence for:, Collaboration Solutions for:, ~ Education (13), ~ Education (13)

Company Name: Offerial
Description: Offerial is a hospitality tech startup helping hotels improve sales, marketing, customer satisfaction and loyalty through personalization.
Website: http://offerial.com
Phone: **Email:** hellohotel@offerial.com
City: Athens **State:** Attiki **PC:** **Country:** GREECE
Year Established: **Status 2020:** Active
Industries: Analytics for:, Artificial Intelligence for:, Big Data and Analytics for:, E-Commerce for:, ~ Hospitality (23), Machine Learning for:, ~ Media-Communications (41), ~ Travel and Transportation (58)

Company Name: Orange Click Media
Description: Digital Transformation Agency focusing on AI & Data Driven Solutions
Website: http://www.ocm.media
Phone: 7498200437 **Email:** galinos@orangeclickmedia.com
City: Athens **State:** Attiki **PC:** **Country:** GREECE
Year Established: 2014 **Status 2020:** Active
Industries: Machine Learning

Company Name: Publisto
Description: Web and native app design and development, machine learning, analytics and data mining services for full mobile solutions.
Website: http://www.publisto.com
Phone: 30 213 0038 247 **Email:** info@publisto.com
City: Athens **State:** Attiki **PC:** **Country:** GREECE
Year Established: 2010 **Status 2020:** Active
Industries: Analytics for:, Artificial Intelligence for:, Web

Company Name: Purposeful
Description: Discover alternative effects for existing drugs using its advanced computational workflow.
Website: http://www.purposeful.eu/
Phone: **Email:** info@purposeful.eu
City: Athens **State:** Attiki **PC:** **Country:** GREECE
Year Established: 2018 **Status 2020:** Active
Industries: Artificial Intelligence for:, Databases

Company Name: Spotawheel
Description: Spotawheel is a tech-driven used cars dealership platform that takes customer trust to a whole new level
Website: http://www.spotawheel.com
Phone: 30 21 17809015 **Email:** hello@spotawheel.: Greece
City: Athens **State:** Attiki **PC:** **Country:** GREECE
Year Established: 2016 **Status 2020:** Active
Industries: ~ Automotive (5), Predictive Analytics

Company Name: Suibee
Description: Suibee is a user-generated content aggregator that attempts a personality analysis based on Facebook user information.
Website: http://www.suibee.com
Phone: **Email:** admin@suibee.com
City: Athens **State:** Attiki **PC:** **Country:** GREECE
Year Established: 2012 **Status 2020:** Active
Industries: Predictive Analytics for:, ~ Social Assistance-Non-Profits (53)

Company Name: Synasource
Description: Synasource is a tech startup specialised in Machine Learning Predictive Algorithms for the Sports and Sports Betting industry.
Website: http://www.getthebet.co
Phone: **Email:** info@synasource.com
City: Athens **State:** Attiki **PC:** **Country:** GREECE
Year Established: **Status 2020:** Active
Industries:

Company Name: Trafisense
Description: Trafisense operates as a monitoring service for dry-type power transformers based on proprietary machine-learning technology.
Website: http://trafisense.com/
Phone: **Email:** 37552@reference-encyclopedia-ai.net
City: Athens **State:** Attiki **PC:** **Country:** GREECE
Year Established: 2016 **Status 2020:** Active
Industries: IT Managed Services for:, IT Managed Services for:, Machine Learning

Company Name: VesselBot
Description: AI supported marketplace matching Cargoes and Vessels based on a broad number of technical, and commercial facto: Serbia
Website: http://www.vesselbot.com
Phone: 30 2114016523 **Email:** info@vesselbot.com
City: Athens **State:** Attiki **PC:** **Country:** GREECE
Year Established: 2015 **Status 2020:** Active
Industries: Artificial Intelligence for:, ~ Automotive (5), IT Managed Services for:, ~ Telecommunications (56)

Company Name: Workathlon
Description: Workathlon is an AI-powered hospitality recruitment solution to help companies find, nurture, and hire the very best talent.
Website: http://www.workathlon.com
Phone: **Email:** katerina@workathlon.com
City: Athens **State:** Attiki **PC:** **Country:** GREECE
Year Established: 2017 **Status 2020:** Active
Industries: Artificial Intelligence

Company Name: appweevr
Description: Appweevr is a consulting company that helps online content publishers better understand their audience and create more engaging content.
Website: http://www.appweevr.com
Phone: **Email:** sales@appweevr.com
City: Attikí **State:** Attiki **PC:** **Country:** GREECE
Year Established: 2011 **Status 2020:** Active
Industries: Analytics for:, Big Data and Analytics for:, Natural Language Processing

Company Name: Pulse and Opinion S.A.
Description: big data extraction and analysis on social media, sentiment analysis, , coreml algorithms, AI algorithms
Website: http://www.pno.systems
Phone: 30 212 0002 766 **Email:** office@pno.systems
City: Melissia **State:** Attiki **PC:** **Country:** GREECE
Year Established: **Status 2020:** Active
Industries: Analytics for:, Artificial Intelligence for:, Big Data and Analytics for:, Machine Learning for:, Natural Language Processing

Company Name: Novocaptis
Description: Novocaptis Cognitive Systems & Robotics is focused on the research and development of artificial intelligence technologies and robotics.
Website: http://www.novocaptis.com/
Phone: 30 231 08 04 970 **Email:** info@novocaptis.com
City: Thessaloníki **State:** Thessaloniki **PC:** **Country:** GREECE
Year Established: 2010 **Status 2020:** Active
Industries: Robotics

Company Name: Gnosis Data Analys
Description: Complete spectrum of data-analysis service
Website: http://www.gnosisda.gr/
Phone: **Email:** contact@gnosisda.: Greece
City: Heraklion **State:** Iraklion **PC:** **Country:** GREECE
Year Established: 2013 **Status 2020:** Active
Industries: Analytics for:, Machine Learning for:, Predictive Analytics

Company Name: Geab:
Description: Geabit is the first AI-based monitoring system for agriculture dedicated to crop yield enhancement.
Website: http://geabit.com
Phone: **Email:** info@geabit.com
City: Trikala **State:** Trikala **PC:** **Country:** GREECE
Year Established: 2016 **Status 2020:** Active
Industries: ~ Agriculture (3), Artificial Intelligence for:, Machine Learning for:, Virtual Reality (VR)

Honduras

Company Name: Spicy Rocket
Description: We are a web design platform.
Website: http://spicyrocket.com
Phone: 504 8766-3153 **Email:** hola@spicyrocket.com
City: Tegucigalpa **State:** Francisco Morazán Department **PC:** **Country:** HONDURAS
Year Established: 2018 **Status 2020:** Active
Industries: Application Services for:, E-Commerce for:, Web

Hong Kong

Company Name: Delvify
Description: Delvify builds and runs AI predictive models for business: Spain
Website: http://delvify.io/
Phone: 852 2870 0989 **Email:** hello@delvify.io
City: Causeway Bay **State:** Hong Kong Island **PC:** **Country:** HONG KONG
Year Established: 2019 **Status 2020:** Active
Industries: Artificial Intelligence for:, Computer Vision for:, E-Commerce for:, IT Managed Services for:, Machine Learning for:, Natural Language Processing

Company Name: MindLayer
Description: MindLayer provide a powerful and easy-to-use backend to build AI models and various client Software Development Kits.
Website: http://www.mindlayer.io
Phone: 852 3500 3910 **Email:** hello@mindlayer.io
City: Causeway Bay **State:** Hong Kong Island **PC:** **Country:** HONG KONG
Year Established: 2015 **Status 2020:** Active
Industries: Artificial Intelligence for:, Web

Company Name: Object AI
Description: Object detection in images and video, powered by artificial intelligence.
Website: http://www.objectai.com/
Phone: **Email:** hello@objectai.com
City: Causeway Bay **State:** Hong Kong Island **PC:** **Country:** HONG KONG
Year Established: 2016 **Status 2020:** Active
Industries: Artificial Intelligence for:, Computer Vision

Company Name: Think Col
Description: ThinkCol is a data science consulting firm based in Hong Kong promoting self-sustaining data solutions to corporations.
Website: http://thinkcol.com
Phone: 852 3705 1019 **Email:** info@thinkcol.com
City: Causeway Bay **State:** Hong Kong Island **PC:** **Country:** HONG KONG
Year Established: 2016 **Status 2020:** Active
Industries:

Company Name: Artificial Intelligence Society of Hong Kong
Description: Artificial Intelligence Society of Hong Kong is dedicated to the further development of AI technologies and adoption.
Website: http://aisociety.hk/
Phone: **Email:** 36089@reference-encyclopedia-ai.net
City: Central **State:** Hong Kong Island **PC:** **Country:** HONG KONG
Year Established: 2016 **Status 2020:** Active
Industries:

Company Name: Blockpass
Description:
Website: https://www.blockpass.org
Phone: 85297334935 **Email:** caitlin.betts@blockpass.org
City: Central **State:** Hong Kong Island **PC:** **Country:** HONG KONG
Year Established: **Status 2020:** Active
Industries: Blockchain

Company Name: China Money Network
Description: China Money Network is an AI-powered platform tracking China's smart investments and technology innovation.
Website: http://www.ChinaMoneyNetwork.com
Phone: **Email:** 36270@reference-encyclopedia-ai.net
City: Central **State:** Hong Kong Island **PC:** **Country:** HONG KONG
Year Established: 2011 **Status 2020:** Active
Industries: Artificial Intelligence for:, Digital Media for:, ~ Banking and Financial Markets-Services (7)

Company Name: FOOD FINANCE
Description: Platform to finance: production, distribution, sales and development of new and existing types of food.
Website: http://www.food.finance
Phone: **Email:** info@food.finance
City: Central **State:** Hong Kong Island **PC:** **Country:** HONG KONG
Year Established: **Status 2020:** Active
Industries: Artificial Intelligence for:, Big Data and Analytics for:, ~ Banking and Financial Markets-Services (7), ~ Food and Beverage (17)

Company Name: Gum
Description: Gum launches/incubates computer vision/deep learning products as cloud services.
Website: http://www.getgum.com
Phone: (8529) 136-6995 **Email:** info@getgum.com
City: Central **State:** Hong Kong Island **PC:** **Country:** HONG KONG
Year Established: 2016 **Status 2020:** Active
Industries: Artificial Intelligence for:, Databases for:, Enterprise Application Services

Company Name: mlytics
Description: We envision a more reliable, faster, and safer internet world with options and transparency.
Website: http://mlytics.com
Phone: **Email:** marketing@mlytics.com
City: Central **State:** Hong Kong Island **PC:** **Country:** HONG KONG
Year Established: 2017 **Status 2020:** Active
Industries: Artificial Intelligence for:, Big Data and Analytics for:, ~ Media-Communications (41), Cyber Security for:, IT Managed Services for:, Web for:, Business Software as a Service Apps (SaaS Apps)

Company Name: Portier Technologies
Description: Portier actions the world's richest traveler data via an eco-system that's built around Portier Phones placed in hotel rooms.
Website: http://www.goportier.com
Phone: **Email:** contact@goportier.com
City: Central **State:** Hong Kong Island **PC:** **Country:** HONG KONG
Year Established: 2016 **Status 2020:** Active
Industries: Artificial Intelligence for:, Big Data and Analytics for:, Enterprise Application Services for:, Business Software as a Service Apps (SaaS Apps)

Company Name: Soteria AI
Description: Soteria AI is developing the next generation of artificial intelligence.
Website: http://www.natasha-ai.com/
Phone: **Email:** 34550@reference-encyclopedia-ai.net
City: Central **State:** Hong Kong Island **PC:** **Country:** HONG KONG
Year Established: 2019 **Status 2020:** Active
Industries: Artificial Intelligence

Company Name: TIANCAI
Description: Tiancai is a software development platform where the engineers, project managers and designers gather to build your next software project.
Website: http://tiancai.p: Romania
Phone: 852-3103-1093 **Email:** support@tiancai.p: Romania
City: Central **State:** Hong Kong Island **PC:** **Country:** HONG KONG
Year Established: **Status 2020:** Active
Industries: Artificial Intelligence for:, Machine Learning for:, ~ Professional Services (48)

Company Name: Emotics
Description: Emotics is a RegTech company that measures engagement with online training to reduce the cost of compliance for highly regulated industries.
Website: http://emotics.co
Phone: 852 5995 1391 **Email:** hello@emotics.co
City: Central and Western **State:** Hong Kong Island **PC:** **Country:** HONG KONG
Year Established: 2017 **Status 2020:** Active
Industries: Artificial Intelligence for:, IT Managed Services

Company Name: HomeKong
Description: HomeKong is your personal real estate assistant.
Website: http://www.homekong.ai/
Phone: **Email:** info@homekong.ai
City: Central and Western **State:** Hong Kong Island **PC:** **Country:** HONG KONG
Year Established: 2018 **Status 2020:** Active
Industries: Artificial Intelligence

Company Name: Accrue
Description: Accrue is a financial analytics company that builds deep learning technology.
Website: http://www.accrue.com/
Phone: **Email:** team@accrue.com
City: Cyberport **State:** Hong Kong Island **PC:** **Country:** HONG KONG
Year Established: **Status 2020:** Active
Industries: Analytics for:, Artificial Intelligence for:, Cloud for:, Enterprise Application Services for:, ~ Banking and Financial Markets-Services (7), ~ Banking and Financial Markets-Services (7), Machine Learning for:, Risk Management for:, ~ Professional Services (48), F

Company Name: SleekFlow
Description: SleekFlow develops cloud-based automation software of sales, marketing and service hub for all messaging apps.
Website: http://sleekflow.io
Phone: 85239053590 **Email:** hi@sleekflow.io
City: Cyberport **State:** Hong Kong Island **PC:** **Country:** HONG KONG
Year Established: 2019 **Status 2020:** Active
Industries: Artificial Intelligence for:, Business Software as a Service Apps (SaaS Apps) for:, Automation

Company Name: Wizpresso
Description: Alternative Data, Financial Research, Research Technology
Website: http://wizpresso.com
Phone: 852-36185854 **Email:** hello@wizpresso.com
City: Cyberport **State:** Hong Kong Island **PC:** **Country:** HONG KONG
Year Established: 2018 **Status 2020:** Active
Industries: Analytics for:, Artificial Intelligence for:, IT Managed Services

Company Name: Aidyia
Description: Aidyia Limited was the wholly owned advisor to Aidyia Holdings Limited, a Cayman Island company.
Website: http://www.aidyia.com
Phone: **Email:** info@aidyia.com
City: Hong Kong **State:** Hong Kong Island **PC:** **Country:** HONG KONG
Year Established: **Status 2020:** Active
Industries:

Company Name: alphabase.ai
Description: The Investment Management Platform Powered by Global AI Talents
Website: http://alphabase.ai
Phone: **Email:** info@alphabase.ai
City: Hong Kong **State:** Hong Kong Island **PC:** **Country:** HONG KONG
Year Established: **Status 2020:** Active
Industries: Artificial Intelligence for:, Big Data and Analytics for:, ~ Banking and Financial Markets-Services (7), Machine Learning

Company Name: Block Aero Technologies
Description: Block Aero Technologies is an aerospace blockchain start-up using artificial intelligence to automate aviation asset management process: Spain
Website: http://www.block.ae: Romania
Phone: **Email:** info@block.ae: Romania
City: Hong Kong **State:** Hong Kong Island **PC:** **Country:** HONG KONG
Year Established: **Status 2020:** Active
Industries: ~ Aerospace and Defense (2), Artificial Intelligence for:, ~ Banking and Financial Markets-Services (7), Blockchain for:, Supply Chain Management

Company Name: Blue Fire AI
Description: Blue Fire AI focuses on providing revenue generating signals for the capital markets industry.
Website: http://www.bluefireai.com/
Phone: **Email:** 36178@reference-encyclopedia-ai.net
City: Hong Kong **State:** Hong Kong Island **PC:** **Country:** HONG KONG
Year Established: 2016 **Status 2020:** Active
Industries: IT Managed Services

Company Name: BUN: SWITZERLAND
Description: A modern outsourcing house for high-growth tech compani: Spain
Website: http://www.meetbunch.com
Phone: 63 915 957 8559 **Email:** sales@meetbunch.com
City: Hong Kong **State:** Hong Kong Island **PC:** **Country:** HONG KONG
Year Established: **Status 2020:** Active
Industries: Artificial Intelligence for:, ~ Banking and Financial Markets-Services (7), Web for:, Business Process and Operations for:, Business Process and Operations

Company Name: Chain of Demand
Description: Chain of Demand uses AI and big data to track and predict sales demand for fashion brands
Website: http://www.chainofdemand.co
Phone: 852 6142 1566 **Email:** info@chainofdemand.co
City: Hong Kong **State:** Hong Kong Island **PC:** **Country:** HONG KONG
Year Established: 2017 **Status 2020:** Active
Industries: Artificial Intelligence for:, Business Applications for:, Big Data and Analytics for:, ~ Fashion (16), IT Managed Services for:, Machine Learning for:, Predictive Analytics for:, Business Software as a Service Apps (SaaS Apps)

Company Name: Clare.AI
Description: Clare.ai builds white-label chatbot to help financial institutions provide a more personalized experience for your customers.
Website: http://www.clare.ai
Phone: 85281929363 **Email:** hello@clare.ai
City: Hong Kong **State:** Hong Kong Island **PC:** **Country:** HONG KONG
Year Established: **Status 2020:** Active
Industries: Artificial Intelligence for:, ~ Banking and Financial Markets-Services (7)

Company Name: CoinCheckup
Description: Coincheckup is a cryptocurrency analysis and research platform designed to offer you transparent information on each cryptocurrency.
Website: http://coincheckup.com
Phone: 852 8193 3394 **Email:** contact@coincheckup.com
City: Hong Kong **State:** Hong Kong Island **PC:** **Country:** HONG KONG
Year Established: 2017 **Status 2020:** Active
Industries: Blockchain for:, ~ Banking and Financial Markets-Services (7), Predictive Analytics for:, Business Intelligence

Company Name: Daily Food
Description: FOOD 4.0 SERVICE
Website: http://www.dailyfood.hk/
Phone: **Email:** info@dailyfood.: Hong Kong
City: Hong Kong **State:** Hong Kong Island **PC:** **Country:** HONG KONG
Year Established: **Status 2020:** Active
Industries: Artificial Intelligence for:, E-Commerce for:, ~ Transportation and Logistics (57), ~ Social Media (54), ~ Media-Communications (41)

Company Name: Find Solution Ai
Description: FS develops artificial intelligence and data analysis technologies for education, medical diagnostics, and e-commerce sectors.
Website: http://www.findsolutionai.com/
Phone: 85225283322 **Email:** info@findsolutiongroup.com
City: Hong Kong **State:** Hong Kong Island **PC:** **Country:** HONG KONG
Year Established: **Status 2020:** Active
Industries: Artificial Intelligence for:, Big Data and Analytics for:, ~ Education (13), ~ Education (13), Facial Recognition for:, ~ Arts-Entertainment-Recreation (4)

Company Name: Fintica
Description: Fintica develops technology that addresses financial industry domains.
Website: http://www.fintica-ai.com/
Phone: **Email:** 36569@reference-encyclopedia-ai.net
City: Hong Kong **State:** Hong Kong Island **PC:** **Country:** HONG KONG
Year Established: 2019 **Status 2020:** Active
Industries: Artificial Intelligence for:, ~ Automotive (5), IT Managed Services for:, Predictive Analytics

Company Name: House Panda
Description: The world's first tokenized supercomputer processing power and HPC-powered app marketplace from a startup incubated by NVIDIA Inception
Website: http://www.housepanda.eu
Phone: **Email:** sa@housepanda.eu
City: Hong Kong **State:** Hong Kong Island **PC:** **Country:** HONG KONG

Year Established: **Status 2020:** Active
Industries: Artificial Intelligence for:, Blockchain for:, Cloud

Company Name: Insilico Medicine
Description: Insilico Medicine is dedicated to develop high-performance AI platform for drug development to treat cancer and age-related diseas: Spain
Website: http://www.insilico.com/
Phone: 1 240 641 6266 **Email:** ai@insilico.com
City: Hong Kong **State:** Hong Kong Island **PC:** **Country:** HONG KONG
Year Established: 2014 **Status 2020:** Active
Industries: Artificial Intelligence for:, ~ Biotechnology (9), ~ Healthcare (20)

Company Name: Knbor
Description: Knbor Technology is a innovative company, focused on smart ligting, to bring us to intelligent life.
Website: http://www.knbor.com
Phone: **Email:** ada.liu@knbor.com
City: Hong Kong **State:** Hong Kong Island **PC:** **Country:** HONG KONG
Year Established: 2015 **Status 2020:** Active
Industries: Artificial Intelligence for:, ~ Healthcare (20), IT Managed Services for:, Internet of Things (IoT)

Company Name: KomraVision
Description: Brining AI into hyperspectal analys
Website: http://www.komravision.com/
Phone: **Email:** contact@komravision.com
City: Hong Kong **State:** Hong Kong Island **PC:** **Country:** HONG KONG
Year Established: 2018 **Status 2020:** Active
Industries:

Company Name: Krunch Ltd
Description: Krunch helps you understand the developer world through data
Website: http://krunchdata.io
Phone: **Email:** jordan.chung@krunchdata.io
City: Hong Kong **State:** Hong Kong Island **PC:** **Country:** HONG KONG
Year Established: 2018 **Status 2020:** Active
Industries: Artificial Intelligence

Company Name: LalaChat.ai
Description: Artificial Intelligence Chatbot for Innovative Use Ca: Sweden
Website: http://www.lalachat.ai
Phone: **Email:** jack.lee@lalachat.ai
City: Hong Kong **State:** Hong Kong Island **PC:** **Country:** HONG KONG
Year Established: 2017 **Status 2020:** Active
Industries: Artificial Intelligence for:, IT Managed Services

Company Name: Latticespace
Description: Latticespace is a tailored chatbot maker for enterprise.
Website: http://www.whatsquare.com
Phone: 852 3957 1987 **Email:** hi@latticespace.com
City: Hong Kong **State:** Hong Kong Island **PC:** **Country:** HONG KONG
Year Established: **Status 2020:** Active
Industries: Artificial Intelligence for:, Enterprise Application Services for:, ~ Media-Communications (41)

Company Name: LUXSENS
Description: LUXSENS is an AI technology company connecting luxury merchants to consumers.
Website: http://www.luxsens.com
Phone: 0755-26929153 **Email:** info@luxsens.com
City: Hong Kong **State:** Hong Kong Island **PC:** **Country:** HONG KONG
Year Established: **Status 2020:** Active
Industries: Artificial Intelligence for:, ~ Retail and Consumer Products (52), Cyber Security for:, ~ Travel and Transportation (58)

Company Name: Mapxus (Maphive Technology Limited)
Description: Mapxus is a thriving indoor map technology platform that provides state-of-the-art indoor map services for global applications.
Website: http://www.mapxus.com
Phone: 852 3709 6860 **Email:** info@mapxus.com
City: Hong Kong **State:** Hong Kong Island **PC:** **Country:** HONG KONG
Year Established: **Status 2020:** Active
Industries: Analytics for:, Artificial Intelligence for:, Big Data and Analytics for:, IT Managed Services for:, Machine Learning for:, ~ Professional Services (48), ~ Transportation and Logistics (57)

Company **Name:** Marketplace Assist
Description: AI platform for factories to launch D2C brands on global ecommerce channels, without middlemen.
Website: http://marketplaceassist.com/
Phone: **Email:** hello@marketplaceassist.com
City: Hong Kong **State:** Hong Kong Island **PC:** **Country:** HONG KONG
Year Established: **Status 2020:** Active
Industries: Artificial Intelligence for:, Blockchain for:, E-Commerce

Company Name: MATRIX Foundation
Description: MATRIX is an open-source blockchain platform.
Website: http://www.matrixchain.io/
Phone: **Email:** public@matrix.space
City: Hong Kong **State:** Hong Kong Island **PC:** **Country:** HONG KONG
Year Established: 2016 **Status 2020:** Active
Industries: Blockchain for:, Application Services for:, Web

Company Name: Mi: Romania
Description: Miro brings AI SUPERPOWERS to atheletes & brands in Running Sport Industry.
Website: http://www.miro.io
Phone: 852 9136 6995 **Email:** jackie@miro.io
City: Hong Kong **State:** Hong Kong Island **PC:** **Country:** HONG KONG
Year Established: **Status 2020:** Active
Industries: Artificial Intelligence for:, ~ Event Management (15), ~ Arts-Entertainment-Recreation (4), Computer Vision

Company Name: Murcul
Description: AI based coding as a service
Website: http://murcul.com
Phone: **Email:** hello@murcul.com
City: Hong Kong **State:** Hong Kong Island **PC:** **Country:** HONG KONG
Year Established: **Status 2020:** Active
Industries: Artificial Intelligence for:, Enterprise Application Services for:, Application Services for:, ~ Professional Services (48), ~ Professional Services (48), Cyber Security

Company Name: NUSIC
Description: Self-mixing music
Website: http://nusic.com.cn
Phone: 86 158 1388 1787 **Email:** hello@nusic.com.cn
City: Hong Kong **State:** Hong Kong Island **PC:** **Country:** HONG KONG
Year Established: **Status 2020:** Active
Industries: Artificial Intelligence for:, ~ Automotive (5), ~ Arts-Entertainment-Recreation (4)

Company Name: Olasso
Description: Olasso is a SaaS return management platform that delivers premium post-purchase services through AI.
Website:
Phone: **Email:** hello@olasso.com
City: Hong Kong **State:** Hong Kong Island **PC:** **Country:** HONG KONG
Year Established: 2018 **Status 2020:** Active
Industries: Artificial Intelligence for:, IT Managed Services for:, ~ Telecommunications (56), Business Software as a Service Apps (SaaS Apps) for:, Business Software as a Service Apps (SaaS Apps) for:, ~ Transportation and Logistics (57), Supply Chain Management

Company Name: Olivex
Description: Olivex is a health care app that provides artificial intelligence (AI) and gamification to improve users' health and fitness.
Website: http://www.olivex.ai/
Phone: **Email:** 37097@reference-encyclopedia-ai.net
City: Hong Kong **State:** Hong Kong Island **PC:** **Country:** HONG KONG
Year Established: 2017 **Status 2020:** Active
Industries: Artificial Intelligence for:, ~ Healthcare (20), Machine Learning

Company Name: Omnibloc
Description: Blockchain and AI recruitment technology.
Website: http://omnibloc.com
Phone: 85297603982 **Email:** matthewchadderdon@omnibloc.com
City: Hong Kong **State:** Hong Kong Island **PC:** **Country:** HONG KONG
Year Established: **Status 2020:** Active
Industries: Artificial Intelligence for:, Blockchain for:, Blockchain for:, ~ Human Resources (24), Machine Learning for:, ~ Human Resources (24)

Company Name: Onlan Capital Ventur: Spain
Description: Venture capital investing; Asian business development services; technical services (e.g. software development)
Website: http://www.onlan.vc
Phone: **Email:** 37106@reference-encyclopedia-ai.net
City: Hong Kong **State:** Hong Kong Island **PC:** **Country:** HONG KONG
Year Established: 2015 **Status 2020:** Active
Industries:

Company Name: Parle
Description: Parle is a browser extension that curates and pins discussions on relevant sites across the web from sources like Reddit and Hacker News.
Website: http://parle.co
Phone: **Email:** contactus@parle.co
City: Hong Kong **State:** Hong Kong Island **PC:** **Country:** HONG KONG
Year Established: **Status 2020:** Active
Industries: Artificial Intelligence for:, Application Services for:, Machine Learning for:, Cyber Security

Company Name: Playnote
Description: Playnote is a provider of music education products for music schools, institutes and individual music teachers.
Website: http://www.playnote.com
Phone: 852 2210 7007 **Email:** info@playnote.com
City: Hong Kong **State:** Hong Kong Island **PC:** **Country:** HONG KONG
Year Established: **Status 2020:** Active
Industries: Artificial Intelligence for:, Data Management for:, IT Managed Services for:, ~ Education (13), ~ Professional Services (48)

Company Name: Pulse iD
Description: Deepen and protect customer relationships with precise location.
Website: www.pulseid.com
Phone: **Email:** contact@pulseid.com
City: Hong Kong **State:** Hong Kong Island **PC:** **Country:** HONG KONG
Year Established: **Status 2020:** Active
Industries: Artificial Intelligence for:, ~ Banking and Financial Markets-Services (7), Machine Learning

Company Name: Raven Protocol
Description: Raven Protocol is a decentralised and distributed deep-learning training protocol
Website: http://www.ravenprotocol.com/
Phone: **Email:** 37263@reference-encyclopedia-ai.net
City: Hong Kong **State:** Hong Kong Island **PC:** **Country:** HONG KONG
Year Established: 2017 **Status 2020:** Active
Industries: Blockchain for:, ~ Banking and Financial Markets-Services (7), Machine Learning

Company Name: ReignDesign
Description: Consulting. Design. Apps.
Website: http://www.reigndesign.com
Phone: 86 21 5352 1288 **Email:** info@reigndesign.com
City: Hong Kong **State:** Hong Kong Island **PC:** **Country:** HONG KONG
Year Established: **Status 2020:** Active
Industries: Application Services for:, Artificial Intelligence for:, Mobile for:, ~ Professional Services (48)

Company **Name:** Revsmart Wearable HK Company Limited
Description: Consumer Electronics
Website: http://www.revsmarttech.com/
Phone: 91-9597258032 **Email:** sunder@revsmartasia.com
City: Hong Kong **State:** Hong Kong Island **PC:** **Country:** HONG KONG
Year Established: **Status 2020:** Active
Industries: Artificial Intelligence for:, ~ Telecommunications (56), ~ Manufacturing-Electronic (30), ~ Manufacturing-Electronic (30)

Company Name: Rocco
Description: Rocco is an AI-powered social media marketing assistant.
Website: http://www.rocco.ai
Phone: **Email:** 37307@reference-encyclopedia-ai.net
City: Hong Kong **State:** Hong Kong Island **PC:** **Country:** HONG KONG
Year Established: 2016 **Status 2020:** Active
Industries: Application Services for:, Artificial Intelligence for:, ~ Social Assistance-Non-Profits (53)

Company Name: Rocketbots
Description: Rocketbots is an AI chat automation platform. Launch on platforms like Facebook Messenger, website, SMS, Wechat mobile apps and more.
Website: http://respond.io/
Phone: **Email:** 37309@reference-encyclopedia-ai.net
City: Hong Kong **State:** Hong Kong Island **PC:** **Country:** HONG KONG
Year Established: 2018 **Status 2020:** Active
Industries: Artificial Intelligence for:, ~ Customer Relationship Management (11), IT Managed Services for:, Application Services for:, Automation

Company Name: Samanta
Description: Samanta is a Virtual Human Intelligence App.
Website: http://www.hisamanta.com
Phone: **Email:** say@hisamanta.com
City: Hong Kong **State:** Hong Kong Island **PC:** **Country:** HONG KONG

Year Established: **Status 2020:** Active
Industries: Artificial Intelligence for:, Human Computer Interaction for:, Application Services

Company Name: Sen
Description: Senno is a blockchain based decision-making network that utilizes sentiment analysis to create a real-time crowd wisdom ecosystem.
Website: http://senno.io/
Phone: **Email:** info@senno.io
City: Hong Kong **State:** Hong Kong Island **PC:** **Country:** HONG KONG
Year Established: 2017 **Status 2020:** Active
Industries: Analytics for:, Artificial Intelligence for:, Blockchain for:, IT Managed Services

Company Name: SmoothWeb
Description: TRANSFORMATION: AI, AR, Mobile; ENGAGEMENT: Realtime recognition, Interactive touch, INTELLIGENCE: Data collection, Insights
Website: http://smoothweb.com
Phone: 852 6114 1900 **Email:** info@smoothweb.com
City: Hong Kong **State:** Hong Kong Island **PC:** **Country:** HONG KONG
Year Established: **Status 2020:** Active
Industries: Artificial Intelligence for:, Digital Media for:, ~ Media-Communications (41), ~ Event Management (15)

Company Name: Squared-S Artificial Intelligence
Description: Squared-S is an AI driven B2B FinTech, providing Portfolio Optimisation, Risk Forecasting, Credit Analysis & other Customised AI Solutions
Website: http://www.squared-s.com
Phone: **Email:** info@squared-s.com
City: Hong Kong **State:** Hong Kong Island **PC:** **Country:** HONG KONG
Year Established: **Status 2020:** Active
Industries: Artificial Intelligence for:, Big Data and Analytics for:, IT Managed Services for:, Machine Learning

Company Name: Sugar AI
Description: Sugar's tailor-made solutions for our digital partners aim to mitigate frictions with online transactions.
Website: http://www.sugarai.com
Phone: 852 3705 5389 **Email:** hello@sugarai.com
City: Hong Kong **State:** Hong Kong Island **PC:** **Country:** HONG KONG
Year Established: **Status 2020:** Active
Industries: Artificial Intelligence for:, ~ Banking and Financial Markets-Services (7), Machine Learning

Company Name: Talvala
Description: Speech Analytics and Human/Machine Interfaces
Website: http://talvala.com
Phone: **Email:** olivier.jeudy@talvala.com
City: Hong Kong **State:** Hong Kong Island **PC:** **Country:** HONG KONG
Year Established: **Status 2020:** Active
Industries:

Company Name: Telkie
Description: Built with artificial intelligence, Telkie answers to servicing, bookings and requests made by travelers with an automation workflow.
Website: http://www.telkie.com
Phone: **Email:** team@telkie.com
City: Hong Kong **State:** Hong Kong Island **PC:** **Country:** HONG KONG
Year Established: **Status 2020:** Active
Industries: Artificial Intelligence for:, ~ Travel and Transportation (58)

Company Name: TravelFlan
Description: TravelFlan utilizes Artificial Technology (AI), Big Data, and Machine Learning technologies to provide end-2-end digital solutions.
Website: http://www.travelflan.com/
Phone: 852 8174 2554 **Email:** info@travelflan.com
City: Hong Kong **State:** Hong Kong Island **PC:** **Country:** HONG KONG
Year Established: 2015 **Status 2020:** Active
Industries: Analytics for:, Artificial Intelligence for:, Big Data and Analytics for:, IT Managed Services for:, Machine Learning for:, Supply Chain Management

Company Name: YIWU MARKET
Description: INTERNATIONAL TRADE PLATFORM FOR CONSUMER GOODS BASED IN AI
Website: http://www.yiwu.market
Phone: **Email:** info@yiwu.market
City: Hong Kong **State:** Hong Kong Island **PC:** **Country:** HONG KONG
Year Established: **Status 2020:** Active
Industries: Artificial Intelligence for:, Finance and Accounting

Company Name: Youth Laboratori: Spain
Description: Artificial Intelligence for the impartial analysis of skin health & testing the efficiency of anti-aging products
Website: http://beauty.ai/
Phone: **Email:** team@beauty.ai
City: Hong Kong **State:** Hong Kong Island **PC:** **Country:** HONG KONG
Year Established: 2015 **Status 2020:** Active
Industries: Artificial Intelligence for:, ~ Beauty (8), ~ Biotechnology (9), ~ Beauty (8), ~ Healthcare (20), IT Managed Services for:, ~ Healthcare (20), ~ Healthcare (20), ~ Healthcare (20)

Company Name: Zero One Network International Limited
Description: The product - Brand Pit is developed for in-depth insights into their customer behaviour, by using cutting edge image recognition.
Website:
Phone: **Email:** 37734@reference-encyclopedia-ai.net
City: Hong Kong **State:** Hong Kong Island **PC:** **Country:** HONG KONG
Year Established: 2013 **Status 2020:** Active
Industries: ~ Education (13), Machine Learning for:, ~ Social Assistance-Non-Profits (53)

Company **Name:** Block AI
Description: Block AI is a company that focus on both software development and marketing for blockchain and A.I. related project.
Website: http://www.blockchainaitech.co/
Phone: **Email:** contact@blockchainaitech.co
City: Quarry Bay **State:** Hong Kong Island **PC:** **Country:** HONG KONG
Year Established: 2018 **Status 2020:** Active
Industries: Artificial Intelligence for:, Web

Company Name: Biorna Quantics
Description: Biorna Quantics provides a digital intelligence solution for the future of human optimization.
Website: http://www.biorna-quantics.com
Phone: 852 2882-6239 **Email:** info@biorna-quantics.com
City: Sai Wan **State:** Hong Kong Island **PC:** **Country:** HONG KONG
Year Established: 2015 **Status 2020:** Active
Industries: Analytics for:, Artificial Intelligence for:, ~ Healthcare (20), ~ Healthcare (20), ~ Healthcare (20), IT Managed Services for:, Application Services for:, ~ Healthcare (20)

Company Name: AimMatic
Description: Turn voice into data
Website: http://www.aimmatic.com
Phone: 852-8191-6725 **Email:** solution.desk@aimmatic.com
City: Sheung Wan **State:** Hong Kong Island **PC:** **Country:** HONG KONG

Year Established: **Status 2020:** Active
Industries: Analytics for:, Artificial Intelligence for:, Big Data and Analytics for:, Business Intelligence for:, Data Management for:, Enterprise Application Services for:, Machine Learning for:, ~ Media-Communications (41), Natural Language Processing for:, Speech Recogn: Italy

Company Name: Backhome
Description: An AI-Powered Real Estate Consultancy
Website: http://www.backhome.: Hong Kong
Phone: **Email:** contact@backhome.: Hong Kong
City: Sheung Wan **State:** Hong Kong Island **PC:** **Country:** HONG KONG
Year Established: 2017 **Status 2020:** Active
Industries: Artificial Intelligence

Company Name: BrandCrafter
Description: BrandCrafter is a a real-time tool using machine learning to get a global and local views of brand activities based on digital data.
Website: http://www.brandcrafter.com
Phone: 852 3956 4853 **Email:** info@brandcrafter.com
City: Sheung Wan **State:** Hong Kong Island **PC:** **Country:** HONG KONG
Year Established: 2017 **Status 2020:** Active
Industries: Artificial Intelligence for:, IT Managed Services for:, Machine Learning

Company Name: Imago
Description: Imago delivers AI solutions for natural language processing and chatbots.
Website: http://www.imago.ai/
Phone: **Email:** enquiry@imago.ai
City: Sheung Wan **State:** Hong Kong Island **PC:** **Country:** HONG KONG
Year Established: 2016 **Status 2020:** Active
Industries: Artificial Intelligence for:, IT Managed Services

Company Name: imimr
Description: imimr provides artificial intelligence business solutions to corporations for great customer experience and business performance.
Website: http://www.imimr.biz/
Phone: (852) 31881788 **Email:** cs@imimr.net
City: Sheung Wan **State:** Hong Kong Island **PC:** **Country:** HONG KONG
Year Established: 2015 **Status 2020:** Active
Industries: Application Services for:, Artificial Intelligence for:, Machine Learning

Company Name: Ipselex
Description: Making patent lawyers redundant with AI
Website: http://www.ipselex.com
Phone: **Email:** contact@ipselex.com
City: Sheung Wan **State:** Hong Kong Island **PC:** **Country:** HONG KONG
Year Established: **Status 2020:** Active
Industries: Artificial Intelligence for:, ~ Law-Legal Services (26), Machine Learning

Company Name: MioTech
Description: MioTech is an artificial intelligence platform that empowers financial institutions to draw actionable insights on their data.
Website: http://www.miotech.com/
Phone: **Email:** pr@mioying.com
City: Sheung Wan **State:** Hong Kong Island **PC:** **Country:** HONG KONG
Year Established: 2016 **Status 2020:** Active
Industries:

Company Name: Pathship
Description: Pathship is an intelligent learning platform connecting your employees with experts across the globe.
Website: http://pathship.com
Phone: 85264453986 **Email:** hello@pathship.com
City: Sheung Wan **State:** Hong Kong Island **PC:** **Country:** HONG KONG
Year Established: 2014 **Status 2020:** Closed
Industries: Artificial Intelligence for:, ~ Education (13), ~ Education (13)

Company Name: C&R
Description: C&R is a product innovation team that use AI to make cities smarter and to create thoughtful and new experiences.
Website: http://cnr.ai
Phone: 852 3582 4232 **Email:** findus@cnr.ai
City: Wan Chai **State:** Hong Kong Island **PC:** **Country:** HONG KONG
Year Established: 2017 **Status 2020:** Active
Industries: Artificial Intelligence for:, IT Managed Services

Company Name: Carnot Innovations
Description: Carnot Innovations is an AI based predictive maintenance platform
Website: http://carnot-innovations.com/
Phone: **Email:** contact@business.com
City: Wan Chai **State:** Hong Kong Island **PC:** **Country:** HONG KONG
Year Established: 2018 **Status 2020:** Active
Industries: Artificial Intelligence

Company Name: Fund Kernel
Description: FundKernel is a tokenized investment platform that allows wealth managers to invest as in funds, private equity, and structured investment.
Website: http://fundkernel.com/
Phone: **Email:** info@fundkernel.com
City: Wan Chai **State:** Hong Kong Island **PC:** **Country:** HONG KONG
Year Established: **Status 2020:** Active
Industries: Artificial Intelligence for:, Blockchain for:, ~ Banking and Financial Markets-Services (7), ~ Banking and Financial Markets-Services (7), ~ Professional Services (48)

Company Name: Miro AI
Description: Miro uses AI & computer vision to analyze bodies in motion.
Website: http://www.miro.io
Phone: (1248) 345-7700 **Email:** team@miro.io
City: Wan Chai **State:** Hong Kong Island **PC:** **Country:** HONG KONG
Year Established: 2017 **Status 2020:** Active
Industries: Artificial Intelligence for:, Big Data and Analytics for:, Computer Vision for:, ~ Arts-Entertainment-Recreation (4), ~ Event Management (15), ~ Healthcare (20), ~ Arts-Entertainment-Recreation (4)

Company **Name:** Quokka
Description: Quokka is a SaaS staff engagement platform which helps company recognize their staff and build a happy workplace
Website: http://www.quokkareward.com
Phone: 852-96538757 **Email:** hr@quokkareward.com
City: Wan Chai **State:** Hong Kong Island **PC:** **Country:** HONG KONG
Year Established: 2019 **Status 2020:** Active
Industries: Predictive Analytics

Company Name: Apoidea
Description: Apoidea Group is a technology company which focuses on identifying and presenting valuable business information.
Website: http://www.apoidea.ai/
Phone: **Email:** info@apoidea.ai
City: Kowloon City **State:** Kowloon **PC:** **Country:** HONG KONG

Year Established: 2017 **Status 2020:** Active
Industries: Artificial Intelligence for:, IT Managed Services

Company Name: Apptilaus
Description: Subscription Analytics and Reporting for Mobile Ap: Palestine
Website: http://apptilaus.com
Phone: **Email:** info@apptilaus.com
City: Kowloon City **State:** Kowloon **PC:** **Country:** HONG KONG
Year Established: 2018 **Status 2020:** Active
Industries: Analytics for:, Application Services for:, E-Commerce for:, Mobile for:, Application Services for:, Predictive Analytics for:, Business Software as a Service Apps (SaaS Apps) for:, Business Software as a Service Apps (SaaS Apps)

Company Name: August Robotics
Description: August Robotics is a global robotics and artificial intelligence company.
Website: http://www.augustrobotics.com
Phone: **Email:** info@augustrobotics.com
City: Kowloon City **State:** Kowloon **PC:** **Country:** HONG KONG
Year Established: 2017 **Status 2020:** Active
Industries: Artificial Intelligence for:, Robotics

Company Name: Chatboy
Description: Chatboy provides a chatbot service that allows auto answering and provides sales suggestions, and customer update subscription services.
Website: http://www.chatboy.xyz
Phone: **Email:** 36260@reference-encyclopedia-ai.net
City: Kowloon City **State:** Kowloon **PC:** **Country:** HONG KONG
Year Established: 2015 **Status 2020:** Active
Industries: Artificial Intelligence for:, Human Computer Interaction for:, Machine Learning

Company Name: Onanoff
Description: Onanoff is an audio technology company.
Website: http://www.onanoff.com/
Phone: **Email:** info@onanoff.net
City: Kowloon City **State:** Kowloon **PC:** **Country:** HONG KONG
Year Established: 2014 **Status 2020:** Active
Industries: Application Services

Company Name: Set Sail Software
Description: Set Sail Software is a Hong Kong-based development company, founded by a group of IT professionals.
Website: http://chatbot.com.: Hong Kong
Phone: 852 6688 0053 **Email:** info@setsailsoftware.com
City: Kowloon City **State:** Kowloon **PC:** **Country:** HONG KONG
Year Established: 2015 **Status 2020:** Active
Industries: Artificial Intelligence for:, IT Managed Services for:, Application Services for:, Robotics for:, ~ Social Assistance-Non-Profits (53)

Company Name: Vfluencer
Description: Vfluencer is an AI-powered micro-influencer marketing platform.
Website: http://www.vfluencer.com
Phone: **Email:** hello@vfluencer.com
City: Kowloon City **State:** Kowloon **PC:** **Country:** HONG KONG
Year Established: 2017 **Status 2020:** Active
Industries: Analytics for:, Artificial Intelligence for:, Big Data and Analytics for:, ~ Customer Relationship Management (11), Web

Company Name: Sanuker
Description: Sanuker develops chatbot builder and push panel for you to design your own chatbot.
Website: http://www.sanuker.com/
Phone: **Email:** hello@sanuker.com
City: Kwun Tong **State:** Kowloon **PC:** **Country:** HONG KONG
Year Established: 2015 **Status 2020:** Active
Industries:

Company Name: Zapevo Limited
Description: Zapevo is a data-driven platform for luxury goods (new & pre owned) and services, empowering customers with an AI driven valuation tool.
Website: http://watchsignals.com
Phone: **Email:** founders@watchsignals.com
City: Kwun Tong **State:** Kowloon **PC:** **Country:** HONG KONG
Year Established: 2018 **Status 2020:** Active
Industries: Artificial Intelligence for:, E-Commerce

Company Name: BitRefine Group
Description: Bitrefine group solves clients' toughest challenges in the field of machine learning and computer vision.
Website: http://bitrefine.group/
Phone: (8528) 197-4631 **Email:** hello@bitrefine.group
City: Mong Kok **State:** Kowloon **PC:** **Country:** HONG KONG
Year Established: 2013 **Status 2020:** Active
Industries: Artificial Intelligence for:, Big Data and Analytics for:, IT Managed Services for:, Machine Learning

Company Name: Dayta AI Limited
Description: Dayta provides tailor-made AI implementation services to your business and empowers your business with machine learning at ease.
Website: http://dayta.ai
Phone: 852 9862 8809 **Email:** patricktu@dayta.ai
City: Wong Tai Sin **State:** Kowloon **PC:** **Country:** HONG KONG
Year Established: **Status 2020:** Active
Industries: Analytics for:, Artificial Intelligence for:, Big Data and Analytics for:, Databases for:, Image Recognition for:, Machine Learning for:, Data Management

Company Name: HOPEHASH
Description: HOPEHASH is a cloud mining service provider company.
Website: http://hopehash.com
Phone: **Email:** 36703@reference-encyclopedia-ai.net
City: Kwai Tsing **State:** New Territories **PC:** **Country:** HONG KONG
Year Established: 2017 **Status 2020:** Active
Industries: Artificial Intelligence for:, Cloud for:, Databases

Company Name: MAD Gaze
Description: MAD Gaze manufactures augmented reality smart glasses and build ecosystem truly for enterprise and consumers.
Website: http://www.madgaze.com
Phone: 852 3998 3180 **Email:** info@madgaze.com
City: Kwai Tsing **State:** New Territories **PC:** **Country:** HONG KONG
Year Established: 2013 **Status 2020:** Active
Industries: Artificial Intelligence for:, Augmented Reality for:, IT Managed Services for:, Internet of Things (IoT)

Company Name: Neoma
Description: World's 1st AI assistant for hotel staff
Website: http://gaiahospitality.com/
Phone: (852) 3970 5670 **Email:** info@gaiahospitality.com
City: New Territories **State:** New Territories **PC:** **Country:** HONG KONG
Year Established: 2014 **Status 2020:** Active
Industries: Artificial Intelligence for:, Cloud for:, IT Managed Services

Company Name: Asiabots
Description: An A.I. company focusing on Natural Language processing (NLP), Natural humanlike voice TTS and chatbot on mobile or phone call .
Website: http://www.asiabots.com
Phone: 852-35983639 **Email:** info@asiabots.com
City: Sha Tin **State:** New Territories **PC:** **Country:** HONG KONG
Year Established: 2017 **Status 2020:** Active
Industries: Artificial Intelligence

Company Name: Axon Labs Limited
Description: A Hong Kong-based machine intelligence research and development company
Website: http://www.axon-labs.com
Phone: **Email:** info@axon-labs.com
City: Sha Tin **State:** New Territories **PC:** **Country:** HONG KONG
Year Established: 2011 **Status 2020:** Active
Industries: Artificial Intelligence for:, IT Managed Services for:, Machine Learning

Company Name: Chain Technology
Description: Data Management Platform for Smart City & Digital Tw: India
Website: http://chaintechdev.com
Phone: **Email:** info@chaintechdev.com
City: Sha Tin **State:** New Territories **PC:** **Country:** HONG KONG
Year Established: 2016 **Status 2020:** Active
Industries: Artificial Intelligence for:, ~ Construction (10), IT Managed Services for:, Internet of Things (IoT) for:, Business Software as a Service Apps (SaaS Apps) for:, ~ Construction (10), ~ Construction (10)

Company Name: Dayta AI
Description: Dayta AI provides data analytics and artificial intelligence solutions.
Website: http://dayta.ai
Phone: 852 9862 8809 **Email:** info@dayta.ai
City: Sha Tin **State:** New Territories **PC:** **Country:** HONG KONG
Year Established: **Status 2020:** Active
Industries: Analytics for:, Artificial Intelligence for:, Big Data and Analytics for:, Databases for:, Facial Recognition for:, Image Recognition for:, Machine Learning for:, Data Management

Company Name: Easychat
Description: Easychat is an conversational AI platform for eCommerce.
Website: http://www.easychat.co
Phone: **Email:** teams@easychat.co
City: Sha Tin **State:** New Territories **PC:** **Country:** HONG KONG
Year Established: **Status 2020:** Active
Industries: Artificial Intelligence for:, E-Commerce for:, IT Managed Services

Company Name: Fano Labs
Description: Fano Labs specializes in speech and NLP technologies to help enterprises with customer service, compliance and other lines of business.
Website: http://www.fano.ai
Phone: 852 3543 1189 **Email:** hello@fano.ai
City: Sha Tin **State:** New Territories **PC:** **Country:** HONG KONG
Year Established: 2015 **Status 2020:** Active
Industries: Artificial Intelligence for:, ~ Customer Relationship Management (11), Natural Language Processing for:, Speech Recognition

Company Name: Hanson Robotics Limited
Description: Founded in 2013, we're an AI research and robotics company. From Sophia the Robot to Bina48, we bring remarkable humanoid robots to life.
Website: http://www.hansonrobotics.com
Phone: 852 3563 9201 **Email:** info@hansonrobotics.com
City: Sha Tin **State:** New Territories **PC:** **Country:** HONG KONG
Year Established: **Status 2020:** Active
Industries: Artificial Intelligence for:, ~ Manufacturing-Electronic (30), ~ Education (13), ~ Healthcare (20), Robotics for:, ~ Customer Relationship Management (11)

Company Name: Insight Robotics
Description: Automated data collection and geographic analysis for industry to quantify risks, make decisions and prevent disasters.
Website: http://www.insightrobotics.com
Phone: 852-23252777 **Email:** info@insightrobotics.com
City: Sha Tin **State:** New Territories **PC:** **Country:** HONG KONG
Year Established: **Status 2020:** Active
Industries:

Company Name: King City Technology Limited
Description: King City is a Hong Kong based hardware startup which focuses on developing the radar based gesture recognition technology.
Website: http://www.kingcitytech.com
Phone: **Email:** info@kingcitytech.com
City: Sha Tin **State:** New Territories **PC:** **Country:** HONG KONG
Year Established: 2016 **Status 2020:** Active
Industries: Artificial Intelligence for:, Virtual Reality (VR)

Company Name: Neufast
Description: Neufast is developing an app that provides step-by-step training in interviews for the user's dream job, company and industry.
Website: http://www.neufast.com/
Phone: 852-5987-6904 **Email:** info@neufast.com
City: Sha Tin **State:** New Territories **PC:** **Country:** HONG KONG
Year Established: **Status 2020:** Active
Industries: Artificial Intelligence for:, ~ Human Resources (24), ~ Human Resources (24), ~ Professional Services (48)

Company Name: Neufast Limited
Description: Neufast is an AI-powered video interviewing solution provider for faster and cheaper talent assessment in APAC & China.
Website: http://www.neufast.com/
Phone: **Email:** customer-service@neufast.com
City: Sha Tin **State:** New Territories **PC:** **Country:** HONG KONG
Year Established: 2018 **Status 2020:** Active
Industries: Artificial Intelligence for:, Natural Language Processing for:, Predictive Analytics

Company Name: PopSquare
Description: PopSquare is an O2O AI-enabled pop-up marketplace and products experience platform.
Website: http://www.popsquare.io/
Phone: (852) 3188 7418 **Email:** info@popsquare.io
City: Sha Tin **State:** New Territories **PC:** **Country:** HONG KONG
Year Established: 2017 **Status 2020:** Active
Industries: Artificial Intelligence

Company Name: Visiona MedTech
Description: Visiona MedTech is a developing AI-enabled analytic application for auto detection of sight-threatening diseases in retinal images.
Website: http://visionamed.com/
Phone: **Email:** info@visionamed.com
City: Sha Tin **State:** New Territories **PC:** **Country:** HONG KONG
Year Established: 2013 **Status 2020:** Active
Industries: Artificial Intelligence for:, ~ Healthcare (20), ~ Healthcare (20)

Company **Name:** Hanson Robotics
Description: Hanson Robotics is an AI and robotics company dedicated to creating socially intelligent machines that enrich the quality of our lives.
Website: http://www.hansonrobotics.com/
Phone: 852 3563 9201 **Email:** info@hansonrobotics.com
City: Tai Po **State:** New Territories **PC:** **Country:** HONG KONG

Year Established: 2013 **Status 2020:** Active
Industries: Artificial Intelligence for:, Robotics

Hungary

Company Name: LetSee
Description: LetSee is an application to help visually impaired people.
Website: http://letseeapp.com/
Phone: **Email:** csanad.egervari@letseeapp.com
City: **State:** **PC:** **Country:** HUNGARY
Year Established: **Status 2020:** Active
Industries: Application Services for:, Artificial Intelligence for:, Computer Vision for:, Machine Learning

Company Name: Givme Analytics Kft
Description: Givme Analytics Kft
Website:
Phone: **Email:** 36625@reference-encyclopedia-ai.net
City: Pecs **State:** Pecs **PC:** **Country:** HUNGARY
Year Established: 2017 **Status 2020:** Active
Industries: Artificial Intelligence

Company Name: Almotive
Description: Almotive is gearing up to be the leading provider of camera-first, AI-powered, Level 5 self-driving technology.
Website: http://aimotive.com/
Phone: (361) 336-0033 **Email:** info@aimotive.com
City: Budapest **State:** BUD **PC:** **Country:** HUNGARY
Year Established: **Status 2020:** Active
Industries: Artificial Intelligence for:, ~ Automotive (5), Cloud for:, Computer Vision for:, Data Management for:, ~ Manufacturing-Electronic (30), IT Managed Services for:, Robotics for:, ~ Professional Services (48)

Company Name: Analogy Co.
Description: Analogy Co. provides a tool for corporations and communities to access aggregated knowledge of thousands of cases as if it was a consultant.
Website: http://www.analogy.co/
Phone: 36 30 725 4282 **Email:** info@analogy.co
City: Budapest **State:** BUD **PC:** **Country:** HUNGARY
Year Established: **Status 2020:** Active
Industries: Artificial Intelligence for:, ~ Gaming (18)

Company Name: Banding
Description: Smart matchmaking app for bands and DJ's to discover their potential fans all over the world through exchange gigs and collaborations.
Website: http://banding.app
Phone: **Email:** info@banding.app
City: Budapest **State:** BUD **PC:** **Country:** HUNGARY
Year Established: **Status 2020:** Active
Industries: Artificial Intelligence for:, Machine Learning for:, ~ Arts-Entertainment-Recreation (4), ~ Arts-Entertainment-Recreation (4)

Company Name: Bonomi
Description: SAAS - AI Messaging Assistants for hotels & resorts
Website: http://www.bonomi.io
Phone: **Email:** info@bonomi.io
City: Budapest **State:** Budapest **PC:** **Country:** HUNGARY
Year Established: 2017 **Status 2020:** Active
Industries: Artificial Intelligence

Company Name: Chatler AI Informatikai es Szolgaltato Kft
Description: Chatler AI Informatikai es Szolgltat Kft
Website:
Phone: **Email:** 36261@reference-encyclopedia-ai.net
City: Budapest **State:** Budapest **PC:** **Country:** HUNGARY
Year Established: 2017 **Status 2020:** Active
Industries: Artificial Intelligence

Company Name: Chatler.ai
Description: Machine learning powered response recommendation engine for chat agents
Website: http://chatler.ai/
Phone: **Email:** info@chatler.ai
City: Budapest **State:** BUD **PC:** **Country:** HUNGARY
Year Established: **Status 2020:** Active
Industries:

Company Name: Dakai
Description: We modernize and optimize businesses with the power of modern technologies such as Machine Learning, Blockchain and smart decisions.
Website: http://dakai.io
Phone: **Email:** info@dakai.io
City: Budapest **State:** Budapest **PC:** **Country:** HUNGARY
Year Established: 2017 **Status 2020:** Active
Industries: Web

Company Name: Eva Vision
Description: Eva Vision provides a voice controlled eyewear for the visually impaired.
Website: http://www.eva.vision/
Phone: 36 30 231 9648 **Email:** info@eva.vision
City: Budapest **State:** BUD **PC:** **Country:** HUNGARY
Year Established: **Status 2020:** Active
Industries: Artificial Intelligence for:, ~ Healthcare (20), IT Managed Services for:, ~ Professional Services (48)

Company Name: EvoAld
Description: sensor and deep neural network based software
Website: http://www.evoaid.com/en/home/
Phone: 36208044744 **Email:** gergo.nagy@evoaid.com
City: Budapest **State:** Budapest **PC:** **Country:** HUNGARY
Year Established: 2016 **Status 2020:** Active
Industries: Artificial Intelligence for:, ~ Healthcare (20), Machine Learning for:, Application Services

Company Name: Family Financ: Spain
Description: Design-driven mobile banking apps for banks with a special focus on younger customers including boxed solutions and E2E product development.
Website: http://www.familyfinances.: Hungary
Phone: (3630) 336-7412 **Email:** hello@familyfinances.: Hungary
City: Budapest **State:** Budapest **PC:** **Country:** HUNGARY
Year Established: 2017 **Status 2020:** Active
Industries: Artificial Intelligence for:, ~ Education (13), ~ Banking and Financial Markets-Services (7), ~ Banking and Financial Markets-Services (7), ~ Banking and Financial Markets-Services (7), IT Managed Services for:, ~ Banking and Financial Markets-Services (7), Fina

Company Name: fastrrr
Description: Science behind sailing
Website: http://fastrrr.com
Phone: (3670) 608-0692 **Email:** info@fastrrr.com
City: Budapest **State:** Budapest **PC:** **Country:** HUNGARY
Year Established: 2017 **Status 2020:** Active
Industries: Artificial Intelligence for:, Big Data and Analytics for:, IT Managed Services for:, Machine Learning for:, ~ Arts-Entertainment-Recreation (4)

Company **Name:** HubScience
Description: HubScience offers hybrid solution that boosts the human literature reading by combining of manual curation with the speed of AI.
Website: http://hubscience.com
Phone: **Email:** hello@hubsience.com
City: Budapest **State:** Budapest **PC:** **Country:** HUNGARY
Year Established: 2015 **Status 2020:** Active
Industries: Artificial Intelligence for:, Web

Company Name: MAPCAT.com
Description: Custom-made, OSM-based worldwide map API for public websites, internal systems or mobile apps to let your location-based info come to life.
Website: http://www.mapcat.com
Phone: **Email:** info@mapcat.com
City: Budapest **State:** BUD **PC:** **Country:** HUNGARY
Year Established: **Status 2020:** Active
Industries: Artificial Intelligence for:, ~ Professional Services (48)

Company Name: Neticle
Description: Neticle is a SaaS-based listening and survey solution for enterprises applying market-leading NLP algorithms.
Website: http://www.neticle.com/
Phone: 36 70 701 6488 **Email:** peter.szekeres@neticle.com
City: Budapest **State:** BU **PC:** **Country:** HUNGARY
Year Established: 2012 **Status 2020:** Active
Industries: Natural Language Processing for:, Business Software as a Service Apps (SaaS Apps) for:, ~ Social Assistance-Non-Profits (53), Data Management

Company Name: Omnicoa: Switzerland
Description: Omnicoach is designed to be the most practical AI Coach for esport games.
Website: http://omnicoach.gg/
Phone: **Email:** info@omnicoach.gg
City: Budapest **State:** Budapest **PC:** **Country:** HUNGARY
Year Established: 2018 **Status 2020:** Active
Industries: ~ Education (13), ~ Arts-Entertainment-Recreation (4), IT Managed Services for:, Machine Learning for:, ~ Arts-Entertainment-Recreation (4), ~ Arts-Entertainment-Recreation (4)

Company Name: OnePrice
Description: Provides price targets for retail investors based on AI forecasted key financials
Website: http://www.oneprice.me/
Phone: **Email:** info@oneprice.me
City: Budapest **State:** BUD **PC:** **Country:** HUNGARY
Year Established: **Status 2020:** Active
Industries: Artificial Intelligence for:, Machine Learning for:, Predictive Analytics for:, ~ Banking and Financial Markets-Services (7)

Company Name: Scarab Research:
Description: Recommendation & Personalization
Website: http://www.scarabresearch.com
Phone: 1 302 SCARAB0 **Email:** sales@scarabresearch.com
City: Budapest **State:** BUD **PC:** **Country:** HUNGARY
Year Established: **Status 2020:** Active
Industries: Artificial Intelligence for:, Cloud for:, E-Commerce for:, Machine Learning for:, ~ Media-Communications (41), ~ Retail and Consumer Products (52), ~ Professional Services (48)

Company Name: SequenceIQ, Inc.
Description: Turn your data into actionable insights
Website: http://sequenceiq.com/
Phone: 36703754112 **Email:** info@sequenceiq.com
City: Budapest **State:** Budapest **PC:** **Country:** HUNGARY
Year Established: 2014 **Status 2020:** Active
Industries: Big Data and Analytics for:, Application Program Interfaces (APIs) for:, Predictive Analytics

Company Name: SignAll
Description: SignAll is pioneering the first automated sign language translation solution.
Website: http://www.signall.us
Phone: **Email:** hello@signall.us
City: Budapest **State:** Budapest **PC:** **Country:** HUNGARY
Year Established: 2016 **Status 2020:** Active
Industries: Computer Vision for:, Natural Language Processing for:, Compute

Company Name: Synetiq
Description: Synetiq helps brands & media producers create high performing video ads from based on biometric data from their target audience.
Website: http://synetiq.net
Phone: 36205444804 **Email:** info@synetiq.net
City: Budapest **State:** BUD **PC:** **Country:** HUNGARY
Year Established: **Status 2020:** Active
Industries:

Company Name: Turbine
Description: Turbine's platform understands the inner mechanisms of cancer enabling the discovery of novel targets & precision medicinal therapies.
Website: http://turbine.ai/
Phone: 36304193891 **Email:** info@turbine.ai
City: Budapest **State:** Budapest **PC:** **Country:** HUNGARY
Year Established: 2015 **Status 2020:** Active
Industries: Artificial Intelligence for:, ~ Biotechnology (9)

Company Name: Ultinous
Description: Ultinous provides advanced video analytics technology.
Website: http://ultinous.com/
Phone: **Email:** info@ultinous.com
City: Budapest **State:** Budapest **PC:** **Country:** HUNGARY
Year Established: 2014 **Status 2020:** Active
Industries: Analytics for:, Artificial Intelligence for:, Image Recognition

Company Name: Xdroid
Description: Xdroid offers best-of-breed innovative artificial intelligence solutions in the field of machine learning.
Website: http://www.xdroids.com/
Phone: **Email:** info@xdroid.com
City: Budapest **State:** BUD **PC:** **Country:** HUNGARY
Year Established: **Status 2020:** Active
Industries: Artificial Intelligence

Company Name: Vivelab Ergo Kft.
Description: ViveLab Ergo does virtual testing and verification of product plans and simulate interactions between human and machine.
Website: http://www.vivelab.cloud
Phone: **Email:** info@vivelabergo.com
City: Székesfehérvár **State:** Fejer **PC:** **Country:** HUNGARY
Year Established: 2017 **Status 2020:** Active
Industries: Analytics for:, Artificial Intelligence for:, IT Managed Services

Company Name: OISYS
Description: OISYS is the tool to monitor your production in real time. It facilitates decision making through big data analytics.
Website: http://oisys.co
Phone: 36309531517 **Email:** peter.kiss@oisys.co
City: Budaörs **State:** Pest **PC:** **Country:** HUNGARY
Year Established: 2015 **Status 2020:** Active
Industries: Analytics for:, Big Data and Analytics for:, Internet of Things (IoT) for:, Machine Learning

Iceland

Company Name: Activity Stream
Description: Activity Stream makes client's organization better by turning business data into actionable intelligence and insights.
Website: http://www.activitystream.com/
Phone: **Email:** einar@activitystream.com
City: Reykjavik **State:** Gullbringusysla **PC:** **Country:** Iceland
Year Established: 2013 **Status 2020:** Active
Industries: Analytics for:, Big Data and Analytics for:, Enterprise Application Services for:, Predictive Analytics

Company Name: Lucinity
Description: Lucinity is the Intelligent AML solution company that empowers clients to detect suspicious behavior patterns and improve review efficiency.
Website:
Phone: **Email:** 4413@reference-encyclopedia-ai.net
City: Reykjavik **State:** Gullbringusysla **PC:** **Country:** ICELAND
Year Established: **Status 2020:** Active
Industries: Artificial Intelligence for:, ~ Professional Services (48)

Company Name: Marsyn
Description: Marsyn ehf provides accurate and up-to-date information on oceanic condition for the fishing industry.
Website: http://www.marsyn.: Iceland
Phone: **Email:** runam@hi.: Iceland
City: Reykjavik **State:** Gullbringusysla **PC:** **Country:** ICELAND
Year Established: 2012 **Status 2020:** Active
Industries: Application Services

Company Name: MyID.is Certified
Description: MyID.is a digital ID certification platform. MyID.is trying to solve the problem of how to provide users with a digital ID that has been
Website: http://myid.: Iceland
Phone: **Email:** charles@myid.: Iceland
City: Reykjavik **State:** Gullbringusysla **PC:** **Country:** ICELAND
Year Established: **Status 2020:** Active
Industries: Artificial Intelligence for:, Identity for:, ~ Social Media (54)

Company Name: Seafood IQ
Description: Seafood IQ develops the only data platform that combines IoT/RFID, Blockchain, and artificial intelligence.
Website: http://seafoodiq.com/
Phone: 354 7873737 **Email:** Info@seafoodiq.com
City: Reykjavik **State:** Gullbringusysla **PC:** **Country:** ICELAND
Year Established: 2015 **Status 2020:** Active
Industries: Artificial Intelligence for:, IT Managed Services

Company Name: Viska
Description: Viska is an AI powered knowledge game on mobile
Website: http://www.viska.com/
Phone: **Email:** hello@viska.com
City: Reykjavik **State:** Gullbringusysla **PC:** **Country:** ICELAND
Year Established: 2017 **Status 2020:** Active
Industries: Artificial Intelligence for:, ~ Education (13), ~ Education (13), Mobile

Company Name: Medilync
Description: Medilync was founded with the goal of revolutionizing the way diabetes is managed and treated in a value-based care landscape.
Website: http://www.medilync.com
Phone: 354 840 6944 **Email:** sigurjon@medilync.com
City: Vestmannaeyjar **State:** Rangarvallasysla **PC:** **Country:** ICELAND
Year Established: 2012 **Status 2020:** Active
Industries: Analytics for:, Artificial Intelligence for:, ~ Healthcare (20), Internet of Things (IoT) for:, Machine Learning for:, Predictive Analytics

India

Company Name: HCL Technologies - IoT WoRKS
Description: IoT
Website: www.hcltech.com
Phone: **Email:** iotworks@hcl.com
City: **State:** **PC:** **Country:** India
Year Established: **Status 2020:** Active
Industries:

Company Name: Pinoty
Description: Pinoty is a medical technology company committed to transforming cardiac care by utilizing medical grade AI, IoT and Cloud technology.
Website: http://pinoty.com
Phone: 91 8125205678 **Email:** champions@pinoty.com
City: Madhapur **State:** AP **PC:** **Country:** India
Year Established: 2018 **Status 2020:** Active
Industries:

Company Name: Codestrek AI
Description: Committed to significantly improving the lives of as many people as possible.
Website: http://www.codestrek.com
Phone: **Email:** care@codestrek.com
City: Secunderabad **State:** AP **PC:** **Country:** India
Year Established: 2017 **Status 2020:** Active
Industries: IT Managed Services

Company Name: Cenacle
Description: Cenacle provides research-based consulting services for next generation technologies, helping clients in early adoption strategi: Spain
Website: http://cenacle.co.: India
Phone: 866-244-4707 **Email:** 36248@reference-encyclopedia-ai.net
City: Vijayawada **State:** AP **PC:** **Country:** India
Year Established: 2012 **Status 2020:** Active
Industries: Big Data and Analytics for:, IT Managed Services for:, Predictive Analytics for:, Business Intelligence

Company Name: AutomataPi
Description: AutomataPi is a next generation cognitive business process automation engine.
Website: http://www.automatapi.com
Phone: 022 4970 6994 **Email:** auto@automatapi.com
City: Powai **State:** AS **PC:** **Country:** India
Year Established: 2017 **Status 2020:** Active
Industries: Automation for:, IT Managed Services for:, Machine Learning

Company Name: WNNA
Description: AI Powered Personal Shortcut To Travel & Daily Life Actions From Around The Web.
Website: http://wnna.co
Phone: 1(650)383-0003 **Email:** hello@wnna.co
City: **State: Bahra** **PC:** **Country:** India
Year Established: **Status 2020:** Active
Industries: Artificial Intelligence for:, Mobile for:, ~ Media-Communications (41), Cyber Security for:, Content

Company Name: Nural
Description: Start here, build everywhere! Create a smarter, more connected digital world, and empower people to do more, all in one place.
Website: http://www.nural.me
Phone: **Email:** hamad@nural.me
City: Manama **State: Bahra PC:** **Country:** India
Year Established: **Status 2020:** Active
Industries: Artificial Intelligence for:, Machine Learning for:, ~ Professional Services (48)

Company Name: Advenio
Description: Advenio is a team of technology led social entrepreneurs focused on technology equity in critical sectors.
Website: https://www.adveniotecnosys.com/
Phone: **Email:** hr@adveniotecnosys.com
City: Chandigarh **State:** CH **PC:** **Country:** India
Year Established: 2010 **Status 2020:** Active
Industries:

Company Name: DataToBiz
Description: Data Analytics & AI Consulting services firm providing complete end to end data solutions from data warehousing to Predictive ML analytics
Website: http://DataToBiz.com
Phone: **Email:** hi@datatobiz.com
City: Chandigarh **State:** CH **PC:** **Country:** India
Year Established: 2018 **Status 2020:** Active
Industries: Artificial Intelligence

Company Name: Etasens Technologies
Description: Etasens is a service based company delivering new age solutions focused on Enterprise Solutions, Cloud Solutions and Machine Learning.
Website: http://www.etasens.com
Phone: **Email:** contact@etasens.com
City: Chandigarh **State:** CH **PC:** **Country:** India
Year Established: 2018 **Status 2020:** Active
Industries: Cloud for:, Cloud for:, Enterprise Application Services for:, Machine Learning

Company Name: Labellerr
Description: A cloud-based(SaaS) enterprise data annotation tool for computer vision teams to build AI/ML models faster.
Website: http://www.labellerr.com/home
Phone: (999) 044-1155 **Email:** support@tensormatics.com
City: Chandigarh **State:** CH **PC:** **Country:** India
Year Established: 2019 **Status 2020:** Active
Industries: Artificial Intelligence for:, IT Managed Services for:, Machine Learning for:, Business Software as a Service Apps (SaaS Apps)

Company Name: Alpha Bots
Description: We specializes in create Messenger based Chatbots, enhanced with AI & ML to help businesses tap into their potential & boost their growth!
Website: https://www.alpha-bot.com/
Phone: **Email:** support@alpha-bot.com
City: Delhi **State:** DL **PC:** **Country:** India
Year Established: 2019 **Status 2020:** Active
Industries: Web

Company Name: Andor Communications Private Limited
Description: An imaging and AI enabler technology company working on next level of mobile solutions.
Website: http://lightxapp.com/
Phone: **Email:** support@lightxapp.com
City: Delhi **State:** DL **PC:** **Country:** India
Year Established: 2015 **Status 2020:** Active
Industries: Application Services

Company Name: Applicate
Description: Applicate makes it simple to act up on complex business gaps and opportunities .
Website: http://www.applicatetechnology.com/
Phone: **Email:** ranjeet@applicatetechnology.com
City: Delhi **State:** DL **PC:** **Country:** India
Year Established: **Status 2020:** Active
Industries: Artificial Intelligence for:, IT Managed Services for:, IT Managed Services

Company Name: Attentive AI
Description: SaaS, DaaS
Website: http://attentive.ai
Phone: **Email:** info@attentive.ai
City: Delhi **State:** DL **PC:** **Country:** India
Year Established: 2017 **Status 2020:** Active
Industries: Artificial Intelligence for:, IT Managed Services

Company Name: Ayata Intelligence
Description: Ayata Intelligence is an Artificial Intelligence company that strives to make products and services.
Website: http://ayataintelligence.com/
Phone: **Email:** hiring@ayataintelligence.com
City: Delhi **State:** DL **PC:** **Country:** India
Year Established: **Status 2020:** Active
Industries: Artificial Intelligence for:, ~ Manufacturing-Electronic (30)

Company Name: Couch Fashion - The AI Fashion Assistant -
Description: CouchFashion is an A.I. Fashion Assistant. The answers given by the bot are always personalized to users body type and other preferences.
Website:
Phone: **Email:** 36342@reference-encyclopedia-ai.net
City: Delhi **State:** DL **PC:** **Country:** India
Year Established: 2017 **Status 2020:** Closed
Industries: Artificial Intelligence for:, E-Commerce for:, ~ Fashion (16)

Company Name: ERA.AI
Description: AI, Marketing Tech, Publisher Tech
Website: http://era.ai
Phone: **Email:** hello@era.ai
City: Delhi **State:** DL **PC:** **Country:** India
Year Established: **Status 2020:** Active
Industries:

Company Name: Fashinscoop
Description: SHOP | STYLE | DISCOVER - Exclusive Fashion
Website: http://www.fashinscoop.com
Phone: (797)717-9745 **Email:** hello@fashinscoop.com
City: Delhi **State:** DL **PC:** **Country:** India
Year Established: **Status 2020:** Active
Industries: Artificial Intelligence for:, ~ Fashion (16), ~ Retail and Consumer Products (52)

Company Name: Hello Vinci
Description: AI Powered and Voice Enabled Price Comparison Platform for Online Shopping
Website: http://www.hellovinci.com
Phone: **Email:** ankur.dhamija@hellovinci.com
City: Delhi **State:** DL **PC:** **Country:** India
Year Established: **Status 2020:** Active
Industries: Artificial Intelligence for:, E-Commerce for:, Mobile for:, Natural Language Processing for:, ~ Retail and Consumer Products (52)

Company Name: Inclick Track
Description: Social Media Analytics for Brands and Agenci: Spain
Website: http://inclick.co/
Phone: **Email:** contact@inclick.co
City: Delhi **State:** DL **PC:** **Country:** India
Year Established: **Status 2020:** Active
Industries: ~ Media-Communications (41), Analytics for:, Artificial Intelligence for:, ~ Social Media (54)

Company Name: Instahyre
Description: Instahyre is an advanced hiring platform based on AI and machine learning algorithms, enabling recruiters to hire top talent effortlessly.
Website: http://www.instahyre.com
Phone: **Email:** info@instahyre.com
City: Delhi **State:** DL **PC:** **Country:** India
Year Established: **Status 2020:** Active
Industries: Artificial Intelligence for:, Machine Learning for:, ~ Human Resources (24)

Company Name: Kid Closet
Description: We make kids wear shopping smart and simple experience for parents.
Website: http://kidcloset.: India
Phone: 9873772629 **Email:** ankit@budstrends.com
City: Delhi **State:** DL **PC:** **Country:** India
Year Established: **Status 2020:** Active
Industries: Analytics for:, Artificial Intelligence for:, E-Commerce for:, ~ Fashion (16), ~ Media-Communications (41)

Company **Name:** Nearify

Description: Nearify is an artificially intelligent event discovery platform that brings you your kind of event at your current location globally.
Website: http://www.nearify.com
Phone: 91 8335971023 **Email:** hello@nearify.com
City: Delhi **State:** DL **PC:** **Country:** India
Year Established: 2012 **Status 2020:** Active
Industries: Artificial Intelligence

Company Name: Psynaptech.ai
Description: Providing AI solutions for customer care services.
Website:
Phone: 91-8802790769 **Email:** udapra@gmail.com
City: Delhi **State:** DL **PC:** **Country:** India
Year Established: **Status 2020:** Active
Industries: Artificial Intelligence

Company Name: Rank Me Online
Description: SAAS for AI driven Social Listening, Online Reputation Management, and End to End Influencer marketing.
Website: http://www.rankmeonline.com
Phone: 91 88004 94904 **Email:** info@rankmeonline.com
City: Delhi **State:** DL **PC:** **Country:** India
Year Established: 2017 **Status 2020:** Active
Industries: Artificial Intelligence for:, Digital Marketing for:, IT Managed Services for:, Business Software as a Service Apps (SaaS Apps) for:, ~ Social Assistance-Non-Profits (53)

Company Name: Rekrutify.com
Description: AI- based recruitment platform for employers to find right talent by doing a matchmaking using our proprietary algorithm.
Website: http://www.rekrutify.com
Phone: 8448510097 **Email:** info@rekrutify.com
City: Delhi **State:** DL **PC:** **Country:** India
Year Established: 2017 **Status 2020:** Active
Industries: Artificial Intelligence for:, Web

Company Name: StrollUp
Description: StrollUp serves as a chatbot that helps users find best events and activities in the city.
Website: http://www.strollup.in/
Phone: 9899537201 **Email:** connect@strollup.: India
City: Delhi **State:** DL **PC:** **Country:** India
Year Established: **Status 2020:** Active
Industries: Artificial Intelligence for:, ~ Event Management (15)

Company Name: TradeIQ.ai
Description: Providing AI powered asset management solutions
Website: http://www.tradeiq.ai/
Phone: **Email:** info@tradeiq.ai
City: Delhi **State:** DL **PC:** **Country:** India
Year Established: 2019 **Status 2020:** Active
Industries: Artificial Intelligence for:, Machine Learning for:, Compute

Company Name: Webnot: Switzerland
Description: India based Data Analytics company
Website: http://webnotch.in/
Phone: **Email:** webnotchofficial@gmail.com
City: Delhi **State:** DL **PC:** **Country:** India
Year Established: 2019 **Status 2020:** Active
Industries: Analytics for:, IT Managed Services for:, Machine Learning

Company Name: 98F: Italy
Description: 98Fit is an effortless fitness platform that behaves just like a human coach analyzing every minute aspect of user's life.
Website: http://www.98fit.com/
Phone: **Email:** info@98fit.com
City: New Delhi **State:** DL **PC:** **Country:** India
Year Established: 2016 **Status 2020:** Active
Industries: Application Services for:, Artificial Intelligence for:, Big Data and Analytics for:, ~ Healthcare (20), Mobile for:, Mobile for:, Application Services for:, ~ Arts-Entertainment-Recreation (4)

Company Name: Abhiwan Technologies
Description: Content Development in Virtual Reality , Augmented Reality and Mixed Reality.
Website: http://www.abhiwan.com
Phone: 9910918980 **Email:** abhishek@abhiwan.com
City: New Delhi **State:** DL **PC:** **Country:** India
Year Established: **Status 2020:** Active
Industries:

Company Name: Adiam
Description: Adiam is a company that provides app design, development and deployment services for new age mobile technologies.
Website: http://www.adiamtech.com/
Phone: (707) 902-3427 **Email:** sales@adiamtech.com
City: New Delhi **State:** DL **PC:** **Country:** India
Year Established: 2013 **Status 2020:** Active
Industries: Application Services for:, ~ Biotechnology (9), Mobile for:, Natural Language Processing for:, Robotics

Company Name: AIRMESH
Description: Creating a Global Ecosystem to Enable Connected Life
Website: http://www.airmesh.com/
Phone: **Email:** corp.sg@airmesh.group
City: New Delhi **State:** DL **PC:** **Country:** India
Year Established: 2015 **Status 2020:** Active
Industries: Artificial Intelligence for:, Web

Company Name: AiroCorp
Description: We're building the world's first Artificial Intelligence Operating System
Website: http://airocorp.com/
Phone: 7838996573 **Email:** contact@airocorp.com
City: New Delhi **State:** DL **PC:** **Country:** India
Year Established: 2013 **Status 2020:** Active
Industries: Application Services for:, Artificial Intelligence for:, IT Managed Services

Company Name: AppWharf
Description: Appwharf is an intelligent assistant that helps find you the best-fit SaaS for your business.
Website: http://www.appwharf.com/
Phone: **Email:** abhishek@appwharf.com
City: New Delhi **State:** DL **PC:** **Country:** India
Year Established: **Status 2020:** Active
Industries: Artificial Intelligence for:, Business Intelligence for:, ~ Customer Relationship Management (11), ~ Professional Services (48)

Company Name: AutoGenerate.ai
Description: SaaS solution for AI-Generated Fashion Designs
Website: http://autogenerate.ai
Phone: **Email:** sukrit@autogenerate.ai
City: New Delhi **State:** DL **PC:** **Country:** India
Year Established: 2019 **Status 2020:** Active
Industries: Artificial Intelligence for:, ~ Fashion (16), Business Software as a Service Apps (SaaS Apps)

Company Name: Captain Grocer
Description: Captaingrocer is a fully personalised grocery store for Indian Consumers, powered by data science and analytics.
Website: http://captaingrocer.com
Phone: **Email:** 36229@reference-encyclopedia-ai.net
City: New Delhi **State:** DL **PC:** **Country:** India
Year Established: 2015 **Status 2020:** Closed
Industries: Analytics for:, Artificial Intelligence

Company Name: Corseco Technologies Private Limited
Description: End To End AI Based Solutions for the enterpri: Sweden
Website: http://www.corsecotech.com
Phone: 91-9818004499 **Email:** info@corsecotech.com
City: New Delhi **State:** DL **PC:** **Country:** India
Year Established: **Status 2020:** Active
Industries: Artificial Intelligence

Company Name: Cosmic Info Ventur: Spain
Description: Creative Technology Studio, Innovation Consultancy, Brand Strategy, Digital Marketing
Website: http://www.cosmicinfoventures.com/
Phone: 310-402-1717 **Email:** aditya@cosmicinfoventures.com
City: New Delhi **State:** DL **PC:** **Country:** India
Year Established: **Status 2020:** Active
Industries: Artificial Intelligence for:, Blockchain for:, Cloud for:, ~ Arts-Entertainment-Recreation (4), ~ Administrative and Support Services (1)

Company Name: Curie Labs
Description: Curie Labs, operated by Delhi-based Predictive Labs Pvt. Ltd, helps building owners and malls save on power
Website:
Phone: **Email:** 36361@reference-encyclopedia-ai.net
City: New Delhi **State:** DL **PC:** **Country:** India
Year Established: 2016 **Status 2020:** Closed
Industries: ~ Energy and Utilities (14), Predictive Analytics

Company Name: EagletFly
Description: IT Technologies Education Startup in India. At EagletFly we teach Big Data, Data Science, Data Analytics, Data Analyst with Python & R
Website: http://eagletflysolutions.com/
Phone: (981) 143-4634 **Email:** Eagletflydelhi@gmail.com
City: New Delhi **State:** DL **PC:** **Country:** India
Year Established: 2019 **Status 2020:** Active
Industries: Artificial Intelligence for:, Big Data and Analytics for:, ~ Education (13), IT Managed Services for:, Virtual Reality (VR)

Company Name: EasyLeadz
Description: An AI sales assistant which finds B2B leads for you 24/7
Website: http://www.easyleadz.com
Phone: **Email:** shreyaa@easyleadz.com
City: New Delhi **State:** DL **PC:** **Country:** India
Year Established: 2016 **Status 2020:** Active
Industries: Artificial Intelligence for:, IT Managed Services for:, Robotics for:, Business Software as a Service Apps (SaaS Apps)

Company Name: Econolytics
Description: Econolytics is simple and driven to make the most efficient data analytic marketplace.
Website: http://www.econolytics.: India
Phone: 91 9899112471 **Email:** info@econolytics.: India
City: New Delhi **State:** DL **PC:** **Country:** India
Year Established: 2018 **Status 2020:** Active
Industries: Analytics for:, Machine Learning

Company Name: Edureify
Description: AI , Web, Mobile, Personalized learning Edtech
Website: http://edureify.com/
Phone: **Email:** Social@edureify.com
City: New Delhi **State:** DL **PC:** **Country:** India
Year Established: **Status 2020:** Active
Industries: Artificial Intelligence for:, ~ Education (13), Web for:, ~ Personal-Religious-Civic (45), Machine Learning for:, ~ Media-Communications (41)

Company Name: Ela Cancer
Description: Best Cancer Treatment Clinic or Hospitals and Oncology Specialist in India for Breast Cancer, Prostate Cancer, Lung Cancer, Oral Cancer...
Website: http://www.elacancer.com
Phone: 8929020600 **Email:** contact@elacancer.com
City: New Delhi **State:** DL **PC:** **Country:** India
Year Established: **Status 2020:** Active
Industries:

Company Name: Fitho
Description: Health technology company, focused on building products that help people live healthier
Website: http://www.fitho.: India
Phone: **Email:** fitness@fitho.: India
City: New Delhi **State:** DL **PC:** **Country:** India
Year Established: **Status 2020:** Active
Industries: Artificial Intelligence for:, ~ Healthcare (20), IT Managed Services for:, Web for:, ~ Healthcare (20)

Company Name: Gobasco
Description: Employ real-time data analytics on data-streams.
Website: http://gobasco.com/
Phone: **Email:** INFO@GOBASCO.COM
City: New Delhi **State:** DL **PC:** **Country:** India
Year Established: 2017 **Status 2020:** Active
Industries: ~ Agriculture (3), Artificial Intelligence for:, ~ Telecommunications (56), Supply Chain Management

Company Name: HealthM
Description: HealthMir is a Artificial intelligence-driven health content.
Website: http://www.healthmir.com/
Phone: (704)281-4019 **Email:** founders@healthmir.com
City: New Delhi **State:** DL **PC:** **Country:** India
Year Established: 2015 **Status 2020:** Active
Industries: Artificial Intelligence for:, ~ Healthcare (20), ~ Healthcare (20), ~ Healthcare (20)

Company Name: HopeQure Wellness Solutions Pvt Ltd
Description: HopeQure is an online video counseling platform used by thousands of Clients and 650 Psychologists for improved delivering Mental Health.
Website: http://www.hopequre.com
Phone: **Email:** vivek@hopequre.com
City: New Delhi **State:** DL **PC:** **Country:** India
Year Established: 2017 **Status 2020:** Active
Industries: Artificial Intelligence for:, ~ Healthcare (20), ~ Healthcare (20)

Company Name: Hostmud
Description: Product Engineering at Scale
Website: http://www.hostmud.com
Phone: **Email:** hello@hostmud.com
City: New Delhi **State:** DL **PC:** **Country:** India
Year Established: **Status 2020:** Active
Industries: Artificial Intelligence for:, Cloud for:, Cloud for:, Cloud for:, Enterprise Application Services for:, Enterprise Application Services for:, Machine Learning for:, Cloud

Company Name: Hyperhire
Description: Hyperhire is a B2B End to End HR Solutions Platform that leverages Artificial Intelligence.
Website: http://www.hyperhire.in/
Phone: 91 11669 61000 **Email:** contact@hyperhire.: India
City: New Delhi **State:** DL **PC:** **Country:** India
Year Established: 2016 **Status 2020:** Active
Industries: Artificial Intelligence

Company Name: iGloble Software Solutions
Description: An innovative company delivering products & ML based platforms to transform data into usable information for faster & smarter insights
Website: http://www.igloble.com/
Phone: **Email:** sales@igloble.com
City: New Delhi **State:** DL **PC:** **Country:** India
Year Established: 2016 **Status 2020:** Active
Industries: IT Managed Services for:, Machine Learning for:, Predictive Analytics

Company Name: iNICU
Description: iNICU is a Medical Devices Technology Company.
Website: http://inicucloud.com/
Phone: **Email:** info@inicucloud.com
City: New Delhi **State:** DL **PC:** **Country:** India
Year Established: 2016 **Status 2020:** Active
Industries: Artificial Intelligence for:, ~ Healthcare (20), ~ Healthcare (20)

Company Name: Leverage Edu
Description: AI-enabled marketplace designed to help students with their higher education and career growth plans
Website: http://www.leverageedu.com
Phone: **Email:** myawesomecareer@leverageedu.com
City: New Delhi **State:** DL **PC:** **Country:** India
Year Established: 2017 **Status 2020:** Active
Industries: ~ Education (13), ~ Education (13), Web

Company Name: Localpeep
Description: Affiliate Marketing for brick and mortar reta: Israel
Website: http://localpeep.com
Phone: **Email:** info@localpeep.com
City: New Delhi **State:** DL **PC:** **Country:** India
Year Established: 2015 **Status 2020:** Active
Industries: E-Commerce for:, ~ Retail and Consumer Products (52), Mobile for:, Predictive Analytics

Company Name: Lucideus
Description: Lucideus is an Enterprise Cyber Security platforms company. It protects Fortune 500 companies around the world with it's SAFE Platform.
Website: http://lucideus.com/
Phone: 91 11 2632 2632 **Email:** info@lucideustech.com
City: New Delhi **State:** DL **PC:** **Country:** India
Year Established: 2012 **Status 2020:** Active
Industries: Artificial Intelligence for:, Cyber Security for:, Security

Company Name: MINDZ TECHNOLOGY
Description: Mindz Technology is a globally recognized IT Services company providing corporate solutions.
Website: http://www.mindztechnology.com
Phone: 011-48912579 **Email:** info@mindztechnology.com
City: New Delhi **State:** DL **PC:** **Country:** India
Year Established: **Status 2020:** Active
Industries: Artificial Intelligence for:, Augmented Reality for:, Enterprise Application Services for:, ~ Human Resources (24), Machine Learning for:, ~ Professional Services (48), Cyber Security

Company Name: Muoro.io
Description: Muoro Turns Data into Decisions, with AI and Analytics
Website: http://muoro.io
Phone: **Email:** hello@muoro.io
City: New Delhi **State:** DL **PC:** **Country:** India
Year Established: 2016 **Status 2020:** Active
Industries: Artificial Intelligence for:, IT Managed Services for:, Machine Learning for:, Robotics

Company Name: Neuron
Description: Neuron is a machine learning platform for Natural language processing.
Website: http://neuronme.com/
Phone: **Email:** veer@neuronme.com
City: New Delhi **State:** DL **PC:** **Country:** India
Year Established: 2014 **Status 2020:** Active
Industries:

Company Name: NullPointer
Description: SaaS
Website: http://nullpointer.: India
Phone: 91-8826009272 **Email:** bala@nullpointer.: India
City: New Delhi **State:** DL **PC:** **Country:** India
Year Established: **Status 2020:** Active
Industries: Artificial Intelligence for:, ~ Banking and Financial Markets-Services (7), Machine Learning for:, ~ Media-Communications (41), ~ Arts-Entertainment-Recreation (4)

Company Name: Propertytrees
Description: Real Estate portal based on Machine Learning and Blockcha: India
Website: http://propertytrees.com
Phone: **Email:** info@propertytrees.com
City: New Delhi **State:** DL **PC:** **Country:** India
Year Established: **Status 2020:** Active
Industries: Artificial Intelligence for:, Blockchain for:, Machine Learning for:, ~ Real Estate (49)

Company Name: Quovantis Technologies
Description: We help leading product companies and innovative startups to build delightful digital experiences.
Website: http://www.quovantis.com
Phone: (408)639-8268 **Email:** info@quovantis.com
City: New Delhi **State:** DL **PC:** **Country:** India
Year Established: 2010 **Status 2020:** Active
Industries: Big Data and Analytics for:, IT Managed Services for:, Mobile for:, Business Process and Operations for:, Predictive Analytics

Company Name: RAAV Tech
Description: RAAV Tech is a quality instruments and analytics company that uses artificial intelligence and deep learning.
Website: http://www.raavtechlabs.com/
Phone: **Email:** info@raav.: India
City: New Delhi **State:** DL **PC:** **Country:** India
Year Established: 2018 **Status 2020:** Active
Industries: Analytics for:, Artificial Intelligence for:, Machine Learning

Company Name: Stri: Kenya
Description: STRIKE builds solar cum electric vehicl: Spain
Website: http://www.strikemotors.net/
Phone: (882)628-2168 **Email:** taranpreetsinghbabbar@gmail.com
City: New Delhi **State:** DL **PC:** **Country:** India
Year Established: **Status 2020:** Active
Industries: Artificial Intelligence for:, ~ Automotive (5), ~ Energy and Utilities (14), ~ Energy and Utilities (14), ~ Energy and Utilities (14), ~ Transportation and Logistics (57)

Company **Name:** talkRecruit
Description: Video & AI Based Recruitment Platform
Website: http://www.talkrecruit.com
Phone: 9818553338 **Email:** hello@talkrecruit.com
City: New Delhi **State:** DL **PC:** **Country:** India
Year Established: **Status 2020:** Active
Industries: Artificial Intelligence for:, ~ Human Resources (24), Machine Learning for:, ~ Media-Communications (41)

Company Name: Unreal AI
Description: Saas, Security, AI
Website: http://unrealai.xyz
Phone: **Email:** saurabh@unrealai.xyz
City: New Delhi **State:** DL **PC:** **Country:** India

Year Established: **Status 2020:** Active
Industries: Artificial Intelligence for:, ~ Biotechnology (9), IT Managed Services for:, Security

Company Name: Vanido
Description: Vanido is your AI singing teacher.
Website: http://vanido.io
Phone: **Email:** founders@vanido.io
City: New Delhi **State:** DL **PC:** **Country:** India
Year Established: 2016 **Status 2020:** Active
Industries: Application Services for:, ~ Education (13)

Company Name: Vis: Italy
Description: AI driven chatbot to provide health advice within minutes.
Website: http://getvisitapp.com
Phone: **Email:** hello@getvisitapp.com
City: New Delhi **State:** DL **PC:** **Country:** India
Year Established: **Status 2020:** Active
Industries: Artificial Intelligence for:, ~ Healthcare (20), Machine Learning for:, ~ Healthcare (20)

Company Name: wellOwi: Sweden
Description: We quantify health using unique biological data points to give actionable insights and personalised interventions.
Website: http://www.wellowise.com
Phone: **Email:** manish@wellowise.com
City: New Delhi **State:** DL **PC:** **Country:** India
Year Established: **Status 2020:** Active
Industries: Artificial Intelligence for:, Big Data and Analytics for:, ~ Healthcare (20), ~ Healthcare (20), ~ Healthcare (20)

Company Name: Alluvium
Description: Alluvium connect factories with IoT and AI to improve worker safety, productivity and compliance of workers and assets.
Website: http://www.alluvium.io/
Phone: 079-26402005/06 **Email:** info@alluvium.io
City: Ahmedabad **State:** GJ **PC:** **Country:** India
Year Established: 2015 **Status 2020:** Active
Industries: Artificial Intelligence for:, Industrial Solutions for:, Internet of Things (IoT) for:, Application Services

Company Name: Alluvium IoT Solutions
Description: Alluvium IoT Solutions connect factories with IoT & AI to enhance worker safety, productivity & compliance of workers and assets.
Website: http://alluvium.in/
Phone: 079-26402005/06 **Email:** support@alluvium.: India
City: Ahmedabad **State:** GJ **PC:** **Country:** India
Year Established: **Status 2020:** Active
Industries: Artificial Intelligence for:, Industrial Solutions

Company Name: Brainasoft
Description: Brainasoft is an Artificial Intelligence (AI) startup focusing on natural language processing, machine learning, & human-computer interface.
Website: http://www.brainasoft.com
Phone: **Email:** 36202@reference-encyclopedia-ai.net
City: Ahmedabad **State:** GJ **PC:** **Country:** India
Year Established: 2013 **Status 2020:** Active
Industries: Artificial Intelligence

Company Name: Byte Prophecy
Description: Byte Prophecy is an Enterprise AI company that delivers the last-mile of analytics i.e. insights that drive action
Website: http://www.byteprophecy.com
Phone: **Email:** contact@byteprophecy.com
City: Ahmedabad **State:** GJ **PC:** **Country:** India
Year Established: **Status 2020:** Active
Industries:

Company Name: DataOne Innovation Labs
Description: SaaS, Big Data Analytics, Machine Learning, Artificial Intelligence
Website: http://dataone.io
Phone: **Email:** contact@dataone.io
City: Ahmedabad **State:** GJ **PC:** **Country:** India
Year Established: 2016 **Status 2020:** Active
Industries: Analytics for:, Artificial Intelligence for:, Big Data and Analytics for:, Enterprise Application Services for:, IT Managed Services for:, Machine Learning for:, Business Software as a Service Apps (SaaS Apps)

Company Name: DKM Machines
Description: DKM Machines is Autotech on road safety company.
Website: http://dkmachines.io
Phone: **Email:** dikshitkumarmodi@dkmachines.io
City: Ahmedabad **State:** GJ **PC:** **Country:** India
Year Established: 2017 **Status 2020:** Active
Industries: Artificial Intelligence for:, ~ Automotive (5), Blockchain for:, Machine Learning

Company Name: Enpacto
Description: We are helping businesses and individuals with Conversational AI.
Website: http://enpacto.tech
Phone: (814) 033-1774 **Email:** hello@enpacto.tech
City: Ahmedabad **State:** GJ **PC:** **Country:** India
Year Established: 2020 **Status 2020:** Active
Industries: Artificial Intelligence

Company Name: Plutomen Technologi
Description: We are one of the brightest company working in AR VR having some of the most experienced resources with 5 years experience.
Website: http://pluto-men.com/
Phone: 91 079 49009400 **Email:** info@pluto-men.com
City: Ahmedabad **State:** GJ **PC:** **Country:** India
Year Established: 2016 **Status 2020:** Active
Industries: Artificial Intelligence for:, Augmented Reality for:, Application Services for:, Virtual Reality (VR) for:, Virtual Reality (VR)

Company Name: Pragnakalp Techlabs
Description: Chatbots Development, Python Programming, Natural Language Processing (NLP), Machine Learning Solutions
Website: http://www.pragnakalp.com/
Phone: **Email:** letstalk@pragnakalp.com
City: Ahmedabad **State:** GJ **PC:** **Country:** India
Year Established: 2018 **Status 2020:** Active
Industries: Artificial Intelligence for:, IT Managed Services for:, Machine Learning

Company Name: Shabrus Software
Description: Shabrus is a digital-first professional services firm.
Website: http://www.shabrus.com
Phone: 91 8128260867 **Email:** sales@shabrus.com
City: Ahmedabad **State:** GJ **PC:** **Country:** India
Year Established: **Status 2020:** Active
Industries:

Company Name: Space-O Technologies
Description: A Leading Mobile App Development Company with Distinction
Website: http://www.spaceotechnologies.com/
Phone: (650) 666-3071 **Email:** sales@spaceotechnologies.com
City: Ahmedabad **State:** GJ **PC:** **Country:** India
Year Established: **Status 2020:** Active
Industries: Artificial Intelligence for:, Augmented Reality for:, Blockchain for:, Machine Learning for:, Mobile for:, Cyber Security for:, Cyber Security

Company Name: Sprout Matrix
Description: Creating MVP backed with AI.
Website: http://sproutmatrix.com
Phone: **Email:** hola@sproutmatrix.com
City: Ahmedabad **State:** GJ **PC:** **Country:** India
Year Established: 2019 **Status 2020:** Active
Industries: Artificial Intelligence for:, IT Managed Services for:, Web

Company Name: Version Labs
Description: Version Labs is a software development and new age digital marketing firm that specializes in chatbots.
Website: http://versionlabs.co/
Phone: **Email:** hello@versionlabs.co
City: Ahmedabad **State:** GJ **PC:** **Country:** India
Year Established: 2018 **Status 2020:** Active
Industries: Artificial Intelligence for:, Digital Marketing

Company Name: Virtual Code: Serbia
Description: Virtual Coders is offering next-gen digital transformation, enterprise IT and product engineering services.
Website: http://www.virtualcoders.in/
Phone: 97148-67090 **Email:** dm@virtualcoders.: India
City: Ahmedabad **State:** GJ **PC:** **Country:** India
Year Established: **Status 2020:** Active
Industries: Artificial Intelligence for:, Machine Learning for:, Application Services

Company Name: CoRygbee Pvt. Ltd
Description: A personal smart idea guide, that behaves like an AI-boosted intellectual partner for user to jot down and pursue their ideas.
Website:
Phone: **Email:** 36339@reference-encyclopedia-ai.net
City: Gandhinagar **State:** GJ **PC:** **Country:** India
Year Established: 2016 **Status 2020:** - Closed
Industries: Artificial Intelligence for:, Application Services

Company Name: KshatraInfotech
Description: KshatraInfotech is an AI, image processing and app development company.
Website: http://www.kshatrainfotech.com/
Phone: 91 94095 25981 **Email:** info@kshatrainfotech.com
City: Gandhinagar **State:** GJ **PC:** **Country:** India
Year Established: 2015 **Status 2020:** Active
Industries: Application Services for:, Artificial Intelligence for:, IT Managed Services

Company Name: Inbox Infotech
Description: Inbox Infotech provides IT support and solutions in the field of cybersecurity, artificial intelligence, and IoT.
Website: http://inboxtechs.com/
Phone: 0265-2371137 **Email:** info@inboxtechs.com
City: Vadodara **State:** GJ **PC:** **Country:** India
Year Established: 2016 **Status 2020:** Active
Industries: Artificial Intelligence for:, Cyber Security for:, Internet of Things (IoT)

Company Name: Umwelt PeopleTech Solutions Private Limited
Description: SaaS based Platform
Website: http://umwelt.ai
Phone: 91-9873665877 **Email:** sales@umwelt.ai
City: Faridabad **State:** HR **PC:** **Country:** India
Year Established: **Status 2020:** Active
Industries:

Company Name: AdStair
Description: India's First AI Enabled Ads Optimisation Company
Website: https://www.adstair.com/
Phone: 33 1 40 40 22 90 **Email:** 35957@reference-encyclopedia-ai.net
City: Gurgaon **State:** HR **PC:** **Country:** India
Year Established: 2017 **Status 2020:** Active
Industries: Artificial Intelligence

Company Name: Auliv
Description: Auliv uses Computer Vision & AI to generate your 2D & 3D(in development) personalized emoji avatars instantly from a single selfie.
Website: http://www.aulivtech.com
Phone: **Email:** Info@aulivtech.com
City: Gurgaon **State:** HR **PC:** **Country:** India
Year Established: 2018 **Status 2020:** Active
Industries: Artificial Intelligence for:, ~ Arts-Entertainment-Recreation (4), ~ Arts-Entertainment-Recreation (4), Application Services

Company Name: BASH.ai
Description: BASH.ai is an intelligent chatbot which implements Machine Learning Algorithms to improve employee productivity.
Website: http://bash.ai/
Phone: **Email:** info@bash.ai
City: Gurgaon **State:** HR **PC:** **Country:** India
Year Established: **Status 2020:** Active
Industries: Artificial Intelligence for:, ~ Human Resources (24), Web for:, Machine Learning for:, Natural Language Processing for:, Predictive Analytics

Company Name: Blue Sky Analytics
Description: Geospatial Data Intelligence company using ML/AI to build an environmental data stack
Website: http://blueskyhq.in/
Phone: **Email:** abhilasha@breezo.: India
City: Gurgaon **State:** HR **PC:** **Country:** India
Year Established: 2018 **Status 2020:** Active
Industries: Artificial Intelligence for:, Big Data and Analytics for:, Internet of Things (IoT) for:, Machine Learning

Company Name: Bobble AI
Description: Smarter Phone Experience with Bobble's Artificial Intelligence
Website: http://bobble.ai
Phone: 91 11 30018074 **Email:** hello@bobble.ai
City: Gurgaon **State:** HR **PC:** **Country:** India
Year Established: 2015 **Status 2020:** Active
Industries: Artificial Intelligence

Company Name: Bobble App
Description: Bobble App is a computer software platform.
Website: http://www.bobble.ai/en/home
Phone: **Email:** nimit.pahwa@bobble.ai
City: Gurgaon **State:** HR **PC:** **Country:** India
Year Established: 2015 **Status 2020:** Active
Industries: Artificial Intelligence

Company Name: ChironX
Description: ChironX is a deep tech company solving healthcare diagnostics using AI, data science and advanced image processing.
Website: http://www.chironx.ai/
Phone: **Email:** hello@chironx.ai
City: Gurgaon **State:** HR **PC:** **Country:** India
Year Established: 2017 **Status 2020:** Active
Industries: Artificial Intelligence for:, ~ Healthcare (20), ~ Healthcare (20), Image Recognition for:, IT Managed Services

Company Name: ClickPost
Description: ClickPost is a Logistics Intelligence Platform that helps companies use data science to optimize supply chain performance
Website: http://www.clickpost.in/
Phone: **Email:** founders@clickpost.: India
City: Gurgaon **State:** HR **PC:** **Country:** India
Year Established: 2015 **Status 2020:** Active
Industries: Enterprise Application Services for:, ~ Telecommunications (56), Machine Learning for:, Business Software as a Service Apps (SaaS Apps)

Company Name: Crystal Analytix
Description: We function as a premier data science training centre, where both corporate professionals and students advance their technical skills.
Website: http://www.crystalanalytix.com/
Phone: (971) 753-3401 **Email:** info@crystalanalytix.com
City: Gurgaon **State:** HR **PC:** **Country:** India
Year Established: 2017 **Status 2020:** Active
Industries: Analytics for:, Business Intelligence for:, Application Services

Company Name: DEWII
Description: Technology enabled background verification
Website: http://www.DEWII.: India
Phone: **Email:** info@DEWII.: India
City: Gurgaon **State:** HR **PC:** **Country:** India
Year Established: 2017 **Status 2020:** Active
Industries: Artificial Intelligence for:, IT Managed Services

Company Name: Dieatto
Description: Dieatto is an AI powered diet bot using machine learning to tailor and track diet plans.
Website: http://dieatto.com/
Phone: (779) 922-7544 **Email:** contact@dieatto.com
City: Gurgaon **State:** HR **PC:** **Country:** India
Year Established: 2018 **Status 2020:** Active
Industries: Artificial Intelligence for:, ~ Healthcare (20), ~ Healthcare (20)

Company Name: EnrichAI
Description: A cloud based plug and play platform for collecting and processing Internet of Things (IoT) data and churning insights from : Italy
Website: http://www.enrichai.com
Phone: **Email:** contact@enrichai.com
City: Gurgaon **State:** HR **PC:** **Country:** India
Year Established: 2017 **Status 2020:** Active
Industries: Enterprise Application Services for:, IT Managed Services for:, Internet of Things (IoT) for:, Predictive Analytics

Company Name: Famepilot Internet Private Limited
Description: SAAS, ONLINE REPUTATION MANAGEMENT PLATFORM, AUTOMATED AUTHENTIC REVIEW GENERATION, CUSTOMER EXPERIENCE & ENGAGEMENT PLATFORM
Website: http://famepilot.com/
Phone: 935 404 4413 **Email:** info@famepilot.com
City: Gurgaon **State:** HR **PC:** **Country:** India
Year Established: 2018 **Status 2020:** Active
Industries: Artificial Intelligence for:, IT Managed Services for:, Web for:, Business Software as a Service Apps (SaaS Apps)

Company Name: fleetx.io
Description: Fleetx is an intelligent data platform which uses AI, machine learning, sensors and predictive analytics to help fleet owners.
Website: http://www.fleetx.io
Phone: **Email:** contact@fleetx.io
City: Gurgaon **State:** HR **PC:** **Country:** India
Year Established: 2017 **Status 2020:** Active
Industries:

Company Name: Flixstock
Description: Flixstock is a technology startup, working on programmatic image generation through machine learning & Artificial intelligence for eCommerce companies.
Website: https://flixstock.com
Phone: **Email:** sales@flixstock.com
City: Gurgaon **State:** HR **PC:** **Country:** India
Year Established: **Status 2020:** Active
Industries: Artificial Intelligence for:, ~ Retail and Consumer Products (52), Automation for:, ~ E-Commerce (378), Business Applications for:, ~ E-Commerce (622), Business Process and Operations for:, ~ E-Commerce (744), Business Resiliency Services for:, E-Commerce for:, Mac

Company Name: Globlal Technology Solutions
Description: Global Technology Solutions (GTS) is a leading expert in data annotation, speech data collection, and dataset provider.
Website: http://gts.ai/
Phone: 91 8824335106 **Email:** info@gts.ai
City: Gurgaon **State:** HR **PC:** **Country:** India
Year Established: 2015 **Status 2020:** Active
Industries: Artificial Intelligence for:, Facial Recognition for:, IT Managed Services for:, Machine Learning

Company Name: goFlatmates.com
Description: AI based Matching Engine connecting bachelors looking for flatmat: Spain
Website: http://www.goflatmates.com
Phone: 91 9810612712 **Email:** anshul@goflatmates.com
City: Gurgaon **State:** HR **PC:** **Country:** India
Year Established: 2019 **Status 2020:** Active
Industries: Artificial Intelligence

Company Name: GoVocal.AI
Description: Platform to Build Voice Activated & AI Powered Apps for digital assistants like Amazon Alexa, Goggle Assistant and for IOT devic: Spain
Website: http://GoVocal.AI
Phone: **Email:** contactus@govocal.ai
City: Gurgaon **State:** HR **PC:** **Country:** India
Year Established: **Status 2020:** Active
Industries: Artificial Intelligence for:, Enterprise Application Services for:, Machine Learning for:, Natural Language Processing for:, Speech Recognition

Company Name: HAL Robotics
Description: HAL Robotics with its home-grown AI-powered IoT smart devices enabling enterprises to become #ResourceSmart.
Website: http://www.halrobotics.net/
Phone: 91 9810350101 **Email:** connect@halrobotics.net
City: Gurgaon **State:** HR **PC:** **Country:** India
Year Established: **Status 2020:** Active
Industries: Artificial Intelligence for:, Big Data and Analytics for:, Machine Learning for:, Compute

Company Name: HOOPOUN
Description: Hoopoun enables true Digitization through Digital Receipts, Payments & Unified Loyalty Rewards using blockchain and Artificial Intellingence
Website: https://www.hoopoun.io/
Phone: **Email:** 36702@reference-encyclopedia-ai.net
City: Gurgaon **State:** HR **PC:** **Country:** India
Year Established: 1999 **Status 2020:** Active
Industries: Application Services for:, Artificial Intelligence for:, Blockchain for:, IT Managed Services for:, Web for:, Mobile for:, ~ Banking and Financial Markets-Services (7)

Company Name: Hora.AI
Description: Hora.ai is an Indian fintech lending startup that gives microloans to underserved blue collar skilled workers on a smartphone app.
Website: http://www.hora.ai/
Phone: **Email:** hello@hora.ai
City: Gurgaon **State:** HR **PC:** **Country:** India
Year Established: 2017 **Status 2020:** Active
Industries: Artificial Intelligence for:, ~ Banking and Financial Markets-Services (7), ~ Banking and Financial Markets-Services (7)

Company Name: iDelivr
Description: iDelivr is an Artificial Intelligence (AI) chatbot company.
Website: http://idelivr.ai/
Phone: **Email:** vs@idelivr.ai
City: Gurgaon **State:** HR **PC:** **Country:** India

Year Established: 2015 **Status 2020:** Active
Industries: Artificial Intelligence for:, IT Managed Services for:, Web for:, Mobile for:, Application Services

Company Name: Ikarus
Description: AI tech startup working in the domain of enterprise process automation
Website: http://www.ikarus.ai/
Phone: 91 97172 68697 **Email:** info@ikarus.ai
City: Gurgaon **State:** HR **PC:** **Country:** India
Year Established: 2016 **Status 2020:** Active
Industries: Artificial Intelligence for:, Enterprise Application Services for:, Machine Learning

Company Name: ImagoAI
Description: Image based Phenotyping in Plant Breeding using Artificial Intelligence
Website: http://www.imagoai.com
Phone: **Email:** abhishek@imagoai.com
City: Gurgaon **State:** HR **PC:** **Country:** India
Year Established: **Status 2020:** Active
Industries: ~ Agriculture (3), ~ Agriculture (3), Artificial Intelligence for:, ~ Biotechnology (9), Machine Learning

Company Name: inFeedo
Description: A 5 year old Predictive People Analytics company helping employees in 60 companies (and counting) and making them feel heard and valued.
Website: http://www.infeedo.com/
Phone: **Email:** tanmaya@infeedo.com
City: Gurgaon **State:** HR **PC:** **Country:** India
Year Established: **Status 2020:** Active
Industries: Artificial Intelligence for:, Enterprise Application Services for:, ~ Human Resources (24), Machine Learning for:, Natural Language Processing for:, Predictive Analytics

Company Name: Insino Ventur: Spain
Description: We're simply amending the next big in tech to make sure the world stays at par.
Website: http://insinoventures.com/
Phone: 91 9785468738 **Email:** hello@insinoventures.com
City: Gurgaon **State:** HR **PC:** **Country:** India
Year Established: **Status 2020:** Active
Industries: Artificial Intelligence for:, Augmented Reality for:, Blockchain for:, Machine Learning for:, Cyber Security for:, Cyber Security for:, Cyber Security for:, Cyber Security

Company Name: IntelliTicks
Description: IntelliTicks is an AI-powered live chat platform for increasing conversions and lead generation.
Website: http://www.intelliticks.com/
Phone: 7709-527-736 **Email:** sales@intelliticks.com
City: Gurgaon **State:** HR **PC:** **Country:** India
Year Established: 2017 **Status 2020:** Active
Industries: Artificial Intelligence for:, Application Services

Company Name: KarnaAI
Description: ParallelDots is a technology company that develops artificial intelligence solutions for developers, startups, and enterprises.
Website: http://www.paralleldots.xyz
Phone: 9820353142 **Email:** kushank@paralleldots.com
City: Gurgaon **State:** HR **PC:** **Country:** India
Year Established: **Status 2020:** Active
Industries:

Company Name: Leena AI
Description: Leena is smart AI powered HR companion dedicated towards engaging employees.
Website: http://www.leena.ai/
Phone: 1-650-417-8550 **Email:** adit@chatteron.io
City: Gurgaon **State:** HR **PC:** **Country:** India
Year Established: **Status 2020:** Active
Industries: Artificial Intelligence for:, ~ Human Resources (24), IT Managed Services for:, IT Managed Services

Company Name: Litifer
Description: Litifer is a startup working in the AI-IOT field for the last 2 years.
Website: http://www.litifer.com
Phone: **Email:** contact@litifer.com
City: Gurgaon **State:** HR **PC:** **Country:** India
Year Established: 2016 **Status 2020:** Active
Industries: Artificial Intelligence for:, IT Managed Services for:, IT Managed Services for:, Internet of Things (IoT)

Company Name: Lokll
Description: Consumer Internet, Marketplace, Travel
Website: http://lokll.com
Phone: (987) 391-5513 **Email:** team@lokll.com
City: Gurgaon **State:** HR **PC:** **Country:** India
Year Established: 2019 **Status 2020:** Active
Industries: Artificial Intelligence for:, E-Commerce

Company Name: Lynette AI
Description: Connects hoteliers to their guests on all communication channels throgh conversational AI.
Website: http://www.lynetteai.com/
Phone: **Email:** info@lynetteai.com
City: Gurgaon **State:** HR **PC:** **Country:** India
Year Established: 2018 **Status 2020:** Active
Industries: Artificial Intelligence for:, Big Data and Analytics for:, IT Managed Services

Company Name: ManageSmart.AI
Description: AI, Data Analytics, Machine Learning and Blockchain Tech Startup
Website: http://www.managesmart.ai
Phone: **Email:** contact@managesmart.ai
City: Gurgaon **State:** HR **PC:** **Country:** India
Year Established: 2015 **Status 2020:** Active
Industries: Analytics for:, Artificial Intelligence for:, Blockchain for:, Machine Learning for:, Business Software as a Service Apps (SaaS Apps)

Company Name: Metvy
Description: AI driven networking platform for individuals and organisations which aims to provided a seamless end to end networking experience.
Website: http://www.metvy.com
Phone: 91 9821964864 **Email:** shawrya@metvy.com
City: Gurgaon **State:** HR **PC:** **Country:** India
Year Established: 2018 **Status 2020:** Active
Industries: Artificial Intelligence for:, IT Managed Services for:, Web

Company Name: MikeLegal
Description: MikeLegal is Asia's first Artificially Intelligent legal associate.
Website: http://www.mikelegal.com/
Phone: (874) 392-2707 **Email:** team@mikelegal.com
City: Gurgaon **State:** HR **PC:** **Country:** India
Year Established: 2017 **Status 2020:** Active
Industries:

Company Name: nimoy.ai
Description: Artificial Intelligence product company
Website: http://www.nimoy.ai/
Phone: **Email:** info@nimoy.ai
City: Gurgaon **State:** HR **PC:** **Country:** India
Year Established: **Status 2020:** Active
Industries: Artificial Intelligence for:, Machine Learning

Company Name: One Labs
Description: One Labs is consumer technology and artificial intelligence based startup
Website: http://onelabs.in/
Phone: **Email:** 37102@reference-encyclopedia-ai.net
City: Gurgaon **State:** HR **PC:** **Country:** India
Year Established: 2015 **Status 2020:** Active
Industries: Artificial Intelligence

Company Name: OrDekho
Description: Ordekho helps the user to design, print & promote product now at one place using our smart AI recognition system and webapp.
Website: http://www.ordekho.com
Phone: 9975162987 **Email:** info@ordekho.com
City: Gurgaon **State:** HR **PC:** **Country:** India
Year Established: 2017 **Status 2020:** Active
Industries: Artificial Intelligence for:, ~ Media-Communications (41)

Company Name: ParallelDots
Description: ParallelDots is a technology company that develops artificial intelligence solutions for developers, startups, and enterprises.
Website: http://www.paralleldots.com/
Phone: 1 (315) 215-1558 **Email:** contact@paralleldots.com
City: Gurgaon **State:** HR **PC:** **Country:** India
Year Established: 2017 **Status 2020:** Active
Industries: Artificial Intelligence for:, Machine Learning for:, Natural Language Processing for:, Content

Company Name: Prizmatics
Description: Prizmatics is working in the field of AI based Analytics, Data Management and Big Data
Website: http://www.prizmatics.com/
Phone: 9899300519 **Email:** info@prizmatics.com
City: Gurgaon **State:** HR **PC:** **Country:** India
Year Established: **Status 2020:** Active
Industries: Analytics for:, Artificial Intelligence for:, Big Data and Analytics for:, Business Intelligence for:, Image Recognition for:, Data Management

Company Name: QuillHash Technologies
Description: QuillHash Technologies offers private and public blockchain development, blockchain audits, smart contract development, and dex development.
Website: http://www.quillhash.com
Phone: 8130096886 **Email:** hello@quillhash.com
City: Gurgaon **State:** HR **PC:** **Country:** India
Year Established: 2018 **Status 2020:** Active
Industries: Artificial Intelligence for:, Blockchain for:, ~ Banking and Financial Markets-Services (7), Virtual Reality (VR)

Company Name: Rj
Description: PayOOM is India's fastest growing and most loved affiliate network.
Website: http://www.awefashion.unaux.com/awefashion/index.php
Phone: 6391175689 **Email:** contact@PayOOM.com
City: Gurgaon **State:** HR **PC:** **Country:** India
Year Established: **Status 2020:** Active
Industries:

Company Name: Samatrix
Description: Samatrix is one of the leading artificial intelligence and machine learning consulting firms.
Website: http://samatrix.io/
Phone: 91 124 436 8900 **Email:** contact@samatrix.io
City: Gurgaon **State:** HR **PC:** **Country:** India
Year Established: **Status 2020:** Active
Industries: Artificial Intelligence for:, IT Managed Services for:, Machine Learning for:, ~ Professional Services (48)

Company Name: Shipsy
Description: Shipsy's platform enables data driven decision making enhancing visibility and operational efficiency for Supply Chain industry
Website: http://shipsy.: India
Phone: **Email:** contact@shipsy.co.: India
City: Gurgaon **State:** HR **PC:** **Country:** India
Year Established: 2015 **Status 2020:** Active
Industries: Big Data and Analytics for:, Internet of Things (IoT) for:, ~ Telecommunications (56), Machine Learning for:, Supply Chain Management

Company Name: Silversparro Technologies Pvt. Ltd
Description: Silversparro is a deep learning technology solution provider for enterprises in Manufacturing, Retail and BFSI Sector.
Website: http://www.sparrosense.com
Phone: **Email:** contact@sparrosense.com
City: Gurgaon **State:** HR **PC:** **Country:** India
Year Established: **Status 2020:** Active
Industries: Artificial Intelligence for:, Computer Vision for:, Enterprise Application Services for:, Machine Learning for:, Natural Language Processing for:, Speech Recognition

Company Name: Simultaneous Geographical Reality Labs
Description: SGR offers Data Visualisation and Analytics services using Image , Video & 3D data.
Website: http://sgrlabs.co.: India
Phone: 8860276440 **Email:** rajan.s@sgrlabs.co.: India
City: Gurgaon **State:** HR **PC:** **Country:** India
Year Established: 2018 **Status 2020:** Active
Industries: Artificial Intelligence for:, IT Managed Services

Company Name: SMILE INTERNET TECHNOLOGIES PRIVATE LIMITED
Description: GetVid.ai is on mission to help Video Creators become more efficient
Website: http://www.getvid.ai
Phone: 91 99861 86194 **Email:** vaibhav.p@getvid.ai
City: Gurgaon **State:** HR **PC:** **Country:** India
Year Established: 2018 **Status 2020:** Active
Industries: Artificial Intelligence for:, Digital Media for:, Web

Company Name: Sorted AI - Personal Assistant
Description: An Assistant to make you more productive - Block Notifications, Setup Reminders, Search & Organize Documents, automatically.
Website: http://www.sortedai.com
Phone: 9818267291 **Email:** hello@sortedai.com
City: Gurgaon **State:** HR **PC:** **Country:** India
Year Established: 2019 **Status 2020:** Active
Industries: Artificial Intelligence for:, Data Management for:, Application Services for:, Application Services

Company Name: Splice Global
Description: Splice Global is a software development company specialized in providing GPS and AI-enabled technology solutions.
Website: http://www.spliceglobal.com/
Phone: 91-9599509350 **Email:** info@spliceglobal.com
City: Gurgaon **State:** HR **PC:** **Country:** India
Year Established: 2016 **Status 2020:** Active
Industries: Artificial Intelligence for:, ~ Telecommunications (56)

Company Name: SynergyLabs
Description: SynergyLabs offers artificial intelligence and machine learning services.
Website: http://synlabs.io
Phone: 0124-400-6215 **Email:** info@synlabs.io
City: Gurgaon **State:** HR **PC:** **Country:** India
Year Established: 2016 **Status 2020:** Active
Industries: Artificial Intelligence for:, Machine Learning

Company Name: Talocity
Description: Asynchronous Video Interview powered vertical SaaS recruitment platform based on Artificial Intelligence matching and predictive analysis.
Website: http://talocity.: India
Phone: **Email:** tse@talocity.: India
City: Gurgaon **State:** HR **PC:** **Country:** India
Year Established: 2015 **Status 2020:** Active
Industries: Artificial Intelligence for:, Web for:, Business Software as a Service Apps (SaaS Apps)

Company Name: The Hi-Tech Robotic Systemz
Description: Autonomous & Driver Assitive Systems for commercial and industrial vehicles.
Website: http://hitechroboticsystemz.com/
Phone: **Email:** marketing@hitechroboticsystemz.com
City: Gurgaon **State:** HR **PC:** **Country:** India
Year Established: **Status 2020:** Active
Industries: Analytics for:, Artificial Intelligence for:, ~ Automotive (5), Robotics

Company Name: ThirdWat: Switzerland
Description: Thirdwatch prevents fraud in digital, banking and e-commerce transactions in real time using AI. https://www.youtube.com/watch?v=_0BeScGNp8A
Website: http://www.thirdwatch.ai/
Phone: **Email:** hello@thirdwatch.ai
City: Gurgaon **State:** HR **PC:** **Country:** India
Year Established: 2016 **Status 2020:** Active
Industries: Artificial Intelligence for:, E-Commerce for:, ~ Banking and Financial Markets-Services (7), Security

Company Name: ThirdWatch, Stopping Fraud and RTO using AI
Description: Thirdwatch prevents fraud in digital, banking and e-commerce transactions in real time using AI. https://www.youtube.com/watch?v=_0BeScGNp8A
Website: http://www.thirdwatch.ai/
Phone: **Email:** hello@thirdwatch.ai
City: Gurgaon **State:** HR **PC:** **Country:** India
Year Established: **Status 2020:** Active
Industries: Artificial Intelligence for:, E-Commerce for:, ~ Banking and Financial Markets-Services (7), Security

Company Name: Transporter.city
Description: Transporter.city is an artificial intelligence (AI) enabled logistics platform.
Website: http://www.transporter.city/
Phone: **Email:** care@transporter.city
City: Gurgaon **State:** HR **PC:** **Country:** India
Year Established: 2016 **Status 2020:** Active
Industries: Artificial Intelligence for:, ~ Telecommunications (56), ~ Telecommunications (56)

Company Name: Veda Labs
Description: AI platform for brick and mortar stores to get offline business analytics online!
Website: http://www.vedalabs.: India
Phone: **Email:** veer@vedalabs.: India
City: Gurgaon **State:** HR **PC:** **Country:** India
Year Established: 2017 **Status 2020:** Active
Industries:

Company Name: Webragger
Description: AI powered Digital & Influencer Marketing Platform
Website: http://www.webragger.com
Phone: **Email:** info@webragger.com
City: Gurgaon **State:** HR **PC:** **Country:** India
Year Established: 2014 **Status 2020:** Active
Industries: Artificial Intelligence

Company Name: Xane.ai
Description: Xane.ai develops an artificially Intelligent chatbot aimed at revolutionizing 'people experience' in organizations.
Website: http://xane.ai/
Phone: 91 98734 93987 **Email:** xane@xane.ai
City: Gurgaon **State:** HR **PC:** **Country:** India
Year Established: 2017 **Status 2020:** Active
Industries: Artificial Intelligence for:, Machine Learning

Company Name: Yana
Description: Yana is a human powered personal assistant on your mobile.
Website: http://getyana.com/
Phone: (801) 089-0890 **Email:** connect@getyana.com
City: Gurgaon **State:** HR **PC:** **Country:** India
Year Established: 2015 **Status 2020:** Active
Industries: Application Services for:, Artificial Intelligence for:, Application Services

Company Name: Zvesta
Description: Zvesta provides smart and easily accessible digital products for the buyer to minimize the real-estate complexity.
Website: http://zvesta.com
Phone: **Email:** support@zvesta.com
City: Gurgaon **State:** HR **PC:** **Country:** India
Year Established: 2015 **Status 2020:** Active
Industries: Artificial Intelligence for:, Predictive Analytics

Company Name: zvesta.com
Description: zVesta is the developer of PA & AI in Real Estate with SaaS solution & standard ERP for builders with centralized engine & hosting inventory
Website: http://zvesta.com
Phone: **Email:** support@zvesta.com
City: Gurgaon **State:** HR **PC:** **Country:** India
Year Established: **Status 2020:** Active
Industries: Artificial Intelligence for:, Predictive Analytics for:, ~ Real Estate (49)

Company **Name:** Intello Labs
Description: Intello Labs uses image matching and machine learning to measure the quality of crops.
Website: http://www.intellolabs.com
Phone: **Email:** contact@intellolabs.com
City: Haryana **State:** HR **PC:** **Country:** India
Year Established: 2016 **Status 2020:** Active
Industries: ~ Agriculture (3), Artificial Intelligence for:, Big Data and Analytics for:, ~ Customer Relationship Management (11), Image Recognition for:, IT Managed Services for:, Machine Learning

Company Name: Surbo
Description: Surbo helps you to capture consumer feedback and conduct surveys using a chat interface.
Website: http://www.surbo.io
Phone: 087505 80630 **Email:** support@surbo.io
City: Haryana **State:** HR **PC:** **Country:** India
Year Established: **Status 2020:** Active
Industries: Artificial Intelligence for:, IT Managed Services for:, IT Managed Services for:, ~ Professional Services (48)

Company Name: Tosh Innovations
Description: Certification Authorities, Deeptech Certifications, Online Training
Website: http://www.toshinnovations.com/
Phone: **Email:** hello@toshinnovations.com
City: Haryana **State:** HR **PC:** **Country:** India
Year Established: 2016 **Status 2020:** Active
Industries: Artificial Intelligence for:, Internet of Things (IoT) for:, Machine Learning for:, ~ Education (13)

Company Name: Zenatix
Description: Zenatix is an energy data analytics company that provides energy management and analytics solutions.
Website: http://zenatix.com/
Phone: (995) 896-4442 **Email:** info@zenatix.com
City: Haryana **State:** HR **PC:** **Country:** India
Year Established: **Status 2020:** Active
Industries: Artificial Intelligence for:, ~ Energy and Utilities (14), ~ Retail and Consumer Products (52)

Company Name: TechXila
Description: Business & Technology Consulting , IT Consulting, Data Analytics
Website: http://www.techxila.com
Phone: **Email:** sales@techxila.com
City: Jamshedpur **State:** JH **PC:** **Country:** India
Year Established: 2018 **Status 2020:** Active
Industries: Machine Learning

Company Name: ActOnMagic
Description: Helps Enterprises and MSPs to achieve infinite scale without infinite cost.
Website: http://www.actoncloud.com/
Phone: 91 96 63 367468 **Email:** cloud@actonmagic.com
City: Bangalore **State:** KA **PC:** **Country:** India
Year Established: 2014 **Status 2020:** Active
Industries: Cloud for:, Cloud for:, Predictive Analytics

Company Name: Agilean Solutions Private Limited
Description: Agilean is NLP and AI based SaaS Enterprise automated work-flow management tool for small and medium IT company for different verticals
Website: agilean.in/
Phone: **Email:** sarmabkp@agilean.: India
City: Bangalore **State:** KA **PC:** **Country:** India
Year Established: **Status 2020:** Active
Industries: Artificial Intelligence for:, Enterprise Application Services for:, Natural Language Processing for:, ~ Professional Services (48)

Company Name: Aibo
Description: Aibono uses comprehensive data instruments, predictive analytics, and process improvements to help farmers improve yields.
Website: http://www.aibono.com/
Phone: **Email:** contact@airwood.: India
City: Bangalore **State:** KA **PC:** **Country:** India
Year Established: 2014 **Status 2020:** Active
Industries: ~ Agriculture (3), ~ Agriculture (3), IT Managed Services for:, Predictive Analytics

Company Name: Aimliot
Description: Aimliot stands for AI, ML and IoT. Basically, Artificial Intelligence, Machine Learning and Internet of Things.
Website: http://aimliot.com/
Phone: 91 7019083516 **Email:** amit@aimliot
City: Bangalore **State:** KA **PC:** **Country:** India
Year Established: 2017 **Status 2020:** Active
Industries:

Company Name: AirCTO
Description: AirCTO is an AI-powered recruitment platform that helps companies recruit top developers.
Website: https://aircto.com/
Phone: **Email:** contact@aircto.com
City: Bangalore **State:** KA **PC:** **Country:** India
Year Established: 2016 **Status 2020:** Active
Industries: Artificial Intelligence

Company Name: Almug Technologies
Description: Almug provides structured/unstructured data management solutions using AI, enabling businesses to recognize the value inherent in their data.
Website: http://almug.ai
Phone: 91 80 6753 0800 **Email:** info@almugtech.com
City: Bangalore **State:** KA **PC:** **Country:** India
Year Established: **Status 2020:** Active
Industries: Artificial Intelligence for:, Natural Language Processing for:, Predictive Analytics

Company Name: Ammras
Description: Cloud-Based Business Solutions for the Global Life Sciences Industry.
Website: http://ammras.com/
Phone: 9562242266 **Email:** bewithus@ammras.com
City: Bangalore **State:** KA **PC:** **Country:** India
Year Established: 2016 **Status 2020:** Active
Industries: Artificial Intelligence for:, ~ Biotechnology (9), ~ Healthcare (20), IT Managed Services

Company Name: Analyttica
Description: Analyttica launches learning and data exploration platform.
Website: http://www.analyttica.com/
Phone: 080-4650-7300 **Email:** info@analyttica.com
City: Bangalore **State:** KA **PC:** **Country:** India
Year Established: 2012 **Status 2020:** Active
Industries: Analytics for:, IT Managed Services for:, Predictive Analytics

Company Name: Anvaya Analytics
Description: Anvaya Analytics is a data solutions company
Website: http://www.anvayaanalytics.com
Phone: **Email:** contact@anvayaanalytics.com
City: Bangalore **State:** KA **PC:** **Country:** India
Year Established: 2015 **Status 2020:** Active
Industries: Analytics for:, Big Data and Analytics for:, Machine Learning

Company Name: Appaie
Description: Platform to Automate App development using coding bots
Website: http://www.appaie.com/
Phone: **Email:** 36074@reference-encyclopedia-ai.net
City: Bangalore **State:** KA **PC:** **Country:** India
Year Established: 2014 **Status 2020:** Active
Industries: Artificial Intelligence for:, IT Managed Services

Company Name: Appnings Software Solutions Pvt Ltd
Description: Website & Mobile App Development Company in India & U: SAUDI ARABIA
Website: http://www.appnings.com
Phone: (767)676-9955 **Email:** info@appnings.com
City: Bangalore **State:** KA **PC:** **Country:** India
Year Established: **Status 2020:** Active
Industries: Application Services for:, Application Services for:, Application Services for:, Artificial Intelligence for:, Augmented Reality for:, Application Services for:, Digital Marketing for:, Enterprise Application Services for:, ~ Professional Services (48), Mobile for

Company Name: Artivatic.ai
Description: Artivatic's patent pending technology solves complex problems in Insurance for On-boarding, Fraud, Risk Profiling, Underwriting & claims.
Website: http://artivatic.ai
Phone: **Email:** layak@artivatic.ai
City: Bangalore **State:** KA **PC:** **Country:** India
Year Established: 2017 **Status 2020:** Active
Industries: Artificial Intelligence for:, Application Program Interfaces (APIs) for:, ~ Banking and Financial Markets-Services (7), ~ Healthcare (20), Internet of Things (IoT) for:, Machine Learning for:, Machine Learning

Company Name: AskSid Technology Solutions
Description: AskSid Technology Solutions is a specialist Conversational AI solution for retail and consumer goods.
Website: http://www.asksid.ai/
Phone: **Email:** curiousmuch@asksid.ai
City: Bangalore **State:** KA **PC:** **Country:** India
Year Established: 2017 **Status 2020:** Active
Industries: Artificial Intelligence for:, Computer Vision for:, E-Commerce for:, Machine Learning

Company Name: Asteria Aerospace
Description: Asteria Aerospace is a robotics and artificial intelligence company.
Website: http://www.asteria.co.in/
Phone: **Email:** info@asteria.co.: India
City: Bangalore **State:** KA **PC:** **Country:** India
Year Established: 2011 **Status 2020:** Active
Industries: ~ Aerospace and Defense (2), Artificial Intelligence

Company Name: Athena Wisdom
Description: Athena Wisdom understands, predicts, and influences the dynamics of human behavior.
Website: http://athenawisdom.com/
Phone: **Email:** info@athenawisdom.com
City: Bangalore **State:** KA **PC:** **Country:** India
Year Established: 2013 **Status 2020:** Active
Industries: Artificial Intelligence for:, Human Computer Interaction

Company Name: BevyJobs.com & BevyTalent.com
Description: Leveraging data and machine learning to connect candidates with companies faster, smarter, and less expensive than ever before.
Website: http://www.bevyjobs.com/
Phone: **Email:** india@bevy.
City: Bangalore **State:** KA **PC:** **Country:** India
Year Established: **Status 2020:** Active
Industries: Analytics for:, Artificial Intelligence for:, Machine Learning for:, Mobile for:, ~ Human Resources (24)

Company Name: Bewgle, Inc
Description: We read reviews, so you don't have to
Website: http://www.bewgle.com
Phone: **Email:** info@bewgle.com
City: Bangalore **State:** KA **PC:** **Country:** India
Year Established: 2017 **Status 2020:** Active
Industries: Machine Learning

Company Name: Bicycle AI
Description: Bicycle is a full-stack customer support service provider.
Website: http://bicycleai.com/
Phone: **Email:** hello@bicycleai.com
City: Bangalore **State:** KA **PC:** **Country:** India
Year Established: 2016 **Status 2020:** Active
Industries:

Company Name: Big Data BizViz
Description: BDB is a data analytics platform that provides real-time analytics solution on cloud and on-premise.
Website: http://www.bdb.ai/
Phone: 91 90360 03432 **Email:** sales@bdb.ai
City: Bangalore **State:** KA **PC:** **Country:** India
Year Established: 2015 **Status 2020:** Active
Industries: Analytics for:, Artificial Intelligence for:, Big Data and Analytics for:, Machine Learning for:, Business Software as a Service Apps (SaaS Apps)

Company Name: Bigthinx
Description: Human AI for online shopping, fitness and health.
Website: http://bigthinx.com
Phone: **Email:** info@bigthinx.com
City: Bangalore **State:** KA **PC:** **Country:** India
Year Established: 2015 **Status 2020:** Active
Industries: Artificial Intelligence for:, Big Data and Analytics for:, E-Commerce for:, ~ Fashion (16), Web

Company Name: Bitgram
Description: Bitgram is a data sovereignty and consumer data protection platform.
Website: http://www.bitgram.in/index.html
Phone: 91-9880935976 **Email:** rohit@bitgram.: India
City: Bangalore **State:** KA **PC:** **Country:** India
Year Established: **Status 2020:** Active
Industries: Artificial Intelligence for:, IT Managed Services for:, Cyber Security for:, Security

Company Name: BRIDGEi2i Analytics Solutions
Description: CEO & Founder, BRIDGEi2i Analytics Solutions
Website: http://www.bridgei2i.com
Phone: 91 80 67 422100 **Email:** sandip.saha@bridgei2i.com
City: Bangalore **State:** KA **PC:** **Country:** India
Year Established: 2011 **Status 2020:** Active
Industries: Predictive Analytics

Company Name: CamCom
Description: CamCom in an artificial intelligence- and deep learning-based startup that is focussed on quality assessment, defect and damage detection.
Website: http://camcom.ai
Phone: **Email:** umesh@camcom.ai
City: Bangalore **State:** KA **PC:** **Country:** India
Year Established: 2017 **Status 2020:** Active
Industries: Artificial Intelligence for:, ~ Automotive (5)

Company **Name:** Claire.ai
Description: Building Products for Productivity using Natural Language Processing & Machine Learning
Website: http://claire.ai
Phone: **Email:** Claire@claire.ai
City: Bangalore **State:** KA **PC:** **Country:** India
Year Established: 2015 **Status 2020:** Active
Industries: Artificial Intelligence for:, IT Managed Services for:, Business Software as a Service Apps (SaaS Apps)

Company Name: Clutch.AI
Description: 4 tools & 1 service that make AI accessible to everyone across industries!
Website: http://www.clutch.ai
Phone: 080-46661029 **Email:** contact@clutch.ai
City: Bangalore **State:** KA **PC:** **Country:** India
Year Established: **Status 2020:** Active
Industries: Artificial Intelligence for:, ~ Professional Services (48)

Company Name: Codeground
Description: Saas based online assessment platform. Aimed to bring in automation & accuracy in the recruitment process
Website: http://codeground.: India
Phone: **Email:** hemant.agrawal@codeground.: India
City: Bangalore **State:** KA **PC:** **Country:** India
Year Established: **Status 2020:** Active
Industries: Artificial Intelligence for:, ~ Education (13), ~ Human Resources (24), ~ Human Resources (24)

Company Name: CollPoll
Description: World-class Enterprise System for Education.
Website: http://www.collpoll.com
Phone: **Email:** team@collpoll.com
City: Bangalore **State:** KA **PC:** **Country:** India
Year Established: **Status 2020:** Active
Industries: Artificial Intelligence for:, ~ Education (13), ~ Education (13)

Company Name: Couture.ai
Description: Vertical targeted AI platform for scale.
Website: http://www.couture.ai/
Phone: **Email:** info@couture.ai
City: Bangalore **State:** KA **PC:** **Country:** India

Year Established: **Status 2020:** Active
Industries: Artificial Intelligence for:, Big Data and Analytics for:, Computer Vision for:, Application Services for:, Machine Learning for:, Natural Language Processing for:, Predictive Analytics for:, ~ Retail and Consumer Products (52)

Company Name: CronJ IT Technologies Private Limited
Description: CronJ develops product on Blockchain, Computer Vision, Industry 4.0, Industrial Automation, Iot and supply Chain management.
Website: http://www.cronj.com
Phone: 91 7093 801 977 **Email:** contact@cronj.com
City: Bangalore **State:** KA **PC:** **Country:** India
Year Established: **Status 2020:** Active
Industries: Artificial Intelligence for:, Blockchain for:, Computer Vision for:, Automation for:, Predictive Analytics

Company Name: CustomFit.ai
Description: CustomFit.ai transforms your website/app into #1 Growth Engine / #1 Salesperson by personalizing for each visitor.
Website: http://customfit.ai
Phone: **Email:** reach@customfit.ai
City: Bangalore **State:** KA **PC:** **Country:** India
Year Established: 2019 **Status 2020:** Active
Industries: Artificial Intelligence for:, E-Commerce for:, Enterprise Application Services for:, IT Managed Services for:, Web for:, Internet of Things (IoT) for:, Application Services for:, Business Software as a Service Apps (SaaS Apps)

Company Name: CynLr
Description: CynLr is a visual object intelligence platform.
Website: http://www.cynlr.com
Phone: **Email:** nikhil@cynlr.com
City: Bangalore **State:** KA **PC:** **Country:** India
Year Established: 2015 **Status 2020:** Active
Industries: Artificial Intelligence for:, Computer Vision for:, Robotics

Company Name: Datacogin
Description: Artificial Intelligent solutions for Healthcare.
Website:
Phone: 91 9591158035 **Email:** 36392@reference-encyclopedia-ai.net
City: Bangalore **State:** KA **PC:** **Country:** India
Year Established: 2016 **Status 2020:** - Closed
Industries:

Company Name: DataTurks
Description: Making Machine Learning Accessible to Everyone
Website: http://dataturks.com/
Phone: **Email:** contact@dataturks.com
City: Bangalore **State:** KA **PC:** **Country:** India
Year Established: **Status 2020:** Active
Industries: Artificial Intelligence for:, Machine Learning for:, Natural Language Processing

Company Name: Datoin
Description: Datoin is an automation platform which helps enterprises to automate by leveraging enterprise's data, AI, and component-based engineering.
Website: http://datoin.com/
Phone: **Email:** contact@datoin.com
City: Bangalore **State:** KA **PC:** **Country:** India
Year Established: 2015 **Status 2020:** Active
Industries: Artificial Intelligence for:, IT Managed Services for:, Mobile for:, Application Services for:, Business Software as a Service Apps (SaaS Apps) for:, Business Software as a Service Apps (SaaS Apps)

Company Name: DeepBrai: New Zealand
Description: DeepBrainz, A DPIIT/DIPP Recognized AI & Technology Startup Company: An End-to-End Deep Learning, AI Platform & AI-first SaaS for Everyone
Website: http://www.deepbrainz.com
Phone: **Email:** arunkumarramanan@deepbrainz.com
City: Bangalore **State:** KA **PC:** **Country:** India
Year Established: 2015 **Status 2020:** Active
Industries: Artificial Intelligence for:, ~ Automotive (5), Big Data and Analytics for:, Cloud for:, Databases for:, ~ Healthcare (20), Application Services for:, Web for:, Web for:, Machine Learning

Company Name: DeepBrainz Intelligent Systems
Description: A Future Revolutionary Technology Startup in World Industries, Advancing Tomorrow's State-of-the-art AI, "Empowering Humanity Universally!"
Website: http://www.deepbrainz.wordpress.com
Phone: 8072559165 **Email:** deepbrainz.ai@gmail.com
City: Bangalore **State:** KA **PC:** **Country:** India
Year Established: **Status 2020:** Active
Industries: Artificial Intelligence for:, Blockchain for:, Cloud for:, IT Managed Services for:, Computer Vision for:, Cyber Security for:, Application Services for:, Application Services for:, ~ Manufacturing-Electronic (30), Human Computer Interaction for:, IT Managed Servic

Company Name: DeltaX
Description: DeltaX is the pioneering cross-channel digital advertising platform.
Website: http://deltax.com
Phone: 1 855 5 DELTAX **Email:** contact@deltax.com
City: Bangalore **State:** KA **PC:** **Country:** India
Year Established: 2012 **Status 2020:** Active
Industries: ~ Retail and Consumer Products (52), Machine Learning

Company Name: DheeYantra Research Labs
Description: DheeYantra is building a cognitive conversational chatbot platform by name "dhee.ai" for English and vernacular languag: Spain
Website: http://www.dheeyantra.com
Phone: 9980879343 **Email:** contact@dheeyantra.com
City: Bangalore **State:** KA **PC:** **Country:** India
Year Established: **Status 2020:** Active
Industries: Artificial Intelligence

Company Name: Dressire
Description: Dressire is a tech startup that offers artificial intelligence and advanced analytics based solutions for malls, retailers, and brands.
Website: http://dressire.com
Phone: **Email:** ashish@dressire.com
City: Bangalore **State:** KA **PC:** **Country:** India
Year Established: 2012 **Status 2020:** Active
Industries: Artificial Intelligence for:, Business Software as a Service Apps (SaaS Apps)

Company Name: Eder AI Inc
Description: A deeptech start-up based out of Bangalore building a private machine learning platform for secure AI
Website: http://www.eder.io/
Phone: **Email:** hello@eder.io
City: Bangalore **State:** KA **PC:** **Country:** India
Year Established: **Status 2020:** Active
Industries:

Company Name: Eder Labs
Description: A deeptech start-up in Bangalore enabling enterprises scale AI adoption securely, with data privacy
Website: http://eder.io/
Phone: **Email:** sharat@eder.io
City: Bangalore **State:** KA **PC:** **Country:** India
Year Established: 2018 **Status 2020:** Active
Industries: Artificial Intelligence for:, Web for:, Cyber Security

Company Name: EdGE Networks
Description: EdGE Networks provides nextGen technology solutions for workforce transformation powered by data science and artificial intelligence.
Website: http://www.edgenetworks.: India
Phone: 91 80 4114 8049 **Email:** info@edgenetworks.: India
City: Bangalore **State:** KA **PC:** **Country:** India
Year Established: **Status 2020:** Active
Industries: Analytics for:, Artificial Intelligence for:, ~ Human Resources (24), IT Managed Services for:, ~ Human Resources (24), ~ Professional Services (48)

Company Name: Edisn.ai
Description: Edisn.ai is an AI powered fan engagement platform with state-of-the-art player recognition and contextual content delivery
Website: http://edisn.ai/
Phone: **Email:** contact@edisn.ai
City: Bangalore **State:** KA **PC:** **Country:** India
Year Established: 2018 **Status 2020:** Active
Industries: ~ Arts-Entertainment-Recreation (4)

Company Name: elth.ai
Description: elth.ai The future of health care is here.
Website: http://elth.ai/
Phone: **Email:** contact@elth.ai
City: Bangalore **State:** KA **PC:** **Country:** India
Year Established: **Status 2020:** Active
Industries: Artificial Intelligence for:, ~ Healthcare (20), ~ Healthcare (20)

Company Name: Esthan Group
Description: Esthan is a full fledged digital PR agency which focusses on growing IoT, M2M and Big Data and SaaS businesses.
Website: http://esthan.com
Phone: **Email:** contact@esthan.com
City: Bangalore **State:** KA **PC:** **Country:** India
Year Established: 2017 **Status 2020:** Active
Industries: Analytics for:, Artificial Intelligence for:, ~ Customer Relationship Management (11)

Company Name: EtaPro Technologies
Description: AI driven manufacturing technology platform empowering manufactures to reduce time to market with high quality products.
Website: http://www.lioncircuits.com/
Phone: **Email:** hellolion@lioncircuits.com
City: Bangalore **State:** KA **PC:** **Country:** India
Year Established: 2016 **Status 2020:** Active
Industries:

Company Name: Euphoric Thought Technologies
Description: Outsourced IT Product Development Company with Specialization in Blockchain, Cloud, Web Application Development and Artificial Intelligence.
Website: http://www.euphoricthought.com/
Phone: **Email:** manu@euphoricthought.com
City: Bangalore **State:** KA **PC:** **Country:** India
Year Established: **Status 2020:** Active
Industries: Artificial Intelligence for:, Blockchain for:, IT Managed Services for:, ~ Professional Services (48), ~ Professional Services (48), Cyber Security

Company Name: EvenRank
Description: EvenRank is a personalized career and coaching platform that uses data science to make job recommendations.
Website: http://www.evenrank.com
Phone: **Email:** r@evenrank.com
City: Bangalore **State:** KA **PC:** **Country:** India
Year Established: 2016 **Status 2020:** Active
Industries: Analytics for:, Artificial Intelligence for:, Application Services for:, ~ Education (13), Web for:, Mobile

Company Name: Faasthelp
Description: Faasthelp is an artificial intelligence powered sales and customer support software.
Website: http://faasthelp.com
Phone: **Email:** contact@faasthelp.com
City: Bangalore **State:** KA **PC:** **Country:** India
Year Established: 2013 **Status 2020:** Active
Industries: Artificial Intelligence for:, IT Managed Services for:, Business Software as a Service Apps (SaaS Apps)

Company Name: Factana Computing Pvt Ltd
Description: We are with a mission of building Cognitive Internet of Things (IoT) products and platform that will enhance human experience.
Website: http://factana.com/
Phone: **Email:** info@factana.com
City: Bangalore **State:** KA **PC:** **Country:** India
Year Established: 2017 **Status 2020:** Active
Industries: Artificial Intelligence for:, Automation for:, IT Managed Services for:, Web for:, Internet of Things (IoT) for:, Machine Learning

Company Name: Farebond
Description: Builds simple solutions that are useful in travel planning or booking process
Website: http://farebond.com
Phone: **Email:** hello@farebond.com
City: Bangalore **State:** KA **PC:** **Country:** India
Year Established: 2016 **Status 2020:** Active
Industries: Artificial Intelligence for:, Big Data and Analytics for:, Machine Learning for:, Predictive Analytics

Company Name: Fedo
Description: Artificial Intelligence based Credit Score for Heal:Thailand
Website: http://fedo.ai
Phone: **Email:** prasanth@fedo.: India
City: Bangalore **State:** KA **PC:** **Country:** India
Year Established: 2017 **Status 2020:** Active
Industries: Analytics for:, Artificial Intelligence for:, ~ Healthcare (20)

Company Name: FinBox
Description: FinBox digitizes customer journeys for Banks and NBFCs & to help them underwrite NTC customers using alternative data from the smartphone.
Website: http://www.finbox.in/
Phone: **Email:** support@finbox.: India
City: Bangalore **State:** KA **PC:** **Country:** India
Year Established: 2015 **Status 2020:** Active
Industries: Artificial Intelligence for:, ~ Banking and Financial Markets-Services (7), ~ Banking and Financial Markets-Services (7), ~ Banking and Financial Markets-Services (7)

Company Name: Flux Auto
Description: Flux Auto develops modular autonomous driving technology for trucks.
Website: http://www.fluxauto.xyz/
Phone: 91 8722445111 **Email:** contact@fluxauto.xyz
City: Bangalore **State:** KA **PC:** **Country:** India
Year Established: **Status 2020:** Active
Industries: Artificial Intelligence for:, ~ Automotive (5), ~ Automotive (5), Machine Learning

Company Name: Foore
Description: Customer Messaging Platform for Brick and Mortar Businesses.
Website: http://www.foore.: India
Phone: **Email:** contact@foore.: India
City: Bangalore **State:** KA **PC:** **Country:** India
Year Established: 2018 **Status 2020:** Active
Industries: Enterprise Application Services for:, Natural Language Processing for:, Business Software as a Service Apps (SaaS Apps)

Company Name: FORMCE: PORTUGAL
Description: FORMCEPT is an effort to make content analysis accessible to everyone, be it an enterprise, an individual or a device.
Website: http://www.formcept.com
Phone: 91 80 4204 2308 **Email:** contactus@formcept.com
City: Bangalore **State:** KA **PC:** **Country:** India
Year Established: 2011 **Status 2020:** Active
Industries: Analytics for:, Big Data and Analytics for:, Databases for:, Predictive Analytics for:, Business Software as a Service Apps (SaaS Apps)

Company Name: Fortraiz
Description: AI First Company trying to solve security challenges in Internet
Website: http://fortraiz.com
Phone: **Email:** rahul@fortraiz.com
City: Bangalore **State:** KA **PC:** **Country:** India
Year Established: 2016 **Status 2020:** Active
Industries: Artificial Intelligence for:, Cyber Security for:, IT Managed Services for:, Web for:, Security

Company Name: Frrole
Description: Frrole is an AI-Powered Next-Gen Consumer Intelligence platform for marketers, analysts, product owners, recruiters, and sales folks.
Website: http://frrole.ai
Phone: 91 96 8686 2350 **Email:** contact@frrole.com
City: Bangalore **State:** KA **PC:** **Country:** India
Year Established: **Status 2020:** Active
Industries: Analytics for:, Artificial Intelligence for:, Big Data and Analytics for:, Business Intelligence for:, Machine Learning for:, Natural Language Processing for:, Predictive Analytics for:, ~ Human Resources (24), ~ Human Resources (24), ~ Social Media (54)

Company Name: Fulassure
Description: Actionable Intelligence Platform for IOT Networks
Website: http://www.fulassure.io
Phone: **Email:** contact@fulassure.io
City: Bangalore **State:** KA **PC:** **Country:** India
Year Established: 2017 **Status 2020:** Active
Industries: Artificial Intelligence for:, IT Managed Services

Company Name: FullThrottle Labs Private Limited
Description: Information Technology
Website: http://www.fullthrottlelabs.com/
Phone: 090056 71616 **Email:** harpreet@fullthrottlelabs.com
City: Bangalore **State:** KA **PC:** **Country:** India
Year Established: **Status 2020:** Active
Industries:

Company Name: GeoIQ.io
Description: Map-based intelligent platform with single-click access to street-level location data - demographics, competitions, movements - for retail.
Website: http://www.geoiq.io
Phone: **Email:** dev@geoiq.io
City: Bangalore **State:** KA **PC:** **Country:** India
Year Established: 2018 **Status 2020:** Active
Industries: Big Data and Analytics for:, Data Management

Company Name: GetPY Analytics
Description: Build Customer Data Management System via digital receipt, Analytics, Actionable Insights (ML, AI), Forecasting & Recommended Actions,
Website: http://www.getpy.biz
Phone: (998) 011-6948 **Email:** kirtis@pytechno.com
City: Bangalore **State:** KA **PC:** **Country:** India
Year Established: 2017 **Status 2020:** Active
Industries: Analytics for:, Artificial Intelligence for:, Big Data and Analytics for:, IT Managed Services for:, Web

Company Name: GetPY Analytics Private Limited
Description: Build Customer Data Management System via digital receipt, Analytics, Actionable Insights (ML, AI), Forecasting & Recommended Actions,
Website: http://www.pytechno.com
Phone: 9980116948 **Email:** kirtis@pytechno.com
City: Bangalore **State:** KA **PC:** **Country:** India
Year Established: **Status 2020:** Active
Industries: Analytics for:, Artificial Intelligence for:, Big Data and Analytics for:, IT Managed Services for:, Web

Company Name: Gnani.ai
Description: Speech to Text, AI, NLP, Speech Analytics
Website: http://gnani.ai/
Phone: 91 99160 08309 **Email:** operations@gnani.ai
City: Bangalore **State:** KA **PC:** **Country:** India
Year Established: 2016 **Status 2020:** Active
Industries: Artificial Intelligence for:, IT Managed Services for:, Machine Learning

Company Name: Grow F: Italy
Description: Grow Fit is a mobile health companion that uses artificial intelligence.
Website: http://www.getgrowfit.com/
Phone: (803)965-8868 **Email:** hello@getgrowapp.com
City: Bangalore **State:** KA **PC:** **Country:** India
Year Established: 2015 **Status 2020:** Active
Industries: Artificial Intelligence for:, ~ Healthcare (20), Application Services for:, ~ Healthcare (20)

Company **Name:** Hashresearch
Description: Convert the data into consumable and understandable.
Website: http://hashresearch.com/
Phone: 91 80 56 509614 **Email:** hashresearch@gmail.com
City: Bangalore **State:** KA **PC:** **Country:** India
Year Established: 2013 **Status 2020:** Active
Industries: Data Management for:, Predictive Analytics

Company Name: Health Vecto: Serbia
Description: Revolutionizing personal health, providing people clinically relevant clarity and simple actionable insights via predictive analytics
Website: http://www.360hvpl.com
Phone: **Email:** support@360hvpl.com
City: Bangalore **State:** KA **PC:** **Country:** India
Year Established: 2011 **Status 2020:** Active
Industries: Analytics for:, ~ Healthcare (20), Predictive Analytics

Company Name: Holo
Description: Holo is a location bases mobile app that allows users to leave messages to friends at various locations.
Website: http://holo.host
Phone: 350 56004529 **Email:** info@holo.host
City: Bangalore **State:** KA **PC:** **Country:** India
Year Established: 2017 **Status 2020:** Active
Industries: ~ Media-Communications (41)

Company Name: HopOn
Description: Smart employee transportation to transform urban mobility
Website: http://www.hopon.co.: India
Phone: 91 8884 114 220 **Email:** info@hopon.co.: India
City: Bangalore **State:** KA **PC:** **Country:** India
Year Established: 2013 **Status 2020:** Active
Industries: Cloud for:, IT Managed Services for:, Application Services

Company Name: Hotelplex
Description: Hotelplex is a set of AI based revenue management tools for hoteliers and hotel management companies to maximize their revenues.
Website: http://hotelplex.co
Phone: **Email:** hello@hotelplex.co
City: Bangalore **State:** KA **PC:** **Country:** India

Year Established: 2018 **Status 2020:** Active
Industries: Artificial Intelligence for:, IT Managed Services

Company Name: Huew
Description: Huew is a mobile/web app that makes fashion search & discovery absolutely easy and fun for women online shoppers in India.
Website: http://huew.co
Phone: **Email:** anand@huew.co
City: Bangalore **State:** KA **PC:** **Country:** India
Year Established: **Status 2020:** Active
Industries: Application Services for:, Artificial Intelligence for:, E-Commerce for:, ~ Fashion (16)

Company Name: Infilect
Description: Infilect is a B2B SaaS company that helps global retail brands and retailers with deep visual intelligence
Website: http://infilect.com
Phone: **Email:** anand@infilect.com
City: Bangalore **State:** KA **PC:** **Country:** India
Year Established: 2015 **Status 2020:** Active
Industries: Artificial Intelligence for:, Business Applications for:, Computer Vision for:, Business Software as a Service Apps (SaaS Apps)

Company Name: InstaFinancials
Description: InstaFinancials is an award winning Corporate Intelligence Platform & Early Warning System.
Website: http://www.instafinancials.com
Phone: 91 7879 776 776 **Email:** Raji@InstaFinancials.com
City: Bangalore **State:** KA **PC:** **Country:** India
Year Established: **Status 2020:** Active
Industries: Artificial Intelligence for:, Business Applications for:, ~ Banking and Financial Markets-Services (7), IT Managed Services

Company Name: Insteract
Description: Automate your travel desk. Insteract makes business trip planning transparent and personlised.
Website: http://www.insteract.com
Phone: (994) 012-6711 **Email:** helloinsteract@insteract.com
City: Bangalore **State:** KA **PC:** **Country:** India
Year Established: 2015 **Status 2020:** Active
Industries:

Company Name: Invento Robotics
Description: Invento makes the Mitra robot a humanoid to automate retail store experience.
Website: http://www.mitrarobot.com
Phone: 1 8448449054 **Email:** info@mitrarobot.com
City: Bangalore **State:** KA **PC:** **Country:** India
Year Established: 2016 **Status 2020:** Active
Industries: Artificial Intelligence for:, Robotics

Company Name: Inventrom Pvt.Ltd. (Bolt IoT)
Description: Inventrom Pvt. Ltd is the creator of the award winning Bolt Internet of Things Platform for develope: Serbia
Website: http://www.boltiot.com
Phone: **Email:** contactus@boltiot.com
City: Bangalore **State:** KA **PC:** **Country:** India
Year Established: 2016 **Status 2020:** Active
Industries: Data Management for:, Internet of Things (IoT) for:, Machine Learning

Company Name: IOT Pot
Description: IOT Pot is a Connected Cooking Platform startup with IoT and Voice Assisted and Machine Learning solutions that helps in cooking.
Website: http://www.iotpot.com
Phone: **Email:** bvshete@iotpot.com
City: Bangalore **State:** KA **PC:** **Country:** India
Year Established: 2016 **Status 2020:** Active
Industries: ~ Food and Beverage (17), Internet of Things (IoT) for:, Machine Learning

Company Name: iyotta Software
Description: iyotta Software is an Indian startup focused on social media analysis for e-commerce and news discovery.
Website: http://iyottasoft.com
Phone: 91 80 4130 4190 **Email:** info@iyottasoft.com
City: Bangalore **State:** KA **PC:** **Country:** India
Year Established: 2010 **Status 2020:** Active
Industries: Big Data and Analytics for:, E-Commerce for:, Machine Learning for:, Natural Language Processing for:, ~ Social Assistance-Non-Profits (53)

Company Name: Jiffy RPA
Description: Jiffy RPA is an integrated automation platform that delivers impact on productivity, efficiency, and profitability for enterprises.
Website: http://www.jiffyrpa.com
Phone: **Email:** marketing@jiffy.ai
City: Bangalore **State:** KA **PC:** **Country:** India
Year Established: 2012 **Status 2020:** Active
Industries: Analytics for:, Artificial Intelligence for:, Data Management for:, Application Services for:, Robotics

Company Name: Jungroo Learning
Description: AI powered companion for students and educato: Serbia
Website: http://www.jungroo.com
Phone: **Email:** sethu@jungroo.com
City: Bangalore **State:** KA **PC:** **Country:** India
Year Established: **Status 2020:** Active
Industries: Artificial Intelligence for:, ~ Education (13), ~ Education (13)

Company Name: Kenome
Description: Kenome is a core AI company helping enterprises make sense of dark data using cutting-edge Machine Learning NLP and Knowledge Graphs
Website: http://www.kenome.io
Phone: **Email:** ppt@kenome.io
City: Bangalore **State:** KA **PC:** **Country:** India
Year Established: 2017 **Status 2020:** Active
Industries:

Company Name: Khidki
Description: Khidki is a vernacular social network localized by town. Users create and consume content in their local language mostly related to the town
Website: http://get.khidkiapp.com
Phone: 7411752995 **Email:** contact@khidkiapp.com
City: Bangalore **State:** KA **PC:** **Country:** India
Year Established: **Status 2020:** Active
Industries: Artificial Intelligence

Company Name: Kidovators (by GyanLab)
Description: Building future human capital through 21st Century Skills programs for K-12 | Initiative by GyanLab
Website: http://kidovators.com/
Phone: (819) 739-2069 **Email:** kidovators@addongyan.com
City: Bangalore **State:** KA **PC:** **Country:** India
Year Established: 2011 **Status 2020:** - Closed
Industries: Big Data and Analytics for:, ~ Education (13), Machine Learning

Company Name: KloveChef (IOK Labs)
Description: A Voice Guided Connected Cooking platform with IOT ML AI technology to help the cooks to cook better
Website: http://www.klovechef.ai/
Phone: **Email:** bahubali@klovechef.com
City: Bangalore **State:** KA **PC:** **Country:** India
Year Established: 2016 **Status 2020:** Active
Industries: Artificial Intelligence for:, ~ Food and Beverage (17)

Company Name: KrishiHub
Description: KrishiHub is an agri-tech startup building technology-driven agricultural ecosystem for Indian farmers.
Website: http://krishihub.com
Phone: 1800 200 9261 **Email:** contact@krishihub.co.: India
City: Bangalore **State:** KA **PC:** **Country:** India
Year Established: 2016 **Status 2020:** Active
Industries: ~ Agriculture (3), ~ Agriculture (3), Artificial Intelligence for:, Web

Company Name: Logistimo
Description: Supply chain & logistics platform (cloud, mobile, social, IoT and AI-enabled web service) for low-resource rural emerging markets
Website: http://logistimo.com
Phone: 91 80 4202 4381 **Email:** info@logistimo.com
City: Bangalore **State:** KA **PC:** **Country:** India
Year Established: **Status 2020:** Active
Industries: Artificial Intelligence for:, ~ Transportation and Logistics (57), Machine Learning for:, ~ Professional Services (48), Supply Chain Management for:, Cyber Security for:, Cyber Security

Company Name: LucentAI
Description: LucentAI provides technology solutions powered by AI.
Website: http://lucent.ai/
Phone: **Email:** 36919@reference-encyclopedia-ai.net
City: Bangalore **State:** KA **PC:** **Country:** India
Year Established: 2017 **Status 2020:** Active
Industries: Artificial Intelligence

Company Name: Manthan
Description: Manthan Software Services offers a portfolio of business-ready products in advanced analytics and big data for consumer industries.
Website: http://www.manthan.com
Phone: 1(800)746-9370 **Email:** info@manthan.com
City: Bangalore **State:** KA **PC:** **Country:** India
Year Established: **Status 2020:** Active
Industries:

Company Name: Mate Labs
Description: Mate Labs is a machine learning solutions platform for beginners.
Website: http://matelabs.in/
Phone: **Email:** mate@matelabs.: India
City: Bangalore **State:** KA **PC:** **Country:** India
Year Established: **Status 2020:** Active
Industries: Artificial Intelligence for:, Machine Learning for:, Enterprise Application Services

Company Name: MegaExams
Description: MegaExams' SaaS platform automates exam creation and evaluation to help schools improve learning outcomes while saving their time and money.
Website: http://www.megaexams.com
Phone: **Email:** 36959@reference-encyclopedia-ai.net
City: Bangalore **State:** KA **PC:** **Country:** India
Year Established: 2015 **Status 2020:** Active
Industries: Artificial Intelligence for:, Big Data and Analytics for:, ~ Education (13), Business Software as a Service Apps (SaaS Apps)

Company Name: MeTripping
Description: Intelligent Travel Sear: Switzerland
Website: http://www.metripping.com
Phone: **Email:** varun@metripping.com
City: Bangalore **State:** KA **PC:** **Country:** India
Year Established: **Status 2020:** Active
Industries: Artificial Intelligence for:, Content for:, ~ Travel and Transportation (58)

Company Name: ModelChimp
Description: Performance tracking of machine learning experiments
Website: http://modelchimp.com/
Phone: **Email:** 37001@reference-encyclopedia-ai.net
City: Bangalore **State:** KA **PC:** **Country:** India
Year Established: 2018 **Status 2020:** Active
Industries: Artificial Intelligence for:, Big Data and Analytics for:, ~ Education (13), Machine Learning

Company Name: MoneyOnClick
Description: Social Fintech Lending for underserved lower-middle income families in small citi: Spain
Website: http://www.moneyonclick.com
Phone: **Email:** 37010@reference-encyclopedia-ai.net
City: Bangalore **State:** KA **PC:** **Country:** India
Year Established: 2018 **Status 2020:** Active
Industries: Artificial Intelligence for:, ~ Banking and Financial Markets-Services (7), Web for:, ~ Banking and Financial Markets-Services (7), Machine Learning

Company Name: NearLearn
Description: Near Learn is best Online Corporate Training providing Company in Bangalore, India. Offers Online Classroom and Training courses.
Website: http://nearlearn.com
Phone: 91-6360148867 **Email:** info@nearlearn.com
City: Bangalore **State:** KA **PC:** **Country:** India
Year Established: **Status 2020:** Active
Industries: Artificial Intelligence for:, Blockchain for:, Business Intelligence for:, Cloud for:, ~ Education (13), Data Management for:, Machine Learning for:, Finance and Accounting for:, ~ Education (13), Cyber Security

Company Name: Nettoraid
Description: Nettoraid is a desktop and mobile web based artifical intelligence solutions developer.
Website: http://www.nettoraid.com
Phone: 91 88 91 122554 **Email:** support@nettoraid.com
City: Bangalore **State:** KA **PC:** **Country:** India
Year Established: 2010 **Status 2020:** Active
Industries: Artificial Intelligence for:, Web for:, Mobile

Company Name: Niki
Description: Har Ghar Ki Local Agent! Building Internet commerce in the style that's most natural to Bharat.
Website: http://niki.ai
Phone: **Email:** info@niki.ai
City: Bangalore **State:** KA **PC:** **Country:** India
Year Established: 2015 **Status 2020:** Active
Industries: E-Commerce for:, Machine Learning for:, Natural Language Processing

Company Name: nTalents.ai
Description: nTalents.ai is an Artificial Intelligence enabled Talent Management Tool which provides unparalleled accuracy in competency measurements.
Website: http://ntalents.ai/
Phone: 9560833909 **Email:** admin@ntalents.ai
City: Bangalore **State:** KA **PC:** **Country:** India
Year Established: 2017 **Status 2020:** Active
Industries: Artificial Intelligence for:, ~ Education (13), Business Software as a Service Apps (SaaS Apps)

Company Name: Oleic
Description: Game based AI learning platform.
Website: http://www.oleic.co
Phone: **Email:** hi@stemai.org
City: Bangalore **State:** KA **PC:** **Country:** India
Year Established: 2019 **Status 2020:** Active
Industries: Artificial Intelligence

Company Name: Option3
Description: Automation
Website: www.jiffyrpa.com
Phone: 855-787-7885 **Email:** 27246@reference-encyclopedia-ai.net
City: Bangalore **State:** KA **Zip:** 560103 **Country:** India
Year Established: **Status 2020:** Active
Industries:

Company Name: Option3
Description:
Website: www.option3.io
Phone: 302-451-9994 **Email:** sudhir.sen@option3.io
City: Bangalore **State:** KA **Zip:** 560102 **Country:** India
Year Established: **Status 2020:** Active
Industries:

Company Name: Pexitics
Description: Pexitics is an Analytics firm specializing in HR Analytics and BFSI Analytics. It launched its product PexiScore in 2017.
Website: http://pexitics.com/
Phone: **Email:** score@pexitics.com
City: Bangalore **State:** KA **PC:** **Country:** India
Year Established: 2016 **Status 2020:** Active
Industries: Predictive Analytics for:, Data Management

Company Name: Play Shifu
Description: An Educational games startup.
Website: http://www.playshifu.com/
Phone: 1 650-485-1702 **Email:** info@playshifu.com
City: Bangalore **State:** KA **PC:** **Country:** India
Year Established: **Status 2020:** Active
Industries:

Company Name: Playment
Description: Playment is a fully managed data labeling platform generating training data for computer vision models at scale.
Website: http://playment.io
Phone: 9830439500 **Email:** marketing@playment.: India
City: Bangalore **State:** KA **PC:** **Country:** India
Year Established: **Status 2020:** Active
Industries: Artificial Intelligence for:, ~ Automotive (5), Computer Vision for:, Enterprise Application Services for:, Machine Learning for:, Business Process and Operations

Company Name: Prakshep
Description: Prakshep offers data services for crop health monitoring and assessment using satellite imagery, machine learning, and big data analytics.
Website: http://www.prakshep.com/
Phone: **Email:** vama@prakshep.com
City: Bangalore **State:** KA **PC:** **Country:** India
Year Established: 2016 **Status 2020:** Active
Industries: Analytics for:, Big Data and Analytics for:, ~ Healthcare (20), Internet of Things (IoT) for:, Machine Learning

Company Name: Predible Heal:Thailand
Description: Artificial Intelligence in Radiolgy, tailored for Specialists
Website: http://www.prediblehealth.com
Phone: **Email:** suthirth@predible.co
City: Bangalore **State:** KA **PC:** **Country:** India
Year Established: 2016 **Status 2020:** Active
Industries: Artificial Intelligence

Company Name: Predict22 Sports Analytics
Description: AI Sports Analytics
Website: http://www.predict22.com/
Phone: **Email:** contact@predict22.com
City: Bangalore **State:** KA **PC:** **Country:** India
Year Established: 2017 **Status 2020:** Active
Industries: Artificial Intelligence for:, ~ Arts-Entertainment-Recreation (4), IT Managed Services for:, ~ Arts-Entertainment-Recreation (4)

Company Name: Predictive Research:
Description: Predictive Research is in quantitative financial business services, business intelligence, data mining techniques and predictive modeling.
Website: http://www.predictiveresearch.in/
Phone: **Email:** info@predictiveresearch.co.: India
City: Bangalore **State:** KA **PC:** **Country:** India
Year Established: 2011 **Status 2020:** Active
Industries: ~ Banking and Financial Markets-Services (7), Predictive Analytics

Company Name: Predictly Tech Labs
Description: Our objective is to simplify the highly sophisticated interplay of marketing processes, technology and the data for the marketers.
Website: http://www.predictly.co/
Phone: **Email:** info@predictly.co
City: Bangalore **State:** KA **PC:** **Country:** India
Year Established: **Status 2020:** Active
Industries: Analytics for:, Artificial Intelligence for:, Machine Learning for:, Predictive Analytics

Company Name: Pris
Description: At Pristech, they utilize the best analytics tools and methods.
Website: http://www.pparke.in/
Phone: 91 99 02 122448 **Email:** pparkesupport@pristech.: India
City: Bangalore **State:** KA **PC:** **Country:** India
Year Established: 2013 **Status 2020:** Active
Industries: Analytics for:, Data Management for:, IT Infrastructure for:, Application Services for:, ~ Travel and Transportation (58), Predictive Analytics

Company Name: Qualyon
Description: Virtual Agent, Chatbot, BFSI, AI, NLU, CRM
Website: http://www.qualyon.com
Phone: **Email:** satish@qualyon.com
City: Bangalore **State:** KA **PC:** **Country:** India
Year Established: **Status 2020:** Active
Industries: Artificial Intelligence for:, Natural Language Processing

Company Name: Racetrack
Description: Racetrack is a sales and support-focused AI-driven platform designed for education, real estate, and e-commerce sectors.
Website: http://racetrack.ai
Phone: 91 97413 19333 **Email:** info@racetrack.ai
City: Bangalore **State:** KA **PC:** **Country:** India
Year Established: **Status 2020:** Active
Industries: Artificial Intelligence for:, Cloud for:, ~ Media-Communications (41)

Company Name: Rare Mile Technologies
Description: Big Data, Unstructured Data Analytics, Algorithms & Machine Learning Solutions Provider
Website: http://www.raremile.com
Phone: 1(408) 216-8844 **Email:** us@raremile.com
City: Bangalore **State:** KA **PC:** **Country:** India
Year Established: 2011 **Status 2020:** Active
Industries: Analytics

Company Name: RecoSense Infosolutions Pvt Ltd
Description: RecoSense offers SaaS-based data intelligence platform.
Website: http://recosenselabs.com
Phone: **Email:** info@recosenselabs.com
City: Bangalore **State:** KA **PC:** **Country:** India

Year Established: 2014 **Status 2020:** Active
Industries: Artificial Intelligence for:, Automation for:, Digital Media for:, IT Managed Services for:, Machine Learning for:, Business Software as a Service Apps (SaaS Apps)

Company Name: Retigence Software
Description: Retigence Software offers SAP HANA solution that optimizes supply chain inventory with real-time actionable insights.
Website: http://www.retigence.com
Phone: (990) 051-7488 **Email:** srinibas.behera@retigence.com
City: Bangalore **State:** KA **PC:** **Country:** India
Year Established: 2010 **Status 2020:** Active
Industries: Analytics for:, IT Managed Services for:, Predictive Analytics

Company Name: Saarthi.ai
Description: Multilingual Conversational Enterprise AI Platform for omnichannel automation of customer journeys in the user's native language.
Website: http://saarthi.ai
Phone: 91-8108832736 **Email:** hello@saarthi.ai
City: Bangalore **State:** KA **PC:** **Country:** India
Year Established: 2017 **Status 2020:** Active
Industries: Analytics for:, Artificial Intelligence for:, ~ Customer Relationship Management (11), Application Program Interfaces (APIs) for:, IT Managed Services for:, Web for:, Business Software as a Service Apps (SaaS Apps) for:, Internet of Things (IoT)

Company Name: Salesken
Description: Salesken is gives you incredible insights into the last mile of customer-salesperson interactions.
Website: http://salesken.ai/
Phone: **Email:** 37329@reference-encyclopedia-ai.net
City: Bangalore **State:** KA **PC:** **Country:** India
Year Established: 2018 **Status 2020:** Active
Industries:

Company Name: Saturam
Description: Saturam is a data-driven digital transformation company which provides streaming data pipelines for embedded analytics & IoT.
Website: http://www.saturam.com/
Phone: 080 2353 9800 **Email:** contact@saturam.com
City: Bangalore **State:** KA **PC:** **Country:** India
Year Established: **Status 2020:** Active
Industries: Analytics for:, Artificial Intelligence for:, Big Data and Analytics for:, Data Management for:, Data Management for:, Automation for:, Machine Learning

Company Name: Scientist Technologies
Description: AI solutions company in retail, mobility and cyber security
Website: http://www.scientisttechnologies.com
Phone: 9916695156 **Email:** team@scientisttechnologies.com
City: Bangalore **State:** KA **PC:** **Country:** India
Year Established: 2016 **Status 2020:** Active
Industries: Artificial Intelligence

Company Name: Seconize
Description: Seconize is intelligence driven next generation cyber risk management platform.
Website: http://seconize.co/
Phone: **Email:** hello@seconize.co
City: Bangalore **State:** KA **PC:** **Country:** India
Year Established: 2017 **Status 2020:** Active
Industries: Artificial Intelligence for:, Cyber Security for:, IT Managed Services for:, Security

Company Name: Securtime
Description: Securtime is a software company that provides attendance management solutions in global markets.
Website: http://www.securtime.com/
Phone: **Email:** bangalore@securax.: India
City: Bangalore **State:** KA **PC:** **Country:** India
Year Established: 2012 **Status 2020:** Active
Industries: Cloud for:, IT Managed Services for:, Application Services for:, Security

Company Name: SigTuple
Description: SigTuple builds intelligent solutions for medical diagnosis using state of the art machine learning techniques.
Website: http://www.sigtuple.com
Phone: **Email:** info@sigtuple.com
City: Bangalore **State:** KA **PC:** **Country:** India
Year Established: 2015 **Status 2020:** Active
Industries: Analytics for:, Artificial Intelligence for:, Big Data and Analytics for:, ~ Healthcare (20), Machine Learning

Company Name: SimplyFI Softech India Pvt. Ltd.
Description: SimplyFI Softech Pvt. Ltd. is a Product Development Company developing solutions on Blockchain and Artificial Intelligence.Visit our website
Website: http://simplyfi.tech/
Phone: **Email:** info@simplyfi.tech
City: Bangalore **State:** KA **PC:** **Country:** India
Year Established: 2016 **Status 2020:** Active
Industries: Artificial Intelligence for:, Blockchain for:, IT Managed Services

Company Name: Skyfire Applied Intelligence Pvt Ltd
Description: Our mission is to make healthcare affordable, accessible and efficient for everyone, using technology such as AI and Robotics.
Website: http://atom360.io/
Phone: 91-7829743210 **Email:** discover@atom360.io
City: Bangalore **State:** KA **PC:** **Country:** India
Year Established: **Status 2020:** Active
Industries: Artificial Intelligence for:, ~ Healthcare (20)

Company Name: Smartco: India
Description: Providing financial access to the millions of mobile users in India using alternative credit assessment
Website: http://smartcoin.co.: India
Phone: **Email:** contact@smartcoin.co.: India
City: Bangalore **State:** KA **PC:** **Country:** India
Year Established: 2015 **Status 2020:** Active
Industries: Big Data and Analytics for:, ~ Banking and Financial Markets-Services (7), Machine Learning for:, Predictive Analytics

Company Name: SprintAI
Description: SprintAI is an Enterprise AI company.
Website:
Phone: **Email:** 37460@reference-encyclopedia-ai.net
City: Bangalore **State:** KA **PC:** **Country:** India
Year Established: 2018 **Status 2020:** - Closed
Industries:

Company Name: Str8bat Sport Tech Solutions
Description: Sports Wearable Company to help player improve everyday and play better
Website: http://www.str8bat.com
Phone: **Email:** contact@str8bat.com
City: Bangalore **State:** KA **PC:** **Country:** India
Year Established: 2017 **Status 2020:** Active
Industries: Cloud for:, Internet of Things (IoT) for:, Machine Learning for:, ~ Arts-Entertainment-Recreation (4)

Company Name: Streamingo Solutions
Description: An innovative, scalable and versatile AI platform to boost productivity and enhance engagement of the online video experience
Website: http://streamingo.ai/
Phone: **Email:** info@streamingo.ai
City: Bangalore **State:** KA **PC:** **Country:** India
Year Established: 2015 **Status 2020:** Active
Industries: Artificial Intelligence for:, Big Data and Analytics for:, Web for:, Machine Learning

Company Name: Synapsica
Description: Artificial intelligence and computer vision enabled smart medical diagnostic assistance
Website: http://www.synapsica.com
Phone: **Email:** info@synapsica.com
City: Bangalore **State:** KA **PC:** **Country:** India
Year Established: **Status 2020:** Active
Industries: Artificial Intelligence for:, ~ Healthcare (20), ~ Healthcare (20), IT Managed Services for:, Machine Learning for:, ~ Healthcare (20), Natural Language Processing for:, Predictive Analytics for:, ~ Professional Services (48)

Company Name: TalentRecru: Italy
Description: TalentRecruit is an advanced talent acquisition software suite.
Website: http://talentrecruit.com/
Phone: 91 9620 666 066 **Email:** alok@talentrecruit.com
City: Bangalore **State:** KA **PC:** **Country:** India
Year Established: 2014 **Status 2020:** Active
Industries: Artificial Intelligence for:, IT Managed Services for:, Machine Learning for:, Business Software as a Service Apps (SaaS Apps)

Company Name: TARDID Technologies.
Description: TARDID is a industry specific augmented intelligence platform
Website: http://www.tardidtech.com/
Phone: 91-80430-07374 **Email:** info@tardidtech.com
City: Bangalore **State:** KA **PC:** **Country:** India
Year Established: 2016 **Status 2020:** Active
Industries:

Company Name: TARS
Description: Automating Conversations between Enterprises and Custome: Serbia
Website: http://hellotars.com/
Phone: 91-9980835840 **Email:** hi@hellotars.com
City: Bangalore **State:** KA **PC:** **Country:** India
Year Established: **Status 2020:** Active
Industries: Artificial Intelligence for:, E-Commerce for:, Enterprise Application Services for:, Mobile

Company Name: TartanSense
Description: TartanSense is an AI powered robotics solutions provider empowering small farm holders.
Website: http://www.tartansense.com/
Phone: 91 9840 6856 91 **Email:** info@tartansense.com
City: Bangalore **State:** KA **PC:** **Country:** India
Year Established: **Status 2020:** Active
Industries: Artificial Intelligence for:, ~ Agriculture (3)

Company Name: Techiexpert
Description: Techiexpert.com - Emerging technologies & Startup News
Website: http://www.techiexpert.com/
Phone: **Email:** admin@techiexpert.com
City: Bangalore **State:** KA **PC:** **Country:** India
Year Established: **Status 2020:** Active
Industries: Analytics for:, Artificial Intelligence for:, Big Data and Analytics for:, Cloud for:, Databases for:, ~ Banking and Financial Markets-Services (7), ~ Healthcare (20), Machine Learning

Company Name: Techl33t Infosystems Private Limited
Description: Deep Tech, Agile Digital, Analytics
Website: http://www.techl33t.: India
Phone: **Email:** 37511@reference-encyclopedia-ai.net
City: Bangalore **State:** KA **PC:** **Country:** India
Year Established: 2016 **Status 2020:** Active
Industries: Artificial Intelligence for:, IT Managed Services

Company Name: TechLeer
Description: Stay Enlightened on AI, VR, AR
Website: http://www.techleer.com
Phone: **Email:** teamtechleer@gmail.com
City: Bangalore **State:** KA **PC:** **Country:** India

Year Established: **Status 2020:** Active
Industries: Artificial Intelligence for:, Augmented Reality for:, ~ Personal-Religious-Civic (45), ~ Arts-Entertainment-Recreation (4)

Company **Name:** Tercept Inc
Description: Machine Learning Driven Programmatic Yield Analytics & Optimization
Website: http://www.tercept.com
Phone: 91 9916327821 **Email:** hello@tercept.com
City: Bangalore **State:** KA **PC:** **Country:** India
Year Established: 2017 **Status 2020:** Active
Industries: Artificial Intelligence for:, ~ Education (13), Machine Learning

Company Name: Tophyre technologies private limited
Description: SaaS based intelligent Screening engine
Website: http://www.tophyre.com
Phone: 9611692266 **Email:** ramesh.poolakkil@tophyre.com
City: Bangalore **State:** KA **PC:** **Country:** India
Year Established: 2018 **Status 2020:** Active
Industries: Artificial Intelligence for:, IT Managed Services for:, Business Software as a Service Apps (SaaS Apps)

Company Name: TradeLab
Description: Tradelab Software Private Limited is a start-up in capital market
Website: http://tradelab.: India
Phone: **Email:** info@tradelab.: India
City: Bangalore **State:** KA **PC:** **Country:** India
Year Established: 2012 **Status 2020:** Active
Industries: Artificial Intelligence for:, ~ Banking and Financial Markets-Services (7)

Company Name: Traxroot | Intelligent Telematics
Description: Traxroot | Intelligent Telematics is a data analytics company which focuses mainly in telematics
Website: http://www.traxroot.com/
Phone: 91 888 466 0033 **Email:** sales@traxroot.com
City: Bangalore **State:** KA **PC:** **Country:** India
Year Established: 2016 **Status 2020:** Active
Industries: ~ Telecommunications (56), ~ Telecommunications (56)

Company Name: Trendwise Analytics
Description: Trendwise Analytics is a Bangalore - based AI and ML Company, providing Training and Consulting Services.
Website: http://trendwiseanalytics.com
Phone: **Email:** info@trendwiseanalytics.com
City: Bangalore **State:** KA **PC:** **Country:** India
Year Established: 2011 **Status 2020:** Active
Industries: Analytics for:, Artificial Intelligence for:, Big Data and Analytics for:, Machine Learning

Company Name: Unbox Robotics
Description: Unbox Robotics builds on-demand AI-driven warehouse robotics solutions, which can be deployed using limited foot-print, time, and capital.
Website: http://unboxrobotics.com/
Phone: 91 9740227165 **Email:** hello@unboxrobotics.com
City: Bangalore **State:** KA **PC:** **Country:** India
Year Established: 2019 **Status 2020:** Active
Industries: Artificial Intelligence for:, Business Applications for:, Automation for:, Internet of Things (IoT) for:, ~ Telecommunications (56), Robotics for:, Supply Chain Management

Company Name: Uncanny Vision
Description: Uncanny Vision is an award-winning AI-based Vision startup making IoT devices (like Surveillance cameras) smarter.
Website: http://www.uncannyvision.com
Phone: 91-79752 73291 **Email:** sales@uncannyvision.com
City: Bangalore **State:** KA **Zip:** 560008 **Country:** India
Year Established: **Status 2020:** Active
Industries: Analytics for:, ~ Construction (132), ~ Retail and Consumer Products (174), Artificial Intelligence for:, ~

Administrative and Support Services (1), Collections for:, ~ Government (1239), ~ Home (1242), ~ Real Estate (1269), ~ Retail and Consumer Products (1272),

Company Name: UnoTag
Description: SaaS to verify counterfe: Italy
Website: http://www.unotag.: India
Phone: 91-953535-3738 **Email:** info@unotag.: India
City: Bangalore **State:** KA **PC:** **Country:** India
Year Established: **Status 2020:** Active
Industries: Artificial Intelligence

Company Name: UtilizeAI
Description: NLP/NLU Research and Product Start-up
Website: http://www.utilize.ai/
Phone: 8971622711 **Email:** info@utilize.ai
City: Bangalore **State:** KA **PC:** **Country:** India
Year Established: **Status 2020:** Active
Industries:

Company Name: Vaultedge
Description: Vaultedge is a legal tech company that helps law firms organize and find documents easier.
Website: http://www.vaultedge.com
Phone: 1 97314 66111 **Email:** sales@vaultedge.com
City: Bangalore **State:** KA **PC:** **Country:** India
Year Established: 2015 **Status 2020:** Active
Industries: Artificial Intelligence for:, Cloud for:, Data Management for:, Data Management for:, Web for:, Risk Management

Company Name: Vernacular.ai
Description: Vernacular.ai, a multilingual artificial intelligence platform for business: Spain
Website: http://vernacular.ai
Phone: **Email:** hello@vernacular.ai
City: Bangalore **State:** KA **PC:** **Country:** India
Year Established: 2016 **Status 2020:** Active
Industries: Artificial Intelligence for:, Web for:, Internet of Things (IoT)

Company Name: VisioLucid
Description: They assist enterprises transform & thrive in a changing world by providing solutions on big data, web/cloud computing & machine vision.
Website: http://www.visiolucid.com
Phone: 91 (080)-41149552 **Email:** contactus@visiolucid.com
City: Bangalore **State:** KA **PC:** **Country:** India
Year Established: 2013 **Status 2020:** Active
Industries: Artificial Intelligence for:, Big Data and Analytics for:, Cloud for:, Enterprise Application Services for:, IT Managed Services

Company Name: visionbot.com
Description: Computer Vision as Service Platform
Website: http://www.visionbot.io
Phone: 91-733 773 0600 **Email:** info@visionbot.io
City: Bangalore **State:** KA **PC:** **Country:** India
Year Established: 2016 **Status 2020:** Active
Industries: Artificial Intelligence for:, Computer Vision for:, Facial Recognition for:, Image Recognition for:, Machine Learning for:, Business Software as a Service Apps (SaaS Apps)

Company Name: Vyuti
Description: Product and Solutions involving robotics, machine vision and machine learning
Website: http://www.vyuti.com
Phone: **Email:** nikhil.r@vyuti.com
City: Bangalore **State:** KA **PC:** **Country:** India
Year Established: **Status 2020:** Active
Industries: Artificial Intelligence for:, Computer Vision for:, ~ Manufacturing-Miscellaneous (34), Robotics

Company Name: Wysa
Description: Wysa is an AI conversational agent that has been shown to help improve mental heal:Thailand
Website: http://www.wysa.io/
Phone: 91 7411004366 **Email:** hello@wysa.ai
City: Bangalore **State:** KA **PC:** **Country:** India
Year Established: 2015 **Status 2020:** Active
Industries: Artificial Intelligence for:, ~ Healthcare (20), ~ Healthcare (20), Machine Learning for:, ~ Healthcare (20), ~ Healthcare (20)

Company Name: Yellow Messenger
Description: Conversational AI Platform for Enterpris: Spain
Website: http://www.yellowmessenger.com
Phone: **Email:** raghu@yellowmessenger.com
City: Bangalore **State:** KA **PC:** **Country:** India
Year Established: 2016 **Status 2020:** Active
Industries: Artificial Intelligence for:, ~ Customer Relationship Management (11), Enterprise Application Services

Company Name: YellowAnt
Description: Intelligent bot assistant for the workplace
Website: http://www.yellowant.com
Phone: **Email:** 37710@reference-encyclopedia-ai.net
City: Bangalore **State:** KA **PC:** **Country:** India
Year Established: 2016 **Status 2020:** Active
Industries: Artificial Intelligence

Company Name: YUGASYS PRIVATE LIMITED
Description: Yugasys believes in the power of Artificial Intelligence to solve the most unique and biggest problems existing in our daily routines.
Website: http://www.yugasys.com
Phone: 080 2665 1617 **Email:** support@yugasys.com
City: Bangalore **State:** KA **PC:** **Country:** India
Year Established: **Status 2020:** Active
Industries: Artificial Intelligence for:, Machine Learning for:, Application Services for:, Natural Language Processing

Company Name: YunoWorld Technologies Pvt Ltd
Description: YunoWorld Technologies is a web data driven company focussed on solving customer challenges in web data discovery and extraction space.
Website: http://www.yunoworldtech.com
Phone: **Email:** info@yunoworldtech.com
City: Bangalore **State:** KA **PC:** **Country:** India
Year Established: 2015 **Status 2020:** Active
Industries: Analytics for:, Artificial Intelligence for:, Big Data and Analytics for:, IT Managed Services for:, Web for:, Machine Learning

Company Name: ZORT
Description: A smart SMS Messenger and Personal Assistant
Website: http://www.zort.io
Phone: **Email:** info@zort.io
City: Bangalore **State:** KA **PC:** **Country:** India
Year Established: 2018 **Status 2020:** Active
Industries: Web for:, Machine Learning for:, Application Services

Company Name: AppiVa Software
Description: ezTask.io is an AI enabled sales management and collaboration platform for enterprise to simplify and automate sales workflow
Website: http://eztask.io
Phone: **Email:** social@eztask.io
City: Bangalore City **State:** KA **PC:** **Country:** India
Year Established: 2016 **Status 2020:** Active
Industries:

Company Name: Cogxar Reseach and Solutions
Description: Cogxar is a research and development center for artificial intelligence, focused at evolutionary and adaptive systems.
Website: http://www.cogxar.com
Phone: **Email:** info@cogxar.com
City: Bangalore City **State:** KA **PC:** **Country:** India

Year Established: 2012 **Status 2020:** Active
Industries: Artificial Intelligence

Company Name: Hypermine
Description: Blockchain, Digital Security, Decentralized Applications
Website: http://www.hypermine.: India
Phone: 91-7899-122-222 **Email:** irfan@hypermine.: India
City: Bangalore City **State:** KA **PC:** **Country:** India
Year Established: **Status 2020:** Active
Industries:

Company Name: KayaDev AI
Description: AI & Automation Services Company
Website: http://www.kayadev.ai
Phone: (962) 021-6988 **Email:** info@kayadev.com
City: Bangalore City **State:** KA **PC:** **Country:** India
Year Established: 2018 **Status 2020:** Active
Industries: IT Managed Services for:, Machine Learning

Company Name: Maxrev.pro
Description: Maxrev.pro is a set of AI based revenue management tools for hoteliers and hotel management companies to maximize their revenues.
Website: http://maxrev.p: Romania
Phone: **Email:** support@maxrev.p: Romania
City: Bangalore City **State:** KA **PC:** **Country:** India
Year Established: 2019 **Status 2020:** Active
Industries: Analytics for:, Artificial Intelligence for:, IT Managed Services

Company Name: Praydus Kaisha
Description: Agritech
Website: http://www.mobifarm.net
Phone: 8884424013 **Email:** prayduskaisha@gmail.com
City: Bangalore City **State:** KA **PC:** **Country:** India
Year Established: **Status 2020:** Active
Industries: ~ Agriculture (3), Artificial Intelligence for:, E-Commerce for:, ~ Banking and Financial Markets-Services (7), Supply Chain Management

Company Name: Restog: Romania
Description: Restogro is an advanced suite of SaaS solutions built for restaurants, POS & consultants with the vision to evolve how they work
Website: http://www.restogro.com
Phone: 9629749609 **Email:** admin@restogro.com
City: Bangalore City **State:** KA **PC:** **Country:** India
Year Established: 2019 **Status 2020:** Active
Industries: ~ Food and Beverage (17), Machine Learning for:, Business Software as a Service Apps (SaaS Apps)

Company Name: RoadMetrics
Description: Mapping Road Conditions at Scale
Website: http://roadmetrics.in/
Phone: 9909036704 **Email:** info@roadmetrics.: India
City: Bangalore City **State:** KA **PC:** **Country:** India
Year Established: 2019 **Status 2020:** Active
Industries: Enterprise Application Services for:, IT Managed Services for:, Machine Learning

Company Name: Telestratum Networks
Description: Analytics powered Self Optimization solutions for Telecom Networks
Website: http://telestratum.com
Phone: **Email:** info@telestratum.com
City: Bangalore City **State:** KA **PC:** **Country:** India
Year Established: 2013 **Status 2020:** Active
Industries: Internet of Things (IoT) for:, Predictive Analytics

Company Name: Thinklytics
Description: We deliver business centric dashboards for businesses and individuals. Thinklytics is the modern platform for building visualizations.
Website: http://www.thinklytics.io
Phone: 91-97842-66896 **Email:** gaurav@thinklytics.io
City: Bangalore City **State:** KA **PC:** **Country:** India
Year Established: **Status 2020:** Active
Industries: Analytics for:, Artificial Intelligence for:, IT Managed Services for:, Machine Learning for:, ~ Professional Services (48)

Company Name: Acrobee India Private Limited
Description: Analytics , AI & Machine Learning
Website: http://acrobee.com
Phone: **Email:** info@acrobee.com
City: Bengaluru **State:** KA **PC:** **Country:** India
Year Established: **Status 2020:** Active
Industries: Analytics for:, Artificial Intelligence for:, ~ Education (13)

Company Name: Afthonia Lab Pvt. Ltd.
Description: Afthonia focusses on early stage startups in Fintech and provides them with a trusted ecosystem to grow and succeed.
Website: http://www.afthonialab.com/
Phone: 7387683645 **Email:** anna@afthonialab.com
City: Bengaluru **State:** KA **PC:** **Country:** India
Year Established: **Status 2020:** Active
Industries: Artificial Intelligence for:, ~ Banking and Financial Markets-Services (7), ~ Banking and Financial Markets-Services (7), ~ Banking and Financial Markets-Services (7), ~ Administrative and Support Services (1), ~ Insurance (25), Machine Learning for:, ~ Banking

Company Name: Agara
Description: Agara is an autonomous virtual voice agent designed for natural conversations with customers without any human assistance.
Website: https://agara.ai/
Phone: **Email:** abhimanyu@agaralabs.com
City: Bengaluru **State:** KA **PC:** **Country:** India
Year Established: **Status 2020:** Active
Industries: Artificial Intelligence for:, ~ Administrative and Support Services (1), ~ Automotive (5), ~ Banking and Financial Markets-Services (7), ~ Beauty (8), ~ E-Commerce (12), ~ Energy and Utilities (14), ~ Food and Beverage (17), ~ Healthcare (20), ~ Hospitality (23), ~

Company Name: Aidapp
Description: At Aidapp, we are building products that simplify living. We design technology to be really enjoyable to use - and get work done.
Website: http://www.aidapp.: India
Phone: 91 9901257384 **Email:** hello@aidapp.: India
City: Bengaluru **State:** KA **PC:** **Country:** India
Year Established: **Status 2020:** Active
Industries: Artificial Intelligence for:, IT Managed Services for:, Machine Learning for:, Mobile for:, ~ Professional Services (48)

Company Name: Aindra
Description: Aindra is working in domain of Artificial Intelligence and specifically in the area of Computer Vision.
Website: https://www.aindra.in/
Phone: **Email:** contactus@aindra.: India
City: Bengaluru **State:** KA **PC:** **Country:** India
Year Established: 2012 **Status 2020:** Active
Industries: Artificial Intelligence for:, ~ Healthcare (20), Machine Learning

Company Name: Akaike Technologies
Description: Data Science, Data Analytics, Artificial Intelligence
Website: http://www.akaiketech.com/
Phone: (91)99021 04302 **Email:** contact@akaiketech.com
City: Bengaluru **State:** KA **PC:** **Country:** India

Year Established: 2018 **Status 2020:** Active
Industries: Artificial Intelligence for:, Big Data and Analytics for:, IT Managed Services for:, Machine Learning

Company Name: Alisense.ai
Description: Saas Platform, Blockcha: India
Website:
Phone: 7900711101 **Email:** Alisense.ai@rediffmail.com
City: Bengaluru **State:** KA **PC:** **Country:** India
Year Established: **Status 2020:** Active
Industries:

Company Name: alphaics Corporation
Description: AlphaICs is capitalizing on this opportunity to deliver the next generation of AI compute.
Website: http://www.alphaics.ai/
Phone: **Email:** info@alphaics.com
City: Bengaluru **State:** KA **PC:** **Country:** India
Year Established: 2016 **Status 2020:** Active
Industries: Artificial Intelligence

Company Name: AnswerWise
Description: AnswerWise is an AI platform that automates your customer support with a Human AI approach.
Website: http://www.answerwise.io/
Phone: **Email:** hello@answerwise.io
City: Bengaluru **State:** KA **PC:** **Country:** India
Year Established: 2019 **Status 2020:** Active
Industries: Artificial Intelligence for:, Business Software as a Service Apps (SaaS Apps)

Company Name: AppKompute
Description: AppKompute is an Artificial Intelligence and Automation solutions provider that offers a suite of Engineered products.
Website: http://appkompute.com
Phone: **Email:** support@appkompute.com
City: Bengaluru **State:** KA **PC:** **Country:** India
Year Established: **Status 2020:** Active
Industries: Analytics for:, Artificial Intelligence for:, Big Data and Analytics for:, Automation for:, IT Managed Services for:, Predictive Analytics for:, Robotics

Company Name: AuthMe Id Service
Description: AuthMe Id Services develops and offers artificial intelligence (AI) solutions to resolve customer complaints and queries.
Website: http://www.callup.ai/
Phone: **Email:** sales@callup.ai
City: Bengaluru **State:** KA **PC:** **Country:** India
Year Established: 2017 **Status 2020:** Active
Industries: Artificial Intelligence

Company Name: Awesummly
Description: Awesummly is an Artificial intelligence powered relevant content discovery and shortening app
Website: http://www.awesummly.com/
Phone: (882) 667-4702 **Email:** info@awesummly.com
City: Bengaluru **State:** KA **PC:** **Country:** India
Year Established: 2015 **Status 2020:** Active
Industries: Artificial Intelligence for:, Application Services for:, Compute

Company Name: Bigclozet
Description: Fashion discovery that actually makes sense, amalgamating Data Science and Technology into clothing and lifestyle product discovery.
Website: http://www.bigclozet.com
Phone: **Email:** 36155@reference-encyclopedia-ai.net
City: Bengaluru **State:** KA **PC:** **Country:** India
Year Established: 2015 **Status 2020:** Active
Industries: Artificial Intelligence for:, E-Commerce for:, ~ Fashion (16)

Company Name: boxx.ai
Description: We use Artificial Intelligence to democratize analytics
Website: http://boxx.ai
Phone: 91 888 4535 222 **Email:** accounts@boxx.ai
City: Bengaluru **State:** KA **PC:** **Country:** India
Year Established: 2016 **Status 2020:** Active
Industries:

Company Name: CamfyVision
Description: CamfyVision develops intelligent computer vision algorithms using the combination of AI and deep learning.
Website: http://www.camfyvision.com/
Phone: 91-91086 28001 **Email:** vedpalsingh@camfyvision.co
City: Bengaluru **State:** KA **PC:** **Country:** India
Year Established: 2017 **Status 2020:** Active
Industries:

Company Name: CarX
Description: An AI-powered connected-car platform, SaaS, Fleet Management, ADAS, Driving Safety
Website: http://www.carx.io
Phone: **Email:** contact@carx.io
City: Bengaluru **State:** KA **PC:** **Country:** India
Year Established: 2016 **Status 2020:** Active
Industries: Application Services for:, Artificial Intelligence for:, ~ Automotive (5), ~ Telecommunications (56), ~ Telecommunications (56), Business Software as a Service Apps (SaaS Apps)

Company Name: Charmboard
Description: Charmboard is the world's leading in-video discovery platform.
Website: http://www.charmboard.com
Phone: **Email:** marketing@charmboard.com
City: Bengaluru **State:** KA **PC:** **Country:** India
Year Established: **Status 2020:** Active
Industries: Artificial Intelligence for:, Computer Vision for:, E-Commerce for:, ~ Fashion (16), ~ Arts-Entertainment-Recreation (4), ~ Social Media (54), ~ Professional Services (48), ~ Media-Communications (41)

Company Name: Chillycon
Description: Your AI Personal Advisor
Website: http://www.chillycon.com
Phone: **Email:** contact@chillycon.com
City: Bengaluru **State:** KA **PC:** **Country:** India
Year Established: 2017 **Status 2020:** Active
Industries: Artificial Intelligence

Company Name: Ciafo
Description: Ciafo is an Indian technology-driven startup that provides web-based consumer products for its customers.
Website: http://ciafo.com
Phone: **Email:** marketing@ciafo.com
City: Bengaluru **State:** KA **PC:** **Country:** India
Year Established: 2010 **Status 2020:** Active
Industries: Artificial Intelligence for:, Enterprise Application Services for:, Mobile for:, Web

Company Name: CloudSEK
Description: Cloudsek is an Infosec Risk assessment company which provides intelligence needed to tackle online threats.
Website: http://www.cloudsek.com
Phone: **Email:** rahul.sasi@cloudsek.com
City: Bengaluru **State:** KA **PC:** **Country:** India
Year Established: 2015 **Status 2020:** Active
Industries: Artificial Intelligence for:, IT Managed Services for:, Machine Learning for:, Business Software as a Service Apps (SaaS Apps) for:, Security

Company Name: Codecafe
Description: AI, ML, Custom Software
Website: http://www.codecafegroup.com
Phone: 8197508050 **Email:** reach@codecafegroup.com
City: Bengaluru **State:** KA **PC:** **Country:** India

Year Established: **Status 2020:** Active
Industries:

Company Name: CoRover
Description: CoRover is an award winning platform based on AI, ML & NLP, provides ChatBots, to improve sales, save cost & improve customer satisfaction
Website: http://CoRover.ai
Phone: (9198) 001-1208 **Email:** email@CoRover.mobi
City: Bengaluru **State:** KA **PC:** **Country:** India
Year Established: 2016 **Status 2020:** Active
Industries: Artificial Intelligence for:, IT Managed Services

Company Name: Crediwatch
Description: Amplified Intelligence for Business and Enterprise.
Website: http://www.crediwatch.com/
Phone: 91 (80) 2663 2121 **Email:** info@crediwatch.com
City: Bengaluru **State:** KA **PC:** **Country:** India
Year Established: 2016 **Status 2020:** Active
Industries: Artificial Intelligence for:, ~ Banking and Financial Markets-Services (7), IT Managed Services

Company Name: Crop: India
Description: CropIn is a leading AI and Data-led agri-tech organization that provides SaaS solutions to agribusinesses globally using deep learning.
Website: http://www.cropin.com/
Phone: **Email:** marketing@cropin.com
City: Bengaluru **State:** KA **PC:** **Country:** India
Year Established: 2010 **Status 2020:** Active
Industries: Analytics for:, Artificial Intelligence for:, ~ Agriculture (3), ~ Agriculture (3), IT Managed Services for:, IT Managed Services for:, Machine Learning for:, Predictive Analytics for:, Predictive Analytics for:, Business Software as a Service Apps (SaaS Apps) for

Company Name: CrowdShakti
Description: CrowdShakti is an artificial intelligence and software company.
Website: http://www.crowdshakti.com/
Phone: 91 8074136872 **Email:** info@crowdshakti.com
City: Bengaluru **State:** KA **PC:** **Country:** India
Year Established: 2017 **Status 2020:** Active
Industries: Artificial Intelligence for:, Machine Learning

Company Name: CultYvate
Description: CultYvate is an Ag-Tech company that provides farming solutions built on artificial intelligence and the internet of things.
Website: http://www.cultyvate.com
Phone: **Email:** 36359@reference-encyclopedia-ai.net
City: Bengaluru **State:** KA **PC:** **Country:** India
Year Established: 2016 **Status 2020:** Active
Industries: ~ Agriculture (3), ~ Agriculture (3), Artificial Intelligence for:, ~ Agriculture (3)

Company **Name:** DATAIKEN
Description: DATAIKEN is an integrated platform to design and automate AI & ML pipelines and processes and governance, as SaaS or On-premises.
Website: http://dataiken.com
Phone: **Email:** solutions@dataiken.com
City: Bengaluru **State:** KA **PC:** **Country:** India
Year Established: 2012 **Status 2020:** Active
Industries: Analytics for:, Business Intelligence for:, Data Management for:, Data Management for:, Application Program Interfaces (APIs) for:, Application Services for:, Application Services for:, Machine Learning for:, Machine Learning for:, Natural Language Processing

Company Name: Dave.AI
Description: Dave.AI is a Sociograph's patent pending artificial intelligence platform
Website: http://www.iamdave.ai/
Phone: (91) 9663399230 **Email:** info@iamdave.ai
City: Bengaluru **State:** KA **PC:** **Country:** India
Year Established: 2016 **Status 2020:** Active
Industries: Artificial Intelligence for:, Big Data and Analytics for:, IT Managed Services for:, IT Managed Services for:, Machine Learning

Company Name: Deepnews.io
Description: Stock price forecasting AI algorithm
Website: http://deepnews.io
Phone: **Email:** support@deepnews.io
City: Bengaluru **State:** KA **PC:** **Country:** India
Year Established: 2019 **Status 2020:** Active
Industries: Machine Learning for:, ~ Banking and Financial Markets-Services (7)

Company Name: DeepSync
Description: We have pioneered Human voice Cloning to deploy them at radical scale.
Website: http://www.deepsync.co
Phone: 91 9980687262 **Email:** ishansan38@gmail.com
City: Bengaluru **State:** KA **PC:** **Country:** India
Year Established: **Status 2020:** Active
Industries:

Company Name: Deuglo
Description: Deuglo provides mobile apps and AI software development services.
Website: http://www.deuglo.com/
Phone: 91-8041222824 **Email:** contact@deuglo.com
City: Bengaluru **State:** KA **PC:** **Country:** India
Year Established: 2014 **Status 2020:** Active
Industries: Artificial Intelligence for:, Application Services

Company Name: DigiConnectt
Description: Digitizing sales conversations to optimize sales performance and increase sales revenue.
Website: http://lconnectt.com/
Phone: **Email:** sales@lconnectt.com
City: Bengaluru **State:** KA **PC:** **Country:** India
Year Established: 2016 **Status 2020:** Active
Industries: Analytics for:, Artificial Intelligence for:, IT Managed Services for:, Business Software as a Service Apps (SaaS Apps) for:, Automation

Company Name: DrumUp
Description: DrumUp is a social media virtual assistant for businesses and professionals to discover & post great content on Twitter and Facebook pages.
Website: http://drumup.io/
Phone: **Email:** 36460@reference-encyclopedia-ai.net
City: Bengaluru **State:** KA **PC:** **Country:** India
Year Established: 2015 **Status 2020:** Active
Industries: Application Services for:, Mobile for:, Natural Language Processing for:, Business Software as a Service Apps (SaaS Apps) for:, ~ Social Assistance-Non-Profits (53), ~ Social Assistance-Non-Profits (53)

Company Name: Entropik Technology
Description: The boundaries between Human and Machines are shrinking fast.
Website: http://entropika.space/
Phone: **Email:** info@entropika.space
City: Bengaluru **State:** KA **PC:** **Country:** India
Year Established: **Status 2020:** Active
Industries: Artificial Intelligence for:, IT Managed Services for:, Machine Learning

Company Name: eXabit Systems
Description: Exabit is an AgTech IoT platform for sustainable agriculture.
Website: http://www.exabit.: India
Phone: 91 8025614900 **Email:** contactus@exabit.: India
City: Bengaluru **State:** KA **PC:** **Country:** India
Year Established: 2014 **Status 2020:** Active
Industries:

Company Name: eXabit Systems Private Limited
Description: An AgTech IoT platform for sustainable agriculture.
Website: http://www.exabit.: India
Phone: **Email:** info@exabit.: India
City: Bengaluru **State:** KA **PC:** **Country:** India
Year Established: **Status 2020:** Active
Industries: ~ Agriculture (3), Artificial Intelligence for:, Machine Learning

Company Name: Expertrec
Description: Use machine learning to drive more sales through search , product recommendations and other customer interaction points
Website: http://www.expertrec.com
Phone: **Email:** 36536@reference-encyclopedia-ai.net
City: Bengaluru **State:** KA **PC:** **Country:** India
Year Established: 2014 **Status 2020:** Active
Industries: Enterprise Application Services for:, Machine Learning for:, Business Intelligence for:, Web for:, Content

Company Name: Fasal
Description: Climate Smart Precision Agriculture Platform
Website: http://fasal.co
Phone: 91-8904470724 **Email:** connect@wolkus.com
City: Bengaluru **State:** KA **PC:** **Country:** India
Year Established: **Status 2020:** Active
Industries: ~ Agriculture (3), ~ Agriculture (3), Artificial Intelligence for:, Machine Learning

Company Name: Fingage
Description: SAAS, FinTech, India, Compliance, Lending
Website: http://www.getfingage.com
Phone: **Email:** hello@getfingage.com
City: Bengaluru **State:** KA **PC:** **Country:** India
Year Established: **Status 2020:** Active
Industries:

Company Name: FireCompass
Description: FireCompass is an AI Platform for Discovering Your Attack Surface-Shadow IT Discovery |Dark Web Monitoring |3rd Party Vendor Risk Management
Website: http://www.firecompass.com
Phone: **Email:** contact@firecompass.com
City: Bengaluru **State:** KA **PC:** **Country:** India
Year Established: 2019 **Status 2020:** Active
Industries: Artificial Intelligence for:, Big Data and Analytics for:, Cyber Security for:, IT Managed Services for:, Web

Company Name: Fyle
Description: Fyle is an intelligent expense management platform for enterprises.
Website: http://www.fylehq.com
Phone: **Email:** hello@fylehq.com
City: Bengaluru **State:** KA **PC:** **Country:** India
Year Established: 2016 **Status 2020:** Active
Industries: Finance and Accounting for:, Artificial Intelligence for:, Business Applications for:, ~ Banking and Financial Markets-Services (7), Business Software as a Service Apps (SaaS Apps)

Company Name: Fyllo
Description: Fyllo is an IoT and AI based precision agriculture service company
Website: http://www.fyllo.: India
Phone: 91 8105821019 **Email:** contact@fyllo.: India
City: Bengaluru **State:** KA **PC:** **Country:** India
Year Established: 2019 **Status 2020:** Active
Industries: ~ Agriculture (3), ~ Agriculture (3), Artificial Intelligence for:, Internet of Things (IoT)

Company Name: Gamasome Interactive LLP
Description: AI and Technology Solutions Company
Website: http://www.gamasome.com
Phone: **Email:** contact@gamasome.com
City: Bengaluru **State:** KA **PC:** **Country:** India
Year Established: 2015 **Status 2020:** Active
Industries:

Company Name: Glance
Description: Glance is a screen zero platform that consumers use across connected devices to experience the Internet.
Website: http://www.glance.: Sweden
Phone: **Email:** michael@glance.: Sweden
City: Bengaluru **State:** KA **PC:** **Country:** India
Year Established: 2016 **Status 2020:** Active
Industries: Application Services for:, Artificial Intelligence for:, Web

Company Name: HappyLocate
Description: HappyLocate is a platform that helps corporate automate and manage end to end employee relocations.
Website: http://www.happylocate.com/
Phone: 088844 47224 **Email:** reachus@happylocate.com
City: Bengaluru **State:** KA **PC:** **Country:** India
Year Established: 2016 **Status 2020:** Active
Industries: Artificial Intelligence for:, Web

Company Name: Impact Micro Ventures (IMV)
Description: AI based platform for 'no-file' & 'thin-file' micro-enterprise financing
Website: http://impaact.in/
Phone: **Email:** pranay@impaact.: India
City: Bengaluru **State:** KA **PC:** **Country:** India
Year Established: 2017 **Status 2020:** Active
Industries: Artificial Intelligence for:, ~ Banking and Financial Markets-Services (7), ~ Banking and Financial Markets-Services (7), Machine Learning

Company Name: Insight Jedi
Description: Insight Jedi helps users algorithmically build predictive models, unearth insights and make decisions.
Website: http://www.insightjedi.com/
Phone: **Email:** 36774@reference-encyclopedia-ai.net
City: Bengaluru **State:** KA **PC:** **Country:** India
Year Established: 2014 **Status 2020:** Active
Industries: Big Data and Analytics for:, Web for:, Machine Learning for:, Predictive Analytics

Company Name: iSAN DATA SYSTEMS
Description: iSAN DATA SYSTEMS specializes in artificial intelligence, machine learning, cloud implementation and consulting.
Website: http://www.isandatasystems.com/
Phone: 91 9845561399 **Email:** support@isandatasystems.com
City: Bengaluru **State:** KA **PC:** **Country:** India
Year Established: 2016 **Status 2020:** Active
Industries:

Company Name: Jhaiho
Description: Saas, Mobile App, Online market place, AI
Website: http://jhaiho.com
Phone: **Email:** gagfux@jhaiho.com
City: Bengaluru **State:** KA **PC:** **Country:** India
Year Established: 2016 **Status 2020:** Active
Industries:

Company Name: Jovian.ml
Description: Jovian.ml is a platform for data scientists to track and reproduce machine learning experiments.
Website: http://www.jovian.ml
Phone: **Email:** hello@jovian.ml
City: Bengaluru **State:** KA **PC:** **Country:** India
Year Established: 2019 **Status 2020:** Active
Industries: Machine Learning

Company Name: Koinearth
Description: Koinearth is a stealth mode startup working at the intersection of blockchains, machine learning and mechanism design
Website: http://koinearth.com/
Phone: 91 9986073402 **Email:** info@koinearth.com
City: Bengaluru **State:** KA **PC:** **Country:** India
Year Established: 2018 **Status 2020:** Active
Industries: Blockchain for:, Machine Learning

Company Name: Koshex
Description: Wealthtech, AI & ML
Website: http://koshex.com
Phone: **Email:** kosh@koshex.com
City: Bengaluru **State:** KA **PC:** **Country:** India
Year Established: 2018 **Status 2020:** Active
Industries: Artificial Intelligence for:, Machine Learning for:, ~ Banking and Financial Markets-Services (7)

Company Name: Leadsprofessionals
Description: SaaS
Website: http://leadsprofessionals.com/
Phone: **Email:** MohanKapoor@leadsprofessionals.com
City: Bengaluru **State:** KA **PC:** **Country:** India
Year Established: 2017 **Status 2020:** Active
Industries: Big Data and Analytics for:, Machine Learning

Company Name: Liv.ai
Description: Liv.ai's mission is to give voice to a billion Indians.
Website: http://liv.ai
Phone: **Email:** hello@liv.ai
City: Bengaluru **State:** KA **PC:** **Country:** India
Year Established: **Status 2020:** Active
Industries: Artificial Intelligence for:, Machine Learning for:, Speech Recognition

Company Name: Machstatz
Description: Industrial IOT , Data Analytics, Process optimisation, Machine failure prediction, Condition based monitoring, Plug and play IOT device
Website: http://www.machstatz.com
Phone: (981) 804-7258 **Email:** info@machstatz.com
City: Bengaluru **State:** KA **PC:** **Country:** India
Year Established: 2017 **Status 2020:** Active
Industries: Artificial Intelligence for:, IT Managed Services

Company Name: Merak Software Solutions
Description: Merak.ai is a product suite comprising of tailor-made machine learning solutions to help businesses grow.
Website: http://www.merak.ai
Phone: 91 9999367504 **Email:** vibhor@merak.ai
City: Bengaluru **State:** KA **PC:** **Country:** India
Year Established: 2017 **Status 2020:** Active
Industries: Artificial Intelligence for:, IT Managed Services for:, Machine Learning

Company Name: MINDSET
Description: MINDSET is an artificial intelligence company that builds software platform that learns from experience
Website: http://mind---set.com
Phone: **Email:** 36980@reference-encyclopedia-ai.net
City: Bengaluru **State:** KA **PC:** **Country:** India
Year Established: 2016 **Status 2020:** Active
Industries: Artificial Intelligence for:, Machine Learning

Company Name: Monk AI
Description: Human AI solution for business: Spain
Website: http://monk.ai
Phone: **Email:** 37012@reference-encyclopedia-ai.net
City: Bengaluru **State:** KA **PC:** **Country:** India
Year Established: 2016 **Status 2020:** Active
Industries: Artificial Intelligence for:, IT Managed Services for:, Web

Company Name: Myelin Foundry
Description: Myelin Foundry develops Artificial Intelligence algorithms on video, voice, and sensor data, for edge devices.
Website: http://myelinfoundry.com/
Phone: 91 80 6190 4242 **Email:** social@myelinfoundry.com
City: Bengaluru **State:** KA **PC:** **Country:** India
Year Established: 2019 **Status 2020:** Active
Industries: Artificial Intelligence for:, ~ Healthcare (20), Industrial Solutions for:, IT Managed Services for:, IT Managed Services for:, ~ Arts-Entertainment-Recreation (4)

Company Name: NeenOpal Intelligent Solutions Pvt Ltd.
Description: NeenOpal services offers Data Mining, Forecasting, Predictive Statistics, Mathematical Modelling, Optimisation and Big Data Analytics.
Website: http://www.neenopal.com/
Phone: (877) 944-1037 **Email:** himanshu.bahmani@neenopal.com
City: Bengaluru **State:** KA **PC:** **Country:** India
Year Established: 2016 **Status 2020:** Active
Industries: Analytics for:, Big Data and Analytics for:, Predictive Analytics

Company Name: Oloid.ai
Description: Oloid.ai provides facial recognition services.
Website: http://www.oloid.ai/
Phone: (1) 800 711 9123 **Email:** info@oloid.ai
City: Bengaluru **State:** KA **PC:** **Country:** India
Year Established: 2018 **Status 2020:** Active
Industries: Artificial Intelligence for:, Facial Recognition

Company Name: ParentOf
Description: Parentof is a decision sciences organization which provides insights into child growth and decision analytics.
Website: http://www.parentof.com/
Phone: **Email:** nag@prequate.: India
City: Bengaluru **State:** KA **PC:** **Country:** India
Year Established: **Status 2020:** Active
Industries: Artificial Intelligence for:, ~ Education (13), ~ Education (13), Machine Learning for:, ~ Education (13)

Company Name: Pathway.Ai
Description: A simple approach to finding new opportunities, gain job market insights, understand your future prospects.
Website: http://pathway.ai
Phone: **Email:** jobs@pathway.ai
City: Bengaluru **State:** KA **PC:** **Country:** India
Year Established: 2017 **Status 2020:** Active
Industries:

Company Name: Pattem Digital
Description: Pattem Digital is a specialist in strategy consulting, UX research, UI development, mobile apps, big data, and artificial intelligence.
Website: http://pattemdigital.com/
Phone: 9901337558 **Email:** business@pattemdigital.com
City: Bengaluru **State:** KA **PC:** **Country:** India
Year Established: 2018 **Status 2020:** Active
Industries: Artificial Intelligence for:, Application Services for:, Development and Test

Company Name: Pikup.ai
Description: Pikup.ai is a privately held artificial intelligence startup company.
Website: http://www.pikup.ai
Phone: **Email:** 37168@reference-encyclopedia-ai.net
City: Bengaluru **State:** KA **PC:** **Country:** India
Year Established: 2018 **Status 2020:** Active
Industries: Artificial Intelligence

Company Name: PLAiTO | Learning Personalized
Description: A personalized adaptive learning platform that consists of an Artificial Intelligent engine.
Website: http://www.plaito.ai
Phone: 1-800-103-9855 **Email:** contact@plaito.ai
City: Bengaluru **State:** KA **PC:** **Country:** India
Year Established: 2010 **Status 2020:** Active
Industries: Artificial Intelligence

Company Name: Pucho Technology Information Private Limited
Description: A multi-lingual Q&A platform on any device.
Website: http://www.pucho.co/
Phone: 91-9699429836/9110681355 **Email:** vikram@pucho.co
City: Bengaluru **State:** KA **PC:** **Country:** India
Year Established: **Status 2020:** Active
Industries: Artificial Intelligence for:, Blockchain for:, Computer Vision for:, ~ Education (13), Human Computer Interaction for:, Machine Learning for:, Natural Language Processing for:, ~ Social Media (54), Speech Recognition

Company Name: QGra: Philippin: Spain
Description: Beautiful Segment-of-One Marketing powered by AI
Website: http://qgraph.io/
Phone: **Email:** app@qgraph.io
City: Bengaluru **State:** KA **PC:** **Country:** India
Year Established: **Status 2020:** Active
Industries: Artificial Intelligence for:, ~ Media-Communications (41), Mobile

Company Name: RayEye
Description: A computer vision company building shopper focused solution for retail to evaluate and enhance shopper experience using in-store cameras
Website: http://rayeye.: India
Phone: 7753838089 **Email:** info@rayeye.: India
City: Bengaluru **State:** KA **PC:** **Country:** India
Year Established: 2019 **Status 2020:** Active
Industries:

Company Name: Rivi
Description: Rivi is an intelligent travel product that better understands the users and shares personalised travel suggestions using Machine Learning.
Website: http://rivi.co
Phone: **Email:** hello@rivi.co
City: Bengaluru **State:** KA **PC:** **Country:** India
Year Established: 2017 **Status 2020:** Active
Industries: Machine Learning for:, Mobile

Company Name: RobotsAlive
Description: Robots Alive engages in design and development of robotic and automation technologies.
Website: http://www.robots-alive.com
Phone: **Email:** info@robots-alive.com
City: Bengaluru **State:** KA **PC:** **Country:** India
Year Established: **Status 2020:** Active
Industries: Artificial Intelligence for:, ~ Manufacturing-Electronic (30), Robotics for:, ~ Professional Services (48)

Company Name: SapientRazorfish
Description:
Website: http://www.sapientrazorfish.com
Phone: 90 222 236 15 90 **Email:** 12747@reference-encyclopedia-ai.net
City: Bengaluru **State:** KA **Zip:** 560037 **Country:** India
Year Established: **Status 2020:** Active
Industries:

Company Name: Save Mom
Description: Save Mom offers wearable-based connected solutions, making a way for predictive healthcare systems.
Website: http://www.savemom.in/
Phone: 91 9361513147 **Email:** info@savemom.: India
City: Bengaluru **State:** KA **PC:** **Country:** India
Year Established: 2016 **Status 2020:** Active
Industries: ~ Healthcare (20), ~ Retail and Consumer Products (52), Predictive Analytics

Company Name: Sensefor:Thailand
Description: Senseforth is a leading Conversational AI solutions Company.
Website: http://www.senseforth.ai
Phone: **Email:** hi@senseforth.com
City: Bengaluru **State:** KA **PC:** **Country:** India
Year Established: 2017 **Status 2020:** Active
Industries: Artificial Intelligence for:, Application Services for:, Web for:, Machine Learning for:, Natural Language Processing for:, Natural Language Processing

Company Name: Senseforth Technologies Pvt Ltd
Description: Senseforth is a comprehensive bot platform built on AI
Website: http://www.senseforth.ai
Phone: **Email:** admin@senseforth.com
City: Bengaluru **State:** KA **PC:** **Country:** India
Year Established: **Status 2020:** Active
Industries: Artificial Intelligence for:, Enterprise Application Services for:, Application Services for:, Machine Learning for:, Natural Language Processing

Company Name: SensoVision Systems
Description: SensoVision is a technology development and consulting start-up in the domain of Computer Vision, Machine Learning & Drone Autonomy.
Website: http://sensoviz.com/index.html
Phone: 91 9880135487 **Email:** info@sensoviz.com
City: Bengaluru **State:** KA **PC:** **Country:** India
Year Established: 2015 **Status 2020:** Active
Industries: Computer Vision for:, Automation for:, Machine Learning

Company Name: Singulariti.ai
Description: Singulariti is an analytics company that uses machine learning and artificial intelligence to solve hard industry problems.
Website: http://www.singulariti.: India
Phone: **Email:** contact@singulariti.: India
City: Bengaluru **State:** KA **PC:** **Country:** India
Year Established: **Status 2020:** Active
Industries:

Company Name: Skillate
Description: Skillate optimises the recruitment cycle of enterprises using Artificial Intelligence.
Website: http://www.skillate.com
Phone: 91 9731502879 **Email:** contact@skillate.com
City: Bengaluru **State:** KA **PC:** **Country:** India
Year Established: **Status 2020:** Active
Industries: Artificial Intelligence for:, ~ Human Resources (24), Web for:, ~ Human Resources (24)

Company Name: Someshwara Software
Description: Someshwara Software provides AI, AR & VR and digital services.
Website: http://someshwara.com/
Phone: 91-9632159466 **Email:** hello@someshwara.com
City: Bengaluru **State:** KA **PC:** **Country:** India

Year Established: 2014 **Status 2020:** Active
Industries: Artificial Intelligence for:, Augmented Reality for:, Virtual Reality (VR)

Company Name: Spektacom
Description: Spektacom is a technology company that aims to revolutionize sports using sensor technologies.
Website: http://spektacom.com
Phone: **Email:** info@spektacom.com
City: Bengaluru **State:** KA **PC:** **Country:** India
Year Established: 2017 **Status 2020:** Active
Industries: Analytics for:, Machine Learning for:, ~ Arts-Entertainment-Recreation (4)

Company Name: Spookfish Innovations
Description: Computer Vision and Industrial Automation
Website: http://www.spookfish.: India
Phone: **Email:** connect@spookfish.: India
City: Bengaluru **State:** KA **PC:** **Country:** India
Year Established: 2015 **Status 2020:** Active
Industries: Artificial Intelligence for:, Computer Vision for:, Automation for:, Machine Learning for:, ~ Manufacturing-General (31)

Company Name: Startup Planner
Description: Startup Planner is an online self-incubator for the startup. This AI powered tool helps entrepreneurs to build a market fit product.
Website: http://www.startupplanner.io/
Phone: 91 9901622788 **Email:** satisha@leangears.com
City: Bengaluru **State:** KA **PC:** **Country:** India
Year Established: **Status 2020:** Active
Industries: Artificial Intelligence for:, ~ Professional Services (48)

Company **Name:** Stodict
Description: AI Powered Real-Time hyperlocal Information Discovery Platform
Website: http://www.stodict.com/
Phone: 8543048894 **Email:** sales@stodict.com
City: Bengaluru **State:** KA **PC:** **Country:** India
Year Established: **Status 2020:** Active
Industries: Artificial Intelligence

Company Name: Stylumia Intelligence Technology
Description: Stylumia enables boosting full-price sales, profit and reduce inventory using real-time fashion intelligence tools.
Website: http://www.stylumia.com/
Phone: 91-95828-05661 **Email:** sales@stylumia.com
City: Bengaluru **State:** KA **PC:** **Country:** India
Year Established: 2015 **Status 2020:** Closed
Industries: Artificial Intelligence

Company Name: Supertext
Description: Supertext helps Businesses/Brands automate customer support and service using custom chatbots
Website: http://supertextnow.com/
Phone: **Email:** engage@supertextnow.com
City: Bengaluru **State:** KA **PC:** **Country:** India
Year Established: **Status 2020:** Active
Industries: Artificial Intelligence for:, Business Applications for:, Application Services for:, Machine Learning for:, Mobile for:, Natural Language Processing

Company Name: SwitchOn
Description: SwitchOn is an Edge-AI enabled Industrial IoT company
Website: http://switchon.io/
Phone: 91 8105006717 **Email:** info@switchon.io
City: Bengaluru **State:** KA **PC:** **Country:** India
Year Established: 2017 **Status 2020:** Active
Industries: Artificial Intelligence for:, ~ Automotive (5), Automation for:, ~ Manufacturing-General (31), Internet of Things (IoT)

Company Name: Synapptra
Description: Synapptra places human occupants, their well-being and comfort as the focal point of commercial spaces.
Website: http://www.synapptra.com/
Phone: 91 98453 16810 **Email:** sales@synapptra.com
City: Bengaluru **State:** KA **PC:** **Country:** India
Year Established: 2017 **Status 2020:** Active
Industries: Artificial Intelligence for:, ~ Energy and Utilities (14), Automation for:, Business Software as a Service Apps (SaaS Apps)

Company Name: Team Indus
Description: TeamIndus builds a privately funded spacecraft capable of soft landing on the moon by 2017.
Website: http://www.teamindus.in/
Phone: 91 80 4666 7100 **Email:** peoplecapital@teamindus.: India
City: Bengaluru **State:** KA **PC:** **Country:** India
Year Established: **Status 2020:** Active
Industries: ~ Aerospace and Defense (2), Artificial Intelligence for:, ~ Aerospace and Defense (2)

Company Name: Thunder Products
Description: Machine Learning and AI
Website: http://www.thunderproducts.co
Phone: 9177854477 **Email:** contact@thunderbuzz.net
City: Bengaluru **State:** KA **PC:** **Country:** India
Year Established: 2019 **Status 2020:** Active
Industries: ~ Banking and Financial Markets-Services (7), Machine Learning

Company Name: Trialkart
Description: Trialkart is virtual trial and deep learning company providing various proprietary technology solutions and experiences to its customers.
Website: http://trialkart.com
Phone: **Email:** jaya@trialkart.com
City: Bengaluru **State:** KA **PC:** **Country:** India
Year Established: 2015 **Status 2020:** Active
Industries: Artificial Intelligence for:, ~ Education (13), IT Managed Services

Company Name: TriOcula Technologies
Description: AR and AI based Surgical Navigation and Simulato: Serbia
Website: http://triocula.com
Phone: **Email:** hello@triocula.com
City: Bengaluru **State:** KA **PC:** **Country:** India
Year Established: 2016 **Status 2020:** Active
Industries:

Company Name: Tripeur
Description: Conversational Commerce in Enterprise Travel
Website: http://www.tripeur.com/
Phone: 91 9845101570 **Email:** sajit@tripeur.com
City: Bengaluru **State:** KA **PC:** **Country:** India
Year Established: 2015 **Status 2020:** Active
Industries: Artificial Intelligence for:, IT Managed Services for:, Machine Learning

Company Name: TrustCheckr
Description: A Bengaluru-based fraud analytics solution provider .
Website: http://www.trustcheckr.com
Phone: **Email:** hello@trustcheckr.com
City: Bengaluru **State:** KA **PC:** **Country:** India
Year Established: 2017 **Status 2020:** Active
Industries: Artificial Intelligence for:, Security for:, IT Managed Services for:, Web

Company Name: Twixor
Description: Twixor : An Actionable Messaging solution platform for Enterprises backed by a powerful workflow automation engine.
Website: http://www.twixor.com
Phone: (91) 44 6888 8010 **Email:** info@twixor.com
City: Bengaluru **State:** KA **PC:** **Country:** India

Year Established: **Status 2020:** Active
Industries: Artificial Intelligence for:, ~ Telecommunications (56)

Company Name: Wipro Technologies
Description:
Website: http://www.wipro.com
Phone: 7 495 540 50 55 (RU) **Email:** n.semenov@yadro.com
City: Bengaluru **State:** KA **Zip:** 560 035 **Country:** India
Year Established: **Status 2020:** Active
Industries:

Company Name: Zoyo AI
Description: Your Intelligent Shopping Assistant On Chat
Website: http://zoyo.ai/
Phone: **Email:** 37744@reference-encyclopedia-ai.net
City: Bengaluru **State:** KA **PC:** **Country:** India
Year Established: 2015 **Status 2020:** Active
Industries: Artificial Intelligence for:, E-Commerce

Company Name: AlienHu
Description: An AI Driven Virtual Neutral Network of Suppliers, Merchants & Consumers for Local Market or Offline Market.
Website: http://alienhu.com/
Phone: **Email:** support@alienhu.com
City: Dandeli **State:** KA **PC:** **Country:** India
Year Established: 2016 **Status 2020:** Active
Industries: Artificial Intelligence for:, IT Managed Services for:, Web

Company Name: Bankbuddy.ai
Description: Financial Technology providing Artificial Intelligence solutions to help FI's Automate, Analyze & Assist stakeholder interactions
Website: http://www.bankbuddy.ai/
Phone: **Email:** info@bankbuddy.ai
City: Dubai **State:** KA **PC:** **Country:** India
Year Established: **Status 2020:** Active
Industries: Artificial Intelligence for:, Enterprise Application Services for:, ~ Banking and Financial Markets-Services (7), ~ Insurance (25), Machine Learning for:, Natural Language Processing for:, ~ Professional Services (48)

Company Name: Docketrun
Description: Docketrun is an AI platform that makes it Easy to Activate, Use, and Deploy AI-based API Services to build Intelligent Applications.
Website: http://www.docketrun.com/
Phone: **Email:** tech@docketrun.com
City: Hubli **State:** KA **PC:** **Country:** India
Year Established: 2018 **Status 2020:** Active
Industries: Artificial Intelligence for:, Application Program Interfaces (APIs) for:, IT Managed Services

Company Name: Kooki
Description: Kooki is an AI startup developing multilingual speech recognition and NLP for next billion people.
Website: http://www.kooki.com
Phone: **Email:** support@kooki.com
City: Hubli **State:** KA **PC:** **Country:** India
Year Established: **Status 2020:** Active
Industries: Artificial Intelligence for:, ~ Manufacturing-Electronic (30)

Company Name: PhotographAI
Description: PhotographAI is a technology platform with ready-to-use machine learning solutions for businesses.
Website: http://www.photographai.com
Phone: **Email:** 37164@reference-encyclopedia-ai.net
City: Kormangala **State:** KA **PC:** **Country:** India
Year Established: 2017 **Status 2020:** Active
Industries: IT Managed Services for:, Machine Learning

Company Name: Vanora Robots
Description: Vanora Robots is a technology company developing products and technology for automated homes.
Website: http://www.vanorarobots.com
Phone: **Email:** info@vanorarobots.com
City: Mangalore **State:** KA **PC:** **Country:** India
Year Established: **Status 2020:** Active
Industries: Artificial Intelligence for:, ~ Manufacturing-Electronic (30), Robotics

Company Name: ElkanIO Research Labs
Description: ElkanIO Research Labs provides AI chatbot, advanced data analytics, and RPA solutions.
Website: http://www.elkanio.com/
Phone: 91-94 00 74 74 84 **Email:** hello@elkanio.com
City: Cochin **State:** KL **PC:** **Country:** India
Year Established: 2017 **Status 2020:** Active
Industries: Artificial Intelligence for:, IT Managed Services for:, Machine Learning

Company Name: ZappyHire
Description: ZappyHire serves as an AI-driven hiring platform.
Website: http://www.zappyhire.com/
Phone: 9901276899 **Email:** admin@zappyhire.com
City: Cochin **State:** KL **PC:** **Country:** India
Year Established: 2018 **Status 2020:** Active
Industries: Artificial Intelligence

Company Name: Dexlock
Description: Dexlock offers specialized services in Big Data, Machine Learning, Android, iOS development and Cloud services.
Website: http://www.dexlock.com
Phone: (484) 404-2222 **Email:** info@dexlock.com
City: Ernakulam **State:** KL **PC:** **Country:** India
Year Established: 2012 **Status 2020:** Active
Industries:

Company Name: Articbot
Description: Articbot is a conversational AI platform for automated customer support and lead generation
Website: http://www.articbot.com/
Phone: **Email:** agent@articbot.com
City: Kannur **State:** KL **PC:** **Country:** India
Year Established: 2017 **Status 2020:** Active
Industries: Artificial Intelligence for:, IT Managed Services

Company Name: Accubits Technoogies Inc
Description: Accubits is an AI and BLOCKCHAIN focused development and solutions company.
Website: http://www.accubits.com/
Phone: **Email:** jithinvg@accubits.com
City: Kochi **State:** KL **PC:** **Country:** India
Year Established: 2012 **Status 2020:** Active
Industries:

Company Name: IntelliOak Technologies
Description: IntelliOak Technologies is an AI Based Intelligent Recruitment Platform
Website:
Phone: **Email:** 36792@reference-encyclopedia-ai.net
City: Kochi **State:** KL **PC:** **Country:** India
Year Established: 2018 **Status 2020:** Active
Industries: Artificial Intelligence for:, Machine Learning

Company Name: Peergauge
Description: Peergauge is a cloud-based people analytics platform which helps organizations to measure, analyze and improve employee engagement.
Website: http://peergauge.com/
Phone: 91 9633446762 **Email:** contact@peergauge.com
City: Kochi **State:** KL **PC:** **Country:** India
Year Established: 2017 **Status 2020:** Active
Industries: Analytics for:, Predictive Analytics

Company Name: PixDynamics
Description: PixDynamics is IT solutions and services ensures that customers are smoothly transitioned to the new paradigm of Software development.
Website: http://pixdynamics.com/
Phone: 91 8089 992 111 **Email:** connect@pixdynamics.com
City: Kochi **State:** KL **PC:** **Country:** India
Year Established: 2017 **Status 2020:** Active
Industries: Artificial Intelligence for:, IT Managed Services for:, IT Managed Services for:, IT Managed Services

Company Name: Riafy Technologies
Description: Riafy uses Relational Intelligence on Big Data to predict the future.
Website: http://www.riafy.me/
Phone: **Email:** 37299@reference-encyclopedia-ai.net
City: Kochi **State:** KL **PC:** **Country:** India
Year Established: 2013 **Status 2020:** Active
Industries: Predictive Analytics

Company Name: Technisanct
Description: Big Data and Cyber Security Startup
Website: http://www.goldeneagleai.com/
Phone: **Email:** GDurendal@gmail.com
City: Kochi **State:** KL **PC:** **Country:** India
Year Established: **Status 2020:** Active
Industries: Artificial Intelligence for:, Big Data and Analytics for:, Cyber Security for:, Machine Learning

Company Name: Callbell Security
Description: AI Cyber Security Company
Website: http://www.callbellsecurity.com
Phone: (907) 435-5803 **Email:** info@callbellsecurity.com
City: Kozhikode **State:** KL **PC:** **Country:** India
Year Established: 2017 **Status 2020:** Active
Industries: Artificial Intelligence for:, Big Data and Analytics for:, Cyber Security

Company Name: Klowdx
Description: We are an Indian startup company focusing on app development and digital marketing.
Website: http://www.klowdx.io
Phone: **Email:** adil@klowdx.io
City: Kozhikode **State:** KL **PC:** **Country:** India
Year Established: **Status 2020:** Active
Industries: Artificial Intelligence for:, Digital Marketing for:, Machine Learning for:, Application Services for:, ~ Social Media (54), ~ Social Media (54), ~ Social Media (54), Cyber Security

Company Name: Wudi
Description: Wudi is a social tech start-up with a mission to create affordable Artificial Intelligence (AI) driven systems & free educational softwares.
Website: http://www.datawudi.com/
Phone: **Email:** team@datawudi.com
City: Kunnamangalam **State:** KL **PC:** **Country:** India
Year Established: 2017 **Status 2020:** Active
Industries: Artificial Intelligence for:, IT Managed Services for:, IT Managed Services for:, Robotics

Company Name: Cogniphi Technologies
Description: Cogniphi Technologies is technology company that enables customers to achieve transformational outcomes through cognitive digital solutions.
Website: http://www.cogniphi.com/
Phone: 0471 2700060 **Email:** connect@cogniphi.com
City: Trivandrum **State:** KL **PC:** **Country:** India
Year Established: 2015 **Status 2020:** Active
Industries: Artificial Intelligence for:, IT Managed Services

Company Name: GenRobotic
Description: A Robotic Company.
Website: http://www.genrobotics.org/
Phone: **Email:** info@genrobotics.org
City: Trivandrum **State:** KL **PC:** **Country:** India
Year Established: 2015 **Status 2020:** Active
Industries: Artificial Intelligence

Company Name: CUREORE
Description: Cureore is consultant in healthcare and wellness industry helping user and their family to mitigate healthcare maze.
Website: http://www.cureore.com
Phone: 9333109333 **Email:** info@cureore.com
City: Bhopal **State:** MP **PC:** **Country:** India
Year Established: **Status 2020:** Active
Industries: Artificial Intelligence for:, ~ Healthcare (20), ~ Healthcare (20), ~ Healthcare (20), ~ Healthcare (20)

Company Name: Finchfly
Description: Finchfly simplifies advertising with social media influencers using it's Artificial Intelligence Technology.
Website: http://www.finchfly.com
Phone: 91 700-084-7396 **Email:** hello@finchfly.com
City: Bhopal **State:** MP **PC:** **Country:** India
Year Established: 2018 **Status 2020:** Active
Industries:

Company Name: Vizzbee
Description: Autonomous Drone Solutions for last mile delivery as well as search and rescue
Website: http://vizzbee.com
Phone: 91-91784 17068 **Email:** info@vizzbee.com
City: Bhopal **State:** MP **PC:** **Country:** India
Year Established: **Status 2020:** Active
Industries: Artificial Intelligence for:, ~ Transportation and Logistics (57), ~ Transportation and Logistics (57), ~ Transportation and Logistics (57), Robotics

Company Name: accession
Description: UX, UI, Web and Mobile Application Development Services, Artificial Intelligence, IoT
Website: https://www.accessionn.com/
Phone: **Email:** sales@accessionsoftware.com
City: Indore **State:** MP **PC:** **Country:** India
Year Established: 2018 **Status 2020:** Active
Industries: Artificial Intelligence for:, IT Managed Services

Company Name: Annova Solutions Pvt Ltd
Description: Your growth partner in AI and Machine Learning, Healthcare Operations, Computer Vision Services and more...
Website: http://annovasolutions.com/
Phone: **Email:** 36063@reference-encyclopedia-ai.net
City: Indore **State:** MP **PC:** **Country:** India
Year Established: 2016 **Status 2020:** Active
Industries: Artificial Intelligence for:, ~ Customer Relationship Management (11), ~ Healthcare (20), Machine Learning for:, Business Process and Operations

Company Name: Aphelion Labs
Description: A consulting company that leverages AI and deep analytical technologies for marketing, insights & business growth.
Website: http://www.aphelion.: India
Phone: **Email:** hi@aphelion.: India
City: Indore **State:** MP **PC:** **Country:** India
Year Established: 2016 **Status 2020:** Active
Industries: Analytics for:, Artificial Intelligence for:, Business Intelligence for:, Enterprise Application Services for:, Machine Learning

Company Name: Bingage
Description: Ai-enabled Marketing suite for restaurants to increase ROI.
Website: http://bingage.com/
Phone: (750) 902-5257 **Email:** info@bingage.com
City: Indore **State:** MP **PC:** **Country:** India
Year Established: 2017 **Status 2020:** Active
Industries: ~ Retail and Consumer Products (52), Machine Learning for:, ~ Food and Beverage (17), Business Software as a Service Apps (SaaS Apps)

Company Name: Codiant Software Technologies Pvt. Ltd.
Description: Codiant is one of the leading web and mobile app development company with regional offices in USA, UK and India.
Website: http://www.codiant.com
Phone: (309)278-0633 **Email:** im@codiant.com
City: Indore **State:** MP **PC:** **Country:** India
Year Established: **Status 2020:** Active
Industries: Application Services for:, Artificial Intelligence for:, Augmented Reality for:, Big Data and Analytics for:, Cloud for:, E-Commerce for:, Enterprise Application Services for:, IT Managed Services for:, Application Services for:, ~ Professional Services (48), Cyber

Company Name: FintastIQ
Description: FintastIQ is world's first and largest Trading Strategy Marketplace. We provide AI based and ML enabled solution to investors.
Website: http://www.fintastiq.com
Phone: 91 8085 999 333 **Email:** marketing@capitalvia.com
City: Indore **State:** MP **PC:** **Country:** India
Year Established: 2019 **Status 2020:** Active
Industries: Artificial Intelligence for:, ~ Banking and Financial Markets-Services (7)

Company Name: NeuraTech Innovations
Description: Innovating today, for a better tomorrow.
Website: http://www.neuratech.co
Phone: 994-330-6662 **Email:** contact@neuratech.co
City: Indore **State:** MP **PC:** **Country:** India
Year Established: **Status 2020:** Active
Industries: Artificial Intelligence for:, Human Computer Interaction for:, ~ Professional Services (48)

Company Name: Pwave Technologies
Description: Pwave Technologies provides medical software based services.
Website: http://pwavetech.com
Phone: 91-916-5640007 **Email:** info@pwavetech.com
City: Indore **State:** MP **PC:** **Country:** India
Year Established: **Status 2020:** Active
Industries: Artificial Intelligence for:, ~ Healthcare (20), ~ Professional Services (48)

Company Name: Techrefic Technologies Private Limited
Description: Techrefic is redefining the technologies like AI, ML, NLP, RPA, IPA, IOT, Web/Mobile Development, PG Integrations Technology Integrations.
Website: http://www.techrefic.com
Phone: **Email:** info@techrefic.com
City: Indore **State:** MP **PC:** **Country:** India
Year Established: 2017 **Status 2020:** Active
Industries: Artificial Intelligence for:, IT Managed Services for:, Robotics

Company Name: ThePolitics.: India
Description: A platform for disseminating knowledge about the polity, politics & policies with the aim of strengthening the democracy.
Website: http://thepolitics.: India
Phone: 91-731-4975323 **Email:** info@thepolitics.: India
City: Indore **State:** MP **PC:** **Country:** India
Year Established: **Status 2020:** Active
Industries: Artificial Intelligence for:, Big Data and Analytics for:, Business Intelligence for:, Machine Learning for:, Natural Language Processing for:, ~ Politics (47)

Company Name: Cloud: Ireland
Description: India's First Super App
Website: http://cloudie.co.in/
Phone: 7038685635 **Email:** mohitdhanwani12345@gmail.com
City: Akola **State:** MH **PC:** **Country:** India
Year Established: **Status 2020:** Active
Industries: Artificial Intelligence for:, Content for:, E-Commerce for:, Mobile for:, ~ Social Media (54)

Company Name: aPLS Web Development
Description: Web Development, App Development, Software Development, Data Analytics, Data Science, IOT
Website: http://apls.work
Phone: **Email:** nb@apls.work
City: Aurangabad **State:** MH **PC:** **Country:** India
Year Established: 2014 **Status 2020:** Active
Industries: Artificial Intelligence

Company Name: PeAr Technologi
Description: PeAr Technologies is a deep-tech and artificial intelligence-focussed startup
Website: http://www.peartechnologies.biz/
Phone: **Email:** infopeartechnologies@gmail.com
City: Ghatkopar **State:** MH **PC:** **Country:** India
Year Established: 2018 **Status 2020:** Active
Industries:

Company Name: Superbot
Description: Superbot is an AI to get things done and discover things nearby
Website: http://superbotapp.com/
Phone: **Email:** contact@voverosoftware.com
City: Jalgaon **State:** MH **PC:** **Country:** India
Year Established: **Status 2020:** Active
Industries: Application Services for:, Artificial Intelligence for:, Mobile

Company Name: Altorise
Description: A creative tech startup - we help brands grow online from better digital branding, stronger customer relationships, and data insights.
Website: http://altorise.com/
Phone: 91 22 3996 7473 **Email:** hi@altorise.com
City: Kandivli **State:** MH **PC:** **Country:** India
Year Established: 2014 **Status 2020:** Active
Industries: Artificial Intelligence for:, Big Data and Analytics for:, IT Managed Services for:, Machine Learning for:, ~ Social Assistance-Non-Profits (53)

Company Name: 1 Martian Way
Description: 1 Martian Way (1MW) is an Artificial Intelligence company based in Mumbai, India
Website: http://1martianway.com/
Phone: **Email:** sales@1martianway.com
City: Mumbai **State:** MH **PC:** **Country:** India
Year Established: 2014 **Status 2020:** Active
Industries: Artificial Intelligence for:, Robotics

Company Name: Accelo Innovation
Description: Accelo Innovation is an artificial intelligence firm.
Website: http://www.accelo.io/
Phone: **Email:** 35940@reference-encyclopedia-ai.net
City: Mumbai **State:** MH **PC:** **Country:** India
Year Established: 2016 **Status 2020:** Active
Industries: Artificial Intelligence for:, IT Managed Services

Company Name: Adoro Marketplace
Description: An Artificial Intelligence based hyper-personal shopping platform
Website: http://www.adoro.: India
Phone: **Email:** care@adoro.: India
City: Mumbai **State:** MH **PC:** **Country:** India
Year Established: **Status 2020:** Active
Industries: Artificial Intelligence for:, E-Commerce for:, ~ Fashion (16), ~ Media-Communications (41), ~ Social Media (54)

Company **Name:** Aiozium
Description: Aiozium - SaaS-Based Marketing Intelligence Tool Powered by AI
Website: http://www.aiozium.com/
Phone: 91-99208-31975 **Email:** hello@aiozium.com
City: Mumbai **State:** MH **PC:** **Country:** India
Year Established: **Status 2020:** Active
Industries: Artificial Intelligence

Company Name: AllinCall
Description: FinTech, SaaS, Technology
Website: http://www.allincall.in/
Phone: **Email:** aman@allincall.: India
City: Mumbai **State:** MH **PC:** **Country:** India
Year Established: 2017 **Status 2020:** Active
Industries: Artificial Intelligence for:, ~ Banking and Financial Markets-Services (7), Business Software as a Service Apps (SaaS Apps)

Company Name: Ananto
Description: Big Data Analytics Solutions & Service
Website: http://www.ananto.com
Phone: 91 80 80 701234 **Email:** ashima.suri@ananto.com
City: Mumbai **State:** MH **PC:** **Country:** India
Year Established: 2013 **Status 2020:** Active
Industries: Analytics for:, Big Data and Analytics for:, Business Intelligence for:, Predictive Analytics

Company Name: Apex Infosys India
Description: Apex Infosys India is a global technology and innovation company that specializes in IoT-related services and products.
Website: http://www.apexinfosys.: India
Phone: **Email:** info@apexinfosys.: India
City: Mumbai **State:** MH **PC:** **Country:** India
Year Established: 2017 **Status 2020:** Active
Industries: Artificial Intelligence for:, Digital Marketing for:, Internet of Things (IoT)

Company Name: Appectual IT Solutions - Mobile App Development
Description: Mobile App Development Company - Appectual IT Solutions based in Mumbai that delivers Android & IOS App Designs and Development services.
Website: http://www.appectual.com
Phone: 91 7738 14 15 39 **Email:** info@appectual.com
City: Mumbai **State:** MH **PC:** **Country:** India
Year Established: **Status 2020:** Active
Industries: Artificial Intelligence for:, Machine Learning for:, Application Services for:, Cyber Security

Company Name: ArrowAI
Description: ArrowAI Bot Based Applications can be used for various things like Automating Processes, Executing Workflows, Reporting.
Website: http://arrowai.com
Phone: 91 993-633-9580 **Email:** contact@arrowai.comv
City: Mumbai **State:** MH **PC:** **Country:** India
Year Established: 2016 **Status 2020:** Active
Industries: Artificial Intelligence for:, IT Managed Services

Company Name: Arya.ai
Description: Arya.ai is a Deep Learning platform offering multiple tools to build, manage and scale complex Deep Learning applications.
Website: http://arya.ai
Phone: **Email:** 36093@reference-encyclopedia-ai.net
City: Mumbai **State:** MH **PC:** **Country:** India
Year Established: 2013 **Status 2020:** Active
Industries: Artificial Intelligence for:, Internet of Things (IoT)

Company Name: AspectWi: Sweden
Description: Find the right products for the qualities that matter to you, using combined intelligence from opinions of real users.
Website: http://www.aspectwise.: India
Phone: **Email:** 36100@reference-encyclopedia-ai.net
City: Mumbai **State:** MH **PC:** **Country:** India
Year Established: 2016 **Status 2020:** Active
Industries: Artificial Intelligence for:, Big Data and Analytics for:, ~ Social Assistance-Non-Profits (53)

Company Name: Autosys Industrial Solutions Private Limited
Description: Industrial Automation Solutions
Website: http://www.autosys.xyz
Phone: 91-961-969-5774 **Email:** info@autosys.xyz
City: Mumbai **State:** MH **PC:** **Country:** India
Year Established: **Status 2020:** Active
Industries:

Company Name: Ayu Devices
Description: Hear between the beats with AI-enabled digital stethosco:
Website: http://ayudevices.com
Phone: -8369059491 **Email:** contact@ayudevices.som
City: Mumbai **State:** MH **PC:** **Country:** India
Year Established: **Status 2020:** Active
Industries: Artificial Intelligence for:, ~ Healthcare (20), ~ Healthcare (20), ~ Healthcare (20), Machine Learning for:, ~ Healthcare (20), ~ Manufacturing-Medical Equipment-Supplies (33), ~ Healthcare (20)

Company Name: BindasJobs
Description: Bindas Jobs is an employment and skilling marketplace which connects companies and blue collar job seekers.
Website: http://bindasjobs.com/
Phone: 91 99202 58866 **Email:** support@bindasjobs.com
City: Mumbai **State:** MH **PC:** **Country:** India
Year Established: 2016 **Status 2020:** Active
Industries:

Company Name: Bizlem
Description: Bizlem is a web social business platform specializing in the area of artificial intelligence and natural language processing.
Website: http://bizlem.com
Phone: **Email:** devna@bizlem.com
City: Mumbai **State:** MH **PC:** **Country:** India
Year Established: 2017 **Status 2020:** Active
Industries: Artificial Intelligence for:, IT Managed Services for:, Machine Learning for:, Natural Language Processing

Company Name: Blubyn
Description: We are an AI powered travel portal where you can discover, search and book flights, hotels and experiences by just sending a message.
Website: http://www.blubyn.com
Phone: **Email:** ankit@blubyn.com
City: Mumbai **State:** MH **PC:** **Country:** India
Year Established: **Status 2020:** Active
Industries: Artificial Intelligence for:, Natural Language Processing for:, ~ Travel and Transportation (58), Web

Company Name: Capshun
Description: Mobile App
Website: http://www.capshun.co/
Phone: 91-9987782216 **Email:** info@capshun.co
City: Mumbai **State:** MH **PC:** **Country:** India
Year Established: **Status 2020:** Active
Industries: Artificial Intelligence for:, Content for:, Machine Learning for:, ~ Social Media (54)

Company **Name:** CarrotBox Technologies
Description: SaaS, Marketing AI, Customer Engagement, Rewards & Loyalty
Website:
Phone: **Email:** 4951@reference-encyclopedia-ai.net
City: Mumbai **State:** MH **PC:** **Country:** India
Year Established: **Status 2020:** Active
Industries: Artificial Intelligence for:, ~ Media-Communications (41), ~ Retail and Consumer Products (52)

Company Name: CVViZ
Description: CVViZ is an Artificial Intelligence powered, cloud based solution for your recruitment.
Website: http://www.cvviz.com
Phone: 91-9860736361 **Email:** amit.gawande@cvviz.com
City: Mumbai **State:** MH **PC:** **Country:** India
Year Established: **Status 2020:** Active
Industries: Artificial Intelligence for:, IT Managed Services for:, Machine Learning

Company Name: Deep Trading
Description: Utilizing mass deep learning algorithms in finance
Website: http://www.deeptrading.com
Phone: **Email:** info@deeptrading.com
City: Mumbai **State:** MH **PC:** **Country:** India
Year Established: 2016 **Status 2020:** Active
Industries: Artificial Intelligence for:, ~ Education (13), ~ Banking and Financial Markets-Services (7), ~ Banking and Financial Markets-Services (7)

Company Name: Dinomeals
Description: DinoMeals is a technology company bringing Artificial Intelligence & Virtual Reality to the Hospitality Industry, the first in the segment.
Website: http://dinomeals.com
Phone: **Email:** support@dinomeals.com
City: Mumbai **State:** MH **PC:** **Country:** India
Year Established: **Status 2020:** Active
Industries: Artificial Intelligence for:, ~ Hospitality (23), IT Managed Services for:, Web for:, ~ Food and Beverage (17)

Company Name: Doc Care
Description: Doc Care is the healthcare Technology company providing healthcare Solutions & services by employing tech innovation to Indian market.
Website: http://www.doccare.co.: India
Phone: **Email:** jk.singha@docareathome.com
City: Mumbai **State:** MH **PC:** **Country:** India
Year Established: **Status 2020:** Active
Industries: Artificial Intelligence for:, ~ Healthcare (20), ~ Healthcare (20), ~ Healthcare (20), IT Managed Services for:, ~ Healthcare (20)

Company Name: Docsumo
Description: Docsumo automates data entry and provides a fast, accurate & simple way to convert PDF & image documents to digitized data.
Website: http://www.docsumo.com/
Phone: **Email:** hello@docsumo.com
City: Mumbai **State:** MH **PC:** **Country:** India
Year Established: **Status 2020:** Active
Industries: Finance and Accounting for:, Artificial Intelligence for:, ~ Professional Services (48), Cyber Security

Company Name: Firmway
Description: Firmway is a platform that digitizes balance confirmation and reconciliation process.
Website: http://firmway.: India
Phone: (91) 9769 599848 **Email:** support@firmway.: India
City: Mumbai **State:** MH **PC:** **Country:** India
Year Established: 2016 **Status 2020:** Active
Industries: ~ Banking and Financial Markets-Services (7), Machine Learning for:, IT Managed Services

Company Name: Fisheyebox
Description: Fisheyebox is to creates music with Artificial Intelligence.
Website: http://www.fisheyebox.com
Phone: 91 7506590059 **Email:** info@fisheyebox.com
City: Mumbai **State:** MH **PC:** **Country:** India
Year Established: 2013 **Status 2020:** Active
Industries: Artificial Intelligence for:, ~ Arts-Entertainment-Recreation (4)

Company Name: FitCircle
Description: Start your journey to #aBetterYou with Clean Nutrition Products and an AI Powered Fitness Companion
Website: http://www.fitcircle.in/
Phone: **Email:** stayfit@fitcircle.: India
City: Mumbai **State:** MH **PC:** **Country:** India
Year Established: 2014 **Status 2020:** Active
Industries:

Company Name: FitPhilia Solutions Private Limited
Description: We help people make fitness a habit by driving behavioral change towards fitness
Website: http://fitphilia.com
Phone: 91 7829-117-991 **Email:** nirav@fitphilia.com
City: Mumbai **State:** MH **PC:** **Country:** India
Year Established: 2015 **Status 2020:** Active
Industries: Artificial Intelligence for:, ~ Healthcare (20)

Company Name: Flickbay
Description: Flickbay is Bollywood's only official app
Website: http://flickbay.com/
Phone: **Email:** 36581@reference-encyclopedia-ai.net
City: Mumbai **State:** MH **PC:** **Country:** India
Year Established: 2012 **Status 2020:** Active
Industries: Artificial Intelligence for:, IT Managed Services for:, Machine Learning

Company Name: Flickstree
Description: Flickstree is a AI-enabled video publisher network that allows the user to engage and monetize their traffic.
Website: http://www.flickstree.com
Phone: **Email:** saurabh@flickstree.com
City: Mumbai **State:** MH **PC:** **Country:** India
Year Established: 2014 **Status 2020:** Active
Industries: ~ E-Commerce (12), Artificial Intelligence for:, ~ Media-Communications (41), ~ Media-Communications (41)

Company Name: FreightB: Romania
Description: Software for the new-age freight
Website: http://www.freightbro.com
Phone: (978)956-6668 **Email:** zakkiria@freightbro.com
City: Mumbai **State:** MH **PC:** **Country:** India
Year Established: **Status 2020:** Active
Industries: ~ Travel and Transportation (58), Application Services for:, Artificial Intelligence for:, Business Applications for:, Blockchain for:, E-Commerce for:, ~ Transportation and Logistics (57), ~ Transportation and Logistics (57), ~ Transportation and Logistics (57),

Company Name: Gade Autonomous Systems
Description: Gade Autonomous Systems aim to become a world leader in robotics domain by introducing state-of-the-art social and service robots.
Website: http://www.autonomous-systems.in/
Phone: 91 22 42957058 **Email:** 36606@reference-encyclopedia-ai.net
City: Mumbai **State:** MH **PC:** **Country:** India
Year Established: 2010 **Status 2020:** Active
Industries: Artificial Intelligence for:, Robotics

Company Name: GenieTalk
Description: GenieTalk as a virtual assistant uses AI to bring conversation commerce with a personalised experience on the app.
Website: http://genietalk.com/
Phone: **Email:** info@genietalk.com
City: Mumbai **State:** MH **PC:** **Country:** India
Year Established: **Status 2020:** Active
Industries: Artificial Intelligence for:, Machine Learning for:, ~ Travel and Transportation (58)

Company Name: GoHero.ai
Description: Hi! We're GoHero.ai . A personal concierge app with artificial human intelligence to find, plan and book all your travel needs on chat.
Website: http://www.gohero.ai/
Phone: 91 9920227244 **Email:** hello@gohero.ai
City: Mumbai **State:** MH **PC:** **Country:** India
Year Established: 2015 **Status 2020:** Active
Industries: Artificial Intelligence for:, ~ Arts-Entertainment-Recreation (4), ~ Travel and Transportation (58)

Company Name: GovEVA
Description: GovEVA provides end-to-end ESGC (Environment, Social, Governance, Compliance) solutions to drive superior outcom: Spain
Website: http://www.goveva.com/
Phone: 022 2481 1302 **Email:** office@intuit-consulting.com
City: Mumbai **State:** MH **PC:** **Country:** India
Year Established: 2016 **Status 2020:** Active
Industries: Artificial Intelligence for:, Enterprise Application Services for:, ~ Government (19), IT Managed Services for:, Web for:, Business Process and Operations

Company Name: G-Square Solutions Pvt. Ltd.
Description: Providing AI driven business analytics
Website: http://g-square.: India
Phone: 91 22 4347 0408 **Email:** info@g-square.: India
City: Mumbai **State:** MH **PC:** **Country:** India
Year Established: 2014 **Status 2020:** Active
Industries:

Company Name: Happy
Description: Happy is a digital lending platform offering short term loans using alternate data to micro-enterprises in India
Website: http://happyness.net/
Phone: **Email:** mk@happyness.net
City: Mumbai **State:** MH **PC:** **Country:** India
Year Established: 2016 **Status 2020:** Active
Industries: Artificial Intelligence for:, ~ Banking and Financial Markets-Services (7), ~ Banking and Financial Markets-Services (7)

Company Name: Haptik
Description: Conversational AI Platform
Website: http://haptik.ai/
Phone: **Email:** hello@haptik.co
City: Mumbai **State:** MH **PC:** **Country:** India
Year Established: 2013 **Status 2020:** Active
Industries: Artificial Intelligence for:, ~ Customer Relationship Management (11), Machine Learning for:, Compute

Company Name: HealWell24
Description: HealWell24 is India's emerging technology-Enabled healthcare company, providing Doctors, Diagnostics /Blood tests, B2B Digitised Healthcare.
Website: http://www.healwell24.com/
Phone: **Email:** care@healwell24.com
City: Mumbai **State:** MH **PC:** **Country:** India
Year Established: 2017 **Status 2020:** Active
Industries: Artificial Intelligence for:, ~ Healthcare (20), ~ Healthcare (20), Web

Company Name: Homeguard Securiti: Spain
Description: Better & Safer living through digitalising security of gated community (Society).
Website: http://www.homeguard.co.: India
Phone: 91-7838981669 **Email:** homeguard.society@gmail.com
City: Mumbai **State:** MH **PC:** **Country:** India
Year Established: **Status 2020:** Active
Industries: Artificial Intelligence for:, IT Managed Services for:, Application Services for:, ~ Real Estate (49), Security

Company Name: iKen Solutions Pvt. Ltd.
Description: iKen Solutions is a software product company specializing in consumer analytics products with Mooga as its flagship product.
Website: http://www.ikensolutions.com
Phone: (226) 518-2059 **Email:** iken@ikensolutions.com
City: Mumbai **State:** MH **PC:** **Country:** India
Year Established: **Status 2020:** Active
Industries:

Company Name: IntelliDataLytics
Description: Data Analytics, Database Solutions , Mobile apps , Web Solutions , Digital Marketing
Website: http://www.intellidatalytics.com
Phone: 91 9769859993 **Email:** info@intellidatalytics.com
City: Mumbai **State:** MH **PC:** **Country:** India
Year Established: 2015 **Status 2020:** Active
Industries: Analytics for:, Databases for:, Data Management for:, Databases for:, Digital Marketing for:, IT Managed Services for:, Application Services for:, Application Services for:, Predictive Analytics for:, Data Management

Company Name: Intelligence Node
Description: Price intelligence that redefines retail profitability.
Website: http://www.intelligencenode.com/
Phone: **Email:** contactus@intelligencenode.com
City: Mumbai **State:** MH **PC:** **Country:** India
Year Established: 2012 **Status 2020:** Active
Industries: Artificial Intelligence for:, Big Data and Analytics for:, Business Intelligence for:, E-Commerce for:, Machine Learning for:, Business Software as a Service Apps (SaaS Apps) for:, Business Software as a Service Apps (SaaS Apps)

Company Name: Intelligent Industrial Internet Systems Private Limited
Description: Data Analytics, Machine Learning, Natural Language Processing, Insurance Underwriting, Insurance Fraud Detection, Diagnostics Intelligence
Website: http://www.i3systems.in/
Phone: **Email:** contact@i3systems.: India
City: Mumbai **State:** MH **PC:** **Country:** India
Year Established: **Status 2020:** Active
Industries: Analytics for:, Artificial Intelligence for:, ~ Insurance (25), Machine Learning for:, Natural Language Processing

Company Name: Intusen Analytics
Description: Intusen Analytics is a Solve production issues 3X faster using a combination of anomaly detection in system data
Website: http://www.intusen.com/
Phone: **Email:** j.raynerk@gmail.com
City: Mumbai **State:** MH **PC:** **Country:** India
Year Established: 2017 **Status 2020:** Active
Industries: Artificial Intelligence for:, IT Managed Services for:, Web

Company Name: InvenZone
Description: InvenZone, niche social platform and vertical search for researchers and high end academic data.
Website: http://www.invenzone.com/
Phone: **Email:** info@invenzone.com
City: Mumbai **State:** MH **PC:** **Country:** India
Year Established: 2013 **Status 2020:** Closed
Industries: Artificial Intelligence for:, Web for:, Content for:, ~ Social Assistance-Non-Profits (53)

Company **Name:** IPHawk
Description: A transformation in which artificial-intelligence platforms dramatically affect how legal work gets done.
Website: http://www.iphawk.com/
Phone: 91.9890.891982 **Email:** 36808@reference-encyclopedia-ai.net
City: Mumbai **State:** MH **PC:** **Country:** India
Year Established: 2017 **Status 2020:** Active
Industries: Artificial Intelligence for:, ~ Automotive (5), Internet of Things (IoT) for:, Finance and Accounting

Company Name: Kyte
Description: Kyte is an intelligent SMS inbox.
Website: http://kyte.ai
Phone: **Email:** careers@kyte.ai
City: Mumbai **State:** MH **PC:** **Country:** India
Year Established: **Status 2020:** Active
Industries: Artificial Intelligence for:, Machine Learning for:, ~ Telecommunications (56)

Company Name: Miko
Description: Miko is an advanced robotics startup founded by three IIT Bombay post-graduates on the pillars of robotics, AI & IoT.
Website: http://www.miko.ai/
Phone: **Email:** careers@emotix.: India
City: Mumbai **State:** MH **PC:** **Country:** India
Year Established: 2015 **Status 2020:** Active
Industries: Artificial Intelligence for:, Robotics

Company Name: MockRabb: Italy
Description: MockRabbit, the world's first Natural Language Processing, Artificial Intelligence and Machine Learning based mock interview practice app.
Website: http://mockrabbit.com
Phone: 22-43435200 **Email:** info@mockrabbit.com
City: Mumbai **State:** MH **PC:** **Country:** India
Year Established: 2018 **Status 2020:** Active
Industries: Artificial Intelligence for:, ~ Education (13), Application Services

Company Name: Netcore Solutions
Description: Netcore offers AI Powered Growth Marketing Suite, Marketing Automation Solution, Marketing & Customer Analytics Solutions for enterprises.
Website: http://netcore.: India
Phone: 2266628100 **Email:** sales@netcore.co.: India
City: Mumbai **State:** MH **PC:** **Country:** India
Year Established: **Status 2020:** Active
Industries: Analytics for:, Artificial Intelligence for:, Cloud for:, Digital Marketing for:, ~ Media-Communications (41), Enterprise Application Services for:, ~ Media-Communications (41), ~ Media-Communications (41), Predictive Analytics for:, ~ Telecommunications (56)

Company Name: Newzz
Description: AI -based headlines aggregator website.
Website: http://newzz.: India
Phone: **Email:** newzz.care@gmail.com
City: Mumbai **State:** MH **PC:** **Country:** India
Year Established: 2019 **Status 2020:** Active
Industries: Artificial Intelligence for:, IT Managed Services

Company Name: Nuclete:
Description: Nucletech - Conversational Chatbot
Website: http://www.nucletech.com
Phone: **Email:** hello@nucletech.com
City: Mumbai **State:** MH **PC:** **Country:** India
Year Established: 2019 **Status 2020:** Active
Industries: Artificial Intelligence for:, IT Managed Services for:, Web for:, Mobile

Company Name: Occipital Tech
Description: Automating quality control in agriculture using computer vision and machine learning
Website: http://www.occipitaltech.com
Phone: **Email:** contact@occipitaltech.com
City: Mumbai **State:** MH **PC:** **Country:** India
Year Established: 2017 **Status 2020:** Active
Industries: Computer Vision for:, Automation for:, Machine Learning

Company Name: Orbo.ai
Description: Orbo is a computer vision and deep facial technology company.
Website: http://orbo.ai/
Phone: 91 8369 27 25 26 **Email:** support@orbo.ai
City: Mumbai **State:** MH **PC:** **Country:** India
Year Established: 2016 **Status 2020:** Active
Industries:

Company Name: ovonts
Description: An unified experiences, media and communication platform
Website: http://ovonts.com/
Phone: **Email:** manish@ovonts.com
City: Mumbai **State:** MH **PC:** **Country:** India
Year Established: 2019 **Status 2020:** Active
Industries: Big Data and Analytics for:, Content for:, ~ Event Management (15), IT Managed Services for:, Application Services

Company Name: Paletly
Description: Transform images into shopping windows.
Website: http://paletly.com
Phone: **Email:** suma@paletly.com
City: Mumbai **State:** MH **PC:** **Country:** India
Year Established: 2012 **Status 2020:** Active
Industries: E-Commerce for:, ~ Fashion (16), Image Recognition for:, Machine Learning for:, Web

Company Name: Pensieve
Description: Pensieve is an AI-based legal research platform that helps users draft, review, and analyze legal documents.
Website: http://www.pensieve.co.in/
Phone: **Email:** contact@pensieve.co.: India
City: Mumbai **State:** MH **PC:** **Country:** India
Year Established: 2016 **Status 2020:** Active
Industries: Artificial Intelligence for:, Machine Learning for:, Natural Language Processing

Company Name: Pentation Analytics
Description: Pentation as an Insurtech enables insurers and intermediaries with our Insurance Analytics Suite- an Insurance specific AI/ML Software Suite
Website: http://www.pentationanalytics.com/
Phone: 022 28583386 **Email:** contact@pentationanalytics.com
City: Mumbai **State:** MH **PC:** **Country:** India
Year Established: 2015 **Status 2020:** Active
Industries: Artificial Intelligence for:, IT Managed Services for:, IT Managed Services

Company Name: Pictor Imaging
Description: At Pictor, all come to work every day because we want to solve the biggest problem in product imaging.
Website: http://www.getpictor.com/
Phone: 2265366999 **Email:** siddharth@getpictor.com
City: Mumbai **State:** MH **PC:** **Country:** India
Year Established: 2015 **Status 2020:** Active
Industries: Computer Vision for:, Machine Learning

Company Name: Presciente.com
Description: Presciente is a technology startup focused on providing machine learning, IOT and data science service to customers.
Website: http://www.presciente.com
Phone: **Email:** 37203@reference-encyclopedia-ai.net
City: Mumbai **State:** MH **PC:** **Country:** India
Year Established: 2016 **Status 2020:** Active
Industries: Business Intelligence for:, Databases for:, Machine Learning for:, Natural Language Processing

Company Name: Quantta Analytics
Description: Quantta is passionate about using big data and artificial intelligence to understand and predict human behavior.
Website: http://www.quantta.com
Phone: **Email:** consult.us@quantta.com
City: Mumbai **State:** MH **PC:** **Country:** India

Year Established: 2012 **Status 2020:** Active
Industries: Business Software as a Service Apps (SaaS Apps)

Company Name: Quickwork
Description: Business Automation using Artifical Intelligence and Chatbots. Quickly!
Website: http://www.quickwork.co
Phone: **Email:** marketing@quickwork.co
City: Mumbai **State:** MH **PC:** **Country:** India
Year Established: **Status 2020:** Active
Industries: Artificial Intelligence for:, Enterprise Application Services for:, ~ Media-Communications (41), Automation

Company Name: Qure AI
Description: build deep learning solutions that aid physicians with routine diagnosis and treatment, allowing them to spend more time with patients
Website: http://qure.ai/
Phone: **Email:** careers@qure.ai
City: Mumbai **State:** MH **PC:** **Country:** India
Year Established: 2016 **Status 2020:** Active
Industries: Artificial Intelligence for:, ~ Healthcare (20), ~ Healthcare (20)

Company Name: Recommender Labs
Description: Recommender Labs design meets technology to create machine learning-based applications that generate personalized recommendations.
Website: http://www.recommenderlabs.com/
Phone: **Email:** sales@recommenderlabs.com
City: Mumbai **State:** MH **PC:** **Country:** India
Year Established: 2016 **Status 2020:** Active
Industries: Application Services for:, Artificial Intelligence for:, IT Managed Services

Company Name: SBS Dimensions - India
Description: Sales Execution Consulting | Technology Solutions
Website: http://www.sbsdimensions.com
Phone: **Email:** info@sbsdimensions.com
City: Mumbai **State:** MH **PC:** **Country:** India
Year Established: 2017 **Status 2020:** Active
Industries: ~ Construction (10), Application Services

Company Name: Scholr
Description: Scholr provides on-demand homework help and personal learning assistance to school students through artificial intelligence and real tutors.
Website: http://www.scholr.com
Phone: 022-30266182 **Email:** info@scholr.com
City: Mumbai **State:** MH **PC:** **Country:** India
Year Established: **Status 2020:** Active
Industries: Artificial Intelligence for:, ~ Education (13), ~ Education (13)

Company Name: Sciative Solutions
Description: Sciative Solutions is develops automated dynamic price optimisation systems through big data, AI and Machine-to-Machine interactions.
Website: http://www.sciative.com/
Phone: **Email:** 37345@reference-encyclopedia-ai.net
City: Mumbai **State:** MH **PC:** **Country:** India
Year Established: 2016 **Status 2020:** Active
Industries: Artificial Intelligence for:, Big Data and Analytics

Company Name: SegmentOne
Description: SegmentOne is an AI-based customer growth automation platform that helps online businesses target each customer uniquely.
Website: http://www.f6s.com/segmentone
Phone: **Email:** 37357@reference-encyclopedia-ai.net
City: Mumbai **State:** MH **PC:** **Country:** India
Year Established: 2016 **Status 2020:** Active
Industries:

Company Name: Selekt.in
Description: An intelligent assistant for product discovery. It can interact, understand and guide customers in selecting products that suit their needs
Website: http://www.selekt.: India
Phone: **Email:** info@selekt.: India
City: Mumbai **State:** MH **PC:** **Country:** India
Year Established: 2016 **Status 2020:** Active
Industries: Artificial Intelligence for:, E-Commerce

Company Name: SMECorner
Description: SMEcorner is a financial lending firm that focuses on providing services to small and medium enterprises.
Website: http://www.smecorner.com/
Phone: 18001037382 **Email:** service@smecorner.com
City: Mumbai **State:** MH **PC:** **Country:** India
Year Established: 2014 **Status 2020:** Active
Industries: Artificial Intelligence for:, ~ Banking and Financial Markets-Services (7), ~ Banking and Financial Markets-Services (7), ~ Banking and Financial Markets-Services (7), Machine Learning

Company Name: Socioboard Technologies Private Limited
Description: Socioboard is an advanced, easy, versatile, customizable and scalable open-source social media marketing tool.
Website: http://socioboard.com/
Phone: **Email:** 37425@reference-encyclopedia-ai.net
City: Mumbai **State:** MH **PC:** **Country:** India
Year Established: 2013 **Status 2020:** Active
Industries: Business Applications for:, Digital Media for:, Enterprise Application Services for:, Mobile for:, Predictive Analytics

Company Name: SPOCTO
Description: Spocto is a multi channel customer engagement platform that helps marketers to interact with customers.
Website: http://www.spocto.com
Phone: **Email:** hello@spocto.com
City: Mumbai **State:** MH **PC:** **Country:** India
Year Established: **Status 2020:** Active
Industries: Analytics for:, Artificial Intelligence for:, Big Data and Analytics for:, ~ Administrative and Support Services (1), Digital Media for:, Web for:, Machine Learning for:, Mobile for:, Predictive Analytics for:, ~ Real Estate (49)

Company Name: Square Off
Description: Building next gen games & toys with robotics & AI
Website: http://squareoffnow.com/
Phone: **Email:** contact@infivention.com
City: Mumbai **State:** MH **PC:** **Country:** India
Year Established: 2015 **Status 2020:** Active
Industries: Artificial Intelligence for:, Internet of Things (IoT) for:, Robotics

Company Name: SuperFan.Ai
Description: SuperFan.ai revolutionses the way an influencer connects with an engaged community around his passion using AI powered chat bots
Website: http://www.superfan.ai
Phone: **Email:** hello@superfan.ai
City: Mumbai **State:** MH **PC:** **Country:** India
Year Established: **Status 2020:** Active
Industries: Artificial Intelligence for:, Enterprise Application Services for:, Machine Learning for:, ~ Arts-Entertainment-Recreation (4)

Company Name: Thunderpod
Description: Thunderpod is a social health and fitness platform where users consume content made by creators in the form of interactive challenges.
Website: http://www.thunderpod.com/
Phone: 9769314368 **Email:** hello@thunderpod.com
City: Mumbai **State:** MH **PC:** **Country:** India

Year Established: 2018 **Status 2020:** Active
Industries: Artificial Intelligence for:, ~ Healthcare (20), ~ Healthcare (20)

Company Name: UnFound
Description: India's only AI platform to combat misinformation
Website:
Phone: **Email:** 37591@reference-encyclopedia-ai.net
City: Mumbai **State:** MH **PC:** **Country:** India
Year Established: 2018 **Status 2020:** Closed
Industries: Artificial Intelligence for:, Application Program Interfaces (APIs) for:, Machine Learning for:, Natural Language Processing

Company Name: UnoLigo Solutions
Description: UnoLigo runs an omnichannel bot-based customer transmigration platform that uses artificial intelligence and machine learning.
Website:
Phone: **Email:** 37596@reference-encyclopedia-ai.net
City: Mumbai **State:** MH **PC:** **Country:** India
Year Established: 2019 **Status 2020:** Active
Industries: Artificial Intelligence for:, Enterprise Application Services for:, Machine Learning

Company Name: Vicit Infot Tech Pvt Ltd
Description: Creators of successful online social change platform Thappad and futuristic Celebrity Bot project.
Website: http://iconic.wtf
Phone: **Email:** hello@iconic.wtf
City: Mumbai **State:** MH **PC:** **Country:** India
Year Established: **Status 2020:** Active
Industries: Artificial Intelligence for:, ~ Arts-Entertainment-Recreation (4), ~ Telecommunications (56)

Company Name: vPhra: Sweden
Description: They help companies communicate insights from their data, in a personalised way, at scale.
Website: http://phrazor.ai/
Phone: **Email:** contact@vphrase.com
City: Mumbai **State:** MH **PC:** **Country:** India
Year Established: 2015 **Status 2020:** Active
Industries: Analytics for:, Artificial Intelligence for:, Big Data and Analytics for:, IT Managed Services

Company Name: vPhrase Analytics Solutions Pvt. Ltd.
Description: They help companies communicate insights from their data, in a personalised way, at scale.
Website: http://www.vphrase.com
Phone: 91 8108865848 **Email:** deepthi.udyawar@vphrase.com
City: Mumbai **State:** MH **PC:** **Country:** India
Year Established: **Status 2020:** Active
Industries: Analytics for:, Artificial Intelligence for:, Big Data and Analytics for:, IT Managed Services

Company Name: Worlzen
Description: An intelligent networking portal designed to help people plan meetups with anyone, anywhere,
Website: http://www.worlzen.com
Phone: **Email:** hello@worlzen.com
City: Mumbai **State:** MH **PC:** **Country:** India
Year Established: **Status 2020:** Active
Industries: Application Services for:, Artificial Intelligence for:, ~ Personal-Religious-Civic (45), ~ Arts-Entertainment-Recreation (4), ~ Social Media (54)

Company Name: Yobee Research:
Description: Applying AI to Financial Markets
Website: http://yobee.co.: India
Phone: **Email:** hello@yobee.co.: India
City: Mumbai **State:** MH **PC:** **Country:** India
Year Established: 2019 **Status 2020:** Active
Industries:

Company Name: Zenkast.com
Description: Customer Engagement and Insights through game of Predictions
Website: http://www.zenkast.com
Phone: 91 99 75 721991 **Email:** vijay@zenkast.com
City: Mumbai **State:** MH **PC:** **Country:** India
Year Established: 2014 **Status 2020:** Active
Industries: Databases for:, Predictive Analytics

Company Name: Zommoz
Description: Customer Assistance With Intelligence
Website: http://zommoz.in/
Phone: **Email:** 37743@reference-encyclopedia-ai.net
City: Mumbai **State:** MH **PC:** **Country:** India
Year Established: 2015 **Status 2020:** Active
Industries: ~ Customer Relationship Management (11), Machine Learning for:, Natural Language Processing

Company Name: COJAG
Description: Drone Technology, Geophysical Services, Data Analytics, IoT and Co-Working Space
Website: http://www.cojagtech.com/
Phone: **Email:** informcojag@gmail.com
City: Nagpur **State:** MH **PC:** **Country:** India
Year Established: 2016 **Status 2020:** Active
Industries: Artificial Intelligence for:, Big Data and Analytics for:, ~ Metals and Mining (42)

Company Name: NagStud
Description: Digital Reach - Web Design & Development, SEO, Digital Marketing, Artificial Intelligence, Innovation
Website: http://www.nagstud.com
Phone: 91 869-869-2089 **Email:** contact@nagstud.com
City: Nagpur **State:** MH **PC:** **Country:** India
Year Established: **Status 2020:** Active
Industries: Artificial Intelligence for:, IT Managed Services for:, ~ Media-Communications (41), ~ Professional Services (48)

Company Name: YouBotics
Description: YouBotics has innovated Technology Expert bot that conducts Technical Video Interviews with Automatic Evaluation
Website: http://www.youbotics.ai
Phone: 91 93735 92412 **Email:** parikshit@youbotics.ai
City: Nagpur **State:** MH **PC:** **Country:** India
Year Established: **Status 2020:** Active
Industries: Artificial Intelligence for:, ~ Human Resources (24), IT Managed Services for:, Machine Learning for:, Natural Language Processing for:, ~ Human Resources (24), ~ Human Resources (24)

Company **Name:** Tinker Bot
Description: Tinker Bot is an AI based Chat Bot that helps to learn new things by chatting with it.
Website: http://www.tinkerbot.: India
Phone: 91 7507112371 **Email:** ceo@tinkerbot.: India
City: Nasik **State:** MH **PC:** **Country:** India
Year Established: 2017 **Status 2020:** Active
Industries: Artificial Intelligence for:, ~ Education (13), ~ Education (13), Machine Learning

Company Name: AmplifyRea: Switzerland
Description: Conversational AI Automation Platform for Sales, Marketing & Support Teams
Website: http://www.AmplifyReach.com/
Phone: **Email:** kick-start@amplifyreach.com
City: Pune **State:** MH **PC:** **Country:** India
Year Established: 2017 **Status 2020:** Active
Industries: Artificial Intelligence for:, ~ Customer Relationship Management (11), Machine Learning for:, Natural Language Processing for:, Predictive Analytics for:, Internet of Things (IoT)

Company Name: Aztrino Anthrobotics
Description: In the business of providing easy solutions to difficult problems, through merging human consciousness with machine intelligence.
Website: http://iva.to
Phone: **Email:** support@iva.to
City: Pune **State:** MH **PC:** **Country:** India
Year Established: **Status 2020:** Active
Industries: Artificial Intelligence for:, E-Commerce

Company Name: BotSpace
Description: BotSpace is SaaS platform that helps businesses deploy chat solutions to automate support & engagement without training.
Website: http://www.botspace.me
Phone: 7875480555 **Email:** contact@botspace.me
City: Pune **State:** MH **PC:** **Country:** India
Year Established: **Status 2020:** Active
Industries: Artificial Intelligence for:, Natural Language Processing

Company Name: Cadence Data Soft Pvt. Ltd.
Description: Software Development Services Company
Website: http://www.cadencedatasoft.com
Phone: 877-778-8979 **Email:** banand@cadencedatasoft.com
City: Pune **State:** MH **PC:** **Country:** India
Year Established: **Status 2020:** Active
Industries: Application Services for:, Artificial Intelligence for:, Cloud for:, Cloud for:, Machine Learning for:, Application Services for:, ~ Professional Services (48)

Company Name: CleomeSoft Technologies
Description: CleomeSoft helps start-ups and enterprises build innovative software solutions by bringing together UX, Big Data and ML
Website: http://www.cleomesoft.com/
Phone: 1 (214) 660-5586 **Email:** hello@cleomesoft.com
City: Pune **State:** MH **PC:** **Country:** India
Year Established: 2018 **Status 2020:** Active
Industries: Artificial Intelligence for:, Big Data and Analytics for:, IT Managed Services for:, Internet of Things (IoT) for:, Machine Learning for:, Development and Test

Company Name: Clodura
Description: Clodura is an Automated LeadGen platform which uses machine learning to find high value prospects which are more likely to close.
Website: http://www.clodura.com/
Phone: **Email:** kapil@clodura.com
City: Pune **State:** MH **PC:** **Country:** India
Year Established: 2015 **Status 2020:** Active
Industries: Artificial Intelligence for:, IT Managed Services for:, IT Managed Services for:, Web

Company Name: cloudmantra
Description: cloudmantra offers top-class Cloud Consulting, Cloud-Native App Development and Machine Learning/Data Science services to its clients.
Website: http://www.cloudmantra.net
Phone: (425) 365-4250 **Email:** info@cloudmantra.net
City: Pune **State:** MH **PC:** **Country:** India
Year Established: 2014 **Status 2020:** Active
Industries: Cloud for:, Cloud for:, Cloud for:, Internet of Things (IoT) for:, Machine Learning

Company Name: Cloudzi: Spain
Description: Cloudzies is a AI and cloud-based digital marketing platform that improves advertising and ad-creation with data driven approach.
Website: http://cloudzies.com
Phone: **Email:** hello@cloudzies.com
City: Pune **State:** MH **PC:** **Country:** India
Year Established: 2019 **Status 2020:** Active
Industries:

Company Name: CoalesceFlow
Description: SaaS, Mobile App, Artificial Intelligence, Computer Vision, DSaas, Android
Website: http://www.coalesceflow.com/
Phone: **Email:** rohan@coalesceflow.com
City: Pune **State:** MH **PC:** **Country:** India
Year Established: 2018 **Status 2020:** Active
Industries: Artificial Intelligence for:, IT Managed Services

Company Name: Cordnex Technologies
Description: Artificial Intelligence build AI voice
Website: http://cordnex.ai
Phone: **Email:** support@cordnex.ai
City: Pune **State:** MH **PC:** **Country:** India
Year Established: 2012 **Status 2020:** Active
Industries: Artificial Intelligence

Company Name: Covanix Systems
Description: Integrate. Orchestrate. Effectuate.
Website: http://www.covanix.com/
Phone: **Email:** info@covanix.com
City: Pune **State:** MH **PC:** **Country:** India
Year Established: **Status 2020:** Active
Industries: Analytics for:, Artificial Intelligence for:, Enterprise Application Services for:, ~ Retail and Consumer Products (52), ~ Media-Communications (41), ~ Retail and Consumer Products (52), Predictive Analytics for:, ~ Retail and Consumer Products (52)

Company Name: Cuelogic Technologies Pvt. Ltd.
Description: Outsourced Product Development for leading edge startups and Fortune 500 enterprises looking to compete with unicorns.
Website: http://www.cuelogic.com
Phone: 347 374 8437 **Email:** cuetechsubmission@gmail.com
City: Pune **State:** MH **PC:** **Country:** India
Year Established: **Status 2020:** Active
Industries: Analytics for:, Artificial Intelligence for:, Big Data and Analytics for:, ~ Education (13), ~ Banking and Financial Markets-Services (7), Machine Learning for:, Mobile for:, Application Services for:, ~ Professional Services (48), Cyber Security

Company Name: CutShort
Description: AI-based recruitment platform and SaaS software used by 8000 companies, from startups to product giants like Google.
Website: http://cutshort.io
Phone: 98508-97523 **Email:** hello@cutshort.io
City: Pune **State:** MH **PC:** **Country:** India
Year Established: 2015 **Status 2020:** Active
Industries: Artificial Intelligence for:, Web for:, Machine Learning for:, Business Software as a Service Apps (SaaS Apps)

Company Name: Data Synopsis
Description: Data Synopsis offer solutions to help organizations capitalize on the potential of big data and get actionable insights from their data.
Website: http://www.data-synopsis.com
Phone: 91 93 71 214640 **Email:** info@data-synopsis.com
City: Pune **State:** MH **PC:** **Country:** India
Year Established: 2012 **Status 2020:** Active
Industries: Analytics for:, Artificial Intelligence for:, IT Managed Services

Company Name: drivebuddyAI
Description: ADAS, Artificial Intelligence, IoT, Automotive
Website: http://www.drivebuddyai.com
Phone: **Email:** connect@drivebuddyai.com
City: Pune **State:** MH **PC:** **Country:** India
Year Established: 2018 **Status 2020:** Active
Industries: Artificial Intelligence for:, ~ Automotive (5), ~ Telecommunications (56), Internet of Things (IoT)

Company Name: Eatby
Description: Food intelligence to grow restaurants business.
Website: http://www.eatby.: India
Phone: **Email:** info@eatby.: India
City: Pune **State:** MH **PC:** **Country:** India
Year Established: 2015 **Status 2020:** Active
Industries: Predictive Analytics for:, ~ Food and Beverage (17)

Company Name: EMERGENTECK
Description: RPA, Data Science, ML. AI Training and Service
Website: http://www.kausalvikash.in/
Phone: (735) 007-0755 **Email:** info@kausalvikash.: India
City: Pune **State:** MH **PC:** **Country:** India
Year Established: 2018 **Status 2020:** Active
Industries: Artificial Intelligence for:, ~ Education (13), IT Managed Services for:, Machine Learning

Company Name: Engazify
Description: Engazify is an AI powered HR bot which makes it easy for employees to appreciate hard work & share real-time feedback with their co-workers.
Website: http://engazify.com
Phone: **Email:** contact@engazify.com
City: Pune **State:** MH **PC:** **Country:** India
Year Established: 2015 **Status 2020:** Active
Industries: Artificial Intelligence for:, Business Applications for:, Application Services for:, Business Software as a Service Apps (SaaS Apps)

Company Name: ENLYFT DIGITAL SOLUTIONS PRIVATE LIMITED
Description: Digital Marketing Agency
Website: http://www.enlyft.co.: India
Phone: 9120 4906 7869 **Email:** info@enlyft.co.: India
City: Pune **State:** MH **PC:** **Country:** India
Year Established: **Status 2020:** Active
Industries:

Company Name: ExtraaEdge
Description: Data Science powered - Admission & Marketing CRM Automation for Education Enrolments
Website: http://www.extraaedge.com
Phone: **Email:** info@theextraaedge.com
City: Pune **State:** MH **PC:** **Country:** India
Year Established: 2015 **Status 2020:** Active
Industries: Artificial Intelligence for:, ~ Customer Relationship Management (11), ~ Education (13)

Company Name: Glimpse Analytics
Description: Glimpse uses your existing CCTV camera, and adds Artificial Intelligence, to bring advance customer analytics to brick-and-mortar retailers!
Website: http://glimpseanalytics.com
Phone: 91 96198 51161 **Email:** hello@glimpseanalytics.com
City: Pune **State:** MH **PC:** **Country:** India
Year Established: 2019 **Status 2020:** Active
Industries: Artificial Intelligence for:, IT Managed Services

Company Name: Hartley Lab
Description: Hartley Lab is a product development consultancy.
Website: http://www.hartleylab.com
Phone: 91-9923433599 **Email:** hello@hartleylab.com
City: Pune **State:** MH **PC:** **Country:** India
Year Established: **Status 2020:** Active
Industries:

Company Name: IdeaClicks
Description: AI based Digital Marketing
Website: http://IdeaClicks.: India
Phone: 91 702 802 0321 **Email:** digital@IdeaClicks.: India
City: Pune **State:** MH **PC:** **Country:** India
Year Established: 2015 **Status 2020:** Active
Industries: Artificial Intelligence for:, Digital Marketing for:, IT Managed Services for:, ~ Administrative and Support Services (1)

Company Name: iKnowlation
Description: iKnowlation provides machine learning and AI models that enable customers to deal with data problems.
Website: http://www.iknowlation.com
Phone: **Email:** contactus@iknowlation.com
City: Pune **State:** MH **PC:** **Country:** India
Year Established: 2015 **Status 2020:** Active
Industries: Artificial Intelligence for:, IT Managed Services for:, Machine Learning

Company Name: Journey360
Description: AI-powered Customer Data Platform
Website: http://journey360.ai/
Phone: **Email:** 36833@reference-encyclopedia-ai.net
City: Pune **State:** MH **PC:** **Country:** India
Year Established: 2019 **Status 2020:** Active
Industries: Artificial Intelligence for:, IT Managed Services

Company Name: Keito
Description: Building an Intelligent Digital Assistant.
Website: https://www.keito.works/
Phone: **Email:** hr@keito.works
City: Pune **State:** MH **PC:** **Country:** India
Year Established: **Status 2020:** Active
Industries: Artificial Intelligence for:, Machine Learning

Company Name: Light Information Systems
Description: NLPBOTS- Automating enterprise processes & conversations with AI NLP.
Website: http://www.nlpbots.com
Phone: (937) 105-2898 **Email:** animesh@lightinfosys.com
City: Pune **State:** MH **PC:** **Country:** India
Year Established: 2012 **Status 2020:** Active
Industries: Artificial Intelligence for:, Enterprise Application Services for:, IT Managed Services for:, IT Managed Services for:, Natural Language Processing

Company Name: maice
Description: Content Marketing
Website: http://www.maice.co
Phone: **Email:** ceo@maice.co
City: Pune **State:** MH **PC:** **Country:** India
Year Established: 2018 **Status 2020:** Active
Industries: Analytics for:, Artificial Intelligence

Company Name: MARSIAN Technologies
Description: MARSIAN provides IT services, solutions, consulting and training on niche IT skills on data science, artificial intelligence and big data.
Website: http://marsiantech.com/
Phone: 070280-52111 **Email:** learning@marsiantech.com
City: Pune **State:** MH **PC:** **Country:** India
Year Established: 2014 **Status 2020:** Active
Industries: Artificial Intelligence for:, IT Managed Services for:, IT Managed Services

Company Name: Megdap
Description: Megdap is an AI platform for language processing, allowing enterprises talk with customers in a language of their choice.
Website: http://www.megdap.com/index.html
Phone: 91 8087711283 **Email:** shekharmenon@megdap.com
City: Pune **State:** MH **PC:** **Country:** India
Year Established: 2015 **Status 2020:** Active
Industries: Artificial Intelligence for:, Cloud for:, Natural Language Processing

Company Name: Persistent
Description: Software Development
Website: www.persistent.com
Phone: 91 (20) 670 30000 **Email:** vijesh_rangaswami@persistent.com
City: Pune **State:** MH **Zip:** 411016 **Country:** India

Year Established: **Status 2020:** Active
Industries:

Company Name: Pro Recce
Description: Pro Recce is your destination for locations, a first of its kind Location Scouting and Listing platform
Website: http://www.prorecce.com
Phone: 9970051961 **Email:** info@prorecce.com
City: Pune **State:** MH **PC:** **Country:** India
Year Established: **Status 2020:** Active
Industries:

Company Name: Robolab Technologies Pvt Ltd
Description: RoboLab – The Perfect Platform To Explore, Learn & Build Robots.
Website: http://www.robolab.: India
Phone: 7249422053 **Email:** connect@robolab.: India
City: Pune **State:** MH **PC:** **Country:** India
Year Established: 2013 **Status 2020:** Active
Industries: Artificial Intelligence for:, ~ Education (13), Automation for:, Robotics

Company Name: Schoolbox
Description: Schoolbox provides evaluative AI education and training automation services.
Website: http://schoolbox.org/
Phone: 91-70040 90585 **Email:** contact@schoolbox.org
City: Pune **State:** MH **PC:** **Country:** India
Year Established: 2016 **Status 2020:** Active
Industries: Artificial Intelligence for:, ~ Education (13), ~ Education (13)

Company Name: Scorg Technologies
Description: SCORG Technologies is a global software development and technology services company with experience in multiple industry verticals.
Website: http://www.scorgtechnologies.com/
Phone: 91 20 6680 0000 **Email:** enquiry@scorgtechnologies.com
City: Pune **State:** MH **PC:** **Country:** India
Year Established: **Status 2020:** Active
Industries: Artificial Intelligence for:, Big Data and Analytics for:, ~ Healthcare (20), IT Managed Services for:, ~ Professional Services (48), ~ Professional Services (48)

Company Name: SENSE IT OUT INTELLIGENT SOLUTIONS PVT LTD
Description: An Agri-tech startup with a sensor based IOT product, which maximizes yield by automation to optimize the use of water & fertilizers.
Website: http://senseitout.com/
Phone: **Email:** info@senseitout.com
City: Pune **State:** MH **PC:** **Country:** India
Year Established: **Status 2020:** Active
Industries:

Company Name: Sucoso
Description: Solution Engineering for Enterprise Blockchain, Industrial IoT and Business Artificial Intelligence
Website: http://www.sucoso.com/
Phone: **Email:** connect@sucoso.com
City: Pune **State:** MH **PC:** **Country:** India
Year Established: **Status 2020:** Active
Industries: Artificial Intelligence for:, Data Management for:, Enterprise Application Services for:, Automation for:, ~ Management of Companies (28)

Company Name: TECHNOGEEKS
Description: Bigdata Hadoop, ETL Testing, Selenium, Informatica, Java, Python, Hadoop Admin, Bigdata Admin Training Pune
Website: http://technogeekscs.com/
Phone: 860-099-8107 **Email:** contact@technogeekscs.co.: India
City: Pune **State:** MH **PC:** **Country:** India

Year Established: **Status 2020:** Active
Industries: Artificial Intelligence for:, Big Data and Analytics for:, ~ Education (13), ~ Education (13)

Company Name: Utter
Description: Utter is an English learning app that allows learners to pick topics of their interest and converse with chat bots and live tuto: Serbia
Website: http://www.utter.in/
Phone: **Email:** hey@utter.: India
City: Pune **State:** MH **PC:** **Country:** India
Year Established: 2015 **Status 2020:** Active
Industries: Application Services for:, ~ Education (13), ~ Education (13), ~ Education (13), Natural Language Processing for:, ~ Education (13)

Company Name: YuktaMedia
Description: YuktaMedia is provider of YuktaOne Ad & Revenue Ops Management Platform for Publisher, Agencies and Advertisers.
Website: http://yuktamedia.com
Phone: **Email:** info@yuktamedia.com
City: Pune **State:** MH **PC:** **Country:** India
Year Established: 2014 **Status 2020:** Active
Industries: Analytics for:, Business Applications for:, IT Managed Services for:, Enterprise Application Services for:, Predictive Analytics for:, Business Software as a Service Apps (SaaS Apps)

Company Name: TAARAKA
Description: Building a path-breaking prediction machine!
Website: http://www.taaraka.com
Phone: **Email:** support@taaraka.com
City: Thane **State:** MH **PC:** **Country:** India
Year Established: 2015 **Status 2020:** Active
Industries: Analytics for:, Artificial Intelligence for:, Digital Media for:, Web for:, Machine Learning

Company Name: Ibnus
Description: Ibnus is a leading, global software solution provider delivering high quality and cost effective products and IT solutions.
Website: http://ibnus.io
Phone: 91-9040033118 **Email:** contact@ibnus.io
City: Bhubaneshwar **State:** OR **PC:** **Country:** India
Year Established: **Status 2020:** Active
Industries: Artificial Intelligence for:, Blockchain for:, IT Managed Services for:, Machine Learning

Company Name: Arrelic
Description: Transforming Manufacturing with Industry 4.0 and IIoT
Website: http://arrelic.com/
Phone: 91 674 2302050 **Email:** info@arrelic.com
City: Bhubaneswar **State:** OR **PC:** **Country:** India
Year Established: 2016 **Status 2020:** Active
Industries: Artificial Intelligence for:, Big Data and Analytics for:, Automation for:, Machine Learning for:, Predictive Analytics for:, Predictive Analytics

Company Name: Blink: India
Description: BlinkIn is a SaaS based product that provides an intelligent and smart visual support which help you solve your problem visually.
Website: http://blinkin.de/
Phone: **Email:** info@blinkin.io
City: Bhubaneswar **State:** OR **PC:** **Country:** India
Year Established: 2016 **Status 2020:** Active
Industries: Artificial Intelligence for:, Business Software as a Service Apps (SaaS Apps)

Company Name: Ziplr
Description: URL Shortening and Digital Marketing Analytics Application
Website: http://ziplr.io/
Phone: **Email:** contact@ziplr.io
City: Bhubaneswar **State:** OR **PC:** **Country:** India

Year Established: 2015 **Status 2020:** Active
Industries: Predictive Analytics

Company Name: Hopsticks
Description: Patent Pending Visual Food Discovery App (B2C) and SaaS Platform for Restaurants (B2B) utilising Machine Learning, IOT & Virtual Currenci: Spain
Website: http://www.hopsticks.com
Phone: **Email:** hello@hopsticks.com
City: Pondicherry **State:** PY **PC:** **Country:** India
Year Established: 2019 **Status 2020:** Active
Industries: Web for:, Internet of Things (IoT) for:, Machine Learning for:, Mobile for:, Application Services for:, Business Software as a Service Apps (SaaS Apps)

Company Name: AgNext Technologies
Description: AgNext is working at the intersection of hardware, software and analytics for quality estimation in agriculture and food.
Website: https://www.agnext.com/
Phone: **Email:** contact@agnext.: India
City: Mohali **State:** PB **PC:** **Country:** India
Year Established: 2016 **Status 2020:** Active
Industries: Analytics for:, Artificial Intelligence for:, Computer Vision for:, ~ Agriculture (3), ~ Food and Beverage (17), Machine Learning for:, Predictive Analytics for:, ~ Administrative and Support Services (1), ~ Administrative and Support Services (1)

Company Name: Hocrox Technologies
Description: Global digital consultancy that helps brands leverage design, analytics and engineering.
Website: http://hocrox.com/
Phone: **Email:** info@hocrox.com
City: Mohali **State:** PB **PC:** **Country:** India
Year Established: **Status 2020:** Active
Industries: Analytics for:, Artificial Intelligence for:, Big Data and Analytics

Company Name: Smarter.Cod: Spain
Description: Smarter.Codes provides an AI-driven content analysis solutions.
Website: http://smarter.codes/
Phone: 91-9888-949-988 **Email:** hello@smarter.cod: Spain
City: Mohali **State:** PB **PC:** **Country:** India
Year Established: 2014 **Status 2020:** Active
Industries: Analytics for:, Artificial Intelligence for:, Content

Company Name: The Expert Community
Description: The Expert Community (TEC) is an Indian IT technologies firm providing unique platform for service providers and service seekers.
Website: http://theexpertcommunity.org/
Phone: **Email:** info@theexpertcommunity.org
City: Mohali **State:** PB **PC:** **Country:** India
Year Established: **Status 2020:** Active
Industries:

Company Name: ToXSL Technologies Pvt Ltd.
Description: ToXSL Technologies is a Mobile and Web Application Development Company.
Website: http://toxsl.com/
Phone: 95691 27788 **Email:** sales@toxsl.com
City: Mohali **State:** PB **PC:** **Country:** India
Year Established: 2012 **Status 2020:** Active
Industries: Artificial Intelligence for:, Application Services for:, Web for:, Web

Company Name: ClickByte Media
Description: AdTech
Website: http://www.clickbytemedia.com/
Phone: (971) 797-6520 **Email:** contact@mytokri.com
City: Alwar **State:** RJ **PC:** **Country:** India
Year Established: 2013 **Status 2020:** Active
Industries: Artificial Intelligence for:, Web

Company Name: A2DWEB
Description: An Innovative platform which will offer news, gadgets, inventions, innovations, tutorials etc in an simplified way by using AI to manage it.
Website: https://www.a2dweb.com/
Phone: **Email:** adangi@live.com
City: Bhilwara **State:** RJ **PC:** **Country:** India
Year Established: 2017 **Status 2020:** Active
Industries: Artificial Intelligence for:, IT Managed Services for:, Web for:, ~ Social Assistance-Non-Profits (53)

Company Name: Asnp: Romania
Description: Asnpro is a outsourcing Service Provider is a data-based platform that offers services for Artificial Intelligence Training Data.
Website: http://asnpro.: India
Phone: **Email:** plpraphool@gmail.com
City: Dungarpur **State:** RJ **Zip:** 314001 **Country:** India
Year Established: **Status 2020:** Active
Industries: Artificial Intelligence for:, ~ E-Commerce (12), Cyber Security

Company Name: Guitaa.com
Description: AI backed Immersive Music Learning Platform
Website: http://www.guitaa.com
Phone: **Email:** hi@guitaa.com
City: Jaipur **State:** RJ **PC:** **Country:** India
Year Established: 2017 **Status 2020:** Active
Industries: Big Data and Analytics for:, ~ Education (13), Machine Learning for:, ~ Arts-Entertainment-Recreation (4), ~ Social Assistance-Non-Profits (53)

Company **Name:** Loop Digital Hotels
Description: Loop digital Hotels provides hotels with technological support in increasing revenue with the help of Data Analytics and AI.
Website: http://www.loopdigitalhotels.com
Phone: 91 141 4010545 **Email:** info@loopdigital.com
City: Jaipur City **State:** RJ **PC:** **Country:** India
Year Established: **Status 2020:** Active
Industries: Artificial Intelligence for:, ~ Hospitality (23), Machine Learning for:, Predictive Analytics

Company Name: zoogaad
Description: zoogaad offers a news site that uses artificial intelligence to provide news stories.
Website: http://zoogaad.com/
Phone: **Email:** info@zoogaad.com
City: Jodhpur **State:** RJ **PC:** **Country:** India
Year Established: **Status 2020:** Active
Industries: Artificial Intelligence for:, ~ Media-Communications (41), ~ Media-Communications (41)

Company Name: ArcGate
Description: ArcGate is a BPO company helping high growth companies with data management.
Website: http://www.arcgate.com
Phone: (512) 535-6494 **Email:** info@arcgate.com
City: Udaipur City **State:** RJ **PC:** **Country:** India
Year Established: **Status 2020:** Active
Industries: Artificial Intelligence for:, Big Data and Analytics for:, Mobile for:, Business Process and Operations

Company Name: AgriBot
Description: Virtual Assistant for Agri Businesses and Farmers, AgriBot is available 24/7 to bring enormous agriculture knowledge at the fingertips.
Website: https://agri.bot/
Phone: 8098320006 **Email:** contact@agri.bot
City: Chennai **State:** TN **PC:** **Country:** India
Year Established: 2019 **Status 2020:** Active
Industries: ~ Agriculture (3), Artificial Intelligence for:, IT Managed Services for:, Machine Learning

Company Name: Aifosys
Description: We are Developing AI based ERP applications for Automobile, Manufacturing, Oil & Gas, Pharma, Institutions, Hospitals, Retail Industries.
Website: http://www.aifosys.com/
Phone: **Email:** info@aifosys.com
City: Chennai **State:** TN **PC:** **Country:** India
Year Established: 2013 **Status 2020:** Active
Industries: Artificial Intelligence for:, Automation for:, ~ Education (13), IT Managed Services

Company Name: ARGICK
Description: ARGICK is a dedicated AR/MR and VR , IoT and Computer Vision service provider.
Website: http://www.argick.com
Phone: 91 - 95380 72423 **Email:** hisham.sheik@argick.com
City: Chennai **State:** TN **PC:** **Country:** India
Year Established: **Status 2020:** Active
Industries: Analytics for:, Artificial Intelligence for:, Augmented Reality for:, Computer Vision for:, Machine Learning

Company Name: Autointelli
Description: Autointelli is one of the leading AIOps platform & solutions providers in India.
Website: http://www.autointelli.com/
Phone: 4422541017 **Email:** sales@autointelli.com
City: Chennai **State:** TN **PC:** **Country:** India
Year Established: 2018 **Status 2020:** Active
Industries: Artificial Intelligence for:, Cloud for:, Automation for:, IT Managed Services for:, IT Infrastructure for:, Machine Learning

Company Name: Botminds
Description: Botminds is an AI company for document process automation.
Website: http://www.botminds.ai/
Phone: 91 9789058220 **Email:** hello@botminds.ai
City: Chennai **State:** TN **PC:** **Country:** India
Year Established: 2015 **Status 2020:** Active
Industries: Artificial Intelligence for:, Data Management

Company Name: Crux IQ
Description: Crux IQ is a platform that helps you analyze legal contracts, extract important information and summarize as per your requirement.
Website: http://www.cruxiq.com/
Phone: 91-44-4360-3789 **Email:** contact@cruxiq.com
City: Chennai **State:** TN **PC:** **Country:** India
Year Established: **Status 2020:** Active
Industries:

Company Name: CustomerLabs Inc
Description: Customer Lifecycle sales and digital marketing stack for SMBs, the Digital Marketers' Wingman.
Website: http://www.customerlabs.co/
Phone: **Email:** founders@customerlabs.co
City: Chennai **State:** TN **PC:** **Country:** India
Year Established: 2013 **Status 2020:** Active
Industries: Predictive Analytics for:, Business Software as a Service Apps (SaaS Apps) for:, Automation

Company Name: Dartexon Consulting Services
Description: Dartexon Consulting Services is an experienced team of engineers, thinkers, and entrepreneu: Serbia
Website: http://dartexon.com
Phone: 91 89398 98636 **Email:** info@dartexon.com
City: Chennai **State:** TN **PC:** **Country:** India
Year Established: 2017 **Status 2020:** Active
Industries: Artificial Intelligence for:, Blockchain for:, Application Services

Company Name: Datachain Inc
Description: Consumer Identity and Intelligence Platform for APAC, built on Blockcha: India
Website:
Phone: **Email:** 36389@reference-encyclopedia-ai.net
City: Chennai **State:** TN **PC:** **Country:** India
Year Established: 2018 **Status 2020:** Closed
Industries: IT Managed Services for:, Web for:, Machine Learning

Company Name: Delium Technologies
Description: AI and ML to solve the age-old unsolved problem in inventory for retaile: Serbia
Website: http://www.delium.co
Phone: 9500025826 **Email:** info@delium.co
City: Chennai **State:** TN **PC:** **Country:** India
Year Established: **Status 2020:** Active
Industries: Artificial Intelligence for:, Machine Learning for:, ~ Retail and Consumer Products (52)

Company Name: Finologic Technologies Private Limited
Description: We are a gaming & entertainment startup. We do awesome games, Gaming as a Service, AI on Games, VR-AR
Website: http://www.finologic.co
Phone: 91 93 60 309925 **Email:** contact@finologic.co
City: Chennai **State:** TN **PC:** **Country:** India
Year Established: **Status 2020:** Active
Industries: Artificial Intelligence for:, Machine Learning for:, Mobile

Company Name: Franc
Description: SaaS
Website: http://franctechnologies.com
Phone: **Email:** hello@franctechnologies.com
City: Chennai **State:** TN **PC:** **Country:** India
Year Established: 2018 **Status 2020:** Active
Industries: Artificial Intelligence for:, Big Data and Analytics for:, Machine Learning for:, Predictive Analytics for:, Business Software as a Service Apps (SaaS Apps)

Company Name: HILAK TECHNOLOGY PRIVATE LIMITED
Description: Established in 2017, HILAK TECHNOLOGY PRIVATE LIMITED founded with the mission of building world class cloud based products & solutions.
Website: http://hilak-technology.com
Phone: 91 9884925355 **Email:** sakthi.sekar@hilak-technology.com
City: Chennai **State:** TN **PC:** **Country:** India
Year Established: **Status 2020:** Active
Industries: Artificial Intelligence for:, Cloud for:, ~ Education (13), ~ Banking and Financial Markets-Services (7), ~ Healthcare (20), Application Services for:, ~ Human Resources (24)

Company Name: Hueint
Description: Hueint is a deep tech start-up focusing on artificial intelligence, computer vision, and emerging technologies.
Website: http://hueint.com
Phone: **Email:** info@hueint.com
City: Chennai **State:** TN **PC:** **Country:** India
Year Established: 2018 **Status 2020:** Active
Industries: Artificial Intelligence for:, Augmented Reality for:, IT Managed Services

Company Name: infoMicroF: India
Description: SaaS Banking Platform
Website: http://infomicrofin.com/
Phone: 9176593410 **Email:** santhoshvkumar@whileofone.com
City: Chennai **State:** TN **PC:** **Country:** India
Year Established: **Status 2020:** Active
Industries: Artificial Intelligence for:, ~ Banking and Financial Markets-Services (7), IT Managed Services for:, Web for:, Robotics

Company Name: Inta: India
Description: Intain is a research based technology venture that combines the powers of AI and Blockchain.
Website: http://www.intainft.com
Phone: **Email:** explore@intainft.com
City: Chennai **State:** TN **PC:** **Country:** India
Year Established: 2018 **Status 2020:** Active
Industries: Artificial Intelligence for:, ~ Banking and Financial Markets-Services (7), IT Managed Services

Company Name: IYANTRAS
Description: IYANTRAS is a global artificial intelligence and robotics consulting and services firm empowered by design thinking.
Website: http://www.iyantras.com
Phone: 91 7338766066 **Email:** support@iyantras.com
City: Chennai **State:** TN **PC:** **Country:** India
Year Established: 2016 **Status 2020:** Active
Industries: Robotics

Company Name: Mitosis Technologies
Description: Mitosis Technologies is an agile Software Development Company. Our domain expertise and technical excellence help customers.
Website: http://www.mitosistech.com/
Phone: 91 7824035173 **Email:** hello@mitosistech.com
City: Chennai **State:** TN **PC:** **Country:** India
Year Established: 2013 **Status 2020:** Active
Industries: Artificial Intelligence for:, Big Data and Analytics for:, Blockchain for:, ~ Banking and Financial Markets-Services (7), Data Management for:, Machine Learning for:, Predictive Analytics for:, Web

Company Name: NaturalText
Description: Text Understanding using Artifical Learning. Products include Learning and Reasoning, Conextual Word mining, Search, Bioinformatics
Website: http://naturaltext.com
Phone: **Email:** rajasankar@naturaltext.com
City: Chennai **State:** TN **PC:** **Country:** India
Year Established: **Status 2020:** Active
Industries: Artificial Intelligence for:, ~ Biotechnology (9), Machine Learning for:, Natural Language Processing

Company Name: OptaCred: Italy
Description: OptaCredit is an artificial intelligence-powered, data-driven online lender
Website: http://www.optacredit.com/
Phone: **Email:** media@optacredit.com
City: Chennai **State:** TN **PC:** **Country:** India
Year Established: 2016 **Status 2020:** Active
Industries:

Company Name: Orbuculum
Description: A artificial intelligent system used for disease diagnosis of disease.
Website:
Phone: **Email:** 37119@reference-encyclopedia-ai.net
City: Chennai **State:** TN **PC:** **Country:** India
Year Established: 2017 **Status 2020:** Active
Industries: Artificial Intelligence for:, ~ Biotechnology (9), ~ Healthcare (20)

Company Name: Purpleslate
Description: Conversational Simplified!
Website: http://www.purpleslate.: India
Phone: 91 9500013461 **Email:** sidharth@purpleslate.: India
City: Chennai **State:** TN **PC:** **Country:** India
Year Established: 2017 **Status 2020:** Active
Industries: Artificial Intelligence for:, IT Managed Services

Company Name: Sedin Technologies
Description:
Website: http://www.sedintechnologies.com
Phone: **Email:** 12752@reference-encyclopedia-ai.net
City: Chennai **State:** TN **Zip:** 600083 **Country:** India
Year Established: **Status 2020:** Active
Industries:

Company Name: Sensigo Technologies
Description: We specialize in Blockchain development, Artificial Intelligence, DevOps, Mobile App development, Web App development.
Website: http://sensigotech.com/
Phone: 8220862740 **Email:** techsensigo@gmail.com
City: Chennai **State:** TN **PC:** **Country:** India
Year Established: 2016 **Status 2020:** Active
Industries: Artificial Intelligence for:, IT Managed Services for:, Application Services for:, Web

Company Name: Skcri: Portugal
Description: Our company's mission is simple: Strive for perfection. Craft things that don't exist and settle down only when its perfect.
Website: http://www.skcript.com/
Phone: **Email:** business@skcript.com
City: Chennai **State:** TN **PC:** **Country:** India
Year Established: 2013 **Status 2020:** Active
Industries: Blockchain for:, Computer Vision for:, Data Management for:, Automation for:, Predictive Analytics

Company Name: Softence
Description: Softence specializes in AI, machine learning, automation, and big data analytics services.
Website: http://softence.com/
Phone: 044 4286 9090 **Email:** info@softence.com
City: Chennai **State:** TN **PC:** **Country:** India
Year Established: 2015 **Status 2020:** Active
Industries: Artificial Intelligence for:, Big Data and Analytics for:, Machine Learning

Company Name: SP Robotic Works Pvt Ltd
Description: A platform to learn, build and showcase Robotics, IoT, Image Processing, Virtual Reality (VR) and other next generation skills
Website: http://www.sproboticworks.com/
Phone: 1800 121 2135 **Email:** info@sproboticworks.com
City: Chennai **State:** TN **PC:** **Country:** India
Year Established: 2012 **Status 2020:** Active
Industries: ~ Education (13), Internet of Things (IoT) for:, Machine Learning for:, Robotics

Company Name: Surukam
Description: Surukam helps corporate legal teams automate their workflows & the decision-making process by implementing next-gen Artificial Intelligence.
Website: http://www.surukam.com/
Phone: **Email:** contact@surukam.com
City: Chennai **State:** TN **PC:** **Country:** India
Year Established: 2014 **Status 2020:** Active
Industries:

Company Name: Takvaviya Analytics
Description: AI Driven Image Analytics Company offering asset management & productivity improvement solutions across various secto: Serbia
Website: http://takvaviya.com
Phone: **Email:** contact@takvaviya.com
City: Chennai **State:** TN **PC:** **Country:** India
Year Established: 2017 **Status 2020:** Active
Industries: Artificial Intelligence for:, IT Managed Services

Company Name: Tango : ITALY
Description: Information Technology,
Website: http://www.tangotech.co.in/
Phone: 91 73388 26885 **Email:** suren@tangotech.co.: India
City: Chennai **State:** TN **PC:** **Country:** India
Year Established: 2017 **Status 2020:** Active
Industries: Artificial Intelligence for:, IT Managed Services for:, IT Managed Services

Company Name: UnderstandBetter
Description: UnderstandBetter is a personalised employee feedback platform that gives managers insights to take action on
Website: http://understandbetter.co
Phone: 1 (256) 615-8438 **Email:** support@understandbetter.co
City: Chennai **State:** TN **PC:** **Country:** India
Year Established: 2016 **Status 2020:** Active
Industries: Artificial Intelligence

Company Name: VRapido Technologies
Description: Highly advance technology solutions Chat-Bots, AI, Analytics & Managed Service
Website: http://www.vrapido.: India
Phone: **Email:** barath@vrapido.: India
City: Chennai **State:** TN **PC:** **Country:** India
Year Established: **Status 2020:** Active
Industries: Analytics for:, Artificial Intelligence for:, Enterprise Application Services for:, Enterprise Application Services for:, Machine Learning for:, Application Services for:, ~ Professional Services (48), Cyber Security

Company Name: YOOPHA
Description: YOOPHA, Next Generation Digital Healthcare Services driven by AI, connecting Doctors, Labs, Pharmacies & Patients under YOOPHA SuperApp
Website: http://www.yoopha.com/
Phone: 91 909 419 5657 **Email:** ajr@yoopha.com
City: Chennai **State:** TN **PC:** **Country:** India
Year Established: 2018 **Status 2020:** Active
Industries: Application Services for:, Artificial Intelligence for:, ~ Healthcare (20), IT Managed Services for:, Machine Learning for:, ~ Healthcare (20)

Company Name: Brainak System Technologies
Description: Brainak System Technologies develops mobile apps using artificial intelligence.
Website: http://www.brainak.com/
Phone: (887) 056-1064 **Email:** brainakinfo@gmail.com
City: Coimbatore **State:** TN **PC:** **Country:** India
Year Established: 2017 **Status 2020:** Active
Industries:

Company Name: FindDate
Description: Chat app network, dating, social, AI
Website: http://finddate.co
Phone: **Email:** contact@finddate.co
City: Coimbatore **State:** TN **PC:** **Country:** India
Year Established: 2017 **Status 2020:** Active
Industries: Artificial Intelligence for:, ~ Event Management (15), IT Managed Services for:, Machine Learning

Company Name: NeoTrack
Description: NeoTrack is an exclusive Artificial Intelligence (coupled with GPS) based School Bus Tracking solution which can think and act itself.
Website: http://www.neotrackweb.com/
Phone: (875) 435-5558 **Email:** sales@neotrackweb.com
City: Coimbatore **State:** TN **PC:** **Country:** India
Year Established: 2014 **Status 2020:** Active
Industries:

Company Name: Teplar Solutions
Description: Business Intelligence and Software Development Company
Website: http://www.teplar.com
Phone: 0422-4972112 **Email:** contact@teplar.com
City: Coimbatore **State:** TN **PC:** **Country:** India
Year Established: 2017 **Status 2020:** Active
Industries: Artificial Intelligence for:, Blockchain for:, Business Intelligence for:, IT Managed Services for:, Application Services for:, Internet of Things (IoT) for:, Web for:, Web for:, Web

Company Name: 945signals
Description: 945signals is a researcher and developer of intelligent search, Data/Web mining and big data solutions.
Website: http://945signals.com/
Phone: 91 94 88 471212 **Email:** saran@945signals.com
City: Erode **State:** TN **PC:** **Country:** India
Year Established: 2011 **Status 2020:** Active
Industries: Application Program Interfaces (APIs) for:, Machine Learning for:, Natural Language Processing for:, Web for:, Content

Company Name: AI-Techservice
Description: AI-Techservices is an artificial intelligence software development company.
Website: https://www.ai-techservices.com/
Phone: 80152 04845 **Email:** support@ai-techservices.com
City: Madurai **State:** TN **PC:** **Country:** India
Year Established: 2014 **Status 2020:** Active
Industries: Artificial Intelligence for:, IT Managed Services

Company Name: Contentop
Description: An NLP startup building a next-gen engine for content generation
Website: http://contentop.com
Phone: **Email:** web@contentop.com
City: Nagercoil **State:** TN **PC:** **Country:** India
Year Established: **Status 2020:** Active
Industries: Artificial Intelligence for:, Content for:, Databases for:, Machine Learning for:, Natural Language Processing

Company Name: Alpha Cloud Labs
Description: AlphaCloud Labs provides a cloud and deep learning-based unstructured data management, collaboration and content analytics platform.
Website: http://www.alphacloudlabs.com/
Phone: (512) 828-6806 **Email:** info@alphacloudlabs.com
City: Perungudi **State:** TN **PC:** **Country:** India
Year Established: 2010 **Status 2020:** Active
Industries: Analytics for:, Artificial Intelligence for:, Big Data and Analytics for:, Cloud

Company Name: Virtual Scree: New Zealand
Description: Virtual Screenz is an innovative fashion creators, augmented reality technology, virtual dressing room and virtual jewellery room.
Website: http://virtualscreenz.com
Phone: 91 4562 276944 **Email:** info@virtualscreenz.com
City: Sivakasi **State:** TN **PC:** **Country:** India
Year Established: **Status 2020:** Active
Industries: Artificial Intelligence for:, E-Commerce for:, ~ Media-Communications (41), Application Services for:, ~ Professional Services (48), Cyber Security

Company Name: Blockchain App Factory
Description:
Website: https://www.blockchainappfactory.com/
Phone: 1 484 823 08002 **Email:** suresh@blockchainappfactory.com
City: Tamil Nadu **State:** TN **Zip:** 600006 **Country:** India
Year Established: **Status 2020:** Active
Industries: Blockchain

Company Name: Param.ai
Description: Param.ai is a predictive intelligence recruitment solution.
Website: param.ai
Phone: **Email:** hello@param.ai
City: Gachibowli **State:** Telangana **Zip:** 500032 **Country:** India
Year Established: **Status 2020:** Active
Industries: Artificial Intelligence for:, ~ Human Resources (24)

Company Name: 3LOQ Labs
Description: 3LOQ enables brands and retailers to understand individual customer's behaviour, based on past action and context, using its advanced
Website: http://3loq.com/
Phone: 91 22 6687 9696 **Email:** info@3loq.com
City: Hyderabad **State:** TG **PC:** **Country:** India
Year Established: 2012 **Status 2020:** Active
Industries: Analytics for:, Big Data and Analytics for:, Predictive Analytics

Company Name: 3RDFlix
Description: 3RDFlix is an immersive experiences company
Website: https://3rdflix.com/
Phone: 91 90903 45555 **Email:** info@3rdflix.com
City: Hyderabad **State:** AP **PC:** **Country:** India
Year Established: 2018 **Status 2020:** Active
Industries: Artificial Intelligence for:, Machine Learning

Company Name: Agilitix AI
Description: Agilitix AI
Website: https://agilitix.ai/
Phone: **Email:** hello@agilitix.ai
City: Hyderabad **State:** TG **PC:** **Country:** India
Year Established: 2017 **Status 2020:** Active
Industries:

Company Name: AIBridge ML Pvt Ltd
Description: An Artificial Intelligence Company
Website: https://www.aibridgeml.ai/
Phone: 040-4640-0400 **Email:** aiml-sales@aibridgeml.com
City: Hyderabad **State:** TG **PC:** **Country:** India
Year Established: 2019 **Status 2020:** Active
Industries:

Company Name: AlgoLeap
Description: AlgoLeap is an advanced analytics firm specializing in the application.
Website: http://www.algoleap.com/
Phone: 91 9010627282 **Email:** info@algoleap.com
City: Hyderabad **State:** TG **PC:** **Country:** India
Year Established: 2017 **Status 2020:** Active
Industries: Artificial Intelligence for:, Security for:, Predictive Analytics

Company Name: Amber Flux Pvt Ltd
Description: Amber Flux is an AI, edge computing tech company. Have multiple granted patents in USA in AI. Edge Micro services for Industrial IOT, 5G.
Website: http://www.amberflux.com
Phone: **Email:** goparajum@amberflux.com
City: Hyderabad **State:** TG **PC:** **Country:** India
Year Established: 2013 **Status 2020:** Active
Industries: Artificial Intelligence for:, Cloud for:, IT Managed Services for:, Mobile for:, ~ Education (13)

Company Name: Ayasta Technologies
Description: We help large enterprises reduce operational risk and improve productivity by digitising electrical workflows using sensors and analytics.
Website: http://www.ayasta.com/
Phone: **Email:** hello@ayasta.com
City: Hyderabad **State:** TG **PC:** **Country:** India
Year Established: 2017 **Status 2020:** Active
Industries: Computer Vision for:, Enterprise Application Services for:, Internet of Things (IoT) for:, Machine Learning for:, Predictive Analytics

Company Name: Bitcoin India
Description: Bitcoin India - a SUPER FAST Trading Engine (Exchange), wallet (23 Digital/Crypto Assets) & mining pool.
Website: http://www.bitcoin-india.org/
Phone: **Email:** sykam.reddy@bitcoin-india.org
City: Hyderabad **State:** AP **PC:** **Country:** India
Year Established: **Status 2020:** Active
Industries: Artificial Intelligence for:, ~ Banking and Financial Markets-Services (7), ~ Banking and Financial Markets-Services (7), ~ Banking and Financial Markets-Services (7), ~ Metals and Mining (42), ~ Metals and Mining (42), ~ Professional Services (48)

Company Name: Broadcast Wearables Pvt Ltd
Description: Worlds 1st Programmable Tshirt, World's 1st Fitness Jersey with Functions of a Fitness Band, World's 1st Cycling Jersey LEDTurn Indicato: Serbia
Website: http://www.broadcastwear.com/
Phone: **Email:** saumil@broadcastwear.com
City: Hyderabad **State:** TG **PC:** **Country:** India
Year Established: 2016 **Status 2020:** Active
Industries: Internet of Things (IoT) for:, ~ Arts-Entertainment-Recreation (4), ~ Arts-Entertainment-Recreation (4), Internet of Things (IoT)

Company Name: Brontobyte Analytics
Description: Brontobyte Analytics is an AI-based company
Website: http://www.brontobyteanalytics.com/
Phone: 91 8008333336 **Email:** info@brontobyteanalytics.com
City: Hyderabad **State:** TG **PC:** **Country:** India
Year Established: 2016 **Status 2020:** Active
Industries: Analytics

Company Name: C3C
Description: C3C- App to make City Commute Happier. C3C is Chic Carpool, Cabpool, Public transport, Social app for mitigating traffic &Pollution
Website: http://www.c3c.in/a
Phone: **Email:** admin@c3c.: India
City: Hyderabad **State:** AP **PC:** **Country:** India
Year Established: **Status 2020:** Active
Industries: Artificial Intelligence for:, ~ Social-Environmental-Physical-Engineering Sciences (55), Application Services for:, ~ Transportation and Logistics (57)

Company Name: CaroCure Discovery Solutions Private Limited
Description: CaroCure is a rational drug discovery company employing innovative technologies to design and create best-in-class drug candidat: Spain
Website: http://carocure.com/
Phone: (996) 636-4176 **Email:** kranthi.k@carocure.com
City: Hyderabad **State:** AP **PC:** **Country:** India
Year Established: 2017 **Status 2020:** Active
Industries: Artificial Intelligence for:, ~ Biotechnology (9)

Company Name: Cognier Insights
Description: Cognier Insights is Simplified Blockchain Solutions.
Website: http://www.cognierblock.com/
Phone: 0091-916 000 0748 **Email:** info@cognier.co
City: Hyderabad **State:** TG **PC:** **Country:** India
Year Established: 2017 **Status 2020:** Active
Industries: IT Managed Services for:, IT Managed Services for:, Machine Learning

Company Name: CUSMAT Technology
Description: Saas, Virtual reality , Heavy Industry
Website: http://www.CUSMAT.COM
Phone: **Email:** soumyaranjan@cusmat.com
City: Hyderabad **State:** TG **PC:** **Country:** India

Year Established: 2016 **Status 2020:** Active
Industries: Artificial Intelligence for:, ~ Education (13), IT Managed Services

Company Name: Deta
Description: Deta is a proprietary AI Engine to provide intelligent insights for varying market intelligence needs of clients.
Website: http://www.deta.ai
Phone: 1-614-588-8538 **Email:** sales@deta.ai
City: Hyderabad **State:** AP **PC:** **Country:** India
Year Established: **Status 2020:** Active
Industries: Artificial Intelligence for:, Machine Learning

Company Name: EHNOTE
Description: EHNOTE offers cloud based solutions for Clinic Management, Electronic Medical Records, as well as Clinical Analytics for Hospitals.
Website: http://www.ehnote.com/
Phone: **Email:** Ehnoteseo@gmail.com
City: Hyderabad **State:** TG **PC:** **Country:** India
Year Established: 2016 **Status 2020:** Active
Industries: Artificial Intelligence for:, Big Data and Analytics for:, ~ Healthcare (20), IT Managed Services

Company Name: Elephanta AI
Description: Machine learning at speed and scale - Elephanta AI provides deployment-ready enterprise AI solutions for data-driven organizations.
Website: http://elephanta.ai/
Phone: 91 6303950724 **Email:** contact@elephanta.ai
City: Hyderabad **State:** TG **PC:** **Country:** India
Year Established: 2019 **Status 2020:** Active
Industries: Analytics for:, Artificial Intelligence for:, Big Data and Analytics for:, Data Management for:, Enterprise Application Services for:, Machine Learning

Company Name: Endless Robotics
Description: Endless Robotics is build intelligent robots to solve dull and dirty problems for construction, maintenance and smart city management.
Website: http://endlessrobotics.com/
Phone: **Email:** help@endlessrobotics.com
City: Hyderabad **State:** TG **PC:** **Country:** India
Year Established: 2015 **Status 2020:** Active
Industries:

Company Name: ENIXTA Innovations Pvt Ltd
Description: ENIXTA (anagram of Next AI) is an artificial intelligence company - aiming to use AI to help consumers make better buying decisions
Website: http://www.enixta.com
Phone: **Email:** marketing@buysmaart.com
City: Hyderabad **State:** AP **PC:** **Country:** India
Year Established: **Status 2020:** Active
Industries: Artificial Intelligence for:, Business Intelligence

Company Name: Enmovil
Description: Enmovil delivers a Business Intelligence Platform.
Website: http://www.enmovil.in/aboutus
Phone: **Email:** info@enmovil.: India
City: Hyderabad **State:** TG **PC:** **Country:** India
Year Established: 2015 **Status 2020:** Active
Industries: ~ Telecommunications (56), IT Managed Services for:, Machine Learning

Company Name: Fabulyst
Description: Fabulyst is an AI engine that works as a virtual personal stylist, solving modern women's style aspirations.
Website: http://www.fabulyst.com
Phone: (99) 123-4286 **Email:** support@mail.net
City: Hyderabad **State:** TG **PC:** **Country:** India
Year Established: 2016 **Status 2020:** Active
Industries: Artificial Intelligence for:, E-Commerce for:, Web for:, ~ Retail and Consumer Products (52)

Company Name: Facillizence
Description: Facillizence is a Commercial Real Estate company
Website: http://facillizence.com/
Phone: 91 - 897 818 8734 **Email:** info@indriyn.com
City: Hyderabad **State:** TG **PC:** **Country:** India
Year Established: 2015 **Status 2020:** Active
Industries: Artificial Intelligence for:, ~ Real Estate (49)

Company Name: Farmioc
Description: Global Agriculture Data Company
Website: http://farmioc.com
Phone: 91 78937 32513 **Email:** contact@farmioc.com
City: Hyderabad **State:** TG **PC:** **Country:** India
Year Established: 2018 **Status 2020:** Active
Industries: ~ Agriculture (3), Analytics for:, Big Data and Analytics for:, ~ Agriculture (3), Machine Learning for:, Predictive Analytics

Company Name: FastCollab
Description: FastCollab is an Artificial Intelligence Powered Corporate Travel Assistant.
Website: http://www.fastcollab.com/
Phone: 91 80 3063 6063 **Email:** customercare@fastcollab.com
City: Hyderabad **State:** TG **PC:** **Country:** India
Year Established: 2016 **Status 2020:** Active
Industries: Artificial Intelligence for:, IT Managed Services

Company Name: Gamooga
Description: Omni-channel customer engagement platform backed by a powerful predictive analytics engine
Website: http://www.gamooga.com/
Phone: **Email:** contact@gamooga.com
City: Hyderabad **State:** AP **PC:** **Country:** India
Year Established: 2014 **Status 2020:** Active
Industries: Analytics for:, Predictive Analytics

Company Name: Genylabs
Description: Genylabs is an artificial intelligence company.
Website: http://genylabs.io/
Phone: **Email:** hello@genylabs.io
City: Hyderabad **State:** TG **PC:** **Country:** India
Year Established: 2016 **Status 2020:** Active
Industries: Artificial Intelligence for:, ~ Education (13)

Company Name: GEO-I
Description: Geo-I is an intelligent and affordable software company.
Website: http://www.geoidentify.com
Phone: **Email:** 36616@reference-encyclopedia-ai.net
City: Hyderabad **State:** TG **PC:** **Country:** India
Year Established: 2014 **Status 2020:** Active
Industries: IT Managed Services for:, Application Services

Company Name: Grene Robotics
Description: SAAS, AI & Machine Learning
Website: http://www.grenerobotics.com
Phone: 718-404-7489 **Email:** kiran@desker.co
City: Hyderabad **State:** AP **PC:** **Country:** India
Year Established: **Status 2020:** Active
Industries: Artificial Intelligence for:, Cloud for:, Enterprise Application Services for:, Machine Learning

Company Name: Helical Insight
Description: Helical Insight is an open source developer friendly API-driven Business Intelligence framework.
Website: http://helicalinsight.com
Phone: **Email:** support@helicalinsight.com
City: Hyderabad **State:** TG **PC:** **Country:** India
Year Established: 2012 **Status 2020:** Active
Industries: Analytics for:, Business Intelligence for:, Data Management for:, IT Managed Services for:, Machine Learning for:, Application Services

Company Name: Hyperdata.IO
Description: Hyperdata combines advanced machine learning with human intelligence.
Website: http://www.hyperdata.io/
Phone: **Email:** support@hyperlinq.io
City: Hyderabad **State:** TG **PC:** **Country:** India
Year Established: 2017 **Status 2020:** Active
Industries: Business Applications for:, Machine Learning

Company Name: Ifelseloop
Description: Ifelseloop.com is a tutorial site for computer programme: Serbia
Website: http://www.ifelseloop.com/
Phone: 9494286811 **Email:** myifelseloop@gmail.com
City: Hyderabad **State:** AP **PC:** **Country:** India
Year Established: **Status 2020:** Active
Industries:

Company Name: Innomatics Research labs
Description: We are a AI driven company focusing on building products and consulting. We also have a training brand - Innomatics Research Labs
Website: http://www.zeominds.com/
Phone: **Email:** VISHWANATH.NYATHANI@ZEOMINDS.COM
City: Hyderabad **State:** TG **PC:** **Country:** India
Year Established: 2019 **Status 2020:** Active
Industries:

Company Name: INSOFE
Description: International School of Engineering
Website: http://www.insofe.edu.: India
Phone: **Email:** info@insofe.edu.: India
City: Hyderabad **State:** TG **PC:** **Country:** India
Year Established: 2010 **Status 2020:** Active
Industries: Big Data and Analytics for:, ~ Education (13), ~ Education (13), Predictive Analytics

Company Name: Kenyt Technologies Pvt Ltd
Description: Kenyt.AI builds virtual assistants for variety of businesses with aim to capture more leads and improve user retention.
Website: http://www.kenyt.ai
Phone: 78937 68516 **Email:** contact@kenyt.ai
City: Hyderabad **State:** TG **PC:** **Country:** India
Year Established: 2015 **Status 2020:** Active
Industries: Analytics for:, Artificial Intelligence for:, IT Managed Services for:, Mobile for:, Robotics

Company Name: LEAP ROBOTS
Description: A platform to learn and build Robotics, 3D printing, Internet of Things (IOT), Artificial Intelligence (AI) and other next generation tech.
Website: http://leaprobots.com
Phone: 91 8074143384 **Email:** info@leaprobots.com
City: Hyderabad **State:** TG **PC:** **Country:** India
Year Established: 2016 **Status 2020:** Active
Industries: Artificial Intelligence for:, ~ Arts-Entertainment-Recreation (4), Internet of Things (IoT) for:, Robotics for:, ~ Education (13)

Company Name: LearnerScri: Portugal
Description: We report everything you do on Moodle
Website: http://learnerscript.com
Phone: 1 (469) 381-1227 **Email:** info@learnerscript.com
City: Hyderabad **State:** TG **PC:** **Country:** India
Year Established: 2018 **Status 2020:** Active
Industries: Analytics for:, ~ Education (13), ~ Education (13), Predictive Analytics

Company Name: Livo
Description: Reenvisioning blood diagnostics to make them accessible and affordable at the point of care.
Website: http://www.livo.ai
Phone: **Email:** info@livo.ai
City: Hyderabad **State:** TG **PC:** **Country:** India
Year Established: 2018 **Status 2020:** Active
Industries: Artificial Intelligence for:, ~ Healthcare (20), Machine Learning

Company Name: Loop Reality
Description: Loop Reality is a technology company building immersive products and experience using disruptive technologies (VR, AR, IoT, Analytics).
Website: http://www.loopreality.com
Phone: **Email:** info@loopreality.com
City: Hyderabad **State:** AP **PC:** **Country:** India
Year Established: **Status 2020:** Active
Industries: Analytics for:, Artificial Intelligence for:, ~ Human Resources (24), ~ Life Sciences (27), ~ Healthcare (20), ~ Human Resources (24)

Company Name: Machintelli
Description: A product development organization
Website: http://www.machintelli.com
Phone: **Email:** praveen@machintelli.com
City: Hyderabad **State:** TG **PC:** **Country:** India
Year Established: 2016 **Status 2020:** Active
Industries: Artificial Intelligence for:, E-Commerce for:, IT Managed Services for:, Machine Learning

Company Name: MARUT Dron: Spain
Description: MARUT Drones is a research and product development company using drone technology to curb mosquito menace.
Website: http://marutdrones.com/
Phone: **Email:** prem@marutdrones.com
City: Hyderabad **State:** AP **PC:** **Country:** India
Year Established: 2019 **Status 2020:** Active
Industries: Artificial Intelligence for:, IT Managed Services

Company Name: minto.ai
Description: Smart and Real-Time condition monitoring platform for rotating machin: Spain
Website: http://www.minto.ai/
Phone: **Email:** zerodowntime@minto.ai
City: Hyderabad **State:** TG **PC:** **Country:** India
Year Established: 2018 **Status 2020:** Active
Industries: Artificial Intelligence for:, Big Data and Analytics for:, Automation for:, Internet of Things (IoT) for:, Predictive Analytics

Company Name: Mobiport
Description: Mobiport is a platform to create conversational apps for platforms like Amazon Alexa, Google Assistant and Microsoft Cortana.
Website: http://mobiport.io
Phone: **Email:** hello@mobiport.io
City: Hyderabad **State:** TG **PC:** **Country:** India
Year Established: 2016 **Status 2020:** Active
Industries: Application Services for:, Artificial Intelligence for:, Big Data and Analytics for:, IT Managed Services for:, Machine Learning

Company Name: NicheAI
Description: Early stage Artificial Intelligence (AI) start up.
Website: http://studio.nicheai.com/
Phone: **Email:** careers@nicheai.com
City: Hyderabad **State:** AP **PC:** **Country:** India
Year Established: **Status 2020:** Active
Industries: Artificial Intelligence

Company Name: Nitty-Gritty Software Solutions Private Limited
Description: Focused on building future technologies in learning doma: India
Website:
Phone: **Email:** 37067@reference-encyclopedia-ai.net
City: Hyderabad **State:** TG **PC:** **Country:** India
Year Established: 2015 **Status 2020:** Active
Industries: Artificial Intelligence for:, ~ Education (13), IT Managed Services for:, Web for:, Machine Learning

Company Name: Ntwist
Description: NTWIST helps enterprises leverage machine learning and Artificial Intelligence.
Website: http://ntwist.com/
Phone: **Email:** info@ntwist.com
City: Hyderabad **State:** TG **PC:** **Country:** India
Year Established: 2016 **Status 2020:** Active
Industries: Artificial Intelligence for:, Computer Vision

Company Name: Nuacem
Description: A Next-gen, AI Powered Omnichannel Digital Customer Engagement Platform.
Website: http://nuacem.com
Phone: 91 863 994 5832 **Email:** info@nuacem.com
City: Hyderabad **State:** AP **PC:** **Country:** India
Year Established: 2018 **Status 2020:** Active
Industries:

Company Name: Onward Asslst
Description: Oncology AI platform for better treatment decisions
Website: http://www.onwardhealth.ai
Phone: **Email:** dinesh@onwardhealth.co
City: Hyderabad **State:** AP **PC:** **Country:** India
Year Established: **Status 2020:** Active
Industries: Artificial Intelligence for:, ~ Healthcare (20), ~ Healthcare (20), Machine Learning for:, Predictive Analytics

Company Name: Perfhack
Description: Measuring Perceived Performance of any Website
Website: http://www.perfhack.com
Phone: 091-733-075-9777 **Email:** contact@perfhack.com
City: Hyderabad **State:** TG **PC:** **Country:** India
Year Established: 2017 **Status 2020:** Active
Industries: Application Services for:, Artificial Intelligence

Company Name: PerspectAI
Description: Our SaaS platform enables organizations to attract, hire, & retain top talent, bias-free, using a blend of VR, Mobile, Games & AI Interview.
Website: http://perspect.ai
Phone: **Email:** info@perspect.ai
City: Hyderabad **State:** AP **PC:** **Country:** India
Year Established: **Status 2020:** Active
Industries: Analytics for:, Artificial Intelligence for:, ~ Human Resources (24), ~ Life Sciences (27), ~ Healthcare (20), ~ Human Resources (24)

Company Name: Proxzar
Description: Proxzar is an Artificial Intelligence powered platform on cloud to create, train and host proxies.
Website: http://www.proxzar.ai/
Phone: 086394 87984 **Email:** info@proxzar.ai
City: Hyderabad **State:** TG **PC:** **Country:** India
Year Established: 2018 **Status 2020:** Active
Industries: Artificial Intelligence for:, IT Managed Services

Company Name: Quadratic
Description: Quadratyx is a AI and data Science company.
Website: http://quadratyx.com
Phone: 040-2970-2383 **Email:** engage@quadratyx.com
City: Hyderabad **State:** TG **PC:** **Country:** India
Year Established: 2014 **Status 2020:** Active
Industries: Artificial Intelligence

Company Name: Saanketh AI Systems Pvt Ltd.
Description: Artificial Intelligence, Deep Learning, Machine Learning, Applied Ai, Research & Product Development
Website: http://www.saanketh.ai
Phone: 91 40 40171695 **Email:** info@saanketh.ai
City: Hyderabad **State:** AP **PC:** **Country:** India
Year Established: **Status 2020:** Active
Industries: Artificial Intelligence for:, Business Intelligence for:, IT Managed Services for:, IT Managed Services for:, Machine Learning for:, Business Intelligence

Company Name: SAYINT
Description: Smart Insights from Conversations
Website: http://www.sayint.ai
Phone: **Email:** contact@sayint.ai
City: Hyderabad **State:** TG **PC:** **Country:** India
Year Established: 2016 **Status 2020:** Active
Industries: IT Managed Services for:, Machine Learning

Company Name: Seethos
Description: A.I. as a Service
Website: http://www.seethos.com
Phone: 1 (646) 895-6080 **Email:** nfo@seethos.com
City: Hyderabad **State:** TG **PC:** **Country:** India
Year Established: 2017 **Status 2020:** Active
Industries: Artificial Intelligence for:, Web

Company Name: SelectDine
Description: SelectDine focus on Restaurant Setup/Franchise, Restaurant Hiring Solutions, Restaurant Supply Chain Management and AI to manage Restaurant.
Website: http://www.selectdine.com/
Phone: **Email:** admin@selectdine.com
City: Hyderabad **State:** TG **PC:** **Country:** India
Year Established: 2017 **Status 2020:** Active
Industries: IT Managed Services for:, Business Software as a Service Apps (SaaS Apps)

Company Name: Sigmalytics
Description: Helping enterprises to integrate AI into their core business model by providing BPO service
Website: http://www.thesigmalytics.com
Phone: **Email:** admin@thesigmalytics.com
City: Hyderabad **State:** TG **PC:** **Country:** India
Year Established: 2019 **Status 2020:** Active
Industries: Artificial Intelligence for:, IT Managed Services for:, Machine Learning for:, Predictive Analytics

Company Name: Smartron
Description: Smartron is a global technology OEM brand offering intelligent experiences through tronX, the AI powered IoT platform.
Website: http://www.smartron.com/
Phone: 040 6999 1775 **Email:** info@smartron.com
City: Hyderabad **State:** TG **PC:** **Country:** India
Year Established: 2014 **Status 2020:** Active
Industries: Artificial Intelligence

Company Name: SMATSUITE
Description: Have two AI products SmatBot (A chatbot for websites, messenger for lead generation etc) and SmatSocial (An Assistant for SMM automation)
Website: http://www.SmatSuite.com
Phone: 7207982810 **Email:** santosh@smatsocial.com
City: Hyderabad **State:** TG **PC:** **Country:** India
Year Established: 2015 **Status 2020:** Active
Industries: Artificial Intelligence for:, IT Managed Services for:, IT Managed Services

Company Name: Soulpage IT Solutions
Description: Soulpage IT Solutions is a Data Science Technology company specializing in AI, Machine Learning, NLP and Deep Learning etc.
Website: http://soulpageit.com/
Phone: 91 9032334488 **Email:** contact@soulpageit.com
City: Hyderabad **State:** AP **PC:** **Country:** India
Year Established: **Status 2020:** Active
Industries: Analytics for:, Artificial Intelligence for:, Big Data and Analytics for:, IT Managed Services for:, Machine Learning for:, Natural Language Processing for:, ~ Professional Services (48)

Company Name: thirdleap
Description: Thirdleap is a Leap Of Faith With Technology.
Website: http://www.thirdleap.ai
Phone: **Email:** info@thirdleap.ai
City: Hyderabad **State:** TG **PC:** **Country:** India

Year Established: 2015 **Status 2020:** Active
Industries:

Company Name: Tresm Labs
Description: AI Focussed Company Building Solutions For Enterprises.
Website: http://tresmlabs.ai
Phone: **Email:** info@tresmlabs.com
City: Hyderabad **State:** AP **PC:** **Country:** India
Year Established: 2016 **Status 2020:** Active
Industries: Artificial Intelligence for:, IT Managed Services

Company Name: TrionCube
Description: TrionCube is an early stage technology product company that provides solutions to sales industry.
Website: http://trioncube.com
Phone: **Email:** hello@trioncube.com
City: Hyderabad **State:** AP **PC:** **Country:** India
Year Established: **Status 2020:** Active
Industries: Artificial Intelligence for:, Big Data and Analytics for:, Enterprise Application Services

Company Name: tuplejump
Description: tuplejump offers big data solutions that enable businesses to capture and analyze data.
Website: http://www.tuplejump.com
Phone: **Email:** info@tuplejump.com
City: Hyderabad **State:** AP **PC:** **Country:** India
Year Established: **Status 2020:** Active
Industries: Analytics for:, Artificial Intelligence for:, Big Data and Analytics for:, Data Management for:, Machine Learning for:, ~ Professional Services (48)

Company Name: TurboHire Technologies Pvt Ltd
Description: Turbo Hire delivers highly intelligent Applicant Tracking System Powered by Simplicity of JustDropYourResume.com for Job Applications.
Website: http://Turbohire.co
Phone: **Email:** deepak.ag@turbohire.co
City: Hyderabad **State:** AP **PC:** **Country:** India
Year Established: **Status 2020:** Active
Industries: Artificial Intelligence for:, ~ Human Resources (24), Machine Learning for:, Natural Language Processing for:, ~ Human Resources (24)

Company Name: Vihik cabs
Description: Vihik (Vehicle Aggregator) is artificial intelligent application for booking vehicles at cheaper rate in city and outstation.
Website: http://vihik.com/
Phone: **Email:** support@vihik.com
City: Hyderabad **State:** TG **PC:** **Country:** India
Year Established: 2016 **Status 2020:** Active
Industries: Artificial Intelligence

Company Name: Vitwit
Description: Vitwit specializes in AI, blockchain and cloud solutions.
Website: http://www.vitwit.com/
Phone: 91 630 0946153 **Email:** contact@vitwit.com
City: Hyderabad **State:** TG **PC:** **Country:** India
Year Established: 2015 **Status 2020:** Active
Industries: Artificial Intelligence for:, Blockchain

Company Name: Workru: Italy
Description: Workruit, an on-the-go mobile app that simplifies recruitment using AI. Get our free app today!
Website: http://workruit.com
Phone: 8639217011 **Email:** info@workruit.com
City: Hyderabad **State:** TG **PC:** **Country:** India
Year Established: 2016 **Status 2020:** Active
Industries: Artificial Intelligence for:, Web

Company Name: Xmachin: Spain
Description: Xmachines is a Robotics company located in Hyderabad .
Website: http://xmachines.ai/
Phone: 8247476933 **Email:** support@xmachines.ai
City: Hyderabad **State:** TG **PC:** **Country:** India
Year Established: 2017 **Status 2020:** Active
Industries: Artificial Intelligence for:, Automation for:, Machine Learning for:, Robotics

Company Name: Yuthivara Analytics
Description: Software & Advanced Analytics Solutions
Website: http://www.yuthivaraanalytics.com
Phone: **Email:** hr@yuthivaraanalytics.com
City: Hyderabad **State:** TG **PC:** **Country:** India
Year Established: 2017 **Status 2020:** Active
Industries: Predictive Analytics

Company Name: Yuvtar Inc
Description: Yuvtar lets a user create his or her online avatar. The avatar grows with the user with time, learning & mimicking the user.
Website:
Phone: **Email:** hello@yuvtar.me
City: Hyderabad **State:** AP **PC:** **Country:** India
Year Established: **Status 2020:** Active
Industries: Artificial Intelligence for:, Machine Learning for:, ~ Social Media (54)

Company Name: Tech Lurn
Description: TechLurn provides trending stories from Science & Technology, Artificial Intelligence, Gadgets and Digital Marketing.
Website: http://techlurn.com
Phone: 8919885200 **Email:** contact@techlurn.com
City: Warangal **State:** TG **PC:** **Country:** India
Year Established: 2016 **Status 2020:** Active
Industries: Artificial Intelligence for:, Digital Media

Company Name: Dhonor
Description: Dhonor is a blockchain verification application empowers patients to self-verify pharmaceuticals and other healthcare products.
Website: http://dhonor.org/
Phone: **Email:** wassim.merheby@dhonor.org
City: Dubai **State:** UP **PC:** **Country:** India
Year Established: **Status 2020:** Active
Industries: Artificial Intelligence for:, Big Data and Analytics for:, ~ Banking and Financial Markets-Services (7), ~ Banking and Financial Markets-Services (7), ~ Healthcare (20), ~ Healthcare (20)

Company Name: Quanterium BlockChain Solutions
Description: Quanterium Blockchain Solutions is a developer of cutting-edge tech solutions combining Blockchain and AI.
Website: www.quanterium.net
Phone: **Email:** info@quanterium.net
City: Dubai **State:** UP **PC:** **Country:** India
Year Established: **Status 2020:** Active
Industries: Artificial Intelligence for:, Business Applications for:, Blockchain for:, E-Commerce for:, ~ Healthcare (20), ~ Social Assistance-Non-Profits (53), ~ Social-Environmental-Physical-Engineering Sciences (55)

Company Name: BotMyWork
Description: Organise and Automate actions at your professional front with Chatbots
Website: http://botmywork.com
Phone: 0522-407-7802 **Email:** support@botmywork.com
City: Lucknow **State:** UP **PC:** **Country:** India
Year Established: **Status 2020:** Active
Industries:

Company Name: Brainpan Innovations
Description: 1. Doctor's Diary: Doctor's Diary is an Electronic Health Record (EHR) application that promises 'one patient, one record' for 1.
Website: http://www.brainpan.co/
Phone: (999) 082-5238 **Email:** amrit.ravi@brainpan.co
City: Lucknow **State:** UP **PC:** **Country:** India
Year Established: 2015 **Status 2020:** Active
Industries: Big Data and Analytics for:, ~ Healthcare (20), ~ Healthcare (20), ~ Healthcare (20), Management Information Systems for:, ~ Healthcare (20), Predictive Analytics

Company Name: Medma Infomatix Pvt. Ltd.
Description: IT Software Development Company.
Website: http://medma.net
Phone: 213-814-0722 **Email:** info@medma.net
City: Lucknow **State:** UP **PC:** **Country:** India
Year Established: **Status 2020:** Active
Industries: Artificial Intelligence for:, Cloud for:, E-Commerce for:, Enterprise Application Services for:, IT Managed Services for:, Mobile for:, ~ Professional Services (48), Cyber Security

Company Name: WikQik
Description: Advancing AI for Everyone
Website: http://www.wikqik.com
Phone: 9519696660 **Email:** care@wikqik.com
City: Lucknow **State:** UP **PC:** **Country:** India
Year Established: 2019 **Status 2020:** Active
Industries: Artificial Intelligence for:, ~ Banking and Financial Markets-Services (7), ~ Retail and Consumer Products (52), ~ Social Assistance-Non-Profits (53)

Company Name: 4Bell Technology
Description: 4Bell is a technology and consulting company where we major providing the services in to the recruitment industry.
Website: http://4bell.com/
Phone: 7217860087 **Email:** vibhanshu@4bell.com
City: Noida **State:** UP **PC:** **Country:** India
Year Established: 2016 **Status 2020:** Active
Industries: Web

Company Name: Agsmartic Technologies Pvt. Ltd.
Description: AgriTech, IoT, Machine Learning, Smart Irrigation
Website: http://www.agsmartic.com
Phone: 0120-6600506 **Email:** info@agsmartic.com
City: Noida **State:** UP **PC:** **Country:** India
Year Established: **Status 2020:** Active
Industries: ~ Agriculture (3), ~ Agriculture (3), Artificial Intelligence

Company Name: Ajoopa
Description: Mobile App, Productivity, Artificial Intelligence
Website: http://www.ajoopa.com
Phone: **Email:** support@ajoopa.com
City: Noida **State:** UP **PC:** **Country:** India
Year Established: **Status 2020:** Active
Industries: Application Services for:, Artificial Intelligence for:, Machine Learning

Company Name: Algoscale Technologies, Inc.
Description: Algoscale's platform Data Hub works across the Big Data Analytics value chain offering analysis and technology infrastructure under one roof
Website: https://algoscale.com/
Phone: **Email:** askus@algoscale.com
City: Noida **State:** UP **PC:** **Country:** India
Year Established: 2014 **Status 2020:** Active
Industries: Analytics for:, Artificial Intelligence for:, Big Data and Analytics for:, Business Intelligence for:, IT Managed Services for:, Machine Learning

Company Name: Anolytics
Description: Anolytics offers data and image annotation service for computer vision and machine learning process.
Website: http://www.anolytics.ai/
Phone: 516-342-5749 **Email:** info@anolytics.ai
City: Noida **State:** UP **PC:** **Country:** India
Year Established: 2018 **Status 2020:** Active
Industries: Artificial Intelligence for:, Image Recognition for:, IT Managed Services for:, Machine Learning

Company Name: Boltt Sports Technologies
Description: AI based mobile health and fitness coaching
Website: http://boltt.com/
Phone: **Email:** info@boltt.com
City: Noida **State:** UP **PC:** **Country:** India
Year Established: **Status 2020:** Active
Industries: Artificial Intelligence for:, ~ Healthcare (20)

Company Name: Bytescare
Description: Bytescare is an intelligent system to detect and monitor the piracy of copyright media on the internet
Website: http://www.bytescare.com/
Phone: 91 9871442583 **Email:** contact@bytescare.com
City: Noida **State:** UP **PC:** **Country:** India
Year Established: 2017 **Status 2020:** Active
Industries: Artificial Intelligence for:, IT Managed Services for:, Web

Company Name: CampuStori: Spain
Description: CampuStories helps you effortlessly manage the activities of your institute in one place and makes it easier than ever to track them.
Website: http://www.campustories.com
Phone: **Email:** 4965@reference-encyclopedia-ai.net
City: Noida **State:** UP **PC:** **Country:** India
Year Established: **Status 2020:** Active
Industries: Analytics for:, Artificial Intelligence for:, ~ Education (13), IT Managed Services

Company Name: Casemine
Description: CaseMine leveraging AI to unearth latent linkages between case laws thereby making legal research more in-depth and comprehensive.
Website: http://www.casemine.com/home
Phone: 0120 650 0618 **Email:** hello@casemine.com
City: Noida **State:** UP **PC:** **Country:** India
Year Established: 2013 **Status 2020:** Active
Industries:

Company Name: Clear-Data Analytics
Description: Clear-Data Analytics provides companies with marketing and analytics solutions.
Website: http://www.clear-data.: India
Phone: **Email:** make.sense@clear-data.: India
City: Noida **State:** UP **PC:** **Country:** India
Year Established: 2013 **Status 2020:** Active
Industries: Analytics

Company Name: Codefire Technologies Pvt. Ltd.
Description: CodeFire is technology company having core expertise in solving complex and hard to crack problems and developing applications.
Website: http://www.codefire.org
Phone: (530) 377-0678 **Email:** contact@codefire.: India
City: Noida **State:** UP **PC:** **Country:** India
Year Established: **Status 2020:** Active
Industries:

Company Name: Devnagri
Description: Devnagri is an AI-powered Human translation Platform to help businesses reach 500 M Indian Internet users in their regional languages.
Website: http://www.devnagri.com
Phone: **Email:** namaste@devnagri.com
City: Noida **State:** UP **PC:** **Country:** India

Year Established: 2017 **Status 2020:** Active
Industries: Artificial Intelligence for:, IT Managed Services for:, Natural Language Processing for:, Business Software as a Service Apps (SaaS Apps)

Company Name: DoctorKePaas
Description: CLINICAL ASSISTANCE PLATFORM to empower health workers and practitione: Serbia
Website: http://www.doctorkepaas.com/
Phone: 91 8755 8466 48 **Email:** contact@doctorkepaas.com
City: Noida **State:** UP **PC:** **Country:** India
Year Established: **Status 2020:** Active
Industries: Artificial Intelligence for:, ~ Healthcare (20), Machine Learning for:, ~ Healthcare (20), Enterprise Application Services

Company Name: HCL Technologies Ltd.
Description: Digital Transformation
Website: http://www.hcltech.com
Phone: 770-833-8247 **Email:** zdwhigham@us.ibm.com
City: Noida **State:** UP **Zip:** 201304 **Country:** India
Year Established: **Status 2020:** Active
Industries:

Company Name: Korbose Technology
Description: Korbose Technology provides new-age business solutions to meet the challenges of ever changing business demands.
Website: http://www.korbose.com/
Phone: 0120-4750223 **Email:** info@korbose.com
City: Noida **State:** UP **PC:** **Country:** India
Year Established: 2010 **Status 2020:** Active
Industries: Artificial Intelligence for:, IT Managed Services

Company Name: Kosh
Description: Kosh is a financial services platform designed for service providers.
Website: http://getkosh.com/
Phone: 91 8882381176 **Email:** public@getkosh.com
City: Noida **State:** UP **PC:** **Country:** India
Year Established: 2019 **Status 2020:** Active
Industries: ~ Banking and Financial Markets-Services (7), Machine Learning

Company Name: Nube Technologies
Description: Nube helps discover, enhance and consolidate business data.
Website: http://nubetech.co
Phone: 747-999-8330 **Email:** info@nubetech.co
City: Noida **State:** UP **PC:** **Country:** India
Year Established: 2010 **Status 2020:** Active
Industries: Analytics for:, Big Data and Analytics

Company Name: Prithvi.ai
Description: Prithvi.ai is a seed stage accelerator program.
Website: http://prithvi.ai/
Phone: **Email:** info@mysite.com
City: Noida **State:** UP **PC:** **Country:** India
Year Established: 2018 **Status 2020:** Active
Industries: Artificial Intelligence for:, Databases

Company Name: Project42 Labs
Description: Project42 Labs is an AI and machine learning company.
Website: http://www.project42labs.com/
Phone: 91 988 678 2956 **Email:** sales@project42labs.com
City: Noida **State:** UP **PC:** **Country:** India
Year Established: 2018 **Status 2020:** Active
Industries: Artificial Intelligence for:, Machine Learning

Company Name: PS Quick: ITALY
Description: PS QuickIT has extensive experience building mobile app, web app and desktop application at enterprise and mid label.
Website: http://www.psquickit.com/
Phone: 91-120-4151444 **Email:** info@psquickit.com
City: Noida **State:** UP **PC:** **Country:** India
Year Established: 2012 **Status 2020:** Active
Industries: Application Services for:, Artificial Intelligence for:, Cloud for:, ~ Customer Relationship Management (11)

Company Name: RealBox Data Analytics
Description: We build Voice Assistants for Large Enterprises to do analytics, dashboard & machine Learning with Alexa, Cortana & Google Assistant
Website: http://www.realbox.: India
Phone: **Email:** support@realbox.: India
City: Noida **State:** UP **PC:** **Country:** India
Year Established: 2015 **Status 2020:** Active
Industries: Analytics for:, Business Intelligence for:, Predictive Analytics for:, Internet of Things (IoT)

Company Name: Siftr Labs
Description: Siftr is a computer vision platform to analyse images in user generated content.
Website: http://siftr.co/
Phone: **Email:** 37387@reference-encyclopedia-ai.net
City: Noida **State:** UP **PC:** **Country:** India
Year Established: 2015 **Status 2020:** Active
Industries: Artificial Intelligence for:, ~ Media-Communications (41), ~ Social Assistance-Non-Profits (53)

Company Name: Skilancer Solar
Description: Skilancer is a centrally controlled, self-powered, robot for automatic cleaning of solar panels with elements of Artificial Intelligence.
Website: http://www.skilancersolar.com/
Phone: 91 9971045274 **Email:** neeraj@skilancer.com
City: Noida **State:** UP **PC:** **Country:** India
Year Established: 2017 **Status 2020:** Active
Industries: Artificial Intelligence for:, ~ Energy and Utilities (14), ~ Energy and Utilities (14)

Company Name: SpotDraft
Description: SpotDraft develops an artificial intelligence-powered platform to draft and execute legal contracts.
Website: http://www.spotdraft.com/
Phone: **Email:** team@spotdraft.com
City: Noida **State:** UP **PC:** **Country:** India
Year Established: 2017 **Status 2020:** Active
Industries:

Company Name: tail.re
Description: Intuitive replenishments for frequently consumed products
Website: http://tail.re
Phone: **Email:** scientists@tail.re
City: Noida **State:** UP **PC:** **Country:** India
Year Established: 2015 **Status 2020:** Active
Industries:

Company Name: The Tarzan Way
Description: AI Based Travel Consultant, Experiential Travel Provider
Website: http://www.thetarzanway.com
Phone: **Email:** info@thetarzanway.com
City: Noida **State:** UP **PC:** **Country:** India
Year Established: 2018 **Status 2020:** Active
Industries: Artificial Intelligence for:, Business Applications for:, ~ Travel and Transportation (58)

Company Name: Valiance Solutions
Description: Valiance Solutions is a data analytics firm that uses advanced analytics to build products and make decisions.
Website: http://valiancesolutions.com
Phone: 8750068961 **Email:** vikas.kamra@valiancesolutions.com
City: Noida **State:** UP **PC:** **Country:** India
Year Established: 2012 **Status 2020:** Active
Industries: Analytics for:, Business Intelligence for:, Predictive Analytics

Company Name: WITO: NIGERIA
Description: Witoni offers automation, monitoring and security solutions.
Website: http://www.witoni.com/
Phone: 098738 22561 **Email:** enquiry@witoni.com
City: Noida **State:** UP **PC:** **Country:** India
Year Established: 2015 **Status 2020:** Active
Industries: Artificial Intelligence for:, Cyber Security for:, IT Managed Services

Company Name: Xotiv Technologies
Description: Xotiv Technologies is all about Passion, Excellence, and Flexibility in the software development services and solutions.
Website: http://xotiv.com/
Phone: 0120-4543329 **Email:** info@xotiv.com
City: Noida **State:** UP **PC:** **Country:** India
Year Established: **Status 2020:** Active
Industries: Analytics for:, Application Services for:, Artificial Intelligence for:, Big Data and Analytics for:, Digital Marketing for:, ~ Professional Services (48), IT Managed Services for:, Machine Learning for:, Business Process and Operations for:, Business Process and

Company Name: Acroalias
Description: Acroalias is company moving towards future with the aim of fixing the social healthcare problems with algorithms using various technologies.
Website: http://www.acroalias.com/
Phone: 91 8240369098 **Email:** acroalias@gmail.com
City: Kolkata **State:** WB **PC:** **Country:** India
Year Established: **Status 2020:** Active
Industries: Artificial Intelligence for:, ~ Healthcare (20), ~ Healthcare (20), Machine Learning for:, ~ Healthcare (20)

Company **Name:** Autogram
Description: AI-enabled customized video-interviewing platform, helping corporates hire efficiently using Personality, Cognitive and Emotion analysis.
Website: http://autogram.ai
Phone: 7044055484 **Email:** aditya@myautogram.com
City: Kolkata **State:** WB **PC:** **Country:** India
Year Established: 2017 **Status 2020:** Active
Industries: Artificial Intelligence for:, Web

Company Name: Biogenick
Description: Biogenick Life is an AI driven app that can decode the mystery of health by translating genomic, health IoT, clinical and lifestyle data.
Website: http://www.biogenick.com/
Phone: **Email:** animikh.ray@biogenick.com
City: Kolkata **State:** WB **PC:** **Country:** India
Year Established: 2017 **Status 2020:** Active
Industries: ~ Biotechnology (9), ~ Healthcare (20), Machine Learning

Company Name: Firdekho Heal:Thailand
Description: Our mission is to help Peoples find the right doctors and the right hospitals, for the right care.
Website: http://health.firdekho.com
Phone: 91 9999 877 688 **Email:** healthcare@firdekho.com
City: Kolkata **State:** WB **PC:** **Country:** India
Year Established: **Status 2020:** Active
Industries: Artificial Intelligence for:, ~ Healthcare (20), ~ Healthcare (20)

Company Name: instaHop
Description: instaHop is an India-based AI-driven mass transit system that offers its users with economical and convenient ride options.
Website:
Phone: **Email:** 36779@reference-encyclopedia-ai.net
City: Kolkata **State:** WB **PC:** **Country:** India
Year Established: 2016 **Status 2020:** Closed
Industries: Artificial Intelligence for:, Machine Learning

Company Name: Mihup Communications
Description: Intelligence-based personal mobile assistant app
Website: http://www.mihup.com/
Phone: (983) 030-9240 **Email:** officials@mihup.com
City: Kolkata **State:** WB **PC:** **Country:** India
Year Established: 2016 **Status 2020:** Active
Industries: Artificial Intelligence for:, IT Managed Services for:, Machine Learning for:, Speech Recognition

Company Name: Rplanx Technology
Description: Seamless Technology Frontie: Serbia
Website: http://rplanx.com/
Phone: 778-363-6773 **Email:** info@rplanx.com
City: Kolkata **State:** WB **PC:** **Country:** India
Year Established: 2016 **Status 2020:** Active
Industries: Artificial Intelligence for:, ~ Banking and Financial Markets-Services (7)

Company Name: StepUp Analytics
Description: StepUp Analytics is a Community of creative, high-energy Data Science and Analytics Professionals and Data Enthusiast.
Website: http://stepupanalytics.com/
Phone: 91 990-204-6528 **Email:** info@stepupanalytics.com
City: Kolkata **State:** WB **PC:** **Country:** India
Year Established: 2015 **Status 2020:** Active
Industries: ~ Personal-Religious-Civic (45), ~ Education (13), Machine Learning

Company Name: Ascentspark Software
Description: Premiere software development company offering solutions in web development, mobile apps, augmented reality, IoT and artificial intelligence
Website: http://www.ascentspark.com
Phone: **Email:** partha@ascentspark.com
City: Salt Lake City **State:** WB **PC:** **Country:** India
Year Established: 2012 **Status 2020:** Active
Industries: Artificial Intelligence for:, Augmented Reality for:, E-Commerce for:, IT Managed Services for:, Machine Learning for:, Application Services for:, Predictive Analytics for:, Web for:, Web

Company Name: Data Sutram
Description: Data Sutram is a data-science company that aims to provide a data-driven solutions to Corporate, Social Sector, Government & the People.
Website: http://www.datasutram.com/
Phone: 91 98310 74382 **Email:** founders@datasutram.com
City: Salt Lake City **State:** WB **PC:** **Country:** India
Year Established: 2018 **Status 2020:** Active
Industries:

Indonesia

Company Name: Eddemy
Description: Eddemy is a data analytic company for K-12 school and Higher Ed all around Indonesia.
Website: http://eddemy.com
Phone: **Email:** info@eddemy.com
City: Serpong **State:** Banten **Zip:** **Country:** **Indonesia**
Year Established: 2018 **Status 2020:** Active
Industries: ~ Education (13), Machine Learning

Company Name: Lenna.ai
Description: Lenna.ai is a customer-centric AI company that specializes in innovative AI Powered Customer Support Platform for individual and enterprise.
Website: http://Lenna.ai/
Phone: **Email:** info@lenna.ai
City: Tangerang **State:** Banten **PC:** **Country:** Indonesia
Year Established: 2017 **Status 2020:** Active
Industries: Artificial Intelligence for:, Machine Learning for:, Internet of Things (IoT)

Company Name: Lightora
Description: Lightora is a software company focus in retail analytics.
Website: http://www.lightora.com/
Phone: **Email:** info@lightora.com
City: Tangerang **State:** Banten **PC:** **Country: Indonesia**
Year Established: **Status 2020:** Active
Industries: Analytics for:, Artificial Intelligence for:, ~ Professional Services (48)

Company Name: SD Technologies
Description: SDTech is company who using AI technology by providing Virtual Assistant application for individual and enterprise business purposes.
Website: http://sdtech.co.id/
Phone: 021-22213200 **Email:** info@sdtech.co.id
City: Tangerang **State:** Banten **PC:** **Country: Indonesia**
Year Established: **Status 2020:** Active
Industries: Artificial Intelligence for:, Machine Learning

Company Name: Halos
Description: Halosis is building AI (Artificial Intelligence) technology.
Website: http://www.halosis.co.id/
Phone: **Email:** 36664@reference-encyclopedia-ai.net
City: Cengkareng **State:** Jakarta **PC:** **Country: Indonesia**
Year Established: 2017 **Status 2020:** Active
Industries: Artificial Intelligence

Company Name: Datanest
Description: Data Science as a Service startup providing with AI-based API for Enterprises.
Website: http://Datanest.io
Phone: **Email:** hello@datanest.io
City: Dki Jakarta **State:** Jakarta **PC:** **Country: Indonesia**
Year Established: 2017 **Status 2020:** Active
Industries: Artificial Intelligence for:, Big Data and Analytics for:, Machine Learning for:, Business Software as a Service Apps (SaaS Apps) for:, Automation

Company Name: AI Collective
Description: AI Collective provides an analytic infrastructure that transforms the way an enterprise structure and analyse their data.
Website: http://arkana.ai/
Phone: **Email:** hello@arkana.ai
City: Jakarta **State:** Jakarta **PC:** **Country: Indonesia**
Year Established: **Status 2020:** Active
Industries: Artificial Intelligence for:, Big Data and Analytics for:, Blockchain for:, Business Intelligence for:, Databases for:, IT Managed Services for:, Predictive Analytics for:, ~ Professional Services (48)

Company Name: AiSensum
Description: AiSensum use artificial intelligence and big data analytics to offer intuitive insights for impactful decision making.
Website: https://aisensum.com/
Phone: 62 (0) 21 2251 3220 **Email:** indonesia@aisensum.com
City: Jakarta **State:** Jakarta **PC:** **Country: Indonesia**
Year Established: 2018 **Status 2020:** Active
Industries: Analytics for:, Artificial Intelligence for:, Big Data and Analytics

Company Name: Algoritma Data Science Acade: Malaysia
Description: Algoritma is a data science school that conducts best-in-class training for individuals and companies in SEA.
Website: https://algorit.ma/
Phone: **Email:** community@algorit.: Morocco
City: Jakarta **State:** Jakarta **PC:** **Country: Indonesia**
Year Established: 2017 **Status 2020:** Active
Industries: Big Data and Analytics for:, ~ Education (13), Databases for:, Data Management for:, ~ Education (13), Machine Learning for:, ~ Education (13)

Company Name: Bahasa.ai
Description: Bahasa.ai is an AI as a service company whose mission is to build the most robust NLP/NLU modules for Bahasa Indonesia.
Website: http://bahasa.ai
Phone: **Email:** bisnis@bahasa.ai
City: Jakarta **State:** Jakarta **PC:** **Country: Indonesia**
Year Established: 2017 **Status 2020:** Active
Industries: Artificial Intelligence for:, IT Managed Services for:, Machine Learning

Company Name: BJTech
Description: Artificial Intelligence conversation platform designed for SMEs and Businesses who want to enhance their customer care experience
Website: http://bjtech.io/
Phone: **Email:** joni@bjtech.com
City: Jakarta **State:** Jakarta **PC:** **Country: Indonesia**
Year Established: **Status 2020:** Active
Industries: Artificial Intelligence

Company Name: Eureka
Description: Eureka is an information technology company that specializes in data analytics, big data, and artificial intelligence.
Website: http://eureka.ai/
Phone: 62 21230 1860 **Email:** info@eureka.ai
City: Jakarta **State:** JK **PC:** **Country: Indonesia**
Year Established: 2016 **Status 2020:** Active
Industries: Analytics for:, Artificial Intelligence for:, Big Data and Analytics for:, Machine Learning

Company Name: Kata.ai
Description: Kata.ai is a Conversational Artificial Intelligence company, providing the ultimate toolset for developers to build sophisticated chatbots.
Website: http://kata.ai/
Phone: **Email:** business@kata.ai
City: Jakarta **State:** Jakarta **PC:** **Country: Indonesia**
Year Established: **Status 2020:** Active
Industries: Artificial Intelligence for:, Machine Learning for:, Natural Language Processing for:, Enterprise Application Services

Company Name: LEGALNEXT
Description: We are Virtual Legal Assistant
Website: http://legalnext.id
Phone: 82221868122 **Email:** id.legalnext@gmail.com
City: Jakarta **State:** Jakarta **PC:** **Country: Indonesia**
Year Established: **Status 2020:** Active
Industries:

Company Name: LYKE
Description: Fashion discovery app, enabling users to find styles using AI-enabled visual recognition technology. Acquired by Jollychic in March 2018.
Website: http://www.lyke.co.id/
Phone: **Email:** hello@lykehq.com
City: Jakarta **State:** Jakarta **PC:** **Country: Indonesia**
Year Established: **Status 2020:** Active
Industries: Artificial Intelligence for:, ~ Beauty (8), E-Commerce for:, ~ Fashion (16), Computer Vision

Company Name: Nodeflux
Description: Nodeflux is a start-up technology company, creating a distributed computation platform
Website: http://www.nodeflux.io/
Phone: **Email:** hi@nodeflux.io
City: Jakarta **State:** Jakarta **PC:** **Country: Indonesia**
Year Established: 2016 **Status 2020:** Active
Industries: Artificial Intelligence for:, Computer Vision for:, IT Managed Services for:, Machine Learning

Company Name: Sonar Platform
Description: Sonar Platform generates automated and personalized insights from social media conversations
Website: http://www.sonarplatform.com
Phone: 62 21 719 8328 **Email:** info@sonar.id
City: Jakarta **State:** Jakarta **PC:** **Country: Indonesia**
Year Established: 2015 **Status 2020:** Active
Industries: Analytics for:, Big Data and Analytics for:, Machine Learning for:, ~ Social Assistance-Non-Profits (53)

Company Name: SOYAKA Artificial Intelligence Science and Technology Co Ltd
Description: Trading of goods and technology, e-commerce, international sales for artificial intelligence and robotics.
Website: http://soyakaai.com
Phone: **Email:** 37443@reference-encyclopedia-ai.net
City: Jakarta **State:** JK **PC:** **Country: Indonesia**
Year Established: 2018 **Status 2020:** Active
Industries: Artificial Intelligence for:, E-Commerce for:, Web

Company Name: SurveySensum
Description: SurveySensum is an AI-enabled experience management platform.
Website: http://www.surveysensum.com/
Phone: 91 9999062749 **Email:** support@surveysensum.com
City: Jakarta **State:** Jakarta **PC:** **Country: Indonesia**
Year Established: 2019 **Status 2020:** Active
Industries: Artificial Intelligence for:, Business Software as a Service Apps (SaaS Apps)

Company Name: Verihubs
Description: Verihubs is a artificial intelligence company located in South Jakarta.
Website: http://verihubs.com/
Phone: **Email:** contactus@verihubs.com
City: Jakarta **State:** Jakarta **PC:** **Country: Indonesia**
Year Established: 2019 **Status 2020:** Active
Industries: Artificial Intelligence for:, Application Services for:, Digital Media

Company Name: Techinlabs
Description: A hiring platform that connecting tech company to their future perfect match tech talent in Southeast Asia.
Website: http://techinlabs.co
Phone: **Email:** hello@techinlabs.co
City: Jakarta Pusat **State:** Jakarta **PC:** **Country: Indonesia**
Year Established: **Status 2020:** Active
Industries: Artificial Intelligence for:, Application Services for:, IT Managed Services for:, ~ Professional Services (48), ~ Human Resources (24)

Company Name: Botika
Description: Botika develops virtual assistants with the use of artificial intelligent and machine learning technology solutions.
Website: http://botika.online/
Phone: **Email:** admin@botika.online
City: Yogyakarta **State:** Jogja **PC:** **Country: Indonesia**
Year Established: 2016 **Status 2020:** Active
Industries: Artificial Intelligence for:, ~ Customer Relationship Management (11), E-Commerce for:, ~ Social Assistance-Non-Profits (53), ~ Travel and Transportation (58), Internet of Things (IoT)

Company Name: Neurabot
Description: Neurabot : Digital Laboratory Platform #1 with AI for BioTechnology
Website: http://neurabot.io
Phone: **Email:** lab@neurabot.io
City: Yogyakarta **State:** Jogja **PC:** **Country: Indonesia**
Year Established: **Status 2020:** Active
Industries: Artificial Intelligence for:, Big Data and Analytics for:, ~ Biotechnology (9), ~ Healthcare (20), Predictive Analytics

Company Name: Elektronik Virtual Asisten (EVA.id)
Description: EVA develop an Artificial Intelligence as a chat bot to perform online activities through chatting platforms, such as Telegram and FB Msgr.
Website: http://www.eva.id/
Phone: **Email:** via@eva.id
City: Bandung **State:** West Java **PC:** **Country: Indonesia**
Year Established: **Status 2020:** Active
Industries: Artificial Intelligence for:, IT Managed Services for:, Natural Language Processing for:, Application Services

Company Name: IMD Global Service
Description: IMD Global Services is a software and mobile application development company.
Website: http://www.imdglobalservices.com/
Phone: 62 813-2002-1766 **Email:** san.emirza@imdglobalservices.com
City: Bandung **State:** West Java **PC:** **Country: Indonesia**
Year Established: 2017 **Status 2020:** Active
Industries: Machine Learning for:, Application Services

Company Name: Pleasure Ventura
Description: Pleasure Ventura is a startup studio or venture builder which aim to building the future by creating startups together smart entrepreneurs.
Website: http://pleasurra.com
Phone: **Email:** jume@pleasurra.com
City: Bandung **State:** West Java **PC:** **Country: Indonesia**
Year Established: **Status 2020:** Active
Industries: Artificial Intelligence

Company Name: Prosa.ai
Description: AI-Powered Natural Language and Speech Processing for Bahasa Indonesia
Website: http://www.prosa.ai
Phone: **Email:** business@prosa.ai
City: Bandung **State:** West Java **PC:** **Country: Indonesia**
Year Established: **Status 2020:** Active
Industries: Analytics for:, Artificial Intelligence for:, ~ Biotechnology (9), IT Managed Services for:, Machine Learning for:, Natural Language Processing for:, ~ Professional Services (48)

Company Name: EIRR
Description: Trusted Media Internet Group Company
Website: http://www.eirr.net
Phone: 022-206-60110 **Email:** hi@eirr.net
City: Cimahi **State:** West Java **PC:** **Country: Indonesia**
Year Established: **Status 2020:** Active
Industries:

Company Name: Neurosensum
Description: Neurosensum is a neuroscience and AI-based company that uses neuroscience tools in understanding consumers' subconscious response.
Website: http://neurosensum.com/
Phone: 62 21 2251 3883 **Email:** indonesia@neurosensum.com
City: Kuningan **State:** JK **PC:** **Country: Indonesia**
Year Established: 2017 **Status 2020:** Active
Industries:

Iran

Company Name: Retruster Ltd
Description: Retruster stops phishing, fraud and ransomware. Leveraging AI and advanced algorithms to keep you protected.
Website: http://www.retruster.com
Phone: **Email:** michael.snape@retruster.com
City: Bostan **State:** Khuzestan Province **PC:** **Country:** IRAN
Year Established: 2017 **Status 2020:** Active
Industries: Artificial Intelligence for:, Big Data and Analytics for:, Cyber Security for:, IT Managed Services for:, Web

Company Name: AKO Smart Technologies
Description: Smart Health-care Solutions
Website: http://www.ako.technology/
Phone: 98 935 391 7352 **Email:** contact@ako.technology
City: Tehran **State:** Tehran Province **PC:** **Country:** IRAN
Year Established: 2015 **Status 2020:** Active
Industries: Artificial Intelligence for:, ~ Healthcare (20), ~ Healthcare (20)

Company Name: Arezome
Description: Arezome offers a range of creative services from Mobile Application Development to Machine Learning and AI.
Website: http://Arezo.me
Phone: **Email:** support@arezo.me
City: Tehran **State:** Tehran Province **PC:** **Country:** IRAN
Year Established: 2017 **Status 2020:** Active
Industries: Application Services for:, Artificial Intelligence for:, Web

Company Name: Diaalog
Description: Diaalog is a Coversational AI platform for automation of customer support and sales conversations for business: Spain
Website: http://diaalog.: Iran
Phone: **Email:** hi@diaalog.: Iran
City: Tehran **State:** Tehran Province **PC:** **Country:** IRAN
Year Established: 2016 **Status 2020:** Active
Industries: Artificial Intelligence for:, ~ Customer Relationship Management (11), Machine Learning

Company Name: Dialog
Description: Dialog virtual operator is an Intelligent ChatBot that learn from Operators & users conversation for automatically response to users issu: Spain
Website: http://dlg.: Isle of Man
Phone: **Email:** info@dlg.: Isle of Man
City: Tehran **State:** Tehran Province **PC:** **Country:** IRAN
Year Established: 2016 **Status 2020:** Active
Industries: Artificial Intelligence for:, ~ Customer Relationship Management (11), Machine Learning for:, Natural Language Processing

Company Name: Luxin Tech
Description: Smart Home, IoT
Website: http://luxintech.com/
Phone: **Email:** info@luxintech.com
City: Tehran **State:** Tehran Province **PC:** **Country:** IRAN
Year Established: 2015 **Status 2020:** Active
Industries: Artificial Intelligence for:, Internet of Things (IoT) for:, ~ Construction (10)

Company Name: Matin International Group
Description: Matin has created a future-proof AI platform that transforms industries to create actionable intelligence of data.
Website: http://matinint.com
Phone: **Email:** info@matinint.com
City: Tehran **State:** Tehran Province **PC:** **Country:** IRAN
Year Established: **Status 2020:** Active
Industries: Artificial Intelligence for:, Application Services for:, Machine Learning for:, Natural Language Processing

Company Name: Nullatech
Description: Our prediction service gives you important insights to overcome risks of trading and investment caused by uncertainty of the future market.
Website: http://www.nullatech.com/
Phone: **Email:** info@nullatech.com
City: Tehran **State:** Tehran Province **PC:** **Country:** IRAN
Year Established: 2017 **Status 2020:** Active
Industries: Analytics for:, Artificial Intelligence for:, IT Managed Services

Company Name: Paklean
Description: Online laundry and dry cleaning
Website: http://paklean.com
Phone: **Email:** info@paklean.com
City: Tehran **State:** Tehran Province **PC:** **Country:** IRAN
Year Established: **Status 2020:** Active
Industries: Artificial Intelligence for:, IT Managed Services for:, ~ Personal-Religious-Civic (45), Mobile

Company Name: Tab: Romania
Description: Tabro is an Intelligent advertisement platform for any vehicle
Website: http://www.tabro.: Iran
Phone: **Email:** hi@tabro.: Iran
City: Tehran **State:** Tehran Province **PC:** **Country:** IRAN
Year Established: 2017 **Status 2020:** Active
Industries: Artificial Intelligence for:, ~ Automotive (5), ~ Telecommunications (56)

Ireland

Company Name: Apridata
Description: Provider of analytics platform for distributors and manufacture: Serbia
Website: http://www.apridata.com
Phone: 353 49 4361800 **Email:** info@apridata.com
City: Cavan **State:** CN **PC:** **Country: Ireland**
Year Established: 2013 **Status 2020:** Active
Industries: Analytics for:, Machine Learning for:, Predictive Analytics

Company Name: Gigliotti.Co Limited
Description: SmartDrinx, a smart, interactive, autonomous IoT beverage dispensing system
Website: http://gigliotti.co/
Phone: **Email:** info@gigliotti.co
City: Mountshannon **State:** CE **PC:** **Country: Ireland**
Year Established: 2015 **Status 2020:** Active
Industries: Application Services for:, Big Data and Analytics for:, ~ Food and Beverage (17), Internet of Things (IoT) for:, Predictive Analytics

Company Name: ApisProtect
Description: ApisProtect develops an agricultural technology designed for the management and care of bees.
Website: http://www.apisprotect.com/
Phone: **Email:** enquiries@apisprotect.com
City: Cork **State:** CO **PC:** **Country: Ireland**
Year Established: 2017 **Status 2020:** Active
Industries:

Company Name: fourTheorem
Description: fourTheorem is a non-traditional software design and development business.
Website: http://www.fourtheorem.com/
Phone: **Email:** hello@fourtheorem.com
City: Cork **State:** CO **PC:** **Country: Ireland**
Year Established: 2017 **Status 2020:** Active
Industries: Machine Learning for:, Application Services

Company Name: Galactica Biotech
Description: Galactica Biotech develops a cutting edge proprietary machine learning method that is able to identify new applications for molecules.
Website:
http://www.galacticabiotech.cominfo@galacticabiotech.com
Phone: **Email:** info@galacticabiotech.com
City: Cork **State:** CO **PC:** **Country: Ireland**
Year Established: 2017 **Status 2020:** Active
Industries: Artificial Intelligence for:, ~ Biotechnology (9)

Company Name: Getvisibility
Description: Getvisibility operates as an AI Security Company.
Website: http://www.getvisibility.com/
Phone: **Email:** 36619@reference-encyclopedia-ai.net
City: Cork **State:** CO **PC:** **Country: Ireland**
Year Established: 2017 **Status 2020:** Active
Industries: Artificial Intelligence for:, Cyber Security for:, Security

Company Name: Keelvar
Description: Advanced eSourcing Enterprise SaaS provider
Website: www.keelvar.com
Phone: **Email:** info@keelvar.com
City: Cork **State:** County Cork **PC:** **Country: Ireland**
Year Established: **Status 2020:** Active
Industries: Artificial Intelligence for:, ~ Administrative and Support Services (1), ~ Professional Services (48)

Company Name: PURPLEMIND
Description: SaaS, Data Visualisation & Predictive Analytics
Website: http://www.purplemind.io
Phone: **Email:** 37228@reference-encyclopedia-ai.net
City: Cork **State:** CO **PC:** **Country: Ireland**
Year Established: 2017 **Status 2020:** Active
Industries: Analytics for:, Data Management for:, Machine Learning for:, ~ Education (13), Predictive Analytics

Company Name: Roborzoid
Description: Roborzoid is a platform for managing voice and gesture.
Website: http://www.roborzoid.com
Phone: **Email:** info@roborzoid.com
City: Cork **State:** County Cork **PC:** **Country: Ireland**
Year Established: **Status 2020:** Active
Industries: Artificial Intelligence for:, ~ Automotive (5)

Company Name: Tip Tap Tap
Description: Tip tap tap is an educational platform that uses interactive touch-sensing technologies on school desks to improve teaching methods.
Website: http://tiptaptap.: Ireland
Phone: **Email:** info@tiptaptap.: Ireland
City: Cork **State:** CO **PC:** **Country: Ireland**
Year Established: 2015 **Status 2020:** Active
Industries: ~ Education (13), ~ Education (13), ~ Education (13), Machine Learning

Company Name: Trustev
Description: Trustev increases sales and stops fraud for e-commerce and financial companies.
Website: http://www.trustev.com
Phone: 353 87 204 9121 **Email:** pat.phelan@trustev.com
City: Cork **State:** County Cork **PC:** **Country: Ireland**
Year Established: **Status 2020:** Active
Industries: Artificial Intelligence for:, E-Commerce for:, Security for:, Security for:, ~ Professional Services (48)

Company Name: TIC ~ BizTweet
Description: We provide airports with the ability to communicate effectively in real-time to passengers via social media, using AI.
Website: http://www.biztweet.ae: Romania
Phone: **Email:** 37539@reference-encyclopedia-ai.net
City: Kinsale **State:** CO **PC:** **Country: Ireland**
Year Established: 2011 **Status 2020:** Active
Industries: Artificial Intelligence

Company Name: Flock Data Analytics Ltd.
Description: Big data analytics for event-driven investment
Website: http://www.flockpit.com
Phone: **Email:** 36583@reference-encyclopedia-ai.net
City: Mallow **State:** CO **PC:** **Country: Ireland**
Year Established: 2015 **Status 2020:** Active
Industries: Analytics for:, ~ Banking and Financial Markets-Services (7), Machine Learning for:, ~ Social Assistance-Non-Profits (53)

Company Name: Cx MOMENTS
Description: Machine Learning Text Analytics for customer surveys, CRM records, knowledge-base, webchat and chatbot optimisation.
Website: http://www.cxmoments.com
Phone: **Email:** 36366@reference-encyclopedia-ai.net
City: Blackrock **State:** D **PC:** **Country: Ireland**
Year Established: 2016 **Status 2020:** Active
Industries: Analytics for:, Machine Learning for:, Natural Language Processing for:, Data Management

Company Name: Eiratech Robotics
Description: goods-to-person robotics platform for multiple applications, e.g. e-fulfilment, material handling, Industry 4.0, retail and self-storage
Website: http://www.eiratech.com
Phone: (3531) 809-6241 **Email:** info@eiratech.com
City: Blanchardstown **State:** D **PC:** **Country: Ireland**
Year Established: 2014 **Status 2020:** Active
Industries: Artificial Intelligence for:, Automation for:, ~ Telecommunications (56), Robotics for:, Supply Chain Management for:, ~ Transportation and Logistics (57)

Company Name: 4Securitas
Description: 4Securitas simplify security - monitoring and protecting critical servers for enterprises large and small.
Website: http://www.4securitas.com/
Phone: **Email:** 35924@reference-encyclopedia-ai.net
City: Dublin **State:** D **PC:** **Country: Ireland**
Year Established: 2017 **Status 2020:** Active
Industries: Artificial Intelligence for:, Cyber Security for:, IT Managed Services for:, Security

Company Name: Ad World Maste: Serbia
Description: Worldwide Agency Ranking Powered by AI!
Website: http://adworldmasters.com
Phone: **Email:** contact@adworldmasters.com
City: Dublin **State:** County Dublin **PC:** **Country: Ireland**
Year Established: **Status 2020:** Active
Industries:

Company Name: AID:Tech
Description: AID:Tech is a digital identity and seamless access to life's services through Blockchain and artificial intelligence.
Website: https://aid.technology/
Phone: **Email:** info@aid.technology
City: Dublin **State:** D **PC:** **Country: Ireland**
Year Established: 2016 **Status 2020:** Active
Industries: Artificial Intelligence for:, Blockchain for:, Enterprise Application Services for:, ~ Government (19), IT Managed Services

Company Name: Alldus International
Description: Alldus International is taking a holistic approach to AI Workforce Solutions.
Website: https://alldus.com/
Phone: **Email:** info@alldus.com
City: Dublin **State:** D **PC:** **Country: Ireland**
Year Established: 2018 **Status 2020:** Active
Industries: Artificial Intelligence

Company Name: Artomatix
Description: Artomatix is a software company that uses Artificial Intelligence to create realistic 3D art creation.
Website: http://artomatix.com/
Phone: **Email:** Contact@Artomatix.com
City: Dublin **State:** County Dublin **PC:** **Country: Ireland**
Year Established: **Status 2020:** Active
Industries: ~ Arts-Entertainment-Recreation (4), Artificial Intelligence for:, ~ Professional Services (48)

Company Name: AYLIEN
Description: AYLIEN is an artificial intelligence startup that focuses on creating technologies that help machines understand human languages better.
Website: http://aylien.com
Phone: 35315983168 **Email:** hello@aylien.com
City: Dublin **State:** County Dublin **PC:** **Country: Ireland**
Year Established: **Status 2020:** Active
Industries: Artificial Intelligence for:, Big Data and Analytics for:, Machine Learning for:, Natural Language Processing for:, Data Management

Company Name: Beautifeye
Description: Beautifeye is an image analysis SaaS platform capable of automatically extracting marketing insights from social network photos.
Website: http://www.beautifeye.co
Phone: **Email:** luca@beautifeye.co
City: Dublin **State:** D **PC:** **Country: Ireland**
Year Established: 2013 **Status 2020:** Active
Industries: Machine Learning for:, Business Software as a Service Apps (SaaS Apps)

Company Name: bizbaze
Description: Bizbaze is a collaborative social-commerce platform for digital banking.
Website: http://www.bizbaze.com
Phone: **Email:** info@bizbaze.com
City: Dublin **State:** County Dublin **PC:** **Country: Ireland**
Year Established: **Status 2020:** Active
Industries: Artificial Intelligence for:, ~ Banking and Financial Markets-Services (7), E-Commerce

Company Name: BrainRex
Description: A single API for crypto data and analytics.
Website: http://brainrex.com
Phone: (650) 507-9263 **Email:** hello@brainrex.com
City: Dublin **State:** D **PC:** **Country: Ireland**
Year Established: 2018 **Status 2020:** Active
Industries: Artificial Intelligence for:, Blockchain for:, ~ Banking and Financial Markets-Services (7), Data Management for:, ~ Education (13), Machine Learning

Company Name: Chad Agate, LLC
Description: Internet application development, UI/UX design, web design/development, data science, machine learning, and eCommerce.
Website:
Phone: **Email:** 36252@reference-encyclopedia-ai.net
City: Dublin **State:** D **PC:** **Country: Ireland**
Year Established: 2017 **Status 2020:** Active
Industries: Application Services for:, Artificial Intelligence for:, E-Commerce for:, Web for:, Machine Learning

Company Name: ChannelSight
Description: ChannelSight's B2B SaaS eCommerce platform enables brands, publishers and broadcasters to generate new revenue streams from digital content
Website: http://www.channelsight.com
Phone: 3531 902 2822 **Email:** ross@channelsight.com
City: Dublin **State:** County Dublin **PC:** **Country: Ireland**
Year Established: **Status 2020:** Active
Industries: ~ Media-Communications (41), Analytics for:, Artificial Intelligence for:, Augmented Reality for:, Big Data and Analytics for:, ~ Media-Communications (41), Digital Marketing for:, E-Commerce for:, E-Commerce for:, ~ E-Commerce (12), Predictive Analytics

Company Name: CoalFace
Description: CoalFace is a FinTech company that focuses on modelling of big data and AI techniques application.
Website: http://www.coalfacecapital.com
Phone: **Email:** info@coalfacecapital.com
City: Dublin **State:** D **PC:** **Country: Ireland**
Year Established: 2015 **Status 2020:** Active
Industries: Artificial Intelligence for:, Big Data and Analytics for:, ~ Banking and Financial Markets-Services (7), Machine Learning

Company Name: Conker
Description: Conker provides a behavioral and predictive analytics tool that automates the analytical process of enterprises.
Website: http://www.conker.io
Phone: **Email:** info@conker.io
City: Dublin **State:** D **PC:** **Country: Ireland**
Year Established: 2012 **Status 2020:** Active
Industries: Analytics for:, Big Data and Analytics for:, Enterprise Application Services for:, Predictive Analytics

Company Name: Cosmosa: Iran
Description: Aircraft Design, 3D Flight Simulation, Flight systems, Flight training, Aerospace Engineering, Artificial Intelligence, AI, Flight Dynamics
Website: http://cosmosair.net
Phone: **Email:** info@cosmosair.net
City: Dublin **State:** County Dublin **PC:** **Country: Ireland**
Year Established: **Status 2020:** Active
Industries: ~ Aerospace and Defense (2), ~ Travel and Transportation (58), Artificial Intelligence for:, Augmented Reality for:, ~ Transportation and Logistics (57), Embedded for:, Application Services for:, Predictive Analytics

Company Name: Decision Point AI™ Euro:
Description: Professional services consulting for business key decision making solutions
Website: http://decision-point-ai.eu
Phone: 353 1 254 4342 **Email:** marketing19@decision-point.info
City: Dublin **State:** D **PC:** **Country: Ireland**
Year Established: 2019 **Status 2020:** Active
Industries: Predictive Analytics

Company Name: Digifeye
Description: Digifeye is a discovery and sales platform which turns digital imagery into shoppable content.
Website: http://www.digifeye.com/
Phone: 353 1 542 4172 **Email:** info@ndrc.: Ireland
City: Dublin **State:** D **PC:** **Country: Ireland**
Year Established: 2013 **Status 2020:** Active
Industries:

Company Name: EdgeTier
Description: Human-Centric Artificial Intelligence
Website: http://www.edgetier.com/
Phone: **Email:** info@edgetier.com
City: Dublin **State:** D **PC:** **Country: Ireland**
Year Established: 2015 **Status 2020:** Active
Industries: Artificial Intelligence for:, IT Managed Services for:, Machine Learning

Company Name: Empiric Logic
Description: Secure, explainable AI SaaS company whose phenotype mapping and analysis platform is used by pharma, pharma services, and biotech companies.
Website: http://empiriclogic.com
Phone: **Email:** info@empiriclogic.com
City: Dublin **State:** D **PC:** **Country: Ireland**
Year Established: 2018 **Status 2020:** Active
Industries: Artificial Intelligence for:, ~ Biotechnology (9)

Company Name: Fabrikatyr Analytics
Description: Fabrikatyr Analytics Uncovering tangible truths from modern media.
Website:
Phone: **Email:** 36544@reference-encyclopedia-ai.net
City: Dublin **State:** D **PC:** **Country: Ireland**
Year Established: 2012 **Status 2020:** Closed
Industries: Analytics for:, Artificial Intelligence

Company Name: GameX
Description: A Cross-Platform Recommendation Engine for the Gaming Industry
Website: http://gamex.io
Phone: (086)272-3313 **Email:** info@gamex.io
City: Dublin **State:** County Dublin **PC:** **Country: Ireland**
Year Established: **Status 2020:** Active
Industries: Artificial Intelligence for:, ~ Gaming (18), Industrial Solutions for:, ~ Arts-Entertainment-Recreation (4)

Company Name: HeyStaks
Description: HeyStacks is a mobile intent analytics platform.
Website: http://www.heystaks.com
Phone: 353-1-716-3565 **Email:** maurice.coyle@heystaks.com
City: Dublin **State:** County Dublin **PC:** **Country: Ireland**
Year Established: **Status 2020:** Active
Industries: ~ Media-Communications (41), ~ Media-Communications (41), Analytics for:, Artificial Intelligence for:, Big Data and Analytics for:, E-Commerce for:, ~ Media-Communications (41), Cyber Security

Company Name: Inboarding
Description: A new way to create an inclusive workplace where everyone belongs
Website: http://www.inboarding.co
Phone: **Email:** hello@inboarding.co
City: Dublin **State:** D **PC:** **Country: Ireland**
Year Established: 2019 **Status 2020:** Active
Industries: Artificial Intelligence for:, Business Applications for:, IT Managed Services for:, Business Software as a Service Apps (SaaS Apps) for:, Collaboration Solutions

Company Name: Intouch.com
Description: AI-Powered platform for retailers to intelligently target shoppers with personalized offerings in-store.
Website: http://www.intouch.com
Phone: (3531) 969-5555 **Email:** founders@intouch.com
City: Dublin **State:** D **PC:** **Country: Ireland**
Year Established: 2015 **Status 2020:** Active
Industries: Artificial Intelligence for:, Data Management for:, E-Commerce for:, IT Managed Services for:, Machine Learning

Company Name: Kids Speech Labs
Description: Kids Speech Labs is a digital health company building AI driven solutions to disrupt this industry, improving access.
Website: http://www.kidssspeechlabs.com/
Phone: **Email:** 36853@reference-encyclopedia-ai.net
City: Dublin **State:** D **PC:** **Country: Ireland**
Year Established: 2018 **Status 2020:** Active
Industries:

Company Name: Kitman Labs
Description: The World's First Athlete Optimization System
Website: http://kitmanlabs.com
Phone: (650) 462-2022 **Email:** info@kitmanlabs.com
City: Dublin **State:** County Dublin **PC:** **Country: Ireland**
Year Established: **Status 2020:** Active
Industries: Artificial Intelligence for:, ~ Healthcare (20), Predictive Analytics for:, ~ Arts-Entertainment-Recreation (4)

Company Name: Knog: India
Description: Knogin delivers the entire Security Monitoring stack in a single tool without the need for a large Security Operations Team
Website: http://knogin.com
Phone: 833-5664461 **Email:** support@knogin.com
City: Dublin **State:** D **PC:** **Country: Ireland**
Year Established: 2018 **Status 2020:** Active
Industries: Analytics for:, Big Data and Analytics for:, Cyber Security for:, IT Managed Services for:, Predictive Analytics for:, Business Software as a Service Apps (SaaS Apps)

Company Name: LogoGrab
Description: LogoGrab is an image recognition technology provider for detecting logos and SKUs in images and videos.
Website: http://www.logograb.com
Phone: 35315583155 **Email:** enquiries@logograb.com
City: Dublin **State:** County Dublin **PC:** **Country: Ireland**
Year Established: **Status 2020:** Active
Industries: Artificial Intelligence for:, Augmented Reality for:, ~ Media-Communications (41), Computer Vision for:, Image Recognition

Company Name: Mindfule
Description: Mindfule is the personalised nutrition tracking app, guiding people towards healthy and strong minds through AI and Machine Learning.
Website: http://Mindfule.app
Phone: **Email:** hello@mindfule.app
City: Dublin **State:** County Dublin **PC:** **Country: Ireland**
Year Established: **Status 2020:** Active
Industries: Artificial Intelligence for:, Machine Learning for:, ~ Life Sciences (27), ~ Healthcare (20), ~ Healthcare (20), ~ Healthcare (20)

Company Name: NadiF: India
Description: NadiFin is a FinTech accelerator program for cutting-edge startups.
Website: http://www.nadifin.com/
Phone: **Email:** 37035@reference-encyclopedia-ai.net
City: Dublin **State:** D **PC:** **Country: Ireland**
Year Established: 2019 **Status 2020:** Active
Industries: Artificial Intelligence for:, Blockchain for:, ~ Banking and Financial Markets-Services (7), Machine Learning

Company Name: NewsWhip
Description: NewsWhip is the world's largest engagement database, giving customers an understanding of what's interesting their audience right now.
Website: http://www.newswhip.com
Phone: (212) 882-1360 **Email:** hello@newswhip.com
City: Dublin **State:** County Dublin **PC:** **Country: Ireland**
Year Established: **Status 2020:** Active
Industries:

Company Name: Nuritas
Description: Nuritas combines artificial intelligence and genomics to discover and unlock natural bioactive peptides with extraordinary health benefits
Website: http://www.nuritas.com
Phone: 353 (0) 1-430-1290 **Email:** info@nuritas.com
City: Dublin **State:** County Dublin **PC:** **Country: Ireland**
Year Established: **Status 2020:** Active
Industries: Artificial Intelligence for:, ~ Biotechnology (9), ~ Biotechnology (9), Databases

Company Name: Openet
Description: Openet develops software used by telecommunications service providers to commercialize and analyze activity on their network.
Website: http://www.openet.com
Phone: 703 435 0730 **Email:** Info@openet.com
City: Dublin **State:** County Dublin **PC:** **Country: Ireland**
Year Established: **Status 2020:** Active
Industries: Artificial Intelligence for:, ~ Telecommunications (56), ~ Professional Services (48), ~ Telecommunications (56)

Company Name: Opening.io
Description: Opening.io is AI-powered talent recommender engine for HR tech vendors, enterprises, and staffing agencies.
Website: http://www.opening.io
Phone: **Email:** andreea@opening.io
City: Dublin **State:** D **PC:** **Country: Ireland**
Year Established: 2015 **Status 2020:** Active
Industries:

Company Name: OptimizMe
Description: Accelerated Learning Platform using Artificial Intelligence
Website: http://www.optimizme.com
Phone: **Email:** thomas@optimizme.com
City: Dublin **State:** D **PC:** **Country: Ireland**
Year Established: 2018 **Status 2020:** Active
Industries: Artificial Intelligence for:, ~ Education (13), ~ Education (13), ~ Education (13)

Company Name: Overcast HQ
Description: Overcast provides powerful video management solutions that streamline how businesses review, approve and collaborate on video using AI.
Website: http://www.overcasthq.com/
Phone: **Email:** info@overcasthq.com
City: Dublin **State:** County Dublin **PC:** **Country: Ireland**
Year Established: **Status 2020:** Active
Industries: Artificial Intelligence for:, Collaboration Solutions for:, ~ Media-Communications (41)

Company **Name:** Pryml
Description: Pryml is a secure way to develop innovative solutions on confidential data without compromising privacy.
Website: http://pryml.io/
Phone: **Email:** hello@pryml.io
City: Dublin **State:** D **PC:** **Country: Ireland**
Year Established: 2019 **Status 2020:** Active
Industries: Analytics for:, Artificial Intelligence for:, Big Data and Analytics for:, IT Managed Services for:, Cyber Security for:, Security

Company Name: RecommenderX
Description: RecommenderX is an A.I. Recommendation as a Service (RaaS) cloud platform company.
Website: http://www.recommenderx.com
Phone: **Email:** info@recommenderx.com
City: Dublin **State:** County Dublin **PC:** **Country: Ireland**
Year Established: **Status 2020:** Active
Industries: Analytics for:, Artificial Intelligence for:, Business Intelligence for:, Data Management for:, ~ Banking and Financial Markets-Services (7), ~ Banking and Financial Markets-Services (7), ~ Media-Communications (41)

Company Name: SBDA Group
Description: SBDA Group is an AI company that provides retail banks with solutions for boosting customer engagement.
Website: http://sbdagroup.com
Phone: **Email:** info@sbdagroup.com
City: Dublin **State:** D **PC:** **Country: Ireland**
Year Established: 2014 **Status 2020:** Active
Industries: Artificial Intelligence for:, ~ Banking and Financial Markets-Services (7), ~ Banking and Financial Markets-Services (7)

Company Name: Shopbra: India
Description: Shopbrain is a powerful AI shopping assistant that helps shoppers find the best price while they shop online.
Website: http://www.shopbrain.com/
Phone: **Email:** marketing@shopbrain.com
City: Dublin **State:** D **PC:** **Country: Ireland**
Year Established: 2015 **Status 2020:** Active
Industries: Artificial Intelligence for:, E-Commerce for:, ~ Retail and Consumer Products (52)

Company Name: Shryne
Description: Social AI services, including social data archiving, analytics, and health prediction.
Website: http://www.shryne.com
Phone: **Email:** hello@shryne.com
City: Dublin **State:** County Dublin **PC:** **Country: Ireland**
Year Established: **Status 2020:** Active
Industries: Analytics for:, Artificial Intelligence for:, Cloud

Company Name: Simply Connected
Description: Cloud based platform for IoT
Website: http://www.nthenergy.com
Phone: **Email:** 37396@reference-encyclopedia-ai.net
City: Dublin **State:** D **PC:** **Country: Ireland**
Year Established: 2012 **Status 2020:** Active
Industries: IT Managed Services for:, Machine Learning

Company Name: Skylads
Description: Skylads is a R&D lab specializing in the field of machine learning and artificial intelligence.
Website: http://www.skylads.com
Phone: **Email:** support@skylads.com
City: Dublin **State:** County Dublin **PC:** **Country: Ireland**
Year Established: **Status 2020:** Active
Industries: ~ Media-Communications (41), ~ Media-Communications (41), Artificial Intelligence for:, ~ Professional Services (48)

Company Name: Soapbox Labs
Description: SoapBox Labs develops a cloud-based platform for children's speech recognition.
Website: http://soapboxlabs.com/
Phone: **Email:** info@soapboxlabs.com
City: Dublin **State:** County Dublin **PC:** **Country: Ireland**
Year Established: **Status 2020:** Active
Industries: Artificial Intelligence for:, IT Managed Services for:, Speech Recognition

Company Name: Talivest
Description: Talivest is a people analytics SaaS company, specialising in employee engagement through innovative technology solutions.
Website: http://www.talivest.com/
Phone: **Email:** info@talivest.com
City: Dublin **State:** D **PC:** **Country: Ireland**
Year Established: 2013 **Status 2020:** Active
Industries:

Company Name: thinkHRX
Description: SaaS platform that utilises AI and Predictive Analytics to make hiring and recruiting significantly more effective and accurate.
Website: http://thinkhrx.com
Phone: **Email:** engage@thinkhrx.com
City: Dublin **State:** County Dublin **PC:** **Country: Ireland**
Year Established: **Status 2020:** Active
Industries: Artificial Intelligence for:, Blockchain for:, ~ Human Resources (24), Web for:, Machine Learning for:, Predictive Analytics for:, ~ Human Resources (24)

Company Name: Unravel Analytics
Description: Unravel tests web applications using machine learning and AI expert systems.
Website: http://unravel.io
Phone: (415) 503-9055 **Email:** mail@unravel.io
City: Dublin **State:** D **PC:** **Country: Ireland**
Year Established: 2012 **Status 2020:** Active
Industries: Artificial Intelligence for:, Machine Learning for:, Web

Company Name: UrbanFox
Description: UrbanFox turns customer data into sales.
Website: http://www.urbanfox.io
Phone: (415)513-0133 **Email:** daniel@urbanfox.: Ireland
City: Dublin **State:** County Dublin **PC:** **Country: Ireland**
Year Established: **Status 2020:** Active
Industries: Artificial Intelligence for:, ~ Media-Communications (41), ~ Media-Communications (41)

Company Name: Verge.Capital
Description: Credit score re-invented. Driving fair access to credit.
Website: http://verge.capital/
Phone: **Email:** 4407@reference-encyclopedia-ai.net
City: Dublin **State:** County Dublin **PC:** **Country: Ireland**

Year Established: **Status 2020:** Active
Industries: Artificial Intelligence for:, ~ Banking and Financial Markets-Services (7), ~ Banking and Financial Markets-Services (7), Machine Learning for:, Risk Management

Company Name: Vivagogy Limited
Description: Vivagogy is changing learning by creating differentiated learning paths and competency assessments with blockchain credentialling .
Website: http://www.vivagogy.com
Phone: 33638807444 **Email:** chris@vivagogy.com
City: Dublin **State:** County Dublin **PC:** **Country: Ireland**
Year Established: **Status 2020:** Active
Industries: Artificial Intelligence for:, Blockchain for:, ~ Education (13), IT Managed Services for:, Machine Learning for:, ~ Social-Environmental-Physical-Engineering Sciences (55), ~ Social Media (54)

Company **Name:** Voysis
Description: Voysis develops tech that makes it easier for digital voice assistants to understand a user's natural language.
Website: http://voysis.com/
Phone: **Email:** 37645@reference-encyclopedia-ai.net
City: Dublin **State:** D **PC:** **Country: Ireland**
Year Established: 2012 **Status 2020:** Active
Industries: Artificial Intelligence for:, Natural Language Processing

Company Name: Webio
Description: The Conversational Middleware Company
Website: http://www.crunchbase.com/organization/webio
Phone: 35315310447 **Email:** info@webio.com
City: Dublin **State:** County Dublin **PC:** **Country: Ireland**
Year Established: **Status 2020:** Active
Industries: Artificial Intelligence for:, ~ Social Media (54), ~ Telecommunications (56), ~ Social Media (54)

Company Name: WECOFIX
Description: Providing Data-driven market-entry insights to target untapped markets.
Website: http://www.wecofix.com
Phone: 353 94 98 98 49 **Email:** info@wecofix.com
City: Dublin **State:** D **PC:** **Country: Ireland**
Year Established: 2017 **Status 2020:** Active
Industries: Analytics for:, Application Services for:, ~ Banking and Financial Markets-Services (7), Enterprise Application Services for:, Predictive Analytics

Company Name: WeFindX Foundation
Description: Public Intelligence
Website: http://wefindx.com
Phone: **Email:** ideas@wefindx.com
City: Dublin **State:** County Dublin **PC:** **Country: Ireland**
Year Established: **Status 2020:** Active
Industries: Artificial Intelligence for:, Blockchain for:, ~ Telecommunications (56), Application Services

Company Name: Xpanse Analytics
Description: Saas Automated Predictive Analytics from raw data
Website: http://xpanse.ai
Phone: **Email:** info@xpanseanalytics.com
City: Dublin **State:** County Dublin **PC:** **Country: Ireland**
Year Established: **Status 2020:** Active
Industries: Artificial Intelligence for:, Databases for:, ~ Media-Communications (41), Predictive Analytics

Company Name: Chatspace
Description: Chatspace is an AI Answers & Insights Platform for Enterprise companies to grow capabilities out of reach for traditional teams
Website: http://chatspace.ai
Phone: **Email:** info@chatspace.ai
City: Galway **State:** G **PC:** **Country: Ireland**
Year Established: 2017 **Status 2020:** Active
Industries: Artificial Intelligence for:, Big Data and Analytics for:, Machine Learning

Company Name: CitySwift
Description: Data-Driven Bus Scheduling
Website: http://cityswift.com
Phone: 353 913 93255 **Email:** info@cityswift.com
City: Galway **State:** G **PC:** **Country: Ireland**
Year Established: 2016 **Status 2020:** Active
Industries: Artificial Intelligence

Company Name: Luna Connect
Description: Luna Connect is a technology platform that profitably delivers the digital efficiencies that borrowers expect.
Website: http://lunaconnect.io/
Phone: **Email:** hello@lunaconnect.io
City: Galway **State:** G **PC:** **Country: Ireland**
Year Established: 2017 **Status 2020:** Active
Industries: IT Managed Services

Company Name: RealSpeaker
Description: RealSpeaker'™s AI-based multi-lingual transcription platform. It has the ability to machine transcribe any kind of media files or URL links
Website: http://realspeaker.net
Phone: 33626326843 **Email:** viktor@realspeaker.me
City: Galway **State:** County Galway **PC:** **Country: Ireland**
Year Established: **Status 2020:** Active
Industries:

Company Name: Siren
Description: Siren is a software company that provides an Investigative Intelligence platform to complex organizations and derive business value.
Website: http://siren.io/
Phone: 353 91 704 885 **Email:** info@siren.io
City: Galway **State:** G **PC:** **Country: Ireland**
Year Established: 2014 **Status 2020:** Active
Industries: Analytics for:, Big Data and Analytics for:, Data Management for:, Application Services for:, Web

Company Name: Standard Access
Description: Our Data Over Sound via your phone unlocks doors to real estate, our ERP/hardware/smartlock combo delivers, data analytics, secure access
Website: http://standardaccess.co
Phone: **Email:** info@standardaccess.co
City: Dingle **State:** KY **PC:** **Country: Ireland**
Year Established: 2014 **Status 2020:** Active
Industries: Cloud for:, Data Management for:, Internet of Things (IoT) for:, Predictive Analytics for:, Robotics for:, Robotics

Company Name: Sentenai Inc.
Description:
Website: http://www.sentenai.com
Phone: 353-1-629-2141 **Email:** 12285@reference-encyclopedia-ai.net
City: Maynooth **State:** County Kildare **PC:** **Country: Ireland**
Year Established: **Status 2020:** Active
Industries: Cloud for:, Cloud for:, IT Infrastructure for:, Machine Learning for:, ~ Professional Services (48)

Company Name: CIS Force
Description: Hire tech talents hourly, fair!
Website: http://cisforce.com/
Phone: **Email:** contact@cisforce.com
City: Naas **State:** County Kildare **PC:** **Country: Ireland**
Year Established: **Status 2020:** Active
Industries: Artificial Intelligence for:, Business Applications for:, ~ Human Resources (24), IT Managed Services for:, Web

Company Name: Emotion Reader
Description: Emotion Reader uses algorithms to analyze facial expressions around video content.
Website: http://www.emotionreader.io
Phone: **Email:** info@emotionreader.io
City: Limerick **State:** LK **PC:** **Country: Ireland**
Year Established: 2017 **Status 2020:** Active
Industries: Facial Recognition for:, IT Managed Services for:, Machine Learning

Company Name: NVMdurance
Description: NVMdurance is accelerating the adoption of 3D NAND.
Website: http://nvmdurance.com
Phone: (408) 641-3884 **Email:** pearse.coyle@nvmdurance.com
City: Limerick **State:** County Limerick **PC:** **Country: Ireland**
Year Established: **Status 2020:** Active
Industries: Artificial Intelligence for:, Storage for:, Machine Learning for:, ~ Transportation and Logistics (57), ~ Professional Services (48)

Company Name: Sanctum Technologies
Description: Sanctum is a solutions provider of high-performance multi-core processor platforms and systems that support high compute applications.
Website: http://sanctum-networks.com/
Phone: **Email:** contact@sanctumnetworks.com
City: Louth **State:** County Louth **PC:** **Country: Ireland**
Year Established: **Status 2020:** Active
Industries: Artificial Intelligence for:, Cloud for:, ~ Professional Services (48)

Company Name: ServisBOT
Description: SaaS platform for Conversational AI solutions
Website: http://www.servisbot.com
Phone: (617) 819-5336 **Email:** info@servisbot.com
City: Waterford **State:** WD **PC:** **Country: Ireland**
Year Established: 2016 **Status 2020:** Active
Industries: Analytics for:, Artificial Intelligence for:, IT Managed Services for:, Robotics for:, Business Software as a Service Apps (SaaS Apps)

Isle of Man

Company Name: Bluedog Security Monitoring
Description: Cyber Security
Website: http://www.bluedog-security.com/
Phone: **Email:** info@bluedog-security.com
City: Douglas **State:** NA - Isle of Man **PC:** **Country:** ISLE OF MAN
Year Established: **Status 2020:** Active
Industries: Artificial Intelligence for:, Cyber Security

Israel

Company Name: AlgoTrace
Description: AI ML Prediction Analytics Solutions provider
Website: http://algotrace.com/
Phone: **Email:** info@algotrace.com
City: Bet Dagan **State:** Center District **PC:** **Country:** Israel
Year Established: 2017 **Status 2020:** Active
Industries: Artificial Intelligence for:, IT Managed Services

Company Name: DigitalRobotix
Description: DigitalRobotix develops an angel investor adviser bot that enables startups to find the right angel for their venture.
Website: http://www.digitalrobotix.com
Phone: 972 58 6757872 **Email:** info@DigitalRobotiX.com
City: Bet Dagan **State:** Center District **PC:** **Country:** Israel
Year Established: 2016 **Status 2020:** Active
Industries: Artificial Intelligence for:, ~ Banking and Financial Markets-Services (7), ~ Banking and Financial Markets-Services (7), ~ Banking and Financial Markets-Services (7)

Company Name: figr Communications Ltd
Description: AI powered messaging, boosting user engagement
Website: http://figr.me/
Phone: **Email:** contact@figr.me
City: Bet Herut **State:** Center District **PC:** **Country:** Israel
Year Established: 2017 **Status 2020:** Active
Industries: Artificial Intelligence for:, IT Managed Services for:, Application Services

Company Name: Pellesus
Description: Pellesus provides a Horse Wellness Monitoring and Performance Solution.
Website: http://pellesus.com
Phone: **Email:** contact@pellesus.com
City: Hadasim **State:** Center District **PC:** **Country:** Israel
Year Established: 2017 **Status 2020:** Active
Industries: Analytics for:, Artificial Intelligence for:, ~ Banking and Financial Markets-Services (7), ~ Healthcare (20), Internet of Things (IoT)

Company Name: Zoo: Moldova
Description: Zoomd is a MarTech company dedicated to helping advertisers and publishers with a patented, performance-based advertising platform.
Website: http://zoomd.com
Phone: **Email:** info@zoomd.com
City: Hasharon **State:** Center District **PC:** **Country:** Israel
Year Established: 2012 **Status 2020:** Active
Industries:

Company Name: AiQOO
Description: AIQOO is an AI and Big-Data powered value maximization platform that tailors the needs and challenges of small and mid-size businesses.
Website: https://www.aiqoo.com/
Phone: **Email:** office@aiqoo.com
City: Hod Hasharon **State:** Center District **PC:** **Country:** Israel
Year Established: 2017 **Status 2020:** Active
Industries: Artificial Intelligence for:, Big Data and Analytics for:, Digital Marketing

Company Name: FSIGHT
Description: FSIGHT is an energy artifical intelligence platform based in Hod Hasharon, Israel.
Website: http://www.fsight.io/
Phone: 972.73.394.6131 **Email:** 36599@reference-encyclopedia-ai.net
City: Hod Hasharon **State:** Center District **PC:** **Country:** Israel
Year Established: 2014 **Status 2020:** Active
Industries: Artificial Intelligence for:, Big Data and Analytics for:, ~ Energy and Utilities (14), ~ Energy and Utilities (14)

Company Name: MinerEye
Description: You can't protect what you can't see
Website: http://minereye.com/
Phone: (9729) 765-3712 **Email:** info@minereye.com
City: Hod Hasharon **State:** Center District **PC:** **Country:** Israel
Year Established: 2014 **Status 2020:** Active
Industries: Artificial Intelligence for:, Compliance for:, Cyber Security for:, Security

Company Name: NeuroBlade
Description: Fabless semiconductor company
Website: http://www.neuroblade.ai/
Phone: 972 988 64966 **Email:** info@neuroblade.ai
City: Hod Hasharon **State:** Center District **PC:** **Country:** Israel
Year Established: 2017 **Status 2020:** Active
Industries:

Company Name: Novarize
Description: Novarize is a platform that delivers a ranked feed of potential opportunities unique to the user's brand, market, and competitive landscape.
Website: http://novarize.com
Phone: **Email:** 37074@reference-encyclopedia-ai.net
City: Hod Hasharon **State:** Center District **PC:** **Country:** Israel
Year Established: 2018 **Status 2020:** Active
Industries: Artificial Intelligence for:, Big Data and Analytics for:, Machine Learning

Company Name: YieldsApp
Description: YieldsApp is an innovative machine-learning platform developing AI-based agricultural management software.
Website: http://www.yieldsapp.com
Phone: 972 52-359-7964 **Email:** 37712@reference-encyclopedia-ai.net
City: Hod Hasharon **State:** Center District **PC:** **Country:** Israel
Year Established: 2018 **Status 2020:** Active
Industries: ~ Agriculture (3), ~ Agriculture (3), Artificial Intelligence for:, ~ Agriculture (3), Machine Learning

Company Name: BioEye
Description: BioEye is a mobile eye-tracking application for monitoring cognitive state.
Website: http://www.bioeye.com
Phone: **Email:** eran.ferri@bioeyetech.com
City: Hofit **State:** Center District **PC:** **Country:** Israel
Year Established: 2017 **Status 2020:** Active
Industries: Analytics for:, Artificial Intelligence for:, Big Data and Analytics for:, ~ Healthcare (20), ~ Healthcare (20)

Company Name: Keyma: South Korea
Description: Keymakr specializes in adapting technology solutions for the accurate use of video analytics to various semantics.
Website: http://keymakr.com
Phone: **Email:** hello@keymakr.com
City: Holon **State:** Center District **PC:** **Country:** Israel
Year Established: 2015 **Status 2020:** Active
Industries: Analytics for:, Artificial Intelligence for:, Machine Learning

Company Name: Preciate
Description: Preciate provides a customer engagement platform that uses the latest in facial recognition.
Website: http://preciate.me/
Phone: 972.3.7371110 **Email:** 37195@reference-encyclopedia-ai.net
City: Holon **State:** Center District **PC:** **Country:** Israel
Year Established: 2018 **Status 2020:** Active
Industries: Analytics for:, Artificial Intelligence for:, Facial Recognition for:, IT Managed Services

Company Name: Tactiga
Description: Tactiga developed artificial intelligence software based on unique system for analyzing.
Website:
Phone: **Email:** 37505@reference-encyclopedia-ai.net
City: Holon **State:** Center District **PC:** **Country:** Israel
Year Established: 2012 **Status 2020:** Closed
Industries: Analytics for:, Artificial Intelligence for:, Big Data and Analytics

Company Name: Colibri Sen: Sweden
Description: Colibri Sense is developing drone based SaaS, for civil security solutions.
Website: http://colibrisense.com
Phone: **Email:** gilead@colibrisense.com
City: Kefar Sirkin **State:** Center District **PC:** **Country:** Israel
Year Established: 2016 **Status 2020:** Active
Industries: Artificial Intelligence for:, Cyber Security for:, Business Software as a Service Apps (SaaS Apps) for:, Security

Company Name: 3d Signals
Description: Fast forward to Industry 4.0 with 3d Signals Asset Performance Monitoring solution.
Website: https://3dsig.com/
Phone: **Email:** info@3dsignals.com
City: Kfar Saba **State:** Center District **PC:** **Country:** Israel
Year Established: 2015 **Status 2020:** Active
Industries: Artificial Intelligence for:, Industrial Solutions for:, Automation

Company Name: DeePathology
Description: DeePathology is a medical practice that covers the areas of AI and deep learning to digital pathology.
Website: http://deepathology.ai
Phone: **Email:** info@deepathology.ai
City: Kfar Saba **State:** Center District **PC:** **Country:** Israel
Year Established: **Status 2020:** Active
Industries: Artificial Intelligence for:, Computer Vision

Company Name: Fixefy
Description: Fixefy is an AI driven integration platform that solves supply chain finance data asymmetry.
Website: http://www.fixefy.com/
Phone: 972-3-5168200 **Email:** contact@fixefy.com
City: Kfar Saba **State:** Center District **PC:** **Country:** Israel
Year Established: 2018 **Status 2020:** Active
Industries:

Company Name: inter-act now
Description: Inter-act is disrupting digital advertising, adTech, and chatbot technology to introduce engagement-based ad-network.
Website: http://inter-act.io
Phone: **Email:** 36795@reference-encyclopedia-ai.net
City: Kfar Saba **State:** Center District **PC:** **Country:** Israel
Year Established: 2017 **Status 2020:** Active
Industries: Artificial Intelligence

Company Name: Kamidoo
Description: Kamidoo is a text-to-storytelling platform that enables publishers to automatically deliver visual-interactive experiences to their audience
Website: http://www.kamidoo.com
Phone: **Email:** 36838@reference-encyclopedia-ai.net
City: Kfar Saba **State:** Center District **PC:** **Country:** Israel
Year Established: 2017 **Status 2020:** Active
Industries: Artificial Intelligence for:, IT Managed Services for:, ~ Arts-Entertainment-Recreation (4), Natural Language Processing

Company Name: Keotic Networks
Description: Keotic Networks is an artificial intelligence company
Website: http://www.keotic.com
Phone: **Email:** info@keotic.com
City: Kfar Saba **State:** Center District **PC:** **Country:** Israel
Year Established: 2015 **Status 2020:** Active
Industries: Artificial Intelligence for:, Machine Learning

Company Name: RoundU
Description: RoundU uses artificial intelligence and deep machine learning to match social media ads with consumer profiles and online behavior.
Website: http://roundu.co/
Phone: **Email:** info@roundu.co
City: Kfar Saba **State:** Center District **PC:** **Country:** Israel
Year Established: 2017 **Status 2020:** Active
Industries: Artificial Intelligence for:, IT Managed Services

Company Name: Tokabot
Description: An engagement platform for fans in the sports & entertainment domain. Chatbot @ user side - and a marketing platform @ business side.
Website: http://www.tokabot.com/
Phone: **Email:** football@tokabot.com
City: Kfar Saba **State:** Center District **PC:** **Country:** Israel

Year Established: 2017 **Status 2020:** Active
Industries: Analytics for:, Artificial Intelligence for:, Content for:, Web for:, Machine Learning for:, ~ Arts-Entertainment-Recreation (4), ~ Arts-Entertainment-Recreation (4), ~ Arts-Entertainment-Recreation (4)

Company **Name:** VoicEncode
Description: VoicEncode is an Artificial Intelligence that recognizes all users in any language.
Website: http://www.voicencode.com
Phone: **Email:** 37641@reference-encyclopedia-ai.net
City: Kfar Saba **State:** Center District **PC:** **Country:** Israel
Year Established: 2019 **Status 2020:** Active
Industries: Artificial Intelligence for:, IT Managed Services for:, Machine Learning

Company Name: Zebra Medical Vision, Inc.
Description: Healthcare
Website: www.zebra-med.com
Phone: **Email:** info@zebra-med.com
City: Kibbutz Shefayim **State:** Center District **Zip:** 6099000
Country: Israel
Year Established: **Status 2020:** Active
Industries: Artificial Intelligence for:, Big Data and Analytics for:, Computer Vision for:, ~ Healthcare (20), ~ Healthcare (20), ~ Healthcare (20)

Company Name: SafetyFirst
Description: SafetyFirst helps workers and their managers prevent accidents and injuries before they happen.
Website: http://margad.wixsite.com/safetyfirst
Phone: **Email:** 37326@reference-encyclopedia-ai.net
City: Lod **State:** Center District **PC:** **Country:** Israel
Year Established: 2018 **Status 2020:** Active
Industries: Artificial Intelligence for:, Cloud for:, IT Managed Services for:, Internet of Things (IoT)

Company Name: VitAlerter
Description: VitAlerter provides a medical solution that enables a safe and secure environment.
Website: http://www.vitalerter.com
Phone: **Email:** info@vitalerter.com
City: Lod **State:** Center District **PC:** **Country:** Israel
Year Established: 2017 **Status 2020:** Active
Industries: Artificial Intelligence for:, Cloud for:, ~ Healthcare (20)

Company Name: Seed-X
Description: Agriculture, Deep Learning, Machine Learning, Seeds, Phenotype to Genotype, AI
Website: https://www.seed-x.com/
Phone: **Email:** info@seed-x.com
City: Magshimim **State:** Center District **PC:** **Country:** Israel
Year Established: 2016 **Status 2020:** Active
Industries: ~ Agriculture (3), Artificial Intelligence for:, IT Managed Services for:, Machine Learning

Company Name: Emedgene
Description: Emedgene uses AI to automatically interpret genetic tests, so that health organizations can scale personalized care to wider populations.
Website: http://www.emedgene.com
Phone: **Email:** info@emedgene.com
City: Mazor **State:** Center District **PC:** **Country:** Israel
Year Established: 2015 **Status 2020:** Active
Industries: Artificial Intelligence for:, ~ Healthcare (20), ~ Healthcare (20), ~ Healthcare (20), IT Managed Services for:, ~ Healthcare (20)

Company Name: EcoPlant
Description: EcoPlant is a cloud based platform.
Website: http://www.ecoplant.co/
Phone: 972.50.4433582 **Email:** info@ecoplant.co
City: Modi'in **State:** Center District **PC:** **Country:** Israel
Year Established: 2016 **Status 2020:** Active
Industries: Artificial Intelligence for:, Cloud for:, Automation for:, Internet of Things (IoT)

Company Name: Findings
Description: Findings provides a scalable platform of assessment powered by artificial intelligence.
Website: http://findings.co/
Phone: **Email:** 36566@reference-encyclopedia-ai.net
City: Modi'in **State:** Center District **PC:** **Country:** Israel
Year Established: 2018 **Status 2020:** Active
Industries: Artificial Intelligence for:, Automation for:, IT Managed Services for:, Security for:, Supply Chain Management

Company Name: i4drive
Description: AI software for fully connected autonomous vehicl: Spain
Website: http://www.i4drive.com/
Phone: (9723) 720-7706 **Email:** info@i4drive.com
City: Modi'in **State:** Center District **PC:** **Country:** Israel
Year Established: 2014 **Status 2020:** Active
Industries:

Company Name: Sage Pair Ltd.
Description: Saas face-to-face video conferencing platform for one-to-one personalized learning sessions in a variety of professional fields.
Website: http://www.sagepair.com/
Phone: 972-58-402-0735 / 323-739-1546 **Email:** azi@sagepair.com
City: Modi'in **State:** Center District **PC:** **Country:** Israel
Year Established: **Status 2020:** Active
Industries:

Company Name: TrenDemon
Description: Uncovering how soft marketing efforts impact hard business objectives.
Website: http://trendemon.com
Phone: 972 72-240-2999 **Email:** team@trendemon.com
City: Natanya **State:** Center District **PC:** **Country:** Israel
Year Established: 2015 **Status 2020:** Active
Industries: Analytics for:, Business Intelligence for:, Content for:, Data Management for:, Predictive Analytics for:, Predictive Analytics

Company Name: EchoCare
Description: EchoCare develops a non-wearable home-monitoring system for senior care that automatically provides alerts.
Website: http://www.echocare-tech.com/
Phone: **Email:** info@echocare-tech.com
City: Ness Ziona **State:** Center District **PC:** **Country:** Israel
Year Established: 2015 **Status 2020:** Active
Industries: Big Data and Analytics for:, Cloud for:, ~ Healthcare (20), ~ Healthcare (20), Machine Learning

Company Name: Endotech
Description: EndoTech is an information technology company that focuses on artificial intelligence and machine learning.
Website: http://endotech.io
Phone: **Email:** 36508@reference-encyclopedia-ai.net
City: Ness Ziona **State:** Center District **PC:** **Country:** Israel
Year Established: 2012 **Status 2020:** Active
Industries: Artificial Intelligence for:, ~ Banking and Financial Markets-Services (7), ~ Banking and Financial Markets-Services (7)

Company Name: Eye-Net Mobile
Description: cellular-based V2X accident prevention solutions.
Website: http://www.eyenet-mobile.com/
Phone: 972 77 9709030 **Email:** info@eyenet-mobile.com
City: Ness Ziona **State:** Center District **PC:** **Country:** Israel

Year Established: **Status 2020:** Active
Industries: Analytics for:, Artificial Intelligence for:, ~ Automotive (5), Big Data and Analytics for:, Cloud for:, Machine Learning for:, Application Services

Company Name: PrintSyst
Description: PrintSyst developing a one-Button 3D Printing software solution Aerospace AM and Scaling Production with AI & Machine Learning.
Website: http://www.printsyst.ai
Phone: **Email:** info@printsyst.com
City: Ness Ziona **State:** Center District **PC:** **Country:** Israel
Year Established: 2017 **Status 2020:** Active
Industries: Artificial Intelligence for:, Automation for:, Machine Learning

Company Name: Click-Ins
Description: Next-generation platform that inspects vehicles and detects damages with just a click of a digital camera.
Website: http://click-ins.com/
Phone: **Email:** info@click-ins.com
City: Netanya **State:** Center District **PC:** **Country:** Israel
Year Established: 2014 **Status 2020:** Active
Industries: Cyber Security for:, ~ Banking and Financial Markets-Services (7), Security for:, Application Services for:, Security

Company Name: Etugo
Description: Etugo develops an electric power operating system intended to make any electric infrastructure autonomous.
Website:
Phone: **Email:** 36522@reference-encyclopedia-ai.net
City: Netanya **State:** Center District **PC:** **Country:** Israel
Year Established: 2015 **Status 2020:** Active
Industries: Artificial Intelligence for:, Internet of Things (IoT)

Company Name: IDEE: SOUTH AFRICA
Description: SaaS, IoT development, developer tools, Artificial Intelligence, Internet of Things
Website: http://ideeza.com
Phone: **Email:** 36737@reference-encyclopedia-ai.net
City: Netanya **State:** Center District **PC:** **Country:** Israel
Year Established: 2017 **Status 2020:** Active
Industries: Artificial Intelligence for:, IT Managed Services for:, Business Software as a Service Apps (SaaS Apps)

Company Name: Nimblix
Description: Nimblix is a smart AI tool that provides personal frictionless shopping experience in brick and mortar stores.
Website: http://www.nimblix.net
Phone: **Email:** info@nimblix.net
City: Netanya **State:** Center District **PC:** **Country:** Israel
Year Established: 2018 **Status 2020:** Active
Industries: Artificial Intelligence for:, Big Data and Analytics for:, Machine Learning for:, ~ Retail and Consumer Products (52)

Company Name: Stog
Description: Stog is a resource efficient AI augmented platform for aeroponic farming.
Website: http://stog.io
Phone: **Email:** roman.chachanashvili@stog.io
City: Netanya **State:** Center District **PC:** **Country:** Israel
Year Established: 2017 **Status 2020:** Active
Industries: ~ Agriculture (3), ~ Agriculture (3), Artificial Intelligence for:, Industrial Solutions

Company Name: Videocit: Spain
Description: Videocites introduces a collection of novel AI-based SaaS products for Video tracking and handling throughout the web and huge archives.
Website: http://www.videocites.com
Phone: **Email:** info@videocites.com
City: Netanya **State:** Center District **PC:** **Country:** Israel
Year Established: 2014 **Status 2020:** Active
Industries: Analytics for:, Artificial Intelligence for:, Big Data and Analytics for:, Web for:, Business Software as a Service Apps (SaaS Apps)

Company Name: 1.21 Gigawatts
Description: 1.21GW is developing an autonomous traffic controller for preventing collisions and organizing traffic flow.
Website: http://121gw.tech/
Phone: **Email:** ronidulgerg@121GW.Tech
City: Petah Tikwah **State:** Center District **PC:** **Country:** Israel
Year Established: 2017 **Status 2020:** Active
Industries: ~ Automotive (5), Predictive Analytics

Company Name: 4Cast
Description: 4Cast is a solutions provider in the defense, security, enterprise, and healthcare market.
Website: https://4cast-solutions.com/
Phone: **Email:** 35922@reference-encyclopedia-ai.net
City: Petah Tikwah **State:** Center District **PC:** **Country:** Israel
Year Established: 2018 **Status 2020:** Active
Industries:

Company Name: AlltypesAI
Description: AlltypesAI provides a software solution for the customs clearance process.
Website: https://alltypes.ai/
Phone: **Email:** info@alltypes.ai
City: Petah Tikwah **State:** Center District **PC:** **Country:** Israel
Year Established: 2017 **Status 2020:** Active
Industries: Analytics for:, Artificial Intelligence for:, ~ Transportation and Logistics (57)

Company Name: AudaScience
Description: AuDaScience develops automated data science and machine learning applications for the B2C enterprise market.
Website: http://audascience.com
Phone: **Email:** office@audascience.com
City: Petah Tikwah **State:** Center District **PC:** **Country:** Israel
Year Established: 2017 **Status 2020:** Active
Industries: Big Data and Analytics for:, Automation for:, Machine Learning

Company Name: Qbiq
Description: Qbiq develops an AI-powered platform that automates and optimizes architectural services for the real estate market.
Website: http://www.qbiq.ai
Phone: **Email:** 37230@reference-encyclopedia-ai.net
City: Petah Tikwah **State:** Center District **PC:** **Country:** Israel
Year Established: 2018 **Status 2020:** Active
Industries: Artificial Intelligence for:, Finance and Accounting

Company Name: Sirona Portal
Description: Sirona is a health and fitness company that features an AI-based platform designed for individual workouts outside the gym or clinic.
Website: http://sirona.ai
Phone: **Email:** info@sirona.ai
City: Petah Tikwah **State:** Center District **PC:** **Country:** Israel
Year Established: 2017 **Status 2020:** Active
Industries: Artificial Intelligence for:, Augmented Reality for:, ~ Healthcare (20), ~ Arts-Entertainment-Recreation (4)

Company Name: DreaMed Diabet: Spain
Description: DreaMed Diabetes offers AI solutions and personalized support for optimized insulin therapy.
Website: http://dreamed-diabetes.com/
Phone: **Email:** info@dreamed.ai
City: Petah Tiqva **State:** Center District **PC:** **Country:** Israel
Year Established: 2014 **Status 2020:** Active
Industries: Artificial Intelligence for:, ~ Healthcare (20), Enterprise Application Services for:, ~ Healthcare (20)

Company **Name:** Kitov

Description: Kitov develops a platform for automated visual inspection based on artificial intelligence.
Website: http://www.kitov.ai/
Phone: **Email:** info@kitovsystems.com
City: Petah Tiqva **State:** Center District **PC:** **Country:** Israel
Year Established: 2014 **Status 2020:** Active
Industries: Artificial Intelligence for:, Computer Vision for:, Automation for:, IT Managed Services

Company Name: SENSILIZE
Description: Empowering farmers with data
Website: http://sensilize.ag/
Phone: 97233741346 **Email:** info@sensilize.com
City: Petah Tiqva **State:** Center District **PC:** **Country:** Israel
Year Established: 2013 **Status 2020:** Active
Industries: ~ Agriculture (3), ~ Agriculture (3), Artificial Intelligence for:, Big Data and Analytics for:, Machine Learning for:, Robotics for:, Business Software as a Service Apps (SaaS Apps) for:, Business Software as a Service Apps (SaaS Apps) for:, ~ Social-Environment

Company Name: Softimize
Description: Softimize is the provider of TBBTM , the quickest path of medical device manufacturers to their own medical device cloud and applications
Website: http://www.softimize.co
Phone: 972 74-702-4735 **Email:** info@softimize.co
City: Petah Tiqva **State:** Center District **PC:** **Country:** Israel
Year Established: 2011 **Status 2020:** Active
Industries: ~ Healthcare (20), IT Managed Services for:, Web for:, Machine Learning

Company Name: MedAware Ltd
Description:
Website: http://www.medaware.com
Phone: 617-648-0349 **Email:** info@medaware.com
City: Raanana **State:** Center District **PC:** **Country:** Israel
Year Established: **Status 2020:** Active
Industries: Analytics for:, Big Data and Analytics for:, ~ Healthcare (20), ~ Healthcare (20)

Company Name: Anodot
Description: We use AI to constantly monitor and forecast business performance in FinTech, AdTech, Gaming, Telco and eComm custome: Serbia
Website: http://www.anodot.com/
Phone: 97297718707 **Email:** info@anodot.com
City: Ra'anana **State:** Center District **PC:** **Country:** Israel
Year Established: 2014 **Status 2020:** Active
Industries: Analytics for:, Artificial Intelligence for:, Big Data and Analytics for:, Business Intelligence for:, Machine Learning

Company Name: iMedis Medical
Description: IMedis is an artificial intelligence company focused on early cancer detection.
Website: http://www.imedis-medical.com/
Phone: **Email:** info@imedis-medical.com
City: Ra'anana **State:** Center District **PC:** **Country:** Israel
Year Established: **Status 2020:** Active
Industries: Artificial Intelligence for:, ~ Healthcare (20), ~ Manufacturing-Medical Equipment-Supplies (33)

Company Name: IMNA Solutions
Description: IMNA Solutions is a privacy and security phone based communications through critical and immediate real-time alerts.
Website: http://www.listenapp.com
Phone: **Email:** info@listenapp.net
City: Ra'anana **State:** Center District **PC:** **Country:** Israel
Year Established: 2014 **Status 2020:** Active
Industries: ~ Customer Relationship Management (11), ~ Healthcare (20), Mobile for:, Predictive Analytics for:, Security

Company Name: Naval Dome
Description: Naval Dome specializes in providing cyber defense solutions specifically for shipboard use.
Website: http://www.navaldome.com
Phone: 1 2134230795 **Email:** info@navaldome.com
City: Ra'anana **State:** Center District **PC:** **Country:** Israel
Year Established: 2016 **Status 2020:** Active
Industries: ~ Automotive (5), Cloud for:, Cyber Security for:, Application Services for:, ~ Transportation and Logistics (57), Security

Company Name: Rayven.io
Description: Rayven is a codeless platform for deploying IOT, machine learning and predictive analytics solutions.
Website: http://www.rayven.io
Phone: **Email:** sales@rayven.io
City: Ra'anana **State:** Center District **PC:** **Country:** Israel
Year Established: 2016 **Status 2020:** Active
Industries:

Company Name: RFISee
Description: RFISee is developing 4D imaging-radar-on-1-chip, providing the next generation ears and eyes for autonomous vehicles, drones, robots etc.
Website: http://rfisee.com
Phone: 972 3-55 00 743 **Email:** info@rfisee.com
City: Ra'anana **State:** Center District **PC:** **Country:** Israel
Year Established: 2015 **Status 2020:** Active
Industries: Artificial Intelligence for:, ~ Automotive (5), ~ Automotive (5)

Company Name: Soltell Systems
Description: Soltell introduces Industrial IoT-powered automation to enhance operation & management of distributed solar photovoltaic (PV) faciliti: Spain
Website: http://www.soltell.com
Phone: 972-546690888 **Email:** info@soltell.com
City: Ra'anana **State:** Center District **PC:** **Country:** Israel
Year Established: **Status 2020:** Active
Industries: Artificial Intelligence for:, ~ Energy and Utilities (14), Automation for:, Predictive Analytics for:, ~ Construction (10), ~ Energy and Utilities (14)

Company Name: Spatial Logic
Description: Spatial Logic develops a new class of AI based Visual Positioning System (VPS) delivering positioning and pose accuracy far superior to GPS.
Website: http://www.splogic.ai/
Phone: **Email:** info@spatiallogic-ai.com
City: Ra'anana **State:** Center District **PC:** **Country:** Israel
Year Established: 2017 **Status 2020:** Active
Industries: Artificial Intelligence for:, ~ Automotive (5), Computer Vision for:, IT Managed Services

Company Name: Stargo
Description: We revolutionize the freight forwarding and cargo industry via guaranteed payment, automating and optimizing routing & pricing in real-time.
Website: http://www.stargo.co/
Phone: 972.54.467.6730 **Email:** marketing@stargo.co
City: Ra'anana **State:** Center District **PC:** **Country:** Israel
Year Established: 2010 **Status 2020:** Active
Industries: Artificial Intelligence for:, Business Applications for:, ~ Telecommunications (56), Machine Learning for:, ~ Banking and Financial Markets-Services (7), Business Software as a Service Apps (SaaS Apps) for:, ~ Transportation and Logistics (57), Supply Chain Mana

Company Name: WeSnapp
Description: WeSnapp uses artificial intelligence to leverage the post-production image editing process.
Website: http://wesnapp.io/
Phone: 97236434347 **Email:** contact@wesnapp.io
City: Ra'anana **State:** Center District **PC:** **Country:** Israel

Year Established: 2016 **Status 2020:** Active
Industries: Artificial Intelligence for:, ~ Arts-Entertainment-Recreation (4), Application Services for:, Machine Learning for:, ~ Media-Communications (41)

Company **Name:** WallSensor Technologies Ltd.
Description: Smart Home DIY sensors for termites infestation early detection
Website: http://www.wallsensor.com
Phone: **Email:** info@wallsensor.com
City: Ramot Hashavim **State:** Center District **PC:** **Country:** Israel
Year Established: 2015 **Status 2020:** Active
Industries: Artificial Intelligence for:, Big Data and Analytics for:, Internet of Things (IoT)

Company Name: AgPlenus
Description: AgPlenus leverages computational algorithms and artificial intelligence models for analysis of molecules for agricultural products.
Website: http://www.agplenus.com/
Phone: **Email:** 35976@reference-encyclopedia-ai.net
City: Rehovot **State:** Center District **PC:** **Country:** Israel
Year Established: 2018 **Status 2020:** Active
Industries: ~ Agriculture (3), Artificial Intelligence for:, ~ Manufacturing-Petroleum-Coal-Chemicals-Plastics-Rubber (37)

Company Name: AiDock
Description: Document processing as a service
Website: http://aidock.net/
Phone: 972-54-644-9996 **Email:** info@aidock.net
City: Rehovot **State:** Center District **PC:** **Country:** Israel
Year Established: **Status 2020:** Active
Industries: Artificial Intelligence for:, Data Management for:, Knowledge Management for:, ~ Transportation and Logistics (57), Machine Learning for:, ~ Transportation and Logistics (57)

Company Name: Deep Heal:Thailand
Description: Deep Health is a medical device manufacturing company that features a spine navigation system.
Website: http://deep-health.co
Phone: **Email:** 36408@reference-encyclopedia-ai.net
City: Rehovot **State:** Center District **PC:** **Country:** Israel
Year Established: 2018 **Status 2020:** Active
Industries: Artificial Intelligence for:, Automation

Company Name: Emnotion LTD
Description: Climate risks solutions market place
Website: http://www.emnotion.com/
Phone: **Email:** info@emnotion.com
City: Rehovot **State:** Center District **PC:** **Country:** Israel
Year Established: 2016 **Status 2020:** Active
Industries: Analytics for:, Artificial Intelligence for:, IT Managed Services for:, Machine Learning

Company Name: PickPack
Description: Pickpack provides end-to-end SaaS and crowdsourced delivery logistic platforms based on intelligent AI and machine learning.
Website: http://pickpackage.com
Phone: 972-525837207 **Email:** meir@pickpackage.com
City: Rehovot **State:** Center District **PC:** **Country:** Israel
Year Established: 2016 **Status 2020:** Active
Industries: Artificial Intelligence for:, Enterprise Application Services for:, ~ Transportation and Logistics (57), ~ Telecommunications (56), Business Software as a Service Apps (SaaS Apps) for:, Supply Chain Management

Company Name: Noviopus
Description: Noviopus is develops the next generation of recruitment and finding a job systems.
Website: http://noviopus.com/
Phone: (972) 3-6424438 **Email:** 37076@reference-encyclopedia-ai.net
City: Rishon Le Zion **State:** Center District **PC:** **Country:** Israel
Year Established: 2015 **Status 2020:** Active
Industries: Big Data and Analytics for:, Machine Learning

Company Name: Onedeck
Description: Onedeck is a SaaS for trading and tracking crypto assets.
Website: http://onedeck.cc
Phone: **Email:** cc@onedeck.cc
City: Rishon Le Zion **State:** Center District **PC:** **Country:** Israel
Year Established: 2019 **Status 2020:** Closed
Industries: Analytics for:, Artificial Intelligence for:, Big Data and Analytics for:, Blockchain for:, ~ Banking and Financial Markets-Services (7), Business Software as a Service Apps (SaaS Apps) for:, Finance and Accounting for:, Finance and Accounting

Company Name: Kannita
Description: Kannita is improve their business results with in-store operations predictive analysis and maximize store ROI.
Website: http://kannita.com/
Phone: **Email:** contact@kannita.com
City: Rishpon **State:** Center District **PC:** **Country:** Israel
Year Established: 2015 **Status 2020:** Active
Industries:

Company Name: CogniFiber
Description: CogniFiber implements machine-learning and deep-learning algorithms to develops photonic computing hardware.
Website: http://www.cognifiber.com/
Phone: **Email:** 36302@reference-encyclopedia-ai.net
City: Rosh Ha'ayin **State:** Center District **PC:** **Country:** Israel
Year Established: 2019 **Status 2020:** Active
Industries: Machine Learning

Company Name: Talenya
Description: Talenya uses artificial intelligence to help talent acquisition teams fill jobs faster.
Website: http://talenya.com
Phone: **Email:** talenyajobs@talenya.com
City: Rosh Ha'ayin **State:** Center District **PC:** **Country:** Israel
Year Established: 2016 **Status 2020:** Active
Industries:

Company Name: Zebra Medical Vision
Description: Zebra Medical Vision is a medical imaging insights platform.
Website: http://www.zebra-med.com
Phone: 972 9-882-7795 **Email:** info@zebra-med.com
City: Shefayim **State:** Center District **PC:** **Country:** Israel
Year Established: 2014 **Status 2020:** Active
Industries: Artificial Intelligence for:, ~ Healthcare (20), ~ Healthcare (20), Machine Learning for:, ~ Healthcare (20)

Company Name: Padth.ai
Description: Padth.ai builds custom machine learning and predictive models.
Website: http://padth.ai/
Phone: 972-54-4545097 **Email:** info@padth.ai
City: Tel Mond **State:** Center District **PC:** **Country:** Israel
Year Established: 2016 **Status 2020:** Active
Industries: Artificial Intelligence for:, Machine Learning

Company Name: Comigo
Description: Comigo is the creator of the Experience Intelligence class solutions, thus, creating TV that understands with the first ever TV AI offering.
Website: http://www.comigo.com/
Phone: 972 9-771-5090 **Email:** jobs@comigo.com
City: Yarqona **State:** Center District **PC:** **Country:** Israel
Year Established: 2011 **Status 2020:** Active
Industries: Artificial Intelligence for:, Big Data and Analytics for:, Content for:, ~ Arts-Entertainment-Recreation (4)

Company **Name:** LIVEgg

Description: LIVEgg is a biotechnology company that develops digital solutions for the poultry industry to create and lead the smart hatcheries arena.
Website: http://livegg.co.: Israel
Phone: 972.4.6375534 **Email:** info@livegg.com
City: Barkai **State:** Haifa District **PC:** **Country:** Israel
Year Established: 2015 **Status 2020:** Active
Industries: Analytics for:, Big Data and Analytics for:, ~ Biotechnology (9), Machine Learning

Company Name: BeeEye
Description: Machine-learning, data science, decision-grade financial indicators, data enrichment, prediction models and big-data analysis.,
Website: http://www.beeeye.com
Phone: **Email:** assaf@beeeye.com
City: Binyamina **State:** Haifa District **PC:** **Country:** Israel
Year Established: 2015 **Status 2020:** Active
Industries: Analytics for:, Artificial Intelligence for:, Big Data and Analytics for:, IT Managed Services for:, Machine Learning

Company Name: ARpalus
Description: ARpalus is a B2B SaaS company that helps CPG & Retailers in optimizing their in-store operations using real-time computer-vision
Website: http://www.arpalus.com
Phone: **Email:** ofir@arpalus.com
City: Caesarea **State:** Haifa District **PC:** **Country:** Israel
Year Established: 2019 **Status 2020:** Active
Industries: Artificial Intelligence for:, Computer Vision for:, Machine Learning for:, Predictive Analytics for:, Business Software as a Service Apps (SaaS Apps)

Company Name: Deep AI Technologies
Description: Deep AI accelerates neural networks to help AI vendors develop their applications faster and cheaper.
Website: http://deep-aitech.com
Phone: 972 52-266-1115 **Email:** info@deep-aitech.com
City: Caesarea **State:** Haifa District **PC:** **Country:** Israel
Year Established: 2017 **Status 2020:** Active
Industries:

Company Name: Moodify
Description: Moodify offers a platform that uses Artificial Empathy to provide live behavioral and cognitive guidance.
Website: http://moodify.today/
Phone: 972-54-7465321 **Email:** OFFICE@MOODIFY.TODAY
City: Caesarea **State:** Haifa District **PC:** **Country:** Israel
Year Established: 2017 **Status 2020:** Active
Industries: Artificial Intelligence for:, ~ Automotive (5), ~ Automotive (5), IT Managed Services

Company Name: NeuReality
Description: NeuReality is a semiconductor start-up that designs AI-as-a-service infrastructure.
Website: http://neureality-ai.com
Phone: **Email:** 37051@reference-encyclopedia-ai.net
City: Caesarea **State:** Haifa District **PC:** **Country:** Israel
Year Established: 2018 **Status 2020:** Active
Industries: Artificial Intelligence for:, Machine Learning

Company Name: RevenueWize
Description: RevenueWize is an AI-powered platform that allows sellers to increase their profits and sales on online marketplaces.
Website: http://www.revenuewize.com
Phone: **Email:** info@revenuewize.com
City: Caesarea **State:** Haifa District **PC:** **Country:** Israel
Year Established: 2018 **Status 2020:** Active
Industries: Artificial Intelligence for:, Business Software as a Service Apps (SaaS Apps)

Company Name: R-Go Robotics
Description: R-Go Robotics is a robotics company that enables mobile robots to understand complex surroundings and operate autonomously.
Website: http://www.r-gorobotics.com/
Phone: **Email:** info@r-go.io
City: Caesarea **State:** HA **PC:** **Country:** Israel
Year Established: 2018 **Status 2020:** Active
Industries: Artificial Intelligence for:, IT Managed Services for:, Machine Learning for:, Robotics

Company Name: Simpool
Description: We use AI to help companies predict and maximize user LTV through endless Game Economy scenario simulations
Website: http://simpool.io/
Phone: **Email:** guy@simpool.io
City: Caesarea **State:** HA **PC:** **Country:** Israel
Year Established: 2018 **Status 2020:** Active
Industries:

Company Name: WalkOut
Description: WalkOut developed a proprietary artificial intelligence system for highly accurate real-time product identification.
Website: http://walkout.co
Phone: **Email:** info@walkout.co
City: Caesarea **State:** Haifa District **PC:** **Country:** Israel
Year Established: 2017 **Status 2020:** Active
Industries: Artificial Intelligence for:, Computer Vision for:, ~ Retail and Consumer Products (52)

Company Name: ai.type
Description: ai.type offers a revolutionary solution for typing on touchscreen devices.
Website: http://aitype.com/
Phone: **Email:** 35999@reference-encyclopedia-ai.net
City: Hadera **State:** Haifa District **PC:** **Country:** Israel
Year Established: 2010 **Status 2020:** Active
Industries: Application Services for:, Natural Language Processing

Company Name: Coral Detection Systems
Description: Coral Detection Systems is an AI-based drowning detection system for residential swimming pools.
Website: http://coraldrowningdetection.com
Phone: **Email:** info@coraldrwoningdetection.com
City: Hahotrim **State:** HA **PC:** **Country:** Israel
Year Established: 2014 **Status 2020:** Active
Industries: Artificial Intelligence for:, Computer Vision for:, Machine Learning for:, ~ Government (19)

Company Name: AIFortify
Description: AIFortify is an early-stage startup that develops AI-powered decision automation and management platform.
Website: https://aifortify.com/
Phone: **Email:** contact@aifortify.com
City: Haifa **State:** Haifa District **PC:** **Country:** Israel
Year Established: 2016 **Status 2020:** Active
Industries: Artificial Intelligence for:, IT Managed Services for:, Web for:, Machine Learning for:, Web

Company Name: C-Robotics
Description: C-Robotics develops a unique robot that is programmed to clean restrooms.
Website: http://www.c-robotics.info
Phone: **Email:** 36347@reference-encyclopedia-ai.net
City: Haifa **State:** Haifa District **PC:** **Country:** Israel
Year Established: 2017 **Status 2020:** Active
Industries: Artificial Intelligence for:, Augmented Reality for:, Robotics

Company Name: EazyTrain
Description: EazyTrain designs a train passenger flow and positioning management software system that improves the passenger experience.
Website: http://www.eazytrain.com/

Phone: **Email:** info@eazytrain.com
City: Haifa **State:** Haifa District **PC:** **Country:** Israel
Year Established: 2017 **Status 2020:** Active
Industries: IT Managed Services for:, Application Services

Company Name: Healthymize
Description: Healthymize provides AI based voice monitoring to predict flare ups in voice affecting diseases.
Website: http://healthymize.com/
Phone: **Email:** contact@healthymize.com
City: Haifa **State:** Haifa District **PC:** **Country:** Israel
Year Established: 2016 **Status 2020:** Active
Industries: Artificial Intelligence for:, ~ Healthcare (20), ~ Healthcare (20)

Company Name: INTSITE
Description: AI, Computer vision, ML, DL, Aerospace technology, Robotics, SaaS
Website: http://www.intsite.ai
Phone: 972 (4) 643-5813 **Email:** office@intsite.ai
City: Haifa **State:** Haifa District **PC:** **Country:** Israel
Year Established: 2017 **Status 2020:** Active
Industries: ~ Agriculture (3), Artificial Intelligence for:, Computer Vision for:, ~ Construction (10), IT Infrastructure for:, ~ Telecommunications (56), Machine Learning for:, ~ Metals and Mining (42), ~ Metals and Mining (42)

Company Name: kmoEye
Description: kmoeye's goal is to provide an artificial vision technology. This technology is an outcome of research in neurophysiology and holography.
Website: http://www.kmoeye.com/
Phone: **Email:** 36857@reference-encyclopedia-ai.net
City: Haifa **State:** Haifa District **PC:** **Country:** Israel
Year Established: 2012 **Status 2020:** Active
Industries: Artificial Intelligence for:, ~ Automotive (5), ~ Automotive (5), Computer Vision for:, Robotics

Company Name: Lofic
Description: Lofic is a collaborative music creation platform that connects wit musicians around the world to play & record music.
Website: http://www.lofic.net
Phone: **Email:** info@lofic.net
City: Haifa **State:** Haifa District **PC:** **Country:** Israel
Year Established: 2016 **Status 2020:** Active
Industries: Artificial Intelligence for:, Application Services for:, Machine Learning for:, ~ Arts-Entertainment-Recreation (4), ~ Arts-Entertainment-Recreation (4)

Company Name: Lynxight
Description: Lynxight creates computer vision applications for underwater operations to manage safety risks and improve operational performance.
Website: http://lynxight.com
Phone: **Email:** info@lynxight.com
City: Haifa **State:** Haifa District **PC:** **Country:** Israel
Year Established: 2018 **Status 2020:** Active
Industries: Analytics for:, Artificial Intelligence for:, Predictive Analytics for:, ~ Waste Management and Remediation Services (59)

Company Name: mediTective
Description: MediTective is an artificial intelligence system that detects polyps in gastrointestinal procedures.
Website: http://www.meditective.com
Phone: **Email:** info@meditective.com
City: Haifa **State:** Haifa District **PC:** **Country:** Israel
Year Established: 2019 **Status 2020:** Active
Industries: Artificial Intelligence for:, Big Data and Analytics for:, ~ Healthcare (20), ~ Healthcare (20)

Company Name: Mirrori
Description: Mirrori is a virtual beauty assistant providing advice to women based on their facial features and their own inventory of beauty products.
Website: http://www.mirrori.co
Phone: **Email:** 36989@reference-encyclopedia-ai.net
City: Haifa **State:** Haifa District **PC:** **Country:** Israel
Year Established: 2018 **Status 2020:** Active
Industries: Artificial Intelligence for:, Computer Vision for:, Machine Learning

Company Name: Newt
Description: Newt is creating an AI-powered personal sports nutritionist.
Website: http://www.newtfit.com
Phone: **Email:** gil@newtfit.com
City: Haifa **State:** Haifa District **PC:** **Country:** Israel
Year Established: 2019 **Status 2020:** Active
Industries:

Company Name: Omika Vision
Description: Omika Vision creates tools for deploying AI-powered machine vision to any industry.
Website: http://www.omika-vision.com/
Phone: **Email:** 37099@reference-encyclopedia-ai.net
City: Haifa **State:** HA **PC:** **Country:** Israel
Year Established: 2019 **Status 2020:** Active
Industries: Artificial Intelligence for:, Automation for:, IT Managed Services for:, Machine Learning

Company Name: OutOfScreens
Description: OutOfScreens designs and manufactures a 3D printing machine for creating and crafting physical objects.
Website: http://outofscreens.com
Phone: 052-5 242 293 **Email:** contact@outofscreens.com
City: Haifa **State:** HA **PC:** **Country:** Israel
Year Established: 2018 **Status 2020:** Active
Industries: Artificial Intelligence

Company Name: PG Medical
Description: PG Medical harnesses machine learning algorithms to provide physicians with a virtual pain expert at the palm of their hands.
Website: http://pgmeds.com/
Phone: **Email:** info@pgmeds.com
City: Haifa **State:** Haifa District **PC:** **Country:** Israel
Year Established: 2018 **Status 2020:** Active
Industries: Automation for:, ~ Healthcare (20), IT Managed Services for:, Machine Learning

Company Name: PHASE3 Technologies
Description: Predictive Maintenance & Monitoring of Power Generato: Serbia
Website: http://www.phase3-tech.com/
Phone: 972 4 847 0100 **Email:** nfo@phase3-tech.com
City: Haifa **State:** Haifa District **PC:** **Country:** Israel
Year Established: 2011 **Status 2020:** Active
Industries: ~ Energy and Utilities (14), IT Managed Services for:, Application Services

Company Name: Presenso
Description: AI Driven Industrial Intelligence
Website: http://www.presenso.com/
Phone: 97249821199 **Email:** info@presenso.com
City: Haifa **State:** Haifa District **PC:** **Country:** Israel
Year Established: 2015 **Status 2020:** Active
Industries: **Company Name:** Pruvo
Description: Pruvo is an AI-driven solution company that increases profitability for travelers and travel companies.
Website: http://www.pruvo.com
Phone: **Email:** info@pruvo.net
City: Haifa **State:** Haifa District **PC:** **Country:** Israel
Year Established: 2016 **Status 2020:** Active
Industries: Artificial Intelligence for:, E-Commerce for:, Web for:, ~ Travel and Transportation (58)

Company Name: Sonar
Description: Sonaris is making vital ultrasound screening tests available in every clinic, by providing an AI-powered imaging workflow
Website: http://www.sonaris.co/
Phone: **Email:** info@sonaris.co
City: Haifa **State:** Haifa District **PC:** **Country:** Israel
Year Established: 2017 **Status 2020:** Active
Industries: Artificial Intelligence for:, Computer Vision for:, ~ Healthcare (20), ~ Healthcare (20), Machine Learning

Company Name: TankU
Description: TankU is a technology and services company for reshaping on-the-road mobile payment one-tap secure fueling.
Website: http://www.tanku.com
Phone: **Email:** info@tanku.com
City: Haifa **State:** Haifa District **PC:** **Country:** Israel
Year Established: 2014 **Status 2020:** Active
Industries: Application Services for:, Artificial Intelligence for:, ~ Automotive (5), ~ Automotive (5), ~ Energy and Utilities (14)

Company Name: TheWhollySee
Description: Deep learning training data for autonomous vehicl: Spain
Website: http://tws.ai
Phone: **Email:** info@thewhollysee.com
City: Haifa **State:** Haifa District **PC:** **Country:** Israel
Year Established: 2016 **Status 2020:** Active
Industries: Artificial Intelligence for:, ~ Automotive (5), ~ Automotive (5), Business Applications for:, Image Recognition for:, Machine Learning

Company Name: Whee: Romania
Description: Wheero provides holistic bicycle safety equipment installed on the bicycle.
Website: http://www.wheero.com
Phone: **Email:** 37665@reference-encyclopedia-ai.net
City: Haifa **State:** Haifa District **PC:** **Country:** Israel
Year Established: 2017 **Status 2020:** Active
Industries: Artificial Intelligence for:, ~ Automotive (5)

Company Name: Nanovel
Description: Nanovel builds a fully-automatic machine to help in the manual process of agricultural work.
Website: http://www.nanovel.co.: Israel
Phone: 054-449-2724 **Email:** liat@nanovel.co.: Israel
City: Nesher **State:** Haifa District **PC:** **Country:** Israel
Year Established: 2018 **Status 2020:** Active
Industries: ~ Agriculture (3), ~ Agriculture (3), Artificial Intelligence for:, ~ Agriculture (3), Machine Learning

Company Name: Precognize
Description: Precognize is a predictive maintenance software for the heavy industry (Chemical, Petrochemical, Refineries, Energy)
Website: http://www.precog.co
Phone: **Email:** info@precog.co
City: Tirat Carmel **State:** Haifa District **PC:** **Country:** Israel
Year Established: 2011 **Status 2020:** Active
Industries: Artificial Intelligence for:, Enterprise Application Services for:, Internet of Things (IoT) for:, Machine Learning

Company Name: Carallarm
Description: Carallarm is a revolutionary artificial intelligence app that alarms users whenever they forget children in cars.
Website: http://www.carallarm.com
Phone: **Email:** carallarm@gmail.com
City: Bat Hefer **State:** HaMerkaz **PC:** **Country:** Israel
Year Established: 2017 **Status 2020:** Active
Industries: Application Services for:, Artificial Intelligence for:, Application Services

Company Name: Academix Bio
Description: Academix creates proprietary machine learning algorithms that help to find the right collaboration for user's specific R&D needs.
Website: https://academix.bio/
Phone: **Email:** contact@academix.bio
City: Jerusalem **State:** Jerusalem District **PC:** **Country:** Israel
Year Established: 2017 **Status 2020:** Active
Industries:

Company Name: Autonomeye
Description: Developing smart glasses for blind people
Website: http://www.autonomeye.co/
Phone: **Email:** shmielatme@gmail.com
City: Jerusalem **State:** Jerusalem District **PC:** **Country:** Israel
Year Established: **Status 2020:** Active
Industries: Artificial Intelligence for:, ~ Healthcare (20)

Company Name: BrainQ
Description: BrainQ develops Artificial Intelligence-powered technologies to treat neuro-disorders in innovative ways.
Website: http://brainqtech.com/
Phone: **Email:** info@brainqtech.com
City: Jerusalem **State:** Jerusalem District **PC:** **Country:** Israel
Year Established: 2011 **Status 2020:** Active
Industries: Artificial Intelligence for:, ~ Healthcare (20)

Company Name: Ception
Description: Ception is an automotive company for precise localization, based on advanced computer vision and deep learning algorithms.
Website: http://www.ception.ai
Phone: **Email:** info@ception.ai
City: Jerusalem **State:** Jerusalem District **PC:** **Country:** Israel
Year Established: 2018 **Status 2020:** Active
Industries: Artificial Intelligence for:, ~ Automotive (5), ~ Automotive (5)

Company Name: cnvrg.io
Description: cnvrg.io is a full stack data science platform that helps teams manage models, and build auto-adaptive machine learning pipelin: Spain
Website: http://cnvrg.io/
Phone: **Email:** hi@cnvrg.io
City: Jerusalem **State:** Jerusalem District **PC:** **Country:** Israel
Year Established: 2016 **Status 2020:** Active
Industries: Artificial Intelligence for:, Enterprise Application Services for:, Machine Learning for:, Predictive Analytics for:, Business Software as a Service Apps (SaaS Apps)

Company Name: CogAid
Description: CogAid is an assistive tool for Workers and Professionals with Cognitive Disabilities.
Website: http://cogaid.com
Phone: 972 53 221 8832 **Email:** info@cogaid.com
City: Jerusalem **State:** JM **PC:** **Country:** Israel
Year Established: 2015 **Status 2020:** Active
Industries: Artificial Intelligence for:, ~ Healthcare (20)

Company **Name:** Convizit
Description: The Next Generation of User Behavior Analytics
Website: http://convizit.com/
Phone: **Email:** info@convizit.com
City: Jerusalem **State:** Jerusalem District **PC:** **Country:** Israel
Year Established: 2017 **Status 2020:** Active
Industries: Analytics for:, Artificial Intelligence for:, Big Data and Analytics for:, Web for:, Machine Learning

Company Name: Correlor
Description: Predictive analytics for the industrial world
Website: http://www.correlor.com
Phone: **Email:** info@correlor.com
City: Jerusalem **State:** Jerusalem District **PC:** **Country:** Israel

Year Established: 2015 **Status 2020:** Active
Industries: Analytics for:, Machine Learning for:, Business Software as a Service Apps (SaaS Apps)

Company Name: CyberTraits
Description: Cyber Traits is a candidate-position fit evaluation system for HR and HLS markets.
Website: http://cybertraits.com
Phone: 972 54 4660-556 **Email:** administrator@cybertraits.com
City: Jerusalem **State:** Jerusalem District **PC:** **Country:** Israel
Year Established: 2014 **Status 2020:** Active
Industries: Automation for:, Cyber Security for:, IT Managed Services for:, Application Services for:, ~ Government (19)

Company Name: Datacrushe: Serbia
Description: SaaS eCommerce Revenue Discovery Platform
Website: http://www.datacrushers.com
Phone: 323-473-3032 **Email:** sales@datacrushers.com
City: Jerusalem **State:** Jerusalem District **PC:** **Country:** Israel
Year Established: 2014 **Status 2020:** Active
Industries: Analytics for:, Artificial Intelligence for:, E-Commerce for:, Machine Learning for:, Predictive Analytics for:, Predictive Analytics for:, Business Software as a Service Apps (SaaS Apps)

Company Name: DataToCapital
Description: DataToCapital is a boutique management consulting firm that offers its services to tier-1 firms and start-ups operating in Israel.
Website: http://www.datatocapital.com/
Phone: (9725) 478-5227 **Email:** yohan.albo@datatocapital.com
City: Jerusalem **State:** Jerusalem District **PC:** **Country:** Israel
Year Established: 2015 **Status 2020:** Active
Industries: Predictive Analytics for:, Business Process and Operations for:, Business Process and Operations

Company Name: DMWAY Analytics
Description: DMWAY makes predictive analytics accessible and affordable for everyone!
Website: http://dmway.com/
Phone: (9723) 670-2551 **Email:** info@dmway.com
City: Jerusalem **State:** JM **PC:** **Country:** Israel
Year Established: 2013 **Status 2020:** Active
Industries: Analytics for:, Predictive Analytics

Company Name: Dolphin Vision
Description: AI-based visual surveillance technology for Water environments
Website: http://dolphinvision.net
Phone: 972-523-411000 **Email:** info@dolphinvision.net
City: Jerusalem **State:** Jerusalem District **PC:** **Country:** Israel
Year Established: 2018 **Status 2020:** Active
Industries: Artificial Intelligence for:, ~ Transportation and Logistics (57), Security

Company Name: DrizzleX
Description: DrizzleX provides a water-metering solution that enables water conservation in residential buildings without individual apartment meters.
Website: http://www.drizzlex.com/
Phone: 972 54-764-3311 **Email:** contact@drizzlex.com
City: Jerusalem **State:** Jerusalem District **PC:** **Country:** Israel
Year Established: 2016 **Status 2020:** Active
Industries: Artificial Intelligence for:, ~ Energy and Utilities (14), Internet of Things (IoT)

Company Name: EDas Healthcare
Description: EDas Healthcare enables the real-time diagnosis of infectious diseases using machine learning and a dynamic algorithm.
Website: http://www.edashealthcare.com/
Phone: **Email:** info@edashealthcare.com
City: Jerusalem **State:** JM **PC:** **Country:** Israel
Year Established: 2018 **Status 2020:** Active
Industries:

Company Name: EnsoGuard
Description: EnsoGuard is a computer software that features automatic monitoring of target system.
Website: http://www.ensoguard.com
Phone: **Email:** 36512@reference-encyclopedia-ai.net
City: Jerusalem **State:** Jerusalem District **PC:** **Country:** Israel
Year Established: 2018 **Status 2020:** Active
Industries: Artificial Intelligence for:, Cyber Security for:, IT Managed Services for:, Web

Company Name: Evan Spero
Description: Asssitive Domotics
Website: http://www.Vectored-Photonics.com
Phone: **Email:** evan@Vectored-Photonics.com
City: Jerusalem **State:** Jerusalem District **PC:** **Country:** Israel
Year Established: 2016 **Status 2020:** Active
Industries: Artificial Intelligence for:, ~ Healthcare (20)

Company Name: Flame
Description: Flame develops an unmanned intelligent glider to deploy a fire-retardant payload at precise locations at any time of the day or night.
Website: http://www.flamegliders.com/
Phone: **Email:** gilad@flamegliders.com
City: Jerusalem **State:** JM **PC:** **Country:** Israel
Year Established: 2017 **Status 2020:** Active
Industries: ~ Manufacturing-General (31), Application Services

Company Name: geekAp: Palestine
Description: geekApps - All in One is a full solution platform for DIY mobile app building, digital advertising & business growth tools.
Website: http://www.geekapps.com
Phone: 972-50-533-9933 **Email:** adi@geekapps.com
City: Jerusalem **State:** JM **PC:** **Country:** Israel
Year Established: 2016 **Status 2020:** Active
Industries: Artificial Intelligence for:, Application Services

Company Name: Lightkey
Description: Lightkey is the world's only non-cloud-based AI-powered predictive typing software for Windows
Website: http://www.lightkey.io/
Phone: **Email:** eran@lightkey.io
City: Jerusalem **State:** JM **PC:** **Country:** Israel
Year Established: 2016 **Status 2020:** Active
Industries: Artificial Intelligence for:, Machine Learning for:, Predictive Analytics for:, Application Services for:, Data Management

Company Name: Lightricks
Description: Lightricks integrates advanced technologies from computer vision, computer graphics, and image processing into mobile products.
Website: http://www.lightricks.com
Phone: **Email:** contact@lightricks.com
City: Jerusalem **State:** Jerusalem District **PC:** **Country:** Israel
Year Established: 2013 **Status 2020:** Active
Industries: Application Services for:, Artificial Intelligence for:, Application Services for:, ~ Media-Communications (41)

Company Name: MADA Analytics
Description: MADA Analytics develops an artificial intelligence software to optimize the financial returns on investments in renewable power plants.
Website: http://madaanalytics.com
Phone: **Email:** 36927@reference-encyclopedia-ai.net
City: Jerusalem **State:** Jerusalem District **PC:** **Country:** Israel
Year Established: 2017 **Status 2020:** Active
Industries: Artificial Intelligence for:, Big Data and Analytics for:, ~ Energy and Utilities (14), ~ Banking and Financial Markets-Services (7)

Company Name: Modal AI
Description: Modal AI specializes in the development of core knowledge representation and reasoning technology.
Website: http://www.modalai.co
Phone: **Email:** grossd@modalai.co
City: Jerusalem **State:** Jerusalem District **PC:** **Country:** Israel
Year Established: 2018 **Status 2020:** Active
Industries: Artificial Intelligence for:, ~ Automotive (5), Internet of Things (IoT)

Company Name: MYOR
Description: MYOR uses skin-surface noninvasive monitoring technologies to adjust nutrition and enable health.
Website: http://myor.me/
Phone: **Email:** info@myor.me
City: Jerusalem **State:** JM **PC:** **Country:** Israel
Year Established: 2018 **Status 2020:** Active
Industries: Artificial Intelligence for:, Big Data and Analytics for:, ~ Biotechnology (9), ~ Healthcare (20), ~ Healthcare (20)

Company Name: Native Alpha
Description: Native Alpha is a data-centric startup, building algorithmic trading strategies.
Website: http://www.nativealpha.com
Phone: **Email:** 37040@reference-encyclopedia-ai.net
City: Jerusalem **State:** Jerusalem District **PC:** **Country:** Israel
Year Established: 2016 **Status 2020:** Active
Industries: Artificial Intelligence for:, ~ Banking and Financial Markets-Services (7)

Company Name: NUA Robotics
Description: Their vision is to give the things they use everyday a human-like behavior, and by that allowing them to become their personal assistants.
Website: http://unbouncepages.com/nuarobotics/
Phone: **Email:** founders@nuarobotics.com
City: Jerusalem **State:** Jerusalem District **PC:** **Country:** Israel
Year Established: 2015 **Status 2020:** Closed
Industries: Artificial Intelligence for:, Computer Vision for:, Internet of Things (IoT) for:, Machine Learning for:, Robotics

Company Name: Oddetect
Description: Oddetect develops video analytics software for surveillance systems
Website: http://oddetect.com/
Phone: **Email:** info@oddetect.com
City: Jerusalem **State:** Jerusalem District **PC:** **Country:** Israel
Year Established: 2018 **Status 2020:** Active
Industries: Analytics for:, Artificial Intelligence for:, IT Managed Services for:, Machine Learning

Company Name: PeopleBroadcasting
Description: PeopleBroadcasting is developing a platform that enables high content monitoring and filtering to prevent inappropriate content.
Website: http://peoplebroadcasting.org
Phone: **Email:** 37153@reference-encyclopedia-ai.net
City: Jerusalem **State:** Jerusalem District **PC:** **Country:** Israel
Year Established: 2016 **Status 2020:** Active
Industries: Artificial Intelligence for:, Web for:, Machine Learning

Company Name: Pepticom Ltd.
Description: Pepticom is an Artificial Intelligence (AI) company for the discovery of novel molecules in the Pharmaceutical and Agricultural markets.
Website: http://www.pepticom.com
Phone: **Email:** maayan.elias@pepticom.com
City: Jerusalem **State:** Jerusalem District **PC:** **Country:** Israel
Year Established: 2011 **Status 2020:** Active
Industries:

Company Name: Personity.ai
Description: Personity develops a machine learning based Personality-as-aService platform that deduces user's personality.
Website: http://personity.ai
Phone: (888)497-3411 **Email:** support@personity.ai
City: Jerusalem **State:** Jerusalem District **PC:** **Country:** Israel
Year Established: 2012 **Status 2020:** Active
Industries: Artificial Intelligence for:, Machine Learning for:, Enterprise Application Services

Company Name: Pollight
Description: Pollight develops a wireless building automation system based on a secure and scalable network.
Website: http://pollights.com
Phone: **Email:** contact@pollights.com
City: Jerusalem **State:** Jerusalem District **PC:** **Country:** Israel
Year Established: 2012 **Status 2020:** Active
Industries: Artificial Intelligence for:, Internet of Things (IoT)

Company Name: Pomicell
Description: Pomicell is an AI-powered machine learning platform making big data usable for biotech compani: Spain
Website: http://www.pomicell.com
Phone: **Email:** info@pomicell.com
City: Jerusalem **State:** Jerusalem District **PC:** **Country:** Israel
Year Established: 2015 **Status 2020:** Active
Industries: Artificial Intelligence for:, Big Data and Analytics for:, ~ Biotechnology (9), Machine Learning

Company Name: Prodictive Israel
Description: Prodictive is developing an artificial intelligence solutions.
Website: http://prodictive.com
Phone: **Email:** 37211@reference-encyclopedia-ai.net
City: Jerusalem **State:** JM **PC:** **Country:** Israel
Year Established: 2016 **Status 2020:** Active
Industries: Artificial Intelligence for:, Machine Learning

Company Name: Proto-Me: Switzerland
Description: Proto-Mech is developing innovative technology and approach for Human-Computer Interaction using Natural Language Understanding.
Website: http://proto-mech.com
Phone: **Email:** 37218@reference-encyclopedia-ai.net
City: Jerusalem **State:** Jerusalem District **PC:** **Country:** Israel
Year Established: 2013 **Status 2020:** Active
Industries: Machine Learning for:, Natural Language Processing

Company Name: Psytient
Description: Psytient develops an Artificial intelligence-based solution to reduce and prevent hospital re-admissions.
Website: http://www.psytient.com
Phone: **Email:** info@psytient.com
City: Jerusalem **State:** Jerusalem District **PC:** **Country:** Israel
Year Established: 2019 **Status 2020:** Active
Industries: Artificial Intelligence for:, ~ Healthcare (20), ~ Healthcare (20)

Company Name: Quze.ai
Description: Time optimization & Utilization for service providers and custome: Serbia
Website: http://www.quze.ai
Phone: 972 54 9446170 **Email:** efaim@quze.ai
City: Jerusalem **State:** Jerusalem District **PC:** **Country:** Israel
Year Established: 2016 **Status 2020:** Active
Industries: Artificial Intelligence for:, Machine Learning

Company Name: Sweet: Switzerland
Description: Sweetch is an artificial intelligence based platform for large scale prediction, prevention and outcome improvement.
Website: http://sweetch.com/
Phone: **Email:** support@sweetch.com
City: Jerusalem **State:** Jerusalem District **PC:** **Country:** Israel

Year Established: 2013 **Status 2020:** Active
Industries: Artificial Intelligence for:, ~ Healthcare (20), ~ Healthcare (20), Application Services

Company Name: WriteOn
Description: WriteOn is developing software that will analyzes handwriting analysis using image processing.
Website:
Phone: **Email:** 37688@reference-encyclopedia-ai.net
City: Jerusalem **State:** Jerusalem District **PC:** **Country:** Israel
Year Established: 2016 **Status 2020:** Active
Industries: Analytics for:, Artificial Intelligence

Company Name: ProSen: Sweden
Description: ProSense is developing software that produces forecasts for failures in Big Data industrial cooling systems.
Website: http://www.prosense.co
Phone: 054-6490248 **Email:** amatzya@prosense.co
City: Mevo Beitar **State:** Jerusalem District **PC:** **Country:** Israel
Year Established: 2018 **Status 2020:** Active
Industries: Big Data and Analytics for:, Industrial Solutions for:, Machine Learning

Company Name: GoArc
Description: GoArc provides recommendation system to improve safety in industrial organizations.
Website: http://www.go-arc.com/
Phone: **Email:** office@go-arc.com
City: Moza **State:** Jerusalem District **PC:** **Country:** Israel
Year Established: 2015 **Status 2020:** Active
Industries: Industrial Solutions for:, Internet of Things (IoT) for:, Predictive Analytics for:, Business Software as a Service Apps (SaaS Apps) for:, Security

Company Name: Illumigyn
Description: Illumigyn incorporates existing machine vision technologies into a compact imaging colposcope for medical applications.
Website: http://illumigyn.com/
Phone: **Email:** 36744@reference-encyclopedia-ai.net
City: Neve Ilan **State:** JM **PC:** **Country:** Israel
Year Established: 2012 **Status 2020:** Active
Industries: Artificial Intelligence for:, ~ Healthcare (20), ~ Healthcare (20)

Company Name: SupPlant
Description: SupPlant is the world's leading provider of Growth-Based Irrigation technology and products.
Website: http://supplant.me
Phone: 972-4-953-4062 **Email:** info@supplant.me
City: Affula **State:** North District **PC:** **Country:** Israel
Year Established: 2012 **Status 2020:** Active
Industries: ~ Agriculture (3), IT Managed Services for:, Internet of Things (IoT) for:, Machine Learning for:, Robotics for:, Robotics

Company Name: Neural Flow
Description: Neural Flow is a software platform that is designed to optimize the performance of continuously stirred tank reactors.
Website: http://neural-flow.com
Phone: **Email:** info@neural-flow.com
City: Ma'alot **State:** North District **PC:** **Country:** Israel
Year Established: 2017 **Status 2020:** Active
Industries:

Company Name: Agwa
Description: Vegetables as a Service - fresh salad bowl a day with minimal efforts on your backyard
Website: https://www.agwafarm.com/
Phone: **Email:** niv@agwafarm.com
City: Misgav **State:** North District **PC:** **Country:** Israel
Year Established: 2020 **Status 2020:** Active
Industries: ~ Agriculture (3), Artificial Intelligence

Company Name: Datarum
Description: Datarum offers artificial intelligence services for the health and agriculture industries.
Website:
Phone: **Email:** 36398@reference-encyclopedia-ai.net
City: Misgav **State:** North District **PC:** **Country:** Israel
Year Established: 2015 **Status 2020:** Active
Industries: ~ Agriculture (3), Artificial Intelligence for:, ~ Healthcare (20)

Company Name: NanoScent
Description: Making Scents Readable. VOC detection for environmental protection, process control and employee safety in Industry 4.0
Website: http://www.nanoscentlabs.com
Phone: **Email:** contact@nanoscentlabs.com
City: Misgav **State:** North District **PC:** **Country:** Israel
Year Established: 2017 **Status 2020:** Active
Industries: Artificial Intelligence for:, Big Data and Analytics for:, ~ Energy and Utilities (14), Industrial Solutions for:, IT Managed Services

Company Name: Ainovia
Description: Ainovia is an artificial intelligence technologies company that develops relevant products & technologies that commercializes.
Website: https://ainovia.com/
Phone: **Email:** 36016@reference-encyclopedia-ai.net
City: Moshava **State:** North District **PC:** **Country:** Israel
Year Established: 2018 **Status 2020:** Active
Industries: Artificial Intelligence for:, IT Managed Services

Company Name: iDRiSi Tech
Description: iDRiSi Tech develops indoor location and asset-tracking solutions.
Website: http://www.idrisi.tech/
Phone: **Email:** 36740@reference-encyclopedia-ai.net
City: Nazareth **State:** North District **PC:** **Country:** Israel
Year Established: 2018 **Status 2020:** Active
Industries: Artificial Intelligence for:, Internet of Things (IoT) for:, ~ Telecommunications (56), Internet of Things (IoT) for:, IT Managed Services

Company Name: Shield34
Description: Shield34 provides an AI-based solution for Selenium coders.
Website: http://www.shield34.com
Phone: **Email:** mail@shield34.com
City: Nazareth **State:** North District **PC:** **Country:** Israel
Year Established: 2017 **Status 2020:** Active
Industries:

Company Name: Let-Lab
Description: Israel's 1st Industry 4.0 Innovation Lab
Website: http://www.let-lab.com
Phone: 972 50 6595963 **Email:** letlab@ham-let.com
City: Nazareth Illit **State:** North District **PC:** **Country:** Israel
Year Established: **Status 2020:** Active
Industries: Artificial Intelligence for:, Big Data and Analytics for:, Blockchain for:, Automation for:, ~ Manufacturing-General (31), Machine Learning

Company Name: Realspections
Description: Real-time automatic AI powered vehicle damage recognition
Website: http://www.realspections.com
Phone: **Email:** david@realspections.com
City: Ramat Yishai **State:** North District **PC:** **Country:** Israel
Year Established: 2019 **Status 2020:** Active
Industries: Artificial Intelligence for:, ~ Automotive (5)

Company Name: IR-MED
Description: IR-MED is a medical device company that focuses in infrared light-based diagnostics.
Website: http://www.ir-medical.com
Phone: **Email:** info@ir-medical.com
City: Rosh Pinna **State:** North District **PC:** **Country:** Israel
Year Established: 2012 **Status 2020:** Active
Industries: Big Data and Analytics for:, ~ Healthcare (20), Machine Learning for:, Compute

Company Name: YORAN Imaging
Description: YORAN Imaging is a disruptive startup that enables the heat sealing process by using thermal imaging technology.
Website: http://www.yoran-imaging.com
Phone: **Email:** Info@yoran-imaging.com
City: Timrat **State:** North District **PC:** **Country:** Israel
Year Established: 2016 **Status 2020:** Active
Industries: Artificial Intelligence for:, ~ Food and Beverage (17), Industrial Solutions for:, Automation for:, ~ Transportation and Logistics (57)

Company Name: Onvego
Description: Onvego is a vibrant young company, with a goal to make speech and multimodality the leading interfaces of smart mobile apps.
Website: http://www.onvego.com
Phone: **Email:** info@onvego.com
City: Yoqn`am **State:** North District **PC:** **Country:** Israel
Year Established: 2015 **Status 2020:** Active
Industries: Artificial Intelligence for:, IT Managed Services for:, IT Managed Services

Company Name: Adasky
Description: AdaSky is a small team of experienced vets from the Israel high-tech industry who are now bringing FIR technology to the automotive market.
Website: http://www.adasky.com/
Phone: (401) 792-7080 **Email:** contact@adasky.com
City: Yoqne`am `illit **State:** North District **PC:** **Country:** Israel
Year Established: 2015 **Status 2020:** Active
Industries: Artificial Intelligence for:, ~ Automotive (5), ~ Automotive (5), Computer Vision

Company Name: Augmedics
Description: Augmedics develops a smart surgical system.
Website: http://www.augmedics.com/
Phone: **Email:** nissan@augmedics.com
City: Yoqne`am `illit **State:** North District **PC:** **Country:** Israel
Year Established: 2014 **Status 2020:** Active
Industries: Augmented Reality for:, Machine Learning

Company Name: ciValue
Description: Customer Centric AI & Monetization Solutions for FMCG Reta: Israel
Website: http://www.civalue.com/
Phone: 1 917 338 3350 **Email:** info@civalue.com
City: Yoqne`am `illit **State:** North District **PC:** **Country:** Israel
Year Established: 2014 **Status 2020:** Active
Industries:

Company Name: N Join
Description: N-Join is a technology development company focused on the industrial market.
Website: http://www.n-join.com/
Phone: **Email:** 37034@reference-encyclopedia-ai.net
City: Yoqne`am `illit **State:** North District **PC:** **Country:** Israel
Year Established: 2014 **Status 2020:** Closed
Industries: Industrial Solutions for:, IT Managed Services for:, Machine Learning

Company Name: Timing
Description: Timing is an AI-driven Dynamic Scheduling platform for service organizations
Website: http://www.timing.tech
Phone: **Email:** info@timing.tech
City: Yoqne`am `illit **State:** North District **PC:** **Country:** Israel
Year Established: 2016 **Status 2020:** Active
Industries: Artificial Intelligence for:, Enterprise Application Services for:, ~ Telecommunications (56), Business Software as a Service Apps (SaaS Apps) for:, ~ Customer Relationship Management (11)

Company Name: Uppspace
Description: Uppspace develops a performance monitoring and crash prevention system for cloud and big data consumer websites.
Website: http://www.uppspace.com
Phone: 972 5 48058508 **Email:** info@uppspace.com
City: Yoqne`am `illit **State:** North District **PC:** **Country:** Israel
Year Established: 2012 **Status 2020:** Active
Industries: Cloud for:, Predictive Analytics for:, Business Software as a Service Apps (SaaS Apps)

Company Name: Wearable Devic: Spain
Description: Developing Mudra, a Brain-Computer Interface wristband that uses neural impulses as input to control digital devic: Spain
Website: http://www.wearabledevices.co.: Israel
Phone: **Email:** shmuel.barel@wearabledevices.co.: Israel
City: Yoqne`am `illit **State:** North District **PC:** **Country:** Israel
Year Established: 2014 **Status 2020:** Active
Industries: Augmented Reality for:, Human Computer Interaction for:, Machine Learning for:, Virtual Reality (VR) for:, Internet of Things (IoT)

Company Name: Angarish - Closed
Description: Angarish is a fintech startup that provides data enrichment and insights for businesses.
Website:
Phone: **Email:** 36059@reference-encyclopedia-ai.net
City: Ashdod **State:** South District **PC:** **Country:** Israel
Year Established: 2016 **Status 2020:** Active
Industries: Artificial Intelligence for:, Databases for:, Databases for:, ~ Banking and Financial Markets-Services (7), IT Managed Services for:, Machine Learning

Company Name: Deep Learning Robotics
Description: Deep Learning Robotics is a technology company specializing in robotics, computer vision and machine learning.
Website: http://www.dlrob.com
Phone: **Email:** info@dlrob.com
City: Ashdod **State:** South District **PC:** **Country:** Israel
Year Established: 2015 **Status 2020:** Active
Industries:

Company Name: MyFavorEats
Description: MyFavorEats is a platform that helps users to create personalized recipes.
Website: http://myfavoreats.com
Phone: **Email:** info@myfavoreats.com
City: Ashdod **State:** South District **PC:** **Country:** Israel
Year Established: 2016 **Status 2020:** Active
Industries: Artificial Intelligence for:, ~ Food and Beverage (17), Machine Learning for:, ~ Healthcare (20)

Company Name: Sensority
Description: Sensority is the sole multi-disciplinary video analytics solution that relies on the human Psychophysiology Autonomic Nervous System.
Website: http://www.sensority.net
Phone: 972 50 300 6384 **Email:** contact@sensority.net
City: Ashdod **State:** South District **PC:** **Country:** Israel
Year Established: 2014 **Status 2020:** Active
Industries:

Company Name: Breathevision
Description: BreatheVision develops a method for early detection of breathing deterioration in patients under conscious sedation.
Website: http://www.breathevision.com
Phone: 972-(0) 8-672-0512 **Email:** info@breathevision.com
City: Ashkelon **State:** South District **PC:** **Country:** Israel
Year Established: 2013 **Status 2020:** Active
Industries: Artificial Intelligence for:, Computer Vision for:, ~ Healthcare (20), Machine Learning for:, ~ Healthcare (20), ~ Healthcare (20)

Company Name: InElint Security
Description: InElint Security is a network of cyber-attack intelligence that helps organizations handle known and unknown cyber attacks.
Website: http://inelint.com/
Phone: **Email:** 36757@reference-encyclopedia-ai.net
City: Ashkelon **State:** South District **PC:** **Country:** Israel
Year Established: 2018 **Status 2020:** Active
Industries: Artificial Intelligence for:, Cyber Security for:, Machine Learning for:, Security

Company Name: LVision
Description: LVision converts live streaming into data with machine learning algorithms, computer vision, and deep learning.
Website: http://www.lvision.io
Phone: 972 8 6725565 **Email:** support@lvision.io
City: Ashkelon **State:** South District **PC:** **Country:** Israel
Year Established: 2018 **Status 2020:** Active
Industries: Analytics for:, Artificial Intelligence for:, Computer Vision for:, Machine Learning

Company Name: CardForest
Description: CardForest is an Israel-based company that provides a wide range of card games and empowers its users to add AI and build communities.
Website: http://www.cardforest.com/
Phone: **Email:** contact@cardforest.com
City: Be'er Sheva **State:** South District **PC:** **Country:** Israel
Year Established: 2013 **Status 2020:** Active
Industries: Artificial Intelligence for:, Digital Media

Company Name: SIGA OT Solutions
Description: SIGA provides an OT anomaly detection solution by real-time monitoring the raw electric signals of critical industrial assets.
Website: http://www.sigasec.com
Phone: **Email:** info@sigasec.com
City: Be'er Sheva **State:** South District **PC:** **Country:** Israel
Year Established: 2014 **Status 2020:** Active
Industries: Cyber Security for:, ~ Manufacturing-General (31), IT Infrastructure for:, Machine Learning

Company Name: B24Chat
Description: B24Chat is an AI-based service for virtual communication companies.
Website: http://b24chat.com
Phone: **Email:** 36130@reference-encyclopedia-ai.net
City: Beersheba **State:** South District **PC:** **Country:** Israel
Year Established: 2019 **Status 2020:** Active
Industries:

Company Name: IVO Driver Robot
Description: IVO Driver Robot provides an autonomous robot that can convert any vehicle into an autonomous one.
Website: http://www.lar-bgu.com/ivo
Phone: **Email:** 36815@reference-encyclopedia-ai.net
City: Beersheba **State:** South District **PC:** **Country:** Israel
Year Established: 2017 **Status 2020:** Active
Industries: Artificial Intelligence for:, ~ Automotive (5), Robotics

Company Name: Sightbit
Description: Sightbit is a complete smart AI beach system-for drowning prevention and data-powered management.
Website: http://sightbit.com
Phone: **Email:** Info@sightbit.com
City: Beersheba **State:** South District **PC:** **Country:** Israel
Year Established: 2019 **Status 2020:** Active
Industries: Analytics for:, Artificial Intelligence

Company Name: Soos Technology
Description: Soos develops an incubation system that affects the sex development process and turns genetic males into functional female chicks.
Website: http://www.soos.org.: Israel
Phone: **Email:** alon@soos.org.: Israel
City: Beersheba **State:** South District **PC:** **Country:** Israel
Year Established: 2017 **Status 2020:** Active
Industries: ~ Agriculture (3), Artificial Intelligence for:, ~ Biotechnology (9)

Company Name: Ultraw
Description: UltraWis offers a software platform that utilizes augmented reality, machine learning, and artificial intelligence.
Website: http://www.ultrawis.com
Phone: **Email:** info@ultrawis.com
City: Beersheba **State:** South District **PC:** **Country:** Israel
Year Established: 2019 **Status 2020:** Active
Industries: Artificial Intelligence for:, Augmented Reality for:, ~ Automotive (5)

Company Name: BionicHive
Description: BionicHIVE is developing an automated warehouse solution.
Website: http://www.bionichive.com
Phone: **Email:** info@BionicHIVE.com
City: Mishmar Hanegev **State:** South District **PC:** **Country:** Israel
Year Established: 2014 **Status 2020:** Active
Industries: Artificial Intelligence for:, ~ Automotive (5), IT Managed Services for:, Robotics

Company Name: CloudERP
Description: CloudERP allows distributed organizations to give each user an online connection to the management.
Website: http://clouderp.co.il/
Phone: 972-77-22-000-63 **Email:** clouderp@clouderp.io
City: Netivot **State:** South District **PC:** **Country:** Israel
Year Established: 2014 **Status 2020:** Active
Industries: Cloud for:, Cloud for:, Application Services

Company Name: Youtiligent
Description: Youtiligent is a software company that uses Machine Learning to Learn Machines.
Website: http://www.youtiligent.com
Phone: **Email:** avichaib@youtilligent.com
City: Nir`am **State:** South District **PC:** **Country:** Israel
Year Established: 2018 **Status 2020:** Active
Industries: Artificial Intelligence for:, Internet of Things (IoT) for:, ~ Telecommunications (56), ~ Construction (10)

Company Name: Cambium
Description: Cambium is a software development company that specializes in customized software development.
Website: http://cambium.co.: Israel
Phone: **Email:** shira@cambium.co.: Israel
City: Yeruham **State:** South District **PC:** **Country:** Israel
Year Established: 2010 **Status 2020:** Active
Industries: Application Services for:, Artificial Intelligence for:, Big Data and Analytics

Company Name: ConfirmU
Description: ConfirmU is a data analytics startup specializing in alternative credit scoring services for lenders.
Website: http://confirmu.com
Phone: **Email:** info@confirmu.com
City: Giv'atayim **State:** TA **PC:** **Country:** Israel
Year Established: 2016 **Status 2020:** Active
Industries: Analytics for:, Artificial Intelligence for:, ~ Banking and Financial Markets-Services (7), Machine Learning

Company Name: Netz View
Description: Netz View develops an AI-based solution for medical image decoding.
Website: http://www.netzview.ai
Phone: **Email:** info@netzview.ai
City: Giv'atayim **State:** Tel Aviv District **PC:** **Country:** Israel
Year Established: 2018 **Status 2020:** Active
Industries: Artificial Intelligence for:, Machine Learning for:, ~ Healthcare (20)

Company Name: Referral-AI
Description: Relationship Intelligence by Referral-AI. Prospecting Reimaging. Gain warm introductions by mutual interests. Unlock pipelines.
Website: http://referral-ai.com/
Phone: **Email:** doron.herzlich@referral-ai.com
City: Giv'atayim **State:** TA **PC:** **Country:** Israel
Year Established: 2016 **Status 2020:** Active
Industries: Web

Company Name: SNDBOX
Description: SNDBOX is an AI malware research platform, offering malware analysis visibility.
Website: http://www.sndbox.com/
Phone: **Email:** contact@sndbox.com
City: Giv'atayim **State:** Tel Aviv District **PC:** **Country:** Israel
Year Established: 2017 **Status 2020:** Active
Industries: Artificial Intelligence

Company Name: WSC Sports
Description: WSC Sports provides an innovative workflow automation solution for sports media-right owners.
Website: http://wsc-sports.com/
Phone: 972-3-773-1660 **Email:** contact@wsc-sports.com
City: Giv'atayim **State:** Tel Aviv District **PC:** **Country:** Israel
Year Established: 2011 **Status 2020:** Active
Industries: Artificial Intelligence for:, Content for:, Digital Media for:, ~ Arts-Entertainment-Recreation (4)

Company Name: Aiola
Description: Deploying 'virtual AI experts' into core enterprise business process: Spain
Website: http://aiola.com/
Phone: 972-54-6247055 **Email:** anat@aiola.com
City: Herzliya **State:** Tel Aviv District **PC:** **Country:** Israel
Year Established: 2019 **Status 2020:** Active
Industries:

Company Name: AI-PREDATOR
Description: SaaS - A Pro active AI that identifies and targets cyber crimes on the Social media and Gaming platform
Website: http://www.ai-predator.com/
Phone: **Email:** info@ai-predator.com
City: Herzliya **State:** Tel Aviv District **PC:** **Country:** Israel
Year Established: 2019 **Status 2020:** Active
Industries: Artificial Intelligence

Company Name: Albo Systems
Description: Albo Systems is an artificial intelligence company that uses deep learning algorithms to prevent the transmission of diseases by mosquitoes.
Website: https://www.albosys.com/
Phone: 972 (0) 52 619 4126 **Email:** jacques.amselem@albosys.com
City: Herzliya **State:** Tel Aviv District **PC:** **Country:** Israel
Year Established: 2019 **Status 2020:** Active
Industries: Artificial Intelligence for:, Computer Vision for:, Image Recognition for:, Machine Learning

Company Name: Awonna
Description: Awonna develops a platform API to help e-commerce organizations create additional revenue channels.
Website: http://awonna.com/
Phone: **Email:** shachar@awonna.com
City: Herzliya **State:** Tel Aviv District **PC:** **Country:** Israel
Year Established: 2015 **Status 2020:** Active
Industries: Artificial Intelligence for:, Databases for:, E-Commerce for:, IT Managed Services

Company Name: Bond: ITALY
Description: BondIT is an algorithm-advice solution for bond portfolio managers and advisers.
Website: http://www.bonditglobal.com
Phone: **Email:** info@bonditglobal.com
City: Herzliya **State:** Tel Aviv District **PC:** **Country:** Israel
Year Established: 2012 **Status 2020:** Active
Industries: ~ Banking and Financial Markets-Services (7), ~ Banking and Financial Markets-Services (7), ~ Banking and Financial Markets-Services (7), IT Managed Services for:, Machine Learning

Company Name: BOTS101
Description: BOTS101 is an internet company that specializes in artificial intelligence-based software.
Website: http://www.bots101.com
Phone: **Email:** 36196@reference-encyclopedia-ai.net
City: Herzliya **State:** Tel Aviv District **PC:** **Country:** Israel
Year Established: 2017 **Status 2020:** Active
Industries: Artificial Intelligence for:, ~ Media-Communications (41)

Company **Name:** Coneuron
Description: A Tel Aviv, Israel-based Artificial Intelligence startup.
Website: http://coneuron.com/
Phone: **Email:** info@coneuron.com
City: Herzliya **State:** Tel Aviv District **PC:** **Country:** Israel
Year Established: 2017 **Status 2020:** Active
Industries:

Company Name: Dataloop AI
Description: DataLoop's data management and annotation platform streamlines the process of generating machine consumable datasets out of raw visual data.
Website: http://www.dataloop.ai/
Phone: **Email:** info@dataloop.ai
City: Herzliya **State:** Tel Aviv District **PC:** **Country:** Israel
Year Established: 2017 **Status 2020:** Active
Industries: Artificial Intelligence for:, Computer Vision for:, Machine Learning for:, Business Software as a Service Apps (SaaS Apps)

Company Name: Dxplorer
Description: Dxplorer designs a self-service data discovery platform that enables fast and accurate discovery and analysis of enterprise data.
Website: http://www.xplore.io/
Phone: **Email:** contact@xplore.io
City: Herzliya **State:** Tel Aviv District **PC:** **Country:** Israel
Year Established: 2015 **Status 2020:** Active
Industries: Analytics for:, Artificial Intelligence for:, Business Applications for:, IT Managed Services

Company Name: Firefly.ai
Description: Firefly.ai is an automated machine learning platform for business impact.
Website: http://www.firefly.ai/
Phone: **Email:** info@firefly.ai
City: Herzliya **State:** Tel Aviv District **PC:** **Country:** Israel

Year Established: 2016 **Status 2020:** Active
Industries: Artificial Intelligence for:, Enterprise Application Services for:, Machine Learning

Company Name: Firmus
Description: Firmus helps construction companies learn from their mistakes and detect design and coordination issues.
Website: http://www.firmus.ai
Phone: **Email:** 36572@reference-encyclopedia-ai.net
City: Herzliya **State:** Tel Aviv District **PC:** **Country:** Israel
Year Established: 2019 **Status 2020:** Active
Industries: Artificial Intelligence for:, ~ Construction (10), IT Managed Services for:, IT Managed Services

Company Name: GetAlert
Description: GetAlert Security Camera powered by AI
Website: http://www.getalert.com/
Phone: 972 (54) 666-0999 **Email:** info@getalert.com
City: Herzliya **State:** Tel Aviv District **PC:** **Country:** Israel
Year Established: 2015 **Status 2020:** Active
Industries: Artificial Intelligence for:, ~ Biotechnology (9), Computer Vision for:, Security

Company Name: Iguazio
Description: The Iguazio Data Science Platform enables you to develop, deploy and manage AI applications at scale and in real-time.
Website: http://www.iguazio.com/
Phone: **Email:** info@iguazio.com
City: Herzliya **State:** Tel Aviv District **PC:** **Country:** Israel
Year Established: 2014 **Status 2020:** Active
Industries: Analytics for:, Artificial Intelligence for:, Big Data and Analytics for:, Machine Learning for:, Enterprise Application Services for:, Compute for:, Business Software as a Service Apps (SaaS Apps)

Company Name: InnerEye
Description: Combining Human Intelligence with Artificial Intelligence
Website: http://www.innereye.ai
Phone: **Email:** uri@innereye.ai
City: Herzliya **State:** Tel Aviv District **PC:** **Country:** Israel
Year Established: 2014 **Status 2020:** Active
Industries: Artificial Intelligence for:, IT Managed Services for:, Internet of Things (IoT)

Company Name: MDAlgorithms
Description: MDAlgorithms uses smart algorithms and computer vision to provide real time mobile tools for people with health disorders.
Website: http://www.mdalgorithms.com
Phone: **Email:** 36948@reference-encyclopedia-ai.net
City: Herzliya **State:** Tel Aviv District **PC:** **Country:** Israel
Year Established: 2015 **Status 2020:** Active
Industries:

Company Name: Movez Analytics
Description: Movez is a computer software company that develops a sports analytics platform based on artificial intelligence and machine learning.
Website: http://movez.ai
Phone: **Email:** Info@movez.ai
City: Herzliya **State:** Tel Aviv District **PC:** **Country:** Israel
Year Established: 2018 **Status 2020:** Active
Industries: Analytics for:, Artificial Intelligence for:, Machine Learning

Company Name: MyndYou
Description: MyndYou is an AI-based platform that empowers practitioners to deliver personalized and data-driven cognitive care to seniors.
Website: http://www.myndyou.com/
Phone: **Email:** info@myndyou.com
City: Herzliya **State:** Tel Aviv District **PC:** **Country:** Israel
Year Established: 2016 **Status 2020:** Active
Industries: Artificial Intelligence for:, ~ Healthcare (20), ~ Healthcare (20), ~ Healthcare (20), ~ Healthcare (20)

Company Name: Ola.co
Description: GetAlert provides an artificial intelligence-powered security camera.
Website: http://www.ola.co
Phone: 972 (54) 666-0999 **Email:** 37095@reference-encyclopedia-ai.net
City: Herzliya **State:** Tel Aviv District **PC:** **Country:** Israel
Year Established: 2015 **Status 2020:** Active
Industries: Artificial Intelligence for:, Automation for:, Enterprise Application Services for:, IT Managed Services

Company Name: Order Chat
Description: Order Chat provides a free 60-second chat service to find and book a table at any restaurant in the world.
Website: http://order.chat/
Phone: **Email:** 37122@reference-encyclopedia-ai.net
City: Herzliya **State:** Tel Aviv District **PC:** **Country:** Israel
Year Established: 2018 **Status 2020:** Active
Industries: Artificial Intelligence for:, Internet of Things (IoT) for:, IT Managed Services for:, ~ Travel and Transportation (58), ~ Food and Beverage (17)

Company Name: PolicyPup
Description: Changing the way drivers purchase and interact with auto insurance, powered by Ai, & driven by customer experience
Website: http://www.policypup.io/
Phone: **Email:** Alex@policypup.com
City: Herzliya **State:** TA **PC:** **Country:** Israel
Year Established: **Status 2020:** Active
Industries: Artificial Intelligence for:, ~ Insurance (25), Blockchain for:, ~ Insurance (25)

Company **Name:** PuliSec Labs
Description: Pulisec Labs is a stealth Israeli Cyber-Security and AI startup company that fixes small businesses' cyber security problems.
Website: http://www.pulisec.com
Phone: **Email:** 37223@reference-encyclopedia-ai.net
City: Herzliya **State:** Tel Aviv District **PC:** **Country:** Israel
Year Established: 2018 **Status 2020:** Active
Industries: Artificial Intelligence for:, Cyber Security

Company Name: Recongate
Description: ReconGate lets you fuse diverse data sources and apply state of the art machine learning.
Website: http://recongate.com/
Phone: **Email:** 37275@reference-encyclopedia-ai.net
City: Herzliya **State:** Tel Aviv District **PC:** **Country:** Israel
Year Established: 2016 **Status 2020:** Active
Industries: Analytics for:, Artificial Intelligence for:, Big Data and Analytics for:, Cyber Security

Company Name: RideVision
Description: Ride Vision develops autonomous driving software for motorcycles.
Website: http://ride.vision/
Phone: **Email:** ask@ride.vison
City: Herzliya **State:** TA **PC:** **Country:** Israel
Year Established: **Status 2020:** Active
Industries: Artificial Intelligence for:, ~ Automotive (5), ~ Automotive (5), Computer Vision for:, Machine Learning for:, ~ Professional Services (48)

Company Name: SnatchBot
Description: SnatchBot is a free cloud-based chatbot platform to build bots for Facebook messenger, Skype, Slack, SMS, Twitter, WeChat and others...
Website: http://snatchbot.me
Phone: **Email:** team@snatchbot.me
City: Herzliya **State:** TA **PC:** **Country:** Israel

Year Established: 2015 **Status 2020:** Active
Industries: Artificial Intelligence for:, Embedded for:, Human Computer Interaction for:, Machine Learning for:, Natural Language Processing for:, Business Software as a Service Apps (SaaS Apps) for:, Business Strategy and Design for:, Business Strategy and Design

Company Name: Talamoos
Description: Talamoos allows users to predict their customers next actions with real-time machine learning.
Website: http://www.talamoos.com
Phone: **Email:** info@talamoos.com
City: Herzliya **State:** Tel Aviv District **PC:** **Country:** Israel
Year Established: 2014 **Status 2020:** Active
Industries: Artificial Intelligence for:, Web

Company Name: TechSee
Description: TechSee builds smart visual platforms that enable service providers to interact with the customer via a live virtual channel.
Website: http://www.techsee.me
Phone: **Email:** 37512@reference-encyclopedia-ai.net
City: Herzliya **State:** Tel Aviv District **PC:** **Country:** Israel
Year Established: 2015 **Status 2020:** Active
Industries: Artificial Intelligence for:, Augmented Reality for:, Mobile for:, Compute

Company Name: Triptimize
Description: Optimizing Travel Sear: Switzerland
Website: http://triptimize.me/Landing/
Phone: **Email:** 37571@reference-encyclopedia-ai.net
City: Herzliya **State:** Tel Aviv District **PC:** **Country:** Israel
Year Established: 2014 **Status 2020:** Active
Industries: Machine Learning for:, Web

Company Name: Upstream Security
Description: Upstream Security is a Centralized Security & Analytics Platform for Connected & Autonomous Vehicle Fleets.
Website: http://www.upstream.auto
Phone: 1-800-832-3406 **Email:** hello@upstreamsecurity.com
City: Herzliya **State:** Tel Aviv District **PC:** **Country:** Israel
Year Established: 2017 **Status 2020:** Active
Industries: ~ Automotive (5), Cyber Security for:, Machine Learning for:, Security for:, Business Software as a Service Apps (SaaS Apps)

Company Name: vHive
Description: vHive develops a cloud-based AI that enables enterprises to deploy autonomous drone hives.
Website: https://www.vhive.ai/
Phone: **Email:** 37623@reference-encyclopedia-ai.net
City: Herzliya **State:** Tel Aviv District **PC:** **Country:** Israel
Year Established: 2016 **Status 2020:** Active
Industries:

Company Name: Voca.ai
Description: Delivering Happier Customers at Scale with Voice AI Agents
Website: http://www.voca.ai
Phone: (917) 444-9909 **Email:** hi-voca@voca.ai
City: Herzliya **State:** Tel Aviv District **PC:** **Country:** Israel
Year Established: 2017 **Status 2020:** Active
Industries: Analytics for:, Artificial Intelligence for:, Machine Learning for:, Business Software as a Service Apps (SaaS Apps)

Company Name: CoreAI
Description: CoreAI provides artificial intelligence, machine and deep learning services.
Website: http://www.coreai.ai/
Phone: 972 54 4976198 **Email:** 36337@reference-encyclopedia-ai.net
City: Qiryat Ono **State:** Tel Aviv District **PC:** **Country:** Israel
Year Established: 2018 **Status 2020:** Active
Industries: Artificial Intelligence for:, Machine Learning

Company Name: Privacy Rating
Description: Privacy Rating is a regtech start-up enabling enterprises to work with third-party solutions for safely and privately.
Website: http://www.qprivacy.com
Phone: **Email:** 37209@reference-encyclopedia-ai.net
City: Qiryat Ono **State:** Tel Aviv District **PC:** **Country:** Israel
Year Established: 2018 **Status 2020:** Active
Industries: Artificial Intelligence for:, Big Data and Analytics

Company Name: 4Dentity
Description: 4Dentity is a secret gesture password technology empowered by Artificial Intelligence tools.
Website: http://4dentity.com/
Phone: **Email:** 35923@reference-encyclopedia-ai.net
City: Ramat Gan **State:** TA **PC:** **Country:** Israel
Year Established: 2016 **Status 2020:** Active
Industries: Artificial Intelligence for:, ~ Biotechnology (9), Cyber Security for:, Security

Company Name: Bidalgo
Description: The leading provider of AI solutions to help app marketers scale across Facebook, Instagram, Pinterest and other platforms.
Website: http://www.bidalgo.com/
Phone: 972 3-728-5011 **Email:** 36152@reference-encyclopedia-ai.net
City: Ramat Gan **State:** Tel Aviv District **PC:** **Country:** Israel
Year Established: 2010 **Status 2020:** Active
Industries: Artificial Intelligence for:, Predictive Analytics for:, Business Software as a Service Apps (SaaS Apps) for:, ~ Social Assistance-Non-Profits (53)

Company **Name:** Botson.ai
Description: Botson.ai is an e-commerce company
Website: http://botson.ai
Phone: **Email:** 36197@reference-encyclopedia-ai.net
City: Ramat Gan **State:** TA **PC:** **Country:** Israel
Year Established: 2016 **Status 2020:** Active
Industries: Artificial Intelligence for:, Machine Learning for:, ~ Social Assistance-Non-Profits (53)

Company Name: ClickSpree
Description: Boost Video Marketing ROI
Website: http://clickspree.com
Phone: **Email:** 36288@reference-encyclopedia-ai.net
City: Ramat Gan **State:** Tel Aviv District **PC:** **Country:** Israel
Year Established: 2013 **Status 2020:** Active
Industries: Artificial Intelligence for:, Content for:, ~ E-Commerce (12), ~ E-Commerce (12), Machine Learning for:, Predictive Analytics

Company Name: ConMa: Gibraltar
Description: ConMagi specializes in providing solutions in machine learning and data mining.
Website: http://www.conmagi.com
Phone: **Email:** info@conmagi.com
City: Ramat Gan **State:** Tel Aviv District **PC:** **Country:** Israel
Year Established: 2017 **Status 2020:** Active
Industries: Artificial Intelligence for:, Databases for:, Machine Learning for:, Speech Recognition

Company Name: Convi Technology
Description: Convi Technology develops an AI based platform for small and medium-sized enterprises in the global market.
Website: http://www.convi.info
Phone: **Email:** 36332@reference-encyclopedia-ai.net
City: Ramat Gan **State:** Tel Aviv District **PC:** **Country:** Israel
Year Established: 2019 **Status 2020:** Active
Industries: Artificial Intelligence for:, Application Services

Company Name: CyTwist
Description: CyTwist is an artificial intelligence cyber technology company.
Website: http://www.cytwist.com/
Phone: **Email:** 36372@reference-encyclopedia-ai.net
City: Ramat Gan **State:** Tel Aviv District **PC:** **Country:** Israel
Year Established: 2015 **Status 2020:** Active
Industries: Artificial Intelligence for:, Cyber Security for:, IT Managed Services

Company Name: D&C Algo
Description: D&C Algo is an outsourcing company that specializes in AI solutions for small-medium companies.
Website:
Phone: **Email:** 36374@reference-encyclopedia-ai.net
City: Ramat Gan **State:** Tel Aviv District **PC:** **Country:** Israel
Year Established: 2019 **Status 2020:** Closed
Industries: Artificial Intelligence for:, IT Managed Services for:, Business Process and Operations

Company Name: DeepCoding
Description: DeepCoding has created the first Delivery Intelligence Platform.
Website: http://deepcoding.ai/
Phone: **Email:** info@deepcoding.ai
City: Ramat Gan **State:** TA **PC:** **Country:** Israel
Year Established: **Status 2020:** Active
Industries: Artificial Intelligence for:, Business Intelligence for:, Data Management for:, IT Managed Services for:, IT Managed Services for:, Machine Learning for:, Predictive Analytics for:, ~ Professional Services (48)

Company Name: HoopsAI
Description: HoopsAI is a sports technology company that utilizes advanced artificial-intelligence methods to understand sports better.
Website: http://www.hoopsai.com/
Phone: **Email:** info@hoopsai.com
City: Ramat Gan **State:** Tel Aviv District **PC:** **Country:** Israel
Year Established: 2018 **Status 2020:** Active
Industries: Analytics for:, Artificial Intelligence for:, IT Managed Services for:, ~ Arts-Entertainment-Recreation (4)

Company Name: iKNOWtice
Description: An AI-powered Personalisation and Intent Identification Engine for Mobile and Web E-Commerce Publishers obviating any need for login.
Website: http://www.iknowtice.com/
Phone: **Email:** 36743@reference-encyclopedia-ai.net
City: Ramat Gan **State:** TA **PC:** **Country:** Israel
Year Established: 2016 **Status 2020:** Active
Industries:

Company Name: Indoor Robotics
Description: Indoor Robotics develops stealth mode robotics.
Website: http://indoor.website
Phone: **Email:** hello@indoor-robotics.com
City: Ramat Gan **State:** TA **PC:** **Country:** Israel
Year Established: **Status 2020:** Active
Industries: Artificial Intelligence for:, Cloud for:, Machine Learning for:, Robotics

Company Name: Intuition Robotics
Description: Intuition designs social companion technologies that positively impacts the lives of older adults.
Website: http://www.intuitionrobotics.com/
Phone: **Email:** info@intuitionrobotics.com
City: Ramat Gan **State:** Tel Aviv District **PC:** **Country:** Israel
Year Established: 2015 **Status 2020:** Active
Industries: Artificial Intelligence for:, Human Computer Interaction

Company Name: Litigation Master
Description: Litigation Master is an AI startup that developed software with contextual analysis to review legal documents and financial statements.
Website: http://litigationmaster.com
Phone: **Email:** 36905@reference-encyclopedia-ai.net
City: Ramat Gan **State:** Tel Aviv District **PC:** **Country:** Israel
Year Established: 2014 **Status 2020:** Active
Industries: Analytics for:, Artificial Intelligence for:, Big Data and Analytics

Company Name: Over.ai
Description: Voice AI-powered agent with natural conversational abilities in multiple languages for business and call centers.
Website: http://over.ai/
Phone: **Email:** info@over.ai
City: Ramat Gan **State:** Tel Aviv District **PC:** **Country:** Israel
Year Established: 2018 **Status 2020:** Active
Industries: Artificial Intelligence for:, IT Managed Services for:, Internet of Things (IoT)

Company Name: RemitRix
Description: Risk and regulation solutions
Website: http://www.remitrix.com
Phone: 44 20 3608 3987 **Email:** info@remitrix.com
City: Ramat Gan **State:** TA **PC:** **Country:** Israel
Year Established: **Status 2020:** Active
Industries: Artificial Intelligence for:, ~ Insurance (25), Machine Learning

Company Name: RunMaxi
Description: RunMaxi is an AI digital property management solution.
Website: http://runmaxi.co.il/
Phone: 972-79-969-0330 **Email:** help@runmaxi.co.: Israel
City: Ramat Gan **State:** Tel Aviv District **PC:** **Country:** Israel
Year Established: 2014 **Status 2020:** Active
Industries: Artificial Intelligence for:, ~ Real Estate (49)

Company Name: Shield.
Description: A cross-regulation AI powered compliance platform that provides a 360 view on eComms, trade & financial data
Website: http://hubs.ly/H0qC7CQ0
Phone: **Email:** info@shieldfc.com
City: Ramat Gan **State:** TA **PC:** **Country:** Israel
Year Established: 2018 **Status 2020:** Active
Industries: Artificial Intelligence for:, Big Data and Analytics for:, Compliance for:, Data Management for:, ~ Banking and Financial Markets-Services (7), ~ Banking and Financial Markets-Services (7), Machine Learning for:, Natural Language Processing for:, Natural Language

Company Name: Spe: Tanzania
Description: Spetz is an AI direct-message hiring chatbot providing corporates with a way to engage talent where they're most active
Website: http://www.spetz.io
Phone: **Email:** info@spetz.io
City: Ramat Gan **State:** Tel Aviv District **PC:** **Country:** Israel
Year Established: 2017 **Status 2020:** Active
Industries: Artificial Intelligence for:, Big Data and Analytics

Company Name: SupeRevenue
Description: SupeRevenue designs and develops solutions to predict the behavior of customers in the industry of insurance.
Website: http://superevenue.com/
Phone: **Email:** 37482@reference-encyclopedia-ai.net
City: Ramat Gan **State:** TA **PC:** **Country:** Israel
Year Established: 2016 **Status 2020:** Active
Industries: ~ Banking and Financial Markets-Services (7), Machine Learning

Company Name: Suridata.ai
Description: AI Based Privacy Compliance (GDPR, CCPA) and Data Governance
Website: http://www.suridata.ai
Phone: **Email:** info@suridata.ai
City: Ramat Gan **State:** Tel Aviv District **PC:** **Country:** Israel
Year Established: 2019 **Status 2020:** Active
Industries: Big Data and Analytics for:, Cyber Security for:, IT Managed Services for:, Natural Language Processing for:, Cyber Security

Company Name: Tie - Predictive Analytics
Description: Tie is a predictive analytics platform for sales & marketing in the mobile ecosystem.
Website: http://thetie.co/
Phone: **Email:** 37540@reference-encyclopedia-ai.net
City: Ramat Gan **State:** Tel Aviv District **PC:** **Country:** Israel
Year Established: 2016 **Status 2020:** Active
Industries: Artificial Intelligence for:, Big Data and Analytics for:, Business Intelligence for:, Machine Learning for:, Mobile

Company Name: Tie Technologies
Description: Tie Technologies is an automatic networking platform that creates effective business connections based on mutual needs.
Website:
Phone: **Email:** 37541@reference-encyclopedia-ai.net
City: Ramat Gan **State:** TA **PC:** **Country:** Israel
Year Established: 2016 **Status 2020:** Closed
Industries: Predictive Analytics

Company Name: Tpredict
Description: Tpredict designes a solution that helps physicians make smarter, faster, and more accurate treatment decisions.
Website: http://tpredict.com/
Phone: 6099480607 **Email:** 37550@reference-encyclopedia-ai.net
City: Ramat Gan **State:** Tel Aviv District **PC:** **Country:** Israel
Year Established: 2016 **Status 2020:** Active
Industries: Artificial Intelligence for:, ~ Healthcare (20), IT Managed Services for:, Predictive Analytics

Company Name: Transfote
Description: Transfotech is a technology company that drives corporate innovation with custom AI-powered solutions and strategic consulting.
Website: http://www.transfotech.com
Phone: **Email:** info@transfotech.com
City: Ramat Gan **State:** Tel Aviv District **PC:** **Country:** Israel
Year Established: 2012 **Status 2020:** Active
Industries:

Company Name: Trip Expert
Description: Trip Expert provides a platform for rapid developing portals for large cities with a planner of trips based on artificial intelligence.
Website: http://trip.expert/
Phone: **Email:** 37569@reference-encyclopedia-ai.net
City: Ramat Gan **State:** Tel Aviv District **PC:** **Country:** Israel
Year Established: 2018 **Status 2020:** Active
Industries: Artificial Intelligence for:, IT Managed Services for:, Machine Learning

Company Name: White Raven
Description: Automotive Visual Positioning
Website: http://www.whiteraven.ai
Phone: **Email:** contact@whiteraven.ai
City: Ramat Gan **State:** Tel Aviv District **PC:** **Country:** Israel
Year Established: 2013 **Status 2020:** Active
Industries: Artificial Intelligence for:, Computer Vision

Company Name: Yeda Education
Description: K-12 Low Touch Ongoing Learning & Diagnostic Assessment
Website: http://www.yedaeducation.com/
Phone: **Email:** office@yedaeducation.com
City: Ramat Gan **State:** Tel Aviv District **PC:** **Country:** Israel
Year Established: 2019 **Status 2020:** Active
Industries: Artificial Intelligence for:, ~ Education (13)

Company Name: Zero Energy Solutions
Description: Zero Energy Solutions developes a Climate Intelligence platform, that senses, analyzes and automates climate comfort in every room
Website: http://www.zero.energy/
Phone: 97237744118 **Email:** office@zero.energy
City: Ramat Gan **State:** Tel Aviv District **PC:** **Country:** Israel
Year Established: 2015 **Status 2020:** Active
Industries: Artificial Intelligence for:, ~ Energy and Utilities (14), ~ Energy and Utilities (14), ~ Energy and Utilities (14)

Company Name: Atvisor
Description: Atvisor is an AI-based digital platform for people with disabilities and assistive technology consultation.
Website: http://www.innitie.com
Phone: **Email:** contact@atvisor.ai
City: Ramat Hasharon **State:** Tel Aviv District **PC:** **Country:** Israel
Year Established: 2016 **Status 2020:** Active
Industries: Artificial Intelligence for:, ~ Healthcare (20), ~ Healthcare (20)

Company **Name:** HiClient
Description: HiClient is chatting automatically with website visitors 24/7 with an AI Technology.
Website: http://www.hiclient.com/
Phone: 054 123 4567 **Email:** contact@upsite.co.: Israel
City: Ramat Hasharon **State:** Tel Aviv District **PC:** **Country:** Israel
Year Established: 2011 **Status 2020:** Active
Industries: Artificial Intelligence for:, Web for:, Web

Company Name: Jurn.io
Description: Jurn.io provides a video and virtual-reality content layer by analyzing and integrating influencer content.
Website: http://www.jurn.io
Phone: **Email:** hello@jurn.io
City: Ramat Hasharon **State:** Tel Aviv District **PC:** **Country:** Israel
Year Established: 2017 **Status 2020:** Active
Industries: Big Data and Analytics for:, Content for:, Machine Learning

Company Name: Selfit Medical
Description: Selfit Medical is a smart digital therapy platform for the aging population.
Website: http://www.selfitmedical.com
Phone: **Email:** info@selfitmedical.com
City: Ramat Hasharon **State:** Tel Aviv District **PC:** **Country:** Israel
Year Established: 2017 **Status 2020:** Active
Industries: Artificial Intelligence for:, Augmented Reality for:, Big Data and Analytics for:, ~ Healthcare (20)

Company Name: Sigmento
Description: Sigmento offers product data automation for retailers and manufacturers at scale.
Website: http://sigmento.com/
Phone: 1 (855) 505-7357 **Email:** info@sigmento.com
City: Ramat Hasharon **State:** Tel Aviv District **PC:** **Country:** Israel
Year Established: 2015 **Status 2020:** Active
Industries: Big Data and Analytics for:, E-Commerce for:, E-Commerce for:, Machine Learning for:, Natural Language Processing

Company Name: Skyx
Description: Skyx is an agricultural-robotics technology company enabling a modular swarm of autonomous drones for spraying.
Website: http://skyx.solutions
Phone: **Email:** skyx.web@gmail.com
City: Ramat Hasharon **State:** Tel Aviv District **PC:** **Country:** Israel
Year Established: 2017 **Status 2020:** Active
Industries: ~ Agriculture (3), ~ Agriculture (3), Artificial Intelligence for:, Robotics

Company Name: 24me
Description: 24me is a tech company building the next generation digital personal assistant for everyone.
Website: http://www.twentyfour.me/
Phone: **Email:** info@twentyfour.me
City: Tel Aviv **State:** Tel Aviv District **PC:** **Country:** Israel
Year Established: 2012 **Status 2020:** Active
Industries: Artificial Intelligence for:, Big Data and Analytics for:, Internet of Things (IoT)

Company Name: ACC
Description: ACC develops data tools for financial institutions working in Cryptocurrency market investment and risk management.
Website: http://accrypto.io
Phone: **Email:** inquiries@accrypto.io
City: Tel Aviv **State:** Tel Aviv District **PC:** **Country:** Israel
Year Established: 2017 **Status 2020:** Active
Industries: Artificial Intelligence for:, Big Data and Analytics for:, Blockchain for:, ~ Banking and Financial Markets-Services (7), IT Managed Services for:, Risk Management

Company Name: Adminz.io
Description: Adminz.io develops customer support platform designed to perform repetitive tasks for insurance and law firms.
Website: https://adminz.io/
Phone: **Email:** 35955@reference-encyclopedia-ai.net
City: Tel Aviv **State:** Tel Aviv District **PC:** **Country:** Israel
Year Established: 2019 **Status 2020:** Active
Industries: Artificial Intelligence for:, Application Services

Company Name: Agronnabis
Description: Agronnabis specializes in developing artificial intelligence pest decision-making tools.
Website:
Phone: **Email:** 35977@reference-encyclopedia-ai.net
City: Tel Aviv **State:** TA **PC:** **Country:** Israel
Year Established: 2018 **Status 2020:** Closed
Industries:

Company Name: AI21 Labs
Description: AI21 is bringing AI into the 21st century, developing AI systems with an unprecedented capacity to understand and generate natural language.
Website: http://www.ai21.com/
Phone: **Email:** info@i21.com
City: Tel Aviv **State:** Tel Aviv District **PC:** **Country:** Israel
Year Established: 2017 **Status 2020:** Active
Industries: Artificial Intelligence

Company Name: AiroAv
Description: Malware protection platform focused solely on Mac
Website: http://www.airoav.com
Phone: **Email:** info@airoav.com
City: Tel Aviv **State:** TA **PC:** **Country:** Israel
Year Established: **Status 2020:** Active
Industries: Artificial Intelligence for:, Cyber Security for:, Predictive Analytics

Company Name: Airwayz
Description: Airwayz is a provider of management system for unmanned traffic management (UTM) and drone fleets.
Website: https://www.airwayz.co/
Phone: **Email:** contact@airwayz.co
City: Tel Aviv **State:** Tel Aviv District **PC:** **Country:** Israel
Year Established: 2018 **Status 2020:** Active
Industries: Artificial Intelligence for:, ~ Automotive (5), Cloud for:, ~ Telecommunications (56)

Company Name: AiVF
Description: AIVF is an artificial intelligence support platform for IVF treatments.
Website: http://www.aivf.co/
Phone: **Email:** 36024@reference-encyclopedia-ai.net
City: Tel Aviv **State:** Tel Aviv District **PC:** **Country:** Israel
Year Established: 2018 **Status 2020:** Active
Industries: Artificial Intelligence for:, Big Data and Analytics for:, ~ Healthcare (20)

Company Name: AlvIA Israel
Description: AlvIA develops technology that identifies Patterns of Behavior and Anomaly Detection transforming video streams to numerical data.
Website: https://ai-ia.ai/
Phone: **Email:** info@ai-ia.ai
City: Tel Aviv **State:** Tel Aviv District **PC:** **Country:** Israel
Year Established: 2018 **Status 2020:** Active
Industries: Artificial Intelligence for:, ~ Arts-Entertainment-Recreation (4), ~ Construction (10)

Company **Name:** Albe
Description: Albe offers an entirely new way to evaluate credit applications and monitor credit payment.
Website: http://albe.io/
Phone: **Email:** info@labe.io
City: Tel Aviv **State:** Tel Aviv District **PC:** **Country:** Israel
Year Established: 2019 **Status 2020:** Active
Industries: Artificial Intelligence for:, ~ Banking and Financial Markets-Services (7), ~ Banking and Financial Markets-Services (7)

Company Name: AlgoREIT
Description: Technology driven real estate market analys
Website:
Phone: **Email:** 36035@reference-encyclopedia-ai.net
City: Tel Aviv **State:** Tel Aviv District **PC:** **Country:** Israel
Year Established: **Status 2020:** - Closed
Industries: Analytics for:, Big Data and Analytics for:, Machine Learning

Company Name: Algosave
Description: Algosave leverages big data, machine learning and the power of cloud computing to save bank capital.
Website: http://algosave.com/
Phone: **Email:** david@algosave.com
City: Tel Aviv **State:** Tel Aviv District **PC:** **Country:** Israel
Year Established: 2015 **Status 2020:** Active
Industries: ~ Banking and Financial Markets-Services (7), ~ Banking and Financial Markets-Services (7), ~ Banking and Financial Markets-Services (7), Machine Learning

Company Name: Allegro.AI
Description: Allegro AI helps companies develop, deploy and manage DL & ML based solutions with a focus on unstructured data.
Website: http://allegro.ai/
Phone: **Email:** info@allegro.ai
City: Tel Aviv **State:** Tel Aviv District **PC:** **Country:** Israel
Year Established: 2016 **Status 2020:** Active
Industries: Machine Learning

Company Name: Altimo
Description: We commercialize artificial intelligence.
Website: http://www.altimo.io
Phone: **Email:** partnerships@altimo.io
City: Tel Aviv **State:** TA **PC:** **Country:** Israel
Year Established: **Status 2020:** Active
Industries: Artificial Intelligence for:, E-Commerce for:, Web

Company Name: Amigo
Description: Amigo is a mobile application platform for individuals who wish to find new partners for any purpose.
Website: http://hadarkeidar.wixsite.com/amigo
Phone: **Email:** amigo.official.team@gmail.com
City: Tel Aviv **State:** Tel Aviv District **PC:** **Country:** Israel
Year Established: 2018 **Status 2020:** Active
Industries: Machine Learning for:, Application Services for:, ~ Social Assistance-Non-Profits (53)

Company Name: Anagog
Description: Revolutionizing the way you know your customers to craft the most personal customer experience.
Website: http://www.anagog.com
Phone: **Email:** info@anagog.com
City: Tel Aviv **State:** Tel Aviv District **PC:** **Country:** Israel
Year Established: 2010 **Status 2020:** Active
Industries: Application Services for:, Artificial Intelligence for:, ~ Banking and Financial Markets-Services (7), Business Intelligence

Company Name: Anima.ey
Description: Anima is an AI tool aiming to provide professionals initial information concerning sexual abuse experience through self-figure drawings.
Website: http://anima-ey.com
Phone: **Email:** info@anima-ey.com
City: Tel Aviv **State:** Tel Aviv District **PC:** **Country:** Israel
Year Established: 2017 **Status 2020:** Active
Industries: Artificial Intelligence

Company Name: AnyVision
Description: AnyVision is an AI design and development company that specializes in face, object and human recognition in mass crowd events.
Website: http://anyvision.co
Phone: **Email:** info@anyvision.co
City: Tel Aviv **State:** Tel Aviv District **PC:** **Country:** Israel
Year Established: 2015 **Status 2020:** Active
Industries:

Company Name: Arcadia
Description: Boost construction site productivity with AI and mobile Localization
Website: http://arcadia.ai
Phone: **Email:** contact@arcadia.ai
City: Tel Aviv **State:** Tel Aviv District **PC:** **Country:** Israel
Year Established: 2016 **Status 2020:** Active
Industries: Augmented Reality for:, Machine Learning for:, Mobile for:, Application Services

Company Name: Arpeely
Description: Arpeely develops machine learning based media acquisition algorithms for managed and RTB environments.
Website: http://arpeely.com
Phone: **Email:** hi@arpeely.com
City: Tel Aviv **State:** Tel Aviv District **PC:** **Country:** Israel
Year Established: 2016 **Status 2020:** Active
Industries: ~ Automotive (5), Digital Media for:, Web for:, Machine Learning for:, ~ Arts-Entertainment-Recreation (4)

Company Name: Artbra: India
Description: Artbrain is an art-focused technology company.
Website: http://www.artbrain.co/
Phone: **Email:** hello@artbrain.co
City: Tel Aviv **State:** Tel Aviv District **PC:** **Country:** Israel
Year Established: 2018 **Status 2020:** Active
Industries: ~ Arts-Entertainment-Recreation (4), Machine Learning for:, ~ Banking and Financial Markets-Services (7)

Company Name: Aspectiva
Description: Turn Product Reviews into a Smarter Shopping Experience
Website: http://www.aspectiva.com
Phone: **Email:** info@aspectiva.com
City: Tel Aviv **State:** Tel Aviv District **PC:** **Country:** Israel
Year Established: 2013 **Status 2020:** Active
Industries: Artificial Intelligence for:, E-Commerce for:, Web for:, Machine Learning for:, Natural Language Processing

Company Name: Astralink
Description: Augmented Reality Platform for Construction Sit: Spain
Website: http://www.astralink.io
Phone: **Email:** hello@astralink.io
City: Tel Aviv **State:** Tel Aviv District **PC:** **Country:** Israel
Year Established: 2015 **Status 2020:** Active
Industries: Artificial Intelligence for:, Augmented Reality for:, Computer Vision for:, ~ Construction (10), Enterprise Application Services for:, Machine Learning for:, Mobile for:, Mobile

Company Name: Augmind
Description: Augmented Reality
Website: http://www.augmind.me/
Phone: 972 54-818-3132 **Email:** info@augmind.me
City: Tel Aviv **State:** TA **PC:** **Country:** Israel
Year Established: **Status 2020:** Active
Industries: Artificial Intelligence for:, IT Managed Services for:, ~ Professional Services (48), ~ Arts-Entertainment-Recreation (4)

Company Name: AXON Vision
Description: Axon Vision empowers the Next-Gen Defense & HLS Systems with Artificial Intelligence.
Website: http://axon-vision.com
Phone: **Email:** info@axon-vision.com
City: Tel Aviv **State:** Tel Aviv District **PC:** **Country:** Israel
Year Established: 2017 **Status 2020:** Active
Industries: Artificial Intelligence for:, Machine Learning

Company Name: BeaconCure
Description: Scientific Intelligence for healthcare
Website: http://beaconcure.com/
Phone: **Email:** hello@beaconcure.com
City: Tel Aviv **State:** Tel Aviv District **PC:** **Country:** Israel
Year Established: 2015 **Status 2020:** Active
Industries: Analytics for:, Artificial Intelligence for:, ~ Biotechnology (9), ~ Healthcare (20)

Company Name: Beam Travel Technology
Description: Beam Travel Technology created an intelligent and social travel-planning platform.
Website: http://www.beam.travel/
Phone: **Email:** 36142@reference-encyclopedia-ai.net
City: Tel Aviv **State:** Tel Aviv District **PC:** **Country:** Israel
Year Established: 2019 **Status 2020:** Active
Industries: Artificial Intelligence for:, IT Managed Services for:, Web for:, Machine Learning

Company Name: Beewizer
Description: Beewizer is a smart payment accelerator based on unique AI technology that provides accounting services.
Website: http://www.beewizer.com/
Phone: **Email:** info@beewizer.com
City: Tel Aviv **State:** Tel Aviv District **PC:** **Country:** Israel
Year Established: 2018 **Status 2020:** Active
Industries: Finance and Accounting for:, Artificial Intelligence for:, ~ Banking and Financial Markets-Services (7)

Company Name: Behave
Description: Behave helps customers drive business growth through data.
Website: http://behave.ai/
Phone: **Email:** 36143@reference-encyclopedia-ai.net
City: Tel Aviv **State:** TA **PC:** **Country:** Israel
Year Established: 2017 **Status 2020:** Active
Industries: Artificial Intelligence for:, Business Intelligence for:, IT Managed Services

Company Name: Bestpractix
Description: Providing lawyers with a platform that seamlessly leverages and embeds organizational knowledge into the contract drafting process.
Website: http://bestpractix.com
Phone: **Email:** omer@bestpractix.com
City: Tel Aviv **State:** Tel Aviv District **PC:** **Country:** Israel
Year Established: 2018 **Status 2020:** Active
Industries: IT Managed Services for:, Natural Language Processing

Company Name: Better Impression
Description: Better Impression helps tens of millions of unique B2B and B2C users from around the world make better-informed decisions online.
Website: http://www.bimpression.com
Phone: **Email:** hr@bimpression.com
City: Tel Aviv **State:** Tel Aviv District **PC:** **Country:** Israel
Year Established: 2012 **Status 2020:** Active
Industries: Analytics for:, Big Data and Analytics for:, IT Managed Services for:, Machine Learning for:, Business Software as a Service Apps (SaaS Apps)

Company Name: Beyond Verbal
Description: Beyond Verbal uses Voice and AI to revolutionize Healthcare, Well-being and Emotional Understanding.
Website: http://beyondverbal.com
Phone: (972) 357-5877 **Email:** Info@beyondverbal.com
City: Tel Aviv **State:** TA **PC:** **Country:** Israel
Year Established: 2012 **Status 2020:** Active
Industries:

Company Name: BeyondMinds
Description: BeyondMinds is an AI research company enabling AI transformations together with data-driven organizations
Website: http://www.beyondminds.ai/
Phone: **Email:** info@beyondminds.ai
City: Tel Aviv **State:** Tel Aviv District **PC:** **Country:** Israel
Year Established: 2018 **Status 2020:** Active
Industries:

Company Name: BigaBid
Description: Bigabid is a mobile UA & Re-Engagement technology company. 100% Programatic. 100% Performance based.
Website: http://www.bigabid.com/
Phone: 1(164)693-46994 **Email:** info@bigabid.com
City: Tel Aviv **State:** Tel Aviv District **PC:** **Country:** Israel
Year Established: 2016 **Status 2020:** Active
Industries: Big Data and Analytics for:, Machine Learning for:, Mobile for:, ~ Media-Communications (41)

Company Name: binah.ai
Description: Combining signal processing, machine learning, and AI to solve real-world business challenges.
Website: http://www.binah.ai/
Phone: **Email:** 36157@reference-encyclopedia-ai.net
City: Tel Aviv **State:** Tel Aviv District **PC:** **Country:** Israel
Year Established: 2016 **Status 2020:** Active
Industries: Artificial Intelligence for:, Big Data and Analytics for:, Business Intelligence for:, Machine Learning

Company Name: BioGaming
Description: Home Health Physical Therapy solution for Better Compliance
Website: http://www.biogaming.com/
Phone: **Email:** 36159@reference-encyclopedia-ai.net
City: Tel Aviv **State:** Tel Aviv District **PC:** **Country:** Israel
Year Established: 2011 **Status 2020:** Active
Industries: ~ Healthcare (20), ~ Healthcare (20), Machine Learning for:, ~ Healthcare (20)

Company Name: Blaick Technologies
Description: Blaick is a cyber-security company which deploys proprietary Artificial Intelligence threats detection technology to prevent cyber crime.
Website: http://blaick.com
Phone: **Email:** 36172@reference-encyclopedia-ai.net
City: Tel Aviv **State:** Tel Aviv District **PC:** **Country:** Israel
Year Established: 2016 **Status 2020:** Active
Industries: Artificial Intelligence for:, Cyber Security for:, Security for:, Security

Company Name: Bonobo AI
Description: Bonobo.ai is a platform for Marketing Automation and Behavioral Insights for Conversational Human-Machine Interactions.
Website: http://www.bonobo.ai
Phone: **Email:** hello@bonobo.ai
City: Tel Aviv **State:** Tel Aviv District **PC:** **Country:** Israel
Year Established: 2017 **Status 2020:** Active
Industries: Artificial Intelligence for:, Web

Company Name: Booth Gu: Russia
Description: Booth Guru provides B2B trade-show exhibitors an AI based SaaS platform for managing every step of an event.
Website: http://booth.gu: Russia
Phone: **Email:** info@booth.gu: Russia
City: Tel Aviv **State:** Tel Aviv District **PC:** **Country:** Israel
Year Established: 2016 **Status 2020:** Active
Industries: Artificial Intelligence for:, Big Data and Analytics for:, ~ Event Management (15), Machine Learning for:, Business Software as a Service Apps (SaaS Apps)

Company Name: Bosco
Description: Bosco is an AI-powered parenting app that predicts and prevents threats to children.
Website: http://www.boscoapp.com/
Phone: **Email:** enonl@s-fbi.com
City: Tel Aviv **State:** Tel Aviv District **PC:** **Country:** Israel
Year Established: 2015 **Status 2020:** Active
Industries: Application Services for:, Artificial Intelligence

Company Name: Braincast
Description: General Purpose Machine Learning API for Develope: Serbia
Website: http://braincast.ai/
Phone: **Email:** lior@braincast.ai
City: Tel Aviv **State:** Tel Aviv District **PC:** **Country:** Israel
Year Established: 2019 **Status 2020:** Active
Industries: Artificial Intelligence for:, Cloud for:, Cloud for:, Databases for:, Application Program Interfaces (APIs) for:, Application Services for:, Application Services for:, Machine Learning for:, Machine Learning for:, Business Software as a Service Apps (SaaS Apps) fo

Company Name: BrainPal
Description: Machine learning platform for website personalization.
Website: http://brainpal.io
Phone: **Email:** 36203@reference-encyclopedia-ai.net
City: Tel Aviv **State:** Tel Aviv District **PC:** **Country:** Israel
Year Established: 2016 **Status 2020:** Closed
Industries: Artificial Intelligence for:, ~ Education (13), Web

Company Name: Brainvivo
Description: Brainvivo is the first company to digitize the human brain's abilities and make them universally accessible
Website: http://www.brainvivo.com
Phone: **Email:** info@brainvivo.com
City: Tel Aviv **State:** TA **PC:** **Country:** Israel
Year Established: 2016 **Status 2020:** Active
Industries: Artificial Intelligence

Company Name: Bravo.ai
Description: Bravo.ai is an agile management app for manual work in labor intensive businesses.
Website: http://www.bravo.ai
Phone: **Email:** 36204@reference-encyclopedia-ai.net
City: Tel Aviv **State:** TA **PC:** **Country:** Israel
Year Established: 2016 **Status 2020:** Active
Industries: Artificial Intelligence for:, Application Services for:, Application Services for:, Business Process and Operations

Company Name: Brodmann17
Description: Brodmann17 delivers the next generation of ADAS and automted driving
Website: http://brodmann17.com
Phone: **Email:** partners@brodmann17.com
City: Tel Aviv **State:** Tel Aviv District **PC:** **Country:** Israel
Year Established: 2016 **Status 2020:** Active
Industries: Artificial Intelligence for:, ~ Automotive (5), Computer Vision for:, Machine Learning

Company Name: Brow: Slovakia
Description: Browsi helps publishers meet any advertiser expectation by putting AI behind their ad inventory.
Website: http://gobrowsi.com
Phone: **Email:** 36212@reference-encyclopedia-ai.net
City: Tel Aviv **State:** Tel Aviv District **PC:** **Country:** Israel
Year Established: 2013 **Status 2020:** Active
Industries:

Company Name: Bumblebee
Description: Bumblebee is an AI pollination solution for crops which pollination is a limiting factor for their yield.
Website: http://pollination.ai
Phone: 972 54-633-6372 **Email:** contact@pollination.ai
City: Tel Aviv **State:** TA **PC:** **Country:** Israel
Year Established: 2019 **Status 2020:** Active
Industries: ~ Agriculture (3), Artificial Intelligence for:, Computer Vision for:, ~ Agriculture (3)

Company Name: Cannalyze
Description: Cannalyze provides cannabis test data accessible to humans and discover strains unique cannabinoids.
Website: http://cannalyze.co
Phone: **Email:** info@cannalyze.co
City: Tel Aviv **State:** Tel Aviv District **PC:** **Country:** Israel
Year Established: 2019 **Status 2020:** Active
Industries: ~ Healthcare (20), Artificial Intelligence for:, ~ Agriculture (3), ~ Healthcare (20), ~ Healthcare (20)

Company Name: Canny AI
Description: Canny AI is a Deep Tech startup working to create the perfect lip-sync between video and audio.
Website: http://cannyai.com
Phone: **Email:** info@cannyai.com
City: Tel Aviv **State:** TA **PC:** **Country:** Israel
Year Established: 2017 **Status 2020:** Active
Industries: Artificial Intelligence for:, ~ Media-Communications (41), ~ Arts-Entertainment-Recreation (4)

Company Name: Carpe Diem Solutions
Description: IoT developer of real-time and AI-powered sensor-fusion and signal processing for connectivity, tracking, edge, positioning and navigation.
Website: http://www.carpe-diem.solutions/
Phone: 972 52 542 7575 **Email:** info@carpe-diem.solutions
City: Tel Aviv **State:** Tel Aviv District **PC:** **Country:** Israel
Year Established: 2018 **Status 2020:** Active
Industries: ~ Energy and Utilities (14), IT Managed Services for:, Machine Learning for:, ~ Social-Environmental-Physical-Engineering Sciences (55), Virtual Reality (VR) for:, Virtual Reality (VR) for:, Internet of Things (IoT)

Company Name: Cartica AI
Description: Cartica AI is a Solutions for the Next Generation of Vehicles and Mobility
Website: http://cartica.ai/
Phone: **Email:** 36238@reference-encyclopedia-ai.net
City: Tel Aviv **State:** Tel Aviv District **PC:** **Country:** Israel
Year Established: 2019 **Status 2020:** Active
Industries: Artificial Intelligence for:, ~ Automotive (5)

Company **Name:** ChameleonX
Description: ChameleonX provides AI-powered Runtime Web Application Self-protection (RWASP) solution.
Website: http://chameleonx.com
Phone: **Email:** info@chameleonx.com
City: Tel Aviv **State:** Tel Aviv District **PC:** **Country:** Israel
Year Established: 2016 **Status 2020:** Active
Industries: Artificial Intelligence for:, Cyber Security

Company Name: Chatbot Summ: Italy
Description: We are the world's leading international conference for people who believe that natural language interactions are next curve in digital.
Website: http://www.chatbotsummit.com
Phone: **Email:** info@chatbotsummit.com
City: Tel Aviv **State:** Tel Aviv District **PC:** **Country:** Israel
Year Established: 2016 **Status 2020:** Active
Industries: Application Services for:, Artificial Intelligence for:, ~ Event Management (15), IT Managed Services

Company Name: CHEQ
Description: CHEQ is an AI-driven cybersecurity company disrupting the ad-verification space.
Website: http://www.cheq.ai/
Phone: **Email:** info@cheq.com
City: Tel Aviv **State:** Tel Aviv District **PC:** **Country:** Israel
Year Established: 2016 **Status 2020:** Active
Industries: Artificial Intelligence for:, Cyber Security for:, Machine Learning

Company Name: Clair Labs
Description: Clair Labs is dedicated to helping people live happier, healthier lives by making high quality sleep healthcare more accessible than ever.
Website: http://www.clairlabs.com/
Phone: **Email:** contact@clairlabs.com
City: Tel Aviv **State:** Tel Aviv District **PC:** **Country:** Israel
Year Established: 2018 **Status 2020:** Active
Industries: Artificial Intelligence for:, Big Data and Analytics for:, Computer Vision for:, ~ Healthcare (20)

Company Name: Cla: New Zealand
Description: Pioneering, audio-based solution to detect increased risk of maltreatment of vulnerable, helpless individuals.
Website: http://clanz.io
Phone: **Email:** Romi@Clanz.io
City: Tel Aviv **State:** Tel Aviv District **PC:** **Country:** Israel
Year Established: 2019 **Status 2020:** Active
Industries: ~ Social Assistance-Non-Profits (53), ~ Healthcare (20), ~ Healthcare (20), Natural Language Processing for:, ~ Administrative and Support Services (1), Security for:, Speech Recognition

Company Name: CliClap
Description: CliClap is an AI-powered, autonomous content marketing solution that generates more qualified leads, increasing conversions by 150%
Website: http://www.cliclap.com/
Phone: **Email:** hello@cliclap.com
City: Tel Aviv **State:** Tel Aviv District **PC:** **Country:** Israel

Year Established: 2016 **Status 2020:** Active
Industries: Artificial Intelligence for:, Business Applications for:, Content for:, Web for:, ~ E-Commerce (12), ~ Social Assistance-Non-Profits (53), ~ Social Assistance-Non-Profits (53)

Company Name: Coach The Bot
Description: Coach The Bot develops an AI assistant intended to connect, control, and protect chatbot stack.
Website: http://www.coachthebot.ai
Phone: **Email:** 36295@reference-encyclopedia-ai.net
City: Tel Aviv **State:** Tel Aviv District **PC:** **Country:** Israel
Year Established: 2018 **Status 2020:** Active
Industries: Artificial Intelligence for:, IT Managed Services for:, Natural Language Processing

Company Name: codingintelligence.com
Description: Codota understands the world's code and provides you with the right suggestion at the right time
Website: http://www.codota.com
Phone: **Email:** info@codota.com
City: Tel Aviv **State:** Tel Aviv District **PC:** **Country:** Israel
Year Established: 2013 **Status 2020:** Active
Industries: Artificial Intelligence for:, Application Services for:, Business Software as a Service Apps (SaaS Apps) for:, Web

Company Name: CognitiveID
Description: CognitiveID provides a continuous behavioural and cognitive user identification solution that minimizes online identity theft.
Website: http://www.cognitive-id.com
Phone: **Email:** contact@cognitive-id.com
City: Tel Aviv **State:** Tel Aviv District **PC:** **Country:** Israel
Year Established: 2016 **Status 2020:** Active
Industries:

Company Name: Comvert
Description: Comvert automatically adapts the content and design of a website in real-time.
Website: http://www.comvert.io
Phone: **Email:** 36318@reference-encyclopedia-ai.net
City: Tel Aviv **State:** Tel Aviv District **PC:** **Country:** Israel
Year Established: 2018 **Status 2020:** Active
Industries: Artificial Intelligence for:, Automation

Company Name: Congnni
Description: Autonomous Insights for cloud security
Website: http://cognni.ai/
Phone: 1-516-321-1158 **Email:** info@shieldox.ai
City: Tel Aviv **State:** TA **PC:** **Country:** Israel
Year Established: 2017 **Status 2020:** Active
Industries: Artificial Intelligence for:, Cyber Security

Company Name: Const: Russia
Description: Constru Artificial Vision in Construction
Website: http://www.constru.ai/
Phone: **Email:** info@constru.ai
City: Tel Aviv **State:** Tel Aviv District **PC:** **Country:** Israel
Year Established: 2017 **Status 2020:** Active
Industries: Artificial Intelligence for:, Computer Vision for:, ~ Construction (10)

Company Name: Copula AI
Description: Copula AI provides solutions in natural language processing and related areas.
Website: http://www.copula.ai
Phone: **Email:** 36335@reference-encyclopedia-ai.net
City: Tel Aviv **State:** Tel Aviv District **PC:** **Country:** Israel
Year Established: 2017 **Status 2020:** Active
Industries: Artificial Intelligence for:, Machine Learning for:, Natural Language Processing

Company Name: Crazy SOB
Description: Crazy SOB develops a platform that uses natural language processing to translate online recipes from various media sources.
Website: http://www.crazy-sob.com
Phone: **Email:** 36344@reference-encyclopedia-ai.net
City: Tel Aviv **State:** Tel Aviv District **PC:** **Country:** Israel
Year Established: 2016 **Status 2020:** Active
Industries: Artificial Intelligence for:, ~ Food and Beverage (17)

Company **Name:** Crosswise
Description: Cross-Device Identification Mapping
Website: http://www.crosswise.com
Phone: **Email:** info@crosswise.com
City: Tel Aviv **State:** Tel Aviv District **PC:** **Country:** Israel
Year Established: 2013 **Status 2020:** Active
Industries: Analytics for:, Artificial Intelligence for:, Big Data and Analytics for:, Identity for:, Machine Learning for:, Mobile

Company Name: CrowdSen: Sweden
Description: CrowdSense is an automated intelligence agency platform focusing on early detection and smart filtering of market moving events
Website: http://www.crowdsense.ai
Phone: **Email:** info@crowdsense.ai
City: Tel Aviv **State:** Tel Aviv District **PC:** **Country:** Israel
Year Established: 2019 **Status 2020:** Active
Industries: Artificial Intelligence for:, Big Data and Analytics for:, Automation for:, Machine Learning for:, Natural Language Processing

Company Name: Cuma Financial
Description: Cuma Financial is a technology company specializing in data gathering and analysis geared towards creating exceptional financial tools.
Website: http://cumafinancial.com/index.html
Phone: **Email:** cuma@cuma.capital
City: Tel Aviv **State:** Tel Aviv District **PC:** **Country:** Israel
Year Established: 2017 **Status 2020:** Active
Industries: Artificial Intelligence for:, ~ Banking and Financial Markets-Services (7), ~ Banking and Financial Markets-Services (7)

Company Name: Curve
Description: Curve is a cross-organizational and actionable platform that provides enterprise retailers with accurate sales predictions.
Website: http://curve.tech
Phone: **Email:** info@curve.tech
City: Tel Aviv **State:** Tel Aviv District **PC:** **Country:** Israel
Year Established: 2017 **Status 2020:** Active
Industries: E-Commerce for:, Machine Learning

Company Name: Cyabra
Description: Cyabra protects from disinformation and deepfakes (a.k.a fake news).
Website: http://www.cyabra.com
Phone: **Email:** info@cyabra.com
City: Tel Aviv **State:** Tel Aviv District **PC:** **Country:** Israel
Year Established: 2018 **Status 2020:** Active
Industries: Cyber Security for:, IT Managed Services for:, Natural Language Processing for:, ~ Social Assistance-Non-Profits (53)

Company Name: Cyberfish
Description: Cyberfish is developing next-generation anti-phishing protection that combines machine learning, computer vision, and AI technology.
Website: http://cyberfish.io
Phone: 1 (877) 242 0433 **Email:** team@cyberfish.io
City: Tel Aviv **State:** Tel Aviv District **PC:** **Country:** Israel
Year Established: 2018 **Status 2020:** Active
Industries: Computer Vision for:, Cyber Security for:, Machine Learning for:, Security

Company Name: Cyberwrite
Description: Cyberwrite provides cyber insurance technologies to the insurance eco-system.
Website: http://www.cyberwrite.com
Phone: **Email:** info@cyberwrite.com
City: Tel Aviv **State:** Tel Aviv District **PC:** **Country:** Israel
Year Established: 2016 **Status 2020:** Active
Industries: Cyber Security for:, Machine Learning

Company Name: Cybord
Description: Cybord is an electronic manufacturing company that developed a non-destructive testing system.
Website: http://www.cy-bord.com/
Phone: **Email:** 36370@reference-encyclopedia-ai.net
City: Tel Aviv **State:** Tel Aviv District **PC:** **Country:** Israel
Year Established: 2018 **Status 2020:** Active
Industries: Artificial Intelligence for:, Big Data and Analytics for:, Internet of Things (IoT) for:, Machine Learning

Company Name: Cyb-Org
Description: Cyb-Org developed an information system for smooth and complete management and control of retail and wholesale organizations.
Website: http://cyb-org.com
Phone: **Email:** Info@cyb-org.com
City: Tel Aviv **State:** TA **PC:** **Country:** Israel
Year Established: 2016 **Status 2020:** Active
Industries:

Company Name: Cytegic
Description: Cytegic- Automated Cyber Risk Officer
Website: http://www.cytegic.com/
Phone: 1.646.844.5977 **Email:** elon.kaplan@cytegic.com
City: Tel Aviv **State:** Tel Aviv District **PC:** **Country:** Israel
Year Established: 2012 **Status 2020:** Active
Industries: Cyber Security for:, Application Services for:, Risk Management for:, Security

Company Name: CytoReason
Description: CytoReason: Re-defining the context of the immune system at a cellular level to better understand disease & guide more effective drug R&D.
Website: http://www.cytoreason.com/
Phone: **Email:** rob@cytoreason.com
City: Tel Aviv **State:** Tel Aviv District **PC:** **Country:** Israel
Year Established: 2016 **Status 2020:** Active
Industries: Artificial Intelligence for:, ~ Biotechnology (9), ~ Biotechnology (9), ~ Healthcare (20), ~ Healthcare (20), Machine Learning

Company Name: DAGsHub
Description: DAGsHub is a platform for data version control and collaboration for data scientists and machine learning engineers.
Website: http://dagshub.com
Phone: **Email:** contact@dagshub.com
City: Tel Aviv **State:** Tel Aviv District **PC:** **Country:** Israel
Year Established: 2019 **Status 2020:** Active
Industries: Artificial Intelligence for:, IT Managed Services for:, Machine Learning

Company Name: Data Science Group
Description: Data Science Group offers data science consulting, scientific modeling, predictive analysis, big data analytics, and machine learning.
Website: http://www.datascience.co.il/
Phone: 972-54-440-8089 **Email:** info@datascience.co.: Israel
City: Tel Aviv **State:** Tel Aviv District **PC:** **Country:** Israel
Year Established: 2015 **Status 2020:** Active
Industries: Databases for:, IT Managed Services for:, Machine Learning

Company Name: Databand
Description: Databand provides a software platform for agile machine learning development.
Website: http://databand.ai/
Phone: **Email:** 36387@reference-encyclopedia-ai.net
City: Tel Aviv **State:** Tel Aviv District **PC:** **Country:** Israel
Year Established: 2018 **Status 2020:** Active
Industries: Data Management for:, Data Management for:, IT Managed Services for:, Machine Learning

Company Name: DataGen Technologies
Description: Creating photorealistic synthetic data to train neural networks to solve real-world computer vision tasks.
Website: http://datagen.tech/
Phone: **Email:** hello@datagen.tech
City: Tel Aviv **State:** Tel Aviv District **PC:** **Country:** Israel
Year Established: 2018 **Status 2020:** Active
Industries: Artificial Intelligence for:, Computer Vision

Company Name: DatsMi
Description: DatsMi is an events services company that utilizes artificial intelligence and internet of things.
Website: http://www.datsmi.me
Phone: **Email:** 36400@reference-encyclopedia-ai.net
City: Tel Aviv **State:** Tel Aviv District **PC:** **Country:** Israel
Year Established: 2018 **Status 2020:** Active
Industries: Analytics for:, Artificial Intelligence for:, Internet of Things (IoT)

Company Name: DeepCube
Description: DeepCube features a proprietary platform that generates neural networks that use processing power and memory.
Website: http://www.deepcube.com
Phone: **Email:** partnerships@deepcube.com
City: Tel Aviv **State:** Tel Aviv District **PC:** **Country:** Israel
Year Established: 2017 **Status 2020:** Active
Industries: Artificial Intelligence for:, IT Managed Services for:, Machine Learning

Company Name: DeepNen
Description: DeepNen is an internet company that features a web-based application using the power of deep convolutional networks.
Website: http://www.deepnen.com
Phone: **Email:** david@deepnen.com
City: Tel Aviv **State:** Tel Aviv District **PC:** **Country:** Israel
Year Established: 2018 **Status 2020:** Active
Industries: Artificial Intelligence for:, Augmented Reality for:, Machine Learning

Company Name: DeepOncology AI
Description: DeepOncology is an AI-based company that features deep learning and AI to cover the fields of oncology & radiology.
Website: http://www.deeponcology.ai
Phone: **Email:** shlomo@deeponcology.ai
City: Tel Aviv **State:** Tel Aviv District **PC:** **Country:** Israel
Year Established: 2018 **Status 2020:** Active
Industries: Artificial Intelligence for:, Computer Vision

Company Name: DermaDetect
Description: AI based diagnosis & treatment of skin disorde: Serbia
Website: http://www.dermadetect.com
Phone: **Email:** eugene@dermadetect.com
City: Tel Aviv **State:** Tel Aviv District **PC:** **Country:** Israel
Year Established: 2017 **Status 2020:** Active
Industries: Artificial Intelligence for:, ~ Healthcare (20), ~ Healthcare (20), ~ Healthcare (20), ~ Healthcare (20)

Company Name: Diagnostic Robotics
Description: Diagnostic Robotic develops a signal-agnostic artificial intelligence system for healthcare insurers, providers, and patients.
Website: http://www.diagnosticrobotics.com
Phone: **Email:** contact@diagnosticrobotics.com
City: Tel Aviv **State:** Tel Aviv District **PC:** **Country:** Israel
Year Established: 2017 **Status 2020:** Active
Industries: Analytics for:, Artificial Intelligence for:, ~ Healthcare (20), ~ Healthcare (20), Robotics

Company Name: Diagsen: Sweden
Description: DiagSense is working on the field of algorithm development for predicting failures or abnormal behavior in mechanical systems and pipelines.
Website: http://www.diagsense.com
Phone: 972-77-7123303 **Email:** info@diagsense.com
City: Tel Aviv **State:** Tel Aviv District **PC:** **Country:** Israel
Year Established: 2013 **Status 2020:** Active
Industries: Artificial Intelligence

Company Name: Dialogue
Description: Dialogue personalizes customer experiences through AI-powered messages creation.
Website: http://nowdialogue.com
Phone: **Email:** omri@nowdialogue.com
City: Tel Aviv **State:** TA **PC:** **Country:** Israel
Year Established: **Status 2020:** Active
Industries:

Company Name: D-ID
Description: D-ID is an artificial intelligence company that develops a solution protecting identities from face recognition.
Website: http://www.deidentification.co/
Phone: **Email:** info@d-id.com
City: Tel Aviv **State:** Tel Aviv District **PC:** **Country:** Israel
Year Established: 2017 **Status 2020:** Active
Industries: Artificial Intelligence for:, Facial Recognition for:, Cyber Security

Company Name: Digitall
Description: Digitall provides conversational AI solutions.
Website: http://digitall.ai/
Phone: **Email:** sales@digitall.ai
City: Tel Aviv **State:** Tel Aviv District **PC:** **Country:** Israel
Year Established: 2017 **Status 2020:** Active
Industries: Artificial Intelligence for:, IT Managed Services

Company Name: DigitalOwl
Description: AI for Underwriters and Claim adjuste: Serbia
Website: http://www.digitalowl.com/
Phone: **Email:** info@digitalowl.com
City: Tel Aviv **State:** Tel Aviv District **PC:** **Country:** Israel
Year Established: 2018 **Status 2020:** Active
Industries: Artificial Intelligence for:, ~ Insurance (25), Natural Language Processing

Company Name: DoQme
Description: DoQme is an artificial intelligence health solution company.
Website: http://www.doqme.com/
Phone: **Email:** doqmesocial@gmail.com
City: Tel Aviv **State:** Tel Aviv District **PC:** **Country:** Israel
Year Established: 2016 **Status 2020:** Active
Industries: Artificial Intelligence for:, Cloud for:, Cloud for:, ~ Healthcare (20), ~ Healthcare (20), IT Managed Services

Company Name: DRIVE T: LATVIA
Description: DRIVE is the place for entrepreneurs that are looking to apply their ideas and products to the smart mobility field.
Website: http://www.drivetlv.com
Phone: **Email:** boaz@drivetlv.com
City: Tel Aviv **State:** Tel Aviv District **PC:** **Country:** Israel
Year Established: 2017 **Status 2020:** Active
Industries: Analytics for:, Artificial Intelligence for:, IT Managed Services for:, Machine Learning

Company Name: Dzomo
Description: Dzomo provides a platform powered by artificial intelligence that customizes photos for marketers and content creators.
Website: http://www.dzomo.ai/
Phone: **Email:** 36465@reference-encyclopedia-ai.net
City: Tel Aviv **State:** Tel Aviv District **PC:** **Country:** Israel
Year Established: 2019 **Status 2020:** Active
Industries: Artificial Intelligence for:, ~ Media-Communications (41), ~ Media-Communications (41)

Company Name: Emelai
Description: Emelai is a technology startup using Artificial Intelligence cognitive computing to create automated Habit Formation digital platforms.
Website: http://www.emelai.io
Phone: 972 50 393 3995 **Email:** info@emelai.io
City: Tel Aviv **State:** TA **PC:** **Country:** Israel
Year Established: 2016 **Status 2020:** Active
Industries: Artificial Intelligence for:, IT Managed Services for:, IT Managed Services

Company Name: Empirical Hire
Description: Empirical Hire offers a software platform that specializes in hiring process and machine learning algorithms.
Website: http://www.empirical.app
Phone: **Email:** 36504@reference-encyclopedia-ai.net
City: Tel Aviv **State:** Tel Aviv District **PC:** **Country:** Israel
Year Established: 2017 **Status 2020:** Active
Industries: Artificial Intelligence for:, Machine Learning

Company Name: Endor
Description: Predictive software platform that lets business users ask any predictive question and get high-quality results in minutes instead of months.
Website: http://www.endor.com
Phone: **Email:** 36507@reference-encyclopedia-ai.net
City: Tel Aviv **State:** Tel Aviv District **PC:** **Country:** Israel
Year Established: 2014 **Status 2020:** Active
Industries: Big Data and Analytics for:, Machine Learning for:, Predictive Analytics

Company Name: eSistence Virtual Interaction
Description: ESistence Virtual Interaction offers a free dialogue chatbot.
Website: http://www.esistence.com
Phone: **Email:** asher.polani@esistence.com
City: Tel Aviv **State:** Tel Aviv District **PC:** **Country:** Israel
Year Established: 2012 **Status 2020:** Active
Industries: Artificial Intelligence for:, Databases for:, ~ Customer Relationship Management (11), Machine Learning

Company Name: Esthetic Eye
Description: Esthetic Eye is a system that creates aesthetic, designed, and ready-to-print photo books.
Website: http://www.estheticeye.com
Phone: **Email:** chloe@estheticeye.com
City: Tel Aviv **State:** Tel Aviv District **PC:** **Country:** Israel
Year Established: 2018 **Status 2020:** Active
Industries: Artificial Intelligence for:, Computer Vision

Company Name: EverThere
Description: Everthere's data applications provide live and personalized human-expert-level market insights, making 'research' as we know it obsolete.
Website: http://everthere.co
Phone: **Email:** info@everthere.co
City: Tel Aviv **State:** Tel Aviv District **PC:** **Country:** Israel

Year Established: 2019 **Status 2020:** Active
Industries: Business Intelligence for:, Natural Language Processing for:, Predictive Analytics

Company Name: EverythingMe
Description: EverythingMe is a launcher for Android devices that adds contextual capabilities to mobile phones.
Website: http://everything.me
Phone: 415-250-2382 **Email:** info@everything.me
City: Tel Aviv **State:** TA **PC:** **Country:** Israel
Year Established: 2010 **Status 2020:** Closed
Industries: Machine Learning for:, Mobile for:, Web

Company Name: Evo.Do
Description: Evo.Do is a codeless test automation for interactive products and other digital products.
Website: http://www.evo.do/
Phone: **Email:** 36528@reference-encyclopedia-ai.net
City: Tel Aviv **State:** Tel Aviv District **PC:** **Country:** Israel
Year Established: 2018 **Status 2020:** Active
Industries:

Company Name: Explority
Description: Explority is an AI-powered enterprise SaaS platform that helps stakeholders to grow.
Website: http://www.explority.com
Phone: **Email:** 36537@reference-encyclopedia-ai.net
City: Tel Aviv **State:** Tel Aviv District **PC:** **Country:** Israel
Year Established: 2016 **Status 2020:** Active
Industries: Artificial Intelligence for:, Machine Learning for:, Business Software as a Service Apps (SaaS Apps) for:, Web

Company Name: Explorium
Description: Automated Data and Feature Discovery Platform
Website: http://www.explorium.ai/
Phone: **Email:** info@explorium.ai
City: Tel Aviv **State:** Tel Aviv District **PC:** **Country:** Israel
Year Established: 2017 **Status 2020:** Active
Industries: Analytics for:, Artificial Intelligence for:, Machine Learning for:, Predictive Analytics

Company Name: EyeSafe Labs
Description: EyeSafe specializes in providing camera monitoring to the security industry, .
Website:
Phone: **Email:** 36540@reference-encyclopedia-ai.net
City: Tel Aviv **State:** Tel Aviv District **PC:** **Country:** Israel
Year Established: 2016 **Status 2020:** Closed
Industries: Artificial Intelligence for:, Computer Vision for:, Security

Company Name: Eyezon
Description: Eyezon provides checkout process services that utilize deep learning and advanced computer vision technologies to track shoppers.
Website: http://www.eyezon.ai
Phone: **Email:** info@eyezon.ai
City: Tel Aviv **State:** Tel Aviv District **PC:** **Country:** Israel
Year Established: 2018 **Status 2020:** Active
Industries: Artificial Intelligence for:, Computer Vision for:, ~ Banking and Financial Markets-Services (7)

Company Name: Faception
Description: Faception is a facial personality profiling company.
Website: http://www.faception.com/
Phone: **Email:** info@faception.com
City: Tel Aviv **State:** Tel Aviv District **PC:** **Country:** Israel
Year Established: 2014 **Status 2020:** Active
Industries: Analytics for:, Computer Vision for:, Machine Learning

Company Name: Facetrom
Description: Facetroom is developing a technology that analyzes facial features and to build an accurate and detailed profile.
Website: http://www.facetrom.com
Phone: **Email:** 36547@reference-encyclopedia-ai.net
City: Tel Aviv **State:** Tel Aviv District **PC:** **Country:** Israel
Year Established: 2015 **Status 2020:** Active
Industries: Artificial Intelligence for:, Computer Vision for:, Business Software as a Service Apps (SaaS Apps)

Company Name: FamilyKeeper
Description: FamilyKeeper is the world's most advanced AI-Powered online child protection app
Website: http://www.familykeeper.co
Phone: **Email:** bar@familykeeper.co
City: Tel Aviv **State:** Tel Aviv District **PC:** **Country:** Israel
Year Established: 2017 **Status 2020:** Active
Industries: Artificial Intelligence

Company Name: Famuza
Description: A fashion tech startup
Website:
Phone: **Email:** 36551@reference-encyclopedia-ai.net
City: Tel Aviv **State:** Tel Aviv District **PC:** **Country:** Israel
Year Established: 2014 **Status 2020:** Closed
Industries: ~ Fashion (16), Predictive Analytics

Company Name: Fantasy Advantage
Description: Fantasy Advantage explores ways to harness natural-language processing and other technologies to provide sports analysis.
Website: http://www.fantasyadvantage.com
Phone: **Email:** 36553@reference-encyclopedia-ai.net
City: Tel Aviv **State:** Tel Aviv District **PC:** **Country:** Israel
Year Established: 2017 **Status 2020:** Active
Industries: Artificial Intelligence for:, ~ Arts-Entertainment-Recreation (4), Machine Learning for:, ~ Arts-Entertainment-Recreation (4)

Company Name: Fides.ai
Description: Fides allows companies to accelerate AI adoption by adding a layer of monitoring.
Website: http://itayc6.wixsite.com/website
Phone: **Email:** itayc@outlook.com
City: Tel Aviv **State:** Tel Aviv District **PC:** **Country:** Israel
Year Established: 2019 **Status 2020:** Active
Industries: Artificial Intelligence for:, IT Managed Services

Company Name: Fifth Dimension
Description: Fifth Dimension offers comprehensive investigation platform for Law Enforcement and Police agencies leveraging AI and Deep Learning
Website: http://www.5dimension.com/
Phone: 972 (3) 543-1900 **Email:** contact@5dimension.com
City: Tel Aviv **State:** Tel Aviv District **PC:** **Country:** Israel
Year Established: 2014 **Status 2020:** Active
Industries: Artificial Intelligence for:, IT Managed Services for:, Machine Learning

Company Name: FinityX
Description: FinityX is an asset management startup that develops an AI data driven investment management solution.
Website: http://www.finityx.com
Phone: **Email:** Sapir@finityx.com
City: Tel Aviv **State:** Tel Aviv District **PC:** **Country:** Israel
Year Established: 2018 **Status 2020:** Active
Industries: Artificial Intelligence for:, ~ Banking and Financial Markets-Services (7), Big Data and Analytics for:, Data Management for:, ~ Banking and Financial Markets-Services (7)

Company Name: FitV
Description: FitV provides a machine vision system platform for effective and personalized workouts.
Website: http://www.fitv.ai
Phone: **Email:** contact@fitv.ai
City: Tel Aviv **State:** Tel Aviv District **PC:** **Country:** Israel
Year Established: 2018 **Status 2020:** Active
Industries: Artificial Intelligence for:, Computer Vision for:, ~ Healthcare (20), Machine Learning for:, Compute

Company Name: Five Sig: Morocco
Description: Five Sigma is a B2B insurtech start-up which changes the way claims are being managed.
Website: http://www.fivesigmalabs.com
Phone: **Email:** contact@fivesigmalabs.com
City: Tel Aviv **State:** Tel Aviv District **PC:** **Country:** Israel
Year Established: 2017 **Status 2020:** Active
Industries:

Company Name: FOCUUS
Description: Performance marketing tracking & BI solution
Website: http://www.focuus.com/
Phone: **Email:** contactus@focuus.com
City: Tel Aviv **State:** Tel Aviv District **PC:** **Country:** Israel
Year Established: 2015 **Status 2020:** Active
Industries: Business Intelligence for:, Machine Learning for:, Predictive Analytics

Company Name: galigu
Description: galigu is rediscovering VR-search to unleash the power of virtual reality.
Website: http://galigu.com
Phone: **Email:** info@galigu.com
City: Tel Aviv **State:** Tel Aviv District **PC:** **Country:** Israel
Year Established: 2016 **Status 2020:** Closed
Industries: Content for:, Human Computer Interaction for:, Machine Learning for:, Web for:, Virtual Reality (VR) for:, Compute

Company Name: Gemina Israel
Description: Gemina Israel provides a platform for automated Business Document Analysis based on Artificial Intelligence.
Website: http://www.gemina.co.il/
Phone: **Email:** info@gemina.co.: Israel
City: Tel Aviv **State:** Tel Aviv District **PC:** **Country:** Israel
Year Established: 2017 **Status 2020:** Active
Industries: Finance and Accounting for:, Artificial Intelligence

Company Name: Gooster
Description: The A.I. concierge chatbot, helping urban hotels rediscover their guests, while they discover the city, through messaging.
Website: http://www.gooster.net
Phone: **Email:** ardon@gooster.net
City: Tel Aviv **State:** Tel Aviv District **PC:** **Country:** Israel
Year Established: 2016 **Status 2020:** Active
Industries: Artificial Intelligence

Company Name: Granulate
Description: Granulate is an AI-powered optimization software that improves performance by creating a streamlined environment for any app.
Website: http://www.granulate.io
Phone: **Email:** info@granulate.io
City: Tel Aviv **State:** Tel Aviv District **PC:** **Country:** Israel
Year Established: 2018 **Status 2020:** Active
Industries: Artificial Intelligence for:, Cloud for:, IT Managed Services

Company Name: Greeneye Technology
Description: Greeneye's mission is to dramatically reduce chemical usage while increasing productivity and profitability for farmers.
Website: http://www.greeneye.ag
Phone: **Email:** info@greeneye.ag
City: Tel Aviv **State:** Tel Aviv District **PC:** **Country:** Israel
Year Established: 2017 **Status 2020:** Active
Industries: ~ Agriculture (3), ~ Agriculture (3), Artificial Intelligence for:, Big Data and Analytics for:, ~ Agriculture (3), Internet of Things (IoT)

Company Name: Guardian Key
Description: Guardian Key is an AI company that provides parents with an advanced child monitoring app.
Website: http://www.guardiankey.app
Phone: **Email:** guardiankeyapp@gmail.com
City: Tel Aviv **State:** Tel Aviv District **PC:** **Country:** Israel
Year Established: 2018 **Status 2020:** Active
Industries: Artificial Intelligence for:, IT Managed Services for:, Web for:, Machine Learning

Company Name: Gymex
Description: Artificial Intelligence Soccer Predictor
Website: http://www.gymex.com/
Phone: **Email:** 36659@reference-encyclopedia-ai.net
City: Tel Aviv **State:** Tel Aviv District **PC:** **Country:** Israel
Year Established: 2010 **Status 2020:** Active
Industries: Artificial Intelligence for:, IT Managed Services for:, Machine Learning

Company Name: Hailo
Description: Hailo has developed a specialized deep learning processor that delivers the performance of a data center-class computer to edge devices.
Website: http://hailo.ai/
Phone: **Email:** contact@hailo.ai
City: Tel Aviv **State:** Tel Aviv District **PC:** **Country:** Israel
Year Established: 2017 **Status 2020:** Active
Industries: Artificial Intelligence for:, Augmented Reality for:, ~ Automotive (5), Cloud for:, Embedded for:, Internet of Things (IoT) for:, Machine Learning for:, Machine Learning

Company Name: Heat Intelligence
Description: Heat is a cloud service for intelligence on demand, providing cognitive services in real time by a hybrid cloud of humans and AI.
Website: http://heatintelligence.com
Phone: **Email:** info@heatintelligence.com
City: Tel Aviv **State:** Tel Aviv District **PC:** **Country:** Israel
Year Established: 2016 **Status 2020:** Active
Industries:

Company Name: HI4AI
Description: Scale Up Data Labeling with Dedicated Expertise Computer Vision, Machine Learning, Artificial Intelligence
Website: http://www.hi4.ai
Phone: **Email:** roberto@hi4.ai
City: Tel Aviv **State:** Tel Aviv District **PC:** **Country:** Israel
Year Established: 2020 **Status 2020:** Active
Industries: Artificial Intelligence

Company Name: Huma: New Zealand
Description: Data Driven, Programmatic platform for Micro Influencers Campaigns.
Website: http://www.humanz.ai
Phone: 972 (052) - 8675541 **Email:** dror@humanz.ai
City: Tel Aviv **State:** Tel Aviv District **PC:** **Country:** Israel
Year Established: 2017 **Status 2020:** Active
Industries: Artificial Intelligence for:, Big Data and Analytics for:, Digital Marketing for:, Machine Learning

Company Name: Hunters.AI
Description: The first autonomous threat hunting machine, helping organizations detect, identify and remediate sophisticated cyber attacks.
Website: http://www.hunters.ai
Phone: **Email:** info@hunters.ai
City: Tel Aviv **State:** TA **PC:** **Country:** Israel
Year Established: **Status 2020:** Active
Industries: Artificial Intelligence for:, Cyber Security for:, Machine Learning for:, Security

Company Name: Hybrid Security
Description: Hybrid Security is a cyber-security company that offers behavior-based web fraud detection.
Website: http://www.hybridsec.com
Phone: **Email:** 36726@reference-encyclopedia-ai.net
City: Tel Aviv **State:** Tel Aviv District **PC:** **Country:** Israel
Year Established: 2010 **Status 2020:** Closed
Industries:

Company Name: ImmunAI
Description: ImmunAI provides a platform that combines biology with machine-learning to unravel the immune system.
Website: http://www.immunai.com/
Phone: **Email:** press@immunai.com
City: Tel Aviv **State:** Tel Aviv District **PC:** **Country:** Israel
Year Established: 2019 **Status 2020:** Active
Industries: Analytics for:, Artificial Intelligence for:, ~ Biotechnology (9), IT Managed Services

Company Name: InFASH
Description: InFASH provides a fashion social-commerce platform that allows users to post stylish looks.
Website: http://www.infash.com/
Phone: **Email:** 36758@reference-encyclopedia-ai.net
City: Tel Aviv **State:** TA **PC:** **Country:** Israel
Year Established: 2017 **Status 2020:** Active
Industries: Artificial Intelligence for:, ~ Banking and Financial Markets-Services (7), ~ Fashion (16), IT Managed Services

Company Name: infiBond
Description: Infi's technology enables machines to process emotion and replicate the psychological functioning of the human brain.
Website: http://www.infibond.com
Phone: 972.3.576.9961 **Email:** contact@infibond.com
City: Tel Aviv **State:** Tel Aviv District **PC:** **Country:** Israel
Year Established: 2013 **Status 2020:** Active
Industries: Artificial Intelligence for:, Machine Learning for:, ~ Healthcare (20)

Company Name: InfiniGrow
Description: InfiniGrow is an AI-driven marketing planning platform that enables marketers to optimally allocate their budget to achieve their KPIs.
Website: http://infinigrow.com
Phone: **Email:** info@infinigrow.com
City: Tel Aviv **State:** Tel Aviv District **PC:** **Country:** Israel
Year Established: 2017 **Status 2020:** Active
Industries: Analytics for:, Artificial Intelligence for:, Big Data and Analytics for:, Business Software as a Service Apps (SaaS Apps)

Company Name: Innoviz Technologies
Description: Innoviz delivers the vision and intelligence required for the mass-production of autonomous vehicles.
Website: http://www.innoviz.tech/
Phone: (9729) 955-9218 **Email:** info@innoviz.tech
City: Tel Aviv **State:** Tel Aviv District **PC:** **Country:** Israel
Year Established: 2016 **Status 2020:** Active
Industries: Artificial Intelligence for:, ~ Automotive (5), ~ Automotive (5), ~ Telecommunications (56), Robotics

Company Name: Intelici
Description: Intelici is a network security company specializing in cyber Intelligence detection and protection system.
Website: http://www.intelici.com/
Phone: **Email:** info@intelici.com
City: Tel Aviv **State:** Tel Aviv District **PC:** **Country:** Israel
Year Established: 2016 **Status 2020:** Active
Industries: Big Data and Analytics for:, Cyber Security for:, Machine Learning for:, Security

Company Name: Intelligent Smart Ideas
Description: Intelligent Smart Ideas creates technological solutions for life-endangering incidents with an innovative approach and powerful design.
Website: http://intelligentsmartid.wix.com/intelligentsmartidea
Phone: **Email:** 36790@reference-encyclopedia-ai.net
City: Tel Aviv **State:** Tel Aviv District **PC:** **Country:** Israel
Year Established: 2015 **Status 2020:** Active
Industries: Artificial Intelligence for:, ~ Government (19), ~ Construction (10)

Company Name: Intelligent Traffic Control
Description: Traffic management solutions
Website: http://itc-israel.co.il/
Phone: 972-077-6021160 **Email:** info@itc-israel.co.: Israel
City: Tel Aviv **State:** Tel Aviv District **PC:** **Country:** Israel
Year Established: 2019 **Status 2020:** Active
Industries: Artificial Intelligence for:, ~ Automotive (5), Machine Learning for:, ~ Construction (10)

Company Name: Intelligo Heal:Thailand
Description: Intelligo Health is developing an automated intelligence.
Website: http://intelligo-health.com
Phone: **Email:** info@Intelligo-health.com
City: Tel Aviv **State:** Tel Aviv District **PC:** **Country:** Israel
Year Established: 2016 **Status 2020:** Active
Industries: Artificial Intelligence for:, ~ Healthcare (20)

Company Name: Interactbot
Description: Interactbot develops an innovative enterprise chatbot platform that unlike its competitors.
Website:
Phone: **Email:** 36796@reference-encyclopedia-ai.net
City: Tel Aviv **State:** TA **PC:** **Country:** Israel
Year Established: 2016 **Status 2020:** Closed
Industries:

Company Name: Intervyo
Description: Intervyo is the world's first automated interviewing system, that screens candidates for recruiters and accurately predicts job suitability.
Website: http://www.intervyo.com
Phone: **Email:** contact@intervyo.com
City: Tel Aviv **State:** Tel Aviv District **PC:** **Country:** Israel
Year Established: 2014 **Status 2020:** Active
Industries: Predictive Analytics

Company Name: Inthegame
Description: Inthegame builds apps gamifying the viewing experience of eSports and live broadcast, powered by computer vision & AI
Website: http://www.inthegame.io
Phone: **Email:** aviram@inthegame.io
City: Tel Aviv **State:** Tel Aviv District **PC:** **Country:** Israel
Year Established: 2017 **Status 2020:** Active
Industries: Artificial Intelligence for:, ~ Arts-Entertainment-Recreation (4)

Company Name: iXDen
Description: Securing IoT devices of ICS systems. Invented "biometric-like" IoT Device Identity and Authentication using mathematics and AI
Website: http://www.ixden.com
Phone: **Email:** Zion.Harel@iXDen.com
City: Tel Aviv **State:** Tel Aviv District **PC:** **Country:** Israel
Year Established: 2017 **Status 2020:** Active
Industries: Artificial Intelligence for:, Cyber Security for:, Internet of Things (IoT)

Company Name: Jenna AI
Description: SaaS AI driven solution that automatically questions and screens candidates allowing better hiring process
Website: http://www.jenna.ai
Phone: **Email:** 36825@reference-encyclopedia-ai.net
City: Tel Aviv **State:** Tel Aviv District **PC:** **Country:** Israel
Year Established: 2018 **Status 2020:** Active
Industries:

Company Name: JoVo App Ltd.
Description: Mobile app helping companies to optimize their recruiting processes with big data analytics and machine learning
Website: http://www.jovoapp.com
Phone: 917-809-5100 **Email:** hello@jovoapp.com
City: Tel Aviv **State:** Tel Aviv District **PC:** **Country:** Israel
Year Established: 2016 **Status 2020:** Active
Industries: Analytics for:, Machine Learning for:, Application Services

Company Name: Juno.AI
Description: Juno.AI develops an advanced technology for child protection in education facilities.
Website: http://www.junoai.co
Phone: **Email:** 36834@reference-encyclopedia-ai.net
City: Tel Aviv **State:** Tel Aviv District **PC:** **Country:** Israel
Year Established: 2019 **Status 2020:** Active
Industries: Artificial Intelligence for:, ~ Social Assistance-Non-Profits (53), ~ Administrative and Support Services (1), ~ Government (19), Security

Company Name: Kaleidoo
Description: Kaleidoo improves actionable business insights via advanced AI technology, products and services.
Website: http://www.kaleidoo.co/
Phone: **Email:** 36837@reference-encyclopedia-ai.net
City: Tel Aviv **State:** Tel Aviv District **PC:** **Country:** Israel
Year Established: 2019 **Status 2020:** Active
Industries: Artificial Intelligence for:, Big Data and Analytics

Company Name: Kami
Description: Kami develops an emotionally enabled, conversational AI for voice platforms.
Website: http://kamicomputing.com/
Phone: **Email:** info@kamicomputing.com
City: Tel Aviv **State:** Tel Aviv District **PC:** **Country:** Israel
Year Established: 2016 **Status 2020:** Active
Industries: Artificial Intelligence for:, Web

Company Name: KanduAI
Description: AI as a Service on edge devices, focused on commercial IoT
Website: http://www.kanduai.com
Phone: 972-73-374-2863 **Email:** contact@kanduai.com
City: Tel Aviv **State:** TA **PC:** **Country:** Israel
Year Established: **Status 2020:** Active
Industries: Artificial Intelligence for:, Facial Recognition for:, Image Recognition for:, Machine Learning

Company Name: Katif
Description: Autonomous, Robotic and Vertical farms for Cannabis and food cro: Palestine
Website: http://www.katif.com
Phone: **Email:** info@katif.com
City: Tel Aviv **State:** TA **PC:** **Country:** Israel
Year Established: **Status 2020:** Active
Industries: ~ Agriculture (3), ~ Agriculture (3), Artificial Intelligence for:, ~ Agriculture (3), ~ Agriculture (3), Robotics

Company Name: Knowsome
Description: Knowsome harnesses AI to identify learning opportunities and turn them into a personal Life Long Learning journey
Website: http://www.itsknowsome.com/
Phone: **Email:** info@itsknowsome.com
City: Tel Aviv **State:** TA **PC:** **Country:** Israel
Year Established: 2017 **Status 2020:** Active
Industries: Artificial Intelligence for:, ~ Education (13)

Company Name: Komoona
Description: Komoona is a dynamic yield optimization platform.
Website: http://www.komoona.com
Phone: **Email:** feedback@komoona.com
City: Tel Aviv **State:** Tel Aviv District **PC:** **Country:** Israel
Year Established: 2011 **Status 2020:** Active
Industries: IT Managed Services for:, Web for:, Machine Learning for:, Mobile

Company Name: Landly.AI
Description: AI-driven Realtor
Website: http://landly.ai
Phone: **Email:** ping@landly.ai
City: Tel Aviv **State:** Tel Aviv District **PC:** **Country:** Israel
Year Established: 2019 **Status 2020:** Active
Industries: Web for:, Machine Learning for:, ~ Real Estate (49), ~ Real Estate (49), ~ Real Estate (49)

Company Name: LawGeex
Description: LawGeex is an Israel-based contract review platform that helps businesses by using AI.
Website: http://www.lawgeex.com/
Phone: (929) 503 9093 **Email:** hello@lawgeex.com
City: Tel Aviv **State:** Tel Aviv District **PC:** **Country:** Israel
Year Established: 2014 **Status 2020:** Active
Industries: Analytics for:, Artificial Intelligence for:, Big Data and Analytics for:, Machine Learning for:, Business Software as a Service Apps (SaaS Apps)

Company Name: Leadgence
Description: Leadgence uses big data and AI to identify customers in the buying window and dramatically improve B2B sales performance.
Website: http://www.leadgence.com
Phone: **Email:** contact@leadgence.com
City: Tel Aviv **State:** Tel Aviv District **PC:** **Country:** Israel
Year Established: 2018 **Status 2020:** Active
Industries: Artificial Intelligence for:, Predictive Analytics

Company Name: Leaperr
Description: Leaperr is a smart AI autonomous Interior Design system capable of designing interior spaces by itself
Website: http://leaperr.com/
Phone: **Email:** info@leaperr.com
City: Tel Aviv **State:** TA **PC:** **Country:** Israel
Year Established: **Status 2020:** Active
Industries: Artificial Intelligence for:, Big Data and Analytics for:, E-Commerce for:, Image Recognition for:, ~ Professional Services (48)

Company Name: Legal Automation
Description: Legal Automation is a software company that focuses on providing products intended for Underwriting and Claim Adjustment.
Website: http://www.paralegal.io/
Phone: **Email:** info@paralegal.io
City: Tel Aviv **State:** Tel Aviv District **PC:** **Country:** Israel
Year Established: 2017 **Status 2020:** Active
Industries: Artificial Intelligence

Company Name: Legally
Description: AI-powered marketplace for lawyers and customers that transforms legalese to plain language.
Website: http://www.legally.space
Phone: **Email:** contact@legally.space
City: Tel Aviv **State:** Tel Aviv District **PC:** **Country:** Israel
Year Established: 2017 **Status 2020:** Active
Industries:

Company Name: LitiGate
Description: AI-Powered Litigation Platform
Website: http://www.litigate.ai
Phone: **Email:** hello@litigate.ai
City: Tel Aviv **State:** TA **PC:** **Country:** Israel
Year Established: 2017 **Status 2020:** Active
Industries: Artificial Intelligence for:, Machine Learning for:, Data Management

Company Name: LIVV
Description: LIVV is a rental apartment search app developing an AI-powered real estate agent app.
Website: http://www.livv.co
Phone: **Email:** community@livv.co
City: Tel Aviv **State:** Tel Aviv District **PC:** **Country:** Israel
Year Established: 2018 **Status 2020:** Active
Industries: Application Services for:, Artificial Intelligence for:, Big Data and Analytics for:, Web for:, Machine Learning

Company Name: Magic Square
Description: Magic Square provides systematic trading powered by artificial intelligence with zero coding.
Website: http://www.msq.ai
Phone: **Email:** 36931@reference-encyclopedia-ai.net
City: Tel Aviv **State:** Tel Aviv District **PC:** **Country:** Israel
Year Established: 2019 **Status 2020:** Active
Industries: Artificial Intelligence for:, IT Managed Services for:, Predictive Analytics

Company Name: Manto AI
Description: Manto AI predicts which employees might resign, when and why, using a unique combination of AI algorithms, and domain expertise.
Website: http://www.manto-ai.com
Phone: **Email:** guy@manto-ai.com
City: Tel Aviv **State:** Tel Aviv District **PC:** **Country:** Israel
Year Established: 2018 **Status 2020:** Active
Industries: Analytics for:, Artificial Intelligence for:, Enterprise Application Services for:, Machine Learning for:, Predictive Analytics for:, Business Software as a Service Apps (SaaS Apps)

Company Name: MDI Heal:Thailand
Description: MDI Health offers an AI-powered platform that provides unique decision support tools for personalized drug treatments.
Website: http://www.mdi.health/
Phone: **Email:** 36949@reference-encyclopedia-ai.net
City: Tel Aviv **State:** TA **PC:** **Country:** Israel
Year Established: 2019 **Status 2020:** Active
Industries: Artificial Intelligence for:, ~ Healthcare (20), Machine Learning for:, ~ Healthcare (20)

Company **Name:** MedHub-AI
Description: MedHub-AI develops deep-learning video analysis algorithms that provide accurate diagnostic insights and practical guidance for physicians.
Website: http://www.medhub-ai.com/
Phone: 972 (52) 5832020 **Email:** hello@medhub-ai.com
City: Tel Aviv **State:** Tel Aviv District **PC:** **Country:** Israel
Year Established: 2017 **Status 2020:** Active
Industries: Artificial Intelligence for:, IT Managed Services for:, Machine Learning for:, ~ Healthcare (20)

Company Name: Medint Medical Intelligence ltd.
Description: MedInt developed a unique algorithm-based technology system to identify and analyze health data insights to patients with chronic diseases.
Website: http://www.medint.io
Phone: (1628) 227-0024 **Email:** info@medint.io
City: Tel Aviv **State:** Tel Aviv District **PC:** **Country:** Israel
Year Established: 2016 **Status 2020:** Active
Industries: Artificial Intelligence for:, Big Data and Analytics for:, ~ Biotechnology (9), ~ Customer Relationship Management (11), ~ Healthcare (20), IT Managed Services for:, Machine Learning for:, ~ Healthcare (20), ~ Healthcare (20), Natural Language Processing

Company Name: Medorion
Description: Medorion solves health communication problems by incorporating AI, behavioral science, and marketing Technologies
Website: http://www.medorion.com
Phone: **Email:** info@medorion.com
City: Tel Aviv **State:** Tel Aviv District **PC:** **Country:** Israel
Year Established: 2017 **Status 2020:** Active
Industries: Artificial Intelligence for:, ~ Healthcare (20), ~ Healthcare (20)

Company Name: Meteo-Logic
Description: Meteo-Logic is a data analytics company; bringing unique algo-trading and weather prediction capabilities into the energy commodity market.
Website: http://www.meteo-logic.com
Phone: (9729) 742-6755 **Email:** info@meteo-logic.com
City: Tel Aviv **State:** Tel Aviv District **PC:** **Country:** Israel
Year Established: 2011 **Status 2020:** Active
Industries: Big Data and Analytics for:, ~ Energy and Utilities (14), Machine Learning

Company Name: Metis-BK
Description: Metis-BK provides platform that big knowledge that changes how organizations create knowledge.
Website: http://www.metismart.com/
Phone: **Email:** info@metis-intelligence.com
City: Tel Aviv **State:** TA **PC:** **Country:** Israel
Year Established: 2016 **Status 2020:** Active
Industries: Analytics for:, Artificial Intelligence for:, IT Managed Services for:, Machine Learning

Company Name: Minta
Description: Minta is an Artificial intelligence-driven video creation chatbot.
Website: http://www.withminta.com
Phone: **Email:** 36983@reference-encyclopedia-ai.net
City: Tel Aviv **State:** Tel Aviv District **PC:** **Country:** Israel
Year Established: 2018 **Status 2020:** Active
Industries: Artificial Intelligence

Company Name: Miron Derchansky
Description: Partner at iLab Ventures and Head of iLab Israel
Website: http://leoinnovationlab.com/
Phone: **Email:** miron@leoilab.com
City: Tel Aviv **State:** Tel Aviv District **PC:** **Country:** Israel
Year Established: 2015 **Status 2020:** Active
Industries: Computer Vision for:, ~ Healthcare (20), Machine Learning

Company Name: Mizo Tech
Description: Mizo is a company that provides needed tools in one click and gives the possibility of performing any action easily.
Website: http://www.mizo-wiz.com
Phone: **Email:** 36994@reference-encyclopedia-ai.net
City: Tel Aviv **State:** Tel Aviv District **PC:** **Country:** Israel
Year Established: 2010 **Status 2020:** Active
Industries: Predictive Analytics

Company Name: mmuze
Description: The leading voice shopping platform for reta: Israel
Website: http://www.mmuze.com
Phone: **Email:** info@mmuze.com
City: Tel Aviv **State:** Tel Aviv District **PC:** **Country:** Israel
Year Established: 2014 **Status 2020:** Active
Industries:

Company Name: Moonshot Marketing
Description: Moonshot is a technology-driven, online marketing company
Website: http://www.moonshot-marketing.com
Phone: 972-77-460-4472 **Email:** info@moonshot.co.: Israel
City: Tel Aviv **State:** Tel Aviv District **PC:** **Country:** Israel

Year Established: 2014 **Status 2020:** Active
Industries: Artificial Intelligence for:, Big Data and Analytics

Company Name: MyPart
Description: A game changing AI platform 'leapfrogging' song search within the Music Industry, allowing instant discovery of songs
Website: http://mypart.com
Phone: **Email:** my_art@mypart.com
City: Tel Aviv **State:** Tel Aviv District **PC:** **Country:** Israel
Year Established: 2017 **Status 2020:** Active
Industries: ~ Arts-Entertainment-Recreation (4), Artificial Intelligence for:, Machine Learning for:, ~ Arts-Entertainment-Recreation (4)

Company Name: Neefla Technologies Ltd.
Description: Automatic Bidding Platform For Advertisers using AI and ML algorithms
Website: http://www.neefla.com
Phone: (917) 387-4532 **Email:** sales@neefla.com
City: Tel Aviv **State:** Tel Aviv District **PC:** **Country:** Israel
Year Established: 2017 **Status 2020:** Active
Industries: Artificial Intelligence

Company Name: Neomatix
Description: Automated Tire Monitoring and Management for Vehicle Fleets
Website: http://www.neomatix.com/
Phone: 972 5 4653 4030 **Email:** info@neo-matix.com
City: Tel Aviv **State:** Tel Aviv District **PC:** **Country:** Israel
Year Established: 2011 **Status 2020:** Active
Industries: Computer Vision for:, IT Managed Services for:, Machine Learning

Company Name: Neowize
Description: NeoWize develops and provides e-commerce personalization solutions
Website: http://www.neowize.com
Phone: 1(925)392-5925 **Email:** contactus@neowize.com
City: Tel Aviv **State:** Tel Aviv District **PC:** **Country:** Israel
Year Established: 2016 **Status 2020:** Active
Industries: E-Commerce for:, IT Managed Services for:, Machine Learning

Company Name: NetOp CLD
Description: NetOp CLD develops an autonomous network operation SaaS that simplifies the operations of enterprise networking architecture.
Website: http://www.netop.cloud
Phone: **Email:** 37048@reference-encyclopedia-ai.net
City: Tel Aviv **State:** Tel Aviv District **PC:** **Country:** Israel
Year Established: 2019 **Status 2020:** Active
Industries: ~ Automotive (5), Machine Learning for:, Business Software as a Service Apps (SaaS Apps)

Company Name: Neuledge
Description: Helps business and corporations to convert their data to a private and reliable knowledge-base.
Website: http://neuledge.com/
Phone: **Email:** hi@neuledge.com
City: Tel Aviv **State:** TA **PC:** **Country:** Israel
Year Established: **Status 2020:** Active
Industries: Artificial Intelligence for:, Big Data and Analytics for:, Natural Language Processing for:, Cyber Security for:, Content for:, Cyber Security

Company Name: NeuraLegion
Description: SaaS, Cyber-Security, Machine Learning
Website: http://www.neuralegion.com/
Phone: **Email:** info@NeuraLegion.com
City: Tel Aviv **State:** TA **PC:** **Country:** Israel
Year Established: **Status 2020:** Active
Industries: Artificial Intelligence for:, Cyber Security for:, IT Managed Services for:, Security for:, Security

Company Name: Neuron Vision
Description: Neuron Vision is building deep learning rapid POC and solutions for startup companies.
Website: http://www.neuron.vision/
Phone: 972-054-7629366 **Email:** contact@neuron.vision
City: Tel Aviv **State:** Tel Aviv District **PC:** **Country:** Israel
Year Established: 2016 **Status 2020:** Active
Industries: Artificial Intelligence for:, IT Managed Services

Company Name: Nibi
Description: Nibi is an artificial intelligence engine that translates the natural language to SQL.
Website: http://nibi.ai
Phone: **Email:** 37064@reference-encyclopedia-ai.net
City: Tel Aviv **State:** Tel Aviv District **PC:** **Country:** Israel
Year Established: 2018 **Status 2020:** Active
Industries: Artificial Intelligence for:, IT Managed Services for:, Security

Company Name: NoTraffic
Description: Traffic management platform based on smart sensors which prepares the road infrastructure for the connected and autonomous era.
Website: http://notraffic.tech
Phone: **Email:** Contact@notraffic.tech
City: Tel Aviv **State:** TA **PC:** **Country:** Israel
Year Established: **Status 2020:** Active
Industries: Artificial Intelligence for:, ~ Automotive (5), Web for:, ~ Government (19), ~ Transportation and Logistics (57), ~ Manufacturing-Electronic (30), ~ Construction (10), ~ Transportation and Logistics (57)

Company Name: NSure.ai
Description: NSure.ai uses an advanced AI technology to provide insurance-backed protection against digital gift-card fraud.
Website: http://www.nsureai.com
Phone: **Email:** Info@nsure.ai.com
City: Tel Aviv **State:** Tel Aviv District **PC:** **Country:** Israel
Year Established: 2019 **Status 2020:** Active
Industries: Artificial Intelligence for:, Security for:, Machine Learning for:, Security

Company Name: Nucleai
Description: Nucleai is an AI Healthcare startup in the pathology domain.
Website: http://www.nucleaimd.com
Phone: **Email:** pharma@nucleaimd.com
City: Tel Aviv **State:** Tel Aviv District **PC:** **Country:** Israel
Year Established: 2017 **Status 2020:** Active
Industries: Artificial Intelligence for:, ~ Healthcare (20), Machine Learning

Company Name: Octopus Heal:Thailand
Description: Octopus.Health is a patient engagement platform for proactive population health.
Website: http://www.octopus.heal:Thailand
Phone: **Email:** info@octopus.heal:Thailand
City: Tel Aviv **State:** Tel Aviv District **PC:** **Country:** Israel
Year Established: 2017 **Status 2020:** Active
Industries:

Company Name: OMGwhen
Description: OMGwhen is a web & mobile platform where users can find near by events.
Website: http://omgwhen.com/
Phone: **Email:** 37098@reference-encyclopedia-ai.net
City: Tel Aviv **State:** Tel Aviv District **PC:** **Country:** Israel
Year Established: 2014 **Status 2020:** Active
Industries: Application Services for:, ~ Event Management (15), Machine Learning

Company Name: Optibus
Description: Optibus is a SaaS platform for planning and running mass transportation through advanced artificial intelligence and algorithms.
Website: http://www.optibus.com
Phone: **Email:** info@optibus.com
City: Tel Aviv **State:** Tel Aviv District **PC:** **Country:** Israel
Year Established: 2014 **Status 2020:** Active
Industries: Artificial Intelligence for:, ~ Government (19), ~ Transportation and Logistics (57), Business Software as a Service Apps (SaaS Apps)

Company Name: Otaiot
Description: Otaiot specializes in over the air AI and IOT controllers programming.
Website: http://www.ota-iot.com
Phone: **Email:** eladkaner@gmail.com
City: Tel Aviv **State:** Tel Aviv District **PC:** **Country:** Israel
Year Established: 2018 **Status 2020:** Active
Industries: Artificial Intelligence for:, IT Managed Services for:, Internet of Things (IoT) for:, Application Services

Company Name: Otica.ai
Description: Otica is a LegalTech platform designed to help legal professionals share and monetize their knowledge.
Website: http://www.otica.ai
Phone: **Email:** info@otica.ai
City: Tel Aviv **State:** Tel Aviv District **PC:** **Country:** Israel
Year Established: 2017 **Status 2020:** Active
Industries: Artificial Intelligence for:, Big Data and Analytics for:, Web

Company Name: OurCart
Description: OurCart helps CPG marketers collect offline purchase data to gain insights into shopper behavior across channels.
Website: http://ourcart.com
Phone: **Email:** contact@ourcart.com
City: Tel Aviv **State:** Tel Aviv District **PC:** **Country:** Israel
Year Established: 2013 **Status 2020:** Active
Industries: Artificial Intelligence for:, IT Managed Services for:, Mobile for:, ~ Retail and Consumer Products (52)

Company **Name:** Outermeasure
Description: Outermeasure develops sustainable solutions for business growth, supply chain analytics, and AI consulting.
Website: http://www.outermeasure.com
Phone: **Email:** 37129@reference-encyclopedia-ai.net
City: Tel Aviv **State:** Tel Aviv District **PC:** **Country:** Israel
Year Established: 2018 **Status 2020:** Active
Industries: Analytics

Company Name: OwnHeal:Thailand
Description: Developing unique electro-optic technologies designed to allow home diagnostics.
Website:
Phone: **Email:** 37132@reference-encyclopedia-ai.net
City: Tel Aviv **State:** Tel Aviv District **PC:** **Country:** Israel
Year Established: 2013 **Status 2020:** Active
Industries: ~ Healthcare (20), Machine Learning for:, Mobile

Company Name: Ozen Solutions
Description: Sound-based, real-time detection and prediction of mechanical faults in advance
Website: http://www.ozen.solutions
Phone: **Email:** info@ozen.solutions
City: Tel Aviv **State:** Tel Aviv District **PC:** **Country:** Israel
Year Established: 2016 **Status 2020:** Active
Industries: Artificial Intelligence for:, IT Managed Services for:, ~ Telecommunications (56), Machine Learning

Company Name: Package.ai
Description: PACKAGE.AI is a software and Artificial Intelligence (AI) for optimizing last-mile delivery operations and experiences.
Website: http://package.ai/
Phone: **Email:** 37135@reference-encyclopedia-ai.net
City: Tel Aviv **State:** Tel Aviv District **PC:** **Country:** Israel
Year Established: 2016 **Status 2020:** Active
Industries: Artificial Intelligence for:, ~ Customer Relationship Management (11), ~ Transportation and Logistics (57), ~ Telecommunications (56)

Company Name: Pagaya Investments
Description: Pagaya is a fin-tech company that aims to reshape the asset management space using machine learning and big data analytics.
Website: http://www.pagaya.com/
Phone: 347.884.5589 **Email:** info@pagaya-inv.com
City: Tel Aviv **State:** TA **PC:** **Country:** Israel
Year Established: 2016 **Status 2020:** Active
Industries: Artificial Intelligence for:, Big Data and Analytics for:, ~ Banking and Financial Markets-Services (7), ~ Banking and Financial Markets-Services (7), Machine Learning

Company Name: Pairsonal
Description: Pairsonal is an innovative authentication platform that provides issuers the ability to prevent all types of fraud and misuse in fuel cards.
Website: http://www.pairsonal.com
Phone: **Email:** support@pairsonal.com
City: Tel Aviv **State:** Tel Aviv District **PC:** **Country:** Israel
Year Established: 2017 **Status 2020:** Active
Industries: ~ Telecommunications (56), Machine Learning for:, Security

Company Name: PAI-TECH
Description: PAI-TECH has developed a brand-new Bot Operating System Standard which provides a digital workforce of intelligent bots.
Website: http://pai-tech.org/
Phone: **Email:** contact@pai-tech.org
City: Tel Aviv **State:** Tel Aviv District **PC:** **Country:** Israel
Year Established: 2018 **Status 2020:** Active
Industries: Artificial Intelligence for:, IT Managed Services for:, Web

Company Name: ParaGroup
Description: ParaGroup implements Artificial Intelligence in the infrastructure industries that aim for optimization of execution at early design stages.
Website: http://www.paragroup.org
Phone: **Email:** 37140@reference-encyclopedia-ai.net
City: Tel Aviv **State:** Tel Aviv District **PC:** **Country:** Israel
Year Established: 2012 **Status 2020:** Active
Industries: Artificial Intelligence for:, Machine Learning

Company Name: Pecan
Description: The Pecan Platform automates the entire predictive analytics process, reducing "time-to-model" from months to days.
Website: http://www.pecan.ai
Phone: **Email:** info@pecan.ai
City: Tel Aviv **State:** Tel Aviv District **PC:** **Country:** Israel
Year Established: 2016 **Status 2020:** Active
Industries:

Company Name: Pentom
Description: Pentom provides intelligent automated penetration testing solutions.
Website: http://pentom.herokuapp.com
Phone: 972 52 8136 894 **Email:** help.pentom@gmail.com
City: Tel Aviv **State:** Tel Aviv District **PC:** **Country:** Israel
Year Established: 2017 **Status 2020:** Active
Industries: Cyber Security for:, ~ Education (13), Machine Learning

Company Name: Perceptive AI
Description: Machine Learning Customer Success = <3
Website: http://www.prcptv.ai
Phone: **Email:** guy@prcptv.ai
City: Tel Aviv **State:** TA **PC:** **Country:** Israel
Year Established: 2017 **Status 2020:** Active
Industries: Analytics for:, Artificial Intelligence for:, Business Applications for:, Predictive Analytics for:, Business Software as a Service Apps (SaaS Apps)

Company Name: Phi-G
Description: Phi-G develops precision management and targeting sleeping disorder that takes all the multi-disturbing actors stimulant.
Website: http://www.phi-g.com
Phone: **Email:** assaf@phi-g.com
City: Tel Aviv **State:** TA **PC:** **Country:** Israel
Year Established: 2018 **Status 2020:** Active
Industries: Artificial Intelligence for:, ~ Healthcare (20), Machine Learning

Company Name: Phish.AI
Description: Next-Generation Anti-Phishing Platform Powered by AI & Computer Vision
Website: http://www.phish.ai
Phone: **Email:** info@phish.ai
City: Tel Aviv **State:** Tel Aviv District **PC:** **Country:** Israel
Year Established: 2018 **Status 2020:** Active
Industries:

Company Name: Picup
Description: PicUP is an AI based visualization, optimization and personalization platform for outbound calls.
Website: http://picup.io
Phone: **Email:** contact@picup.io
City: Tel Aviv **State:** Tel Aviv District **PC:** **Country:** Israel
Year Established: 2017 **Status 2020:** Active
Industries: Artificial Intelligence for:, ~ Customer Relationship Management (11)

Company **Name:** PlainSight Intel LLC
Description: Our technology powers a new generation of competitive intelligence solutions. Say goodbye to Google Alerts and endless Google Searches!
Website: http://www.plainsightintel.com
Phone: 214-499-8973 **Email:** sales@plainsightintel.com
City: Tel Aviv **State:** Tel Aviv District **PC:** **Country:** Israel
Year Established: 2015 **Status 2020:** Active
Industries: IT Managed Services for:, Internet of Things (IoT) for:, Machine Learning

Company Name: Platica
Description: Vertical uses language technology to help brands offer top of the line support while building meaningful relationships with their customers.
Website: http://www.platica.com
Phone: **Email:** hello@platica.com
City: Tel Aviv **State:** Tel Aviv District **PC:** **Country:** Israel
Year Established: 2015 **Status 2020:** Active
Industries: Artificial Intelligence for:, ~ Customer Relationship Management (11), IT Managed Services for:, Mobile for:, Business Software as a Service Apps (SaaS Apps)

Company Name: Powhere
Description: Powhere develops a solution for electric vehicle drivers to manage the way they charge their cars.
Website: http://www.powhere.co
Phone: 972 52-696-4455 **Email:** info@powhere.co
City: Tel Aviv **State:** Tel Aviv District **PC:** **Country:** Israel
Year Established: 2017 **Status 2020:** Active
Industries: Artificial Intelligence for:, ~ Automotive (5), ~ Automotive (5), Machine Learning

Company Name: PREDICTA MED
Description: PREDICTA MED offers solutions for the treatment of autoimmune diseases by artificial intelligence.
Website: http://www.predicta-med.com/
Phone: **Email:** 37197@reference-encyclopedia-ai.net
City: Tel Aviv **State:** Tel Aviv District **PC:** **Country:** Israel
Year Established: 2020 **Status 2020:** Active
Industries: Artificial Intelligence for:, ~ Healthcare (20), ~ Healthcare (20)

Company Name: ProBot
Description: ProBot is an Artificial Intelligence start up that talks about business applications.
Website:
Phone: **Email:** 37210@reference-encyclopedia-ai.net
City: Tel Aviv **State:** TA **PC:** **Country:** Israel
Year Established: 2016 **Status 2020:** Closed
Industries: Application Services for:, Artificial Intelligence

Company Name: Pudding.ai
Description: Machine Learning for Better Creative
Website: http://pudding.ai
Phone: **Email:** 37747@reference-encyclopedia-ai.net
City: Tel Aviv **State:** Tel Aviv District **PC:** **Country:** Israel
Year Established: 2017 **Status 2020:** Active
Industries: Artificial Intelligence for:, Big Data and Analytics for:, Machine Learning

Company Name: Pulsee
Description: Predictive People Analytics Platform
Website: http://www.pulsee.io/
Phone: **Email:** 37226@reference-encyclopedia-ai.net
City: Tel Aviv **State:** Tel Aviv District **PC:** **Country:** Israel
Year Established: 2018 **Status 2020:** Active
Industries: Analytics for:, Artificial Intelligence for:, IT Managed Services for:, Machine Learning

Company Name: Pzartech
Description: Pzartech reduces downtime through the visual recognition of mechanical spare parts.
Website: http://www.pzartech.com/
Phone: **Email:** info@pzartech.com
City: Tel Aviv **State:** Tel Aviv District **PC:** **Country:** Israel
Year Established: 2015 **Status 2020:** Active
Industries: ~ Aerospace and Defense (2), Artificial Intelligence for:, Image Recognition for:, ~ Manufacturing-General (31), IT Managed Services for:, IT Managed Services for:, Machine Learning for:, Computer Vision for:, Computer Vision

Company Name: Q.AI
Description: Q.AI is an intelligent healthcare resource management system.
Website: http://www.queueai.com
Phone: **Email:** 37229@reference-encyclopedia-ai.net
City: Tel Aviv **State:** Tel Aviv District **PC:** **Country:** Israel
Year Established: 2019 **Status 2020:** Active
Industries:

Company Name: Qsee
Description: Qsee offers real-time predictive insights solutions to prevent defective products.
Website: http://www.qsee.io
Phone: 1 (646) 480-0026 **Email:** info@qsee.io
City: Tel Aviv **State:** Tel Aviv District **PC:** **Country:** Israel
Year Established: 2017 **Status 2020:** Active
Industries: Artificial Intelligence for:, Internet of Things (IoT) for:, Predictive Analytics for:, Business Process and Operations

Company Name: Quali.fit
Description: Quali.fit is an AI assistant for recruiting and staffing firms EI4474(SaaS, B2b)
Website: http://www.quali.f: Italy
Phone: 972 545 875 200 **Email:** info@quali.f: Italy
City: Tel Aviv **State:** Tel Aviv District **PC:** **Country:** Israel

Year Established: 2016 **Status 2020:** Active
Industries: Artificial Intelligence

Company Name: RAD-ACE
Description: RAD-ACE develops an application performance management tool based on wire data analytics and machine learning.
Website: http://www.rad-ace.com
Phone: **Email:** 37253@reference-encyclopedia-ai.net
City: Tel Aviv **State:** Tel Aviv District **PC:** **Country:** Israel
Year Established: 2016 **Status 2020:** Active
Industries: Analytics for:, Artificial Intelligence for:, IT Managed Services for:, Machine Learning

Company Name: Random Forest Ltd
Description: Random Forest VC is an early-stage VC focusing on market disruptive ventures, based on cutting-edge Machine Learning and Artificial Intelligence.
Website: http://www.randomforestvc.com/
Phone: **Email:** sigal@randomforestvc.com
City: Tel Aviv **State:** TA **PC:** **Country:** Israel
Year Established: **Status 2020:** Active
Industries: Artificial Intelligence for:, ~ Banking and Financial Markets-Services (7), Databases for:, Machine Learning

Company Name: Raycat: Switzerland
Description: Pure SaaS product that provides actionable insights to operators & owners of solar plants that can significantly enhance the project yield.
Website: http://www.raycatch.com
Phone: **Email:** info@raycatch.com
City: Tel Aviv **State:** Tel Aviv District **PC:** **Country:** Israel
Year Established: 2015 **Status 2020:** Active
Industries: Analytics for:, Artificial Intelligence for:, Big Data and Analytics for:, ~ Energy and Utilities (14), ~ Energy and Utilities (14), Predictive Analytics for:, ~ Energy and Utilities (14), Business Software as a Service Apps (SaaS Apps) for:, Business Software as Service

Company Name: RayGo
Description: A "handsfree for apps" based on technology developed for the blind
Website:
Phone: **Email:** 37264@reference-encyclopedia-ai.net
City: Tel Aviv **State:** Tel Aviv District **PC:** **Country:** Israel
Year Established: 2013 **Status 2020:** Closed
Industries: ~ Customer Relationship Management (11), Application Services for:, Internet of Things (IoT) for:, ~ Government (19)

Company Name: Razor Labs
Description: Razor Labs is a leader in the AI industry and is your partner on the journey to ROI from AI.
Website: http://www.razor-labs.com/
Phone: 972.3.561.0901 **Email:** office@razor-labs.com
City: Tel Aviv **State:** Tel Aviv District **PC:** **Country:** Israel
Year Established: 2016 **Status 2020:** Active
Industries: Artificial Intelligence for:, Computer Vision for:, Automation for:, Machine Learning

Company Name: RealFace
Description: Realface is innovating user authentication with the worlds leading face recognition technology
Website: http://www.realfacetech.com
Phone: **Email:** info@realfacetech.com
City: Tel Aviv **State:** Tel Aviv District **PC:** **Country:** Israel
Year Established: 2014 **Status 2020:** Active
Industries: Application Services for:, Computer Vision for:, Machine Learning for:, ~ Social Assistance-Non-Profits (53)

Company Name: RealFriend
Description: RealFriend is developing an A.I. personal assistant for all things real estate.
Website: http://www.realfriend.ai
Phone: **Email:** 37270@reference-encyclopedia-ai.net
City: Tel Aviv **State:** Tel Aviv District **PC:** **Country:** Israel
Year Established: 2018 **Status 2020:** Active
Industries: Artificial Intelligence

Company Name: Rephraser.ai
Description: Rephraser is a language learning platform that develops a business solution that translates languages.
Website: http://www.rephraser.ai
Phone: **Email:** 37288@reference-encyclopedia-ai.net
City: Tel Aviv **State:** Tel Aviv District **PC:** **Country:** Israel
Year Established: 2019 **Status 2020:** Active
Industries: Artificial Intelligence for:, ~ Education (13), ~ Education (13)

Company Name: Reps AI
Description: Reps AI increases customer satisfaction for across the different customers' service touchpoints with our realtime assistant
Website: http://www.reps.ai
Phone: **Email:** info@reps.ai
City: Tel Aviv **State:** Tel Aviv District **PC:** **Country:** Israel
Year Established: 2017 **Status 2020:** Active
Industries: Artificial Intelligence for:, ~ Customer Relationship Management (11), IT Managed Services

Company Name: Rewire
Description: Rewire is an artificial intelligence company that helps to overcome the difficulties associated with migraines.
Website: http://www.rewiredigitalhealth.com
Phone: **Email:** info@rewiredigitalhealth.com
City: Tel Aviv **State:** Tel Aviv District **PC:** **Country:** Israel
Year Established: 2016 **Status 2020:** Active
Industries: Artificial Intelligence for:, ~ Healthcare (20), ~ Healthcare (20)

Company Name: Rise.ai
Description: Rise.ai provides automated branded currency solutions for brands and retailers.
Website: http://www.rise-ai.com
Phone: 1-646-878-6419 **Email:** info@rise-ai.com
City: Tel Aviv **State:** Tel Aviv District **PC:** **Country:** Israel
Year Established: 2015 **Status 2020:** Active
Industries: Analytics for:, Artificial Intelligence for:, Web

Company Name: Riskified
Description: Riskified designs an e-commerce fraud-prevention technology that turns fraud management into a growth engine for online retailers.
Website: http://www.riskified.com/
Phone: 1(855)622-5868 **Email:** sales@riskified.com
City: Tel Aviv **State:** Tel Aviv District **PC:** **Country:** Israel
Year Established: 2012 **Status 2020:** Active
Industries:

Company Name: Roby.AI
Description: Roby offers an artificial intelligence assistant for rental agencies and property managers.
Website: http://roby.ai
Phone: **Email:** roby@roby.ai
City: Tel Aviv **State:** Tel Aviv District **PC:** **Country:** Israel
Year Established: 2017 **Status 2020:** Active
Industries: Artificial Intelligence for:, ~ Healthcare (20)

Company Name: Rootclaim
Description: Rootclaim is a collaborative analysis platform that change the way people understand complex issues.
Website: http://www.rootclaim.com
Phone: **Email:** 37314@reference-encyclopedia-ai.net
City: Tel Aviv **State:** Tel Aviv District **PC:** **Country:** Israel

Year Established: 2014 **Status 2020:** Active
Industries: Analytics for:, Artificial Intelligence for:, Augmented Reality

Company Name: Roundforest
Description: Roundforest empowers consumers with big data solutions.
Website: http://www.roundforest.com
Phone: **Email:** contact@roundforest.com
City: Tel Aviv **State:** Tel Aviv District **PC:** **Country:** Israel
Year Established: 2014 **Status 2020:** Active
Industries: Analytics for:, Big Data and Analytics for:, E-Commerce for:, Web for:, Machine Learning for:, Natural Language Processing for:, Predictive Analytics

Company Name: Roya Music
Description: Roya Music develops a digital radio music service based on free and personal taste and localization.
Website: http://shimon828.wix.com/roya
Phone: **Email:** 37317@reference-encyclopedia-ai.net
City: Tel Aviv **State:** Tel Aviv District **PC:** **Country:** Israel
Year Established: 2015 **Status 2020:** Active
Industries: Business Intelligence for:, ~ Arts-Entertainment-Recreation (4), ~ Arts-Entertainment-Recreation (4), Predictive Analytics

Company Name: RubiQ
Description: RubiQ empowers passengers to self manage disruptions through Artificial intelligence-based real-time communication.
Website: http://www.rubiq.tech
Phone: **Email:** amos.bj@rubiq.tech
City: Tel Aviv **State:** Tel Aviv District **PC:** **Country:** Israel
Year Established: 2018 **Status 2020:** Active
Industries: Artificial Intelligence for:, Machine Learning

Company Name: Rumble
Description: Rumble is an information technology company that provides managment solutions for media, retail, travel, and ad-tech companies.
Website:
Phone: **Email:** marketing@rumble.me
City: Tel Aviv **State:** Tel Aviv District **PC:** **Country:** Israel
Year Established: 2011 **Status 2020:** Active
Industries: Application Services for:, Data Management for:, Enterprise Application Services for:, IT Managed Services for:, Predictive Analytics

Company Name: Run:AI
Description: Run:AI develops an automated distributed training technology that virtualizes and accelerates deep learning.
Website: http://www.run.ai/
Phone: **Email:** info@run.ai
City: Tel Aviv **State:** TA **PC:** **Country:** Israel
Year Established: **Status 2020:** Active
Industries: Artificial Intelligence for:, IT Managed Services for:, ~ Education (13), ~ Manufacturing-Electronic (30), ~ Professional Services (48), ~ Education (13)

Company Name: Sage AI
Description: Sage AI develops an chatbot powered by artificial intelligence for customer service.
Website: http://www.sagetalk.io/
Phone: **Email:** support@sagetalk.io
City: Tel Aviv **State:** Tel Aviv District **PC:** **Country:** Israel
Year Established: 2017 **Status 2020:** Active
Industries: Artificial Intelligence for:, Automation for:, IT Managed Services

Company Name: Saillog
Description: Saillog is an artificial intelligence-based solution that enables farmers to identify and treat plant diseases and pests.
Website: http://www.saillog.co/
Phone: **Email:** nessi@saillog.co
City: Tel Aviv **State:** Tel Aviv District **PC:** **Country:** Israel
Year Established: 2017 **Status 2020:** Active
Industries: ~ Agriculture (3), ~ Agriculture (3), Artificial Intelligence for:, Computer Vision for:, ~ Agriculture (3), Application Services

Company Name: SAI
Description: SAIPS is a world-class provider of customized algorithmic solutions in the fields of computer vision and machine learning.
Website: http://www.saips.co.il/
Phone: **Email:** info@saips.co.: Israel
City: Tel Aviv **State:** Tel Aviv District **PC:** **Country:** Israel
Year Established: 2013 **Status 2020:** Active
Industries: Artificial Intelligence for:, Computer Vision for:, Enterprise Application Services for:, Machine Learning

Company Name: Salead
Description: Salead offers a business-to-business networking platform that creates qualified business opportunities and marketing business intelligence.
Website: http://gosalead.com
Phone: **Email:** info@gosalead.com
City: Tel Aviv **State:** Tel Aviv District **PC:** **Country:** Israel
Year Established: 2012 **Status 2020:** Active
Industries: Artificial Intelligence for:, Business Applications for:, IT Managed Services

Company Name: Scalez
Description: Conversational AI Platforms for Personalized Expert Advice Experienc: Spain
Website: http://www.scalez.ai
Phone: **Email:** hello@scalez.ai
City: Tel Aviv **State:** Tel Aviv District **PC:** **Country:** Israel
Year Established: 2019 **Status 2020:** Active
Industries: Artificial Intelligence for:, E-Commerce for:, Web for:, Machine Learning for:, Natural Language Processing

Company Name: Scientra
Description: Scientra is a unique startup that is redefining the frontiers of real-time prediction in a challenging market.
Website: http://www.scientra.com
Phone: **Email:** 37348@reference-encyclopedia-ai.net
City: Tel Aviv **State:** Tel Aviv District **PC:** **Country:** Israel
Year Established: 2013 **Status 2020:** Active
Industries: Analytics for:, Machine Learning

Company Name: Search: India
Description: Searchin is an AI powered talent sourcer discovering & analyzing candidates by skills, personality & company culture – all within minut: Spain
Website: http://searchinco.co
Phone: **Email:** team@searchinco.co
City: Tel Aviv **State:** Tel Aviv District **PC:** **Country:** Israel
Year Established: 2015 **Status 2020:** Active
Industries:

Company Name: Seekuence Labs
Description: Seekuence Labs is an AI platform offering an end-to-end solution for cloud simulations, data collections, and a real-time interception.
Website:
Phone: **Email:** 37355@reference-encyclopedia-ai.net
City: Tel Aviv **State:** Tel Aviv District **PC:** **Country:** Israel
Year Established: 2018 **Status 2020:** Closed
Industries: Analytics for:, Artificial Intelligence for:, Business Intelligence for:, Cyber Security for:, Enterprise Application Services

Company Name: SeeTrue
Description: SeeTrue is an AI-based automatic threat detection platform for security screening.
Website: http://www.seetrue.ai
Phone: 972 (074) 7366245 **Email:** info@seetrue.ai
City: Tel Aviv **State:** Tel Aviv District **PC:** **Country:** Israel

Year Established: 2018 **Status 2020:** Active
Industries: Artificial Intelligence for:, Machine Learning for:, Security

Company Name: SellerO: Palestine
Description: Helping online businesses sell better with artificial intelligence and human collaboration
Website: http://www.sellerops.com
Phone: **Email:** Contact@sellerops.com
City: Tel Aviv **State:** TA **PC:** **Country:** Israel
Year Established: **Status 2020:** Active
Industries: Artificial Intelligence for:, Business Applications for:, E-Commerce for:, ~ Media-Communications (41)

Company Name: Semantic Interfaces
Description: Semantic Interfaces is a software platform that translates language text and voice commands into application specific command language.
Website: http://semanticinterfaces.com
Phone: **Email:** 37359@reference-encyclopedia-ai.net
City: Tel Aviv **State:** Tel Aviv District **PC:** **Country:** Israel
Year Established: 2011 **Status 2020:** Active
Industries: Artificial Intelligence for:, Machine Learning for:, Speech Recognition

Company Name: Sense
Description: SenseIT is a web testing tool that provides accessibility solutions for public and private sector organizations.
Website: http://www.senseit360.com
Phone: **Email:** 37365@reference-encyclopedia-ai.net
City: Tel Aviv **State:** Tel Aviv District **PC:** **Country:** Israel
Year Established: 2019 **Status 2020:** Active
Industries: Analytics for:, Artificial Intelligence for:, Business Software as a Service Apps (SaaS Apps)

Company Name: Sentry Parental Control
Description: Sentry developed the best parental control app, which is nonintrusive on one hand and has the be
Website: http://www.sntry.io
Phone: **Email:** support@sntry.io
City: Tel Aviv **State:** Tel Aviv District **PC:** **Country:** Israel
Year Established: 2017 **Status 2020:** Active
Industries: Machine Learning for:, Mobile for:, ~ Education (13)

Company Name: Serendi Systems
Description: Serendi is a machine learning tool that specializes in analyzing handwritten paragraphs and converting it into a document file.
Website: http:// www.serendi.me/
Phone: **Email:** contact@serendi.me
City: Tel Aviv **State:** Tel Aviv District **PC:** **Country:** Israel
Year Established: 2016 **Status 2020:** Active
Industries: Application Services for:, Artificial Intelligence for:, Machine Learning for:, Web

Company Name: Servicefriend
Description: Servicefriend is a customer service bot for messaging.
Website: http://www.servicefriend.com/
Phone: **Email:** sales@servicefriend.com
City: Tel Aviv **State:** Tel Aviv District **PC:** **Country:** Israel
Year Established: 2015 **Status 2020:** Active
Industries: Artificial Intelligence for:, ~ Customer Relationship Management (11)

Company Name: Shibumi
Description: Shibumi provides data science solutions with artificial intelligence.
Website: http://www.shibumi-ai.com/
Phone: 972-054-309-1944 **Email:** info@shibumi-ai.com
City: Tel Aviv **State:** Tel Aviv District **PC:** **Country:** Israel
Year Established: 2016 **Status 2020:** Active
Industries: Artificial Intelligence

Company Name: Shieldren
Description: Providing protection for children by using advanced machine learning technology for the detection, prevention & prediction of online threats
Website:
Phone: **Email:** 37378@reference-encyclopedia-ai.net
City: Tel Aviv **State:** Tel Aviv District **PC:** **Country:** Israel
Year Established: 2017 **Status 2020:** - Closed
Industries: Web for:, Machine Learning for:, Application Services for:, ~ Education (13)

Company Name: Shoodoo Analytics
Description: Professional Predictive Analytics for Business Use: Serbia
Website: http://www.shoodoo.com/
Phone: **Email:** amir.raskin@shoodoo.com
City: Tel Aviv **State:** TA **PC:** **Country:** Israel
Year Established: 2015 **Status 2020:** Active
Industries: Analytics for:, Artificial Intelligence for:, Big Data and Analytics for:, Cloud for:, IT Managed Services for:, Machine Learning for:, Predictive Analytics

Company Name: Shopix
Description: Visual Content Made Shoppable
Website: http://shopixai.com/
Phone: **Email:** 37381@reference-encyclopedia-ai.net
City: Tel Aviv **State:** Tel Aviv District **PC:** **Country:** Israel
Year Established: 2018 **Status 2020:** Active
Industries: Artificial Intelligence for:, Computer Vision for:, E-Commerce for:, Business Software as a Service Apps (SaaS Apps) for:, Web for:, Computer Vision

Company Name: Shopta: Greece
Description: Your Personal Shopping Assistant
Website: http://shoptagr.com
Phone: **Email:** Jonathan@Shoptagr.com
City: Tel Aviv **State:** Tel Aviv District **PC:** **Country:** Israel
Year Established: 2013 **Status 2020:** Active
Industries: Application Services for:, Artificial Intelligence for:, E-Commerce for:, Application Services

Company Name: Sight Diagnostics
Description: Sight Diagnostics is a medical device company bringing affordable, accurate diagnostics to the point-of-care.
Website: http://www.sightdx.com/
Phone: **Email:** info@sightdx.com
City: Tel Aviv **State:** TA **PC:** **Country:** Israel
Year Established: 2011 **Status 2020:** Active
Industries:

Company Name: Sightec
Description: Computer Vision & AI for autonomous flights
Website: http://www.sightec.com
Phone: **Email:** Roy.Shmuel@sightec.com
City: Tel Aviv **State:** Tel Aviv District **PC:** **Country:** Israel
Year Established: 2010 **Status 2020:** Active
Industries: Artificial Intelligence for:, Computer Vision for:, Image Recognition for:, Machine Learning for:, Compute

Company Name: silverback.ai
Description: Silverback empowers online retailers to outsmart their competition and lead, presenting a predictive sales decisions hub for retailers.
Website: http://www.silverback.ai
Phone: **Email:** hello@silverback.ai
City: Tel Aviv **State:** Tel Aviv District **PC:** **Country:** Israel
Year Established: 2014 **Status 2020:** Active
Industries: Artificial Intelligence for:, Business Applications for:, E-Commerce for:, Machine Learning for:, Predictive Analytics for:, Business Intelligence for:, Business Intelligence for:, Business Software as a Service Apps (SaaS Apps)

Company Name: Similari
Description: Similari enables enterprises to easily find patents and technologies using AI and deep learning engine.
Website: http://similari.com
Phone: **Email:** 37394@reference-encyclopedia-ai.net
City: Tel Aviv **State:** Tel Aviv District **PC:** **Country:** Israel
Year Established: 2018 **Status 2020:** Active
Industries: Artificial Intelligence for:, Big Data and Analytics for:, Databases for:, Data Management for:, IT Managed Services for:, Machine Learning for:, Natural Language Processing

Company Name: SIMP
Description: SIMP Investments is a data-driven investment platform that specializes in locating and buying single-family homes.
Website: http://simphomes.com
Phone: **Email:** info@simp.hom: Spain
City: Tel Aviv **State:** Tel Aviv District **PC:** **Country:** Israel
Year Established: 2019 **Status 2020:** Active
Industries: Big Data and Analytics for:, ~ Banking and Financial Markets-Services (7), Machine Learning

Company Name: Sixgill
Description: Sixgill is a deep & dark web threat intelligence provider that helps BFSI's, MSSPs & F500 companies to fight cyber crime.
Website: http://cybersixgill.com/
Phone: **Email:** info@cybersixgill.com
City: Tel Aviv **State:** Tel Aviv District **PC:** **Country:** Israel
Year Established: 2014 **Status 2020:** Active
Industries: Artificial Intelligence for:, Business Intelligence for:, Cyber Security for:, Machine Learning for:, Security

Company Name: Smellio
Description: no plea: Sweden
Website: http://scalez.io
Phone: **Email:** 37419@reference-encyclopedia-ai.net
City: Tel Aviv **State:** Tel Aviv District **PC:** **Country:** Israel
Year Established: 2018 **Status 2020:** Active
Industries: Artificial Intelligence

Company Name: Snapland
Description: Snapland is a real estate tech startup that develops an AI engine specializing in zoning and planning.
Website: http://snap.land
Phone: **Email:** team@snap.land
City: Tel Aviv **State:** Tel Aviv District **PC:** **Country:** Israel
Year Established: 2017 **Status 2020:** Active
Industries: Artificial Intelligence for:, IT Managed Services

Company Name: SNEEZZ
Description: Search Engine on People.
Website: http://www.sneezz.com/snz/
Phone: **Email:** eitan@oracall.com
City: Tel Aviv **State:** Tel Aviv District **PC:** **Country:** Israel
Year Established: 2015 **Status 2020:** Active
Industries: Artificial Intelligence for:, IT Managed Services for:, Web for:, Web

Company Name: Sogo Service
Description: Sogo Services is an IT company that specializes in delivering software solutions based on NLP, machine learning and rule-based programming.
Website: http://sogoservices.com/
Phone: **Email:** sales@sogoservices.com
City: Tel Aviv **State:** Tel Aviv District **PC:** **Country:** Israel
Year Established: 2015 **Status 2020:** Active
Industries: Machine Learning

Company Name: Solume.io
Description: Monitoring all crypto online media, real time and historically, in order to deliver risk assessment, asset ranking and event discovery
Website: http://solume.io
Phone: **Email:** contact@solume.io
City: Tel Aviv **State:** Tel Aviv District **PC:** **Country:** Israel
Year Established: 2017 **Status 2020:** Active
Industries: ~ Banking and Financial Markets-Services (7), Natural Language Processing

Company Name: SoundTrack AI Inc.
Description: Acoustic based, AI enabled, SAAS platform, monitoring mechanical systems for industrial compani: Spain
Website: http://www.soundtrackAI.com
Phone: **Email:** 37442@reference-encyclopedia-ai.net
City: Tel Aviv **State:** Tel Aviv District **PC:** **Country:** Israel
Year Established: 2019 **Status 2020:** Active
Industries: Artificial Intelligence for:, Machine Learning

Company Name: Spartans AI
Description: Creating innovative solutions and products utilizing VR, AR and Artificial Intelligence
Website: http://www.spartans.tech
Phone: **Email:** contact@spartans.tech
City: Tel Aviv **State:** Tel Aviv District **PC:** **Country:** Israel
Year Established: 2017 **Status 2020:** Active
Industries: Artificial Intelligence for:, IT Managed Services for:, Virtual Reality (VR)

Company Name: Spree
Description: Spree is a Content Intelligence Platform for the Enterpri: Sweden
Website: http://www.spree.co
Phone: **Email:** Danielle@spree.co
City: Tel Aviv **State:** Tel Aviv District **PC:** **Country:** Israel
Year Established: 2015 **Status 2020:** Active
Industries: Artificial Intelligence for:, Big Data and Analytics for:, Machine Learning for:, Natural Language Processing for:, Business Software as a Service Apps (SaaS Apps)

Company Name: Steller: Romania
Description: Stellerro is the first STO predictive analytics AI Index, based on Optimized Tokenomics via Reinforced Learning and Simulating modeling.
Website: http://www.stellerro.com/
Phone: **Email:** Info@Stellerro.com
City: Tel Aviv **State:** Tel Aviv District **PC:** **Country:** Israel
Year Established: 2018 **Status 2020:** Active
Industries:

Company Name: StreetSmart
Description: StreetSmart offers a decision support system for drivers in all car services.
Website: http://streetsm4rt.com/
Phone: 972 (0) 36930925 **Email:** info@streetsm4rt.com
City: Tel Aviv **State:** Tel Aviv District **PC:** **Country:** Israel
Year Established: 2015 **Status 2020:** Active
Industries: Artificial Intelligence for:, ~ Automotive (5), IT Managed Services for:, Web for:, Machine Learning

Company Name: Substrata
Description: Machine Learning B2B Solutions to help Organizations Grow and Thrive
Website: http://substrata.me/
Phone: **Email:** ori@substrata.me
City: Tel Aviv **State:** Tel Aviv District **PC:** **Country:** Israel
Year Established: 2019 **Status 2020:** Active
Industries: Artificial Intelligence for:, Business Applications for:, IT Managed Services for:, Machine Learning for:, Natural Language Processing for:, Business Software as a Service Apps (SaaS Apps)

Company Name: Super Signal
Description: Super Signal is an investment management company that features a data-driven investment manager powered by AI-technology.
Website: http://www.supersignalcapital.com
Phone: **Email:** 37481@reference-encyclopedia-ai.net
City: Tel Aviv **State:** Tel Aviv District **PC:** **Country:** Israel
Year Established: 2017 **Status 2020:** Active
Industries: Artificial Intelligence for:, ~ Banking and Financial Markets-Services (7), ~ Banking and Financial Markets-Services (7)

Company Name: SuperCO
Description: SuperCO develops a platform for leaders of cities to engage their communities to build thriving neighborhoods.
Website: http://coing.co/
Phone: **Email:** adi@coing.co
City: Tel Aviv **State:** Tel Aviv District **PC:** **Country:** Israel
Year Established: 2019 **Status 2020:** Active
Industries: Artificial Intelligence for:, ~ Government (19), IT Managed Services for:, ~ Construction (10)

Company Name: Superfy
Description: Superfy gets what you need and automagically finds people that can help you by chat.
Website: http://www.asksuperfy.com
Phone: **Email:** info@superfy.co
City: Tel Aviv **State:** Tel Aviv District **PC:** **Country:** Israel
Year Established: 2015 **Status 2020:** Active
Industries: Artificial Intelligence for:, Application Services

Company Name: superQuery
Description: AI-powered IDE designed for serverless big data services by Google, AWS, Microsoft and Oracle. Increase speed & reduce costs by 60%
Website: http://web.superquery.io/
Phone: 97252635343 **Email:** ido@superquery.io
City: Tel Aviv **State:** Tel Aviv District **PC:** **Country:** Israel
Year Established: 2017 **Status 2020:** Active
Industries: Artificial Intelligence for:, Big Data and Analytics

Company Name: Swapp
Description: Swapp aims to disrupt the current planning methodologies by providing an automated end-to-end planning service.
Website: http://www.swapp.net/
Phone: **Email:** info@swapp.net
City: Tel Aviv **State:** Tel Aviv District **PC:** **Country:** Israel
Year Established: 2019 **Status 2020:** Active
Industries: Artificial Intelligence for:, Big Data and Analytics for:, ~ Construction (10), IT Managed Services

Company Name: Syte
Description: Syte powers image search for e-commerce, improving site navigation, product discovery, and user experience that engage and convert shoppers.
Website: http://www.syte.ai/
Phone: **Email:** info@syte.ai
City: Tel Aviv **State:** Tel Aviv District **PC:** **Country:** Israel
Year Established: 2015 **Status 2020:** Active
Industries: Artificial Intelligence for:, E-Commerce for:, Business Software as a Service Apps (SaaS Apps) for:, Computer Vision

Company Name: TA9
Description: TA9 is a data analysis and big data intelligence platform for producing valuable, real-time insights from mass of data.
Website: http://www.t-a9.com
Phone: 972-73-2802266 **Email:** info@t-a9.com
City: Tel Aviv **State:** TA **PC:** **Country:** Israel
Year Established: 2014 **Status 2020:** Active
Industries: Analytics for:, Artificial Intelligence

Company Name: Taliaz
Description: Taliaz has developed a highly-accurate decision support tool, to help clinicians identify the right treatment for their individual patients.
Website: http://www.taliazhealth.com/
Phone: **Email:** office@taliazhealth.com
City: Tel Aviv **State:** Tel Aviv District **PC:** **Country:** Israel
Year Established: 2012 **Status 2020:** Active
Industries: Analytics for:, Artificial Intelligence for:, Big Data and Analytics for:, ~ Biotechnology (9), ~ Healthcare (20), Machine Learning for:, ~ Healthcare (20)

Company Name: Taran
Description: Taranis offers a precision intelligence platform for agriculture.
Website: http://taranis.ag/
Phone: 1 715 443 5006 **Email:** info@taranis.ag
City: Tel Aviv **State:** Tel Aviv District **PC:** **Country:** Israel
Year Established: 2014 **Status 2020:** Active
Industries: ~ Agriculture (3), ~ Agriculture (3), Analytics for:, Big Data and Analytics for:, ~ Agriculture (3), Predictive Analytics

Company Name: Tastewi: Sweden
Description: Tastewise is a data, analytics and insights platform for restaurants, food brands and hospitality.
Website: http://www.tastewise.io
Phone: **Email:** info@tastewise.io
City: Tel Aviv **State:** Tel Aviv District **PC:** **Country:** Israel
Year Established: 2017 **Status 2020:** Active
Industries: Artificial Intelligence for:, Big Data and Analytics for:, ~ Retail and Consumer Products (52), ~ Food and Beverage (17), Predictive Analytics for:, ~ Food and Beverage (17)

Company Name: The Elegant Monkeys
Description: The makers of Kenko Technology, a science driven AI algorithms that translate physiological data to human emotions.
Website: http://www.elegantmonkeys.com
Phone: **Email:** contact@elegantmonkeys.com
City: Tel Aviv **State:** Tel Aviv District **PC:** **Country:** Israel
Year Established: 2014 **Status 2020:** Closed
Industries: Artificial Intelligence for:, ~ Healthcare (20), IT Managed Services for:, Internet of Things (IoT) for:, Internet of Things (IoT)

Company Name: timbr.ai
Description: timbr.ai - the SQL Knowledge Graph™ implements the Semantic Web in SQL to turn databases into knowledge graphs with semantic reasoning
Website: http://timbr.ai
Phone: 1 (832) 998-8697 **Email:** contact@timbr.ai
City: Tel Aviv **State:** Tel Aviv District **PC:** **Country:** Israel
Year Established: 2018 **Status 2020:** Active
Industries:

Company Name: Tiv.ai
Description: Tiv.ai's aim to balance our daily mental overload and help families live a more peaceful and productive life.
Website: http://tiv.ai
Phone: **Email:** assaf@tiv.ai
City: Tel Aviv **State:** TA **PC:** **Country:** Israel
Year Established: 2017 **Status 2020:** Active
Industries: Internet of Things (IoT)

Company Name: TOPeration
Description: TOPeration provides an operation management SaaS for food and hospitality enterprises.
Website: http://www.toperation.co/
Phone: **Email:** 37545@reference-encyclopedia-ai.net
City: Tel Aviv **State:** Tel Aviv District **PC:** **Country:** Israel
Year Established: 2017 **Status 2020:** Active
Industries: Artificial Intelligence for:, IT Managed Services for:, Machine Learning for:, Business Software as a Service Apps (SaaS Apps)

Company Name: Track160
Description: Track160 is quantifies performance and tactics metrics in team sports.
Website: http://www.track160.com/
Phone: **Email:** info@track160.com
City: Tel Aviv **State:** Tel Aviv District **PC:** **Country:** Israel
Year Established: 2017 **Status 2020:** Active
Industries: Analytics for:, Artificial Intelligence for:, Machine Learning for:, ~ Arts-Entertainment-Recreation (4)

Company Name: Trekeye
Description: Trekeye is an IoT technology that provides real-time operational intelligence for traditional Industries.
Website: http://www.trekeye.com
Phone: **Email:** 37564@reference-encyclopedia-ai.net
City: Tel Aviv **State:** Tel Aviv District **PC:** **Country:** Israel
Year Established: 2015 **Status 2020:** Active
Industries: Artificial Intelligence for:, Business Intelligence

Company Name: Trell
Description: AI to make the food value chainmore profitable, sustainable and efficient.
Website: http://www.trellis.ag
Phone: 97252311115 **Email:** info@trellis.ag
City: Tel Aviv **State:** Tel Aviv District **PC:** **Country:** Israel
Year Established: 2016 **Status 2020:** Active
Industries: ~ Agriculture (3), Analytics for:, Artificial Intelligence for:, Cloud for:, ~ Food and Beverage (17), Business Software as a Service Apps (SaaS Apps)

Company Name: Trenario
Description: Improving performance and compliance with an artificial intelligence platform.
Website: http://www.trenario.com
Phone: **Email:** contact@trenario.com
City: Tel Aviv **State:** Tel Aviv District **PC:** **Country:** Israel
Year Established: 2015 **Status 2020:** Active
Industries: Artificial Intelligence for:, Compliance for:, ~ Education (13), Enterprise Application Services for:, Enterprise Application Services for:, Machine Learning for:, Mobile for:, Predictive Analytics for:, Predictive Analytics for:, Business Software as a Service Ap

Company Name: Truvi
Description: Truvi is an AI-based platform that enables responders, aid organizations and municipalities for disaster preparedness and response.
Website: http://www.truvi.io
Phone: **Email:** 37574@reference-encyclopedia-ai.net
City: Tel Aviv **State:** Tel Aviv District **PC:** **Country:** Israel
Year Established: 2018 **Status 2020:** Active
Industries: Artificial Intelligence for:, IT Managed Services

Company Name: Twiggle
Description: AI-Powered Search, Discovery, and Merchandising Solutions for E-Commerce
Website: http://www.twiggle.com
Phone: 97235069255 **Email:** info@twiggle.com
City: Tel Aviv **State:** TA **PC:** **Country:** Israel
Year Established: 2014 **Status 2020:** Active
Industries: Artificial Intelligence for:, E-Commerce for:, Machine Learning for:, Natural Language Processing for:, Business Intelligence

Company Name: UNIQAI Systems
Description: UNIQAI Systems provides Artificial Intelligence based planning, decision making and risk analysis solutions
Website: http://www.uniqai.com
Phone: 972-52-3277256 **Email:** nadav@uniqai.com
City: Tel Aviv **State:** Tel Aviv District **PC:** **Country:** Israel
Year Established: 2016 **Status 2020:** Active
Industries: Robotics

Company Name: Unitycom
Description: Unitycom is an Artificial Intelligence company that focuses on SaaS, marketing automation, and artificial intelligence.
Website: http://www.byunitycom.com
Phone: **Email:** 37593@reference-encyclopedia-ai.net
City: Tel Aviv **State:** Tel Aviv District **PC:** **Country:** Israel
Year Established: 2019 **Status 2020:** Active
Industries: Artificial Intelligence for:, Business Software as a Service Apps (SaaS Apps)

Company Name: Valerann
Description: Valerann is developing an autonomous traffic control and management system.
Website: http://www.valerann.com/
Phone: **Email:** info@valerann.com
City: Tel Aviv **State:** Tel Aviv District **PC:** **Country:** Israel
Year Established: 2016 **Status 2020:** Active
Industries: ~ Automotive (5), Application Services for:, Internet of Things (IoT)

Company Name: Vayo
Description: Vayo's platform enables SaaS companies to grow their business by turning cross-organizational customer data into actionable insights.
Website: http://www.vayo.io/
Phone: **Email:** info@vayo.io
City: Tel Aviv **State:** TA **PC:** **Country:** Israel
Year Established: **Status 2020:** Active
Industries: Analytics for:, Artificial Intelligence for:, Business Applications for:, Enterprise Application Services for:, Application Services for:, ~ Professional Services (48)

Company Name: vBrand
Description: Artificial Intelligence Platform for Brand Sponsorship
Website: http://www.vbrandsports.com
Phone: **Email:** contact@vbrandsports.com
City: Tel Aviv **State:** Tel Aviv District **PC:** **Country:** Israel
Year Established: 2013 **Status 2020:** Active
Industries: Artificial Intelligence for:, Facial Recognition for:, Image Recognition for:, ~ Arts-Entertainment-Recreation (4)

Company Name: Viewly
Description: Viewly offers an AI engine for non-profit websites which independently personalizes the donation process for each individual donor.
Website: http://www.viewly.com/
Phone: **Email:** info@viewly.com
City: Tel Aviv **State:** Tel Aviv District **PC:** **Country:** Israel
Year Established: 2015 **Status 2020:** Active
Industries:

Company Name: viisights
Description: viisights is a leading provider of behavioral understanding systems by artificial intelligence
Website: http://www.viisights.com
Phone: **Email:** info@viisight.com
City: Tel Aviv **State:** Tel Aviv District **PC:** **Country:** Israel
Year Established: 2014 **Status 2020:** Active
Industries: Analytics for:, Artificial Intelligence for:, ~ Automotive (5), ~ Automotive (5), Big Data and Analytics for:, Computer Vision for:, Cyber Security for:, Machine Learning for:, Machine Learning for:, ~ Government (19), ~ Media-Communications (41)

Company Name: VirtHues Labs
Description: Software Consultancy
Website:
Phone: **Email:** contact@virthues.com
City: Tel Aviv **State:** Tel Aviv District **PC:** **Country:** Israel
Year Established: 2017 **Status 2020:** Active
Industries: Databases for:, IT Managed Services for:, Machine Learning for:, Compute for:, Business Process and Operations for:, Business Process and Operations

Company Name: Viscera AI
Description: Viscera AI provides a platform based on artificial intelligence to help serve the needs of dentists.
Website:
Phone: **Email:** 37632@reference-encyclopedia-ai.net
City: Tel Aviv **State:** Tel Aviv District **PC:** **Country:** Israel
Year Established: 2019 **Status 2020:** Closed
Industries: Artificial Intelligence for:, ~ Healthcare (20), ~ Healthcare (20), Machine Learning

Company Name: Voiceitt
Description: Automatic speech recognition technology designed to recognize non-standard speech patterns of people with disabiliti: Spain
Website: http://www.voiceitt.com/
Phone: 972 54-235-7727 **Email:** danny@voiceitt.com
City: Tel Aviv **State:** Tel Aviv District **PC:** **Country:** Israel
Year Established: 2012 **Status 2020:** Active
Industries: Artificial Intelligence for:, ~ Healthcare (20), Enterprise Application Services for:, ~ Banking and Financial Markets-Services (7), Machine Learning for:, ~ Healthcare (20), Application Services for:, Speech Recognition for:, Internet of Things (IoT)

Company Name: WannA
Description: WannA matches needs, locally. Automatically connecting users with shared needs directly with corresponding users' offers.
Website: http://wanna-mobile.com
Phone: **Email:** jonthan@wanna-mobile.com
City: Tel Aviv **State:** TA **PC:** **Country:** Israel
Year Established: 2014 **Status 2020:** Closed
Industries: Mobile for:, Natural Language Processing for:, ~ Education (13)

Company **Name:** Wasteless
Description: Wasteless provides machine learning and real-time tracking solution for grocery stores.
Website: http://www.wasteless.co
Phone: **Email:** hello@wasteless.co
City: Tel Aviv **State:** Tel Aviv District **PC:** **Country:** Israel
Year Established: 2016 **Status 2020:** Active
Industries: Artificial Intelligence for:, Web for:, Machine Learning for:, Supply Chain Management for:, ~ Waste Management and Remediation Services (59)

Company Name: Whizar Artificial Intelligence
Description: Whizar Artificial Intelligence is an airfare optimization SaaS company for travel agencies.
Website: http://www.whizar.com/
Phone: **Email:** contact@whizar.com
City: Tel Aviv **State:** TA **PC:** **Country:** Israel
Year Established: 2017 **Status 2020:** Active
Industries: Artificial Intelligence for:, IT Managed Services for:, Business Software as a Service Apps (SaaS Apps)

Company Name: Whizzco
Description: Yield Management Tool for Content Recommendation
Website: http://whizzco.com/
Phone: **Email:** Hello@whizzco.com
City: Tel Aviv **State:** Tel Aviv District **PC:** **Country:** Israel
Year Established: 2017 **Status 2020:** Active
Industries: Artificial Intelligence for:, Web for:, Internet of Things (IoT) for:, ~ Social Assistance-Non-Profits (53)

Company Name: Wispa
Description: Wispa is a start-up that develops an innovative technology that understands what people write on social networks
Website: http://www.wispa.com
Phone: **Email:** 37678@reference-encyclopedia-ai.net
City: Tel Aviv **State:** Tel Aviv District **PC:** **Country:** Israel
Year Established: 2012 **Status 2020:** Active
Industries: Databases for:, Mobile for:, Natural Language Processing

Company Name: XTEND LTD
Description: XTEND - Extending Reality Skywards
Website: www.xtend.me
Phone: **Email:** hello@xtend.me
City: Tel Aviv **State:** TA **PC:** **Country:** Israel
Year Established: **Status 2020:** Active
Industries: ~ Transportation and Logistics (57), ~ Transportation and Logistics (57)

Company Name: Zencity
Description: Data-driven Decision Making for Local Government
Website: http://zencity.io
Phone: **Email:** info@zencity.io
City: Tel Aviv **State:** Tel Aviv District **PC:** **Country:** Israel
Year Established: 2015 **Status 2020:** Active
Industries: Analytics for:, Artificial Intelligence for:, ~ Government (19), ~ Government (19), ~ Government (19), Machine Learning for:, ~ Social Assistance-Non-Profits (53)

Company Name: AbiliSen: Sweden
Description: AbiliSense develops an AI sound recognition technology that empowers IoT devices by smart listening abilities.
Website: https://www.abilisense.com/
Phone: **Email:** info@abilisense.com
City: Tel Aviv-yafo **State:** Tel Aviv District **PC:** **Country:** Israel
Year Established: 2015 **Status 2020:** Active
Industries: Artificial Intelligence for:, Voice Recognition for:, ~ Automotive (5), ~ Healthcare (20), Cyber Security for:, IT Managed Services for:, Application Services for:, Internet of Things (IoT) for:, Internet of Things (IoT)

Company Name: Algoreta: Israel
Description: Algoretail is a retail platform building a fully automated self-operating system for retailers.
Website: https://www.algoretail.co.il/
Phone: **Email:** office@algoretail.co.: Israel
City: Tel Aviv-yafo **State:** TA **PC:** **Country:** Israel
Year Established: 2018 **Status 2020:** Active
Industries: Artificial Intelligence for:, Business Intelligence for:, Automation for:, Supply Chain Management

Company Name: ArcusTeam
Description: ArcusTeam has developed an Automated Platform for Detecting Vulnerabilities on ANY IoT Software
Website: http://www.arcusteam.com/
Phone: **Email:** contact@arcusteam.com
City: Tel Aviv-yafo **State:** TA **PC:** **Country:** Israel
Year Established: **Status 2020:** Active
Industries:

Company Name: Aurora Labs
Description: Aurora Labs offers a self-healing platform for connected vehicle software.
Website: http://www.auroralabs.com/
Phone: **Email:** info@auroralabs.com
City: Tel Aviv-yafo **State:** Tel Aviv District **PC:** **Country:** Israel
Year Established: 2016 **Status 2020:** Active
Industries: Artificial Intelligence for:, ~ Automotive (5), ~ Automotive (5), Application Services for:, Machine Learning for:, Predictive Analytics

Company Name: Axonize
Description: Axonize makes large scale IoT projects easy by automating deployment at a fraction of the time and cost.
Website: http://www.axonize.com/
Phone: **Email:** hello@axonize.com
City: Tel Aviv-yafo **State:** Tel Aviv District **PC:** **Country:** Israel
Year Established: 2016 **Status 2020:** Active
Industries: Analytics for:, Artificial Intelligence for:, Cloud for:, Data Management for:, Internet of Things (IoT)

Company Name: BUILD: India
Description: Blockchain Based Fair-Play Financial Services Marketplace for Real-Estate
Website: http://www.buildin.io
Phone: **Email:** info@buildin.io
City: Tel Aviv-yafo **State:** Tel Aviv District **PC:** **Country:** Israel
Year Established: 2016 **Status 2020:** Active
Industries: Artificial Intelligence for:, Blockchain for:, ~ Banking and Financial Markets-Services (7)

Company Name: Cellosco:
Description: Celloscope utilizes state-of-the-art sensor and AI technologies that turns smartphone into a medical monitor.
Website: http://www.celloscope.com/
Phone: **Email:** 36246@reference-encyclopedia-ai.net
City: Tel Aviv-yafo **State:** Tel Aviv District **PC:** **Country:** Israel
Year Established: 2018 **Status 2020:** Active
Industries: Analytics for:, Artificial Intelligence for:, ~ Healthcare (20)

Company Name: cignal.io Ltd.
Description: Cignal.io develop data-driven algorithms and optimization engines to help brands connect with their audiences at scale.
Website: http://cignal.io
Phone: 972 3 6930900 **Email:** info@cignal.io
City: Tel Aviv-yafo **State:** Tel Aviv District **PC:** **Country:** Israel
Year Established: 2016 **Status 2020:** Active
Industries: Artificial Intelligence for:, Machine Learning

Company Name: CVAid Medical
Description: CVAid Medical develops an innovative AI based stroke detection technological platform.
Website: http://www.cvaidmedical.com/
Phone: **Email:** 36365@reference-encyclopedia-ai.net
City: Tel Aviv-yafo **State:** Tel Aviv District **PC:** **Country:** Israel
Year Established: 2018 **Status 2020:** Active
Industries: Artificial Intelligence for:, ~ Healthcare (20)

Company Name: Data2Life
Description: Data2Life focuses on using real world data to address clinical and health related challenges.
Website: http://Data2Life.com
Phone: (9723) 602-0264 **Email:** media@data2life.com
City: Tel Aviv-yafo **State:** Tel Aviv District **PC:** **Country:** Israel
Year Established: 2014 **Status 2020:** Active
Industries: Artificial Intelligence for:, Big Data and Analytics for:, ~ Biotechnology (9), ~ Healthcare (20)

Company Name: GuestsAI
Description: GuestsAI is a engine analyzes hotel guest behavior using artificial intelligence and detects hidden rooms.
Website: http://guestsai.com/index.html
Phone: **Email:** 36656@reference-encyclopedia-ai.net
City: Tel Aviv-yafo **State:** Tel Aviv District **PC:** **Country:** Israel
Year Established: 2017 **Status 2020:** Active
Industries: Artificial Intelligence for:, ~ Travel and Transportation (58)

Company Name: HiGrade
Description: HiGrade provides mobile cannabis testing for consumers and patients, using patent-pending AI technology.
Website: http://www.gethigrade.com
Phone: 972 54 700 2755 **Email:** info@gethigrade.com
City: Tel Aviv-yafo **State:** Tel Aviv District **PC:** **Country:** Israel
Year Established: 2016 **Status 2020:** Active
Industries: Artificial Intelligence

Company Name: Ibex Medical Analytics
Description: IBEX develops a product suite to improve clinical decision-making and to streamline pathology laboratory workflows.
Website: http://ibex-ai.com/
Phone: **Email:** info@ibex-ai.com
City: Tel Aviv-yafo **State:** Tel Aviv District **PC:** **Country:** Israel
Year Established: 2016 **Status 2020:** Active
Industries: Analytics for:, Artificial Intelligence for:, ~ Healthcare (20)

Company Name: ICV
Description: ICV is building and providing HR tools for HR teams to source, sort, filter and match the best candidate for every position, every time.
Website: http://www.geticv.com
Phone: 050 667 8856 **Email:** ron@geticv.com
City: Tel Aviv-yafo **State:** TA **PC:** **Country:** Israel
Year Established: 2015 **Status 2020:** Active
Industries: Machine Learning

Company Name: Inflowz
Description: Inflowz is the artificial intelligence sales process optimization platform for velocity sales leaders.
Website: http://www.inflowz.com
Phone: **Email:** 34874@reference-encyclopedia-ai.net
City: Tel Aviv-yafo **State:** Tel Aviv District **PC:** **Country:** Israel
Year Established: 2017 **Status 2020:** Active
Industries:

Company Name: Librimind
Description: Librimind creates sustainable industrial solutions powered by AI and IoT
Website: http://www.librimind.com
Phone: **Email:** hello@librimind.com
City: Tel Aviv-yafo **State:** Tel Aviv District **PC:** **Country:** Israel
Year Established: 2017 **Status 2020:** Active
Industries: Analytics for:, Artificial Intelligence for:, Big Data and Analytics for:, Automation for:, ~ Metals and Mining (42), Predictive Analytics for:, Predictive Analytics for:, Application Services

Company Name: Mystore-E
Description: We help retailers get things done!
Website: http://mystore-e.com/
Phone: **Email:** info@mystore-e.com
City: Tel Aviv-yafo **State:** Tel Aviv District **PC:** **Country:** Israel
Year Established: 2016 **Status 2020:** Active
Industries:

Company Name: Orca AI
Description: Orca AI is a Boat collision avoidance system maker
Website: http://www.orca-ai.io/
Phone: **Email:** 37120@reference-encyclopedia-ai.net
City: Tel Aviv-yafo **State:** Tel Aviv District **PC:** **Country:** Israel
Year Established: 2018 **Status 2020:** Active
Industries: Artificial Intelligence for:, Industrial Solutions for:, Application Services for:, ~ Transportation and Logistics (57), ~ Government (19), ~ Transportation and Logistics (57)

Company Name: OrderBoard
Description: OrderBoard provides IT, cyber security and artificial intelligence solutions.
Website: http://orderboard.ai/
Phone: 833-936-7337 **Email:** info@orderboard.ai
City: Tel Aviv-yafo **State:** Tel Aviv District **PC:** **Country:** Israel
Year Established: 2018 **Status 2020:** Active
Industries: Artificial Intelligence for:, Cyber Security for:, IT Managed Services

Company Name: Phrasetech
Description: Automated text creation, control and optimization for enterprise compani: Spain
Website: http://www.phrasetech.com
Phone: 1-646-396-557 **Email:** info@phrasetech.com
City: Tel Aviv-yafo **State:** Tel Aviv District **PC:** **Country:** Israel
Year Established: 2013 **Status 2020:** Active
Industries: Analytics for:, Artificial Intelligence for:, Business Applications for:, Content for:, IT Managed Services for:, Natural Language Processing

Company Name: Radiomize
Description: Radiomize, a touch-enabled steering wheel cover and personal music and genre-based news discovery app, provide a connected car driving.
Website: http://www.radiomize.com
Phone: (972) 52-8395412 **Email:** INFO@JUSTDRIVE.AI
City: Tel Aviv-yafo **State:** Tel Aviv District **PC:** **Country:** Israel
Year Established: 2015 **Status 2020:** Active
Industries: Analytics for:, Application Services for:, Artificial Intelligence

Company Name: Rewardpod
Description: Rewardpod is a Israeli app customer predictive analytics company.
Website: http://rewardpod.com
Phone: **Email:** 37297@reference-encyclopedia-ai.net
City: Tel Aviv-yafo **State:** Tel Aviv District **PC:** **Country:** Israel
Year Established: 2013 **Status 2020:** Active
Industries: Analytics for:, Web for:, Predictive Analytics

Company Name: Seebo
Description: Seebo empowers manufacturers with process-based Industrial AI solutions for predicting and preventing manufacturing disruptions.
Website: http://www.seebo.com
Phone: 972 73-272-5188 **Email:** info@seebo.com
City: Tel Aviv-yafo **State:** Tel Aviv District **PC:** **Country:** Israel
Year Established: 2012 **Status 2020:** Active
Industries: Artificial Intelligence for:, Automation for:, Internet of Things (IoT) for:, Machine Learning for:, Predictive Analytics

Company Name: Singulai
Description: Singulai develops human-centred machine intelligence.
Website: http://www.singulai.com/
Phone: **Email:** info@singulai.com
City: Tel Aviv-yafo **State:** Tel Aviv District **PC:** **Country:** Israel
Year Established: 2017 **Status 2020:** Active
Industries: Artificial Intelligence for:, Robotics

Company Name: Stardat
Description: Stardat provides machine learning based artificial intelligence solutions.
Website: http://www.stardat.net/
Phone: **Email:** 37466@reference-encyclopedia-ai.net
City: Tel Aviv-yafo **State:** Tel Aviv District **PC:** **Country:** Israel
Year Established: 2019 **Status 2020:** Active
Industries: Artificial Intelligence for:, Machine Learning

Company Name: Tomobox
Description: Conversational engines for the messaging age
Website: http://tomobox.co/
Phone: **Email:** info@tomobox.co
City: Tel Aviv-yafo **State:** Tel Aviv District **PC:** **Country:** Israel
Year Established: 2015 **Status 2020:** Active
Industries: Analytics for:, Artificial Intelligence for:, Big Data and Analytics for:, Cloud for:, ~ Customer Relationship Management (11), Machine Learning

Company Name: Treebute.io
Description: Treebute is A global SaaS and AI platform for preservation and trade of scientific knowledge
Website: http://www.treebute.io/
Phone: **Email:** info@treebute.io
City: Tel Aviv-yafo **State:** Tel Aviv District **PC:** **Country:** Israel
Year Established: 2018 **Status 2020:** Active
Industries: Artificial Intelligence for:, Business Intelligence for:, IT Managed Services for:, ~ Administrative and Support Services (1)

Company Name: Wis2Biz
Description: AI platform for medical centers and weight loss companies, that predicts and prevents dropouts ahead of time
Website: http://www.wis2biz.com/
Phone: **Email:** lior@wis2biz.com
City: Tel Aviv-yafo **State:** TA **PC:** **Country:** Israel
Year Established: 2017 **Status 2020:** Active
Industries: Artificial Intelligence for:, ~ Healthcare (20)

Company Name: Zest
Description: Zest solves the pain of modern professional extinction by keeping their knowledge current
Website: http://zest.
Phone: **Email:** business@zest.
City: Tel Aviv-yafo **State:** Tel Aviv District **PC:** **Country:** Israel
Year Established: 2018 **Status 2020:** Active
Industries: Artificial Intelligence for:, ~ Personal-Religious-Civic (45), Content for:, Digital Marketing for:, IT Managed Services for:, Machine Learning for:, ~ Peer to Peer (44)

Company Name: Flowless
Description: Smart Solutions for Comprehensive & Sustainable Water Resources Management
Website: http://www.flowless.co
Phone: **Email:** info@flowless.co
City: Ramallah **State:** West Bank **PC:** **Country:** Israel
Year Established: 2019 **Status 2020:** Active
Industries: Artificial Intelligence for:, ~ Banking and Financial Markets-Services (7), IT Infrastructure for:, Machine Learning for:, ~ Social-Environmental-Physical-Engineering Sciences (55), ~ Waste Management and Remediation Services (59)

Italy

Company Name: MainAd
Description: International ad tech company, focusing on performance results, accomplished through our programmatic know-how & proprietary tech, Logico.
Website: http://www.mainad.com
Phone: 39 085 65149 **Email:** sales@mainad.com
City: Pescara **State:** Abruzzo **PC:** **Country:** ITALY
Year Established: **Status 2020:** Active
Industries: ~ Media-Communications (41), ~ Media-Communications (41), ~ Media-Communications (41), Artificial Intelligence for:, Big Data and Analytics for:, E-Commerce for:, Machine Learning for:, ~ Media-Communications (41), Predictive Analytics

Company Name: Quintetto
Description: Quintetto is a software and infrastructure provider with 12 years of technology development and market lead.
Website: http://www.quintetto.: Italy
Phone: 0165 18.45.290 **Email:** info@quintetto.: Italy
City: Pont-saint-martin **State:** Aosta **PC:** **Country:** ITALY
Year Established: **Status 2020:** Active
Industries:

Company Name: Nextome
Description: Nextome is the indoor positioning and navigation system.
Website: www.nextome.net
Phone: **Email:** info@nextome.net
City: Conversano **State:** Apulia **PC:** **Country:** ITALY
Year Established: **Status 2020:** Active
Industries: Artificial Intelligence for:, Mobile for:, ~ Transportation and Logistics (57), ~ Professional Services (48)

Company Name: Altosight
Description: The most accurate AI-backed price tracker for manufacturers and ecommerce stores.
Website: https://altosight.com/
Phone: **Email:** info@altosight.com
City: Monteroni Di Lecce **State:** Apulia **PC:** **Country:** ITALY
Year Established: 2017 **Status 2020:** Active
Industries: Artificial Intelligence for:, E-Commerce for:, Enterprise Application Services for:, Business Software as a Service Apps (SaaS Apps)

Company Name: Holsys
Description: New era of Artificial Intelligence solutions
Website: http://www.holsys.com
Phone: **Email:** c.martines@holsys.com
City: Taranto **State:** Apulia **PC:** **Country:** ITALY
Year Established: **Status 2020:** Active
Industries: Artificial Intelligence for:, Machine Learning

Company Name: Youbiquo
Description: Youbiquo is an Italian company that offers users Augmented Reality Smart Glasses for enterprises, for maintenance and logistic activities.
Website: http://www.youbiquo.eu
Phone: 39.089.0976534 **Email:** info@youbiquo.eu
City: Cava De' Tirreni **State:** Campania **PC:** **Country:** ITALY
Year Established: 2013 **Status 2020:** Active
Industries: Artificial Intelligence for:, Internet of Things (IoT)

Company Name: Evja
Description: Evja is revolutionizing agriculture by combining Artificial Intelligence, Internet of Things and Agronomic Models.
Website: http://www.evja.eu/
Phone: **Email:** info@evja.eu
City: Naples **State:** Campania **PC:** **Country:** ITALY
Year Established: 2015 **Status 2020:** Active
Industries: ~ Agriculture (3), ~ Agriculture (3), Artificial Intelligence for:, Big Data and Analytics for:, IT Managed Services for:, Web

Company Name: Remocean
Description: Remocean offers a real-time monitoring system with hardware and software that employs X-band razors to analyze sea state parameters.
Website: http://www.remocean.: Italy
Phone: **Email:** info@remocean.com
City: Napoli **State:** Campania **PC:** **Country:** ITALY
Year Established: 2010 **Status 2020:** Active
Industries: Internet of Things (IoT) for:, Predictive Analytics

Company Name: AILabs
Description: AI made by humans
Website: http://www.ailabs.it/
Phone: **Email:** 36010@reference-encyclopedia-ai.net
City: Bologna **State:** Emilia-Romagna **PC:** **Country:** ITALY
Year Established: 2017 **Status 2020:** Active
Industries: Artificial Intelligence for:, Big Data and Analytics for:, Machine Learning

Company Name: Awhy
Description: SaaS
Website: http://www.awhy.: Italy
Phone: 39 3889948244 **Email:** nabil.arafin@awhy.: Italy
City: Bologna **State:** Emilia-Romagna **PC:** **Country:** ITALY
Year Established: 2015 **Status 2020:** Active
Industries: Artificial Intelligence for:, Business Software as a Service Apps (SaaS Apps)

Company Name: Musixmat: Switzerland
Description: Musixmatch is a Music AI company developing algorithms and tools for music discovery, reccomandation, search trough the power of lyrics
Website: http://www.musixmatch.com
Phone: **Email:** info@musixmatch.com
City: Bologna **State:** Emilia-Romagna **PC:** **Country:** ITALY
Year Established: 2010 **Status 2020:** Active
Industries: Application Services for:, Artificial Intelligence for:, Machine Learning for:, ~ Arts-Entertainment-Recreation (4), ~ Arts-Entertainment-Recreation (4), Natural Language Processing

Company Name: REJOINT
Description: Rejoint develops Artificial Intelligence driven 3D printed personalized knee replacement.
Website: http://www.rejoint.life
Phone: 39 335 5424542 **Email:** info@rejoint.life
City: Bologna **State:** Emilia-Romagna **PC:** **Country:** ITALY
Year Established: 2015 **Status 2020:** Active
Industries: Artificial Intelligence for:, ~ Healthcare (20), ~ Healthcare (20)

Company Name: GETCOO
Description: Artificial Intelligence based Computer Vision solutions for industry
Website: http://www.getcoo.com/en
Phone: 39 335 283002 **Email:** info@getcoo.com
City: Faenza **State:** Emilia-Romagna **PC:** **Country:** ITALY
Year Established: **Status 2020:** Active
Industries: Artificial Intelligence for:, Computer Vision for:, Automation for:, Computer Vision

Company Name: Axyon AI
Description: Axyon AI leverages the most recent advancements in deep learning to create bespoke business applications for capital markets.
Website: http://www.axyon.ai/
Phone: 39 059 7880067 **Email:** info@axyon.ai
City: Modena **State:** Emilia-Romagna **PC:** **Country:** ITALY
Year Established: 2016 **Status 2020:** Active
Industries: Artificial Intelligence for:, ~ Banking and Financial Markets-Services (7), ~ Banking and Financial Markets-Services (7)

Company Name: Axyon AI SRL
Description: Deep Learning for Banks and Financial Institutions
Website: http://www.axyon.ai/
Phone: 39 059 815602 **Email:** jobs@axyon.ai
City: Modena **State:** Emilia-Romagna **PC:** **Country:** ITALY
Year Established: **Status 2020:** Active
Industries: Artificial Intelligence for:, ~ Banking and Financial Markets-Services (7), ~ Banking and Financial Markets-Services (7)

Company Name: Expert System
Description: Expert System develops software that understands the meaning of written language.
Website: http://www.expertsystem.com
Phone: **Email:** info@expertsystem.com
City: Modena **State:** Emilia-Romagna **PC:** **Country:** ITALY
Year Established: **Status 2020:** Active
Industries:

Company Name: Pikkart
Description: Pikkart AR
Website: http://www.pikkart.com
Phone: 39 059 710854 **Email:** niccolo.barone@pikkart.com
City: Modena **State:** Emilia-Romagna **PC:** **Country:** ITALY
Year Established: **Status 2020:** Active
Industries: Artificial Intelligence for:, Augmented Reality for:, Machine Learning

Company Name: AI Parts
Description: AI Machine Learning Predictive Maintenance in Automotive Industry. Predicting car replacements before fault.
Website: http://www.aiparts.: Italy
Phone: **Email:** hello@aiparts.: Italy
City: Parma **State:** Emilia-Romagna **PC:** **Country:** ITALY
Year Established: **Status 2020:** Active
Industries: Artificial Intelligence for:, ~ Automotive (5), Machine Learning

Company Name: NeveXN
Description: NeveXN is a developer of green technology for artificial snowmaking.
Website: http://www.nevexn.com/en/
Phone: (223) 680-0229 **Email:** info@nevexn.com
City: Rovereto **State:** Emilia-Romagna **PC:** **Country:** ITALY
Year Established: 2012 **Status 2020:** Active
Industries: Artificial Intelligence for:, ~ Manufacturing-Petroleum-Coal-Chemicals-Plastics-Rubber (37), Industrial Solutions for:, IT Managed Services

Company Name: Novalabs
Description: Nova Labs provides innovative technology for robot development.
Website: http://www.novalabs.io
Phone: **Email:** info@novalabs.io
City: Rovereto **State:** Emilia-Romagna **PC:** **Country:** ITALY
Year Established: 2015 **Status 2020:** Active
Industries: Artificial Intelligence for:, Robotics

Company Name: NUWA Technologies
Description: It develops innovative solutions such as cloud services, software and apps for Music Industry.
Website: http://www.nuwatech.com/
Phone: **Email:** info@nuwatech.com
City: Pordenone **State:** Friuli-Venezia Giulia **PC:** **Country:** ITALY
Year Established: 2016 **Status 2020:** Active
Industries: Artificial Intelligence for:, ~ Event Management (15), IT Managed Services for:, IT Managed Services for:, Machine Learning for:, ~ Arts-Entertainment-Recreation (4), ~ Arts-Entertainment-Recreation (4), Predictive Analytics for:, Predictive Analytics

Company Name: Kaitiaki
Description: We use artificial intelligence to analyze conversations of kids on social networks and alert you in case of threat, respecting their privacy
Website: http://www.kaitiaki.: Italy
Phone: **Email:** info@kaitiaki.: Italy
City: Udine **State:** Friuli-Venezia Giulia **PC:** **Country:** ITALY
Year Established: 2017 **Status 2020:** Active
Industries: Artificial Intelligence for:, ~ Social Assistance-Non-Profits (53)

Company Name: Kaitiaki Srl
Description: Behavioral analysis on social network profiles based on artificial intelligence
Website: http://www.kaitiaki.: Italy
Phone: **Email:** info@kaitiaki.: Italy
City: Udine **State:** Friuli-Venezia Giulia **PC:** **Country:** ITALY
Year Established: **Status 2020:** Active
Industries: Artificial Intelligence for:, ~ Social Assistance-Non-Profits (53)

Company Name: Allelica
Description: Allelica is a software company that develops algorithms to predict human traits and diseases based on genomics data.
Website: https://www.allelica.com/
Phone: **Email:** info@allelica.com
City: Roma **State:** Lazio **PC:** **Country:** ITALY
Year Established: 2018 **Status 2020:** Active
Industries: ~ Biotechnology (9), ~ Healthcare (20), ~ Healthcare (20), Predictive Analytics

Company Name: Datalytics
Description: Datalytics provides real-time solution to understand and improve brand reputation and social media engagement
Website: http://www.datalytics.it/
Phone: 39 393 9024604 **Email:** info@datalytics.: Italy
City: Roma **State:** Lazio **PC:** **Country:** ITALY
Year Established: **Status 2020:** Active
Industries: Analytics for:, Artificial Intelligence for:, ~ Arts-Entertainment-Recreation (4), Digital Marketing for:, Predictive Analytics for:, Compute for:, Cyber Security for:, ~ Social Media (54), ~ Social Media (54)

Company Name: Deep Learning Italia
Description: Deep Learning Italia is a community to share knowledge on the Deep Learning and Machine Learning area.
Website: http://www.deeplearningitalia.com
Phone: **Email:** info@deeplearningitalia.com
City: Roma **State:** Lazio **PC:** **Country:** ITALY
Year Established: 2016 **Status 2020:** Active
Industries: Artificial Intelligence for:, ~ Education (13), IT Managed Services for:, Machine Learning

Company Name: Innovaetica
Description: Innovaetic is an Italian company with expertise in blockchain, cryptographic technologies and AI.
Website: http://www.innovaetica.com/
Phone: **Email:** 36769@reference-encyclopedia-ai.net
City: Roma **State:** Lazio **PC:** **Country:** ITALY
Year Established: 2012 **Status 2020:** Active
Industries:

Company Name: InsideOut10
Description: At InsideOut10, we believe that the open exchange of ideas has a positive global impact. Every day we are inspired by stories of people.
Website: http://www.insideout.io
Phone: **Email:** info@insideout.io
City: Roma **State:** Lazio **PC:** **Country:** ITALY
Year Established: 2011 **Status 2020:** Active
Industries: Artificial Intelligence for:, Augmented Reality for:, Web

Company Name: Nextwin Srl
Description: Nextwin is company creating solutions for sport passionate using big data and gamification
Website: http://www.invictus.bet
Phone: **Email:** info@nextwin.com
City: Roma **State:** Lazio **PC:** **Country:** ITALY
Year Established: **Status 2020:** Active
Industries: Artificial Intelligence for:, Big Data and Analytics for:, Web for:, Mobile for:, ~ Education (13)

Company Name: Pathflow
Description: Pathflow is a business intelligence system that analyzes customers' behavior in stores to quantitatively measure their shopping experience.
Website: http://pathflow.co
Phone: **Email:** info@pathflow.co
City: Roma **State:** Lazio **PC:** **Country:** ITALY
Year Established: 2012 **Status 2020:** Closed
Industries:

Company Name: Poleecy
Description: Instant Insurance, Insurtech, Blockcha: India
Website: www.poleecy.com
Phone: **Email:** info@poleecy.com
City: Roma **State:** Lazio **PC:** **Country:** ITALY
Year Established: **Status 2020:** Active
Industries: ~ Insurance (25)

Company Name: UNFRAUD
Description: UNFRAUD is a software platform that prevents potential online fraud scenarios.
Website: http://unfraud.com/
Phone: **Email:** admin@unfraud.com
City: Roma **State:** Lazio **PC:** **Country:** ITALY
Year Established: **Status 2020:** Active
Industries: Artificial Intelligence for:, Security for:, IT Managed Services

Company Name: Airgloss
Description: Airgloss develops advanced devices aimed at improving indoor environmental comfort using a proprietary AI based sensing technology.
Website: http://www.airglossproject.com/
Phone: **Email:** info@airgloss.com
City: Rome **State:** Lazio **PC:** **Country:** ITALY
Year Established: 2014 **Status 2020:** Active
Industries: Artificial Intelligence for:, Big Data and Analytics for:, ~ Construction (10), ~ Healthcare (20), IT Managed Services for:, ~ Construction (10)

Company Name: AISE.ai
Description: AI System Engineering - a platform and tools for Machine Learning and Big Data
Website: http://aise.ai
Phone: **Email:** cv-c@aise.ai
City: Rome **State:** Lazio **PC:** **Country:** ITALY
Year Established: **Status 2020:** Active
Industries: Analytics for:, Artificial Intelligence for:, Big Data and Analytics for:, Cloud for:, Cloud for:, Enterprise Application Services for:, Machine Learning for:, Application Services

Company Name: Atoo: Morocco
Description: Atooma created Resonance: it uses the IoT to create contextual predictions and automations based on user liv: Spain
Website: http://www.atooma.com
Phone: **Email:** 36108@reference-encyclopedia-ai.net
City: Rome **State:** Lazio **PC:** **Country:** ITALY
Year Established: 2012 **Status 2020:** Active
Industries: Artificial Intelligence for:, ~ Automotive (5), Cloud for:, Automation for:, Internet of Things (IoT)

Company Name: Cogisen
Description: Cogisen has AI Technology to extract context and intent from videos.
Website: http://www.cogisen.com/
Phone: **Email:** info@cogisen.com
City: Rome **State:** Lazio **PC:** **Country:** ITALY
Year Established: **Status 2020:** Active
Industries: Artificial Intelligence for:, Computer Vision for:, Image Recognition for:, ~ Life Sciences (27)

Company Name: Eggup
Description: Soft skills analytics for teams and individuals
Website: http://home.eggup.co/
Phone: **Email:** cristian.demitri@eggup.net
City: Rome **State:** Lazio **PC:** **Country:** ITALY
Year Established: 2013 **Status 2020:** Active
Industries: Predictive Analytics

Company Name: GenomeUp
Description: A.I. for precision medicine
Website: http://www.genomeup.com
Phone: **Email:** info@genomeup.com
City: Rome **State:** Lazio **PC:** **Country:** ITALY
Year Established: **Status 2020:** Active
Industries: Artificial Intelligence for:, ~ Biotechnology (9), ~ Healthcare (20), ~ Healthcare (20)

Company Name: INNAAS
Description: Starting from datasets INNAAS builds Smart Advisors capable of streamlining business processes and helping users to save time through AI.
Website: http://www.innaas.com
Phone: 3494064986 **Email:** info@innaas.com
City: Rome **State:** Lazio **PC:** **Country:** ITALY
Year Established: **Status 2020:** Active
Industries: Analytics for:, Artificial Intelligence for:, Big Data and Analytics

Company Name: IPERVOX.COM
Description: The SaaS platform that allow everyone to build voice apps (Alexa Skills, Google Actions, et) without any technical knowledge
Website: http://ipervox.com
Phone: **Email:** info@ipervox.com
City: Rome **State:** Lazio **PC:** **Country:** ITALY
Year Established: 2019 **Status 2020:** Active
Industries: Content for:, Natural Language Processing for:, Business Software as a Service Apps (SaaS Apps)

Company Name: Mr. Doc
Description: Mr. Doc is an AI platform able to diagnose a wide range of non-communicable disease.
Website: http://www.mrdoc.ai/
Phone: **Email:** kasiaparys@mrdoc.ai
City: Rome **State:** Lazio **PC:** **Country:** ITALY
Year Established: 2017 **Status 2020:** Active
Industries: Artificial Intelligence for:, ~ Healthcare (20)

Company Name: PASTO
Description: The voice driven cooking assistant.
Website: http://www.mypasto.com/
Phone: **Email:** info@mypasto.com
City: Rome **State:** Lazio **PC:** **Country:** ITALY
Year Established: **Status 2020:** Active
Industries: Artificial Intelligence for:, ~ Food and Beverage (17), Machine Learning

Company Name: Revotree
Description: Scalable IoT system for Agtech to monitor water needs in large rural areas, manage water supply and save resources thanks to AI.
Website: http://revotree.it/en/invest
Phone: 39 329-965-2259 **Email:** info@revotree.: Italy
City: Rome **State:** Lazio **PC:** **Country:** ITALY
Year Established: **Status 2020:** Active
Industries: ~ Agriculture (3), ~ Agriculture (3), Artificial Intelligence for:, ~ Social-Environmental-Physical-Engineering Sciences (55)

Company Name: TrueYou
Description: TrueYou is a dating apps aggregator using artificial intelligence to improve digital communication and quality of matches.
Website: http://www.trueyou.: Italy
Phone: **Email:** andrea@trueyou.: Italy
City: Rome **State:** Lazio **PC:** **Country:** ITALY
Year Established: **Status 2020:** Active
Industries:

Company Name: WordLift
Description: WordLift is the Artificial Intelligence you need to grow your audience. A WordPress Plugin that does what an SEO expert would do.
Website: http://wordlift.io/
Phone: 39 06 6821 0190 **Email:** andrea@wordlift.io
City: Rome **State:** Lazio **PC:** **Country:** ITALY
Year Established: **Status 2020:** Active
Industries: Artificial Intelligence for:, Content for:, Digital Marketing for:, ~ Professional Services (48)

Company Name: SurgiQ
Description: Real-time assistant supporting healthcare performanc: Spain
Website: http://www.surgiq.com
Phone: **Email:** learn@surgiq.com
City: Genoa **State:** Liguria **PC:** **Country:** ITALY
Year Established: 2016 **Status 2020:** Active
Industries: Artificial Intelligence for:, ~ Healthcare (20), ~ Healthcare (20)

Company Name: BetBox.ai
Description: BetBox is the world's first AI-driven Hedge Fund bringing the power of Machine Learning
Website: http://betbox.ai/
Phone: **Email:** hello@betbox.ai
City: Genova **State:** Liguria **PC:** **Country:** ITALY
Year Established: **Status 2020:** Active
Industries: Artificial Intelligence

Company Name: Kellify
Description: Make your passion be worth. Invest easily in passion assets or care for your collection driven by AI.
Website: http://kellify.com/
Phone: **Email:** we@kellify.com
City: Genova **State:** Liguria **PC:** **Country:** ITALY

Year Established: 2017 **Status 2020:** Active
Industries: Artificial Intelligence for:, ~ Banking and Financial Markets-Services (7), ~ Banking and Financial Markets-Services (7), Machine Learning

Company Name: THE TACTIGON
Description: Gesture Controller for AR/VR, Robotics, Gaming applications with Ardui
Website: http://www.thetactigon.com/landing/
Phone: **Email:** info@thetactigon.com
City: Inzago **State:** Lombardia **PC:** **Country:** ITALY
Year Established: 2014 **Status 2020:** Active
Industries: Artificial Intelligence for:, Augmented Reality for:, Human Computer Interaction for:, Machine Learning for:, Virtual Reality (VR) for:, Internet of Things (IoT)

Company Name: Ds4
Description: Ds4 develops, designs, and builds automation systems on demand.
Website: http://www.ds4.it/
Phone: 39 035 661 140 **Email:** info@ds4.: Italy
City: Bergamo **State:** Lombardy **PC:** **Country:** ITALY
Year Established: **Status 2020:** Active
Industries: Artificial Intelligence for:, ~ Manufacturing-Electronic (30), ~ Social-Environmental-Physical-Engineering Sciences (55)

Company Name: Socialbeat
Description: SaaS, Artificial Intelligence, Content monitoring
Website: http://www.socialbeat.io
Phone: 39 366 387 3490 **Email:** info@socialbeat.io
City: Bergamo **State:** Lombardy **PC:** **Country:** ITALY
Year Established: 2017 **Status 2020:** Active
Industries: Artificial Intelligence for:, Content for:, Business Software as a Service Apps (SaaS Apps)

Company Name: Neosperience
Description: Neosperience helps organizations understand, engage and delight customers, using personalization to deliver relevant experiences.
Website: http://www.neosperience.com
Phone: **Email:** info@neosperience.com
City: Brescia **State:** Lombardy **PC:** **Country:** ITALY
Year Established: **Status 2020:** Active
Industries: Analytics for:, Artificial Intelligence for:, Cloud for:, Digital Marketing for:, Mobile

Company Name: GetDayOffer
Description: Search and book special offers, local and typical dishes in the nearest restaurants with personal preferences (AI)
Website: http://www.getdayoffer.com
Phone: **Email:** info@getdayoffer.com
City: Lodi **State:** Lombardy **PC:** **Country:** ITALY
Year Established: **Status 2020:** Active
Industries: Artificial Intelligence for:, ~ Food and Beverage (17), Machine Learning

Company Name: Agilize Europe Srl
Description: Agilize is a company that offers a comprehensive accounting service based on software and automated business processes.
Website: http://agilize.it/
Phone: 40 208283 **Email:** contatto@agilize.: Italy
City: Milan **State:** Lombardy **PC:** **Country:** ITALY
Year Established: 2016 **Status 2020:** Active
Industries: Finance and Accounting for:, Enterprise Application Services for:, Enterprise Application Services for:, Web for:, Machine Learning

Company Name: Akamas
Description: AI-driven full-stack solution for continuous performance optimization.
Website: https://www.akamas.io/
Phone: **Email:** info@akamas.io
City: Milan **State:** Lombardy **PC:** **Country:** ITALY
Year Established: 2017 **Status 2020:** Active
Industries: Application Services for:, Artificial Intelligence for:, Enterprise Application Services for:, Machine Learning

Company Name: Bra: India
Description: Brain is a research company that develops proprietary signals based on alternative data and algorithms for investment.
Website: http://braincompany.co/
Phone: **Email:** contacts@braincompany.co
City: Milan **State:** Lombardy **PC:** **Country:** ITALY
Year Established: 2016 **Status 2020:** Active
Industries: Artificial Intelligence for:, ~ Banking and Financial Markets-Services (7), Machine Learning

Company Name: CarBra: India
Description: CarBrain is a smart cars, IoT company. We make every car a smart car with AI, nlp, computer vision.
Website: http://carbrain.net
Phone: **Email:** info@carbrain.net
City: Milan **State:** Lombardy **PC:** **Country:** ITALY
Year Established: 2016 **Status 2020:** Active
Industries: Artificial Intelligence for:, ~ Automotive (5)

Company Name: Cardo AI
Description: Cardo AI is uses Artificial Intelligence algorithms and advanced integrated platform to provide access to institutional investors.
Website: http://cardoai.com/
Phone: **Email:** info@cardoai.com
City: Milan **State:** Lombardy **PC:** **Country:** ITALY
Year Established: **Status 2020:** Active
Industries:

Company Name: dilium
Description: Technologies for ideas
Website: http://dilium.com
Phone: **Email:** hello@dilium.com
City: Milan **State:** Lombardy **PC:** **Country:** ITALY
Year Established: 2017 **Status 2020:** Active
Industries: Artificial Intelligence for:, Augmented Reality for:, IT Managed Services

Company Name: Elif Lab
Description: We are an innovative company that operates in the field of data science.
Website: http://www.eliflab.com
Phone: **Email:** info@eliflab.com
City: Milan **State:** Lombardy **PC:** **Country:** ITALY
Year Established: 2016 **Status 2020:** Active
Industries: Artificial Intelligence for:, Big Data and Analytics for:, Business Intelligence for:, Databases for:, Data Management for:, ~ Government (19), Predictive Analytics for:, Predictive Analytics for:, Data Management

Company Name: ELSE Corp
Description: ELSE Corp is an Italian B2B and B2B2C startup, designing new technological solutions for Virtual Retail and Cloud Manufacturing
Website: http://www.else-corp.com
Phone: **Email:** info@else-corp.: Italy
City: Milan **State:** Lombardy **PC:** **Country:** ITALY
Year Established: **Status 2020:** Active
Industries: Artificial Intelligence for:, Cloud for:, ~ Fashion (16), ~ Retail and Consumer Products (52)

Company Name: Fluida Euro:
Description: Liquid Workforce Management Platform
Website: http://www.fluida.io
Phone: **Email:** info@e-gva.: Italy
City: Milan **State:** Lombardy **PC:** **Country:** ITALY
Year Established: **Status 2020:** Active
Industries: Analytics for:, Artificial Intelligence for:, Blockchain for:, ~ Human Resources (24)

Company Name: Igreg Studio srl
Description: Professional Photography and video on Demand
Website: http://www.igregstudio.com
Phone: 39 02 8715 9191 **Email:** info@igregstudio.com
City: Milan **State:** Lombardy **PC:** **Country:** ITALY
Year Established: **Status 2020:** Active
Industries: Artificial Intelligence for:, Machine Learning for:, ~ Media-Communications (41), ~ Media-Communications (41)

Company **Name:** InsightSensor
Description: AI controlled sensors to help hobbyists taking care of their garden
Website: http://insightsensor.com
Phone: **Email:** contact@insightsensor.com
City: Milan **State:** Lombardy **PC:** **Country:** ITALY
Year Established: 2017 **Status 2020:** Active
Industries: ~ Agriculture (3), Artificial Intelligence for:, ~ Healthcare (20)

Company Name: LIFEdata AI
Description: LIFEdata is an AI Voice SaaS platform that turns speech (and instant messaging) into action, powering the Omni-Channel User Experience.
Website: http://lifedata.ai
Phone: **Email:** info@lifedata.ai
City: Milan **State:** Lombardy **PC:** **Country:** ITALY
Year Established: 2019 **Status 2020:** Active
Industries: Artificial Intelligence for:, Big Data and Analytics for:, E-Commerce for:, Application Program Interfaces (APIs) for:, Natural Language Processing for:, Predictive Analytics for:, Application Services for:, Application Services for:, Business Software as a Servi

Company Name: Mercurius BI Srl
Description: Mercurius combines machine learning and risk management techniques in order to transform sports betting into a new asset class.
Website: http://mercurius.io/
Phone: **Email:** info@mercurius.io
City: Milan **State:** Lombardy **PC:** **Country:** ITALY
Year Established: 2017 **Status 2020:** Active
Industries: Artificial Intelligence for:, ~ Banking and Financial Markets-Services (7), Machine Learning for:, ~ Banking and Financial Markets-Services (7), Predictive Analytics for:, ~ Arts-Entertainment-Recreation (4)

Company Name: Namu
Description: Namu develops CDM for Sales & Marketing
Website: http://namu.io
Phone: **Email:** 37038@reference-encyclopedia-ai.net
City: Milan **State:** Lombardy **PC:** **Country:** ITALY
Year Established: 2017 **Status 2020:** Active
Industries: Artificial Intelligence for:, ~ Customer Relationship Management (11), Predictive Analytics for:, Automation

Company Name: Pred: Italy
Description: PREDIT offers a Cloud AI solution helping Fashion & Retail brands improve profitability of assortments and reducing related risks and costs
Website: http://www.predit.it/
Phone: **Email:** info@predit.: Italy
City: Milan **State:** Lombardy **PC:** **Country:** ITALY
Year Established: 2016 **Status 2020:** Active
Industries: Artificial Intelligence for:, Business Intelligence for:, ~ Fashion (16), IT Managed Services for:, IT Managed Services for:, Machine Learning for:, Predictive Analytics

Company Name: Radicalb: Italy
Description: Radicalbit is a deep tech company specialized in Real-Time Advanced Analytics and Artificial Intelligence
Website: http://radicalbit.io/
Phone: 39 (0)422 1600025 **Email:** sales@radicalbit.io
City: Milan **State:** Lombardy **PC:** **Country:** ITALY
Year Established: 2015 **Status 2020:** Active
Industries: Analytics for:, Artificial Intelligence for:, Big Data and Analytics for:, Data Management for:, IT Managed Services for:, Machine Learning for:, Natural Language Processing for:, Predictive Analytics for:, Predictive Analytics

Company Name: Sequitur Capital
Description: Investment Management, Venture Capital, Club deals, Scale-ups, Deep Tech
Website: http://www.sequitur-capital.com
Phone: **Email:** info@sequitur-capital.com
City: Milan **State:** Lombardy **PC:** **Country:** ITALY
Year Established: **Status 2020:** Active
Industries: Artificial Intelligence for:, Augmented Reality for:, Business Applications for:, Machine Learning for:, ~ Construction (10), ~ Professional Services (48), ~ Banking and Financial Markets-Services (7)

Company Name: Smart Robots S.r.l.
Description: Smart Robots products provide robots with advanced cognitive skills to improve work processes where humans and robots work side by side.
Website: http://www.smartrobots.it/
Phone: 39 02 4590 2000 **Email:** info@smartrobots.: Italy
City: Milan **State:** Lombardy **PC:** **Country:** ITALY
Year Established: **Status 2020:** Active
Industries: Artificial Intelligence for:, ~ Manufacturing-General (31), Robotics

Company Name: smartFAB
Description: Actionable Analytics
Website: http://www.smartfab.ai
Phone: 39 335 7007119 **Email:** ann@smartfab.ai
City: Milan **State:** Lombardy **PC:** **Country:** ITALY
Year Established: **Status 2020:** Active
Industries:

Company Name: Userbot
Description: Userbot is an AI powered customer interaction platform based in UK .
Website: http://userbot.ai/
Phone: **Email:** ciao@userbot.ai
City: Milan **State:** Lombardy **PC:** **Country:** ITALY
Year Established: 2017 **Status 2020:** Active
Industries: Artificial Intelligence for:, ~ Customer Relationship Management (11), IT Managed Services

Company Name: Volvero
Description: Wego is a blockchain based innovative startups in the sustainable mobility.
Website: http://volvero.com/
Phone: 1 3127610516 **Email:** info@volvero.com
City: Milan **State:** Lombardy **PC:** **Country:** ITALY
Year Established: **Status 2020:** Active
Industries: Application Services for:, Artificial Intelligence for:, ~ Construction (10), ~ Energy and Utilities (14), ~ Social-Environmental-Physical-Engineering Sciences (55), ~ Transportation and Logistics (57), Big Data and Analytics for:, Blockchain

Company Name: Walllabi: Spain
Description: We're bringing in the sport the recent developments in the training of the artificial neural networks and machine learning techniques.
Website: http://www.wallabies.it/
Phone: 39 3397492510 **Email:** info@wallabies.: Italy
City: Milan **State:** Lombardy **PC:** **Country:** ITALY
Year Established: 2016 **Status 2020:** Active
Industries: Artificial Intelligence for:, ~ Arts-Entertainment-Recreation (4), ~ Arts-Entertainment-Recreation (4), IT Managed Services for:, Machine Learning for:, ~ Arts-Entertainment-Recreation (4), ~ Arts-Entertainment-Recreation (4), ~ Arts-Entertainment-Recreation (4)

Company Name: Audiens
Description: Customer Data Platform as a Service
Website: http://www.audiens.com
Phone: **Email:** sales@audiens.com
City: Milano **State:** Lombardy **PC:** **Country:** ITALY
Year Established: 2015 **Status 2020:** Active
Industries: Big Data and Analytics for:, Data Management for:, Digital Marketing for:, Machine Learning for:, Enterprise Application Services

Company Name: BOOM IMAGE STUDIO
Description: On demand photography service driven by artificial intelligence
Website: http://boomimagestudio.com/
Phone: 02 4969 3763 **Email:** info@boomimagestudio.com
City: Milano **State:** Lombardy **PC:** **Country:** ITALY
Year Established: **Status 2020:** Active
Industries: Artificial Intelligence for:, ~ Personal-Religious-Civic (45), Computer Vision for:, Machine Learning for:, ~ Media-Communications (41)

Company **Name:** BOOM imagestudio
Description: On demand photography service driven by artificial intelligence
Website: http://boomimagestudio.com/
Phone: 02 4969 3763 **Email:** info@boomimagestudio.com
City: Milano **State:** Lombardy **PC:** **Country:** ITALY
Year Established: 2018 **Status 2020:** Active
Industries: Artificial Intelligence for:, Computer Vision for:, Machine Learning

Company Name: Emotiva
Description: Emotion AI, Emotion Recognition, Affective Computing, Emotion Artificial Intelligence to understand human behaviors.
Website: http://www.emotiva.: Italy
Phone: 39 0287189207 **Email:** info@emotiva.: Italy
City: Milano **State:** Lombardy **PC:** **Country:** ITALY
Year Established: 2017 **Status 2020:** Active
Industries: Analytics for:, Artificial Intelligence for:, IT Managed Services for:, Machine Learning

Company Name: HITBYT: SPAIN
Description: AI-Powered Startup | Chatbot and Voice Apps Development
Website: http://hitbytes.io/
Phone: 1 408 692 5909 **Email:** info@hitbytes.io
City: Milano **State:** Lombardy **PC:** **Country:** ITALY
Year Established: **Status 2020:** Active
Industries: Artificial Intelligence for:, Machine Learning for:, ~ Media-Communications (41), Development and Test

Company Name: Indigo.ai
Description: We combine language and science to build meaningful AI.
Website: http://indigo.ai/
Phone: 39 342 3271299 **Email:** g@indigo.ai
City: Milano **State:** Lombardy **PC:** **Country:** ITALY
Year Established: 2016 **Status 2020:** Active
Industries: Artificial Intelligence for:, IT Managed Services for:, Internet of Things (IoT) for:, Machine Learning

Company Name: kpi6
Description: KPI6 monitors the flow of information generated on social media in order to help companies to make better decisions, quicker.
Website: http://kpi6.com
Phone: **Email:** info@kpi6.com
City: Milano **State:** Lombardy **PC:** **Country:** ITALY
Year Established: 2015 **Status 2020:** Active
Industries: Artificial Intelligence for:, Data Management for:, Predictive Analytics for:, ~ Social Assistance-Non-Profits (53)

Company Name: Math&Sport
Description: Math&Sport focuses on the optimization of the athlete performance and game tactics through the use of mathematics and data science.
Website: http://www.mathandsport.com/
Phone: **Email:** 36944@reference-encyclopedia-ai.net
City: Milano **State:** Lombardy **PC:** **Country:** ITALY
Year Established: 2016 **Status 2020:** Active
Industries: Analytics for:, Machine Learning for:, ~ Arts-Entertainment-Recreation (4)

Company Name: MDOTM
Description: MDOTM develops AI-driven investment strategies for the financial markets.
Website: http://www.mdotm.eu
Phone: **Email:** info@mdotm.eu
City: Milano **State:** Lombardy **PC:** **Country:** ITALY
Year Established: 2015 **Status 2020:** Active
Industries: Artificial Intelligence for:, ~ Banking and Financial Markets-Services (7), ~ Banking and Financial Markets-Services (7), ~ Banking and Financial Markets-Services (7), ~ Banking and Financial Markets-Services (7), Machine Learning

Company Name: Metaliquid
Description: Metaliquid is a video content semantic analysis startup that applies deep learning technology to video content comprehension
Website: http://www.meta-liquid.com/
Phone: **Email:** info@meta-liquid.com
City: Milano **State:** Lombardy **PC:** **Country:** ITALY
Year Established: **Status 2020:** Active
Industries: Artificial Intelligence for:, Computer Vision

Company Name: NamiLab
Description: NamiLab is a software applications development company.
Website: http://www.nami-lab.com
Phone: **Email:** info@nami-lab.com
City: Milano **State:** Lombardy **PC:** **Country:** ITALY
Year Established: **Status 2020:** Active
Industries:

Company Name: Robonica Srl
Description: Intelligent Home Growing Systems
Website: http://robonica.it/
Phone: **Email:** info@robonica.: Italy
City: Milano **State:** Lombardy **PC:** **Country:** ITALY
Year Established: **Status 2020:** Active
Industries: Artificial Intelligence for:, Machine Learning for:, ~ Healthcare (20), ~ Food and Beverage (17)

Company Name: Socialangel
Description: Socialangel offer a smart virtual social media manager helping companies achieving their goals on Facebook.
Website: http://www.socialangel.io
Phone: **Email:** info@socialangel.io
City: Milano **State:** Lombardy **PC:** **Country:** ITALY
Year Established: **Status 2020:** Active
Industries: Artificial Intelligence for:, Big Data and Analytics for:, ~ Social Media (54), ~ Social Media (54)

Company Name: SweetHive
Description: The Context Sharing Platform, one solution to manage schools, enterprises, houses and services. Just add a new place to you hive!
Website: http://sweethive.com/
Phone: **Email:** info@sweethive.com
City: Milano **State:** Lombardy **PC:** **Country:** ITALY
Year Established: **Status 2020:** Active
Industries: Artificial Intelligence for:, Cloud for:, Cloud for:, Collaboration Solutions for:, Management Information Systems

Company Name: VUIX
Description: Vuix is the ultimate and ease-to-use visual interface to create voice apps for Amazon Alexa or Google Assistant. Without code.
Website: http://vuix.io
Phone: **Email:** hello@vuix.io
City: Milano **State:** Lombardy **PC:** **Country:** ITALY
Year Established: **Status 2020:** Active
Industries: Artificial Intelligence

Company Name: WAVENURE
Description: Al-based investments' and funds' performance enhancer
Website: http://wavenure.ai
Phone: **Email:** info@wavenure.com
City: Milano **State:** Lombardy **PC:** **Country:** ITALY
Year Established: 2016 **Status 2020:** Active
Industries: Artificial Intelligence for:, ~ Banking and Financial Markets-Services (7), ~ Banking and Financial Markets-Services (7), IT Managed Services for:, Machine Learning

Company Name: White Rabbit Srl
Description: White Rabbit - The Happy Business Suite
Website:
Phone: 39 0854549825 **Email:** barbarossa@whiterabbit.cloud
City: Monza **State:** Lombardy **PC:** **Country:** ITALY
Year Established: **Status 2020:** Active
Industries: ~ Media-Communications (41), ~ Media-Communications (41), Analytics for:, Artificial Intelligence for:, Business Intelligence for:, Content for:, Content for:, E-Commerce for:, ~ Media-Communications (41), ~ Media-Communications (41), Predictive Analytics for:, ~ So

Company Name: MIPU
Description: MIPU provides AI and predictive analysis solutions to optimize industrial processes and operations.
Website: http://mipu.it/
Phone: 0365 520098 **Email:** info@mipu.eu
City: Salo **State:** Lombardy **PC:** **Country:** ITALY
Year Established: 2012 **Status 2020:** Active
Industries: Analytics

Company Name: ELSE Tech (ATOM Group)
Description: Is a technological arm of the group of partners, ELSE Corp, ATOM Group and ShoeMaster, dedicated to software development and integration
Website: http://www.else-tech.: Italy
Phone: **Email:** info@else-tech.: Italy
City: Vigevano **State:** Lombardy **PC:** **Country:** ITALY
Year Established: 2018 **Status 2020:** Closed
Industries: Artificial Intelligence for:, Cloud for:, Computer Vision for:, Internet of Things (IoT)

Company Name: FERT experienced solutions
Description: FERT experienced solutions on creating A.I. algorithms applied to predictions and sentiment analysis.
Website: http://www.fertes.eu
Phone: **Email:** 36560@reference-encyclopedia-ai.net
City: Asti **State:** Piedmont **PC:** **Country:** ITALY
Year Established: 2018 **Status 2020:** Active
Industries: Artificial Intelligence for:, Big Data and Analytics for:, Machine Learning

Company Name: AIKO - Autonomous Space Missions
Description: AIKO develops and commercialize algorithms based on Artificial Intelligence to increase the autonomy of small satellite missions.
Website: https://www.aikospace.com/
Phone: **Email:** info@aikospace.com
City: Torino **State:** Piedmont **PC:** **Country:** ITALY
Year Established: 2017 **Status 2020:** Active
Industries: ~ Aerospace and Defense (2), Artificial Intelligence for:, Automation

Company Name: Nextatlas
Description: Nextatlas helps brands easily visualize emerging trends by meshing together data from a wide variety of sources into actionable insights.
Website: http://www.nextatlas.com
Phone: **Email:** info@nextatlas.com
City: Torino **State:** Piedmont **PC:** **Country:** ITALY
Year Established: **Status 2020:** Active
Industries: Analytics for:, Artificial Intelligence for:, Big Data and Analytics

Company Name: Prometheus
Description: Prometheus is an online platform that uses AI and Machine Learning to help students make better career choices.
Website: http://prometheus-en.strikingly.com/
Phone: 55 12 981480884 **Email:** prometheusplat@gmail.com
City: Torino **State:** Piedmont **PC:** **Country:** ITALY
Year Established: **Status 2020:** Active
Industries: Artificial Intelligence for:, Big Data and Analytics for:, ~ Education (13), ~ Education (13), Machine Learning for:, ~ Education (13)

Company Name: Technology & Cognition
Description: We developed AIDA (Artificial Intelligence for Document Automation), a SaaS solution to recognize and extract informations from documents
Website: http://www.tclab.: Italy
Phone: 115695659 **Email:** info@tclab.: Italy
City: Torino **State:** Piedmont **PC:** **Country:** ITALY
Year Established: 2016 **Status 2020:** Active
Industries: Artificial Intelligence for:, Cloud for:, Data Management for:, IT Managed Services for:, Web for:, Machine Learning for:, Business Software as a Service Apps (SaaS Apps)

Company Name: You Are My Guide
Description: You Are My Guide can help you improve your profitability and expand your business.
Website: http://youaremyguide.com
Phone: **Email:** info@youaremyguide.com
City: Torino **State:** Piedmont **PC:** **Country:** ITALY
Year Established: 2014 **Status 2020:** Active
Industries:

Company Name: ClearBox AI Solutions
Description: SaaS: Explainable AI engine that enables trustworthy and human-centric AI model deployment in enterprises at scale
Website: http://clearbox.ai/
Phone: **Email:** info@clearbox.ai
City: Turin **State:** Piedmont **PC:** **Country:** ITALY
Year Established: 2019 **Status 2020:** Active
Industries: Artificial Intelligence for:, IT Managed Services for:, Business Software as a Service Apps (SaaS Apps)

Company Name: Omnidermal
Description: Omnidermal specialized in the realization of devices equipped with artificial intelligence algorithms applied to applied to dermatology.
Website: http://www.omnidermal.com/
Phone: (39) 3807342667 **Email:** info@omnidermal.com
City: Turin **State:** Piedmont **PC:** **Country:** ITALY
Year Established: 2017 **Status 2020:** Active
Industries: Artificial Intelligence

Company Name: Sport Grand Tour
Description: Orangogo allows you to discover your talent
Website: http://www.orangogo.: Italy
Phone: 39.327.7745292 **Email:** info@orangogo.: Italy
City: Turin **State:** Piedmont **PC:** **Country:** ITALY
Year Established: 2017 **Status 2020:** Active
Industries: Artificial Intelligence for:, ~ Arts-Entertainment-Recreation (4)

Company Name: Athlos s.r.l.
Description: Athlos provide an advanced tool that allow developers to integrate italian natural language processing
Website: http://www.athlos.biz
Phone: **Email:** info@athlos.biz
City: Cagliari **State:** Sardinia **PC:** **Country:** ITALY
Year Established: **Status 2020:** Active
Industries: Artificial Intelligence for:, ~ Education (13), Natural Language Processing

Company Name: Pluribus One
Description: Research-intensive start-up
Website: http://www.pluribus-one.: Italy
Phone: **Email:** info@pluribus-one.: Italy
City: Cagliari **State:** Sardinia **PC:** **Country:** ITALY
Year Established: 2015 **Status 2020:** Active
Industries: Computer Vision for:, Cyber Security for:, Image Recognition for:, Machine Learning

Company Name: WonderStore
Description: WonderStore is a computer vision platform for retail that satisfies the strategic need to know the shop visitors.
Website: http://www.wonderstore.ai
Phone: 39 331 6387336 **Email:** lcrudele@wonderstore.ai
City: Cagliari **State:** Sardinia **PC:** **Country:** ITALY
Year Established: 2017 **Status 2020:** Active
Industries: Analytics for:, Artificial Intelligence for:, Big Data and Analytics for:, Business Intelligence for:, Cloud for:, Computer Vision for:, Facial Recognition for:, Machine Learning for:, Machine Learning

Company Name: SharkPick
Description: SharkPick combines AI and collective intelligence for financial forecasting that offers its results in a single application.
Website: http://www.sharkpick.com/
Phone: **Email:** 37375@reference-encyclopedia-ai.net
City: Sassari **State:** Sardinia **PC:** **Country:** ITALY
Year Established: 2016 **Status 2020:** Active
Industries: Artificial Intelligence for:, Machine Learning for:, Mobile for:, Application Services for:, Finance and Accounting

Company Name: Morpheos
Description: Morpheos creates innovative technology in high quality products and services that are easy to use and affordable.
Website: http://www.morpheos.eu
Phone: **Email:** info@morpheos.eu
City: Catania **State:** Sicily **PC:** **Country:** ITALY
Year Established: **Status 2020:** Active
Industries: Artificial Intelligence for:, IT Managed Services

Company Name: Motorsquare
Description: We will help our customers to better know their customers.
Website: http://www.motorsquare.eu
Phone: 39 3478689931 **Email:** info@motorsquare.eu
City: Catania **State:** Sicily **PC:** **Country:** ITALY
Year Established: 2015 **Status 2020:** Active
Industries: ~ Automotive (5), Big Data and Analytics for:, IT Managed Services for:, Predictive Analytics

Company Name: Smartisland Group
Description: Smartisland Group is a startup whose mission is to develop visual and visual hardware and software technologies for the IoT.
Website:
Phone: 39 38 83 69 27 18 **Email:** 37416@reference-encyclopedia-ai.net
City: Niscemi **State:** Sicily **PC:** **Country:** ITALY
Year Established: 2016 **Status 2020:** Closed
Industries: Artificial Intelligence

Company Name: Coderblock
Description: Coderblock is the first AI Italian marketplace dedicated to recruitment that favors the encounter between companies and digital freelancers.
Website: http://coderblock.com/en
Phone: **Email:** info@coderblock.com
City: Palermo **State:** Sicily **PC:** **Country:** ITALY
Year Established: 2016 **Status 2020:** Active
Industries: Artificial Intelligence for:, IT Managed Services for:, IT Managed Services

Company Name: AUREOO
Description: Aureoo is a collective intelligence platform that reinvents the way users read and find information in the web era.
Website: http://www.aureoo.com/about/
Phone: **Email:** info@aureoo.com
City: Trento **State:** Trentino-South Tyrol **PC:** **Country:** ITALY
Year Established: 2014 **Status 2020:** Active
Industries: Artificial Intelligence for:, ~ Education (13), ~ Education (13), IT Managed Services for:, IT Managed Services

Company Name: HPA - High Performance Analytics
Description: HPA is an innovative startup that stems from the passion and skill of a team of maths and machine learning experts.
Website: http://www.hpa.ai
Phone: **Email:** info@hpa.ai
City: Trento **State:** Trentino-South Tyrol **PC:** **Country:** ITALY
Year Established: 2017 **Status 2020:** Active
Industries: Analytics for:, Machine Learning

Company Name: SpazioDati
Description: SpazioDati builds a high-quality knowledge-graph that powers Dandelion API and Atoka.
Website: spaziodati.eu
Phone: **Email:** info@spaziodati.eu
City: Trento **State:** Trentino-South Tyrol **PC:** **Country:** ITALY
Year Established: **Status 2020:** Active
Industries:

Company Name: Cynny
Description: Cynny develops MorphCast, a new adaptive video format that delivers face recognition in a smartphone without the need for an app or plugin.
Website: http://www.morphcast.com/
Phone: **Email:** info@cynny.com
City: Firenze **State:** Tuscany **PC:** **Country:** ITALY
Year Established: 2013 **Status 2020:** Active
Industries: Artificial Intelligence for:, Blockchain for:, Digital Marketing for:, Digital Media for:, Facial Recognition for:, Human Computer Interaction for:, IT Managed Services

Company Name: Cynny S.p.a.
Description: Cynny develops MorphCast, a new adaptive video format that delivers face recognition in a smartphone without the need for an app or plugin.
Website: http://www.morphcast.com/
Phone: **Email:** info@morphcast.com
City: Firenze **State:** Tuscany **PC:** **Country:** ITALY
Year Established: **Status 2020:** Active
Industries: Artificial Intelligence for:, Blockchain for:, Digital Marketing for:, Digital Media for:, Facial Recognition for:, Human Computer Interaction for:, IT Managed Services for:, ~ Media-Communications (41)

Company Name: Travel Appeal
Description: Travel Appeal reads and processes millions of data to turn them in plain insights and smart suggestions for your business.
Website: http://www.travelappeal.com/
Phone: **Email:** info@travelappeal.com
City: Firenze **State:** Tuscany **PC:** **Country:** ITALY
Year Established: **Status 2020:** Active
Industries: Analytics for:, Artificial Intelligence for:, Big Data and Analytics for:, Predictive Analytics

Company Name: Istella
Description: Istella develops systems for Big Data Search and Analytics, Robotic Process Automation and Artificial Intelligence.
Website: http://www.istella.ai
Phone: 0039 050 3190250 **Email:** info@istella.ai
City: Pisa **State:** Tuscany **PC:** **Country:** ITALY
Year Established: **Status 2020:** Active
Industries: Analytics for:, ~ Telecommunications (178), Artificial Intelligence for:, ~ Administrative and Support Services (1), ~ Banking and Financial Markets-Services (7), ~ Customer Relationship Management (11), ~ E-Commerce (12), ~ Government (19), ~ Telecommunications

Company Name: VRMedia
Description: developing innovative hardware/software products and solutions using virtual and augmented reality
Website: http://www.kiberhelmet.com
Phone: 0039 0587 274813 **Email:** info@vrmedia.: Italy
City: Pisa **State:** Tuscany **PC:** **Country:** ITALY
Year Established: **Status 2020:** Active
Industries: Artificial Intelligence for:, ~ Manufacturing-Electronic (30), ~ Professional Services (48)

Company **Name:** BRAINCONTROL
Description: BrainControl is a platform based on Artificial Intelligence for human-machine interaction through bio-feedback
Website: http://www.braincontrol.com/
Phone: 39 0577 1916187 **Email:** info@braincontrol.: Italy
City: Siena **State:** Tuscany **PC:** **Country:** ITALY
Year Established: 2010 **Status 2020:** Active
Industries: Artificial Intelligence for:, ~ Biotechnology (9), ~ Healthcare (20), IT Managed Services

Company Name: Agricolus
Description: Making Precision farming easier! Agricolus® makes agTech tools accessible to worldwide farmers to improve production reducing wastes.
Website: http://www.agricolus.com/
Phone: **Email:** accounting@agricolus.com
City: Perugia **State:** Umbria **PC:** **Country:** ITALY
Year Established: 2017 **Status 2020:** Active
Industries: ~ Agriculture (3), ~ Agriculture (3), Internet of Things (IoT) for:, Machine Learning for:, Predictive Analytics for:, Business Software as a Service Apps (SaaS Apps)

Company Name: Sentetic
Description: Sentetic is a new, data-driven approach to condition monitoring which doesn't require years of model-building before you get value.
Website:
Phone: **Email:** 37368@reference-encyclopedia-ai.net
City: Perugia **State:** Umbria **PC:** **Country:** ITALY
Year Established: 2015 **Status 2020:** Active
Industries: Automation for:, Machine Learning for:, Predictive Analytics

Company Name: Enodron
Description: Enodron e una startup innovativa della provincia di Treviso che offre servizi avanzati di viticoltura di precisione tramite dro: Nigeria
Website: http://www.enodron.: Italy
Phone: **Email:** info@enodron.: Italy
City: Follina **State:** Veneto **PC:** **Country:** ITALY
Year Established: **Status 2020:** Active
Industries: ~ Agriculture (3), Artificial Intelligence for:, ~ Transportation and Logistics (57), Robotics

Company Name: PatchAI
Description: PatchAI is the first empathetic AI-powered virtual assistant for collection and predictive analytics of Real World Data in Clinical Trials.
Website: http://www.patchai.io
Phone: **Email:** info@patchai.io
City: Padova **State:** Veneto **PC:** **Country:** ITALY
Year Established: **Status 2020:** Active
Industries: Artificial Intelligence for:, Big Data and Analytics for:, Cloud for:, ~ Manufacturing-Medical Equipment-Supplies (33), ~ Healthcare (20), ~ Pharmaceuticals (46), Predictive Analytics

Company Name: MadeUp
Description: MadeUp is the solution for the companies that want to guarantee the authenticity of their product and provide a unique customer experience
Website: http://www.made-up.: Italy
Phone: (346) 158-0550 **Email:** info@made-up.: Italy
City: Treviso **State:** Veneto **PC:** **Country:** ITALY
Year Established: 2014 **Status 2020:** Active
Industries: E-Commerce for:, ~ Fashion (16), Mobile for:, Internet of Things (IoT) for:, Predictive Analytics

Company Name: AdsHotel
Description: Artificial Intelligence hotel distribution via ready-to-book price ads
Website: http://adshotel.com
Phone: 39.041.5095001 **Email:** partner@adshotel.com
City: Venezia **State:** Veneto **PC:** **Country:** ITALY
Year Established: **Status 2020:** Active
Industries: ~ Media-Communications (41), Artificial Intelligence for:, Blockchain for:, ~ Hospitality (23), ~ Hospitality (23), Machine Learning for:, ~ Travel and Transportation (58)

Japan

Company Name: Worksbot
Description: Worksbot is to provide AI based Erp softwares, Engineering designing, Digital lead Generation and RPO business to the all kind of industry.
Website: http://www.worksbot.com
Phone: 4448587356 **Email:** info@worksbot.com
City: Akasaka **State:** Aichi **PC:** **Country: Japan**
Year Established: 2011 **Status 2020:** Active
Industries: Artificial Intelligence for:, Big Data and Analytics for:, Enterprise Application Services for:, IT Managed Services for:, Robotics for:, Web for:, Web

Company Name: AgreeB: Italy
Description: AgreeBit provides AI agent technology.
Website: https://agreebit.jp/
Phone: **Email:** info@agreebit.: Japan
City: Nagoya **State:** Aichi **PC:** **Country: Japan**
Year Established: 2019 **Status 2020:** Active
Industries:

Company Name: KYSMO
Description: KYSMO is an Artificial Intelligence start up.
Website: http://www.kysmo.tech
Phone: **Email:** 36872@reference-encyclopedia-ai.net
City: Nagoya **State:** Aichi **PC:** **Country: Japan**
Year Established: 2017 **Status 2020:** Active
Industries: Artificial Intelligence

Company Name: NEF Communications
Description: NEF Communications is Solving business issues through statistics, machine learning and deep learning
Website: http://nef-com.jp/
Phone: **Email:** 37046@reference-encyclopedia-ai.net
City: Nagoya **State:** Aichi **PC:** **Country: Japan**
Year Established: 2013 **Status 2020:** Active
Industries: Machine Learning for:, Web

Company Name: OPTIMIND
Description: OPTIMIND is a tech venture company from Nagoya University.
Website: http://www.optimind.tech/
Phone: **Email:** 37116@reference-encyclopedia-ai.net
City: Nagoya **State:** Aichi **PC:** **Country: Japan**

Year Established: 2015 **Status 2020:** Active
Industries: IT Managed Services for:, Machine Learning

Company Name: SEO-NEXT
Description: SEO-NEXT is providing an SEO countermeasure service that uses artificial intelligence and does not take a one second delay
Website: http://www.seo-next.jp/
Phone: **Email:** 37369@reference-encyclopedia-ai.net
City: Nagoya **State:** Aichi **PC:** **Country: Japan**
Year Established: 2014 **Status 2020:** Active
Industries: Artificial Intelligence

Company Name: TRYETING
Description: TRYETING provides an AI platform that integrates various types of software.
Website: http://www.tryeting.: Japan
Phone: 052-979-2110 **Email:** 30966@reference-encyclopedia-ai.net
City: Nagoya **State:** Aichi **PC:** **Country: Japan**
Year Established: 2016 **Status 2020:** Active
Industries: Artificial Intelligence for:, Business Intelligence

Company Name: LiveYourDreams
Description: LiveYourDreams offers video media, robotics workshop and AI technology services.
Website: http://www.liveyourdreams.tv/
Phone: 03-4400-1188 **Email:** contact@liveyourdreams.tv
City: Odate **State:** Akita **PC:** **Country: Japan**
Year Established: 2019 **Status 2020:** Active
Industries: Artificial Intelligence for:, Robotics

Company Name: T&T
Description: Provider of Travel Time Prediction, enabling each traveler or handler of a package to reduce his/her waiting time.
Website: http://www.tandtis.com/home-e/
Phone: **Email:** 37503@reference-encyclopedia-ai.net
City: Chiba **State:** Chiba **PC:** **Country: Japan**
Year Established: 2013 **Status 2020:** Active
Industries: ~ Transportation and Logistics (57), IT Managed Services for:, Internet of Things (IoT) for:, ~ Banking and Financial Markets-Services (7), Predictive Analytics

Company Name: Smart119
Description: Improving emergency and critical care by computer science and artificial intelligence.
Website: http://smart119.biz/en/
Phone: **Email:** info@smart119.biz
City: Chiba-shi **State:** Chiba **PC:** **Country: Japan**
Year Established: 2018 **Status 2020:** Active
Industries: Artificial Intelligence for:, ~ Healthcare (20), Machine Learning for:, ~ Healthcare (20)

Company Name: Liberaware
Description: Liberaware is a machine learning and artificial intelligence company.
Website: http://liberaware.co.jp/index.html
Phone: 043-497-5740 **Email:** 36894@reference-encyclopedia-ai.net
City: Togawa **State:** Chiba **PC:** **Country: Japan**
Year Established: 2016 **Status 2020:** Active
Industries: Artificial Intelligence

Company Name: Fukuoka Prefectural Office
Description:
Website:
Phone: 81-92-643-3214 **Email:** kumamoto-a6518@pref.fukuoka.lg.: Japan
City: Fukuoka **State:** Fukuoka **Zip:** 812-8577 **Country: Japan**
Year Established: **Status 2020:** Active
Industries:

Company Name: INFONEX
Description: INFONEX strive to improve quality by setting checkpoints in the following processes.
Website: http://www.infonex.jp/
Phone: **Email:** info@infonex.: Japan
City: Fukuoka **State:** Fukuoka **PC:** **Country: Japan**
Year Established: 2016 **Status 2020:** Active
Industries: Application Services for:, ~ Administrative and Support Services (1)

Company Name: Medma: India
Description: Medmain's mission is to solve the global shortage of pathologists and the slow turnaround time associated with pathologic diagnoses.
Website: http://en.medmain.com/
Phone: **Email:** info@medmain.com
City: Fukuoka **State:** Fukuoka **PC:** **Country: Japan**
Year Established: 2018 **Status 2020:** Active
Industries: Artificial Intelligence for:, ~ Healthcare (20), IT Managed Services for:, ~ Healthcare (20)

Company Name: 101design
Description: 101design accepts general website production from new production to renewal.
Website: http://101de-sign.com/
Phone: **Email:** 35910@reference-encyclopedia-ai.net
City: Fukuoka-shi **State:** Fukuoka **PC:** **Country: Japan**
Year Established: 2014 **Status 2020:** Active
Industries: Artificial Intelligence for:, Machine Learning for:, Web for:, Web

Company Name: LINE Fukuoka
Description: We conduct all kinds of work such as development, creative, management and business planning of LINE and related services.
Website: http://linefukuoka.co.jp/ja/
Phone: **Email:** 36900@reference-encyclopedia-ai.net
City: Hakata **State:** Fukuoka **PC:** **Country: Japan**
Year Established: 2013 **Status 2020:** Active
Industries:

Company Name: QUANDO
Description: Quando is an Business development company utilizing IoT / AI
Website: http://quando.jp/
Phone: **Email:** 37237@reference-encyclopedia-ai.net
City: Kitakyushu **State:** Fukuoka **PC:** **Country: Japan**
Year Established: 2017 **Status 2020:** Active
Industries: Artificial Intelligence for:, ~ Banking and Financial Markets-Services (7), Business Process and Operations

Company Name: JSW
Description:
Website: http://www.jsw.co.: Japan
Phone: 81-82-822-3231 **Email:** satoru_nakamura@jsw.co.: Japan
City: Hiroshima **State:** Hiroshima **Zip:** 736-8602 **Country: Japan**
Year Established: **Status 2020:** Active
Industries:

Company Name: Luce Sear: Switzerland
Description: Luce Search is Surveying with moving objects Image processing analysis Development and operation of UAV or various robots
Website: http://www.lucd.ai
Phone: 1 615-651-7327 **Email:** info@lucd.ai
City: Hiroshima **State:** Hiroshima **PC:** **Country: Japan**
Year Established: 2017 **Status 2020:** Active
Industries: Cloud for:, Image Recognition for:, Application Services

Company Name: Al Hayabu: Saudi Arabia
Description: Al Hayabusa specializes in visual inspection and existing image processing using machine learning technology.
Website: https://aihayabusa.co.jp/aihayabusa/
Phone: 0138-76-4659 **Email:** 35985@reference-encyclopedia-ai.net
City: Hakodate **State:** Hokkaido **PC:** **Country: Japan**
Year Established: 2017 **Status 2020:** Active
Industries: Artificial Intelligence for:, IT Managed Services

Company Name: Aiku Lab
Description: Aiku Lab provides business with artificial intelligence solutions.
Website: https://aiku.co.jp/
Phone: 011-512-1900 **Email:** 36009@reference-encyclopedia-ai.net
City: Sapporo **State:** Hokkaido **PC:** **Country: Japan**
Year Established: 2016 **Status 2020:** Active
Industries: Company Name: Device Lab
Description: evice Lab Inc. is a spin-off company from University of Tsukuba (EN/JP).
Website: http://www.devicelab.co.jp/
Phone: **Email:** 28467@reference-encyclopedia-ai.net
City: Tsukuba **State:** Ibaraki **PC:** **Country: Japan**
Year Established: 2017 **Status 2020:** Active
Industries: Predictive Analytics

Company Name: SUIM: India
Description: S'UIMIN is a developer of sleep study services that leverage electroencephalography (brain wave) devices and AI technology.
Website: http://www.suimin.co.jp/
Phone: 029-853-3853 **Email:** contact@suimin.co.: Japan
City: Tsukuba **State:** Ibaraki **PC:** **Country: Japan**
Year Established: 2017 **Status 2020:** Active
Industries: Artificial Intelligence for:, ~ Healthcare (20)

Company Name: REXEV
Description: REXEV is a company that combines next-generation technologies such as AI, IoT, and autonomous driving with energy management technology.
Website: http://rexev.co.: Japan
Phone: 03.3525.8008 **Email:** info@rexev.co.: Japan
City: Odawara **State:** Kanagawa **PC:** **Country: Japan**
Year Established: 2019 **Status 2020:** Active
Industries: Artificial Intelligence for:, Internet of Things (IoT)

Company Name: AI Messenger
Description: AI Messenger is an AI chatbot tool for customer support business.
Website: https://www.ai-messenger.jp/
Phone: **Email:** 35992@reference-encyclopedia-ai.net
City: Shibuya **State:** Kanagawa **PC:** **Country: Japan**
Year Established: 2016 **Status 2020:** Active
Industries: Artificial Intelligence

Company Name: Axiver: Sweden
Description: Axiverse creates an environment where people can play an active role and create a better society.
Website: http://axiverse.co.: Japan
Phone: **Email:** 36129@reference-encyclopedia-ai.net
City: Shibuya **State:** Kanagawa **PC:** **Country: Japan**
Year Established: 2015 **Status 2020:** Active
Industries: IT Managed Services for:, Machine Learning

Company Name: Avinton
Description: Avinton is a technology-focused, academically oriented, and independent IT, AI, and Big Data consultancy.
Website: http://avinton.com/
Phone: 81 (0)3 5530 8976 **Email:** jobs@avinton.com
City: Yokohama **State:** Kanagawa **PC:** **Country: Japan**
Year Established: 2010 **Status 2020:** Active
Industries: Analytics for:, Artificial Intelligence for:, Big Data and Analytics for:, IT Managed Services for:, Machine Learning

Company Name: dataremer
Description: Dataremer is a data collection service for AI technology development.
Website: http://www.dataremer.com/
Phone: **Email:** 36397@reference-encyclopedia-ai.net
City: Kochi **State:** Kochi **PC:** **Country: Japan**
Year Established: 2016 **Status 2020:** Active
Industries: Artificial Intelligence for:, Cloud for:, Web

Company Name: Fantas
Description: Fantas Tech is a company of property re-commerce site Hayagai.
Website: http://fantas-tech.co.jp/
Phone: 03-4577-2000 **Email:** info@fantas-tech.co.: Japan
City: Shioya **State:** Kumamoto **PC:** **Country: Japan**
Year Established: 2010 **Status 2020:** Active
Industries: Artificial Intelligence

Company Name: SpeakGlobal
Description: SpeakGlobal makes innovative language learning software with virtual tutors - "The tennis ball machine for English conversation"
Website: http://www.kaiwabox.com
Phone: **Email:** inquiry@speakglobal.co.: Japan
City: Kobe **State:** Kyoto **PC:** **Country: Japan**
Year Established: **Status 2020:** Active
Industries:

Company Name: 1-10 IMAGINE
Description: 1-10 IMAGINE is an entertainment creative studio that provides cyber wheel, anatome, and cyber boccia.
Website: https://1-10imagine.com/
Phone: 075-371-2017 **Email:** 35915@reference-encyclopedia-ai.net
City: Kyoto **State:** Kyoto **PC:** **Country: Japan**
Year Established: 2016 **Status 2020:** Active
Industries: Artificial Intelligence for:, ~ Arts-Entertainment-Recreation (4)

Company Name: Amirobo tech
Description: Amirobo tech provides services such as ICT, robot technology, and application development technology.
Website: http://www.amirobo.tech
Phone: **Email:** amirobotech@gmail.com
City: Kyoto **State:** Kyoto **PC:** **Country: Japan**
Year Established: 2017 **Status 2020:** Active
Industries: Artificial Intelligence for:, IT Managed Services for:, IT Managed Services for:, Robotics

Company Name: DataGrid Japan
Description: Creative AI development, AI related system development and consulting
Website: http://datagrid.co.jp/
Phone: **Email:** info@datagrid.co.: Japan
City: Kyoto **State:** Kyoto **PC:** **Country: Japan**
Year Established: 2017 **Status 2020:** Active
Industries: Artificial Intelligence for:, Content

Company Name: Hacarus
Description: Hacarus is an AI startup providing solutions for medical and manufacturing industries via SaaS, embedded system and FPGA.
Website: http://hacarus.com
Phone: 81757085516 **Email:** info@hacarus.com
City: Kyoto **State:** Kyoto **PC:** **Country: Japan**
Year Established: **Status 2020:** Active
Industries: Artificial Intelligence for:, ~ Life Sciences (27), Machine Learning for:, ~ Manufacturing-Miscellaneous (34), ~ Healthcare (20)

Company Name: Innovotion
Description: Innovotion ia a mathematical knowledge and machine learning technology company
Website: http://www.innovotion.co.jp/
Phone: **Email:** 36770@reference-encyclopedia-ai.net
City: Kyoto **State:** Kyoto **PC:** **Country: Japan**
Year Established: 2011 **Status 2020:** Active
Industries: Machine Learning

Company Name: Patentfield
Description: Patentfield is a patents search and analysis platform that combines advanced search, data visualization, and AI functions.
Website: http://en.patentfield.com/
Phone: 075-751-960 **Email:** 37143@reference-encyclopedia-ai.net
City: Kyoto **State:** Kyoto **PC:** **Country: Japan**
Year Established: 2017 **Status 2020:** Active
Industries: Artificial Intelligence for:, IT Managed Services for:, Web for:, Web

Company Name: AI Si
Description: AI Silk are innovative conductive fibers produced with a dyeing technique.
Website: http://www.ai-silk.com/
Phone: **Email:** 35993@reference-encyclopedia-ai.net
City: Sendai-shi **State:** Miyagi **PC:** **Country: Japan**
Year Established: 2015 **Status 2020:** Active
Industries: Artificial Intelligence for:, ~ Fashion (16), ~ Healthcare (20)

Company Name: NAIL (Niigata Artificial Intelligence Laboratory)
Description: NAIL Niigata Artificial Intelligence Laboratory is analyzing big data extensively using AI technology.
Website: http://www.nai-lab.com
Phone: **Email:** 37036@reference-encyclopedia-ai.net
City: Niigata **State:** Niigata **PC:** **Country: Japan**
Year Established: 2017 **Status 2020:** Active
Industries: Artificial Intelligence for:, Application Services for:, Machine Learning

Company Name: Daiya Industry
Description:
Website: https://www.daiyak.co.jp/
Phone: 81-86-282-1245 **Email:** watanabe@daiyak.co.: Japan
City: Okayama **State:** Okayama **Zip:** 701-0203 **Country: Japan**
Year Established: **Status 2020:** Active
Industries: Artificial Intelligence

Company Name: Okinawa Protein Tomography
Description: Okinawa Protein Tomography is an Innovative Protein Molecular Structural Analysis company.
Website: http://www.okinawa-pt.com/index.html
Phone: **Email:** info@okinawa-pt.com
City: Onna **State:** Okinawa **PC:** **Country: Japan**
Year Established: 2014 **Status 2020:** Active
Industries: Predictive Analytics for:, ~ Banking and Financial Markets-Services (7)

Company Name: Bacallln
Description: Bacallln is an artificial intelligence and system development company.
Website: http://bacallan.club/
Phone: 06-6645-9000 **Email:** bacallan1@gmail.com
City: Osaka **State:** Osaka **PC:** **Country: Japan**
Year Established: 2013 **Status 2020:** Active
Industries: Artificial Intelligence for:, IT Managed Services for:, IT Managed Services

Company Name: Cofame
Description: Conversational bot to get to know about perople around you.
Website: http://keiko.ai/
Phone: **Email:** keiko@cofame.com
City: Osaka **State:** Osaka **PC:** **Country: Japan**
Year Established: **Status 2020:** Active
Industries: Artificial Intelligence for:, Identity

Company Name: PLENGoer Robotics
Description: PLENGoer Robotics develops personal service robots.
Website: http://plengoer.com/en/
Phone: **Email:** info@plengoer.com
City: Osaka **State:** Osaka **PC:** **Country: Japan**
Year Established: 2016 **Status 2020:** Active
Industries: Artificial Intelligence for:, Machine Learning for:, Robotics

Company Name: RT.WORKS
Description: RT.Works is an Encore Smart Robot technology to enrich your second life
Website: http://www.rtworks.co.jp/
Phone: **Email:** support-rtw@rtworks.co.: Japan
City: Osaka **State:** Osaka **PC:** **Country: Japan**
Year Established: 2014 **Status 2020:** Active
Industries:

Company Name: Silver Egg Technology
Description: Provider of web marketing ASP services based on AI technology
Website: http://www.silveregg.co.: Japan
Phone: 81 3-5357-1255 **Email:** inquiry@silveregg.co.: Japan
City: Osaka **State:** **PC:** **Country: Japan**
Year Established: **Status 2020:** Active
Industries: Artificial Intelligence for:, Web for:, ~ Media-Communications (41), ~ Professional Services (48)

Company Name: EAMS LAB
Description: EAMS LAB is developes industrial unmanned aircraft control development using artificial intelligence.
Website: http://elab.co.jp/
Phone: **Email:** info@elab.co.: Japan
City: Saitama **State:** Saitama **PC:** **Country: Japan**
Year Established: 2017 **Status 2020:** Active
Industries: Artificial Intelligence for:, Industrial Solutions

Company Name: Linkwiz
Description: LinkWiz offers software that solves something about robots that is a bit difficult to use.
Website: http://linkwiz.co.jp/
Phone: 81 53-401-3450 **Email:** contact@linkwiz.co.: Japan
City: Hamamatsu **State:** Shizuoka **PC:** **Country: Japan**
Year Established: 2015 **Status 2020:** Active
Industries: Artificial Intelligence for:, Robotics

Company Name: Mold Giken Co., Ltd.
Description:
Website: http://moldgiken.co.jp/
Phone: 81-53-582-2422 **Email:** mold-ariumi@za.tnc.ne.: Japan
City: Shizuoka **State:** Shizuoka **Zip:** 434-0002 **Country: Japan**
Year Established: **Status 2020:** Active
Industries: Blockchain

Company Name: voiceware
Description: voiceware specializes in research and development of products using voice conversion technology, and sales.
Website: http://voiceware.co.jp/
Phone: 03-6869-0230 **Email:** contact@voiceware.co.: Japan
City: Chofu **State:** Tokyo **PC:** **Country: Japan**
Year Established: 2017 **Status 2020:** Active
Industries: Artificial Intelligence for:, IT Managed Services

Company Name: MITech
Description: MITech specializes in applied machine learning and developed machine learning algorithms.
Website: http://mitech.: Japan
Phone: **Email:** 36992@reference-encyclopedia-ai.net
City: Fuchu **State:** Tokyo **PC:** **Country: Japan**

Year Established: 2018 **Status 2020:** Active
Industries: Artificial Intelligence for:, Embedded for:, Image Recognition for:, Machine Learning

Company Name: Aide: Malaysia
Description: Aidemy is a web service where you can learn AI programming online.
Website: https://aidemy.net/
Phone: **Email:** support@aidemy.net
City: Hongo **State:** Tokyo **PC:** **Country: Japan**
Year Established: 2016 **Status 2020:** Active
Industries: Artificial Intelligence for:, ~ Education (13), Web

Company Name: DeepEyeVision
Description: DeepEyeVision is a cloud-based AI diagnosis support solution.
Website: http://deepeyevision.com
Phone: 81.90.7175.9433 **Email:** info@deepeyevision.com
City: Hongo **State:** Tokyo **PC:** **Country: Japan**
Year Established: 2016 **Status 2020:** Active
Industries: Artificial Intelligence for:, ~ Healthcare (20), ~ Healthcare (20)

Company Name: ChillStack
Description: ChillStack provides information on AI, security, and development.
Website: http://chillstack.com
Phone: **Email:** 36269@reference-encyclopedia-ai.net
City: Koganei **State:** Tokyo **PC:** **Country: Japan**
Year Established: 2018 **Status 2020:** Active
Industries: Artificial Intelligence for:, Security

Company Name: Artificial Intelligence Research Center
Description: AIRC wants to create a "space" for open innovation that connects industry, academia, and government together.
Website: http://www.airc.aist.go.jp/en/
Phone: **Email:** airc-info-ml@aist.go.: Japan
City: Koto **State:** Tokyo **PC:** **Country: Japan**
Year Established: 2015 **Status 2020:** Active
Industries: Artificial Intelligence for:, IT Managed Services

Company Name: SOINN
Description: SOINN is an Intelligent various devices, devices and information systems utilizing advanced AI technology including patented technology.
Website: http://soinn.com/
Phone: **Email:** 37431@reference-encyclopedia-ai.net
City: Machida **State:** Tokyo **PC:** **Country: Japan**
Year Established: 2014 **Status 2020:** Active
Industries: Artificial Intelligence for:, Content for:, IT Managed Services

Company Name: ATLAB
Description: ATLAB, a tech company, provides services and products with an innovative approach that focuses on the field of Robotic Process Automation.
Website: http://atlab-ai.jp/
Phone: 03-5772-2717 **Email:** info@atlab-ai.: Japan
City: Minami **State:** Tokyo **PC:** **Country: Japan**
Year Established: 2017 **Status 2020:** Active
Industries: Artificial Intelligence for:, ~ Fashion (16), Robotics

Company Name: Atlas Associat: Spain
Description: Aiming to build an ecosystem centered on the world of social networks existing on www and create markets
Website: http://www.atlasassociates.io/
Phone: **Email:** support@atlasassociates.io
City: Minami-aoyama **State:** Tokyo **PC:** **Country: Japan**
Year Established: 2019 **Status 2020:** Active
Industries: Artificial Intelligence for:, Digital Marketing for:, IT Managed Services for:, Web for:, ~ Social Assistance-Non-Profits (53), ~ Social Assistance-Non-Profits (53)

Company Name: iVOICE
Description: iVOICE specializes in social implementation of speech analysis AI.
Website: http://ivoice.co.: Japan
Phone: **Email:** 36816@reference-encyclopedia-ai.net
City: Minami-shinagawa **State:** Tokyo **PC:** **Country: Japan**
Year Established: 2020 **Status 2020:** Active
Industries:

Company Name: LaiBlitz
Description: LaiBlitz uses AI and IoT technologies to maximize the value of the sports business from the management, business and IT perspectives.
Website: http://laiblitz.co.jp/
Phone: **Email:** info@laiblitz.co.: Japan
City: Minami-shinagawa **State:** Tokyo **PC:** **Country: Japan**
Year Established: 2011 **Status 2020:** Active
Industries: Artificial Intelligence for:, IT Managed Services for:, ~ Arts-Entertainment-Recreation (4)

Company Name: AHACRAFT
Description: AHACRAFT is a technology group that specializes in the search for knowledge and the depth of knowledge.
Website: https://ahacraft.co.jp/
Phone: **Email:** 35979@reference-encyclopedia-ai.net
City: Nibancho **State:** Tokyo **PC:** **Country: Japan**
Year Established: 2015 **Status 2020:** Active
Industries:

Company Name: CCReB Adviso: Serbia
Description: CCReB Advisors provides planning, creation and sales of CRE sales support tools using AI IoT.
Website: http://ccreb.: Japan
Phone: **Email:** 36242@reference-encyclopedia-ai.net
City: Nibancho **State:** Tokyo **PC:** **Country: Japan**
Year Established: 2019 **Status 2020:** Active
Industries: Artificial Intelligence for:, Internet of Things (IoT)

Company Name: AI Samurai
Description: AI Samurai is a patent examination simulation system that helps solve issues and problems faced by inventors.
Website: https://aisamurai.co.jp/
Phone: 03-6270-5577 **Email:** info@aisamurai.co.: Japan
City: Otemachi **State:** Tokyo **PC:** **Country: Japan**
Year Established: 2015 **Status 2020:** Active
Industries: Artificial Intelligence for:, IT Managed Services for:, Business Intelligence

Company Name: Preferred Networks
Description: Preferred Networks applies cutting-edge deep learning technology to applications in the the Internet of things.
Website: http://preferred.jp/en/
Phone: **Email:** pfn-pr@preferred.: Japan
City: Otemachi **State:** Tokyo **PC:** **Country: Japan**
Year Established: 2014 **Status 2020:** Active
Industries: Artificial Intelligence for:, ~ Biotechnology (9), Internet of Things (IoT) for:, Machine Learning for:, Robotics

Company Name: Preferred Networks, Inc
Description: Preferred Networks applies cutting-edge deep learning technology to applications in the the Internet of Things
Website: http://www.preferred-networks.jp/en/
Phone: **Email:** pfn-info@preferred.: Japan
City: Otemachi **State:** Tokyo **PC:** **Country: Japan**
Year Established: **Status 2020:** Active
Industries: Artificial Intelligence for:, ~ Biotechnology (9), ~ Healthcare (20), Machine Learning for:, ~ Manufacturing-Miscellaneous (34), Robotics for:, ~ Professional Services (48)

Company Name: Ubiden
Description: Ubiden offers mobile network and IoT/AI technology services.
Website: http://www.ubiden.com
Phone: **Email:** info@ubiden.com
City: Roppongi **State:** Tokyo **PC:** **Country: Japan**

Year Established: 2019 **Status 2020:** Active
Industries: Artificial Intelligence for:, Internet of Things (IoT) for:, Mobile

Company Name: IDEAAI
Description: IDEAAI specializes in AI and image processing technology.
Website: http://ideaai.co.jp/
Phone: 03-5778-5276 **Email:** contact@ideaai.co.: Japan
City: Sarugaku **State:** Tokyo **PC:** **Country: Japan**
Year Established: 2019 **Status 2020:** Active
Industries: Artificial Intelligence for:, Augmented Reality for:, IT Managed Services

Company Name: J.Score
Description: J.Score is a mobile application for AI score diagnosis.
Website: http://www.jscore.co.jp/
Phone: **Email:** jscore-support@em.jscore.co.: Japan
City: Sarugaku **State:** Tokyo **PC:** **Country: Japan**
Year Established: 2016 **Status 2020:** Active
Industries: Artificial Intelligence for:, Application Services

Company Name: Lis: Sweden
Description: Lisse offers legal business innovation through the use of AI.
Website: http://lisse-law.com/
Phone: 03-5789-5290 **Email:** info@lisse-law.co
City: Sarugaku **State:** Tokyo **PC:** **Country: Japan**
Year Established: 2018 **Status 2020:** Active
Industries: Artificial Intelligence

Company Name: Empa:Thailand
Description: Empath is Emotion AI, which can identify emotion from the voice in real-time regardless of language.
Website: http://webempath.com
Phone: 81-(0)3-6450-5518 **Email:** 36503@reference-encyclopedia-ai.net
City: Setagaya **State:** Tokyo **PC:** **Country: Japan**
Year Established: 2017 **Status 2020:** Active
Industries: Artificial Intelligence for:, ~ Arts-Entertainment-Recreation (4), Compute

Company Name: Morikatron
Description: Morikatron is an AI game company.
Website: http://morikatron.com/
Phone: **Email:** 37019@reference-encyclopedia-ai.net
City: Setagaya **State:** Tokyo **PC:** **Country: Japan**
Year Established: 2017 **Status 2020:** Active
Industries: Artificial Intelligence

Company Name: monoAI technology
Description: monoAI technology develop and operate network games and conduct technology research and content development for VR and AR content.
Website: http://monoai.co.: Japan
Phone: 050-3640-7964 **Email:** vs.marketing@veriserve.co.: Japan
City: Tokio **State:** Tokyo **PC:** **Country: Japan**
Year Established: 2013 **Status 2020:** Active
Industries: Artificial Intelligence

Company Name: 9DW
Description: 9DW is focused on AI development.
Website: https://9dw.jp/
Phone: 81 3-6807-4307 **Email:** 35929@reference-encyclopedia-ai.net
City: Tokyo **State:** Tokyo **PC:** **Country: Japan**
Year Established: 2016 **Status 2020:** Active
Industries:

Company Name: A.N.Lab
Description: A.N.Lab is a Tokyo based software development firm.
Website: http://anlab.jp/
Phone: 81.3.4360.5655 **Email:** info@anlab.: Japan
City: Tokyo **State:** Tokyo **PC:** **Country: Japan**
Year Established: 2017 **Status 2020:** Active
Industries: Artificial Intelligence for:, Web

Company Name: ABEJA
Description: ABEJA develops AI business solutions utilizing deep learning.
Website: http://abejainc.com
Phone: 81364528848 **Email:** info@abejainc.com
City: Tokyo **State:** Tokyo **PC:** **Country: Japan**
Year Established: **Status 2020:** Active
Industries: Analytics for:, Artificial Intelligence for:, Big Data and Analytics for:, Machine Learning

Company Name: Accel Lab
Description: Accel Lab is a real estate tech consultant that offers a service platform that makes a property or space more attractive.
Website: https://accel-lab.com/
Phone: 03-6674-0338 **Email:** 35937@reference-encyclopedia-ai.net
City: Tokyo **State:** Tokyo **PC:** **Country: Japan**
Year Established: 2017 **Status 2020:** Active
Industries: Artificial Intelligence for:, IT Managed Services for:, Internet of Things (IoT) for:, ~ Real Estate (49), ~ Real Estate (49)

Company Name: ACES Japan
Description: ACES is providing image recognition algorithms such as object recognition and face and expression recognition
Website: https://acesinc.co.jp/
Phone: **Email:** marketing@acespower.com
City: Tokyo **State:** Tokyo **PC:** **Country: Japan**
Year Established: 2017 **Status 2020:** Active
Industries: Artificial Intelligence for:, ~ Banking and Financial Markets-Services (7)

Company Name: Action Index inc.
Description: VR
Website: http://www.actionindex.jp/
Phone: (424) 777-2215 **Email:** info@actionindex.: Japan
City: Tokyo **State:** Tokyo **PC:** **Country: Japan**
Year Established: 2016 **Status 2020:** Active
Industries: Artificial Intelligence for:, ~ Arts-Entertainment-Recreation (4), ~ Media-Communications (41), Virtual Reality (VR)

Company Name: ActiValues
Description: ActiValues develops and offers an artificial intelligence based multilingual communication application called talkappi.
Website: https://activalues.com/
Phone: **Email:** info@activalues.com
City: Tokyo **State:** Tokyo **PC:** **Country: Japan**
Year Established: 2016 **Status 2020:** Active
Industries: Artificial Intelligence for:, IT Managed Services for:, Natural Language Processing

Company Name: AI CROSS
Description: AI CROSS is an internet company that uses artificial intelligence (AI) to help enterprises communicate through mobile with their customers.
Website: https://aicross.co.jp/
Phone: **Email:** 35983@reference-encyclopedia-ai.net
City: Tokyo **State:** Tokyo **PC:** **Country: Japan**
Year Established: 2015 **Status 2020:** Active
Industries: Artificial Intelligence for:, IT Managed Services for:, Web for:, Application Services for:, ~ Social Assistance-Non-Profits (53)

Company Name: AI inside
Description: AI inside specializes in software development and artificial intelligence business.
Website: https://inside.ai/index.html
Phone: 03-5468-5041 **Email:** 35986@reference-encyclopedia-ai.net
City: Tokyo **State:** Tokyo **PC:** **Country: Japan**
Year Established: 2015 **Status 2020:** Active
Industries: Artificial Intelligence for:, IT Managed Services

Company Name: AI Squared
Description: AI Squared provides various IT services and consulting using artificial intelligence.
Website: https://www.ai2-jp.com/
Phone: 03-5835-3155 **Email:** info@ai2-jp.com
City: Tokyo **State:** Tokyo **PC:** **Country: Japan**
Year Established: 2015 **Status 2020:** Active
Industries:

Company Name: AI TOKYO LAB
Description: AI TOKYO LAB is an AI-specialized technology company that develops AI and IoT solutions.
Website: https://aitokyolab.com/
Phone: 03-6380-8669 **Email:** 35998@reference-encyclopedia-ai.net
City: Tokyo **State:** Tokyo **PC:** **Country: Japan**
Year Established: 2019 **Status 2020:** Active
Industries: Artificial Intelligence for:, IT Managed Services

Company Name: Aill
Description: Aillis specializes in the development of testing methods for Influenza using artificial intelligence technology.
Website: https://aillis.jp/
Phone: **Email:** 36012@reference-encyclopedia-ai.net
City: Tokyo **State:** Tokyo **PC:** **Country: Japan**
Year Established: 2017 **Status 2020:** Active
Industries: Artificial Intelligence for:, IT Managed Services for:, ~ Healthcare (20)

Company Name: Aipore
Description: Aipore is a technology company specializing in the area of nanopore sensor using semiconductor Si microfabrication technology.
Website: http://aipore.com/
Phone: **Email:** support-hp@aipore.com
City: Tokyo **State:** Tokyo **PC:** **Country: Japan**
Year Established: 2018 **Status 2020:** Active
Industries: Artificial Intelligence for:, IT Managed Services

Company Name: AIQ Japan
Description: AIQ is a Artificial intelligence technology development
Website: http://aiqlab.com/
Phone: **Email:** 36018@reference-encyclopedia-ai.net
City: Tokyo **State:** Tokyo **PC:** **Country: Japan**
Year Established: 2017 **Status 2020:** Active
Industries: Artificial Intelligence for:, Web

Company Name: al
Description: Alt Inc. commence the distribution of the world's first Personalized Artificial Intelligence.
Website: https://alt.ai/
Phone: 81(3)-6380-7076 **Email:** info@alt.ai
City: Tokyo **State:** Tokyo **PC:** **Country: Japan**
Year Established: 2014 **Status 2020:** Active
Industries:

Company Name: AlpacaJapan
Description: Building cutting-edge capital markets AI technology working with number of financial institutions
Website: http://www.alpaca.ai/
Phone: **Email:** info@alpaca.ai
City: Tokyo **State:** Tokyo **PC:** **Country: Japan**
Year Established: **Status 2020:** Active
Industries: Artificial Intelligence for:, ~ Banking and Financial Markets-Services (7), Machine Learning

Company Name: Alternative Machine
Description: Alternative Machine applies technology generated by ALife research which explores the principle of every life phenomenon.
Website: https://alternativemachine.co.jp/
Phone: **Email:** media@alternativemachine.co.: Japan
City: Tokyo **State:** Tokyo **PC:** **Country: Japan**
Year Established: 2017 **Status 2020:** Active
Industries: Artificial Intelligence for:, IT Managed Services for:, Machine Learning for:, Predictive Analytics for:, Business Intelligence

Company Name: Amadeus Code
Description: Amadeus Code is an artificial intelligence powered songwriting assistant.
Website: http://amadeuscode.com/
Phone: **Email:** contact@amadeuscode.com
City: Tokyo **State:** Tokyo **PC:** **Country: Japan**
Year Established: **Status 2020:** Active
Industries: Artificial Intelligence for:, Voice Recognition for:, ~ Arts-Entertainment-Recreation (4), ~ Arts-Entertainment-Recreation (4), ~ Professional Services (48)

Company Name: Amanogi Space
Description: Tokyo Tech spin-off working on proprietary satellite that interprets space data at petabyte scale to unlock space data analysis.
Website: http://amanogi.space/
Phone: **Email:** 36052@reference-encyclopedia-ai.net
City: Tokyo **State:** Tokyo **PC:** **Country: Japan**
Year Established: 2016 **Status 2020:** Active
Industries: Artificial Intelligence for:, IT Managed Services

Company Name: Amplified.ai
Description: Amplified.ai offers simple, instant, and reliable artificial intelligence systems that help humans innovate faster.
Website: http://www.amplified.ai/
Phone: **Email:** 36057@reference-encyclopedia-ai.net
City: Tokyo **State:** Tokyo **PC:** **Country: Japan**
Year Established: 2017 **Status 2020:** Active
Industries: Artificial Intelligence for:, Big Data and Analytics for:, IT Managed Services for:, Machine Learning for:, Virtual Reality (VR)

Company Name: ANAP Lab
Description: ANAP Lab provides machine learning, IoT, AI, and AR / VR technologies for fashion industry.
Website: http://anaplab.com/
Phone: **Email:** info@anaplab.com
City: Tokyo **State:** Tokyo **PC:** **Country: Japan**
Year Established: 2017 **Status 2020:** Active
Industries: Artificial Intelligence for:, ~ Fashion (16), Machine Learning

Company Name: AnyTech
Description: AnyTech is a freelance network and artificial intelligence company.
Website: http://www.anytech.io/
Phone: **Email:** info@brightview.: Japan
City: Tokyo **State:** Tokyo **PC:** **Country: Japan**
Year Established: 2015 **Status 2020:** Active
Industries: Artificial Intelligence

Company Name: ARAYA
Description: ARAYA is an AI services provider that utilizes machine learning algorithms including deep learning to meet the diverse needs of customers.
Website: http://www.araya.org
Phone: **Email:** support@araya.org
City: Tokyo **State:** Tokyo **PC:** **Country: Japan**

Year Established: 2013 **Status 2020:** Active
Industries: Artificial Intelligence for:, Facial Recognition for:, Internet of Things (IoT) for:, Machine Learning

Company Name: Arbito
Description: Arbito provides image inspection, analysis, and repair service using AI.
Website: http://www.arbito.co.: Japan
Phone: **Email:** info@arbito.co.: Japan
City: Tokyo **State:** Tokyo **PC:** **Country: Japan**
Year Established: 2019 **Status 2020:** Active
Industries: Analytics for:, Artificial Intelligence for:, Internet of Things (IoT)

Company Name: ARISE Analytics
Description: ARISE Analytics provides data analysis, algorithm development, and analytic services such as DMP, AI, and IoT solution introduction support.
Website: http://ariseanalytics.com/
Phone: 03-6365-6363 **Email:** 36083@reference-encyclopedia-ai.net
City: Tokyo **State:** Tokyo **PC:** **Country: Japan**
Year Established: 2017 **Status 2020:** Active
Industries: Artificial Intelligence for:, IT Managed Services for:, IT Managed Services

Company Name: Arise Innovation
Description: Arise Innovation utilizes IT such as IoT/AI/RPA to address the shortage of human resources coming from the decline in population.
Website: http://www.ariseinnovation.co.jp/
Phone: **Email:** info@ariseinnovation.co.: Japan
City: Tokyo **State:** Tokyo **PC:** **Country: Japan**
Year Established: 2016 **Status 2020:** Active
Industries: Artificial Intelligence for:, IT Managed Services

Company Name: Ascent Robotics
Description: Ascent Robotics is an AI startup developing intelligent solutions in industrial robotics and autonomous vehicles.
Website: http://ascent.ai
Phone: **Email:** hello@ascent.ai
City: Tokyo **State:** Tokyo **PC:** **Country: Japan**
Year Established: 2016 **Status 2020:** Active
Industries: Artificial Intelligence for:, ~ Automotive (5), Enterprise Application Services for:, Machine Learning for:, Robotics

Company Name: Ascent Robotics, Inc.
Description: Ascent builds end-to-end AI's for robotic systems.
Website: http://ascent.ai
Phone: **Email:** hello@ascent.ai
City: Tokyo **State:** Tokyo **PC:** **Country: Japan**
Year Established: **Status 2020:** Active
Industries: Artificial Intelligence for:, ~ Automotive (5), Enterprise Application Services for:, Machine Learning for:, Robotics

Company Name: Asilla
Description: Asilla develops and provides AI specialized in image and video analysis.
Website: http://www.asilla.: Japan
Phone: **Email:** 36095@reference-encyclopedia-ai.net
City: Tokyo **State:** Tokyo **PC:** **Country: Japan**
Year Established: 2015 **Status 2020:** Active
Industries:

Company Name: atama plus
Description: atama plus is an Edtech startup company that utilizes artificial intelligence for middle and high school students.
Website: http://www.atama.plus/
Phone: **Email:** info@atama.plus
City: Tokyo **State:** Tokyo **PC:** **Country: Japan**
Year Established: 2017 **Status 2020:** Active
Industries: Artificial Intelligence for:, ~ Education (13), ~ Education (13), IT Managed Services

Company Name: Autify
Description: Autify is a software testing automation platform powered by AI.
Website: http://autify.com
Phone: **Email:** 36114@reference-encyclopedia-ai.net
City: Tokyo **State:** Tokyo **PC:** **Country: Japan**
Year Established: 2016 **Status 2020:** Active
Industries: Analytics for:, Artificial Intelligence for:, IT Managed Services

Company Name: Automa: Gibraltar
Description: Automagi develops and provides artificial intelligence (AI), knowledge database, and machine learning solution.
Website: http://www.automagi.jp/
Phone: 03-5333-6131 **Email:** 36116@reference-encyclopedia-ai.net
City: Tokyo **State:** Tokyo **PC:** **Country: Japan**
Year Established: 2010 **Status 2020:** Active
Industries: Artificial Intelligence for:, Business Intelligence for:, IT Managed Services for:, IT Managed Services

Company Name: AWL
Description: AWL provides AI camera solutions to solve retail store issues and increase value.
Website: http://awl.co.: Japan
Phone: 81.3.6380.8669 **Email:** 36127@reference-encyclopedia-ai.net
City: Tokyo **State:** Tokyo **PC:** **Country: Japan**
Year Established: 2016 **Status 2020:** Active
Industries: Artificial Intelligence for:, Security

Company Name: Bespo: Kenya
Description: Bespoke is a developer of Artificial Intelligence (AI) technology dedicated to multilingual guest services.
Website: http://www.be-spoke.io
Phone: **Email:** info@be-spoke.io
City: Tokyo **State:** Tokyo **PC:** **Country: Japan**
Year Established: 2015 **Status 2020:** Active
Industries: Artificial Intelligence for:, IT Managed Services for:, ~ Arts-Entertainment-Recreation (4), Machine Learning

Company Name: Bisu
Description: Every day 7bn people flush terabytes of health data down the toilet. Bisu helps people capture these data and lead healthier, happier lives.
Website: http://www.bisu.bio
Phone: **Email:** daniel@bisu.bio
City: Tokyo **State:** Tokyo **PC:** **Country: Japan**
Year Established: 2015 **Status 2020:** Active
Industries: Big Data and Analytics for:, ~ Healthcare (20), ~ Healthcare (20), Internet of Things (IoT) for:, Machine Learning for:, ~ Healthcare (20)

Company Name: bitgr: Italy
Description: Democratic AI
Website: http://bitgrit.net
Phone: **Email:** 36166@reference-encyclopedia-ai.net
City: Tokyo **State:** Tokyo **PC:** **Country: Japan**
Year Established: 2017 **Status 2020:** Active
Industries: Artificial Intelligence for:, IT Managed Services

Company Name: Change Value
Description: For the world, creating a business useful for people.
Website: http://changevalue.: Japan
Phone: **Email:** 36255@reference-encyclopedia-ai.net
City: Tokyo **State:** Tokyo **PC:** **Country: Japan**
Year Established: 2015 **Status 2020:** Active
Industries: Predictive Analytics

Company Name: Cinnamon
Description: Cinnamon is an AI company to enable AI-empowered enterprise with Natural Language Understanding.
Website: http://www.cinnamon.
Phone: 84 89 986 60 03 **Email:** 36278@reference-encyclopedia-ai.net
City: Tokyo **State:** Tokyo **PC:** **Country: Japan**
Year Established: 2012 **Status 2020:** Active
Industries: Artificial Intelligence for:, Machine Learning

Company Name: Cogent Labs
Description: Cogent Labs is solving for practical artificial intelligence.
Website: http://cogent.co.: Japan
Phone: **Email:** contact@cogent.co.: Japan
City: Tokyo **State:** Tokyo **PC:** **Country: Japan**
Year Established: **Status 2020:** Active
Industries: Artificial Intelligence for:, Enterprise Application Services for:, Machine Learning for:, ~ Professional Services (48)

Company Name: COGNIROBO
Description: Cognirobo is fully aware of the social mission of protecting all personal information handled by the Company.
Website: http://www.cognirobo.com/
Phone: **Email:** 36303@reference-encyclopedia-ai.net
City: Tokyo **State:** Tokyo **PC:** **Country: Japan**
Year Established: 2016 **Status 2020:** Active
Industries: IT Managed Services for:, IT Managed Services for:, Application Services

Company Name: CollabWiz
Description: CollabWiz is an AI technology based platform.
Website: http://www.collabwiz.co.: Japan
Phone: **Email:** tomoya.suzuki@collabwiz.co.: Japan
City: Tokyo **State:** Tokyo **PC:** **Country: Japan**
Year Established: 2018 **Status 2020:** Active
Industries: Application Services for:, Machine Learning

Company Name: Cooori
Description: We are an ed-tech artificial intelligence-driven platform focusing on language learning products.
Website: http://www.cooori.com
Phone: **Email:** s.endo@cooori.com
City: Tokyo **State:** Tokyo **PC:** **Country: Japan**
Year Established: 2015 **Status 2020:** Active
Industries: Artificial Intelligence for:, ~ Education (13), ~ Education (13)

Company Name: CS-C
Description: CS-C is an AI marketing engine development "C-mo" series Media development and operation system.
Website: http://s-cs-c.com/
Phone: **Email:** 36356@reference-encyclopedia-ai.net
City: Tokyo **State:** Tokyo **PC:** **Country: Japan**
Year Established: 2011 **Status 2020:** Active
Industries:

Company Name: DataCook
Description: Health Tech, AI
Website: http://datacook.: Japan
Phone: **Email:** info@datacook.: Japan
City: Tokyo **State:** Tokyo **PC:** **Country: Japan**
Year Established: 2013 **Status 2020:** Active
Industries: Artificial Intelligence for:, ~ Healthcare (20)

Company Name: DeepX
Description: DeepX offers automation of every machine using advanced artificial intelligence.
Website: http://www.deepx.co.jp/
Phone: 81 3-6240-0261 **Email:** info@deepx.co.: Japan
City: Tokyo **State:** Tokyo **PC:** **Country: Japan**
Year Established: 2016 **Status 2020:** Active
Industries: Artificial Intelligence for:, Automation for:, Machine Learning

Company Name: DIGITAL ATTENDANT
Description: DIGITAL ATTENDANT is an AI venture founded with the vision of reducing the benefits of AI technology.
Website: http://digitalattendant.co.jp/
Phone: **Email:** 36435@reference-encyclopedia-ai.net
City: Tokyo **State:** Tokyo **PC:** **Country: Japan**
Year Established: 2014 **Status 2020:** Active
Industries: Artificial Intelligence for:, IT Managed Services for:, IT Managed Services for:, Application Services

Company Name: Dimension
Description: Cyberian Lives Matter
Website: http://dimension.: Isle of Man
Phone: **Email:** info@dimension.: Isle of Man
City: Tokyo **State:** Tokyo **PC:** **Country: Japan**
Year Established: **Status 2020:** Active
Industries: Artificial Intelligence for:, Big Data and Analytics for:, Blockchain for:, Natural Language Processing for:, Cyber Security for:, Security

Company Name: DT Lab
Description: DT Lab is an Internship for data analysis and machine learning company.
Website: http://dt-labo.co.: Japan
Phone: **Email:** 36461@reference-encyclopedia-ai.net
City: Tokyo **State:** Tokyo **PC:** **Country: Japan**
Year Established: 2016 **Status 2020:** Active
Industries: Analytics for:, Big Data and Analytics for:, Machine Learning

Company Name: EAGLYS
Description: EAGLYS provides Secure Computing Platform to perform encrypted data sharing, storing, analyzing, and machine learning over encrypted data
Website: http://eaglys.co.jp/en/
Phone: **Email:** info@eaglys.co.: Japan
City: Tokyo **State:** Tokyo **PC:** **Country: Japan**
Year Established: 2016 **Status 2020:** Active
Industries: Cloud for:, Cyber Security for:, Machine Learning for:, Security

Company Name: Edge consulting Japan
Description: Edge Consulting is an Artificial intelligence company
Website: https://www.edge-tech.co.: Japan
Phone: **Email:** kaizen@edge-tech.co.: Japan
City: Tokyo **State:** Tokyo **PC:** **Country: Japan**
Year Established: 2014 **Status 2020:** Active
Industries: Artificial Intelligence for:, Business Process and Operations

Company Name: Edgecortix
Description: Edgecortix is a deeptech startup automating machine learning driven hardware & software co-design and deep learning acceleration at the edge
Website: http://www.edgecortix.com
Phone: **Email:** info@edgecortix.com
City: Tokyo **State:** Tokyo **PC:** **Country: Japan**
Year Established: 2019 **Status 2020:** Active
Industries: Artificial Intelligence for:, Internet of Things (IoT)

Company Name: Edgematrix
Description: EDGEMATRIX is a startup spun out from the AI project team of a global venture company .
Website: http://edgematrix.com/
Phone: 03-6778-8525 **Email:** info@edgematrix.com
City: Tokyo **State:** Tokyo **PC:** **Country: Japan**
Year Established: 2019 **Status 2020:** Active
Industries: Artificial Intelligence

Company Name: Elix
Description: Elix is research-oriented technology company specialized in deep learning.
Website: http://www.elix-inc.com/
Phone: **Email:** 36492@reference-encyclopedia-ai.net
City: Tokyo **State:** Tokyo **PC:** **Country: Japan**

Year Established: 2016 **Status 2020:** Active
Industries: IT Managed Services for:, Machine Learning

Company Name: Elvez
Description: Elves Ups is a collaborative AI dialogue system development tool.
Website: http://elvez.jp/
Phone: **Email:** 36496@reference-encyclopedia-ai.net
City: Tokyo **State:** Tokyo **PC:** **Country: Japan**
Year Established: 2016 **Status 2020:** Active
Industries: Artificial Intelligence for:, Content for:, ~ Arts-Entertainment-Recreation (4)

Company Name: Emerada
Description: Emerada is a bank account aggregation & cashflow analytics platform to SMEs and banks for enhancing lending activity in Japan.
Website: http://emerada-bank.com/
Phone: **Email:** emerada-support@emeradaco.com
City: Tokyo **State:** Tokyo **PC:** **Country: Japan**
Year Established: **Status 2020:** Active
Industries: Artificial Intelligence for:, ~ Banking and Financial Markets-Services (7), ~ Banking and Financial Markets-Services (7)

Company Name: emol
Description: emol is an application that records emotions and talks with AI robots.
Website: http://emol.jp/
Phone: **Email:** 36500@reference-encyclopedia-ai.net
City: Tokyo **State:** Tokyo **PC:** **Country: Japan**
Year Established: 2019 **Status 2020:** Active
Industries: Application Services for:, Artificial Intelligence

Company Name: Emotion Intelligence
Description: Emotion Intelligence, Inc. (Emotion intelligence abbreviation "emin") is company performs "congnitive emotional interaction design".
Website: http://www.emin.co.jp/en/
Phone: **Email:** 36501@reference-encyclopedia-ai.net
City: Tokyo **State:** Tokyo **PC:** **Country: Japan**
Year Established: 2011 **Status 2020:** Active
Industries:

Company Name: Empath Inc.
Description: Empath Inc. develops Emotion AI Empath, which can identify emotion from the voice in real-time regardless of language.
Website: http://webempath.net/lp-eng/
Phone: **Email:** info@webempath.com
City: Tokyo **State:** Tokyo **PC:** **Country: Japan**
Year Established: 2017 **Status 2020:** Active
Industries: Artificial Intelligence

Company Name: Epicbase
Description: Epicbase is an AI-based automatic voice transcription service based on voice recognition technology.
Website: http://www.epicbase.co.: Japan
Phone: **Email:** 36516@reference-encyclopedia-ai.net
City: Tokyo **State:** Tokyo **PC:** **Country: Japan**
Year Established: 2020 **Status 2020:** Active
Industries: Artificial Intelligence

Company Name: FiNC
Description: FiNC, combines data analysis, rich content & social elements to help users log, understand, manage and improve their health & wellness.
Website: http://www.finc.com
Phone: (8136) 206-3480 **Email:** 36564@reference-encyclopedia-ai.net
City: Tokyo **State:** Tokyo **PC:** **Country: Japan**
Year Established: 2012 **Status 2020:** Active
Industries: Artificial Intelligence for:, ~ Healthcare (20), ~ Healthcare (20), Machine Learning for:, ~ Healthcare (20), ~ Healthcare (20)

Company Name: Flitto Japan
Description: Flitto Japan provides artificial intelligence, crowdsourcing service.
Website: http://www.flitto.: Japan
Phone: 81.03.4500.1794 **Email:** flittojapan@flitto.com
City: Tokyo **State:** Tokyo **PC:** **Country: Japan**
Year Established: 2018 **Status 2020:** Active
Industries: Artificial Intelligence

Company Name: Frontier Field
Description: Frontier Field uses AI and big data in the medical and healthcare fields to create mechanisms and services.
Website: http://www.frontierfield.co.jp/
Phone: 03-6268-9071 **Email:** 36598@reference-encyclopedia-ai.net
City: Tokyo **State:** Tokyo **PC:** **Country: Japan**
Year Established: 2016 **Status 2020:** Active
Industries: Artificial Intelligence for:, Big Data and Analytics for:, ~ Healthcare (20)

Company **Name:** GAUSS Japan
Description: GAUSS is a company that develops AI algorithms
Website: http://gauss-ai.jp/
Phone: **Email:** 36609@reference-encyclopedia-ai.net
City: Tokyo **State:** Tokyo **PC:** **Country: Japan**
Year Established: 2017 **Status 2020:** Active
Industries: Artificial Intelligence for:, Machine Learning

Company Name: GHELIA
Description: GHELIA aims to utilize AI technologies not only for business enterprises but also for human enhancement.
Website: http://ghelia.com/en
Phone: **Email:** 36620@reference-encyclopedia-ai.net
City: Tokyo **State:** Tokyo **PC:** **Country: Japan**
Year Established: 2017 **Status 2020:** Active
Industries:

Company Name: GITAI
Description: GITAI specializes in artificial intelligence and robotic research.
Website: http://gitai.tech/
Phone: **Email:** 36623@reference-encyclopedia-ai.net
City: Tokyo **State:** Tokyo **PC:** **Country: Japan**
Year Established: 2016 **Status 2020:** Active
Industries: Artificial Intelligence for:, Robotics

Company Name: Graffity
Description: New AR communication app
Website: http://graffity.: Japan
Phone: 03-6447-2515 **Email:** contact@graffity.: Japan
City: Tokyo **State:** Tokyo **PC:** **Country: Japan**
Year Established: **Status 2020:** Active
Industries: Artificial Intelligence for:, Augmented Reality for:, Machine Learning for:, ~ Social Media (54)

Company Name: GROUND Inc.
Description: Logistics, Technology, Robotics, Logitech, AI, Warehouse, Supply Chain, Data Science
Website: http://www.groundinc.co.: Japan
Phone: **Email:** info@groundinc.co.: Japan
City: Tokyo **State:** Tokyo **PC:** **Country: Japan**
Year Established: **Status 2020:** Active
Industries: Artificial Intelligence for:, Big Data and Analytics for:, ~ Transportation and Logistics (57), Predictive Analytics for:, Robotics for:, Supply Chain Management

Company Name: Gruff
Description: Gruff is an Artificial Intelligence company.
Website: http://gruff.co.jp/
Phone: **Email:** 36652@reference-encyclopedia-ai.net
City: Tokyo **State:** Tokyo **PC:** **Country: Japan**
Year Established: 2015 **Status 2020:** Active
Industries: Artificial Intelligence for:, Application Services for:, Machine Learning

Company Name: GVA TECH Japan
Description: GVA TECH is a development and provision of AI-CON series many of the current Legal Services are highly specialized.
Website: http://gvatech.co.jp/
Phone: **Email:** contact@gvatech.co.: Japan
City: Tokyo **State:** Tokyo **PC:** **Country: Japan**
Year Established: 2017 **Status 2020:** Active
Industries: Artificial Intelligence for:, Business Process and Operations

Company Name: HERBIO
Description: HERBIO is a medical device development company.
Website: http://herbio.co.jp/
Phone: **Email:** 36686@reference-encyclopedia-ai.net
City: Tokyo **State:** Tokyo **PC:** **Country: Japan**
Year Established: 2017 **Status 2020:** Active
Industries: Business Intelligence for:, Application Services

Company Name: HONNMO:
Description: HONNMONO is a Business Intelligence based company.
Website: http://honnmono.jp/
Phone: **Email:** 36700@reference-encyclopedia-ai.net
City: Tokyo **State:** Tokyo **PC:** **Country: Japan**
Year Established: 2012 **Status 2020:** Active
Industries:

Company Name: HORBAL
Description: HORBAL is Aiming to create a system that realizes the worldview through business assets.
Website: http://www.horbal.jp/
Phone: **Email:** 36704@reference-encyclopedia-ai.net
City: Tokyo **State:** Tokyo **PC:** **Country: Japan**
Year Established: 2011 **Status 2020:** Active
Industries: Big Data and Analytics for:, Application Services

Company Name: Human Intelligence
Description: Your personal Artificial Intelligence
Website: http://humanintelligence.store
Phone: **Email:** support@humanintelligence.store
City: Tokyo **State:** Tokyo **PC:** **Country: Japan**
Year Established: **Status 2020:** Active
Industries: Artificial Intelligence for:, Cloud for:, ~ Life Sciences (27), Compute for:, Content

Company Name: iChain, Inc.
Description: iChain is Japanese leading InsurTech startup that innovates the insurance industry based on Blockchain Technology (Distributed Ledger Tech).
Website: http://www.ichain.co.: Japan
Phone: 81 3 5542 0005 **Email:** ichain-inquiry@ichain.co.: Japan
City: Tokyo **State:** Tokyo **PC:** **Country: Japan**
Year Established: **Status 2020:** Active
Industries: Artificial Intelligence for:, Blockchain for:, ~ Insurance (25), ~ Insurance (25)

Company Name: ID Crui: Sweden
Description: ID Cruise is a media and artificial intelligence based psychology company.
Website: http://www.id-cruise.co.jp/
Phone: 03-6865-6584 **Email:** 36736@reference-encyclopedia-ai.net
City: Tokyo **State:** Tokyo **PC:** **Country: Japan**
Year Established: 2017 **Status 2020:** Active
Industries: Artificial Intelligence for:, IT Managed Services for:, ~ Arts-Entertainment-Recreation (4)

Company Name: Ide: India
Description: Idein seeks to enable all real-world events to be handled by software.
Website: http://idein.jp/
Phone: **Email:** info@idein.: Japan
City: Tokyo **State:** Tokyo **PC:** **Country: Japan**
Year Established: 2015 **Status 2020:** Active
Industries: Computer Vision for:, Application Services for:, Internet of Things (IoT) for:, Machine Learning

Company Name: Idrasys
Description: Idrasys is an artificial intelligence business.
Website: http://idrasys.co.jp/
Phone: **Email:** 36739@reference-encyclopedia-ai.net
City: Tokyo **State:** Tokyo **PC:** **Country: Japan**
Year Established: 2018 **Status 2020:** Active
Industries: Artificial Intelligence for:, Cloud for:, Natural Language Processing

Company Name: Insight Tech Japan
Description: Insight Tech is a Marketing surveys and report creation Data analysis contracts using artificial intelligence
Website: http://insight-tech.co.jp/
Phone: **Email:** 36775@reference-encyclopedia-ai.net
City: Tokyo **State:** Tokyo **PC:** **Country: Japan**
Year Established: 2012 **Status 2020:** Active
Industries: Artificial Intelligence for:, Business Process and Operations

Company Name: intronworks
Description: Intronworks is a data analysis company specializing in natural language processing
Website: http://intronworks.jp/
Phone: **Email:** 36803@reference-encyclopedia-ai.net
City: Tokyo **State:** Tokyo **PC:** **Country: Japan**
Year Established: 2011 **Status 2020:** Active
Industries: Analytics for:, Machine Learning for:, Web

Company Name: JAI: ROMANIA
Description: JAIRO realize general-purpose artificial intelligence that can be used for a wide range of purposes.
Website: http://www.jairo.org/
Phone: **Email:** info@jairo.org
City: Tokyo **State:** Tokyo **PC:** **Country: Japan**
Year Established: 2016 **Status 2020:** Active
Industries: Artificial Intelligence for:, Application Services for:, Natural Language Processing

Company Name: Japan Data Science Consortium
Description: Japan Data Science Consortium (JDSC) is an AI company that provides solutions for the medical, education and retail areas.
Website: http://jdsc.ai/
Phone: **Email:** 36822@reference-encyclopedia-ai.net
City: Tokyo **State:** Tokyo **PC:** **Country: Japan**
Year Established: 2018 **Status 2020:** Active
Industries: Application Services for:, Machine Learning for:, Predictive Analytics

Company Name: Japan Legal System Institute
Description: Legal Technology, Legal Tech, Artificial Intelligence, AI, Document, SaaS, Smart Contract App.
Website: http://j-legal-system.com
Phone: **Email:** e.hong@j-legalsystem.com
City: Tokyo **State:** Tokyo **PC:** **Country: Japan**
Year Established: 2018 **Status 2020:** Active
Industries: Mobile for:, Application Services

Company Name: KARAKURI Japan
Description: Karakuri is an SaaS business, AI solution business and AI Business Development.
Website: http://www.karakuri.ai/
Phone: **Email:** 36843@reference-encyclopedia-ai.net
City: Tokyo **State:** Tokyo **PC:** **Country: Japan**
Year Established: 2018 **Status 2020:** Active
Industries: Artificial Intelligence for:, Business Software as a Service Apps (SaaS Apps) for:, Business Process and Operations

Company Name: Kenpal Inc.
Description: Driver safety solution that monitors the driver's brain waves for signs of drowsiness
Website: http://www.kenpalinc.com/
Phone: **Email:** sales@keweitai.com
City: Tokyo **State:** Tokyo **PC:** **Country: Japan**
Year Established: 2012 **Status 2020:** Active
Industries: Artificial Intelligence for:, ~ Automotive (5)

Company Name: Kobelco
Description:
Website: https://www.kobelcocm-global.com/
Phone: 81-3-5789-2118 **Email:** sasaoka.yoshio@kobelco.com
City: Tokyo **State:** Tokyo **Zip:** 141-8626 **Country: Japan**
Year Established: **Status 2020:** Active
Industries:

Company Name: Kudan
Description: Kudan is accelerating evolution of AR/MR/VR and automobile/drone/robot by developing computer software algorithms as Artificial Perception.
Website: http://www.kudan.io
Phone: **Email:** hello@kudan.eu
City: Tokyo **State:** Tokyo **PC:** **Country: Japan**
Year Established: 2011 **Status 2020:** Active
Industries: Artificial Intelligence for:, Computer Vision

Company Name: Laboro.AI
Description: Solution development business using artificial intelligence technology .
Website: http://laboro.ai/
Phone: **Email:** 36873@reference-encyclopedia-ai.net
City: Tokyo **State:** Tokyo **PC:** **Country: Japan**
Year Established: 2016 **Status 2020:** Active
Industries: Artificial Intelligence for:, Business Applications for:, Cloud

Company Name: LAPRAS
Description: LAPRASis an Artificial Intelligence company.
Website: http://lapras.com/
Phone: **Email:** 36879@reference-encyclopedia-ai.net
City: Tokyo **State:** Tokyo **PC:** **Country: Japan**
Year Established: 2016 **Status 2020:** Active
Industries:

Company Name: Latona
Description: IoT/Edge Computing, Artificial Intelligence
Website: http://latona.io/
Phone: **Email:** info@latona.io
City: Tokyo **State:** Tokyo **PC:** **Country: Japan**
Year Established: 2018 **Status 2020:** Active
Industries:

Company Name: LeapMind
Description: LeapMind makes deep learning 'small and compact' and accessible across a broad spectrum of applications, evolving the Internet of Things.
Website: http://leapmind.io/
Phone: **Email:** info@leapmind.io
City: Tokyo **State:** Tokyo **PC:** **Country: Japan**
Year Established: 2012 **Status 2020:** Active
Industries: Artificial Intelligence for:, Machine Learning

Company Name: LeapMind, Inc.
Description: We are carrying out research on original chip architectures in order to implement Neural Networks on a circuit with low power.
Website: http://leapmind.io/
Phone: **Email:** info@leapmind.io
City: Tokyo **State:** Tokyo **PC:** **Country: Japan**
Year Established: **Status 2020:** Active
Industries: Artificial Intelligence for:, ~ Manufacturing-Electronic (30), ~ Manufacturing-Electronic (30), Machine Learning for:, ~ Professional Services (48)

Company Name: Ledge Japan
Description: Ledge is an AI-specialized web media with the concept of connecting ideas and implementation
Website: http://ledge.ai/aboutus/
Phone: **Email:** 36883@reference-encyclopedia-ai.net
City: Tokyo **State:** Tokyo **PC:** **Country: Japan**
Year Established: 2017 **Status 2020:** Active
Industries: Artificial Intelligence for:, ~ Arts-Entertainment-Recreation (4), Web

Company Name: Leeways
Description: Leeways is an artificial intelligence start up.
Website: http://leeways.co.jp/
Phone: **Email:** info@leeways.co.: Japan
City: Tokyo **State:** Tokyo **PC:** **Country: Japan**
Year Established: 2014 **Status 2020:** Active
Industries: Artificial Intelligence for:, Content for:, ~ Arts-Entertainment-Recreation (4)

Company Name: LegalForce Japan
Description: LegalForce is an AI that reduces the workload while improving the accuracy of contract review .
Website: http://www.legalforce.co.jp/
Phone: **Email:** 36886@reference-encyclopedia-ai.net
City: Tokyo **State:** Tokyo **PC:** **Country: Japan**
Year Established: 2017 **Status 2020:** Active
Industries: Artificial Intelligence for:, Business Process and Operations

Company Name: Life Log Technology
Description: Life Log is a healthcare technology company composed of dietitians, engineers, data scientists, and artificial intelligence researchers.
Website: http://calomeal.com/
Phone: **Email:** info@calomeal. Om
City: Tokyo **State:** Tokyo **PC:** **Country: Japan**
Year Established: 2016 **Status 2020:** Active
Industries: Artificial Intelligence for:, ~ Beauty (8), ~ Food and Beverage (17), ~ Healthcare (20)

Company Name: Lifestyle Design Co., Ltd.
Description: Lifestyle Design Co., Ltd. is a Japanese startup that specializes in the planning, developments, and operation of LaFabric.
Website: http://lifestyledesign.co.jp/
Phone: 201612-1024 **Email:** contact@lifestyledesign.co.: Japan
City: Tokyo **State:** Tokyo **PC:** **Country: Japan**
Year Established: **Status 2020:** Active
Industries: Artificial Intelligence for:, Big Data and Analytics for:, E-Commerce for:, ~ Fashion (16), ~ Media-Communications (41)

Company Name: Lightblue Technology
Description: Lightblue Technology is an AI startup.
Website: http://www.lightblue-tech.com/
Phone: 03-6801-8990 **Email:** office@lightblue-tech.com
City: Tokyo **State:** Tokyo **PC:** **Country: Japan**
Year Established: 2018 **Status 2020:** Active
Industries: Artificial Intelligence

Company Name: Little Cloud
Description: Little Cloud is an AI platform
Website: http://little-cloud.co.jp/
Phone: **Email:** info@little-cloud.: Japan
City: Tokyo **State:** Tokyo **PC:** **Country: Japan**
Year Established: 2013 **Status 2020:** Active
Industries: Artificial Intelligence for:, Cloud for:, Web

Company Name: localio
Description: Locario is a local and small business support company.
Website: http://www.localio.co.: Japan
Phone: **Email:** 36907@reference-encyclopedia-ai.net
City: Tokyo **State:** Tokyo **PC:** **Country: Japan**

Year Established: 2012 **Status 2020:** Active
Industries:

Company Name: Machine Learning Solutions
Description: Machine Learning Solutions is a Artificial Intelligence platform.
Website: http://machine-learning.co.jp/
Phone: **Email:** contact@machine-learning.co.: Japan
City: Tokyo **State:** Tokyo **PC:** **Country: Japan**
Year Established: 2017 **Status 2020:** Active
Industries: Artificial Intelligence for:, Application Services for:, Machine Learning for:, Predictive Analytics

Company Name: MeeCap
Description: We develop and provide software called MeeCap.MeeCap is a process mining solution using AI.
Website: http://www.mee-cap.com/
Phone: **Email:** info@mee-cap.com
City: Tokyo **State:** Tokyo **PC:** **Country: Japan**
Year Established: 2018 **Status 2020:** Active
Industries: Artificial Intelligence for:, IT Managed Services

Company Name: MeeCap, Inc.
Description: MeeCap is a Office device data collection and analysis solution utilizing AI.
Website: http://www.mee-cap.com/
Phone: **Email:** info@mee-cap.com
City: Tokyo **State:** Tokyo **PC:** **Country: Japan**
Year Established: **Status 2020:** Active
Industries: Artificial Intelligence for:, IT Managed Services

Company Name: MetaCube
Description: MetaCube is an information collaboration with global standard technologies, artificial intelligence, and IoT technologies.
Website: http://metacube.jp/
Phone: **Email:** 36967@reference-encyclopedia-ai.net
City: Tokyo **State:** Tokyo **PC:** **Country: Japan**
Year Established: 2012 **Status 2020:** Active
Industries: Artificial Intelligence for:, ~ Healthcare (20), Business Process and Operations

Company Name: METRICA Japan
Description: METRICA is Combining medical care and nursing care with technology such as machine learning and deep learning.
Website: http://metrica.me/
Phone: **Email:** info@metrica.co.: Japan
City: Tokyo **State:** Tokyo **PC:** **Country: Japan**
Year Established: 2018 **Status 2020:** Active
Industries: Artificial Intelligence for:, Application Services for:, Predictive Analytics

Company Name: Mimir Japan
Description: Mimir is a market research company
Website: http://mimir-inc.biz/
Phone: **Email:** 36978@reference-encyclopedia-ai.net
City: Tokyo **State:** Tokyo **PC:** **Country: Japan**
Year Established: 2017 **Status 2020:** Active
Industries: Predictive Analytics

Company Name: Miraiapuri
Description: Miraiapuri is an Artificial Intelligence start up.
Website: http://miraiapuri.co.jp/
Phone: **Email:** 36987@reference-encyclopedia-ai.net
City: Tokyo **State:** Tokyo **PC:** **Country: Japan**
Year Established: 2011 **Status 2020:** Active
Industries: Artificial Intelligence

Company Name: Moneytree
Description: Moneytree is Japan's #1 financial data aggregation platform, providing financial data API services (B2E) and personal finance apps (B2C)
Website: http://moneytreehq.com
Phone: 81 3 5962 7732 **Email:** support@moneytreehq.com
City: Tokyo **State:** Tokyo **PC:** **Country: Japan**
Year Established: **Status 2020:** Active
Industries: Analytics for:, Artificial Intelligence for:, ~ Banking and Financial Markets-Services (7), Big Data and Analytics for:, ~ Banking and Financial Markets-Services (7), ~ Banking and Financial Markets-Services (7), ~ Banking and Financial Markets-Services (7), F: India

Company Name: MUJIN, Inc.
Description: MUJIN develops automation solutions for industrial robots to simplify factory automation and increase worldwide manufacturing productivity.
Website: http://www.mujin.co.: Japan
Phone: 81 3-4577-7638 **Email:** info@mujin.co.: Japan
City: Tokyo **State:** Tokyo **PC:** **Country: Japan**
Year Established: **Status 2020:** Active
Industries: Artificial Intelligence for:, ~ Automotive (5), Computer Vision for:, Enterprise Application Services for:, Automation for:, ~ Transportation and Logistics (57), ~ Manufacturing-Miscellaneous (34), Robotics

Company Name: Net Smile, Inc.
Description: NetSmile is leading company of artificial intelligence development.
Website: https://aiocr.ai/lp_en/
Phone: **Email:** info@netsmile.: Japan
City: Tokyo **State:** Tokyo **PC:** **Country: Japan**
Year Established: **Status 2020:** Active
Industries: Analytics for:, ~ Administrative and Support Services (123), Application Program Interfaces for:, ~ Administrative and Support Services (184), Artificial Intelligence for:, ~ Food and Beverage (17), ~ Government (19), ~ Healthcare (20), ~ Human Resources (24), ~

Company Name: Neural Pocket
Description: Neural Pocket is analyzed with adedicated data analytics program, and spatial information.
Website: http://www.neuralpocket.com/
Phone: **Email:** contact@neuralpocket.com
City: Tokyo **State:** Tokyo **PC:** **Country: Japan**
Year Established: 2018 **Status 2020:** Active
Industries: Artificial Intelligence for:, Big Data and Analytics for:, ~ Fashion (16)

Company Name: Nextremer
Description: Using AI to make cars and other connected hardware conversational
Website: http://www.nextremer.com/en/
Phone: 81039156447 **Email:** info@nextremer.com
City: Tokyo **State:** Tokyo **PC:** **Country: Japan**
Year Established: **Status 2020:** Active
Industries: Artificial Intelligence for:, Computer Vision for:, Machine Learning for:, Natural Language Processing

Company Name: Nippon Computer Vision
Description: Nippon Computer Vision is a leading AI technology company located in japan
Website: http://www.japancv.co.: Japan
Phone: **Email:** 37065@reference-encyclopedia-ai.net
City: Tokyo **State:** Tokyo **PC:** **Country: Japan**
Year Established: 2019 **Status 2020:** Active
Industries:

Company Name: NOBORDER Inc.
Description: HRtech startup that has AI, chatbot technology.
Website: http://noborderinc.com
Phone: **Email:** info@noborderinc.com
City: Tokyo **State:** Tokyo **PC:** **Country: Japan**
Year Established: **Status 2020:** Active
Industries:

Company Name: OneStone
Description: Onestone is agood artificial intelligence can take away human work, an ideal product for someone can be poison for someone.
Website: http://one-stone.co.jp/
Phone: **Email:** 37105@reference-encyclopedia-ai.net
City: Tokyo **State:** Tokyo **PC:** **Country: Japan**
Year Established: 2016 **Status 2020:** Active
Industries: Artificial Intelligence for:, ~ Arts-Entertainment-Recreation (4)

Company Name: Opendoors
Description: Opendoors designs multi-sided frictionless markeplaces where humans and AI complement each others.
Website: http://www.opendoo.: Serbia
Phone: **Email:** feedback@opendoo.: Serbia
City: Tokyo **State:** Tokyo **PC:** **Country: Japan**
Year Established: 2017 **Status 2020:** Active
Industries: Artificial Intelligence for:, Application Services

Company Name: Palsbots
Description: Palsbots is a robort software specialists company.
Website: http://palsbots.net/
Phone: 03-6407-8852 **Email:** 37137@reference-encyclopedia-ai.net
City: Tokyo **State:** Tokyo **PC:** **Country: Japan**
Year Established: 2015 **Status 2020:** Active
Industries: Artificial Intelligence for:, Robotics for:, Web

Company Name: PGV
Description: PGV is willing to move forward to create a bright future with these thoughts .
Website: http://www.pgv.co.jp/
Phone: **Email:** 37160@reference-encyclopedia-ai.net
City: Tokyo **State:** Tokyo **PC:** **Country: Japan**
Year Established: 2016 **Status 2020:** Active
Industries: Artificial Intelligence

Company Name: Phybb: Italy
Description: Introducing SpiderAF - Advanced AI-Powered Digital Ad Fraud Detection and Reporting for Everyone.
Website: http://spideraf.com
Phone: 81364197946 **Email:** sales@spideraf.com
City: Tokyo **State:** Tokyo **PC:** **Country: Japan**
Year Established: 2011 **Status 2020:** Active
Industries: Analytics for:, Artificial Intelligence for:, Security for:, Web for:, ~ Arts-Entertainment-Recreation (4), ~ Media-Communications (41)

Company **Name:** PLANTIO
Description: PLANTIO offers AI and IoT based plantation services, enabling customers to get sustainably harvested food.
Website: http://www.plantio.co.jp/
Phone: **Email:** 37176@reference-encyclopedia-ai.net
City: Tokyo **State:** Tokyo **PC:** **Country: Japan**
Year Established: 2015 **Status 2020:** Active
Industries: ~ Agriculture (3), Artificial Intelligence for:, Internet of Things (IoT)

Company Name: ProEver
Description: ProEver is a knowledge &talent management system created using artificial intelligence that supports intra-organizational knowledge sharing.
Website: http://www.proever.pm/
Phone: **Email:** 37214@reference-encyclopedia-ai.net
City: Tokyo **State:** Tokyo **PC:** **Country: Japan**
Year Established: 2015 **Status 2020:** Active
Industries: Artificial Intelligence for:, Business Intelligence

Company Name: PSYGIG
Description: PSYGIG helps engineers make safer Mobility IoT by accelerating the development of autonomous devices.
Website: http://psygig.com/
Phone: **Email:** info@psygig.com
City: Tokyo **State:** Tokyo **PC:** **Country: Japan**
Year Established: 2017 **Status 2020:** Active
Industries: Artificial Intelligence for:, IT Infrastructure for:, Business Software as a Service Apps (SaaS Apps)

Company Name: Qlonolink
Description: Qlonolink provides an integrated analysis platform for five major marketing data.
Website: http://qlonolink.com/
Phone: **Email:** 37232@reference-encyclopedia-ai.net
City: Tokyo **State:** Tokyo **PC:** **Country: Japan**
Year Established: 2014 **Status 2020:** Active
Industries: Application Services for:, Machine Learning

Company Name: Qubena Japan
Description: Qubena is an AI platform that analyzes each child's strengths and weaknesses.
Website: http://qubena.com/
Phone: **Email:** 37250@reference-encyclopedia-ai.net
City: Tokyo **State:** Tokyo **PC:** **Country: Japan**
Year Established: 2010 **Status 2020:** Active
Industries: Artificial Intelligence for:, ~ Education (13)

Company Name: REACT Japan
Description: REACT are devoting every day with the mission of "zero communication costs between people".
Website: http://react.tokyo/
Phone: **Email:** info@react.tokyo
City: Tokyo **State:** Tokyo **PC:** **Country: Japan**
Year Established: 2015 **Status 2020:** Active
Industries: Artificial Intelligence for:, Content

Company Name: Rei-Frontier
Description: Analysis and research business about human behavior, using AI.
Website: http://www.rei-frontier.: Japan
Phone: **Email:** info@rei-frontier.: Japan
City: Tokyo **State:** Tokyo **PC:** **Country: Japan**
Year Established: **Status 2020:** Active
Industries: Analytics for:, Artificial Intelligence

Company Name: Ridge-i
Description: Ridge-i provide AI technology optimized for business needs.
Website: http://ridge-i.com/
Phone: **Email:** contact@ridge-i.com
City: Tokyo **State:** Tokyo **PC:** **Country: Japan**
Year Established: 2016 **Status 2020:** Active
Industries: Artificial Intelligence for:, Security for:, Automation

Company Name: Roboken
Description: Roboken is a Robotics AI and SES Company.
Website: http://robo-ken.jp/
Phone: **Email:** 37305@reference-encyclopedia-ai.net
City: Tokyo **State:** Tokyo **PC:** **Country: Japan**
Year Established: 2014 **Status 2020:** Active
Industries:

Company Name: SALTO Japan
Description: Salto is a Artificial Intelligence.
Website: http://www.salto.site/
Phone: **Email:** 37334@reference-encyclopedia-ai.net
City: Tokyo **State:** Tokyo **PC:** **Country: Japan**
Year Established: 2015 **Status 2020:** Active
Industries: Artificial Intelligence for:, Application Services for:, Machine Learning for:, Predictive Analytics

Company Name: SCHOL
Description: SCHOL provides solutions using distributed ledger technology and machine learning technology.
Website: http://www.schol.co.jp/
Phone: **Email:** contact@schol.co.: Japan
City: Tokyo **State:** Tokyo **PC:** **Country: Japan**
Year Established: 2019 **Status 2020:** Active
Industries: IT Managed Services for:, Machine Learning

Company Name: SE4
Description: SE4™ Is a startup robotics company specializing in remote robotics.
Website: http://www.se4.io
Phone: **Email:** contact@se4.space
City: Tokyo **State:** Tokyo **PC:** **Country: Japan**
Year Established: 2018 **Status 2020:** Active
Industries: Artificial Intelligence for:, IT Managed Services for:, Robotics for:, ~ Aerospace and Defense (2)

Company Name: Sense Of Wonder
Description: Sense of Wonder is an AI (artificial intelligence) system development business company
Website: http://www.senseofwonder.co.jp/index.html
Phone: **Email:** 37363@reference-encyclopedia-ai.net
City: Tokyo **State:** Tokyo **PC:** **Country: Japan**
Year Established: 2014 **Status 2020:** Active
Industries: Artificial Intelligence for:, Business Applications for:, Content

Company Name: Sigfoss
Description: Sigfoss is an AI solution provider.
Website: http://www.sigfoss.com
Phone: 81.3.5809.1637 **Email:** 37389@reference-encyclopedia-ai.net
City: Tokyo **State:** Tokyo **PC:** **Country: Japan**
Year Established: 2014 **Status 2020:** Active
Industries: Company Name: sinewave Japan
Description: Language Education business;Voice / AI (voice / artificial intelligence);R & D business;Software development business;
Website: http://www.sinewave.co.: Japan
Phone: **Email:** 37399@reference-encyclopedia-ai.net
City: Tokyo **State:** Tokyo **PC:** **Country: Japan**
Year Established: 2010 **Status 2020:** Active
Industries: Artificial Intelligence for:, ~ Education (13), ~ Education (13)

Company Name: SmartHacks
Description: The largest database for AI speakers such as Google Home, Amazon Echo, Homepod, Cortana, etc.
Website: http://smarthacks.io/
Phone: **Email:** info@smarthacks.io
City: Tokyo **State:** Tokyo **PC:** **Country: Japan**
Year Established: **Status 2020:** Active
Industries: Analytics for:, Artificial Intelligence for:, ~ Personal-Religious-Civic (45), ~ Social Media (54)

Company Name: Sports AI
Description: Sports AI is a Club team support project utilizing AI and data
Website: http://sports-ai.: Japan
Phone: **Email:** info@sports-ai.: Japan
City: Tokyo **State:** Tokyo **PC:** **Country: Japan**
Year Established: 2017 **Status 2020:** Active
Industries: Artificial Intelligence for:, Web for:, ~ Arts-Entertainment-Recreation (4)

Company Name: Spotech, Inc.
Description: The AI matches clients with global IT freelancers who can work a side job remotely.
Website: http://spotech.io/en/
Phone: **Email:** info@spotech.io
City: Tokyo **State:** Tokyo **PC:** **Country: Japan**
Year Established: 2018 **Status 2020:** Active
Industries: Artificial Intelligence for:, Web

Company Name: STANDAGE
Description: STANDAGE is a developer of next-generation infrastructure based on Blockchain & AI technologies.
Website: http://standage.co.: Japan
Phone: 03.6435.3371 **Email:** 37465@reference-encyclopedia-ai.net
City: Tokyo **State:** Tokyo **PC:** **Country: Japan**
Year Established: 2017 **Status 2020:** Active
Industries: Artificial Intelligence for:, Blockchain

Company Name: Sumaita
Description: Sumiai Talk is a tech company with the latest AI technology.
Website: http://corp.sumaitalk.com/
Phone: **Email:** 37478@reference-encyclopedia-ai.net
City: Tokyo **State:** Tokyo **PC:** **Country: Japan**
Year Established: 2018 **Status 2020:** Active
Industries: Artificial Intelligence for:, IT Managed Services

Company Name: talent and assessment
Description: talent and assessment is a company based on Career Planning
Website: http://www.taleasse.co.jp/
Phone: 03-6435-8621 **Email:** info@taleasse.com
City: Tokyo **State:** Tokyo **PC:** **Country: Japan**
Year Established: 2014 **Status 2020:** Active
Industries:

Company Name: Tamecco
Description: Tamecco specializes in Real-Time Location Services (RTLS) for major retail brands, industrial, manufacturing & semi-conductor companies.
Website: http://tamecco.: Japan
Phone: 81364355558 **Email:** info@tamecco.: Japan
City: Tokyo **State:** Tokyo **PC:** **Country: Japan**
Year Established: **Status 2020:** Active
Industries: Analytics for:, Artificial Intelligence for:, Big Data and Analytics for:, Mobile for:, ~ Transportation and Logistics (57), Predictive Analytics

Company Name: Tecnos Data Science Engineering
Description: Tecnos Data Science Engineering is a Provision of solutions utilizing big data and artificial intelligence (AI) and provision of AI products
Website: http://www.tdse.jp/
Phone: **Email:** 37513@reference-encyclopedia-ai.net
City: Tokyo **State:** Tokyo **PC:** **Country: Japan**
Year Established: 2013 **Status 2020:** Active
Industries:

Company Name: TENTIAL
Description: TENTIAL analyzes detailed purchasing behavior and attributes online and aim to deliver products based on information.
Website: http://corp.tential.jp/
Phone: **Email:** info@aspole.: Japan
City: Tokyo **State:** Tokyo **PC:** **Country: Japan**
Year Established: 2018 **Status 2020:** Active
Industries: Artificial Intelligence for:, Internet of Things (IoT) for:, ~ Arts-Entertainment-Recreation (4)

Company Name: tripla
Description: Travel, AI
Website: http://corp.tripla.: Japan
Phone: **Email:** support@tripla.: Japan
City: Tokyo **State:** Tokyo **PC:** **Country: Japan**
Year Established: 2015 **Status 2020:** Active
Industries: Artificial Intelligence

Company Name: UsideU
Description: UsideU is developing and providing service robots in which people and robots collaborate.
Website: http://www.usideu.com/
Phone: **Email:** 37606@reference-encyclopedia-ai.net
City: Tokyo **State:** Tokyo **PC:** **Country: Japan**
Year Established: 2017 **Status 2020:** Active
Industries: Artificial Intelligence for:, Robotics

Company Name: Vernax
Description: Audrey allows anyone to train their intelligent assistant and integrate it around apps and services.
Website: http://www.getaudrey.com
Phone: 31 404 300 443 **Email:** davidyap@vernax.com
City: Tokyo **State:** Tokyo **PC:** **Country: Japan**
Year Established: **Status 2020:** Active
Industries: Artificial Intelligence for:, Speech Recognition

Company Name: Woz
Description: WOZ is a digital studio that develops web services, smartphone apps, and AI systems.
Website: http://woz-inc.com
Phone: **Email:** 37687@reference-encyclopedia-ai.net
City: Tokyo **State:** Tokyo **PC:** **Country: Japan**
Year Established: 2015 **Status 2020:** Active
Industries: Artificial Intelligence for:, Business Intelligence for:, Web

Company Name: xenodata lab
Description: xenodata lab is a developing an AI-powered finance data analytics leveraging Natural Language Processing (NLP).
Website: http://www.xenodata-lab.com/
Phone: **Email:** inquiry@xenodata-lab.com
City: Tokyo **State:** Tokyo **PC:** **Country: Japan**
Year Established: 2016 **Status 2020:** Active
Industries: Artificial Intelligence for:, ~ Banking and Financial Markets-Services (7), ~ Banking and Financial Markets-Services (7), ~ Banking and Financial Markets-Services (7)

Company Name: Xrosriver inc.
Description: Xrosriver is an entertainment technology company.
Website: http://xrosriver.com/
Phone: 81368696925 **Email:** info@xrosriver.com
City: Tokyo **State:** Tokyo **PC:** **Country: Japan**
Year Established: **Status 2020:** Active
Industries: Artificial Intelligence for:, ~ Arts-Entertainment-Recreation (4)

Company Name: XTREME-D Inc.
Description: XTREME-D is an startup whose mission is to make HPC cloud computing access easy, fast, efficient, and economical for every customer.
Website: http://xtreme-d.net/en
Phone: **Email:** info@xd-lab.net
City: Tokyo **State:** Tokyo **PC:** **Country: Japan**
Year Established: 2015 **Status 2020:** Active
Industries: Artificial Intelligence for:, Big Data and Analytics for:, Cloud for:, IT Managed Services for:, IT Managed Services

Company Name: YOKOZUNA data
Description: Yokozuna Data has developed a state-of-the-art data science platform to predict individual behavior for video game players.
Website: http://www.yokozunadata.com
Phone: **Email:** info@yokozunadata.com
City: Tokyo **State:** Tokyo **PC:** **Country: Japan**
Year Established: 2015 **Status 2020:** Active
Industries: Analytics for:, Artificial Intelligence for:, Big Data and Analytics for:, Machine Learning for:, Mobile for:, Predictive Analytics for:, Predictive Analytics for:, ~ Arts-Entertainment-Recreation (4)

Company Name: ZAISAN Net
Description: ZAISAN Net is a AI-Fintech startup specializing in stock price movement.
Website: http://zaisan.net/
Phone: **Email:** cs@zaisan.net
City: Tokyo **State:** Tokyo **PC:** **Country: Japan**
Year Established: 2015 **Status 2020:** Active
Industries: Artificial Intelligence for:, ~ Banking and Financial Markets-Services (7), ~ Banking and Financial Markets-Services (7), Machine Learning for:, Natural Language Processing for:, ~ Banking and Financial Markets-Services (7)

Company Name: ZAISAN Net, Inc.
Description: AI-Fintech startup specializing in stock price movement
Website: http://zaisan.net/
Phone: **Email:** cs@zaisan.net
City: Tokyo **State:** Tokyo **PC:** **Country: Japan**
Year Established: **Status 2020:** Active
Industries: Artificial Intelligence for:, ~ Banking and Financial Markets-Services (7), Machine Learning for:, Natural Language Processing for:, ~ Banking and Financial Markets-Services (7)

Company Name: AI Medical Service
Description: AI Medical Service is a Tokyo-based company developing AI software to help detect gastric cancer.
Website: https://www.ai-ms.com/en/
Phone: **Email:** info@ai-ms.com
City: Toshima **State:** Tokyo **PC:** **Country: Japan**
Year Established: 2017 **Status 2020:** Active
Industries: Artificial Intelligence for:, ~ Healthcare (20), ~ Healthcare (20)

Jordon

Company Name: Arabot
Description: arabot an intelligent chatbot, A.I and Machine Learning Company
Website: http://arabot.io/
Phone: **Email:** info@arabot.io
City: Amman **State:** Amman Governorate **PC:** **Country:** JORDAN
Year Established: 2016 **Status 2020:** Active
Industries: Artificial Intelligence for:, IT Managed Services for:, Web for:, Machine Learning

Company Name: Autism4AI
Description: AI4Autism treatment using AR, Data mining, and patterned assistive sensory tech digital sensory room & digital sensory hologram
Website: http://www.mashrou3na.com/
Phone: **Email:** info@mashrou3na.com
City: Amman **State:** Amman Governorate **PC:** **Country:** JORDAN
Year Established: **Status 2020:** Active
Industries:

Company Name: Harreef.ai
Description: Harreef.ai is a Virtual personal assistant.
Website: http://harreef.ai/
Phone: 962 7 8668 0318 **Email:** info@harreef.ai
City: Amman **State:** Amman Governorate **PC:** **Country:** JORDAN
Year Established: 2017 **Status 2020:** Active
Industries: Artificial Intelligence

Kazakhstan

Company Name: Aitec.one
Description: AI, Loyalty, Payment
Website: https://aitec.one/
Phone: 7 (727) 339 30 56 **Email:** a@aitec.one
City: Almaty **State:** Almaty Province **PC:** **Country:** KAZAKHSTAN
Year Established: 2017 **Status 2020:** Active
Industries: Artificial Intelligence for:, Mobile

Company Name: VeriGram
Description: VeriGram is an AI company that provides computer vision and machine learning software to companies for solving business process.
Website:
Phone: 77777870657 **Email:** Askar@verigram.: Kazakhstan
City: Almaty **State:** Almaty Province **PC:** **Country:** KAZAKHSTAN

Year Established: 2017 **Status 2020:** Active
Industries: Artificial Intelligence for:, IT Managed Services

Company Name: BeInTech
Description: Technology company disrupting real estate industry and other business: Spain
Website: http://bein.tech
Phone: 77075557292 **Email:** disrupt@bein.tech
City: Astana **State:** Astana **PC:** **Country:** KAZAKHSTAN
Year Established: **Status 2020:** Active
Industries: Artificial Intelligence for:, IT Managed Services for:, ~ Real Estate (49), Robotics

Kenya

Company Name: Apollo Agriculture
Description: Apollo Agriculture's mission is to deliver modern farming everywhere
Website: http://www.apolloagriculture.com
Phone: **Email:** founders@apolloagriculture.com
City: Nairobi **State:** Nairobi County **PC:** **Country:** KENYA
Year Established: 2016 **Status 2020:** Active
Industries: ~ Agriculture (3), ~ Agriculture (3), ~ Banking and Financial Markets-Services (7), Machine Learning

Company Name: BlockchainCybertech Limited
Description: Develops smart blockchain solutions for Supply chain and Financial service
Website: http://blockchaincybertech.com/
Phone: **Email:** info@blockchaincybertech.com
City: Nairobi **State:** Nairobi County **PC:** **Country:** KENYA
Year Established: **Status 2020:** Active
Industries: Artificial Intelligence for:, Blockchain for:, ~ Banking and Financial Markets-Services (7), ~ Banking and Financial Markets-Services (7), Supply Chain Management

Company Name: Brave Venture Labs
Description: Brave Venture Labs is a network science lab that matches talent with the right job opportunities using artificial intelligence.
Website: http://braveventurelabs.com/
Phone: 254 720 638567 **Email:** info@braveventurelabs.com
City: Nairobi **State:** Nairobi County **PC:** **Country:** KENYA
Year Established: 2016 **Status 2020:** Active
Industries:

Company Name: Digital Uniq Limited
Description: AI & Advanced Analytics company
Website: http://www.digitaluniq.ai
Phone: **Email:** info@digitaluniq.ai
City: Nairobi **State:** Nairobi County **PC:** **Country:** KENYA
Year Established: 2014 **Status 2020:** Active
Industries: Analytics for:, Artificial Intelligence for:, Machine Learning

Company Name: HydroIQ
Description: HydroIQ is the Virtual Water Network Operator (VWNO).
Website: http://hydroiq.africa
Phone: 254 (0) 20 7853 011 **Email:** info@hydroiq.co.: Kenya
City: Nairobi **State:** Nairobi County **PC:** **Country:** KENYA
Year Established: 2017 **Status 2020:** Active
Industries: Analytics for:, Application Services for:, ~ Waste Management and Remediation Services (59)

Company Name: irisX
Description: A SaaS company that provides a social crediting system for companies and cities worldwide
Website: http://irisx.blanqx.com
Phone: **Email:** irisx@blanqx.com
City: Nairobi **State:** Nairobi County **PC:** **Country:** KENYA
Year Established: **Status 2020:** Active
Industries: Artificial Intelligence for:, Security

Company Name: Jobonics
Description: Jobonics is an all in one recruiting solution for employers in Africa to find, screen and hire talent in an easy and fast way.
Website: http://www.jobonics.com
Phone: **Email:** support@jobonics.com
City: Nairobi **State:** Nairobi County **PC:** **Country:** KENYA
Year Established: **Status 2020:** Active
Industries: Artificial Intelligence for:, Business Applications for:, ~ Human Resources (24), ~ Professional Services (48)

Company Name: Kanjwa
Description: Kanjwa is an online platform that talks about finance and money in Kenya.
Website: http://www.kanjwa.com
Phone: **Email:** info@kanjwa.com
City: Nairobi **State:** Nairobi County **PC:** **Country:** KENYA
Year Established: **Status 2020:** Active
Industries:

Company Name: KaziQuest
Description: KaziQuest is on a mission to change the way organisations in Africa recruit and manage talent.
Website: http://kaziquest.com/
Phone: **Email:** hello@kaziquest.com
City: Nairobi **State:** Nairobi County **PC:** **Country:** KENYA
Year Established: 2018 **Status 2020:** Active
Industries: Artificial Intelligence for:, IT Managed Services

Company Name: Kazisha
Description: Hr recruitment consultancy firm and services, AI & data driven
Website: http://www.kazisha.net
Phone: **Email:** kazishastartup@gmail.com
City: Nairobi **State:** Nairobi County **PC:** **Country:** KENYA
Year Established: **Status 2020:** Active
Industries:

Company Name: Notonlab
Description: Software, Chatbots, Verification
Website: http://notonlab.com/
Phone: 254-780161136 **Email:** info@notonlab.com
City: Nairobi **State:** Nairobi County **PC:** **Country:** KENYA
Year Established: 2015 **Status 2020:** Active
Industries: Application Services for:, Artificial Intelligence for:, ~ Banking and Financial Markets-Services (7), IT Managed Services

Company Name: PesaBot
Description: We help companies enhance their customer support through instant messaging powered by AI and make it easy for them to collect payments.
Website: http://pesabot.com
Phone: **Email:** hello@pesabot.com
City: Nairobi **State:** Nairobi County **PC:** **Country:** KENYA
Year Established: 2016 **Status 2020:** Active
Industries: Artificial Intelligence for:, IT Managed Services for:, ~ Banking and Financial Markets-Services (7)

Company Name: Ryanada Limited
Description: Big Data Company on Mission to Empower People via Technology. Ryanada leverages on Cloud Computing, IoT and AI Technologies to empower SMEs.
Website: http://www.ryanada.com
Phone: **Email:** info@ryanada.com
City: Nairobi **State:** Nairobi County **PC:** **Country:** KENYA
Year Established: 2011 **Status 2020:** Active
Industries: Artificial Intelligence for:, IT Managed Services

Company Name: SUPERFLUID LABS
Description: Superfluid Labs delivers Africa's Consumer Credit Risk Analytics platform using AI technologies and alternative data sets
Website: http://www.superfluid.io
Phone: **Email:** info@superfluid.io
City: Nairobi **State:** Nairobi County **PC:** **Country:** KENYA

Year Established: 2015 **Status 2020:** Active
Industries: Analytics for:, Artificial Intelligence for:, Business Intelligence for:, Databases for:, ~ Banking and Financial Markets-Services (7), Finance and Accounting

Company Name: TalkLift
Description: SAAS, AI Chatbots,
Website: http://talklift.com/
Phone: **Email:** moses@talklift.com
City: Nairobi **State:** Nairobi County **PC:** **Country:** KENYA
Year Established: 2017 **Status 2020:** Active
Industries: Artificial Intelligence for:, Enterprise Application Services for:, IT Managed Services for:, IT Managed Services for:, Business Software as a Service Apps (SaaS Apps) for:, ~ Social Assistance-Non-Profits (53)

Company **Name:** UjuziKilimo
Description: UjuziKilimo collects & analyzes data to provide actionable insights that inform the agriculture industry.
Website: http://www.ujuzikilimo.com/
Phone: 254 (0) 20 2611 248 **Email:** info@ujuzikilimo.com
City: Nairobi **State:** Nairobi County **PC:** **Country:** KENYA
Year Established: 2016 **Status 2020:** Active
Industries: ~ Agriculture (3), Analytics for:, Big Data and Analytics for:, ~ Agriculture (3), Internet of Things (IoT) for:, Predictive Analytics

Company Name: umba
Description: Utilizing AI to bring Financial Inclusion to Emerging Markets
Website: http://www.umba.com
Phone: **Email:** invest@umba.com
City: Nairobi **State:** Nairobi County **PC:** **Country:** KENYA
Year Established: 2017 **Status 2020:** Active
Industries: ~ Banking and Financial Markets-Services (7), ~ Banking and Financial Markets-Services (7), Machine Learning for:, ~ Banking and Financial Markets-Services (7), Application Services

Kuwait

Company Name: Kait Technologi
Description: Customer service platform
Website: http://www.kait.ai
Phone: **Email:** Office@kait.ai
City: Kuwait **State:** Al Asimah Governate **PC:** **Country:** KUWAIT
Year Established: **Status 2020:** Active
Industries: Artificial Intelligence for:, Machine Learning

Company Name: Nabta Heal:
Description: Nabta is the first dedicated platform for women's health in the Middle East and North Africa.
Website: http://twitter.com/NabtaHeal:Thailand
Phone: 965-666-7898 **Email:** yalla@nabtahealth.com
City: Kuwait **State:** Al Asimah Governate **PC:** **Country:** KUWAIT
Year Established: **Status 2020:** Active
Industries: Artificial Intelligence for:, ~ Healthcare (20), ~ Healthcare (20), ~ Healthcare (20)

Latvia

Company Name: Alpha Visum
Description: Big Data & Artificial Intelligence solutions in investment analysis.
Website: http://www.alphavisum.com
Phone: 371 29129292 **Email:** info@alphavisum.com
City: Jurmala **State:** Riga **PC:** **Country:** LATVIA
Year Established: **Status 2020:** Active
Industries: Analytics for:, Artificial Intelligence for:, Big Data and Analytics for:, Machine Learning

Company Name: 4SmartStreets
Description: WE PROVIDE ACCURATE DATA ABOUT THE CITIES AND STREETS USING STATE OF THE ART ADVANCES IN A.I. AND COMPUTER VISION
Website: http://www.4smartstreets.com/home
Phone: **Email:** info@4smartstreets.com
City: Riga **State:** Riga **PC:** **Country:** LATVIA
Year Established: 2016 **Status 2020:** Active
Industries: Artificial Intelligence

Company Name: AirQualityTree
Description: Modular air quality monitoring unit that can help people with asthma and other allergic illnesses that can be caused by bad microclimate.
Website:
Phone: **Email:** 36020@reference-encyclopedia-ai.net
City: Riga **State:** Riga **PC:** **Country:** LATVIA
Year Established: 2017 **Status 2020:** Active
Industries: Artificial Intelligence for:, ~ Healthcare (20)

Company Name: Ardora
Description: Digital assistant for people taking care of relatives with dementia.
Website: http://www.ardora.co/
Phone: **Email:** info@ardora.co
City: Riga **State:** Riga **PC:** **Country:** LATVIA
Year Established: **Status 2020:** Active
Industries: Artificial Intelligence for:, ~ Healthcare (20), ~ Healthcare (20), ~ Professional Services (48)

Company Name: asya
Description: Asya is an AI powered app that help people pratice mindful communication.
Website: http://asya.ai
Phone: **Email:** ariel@asya.app
City: Riga **State:** Riga **PC:** **Country:** LATVIA
Year Established: **Status 2020:** Active
Industries:

Company Name: asya.ai
Description: Asya is an app for mindful conversation powered by Ethical AI
Website: http://asya.ai
Phone: **Email:** info@asya.ai
City: Riga **State:** Riga **PC:** **Country:** LATVIA
Year Established: **Status 2020:** Active
Industries: Application Services for:, Artificial Intelligence for:, Machine Learning

Company Name: BT8 Group
Description: BT8 Group is the holding company of Auctee, and other Auctee-related initiatives.
Website: http://www.bt8group.com
Phone: **Email:** office@bt8group.com
City: Riga **State:** Riga **PC:** **Country:** LATVIA
Year Established: **Status 2020:** Active
Industries:

Company Name: Citintelly
Description: Intelligent Street Lighting Control for the Smart City
Website: http://www.citintelly.com
Phone: 371 26371717 **Email:** office@citintelly.com
City: Riga **State:** Riga **PC:** **Country:** LATVIA
Year Established: 2016 **Status 2020:** Active
Industries: ~ Energy and Utilities (14), IT Managed Services for:, Application Services for:, IT Infrastructure for:, ~ Construction (10), ~ Construction (10), ~ Construction (10)

Company Name: Forex Team
Description: Automated forex trading mobile solutions
Website: http://www.forexteam.com
Phone: **Email:** info@forexteam.com
City: Riga **State:** Riga **PC:** **Country:** LATVIA

Year Established: **Status 2020:** Active
Industries: Analytics for:, Artificial Intelligence for:, ~ Banking and Financial Markets-Services (7), ~ Banking and Financial Markets-Services (7), Application Services

Company Name: KleinTech Service
Description: KleinTech specializes in application of deep learning and machine vision technologies to logistics industry by replacing human labor.
Website: http://www.kleintech.net
Phone: 371 67 704 670 **Email:** kleintech@kleintech.net
City: Riga **State:** Riga **PC:** **Country:** LATVIA
Year Established: 2010 **Status 2020:** Active
Industries: Artificial Intelligence for:, Big Data and Analytics

Company Name: Maintenel Automation
Description: Reducing Operating and Maintenance Costs of Your Equipment
Website: http://www.maintenel.com/
Phone: **Email:** info@maintenel.com
City: Riga **State:** Riga **PC:** **Country:** LATVIA
Year Established: 2013 **Status 2020:** Active
Industries: ~ Telecommunications (56), Automation for:, Predictive Analytics

Company Name: Phonal AI
Description: Speech Analytics AI for Customer Service and Education
Website: http://phonal.ai
Phone: **Email:** support@phonal.ai
City: Riga **State:** Riga **PC:** **Country:** LATVIA
Year Established: 2019 **Status 2020:** Active
Industries: Artificial Intelligence for:, Big Data and Analytics for:, ~ Customer Relationship Management (11), ~ Education (13), Speech Recognition

Company Name: Recorn
Description:
Website: http://recorn.app
Phone: **Email:** info@recorn.app
City: Riga **State:** Riga **PC:** **Country:** LATVIA
Year Established: **Status 2020:** Active
Industries:

Company Name: SimpleMediaCode
Description: Simple Media Code will create new web site, improve your existing website or consult about web page optimization.
Website: http://simplemediacode.com
Phone: 371 29 996 832 **Email:** info@simplemediacode.com
City: Riga **State:** Riga **PC:** **Country:** LATVIA
Year Established: 2018 **Status 2020:** Active
Industries: Digital Marketing for:, Predictive Analytics for:, Web for:, Web

Company Name: Smartsub
Description: Smartsub is a digital marketing assistant powered by artificial intelligence that helps to find the best keywords.
Website: http://smartsub.co/
Phone: **Email:** hello@smartsub.co
City: Riga **State:** Riga **PC:** **Country:** LATVIA
Year Established: 2016 **Status 2020:** Active
Industries: Artificial Intelligence for:, Digital Marketing

Company Name: XOResearch:
Description: XOresearch is a company focused on providing deep learning technology to Healthcare.
Website: http://www.xoresearch.com
Phone: 37167305084 **Email:** getintouch@xoresearch.com
City: Riga **State:** Riga **PC:** **Country:** LATVIA
Year Established: **Status 2020:** Active
Industries: Artificial Intelligence for:, ~ Healthcare (20), ~ Healthcare (20), Machine Learning for:, ~ Healthcare (20), ~ Professional Services (48)

Lebanon

Company Name: 3P - PASS PAY PARTY
Description: 3P is a nightlife application for booking your tickets, buying your drinks and socializing with the party community.Clubbers think no more!
Website: http://www.passpayparty.com
Phone: **Email:** jennifer@passpayparty.com
City: Beirut **State:** Beirut Governorate **PC:** **Country:** LEBANON
Year Established: **Status 2020:** Active
Industries:

Company Name: dox
Description: dox is providing a battery predictive maintenance platform helping EV OEMs reduce warranty costs, battery waste, and sudden failur: Spain
Website: http://dox.tech
Phone: **Email:** info@dox.tech
City: Beirut **State:** Beirut Governorate **PC:** **Country:** LEBANON
Year Established: 2017 **Status 2020:** Active
Industries: ~ Energy and Utilities (14), ~ Telecommunications (56), Machine Learning for:, Predictive Analytics

Company Name: Fallound
Description: Making every commute worth your time
Website: http://fallound.com
Phone: 96178869950 **Email:** support@fallound.com
City: Beirut **State:** Beirut Governorate **PC:** **Country:** LEBANON
Year Established: **Status 2020:** Active
Industries:

Company Name: Fig
Description: Fig offers businesses a chatbot development platform for non techies. No coding and no conversational design knowledge needed
Website: http://www.figbots.ai
Phone: **Email:** info@figbots.ai
City: Beirut **State:** Beirut Governorate **PC:** **Country:** LEBANON
Year Established: 2017 **Status 2020:** Active
Industries: Artificial Intelligence for:, Big Data and Analytics for:, Machine Learning for:, Natural Language Processing

Company Name: Figurit
Description: Figurit is a content discovery platform that helps content creators looking for fresh and exciting stories to write about.
Website: http://www.figur.: Italy
Phone: 961 3 421260 **Email:** contact@figur.: Italy
City: Beirut **State:** Beirut Governorate **PC:** **Country:** LEBANON
Year Established: 2016 **Status 2020:** Active
Industries: Big Data and Analytics for:, Content for:, Content for:, ~ Media-Communications (41), Predictive Analytics for:, Web for:, Web for:, Data Management

Company Name: Lexyom
Description: Lexyom is an online platform providing its users with smart legal answers and tailored legal services using artificial intelligence.
Website: http://www.lexyom.com
Phone: **Email:** hello@lexyom.com
City: Beirut **State:** Beirut Governorate **PC:** **Country:** LEBANON
Year Established: 2016 **Status 2020:** Active
Industries: Artificial Intelligence

Company Name: MAJ Solution
Description: Digital construction flows - SaaS - International
Website: http://www.majsolution.com
Phone: 961-3-455576 **Email:** maj@interactivelife.com
City: Beirut **State:** Beirut Governorate **PC:** **Country:** LEBANON
Year Established: **Status 2020:** Active
Industries: Analytics for:, Artificial Intelligence for:, Big Data and Analytics for:, IT Managed Services for:, Mobile for:, ~ Professional Services (48)

Company Name: Oreyeon
Description: Oreyeon develops solutions enabling airports to optimize their safety procedures.
Website: http://oreyeon.com/
Phone: 961 70 609 630 **Email:** 37124@reference-encyclopedia-ai.net
City: Beirut **State:** Beirut Governorate **PC:** **Country:** LEBANON
Year Established: 2018 **Status 2020:** Active
Industries: Machine Learning for:, ~ Government (19)

Company **Name:** Personafier SAL
Description: Personafier is an affordable subscription based content intelligence platform that gives you real time insights on your target persona.
Website: http://www.personafier.com
Phone: 96170059975 **Email:** ihab@personafier.com
City: Beirut **State:** Beirut Governorate **PC:** **Country:** LEBANON
Year Established: 2018 **Status 2020:** Active
Industries: Analytics for:, Artificial Intelligence for:, Content for:, Content for:, Content for:, ~ Event Management (15), ~ Social Assistance-Non-Profits (53), ~ Social Assistance-Non-Profits (53)

Company Name: Tummy
Description: Tummy eliminates patient's stress by securely aggregating wearables, digital labs and healthcare professionals' information.
Website:
Phone: **Email:** 37577@reference-encyclopedia-ai.net
City: Beirut **State:** Beirut Governorate **PC:** **Country:** LEBANON
Year Established: 2014 **Status 2020:** Closed
Industries: ~ Healthcare (20), ~ Healthcare (20), IT Managed Services for:, ~ Healthcare (20), ~ Banking and Financial Markets-Services (7), Enterprise Application Services for:, Predictive Analytics

Company Name: Yakshof
Description: Track, Analyze, Act and Control the conversation
Website: http://www.yakshof.com
Phone: 961 1 742 185 **Email:** info@yakshof.com
City: Beirut **State:** Beirut Governorate **PC:** **Country:** LEBANON
Year Established: 2012 **Status 2020:** Active
Industries: Analytics for:, Data Management for:, Machine Learning

Company Name: Yayy
Description: Video Game Company
Website: http://www.yayygames.com
Phone: 96170624916 **Email:** ziad@yayygames.com
City: Beirut **State:** Beirut Governorate **PC:** **Country:** LEBANON
Year Established: **Status 2020:** Active
Industries:

Company Name: Neotic
Description: Neotic creates Artificial Intelligence technologies for advanced investment decisions
Website: http://neotic.ai
Phone: **Email:** info@neotic.ai
City: Tripoli **State:** North Governorate **PC:** **Country:** LEBANON
Year Established: 2017 **Status 2020:** Active
Industries: Artificial Intelligence for:, ~ Banking and Financial Markets-Services (7), ~ Banking and Financial Markets-Services (7), Machine Learning for:, Risk Management

Liechtenstein

Company Name: EQUITY-AI
Description: Solving AI suppression of minority voices. EQUITY-AI ships equity tools that remove implicit biases from deep learning models.
Website: http://equity-ai.com
Phone: **Email:** team@equity-ai.com
City: Vaduz **State:** Vaduz **PC:** **Country:** Liechtenstein
Year Established: 2019 **Status 2020:** Active
Industries: Artificial Intelligence for:, IT Managed Services for:, Natural Language Processing

Company Name: TV-TWO
Description: Blockchain Transparency for Cross-Device Video Entertainment (Watch & Earn Crypto)
Website: http://tv-two.com/
Phone: **Email:** team@tv-two.com
City: Vaduz **State:** Vaduz **PC:** **Country:** Liechtenstein
Year Established: **Status 2020:** Active
Industries: Artificial Intelligence for:, Blockchain for:, ~ Banking and Financial Markets-Services (7), Machine Learning for:, ~ Arts-Entertainment-Recreation (4)

Lithuania

Company Name: Satalia Lithuania (previously Data Dog)
Description: AI and data science company that revolutionise resource planning, supply chain, sales and customer service operations.
Website: http://data.dog/
Phone: 370 37 211949 **Email:** info@datadog.lt
City: Kaunas **State:** Kaunas County **PC:** **Country: Lithuania**
Year Established: 2012 **Status 2020:** Active
Industries: Artificial Intelligence for:, Big Data and Analytics for:, IT Managed Services for:, ~ Telecommunications (56), Machine Learning for:, Supply Chain Management

Company Name: bitREC
Description: Builds state of the art recommender systems for smart retailers.
Website: http://www.bitrec.com
Phone: **Email:** info@bitrec.com
City: Vilnius **State:** Vilnius County **PC:** **Country: Lithuania**
Year Established: 2012 **Status 2020:** Active
Industries:

Company Name: Devs.LT
Description: A platform, that uses AI and machine learning to help companies hire their perfect match from the pool of pre-screened IT-talents worldwide.
Website: http://devs.lt
Phone: 37067114039 **Email:** a@devs.lt
City: Vilnius **State:** Vilnius County **PC:** **Country: Lithuania**
Year Established: **Status 2020:** Active
Industries: Artificial Intelligence for:, ~ Human Resources (24), Machine Learning

Company Name: Exacaster
Description: A big data predictive analytics technology company.
Website: http://www.exacaster.com
Phone: (3706) 850-6502 **Email:** hello@exacaster.com
City: Vilnius **State:** Vilnius County **PC:** **Country: Lithuania**
Year Established: 2011 **Status 2020:** Active
Industries: Analytics for:, Business Applications for:, Enterprise Application Services for:, Machine Learning for:, Predictive Analytics for:, Business Software as a Service Apps (SaaS Apps) for:, Business Software as a Service Apps (SaaS Apps)

Company Name: Feedpresso
Description: News in any language, automatically personalised using artificial intelligence.
Website: http://www.feedpresso.com
Phone: **Email:** tadas.subonis@feedpresso.com
City: Vilnius **State:** Vilnius County **PC:** **Country: Lithuania**
Year Established: 2014 **Status 2020:** Active
Industries: Application Services for:, Artificial Intelligence for:, Digital Media for:, IT Managed Services for:, Machine Learning

Company Name: GOSU Data Lab
Description: GOSU Data Lab is a company with a focus on GAMING DATA and AI
Website: http://www.gosu.ai
Phone: **Email:** a@gosu.ai
City: Vilnius **State:** Vilnius County **PC:** **Country: Lithuania**
Year Established: **Status 2020:** Active
Industries: Artificial Intelligence for:, Big Data and Analytics for:, Machine Learning

Company Name: MANU
Description: MANU makes personalized business decisions based on behavioral analytics profiling.
Website: http://www.manu.lt/
Phone: 370 615 83773 **Email:** labas@manu.lt
City: Vilnius **State:** Vilnius County **PC:** **Country: Lithuania**
Year Established: 2016 **Status 2020:** Active
Industries: Analytics for:, Artificial Intelligence for:, ~ Banking and Financial Markets-Services (7)

Company **Name:** Mobylogix
Description: Data-driven creative digital agency that builds custom engaging digital products and marketing campaigns.
Website: http://www.mobylogix.com
Phone: 37063982829 **Email:** hello@mobylogix.com
City: Vilnius **State:** Vilnius County **PC:** **Country: Lithuania**
Year Established: **Status 2020:** Active
Industries: Artificial Intelligence for:, Enterprise Application Services for:, Machine Learning for:, Application Services

Company Name: Musical Blockcha: India
Description: World's #1 Creative approach to Blockchain. Longstoryshort: we created a solution that converts img/txt/data into music using AI Blockchain.
Website: http://musicalblockchain.com
Phone: 37060778511 **Email:** king@musicalblockchain.com
City: Vilnius **State:** Vilnius County **PC:** **Country: Lithuania**
Year Established: **Status 2020:** Active
Industries: ~ Arts-Entertainment-Recreation (4), Artificial Intelligence for:, Blockchain for:, ~ Education (13), ~ Social-Environmental-Physical-Engineering Sciences (55), ~ Manufacturing-Electronic (30), ~ Arts-Entertainment-Recreation (4), ~ Professional Services (48), : Morocco

Company Name: NAMERIGHT
Description: NAMERIGHT powers humans intuition with machine intelligence to enable them choose the right name
Website: http://www.nameright.com/
Phone: **Email:** founders@nameright.com
City: Vilnius **State:** Vilnius County **PC:** **Country: Lithuania**
Year Established: **Status 2020:** Active
Industries: Artificial Intelligence for:, Natural Language Processing for:, ~ Life Sciences (27), ~ Professional Services (48)

Company Name: Oxip: Italy
Description: AI-Powered medical image analys
Website: http://www.oxipit.ai/
Phone: 37062599148 **Email:** info@oxipit.ai
City: Vilnius **State:** Vilnius County **PC:** **Country: Lithuania**
Year Established: **Status 2020:** Active
Industries: Artificial Intelligence for:, Business Applications for:, Computer Vision for:, ~ Healthcare (20), ~ Healthcare (20), Machine Learning

Company Name: Perfection42
Description: Empowering creators to perfect their work by freeing their minds from repetitiveness.
Website: http://www.Perfection42.com
Phone: 37060008900 **Email:** simona@perfection42.com
City: Vilnius **State:** Vilnius County **PC:** **Country: Lithuania**
Year Established: 2018 **Status 2020:** Active
Industries: ~ Arts-Entertainment-Recreation (4), Artificial Intelligence for:, Augmented Reality for:, IT Managed Services for:, Web for:, Virtual Reality (VR)

Company Name: PIXEVIA
Description: PIXEVIA - artificial intelligence for reta: Israel
Website: http://www.pixevia.com/
Phone: 37068526284 **Email:** info@magma.lt
City: Vilnius **State:** Vilnius County **PC:** **Country: Lithuania**
Year Established: 2015 **Status 2020:** Active
Industries: ~ Construction (10)

Company Name: Reekon
Description: Semi-autonomous customer service automation platform that handles E-commerce and IT customer inquiries via emails, phone calls and live chat
Website: http://reekon.net/
Phone: **Email:** reekon@yellowhmk.com
City: Vilnius **State:** Vilnius County **PC:** **Country: Lithuania**
Year Established: 2020 **Status 2020:** Active
Industries: Artificial Intelligence for:, ~ Customer Relationship Management (11), Machine Learning for:, IT Managed Services

Company Name: Sendato
Description: Sendato offers its commercial customers with e-marketing automation and multi-channel communication solutions.
Website: http://www.sendato.com/
Phone: **Email:** 37362@reference-encyclopedia-ai.net
City: Vilnius **State:** Vilnius County **PC:** **Country: Lithuania**
Year Established: 2016 **Status 2020:** Active
Industries: Artificial Intelligence for:, IT Managed Services for:, Business Software as a Service Apps (SaaS Apps)

Company Name: SKETCHAR
Description: SketchAR is a fully-fledged tool for teaching drawing using augmented reality, machine learning, and neural networks.
Website: sketchar.tech
Phone: **Email:** marketing@thron.com
City: Vilnius **State:** Vilnius County **PC:** **Country: Lithuania**
Year Established: **Status 2020:** Active
Industries:

Company Name: Telesoftas
Description: TeleSoftas is a consulting and product engineering service company, providing high-end bespoke software engineering solutions.
Website: http://www.telesoftas.com
Phone: 370 694 20374 **Email:** info@telesoftas.com
City: Vilnius **State:** Vilnius County **PC:** **Country: Lithuania**
Year Established: **Status 2020:** Active
Industries: Artificial Intelligence for:, Augmented Reality for:, Big Data and Analytics for:, ~ Professional Services (48), Application Services for:, ~ Customer Relationship Management (11), ~ Professional Services (48), ~ Professional Services (48), Development and Test f

Company Name: Vecticum
Description: Time saving tools for daily business tasks
Website: http://www.vecticum.com
Phone: 37068686361 **Email:** info@vecticum.com
City: Vilnius **State:** Vilnius County **PC:** **Country: Lithuania**
Year Established: **Status 2020:** Active
Industries: Artificial Intelligence for:, Machine Learning for:, ~ Professional Services (48)

Luxembourg

Company Name: Aiva Technologies
Description: Aiva is an Artificial Intelligence capable of composing emotional soundtracks for films, video games, tv shows and commercials.
Website: http://www.aiva.ai/
Phone: **Email:** contact@aiva.ai
City: **State:** **PC:** **Country:** Luxembourg
Year Established: **Status 2020:** Active
Industries: Artificial Intelligence for:, Machine Learning for:, ~ Arts-Entertainment-Recreation (4)

Company Name: ALPHA10X
Description: AI that connects the people, capital, and ideas that promise to solve the world's greatest challenges.
Website: http://alpha10x.com/
Phone: **Email:** info@alpha10x.com
City: Luxembourg **State:** Luxembourg **PC:** **Country:** Luxembourg
Year Established: 2018 **Status 2020:** Active
Industries: Artificial Intelligence for:, ~ Banking and Financial Markets-Services (7)

Company Name: DataThings
Description: DataThings is a Luxembourgish company aiming at delivering machine learning and live data analytics to many business: Spain
Website: http://www.datathings.com
Phone: (3522) 060-0315 **Email:** contact@datathings.com
City: Luxembourg **State:** Luxembourg **PC:** **Country:** Luxembourg
Year Established: 2017 **Status 2020:** Active
Industries: Analytics for:, Artificial Intelligence for:, Big Data and Analytics for:, IT Managed Services for:, Machine Learning for:, ~ Construction (10)

Company **Name:** LuxAI
Description: LuxAI is an innovative startup specialized in disruptive robotic solutions for education, health-care and entertainment.
Website: http://www.luxai.eu/
Phone: (3522) 899-8465 **Email:** info@luxai.eu
City: Luxembourg **State:** Luxembourg **PC:** **Country:** Luxembourg
Year Established: 2016 **Status 2020:** Active
Industries: ~ Healthcare (20), Robotics for:, ~ Healthcare (20)

Company Name: SCROBLE
Description: Creating new Fashion Shopping Reality & reinventing brick-and-mortar
Website: http://www.scroble.com/
Phone: **Email:** 37350@reference-encyclopedia-ai.net
City: Luxembourg **State:** Luxembourg **PC:** **Country:** Luxembourg
Year Established: 2018 **Status 2020:** Active
Industries: Artificial Intelligence for:, E-Commerce for:, ~ Fashion (16), IT Managed Services

Company Name: Kleos Space
Description: Kleos Space develop the Geolocation Intelligence Data Service and over a longer term market disruptive in-Space technologies.
Website: http://www.kleos.space
Phone: 352 2088 2290 **Email:** office@kleos.space
City: Esch-sur-alzette **State:** Luxembourg District **PC:** **Country:** Luxembourg
Year Established: 2017 **Status 2020:** Active
Industries: Analytics for:, Artificial Intelligence for:, Internet of Things (IoT) for:, ~ Telecommunications (56)

Company Name: HAPPENING TECHNOLOGIES : SAUDI ARABIA
Description: SaaS
Website: http://www.happening.media
Phone: 33609475181 **Email:** denis@happening.media
City: Luxembourg **State:** Luxembourg District **PC:** **Country:** Luxembourg
Year Established: **Status 2020:** Active
Industries: ~ Arts-Entertainment-Recreation (4), Artificial Intelligence for:, Big Data and Analytics for:, Data Management for:, ~ Banking and Financial Markets-Services (7), Machine Learning

Company Name: Talkwalker
Description: Talkwalker is a listening and analytics company that empowers over 1, 000 brands to optimize the impact of their communication efforts.
Website: http://www.talkwalker.com
Phone: 1(646)712-9441 **Email:** contact@talkwalker.com
City: Luxembourg **State:** Luxembourg District **PC:** **Country:** Luxembourg
Year Established: **Status 2020:** Active
Industries: Analytics for:, Artificial Intelligence for:, Machine Learning for:, Web for:, Cyber Security for:, ~ Social Media (54), Data Management

Malaysia

Company Name: Upal
Description: UPal (UPal.com.my & Mobile App) is The Largest & Most Reliable University Student Part Time & Internship Job Matching Portal in Malaysia
Website: http://www.upal.com.: Malaysia
Phone: 60123835993 **Email:** weiming@upoal.com.: Malaysia
City: Kuala Lumpor **State:** Federal Territory of Kuala Lumpur **PC:** **Country:** Malaysia
Year Established: **Status 2020:** Active
Industries: Artificial Intelligence for:, ~ Human Resources (24), ~ Education (13)

Company Name: Artemiz Innovations Sdn Bhd
Description: Geospatial-Intelligence-As-A-Service; Patented Software for Joint Command & Control of Satellites & Drones.
Website: http://www.artemiz.org/
Phone: **Email:** admin@artemiz.ca
City: Kuala Lumpur **State:** Federal Territory of Kuala Lumpur **PC:** **Country:** Malaysia
Year Established: **Status 2020:** Active
Industries: ~ Aerospace and Defense (2), Artificial Intelligence for:, Machine Learning

Company Name: Custlr
Description: Custlr is an Android app which has a "fitting algorithm" to eliminate -guesswork when buying shirts without trying it out first.
Website: http://custlr.com/
Phone: 60 18-221 3226 **Email:** admin@custlr.com
City: Kuala Lumpur **State:** Federal Territory of Kuala Lumpur **PC:** **Country:** Malaysia
Year Established: **Status 2020:** Active
Industries: Application Services for:, Artificial Intelligence for:, E-Commerce for:, Machine Learning

Company Name: dahmakan
Description: dahmakan uses artificial intelligence in logistics and production to conquer the Asian takeout market.
Website: http://www.dahmakan.com
Phone: 60377732730 **Email:** care@dahmakan.com
City: Kuala Lumpur **State:** Federal Territory of Kuala Lumpur **PC:** **Country:** Malaysia
Year Established: **Status 2020:** Active
Industries:

Company Name: Ebizu
Description: Ebizu is retail and advertising technology provider targeted at helping brands reach and engage the connected consumer.
Website: http://www.ebizu.com/
Phone: (6032) 242-2667 **Email:** info@ebizu.com
City: Kuala Lumpur **State:** Federal Territory of Kuala Lumpur **PC:** **Country:** Malaysia
Year Established: 2013 **Status 2020:** Active
Industries: Business Applications for:, Big Data and Analytics for:, ~ Media-Communications (41), ~ Retail and Consumer Products (52), Predictive Analytics for:, Predictive Analytics

Company Name: Grainer
Description: General IT company with expertise in Blockchain & AI
Website: http://www.grainer.io
Phone: (6012) 244-1566 **Email:** info@grainer.io
City: Kuala Lumpur **State:** Federal Territory of Kuala Lumpur **PC:**
Country: Malaysia
Year Established: 2020 **Status 2020:** Active
Industries: Artificial Intelligence for:, Blockchain for:, IT Managed Services

Company Name: Growthbotics
Description: Growthbotics offers the best AI chatbots & blockchain solutions for the Finance, Banking, and Insurance Industry.
Website: http://www.growthbotics.com/
Phone: 1 919 641 1442 **Email:** support@growthbotics.com
City: Kuala Lumpur **State:** Federal Territory of Kuala Lumpur **PC:**
Country: Malaysia
Year Established: 2017 **Status 2020:** Active
Industries: Artificial Intelligence for:, ~ Banking and Financial Markets-Services (7), ~ Banking and Financial Markets-Services (7), ~ Banking and Financial Markets-Services (7)

Company Name: Hyperlab
Description: Conversational AI built for visionary enterpris: Spain
Website: http://hyperlab.xyz/
Phone: **Email:** hello@hyperlab.xyz
City: Kuala Lumpur **State:** Federal Territory of Kuala Lumpur **PC:**
Country: Malaysia
Year Established: **Status 2020:** Active
Industries: Artificial Intelligence for:, Enterprise Application Services for:, Natural Language Processing

Company Name: Insuradar
Description: Intelligent Cognitive Enterprising Ai. Disrupting industries with Artificial Intelligence.
Website: http://insuradar.com/
Phone: 60 3-2276 4774 **Email:** contact-us@insuradar.com
City: Kuala Lumpur **State:** Federal Territory of Kuala Lumpur **PC:**
Country: Malaysia
Year Established: 2018 **Status 2020:** Active
Industries: Artificial Intelligence for:, Enterprise Application Services for:, Enterprise Application Services for:, Web

Company Name: KATSANA Holdings Sdn Bhd
Description: KATSANA is a data company focusing on connected cars, telematics and usage-based insurance.
Website: http://www.katsana.com
Phone: (601) 828-3114 **Email:** contact@katsana.com
City: Kuala Lumpur **State:** Federal Territory of Kuala Lumpur **PC:**
Country: Malaysia
Year Established: 2013 **Status 2020:** Active
Industries: ~ Automotive (5), ~ Telecommunications (56)

Company Name: Loosely Coupled Technologies
Description: Loosely Coupled Technologies is a data analytics company
Website: http://www.looselycoupled.org/
Phone: 603 8408 1341 **Email:** info@looselycoupled.org
City: Kuala Lumpur **State:** Federal Territory of Kuala Lumpur **PC:**
Country: Malaysia
Year Established: 2017 **Status 2020:** Active
Industries:

Company Name: Monster Alliance
Description: Modern Media Company with Artificial Intelligence
Website: http://www.monsteralliance.co
Phone: (6010) 249-8213 **Email:** sean@monsteralliance.co
City: Kuala Lumpur **State:** Federal Territory of Kuala Lumpur **PC:**
Country: Malaysia
Year Established: 2016 **Status 2020:** Active
Industries: Artificial Intelligence for:, Digital Media for:, IT Managed Services for:, Web for:, Internet of Things (IoT) for:, ~ Media-Communications (41), ~ Arts-Entertainment-Recreation (4), ~ Arts-Entertainment-Recreation (4), ~ Social Assistance-Non-Profits (53)

Company Name: Omega Prime Group
Description: Omega Prime Group Hashtechz is AI-Driven Crypto Bot is refined over time by feedback mechanisms.
Website: http://omegaprimegroup.com/
Phone: 173310237 **Email:** info@omegaprimegroup.com
City: Kuala Lumpur **State:** Federal Territory of Kuala Lumpur **PC:**
Country: Malaysia
Year Established: 2016 **Status 2020:** Active
Industries: Artificial Intelligence for:, IT Managed Services for:, Finance and Accounting

Company Name: Peasy.AI
Description: SaaS AI Marketing Platform
Website: http://peasy.ai
Phone: 603-2713-7116 **Email:** benjamin.fong@peasy.ai
City: Kuala Lumpur **State:** Federal Territory of Kuala Lumpur **PC:**
Country: Malaysia
Year Established: 2018 **Status 2020:** Active
Industries: Artificial Intelligence for:, IT Managed Services for:, Machine Learning

Company Name: ReferDoc
Description: ReferDoc is secure and seamless referral management platform for healthcare providers to make and keep track of patient referrals.
Website: http://www.referdoc.com
Phone: **Email:** raymondfoo.cc@gmail.com
City: Kuala Lumpur **State:** Federal Territory of Kuala Lumpur **PC:**
Country: Malaysia
Year Established: **Status 2020:** Active
Industries:

Company Name: SensQ
Description: One-off ('ad-hoc') Cross-Channel Social Media Audit Report in 72 Hou: Serbia
Website: http://sensq.com/
Phone: **Email:** support@sensq.com
City: Kuala Lumpur **State:** Federal Territory of Kuala Lumpur **PC:**
Country: Malaysia
Year Established: 2017 **Status 2020:** Active
Industries: Analytics for:, Predictive Analytics for:, ~ Social Assistance-Non-Profits (53), ~ Social Assistance-Non-Profits (53), ~ Social Assistance-Non-Profits (53), Data Management

Company Name: SmartBite
Description: SmartBite's innovative approach to food delivery is delighting office workers, restaurants and corporations all at the same time
Website: http://trysmartbite.com/
Phone: **Email:** info@trysmartbite.com
City: Kuala Lumpur **State:** Federal Territory of Kuala Lumpur **PC:**
Country: Malaysia
Year Established: **Status 2020:** Active
Industries: Artificial Intelligence for:, ~ Transportation and Logistics (57), ~ Transportation and Logistics (57)

Company Name: Supahands
Description: Supahands provides businesses with data management, content moderation and data training solutions using technology and a large workforce.
Website: www.supahands.com/
Phone: **Email:** hello@supahands.com
City: Kuala Lumpur **State:** Federal Territory of Kuala Lumpur **PC:**
Country: Malaysia
Year Established: **Status 2020:** Active
Industries:

Company Name: TransferFriend
Description: Online money transfer with AI powered financial education
Website: http://www.transferfriend.com
Phone: **Email:** hello@transferfriend.com
City: Kuala Lumpur **State:** Federal Territory of Kuala Lumpur **PC:** **Country:** Malaysia
Year Established: **Status 2020:** Active
Industries: Artificial Intelligence for:, ~ Banking and Financial Markets-Services (7), ~ Banking and Financial Markets-Services (7), ~ Banking and Financial Markets-Services (7), ~ Banking and Financial Markets-Services (7), ~ Banking and Financial Markets-Services (7)

Company Name: Wonderland Technologies Sdn Bhd
Description: Sci-Fi solutions provider in AI (artificial intelligence), Hologram display, VR, AR and interactive screens
Website: http://www.wonderland.: Malaysia
Phone: 60173934084 **Email:** info@wonderland.: Malaysia
City: Kuala Lumpur **State:** Federal Territory of Kuala Lumpur **PC:** **Country:** Malaysia
Year Established: **Status 2020:** Active
Industries: Artificial Intelligence for:, Augmented Reality for:, IT Managed Services for:, ~ Manufacturing-Electronic (30), Human Computer Interaction

Company Name: Workspez
Description: Artificial Intelligence Accounting System
Website: http://workspez.com
Phone: 386051191 **Email:** info@workspez.com
City: Kuala Lumpur **State:** Federal Territory of Kuala Lumpur **PC:** **Country:** Malaysia
Year Established: **Status 2020:** Active
Industries: Finance and Accounting for:, Artificial Intelligence for:, Big Data and Analytics for:, Machine Learning

Company Name: Centaurus Technology
Description: Aerospace - Unmanned Aerial Vehicle
Website: http://www.CentaurusTechnology.com
Phone: 60129774983 **Email:** info@centaurustechnology.com
City: Kuantan **State:** PHG **PC:** **Country:** Malaysia
Year Established: **Status 2020:** Active
Industries: Artificial Intelligence for:, Enterprise Application Services

Company Name: WyseTime
Description: WyseTime provide excellent image and video analytic solution using AI technology.
Website: http://www.wysetime.com/
Phone: 6011-1642-6314 **Email:** info@mysite.com
City: George Town **State:** Penang **PC:** **Country:** Malaysia
Year Established: 2018 **Status 2020:** Active
Industries: Artificial Intelligence for:, IT Managed Services

Company Name: Food Market Hub
Description: Supply Chain Platform For Horeca (Restaurants, Central Kitchen, Hotel, Marine Supply, Canteen, Cafe).
Website: http://www.foodmarkethub.com/cloud
Phone: (6019) 470-3321 **Email:** anthony@foodmarkethub.com
City: Penang **State:** Penang **PC:** **Country:** Malaysia
Year Established: 2017 **Status 2020:** Active
Industries: Artificial Intelligence for:, E-Commerce for:, Enterprise Application Services for:, ~ Food and Beverage (17), IT Managed Services for:, Application Services for:, ~ Administrative and Support Services (1), ~ Food and Beverage (17), ~ Food and Beverage (17), Sup: Poland

Company Name: Ombré
Description: Personal fashion styling app that helps to determine the outfit suitable for users based on their physical traits.
Website: http://ombre.me
Phone: (012)552-1052 **Email:** hello@ombre.me
City: **State:** Selangor **PC:** **Country:** Malaysia
Year Established: **Status 2020:** Active
Industries: Artificial Intelligence for:, ~ Fashion (16)

Company Name: 1U: Nigeria
Description: 1UNi is an online school search, compare and application platform for students searching for study opportunities in Malaysia.
Website: http://1uni.net
Phone: 603-7621 4349 **Email:** info@1uni.net
City: Petaling Jaya **State:** SGR **PC:** **Country:** Malaysia
Year Established: **Status 2020:** Active
Industries: Artificial Intelligence for:, Blockchain for:, ~ Education (13), ~ Education (13), ~ Education (13), Cyber Security

Company Name: Predictry
Description: Predictry provides its clients with predictive behavior, machine learning, and artificial intelligence services.
Website: http://www.predictry.com
Phone: 82-10-63165683 **Email:** hello@predictry.com
City: Petaling Jaya **State:** SGR **PC:** **Country:** Malaysia
Year Established: **Status 2020:** Active
Industries: Analytics for:, Artificial Intelligence for:, Big Data and Analytics for:, Machine Learning

Company Name: ReGov Technologies
Description: We are a fast-growing information technology venture and an early adopter of blockchain technology in Malaysia.
Website: http://www.regovtech.com
Phone: 03-76114793 **Email:** hello@regovtech.com
City: Petaling Jaya **State:** SGR **PC:** **Country:** Malaysia
Year Established: **Status 2020:** Active
Industries: Artificial Intelligence for:, Big Data and Analytics for:, Blockchain for:, ~ Banking and Financial Markets-Services (7), IT Managed Services for:, Web for:, Machine Learning

Company Name: Tide Analytics
Description: Tide Analytics provides businesses with analytics and insights that enable them to measure their marketing campaigns' success.
Website: http://tideanalytics.com
Phone: **Email:** hello@tideanalytics.com
City: Petaling Jaya **State:** Selangor **PC:** **Country:** Malaysia
Year Established: 2014 **Status 2020:** Active
Industries: Analytics for:, Big Data and Analytics for:, Predictive Analytics

Company Name: Blocklime Technologies Sdn. Bhd.
Description: Blocklime is Distributed Ledger Technology (DLT) Enabler based in Cyberjaya, Malaysia.
Website: http://www.blocklime.com/
Phone: **Email:** hello@blocklime.com
City: Selangor **State:** Selangor **PC:** **Country:** Malaysia
Year Established: 2017 **Status 2020:** Active
Industries: Blockchain for:, ~ Banking and Financial Markets-Services (7), IT Managed Services for:, Application Services

Company Name: MachinesHub
Description: Global Market Place to Sell-Rent-Buy-Review - Construction Machinery
Website: http://www.machineshub.com/
Phone: 65 8102 2144 **Email:** ceo@machineshub.com
City: Selangor **State:** Selangor **PC:** **Country:** Malaysia
Year Established: 2014 **Status 2020:** Active
Industries: ~ Construction (10), Machine Learning

Company Name: Poladrone
Description: Poladrone utilise machine learning algorithms to provide aerial insights for plantations.
Website: http://www.poladrone.com/
Phone: 60173008660 **Email:** hello@poladrone.com
City: Selangor **State:** Selangor **PC:** **Country:** Malaysia
Year Established: 2016 **Status 2020:** Active
Industries:

Company Name: Soding
Description: Soding an AI recruitment evaluation platform for tech candidates.
Website: http://soding.com.my/
Phone: **Email:** 37428@reference-encyclopedia-ai.net
City: Shah Alam **State:** Selangor **PC:** **Country:** Malaysia
Year Established: 2016 **Status 2020:** Active
Industries: Artificial Intelligence

Malta

Company Name: DiscoveryIoT
Description: Information Technology & Service
Website: http://discoveryiot.io/
Phone: **Email:** 36441@reference-encyclopedia-ai.net
City: Birkirkara **State:** NA - Malta **PC:** **Country:** Malta
Year Established: 2016 **Status 2020:** Active
Industries: Artificial Intelligence for:, IT Managed Services

Company Name: EBO
Description: EBO is a combine the power of Artificial Intelligence with the flexibility of language and the scalability of the cloud,
Website: http://www.ebo.ai
Phone: **Email:** hello@ebo.ai
City: Birkirkara **State:** NA - Malta **PC:** **Country:** Malta
Year Established: 2017 **Status 2020:** Active
Industries: Artificial Intelligence

Company Name: Umana Medical Technologies
Description: Umana build technologies that make a true impact on people's lives.
Website: http://umanamedical.com
Phone: 356 27639710 **Email:** info@umanamedical.com
City: Birkirkara **State:** NA - Malta **PC:** **Country:** Malta
Year Established: 2017 **Status 2020:** Active
Industries: Artificial Intelligence for:, ~ Healthcare (20), IT Managed Services for:, ~ Healthcare (20)

Company Name: Novofina
Description: Algorithm-based Wealth Management FinTech/WealthTech New Finance
Website: http://www.novofina.com
Phone: 43 1 361 77 77 **Email:** info@novofina.com
City: Mosta **State:** NA - Malta **PC:** **Country:** Malta
Year Established: **Status 2020:** Active
Industries: Artificial Intelligence for:, ~ Banking and Financial Markets-Services (7), ~ Banking and Financial Markets-Services (7), ~ Banking and Financial Markets-Services (7)

Company **Name:** Aryia Technologies
Description: The First Blockchain-Powered Smart Speaker That Doesn't Spy On You
Website: http://aryia.ai
Phone: 5712012316 **Email:** contact@aryia.ai
City: Sliema **State:** NA - Malta **PC:** **Country:** Malta
Year Established: **Status 2020:** Active
Industries: Artificial Intelligence for:, Blockchain for:, ~ Manufacturing-Electronic (30)

Company Name: BetMagician
Description: Sports predictions generated by Artificial Intelligence
Website: http://betmagician.com/
Phone: **Email:** 36149@reference-encyclopedia-ai.net
City: Sliema **State:** NA - Malta **PC:** **Country:** Malta
Year Established: 2016 **Status 2020:** Active
Industries: Artificial Intelligence for:, ~ Arts-Entertainment-Recreation (4)

Company Name: Cognitive Technology
Description: We find the missing links in Information Management.
Website: http://www.cognitive.com.: Malta
Phone: (3562) 740-0888 **Email:** info@cognitive.com.: Malta
City: Sliema **State:** NA - Malta **PC:** **Country:** Malta
Year Established: 2013 **Status 2020:** Active
Industries: Analytics for:, Data Management for:, Predictive Analytics

Company Name: GVZH Advocat: Spain
Description:
Website: https://www.gvzh.com.mt/
Phone: 356 2122 8888 **Email:** andrew.zammit@gvzh.com.: Malta
City: Valletta **State:** **Zip:** VLT 1455 **Country:** Malta
Year Established: **Status 2020:** Active
Industries: Blockchain

Company Name: ReaQta
Description: ReaQta offers cyber threat protection solutions based on real-time behavioral analysis.
Website: http://reaqta.com
Phone: 35677489802 **Email:** info@reaqta.com
City: Valletta **State:** NA - Malta **PC:** **Country:** Malta
Year Established: 2014 **Status 2020:** Active
Industries: Analytics for:, Artificial Intelligence for:, Cyber Security for:, Security for:, Compute

Company Name: PeaCounts
Description: PeaCounts is reinventing work with its blockchain payroll solution that revolutionizes how work is measured and people are paid.
Website: http://www.peacounts.com/
Phone: 310-739-7699 **Email:** kopper@peacounts.com
City: Zebbug **State:** NA - Malta **PC:** **Country:** Malta
Year Established: **Status 2020:** Active
Industries: Application Services for:, Artificial Intelligence for:, ~ Banking and Financial Markets-Services (7), Blockchain for:, Business Intelligence for:, ~ Banking and Financial Markets-Services (7), Application Services for:, Blockchain for:, ~ Professional Services

Mexico

Company Name: H3 System
Description: Hotel AI and Management
Website:
Phone: (322) 140-1779 **Email:** 36660@reference-encyclopedia-ai.net
City: Tuxtla Gutierres **State:** Chis. **PC:** **Country:** Mexico
Year Established: 2019 **Status 2020:** Closed
Industries: Artificial Intelligence for:, IT Managed Services

Company Name: Intuaition
Description: Intuaition is an AI-assisted NLP social analytics tool that extracts, analyzes and interprets social data.
Website: http://www.intuaition.com/
Phone: 52 (1) 55 55 50 84 50 **Email:** info@intuaition.com
City: San Angel **State:** Gto. **PC:** **Country:** Mexico
Year Established: 2018 **Status 2020:** Active
Industries: Artificial Intelligence for:, Big Data and Analytics for:, Machine Learning

Company Name: Axenda
Description: Axenda is the cloud platform designed to help companies that want to efficiently control the management of their projects.
Website: http://axenda.mx/
Phone: 52 1 333 191 2278 **Email:** contact@axenda.: Mexico
City: Guadalajara **State:** Jal. **PC:** **Country:** Mexico
Year Established: 2017 **Status 2020:** Active
Industries:

Company Name: ChocolatTUX User eXperience Research & Design
Description: User Experience (UX) Agency
Website: http://chocolatux.com
Phone: 52 33 23041348 **Email:** ruben@chocolatux.com
City: Guadalajara **State:** Jal. **PC:** **Country:** Mexico

Year Established: 2015 **Status 2020:** Active
Industries: Artificial Intelligence for:, Application Services for:, ~ Education (13), Development and Test for:, Development and Test for:, Web

Company Name: Coophi
Description: Web based project/task management SaaS that gives you full visibility of your projects and helps you create your own execution methodology.
Website: http://coophi.com
Phone: 3313607178 **Email:** hi@coophi.com
City: Guadalajara **State:** Jal. **PC:** **Country:** Mexico
Year Established: **Status 2020:** Active
Industries: Application Services for:, Artificial Intelligence for:, Collaboration Solutions for:, Enterprise Application Services for:, Machine Learning for:, Natural Language Processing

Company Name: Indacar
Description: Retention and Loyalty service to autodealers and OEM's
Website: http://indacar.io/
Phone: **Email:** rodrigo@indacar.io
City: Guadalajara **State:** Jal. **PC:** **Country:** Mexico
Year Established: 2014 **Status 2020:** Active
Industries: Artificial Intelligence for:, ~ Automotive (5)

Company Name: Retewi
Description: Retewi seeks to create the largest health information channel knowledge through a system of artificial intelligence.
Website: http://www.retewi.com/
Phone: **Email:** 37294@reference-encyclopedia-ai.net
City: Guadalajara **State:** Jal. **PC:** **Country:** Mexico
Year Established: 2011 **Status 2020:** Closed
Industries: Artificial Intelligence for:, ~ Healthcare (20), ~ Healthcare (20)

Company Name: Sign Accessible Technologies
Description: Company that creates technologies to tend bridges between Deaf and hearing people, using a virtual character as a mediator
Website: http://signamy.com/
Phone: **Email:** info@sign-accessible.com
City: Guadalajara **State:** Jal. **PC:** **Country:** Mexico
Year Established: **Status 2020:** Active
Industries: Application Services for:, Artificial Intelligence for:, Computer Vision for:, ~ Education (13), Application Services

Company Name: Omen Health
Description: Blockchain and ai company focused in developing universal medical record and democratization of healthcare through dapps.
Website: http://omenhealth.com
Phone: 3315454611 **Email:** contacto@omencorp.com
City: Zapopan **State:** Jal. **PC:** **Country:** Mexico
Year Established: **Status 2020:** Active
Industries: Artificial Intelligence for:, ~ Biotechnology (9), ~ Healthcare (20), ~ Life Sciences (27), ~ Healthcare (20)

Company Name: SOA Professionals
Description: Cognitive
Website: http://www.soapros.com
Phone: 248 522 6920 **Email:** info@softpathtech.com
City: Ciudad de Mexico **State:** C.P. **Zip:** 6600 **Country:** Mexico
Year Established: **Status 2020:** Active
Industries:

Company Name: Agrosphere
Description: Precicion Agriculture powered by Machine Learning
Website: http://www.flyx.systems/
Phone: **Email:** 35978@reference-encyclopedia-ai.net
City: Mexico City **State:** CDMX **PC:** **Country:** Mexico
Year Established: 2015 **Status 2020:** Active
Industries: ~ Aerospace and Defense (2), Artificial Intelligence for:, Internet of Things (IoT)

Company Name: Artificial Nerds
Description: Conversational Commerce: Helping businesses convert chats in sells.
Website: http://nerds.ai
Phone: **Email:** contacto@nerds.ai
City: Mexico City **State:** CDMX **PC:** **Country:** Mexico
Year Established: 2017 **Status 2020:** Active
Industries: Artificial Intelligence for:, E-Commerce for:, Natural Language Processing

Company Name: Atexto
Description: Speech Recognition Training Service
Website: http://atexto.com
Phone: 1 (786) 374-2793 **Email:** info@atexto.com
City: Mexico City **State:** CDMX **PC:** **Country:** Mexico
Year Established: 2018 **Status 2020:** Active
Industries: ~ Customer Relationship Management (11), Databases for:, Application Program Interfaces (APIs) for:, Human Computer Interaction for:, IT Managed Services for:, Machine Learning for:, Natural Language Processing for:, Speech Recognition for:, Speech Recognition fo

Company Name: Bayonet
Description: Bayonet is a Machine Learning company that helps e-commerce merchants protect against fraud with 15x less resources than existing solutions.
Website: http://bayonet.io
Phone: **Email:** info@bayonet.io
City: Mexico City **State:** CDMX **PC:** **Country:** Mexico
Year Established: 2016 **Status 2020:** Active
Industries: Analytics for:, Big Data and Analytics for:, E-Commerce for:, Machine Learning

Company Name: Blank!t
Description: Making Hospitals and Homes smarter for better health.
Website: http://www.blankit.com.: Mexico
Phone: **Email:** contacto@blankit.com.: Mexico
City: Mexico City **State:** CDMX **PC:** **Country:** Mexico
Year Established: 2018 **Status 2020:** Active
Industries: Big Data and Analytics for:, Cloud for:, Data Management for:, ~ Healthcare (20), Internet of Things (IoT) for:, Machine Learning

Company Name: BlueMessaging
Description: BlueMessaging is an artificial intelligence self-service platform enabling companies to build chatbots.
Website: http://bluemessaging.com
Phone: **Email:** info@bluemessaging.com
City: Mexico City **State:** CDMX **PC:** **Country:** Mexico
Year Established: 2010 **Status 2020:** Active
Industries: Artificial Intelligence for:, IT Managed Services

Company Name: Crowdsquad
Description: People trust people not ads. Using AI, Crowdsquad connects your brand with people like you and me that have a high influence in market nich: Spain
Website: http://crowdsquad.: Mexico
Phone: **Email:** 36352@reference-encyclopedia-ai.net
City: Mexico City **State:** CDMX **PC:** **Country:** Mexico
Year Established: 2017 **Status 2020:** Active
Industries:

Company Name: Descifra
Description: Descifra uses Big Data and Machine Learning to solve location problems and predict client's sales, helping them create better strategies.
Website: http://www.descifra.global/
Phone: **Email:** hola@descifra.: Mexico
City: Mexico City **State:** CDMX **PC:** **Country:** Mexico
Year Established: 2012 **Status 2020:** Active
Industries: Big Data and Analytics for:, Internet of Things (IoT) for:, Business Software as a Service Apps (SaaS Apps)

Company Name: Diagnostikare
Description: mHealth startup based on AI.
Website: http://www.diagnostikare.com
Phone: **Email:** info@diagnostikare.com
City: Mexico City **State:** CDMX **PC:** **Country:** Mexico
Year Established: 2018 **Status 2020:** Active
Industries: Artificial Intelligence for:, ~ Healthcare (20), ~ Healthcare (20), ~ Healthcare (20), ~ Healthcare (20), Internet of Things (IoT)

Company Name: DILE
Description: DILE is a startup building Artificial Intelligence as a Service for Retail, Insurance, Telecommunication and Banking Industri: Spain
Website: http://www.dile.co/
Phone: **Email:** support@dile.co
City: Mexico City **State:** CDMX **PC:** **Country:** Mexico
Year Established: 2017 **Status 2020:** Active
Industries: Predictive Analytics

Company Name: Docademic
Description: 2 services: Worlds largest Free Video-Telemedicine Service App & Platform for Doctors with tools, social network. Uses AI and blockchain.
Website: http://www.docademic.com
Phone: **Email:** contacto@docademic.com
City: Mexico City **State:** CDMX **PC:** **Country:** Mexico
Year Established: 2012 **Status 2020:** Active
Industries: Application Services for:, Artificial Intelligence for:, Blockchain for:, ~ Healthcare (20)

Company Name: Elion AI
Description: Health analytics startup focused on improving primary care and health management through data.
Website: http://www.elion.ai
Phone: **Email:** akimura@elion.ai
City: Mexico City **State:** CDMX **PC:** **Country:** Mexico
Year Established: 2018 **Status 2020:** Active
Industries: Big Data and Analytics for:, ~ Healthcare (20), ~ Healthcare (20), Machine Learning

Company Name: Getin
Description: Platform of retail analytics
Website: http://getin.mx/
Phone: 55 59299109 **Email:** contacto@getin.: Mexico
City: Mexico City **State:** CDMX **PC:** **Country:** Mexico
Year Established: 2016 **Status 2020:** Active
Industries: Analytics for:, Big Data and Analytics for:, Business Intelligence for:, Predictive Analytics

Company Name: GP Avanttia
Description: Comprehensive collection platform that allows you to optimize and automate the recovery of receivables.
Website: http://www.avanttia.com/
Phone: **Email:** hola@avanttia.com
City: Mexico City **State:** CDMX **PC:** **Country:** Mexico
Year Established: 2016 **Status 2020:** Active
Industries: Business Applications for:, ~ Banking and Financial Markets-Services (7), IT Managed Services

Company Name: GTN Medical
Description: Connecting patients and doctors around the world using AI.
Website: http://gtnmedical.com
Phone: **Email:** info@gtnmedical.com
City: Mexico City **State:** CDMX **PC:** **Country:** Mexico
Year Established: 2013 **Status 2020:** Active
Industries: Artificial Intelligence for:, ~ Healthcare (20)

Company Name: Gus Chat
Description: Gus Chat is a company dedicated to the development of intelligent chatbots.
Website: http://gus.chat/
Phone: 52 1 55 6673 9612 **Email:** marketing@gus.chat
City: Mexico City **State:** CDMX **PC:** **Country:** Mexico
Year Established: 2015 **Status 2020:** Active
Industries: Artificial Intelligence for:, Web

Company Name: Hexgrid Consulting
Description: Tech & Product Consulting
Website: http://www.hexgrid.io
Phone: **Email:** hello@hexgrid.io
City: Mexico City **State:** CDMX **PC:** **Country:** Mexico
Year Established: 2017 **Status 2020:** Active
Industries: Digital Marketing for:, Human Computer Interaction for:, Machine Learning for:, Application Services for:, Web for:, Web

Company Name: Hubex
Description: Process Automation as a Service Marketplace for Banks and Insure: Serbia
Website: http://www.hubex.tech
Phone: (506) 2201-3587 **Email:** info@hubex.tech
City: Mexico City **State:** CDMX **PC:** **Country:** Mexico
Year Established: 2019 **Status 2020:** Active
Industries: Artificial Intelligence for:, IT Managed Services for:, Robotics

Company Name: Insaite
Description: AI - Artificial Intelligence solutions
Website: http://insaite.io/
Phone: **Email:** info@insaite.io
City: Mexico City **State:** CDMX **PC:** **Country:** Mexico
Year Established: 2018 **Status 2020:** Active
Industries: Artificial Intelligence

Company Name: KarmaPul: Sweden
Description: Karmapulse helps brands, companies, agencies and entrepreneurs to translate social data in to human experiences.
Website: http://www.karmapulse.com
Phone: **Email:** 36845@reference-encyclopedia-ai.net
City: Mexico City **State:** CDMX **PC:** **Country:** Mexico
Year Established: 2014 **Status 2020:** Active
Industries: Analytics for:, Natural Language Processing for:, ~ Social Assistance-Non-Profits (53)

Company Name: Klustera
Description: Klustera is an AI-enabled retargeting platform that allows companies to target users online, based on their behaviour in the real world.
Website: http://klustera.com/
Phone: **Email:** hello@klustera.com
City: Mexico City **State:** CDMX **PC:** **Country:** Mexico
Year Established: 2014 **Status 2020:** Active
Industries:

Company Name: Mariachi IO
Description: Mariachi IO is a technology company that provides customized software focused on artificial intelligence & digital transformation business.
Website: http://www.mariachi.io/
Phone: 52 1 55 2569 7362 **Email:** adrian@mariachi.io
City: Mexico City **State:** CDMX **PC:** **Country:** Mexico
Year Established: 2015 **Status 2020:** Active
Industries: Artificial Intelligence for:, Big Data and Analytics for:, Business Intelligence for:, ~ Agriculture (3), IT Managed Services for:, Internet of Things (IoT) for:, Mobile for:, Business Process and Operations for:, Business Process and Operations

Company Name: Ovrmind
Description: A Full Service Digital Agency, Specialize in performance models, ppc and automated media buying helping our clients to generate convertions.
Website: http://www.ovrmind.com
Phone: **Email:** info@ovrmind.com
City: Mexico City **State:** CDMX **PC:** **Country:** Mexico
Year Established: 2012 **Status 2020:** Active
Industries: Artificial Intelligence for:, Digital Marketing

Company Name: Polls: Turkey
Description: Training sets for your AI - SaaS
Website: http://pollstr.io
Phone: **Email:** contact@pollstr.io
City: Mexico City **State:** CDMX **PC:** **Country:** Mexico
Year Established: 2016 **Status 2020:** Active
Industries: Artificial Intelligence for:, Big Data and Analytics for:, Machine Learning for:, Business Software as a Service Apps (SaaS Apps) for:, Data Management

Company Name: Quantum Labs
Description: Quantum Labs is a Mexico City based company developing artificial intelligence solutions for supply chain management
Website: http://quantumlabs.ai/
Phone: 52 1 5541437297 **Email:** malvarado@quantumlabs.ai
City: Mexico City **State:** CDMX **PC:** **Country:** Mexico
Year Established: **Status 2020:** Active
Industries: Artificial Intelligence for:, Computer Vision for:, Supply Chain Management

Company Name: Quark: Morocco
Description: Quarkma is a natural language processing company based in Mexico City devoted to dialog systems and document information extraction
Website: http://quarkma.com/
Phone: 52 1 5529532422 **Email:** font@quarkma.com
City: Mexico City **State:** CDMX **PC:** **Country:** Mexico
Year Established: **Status 2020:** Active
Industries: Artificial Intelligence for:, Computer Vision for:, Natural Language Processing

Company Name: SinCola
Description: Sincola is the solution to the long lines and wait times.
Website: http://www.sin-cola.com/
Phone: 52 55 7587-6534 **Email:** info@sin-cola.com
City: Mexico City **State:** CDMX **PC:** **Country:** Mexico
Year Established: 2012 **Status 2020:** Active
Industries: Business Applications for:, ~ Customer Relationship Management (11), Application Services

Company Name: Smart Drone
Description: We develop drones that can broadcast video and control troght internet
Website: http://www.smartdrone.com.: Mexico
Phone: **Email:** qhuevik@smartdrone.com.: Mexico
City: Mexico City **State:** CDMX **PC:** **Country:** Mexico
Year Established: 2013 **Status 2020:** Active
Industries: ~ Aerospace and Defense (2), Artificial Intelligence

Company Name: Tedcare
Description: Tedcare is a baby smart monitor that measures blood oxyge and pulse rate.
Website: http://ted.care/
Phone: 52 228 194 1116 **Email:** staff@ted.care
City: Mexico City **State:** CDMX **PC:** **Country:** Mexico
Year Established: 2014 **Status 2020:** Active
Industries: ~ Healthcare (20), Internet of Things (IoT) for:, Mobile for:, Predictive Analytics for:, Internet of Things (IoT)

Company Name: Ther: Malaysia
Description: We develop a screening tool for the early breast cancer detection using Machine Learning and Thermograms.
Website: http://thermy.com.mx/
Phone: 521 (55) 4020 1607 **Email:** hola@thermy.com.: Mexico
City: Mexico City **State:** CDMX **PC:** **Country:** Mexico
Year Established: 2016 **Status 2020:** Active
Industries: Artificial Intelligence for:, Machine Learning

Company Name: Yaydoo
Description: Yaydoo is a procurement platform that streamlines business purchasing using a cloud-based e-procurement software and AI.
Website: http://yaydoo.com/en/
Phone: 1 (347) 427 5557 **Email:** info@yaydoo.com
City: Mexico City **State:** CDMX **PC:** **Country:** Mexico
Year Established: 2017 **Status 2020:** Active
Industries: Artificial Intelligence for:, Business Applications for:, Enterprise Application Services for:, ~ Administrative and Support Services (1), ~ Administrative and Support Services (1), Business Software as a Service Apps (SaaS Apps)

Company Name: Intelimetrica
Description: Intelimetrica is a company focuses on quantitative analysis and data mining.
Website: http://intelimetrica.com/
Phone: 52 (55) 6823 0441 **Email:** contacto@intelimetrica.com
City: Miguel Hidalgo **State:** CDMX **PC:** **Country:** Mexico
Year Established: 2011 **Status 2020:** Active
Industries: Artificial Intelligence for:, ~ Customer Relationship Management (11), Databases

Company Name: Nowports
Description: Nowports is a digital freight forwarder that helps companies improve import process.
Website: http://nowports.com/
Phone: **Email:** maximiliano.casal@nowports.com
City: Monterrey **State:** N.L. **PC:** **Country:** Mexico
Year Established: 2018 **Status 2020:** Active
Industries: Artificial Intelligence for:, ~ Telecommunications (56), ~ Transportation and Logistics (57)

Company Name: Pulpai
Description: SaaS
Website: http://www.pulpai.co
Phone: 52 (81) 2719 0459 **Email:** daniela@pulpai.co
City: Monterrey **State:** N.L. **PC:** **Country:** Mexico
Year Established: **Status 2020:** Active
Industries: Artificial Intelligence for:, ~ Retail and Consumer Products (52)

Company Name: SENSAI - Empower Success
Description: Is an augmented productivity platform that empowers operations teams through real-time asset insights, enabling accurate & fast decisions.
Website: http://sensai.net/
Phone: 1 (248) 863 2631 **Email:** hello@sensai.net
City: Monterrey **State:** N.L. **PC:** **Country:** Mexico
Year Established: 2017 **Status 2020:** Closed
Industries:

Company Name: Lytica
Description: In a world full of information we are a data-driven company who seeks to solve day to day challenges with A.I. and data analysis.
Website: http://lytica.ai
Phone: 52 55 4890 2654 **Email:** contact@lytica.ai
City: San Pedro **State:** N.L. **PC:** **Country:** Mexico
Year Established: 2019 **Status 2020:** Active
Industries: Analytics for:, Artificial Intelligence for:, IT Managed Services

Company Name: NULLSEC
Description: Ethical Hacking, Security, Pentesting, Security Software
Website: http://nullsec.site
Phone: **Email:** 37084@reference-encyclopedia-ai.net
City: San Pedro **State:** N.L. **PC:** **Country:** Mexico
Year Established: 2014 **Status 2020:** Active
Industries: Cloud for:, Cyber Security for:, Predictive Analytics

Company Name: HeyBOB
Description: Your online personal assistant
Website: http://www.heybob.mx/
Phone: **Email:** omar@heybob.: Mexico
City: Puebla De Zaragoza **State:** Pue. **PC:** **Country:** Mexico
Year Established: 2016 **Status 2020:** Active
Industries: Artificial Intelligence for:, Internet of Things (IoT)

Company Name: Contaayuda
Description: Accounting services in a Saas model. We use BI to detect risks and Machine learning to keep cost low.
Website: http://contaayuda.com
Phone: 442-250-1780 **Email:** hola@contaayuda.com
City: Queretaro **State:** Qro. **PC:** **Country:** Mexico
Year Established: 2016 **Status 2020:** Active
Industries: IT Managed Services for:, Machine Learning for:, Business Software as a Service Apps (SaaS Apps)

Company Name: TheGuruCompany
Description: We create SaaS business that can change the way SMB's make businesses through technology and AI algorithms.
Website: http://thegurucompany.com
Phone: 52 442 477 8293 **Email:** roger@thegurucompany.com
City: Querétaro **State:** Qro. **PC:** **Country:** Mexico
Year Established: 2017 **Status 2020:** Active
Industries: Artificial Intelligence for:, Enterprise Application Services for:, Business Software as a Service Apps (SaaS Apps)

Company Name: Luxelare
Description: Luxelare develops products and services that deliver information to help with decision making in the agriculture sector.
Website: http://www.luxelare.com
Phone: **Email:** contacto@luxelare.com
City: Los Mochis **State:** Sin. **PC:** **Country:** Mexico
Year Established: 2015 **Status 2020:** Active
Industries: ~ Agriculture (3), ~ Agriculture (3), Big Data and Analytics for:, IT Managed Services for:, Predictive Analytics

Company Name: Livestock Analytics
Description: Livestock Analytics is a system that helps you make better decisions by acquiring and analyzing individual data from your cattle.
Website: http://www.livestockanalytics.com/
Phone: (480)626-0199 **Email:** info@tisconsulting.org
City: Hermosillo **State:** Son. **PC:** **Country:** Mexico
Year Established: 2014 **Status 2020:** Active
Industries: Analytics for:, Artificial Intelligence for:, ~ Agriculture (3)

Company Name: SoldAI
Description: Through our AI platform, we create chatbots and telephone assistants that interact with customers and employees of companies.
Website: http://soldai.com/
Phone: **Email:** info@soldai.com
City: Mérida **State:** Yuc. **PC:** **Country:** Mexico
Year Established: 2015 **Status 2020:** Active
Industries: Artificial Intelligence for:, ~ Customer Relationship Management (11), Enterprise Application Services for:, Business Software as a Service Apps (SaaS Apps) for:, Internet of Things (IoT)

Moldova

Company Name: Advanced Technologies & Engineering
Description: Computer Vision, Security, Face Recognition
Website: http://adtech.md/
Phone: **Email:** 35958@reference-encyclopedia-ai.net
City: Chisinau **State:** Chisinau **PC:** **Country:** Moldova
Year Established: 2010 **Status 2020:** Active
Industries: Artificial Intelligence for:, Computer Vision for:, Facial Recognition for:, Machine Learning for:, Security

Company Name: nemo.ai
Description: Next generation product search and recommendation engine for e-commerce shops.
Website: http://nemo.ai
Phone: **Email:** sciumac@nemo.ai
City: Chisinau **State:** Chisinau **PC:** **Country:** Moldova
Year Established: 2017 **Status 2020:** Active
Industries: Artificial Intelligence for:, E-Commerce for:, Web

Mongolia

Company Name: AND SYSTEMS Tech LLC
Description: We leverage the latest technological innovations to overcome the multiple challenges of serving the under-banked.
Website: http://andsystems.net/index.html
Phone: **Email:** people@andsystems.net
City: Ulaanbaatar **State:** Ulaanbaatar **PC:** **Country:** Mongolia
Year Established: 2015 **Status 2020:** Active
Industries: Artificial Intelligence for:, Big Data and Analytics for:, Blockchain for:, ~ Banking and Financial Markets-Services (7), IT Managed Services for:, ~ Banking and Financial Markets-Services (7), ~ Banking and Financial Markets-Services (7)

Company Name: Anduud Lab
Description: Artificial Intelligence, Chatbot, Virtual Assistant, Business Intelligence, Knowledge Gra: Philippin: Spain
Website: http://anduud.ai
Phone: 976-95951370 **Email:** contact@anduud.ai
City: Ulaanbaatar **State:** Ulaanbaatar **PC:** **Country:** Mongolia
Year Established: 2018 **Status 2020:** Active
Industries: Artificial Intelligence for:, Business Intelligence for:, Application Services for:, Application Program Interfaces (APIs) for:, Natural Language Processing for:, Content

Company Name: LendMN NBFI
Description: "LendMN NBFI" JSC is a non-collateralized low-cost, consumer micro-loan service provider through LendMN application in Mongolia.
Website: http://lend.mn/en/index.html
Phone: 976-77070101 **Email:** service@lend.: Mongolia
City: Ulaanbaatar **State:** Ulaanbaatar **PC:** **Country:** MONGOLIA
Year Established: **Status 2020:** Active
Industries: Artificial Intelligence for:, ~ Banking and Financial Markets-Services (7), ~ Banking and Financial Markets-Services (7)

Company Name: Shoppy
Description: Shoppy.mn is an online artificial intelligence based eCommerce platform.
Website: http://shoppy.mn/
Phone: 7777-8985 **Email:** info@shoppy.: Mongolia
City: Ulaanbaatar **State:** Ulaanbaatar **PC:** **Country:** MONGOLIA
Year Established: 2017 **Status 2020:** Active
Industries:

Morocco

Company Name: DeepLogik
Description: AI, ML, Finance, Banking, Saas, Mobile
Website: http://www.deeplogik.com
Phone: **Email:** elmehdi.eljair@deeplogik.com
City: Casablanca **State:** Casablanca-Settat **PC:** **Country:** Morocco
Year Established: 2019 **Status 2020:** Active
Industries: Artificial Intelligence for:, ~ Banking and Financial Markets-Services (7), ~ Banking and Financial Markets-Services (7), IT Managed Services for:, Web for:, Machine Learning for:, Mobile

Company Name: Meolink
Description: Meolink develops machine-to-machine software products.
Website: http://www.meolink.com/
Phone: 212 522 21 81 80 **Email:** 30933@reference-encyclopedia-ai.net
City: Casablanca **State:** Casablanca-Settat **PC:** **Country:** Morocco
Year Established: 2011 **Status 2020:** Active
Industries: Enterprise Application Services for:, Machine Learning for:, ~ Customer Relationship Management (11)

Company Name: Nour
Description: Nour is messagering service based on artificial intelligence.
Website: http://nour.: Morocco
Phone: **Email:** hello@nour.: Morocco
City: Casablanca **State:** Casablanca-Settat **PC:** **Country:** Morocco
Year Established: 2016 **Status 2020:** Active
Industries: Artificial Intelligence for:, ~ Education (13)

Company Name: Casky
Description: MaaS, IoT, Blockchain, Dapp, Big-Data, Road Safety, AI, Transportation, Mobile Application
Website: http://casky.io/uk
Phone: **Email:** ja@casky.io
City: Marrakech **State:** Marrakesh-Safi **PC:** **Country:** Morocco
Year Established: **Status 2020:** Active
Industries: Artificial Intelligence for:, Blockchain for:, ~ Manufacturing-Electronic (30), Application Services for:, ~ Transportation and Logistics (57)

Company Name: Atlan Space
Description: Building Artificial Intelligence to autonomously pilot any fixed wing drone, to monitor and take measures over very large areas
Website: http://atlanspace.com
Phone: **Email:** contact@atlanspace.com
City: Rabat **State:** Rabat-Salé-Kénitra **PC:** **Country:** Morocco
Year Established: 2016 **Status 2020:** Active
Industries: Artificial Intelligence for:, Robotics

Company Name: GreeEyes
Description: We are a startup specialized in the precision agriculture, we combine between IOT and AI to predict and process different diseas: Spain
Website:
Phone: **Email:** 36645@reference-encyclopedia-ai.net
City: Rabat **State:** Rabat-Salé-Kénitra **PC:** **Country:** Morocco
Year Established: 2015 **Status 2020:** Active
Industries: ~ Agriculture (3), Artificial Intelligence

Myanmar

Company Name: Bagan Innovation Technology
Description: Digital Agency
Website: http://www.bitmyanmar.com.mm/
Phone: 959 5107278 **Email:** thetlynnhan@baganit.com
City: Yangon **State:** Yangon Region **PC:** **Country:** Myanmar
Year Established: **Status 2020:** Active
Industries: Artificial Intelligence for:, Big Data and Analytics for:, Cloud for:, Content for:, Machine Learning for:, Application Services

Nepal

Company Name: Eydean
Description: Artificial Intelligence As A Service
Website: http://eydean.com
Phone: 977 9840067049 **Email:** info@eydean.com
City: Kathmandu **State:** BA **PC:** **Country:** Nepal
Year Established: **Status 2020:** Active
Industries: Artificial Intelligence for:, IT Managed Services for:, Machine Learning for:, ~ Professional Services (48)

Company Name: Unelma Platforms
Description: Unelma platforms aims to deliver state-of-the-art software to empower people
Website: http://www.unelmaplatforms.com/
Phone: 977 56-560267 **Email:** info@unelmaplatforms.com
City: **State:** Narayani **PC:** **Country:** Nepal
Year Established: **Status 2020:** Active
Industries: Analytics for:, Artificial Intelligence for:, Cloud for:, Enterprise Application Services for:, ~ Healthcare (20), ~ Education (13), Human Computer Interaction for:, Cyber Security

Netherlands

Company Name: Flow.ai
Description: Flow.ai is an easy to use complete toolbox to create Chatbots, AI assistants, Customer service or conversational commerce solutions.
Website: http://flow.ai
Phone: (061)302-6466 **Email:** hello@flow.ai
City: **State:** **PC:** **Country: Netherlands**
Year Established: **Status 2020:** Active
Industries: Artificial Intelligence for:, ~ Media-Communications (41), ~ Social Media (54), ~ Professional Services (48), Development and Test

Company Name: Climate Connect Technologies
Description: Data Science and ML based forecasting and analytics for the energy sector - weather, generation, demand, power markets trading
Website: http://climate-connect.com/
Phone: 44 7932730 229 **Email:** niladri.roy@climate-connect.com
City: den Bosch **State:** Drenthe **PC:** **Country:** Netherlands
Year Established: 2017 **Status 2020:** Active
Industries: Artificial Intelligence for:, ~ Energy and Utilities (14), Machine Learning

Company Name: Huxley
Description: Huxley combines machine learning, computer vision and an augmented reality interface to essentially allow anyone to be a master farmer.
Website: http://www.huxley.io/
Phone: **Email:** 36725@reference-encyclopedia-ai.net
City: Nieuw-amsterdam **State:** Drenthe **PC:** **Country:** Netherlands
Year Established: 2016 **Status 2020:** Active
Industries: Artificial Intelligence

Company Name: FactoryHub
Description: Manufacturing Operations Platform, SaaS, IoT, MaaS, Edge Computing
Website: http://factoryhub.co
Phone: 31(0)88 0068 300 **Email:** hello@factoryhub.co
City: Almere **State:** Flevoland **PC:** **Country:** Netherlands
Year Established: 2019 **Status 2020:** Closed
Industries: Artificial Intelligence for:, Big Data and Analytics for:, IT Managed Services for:, Web

Company Name: Hydrowashr
Description: Hydrowashr is a smart integration of hand washing and drying in one device.
Website: http://hydrowashr.com/
Phone: 058 2896672 **Email:** info@hydrowashr.: Netherlands
City: Leeuwarden **State:** Friesland **PC:** **Country:** Netherlands
Year Established: 2012 **Status 2020:** Active
Industries:

Company Name: Sqriba
Description: Robotica and artificial intelligence for education
Website: http://www.sqriba.com
Phone: 31341266345 **Email:** info@sqriba.com
City: Ermelo **State:** Gelderland **PC:** **Country:** Netherlands
Year Established: 2018 **Status 2020:** Active
Industries: Artificial Intelligence for:, ~ Education (13), Machine Learning for:, Robotics

Company Name: Illuminoo
Description: Illuminoo is a high-tech software company.
Website: http://illuminoo.com/
Phone: (3164) 021-1500 **Email:** info@illuminoo.com
City: Geldermalsen **State:** Gelderland **PC:** **Country:** Netherlands
Year Established: 2016 **Status 2020:** Active
Industries: Artificial Intelligence for:, IT Managed Services

Company Name: Virtual Assistant
Description: Virtask is into AI that provides virtual assistants in the field of healthcare, educational institutions, and organizations.
Website: http://www.virtask.: Netherlands
Phone: **Email:** info@virtask.: Netherlands
City: Harfsen **State:** Gelderland **PC:** **Country:** Netherlands
Year Established: 2011 **Status 2020:** Active
Industries: Artificial Intelligence for:, Internet of Things (IoT)

Company Name: deepdee
Description: AI/ML based platform for automated qualified medical diagnosis.
Website: http://deepdee.org
Phone: 31 618 513 270 **Email:** info@deepdee.org
City: Nijmegen **State:** GE **PC:** **Country:** Netherlands
Year Established: **Status 2020:** Active
Industries: Artificial Intelligence for:, ~ Healthcare (20), IT Managed Services

Company Name: ReSnap
Description:
Website: https://www.resnap.com/
Phone: **Email:** 27304@reference-encyclopedia-ai.net
City: Nijmegen **State:** Gelderland **Zip:** 6511EV **Country:** Netherlands
Year Established: **Status 2020:** Active
Industries: **Company Name:** ReSnap
Description: ReSnap develops an image selection technology based on artificial intelligence.
Website: http://www.resnap.com
Phone: **Email:** mail@resnap.com
City: Nijmegen **State:** GE **PC:** **Country:** Netherlands
Year Established: **Status 2020:** Active
Industries: Artificial Intelligence for:, Image Recognition for:, Application Services for:, Machine Learning for:, ~ Social Media (54)

Company Name: ScreenPoint Medical
Description: ScreenPoint develops Deep Learning and image analysis technology for automated reading of mammograms.
Website: http://www.screenpoint-medical.com
Phone: 31 242020020 **Email:** info@screenpointmed.com
City: Nijmegen **State:** Gelderland **PC:** **Country:** Netherlands
Year Established: 2014 **Status 2020:** Active
Industries: Artificial Intelligence for:, IT Managed Services for:, ~ Healthcare (20)

Company Name: Yuras
Description: Yuras provides legal professionals with intelligent tools for discovery, based on state of the art machine learning technology.
Website: http://www.yuras.: Netherlands
Phone: **Email:** stephan@yuras.: Netherlands
City: Nijmegen **State:** Gelderland **PC:** **Country:** Netherlands
Year Established: 2016 **Status 2020:** Active
Industries:

Company Name: Alledaags NL (Everyday)
Description: Alledaags NL makes customized learning solutions for large SMEs or institutions
Website: http://www.alledaags.nl/
Phone: 050 - 76 76 066 **Email:** info@alledaags.: Netherlands
City: Groningen **State:** GR **PC:** **Country:** Netherlands
Year Established: **Status 2020:** Active
Industries: Artificial Intelligence for:, IT Managed Services for:, ~ Media-Communications (41), Application Services for:, ~ Professional Services (48)

Company Name: Crowdynews
Description: Crowdynews offers an AI-driven content curation platform that helps publishers and brands increase visitor engagement, conversion & revenue.
Website: http://www.crowdynews.com
Phone: 31 50 820 0220 **Email:** hello@crowdynews.com
City: Groningen **State:** GR **PC:** **Country:** Netherlands
Year Established: **Status 2020:** Active
Industries: Artificial Intelligence for:, Content for:, ~ Media-Communications (41), ~ Media-Communications (41), ~ Social Media (54)

Company Name: Radient
Description: Saas, Web App
Website: http://www.radient.io
Phone: 31657534896 **Email:** engineering@iamclair.com
City: Groningen **State:** GR **PC:** **Country:** Netherlands
Year Established: **Status 2020:** Active
Industries:

Company Name: Token Agency
Description:
Website: http://www.token.agency/
Phone: 31 (0) 639583979 **Email:** theron@token.agency
City: Groningen **State:** GR **Zip:** 9752HE **Country:** Netherlands
Year Established: **Status 2020:** Active
Industries: Blockchain

Company Name: BodyGra: Philippin: Spain
Description: Healthcare Technologies
Website: http://www.body-graph.com
Phone: 31852735893 **Email:** Info@body-graph.com
City: Baexem **State:** LI **PC:** **Country:** Netherlands
Year Established: **Status 2020:** Active
Industries: Artificial Intelligence for:, ~ Healthcare (20), ~ Healthcare (20), Machine Learning for:, ~ Healthcare (20), ~ Professional Services (48), ~ Arts-Entertainment-Recreation (4)

Company Name: Smart Robotics
Description: Smart Robotics, the agency for robots, delivers flexible robotic solutions.
Website: http://smart-robotics.: Netherlands
Phone: (407)440-448 **Email:** info@smart-robotics.: Netherlands
City: Best **State:** Noord-Brabant **PC:** **Country:** Netherlands
Year Established: 2015 **Status 2020:** Active
Industries:

Company Name: CheckandPack
Description: CheckandPack helps users prepare for their holidays in the most innovative way.
Website: http://checkandpack.com/
Phone: 31 76 820 0200 **Email:** 36263@reference-encyclopedia-ai.net
City: Breda **State:** Noord-Brabant **PC:** **Country:** Netherlands
Year Established: 2010 **Status 2020:** Active
Industries: ~ Transportation and Logistics (57), Predictive Analytics for:, ~ Travel and Transportation (58)

Company Name: Datametrics
Description: Datametrics is insurance & banking consulting agency that helps firms from financial sector with data science & intelligence units.
Website: http://www.datametrics.nl/
Phone: 31-762051000 **Email:** info@datametrics.: Netherlands
City: Breda **State:** Noord-Brabant **PC:** **Country:** Netherlands
Year Established: 2013 **Status 2020:** Active
Industries: Artificial Intelligence for:, ~ Banking and Financial Markets-Services (7)

Company Name: SphereMall
Description: SphereMall puts shoppers at the center and builds a personalized shopping mall around them based upon their preferences and needs
Website: http://www.spheremall.com
Phone: 31 85 888 99 71 **Email:** info@spheremall.com
City: Breda **State:** Noord-Brabant **PC:** **Country:** Netherlands
Year Established: 2014 **Status 2020:** Active
Industries: Business Applications for:, Business Applications for:, Big Data and Analytics for:, E-Commerce for:, Machine Learning for:, ~ Retail and Consumer Products (52)

Company Name: Medvice Digital Heal:Thailand
Description: Machine Learning Supported Automated Medical Interview Systems
Website: http://www.medvice.io
Phone: (3168) 115-1675 **Email:** ziyaad@medvice.io
City: Den Bosch **State:** Noord-Brabant **PC:** **Country:** Netherlands
Year Established: 2016 **Status 2020:** Active
Industries: Artificial Intelligence for:, ~ Healthcare (20), ~ Healthcare (20), Application Services for:, Machine Learning

Company Name: Pixyle.ai
Description: Visual AI for Fashion Reta: Israel
Website: http://www.pixyle.ai/
Phone: **Email:** hello@pixyle.ai
City: Den Bosch **State:** Noord-Brabant **PC:** **Country:** Netherlands
Year Established: 2018 **Status 2020:** Active
Industries: Artificial Intelligence

Company Name: StyleScript, tradename of StyleCompass BV
Description: An Artificial Intelligence powered API that boosts sales for eCommerce sites through a personalized style advisor
Website: http://StyleScript.com
Phone: 31 (0)73 623 35 25 **Email:** info@stylescript.com
City: Den Bosch **State:** Noord-Brabant **PC:** **Country:** Netherlands
Year Established: 2016 **Status 2020:** Active
Industries: Artificial Intelligence for:, E-Commerce for:, IT Managed Services for:, Web

Company Name: AI in Motion | AI: ISLE OF MAN
Description: We add intelligence to perception, localization and mapping for use in automated guided vehicles, unmanned ground vehicles, and dron: Spain
Website: https://www.aiim.ai/
Phone: 31 40 7113500 **Email:** info@aiim.ai
City: Eindhoven **State:** Noord-Brabant **PC:** **Country:** Netherlands
Year Established: 2019 **Status 2020:** Active
Industries: Artificial Intelligence for:, ~ Automotive (5), Computer Vision for:, Internet of Things (IoT) for:, Machine Learning

Company Name: BStriker
Description: BStriker develops a platform that identifies defects in a software application.
Website: http://www.bstriker.com/
Phone: **Email:** info@bstriker.com
City: Eindhoven **State:** Noord-Brabant **PC:** **Country:** Netherlands
Year Established: 2013 **Status 2020:** Active
Industries: Application Services for:, Predictive Analytics

Company Name: Hairmod
Description: Hairmod is an Intelligent Personal Beauty Assistant which recommends beauty services and products match only to user's taste and preferenc: Spain
Website: http://hairmod.co
Phone: **Email:** info@mysite.com
City: Eindhoven **State:** Noord-Brabant **PC:** **Country:** Netherlands
Year Established: 2015 **Status 2020:** Active
Industries: Application Services for:, Artificial Intelligence for:, ~ Beauty (8)

Company Name: Joint Robotics
Description: Joint Robotics is a technology startup that will kick-start this revolution by introducing an accessible and open autonomous robot platform.
Website:
Phone: 31 61 33 999 77 **Email:** 36832@reference-encyclopedia-ai.net
City: Eindhoven **State:** Noord-Brabant **PC:** **Country:** Netherlands
Year Established: 2015 **Status 2020:** Closed
Industries: Artificial Intelligence for:, Robotics

Company Name: Navinfo Euro:
Description: NavInfo Europe incorporates the European Advanced Research Lab and Corporate Development activities for NavInfo
Website: http://www.navinfo.eu/
Phone: 31 (0) 40 231 34 00 **Email:** info@navinfo.eu
City: Eindhoven **State:** Noord-Brabant **PC:** **Country:** Netherlands
Year Established: 2014 **Status 2020:** Active
Industries: Artificial Intelligence for:, Computer Vision for:, IT Managed Services

Company Name: SPOSEA BV
Description: We simplify dynamic pricing for SAP Clients and E-Commerce retaile: Serbia
Website: http://www.sposea.com
Phone: 3140 3046402 **Email:** anjo@alm-ventures.com
City: Eindhoven **State:** Noord-Brabant **PC:** **Country:** Netherlands
Year Established: 2016 **Status 2020:** Active
Industries: E-Commerce for:, Enterprise Application Services for:, Enterprise Application Services for:, Predictive Analytics for:, Compute for:, Business Software as a Service Apps (SaaS Apps) for:, Web

Company Name: YaDo-VR BV
Description: Capturing Reality Through automated LIDAR data processing, automated classification resulting in DYNAMIC TRUE 3D IMAGERY
Website: http://www.yadovr.com
Phone: 31408517530 **Email:** info@yadovr.com
City: Eindhoven **State:** Noord-Brabant **PC:** **Country:** Netherlands
Year Established: 2016 **Status 2020:** Active
Industries: Artificial Intelligence for:, ~ Automotive (5)

Company Name: ClearPredictions
Description: ClearPredictions.com is an easy to use online predictive analytics platform
Website: http://www.clearpredictions.com
Phone: **Email:** info@ClearPredictions.com
City: 's-hertogenbosch **State:** Noord-Brabant **PC:** **Country:** Netherlands
Year Established: 2015 **Status 2020:** Active
Industries:

Company Name: Table Duck
Description: AI Driven Self Ordering Hospitality Chatbot
Website: http://www.tableduck.com
Phone: 31629193118 **Email:** info@tableduck.com
City: Alkmaar **State:** Noord-Holland **PC:** **Country:** Netherlands
Year Established: 2017 **Status 2020:** Active
Industries: Artificial Intelligence for:, Machine Learning

Company Name: GROW Labs
Description: Using AI and Machine Learning, our smart platform matches innovative companies with the best development agencies worldwide.
Website: http://growlabs.tech
Phone: **Email:** info@growlabs.tech
City: Amstelveen **State:** Noord-Holland **PC:** **Country:** Netherlands
Year Established: 2015 **Status 2020:** Active
Industries: Artificial Intelligence for:, Big Data and Analytics for:, IT Managed Services for:, Application Services for:, ~ Banking and Financial Markets-Services (7), ~ Banking and Financial Markets-Services (7)

Company Name: VATBox
Description: VATBox has successfully digitised the VAT/GST recovery workflow with its cloud-based enterprise recovery solution, using AI.
Website: http://www.vatbox.com/
Phone: **Email:** liata@vatbox.com
City: Amstelveen **State:** Noord-Holland **PC:** **Country:** Netherlands
Year Established: 2013 **Status 2020:** Active
Industries: Artificial Intelligence for:, Enterprise Application Services for:, ~ Banking and Financial Markets-Services (7), ~ Banking and Financial Markets-Services (7), IT Managed Services for:, Machine Learning for:, Business Software as a Service Apps (SaaS Apps)

Company Name: 904Labs
Description: Boost customer engagement and increase revenue through self-learning onsite search.
Website: http://904labs.com/
Phone: 31-85-303-7256 **Email:** info@904labs.com
City: Amsterdam **State:** Noord-Holland **PC:** **Country:** Netherlands
Year Established: 2014 **Status 2020:** Active
Industries: Artificial Intelligence for:, E-Commerce for:, IT Managed Services for:, IT Managed Services for:, Machine Learning for:, Web for:, Content

Company Name: AdGoji
Description: AdGoji is a data-driven mobile customer acquisition company that delivers customers to m-commerce organizations.
Website: http://www.adgoji.com/
Phone: **Email:** info@adgoji.com
City: Amsterdam **State:** Noord-Holland **PC:** **Country:** Netherlands
Year Established: 2012 **Status 2020:** Active
Industries: IT Managed Services for:, Machine Learning

Company Name: AdVerif.ai
Description: AdVerif.ai is an artificial intelligence company providing content verification solutions for advertisers, publishers and ad networks
Website: http://adverifai.com/
Phone: **Email:** info@adverifai.com
City: Amsterdam **State:** Noord-Holland **PC:** **Country:** Netherlands
Year Established: 2017 **Status 2020:** Active
Industries: Artificial Intelligence

Company Name: Aidence
Description: Aidence is improving healthcare using Computer-Aided Diagnostics.
Website: http://aidence.com/
Phone: **Email:** info@aidence.com
City: Amsterdam **State:** Noord-Holland **PC:** **Country:** Netherlands
Year Established: 2015 **Status 2020:** Active
Industries: Artificial Intelligence for:, ~ Healthcare (20), ~ Healthcare (20), IT Managed Services for:, ~ Healthcare (20)

Company Name: ApexQub: Italy
Description: ApexQubit is a biotech startup harnessing AI and quantum machine learning for discovery of new medicines and better health for humanity.
Website: http://www.apexqubit.com/
Phone: **Email:** info@apexqubit.com
City: Amsterdam **State:** Noord-Holland **PC:** **Country:** Netherlands
Year Established: 2018 **Status 2020:** Active
Industries: Artificial Intelligence for:, Business Applications for:, ~ Biotechnology (9), IT Managed Services for:, ~ Education (13)

Company Name: betterlAIfe
Description: BetterlAIfe specializes in AI technologies to develop solutions aimed at improving the quality of life using data in healthcare.
Website: http://www.betterlaife.com
Phone: (3164) 917-5080 **Email:** contact@betterlaife.com
City: Amsterdam **State:** Noord-Holland **PC:** **Country:** Netherlands
Year Established: 2017 **Status 2020:** Active
Industries: Artificial Intelligence for:, ~ Healthcare (20), IT Managed Services for:, Machine Learning

Company Name: Chargetrip
Description: Chargetrip offers smart navigation for Electric Vehicles as an API based SaaS platform.
Website: http://www.chargetrip.com
Phone: 31 6 48 47 59 65 **Email:** info@chargetrip.com
City: Amsterdam **State:** Noord-Holland **PC:** **Country:** Netherlands
Year Established: 2017 **Status 2020:** Active
Industries: ~ Automotive (5), Predictive Analytics

Company Name: City.AI
Description: Global Applied AI Community
Website: http://city.ai/
Phone: **Email:** 36283@reference-encyclopedia-ai.net
City: Amsterdam **State:** Noord-Holland **PC:** **Country:** Netherlands
Year Established: 2015 **Status 2020:** Active
Industries: Artificial Intelligence for:, Digital Media for:, ~ Event Management (15)

Company Name: Cleeng
Description: Cleeng is the leader in Subscriber Retention Management (SRM). It's a SaaS, modular, API-based solution made for subscription businesses.
Website: http://cleeng.com
Phone: **Email:** bguichard@cleeng.com
City: Amsterdam **State:** Noord-Holland **PC:** **Country:** Netherlands
Year Established: 2011 **Status 2020:** Active
Industries: Analytics for:, Finance and Accounting for:, ~ Customer Relationship Management (11), Web for:, Predictive Analytics for:, Business Software as a Service Apps (SaaS Apps)

Company Name: Contexta
Description: Contexta is provides solutions to enhance your growing enterprise.
Website: http://www.contexta-solutions.io/
Phone: 31 64 128 1019 **Email:** 36329@reference-encyclopedia-ai.net
City: Amsterdam **State:** Noord-Holland **PC:** **Country:** Netherlands
Year Established: 2016 **Status 2020:** Active
Industries: Artificial Intelligence for:, IT Managed Services

Company Name: Contexta360
Description: Contexta360 Provides speech intelligence.
Website: http://contexta360.com/
Phone: **Email:** 28466@reference-encyclopedia-ai.net
City: Amsterdam **State:** Noord-Holland **PC:** **Country:** Netherlands
Year Established: 2016 **Status 2020:** Active
Industries:

Company Name: Converling
Description: Converling is an online social marketplace for translators and people who are in need of translations.
Website: http://www.converling.com
Phone: (3120) 308-0020 **Email:** info@converling.com
City: Amsterdam **State:** Noord-Holland **PC:** **Country:** Netherlands
Year Established: 2013 **Status 2020:** Active
Industries: Natural Language Processing for:, Web

Company Name: Cubonacci
Description: Cubonacci helps organizations on developing custom machine learning models without worrying about peripheral matters.
Website: http://www.cubonacci.com/
Phone: 31(0)20 308 43 90 **Email:** info@cubonacci.com
City: Amsterdam **State:** Noord-Holland **PC:** **Country:** Netherlands
Year Established: 2018 **Status 2020:** Active
Industries: Application Services for:, Machine Learning for:, Application Services

Company Name: DAN DNA
Description: DNA is the central data unit for Dentsu Aegis Network Netherlands - combining all online and offline data service
Website: http://www.dan-dna.nl/
Phone: **Email:** info.nl@dentsuaegis.com
City: Amsterdam **State:** Noord-Holland **PC:** **Country:** Netherlands
Year Established: 2015 **Status 2020:** Active
Industries: Analytics for:, Big Data and Analytics for:, Data Management for:, Predictive Analytics

Company Name: Dealteq
Description: Your deal acceleration platform.
Website: http://dealteq.com
Phone: **Email:** info@dealteq.com
City: Amsterdam **State:** Noord-Holland **PC:** **Country:** Netherlands
Year Established: 2015 **Status 2020:** Active
Industries: ~ Banking and Financial Markets-Services (7), Predictive Analytics

Company Name: Deepdesk
Description: AI for CX
Website: http://deepdesk.com
Phone: (3120) 895-0251 **Email:** hello@deepdesk.com
City: Amsterdam **State:** Noord-Holland **PC:** **Country:** Netherlands
Year Established: 2019 **Status 2020:** Active
Industries: Artificial Intelligence for:, ~ Customer Relationship Management (11), Enterprise Application Services for:, Machine Learning

Company Name: Deeptrace
Description: The anti-virus for deepfakes. Deep learning solutions for monitoring and detecting synthetic media.
Website: http://www.deeptracelabs.com
Phone: **Email:** info@deeptracelabs.com
City: Amsterdam **State:** Noord-Holland **PC:** **Country:** Netherlands
Year Established: 2018 **Status 2020:** Active
Industries: Artificial Intelligence for:, Computer Vision

Company Name: Dropsear: Switzerland
Description: Dropsearch provides a single search interface for all your cloud platforms powered by AI for indexing and providing relevant results.
Website: http://dropsearch.net
Phone: **Email:** 36459@reference-encyclopedia-ai.net
City: Amsterdam **State:** Noord-Holland **PC:** **Country:** Netherlands
Year Established: 2017 **Status 2020:** Active
Industries: Artificial Intelligence for:, IT Managed Services for:, Web for:, Web

Company Name: Emerging Horizons
Description: Emerging Horizons provides services to help companies be prepared for upcoming technologies.
Website: http://emerginghorizons.: Netherlands
Phone: 31 6 113 94 292 **Email:** o.k.rikken@gmail.com
City: Amsterdam **State:** Noord-Holland **PC:** **Country:** Netherlands
Year Established: 2019 **Status 2020:** Active
Industries: Artificial Intelligence for:, Big Data and Analytics for:, Blockchain

Company Name: Emplysight
Description: Emplysight uses analytics to help organizations get a better understanding in their current and future workforce.
Website: http://emplysight.com/
Phone: **Email:** info@emplysight.com
City: Amsterdam **State:** Noord-Holland **PC:** **Country:** Netherlands
Year Established: 2017 **Status 2020:** Active
Industries: Analytics for:, Artificial Intelligence for:, Machine Learning for:, Predictive Analytics

Company Name: FINDEST
Description: Scout technologies using IGOR AI
Website: http://www.findest.eu
Phone: (3120) 893-2700 **Email:** igor@findest.eu
City: Amsterdam **State:** Noord-Holland **PC:** **Country:** Netherlands
Year Established: 2016 **Status 2020:** Active
Industries: Artificial Intelligence for:, IT Managed Services

Company Name: Frosha
Description: Frosha builds real-time platform that structures customer data into a single format.
Website: http://frosha.io/
Phone: 31 6 166 00 694 **Email:** info@frosha.io
City: Amsterdam **State:** Noord-Holland **PC:** **Country:** Netherlands
Year Established: 2016 **Status 2020:** Active
Industries: Big Data and Analytics for:, ~ Customer Relationship Management (11), IT Managed Services for:, Machine Learning for:, Compute

Company Name: holler.live
Description: holler.live is a SaaS solution disrupting the market research industry by taking it to true scale, real-time and automation.
Website: http://business.holler.live
Phone: (3164) 388-4770 **Email:** hi@holler.live
City: Amsterdam **State:** Noord-Holland **PC:** **Country:** Netherlands
Year Established: 2017 **Status 2020:** Active
Industries: Analytics for:, Big Data and Analytics for:, Business Intelligence for:, Learning and Marketing Communications Services

(MarComm) for:, ~ Customer Relationship Management (11), Predictive Analytics for:, ~ Media-Communications (41), ~ Media-Communications (41)

Company Name: Kaizo
Description: Employee Performance Management software using gamification and AI to improve KPIs and OK: Serbia
Website: http://kaizo.com
Phone: **Email:** hello@kaizo.com
City: Amsterdam **State:** Noord-Holland **PC:** **Country:** Netherlands
Year Established: 2018 **Status 2020:** Active
Industries: Artificial Intelligence for:, ~ Customer Relationship Management (11), Machine Learning for:, Business Software as a Service Apps (SaaS Apps)

Company Name: Machine2Learn
Description: AI for Manufacturing, Smart Edge
Website: http://www.machine2learn.com
Phone: **Email:** info@machine2learn.com
City: Amsterdam **State:** Noord-Holland **PC:** **Country:** Netherlands
Year Established: 2017 **Status 2020:** Active
Industries:

Company Name: MadeVivid
Description: MadeVivid is a content agency for tech and science companies.
Website: http://www.madevivid.com
Phone: **Email:** ciara@madevivid.com
City: Amsterdam **State:** Noord-Holland **PC:** **Country:** Netherlands
Year Established: 2016 **Status 2020:** Active
Industries: Machine Learning for:, Robotics

Company Name: Media Distillery
Description: Media Distillery is an artificial intelligence to understand what's inside video.
Website: http://www.mediadistillery.com/
Phone: 31 20 235 1430 **Email:** hello@mediadistillery.com
City: Amsterdam **State:** Noord-Holland **PC:** **Country:** Netherlands
Year Established: 2014 **Status 2020:** Active
Industries: Artificial Intelligence for:, IT Managed Services for:, Web for:, Web

Company Name: Mi8 Marketing Cloud
Description: Mi8 shapes the future of marketing & sal: Spain
Website: http://www.mi8.marketing
Phone: (3162) 282-3677 **Email:** support@mi8.marketing
City: Amsterdam **State:** Noord-Holland **PC:** **Country:** Netherlands
Year Established: 2014 **Status 2020:** Active
Industries: Analytics for:, IT Managed Services for:, Predictive Analytics

Company Name: Mobile Professionals
Description: Mobile advertising agency powered by home-bred DSP technology
Website: http://mobpro.com
Phone: (3120) 702-8200 **Email:** contact@mobpro.com
City: Amsterdam **State:** Noord-Holland **PC:** **Country:** Netherlands
Year Established: 2011 **Status 2020:** Active
Industries: Machine Learning for:, Mobile

Company Name: NeoSound Intelligence
Description: AI tech company providing speech analytics solutions for Call Centr: Spain
Website: http://www.neosound.eu
Phone: 31 70 700 6169 **Email:** contact@neosound.eu
City: Amsterdam **State:** Noord-Holland **PC:** **Country:** Netherlands
Year Established: 2018 **Status 2020:** Active
Industries: Artificial Intelligence for:, IT Managed Services for:, Machine Learning for:, Business Software as a Service Apps (SaaS Apps)

Company Name: NewsOgram
Description: NewsOgram is a personalised news based on artificial intelligence.
Website: http://newsogram.com
Phone: **Email:** 37059@reference-encyclopedia-ai.net
City: Amsterdam **State:** Noord-Holland **PC:** **Country:** Netherlands
Year Established: 2017 **Status 2020:** Active
Industries: Artificial Intelligence for:, Machine Learning

Company Name: Orchest
Description: Orchest is an open source end-to-end machine learning platform.
Website: http://www.orchest.io
Phone: **Email:** info@orchest.io
City: Amsterdam **State:** Noord-Holland **PC:** **Country:** Netherlands
Year Established: 2020 **Status 2020:** Active
Industries: Machine Learning

Company Name: Phyramid
Description: We're a software development firm, with roots in artificial intelligence and data visualisation.
Website: http://www.phyramid.com
Phone: **Email:** business@phyramid.com
City: Amsterdam **State:** Noord-Holland **PC:** **Country:** Netherlands
Year Established: 2012 **Status 2020:** Active
Industries: Artificial Intelligence for:, Web for:, Web

Company Name: Playpost
Description: Playpost transforms articles on the web into audio using artificial intelligence to create natural-sounding audio. Just like audiobooks.
Website: http://playpost.app
Phone: **Email:** info@playpost.app
City: Amsterdam **State:** Noord-Holland **PC:** **Country:** Netherlands
Year Established: 2019 **Status 2020:** Active
Industries: Application Services for:, Artificial Intelligence for:, Natural Language Processing

Company Name: RapidPricer B.V.
Description: RapidPricer helps retailers to increase margins and reduce waste by automating pricing and promotions .
Website: http://www.rapidpricer.nl/
Phone: **Email:** info@rapidpricer.: Netherlands
City: Amsterdam **State:** Noord-Holland **PC:** **Country:** Netherlands
Year Established: 2018 **Status 2020:** Active
Industries:

Company Name: Reason.ai
Description: Reason.ai is an NLU and Visual Dialog Modeling Engine for powering complex goal-oriented dialogs between organizations and their clients.
Website: http://reason.ai/
Phone: **Email:** 37273@reference-encyclopedia-ai.net
City: Amsterdam **State:** Noord-Holland **PC:** **Country:** Netherlands
Year Established: 2015 **Status 2020:** Active
Industries:

Company Name: Recommendme.online
Description: Virtual assistant for Google AdWords advertisers aimed to help them prevent budget drain/improve performance using automated recommendations
Website: http://recommendme.online
Phone: 31208932445 **Email:** report@recommendme.online
City: Amsterdam **State:** Noord-Holland **PC:** **Country:** Netherlands
Year Established: 2017 **Status 2020:** Active
Industries: Analytics for:, Artificial Intelligence for:, Machine Learning

Company Name: RemIQz Football
Description: RemIQz Football specializes in predictive football analytics.
Website: http://www.remiqz.com/
Phone: 31(0) 6 2937 9908 **Email:** info@remiqz.com
City: Amsterdam **State:** Noord-Holland **PC:** **Country:** Netherlands
Year Established: 2016 **Status 2020:** Active
Industries: Application Services for:, Predictive Analytics for:, ~ Arts-Entertainment-Recreation (4), ~ Arts-Entertainment-Recreation (4)

Company Name: Reynen Court
Description: Service Automation platform for Law Firms
Website: http://www.reynencourt.com
Phone: 31 6 236 603 10 **Email:** info@reynencourt.com
City: Amsterdam **State:** Noord-Holland **PC:** **Country:** Netherlands
Year Established: 2018 **Status 2020:** Active
Industries:

Company Name: Rockstart
Description: Rockstart supports startups in becoming scalable by providing them with access to the market, capital, expertise, and community.
Website: http://www.rockstart.com/
Phone: **Email:** accelerator@rockstart.com
City: Amsterdam **State:** Noord-Holland **PC:** **Country:** Netherlands
Year Established: 2011 **Status 2020:** Active
Industries: ~ Agriculture (3), ~ Agriculture (3), Artificial Intelligence for:, ~ Energy and Utilities (14), ~ Food and Beverage (17), ~ Healthcare (20), Machine Learning for:, ~ Energy and Utilities (14)

Company Name: Science Rockstars
Description: Behavioural science meets marketing
Website: http://www.sciencerockstars.com
Phone: **Email:** q@sciencerockstars.com
City: Amsterdam **State:** Noord-Holland **PC:** **Country:** Netherlands
Year Established: 2012 **Status 2020:** Active
Industries: Analytics for:, Big Data and Analytics for:, Machine Learning

Company Name: Scyfer
Description: Scyfer is a spin off of the University of Amsterdam specialised in machine learning solutions.
Website: http://www.scyfer.: Netherlands
Phone: 31 6 22807457 **Email:** info@scyfer.: Netherlands
City: Amsterdam **State:** Noord-Holland **PC:** **Country:** Netherlands
Year Established: 2013 **Status 2020:** Active
Industries:

Company Name: Semiotic Labs
Description: Condition Monitoring service based on Machine Learning and proprietary sensors.
Website: http://www.semioticlabs.com/
Phone: **Email:** info@semioticlabs.com
City: Amsterdam **State:** Noord-Holland **PC:** **Country:** Netherlands
Year Established: 2015 **Status 2020:** Active
Industries: Enterprise Application Services for:, IT Managed Services for:, Machine Learning

Company Name: SingularityNET
Description: SingularityNET is a decentralized marketplace for AI algorithms.
Website: http://singularitynet.io/
Phone: **Email:** info@singularitynet.io
City: Amsterdam **State:** Noord-Holland **PC:** **Country:** Netherlands
Year Established: 2017 **Status 2020:** Active
Industries: Artificial Intelligence

Company Name: SKACE
Description: Instant people feedback & performance management app.
Website: http://getskace.com/
Phone: **Email:** info@getskace.com
City: Amsterdam **State:** Noord-Holland **PC:** **Country:** Netherlands
Year Established: 2015 **Status 2020:** Active
Industries: Application Services for:, Artificial Intelligence for:, ~ Banking and Financial Markets-Services (7)

Company Name: Stormly
Description: AI- powered analytics platform
Website: http://www.stormly.com/
Phone: **Email:** aleks@stormly.com
City: Amsterdam **State:** Noord-Holland **PC:** **Country:** Netherlands
Year Established: 2017 **Status 2020:** Active
Industries: Artificial Intelligence

Company Name: SurveyAuto
Description: SurveyAuto uses machine learning on satellite imagery to accurately identify survey targets, tracks and monitors enumerators in real-time.
Website: http://www.surveyauto.com/
Phone: 617 430 5048 **Email:** info@surveyauto.com
City: Amsterdam **State:** Noord-Holland **PC:** **Country:** Netherlands
Year Established: 2019 **Status 2020:** Active
Industries: Artificial Intelligence for:, IT Managed Services for:, Machine Learning

Company Name: Talkalyze
Description: Real time AI call coa: Switzerland
Website: http://talkalyze.com
Phone: **Email:** rogier@talkalyze.com
City: Amsterdam **State:** Noord-Holland **PC:** **Country:** Netherlands
Year Established: 2019 **Status 2020:** Active
Industries: Artificial Intelligence

Company Name: ThirdSight
Description: Computer vision technology company
Website: http://thirdsight.co
Phone: 31 207 07 05 14 **Email:** marketing@thirdsight.co
City: Amsterdam **State:** Noord-Holland **PC:** **Country:** Netherlands
Year Established: 2010 **Status 2020:** Active
Industries: Augmented Reality for:, Computer Vision for:, Machine Learning

Company Name: Unless
Description: Unless is a predictive personalization platform for websites.
Website: http://unless.com
Phone: 31(0)20 7009345 **Email:** press@unless.com
City: Amsterdam **State:** Noord-Holland **PC:** **Country:** Netherlands

Year Established: 2016 **Status 2020:** Active
Industries: Artificial Intelligence for:, Machine Learning for:, Business Software as a Service Apps (SaaS Apps)

Company Name: VentureBuilde: Serbia
Description: VentureBuilders is a hands-on European venture capital fund, focused on AI, data and general SaaS companies.
Website: http://www.venturebuilders.capital/
Phone: **Email:** 37616@reference-encyclopedia-ai.net
City: Amsterdam **State:** Noord-Holland **PC:** **Country:** Netherlands
Year Established: 2012 **Status 2020:** Active
Industries: Artificial Intelligence for:, Business Software as a Service Apps (SaaS Apps) for:, ~ Banking and Financial Markets-Services (7)

Company Name: VisionLabs B.V.
Description: VisionLabs is a world-leading visual recognition company
Website: http://www.visionlabs.ai
Phone: 31 20 369 0493 **Email:** pr@visionlabs.ai
City: Amsterdam **State:** Noord-Holland **PC:** **Country:** Netherlands
Year Established: 2012 **Status 2020:** Active
Industries: ~ Biotechnology (9), Computer Vision for:, Facial Recognition for:, Image Recognition for:, IT Managed Services for:, Machine Learning for:, Robotics

Company Name: WeAreBra: India
Description: Forming successful technology teams for the digital era
Website: http://www.wearebrain.com/
Phone: **Email:** sayhello@wearebrain.com
City: Amsterdam **State:** Noord-Holland **PC:** **Country:** Netherlands
Year Established: 2015 **Status 2020:** Active
Industries:

Company Name: wedoido
Description: Planning your wedding should be fun and easy. Our Wedding Assistants create your perfect marriage by using smart tech.
Website: http://wedoido.com
Phone: **Email:** yes@wedoido.com
City: Amsterdam **State:** Noord-Holland **PC:** **Country:** Netherlands
Year Established: 2019 **Status 2020:** Active
Industries: Artificial Intelligence for:, E-Commerce for:, Web for:, ~ Event Management (15)

Company Name: Wizenoze
Description: At the heart of the WizeNoze platform is a set of powerful classification algorithms.
Website: http://wizenoze.com/
Phone: 31 6 51324466 **Email:** diane@wizenoze.com
City: Amsterdam **State:** Noord-Holland **PC:** **Country:** Netherlands
Year Established: 2013 **Status 2020:** Active
Industries: Artificial Intelligence for:, ~ Education (13), IT Managed Services for:, Machine Learning for:, Web

Company Name: Wonderflow
Description: Advanced Consumer Feedback Analytics
Website: http://wonderflow.co
Phone: 31203639266 **Email:** hello@wonderflow.co
City: Amsterdam **State:** Noord-Holland **PC:** **Country:** Netherlands
Year Established: 2013 **Status 2020:** Active
Industries: Artificial Intelligence for:, Big Data and Analytics for:, Business Intelligence for:, Learning and Marketing Communications Services (MarComm) for:, Natural Language Processing for:, Data Management

Company Name: Zapplied
Description: Zapplied Platform combines technology and artificial intelligence with document & deal automation.
Website: http://www.zappliedplatform.com/
Phone: 31 20 - 305 49 69 **Email:** info@zapplied.com
City: Amsterdam **State:** Noord-Holland **PC:** **Country:** Netherlands
Year Established: 2010 **Status 2020:** Active
Industries: Artificial Intelligence

Company Name: AzioBot
Description: Aziobot builds autonomous cleaning robots for businesses.
Website: http://www.aziobot.com
Phone: **Email:** contact@aziobot.com
City: Den Bosch **State:** NB **PC:** **Country:** Netherlands
Year Established: **Status 2020:** Active
Industries: Artificial Intelligence for:, Robotics

Company Name: nFold
Description: nFold uses speech to text technology to provide a more comprehensive and intuitive view of candidates to hiring managers and recruite: Serbia
Website: http://nfold.ai
Phone: **Email:** hello@nfold.ai
City: Den Bosch **State:** NB **PC:** **Country:** Netherlands
Year Established: **Status 2020:** Active
Industries: Artificial Intelligence for:, ~ Human Resources (24), Machine Learning for:, Natural Language Processing for:, ~ Human Resources (24), Speech Recognition

Company Name: Recht Direct
Description: Right Direct is the advantageous legal subscription for the entrepreneur who opts for prevention.
Website: http://www.rechtdirect.: Netherlands
Phone: 0493-326688 **Email:** info@rechtdirect.: Netherlands
City: Deurne **State:** NB **PC:** **Country:** Netherlands
Year Established: **Status 2020:** Active
Industries: Artificial Intelligence for:, ~ Law-Legal Services (26)

Company Name: Darwin Pricing B.V.
Description: Dynamic Geo-Pricing services for eCommerce professionals. World's first Dynamic Pricing engine based on AI and Deep Learning technologies.
Website: http://www.darwinpricing.com
Phone: (310)408-51753 **Email:** anjo@sposea.com
City: Eindhoven **State:** NB **PC:** **Country:** Netherlands
Year Established: **Status 2020:** Active
Industries: Artificial Intelligence for:, E-Commerce for:, Enterprise Application Services for:, ~ Media-Communications (41), Predictive Analytics for:, ~ Retail and Consumer Products (52), ~ Retail and Consumer Products (52)

Company Name: FOBISS
Description: Creating proprietary Intelligent Business Operation (IBO) systems for global clients
Website: http://www.fobiss.com
Phone: 31 85 0090515 **Email:** info@fobiss.com
City: Eindhoven **State:** NB **PC:** **Country:** Netherlands
Year Established: **Status 2020:** Active
Industries: Artificial Intelligence for:, Business Applications for:, Business Intelligence for:, Predictive Analytics

Company Name: Fullcircle
Description: Fullcircle builds tailor-made, data-driven software products using state of the art machine learning algorithms.
Website:
Phone: **Email:** 4950@reference-encyclopedia-ai.net
City: Eindhoven **State:** NB **PC:** **Country:** Netherlands
Year Established: **Status 2020:** Active
Industries: Artificial Intelligence for:, Enterprise Application Services for:, IT Managed Services for:, Machine Learning for:, Predictive Analytics for:, ~ Professional Services (48)

Company Name: Orien: Sweden
Description: Oriense develops assisting devices for the blind and the visually impaired.
Website: http://oriense.com
Phone: 31614909460 **Email:** hello@oriense.com
City: Eindhoven **State:** NB **PC:** **Country:** Netherlands
Year Established: **Status 2020:** Active
Industries: Artificial Intelligence for:, ~ Healthcare (20), Augmented Reality for:, Computer Vision for:, ~ Manufacturing-Electronic (30), Embedded for:, ~ Transportation and Logistics (57)

Company Name: Dendri Systems
Description: Dendri Systems is specializes in researching, developing and selling software and hardware in the field of artificial intelligence.
Website: http://www.dendrisystems.com/
Phone: 31 6 2900 7652 **Email:** info@dendrisystems.com
City: Prinsenbeek **State:** NB **PC:** **Country:** Netherlands
Year Established: **Status 2020:** Active
Industries: Artificial Intelligence for:, ~ Banking and Financial Markets-Services (7), IT Managed Services

Company Name: 100grams
Description: Mobile & Web Application Development Company | Amsterdam, : Netherlands
Website: http://100grams.io
Phone: **Email:** hello@100grams.: Netherlands
City: Amsterdam **State:** NH **PC:** **Country:** Netherlands
Year Established: **Status 2020:** Active
Industries: Artificial Intelligence for:, Augmented Reality for:, E-Commerce for:, Application Services for:, Cyber Security for:, Cyber Security

Company Name: Aiir Innovations
Description: Aiir Innovations creates advanced software solutions to make aircraft engine inspection faster, more efficient and safer.
Website: http://aiir.: Netherlands
Phone: **Email:** hello@aiir.: Netherlands
City: Amsterdam **State:** NH **PC:** **Country:** Netherlands
Year Established: **Status 2020:** Active
Industries:

Company Name: AmberScript
Description: We take away the pain of manual transcription by offering AI driven automatic transcription and an online editor resulting in 100% accuracy
Website: http://www.amberscript.com/
Phone: **Email:** info@amberscript.com
City: Amsterdam **State:** NH **PC:** **Country:** Netherlands
Year Established: **Status 2020:** Active
Industries: Artificial Intelligence for:, Machine Learning for:, Application Services for:, Speech Recognition

Company Name: BrainCreators
Description: BrainCreators delivers enterprise AI solutions
Website: http://www.braincreators.com
Phone: 31 (0)20 369 7260 **Email:** info@braincreators.com
City: Amsterdam **State:** NH **PC:** **Country:** Netherlands
Year Established: **Status 2020:** Active
Industries: Artificial Intelligence for:, Enterprise Application Services for:, Enterprise Application Services for:, Machine Learning for:, ~ Professional Services (48), ~ Professional Services (48)

Company Name: Brainginee: Serbia
Description: Combining Neuroscience & Machine Learning in an Emotion Analytics platform
Website: http://www.braingineers.com
Phone: 31 20 261 2438 **Email:** info@braingineers.com
City: Amsterdam **State:** NH **PC:** **Country:** Netherlands
Year Established: **Status 2020:** Active
Industries: Artificial Intelligence for:, Machine Learning for:, ~ Media-Communications (41), ~ Life Sciences (27), Development and Test

Company Name: Bundle
Description: Bundle is the fastest way to organize the photo mess in your camera roll into a beautiful shared photo gallery.
Website: http://bundleapp.co/
Phone: **Email:** hello@bundleapp.co
City: Amsterdam **State:** NH **PC:** **Country:** Netherlands
Year Established: **Status 2020:** Active
Industries: Application Services for:, Artificial Intelligence for:, Image Recognition for:, Machine Learning for:, ~ Social Media (54), Business Intelligence

Company Name: Connecterra
Description: Rewiring humankinds' relationship with nature.
Website: http://connecterra.io
Phone: 31850667040 **Email:** info@connecterra.io
City: Amsterdam **State:** NH **PC:** **Country:** Netherlands
Year Established: **Status 2020:** Active
Industries: ~ Agriculture (3), Artificial Intelligence for:, Machine Learning

Company Name: Crobox
Description: Crobox Persuasion Profiling Technology helps eCommerce brands better understand and act on their shoppers behaviour in real time.
Website: http://crobox.com
Phone: **Email:** rodger@crobox.com
City: Amsterdam **State:** NH **PC:** **Country:** Netherlands
Year Established: **Status 2020:** Active
Industries: Analytics for:, Artificial Intelligence for:, Big Data and Analytics for:, Machine Learning for:, Predictive Analytics

Company Name: Cupenya
Description: AI powered solution for next generation Customer Service
Website: http://www.cupenya.com
Phone: 31 6 49136188 **Email:** info@cupenya.com
City: Amsterdam **State:** NH **PC:** **Country:** Netherlands
Year Established: **Status 2020:** Active
Industries: Analytics for:, Artificial Intelligence for:, Business Applications for:, Enterprise Application Services for:, ~ Professional Services (48)

Company Name: Dashmote
Description: Turn Images into Insights.
Website: http://dashmote.com/
Phone: **Email:** marketing@dashmote.com
City: Amsterdam **State:** NH **PC:** **Country:** Netherlands
Year Established: **Status 2020:** Active
Industries: Artificial Intelligence for:, Computer Vision for:, Enterprise Application Services for:, Image Recognition for:, ~ Media-Communications (41), ~ Professional Services (48)

Company Name: effect.ai
Description: A decentralized network for artificial intelligence.
Website: http://effect.ai/
Phone: **Email:** hello@effect.ai
City: Amsterdam **State:** NH **PC:** **Country:** Netherlands
Year Established: **Status 2020:** Active
Industries: Artificial Intelligence for:, Blockchain for:, IT Managed Services

Company Name: Findest B.V.
Description: Artificial Intelligence technology scouting SaaS company
Website: http://www.findest.eu
Phone: 31208932700 **Email:** igor@findest.eu
City: Amsterdam **State:** NH **PC:** **Country:** Netherlands
Year Established: **Status 2020:** Active
Industries: Artificial Intelligence

Company Name: Genezix
Description: AI Network
Website: http://genezix.com/
Phone: 31 23 204 7474 **Email:** bs@genezix.com
City: Amsterdam **State:** NH **PC:** **Country:** Netherlands

Year Established: **Status 2020:** Active
Industries: Artificial Intelligence for:, Cloud

Company Name: GeoSpark
Description: Location Intelligence Platform
Website: http://geospark.co
Phone: **Email:** support@geospark.co
City: Amsterdam **State:** NH **PC:** **Country:** Netherlands
Year Established: **Status 2020:** Active
Industries: Artificial Intelligence for:, Machine Learning for:, ~ Professional Services (48)

Company Name: Grip QA
Description: Grip is a data analytics-based software development company.
Website: http://grip.qa
Phone: **Email:** info@grip.qa
City: Amsterdam **State:** NH **PC:** **Country:** Netherlands
Year Established: **Status 2020:** Active
Industries: Artificial Intelligence for:, Enterprise Application Services for:, Machine Learning for:, Predictive Analytics

Company Name: HAL24K
Description: HAL24K is a Data Intelligence Research Lab based in Amsterdam, San Francisco and London
Website: http://www.hal24k.com
Phone: **Email:** hiring@hal24k.com
City: Amsterdam **State:** NH **PC:** **Country:** Netherlands
Year Established: **Status 2020:** Active
Industries:

Company Name: Healthplus.ai B.V.
Description: Heathplus.ai creates, develops and scales AI tools that solve real health and health care problems.
Website: http://www.healthplus.ai
Phone: 31 (0) 646 283 305 **Email:** info@healthplus.ai
City: Amsterdam **State:** NH **PC:** **Country:** Netherlands
Year Established: **Status 2020:** Active
Industries: Artificial Intelligence for:, ~ Healthcare (20)

Company Name: Internet of Thinkers
Description: The Intelligence Crowd in the Cloud - we provide the power to help you make great decisions.
Website: http://www.internetofthinkers.com
Phone: **Email:** contactus@internet-of-thinkers.com
City: Amsterdam **State:** NH **PC:** **Country:** Netherlands
Year Established: **Status 2020:** Active
Industries: Artificial Intelligence for:, Business Intelligence for:, Databases for:, Application Services for:, ~ Media-Communications (41)

Company Name: Kepler Vision Technologies
Description: Body language recognition
Website: http://www.keplervision.eu
Phone: **Email:** h.stokman@keplervision.eu
City: Amsterdam **State:** NH **PC:** **Country:** Netherlands
Year Established: **Status 2020:** Active
Industries: Artificial Intelligence for:, Computer Vision for:, Machine Learning

Company Name: letz.do
Description: Letz is a multiplatform productivity app that strives to make your life easier and make you enjoy productivity.
Website: http://letz.do/
Phone: 38926151283 **Email:** contact@letz.do
City: Amsterdam **State:** NH **PC:** **Country:** Netherlands
Year Established: **Status 2020:** Active
Industries: Artificial Intelligence for:, Application Services for:, Application Services

Company Name: MeterQubes Solutions
Description: Trade Digital Assets with an Edge
Website: http://meterqubes.io/
Phone: (968) 9965 0205 **Email:** Ahmed@meterqubes.io
City: Amsterdam **State:** NH **PC:** **Country:** Netherlands
Year Established: **Status 2020:** Active
Industries: Artificial Intelligence for:, Blockchain for:, Finance and Accounting

Company Name: nwzer
Description: Artificial Intelligence & Blockchain powered Citizen Journalism
Website: http://nwzer.com
Phone: **Email:** contact@nwzer.com
City: Amsterdam **State:** NH **PC:** **Country:** Netherlands
Year Established: **Status 2020:** Active
Industries: Artificial Intelligence for:, Blockchain for:, ~ Media-Communications (41)

Company Name: OkiDoki messenger (AKA PopAppFactory)
Description: We make innovative and aesthetically perfect mobile apps for kids that shift mobile experience from entertainment to education.
Website: http://www.popappfactory.com
Phone: 31616549063 **Email:** info@popappfactory.com
City: Amsterdam **State:** NH **PC:** **Country:** Netherlands
Year Established: **Status 2020:** Active
Industries: Application Services for:, Artificial Intelligence for:, ~ Education (13), ~ Arts-Entertainment-Recreation (4), Mobile for:, ~ Education (13), ~ Social Media (54), ~ Professional Services (48)

Company Name: OneWatt
Description: OneWatt is an AI company providing a non-invasive, non-contact predictive motor health maintenance system using sound.
Website: http://www.onewatt.eu
Phone: **Email:** hi@onewatt.eu
City: Amsterdam **State:** NH **PC:** **Country:** Netherlands
Year Established: **Status 2020:** Active
Industries: Artificial Intelligence for:, Automation for:, Predictive Analytics

Company Name: Owl: India
Description: Turn News into Actionable Intelligence
Website: http://www.owlin.com
Phone: **Email:** berjan@owlin.com
City: Amsterdam **State:** NH **PC:** **Country:** Netherlands
Year Established: **Status 2020:** Active
Industries: Analytics for:, Artificial Intelligence for:, Big Data and Analytics for:, ~ Banking and Financial Markets-Services (7), Machine Learning for:, Natural Language Processing

Company Name: Pact Care
Description: Enabling trustful collaborations in healthcare
Website: http://pact.care/
Phone: 31 20 893 4143 **Email:** info@pact.care
City: Amsterdam **State:** NH **PC:** **Country:** Netherlands
Year Established: **Status 2020:** Active
Industries: Artificial Intelligence for:, Blockchain for:, ~ Healthcare (20), IT Managed Services for:, Robotics

Company Name: Pimmr
Description: Genius A.I. that discovers things you will love
Website: http://www.pimmr.com/
Phone: **Email:** hello@pimmr.com
City: Amsterdam **State:** NH **PC:** **Country:** Netherlands
Year Established: **Status 2020:** Active
Industries: Artificial Intelligence for:, Mobile for:, ~ Food and Beverage (17)

Company Name: Pyramid Analytics
Description: Pyramid Analytics provides trusted insights for every employee across your organization with enterprise-level business analytics software.
Website: http://www.pyramidanalytics.com
Phone: 1(203) 202-3500 **Email:** info@pyramidanalytics.com
City: Amsterdam **State:** NH **PC:** **Country:** Netherlands

Year Established: **Status 2020:** Active
Industries: Analytics for:, Artificial Intelligence for:, Business Applications for:, Business Intelligence for:, Enterprise Application Services

Company Name: Roader
Description: Roader creates new ways of capturing and sharing video
Website: http://www.roader.com
Phone: 31208006459 **Email:** info@roader.com
City: Amsterdam **State:** NH **PC:** **Country:** Netherlands
Year Established: **Status 2020:** Active
Industries: Application Services for:, Artificial Intelligence for:, ~ Manufacturing-Electronic (30), Machine Learning for:, ~ Arts-Entertainment-Recreation (4), ~ Professional Services (48), ~ Media-Communications (41)

Company Name: Rockstart Accelerator
Description: Rockstart Accelerator supports startups in becoming scalable by providing them with access to the market, capital, expertise, and community.
Website: http://www.rockstart.com/accelerator
Phone: **Email:** accelerator@rockstart.com
City: Amsterdam **State:** NH **PC:** **Country:** Netherlands
Year Established: **Status 2020:** Active
Industries:

Company Name: Scitodate
Description: Scitodate a group of passionate scientists building a new generation of research engine.
Website: http://www.scitodate.com
Phone: **Email:** info@scitodate.com
City: Amsterdam **State:** NH **PC:** **Country:** Netherlands
Year Established: **Status 2020:** Active
Industries: Artificial Intelligence for:, Business Intelligence for:, ~ Manufacturing-Miscellaneous (34)

Company Name: Seedlink
Description: Seedlink employs AI to empower organizations to make better people and human resource decisions
Website: http://www.seedlinktech.com/
Phone: 31 20 810 2230 **Email:** info@seedlinktech.com
City: Amsterdam **State:** NH **PC:** **Country:** Netherlands
Year Established: **Status 2020:** Active
Industries: Artificial Intelligence for:, ~ Human Resources (24), IT Managed Services for:, Natural Language Processing for:, Predictive Analytics for:, Data Management

Company Name: Sightcorp
Description: Sightcorp is an AI software company specializing in face analysis software. We analyze faces in images, videos, and in real-life environment
Website: http://www.sightcorp.com
Phone: 31207051590 **Email:** info@sightcorp.com
City: Amsterdam **State:** NH **PC:** **Country:** Netherlands
Year Established: **Status 2020:** Active
Industries: Artificial Intelligence for:, Computer Vision for:, Application Services for:, ~ Media-Communications (41), Machine Learning for:, ~ Retail and Consumer Products (52), ~ Professional Services (48)

Company Name: Si
Description: Silk is a cloud-based application that enables users to visualize their data online by the way of interactive web pages.
Website: http://www.silk.co
Phone: **Email:** info@silk.co
City: Amsterdam **State:** NH **PC:** **Country:** Netherlands
Year Established: **Status 2020:** Active
Industries: Artificial Intelligence for:, Data Management for:, Application Services for:, ~ Professional Services (48)

Company Name: Ticketless
Description: Customer Service Agent focused AI-software that improves agent performance
Website: http://ticketless.ai
Phone: **Email:** hello@ticketless.ai
City: Amsterdam **State:** NH **PC:** **Country:** Netherlands
Year Established: **Status 2020:** Active
Industries: Artificial Intelligence for:, Machine Learning

Company Name: trakkies
Description: trakkies international is an intelligence platform that provides products and services designed for human-centered relationships.
Website: http://www.trakkies.com
Phone: **Email:** info@trakkies.com
City: Amsterdam **State:** NH **PC:** **Country:** Netherlands
Year Established: **Status 2020:** Active
Industries: Analytics for:, Artificial Intelligence for:, Big Data and Analytics for:, Cloud for:, Cloud for:, Embedded for:, ~ Administrative and Support Services (1)

Company Name: Tur.ai
Description: Robotic Process Automation
Website: http://tur.ai
Phone: **Email:** sayhello@wearebrain.com
City: Amsterdam **State:** NH **PC:** **Country:** Netherlands
Year Established: **Status 2020:** Active
Industries: Artificial Intelligence for:, Automation for:, Natural Language Processing for:, ~ Administrative and Support Services (1), ~ Professional Services (48), Robotics for:, Automation

Company Name: Ub Technologies
Description: End-to-end portfolio & risk analytics for financial institutions
Website: http://www.ubtechnologies.nl/
Phone: **Email:** info@ubtechnologies.: Netherlands
City: Amsterdam **State:** NH **PC:** **Country:** Netherlands
Year Established: **Status 2020:** Active
Industries: Analytics for:, Artificial Intelligence for:, ~ Banking and Financial Markets-Services (7), ~ Banking and Financial Markets-Services (7), ~ Banking and Financial Markets-Services (7), Machine Learning for:, ~ Professional Services (48)

Company Name: U: Netherlands
Description: The Internet of Plac: Spain
Website: http://unl.global
Phone: **Email:** hi@unl.global
City: Amsterdam **State:** NH **PC:** **Country:** Netherlands
Year Established: **Status 2020:** Active
Industries: Artificial Intelligence for:, Blockchain for:, E-Commerce for:, ~ Transportation and Logistics (57), ~ Transportation and Logistics (57), ~ Transportation and Logistics (57), ~ Construction (10)

Company Name: Unless.com
Description: Unless is a personalization platform for websites.
Website: http://unless.com/
Phone: 31(0)20 7009345 **Email:** press@unless.com
City: Amsterdam **State:** NH **PC:** **Country:** Netherlands
Year Established: **Status 2020:** Active
Industries: Artificial Intelligence for:, Machine Learning for:, ~ Media-Communications (41), ~ Media-Communications (41)

Company Name: Vartion
Description: Applied Data Intelligence for Finance and Life Scienc: Spain
Website: http://vartion.com
Phone: **Email:** info@vartion.com
City: Amsterdam **State:** NH **PC:** **Country:** Netherlands
Year Established: **Status 2020:** Active
Industries: Artificial Intelligence for:, Big Data and Analytics for:, ~ Biotechnology (9)

Company Name: We-Assist
Description: We-assist is a Dutch tech company develops customer service software and helps organisations set up their helpdesk more efficiently.
Website: http://we-assist.com
Phone: 31 (0)85-065 5352 **Email:** sales@we-assist.com
City: Amsterdam **State:** NH **PC:** **Country:** Netherlands
Year Established: **Status 2020:** Active
Industries: Artificial Intelligence for:, Cloud for:, ~ Professional Services (48)

Company Name: Wercker
Description: Wercker is a platform and tool to rapidly develop, build, and deploy containerized applications and microservices for the modern cloud.
Website: http://wercker.com
Phone: **Email:** pleasemailus@wercker.com
City: Amsterdam **State:** NH **PC:** **Country:** Netherlands
Year Established: **Status 2020:** Active
Industries: Artificial Intelligence for:, Cloud for:, Enterprise Application Services for:, ~ Professional Services (48)

Company Name: Wonderkind
Description: Wonderkind is a fully automated job advertising platform.
Website: http://wonderkind.com/
Phone: 31(0)20 820 3323 **Email:** hello@wonderkind.com
City: Amsterdam **State:** NH **PC:** **Country:** Netherlands
Year Established: **Status 2020:** Active
Industries:

Company Name: X2AI
Description: Automated Mental Healthcare using Emotional Artificial Intelligence
Website: x2.ai
Phone: **Email:** hello@x2ai.com
City: Amsterdam **State:** NH **PC:** **Country:** Netherlands
Year Established: **Status 2020:** Active
Industries: Artificial Intelligence for:, ~ Healthcare (20), ~ Healthcare (20)

Company Name: SaySimple
Description: Social Messaging Automation Platform
Website: http://www.saysimple.com/
Phone: 31 (0) 23 554 67 66 **Email:** info@saysimple.com
City: Haarlem **State:** NH **PC:** **Country:** Netherlands
Year Established: **Status 2020:** Active
Industries: Artificial Intelligence for:, IT Managed Services for:, ~ Social Media (54)

Company Name: IoT-Shops.com
Description: IoT sensors, gateways, kits marketplace.
Website: http://www.iot-shops.com
Phone: **Email:** 4861@reference-encyclopedia-ai.net
City: Marken **State:** NH **PC:** **Country:** Netherlands
Year Established: **Status 2020:** Active
Industries: Artificial Intelligence for:, Machine Learning for:, ~ Manufacturing-Electronic (30), ~ Construction (10), ~ Construction (10)

Company Name: 360 Sports Intelligence
Description: 360SportsIntelligence an effective, efficient & user-friendly online tool for automated recording, viewing, coding & presentation of team.
Website: http://360sportsintelligence.com/
Phone: **Email:** info@360sportsintelligence.com
City: Enschede **State:** Overste **PC:** **Country:** Netherlands
Year Established: **Status 2020:** Active
Industries: Artificial Intelligence for:, ~ Professional Services (48), ~ Arts-Entertainment-Recreation (4)

Company Name: SciSports
Description: SciSports uses data intelligence to understand football.
Website: https://www.scisports.com
Phone: **Email:** j.leenders@scisports.com
City: Enschede **State:** Overste **PC:** **Country:** Netherlands
Year Established: **Status 2020:** Active
Industries: Analytics for:, Artificial Intelligence for:, ~ Arts-Entertainment-Recreation (4)

Company **Name:** Serious VR
Description: Virtual training and performance data
Website: http://www.serious-vr.com
Phone: 31645034433 **Email:** info@serious-vr.com
City: Enschede **State:** Overijssel **PC:** **Country:** Netherlands
Year Established: 2016 **Status 2020:** Active
Industries: Analytics for:, Artificial Intelligence for:, IT Managed Services for:, Machine Learning for:, Machine Learning

Company Name: Evidencio
Description: Medical Decision Support based on Medical Prediction Models & AI
Website: http://www.evidencio.com
Phone: 31 53 4787529 **Email:** info@evidencio.com
City: Haaksbergen **State:** Overste **PC:** **Country:** Netherlands
Year Established: **Status 2020:** Active
Industries: Artificial Intelligence for:, Cloud for:, Machine Learning for:, ~ Healthcare (20), Predictive Analytics

Company Name: OSAsen: Sweden
Description: Sleep Apnea screening solution
Website: http://www.osasense.com
Phone: 31 53 478 75 29 **Email:** info@osasense.com
City: Haaksbergen **State:** Overste **PC:** **Country:** Netherlands
Year Established: **Status 2020:** Active
Industries: Artificial Intelligence for:, Machine Learning for:, ~ Healthcare (20), ~ Manufacturing-Medical Equipment-Supplies (33), Predictive Analytics

Company Name: Safesize
Description: Safesize revolutionize the way people buy shoes anytime, anywhere.
Website: http://www.safesize.com/
Phone: **Email:** hello@safesize.com
City: Nijverdal **State:** Overijssel **PC:** **Country:** Netherlands
Year Established: 2013 **Status 2020:** Active
Industries: E-Commerce for:, IT Managed Services for:, IT Managed Services for:, Machine Learning for:, ~ Retail and Consumer Products (52)

Company Name: 9signals
Description: 9signals deeply integrates Artificial Intelligence with Graph Technology to structure, search, analyze, and enrich data.
Website: http://9signals.com/
Phone: 31853037840 **Email:** friends@9signals.com
City: Delft **State:** South Holland **PC:** **Country:** Netherlands
Year Established: 2019 **Status 2020:** Active
Industries: Analytics for:, Artificial Intelligence for:, Data Management

Company Name: BRISE Care B.V.
Description: BRISE is the world's first air purifier with A.I. technology
Website: http://www.Brisecare.com
Phone: (015)800-0240 **Email:** kchang@Brisecare.com
City: Delft **State:** ZH **PC:** **Country:** Netherlands
Year Established: **Status 2020:** Active
Industries: Artificial Intelligence for:, ~ Healthcare (20), ~ Healthcare (20), ~ Healthcare (20)

Company Name: Dutch Analytics
Description: Dutch Analytics is developed an artificial intelligence platform.
Website: http://dutchanalytics.com
Phone: 015 2024002 **Email:** info@dutchanalytics.com
City: Delft **State:** South Holland **PC:** **Country:** Netherlands
Year Established: 2016 **Status 2020:** Active
Industries: Analytics for:, Artificial Intelligence for:, IT Managed Services

Company Name: Fizyr
Description: Fizyr is enables the automating of human tasks in logistics using AI.
Website: http://fizyr.com/
Phone: 31 15 760 1686 **Email:** info@fizyr.com
City: Delft **State:** South Holland **PC:** **Country:** Netherlands
Year Established: 2014 **Status 2020:** Active
Industries: Artificial Intelligence for:, Automation for:, ~ Telecommunications (56)

Company Name: jungle.ai
Description: Provides predictive intelligence by leveraging high-volume complex data, distributed computing, machine learning and genetic optimisation.
Website: jungle.ai/
Phone: **Email:** hello@jungle.ai
City: Delft **State:** ZH **PC:** **Country:** Netherlands
Year Established: **Status 2020:** Active
Industries:

Company Name: Next Ocean BV
Description: Next Ocean predicts the actual time traces of waves approaching the ship and the resulting ship motion response.
Website: http://www.nextocean.nl/
Phone: **Email:** info@nextocean.: Netherlands
City: Delft **State:** South Holland **PC:** **Country:** Netherlands
Year Established: 2016 **Status 2020:** Active
Industries: Predictive Analytics for:, Business Process and Operations

Company Name: Somnox
Description: Somnox is world's first sleeprobot to help you fall asleep, experience a better night's rest and wake up more energized.
Website: http://meetsomnox.com/
Phone: 316 82 42 10 37 **Email:** info@somnox.: Netherlands
City: Delft **State:** South Holland **PC:** **Country:** Netherlands
Year Established: 2014 **Status 2020:** Active
Industries: Application Services for:, Artificial Intelligence for:, ~ Healthcare (20), Robotics for:, ~ Healthcare (20)

Company Name: Sparksheet
Description: Sparksheet is a probabilistic metaprogramming platform that generates Spark apps and Data Science AI assistants from spreadsheet models.
Website: http://www.sparksheet.io
Phone: **Email:** ocastaneda@sparksheet.io
City: Delft **State:** South Holland **PC:** **Country:** Netherlands
Year Established: 2016 **Status 2020:** Active
Industries: Application Services for:, Artificial Intelligence

Company Name: Wavyr
Description: A SaaS company focussed on providing Conversational AI solutions
Website: http://wavyr.: Netherlands
Phone: 3120 893 2947 **Email:** thijs@wavyr.: Netherlands
City: Delft **State:** South Holland **PC:** **Country:** Netherlands
Year Established: 2017 **Status 2020:** Active
Industries: Artificial Intelligence

Company Name: AI Lab One
Description: Artificial Intelligence consulting agency focused on AI for Government, AI for Healthcare, AI for Marketing, AI for Good.
Website: https://ailab.one/
Phone: **Email:** hello@ailab.one
City: Den Haag **State:** South Holland **PC:** **Country:** Netherlands
Year Established: 2018 **Status 2020:** Active
Industries: Machine Learning

Company Name: EyeSense
Description: EyeSense creates smart solutions that interpret the visual world and speak it out to you in real time.
Website:
Phone: **Email:** 36541@reference-encyclopedia-ai.net
City: Den Haag **State:** South Holland **PC:** **Country:** Netherlands
Year Established: 2016 **Status 2020:** Closed
Industries: Artificial Intelligence for:, Augmented Reality

Company Name: Octo
Description: OCTO is a forward way of thinking-- adaptable, energetic and inspiring mutual innovation with our companies to optimise problem solving.
Website:
Phone: 31 85 0605 906 **Email:** 37091@reference-encyclopedia-ai.net
City: Den Haag **State:** South Holland **PC:** **Country:** Netherlands
Year Established: 2015 **Status 2020:** Closed
Industries: Artificial Intelligence for:, Big Data and Analytics for:, IT Managed Services

Company Name: TheAIGam: Spain
Description: Challenge people worldwide by coding bots in awesome gam: Spain
Website: http://theaigames.com/
Phone: **Email:** developers@theaigames.com
City: Den Haag **State:** ZH **PC:** **Country:** Netherlands
Year Established: **Status 2020:** Active
Industries: Artificial Intelligence for:, ~ Personal-Religious-Civic (45), Application Services for:, Machine Learning for:, Robotics

Company Name: XGear
Description: XGear is a data aggregation and predictive analysis platform for the connected car of the future! XGear delivers unparalleled real-time : India
Website: http://www.xgear.io
Phone: 31611221102 **Email:** ahmed@xgear.io
City: Den Haag **State:** South Holland **PC:** **Country:** Netherlands
Year Established: 2014 **Status 2020:** Active
Industries: ~ Automotive (5), Predictive Analytics

Company Name: BotBoys
Description: BotBoys
Website: http://botboys.com
Phone: **Email:** vinc@botboys.com
City: Leiden **State:** ZH **PC:** **Country:** Netherlands
Year Established: **Status 2020:** Active
Industries: Artificial Intelligence for:, ~ Telecommunications (56), Natural Language Processing

Company Name: CashRocket
Description: CashRocket develops a Predictive Cash Flow Analytics SaaS - using ESA's artificial intelligence.
Website: http://www.cashrocket.io
Phone: **Email:** info@cashrocket.io
City: Noordwijk **State:** South Holland **PC:** **Country:** Netherlands
Year Established: 2016 **Status 2020:** Active
Industries: Artificial Intelligence

Company Name: Captain AI
Description: Captain AI develops an autonomous shipping solution using high-fidelity simulation, sensors, and state-of-the-art deep learning techniques.
Website: http://www.captainai.com/
Phone: (3161) 450-4307 **Email:** info@captainai.com
City: Rotterdam **State:** South Holland **PC:** **Country:** Netherlands
Year Established: 2018 **Status 2020:** Active
Industries: Artificial Intelligence

Company Name: CheckData
Description: People | Data | Value We believe in the power of data and even more in the power of people using it.
Website: http://www.checkdata.: Netherlands
Phone: 31 10 333 0888 **Email:** info@checkdata.: Netherlands
City: Rotterdam **State:** South Holland **PC:** **Country:** Netherlands
Year Established: 2014 **Status 2020:** Active
Industries: Analytics for:, Artificial Intelligence for:, Big Data and Analytics for:, IT Managed Services

Company Name: Clockworks
Description: Clockworks is a deep learning software Company.
Website: http://www.clockworks.co/
Phone: **Email:** hello@clockworks.co
City: Rotterdam **State:** South Holland **PC:** **Country:** Netherlands
Year Established: 2017 **Status 2020:** Active
Industries:

Company Name: DoBots
Description: DoBots specializes in software where we come from the perspective of robotics.
Website: http://www.dobots.: Netherlands
Phone: 31 10 404 9444 **Email:** info@dobots.: Netherlands
City: Rotterdam **State:** South Holland **PC:** **Country:** Netherlands
Year Established: 2011 **Status 2020:** Active
Industries: Artificial Intelligence for:, Robotics

Company Name: E-Tail Genius
Description: E-Tail Genius develops an AI-powered platform that boosts decision making in pricing, assortment optimization, and demand forecasting.
Website: http://www.etailgenius.com/
Phone: (10) 307-6639 **Email:** 36520@reference-encyclopedia-ai.net
City: Rotterdam **State:** South Holland **PC:** **Country:** Netherlands
Year Established: 2017 **Status 2020:** Active
Industries: Analytics for:, Artificial Intelligence for:, Big Data and Analytics for:, IT Managed Services for:, Machine Learning for:, Application Services

Company Name: EventX
Description: Blockchain, NFC, AI
Website: http://eventx.network
Phone: **Email:** info@eventx.network
City: Rotterdam **State:** ZH **PC:** **Country:** Netherlands
Year Established: **Status 2020:** Active
Industries: Artificial Intelligence for:, Blockchain for:, ~ Banking and Financial Markets-Services (7), ~ Event Management (15), ~ Event Management (15), ~ Media-Communications (41), ~ Banking and Financial Markets-Services (7), ~ Banking and Financial Markets-Services (7)

Company Name: FabMetrics
Description: SaaS solution for utilizing IIoT data of manufactures. Developing algorithms to improve efficiency of production lines.
Website: http://www.fabmetrics.net
Phone: **Email:** 30965@reference-encyclopedia-ai.net
City: Rotterdam **State:** South Holland **PC:** **Country:** Netherlands
Year Established: 2017 **Status 2020:** Active
Industries: Cloud for:, Data Management for:, Automation for:, Internet of Things (IoT) for:, Machine Learning for:, Business Software as a Service Apps (SaaS Apps)

Company Name: Flamingo.report
Description: Data, real estate, proptech, realtech, AI
Website: http://www.flamingo.report
Phone: **Email:** hello@flamingo.report
City: Rotterdam **State:** ZH **PC:** **Country:** Netherlands
Year Established: **Status 2020:** Active
Industries: Artificial Intelligence for:, IT Managed Services for:, IT Managed Services for:, Web

Company Name: get-art.work
Description: Translate any picture into art with the visual language of your favorite masterpiece
Website: http://get-art.work
Phone: 31646904002 **Email:** sjoerd@get-art.work
City: Rotterdam **State:** ZH **PC:** **Country:** Netherlands
Year Established: **Status 2020:** Active
Industries: ~ Arts-Entertainment-Recreation (4), Artificial Intelligence for:, ~ Professional Services (48)

Company Name: Optimal.ag
Description: Optimal.ag applies reinforcement learning to solve valuable decision-making problems in highly uncertain environments.
Website: http://optimal.ag/
Phone: **Email:** contact@optimal.ag
City: Rotterdam **State:** South Holland **PC:** **Country:** Netherlands
Year Established: 2016 **Status 2020:** Active
Industries: ~ Agriculture (3), Artificial Intelligence for:, Machine Learning

Company Name: Quantib
Description: Quantib is a healthcare AI company providing groundbreaking technology for faster and more accurate diagnosis of disea: Sweden
Website: http://www.quantib.com/
Phone: (31) 108 41 17 49 **Email:** services@quantib.com
City: Rotterdam **State:** South Holland **PC:** **Country:** Netherlands
Year Established: 2012 **Status 2020:** Active
Industries: Artificial Intelligence for:, ~ Healthcare (20), Machine Learning for:, ~ Healthcare (20), ~ Healthcare (20)

Company Name: Recruitsos
Description: Recruitsos is recruitment automation.
Website: http://www.recruitsos.io
Phone: **Email:** hello@recruitsos.io
City: Rotterdam **State:** ZH **PC:** **Country:** Netherlands
Year Established: **Status 2020:** Active
Industries: Artificial Intelligence for:, Big Data and Analytics for:, ~ Human Resources (24), IT Managed Services for:, Machine Learning for:, ~ Media-Communications (41), ~ Social Media (54), ~ Professional Services (48), ~ Media-Communications (41)

Company Name: Travis the Translator
Description: Travis is the Original Creators of Pocket Translators. Understand the World. NEW : Travis Travel, Travis Business, Travis Tou: Switzerland
Website: http://www.travistranslator.com/
Phone: **Email:** hello@travistranslator.com
City: Rotterdam **State:** South Holland **PC:** **Country:** Netherlands
Year Established: 2017 **Status 2020:** Active
Industries: Artificial Intelligence for:, Mobile

Company Name: UXH
Description: Artificial intelligence in Yachting
Website: http://www.uxh.space
Phone: **Email:** info@uxh.space
City: Rotterdam **State:** ZH **PC:** **Country:** Netherlands

Year Established: **Status 2020:** Active
Industries: Artificial Intelligence for:, ~ Hospitality (23), ~ Government (19)

Company Name: Volareo
Description: World's 1st Smart Voice Speaker as a Hub, for Decentralized Music & Commerce
Website: http://www.volareo.live
Phone: **Email:** hello@volareo.live
City: Rotterdam **State:** South Holland **PC:** **Country:** Netherlands
Year Established: 2018 **Status 2020:** Active
Industries: Blockchain for:, ~ Banking and Financial Markets-Services (7), E-Commerce for:, Human Computer Interaction for:, ~ Arts-Entertainment-Recreation (4), ~ Arts-Entertainment-Recreation (4), Natural Language Processing for:, Internet of Things (IoT)

Company Name: Widget Bra: India
Description: Offices in Rotterdam (Netherlands), Canberra (Australia), and Burlington VT (United States)
Website: http://www.widgetbrain.com
Phone: (267)282-1478 **Email:** hello@widgetbrain.com
City: Rotterdam **State:** South Holland **PC:** **Country:** Netherlands
Year Established: 2015 **Status 2020:** Active
Industries: Artificial Intelligence for:, IT Managed Services for:, Web for:, Machine Learning for:, Robotics

Company Name: Eastsource
Description: Software Development Consultancy and Outsourcing to Eastern Euro:
Website: http://eastsource.tech
Phone: **Email:** info@eastsource.tech
City: The Hague **State:** South Holland **PC:** **Country:** Netherlands
Year Established: 2016 **Status 2020:** Active
Industries:

Company Name: Envision
Description: Envision builds AI based tools that enable visually impaired people to access visual information around them independently.
Website: http://www.LetsEnvision.com
Phone: (65) 167-0827 **Email:** support@letsenvision.com
City: The Hague **State:** South Holland **PC:** **Country:** Netherlands
Year Established: 2017 **Status 2020:** Active
Industries: Artificial Intelligence for:, Big Data and Analytics

Company Name: Finturi
Description: Making invoice financing secure, low-cost, quick and easy using blockchain and artificial intelligence
Website: http://www.finturi.com/
Phone: **Email:** info@finturi.com
City: The Hague **State:** South Holland **PC:** **Country:** Netherlands
Year Established: 2018 **Status 2020:** Active
Industries: Artificial Intelligence for:, ~ Banking and Financial Markets-Services (7), ~ Banking and Financial Markets-Services (7)

Company Name: Olympian
Description: An online education company that teaches artificial intelligence through bite-sized videos, workshops and games.
Website: http://olympian.ai
Phone: 31613956028 **Email:** team@olympian.ai
City: The Hague **State:** South Holland **PC:** **Country:** Netherlands
Year Established: 2018 **Status 2020:** Active
Industries: Artificial Intelligence for:, ~ Education (13)

Company Name: Scoopexpert
Description: We help people and companies worldwide to discover what is happening around them: biggest database of events and activiti: Spain
Website: http://scoopexpert.com
Phone: **Email:** info-crunch@scoopexpert.com
City: The Hague **State:** South Holland **PC:** **Country:** Netherlands
Year Established: 2015 **Status 2020:** Active
Industries: Analytics for:, Artificial Intelligence for:, Big Data and Analytics for:, IT Managed Services for:, Predictive Analytics

Company Name: TiNC Works!
Description: Determine and manage the health of your network - even if it stretches into the cloud...
Website: http://www.tinc.works
Phone: 31643439268 **Email:** akker@tinc.works
City: The Hague **State:** ZH **PC:** **Country:** Netherlands
Year Established: **Status 2020:** Active
Industries: Artificial Intelligence for:, Augmented Reality for:, Cloud for:, ~ Media-Communications (41), Automation for:, ~ Banking and Financial Markets-Services (7), Automation for:, IT Managed Services for:, Machine Learning for:, ~ Manufacturing-Electronic (30), Security

Company Name: Modellengenerator
Description: The Model Generator is an online service that allows you to easily generate automated documents.
Website: http://modellengenerator.: Netherlands
Phone: 31 (0) 6 835 959 46 **Email:** cvanbeusekom@ict-concept.: Netherlands
City: Amersfoort **State:** UT **PC:** **Country:** Netherlands
Year Established: **Status 2020:** Active
Industries: Artificial Intelligence for:, ~ Law-Legal Services (26)

Company Name: Qlouder
Description: IT solutions you need, yet never imagined
Website: http://www.qlouder.com/
Phone: 31203337500 **Email:** info@qlouder.com
City: Maarssen **State:** Utrecht **PC:** **Country:** Netherlands
Year Established: 2012 **Status 2020:** Active
Industries: Big Data and Analytics for:, Cloud for:, Data Management for:, Web for:, Machine Learning for:, Web

Company Name: Flytxt
Description: Driving digital customer engagement through Artificial Intelligence and Marketing Automation
Website: http://www.flytxt.com
Phone: 88 02 871 1879 **Email:** marketing@flytxt.com
City: Nieuwegein **State:** UT **PC:** **Country:** Netherlands
Year Established: **Status 2020:** Active
Industries: Analytics for:, Artificial Intelligence for:, ~ Media-Communications (41)

Company Name: Nori Heal:Thailand
Description: Chatbot coach for chronic disease management
Website: http://norihealth.com
Phone: **Email:** roeland@norihealth.com
City: Nieuwegein **State:** UT **PC:** **Country:** Netherlands
Year Established: **Status 2020:** Active
Industries: Artificial Intelligence for:, ~ Healthcare (20), Natural Language Processing

Company Name: advocaatzoeken.: Netherlands
Description: advocaatzoeken.nl is the online platform for lawyers and clients.
Website: http://www.advocaatzoeken.: Netherlands
Phone: 088 - 833 88 88 **Email:** info@advocaatzoeken.: Netherlands
City: Utrecht **State:** UT **PC:** **Country:** Netherlands
Year Established: **Status 2020:** Active
Industries: Artificial Intelligence for:, ~ Government (19), ~ Law-Legal Services (26)

Company Name: Algoritmica
Description: Algoritmica makes predictive maintenance software that predicts asset failures using machine data and deep learning.
Website: http://www.crunchbase.com/organization/algoritmica
Phone: **Email:** info@algoritmica.: Netherlands
City: Utrecht **State:** UT **PC:** **Country:** Netherlands
Year Established: **Status 2020:** Active
Industries: Analytics for:, Artificial Intelligence for:, Big Data and Analytics for:, ~ Energy and Utilities (14), ~ Energy and Utilities (14), Predictive Analytics

Company Name: Brainial | AI Experts & Solutions
Description: Brainial AI Experts and Solutions provides AI-powered solutions and services to transform enterprises into great AI companies.
Website: http://brainial.com
Phone: 31 6 44334473 **Email:** taco@brainial.com
City: Utrecht **State:** Utrecht **PC:** **Country:** Netherlands
Year Established: 2019 **Status 2020:** Active
Industries: Artificial Intelligence for:, Machine Learning for:, Natural Language Processing

Company Name: Feli
Description: Feli is a technology platform for the future of e-commerce.
Website: http://www.meetfeli.com
Phone: 31(0)652504763 **Email:** 36559@reference-encyclopedia-ai.net
City: Utrecht **State:** Utrecht **PC:** **Country:** Netherlands
Year Established: 2016 **Status 2020:** Active
Industries: Artificial Intelligence for:, E-Commerce for:, E-Commerce

Company Name: Innerdoc
Description: Deep Text Search. Made Intelligent.
Website: http://www.innerdoc.com
Phone: **Email:** hey@innerdoc.com
City: Utrecht **State:** Utrecht **PC:** **Country:** Netherlands
Year Established: 2019 **Status 2020:** Active
Industries:

Company Name: Moveshelf
Description: Motion intelligence, 3D Character Animation, Movement Science, SaaS
Website: http://moveshelf.com
Phone: **Email:** info@moveshelf.com
City: Utrecht **State:** Utrecht **PC:** **Country:** Netherlands
Year Established: 2018 **Status 2020:** Active
Industries: Analytics for:, Artificial Intelligence for:, IT Managed Services for:, Business Software as a Service Apps (SaaS Apps)

Company Name: Neurolytics
Description: SaaS Computer Vision
Website: http://www.neurolytics.ai/
Phone: 31 6 4220 3117 **Email:** info@neurolytics.ai
City: Utrecht **State:** Utrecht **PC:** **Country:** Netherlands
Year Established: 2018 **Status 2020:** Active
Industries: Computer Vision for:, Predictive Analytics for:, ~ Healthcare (20)

Company Name: Oddity.ai
Description: Video Surveillance Automation
Website: http://oddity.ai
Phone: 31650618507 **Email:** info@oddity.ai
City: Utrecht **State:** UT **PC:** **Country:** Netherlands
Year Established: **Status 2020:** Active
Industries: Artificial Intelligence for:, IT Managed Services for:, Machine Learning for:, ~ Government (19), ~ Professional Services (48)

Company Name: Qualitas Global Services LLP
Description: Qualitas Global was founded in August 2014 by Neville Patel, a creative entrepreneur, strategic thinker and technology enthusiast.
Website: http://www.qualitasglobal.com/
Phone: (91) 20 4622 6500 **Email:** info@qualitasglobal.com
City: Utrecht **State:** Utrecht **PC:** **Country:** Netherlands
Year Established: 2014 **Status 2020:** Active
Industries: Artificial Intelligence for:, IT Managed Services for:, IT Managed Services for:, Machine Learning for:, ~ Arts-Entertainment-Recreation (4)

Company Name: Simreka
Description: Simreka is a simulation software that accelerates materials driven product and manufacturing process innovation using AI
Website: http://simreka.com/
Phone: **Email:** info@magenta-technology.com
City: Utrecht **State:** Utrecht **PC:** **Country:** Netherlands
Year Established: 2017 **Status 2020:** Active
Industries: Artificial Intelligence

Company Name: Synkick
Description: Synkick is an automated music system that uses AI to create the best playlist suitable for any situation to increase hospitality
Website: http://Synkick.com
Phone: **Email:** 37498@reference-encyclopedia-ai.net
City: Utrecht **State:** Utrecht **PC:** **Country:** Netherlands
Year Established: 2014 **Status 2020:** Active
Industries: Artificial Intelligence for:, ~ Arts-Entertainment-Recreation (4)

Company Name: Withthegrid
Description: Monitoring and optimising energy grids
Website: http://withthegrid.com/
Phone: **Email:** info@withthegrid.com
City: Utrecht **State:** Utrecht **PC:** **Country:** Netherlands
Year Established: 2016 **Status 2020:** Active
Industries: Analytics for:, Artificial Intelligence for:, ~ Energy and Utilities (14)

Company Name: Worldwatch.ai | AI Powered Market Intelligence
Description: AI Powered Market, Competitor & Customer Intelligence. Become Well Informed, Opportunity Driven and Sales Centered!
Website: http://worldwatch.ai
Phone: **Email:** info@worldwatch.ai
City: Utrecht **State:** Utrecht **PC:** **Country:** Netherlands
Year Established: 2019 **Status 2020:** Closed
Industries: Artificial Intelligence for:, ~ E-Commerce (12), Machine Learning for:, Natural Language Processing for:, Predictive Analytics for:, Business Intelligence

New Zealand

Company Name: Aider International Ltd
Description: Aider is a mobile digital assistant that uses conversational AI to help small businesses be more successful data-led actionable insights.
Website: http://www.aider.ai/
Phone: 64 21 345 124 **Email:** pete@aider.ai
City: Auckland **State:** Auckland **PC:** **Country:** New Zealand
Year Established: **Status 2020:** Active
Industries: Artificial Intelligence for:, Business Intelligence for:, ~ Banking and Financial Markets-Services (7), ~ Professional Services (48)

Company Name: ako
Description: ako solves real business problems using artificial intelligence.
Website: https://www.ako.ai/
Phone: **Email:** info@ako.ai
City: Auckland **State:** Auckland **PC:** **Country:** New Zealand

Year Established: 2017 **Status 2020:** Active
Industries: Artificial Intelligence

Company Name: A: Malaysia
Description: Amy is an AI powered private maths tutor which integrates into your online learning management system.
Website: http://www.amy.app/
Phone: **Email:** hello@amy.app
City: Auckland **State:** Auckland **PC:** **Country:** New Zealand
Year Established: 2016 **Status 2020:** Active
Industries: Artificial Intelligence for:, ~ Education (13)

Company Name: Autogrow Systems Ltd
Description: IoT, Crop Science, and AI autonomy for Controlled Environment Agriculture
Website: http://autogrow.com/
Phone: **Email:** darryn.keiller@autogrow.com
City: Auckland **State:** Auckland **PC:** **Country:** New Zealand

Year Established: 2016 **Status 2020:** Active
Industries: ~ Agriculture (3), Artificial Intelligence for:, ~ Agriculture (3), IT Managed Services for:, IT Managed Services

Company Name: Cove
Description: Insurance. Simple.
Website: http://www.coveinsurance.co.: New Zealand
Phone: 0800 268 347 **Email:** info@coveinsurance.co.: New Zealand
City: Auckland **State:** Auckland **PC:** **Country:** New Zealand
Year Established: **Status 2020:** Active
Industries: Artificial Intelligence for:, ~ Banking and Financial Markets-Services (7), ~ Banking and Financial Markets-Services (7), ~ Insurance (25), ~ Insurance (25)

Company Name: Datamine Limited
Description: Datamine is a leading analytics consultancy dedicated to helping businesses implement smart, data-driven decisions.
Website: http://www.datamine.com/
Phone: 64 9 303 2300 **Email:** web@datamine.com
City: Auckland **State:** Auckland **PC:** **Country:** New Zealand
Year Established: **Status 2020:** Active
Industries:

Company Name: FaceMe
Description: FaceMe is a software company creating AI powered Digital Employees for next generation Customer Experiences.
Website: http://www.faceme.com
Phone: 415 633 8808 **Email:** info@faceme.com
City: Auckland **State:** Auckland **PC:** **Country:** New Zealand
Year Established: 2010 **Status 2020:** Active
Industries: Artificial Intelligence

Company Name: Flossie
Description: Flossie is the leading mobile app to book Tried and Tested, premium beauty services in seconds. Available on both iOS and Android.
Website: http://www.flossie.com
Phone: 0800 435 677 **Email:** info@flossie.com
City: Auckland **State:** Auckland **PC:** **Country:** New Zealand
Year Established: **Status 2020:** Active
Industries: Application Services for:, Application Services for:, Application Services for:, Artificial Intelligence for:, ~ Beauty (8), Content for:, Application Services for:, ~ Retail and Consumer Products (52), ~ Retail and Consumer Products (52)

Company Name: Formus Labs
Description: Formus Labs is a biotechnology platform that provides a cloud-platform for surgeons and engineers.
Website: http://www.formuslabs.com
Phone: 64 22 605 3001 **Email:** info@formuslabs.com
City: Auckland **State:** Auckland **PC:** **Country:** New Zealand
Year Established: 2016 **Status 2020:** Active
Industries: ~ Biotechnology (9), Machine Learning

Company Name: InsightNG
Description: InsightNG is a platform for visual learning and intelligent knowledge discovery to enhance and augment 21st century learning.
Website: http://www.insightng.com
Phone: **Email:** info@insightng.com
City: Auckland **State:** Auckland **PC:** **Country:** New Zealand
Year Established: **Status 2020:** Active
Industries: Artificial Intelligence for:, Collaboration Solutions for:, Content for:, Data Management for:, ~ Education (13), Machine Learning for:, Cyber Security

Company Name: Insite AI
Description: Cloud-based AI & ML decision engine for large CPGs & retailers. We underpin category management & merchandising actions worth 7-10 figures.
Website: http://www.insite.ai
Phone: **Email:** sales@insite.ai
City: Auckland **State:** Auckland **PC:** **Country:** New Zealand
Year Established: 2018 **Status 2020:** Active
Industries: Artificial Intelligence for:, Machine Learning

Company Name: McCarthyFinch
Description: Artificial Intelligence to improve the practice of law
Website: http://www.mccarthyfinch.com
Phone: **Email:** contact@mccarthyfinch.com
City: Auckland **State:** Auckland **PC:** **Country:** New Zealand
Year Established: **Status 2020:** Active
Industries: Artificial Intelligence

Company Name: Mooven
Description: Mooven provides products for the transport sector to help drive efficiency through the use of proactive, real-time decision tools.
Website: http://www.mooven.io
Phone: **Email:** sales@mooven.io
City: Auckland **State:** Auckland **PC:** **Country:** New Zealand
Year Established: 2017 **Status 2020:** Active
Industries: IT Managed Services for:, Application Services

Company Name: Narrative Mu: Sweden
Description: Narrative Muse is an artificial intelligence company that engages audiences and predicts demand for women-focused content.
Website: http://hello@narrativemuse.co
Phone: **Email:** hello@narrativemuse.co
City: Auckland **State:** Auckland **PC:** **Country:** New Zealand
Year Established: 2018 **Status 2020:** Active
Industries: Artificial Intelligence

Company Name: Performance Lab
Description: Performance Lab is a product and technology development company.
Website: http://www.performancelab.co.nz/
Phone: 206 499 3089 **Email:** careers@performancelab.co.: New Zealand
City: Auckland **State:** Auckland **PC:** **Country:** New Zealand
Year Established: **Status 2020:** Active
Industries: Artificial Intelligence for:, ~ Healthcare (20), ~ Healthcare (20)

Company Name: Soul Machin: Spain
Description: Soul Machines designs intelligent and emotionally responsive avatars that changes the way people interact with machines.
Website: http://soulmachines.com/
Phone: **Email:** sales@soulmachines.com
City: Auckland **State:** Auckland **PC:** **Country:** New Zealand
Year Established: 2016 **Status 2020:** Active
Industries: Artificial Intelligence for:, ~ Education (13), IT Managed Services for:, Virtual Reality (VR)

Company Name: Spark 64
Description: Spark 64 is a technology start up building Chatbots, Ai, and mobile apps.
Website: http://www.spark64.com
Phone: **Email:** enquiries@spark64.com
City: Auckland **State:** Auckland **PC:** **Country:** New Zealand
Year Established: **Status 2020:** Active
Industries: Artificial Intelligence for:, Application Services for:, ~ Professional Services (48)

Company Name: TaskPace
Description: TaskPace - AI sales management assistant for your CRM
Website: http://www.taskpace.com
Phone: **Email:** contact@taskpace.com
City: Auckland **State:** Auckland **PC:** **Country:** New Zealand
Year Established: **Status 2020:** Active
Industries: Artificial Intelligence for:, ~ Media-Communications (41), Automation

Company Name: The Clinician
Description: The Clinician is changing the way healthcare is measured and delivered.
Website: http://www.theclinician.com
Phone: 6493910034 **Email:** info@theclinician.com
City: Auckland **State:** Auckland **PC:** **Country:** New Zealand
Year Established: **Status 2020:** Active
Industries: Artificial Intelligence for:, ~ Healthcare (20), Data Management for:, Data Management for:, ~ Healthcare (20), ~ Healthcare (20), ~ Healthcare (20), ~ Healthcare (20)

Company Name: Vital
Description: Modern cloud-based Emergency Department SaaS
Website: http://vitaler.com
Phone: (800) 886-9125 **Email:** info@vitaler.com
City: Auckland **State:** Auckland **PC:** **Country:** New Zealand
Year Established: 2017 **Status 2020:** Active
Industries:

Company Name: Komodo Monitr
Description: Athlete monitoring for every sporting level
Website: http://www.komodomonitr.com
Phone: **Email:** contact@komodomonitr.com
City: Christchurch **State:** Canterbury **PC:** **Country:** New Zealand
Year Established: 2018 **Status 2020:** Active
Industries: Analytics for:, Data Management for:, Predictive Analytics for:, ~ Arts-Entertainment-Recreation (4)

Company Name: ContentForest
Description: Data-Science and AI powered marketing insights platform
Website: http://www.contentforest.com
Phone: **Email:** contact@contentforest.com
City: Richmond **State:** Canterbury **PC:** **Country:** New Zealand
Year Established: 2012 **Status 2020:** Active
Industries: Analytics for:, Artificial Intelligence for:, Enterprise Application Services

Company Name: BitBank.: New Zealand
Description: Live Crypto Market Predictions With Deep Learning
Website: http://bitbank.: New Zealand
Phone: **Email:** leepenkman@bitbank.: New Zealand
City: Wellington **State:** Wellington **PC:** **Country:** New Zealand
Year Established: **Status 2020:** Active
Industries: Artificial Intelligence for:, ~ Education (13), Machine Learning for:, ~ Professional Services (48)

Company Name: Facenition
Description: Retail analytics powered by face recognition and AI
Website: http://www.facenition.com
Phone: **Email:** info@facenition.com
City: Wellington **State:** Wellington **PC:** **Country:** New Zealand
Year Established: 2019 **Status 2020:** Active
Industries: Analytics for:, Artificial Intelligence for:, Computer Vision for:, Facial Recognition for:, Machine Learning for:, Predictive Analytics

Company Name: Intela AI
Description: Intela AI build products and platforms for machine learning, machine vision, NLP, real time analytics and speech.
Website: http://www.intela.ai
Phone: **Email:** 36783@reference-encyclopedia-ai.net
City: Wellington **State:** Wellington **PC:** **Country:** New Zealand
Year Established: 2016 **Status 2020:** Active
Industries: Artificial Intelligence for:, Machine Learning for:, Compute

Company Name: JRNY
Description: We help insurance providers protect people better.
Website: http://www.jrny.ai
Phone: **Email:** letschat@jrny.ai
City: Wellington **State:** Wellington **PC:** **Country:** New Zealand
Year Established: 2016 **Status 2020:** Active
Industries: Enterprise Application Services for:, ~ E-Commerce (12), Natural Language Processing for:, Automation

Company Name: Montoux
Description: Montoux transforms pricing for life insurers.
Website: http://montoux.com
Phone: 1 (646) 204 1932 **Email:** hello@montoux.com
City: Wellington **State:** Wellington **PC:** **Country:** New Zealand
Year Established: 2012 **Status 2020:** Active
Industries: ~ Insurance (25), Predictive Analytics

Company Name: Prime Tenancy
Description: Intelligent solution for the property management role of real estate ownership.
Website: http://primetenancy.com/
Phone: **Email:** info@primetenancy.com
City: Wellington **State:** Wellington **PC:** **Country:** New Zealand
Year Established: **Status 2020:** Active
Industries: Artificial Intelligence for:, ~ Banking and Financial Markets-Services (7), Machine Learning for:, Mobile for:, Application Services for:, Predictive Analytics for:, ~ Real Estate (49), ~ Real Estate (49)

Company Name: Whyd
Description: AI powered insights platform where consumers can find out what is good or bad about a product.
Website: http://whydis.com
Phone: **Email:** hello@whydis.com
City: Wellington **State:** Wellington **PC:** **Country:** New Zealand
Year Established: 2018 **Status 2020:** Active
Industries: Artificial Intelligence for:, Business Intelligence for:, Learning and Marketing Communications Services (MarComm) for:, E-Commerce

Nigeria

Company Name: MyEvendor.ng
Description: Find and book vendors for your events and entertainment needs.
Website: http://www.myevendor.ng
Phone: **Email:** hello@myevendor.ng
City: Uyo **State:** AK **PC:** **Country: Nigeria**
Year Established: **Status 2020:** Active
Industries:

Company Name: Croft Ecosystems
Description: Solving Africa's problems with AI, IOT, and robotics.
Website: http://croftecosystems.com
Phone: 234 816 395 1800 **Email:** info@croftecosystems.com
City: Warri **State:** DE **PC:** **Country: Nigeria**
Year Established: 2017 **Status 2020:** Active
Industries: Artificial Intelligence for:, IT Infrastructure

Company Name: Numbe: Serbia
Description: Security, Artificial Intelligence, Machine Learning, Data Science, Surveillance
Website: http://numbers.xigma.org
Phone: 9051215259 **Email:** contact@numbers.xigma.org
City: Benin City **State:** ED **PC:** **Country: Nigeria**
Year Established: **Status 2020:** Active
Industries: Artificial Intelligence for:, Big Data and Analytics for:, Machine Learning for:, Security

Company Name: Xigma Inc
Description: Xigma is a high technological research company with focus areas in | Space Science | Nanotechnology | Robotics & AI | for Commercialisation.
Website: http://www.xigma.org
Phone: 234 7066614627 **Email:** xigmaofficial@gmail.com
City: Benin City **State:** ED **PC:** **Country: Nigeria**
Year Established: 2015 **Status 2020:** Active
Industries: Artificial Intelligence for:, IT Managed Services for:, Robotics for:, ~ Aerospace and Defense (2)

Company Name: banta
Description: Banta is an AI content creator from anonymous community collaborato: Serbia
Website: http://getbanta.com
Phone: **Email:** info@getbanta.com
City: Abuja **State:** Federal Capital Territory **PC:** **Country: Nigeria**
Year Established: 2017 **Status 2020:** Active
Industries:

Company Name: KiaKia
Description: AI powered online market place for credit scoring and matching lenders with borrowers in real-time
Website: http://www.kiakia.co
Phone: (803)810-0159 **Email:** olajide@kiakia.co
City: Abuja **State:** Federal Capital Territory **PC:** **Country: Nigeria**
Year Established: 2015 **Status 2020:** Active
Industries: Artificial Intelligence for:, ~ Banking and Financial Markets-Services (7), ~ Banking and Financial Markets-Services (7), ~ Banking and Financial Markets-Services (7), Machine Learning for:, Predictive Analytics

Company Name: Provider
Description: AI-powered conversational food and condiments chatbot
Website: http://provider.com.ng/
Phone: **Email:** help@provider.com.ng
City: Abuja **State:** Federal Capital Territory **PC:** **Country: Nigeria**
Year Established: **Status 2020:** Active
Industries: Artificial Intelligence for:, ~ Social Media (54), ~ Transportation and Logistics (57), ~ Telecommunications (56), Natural Language Processing for:, ~ Retail and Consumer Products (52)

Company Name: Sendroid AI
Description: Sendroid helps businesses open chat conversations from Facebook or Instagram ad clicks.
Website: http://sendroid.co/
Phone: 8064117751 **Email:** hello@sendroid.co
City: Abuja **State:** Federal Capital Territory **PC:** **Country: Nigeria**
Year Established: **Status 2020:** Active
Industries: ~ Media-Communications (41), Artificial Intelligence for:, Digital Marketing for:, E-Commerce

Company Name: SpearGate Consulting LTD
Description: Advanced Technology Consulting and Development
Website: http://www.speargateltd.com
Phone: 7088289121 **Email:** contact@speargateltd.com
City: Abuja **State:** Federal Capital Territory **PC:** **Country: Nigeria**
Year Established: 2016 **Status 2020:** Active
Industries: Analytics for:, Artificial Intelligence

Company Name: Advancer™
Description: Nigerias' trendy salary advance platform.We are an alternative lender offering unsecured loans to millennials and blue/white collar workers;
Website: http://www.theadvancer.online
Phone: (234)803-30144 **Email:** info@theadvancer.online
City: Lagos **State:** LA **PC:** **Country: Nigeria**
Year Established: 2016 **Status 2020:** Active
Industries: ~ Banking and Financial Markets-Services (7), ~ Banking and Financial Markets-Services (7), Predictive Analytics

Company Name: AI Commons Global Limited
Description: We develop technologies to empower companies and developers to easily adopt and deploy state-of-the-art Artificial Intelligence.
Website: http://www.aicommons.science
Phone: 234 7038062925 **Email:** info@aicommons.science
City: Lagos **State:** LA **PC:** **Country: Nigeria**
Year Established: **Status 2020:** Active
Industries: Artificial Intelligence for:, Cloud for:, Computer Vision for:, Machine Learning

Company Name: Aitech: Morocco
Description: Software Development, Machine Learning, Artificial Intelligence, Consultancy
Website: https://aitechma.com/
Phone: 234-814-998-5876 **Email:** info@aitechma.com
City: Lagos **State:** LA **PC:** **Country: Nigeria**
Year Established: 2017 **Status 2020:** Active
Industries: Web for:, Application Services

Company Name: Chekk: Italy
Description: Chekkit is an ethereum blockchain powered anti-counterfeiting solution for food and drug supply chain tracking.
Website: http://chekkitapp.com/
Phone: (705) 604-9656 **Email:** dare@chekkitapp.com
City: Lagos **State:** LA **PC:** **Country: Nigeria**
Year Established: 2018 **Status 2020:** Active
Industries: Artificial Intelligence for:, Blockchain for:, Application Program Interfaces (APIs) for:, ~ Healthcare (20), Web for:, ~ Telecommunications (56)

Company Name: Dochase Ads
Description: Dochase connects global businesses to customers in Africa using data analytics, robust targeting on mobile, web , social media and telecom.
Website: http://www.dochase.com
Phone: 234 803-441-0381 **Email:** info@dochase.com
City: Lagos **State:** LA **PC:** **Country: Nigeria**
Year Established: 2015 **Status 2020:** Active
Industries: Analytics for:, Artificial Intelligence for:, Artificial Intelligence for:, Digital Marketing for:, ~ Media-Communications (41), ~ Media-Communications (41), ~ Social Assistance-Non-Profits (53)

Company Name: Entraded
Description: An AI Powered Algorithmic Crypto Trading Platform
Website: http://www.entraded.com
Phone: **Email:** hello@entraded.com
City: Lagos **State:** LA **PC:** **Country: Nigeria**
Year Established: 2019 **Status 2020:** Active
Industries: Artificial Intelligence for:, ~ Banking and Financial Markets-Services (7), ~ Banking and Financial Markets-Services (7), ~ Banking and Financial Markets-Services (7), Web for:, Machine Learning for:, Predictive Analytics for:, Finance and Accounting for:, Financ

Company Name: Infusion Lawye: Serbia
Description: a virtual intellectual property (IP) & information technology (IT) law firm for the knowledge economy and the digital age.
Website: http://infusionlawyers.com
Phone: 234816 995 1792 **Email:** info@infusionlawyers.com
City: Lagos **State:** LA **PC:** **Country: Nigeria**
Year Established: 2017 **Status 2020:** Active
Industries: ~ Media-Communications (41)

Company Name: Jock Sport Ltd
Description: Jock sport Ltd is a smart watch company that provides smart watches that's helps you automate your healthy status.
Website: http://jocksports.ca
Phone: **Email:** 36830@reference-encyclopedia-ai.net
City: Lagos **State:** LA **PC:** **Country: Nigeria**
Year Established: 2017 **Status 2020:** Active
Industries: Application Services for:, ~ Arts-Entertainment-Recreation (4), ~ Healthcare (20)

Company Name: Kudi
Description: Kudi is a financial service provider that focuses on providing access to electronic banking and financial services.
Website: http://kudi.ai/
Phone: **Email:** hello@kudi.ai
City: Lagos **State:** LA **PC:** **Country: Nigeria**
Year Established: 2016 **Status 2020:** Active
Industries: Artificial Intelligence for:, ~ Banking and Financial Markets-Services (7), ~ Banking and Financial Markets-Services (7), ~ Banking and Financial Markets-Services (7), ~ Banking and Financial Markets-Services (7)

Company Name: Kynect Heal:Thailand
Description: Using deep learning to solve the world's biggest health problems and make healthcare affordable and better for all
Website:
Phone: **Email:** 4952@reference-encyclopedia-ai.net
City: Lagos **State:** LA **PC:** **Country: Nigeria**
Year Established: **Status 2020:** Active
Industries:

Company Name: Lush Plans
Description: Event management app that for managing a wedding with the click of a button. Budget Event info = Wedding package
Website: http://lushplans.com
Phone: (647) 952-0729 **Email:** info@lushplans.com
City: Lagos **State:** LA **PC:** **Country: Nigeria**
Year Established: 2018 **Status 2020:** Active
Industries: Big Data and Analytics for:, ~ Event Management (15), ~ Event Management (15), Machine Learning for:, Application Services for:, ~ Event Management (15)

Company Name: NEXTdata
Description: NEXTdata creates artificial life from data. Our algorithms are one of their kind and able to learn for themselves.
Website: http://www.nextdata.xyz
Phone: **Email:** nextdata@edaqs.com
City: Lagos **State:** LA **PC:** **Country: Nigeria**
Year Established: 2014 **Status 2020:** Active
Industries: Artificial Intelligence

Company Name: Sela
Description: The Sela platform fosters transparency, measurement, and community for development projects.
Website: http://sela-labs.co/
Phone: **Email:** info@sela-labs.co
City: Lagos **State:** LA **PC:** **Country: Nigeria**
Year Established: 2017 **Status 2020:** Active
Industries: Artificial Intelligence for:, Blockchain for:, Computer Vision

Company Name: Skiibo
Description: Skiibo - chat, date and meet new people in Africa and around the world
Website: http://skiibo.com
Phone: **Email:** info@skiibo.com
City: Lagos **State:** LA **PC:** **Country: Nigeria**
Year Established: 2018 **Status 2020:** Active
Industries: Artificial Intelligence for:, Business Process and Operations for:, ~ Social Assistance-Non-Profits (53)

Company Name: SNAPRA
Description: SNAPRA is the visual search technology company of Africa using computer vision to make online shopping experience more user friendly.
Website: http://www.snapra.net/
Phone: 2024927324 **Email:** info@snapra.net
City: Lagos **State:** LA **PC:** **Country: Nigeria**
Year Established: 2017 **Status 2020:** Active
Industries: Artificial Intelligence for:, E-Commerce for:, Computer Vision

Company Name: Tringoo
Description: Web App
Website: http://tringoo.com
Phone: **Email:** info@tringoo.com
City: Lagos **State:** LA **PC:** **Country: Nigeria**
Year Established: **Status 2020:** Active
Industries: Artificial Intelligence for:, Digital Media for:, ~ Arts-Entertainment-Recreation (4), ~ Media-Communications (41), ~ Social Media (54), ~ Media-Communications (41)

Company Name: Versus Africa
Description: Versus combines online and offline consumer data to give brands actionable and competitive insight for the African market.
Website: http://www.versus.africa/
Phone: **Email:** info@versus.africa
City: Lagos **State:** LA **PC:** **Country: Nigeria**
Year Established: 2014 **Status 2020:** Active
Industries: Learning and Marketing Communications Services (MarComm) for:, Predictive Analytics

Company Name: Tata
Description: An Artificial Intelligent assistant for university students.
Website: http://tatafo.tech4herafrica.com
Phone: **Email:** tatafo@tech4herafrica.com
City: Ogudu **State:** LA **PC:** **Country: Nigeria**
Year Established: 2018 **Status 2020:** Active
Industries: Artificial Intelligence for:, ~ Education (13)

Company Name: Toursom
Description: Toursom is an online platform that uses machine learning to book personalised vacation packages to Africa.
Website: http://www.toursom.com/
Phone: **Email:** info@toursom.com
City: Yaba **State:** LA **PC:** **Country: Nigeria**
Year Established: 2018 **Status 2020:** Active
Industries: Artificial Intelligence for:, ~ Arts-Entertainment-Recreation (4), ~ Travel and Transportation (58)

Company Name: Honey Flow Africa
Description: Honey Flow Africa optimizes beekeeping operations by digitizing and bringing the power of IoT and AI
Website:
http://www.honeyflowafrica.cominfo@honeyflowafrica.com
Phone: **Email:** info@honeyflowafrica.com
City: Port Harcourt **State:** RV **PC:** **Country: Nigeria**
Year Established: 2018 **Status 2020:** Active
Industries: ~ Agriculture (3), ~ Agriculture (3), Artificial Intelligence for:, ~ Agriculture (3), ~ Food and Beverage (17), ~ Food and Beverage (17)

Company Name: Touchabl Pictur: Spain
Description: 'Shazam' for fashion discovery. Making buying & selling of fashion stress-free in Africa; just touch or snap it to buy instantly.
Website: http://about.touchabl.com
Phone: **Email:** teamtouchabl@gmail.com
City: Port Harcourt **State:** RV **PC:** **Country: Nigeria**
Year Established: 2017 **Status 2020:** Active
Industries: Artificial Intelligence for:, Machine Learning for:, ~ Social Assistance-Non-Profits (53)

Norway

Company Name: Anzyz Technologi
Description: Anzyz is an Artificial Intelligence company, which uniquely integrates supervised, unsupervised and manual rule based learning.
Website: http://www.anzyz.com/
Phone: 47) 982 28 121 **Email:** contact@anzyz.com
City: Grimstad **State:** Agder **PC:** **Country:** Norway
Year Established: 2014 **Status 2020:** Active
Industries: Artificial Intelligence for:, ~ Education (13), IT Managed Services for:, Machine Learning

Company Name: VOCA AS
Description: VOCA AS is an innovative robot vision and artificial intelligence technology platform has been developed for offshore industry applications.
Website: http://voca.no/
Phone: 47 38 19 83 44 **Email:** post@voca.
City: Kristiansand **State:** Agder **PC:** **Country:** Norway
Year Established: **Status 2020:** Active
Industries: Artificial Intelligence for:, Web for:, Machine Learning for:, Robotics

Company Name: Status
Description: Status offers communication solutions that enable individuals to keep track of where their friends are and what they are doing.
Website: http://statushq.com
Phone: **Email:** support@statushq.com
City: Vestol **State:** Agder **PC:** **Country:** Norway
Year Established: **Status 2020:** Active
Industries:

Company Name: CloudXtract
Description: SaaS, BigData, AI, Artificiel Intelligence, B2B, SMB, Small Business
Website: http://www.cloudxtract.com
Phone: (479) 262-9080 **Email:** rune.elvrum@cloudxtract.com
City: Gjovik **State:** Innlandet **PC:** **Country:** Norway
Year Established: 2016 **Status 2020:** Active
Industries: Artificial Intelligence

Company Name: Abelee
Description: Abelee provides investment services based on adaptive data-driven models and strategies.
Website: https://www.abelee.com/
Phone: **Email:** 35934@reference-encyclopedia-ai.net
City: Oslo **State:** Oslo **PC:** **Country:** Norway
Year Established: 2017 **Status 2020:** Active
Industries: Artificial Intelligence for:, ~ Banking and Financial Markets-Services (7), IT Managed Services for:, Machine Learning

Company Name: AIA Science
Description: AIA Science offers software for data analysis and artificial intelligence solutions.
Website: http://www.aiascience.com/
Phone: **Email:** contact@aiascience.com
City: Oslo **State:** Oslo **PC:** **Country:** Norway
Year Established: 2016 **Status 2020:** Active
Industries: Artificial Intelligence for:, IT Managed Services

Company Name: AIMS Innovation
Description: Application Performance Monitoring
Website: http://www.aims.ai
Phone: 47 48 22 34 24 **Email:** ivar.sagemo@aims.ai
City: Oslo **State:** Oslo **PC:** **Country:** Norway
Year Established: **Status 2020:** Active
Industries: Analytics for:, Artificial Intelligence for:, Enterprise Application Services for:, Machine Learning

Company Name: Ardoq
Description: Ardoq is an Enterprise Intelligence Graph for Compliance, Governance, and Digital Transformation.
Website: http://ardoq.com/
Phone: 4745812134 **Email:** contact@ardoq.com
City: Oslo **State:** Oslo **PC:** **Country:** Norway
Year Established: **Status 2020:** Active
Industries: Artificial Intelligence for:, Enterprise Application Services for:, ~ Professional Services (48)

Company **Name:** ayfie Group
Description: ayfie Group offers search and text analytics solutions that bring structure to unstructured data.
Website: http://www.ayfie.com
Phone: 1 917 777-0733 **Email:** marketing@ayfie.com
City: Oslo **State:** Oslo **PC:** **Country:** Norway
Year Established: 2016 **Status 2020:** Active
Industries: Analytics for:, Artificial Intelligence for:, Big Data and Analytics for:, Application Program Interfaces (APIs) for:, Machine Learning for:, Natural Language Processing for:, ~ Banking and Financial Markets-Services (7), Web for:, Web for:, Content for:, Data Mana

Company Name: BuiltOn
Description: BuiltOn is a SaaS Backend with integrated ML tools for web and app developers building smart digital products and experiences.
Website: http://www.builton.dev/
Phone: 0047 948 74 377 **Email:** hello@builton.dev
City: Oslo **State:** Oslo **PC:** **Country:** Norway
Year Established: 2016 **Status 2020:** Active
Industries: E-Commerce for:, Enterprise Application Services for:, IT Managed Services for:, Machine Learning for:, Business Software as a Service Apps (SaaS Apps)

Company Name: Connected.ART
Description: Information technology for the art industry
Website: http://www.connected.art
Phone: **Email:** hello@connected.art
City: Oslo **State:** Oslo **PC:** **Country:** Norway
Year Established: **Status 2020:** Active
Industries: ~ Arts-Entertainment-Recreation (4), Artificial Intelligence for:, ~ Arts-Entertainment-Recreation (4), IT Managed Services for:, ~ Arts-Entertainment-Recreation (4)

Company Name: Credit Morgan
Description: Credit Morgan is an online SME loan and investing platform who connects investors with creditworthy British and Norwegian businesses.
Website: http://creditmorgan.com
Phone: **Email:** info@creditmorgan.com
City: Oslo **State:** Oslo **PC:** **Country:** Norway
Year Established: **Status 2020:** Active
Industries: Artificial Intelligence for:, ~ Banking and Financial Markets-Services (7), Network

Company Name: Epigram AI
Description: Epigram is one of agencies in machine learning.
Website: http://epigram.ai/
Phone: 47 906 86 502 **Email:** hello@epigram.ai
City: Oslo **State:** Oslo **PC:** **Country:** Norway
Year Established: 2017 **Status 2020:** Active
Industries: Artificial Intelligence for:, Machine Learning

Company Name: Exabel
Description: Artificial intelligence for human investo: Serbia
Website: http://www.exabel.com/
Phone: 4748196691 **Email:** contact@exabel.com
City: Oslo **State:** Oslo **PC:** **Country:** Norway
Year Established: **Status 2020:** Active
Industries: Analytics for:, Artificial Intelligence for:, Cloud for:, ~ Banking and Financial Markets-Services (7), ~ Banking and Financial Markets-Services (7), Machine Learning

Company Name: Globus.ai
Description: Globus.ai is a privately held company that is specializes in artificial intelligence, machine learning including reinforcement learning.
Website: http://www.globus.ai/
Phone: 47 454 75 921 **Email:** contact@globus.ai
City: Oslo **State:** Oslo **PC:** **Country:** Norway
Year Established: 2017 **Status 2020:** Active
Industries: Artificial Intelligence for:, Machine Learning

Company Name: Greenbird Integration Technology
Description: Hybrid cloud platform for big data integrations empowering Smart Grid, Smart City and the industrial Internet-of-Things.
Website: www.greenbird.com
Phone: **Email:** info@greenbird.com
City: Oslo **State:** Oslo **PC:** **Country:** Norway
Year Established: **Status 2020:** Active
Industries: Analytics for:, Artificial Intelligence for:, Big Data and Analytics for:, Data Management for:, ~ Professional Services (48)

Company Name: GreyOcean Invest
Description: GreyOcean is a digital ethical investment platform.
Website: http://www.greyocean.co.uk
Phone: **Email:** info@greyocean.co.uk
City: Oslo **State:** Oslo **PC:** **Country:** Norway
Year Established: **Status 2020:** Active
Industries:

Company Name: Huddly
Description: Huddly was created to elevate communication with compelling and intelligent vision products for everybody.
Website: http://www.huddly.com
Phone: **Email:** contact@huddly.com
City: Oslo **State:** Oslo **PC:** **Country:** Norway
Year Established: **Status 2020:** Active
Industries: Artificial Intelligence for:, Collaboration Solutions for:, Computer Vision for:, ~ Manufacturing-Electronic (30), Machine Learning for:, ~ Manufacturing-Miscellaneous (34), ~ Media-Communications (41)

Company Name: Intelecy
Description: Intelecy is a fast-growing Norwegian technology company.
Website: http://www.intelecy.com
Phone: **Email:** contact@intelecy.com
City: Oslo **State:** Oslo **PC:** **Country:** Norway
Year Established: 2016 **Status 2020:** Active
Industries: Industrial Solutions for:, IT Managed Services for:, Machine Learning

Company Name: Iris.ai
Description: Iris is an AI Science Assistant, helping R&D double productivity when seeking out new opportunities in published research.
Website: http://iris.ai
Phone: **Email:** anita@iris.ai
City: Oslo **State:** Oslo **PC:** **Country:** Norway
Year Established: **Status 2020:** Active
Industries: Artificial Intelligence for:, ~ Healthcare (20), ~ Education (13), ~ Administrative and Support Services (1), Business Intelligence for:, Computer Vision

Company Name: Luca Labs
Description: Artificial intelligence for accounting.
Website: http://www.lucalabs.com
Phone: 47 904 79 559 **Email:** post@lucalabs.com
City: Oslo **State:** Oslo **PC:** **Country:** Norway
Year Established: 2016 **Status 2020:** Active
Industries: Artificial Intelligence

Company Name: Lucidtech
Description: Lucidtech is a Norwegian company that develops machine learning technology to automate business processes.
Website: http://lucidtech.io/
Phone: **Email:** hello@lucidtech.ai
City: Oslo **State:** Oslo **PC:** **Country:** Norway
Year Established: 2016 **Status 2020:** Active
Industries: Analytics for:, Artificial Intelligence for:, IT Managed Services for:, Machine Learning for:, Robotics

Company Name: LumiNode AI
Description: The Next Generation Marketing Automation Tool - Optimize and Automate Your Campaign Management with Artificial Intelligence
Website: http://www.luminode.ai
Phone: **Email:** info@luminode.ai
City: Oslo **State:** Oslo **PC:** **Country:** Norway
Year Established: **Status 2020:** Active
Industries: Analytics for:, Artificial Intelligence for:, ~ Retail and Consumer Products (52), ~ Retail and Consumer Products (52)

Company Name: Memory
Description: Memory is a Norwegian startup that builds tools for the future of work.
Website: http://memory.ai/
Phone: **Email:** hello@memory.ai
City: Oslo **State:** Oslo **PC:** **Country:** Norway
Year Established: 2013 **Status 2020:** Active
Industries: Artificial Intelligence for:, Machine Learning

Company Name: Movi
Description: Movi is the worlds most powerful Mobile Video SDK
Website: http://movi.ai
Phone: **Email:** post@movi.ai
City: Oslo **State:** Oslo **PC:** **Country:** Norway
Year Established: **Status 2020:** Active
Industries: Artificial Intelligence for:, Big Data and Analytics for:, Mobile for:, ~ Media-Communications (41), ~ Media-Communications (41)

Company Name: Narrafy
Description: Path to AI.
Website: http://www.narrafy.io
Phone: **Email:** contact@narrafy.io
City: Oslo **State:** Oslo **PC:** **Country:** Norway
Year Established: 2017 **Status 2020:** Active
Industries: Artificial Intelligence for:, Machine Learning

Company Name: Oivi
Description: Oivi develops an easy and affordable AI-camera and platform that will identifies diabetic eye-disease.
Website: http://www.oivi.co/
Phone: 47 9974 7277 **Email:** contact@oivi.co
City: Oslo **State:** Oslo **PC:** **Country:** Norway
Year Established: 2017 **Status 2020:** Active
Industries: Artificial Intelligence for:, ~ Healthcare (20)

Company Name: Omnicus
Description: Omnichannel cloud-based Contact Center & Ticketing System
Website: http://omnicus.com
Phone: 4797059682 **Email:** ejonassen@omnicus.com
City: Oslo **State:** Oslo **PC:** **Country:** Norway
Year Established: 2016 **Status 2020:** Active
Industries: Artificial Intelligence for:, ~ Customer Relationship Management (11), ~ Customer Relationship Management (11),

Enterprise Application Services for:, Machine Learning for:, Business Software as a Service Apps (SaaS Apps)

Company Name: Semine
Description: Semine is one of the fastest growing startups in the Nordic area. First mover in full automation in accounting using AI (Hyper automation).
Website: http://www.semine.com/
Phone: **Email:** 37361@reference-encyclopedia-ai.net
City: Oslo **State:** Oslo **PC:** **Country:** Norway
Year Established: 2016 **Status 2020:** Active
Industries: Finance and Accounting for:, Artificial Intelligence for:, IT Managed Services for:, Robotics

Company Name: Simplifai
Description: Simplifai is bringing order to the chaos of modern traffic systems, using artificial intelligence.
Website: http://www.simplifai.ai/
Phone: (47) 415 03 263 **Email:** hello@simplifai.ai
City: Oslo **State:** Oslo **PC:** **Country:** Norway
Year Established: 2017 **Status 2020:** Active
Industries: Artificial Intelligence for:, Machine Learning

Company Name: Solution Seeker
Description: Solution Seeker are developing ProductionCompass AI, the world's first artificial intelligence for upstream oil & gas production.
Website: http://www.solutionseeker.no/
Phone: **Email:** contact@solutionseeker.: Norway
City: Oslo **State:** Oslo **PC:** **Country:** Norway
Year Established: 2013 **Status 2020:** Active
Industries:

Company Name: Spacemaker AI
Description: Spacemaker AI develops a game changing AI technology that discovers the smartest ways to maximize the value of any building site.
Website: http://spacemaker.ai/
Phone: **Email:** hello@spacemaker.ai
City: Oslo **State:** Oslo **PC:** **Country:** Norway
Year Established: 2016 **Status 2020:** Active
Industries: Artificial Intelligence for:, IT Managed Services for:, IT Managed Services

Company Name: Unloc AI
Description: Unloc AI provides more freedom with open doors via sharing digital keys.
Website: http://unloc.app
Phone: **Email:** info@unloc.app
City: Oslo **State:** Oslo **PC:** **Country:** Norway
Year Established: 2017 **Status 2020:** Active
Industries: Artificial Intelligence

Company Name: Vilect AI
Description: AI recruitment assistant that helps non-hr managers run high quality processes and hire the best candidates in record time
Website: http://www.vilect.ai
Phone: **Email:** hallo@vilect.com
City: Oslo **State:** Oslo **PC:** **Country:** Norway
Year Established: **Status 2020:** Active
Industries: Artificial Intelligence for:, ~ Human Resources (24), ~ Human Resources (24)

Company Name: Viva Labs
Description: Artificial Intelligence for Hom: Spain
Website: http://meetviva.com
Phone: 4797799546 **Email:** henrik@meetviva.com
City: Oslo **State:** Oslo **PC:** **Country:** Norway
Year Established: **Status 2020:** Active
Industries: Artificial Intelligence for:, ~ Energy and Utilities (14)

Company Name: Xigrid
Description: ML technology for HVAC control
Website:
Phone: 4748046371 **Email:** info@xigrid.com
City: Oslo **State:** Oslo **PC:** **Country:** Norway
Year Established: 2018 **Status 2020:** Active
Industries: Machine Learning for:, ~ Energy and Utilities (14)

Company **Name:** Boost AI
Description: Boost AI has created the James platform - The World'S Most Robust Virtual Agent Platform.
Website: http://boost.ai/
Phone: **Email:** contact@boost.ai
City: Sandnes **State:** Rogaland **PC:** **Country:** Norway
Year Established: **Status 2020:** Active
Industries: Artificial Intelligence for:, IT Managed Services for:, Machine Learning

Company Name: Earth Science Analytics
Description: Earth Science Analytics is an Artificial Intelligence petroleum geoscience software provider
Website: http://earthanalytics.ai/
Phone: **Email:** contact@earthanalytics.: Norway
City: Stavanger **State:** Rogaland **PC:** **Country:** Norway
Year Established: 2016 **Status 2020:** Active
Industries: Artificial Intelligence for:, ~ Energy and Utilities (14)

Company Name: EIR of Norway
Description: EIR of Norway is a digital seafood company. Using premium arctic seafood delicacies, that are sustainably sourced and digitally certified.
Website: http://www.eirofnorway.com
Phone: **Email:** post@eirofnorway.com
City: Stavanger **State:** Rogaland **PC:** **Country:** Norway
Year Established: **Status 2020:** Active
Industries: Artificial Intelligence for:, Blockchain for:, ~ Food and Beverage (17)

Company Name: Foodback
Description: Food Tech, Feedback, Customer Engagement, SaaS, Data Driven, Cloud, AI
Website: http://www.foodback.com
Phone: 47 909 30 177 **Email:** hello@foodback.com
City: Stavanger **State:** Rogaland **PC:** **Country:** Norway
Year Established: 2013 **Status 2020:** Active
Industries: Artificial Intelligence for:, Data Management for:, ~ Food and Beverage (17), Business Software as a Service Apps (SaaS Apps)

Company Name: Memkite
Description: On-device Image Recognition Search for iOS
Website: http://memkite.com
Phone: **Email:** info@memkite.com
City: Trondheim **State:** Trondelag **PC:** **Country:** Norway
Year Established: **Status 2020:** Active
Industries: Artificial Intelligence for:, Image Recognition for:, Mobile for:, Cyber Security

Company Name: Capeesh
Description: Capeesh is language learning based on machine intelligence. The software teaches you industry terminology and pronunciation in a fun way.
Website: http://www.capeesh.com/
Phone: 47 924 09 439 **Email:** contact@capeesh.com
City: Trondheim **State:** Trøndelag **PC:** **Country:** Norway
Year Established: 2017 **Status 2020:** Active
Industries: ~ Education (13), Natural Language Processing

Company Name: RagnaRock Geo
Description: RagnaRock Geo is an artificial intelligent software intended to interpret seismic data company.
Website: http://www.ragnarockgeo.com/
Phone: **Email:** rrg@ragnarockgeo.com
City: Trondheim **State:** Trøndelag **PC:** **Country:** Norway

Year Established: 2018 **Status 2020:** Active
Industries: Analytics for:, Artificial Intelligence for:, Data Management

Company Name: Showtag
Description: Showtag is aiming to connect brand and audiences through the seamless integration of product placement for streaming media.
Website: http://showtagenabled.com/
Phone: 47 4540 2552 **Email:** ewald.bos@showtag.tv
City: Trondheim **State:** Trøndelag **PC:** **Country:** Norway
Year Established: 2016 **Status 2020:** Active
Industries: Artificial Intelligence for:, Machine Learning

Company Name: UBIQ Aerospace
Description: UBIQ Aerospace is an autonomy enabler devoted to building solutions that expand aircraft capabilities.
Website: http://www.ubiqaerospace.com/
Phone: **Email:** contact@ubiqaerospace.com
City: Trondheim **State:** Trøndelag **PC:** **Country:** Norway
Year Established: 2017 **Status 2020:** Active
Industries:

Company Name: Way Trafikkskole
Description: Way is digitizing the world of traffic training, using virtual environments and intelligent assessments to make an AI based traffic teacher.
Website: http://way.no/
Phone: 47 98831706 **Email:** patrick@way.: Norway
City: Trondheim **State:** Trøndelag **PC:** **Country:** Norway
Year Established: 2015 **Status 2020:** Active
Industries: Artificial Intelligence for:, ~ Automotive (5), ~ Education (13)

Company Name: Manolin
Description: Manolin empowers the aquaculture industry to improve fish, farm, and ocean health through advanced data analytics and risk forecasting.
Website: http://manolinaqua.com/
Phone: **Email:** tony@manolinaqua.com
City: Bergen **State:** Vestland **PC:** **Country:** Norway
Year Established: 2018 **Status 2020:** Active
Industries: Analytics for:, ~ Agriculture (3), Big Data and Analytics for:, Predictive Analytics

Company Name: Quantfolio
Description: Quantfolio has developed a machine learning software for selecting the best savings products.
Website: http://www.quantfol.io/
Phone: **Email:** 37241@reference-encyclopedia-ai.net
City: Bergen **State:** Vestland **PC:** **Country:** Norway
Year Established: 2015 **Status 2020:** Active
Industries: ~ Banking and Financial Markets-Services (7), Machine Learning

Company Name: Sensee AS
Description: Internet of Things as a Service for small and medium sized businesses - unlocking the IoT value currently only available to large companies.
Website: http://www.sensee.io
Phone: 47 917 54 540 **Email:** danielle.glenn@sensee.io
City: Asker **State:** Viken **PC:** **Country:** Norway
Year Established: **Status 2020:** Active
Industries: Artificial Intelligence for:, Big Data and Analytics for:, Cloud for:, Application Services for:, Enterprise Application Services

Company Name: Halodi Robotics
Description: Halodi Robotics is the start of the home robot revolution.
Website: http://halodi.com
Phone: 47 902 90 427 **Email:** pal@halodi.: Norway
City: Dilling **State:** Viken **PC:** **Country:** Norway
Year Established: 2015 **Status 2020:** Active
Industries: Artificial Intelligence for:, Robotics

Company Name: Target Circle
Description: We are the first UA automation platform, powered by AI and focused on everything outside of social and search.
Website: http://targetcircle.com/en/home/
Phone: 44 2035 147 822 **Email:** sales@targetcircle.com
City: Lillestrøm **State:** Viken **PC:** **Country:** Norway
Year Established: 2014 **Status 2020:** Active
Industries: Analytics for:, Artificial Intelligence for:, Big Data and Analytics for:, Data Management for:, Security for:, Mobile for:, Mobile for:, ~ Media-Communications (41), Business Software as a Service Apps (SaaS Apps)

Company Name: AIHAND
Description: AIHAND is a place where perfect companies can find their perfect employees, we're focused on artificial intelligence jobs.
Website: http://aihand.io
Phone: 48731385460 **Email:** admin@aihand.io
City: Lysaker **State:** Viken **PC:** **Country:** Norway
Year Established: **Status 2020:** Active
Industries: Artificial Intelligence for:, Machine Learning for:, ~ Human Resources (24)

Company Name: Cognite
Description: Cognite develops industrial IOT data platform.
Website: http://www.cognite.com/
Phone: 47 95 09 21 00 **Email:** contact@cognite.com
City: Lysaker **State:** Viken **PC:** **Country:** Norway
Year Established: 2016 **Status 2020:** Active
Industries: Artificial Intelligence for:, Data Management for:, IT Managed Services for:, Internet of Things (IoT) for:, Machine Learning for:, Business Software as a Service Apps (SaaS Apps)

Company Name: Iris AI
Description:
Website: https://iris.ai/
Phone: **Email:** founders@iris.ai
City: Stabekk **State:** Viken **PC:** **Country:** Norway
Year Established: **Status 2020:** Active
Industries:

Pakistan

Company Name: AI Bots
Description: Artificial Intelligence Bots is a Pakistan based private company that provides Ai based bots to SMEs to gain maximum productivity.
Website: http://ai.com.: Pakistan
Phone: 92812872247 **Email:** info@ai.com.: Pakistan
City: Quetta **State:** Balochistan **PC:** **Country: Pakistan**
Year Established: **Status 2020:** Active
Industries: Artificial Intelligence for:, IT Managed Services for:, Machine Learning for:, Robotics for:, ~ Professional Services (48)

Company Name: DealSmash
Description: A mobile app for in-store shoppers offering them personalized deals and discounts based on their interests and buying patterns.
Website: http://www.dealsmash.co
Phone: 17324271100 **Email:** info@dealsmash.co
City: Islamabad **State:** Islamabad Capital Territory **PC:** **Country: Pakistan**
Year Established: **Status 2020:** Active
Industries: Analytics for:, Artificial Intelligence for:, ~ Retail and Consumer Products (52)

Company Name: Geekviews
Description: Publish news related to Cyber Security, Artificial intelligence, social media, and newly launched gadgets.
Website: http://geekviews.tech/
Phone: **Email:** Geekviews.tech@gmail.com
City: Islamabad **State:** Islamabad Capital Territory **PC:** **Country: Pakistan**

Year Established: 2017 **Status 2020:** Active
Industries: Artificial Intelligence for:, Big Data and Analytics for:, IT Managed Services

Company Name: Techlets Pvt. Ltd.
Description: WALEE - an everyday trade app that connects businesses looking to selling online and social influencers who can resell through AI.
Website: http://techletspk.com/
Phone: 92 346 5346326 **Email:** ahsan.tahir@techletspk.com
City: Islamabad **State:** Islamabad Capital Territory **PC:** **Country: Pakistan**
Year Established: 2015 **Status 2020:** Active
Industries: Artificial Intelligence for:, IT Managed Services

Company Name: Datics.ai
Description: Where Data Meets Analytics & AI.
Website: http://datics.ai/
Phone: (333) 492-9891 **Email:** sidra.sial@datics.ai
City: Lahore **State:** PB **PC:** **Country: Pakistan**
Year Established: 2018 **Status 2020:** Active
Industries:

Company Name: Eyedeus
Description: Eyedeus Labs, is a spin-off from Computer Vision Lab (CV Lab) LUMS School of Science and Engineering, Lahore Pakistan.
Website: http://eyedeus.com/
Phone: 92 42 37100864 **Email:** info@groopic.com
City: Lahore **State:** Punjab **PC:** **Country: Pakistan**
Year Established: 2012 **Status 2020:** Closed
Industries: Artificial Intelligence for:, IT Managed Services

Company Name: Fotisto
Description: Fotisto is a marketplace that uses AI and Cloud-based tools to bridge clients with photographers/videographers.
Website: http://www.fotisto.pk/
Phone: **Email:** info@fotisto.: Pakistan
City: Lahore **State:** PB **PC:** **Country: Pakistan**
Year Established: 2018 **Status 2020:** Active
Industries: Artificial Intelligence for:, ~ Customer Relationship Management (11), E-Commerce for:, Business Software as a Service Apps (SaaS Apps)

Company Name: Ingrain Media
Description: Ingrain Media creates machine vision technology that enables AR experiences beyond the range of depth sensors.
Website: http://ingrain.io
Phone: (92) 345.908.6088 **Email:** hello@ingrain.io
City: Lahore **State:** Punjab **PC:** **Country: Pakistan**
Year Established: 2012 **Status 2020:** Active
Industries: Artificial Intelligence for:, Augmented Reality for:, Computer Vision for:, Machine Learning for:, Virtual Reality (VR)

Company Name: Lastingsal: Spain
Description: Jarvis for sales (Intelligent Sales Engine)
Website: http://lastingsales.com
Phone: **Email:** no-reply@domain.com
City: Lahore **State:** Punjab **PC:** **Country: Pakistan**
Year Established: 2016 **Status 2020:** Active
Industries: Artificial Intelligence for:, ~ Customer Relationship Management (11), IT Managed Services

Company Name: UmerQaiser.com | Tech Solutions
Description: Software Products & Services based on AI, Cloud, RPA, AR & Microsoft .NET.
Website: http://www.UmerQaiser.com
Phone: **Email:** contact@umerqaiser.com
City: Lahore **State:** Punjab **PC:** **Country: Pakistan**
Year Established: 2018 **Status 2020:** Active
Industries: Artificial Intelligence for:, IT Managed Services for:, Web

Company Name: Snapthat
Description: Snapthat is personalized visual search engine for fashion that helps people find their favorite dress.
Website: http://www.snapthat.ai
Phone: 92 335 5533318 **Email:** haris@snapthat.ai
City: Rawalpindi **State:** Punjab **PC:** **Country: Pakistan**
Year Established: 2019 **Status 2020:** Active
Industries: Artificial Intelligence for:, ~ Fashion (16), Computer Vision

Company Name: Baseh Technologi
Description: Baseh Technologies is a group of individuals who are designing the future.
Website: http://www.base-h.com
Phone: **Email:** dante@base-h.com
City: Karachi **State:** Sindh **PC:** **Country: Pakistan**
Year Established: 2017 **Status 2020:** Active
Industries: Artificial Intelligence for:, IT Managed Services for:, ~ Arts-Entertainment-Recreation (4)

Company Name: Botsify
Description: Build chatbots for messenger without any coding knowledge.
Website: http://www.botsify.com
Phone: **Email:** usama@botsify.com
City: Karachi **State:** Sindh **PC:** **Country: Pakistan**
Year Established: 2016 **Status 2020:** Active
Industries: Application Services for:, Artificial Intelligence for:, IT Managed Services for:, Application Program Interfaces (APIs)

Company Name: ByteCorp
Description: AI Solutions and Prooducts
Website: http://www.bytecorp.io
Phone: **Email:** info@bytecorp.io
City: Karachi **State:** Sindh **PC:** **Country: Pakistan**
Year Established: 2019 **Status 2020:** Active
Industries: Artificial Intelligence for:, Computer Vision for:, ~ Healthcare (20), IT Managed Services

Company Name: Healthcare Matrix
Description: Healthcare Matrix provides healthcare facilities to underserved communities via intelligent medical kiosk & automated medicine dispenser.
Website: http://healthcare-matrix.com/
Phone: **Email:** info@healthcare-matrix.com
City: Karachi **State:** Sindh **PC:** **Country: Pakistan**
Year Established: 2016 **Status 2020:** Active
Industries: Artificial Intelligence for:, ~ Healthcare (20), ~ Healthcare (20), ~ Healthcare (20)

Company Name: Odd Technologies (Pvt) Ltd
Description: Odd Technologies (Pvt) Ltd is a fast growing software company in the field of Artificial Intelligence in Karachi, Pakistan.
Website: http://oddtechnologies.com
Phone: 92 346 314 9752 **Email:** info@oddtechnologies.com
City: Karachi **State:** Sindh **PC:** **Country: Pakistan**
Year Established: 2019 **Status 2020:** Active
Industries: Artificial Intelligence for:, IT Managed Services

Peru

Company Name: Gainmers
Description: Gainmers is a P2P Sportsbook based on AI that runs on the Ethereum Network.
Website:
Phone: **Email:** 36607@reference-encyclopedia-ai.net
City: Lima **State:** Callao Region **PC:** **Country:** Peru
Year Established: 2017 **Status 2020:** Closed
Industries: Artificial Intelligence for:, ~ Arts-Entertainment-Recreation (4), Blockchain for:, ~ Arts-Entertainment-Recreation (4)

Company Name: Suruna
Description: Suruna is AI tool for video personalization. Creating a video feed using Emotion AI.
Website: http://suruna.com
Phone: (511) 449-2541 **Email:** 37488@reference-encyclopedia-ai.net
City: Lima **State:** Callao Region **PC:** **Country:** Peru
Year Established: 2013 **Status 2020:** Active
Industries:

Company Name: FractalUp
Description: SaaS OTT for 13-20y/teachers/directors. Integral Personalized EdTech (AI) w. our Natural Knowledge Fractals Method (paths w. neuroscience)
Website: http://www.fractalup.com
Phone: 51 951385676 **Email:** marcos.vargas@fractalup.com
City: Trujillo **State:** La Libertad **PC:** **Country:** Peru
Year Established: 2013 **Status 2020:** Active
Industries: Artificial Intelligence for:, Big Data and Analytics for:, ~ Education (13), ~ Education (13), Business Software as a Service Apps (SaaS Apps) for:, Virtual Reality (VR)

Company Name: Quantum Talent
Description: Quantum Talent is a SaaS startup that offers HR solutions by reducing turnover and increasing employee productivity.
Website: http://quantum-talent.com
Phone: **Email:** cganoza@quantum-talent.com
City: San Isidro **State:** Municipalidad Metropolitana de Lima **PC:** **Country:** Peru
Year Established: 2016 **Status 2020:** Active
Industries: Artificial Intelligence for:, Big Data and Analytics for:, ~ Education (13), Machine Learning for:, Business Software as a Service Apps (SaaS Apps)

Phillipines

Company Name: Lorax AI
Description: Lorax AI helps local governments in digitizing data and gives instant visual analysis.
Website: http://lorax.ph/
Phone: **Email:** 36914@reference-encyclopedia-ai.net
City: Mandaue City **State:** Central Visayas **PC:** **Country:** **Phillipines**
Year Established: 2012 **Status 2020:** Active
Industries: Artificial Intelligence for:, IT Managed Services

Company Name: HiDok Inc.
Description: A platform that integrates EMR and lifestyle monitoring features with the goal of gamifying health awareness and incentivizing users.
Website: http://www.hidok
Phone: 082-293-2132 **Email:** contact@hidok.: Country **City:** Davao City **State:** Davao Region **PC:** **Country: Philippines**
Year Established: 2017 **Status 2020:** Active
Industries: ~ Healthcare (20), IT Managed Services for:, Application Services for:, Application Services

Company Name: IMARK International
Description: IMARK International is a global provider of Internet Marketing, Digital Marketing, Ecommerce, and Software.
Website: http://www.imarkintl.com/
Phone: 63-921-643-1323 **Email:** business@imarkintl.com
City: Makati **State:** NCR **PC:** **Country: Philippines**
Year Established: **Status 2020:** Active
Industries: Artificial Intelligence for:, Digital Marketing for:, E-Commerce for:, ~ Professional Services (48), Cyber Security for:, Cyber Security

Company Name: Senti AI
Description: The pioneering Artificial Intelligence company in the Philippin: Spain
Website: http://www.senti.ai
Phone: **Email:** ralph@senti.com.: Philippin: Spain
City: Makati **State:** NCR **PC:** **Country: Philippines**
Year Established: 2015 **Status 2020:** Active
Industries: Artificial Intelligence for:, Big Data and Analytics for:, Machine Learning

Company Name: Enguest
Description: Enguest is a rewards app that transforms guests into hotel influencers.
Website: http://www.enguest.com/
Phone: **Email:** rewards@enguest.com
City: Manila **State:** NCR **Zip:**
Year Established: 2016 **Status 2020:** Active
Industries: Artificial Intelligence

Company Name: Kaleidoscope IoT
Description: Kaleidoscope is a Cloud based IoT platform enabling end-to-end IoT solutions, driving digital transformations globally.
Website: http://kaleidoscopeiot.com/
Phone: **Email:** press@kaleidoscopeiot.com
City: Manila **State:** NCR **PC:** **Country: Philippines**
Year Established: 2017 **Status 2020:** Active
Industries: ~ Agriculture (3), Artificial Intelligence for:, Cloud for:, Cloud for:, Computer Vision for:, Automation for:, Internet of Things (IoT) for:, Machine Learning for:, Machine Learning

Company Name: Maonos
Description: SaaS Business Intelligence Artificial Intelligence
Website: http://www.maonos.com
Phone: 6325000826 **Email:** ask@maonos.com
City: Manila **State:** NCR **PC:** **Country: Philippines**
Year Established: **Status 2020:** Active
Industries: Artificial Intelligence for:, ~ Media-Communications (41), Business Intelligence

Company Name: Orbotics
Description: Redesigning innovations
Website: http://orbotics.info/
Phone: 51434085175 **Email:** carlomarkk@orbotics.info
City: Manila **State:** NCR **PC:** **Country: Philippines**
Year Established: **Status 2020:** Active
Industries: Artificial Intelligence for:, ~ Telecommunications (56), ~ Manufacturing-Electronic (30), ~ Transportation and Logistics (57), ~ Education (13), Mobile for:, Security

Company Name: Chatbot: PHILIPPIN: SPAIN
Description: ChatbotPH is an artificial intelligence-powered chatbot startup.
Website: http://www.chatbot.ph/
Phone: **Email:** hello@chatbot.: Philippin: Spain
City: Muntinlupa **State:** NCR **PC:** **Country: Philippines**
Year Established: 2017 **Status 2020:** Active
Industries: Artificial Intelligence for:, IT Managed Services for:, IT Managed Services

Company Name: Rumarocket
Description: Using machine learning algorithms to help companies hire faster, better and smarter
Website: http://www.rumarocket.com
Phone: (632)798-8176 **Email:** info@rumarocket.com
City: Pasig **State:** NCR **PC:** **Country: Philippines**
Year Established: 2013 **Status 2020:** Active
Industries: IT Managed Services for:, IT Managed Services for:, Web for:, Machine Learning

Company Name: Thinking Machin: Spain
Description: Thinking Machines is a data science company operating at the intersection of AI and Data Design.
Website: http://thinkingmachin.es/
Phone: **Email:** hello@thinkingmachin.: Spain
City: Taguig **State:** NCR **PC:** **Country: Philippines**

Year Established: **Status 2020:** Active
Industries: Artificial Intelligence for:, IT Managed Services for:, IT Managed Services

Poland

Company Name: Aether Biomedical
Description: Aether Biomedical is a rehabiliation robotics startup focused on building bionic limbs for upper limb ampute: Spain
Website: https://www.aetherbiomedical.com/
Phone: **Email:** info@aetherbiomedical.com
City: Poznan **State:** Greater Poland Voivodeship **PC:** **Country: Poland**
Year Established: 2017 **Status 2020:** Active
Industries:

Company Name: IC Solutions
Description: ICSolutions is a company specializing in solutions of artificial intelligence and alternative methods of communicating with computers.
Website: http://icsolutions.pl/
Phone: 48 696 00 89 57 **Email:** biuro@icsolutions.: Poland
City: Poznan **State:** WP **PC:** **Country: Poland**
Year Established: **Status 2020:** Active
Industries: Artificial Intelligence for:, IT Managed Services

Company Name: MNM Diagnostics
Description: Welcome to the future of personalized diagnostics.
Website: http://mnm.bio
Phone: 48 61 829 50 75 **Email:** contact@mnm.bio
City: Poznan **State:** Greater Poland Voivodeship **PC:** **Country: Poland**
Year Established: 2018 **Status 2020:** Active
Industries: Artificial Intelligence for:, ~ Biotechnology (9), ~ Healthcare (20), ~ Healthcare (20)

Company Name: StethoMe
Description: AI-powered healthcare. Automatic and remote lung and heart screening
Website: http://StethoMe.com/
Phone: 48 577 675 723 **Email:** media@StethoMe.com
City: Poznan **State:** Greater Poland Voivodeship **PC:** **Country: Poland**
Year Established: 2015 **Status 2020:** Active
Industries: Artificial Intelligence for:, ~ Healthcare (20), ~ Healthcare (20)

Company Name: text2data.com
Description: At text2data, we believe Artificial intelligence and NLP are the future! We provide cloud based text and sentiment analysis services.
Website: http://www.texti.ai/
Phone: **Email:** 37521@reference-encyclopedia-ai.net
City: Poznan **State:** Greater Poland Voivodeship **PC:** **Country: Poland**
Year Established: 2014 **Status 2020:** Active
Industries: Artificial Intelligence for:, Databases for:, Application Program Interfaces (APIs) for:, IT Managed Services for:, Machine Learning for:, Natural Language Processing for:, Business Software as a Service Apps (SaaS Apps) for:, Data Management

Company Name: Reliability Solutions
Description: Predictive Maintenance system powered by Deep Learning algorithms and advanced analytical tools
Website: http://reliasol.pl/en/
Phone: 48 (12) 394-11-21 **Email:** office@relia-sol.: Poland
City: Cracow **State:** Lesser Poland Voivodeship **PC:** **Country: Poland**
Year Established: 2014 **Status 2020:** Active
Industries: Analytics for:, Artificial Intelligence for:, ~ Biotechnology (9), IT Managed Services for:, Machine Learning for:, Predictive Analytics

Company Name: AA Software Solutions
Description: Outsource and Software Development.
Website: http://www.aasoftwaresolution.com
Phone: 48 570 74 35 88 **Email:** ceo@aasoftwaresolution.com
City: Krakow **State:** ML **PC:** **Country: Poland**
Year Established: **Status 2020:** Active
Industries: ~ Professional Services (48), Artificial Intelligence for:, IT Managed Services for:, Web for:, Business Process and Operations for:, ~ Professional Services (48), ~ Professional Services (48), Cyber Security

Company Name: Airly
Description: Airly builds networks of air quality sensors that can be deployed across entire cities to enable real-time monitoring via map.airly.eu
Website: http://airly.eu/en/
Phone: **Email:** contact@airly.eu
City: Krakow **State:** ML **PC:** **Country: Poland**
Year Established: **Status 2020:** Active
Industries: Artificial Intelligence for:, ~ Energy and Utilities (14), ~ Manufacturing-Electronic (30), ~ Construction (10)

Company Name: AVSystem
Description:
Website: https://www.avsystem.com/
Phone: 48 12 619 47 00 **Email:** w.yan@avsystem.com
City: Krakow **State:** Lesser Poland Voivodeship **Zip:** 31-315 **Country: Poland**
Year Established: **Status 2020:** Active
Industries: Blockchain

Company Name: Cardiomatics
Description: Analytics SaaS for Cardiology
Website: http://cardiomatics.com
Phone: **Email:** office@cardiomatics.com
City: Krakow **State:** Lesser Poland Voivodeship **PC:** **Country: Poland**
Year Established: 2017 **Status 2020:** Active
Industries: Artificial Intelligence for:, ~ Healthcare (20)

Company Name: CODEST
Description: Online products design and development, Internet Advertising, Web development, E-commerce.
Website: http://codesthq.com/
Phone: 48507095252 **Email:** hello@codesthq.com
City: Krakow **State:** ML **PC:** **Country: Poland**
Year Established: **Status 2020:** Active
Industries: ~ Media-Communications (41), ~ Media-Communications (41), ~ Media-Communications (41), Artificial Intelligence for:, Digital Media for:, Enterprise Application Services for:, ~ Professional Services (48), Cyber Security

Company Name: Craftinity
Description: Craftinity brings together the research oriented field of deep learning to your business.
Website: http://craftinity.com
Phone: 48 601 187 742 **Email:** contact@craftinity.com
City: Krakow **State:** ML **PC:** **Country: Poland**
Year Established: **Status 2020:** Active
Industries: Artificial Intelligence for:, Machine Learning

Company Name: edrone
Description: First eCRM for eCommerce. Collects and proccesses customer data, consumer behaviours in order to engage store visitors and buyers.
Website: http://edrone.me/en/
Phone: (4851) 004-3827 **Email:** hello@edrone.me
City: Krakow **State:** Lesser Poland Voivodeship **PC:** **Country: Poland**
Year Established: 2014 **Status 2020:** Active
Industries: Analytics for:, Artificial Intelligence for:, Big Data and Analytics for:, Databases for:, E-Commerce for:, Business Software as a Service Apps (SaaS Apps) for:, Business Software as a Service Apps (SaaS Apps) for:, Automation for:, ~ Social Assistance-Non-Prof: Italy

Company Name: Intelliseq sp. z o.o.
Description: Intelliseq is a genome informatics company established in 2014 by a group of scientists fascinated with pharmacogenomics and transcriptomics
Website: http://intelliseq.pl/
Phone: 48 696622014 **Email:** contact@intelliseq.: Poland
City: Krakow **State:** Lesser Poland Voivodeship **PC:** **Country: Poland**
Year Established: 2014 **Status 2020:** Active
Industries: Analytics for:, Artificial Intelligence for:, ~ Biotechnology (9), ~ Healthcare (20)

Company Name: Syneri: Sweden
Description: Next-gen omnichannel marketing & customer intelligence capabilities at scale.
Website: http://synerise.com
Phone: 48507760147 **Email:** info@synerise.com
City: Krakow **State:** ML **PC:** **Country: Poland**
Year Established: **Status 2020:** Active
Industries:

Company Name: The Eye
Description: The Eye is an algorithms of artificial intelligence.
Website: http://theeyesee.: Italy
Phone: 48123941121 **Email:** office@relia-sol.: Poland
City: Krakow **State:** ML **PC:** **Country: Poland**
Year Established: **Status 2020:** Active
Industries: Artificial Intelligence

Company Name: Untitled Kingdom
Description: Software Development Studio, crafting custom apps for iOS, AppleWatch, iBeacons, IoT, Android and Web.
Website: http://www.untitledkingdom.co
Phone: **Email:** hello@untitledkingdom.co
City: Krakow **State:** ML **PC:** **Country: Poland**
Year Established: **Status 2020:** Active
Industries: Application Services for:, Artificial Intelligence for:, Machine Learning for:, Mobile for:, ~ Professional Services (48)

Company Name: Ardigen
Description: Ardigen is a life science computational partner in the era of Artificial Intelligence.
Website: http://www.ardigen.com
Phone: 48 12 340 20 40 **Email:** ardigen@ardigen.com
City: Kraków **State:** Lesser Poland Voivodeship **PC:** **Country: Poland**
Year Established: 2015 **Status 2020:** Active
Industries: Artificial Intelligence for:, ~ Biotechnology (9), ~ Healthcare (20), IT Managed Services

Company Name: NovaKid
Description: Next-generation English Leaning For Kids
Website: http://www.novakidschool.com
Phone: **Email:** max@novakidschool.com
City: Kraków **State:** Lesser Poland Voivodeship **PC:** **Country: Poland**
Year Established: 2017 **Status 2020:** Active
Industries: Artificial Intelligence for:, ~ Education (13), ~ Education (13)

Company Name: Prisma: Kenya
Description: Software House built around a core idea to design and create best products for mobile devices. We do Machine Learning as well.
Website: http://www.prismake.com
Phone: **Email:** hello@prismake.com
City: Kraków **State:** Lesser Poland Voivodeship **PC:** **Country: Poland**
Year Established: 2014 **Status 2020:** Active
Industries: Artificial Intelligence for:, Business Process and Operations

Company Name: S-LABS
Description: Advanced Data Science analytics obtained from IoT sensors and external information sources, dedicated for Energy sector
Website: http://slabs.: Poland
Phone: 48 516 910 131 **Email:** leszek.trzepla@slabs.: Poland
City: Kraków **State:** Lesser Poland Voivodeship **PC:** **Country: Poland**
Year Established: 2015 **Status 2020:** Active
Industries: Analytics for:, Artificial Intelligence for:, ~ Energy and Utilities (14), IT Managed Services for:, Internet of Things (IoT) for:, ~ Energy and Utilities (14)

Company Name: Enigma Pattern
Description: Customised, applied AI solutions.
Website: http://www.enigmapattern.com
Phone: 48 507 795 265 **Email:** hello@enigmapattern.com
City: Lodz **State:** Łódź Voivodeship **PC:** **Country: Poland**
Year Established: 2017 **Status 2020:** Active
Industries: Artificial Intelligence for:, Computer Vision for:, Image Recognition for:, IT Managed Services for:, Machine Learning

Company Name: Finphare
Description: Fintech SaaS company providing Media Coverage Discovery and Analytics Tools for Financial Markets
Website: http://finphare.com/
Phone: (4857) 510-2760 **Email:** contact@finphare.com
City: Lodz **State:** Łódź Voivodeship **PC:** **Country: Poland**
Year Established: 2019 **Status 2020:** Active
Industries: Artificial Intelligence for:, ~ Banking and Financial Markets-Services (7), Digital Media for:, ~ Banking and Financial Markets-Services (7), Machine Learning for:, Business Software as a Service Apps (SaaS Apps) for:, ~ Banking and Financial Markets-Services (

Company Name: Sara AI
Description: Sara AI provides projects of strong artificial intelligence.
Website: http://saraai.com/
Phone: 48 505 243 394 **Email:** info@allplayer.org
City: Lodz **State:** Łódź Voivodeship **PC:** **Country: Poland**
Year Established: 2019 **Status 2020:** Active
Industries: Artificial Intelligence for:, IT Managed Services for:, Web for:, Machine Learning

Company Name: Alphamoon
Description: Custom-tailored AI solutions
Website: http://alphamoon.ai
Phone: **Email:** contact@alphamoon.ai
City: Wroclaw **State:** DO **PC:** **Country: Poland**
Year Established: **Status 2020:** Active
Industries: Artificial Intelligence for:, Big Data and Analytics for:, Machine Learning for:, Cyber Security

Company Name: ChallengeRocket
Description: AI-powered recruitment. Reach & assess hidden programming talents with programming challenges.
Website: http://www.challengeRocket.com
Phone: 48 695 520 111 **Email:** office@challengerocket.com
City: Wroclaw **State:** Lower Silesian Voivodeship **PC:** **Country: Poland**
Year Established: 2016 **Status 2020:** Active
Industries: Artificial Intelligence for:, Databases for:, Predictive Analytics

Company Name: Code Poets
Description: Code Poet is a software development company
Website: http://codepoets.it?utm_source=clutch.co&utm_medium=re...
Phone: 48 696 784 716 **Email:** contact@codepoets.: Italy
City: Wroclaw **State:** Lower Silesian Voivodeship **PC:** **Country: Poland**
Year Established: 2013 **Status 2020:** Active
Industries: ~ Biotechnology (9), Machine Learning

Company Name: Deepstributed
Description: AI, Machine Learning, Deep Learning, IaaS, PaaS, SaaS
Website: http://deepstributed.com
Phone: 48503064414 **Email:** contact@deepstributed.com
City: Wroclaw **State:** DO **PC:** **Country: Poland**
Year Established: **Status 2020:** Active
Industries: Artificial Intelligence for:, Cloud for:, Cloud for:, Machine Learning for:, Enterprise Application Services

Company Name: Dspot
Description: DSpot is a web development company that specializes in developing IT solutions through the web, mobile, and AI expertise.
Website: http://www.dspot.com.: Poland
Phone: 48 730 576 348 **Email:** info@dspot.com.: Poland
City: Wroclaw **State:** Lower Silesian Voivodeship **PC:** **Country: Poland**
Year Established: 2015 **Status 2020:** Active
Industries:

Company Name: Dumpling
Description: Multi-purpose NMR platform that accelerates all aspects of spectra analys
Website: http://dumpling.bio
Phone: **Email:** contact@dumpling.bio
City: Wroclaw **State:** Lower Silesian Voivodeship **PC:** **Country: Poland**
Year Established: 2017 **Status 2020:** Active
Industries: ~ Biotechnology (9), Machine Learning

Company Name: Infermedica
Description: Infermedica uses artificial intelligence for medical diagnosis and patient triage.
Website: http://infermedica.com
Phone: **Email:** office@infermedica.com
City: Wroclaw **State:** DO **PC:** **Country: Poland**
Year Established: **Status 2020:** Active
Industries: Artificial Intelligence for:, ~ Healthcare (20), Machine Learning

Company Name: Microscope: Italy
Description: MicroscopeIT is a software company that specializes in advanced image analysis, microscopy, cloud, and machine and deep learning.
Website: http://www.microscopeit.com/
Phone: 48 538 212 600 **Email:** info@microscopeit.com
City: Wroclaw **State:** Lower Silesian Voivodeship **PC:** **Country: Poland**
Year Established: 2011 **Status 2020:** Active
Industries: Image Recognition for:, Machine Learning

Company Name: NeuroSYS
Description: Software development studio specializing in artificial intelligence and custom IT solutions.
Website: http://neurosys.com
Phone: 1 (800) 601-9750 **Email:** hello@neurosys.com
City: Wroclaw **State:** Lower Silesian Voivodeship **PC:** **Country: Poland**
Year Established: 2010 **Status 2020:** Active
Industries: Artificial Intelligence for:, Big Data and Analytics for:, Business Intelligence for:, Databases for:, Enterprise Application Services for:, Machine Learning for:, Web

Company Name: rebug.io
Description: Web service which record user's activities and notifies you about every bug and error in your software to repair them faster and better.
Website: http://rebug.io
Phone: 48 71 707 03 71 **Email:** hello@rebug.io
City: Wroclaw **State:** Lower Silesian Voivodeship **PC:** **Country: Poland**
Year Established: 2016 **Status 2020:** Active
Industries: Application Services for:, Predictive Analytics for:, Development and Test for:, Web

Company Name: Surveily
Description: Surveily applies Artificial Intelligence to increase safety in manufacturing plants.
Website: http://surveily.com/
Phone: 48 664 034 361 **Email:** info@surveily.com
City: Wroclaw **State:** Lower Silesian Voivodeship **PC:** **Country: Poland**
Year Established: 2018 **Status 2020:** Active
Industries: Artificial Intelligence for:, Machine Learning for:, ~ Government (19), Security

Company Name: Tooploox
Description: Tooploox is a software development studio specializing in artificial intelligence, mobile and web development.
Website: http://www.tooploox.com
Phone: 48733888088 **Email:** hello@tooploox.com
City: Wroclaw **State:** DO **PC:** **Country: Poland**
Year Established: **Status 2020:** Active
Industries: Artificial Intelligence for:, Blockchain for:, Application Services for:, ~ Professional Services (48), Robotics for:, ~ Professional Services (48), Cyber Security for:, Cyber Security

Company Name: Seodity
Description: Completely new SEO tools for content and technical SEO analysis.
Website: http://www.seodity.com
Phone: **Email:** support@seodity.com
City: Gorzow Wielkopolski **State:** LU **PC:** **Country: Poland**
Year Established: **Status 2020:** Active
Industries:

Company Name: Usarya
Description: The best stone picking machine on the market.
Website: http://usarya-polska.pl/
Phone: **Email:** usarya.polska@gmail.com
City: Lomianki **State:** Masovian Voivodeship **PC:** **Country: Poland**
Year Established: 2017 **Status 2020:** Active
Industries: Artificial Intelligence for:, Machine Learning

Company Name: Addepto
Description: Addepto is a machine learning and business intelligence software house developing custom solutions for Global Startups and Large Enterpris: Spain
Website: https://www.addepto.com/
Phone: **Email:** contact@addepto.com
City: Warsaw **State:** Masovian Voivodeship **PC:** **Country: Poland**
Year Established: 2017 **Status 2020:** Active
Industries: Analytics for:, Artificial Intelligence for:, Big Data and Analytics for:, Business Intelligence for:, Data Management for:, Databases for:, Data Management for:, Machine Learning for:, Machine Learning

Company Name: AIDA Diagnostics
Description: AIDA Diagnostics is a software based on machine learning algorithms which optimizing blood transfusions in hospital.
Website: https://aidadx.io/
Phone: 518927701 **Email:** contact@aidadx.io
City: Warsaw **State:** Masovian Voivodeship **PC:** **Country: Poland**
Year Established: 2019 **Status 2020:** Active
Industries: Artificial Intelligence for:, ~ Healthcare (20), Machine Learning

Company Name: Applica
Description: Applica's proprietary AI automates text-intensive work by extracting meaning from unstructured and semi-structured documents.
Website: http://www.applica.ai
Phone: 646-944-1046 **Email:** contact@applica.ai
City: Warsaw **State:** Masovian Voivodeship **PC:** **Country: Poland**

Year Established: 2013 **Status 2020:** Active
Industries: Artificial Intelligence for:, IT Managed Services for:, Application Services for:, Machine Learning for:, Natural Language Processing

Company Name: Appsilon Data Science
Description: Appsilon offers data science consulting, custom dashboards, deep learning solutions and technical support.
Website: http://appsilon.com/
Phone: **Email:** hello@appsilon.com
City: Warsaw **State:** MZ **PC:** **Country: Poland**
Year Established: **Status 2020:** Active
Industries: Artificial Intelligence for:, Application Services

Company Name: Boringowl
Description: BoringOwl is delivering custom analytics, web applications and AI solutions
Website: http://www.boringowl.io
Phone: 48 509 280 539 **Email:** HELLO@BORINGOWL.IO
City: Warsaw **State:** Masovian Voivodeship **PC:** **Country: Poland**
Year Established: 2019 **Status 2020:** Active
Industries:

Company Name: CashDirector
Description: CashDirector SA is a technology company providing banks with Virtual CFO & real-time accounting platforms for SME clients.
Website: http://www.cashDirector.com/
Phone: 1 408 8444 310 **Email:** info@cashdirector.com
City: Warsaw **State:** Masovian Voivodeship **PC:** **Country: Poland**
Year Established: 2012 **Status 2020:** Active
Industries: Finance and Accounting for:, Enterprise Application Services for:, ~ Banking and Financial Markets-Services (7), IT Managed Services for:, Machine Learning

Company Name: CashDirector SA
Description: CashDirector SA is a technology company providing banks with Virtual CFO & real-time accounting platforms for SME clients.
Website: http://www.cashDirector.com/
Phone: 48 606 296844 **Email:** rstrzelecki@cashDirector.com
City: Warsaw **State:** MZ **Zip:** 807 **Country: Poland**
Year Established: **Status 2020:** Active
Industries: Artificial Intelligence for:, ~ Banking and Financial Markets-Services (7), Automation for:, ~ Administrative and Support Services (367), ~ Banking and Financial Markets-Services (373), ~ Management of Companies (394), ~ Professional Services (414), Business App

Company Name: Cla: Iran
Description: Hardware, AI, CleanTech, Health Care, Wellness, Smart City, Smart Home
Website: http://claircity.com
Phone: (4857) 069-1639 **Email:** info@claircity.com
City: Warsaw **State:** Masovian Voivodeship **PC:** **Country: Poland**
Year Established: 2018 **Status 2020:** Active
Industries: Artificial Intelligence for:, ~ Healthcare (20), Machine Learning

Company Name: CodersFirst
Description: A whole new way of meritocratic hiring based on data.
Website: http://www.codersfirst.com
Phone: **Email:** info@codersfirst.com
City: Warsaw **State:** MZ **PC:** **Country: Poland**
Year Established: **Status 2020:** Active
Industries: Artificial Intelligence for:, Big Data and Analytics for:, Machine Learning for:, ~ Human Resources (24)

Company Name: Cognibe
Description: Cognibe provides learning solutions, data analytics, and process automation to enhance the advantage of increasing client's ROI.
Website: http://Www.cognibe.com
Phone: 48 507 655 992 **Email:** info.pl@cognibe.com
City: Warsaw **State:** Masovian Voivodeship **PC:** **Country: Poland**
Year Established: 2012 **Status 2020:** Active
Industries: Analytics for:, Artificial Intelligence for:, Robotics

Company Name: Cognitum
Description: Cognitum is a Semantic Tech vendors delivering innovative, scalable solutions for data acquisition, storage, searching and processing.
Website: http://www.cognitum.eu/
Phone: **Email:** office@cognitum.eu
City: Warsaw **State:** MZ **PC:** **Country: Poland**
Year Established: **Status 2020:** Active
Industries: Artificial Intelligence for:, Big Data and Analytics for:, Content for:, ~ Professional Services (48)

Company Name: ConnectPoint
Description: ConnectPoint is an IT Solutions Provider and Data Specialist for Utilities and Industry.
Website: http://connectpoint.pl/en
Phone: (4860) 692-0356 **Email:** biuro@connectpoint.: Poland
City: Warsaw **State:** Masovian Voivodeship **PC:** **Country: Poland**
Year Established: 2010 **Status 2020:** Active
Industries: Business Intelligence for:, IT Managed Services for:, Internet of Things (IoT) for:, Machine Learning

Company Name: Creamfinance
Description: Creamfinance is a financial services company based on cutting edge financial technology instruments.
Website: http://www.creamfinance.com/
Phone: (3712) 773-7573 **Email:** info@creamfinance.com
City: Warsaw **State:** Masovian Voivodeship **PC:** **Country: Poland**
Year Established: 2012 **Status 2020:** Active
Industries: ~ Banking and Financial Markets-Services (7), ~ Banking and Financial Markets-Services (7), ~ Banking and Financial Markets-Services (7), Machine Learning

Company Name: Daftcode
Description: A venture building company. We create and launch our own projects, from concept stages, through development and up to market launch.
Website: http://www.daftcode.com
Phone: (4822) 100-5558 **Email:** hello@daftcode.com
City: Warsaw **State:** Masovian Voivodeship **PC:** **Country: Poland**
Year Established: 2011 **Status 2020:** Active
Industries: Artificial Intelligence for:, ~ Education (13), Security for:, ~ Banking and Financial Markets-Services (7), Business Software as a Service Apps (SaaS Apps) for:, Business Software as a Service Apps (SaaS Apps)

Company Name: E-contenta
Description: AI driven platform that help brands to distribute their editorials in the format of native advertising
Website: http://e-contenta.com/en/
Phone: 7(921)8629604 **Email:** zoya@e-contenta.com
City: Warsaw **State:** Masovian Voivodeship **PC:** **Country: Poland**
Year Established: 2016 **Status 2020:** Active
Industries: Analytics for:, Content for:, Content for:, Digital Marketing for:, Predictive Analytics

Company Name: eDream Data
Description: The main aim of the project is to create and implement software for a database which will analyse the data.
Website:
Phone: **Email:** 36476@reference-encyclopedia-ai.net
City: Warsaw **State:** Masovian Voivodeship **PC:** **Country:** **Poland**
Year Established: 2015 **Status 2020:** Active
Industries: Artificial Intelligence for:, Databases

Company Name: Emplobot
Description: Emplocity unlocks passive candidates' potential with an AI-powered Emplobot that applies for jobs on their behalf.
Website: http://www.emplobot.com/
Phone: **Email:** chris@emplocity.com
City: Warsaw **State:** Masovian Voivodeship **PC:** **Country:** **Poland**
Year Established: 2013 **Status 2020:** Active
Industries: Artificial Intelligence for:, IT Managed Services for:, Business Software as a Service Apps (SaaS Apps)

Company Name: Filmaster
Description: Filmaster provides Netflix-like personalization and analytics solutions for the entertainment industry.
Website: http://filmaster.tv
Phone: 48 795 158 581 **Email:** filmaster@filmaster.com
City: Warsaw **State:** Masovian Voivodeship **PC:** **Country:** **Poland**
Year Established: 2010 **Status 2020:** Active
Industries: Predictive Analytics

Company Name: Hotailors.com
Description: Corporate SaaS for business travel
Website: http://www.hotailors.com
Phone: 48609009959 **Email:** info@hotailors.com
City: Warsaw **State:** MZ **PC:** **Country: Poland**
Year Established: **Status 2020:** Active
Industries:

Company Name: Infinite Data
Description: Infinite data is the evolution of automated IT processes.
Website: http://infinitedata.com/
Phone: 48 22 245 23 02 **Email:** 36759@reference-encyclopedia-ai.net
City: Warsaw **State:** Masovian Voivodeship **PC:** **Country:** **Poland**
Year Established: 2014 **Status 2020:** Active
Industries: IT Managed Services for:, Machine Learning

Company Name: INGRID Ventures
Description: Invests & incubates compani: Spain
Website: http://ingridx.com
Phone: **Email:** hello@ingridx.com
City: Warsaw **State:** Masovian Voivodeship **PC:** **Country:** **Poland**
Year Established: 2016 **Status 2020:** Active
Industries: Artificial Intelligence for:, IT Managed Services

Company Name: Inteliclinic
Description: Inteliclinic is an engineering studio specializing in artificial intelligence technologies and biological signal processing systems.
Website: http://inteliclinic.com/
Phone: **Email:** contact@inteliclinic.com
City: Warsaw **State:** Masovian Voivodeship **PC:** **Country:** **Poland**
Year Established: 2013 **Status 2020:** Closed
Industries: Artificial Intelligence for:, Internet of Things (IoT)

Company Name: Liber Finance Group
Description: Liber Finance Group is a financial technology company that operates multiple AI-driven marketplaces across Europe for consumer finance
Website: http://www.liberfinancegroup.com
Phone: **Email:** info@liberfinancegroup.com
City: Warsaw **State:** MZ **PC:** **Country: Poland**
Year Established: **Status 2020:** Active
Industries: Artificial Intelligence for:, ~ Banking and Financial Markets-Services (7), ~ Banking and Financial Markets-Services (7), Machine Learning

Company Name: Loglab
Description: Loglab is a group of programmers and scientists with many years of experience in the field of artificial intelligence and data analysis.
Website: http://loglab.pl/
Phone: **Email:** 36911@reference-encyclopedia-ai.net
City: Warsaw **State:** Masovian Voivodeship **PC:** **Country:** **Poland**
Year Established: 2016 **Status 2020:** Active
Industries: Artificial Intelligence

Company Name: Metis.finance
Description: Providing intelligent cash flow management for small and medium sized compani: Spain
Website: http://metis.finance
Phone: (4878) 255-6706 **Email:** contact@metis.finance
City: Warsaw **State:** Masovian Voivodeship **PC:** **Country:** **Poland**
Year Established: 2017 **Status 2020:** Active
Industries: Artificial Intelligence for:, ~ Banking and Financial Markets-Services (7)

Company Name: MLJAR
Description: MLJAR is a platform for rapid prototyping, development and deploying pattern recognition algorithms.
Website: http://mljar.com
Phone: **Email:** contact@mljar.com
City: Warsaw **State:** MZ **PC:** **Country: Poland**
Year Established: **Status 2020:** Active
Industries: Artificial Intelligence for:, Computer Vision for:, Machine Learning for:, Predictive Analytics

Company Name: Molecule.one
Description: AI-powered software for organic synthesis design
Website: http://molecule.one
Phone: **Email:** hello@molecule.one
City: Warsaw **State:** Masovian Voivodeship **PC:** **Country:** **Poland**
Year Established: 2016 **Status 2020:** Active
Industries: Artificial Intelligence

Company Name: neptune.ai
Description: The most lightweight experiment management tool that fits any workflow.
Website: http://neptune.ai/
Phone: **Email:** contact@neptune.ai
City: Warsaw **State:** Masovian Voivodeship **PC:** **Country:** **Poland**
Year Established: 2017 **Status 2020:** Active
Industries: Analytics for:, Artificial Intelligence for:, IT Managed Services for:, Web

Company Name: neptune.ml
Description: Platform built for data scientists to make machine learning models development fast and reliable.
Website: http://neptune.ml/
Phone: **Email:** contact@neptune.ml
City: Warsaw **State:** MZ **PC:** **Country: Poland**
Year Established: **Status 2020:** Active
Industries: Analytics for:, Artificial Intelligence for:, IT Managed Services for:, Web for:, ~ Professional Services (48)

Company Name: Nethone
Description: Nethone is A.I.-powered KYU (Know Your Users) solutions that help convert threats and challenges into well-informed, profitable decisions.
Website: http://www.nethone.com
Phone: 48 22 112 15 15 **Email:** contact@nethone.com
City: Warsaw **State:** MZ **PC:** **Country: Poland**
Year Established: **Status 2020:** Active
Industries: Artificial Intelligence for:, Big Data and Analytics for:, Business Intelligence for:, Cyber Security for:, Security for:, Machine Learning for:, Risk Management

Company Name: Nomagic
Description: Nomagic provides smart pick and place robotic solutions for order fulfillment.
Website: http://nomagic.ai/
Phone: **Email:** info@nomagic.ai
City: Warsaw **State:** Masovian Voivodeship **PC:** **Country: Poland**
Year Established: 2017 **Status 2020:** Active
Industries: Artificial Intelligence for:, Cloud for:, ~ Telecommunications (56), Robotics

Company Name: NOXAI
Description: NOXAI - Artificial Intelligence for People
Website: http://noxai.com
Phone: **Email:** info@brandbucket.com
City: Warsaw **State:** Masovian Voivodeship **PC:** **Country: Poland**
Year Established: 2015 **Status 2020:** Active
Industries: Artificial Intelligence for:, IT Managed Services

Company Name: Placeme
Description: Placeme is an online tool that enables predict potential sales at specific address.
Website: http://placeme.pl/
Phone: 49 793 345 678 **Email:** hello@placeme.: Poland
City: Warsaw **State:** Masovian Voivodeship **PC:** **Country: Poland**
Year Established: 2017 **Status 2020:** Active
Industries:

Company Name: PlatformX
Description: PlatformX - the artificial intelligence that automates software development.
Website: http://platformx.ai/
Phone: **Email:** 37177@reference-encyclopedia-ai.net
City: Warsaw **State:** Masovian Voivodeship **PC:** **Country: Poland**
Year Established: 2017 **Status 2020:** Active
Industries: Artificial Intelligence for:, IT Managed Services

Company Name: Pragmasoft
Description: Pragmasoft is an AI based real time space tracking tool, dedicated to human behaviour and space usage detection.
Website: http://pragmasoft.pl/en
Phone: 48665063629 **Email:** kontakt@pragmasoft.: Poland
City: Warsaw **State:** Masovian Voivodeship **PC:** **Country: Poland**
Year Established: 2014 **Status 2020:** Active
Industries: Artificial Intelligence for:, IT Managed Services

Company Name: QuarticON
Description: QuarticON is a fully automated, personalized product recommendation system for e-commerce market.
Website: http://www.quarticon.com/
Phone: 48 22 844 02 51 **Email:** contact@quarticon.com
City: Warsaw **State:** Masovian Voivodeship **PC:** **Country: Poland**
Year Established: 2011 **Status 2020:** Active
Industries: Artificial Intelligence for:, E-Commerce

Company Name: REKTRA Network
Description: SaaS, Blockchain, Algorithmic Trading, Artficitial Intelligence
Website: http://rektra.network
Phone: **Email:** rektra.network@protonmail.com
City: Warsaw **State:** MZ **PC:** **Country: Poland**
Year Established: **Status 2020:** Active
Industries: Artificial Intelligence for:, Blockchain for:, Web for:, ~ Professional Services (48), Finance and Accounting

Company Name: RoomSage
Description: An advanced, AI-based revenue-enhancement technology platform developed specifically for the hospitality industry
Website: http://roomsage.com
Phone: 650-400-8328 **Email:** dariusz.wiatr@roomsage.com
City: Warsaw **State:** MZ **PC:** **Country: Poland**
Year Established: **Status 2020:** Active
Industries: ~ Media-Communications (41), Artificial Intelligence for:, ~ Hospitality (23), Machine Learning

Company Name: RTB House
Description: Technology Powered by Deep Learning
Website: http://www.rtbhouse.com
Phone: 48 22 188 12 71 **Email:** rtbhouse@rtbhouse.com
City: Warsaw **State:** Masovian Voivodeship **PC:** **Country: Poland**
Year Established: 2012 **Status 2020:** Active
Industries: Artificial Intelligence

Company Name: SAG Sport
Description: SportsTech company, focused on delivering value to football coaches, academies and football clubs with its AI-based analytics system.
Website: http://sagsport.com
Phone: (0048) 534-155-165 **Email:** contact@sagsport.com
City: Warsaw **State:** Masovian Voivodeship **PC:** **Country: Poland**
Year Established: 2017 **Status 2020:** Active
Industries: Artificial Intelligence for:, ~ Arts-Entertainment-Recreation (4)

Company Name: SAMITO
Description: Marketing Automation (SaaS) powered by Big Data with advanced personalization, recommendation system and targeting capabilities.
Website: http://www.samito.co/
Phone: 48 501519533 **Email:** contact@samito.co
City: Warsaw **State:** Masovian Voivodeship **PC:** **Country: Poland**
Year Established: 2014 **Status 2020:** Active
Industries: Artificial Intelligence for:, E-Commerce for:, IT Managed Services for:, Business Software as a Service Apps (SaaS Apps) for:, Business Software as a Service Apps (SaaS Apps)

Company Name: Scanbots
Description: Scanbots executes aerial monitoring of linear infrastructure with UAVs and develops solutions for data collection, analytics and exploitation
Website: http://www.scanbots.net/
Phone: **Email:** info@scanbots.net
City: Warsaw **State:** MZ **PC:** **Country: Poland**
Year Established: **Status 2020:** Active
Industries: Analytics for:, Artificial Intelligence for:, ~ Energy and Utilities (14), ~ Transportation and Logistics (57), ~ Energy and Utilities (14), Machine Learning for:, ~ Oil and Gas (43)

Company Name: SmartLife Robotics
Description: Introducing the New Generation Robots to socialize, educate and care.
Website: http://smartlife.global/
Phone: **Email:** office@smartlife.global
City: Warsaw **State:** Masovian Voivodeship **PC:** **Country: Poland**

Year Established: 2017 **Status 2020:** Active
Industries: Artificial Intelligence for:, ~ Education (13), IT Managed Services for:, Robotics

Company Name: Sparkb: Italy
Description: Bespoke software solution for your business
Website: http://www.sparkbit.: Poland
Phone: 601-863-388 **Email:** contact@sparkbit.: Poland
City: Warsaw **State:** Masovian Voivodeship **PC:** **Country:** **Poland**
Year Established: 2014 **Status 2020:** Active
Industries: Artificial Intelligence for:, IT Managed Services for:, IT Managed Services for:, Internet of Things (IoT) for:, Machine Learning

Company Name: Square Data S.A.
Description: CEM Platform & Omnichannel solution including machine learning for Marketing departments
Website: http://squaredata.pl/
Phone: **Email:** tj@squaredata.: Poland
City: Warsaw **State:** Masovian Voivodeship **PC:** **Country:** **Poland**
Year Established: 2016 **Status 2020:** Active
Industries: E-Commerce for:, Machine Learning for:, Business Software as a Service Apps (SaaS Apps)

Company Name: Startup development Hou: Sweden
Description: Startup development House is a digital product and software development house based in Warsaw.
Website: http://start-up.house/
Phone: 48 661 910 176 **Email:** office@start-up.hou: Sweden
City: Warsaw **State:** Masovian Voivodeship **PC:** **Country:** **Poland**
Year Established: 2015 **Status 2020:** Active
Industries: Internet of Things (IoT) for:, Machine Learning for:, Web

Company Name: Tiramisu Web Ap:
Description: Software Hou: Sweden
Website: http://www.tirasu.com
Phone: 1(202)527-9499 **Email:** contact@tirasu.com
City: Warsaw **State:** Masovian Voivodeship **PC:** **Country:** **Poland**
Year Established: 2014 **Status 2020:** Active
Industries:

Company Name: Togetherdata
Description: TogetherData is a data science company that specializes in integrated big data analytics activities.
Website: http://togetherdata.pl/
Phone: 48 22 417 34 52 **Email:** office@togetherdata.com
City: Warsaw **State:** Masovian Voivodeship **PC:** **Country:** **Poland**
Year Established: 2016 **Status 2020:** Active
Industries: Analytics for:, Big Data and Analytics for:, Machine Learning

Company Name: ulam.ai
Description: Text-processing machine learning solutions
Website: http://www.ulam.ai
Phone: **Email:** office@ulam.ai
City: Warsaw **State:** Masovian Voivodeship **PC:** **Country:** **Poland**
Year Established: 2017 **Status 2020:** Active
Industries: Artificial Intelligence for:, Databases for:, Data Management for:, Machine Learning for:, Business Software as a Service Apps (SaaS Apps) for:, Data Management

Company Name: United Robots
Description: United Robots is a technology company operating in the robotics and artificial intelligence industry.
Website: http://www.unitedrobots.co
Phone: 48 502 130 072 **Email:** info@unitedrobots.co
City: Warsaw **State:** Masovian Voivodeship **PC:** **Country:** **Poland**
Year Established: 2016 **Status 2020:** Active
Industries: Artificial Intelligence for:, IT Managed Services for:, Robotics

Company Name: Varstadt
Description: Product Design, Documentation and Consulting for Tech Startu: Palestine
Website: http://www.varstadt.com
Phone: **Email:** contact@varstadt.com
City: Warsaw **State:** MZ **PC:** **Country: Poland**
Year Established: **Status 2020:** Active
Industries: Artificial Intelligence for:, ~ Media-Communications (41), Business Intelligence for:, Application Services for:, ~ Media-Communications (41), Knowledge Management for:, Automation for:, ~ Manufacturing-General (31), Machine Learning for:, ~ Professional Service

Company Name: WindAlly
Description: Modern software for wind asset management. Looking for a seed investment and an opportunity to start a pilot project.
Website: http://windally.io
Phone: 48661490944 **Email:** filip@windally.io
City: Warsaw **State:** Masovian Voivodeship **PC:** **Country:** **Poland**
Year Established: 2018 **Status 2020:** Active
Industries: Artificial Intelligence for:, Big Data and Analytics for:, Enterprise Application Services for:, Machine Learning for:, ~ Energy and Utilities (14), ~ Energy and Utilities (14)

Company **Name:** Yosh.AI
Description: Yosh.AI develops voice assistant for retailers enabling them to enter voice commerce on platforms like Google Assistant and Alexa.
Website: http://yosh.ai/
Phone: **Email:** hello@yosh.ai
City: Warsaw **State:** Masovian Voivodeship **PC:** **Country:** **Poland**
Year Established: 2016 **Status 2020:** Active
Industries: Artificial Intelligence for:, E-Commerce for:, IT Managed Services for:, Machine Learning for:, Internet of Things (IoT) for:, Computer Vision

Company Name: AIQA Technologies
Description: AIQA offers solution for web-driven projects that already uses test automation.
Website:
Phone: **Email:** 4453@reference-encyclopedia-ai.net
City: Warszawa **State:** MZ **PC:** **Country: Poland**
Year Established: **Status 2020:** Active
Industries: Artificial Intelligence for:, Application Services for:, Machine Learning for:, Business Process and Operations for:, ~ Professional Services (48)

Company Name: Algolytics
Description: Algolytics provides award winning software solutions for predictive analytics and Big Data.
Website: http://www.algolytics.com/
Phone: 48 22 353 61 30 **Email:** marketing@algolytics.com
City: Warszawa **State:** Masovian Voivodeship **PC:** **Country:** **Poland**
Year Established: 2014 **Status 2020:** Active
Industries: Analytics for:, Big Data and Analytics for:, Databases for:, Predictive Analytics

Company Name: Bring
Description: Same day delivery, logistics, chatbots, AI, personal assistant
Website: http://www.bring.ai
Phone: **Email:** office@bring.ai
City: Warszawa **State:** MZ **PC:** **Country: Poland**
Year Established: **Status 2020:** Active
Industries: Artificial Intelligence for:, ~ Transportation and Logistics (57), ~ Transportation and Logistics (57)

Company Name: Dclog
Description: DCLOG specializes in providing IT solutions and automatic identification (AI) for logistics and production companies.
Website: http://www.dclog.: Poland
Phone: 48-664174134 **Email:** biuro@dclog.: Poland
City: Warszawa **State:** Masovian Voivodeship **PC:** **Country:** **Poland**
Year Established: 2011 **Status 2020:** Active
Industries: Artificial Intelligence for:, IT Managed Services for:, ~ Telecommunications (56)

Company Name: Execon
Description: Execon provides world-class and real time actionable analytics for headless commerce, boosting your business through advanced optimisation.
Website: http://www.execon.pl/en/
Phone: 48 22 211 22 32 **Email:** info@execon.: Poland
City: Warszawa **State:** Masovian Voivodeship **PC:** **Country:** **Poland**
Year Established: 2012 **Status 2020:** Active
Industries: Analytics for:, Big Data and Analytics for:, Business Intelligence for:, E-Commerce for:, Predictive Analytics for:, Web for:, Web for:, Web

Company Name: KERRIS : ITALY
Description: Complete toolbox for software-house & agencies based on years of research and AI.
Website: http://www.kerrisit.com
Phone: (4822) 378-2838 **Email:** hello@kerrisit.com
City: Warszawa **State:** Masovian Voivodeship **PC:** **Country:** **Poland**
Year Established: 2019 **Status 2020:** Active
Industries: Artificial Intelligence

Company Name: Marvtek
Description: Digital marketing company powered by machine learning - offering sophisticated and advanced solutions to customers on the go.
Website: http://www.marvtek.com
Phone: 48 736 658 632 **Email:** contact@marvtek.com
City: Warszawa **State:** Masovian Voivodeship **PC:** **Country:** **Poland**
Year Established: 2018 **Status 2020:** Active
Industries: Digital Marketing for:, Machine Learning

Company Name: Semantive
Description: Semantive is a digital transformation company that offers services in pilot projects, AI use case ideation, and data readiness assessment.
Website: http://semantive.com/
Phone: **Email:** contact@semantive.com
City: Warszawa **State:** Masovian Voivodeship **PC:** **Country:** **Poland**
Year Established: 2012 **Status 2020:** Active
Industries:

Company Name: Sigdelta
Description: SigDelta is a team of data experts that offers data analysis, machine learning, and big data.
Website: http://sigdelta.com/
Phone: 48 22 203 56 00 **Email:** office@sigdelta.com
City: Warszawa **State:** Masovian Voivodeship **PC:** **Country:** **Poland**
Year Established: 2016 **Status 2020:** Active
Industries: Big Data and Analytics for:, Machine Learning

Company Name: Zillin
Description: Zillin.io makes Machine Learning data preparation simple by enabling flawless team collaboration.
Website: http://zillin.io/
Phone: (48) 533 307 587 **Email:** hello@zillin.io
City: Opole **State:** Opole Voivodeship **PC:** **Country: Poland**
Year Established: 2019 **Status 2020:** Active
Industries: Machine Learning

Company Name: enkids
Description: online english school
Website: http://enkids.co
Phone: 48 22 389 52 58 **Email:** info@enkids.co
City: Bialystok **State:** Podlaskie Voivodeship **PC:** **Country:** **Poland**
Year Established: 2019 **Status 2020:** Active
Industries: Artificial Intelligence for:, ~ Education (13), ~ Education (13), ~ Education (13)

Company Name: AdEmotion
Description: Automated creation of personalized digital advertising based on psychographics and visual preferences.
Website: http://www.ademotion.pl/
Phone: 48 518 638 681 **Email:** k.rokita@ademotion.: Poland
City: Gdansk **State:** Pomeranian Voivodeship **PC:** **Country:** **Poland**
Year Established: 2017 **Status 2020:** Active
Industries: Artificial Intelligence for:, Digital Marketing for:, ~ Healthcare (20)

Company Name: Pin Your Client
Description: Pin Your Client offers a range of predictive analytics software solutions for SaaS-based platforms.
Website: http://pinyourclient.com/
Phone: **Email:** kuba@pinyourclient.com
City: Gdansk **State:** Pomeranian Voivodeship **PC:** **Country:** **Poland**
Year Established: 2014 **Status 2020:** Active
Industries: Artificial Intelligence for:, IT Managed Services for:, Machine Learning for:, Predictive Analytics for:, Business Software as a Service Apps (SaaS Apps)

Company Name: SentiOne
Description: Conversational AI Platform - Discover customer service automation with next-generation chatbots
Website: http://sentione.com
Phone: 48 881609010 **Email:** contact@sentione.com
City: Gdansk **State:** Pomeranian Voivodeship **PC:** **Country:** **Poland**
Year Established: 2011 **Status 2020:** Active
Industries: Analytics for:, Artificial Intelligence for:, Big Data and Analytics for:, ~ Customer Relationship Management (11), Machine Learning for:, Natural Language Processing

Company Name: Haxtron
Description: Robotics and Autonomous Systems
Website: http://haxtron.com/
Phone: **Email:** info@haxtron.com
City: Gdynia **State:** Pomeranian Voivodeship **PC:** **Country:** **Poland**
Year Established: 2018 **Status 2020:** Active
Industries: ~ Automotive (5), Embedded for:, ~ Manufacturing-General (31), ~ Social-Environmental-Physical-Engineering Sciences (55), Robotics

Company Name: Tagtog
Description: tagtog is a Web-based SaaS text annotation tool to train AI
Website: http://tagtog.net
Phone: **Email:** info@tagtog.net
City: **State:** ZA **PC:** **Country: Poland**
Year Established: **Status 2020:** Active
Industries: Artificial Intelligence for:, Databases for:, IT Managed Services for:, Machine Learning for:, ~ Professional Services (48), Data Management

Company Name: CTAdventure
Description: Machine Learning, Image Processing, Artificial Intelligence, Augmented Reality, Virtual Reality
Website: http://ctadventure.com
Phone: 48502436544 **Email:** contact@ctadventure.com
City: Gdansk **State:** PM **PC:** **Country: Poland**

Year Established: **Status 2020:** Active
Industries: Artificial Intelligence for:, Augmented Reality for:, Image Recognition for:, Machine Learning for:, ~ Manufacturing-Medical Equipment-Supplies (33)

Company Name: Neoteric
Description: End-to-end software product development for startups and enterpris: Spain
Website: http://www.neoteric.eu
Phone: 570044322 **Email:** cslowik@neoteric.eu
City: Gdansk **State:** PM **PC:** **Country: Poland**
Year Established: **Status 2020:** Active
Industries: Artificial Intelligence for:, Blockchain for:, IT Managed Services for:, Machine Learning for:, Business Process and Operations for:, Predictive Analytics for:, ~ Professional Services (48), ~ Professional Services (48)

Company Name: Brainhint
Description: Brainhint offers AI systems based on an internally developed platform for automation of operational decision making in large organizations.
Website: http://brainhint.com
Phone: (4873) 001-4646 **Email:** contact@brainhint.com
City: Chorzow **State:** Silesian Voivodeship **PC:** **Country: Poland**
Year Established: 2017 **Status 2020:** Active
Industries: Artificial Intelligence for:, IT Managed Services for:, IT Managed Services

Company Name: Digital Fingerprints
Description: Digital Fingerprints is a continuous authentication solution based on behavioural biometrics compliant with PSD2 and GD: PUERTO RICO
Website: http://fingerprints.digital
Phone: **Email:** contact@fingerprints.digital
City: Katowice **State:** Silesian Voivodeship **PC:** **Country: Poland**
Year Established: 2017 **Status 2020:** Active
Industries: Artificial Intelligence for:, Big Data and Analytics for:, ~ Biotechnology (9), Cyber Security for:, Security for:, Machine Learning for:, Risk Management

Company Name: VEMMIO
Description: VEMMIO is groundbreaking Smart Home system. We make things easy. Helping people live in comfort and save money.
Website: http://www.vemmio.com
Phone: 48606601006 **Email:** office@vemmio.com
City: Katowice **State:** Silesian Voivodeship **PC:** **Country: Poland**
Year Established: 2013 **Status 2020:** Active
Industries: Artificial Intelligence for:, Internet of Things (IoT) for:, ~ Construction (10)

Company Name: Enteye
Description: Develop and deploy scalable predictive maintenance solutions for industry machines.
Website: http://enteye.com
Phone: **Email:** contact@enteye.com
City: Ruda Slaska **State:** Silesian Voivodeship **PC:** **Country: Poland**
Year Established: 2013 **Status 2020:** Active
Industries:

Company Name: LETME.ai
Description: #thesearchisover. Let AI find it for you.
Website: http://www.letme.ai
Phone: **Email:** hi@letme.ai
City: Kielce **State:** Świętokrzyskie Voivodeship **PC:** **Country: Poland**
Year Established: 2016 **Status 2020:** Active
Industries: Artificial Intelligence for:, Web

Portugal

Company Name: Klugit Energy
Description: Klugit converts your current electric water heater into a smart, Wi-Fi and smart-grid ready product.
Website: http://klugitenergy.com
Phone: **Email:** info@klugitenergy.com
City: Aveiro **State:** Aveiro District **PC:** **Country: Portugal**
Year Established: 2018 **Status 2020:** Active
Industries:

Company Name: Anybra: India
Description: Anybrain is a artificial intelligence and data processing firm.
Website:
Phone: 351 253 216 254 **Email:** info@anybrain.gg
City: Braga **State:** Braga **PC:** **Country: Portugal**
Year Established: 2015 **Status 2020:** Active
Industries: Artificial Intelligence for:, IT Managed Services for:, IT Managed Services

Company Name: NeuroPsyAI
Description: NeuroPsyCAD provides clinicians with patient-personalized reports for early and accurate diagnoses of neuropsychiatric disorders.
Website: http://neuropsycad.com/
Phone: 966595936 **Email:** diana@neuropsycad.com
City: Braga **State:** Braga **PC:** **Country: Portugal**
Year Established: **Status 2020:** Active
Industries: Analytics for:, Artificial Intelligence for:, ~ Healthcare (20), ~ Healthcare (20), ~ Life Sciences (27)

Company Name: Performetric
Description: Real-time, adaptive system that monitors and manages mental fatigue in a non-invasive and non-intrusive way.
Website: http://performetric.net
Phone: 351 308804032 **Email:** geral@performetric.net
City: Braga **State:** Braga **PC:** **Country: Portugal**
Year Established: **Status 2020:** Active
Industries: Artificial Intelligence for:, Machine Learning for:, ~ Professional Services (48)

Company **Name:** Empire Puzzle
Description:
Website:
Phone: **Email:** 12486@reference-encyclopedia-ai.net
City: Castelo Branco **State:** Castelo Branco **Zip:** 6000-767
Country: Portugal
Year Established: **Status 2020:** Active
Industries:

Company Name: MATEREO
Description: MATEREO develops advanced data analytics for predictive and more reliable structural maintenance operations on bridges and overpasses. #SaaS
Website: http://matereo.com/
Phone: 351 239 700 300 **Email:** matereo@matereo.com
City: Coimbra **State:** Coimbra District **PC:** **Country: Portugal**
Year Established: 2014 **Status 2020:** Active
Industries: Artificial Intelligence for:, IT Managed Services

Company Name: Stratio Automotive
Description: Stratio Automotive transforms vehicle data into predictive intelligence.
Website: http://stratioautomotive.com/
Phone: 351 239 196 692 **Email:** business@stratioautomotive.com
City: Coimbra **State:** Coimbra District **PC:** **Country: Portugal**
Year Established: **Status 2020:** Active
Industries: Artificial Intelligence for:, ~ Automotive (5), ~ Social-Environmental-Physical-Engineering Sciences (55), ~ Professional Services (48)

Company Name: Wizdee
Description: Natural Language Self-Service Data Search and Discovery
Website: http://www.wizdee.com
Phone: **Email:** info@wizdee.com
City: Coimbra **State:** Coimbra District **PC:** **Country: Portugal**
Year Established: 2012 **Status 2020:** Active
Industries: Analytics for:, Artificial Intelligence for:, Big Data and Analytics for:, Business Intelligence for:, IT Managed Services

Company Name: Opz.io
Description: Opz.io is an intelligent time tracking solution that provides real-time analytics and reporting to individuals and companies.
Website: http://www.opz.io/
Phone: **Email:** info@opz.io
City: Faro **State:** Faro District **PC:** **Country: Portugal**
Year Established: **Status 2020:** Active
Industries: Analytics for:, Artificial Intelligence for:, Compute for:, ~ Professional Services (48)

Company Name: agriw
Description: Agriculture predictive systems with AI virtual assistant, based on big data algorithms, satellite imagery, and wireless sensor networks.
Website: http://www.agriw.: Portugal
Phone: **Email:** info@agriw.: Portugal
City: Obidos **State:** Leiria **PC:** **Country: Portugal**
Year Established: **Status 2020:** Active
Industries: Artificial Intelligence

Company Name: Bitcliq
Description: Bitcliq is a platform with blockchain technology that gathers fishing fleets and its custome: Serbia
Website: http://www.bitcliq.com/
Phone: 351 262 838 156 **Email:** hello@bitcliq.com
City: Caldas Da Rainha **State:** Leiria District **PC:** **Country: Portugal**
Year Established: 2013 **Status 2020:** Active
Industries: Artificial Intelligence for:, Blockchain for:, IT Managed Services for:, Internet of Things (IoT)

Company Name: Tesselo
Description: Planet B is too far away.
Website: http://tesselo.com
Phone: **Email:** hello@tesselo.com
City: Alcabideche **State:** Lisbon **PC:** **Country: Portugal**
Year Established: 2017 **Status 2020:** Active
Industries: Artificial Intelligence for:, IT Managed Services for:, ~ Social Assistance-Non-Profits (53)

Company Name: Botly
Description: A chatbot studio, developing automated agents with propertary algorithms to advise, recommend and sell insurance and financial products.
Website: http://www.botlystudio.ai
Phone: 351 927343915 **Email:** info@botlystudio.ai
City: Lisboa **State:** Lisbon **PC:** **Country: Portugal**
Year Established: 2016 **Status 2020:** Active
Industries:

Company Name: Reckon.ai
Description: Reckon uses AI and image recognition for helping retailers track and optimize their pricing strategies against their competition.
Website: http://reckon.ai/
Phone: **Email:** hello@reckon.ai
City: Lisboa **State:** Lisbon **PC:** **Country: Portugal**
Year Established: 2017 **Status 2020:** Active
Industries: Artificial Intelligence for:, Big Data and Analytics for:, Image Recognition for:, Business Software as a Service Apps (SaaS Apps)

Company Name: Talenteo
Description: Talenteo is the platform to recruit IT oriented people using the most recent technology.
Website: http://www.talenteo.co.uk/
Phone: **Email:** info@talenteo.co.uk
City: Lisboa **State:** Lisbon **PC:** **Country: Portugal**
Year Established: **Status 2020:** Active
Industries: Analytics for:, Artificial Intelligence for:, ~ Human Resources (24), Machine Learning for:, ~ Arts-Entertainment-Recreation (4), ~ Human Resources (24)

Company Name: Transend LDA
Description: Transend LDA is an Artificial Intelligence Platform for intelligent systems.
Website: http://www.transend.pt/trsendEN/
Phone: **Email:** contact@transend.: Portugal
City: Lisboa **State:** Lisbon **PC:** **Country: Portugal**
Year Established: 2016 **Status 2020:** Active
Industries: Artificial Intelligence for:, Databases for:, IT Managed Services for:, Machine Learning

Company Name: 20tree.ai
Description: Creating planet intelligence.
Website: http://www.20tree.ai
Phone: **Email:** info@20tree.ai
City: Lisbon **State:** Lisbon **PC:** **Country: Portugal**
Year Established: **Status 2020:** Active
Industries: Artificial Intelligence for:, Big Data and Analytics for:, Machine Learning for:, ~ Professional Services (48)

Company Name: Build Up Labs
Description: A startup studio, that repeatedly ideate, build and grow several startups in parallel
Website: http://www.builduplabs.com/
Phone: **Email:** rui@builduplabs.com
City: Lisbon **State:** Lisbon **PC:** **Country: Portugal**
Year Established: 2014 **Status 2020:** Active
Industries: Machine Learning for:, Business Software as a Service Apps (SaaS Apps) for:, ~ Social Assistance-Non-Profits (53)

Company **Name:** Builtrix
Description: Your trusted partner to improve Water & Energy Management, Operation Performance and Financial Health of your Building.
Website: http://builtrix.tech
Phone: **Email:** info@builtrix.tech
City: Lisbon **State:** Lisbon **PC:** **Country: Portugal**
Year Established: **Status 2020:** Active
Industries: Artificial Intelligence for:, Big Data and Analytics for:, Data Management for:, Data Management for:, ~ Real Estate (49), ~ Professional Services (48)

Company Name: Climber Hotel
Description: Climber is a Revenue Management Software for small hotel chains.
Website: http://www.climberhotel.com
Phone: **Email:** sales@climberhotel.com
City: Lisbon **State:** Lisbon **PC:** **Country: Portugal**
Year Established: **Status 2020:** Active
Industries: Analytics for:, Artificial Intelligence for:, ~ Hospitality (23), Machine Learning

Company Name: Climber RMS
Description: Climber is a Revenue Management Software for small hotel chains.
Website: http://climberrms.com
Phone: **Email:** sales@climberhotel.com
City: Lisbon **State:** Lisbon **PC:** **Country: Portugal**
Year Established: 2015 **Status 2020:** Active
Industries: Analytics for:, Artificial Intelligence for:, Business Software as a Service Apps (SaaS Apps)

Company Name: Daimler Trucks and Buses Tech and Data Hub
Description: Daimler Trucks and Buses Tech and Data Hub creates value from real-time data by leveraging the power of machine learning and big data.
Website: http://techhublisbon.io/
Phone: **Email:** techhublisbon@daimler.com
City: Lisbon **State:** Lisbon **PC:** **Country: Portugal**
Year Established: 2018 **Status 2020:** Active
Industries: Artificial Intelligence for:, Big Data and Analytics for:, IT Managed Services for:, Machine Learning

Company Name: DareData Engineering
Description: DareData Engineering is a data science consultancy and contractor with aims to bootstrap a product.
Website: http://daredata.engineering/
Phone: **Email:** contact@daredata.engineering
City: Lisbon **State:** Lisbon **PC:** **Country: Portugal**
Year Established: 2017 **Status 2020:** Active
Industries: Robotics

Company Name: dDataMarket
Description: Enabling organizations to use AI, by providing them with the tools and the data to train machine learning models efficiently.
Website:
Phone: **Email:** 4934@reference-encyclopedia-ai.net
City: Lisbon **State:** Lisbon **PC:** **Country: Portugal**
Year Established: **Status 2020:** Active
Industries: Artificial Intelligence for:, Big Data and Analytics for:, Cloud for:, Machine Learning

Company Name: DocDigitizer
Description: DocDigitizer is teaching machines to read documents that humans don't want to read.
Website: http://docdigitizer.com
Phone: 351 214 139 860 **Email:** 36447@reference-encyclopedia-ai.net
City: Lisbon **State:** Lisbon **PC:** **Country: Portugal**
Year Established: 2017 **Status 2020:** Active
Industries: Artificial Intelligence for:, ~ Automotive (5), Machine Learning

Company Name: EyeSee Solutions
Description: Artificial Intelligence Applications for Mobile and Video Advertising
Website: http://www.EyeSeeSolutions.com
Phone: **Email:** info@eyeseesolutions.com
City: Lisbon **State:** Lisbon **PC:** **Country: Portugal**
Year Established: 2011 **Status 2020:** Active
Industries: Artificial Intelligence for:, Digital Media

Company Name: GOVWI: SWEDEN
Description: GOVWISE is the sales prediction tool for companies that sell to the public sector.
Website: http://en.govwise.biz/
Phone: **Email:** info@govwise.biz
City: Lisbon **State:** Lisbon **PC:** **Country: Portugal**
Year Established: **Status 2020:** Active
Industries:

Company Name: Heptasense
Description: SaaS platform for people behavior analytics through security cameras.
Website: http://www.heptasense.com
Phone: **Email:** info@heptasense.com
City: Lisbon **State:** Lisbon **PC:** **Country: Portugal**
Year Established: **Status 2020:** Active
Industries: Analytics for:, Artificial Intelligence for:, Cloud for:, Computer Vision for:, Automation for:, Machine Learning for:, Predictive Analytics

Company Name: HiJiffy
Description: Messenger Concierge for the hospitality sector
Website: http://hijiffy.com
Phone: 351 91 739 01 52 **Email:** info@hijiffy.: Portugal
City: Lisbon **State:** Lisbon **PC:** **Country: Portugal**
Year Established: 2015 **Status 2020:** Active
Industries: Application Services for:, Artificial Intelligence

Company Name: IBSHURANCE
Description: IBSHURANCE help insurance companies to automate claims, manage all providers, reduce costs and improve customer experience
Website: http://ibshurance.com/
Phone: 351 967 570 432 **Email:** hello@ibshurance.com
City: Lisbon **State:** Lisbon **PC:** **Country: Portugal**
Year Established: 2017 **Status 2020:** Active
Industries: Machine Learning

Company Name: K1 Digital
Description: K1 Digital develops solutions with the use of intelligent technologies, helping organizations in their digital transformation.
Website: http://www.k-1-digital.com/
Phone: 351 213 860 992 **Email:** contact@k-1-digital.com
City: Lisbon **State:** Lisbon **PC:** **Country: Portugal**
Year Established: 2017 **Status 2020:** Active
Industries: IT Managed Services for:, Application Services for:, Machine Learning for:, Application Services

Company Name: Liquid
Description: Automated growth marketing for mobile ap: Palestine
Website: http://www.onliquid.com
Phone: **Email:** info@onliquid.com
City: Lisbon **State:** Lisbon **PC:** **Country: Portugal**
Year Established: **Status 2020:** Active
Industries: Analytics for:, Artificial Intelligence for:, Machine Learning for:, ~ Media-Communications (41), Mobile for:, ~ Media-Communications (41)

Company **Name:** Meta Innovation Consulting Group
Description: MetaICG helps businesses deliver technology products and services to market quickly, reliably, and cost-effectively.
Website: http://www.meta-icg.com
Phone: 351 211 306 718 **Email:** info@meta-icg.com
City: Lisbon **State:** Lisbon **PC:** **Country: Portugal**
Year Established: 2014 **Status 2020:** Active
Industries: Analytics for:, Artificial Intelligence for:, IT Managed Services for:, IT Managed Services for:, Internet of Things (IoT) for:, ~ Customer Relationship Management (11)

Company Name: muse.ai
Description: muse.ai is an international company that is building an Advanced Artificial Intelligence for understanding the world's video content.
Website: http://muse.ai/
Phone: **Email:** info@muse.ai
City: Lisbon **State:** Lisbon **PC:** **Country: Portugal**
Year Established: 2015 **Status 2020:** Active
Industries: Artificial Intelligence

Company Name: Muzzley
Description: Muzzley is a single intelligent entry point for connected devices, and a complete SaaS and PaaS solution for consumer IoT.
Website: http://muzzley.com/muzzleyforbusiness
Phone: 351 96 760 2782 **Email:** we@muzzley.com
City: Lisbon **State:** Lisbon **PC:** **Country: Portugal**
Year Established: 2012 **Status 2020:** Active
Industries: IT Managed Services for:, Internet of Things (IoT) for:, Machine Learning for:, Business Software as a Service Apps (SaaS Apps)

Company Name: Planless.io
Description: Saas intelligent project management
Website: http://planless.io
Phone: **Email:** hello@planless.io
City: Lisbon **State:** Lisbon **PC:** **Country: Portugal**
Year Established: 2017 **Status 2020:** Active
Industries: Artificial Intelligence for:, Business Process and Operations

Company Name: Sensei
Description: Sensei is a business intelligence platform for retail, it captures and relates in-store with digital raw data for business optimisation.
Website: http://www.sensei.tech
Phone: **Email:** info@sensei.tech
City: Lisbon **State:** Lisbon **PC:** **Country: Portugal**
Year Established: **Status 2020:** Active
Industries: Analytics for:, Artificial Intelligence for:, Computer Vision for:, ~ Retail and Consumer Products (52)

Company Name: Twihive Digital
Description: Artificial Intelligence for Designers: Saving time, effort and money
Website: http://www.digital.twihive.com
Phone: **Email:** digital@twihive.com
City: Lisbon **State:** Lisbon **PC:** **Country: Portugal**
Year Established: 2019 **Status 2020:** Active
Industries: ~ Arts-Entertainment-Recreation (4), Artificial Intelligence for:, IT Managed Services for:, Machine Learning

Company Name: Virtuleap
Description: VR Brain Training for Cognitive Heal:Thailand
Website: http://www.virtuleap.com
Phone: **Email:** amir@virtuleap.com
City: Lisbon **State:** Lisbon **PC:** **Country: Portugal**
Year Established: 2018 **Status 2020:** Active
Industries: Application Services for:, Artificial Intelligence for:, Big Data and Analytics for:, ~ Biotechnology (9), ~ Education (13), ~ Arts-Entertainment-Recreation (4), ~ Healthcare (20), ~ Healthcare (20), ~ Healthcare (20), ~ Healthcare (20), ~ Healthcare (20)

Company Name: Visor.ai
Description: Visor.ai helps companies to automate interactions using artificial inteligence and chatbots.
Website: http://www.visor.ai
Phone: 351 913 566 776 **Email:** info@visor.ai
City: Lisbon **State:** Lisbon **PC:** **Country: Portugal**
Year Established: **Status 2020:** Active
Industries: Artificial Intelligence for:, Machine Learning

Company Name: YData
Description: Elevating data privacy in a world moving towards AI
Website: http://ydata.ai
Phone: **Email:** hello@ydata.ai
City: Lisbon **State:** Lisbon **PC:** **Country: Portugal**
Year Established: 2019 **Status 2020:** Active
Industries:

Company Name: Zecoda
Description: SaaS platform that turns design files into code automatically
Website: http://zecoda.com
Phone: **Email:** contact@zecoda.com
City: Lisbon **State:** Lisbon **PC:** **Country: Portugal**
Year Established: 2019 **Status 2020:** Active
Industries: Artificial Intelligence for:, Enterprise Application Services for:, Machine Learning for:, Business Software as a Service Apps (SaaS Apps)

Company Name: GitScrum
Description: GitScrum is an application to task management of the day-to-day. Git Scrum = Team More Productive
Website: http://gitscrum.com
Phone: **Email:** renato.marinho@gitscrum.com
City: Sintra **State:** Lisbon **PC:** **Country: Portugal**
Year Established: **Status 2020:** Active
Industries: Artificial Intelligence for:, Application Services

Company Name: Adaptive
Description: Adaptive researches and develops projects in Artificial Intelligence, Communication Security, Electronic Transaction Systems, Adaptive
Website: http://www.adaptive.: Portugal
Phone: 351-291098007 **Email:** info@adaptive.: Portugal
City: Funchal **State:** Madeira **PC:** **Country: Portugal**
Year Established: **Status 2020:** Active
Industries: Artificial Intelligence for:, Security for:, IT Managed Services

Company Name: Alientech.com
Description: Alientech.com offers website analytics tools that provide the users with real time statistics.
Website: https://alientech.com/
Phone: **Email:** 36040@reference-encyclopedia-ai.net
City: Porto **State:** Porto **PC:** **Country: Portugal**
Year Established: 2016 **Status 2020:** Active
Industries: Analytics for:, Predictive Analytics

Company Name: Bandora Systems
Description: Artificial Intelligence platform for Energy Efficiency in Buildings
Website: http://www.bandorasystems.com
Phone: (351)918221853 **Email:** marciafspereira@gmail.com
City: Porto **State:** Porto **PC:** **Country: Portugal**
Year Established: **Status 2020:** Active
Industries: Artificial Intelligence for:, Big Data and Analytics for:, ~ Energy and Utilities (14), Machine Learning for:, ~ Professional Services (48)

Company **Name:** HealthyRoad
Description: HealthyRoad is a technology company that develops AI facial biometric software for the automotive industry.
Website: www.healthyroad.: Portugal
Phone: **Email:** geral@healthyroad.: Portugal
City: Porto **State:** Porto **PC:** **Country: Portugal**
Year Established: **Status 2020:** Active
Industries: Artificial Intelligence for:, ~ Automotive (5), ~ Biotechnology (9), ~ Transportation and Logistics (57), Machine Learning for:, Risk Management for:, ~ Professional Services (48)

Company Name: InovReta: Israel
Description: Inovretail is a Predictive Analytics company focused on helping retailers predictict promotional impact, stockouts and sales baselines.
Website: http://www.inovretail.com/
Phone: **Email:** info@inovretail.com
City: Porto **State:** Porto **PC:** **Country: Portugal**
Year Established: 2011 **Status 2020:** Active
Industries: Predictive Analytics

Company Name: Luna.ai
Description: Luna.ai is Customer interactions automation, for marketing, support and sales,
Website: http://luna.ai
Phone: **Email:** 36897103@qq.com
City: Porto **State:** Porto **PC:** **Country: Portugal**
Year Established: 2016 **Status 2020:** Active
Industries: Artificial Intelligence for:, ~ Social Media (54)

Company Name: Movvo
Description: Movvo is a global technology company strategically positioned at the intersection of the retail industry, artificial intelligence and custom
Website: http://www.movvo.com
Phone: 351 22 243 0089 **Email:** hello@movvo.com
City: Porto **State:** Porto **PC:** **Country: Portugal**

Year Established: **Status 2020:** Active
Industries: Analytics for:, Artificial Intelligence for:, Business Intelligence for:, ~ Real Estate (49), Machine Learning for:, ~ Real Estate (49), ~ Professional Services (48)

Company Name: Nemobile Applications Worldwide
Description: Become an AI-driven Business, empower your sales and achieve real ROI.
Website: http://nemobile.app
Phone: **Email:** info@nemobile.app
City: Porto **State:** Porto **PC:** **Country: Portugal**
Year Established: 2019 **Status 2020:** Active
Industries: Artificial Intelligence for:, ~ Automotive (5), IT Managed Services for:, Machine Learning for:, Business Software as a Service Apps (SaaS Apps)

Company Name: NILG.AI
Description: Artificial Intelligence, Data Science, Computer Vision
Website: http://www.nilg.ai
Phone: **Email:** info@nilg.ai
City: Porto **State:** Porto **PC:** **Country: Portugal**
Year Established: 2018 **Status 2020:** Active
Industries: Artificial Intelligence for:, Computer Vision for:, Machine Learning for:, Natural Language Processing for:, Predictive Analytics

Company Name: Nimest Tech
Description: Nimest Tech is a travel assistant, powered with AI, AR and Storytelling techniques.
Website: http://www.nimest.co
Phone: 351 920 333 697 **Email:** info@nimest.co
City: Porto **State:** Porto **PC:** **Country: Portugal**
Year Established: 2017 **Status 2020:** Active
Industries: ~ Arts-Entertainment-Recreation (4), Artificial Intelligence for:, Augmented Reality for:, ~ Travel and Transportation (58)

Company Name: Shelf.AI
Description: Shelf.AI bring AI to e-commerce and empower retailers to engage with customers in truly personalised shopping experience.
Website: http://www.shelf.ai/
Phone: 351 22 0933931 **Email:** info@shelf.ai
City: Porto **State:** Porto **PC:** **Country: Portugal**
Year Established: **Status 2020:** Active
Industries: Artificial Intelligence for:, E-Commerce for:, ~ Retail and Consumer Products (52)

Company Name: SWORD Heal:Thailand
Description: SWORD Health is a medical company that created the first AI-powered digital physical therapist, shifting healthcare from analog to digital.
Website: http://www.swordhealth.com
Phone: 351 22 324 8286 **Email:** hello@swordhealth.com
City: Porto **State:** Porto **PC:** **Country: Portugal**
Year Established: **Status 2020:** Active
Industries:

Company Name: Wisecrop
Description: Wisecrop is an online Agricultural Operating System that provides predictive indicators and business management tools.
Website: http://www.wisecrop.com
Phone: **Email:** info@wisecrop.com
City: Porto **State:** Porto **PC:** **Country: Portugal**
Year Established: 2012 **Status 2020:** Active
Industries: ~ Agriculture (3), Business Intelligence for:, IT Managed Services for:, Internet of Things (IoT) for:, Predictive Analytics

Company Name: zenPrice
Description: Competitive intelligence pricing SaaS for Communication Service Providers. It enables better decisions for your pricing strategy
Website: http://zenprice.com
Phone: **Email:** info@zenprice.com
City: Porto **State:** Porto **PC:** **Country: Portugal**
Year Established: 2019 **Status 2020:** Active
Industries: Artificial Intelligence for:, Business Software as a Service Apps (SaaS Apps)

Company Name: HUUB
Description: HUUB is democratising Supply Chain through Technology by allowing Fashion Brands to manage its physical and data flow in a unified ecosystem
Website: http://thehuub.co/
Phone: **Email:** hello@thehuub.co
City: Maia **State:** Porto District **PC:** **Country: Portugal**
Year Established: 2015 **Status 2020:** Active
Industries: Artificial Intelligence for:, Business Intelligence for:, E-Commerce for:, ~ Telecommunications (56), ~ Transportation and Logistics (57), Supply Chain Management

Company Name: Cmantix
Description: SaaS
Website: http://cmantix.com/
Phone: **Email:** media@cmantix.com
City: Oporto **State:** Porto District **PC:** **Country: Portugal**
Year Established: **Status 2020:** Active
Industries: Artificial Intelligence for:, Machine Learning for:, Natural Language Processing for:, Content for:, Cyber Security for:, Data Management

Company Name: ShopAI.co
Description: We are harnessing AI for building image based search engines for fashion brands. See, shoot, search and buy.
Website: http://shopai.co/
Phone: **Email:** hello@shopai.co
City: Oporto **State:** Porto District **PC:** **Country: Portugal**
Year Established: **Status 2020:** Active
Industries: Artificial Intelligence for:, Big Data and Analytics for:, E-Commerce for:, ~ Fashion (16), ~ Retail and Consumer Products (52)

Company **Name:** Immersive Lives
Description: Immersive Lives expanding reality through people-centric solutions.
Website: http://immersivelives.: Portugal
Phone: (351) 966 057 132 **Email:** research@immersivelives.: Portugal
City: Obidos **State:** Santarem **PC:** **Country: Portugal**
Year Established: 2016 **Status 2020:** Active
Industries: Artificial Intelligence for:, Virtual Reality (VR)

Company Name: Plicca
Description: Deep Learning Saas
Website: http://plicca.com
Phone: **Email:** 37180@reference-encyclopedia-ai.net
City: Almada **State:** Setubal **PC:** **Country: Portugal**
Year Established: 2018 **Status 2020:** Active
Industries: IT Managed Services for:, Machine Learning for:, Data Management

Company Name: Enging
Description: Enging provides smart online monitoring solutions based on predictive maintenance for industrial electrical machines.
Website: http://enging.pt/
Phone: 351 913 887 000 **Email:** geral@enging.: Portugal
City: Lagares **State:** Viseu **PC:** **Country: Portugal**
Year Established: 2012 **Status 2020:** Active
Industries: IT Managed Services for:, Internet of Things (IoT) for:, Predictive Analytics

Puerto Rico

Company Name: Migo IQ
Description: Migo IQ is a real-world recommendation engine.
Website: http://www.migoiq.com/
Phone: (888)292-8689 **Email:** info@migoIQ.com
City: San Juan **State:** San Juan **PC:** **Country:** Puerto Rico RICO
Year Established: 2014 **Status 2020:** Active
Industries: Machine Learning

Romania

Company Name: Logistix Cloud
Description: AI powered Transportation Management Software
Website: http://www.logistix-cloud.com/en/home/
Phone: **Email:** info@ghb-software.com
City: Oradea **State:** BH **PC:** **Country: Romania**
Year Established: 2017 **Status 2020:** Active
Industries: Artificial Intelligence for:, IT Managed Services for:, ~ Telecommunications (56), Business Software as a Service Apps (SaaS Apps)

Company Name: Mondly
Description: Mondly helps over 50 million people learn 33 languages @ VR, iOS, Android, Web | "App of the Year" in 2017 by Facebook in EMEA
Website: http://www.mondly.com
Phone: (4073) 396-9116 **Email:** contact@mondly.com
City: Brasov **State:** BV **PC:** **Country: Romania**
Year Established: 2013 **Status 2020:** Active
Industries: Application Services for:, Augmented Reality for:, ~ Education (13), ~ Education (13), Machine Learning for:, Application Services for:, Speech Recognition for:, Speech Recognition for:, Virtual Reality (VR) for:, Web

Company Name: Hubgets
Description: Instant communication & collaboration that makes your business more profitable. Boost your team's productivity now!
Website: http://www.hubgets.com
Phone: (302)353-4432 **Email:** social@hubgets.com
City: Bucarest **State:** Bucharest **PC:** **Country: Romania**
Year Established: 2011 **Status 2020:** Active
Industries: Artificial Intelligence for:, Collaboration Solutions for:, Enterprise Application Services for:, IT Managed Services for:, Application Services for:, Business Software as a Service Apps (SaaS Apps) for:, Business Strategy and Design

Company Name: AQUASoft
Description: Our special care for top notch people and innovative technologies placed us as premier provider in software industry.
Website: http://www.aquasoft.: Romania
Phone: (021) 313-3930 **Email:** office@aquasoft.: Romania
City: Bucharest **State:** Bucharest **PC:** **Country: Romania**
Year Established: **Status 2020:** Active
Industries: Application Services for:, Artificial Intelligence for:, Business Applications for:, Application Services for:, Enterprise Application Services for:, ~ Administrative and Support Services (1), ~ Retail and Consumer Products (52), ~ Professional Services (48)

Company Name: DeviceHub
Description: DeviceHub is an integrated PaaS (Platform as a Service) for IoT solutions, in order to integrate both hardware and web technologies.
Website: http://www.devicehub.net
Phone: 40721262666 **Email:** contact@devicehub.net
City: Bucharest **State:** Bucharest **PC:** **Country: Romania**
Year Established: **Status 2020:** Active
Industries:

Company Name: DRUID
Description: DRUID is an AI-powered enterprise chatbot platform that allows easy development of chat or voice-enabled intelligent virtual assistants
Website: http://www.druidai.com
Phone: (004) 031 06 99 256 **Email:** marketing@druidai.com
City: Bucharest **State:** Bucharest **PC:** **Country: Romania**
Year Established: 2018 **Status 2020:** Active
Industries: Artificial Intelligence for:, Enterprise Application Services for:, IT Managed Services for:, Machine Learning for:, Collaboration Solutions

Company Name: Femyo
Description: Europe's first medical marketplace dedicated to women.
Website: http://www.femyo.co.uk
Phone: **Email:** support@femyo.co.uk
City: Bucharest **State:** Bucharest **PC:** **Country: Romania**
Year Established: **Status 2020:** Active
Industries: Artificial Intelligence for:, E-Commerce for:, Application Services

Company Name: Footprints for Reta: Israel
Description: The most advanced marketing automation tool to act on what your shoppers want and except in your shopping centers.
Website: http://footprintsforretail.com/
Phone: (4074) 520-1896 **Email:** dan.marculescu@footprintsforretail.com
City: Bucharest **State:** Bucharest **PC:** **Country: Romania**
Year Established: 2014 **Status 2020:** Active
Industries: Big Data and Analytics for:, ~ Customer Relationship Management (11), Data Management for:, ~ Media-Communications (41), Application Services for:, Application Services for:, Predictive Analytics

Company Name: KFactory
Description: KFactory applies IoT and machine learning in manufacturing, boosting performance on production.
Website: http://www.kfactory.eu
Phone: **Email:** 36851@reference-encyclopedia-ai.net
City: Bucharest **State:** Bucharest **PC:** **Country: Romania**
Year Established: 2017 **Status 2020:** Active
Industries: Databases for:, IT Managed Services for:, Internet of Things (IoT) for:, Machine Learning for:, Application Services

Company Name: Q-intell
Description: The prize goes to the person who sees the future the quickest!
Website: http://www.Q-intell.com
Phone: **Email:** contact@q-intell.com
City: Bucharest **State:** Bucharest **PC:** **Country: Romania**
Year Established: 2016 **Status 2020:** Active
Industries: Analytics for:, Business Intelligence for:, Data Management for:, Predictive Analytics

Company Name: ScentSee
Description: ScentSee is an API that helps customers find a scent that they are interested in.
Website: http://get.scentSee.com
Phone: 40 724 714 234 **Email:** bogdan@scentsee.com
City: Bucharest **State:** Bucharest **PC:** **Country: Romania**
Year Established: 2015 **Status 2020:** Active
Industries: Databases for:, Application Program Interfaces (APIs) for:, Machine Learning

Company Name: SecurifAI
Description: SecurifAI develop AI systems for real-time video analysis.
Website: http://www.securifai.: Romania
Phone: 40 744 55 97 38 **Email:** contact@securifai.: Romania
City: Bucharest **State:** Bucharest **PC:** **Country: Romania**
Year Established: **Status 2020:** Active
Industries: Artificial Intelligence for:, Compute for:, ~ Media-Communications (41)

Company Name: Sether
Description: Sether is the new smart contract developer tool to use the power of social media.
Website: http://sether.com/
Phone: 4031 428 2612 **Email:** contact@sether.com
City: Bucharest **State:** Bucharest **PC:** **Country: Romania**
Year Established: **Status 2020:** Active
Industries: Artificial Intelligence for:, Big Data and Analytics for:, Blockchain for:, Security

Company Name: VisageCloud
Description: Face recognition meets big data. In-cloud or on-premise.
Website: http://visagecloud.com
Phone: **Email:** 37631@reference-encyclopedia-ai.net
City: Bucharest **State:** Bucharest **PC:** **Country: Romania**
Year Established: 2016 **Status 2020:** Active
Industries: Analytics for:, Artificial Intelligence for:, Big Data and Analytics for:, Computer Vision for:, Application Program Interfaces (APIs) for:, IT Managed Services

Company Name: Optimus Digital
Description: Electronics and Information Technology
Website: http://www.optimusdigital.com
Phone: 44 772172343 **Email:** bogdan.florea@optimusdigital.com
City: Buzau **State:** BZ **PC:** **Country: Romania**
Year Established: **Status 2020:** Active
Industries: Artificial Intelligence for:, ~ Manufacturing-Electronic (30), Embedded for:, IT Managed Services for:, Machine Learning

Company Name: MediaServista
Description: MediaServista is a content curation platform for advertisers and publishers.
Website: http://www.mediaservista.com
Phone: 40752200344 **Email:** george.bara@24cloud.: Romania
City: Cluj **State:** CJ **PC:** **Country: Romania**
Year Established: **Status 2020:** Active
Industries: Artificial Intelligence for:, ~ Life Sciences (27), Predictive Analytics for:, ~ Media-Communications (41), ~ Professional Services (48)

Company Name: Tembo Cafe
Description: Tembo is a coffee house franchise with a machine learning driven coffee ordering app.
Website: http://www.tembo.cafe
Phone: **Email:** hello@tembo.cafe
City: Cluj **State:** CJ **PC:** **Country: Romania**
Year Established: 2017 **Status 2020:** Active
Industries: Application Services for:, Business Applications for:, Business Applications for:, ~ Agriculture (3), E-Commerce for:, Machine Learning for:, Enterprise Application Services

Company Name: teleportHQ
Description: AI-powered Visual Development Platform
Website: http://teleporthq.io/
Phone: **Email:** hello@teleporthq.io
City: Cluj-napoca **State:** CJ **PC:** **Country: Romania**
Year Established: 2017 **Status 2020:** Active
Industries: IT Managed Services for:, Web for:, Machine Learning

Company Name: Tralio
Description: Tralio is an intelligent agent that specializes in AI solutions for the financial services and other sectors.
Website: http://www.tralio.ai
Phone: **Email:** 37556@reference-encyclopedia-ai.net
City: Cluj-napoca **State:** CJ **PC:** **Country: Romania**
Year Established: 2017 **Status 2020:** Closed
Industries:

Company Name: Digitalya OPS
Description: Digital product development for innovative startups using the less is more methodology.
Website: http://digitalya.co
Phone: 40 726 216 174 **Email:** ovidiu@digitalya.co
City: Iasi **State:** IS **PC:** **Country: Romania**
Year Established: **Status 2020:** Active
Industries: Artificial Intelligence for:, Big Data and Analytics for:, Web for:, Cyber Security

Company Name: GreenSoft
Description: GreenSoft is a software service provider that incorporates innovation and technology from AI to improve client competitiveness on market.
Website: http://www.greensoft.com.: Romania
Phone: **Email:** adi.brezulianu@greensoft.com.: Romania
City: Iasi **State:** IS **PC:** **Country: Romania**
Year Established: **Status 2020:** Active
Industries: Artificial Intelligence for:, Enterprise Application Services for:, ~ Professional Services (48)

Company Name: Marionette Studio
Description: Animate Everything Online
Website: http://marionettestudio.com/
Phone: 40727308676 **Email:** feedback@marionettestudio.com
City: Iasi **State:** IS **PC:** **Country: Romania**
Year Established: **Status 2020:** Active
Industries: ~ Arts-Entertainment-Recreation (4), ~ Arts-Entertainment-Recreation (4), Artificial Intelligence for:, ~ Media-Communications (41), ~ Arts-Entertainment-Recreation (4), ~ Professional Services (48), ~ Media-Communications (41), ~ Arts-Entertainment-Recreation (

Company Name: Nurss
Description: Nurss enables user to precise diagnostic predictions in order to avoid the occurrence and aggravation of diseases.
Website:
Phone: **Email:** 37086@reference-encyclopedia-ai.net
City: Iasi **State:** IS **PC:** **Country: Romania**
Year Established: 2014 **Status 2020:** Closed
Industries: Big Data and Analytics for:, ~ Healthcare (20), IT Managed Services for:, Internet of Things (IoT) for:, ~ Healthcare (20), Mobile for:, Predictive Analytics for:, Predictive Analytics

Company Name: Happy Recruiter
Description: Happy Recruiter is the Recruitment Robot will recruit for all the projects you have.
Website: http://happyrecruiter.com/en/
Phone: 40 738 766 894 **Email:** office@happyrecruiter.com
City: Targu-mures **State:** MS **PC:** **Country: Romania**
Year Established: **Status 2020:** Active
Industries: Artificial Intelligence for:, Robotics

Company Name: Estesis
Description: Estesis offers software development using artificial intelligence and data science services.
Website: http://estesis.tech
Phone: 7.991.369.9758 **Email:** sales@estesis.tech
City: Barnaul **State:** Altai Krai **PC:** **Country:** Russia
Year Established: 2019 **Status 2020:** Active
Industries: Artificial Intelligence

Russia

Company Name: Cashee
Description: Cashee is a smart recommendation system based on customer face recognition.
Website: http://cashee.: Russia
Phone: 7 921 073 37 07 **Email:** sales@cashee.: Russia
City: Arkhangelsk **State:** Arkhangelsk Oblast **PC:** **Country:** Russia

Year Established: 2017 **Status 2020:** Active
Industries: Artificial Intelligence for:, IT Managed Services for:, Web

Company Name: Exciting Reality
Description: Exciting Reality offers application development with AR, VR and MR services.
Website: http://funreality.: Russia
Phone: 7.834.230.5138 **Email:** info@funreality.: Russia
City: Saransk **State:** Mordovia Republic **PC:** **Country:** Russia
Year Established: 2011 **Status 2020:** Active
Industries: Artificial Intelligence

Company Name: RILOS
Description: Rilos is the owner of Geomatrix solution, a proptech online SaaS predictive analytics for retailers operating in 65 countri: Spain
Website: http://www.rilos.ru/en
Phone: 74996382414 **Email:** geomatrix@rilos.: Russia
City: Moscou **State:** Moscow City **PC:** **Country:** Russia
Year Established: 2010 **Status 2020:** Active
Industries: ~ Retail and Consumer Products (52), Predictive Analytics for:, Business Software as a Service Apps (SaaS Apps)

Company Name: Agrosputnik
Description: Analytical software for crop monitoring powered by machine learning
Website: https://agrosputnik.com/
Phone: **Email:** team@agrosputnik.com
City: Moscow **State:** Moscow City **PC:** **Country:** Russia
Year Established: 2016 **Status 2020:** Active
Industries: ~ Agriculture (3), Artificial Intelligence for:, Machine Learning

Company Name: Akeso
Description: Aeso is a startup that engages in the analysis of medical data using machine learning.
Website: https://www.akesomed.ru/
Phone: **Email:** info@akesomed.: Russia
City: Moscow **State:** Moscow City **PC:** **Country:** Russia
Year Established: 2017 **Status 2020:** Active
Industries: Artificial Intelligence for:, ~ Healthcare (20), Machine Learning

Company Name: Alpha Smart Systems
Description: Alpha Smart Systems is an international developer of robots and robotized ecosystem, innovative solutions and artificial intelligence.
Website: http://alpha-smart.com/
Phone: (646) 666-9994 **Email:** info@alpha-smart.com
City: Moscow **State:** Moscow City **PC:** **Country:** Russia
Year Established: 2011 **Status 2020:** Active
Industries: Artificial Intelligence for:, IT Managed Services for:, IT Managed Services for:, Robotics

Company Name: Antip.io
Description: AI platform for BTL and retail audience analysis.
Website: http://antip.io
Phone: **Email:** mike@antip.io
City: Moscow **State:** Moscow City **PC:** **Country:** Russia
Year Established: 2019 **Status 2020:** Active
Industries: Analytics for:, Artificial Intelligence for:, Facial Recognition for:, IT Managed Services

Company Name: ARMAKS GROUP
Description: Smart Governance Platform
Website: http://armaksgroup.com
Phone: 79060643333 **Email:** maxim@armaksgroup.com
City: Moscow **State:** Moscow City **PC:** **Country:** Russia
Year Established: 2016 **Status 2020:** Active
Industries:

Company Name: AVATARIKA
Description: SaaS AI virtual assistance for b2b2b
Website: http://avatarika.com/
Phone: (7926) 532-9726 **Email:** yura@avatarika.com
City: Moscow **State:** Moscow City **PC:** **Country:** Russia
Year Established: 2020 **Status 2020:** Active
Industries: Artificial Intelligence for:, Machine Learning for:, Business Software as a Service Apps (SaaS Apps) for:, Automation

Company Name: BestFitMe
Description: BestFitMe is an Artificial intelligence and computer vision for psychological profiling of candidates and employee.
Website: http://job.bestfitme.ru/
Phone: 7 (499) 391 4596 **Email:** hello@bestfitme.: Russia
City: Moscow **State:** Moscow City **PC:** **Country:** Russia
Year Established: 2013 **Status 2020:** Active
Industries: Artificial Intelligence

Company Name: BestPlace
Description: BestPlace is a B2B geo-information service for an accurate forecast of the revenue of a new outlet based on machine learning algorithms.
Website: http://bestplace.pro/
Phone: 7 (495) 803-35-96 **Email:** box@bestplace.p: Romania
City: Moscow **State:** Moscow City **PC:** **Country:** Russia
Year Established: 2016 **Status 2020:** Active
Industries: Artificial Intelligence for:, Internet of Things (IoT) for:, Machine Learning

Company Name: BINDX.AI
Description: B2B sales acceleration service using predictive analytics based on AI focused on emerging economies.
Website: http://bindx.ai
Phone: 7 499 110-01-50 **Email:** info@bindx.ai
City: Moscow **State:** Moscow City **PC:** **Country:** Russia
Year Established: 2017 **Status 2020:** Active
Industries: Artificial Intelligence for:, Big Data and Analytics for:, E-Commerce for:, Automation

Company Name: Botkin.AI
Description: Artificial Intelligence to build and use mathematical patient representation models for diagnostics and desease risk assessment
Website: http://botkin.ai/
Phone: **Email:** info@botkin.ai
City: Moscow **State:** Moscow City **PC:** **Country:** Russia
Year Established: 2017 **Status 2020:** Active
Industries: Analytics for:, Artificial Intelligence for:, ~ Healthcare (20)

Company **Name:** CERA
Description: AI-based and Computer vision Retail analytics platform.
Website: http://www.ceremarketing.com/
Phone: 7-499-640-99-10 **Email:** office@ceramarketing.com
City: Moscow **State:** Moscow City **PC:** **Country:** Russia
Year Established: 2013 **Status 2020:** Active
Industries: Analytics for:, Artificial Intelligence for:, Computer Vision for:, Image Recognition for:, IT Managed Services for:, IT Managed Services for:, Predictive Analytics

Company Name: ChatFirst
Description: AI Virtual Assistants for employees of your company
Website: http://chatfirst.co/
Phone: **Email:** info@chatfirst.co
City: Moscow **State:** Moscow City **PC:** **Country:** Russia
Year Established: 2016 **Status 2020:** Active
Industries: Artificial Intelligence for:, Business Applications

Company Name: Clover Group
Description: Innovative company with diversified prognostics-based product portfolio, which employs hybrid approcaches for equipment behavior estimation
Website: http://clover.global/
Phone: **Email:** info@clover.global
City: Moscow **State:** Moscow City **PC:** **Country:** Russia
Year Established: 2016 **Status 2020:** Active
Industries: ~ Banking and Financial Markets-Services (7), Enterprise Application Services for:, Industrial Solutions for:, Automation for:, Machine Learning for:, Predictive Analytics for:, Risk Management for:, Robotics for:, Robotics

Company Name: Dataplex
Description: Dataplex is cloud-based computer vision service for business and home usage. It allows everybody employing ai tech using usual IP video cam
Website: http://www.dataplex.ai
Phone: 79035975592 **Email:** o.naidenov@dataplex.ai
City: Moscow **State:** Moscow City **PC:** **Country:** Russia
Year Established: **Status 2020:** Active
Industries: Artificial Intelligence for:, Computer Vision for:, Machine Learning for:, ~ Media-Communications (41)

Company Name: Dbra: India
Description: A tool to label data and build narrow AI for business
Website: http://dbrain.io
Phone: **Email:** hello@dbrain.io
City: Moscow **State:** Moscow City **PC:** **Country:** Russia
Year Established: **Status 2020:** Active
Industries: Artificial Intelligence for:, Blockchain for:, IT Managed Services for:, Machine Learning

Company Name: Deep Systems
Description: Artificial intelligence for real problems.
Website: http://deepsystems.ai
Phone: (408)410-7156 **Email:** inbox@deepsystems.ai
City: Moscow **State:** Moscow City **PC:** **Country:** Russia
Year Established: 2015 **Status 2020:** Active
Industries: Artificial Intelligence

Company Name: Diagnocat
Description: Diagnocat AI analyzes dental 3D x-rays, recognizes anatomical areas and detects various pathologies of maxillo-facial area.
Website: http://diagnocat.com
Phone: **Email:** va@diagnocat.com
City: Moscow **State:** Moscow City **PC:** **Country:** Russia
Year Established: 2017 **Status 2020:** Active
Industries: Artificial Intelligence for:, ~ Healthcare (20)

Company Name: DigRate
Description: Digital Rating Agency is the first professional provider of independent evaluation of ICO projects, digital assets and cryptocurrencies.
Website: http://digrate.com/en
Phone: 41 21 588 02 23 **Email:** info@digrate.com
City: Moscow **State:** Moscow City **PC:** **Country:** Russia
Year Established: 2017 **Status 2020:** Active
Industries: Analytics for:, Blockchain for:, ~ Banking and Financial Markets-Services (7), ~ Banking and Financial Markets-Services (7), ~ Banking and Financial Markets-Services (7), Predictive Analytics

Company Name: Doct
Description: Doctis is developing a universal telemedicine platform using predictive medical technologies and artificial intelligence.
Website: http://www.doctis.ru/
Phone: **Email:** 36448@reference-encyclopedia-ai.net
City: Moscow **State:** Moscow City **PC:** **Country:** Russia
Year Established: 2016 **Status 2020:** Active
Industries:

Company Name: Emotian
Description: Emotian analyze how emotions correlate with individual behavior and create adjusted customer profiles.
Website: http://emotian.at/
Phone: (7926) 228-3420 **Email:** team@emotian.at
City: Moscow **State:** Moscow City **PC:** **Country:** Russia
Year Established: 2016 **Status 2020:** Active
Industries: Artificial Intelligence for:, Big Data and Analytics

Company Name: EORA
Description: EORA is a solutions based on artificial intelligence company.
Website: http://eora.ru/
Phone: 7 800 500 16 86 **Email:** hello@eora.: Russia
City: Moscow **State:** Moscow City **PC:** **Country:** Russia
Year Established: 2014 **Status 2020:** Active
Industries: Artificial Intelligence

Company Name: Evercity
Description: Digital platform for impact measurement, management & investment
Website: http://evercity.io/
Phone: **Email:** info@evercity.io
City: Moscow **State:** Moscow City **PC:** **Country:** Russia
Year Established: 2018 **Status 2020:** Active
Industries: Artificial Intelligence for:, Blockchain for:, ~ Energy and Utilities (14), ~ Banking and Financial Markets-Services (7), ~ Social-Environmental-Physical-Engineering Sciences (55)

Company Name: Find Your Stamps Value
Description: FYSV - online service for identification and valuation of postage stamps through AI-powered image recognition
Website: http://findyourstampsvalue.com/
Phone: **Email:** info@findyourstampsvalue.com
City: Moscow **State:** Moscow City **PC:** **Country:** Russia
Year Established: 2016 **Status 2020:** Active
Industries: ~ Arts-Entertainment-Recreation (4), Artificial Intelligence for:, E-Commerce for:, Web for:, Web for:, Content for:, Computer Vision

Company Name: Heedbook
Description: Heedbook is an AI-based software for evaluating customer satisfaction in real-time.
Website: http://heedbook.com/
Phone: 1 (424) 442 3173 **Email:** info@heedbook.com
City: Moscow **State:** Moscow City **PC:** **Country:** Russia
Year Established: 2017 **Status 2020:** Active
Industries: Artificial Intelligence for:, Cloud for:, Facial Recognition for:, IT Managed Services for:, Web for:, Internet of Things (IoT) for:, Speech Recognition for:, Speech Recognition

Company Name: Icon8
Description: Icon8 is an artificial intelligence who turns your selfies into pieces of art.
Website: http://geticon8.com
Phone: **Email:** support@geticon8.com
City: Moscow **State:** Moscow City **PC:** **Country:** Russia
Year Established: 2016 **Status 2020:** Active
Industries: Artificial Intelligence for:, Digital Media

Company Name: Inleksys
Description: Inleksys concentrates on research and development of BI solutions in the area of data science, data quality and machine learning.
Website: http://inleksys.: Russia
Phone: (7905) 716-5446 **Email:** clients@inleksys.: Russia
City: Moscow **State:** Moscow City **PC:** **Country:** Russia
Year Established: 2016 **Status 2020:** Active
Industries: Artificial Intelligence for:, Business Applications for:, Big Data and Analytics

Company Name: Jetlex
Description: Jetlex is a program based on AI for automatic extraction of data from documents and for entering the extracted information into databases.
Website: http://jetlex.ai
Phone: **Email:** info@jetlex.ai
City: Moscow **State:** Moscow City **PC:** **Country:** Russia
Year Established: 2018 **Status 2020:** Active
Industries: Artificial Intelligence for:, IT Managed Services for:, IT Managed Services for:, Machine Learning

Company Name: LoyaltyLab
Description: Reinventing personal communication in traditional reta: Israel
Website: http://loyaltylab.co/en
Phone: (7909) 981-2208 **Email:** kmurashov@loyaltylab.co
City: Moscow **State:** Moscow City **PC:** **Country:** Russia
Year Established: 2018 **Status 2020:** Active
Industries: Analytics for:, Big Data and Analytics for:, IT Managed Services for:, Predictive Analytics

Company Name: Luden.io
Description: Luden.io is an independent game developer focused on meaningful and educational games.
Website: http://www.luden.io
Phone: **Email:** info@luden.io
City: Moscow **State:** Moscow City **PC:** **Country:** Russia
Year Established: 2015 **Status 2020:** Active
Industries: Augmented Reality for:, ~ Education (13), ~ Education (13), Machine Learning for:, ~ Arts-Entertainment-Recreation (4), Virtual Reality (VR)

Company Name: Lutrovnik
Description: Lutrovnik is an algorithmic bureau, using data science, AI and ML to solve hard problems facing ecommerce and online travel businesses.
Website: http://www.lutrovnik.com/
Phone: (1616) 328-5559 **Email:** is@lutrovnik.com
City: Moscow **State:** Moscow City **PC:** **Country:** Russia
Year Established: 2015 **Status 2020:** Active
Industries: Artificial Intelligence for:, E-Commerce

Company Name: Magneta
Description: Magneta is a messaging customer care & support system with AI for enterprises.
Website: http://magneta.ai/
Phone: **Email:** info@magenta-technology.com
City: Moscow **State:** Moscow City **PC:** **Country:** Russia
Year Established: 2015 **Status 2020:** Closed
Industries: Artificial Intelligence for:, ~ Customer Relationship Management (11), Enterprise Application Services

Company Name: Metrix.AI
Description: Scaling digital ad efficiency combining science and AI
Website: http://metrix.ai/
Phone: (7915) 227-4710 **Email:** denis@metrix.ai
City: Moscow **State:** Moscow City **PC:** **Country:** Russia
Year Established: 2017 **Status 2020:** Active
Industries: Artificial Intelligence for:, Digital Marketing

Company Name: Mr. Chatbot
Description: Mr. Chatbot allows ecommerce shops to create their own helpful chatbot.
Website:
Phone: **Email:** i@cherevko.net
City: Moscow **State:** Moscow City **PC:** **Country:** Russia
Year Established: 2016 **Status 2020:** Closed
Industries:

Company Name: NTechLab
Description: NTechLab develops software products using techniques in the fields of artificial neural networks and machine learning.
Website: http://ntechlab.com/
Phone: 74991102254 **Email:** info@ntechlab.: Russia
City: Moscow **State:** Moscow City **PC:** **Country:** Russia
Year Established: 2015 **Status 2020:** Active
Industries: Artificial Intelligence for:, Machine Learning

Company Name: Ocutri
Description: We offer full cycle custom software development and R&D for non-standard and science intensive tasks.
Website: http://www.ocutri.com
Phone: 79264389975 **Email:** info@ocutri.com
City: Moscow **State:** Moscow City **PC:** **Country:** Russia
Year Established: 2014 **Status 2020:** Active
Industries: Artificial Intelligence for:, Augmented Reality for:, Big Data and Analytics for:, Computer Vision for:, Machine Learning for:, Virtual Reality (VR) for:, Virtual Reality (VR)

Company Name: OhMyBet!
Description: OhMyBet! is an Artificial Intelligence tool for sports bettors that predicts outcomes of tennis matches using machine learning algorithms
Website: http://ohmybet.com
Phone: **Email:** general@ohmybet.com
City: Moscow **State:** Moscow City **PC:** **Country:** Russia
Year Established: 2016 **Status 2020:** Active
Industries: Artificial Intelligence for:, Machine Learning for:, Predictive Analytics

Company Name: Opiner
Description: Artificial intelligence for collection and aggregation of people opinions from web.
Website: http://opiner.: Russia
Phone: 7 926 435-73-02 **Email:** info@opiner.: Russia
City: Moscow **State:** Moscow City **PC:** **Country:** Russia
Year Established: 2013 **Status 2020:** Active
Industries: Artificial Intelligence for:, Big Data and Analytics for:, E-Commerce

Company Name: Psychologist OnLine
Description: Psychologist OnLine is a fast provision of psychological support online in different variations using artificial intelligence.
Website: http://www.psychologistonline.ru/
Phone: **Email:** 37221@reference-encyclopedia-ai.net
City: Moscow **State:** Moscow City **PC:** **Country:** Russia
Year Established: 2017 **Status 2020:** Active
Industries: Artificial Intelligence for:, ~ Healthcare (20), Web

Company Name: RoboCV
Description: RoboCV develops intelligent autopilot systems.
Website: http://www.robocv.com
Phone: 7 495 134 29 77 **Email:** info@robocv.: Russia
City: Moscow **State:** Moscow City **PC:** **Country:** Russia
Year Established: 2012 **Status 2020:** Active
Industries: Artificial Intelligence for:, IT Managed Services for:, Robotics

Company Name: Skychain Global
Description: Blockchain infrastructure aimed to host, train and use artificial intelligence (AI) in healthcare.
Website: http://skychain.global/
Phone: 7 9154808742 **Email:** aoksanenko@wss-consulting.: Russia
City: Moscow **State:** Moscow City **PC:** **Country:** Russia
Year Established: **Status 2020:** Active
Industries: Artificial Intelligence for:, ~ Biotechnology (9), ~ Healthcare (20), ~ Healthcare (20)

Company Name: Smart Engin: Spain
Description: Optical Character Recognition (OCR) Software Company
Website: http://smartengines.com/
Phone: 7 (495) 649-82-60 **Email:** info@smartengines.com
City: Moscow **State:** Moscow City **PC:** **Country:** Russia
Year Established: 2010 **Status 2020:** Active
Industries: Artificial Intelligence for:, Computer Vision for:, Identity for:, Image Recognition for:, Machine Learning

Company Name: SOVA.AI
Description: SOVA - Smart Open Virtual Assistant - is an open platform for creating voice virtual assistants, and the SOVA voice assistant itself.
Website: http://sova.ai/en/
Phone: 79267872637 **Email:** hello@sova.ai
City: Moscow **State:** Moscow City **PC:** **Country:** Russia
Year Established: **Status 2020:** Active
Industries: Artificial Intelligence for:, Blockchain for:, Machine Learning for:, Natural Language Processing

Company Name: sportcamp.club
Description: SaaS Marketplace
Website: http://sportcamp.club
Phone: 79017447042 **Email:** team@sportcamp.club
City: Moscow **State:** Moscow City **PC:** **Country:** Russia
Year Established: **Status 2020:** Active
Industries: Artificial Intelligence for:, ~ Healthcare (20), Web for:, ~ Arts-Entertainment-Recreation (4), ~ Transportation and Logistics (57)

Company Name: Streetbee
Description: Crowdsourcing and Image Recognition provider
Website: http://streetbee.ru/
Phone: 79260957577 **Email:** invest@streetbee.io
City: Moscow **State:** Moscow City **PC:** **Country:** Russia
Year Established: 2013 **Status 2020:** Active
Industries: Artificial Intelligence for:, Databases for:, Image Recognition for:, Machine Learning

Company Name: TalkBank
Description: TalkBank is digital bank in messengers that understands banking commands in natural language.
Website: http://www.talkbank.io/en/
Phone: 8 (495) 005 13 58 **Email:** hello@techfoliance.com
City: Moscow **State:** Moscow City **PC:** **Country:** Russia
Year Established: 2016 **Status 2020:** Active
Industries: Artificial Intelligence for:, ~ Banking and Financial Markets-Services (7), Mobile

Company Name: TehLab AI
Description: TehLab AI creates AI-powered tools for Media and Advertising
Website: http://tehlab.io
Phone: **Email:** 37515@reference-encyclopedia-ai.net
City: Moscow **State:** Moscow City **PC:** **Country:** Russia
Year Established: 2016 **Status 2020:** Active
Industries: Artificial Intelligence for:, ~ Social Assistance-Non-Profits (53)

Company Name: uKit AI
Description: uKit AI is an intelligent system for an instant redesign or a complete technical system.
Website: http://ukit.ai
Phone: **Email:** pr@ukit.com
City: Moscow **State:** Moscow City **PC:** **Country:** Russia
Year Established: 2015 **Status 2020:** Active
Industries:

Company Name: Worki
Description: Worki – mobile-first HR SaaS-enabled classified, leading and most fast growing HR-Tech product in Russia. Powered by AI and Machine Learning
Website: http://worki.: Russia
Phone: **Email:** team@worki.: Russia
City: Moscow **State:** Moscow City **PC:** **Country:** Russia
Year Established: 2016 **Status 2020:** Active
Industries: Artificial Intelligence for:, ~ Agriculture (3), Application Services for:, Business Software as a Service Apps (SaaS Apps) for:, Business Software as a Service Apps (SaaS Apps)

Company Name: Yadro
Description:
Website: https://www.yadro.com/
Phone: 512-851-5541 **Email:** sales@ziften.com
City: Moscow **State:** **Zip:** 123022 **Country:** Russia
Year Established: **Status 2020:** Active
Industries:

Company Name: DeepPavlov
Description: We make research in conversational AI, open source DeepPavlov.ai library for dialogue systems development and apply it to business needs
Website: http://deeppavlov.ai
Phone: (7919) 101-2385 **Email:** kairova@deeppavlov.ai
City: Dolgoprudnyy **State:** MO **PC:** **Country:** Russia
Year Established: 2016 **Status 2020:** Active
Industries: Analytics for:, Artificial Intelligence for:, ~ Customer Relationship Management (11), IT Managed Services

Company Name: Inspector Cloud
Description: AI-powered Saas for retail audits
Website: http://inspector-cloud.com
Phone: 7 962 242 1 777 **Email:** sales@inspector-cloud.com
City: Skolkovo **State:** MO **PC:** **Country:** Russia
Year Established: 2016 **Status 2020:** Active
Industries: Artificial Intelligence for:, Cloud for:, E-Commerce for:, Image Recognition for:, IT Managed Services for:, Business Software as a Service Apps (SaaS Apps) for:, Business Software as a Service Apps (SaaS Apps)

Company Name: Xperience AI
Description: Deep Learning for Computer Vision - optimized for Mobile
Website: http://xperience.ai
Phone: 79527801151 **Email:** hello@xperience.ai
City: Nizhniy Novgorod **State:** Nizhny Novgorod Oblast **PC:** **Country:** Russia
Year Established: 2018 **Status 2020:** Active
Industries: Artificial Intelligence for:, IT Managed Services

Company Name: chatme.ai
Description: AI-powered conversational platform and domain-specific virtual assistants for business process automation
Website: http://chatme.ai/
Phone: 7 926 572 5586 **Email:** info@chatme.ai
City: Novosibirsk **State:** Novosibirsk Oblast **PC:** **Country:** Russia
Year Established: 2017 **Status 2020:** Active
Industries: Artificial Intelligence

Company Name: Radario
Description: Radario is a cloud based marketing and sales platform for ticket sales.
Website: http://radario.co
Phone: (302)313-2001 **Email:** us@radario.co
City: Novosibirsk **State:** Novosibirsk Oblast **PC:** **Country:** Russia
Year Established: 2012 **Status 2020:** Active
Industries: Big Data and Analytics for:, ~ Event Management (15), Predictive Analytics for:, Business Software as a Service Apps (SaaS Apps)

Company Name: SkinCo:
Description: SkinCope offers an AI-powered system for chronic skin conditions.
Website: http://skincope.com/
Phone: **Email:** 37404@reference-encyclopedia-ai.net
City: Novosibirsk **State:** Novosibirsk Oblast **PC:** **Country:** Russia
Year Established: 2017 **Status 2020:** Active
Industries: Artificial Intelligence for:, ~ Healthcare (20), ~ Healthcare (20)

Company Name: Mr Airev
Description: AI-tech tailor-made clothing, at-place looks rental worldwide
Website:
Phone: (7914) 675-6127 **Email:** r.komissarov@gmail.com
City: Vladivostok **State:** Primorsky Krai **PC:** **Country:** Russia
Year Established: 2019 **Status 2020:** Active
Industries: Artificial Intelligence for:, E-Commerce for:, IT Managed Services for:, Machine Learning

Company Name: LIFE2FILM
Description: AI video platform for video create
Website: http://life2film.com/en/
Phone: **Email:** 36895@reference-encyclopedia-ai.net
City: Sterlitamak **State:** Republic of Bashkortostan **PC:** **Country:** Russia
Year Established: 2014 **Status 2020:** Active
Industries: Artificial Intelligence for:, Content for:, ~ Social Assistance-Non-Profits (53)

Company Name: Clevapi
Description: Real-time object recognition powered by artificial intelligence
Website: http://www.clevapi.com
Phone: **Email:** info@clevapi.com
City: Makhachkala **State:** Republic of Dagestan **PC:** **Country:** Russia
Year Established: 2015 **Status 2020:** Active
Industries: Artificial Intelligence

Company Name: Archy
Description: Archy develops high-tech AR for SMB and startups.
Website: http://archy-studio.com
Phone: 7.999.290.2260 **Email:** stas@archy-studio.com
City: Petrozavodsk **State:** Republic of Karelia **PC:** **Country:** Russia
Year Established: 2014 **Status 2020:** Active
Industries: Artificial Intelligence

Company Name: i-Neti
Description: i-Neti provides development & consultancy services for Microsoft dynamics AX/365 and machine learning.
Website: http://www.i-neti.com
Phone: 48 71 710 98 87 **Email:** info@i-neti.com
City: Kazan **State:** Republic of Tatarstan **PC:** **Country:** Russia
Year Established: 2011 **Status 2020:** Active
Industries: IT Managed Services for:, Machine Learning

Company Name: R-Visioneer Easy2See
Description: Conducts advanced research, development and implementation in the field of virtual and real test environments for robots.
Website: http://www.easy2see.me
Phone: **Email:** link@easy2see.me
City: Kazan **State:** Republic of Tatarstan **PC:** **Country:** Russia
Year Established: 2016 **Status 2020:** Active
Industries:

Company Name: Textocat
Description: Products to help businesses extract valuable information from texts.
Website: http://textocat.ru/
Phone: **Email:** info@textocat.com
City: Tatarstan **State:** Republic of Tatarstan **PC:** **Country:** Russia
Year Established: 2014 **Status 2020:** Active
Industries: Artificial Intelligence for:, E-Commerce for:, IT Managed Services for:, Web

Company Name: GraphGrail Ai
Description: GraphGrail Ai - Artificial Intelligence platform on Blockchain built on top of Natural Language Understanding technology
Website: http://graphgrail.com/
Phone: **Email:** ceo@graphgrail.com
City: Rostov-on-don **State:** Rostov Oblast **PC:** **Country:** Russia
Year Established: 2014 **Status 2020:** Active
Industries: Analytics for:, Artificial Intelligence for:, Big Data and Analytics for:, Business Software as a Service Apps (SaaS Apps)

Company Name: CVisionLab
Description: CVisionLab is a leading R&D service provider who develops custom solutions for challenging computer vision and AI problems.
Website: http://www.cvisionlab.com/
Phone: 1 (800) 705-0278 **Email:** info@cvisionlab.com
City: Taganrog **State:** Rostov Oblast **PC:** **Country:** Russia
Year Established: 2011 **Status 2020:** Active
Industries: Artificial Intelligence for:, Computer Vision for:, Machine Learning

Company Name: DataSmart
Description: Company develops client behavior analysis and prediction platform with use of machine learning and conducts research of new AI algorithms
Website: http://www.datasmartproject.com
Phone: (7921) 967-6037 **Email:** office@datasmartproject.com
City: Leningrad **State:** Saint Petersburg City **PC:** **Country:** Russia
Year Established: 2016 **Status 2020:** Active
Industries: Artificial Intelligence for:, Machine Learning

Company Name: FaceApp
Description: FaceApp offers an app that transforms its user's face using artificial intelligence in just one tap.
Website: http://www.faceapp.com/
Phone: **Email:** contact@faceapp.io
City: Saint Petersburg **State:** Saint Petersburg City **PC:** **Country:** Russia
Year Established: 2017 **Status 2020:** Active
Industries: Artificial Intelligence for:, Application Services for:, ~ Media-Communications (41)

Company **Name:** Mycroft Business Solutions
Description: Expert-class automatic purchasing and procurement platform. Business intelligence and business analytic system.
Website: http://mycroft2b.com
Phone: 1(617) 599-8188 **Email:** info@mycroft2b.com
City: Saint Petersburg **State:** Saint Petersburg City **PC:** **Country:** Russia
Year Established: 2014 **Status 2020:** Active
Industries: Analytics for:, Big Data and Analytics for:, Business Intelligence for:, Enterprise Application Services for:, Predictive Analytics for:, Business Software as a Service Apps (SaaS Apps) for:, Automation

Company Name: Pravoved.: Russia
Description: Pravoved is a legal tech company that provides legal service for individuals and creates innovative technologies for business
Website: http://pravoved.: Russia
Phone: 8 8 812 424-15-21 **Email:** support@pravoved.: Russia
City: Saint Petersburg **State:** Saint Petersburg City **PC:**
Country: Russia
Year Established: 2011 **Status 2020:** Active
Industries:

Company Name: Systems of Artificial Intelligence
Description: Systems of Artificial Intelligence is a young company working in the field of Information Technology and Information Security.
Website: http://www.itsai.org
Phone: **Email:** project@itsai.org
City: Sankt Petersburg **State:** Saint Petersburg City **PC:**
Country: Russia
Year Established: 2016 **Status 2020:** Active
Industries: Artificial Intelligence for:, IT Managed Services

Company Name: Ruft Group LC
Description: AI recruiting platform
Website: http://ruftgroup.com/
Phone: 79304748882 **Email:** leshkevich@ruftgroup.com
City: Tambov **State:** Tambov Oblast **PC:** **Country:** Russia
Year Established: **Status 2020:** Active
Industries: Artificial Intelligence for:, IT Managed Services for:, Web for:, ~ Human Resources (24), ~ Professional Services (48)

Company Name: YARP - Yet Another Recruiting Platform
Description: With YARP you can find the right employees in minutes, not weeks!
Website: http://yarpalpha.: Russia
Phone: **Email:** lk@yarpalpha.: Russia
City: Tambov **State:** Tambov Oblast **PC:** **Country:** Russia
Year Established: 2019 **Status 2020:** Active
Industries: Databases for:, IT Managed Services for:, Natural Language Processing for:, Business Software as a Service Apps (SaaS Apps)

Company Name: Biometric Identification Data
Description: FREE online biometric identification service
Website: http://bid.life/
Phone: 79807410491 **Email:** my@bid.life
City: Yaroslavl **State:** Yaroslavl Oblast **PC:** **Country:** Russia
Year Established: **Status 2020:** Active
Industries: Artificial Intelligence for:, ~ Biotechnology (9), Computer Vision for:, IT Managed Services for:, Web for:, Security

Saudi Arabia

Company Name: Taibah Valley
Description: Taibah Valley is a leading one in new technologies, especially in Blockchain, Internet of things and artificial intelligence.
Website: http://www.taibahvalley.com.sa/en/home/
Phone: 148618888 **Email:** info@taibahvalley.com.: Saudi Arabia
City: Medina **State:** Al Madinah Province **PC:** **Country: Saudi Arabia**
Year Established: 2018 **Status 2020:** Active
Industries: Artificial Intelligence for:, Blockchain for:, Internet of Things (IoT)

Company Name: Coursers Learning Platform
Description: it is a learning platform that will be in information technology field that will provide courses by artificial intelligence & Vr & Ar
Website:
Phone: **Email:** contact@thefutureideas.com
City: Dammam **State:** Eastern Province **PC:** **Country:** Saudi Arabia **Year Established:** **Status 2020:** Active
Industries: Artificial Intelligence for:, ~ Education (13), IT Managed Services

Company Name: Mose: Romania
Description: Mosero provides Artificial Intelligence (A.I) solutions to identify rare diseases through a predictive algorithms.
Website:
Phone: **Email:** 37021@reference-encyclopedia-ai.net
City: Jeddah **State:** Makkah Province **PC:** **Country:** Saudi Arabia
Year Established: 2017 **Status 2020:** Active
Industries:

Company Name: Lucidya
Description: Social media analytics tool empowers businesses to make smarter strategic decisions using big data & machine learning technologies.
Website: http://lucidya.com/
Phone: **Email:** see@lucidya.com
City: Riyadh **State:** Riyadh Province **PC:** **Country:** Saudi Arabia
Year Established: 2016 **Status 2020:** Active
Industries: Analytics for:, Artificial Intelligence for:, IT Managed Services for:, ~ Social Assistance-Non-Profits (53)

Company Name: Quant Data & Analytics
Description: Quant Data & Analytics is a tech start-up specializing in data science and providing data analysis and artificial intelligence services.
Website: http://www.quant.sa/
Phone: 966 11 454 6885 **Email:** info@quant.: Saudi Arabia
City: Riyadh **State:** Riyadh Province **PC:** **Country:** SAUDI ARABIA
Year Established: 2015 **Status 2020:** Active
Industries: Analytics for:, Artificial Intelligence for:, IT Managed Services

Serbia

Company Name: Agremo
Description: Agremo is cloud-based software that performs analytics from aerial imagery to provide intelligence for management of agricultural processes.
Website: https://www.agremo.com/
Phone: **Email:** info@agremo.com
City: Beograd **State:** Vojvodina **PC:** **Country: Serbia**
Year Established: 2015 **Status 2020:** Active
Industries: ~ Agriculture (3), Artificial Intelligence for:, Computer Vision for:, Machine Learning for:, Business Software as a Service Apps (SaaS Apps)

Company Name: .nanobile
Description: Internet of Things & Blockchain Software and Hardware Development and Manufacturing Start-Up company.
Website: http://nanobile.com
Phone: **Email:** office@nanobile.com
City: Novi Sad **State:** Vojvodina **PC:** **Country: Serbia**
Year Established: **Status 2020:** Active
Industries: Artificial Intelligence for:, Blockchain for:, ~ Telecommunications (56), IT Managed Services for:, ~ Manufacturing-Miscellaneous (34), ~ Manufacturing-Electronic (30), Robotics for:, ~ Professional Services (48), ~ Professional Services (48)

Company Name: CarAware
Description: CarAware uses deep learning technology to accurately recognize car brand and model in various situations from a single picture.
Website: http://caraware.io
Phone: **Email:** caraware@protech.:
City: Novi Sad **State:** Vojvodina **PC:** **Country: Serbia**
Year Established: 2017 **Status 2020:** Active
Industries: Artificial Intelligence for:, ~ Automotive (5), Computer Vision for:, Machine Learning for:, Application Services

Company Name: Machine Can See
Description: We use AI with Computer Vision to create solutions that help improve the efficiency in retail, transportation and safety
Website: http://www.machinecansee.com
Phone: (3816) 359-3274 **Email:** info@machinecansee.com
City: Novi Sad **State:** Vojvodina **PC:** **Country: Serbia**
Year Established: 2019 **Status 2020:** Active
Industries: Artificial Intelligence for:, Business Applications for:, Computer Vision for:, Image Recognition for:, ~ Travel and Transportation (58), Business Software as a Service Apps (SaaS Apps)

Seychell

Company Name: Invacio AAP Holdings Ltd
Description: INV | Invacio AAP Holdings Ltd tie in to utility driven products driven over blockchain technologies.
Website: http://www.invacio.com
Phone: **Email:** none@none.com
City: **State:** Beau Vallon **PC:** **Country:** Seychell
Year Established: 2017 **Status 2020:** Closed
Industries: Artificial Intelligence

Singapore

Company Name: AIQ Pte Ltd
Description: AIQ offers O2O integrated solutions using our proprietary image recognition, video recognition and visual search technology.
Website: http://aiq.tech/
Phone: 65 6779 5958 **Email:** rachel.ng@aiq.tech
City: Singapore **State:** **PC:** **Country: Singapore**
Year Established: **Status 2020:** Active
Industries: Artificial Intelligence for:, Computer Vision for:, Image Recognition for:, Machine Learning

Company Name: Bambu
Description: Bambu is a global leader in digital wealth technology and machine learning tools.
Website: https://www.bambu.co
Phone: **Email:** marketing@bambu.co
City: Singapore **State:** **Zip:** 79118 **Country: Singapore**
Year Established: **Status 2020:** Active
Industries: Artificial Intelligence for:, ~ Banking and Financial Markets-Services (7)

Company Name: Biofourm
Description: Biofourmis is reinventing remote patient monitoring by detecting personalized patterns predictive of patient's health deterioration
Website: http://www.biofourmis.com
Phone: **Email:** info@biofourmis.com
City: Singapore **State:** **PC:** **Country: Singapore**
Year Established: **Status 2020:** Active
Industries: Artificial Intelligence for:, Machine Learning for:, ~ Healthcare (20), ~ Healthcare (20), Predictive Analytics

Company Name: cover2protect
Description: AI driven predective healthcare solution which is aiming towards decreasing the cost of healthcare by early detection and intervention.
Website: http://cover2protect.com
Phone: 65 9185 8601 **Email:** rajat@cover2protect.com
City: Singapore **State:** **PC:** **Country: Singapore**
Year Established: **Status 2020:** Active
Industries: Artificial Intelligence for:, ~ Healthcare (20), ~ Healthcare (20), ~ Insurance (25), Machine Learning for:, ~ Healthcare (20)

Company Name: Finquest
Description: Finquest provides its customers with information related to investment opportunities, institutional investors and acquirers, and more.
Website: http://www.finquest.com
Phone: **Email:** tanguy.lesselin@finquest.com
City: Singapore **State:** **PC:** **Country: Singapore**
Year Established: **Status 2020:** Active
Industries: Artificial Intelligence for:, Big Data and Analytics for:, ~ Banking and Financial Markets-Services (7)

Company Name: Holmusk
Description: Holmusk is a digital health company providing solutions for complex problems through innovative and scalable behavioural change programmes.
Website: https://holmusk.com
Phone: 65 6250 4233 **Email:** inquiry@holmusk.com
City: Singapore **State:** **PC:** **Country: Singapore**
Year Established: **Status 2020:** Active
Industries: Analytics for:, Artificial Intelligence for:, Big Data and Analytics for:, ~ Healthcare (20), IT Managed Services for:, ~ Healthcare (20), ~ Healthcare (20), ~ Healthcare (20)

Company Name: KAI Square
Description: KAI Square is a high-tech company providing innovative technological solutions covering surveillance, analytics & intelligent monitoring
Website: http://www.kaisquare.com/ Phone: 65 6634 8809
Email: contact@kaisquare.com
City: Singapore **State:** **PC:** **Country: Singapore**
Year Established: **Status 2020:** Active
Industries:

Company Name: OneAnalytix Pte Ltd
Description: OneAnalytix "personalized marketing at scale" uses AI/machine learning to serve retailers, brands and financial services companies.
Website: http://www.oneanalytix.com
Phone: **Email:** info@1analytix.com
City: Singapore **State:** **PC:** **Country: Singapore**
Year Established: **Status 2020:** Active
Industries: ~ Media-Communications (41), Artificial Intelligence for:, Big Data and Analytics for:, ~ Media-Communications (41), Business Intelligence for:, ~ Banking and Financial Markets-Services (7), Machine Learning for:, Predictive Analytics for:, ~ Retail and Consumer

Company Name: Perx Technologies
Description: Perx is a leading loyalty and customer engagement SaaS platform that powers big brands
Website:
Phone: (65) 6816 2711 **Email:** contact@perxtech.com
City: Singapore **State:** **PC:** **Country: Singapore**
Year Established: **Status 2020:** Active
Industries: Artificial Intelligence for:, ~ Retail and Consumer Products (52), ~ Media-Communications (41), ~ Media-Communications (41)

Company Name: praktice.ai
Description: Praktice.ai is serving the biggest hospitals of Singapore and India with its Artificial intelligence solution.
Website: http://praktice.ai/
Phone: **Email:** contact@praktice.ai
City: Singapore **State:** **PC:** **Country: Singapore**
Year Established: **Status 2020:** Active
Industries: Artificial Intelligence for:, ~ Healthcare (20), ~ Healthcare (20), Machine Learning for:, ~ Healthcare (20), Speech Recognition

Company Name: UIB
Description: Simply Communicate. #IoT #AI #Messaging
Website: http://unifiedinbox.com
Phone: 65 6871 4035 **Email:** ken.herron@uib.ai
City: Singapore **State:** **PC:** **Country: Singapore**

Year Established: **Status 2020:** Active
Industries: Analytics for:, Artificial Intelligence for:, Business Applications for:, Big Data and Analytics for:, Cloud for:, ~ Telecommunications (56), Enterprise Application Services for:, Business Strategy and Design

Company Name: AGi Technosys
Description: AGi Technosys provides artificial intelligence solutions to startups and SMEs.
Website: https://www.agitechnosys.com/
Phone: 65 96531921 **Email:** hello@agitechnosys.com
City: Bukit Merah **State:** Central Region **PC:** **Country:** **Singapore**
Year Established: 2018 **Status 2020:** Active
Industries: Artificial Intelligence for:, IT Managed Services

Company Name: AltumV Technology
Description: AltumV Technology provides advancing radiology services and AI medical software.
Website: https://www.altumv.life/
Phone: 65 98005791 **Email:** info@altumv.life
City: Bukit Merah **State:** Central Region **PC:** **Country:** **Singapore**
Year Established: 2017 **Status 2020:** Active
Industries: Artificial Intelligence for:, ~ Healthcare (20)

Company Name: Axension Studios
Description: Axension Studios provides machine learning, web and app development services.
Website: http://www.axensionstudios.com/
Phone: 65 9126 1304 **Email:** info@axensionstudios.com
City: Bukit Merah **State:** Central Region **PC:** **Country:** **Singapore**
Year Established: 2016 **Status 2020:** Active
Industries: Machine Learning for:, Web

Company Name: Kobe
Description: Kobe is an artificial intelligence influencer marketing platform.
Website: http://www.getkobe.com/
Phone: 65 62555662 **Email:** contact@getkobe.com
City: Bukit Merah **State:** Central Region **PC:** **Country:** **Singapore**
Year Established: 2016 **Status 2020:** Active
Industries: Artificial Intelligence for:, IT Managed Services

Company Name: Kooki Singapore
Description: Kooki Singapore builds human capital by augmenting human capabilities using artificial intelligence (AI) technology.
Website: http://hello@kooki.co
Phone: **Email:** 36861@reference-encyclopedia-ai.net
City: Bukit Merah **State:** Central Region **PC:** **Country:** **Singapore**
Year Established: 2015 **Status 2020:** Active
Industries: Artificial Intelligence for:, IT Managed Services for:, Machine Learning

Company Name: Mesh Bio
Description: Mesh Bio is a digital health startup that is transforming chronic disease management through predictive analytics.
Website: http://www.meshbio.com/
Phone: **Email:** contact@meshbio.com
City: Bukit Merah **State:** Central Region **PC:** **Country:** **Singapore**
Year Established: 2018 **Status 2020:** Active
Industries: ~ Biotechnology (9), ~ Healthcare (20), Predictive Analytics

Company Name: mVizn
Description: mVizn is an AI powered machine vision for security, facility management and asset tracking.
Website: http://mvizn.com/index.html
Phone: **Email:** contact@mvizn.com
City: Bukit Merah **State:** Central Region **PC:** **Country:** **Singapore**
Year Established: 2017 **Status 2020:** Active
Industries: Artificial Intelligence for:, Automation for:, Security

Company Name: ProSpace
Description: ProSpace is a B2B tech company that delivers AI enabled workplace analytics platforms to global enterprises.
Website: http://prospace.io/
Phone: 6597530167 **Email:** hello@prospace.io
City: Bukit Merah **State:** Central Region **PC:** **Country:** **Singapore**
Year Established: 2015 **Status 2020:** Active
Industries: Analytics for:, Artificial Intelligence for:, Business Applications

Company Name: Qavar
Description: Qavar is an artificial intelligence company specialized in building apps, systems and chatbots.
Website: http://www.qavar.com/
Phone: 65-6612-5602 **Email:** enquiries@qavar.com
City: Bukit Merah **State:** Central Region **PC:** **Country:** **Singapore**
Year Established: 2014 **Status 2020:** Active
Industries: Application Services for:, Artificial Intelligence

Company Name: Rock Na
Description: Rock Nano designs and builds digital platforms related to the artificial intelligence, robotics, machines, sensors, and motor vehicles.
Website: http://rocknanoholdings.com/
Phone: **Email:** ask@rocknanoglobal.com
City: Bukit Merah **State:** Central Region **PC:** **Country:** **Singapore**
Year Established: 2013 **Status 2020:** Active
Industries:

Company Name: SEACRUX
Description: SEACRUX is an advertising tech company.
Website: http://www.seacrux.com/
Phone: **Email:** 37353@reference-encyclopedia-ai.net
City: Bukit Merah **State:** Central Region **PC:** **Country:** **Singapore**
Year Established: 2018 **Status 2020:** Active
Industries: Artificial Intelligence

Company Name: Shentilium Technologies
Description: Shentilium Technologies is specializing in artificial intelligence and data driven analytics for financial and e-commerce industries.
Website: http://shentilium.com/
Phone: **Email:** contact@shentilium.com
City: Bukit Merah **State:** Central Region **PC:** **Country:** **Singapore**
Year Established: 2016 **Status 2020:** Active
Industries: Analytics for:, Artificial Intelligence

Company Name: SuEtte
Description: Su-Ette delivers end-to-end chatbot solutions, robotic process automation and AI-layer services.
Website: http://www.su-ette.com/
Phone: **Email:** hello@su-ette.com
City: Bukit Merah **State:** Central Region **PC:** **Country:** **Singapore**
Year Established: 2017 **Status 2020:** Active
Industries: Artificial Intelligence for:, IT Managed Services for:, Robotics

Company Name: Neuro10
Description: N10 is a platform that offers intelligent analytics, big data analytics and machine learning on the cloud.
Website: http://www.neuro10.com/
Phone: 65 6513 9219 **Email:** contact@neuro10.com
City: Midview City **State:** Central Region **PC:** **Country:** **Singapore**
Year Established: 2015 **Status 2020:** Active
Industries:

Company Name: 6Estat: Spain
Description: Focus on using AI technology to deliver back office intelligent process automation solution in finance domain.
Website: http://www.6estates.com/
Phone: 56 6777 2757 **Email:** info@6estates.com
City: Singapore **State:** Central Region **PC:** **Country:** **Singapore**
Year Established: 2014 **Status 2020:** Active
Industries: Artificial Intelligence for:, ~ Banking and Financial Markets-Services (7), Natural Language Processing

Company Name: Active.ai
Description: Active.ai is a service platform that connects consumers with their banks via micro conversation.
Website: http://active.ai/
Phone: **Email:** 35947@reference-encyclopedia-ai.net
City: Singapore **State:** Central Region **PC:** **Country:** **Singapore**
Year Established: 2016 **Status 2020:** Active
Industries: Artificial Intelligence for:, ~ Banking and Financial Markets-Services (7), ~ Banking and Financial Markets-Services (7), IT Managed Services

Company Name: ActiveWizards: machine learning company
Description: Helping organizations to implement machine learning, data science and engineering initiatives.
Website: https://activewizards.com/
Phone: **Email:** hello@activewizards.com
City: Singapore **State:** Central Region **PC:** **Country:** **Singapore**
Year Established: 2013 **Status 2020:** Active
Industries: Artificial Intelligence for:, Machine Learning

Company Name: Adaface
Description: Adaface is building a conversational AI for first round tech interviews.
Website: https://www.adaface.com/
Phone: **Email:** 35950@reference-encyclopedia-ai.net
City: Singapore **State:** Central Region **PC:** **Country:** **Singapore**
Year Established: 2018 **Status 2020:** Active
Industries: Artificial Intelligence for:, Machine Learning

Company Name: Adatos A.I
Description: Adatos is a provider of data analysis services.
Website: http://www.adatos.com/
Phone: **Email:** dperez@adatos.com
City: Singapore **State:** Central Region **PC:** **Country:** **Singapore**
Year Established: **Status 2020:** Active
Industries: ~ Agriculture (3), Analytics for:, Artificial Intelligence for:, ~ Banking and Financial Markets-Services (7), Machine Learning

Company Name: ADB: ROMANIA
Description: ADBRO is the premium advertising platform powered by artificial intelligence.
Website: https://adbro.me/en/
Phone: **Email:** hello@adbro.me
City: Singapore **State:** Central Region **PC:** **Country:** **Singapore**
Year Established: 2017 **Status 2020:** Active
Industries: Artificial Intelligence

Company Name: ADDO AI
Description: ADDO means "to add" in Latin and we believe that by adding artificial intelligence.
Website: http://addo.ai/
Phone: **Email:** hr@addo.ai.
City: Singapore **State:** Central Region **PC:** **Country:** **Singapore**
Year Established: 2017 **Status 2020:** Active
Industries: Artificial Intelligence for:, IT Managed Services for:, IT Managed Services

Company Name: ADVANCE.AI
Description: ADVANCE.AI is a data-driven financial technology company with multiple offices in the APAC region.
Website: https://advance.ai/
Phone: **Email:** hrsg@advance.ai
City: Singapore **State:** Central Region **PC:** **Country:** **Singapore**
Year Established: 2014 **Status 2020:** Active
Industries: Artificial Intelligence for:, Big Data and Analytics for:, Security for:, Web for:, Security

Company Name: Affable
Description: Affable is an influencer marketing platform to find authentic and relevant micro-influencers.
Website: http://www.affable.ai/
Phone: 65 9354 5329 **Email:** nisarg@affable.ai
City: Singapore **State:** Central Region **PC:** **Country:** **Singapore**
Year Established: 2017 **Status 2020:** Active
Industries: Artificial Intelligence for:, IT Managed Services for:, IT Managed Services

Company Name: Agorai
Description: Agorai is a global platform that provides the turnkey software solutions, technology, and data needed for any company.
Website: http://www.agorai.ai/
Phone: **Email:** info@agorai.ai
City: Singapore **State:** Central Region **PC:** **Country:** **Singapore**
Year Established: **Status 2020:** Active
Industries:

Company Name: Agrud
Description: Fintech Startup
Website: http://agrud.com
Phone: **Email:** admin@agrud.com
City: Singapore **State:** Central Region **PC:** **Country:** **Singapore**
Year Established: **Status 2020:** Active
Industries: Analytics for:, Artificial Intelligence for:, ~ Banking and Financial Markets-Services (7), ~ Media-Communications (41)

Company Name: Ai Palette
Description: Ai Palette creates successful FMCG product concepts at speed.
Website: https://www.aipalette.com/
Phone: **Email:** info@aipalette.com
City: Singapore **State:** Central Region **PC:** **Country:** **Singapore**
Year Established: 2018 **Status 2020:** Active
Industries: Artificial Intelligence for:, IT Managed Services

Company Name: AI Singapore
Description: AISingapore is Singapore's national AI initiative to accelerate AI research and promote the use of AI in the Singapore ecosystem.
Website: https://www.aisingapore.org/
Phone: **Email:** 35994@reference-encyclopedia-ai.net
City: Singapore **State:** Central Region **PC:** **Country:** **Singapore**
Year Established: 2017 **Status 2020:** Active
Industries: Artificial Intelligence

Company Name: AiChat
Description: AiChat is a chatbot platform that allows businesses to deliver content, automate replies, and engage customers via popular chat apps.
Website: http://www.aichat.co
Phone: **Email:** hi@aichat.co
City: Singapore **State:** Central Region **PC:** **Country:** **Singapore**
Year Established: **Status 2020:** Active
Industries: Artificial Intelligence for:, IT Managed Services for:, Machine Learning for:, ~ Media-Communications (41), ~ Telecommunications (56), Natural Language Processing for:, Predictive Analytics for:, ~ Social Media (54)

Company Name: AIDA
Description: Aida designs and develops an artificial intelligence platform that uses predictive analytics and intelligent systems.
Website: http://aidatech.io/
Phone: **Email:** inquiries@aidatech.io
City: Singapore **State:** Central Region **PC:** **Country:** **Singapore**
Year Established: 2016 **Status 2020:** Active
Industries: Artificial Intelligence for:, IT Managed Services for:, Application Services for:, Machine Learning

Company Name: AIDDT
Description: AIDDT brings artificial intelligence to your In Silico drug design pipeline.
Website: https://aiddt.de/
Phone: **Email:** ritabratamaiti@hiretrex.com
City: Singapore **State:** Central Region **PC:** **Country:** **Singapore**
Year Established: 2019 **Status 2020:** Active
Industries: Artificial Intelligence for:, ~ Biotechnology (9), Application Program Interfaces (APIs) for:, ~ Healthcare (20)

Company Name: AIMLedge
Description: AIMLedge is developing a software platform that automate development and deployment of customized deep learning software.
Website: http://aimledge.com/
Phone: **Email:** 36015@reference-encyclopedia-ai.net
City: Singapore **State:** Central Region **PC:** **Country:** **Singapore**
Year Established: 2018 **Status 2020:** Active
Industries: Artificial Intelligence for:, Enterprise Application Services for:, IT Managed Services for:, Web

Company Name: AIQ
Description: AIQ bridges offline to online media properties with its Computer Vision AI Technology.
Website: http://aiq.tech/
Phone: 65 69049495 **Email:** sales@aiq.tech
City: Singapore **State:** Central Region **PC:** **Country:** **Singapore**
Year Established: 2014 **Status 2020:** Active
Industries: Artificial Intelligence for:, Computer Vision for:, Image Recognition for:, Machine Learning for:, Natural Language Processing for:, Computer Vision

Company Name: AIVON
Description: AIVON is a decentralized blockchain platform and protocol built on an Artificial Intelligence (AI) network.
Website: http://aivon.io
Phone: **Email:** info@aivon.io
City: Singapore **State:** Central Region **PC:** **Country:** **Singapore**
Year Established: **Status 2020:** Active
Industries: Artificial Intelligence for:, ~ Banking and Financial Markets-Services (7), ~ Banking and Financial Markets-Services (7), IT Managed Services for:, ~ Insurance (25), Web

Company Name: Alcheme Skincare
Description: Alchemy is the ancient science of transforming matter into gold.
Website: https://alcheme.one/
Phone: **Email:** 36030@reference-encyclopedia-ai.net
City: Singapore **State:** Central Region **PC:** **Country:** **Singapore**
Year Established: 2017 **Status 2020:** Active
Industries: Artificial Intelligence for:, ~ Beauty (8), ~ Beauty (8), ~ Healthcare (20)

Company Name: Alore CRM
Description: Alore is an AI-powered integrated CRM and inbound marketing platform.
Website: http://alore.io/
Phone: **Email:** support@alore.io
City: Singapore **State:** Central Region **PC:** **Country:** **Singapore**
Year Established: **Status 2020:** Active
Industries: Analytics for:, Artificial Intelligence for:, Web

Company Name: Alore Growth OS
Description: Alore is an AI-powered integrated CRM and inbound marketing platform.
Website: https://alore.io/
Phone: **Email:** support@alore.io
City: Singapore **State:** Central Region **PC:** **Country:** **Singapore**
Year Established: 2017 **Status 2020:** Active
Industries: Analytics for:, Artificial Intelligence for:, ~ Customer Relationship Management (11), Web for:, Business Software as a Service Apps (SaaS Apps) for:, Automation

Company Name: Ampotech
Description: Energy intelligence at the edge: connected hardware company making buildings smarter and more efficient.
Website: http://www.ampotech.com/
Phone: **Email:** info@ampotech.com
City: Singapore **State:** Central Region **PC:** **Country:** **Singapore**
Year Established: 2014 **Status 2020:** Active
Industries: Artificial Intelligence for:, Internet of Things (IoT)

Company Name: AND Global Pte.Ltd
Description: AND GLOBAL Pte.Ltd is a Singapore based True FinTech Company powered by Machine Learning and Brilliant Minds.
Website: http://and.global
Phone: 65 31635349 **Email:** contact@and.global
City: Singapore **State:** Central Region **PC:** **Country:** **Singapore**
Year Established: **Status 2020:** Active
Industries:

Company Name: AntWorks
Description: AntWorks is a global, artificial intelligence (AI) company.
Website: http://ant.works/
Phone: 800-507-8011 **Email:** hello@ant.works
City: Singapore **State:** Central Region **PC:** **Country:** **Singapore**
Year Established: **Status 2020:** Active
Industries: Artificial Intelligence for:, IT Managed Services for:, IT Managed Services

Company Name: Apance
Description: Feelings for machines. AI for creative professionals.
Website: http://www.apance.com
Phone: **Email:** support@apance.com
City: Singapore **State:** Central Region **PC:** **Country:** **Singapore**
Year Established: **Status 2020:** Active
Industries: Artificial Intelligence

Company Name: Apvera
Description: Apvera is an information technology company that offers cyber-security solutions for businesses, firms, and companies.
Website: http://www.apvera.com/
Phone: 415-891-2270 **Email:** info@apvera.com
City: Singapore **State:** Central Region **PC:** **Country:** **Singapore**
Year Established: 2013 **Status 2020:** Active
Industries: Analytics for:, Big Data and Analytics for:, Cyber Security for:, Machine Learning for:, Security

Company Name: Auk Industri: Spain
Description: Auk Industries IIoT system is a scalable end-to-end technology built to provide deep industrial data with ultra-lightweight infrastructure.
Website: http://www.auk.industries/
Phone: 65 6816 3655 **Email:** mail@auk.industri: Spain
City: Singapore **State:** Central Region **PC:** **Country:** **Singapore**
Year Established: 2016 **Status 2020:** Active
Industries: Industrial Solutions for:, Internet of Things (IoT) for:, Machine Learning for:, Internet of Things (IoT)

Company Name: Aureus Analytics
Description: AI Based Analytics Platform for Insurance Carrie: Serbia
Website: http://www.aureusanalytics.com
Phone: 91 22 2570 5445 **Email:** aufinance@aureusanalytics.com
City: Singapore **State:** Central Region **PC:** **Country:** **Singapore**
Year Established: 2013 **Status 2020:** Active
Industries: Artificial Intelligence for:, Machine Learning for:, Predictive Analytics

Company Name: Avanseus
Description: Innovative start up using AI for Enterprise Applications. Current focus is Predictive Maintenance for Telecommunications and IOT.
Website: http://www.avanseus.com/
Phone: 65 69701689 **Email:** info@avanseus.com
City: Singapore **State:** Central Region **PC:** **Country:** **Singapore**
Year Established: 2015 **Status 2020:** Active
Industries: Artificial Intelligence for:, Enterprise Application Services

Company Name: AVANSEUS HOLDINGS PTE LIMITED
Description: Innovative start up using AI for Enterprise Applications. Current focus is Predictive Maintenance for Telecommunications and IOT.
Website: http://www.avanseus.com/
Phone: 65 6701 8501 **Email:** info@avanseus.com
City: Singapore **State:** Central Region **PC:** **Country:** **Singapore**
Year Established: **Status 2020:** Active
Industries: Artificial Intelligence for:, Enterprise Application Services

Company Name: AVEVAI
Description: Electric commercial vehicle and technology
Website: http://www.avevai.com
Phone: **Email:** Contact@avevai.com
City: Singapore **State:** Central Region **PC:** **Country:** **Singapore**
Year Established: 2018 **Status 2020:** Active
Industries: Artificial Intelligence for:, ~ Automotive (5)

Company Name: Basis AI
Description: Basis AI provides artificial intelligence products.
Website: http://www.basis-ai.com/
Phone: **Email:** contact@basis-ai.com
City: Singapore **State:** Central Region **PC:** **Country:** **Singapore**
Year Established: 2018 **Status 2020:** Active
Industries: Machine Learning

Company Name: Bibox
Description: Bibox.com is the first ever AI-driven digital asset trading platform. Embedding AI technology into the trading process for digital ...
Website: http://www.bibox.com/
Phone: **Email:** 36150@reference-encyclopedia-ai.net
City: Singapore **State:** Central Region **PC:** **Country:** **Singapore**
Year Established: 2017 **Status 2020:** Active
Industries: Artificial Intelligence for:, ~ Banking and Financial Markets-Services (7), Blockchain for:, IT Managed Services for:, Web

Company Name: Big.Jobs
Description: Curated careers marketplace where companies meet great candidates Learn more Shubham Garg Srishty Mukherjee Himanshu Geed
Website: http://big.jobs
Phone: 65 9370 3970 **Email:** hello@big.jobs
City: Singapore **State:** Central Region **PC:** **Country:** **Singapore**
Year Established: 2018 **Status 2020:** Active
Industries: Artificial Intelligence for:, Web

Company Name: BIGO Technology
Description: BIGO is a fast-growing Singapore technology company specialising in AI technology.
Website: http://www.bigo.tv/index
Phone: **Email:** press@bigo.: Singapore
City: Singapore **State:** Central Region **PC:** **Country:** **Singapore**
Year Established: 2014 **Status 2020:** Active
Industries: Artificial Intelligence for:, Web for:, ~ Social Assistance-Non-Profits (53)

Company Name: BioMind
Description: BioMind is developed in collaboration with the world's largest hospital for neurological diseases.
Website: http://biomind.ai
Phone: 65 6513 7725 **Email:** consult@biomind.ai
City: Singapore **State:** Central Region **PC:** **Country:** **Singapore**
Year Established: 2017 **Status 2020:** Active
Industries: Artificial Intelligence for:, ~ Healthcare (20)

Company Name: Blink Technologies Pte Ltd
Description: We specialise in Field Force Management Solutions that optimise HR operations.
Website: http://www.blinktech.: Singapore
Phone: 6566028282 **Email:** hello@blinktech.: Singapore
City: Singapore **State:** Central Region **PC:** **Country:** **Singapore**
Year Established: **Status 2020:** Active
Industries:

Company Name: Bolton Remote
Description: Bolton makes scaling easier for companies with remote, global talent.
Website: http://www.boltonremote.com/
Phone: 1 (866) 978-7838 **Email:** info@boltonremote.com
City: Singapore **State:** Central Region **PC:** **Country:** **Singapore**
Year Established: 2013 **Status 2020:** Active
Industries: Cyber Security for:, IT Managed Services for:, Machine Learning for:, Business Process and Operations

Company Name: Botbot.AI
Description: Artificial Intelligence, Chatbot, Machine Learning, RPA, SaaS
Website: http://botbot.ai
Phone: 65 9447 2070 **Email:** chelsea@botbot.ai
City: Singapore **State:** Central Region **PC:** **Country:** **Singapore**
Year Established: **Status 2020:** Active
Industries: Artificial Intelligence for:, Enterprise Application Services for:, Machine Learning for:, Natural Language Processing

Company Name: Browzz: India
Description: An artificial intelligence driven app that turns shoppers into paid influence: Serbia
Website: http://www.browzzin.com
Phone: **Email:** info@browzzin.com
City: Singapore **State:** Central Region **PC:** **Country:** **Singapore**
Year Established: 2016 **Status 2020:** Active
Industries: Artificial Intelligence for:, E-Commerce

Company Name: Bus Uncle
Description: Bus Uncle is a platform of AI based transportation chat bots.
Website: http://www.busuncle.sg/
Phone: **Email:** ah@busuncle.: Singapore
City: Singapore **State:** Central Region **PC:** **Country:** **Singapore**
Year Established: 2017 **Status 2020:** Active
Industries: Artificial Intelligence

Company Name: Butleric
Description: AI-Powered Crowd Enterprise Software
Website: http://www.butleric.com
Phone: 98563969 6598563969 **Email:** ron@butleric.com
City: Singapore **State:** Central Region **PC:** **Country:** **Singapore**
Year Established: **Status 2020:** Active
Industries: Artificial Intelligence for:, Cloud for:, Digital Marketing for:, E-Commerce for:, Enterprise Application Services for:, Machine Learning for:, ~ Retail and Consumer Products (52), ~ Professional Services (48)

Company **Name:** Cardiotrack
Description: Cardiotrack is an AI based diagnostics company that is improving heart health outcomes through early diagnos
Website: http://www.cardiotrack.io
Phone: 91 80 2301 2601 **Email:** info@cardiotrack.io
City: Singapore **State:** Central Region **PC:** **Country:** **Singapore**
Year Established: 2014 **Status 2020:** Active
Industries: Artificial Intelligence for:, ~ Biotechnology (9), ~ Healthcare (20), ~ Healthcare (20)

Company Name: Castella
Description: Fine Art
Website: http://www.castella.art
Phone: (659) 156-4246 **Email:** e@castella.: Singapore
City: Singapore **State:** Central Region **PC:** **Country:** **Singapore**
Year Established: 2018 **Status 2020:** Active
Industries: ~ Arts-Entertainment-Recreation (4), Artificial Intelligence for:, Augmented Reality

Company Name: Centareum
Description: Centareum refining the future of global brick and mortar
Website: http://www.centareum.io/
Phone: 98957428 **Email:** hello@centareum.io
City: Singapore **State:** Central Region **PC:** **Country:** **Singapore**
Year Established: **Status 2020:** Active
Industries: Artificial Intelligence for:, Blockchain for:, ~ Banking and Financial Markets-Services (7), ~ Banking and Financial Markets-Services (7), ~ Media-Communications (41), ~ Banking and Financial Markets-Services (7)

Company Name: ChainTrade
Description: The First Blockchain-based Platform To Trade Food and Raw Materials
Website: http://chaintrade.net/
Phone: **Email:** info@chaintrade.net
City: Singapore **State:** Central Region **PC:** **Country:** **Singapore**
Year Established: **Status 2020:** Active
Industries: Artificial Intelligence for:, ~ Banking and Financial Markets-Services (7), ~ Banking and Financial Markets-Services (7), ~ Food and Beverage (17)

Company Name: CIPHERHUT SOFTWARE SINGAPORE PTE
Description: Blockchain, BaaS, Artificial Intelligence and Internet of Things
Website: http://cipherhut.com
Phone: 1 (404) 795-4609 **Email:** info@cipherhut.com
City: Singapore **State:** Central Region **PC:** **Country:** **Singapore**
Year Established: 2018 **Status 2020:** Active
Industries: Artificial Intelligence for:, Blockchain for:, Internet of Things (IoT)

Company Name: CloudRadigm Pte Ltd
Description: Empowering App Developers with Artificial Intelligence driven Big Data Analytics technology that is easy to adopt and u: Sweden
Website:
Phone: **Email:** contact_us@cloudradigm.com
City: Singapore **State:** Central Region **PC:** **Country:** **Singapore**
Year Established: **Status 2020:** Active
Industries: Analytics for:, Artificial Intelligence for:, Big Data and Analytics for:, Predictive Analytics

Company Name: Cognicept Systems
Description: Cognicept Systems provides tech stack that enables humans to control anywhere globally and resolve issues using machine learning.
Website: http://cognicept.systems/
Phone: 65 9238 3885 **Email:** info@cognicept.systems
City: Singapore **State:** Central Region **PC:** **Country:** **Singapore**
Year Established: 2018 **Status 2020:** Active
Industries: IT Managed Services for:, Machine Learning for:, Robotics

Company Name: Collab
Description: Predictive hiring and human capital development with AI and psychology
Website: http://collab.: Singapore
Phone: **Email:** hello@collab.: Singapore
City: Singapore **State:** Central Region **PC:** **Country:** **Singapore**
Year Established: **Status 2020:** Active
Industries: Artificial Intelligence for:, ~ Human Resources (24), Machine Learning

Company Name: Collab Partnershi: Palestine
Description: AI-powered Marketplace for Partne: Serbia
Website: http://www.collab.: Singapore
Phone: **Email:** super@collab.: Singapore
City: Singapore **State:** Central Region **PC:** **Country:** **Singapore**
Year Established: **Status 2020:** Active
Industries:

Company Name: Compliy
Description: Collaborative AI web-platform with centralized data that simplifies and automates regulatory change processes for compliance teams in APAC.
Website: http://www.compliy.com
Phone: **Email:** info@compliy.com
City: Singapore **State:** Central Region **PC:** **Country:** **Singapore**
Year Established: 2018 **Status 2020:** Active
Industries: Artificial Intelligence for:, ~ Banking and Financial Markets-Services (7), ~ Banking and Financial Markets-Services (7), Risk Management for:, Business Software as a Service Apps (SaaS Apps) for:, Business Software as a Service Apps (SaaS Apps)

Company Name: Connectome
Description: Connectome is the decentralized "AI x AR x Blockchain" technology for Smart Space.
Website: http://connectome.to
Phone: **Email:** 36322@reference-encyclopedia-ai.net
City: Singapore **State:** Central Region **PC:** **Country:** **Singapore**
Year Established: 2018 **Status 2020:** Active
Industries: Artificial Intelligence for:, Blockchain for:, IT Managed Services

Company Name: Contra
Description: Giving a voice to the millennials.
Website: http://contra-app.com/
Phone: 65 9127 3690 **Email:** support@contra-app.com
City: Singapore **State:** Central Region **PC:** **Country:** **Singapore**
Year Established: **Status 2020:** Active
Industries: Application Services for:, Artificial Intelligence

Company Name: Crayon Data
Description: Crayon Data is a growing big data and AI startup with a vision to simplify the world's choices with their personalization engine, maya.ai.
Website: http://www.crayondata.com
Phone: 91 044 66992020 **Email:** media@crayondata.com
City: Singapore **State:** Central Region **PC:** **Country:** **Singapore**
Year Established: 2012 **Status 2020:** Active
Industries: Analytics for:, Artificial Intelligence for:, Big Data and Analytics for:, Databases for:, Application Services for:, Machine Learning for:, Predictive Analytics for:, Predictive Analytics for:, Business Software as a Service Apps (SaaS Apps)

Company Name: CrescoData
Description: CrescoData simplifies the process of managing & scaling product data.
Website: http://www.crescodata.com
Phone: 65 3163 0046 **Email:** sales@crescodata.com
City: Singapore **State:** Central Region **PC:** **Country:** **Singapore**
Year Established: 2014 **Status 2020:** Active
Industries: Artificial Intelligence for:, Cloud for:, Cloud for:, Data Management for:, Digital Marketing for:, Digital Media for:, E-Commerce for:, IT Managed Services for:, IT Managed Services

Company Name: CXA Group
Description: CXA is a AI-powered health and wellness eco-system.
Website: http://www.cxagroup.com
Phone: 65 6659 8082 **Email:** info.sg@cxagroup.com
City: Singapore **State:** Central Region **PC:** **Country:** **Singapore**
Year Established: 2013 **Status 2020:** Active
Industries: Artificial Intelligence for:, ~ Healthcare (20), ~ Healthcare (20), IT Managed Services for:, ~ Healthcare (20)

Company Name: Cyber Intelligence Hou: Sweden
Description: Cyber Intelligence House is a specialist in Cyber Exposure. We bring certainty to an uncertain world.
Website: http://cyberintelligencehouse.com/
Phone: 65 8431 1778 **Email:** ewen@cyberintelligencehouse.com
City: Singapore **State:** Central Region **PC:** **Country:** **Singapore**
Year Established: 2015 **Status 2020:** Active
Industries: Analytics for:, Artificial Intelligence for:, Cyber Security for:, IT Managed Services for:, Compute

Company Name: DataCue
Description: DataCue is a platform for e-commerce stores to automate website personalization with machine learning.
Website: http://www.datacue.co/
Phone: **Email:** 36393@reference-encyclopedia-ai.net
City: Singapore **State:** Central Region **PC:** **Country:** **Singapore**
Year Established: 2017 **Status 2020:** Active
Industries: E-Commerce for:, E-Commerce for:, Web for:, Machine Learning

Company Name: DataVLT
Description: Secure, Affordable, Easier - DataVLT is an on-demand data analytics platform integrated with blockcha: India
Website: http://www.datavlt.com/
Phone: **Email:** info@datavlt.com
City: Singapore **State:** Central Region **PC:** **Country:** **Singapore**
Year Established: **Status 2020:** Active
Industries: Analytics for:, Artificial Intelligence for:, Big Data and Analytics for:, Blockchain for:, Business Intelligence for:, IT Managed Services for:, Web for:, Machine Learning

Company Name: Dataxet
Description: Data Monitoring SaaS Across Asia
Website: http://www.dataxet.com
Phone: **Email:** 36399@reference-encyclopedia-ai.net
City: Singapore **State:** Central Region **PC:** **Country:** **Singapore**
Year Established: 2019 **Status 2020:** Active
Industries: Artificial Intelligence for:, Big Data and Analytics for:, Cyber Security for:, Machine Learning for:, ~ Media-Communications (41), Business Software as a Service Apps (SaaS Apps)

Company Name: Dathena Science
Description: Dathena understands your data privacy and protection needs, and has solved them with our own revolutionary A.I.
Website: http://www.dathena.io
Phone: **Email:** hello@dathena.io
City: Singapore **State:** Central Region **PC:** **Country:** **Singapore**
Year Established: 2016 **Status 2020:** Active
Industries: Artificial Intelligence for:, Big Data and Analytics for:, Cyber Security for:, Machine Learning for:, Natural Language Processing

Company Name: dDriven Solutions Pte Ltd
Description: Industrial Digitalization, Operation Digitalization, Industrial IoT, Analytics
Website: http://www.ddriven.io/
Phone: 65 63853602 **Email:** sales@dDriven.io
City: Singapore **State:** Central Region **PC:** **Country:** **Singapore**
Year Established: 2015 **Status 2020:** Active
Industries: Analytics for:, Big Data and Analytics for:, Internet of Things (IoT) for:, Predictive Analytics

Company Name: Deepdive
Description: We are developing a highly abstracted, yet easy to use machine learning ecosystem to make predictive tools for marketing.
Website: http://www.deepdive.: Singapore
Phone: **Email:** abhinit@deepdive.: Singapore
City: Singapore **State:** Central Region **PC:** **Country:** **Singapore**
Year Established: **Status 2020:** Active
Industries: ~ Media-Communications (41), Analytics for:, Artificial Intelligence for:, ~ Professional Services (48)

Company Name: Deepo
Description: Our mission is to make data science accessible for marketers.
Website: http://www.deepo.io
Phone: **Email:** 36421@reference-encyclopedia-ai.net
City: Singapore **State:** Central Region **PC:** **Country:** **Singapore**
Year Established: 2015 **Status 2020:** Active
Industries:

Company Name: Digital Commerce Intelligence
Description: Digital Commerce Intelligence is a AI-driven online market share data & competitive performance intelligence for brands in southeast Asia.
Website: http://dci.ai
Phone: **Email:** contact@dci.ai
City: Singapore **State:** Central Region **PC:** **Country:** **Singapore**
Year Established: **Status 2020:** Active
Industries: Artificial Intelligence for:, Big Data and Analytics for:, Databases for:, E-Commerce for:, Predictive Analytics

Company Name: DOCLE AI
Description: We try to harness the power of AI to deliver smart transcripts with in-depth speech analysis and predictive intelligence for enterprises.
Website: http://wavel.ai
Phone: **Email:** reachout@wavel.ai
City: Singapore **State:** Central Region **PC:** **Country:** **Singapore**
Year Established: **Status 2020:** Active
Industries: Artificial Intelligence for:, Enterprise Application Services for:, Machine Learning

Company Name: DRNK AR
Description: Go beyond the label with DRNK AR, the future of Wine, Beer and Spirits. Powered by Omniaz.
Website: http://letsdrnk.com
Phone: **Email:** social@letsdrnk.com
City: Singapore **State:** Central Region **PC:** **Country:** **Singapore**
Year Established: 2018 **Status 2020:** Active
Industries: Artificial Intelligence for:, Augmented Reality for:, ~ Food and Beverage (17), ~ Food and Beverage (17)

Company Name: Easy Zippy Pte Ltd
Description: Easy Zippy is a technology company focused on last mile services and solutions
Website: http://www.easyzippy.com
Phone: (659) 336-6957 **Email:** andywee@easyzippy.com
City: Singapore **State:** Central Region **PC:** **Country:** **Singapore**
Year Established: 2015 **Status 2020:** Active
Industries: Application Services for:, ~ Energy and Utilities (14), Application Services for:, Storage

Company Name: Easythingy
Description: Easythingy scours emails automatically and brings in all upcoming trips, hotel bookings, and bills into actionable cards.
Website: http://www.easythingy.com/
Phone: **Email:** info@easythingy.com
City: Singapore **State:** Central Region **PC:** **Country:** **Singapore**
Year Established: **Status 2020:** Active
Industries: Artificial Intelligence for:, ~ Media-Communications (41), Application Services for:, Application Services

Company Name: Edgware Technology
Description: Edgware is a service platform and intrinsically safe optical sensors are typically applicable in the B2B space.
Website: http://www.edgware.tech/
Phone: **Email:** someone@edgwaretech.co
City: Singapore **State:** Central Region **PC:** **Country:** **Singapore**
Year Established: 2018 **Status 2020:** Active
Industries: Machine Learning

Company Name: EKbana Solutions Pte Ltd
Description: Software Development Company
Website: http://www.ekbana.com
Phone: **Email:** info@ekbana.com
City: Singapore **State:** Central Region **PC:** **Country:** **Singapore**
Year Established: 2014 **Status 2020:** Active
Industries: Artificial Intelligence

Company Name: eko.ai
Description: eko.ai is automating the fight against heart disease using machine learning to democratize echo reading and disease prediction.
Website: http://eko.ai/
Phone: **Email:** info@eko.ai
City: Singapore **State:** Central Region **PC:** **Country:** **Singapore**
Year Established: 2017 **Status 2020:** Active
Industries: Artificial Intelligence for:, ~ Healthcare (20), ~ Healthcare (20), Machine Learning

Company Name: Enermo Technology
Description: Enermo Technology is a predictive maintenance and energy management platform that offers predictive maintenance for electrical machinery.
Website: http://www.enermotechnology.com/
Phone: 91-88796-96712 **Email:** connect@enermotechnology.com
City: Singapore **State:** Central Region **PC:** **Country:** **Singapore**
Year Established: 2018 **Status 2020:** Active
Industries: Artificial Intelligence for:, IT Managed Services for:, Internet of Things (IoT) for:, Machine Learning for:, Predictive Analytics

Company Name: Envirean
Description: Machine Learning Software and Hardware for infrastructure & environment monitoring, and automation control at home and enterpri: Sweden
Website: http://www.envirean.com
Phone: **Email:** hello@envirean.com
City: Singapore **State:** Central Region **PC:** **Country:** **Singapore**
Year Established: **Status 2020:** Active
Industries: Artificial Intelligence for:, Data Management for:, ~ Manufacturing-Electronic (30), Application Services for:, Machine Learning

Company Name: envirist.ai
Description: envirist uses artificial intelligence to create strategies for businesses of all sizes to reduce costs and go green.
Website: http://www.codexiastudios.com/archives/envirist
Phone: **Email:** envirist@codexia.org
City: Singapore **State:** Central Region **PC:** **Country:** **Singapore**
Year Established: **Status 2020:** Active
Industries: Artificial Intelligence for:, ~ Social-Environmental-Physical-Engineering Sciences (55), ~ Social-Environmental-Physical-Engineering Sciences (55), ~ Energy and Utilities (14)

Company Name: Envolve.ai
Description: Envolve.ai develops an intelligent analytics platform for retailers and manufacturers to share insights in real-time.
Website: http://envolve.ai/
Phone: 65 8119 5943 **Email:** contact@envolvedata.com
City: Singapore **State:** Central Region **PC:** **Country:** **Singapore**
Year Established: 2018 **Status 2020:** Active
Industries: Analytics for:, Artificial Intelligence for:, Business Intelligence for:, Data Management

Company Name: EtainPower
Description: EtainPower is a blockchain-based energy trading and financing platform powered by AI
Website: http://etainpower.io/
Phone: **Email:** steven@etainpower.io
City: Singapore **State:** Central Region **PC:** **Country:** **Singapore**
Year Established: 2018 **Status 2020:** Active
Industries: Artificial Intelligence for:, IT Managed Services for:, ~ Energy and Utilities (14), ~ Energy and Utilities (14)

Company Name: Ev: Ireland
Description: Intelligent Automation for Intelligent Enterpris: Spain
Website: http://www.evie.ai
Phone: (659) 859-0976 **Email:** hello@evie.ai
City: Singapore **State:** Central Region **PC:** **Country:** **Singapore**
Year Established: 2013 **Status 2020:** Active
Industries:

Company Name: Faladdin
Description: A.I Fortune Teller
Website: http://www.faladdin.com
Phone: **Email:** sertac@faladdin.com
City: Singapore **State:** Central Region **PC:** **Country:** **Singapore**
Year Established: 2017 **Status 2020:** Active
Industries: Artificial Intelligence for:, ~ Arts-Entertainment-Recreation (4)

Company Name: feeders
Description: Feeders, a Machine Learning powered platform to address Electric Utilities challeng: Spain
Website: http://www.ourfeeders.com/
Phone: **Email:** 36556@reference-encyclopedia-ai.net
City: Singapore **State:** Central Region **PC:** **Country:** **Singapore**
Year Established: 2019 **Status 2020:** Active
Industries: ~ Energy and Utilities (14), ~ Energy and Utilities (14), Enterprise Application Services for:, Machine Learning

Company Name: Finbots AI
Description: Finbots AI is an intelligent automation firm focusing on finance, risk and operations area.
Website: http://www.finbots.ai/
Phone: 65 6909 2920 **Email:** client.support@finbots.ai
City: Singapore **State:** Central Region **PC:** **Country:** **Singapore**
Year Established: 2017 **Status 2020:** Active
Industries: Artificial Intelligence for:, ~ Banking and Financial Markets-Services (7), Machine Learning

Company Name: FireVisor
Description: FireVisor provide AI powered software platform that understands manufacturing data to reduce the cost of product failure.
Website: http://firevisor.com
Phone: (1707) 505-9911 **Email:** info@firevisor.com
City: Singapore **State:** Central Region **PC:** **Country:** **Singapore**
Year Established: 2013 **Status 2020:** Active
Industries: Artificial Intelligence for:, Automation for:, Machine Learning

Company Name: Ge: Romania
Description: Gero is a data-driven longevity company developing innovative therapies that will strongly extend human healthspan
Website: http://www.gero.ai/
Phone: 7 (495) 116 03 95 **Email:** info@gero.ai
City: Singapore **State:** Central Region **PC:** **Country:** **Singapore**
Year Established: 2012 **Status 2020:** Active
Industries: Artificial Intelligence for:, ~ Biotechnology (9), ~ Healthcare (20), Machine Learning

Company Name: Glee Trees
Description: Glee Trees develops Gleematic, a robotic process automation or RPA solution enabled by artificial intelligence.
Website: http://www.robotics-process-automation.com/singapore/
Phone: 065-91099419 **Email:** chris.lim@gleetrees.com
City: Singapore **State:** Central Region **PC:** **Country:** **Singapore**
Year Established: 2016 **Status 2020:** Active
Industries: Artificial Intelligence for:, IT Managed Services for:, Machine Learning for:, Robotics

Company Name: H3 Dynamics Holdings
Description: H3 Dynamics is a global maintenance inspection and security automation company.
Website: http://www.h3dynamics.com/
Phone: 65 9710 8445 **Email:** taras@h3dynamics.com
City: Singapore **State:** Central Region **PC:** **Country:** **Singapore**
Year Established: 2015 **Status 2020:** Active
Industries: Artificial Intelligence for:, Business Intelligence for:, ~ Energy and Utilities (14), Cloud for:, ~ Telecommunications (56), ~ Administrative and Support Services (1), Machine Learning for:, Predictive Analytics for:, Predictive Analytics for:, Business Software

Company Name: Hafta
Description: Hafta is creating the world's largest repository of psychometric data.
Website:
Phone: **Email:** 36661@reference-encyclopedia-ai.net
City: Singapore **State:** Central Region **PC:** **Country:** **Singapore**
Year Established: 2016 **Status 2020:** Closed
Industries: ~ Healthcare (20), ~ Banking and Financial Markets-Services (7)

Company Name: Handshak: Spain
Description: Handshakes is an AI-powered SaaS platform that allows users to understand complex corporate relationships.
Website: http://www.handshakes.com.sg/
Phone: (65) 6871 8821 **Email:** enquiries@handshakes.com.: Singapore
City: Singapore **State:** Central Region **PC:** **Country:** **Singapore**
Year Established: 2011 **Status 2020:** Active
Industries: Analytics for:, Artificial Intelligence for:, IT Managed Services for:, Business Software as a Service Apps (SaaS Apps)

Company Name: Healint
Description: Healint helps people who suffer from migraine and other neurological conditions using machine learning, sensor technologies, and analytics.
Website: http://www.healint.com/
Phone: 65 8657 9176 **Email:** contact@healint.com
City: Singapore **State:** Central Region **PC:** **Country:** **Singapore**
Year Established: 2013 **Status 2020:** Active
Industries: Analytics for:, Big Data and Analytics for:, ~ Healthcare (20), Machine Learning for:, ~ Healthcare (20), Mobile

Company Name: Health FX
Description: Health FX harnesses the power of A.I. Machine Learning and Blockchain to empower everyone with their own medical data.
Website: http://hfxtoken.com/
Phone: **Email:** 36678@reference-encyclopedia-ai.net
City: Singapore **State:** Central Region **PC:** **Country:** **Singapore**
Year Established: 2010 **Status 2020:** Active
Industries: Artificial Intelligence for:, Blockchain for:, ~ Healthcare (20), IT Managed Services

Company Name: Hearti
Description: An Smart HRM platform Using A.I & Blockchain to Revolutionize Enterprise Insurance.
Website: http://hearti.io
Phone: **Email:** hello@hearti.io
City: Singapore **State:** Central Region **PC:** **Country:** **Singapore**
Year Established: **Status 2020:** Active
Industries: Artificial Intelligence for:, Blockchain for:, ~ Human Resources (24), ~ Human Resources (24), ~ Insurance (25), Machine Learning

Company Name: HyperGrow:Thailand
Description: HyperGrowth is a technology developer that deliver data solutions to mobile advertisers and e-commerce marketplaces.
Website: http://hypergrowth.co
Phone: **Email:** media@hypergrowth.co
City: Singapore **State:** Central Region **PC:** **Country:** **Singapore**
Year Established: **Status 2020:** Active
Industries: ~ Media-Communications (41), Analytics for:, Artificial Intelligence for:, Big Data and Analytics for:, ~ Media-Communications (41)

Company Name: Imagene Labs
Description: Personalized skin care, nutrition and fitness through genetics
Website: http://www.imagenelabs.com
Phone: 6568172155 **Email:** hello@imagenelabs.com
City: Singapore **State:** Central Region **PC:** **Country:** **Singapore**
Year Established: **Status 2020:** Active
Industries:

Company Name: INSIDER.
Description: Insider is a Growth Management Platform for digital marketers.
Website: http://useinsider.com/
Phone: **Email:** info@useinsider.com
City: Singapore **State:** Central Region **PC:** **Country:** **Singapore**
Year Established: **Status 2020:** Active
Industries: Artificial Intelligence for:, Big Data and Analytics for:, Databases for:, Application Services for:, ~ Media-Communications (41), Predictive Analytics

Company Name: InsureVite
Description: Helping incumbents transform digitally faster and easier through co-creation using AI & Blockchain based platform
Website: http://insurevite.com
Phone: 65-9859-6205 **Email:** contact@insurevite.com
City: Singapore **State:** Central Region **PC:** **Country:** **Singapore**
Year Established: **Status 2020:** Active
Industries: Artificial Intelligence for:, Business Applications for:, Blockchain for:, Collaboration Solutions for:, ~ Banking and Financial Markets-Services (7), IT Managed Services for:, ~ Insurance (25), Application Services

Company Name: Intrepid Technology
Description: AI and blockchain powered ecommerce marketplace for technology service
Website: http://medblox.io
Phone: 877-235-8772 **Email:** info@medblox.io
City: Singapore **State:** Central Region **PC:** **Country:** **Singapore**
Year Established: **Status 2020:** Active
Industries: Artificial Intelligence for:, Business Applications for:, Blockchain for:, E-Commerce for:, ~ Banking and Financial Markets-Services (7), ~ Insurance (25)

Company Name: It's Next Technologies
Description: It's Next Technologies develops AI into the animation and visual effects world.
Website: http://www.its-next.com/
Phone: **Email:** hello@its-next.com
City: Singapore **State:** Central Region **PC:** **Country:** **Singapore**
Year Established: **Status 2020:** Active
Industries: ~ Arts-Entertainment-Recreation (4), Artificial Intelligence

Company Name: JOBHOP
Description: JobHop is a SaaS (Service-as-a Software) that helps companies and candidates engage better in SEA, starting with Vietnam
Website: http://www.jobhop.: Vietnam
Phone: (510) 775-1555 **Email:** hi@jobhop.: India
City: Singapore **State:** Central Region **PC:** **Country:** **Singapore**
Year Established: 2016 **Status 2020:** Active
Industries: Artificial Intelligence for:, Cloud for:, Machine Learning for:, Business Software as a Service Apps (SaaS Apps)

Company Name: JobTech
Description: JobTech collects and analyses labour market data with proprietary AI technologies.
Website: http://jobtech.co
Phone: 65 6908 7656 **Email:** connect@jobtech.co
City: Singapore **State:** Central Region **PC:** **Country:** **Singapore**
Year Established: 2016 **Status 2020:** Active
Industries: Analytics for:, Artificial Intelligence for:, Big Data and Analytics for:, IT Managed Services

Company Name: JointHire
Description: JointHire is a Singapore-based recruitment firm that automates hiring process to help companies hire talents more quickly with better match.
Website: http://www.jointhire.com.sg/
Phone: **Email:** support@jointhire.com.: Singapore
City: Singapore **State:** Central Region **PC:** **Country:** **Singapore**
Year Established: 2017 **Status 2020:** Active
Industries: IT Managed Services for:, Machine Learning for:, Robotics

Company Name: jumper.ai
Description: jumper is the fastest commerce enabler that removes the need to build a website. commerce on and within social media!
Website: http://jumper.ai/
Phone: **Email:** support@jumper.ai
City: Singapore **State:** Central Region **PC:** **Country:** **Singapore**
Year Established: **Status 2020:** Active
Industries: Artificial Intelligence for:, IT Managed Services for:, ~ Social Media (54)

Company Name: Jumpgate Technologies
Description: Jumpgate Technologies represents a new direction in investment management and quant investment technology: working to supplant
Website: http://www.jumpgate.ky
Phone: **Email:** contactus@jumpgate.ky
City: Singapore **State:** Central Region **PC:** **Country:** **Singapore**
Year Established: **Status 2020:** Active
Industries: Analytics for:, Artificial Intelligence for:, ~ Banking and Financial Markets-Services (7), ~ Banking and Financial Markets-Services (7), ~ Banking and Financial Markets-Services (7), Machine Learning for:, Compute

Company Name: Kewmann
Description: KewMann is a data and behavioural science company.
Website: http://www.kewmann.com/
Phone: 65 81390127 **Email:** kyl@kewmann.com
City: Singapore **State:** Central Region **PC:** **Country:** **Singapore**
Year Established: 2014 **Status 2020:** Active
Industries: Artificial Intelligence for:, IT Managed Services

Company Name: Killy
Description: Smart assistant to optimize Tech Dependent, Time Starved Travelers time & experience.
Website: http://www.killy.ai
Phone: 6596531921 **Email:** hello@killy.ai
City: Singapore **State:** Central Region **PC:** **Country:** **Singapore**
Year Established: **Status 2020:** Active
Industries: Artificial Intelligence for:, Machine Learning for:, Mobile for:, Natural Language Processing for:, ~ Media-Communications (41), ~ Travel and Transportation (58), ~ Travel and Transportation (58)

Company Name: Kinship AI
Description: AI powered factory workforce platform
Website: http://kinship.ai/
Phone: **Email:** 36855@reference-encyclopedia-ai.net
City: Singapore **State:** Central Region **PC:** **Country:** **Singapore**
Year Established: 2017 **Status 2020:** Active
Industries: Artificial Intelligence for:, Supply Chain Management

Company Name: Know What's Loved
Description: Data analytics, and data processing solutions for the music industry using Robot Process Automation, AI and Machine Learning technologies.
Website: http://www.knowwhatsloved.com/
Phone: **Email:** info@kwler.com
City: Singapore **State:** Central Region **PC:** **Country:** **Singapore**
Year Established: 2017 **Status 2020:** Active
Industries: Artificial Intelligence for:, Business Intelligence for:, Data Management for:, Machine Learning for:, ~ Arts-Entertainment-Recreation (4), ~ Arts-Entertainment-Recreation (4), ~ Arts-Entertainment-Recreation (4)

Company Name: Konigle
Description: Konigle building the layer of intelligence for traditional small and medium sized businesses using automation and intelligence.
Website: http://www.konigle.com/
Phone: **Email:** info@konigle.com
City: Singapore **State:** Central Region **PC:** **Country:** **Singapore**
Year Established: **Status 2020:** Active
Industries:

Company Name: Kratos Innovation Labs
Description: Kratos is a Singapore tech company with extensive focus on Blockchain, AI & IoT. One of Top 50 hot start-ups by Economic Tim: Spain
Website: http://kratosinnovationlabs.com
Phone: 65 90901423 **Email:** info@kratosinnovationlabs.com
City: Singapore **State:** Central Region **PC:** **Country:** **Singapore**
Year Established: 2017 **Status 2020:** Active
Industries: Artificial Intelligence for:, Blockchain for:, IT Managed Services for:, Internet of Things (IoT) for:, Machine Learning

Company Name: Kristal.AI
Description: Kristal is an AI based asset management platform that gives investors access to independent advisors and portfolio managers.
Website: http://kristal.ai
Phone: **Email:** hello@kristal.ai
City: Singapore **State:** Central Region **PC:** **Country:** **Singapore**
Year Established: 2016 **Status 2020:** Active
Industries: Artificial Intelligence for:, ~ Banking and Financial Markets-Services (7), ~ Banking and Financial Markets-Services (7), ~ Banking and Financial Markets-Services (7), ~ Banking and Financial Markets-Services (7), Finance and Accounting for:, ~ Banking and Fina

Company Name: Kristal.AI (O2O Technologies Pte Ltd)
Description: Kristal is an AI based asset management platform that gives investors access to independent advisors and portfolio managers.
Website: kristal.ai
Phone: **Email:** asheesh@kristal.ai
City: Singapore **State:** Central Region **PC:** **Country:** **Singapore**
Year Established: **Status 2020:** Active
Industries: Artificial Intelligence for:, ~ Banking and Financial Markets-Services (7), Finance and Accounting for:, Scientific Computing for:, ~ Banking and Financial Markets-Services (4460), Web for:, ~ Banking and Financial Markets-Services (5436)

Company Name: KroniKar.ai
Description: KroniKare AI-based system helps with early detection of complications such as infection, undermining and blood circulation problems.
Website: http://www.kronikare.ai/
Phone: (65) 9667 0786 **Email:** info@kronikare.ai
City: Singapore **State:** Central Region **PC:** **Country:** **Singapore**
Year Established: 2017 **Status 2020:** Active
Industries: Artificial Intelligence for:, ~ Biotechnology (9), ~ Healthcare (20), ~ Healthcare (20)

Company Name: Latent
Description: Sales and Productivity CRM to move deals faster for progressive small-to-medium businesses around the world
Website: http://latent.us/
Phone: **Email:** us@rship.us
City: Singapore **State:** Central Region **PC:** **Country:** **Singapore**
Year Established: 2020 **Status 2020:** Active
Industries: ~ Customer Relationship Management (11), Natural Language Processing

Company Name: Leben Care Technologies Pte Ltd
Description: Deep Learning AI healthcare startup in Ophthalmology space, developing solutions to tackle the global problem of avoidable blindness.
Website: http://www.leben.ai
Phone: **Email:** info@leben.ai
City: Singapore **State:** Central Region **PC:** **Country:** **Singapore**
Year Established: **Status 2020:** Active

Industries: Artificial Intelligence for:, ~ Healthcare (20), ~ Healthcare (20), ~ Manufacturing-Medical Equipment-Supplies (33)

Company Name: Lemnis Technologies
Description: Virtual Reality and Augmented Reality without Eye Stra: India
Website: http://www.lemnis.tech
Phone: **Email:** 36889@reference-encyclopedia-ai.net
City: Singapore **State:** Central Region **PC:** **Country:** **Singapore**
Year Established: 2017 **Status 2020:** Active
Industries: Application Services for:, Artificial Intelligence for:, Augmented Reality for:, Computer Vision for:, IT Managed Services for:, Virtual Reality (VR)

Company Name: LydianCo: India
Description: The First A.I. Big Data Marketing Cloud for Blockchain.
Website: http://lydian.io/
Phone: **Email:** Info@lydian.io
City: Singapore **State:** Central Region **PC:** **Country:** **Singapore**
Year Established: 2017 **Status 2020:** Active
Industries: Artificial Intelligence for:, Blockchain for:, Cloud for:, Web

Company Name: Lynx Analytics
Description: Lynx Analytics is a predictive analytics outlet run by quantitative marketing scientists and industry experienced data scientists.
Website: http://www.lynxanalytics.com/
Phone: 65 8198 4052 **Email:** info@lynxanalytics.com
City: Singapore **State:** Central Region **PC:** **Country:** **Singapore**
Year Established: 2010 **Status 2020:** Active
Industries: Analytics for:, Big Data and Analytics for:, IT Managed Services for:, Predictive Analytics

Company Name: Maitian.ai
Description: Maitian.ai is a computer vision powered autonoumous stores that makes the shopping experience even smoother.
Website: http://maitian.ai/
Phone: **Email:** hello@maitian.ai
City: Singapore **State:** Central Region **PC:** **Country:** **Singapore**
Year Established: 2018 **Status 2020:** Active
Industries: E-Commerce

Company Name: Medios Technologies
Description: Medios Technologies builds deep learning software that enables every doctor to detect diabetic retinopathy in the absence of a specialist.
Website: http://mediostech.com/
Phone: **Email:** 36955@reference-encyclopedia-ai.net
City: Singapore **State:** Central Region **PC:** **Country:** **Singapore**
Year Established: 2017 **Status 2020:** Active
Industries: Artificial Intelligence for:, IT Managed Services

Company Name: Medo.ai
Description: Medo.ai envisions the stethoscope of future by bringing expert ultrasound diagnosis to your fingertips.
Website: http://www.medo.ai/
Phone: (1) 780 991 9462 **Email:** masood@medo.ai
City: Singapore **State:** Central Region **PC:** **Country:** **Singapore**
Year Established: **Status 2020:** Active
Industries: Artificial Intelligence for:, ~ Healthcare (20), ~ Professional Services (48), Image Recognition for:, ~ Healthcare (2765), Machine Learning for:, ~ Healthcare (3375)

Company Name: Mei: Romania
Description: Meiro is a Customer Data Platform built in SIngapore with heavy focus on Asian markets, marketing automation and advanced analytics.
Website: http://meiro.io
Phone: **Email:** hello@meiro.io
City: Singapore **State:** Central Region **PC:** **Country:** **Singapore**
Year Established: 2018 **Status 2020:** Active
Industries: Artificial Intelligence for:, Big Data and Analytics for:, IT Managed Services

Company Name: Mogul
Description: Geospatial Real Estate Company
Website:
Phone: **Email:** 4937@reference-encyclopedia-ai.net
City: Singapore **State:** Central Region **PC:** **Country:** **Singapore**
Year Established: **Status 2020:** Active
Industries:

Company Name: Moneythor
Description: Moneythor is a financial technology company delivering better digital banking for customers and enhanced marketing & analytics for banks.
Website: http://www.moneythor.com
Phone: **Email:** info@moneythor.com
City: Singapore **State:** Central Region **PC:** **Country:** **Singapore**
Year Established: 2013 **Status 2020:** Active
Industries: ~ Banking and Financial Markets-Services (7), Application Program Interfaces (APIs) for:, Enterprise Application Services for:, ~ Banking and Financial Markets-Services (7), ~ Banking and Financial Markets-Services (7), Finance and Accounting for:, Predictive A

Company Name: Moovita
Description: Software, Autonomous Driving, AI, auto
Website: http://www.moovita.com/
Phone: (659) 025-6428 **Email:** info@moovita.com2
City: Singapore **State:** Central Region **PC:** **Country:** **Singapore**
Year Established: 2016 **Status 2020:** Active
Industries: Artificial Intelligence for:, ~ Automotive (5), IT Managed Services for:, Machine Learning

Company Name: Movel AI
Description: Movel AI is building solutions for robot navigation based on advanced computer vision and sensor fusion.
Website: http://movel.ai/
Phone: **Email:** contact@movel.ai
City: Singapore **State:** Central Region **PC:** **Country:** **Singapore**
Year Established: **Status 2020:** Active
Industries: Artificial Intelligence for:, Machine Learning for:, Robotics

Company Name: muFusion Social
Description: muFusion Social is an advanced social media analytics platform that offers customized solutions for various business problems.
Website: http://www.mu-sigma.com/analytics/platforms/mufusion/m...
Phone: **Email:** products.support@mu-sigma.com
City: Singapore **State:** Central Region **PC:** **Country:** **Singapore**
Year Established: 2010 **Status 2020:** Active
Industries: Natural Language Processing for:, ~ Social Assistance-Non-Profits (53), ~ Social Assistance-Non-Profits (53)

Company Name: Musiio
Description: Musiio is a Singapore-based startup that uses AI to solve content and curation problems for the music industry.
Website: http://www.musiio.com
Phone: **Email:** info@musiio.com
City: Singapore **State:** Central Region **PC:** **Country:** **Singapore**
Year Established: **Status 2020:** Active
Industries: Artificial Intelligence for:, ~ Arts-Entertainment-Recreation (4), Business Applications for:, IT Managed Services for:, Voice Recognition

Company Name: Myda
Description: Myda provides transforming tools for profitable business in one place.
Website: http://www.mydacloud.com/
Phone: 65 3158 0214 **Email:** info@mydacloud.com
City: Singapore **State:** Central Region **PC:** **Country:** **Singapore**
Year Established: 2015 **Status 2020:** Active
Industries: Big Data and Analytics for:, Business Intelligence for:, Web for:, Predictive Analytics

Company Name: Namahe
Description: Namahe, a leap forward to a sustainable future. First Socially Responsible Supply chain based on Blockchain & Artificial Intelligence
Website: http://www.namahe.com
Phone: **Email:** info@namahe.com
City: Singapore **State:** Central Region **PC:** **Country:** **Singapore**
Year Established: 2010 **Status 2020:** Active
Industries: Artificial Intelligence for:, IT Managed Services

Company Name: Narus Singapore
Description: Narus Singapore provides AI-powered knowledge management solution for organisations.
Website: http://narus.io/
Phone: **Email:** contact@narus.io
City: Singapore **State:** Central Region **PC:** **Country:** **Singapore**
Year Established: 2018 **Status 2020:** Active
Industries: Artificial Intelligence for:, Machine Learning

Company Name: Nd.
Description: AI-powered Design Studio for Presentations
Website:
Phone: **Email:** 37044@reference-encyclopedia-ai.net
City: Singapore **State:** Central Region **PC:** **Country:** **Singapore**
Year Established: 2015 **Status 2020:** Closed
Industries: Web

Company Name: Near
Description: Near is an ambient intelligence platform providing real-time information on places, people, and products.
Website: http://www.near.co
Phone: **Email:** info@near.co
City: Singapore **State:** Central Region **PC:** **Country:** **Singapore**
Year Established: **Status 2020:** Active
Industries: Analytics for:, Artificial Intelligence for:, Digital Marketing

Company Name: Neuri PTE LTD.
Description: Neuri is a Fintech startup that focuses on developing robust and stable AI driven simulation and modeling for automated portfolio management
Website: http://www.neuri.ai
Phone: **Email:** info@neuri.ai
City: Singapore **State:** Central Region **PC:** **Country:** **Singapore**
Year Established: **Status 2020:** Active
Industries: Artificial Intelligence for:, Big Data and Analytics for:, ~ Banking and Financial Markets-Services (7), ~ Banking and Financial Markets-Services (7), Machine Learning

Company Name: Neurobit Technologies
Description: Physiological Data Analytics as a Service
Website: https://www.neurobit.io/
Phone: 65-9062-3184 **Email:** contact@neurobit.io
City: Singapore **State:** Central Region **PC:** **Country:** **Singapore**
Year Established: **Status 2020:** Active
Industries: Artificial Intelligence for:, ~ Healthcare (20), ~ Life Sciences (27), Big Data and Analytics for:, Machine Learning

Company Name: NEWCLEUS
Description: NEWCLEUS provides predictive analytics platform.
Website: http://www.newcleus.co
Phone: **Email:** info@newcleus.co
City: Singapore **State:** Central Region **PC:** **Country:** **Singapore**
Year Established: 2014 **Status 2020:** Active
Industries: Big Data and Analytics for:, ~ Customer Relationship Management (11), Machine Learning for:, Predictive Analytics

Company Name: Nextbillion.ai
Description: Enabling Geospatial AI for the next billion use: Serbia
Website: http://nextbillion.ai/
Phone: (65) 9168 3565 **Email:** hello@nextbillion.ai
City: Singapore **State:** Central Region **PC:** **Country:** **Singapore**
Year Established: 2020 **Status 2020:** Active
Industries:

Company Name: Novatap
Description: Technology automation for people
Website: http://stackhive.com
Phone: **Email:** kshitizshankar@novatap.com
City: Singapore **State:** Central Region **PC:** **Country:** **Singapore**
Year Established: 2012 **Status 2020:** Active
Industries: Artificial Intelligence for:, IT Managed Services for:, Robotics

Company Name: Noviscient
Description: Noviscient
Website: http://www.noviscient.com
Phone: **Email:** info@novicient.com
City: Singapore **State:** Central Region **PC:** **Country:** **Singapore**
Year Established: 2016 **Status 2020:** Active
Industries: ~ Banking and Financial Markets-Services (7), ~ Banking and Financial Markets-Services (7), ~ Banking and Financial Markets-Services (7), IT Managed Services for:, Machine Learning for:, ~ Banking and Financial Markets-Services (7)

Company Name: Nucon
Description: Nucon is an AI engine that helps construction companies to learn from their mistakes.
Website: http://www.nucon.io/
Phone: **Email:** hello@nucon.io
City: Singapore **State:** Central Region **PC:** **Country:** **Singapore**
Year Established: 2018 **Status 2020:** Active
Industries: Artificial Intelligence for:, ~ Construction (10)

Company Name: Nug: Italy
Description: The Data Storytelling Platform for Enterprises and Technology Compani: Spain
Website: nugit.co/
Phone: **Email:** info@nugit.co
City: Singapore **State:** Central Region **PC:** **Country:** **Singapore**

Year Established: **Status 2020:** Active
Industries: ~ Media-Communications (41), Analytics for:, Artificial Intelligence for:, Business Intelligence for:, Digital Media for:, ~ Media-Communications (41)

Company Name: OCTOTRIP
Description: We are a pretty cool company with limitless values. We reinvent the way you will travel for work.
Website: http://octotrip.com/
Phone: **Email:** info@octotrip.com
City: Singapore **State:** Central Region **PC:** **Country:** **Singapore**
Year Established: **Status 2020:** Active
Industries: Artificial Intelligence for:, Big Data and Analytics for:, ~ Travel and Transportation (58), Machine Learning for:, ~ Travel and Transportation (58)

Company **Name:** OpenDNA
Description: OpenDNA is a AI platform technology (leveraging M2M learning, NLP and Neural Networks) that builds dynamic user profiles.
Website: http://opendna.ai
Phone: 6531591381 **Email:** hello@opendna.ai
City: Singapore **State:** Central Region **PC:** **Country:** **Singapore**
Year Established: **Status 2020:** Active
Industries: Analytics for:, Artificial Intelligence for:, Big Data and Analytics for:, Content for:, E-Commerce for:, Web for:, Machine Learning for:, ~ Media-Communications (41), ~ Media-Communications (41), ~ Media-Communications (41)

Company Name: OpenSingularity Foundation Ltd.
Description: Artificial Intelligence, Investments, Deep Learning
Website:
Phone: **Email:** 4863@reference-encyclopedia-ai.net
City: Singapore **State:** Central Region **PC:** **Country:** **Singapore**
Year Established: **Status 2020:** Active
Industries: Artificial Intelligence for:, IT Managed Services for:, Machine Learning

Company Name: OpsmateAI
Description: Opsmate empowers organisations to become more data-driven and bridges the gap towards AI adoption
Website: http://www.opsmate.ai
Phone: **Email:** gautam@opsmate.ai
City: Singapore **State:** Central Region **PC:** **Country:** **Singapore**
Year Established: 2019 **Status 2020:** Active
Industries: Artificial Intelligence for:, IT Managed Services for:, Machine Learning

Company Name: Pand.AI
Description: Pand.AI is an artificial intelligence startup that specialises in deep natural language processing.
Website: http://www.pand.ai
Phone: **Email:** hello@pand.ai
City: Singapore **State:** Central Region **PC:** **Country:** **Singapore**
Year Established: 2016 **Status 2020:** Active
Industries: Artificial Intelligence

Company Name: Payra
Description: Payra harnesses the advantages of a blockchain-enabled platform to bring solution to unbanked personnel.
Website: http://www.payra.io
Phone: **Email:** support@payra.io
City: Singapore **State:** Central Region **PC:** **Country:** **Singapore**
Year Established: 2018 **Status 2020:** Active
Industries: Application Services for:, Big Data and Analytics for:, ~ Banking and Financial Markets-Services (7), ~ Banking and Financial Markets-Services (7), ~ Banking and Financial Markets-Services (7), Mobile for:, ~ Banking and Financial Markets-Services (7), Predictiv

Company Name: Penc: Israel
Description: Pencil is an AI platform that can generate original, pre-optimised ad copy and visuals at scale.
Website: http://trypencil.com/
Phone: **Email:** 37150@reference-encyclopedia-ai.net
City: Singapore **State:** Central Region **PC:** **Country:** **Singapore**
Year Established: 2018 **Status 2020:** Active
Industries: Artificial Intelligence for:, Content for:, Machine Learning

Company Name: PeopleHum
Description: PeopleHum is the next-generation people engagement platform.
Website: http://peoplehum.com
Phone: **Email:** connect@peoplehum.com
City: Singapore **State:** Central Region **PC:** **Country:** **Singapore**
Year Established: 2015 **Status 2020:** Active
Industries: Analytics for:, IT Managed Services for:, Machine Learning

Company Name: Percipient
Description: Percipient is a data technology and analytics company based in Singapore
Website: http://www.percipientcx.com
Phone: **Email:** contactus@percipientcx.com
City: Singapore **State:** Central Region **PC:** **Country:** **Singapore**
Year Established: 2014 **Status 2020:** Active
Industries: Machine Learning

Company Name: photobook.ai
Description: The photobook.ai SDKs for Automatic Photobook creation (Albumstory) and Advanced Face Recognition
Website: http://www.photobook.ai
Phone: **Email:** terence@photobook.ai
City: Singapore **State:** Central Region **PC:** **Country:** **Singapore**
Year Established: 2018 **Status 2020:** Active
Industries:

Company Name: Pilot Automotive Labs
Description: Autonomous transportation for masses by building PILOT, self learning connected plugin device for any car.
Website: http://pilotlab.co
Phone: **Email:** info@pilotlab.co
City: Singapore **State:** Central Region **PC:** **Country:** **Singapore**
Year Established: 2016 **Status 2020:** Active
Industries: Artificial Intelligence for:, ~ Automotive (5), ~ Education (13)

Company Name: PinAlpha
Description: Fully Automated Financial Research & Insights
Website: http://pinalpha.com/
Phone: **Email:** 4693@reference-encyclopedia-ai.net
City: Singapore **State:** Central Region **PC:** **Country:** **Singapore**
Year Established: **Status 2020:** Active
Industries: Artificial Intelligence for:, ~ Banking and Financial Markets-Services (7), IT Managed Services for:, ~ Professional Services (48)

Company Name: PIVOT Fintech
Description: PIVOT Fintech is a transparent digital investment management system based on the fundamentals of Markowitz's Modern Portfolio Theory.
Website: http://www.pivotfintech.com
Phone: **Email:** victor.lye@pivotfintech.com
City: Singapore **State:** Central Region **PC:** **Country:** **Singapore**

Year Established: 2017 **Status 2020:** Active
Industries: Machine Learning

Company Name: Pixibo
Description: Pi from Pixibo, delivers personalised size & fit recommendation in real time for every shopper, for every style.
Website: http://www.wearepixibo.com
Phone: 416 559 6339 **Email:** info@pixibo.com
City: Singapore **State:** Central Region **PC:** **Country:** **Singapore**
Year Established: 2016 **Status 2020:** Active
Industries: E-Commerce for:, ~ Fashion (16), Predictive Analytics

Company Name: PlusMarg: India
Description: PlusMargin combines consumer psychology and machine learning, and persuades users to take action on platforms.
Website: http://plusmargin.com
Phone: 646-863-6073 **Email:** info@plusmargin.com
City: Singapore **State:** Central Region **PC:** **Country:** **Singapore**
Year Established: 2015 **Status 2020:** Active
Industries: IT Managed Services for:, Machine Learning for:, Predictive Analytics

Company Name: Poseidon-AI
Description: Poseidon-AI targets for world food sustainability and revolutionizing the aquaculture industry.
Website: http://www.poseidon-ai.com/
Phone: **Email:** contact@poseidon-ai.com
City: Singapore **State:** Central Region **PC:** **Country:** **Singapore**
Year Established: 2019 **Status 2020:** Active
Industries: Artificial Intelligence for:, ~ Food and Beverage (17)

Company Name: PriceSmartly
Description: Price Discovery Platform with AI
Website: http://pricesmartly.app
Phone: **Email:** contact@pricesmartly.app
City: Singapore **State:** Central Region **PC:** **Country:** **Singapore**
Year Established: 2018 **Status 2020:** Active
Industries: Artificial Intelligence for:, E-Commerce

Company Name: Privyr
Description: Privyr enables sales professionals to deliver the best experiences in every customer interaction.
Website: http://www.privyr.com/
Phone: **Email:** info@privyr.com
City: Singapore **State:** Central Region **PC:** **Country:** **Singapore**
Year Established: **Status 2020:** Active
Industries: Artificial Intelligence for:, Automation

Company Name: PropertyAI
Description: PropertyAI provides Singapore Property Market and economic analysis using artificial intelligence as well as big data mining and analytics.
Website: http://www.propertyai.: Singapore
Phone: **Email:** contact@propertyai.: Singapore
City: Singapore **State:** Central Region **PC:** **Country:** **Singapore**
Year Established: 2016 **Status 2020:** Active
Industries: Artificial Intelligence for:, Big Data and Analytics

Company Name: PropertyQuants
Description: PropertyQuants helps its clients to harness data at scale, to find the best real estate investments globally.
Website: http://propertyquants.com/
Phone: **Email:** info@propertyquants.com
City: Singapore **State:** Central Region **PC:** **Country:** **Singapore**
Year Established: 2018 **Status 2020:** Active
Industries: Analytics for:, Business Intelligence for:, ~ Real Estate (49), Predictive Analytics for:, ~ Real Estate (49)

Company Name: Psion Insights
Description: Psion Insights operates as an AI-powered risk management platform that identifies, analyzes, predicts, and acts on hidden risk signals.
Website: http://www.psioninsights.com
Phone: 65 9648 0041 **Email:** enquiry@psioninsights.com
City: Singapore **State:** Central Region **PC:** **Country:** **Singapore**
Year Established: 2019 **Status 2020:** Active
Industries: Analytics for:, Artificial Intelligence for:, Data Management for:, Machine Learning for:, Risk Management

Company Name: Pulsifi
Description: Pulsifi combines data science, psychology and technology to help organizations identify, retain and develop great people.
Website: http://pulsifi.me/
Phone: **Email:** 37227@reference-encyclopedia-ai.net
City: Singapore **State:** Central Region **PC:** **Country:** **Singapore**
Year Established: 2016 **Status 2020:** Active
Industries: Artificial Intelligence for:, Machine Learning for:, Predictive Analytics for:, Business Software as a Service Apps (SaaS Apps)

Company Name: QNeuron
Description: Creative Contents Management Framework
Website: http://qneuron.us
Phone: **Email:** projects@qneuron.us
City: Singapore **State:** Central Region **PC:** **Country:** **Singapore**
Year Established: 2015 **Status 2020:** Active
Industries: Artificial Intelligence for:, Content for:, ~ Media-Communications (41)

Company Name: Qritive
Description: Qritive makes cancer diagnosis fast, cheap, and accurate.
Website: http://www.qritive.com/
Phone: **Email:** info@qritive.com
City: Singapore **State:** Central Region **PC:** **Country:** **Singapore**
Year Established: 2017 **Status 2020:** Active
Industries:

Company Name: QuantShip
Description: QuantShip helps shipping companies make superior commercial decisions through proprietary machine learning algorithms.
Website: http://www.quantship.ai/
Phone: 65 9897 9663 **Email:** careers@quantship.ai
City: Singapore **State:** Central Region **PC:** **Country:** **Singapore**
Year Established: 2019 **Status 2020:** Active
Industries: Analytics for:, Artificial Intelligence for:, Big Data and Analytics for:, Machine Learning for:, ~ Transportation and Logistics (57)

Company Name: Questo AI
Description: An AI product development company. The app Questo is the world's smartest quizzing app. Snap a photo of your textbook to revise instantly.
Website: http://questo.ai
Phone: **Email:** team@questo.ai
City: Singapore **State:** Central Region **PC:** **Country:** **Singapore**
Year Established: **Status 2020:** Active
Industries: Analytics for:, Artificial Intelligence for:, ~ Education (13), ~ Education (13)

Company Name: Quod AI
Description: Quod AI is an AI platform that explains source code in English.
Website: http://www.quod.ai/
Phone: 65 90385512 **Email:** hello@quod.ai
City: Singapore **State:** Central Region **PC:** **Country:** **Singapore**
Year Established: 2018 **Status 2020:** Active
Industries: Artificial Intelligence

Company Name: Raxel Telematics
Description: White label Mobile telematics platform to run smart insurance and urban transportation
Website: http://raxeltelematics.com
Phone: **Email:** info@raxeltelematics.com
City: Singapore **State:** Central Region **PC:** **Country:** **Singapore**
Year Established: 2013 **Status 2020:** Active
Industries: ~ Automotive (5), Big Data and Analytics for:, Predictive Analytics for:, ~ Construction (10)

Company Name: Red Dot Analytics
Description: Red Dot Analytics is an artificial intelligence technology company for energy savings.
Website: http://rda.ai/
Phone: 65-9893-9590 **Email:** contact@rda.ai
City: Singapore **State:** Central Region **PC:** **Country:** **Singapore**
Year Established: 2016 **Status 2020:** Active
Industries: Artificial Intelligence for:, ~ Energy and Utilities (14)

Company **Name:** Reorder
Description: Enabling autonomous checkout for retailers with computer vision AI.
Website: http://getreorder.com
Phone: **Email:** Hi@reorder.: Singapore
City: Singapore **State:** Central Region **PC:** **Country:** **Singapore**
Year Established: 2018 **Status 2020:** Active
Industries: Artificial Intelligence

Company Name: Responsible Cyber Pte. Ltd.
Description: Hassle Free Smart Security As A Service Platform for Busy Owners With The first AI-powered Virtual Cyber Security Advisor
Website: http://www.responsible-cyber.com
Phone: 65 3157 2141 **Email:** info@responsible-cyber.com
City: Singapore **State:** Central Region **PC:** **Country:** **Singapore**
Year Established: 2016 **Status 2020:** Active
Industries: Artificial Intelligence for:, Cyber Security for:, IT Managed Services for:, Business Software as a Service Apps (SaaS Apps)

Company Name: Resync
Description: Machine Learning and Data Analytics driven Intelligent Energy Management Platform for systems with distributed energy resources.
Website: http://www.resynctech.com/
Phone: **Email:** info@resynctech.com
City: Singapore **State:** Central Region **PC:** **Country:** **Singapore**
Year Established: 2017 **Status 2020:** Active
Industries: Analytics for:, Artificial Intelligence for:, Big Data and Analytics for:, ~ Energy and Utilities (14), ~ Energy and Utilities (14), Internet of Things (IoT) for:, Machine Learning for:, ~ Social-Environmental-Physical-Engineering Sciences (55)

Company Name: Rotimatic
Description: Rotimatic is world's first fully automatic kitchen robot that makes rotis at the press of a button and in under 60 seconds.
Website: http://rotimatic.com/
Phone: **Email:** support@rotimatic.com
City: Singapore **State:** Central Region **PC:** **Country:** **Singapore**
Year Established: **Status 2020:** Active
Industries: Artificial Intelligence for:, ~ Manufacturing-Electronic (30), ~ Food and Beverage (17), ~ Manufacturing-Electronic (30), Robotics for:, ~ Professional Services (48)

Company Name: Saleswhale
Description: Saleswhale uses AI to engage every lead over email, qualify them, and identify leads that are ready to buy.
Website: http://saleswhale.com
Phone: **Email:** gabriel@saleswhale.com
City: Singapore **State:** Central Region **PC:** **Country:** **Singapore**
Year Established: 2015 **Status 2020:** Active
Industries: Artificial Intelligence for:, Business Applications for:, IT Managed Services for:, Automation

Company Name: Saola
Description: The Real-Time Measurement and Intelligence Platform for Streaming TV
Website: http://saola.io
Phone: **Email:** contact@saola.io
City: Singapore **State:** Central Region **PC:** **Country:** **Singapore**
Year Established: **Status 2020:** Active
Industries: Analytics for:, Artificial Intelligence for:, Application Services for:, Enterprise Application Services for:, Machine Learning for:, ~ Media-Communications (41), ~ Media-Communications (41)

Company Name: Sapient Predictive Analytics
Description: Sapient Predictive Analytics provides cutting-edge data science services, predictive analytics and related software.
Website: http://www.sapientswarm.com/
Phone: (65) 8490 4681 **Email:** info@sapientswarm.com
City: Singapore **State:** Central Region **PC:** **Country:** **Singapore**
Year Established: 2018 **Status 2020:** Active
Industries: Predictive Analytics

Company Name: Sassbook AI
Description: Sassbook enables rapid content creation by automating the process via its AI SaaS platform
Website: http://sassbook.com
Phone: **Email:** hello@sassbook.com
City: Singapore **State:** Central Region **PC:** **Country:** **Singapore**
Year Established: 2020 **Status 2020:** Active
Industries: Artificial Intelligence for:, Machine Learning for:, Business Software as a Service Apps (SaaS Apps)

Company Name: SAUCEink
Description: SAUCEink is a media and lifestyle platform to discover and shop.
Website:
Phone: **Email:** enquiries@sauceink.com
City: Singapore **State:** Central Region **PC:** **Country:** **Singapore**
Year Established: 2016 **Status 2020:** Active
Industries:

Company Name: Scry
Description: A Information Technology Company.
Website: http://www.scry.cloud/
Phone: **Email:** contact@scry.cloud
City: Singapore **State:** Central Region **PC:** **Country:** **Singapore**
Year Established: **Status 2020:** Active
Industries: Artificial Intelligence for:, Business Applications for:, IT Managed Services

Company Name: SCX HOLDINGS
Description: Alternative Asset Management, Investment and Intellectual Property
Website: http://www.scx.holdings
Phone: **Email:** andrei@scx.holdings
City: Singapore **State:** Central Region **PC:** **Country:** **Singapore**
Year Established: 2018 **Status 2020:** Active
Industries: Artificial Intelligence for:, ~ Banking and Financial Markets-Services (7), ~ Banking and Financial Markets-Services (7), ~ Banking and Financial Markets-Services (7), ~ Banking and Financial Markets-Services (7)

Company Name: SDhar: Morocco
Description: SDharma is an AI-based decentralized application built upon a blockchain. It uses a behavioural science based Algorithm to guide users.
Website: http://sdharma.org
Phone: **Email:** sdharma@sdharma.org
City: Singapore **State:** Central Region **PC:** **Country:** **Singapore**
Year Established: 2016 **Status 2020:** Active
Industries: Artificial Intelligence for:, Blockchain for:, Machine Learning

Company Name: SEED Vault
Description: SEED Vault is an online platform that provides development tools, Intellectual property, and network for deploying front-ends to AI.
Website:
Phone: **Email:** ask@seedtoken.io
City: Singapore **State:** Central Region **PC:** **Country:** **Singapore**
Year Established: 2017 **Status 2020:** Active
Industries: Artificial Intelligence for:, IT Managed Services for:, ~ Media-Communications (41), Web

Company Name: Sentient.io Pte Ltd
Description: AIaaS, DaaS
Website: http://sentient.io/
Phone: **Email:** enquiry@sentient.io
City: Singapore **State:** Central Region **PC:** **Country:** **Singapore**
Year Established: 2017 **Status 2020:** Active
Industries: Artificial Intelligence

Company Name: Shoffr
Description: Powering customer journeys for new retail.
Website: http://shoffr.io
Phone: 65 83807077 **Email:** abhishek@shoffr.io
City: Singapore **State:** Central Region **PC:** **Country:** **Singapore**
Year Established: **Status 2020:** Active
Industries: Analytics for:, Artificial Intelligence for:, Content for:, Enterprise Application Services for:, ~ Retail and Consumer Products (52)

Company Name: Sigrid
Description: Sigrid.AI is a subscription-based AI managed remote executive assistant service platform.
Website: http://www.sigrid.ai/
Phone: 65-3163-7564 **Email:** info@sigrid.ai
City: Singapore **State:** Central Region **PC:** **Country:** **Singapore**
Year Established: 2016 **Status 2020:** Active
Industries: Artificial Intelligence for:, Business Process and Operations

Company Name: Silent Eight
Description: Silent Eight helps financial institutions manage their compliance and risk obligations using artificial intelligence.
Website: http://www.silenteight.com/
Phone: (967)310-35 **Email:** support@silenteight.com
City: Singapore **State:** Central Region **PC:** **Country:** **Singapore**
Year Established: 2013 **Status 2020:** Active
Industries: Artificial Intelligence for:, ~ Banking and Financial Markets-Services (7), ~ Banking and Financial Markets-Services (7)

Company Name: SimpleCRM.com
Description: SimpleCRM is a comprehensive, robust Enterprise CRM platform with Intelligent Automation capabilities.
Website: http://www.simplecrm.com
Phone: **Email:** sales@simplecrm.com
City: Singapore **State:** Central Region **PC:** **Country:** **Singapore**
Year Established: 2014 **Status 2020:** Active
Industries: Artificial Intelligence for:, ~ Customer Relationship Management (11), IT Managed Services for:, Machine Learning

Company Name: SixSen: Sweden
Description: SixSense is an AI-powered defect analytics platform for smart manufacturing.
Website: http://sixsense.ai/
Phone: 65 9486 0203 **Email:** hello@sixsense.ai
City: Singapore **State:** Central Region **PC:** **Country:** **Singapore**
Year Established: 2018 **Status 2020:** Active
Industries: Artificial Intelligence for:, Automation

Company Name: SmartClean Technologies
Description: SmartClean Technologies is an AI company that offers data-driven cleaning operations designed for facilities.
Website: http://www.smartclean.sg/
Phone: 65 83759830 **Email:** enquiry@smartclean.: Singapore
City: Singapore **State:** Central Region **PC:** **Country:** **Singapore**
Year Established: 2017 **Status 2020:** Active
Industries: Artificial Intelligence for:, Big Data and Analytics for:, ~ Administrative and Support Services (1), Internet of Things (IoT)

Company Name: Smarten Spac: Spain
Description: Smarten Spaces is building management system using state-of-the-art AI and IoT platform.
Website: http://smartenspaces.com/
Phone: 080-61429007 **Email:** business@smartenspaces.com
City: Singapore **State:** Central Region **PC:** **Country:** **Singapore**
Year Established: 2017 **Status 2020:** Active
Industries: Artificial Intelligence for:, IT Managed Services for:, Internet of Things (IoT)

Company Name: Smartfuture Pte Ltd
Description: Smartfuture provides IoT and AI enabled health and wellness solutions.
Website: http://oursmartfuture.com/
Phone: 65 81338717 **Email:** sales@oursmartfuture.com
City: Singapore **State:** Central Region **PC:** **Country:** **Singapore**
Year Established: 2015 **Status 2020:** Active
Industries: Artificial Intelligence for:, ~ Healthcare (20), ~ Healthcare (20), ~ Healthcare (20), ~ Healthcare (20)

Company Name: SmartPeep
Description: We monitor patients and elderly people in ward with cameras, enabling nurses to get notified for emergent situations.
Website: http://www.smartpeep.ai
Phone: **Email:** contactus@smartpeep.ai
City: Singapore **State:** Central Region **PC:** **Country:** **Singapore**
Year Established: **Status 2020:** Active
Industries:

Company Name: Soma Sketch
Description: Soma Sketch simplifies mental health journeys with tools that empower patients and practitioners.
Website: http://www.somasketch.com
Phone: **Email:** hello@somasketch.com
City: Singapore **State:** Central Region **PC:** **Country:** **Singapore**
Year Established: 2019 **Status 2020:** Active
Industries: Computer Vision for:, ~ Healthcare (20), ~ Healthcare (20), Machine Learning

Company Name: SoMin.ai
Description: SoMin.ai is a SaaS platform that combines AI and Behavioral Science for conducting Social Media and Influencer Marketing Campaigns.
Website: http://somin.ai
Phone: 65-912-270-09 **Email:** ask@somin.ai
City: Singapore **State:** Central Region **PC:** **Country:** **Singapore**
Year Established: **Status 2020:** Active
Industries: Artificial Intelligence for:, Content for:, IT Managed Services for:, ~ Media-Communications (41), ~ Social Media (54), ~ Social Media (54)

Company Name: Sparkline Pte Ltd
Description: Digital analytics consultancy focused on analytics implementation, ROI optimisation, and conversion rate optimisation
Website: http://www.sparkline.com
Phone: 65 6557 2543 **Email:** info@sparkline.com
City: Singapore **State:** Central Region **PC:** **Country:** **Singapore**
Year Established: 2012 **Status 2020:** Active
Industries: IT Managed Services for:, Machine Learning

Company Name: Speac.co
Description: Speac.co uses A.I powered Natural Language Processing (NLP) technology to transcribe your audio files.
Website: http://www.speac.co
Phone: 6598774490 **Email:** info@speac.co
City: Singapore **State:** Central Region **PC:** **Country:** **Singapore**
Year Established: 2017 **Status 2020:** Active
Industries: Artificial Intelligence for:, Databases for:, Natural Language Processing for:, Web

Company Name: Spotalpha
Description: Robo-advisor, Capital markets, SaaS, FinTech, ML, AI
Website: http://spotalpha.com
Phone: **Email:** support@spotalpha.com
City: Singapore **State:** Central Region **PC:** **Country:** **Singapore**
Year Established: 2018 **Status 2020:** Active
Industries: ~ Banking and Financial Markets-Services (7), Machine Learning for:, Business Software as a Service Apps (SaaS Apps) for:, ~ Banking and Financial Markets-Services (7)

Company **Name:** SuitApp
Description: virtual stylist technology that provides personalised outfit recommendations
Website: http://suitapp.me/
Phone: 6531381919 **Email:** partners@suitapp.: Malaysia
City: Singapore **State:** Central Region **PC:** **Country:** **Singapore**
Year Established: 2016 **Status 2020:** Active
Industries: Artificial Intelligence for:, E-Commerce for:, ~ Fashion (16)

Company Name: Sup
Description: We are an AI-based social secretary that helps you plan your social calendar
Website: http://suptheapp.com
Phone: **Email:** info@suptheapp.com
City: Singapore **State:** Central Region **PC:** **Country:** **Singapore**
Year Established: **Status 2020:** Active
Industries: Application Services for:, Artificial Intelligence for:, Machine Learning for:, Application Services

Company Name: SweetEsca:
Description: A global AI driven photography platform with tens of thousands of photographers that offers photoshoots for consumers and businesses.
Website: http://www.sweetescape.com/en
Phone: **Email:** executive@sweetescape.com
City: Singapore **State:** Central Region **PC:** **Country:** **Singapore**
Year Established: 2016 **Status 2020:** Active
Industries: Application Services for:, Artificial Intelligence for:, Application Services

Company Name: Symphony
Description: SYMPHONY is a next-generation blockchain-based protocol to empower a data-driven economy.
Website: http://symphonyprotocol.com/
Phone: 65 68722188 **Email:** contact@symphonyprotocol.com
City: Singapore **State:** Central Region **PC:** **Country:** **Singapore**
Year Established: **Status 2020:** Active
Industries: Artificial Intelligence for:, IT Managed Services

Company Name: Synchronous
Description: A.I. for manufacturing
Website: http://synchronous.ai
Phone: **Email:** media@synchronous.ai
City: Singapore **State:** Central Region **PC:** **Country:** **Singapore**
Year Established: 2018 **Status 2020:** Active
Industries: Artificial Intelligence for:, Industrial Solutions

Company Name: TabSquare
Description: TabSquare offers F&B digital ordering systems using AI to make personalised menu recommendations and boost revenues for restaurants.
Website: http://www.tabsquare.ai
Phone: 65 8342 7059 **Email:** marketing@tabsquare.com
City: Singapore **State:** Central Region **PC:** **Country:** **Singapore**
Year Established: 2012 **Status 2020:** Active
Industries: Analytics for:, Artificial Intelligence for:, ~ Food and Beverage (17), ~ Food and Beverage (17)

Company Name: Teach n Learn Pte Ltd
Description: Online Education Marketplace
Website: http://www.teachnlearn.io
Phone: **Email:** Ethan.lim@teachnlearn.io
City: Singapore **State:** Central Region **PC:** **Country:** **Singapore**
Year Established: **Status 2020:** Active
Industries: Artificial Intelligence for:, ~ Education (13), ~ Education (13), Machine Learning

Company Name: TechStorm
Description: TECH STORM - MEDIA REINVENTED. We are the Next-Generation media powerhouse that celebrates Asia's fastest rising stars in Technology .
Website: http://www.techstorm.tv/
Phone: **Email:** hello@techstorm.tv
City: Singapore **State:** Central Region **PC:** **Country:** **Singapore**
Year Established: **Status 2020:** Active
Industries: Artificial Intelligence for:, ~ Media-Communications (41), Digital Media for:, E-Commerce

Company Name: tenqyu
Description: Tenqyu develops mobile applications that enable private and public service providers to offer information and connect with urban residents.
Website: http://www.tenqyu.com
Phone: (865)277-65 **Email:** info@tenqyu.com
City: Singapore **State:** Central Region **PC:** **Country:** **Singapore**
Year Established: **Status 2020:** Active
Industries:

Company Name: Terraview
Description: Terraview is a SaaS-based global image processing startup.
Website: http://www.terraview.co/
Phone: **Email:** hello@terraview.co
City: Singapore **State:** Central Region **PC:** **Country:** **Singapore**
Year Established: 2019 **Status 2020:** Active
Industries: Artificial Intelligence for:, Business Software as a Service Apps (SaaS Apps)

Company Name: The Data Team
Description: The Data Team is a premier consulting company that provides expert consulting services in the areas of big data and data science.
Website: http://www.thedatateam.: India
Phone: **Email:** contact@thedatateam.: India
City: Singapore **State:** Central Region **PC:** **Country:** **Singapore**
Year Established: 2014 **Status 2020:** Active
Industries: Big Data and Analytics for:, Internet of Things (IoT) for:, Machine Learning

Company Name: The Talent Gam: Spain
Description: Gamified Recruitment Solutions
Website: http://thetalentgames.com/
Phone: **Email:** daniyal@thetalentgames.com
City: Singapore **State:** Central Region **PC:** **Country:** **Singapore**
Year Established: 2017 **Status 2020:** Active
Industries: Artificial Intelligence for:, IT Managed Services

Company Name: Tookitaki
Description: Tookitaki provides enterprise software solutions to enable sustainable regulatory compliance programs in financial services industry.
Website: http://tookitaki.ai/
Phone: 65-6250-2620 **Email:** info@tookitaki.com
City: Singapore **State:** Central Region **PC:** **Country:** **Singapore**
Year Established: 2013 **Status 2020:** Active
Industries: Compliance for:, ~ Banking and Financial Markets-Services (7), ~ Banking and Financial Markets-Services (7), Machine Learning for:, Predictive Analytics

Company Name: Trackometrix
Description: Real Time Retail stores Analytics platform using face recognition & motion detection to track, trail, sense & connect with footfalls.
Website: http://trackometrix.com
Phone: **Email:** rd@trackometrix.com
City: Singapore **State:** Central Region **PC:** **Country:** **Singapore**
Year Established: 2014 **Status 2020:** Active
Industries: Analytics for:, Predictive Analytics for:, Compute

Company Name: Trakomatic
Description: Trakomatic enables businesses and organizations to discover the ways people interact using video and sensor technology.
Website: http://trakomatic.com/
Phone: 65 6681 5617 **Email:** contactus@trakomatic.com
City: Singapore **State:** Central Region **PC:** **Country:** **Singapore**
Year Established: 2013 **Status 2020:** Active
Industries: Analytics

Company Name: Transforma Robotics
Description: Transforma Robotics is a spin-off company from Nanyang Technological University (NTU) Singapore.
Website: http://www.transformarobotics.com/
Phone: **Email:** contact@transformarobotics.com
City: Singapore **State:** Central Region **PC:** **Country:** **Singapore**
Year Established: 2016 **Status 2020:** Active
Industries: Artificial Intelligence for:, Application Services for:, Machine Learning for:, Robotics

Company Name: Traverse Technologies
Description: Traverse Technologies is an AI powered professional engineering firm.
Website: http://www.traverse.ai/
Phone: **Email:** hello@traverse.ai
City: Singapore **State:** Central Region **PC:** **Country:** **Singapore**
Year Established: 2018 **Status 2020:** Active
Industries: Artificial Intelligence for:, Internet of Things (IoT) for:, IT Managed Services for:, IT Infrastructure for:, ~ Energy and Utilities (14)

Company Name: Tricog Heal:Thailand
Description: Predictive Healthcare Analytics Company
Website: http://www.tricog.com
Phone: **Email:** connect@tricog.com
City: Singapore **State:** Central Region **PC:** **Country:** **Singapore**
Year Established: 2014 **Status 2020:** Active
Industries: ~ Healthcare (20), ~ Healthcare (20), ~ Healthcare (20), Predictive Analytics

Company Name: TryShifu
Description: Realtime Predictive People Operations
Website: http://tryshifu.com
Phone: **Email:** 37575@reference-encyclopedia-ai.net
City: Singapore **State:** Central Region **PC:** **Country:** **Singapore**
Year Established: 2016 **Status 2020:** Closed
Industries: Big Data and Analytics for:, Predictive Analytics for:, Business Software as a Service Apps (SaaS Apps)

Company Name: TSC - The Stakeholder Company
Description: TSC, an intelligence firm, designs technology and services into stakeholder apps to identify, monitor and engage stakeholder environments.
Website: http://tsc.ai
Phone: 65 9005 2432 **Email:** terence@tsc.ai
City: Singapore **State:** Central Region **PC:** **Country:** **Singapore**
Year Established: **Status 2020:** Active
Industries: Analytics for:, Artificial Intelligence for:, ~ Automotive (5), ~ Banking and Financial Markets-Services (7), ~ Food and Beverage (17), IT Managed Services for:, Machine Learning for:, ~ Oil and Gas (43), Web

Company Name: Tuple Technologies
Description: Find Premium Customers and Multiply their Value with World's first Predictive AI.
Website: http://www.tuple.tech
Phone: **Email:** info@tuple.tech
City: Singapore **State:** Central Region **PC:** **Country:** **Singapore**
Year Established: **Status 2020:** Active
Industries: Analytics for:, Artificial Intelligence for:, Big Data and Analytics

Company Name: uCare.ai
Description: UCare.ai is a Singapore-based Artificial Intelligence-powered healthcare startup.
Website: http://www.ucare.ai/
Phone: **Email:** info@ucare.ai
City: Singapore **State:** Central Region **PC:** **Country:** **Singapore**
Year Established: 2016 **Status 2020:** Active
Industries: Artificial Intelligence for:, ~ Healthcare (20), Predictive Analytics

Company Name: Ui: South Africa
Description: The leading Online Video Platform in Asia
Website: http://uiza.io
Phone: 84-936-331359 **Email:** kevin@uiza.io
City: Singapore **State:** Central Region **PC:** **Country:** **Singapore**
Year Established: **Status 2020:** Active
Industries:

Company Name: UnBlock Analysis
Description: Real-time AI analytics for legitimate compliance and effective transaction monitoring Invested by PwC
Website: http://unblock-analysis.com
Phone: **Email:** company@unblock-analysis.com
City: Singapore **State:** Central Region **PC:** **Country:** **Singapore**
Year Established: 2018 **Status 2020:** Active
Industries: Artificial Intelligence for:, Blockchain for:, Compliance for:, ~ Banking and Financial Markets-Services (7), IT Managed Services

Company Name: Untangle AI
Description: Untangle AI are building a comprehensive platform and developer tools to allow companies.
Website: http://www.untangle.ai
Phone: **Email:** 4554@reference-encyclopedia-ai.net
City: Singapore **State:** Central Region **PC:** **Country:** **Singapore**
Year Established: **Status 2020:** Active
Industries: Artificial Intelligence

Company Name: Uppsala Security
Description: Uppsala Foundation is a threat intelligence platform.
Website: http://www.uppsalasecurity.com
Phone: **Email:** info@uppsalasecurity.com
City: Singapore **State:** Central Region **PC:** **Country:** **Singapore**
Year Established: 2018 **Status 2020:** Active
Industries: Artificial Intelligence for:, Blockchain for:, Cyber Security for:, Security for:, Security for:, Security

Company Name: UrbanAgents
Description: UrbanAgents is a Singapore-based AI-powered property technology (proptech) startup .
Website: http://www.urbanagents.com/
Phone: **Email:** 37602@reference-encyclopedia-ai.net
City: Singapore **State:** Central Region **PC:** **Country:** **Singapore**
Year Established: 2018 **Status 2020:** Active
Industries: Artificial Intelligence for:, IT Managed Services

Company Name: Value3
Description: Value3 is a capital markets AI-platform for independent, predictive and automated credit ratings, research & analytics.
Website: http://www.value3-advisory.com/
Phone: 65 6826 2569 **Email:** office@value3-advisory.com
City: Singapore **State:** Central Region **PC:** **Country:** **Singapore**
Year Established: 2016 **Status 2020:** Active
Industries: Artificial Intelligence for:, ~ Banking and Financial Markets-Services (7)

Company **Name:** Vebits AI
Description: Tackling one of the biggest safety issues facing the industry—the need for AVs to cope with unpredictable human driving behaviour
Website: https://www.vebits.com/
Phone: **Email:** anna@vebits.com
City: Singapore **State:** Central Region **PC:** **Country:** **Singapore**
Year Established: 2017 **Status 2020:** Active
Industries: Artificial Intelligence for:, ~ Automotive (5), ~ Automotive (5), Computer Vision

Company Name: Vigti
Description: Vigti is making gas pipeline safer and smarter
Website: https://www.vigti.com
Phone: **Email:** info@vigti.com
City: Singapore **State:** Central Region **PC:** **Country:** **Singapore**
Year Established: 2019 **Status 2020:** Active
Industries: Web for:, Machine Learning

Company Name: ViSenze
Description: ViSenze simplifies the visual web through artificial intelligence.
Website: http://www.visenze.com
Phone: **Email:** enquiry@visenze.com
City: Singapore **State:** Central Region **PC:** **Country:** **Singapore**
Year Established: **Status 2020:** Active
Industries: Artificial Intelligence for:, Image Recognition for:, Machine Learning for:, Computer Vision

Company Name: ViSenze
Description:
Website: https://www.visenze.com/
Phone: **Email:** 27306@reference-encyclopedia-ai.net
City: Singapore **State:** **PC:** **Country:** Slovakia
Year Established: **Status 2020:** Active
Industries:

Company Name: VokaBee
Description: VokaBee is a digital teaching assistant that increases the efficiency and engagement of learning a new language.
Website: http://vokabee.io/
Phone: 6582813307 **Email:** camil@vokabee.io
City: Singapore **State:** Central Region **PC:** **Country:** **Singapore**
Year Established: **Status 2020:** Active
Industries: Artificial Intelligence for:, ~ Education (13), ~ Education (13), ~ Education (13), Machine Learning for:, ~ Professional Services (48)

Company Name: Wavel.ai
Description: New generation artificial intelligence company focusing on providing Voice AI solutions to enterprises.
Website: http://wavel.ai
Phone: **Email:** reachout@wavel.ai
City: Singapore **State:** Central Region **PC:** **Country:** **Singapore**
Year Established: 2018 **Status 2020:** Active
Industries: Artificial Intelligence for:, Enterprise Application Services for:, Machine Learning

Company Name: WaveScan Technologies Pte. Ltd.
Description: WaveScan is an IoT & AI based Microwave/Millimeter wave sensing NDT company
Website: http://www.wavescan.: Singapore
Phone: 65-81397232 **Email:** kush@wavescan.: Singapore
City: Singapore **State:** Central Region **PC:** **Country:** **Singapore**
Year Established: **Status 2020:** Active
Industries: Analytics for:, Artificial Intelligence for:, ~ Manufacturing-Electronic (30), ~ Manufacturing-Electronic (30), ~ Healthcare (20), IT Managed Services for:, Machine Learning for:, ~ Professional Services (48)

Company Name: Wini: Malaysia
Description: Winimy builds and orchestrates AI-engineered bespoke customer engagement technologies.
Website: http://www.winimy.ai
Phone: 65 97973053 **Email:** 37675@reference-encyclopedia-ai.net
City: Singapore **State:** Central Region **PC: Country: Singapore**
Year Established: 2015 **Status 2020:** Active
Industries: Artificial Intelligence for:, Business Applications for:, ~ Customer Relationship Management (11)

Company Name: WISE AI
Description: WISE AI specialised in facial recognition platform, eKYC and smart city solutions.
Website: http://wiseai.tech/
Phone: Email: info@wiseai.tech
City: Singapore **State:** Central Region **PC: Country: Singapore**
Year Established: Status 2020: Active
Industries:

Company Name: X0PA AI
Description: Artificial Intelligence SAAS platform for talent hiring and retention
Website: http://www.x0pa.com
Phone: 65 81286873 **Email:** info@x0pa.com
City: Singapore **State:** Central Region **PC: Country: Singapore**
Year Established: 2017 **Status 2020:** Active
Industries: Analytics for:, Artificial Intelligence for:, Big Data and Analytics for:, Machine Learning for:, Business Software as a Service Apps (SaaS Apps)

Company Name: X0PA AI Pte Ltd
Description: Chief of Staff at X0PA AI
Website: https://www.x0pa.com
Phone: 6598567010 **Email:** info@x0pa.com
City: Singapore **State:** Central Region **PC: Country: Singapore**
Year Established: Status 2020: Active
Industries: Analytics for:, ~ Human Resources (146), Artificial Intelligence for:, ~ Human Resources (24), Automation for:, ~ Human Resources (390), Big Data and Analytics for:, ~ Human Resources (512), Business Intelligence for:, ~ Human Resources (695), Business Software as

Company Name: Xandar Radar Tech
Description: Radar algorithm with machine learning and AI for smart building IOT solutions, security and ADAS
Website: http://www.xandartech.com
Phone: Email: sam@xandartech.com
City: Singapore **State:** Central Region **PC: Country: Singapore**
Year Established: Status 2020: Active
Industries: Artificial Intelligence for:, IT Managed Services for:, IT Managed Services for:, Web

Company Name: Xjera Labs
Description: Artificial Intelligence (AI) based Image and Video Analytics (VA) solutions for various commercial applications.
Website: http://www.xjeralabs.com/
Phone: Email: enquiry@xjeralabs.com
City: Singapore **State:** Central Region **PC: Country: Singapore**
Year Established: 2013 **Status 2020:** Active
Industries: Artificial Intelligence

Company Name: XRVision Pte. Ltd.
Description: AI-based Enterprise-grade Video Content Analytics (VCA) software
Website: http://www.xrvision.com/
Phone: Email: information@xrvision.ai
City: Singapore **State:** Central Region **PC: Country: Singapore**
Year Established: 2015 **Status 2020:** Active
Industries: Artificial Intelligence for:, Computer Vision for:, Mobile for:, Internet of Things (IoT)

Company Name: Yojee
Description: Yojee is an autonomous next generation logistics platform
Website: http://yojee.com/
Phone: 65 3138 9076 **Email:** info@sendyojee.com
City: Singapore **State:** Central Region **PC: Country: Singapore**
Year Established: Status 2020: Active
Industries: Artificial Intelligence for:, ~ Transportation and Logistics (57), Machine Learning for:, ~ Professional Services (48), Supply Chain Management

Company Name: Zettabyte Pte Ltd
Description: We provide solutions for Higher Education focusing on UI/UX, mobile, web applications, Internet of Things, blockchain and Machine Learning.
Website: http://www.zettabyte.: Singapore
Phone: Email: chris.mugnier@zettabyte.: Singapore
City: Singapore **State:** Central Region **PC: Country: Singapore**
Year Established: 2016 **Status 2020:** Active
Industries: Artificial Intelligence for:, Blockchain for:, Internet of Things (IoT) for:, Application Services for:, Development and Test for:, Web

Company Name: Zimplistic
Description: Zimplistic is a product design company inventing intelligent kitchen appliances that promote healthy eating through simplicity & automation.
Website: http://www.zimplistic.com
Phone: Email: support@zimplistic.com
City: Singapore **State:** Central Region **PC: Country: Singapore**
Year Established: Status 2020: Active
Industries: Artificial Intelligence for:, ~ Manufacturing-Electronic (30), ~ Food and Beverage (17), ~ Manufacturing-Electronic (30), ~ Healthcare (20), ~ Professional Services (48), ~ Professional Services (48)

Company Name: Zumata
Description: Artificial Intelligence Travel Technology * Hotel Distribution API * IBM Watson * Natural Language * Bots *500, 000 Hotels
Website: http://www.zumata.com
Phone: Email: enquiry@zumata.com
City: Singapore **State:** Central Region **PC: Country: Singapore**
Year Established: Status 2020: Active
Industries: Artificial Intelligence for:, ~ Hospitality (23), Machine Learning for:, Natural Language Processing for:, Predictive Analytics for:, ~ Travel and Transportation (58), ~ Travel and Transportation (58), ~ Travel and Transportation (58)

Company Name: Lucid Reality Labs
Description: Lucid Reality Labs offers full-stack spatial technology services.
Website: http://lucidrealitylabs.com/
Phone: 380 68 286 0779 **Email:** info@lucidrealitylabs.com
City: Bedok **State:** East Region **PC: Country: Singapore**
Year Established: 2016 **Status 2020:** Active
Industries: Artificial Intelligence for:, IT Managed Services

Company Name: Lumin(ai)re
Description: Lumin(ai)re is an automated digital ad creatives and publishing company.
Website: http://luminaire-ai.com/
Phone: Email: enquiries@luminaire-ai.com
City: Bedok **State:** East Region **PC: Country: Singapore**
Year Established: 2018 **Status 2020:** Active
Industries: Artificial Intelligence for:, Machine Learning

Company Name: CFB Bots
Description: CFB Bots is a technology service provider specializes in emerging field of robotic process automation and artificial intelligence.
Website: http://www.cfb-bots.com/
Phone: 65 6909 2099 **Email:** enquiries@cfb-bots.com
City: Hougang **State:** North-East Region **PC:** **Country:** **Singapore**
Year Established: 2017 **Status 2020:** Active
Industries: Artificial Intelligence for:, IT Managed Services for:, Robotics

Company Name: Maple Intelligence
Description: Maple Intelligence is a vertically integrated B2B productivity and workflow management platform for property maintenance.
Website: http://www.maple.ai/
Phone: 65 8615 9753 **Email:** enquiries@maple.ai
City: Hougang **State:** North-East Region **PC:** **Country:** **Singapore**
Year Established: 2016 **Status 2020:** Active
Industries: Artificial Intelligence for:, IT Managed Services for:, IT Managed Services

Company Name: AISA Digital
Description: AISA Digital is a technology venture company incorporated in Singapore.
Website: https://www.aisa.digital/
Phone: 65 6681-6632 **Email:** enquiry@www.aisa.digital
City: Jurong West **State:** West Region **PC:** **Country:** **Singapore**
Year Established: 2018 **Status 2020:** Active
Industries:

Slovakia

Company Name: Ingen.io
Description: Ingen.io is an API based framework that extracts meaningful metadata from unstructured text in real-time.
Website: http://ingen.io
Phone: 359 896 863 501 **Email:** api@ingen.io
City: Bratislava **State:** Bratislava Region **PC:** **Country:** **Slovakia**
Year Established: **Status 2020:** Active
Industries: Artificial Intelligence for:, Big Data and Analytics for:, Databases for:, ~ Education (13), Natural Language Processing for:, ~ Life Sciences (27), ~ Professional Services (48)

Company Name: Photoneo
Description: Photoneo was established as a machine vision startup based in Slovakia with a team of visionaries and talented engineers focused on 3D.
Website: http://www.photoneo.com/
Phone: **Email:** info@photoneo.com
City: Bratislava **State:** Bratislava Region **PC:** **Country:** **Slovakia**
Year Established: **Status 2020:** Active
Industries: Artificial Intelligence for:, Machine Learning for:, Robotics

Company Name: MATSUKO
Description: 3D Telepresence in Mixed Reality using a single camera!
Website: http://www.matsuko.com
Phone: **Email:** contact@matsuko.com
City: Kosice **State:** Košice Region **PC:** **Country: Slovakia**
Year Established: **Status 2020:** Active
Industries: Artificial Intelligence for:, Augmented Reality for:, Web for:, Machine Learning for:, ~ Professional Services (48)

Company Name: 7SEGMENTS
Description: 7SEGMENTS is Big Data Analytics solution. Think of it as Google Analytics on steroids for all your data.
Website:
Phone: **Email:** 35928@reference-encyclopedia-ai.net
City: Bratislava **State:** **PC:** **Country: Slovakia**
Year Established: **Status 2020:** Closed
Industries: Analytics for:, Big Data and Analytics for:, Predictive Analytics for:, Business Software as a Service Apps (SaaS Apps)

Company Name: GapData Institute
Description: GapData Institute (GDI) is a nonprofit nonpartisan research institution harnessing the power of data for public good.
Website: http://www.gapdata.org/
Phone: **Email:** info@gapdata.org
City: Bratislava **State:** **PC:** **Country: Slovakia**
Year Established: 2015 **Status 2020:** Active
Industries: ~ Education (13)

Company **Name:** Hilbi
Description: Hilbi is an artificial intelligence (AI)-enhanced, decentralized communication platform that can facilitate instant payments.
Website: http://hilbi.com/
Phone: **Email:** 36692@reference-encyclopedia-ai.net
City: Bratislava **State:** **PC:** **Country: Slovakia**
Year Established: 2015 **Status 2020:** Active
Industries: Artificial Intelligence for:, IT Managed Services

Company Name: iERP.ai
Description: iERP is providing pre-packaged artificial intelligence algorithms to businesses.
Website: http://ierp.ai/
Phone: **Email:** b2b@ierp.ai
City: Bratislava **State:** **PC:** **Country: Slovakia**
Year Established: 2019 **Status 2020:** Active
Industries: Artificial Intelligence

Company Name: Localization Guru (acquired in July 2018)
Description: Localization Guru offers translating websites, mobile apps, marketing materials to technical documentation, and specialized translations.
Website: http://www.localizationguru.com/en/
Phone: **Email:** info@localizationguru.com
City: Bratislava **State:** **PC:** **Country: Slovakia**
Year Established: 2014 **Status 2020:** Active
Industries: ~ Education (13), Mobile for:, Natural Language Processing

Company Name: LURITY
Description: LURITY is a smart shop windows for retail compani: Spain
Website: http://www.lurity.com/
Phone: **Email:** hello@lurity.com
City: Bratislava **State:** **PC:** **Country: Slovakia**
Year Established: 2016 **Status 2020:** Active
Industries: Artificial Intelligence for:, Internet of Things (IoT)

Company Name: Mandarin Solutions
Description: We help companies to build, manage and protect their clouds saving the priceless time on hypothesis tests.
Website: http://mandarin.solutions
Phone: **Email:** marketing@mandarin.solutions
City: Bratislava **State:** **PC:** **Country: Slovakia**
Year Established: 2015 **Status 2020:** Active
Industries: Cloud for:, Cloud for:, Cloud for:, Cloud for:, Cloud for:, Internet of Things (IoT) for:, Predictive Analytics

Company Name: THERE
Description: THERE provides cutting-edge geospatial analytics powered by AI.
Website: http://there.digital
Phone: **Email:** info@there.digital
City: Bratislava **State:** **PC:** **Country: Slovakia**

Year Established: 2018 **Status 2020:** Active
Industries: Artificial Intelligence for:, Big Data and Analytics for:, Internet of Things (IoT) for:, Internet of Things (IoT)

Company Name: YesElf
Description: YesElf is a powerful platform, for providing step-by-step guides for any website or software
Website: http://www.yeself.com
Phone: **Email:** office@yeself.com
City: Bratislava **State:** **PC:** **Country: Slovakia**
Year Established: 2016 **Status 2020:** Active
Industries: Analytics for:, Artificial Intelligence for:, Application Services for:, Application Services

Company Name: Youfirst
Description: YouFirst is an Artificial Intelligence product for Influencers.
Website:
Phone: **Email:** 37718@reference-encyclopedia-ai.net
City: Bratislava **State:** **PC:** **Country: Slovakia**
Year Established: 2017 **Status 2020:** Closed
Industries: Artificial Intelligence for:, Digital Media for:, ~ Arts-Entertainment-Recreation (4)

Company Name: Contextics
Description: Contextics is a provider of free online creative intelligence tool to empower innovation and creativity.
Website: http://www.contextics.com
Phone: **Email:** business@contextics.com
City: Ljubljana **State:** Ljubljana **PC:** **Country: Slovakia**
Year Established: **Status 2020:** Active
Industries:

Company Name: Eligma
Description: AI, machine learning, blockchain, payment, commerce
Website: http://www.eligma.com/
Phone: 386 40 416 193 **Email:** info@eligma.com
City: Ljubljana **State:** Ljubljana **PC:** **Country: Slovakia**
Year Established: **Status 2020:** Active
Industries: Artificial Intelligence for:, Big Data and Analytics for:, Blockchain for:, Machine Learning for:, ~ Banking and Financial Markets-Services (7)

Company Name: Event Registry
Description: Real-time stream of global news content and world events.
Website: http://eventregistry.org/
Phone: **Email:** info@eventregistry.org
City: Ljubljana **State:** Ljubljana **PC:** **Country: Slovakia**
Year Established: **Status 2020:** Active
Industries: Artificial Intelligence for:, Big Data and Analytics for:, Machine Learning for:, Natural Language Processing for:, Data Management

Company Name: HONEYCOMB Colony
Description: Pesonal IoT DataVAULT with organized market place for secure Data lease - earning regular monthly income through data sales/lea: Sweden
Website: http://www.honeycomb-colony.io/
Phone: 00386 70 33 44 55 **Email:** info@honeycomb-colony.io
City: Ljubljana **State:** Ljubljana **PC:** **Country: Slovakia**
Year Established: **Status 2020:** Active
Industries: Artificial Intelligence for:, Big Data and Analytics for:, Blockchain for:, Databases for:, Data Management for:, Machine Learning

Company Name: Horticool
Description: Horticool is a gardening assistant that enables urban people to grow food in apartments.
Website: http://www.horticool.com
Phone: **Email:** info@horticool.com
City: Ljubljana **State:** Ljubljana **PC:** **Country: Slovakia**
Year Established: **Status 2020:** Active
Industries: Artificial Intelligence for:, ~ Home (22)

Company Name: Nervtech
Description: Nervtech is an R&D company specialized in simulations on biometric and cognitive driver evaluation, machine learning, and data integration.
Website: http://www.nervtech.com/
Phone: 386 1 810 91 44 **Email:** info@nervtech.com
City: Ljubljana **State:** Ljubljana **PC:** **Country: Slovakia**
Year Established: 2013 **Status 2020:** Active
Industries: Augmented Reality for:, ~ Automotive (5), Big Data and Analytics for:, ~ Biotechnology (9), Data Management for:, Machine Learning

Company Name: PredictLeads
Description: PredictLeads provides business intelligence via clean APIs.
Website: http://www.predictleads.com
Phone: **Email:** info@predictleads.com
City: Ljubljana **State:** Ljubljana **PC:** **Country: Slovakia**
Year Established: 2015 **Status 2020:** Active
Industries: Artificial Intelligence for:, Business Applications for:, Business Intelligence for:, Application Program Interfaces (APIs)

Company Name: TAIA Translation
Description: Revolutionizing process of ordering translations. With our cloud based application you can order your translations easier and faster.
Website: http://taia.io
Phone: **Email:** info@taia.io
City: Ljubljana **State:** Ljubljana **PC:** **Country: Slovakia**
Year Established: 2017 **Status 2020:** Active
Industries: Artificial Intelligence for:, IT Managed Services for:, Web for:, Internet of Things (IoT) for:, Machine Learning for:, Business Software as a Service Apps (SaaS Apps)

Company Name: Violanto
Description: Violanto builds artificial intelligence to understand eCommerce market changes, consumer behaviour and ACT on it.
Website: http://violanto.com
Phone: (310) 616 5091 **Email:** dean@violanto.com
City: Ljubljana **State:** Ljubljana **PC:** **Country: Slovakia**
Year Established: 2015 **Status 2020:** Active
Industries: Artificial Intelligence for:, E-Commerce

Company Name: Envigence
Description: Envigence is a company dealing with environmental issues and providing solutions.
Website: http://envigence.com
Phone: 00386 (0)5/90-70-451 **Email:** info@envigence.com
City: Solkan **State:** Nova Gorica **PC:** **Country: Slovakia**
Year Established: 2010 **Status 2020:** Active
Industries: Artificial Intelligence for:, IT Managed Services

Company Name: EFOS / Trapview
Description: Trapview automated pest monitoring system is utilizing proprietary IoT AI to revolutionize crop protection decision making
Website: http://www.trapview.com
Phone: 38657577542 **Email:** info@efos.: Slovakia
City: Hrusevje **State:** Postojna **PC:** **Country: Slovakia**
Year Established: **Status 2020:** Active
Industries: ~ Agriculture (3), ~ Agriculture (3), Artificial Intelligence for:, Big Data and Analytics for:, Image Recognition

South Africa

Company Name: Emizen
Description:
Website: http://www.emizen.co.: South Africa
Phone: 27 72 709 9058 **Email:** freddie@emizen.co.: South Africa
City: Boksburg **State:** GP **Zip:** 1459 **Country: South Africa**

Year Established: **Status 2020:** Active
Industries:

Company Name: Gatfol Technology
Description: Gatfol Technology represents a compact, elegant and massively scalable technique for changing keyword search into man-to-machine
Website: http://www.gatfol.com
Phone: 27 82 590 2993 **Email:** info@gatfol.com
City: Centurion **State:** GP **PC:** **Country: South Africa**
Year Established: 2012 **Status 2020:** Active
Industries: Artificial Intelligence for:, Web

Company Name: MineRP
Description:
Website: http://www.minerp.com
Phone: 27 87 980 3100 **Email:** fmegannon@minerp.com
City: Centurion **State:** GP **PC:** **Country: South Africa**
Year Established: **Status 2020:** Active
Industries:

Company Name: Sperosens
Description:
Website: https://www.spero.co.za/
Phone: 27(12) 665 0317 **Email:** info@spero.co.: South Africa
City: Centurion **State:** GP **PC:** **Country: South Africa**
Year Established: **Status 2020:** Active
Industries:

Company Name: Akiba Digital
Description: Financial Services, Mobile, Data Aggregation, Marketplace
Website: http://www.akibadigital.com
Phone: **Email:** info@akibadigital.com
City: Johannesburg **State:** GP **PC:** **Country: South Africa**
Year Established: **Status 2020:** Active
Industries: Artificial Intelligence for:, Big Data and Analytics for:, Data Management for:, ~ Banking and Financial Markets-Services (7), ~ Banking and Financial Markets-Services (7), Machine Learning for:, Mobile for:, ~ Banking and Financial Markets-Services (7)

Company Name: Bankymoon
Description: Bankymoon is a software and consulting firm that provides blockchain powered solutions and services to the financial industry.
Website: http://bankymoon.com
Phone: 27 83 445 1897 **Email:** 36135@reference-encyclopedia-ai.net
City: Johannesburg **State:** GP **PC:** **Country: South Africa**
Year Established: 2015 **Status 2020:** Active
Industries: Application Services for:, Robotics

Company Name: BusinessOptics
Description: BusinessOptics is a prescriptive analytics solution for both real-time decision optimization and scenario analys
Website: http://www.businessoptics.biz
Phone: 1(415) 324-8865 **Email:** info@businessoptics.biz
City: Johannesburg **State:** GP **PC:** **Country: South Africa**
Year Established: 2011 **Status 2020:** Active
Industries: Analytics for:, Cloud for:, Predictive Analytics for:, Supply Chain Management

Company Name: GotBot
Description: GotBot is an artificial intelligence chatbot solution.
Website: http://www.gotbot.co.za/
Phone: (2711) 726-8466 **Email:** info@gotbot.co.: South Africa
City: Johannesburg **State:** GP **PC:** **Country: South Africa**
Year Established: 2016 **Status 2020:** Active
Industries: Artificial Intelligence for:, Business Applications for:, IT Managed Services

Company Name: Ionizr
Description: Ionizr provides analytical insight of physical and online behavior, combining the real time flow of visits to your venue and website.
Website: http://www.ionizr.com/
Phone: 011 051 2800 **Email:** info@ionizr.com
City: Johannesburg **State:** GP **PC:** **Country: South Africa**
Year Established: 2015 **Status 2020:** Active
Industries: Analytics for:, Predictive Analytics

Company Name: LULA
Description: Connecting commuters to private shuttles on their commute to work - freeing up time and saving money
Website: http://www.lulaloop.co.: South Africa
Phone: (2711) 268-2340 **Email:** info@lulaloop.co.: South Africa
City: Johannesburg **State:** GP **PC:** **Country: South Africa**
Year Established: 2016 **Status 2020:** Active
Industries: Big Data and Analytics for:, IT Managed Services for:, Application Services for:, ~ Banking and Financial Markets-Services (7), Predictive Analytics for:, ~ Transportation and Logistics (57), ~ Social Media (54)

Company Name: MomSays
Description: Product Recommendations for moms driven by experienced moms.
Website: http://momsays.co.: South Africa
Phone: **Email:** tribe@momsays.co.: South Africa
City: Johannesburg **State:** GP **PC:** **Country: South Africa**
Year Established: 2018 **Status 2020:** Active
Industries: E-Commerce for:, Predictive Analytics

Company Name: Muzi
Description: Mobile health platform that uses image recognition and AI to make point of care disease screening more accessible, reliable and analyzable.
Website: http://www.muzitech.com
Phone: **Email:** info@muzitech.com
City: Johannesburg **State:** GP **PC:** **Country: South Africa**
Year Established: 2016 **Status 2020:** Active
Industries: Artificial Intelligence for:, ~ Healthcare (20), ~ Healthcare (20), Image Recognition

Company Name: Overscore AI
Description: Overscore AI is a Peer to Peer Jobs Platform that matches you and your friends to open jobs at companies.
Website: http://overscore.co.: South Africa
Phone: (010) 822 2480 **Email:** hello@overscore.co.: South Africa
City: Johannesburg **State:** GP **PC:** **Country: South Africa**
Year Established: 2015 **Status 2020:** Active
Industries:

Company Name: Pragmatic Master
Description: Pragmatic Master combines drones, artificial intelligence and remote sensing tools improve daily business decisions.
Website: http://www.pragmaticmaster.com
Phone: 27769052325 **Email:** info@pragmaticmaster.com
City: Johannesburg **State:** GP **PC:** **Country: South Africa**
Year Established: 2016 **Status 2020:** Active
Industries: Internet of Things (IoT) for:, Robotics

Company Name: Razorthink
Description: Predicting consumer behaviour with AI.
Website: http://www.razorthink.com/
Phone: (866) 972-1122 **Email:** info@razorthink.com
City: Johannesburg **State:** GP **PC:** **Country: South Africa**
Year Established: 2015 **Status 2020:** Active
Industries: Artificial Intelligence for:, IT Managed Services

Company Name: Spookfish
Description: Spookfish uses the latest computer vision technology to predict vehicle repair costs using photos of the damaged vehicle.
Website: http://spookfish.io/
Phone: 27813282725 **Email:** info@spookfish.io
City: Johannesburg **State:** GP **PC:** **Country: South Africa**
Year Established: 2016 **Status 2020:** Active
Industries: Artificial Intelligence for:, IT Managed Services for:, IT Managed Services

Company Name: Strider
Description: They combine strategy, technology, data science and design to solve the most complex business challenges.
Website: http://stridertech.co.za/
Phone: 27 11 568 2553 **Email:** info@stridertech.co.: South Africa
City: Johannesburg **State:** GP **PC:** **Country: South Africa**
Year Established: 2013 **Status 2020:** Active
Industries: Artificial Intelligence for:, Data Management

Company Name: FlowCentric Technologies
Description:
Website: https://www.flowcentric.com/
Phone: 27 (0) 10 020 4488 **Email:** 12545@reference-encyclopedia-ai.net
City: Pretoria **State:** GP **Zip:** 105 **Country: South Africa**
Year Established: **Status 2020:** Active
Industries:

Company Name: Kriterion
Description: Kriterion is a big data and artificial intelligence (AI) startup.
Website: http://kriterion.ai/
Phone: **Email:** info@kriterion.ai
City: Pretoria **State:** GP **PC:** **Country: South Africa**
Year Established: 2018 **Status 2020:** Active
Industries: Artificial Intelligence for:, Industrial Solutions for:, Automation

Company Name: Aerobotics
Description: Aerobotics is a data analytics company, using aerial imagery and machine learning algorithms to help farmers identify pest and disease early
Website: https://www.aerobotics.com/
Phone: 27 21 035 1060 **Email:** info@aerobotics.com
City: Cape Town **State:** WC **PC:** **Country: South Africa**
Year Established: 2014 **Status 2020:** Active
Industries: ~ Agriculture (3), Analytics for:, ~ Agriculture (3), Machine Learning

Company Name: Africa Business Integration
Description: Intelligent Machine Development and Consulting Service
Website: http://www.abi-ai.com
Phone: 630485733 **Email:** afribizintegration@gmail.com
City: Cape Town **State:** WC **PC:** **Country: South Africa**
Year Established: **Status 2020:** Active
Industries: Artificial Intelligence for:, IT Managed Services for:, IT Managed Services

Company Name: AI Media Group
Description: AI Media Group runs Africa's largest B2B trade focused AI community and offers 4IR news, content, insights & consulting services in Africa
Website: https://www.aimediagroup.com/
Phone: (888) 965-5009 **Email:** info@aimediagroup.com
City: Cape Town **State:** WC **PC:** **Country: South Africa**
Year Established: **Status 2020:** Active
Industries: Artificial Intelligence for:, ~ Event Management (15)

Company Name: Atura
Description: Atura is an automated chatbot for asset management compani: Spain
Website: http://atura.ai/
Phone: **Email:** hello@atura.ai
City: Cape Town **State:** WC **PC:** **Country: South Africa**
Year Established: 2016 **Status 2020:** Active
Industries: Artificial Intelligence for:, IT Managed Services for:, IT Managed Services

Company Name: Cortex Logic
Description: Cortex Logic is an AI / Machine Intelligence software & solutions company.
Website: http://cortexlogic.com
Phone: **Email:** info@cortexlogic.com
City: Cape Town **State:** WC **PC:** **Country: South Africa**
Year Established: 2015 **Status 2020:** Active
Industries: Analytics for:, Artificial Intelligence for:, IT Managed Services for:, Security

Company Name: DataProphet
Description: DataProphet is a global leader in Artificial Intelligence (AI) for manufacturing
Website: http://dataprophet.com
Phone: 27 21 300 3555 **Email:** info@dataprophet.com
City: Cape Town **State:** WC **PC:** **Country: South Africa**
Year Established: 2014 **Status 2020:** Active
Industries: Artificial Intelligence for:, ~ Automotive (5), IT Managed Services for:, Internet of Things (IoT) for:, Predictive Analytics for:, Predictive Analytics for:, Business Software as a Service Apps (SaaS Apps)

Company Name: Dolgio
Description: A factoring marketplace for Africa, that provides structure for SMEs to sell their invoices to financial investo: Serbia
Website: http://www.dolg.io
Phone: 27814517157 **Email:** hello@dolgio.com
City: Cape Town **State:** WC **PC:** **Country: South Africa**
Year Established: **Status 2020:** Active
Industries:

Company Name: Explore Data Science Acade: Malaysia
Description: The Explore Data Science Academy will serve the demand for big data analytics skills .
Website: http://www.explore-datascience.net/
Phone: 27 (0)21 555 5555 **Email:** info@explore-datascience.net
City: Cape Town **State:** WC **PC:** **Country: South Africa**
Year Established: 2017 **Status 2020:** Active
Industries: Analytics for:, Artificial Intelligence for:, ~ Education (13), ~ Education (13), ~ Education (13), IT Managed Services

Company Name: Graphflow
Description: Predictive Analytics Suite for WooCommerce
Website: http://graphflow.com
Phone: **Email:** hello@graphflow.com
City: Cape Town **State:** WC **PC:** **Country: South Africa**
Year Established: 2013 **Status 2020:** Active
Industries: Analytics for:, Big Data and Analytics for:, E-Commerce for:, Machine Learning for:, Predictive Analytics

Company Name: Hey Jude
Description: Hey Jude is a mobile assistant app backed up by humans and assisted by AI.
Website: http://www.heyjudeapp.com/
Phone: (2711) 449-7114 **Email:** jude@heyjudeapp.com
City: Cape Town **State:** WC **PC:** **Country: South Africa**
Year Established: 2015 **Status 2020:** Active
Industries:

Company Name: Ixio Analytics
Description: Ixio Analytics specialise in data and management information, advanced analytics and machine learning.
Website: http://www.ixioanalytics.com
Phone: 27 21 140 1595 **Email:** decisions@ixioanalytics.com
City: Cape Town **State:** WC **PC:** **Country: South Africa**
Year Established: 2012 **Status 2020:** Active
Industries: Artificial Intelligence for:, ~ Customer Relationship Management (11), IT Managed Services

Company Name: Mpilo24
Description: Mpilo24 - creator of tech for sport and wellness use cases .
Website:
Phone: **Email:** 4699@reference-encyclopedia-ai.net
City: Cape Town **State:** WC **PC:** **Country: South Africa**
Year Established: **Status 2020:** Active
Industries: Artificial Intelligence for:, Blockchain for:, ~ Healthcare (20), ~ Energy and Utilities (14), ~ Social Assistance-Non-Profits (53), Predictive Analytics for:, ~ Arts-Entertainment-Recreation (4)

Company Name: Ocentric (Pty) Ltd.
Description: Ocentric (Pty) Ltd. is a new Information Technology startup founded in Cape Town, South Africa.
Website:
Phone: 27 78 040 9870 **Email:** 30923@reference-encyclopedia-ai.net
City: Cape Town **State:** WC **PC:** **Country: South Africa**
Year Established: 2017 **Status 2020:** Closed
Industries:

Company Name: Radar Vision
Description: Internet of Things, Artificial Intelligence, Bluetooth 5, Smart sensors, Grid sensors, Self healing sensors, Neural Networks, Swarm Intelligence
Website: http://www.radarvision.org
Phone: 27215553978 **Email:** gerhard@radarvision.co.: South Africa
City: Cape Town **State:** WC **PC:** **Country: South Africa**
Year Established: 2012 **Status 2020:** Active
Industries: Artificial Intelligence for:, Augmented Reality for:, Internet of Things (IoT)

Company Name: Sensorit.io
Description: Sensorit.io is a smart mobility company.
Website: http://sensorit.io
Phone: **Email:** info@sensorit.io
City: Cape Town **State:** WC **PC:** **Country: South Africa**
Year Established: 2017 **Status 2020:** Active
Industries: Artificial Intelligence for:, IT Managed Services

South Korea

Company Name: PharmCADD
Description: Uses AI-based protein structure prediction algorithms, MD simulation, and Quantum calculation to enable faster drug design.
Website: http://www.pharmcadd.com
Phone: **Email:** info@pharmcadd.com
City: Busan **State:** Busan **PC:** **Country: South Korea**
Year Established: 2019 **Status 2020:** Active
Industries: Artificial Intelligence for:, ~ Biotechnology (9)

Company Name: Salad Factory
Description: We are developing a diet app based on artificial intelligence technology.
Website: http://saladfactory.co
Phone: **Email:** team@saladfactory.co
City: Busan **State:** Busan **PC:** **Country: South Korea**
Year Established: 2019 **Status 2020:** Active
Industries: Artificial Intelligence for:, ~ Healthcare (20)

Company Name: Coward Lions
Description: Coward Lions is a company that develops AI and Web platforms.
Website: http://cowardlion.com
Phone: 10-3021-5471 **Email:** mail@korea.:
City: Cheonan **State:** Chungcheongnam-do **PC:** **Country: South Korea**
Year Established: 2016 **Status 2020:** Active
Industries: Artificial Intelligence for:, Web

Company Name: Enercamp
Description: Enercamp specializes in IoT, AI, and ESS charging technology.
Website: http://www.enercamp.com
Phone: 82-(0)53-588-7296 **Email:** jschoi@enercamp.com
City: Daegu **State:** Daegu **PC:** **Country: South Korea**
Year Established: 2017 **Status 2020:** Active
Industries: Artificial Intelligence for:, Internet of Things (IoT)

Company Name: sonnet.ai
Description: sonnet.ai develops autonomous vehicles using deep learning and conventional software technologies.
Website: http://sonnet.ai/
Phone: 6504419771 **Email:** info@sonnet.ai
City: Daegu **State:** Daegu **PC:** **Country: South Korea**
Year Established: 2018 **Status 2020:** Active
Industries: Artificial Intelligence for:, ~ Automotive (5)

Company Name: Deargen
Description: Deargen provides AI-based genome analysis service.
Website: http://www.deargen.me/
Phone: (42) 716-2100 **Email:** contact@deargen.me
City: Daejeon **State:** Daejeon **PC:** **Country: South Korea**
Year Established: 2016 **Status 2020:** Active
Industries: Artificial Intelligence for:, ~ Biotechnology (9)

Company Name: Mimicus
Description: Mimicus provides an unparalleled AI enabled search portal that enables users to unlock hidden solutions from mother nature.
Website: http://mimic.us/
Phone: **Email:** chris.jang@mimic.us
City: Daejeon **State:** Daejeon **PC:** **Country: South Korea**
Year Established: 2016 **Status 2020:** Active
Industries: Machine Learning for:, Natural Language Processing for:, ~ Education (13)

Company Name: Seadronix
Description: Seadronix is a deep learning-based Ship monitoring and autonomous flight control system.
Website: http://www.seadronix.com/
Phone: 042-867-1201 **Email:** www.@seadronix.com
City: Daejeon **State:** Daejeon **PC:** **Country: South Korea**
Year Established: 2015 **Status 2020:** Active
Industries: Artificial Intelligence for:, Machine Learning

Company Name: Hcubed Technology
Description: Hcubed Technology provides software and machine learning systems, measurement systems and training services.
Website: http://www.hcubed.co.kr/
Phone: 042-867-7456 **Email:** hcubed@hcubed.co.: South Korea
City: Yusong **State:** Daejeon **PC:** **Country: South Korea**
Year Established: 2019 **Status 2020:** Active
Industries: Machine Learning for:, ~ Education (13)

Company Name: Pharos iBT
Description: Drug Discovery and Development Biotech Company specializing in collecting and analyzing big data based on IT technology
Website: http://pharosibt.com
Phone: **Email:** 37162@reference-encyclopedia-ai.net
City: Anyang **State:** Gyeonggi-do **PC:** **Country: South Korea**

Year Established: 2016 **Status 2020:** Active
Industries: Artificial Intelligence for:, ~ Biotechnology (9)

Company Name: TECHFLOOR
Description: TECHFLOOR specializes in robot automation and intelligence.
Website: http://techfloor.co.kr/
Phone: 031.422.0778 **Email:** tf@techfloor.co.: South Korea
City: Anyang **State:** Gyeonggi-do **PC:** **Country: South Korea**
Year Established: 2017 **Status 2020:** Active
Industries: Artificial Intelligence for:, Robotics

Company Name: DSLab Global
Description: DSLab Global provides AI automation solutions.
Website: http://dslab.global
Phone: 82-2-1670-1728 **Email:** contact@dslab.global
City: Bundangdong **State:** Gyeonggi-do **PC:** **Country: South Korea**
Year Established: 2020 **Status 2020:** Active
Industries:

Company Name: Naver Labs
Description: Naver Labs is Naver Corp's Research and Development arm with focus on AI, robotics, and autonomous driving.
Website: http://www.naverlabs.com/
Phone: **Email:** 37042@reference-encyclopedia-ai.net
City: Bundangdong **State:** Gyeonggi-do **PC:** **Country: South Korea**
Year Established: 2017 **Status 2020:** Active
Industries: Artificial Intelligence for:, Augmented Reality for:, ~ Automotive (5), Robotics

Company Name: HBsmith
Description: HBsmith provides cloud-based AI QA test automation services.
Website: http://hbsmith.io/
Phone: 010-9166-6855 **Email:** hello@hbsmith.io
City: Dongan **State:** Gyeonggi-do **PC:** **Country: South Korea**
Year Established: 2016 **Status 2020:** Active
Industries: Artificial Intelligence for:, Web for:, Business Process and Operations

Company Name: VSCommunity
Description: VSCommunity provides library management solution.
Website: http://www.vsc.co.: South Korea
Phone: 070-4354-0500 **Email:** vsc@vsc.co.: South Korea
City: Dongan **State:** Gyeonggi-do **PC:** **Country: South Korea**
Year Established: 2016 **Status 2020:** Active
Industries: Artificial Intelligence for:, Big Data and Analytics

Company Name: ELGEN
Description: Elgen is an artificial intelligence consultancy company.
Website: http://www.elgen.co.: South Korea
Phone: 070-8789-2035 **Email:** elgen@elgen.co.: South Korea
City: Gwangmyeong **State:** Gyeonggi-do **PC:** **Country: South Korea**
Year Established: 2014 **Status 2020:** Active
Industries: Artificial Intelligence

Company Name: Spaco: Saudi Arabia
Description:
Website: http://www.spacosa.com
Phone: 82-31-360-3655 **Email:** park@spacosa.com
City: Gyeonggi-do **State:** Gyeonggi-do **Zip:** 14055 **Country: South Korea**
Year Established: **Status 2020:** Active
Industries: Company Name: 2Digit
Description: 2Digit is a Fin-Tech company that provides financial services based on artificial intelligence, blockchain, and financial engineering.
Website: http://2digit.io/
Phone: 031-8038-4877 **Email:** contact@2digit.io
City: Pangyo **State:** Gyeonggi-do **PC:** **Country: South Korea**
Year Established: 2018 **Status 2020:** Active
Industries: Artificial Intelligence for:, Blockchain for:, ~ Banking and Financial Markets-Services (7)

Company Name: BlueBlab
Description: AI System Development with Mobile App
Website: http://blueblab.com
Phone: 82 10 5278 2529 **Email:** tristan.blueblab@gmail.com
City: Pangyo **State:** Gyeonggi-do **PC:** **Country: South Korea**
Year Established: **Status 2020:** Active
Industries: Artificial Intelligence for:, Big Data and Analytics for:, E-Commerce for:, Machine Learning for:, ~ Professional Services (48)

Company Name: NALBI Inc.
Description: NALBI is an leading AI company focusing on research and commercialization of computer vision technology based on deep learning.
Website: http://www.nalbi.ai/
Phone: **Email:** kinajin@nalbi.ai
City: Pangyo **State:** Gyeonggi-do **PC:** **Country: South Korea**
Year Established: **Status 2020:** Active
Industries: Artificial Intelligence for:, Computer Vision

Company Name: Aidentify
Description: Ai.dentify is providing artificial intelligence engines that analyze images and time-series signal data via a cloud API.
Website: http://www.aidentify.io/
Phone: 82 10 8784 0831 **Email:** ejkim@aidentify.io
City: Seongnam **State:** Gyeonggi-do **PC:** **Country: South Korea**
Year Established: **Status 2020:** Active
Industries: Artificial Intelligence

Company Name: AiLeeSoft
Description: AiLeeSoft is an artificial intelligence company that develops AI English conversation platform.
Website: https://www.aileesoft.com/
Phone: 82-31-698-4343 **Email:** biz@aileesoft.com
City: Seongnam **State:** Gyeonggi-do **PC:** **Country: South Korea**
Year Established: 2017 **Status 2020:** Active
Industries: Artificial Intelligence for:, ~ Education (13)

Company Name: Alchera
Description: Alchera provides AI, AR, and big data solutions specializing in visual anomaly detection technology (VADT) using AI-based image recognition.
Website: https://www.alcherainc.com/en_US/
Phone: 070-4681-0173 **Email:** alchera@alcherainc.com
City: Seongnam **State:** Gyeonggi-do **PC:** **Country: South Korea**
Year Established: 2016 **Status 2020:** Active
Industries: Artificial Intelligence for:, Facial Recognition for:, Image Recognition for:, Machine Learning

Company Name: Artificial Intelligence Research Institute
Description: Artificial Intelligence Research Institute offers an internship program.
Website: http://airi.kr/
Phone: 031-8020-8700 **Email:** airi@airi.: South Korea
City: Seongnam **State:** Gyeonggi-do **PC:** **Country: South Korea**
Year Established: 2016 **Status 2020:** Active
Industries: Artificial Intelligence for:, IT Managed Services for:, Web

Company Name: FOUR GRID
Description: Four Grid offers big data and machine learning services.
Website: http://www.4grit.com/
Phone: 031-625-4397 **Email:** biz@4grit.com
City: Seongnam **State:** Gyeonggi-do **PC:** **Country: South Korea**

Year Established: 2015 **Status 2020:** Active
Industries: Big Data and Analytics for:, Machine Learning

Company Name: GoQba technology corporation
Description: AI Health Care
Website: http://www.goqba.com/
Phone: 02-3288-8789 **Email:** goqba@goqba.com
City: Seongnam **State:** Gyeonggi-do **PC:** **Country: South Korea**
Year Established: 2017 **Status 2020:** Active
Industries:

Company Name: Helloapps
Description: Helloapps is artificial intelligence and virtual reality coding education company.
Website: http://www.helloapps.co.kr/
Phone: 070-4417-1559 **Email:** helloapps@naver.com
City: Seongnam **State:** Gyeonggi-do **PC:** **Country: South Korea**
Year Established: 2011 **Status 2020:** Active
Industries: Artificial Intelligence for:, Virtual Reality (VR)

Company Name: Interminds
Description: Interminds is an AI platform for image recognition solutions.
Website: http://intermindsai.com/
Phone: 031-8039-7231 **Email:** admin@interminds.ai
City: Seongnam **State:** Gyeonggi-do **PC:** **Country: South Korea**
Year Established: 2016 **Status 2020:** Active
Industries: Artificial Intelligence for:, Image Recognition

Company Name: Kakao Enterpri: Sweden
Description: Kakao Enterprise specializes in providing AI technology and services.
Website: http://www.kakaoenterprise.com/
Phone: **Email:** contact@kakaoenterprise.com
City: Seongnam **State:** Gyeonggi-do **PC:** **Country: South Korea**
Year Established: 2019 **Status 2020:** Active
Industries: Artificial Intelligence for:, IT Managed Services for:, Machine Learning

Company Name: LaonPeople
Description: LaonPeople is a vision recognition technology company.
Website: http://www.laonpeople.com/
Phone: 02-1899-3058 **Email:** sales@laonpeople.com
City: Seongnam **State:** Gyeonggi-do **PC:** **Country: South Korea**
Year Established: 2010 **Status 2020:** Active
Industries: IT Managed Services for:, Machine Learning

Company Name: mAy-I
Description: mAy-I develops advanced machine vision tracking solution.
Website: http://www.may-i.io
Phone: **Email:** 36947@reference-encyclopedia-ai.net
City: Seongnam **State:** Gyeonggi-do **PC:** **Country: South Korea**
Year Established: 2019 **Status 2020:** Active
Industries: Computer Vision for:, IT Managed Services for:, Machine Learning

Company Name: Mindslab
Description: Mindslab is an artificial intelligence application platform.
Website: http://maum.ai/
Phone: 82 31 625 4340 **Email:** hello@mindslab.ai
City: Seongnam **State:** Gyeonggi-do **PC:** **Country: South Korea**
Year Established: 2014 **Status 2020:** Active
Industries: Application Services for:, Artificial Intelligence for:, IT Managed Services

Company Name: NEXTK
Description: NEXTK is a platform solution company using artificial intelligence technology.
Website: http://www.nextk.co.kr/
Phone: 82 31-718-1618 **Email:** nextk@nextk.co.: South Korea
City: Seongnam **State:** Gyeonggi-do **PC:** **Country: South Korea**
Year Established: 2019 **Status 2020:** Active
Industries: Artificial Intelligence for:, Big Data and Analytics

Company Name: SuperB: India
Description: SuperBin is a company that uses AI to create a culture where our society can share and practice the value of circulating resources.
Website: http://www.superbin.co.: South Korea
Phone: 1600-6217 **Email:** info@superbin.co.: South Korea
City: Seongnam **State:** Gyeonggi-do **PC:** **Country: South Korea**
Year Established: 2015 **Status 2020:** Active
Industries: Artificial Intelligence for:, IT Managed Services

Company Name: ulalaLAB
Description: ulalaLAB, South Korean startup company specializing in Industrial IoT, SaaS and Machine Learning technologies.
Website: http://www.ulalalab.com/
Phone: (822)873-0010 **Email:** mail@ulalaLAB.com
City: Seongnam **State:** Gyeonggi-do **PC:** **Country: South Korea**
Year Established: 2011 **Status 2020:** Active
Industries: Enterprise Application Services for:, Automation for:, IT Managed Services for:, Internet of Things (IoT) for:, Machine Learning for:, Business Software as a Service Apps (SaaS Apps) for:, ~ Customer Relationship Management (11), ~ Customer Relationship Manageme

Company Name: 7meerkat
Description: 7meerkat develops software using artificial intelligence to design a space for new vehicles.
Website: http://7meerkat.com/
Phone: 031-8099-3477 **Email:** 7king@7meerkat.com
City: Sihung **State:** Gyeonggi-do **PC:** **Country: South Korea**
Year Established: 2019 **Status 2020:** Active
Industries: Artificial Intelligence for:, ~ Travel and Transportation (58)

Company Name: BETO Korea Co., Ltd.
Description: BETO Sleep Coach 'The first IoT baby sleep trainer with AI '
Website: http://www.betosleepcoach.com
Phone: 82312140814 **Email:** info@betokorea.com
City: Sowon **State:** Gyeonggi-do **PC:** **Country: South Korea**
Year Established: **Status 2020:** Active
Industries: Artificial Intelligence for:, Robotics

Company Name: 3BIGS
Description: Aims to discover new materials powered by bio big data and AI platform.
Website: http://3bigs.com/
Phone: **Email:** 35919@reference-encyclopedia-ai.net
City: Suwon **State:** Gyeonggi-do **PC:** **Country: South Korea**
Year Established: 2017 **Status 2020:** Active
Industries: Artificial Intelligence for:, ~ Biotechnology (9)

Company Name: INFOTRON
Description: Infotron develops and sells AI speaker modules.
Website: http://infotron.co.: South Korea
Phone: 82 31-374-7808 **Email:** infotron8@gmail.com
City: Suwon **State:** Gyeonggi-do **PC:** **Country: South Korea**
Year Established: 2014 **Status 2020:** Active
Industries: Artificial Intelligence for:, Speech Recognition

Company Name: Laonbud
Description: Laonbud provides solutions for face recognition, object detection, object tracking, visual recognition, and search.
Website: http://www.laonbud.com
Phone: 82-70-8243-2641 **Email:** laonbud@laonbud.com
City: Suwon **State:** Gyeonggi-do **PC:** **Country: South Korea**
Year Established: 2017 **Status 2020:** Active
Industries:

Company Name: NGMsoftware
Description: NGMsoftware develops and supplies solutions for task automation, image analysis, and machine learning.
Website: http://www.ngmaster.net
Phone: 010-9025-7987 **Email:** ngmaster@ngmsoftware.com
City: Suwon **State:** Gyeonggi-do **PC:** **Country: South Korea**
Year Established: 2015 **Status 2020:** Active
Industries: IT Managed Services for:, Machine Learning

Company Name: Augmented Knowledge
Description: Augmented Knowledge is an augmented reality solutions company currently focused on the airline and machinery maintenance industries.
Website: http://www.augmentedk.com
Phone: **Email:** augmentedk@augmentedk.com
City: Incheon **State:** Incheon **PC:** **Country: South Korea**
Year Established: **Status 2020:** Active
Industries: Artificial Intelligence for:, Augmented Reality for:, Computer Vision

Company Name: DeepFine
Description: DeepFine is a sensor fusion solution company that makes life easier with innovative technology.
Website: http://www.deepfine.ai/kor.do
Phone: 070 4633 2487 8 **Email:** help@deepfine.ai
City: Incheon **State:** Incheon **PC:** **Country: South Korea**
Year Established: 2019 **Status 2020:** Active
Industries: Artificial Intelligence for:, Machine Learning

Company Name: Mondrian AI
Description: Mondrian AI is an innovative data science and visualization company.
Website: http://mondrian.ai/
Phone: 032-713-7984 **Email:** contact@mondrian.ai
City: Incheon **State:** Incheon **PC:** **Country: South Korea**
Year Established: 2016 **Status 2020:** Active
Industries: Artificial Intelligence for:, IT Managed Services for:, Machine Learning

Company Name: Neurocle
Description: Neurocle provides a deep learning model which optimized and weight reduced for embedded systems.
Website: http://www.neuro-cle.com/
Phone: 82-2-6952-6898 **Email:** neurocle@neuro-cle.com
City: Daechidong **State:** Seoul **PC:** **Country: South Korea**
Year Established: 2019 **Status 2020:** Active
Industries: Embedded for:, IT Managed Services for:, Machine Learning

Company Name: Lunit Inc.
Description:
Website: http://www.lunit.io
Phone: **Email:** contact@lunit.io
City: Gangnam-gu **State:** Seoul **PC:** **Country: South Korea**
Year Established: **Status 2020:** Active
Industries: Computer Vision for:, ~ Healthcare (20), Image Recognition for:, Machine Learning for:, ~ Professional Services (48)

Company Name: EcoleTree
Description: EcoleTree is an artificial intelligence technology company.
Website: http://ecoletree.com
Phone: **Email:** ecoletree@gmail.com
City: Gasandong **State:** Seoul **PC:** **Country: South Korea**
Year Established: 2017 **Status 2020:** Active
Industries: Artificial Intelligence for:, IT Managed Services

Company Name: Enswers Inc
Description:
Website: http://www.enswers.net
Phone: 82-2-598-5857 **Email:** contact@enswers.net
City: Huam-ro, Jung-gu **State:** Seoul **PC:** **Country: South Korea**
Year Established: **Status 2020:** Active
Industries: Cloud for:, ~ Manufacturing-Electronic (30), Image Recognition for:, IT Managed Services for:, IT Managed Services for:, ~ Professional Services (48)

Company Name: Algorithm LABS
Description: Algorithm LABS is an ed-tech company that researches AI-based algorithms and coding training.
Website: https://www.algorithmlabs.co.kr/
Phone: 02-2651-2650 **Email:** contact@algorithmlabs.co.: South Korea
City: Mapo **State:** Seoul **PC:** **Country: South Korea**
Year Established: 2017 **Status 2020:** Active
Industries: Artificial Intelligence for:, ~ Education (13), IT Managed Services

Company Name: App doctor
Description: App doctor specializes in bug fixing and add-ons for mobile apps.
Website: http://www.appdoctor.co.: South Korea
Phone: 02-6490-1770 **Email:** info@appdr.com
City: Mapo **State:** Seoul **PC:** **Country: South Korea**
Year Established: 2017 **Status 2020:** Active
Industries: Artificial Intelligence for:, Application Services

Company Name: Bluevisor
Description: Bluevior is a fintech company that develops a Robo-advisor system.
Website: http://bluevisor.kr/
Phone: (102) 598-2158 **Email:** ceo@bluevisor.: South Korea
City: Mapo **State:** Seoul **PC:** **Country: South Korea**
Year Established: 2016 **Status 2020:** Active
Industries: Artificial Intelligence for:, ~ Banking and Financial Markets-Services (7), Robotics

Company Name: Dev Unlim: Italy
Description: Dev Unlimit offers AI-based home coach and training application.
Website: http://www.devunlimit.com/
Phone: 82 10 4906 8884 **Email:** root@devunlimit.com
City: Mapo **State:** Seoul **PC:** **Country: South Korea**
Year Established: 2017 **Status 2020:** Active
Industries: Artificial Intelligence

Company Name: Dreamy You:Thailand
Description: Dreamy Youth is an AI-based designer and developer of Chatbot.
Website: http://www.dreamyoungs.com
Phone: 82-70-7012-4230 **Email:** hello@dreamyoungs.com
City: Mapo **State:** Seoul **PC:** **Country: South Korea**
Year Established: 2015 **Status 2020:** Active
Industries: Artificial Intelligence for:, Application Services

Company Name: Illunex
Description: Illunex is an AI enterprise network platform.
Website: http://illunex.com
Phone: 82-31-901-2149 **Email:** manager@illunex.com
City: Mapo **State:** Seoul **PC:** **Country: South Korea**
Year Established: 2018 **Status 2020:** Active
Industries:

Company Name: Medipixel
Description: Medipixel is a healthcare technology company.
Website: http://www.medipixel.io
Phone: 70-4699-0460 **Email:** contact@medipixel.io
City: Mapo **State:** Seoul **PC:** **Country: South Korea**

Year Established: 2017 **Status 2020:** Active
Industries: Artificial Intelligence for:, ~ Healthcare (20), Robotics

Company Name: NUUA
Description: NUUA provides data analysis, marketing and AI services.
Website: http://www.nuua.net
Phone: 02-542-1578 **Email:** hello@nuua.net
City: Mapo **State:** Seoul **PC:** **Country: South Korea**
Year Established: 2012 **Status 2020:** Active
Industries: Analytics for:, Artificial Intelligence

Company Name: Oncocross
Description: Oncocross is a Biopharmaceutical Company.
Website: http://oncocross.com/
Phone: 02-867-9967 **Email:** oncocross@oncocross.com
City: Mapo **State:** Seoul **PC:** **Country: South Korea**
Year Established: 2015 **Status 2020:** Active
Industries: Artificial Intelligence

Company Name: RawlsOn
Description: RawlsOn builds mobile applications with machine learning and AI technology.
Website: http://www.rawls-on.com/
Phone: **Email:** recruit@uirtuslab.com
City: Mapo **State:** Seoul **PC:** **Country: South Korea**
Year Established: 2019 **Status 2020:** Active
Industries: Artificial Intelligence for:, Machine Learning for:, Application Services

Company Name: Spykx
Description: Spykx provides AI and big data services.
Website: http://www.spykx.com/
Phone: 070. 4114. 1106 **Email:** cs@spykx.com
City: Mapo **State:** Seoul **PC:** **Country: South Korea**
Year Established: 2014 **Status 2020:** Active
Industries: Artificial Intelligence for:, Big Data and Analytics

Company Name: Triplet
Description: Triplet provides IoT and AI technology solutions.
Website: http://triplllet.com/
Phone: 82-70-4354-8894 **Email:** help@triplllet.com
City: Mapo **State:** Seoul **PC:** **Country: South Korea**
Year Established: 2012 **Status 2020:** Active
Industries: Artificial Intelligence for:, Internet of Things (IoT)

Company Name: Twigfarm
Description: Twigfarm is an NLP and deep learning tech platform for AI-based translation services.
Website: http://www.twigfarm.net/
Phone: 02-1833-5926 **Email:** support@twigfarm.net
City: Mapo **State:** Seoul **PC:** **Country: South Korea**
Year Established: 2016 **Status 2020:** Active
Industries: Artificial Intelligence for:, Natural Language Processing

Company Name: Kangr: Isle of Man
Description: Kangrim is an AI-based matching algorithm system that proposes individual products based on database to match the taste of consumers/buyers.
Website: http://www.kaangrim.com
Phone: 82-02.318.1750 **Email:** dustwine@ikaan.net
City: Namsandong **State:** Seoul **PC:** **Country: South Korea**
Year Established: 2015 **Status 2020:** Active
Industries: Artificial Intelligence for:, ~ Fashion (16)

Company Name: Neural BC
Description: Neural BC specializes in research and development of artificial intelligence and blockchain technology.
Website: http://www.neuralbc.com/
Phone: **Email:** recruit@neuralbc.com
City: Samseong **State:** Seoul **PC:** **Country: South Korea**
Year Established: 2018 **Status 2020:** Active
Industries: Artificial Intelligence for:, Blockchain for:, IT Managed Services

Company Name: 130T
Description: 130T offers AI based block games for children.
Website: http://www.the130t.com/
Phone: 02.2135.7979 **Email:** contact@the130t.com
City: Seocho **State:** Seoul **PC:** **Country: South Korea**
Year Established: 2018 **Status 2020:** Active
Industries: Artificial Intelligence

Company Name: AI Lab
Description: AI Lab develops artificial intelligence robot that analyzes financial markets and investment stocks.
Website:
Phone: 010-9000-9902 **Email:** 35987@reference-encyclopedia-ai.net
City: Seocho **State:** Seoul **PC:** **Country: South Korea**
Year Established: 2016 **Status 2020:** Closed
Industries: Artificial Intelligence for:, ~ Banking and Financial Markets-Services (7)

Company Name: Alethio
Description: Alethio is an AI technology company.
Website: https://aleth.io/
Phone: **Email:** hi@alphaloan.co
City: Seocho **State:** Seoul **PC:** **Country: South Korea**
Year Established: **Status 2020:** Active
Industries: Artificial Intelligence for:, IT Managed Services

Company Name: CONBUS
Description: CONBUS uses AI technology to bring people closer together.
Website: http://www.conbus.net/
Phone: 070-7720-5600 **Email:** 36319@reference-encyclopedia-ai.net
City: Seocho **State:** Seoul **PC:** **Country: South Korea**
Year Established: 2013 **Status 2020:** Active
Industries: Artificial Intelligence for:, IT Managed Services

Company Name: COOLJA: Myanmar
Description: COOLJAMM develops musical AI engine that composes various styles of music.
Website: http://hum-on.com
Phone: **Email:** contact@cooljamm.com
City: Seocho **State:** Seoul **PC:** **Country: South Korea**
Year Established: 2016 **Status 2020:** Active
Industries:

Company Name: CRE Korea
Description: CRE Korea is a platform of commercial real estate valuations in South Korea by using big data and machine learning.
Website: http://www.cre-korea.com
Phone: **Email:** 36345@reference-encyclopedia-ai.net
City: Seocho **State:** Seoul **PC:** **Country: South Korea**
Year Established: 2017 **Status 2020:** Active
Industries: Big Data and Analytics for:, Machine Learning

Company Name: CTILab
Description: CTILab is an artificial intelligence-based next-generation integrated cyber security platform for IT and OT networks.
Website: http://ctilab.co.kr/
Phone: 02-577-1823 **Email:** recruiting@ctilab.co.: South Korea
City: Seocho **State:** Seoul **PC:** **Country: South Korea**
Year Established: 2015 **Status 2020:** Active
Industries: Artificial Intelligence for:, Cyber Security for:, IT Managed Services

Company Name: danbee
Description: danbee is an information technology company that builds AI chatbot.
Website: http://danbee.ai/
Phone: 02-2088-8018 **Email:** contact@danbee.ai
City: Seocho **State:** Seoul **PC:** **Country: South Korea**

Year Established: 2018 **Status 2020:** Active
Industries: Artificial Intelligence for:, IT Managed Services for:, IT Managed Services

Company Name: DeepNatural
Description: High-quality corpus to train and evaluate your natural language models
Website: http://www.deepnatural.ai
Phone: **Email:** support@deepnatural.ai
City: Seocho **State:** Seoul **PC:** **Country: South Korea**
Year Established: 2017 **Status 2020:** Active
Industries: Artificial Intelligence for:, Databases for:, Machine Learning

Company Name: Fluenty Inc.
Description: We change the way people text via Artificial Intelligence
Website: http://www.fluenty.co
Phone: **Email:** support@fluenty.co
City: Seocho **State:** Seoul **PC:** **Country: South Korea**
Year Established: **Status 2020:** Active
Industries: Artificial Intelligence for:, ~ Social Assistance-Non-Profits (53), IT Managed Services

Company Name: illuni
Description: Iluni specializes in researches and develops machine learning and convergence reality technology.
Website: http://illuni.com
Phone: 82 10 9007 1843 **Email:** admin@illuni.com
City: Seocho **State:** Seoul **PC:** **Country: South Korea**
Year Established: 2018 **Status 2020:** Active
Industries: Machine Learning

Company Name: Intelliz
Description: Intelliz specializes in researching and developing AI solutions for manufacturing industries.
Website: http://intelliz.co.kr/
Phone: **Email:** sales@intelliz.co.: South Korea
City: Seocho **State:** Seoul **PC:** **Country: South Korea**
Year Established: 2016 **Status 2020:** Active
Industries: Artificial Intelligence for:, Computer Vision for:, IT Managed Services for:, Machine Learning

Company Name: Motion Advisor
Description: Motion Advisor is a professional AI service company.
Website: http://motionadvisor.co.kr/
Phone: **Email:** info@motionadvisor.co.: South Korea
City: Seocho **State:** Seoul **PC:** **Country: South Korea**
Year Established: 2019 **Status 2020:** Active
Industries: Artificial Intelligence

Company Name: NCue
Description: NCue provides AI platform services.
Website: http://ncue.net/
Phone: 010-2827-6537 **Email:** dosangyoon@gmail.com
City: Seocho **State:** Seoul **PC:** **Country: South Korea**
Year Established: 2017 **Status 2020:** Active
Industries: Artificial Intelligence for:, IT Managed Services

Company Name: Neurolin: Spain
Description: Neurolines provides artificial intelligence-based cloud services for the chemical industry.
Website: http://neurolines.net/
Phone: 82 2-6956-3377 **Email:** contact@neurolines.net
City: Seocho **State:** Seoul **PC:** **Country: South Korea**
Year Established: 2017 **Status 2020:** Active
Industries: Artificial Intelligence for:, Cloud for:, IT Managed Services

Company Name: Swizzle Global Inc.
Description: The Feedback Interpreters - providing solutions to turn your app store reviews into actionable insights.
Website: http://getswizzle.com
Phone: (703) 996-9124 **Email:** info@getswizzle.com
City: Seocho **State:** Seoul **PC:** **Country: South Korea**
Year Established: **Status 2020:** Active
Industries: Artificial Intelligence for:, Big Data and Analytics for:, ~ Media-Communications (41), Business Intelligence for:, ~ Media-Communications (41), ~ Social Media (54), Data Management

Company Name: Voith: Russia
Description: Voithru is an AI-based crowdsourcing subtitle platform.
Website: http://voithru.com/
Phone: **Email:** sales@voithru.com
City: Seocho **State:** Seoul **PC:** **Country: South Korea**
Year Established: 2018 **Status 2020:** Active
Industries: Artificial Intelligence for:, Databases

Company Name: VoyagerX
Description: VoyagerX develops artificial intelligence software.
Website: http://voyagerx.com
Phone: **Email:** contact@voyagerx.com
City: Seocho **State:** Seoul **PC:** **Country: South Korea**
Year Established: 2017 **Status 2020:** Active
Industries: Artificial Intelligence

Company Name: Wayne Hills Ventur: Spain
Description: Wayne Hills Ventures is a data analytics and AI platform.
Website: http://www.waynehills.co/
Phone: **Email:** waynehills.ventures@gmail.com
City: Seocho **State:** Seoul **PC:** **Country: South Korea**
Year Established: 2017 **Status 2020:** Active
Industries:

Company Name: Wert Intelligence
Description: Wert Intelligence is a patent research center that develops artificial intelligence products.
Website: http://wert.co.kr/
Phone: 02 521 0110 **Email:** wert@wert.co.: South Korea
City: Seocho **State:** Seoul **PC:** **Country: South Korea**
Year Established: 2015 **Status 2020:** Active
Industries: Artificial Intelligence

Company Name: AI Spera
Description: AI Spera is the fraud detection and cyber threat intelligence service company.
Website: https://aispera.com/
Phone: 02-6419-1087 **Email:** support@aispera.com
City: Seongdong **State:** Seoul **PC:** **Country: South Korea**
Year Established: 2017 **Status 2020:** Active
Industries: Artificial Intelligence for:, Cyber Security for:, Security

Company Name: Biz Member Ta
Description: Biz MemberTalk is a business convergence app platform based on big data and artificial intelligence.
Website: http://www.bizmembertalk.com/
Phone: 032-260-1810 **Email:** help@bizmembertalk.com
City: Seongdong **State:** Seoul **PC:** **Country: South Korea**
Year Established: 2018 **Status 2020:** Active
Industries: Artificial Intelligence for:, Business Applications for:, Application Services

Company Name: Exasco:
Description: Exascope is a machine intelligence company that provides computer vision and image processing solutions.
Website: http://www.exascopeinc.com/
Phone: 82-2-469-0111 **Email:** sales@exascopeinc.com
City: Seongdong **State:** Seoul **PC:** **Country: South Korea**
Year Established: 2016 **Status 2020:** Active
Industries: Facial Recognition for:, Image Recognition for:, Machine Learning

Company Name: 42Ma: Russia
Description: 42Maru builds a question answer system that finds a single, specific, correct answer based on Deep Learning
Website: http://www.42maru.com
Phone: 82-10-4850-0016 **Email:** susan@42maru.com
City: Seoul **State:** Seoul **PC:** **Country: South Korea**

Year Established: **Status 2020:** Active
Industries: Artificial Intelligence for:, Machine Learning for:, Robotics

Company Name: Adriel
Description: Adriel is an AI-based digital marketing solution.
Website: http://adriel.ai
Phone: **Email:** contact@adriel.ai
City: Seoul **State:** Seoul **PC:** **Country: South Korea**
Year Established: **Status 2020:** Active
Industries: ~ Media-Communications (41), Artificial Intelligence for:, Digital Marketing

Company Name: AIDAT
Description: AIDAT is a consulting company that provides blockchain technology services.
Website: http://www.aidat.co.kr/
Phone: **Email:** teamaidat@gmail.com
City: Seoul **State:** Seoul **PC:** **Country: South Korea**
Year Established: 2018 **Status 2020:** Active
Industries: Blockchain

Company Name: AIZEN Global
Description: AIZEN is redesigning Digital Banking with AI 'Application Processor' that streamlines banking process with automated feedback loop.
Website: https://www.aizenglobal.com/
Phone: 82 70 7008 0020 **Email:** contact@aizen.co
City: Seoul **State:** Seoul **PC:** **Country: South Korea**
Year Established: 2016 **Status 2020:** Active
Industries: Artificial Intelligence for:, Big Data and Analytics for:, ~ Banking and Financial Markets-Services (7), ~ Banking and Financial Markets-Services (7), IT Managed Services for:, Machine Learning for:, Predictive Analytics

Company Name: Alyce Healthcare
Description: Alyce Healthcare specializes in providing AI rehabilitation solutions.
Website: https://www.alycehealthcare.com/
Phone: **Email:** 36050@reference-encyclopedia-ai.net
City: Seoul **State:** Seoul **PC:** **Country: South Korea**
Year Established: 2018 **Status 2020:** Active
Industries: Artificial Intelligence for:, ~ Healthcare (20), ~ Healthcare (20)

Company Name: AOS Korea
Description: AOS Korea provides legal tech, AI chatbot and intelligent cloud backup services.
Website: http://aoskorea.kr/
Phone: 02-565-5055 **Email:** inc@incircle.: South Korea
City: Seoul **State:** Seoul **PC:** **Country: South Korea**
Year Established: 2015 **Status 2020:** Active
Industries: Artificial Intelligence for:, IT Managed Services

Company Name: askstory
Description: AskStory's mission is to create the most efficient and commercially optimized collective intelligence system.
Website: http://www.askstorygroup.com
Phone: **Email:** fredkwons@askstory.com
City: Seoul **State:** Seoul **PC:** **Country: South Korea**
Year Established: 2013 **Status 2020:** Active
Industries: Artificial Intelligence for:, Big Data and Analytics for:, Databases for:, IT Managed Services for:, Application Services for:, Web

Company Name: BluePrintLab
Description: BluePrintLab specialize in 3D rendering, 3D facial scanning, and AI algorithms to develop solutions that fit.
Website: http://www.blueprint-lab.com
Phone: **Email:** charlie@blueprint-lab.com
City: Seoul **State:** Seoul **PC:** **Country: South Korea**
Year Established: 2017 **Status 2020:** Active
Industries: Artificial Intelligence for:, Augmented Reality for:, Facial Recognition for:, Machine Learning

Company Name: Brunt
Description:
Website: https://brunt.co/
Phone: **Email:** biz@brunt.co
City: Seoul **State:** Seoul **PC:** **Country: South Korea**
Year Established: **Status 2020:** Active
Industries:

Company Name: Calm Island
Description: Calm Island uses unsupervised big data to understand how children learn and how they can be taught more effectively.
Website: http://www.calmid.com
Phone: **Email:** info@calmid.com
City: Seoul **State:** Seoul **PC:** **Country: South Korea**
Year Established: 2011 **Status 2020:** Active
Industries:

Company Name: CHEQUER
Description: CHEQUER is a tech startup company developing Database IDE, SQLGate
Website:
Phone: **Email:** 36266@reference-encyclopedia-ai.net
City: Seoul **State:** Seoul **PC:** **Country: South Korea**
Year Established: 2016 **Status 2020:** Active
Industries: Artificial Intelligence for:, Big Data and Analytics for:, Databases for:, IT Managed Services

Company Name: CICERON inc.
Description: CICERON, provides high quality translation service and customizable machine translator.
Website: http://ciceron.me
Phone: (8226) 441-3838 **Email:** chingoo@ciceron.me
City: Seoul **State:** Seoul **PC:** **Country: South Korea**
Year Established: 2015 **Status 2020:** Active
Industries: IT Managed Services for:, Machine Learning

Company Name: Classting
Description: Classting is an education technology company that serves schools and teachers all over the world for better education.
Website: http://about.classting.com/en/
Phone: **Email:** pr@classting.com
City: Seoul **State:** Seoul **PC:** **Country: South Korea**
Year Established: 2012 **Status 2020:** Active
Industries: ~ Education (13), ~ Education (13), ~ Education (13), Machine Learning

Company Name: Cloubot
Description: Cloubot is AI education service company for students from preschool to K12.
Website: http://www.cloubot.ai
Phone: 1 929 357 4357 **Email:** yjkwon@cloubot.com
City: Seoul **State:** Seoul **PC:** **Country: South Korea**
Year Established: 2017 **Status 2020:** Active
Industries: Artificial Intelligence for:, ~ Education (13), ~ Education (13), IT Managed Services for:, ~ Education (13), Business Software as a Service Apps (SaaS Apps) for:, ~ Education (13)

Company Name: Cochlear.ai
Description: Audio cognition AI startup
Website: http://cochlear.ai
Phone: **Email:** contact@cochlear.ai
City: Seoul **State:** Seoul **PC:** **Country: South Korea**
Year Established: **Status 2020:** Active
Industries: Artificial Intelligence for:, Voice Recognition for:, Cloud for:, IT Managed Services for:, Machine Learning for:, ~ Arts-Entertainment-Recreation (4), ~ Professional Services (48)

Company **Name:** CODE42.AI
Description: CODE42.AI is a TaaS company that develops an urban mobility operating system(UMOS).
Website: http://code42.ai/
Phone: **Email:** ir@code42.ai
City: Seoul **State:** Seoul **PC:** **Country: South Korea**

Year Established: 2019 **Status 2020:** Active
Industries: Artificial Intelligence for:, ~ Automotive (5), Robotics

Company Name: Corne: Serbia
Description:
Website: http://www.corners.co.: South Korea
Phone: 82.2.518.1047 **Email:** sjcha@corners.co.: South Korea
City: Seoul **State:** Seoul **Zip:** 4779 **Country: South Korea**
Year Established: **Status 2020:** Active
Industries:

Company Name: Crowdworks
Description: Crowdworks solves the toughest problem in AI today: Delivering training data sets with next-level accuracy, quality assured.
Website: http://www.crowdworks.: South Korea
Phone: **Email:** marketing@crowdworks.: South Korea
City: Seoul **State:** Seoul **PC:** **Country: South Korea**
Year Established: 2017 **Status 2020:** Active
Industries: Artificial Intelligence for:, Web for:, Machine Learning for:, Web

Company Name: Crowdz Korea
Description: Crowdz operation for Korea and Asia operations
Website:
Phone: **Email:** 36353@reference-encyclopedia-ai.net
City: Seoul **State:** Seoul **PC:** **Country: South Korea**
Year Established: 2014 **Status 2020:** Active
Industries: Business Applications for:, ~ Banking and Financial Markets-Services (7), Blockchain for:, Predictive Analytics for:, Supply Chain Management

Company Name: D&I PARV
Description: SaaS
Website: http://brunel.ai
Phone: 070-51760505 **Email:** official@brunel.ai
City: Seoul **State:** Seoul **PC:** **Country: South Korea**
Year Established: 2018 **Status 2020:** Active
Industries: Artificial Intelligence for:, IT Managed Services for:, Web for:, Natural Language Processing

Company Name: Datacrun: Switzerland
Description: Datacrunch is an analytics based consulting firm.
Website: http://www.datacrunchglobal.com
Phone: **Email:** company@datacrunchglobal.com
City: Seoul **State:** Seoul **PC:** **Country: South Korea**
Year Established: 2016 **Status 2020:** Active
Industries: Artificial Intelligence

Company Name: DAYLI Financial Group
Description: A leading Fintech company in Asia providing data tech solutions, digital wealth management, and lead-generation service
Website: http://daylifg.com/
Phone: **Email:** 36402@reference-encyclopedia-ai.net
City: Seoul **State:** Seoul **PC:** **Country: South Korea**
Year Established: 2015 **Status 2020:** Active
Industries: Artificial Intelligence for:, Big Data and Analytics for:, ~ Banking and Financial Markets-Services (7), ~ Banking and Financial Markets-Services (7), Finance and Accounting for:, ~ Banking and Financial Markets-Services (7)

Company Name: DDH
Description: Artificial Intelligence, Invisible Braces, Clear Aligner, Machine Learning, Healthcare, Dental, Orthodontic,
Website: http://www.ddhinc.net/en/
Phone: 82)-2-742-1704 **Email:** heeungk@ddhinc.net
City: Seoul **State:** Seoul **PC:** **Country: South Korea**
Year Established: **Status 2020:** Active
Industries: Artificial Intelligence for:, ~ Healthcare (20), ~ Healthcare (20), Machine Learning for:, ~ Manufacturing-Medical Equipment-Supplies (33)

Company Name: Deeping Source Inc.
Description: Privacy and Copyright Protection for Machine Learning
Website: http://www.deepingsource.io
Phone: **Email:** contact@deepingsource.io
City: Seoul **State:** Seoul **PC:** **Country: South Korea**
Year Established: 2018 **Status 2020:** Active
Industries:

Company Name: DeepValidation
Description: Deepvalidation is a team of FRESH, FREAKY, GEEKY data scientists and data enginee: Serbia
Website: http://www.deepvalidation.com
Phone: **Email:** info@deepvalidation.com
City: Seoul **State:** Seoul **PC:** **Country: South Korea**
Year Established: 2017 **Status 2020:** Active
Industries: Artificial Intelligence for:, Big Data and Analytics for:, Machine Learning

Company Name: Designovel
Description: Design AI and Fashion Tech
Website: http://www.designovel.com
Phone: **Email:** help@designovel.com
City: Seoul **State:** Seoul **PC:** **Country: South Korea**
Year Established: 2017 **Status 2020:** Active
Industries: Artificial Intelligence for:, ~ Fashion (16), IT Managed Services

Company Name: earlyslo:Thailand
Description: Earlysloth is an AI based survey on the messenger for the enterprise.
Website: http://www.earlysloth.com
Phone: 02-744-0323 **Email:** admin@earlysloth.com
City: Seoul **State:** Seoul **PC:** **Country: South Korea**
Year Established: 2018 **Status 2020:** Active
Industries: Artificial Intelligence

Company Name: Eyedea
Description: Eyedea is a computer vision solution provider.
Website: http://eyedea.co.: South Korea
Phone: **Email:** 36538@reference-encyclopedia-ai.net
City: Seoul **State:** Seoul **PC:** **Country: South Korea**
Year Established: 2015 **Status 2020:** Active
Industries: Artificial Intelligence for:, Computer Vision for:, IT Managed Services for:, Machine Learning for:, Robotics

Company Name: Flitto
Description: Flitto is an integrated platform and language data company that provides diverse translation services.
Website: http://www.flitto.com
Phone: 82 2 512 0142 **Email:** help@flitto.com
City: Seoul **State:** Seoul **PC:** **Country: South Korea**
Year Established: 2012 **Status 2020:** Active
Industries: Artificial Intelligence for:, Databases for:, Databases

Company Name: GDFLab
Description: GDFLab is a video deep learning platform.
Website: http://www.gdflab.com/
Phone: 82 2 6086 1862 **Email:** operation@gdflab.com
City: Seoul **State:** Seoul **PC:** **Country: South Korea**
Year Established: 2018 **Status 2020:** Active
Industries: Artificial Intelligence

Company Name: GomiLabs
Description: GomiLabs is a pet healthcare platform based on AI robot.
Website: http://www.gomilabs.io
Phone: **Email:** vianney.meri@gomilabs.io
City: Seoul **State:** Seoul **PC:** **Country: South Korea**
Year Established: 2015 **Status 2020:** Active
Industries: Artificial Intelligence for:, ~ Healthcare (20), Internet of Things (IoT) for:, ~ Retail and Consumer Products (52)

Company Name: Hyperconnect
Description: Hyperconnect delivers video and AI-powered products designed to generate cultural and social values by connecting people globally.
Website: http://hyperconnect.com/
Phone: **Email:** contact@hpcnt.com
City: Seoul **State:** Seoul **PC:** **Country: South Korea**
Year Established: 2014 **Status 2020:** Active
Industries: Artificial Intelligence for:, IT Managed Services for:, Machine Learning for:, Application Services

Company Name: KnCom
Description: KnCom is a big data, artificial intelligence technology, villa offer, pin tech start up.
Website: http://www.kncom.co.kr/
Phone: (82) 70.7762.9364 **Email:** info@lobig.co.: South Korea
City: Seoul **State:** Seoul **PC:** **Country: South Korea**
Year Established: **Status 2020:** Active
Industries: Artificial Intelligence for:, Big Data and Analytics for:, ~ Professional Services (48)

Company Name: Lablup
Description: Lablup is developing technologies for distributed computing for machine learning researches and applications.
Website: http://www.lablup.com/
Phone: **Email:** contact@lablup.com
City: Seoul **State:** Seoul **PC:** **Country: South Korea**
Year Established: 2015 **Status 2020:** Active
Industries: Cloud for:, IT Managed Services for:, Machine Learning for:, Business Software as a Service Apps (SaaS Apps)

Company Name: Leevi
Description: Leevi develops smart media platform based on intelligent machine learning and natural language processing.
Website: http://leevi.co.: South Korea
Phone: **Email:** contact@leevi.co.: South Korea
City: Seoul **State:** Seoul **PC:** **Country: South Korea**
Year Established: 2013 **Status 2020:** Active
Industries: Artificial Intelligence for:, ~ Education (13), Machine Learning

Company Name: LIONROCKET
Description: LIONROCKET develops deep learning-based voice engine.
Website: http://lionrocket.ai/
Phone: 82 02-6441-4337 **Email:** contact@lionrocket.ai
City: Seoul **State:** Seoul **PC:** **Country: South Korea**
Year Established: 2019 **Status 2020:** Active
Industries: Artificial Intelligence

Company Name: LOLOGEM
Description: AR Software Service Based on ML/AI
Website: http://about.lologem.com/en/
Phone: **Email:** contact@lologem.com
City: Seoul **State:** Seoul **PC:** **Country: South Korea**
Year Established: 2017 **Status 2020:** Active
Industries: Artificial Intelligence for:, Augmented Reality for:, Machine Learning for:, Application Services for:, Business Software as a Service Apps (SaaS Apps)

Company Name: Looxid Labs
Description: Looxid Labs is a tech start-up to seamlessly integrate an emotion recognition system with VR using an eye and brain interface.
Website: http://www.looxidlabs.com
Phone: **Email:** info@looxidlabs.com
City: Seoul **State:** Seoul **PC:** **Country: South Korea**
Year Established: 2015 **Status 2020:** Active
Industries:

Company Name: lululab
Description: Lumini is a personalized AI skin assistant that analyzes the user's skin and recommends the best products and services for each user.
Website: http://www.lulu-lab.com/
Phone: **Email:** lululab@lulu-lab.com
City: Seoul **State:** Seoul **PC:** **Country: South Korea**
Year Established: 2017 **Status 2020:** Active
Industries: Application Services

Company Name: Lunit
Description: Conquering cancer through AI-powered imaging biomarker
Website: http://www.lunit.io
Phone: **Email:** contact@lunit.io
City: Seoul **State:** Seoul **PC:** **Country: South Korea**
Year Established: 2013 **Status 2020:** Active
Industries: Artificial Intelligence for:, Computer Vision for:, ~ Healthcare (20), Image Recognition for:, Machine Learning

Company Name: Magp: Ireland
Description:
Website: http://www.magpie-tech.com
Phone: 82 2-6954-3488 **Email:** hugo@magpie-tech.com
City: Seoul **State:** Seoul **PC:** **Country: South Korea**
Year Established: **Status 2020:** Active
Industries:

Company Name: MakinaRocks
Description: Industrial/Manufacturing AI
Website: http://www.makinarocks.ai/
Phone: **Email:** contact@makinarocks.ai
City: Seoul **State:** Seoul **PC:** **Country: South Korea**
Year Established: 2017 **Status 2020:** Active
Industries:

Company Name: Mathpresso
Description: Mathpresso is an educational data platform where students can ask questions to tutors and search solutions just by taking a photo.
Website: http://mathpresso.com
Phone: **Email:** support.global@mathpresso.com
City: Seoul **State:** Seoul **PC:** **Country: South Korea**
Year Established: 2015 **Status 2020:** Active
Industries: Artificial Intelligence for:, ~ Education (13), ~ Education (13), IT Managed Services for:, Machine Learning for:, ~ Education (13)

Company **Name:** MAXST
Description: On Demand AR Platform for Enterpri: Sweden
Website: http://www.maxst.com
Phone: 82.2.585.9566 **Email:** help@maxst.com
City: Seoul **State:** Seoul **PC:** **Country: South Korea**
Year Established: 2010 **Status 2020:** Active
Industries: Artificial Intelligence for:, Augmented Reality for:, IT Managed Services

Company Name: MeasureChina
Description: MeasureChina is AI powered software for China marketing. It solves challenges in understanding 1.3B Chinese consumers within seconds.
Website: http://measurechina.ai
Phone: **Email:** contact@measurechina.ai
City: Seoul **State:** Seoul **PC:** **Country: South Korea**
Year Established: **Status 2020:** Active
Industries: Artificial Intelligence for:, Big Data and Analytics for:, ~ Professional Services (48)

Company Name: MediRita
Description: AI for drug discovery.
Website: http://www.medirita.com
Phone: **Email:** info@medirita.com
City: Seoul **State:** Seoul **PC:** **Country: South Korea**

Year Established: 2018 **Status 2020:** Active
Industries: Artificial Intelligence for:, ~ Biotechnology (9)

Company Name: MIND AI
Description: MIND AI is an artificial intelligence engine and an ecosystem that was created to offer an entirely new approach to AI.
Website: http://www.mind.ai
Phone: **Email:** info@mind.ai
City: Seoul **State:** Seoul **PC:** **Country: South Korea**
Year Established: 2017 **Status 2020:** Active
Industries: Artificial Intelligence for:, IT Managed Services

Company Name: MindwareWorks
Description: MindwareWorks is an enterprise acting CRM and AI support CRM solution company in Seoul, Korea.
Website: http://www.mindwareworks.com
Phone: 7040426752 **Email:** jay@mindwareworks.com
City: Seoul **State:** Seoul **PC:** **Country: South Korea**
Year Established: **Status 2020:** Active
Industries: Artificial Intelligence for:, ~ Professional Services (48)

Company Name: Minkonet
Description: Minkonet's mission is to change the way we watch and play video games.
Website: http://www.minkonet.com
Phone: **Email:** contact@minkonet.com
City: Seoul **State:** Seoul **PC:** **Country: South Korea**
Year Established: **Status 2020:** Active
Industries: Artificial Intelligence for:, ~ Media-Communications (41), ~ Arts-Entertainment-Recreation (4), ~ Gaming (18), Machine Learning for:, ~ Media-Communications (41)

Company Name: Mixedtek Co., Ltd
Description: we are developing software that reconstruction the AI based 2D image into 3D video.
Website: http://www.mixedtek.com
Phone: **Email:** info@mixedtek.com
City: Seoul **State:** Seoul **PC:** **Country: South Korea**
Year Established: **Status 2020:** Active
Industries: Artificial Intelligence for:, Computer Vision for:, ~ Manufacturing-Electronic (30), ~ Manufacturing-Electronic (30), Machine Learning for:, ~ Media-Communications (41), Compute

Company Name: Moneybra: India
Description: Deep Learning based Conversational AI
Website: http://www.moneybrain.ai
Phone: **Email:** info@moneybrain.ai
City: Seoul **State:** Seoul **PC:** **Country: South Korea**
Year Established: **Status 2020:** Active
Industries: Artificial Intelligence

Company Name: Nearthlab
Description: AI-powered Automated Industrial Inspection Solution Using Autonomous Dron: Spain
Website: http://www.nearthlab.com/
Phone: **Email:** contact@nearthlab.com
City: Seoul **State:** Seoul **PC:** **Country: South Korea**
Year Established: 2015 **Status 2020:** Active
Industries:

Company Name: Neosapience
Description: We make artificial intelligence the people love and enjoy.
Website: http://www.neosapience.com
Phone: **Email:** contact@neosapience.com
City: Seoul **State:** Seoul **PC:** **Country: South Korea**
Year Established: **Status 2020:** Active
Industries: Application Services for:, Artificial Intelligence for:, ~ Professional Services (48)

Company Name: NEUROPHET
Description: NEUROPHET Inc. is a medical SW company using advanced neuroscience and AI technologies for better brain treatment.
Website: http://www.neurophet.com
Phone: **Email:** contact@neurophet.com
City: Seoul **State:** Seoul **PC:** **Country: South Korea**
Year Established: 2016 **Status 2020:** Active
Industries: Artificial Intelligence for:, Machine Learning for:, ~ Healthcare (20)

Company Name: NexCloud
Description: NexClipper is the container monitoring and Artificial Intellgence based operation support solution.
Website: http://www.nexclipper.io
Phone: 82-2-533-8622 **Email:** nexclipper@nexclipper.io
City: Seoul **State:** Seoul **PC:** **Country: South Korea**
Year Established: 2015 **Status 2020:** Active
Industries: Artificial Intelligence for:, IT Managed Services for:, Machine Learning

Company Name: OPENEDGES Technology
Description: OPENEDGES Technology researches AI acceleration technology to contribute to democratizing AI innovation.
Website: http://openedges.com/
Phone: 82 (2) 2038-7507 **Email:** 30928@reference-encyclopedia-ai.net
City: Seoul **State:** Seoul **PC:** **Country: South Korea**
Year Established: 2015 **Status 2020:** Active
Industries: Artificial Intelligence for:, Cloud for:, Internet of Things (IoT) for:, Machine Learning

Company Name: Perfitt
Description: Shoe Size Recommendation Solution, B2B Solution, Retail Technology
Website: http://perfitt.io
Phone: **Email:** ceo@perfitt.io
City: Seoul **State:** Seoul **PC:** **Country: South Korea**
Year Established: 2015 **Status 2020:** Active
Industries: E-Commerce for:, Image Recognition for:, Machine Learning for:, ~ Retail and Consumer Products (52)

Company **Name:** Platfarm Inc. (mojitok)
Description: Platfarm helps messaging services to monetize or/and increase user engagement with the visual communication solution.
Website: http://www.mojitok.com
Phone: 82-70-7560-7002 **Email:** mojitok@platfarm.net
City: Seoul **State:** Seoul **PC:** **Country: South Korea**
Year Established: 2014 **Status 2020:** Active
Industries: Digital Media for:, IT Managed Services for:, Web for:, Machine Learning for:, ~ Social Assistance-Non-Profits (53)

Company Name: POZAlabs
Description: POZAlabs develops music composing assistant using artificial intelligence.
Website: http://www.pozalabs.com
Phone: **Email:** contact@pozalabs.com
City: Seoul **State:** Seoul **PC:** **Country: South Korea**
Year Established: 2018 **Status 2020:** Active
Industries: Artificial Intelligence for:, ~ Arts-Entertainment-Recreation (4)

Company Name: QARA Soft
Description: Fintech start-up that provides online investment advisory and asset management services using deep-learning technology.
Website: http://qara.ai/
Phone: 82-2-6080-8121 **Email:** qara@qarasoft.com
City: Seoul **State:** Seoul **PC:** **Country: South Korea**

Year Established: 2014 **Status 2020:** Active
Industries: Artificial Intelligence for:, ~ Banking and Financial Markets-Services (7), ~ Banking and Financial Markets-Services (7)

Company Name: QARASoft
Description: Fintech start-up that provides online investment advisory and asset management services using deep-learning technology.
Website: http://www.qara.ai
Phone: 82 (0) 2-6080-8121~8122 **Email:** Jameslhn@qarasoft.com
City: Seoul **State:** Seoul **PC: Country: South Korea**
Year Established: Status 2020: Active
Industries: Artificial Intelligence for:, ~ Banking and Financial Markets-Services (7)

Company Name: Qraft Technologies
Description: Qraft Technologies provides AI solutions customized for various uses and has specialties in AI investment solutions.
Website: http://www.qraftec.com
Phone: 82-2-487-8555 **Email:** qraft@qraftec.com
City: Seoul **State:** Seoul **PC: Country: South Korea**
Year Established: Status 2020: Active
Industries: Artificial Intelligence for:, ~ Banking and Financial Markets-Services (7), Machine Learning

Company Name: Qualson Inc
Description: With the slogan, "Rescue people's time", Qualson Inc. develops mobile language learning services.
Website: http://qualson.com
Phone: 070-7015-1703 **Email:** park@qualson.com
City: Seoul **State:** Seoul **PC: Country: South Korea**
Year Established: 2012 **Status 2020:** Active
Industries: ~ Education (13), Machine Learning for:, Mobile

Company Name: Riiid
Description: Riiid develop an AI Tutor platform with our exclusive machine learning technology.
Website: http://riiid.co/
Phone: 82-2-795-1221 **Email:** support@riiid.co
City: Seoul **State:** Seoul **PC: Country: South Korea**
Year Established: Status 2020: Active
Industries: Artificial Intelligence for:, ~ Education (13), Machine Learning for:, ~ Media-Communications (41), ~ Education (13)

Company Name: Roborus
Description: Robotics developing company which creates a new market by differentiating itself through ICT-based cooperation system.
Website: http://www.roborus.ai
Phone: 612-594-2853 **Email:** jkim@roborus.ai
City: Seoul **State:** Seoul **PC: Country: South Korea**
Year Established: 2016 **Status 2020:** Active
Industries: Artificial Intelligence for:, IT Managed Services for:, Robotics

Company Name: Rocky Robots Inc.
Description: Early-stage startup which develops dialogue-based A.I. and a content solution for social robots in the self-improvement context.
Website: www.rockyrobots.com
Phone: Email: info@rockyrobots.com
City: Seoul **State:** Seoul **PC: Country: South Korea**
Year Established: Status 2020: Active
Industries:

Company Name: Rowan
Description:
Website: http://creativerowan.com/
Phone: 82 2 2132 5560 **Email:** solomio0314f@gmail.com
City: Seoul **State:** Seoul **PC: Country: South Korea**
Year Established: Status 2020: Active
Industries: Blockchain

Company Name: Seoul Robotics
Description: Making Robots Intelligent - Building advanced Lidar autonomous perception software for self driving cars and robots
Website: http://seoulrobotics.org
Phone: 82-10-8233-7939 **Email:** hello@seoulrobotics.org
City: Seoul **State:** Seoul **PC: Country: South Korea**
Year Established: Status 2020: Active
Industries: Artificial Intelligence for:, ~ Automotive (5), ~ Transportation and Logistics (57), Robotics for:, ~ Manufacturing-Electronic (30)

Company Name: Sereine Lab
Description: 1:1 Customized Beauty Solution
Website:
Phone: Email: support@sereinelab.com
City: Seoul **State:** Seoul **PC: Country: South Korea**
Year Established: 2016 **Status 2020:** Active
Industries: ~ Beauty (8), Big Data and Analytics for:, Internet of Things (IoT) for:, Machine Learning for:, ~ Healthcare (20)

Company Name: Skelter Labs
Description: Skelter Labs is an artificial intelligence technology company developing innovative machine intelligence technology.
Website: https://www.skelterlabs.com/
Phone: 82-1666-8972 **Email:** mingunseo@wisefour.com
City: Seoul **State:** Seoul **PC: Country: South Korea**
Year Established: Status 2020: Active
Industries: Artificial Intelligence for:, IT Managed Services for:, Machine Learning

Company Name: Smallticket
Description: Smallticket is a financial services company that offers platform that specializes in lifestyle-based insurance products and services.
Website: http://www.smallticket.com/
Phone: 070 8877 0096 **Email:** hello@smallticket.com
City: Seoul **State:** Seoul **PC: Country: South Korea**
Year Established: 2016 **Status 2020:** Active
Industries: Artificial Intelligence for:, ~ Banking and Financial Markets-Services (7), ~ Banking and Financial Markets-Services (7)

Company **Name:** Solidware
Description: Solidware builds Machine Learning-based predictive models for financial services companies to make more profits.
Website: http://www.solidware.io
Phone: Email: contact@solidware.io
City: Seoul **State:** Seoul **PC: Country: South Korea**
Year Established: 2014 **Status 2020:** Active
Industries: Analytics for:, Artificial Intelligence for:, Big Data and Analytics for:, Machine Learning

Company Name: Space Walk
Description: Space Walk is creating innovation in land development based on data and technology.
Website: http://www.spacewalk.tech/
Phone: Email: i@spacewalk.tech
City: Seoul **State:** Seoul **PC: Country: South Korea**
Year Established: 2016 **Status 2020:** Active
Industries:

Company Name: Standigm
Description: Standigm applies cutting-edge AI technologies to drug discovery and development.
Website: http://www.standigm.com
Phone: 82-2-501-8118 **Email:** business@standigm.com
City: Seoul **State:** Seoul **PC: Country: South Korea**
Year Established: Status 2020: Active
Industries: Artificial Intelligence for:, ~ Biotechnology (9), ~ Pharmaceuticals (46)

Company Name: Studio X
Description: Studio X offers blockchain, big data, artificial intelligence and argument reality technology services.
Website: http://studiox.co.: South Korea
Phone: 7051593690 **Email:** contact@studiox.co.: South Korea
City: Seoul **State:** Seoul **PC:** **Country: South Korea**
Year Established: 2018 **Status 2020:** Active
Industries: Artificial Intelligence for:, Blockchain for:, IT Managed Services

Company Name: Sualab
Description: SUALAB researches disruptive innovation technology based on artificial intelligence.
Website: http://www.sualab.com/
Phone: **Email:** 37473@reference-encyclopedia-ai.net
City: Seoul **State:** Seoul **PC:** **Country: South Korea**
Year Established: 2013 **Status 2020:** Active
Industries:

Company Name: Techmaru & Co
Description: Techmaru&Co is a Korean software development company providing global artificial intelligence services.
Website: http://www.zillion.co.kr/techma: Russia
Phone: 031-992-0178 **Email:** tony@techmaru.com
City: Seoul **State:** Seoul **PC:** **Country: South Korea**
Year Established: 2012 **Status 2020:** Active
Industries: Artificial Intelligence for:, IT Managed Services for:, Machine Learning for:, Security

Company Name: Urbanba: Sweden
Description: Urbanbase offers VR/AR tools for architecture and interior design with its patented algorithm and data
Website: http://urbanbase.com
Phone: **Email:** hello@urbanbase.com
City: Seoul **State:** Seoul **PC:** **Country: South Korea**
Year Established: 2014 **Status 2020:** Active
Industries: Artificial Intelligence for:, Cloud for:, Collaboration Solutions for:, Computer Vision for:, ~ Construction (10), Internet of Things (IoT) for:, IT Managed Services

Company Name: Vu
Description: Artificial Intelligence for Doctors and Patients.
Website: http://www.vuno.co/
Phone: 82025156646 **Email:** HELLO@VUNO.CO
City: Seoul **State:** Seoul **PC:** **Country: South Korea**
Year Established: 2014 **Status 2020:** Active
Industries: Artificial Intelligence for:, ~ Healthcare (20), ~ Healthcare (20)

Company Name: Wise Fashion
Description: Wise Fashion analyzes accurate fashion trends using big data and AI technology.
Website: http://wise-fashion.com/
Phone: 070-8656-0064 **Email:** contact@wise-fashion.com
City: Seoul **State:** Seoul **PC:** **Country: South Korea**
Year Established: 2016 **Status 2020:** Active
Industries:

Company Name: WISHUPON, Inc.
Description: WISHUPON is a universal shopping wishlist.
Website: http://www.wishupon.app
Phone: **Email:** hello@wsupon.com
City: Seoul **State:** Seoul **PC:** **Country: South Korea**
Year Established: **Status 2020:** Active
Industries: Application Services for:, Artificial Intelligence for:, E-Commerce for:, ~ Fashion (16), Mobile for:, ~ Retail and Consumer Products (52)

Company Name: Xinapse
Description: Artificial Intelligence, Natural Language Processing, Big Data
Website: http://www.xinapse.ai
Phone: 82 2-6052-5611 **Email:** welcome@xinapse.ai
City: Seoul **State:** Seoul **PC:** **Country: South Korea**
Year Established: 2017 **Status 2020:** Active
Industries: Artificial Intelligence for:, Big Data and Analytics for:, Machine Learning for:, Natural Language Processing

Company Name: Zetabank
Description: Creating an autonomous driving service robot that is sophisticated and easily accessible to customers through AI and speech recognition.
Website: http://www.zetabank.co.: South Korea
Phone: **Email:** yelin@zetabank.co.: South Korea
City: Seoul **State:** Seoul **PC:** **Country: South Korea**
Year Established: 2015 **Status 2020:** Active
Industries: Artificial Intelligence

Company Name: With Mind
Description: With Mind is an app that provides AI mobile interview services.
Website: http://withmind.net
Phone: **Email:** withmind.dev@gmail.com
City: Sinchondong **State:** Seoul **PC:** **Country: South Korea**
Year Established: 2017 **Status 2020:** Active
Industries: Artificial Intelligence for:, Application Services

Company Name: Buzzpole
Description: Buzzpole develops medical software using artificial intelligence.
Website: http://www.buzzpole.com/
Phone: 82-2 6497-8800 **Email:** contact@buzzpole.com
City: Songpadong **State:** Seoul **PC:** **Country: South Korea**
Year Established: 2014 **Status 2020:** Active
Industries: Artificial Intelligence for:, ~ Healthcare (20)

Company **Name:** LiveCare
Description: LiveCare provides IoT and AI-based livestock healthcare services.
Website: http://livecare.xyz/
Phone: 02-3400-0300 **Email:** min@ulikekorea.com
City: Songpadong **State:** Seoul **PC:** **Country: South Korea**
Year Established: 2012 **Status 2020:** Active
Industries: Artificial Intelligence for:, ~ Healthcare (20), ~ Agriculture (3)

Company Name: Namu Planet
Description: Namu Planet specializes in big data and artificial intelligence.
Website: http://www.namuplanet.com/
Phone: 02-462-2553 **Email:** mijinyu@namuplanet.com
City: Songpadong **State:** Seoul **PC:** **Country: South Korea**
Year Established: 2013 **Status 2020:** Active
Industries: Artificial Intelligence for:, Big Data and Analytics for:, IT Managed Services

Company Name: Neurocoms
Description: Neurocoms is a visual data analyzer that converts existing CCTV system into an artificial intelligence surveillance system.
Website: http://neurocoms.com/
Phone: 82-2-424-0126 **Email:** amy@neurocoms.com
City: Songpadong **State:** Seoul **PC:** **Country: South Korea**
Year Established: 2015 **Status 2020:** Active
Industries: Artificial Intelligence for:, Data Management

Company Name: Promedius
Description: Promedius is a cloud-based medical artificial intelligence platform.
Website: http://promedius.ai
Phone: 82-2-423-8511 **Email:** contact@promedius.ai
City: Songpadong **State:** Seoul **PC:** **Country: South Korea**
Year Established: 2019 **Status 2020:** Active
Industries: Artificial Intelligence for:, ~ Healthcare (20)

Company Name: Acryl
Description: Acryl is an artificial intelligence company that specializes in the development of emotion recognition technologies.
Website: http://www.iacryl.com/
Phone: **Email:** info@iacryl.com
City: Yeoksamdong **State:** Seoul **PC:** **Country: South Korea**
Year Established: 2011 **Status 2020:** Active
Industries: Artificial Intelligence

Company Name: adoc
Description: adoc provides medical records, discount medical examination, check AI symptoms and compare hospital expenses services.
Website: http://www.adoc.co.kr/
Phone: 1544-3154 **Email:** contact@adoc.co.: South Korea
City: Yeoksamdong **State:** Seoul **PC:** **Country: South Korea**
Year Established: 2018 **Status 2020:** Active
Industries: Artificial Intelligence for:, ~ Healthcare (20), ~ Healthcare (20)

Company Name: AINE
Description: AINE is a company that provides social platform services using artificial intelligence technology.
Website: http://aine.world/
Phone: 494-87-01302 **Email:** support@aine.world
City: Yeoksamdong **State:** Seoul **PC:** **Country: South Korea**
Year Established: 2019 **Status 2020:** Active
Industries: Artificial Intelligence

Company Name: APROb: Italy
Description: APRObit provides AI and big data embedded exchange services.
Website: http://aprobit.com
Phone: **Email:** aprocs@aprobit.co.: South Korea
City: Yeoksamdong **State:** Seoul **PC:** **Country: South Korea**
Year Established: 2019 **Status 2020:** Active
Industries: Artificial Intelligence for:, Big Data and Analytics

Company Name: Atlas Labs
Description: Atlas Labs develops and delivers language-based AI solutions.
Website: http://www.atlaslabs.ai
Phone: 70-8672-2621 **Email:** support@atlaslabs.ai
City: Yeoksamdong **State:** Seoul **PC:** **Country: South Korea**
Year Established: 2016 **Status 2020:** Active
Industries:

Company Name: Data and Analytics
Description: Data and Analytics is an information technology company.
Website: http://www.dna.uno/
Phone: 02-512-1359 **Email:** dna@dna.u
City: Yeoksamdong **State:** Seoul **PC:** **Country: South Korea**
Year Established: 2013 **Status 2020:** Active
Industries: Big Data and Analytics for:, IT Managed Services for:, Machine Learning

Company Name: DEEP-G
Description: DEEP-G provides technology solutions through AI and big data analytics.
Website: http://www.deep-g.com/
Phone: **Email:** hugh@tfx.ai
City: Yeoksamdong **State:** Seoul **PC:** **Country: South Korea**
Year Established: 2011 **Status 2020:** Active
Industries: Artificial Intelligence for:, Big Data and Analytics

Company Name: gentlep: Ireland
Description: gentlepie is a developer of enterprise AI applications.
Website: http://www.gentlepie.com/
Phone: **Email:** hello@gentlepie.com
City: Yeoksamdong **State:** Seoul **PC:** **Country: South Korea**
Year Established: 2016 **Status 2020:** Active
Industries: Artificial Intelligence for:, IT Managed Services

Company Name: InHandPlus
Description: InHandPlus develops medication-use smartwatch and AI-based medication management platform.
Website: http://www.inhandplus.com
Phone: **Email:** hlee@inhandplus.com
City: Yeoksamdong **State:** Seoul **PC:** **Country: South Korea**
Year Established: 2019 **Status 2020:** Active
Industries: Artificial Intelligence for:, ~ Healthcare (20)

Company Name: Job
Description: Jobis is an accounting management platform by AI.
Website: http://jobis.co/
Phone: 1522-3029 **Email:** help@jobis.co
City: Yeoksamdong **State:** Seoul **PC:** **Country: South Korea**
Year Established: 2015 **Status 2020:** Active
Industries: Finance and Accounting for:, Artificial Intelligence

Company Name: Kaier
Description: Kaier provides optimized solutions by accumulating and developing the latest AI technology.
Website: http://www.kaier.co.kr/
Phone: 82.10.2538.8369 **Email:** admin@kaier.co.: South Korea
City: Yeoksamdong **State:** Seoul **PC:** **Country: South Korea**
Year Established: 2019 **Status 2020:** Active
Industries: Artificial Intelligence for:, Machine Learning

Company Name: Mycelebs
Description: Mycelebs is artificial intelligence (AI) agency that provides AI transformation services.
Website: http://www.mycelebs.com/
Phone: 82-2-6245-7403 **Email:** recruit@mycelebs.com
City: Yeoksamdong **State:** Seoul **PC:** **Country: South Korea**
Year Established: 2014 **Status 2020:** Active
Industries: Artificial Intelligence for:, IT Managed Services for:, Web

Company Name: Piclick
Description: Piclick is an AI platform that matches media content and product details in photographs or videos.
Website: http://www.piclick.me
Phone: 269252108 **Email:** global@piclick.me
City: Yeoksamdong **State:** Seoul **PC:** **Country: South Korea**
Year Established: 2013 **Status 2020:** Active
Industries: Artificial Intelligence for:, Content

Company Name: QUEBON
Description: QUEBON is an AI-based education platform.
Website: http://www.quebon.tv
Phone: 02-562-0701 **Email:** info@quebon.com
City: Yeoksamdong **State:** Seoul **PC:** **Country: South Korea**
Year Established: 2016 **Status 2020:** Active
Industries: Artificial Intelligence for:, ~ Education (13)

Company Name: SDPlex
Description: SDPlex develops software for big data analysis and machine learning systems.
Website: http://sdplex.com/
Phone: 82-2-6203-3114 **Email:** info@sdplex.com
City: Yeoksamdong **State:** Seoul **PC:** **Country: South Korea**
Year Established: 2017 **Status 2020:** Active
Industries: Big Data and Analytics for:, Machine Learning

Company Name: Staping
Description: Staping is an AI-based fashion shopping platform.
Website: http://www.staping.co.: South Korea
Phone: 070-8692-2600 **Email:** kbs601@daum.net
City: Yeoksamdong **State:** Seoul **PC:** **Country: South Korea**
Year Established: 2018 **Status 2020:** Active
Industries: Artificial Intelligence for:, ~ Fashion (16), Application Services

Company Name: VTOU: SWITZERLAND
Description: VTOUCH provides cutting-edge technology using gesture control.
Website: http://vtouch.io/
Phone: 070-4610-3242 **Email:** contact@vtouch.: South Korea
City: Yeoksamdong **State:** Seoul **PC:** **Country: South Korea**
Year Established: 2012 **Status 2020:** Active
Industries: Artificial Intelligence for:, Machine Learning

Company Name: ZPZG
Description: ZPZG offers chatbot service and pyeongchang winter olympics artificial intelligence service.
Website: http://www.zpzgsoft.com
Phone: 02-6953-2515 **Email:** jhkim@zpzgsoft.com
City: Yeoksamdong **State:** Seoul **PC:** **Country: South Korea**
Year Established: 2017 **Status 2020:** Active
Industries: Artificial Intelligence

Company Name: EduHash Global Partne: Serbia
Description: EduHash is an AI enterprise service and educational content platform.
Website: http://eduhashglobal.com/
Phone: (102) 416-3106 **Email:** comm@eduhashglobal.com
City: Yongdungpo **State:** Seoul **PC:** **Country: South Korea**
Year Established: 2018 **Status 2020:** Active
Industries:

Company Name: Underpin
Description: Underpin is a global AI and blockchain company.
Website: http://underpin.kr/
Phone: 070-8095-2048 **Email:** hello@underpin.: South Korea
City: Yongdungpo **State:** Seoul **PC:** **Country: South Korea**
Year Established: 2017 **Status 2020:** Active
Industries: Artificial Intelligence for:, Blockchain

Company Name: Who's Good
Description: Who's Good is an AI-driven ESG insight provider. Who's Good is the first robo-analyst to disclose, compare and analyze non-financial risk and performance of companies for sustainability.
Website: http://www.whosgood.org/
Phone: 82 050 5684 4968 **Email:** info@whosgood.org
City: Yongdungpo **State:** Seoul **PC:** **Country: South Korea**
Year Established: 2014 **Status 2020:** Active
Industries: Analytics for:, Artificial Intelligence for:, IT Managed Services

Company Name: I'mCloud
Description: I'mCloud provides solution for artificial intelligence and big data.
Website: http://www.imcloud.co.kr/
Phone: 82-2-6472-0410 **Email:** imcloud@imcloud.co.: South Korea
City: Youidodong **State:** Seoul **PC:** **Country: South Korea**
Year Established: 2014 **Status 2020:** Active
Industries: Artificial Intelligence for:, Big Data and Analytics

Spain

Company Name: 365looks
Description: Artificial intelligence that "thinks" like a stylist, so it knows how to match clothes and create outfits.
Website: http://365looks.com
Phone: **Email:** info@365looks.com
City: **State:** **PC:** **Country: Spain**
Year Established: **Status 2020:** Active
Industries: Artificial Intelligence for:, ~ Fashion (16)

Company Name: SmartEcoMap
Description: A virtual travel assistant for tourist destinations
Website: http://smartecomap.com/en/
Phone: 34 657 38 77 33 **Email:** contact@smartecomap.com
City: Arrecife **State:** AL **PC:** **Country: Spain**
Year Established: **Status 2020:** Active
Industries: Artificial Intelligence for:, Big Data and Analytics for:, ~ Travel and Transportation (58)

Company **Name:** Galgus
Description: Galgus is a company highly specialized in research and development of wireless optimization software.
Website: http://www.galgus.net/
Phone: (3495) 538-2328 **Email:** hello@galgus.net
City: Camas **State:** AN **PC:** **Country: Spain**
Year Established: 2013 **Status 2020:** Active
Industries: Embedded for:, Internet of Things (IoT) for:, Machine Learning for:, Internet of Things (IoT)

Company Name: Newralers
Description: Newralers creates first-level artificial intelligence, to solve non-complex problems with large amounts of data.
Website:
Phone: 34 650 96 34 44 **Email:** 37058@reference-encyclopedia-ai.net
City: Malaga **State:** AN **PC:** **Country: Spain**
Year Established: 2017 **Status 2020:** Closed
Industries: Artificial Intelligence for:, Big Data and Analytics for:, IT Managed Services

Company Name: Architectur: Spain
Description: Architectures is a cloud-based artificial-intelligence-aided design tool for the residential sector.
Website: http://architechtures.com
Phone: 951 091 451 **Email:** info@architechtures.com
City: Málaga **State:** AN **PC:** **Country: Spain**
Year Established: 2015 **Status 2020:** Active
Industries: Artificial Intelligence

Company Name: Predictiva
Description: Predictiva uses AI to automate quality control processes in call centr: Spain
Website: http://www.predictiva.io
Phone: **Email:** 37198@reference-encyclopedia-ai.net
City: Málaga **State:** AN **PC:** **Country: Spain**
Year Established: 2016 **Status 2020:** Active
Industries: Artificial Intelligence for:, Big Data and Analytics for:, IT Managed Services for:, Web for:, Machine Learning

Company Name: Taalentfy
Description: Taalentfy is an Intelligent Tech Platform gives people and organizations access, manage and recruit the best talent with the best data and tools to take right decisions.
Website: http://www.taalentfy.com
Phone: 34 952 158353 **Email:** hello@knowledgefy.com
City: Málaga **State:** AL **Zip:** 29130 **Country: Spain**
Year Established: **Status 2020:** Active
Industries: Application Services for:, ~ Human Resources (268), Artificial Intelligence for:, ~ Education (13), ~ Human Resources (24), Big Data and Analytics for:, ~ Human Resources (512), Business Applications for:, ~ Human Resources (634), Business Software as a Service Ap

Company Name: Valo
Description: Valo is an all-in-one platform that combines a real-time computation engine and machine learning with big data storage.
Website: http://valo.io/
Phone: 34951255080 **Email:** info@valo.io
City: Málaga **State:** AN **PC:** **Country: Spain**
Year Established: 2015 **Status 2020:** Active
Industries: Big Data and Analytics for:, Machine Learning for:, Compute

Company Name: Stimulus
Description: Stimulus is an interactive software for professional cognitive stimulation and rehabilitation.
Website: http://stimuluspro.com
Phone: **Email:** info@stimuluspro.com
City: Mengibar **State:** AN **PC:** **Country: Spain**

Year Established: 2013 **Status 2020:** Active
Industries: Application Services

Company Name: ec2ce
Description: we are the predictive agriculture
Website: http://www.ec2ce.com
Phone: (3463) 810-9175 **Email:** info@ec2ce.us
City: Sevilla **State:** AN **PC:** **Country: Spain**
Year Established: 2014 **Status 2020:** Active
Industries: ~ Agriculture (3), Artificial Intelligence for:, Big Data and Analytics for:, Machine Learning

Company Name: ec2ce easy to see
Description: ec2ce is artificial intelligence for decision makers.
Website: http://www.ec2ce.com
Phone: 34638109175 **Email:** info@ec2ce.us
City: Sevilla **State:** AL **PC:** **Country: Spain**
Year Established: **Status 2020:** Active
Industries:

Company Name: Educabily
Description: Educabily develops new generation applications for educational environments.
Website: http://educabily.com
Phone: 954 22 49 34 **Email:** info@educabily.com
City: Sevilla **State:** AN **PC:** **Country: Spain**
Year Established: 2017 **Status 2020:** Active
Industries: Application Services for:, ~ Education (13), Machine Learning

Company Name: Gleam AI
Description: Un-intrusive AI-Powered Cybersecurity SaaS platform for Enterprises and Service Provide: Serbia
Website: http://gleam.ai/
Phone: **Email:** hello@gleam.ai
City: Seville **State:** AL **PC:** **Country: Spain**
Year Established: **Status 2020:** Active
Industries: Analytics for:, Artificial Intelligence for:, Big Data and Analytics for:, Cyber Security for:, Machine Learning for:, Security for:, Predictive Analytics

Company Name: Indisys
Description: Indisys develops natural language processing technologies that facilitate intelligent user interaction with computer systems.
Website: http://www.indisys.: Spain
Phone: 34 955 291 396 **Email:** info@indisys.: Spain
City: Seville **State:** AL **PC:** **Country: Spain**
Year Established: **Status 2020:** Active
Industries: Artificial Intelligence for:, Enterprise Application Services for:, Machine Learning for:, ~ Professional Services (48)

Company Name: Fenomat
Description: AI for fertility treatments
Website: http://www.fenomatch.com
Phone: (3497) 623-3905 **Email:** luis.arenaz@fenomatch.com
City: Zaragoza **State:** AR **PC:** **Country: Spain**
Year Established: 2019 **Status 2020:** Active
Industries: Artificial Intelligence for:, ~ Healthcare (20)

Company Name: Incubapps Limited
Description: Incubapps is a big data and artificial intelligence platform for connecting local business and consumers.
Website: http://flashfy.com
Phone: **Email:** 36753@reference-encyclopedia-ai.net
City: Zaragoza **State:** AR **PC:** **Country: Spain**
Year Established: 2015 **Status 2020:** Active
Industries: Artificial Intelligence for:, Big Data and Analytics for:, IT Managed Services for:, ~ Social Assistance-Non-Profits (53), ~ Social Assistance-Non-Profits (53)

Company Name: ZAPIENS
Description: ZAPIENS connects people and knowledge with human-centric Artificial Intelligence systems
Website: http://zapiens.ai
Phone: 34 984 840 864 **Email:** info@zapiens.ai
City: Oviedo **State:** Asturias **PC:** **Country: Spain**
Year Established: **Status 2020:** Active
Industries: Artificial Intelligence for:, Enterprise Application Services for:, Natural Language Processing for:, Application Services

Company Name: Alfred
Description: Alfred allows you to get in touch with your guests in an efficient and immediate way.
Website: https://alfred.repair/
Phone: 7 (495) 150-57-12 **Email:** mail@alfred.repa: Iran
City: Palma **State:** IB **PC:** **Country: Spain**
Year Established: 2017 **Status 2020:** Active
Industries: Artificial Intelligence

Company Name: Alfred - Artificial Intelligence Driven Concierge
Description: Alfred allows you to get in touch with your guests in an efficient and immediate way.
Website: http://alfred-ai.com
Phone: **Email:** info@alfred-ai.com
City: Palma **State:** PM **PC:** **Country: Spain**
Year Established: **Status 2020:** Active
Industries: Artificial Intelligence for:, ~ Hospitality (23), ~ Hospitality (23), Machine Learning

Company Name: MonitorizeMe
Description: We build Big Data, Machine Learning and IA analytical solutions, from Social Media data to Travel Data. Anything you need, we can build it.
Website: http://monitorizeme.com
Phone: (68) 744-4040 **Email:** info@monitorizeme.com
City: Palma **State:** IB **PC:** **Country: Spain**
Year Established: 2011 **Status 2020:** Active
Industries: Analytics for:, Artificial Intelligence for:, Big Data and Analytics for:, Internet of Things (IoT)

Company Name: Flook
Description: Distributed E-Learning, Education Management, Artificial Intelligence, Machine Learning, Predictive Analysis, SaaS, AIaaS, Online Education
Website: http://flook.online
Phone: 34-871-18-0097 **Email:** info@flook.online
City: Palma De Mallorca **State:** PM **PC:** **Country: Spain**
Year Established: **Status 2020:** Active
Industries: Artificial Intelligence for:, ~ Healthcare (20), Data Management for:, ~ Education (13), Machine Learning for:, Management Information Systems for:, Natural Language Processing for:, Predictive Analytics

Company Name: Open Dynamics
Description: Intelligent Systems, Smart Homes, Home Automation, AI, Smart Cities, Smart Villages, Sustainable Living,
Website: http://opendynamics.net/
Phone: **Email:** info@opendynamics.net
City: Palma De Mallorca **State:** PM **PC:** **Country: Spain**
Year Established: **Status 2020:** Active
Industries: ~ Agriculture (3), ~ Professional Services (48), Artificial Intelligence for:, Augmented Reality for:, ~ Agriculture (3), Application Services for:, Predictive Analytics for:, ~ Construction (10)

Company Name: Webgenius
Description: Webhosting, AI Hosting, Dedicated Hosting, VPS Hosting, Cloud Hosting, SaaS, IaaS, PaaS, AIaaS, Assisted Webdesign, Start-Ups Marketplace
Website: http://webgenius.online
Phone: 3-487-118-0097 **Email:** info@webgenius.online
City: Palma De Mallorca **State:** PM **PC:** **Country: Spain**
Year Established: **Status 2020:** Active
Industries: Artificial Intelligence for:, Databases for:, Automation for:, Cloud for:, Machine Learning for:, Enterprise Application Services for:, ~ Social Media (54), ~ Social Media (54), ~ Social Media (54), Cyber Security for:, Cyber Security

Company Name: ASIMOB
Description: ASIMOB develops AI & IoT solutions regarding road safety conditions.
Website: http://asimob.: Spain
Phone: **Email:** info@asimob.: Spain
City: Bilbao **State:** PV **PC:** **Country: Spain**
Year Established: 2016 **Status 2020:** Active
Industries: Artificial Intelligence for:, Internet of Things (IoT)

Company Name: Berba
Description: Berba is a deep interest in technology and artificial intelligence, and an eagerness to ease communication across cultures.
Website: http://berba.net/
Phone: 34 946 66 31 30 **Email:** info@berba.net
City: Bilbao **State:** PV **PC:** **Country: Spain**
Year Established: 2018 **Status 2020:** Active
Industries:

Company Name: ByteHeed
Description: ByteHeed transforms the way a stealthy hypervisor, machine learning algorithms and intelligence are combined to provide protection.
Website: http://www.byteheed.com/
Phone: 34 946 853 437 **Email:** info@byteheed.com
City: Bilbao **State:** PV **PC:** **Country: Spain**
Year Established: 2014 **Status 2020:** Active
Industries: Artificial Intelligence for:, Cyber Security for:, Security

Company Name: Cancerappy
Description: Cancerappy designs and develops a platform that uses big data and artificial intelligence to help research against cancer.
Website: http://cancerappy.com/
Phone: 34 673453865 **Email:** l.martin@cancerappy.com
City: Bilbao **State:** PV **PC:** **Country: Spain**
Year Established: 2019 **Status 2020:** Active
Industries: Artificial Intelligence for:, Big Data and Analytics for:, Application Services for:, Business Intelligence

Company Name: Chicisimo
Description: Chicisimo is automating outfit advice
Website: http://chicisimo.com
Phone: **Email:** aldamiz@chicisimo.com
City: Bilbao **State:** PV **PC:** **Country: Spain**
Year Established: 2010 **Status 2020:** Active
Industries: Artificial Intelligence for:, Big Data and Analytics for:, E-Commerce

Company Name: SHERPA
Description: Sherpa has developed AI-based virtual personal assistant technology with predictive capabilities.
Website: http://www.sher.pa
Phone: **Email:** info@sher.pa
City: Bilbao **State:** PV **PC:** **Country: Spain**
Year Established: **Status 2020:** Active
Industries: Artificial Intelligence for:, Machine Learning for:, Mobile for:, Application Services

Company Name: Sherpa.ai
Description: Sherpa.ai builds AI technology and products: Digital Assistants, Recommenders, and cutting-edge AI technology, such as Federated Learning.
Website: http://sherpa.ai/
Phone: 34 944 630 101 **Email:** info@sher.pa
City: Bilbao **State:** PV **PC:** **Country: Spain**
Year Established: 2012 **Status 2020:** Active
Industries: Artificial Intelligence for:, Internet of Things (IoT) for:, Machine Learning for:, Mobile for:, Application Services for:, Natural Language Processing for:, Predictive Analytics for:, Internet of Things (IoT) for:, Internet of Things (IoT)

Company Name: Alerion
Description: Alerion develops intelligent drones for fully autonomous and automated real-time infrastructure inspections.
Website: http://www.aleriontec.com
Phone: 34 943 55 66 84 **Email:** info@aleriontec.com
City: Donostia-san Sebastian **State:** PV **PC:** **Country: Spain**
Year Established: **Status 2020:** Active
Industries: Artificial Intelligence for:, Computer Vision for:, ~ Transportation and Logistics (57), ~ Transportation and Logistics (57), Robotics

Company Name: Cyber Surgery
Description: Cyber Surgery is an AI company that develops a robotic system for spinal procedures.
Website: http://cyber-surgery.com
Phone: 34 943124627 **Email:** info@cyber-surgery.com
City: San Sebastian **State:** PV **PC:** **Country: Spain**
Year Established: 2017 **Status 2020:** Active
Industries: Artificial Intelligence for:, ~ Healthcare (20), Robotics

Company Name: DAIA Solutions
Description: DAIA is dedicated to the development of applications and data analysis based on artificial intelligence techniques and data mining.
Website: http://daiasolutions.com
Phone: 34 646 87 01 29 **Email:** info@daiasolutions.com
City: San Sebastian **State:** PV **PC:** **Country: Spain**
Year Established: 2012 **Status 2020:** Active
Industries: Artificial Intelligence for:, Databases for:, Enterprise Application Services

Company Name: Irisbond
Description: Irisbond creates a new way for humans to communicate based on precision eye tracking technology.
Website: http://irisbond.com/en
Phone: 34 943 496 622 **Email:** o.martinez@irisbond.com
City: San Sebastian **State:** PV **PC:** **Country: Spain**
Year Established: **Status 2020:** Active
Industries: Artificial Intelligence for:, ~ Healthcare (20), ~ Manufacturing-Electronic (30), ~ Professional Services (48)

Company Name: Erle Robotics
Description: Erle Robotics is a linux-based smart drone with support for the Robot Operating System.
Website: http://erlerobotics.com/
Phone: (3494) 530-6820 **Email:** 36517@reference-encyclopedia-ai.net
City: Vitoria **State:** PV **PC:** **Country: Spain**
Year Established: 2012 **Status 2020:** Active
Industries: Artificial Intelligence for:, ~ Education (13), Application Services for:, Robotics

Company Name: WEUNGRY
Description: WEUNGRY is Powering the Global On-Demand Food Economy. Digital Food Ordering Marketplace & Food Delivery Platform. WEUNGRY Digital Franchi: Sweden
Website: http://weungry.com
Phone: 631WEUNGRY **Email:** customercare@weungry.com
City: Florida **State:** CN **PC:** **Country: Spain**
Year Established: **Status 2020:** Active
Industries: Application Services for:, Artificial Intelligence for:, ~ Transportation and Logistics (57), Application Services for:, Application Services for:, ~ Transportation and Logistics (57), ~ Transportation and Logistics (57), E-Commerce for:, E-Commerce for:, ~ Transp

Company Name: GearTranslations
Description: Translation Management System Leveraged on Machine Learning
Website: http://www.geartranslations.com
Phone: **Email:** info@geartranslations.com
City: Santa Cruz De Tenerife **State:** CN **PC:** **Country: Spain**
Year Established: 2014 **Status 2020:** Active
Industries: Machine Learning

Company Name: Intelnics
Description: Intelnics is a research company which develops artificial intelligence software.
Website: http://www.intelnics.com/
Phone: (3492) 313-3612 **Email:** artelnics@artelnics.com
City: Salamanca **State:** CL **PC:** **Country: Spain**
Year Established: 2014 **Status 2020:** Active
Industries: Artificial Intelligence for:, Databases

Company Name: Artelnics
Description: Artelnics is a company that develops advanced analytics software.
Website: http://www.artelnics.com
Phone: 34923133612 **Email:** artelnics@artelnics.com
City: Santa Marta De Tormes **State:** CL **PC:** **Country: Spain**
Year Established: 2014 **Status 2020:** Active
Industries:

Company Name: Neural Designer
Description: We are a team of scientists and engineers with more than 15 years of experience developing the most advanced machine learning technology.
Website: http://www.neuralbc.com/
Phone: **Email:** recruit@neuralbc.com
City: Villamayor **State:** CL **PC:** **Country: Spain**
Year Established: 2018 **Status 2020:** Active
Industries: Analytics for:, Artificial Intelligence for:, Big Data and Analytics for:, IT Managed Services for:, Machine Learning for:, Predictive Analytics

Company Name: Warden Automation
Description: Warden Automation is a technology-based startup whose mission is to develop disruptive technological solutions for industry and commerce.
Website: http://www.wardenautomation.com/
Phone: (34) 679 58 34 24 **Email:** info@wardenautomation.com
City: Ciudad Real **State:** CM **PC:** **Country: Spain**
Year Established: 2015 **Status 2020:** Active
Industries: Artificial Intelligence for:, Big Data and Analytics for:, Computer Vision for:, IT Managed Services for:, Machine Learning

Company Name: Abalmon
Description: Abalmon is a artificial intelligence platform.
Website:
Phone: **Email:** 35932@reference-encyclopedia-ai.net
City: Barcelona **State:** CT **PC:** **Country: Spain**
Year Established: 2016 **Status 2020:** Active
Industries: Artificial Intelligence for:, IT Managed Services

Company Name: AERVIO
Description: Aervio is a travel management platform for booking process that integrates AI.
Website: http://www.aervio.com/
Phone: **Email:** diego.sanchez@aervio.com
City: Barcelona **State:** CT **PC:** **Country: Spain**
Year Established: 2016 **Status 2020:** Active
Industries: Artificial Intelligence for:, Business Applications for:, Application Services for:, Machine Learning for:, Natural Language Processing for:, Web for:, Predictive Analytics for:, Predictive Analytics for:, Business Software as a Service Apps (SaaS Apps) for:, ~ : Turkey

Company Name: Aimentia HealthTech
Description: Aimentia HealthTech is an artificial intelligence platform created to help professionals and patients for the new era of mental health.
Website: https://www.aimentia.com/
Phone: **Email:** 36014@reference-encyclopedia-ai.net
City: Barcelona **State:** CT **PC:** **Country: Spain**
Year Established: 2019 **Status 2020:** Active
Industries: Artificial Intelligence for:, ~ Healthcare (20), IT Managed Services

Company Name: Alda
Description: Alda - Your AI-powered financial advisor
Website: http://alda.bot/
Phone: 34 665 933 852 **Email:** hello@alda.bot
City: Barcelona **State:** CT **PC:** **Country: Spain**
Year Established: **Status 2020:** Active
Industries: Artificial Intelligence for:, ~ Banking and Financial Markets-Services (7)

Company Name: AllRead Machine Learning Technologies
Description: AllRead Software is a deep learning-based information spotting technology able to read in a single shot.
Website: https://www.allread.ai/
Phone: **Email:** info@allread.ai
City: Barcelona **State:** CT **PC:** **Country: Spain**
Year Established: 2019 **Status 2020:** Active
Industries: Artificial Intelligence for:, Machine Learning

Company Name: Atomian
Description: Cognitive computing NLP = fully understanding of the world => answering all questions you may have
Website: http://www.atomian.com
Phone: 34935040991 **Email:** info@atomian.com
City: Barcelona **State:** CT **PC:** **Country: Spain**
Year Established: 2014 **Status 2020:** Active
Industries: Artificial Intelligence for:, ~ Automotive (5), ~ Administrative and Support Services (1)

Company Name: Awaait Artificial Intelligence S.L.
Description:
Website: www.awaait.com
Phone: **Email:** info@awaait.com
City: Barcelona **State:** CT **PC:** **Country: Spain**
Year Established: **Status 2020:** Active
Industries: Artificial Intelligence for:, ~ Travel and Transportation (58)

Company Name: Badi
Description: Badi is an online room rental platform that allows anyone to publish, find, and securely book rooms.
Website: http://www.badi.com
Phone: **Email:** info@badi.com
City: Barcelona **State:** CT **PC:** **Country: Spain**
Year Established: 2015 **Status 2020:** Active
Industries: Artificial Intelligence for:, Mobile

Company Name: Bee the Data
Description: Bee the Data offers software solutions in the scope of artificial intelligence and machine learning.
Website: http://beethedata.com/
Phone: **Email:** administration@beethedata.com
City: Barcelona **State:** CT **PC:** **Country: Spain**
Year Established: 2014 **Status 2020:** Active
Industries: Artificial Intelligence for:, Big Data and Analytics for:, Computer Vision for:, Machine Learning for:, Natural Language Processing

Company Name: Biel Glass: Spain
Description: Biel Glasses develops smart glasses to improve mobility and personal autonomy of people with low vision.
Website: http://www.bielglasses.com
Phone: **Email:** info@bielglasses.com
City: Barcelona **State:** CT **PC:** **Country: Spain**
Year Established: 2017 **Status 2020:** Active
Industries: Artificial Intelligence for:, ~ Healthcare (20), ~ Healthcare (20)

Company Name: big blue analytics
Description: big blue analytics is an artificial intelligence company.
Website: http://bigblueanalytics.com/
Phone: **Email:** 36153@reference-encyclopedia-ai.net
City: Barcelona **State:** CT **PC:** **Country: Spain**
Year Established: 2016 **Status 2020:** Active
Industries: Artificial Intelligence

Company Name: BitMetrics
Description: Artificial Intelligence
Website: http://www.bitmetrics.: Spain
Phone: 34 93 141 7935 **Email:** info@bitmetrics.: Spain
City: Barcelona **State:** CT **PC:** **Country: Spain**
Year Established: 2017 **Status 2020:** Active
Industries:

Company Name: Bobelo Travel
Description: Bobelo Travel is an intelligent travel agency uses artificial intelligence to create the best business travel itineraries.
Website: http://bobelotravel.com/
Phone: 34 611 404 727 **Email:** 36181@reference-encyclopedia-ai.net
City: Barcelona **State:** CT **PC:** **Country: Spain**
Year Established: 2019 **Status 2020:** Active
Industries: Artificial Intelligence

Company Name: Bookline
Description: Bookline is a company which offers AI-based conversational bots to manage appointments and bookings over the phone.
Website: http://bookline.io
Phone: **Email:** digame@bookline.io
City: Barcelona **State:** CT **PC:** **Country: Spain**
Year Established: 2018 **Status 2020:** Active
Industries: Artificial Intelligence for:, IT Managed Services

Company Name: Brainity
Description: Facebook and Instagram Automatic Retargeting Ads for Shopify.
Website: http://brainity.co/
Phone: **Email:** hello@brainity.co
City: Barcelona **State:** CT **PC:** **Country: Spain**
Year Established: **Status 2020:** Active
Industries: ~ Media-Communications (41), Artificial Intelligence for:, E-Commerce for:, ~ Media-Communications (41)

Company Name: Catchoom
Description: Catchoom is an award-winning image and object recognition provider powering visual search and automatic product tagging solutions.
Website: catchoom.com
Phone: **Email:** rene@catchoom.com
City: Barcelona **State:** CT **PC:** **Country: Spain**
Year Established: **Status 2020:** Active
Industries: Application Services for:, Artificial Intelligence for:, E-Commerce for:, ~ Law-Legal Services (26), Image Recognition for:, ~ Media-Communications (41), ~ Media-Communications (41), ~ Retail and Consumer Products (52), ~ Retail and Consumer Products (52), Compute

Company Name: Citibeats
Description: Citibeats is the AI Advance Analytics Platform unique in identifying social trends and concerns.
Website: http://citibeats.net/
Phone: 34 937 825 152 **Email:** go@citibeats.net
City: Barcelona **State:** CT **PC:** **Country: Spain**
Year Established: 2018 **Status 2020:** Active
Industries: Artificial Intelligence for:, IT Managed Services for:, IT Managed Services

Company Name: Citibeats
Description: Citibeats is an augmented text analytics platform that helps companies and governments understand citizens' needs in real-time.
Website: https://citibeats.com/
Phone: **Email:** ngrau@citibeats.net
City: Barcelona **State:** CT **Zip:** 8005 **Country: Spain**
Year Established: **Status 2020:** Active
Industries: Artificial Intelligence for:, ~ Banking and Financial Markets-Services (7), ~ Government (19), ~ Insurance (25), Enterprise Application Services

Company Name: Clinicgram
Description: Clinicgram is a digital health modular platform that uses artificial intelligence to optimize clinical image on wound management.
Website: http://www.clinicgram.com/
Phone: 34-902 99 53 74 **Email:** info@clinicgram.com
City: Barcelona **State:** CT **PC:** **Country: Spain**
Year Established: 2019 **Status 2020:** Active
Industries: Artificial Intelligence for:, ~ Healthcare (20), Machine Learning

Company Name: Coverfy
Description: Coverfy is an insurtech startup on a mission to make insurance easy for everyone.
Website: http://www.coverfy.com/
Phone: 34 910 05 91 07 **Email:** hola@coverfy.com
City: Barcelona **State:** CT **PC:** **Country: Spain**
Year Established: 2016 **Status 2020:** Active
Industries: Application Services for:, ~ Banking and Financial Markets-Services (7), ~ Banking and Financial Markets-Services (7), Application Services for:, Predictive Analytics

Company Name: crear smart business
Description: crear smart business is a Retail & Real Estate Smart, Innovative, Boutique Consulting company.
Website: http://www.crearsmartbusiness.com/
Phone: **Email:** info@crearsmartbusiness.com
City: Barcelona **State:** CT **PC:** **Country: Spain**
Year Established: 2018 **Status 2020:** Active
Industries: Artificial Intelligence

Company Name: Datancia
Description: Datancia is an innovative start-up in technologies and methods of Advanced Analytics
Website: http://www.datancia.com
Phone: (3463) 072-5232 **Email:** info@datancia.com
City: Barcelona **State:** CT **PC:** **Country: Spain**
Year Established: 2015 **Status 2020:** Active
Industries: Big Data and Analytics for:, Machine Learning

Company Name: DeepSolutions
Description: DeepSolutions specializes in image recognition using state-of-the-art deep neural networks.
Website: http://deepsolutions.io/
Phone: 34 628 842 245 **Email:** bcn@deepsolutions.io
City: Barcelona **State:** CT **PC:** **Country: Spain**
Year Established: 2016 **Status 2020:** Active
Industries: Artificial Intelligence for:, Image Recognition

Company Name: DUNFORCE
Description: The smart collection agent that simplifies and accelerates the payment of your receivables.
Website: www.dunforce.com/
Phone: **Email:** contact@dunforce.io
City: Barcelona **State:** CT **PC:** **Country: Spain**
Year Established: **Status 2020:** Active
Industries: Artificial Intelligence for:, Business Applications for:, ~ Banking and Financial Markets-Services (7), ~ Banking and Financial Markets-Services (7)

Company Name: Earthlab AI System
Description: Making geospatial data accessible and usable
Website: http://earthlab.ai/
Phone: **Email:** hello@earthlab.ai
City: Barcelona **State:** CT **PC:** **Country: Spain**
Year Established: 2020 **Status 2020:** Active
Industries: Analytics for:, Artificial Intelligence

Company Name: Ecomunicat ElectrÃ²nics
Description: Image Artificial Intelligence Tools
Website: http://www.ecomunicat.com
Phone: 34935824530 **Email:** ecomunicat@ecomunicat.com
City: Barcelona **State:** CT **PC:** **Country: Spain**

Year Established: **Status 2020:** Active
Industries:

Company Name: Effilogics Technologies
Description: Effilogics Technologies provides a unique energy management software.
Website: http://www.efficienciaenergetica.com/
Phone: (3493) 151-4652 **Email:** info@effilogics.com
City: Barcelona **State:** CT **PC:** **Country: Spain**
Year Established: 2011 **Status 2020:** Active
Industries: Analytics for:, ~ Energy and Utilities (14), ~ Energy and Utilities (14), Enterprise Application Services for:, Internet of Things (IoT) for:, Predictive Analytics for:, Business Software as a Service Apps (SaaS Apps) for:, ~ Construction (10)

Company Name: Frizbit
Description: Marketing Automation Platform with AI, smartly bringing customers back
Website: http://frizbit.com
Phone: **Email:** info@frizbit.com
City: Barcelona **State:** CT **PC:** **Country: Spain**
Year Established: 2016 **Status 2020:** Active
Industries: Analytics for:, E-Commerce for:, Machine Learning for:, Web

Company Name: Gestoos
Description: Gestoos develops an Artificial Intelligence software that can recognize people'™s gestures and behavior in real-time.
Website: http://www.gestoos.com/
Phone: **Email:** german@gestoos.com
City: Barcelona **State:** CT **PC:** **Country: Spain**
Year Established: **Status 2020:** Active
Industries: Artificial Intelligence for:, ~ Media-Communications (41), Human Computer Interaction for:, ~ Retail and Consumer Products (52)

Company Name: HEXACHORDS
Description: Music Artificial Intelligence
Website: http://www.hexachords.com
Phone: **Email:** 36689@reference-encyclopedia-ai.net
City: Barcelona **State:** CT **PC:** **Country: Spain**
Year Established: 2015 **Status 2020:** Active
Industries: Artificial Intelligence for:, ~ Arts-Entertainment-Recreation (4)

Company Name: Holding Advice and Leadership S.L.
Description: Holding Advice and Leadership S.L. provides real-time solutions in power of current machines and the latest developments in AI and ML.
Website: http://www.hal.cat/
Phone: **Email:** info@hal.cat
City: Barcelona **State:** CT **PC:** **Country: Spain**
Year Established: **Status 2020:** Active
Industries: Artificial Intelligence for:, ~ Professional Services (48), Machine Learning for:, ~ Manufacturing-Machinery (32)

Company **Name:** iMath Research
Description: iMath Research is a math research company that is designed to provide factual data.
Website: http://www.imathresearch.com
Phone: 34 93 586 8743 **Email:** info@imathresearch.com
City: Barcelona **State:** CT **PC:** **Country: Spain**
Year Established: **Status 2020:** Active
Industries: Analytics for:, Artificial Intelligence for:, IT Managed Services

Company Name: INARI
Description: INARI provides blockchain, machine learning and artificial intelligence technologies for the Insurance industry
Website: http://www.inari.io
Phone: **Email:** info@inari.io
City: Barcelona **State:** CT **PC:** **Country: Spain**
Year Established: 2017 **Status 2020:** Active
Industries: Artificial Intelligence for:, Blockchain for:, IT Managed Services for:, IT Managed Services

Company Name: Infantium
Description: Infantium is a mobile app that offers cognitive personalized learning and brain-inspired computing for children in Spain.
Website: http://www.infantium.com
Phone: 34 61 668 96 61 **Email:** hello@infantium.com
City: Barcelona **State:** CT **PC:** **Country: Spain**
Year Established: **Status 2020:** Active
Industries: Artificial Intelligence for:, ~ Education (13), ~ Education (13), Machine Learning

Company Name: Insikt Intelligence
Description: Insikt Intelligence is a deep tech start up leveraging AI and Machine Learning for detection of criminal and radical content.
Website: http://www.insiktintelligence.com/
Phone: **Email:** info@insiktintelligence.com
City: Barcelona **State:** CT **PC:** **Country: Spain**
Year Established: 2016 **Status 2020:** Active
Industries: Artificial Intelligence for:, Big Data and Analytics for:, Cyber Security for:, Databases for:, Security for:, Cyber Security for:, ~ Government (19), Machine Learning for:, Natural Language Processing

Company Name: Intranetum
Description: Intranetum is a SaaS-based self-learning tool that provides its users with information about their businesses.
Website: http://intranetum.com/
Phone: **Email:** 36801@reference-encyclopedia-ai.net
City: Barcelona **State:** CT **PC:** **Country: Spain**
Year Established: 2011 **Status 2020:** Active
Industries: Big Data and Analytics for:, Enterprise Application Services for:, Application Program Interfaces (APIs) for:, Machine Learning

Company Name: ionic AI
Description: Developing next generation solutions that greatly improve performance & battery life of mobile devices.
Website: http://www.ionicai.com/
Phone: 34690720151 **Email:** info@ionicai.com
City: Barcelona **State:** CT **PC:** **Country: Spain**
Year Established: **Status 2020:** Active
Industries: Artificial Intelligence for:, Application Services

Company Name: Kro
Description: Krono is an AI assisted marketplace.
Website: http://krono.ai/
Phone: **Email:** 36867@reference-encyclopedia-ai.net
City: Barcelona **State:** CT **PC:** **Country: Spain**
Year Established: 2018 **Status 2020:** Active
Industries:

Company Name: Marketeer
Description: Marketeer is an automated customer service tool for modern messaging with chatbot for modern companies.
Website: http://marketeer.co
Phone: 34611 217 738 **Email:** hello@marketeer.co
City: Barcelona **State:** CT **PC:** **Country: Spain**
Year Established: 2015 **Status 2020:** Active
Industries: Artificial Intelligence for:, ~ Customer Relationship Management (11), ~ Customer Relationship Management (11), Application Services for:, Internet of Things (IoT) for:, Machine Learning for:, Mobile for:, Business Software as a Service Apps (SaaS Apps) for:, Bus

Company Name: Marketeer.co
Description: Marketeer works for providing customer service bots which efficiency grants customer communication integrating Human and AI.
Website: http://marketeer.co
Phone: 34611 217 738 **Email:** hello@marketeer.co
City: Barcelona **State:** CT **PC:** **Country: Spain**
Year Established: **Status 2020:** Active
Industries:

Company Name: MedicOnline
Description: We're not only a health consult service, we're your new access to unlimited health through medical AI and medical experts.
Website: http://mediconlineapp.com/
Phone: **Email:** 36954@reference-encyclopedia-ai.net
City: Barcelona **State:** CT **PC:** **Country: Spain**
Year Established: 2016 **Status 2020:** Active
Industries: Artificial Intelligence for:, ~ Healthcare (20), ~ Healthcare (20), ~ Healthcare (20), ~ Healthcare (20)

Company Name: Mediktor
Description: The most advanced and accurate sypmtom checker
Website: http://www.mediktor.com/
Phone: (3493) 211-1666 **Email:** info@mediktor.com
City: Barcelona **State:** CT **PC:** **Country: Spain**
Year Established: 2011 **Status 2020:** Active
Industries: Artificial Intelligence for:, ~ Healthcare (20), Machine Learning for:, ~ Healthcare (20)

Company Name: Methinks
Description: Deep learning in neuroimaging
Website: http://www.methinks.es/
Phone: **Email:** 36973@reference-encyclopedia-ai.net
City: Barcelona **State:** CT **PC:** **Country: Spain**
Year Established: 2017 **Status 2020:** Active
Industries: Artificial Intelligence for:, ~ Biotechnology (9), IT Managed Services for:, ~ Healthcare (20)

Company Name: Mind the Byte
Description: Mind the Byte is a bioinformatics company specializing in computational drug design using a pay-per-use SaaS platform.
Website: http://www.mindthebyte.com/
Phone: 34 934 02 09 38 **Email:** info@mindthebyte.com
City: Barcelona **State:** CT **PC:** **Country: Spain**
Year Established: 2011 **Status 2020:** Active
Industries: Artificial Intelligence for:, ~ Biotechnology (9), ~ Biotechnology (9)

Company Name: Neuroelectrics
Description: Neuroelectrics is a digital brain health company that diagnoses and treats brain disorders, and improves overall brain health.
Website: http://www.neuroelectrics.com/
Phone: 34 93 254 03 66 **Email:** info@neuroelectrics.com
City: Barcelona **State:** CT **PC:** **Country: Spain**
Year Established: **Status 2020:** Active
Industries: Artificial Intelligence for:, ~ Biotechnology (9), ~ Healthcare (20), ~ Healthcare (20), ~ Manufacturing-Medical Equipment-Supplies (33), ~ Professional Services (48)

Company **Name:** Nina Capital
Description: Investing in need-driven founders building health tech companies with international ambitions.
Website: http://www.nina.capital/
Phone: **Email:** info@nina.capital
City: Barcelona **State:** CT **PC:** **Country: Spain**
Year Established: 2019 **Status 2020:** Active
Industries: Analytics for:, Artificial Intelligence for:, ~ Healthcare (20), IT Managed Services for:, Internet of Things (IoT) for:, Machine Learning for:, Internet of Things (IoT)

Company Name: Nostrum Biodiscovery
Description: Creating new drugs through AI and supercomputing power
Website: http://www.nostrumbiodiscovery.com
Phone: 34696766027 **Email:** emas@nostrumbiodiscovery.com
City: Barcelona **State:** CT **Zip:** 8028 **Country: Spain**
Year Established: **Status 2020:** Active
Industries: Artificial Intelligence for:, ~ Biotechnology (9), ~ Healthcare (20), ~ Life Sciences (27), ~ Pharmaceuticals (46), Compute for:, ~ Biotechnology (1351), ~ Food and Beverage (1359), ~ Healthcare (1362), ~ Life Sciences (1369), ~ Pharmaceuticals (1388), High Perfor: Morocco

Company Name: oh!bi: Kenya
Description: oh!bike is the lightest e-bike on the market. It is bionic, intuitive and awarded as Best Design of the Year
Website: http://www.kickstarter.com/projects/204802053/ohbike-t...
Phone: 34 931187533 **Email:** aitor.quesada@ohbike.cat
City: Barcelona **State:** CT **PC:** **Country: Spain**
Year Established: **Status 2020:** Active
Industries:

Company Name: Oliver
Description: Platform that through a smart wearable collects and interprets amateur soccer player stats. For players, scouters, and coaches.
Website: http://www.tryoliver.com
Phone: **Email:** hello@tryoliver.com
City: Barcelona **State:** CT **PC:** **Country: Spain**
Year Established: **Status 2020:** Active
Industries: Artificial Intelligence for:, Machine Learning for:, ~ Healthcare (20), ~ Arts-Entertainment-Recreation (4)

Company Name: Optimus Price
Description: Optimus Price is a SaaS that uses Artificial Intelligence to help stores set prices in e-commerce.
Website: http://optimusprice.ai/
Phone: **Email:** hello@optimusprice.ai
City: Barcelona **State:** CT **PC:** **Country: Spain**
Year Established: 2015 **Status 2020:** Active
Industries: Artificial Intelligence for:, Digital Marketing for:, E-Commerce for:, Machine Learning for:, Predictive Analytics for:, Automation

Company Name: PhysicalTech
Description: PhysicalTech is a technology company located in Barcelona, specializing in smart data analysis and computer vision.
Website: http://www.physicaltech.com/
Phone: **Email:** 37166@reference-encyclopedia-ai.net
City: Barcelona **State:** CT **PC:** **Country: Spain**
Year Established: 2016 **Status 2020:** Active
Industries: IT Managed Services

Company Name: Plyzer
Description: We are focused on developing the next-generation AI driven comparison engine
Website: http://www.plyzer.com
Phone: **Email:** hello@plyzer.com
City: Barcelona **State:** CT **PC:** **Country: Spain**
Year Established: **Status 2020:** Active
Industries: Artificial Intelligence for:, Machine Learning

Company Name: Red Points
Description: Red Points is the smart solution for brand protection online
Website: http://www.redpoints.com/
Phone: **Email:** info@redpoints.com
City: Barcelona **State:** CT **PC:** **Country: Spain**
Year Established: **Status 2020:** Active
Industries: Artificial Intelligence for:, Image Recognition for:, ~ Media-Communications (41), ~ Law-Legal Services (26), Machine Learning for:, Security

Company Name: Restb.ai
Description: Restb.ai is the leading computer vision solution for real estate.
Website: http://restb.ai
Phone: **Email:** info@restb.ai
City: Barcelona **State:** CT **PC:** **Country: Spain**
Year Established: 2015 **Status 2020:** Active
Industries:

Company Name: Restb.ai - Cognitive Computer Vision
Description: RestB provides Cognitive Artificial Vision technology, to allow companies fully tailor specialized image recognition models.
Website: http://restb.ai
Phone: **Email:** info@restb.ai
City: Barcelona **State:** CT **PC:** **Country: Spain**
Year Established: **Status 2020:** Active
Industries: Artificial Intelligence for:, Business Applications for:, Computer Vision for:, Image Recognition for:, Machine Learning for:, Computer Vision

Company Name: Review.Network
Description: Transforming how companies do market research, and the way people review products and services through blockchain technology.
Website: http://review.network
Phone: **Email:** hello@review.network
City: Barcelona **State:** CT **PC:** **Country: Spain**
Year Established: **Status 2020:** Active
Industries: Artificial Intelligence for:, Blockchain for:, ~ Media-Communications (41)

Company Name: Sadako Technologies
Description: Sadako Technologies is a Spanish company engaging in artificial intelligence and robotics.
Website: http://www.sadako.: Spain
Phone: 34934900368 **Email:** info@sadako.: Spain
City: Barcelona **State:** CT **PC:** **Country: Spain**
Year Established: **Status 2020:** Active
Industries: Artificial Intelligence for:, ~ Professional Services (48), ~ Social-Environmental-Physical-Engineering Sciences (55), Robotics

Company Name: Sensefields
Description: Advanced Mobility Data Solutions | Accurate Data is Power | We ensure the accuracy. You manage the power.
Website: http://sensefields.com/
Phone: 34 932 50 45 98 **Email:** info@sensefields.com
City: Barcelona **State:** CT **PC:** **Country: Spain**
Year Established: 2011 **Status 2020:** Active
Industries: Artificial Intelligence for:, IT Managed Services for:, Web

Company Name: SimpleML
Description: SimpleML is an online platform that enables individuals to find suitable machine learning algorithms for their datasets.
Website: http://simpleml.com
Phone: 1(415)779-5775 **Email:** hello@simpleml.com
City: Barcelona **State:** CT **PC:** **Country: Spain**
Year Established: **Status 2020:** Active
Industries: Artificial Intelligence for:, Big Data and Analytics for:, Databases for:, Machine Learning

Company Name: Sisu labs
Description: Sisu labs is a technology firm that offers natural language processing and semantic analysis techniques for organizations to sort out data.
Website: http://sisu-labs.com
Phone: **Email:** hello@sisu-labs.com
City: Barcelona **State:** CT **PC:** **Country: Spain**
Year Established: **Status 2020:** Active
Industries: Analytics for:, Artificial Intelligence for:, Big Data and Analytics for:, Natural Language Processing for:, Cyber Security for:, ~ Social Media (54), ~ Social Media (54), ~ Social Media (54), Data Management

Company Name: Smartive
Description: Smartive develops intelligent platforms to improve the operation an efficiency of the energy market.
Website: http://smartive.eu
Phone: 34 93 008 69 85 **Email:** info@smartive.eu
City: Barcelona **State:** CT **PC:** **Country: Spain**
Year Established: **Status 2020:** Active
Industries: Artificial Intelligence for:, Cloud for:, IT Managed Services

Company Name: SmartMonkey
Description: SmartMonkey provides learning AI software solutions for logistics services and field operations.
Website: http://en.smartmonkey.io/
Phone: 34 660 053 865 **Email:** 37418@reference-encyclopedia-ai.net
City: Barcelona **State:** CT **PC:** **Country: Spain**
Year Established: 2015 **Status 2020:** Active
Industries: Artificial Intelligence for:, ~ Telecommunications (56), Supply Chain Management

Company Name: Spaceboost
Description: Spaceboost is a tech platform that lets advertisers turn their data into autonomous, powerful, and profitable ad campaigns on Google & Bing.
Website: http://www.spaceboost.com
Phone: 933 28 31 27 **Email:** nacho@spaceboost.com
City: Barcelona **State:** CT **PC:** **Country: Spain**
Year Established: 2014 **Status 2020:** Active
Industries: Databases for:, Digital Marketing for:, Web for:, Machine Learning for:, Web for:, Web for:, Digital Marketing

Company Name: Talentfy
Description: Talentfy is a Artificial Intelligence & Internet company.
Website: http://www.ytalentfy.com/
Phone: 34 938 54 73 58 **Email:** atencion@ytalentfy.com
City: Barcelona **State:** CT **PC:** **Country: Spain**
Year Established: 2019 **Status 2020:** Active
Industries: Artificial Intelligence for:, IT Managed Services for:, Web

Company Name: Tradler
Description: Tradleoffers utilizes an AI that matches the preferences of a team with the incentive that delivers a quantifiable ROI.
Website: http://www.tradler.co/
Phone: 34611458366 **Email:** info@tradler.co
City: Barcelona **State:** CT **PC:** **Country: Spain**
Year Established: **Status 2020:** Active
Industries: Artificial Intelligence for:, Application Services for:, ~ Human Resources (24)

Company Name: Traveely
Description: Artificial Inteligence to the Trip Planning process
Website: http://www.traveely.com
Phone: **Email:** info@traveely.com
City: Barcelona **State:** CT **PC:** **Country: Spain**
Year Established: 2016 **Status 2020:** Active
Industries: ~ Travel and Transportation (58)

Company Name: Travisy
Description: Travisy is a startup that wants to transform the way travel is planned through the use of Artificial Intelligence.
Website:
Phone: **Email:** 37559@reference-encyclopedia-ai.net
City: Barcelona **State:** CT **PC:** **Country: Spain**
Year Established: 2016 **Status 2020:** Closed
Industries: Artificial Intelligence for:, ~ Travel and Transportation (58), ~ Travel and Transportation (58)

Company Name: Triplist.Me
Description: Travel recommendation platform
Website: http://www.triplist.me
Phone: **Email:** 4794@reference-encyclopedia-ai.net
City: Barcelona **State:** CT **PC:** **Country: Spain**
Year Established: **Status 2020:** Active
Industries:

Company Name: Unblur
Description: Unblur develops an AI software for public emergency services.
Website: http://unblur.co/
Phone: **Email:** info@unblur.co
City: Barcelona **State:** CT **PC:** **Country: Spain**
Year Established: 2015 **Status 2020:** Active
Industries:

Company Name: Unnax
Description: Unnax enables businesses to access financial-related data from customers in a simple and secure way.
Website: http://www.unnax.com
Phone: 902 65 06 51 **Email:** info@unnax.com
City: Barcelona **State:** CT **PC:** **Country: Spain**
Year Established: 2015 **Status 2020:** Active
Industries: ~ Banking and Financial Markets-Services (7), ~ Banking and Financial Markets-Services (7), Identity for:, Application Services for:, ~ Banking and Financial Markets-Services (7)

Company Name: viCloning
Description: viCloning is a sophisticated business tool.
Website: http://www.vicloning.net/
Phone: **Email:** 37626@reference-encyclopedia-ai.net
City: Barcelona **State:** CT **PC:** **Country: Spain**
Year Established: 2013 **Status 2020:** Active
Industries: Artificial Intelligence

Company Name: VIUME
Description: VIUME AI-driven SaaS for online merchandising optimization and product recommendations individualization.
Website: http://www.viume.co
Phone: **Email:** info@viume.co
City: Barcelona **State:** CT **PC:** **Country: Spain**
Year Established: 2017 **Status 2020:** Active
Industries: Artificial Intelligence for:, Computer Vision for:, E-Commerce for:, Natural Language Processing for:, Business Intelligence for:, Business Software as a Service Apps (SaaS Apps) for:, Computer Vision for:, Computer Vision

Company Name: Web360
Description: AI-driven SaaS that provides automatic website creation based on semantic data analysis.
Website: http://web360.: Spain
Phone: **Email:** info@web360.: Spain
City: Barcelona **State:** CT **PC:** **Country: Spain**
Year Established: **Status 2020:** Active
Industries: Artificial Intelligence for:, E-Commerce

Company Name: Websays
Description: Opinion Analytics and Social Media Monitoring, exploiting Machine Learning technology.
Website: http://www.websays.com
Phone: 34 936 67 35 43 **Email:** contact@websays.com
City: Barcelona **State:** CT **PC:** **Country: Spain**
Year Established: 2011 **Status 2020:** Active
Industries: Machine Learning for:, Web for:, ~ Social Assistance-Non-Profits (53), Data Management

Company Name: WeFish - Fishing Diary and Forecast
Description: Mobile App for recreational angle: Serbia
Website: http://wefish.app/en/
Phone: **Email:** info@wefish.app
City: Barcelona **State:** CT **PC:** **Country: Spain**
Year Established: 2017 **Status 2020:** Active
Industries: Big Data and Analytics for:, Machine Learning for:, ~ Arts-Entertainment-Recreation (4)

Company Name: Wide Eyes Technologies
Description: Wide Eyes delivers specific visual search technology that can recognize automatically any kind of fashion article from an image.
Website: http://www.wide-eyes.: Italy
Phone: **Email:** info@wide-eyes.: Italy
City: Barcelona **State:** CT **PC:** **Country: Spain**
Year Established: **Status 2020:** Active
Industries: Artificial Intelligence for:, ~ Fashion (16), Image Recognition for:, ~ Retail and Consumer Products (52)

Company Name: WWWOWWW
Description: Marketplace for Fashion & Beauty Market
Website: http://wwwowww.me
Phone: 34650751085 **Email:** carlos.mas@wwwowww.me
City: Barcelona **State:** CT **PC:** **Country: Spain**
Year Established: 2014 **Status 2020:** Active
Industries: Artificial Intelligence for:, ~ Beauty (8), E-Commerce for:, ~ Fashion (16)

Company Name: Zymvol Biomodeling
Description: Zymvol accelerates the discovery & development of new industrial enzymes through computer simulations
Website: http://zymvol.com/
Phone: 0034 617 927 468 **Email:** info@zymvol.com
City: Barcelona **State:** CT **PC:** **Country: Spain**
Year Established: 2017 **Status 2020:** Active
Industries: Artificial Intelligence for:, ~ Biotechnology (9)

Company Name: Nnergix
Description: Nnergix is a weather analytics startup focused in the renewable energy industry.
Website: http://www.nnergix.com/
Phone: **Email:** info@nnergix.com
City: Castelldefels **State:** CT **PC:** **Country: Spain**
Year Established: 2013 **Status 2020:** Active
Industries: Analytics for:, ~ Energy and Utilities (14), Machine Learning for:, ~ Energy and Utilities (14)

Company Name: Analitza Customer Intelligence
Description: Reduce customer churn and drive cross-sells with Analit: South Africa
Website: http://www.analitza.com/
Phone: **Email:** analitza@analitza.com
City: Girona **State:** CT **PC:** **Country: Spain**
Year Established: **Status 2020:** Active
Industries: Analytics for:, Artificial Intelligence for:, Big Data and Analytics for:, Business Intelligence for:, Machine Learning for:, Predictive Analytics for:, ~ Retail and Consumer Products (52)

Company Name: Maichinery
Description: Maichinery develops projects that are focused on the technological processes within an industry.
Website: http://maichinery.com/
Phone: 611 040 648 **Email:** info@maichinery.com
City: Girona **State:** CT **PC:** **Country: Spain**
Year Established: **Status 2020:** Active
Industries: Artificial Intelligence for:, Automation for:, IT Managed Services

Company Name: Newronia
Description: Newronia is a company that provides logistics information.
Website: http://www.newronia.com
Phone: 34 622 90 33 90 **Email:** info@newronia.com
City: Girona **State:** CT **PC:** **Country: Spain**
Year Established: **Status 2020:** Active
Industries:

Company Name: Braingaze
Description: Braingaze develops next-generation eye tracking software
Website: http://www.braingaze.com/
Phone: 34 93 169 65 72 **Email:** info@braingaze.eu
City: Mataro **State:** CT **PC:** **Country: Spain**
Year Established: 2013 **Status 2020:** Active
Industries: ~ Healthcare (20), Predictive Analytics

Company Name: ConnecThink
Description: Advanced knowledge discovery, transforming data into knowledge experience. A Graph-based semantic framework scoring engine
Website: http://connecthink.eu/
Phone: (606)390-120 **Email:** info@connecthink.eu
City: Sant Cugat Del Valles **State:** CT **PC:** **Country: Spain**
Year Established: **Status 2020:** Active
Industries: Artificial Intelligence for:, Business Applications for:, Big Data and Analytics for:, Business Intelligence for:, Content for:, IT Managed Services for:, ~ Administrative and Support Services (1), Cyber Security

Company Name: Ebotlution Systems
Description: Company determined to develop the most innovative technology in the robotics and AI field applied to Social needs.
Website: http://www.ebotlution.com
Phone: 34 645939038 **Email:** carles.rabaneda@ebotlution.com
City: Viladecans **State:** CT **PC:** **Country: Spain**
Year Established: **Status 2020:** Active
Industries: Artificial Intelligence for:, Robotics for:, ~ Professional Services (48)

Company Name: VidaApp
Description: VidaApp is a digital medicine startup manufacturer of medical devices and Artificial Intelligence ECG Software for cardiovascular health.
Website: http://www.vidaapp.com/
Phone: **Email:** info@vidaapp.com
City: Alcobendas **State:** MD **PC:** **Country: Spain**
Year Established: 2015 **Status 2020:** Active
Industries: Artificial Intelligence for:, ~ Healthcare (20), ~ Healthcare (20), Machine Learning for:, ~ Healthcare (20), ~ Healthcare (20), ~ Healthcare (20), Mobile

Company Name: Doc Foren: Sweden
Description: Doc Forense SL, has been created for demanding clients who, in the same way as our staff, ask for quality, honesty, speed, involvement.
Website: http://www.docforense.com/
Phone: 34 913 620 867 **Email:** info@docforense.com
City: Daganzo De Arriba **State:** Community of Madrid **PC:** **Country: Spain**
Year Established: **Status 2020:** Active
Industries: Artificial Intelligence for:, Databases for:, IT Managed Services

Company Name: Serendeepia
Description: Serendeepia provides machine learning and deep learning services.
Website: http://serendeepia.com/
Phone: **Email:** contact@serendeepia.com
City: Getafe **State:** MD **PC:** **Country: Spain**
Year Established: 2018 **Status 2020:** Active
Industries:

Company Name: Tinsa Digital
Description: Tinsa Digital provides information on the real estate market and automatic valuation models based on artificial intelligence.
Website: http://www.tinsadigital.com
Phone: 913364348 **Email:** hi@tinsadigital.com
City: Las Rozas De Madrid **State:** Community of Madrid **PC:** **Country: Spain**
Year Established: **Status 2020:** Active
Industries: Artificial Intelligence for:, ~ Media-Communications (41)

Company Name: Asociación de Robótica UC3M (ASROB)
Description: We are a group of people with huge interest on the fields of science and technology mainly applied to robotics.
Website: http://asrob.uc3m.: Spain
Phone: **Email:** asrobuc3m@gmail.com
City: Leganes **State:** Community of Madrid **PC:** **Country: Spain**
Year Established: **Status 2020:** Active
Industries: Artificial Intelligence for:, ~ Manufacturing-Electronic (30), Machine Learning for:, Robotics

Company Name: Evidence-Based Behavior
Description: Evidence-Based Behavior (eB2) is a company that develops healthcare solutions for psychiatric patients.
Website: http://eb2.tech/
Phone: **Email:** 36526@reference-encyclopedia-ai.net
City: Leganes **State:** MD **PC:** **Country: Spain**
Year Established: 2017 **Status 2020:** Active
Industries: Artificial Intelligence for:, ~ Healthcare (20), ~ Healthcare (20)

Company Name: Adtuo
Description: Adtuo: Facebook Ads with AI.
Website: http://adtuo.com/
Phone: 34 911 23 34 32 **Email:** info@adtuo.com
City: Madrid **State:** Community of Madrid **PC:** **Country: Spain**
Year Established: **Status 2020:** Active
Industries: ~ Media-Communications (41), Artificial Intelligence for:, Machine Learning for:, ~ Media-Communications (41), ~ Media-Communications (41), ~ Social Media (54), ~ Social Media (54)

Company Name: AI Saturdays
Description: AI Saturdays is an impact organization that empowers individuals to learn AI in a collaborative and project-based way.
Website: https://www.saturdays.ai/
Phone: 34 685 41 25 53 **Email:** info@saturdays.ai
City: Madrid **State:** MD **PC:** **Country: Spain**
Year Established: 2018 **Status 2020:** Active
Industries: Artificial Intelligence for:, ~ Education (13), ~ Education (13), ~ Education (13)

Company Name: AIRTIFICIAL
Description: AIRTIFICIAL is a technology company that specializes in the application of artificial intelligence.
Website: https://www.airtificial.com/
Phone: **Email:** info@airtificial.com
City: Madrid **State:** MD **PC:** **Country: Spain**
Year Established: 2018 **Status 2020:** Active
Industries: Artificial Intelligence for:, IT Managed Services for:, Robotics

Company Name: Altoro Consulting Group SL
Description: Artificial Intelligence & Big Data Analytics Solutions
Website: http://www.altoroanalytics.com/
Phone: 3492 4669780 **Email:** info@altoroanalytics.com
City: Madrid **State:** MD **PC:** **Country: Spain**
Year Established: 2011 **Status 2020:** Active
Industries: Analytics for:, Artificial Intelligence for:, Big Data and Analytics for:, IT Managed Services for:, Machine Learning for:, Data Management

Company Name: Anbotux
Description: Anbotux provides Customer Behaviour Understanding (CBU) & customer-centric analytics for chatbot era using a myriad of data sources & AI.
Website: http://www.anbotux.ai
Phone: **Email:** info@anbotux.ai
City: Madrid **State:** Community of Madrid **PC:** **Country: Spain**

Year Established: **Status 2020:** Active
Industries:

Company Name: AREX Real Estate Technologies
Description: Real Estate. Simplified.
Website: http://www.arexre.com
Phone: 34 677793486 **Email:** miguel.linera@arexre.com
City: Madrid **State:** Community of Madrid **PC:** **Country: Spain**
Year Established: **Status 2020:** Active
Industries: Artificial Intelligence for:, Blockchain for:, ~ Real Estate (49), Machine Learning for:, ~ Real Estate (49)

Company Name: Arus Defence
Description: Arus Defence leverages AI human-machine interfaces and low-code development to create custom solutions for organization.
Website:
Phone: 34661310158 **Email:** 36091@reference-encyclopedia-ai.net
City: Madrid **State:** MD **PC:** **Country: Spain**
Year Established: 2017 **Status 2020:** Closed
Industries: Artificial Intelligence for:, Machine Learning for:, Security

Company Name: Baobab Solucion: Spain
Description: Baobab Soluciones provides customized predictive and prescriptive analytics solutions to large-scale problems to assist companies.
Website: http://baobabsoluciones.es/
Phone: 34 915 337 301 **Email:** info@baobabsoluciones.: Spain
City: Madrid **State:** MD **PC:** **Country: Spain**
Year Established: 2011 **Status 2020:** Active
Industries: Analytics for:, Artificial Intelligence

Company Name: bdeo
Description: Bdeo provides visual intelligence to the insurance industry
Website: http://www.bdeo.io
Phone: 34 910 888 180 **Email:** info@bdeo.: Spain
City: Madrid **State:** Community of Madrid **PC:** **Country: Spain**
Year Established: **Status 2020:** Active
Industries: Artificial Intelligence for:, Augmented Reality for:, Blockchain for:, ~ Media-Communications (41)

Company Name: biicode
Description: biicode is a C and C dependencies manager with a hosting service.
Website: http://www.biicode.com
Phone: **Email:** info@biicode.com
City: Madrid **State:** Community of Madrid **PC:** **Country: Spain**
Year Established: **Status 2020:** Active
Industries: Artificial Intelligence for:, Application Services for:, ~ Manufacturing-Electronic (30), Robotics for:, ~ Professional Services (48), ~ Arts-Entertainment-Recreation (4)

Company **Name:** Botslovers
Description: Botslovers specializes in creating and developing ChatBots with Artificial Intelligence.
Website: http://www.botslovers.com/
Phone: 34 658568561 **Email:** hola@botslovers.com
City: Madrid **State:** MD **PC:** **Country: Spain**
Year Established: 2017 **Status 2020:** Active
Industries: Artificial Intelligence for:, IT Managed Services for:, IT Managed Services for:, Machine Learning

Company Name: Capaball
Description: Capaball is an A.I. tool for the creation of personalized learning plans with the goal of training the workers of the future.
Website: http://capaball.com
Phone: (34) 620 24 27 77 **Email:** sixto@capaball.com
City: Madrid **State:** Community of Madrid **PC:** **Country: Spain**
Year Established: **Status 2020:** Active
Industries: Artificial Intelligence for:, ~ Education (13), ~ Education (13), Machine Learning

Company Name: Clever ecommerce
Description: Create and manage your Google Ads campaigns with the powerful Clever ecommerce tech, based on Artificial Intelligence.
Website: http://www.cleverecommerce.com
Phone: 34 91 017 9993 **Email:** hello@cleverecommerce.com
City: Madrid **State:** MD **PC:** **Country: Spain**
Year Established: 2012 **Status 2020:** Active
Industries: Artificial Intelligence for:, Digital Marketing for:, E-Commerce for:, Automation for:, Digital Marketing for:, Digital Marketing for:, Content

Company Name: Clippingbook
Description: ClippingBook is a personal platform to discover new, relevant content and share it with the world.
Website: http://www.clippingbook.com/
Phone: **Email:** clippingbook@gmail.com
City: Madrid **State:** MD **PC:** **Country: Spain**
Year Established: 2012 **Status 2020:** Closed
Industries: Application Services for:, ~ Social Assistance-Non-Profits (53)

Company Name: Commons
Description: Commons is an advanced chatbot engine, empathic AI, and personal autonomous agents.
Website: http://www.commons.fm/
Phone: **Email:** info@commons.fm
City: Madrid **State:** Community of Madrid **PC:** **Country: Spain**
Year Established: **Status 2020:** Active
Industries: Artificial Intelligence for:, Content for:, IT Managed Services for:, IT Managed Services

Company Name: Delta Ai
Description: Delta AI specializes in business digitalization applications of artificial intelligence.
Website: http://www.delta-ai.com
Phone: (3461) 590-4253 **Email:** founders@wearedeltalabs.com
City: Madrid **State:** MD **PC:** **Country: Spain**
Year Established: 2017 **Status 2020:** Active
Industries: Application Services for:, Artificial Intelligence for:, Web

Company Name: Dietame
Description: Dietame is a AI based platform for personal and online advisory in Nutrition offering custom diet plans and recommendations.
Website: http://dietame.com/
Phone: **Email:** contacto@dietame.com
City: Madrid **State:** MD **PC:** **Country: Spain**
Year Established: 2017 **Status 2020:** Active
Industries: ~ Healthcare (20), Machine Learning for:, ~ Healthcare (20), Internet of Things (IoT) for:, ~ Healthcare (20)

Company Name: DISCOPERI
Description: DISCOPERI is a startup company fighting for making roads safer.
Website: http://www.discoperi.com
Phone: **Email:** general@discoperi.com
City: Madrid **State:** Community of Madrid **PC:** **Country: Spain**
Year Established: **Status 2020:** Active
Industries: Artificial Intelligence for:, ~ Automotive (5), Big Data and Analytics

Company Name: Dive
Description: We are a full stack AI company, enabling businesses to create, "productize" and scale data-driven solutions, quickly and economically
Website: http://dive.tv/
Phone: **Email:** 36443@reference-encyclopedia-ai.net
City: Madrid **State:** MD **PC:** **Country: Spain**

Year Established: 2015 **Status 2020:** Active
Industries:

Company Name: Easyponic
Description: Easyponic is the developer of Nanny, an agricultural intelligence device that takes care of hydroponic cultures.
Website: http://easyponic.com/en/
Phone: **Email:** info@easyponic.com
City: Madrid **State:** Community of Madrid **PC:** **Country: Spain**
Year Established: **Status 2020:** Active
Industries: ~ Agriculture (3), Artificial Intelligence for:, ~ Manufacturing-Electronic (30)

Company Name: Epic Labs
Description: We are experimenting how AI, blockchain and new economies could make a disruptive impact in on-going business, communities and society
Website: http://www.epiclabs.io/
Phone: **Email:** info@epiclabs.io
City: Madrid **State:** MD **PC:** **Country: Spain**
Year Established: 2015 **Status 2020:** Active
Industries: Artificial Intelligence for:, Blockchain for:, Machine Learning for:, ~ Arts-Entertainment-Recreation (4)

Company Name: eSmart: ITALY
Description: ESmartIT is a technology startup that enable entrepreneurs to interact with customers in real time.
Website: http://www.esmartit.: Spain
Phone: **Email:** 36518@reference-encyclopedia-ai.net
City: Madrid **State:** MD **PC:** **Country: Spain**
Year Established: 2018 **Status 2020:** Active
Industries: Analytics for:, Artificial Intelligence for:, Big Data and Analytics for:, IT Managed Services for:, Compute

Company Name: Espaf: Israel
Description: Espafil is developes a tool that allows companies to predict customer behavior in real time by using data they already have.
Website: http://www.espafiltech.com
Phone: **Email:** info@espafiltech.com
City: Madrid **State:** Community of Madrid **PC:** **Country: Spain**
Year Established: **Status 2020:** Active
Industries: Artificial Intelligence for:, Big Data and Analytics for:, E-Commerce for:, Machine Learning for:, ~ Retail and Consumer Products (52), Cyber Security

Company Name: ETHYKA
Description: ETHYKA is an Artificial Intelligence (AI) platform developed to protect artificial intelligence systems and customer channels.
Website: http://www.ethyka.co
Phone: (34) 91 892 47 37 **Email:** info@ethyka.co
City: Madrid **State:** MD **PC:** **Country: Spain**
Year Established: 2017 **Status 2020:** Active
Industries: Artificial Intelligence for:, IT Managed Services

Company Name: FFWD
Description: Fast Forward is a strategic foresight and future anticipation consultancy
Website: http://www.ffwd.is/
Phone: **Email:** hello@ffwd.
City: Madrid **State:** MD **PC:** **Country: Spain**
Year Established: 2015 **Status 2020:** Active
Industries: Business Intelligence for:, Predictive Analytics

Company Name: Findasen: Sweden
Description: Our mission is to innovate and transform the way organizations build relationships with people.
Website: http://www.findasense.com
Phone: 34 911 87 52 32 **Email:** hola@findasense.com
City: Madrid **State:** Community of Madrid **PC:** **Country: Spain**
Year Established: **Status 2020:** Active
Industries: Artificial Intelligence for:, ~ Healthcare (20), IT Managed Services for:, ~ Administrative and Support Services (1), ~ Social Media (54)

Company Name: Frenetic
Description: Frenetic is a disrupting technology created for designing magnetic components using Artificial Intelligence techniques.
Website: http://spfrenetic.com/
Phone: 34 915 29 60 07 **Email:** info@spfrenetic.com
City: Madrid **State:** MD **PC:** **Country: Spain**
Year Established: 2015 **Status 2020:** Active
Industries: Artificial Intelligence for:, ~ Energy and Utilities (14)

Company Name: Geoblink
Description: Geoblink, the Location Intelligence solution specialised in Retail, Real Estate and FMCG.
Website: http://www.geoblink.com
Phone: 34 910 599784 **Email:** info@geoblink.com
City: Madrid **State:** Community of Madrid **PC:** **Country: Spain**
Year Established: **Status 2020:** Active
Industries: Analytics for:, Artificial Intelligence for:, Big Data and Analytics for:, Business Intelligence

Company Name: GoFood: Ireland
Description: Find the best dishes from people you trust
Website: http://gofoodie.app/
Phone: **Email:** info@gofoodie.: Spain
City: Madrid **State:** Community of Madrid **PC:** **Country: Spain**
Year Established: **Status 2020:** Active
Industries: Artificial Intelligence for:, ~ Food and Beverage (17), Machine Learning for:, ~ Food and Beverage (17)

Company Name: Graphext
Description: Automate your AI data science workflow with powerful UIs for your analysts and APIs for your developers.
Website: http://graphext.com
Phone: **Email:** hello@graphext.com
City: Madrid **State:** Community of Madrid **PC:** **Country: Spain**
Year Established: **Status 2020:** Active
Industries: Analytics for:, Artificial Intelligence for:, Business Intelligence for:, Databases for:, Data Management for:, Machine Learning for:, ~ Media-Communications (41), Predictive Analytics for:, Automation

Company Name: Hipoo
Description: Hipoo is the first digital platform for comparison and concession of mortgage loans
Website: http://www.hipoo.com/
Phone: 900 973 270 **Email:** hola@hipoo.com
City: Madrid **State:** Community of Madrid **PC:** **Country: Spain**
Year Established: **Status 2020:** Active
Industries: Artificial Intelligence for:, ~ Banking and Financial Markets-Services (7), Security

Company Name: Human Affinity Platform
Description: Human Affinity Platform (HAP) The power of the new generation of predictive personality algorithms.
Website: http://humanaffinityplatform.com/
Phone: 34 914 578 401 **Email:** hap@humanaffinityplatform.com
City: Madrid **State:** MD **PC:** **Country: Spain**
Year Established: 2017 **Status 2020:** Active
Industries: Big Data and Analytics for:, Web for:, Machine Learning for:, ~ Healthcare (20)

Company Name: IXION
Description: IXION is a highly innovative SME that develops automation solutions and assimilates the most advanced and efficient technologies.
Website: http://ixion.es/en/
Phone: 34914401833 **Email:** info@ixion.: Spain
City: Madrid **State:** Community of Madrid **PC:** **Country: Spain**

Year Established: **Status 2020:** Active
Industries:

Company Name: Jelly Data
Description: Jelly Data is a conversational Business Intelligence Solution allowing non technical people to talk with their data
Website: http://jellydata.io
Phone: **Email:** 36824@reference-encyclopedia-ai.net
City: Madrid **State:** MD **PC:** **Country: Spain**
Year Established: 2018 **Status 2020:** Active
Industries: Analytics for:, Big Data and Analytics for:, IT Managed Services for:, Web for:, Machine Learning

Company Name: Jump into Reality
Description: Jump Into Reality is a technological company awarded in 2018 with the Digital El Espanol Prize in the category of Artificial Intelligence.
Website: http://www.jumpintoreality.com/home
Phone: **Email:** hey@jumpintoreality.com
City: Madrid **State:** MD **PC:** **Country: Spain**
Year Established: 2017 **Status 2020:** Active
Industries: Artificial Intelligence for:, Virtual Reality (VR)

Company Name: JUMP TV SOLUTIONS
Description: A data-as-a-service insights platform that allows video service providers to increase monetization and ROI through business intelligence
Website: http://www.jumptvs.com/
Phone: 34 913 77 62 72 **Email:** info@jumptvs.com
City: Madrid **State:** MD **PC:** **Country: Spain**
Year Established: 2016 **Status 2020:** Active
Industries: Artificial Intelligence for:, Web

Company Name: Knowdle AI
Description: Knowdle AI provides artificial collective intelligence solutions.
Website: http://www.knowdle.ai/
Phone: 34 910 800 000 **Email:** 36858@reference-encyclopedia-ai.net
City: Madrid **State:** MD **PC:** **Country: Spain**
Year Established: 2014 **Status 2020:** Active
Industries: Artificial Intelligence for:, Big Data and Analytics

Company Name: Lang.ai
Description: Provides technologies for semantic understanding of any kind of text. The first unsupervised AI for language understanding.
Website: http://www.lang.ai
Phone: 34910703821 **Email:** jpenalva@lang.ai
City: Madrid **State:** Community of Madrid **PC:** **Country: Spain**
Year Established: **Status 2020:** Active
Industries: Artificial Intelligence for:, ~ Social Media (54)

Company **Name:** LAWERS
Description: The first online marketplace for litigation funding in Spain powered by Machine Learning, Blockchain and Smart Contracts.
Website: http://www.lawers.: Spain
Phone: **Email:** info@lawers.: Spain
City: Madrid **State:** Community of Madrid **PC:** **Country: Spain**
Year Established: **Status 2020:** Active
Industries: Analytics for:, Artificial Intelligence for:, Big Data and Analytics for:, Blockchain for:, ~ Banking and Financial Markets-Services (7), ~ Banking and Financial Markets-Services (7), ~ Insurance (25), Web for:, Machine Learning for:, ~ Professional Services (48)

Company Name: LightFlow
Description: LightFlow, an Epic Labs spin-off, is an AI-driven video optimization platform that helps video publishers to improve Quality of Experience.
Website: http://lightflow.media/
Phone: **Email:** alfonso@epiclabs.io
City: Madrid **State:** MD **PC:** **Country: Spain**
Year Established: 2018 **Status 2020:** Active
Industries: Artificial Intelligence for:, Web for:, Machine Learning for:, ~ Media-Communications (41), ~ Media-Communications (41)

Company Name: Lullaai: Baby Sleep App
Description: Lullaai is a AI assisted baby sleep app.
Website: http://www.lullaai.com
Phone: **Email:** contact@lullaai.com
City: Madrid **State:** MD **PC:** **Country: Spain**
Year Established: 2018 **Status 2020:** Active
Industries: Artificial Intelligence for:, ~ Healthcare (20), ~ Healthcare (20), IT Managed Services for:, Machine Learning for:, ~ Healthcare (20)

Company Name: MedicSen
Description: MedicSen is a start-up dedicated to health care, to technological innovation as a key tool.
Website: http://medicsen.com/
Phone: 34677644510 **Email:** info@medicsen.com
City: Madrid **State:** Community of Madrid **PC:** **Country: Spain**
Year Established: **Status 2020:** Active
Industries: Analytics for:, ~ Biotechnology (131), ~ Healthcare (142), ~ Pharmaceuticals (168), ~ Biotechnology (192), ~ Healthcare (203), ~ Pharmaceuticals (229), Artificial Intelligence for:, ~ Biotechnology (9), ~ Healthcare (20), ~ Manufacturing-Medical Equipment-Suppli: Spain

Company Name: MeetF: Italy
Description: MeetFit is the first startup that connects people in "fitness" world.
Website: http://www.meetfit.eu/
Phone: **Email:** info@active24.cz
City: Madrid **State:** MD **PC:** **Country: Spain**
Year Established: 2018 **Status 2020:** Active
Industries: Artificial Intelligence for:, ~ Healthcare (20), ~ Healthcare (20)

Company Name: Mirubee
Description: Mirubee is the manufacturer Mirubox that allows to save energy intended only to households, knowing your power consumption in real time.
Website: mirubee.com
Phone: **Email:** info@mirubee.com
City: Madrid **State:** Community of Madrid **PC:** **Country: Spain**
Year Established: **Status 2020:** Active
Industries: Artificial Intelligence for:, ~ Energy and Utilities (14)

Company Name: MMG
Description: MMG is an innovative technological start-up focused on creating a global healthcare community and a semantic AI platform.
Website: http://mmg-ai.com
Phone: (3491) 649-2292 **Email:** info@medlabmg.com
City: Madrid **State:** MD **PC:** **Country: Spain**
Year Established: 2015 **Status 2020:** Active
Industries: Artificial Intelligence for:, Business Intelligence for:, ~ Healthcare (20), IT Managed Services for:, Machine Learning for:, ~ Healthcare (20), ~ Healthcare (20), Content for:, Content

Company Name: monoceros.xyz
Description: We are an Innovation Studio focused on Conversational Experienc: Spain
Website: http://monoceros.xyz
Phone: **Email:** hello@monoceros.xyz
City: Madrid **State:** MD **PC:** **Country: Spain**
Year Established: 2017 **Status 2020:** Active
Industries:

Company Name: Nektiu S.L.
Description: Nektiu S.L. is a providing multiple layers of artificial intelligence to the businesses of our clients.
Website: http://nektiu.com/
Phone: 34 910059966 **Email:** customers@nektiu.com
City: Madrid **State:** MD **PC:** **Country: Spain**

Year Established: 2017 **Status 2020:** Active
Industries:

Company Name: Neovis Talents
Description: Neovis Talents develops recruitment software using AI.
Website: http://www.neovistalents.com
Phone: 34-699011148 **Email:** info@neovistalents.com
City: Madrid **State:** MD **PC:** **Country: Spain**
Year Established: 2019 **Status 2020:** Active
Industries: Artificial Intelligence

Company Name: Nextail
Description: A cloud-based platform that combines artificial intelligence and prescriptive analytics to upgrade retailers' inventory management process: Spain
Website: http://nextail.co
Phone: **Email:** info@nextail.co
City: Madrid **State:** MD **PC:** **Country: Spain**
Year Established: 2014 **Status 2020:** Active
Industries: Artificial Intelligence for:, Enterprise Application Services for:, ~ Fashion (16), Mobile for:, Business Software as a Service Apps (SaaS Apps)

Company Name: NUBEPRINT
Description: NUBEPRINT is a service provider of the lean management concepts that control and reduce the costs of managing copiers and printers.
Website: http://nubeprint.com
Phone: 910010247 **Email:** asanchez@nubeprint.com
City: Madrid **State:** MD **PC:** **Country: Spain**
Year Established: 2010 **Status 2020:** Active
Industries: Predictive Analytics for:, ~ Media-Communications (41)

Company Name: O2O - MO2O I Digital Business, Mobile One2One
Description: O2O is specialized on Digital Strategy and Digital Transformation, in areas such as Innovation, Mobility, e-Commerce or Biz Digitalization.
Website: http://www.mo2o.com
Phone: 34 910 609 514 **Email:** info@mo2o.com
City: Madrid **State:** Community of Madrid **PC:** **Country: Spain**
Year Established: **Status 2020:** Active
Industries: Analytics for:, Application Services for:, Artificial Intelligence for:, Big Data and Analytics for:, ~ E-Commerce (12), Digital Marketing for:, E-Commerce for:, Web for:, Machine Learning for:, Mobile for:, ~ Media-Communications (41), ~ Banking and Financial Mar: Kenya

Company Name: OrbitalAds
Description: AI & NLP applied to semantic targeting in Google Ads
Website: http://orbitalads.com
Phone: 692619624 **Email:** founders@orbitalads.com
City: Madrid **State:** MD **PC:** **Country: Spain**
Year Established: 2016 **Status 2020:** Active
Industries: Artificial Intelligence for:, Enterprise Application Services for:, Natural Language Processing

Company Name: Pix Interactive
Description: Pix Interactive is an artificial intelligence-based interactive video platform.
Website: http://pix-videos.com/
Phone: 34 628 89 10 72 **Email:** info@pix-videos.com
City: Madrid **State:** MD **PC:** **Country: Spain**
Year Established: 2016 **Status 2020:** Active
Industries: Artificial Intelligence

Company Name: Pixelabs
Description: Pixelabs provides optimization and automation of healthcare processes in the medical field.
Website: http://pixelabs.es/
Phone: 34 918 265 276 **Email:** info@pixelabs.: Spain
City: Madrid **State:** MD **PC:** **Country: Spain**
Year Established: 2015 **Status 2020:** Active
Industries: Artificial Intelligence for:, ~ Healthcare (20), IT Managed Services for:, Machine Learning

Company Name: Play2Speak
Description: Play2Speak combines digital storytelling with AI to help learner practice speaking a new language in VR
Website: http://play2speak.com/
Phone: **Email:** info@play2speak.com
City: Madrid **State:** Community of Madrid **PC:** **Country: Spain**
Year Established: **Status 2020:** Active
Industries: Artificial Intelligence for:, ~ Education (13), ~ Education (13)

Company Name: Progressive Blue Tech
Description: Progressive Blue Tech is an ICT company specializing in predictive analytics applied to large data volumes "Big Data".
Website: http://www.progressive-blue.es/
Phone: **Email:** info@progressive-blue.: Spain
City: Madrid **State:** MD **PC:** **Country: Spain**
Year Established: 2014 **Status 2020:** Active
Industries: Artificial Intelligence for:, IT Managed Services

Company Name: Quantask
Description: Quantask is an information technology and AI consulting company.
Website: http://quantask.com/
Phone: **Email:** 37240@reference-encyclopedia-ai.net
City: Madrid **State:** MD **PC:** **Country: Spain**
Year Established: 2017 **Status 2020:** Active
Industries: Artificial Intelligence for:, IT Managed Services

Company Name: Recognai
Description: Problems and data come in many forms and shapes. Recognai makes artificial intelligence solutions that fit your problems and data shapes.
Website: http://recogn.ai
Phone: **Email:** contact@recogn.ai
City: Madrid **State:** Community of Madrid **PC:** **Country: Spain**
Year Established: **Status 2020:** Active
Industries: Analytics for:, Artificial Intelligence for:, Predictive Analytics

Company Name: Samsamia Technologies
Description: Samsamia connects fashion brands with their costumers by doing FASHION RECOGNITION.
Website: http://www.samsamia.com
Phone: **Email:** info@samsamia.com
City: Madrid **State:** Community of Madrid **PC:** **Country: Spain**
Year Established: **Status 2020:** Active
Industries: Artificial Intelligence for:, Cloud for:, Computer Vision for:, ~ Fashion (16)

Company Name: Savana
Description: Electronic Health Records reuse, with Clinical Natural Language Processing.
Website: http://savanamed.com/
Phone: **Email:** 37339@reference-encyclopedia-ai.net
City: Madrid **State:** MD **PC:** **Country: Spain**
Year Established: 2014 **Status 2020:** Active
Industries: Artificial Intelligence for:, ~ Healthcare (20)

Company Name: Savelist
Description: Savelist is a platform for shoppers to discover, save and buy products of their interest in one place.
Website: http://savelist.co
Phone: **Email:** hello@savelist.co
City: Madrid **State:** Community of Madrid **PC:** **Country: Spain**
Year Established: **Status 2020:** Active
Industries:

Company Name: Sentimer Technologies
Description: Sentimer is an AI Chatbot platform for customer acquisition, X-selling and customer service through personalized & interactive experience.
Website: http://sentimer.com
Phone: 34 639 11 39 72 **Email:** info@sentimer.com
City: Madrid **State:** MD **PC:** **Country: Spain**
Year Established: 2016 **Status 2020:** Active
Industries: Artificial Intelligence for:, ~ Customer Relationship Management (11), IT Managed Services

Company Name: Sincrolab
Description: Sincrolab offers an Artificial Intelligence digital prescription neuro medicine based on videogames delivered through mobile devices.
Website: http://www.sincrolab.es/
Phone: 34 627 73 68 87 **Email:** info@sincrolab.: Spain
City: Madrid **State:** MD **PC:** **Country: Spain**
Year Established: 2013 **Status 2020:** Active
Industries: Artificial Intelligence for:, ~ Healthcare (20), ~ Healthcare (20)

Company Name: Singularity Experts
Description: Singularity Experts is an artificial intelligence based career counseling company.
Website: http://singularity-experts.com/
Phone: 34 919 036 731 **Email:** info@singularity-experts.com
City: Madrid **State:** MD **PC:** **Country: Spain**
Year Established: 2018 **Status 2020:** Active
Industries:

Company Name: SkanSen: Sweden
Description: SkanSense offers FARSIGHTS a patented technology to locate objects in satellite imagery, even without knowing its size and shape.
Website: http://www.skansense.com/
Phone: **Email:** info@skansense.com
City: Madrid **State:** MD **PC:** **Country: Spain**
Year Established: 2016 **Status 2020:** Active
Industries: ~ Aerospace and Defense (2), Machine Learning for:, ~ Telecommunications (56)

Company Name: SMEBOOK
Description: SMEBOOK is a one-stop shop for technology-based companies and their employe: Spain
Website: http://www.smebook.eu
Phone: 34 912 91 84 53 **Email:** info@smebook.eu
City: Madrid **State:** MD **PC:** **Country: Spain**
Year Established: 2017 **Status 2020:** Active
Industries: Business Intelligence for:, IT Managed Services for:, Natural Language Processing

Company Name: Social-3
Description: Social Network Analysis and Predictive Analytics
Website: http://www.social-3.com/
Phone: **Email:** sales@social-3.com
City: Madrid **State:** MD **PC:** **Country: Spain**
Year Established: 2010 **Status 2020:** Active
Industries: Analytics for:, Predictive Analytics

Company Name: source{d}
Description: Building the first AI that understands code
Website: http://sourced.tech/
Phone: **Email:** hello@sourced.tech
City: Madrid **State:** Community of Madrid **PC:** **Country: Spain**
Year Established: **Status 2020:** Active
Industries: Analytics for:, Artificial Intelligence for:, Machine Learning for:, Application Services for:, ~ Professional Services (48)

Company Name: Spotlab
Description: Spotlab is a medical technology company.
Website: http://www.spotlab.org
Phone: **Email:** info@spotlab.org
City: Madrid **State:** MD **PC:** **Country: Spain**
Year Established: 2017 **Status 2020:** Active
Industries: Artificial Intelligence

Company Name: Taiger
Description: Taiger is an European firm specializing in knowledge access solutions and helps firms solve information access problems.
Website: http://www.taiger.com/
Phone: 6596570242 **Email:** joshua.kwah@taiger.com
City: Madrid **State:** Community of Madrid **PC:** **Country: Spain**
Year Established: **Status 2020:** Active
Industries: Artificial Intelligence for:, IT Managed Services for:, ~ Professional Services (48)

Company Name: The AIBeeHIve Accelerator
Description: We provide a disruptive #AI platform for entrepreneurs that enables effective technology needed to outperform competitors.
Website: http://www.aibeehive.ai/
Phone: 34 910 800 000 **Email:** investors@knowdle.com
City: Madrid **State:** MD **PC:** **Country: Spain**
Year Established: 2011 **Status 2020:** Active
Industries: Artificial Intelligence for:, ~ Banking and Financial Markets-Services (7), IT Managed Services

Company Name: The Sideways Project
Description: The Sideways Project makes autonomous wheelchair with AI.
Website: http://www.thesidewaysproject.com/
Phone: **Email:** marco@thesidewaysproject.com
City: Madrid **State:** MD **PC:** **Country: Spain**
Year Established: 2019 **Status 2020:** Active
Industries: Artificial Intelligence for:, ~ Automotive (5)

Company Name: Triporate
Description: Triporate simplifies Corporate Travel using Artificial Intelligence.
Website: http://www.triporate.com
Phone: 34911233553 **Email:** hello@triporate.com
City: Madrid **State:** Community of Madrid **PC:** **Country: Spain**
Year Established: **Status 2020:** Active
Industries: Artificial Intelligence for:, IT Managed Services for:, ~ Travel and Transportation (58)

Company Name: Unishoper
Description: Unishoper is the artificial intelligence technology that decodes the emotional, bodily and psychological reactions of customers.
Website: http://www.unishoper.com/EN/
Phone: (51) 981 166 709 **Email:** hello@unishoper.com
City: Madrid **State:** MD **PC:** **Country: Spain**
Year Established: 2018 **Status 2020:** Active
Industries: Artificial Intelligence for:, Machine Learning for:, Application Services

Company Name: Urban Data Eye
Description: Urban Data Eye is an analytics platform that provides data to optimize large spaces.
Website: http://www.urbandataeye.com/
Phone: **Email:** info@urbandataeye.com
City: Madrid **State:** MD **PC:** **Country: Spain**
Year Established: 2017 **Status 2020:** Active
Industries:

Company Name: Vaartani
Description: Vaartani provides machine learning as service to businesses to transform product information into trustworthy answers to shoppers' queries.
Website: http://www.vaartani.com/
Phone: **Email:** hello@vaartani.com
City: Madrid **State:** MD **PC:** **Country: Spain**
Year Established: 2018 **Status 2020:** Active
Industries: Web for:, Machine Learning

Company Name: WannaBot
Description: WannaBot is an artificial intelligence technology platform for the development of chatbots.
Website: http://www.wannabot.io
Phone: 34 912 406 458 **Email:** web@wannabot.io
City: Madrid **State:** MD **PC:** **Country: Spain**
Year Established: 2017 **Status 2020:** Active
Industries: Artificial Intelligence for:, IT Managed Services

Company Name: WOOM
Description: WOOM is Data science for Women's and Reproductive Heal:Thailand
Website: http://www.woomfertility.com/
Phone: 34653393310 **Email:** laurence@woomfertility.com
City: Madrid **State:** MD **PC:** **Country: Spain**
Year Established: 2015 **Status 2020:** Active
Industries: Application Services for:, Artificial Intelligence for:, ~ Healthcare (20)

Company Name: EtsFactory
Description: EtsFactory develops artificial intelligence algorithms to make investment decisions based on research and science.
Website: http://www.etsfactory.com/
Phone: 34 91 357 24 71 **Email:** info@etsfactory.com
City: Pozuelo De Alarcon **State:** Community of Madrid **PC:** **Country: Spain**
Year Established: **Status 2020:** Active
Industries: Artificial Intelligence for:, ~ Banking and Financial Markets-Services (7), ~ Banking and Financial Markets-Services (7)

Company Name: wiseri
Description: Wiseri is an online recruitment platform that captivates, guides, and motivates human capital as a resource for enterprises.
Website: http://www.wiseri.com
Phone: 34 63 555 15 41 **Email:** info@wiseri.com
City: San Sebastian De Los Reyes **State:** Community of Madrid **PC:** **Country: Spain**
Year Established: **Status 2020:** Active
Industries: Artificial Intelligence for:, Databases for:, ~ Gaming (18), ~ Human Resources (24), Cyber Security

Company Name: Lurtis Rules
Description: A cloud service that produces complete 3D scenarios out of user constraints
Website: http://www.lurtis.com
Phone: **Email:** investment@lurtis.com
City: Mostoles **State:** Comunidad de Madrid **PC:** **Country: Spain**
Year Established: **Status 2020:** Active
Industries: Artificial Intelligence for:, ~ Arts-Entertainment-Recreation (4), ~ Arts-Entertainment-Recreation (4)

Company Name: Barkibu
Description: Barkibu is is working to prevent pet illnesses and predicting consumer behavior in retail through their robust AI platform
Website: http://www.barkibu.com/
Phone: **Email:** guau@barkibu.com
City: A Coruna **State:** GA **PC:** **Country: Spain**
Year Established: 2013 **Status 2020:** Active
Industries: Artificial Intelligence for:, Machine Learning for:, Mobile for:, ~ Retail and Consumer Products (52), ~ Life Sciences (27)

Company Name: cinfo
Description: automated tv, remote production, cloud production, synthetic video, corporate tv, retail tv, artificial intelligence for video, metadata
Website: http://www.cinfo.: Spain
Phone: (3469) 810-1022 **Email:** decoder@cinfo.: Spain
City: A Coruna **State:** GA **PC:** **Country: Spain**
Year Established: 2015 **Status 2020:** Active
Industries: Artificial Intelligence for:, Computer Vision for:, Web for:, Machine Learning for:, ~ Arts-Entertainment-Recreation (4), ~ Media-Communications (41), ~ Media-Communications (41), Virtual Reality (VR)

Company Name: Improving Metrics
Description: We are a Tech company specialized in digital marketing, data analytics, artificial intelligence, data quality and business optimization.
Website: http://www.improvingmetrics.com
Phone: (34) 881 929 106 **Email:** info@improvingmetrics.com
City: A Coruna **State:** GA **PC:** **Country: Spain**
Year Established: 2011 **Status 2020:** Active
Industries: Analytics for:, Artificial Intelligence for:, Big Data and Analytics for:, IT Managed Services for:, Machine Learning for:, Business Process and Operations

Company Name: Appentra
Description: Deep Tech company creating DevOps tools for the key stages of software development in high performance software applications.
Website: http://www.appentra.com
Phone: 34 881 01 55 56 **Email:** info@appentra.com
City: A Coruña **State:** GA **PC:** **Country: Spain**
Year Established: 2012 **Status 2020:** Active
Industries: Analytics for:, Artificial Intelligence for:, Big Data and Analytics for:, Application Services for:, ~ Education (13)

Company Name: Artabro Tech
Description: Artabro Tech is an information technology and artificial intelligence consulting company.
Website: http://www.artabrotech.com
Phone: 34-981323889 **Email:** info@artabrotech.com
City: Ferrol **State:** GA **PC:** **Country: Spain**
Year Established: 2017 **Status 2020:** Active
Industries: Artificial Intelligence for:, IT Managed Services

Company Name: Emerita Legal
Description: Emerita Legal combines judicial BigData with artificial intelligence to provide a key advantage to lawyers and users of legal services.
Website: http://www.emerita.legal/
Phone: 34 604 00 38 60 **Email:** info@emerita.legal
City: Santiago De Compostela **State:** GA **PC:** **Country: Spain**
Year Established: 2017 **Status 2020:** Active
Industries: Artificial Intelligence for:, IT Managed Services

Company Name: Marexi AI
Description: Marexi AI is a unique platform in Spain for developing and commercializing AI for different industries.
Website:
Phone: **Email:** info@marexi-group.com
City: Vigo **State:** GA **PC:** **Country: Spain**
Year Established: **Status 2020:** Active
Industries: Artificial Intelligence for:, Computer Vision for:, ~ Food and Beverage (17), ~ Healthcare (20), ~ Healthcare (20), Image Recognition for:, Machine Learning for:, ~ Social-Environmental-Physical-Engineering Sciences (55)

Company Name: NORLEAN
Description: Simulation and Digital Twin tool for digital factories (industry 4.0) and business models
Website: http://www.norlean.com
Phone: 34 666 572 965 **Email:** epg@norlean.com
City: Vigo **State:** GA **PC:** **Country: Spain**
Year Established: 2017 **Status 2020:** Active
Industries:

Company Name: Xesol Innovation
Description: Xesol Innovation delivers solutions for autonomous vehicles.
Website: http://www.xesolinnovation.com
Phone: 34986954560 **Email:** info@xesolinnovation.com
City: Vigo **State:** GA **PC:** **Country: Spain**

Year Established: **Status 2020:** Active
Industries: Artificial Intelligence for:, ~ Automotive (5), ~ Automotive (5), Machine Learning for:, ~ Professional Services (48)

Company Name: Techvolucion
Description: Techvolucion provides artificial intelligence and big data services.
Website: http://www.techvolucion.com/
Phone: 34 941 100 061 **Email:** info@techvolucion.com
City: Logroño **State:** RI **PC:** **Country: Spain**
Year Established: 2012 **Status 2020:** Active
Industries: Artificial Intelligence for:, Big Data and Analytics for:, IT Managed Services

Company Name: Traddu
Description: Traddu Translation Agency is a technology and artificial intelligence agency.
Website: http://www.traddu.com
Phone: 34-941 899 745 **Email:** info@traddu.com
City: Logroño **State:** RI **PC:** **Country: Spain**
Year Established: 2015 **Status 2020:** Active
Industries: Artificial Intelligence

Company Name: das-Na
Description: das-Nano is a company of experienced business & industry entrepreneurs offering solutions to industries based on cutting-edge technologies.
Website: http://www.das-nano.com/
Phone: **Email:** info@das-nano.com
City: Tajonar **State:** NC **PC:** **Country: Spain**
Year Established: 2012 **Status 2020:** Active
Industries: Security for:, IT Managed Services

Company Name: Veridas
Description: SaaS
Website: http://www.veridas.com/
Phone: 34 948 246295 **Email:** info@veridas.com
City: Tajonar **State:** NC **PC:** **Country: Spain**
Year Established: 2017 **Status 2020:** Active
Industries: Artificial Intelligence for:, ~ Biotechnology (9), Data Management for:, Identity for:, Machine Learning

Company Name: Aeorum Espana
Description: Aeorum Espana is an engineering company dedicated to the consultancy of R + D + i projects.
Website: http://aeorum.com/
Phone: (34) 951 28 67 73 **Email:** info@aeorum.com
City: Cabanillas **State:** Navarre **PC:** **Country: Spain**
Year Established: **Status 2020:** Active
Industries: Artificial Intelligence for:, IT Managed Services for:, Robotics

Company Name: AI Talentum
Description: AI Talentum develops and implements decision-making computer systems based on statistical techniques and machine learning.
Website: http://www.aitalentum.com/
Phone: 34-868957514 **Email:** info@aitalentum
City: Murcia **State:** MC **PC:** **Country: Spain**
Year Established: 2013 **Status 2020:** Active
Industries: Artificial Intelligence for:, IT Managed Services for:, Machine Learning

Company Name: Compra Activa
Description: Compra Activa is a system whose objective is to optimize the relationship between a Shopping Center and its users.
Website: http://www.compraactiva.me/
Phone: **Email:** 36317@reference-encyclopedia-ai.net
City: Murcia **State:** MC **PC:** **Country: Spain**
Year Established: 2012 **Status 2020:** Active
Industries: Artificial Intelligence

Company Name: Connectif Artificial Intelligence
Description: Connectif Artificial Intelligence is a company offering integrations for different platforms, such as ERPs, CRMs and CMS.
Website: http://www.connectif.ai/
Phone: 34-968 935 520 **Email:** info@connectif.: Spain
City: Murcia **State:** MC **PC:** **Country: Spain**
Year Established: 2018 **Status 2020:** Active
Industries: Artificial Intelligence

Company Name: Minderest
Description: Minderest is a pioneering company of price and assortment intelligence for retailers and manufacturers.
Website: http://www.minderest.com
Phone: 34 868 075 490 **Email:** sales@minderest.com
City: Murcia **State:** MC **PC:** **Country: Spain**
Year Established: 2012 **Status 2020:** Active
Industries: Artificial Intelligence for:, E-Commerce

Company Name: Medbravo
Description: Medbravo empowers health and research organizations with AI solutions and computing technology to transform biomedical data into knowledge.
Website: http://www.medbravo.org/
Phone: 034 618453214 **Email:** contact@business.com
City: Alicante **State:** VC **PC:** **Country: Spain**
Year Established: 2013 **Status 2020:** Active
Industries: Artificial Intelligence for:, ~ Healthcare (20)

Company Name: mypa
Description: The intelligent calling screen that shows you everything you need to know about your contact before you pick up the call.
Website: http://withmypa.com
Phone: (3496) 614-5697 **Email:** helpme@withmypa.com
City: Alicante **State:** VC **PC:** **Country: Spain**
Year Established: 2014 **Status 2020:** Active
Industries: Application Services for:, Artificial Intelligence

Company Name: Aisoy Robotics
Description: Aisoy Robotics creating social robots to bring them into everyday lives. Smart personal robots for making life more fun and easier.
Website: http://www.aisoy.com
Phone: **Email:** info@aisoy.com
City: Elche **State:** Valencian Community **PC:** **Country: Spain**
Year Established: **Status 2020:** Active
Industries: Artificial Intelligence for:, ~ Manufacturing-Electronic (30), ~ Manufacturing-Electronic (30), Robotics for:, ~ Professional Services (48)

Company Name: CallBurn
Description: CallBurn is an AI based SMS & voice messages sending SaaS application.
Website: http://callburn.com/en
Phone: 34 966 602 314 **Email:** admin@callburn.com
City: Elche **State:** VC **PC:** **Country: Spain**
Year Established: 2013 **Status 2020:** Active
Industries:

Company Name: Adele Robots
Description: Adele Robots is a company focused on social robotics and virtual assistants with the main goal of improving business efficiency.
Website: http://www.adelerobots.com/en
Phone: **Email:** info@adelerobots.com
City: Llanera De Ranes **State:** Valencian Community **PC:** **Country: Spain**
Year Established: **Status 2020:** Active
Industries: Artificial Intelligence for:, ~ Manufacturing-Electronic (30), ~ Manufacturing-Electronic (30), ~ Telecommunications (56), Robotics for:, ~ Professional Services (48)

Company Name: Bandness
Description: Bandness is an artificial intelligence system.
Website:
Phone: **Email:** contacto@bandness.com
City: Valencia **State:** VC **PC:** **Country: Spain**
Year Established: 2012 **Status 2020:** Active
Industries: Artificial Intelligence

Company Name: Dekalabs
Description: Dekalabs is a system integrator company that works with blockchain, machine learning, and mobile technologies.
Website: http://dekalabs.com/
Phone: (34) 960 969 701 **Email:** 36426@reference-encyclopedia-ai.net
City: Valencia **State:** VC **PC:** **Country: Spain**
Year Established: 2013 **Status 2020:** Active
Industries: Artificial Intelligence for:, Blockchain for:, Machine Learning

Company Name: GoKoan
Description: GoKoan is a digital teaching and learning tool designed to optimize the way students study using Artificial Intelligence
Website: http://www.gokoan.com/
Phone: **Email:** info@gokoan.com
City: Valencia **State:** VC **PC:** **Country: Spain**
Year Established: 2017 **Status 2020:** Active
Industries: Artificial Intelligence for:, ~ Education (13), ~ Education (13), ~ Education (13), ~ Education (13)

Company Name: Mybrana
Description: MYBRANA is a technology company that has integrated computer vision functionalities, such as face recognition.
Website: http://www.mybrana.com/
Phone: **Email:** mikel.diaz@mybrana.com
City: Valencia **State:** Valencian Community **PC:** **Country: Spain**
Year Established: **Status 2020:** Active
Industries: ~ Media-Communications (41), Artificial Intelligence for:, Augmented Reality for:, Computer Vision for:, ~ Media-Communications (41), ~ Arts-Entertainment-Recreation (4)

Company **Name:** Neuronalbite
Description: It's time to upgrade your e-commerce to our artificial intelligence revolution.
Website: http://www.neuronalbite.com
Phone: 34) 722 271 385 **Email:** hello@neuronalbite.com
City: Valencia **State:** VC **PC:** **Country: Spain**
Year Established: 2017 **Status 2020:** Active
Industries: Artificial Intelligence for:, E-Commerce for:, Web

Company Name: PangeaMT (Machine Technologies)
Description: Language technologies enhaced by artificial intelligence, cognitive companies, institutions, translation professionals, and corporations
Website: http://pangeamt.com
Phone: 34 96 3336333 **Email:** hello@pangeamt.com
City: Valencia **State:** VC **PC:** **Country: Spain**
Year Established: 2019 **Status 2020:** Active
Industries: Artificial Intelligence for:, ~ Education (13), IT Managed Services for:, Web

Company Name: Preseri: Spain
Description: PreSeries takes advantage of Machine Learning to transform startup investing into a successful data-driven practice
Website: http://preseries.com/
Phone: **Email:** info@preseries.com
City: Valencia **State:** VC **PC:** **Country: Spain**
Year Established: 2015 **Status 2020:** Active
Industries: Artificial Intelligence for:, ~ Banking and Financial Markets-Services (7), Machine Learning for:, Predictive Analytics for:, ~ Banking and Financial Markets-Services (7)

Company Name: QUIBIM S.L.
Description: YOUR PRECISION IMAGING COMPANY
Website: http://www.quibim.com
Phone: 34 96 124 32 25 **Email:** info@quibim.com
City: Valencia **State:** Valencian Community **PC:** **Country: Spain**
Year Established: **Status 2020:** Active
Industries: Artificial Intelligence for:, ~ Biotechnology (9), ~ Healthcare (20), ~ Healthcare (20), ~ Healthcare (20), ~ Healthcare (20), ~ Pharmaceuticals (46)

Company Name: Sciling
Description: Sciling offers tools to remove technological barriers and solve inefficiencies of web translation workflows.
Website: http://sciling.com
Phone: 34960067330 **Email:** hello@sciling.com
City: Valencia **State:** Valencian Community **PC:** **Country: Spain**
Year Established: **Status 2020:** Active
Industries: Artificial Intelligence for:, IT Managed Services for:, Natural Language Processing for:, ~ Professional Services (48)

Company Name: Smartaxi
Description: Smartaxi is a mobile application that utilizes artificial intelligence to help taxi drivers predict potential customer locations.
Website: http://smartaxi.me
Phone: **Email:** 37413@reference-encyclopedia-ai.net
City: Valencia **State:** VC **PC:** **Country: Spain**
Year Established: 2012 **Status 2020:** Active
Industries: Artificial Intelligence for:, ~ Customer Relationship Management (11), Application Services for:, ~ Transportation and Logistics (57)

Company Name: szimple
Description: szimple is an all in one media center capable of searching and grabbing the meta info for series and movies with a UX.
Website: http://www.szimple.com
Phone: **Email:** hello@szimple.com
City: Valencia **State:** Valencian Community **PC:** **Country: Spain**
Year Established: **Status 2020:** Active
Industries: Artificial Intelligence for:, ~ Manufacturing-Electronic (30)

Company Name: Taller Innovacion Abierta
Description: Talleria expertise in data analysis on real time, leads to proccess optimization products and services with high economic value.
Website: http://www.talleria.com/
Phone: **Email:** info@talleria.com
City: Valencia **State:** VC **PC:** **Country: Spain**
Year Established: 2010 **Status 2020:** Active
Industries: Analytics for:, Artificial Intelligence for:, Big Data and Analytics

Company Name: Tyris Software
Description: Tyris is specialized in high quality solutions with the latest technology in Computer Vision, Artificial Intelligence and Cloud Services.
Website: http://www.tyris-software.com/en/
Phone: (0034) 961 152 302 **Email:** info@tyris-software.com
City: Valencia **State:** Valencian Community **PC:** **Country: Spain**
Year Established: **Status 2020:** Active
Industries:

Company Name: WITRAC
Description: WITRAC, disruptive Track&Trace Platform Infrastructure based in IoT-AI-5G technologies for Digital Transformation within Industry 4.0
Website: http://witrac.es/en/
Phone: 34630241905 **Email:** info@witrac.: Spain
City: Valencia **State:** VC **PC:** **Country: Spain**

Year Established: 2013 **Status 2020:** Active
Industries: Artificial Intelligence for:, Internet of Things (IoT) for:, Compute for:, Supply Chain Management for:, Internet of Things (IoT)

Sri Lanka

Company Name: Alakazam
Description: Social Media Assistant for SMB
Website: https://alakazam.ai/
Phone: **Email:** dulitha@getalakasam.com
City: Colombo **State:** WP **PC:** **Country: Sri Lanka**
Year Established: **Status 2020:** Active
Industries: Artificial Intelligence for:, Digital Marketing

Company Name: Avantrio
Description: Avantrio is a studio that specializes in providing solutions with blockchain, machine learning and artificial intelligence.
Website: http://avantrio.xyz/
Phone: **Email:** 36122@reference-encyclopedia-ai.net
City: Colombo **State:** WP **PC:** **Country: Sri Lanka**
Year Established: 2018 **Status 2020:** Active
Industries: Artificial Intelligence for:, Blockchain for:, Machine Learning

Company Name: Linear Squared
Description: Linear Squared is specialized in data science and advanced analytics solutions.
Website: http://linearsquared.com/
Phone: 94 11 2 557272 **Email:** info@linearsquared.com
City: Colombo **State:** WP **PC:** **Country: Sri Lanka**
Year Established: 2015 **Status 2020:** Active
Industries: Artificial Intelligence for:, Data Management

Company Name: Zepto
Description: Zepto is a technology startup focused on Self-Service Data Analytics & Visualisation.
Website: http://www.zepto.io
Phone: 94 77 774 3000 **Email:** apurva@zeptolytics.com
City: Colombo **State:** WP **PC:** **Country: Sri Lanka**
Year Established: 2016 **Status 2020:** Active
Industries: Analytics for:, Artificial Intelligence for:, Machine Learning for:, Business Software as a Service Apps (SaaS Apps)

Company Name: ziphio
Description: Ziphio is a software development company that focuses on artificial intelligence, IoT, blockchain, and machine learning.
Website: http://ziphio.com/
Phone: 94 76 618 0751 **Email:** hello@ziphio.com
City: Nugegoda **State:** WP **PC:** **Country: Sri Lanka**
Year Established: 2018 **Status 2020:** Active
Industries: Artificial Intelligence for:, Blockchain

Sweden

Company Name: Univrs
Description: Univrses is a virtual reality software developer specializing in motion tracking for more accurate tracking of movement.
Website: http://univrses.com/
Phone: 46705186900 **Email:** info@univrses.com
City: **State:** **PC:** **Country: Sweden**
Year Established: **Status 2020:** Active
Industries: Artificial Intelligence for:, Compute

Company Name: ATSEDA
Description: Data Science and Analytics
Website: http://atseda.com
Phone: **Email:** contact@atseda.com
City: Alvdalen **State:** Dalarnas Lan **PC:** **Country: Sweden**
Year Established: **Status 2020:** Active
Industries: Artificial Intelligence for:, Machine Learning

Company Name: XIMANT
Description: Intelligent Traffic Solutions for Autonomous Navigation and Congestion avoidance through patent-pending Deep Learning technologies.
Website: http://ximantis.com
Phone: 46317999439 **Email:** inquire@ximantis.com
City: Kungsbacka **State:** Halland County **PC:** **Country: Sweden**
Year Established: **Status 2020:** Active
Industries: Artificial Intelligence for:, ~ Energy and Utilities (14), Machine Learning for:, ~ Transportation and Logistics (57), ~ Transportation and Logistics (57)

Company Name: Ekkono Solutions
Description: Ekkono Solutions provide machine learning for IoT, which takes them from connected to smart.
Website: http://ekkono.ai/
Phone: **Email:** info@ekkono.ai
City: Tvaaker **State:** Hallands län **PC:** **Country: Sweden**
Year Established: 2016 **Status 2020:** Active
Industries: Web for:, Internet of Things (IoT) for:, Machine Learning

Company Name: AIMO
Description: AIMO empowers everyone to take care of their health and optimise fitness.
Website: http://www.aimo-health.com/
Phone: **Email:** info@aimo-health.com
City: Kalmar **State:** Kalmar County **PC:** **Country: Sweden**
Year Established: **Status 2020:** Active
Industries: Artificial Intelligence for:, ~ Healthcare (20), ~ Insurance (25)

Company Name: Apono: Malaysia
Description: Aponomy is a Swedish company that uses information technology to help people improve our society.
Website: http://aponomy.com
Phone: **Email:** info@aponomy.com
City: Kalmar **State:** Kalmar County **PC:** **Country: Sweden**
Year Established: **Status 2020:** Active
Industries: Artificial Intelligence for:, ~ Media-Communications (41), ~ Gaming (18), ~ Human Resources (24), ~ Education (13), ~ Healthcare (20), ~ Healthcare (20), ~ Social-Environmental-Physical-Engineering Sciences (55), ~ Social-Environmental-Physical-Engineering Scienc

Company Name: Arkimera Robotics
Description: Giving software learning power.
Website: http://www.arkimera.: Sweden
Phone: 46 70 634 93 64 **Email:** contact@arkimera.: Sweden
City: Kalmar **State:** Kalmar County **PC:** **Country: Sweden**
Year Established: 2014 **Status 2020:** Active
Industries: Finance and Accounting for:, Enterprise Application Services for:, Machine Learning for:, Robotics for:, Business Software as a Service Apps (SaaS Apps)

Company Name: Edventur: Spain
Description: Edventures is the world's first digital entrepreneurship coach tailored for your specific needs as an entrepreneur.
Website: http://www.edventures.se/
Phone: **Email:** 36481@reference-encyclopedia-ai.net
City: Norrkoping **State:** Östergötland County **PC:** **Country: Sweden**
Year Established: 2017 **Status 2020:** Active
Industries:

Company Name: Zensed
Description: Zensed uses Artificial Intelligence and advanced Machine Learning systems to prevent frauds
Website: http://www.zensed.com
Phone: **Email:** info@zensed.com
City: Angelholm **State:** Skåne County **PC:** **Country: Sweden**
Year Established: **Status 2020:** Active
Industries: Artificial Intelligence for:, Cyber Security for:, Security for:, Machine Learning

Company Name: PeN Chat
Description: An Instant Social Messaging App - Search Google Play, type Pen Chat Calls for Free
Website: http://www.penchat.net
Phone: 46733338896 **Email:** info@penchat.net
City: Helsingborg **State:** Skåne County **PC:** **Country: Sweden**
Year Established: **Status 2020:** Active
Industries: Artificial Intelligence for:, ~ Personal-Religious-Civic (45), E-Commerce for:, ~ Telecommunications (56), ~ Healthcare (20), Application Services for:, ~ Social Media (54)

Company Name: Auranest
Description: Auranest automatically creates & updates profiles on job search services online.
Website: http://www.auranest.com/
Phone: 468-555 21 320 **Email:** contact@auranest.com
City: Lund **State:** Skåne County **PC:** **Country: Sweden**
Year Established: 2014 **Status 2020:** Active
Industries: Web for:, Machine Learning for:, Web

Company Name: Emer: Sweden
Description: Emerse is a Demand Side Platform (DSP) for programmatic media buying.
Website: www.emerse.com
Phone: **Email:** robert.whelan@emerse.com
City: Lund **State:** Skåne County **PC:** **Country: Sweden**
Year Established: **Status 2020:** Active
Industries: ~ Media-Communications (41), ~ Media-Communications (41), ~ Media-Communications (41), ~ Media-Communications (41), ~ Media-Communications (41), Artificial Intelligence for:, ~ Media-Communications (41), Digital Marketing for:, Data Management for:, Machine Lear: Nigeria

Company Name: Hydromesh
Description: Hydromesh's The Hyve is an AI with machine learning acting as a brain of a micro grid that is connected to an energy source and ESS.
Website: http://hydromesh.org
Phone: 46 70 3252383 **Email:** info@hydromesh.org
City: Lund **State:** Skåne County **PC:** **Country: Sweden**
Year Established: 2019 **Status 2020:** Active
Industries: Artificial Intelligence for:, ~ Energy and Utilities (14), ~ Energy and Utilities (14), ~ Energy and Utilities (14), Machine Learning for:, ~ Energy and Utilities (14)

Company **Name:** Parkiro
Description: Parkiro is an Artificial Intelligence "AI" based smart mobility and parking solution.
Website:
Phone: **Email:** 4411@reference-encyclopedia-ai.net
City: Lund **State:** Skåne County **PC:** **Country: Sweden**
Year Established: **Status 2020:** Active
Industries: Analytics for:, Artificial Intelligence for:, ~ Automotive (5), Big Data and Analytics for:, ~ Banking and Financial Markets-Services (7), ~ Travel and Transportation (58)

Company Name: Century Analytics
Description: We trade currencies using artificial intelligence
Website: http://www.century.ai
Phone: **Email:** info@century.ai
City: Malmo **State:** Skåne County **PC:** **Country: Sweden**
Year Established: **Status 2020:** Active
Industries: Artificial Intelligence for:, ~ Banking and Financial Markets-Services (7), ~ Banking and Financial Markets-Services (7), Machine Learning

Company Name: Donna
Description: AI-Powered legal drafting tool for lawyers.
Website: http://donna.legal
Phone: **Email:** info@donna.legal
City: Malmo **State:** Skåne County **PC:** **Country: Sweden**
Year Established: **Status 2020:** Active
Industries: Artificial Intelligence

Company Name: Ifragasatt
Description: Ifragasatt supplies the media industry with cost-efficient products that help them increase traffic, loyalty and user engagement.
Website: http://www.ifragasatt.se/
Phone: 46 (0)46 560 11 60 **Email:** info@ifragasatt.: Sweden
City: Malmo **State:** Skåne County **PC:** **Country: Sweden**
Year Established: 2015 **Status 2020:** Active
Industries: Artificial Intelligence for:, ~ Event Management (15)

Company Name: Lytics
Description: LYTICS is an artificial intelligence company serving the healthcare community in solving complex medical and clinical issues.
Website: http://lytics.ai/
Phone: **Email:** info@lytics.ai
City: Malmo **State:** Skåne County **PC:** **Country: Sweden**
Year Established: **Status 2020:** Active
Industries: Artificial Intelligence for:, Big Data and Analytics for:, ~ Biotechnology (9), ~ Healthcare (20), Databases for:, ~ Healthcare (20), Machine Learning for:, ~ Healthcare (20), Predictive Analytics

Company Name: Mapillary
Description: Mapillary is the street-level imagery platform that scales and automates mapping using collaboration, cameras, and computer vision.
Website: http://www.mapillary.com/
Phone: **Email:** 36940@reference-encyclopedia-ai.net
City: Malmo **State:** Skåne County **PC:** **Country: Sweden**
Year Established: 2013 **Status 2020:** Active
Industries: Artificial Intelligence for:, ~ Automotive (5), Databases for:, Mobile

Company Name: Modcam
Description: Modcam uses computer vision and machine learning on device to track, monitor and analyse people, anonymously!
Website: http://modcam.com/
Phone: 46 70 574 20 55 **Email:** contact@modcam.com
City: Malmo **State:** Skåne County **PC:** **Country: Sweden**
Year Established: 2013 **Status 2020:** Active
Industries: Computer Vision for:, Machine Learning

Company Name: OpenLogger
Description: OpenLogger is an Intelligent IoT monitoring system connecting all lab and hospital devices into one platform.
Website: http://openlogger.se/
Phone: **Email:** 30929@reference-encyclopedia-ai.net
City: Malmo **State:** Skåne County **PC:** **Country: Sweden**
Year Established: 2010 **Status 2020:** Active
Industries: Artificial Intelligence for:, ~ Healthcare (20), IT Managed Services

Company Name: Seavus
Description: Seavus is a software development and consultancy company providing a full line of services for software implementation lifecycles.
Website: http://www.seavus.com
Phone: (464) 030-0940 **Email:** info@seavus.com
City: Malmo **State:** Skåne County **PC:** **Country: Sweden**
Year Established: **Status 2020:** Active
Industries:

Company Name: Sentian.AI
Description: Computer Software
Website: http://www.sentian.ai/
Phone: **Email:** info@sentian.ai
City: Malmo **State:** Skåne County **PC:** **Country: Sweden**
Year Established: 2016 **Status 2020:** Active
Industries: Artificial Intelligence for:, Machine Learning for:, Predictive Analytics

Company Name: DeepMed AB
Description: DeepMed's vision is to redefine the use of X-rays in orthopedics by applying artificial intelligence (AI).
Website: http://deep-med.com/
Phone: 46 (70) 089 12 53 **Email:** info@deep-med.com
City: Danderyd **State:** Stockholm County **PC:** **Country: Sweden**
Year Established: 2016 **Status 2020:** Active
Industries: Artificial Intelligence

Company Name: Inovia Group
Description: Inovia Group is a big data and AI solutions provider.
Website: http://inoviagroup.: Sweden
Phone: 08-35 10 30 **Email:** info@inoviagroup.: Sweden
City: Kista **State:** Stockholm County **PC:** **Country: Sweden**
Year Established: 2012 **Status 2020:** Active
Industries: Artificial Intelligence for:, Big Data and Analytics

Company Name: PerceptiLabs
Description: PerceptiLabs is a research within Machine Learning, and more specifically Deep Learning.
Website: http://www.perceptilabs.com/
Phone: **Email:** 37155@reference-encyclopedia-ai.net
City: Lidingö **State:** Stockholm County **PC:** **Country: Sweden**
Year Established: 2017 **Status 2020:** Active
Industries: Artificial Intelligence for:, Web

Company Name: Adverty
Description: The Next Generation Advertising Platform.
Website: http://www.adverty.com/
Phone: 46703669646 **Email:** nb@adverty.com
City: Stockholm **State:** Stockholm County **PC:** **Country: Sweden**
Year Established: **Status 2020:** Active
Industries: ~ Media-Communications (41), Artificial Intelligence for:, Augmented Reality

Company Name: AIAR EdTech AB
Description: AIAR is democratizing education for the 2.5 billion people in need worldwide by using AI, blockchain and their own utility token.
Website: http://www.aiar.com
Phone: 46760000804 **Email:** info@aiar.com
City: Stockholm **State:** Stockholm County **PC:** **Country: Sweden**
Year Established: **Status 2020:** Active
Industries: Artificial Intelligence for:, Augmented Reality for:, Blockchain for:, Digital Marketing for:, ~ Education (13), ~ Education (13), ~ Education (13), ~ Media-Communications (41), ~ Education (13)

Company Name: Aifloo
Description: Aifloo SmartCare allows your elderly relatives or friends to live independently, free from fear and insecurity.
Website: http://www.aifloo.com/
Phone: 46 (0)8 234 601 **Email:** info@aifloo.com
City: Stockholm **State:** Stockholm County **PC:** **Country: Sweden**

Year Established: **Status 2020:** Active
Industries: Artificial Intelligence for:, ~ Manufacturing-Electronic (30), ~ Healthcare (20), IT Managed Services for:, ~ Professional Services (48)

Company Name: Alex Therapeutics
Description: AI digital CBT therapeutic platform - changing habits, changing heal:Thailand
Website: https://www.alextherapeutics.com/
Phone: 46708830035 **Email:** john@alextherapeutics.com
City: Stockholm **State:** Stockholm County **PC:** **Country: Sweden**
Year Established: 2018 **Status 2020:** Active
Industries: Artificial Intelligence for:, ~ Healthcare (20), ~ Healthcare (20), ~ Healthcare (20), ~ Healthcare (20), ~ Healthcare (20)

Company Name: ami Lab
Description: Ami Lab unveils key facial features through machine learning on a database of models.
Website: http://www.ami-lab.co/
Phone: **Email:** info@ami-lab.co
City: Stockholm **State:** Stockholm County **PC:** **Country: Sweden**
Year Established: 2019 **Status 2020:** Active
Industries: Artificial Intelligence for:, E-Commerce

Company Name: Another Kind of Automation
Description: Another Kind of Automation is a NEW Innovation Management.
Website: http://www.akoa.com/
Phone: **Email:** 36065@reference-encyclopedia-ai.net
City: Stockholm **State:** Stockholm County **PC:** **Country: Sweden**
Year Established: 2016 **Status 2020:** Active
Industries: Artificial Intelligence for:, Robotics

Company Name: Astrid
Description: Astrid is the AI-powered coach for managers and team leaders.
Website: http://www.astrid.ai
Phone: **Email:** training@astrid.ai
City: Stockholm **State:** Stockholm County **PC:** **Country: Sweden**
Year Established: 2019 **Status 2020:** Active
Industries: Analytics for:, Artificial Intelligence for:, Business Applications for:, IT Managed Services

Company Name: Behoover
Description: Request almost anything - Quickly get replies from good and interested compani: Spain
Website: http://www.behoover.com
Phone: **Email:** info@behoover.com
City: Stockholm **State:** Stockholm County **PC:** **Country: Sweden**
Year Established: **Status 2020:** Active
Industries: Artificial Intelligence for:, Content

Company Name: Bitcall
Description: Bitcall is a sales performance solution, powered by AI. Measure, improve and predict your sales activity across all channels.
Website:
Phone: **Email:** 36163@reference-encyclopedia-ai.net
City: Stockholm **State:** Stockholm County **PC:** **Country: Sweden**
Year Established: 2015 **Status 2020:** Closed
Industries: Artificial Intelligence for:, Business Applications for:, Business Software as a Service Apps (SaaS Apps)

Company Name: ContextVision
Description: ContextVision is a medical technology company specializing in image analysis and artificial intelligence.
Website: http://www.contextvision.com
Phone: (468)750-3550 **Email:** info@contextvision.: Sweden
City: Stockholm **State:** Stockholm County **PC:** **Country: Sweden**
Year Established: **Status 2020:** Active
Industries:

Company Name: Dooer
Description: Dooer Fintech is a startup that was founded with the goal of accounting in the future
Website: http://dooer.com/
Phone: (468) 601-0101 **Email:** hej@dooer.com
City: Stockholm **State:** Stockholm County **PC:** **Country:** **Sweden**
Year Established: 2015 **Status 2020:** Active
Industries: Finance and Accounting for:, Artificial Intelligence

Company Name: Echo State
Description: AI, ML, SaaS, Service
Website: http://echostate.: Sweden
Phone: 46 8 520 275 27 **Email:** info@echostate.: Sweden
City: Stockholm **State:** Stockholm County **PC:** **Country:** **Sweden**
Year Established: 2018 **Status 2020:** Active
Industries: Analytics for:, Artificial Intelligence for:, Machine Learning for:, Business Software as a Service Apps (SaaS Apps)

Company Name: Findify
Description: Findify is an intelligent on-site search solution that uses machine learning and big data to increase revenue for ecommerce merchants.
Website: http://www.findify.io/
Phone: **Email:** yourfriends@findify.io
City: Stockholm **State:** Stockholm County **PC:** **Country:** **Sweden**
Year Established: **Status 2020:** Active
Industries: Artificial Intelligence for:, Big Data and Analytics for:, Cyber Security for:, E-Commerce

Company Name: Formulate
Description: Formulate helps retailers transform simple sales data into better merchandising decisions.
Website: http://www.formulate.app/
Phone: (4684) 468-3706 **Email:** info@formulate.app
City: Stockholm **State:** Stockholm County **PC:** **Country:** **Sweden**
Year Established: 2016 **Status 2020:** Active
Industries: Analytics for:, Artificial Intelligence for:, Big Data and Analytics for:, Business Software as a Service Apps (SaaS Apps)

Company Name: Furhat Robotics
Description: Furhat Robotics is a social robotics company based in Sweden.
Website: http://www.furhatrobotics.com/
Phone: **Email:** info@furhatrobotics.com
City: Stockholm **State:** Stockholm County **Zip:** 118 65 **Country:** **Sweden**
Year Established: **Status 2020:** Active
Industries: Artificial Intelligence for:, Computer Vision for:, ~ Administrative and Support Services (1404), ~ Banking and Financial Markets-Services (1410), ~ Event Management (1418), ~ Fashion (1419), ~ Food and Beverage (1420), ~ Gaming (1421), ~ Government (1422), ~ Heal

Company Name: Gavagai
Description: Gavagai is a language technology company.
Website: http://www.gavagai.: Sweden
Phone: 46 72 177 44 50 **Email:** sales@gavagai.io
City: Stockholm **State:** Stockholm County **PC:** **Country:** **Sweden**
Year Established: **Status 2020:** Active
Industries: Analytics for:, Artificial Intelligence for:, Big Data and Analytics for:, Business Intelligence for:, Databases for:, Natural Language Processing for:, ~ Professional Services (48), Data Management

Company Name: Gleechi
Description: Gleechi develops software to enable hand movement and interaction for artificial hands.
Website: http://www.gleechi.com
Phone: (4673) 444-1940 **Email:** jakob.way@gleechi.com
City: Stockholm **State:** Stockholm County **PC:** **Country:** **Sweden**
Year Established: 2014 **Status 2020:** Active
Industries: Artificial Intelligence for:, Augmented Reality for:, Automation for:, Machine Learning for:, ~ Arts-Entertainment-Recreation (4), Robotics for:, ~ Arts-Entertainment-Recreation (4), Virtual Reality (VR)

Company Name: Goava
Description: Goava uses Big Data and Machine Learning to help you discover your best-fit customer prospects.
Website: http://goava.com
Phone: **Email:** johanna.klima@goava.com
City: Stockholm **State:** Stockholm County **PC:** **Country:** **Sweden**
Year Established: 2016 **Status 2020:** Active
Industries: Artificial Intelligence for:, Machine Learning

Company Name: Graviz Telesco:
Description: AI-driven insight platform for creating sustainable grow:Thailand
Website: http://www.graviztelescope.com
Phone: 46700924031 **Email:** hello@graviztelescope.: Sweden
City: Stockholm **State:** Stockholm County **PC:** **Country:** **Sweden**
Year Established: **Status 2020:** Active
Industries: Analytics for:, Artificial Intelligence for:, ~ Management of Companies (28), ~ Media-Communications (41), Predictive Analytics for:, ~ Professional Services (48)

Company Name: HAAARTLAND
Description: AI-inside, IKEA-simple, fun yet powerful platform for key conversations. With prospects, customers, teams, projects, partners...
Website: http://www.haaartland.com/
Phone: 46735000808 **Email:** niklas.lohmann@haaartland.com
City: Stockholm **State:** Stockholm County **PC:** **Country:** **Sweden**
Year Established: **Status 2020:** Active
Industries: Analytics for:, Artificial Intelligence for:, Machine Learning for:, ~ Media-Communications (41), ~ Social Media (54)

Company Name: Happyr
Description: Personal matching for recruiting
Website: http://happyr.com/
Phone: 46 70 452 12 07 **Email:** support@happyr.com
City: Stockholm **State:** Stockholm County **PC:** **Country:** **Sweden**
Year Established: **Status 2020:** Active
Industries: Artificial Intelligence for:, Enterprise Application Services

Company Name: HealthiHabits
Description: Makes behaviour improvements incredibly easy
Website: http://www.healthihabits.com
Phone: 46 (0) 8277213 **Email:** info@healthihabits.com
City: Stockholm **State:** Stockholm County **PC:** **Country:** **Sweden**
Year Established: **Status 2020:** Active
Industries: Artificial Intelligence for:, ~ Healthcare (20), Machine Learning for:, ~ Healthcare (20), ~ Healthcare (20)

Company Name: Imagimob
Description: Imagimob has invented and developed SensorBeat, a technology for real time artificial intelligence on the edge.
Website: http://imagimob.com
Phone: 46 70 5910614 **Email:** anders@imagimob.com
City: Stockholm **State:** Stockholm County **PC:** **Country:** **Sweden**

Year Established: **Status 2020:** Active
Industries: Artificial Intelligence for:, Web for:, Machine Learning for:, ~ Manufacturing-Electronic (30)

Company Name: Instantor
Description: Instantor is a Swedish FinTech that utilises transactional data from bank accounts to make tough calls easy within credit risk management.
Website: http://www.instantor.com
Phone: **Email:** marketing@instantor.com
City: Stockholm **State:** Stockholm County **PC:** **Country:** **Sweden**
Year Established: 2010 **Status 2020:** Active
Industries:

Company Name: Lexi Solutions
Description: Unlock the Hidden Value in Your Supply Chain Data with AI
Website: http://www.lexisolution.com/
Phone: **Email:** info@lexisolution.com
City: Stockholm **State:** Stockholm County **PC:** **Country:** **Sweden**
Year Established: 2012 **Status 2020:** Active
Industries: Artificial Intelligence for:, Machine Learning for:, ~ Administrative and Support Services (1)

Company Name: Lexplore
Description: Using eyetracking and AI to detect dyslexia at the first years in school
Website: http://www.lexplore.com
Phone: **Email:** info@lexplore.com
City: Stockholm **State:** Stockholm County **PC:** **Country:** **Sweden**
Year Established: **Status 2020:** Active
Industries: Artificial Intelligence for:, ~ Education (13), ~ Healthcare (20)

Company Name: Logical Clocks
Description: Logical Clocks provides Enterprise support for the open-source Hopsworks platform to solve the data problem for Deep Learning and AI.
Website: http://www.logicalclocks.com
Phone: **Email:** Info@logicalclocks.com
City: Stockholm **State:** Stockholm County **PC:** **Country:** **Sweden**
Year Established: 2016 **Status 2020:** Active
Industries: Artificial Intelligence for:, IT Managed Services for:, Internet of Things (IoT) for:, Robotics

Company Name: ManoMotion
Description: ManoMotion is a gesture technology company that enables its users to manipulate objects in 3D space with real-life intuitiveness.
Website: http://www.manomotion.com
Phone: 46 73 973 90 63 **Email:** info@manomotion.com
City: Stockholm **State:** Stockholm County **PC:** **Country:** **Sweden**
Year Established: 2015 **Status 2020:** Active
Industries: Artificial Intelligence for:, Augmented Reality for:, Machine Learning for:, Application Services for:, Robotics for:, Virtual Reality (VR) for:, Virtual Reality (VR)

Company Name: Match2One
Description: Match2One makes it easier for advertisers to make automated and hyper-targeted purchases of ad inventory i.e. programmatic marketing
Website: http://www.match2one.com/
Phone: 46 704 382 141 **Email:** hello@match2one.com
City: Stockholm **State:** Stockholm County **PC:** **Country:** **Sweden**
Year Established: 2015 **Status 2020:** Active
Industries: Digital Media for:, Machine Learning

Company Name: Modulai
Description: Modulai is a machine learning agency with a mission to bring the benefits of AI to every organisation.
Website: http://modulai.io
Phone: **Email:** info@modulai.io
City: Stockholm **State:** Stockholm County **PC:** **Country:** **Sweden**
Year Established: **Status 2020:** Active
Industries: Artificial Intelligence for:, Machine Learning

Company Name: My Telesco:
Description: AI-driven insight platform for creating sustainable grow:Thailand
Website: http://www.mytelescope.io
Phone: (4670) 092-4031 **Email:** hello@graviztelescope.: Sweden
City: Stockholm **State:** Stockholm County **PC:** **Country:** **Sweden**
Year Established: 2018 **Status 2020:** Active
Industries: Analytics for:, Predictive Analytics

Company Name: Nectarine Health AB
Description: Transforming elderly care with IoT and Machine Learning
Website: http://nectarinehealth.com/
Phone: 46 101024140 **Email:** info@nectarinehealth.com
City: Stockholm **State:** Stockholm County **PC:** **Country:** **Sweden**
Year Established: **Status 2020:** Active
Industries: Artificial Intelligence for:, ~ Manufacturing-Electronic (30), ~ Healthcare (20), ~ Manufacturing-Electronic (30), ~ Healthcare (20), IT Managed Services for:, Machine Learning for:, ~ Professional Services (48), ~ Professional Services (48)

Company Name: Nordic Artificial Intelligence Institute
Description: Thought leader on Artificial Intelligence and Machine Learning in the Nordics and beyond
Website: http://www.nordicaiinstitute.com
Phone: 46707419945 **Email:** contact@nordicAIinstitute.com
City: Stockholm **State:** Stockholm County **PC:** **Country:** **Sweden**
Year Established: **Status 2020:** Active
Industries: Artificial Intelligence for:, Big Data and Analytics for:, Application Services for:, Machine Learning for:, Natural Language Processing for:, Predictive Analytics for:, Robotics

Company Name: Now Interact
Description: Now Interact creates Predictive Intelligence applications that enhance existing online personalization- and engagement solutions.
Website: http://nowinteract.com/
Phone: **Email:** hello@nowinteract.com
City: Stockholm **State:** Stockholm County **PC:** **Country:** **Sweden**
Year Established: **Status 2020:** Active
Industries: Artificial Intelligence for:, Web for:, Predictive Analytics

Company Name: Pacemaker
Description: Pacemaker lets anyone create and share DJ mixes with Spotify whilst providing a scalable solution for DJ Mixes in music streaming.
Website: http://pacemaker.net
Phone: **Email:** hi@pacemaker.net
City: Stockholm **State:** Stockholm County **PC:** **Country:** **Sweden**
Year Established: **Status 2020:** Active
Industries: Application Services for:, Artificial Intelligence for:, ~ Arts-Entertainment-Recreation (4), ~ Arts-Entertainment-Recreation (4)

Company Name: Peltarion
Description: Unlocking the possibilities of AI. The platform making AI available for everyone. Founded in 2005.
Website: peltarion.com/
Phone: **Email:** oliver@peltarion.com
City: Stockholm **State:** Stockholm County **PC:** **Country:** Sweden
Year Established: **Status 2020:** Active
Industries: Artificial Intelligence for:, Machine Learning for:, ~ Professional Services (48)

Company Name: Project Cosimo
Description: Project Cosimo develops and deploys AI solutions for enterprise administration.
Website: http://www.projectcosimo.com/
Phone: 46707127569 **Email:** contact@projectcosimo.com
City: Stockholm **State:** Stockholm County **PC:** **Country:** Sweden
Year Established: 2016 **Status 2020:** Active
Industries: Artificial Intelligence for:, ~ Administrative and Support Services (1)

Company Name: Racefox
Description: Racefox is a digital skiing coach that analyzes movements, finds one's potential and takes it to the next level.
Website: http://racefox.se/sv/home
Phone: 46 70 564 88 28 **Email:** info@racefox.: Sweden
City: Stockholm **State:** Stockholm County **PC:** **Country:** Sweden
Year Established: 2013 **Status 2020:** Active
Industries:

Company Name: rightprice.ai
Description: RightPrice AI is a company with capabilities in e-commerce pricing, artificial intelligence, and deep learning.
Website: http://www.rightprice.ai/
Phone: **Email:** info@rightprice.ai
City: Stockholm **State:** Stockholm County **PC:** **Country:** Sweden
Year Established: 2017 **Status 2020:** Active
Industries: Analytics for:, Artificial Intelligence for:, E-Commerce for:, Web for:, Machine Learning for:, Business Software as a Service Apps (SaaS Apps)

Company Name: roaring.io
Description: API services for person and company information
Website: http://www.roaring.io
Phone: 08-819820 **Email:** info@roaring.io
City: Stockholm **State:** Stockholm County **PC:** **Country:** Sweden
Year Established: 2016 **Status 2020:** Active
Industries: Big Data and Analytics for:, ~ Banking and Financial Markets-Services (7), Data Management for:, Databases for:, Application Program Interfaces (APIs) for:, Predictive Analytics for:, Data Management

Company Name: Sana Labs
Description: Sana Labs is an artificial intelligence company that exerts breakthroughs in machine learning to personalize educational content.
Website: http://sanalabs.com
Phone: **Email:** info@sanalabs.com
City: Stockholm **State:** Stockholm County **PC:** **Country:** Sweden
Year Established: 2016 **Status 2020:** Active
Industries: Artificial Intelligence for:, ~ Education (13), ~ Education (13)

Company Name: ShimmerCat
Description: ShimmerCat creates faster e-commerce websites with an intelligent IT infrastructure that use HTTP/2 and AI.
Website: http://www.shimmercat.com/
Phone: 46704851947 **Email:** henrik.frienholt@shimmercat.com
City: Stockholm **State:** Stockholm County **PC:** **Country:** Sweden
Year Established: 2014 **Status 2020:** Active
Industries: Artificial Intelligence for:, E-Commerce for:, E-Commerce for:, Enterprise Application Services for:, Web

Company Name: SIFR
Description: SIFR is a company focused on empowering companies using artificial intelligence and big data.
Website: http://www.sifr.ai/
Phone: 37256351267 **Email:** TAAVI.TAMMISTE@SIFR.AI
City: Stockholm **State:** Stockholm County **PC:** **Country:** Sweden
Year Established: **Status 2020:** Active
Industries: Artificial Intelligence for:, Big Data and Analytics for:, Machine Learning

Company Name: Skyqraft
Description: Skyqraft provides autonomous aerial infrastructure inspection.
Website: http://skyqraft.com
Phone: 46 70 417 46 10 **Email:** info@skyqraft.com
City: Stockholm **State:** Stockholm County **PC:** **Country:** Sweden
Year Established: 2019 **Status 2020:** Active
Industries: Artificial Intelligence for:, ~ Automotive (5), Machine Learning for:, ~ Energy and Utilities (14)

Company Name: Space: Portugal
Description: Spacept uses artificial intelligence for space data analytics.
Website: http://www.spacept.com/
Phone: 46 701 738 577 **Email:** info@spacept.com
City: Stockholm **State:** Stockholm County **PC:** **Country:** Sweden
Year Established: 2019 **Status 2020:** Active
Industries: Analytics

Company Name: Spit Lab AB
Description: AI for Infertility
Website: http://www.spitlab.co
Phone: **Email:** contact@spitlab.co
City: Stockholm **State:** Stockholm County **PC:** **Country:** Sweden
Year Established: 2018 **Status 2020:** Active
Industries: Artificial Intelligence for:, ~ Healthcare (20)

Company Name: Starcounter
Description: Starcounteris an in-memory database engine and application server for ultra fast development of high performance business applications.
Website: http://www.starcounter.com
Phone: 46 8428 425 00 **Email:** info@starcounter.com
City: Stockholm **State:** Stockholm County **PC:** **Country:** Sweden
Year Established: **Status 2020:** Active
Industries: Artificial Intelligence for:, Databases for:, Databases for:, Enterprise Application Services for:, ~ Professional Services (48)

Company Name: Strossle
Description: Strossle is a media technology company. We use Artificial Intelligence to help publishers present the most relevant content for each user.
Website: http://www.strossle.com
Phone: 46 73 6257680 **Email:** info@strossle.com
City: Stockholm **State:** Stockholm County **PC:** **Country:** Sweden
Year Established: 2013 **Status 2020:** Active
Industries: Artificial Intelligence for:, Content for:, Content

Company Name: Subtono: Malaysia
Description: Subtonomy is a service monitoring software provider that handles around 11 billion network transactions each day for mobile operators.
Website: http://www.subtonomy.com/
Phone: **Email:** info@subtonomy.com
City: Stockholm **State:** Stockholm County **PC:** **Country: Sweden**
Year Established: 2012 **Status 2020:** Active
Industries: Artificial Intelligence

Company Name: Sumline AB
Description: Sumline is an intelligent mobile app that recommends personalized content to you.
Website: http://www.sumline.com
Phone: 46705335355 **Email:** 37479@reference-encyclopedia-ai.net
City: Stockholm **State:** Stockholm County **PC:** **Country: Sweden**
Year Established: 2013 **Status 2020:** Active
Industries: Mobile

Company Name: Superkicky
Description: A seasoned team, from tech, AI, UX and retail, that aims to reduce the friction in e-commerce.
Website: http://superkicky.com/
Phone: **Email:** 37483@reference-encyclopedia-ai.net
City: Stockholm **State:** Stockholm County **PC:** **Country: Sweden**
Year Established: 2014 **Status 2020:** Active
Industries: Artificial Intelligence for:, E-Commerce for:, Web

Company Name: Vanita: Israel
Description: Use the magic of context and AI to create smart, compelling visuals; Intelligent Motion Stories.
Website: http://www.vanitail.com
Phone: **Email:** info@vanitail.com
City: Stockholm **State:** Stockholm County **PC:** **Country: Sweden**
Year Established: **Status 2020:** Active
Industries:

Company Name: Vionlabs
Description: VionLabs is a media-tech company based in Stockholm, Sweden.
Website: http://www.vionlabs.com/
Phone: 46 8 410 163 16 **Email:** info@vionlabs.com
City: Stockholm **State:** Stockholm County **PC:** **Country: Sweden**
Year Established: 2010 **Status 2020:** Active
Industries: Digital Media for:, Machine Learning for:, ~ Arts-Entertainment-Recreation (4), ~ Arts-Entertainment-Recreation (4)

Company Name: Volumental
Description: Cloud-based platform using 3D for product customization
Website: http://www.volumental.com
Phone: 46-70-875-5901 **Email:** info@volumental.com
City: Stockholm **State:** Stockholm County **PC:** **Country: Sweden**
Year Established: **Status 2020:** Active
Industries: Artificial Intelligence for:, E-Commerce

Company Name: Watty
Description: Watty makes tools to help people understand what's happening at home in real-time, powered by AI.
Website: http://watty.io
Phone: 46 7 04 15 63 62 **Email:** info@watty.io
City: Stockholm **State:** Stockholm County **PC:** **Country: Sweden**
Year Established: **Status 2020:** Active
Industries: Analytics for:, Artificial Intelligence for:, Machine Learning

Company Name: Weld
Description: Programming for non-techies: create websites and apps without coding
Website: http://www.weld.io
Phone: 46 8-509 245 00 **Email:** contact@weld.io
City: Stockholm **State:** Stockholm County **PC:** **Country: Sweden**
Year Established: **Status 2020:** Active
Industries: Application Services for:, Artificial Intelligence for:, Machine Learning for:, Cyber Security

Company Name: Woop
Description: The first workout app that truly sees you.
Website: http://www.stellarworkouts.com
Phone: **Email:** info@stellarworkouts.com
City: Stockholm **State:** Stockholm County **PC:** **Country: Sweden**
Year Established: 2018 **Status 2020:** Active
Industries: Artificial Intelligence for:, Computer Vision for:, ~ Healthcare (20), Application Services for:, ~ Healthcare (20)

Company **Name:** Acumem
Description: Acumem is a provider of intelligent software which analyzes and helps optimizing the computing performance in single- and multi-core
Website: http://www.acumem.com
Phone: 46 18 13 07 00 **Email:** info@acumem.com
City: Uppsala **State:** Uppsala County **PC:** **Country: Sweden**
Year Established: **Status 2020:** Active
Industries: Artificial Intelligence for:, Business Intelligence for:, Application Services for:, ~ Professional Services (48)

Company Name: Aiida by Softrobot
Description: Automate your workflow and get time for important tasks. Aiida is an AI that will revolutionize the way you work with files.
Website: http://www.aiida.: Sweden
Phone: **Email:** axo.sal@softrobot.io
City: Uppsala **State:** Uppsala County **PC:** **Country: Sweden**
Year Established: **Status 2020:** Active
Industries: Finance and Accounting for:, Artificial Intelligence for:, Machine Learning

Company Name: SoftRobot
Description: A software development company specializing in smart technology and artificial intelligence.
Website: http://www.softrobot.io
Phone: **Email:** info@softrobot.io
City: Uppsala **State:** Uppsala County **PC:** **Country: Sweden**
Year Established: 2015 **Status 2020:** Active
Industries: Artificial Intelligence for:, Big Data and Analytics for:, IT Managed Services for:, Machine Learning for:, Internet of Things (IoT)

Company Name: Unibap
Description: Taking intelligent automation and vision perception further
Website: http://unibap.com
Phone: 46 73 390 86 90 **Email:** info@unibap.com
City: Uppsala **State:** Uppsala County **PC:** **Country: Sweden**
Year Established: **Status 2020:** Active
Industries: Artificial Intelligence for:, Industrial Solutions for:, Automation

Company Name: Loogup
Description: First Artificial Intelligent Real Estate Platform
Website: http://www.loogup.ai
Phone: **Email:** randy@loogup.ai
City: Umea **State:** Västerbotten County **PC:** **Country: Sweden**
Year Established: **Status 2020:** Active
Industries: Artificial Intelligence for:, ~ Real Estate (49)

Company Name: Indivd Ai
Description: A patent-pending AI solution The first solution in the world that can get a deep understanding of all store visitors.
Website: http://www.indivd.com
Phone: 46738406527 **Email:** hello@indivd.com
City: Sundsvall **State:** Västernorrland County **PC:** **Country:** **Sweden**
Year Established: **Status 2020:** Active
Industries: Artificial Intelligence for:, Business Applications for:, Enterprise Application Services for:, ~ Human Resources (24), Machine Learning for:, ~ Retail and Consumer Products (52)

Company Name: Ticketbird
Description: SaaS
Website: http://www.ticketbird.com
Phone: 46214411444 **Email:** support@ticketbird.com
City: Västerås **State:** Västmanland County **PC:** **Country:** **Sweden**
Year Established: 2015 **Status 2020:** Active
Industries: Artificial Intelligence for:, ~ Customer Relationship Management (11), Application Program Interfaces (APIs) for:, Machine Learning for:, Business Software as a Service Apps (SaaS Apps) for:, IT Managed Services

Company Name: Bokio
Description: Bokio save time & paperwork, create your payslips online through your mobile, tablet or computer. Bokio is always at hand. Absolutely free.
Website: http://www.bokio.se/
Phone: **Email:** info@bokio.: Sweden
City: Goteborg **State:** Västra Götaland County **PC:** **Country:** **Sweden**
Year Established: **Status 2020:** Active
Industries: Finance and Accounting for:, Artificial Intelligence for:, Web for:, ~ Professional Services (48)

Company Name: Precisely
Description: Precisely supercharges the contract lifecycle by an AI-powered end-to-end contracting platform.
Website: http://precisely.: Sweden
Phone: 46102203490 **Email:** hello@precisely.: Sweden
City: Goteborg **State:** Västra Götaland County **PC:** **Country:** **Sweden**
Year Established: **Status 2020:** Active
Industries:

Company Name: QuiznGifts
Description: SaaS - Digital Entertainment with Real Rewards
Website: http://quizngifts.com/
Phone: **Email:** magnus@weesteer.com
City: Göteborg **State:** Västra Götaland County **PC:** **Country:** **Sweden**
Year Established: 2014 **Status 2020:** Active
Industries: Business Software as a Service Apps (SaaS Apps)

Company Name: adclouds
Description: Adclouds is an A.I. powered advertising platform where you easily produce, manage, and evolve ads.
Website: http://adclouds.io
Phone: **Email:** hello@adclouds.io
City: Gothenburg **State:** Västra Götaland County **PC:** **Country:** **Sweden**
Year Established: **Status 2020:** Active
Industries: ~ Media-Communications (41), ~ Media-Communications (41), Artificial Intelligence

Company Name: ConsumIQ
Description: Consumer ICT, B2C, BCB
Website: http://www.consumiq.com
Phone: **Email:** hello@consumiq.com
City: Gothenburg **State:** Västra Götaland County **PC:** **Country:** **Sweden**
Year Established: 2014 **Status 2020:** Active
Industries: Artificial Intelligence for:, E-Commerce for:, IT Managed Services

Company Name: Eneryield
Description: Machine learning algorithms for advanced energy analytics
Website: http://www.eneryield.com
Phone: (4670) 673-1196 **Email:** hi@eneryield.com
City: Gothenburg **State:** Västra Götaland County **PC:** **Country:** **Sweden**
Year Established: 2019 **Status 2020:** Active
Industries: Artificial Intelligence for:, ~ Energy and Utilities (14), ~ Energy and Utilities (14), Machine Learning for:, Predictive Analytics

Company Name: Irisity AB (publ)
Description: Meet the smartest, most curious, most exact trouble spotter in the surveillance business.
Website: http://www.irisity.com/
Phone: 46 (0)771-41 11 00 **Email:** info@irisity.: Sweden
City: Gothenburg **State:** Västra Götaland County **PC:** **Country:** **Sweden**
Year Established: **Status 2020:** Active
Industries: Artificial Intelligence for:, Security

Company Name: Jobtip
Description: HR Tech company from Sweden using Ai as a recruiting tool leveraging social platforms for employers and recruite: Serbia
Website: http://Jobtip.com
Phone: 1 619-758-4045 **Email:** marketing@jobtip.com
City: Gothenburg **State:** Västra Götaland County **PC:** **Country:** **Sweden**
Year Established: **Status 2020:** Active
Industries: Artificial Intelligence for:, ~ Human Resources (24), Web for:, ~ Human Resources (24)

Company Name: Machine Intelligence Sweden
Description: Machine Intelligence Sweden is an AI garage that builds AI powered startups to solve important problems in society.
Website: http://machineintelligence.se/
Phone: **Email:** info@machineintelligence.: Sweden
City: Gothenburg **State:** Västra Götaland County **PC:** **Country:** **Sweden**
Year Established: 2016 **Status 2020:** Active
Industries: Artificial Intelligence for:, Machine Learning

Company Name: Optisort
Description: Optisort offers computer vision-based sorting solutions for the recycling industry.
Website: http://www.optisort.com
Phone: 46733800371 **Email:** hanseric.melin@optisort.com
City: Gothenburg **State:** Västra Götaland County **PC:** **Country:** **Sweden**
Year Established: **Status 2020:** Active
Industries: Artificial Intelligence for:, ~ Social-Environmental-Physical-Engineering Sciences (55)

Company Name: Refind Technologies
Description: Refind Technologies uses cameras and machine learning software to teach systems to recognize items based on their looks.
Website: http://www.refind.se/
Phone: 46733100362 **Email:** info@refind.: Sweden
City: Gothenburg **State:** Västra Götaland County **PC:** **Country:** **Sweden**
Year Established: 2014 **Status 2020:** Active
Industries: Artificial Intelligence for:, Machine Learning

Company Name: Tablefinder
Description: Tablefinder is a live search and booking engine that enables users to make restaurant reservations.
Website: http://www.tablefinder.com
Phone: 46317805399 **Email:** info@tablefinder.com
City: Gothenburg **State:** Västra Götaland County **PC:** **Country:** **Sweden**
Year Established: **Status 2020:** Active
Industries: Artificial Intelligence for:, ~ Travel and Transportation (58), ~ Food and Beverage (17), Cyber Security

Company Name: Tajitsu Industri: Spain
Description: Tajitsu is a predictive customer analytics platform that helps progressive marketing teams find, engage and retain high value custome: Serbia
Website: http://www.tajitsu.com
Phone: 27 82 333 7096 **Email:** info@tajitsu.com
City: Gothenburg **State:** Västra Götaland County **PC:** **Country:** **Sweden**
Year Established: **Status 2020:** Active
Industries: Artificial Intelligence for:, Big Data and Analytics for:, Machine Learning for:, Mobile for:, Predictive Analytics for:, ~ Professional Services (48)

Company Name: Textual
Description: Textual provides natural language generation for webshops and brands. Provided as a Saas service integrated in Shopify and PIM-systems.
Website: http://www.textual.ai
Phone: 46706806500 **Email:** henrik@textual.ai
City: Gothenburg **State:** Västra Götaland County **PC:** **Country:** **Sweden**
Year Established: 2014 **Status 2020:** Active
Industries: Artificial Intelligence for:, Big Data and Analytics for:, E-Commerce for:, Business Software as a Service Apps (SaaS Apps) for:, ~ Social Assistance-Non-Profits (53)

Company Name: Zalster
Description: Zalster is an agile platform that automates and optimize Facebook and Instagram advertising.
Website: http://zalster.com
Phone: 46733921666 **Email:** hello@zalster.com
City: Gothenburg **State:** Västra Götaland County **PC:** **Country:** **Sweden**
Year Established: 2015 **Status 2020:** Active
Industries: Predictive Analytics

Switzerland

Company Name: Blueshare
Description:
Website: https://www.blueshare.io/
Phone: 359 885 707 514 **Email:** plamen.sakaliyski@blueshare.io
City: **State:** **PC:** **Country: Switzerland**
Year Established: **Status 2020:** Active
Industries:

Company Name: nudgeIT
Description: nudgeIT artificial intelligence makes service management more cost-efficient, productive and responsive to users.
Website: http://www.nudgeit.ch/
Phone: 41 56 544 72 81 **Email:** info@nudgeit.com
City: Baden **State:** AG **PC:** **Country: Switzerland**
Year Established: 2014 **Status 2020:** Active
Industries: Artificial Intelligence for:, IT Managed Services

Company Name: Presspectrum Technologies
Description: Presspectrum Technologies is a startup developing next-generation data analysis technologies for media and e-commerce.
Website:
Phone: 41 44 508 56 52 **Email:** 37205@reference-encyclopedia-ai.net
City: Wettingen **State:** AG **PC:** **Country: Switzerland**
Year Established: 2013 **Status 2020:** Closed
Industries: E-Commerce for:, IT Managed Services for:, Machine Learning

Company Name: Epoque Plus
Description: Leading Artificial Intelligence Trading Services provider for high-net-worth individuals, family offices & institutional investors.
Website: http://www.epoque-plus.ch/
Phone: **Email:** contact@epoque-plus.: Switzerland
City: Herisau **State:** AR **PC:** **Country: Switzerland**
Year Established: **Status 2020:** Active
Industries: Artificial Intelligence for:, ~ Banking and Financial Markets-Services (7)

Company Name: helixstreet.com AG
Description: DNA Sequencing / Precision Medicine / Whole Genome Sequencing / Long Read Sequencing / Machine Learning / Deep Learning / Cryptos / Talents
Website: http://helixstreet.com
Phone: **Email:** info@helixstreet.com
City: Basel **State:** BS **PC:** **Country: Switzerland**
Year Established: 2017 **Status 2020:** Active
Industries: Artificial Intelligence for:, ~ Healthcare (20)

Company Name: Parashift AG
Description: AI based autonomouse Accounting technology
Website: http://www.parashift.io
Phone: 41615087777 **Email:** support@parashift.io
City: Sissach **State:** BL **PC:** **Country: Switzerland**
Year Established: **Status 2020:** Active
Industries: Artificial Intelligence for:, Machine Learning

Company Name: ahead
Description: ahead is an intranet platform that brings your AI-powered digital workplace for SharePoint and Office 365.
Website: https://www.aheadintranet.com/en/
Phone: 41315608880 **Email:** support@isolutions.: Switzerland
City: Bern **State:** BE **PC:** **Country: Switzerland**
Year Established: 2017 **Status 2020:** Active
Industries: Artificial Intelligence for:, IT Managed Services for:, Web for:, Machine Learning for:, Business Software as a Service Apps (SaaS Apps)

Company Name: AI Retailer Systems
Description: Checkout-free solutions based on computer vision and machine learning
Website: http://www.airetailersystems.com/
Phone: **Email:** contact@airetailersystems.com
City: Bern **State:** BE **PC:** **Country: Switzerland**
Year Established: 2019 **Status 2020:** Active
Industries: Artificial Intelligence for:, Computer Vision for:, IT Managed Services for:, Machine Learning

Company Name: Jamie & I
Description: Jamie & I is personal, AI-driven, online stylist.
Website: http://eu.jamieandi.com/
Phone: **Email:** antonia@jamieandi.com
City: Bern **State:** BE **PC:** **Country: Switzerland**
Year Established: 2017 **Status 2020:** Active
Industries: Artificial Intelligence for:, ~ Fashion (16)

Company Name: JobsMarkt
Description: JobsMarkt Connects Employers with Talent Using Intelligent Recruitment
Website: http://www.jobsmarkt.com
Phone: 41(0)31 901 0505 **Email:** welcome@jobsmarkt.com
City: Bern **State:** BE **PC:** **Country: Switzerland**
Year Established: 2015 **Status 2020:** Active
Industries: Artificial Intelligence for:, Enterprise Application Services for:, IT Managed Services for:, Machine Learning for:, Machine Learning for:, Natural Language Processing

Company Name: Retinai
Description: RetinAI optimises and simplifies clinics, research and pharmaceutical workflows to improve healthcare.
Website: http://www.retinai.com
Phone: **Email:** info@retinai.com
City: Bern **State:** BE **PC:** **Country: Switzerland**
Year Established: 2016 **Status 2020:** Active
Industries: Artificial Intelligence for:, Cloud for:, ~ Healthcare (20), ~ Healthcare (20), IT Managed Services for:, Machine Learning

Company Name: Spoud
Description: Spoud is a human centred approach to data-driven enterprises that empower a collaborative data-driven culture.
Website: http://www.spoud.io/
Phone: 031 508 30 60 **Email:** info@spoud.io
City: Bern **State:** BE **PC:** **Country: Switzerland**
Year Established: 2016 **Status 2020:** Active
Industries: Analytics for:, Big Data and Analytics for:, IT Managed Services for:, Machine Learning

Company Name: w hoch 2
Description: w hoch 2 offers applied research, statistical analysis and scientific advice.
Website: http://www.w-hoch2.ch/
Phone: 41 31 558 58 63 **Email:** info@w-hoch2.: Switzerland
City: Bern **State:** BE **PC:** **Country: Switzerland**
Year Established: 2014 **Status 2020:** Active
Industries:

Company Name: Threatray
Description: Threatray produces code-based threat intelligence by making massive malware repositories and feeds searchable and correlatable.
Website: http://threatray.com/
Phone: **Email:** 37537@reference-encyclopedia-ai.net
City: Biel **State:** BE **PC:** **Country: Switzerland**
Year Established: 2018 **Status 2020:** Active
Industries: Artificial Intelligence

Company Name: Wild Tree Tech
Description: Wild Tree Tech is a small company focused on education and independent data-science software.
Website: http://www.wildtreetech.com
Phone: **Email:** hello@wildtreetech.com
City: Brügg **State:** BE **PC:** **Country: Switzerland**
Year Established: 2016 **Status 2020:** Active
Industries:

Company Name: Intelligent Insights
Description: Intelligent Insights are specialized in pattern recognition and machine learning.
Website: http://www.intelligentinsights.: Switzerland
Phone: 41 79 545 58 14 **Email:** info@intelligentinsights.: Switzerland
City: Liebefeld **State:** BE **PC:** **Country: Switzerland**
Year Established: 2014 **Status 2020:** Active
Industries: Artificial Intelligence for:, Machine Learning

Company Name: ADSuisse AG
Description: Discover your customers through data
Website: https://www.adsuisse.com/
Phone: 41445544944 **Email:** r.eck@adsuisse.com
City: Baar **State:** ZG **PC:** **Country: Switzerland**
Year Established: 2017 **Status 2020:** Active
Industries: Artificial Intelligence for:, Big Data and Analytics for:, Content for:, Content for:, ~ Customer Relationship Management (11), Data Management

Company Name: Data Suisse AG
Description: Data Suisse is a deep tech company that helps enterprises boost the quality of their data assets.
Website: http://data-suisse.com
Phone: 41 44 5544 999 **Email:** info@data-suisse.com
City: Baar **State:** ZG **PC:** **Country: Switzerland**
Year Established: 2019 **Status 2020:** Active
Industries: Artificial Intelligence for:, IT Managed Services

Company Name: Veeam Software Corporation
Description:
Website: http://www.veeam.com
Phone: 408-579-4000 **Email:** jim.bahn@virtualinstruments.com
City: Baar **State:** ZG **Zip:** 6340 **Country: Switzerland**
Year Established: **Status 2020:** Active
Industries:

Company Name: BGX
Description: BGX is a multifunctional processing platform.
Website: http://bgx.ai/
Phone: **Email:** info@bgx.ai
City: Zug **State:** ZG **PC:** **Country: Switzerland**
Year Established: 2017 **Status 2020:** Active
Industries: Artificial Intelligence for:, Blockchain for:, ~ Banking and Financial Markets-Services (7), ~ Banking and Financial Markets-Services (7)

Company **Name:** Colendi
Description: Colendi is comprehensive decentralized credit scoring protocol and microcredit platform with blockchain and machine learning Technologies
Website: http://www.colendi.com/
Phone: **Email:** info@colendi.com
City: Zug **State:** ZG **PC:** **Country: Switzerland**
Year Established: 2016 **Status 2020:** Active
Industries: Artificial Intelligence for:, Blockchain for:, Blockchain for:, ~ Banking and Financial Markets-Services (7), Machine Learning

Company Name: Guruvest Ltd.
Description: Guruvest is the next generation investment platform.
Website: http://www.guruvest.io
Phone: **Email:** info@guruvest.io
City: Zug **State:** ZG **PC:** **Country: Switzerland**
Year Established: **Status 2020:** Active
Industries: Artificial Intelligence for:, Blockchain for:, ~ Banking and Financial Markets-Services (7)

Company Name: Mindfire Foundation
Description: Mindfire unites the greatest minds on earth so as to unlock the underlying principles of human intelligence.
Website: http://mindfire.global/
Phone: **Email:** press@mindfire.global
City: Zug **State:** ZG **PC:** **Country: Switzerland**
Year Established: **Status 2020:** Active
Industries: Artificial Intelligence for:, Big Data and Analytics for:, IT Managed Services for:, ~ Social Assistance-Non-Profits (53)

Company Name: Open Packaging Network
Description: Open Source software, 2-Sided AI Driven B2B online marketplace, connects packaging raw materials buyers and sellers directly.
Website: http://www.opnplatform.com/
Phone: 41788589177 **Email:** sergio@opnplatform.com
City: Zug **State:** ZG **PC:** **Country: Switzerland**
Year Established: **Status 2020:** Active
Industries: Artificial Intelligence for:, Business Applications for:, Blockchain for:, IT Managed Services for:, IT Managed Services for:, ~ Professional Services (48)

Company Name: Push.ai LLC
Description: The best shopping experience in your favorite chat app
Website: http://masha.ai
Phone: 4179 873 27 00 **Email:** frederik@masha.ai
City: Zug **State:** ZG **PC:** **Country: Switzerland**
Year Established: 2019 **Status 2020:** Active
Industries: Artificial Intelligence for:, E-Commerce for:, ~ Banking and Financial Markets-Services (7), ~ Retail and Consumer Products (52)

Company Name: Saphirion AG
Description: Saphirion AG is a software company specialize in price analysis software.
Website: http://www.saphirion.com
Phone: **Email:** info@saphirion.com
City: Zug **State:** ZG **PC:** **Country: Switzerland**
Year Established: 2011 **Status 2020:** Active
Industries: Analytics for:, Predictive Analytics

Company Name: StopFakeFood
Description: Food integrity and product authenticity solutions using AI and Spectrometry
Website: http://www.stopfakefood.com/
Phone: **Email:** info@stopfakefood.com
City: Zug **State:** ZG **PC:** **Country: Switzerland**
Year Established: 2017 **Status 2020:** Active
Industries: Analytics for:, Artificial Intelligence for:, Blockchain for:, IT Managed Services

Company Name: SwissCognitive
Description: SwissCognitive–THE Global AI Hub - meet, exchange, connect , according to our core principle 'share for success'.
Website: http://swisscognitive.ch/
Phone: 41 79 200 88 66 **Email:** info@swisscognitive.: Switzerland
City: Zug **State:** ZG **PC:** **Country: Switzerland**
Year Established: 2016 **Status 2020:** Active
Industries: Artificial Intelligence for:, Business Intelligence for:, Computer Vision for:, Databases for:, Facial Recognition for:, Application Services for:, Predictive Analytics for:, Robotics for:, Robotics for:, Speech Recognition for:, Data Management

Company Name: LegalKite
Description: LegalKite is an AI-based search engine for legal content.
Website: http://legalkite.net
Phone: **Email:** info@legalkite.: Switzerland
City: Neyruz **State:** FR **PC:** **Country: Switzerland**
Year Established: **Status 2020:** Active
Industries:

Company Name: DynaMetrics
Description: DynaMetrics is developing an automated credit scoring tool based on big data / analytics & AI.
Website:
Phone: **Email:** 36462@reference-encyclopedia-ai.net
City: Villars-sur-glane **State:** FR **PC:** **Country: Switzerland**
Year Established: 2017 **Status 2020:** Closed
Industries: IT Managed Services

Company Name: ViDi Systems
Description: ViDi is a deep learning-based software dedicated to industrial image analysis.
Website: http://www.vidi-systems.com/
Phone: 41266537230 **Email:** info@vidi-systems.com
City: Villaz-saint-pierre **State:** FR **PC:** **Country: Switzerland**
Year Established: 2012 **Status 2020:** Active
Industries: Artificial Intelligence for:, Computer Vision for:, Machine Learning

Company Name: Aequicens
Description: Artificial Intelligence and Machine Learning Research Lab
Website: http://www.aequicens.com
Phone: **Email:** management@aequicens.com
City: Geneva **State:** GE **PC:** **Country: Switzerland**
Year Established: **Status 2020:** Active
Industries: Artificial Intelligence for:, Databases for:, IT Managed Services for:, Machine Learning for:, ~ Life Sciences (27), Predictive Analytics for:, ~ Social Media (54), ~ Professional Services (48)

Company Name: Faveeo
Description: Faveeo is the first AI-Driven trusted content platform.
Website: http://www.faveeo.com
Phone: 41 76 586 29 27 **Email:** alexis@faveeo.com
City: Geneva **State:** GE **PC:** **Country: Switzerland**
Year Established: 2012 **Status 2020:** Active
Industries: Artificial Intelligence for:, Content for:, Digital Marketing

Company Name: Grydl Analytics
Description: Grydl Analytics are specializing in blockchain, big data and artificial intelligence technologies.
Website: http://www.grydl.com
Phone: (4122) 519-0324 **Email:** contact@grydl.com
City: Geneva **State:** GE **PC:** **Country: Switzerland**
Year Established: 2015 **Status 2020:** Active
Industries: Artificial Intelligence for:, Blockchain for:, ~ Banking and Financial Markets-Services (7), IT Managed Services

Company Name: ImmuniWeb
Description: AI-Enabled Attack Surface Management, Dark Web Monitoring, & Application Penetration Testing solutions tailored to reduce complexity & costs
Website: http://www.immuniweb.com
Phone: 41 22 723 24 24 **Email:** sales@immuniweb.com
City: Geneva **State:** GE **PC:** **Country: Switzerland**
Year Established: 2019 **Status 2020:** Active
Industries: Artificial Intelligence for:, Cyber Security for:, Machine Learning for:, Business Software as a Service Apps (SaaS Apps)

Company Name: Securax
Description: Securaxis leverages new technologies such as AI, data science, ioT to develop security & safety solutions, sp. smart acoustic sensors.
Website: http://www.securaxis.com
Phone: 41788678370 **Email:** gmeleder@securaxis.com
City: Geneva **State:** GE **PC:** **Country: Switzerland**
Year Established: 2015 **Status 2020:** Active
Industries: Artificial Intelligence for:, IT Managed Services for:, IT Managed Services for:, ~ Administrative and Support Services (1), Risk Management

Company Name: Socialea: Sweden
Description: Socialease is AI software that turns SMEs social & digital media communication challenge into a simple and efficient marketing opportunity.
Website: http://socialease.: Switzerland
Phone: 41786200889 **Email:** hello@socialease.: Switzerland
City: Geneve **State:** GE **PC:** **Country: Switzerland**
Year Established: **Status 2020:** Active
Industries: Artificial Intelligence for:, ~ Media-Communications (41), ~ Social Media (54)

Company Name: Andrew Alliance
Description: Andrew Alliance is the Swiss pioneer in robotics for the Life Sciences sector.
Website: http://andrewalliance.com
Phone: 41 22 534 93 40 **Email:** contact@andrewAlliance.com
City: Genève **State:** GE **PC:** **Country: Switzerland**
Year Established: 2011 **Status 2020:** Active
Industries: Artificial Intelligence for:, Robotics

Company Name: Popety.io
Description: Real Estate Technology Company
Website: http://www.popety.io
Phone: **Email:** support@popety.com
City: Plan-les-ouates **State:** GE **PC:** **Country: Switzerland**
Year Established: 2018 **Status 2020:** Active
Industries: Artificial Intelligence

Company Name: HAL9k Capital AG
Description: Venture Capital Investment Holding targeting IoT, AI, Robotics and Cybersecurity ventures with a particular focus on the Machine Economy.
Website: http://hal9k.vc
Phone: **Email:** invest@hal9k.vc
City: Chur **State:** GR **PC:** **Country: Switzerland**
Year Established: 2019 **Status 2020:** Active
Industries: Artificial Intelligence for:, ~ Banking and Financial Markets-Services (7), IT Managed Services

Company Name: OrganizationView
Description: Analytics, Human Resources, SaaS
Website: http://www.organizationview.com
Phone: **Email:** Andrew.marritt@organizationview.com
City: Sankt Moritz **State:** GR **PC:** **Country: Switzerland**
Year Established: 2010 **Status 2020:** Active
Industries: Analytics for:, Artificial Intelligence for:, Robotics for:, Business Software as a Service Apps (SaaS Apps)

Company Name: GEOSAT
Description: Geosatis develops electronic monitoring solutions such as bracelets for the monitoring and reinsertion of offenders.
Website: http://geo-satis.com/
Phone: (4132) 552-0480 **Email:** info@geo-satis.com
City: Le Noirmont **State:** JU **PC:** **Country: Switzerland**
Year Established: 2011 **Status 2020:** Active
Industries: Cyber Security for:, Embedded for:, Internet of Things (IoT) for:, Application Services for:, Predictive Analytics for:, ~ Government (19), ~ Telecommunications (56), ~ Telecommunications (56)

Company Name: AXON VIBE AG
Description: Location-based AI / app tech to enable public transport operators to orchestrate their customers' door to door mobility
Website: http://axonvibe.com
Phone: (4141) 249-2525 **Email:** info@axonvibe.com
City: Luzern **State:** LU **PC:** **Country: Switzerland**
Year Established: 2014 **Status 2020:** Active
Industries:

Company Name: Scailyte
Description: Data-driven biomarker discovery and single-cell precision diagnostics
Website: http://www.scailyte.com
Phone: **Email:** contact@scailyte.com
City: Sursee **State:** LU **PC:** **Country: Switzerland**
Year Established: 2017 **Status 2020:** Active
Industries: Artificial Intelligence for:, ~ Biotechnology (9), ~ Healthcare (20), ~ Healthcare (20)

Company Name: ipQuants AG
Description: Innovation Analytics, Big Data, Legal Analytics
Website: http://ipquants.com/
Phone: **Email:** info@ipQuants.com
City: Schaffhausen **State:** SH **PC:** **Country: Switzerland**
Year Established: **Status 2020:** Active
Industries: Analytics for:, Artificial Intelligence for:, Big Data and Analytics for:, ~ Law-Legal Services (26), Machine Learning

Company Name: Schaffhausen Institute of Technology
Description: Schaffhausen Institute of Technology is an international research-led university that provides research, knowledge, and education.
Website: http://sit.org
Phone: **Email:** admission@sit.org
City: Schaffhausen **State:** SH **PC:** **Country: Switzerland**
Year Established: 2019 **Status 2020:** Active
Industries: Artificial Intelligence for:, ~ Education (13), ~ Education (13), IT Managed Services for:, Machine Learning

Company Name: viso.ai
Description: viso.ai is the world's first online tool that helps businesses use computer vision technology to automate their operations.
Website: http://viso.ai/
Phone: 41 (0)44 500 92 29 **Email:** info@viso.ai
City: Schaffhausen **State:** SH **PC:** **Country: Switzerland**
Year Established: 2017 **Status 2020:** Active
Industries: Artificial Intelligence for:, Computer Vision for:, Internet of Things (IoT) for:, Machine Learning

Company Name: indagia
Description: Indagia is the world's first and only fully integrated audit platform powered by AI!
Website: http://www.indagia.com
Phone: **Email:** info@indagia.com
City: Freienbach **State:** SZ **PC:** **Country: Switzerland**
Year Established: **Status 2020:** Active
Industries: Artificial Intelligence for:, ~ Banking and Financial Markets-Services (7), ~ Banking and Financial Markets-Services (7), ~ Professional Services (48)

Company **Name:** fronttrail Equity Partners
Description: Growth capital investor in European software technology companies in expansion and late stage situations
Website: http://www.fronttrail.com
Phone: 41 44 210 4985 **Email:** requests@fronttrail.com
City: Wollerau **State:** SZ **PC:** **Country: Switzerland**
Year Established: 2016 **Status 2020:** Active
Industries: Artificial Intelligence for:, ~ Banking and Financial Markets-Services (7), IT Managed Services for:, Business Software as a Service Apps (SaaS Apps) for:, ~ Banking and Financial Markets-Services (7)

Company Name: MOOST
Description: Machine Learning as a Service for Smart Home Applications
Website: http://www.moost.io/
Phone: 41 32 510 26 23 **Email:** hello@moost.io
City: Jona **State:** SG **PC:** **Country: Switzerland**
Year Established: 2016 **Status 2020:** Active
Industries: Artificial Intelligence for:, Big Data and Analytics for:, Machine Learning for:, Predictive Analytics for:, ~ Construction (10)

Company Name: PANDY AI
Description: An AI recruitment platform that reduces recruitment costs by 90%, hiring time by 50%, and HR workload by 40%.
Website: http://www.pandy.ai/
Phone: 41 44 53 30 970 **Email:** pandy@pandy.ai
City: Rapperswil **State:** SG **PC:** **Country: Switzerland**
Year Established: 2018 **Status 2020:** Active
Industries: Machine Learning

Company Name: Adverti: Morocco
Description: Advertima creates an artificial intelligence that analyzes people in its surroundings.
Website: https://www.advertima.com/
Phone: **Email:** info@advertima.com
City: Saint Gallen **State:** SG **PC:** **Country: Switzerland**
Year Established: 2016 **Status 2020:** Active
Industries: Artificial Intelligence for:, Human Computer Interaction

Company Name: Mechmine
Description: Predictive Maintenance and Condition Monitoring of machines with IoT, AI and big data, making and selling related HW.
Website: http://mechmine.com
Phone: 41- (0) 76-565-3-161 **Email:** info@mechmine.com
City: Saint Gallen **State:** SG **PC: Country: Switzerland**
Year Established: 2015 **Status 2020:** Active
Industries: Artificial Intelligence for:, IT Managed Services for:, Machine Learning for:, ~ Metals and Mining (42), Predictive Analytics

Company Name: KEMA: ROMANIA
Description: autonomous robotics engineering
Website: http://www.kemaro.: Switzerland
Phone: 41 79 288 8602 **Email:** info@kemaro.: Switzerland
City: Eschlikon **State:** TG **PC: Country: Switzerland**
Year Established: 2016 **Status 2020:** Active
Industries: ~ Telecommunications (56), Robotics

Company Name: ABI Solutions
Description: ABI Solutions is an AI technologies for accounting .
Website: https://abisolutions.ch/
Phone: 4191 210 30 03 **Email:** info@abisolutions.: Switzerland
City: Lugano **State:** TI **PC: Country: Switzerland**
Year Established: 2018 **Status 2020:** Active
Industries: Artificial Intelligence

Company Name: Ingenera : SAUDI ARABIA
Description: 3D full body analysis devices and services for animal phenotyping.
Website: http://www.ingenera.: Switzerland
Phone: 41 91 9500101 **Email:** info@ingenera.: Switzerland
City: Lugano **State:** TI **PC: Country: Switzerland**
Year Established: 2013 **Status 2020:** Active
Industries: Artificial Intelligence for:, ~ Agriculture (3)

Company Name: NNAISEN: SWEDEN
Description: NNAISENSE (pronounced "nascence") is an artificial general intelligence (AGI) and deep learning start-up led by pioneers in the field.
Website: http://nnaisense.com/
Phone: **Email:** info@nnaisense.com
City: Lugano **State:** TI **PC: Country: Switzerland**
Year Established: 2014 **Status 2020:** Active
Industries:

Company Name: SwissLeg
Description: SwissLeg provides affordable artificial limbs to amputees in the developing world.
Website: http://swissleg.com
Phone: **Email:** info@swissleg.com
City: Lugano **State:** TI **PC: Country: Switzerland**
Year Established: 2012 **Status 2020:** Active
Industries: Artificial Intelligence

Company Name: Waterdata
Description: Waterdata is a provider of AI solutions that help retailers to transform their data into profitable automated marketing actions.
Website: http://liquidprice.ai/
Phone: **Email:** waterdata@waterdata.com
City: Lugano **State:** TI **PC: Country: Switzerland**
Year Established: 2016 **Status 2020:** Active
Industries: Analytics for:, Artificial Intelligence for:, E-Commerce for:, Machine Learning

Company Name: Logol
Description: Logol, pioneering specialist in the field of cloud-enabled digital transformation
Website: http://www.logol.com
Phone: 0041 (0)91 210 5827 **Email:** info@logol.com
City: Mendrisio **State:** TI **PC: Country: Switzerland**
Year Established: Status 2020: Active
Industries: Artificial Intelligence for:, IT Managed Services

Company Name: Eyeware
Description: Eyeware offers solutions for using eye tracking information in real-world interactions, by capturing user attention, intention & interest.
Website: http://eyeware.tech
Phone: **Email:** contact@eyeware.tech
City: Martigny **State:** VS **PC: Country: Switzerland**
Year Established: 2016 **Status 2020:** Active
Industries: Artificial Intelligence for:, ~ Automotive (5), ~ Automotive (5), Human Computer Interaction for:, Internet of Things (IoT) for:, Machine Learning

Company Name: recapp
Description: recap offers speech recognition and natural language processing technology solutions to search and access audio contents.
Website: http://www.recapp.
Phone: 41277217776 **Email:** contact@recapp.
City: Martigny **State:** VS **PC: Country: Switzerland**
Year Established: 2014 **Status 2020:** Active
Industries: Analytics for:, IT Managed Services for:, Machine Learning for:, Web

Company Name: Aitonomi TeleRetail
Description: Aitonomi TeleRetail is an autopilot software for driving vehicles.
Website: http://www.aitonomi.com/
Phone: 1 415 335 4480 **Email:** info@teleretail.com
City: Sierre **State:** VS **PC: Country: Switzerland**
Year Established: 2012 **Status 2020:** Active
Industries: Artificial Intelligence for:, ~ Automotive (5), IT Managed Services for:, Robotics

Company Name: Urbio
Description: Urbio is a platform for urban planning combining AI and human expertise.
Website: http://www.urb.io
Phone: **Email:** contact@urb.io
City: Sion **State:** VS **PC: Country: Switzerland**
Year Established: 2019 **Status 2020:** Active
Industries: Artificial Intelligence for:, ~ Energy and Utilities (14), ~ Government (19), IT Managed Services for:, ~ Construction (10)

Company Name: GenLots
Description: GenLots uses machine learning SaaS to optimize the supply chain and reduce total purchasing cost by up to 10%.
Website: http://www.genlots.com/
Phone: **Email:** contact@genlots.com
City: Chexbres **State:** VD **PC: Country: Switzerland**
Year Established: 2017 **Status 2020:** Active
Industries: Artificial Intelligence for:, Machine Learning for:, Business Software as a Service Apps (SaaS Apps) for:, Supply Chain Management

Company Name: Picterra
Description: User-Sourced artificial intelligence for earth imaging
Website: http://www.picterra.ch/
Phone: **Email:** 37167@reference-encyclopedia-ai.net
City: Ecublens **State:** VD **PC: Country: Switzerland**
Year Established: 2016 **Status 2020:** Active
Industries: ~ Aerospace and Defense (2), Artificial Intelligence for:, Computer Vision for:, Internet of Things (IoT) for:, Machine Learning

Company Name: SkAD Labs
Description: Skeleton|CAx™ is an intelligent engineering software reducing the development time of physical products by 50%
Website: http://www.skadlabs.com
Phone: **Email:** contact@skadlabs.com
City: Ecublens **State:** VD **PC: Country: Switzerland**

Year Established: 2016 **Status 2020:** Active
Industries: Artificial Intelligence for:, Cloud for:, Enterprise Application Services for:, ~ Manufacturing-General (31), Machine Learning for:, ~ Manufacturing-General (31), ~ Social-Environmental-Physical-Engineering Sciences (55)

Company Name: DEEP CUBE
Description: DEEP CUBE is an AI startup company doing medical image diagnosis with AI.
Website: http://www.deepcube.: Switzerland
Phone: 41 (0)78 631 50 20 **Email:** chris@deepcube.: Switzerland
City: Epalinges **State:** VD **PC:** **Country: Switzerland**
Year Established: 2018 **Status 2020:** Active
Industries: Artificial Intelligence for:, ~ Healthcare (20)

Company Name: NOVIGENIX
Description: Novigenix is a Swiss molecular diagnostics company leveraging the host immune response & Machine Learning for early detection of cancer
Website: http://www.novigenix.com
Phone: **Email:** nicolas.demierre@novigenix.com
City: Epalinges **State:** VD **PC:** **Country: Switzerland**
Year Established: 2014 **Status 2020:** Active
Industries: Artificial Intelligence for:, ~ Biotechnology (9), ~ Healthcare (20), Machine Learning for:, Predictive Analytics

Company Name: AELER Technologies
Description: AELER is an AI-powered, logistics technology company. They enable full in-transit visibility through next-gen shipping containers.
Website: http://aeler.com
Phone: **Email:** keepintouch@aeler.com
City: Lausanne **State:** VD **PC:** **Country: Switzerland**
Year Established: **Status 2020:** Active
Industries: Artificial Intelligence for:, IT Managed Services for:, IT Managed Services for:, ~ Transportation and Logistics (57), Security for:, ~ Transportation and Logistics (57), Supply Chain Management

Company Name: Agam Security
Description: Agam Security provides a cyber-defense appliance able to automatically detect and block all attacks by using Artificial Intelligence.
Website: https://agamsecurity.ch/
Phone: **Email:** info@agamsecurity.: Switzerland
City: Lausanne **State:** VD **PC:** **Country: Switzerland**
Year Established: 2016 **Status 2020:** Active
Industries:

Company Name: AIcrowd
Description: Crowdsourcing AI to solve real-world problems
Website: https://www.aicrowd.com/
Phone: **Email:** hello@aicrowd.com
City: Lausanne **State:** VD **PC:** **Country: Switzerland**
Year Established: 2018 **Status 2020:** Active
Industries: Artificial Intelligence for:, Machine Learning

Company Name: Akselos
Description: Akselos is the creator of the world's most advanced digital twin technology to protect critical infrastructure today and tomorrow.
Website: http://www.akselos.com/
Phone: **Email:** info@akselos.com
City: Lausanne **State:** VD **PC:** **Country: Switzerland**
Year Established: 2012 **Status 2020:** Active
Industries: Analytics for:, ~ Banking and Financial Markets-Services (7), IT Managed Services for:, IT Infrastructure for:, ~ Social-Environmental-Physical-Engineering Sciences (55)

Company Name: Bright Box
Description: Bright Box is a global corporation that is specialized in solutions and platforms in the Connected Car sector.
Website: http://bright-box.com/
Phone: (4121) 560-5568 **Email:** global@bright-box.com
City: Lausanne **State:** VD **PC:** **Country: Switzerland**
Year Established: 2012 **Status 2020:** Active
Industries: Artificial Intelligence for:, ~ Automotive (5), Big Data and Analytics for:, IT Managed Services for:, Internet of Things (IoT) for:, Mobile

Company Name: ChemAlive : Saudi Arabia
Description: MAchine Learning, Big data and Cloud Driven Automated Quantum Chemistry
Website: http://www.chemalive.com
Phone: 41 (0)78 817 27 36 **Email:** 36265@reference-encyclopedia-ai.net
City: Lausanne **State:** VD **PC:** **Country: Switzerland**
Year Established: 2018 **Status 2020:** Active
Industries: ~ Manufacturing-Petroleum-Coal-Chemicals-Plastics-Rubber (37), Machine Learning

Company Name: GenView
Description: GenView is a Swiss IT Software company.
Website: http://genview3d.com
Phone: (4121) 546-2030 **Email:** 36615@reference-encyclopedia-ai.net
City: Lausanne **State:** VD **PC:** **Country: Switzerland**
Year Established: 2015 **Status 2020:** Active
Industries: IT Managed Services for:, Application Services

Company Name: Iprova
Description: Iprova uses advanced machine learning and other technologies to augment human intelligence.
Website: http://www.iprova.com
Phone: 41 (0) 21 552 0790 **Email:** hello@iprova.com
City: Lausanne **State:** VD **PC:** **Country: Switzerland**
Year Established: 2010 **Status 2020:** Active
Industries:

Company Name: Kido Dynamics
Description: Kido Dynamics uses machine learning and quantum physics techniques to analyse and predict human mobility.
Website: http://www.kidodynamics.com
Phone: **Email:** info@kidodynamics.com
City: Lausanne **State:** VD **PC:** **Country: Switzerland**
Year Established: **Status 2020:** Active
Industries: Analytics for:, Artificial Intelligence for:, Big Data and Analytics for:, Machine Learning for:, ~ Media-Communications (41), ~ Education (13), ~ Travel and Transportation (58), ~ Transportation and Logistics (57)

Company Name: L2F
Description: Creating Space for Meaning
Website: http://www.l2f.ch/
Phone: **Email:** business@l2f.: Switzerland
City: Lausanne **State:** VD **PC:** **Country: Switzerland**
Year Established: 2017 **Status 2020:** Active
Industries: Big Data and Analytics for:, Data Management for:, Databases for:, Machine Learning for:, Predictive Analytics

Company Name: Largo
Description: Largo provides data-driven intelligence to the movie industry with the proprietary technologies.
Website: http://largo.ai/
Phone: **Email:** info@largofilms.: Switzerland
City: Lausanne **State:** VD **PC:** **Country: Switzerland**
Year Established: 2018 **Status 2020:** Active
Industries: Analytics for:, Artificial Intelligence for:, Big Data and Analytics for:, IT Managed Services

Company Name: MindMaze
Description: MindMaze designs an intuitive mind/machine interface through its neuro-inspired computing platform.
Website: http://www.mindmaze.com
Phone: (4121) 552-0801 **Email:** info@mindmaze.com
City: Lausanne **State:** VD **PC:** **Country: Switzerland**
Year Established: 2012 **Status 2020:** Active
Industries: Artificial Intelligence for:, ~ Healthcare (20), IT Managed Services for:, Virtual Reality (VR)

Company Name: SalesWings
Description: SalesWings is the world's most intuitive way for growing sales and marketing teams to track, qualify and prioritize their very best leads.
Website: http://www.saleswingsapp.com
Phone: **Email:** 37333@reference-encyclopedia-ai.net
City: Lausanne **State:** VD **PC:** **Country: Switzerland**
Year Established: **Status 2020:** Active
Industries: Predictive Analytics for:, Automation

Company Name: Sight.io
Description: The key technology and expertise that we have is a set of computer vision algorithms,
Website: http://Sight.io
Phone: **Email:** info@sight.io
City: Lausanne **State:** VD **PC:** **Country: Switzerland**
Year Established: 2011 **Status 2020:** Active
Industries: Artificial Intelligence for:, Computer Vision for:, IT Managed Services for:, Machine Learning for:, Robotics

Company Name: SOPHiA GENETICS
Description: SOPHiA GENETICS combines deep expertise in life sciences and medical disciplines with mathematical capabilities in data computing.
Website: http://www.sophiagenetics.com/home.html
Phone: 41216941060 **Email:** info@sophiagenetics.com
City: Lausanne **State:** VD **PC:** **Country: Switzerland**
Year Established: 2011 **Status 2020:** Active
Industries: Artificial Intelligence for:, Big Data and Analytics for:, ~ Biotechnology (9), ~ Biotechnology (9), ~ Healthcare (20), ~ Healthcare (20), Machine Learning for:, Machine Learning for:, ~ Healthcare (20)

Company Name: Techn
Description: Technis is building the future of connected and interactive flooring. Starting with a new generation of intelligent touch-enabled surface.
Website: http://mytechnis.com
Phone: 41 21 519 05 07 **Email:** info@mytechnis.com
City: Lausanne **State:** VD **PC:** **Country: Switzerland**
Year Established: 2016 **Status 2020:** Active
Industries:

Company Name: Thymio
Description: Thymio is an educational and open-source robot that allows you to discover robotics and programming.
Website: http://www.thymio.org/home-en:home
Phone: **Email:** info@mobsya.org
City: Lausanne **State:** VD **PC:** **Country: Switzerland**
Year Established: 2011 **Status 2020:** Active
Industries: Artificial Intelligence for:, ~ Education (13), Application Services for:, Robotics

Company Name: Unit8
Description: Artificial Intelligence, Machine Learning, Data Science and data engineering service
Website: http://unit8.co/
Phone: **Email:** info@unit8.co
City: Lausanne **State:** VD **PC:** **Country: Switzerland**
Year Established: 2017 **Status 2020:** Active
Industries:

Company Name: VisioSafe
Description: VisioSafe is a software editing firm specialized in artificial intelligence, computer vision, machine learning, video management, and more.
Website: http://www.visiosafe.com/en/index.html
Phone: **Email:** info@visiosafe.com
City: Lausanne **State:** VD **PC:** **Country: Switzerland**
Year Established: 2011 **Status 2020:** Active
Industries: Artificial Intelligence for:, IT Managed Services for:, Machine Learning

Company Name: Gamaya
Description: Gamaya improves efficiency & sustainability of farming by offering compelling agronomy solutions, enabled by hyperspectral imaging and AI.
Website: http://gamaya.com
Phone: (4121) 566-7888 **Email:** info@gamaya.com
City: Morges **State:** VD **PC:** **Country: Switzerland**
Year Established: 2014 **Status 2020:** Active
Industries: ~ Agriculture (3), ~ Agriculture (3), Artificial Intelligence for:, Big Data and Analytics for:, Robotics

Company Name: Anemomind
Description: AngelList is an online platform for start-ups and investors, facilitating all sorts of early-stage technology funding deals.
Website: http://www.anemomind.com/
Phone: 33 682 06 42 70 **Email:** julien@anemomind.com
City: Renens **State:** VD **PC:** **Country: Switzerland**
Year Established: 2014 **Status 2020:** Active
Industries: Artificial Intelligence for:, Finance and Accounting for:, IT Managed Services

Company Name: MachIQ
Description: MachIQ is a two-sided SaaS platform.
Website: http://www.machiq.com
Phone: 41(0)789344838 **Email:** sales@machiq.com
City: Renens **State:** VD **PC:** **Country: Switzerland**
Year Established: 2016 **Status 2020:** Active
Industries: Artificial Intelligence for:, Business Software as a Service Apps (SaaS Apps)

Company Name: Predictive Layer
Description: Predictive Layer is revolutionizing predictive Analytics and forecasting applications.
Website: http://www.predictivelayer.com
Phone: 41 76 690 82 33 **Email:** info@predictivelayer.com
City: Rolle **State:** VD **PC:** **Country: Switzerland**
Year Established: 2014 **Status 2020:** Active
Industries: Artificial Intelligence for:, IT Managed Services

Company Name: FinalSpark
Description: FinalSpark combines generalized neural networks with cutting edge learning methods and evolutionary computation.
Website: http://finalspark.com/
Phone: 41 79 289 3552 **Email:** info@finalspark.com
City: Vevey **State:** VD **PC:** **Country: Switzerland**
Year Established: 2014 **Status 2020:** Active
Industries: Artificial Intelligence

Company Name: Stignergy
Description: Stignergy has been developing Smart Energy Management System (SEMS), an artificial intelligence based on bio-inspired technology.
Website: http://www.stignergy.: Switzerland
Phone: 41 24 557 90 58 **Email:** contact@stignergy.: Switzerland
City: Yverdon-les-bains **State:** VD **PC:** **Country: Switzerland**
Year Established: 2012 **Status 2020:** Active
Industries: Artificial Intelligence for:, IT Managed Services for:, ~ Energy and Utilities (14)

Company Name: RELE.AI
Description: Conversation Intelligence, FinTech
Website: http://rele.ai
Phone: **Email:** info@rele.ai
City: Erlenbach **State:** ZH **PC:** **Country: Switzerland**
Year Established: 2019 **Status 2020:** Active
Industries: Artificial Intelligence for:, ~ Banking and Financial Markets-Services (7), ~ Banking and Financial Markets-Services (7), ~ Banking and Financial Markets-Services (7), IT Managed Services for:, ~ Banking and Financial Markets-Services (7)

Company Name: 1702ai
Description: 1702ai is a real-time threat detection surveillance video platform that uses already installed standard CCTV cameras.
Website: http://www.1702ai.com/
Phone: 41 22 501 73 75 **Email:** 35914@reference-encyclopedia-ai.net
City: Hombrechtikon **State:** ZH **PC:** **Country: Switzerland**
Year Established: 2017 **Status 2020:** Active
Industries: Artificial Intelligence for:, Augmented Reality for:, ~ Government (19), Security for:, Virtual Reality (VR)

Company Name: codiag
Description: codiag is a research-driven company that builds softwares to augment doctors and improve patient outcome.
Website: http://www.codiag.com
Phone: **Email:** info@codiag.com
City: Kusnacht **State:** ZH **PC:** **Country: Switzerland**
Year Established: 2018 **Status 2020:** Active
Industries: Artificial Intelligence for:, ~ Healthcare (20), IT Managed Services

Company Name: Starmind
Description: Starmind infuses artificial intelligence with neuroscience to break the barriers limiting true human and organizational collaboration.
Website: http://starmind.ai/
Phone: 41 58 590 80 00 **Email:** info@starmind.com
City: Kusnacht **State:** ZH **PC:** **Country: Switzerland**
Year Established: 2010 **Status 2020:** Active
Industries: Artificial Intelligence for:, Collaboration Solutions for:, Enterprise Application Services for:, IT Managed Services for:, Application Program Interfaces (APIs) for:, ~ Education (13), Compute for:, Compute for:, Business Software as a Service Apps (SaaS Apps) f

Company Name: SpinningByt: Spain
Description: SpinningBytes develops solutions for automatic text understanding, based on machine learning algorithms and artificial intelligence.
Website: http://www.spinningbytes.com
Phone: 41 (0)44 500 2502 **Email:** info@spinningbytes.com
City: Winterthur **State:** ZH **PC:** **Country: Switzerland**
Year Established: 2015 **Status 2020:** Active
Industries:

Company Name: turicode
Description: turicode transforms unstructured data from PDF documents into valuable information.
Website: http://turicode.com/
Phone: 41 (0)52 520 62 02 **Email:** info@turicode.com
City: Winterthur **State:** ZH **PC:** **Country: Switzerland**
Year Established: 2016 **Status 2020:** Active
Industries: Artificial Intelligence for:, Data Management for:, IT Managed Services for:, Machine Learning

Company Name: AI Ventures
Description: Building, launching and investing in scalable B2C and B2B tech products that utilise advanced Artificial Intelligence
Website: http://www.ai-ventures.co
Phone: **Email:** contact@ai-ventures.co
City: Zurich **State:** ZH **PC:** **Country: Switzerland**
Year Established: **Status 2020:** Active
Industries: Artificial Intelligence for:, IT Managed Services for:, Machine Learning

Company Name: Balza
Description: Balzano develops Software that leverages Artificial Intelligence, enabling your Digital Transformation.
Website: http://balzano.: Switzerland
Phone: 0840 840 365 **Email:** info@balzano.
City: Zurich **State:** ZH **PC:** **Country: Switzerland**
Year Established: 2011 **Status 2020:** Active
Industries: Artificial Intelligence for:, IT Managed Services

Company Name: BinaryEdge
Description: BinaryEdge, build products that help company improve the quality of information security and focus on important data metrics.
Website: http://www.binaryedge.io
Phone: 41 78 713 40 00 **Email:** info@binaryedge.io
City: Zurich **State:** ZH **PC:** **Country: Switzerland**
Year Established: 2015 **Status 2020:** Active
Industries: Artificial Intelligence for:, IT Managed Services for:, Security

Company Name: BlinkLabs
Description: BlinkLabs deliver an easy-to-use software toolkit for visual inspection powered by deep learning.
Website: http://blinklabs.ai/
Phone: **Email:** hello@blinklabs.ai
City: Zurich **State:** ZH **PC:** **Country: Switzerland**
Year Established: 2018 **Status 2020:** Active
Industries:

Company Name: bottish
Description: We are an independent, non-profit organization, run by its members, based in Switzerland
Website: http://www.bottish.org/
Phone: **Email:** thomas@bottish.org
City: Zurich **State:** ZH **PC:** **Country: Switzerland**
Year Established: 2016 **Status 2020:** Active
Industries: Artificial Intelligence for:, ~ Education (13), Robotics for:, ~ Media-Communications (41)

Company Name: BrandFort
Description: Protect your Social Media Brand using Artificial Intelligence
Website: http://www.brandfort.co
Phone: **Email:** contact@brandfort.co
City: Zurich **State:** ZH **PC:** **Country: Switzerland**
Year Established: 2019 **Status 2020:** Active
Industries: Artificial Intelligence

Company Name: b-rayZ
Description: b-rayZTM develops artificial intelligence software for quality management and standardization of clinical procedures in radiology.
Website: http://www.b-rayz.ch/
Phone: **Email:** 36205@reference-encyclopedia-ai.net
City: Zurich **State:** ZH **PC:** **Country: Switzerland**
Year Established: 2019 **Status 2020:** Active
Industries: Analytics for:, Artificial Intelligence for:, ~ Healthcare (20)

Company Name: Caplena
Description: Caplena is a text analysis platform, optimized for open-ended responses.
Website: http://caplena.com/en/
Phone: 41 79 455 52 17 **Email:** info@caplena.com
City: Zurich **State:** ZH **PC:** **Country: Switzerland**
Year Established: 2017 **Status 2020:** Active
Industries: Analytics for:, Artificial Intelligence for:, IT Managed Services

Company Name: CogniPet
Description: CogniPet gives the deep connection between humans and animals a very special digital home.
Website: http://cogni.pet/
Phone: 41 76 690 61 64 **Email:** info@cogni.pet
City: Zurich **State:** ZH **PC:** **Country: Switzerland**
Year Established: 2018 **Status 2020:** Active
Industries: Application Services

Company Name: DeepCode
Description: DeepCode is to change the way they create programs by using powerful artificial intelligence and machine learning techniques.
Website: http://www.deepcode.ai/
Phone: **Email:** boris@deepcode.ai
City: Zurich **State:** ZH **PC:** **Country: Switzerland**
Year Established: 2016 **Status 2020:** Active
Industries: Artificial Intelligence

Company Name: ElectricFeel
Description: ElectricFeel provides the most intelligent platform available to build, run and scale shared electric mobility systems.
Website: http://www.electricfeel.com
Phone: **Email:** contact@electricfeel.com
City: Zurich **State:** ZH **PC:** **Country: Switzerland**
Year Established: 2012 **Status 2020:** Active
Industries: IT Managed Services for:, Application Services

Company Name: EYEFITU
Description: EyeFitU is a software company providing sizing recommendations for the apparel and footwear industry.
Website: http://www.eyefitu.com
Phone: **Email:** info@eyefitu.com
City: Zurich **State:** ZH **PC:** **Country: Switzerland**
Year Established: 2012 **Status 2020:** Active
Industries: Application Services for:, Big Data and Analytics for:, E-Commerce for:, ~ Fashion (16), Machine Learning for:, Mobile for:, ~ Media-Communications (41), Business Software as a Service Apps (SaaS Apps) for:, Business Software as a Service Apps (SaaS Apps)

Company Name: faceshift
Description: Faceshift is a motion capture platform that enables its users to design virtual avatars.
Website: http://www.faceshift.com
Phone: 41 44 633 04 29 **Email:** info@faceshift.com
City: Zurich **State:** ZH **PC:** **Country: Switzerland**
Year Established: 2012 **Status 2020:** Active
Industries:

Company Name: Fashwell
Description: Fashwell automatically recognizes and tags fashion and furniture products in images.
Website: http://www.fashwell.com
Phone: **Email:** hello@fashwell.com
City: Zurich **State:** ZH **PC:** **Country: Switzerland**
Year Established: 2013 **Status 2020:** Active
Industries: Artificial Intelligence for:, Computer Vision for:, E-Commerce for:, Machine Learning for:, ~ Retail and Consumer Products (52), Computer Vision

Company Name: Hades
Description: Hades utilizes artificial intelligence to improve urban drainage systems.
Website: http://hades.ai/
Phone: **Email:** hello@hades.ai
City: Zurich **State:** ZH **PC:** **Country: Switzerland**
Year Established: 2018 **Status 2020:** Active
Industries: Artificial Intelligence for:, IT Managed Services for:, Machine Learning

Company Name: Holodia
Description: HOLOFIT is a VR Fitness Platform that works on all cardio fitness machines.
Website: http://www.holodia.com/
Phone: **Email:** knezevic@holodia.com
City: Zurich **State:** ZH **PC:** **Country: Switzerland**
Year Established: 2017 **Status 2020:** Active
Industries: Artificial Intelligence for:, ~ Healthcare (20), ~ Healthcare (20), Virtual Reality (VR)

Company Name: h-square
Description: h-square provides AI chatbot solutions.
Website: http://www.h-square.io/
Phone: **Email:** 36714@reference-encyclopedia-ai.net
City: Zurich **State:** ZH **PC:** **Country: Switzerland**
Year Established: 2018 **Status 2020:** Active
Industries: Artificial Intelligence for:, Machine Learning

Company Name: Intrepida (Intrepid Analytics)
Description: Intrepida built Ancora.ai, an AI-powered tool to help patients search for and connect to clinical trials. Try it yourself at www.ancora.ai
Website: http://www.ancora.ai
Phone: **Email:** info@intrepida.co
City: Zurich **State:** ZH **PC:** **Country: Switzerland**
Year Established: 2017 **Status 2020:** Active
Industries: Analytics for:, Artificial Intelligence for:, Big Data and Analytics for:, ~ Healthcare (20), ~ Healthcare (20), IT Managed Services for:, ~ Healthcare (20), Natural Language Processing for:, Natural Language Processing

Company Name: Jessie.ai
Description: Jessie.ai is an artificial intelligence (AI) based personal assistant for freelancers.
Website: http://www.jessie.ai/
Phone: 41 78 681 32 63 **Email:** info@jessie.ai
City: Zurich **State:** ZH **PC:** **Country: Switzerland**
Year Established: 2017 **Status 2020:** Active
Industries: Artificial Intelligence

Company Name: KapeIQ
Description: KapeIQ is a deep learning based intelligent fraud detection platform.
Website: http://kapeiq.eun
Phone: **Email:** 36841@reference-encyclopedia-ai.net
City: Zurich **State:** ZH **PC:** **Country: Switzerland**
Year Established: 2015 **Status 2020:** Active
Industries: Artificial Intelligence for:, Security for:, ~ Banking and Financial Markets-Services (7), Predictive Analytics

Company Name: Locatee
Description: Locatee is a workplace analytics solution that transforms data into space utilization insights.
Website: http://www.locatee.com
Phone: 41 43 508 51 23 **Email:** info@locatee.: Switzerland
City: Zurich **State:** ZH **PC:** **Country: Switzerland**
Year Established: 2013 **Status 2020:** Active
Industries: Artificial Intelligence for:, Business Intelligence for:, Data Management for:, ~ Real Estate (49), Business Software as a Service Apps (SaaS Apps) for:, Business Software as a Service Apps (SaaS Apps) for:, ~ Construction (10)

Company Name: Logic Flow
Description: Logic Flow is an automated code translation company that takes care of repetitive technical tasks.
Website: http://www.logic-flow.ch/
Phone: 41 76 513 09 96 **Email:** info@logic-flow.: Switzerland
City: Zurich **State:** ZH **PC:** **Country: Switzerland**
Year Established: 2019 **Status 2020:** Active
Industries: Artificial Intelligence for:, IT Managed Services for:, ~ Telecommunications (56), Application Services

Company Name: Modulos
Description: Modulos is a startup from ETH Zurich working on the full AI Journey.
Website: http://www.modulos.ai
Phone: 41 (0)76 566 05 48 **Email:** contact@modulos.ai
City: Zurich **State:** ZH **PC:** **Country: Switzerland**
Year Established: 2018 **Status 2020:** Active
Industries: Artificial Intelligence for:, IT Managed Services for:, Machine Learning

Company Name: Neuralsight
Description: Neuralsight is a quality problems in the manufacturing industry.
Website: http://neuralsight.ai/
Phone: **Email:** 37050@reference-encyclopedia-ai.net
City: Zurich **State:** ZH **PC:** **Country: Switzerland**
Year Established: 2017 **Status 2020:** Active
Industries: Big Data and Analytics for:, IT Managed Services for:, IT Managed Services for:, Machine Learning

Company Name: nexoya
Description: AI driven Marketing Analytics Platform
Website: http://www.nexoya.com
Phone: **Email:** hello@nexoya.com
City: Zurich **State:** ZH **PC:** **Country: Switzerland**
Year Established: 2018 **Status 2020:** Active
Industries: Analytics for:, Digital Marketing for:, Predictive Analytics

Company Name: Prospera Technologies
Description:
Website: http://www.prospera.ag
Phone: **Email:** info_hq@prospera.ag
City: Zurich **State:** ZH **Zip:** 8005 **Country: Switzerland**
Year Established: **Status 2020:** Active
Industries: ~ Agriculture (3), Artificial Intelligence for:, Computer Vision for:, Data Management for:, Machine Learning

Company Name: The Trip Boutique
Description: Your personal travel advisor. We do the planning. You live the experience
Website: http://www.thetripboutique.co/
Phone: **Email:** hello@thetripboutique.co
City: Zurich **State:** ZH **PC:** **Country: Switzerland**
Year Established: 2017 **Status 2020:** Active
Industries:

Company Name: Traverz
Description: Delivering the ultimate online product search experience
Website: http://www.traverz.com
Phone: **Email:** contact@traverz.com
City: Zurich **State:** ZH **PC:** **Country: Switzerland**
Year Established: 2018 **Status 2020:** Active
Industries: Artificial Intelligence for:, E-Commerce for:, IT Managed Services for:, Machine Learning for:, Business Intelligence

Company Name: 4Quant
Description: Transforming Images to Information
Website: http://4quant.com
Phone: **Email:** info@4quant.com
City: Zürich **State:** ZH **PC:** **Country: Switzerland**
Year Established: 2015 **Status 2020:** Active
Industries: Analytics for:, Artificial Intelligence for:, Big Data and Analytics for:, Image Recognition for:, Compute

Company Name: Acutronic Robotics
Description: Acutronic Robotics delivers high quality real-time compliant modular robot solutions for professional and industrial applications.
Website: https://www.acutronicrobotics.com/
Phone: 34616151561 **Email:** contact@acutronicrobotics.com
City: Zürich **State:** ZH **PC:** **Country: Switzerland**
Year Established: 2016 **Status 2020:** Active
Industries: Artificial Intelligence for:, Automation for:, Machine Learning for:, Compute for:, Robotics

Company Name: Antavi
Description: We digitize the safety service econo: Malaysia
Website: http://antavi.ch/
Phone: **Email:** info@antavi.
City: Zürich **State:** ZH **PC:** **Country: Switzerland**
Year Established: 2015 **Status 2020:** Active
Industries: ~ Event Management (15), Application Services for:, Mobile for:, Business Software as a Service Apps (SaaS Apps)

Company Name: Appetita
Description: Appetita is a friendly AI boosts sales, streamlines service, and delights your customers.
Website: http://www.appetita.ch/
Phone: **Email:** info@appetita.
City: Zürich **State:** ZH **PC:** **Country: Switzerland**
Year Established: 2017 **Status 2020:** Active
Industries: Artificial Intelligence for:, ~ Customer Relationship Management (11), ~ Food and Beverage (17)

Company **Name:** Arbrea Labs
Description: Arbrea Labs develop cutting edge technology, based on visual computing and AI, to create digital human avatars from mobile devices.
Website: http://arbrea-labs.com/
Phone: **Email:** info@arbrea-labs.com
City: Zürich **State:** ZH **PC:** **Country: Switzerland**
Year Established: 2017 **Status 2020:** Active
Industries: Artificial Intelligence for:, ~ Healthcare (20), Machine Learning for:, ~ Healthcare (20), Virtual Reality (VR)

Company Name: Archilyse AG
Description: 1-click holistic architecture analysis as easy to use API solution
Website: http://www.archilyse.com/
Phone: 41 (0)44 633 0994 **Email:** sotier@archilyse.com
City: Zürich **State:** ZH **PC:** **Country: Switzerland**
Year Established: 2017 **Status 2020:** Active
Industries: Analytics for:, ~ Real Estate (49), Business Software as a Service Apps (SaaS Apps)

Company Name: Asimov Medical
Description: Intelligent analysis of medical data. Natural language processing and deep learning or researchers and physicians.
Website: http://www.asimovmed.com
Phone: (415) 707-0515 **Email:** 36096@reference-encyclopedia-ai.net
City: Zürich **State:** ZH **PC:** **Country: Switzerland**
Year Established: 2015 **Status 2020:** Active
Industries: Artificial Intelligence for:, ~ Healthcare (20), ~ Healthcare (20)

Company Name: Assaia
Description: We apply AI to enable time-efficient and affordable air travel over the decades to come.
Website: http://assaia.com
Phone: 41 76 738 88 98 **Email:** hello@assaia.com
City: Zürich **State:** ZH **PC:** **Country: Switzerland**
Year Established: 2018 **Status 2020:** Active
Industries: Artificial Intelligence for:, Computer Vision for:, Machine Learning for:, Predictive Analytics for:, Supply Chain Management

Company Name: Onedot
Description: Onedot is the first intelligent platform for commerce and industry to source, onboard and distribute product data.
Website: http://www.onedot.com
Phone: 41 44 585 22 05 **Email:** info@onedot.com
City: Zürich **State:** ZH **PC:** **Country: Switzerland**

Year Established: 2014 **Status 2020:** Active
Industries: Artificial Intelligence for:, Cloud for:, Data Management for:, Business Software as a Service Apps (SaaS Apps)

Company Name: Oxygen at Work
Description: We help companies reduce health care and energy costs by using data analytics and specific plants to improve office indoor air quality.
Website: http://www.oxygenatwork.org/
Phone: **Email:** hello@oxygenatwork.org
City: Zürich **State:** ZH **PC:** **Country: Switzerland**
Year Established: 2017 **Status 2020:** Active
Industries: Artificial Intelligence for:, Big Data and Analytics for:, ~ Energy and Utilities (14), Machine Learning

Company Name: Parquery
Description: Parquery is a technology spin-off from the Computer Vision Laboratory of ETH Zurich.
Website: http://www.parquery.com/
Phone: **Email:** info@parquery.com
City: Zürich **State:** ZH **PC:** **Country: Switzerland**
Year Established: 2014 **Status 2020:** Active
Industries: Artificial Intelligence for:, Business Applications for:, Computer Vision for:, Image Recognition for:, ~ Travel and Transportation (58)

Company Name: politik.: Switzerland
Description: politik.ch visualizes Swiss Open Politics and Government Data.
Website: http://politik.: Switzerland
Phone: 41 43 443 02 06 **Email:** info@politik.: Switzerland
City: Zürich **State:** ZH **PC:** **Country: Switzerland**
Year Established: 2017 **Status 2020:** Active
Industries: Big Data and Analytics for:, ~ Government (19), Databases for:, Data Management for:, ~ Government (19), Predictive Analytics

Company Name: Pregnolia
Description: Developed an innovative system to accurately assess the stiffness of the cervical tissue of pregnant and non-pregnant women.
Website: http://www.pregnolia.com/
Phone: **Email:** info@pregnolia.com
City: Zürich **State:** ZH **PC:** **Country: Switzerland**
Year Established: 2015 **Status 2020:** Active
Industries:

Company Name: PriceHubble
Description: Leading the development of Data & explainable AI-driven real estate valuations and insights globally
Website: http://www.pricehubble.com/
Phone: **Email:** contact@pricehubble.com
City: Zürich **State:** ZH **PC:** **Country: Switzerland**
Year Established: 2016 **Status 2020:** Active
Industries: Analytics for:, Artificial Intelligence for:, Big Data and Analytics for:, Machine Learning

Company Name: PXL Vision AG
Description: PXL Vision provides unique software solutions powered by latest computer vision, artificial intelligence and VR/AR algorithms.
Website: http://pxl-vision.com/
Phone: **Email:** info@pxl-vision.com
City: Zürich **State:** ZH **PC:** **Country: Switzerland**
Year Established: 2017 **Status 2020:** Active
Industries: Artificial Intelligence for:, Computer Vision for:, Virtual Reality (VR)

Company Name: Raized.AI
Description: Raized.AI builds a data-driven deal sourcing engine for VC investors to find the next unicorn.
Website: http://www.raized.ai/
Phone: **Email:** info@raized.ai
City: Zürich **State:** ZH **PC:** **Country: Switzerland**
Year Established: 2019 **Status 2020:** Active
Industries: ~ Banking and Financial Markets-Services (7), Machine Learning for:, ~ Banking and Financial Markets-Services (7)

Company Name: Riskifier
Description: Riskifier is a RegTech start-up making investment risk profiling simple, fun and insightful with AI powered solution.
Website: http://riskifier.io/
Phone: 41 78 672 32 11 **Email:** info@riskifier.io
City: Zürich **State:** ZH **PC:** **Country: Switzerland**
Year Established: 2017 **Status 2020:** Active
Industries: Artificial Intelligence for:, ~ Banking and Financial Markets-Services (7), ~ Banking and Financial Markets-Services (7), ~ Banking and Financial Markets-Services (7)

Company Name: Seervision
Description: Seervision, a fledgling robotics startup that's meshing machine learning, computer vision, and cinematography
Website: http://seervision.com
Phone: 41 44 632 05 42 **Email:** mail@seervision.com
City: Zürich **State:** ZH **PC:** **Country: Switzerland**
Year Established: 2016 **Status 2020:** Active
Industries: Artificial Intelligence for:, Computer Vision for:, Machine Learning for:, Robotics

Company Name: Sentifi
Description: Leading Crowd-Intelligence for Financial Markets globally
Website: http://www.sentifi.com
Phone: **Email:** contact@sentifi.com
City: Zürich **State:** ZH **PC:** **Country: Switzerland**
Year Established: 2012 **Status 2020:** Active
Industries: Artificial Intelligence

Company Name: SNAQ
Description: SNAQ is a machine learning and computer vision startup active in the medical field.
Website: http://snaq.io/
Phone: **Email:** info@snaq.io
City: Zürich **State:** ZH **PC:** **Country: Switzerland**
Year Established: 2017 **Status 2020:** Active
Industries: Machine Learning

Company Name: Spit
Description: Spitch is the leading provider of speech technology solutions
Website: http://www.spitch.ch/
Phone: 41 44 542 82 66 **Email:** invest@spitch.
City: Zürich **State:** ZH **PC:** **Country: Switzerland**
Year Established: 2014 **Status 2020:** Active
Industries: Analytics for:, Artificial Intelligence for:, ~ Biotechnology (9), ~ Customer Relationship Management (11), Application Services for:, Enterprise Application Services for:, Natural Language Processing for:, Security for:, Security for:, Speech Recognition for:, Int

Company Name: Squir: Romania
Description: Squirro delivers real-time context intelligence by combining structured and unstructured data.
Website: http://squirro.com
Phone: 41 44 586 98 98 **Email:** info@squirro.com
City: Zürich **State:** ZH **PC:** **Country: Switzerland**
Year Established: 2012 **Status 2020:** Active
Industries: Analytics for:, Artificial Intelligence for:, Cloud for:, IT Managed Services for:, Business Software as a Service Apps (SaaS Apps)

Company Name: Swiss Data Science Center
Description: The Swiss Data Science Center is an ETH Domain initiative for Data Science in Switzerland.
Website: http://datascience.: Switzerland
Phone: 41 21 693 79 97 **Email:** contact@datascience.: Switzerland
City: Zürich **State:** ZH **PC:** **Country: Switzerland**

Year Established: 2016 **Status 2020:** Active
Industries: Artificial Intelligence for:, Big Data and Analytics for:, ~ Education (13), IT Managed Services

Company Name: Synthara Technologies
Description: Synthara is an AI company that provides system-level solutions for businesses to enhance their products or services with smart features.
Website: http://www.synthara.ch/
Phone: **Email:** contact-us@synthara.
City: Zürich **State:** ZH **PC:** **Country: Switzerland**
Year Established: 2017 **Status 2020:** Active
Industries: Artificial Intelligence

Company Name: Teralytics
Description: Teralytics' machine learning-based technology provides unrivalled insights into people's mobility needs.
Website: http://www.teralytics.net
Phone: **Email:** info@teralytics.net
City: Zürich **State:** ZH **PC:** **Country: Switzerland**
Year Established: 2012 **Status 2020:** Active
Industries: Artificial Intelligence for:, Business Intelligence for:, Cyber Security for:, Data Management for:, Predictive Analytics

Company Name: Valdon Group GmbH
Description: Consulting Boutique for Quant Finance and Data Science
Website:
Phone: **Email:** contact@valdon.: Switzerland
City: Zürich **State:** ZH **PC:** **Country: Switzerland**
Year Established: 2015 **Status 2020:** Active
Industries: Analytics for:, ~ Banking and Financial Markets-Services (7), Predictive Analytics for:, Predictive Analytics for:, Risk Management

Company Name: VAY Sports
Description: The Real-Time Fitness Coaching App
Website: http://vay.ai
Phone: **Email:** info@vay.ai
City: Zürich **State:** ZH **PC:** **Country: Switzerland**
Year Established: 2019 **Status 2020:** Active
Industries:

Company Name: Veezoo
Description: Veezoo is an Artificial Intelligence that allows you to explore data just by asking questions.
Website: http://www.veezoo.com
Phone: **Email:** info@veezoo.com
City: Zürich **State:** ZH **PC:** **Country: Switzerland**
Year Established: 2016 **Status 2020:** Active
Industries: Artificial Intelligence for:, Big Data and Analytics for:, ~ Customer Relationship Management (11), IT Managed Services for:, Machine Learning

Company Name: Vestun
Description: Quantitative Investment & Big Data
Website: http://www.vestun.com
Phone: **Email:** request@vestun.com
City: Zürich **State:** ZH **PC:** **Country: Switzerland**
Year Established: 2019 **Status 2020:** Active
Industries: Artificial Intelligence

Company Name: Windsor.ai
Description: Windsor.ai offers an integrated marketing analytics platform for marketers to measure and optimize the impact of their campaigns.
Website: http://www.windsor.ai
Phone: 41 (0) 44 523 6060 **Email:** hello@windsor.ai
City: Zürich **State:** ZH **PC:** **Country: Switzerland**
Year Established: 2017 **Status 2020:** Active
Industries: Analytics for:, Artificial Intelligence for:, Business Software as a Service Apps (SaaS Apps)

Company Name: ZENAI
Description: ZENAI provides strategic machine learning services and develops augmented intelligence software.
Website: http://zenai.ch/
Phone: **Email:** info@zenai.
City: Zürich **State:** ZH **PC:** **Country: Switzerland**
Year Established: 2017 **Status 2020:** Active
Industries: ~ Banking and Financial Markets-Services (7), Machine Learning

Company Name: AI Benchmark
Description: AI Benchmark is an android app that measures the speed and memory requirements for several key Computer Vision AI algorithms.
Website: http://ai-benchmark.com
Phone: **Email:** andrey@vision.ee.ethz.
City: Zurich **State:** ZH **PC:** **Country: Switzerland**
Year Established: **Status 2020:** Active
Industries: Application Services for:, Artificial Intelligence

Company Name: Legartis
Description: Legartis is a legal tech startup developing a contract intelligence software. Using ML, NLP and AI, we automate the analysis of contracts.
Website: http://legartis.ai
Phone: **Email:** david@legartis.ai
City: Zurich **State:** ZH **PC:** **Country: Switzerland**
Year Established: **Status 2020:** Active
Industries: Artificial Intelligence for:, Business Applications for:, ~ Law-Legal Services (26), Machine Learning for:, Natural Language Processing for:, ~ Professional Services (48)

Company Name: Mirage
Description: Building delightful AI-powered consumer products.
Website: http://mirage.id
Phone: **Email:** founders@mirage.id
City: Zurich **State:** ZH **PC:** **Country: Switzerland**
Year Established: **Status 2020:** Active
Industries: Artificial Intelligence for:, Computer Vision

Company Name: Visium
Description: AI Consulting
Website: http://visium.: Switzerland
Phone: **Email:** aa@visium.
City: Zurich **State:** ZH **PC:** **Country: Switzerland**
Year Established: **Status 2020:** Active
Industries: Application Services for:, Artificial Intelligence for:, Big Data and Analytics for:, Machine Learning

Taiwan

Company Name: Infinitix Pte Ltd
Description: Infinitix is the software solution provider of Asia's most connected multi/hybrid cloud management platform - CloudFusion.
Website: www.infinitiessoft.com/index.php
Phone: **Email:** marketing@infinitiessoft.com
City: Kaohsiung **State:** Kaohsiung City **PC:** **Country: Taiwan**
Year Established: **Status 2020:** Active
Industries: Artificial Intelligence for:, Cloud for:, Cloud for:, Cloud for:, Automation for:, Enterprise Application Services for:, Cloud for:, IT Managed Services for:, IT Managed Services for:, Machine Learning for:, Application Services for:, Cloud for:, ~ Professional Servi

Company Name: S11 - Information At Your Service
Description: Indie Brand Ownership Simplified. Funnel Factory makes sales funnels easy sustainable and globally scaleable for really small companies.
Website: http://s11.io
Phone: 877-2622488 **Email:** 0@s11.io
City: Kaohsiung **State:** Kaohsiung City **PC:** **Country: Taiwan**

Year Established: 2016 **Status 2020:** Active
Industries: Artificial Intelligence for:, Application Services for:, Internet of Things (IoT)

Company Name: Neousys Technology
Description:
Website: https://www.neousys-tech.com/en/
Phone: **Email:** 12562@reference-encyclopedia-ai.net
City: New Taipei City **State:** New Taipei City **Zip:** 23586
Country: Taiwan
Year Established: **Status 2020:** Active
Industries: Blockchain

Company Name: Minastir Technologies
Description: We develop bespoke and intelligent asset management solutions by harnessing the power of our proprietary, enterprise-grade AI technology
Website: http://www.minastir.com/en/
Phone: 886 960 950 622 **Email:** mp@minastir.com
City: Taipei **State:** **PC:** **Country:**
Year Established: 2015 **Status 2020:** Active
Industries: Artificial Intelligence for:, ~ Banking and Financial Markets-Services (7)

Company Name: LaVida Tec
Description:
Website: https://www.wacare.live
Phone: **Email:** lavidatectw@gmail.com
City: Taichung City 433 **State:** Taichung City **Zip:** 60281433
Country: Taiwan
Year Established: **Status 2020:** Active
Industries:

Company Name: Clef Technology
Description: Gas Pipeline Leak Detection Solution
Website: http://cleftechnology.com/
Phone: **Email:** sales@cleftechnology.com
City: Tainan **State:** Tainan City **PC:** **Country: Taiwan**
Year Established: **Status 2020:** Active
Industries:

Company Name: Yutech
Description: Biomedical wearable devic: Spain
Website: http://innocbic.com/public_html/webtemp/index_en.html
Phone: **Email:** 37727@reference-encyclopedia-ai.net
City: Tainan **State:** Tainan City **PC:** **Country: Taiwan**
Year Established: 2019 **Status 2020:** Active
Industries: Artificial Intelligence for:, ~ Biotechnology (9), ~ Healthcare (20), Internet of Things (IoT) for:, Internet of Things (IoT)

Company Name: AIExplore
Description: International Award Winning AI Platform for smart healthcare, smart manufacturing, smart city and smart agriculture
Website: http://aiexplore.ntust.edu.tw/
Phone: 886-2-27303749 **Email:** aiexplore.tw@gmail.com
City: Taipei **State:** Taipei City **PC:** **Country: Taiwan**

Year Established: 2019 **Status 2020:** Active
Industries: Artificial Intelligence for:, ~ Healthcare (20), IT Managed Services for:, ~ Construction (10)

Company Name: Akohub
Description: Akohub is an intelligent assistant helping ecommerce operators boost conversion rates and generate more sales.
Website: http://www.akohub.com
Phone: **Email:** info@akohub.com
City: Taipei **State:** Taipei City **PC:** **Country: Taiwan**
Year Established: **Status 2020:** Active
Industries: Artificial Intelligence for:, E-Commerce

Company Name: AlphaLoan
Description: AlphaLoan develops AI-based credit scoring systems to help banks and organizations create next-generation financial applications.
Website: https://alphaloan.co/
Phone: **Email:** hi@alphaloan.co
City: Taipei **State:** Taipei City **PC:** **Country: Taiwan**
Year Established: 2016 **Status 2020:** Active
Industries: Artificial Intelligence for:, ~ Banking and Financial Markets-Services (7), ~ Banking and Financial Markets-Services (7)

Company Name: Appier
Description: Appier is a technology company which aims to provide artificial intelligence platform to help enterprises solve their business problems.
Website: http://appier.com
Phone: 1287808891 **Email:** hello@appier.com
City: Taipei **State:** Taipei City **PC:** **Country: Taiwan**
Year Established: **Status 2020:** Active
Industries: Analytics for:, Artificial Intelligence for:, IT Managed Services

Company Name: ATGENOMIX
Description: Genomic informatics platform for connecting people to accurate, early diagnostics tailored uniquely to us.
Website: http://www.atgenomix.com
Phone: **Email:** info@atgenomix.com
City: Taipei **State:** Taipei City **PC:** **Country: Taiwan**
Year Established: 2015 **Status 2020:** Active
Industries: Artificial Intelligence for:, ~ Biotechnology (9), ~ Biotechnology (9), ~ Healthcare (20), ~ Healthcare (20), IT Managed Services

Company Name: Bubbleye
Description: Bubbleye is the most intelligent game targeting in the world.
Website: http://bubbleye.com/ios
Phone: **Email:** contact@bubbleye.com
City: Taipei **State:** Taipei City **PC:** **Country: Taiwan**
Year Established: **Status 2020:** Active
Industries: Artificial Intelligence for:, Machine Learning for:, Mobile

Company Name: Cloud Interactive
Description: Cloud Interactive is a Machine Learning, Engineering, and Design Consulting company.
Website: http://www.cloud-interactive.com/
Phone: 1 415-797-9448 **Email:** info@cloud-interactive.com
City: Taipei **State:** Taipei City **PC:** **Country: Taiwan**
Year Established: 2010 **Status 2020:** Active
Industries: Machine Learning for:, Development and Test for:, Web for:, Web

Company Name: CyCraft
Description: CyCraft is a cybersecurity technology company pioneering artificial intelligence for unmanned SecOps platform
Website: http://www.cycraft.com/
Phone: **Email:** contact@cycraft.com
City: Taipei **State:** Taipei City **PC:** **Country: Taiwan**
Year Established: 2017 **Status 2020:** Active
Industries: Artificial Intelligence for:, Cyber Security for:, Machine Learning

Company Name: DeepWave
Description: Saas, AI, Digital Music, MIR,
Website: http://dwave.cc/
Phone: **Email:** service@dwave.cc
City: Taipei **State:** Taipei City **PC:** **Country: Taiwan**
Year Established: 2019 **Status 2020:** Active
Industries: Artificial Intelligence for:, ~ Arts-Entertainment-Recreation (4), Digital Media for:, IT Managed Services for:, ~ Arts-Entertainment-Recreation (4), ~ Education (13), ~ Arts-Entertainment-Recreation (4)

Company Name: DermAI
Description: Medical AI
Website: http://www.dermai.com.: Taiwan
Phone: 857-930-5158 **Email:** dermaiofficial@gmail.com
City: Taipei **State:** Taipei City **PC:** **Country: Taiwan**
Year Established: 2018 **Status 2020:** Active
Industries: Artificial Intelligence

Company Name: DT42
Description: Trustable AI data solution
Website: http://dt42.io
Phone: **Email:** contact@dt42.io
City: Taipei **State:** Taipei City **PC:** **Country: Taiwan**
Year Established: 2015 **Status 2020:** Active
Industries: Artificial Intelligence for:, Computer Vision for:, IT Managed Services for:, IT Managed Services for:, Machine Learning

Company Name: Fusion360
Description: Saas, Paas, Blockchain & API Economy Platform
Website: http://www.fusions360.com/en/
Phone: **Email:** contactus@fusions360.com
City: Taipei **State:** Taipei City **PC:** **Country: Taiwan**
Year Established: 2016 **Status 2020:** Active
Industries: Artificial Intelligence for:, Blockchain for:, ~ Banking and Financial Markets-Services (7)

Company Name: GliaCloud
Description: GliaCloud is a company disrupting advertising industry with AI.
Website: http://gliacloud.com/
Phone: **Email:** info@gliacloud.com
City: Taipei **State:** Taipei City **PC:** **Country: Taiwan**
Year Established: **Status 2020:** Active
Industries:

Company Name: Glossika
Description: Glossika is a SaaS EduTech platform that trains language fluency via machine learning
Website: http://glossika.com
Phone: **Email:** support@glossika.com
City: Taipei **State:** Taipei City **PC:** **Country: Taiwan**
Year Established: 2012 **Status 2020:** Active
Industries: Artificial Intelligence for:, ~ Education (13), ~ Education (13)

Company Name: HIGH5
Description: High5 is a CRM platform that focus on using artificial intelligence and chatbots.
Website: http://high5.ai
Phone: **Email:** human@high5.ai
City: Taipei **State:** Taipei City **PC:** **Country: Taiwan**
Year Established: **Status 2020:** Active
Industries: Artificial Intelligence

Company Name: HiHedge
Description: HiHedge is a developer of artificial intelligence stock trading software for business clients.
Website: http://www.hihedge.com/
Phone: **Email:** info@kuchi.: Taiwan
City: Taipei **State:** Taipei City **PC:** **Country: Taiwan**
Year Established: 2012 **Status 2020:** Active
Industries: ~ Banking and Financial Markets-Services (7), ~ Banking and Financial Markets-Services (7), ~ Banking and Financial Markets-Services (7), Machine Learning for:, Finance and Accounting

Company Name: iKala
Description: B2B Human-Centered AI marketing technology company providing Digital Transformation and Data-Driven Marketing solutions.
Website: http://ikala.tv/
Phone: **Email:** contact@ikala.tv
City: Taipei **State:** Taipei City **PC:** **Country: Taiwan**
Year Established: 2011 **Status 2020:** Active
Industries: Analytics for:, Artificial Intelligence for:, Cloud for:, Digital Marketing for:, IT Managed Services

Company Name: ioEZ
Description: IoEZ develops AI algorithms for human physiological measurements and fall detection using 3D lidar and radar technology.
Website:
Phone: 886 2-22180545 **Email:** 36807@reference-encyclopedia-ai.net
City: Taipei **State:** Taipei City **PC:** **Country: Taiwan**
Year Established: 2017 **Status 2020:** Closed
Industries: Artificial Intelligence

Company Name: IoNetworks
Description: IoNetworks is an open platform company that develops a video management software.
Website: http://ionetworks.co/
Phone: **Email:** support@ionetworks.co
City: Taipei **State:** Taipei City **PC:** **Country: Taiwan**
Year Established: 2014 **Status 2020:** Active
Industries: Analytics for:, Artificial Intelligence for:, Cloud

Company Name: JARVISH INC.
Description: JARVISH Inc., company of intelligent helmet systems, brings top industry technologists for safer and enjoyable riding experience.
Website: http://www.jarvish.com
Phone: **Email:** services@jarvish.com
City: Taipei **State:** Taipei City **PC:** **Country: Taiwan**
Year Established: **Status 2020:** Active
Industries: Artificial Intelligence for:, Augmented Reality

Company Name: LeadBest
Description: VentureStudio as a services (Digital , BlockChain , Agile , CyberSecurity)
Website: http://leadbestconsultant.com/en/
Phone: **Email:** service@leadbest.io
City: Taipei **State:** Taipei City **PC:** **Country: Taiwan**
Year Established: 2018 **Status 2020:** Active
Industries: Artificial Intelligence for:, ~ Banking and Financial Markets-Services (7)

Company Name: Libgirl
Description: Artificial Intelligence
Website: http://libgirl.com/
Phone: 886-2-2311-9816 **Email:** team@libgirl.com
City: Taipei **State:** Taipei City **PC:** **Country: Taiwan**
Year Established: 2016 **Status 2020:** Active
Industries: Artificial Intelligence for:, IT Managed Services for:, Enterprise Application Services

Company Name: Lona, a Kiipo Company
Description: Lona provides an end-to-end sleep management solution for patients and physicians, from screening, to monitoring, to personalized treatment.
Website: http://www.lonasleep.com
Phone: **Email:** 36913@reference-encyclopedia-ai.net
City: Taipei **State:** Taipei City **PC:** **Country: Taiwan**
Year Established: 2019 **Status 2020:** Active
Industries: Artificial Intelligence for:, ~ Healthcare (20), ~ Healthcare (20), IT Managed Services

Company Name: Make2Real.AI
Description: Make2Real.AI helps innovators and commercial customers make their AI design come true.
Website: http://www.make2real.ai
Phone: **Email:** 36934@reference-encyclopedia-ai.net
City: Taipei **State:** Taipei City **PC:** **Country: Taiwan**
Year Established: 2016 **Status 2020:** Active
Industries: Artificial Intelligence

Company Name: MangaX Technology Co., Ltd.
Description: MangaX develops AI technology that simulates the process of how humans imagine, helping people convert ideas into graphics automatically.
Website: http://www.mangachat.co/
Phone: **Email:** 36938@reference-encyclopedia-ai.net
City: Taipei **State:** Taipei City **PC:** **Country: Taiwan**
Year Established: 2016 **Status 2020:** Active
Industries: Artificial Intelligence for:, IT Managed Services

Company Name: Manli Technology Group Ltd.
Description:
Website: http://www.manli.com/
Phone: 866 2 2555 8881 ext. 56 **Email:** ella@manli.com.: Hong Kong
City: Taipei **State:** Taipei City **Zip:** 10350 **Country: Taiwan**
Year Established: **Status 2020:** Active
Industries: Blockchain

Company Name: Memorence AI
Description: We treasure and guard life and memori: Spain
Website: http://www.memorence.com
Phone: **Email:** hello@memorence.com
City: Taipei **State:** Taipei City **PC:** **Country: Taiwan**
Year Established: 2018 **Status 2020:** Active
Industries:

Company Name: ModernMatchMaker
Description: The eHarmony for the Chinese communities around the world
Website: http://www.modernmatchmaker.net/
Phone: **Email:** global.modernmatchmaker@gmail.com
City: Taipei **State:** Taipei City **PC:** **Country: Taiwan**
Year Established: 2013 **Status 2020:** Active
Industries: ~ Personal-Religious-Civic (45), Machine Learning for:, Mobile

Company Name: NexRetail
Description: AI Solution for Retail Stor: Spain
Website: http://www.nexretail.com
Phone: (323) 834-8988 **Email:** james@nexretail.com
City: Taipei **State:** Taipei City **PC:** **Country: Taiwan**
Year Established: 2016 **Status 2020:** Active
Industries: Analytics for:, Artificial Intelligence for:, Big Data and Analytics

Company Name: Osense Technology Co., Ltd
Description: Indoor Positioning and Navigation, LBS, Computer Vision & Graphics, AR & VR, Application Development, Industry 4.0 software solution
Website: http://osensetech.com/index_english.html
Phone: **Email:** gaoyanhe@osensetech.com
City: Taipei **State:** Taipei City **PC:** **Country: Taiwan**
Year Established: **Status 2020:** Active
Industries: Artificial Intelligence for:, Augmented Reality for:, Computer Vision for:, ~ Professional Services (48)

Company Name: OSENSE TECHNOLOGY CO., LTD.
Description: Artificial intelligence, artificial perception, computer vision, indoor navigation, LBS, and AR & VR
Website: http://www.osensetech.com/
Phone: **Email:** osense@osensetech.com
City: Taipei **State:** Taipei City **PC:** **Country: Taiwan**
Year Established: 2017 **Status 2020:** Active
Industries: Artificial Intelligence for:, Augmented Reality

Company Name: PEEKUR
Description: SaaS, Social Media Analytics, Persona
Website: http://peekur.com/
Phone: **Email:** info@peekur.com
City: Taipei **State:** Taipei City **PC:** **Country: Taiwan**
Year Established: **Status 2020:** Active
Industries: Analytics for:, Artificial Intelligence for:, Digital Marketing

Company Name: RelaJet
Description: RelaJet is a software company. Providing solutions of hearing, trying to make communication between human and machine easier.
Website: http://www.relajet.com
Phone: **Email:** 4727@reference-encyclopedia-ai.net
City: Taipei **State:** Taipei City **PC:** **Country: Taiwan**
Year Established: **Status 2020:** Active
Industries: Artificial Intelligence for:, Blockchain for:, Machine Learning

Company Name: Ret[AI]ling Data Enterpri: Sweden
Description: Ret[AI]ling Data Enterprise is an integrator of artificial internet of things(AIoT) in smart retailing.
Website: http://sites.google.com/view/ret-ai-ling/english
Phone: **Email:** sean@retailingdata.com.: Taiwan
City: Taipei **State:** Taipei City **PC:** **Country: Taiwan**
Year Established: 2019 **Status 2020:** Active
Industries: Artificial Intelligence for:, IT Managed Services

Company Name: Roo: Italy
Description: Rooit is a gamified application that specializes in communication guided by chatbot to facilitate between two users by providing fun games.
Website: http://www.rooit.me
Phone: **Email:** PaulHsu@rooit.me
City: Taipei **State:** Taipei City **PC:** **Country: Taiwan**
Year Established: 2016 **Status 2020:** Active
Industries: Application Services for:, Artificial Intelligence for:, Web for:, ~ Social Assistance-Non-Profits (53), ~ Social Assistance-Non-Profits (53)

Company Name: Rosetta.ai
Description: Rosetta.ai helps fashion e-commerce increase conversion and enlarge order value with deep learning-based technology.
Website: http://www.rosetta.ai
Phone: **Email:** hey@rosetta.ai
City: Taipei **State:** Taipei City **PC:** **Country: Taiwan**
Year Established: 2016 **Status 2020:** Active
Industries: Artificial Intelligence for:, E-Commerce for:, Machine Learning

Company Name: SarMo Technology
Description: SarMo Technology provides the efficient & robust methodology for embedded computer vision systems.
Website: http://sarmotek.com/
Phone: **Email:** yitawu@sarmotek.com
City: Taipei **State:** Taipei City **PC:** **Country: Taiwan**
Year Established: 2013 **Status 2020:** Active
Industries: Artificial Intelligence for:, ~ Government (19), Robotics

Company Name: SHOWHUE
Description: Artificial Intelligence Innovative Application
Website: http://showhue.com
Phone: **Email:** info@showhue.com
City: Taipei **State:** Taipei City **PC:** **Country: Taiwan**
Year Established: **Status 2020:** Active
Industries: Artificial Intelligence for:, Machine Learning for:, ~ Retail and Consumer Products (52)

Company Name: Skymizer
Description: Software, Compiler, Reference designs, turn-key solution
Website: http://skymizer.com/
Phone: **Email:** sales@skymizer.com
City: Taipei **State:** Taipei City **PC:** **Country: Taiwan**
Year Established: 2013 **Status 2020:** Active
Industries: Artificial Intelligence

Company Name: SkyREC Inc.
Description: Data Consulting for In-store Reta: Israel
Website: http://www.skyrec.cc
Phone: 886-2-2752-0550 **Email:** sales@skyrec.cc
City: Taipei **State:** Taipei City **PC:** **Country: Taiwan**

Year Established: **Status 2020:** Active
Industries: Analytics for:, Artificial Intelligence for:, Big Data and Analytics for:, Business Intelligence for:, ~ Retail and Consumer Products (52), ~ Media-Communications (41)

Company Name: Slewell Tech
Description: Sleep analysis, AI, APP service
Website:
Phone: **Email:** fysh711362@gmail.com
City: Taipei **State:** Taipei City **PC:** **Country: Taiwan**
Year Established: 2019 **Status 2020:** Active
Industries:

Company Name: STARWING Technology Co.
Description: Centimeter level Indoor positioning solution provider
Website: http://www.starwing.com.tw/
Phone: 02-2327-9998 **Email:** alice@starwing.com.: Taiwan
City: Taipei **State:** Taipei City **PC:** **Country: Taiwan**
Year Established: **Status 2020:** Active
Industries: Artificial Intelligence

Company Name: StorySense Computing
Description: Artificial Intelligence, Storytelling
Website: http://www.storysensecomputing.com
Phone: **Email:** contact@storysensecomputing.com
City: Taipei **State:** Taipei City **PC:** **Country: Taiwan**
Year Established: **Status 2020:** Active
Industries: Artificial Intelligence for:, ~ Education (13), ~ Professional Services (48)

Company Name: TrustableAI
Description: To promote ethical, trustworthy use of machine learning and artificial intelligence Technologies
Website: http://trustable.ai
Phone: **Email:** hi@trustable.ai
City: Taipei **State:** Taipei City **PC:** **Country: Taiwan**
Year Established: **Status 2020:** Active
Industries: Application Services for:, Artificial Intelligence for:, IT Managed Services

Company Name: ucfunnel
Description: ucfunnel is an AIaaS company in Mar-tech, which has established media marketing solutions from bidder, Ad Exchange, SSP, DMP and to OM SDK.
Website: http://www.ucfunnel.com
Phone: **Email:** sales@ucfunnel.com
City: Taipei **State:** Taipei City **PC:** **Country: Taiwan**
Year Established: 2014 **Status 2020:** Active
Industries: Artificial Intelligence for:, Big Data and Analytics for:, Digital Marketing

Company Name: ULSee
Description: ULSee utilizes computer vision for virtual try-on, augmented reality, and driver safety applications.
Website: http://ulsee.com
Phone: **Email:** marketing_pr@ulsee.com
City: Taipei **State:** Taipei City **PC:** **Country: Taiwan**
Year Established: 2014 **Status 2020:** Active
Industries: Artificial Intelligence for:, Computer Vision for:, Enterprise Application Services for:, Mobile

Company Name: ULSee Inc.
Description: ULSee utilizes computer vision for virtual try-on, augmented reality, and driver safety applications.
Website: http://ulsee.com
Phone: **Email:** Kevin@ulsee.com
City: Taipei **State:** Taipei City **PC:** **Country: Taiwan**
Year Established: **Status 2020:** Active
Industries: Artificial Intelligence for:, Computer Vision for:, Enterprise Application Services for:, Mobile

Company Name: UNH3O
Description: Powering Personalized Relationships Between Human and AI.
Website: http://engaged.ai
Phone: **Email:** keegan@unh3o.com
City: Taipei **State:** Taipei City **PC:** **Country: Taiwan**
Year Established: 2017 **Status 2020:** Active
Industries: Artificial Intelligence for:, Web

Company Name: urAD Co. Ltd
Description: Programmatic advertising- urAD's smart technology platform allows you to take advantage of RTB and buy the impressions you want.
Website: http://www.urad.com.tw/en/
Phone: 886-2-25789887 **Email:** 37600@reference-encyclopedia-ai.net
City: Taipei **State:** Taipei City **PC:** **Country: Taiwan**
Year Established: 2011 **Status 2020:** Active
Industries: Big Data and Analytics for:, IT Managed Services for:, Machine Learning

Company Name: Viscovery
Description: Viscovery is a leading Vision Artificial Intelligence company based on Deep Learning and Computer Vision technology.
Website: http://viscovery.com
Phone: **Email:** marketing@viscovery.com
City: Taipei **State:** Taipei City **PC:** **Country: Taiwan**
Year Established: 2013 **Status 2020:** Active
Industries: Artificial Intelligence for:, Computer Vision for:, IT Managed Services for:, Machine Learning

Company Name: WiBA: SWEDEN
Description: WiBASE is a piloting solution explorer in IIoT application headquartered in Taiwan.
Website: http://www.wibase.com/en/
Phone: **Email:** contactus@wibase.com
City: Taipei **State:** Taipei City **PC:** **Country: Taiwan**
Year Established: 2017 **Status 2020:** Active
Industries: Artificial Intelligence for:, IT Managed Services

Company Name: YOCTOL.AI
Description: YOCTOL.AI - solution-provider in AI Chatbot Ecosystem from the bot-building platform to your most-wanted marketing tool
Website: http://yoctol.ai/
Phone: **Email:** service@yoctol.com
City: Taipei **State:** Taipei City **PC:** **Country: Taiwan**
Year Established: 2015 **Status 2020:** Active
Industries: Analytics for:, Artificial Intelligence for:, ~ Customer Relationship Management (11), IT Managed Services for:, Machine Learning for:, Natural Language Processing for:, Business Software as a Service Apps (SaaS Apps) for:, Business Software as a Service Apps (S

Company Name: AgriTalk Technology Inc.
Description: AgriTalk provide precision agricultural solution by customizing soil microbiome AI and recommend suitable fertilizing decision.
Website: https://www.agritalktech.com/
Phone: **Email:** agritalktech@gmail.com
City: Hsinchu **State:** T'ai-wan **PC:** **Country: Taiwan**
Year Established: 2019 **Status 2020:** Active
Industries: ~ Agriculture (3), ~ Agriculture (3), Artificial Intelligence for:, ~ Biotechnology (9)

Company Name: Algatha
Description: Algatha a popularized artificial intelligence platform
Website: http://www.aigatha.com/company
Phone: **Email:** support@aigatha.com
City: Hsinchu **State:** T'ai-wan **PC:** **Country: Taiwan**
Year Established: **Status 2020:** Active
Industries:

Company Name: FaceHeart
Description: FaceHeart is an AI company that provides services to different users, including smart healthcare, smart transportation, fintech, and so on.
Website: http://www.faceheart.com/
Phone: 886 3 6591088 **Email:** marketing@faceheart.com
City: Hsinchu **State:** T'ai-wan **PC:** **Country: Taiwan**
Year Established: **Status 2020:** Active
Industries:

Company Name: Kapito
Description: Kapito's goal is to empower every production line with AI. We are dedicated to develop world class service on defect inspection.
Website: http://www.fastable.ai/
Phone: **Email:** contact@simplesphere.net.com
City: Hsinchu **State:** T'ai-wan **PC:** **Country: Taiwan**
Year Established: 2017 **Status 2020:** Active
Industries: Artificial Intelligence for:, Automation

Company Name: Taiwan intelltech Manufacturing Co., Ltd.
Description: We provide total solution to help people develop and brew favorite/customized craft beer at home or in business place.
Website: http://www.timc.com.tw/
Phone: **Email:** admin@timc.com.: Taiwan
City: Hsinchu **State:** T'ai-wan **PC:** **Country: Taiwan**
Year Established: 2017 **Status 2020:** Active
Industries: ~ Food and Beverage (17), Application Services

Company Name: aetherAI
Description: Artificial Intelligence, Medical Image, Digital Pathology
Website: http://dysklabs.com/
Phone: 886-915-170-016 **Email:** career@dysklabs.com
City: Tapei **State:** T'ai-wan **PC:** **Country: Taiwan**
Year Established: **Status 2020:** Active
Industries: Artificial Intelligence for:, ~ Manufacturing-Medical Equipment-Supplies (33), ~ Professional Services (48)

Company Name: All Aspect System
Description: Unmanned System for both infrastructure and environmental inspection
Website: https://www.allaspectsystem.com/
Phone: 886(3)2654326 **Email:** cymeuas@gmail.com
City: Taoyüan **State:** Taoyuan City **PC:** **Country: Taiwan**
Year Established: 2018 **Status 2020:** Active
Industries: Embedded for:, Application Services

Tanzania

Company Name: Mtabe
Description: Mtabe is an edtech company that uses articial intelligence to provide education content primarily to students who don't have internet access
Website: http://mtabeapp.com
Phone: **Email:** info@mtabeapp.com
City: Dar Es Salaam **State:** Dar es Salam **PC:** **Country:** Tanzania
Year Established: 2017 **Status 2020:** Active
Industries: Artificial Intelligence for:, ~ Education (13), ~ Education (13), Web

Company Name: Somapps Technologies
Description: Somaapps Technologies is a solution-centric company with a mission to accelerate the advent of mobile software technologies, AI and IoT.
Website: http://somaapps.com/
Phone: 255 683 321 768 **Email:** info@somaapps.com
City: Dar Es Salaam **State:** Dar es Salam **PC:** **Country:** Tanzania
Year Established: 2016 **Status 2020:** Active
Industries: Artificial Intelligence for:, IT Managed Services

Thailand

Company Name: Acaya
Description: A Thai LegalTech startup specializing in legal information retrieval, analytics, and NLP.
Website: https://www.acaya.ai/
Phone: 818890488 **Email:** contact@acaya.ai
City: Bangkok **State:** Bangkok **PC:** **Country:** Thailand
Year Established: 2018 **Status 2020:** Active
Industries: IT Managed Services for:, Natural Language Processing

Company Name: BTC InterGroup
Description: AI-driven Technology for eCommerce Operations Fulfillment
Website: http://www.btcintergroup.com
Phone: **Email:** contact@btcintergroup.com
City: Bangkok **State:** Bangkok **PC:** **Country:** Thailand
Year Established: 2016 **Status 2020:** Active
Industries: Artificial Intelligence for:, E-Commerce

Company Name: Data Wow
Description: Data Wow is Thai-Japanese startups focusing in AI and Machine Learning development and specialize in content moderation.
Website: http://datawow.io
Phone: (2) 024-9119 **Email:** info@datawow.io
City: Bangkok **State:** Bangkok **PC:** **Country: Thailand**
Year Established: 2016 **Status 2020:** Active
Industries: Artificial Intelligence for:, Content for:, IT Managed Services for:, Machine Learning

Company Name: Devcurate
Description: Accelerating impact through career innovation
Website: http://www.devcurate.co
Phone: (6692) 254-0095 **Email:** founder@devcurate.co
City: Bangkok **State:** Bangkok **PC:** **Country: Thailand**
Year Established: 2019 **Status 2020:** Active
Industries: Application Services for:, Machine Learning

Company Name: Divertise Asia
Description: Platform-startup partner.
Website: http://divertise.asia
Phone: **Email:** business@divertise.asia
City: Bangkok **State:** Bangkok **PC:** **Country: Thailand**
Year Established: 2017 **Status 2020:** Active
Industries: Artificial Intelligence for:, Blockchain for:, Machine Learning for:, Application Services for:, Web

Company Name: Hbot.io
Description: Saas
Website: http://www.hbot.io
Phone: (6698) 286-6331 **Email:** contact@hbot.io
City: Bangkok **State:** Bangkok **PC:** **Country: Thailand**
Year Established: 2017 **Status 2020:** Active
Industries: Artificial Intelligence for:, Business Software as a Service Apps (SaaS Apps)

Company Name: HG Robotics Company Limited
Description: HG Robotics is a company that focuses on developing an information and motion management platform for unmanned systems
Website: http://www.hiveground.com
Phone: 66888019585 **Email:** info@hiveground.com
City: Bangkok **State:** Bangkok **PC:** **Country: Thailand**
Year Established: **Status 2020:** Active
Industries: Artificial Intelligence for:, Automation for:, IT Managed Services for:, Robotics

Company Name: iLog.Ai
Description: Cyber security
Website: http://ilog.ai
Phone: (81) 823-4518 **Email:** info@ragnar.co.:Thailand
City: Bangkok **State:** Bangkok **PC:** **Country: Thailand**

Year Established: 2016 **Status 2020:** Active
Industries:

Company Name: Ranked
Description: SEO Powered by Artificial Intelligence
Website: http://www.ranked.ai
Phone: **Email:** support@ranked.ai
City: Bangkok **State:** Bangkok **PC:** **Country: Thailand**
Year Established: 2016 **Status 2020:** Active
Industries: Artificial Intelligence

Company Name: Sertis Co., Ltd.
Description: Custom Data & AI/Machine Learning Solutions
Website: http://sertiscorp.com/company/
Phone: 6620011893 **Email:** info@sertiscorp.com
City: Bangkok **State:** Bangkok **PC:** **Country: Thailand**
Year Established: 2014 **Status 2020:** Active
Industries: Artificial Intelligence for:, Big Data and Analytics for:, Blockchain for:, Computer Vision for:, Databases for:, IT Managed Services for:, Machine Learning for:, Natural Language Processing for:, Natural Language Processing

Company Name: Sharkaroo
Description: Blockchain application development, ICO & STO support
Website: http://www.sharkaroo.io
Phone: 951-551-9410 **Email:** crispin@sharkaroo.io
City: Bangkok **State:** Bangkok **PC:** **Country: Thailand**
Year Established: **Status 2020:** Active
Industries:

Company Name: Skynet Systems CO., LTD.
Description: Social Trading Platform with AI
Website: http://www.skynetsystems.co.:Thailand
Phone: **Email:** pipat@skynetsystems.co.:Thailand
City: Bangkok **State:** Bangkok **PC:** **Country: Thailand**
Year Established: **Status 2020:** Active
Industries: Artificial Intelligence for:, ~ Banking and Financial Markets-Services (7), ~ Banking and Financial Markets-Services (7), ~ Professional Services (48)

Company Name: SUNDAY INS CO., LTD
Description: Smart Insurance. Born Simple. Thailand's "full-stack" Insurtech
Website: http://easysunday.com/
Phone: 6620263355 **Email:** hello@easysunday.com
City: Bangkok **State:** Bangkok **PC:** **Country: Thailand**
Year Established: 2017 **Status 2020:** Active
Industries: Artificial Intelligence for:, ~ Insurance (25), ~ Banking and Financial Markets-Services (7), Machine Learning for:, Machine Learning for:, Predictive Analytics for:, ~ Insurance (25)

Company **Name:** TRENDS Digital
Description: Creative Digital & Tech Innovation partner of Global Fortune 1000 clients across the fast growing AP / ASEAN / SEA Asia
Website: http://www.trendsdigital.com/
Phone: 662115 5953 **Email:** accounts@trendsdigital.com
City: Bangkok **State:** Bangkok **PC:** **Country: Thailand**
Year Established: 2013 **Status 2020:** Active
Industries: Content for:, ~ Education (13), Cyber Security for:, ~ Arts-Entertainment-Recreation (4), Digital Media for:, E-Commerce for:, ~ Administrative and Support Services (1), Application Services for:, Application Services for:, Machine Learning for:, ~ Social Assistanc

Company Name: Wisible
Description: Wisible is the Smart Sales Assistant. We deliver actionable Sales analytic that helps business double sales efficiency.
Website: http://www.wisible.io/en/
Phone: 66630344644 **Email:** support@wisible.io
City: Bangkok **State:** Bangkok **PC:** **Country: Thailand**
Year Established: **Status 2020:** Active
Industries: Artificial Intelligence for:, Business Applications for:, Enterprise Application Services for:, Machine Learning for:, Automation

Company Name: YesMom Pte. Ltd.
Description: YesMom uses machine learning to deliver personalised health insights to women and families.
Website: http://yesmomfertility.com
Phone: **Email:** support@yesmomfertility.com
City: Bangkok **State:** Bangkok **PC:** **Country: Thailand**
Year Established: 2017 **Status 2020:** Active
Industries: Artificial Intelligence for:, ~ Healthcare (20), Machine Learning for:, ~ Healthcare (20)

Company Name: ZWIZ.AI
Description: AI Chatbot and Analytics platform for business
Website: http://www.zwiz.ai
Phone: **Email:** sales@zwiz.ai
City: Bangkok **State:** Bangkok **PC:** **Country: Thailand**
Year Established: **Status 2020:** Active
Industries: Artificial Intelligence for:, ~ Telecommunications (56), ~ Social Media (54)

Company Name: EATLAB
Description: Equipping Restaurants with AI Capability of Facebook
Website: http://www.eatlab.space
Phone: (6687) 337-1808 **Email:** m@eatlab.space
City: Khlong San **State:** Bangkok **PC:** **Country: Thailand**
Year Established: 2018 **Status 2020:** Active
Industries: Artificial Intelligence for:, Predictive Analytics

Company Name: Humaan AI
Description: Applying AI technologies to be unleash everyone capabilities in new exciting ways.
Website: http://humaan.ai
Phone: **Email:** 36721@reference-encyclopedia-ai.net
City: Pathum Wan **State:** Bangkok **PC:** **Country: Thailand**
Year Established: 2019 **Status 2020:** Active
Industries: Artificial Intelligence for:, Enterprise Application Services for:, IT Managed Services for:, Compute

Company Name: Aztrana
Description: AI teaching the world how to understand and serve you.
Website: http://www.aztrana.
Phone: **Email:** hello@aztrana.: Switzerland
City: Chiang Mai **State:** จ.เชียงใหม่ **PC:** **Country: Thailand**
Year Established: **Status 2020:** Active
Industries: Artificial Intelligence for:, Collaboration Solutions for:, ~ Social Media (54)

Company Name: iApp Technology Co., Ltd.
Description: Artificial Intelligence Developers (AI) Focused on Natural Language Processing (NLP)
Website: http://iapp.co.:Thailand
Phone: **Email:** kobkrit@iapp.co.:Thailand
City: Pathum Thani **State:** จ.ปทุมธานี **PC:** **Country: Thailand**
Year Established: 2013 **Status 2020:** Active
Industries: Artificial Intelligence for:, IT Managed Services for:, Machine Learning

Company Name: Invacio Group
Description: Solve intelligence, use it to make the world a better place. Note if looking for INV (Invacio AAP Holdings Ltd) **This is a separate entity*
Website: http://www.invacio.com/
Phone: **Email:** support@invacio.com
City: Phuket **State:** จ.ภูเก็ต **PC:** **Country: Thailand**
Year Established: 2018 **Status 2020:** Closed
Industries:

Tunisia

Company Name: Datavision
Description: Visual Data Analytics & Instant Display Targeting Tool
Website: http://www.datavision.company
Phone: **Email:** contact@datavision.company
City: La Soukra **State:** Ariana **PC:** **Country:** Tunisia
Year Established: **Status 2020:** Active
Industries: Analytics for:, Artificial Intelligence for:, Data Management for:, Image Recognition for:, IT Managed Services for:, Machine Learning for:, ~ Media-Communications (41)

Company Name: National Injection Services
Description: National Injection Services offers big data and cloud solutions that focus on the development of companies through digitalization.
Website: http://www.nationalinjection.servic
Phone: (2165) 524-2400 **Email:** hamza@nationalinjection.service
City: La Marsa **State:** Tunis **PC:** **Country:** Tunisia
Year Established: 2015 **Status 2020:** Active
Industries: Big Data and Analytics for:, Cloud for:, Machine Learning

Company Name: Peaksource Vision
Description: Bringing artificial vision, artificial intelligence and business intelligence to the next level.
Website: http://peaksource.vision
Phone: 216 55 598 124 **Email:** contact@peaksource.vision
City: Tunis **State:** Tunis **PC:** **Country:** Tunisia
Year Established: 2014 **Status 2020:** Active
Industries: Artificial Intelligence for:, Business Intelligence for:, Enterprise Application Services

Company Name: United. Dots
Description: Mobile Apps and IT Solutions
Website: http://www.u4nited.com
Phone: **Email:** welcome@u4nited.com
City: Tunis **State:** Tunis **PC:** **Country:** Tunisia
Year Established: **Status 2020:** Active
Industries:

Company Name: WebRadar.me
Description: Market research, e-reputation & competitive intelligence
Website: http://webradar.me
Phone: 21629657656 **Email:** contact@webradar.me
City: Tunis **State:** Tunis **PC:** **Country:** Tunisia
Year Established: 2011 **Status 2020:** Active
Industries: Analytics for:, Artificial Intelligence for:, Big Data and Analytics for:, Machine Learning

Turkey

Company Name: albabaal.com
Description: hybrid, local classifieds and market place
Website: http://www.albabaal.com
Phone: 90 850 303 30 68 or 90 555 057 00 68 **Email:** talha@albabaal.com
City: Aksaray **State:** Aksaray **PC:** **Country: Turkey**
Year Established: **Status 2020:** Active
Industries:

Company Name: ArgosAI
Description: ArgosAI is a R&D company that develops innovative technologies on computer vision and machine learning applications.
Website: http://www.argosai.com/
Phone: **Email:** info@argosai.com
City: Ankara **State:** Ankara **PC:** **Country: Turkey**
Year Established: 2015 **Status 2020:** Active
Industries: Enterprise Application Services for:, Machine Learning

Company Name: Enhencer
Description: Automated Machine Learning Platform
Website: http://enhencer.com
Phone: 312-286-86-72 **Email:** hello@enhencer.com
City: Ankara **State:** Ankara **PC:** **Country: Turkey**
Year Established: 2017 **Status 2020:** Active
Industries: Artificial Intelligence for:, Business Intelligence for:, IT Managed Services for:, Machine Learning for:, Predictive Analytics for:, Business Software as a Service Apps (SaaS Apps)

Company Name: Gauss Statistical Solutions
Description: Established within METU Technopolis, Gauss Statistical Solutions is the first R&D company of Turkey specialized in statistics.
Website: http://gauss.com.tr/english/
Phone: 312 286 8672 **Email:** info@gauss.com.: Turkey
City: Ankara **State:** Ankara **PC:** **Country: Turkey**
Year Established: 2012 **Status 2020:** Active
Industries: Analytics for:, Predictive Analytics

Company Name: GFDS Inc.
Description: GFDS is a "content factory" producing high quality visual designs and solutions integrated with advanced technology as AR, VR, MR, IoT, AI.
Website: http://www.gfds-inc.com/
Phone: 90 312 285 25 20 **Email:** gfds@gfds-inc.com
City: Ankara **State:** Ankara **PC:** **Country: Turkey**
Year Established: 2013 **Status 2020:** Active
Industries: Artificial Intelligence for:, ~ Education (13), ~ Media-Communications (41), Machine Learning for:, Application Services for:, Development and Test

Company Name: Onlock
Description: Onlock is a smart lock and its ecosystem that allowing people to control their lock remotely and share with anyone and anywhere.
Website: http://www.onlock.io
Phone: 90312 265 00 23 **Email:** iletisim@onlock.io
City: Ankara **State:** Ankara **PC:** **Country: Turkey**
Year Established: 2016 **Status 2020:** Active
Industries: Application Services for:, Internet of Things (IoT) for:, ~ Construction (10)

Company Name: Redev
Description: A tech company.
Website: http://redev.me
Phone: **Email:** hello@redev.me
City: Ankara **State:** Ankara **PC:** **Country: Turkey**
Year Established: 2011 **Status 2020:** Active
Industries: Artificial Intelligence for:, Augmented Reality for:, ~ Education (13), IT Managed Services for:, IT Managed Services for:, Machine Learning for:, Digital Marketing for:, Development and Test for:, Virtual Reality (VR)

Company Name: steth.ai
Description: Steth.ai is an AI-based heart sound diagnostic system for mobile platforms
Website: http://steth.ai
Phone: **Email:** info@mits.com.: Turkey
City: Ankara **State:** Ankara **PC:** **Country: Turkey**
Year Established: 2015 **Status 2020:** Active
Industries: Artificial Intelligence for:, ~ Healthcare (20)

Company Name: DarkBlue Telecommunication Systems
Description: Advanced software and hardware projects with deep learning, mobile telecommunication solutions
Website: http://www.darkbluesystems.com
Phone: **Email:** info@darkbluesystems.com
City: Cankaya **State:** Ankara **PC:** **Country: Turkey**
Year Established: 2014 **Status 2020:** Active
Industries:

Company Name: Milvus Robotics
Description: Milvus Robotics develops mobile robot systems for various application fields.
Website: http://milvusrobotics.com
Phone: 90 850 466 6587 **Email:** info@milvusrobotics.com
City: Yenimahalle **State:** Ankara **PC:** **Country: Turkey**
Year Established: 2011 **Status 2020:** Active
Industries: Artificial Intelligence for:, Automation for:, Robotics

Company Name: TARSENS
Description: Artificial Intelligence for Precision Agriculture
Website: http://tarsens.com
Phone: **Email:** info@tarsens.com
City: Bandirma **State:** Balıkesir **PC:** **Country: Turkey**
Year Established: **Status 2020:** Active
Industries: ~ Agriculture (3), Artificial Intelligence for:, Computer Vision for:, Image Recognition for:, Machine Learning

Company Name: BLG Robotics
Description: Solve to Dynamic Schedueling with Artificial Intellegence for Production Compani: Spain
Website: http://www.blgrobotik.com
Phone: **Email:** info@blgrobotik.com
City: Eskisehir **State:** Eskişehir **PC:** **Country: Turkey**
Year Established: 2016 **Status 2020:** Active
Industries: Artificial Intelligence

Company Name: SAVRONIK
Description:
Website: http://www.savronik.com
Phone: 39 340 6622158 **Email:** massimiliano.silano@sdggroup.com
City: Eskisehir **State:** Eskişehir **PC:** **Country: Turkey**
Year Established: **Status 2020:** Active
Industries:

Company Name: Adalethan: Isle of Man
Description: Adalethanim is a platform working with artificial intelligence that analyzes, interprets, and produces results to help with legal research.
Website: https://adalethanim.com/
Phone: 90 212 809 30 77 **Email:** info@adalethanim.co
City: Besiktas **State:** İstanbul **PC:** **Country: Turkey**
Year Established: 2018 **Status 2020:** Active
Industries: Artificial Intelligence for:, ~ Government (19)

Company **Name:** Fikrimuhal
Description: Fikrimuhal helps enterprises transform into AI companies.
Website: http://www.fikrimuhal.com/
Phone: 90 (505) 804 8186 **Email:** info@fikrimuhal.com
City: Cekmekoy **State:** İstanbul **PC:** **Country: Turkey**
Year Established: 2013 **Status 2020:** Active
Industries: Artificial Intelligence

Company Name: Albert Heal:Thailand
Description: The voice-based health assistant that helps patients to take the right dose at the right time and make life easier for caregivers.
Website: https://albert.health/
Phone: **Email:** contact@albert.heal:Thailand
City: Istanbul **State:** İstanbul **PC:** **Country: Turkey**
Year Established: 2018 **Status 2020:** Active
Industries: ~ Healthcare (20), Machine Learning

Company Name: API PL: UGANDA
Description: API PLUG generates high quality leads from web and social media pages using power of chatbots.
Website: http://apiplug.com
Phone: 90216405112 **Email:** hello@apiplug.com
City: Istanbul **State:** İstanbul **PC:** **Country: Turkey**
Year Established: 2015 **Status 2020:** Active
Industries: Artificial Intelligence for:, Application Program Interfaces (APIs) for:, IT Managed Services for:, ~ E-Commerce (12), Business Software as a Service Apps (SaaS Apps)

Company Name: Communiti
Description: SaaS
Website: http://www.communiti.net
Phone: **Email:** aziz@communiti.net
City: Istanbul **State:** İstanbul **PC:** **Country: Turkey**
Year Established: **Status 2020:** Active
Industries:

Company Name: CONTACT CIRCU:
Description: CONTACT CIRCUIT is a definitive solution for social and business-critical contact management challenges.
Website: http://contactcircuit.com/
Phone: (212)347-2505 **Email:** cagatay@contactcircuit.com
City: Istanbul **State:** İstanbul **PC:** **Country: Turkey**
Year Established: 2016 **Status 2020:** Active
Industries: ~ Customer Relationship Management (11), Application Services for:, Natural Language Processing for:, ~ Social Assistance-Non-Profits (53), Web

Company Name: Digital Living Service
Description: Digital Project Delivery, Cloud Data Services, Aviation, Smart Airports, Building Information Modeling, Infrastructure, Technology Management
Website: http://digitalliving.service
Phone: **Email:** ozan.koseoglu@digitalliving.service
City: Istanbul **State:** İstanbul **PC:** **Country: Turkey**
Year Established: **Status 2020:** Active
Industries: Artificial Intelligence for:, Cloud for:, ~ Construction (10), Data Management for:, Data Management for:, ~ Real Estate (49), ~ Administrative and Support Services (1)

Company Name: Exastax Inc.
Description: Providing innovative and sustainable solutions to accelerate the Digital Transformation of corporates through BigData
Website: http://www.exastax.com
Phone: **Email:** info@exastax.com
City: Istanbul **State:** İstanbul **PC:** **Country: Turkey**
Year Established: 2016 **Status 2020:** Active
Industries: Artificial Intelligence for:, Big Data and Analytics for:, Machine Learning

Company Name: FalconAI Technologies, Inc.
Description: FalconAI is developing cutting edge AI algorithms to reinvent business processes.
Website: http://www.falconai.tech
Phone: **Email:** info@falconai.tech
City: Istanbul **State:** İstanbul **PC:** **Country: Turkey**
Year Established: **Status 2020:** Active
Industries: Artificial Intelligence for:, IT Managed Services for:, ~ Professional Services (48)

Company Name: financiAI
Description: financiAI is a platform for producing revolutionary artificial intelligence solutions for financial problems.
Website:
Phone: **Email:** 36562@reference-encyclopedia-ai.net
City: Istanbul **State:** İstanbul **PC:** **Country: Turkey**
Year Established: 2017 **Status 2020:** Closed
Industries:

Company Name: Forte Partners
Description: Analytics Consulting & Solutions
Website: http://fortepartners.co
Phone: **Email:** info@fortepartners.co
City: Istanbul **State:** İstanbul **PC:** **Country: Turkey**

Year Established: **Status 2020:** Active
Industries: Analytics for:, Artificial Intelligence for:, Big Data and Analytics for:, Business Intelligence for:, Data Management for:, Machine Learning for:, Predictive Analytics

Company Name: Genz Biotech
Description: Genz is an R&D company developing AI solutions in genomic data analysis for personalized medicine for women fighting breast cancer
Website: http://genzbio.com/
Phone: **Email:** umut@genzbio.com
City: Istanbul **State:** İstanbul **PC:** **Country: Turkey**
Year Established: 2015 **Status 2020:** Active
Industries: Artificial Intelligence for:, ~ Biotechnology (9), ~ Healthcare (20), ~ Healthcare (20), ~ Healthcare (20)

Company Name: HiveCDN
Description: HiveCDN reduces video CDN bandwidth usage and improves user experience.
Website: http://www.hivecdn.com
Phone: 90 (850) 885 0992 **Email:** info@hivecdn.com
City: Istanbul **State:** İstanbul **PC:** **Country: Turkey**
Year Established: 2013 **Status 2020:** Active
Industries: Artificial Intelligence for:, Business Applications for:, ~ Media-Communications (41), Business Software as a Service Apps (SaaS Apps) for:, ~ Media-Communications (41)

Company Name: Idverif
Description: Idverif develops 100% authentication artificial intelligence compatible with TC identity, driver's licenses, passports, and bills.
Website: http://idverif.ai/
Phone: (90) 212 483 70 06 **Email:** iletisim@idverif.ai
City: Istanbul **State:** İstanbul **PC:** **Country: Turkey**
Year Established: 2019 **Status 2020:** Active
Industries: Artificial Intelligence for:, ~ Banking and Financial Markets-Services (7)

Company Name: image4io
Description: Full Stack Image Magement (SaaS Product)
Website: http://image4.io
Phone: 90 850 885 4454 **Email:** info@image4.io
City: Istanbul **State:** İstanbul **PC:** **Country: Turkey**
Year Established: 2019 **Status 2020:** Active
Industries: Artificial Intelligence for:, IT Managed Services for:, Web for:, Business Software as a Service Apps (SaaS Apps)

Company Name: Ingenisense
Description: About Ingenisense. It's about the Machine. It's about the Data. It's about You. Ingenisense detects the undetected, sees the unseen, sens: Spain
Website: http://www.ingenisense.com/
Phone: **Email:** hello@ingenisense.com
City: Istanbul **State:** İstanbul **PC:** **Country: Turkey**
Year Established: 2015 **Status 2020:** Active
Industries: Analytics for:, Big Data and Analytics for:, Machine Learning

Company Name: Jetlink
Description: Jetlink is the easiest way to connect with your customers for commerce and support.
Website: http://jetlink.io/
Phone: 90 216 599 0216 **Email:** hello@jetlink.io
City: Istanbul **State:** İstanbul **PC:** **Country: Turkey**
Year Established: 2016 **Status 2020:** Active
Industries: Artificial Intelligence for:, ~ Customer Relationship Management (11), ~ Social Assistance-Non-Profits (53)

Company Name: Lifemote
Description: Lifemote offers AI-driven Wi-Fi analytics that detects home network issues and proactively solves them before the customers complain.
Website: http://www.lifemote.com/
Phone: **Email:** info@lifemote.com
City: Istanbul **State:** İstanbul **PC:** **Country: Turkey**
Year Established: 2017 **Status 2020:** Active
Industries: Analytics for:, Artificial Intelligence for:, Machine Learning

Company Name: Lisa AI
Description: Engagement Predictor for Instagram
Website: http://www.asklisa.ai
Phone: **Email:** hello@asklisa.ai
City: Istanbul **State:** İstanbul **PC:** **Country: Turkey**
Year Established: 2017 **Status 2020:** Active
Industries: Artificial Intelligence for:, Machine Learning for:, ~ Social Assistance-Non-Profits (53)

Company Name: Masraff
Description: AI-powered SaaS platform automating expense management for SMEs and Startups.
Website: http://www.masraff.co/
Phone: **Email:** info@masraff.co
City: Istanbul **State:** İstanbul **PC:** **Country: Turkey**
Year Established: 2017 **Status 2020:** Active
Industries: Artificial Intelligence for:, ~ Banking and Financial Markets-Services (7), Business Software as a Service Apps (SaaS Apps)

Company Name: Milkshake Solutions
Description: Milkshake Solutions provides Artificial Intelligence Company.
Website: http://www.milkshake.solutions/
Phone: 90 212 258 5320 **Email:** info@milkshake.solutions
City: Istanbul **State:** İstanbul **PC:** **Country: Turkey**
Year Established: 2015 **Status 2020:** Active
Industries: Artificial Intelligence for:, Machine Learning for:, Predictive Analytics

Company Name: Ottoo
Description: Ottoo is a connected car and mobility platform powered by artificial intelligence and machine learning.
Website: http://ottoo.com/
Phone: 90 530 116 4009 **Email:** info@ottoo.com
City: Istanbul **State:** İstanbul **PC:** **Country: Turkey**
Year Established: 2016 **Status 2020:** Active
Industries: Artificial Intelligence for:, ~ Automotive (5), Big Data and Analytics for:, ~ Telecommunications (56), Internet of Things (IoT) for:, Machine Learning for:, Machine Learning for:, Mobile

Company Name: Persona.tech
Description: Sophisticated ML/AI from Human Behavior & Dynamics
Website: http://persona.tech
Phone: **Email:** hi@persona.tech
City: Istanbul **State:** İstanbul **PC:** **Country: Turkey**
Year Established: **Status 2020:** Active
Industries: Artificial Intelligence for:, Big Data and Analytics for:, Machine Learning

Company Name: Perzonalization
Description: Real time predictive personalization services for e-commerce
Website: http://www.perzonalization.com
Phone: (650) 720-7488 **Email:** team@perzonalization.com
City: Istanbul **State:** İstanbul **PC:** **Country: Turkey**
Year Established: 2014 **Status 2020:** Active
Industries:

Company Name: Quadro Dynamics
Description: Quadro Dynamics is focused on unmanned systems technology.
Website: http://www.quadrodynamics.com/index.php/en/
Phone: **Email:** 37235@reference-encyclopedia-ai.net
City: Istanbul **State:** İstanbul **PC:** **Country: Turkey**
Year Established: 2014 **Status 2020:** Active
Industries: Application Services for:, IT Managed Services for:, Application Services

Company Name: Sanal Hekim
Description: SanalHekim is newest artificial intelligence in the health systems. Start with your symptoms for diagnosis.
Website:
Phone: **Email:** 37335@reference-encyclopedia-ai.net
City: Istanbul **State:** İstanbul **PC:** **Country: Turkey**
Year Established: 2014 **Status 2020:** Closed
Industries: Artificial Intelligence for:, ~ Healthcare (20), ~ Healthcare (20)

Company Name: Tarentum AI
Description: Tarentum AI develops solutions to critical business needs using machine learning and artificial intelligence technologies.
Website: http://tarentum.io
Phone: **Email:** info@tarentum.io
City: Istanbul **State:** İstanbul **PC:** **Country: Turkey**
Year Established: 2017 **Status 2020:** Active
Industries: Artificial Intelligence

Company Name: Technix Technology (Sayax)
Description: Technix develops energy management solutions for energy suppliers, traders and consumers.
Website: http://www.sayax.com.: Turkey
Phone: **Email:** info@technix.com.: Turkey
City: Istanbul **State:** İstanbul **PC:** **Country: Turkey**
Year Established: 2010 **Status 2020:** Active
Industries: Analytics for:, Artificial Intelligence for:, ~ Energy and Utilities (14), ~ Energy and Utilities (14), ~ Energy and Utilities (14), Enterprise Application Services for:, Machine Learning for:, Enterprise Application Services for:, Enterprise Application Service

Company Name: Uservision
Description: Enterprise SaaS, AI, Qualitative Resear
Website: http://www.user.vision
Phone: **Email:** batukhan@user.vision
City: Istanbul **State:** İstanbul **PC:** **Country: Turkey**
Year Established: 2018 **Status 2020:** Active
Industries: Development and Test

Company Name: Vircon Group Technologies
Description: Vircon Group is currently focused on creating AI & Computer Graphics solutions with a growing team to the numerous high-tech areas
Website: http://vircongroup.com
Phone: **Email:** info@vircongroup.com
City: Istanbul **State:** İstanbul **PC:** **Country: Turkey**
Year Established: 2016 **Status 2020:** Active
Industries: Artificial Intelligence for:, ~ Education (13)

Company Name: Vision Genius
Description: Vision Genius is an artificial intelligence based video analytics platform, designed to meet the challenges of video content extraction.
Website: http://www.visiongenius.ai
Phone: **Email:** info@visiongenius.ai
City: Istanbul **State:** İstanbul **PC:** **Country: Turkey**
Year Established: 2018 **Status 2020:** Active
Industries: Analytics for:, Artificial Intelligence for:, ~ Personal-Religious-Civic (45), Computer Vision for:, IT Managed Services for:, Machine Learning for:, Business Software as a Service Apps (SaaS Apps)

Company Name: Vispera
Description: Vispera is an image recognition and analytics company providing retailers and suppliers with store and team execution insights.
Website: http://vispera.co/
Phone: 90 (212) 268 28 88 **Email:** info@vispera.co
City: Istanbul **State:** İstanbul **PC:** **Country: Turkey**
Year Established: 2014 **Status 2020:** Active
Industries: Analytics for:, Artificial Intelligence for:, Computer Vision for:, Image Recognition for:, Machine Learning

Company Name: WEXT
Description: Proven Approaches Artificial Intelligence = a world-class English language learning experience.
Website: http://wext.com
Phone: **Email:** ali.uzunyolcu@smarteducation.net
City: Istanbul **State:** İstanbul **PC:** **Country: Turkey**
Year Established: 2016 **Status 2020:** Active
Industries: Artificial Intelligence for:, ~ Customer Relationship Management (11), ~ Education (13), ~ Education (13), ~ Education (13), IT Managed Services for:, ~ Education (13)

Company Name: Event Gat: Spain
Description: Event Gates offers AI solutions for security.
Website: http://www.eventgates.com/
Phone: **Email:** 36524@reference-encyclopedia-ai.net
City: Kadikoy **State:** İstanbul **PC:** **Country: Turkey**
Year Established: 2014 **Status 2020:** Active
Industries: Artificial Intelligence for:, ~ Event Management (15), Security

Company Name: Quant Co.
Description: Artificial Intelligence as a Service for Home Energy Management
Website: http://www.quant-co.com/
Phone: **Email:** info@quant-co.com
City: Maslak **State:** Istanbul **PC:** **Country: Turkey**
Year Established: **Status 2020:** Active
Industries: Artificial Intelligence for:, ~ Energy and Utilities (14), ~ Energy and Utilities (14), ~ Energy and Utilities (14), ~ Energy and Utilities (14)

Company Name: CitySpide: Serbia
Description: Advertising, Marketing, AI, Drones, Analytics
Website: http://www.cityspiders.com
Phone: 90 (085) 0390 2051 **Email:** go@cityspiders.com
City: Pendik **State:** İstanbul **PC:** **Country: Turkey**
Year Established: **Status 2020:** Active
Industries:

Company Name: Inoven
Description: Inoven is an artificial intelligence startup focused on visual recognition systems.
Website: http://www.inoven.ai
Phone: 90 216 999 63 62 **Email:** info@inoven.ai
City: Pendik **State:** İstanbul **PC:** **Country: Turkey**
Year Established: 2016 **Status 2020:** Active
Industries: Artificial Intelligence for:, Industrial Solutions for:, IT Managed Services

Company Name: Anatolian Technologies
Description: Anatolian Technologies & Labs focused on developing software and device based new technologies.
Website: http://anatoliantechnologies.com/
Phone: **Email:** info@anatoliantechnologies.com
City: Sariyer **State:** İstanbul **PC:** **Country: Turkey**
Year Established: 2017 **Status 2020:** Active
Industries:

Company Name: MaginTech
Description: MaginTech provides a software which uses Artificial Intelligence for increasing profitability of companies.
Website: http://magintech.com/
Phone: 90 5424863378 **Email:** info@magintech.com
City: Sisli **State:** İstanbul **PC:** **Country: Turkey**
Year Established: 2017 **Status 2020:** Active
Industries: Artificial Intelligence for:, IT Managed Services

Company Name: Udentify
Description: Google Analytics for Brick and Morta: Serbia
Website: http://www.udentify.co
Phone: **Email:** can@udentify.co
City: Sisli **State:** İstanbul **PC:** **Country: Turkey**
Year Established: 2017 **Status 2020:** Active
Industries: Internet of Things (IoT) for:, Machine Learning

Company Name: FlowQ
Description: Predictive Talent Analytics as SaaS
Website: http://www.flowq.com
Phone: **Email:** hi@flowq.com
City: Uskudar **State:** İstanbul **PC:** **Country: Turkey**
Year Established: 2017 **Status 2020:** Active
Industries: Predictive Analytics for:, Business Software as a Service Apps (SaaS Apps)

Company Name: Arya
Description: Arya is a tool for personalized forex trade which increases your profit according to your previous trading statements.
Website: http://aryafinance.com/
Phone: **Email:** info@aryafinance.com
City: Alsancak **State:** İzmir **PC:** **Country: Turkey**
Year Established: 2017 **Status 2020:** Active
Industries: Artificial Intelligence for:, ~ Banking and Financial Markets-Services (7), ~ Banking and Financial Markets-Services (7), Machine Learning

Company Name: Logg: Morocco
Description: SaaS
Website: http://www.solarify.io
Phone: **Email:** info@loggma.com.: Turkey
City: Izmir **State:** Izmir **PC:** **Country: Turkey**
Year Established: **Status 2020:** Active
Industries: Artificial Intelligence for:, ~ Energy and Utilities (14), ~ Professional Services (48), ~ Energy and Utilities (14)

Company **Name:** Bufalo Teknoloji
Description: AI Driven Managed Funds
Website: http://www.bufaloo.com
Phone: **Email:** mcbalta@yahoo.com
City: Gebze **State:** Kocaeli **PC:** **Country: Turkey**
Year Established: **Status 2020:** Active
Industries: Artificial Intelligence for:, ~ Banking and Financial Markets-Services (7), ~ Banking and Financial Markets-Services (7), ~ Banking and Financial Markets-Services (7)

Company Name: E2M2
Description: Software Innovation Company
Website: http://www.e2m2.net
Phone: **Email:** info@e2m2.net
City: Gebze **State:** Kocaeli **PC:** **Country: Turkey**
Year Established: **Status 2020:** Active
Industries: Artificial Intelligence for:, IT Managed Services for:, Machine Learning for:, Application Services for:, Cyber Security

Company Name: EFTA Energy
Description: Solar Photovoltaic Energy Systems
Website: http://www.eftaenerji.com
Phone: 90 332 249 2391 **Email:** bilgi@eftaenerji.com
City: Konya **State:** Konya **PC:** **Country: Turkey**
Year Established: 2015 **Status 2020:** Active
Industries: ~ Energy and Utilities (14), Application Services

Company Name: xMint Software Consultancy
Description: Software solutions and consultancy with a focus on artificial intelligence.
Website: http://xmint.info
Phone: **Email:** melodi.caliskan@xmint.info
City: Yalova **State:** Yalova **PC:** **Country: Turkey**
Year Established: 2019 **Status 2020:** Active
Industries:

Uganda

Company Name: Agric Wallet
Description: Agric Wallet is a FinTech platform using Artificial Intelligence to manage smallholder payment risk in the supply chain.
Website: https://www.agricwallet.com/
Phone: 256 392 912 222 **Email:** liquidity@agricwallet.com
City: Kampala **State:** Central Region **PC:** **Country:** Ugunda
Year Established: 2017 **Status 2020:** Active
Industries: ~ Agriculture (3), Big Data and Analytics for:, ~ Banking and Financial Markets-Services (7), Machine Learning for:, ~ Banking and Financial Markets-Services (7)

Company Name: Feyti limited
Description: Feyti provides software that enables users to identify fake , falsified and counterfeit drugs.
Website: http://www.mfeyti.com
Phone: **Email:** bima.benjamin6@gmail.com
City: Kampala **State:** Central Region **PC:** **Country:** Ugunda
Year Established: 2017 **Status 2020:** Active
Industries: Artificial Intelligence for:, ~ Healthcare (20)

Company Name: LabTECH Engineering Solutions Uganda Limited
Description: Providing machine learning solutions to tackle challenges in key growth sectors in Africa.
Website: http://labtecheng.wixsite.com/labtecheng
Phone: **Email:** alvin.kabwama@gmail.com
City: Kampala **State:** Central Region **PC:** **Country:** Ugunda
Year Established: 2018 **Status 2020:** Active
Industries: Artificial Intelligence for:, ~ Healthcare (20), Internet of Things (IoT) for:, Machine Learning

Company Name: MamaOpe Medicals
Description: MamaOpe designed a Pneumonia diagnosis kit in form of a jacket for children aged below 5 years.
Website: http://mamaope.com/
Phone: **Email:** info@mamaope.com
City: Kampala **State:** Central Region **PC:** **Country:** Ugunda
Year Established: **Status 2020:** Active
Industries: Artificial Intelligence for:, ~ Healthcare (20), ~ Healthcare (20), Machine Learning for:, ~ Healthcare (20), ~ Manufacturing-Medical Equipment-Supplies (33)

Company Name: Ty: Romania
Description: An AI-augmented platform for on-demand delivery of high-quality app development work.
Website:
Phone: **Email:** daisy@tyrohq.com
City: Kampala **State:** Central Region **PC:** **Country:** Ugunda
Year Established: 2018 **Status 2020:** Active
Industries:

Company Name: CHIL AI Lab
Description: Chil AI Lab offers artificial intelligence technology to improve on the access of reproductive health cancer diagnosis.
Website:
Phone: 256 758 403065 **Email:** 36268@reference-encyclopedia-ai.net
City: Mulago **State:** Central Region **PC:** **Country:** Ugunda

Year Established: 2018 **Status 2020:** Closed
Industries: Artificial Intelligence for:, ~ Healthcare (20)

Ukraine

Company Name: Datawiz.io
Description: Datawiz.io provides cloud-based business intelligent and data visualization software specialized in retail industry.
Website: http://datawiz.io/
Phone: **Email:** hello@datawiz.io
City: Chernivtsi **State:** Chernivtsi Oblast **PC:** **Country: United Kingdom**
Year Established: 2013 **Status 2020:** Active
Industries: Artificial Intelligence for:, Business Intelligence for:, Data Management for:, Data Management for:, E-Commerce for:, IT Managed Services for:, Machine Learning for:, Natural Language Processing for:, Natural Language Processing

Company Name: Adloonix
Description: Data-driven Digital Marketing Agency
Website: http://www.adloonix.com
Phone: **Email:** Founder@adloonix.com
City: Dnipropetrovsk **State:** Dnipropetrovsk Oblast **PC:** **Country: United Kingdom**
Year Established: **Status 2020:** Active
Industries:

Company Name: Neural Labs
Description: Neural Labs are a group of developers specializing in Optical Character Recognition, key data extraction, NLP, and machine learning.
Website: http://labsneural.com/
Phone: 38 (095) 011-33-78 **Email:** info@labsneural.com
City: Dnipropetrovsk **State:** Dnipropetrovsk Oblast **PC:** **Country: United Kingdom**
Year Established: 2016 **Status 2020:** Active
Industries: Databases for:, Machine Learning

Company Name: A-listware
Description: A-listware deals with consulting, onboarding and guiding remote teams, AI, mobile, web and embedded development, cloud computing services.
Website: http://www.a-listware.com/
Phone: 38 (099) 132 52 58 **Email:** 36042@reference-encyclopedia-ai.net
City: Kharkiv **State:** Kharkiv Oblast **PC:** **Country: United Kingdom**
Year Established: 2017 **Status 2020:** Active
Industries: Artificial Intelligence for:, Cloud for:, Mobile

Company Name: DevPace
Description: Devpace is a digital agency that delivers technological solutions for the financial, manufacturing and logistics sectors.
Website: http://devpace.net
Phone: 38 095 872 32 11 **Email:** 36431@reference-encyclopedia-ai.net
City: Kharkiv **State:** Kharkiv Oblast **PC:** **Country: United Kingdom**
Year Established: 2017 **Status 2020:** Active
Industries: Artificial Intelligence for:, Big Data and Analytics for:, IT Managed Services

Company Name: Hurma System
Description: HURMA System is a subsidiary and a product by IT Svit.
Website: http://hurma.work/
Phone: 38 0 99 676 90 97 **Email:** info@hurma.work
City: Kharkiv **State:** Kharkiv Oblast **PC:** **Country: United Kingdom**
Year Established: 2017 **Status 2020:** Active
Industries: Analytics for:, Machine Learning for:, Predictive Analytics for:, Business Software as a Service Apps (SaaS Apps)

Company Name: Quantum
Description: Quantum is a software engineering company specializes in Agritech software development for farming and technology companies.
Website: http://quantumobile.com
Phone: 380.50.400.5772 **Email:** 37244@reference-encyclopedia-ai.net
City: Kharkiv **State:** Kharkiv Oblast **PC:** **Country: United Kingdom**
Year Established: 2015 **Status 2020:** Active
Industries: Artificial Intelligence for:, Automation

Company Name: Daze Presentations
Description: Daze Presentations has core mission is to discover, empower, and deliver your ideas to the target audience in the right way.
Website: http://daze.tech
Phone: **Email:** mail@daze.tech
City: Kharkov **State:** Kharkiv Oblast **PC:** **Country: United Kingdom**
Year Established: 2016 **Status 2020:** Active
Industries: Artificial Intelligence for:, Data Management for:, ~ Media-Communications (41)

Company Name: OSDB
Description: Software Development Company
Website: http://osdb.io
Phone: **Email:** bhuriev@osdb.io
City: Kharkov **State:** Kharkiv Oblast **PC:** **Country: United Kingdom**
Year Established: 2017 **Status 2020:** Active
Industries: Artificial Intelligence for:, Blockchain for:, ~ Banking and Financial Markets-Services (7), Internet of Things (IoT) for:, Web

Company Name: 4HIR: SPAIN
Description: 4HIRES - is the next gen career platform, that focused on a talent.
Website: http://www.fourhires.com
Phone: **Email:** info@fourhires.com
City: Kyiv **State:** Kyyiv **PC:** **Country: United Kingdom**
Year Established: **Status 2020:** Active
Industries: Artificial Intelligence for:, Data Management for:, ~ Human Resources (24), ~ Human Resources (24), ~ Human Resources (24)

Company Name: 4ire Labs
Description: Quality, value, schedule - the Holy Trio we believe in.
Website: http://4irelabs.com/
Phone: 19149028110 **Email:** ms@4irelabs.com
City: Kyiv **State:** Kyyiv **PC:** **Country: United Kingdom**
Year Established: 2010 **Status 2020:** Active
Industries: Application Services for:, Artificial Intelligence for:, Blockchain for:, IT Managed Services for:, Machine Learning for:, Application Services

Company Name: AgroBI by Horos.Tech
Description: AgroBI: Decision support system for agribusiness based on machine learning
Website: https://horos.tech/
Phone: **Email:** k.domchenko@horos.tech
City: Kyiv **State:** Kyyiv **PC:** **Country: United Kingdom**
Year Established: 2016 **Status 2020:** Active
Industries: ~ Agriculture (3), ~ Agriculture (3), Artificial Intelligence for:, Big Data and Analytics for:, Business Intelligence for:, Machine Learning for:, Predictive Analytics

Company Name: Captain Grow:Thailand
Description: Captain Growth is the AI-powered app that automates marketing analytics and finds deep insight in your data.
Website: http://captaingrowth.ai/
Phone: **Email:** hello@captaingrowth.ai
City: Kyiv **State:** Kyyiv **PC:** **Country: United Kingdom**

Year Established: 2017 **Status 2020:** Active
Industries:

Company Name: DataRoot Labs
Description: DataRoot Labs (DRL) provides full-service data science & artificial intelligence solutions for startups and enterpris: Spain
Website: http://datarootlabs.com
Phone: **Email:** info@datarootlabs.com
City: Kyiv **State:** Kyyiv **PC:** **Country: United Kingdom**
Year Established: 2016 **Status 2020:** Active
Industries: Analytics for:, Artificial Intelligence for:, Big Data and Analytics for:, IT Managed Services for:, Machine Learning

Company Name: Detrec It
Description: Detrec is an IT company that uses artificial intelligence in neural networks to move the business way forward.
Website: http://www.detrec.ai
Phone: 380-44-2221213 **Email:** info@detrec.ai
City: Kyiv **State:** Kyyiv **PC:** **Country: United Kingdom**
Year Established: 2018 **Status 2020:** Active
Industries: Artificial Intelligence for:, IT Managed Services for:, Compute

Company Name: inCafe
Description: inCafe is an online ordering based on predictive technology. Big Data and AI for each restaurant.
Website: http://www.incafe.co
Phone: 380 (96) 584 22 17 **Email:** info@incafe.co
City: Kyiv **State:** Kyyiv **PC:** **Country: United Kingdom**
Year Established: 2016 **Status 2020:** Active
Industries: Application Services for:, Artificial Intelligence for:, ~ Customer Relationship Management (11), Mobile for:, ~ Food and Beverage (17), Business Software as a Service Apps (SaaS Apps)

Company Name: IoT Factory
Description: IoT factory offers a full range of IT consulting services that include cloud computing, artificial and business intelligence solutions.
Website: http://www.iot-factory.com.: Ukraine
Phone: **Email:** info@iot-factory.com.: Ukraine
City: Kyiv **State:** Kyyiv **PC:** **Country: United Kingdom**
Year Established: 2016 **Status 2020:** Active
Industries: Artificial Intelligence for:, Business Intelligence for:, IT Managed Services

Company Name: K-3 Soft
Description: We build: Education, E-commerce, Robotics, CMS development, etc. React, PHP, JavaScript, Laravel, Node, .Net, iOs, Android development.
Website: http://k-3soft.com
Phone: 38(066)603 30 15 **Email:** djema@k-3soft.com
City: Kyiv **State:** Kyyiv **PC:** **Country: United Kingdom**
Year Established: 2015 **Status 2020:** Active
Industries: Artificial Intelligence for:, Blockchain for:, E-Commerce for:, ~ Education (13), IT Managed Services for:, Business Process and Operations for:, Robotics for:, Web

Company Name: LimpidArmor
Description: LimpidArmor is initially military AR/AI Solution, which is aiming to improve armored vehicle safety.
Website: http://limpidarmor.com
Phone: **Email:** info@limpid.group
City: Kyiv **State:** Kyyiv **PC:** **Country: United Kingdom**
Year Established: 2016 **Status 2020:** Active
Industries: Artificial Intelligence for:, ~ Automotive (5), ~ Government (19), Security

Company Name: Looqme
Description:
Website: http://looqme.io/
Phone: 38 044 384 03 61 **Email:** andriy.gusak@looqme.io
City: Kyiv **State:** **Zip:** 4050 **Country: United Kingdom**
Year Established: **Status 2020:** Active
Industries:

Company Name: Respeecher
Description: We build high fidelity voice cloning (voice conversion) systems using deep neural networks.
Website: http://respeecher.com/
Phone: **Email:** info@respeecher.com
City: Kyiv **State:** Kyyiv **PC:** **Country: United Kingdom**
Year Established: 2018 **Status 2020:** Active
Industries: Artificial Intelligence for:, IT Managed Services

Company Name: RetargetApp
Description: Helping online businesses sell 2x more with AI-powered ads
Website: http://retargetapp.com
Phone: **Email:** hello@retargetapp.com
City: Kyiv **State:** Kyyiv **PC:** **Country: United Kingdom**
Year Established: 2015 **Status 2020:** Active
Industries: Artificial Intelligence for:, Big Data and Analytics for:, E-Commerce

Company Name: ServReality
Description: We are the leading VR/AR/MR and AI software development provider ServReality is all about the latest technologies and innovation
Website: http://ServReality.com
Phone: **Email:** info@servreality.com
City: Kyiv **State:** Kyyiv **PC:** **Country: United Kingdom**
Year Established: 2013 **Status 2020:** Active
Industries: Application Services for:, Artificial Intelligence for:, Augmented Reality for:, Big Data and Analytics for:, Blockchain for:, Computer Vision for:, Computer Vision for:, Enterprise Application Services for:, Application Services for:, Business Process and Operati

Company Name: UniExo
Description: UniExo device reduces recovery period from injuries by assisting and supporting patients outside the healthcare facilities using exoskeleton
Website: http://uniexo.com
Phone: **Email:** info@uniexo.com
City: Kyiv **State:** Kyyiv **PC:** **Country: United Kingdom**
Year Established: 2015 **Status 2020:** Active
Industries: Artificial Intelligence for:, Big Data and Analytics for:, ~ Healthcare (20), Machine Learning for:, Robotics for:, Internet of Things (IoT) for:, Internet of Things (IoT)

Company Name: Widelogics
Description: Chatbot development company
Website:
Phone: **Email:** 4935@reference-encyclopedia-ai.net
City: Kyiv **State:** Kyyiv **PC:** **Country: United Kingdom**
Year Established: **Status 2020:** Active
Industries: Artificial Intelligence for:, Machine Learning for:, ~ Telecommunications (56), Natural Language Processing for:, ~ Professional Services (48)

Company Name: Additive Analytics
Description: Additive Analytics provides analytics for hospitals.
Website: http://www.additiveanalytics.com/
Phone: 380 97 475 0262 **Email:** sales@additiveanalytics.com
City: Kiev **State:** Kyyivs'ka Oblast' **PC:** **Country: United Kingdom**
Year Established: 2013 **Status 2020:** Active
Industries: Analytics for:, ~ Healthcare (20), Machine Learning

Company Name: Arcane Future
Description: Arcane Future delivers analytics, data science, artificial intelligence, and machine learning services for the gaming industry.
Website: http://www.arcanefuture.com
Phone: **Email:** is@arcanefuture.com
City: Kiev **State:** Kyyivs'ka Oblast' **PC:** **Country: United Kingdom**

Year Established: 2018 **Status 2020:** Active
Industries:

Company Name: Esports Charts
Description: Esports Charts is a unique analytical agency collecting all information about esports, streaming and providing actual fact data
Website: http://escharts.com
Phone: **Email:** team@escharts.com
City: Kiev **State:** Kyyivs'ka Oblast' **PC:** **Country: United Kingdom**
Year Established: 2016 **Status 2020:** Active
Industries: Computer Vision for:, ~ Arts-Entertainment-Recreation (4), Predictive Analytics for:, ~ Media-Communications (41)

Company Name: EVE.calls
Description: EVE.calls is a human-like bot that helps companies to support, sell, notify and survey customers.
Website: http://evecalls.com/en/
Phone: 38 044 36 46 846 **Email:** office@evecalls.com
City: Kiev **State:** Kyyivs'ka Oblast' **PC:** **Country: United Kingdom**
Year Established: 2016 **Status 2020:** Active
Industries: Artificial Intelligence for:, ~ Customer Relationship Management (11), Enterprise Application Services for:, Business Software as a Service Apps (SaaS Apps)

Company Name: Leeloo.ai
Description: AI Lead Generation, Support and Sales Automation using Chatbot Customer Journey Automation via Messenge: Serbia
Website: http://leeloo.ai
Phone: **Email:** admin@leeloo.ai
City: Kiev **State:** Kyyivs'ka Oblast' **PC:** **Country: United Kingdom**
Year Established: 2016 **Status 2020:** Active
Industries: Artificial Intelligence for:, IT Managed Services for:, Business Software as a Service Apps (SaaS Apps)

Company Name: Morbax HR
Description: Morbax HR is Digital Talent Management Platform for candidates sourcing, assessment and individual career development.
Website: http://mx@morbax.com
Phone: **Email:** mx@morbax.com
City: Kiev **State:** Kyyivs'ka Oblast' **PC:** **Country: United Kingdom**
Year Established: 2016 **Status 2020:** Active
Industries: Artificial Intelligence for:, Business Applications for:, Big Data and Analytics for:, Machine Learning

Company Name: MorningPag: Spain
Description: AI-powered daily journaling app that tracks of your mental state.
Website: http://morningpages.app/
Phone: **Email:** mornpages@gmail.com
City: Kiev **State:** Kyyivs'ka Oblast' **PC:** **Country: United Kingdom**
Year Established: 2017 **Status 2020:** Active
Industries: Artificial Intelligence for:, Application Services for:, ~ Healthcare (20)

Company **Name:** SoftData
Description: SoftData provides services in the field of data analysis, software development and technological solutions for businesses and institutions.
Website: http://softdatagroup.com
Phone: 38(050)309-30-92 **Email:** hello@softdatagroup.com
City: Kiev **State:** Kyyivs'ka Oblast' **PC:** **Country: United Kingdom**
Year Established: 2013 **Status 2020:** Active
Industries: Artificial Intelligence for:, Databases for:, Internet of Things (IoT)

Company Name: TechHeaven
Description: An AI solution which allows people to recreate themselves in the digital avatars with voice, behavior and movements of a real person.
Website:
Phone: **Email:** 4933@reference-encyclopedia-ai.net
City: Kiev **State:** Kyyivs'ka Oblast' **PC:** **Country: United Kingdom**
Year Established: **Status 2020:** Active
Industries: Artificial Intelligence for:, IT Managed Services

Company Name: Ticketsell.ai
Description: Ticketsell.ai is the AI-empowered platform that provides products suite such as Top Competition, Top Sales, and Top Price.
Website: http://ticketsell.ai
Phone: 38(044) 224 49 49 **Email:** info@ticketsell.ai
City: Kiev **State:** Kyyivs'ka Oblast' **PC:** **Country: United Kingdom**
Year Established: 2018 **Status 2020:** Active
Industries: Artificial Intelligence for:, ~ Event Management (15), Machine Learning for:, Business Software as a Service Apps (SaaS Apps) for:, ~ Arts-Entertainment-Recreation (4)

Company Name: Web-Peppe: Serbia
Description: Drupal development – is one of our main professional activities, we carry out for several years.
Website: http://web-peppers.com
Phone: **Email:** sergey@web-peppers.com
City: Kiev **State:** Kyyivs'ka Oblast' **PC:** **Country: United Kingdom**
Year Established: 2013 **Status 2020:** Active
Industries: Artificial Intelligence for:, Blockchain for:, Machine Learning for:, Mobile for:, Application Services for:, Web

Company Name: BotsCrew
Description: BotsCrew - chatbots development company
Website: http://botscrew.com/
Phone: **Email:** info@botscrew.com
City: Lviv **State:** Lviv Oblast **PC:** **Country: United Kingdom**
Year Established: 2016 **Status 2020:** Active
Industries: Artificial Intelligence for:, ~ Customer Relationship Management (11), Web

Company Name: Chatbots.Studio
Description: Top agency, that builds the great bots for growing businesses. Just message us to get a FREE proof of conce: Portugal
Website: http://Chatbots.Studio
Phone: (38096) 448-8046 **Email:** Igor@chatbots.studio
City: Lviv **State:** Lviv Oblast **PC:** **Country: United Kingdom**
Year Established: 2016 **Status 2020:** Active
Industries: Artificial Intelligence for:, ~ Social Media (54), Machine Learning for:, Natural Language Processing

Company Name: Jappware
Description: Jappware provides high-quality custom software development, integrated and dedicated teams based on the client's care needs.
Website: http://jappware.com
Phone: **Email:** info@jappware.com
City: Lviv **State:** Lviv Oblast **PC:** **Country: United Kingdom**
Year Established: 2017 **Status 2020:** Active
Industries: Cloud for:, Data Management for:, E-Commerce for:, ~ Healthcare (20), Machine Learning for:, Mobile for:, Automation for:, Automation for:, Web for:, Web

Company Name: FlyElephant
Description: FlyElephant is a cloud platform that enables Data Science and Engineering teams to get a ready environment faster with zero setups.
Website: http://flyelephant.net
Phone: **Email:** info@flyelephant.net
City: Odessa **State:** Odessa Oblast **PC:** **Country: United Kingdom**

Year Established: 2014 **Status 2020:** Active
Industries: Analytics for:, Artificial Intelligence for:, Big Data and Analytics for:, Enterprise Application Services for:, IT Infrastructure for:, Machine Learning

Company Name: Singularika
Description: We create intelligent dialog systems based on AI, Natural Language Processing and machine learning.
Website: http://singularika.com/en/
Phone: 78122431430 **Email:** partners@singularika.com
City: Odessa **State:** Odessa Oblast **PC:** **Country: United Kingdom**
Year Established: 2014 **Status 2020:** Active
Industries:

Company Name: Tesoro LTD
Description: Algorithmic trading
Website: http://www.itesoro.com
Phone: **Email:** ceo@itesoro.com
City: Odessa **State:** Odessa Oblast **PC:** **Country: United Kingdom**
Year Established: 2016 **Status 2020:** Active
Industries: Artificial Intelligence for:, ~ Banking and Financial Markets-Services (7)

Company Name: Botodata
Description: Botodata - AI Consulting Company
Website: http://botodata.com/
Phone: 38 063 884 29 77 **Email:** hello@botodata.com
City: Vinnytsya **State:** Vinnytsia Oblast **PC:** **Country: United Kingdom**
Year Established: 2019 **Status 2020:** Active
Industries: Artificial Intelligence for:, IT Managed Services for:, Machine Learning for:, Web

Company Name: Group 42
Description: Group 42 is a United Arab Emirates artificial intelligence (AI) and cloud computing company
Website: http://www.g42.ai/
Phone: **Email:** contact@g42.ai
City: Abu Dhabi **State:** Abu Dhabi **PC:** **Country: United Arab Emirates**
Year Established: 2018 **Status 2020:** Active
Industries: Artificial Intelligence for:, IT Managed Services for:, IT Managed Services

United Arab Emerates

Company Name: Inception Institute of Artificial Intelligence
Description: The Inception Institute of Artificial Intelligence (IIAI) is a national research organization of the UAE.
Website: http://www.inceptioniai.org
Phone: **Email:** contact@inceptioniai.org
City: Abu Dhabi **State:** ABU **PC:** **Country: United Arab Emirates**
Year Established: **Status 2020:** Active
Industries: Artificial Intelligence for:, IT Managed Services

Company Name: Narrativa
Description: Narrativa uses AI techniques to mine big data and generate news stories for its clients' audience at machine scale.
Website: narrativa.com
Phone: **Email:** info@narrativa.com
City: Abu Dhabi **State:** Abu Dhabi **PC:** **Country: United Arab Emirates**
Year Established: **Status 2020:** Active
Industries: Analytics for:, Artificial Intelligence for:, Big Data and Analytics for:, Natural Language Processing

Company Name: Qera
Description: The Abu Dhabi born AI Lab.
Website: http://www.qera.com/
Phone: **Email:** jf@qera.com
City: Abu Dhabi **State:** ABU **PC:** **Country: United Arab Emirates**
Year Established: **Status 2020:** Active
Industries: Artificial Intelligence for:, Business Intelligence for:, Computer Vision for:, ~ Banking and Financial Markets-Services (7), ~ Healthcare (20), Machine Learning for:, ~ Oil and Gas (43)

Company Name: Tuitify
Description: SaaS platform powered by AI to boost your employees' productivity, engagement and work quality by leveraging Knowledge & Experience
Website: http://www.tuitify.com
Phone: **Email:** info@tuitify.com
City: Abu Dhabi **State:** Abu Dhabi **PC:** **Country: United Arab Emirates**
Year Established: 2017 **Status 2020:** Active
Industries: Artificial Intelligence for:, ~ Education (13), Application Program Interfaces (APIs)

Company Name: UAE TOP 10
Description: UAE Top 10 is a prestigious online club of the finest, most exclusive brands in the UAE. USA TOP 10 & UK TOP 10 are some of our Projects.
Website: http://uaet10.com/
Phone: **Email:** joinus@uaet10.com
City: Abu Dhabi **State:** Abu Dhabi **PC:** **Country: United Arab Emirates**
Year Established: 2016 **Status 2020:** Active
Industries: E-Commerce for:, IT Managed Services for:, Predictive Analytics for:, Web

Company Name: Blue Logic
Description: Blue Logic offers artificial intelligence and machine learning services.
Website: http://thatsbluelogic.com/
Phone: 971 4 514 8757 **Email:** hello@thatsbluelogic.com
City: Al Satwa **State:** Dubai **PC:** **Country: United Arab Emirates**
Year Established: 2016 **Status 2020:** Active
Industries: Artificial Intelligence for:, Machine Learning

Company Name: AdsBridge
Description: AdsBridge - intelligent tracking software for affiliate marketers & advertise: Serbia
Website: https://www.adsbridge.com/
Phone: **Email:** support@adsbridge.com
City: Dubai **State:** Dubai **PC:** **Country: United Arab Emirates**
Year Established: 2013 **Status 2020:** Active
Industries: ~ E-Commerce (12), Artificial Intelligence for:, IT Managed Services for:, Robotics for:, Business Software as a Service Apps (SaaS Apps)

Company Name: Affaan Technologies
Description: Affaan Technologies offers artificial intelligence and machine learning consulting services.
Website: http://www.affaan.com/
Phone: 971.4.273.1626 **Email:** info@affaan.com
City: Dubai **State:** Dubai **PC:** **Country: United Arab Emirates**
Year Established: 2010 **Status 2020:** Active
Industries: Artificial Intelligence for:, Machine Learning

Company Name: AffeqtEDU
Description: EdTech, SaaS, International, Big Data, Machine Learning
Website:
Phone: **Email:** bilalsh@affeqtedu.com
City: Dubai **State:** Dubai **PC:** **Country: United Arab Emirates**
Year Established: 2015 **Status 2020:** Active
Industries: Big Data and Analytics for:, ~ Education (13), ~ Education (13), Machine Learning

Company Name: AI Trader
Description: Deep Learning Artificial Intelligence (AI) Automate Crypto Trading
Website: http://www.aitrader.ai/
Phone: **Email:** contact@aitrader.ai
City: Dubai **State:** Dubai **PC:** **Country: United Arab Emirates**
Year Established: 2018 **Status 2020:** Active
Industries: Artificial Intelligence for:, ~ Banking and Financial Markets-Services (7), ~ Banking and Financial Markets-Services (7), Blockchain for:, IT Managed Services for:, Finance and Accounting

Company Name: Audace Labs
Description: Creating Digital Business
Website: http://audacelabs.com
Phone: **Email:** info@audacelabs.com
City: Dubai **State:** DUB **PC:** **Country: United Arab Emirates**
Year Established: **Status 2020:** Active
Industries:

Company Name: Avanza Innovations
Description: Blockchain, Artificial Intelligence, Robotic Process Automation, & Smart City Enablement
Website: http://avanzainnovations.com/
Phone: (9714) 388-7731 **Email:** info@avanzainnovations.com
City: Dubai **State:** Dubai **PC:** **Country: United Arab Emirates**
Year Established: 2018 **Status 2020:** Active
Industries: Artificial Intelligence for:, Blockchain for:, IT Managed Services for:, ~ Construction (10)

Company Name: BitShams Energy Solutions
Description: BitShams Energy Solutions is a company building Blockchain-enabled multi-energy transaction systems using AI algorithms
Website: http://bitshams.com
Phone: **Email:** contact@bitshams.com
City: Dubai **State:** Dubai **PC:** **Country: United Arab Emirates**
Year Established: 2019 **Status 2020:** Active
Industries: Artificial Intelligence for:, Blockchain for:, ~ Energy and Utilities (14)

Company Name: Botler
Description: Botler is a smart messaging platform connecting businesses with customers.
Website: http://www.botler.io/
Phone: **Email:** 36194@reference-encyclopedia-ai.net
City: Dubai **State:** Dubai **PC:** **Country: United Arab Emirates**
Year Established: 2016 **Status 2020:** Active
Industries: Artificial Intelligence for:, E-Commerce

Company Name: BulkWhiz
Description: BulkWhiz is the first ecommerce consumer platform for bulk grocery and home staples powered by next generation AI technology.
Website: http://beta.bulkwhiz.com
Phone: 971 50 333 9104 **Email:** care@bulkwhiz.com
City: Dubai **State:** DUB **PC:** **Country: United Arab Emirates**
Year Established: **Status 2020:** Active
Industries: Artificial Intelligence for:, ~ Retail and Consumer Products (52)

Company Name: Celadon
Description: Software development agency with attitude | Mobile/Web | AI/ML
Website: http://celadonsoft.com/
Phone: (1773) 801-5922 **Email:** hello@celadonsoft.com
City: Dubai **State:** Dubai **PC:** **Country: United Arab Emirates**
Year Established: 2016 **Status 2020:** Active
Industries: Application Services for:, Artificial Intelligence for:, IT Managed Services for:, Application Services for:, Development and Test for:, Web for:, Web for:, Web

Company Name: Cognitev
Description: Cognitev is a big data company that focuses on the intersection of content and commerce.
Website: http://www.cognitev.com
Phone: (023)835-2814 **Email:** info@menacommerce.com
City: Dubai **State:** DUB **PC:** **Country: United Arab Emirates**
Year Established: **Status 2020:** Active
Industries: Artificial Intelligence for:, Content for:, E-Commerce

Company Name: ctAI
Description: Startup developing an AI city-wide traffic management system.
Website: http://ctai.io
Phone: **Email:** info@ctai.io
City: Dubai **State:** DUB **PC:** **Country: United Arab Emirates**
Year Established: **Status 2020:** Active
Industries: Artificial Intelligence for:, ~ Transportation and Logistics (57)

Company Name: Disticha: India
Description: Distichain re-invents global trading with the integration of Block-chain and AI.
Website: http://distichain.com/
Phone: **Email:** info@distichain.com
City: Dubai **State:** DUB **PC:** **Country: United Arab Emirates**
Year Established: **Status 2020:** Active
Industries: Application Services for:, Artificial Intelligence for:, Blockchain for:, E-Commerce for:, IT Managed Services

Company Name: DuLeaf
Description: IoT, AI and Blockcha: India
Website: http://www.duleaf.com/index.html
Phone: **Email:** info@duleaf.com
City: Dubai **State:** DUB **PC:** **Country: United Arab Emirates**
Year Established: **Status 2020:** Active
Industries: Artificial Intelligence for:, Blockchain for:, Computer Vision for:, Mobile for:, ~ Professional Services (48)

Company Name: edusear
Description: We are an EdTech platform for search, compare and enquiring education institutions in its intial phase with a scale up to ML and AI.
Website: http://www.edusearch.: United Arab Emirates
Phone: **Email:** gaurav.verma@edusearch.: United Arab Emirates
City: Dubai **State:** DUB **PC:** **Country: United Arab Emirates**
Year Established: **Status 2020:** Active
Industries:

Company Name: eListG: Uruguay
Description: eListGuy is a Sales Lead Research company, that uses tools backed by human intelligence to harness highly targeted and quality B2B data.
Website: http://www.elistguy.com
Phone: **Email:** info@elistguy.com
City: Dubai **State:** Dubai **PC:** **Country: United Arab Emirates**
Year Established: 2011 **Status 2020:** Active
Industries: Artificial Intelligence for:, IT Managed Services for:, ~ E-Commerce (12)

Company Name: FaceNet
Description: Company that provides data for training of AI models of the human face.
Website:
Phone: **Email:** 36546@reference-encyclopedia-ai.net
City: Dubai **State:** Dubai **PC:** **Country: United Arab Emirates**
Year Established: 2019 **Status 2020:** Closed
Industries: Artificial Intelligence for:, Databases for:, Data Management

Company Name: Fero.Ai
Description: Bringing Unification, Optimization, Automation and Ai enabled coordination to freight transactions, globally.
Website: http://fero.ai/
Phone: (9714) 334-3344 **Email:** aakriti@fero.ai
City: Dubai **State:** Dubai **PC:** **Country: United Arab Emirates**

Year Established: 2018 **Status 2020:** Active
Industries: Artificial Intelligence for:, IT Managed Services for:, ~ Telecommunications (56)

Company Name: iDA
Description: A gamified Career Acceleration Platform for Digital Talent expanding and augmenting the supply pool using Blockchain and AI technologies.
Website: http://idaglobal.org/
Phone: **Email:** admin@idaglobal.org
City: Dubai **State:** Dubai **PC:** **Country: United Arab Emirates**
Year Established: 2019 **Status 2020:** Active
Industries:

Company Name: ILLAMED
Description: Globalizing the healthcare
Website: http://www.illamed.com/
Phone: **Email:** contact@illamed.com
City: Dubai **State:** Dubai **PC:** **Country: United Arab Emirates**
Year Established: 2019 **Status 2020:** Active
Industries: Artificial Intelligence for:, Blockchain for:, ~ Banking and Financial Markets-Services (7), ~ Healthcare (20), IT Managed Services

Company Name: iWire Holding FZ LLC
Description: Investments Holding Company
Website: http://www.iwire.: United Arab Emirates
Phone: **Email:** akhtar@iwiregroup.com
City: Dubai **State:** DUB **PC:** **Country: United Arab Emirates**
Year Established: **Status 2020:** Active
Industries: Analytics for:, Artificial Intelligence for:, ~ Manufacturing-Electronic (30), IT Managed Services for:, ~ Professional Services (48)

Company Name: Jeebly
Description: Jeebly is a highly advanced Tech driven Last Mile Delivery Company.
Website: http://www.jeebly.com/
Phone: (80) 053-3259 **Email:** pr@jeebly.com
City: Dubai **State:** Dubai **PC:** **Country: United Arab Emirates**
Year Established: 2016 **Status 2020:** Active
Industries: Artificial Intelligence for:, IT Managed Services for:, ~ Transportation and Logistics (57), ~ Telecommunications (56), ~ Transportation and Logistics (57)

Company Name: LEAP
Description: Built on AI and cutting-edge technology, LEAP enables candidates to find their dream job while helping companies to reach top talent.
Website: http://www.helloleap.com
Phone: (9714) 512-4080 **Email:** hello@helloleap.com
City: Dubai **State:** Dubai **PC:** **Country: United Arab Emirates**
Year Established: 2017 **Status 2020:** Active
Industries: Artificial Intelligence for:, Web

Company Name: LZine
Description: LZine is an intelligent personal assistant.
Website: http://www.lzine.com
Phone: **Email:** info@lzine.com
City: Dubai **State:** DUB **PC:** **Country: United Arab Emirates**
Year Established: **Status 2020:** Active
Industries: Artificial Intelligence

Company Name: Math-Mathod System
Description: We research and develop automated trading algorithms using advanced Technologies
Website: http://www.math-method.com/
Phone: **Email:** stephen.mathmethod@gmail.com
City: Dubai **State:** Dubai **PC:** **Country: United Arab Emirates**
Year Established: 2016 **Status 2020:** Active
Industries: Artificial Intelligence for:, ~ Biotechnology (9), ~ Banking and Financial Markets-Services (7), IT Managed Services

Company Name: md&lp
Description: AI powered mineral detection & location prediction.
Website: http://www.mdlp.xyz
Phone: **Email:** 4978@reference-encyclopedia-ai.net
City: Dubai **State:** DUB **PC:** **Country: United Arab Emirates**
Year Established: **Status 2020:** Active
Industries: Artificial Intelligence for:, ~ Metals and Mining (42), ~ Social-Environmental-Physical-Engineering Sciences (55), Predictive Analytics

Company Name: MedLab Media MENA
Description: MedLab Media MENA is the Middle East-Northern Africa subsidary of MedLab Media Group.
Website: www.medlabmediagroup.com
Phone: **Email:** mena@medlabmg.com
City: Dubai **State:** Dubai **PC:** **Country: United Arab Emirates**
Year Established: **Status 2020:** Active
Industries: Artificial Intelligence for:, ~ Healthcare (20), IT Managed Services for:, Machine Learning for:, ~ Healthcare (20), ~ Healthcare (20)

Company Name: Modistabox
Description: A fashion tech start-up offering personal styling service that delivers a curated box of products directly to customers across MENA region.
Website: http://Modistabox.com
Phone: **Email:** 37002@reference-encyclopedia-ai.net
City: Dubai **State:** Dubai **PC:** **Country: United Arab Emirates**
Year Established: 2018 **Status 2020:** Active
Industries: Artificial Intelligence for:, E-Commerce for:, ~ Fashion (16), IT Managed Services

Company Name: Mosaikx
Description: Mosaikx designs and develops public health-focused, application-specific software, and wearable hardware.
Website: http://mosaikx.com
Phone: **Email:** hello@mosaikx.com
City: Dubai **State:** DUB **PC:** **Country: United Arab Emirates**
Year Established: **Status 2020:** Active
Industries: Artificial Intelligence for:, ~ Healthcare (20), ~ Healthcare (20)

Company Name: MyFaFo
Description: MyFaFo is an ideal destination for food lovers that uses AI to locate the nearest favorite food stall.
Website: http://www.myfafo.com/
Phone: 970 595 321 095 **Email:** zatari@myfafo.com
City: Dubai **State:** Dubai **PC:** **Country: United Arab Emirates**
Year Established: 2013 **Status 2020:** Closed
Industries: Artificial Intelligence for:, ~ Food and Beverage (17), ~ Food and Beverage (17)

Company Name: Officy
Description: Human-powered personal assistant for work related stuff
Website: http://www.officy.com
Phone: **Email:** 4843@reference-encyclopedia-ai.net
City: Dubai **State:** DUB **PC:** **Country: United Arab Emirates**
Year Established: **Status 2020:** Active
Industries: Artificial Intelligence for:, Big Data and Analytics for:, ~ Human Resources (24), Web for:, Machine Learning for:, ~ Professional Services (48)

Company Name: oneFactor
Description: oneFactor's AI Service Delivery Platform helps telecoms and other data owners to launch AI services as a new digital revenue stream.
Website: http://onefactor.com
Phone: **Email:** sales@onefactor.com
City: Dubai **State:** Dubai **PC:** **Country: United Arab Emirates**
Year Established: 2015 **Status 2020:** Active
Industries: Artificial Intelligence for:, Mobile

Company Name: Play.ht
Description: Create realistic voice over audio using text & AI voic: Spain
Website: http://play.ht/
Phone: **Email:** support@play.ht
City: Dubai **State:** Dubai **PC:** **Country: United Arab Emirates**
Year Established: 2016 **Status 2020:** Active
Industries:

Company Name: Prognica Labs
Description: Prognica is building smart screening solution for early detection of breast cancer using artificial intelligence and machine learning.
Website: http://www.prognica.com/
Phone: 971-56-5391591 **Email:** khalid@prognica.com
City: Dubai **State:** DUB **PC:** **Country: United Arab Emirates**
Year Established: **Status 2020:** Active
Industries: Analytics for:, Artificial Intelligence for:, ~ Healthcare (20), Image Recognition for:, IT Managed Services for:, Machine Learning for:, ~ Professional Services (48)

Company Name: Rangii Studio
Description: Rangiistudio Sell and develop high definition android apps and games solutions with minimum cost
Website: http://www.rangiistudio.com
Phone: **Email:** support@rangiistudio.com
City: Dubai **State:** DUB **PC:** **Country: United Arab Emirates**
Year Established: **Status 2020:** Active
Industries:

Company Name: Safe Driving Network
Description: Safe Driving Network detects the driver's behavior in real-time to prevent collisions, evaluate and coaching the drivers.
Website: http://safedrivingnetwork.com/
Phone: **Email:** info@safedrivingnetwork.com
City: Dubai **State:** DUB **PC:** **Country: United Arab Emirates**
Year Established: **Status 2020:** Active
Industries: Artificial Intelligence for:, ~ Automotive (5), Application Services for:, Application Services for:, ~ Government (19)

Company Name: Sarwa.co
Description: The first hybrid investment platform for young professionals in the region. Sarwa's platform makes expert investing easy and affordable.
Website: www.sarwa.co
Phone: **Email:** mark.chahwan@sarwa.co
City: Dubai **State:** Dubai **PC:** **Country: United Arab Emirates**
Year Established: **Status 2020:** Active
Industries: Artificial Intelligence for:, ~ Banking and Financial Markets-Services (7), ~ Banking and Financial Markets-Services (7)

Company Name: Search: Ireland
Description: The best candidates believe what you believe. We're a talent acquisition platform. We use freelance recruiters & AI to find the best people.
Website: http://searchie.me
Phone: **Email:** info@searchie.me
City: Dubai **State:** DUB **PC:** **Country: United Arab Emirates**
Year Established: **Status 2020:** Active
Industries: Artificial Intelligence for:, ~ Human Resources (24), IT Managed Services for:, Web for:, ~ Human Resources (24)

Company **Name:** Seez
Description: We fully automate the car searching process by searching all car websites, negotiate price down using AI and estimate fair market value.
Website: http://www.seez.co
Phone: **Email:** help@seez.co
City: Dubai **State:** DUB **PC:** **Country: United Arab Emirates**
Year Established: **Status 2020:** Active
Industries: Artificial Intelligence

Company Name: SocialDice
Description: SocialDice is an innovative hiring solution that makes hiring easy, smart and fun tailored for SMEs in the Middle East & North Africa.
Website: http://socialdice.net
Phone: 971 56 454 6539 **Email:** Info@socialdice.net
City: Dubai **State:** Dubai **PC:** **Country: United Arab Emirates**
Year Established: 2013 **Status 2020:** Active
Industries: Artificial Intelligence for:, Business Software as a Service Apps (SaaS Apps)

Company Name: Stylar
Description: Artificial Intelligence, Computer Vision, SaaS
Website: http://www.stylar.me
Phone: **Email:** ahmed@stylar.com
City: Dubai **State:** DUB **PC:** **Country: United Arab Emirates**
Year Established: **Status 2020:** Active
Industries: Artificial Intelligence for:, Computer Vision for:, ~ Fashion (16)

Company Name: The List
Description: Luxury fashion mobile platform connecting people to the right products via intelligence.
Website: http://gothelist.com
Phone: 97144430279 **Email:** customercare@gothelist.com
City: Dubai **State:** Dubai **PC:** **Country: United Arab Emirates**
Year Established: 2016 **Status 2020:** Active
Industries: Artificial Intelligence for:, E-Commerce for:, ~ Fashion (16), Machine Learning for:, Mobile for:, Application Services

Company Name: Training Calendar
Description: Training Calendar is world's first complete platform for skill development and career progression powered by artificial intelligence.
Website: http://www.trainingcalendar.com/
Phone: 971 4 426 4677 **Email:** contact@trainingcalendar.com
City: Dubai **State:** Dubai **PC:** **Country: United Arab Emirates**
Year Established: 2016 **Status 2020:** Active
Industries: Artificial Intelligence for:, ~ Education (13), ~ Education (13)

Company Name: Up Your Game
Description: Realtime employee performance assessment solution, Organization sentiment analytics
Website: http://www.upyourgame.ai
Phone: **Email:** upyourgamedm@gmail.com
City: Dubai **State:** Dubai **PC:** **Country: United Arab Emirates**
Year Established: **Status 2020:** Active
Industries: Artificial Intelligence for:, ~ Human Resources (24), IT Managed Services

Company Name: Virtual i Technologies
Description: Virtual i Technologies enables the insurance industry to move from good faith-based underwriting to data-based dynamic decision making.
Website: http://www.virtualitechnologies.com/
Phone: 971 56 640 7679 **Email:** info@virtualitechnologies.com
City: Dubai **State:** Dubai **PC:** **Country: United Arab Emirates**
Year Established: 2015 **Status 2020:** Active
Industries: Artificial Intelligence for:, ~ Banking and Financial Markets-Services (7), IT Managed Services

Company Name: Votek
Description: Votek is a software company specialized in developing high-tech and innovative solutions based on automatic Arabic speech recognition.
Website: http://votek.me/
Phone: **Email:** info@votek.me
City: Dubai **State:** Dubai **PC:** **Country: United Arab Emirates**
Year Established: 2014 **Status 2020:** Active
Industries: Artificial Intelligence for:, Natural Language Processing for:, Speech Recognition

Company Name: Vuja De Capital
Description: Vuja De Capital is a venture capital firm that seeks to invest in companies operating in the cryptocurrency.
Website: http://www.vujadecapital.com/
Phone: **Email:** 37647@reference-encyclopedia-ai.net
City: Dubai **State:** Dubai **PC:** **Country: United Arab Emirates**
Year Established: 2019 **Status 2020:** Active
Industries:

Company Name: Wasphi
Description: We use proprietary data and advanced technologies to give our clients an intelligence edge
Website:
Phone: **Email:** 37652@reference-encyclopedia-ai.net
City: Dubai **State:** Dubai **PC:** **Country: United Arab Emirates**
Year Established: 2015 **Status 2020:** Closed
Industries: Analytics for:, Artificial Intelligence for:, Big Data and Analytics for:, IT Managed Services

Company Name: Whizkey
Description: Whizkey is an enterprise AI company that builds on-premise and highly customized bespoke AI products with data privacy at the core.
Website: http://whizkey.: United Arab Emirates
Phone: **Email:** hello@whizkey.com
City: Dubai **State:** Dubai **PC:** **Country: United Arab Emirates**
Year Established: 2017 **Status 2020:** Active
Industries: Artificial Intelligence for:, ~ Government (19), Web for:, Machine Learning

Company Name: WiseLetter
Description: Big Data-Driven Predictive Investment Analytics
Website: http://wiseletter.com/
Phone: 971 50 705 1366 **Email:** info@wiseletter.com
City: Dubai **State:** Dubai **PC:** **Country: United Arab Emirates**
Year Established: 2015 **Status 2020:** Active
Industries: Big'Data and Analytics for:, Machine Learning

Company Name: Wrappup
Description: Wrappup is a meeting-based productivity app with intelligent voice recording that helps inside sales managers make better decisions.
Website: http://www.wrappup.ai/sal: Spain
Phone: **Email:** info@wrappup.co
City: Dubai **State:** Dubai **PC:** **Country: United Arab Emirates**
Year Established: 2015 **Status 2020:** Active
Industries: Application Services for:, Artificial Intelligence for:, Business Process and Operations

Company Name: Zettaflow
Description: Comprehensive Data Analytics Environment
Website: http://zettaflow.tech
Phone: **Email:** contact@zettaflow.tech
City: Dubai **State:** Dubai **PC:** **Country: United Arab Emirates**
Year Established: 2019 **Status 2020:** Active
Industries: Analytics for:, Big Data and Analytics for:, Business Intelligence for:, Data Management for:, Data Management for:, Machine Learning for:, Predictive Analytics for:, Business Software as a Service Apps (SaaS Apps) for:, Business Software as a Service Apps (SaaS)

Company Name: Group of Innovative Solutions
Description: Group of Innovative Solutions provides web portal developments and artificial intelligence services.
Website: http://www.gisinter.com/
Phone: 971.044.422.625 **Email:** sales@gisinter.com
City: Jumairah **State:** Dubai **PC:** **Country: United Arab Emirates**
Year Established: 2013 **Status 2020:** Active
Industries: Artificial Intelligence for:, IT Managed Services for:, Web

United Kingdom

Company Name: Artios
Description: Artios uses maths and data science to increase website traffic and improve user experience (UX)
Website: http://artios.io
Phone: 44 (0)20 8213 5872 **Email:** hello@artios.io
City: **State:** **PC:** **Country: United Kingdom**
Year Established: **Status 2020:** Active
Industries: Artificial Intelligence for:, Digital Marketing for:, ~ Media-Communications (41)

Company Name: Beepal
Description: Beepal is a next generation social shopping site, connecting people with products and brands through A.I. recommendation system.
Website: http://beepal.co.uk/
Phone: **Email:** info@beepal.co.uk
City: **State:** **PC:** **Country: United Kingdom**
Year Established: **Status 2020:** Active
Industries: Artificial Intelligence for:, E-Commerce for:, Machine Learning for:, ~ Media-Communications (41), ~ Retail and Consumer Products (52)

Company Name: Digital Clipboard
Description: AI-powered client onboarding for enterpri: Sweden
Website: http://www.digitalclipboard.com/
Phone: 0203 290 8096 **Email:** info@digitalclipboard.com
City: **State:** **PC:** **Country: United Kingdom**
Year Established: **Status 2020:** Active
Industries: Artificial Intelligence for:, ~ Banking and Financial Markets-Services (7)

Company Name: Jellybooks
Description: Jellybooks helps authors and publishers develop traction by identifying and reaching out to the most influential readers.
Website: http://jellybooks.com/
Phone: **Email:** vip@jellybooks.com
City: **State:** **PC:** **Country: United Kingdom**
Year Established: **Status 2020:** Active
Industries: Analytics for:, Artificial Intelligence for:, Databases for:, ~ Media-Communications (41), ~ Media-Communications (41)

Company Name: Loop - The Email Messenger
Description: Loop Email brings teamwork and messaging to your email inbox
Website: http://www.intheloop.io
Phone: **Email:** anamarija@intheloop.io
City: **State:** **PC:** **Country: United Kingdom**
Year Established: **Status 2020:** Active
Industries: Artificial Intelligence for:, Collaboration Solutions for:, ~ Media-Communications (41), ~ Telecommunications (56)

Company Name: Scredible
Description: Scredible is upgrading social media with artificial intelligence.
Website: http://scredible.com/
Phone: **Email:** info@scredible.com
City: **State:** **PC:** **Country: United Kingdom**
Year Established: **Status 2020:** Active
Industries: Artificial Intelligence for:, IT Managed Services for:, IT Managed Services

Company Name: Warwick Analytics
Description: Warwick Analytics offers advanced predictive analytics and process automation.
Website: http://www.warwickanalytics.com
Phone: 44 20 7620 6189 **Email:** info@warwickanalytics.com
City: **State:** **PC:** **Country: United Kingdom**
Year Established: **Status 2020:** Active
Industries: Analytics for:, Artificial Intelligence for:, ~ Professional Services (48)

Company Name: Drone Ag
Description: Practical, hassle-free drone automation and AI for Agriculture
Website: http://droneag.farm
Phone: **Email:** jack@droneag.farm
City: Alnwick **State:** England **PC:** **Country: United Kingdom**
Year Established: 2015 **Status 2020:** Active
Industries:

Company Name: Kerboo
Description: A data intelligence and workflow platform for marketers.
Website: http://kerboo.com/
Phone: (347) 708-0341 **Email:** hello@linkrisk.com
City: Altrincham **State:** England **PC:** **Country: United Kingdom**
Year Established: 2013 **Status 2020:** Active
Industries: Analytics for:, Artificial Intelligence for:, IT Managed Services

Company Name: The Bot Forge
Description: The Bot Forge chatbot agency team works closely with their clients to determine where a chatbot will make the most of their benefits.
Website: http://www.thebotforge.io
Phone: 44 800 061 4082 **Email:** info@thebotforge.io
City: Aylesbury **State:** England **PC:** **Country: United Kingdom**
Year Established: 2018 **Status 2020:** Active
Industries: Artificial Intelligence

Company Name: FLEX Automation
Description: FLEX AI is the product of years of automation development, taking self-service to new heights with the integration of AI chatbot assistants.
Website: http://www.flexautomation.net
Phone: 01256 403 800 **Email:** flex@ics.net
City: Basingstoke **State:** England **PC:** **Country: United Kingdom**
Year Established: 2014 **Status 2020:** Active
Industries: Artificial Intelligence for:, IT Managed Services for:, Robotics

Company Name: InfoSum
Description: InfoSum is driving trusted data collaboration through decentralized technology.
Website: http://www.infosum.com/
Phone: 44 (0)1256 533222 **Email:** hello@infosum.com
City: Basingstoke **State:** England **PC:** **Country: United Kingdom**
Year Established: **Status 2020:** Active
Industries: Analytics for:, Artificial Intelligence for:, Big Data and Analytics for:, Application Services for:, IT Managed Services for:, IT Managed Services

Company Name: JCC Bowe: Serbia
Description: Cobalt Auta delivers the future of transportation.
Website: http://jccbowers.com/
Phone: 44 (0)330 159 8104 **Email:** media@jccbowers.com
City: Basingstoke **State:** England **PC:** **Country: United Kingdom**
Year Established: **Status 2020:** Active
Industries: Artificial Intelligence for:, ~ Automotive (5), ~ Automotive (5), ~ Manufacturing-Electronic (30)

Company **Name:** Aria Networks
Description: Aria is a pioneer in using AI to optimize and automate telecom networks; prescriptive analytics and design automation for telecom and OTT
Website: http://www.aria-networks.com
Phone: 44 1249 454101 **Email:** info@aria-networks.com
City: Bath **State:** England **PC:** **Country: United Kingdom**
Year Established: **Status 2020:** Active
Industries: Analytics for:, Artificial Intelligence for:, ~ Telecommunications (56)

Company Name: Neuro AI
Description: Neuro AI is a startup making hardware for the high speed processing of AI.
Website:
Phone: **Email:** 4415@reference-encyclopedia-ai.net
City: Bath **State:** England **PC:** **Country: United Kingdom**
Year Established: **Status 2020:** Active
Industries: Artificial Intelligence for:, Databases for:, ~ Manufacturing-Electronic (30)

Company Name: Yellow Submarine
Description: SaaS Explainable Machine Learning Platform
Website: http://www.yellowsubmarine.io
Phone: 1234834595 **Email:** justin@yellowsubmarine.io
City: Bedford **State:** England **PC:** **Country: United Kingdom**
Year Established: 2018 **Status 2020:** Active
Industries: Machine Learning

Company Name: Litha Group
Description: AI company focusing on conversational AI and Psychology AI to develop meaningful relationships. First Use Case is an AI Psychotherapist.
Website: http://www.litha.org
Phone: 44(0)7592-350-945 **Email:** hello@litha.org
City: Bidford-on-avon **State:** England **PC:** **Country: United Kingdom**
Year Established: 2019 **Status 2020:** Active
Industries: Artificial Intelligence for:, ~ Healthcare (20), ~ Healthcare (20), ~ Healthcare (20)

Company Name: Capri Healthcare Ltd
Description: Turning NHS Digital first strategy into reality by bringing digital innovation AI/ML
Website: http://caprihealthcare.co.uk
Phone: (333) 321-8999 **Email:** info@caprohealthcare.co.uk
City: Birmingham **State:** England **PC:** **Country: United Kingdom**
Year Established: 2019 **Status 2020:** Active
Industries: Artificial Intelligence for:, ~ Healthcare (20), IT Managed Services for:, ~ Education (13), Machine Learning for:, Natural Language Processing

Company Name: Complygate
Description: HR and COmpliance Management Software
Website: http://complygate.co.uk
Phone: 1216550311 **Email:** info@technowave.co.uk
City: Birmingham **State:** England **PC:** **Country: United Kingdom**
Year Established: **Status 2020:** Active
Industries: Artificial Intelligence for:, Compliance for:, ~ Human Resources (24), IT Managed Services for:, ~ Professional Services (48)

Company Name: Evezy
Description: Evezy is a once-a-month all inclusive payment that allows a hassle-free solution for owning an electric car
Website: http://www.evezy.co.uk/
Phone: 0800 030 6840 **Email:** info@evezy.co.uk
City: Birmingham **State:** England **PC:** **Country: United Kingdom**
Year Established: **Status 2020:** Active
Industries:

Company Name: Feather
Description: Twitter marketing artificial intelligence
Website: http://getfeather.org
Phone: **Email:** greg@getfeather.org
City: Birmingham **State:** England **PC:** **Country: United Kingdom**
Year Established: 2016 **Status 2020:** Active
Industries: Artificial Intelligence for:, ~ Customer Relationship Management (11)

Company Name: FeeLYX
Description: FeeLYX provides AI financial data analysis software for lenders and investors.
Website: http://www.feelyx.com/
Phone: **Email:** 36557@reference-encyclopedia-ai.net
City: Birmingham **State:** England **PC:** **Country: United Kingdom**
Year Established: 2015 **Status 2020:** Active
Industries:

Company Name: Grid Edge
Description: The way we use energy is changing
Website: http://www.gridedge.co.uk/
Phone: **Email:** enquiries@gridedge.co.uk
City: Birmingham **State:** England **PC:** **Country: United Kingdom**
Year Established: 2016 **Status 2020:** Active
Industries: Artificial Intelligence for:, ~ Energy and Utilities (14)

Company Name: iWazat
Description: iWazat is a smart platform that allows event organizers to quickly create web applications for their events.
Website: http://www.iwazat.com
Phone: **Email:** demo@iwaz.at
City: Birmingham **State:** England **PC:** **Country: United Kingdom**
Year Established: **Status 2020:** Active
Industries: Application Services for:, Artificial Intelligence for:, Big Data and Analytics for:, ~ Event Management (15)

Company Name: Link Big
Description: Link Big is a smart link that finally transform general mobile web links to personal user experience links.
Website: http://www.link-big.com/
Phone: **Email:** nadav@link-big.com
City: Birmingham **State:** England **PC:** **Country: United Kingdom**
Year Established: 2014 **Status 2020:** Closed
Industries: Business Applications for:, Cloud for:, Cloud for:, ~ Banking and Financial Markets-Services (7), IT Managed Services for:, Machine Learning for:, ~ Social Assistance-Non-Profits (53)

Company Name: Vitaq.io
Description: Test Automation tool developer: 10x productivity with auto-generation of UI, API and Big Data software tests
Website: http://www.vitaq.io
Phone: **Email:** info@vitaq.io
City: Bletchley **State:** England **PC:** **Country: United Kingdom**
Year Established: 2010 **Status 2020:** Active
Industries: Application Services for:, Artificial Intelligence for:, IT Managed Services for:, Robotics

Company Name: Feebi
Description: Feebi is a social media and website-based chatbot for automating customer service in the hospitality sector.
Website: http://getfeebi.com
Phone: 44 (0) 800 118 2905 **Email:** hello@getfeebi.com
City: Bournemouth **State:** England **PC:** **Country: United Kingdom**
Year Established: **Status 2020:** Active
Industries: Application Services for:, Artificial Intelligence for:, Machine Learning for:, ~ Telecommunications (56)

Company **Name:** Remora
Description: AI engine that learns the unique gestures and behaviours of web visitors to improve engagement
Website: http://www.remora.so
Phone: **Email:** always.listening@ratio.co.uk
City: Bournemouth **State:** England **PC:** **Country: United Kingdom**
Year Established: 2014 **Status 2020:** Active
Industries: Artificial Intelligence for:, IT Managed Services for:, Web

Company Name: velmai
Description: velmai builds fully customisable artificially intelligent avatars. Better chatbots - Next Gen AI Bots that have Emotional Intelligence (EI).
Website: http://www.velmai.com/
Phone: 0044 (0) 7841 913 561 **Email:** md@velmai.com
City: Braunton **State:** England **PC:** **Country: United Kingdom**
Year Established: **Status 2020:** Active
Industries: ~ Media-Communications (41), Artificial Intelligence for:, Augmented Reality for:, Enterprise Application Services for:, Machine Learning for:, ~ Media-Communications (41), ~ Telecommunications (56), Application Services for:, Automation for:, Speech Recognition f

Company Name: Achieve Intelligence
Description: Achieve Intelligence
Website: http://www.achieveintelligence.com/
Phone: 7887 954496 **Email:** guy.garrett@achieveintelligence.com
City: Brighton **State:** England **PC:** **Country: United Kingdom**
Year Established: 2010 **Status 2020:** Active
Industries: Artificial Intelligence for:, IT Managed Services

Company Name: Artlim: Spain
Description: The most innovative global marketplace for art online and a service provider of the most advanced internet Technologies
Website: http://artlimes.com
Phone: **Email:** contact@artlimes.com
City: Brighton **State:** England **PC:** **Country: United Kingdom**
Year Established: **Status 2020:** Active
Industries: ~ Arts-Entertainment-Recreation (4), Artificial Intelligence for:, E-Commerce for:, ~ Professional Services (48), Machine Learning for:, Cyber Security

Company Name: Ducit.ai
Description: Artificial intelligence Open Banking platform delivering intelligent banking for all.
Website: http://www.ducit.ai/
Phone: **Email:** info@ducit.ai
City: Brighton **State:** England **PC:** **Country: United Kingdom**
Year Established: 2018 **Status 2020:** Active
Industries: Artificial Intelligence for:, ~ Banking and Financial Markets-Services (7), ~ Banking and Financial Markets-Services (7), ~ Banking and Financial Markets-Services (7), Machine Learning

Company Name: Emteq Labs
Description: emteq labs is the market-leader in wearable technology to monitor and translate human intent and expression into credible and actionable feedback.
Website: https://www.emteqlabs.com/
Phone: **Email:** info@emteq.net
City: Brighton **State:** England **PC:** **Country: United Kingdom**
Year Established: **Status 2020:** Active
Industries: Artificial Intelligence for:, Augmented Reality for:, Human Computer Interaction

Company Name: StoryStream
Description: StoryStream is the world's most advanced content marketing platform built for automotive brands.
Website: http://www.storystream.ai
Phone: 44 0203 637 1169 **Email:** hello@storystream.ai
City: Brighton **State:** England **PC:** **Country: United Kingdom**
Year Established: **Status 2020:** Active
Industries: Artificial Intelligence for:, Content for:, Content for:, Content for:, Digital Marketing for:, ~ Social Media (54)

Company Name: ClusterHQ
Description: Cluster HQ is a Saas service to make container virtualisation useful for database driven services.
Website: http://clusterhq.com/
Phone: **Email:** info@clusterhq.com
City: Bristol **State:** **PC:** **Country: United Kingdom**

Year Established: **Status 2020:** Active
Industries: Artificial Intelligence for:, Cloud for:, Databases for:, Enterprise Application Services for:, Cloud

Company Name: Graphcore
Description:
Website: https://www.graphcore.ai/
Phone: **Email:** info@graphcore.ai
City: Bristol **State:** England **Zip:** BS1 2PH **Country:** **United Kingdom**
Year Established: **Status 2020:** Active
Industries:

Company Name: Graphcore
Description: Graphcore server hardware system accelerates the processing of complex machine learning models for training and inference.
Website: http://www.graphcore.ai/
Phone: 44 117 927 6004 **Email:** press@graphcore.ai
City: Bristol **State:** **PC:** **Country:** **United Kingdom**
Year Established: **Status 2020:** Active
Industries: Artificial Intelligence for:, ~ Manufacturing-Electronic (30), Machine Learning for:, ~ Manufacturing-Electronic (30)

Company Name: poli
Description: Independent Polling
Website: http://polihq.com/
Phone: **Email:** andy@polihq.com
City: Bristol **State:** **PC:** **Country:** **United Kingdom**
Year Established: **Status 2020:** Active
Industries: Artificial Intelligence

Company Name: Rovco
Description: 3D vision and artificial intelligence applied to subsea robotics, ROV and AUV
Website: http://www.rovco.com
Phone: 44 117 230 0001 **Email:** info@rovco.com
City: Bristol **State:** **PC:** **Country:** **United Kingdom**
Year Established: **Status 2020:** Active
Industries: Artificial Intelligence for:, ~ Automotive (5), ~ Transportation and Logistics (57), Robotics

Company Name: Sigma Polar
Description: Pre-hiring candidate assessment and shortlisting tech. Automates employment processes to increase efficiency, diversity and quality of hire
Website: http://sigmapolaris.com
Phone: 7949764006 **Email:** philip@sigmapolaris.com
City: Bristol **State:** **PC:** **Country:** **United Kingdom**
Year Established: **Status 2020:** Active
Industries: Analytics for:, Artificial Intelligence for:, Business Intelligence for:, ~ Human Resources (24), IT Managed Services for:, Machine Learning for:, ~ Human Resources (24), ~ Professional Services (48)

Company Name: Urban Hawk
Description: Spatial Data Intelligence to boost on real time situation awareness in commercial use cases: mobility, insurance, logistics, retail.
Website: https://urbanhawk.space
Phone: **Email:** robert.sugar@urbanhawk.space
City: Bristol **State:** England **Zip:** BS33BS **Country:** **United Kingdom**
Year Established: **Status 2020:** Active
Industries: Analytics for:, Artificial Intelligence for:, ~ Construction (10), ~ Insurance (25), ~ Transportation and Logistics (57), Augmented Reality for:, ~ Insurance (330), ~ Telecommunications (361), ~ Transportation and Logistics (362), Big Data and Analytics for:, ~ Aut**Company Name:** We Build Bots (Products: IntelAgent)
Description: IntelAgent is a chatbot & analytics platform saving contact centres money, improving customer satisfaction & increasing revenues through AI.
Website: www.intelagent.ai/
Phone: **Email:** info@webuildbots.ai
City: Bristol **State:** England **PC:** **Country:** **United Kingdom**

Year Established: **Status 2020:** Active
Industries: Analytics for:, Artificial Intelligence

Company Name: DAM Good Media Limited
Description: A technology platform helping make live music events more discoverable, and delivers bite-sized technology services to the industry.
Website: http://www.damgoodmedia.com
Phone: **Email:** enquiries@damgoodmedia.com
City: Brockenhurst **State:** England **PC:** **Country:** **United Kingdom**
Year Established: **Status 2020:** Active
Industries: Artificial Intelligence for:, Big Data and Analytics for:, ~ Event Management (15), Machine Learning for:, ~ Arts-Entertainment-Recreation (4), ~ Professional Services (48)

Company Name: AI Holdings Limited
Description: Automated Business Intelligence
Website: http://www.imgeospatial.com
Phone: **Email:** hello@imgeospatial.com
City: Burnham **State:** England **PC:** **Country:** **United Kingdom**
Year Established: **Status 2020:** Active
Industries: Artificial Intelligence for:, IT Managed Services

Company Name: Umbrella
Description: Using AI and data analytics to help corporates tackle bias and improve diversity and inclusion
Website: http://www.umbrellaanalytics.net
Phone: 7961070137 **Email:** nancy@umbrellaanalytics.net
City: Bury Saint Edmunds **State:** England **PC:** **Country:** **United Kingdom**
Year Established: 2018 **Status 2020:** Active
Industries:

Company Name: GigaFare Limited
Description: Machine learning for airfare pricing
Website: http://www.gigafare.co.uk
Phone: **Email:** 36622@reference-encyclopedia-ai.net
City: Bushey **State:** England **PC:** **Country:** **United Kingdom**
Year Established: 2013 **Status 2020:** Closed
Industries: Artificial Intelligence for:, ~ Banking and Financial Markets-Services (7), ~ Banking and Financial Markets-Services (7), Machine Learning for:, ~ Banking and Financial Markets-Services (7)

Company Name: Advanced Security Consulting Limited (JustASC)
Description: Advanced Security Consulting Limited (JustASC) is a specialist business offering consulting and managed services.
Website: http://www.justasc.net/contact/
Phone: 8456437406 **Email:** info@falanx.com
City: Cambridge **State:** England **PC:** **Country:** **United Kingdom**
Year Established: 2012 **Status 2020:** Active
Industries: Application Services for:, Security

Company Name: AI Construct
Description: AI Construct provides the construction industry with AI and seamless integration of robotic equipment.
Website: https://ai-construct.co.uk/
Phone: 44 1223 782 083 **Email:** 35982@reference-encyclopedia-ai.net
City: Cambridge **State:** England **PC:** **Country:** **United Kingdom**
Year Established: 2017 **Status 2020:** Active
Industries: Artificial Intelligence for:, ~ Construction (10)

Company Name: BB1
Description: Machine Learning using deep learning.
Website: http://www.bb1.io
Phone: **Email:** 36136@reference-encyclopedia-ai.net
City: Cambridge **State:** England **PC:** **Country:** **United Kingdom**

Year Established: 2017 **Status 2020:** Active
Industries: Machine Learning

Company Name: BIOS
Description: A full-stack neural interface platform, that uses AI to decode and encode the signals from to the body, to treat chronic health conditions.
Website: http://www.bios.health/
Phone: 44 78 1541 7609 **Email:** info@BIOS.heal:Thailand
City: Cambridge **State:** England **PC:** **Country: United Kingdom**
Year Established: 2015 **Status 2020:** Active
Industries:

Company Name: CamBioScience
Description: Changing the future of eLearning with OBRIZUM, using Ai to create Automated, Adaptive, and Analytic eLearning.
Website: http://www.cambioscience.com/
Phone: **Email:** info@cambioscience.com
City: Cambridge **State:** England **PC:** **Country: United Kingdom**
Year Established: 2015 **Status 2020:** Active
Industries: Artificial Intelligence for:, ~ Education (13)

Company Name: Cambridge Cancer Genomics
Description: Cambridge Cancer Genomics develops precision oncology solutions to transform the way cancer patients are treated.
Website: http://ccg.ai
Phone: **Email:** info@ccg.ai
City: Cambridge **State:** England **PC:** **Country: United Kingdom**
Year Established: 2016 **Status 2020:** Active
Industries: Artificial Intelligence for:, ~ Biotechnology (9), ~ Healthcare (20), ~ Healthcare (20), Machine Learning for:, ~ Healthcare (20)

Company Name: Cambridge Energy Data Lab
Description: CEDL creates intelligent predictive models for energy consumption.
Website: http://camenergydatalab.com/
Phone: 44 1223 365123 **Email:** info@camenergydatalab.com
City: Cambridge **State:** England **PC:** **Country: United Kingdom**
Year Established: **Status 2020:** Active
Industries: Analytics for:, Artificial Intelligence for:, Big Data and Analytics for:, ~ Energy and Utilities (14), ~ Energy and Utilities (14), IT Managed Services for:, Predictive Analytics

Company Name: Cambridge Quantum Computing
Description: CQCL develops tools for the commercialisation of quantum computers by understanding quantum protocols and also quantum algorithms.
Website: http://cambridgequantum.com/
Phone: 44(0)20 33019333 **Email:** info@cambridgequantum.com
City: Cambridge **State:** England **PC:** **Country: United Kingdom**
Year Established: 2014 **Status 2020:** Active
Industries: ~ Education (13)

Company Name: Cambridge Quantum Computing Limited
Description: CQCL develops tools for the commercialisation of quantum computers by understanding quantum protocols and also quantum algorithms.
Website: http://cambridgequantum.com/
Phone: 44(0)20 33019333 **Email:** info@cambridgequantum.com
City: Cambridge **State:** England **PC:** **Country: United Kingdom**
Year Established: **Status 2020:** Active
Industries: Artificial Intelligence for:, IT Managed Services for:, Enterprise Application Services

Company Name: CamIn - Cambridge Innovation Consulting
Description: CamIn provides consulting and expert network services related to emerging technologies.
Website: http://www.camin.com/
Phone: 44 (0)1223 926926 **Email:** info@camin.com
City: Cambridge **State:** England **PC:** **Country: United Kingdom**
Year Established: **Status 2020:** Active
Industries: ~ Aerospace and Defense (2), Artificial Intelligence for:, ~ Automotive (5), Big Data and Analytics for:, ~ Manufacturing-Electronic (30), ~ Energy and Utilities (14), ~ Energy and Utilities (14), IT Managed Services for:, Machine Learning for:, ~ Manufacturing-Mi

Company Name: Conundrum
Description: Conundrum is a platform helps factories to solve the tasks of predictive maintenance.
Website: http://conundrum.ai/
Phone: **Email:** team@conundrum.ai
City: Cambridge **State:** England **PC:** **Country: United Kingdom**
Year Established: 2017 **Status 2020:** Active
Industries: Analytics for:, Artificial Intelligence for:, IT Managed Services for:, Machine Learning

Company Name: CorrosionRADAR
Description: Smarter infrastructure using Industrial Internet of Things and Predictive Analytics
Website: http://www.corrosionradar.com/
Phone: **Email:** info@corrosionradar.com
City: Cambridge **State:** England **PC:** **Country: United Kingdom**
Year Established: 2017 **Status 2020:** Active
Industries: Artificial Intelligence for:, IT Managed Services for:, Internet of Things (IoT) for:, Predictive Analytics

Company Name: Cydar Medical
Description: Cydar Medical has developed computer vision software that produces real-time automated 3D overlays during X-ray guided procedures.
Website: http://www.cydarmedical.com
Phone: **Email:** contact@cydarmedical.com
City: Cambridge **State:** England **PC:** **Country: United Kingdom**
Year Established: **Status 2020:** Active
Industries: Artificial Intelligence for:, Big Data and Analytics for:, Cloud for:, ~ Healthcare (20)

Company Name: dividiti
Description: We automate and accelerate your AI/ML/quantum/systems R&D using our revolutionary "plug&play" components!
Website: http://dividiti.com
Phone: **Email:** anton@dividiti.com
City: Cambridge **State:** England **PC:** **Country: United Kingdom**
Year Established: **Status 2020:** Active
Industries: Artificial Intelligence for:, IT Managed Services for:, Machine Learning for:, ~ Education (13)

Company Name: Ensembl
Description: Ensembl: Powering content aggregation with machine learning and monetizing community intelligence with cryptocurrency.
Website: http://www.ensembl.ai/
Phone: **Email:** 36511@reference-encyclopedia-ai.net
City: Cambridge **State:** England **PC:** **Country: United Kingdom**
Year Established: 2017 **Status 2020:** Active
Industries: Artificial Intelligence for:, ~ Banking and Financial Markets-Services (7), ~ Personal-Religious-Civic (45), ~ Banking and Financial Markets-Services (7), ~ Education (13), ~ Banking and Financial Markets-Services (7), Machine Learning

Company Name: Featurespace
Description: Featurespace is a UK-based provider of adaptive behavioral analytics technology for fraud and risk management in financial services & gaming
Website: http://www.featurespace.com
Phone: **Email:** info@featurespace.com
City: Cambridge **State:** England **PC:** **Country: United Kingdom**
Year Established: **Status 2020:** Active
Industries: Artificial Intelligence for:, ~ Banking and Financial Markets-Services (7), ~ Banking and Financial Markets-Services (7), Security for:, ~ Banking and Financial Markets-Services (7), ~ Professional Services (48)

Company Name: Fetch.ai
Description: Fetch.AI is an artificial intelligence and digital economics company based in Cambridge, Cambridgeshire.
Website: http://fetch.ai/
Phone: 44 1223 750350 **Email:** info@fetch.ai
City: Cambridge **State:** England **PC:** **Country: United Kingdom**
Year Established: **Status 2020:** Active
Industries: Artificial Intelligence for:, Web

Company Name: FiveAI
Description: FiveAI provides a software platform designed for providing a solution in urban mobility in public transport to complex urban environments.
Website: http://five.ai/
Phone: **Email:** info@five.ai
City: Cambridge **State:** England **PC:** **Country: United Kingdom**
Year Established: 2015 **Status 2020:** Active
Industries:

Company Name: Focal Point Positioning
Description: Focal Point has developed next generation navigation and positioning software for smartphones, wearables and autonomous vehicles.
Website: http://www.focalpointpositioning.com/
Phone: **Email:** info@focalpointpositioning.com
City: Cambridge **State:** England **PC:** **Country: United Kingdom**
Year Established: **Status 2020:** Active
Industries: Artificial Intelligence for:, ~ Transportation and Logistics (57)

Company Name: ForecastThis
Description: Deep Learning for Finance & Economics
Website: http://www.forecastthis.com
Phone: (785)145-9388 **Email:** justin@forecastthis.com
City: Cambridge **State:** England **PC:** **Country: United Kingdom**
Year Established: **Status 2020:** Active
Industries: Artificial Intelligence for:, ~ Banking and Financial Markets-Services (7), ~ Banking and Financial Markets-Services (7), Machine Learning

Company Name: GeoSpock
Description: GeoSpock is an extreme-scale spatial big data platform company that provides analytics, visualisation & builds insight.
Website: http://www.geospock.com/en/
Phone: 44 1223 953200 **Email:** info@geospock.com
City: Cambridge **State:** England **PC:** **Country: United Kingdom**
Year Established: 2013 **Status 2020:** Active
Industries: Artificial Intelligence for:, ~ Banking and Financial Markets-Services (7), Databases for:, Internet of Things (IoT) for:, IT Managed Services for:, ~ Telecommunications (56), Mobile for:, Mobile for:, Business Software as a Service Apps (SaaS Apps) for:, ~ Cons: Turkey

Company Name: GeoSpock Ltd.
Description: GeoSpock provides intelligent, software solutions that addresses essential data challenges related to space, time, scale and speed.
Website: http://www.geospock.com
Phone: 44 1223 953200 **Email:** info@geospock.com
City: Cambridge **State:** England **PC:** **Country: United Kingdom**
Year Established: **Status 2020:** Active
Industries: Artificial Intelligence for:, ~ Banking and Financial Markets-Services (7), Databases for:, IT Managed Services for:, ~ Transportation and Logistics (57), Mobile for:, Compute for:, ~ Construction (10)

Company Name: Granta Innovation
Description: Transforming cancer diagnosis with AI and MRI imaging
Website: http://granta.io
Phone: 44-1223-926717 **Email:** hello@grantainnovation.com
City: Cambridge **State:** England **PC:** **Country: United Kingdom**
Year Established: **Status 2020:** Active
Industries: Artificial Intelligence for:, ~ Biotechnology (9), ~ Healthcare (20)

Company **Name:** Handle My Health
Description: Handle My Health are the creators of MIAMI, the web and smartphone based patient intelligence platform.
Website: http://www.handlemyhealth.co.uk
Phone: **Email:** info@handlemyhealth.eu
City: Cambridge **State:** England **PC:** **Country: United Kingdom**
Year Established: 2012 **Status 2020:** Closed
Industries: ~ Healthcare (20), Machine Learning for:, ~ Healthcare (20)

Company Name: Healx
Description: Healx is an AI-powered and patient-inspired technology company, accelerating the discovery and development of rare disease treatments
Website: http://healx.io/
Phone: **Email:** info@healx.io
City: Cambridge **State:** England **PC:** **Country: United Kingdom**
Year Established: 2014 **Status 2020:** Active
Industries: Artificial Intelligence for:, ~ Biotechnology (9), ~ Healthcare (20), ~ Healthcare (20)

Company Name: HFS Research:
Description: It is our mission to provide visionary insight into the major innovations impacting business operations
Website: http://www.hfsresearch.com
Phone: **Email:** insights@hfsresearch.com
City: Cambridge **State:** England **PC:** **Country: United Kingdom**
Year Established: **Status 2020:** Active
Industries: Analytics for:, Artificial Intelligence for:, IT Managed Services for:, ~ Media-Communications (41), ~ Oil and Gas (43), Business Process and Operations for:, ~ Administrative and Support Services (1), Robotics for:, Supply Chain Management

Company Name: Indybo Closed
Description: Indybo is a revolutionary robotics toy that teaches kids the basics of programming and electronics in a fun and intuitive way.
Website: http://www.indybo.com/
Phone: (1510) 849-7098 **Email:** 36756@reference-encyclopedia-ai.net
City: Cambridge **State:** England **PC:** **Country: United Kingdom**
Year Established: 2014 **Status 2020:** Active
Industries: Machine Learning for:, Robotics

Company Name: Intellegens
Description: Cambridge spin out using Deep Learning to train on big, incomplete data. Currently working in drug discovery and material design.
Website: http://intellegens.ai
Phone: (781) 030-3762 **Email:** ben@intellegens.ai
City: Cambridge **State:** England **PC:** **Country: United Kingdom**
Year Established: 2017 **Status 2020:** Active
Industries: Artificial Intelligence for:, ~ Biotechnology (9), Machine Learning

Company Name: itzMe
Description: itzMe is applying cutting-edge Machine Learning & Artificial Intelligence to deep personalisation.
Website: http://www.itzme.ai
Phone: **Email:** 36812@reference-encyclopedia-ai.net
City: Cambridge **State:** England **PC:** **Country: United Kingdom**
Year Established: 2015 **Status 2020:** Active
Industries: Artificial Intelligence for:, Machine Learning

Company Name: Kirontech
Description: Kirontech uses cutting edge machine learning technology to revolutionize the use of healthcare data.
Website: http://www.kirontech.com/
Phone: **Email:** info@kirontech.com
City: Cambridge **State:** England **PC:** **Country: United Kingdom**
Year Established: 2015 **Status 2020:** Active
Industries: Artificial Intelligence for:, ~ Healthcare (20), IT Managed Services for:, Machine Learning for:, IT Managed Services

Company Name: KisanHub
Description: Crop Intelligence Platform
Website: http://www.kisanhub.com
Phone: **Email:** hello@kisanhub.com
City: Cambridge **State:** England **PC:** **Country: United Kingdom**
Year Established: **Status 2020:** Active
Industries: ~ Agriculture (3), Analytics for:, Artificial Intelligence for:, Big Data and Analytics for:, Cloud for:, ~ Agriculture (3), Mobile for:, Predictive Analytics

Company Name: Kristalic
Description: Kristalic is building an AI-powered assistant designed to record your work-related conversations
Website: http://www.kristalic.com/
Phone: **Email:** founders@kristalic.com
City: Cambridge **State:** England **PC:** **Country: United Kingdom**
Year Established: 2018 **Status 2020:** Active
Industries:

Company Name: Leverhulme Centre for the Future of Intelligence
Description: Leverhulme is a research centre exploring the opportunities and challenges to humanity from the development of artificial intelligence.
Website: http://lcfi.ac.uk/
Phone: **Email:** skg41@cam.ac.uk
City: Cambridge **State:** England **PC:** **Country: United Kingdom**
Year Established: **Status 2020:** Active
Industries: Artificial Intelligence

Company Name: Nanna Therapeutics
Description: Nanna Therapeutics is a drug discovery company addressing age-related diseases for which others are failing to provide effective treatments.
Website: http://www.nannatherapeutics.com/
Phone: 44(0)1223 423506 **Email:** info@nannatherapeutics.com
City: Cambridge **State:** England **PC:** **Country: United Kingdom**
Year Established: 2012 **Status 2020:** Active
Industries: Artificial Intelligence for:, ~ Biotechnology (9), ~ Healthcare (20), ~ Healthcare (20), ~ Healthcare (20)

Company Name: Neurence
Description: Neurence provides Intelligent cloud-based recognition engine allowing computers to understand unstructured human environments.
Website: http://neurence.com/
Phone: (207) 887-2641 **Email:** info@neurence.com
City: Cambridge **State:** England **PC:** **Country: United Kingdom**
Year Established: **Status 2020:** Active
Industries: Artificial Intelligence for:, Cloud for:, Image Recognition

Company Name: OKRA Technologies
Description: OKRA is an AI analytics company for healthcare. We combine complex data sets, you get evidence-based insights and predictions in real time.
Website: http://www.okra.ai/
Phone: **Email:** hello@okra.ai
City: Cambridge **State:** England **PC:** **Country: United Kingdom**
Year Established: 2015 **Status 2020:** Active
Industries: Analytics for:, Artificial Intelligence for:, Big Data and Analytics for:, Business Intelligence for:, ~ Healthcare (20), IT Managed Services for:, Machine Learning for:, Predictive Analytics

Company Name: PetaGene
Description: PetaGene'™s mission is to make genomics data cheaper, faster and better.
Website: http://www.petagene.com/
Phone: **Email:** info@petagene.com
City: Cambridge **State:** England **PC:** **Country: United Kingdom**
Year Established: **Status 2020:** Active
Industries: Artificial Intelligence for:, ~ Healthcare (20)

Company **Name:** PORGiESOFT
Description: PORGiESOFT is an EdTech company based in Cambridge that helps students and teachers work smarter in Africa via EdTech AI Assistants.
Website: http://www.porgiesoft.com
Phone: **Email:** contact@porgiesoft.com
City: Cambridge **State:** England **PC:** **Country: United Kingdom**
Year Established: 2018 **Status 2020:** Active
Industries: Artificial Intelligence for:, ~ Education (13), ~ Education (13)

Company Name: ProdX.ai
Description: People Analytics SaaS platform which focus on unleashing team productivity through insights & A.I. powered automated coaching
Website: http://www.prodx.ai
Phone: **Email:** ali@productvx.com
City: Cambridge **State:** England **PC:** **Country: United Kingdom**
Year Established: 2019 **Status 2020:** Active
Industries: Analytics for:, Artificial Intelligence for:, Enterprise Application Services for:, Business Software as a Service Apps (SaaS Apps)

Company Name: PROWLER.io
Description: PROWLER.io is an AI/machine learning platform for building autonomous agents for games and decision-support simulations.
Website: http://www.prowler.io/
Phone: **Email:** info@prowler.io
City: Cambridge **State:** England **PC:** **Country: United Kingdom**
Year Established: 2016 **Status 2020:** Active
Industries: Artificial Intelligence for:, Machine Learning

Company Name: robik.ai
Description: Robik AI builds autonomous vehicles to slash the cost of last-mile delivery.
Website: http://robik.ai/
Phone: **Email:** info@robik.ai
City: Cambridge **State:** England **PC:** **Country: United Kingdom**
Year Established: **Status 2020:** Active
Industries: Artificial Intelligence for:, ~ Social-Environmental-Physical-Engineering Sciences (55), Robotics

Company Name: RoboK
Description: Cambridge University spin-out building cost-effective 3D sensing algorithms optimised for low-power computing platforms
Website: http://www.robok.ai
Phone: **Email:** info@robok.ai
City: Cambridge **State:** England **PC:** **Country: United Kingdom**
Year Established: 2017 **Status 2020:** Active
Industries: Artificial Intelligence for:, ~ Automotive (5), ~ Automotive (5)

Company Name: Spectral Edge
Description: Spectral Edge combines patented Image Fusion tech with Deep Learning to reveal more of the color, detail and clarity in any image.
Website: http://spectraledge.co.uk
Phone: **Email:** INFO@SPECTRALEDGE.CO.UK
City: Cambridge **State:** England **PC:** **Country: United Kingdom**
Year Established: **Status 2020:** Active
Industries: Artificial Intelligence for:, Machine Learning for:, ~ Professional Services (48), ~ Professional Services (48)

Company Name: Tactful
Description: AI-Powered Customer Engagement Platform
Website: http://www.tactful.ai/
Phone: **Email:** info@tactful.ai
City: Cambridge **State:** England **PC:** **Country: United Kingdom**
Year Established: 2016 **Status 2020:** Active
Industries: Artificial Intelligence for:, ~ Customer Relationship Management (11), Enterprise Application Services for:, Natural Language Processing for:, Business Software as a Service Apps (SaaS Apps) for:, Internet of Things (IoT)

Company Name: techspert.io
Description: techspert.io is an AI-driven technology for identifying and sourcing specialist expertise, globally.
Website: http://techspert.io
Phone: 01223 320 560 **Email:** hello@techspert.io
City: Cambridge **State:** England **PC:** **Country: United Kingdom**
Year Established: 2016 **Status 2020:** Active
Industries: Artificial Intelligence

Company Name: Unitary
Description: Unitary is making the internet safer with AI
Website: http://unitary.ai
Phone: **Email:** contact@unitary.ai
City: Cambridge **State:** England **PC:** **Country: United Kingdom**
Year Established: 2019 **Status 2020:** Active
Industries:

Company Name: Wayve
Description: Wayve uses end-to-end deep learning to develop artificial intelligence capable of complex driving.
Website: http://wayve.ai
Phone: **Email:** info@wayve.ai
City: Cambridge **State:** England **PC:** **Country: United Kingdom**
Year Established: 2017 **Status 2020:** Active
Industries: Artificial Intelligence for:, Machine Learning

Company Name: Optalysys Ltd
Description: Pioneering optical AI chi: Palestine
Website: http://www.optalysys.com
Phone: **Email:** info@optalysys.com
City: Castleford **State:** England **PC:** **Country: United Kingdom**
Year Established: 2013 **Status 2020:** Active
Industries: Artificial Intelligence for:, Machine Learning

Company Name: Smiletronix
Description: Delivering AI-powered home dental checkups for easy, affordable and connected dental care.
Website: http://www.smiletronix.com
Phone: **Email:** info@smiletronix.com
City: Cheadle Hulme **State:** England **PC:** **Country: United Kingdom**
Year Established: 2018 **Status 2020:** Active
Industries: Artificial Intelligence for:, ~ Healthcare (20), ~ Healthcare (20), ~ Healthcare (20), ~ Healthcare (20), Web

Company Name: Oxygen Digital Recruitment
Description: Oxygen Digital is an artificial intelligence specialist recruitment company.
Website: http://www.oxygendigitalrecruitment.com/
Phone: 44 20 3239 2223 **Email:** info@oxygendigital.net
City: Chelmsford **State:** England **PC:** **Country: United Kingdom**
Year Established: **Status 2020:** Active
Industries: Artificial Intelligence for:, ~ Human Resources (24)

Company Name: AI Assisted Learning
Description: AI Assisted Learning is a virtual trainer for life goals and ambitions.
Website: https://www.mybrian.app/
Phone: **Email:** 35981@reference-encyclopedia-ai.net
City: Cheltenham **State:** England **PC:** **Country: United Kingdom**
Year Established: 2018 **Status 2020:** Active
Industries: Artificial Intelligence for:, ~ Education (13), IT Managed Services

Company Name: Ripjar
Description: Strategic Intelligence platform for the enterpri: Sweden
Website: http://ripjar.com
Phone: **Email:** jobs@ripjar.com
City: Cheltenham **State:** England **PC:** **Country: United Kingdom**
Year Established: **Status 2020:** Active
Industries: Analytics for:, Artificial Intelligence for:, Cyber Security for:, Data Management for:, Natural Language Processing for:, Predictive Analytics

Company Name: Mindi
Description: Mindi combines the best of human and artificial intelligence.
Website: http://mindi.io
Phone: **Email:** info@mindi.io
City: Covent Garden **State:** England **PC:** **Country: United Kingdom**
Year Established: **Status 2020:** Active
Industries: Artificial Intelligence for:, Machine Learning

Company Name: Mechion
Description: Mechion is a start-up working on creating autonomous patient observation systems.
Website: http://www.mechion.com
Phone: **Email:** info@mechion.com
City: Coventry **State:** England **PC:** **Country: United Kingdom**
Year Established: **Status 2020:** Active
Industries: Artificial Intelligence for:, ~ Healthcare (20), Application Services for:, ~ Healthcare (20), Robotics

Company Name: Ortelio Ltd
Description: Cloud robotics, software development and AI.
Website: http://robotics.ortelio.co.uk
Phone: **Email:** 2013@ortelio.co.uk
City: Coventry **State:** England **PC:** **Country: United Kingdom**
Year Established: 2011 **Status 2020:** Active
Industries: Artificial Intelligence for:, Big Data and Analytics for:, IT Managed Services for:, Robotics

Company Name: Citispotter Limited (UK)
Description: AI Enabled Sentiment Analysis and Insights for the Media Industry
Website: http://citispotter.com/
Phone: **Email:** contact@citispotter.com
City: Cranfield **State:** England **PC:** **Country: United Kingdom**
Year Established: 2019 **Status 2020:** Active
Industries: Artificial Intelligence

Company Name: Somewhere Random Ltd
Description: Somewhere Random is a software consulting firm in artificial intelligence, finance, ecommerce, and advertising.
Website: http://somewhererandom.com
Phone: **Email:** info@somewhererandom.com
City: Cromer **State:** England **PC:** **Country: United Kingdom**
Year Established: 2016 **Status 2020:** Active
Industries:

Company Name: BELOUDEST
Description: BELOUDEST is an AR and VR production agency.
Website: http://beloudest.com/
Phone: 44-0-7725654162 **Email:** info@beloudest.com
City: Croydon **State:** England **PC:** **Country: United Kingdom**
Year Established: 2012 **Status 2020:** Active
Industries: Artificial Intelligence for:, Virtual Reality (VR)

Company Name: Connected Space
Description: We co-create innovative technologies that deliver transformational change
Website: http://www.connected-space.co.uk
Phone: **Email:** 36321@reference-encyclopedia-ai.net
City: Croydon **State:** England **PC:** **Country: United Kingdom**
Year Established: 2013 **Status 2020:** Active
Industries: ~ Automotive (5), IT Infrastructure for:, Web for:, Internet of Things (IoT) for:, Machine Learning for:, Mobile for:, ~ Arts-Entertainment-Recreation (4)

Company Name: Rezatec
Description: Rezatec applies data science to satellite imagery and geospatial data to deliver cloud-based analytics to its global customers.
Website: http://www.rezatec.com/
Phone: **Email:** info@rezatec.com
City: Didcot **State:** England **PC:** **Country: United Kingdom**
Year Established: 2012 **Status 2020:** Active
Industries:

Company Name: Vidrona
Description: Vidrona is ushering in the new era of energy asset management.
Website: http://www.vidrona.com
Phone: **Email:** ashutosh@vidrona.com
City: Didcot **State:** England **PC:** **Country: United Kingdom**
Year Established: 2015 **Status 2020:** Active
Industries: ~ Agriculture (3), Artificial Intelligence for:, Computer Vision for:, Predictive Analytics for:, ~ Energy and Utilities (14), ~ Energy and Utilities (14), ~ Energy and Utilities (14), ~ Energy and Utilities (14)

Company Name: Inlinks
Description: Inlinks automates internal linking of web content using semantic intelligence
Website: http://inlinks.net/home
Phone: (3361) 799-3221 **Email:** fred@inlinks.net
City: Dunstable **State:** England **PC:** **Country: United Kingdom**
Year Established: 2019 **Status 2020:** Active
Industries: Artificial Intelligence for:, Web for:, Internet of Things (IoT) for:, Application Program Interfaces (APIs) for:, Web

Company Name: Intogral
Description: Intogral is developing world leading image analysis software for a global client base working with Artificial Intelligence.
Website: http://intogral.com/
Phone: **Email:** contact@gliff.ai
City: Durham **State:** England **PC:** **Country: United Kingdom**
Year Established: 2018 **Status 2020:** Active
Industries: Artificial Intelligence for:, IT Managed Services

Company Name: Zeno Vision Ltd
Description: We have created an engine for developing imaging software based on high performance computing, computer vision and artificial intelligence.
Website: http://zenovisionltd.com
Phone: **Email:** info@zeno.ai
City: Exeter **State:** England **PC:** **Country: United Kingdom**
Year Established: 2016 **Status 2020:** Active
Industries: Artificial Intelligence for:, ~ Healthcare (20), IT Managed Services

Company Name: Autologyx
Description: Autologyx is the next-generation Fabric Automation Platform for enterprise businesses.
Website: http://www.autologyx.com
Phone: (125) 233-3344 **Email:** 36115@reference-encyclopedia-ai.net
City: Farnborough **State:** England **PC:** **Country: United Kingdom**
Year Established: 2015 **Status 2020:** Active
Industries: Application Services for:, Artificial Intelligence for:, Enterprise Application Services for:, Machine Learning for:, Enterprise Application Services for:, Business Software as a Service Apps (SaaS Apps) for:, Business Software as a Service Apps (SaaS Apps)

Company Name: QiO Technologies
Description: QiO is an Industry 4.0 software company that enables global industrials to quickly improve operational efficiency, productivity and safety.
Website: http://qio.io
Phone: 44 (0) 203 300 0177 **Email:** contactus@qio.io
City: Farnborough **State:** England **PC:** **Country: United Kingdom**
Year Established: **Status 2020:** Active
Industries: Analytics for:, Artificial Intelligence for:, Cloud for:, Application Services for:, Industrial Solutions for:, Machine Learning for:, Predictive Analytics for:, ~ Professional Services (48)

Company Name: Wordnerds
Description: Wordnerds teach computers to understand language, make decisions, and find actionable insights.
Website: http://www.wordnerds.ai/
Phone: 44 191 300 9444 **Email:** hello@wordnerds.ai
City: Gateshead **State:** England **PC:** **Country: United Kingdom**
Year Established: 2017 **Status 2020:** Active
Industries: Artificial Intelligence for:, Web for:, ~ Education (13), Machine Learning

Company Name: Maybe*
Description: Maybe*. The platform that connects the online, offline and social retail journey.
Website: http://www.maybetech.com
Phone: **Email:** 36946@reference-encyclopedia-ai.net
City: Gloucester **State:** England **PC:** **Country: United Kingdom**
Year Established: 2015 **Status 2020:** Active
Industries: Artificial Intelligence for:, ~ Retail and Consumer Products (52)

Company Name: Focal Point VR
Description: Live Streaming VR Video Platform
Website: http://focalpointvr.com/
Phone: **Email:** jonathan@focalpointvr.com
City: Godalming **State:** England **PC:** **Country: United Kingdom**
Year Established: **Status 2020:** Active
Industries: Artificial Intelligence

Company Name: Molinto
Description: Design & development service
Website:
Phone: **Email:** 37007@reference-encyclopedia-ai.net
City: Great Yarmouth **State:** England **PC:** **Country: United Kingdom**
Year Established: 2017 **Status 2020:** Active
Industries: Artificial Intelligence for:, Cloud for:, Application Program Interfaces (APIs) for:, IT Managed Services for:, Machine Learning for:, Natural Language Processing for:, Web

Company Name: Crowd Connected
Description: Pioneering a new generation of big data location intelligence
Website: http://www.crowdconnected.co.uk
Phone: 44 1483 685 970 **Email:** info@crowdconnected.co.uk
City: Guildford **State:** England **PC:** **Country: United Kingdom**
Year Established: 2013 **Status 2020:** Active
Industries: Analytics for:, Predictive Analytics for:, Compute

Company Name: Deputi
Description: Deputi is leveraging AI to help CEOs grow their business by automating day to day operational activities to reduce costs
Website: http://www.deputi.ai
Phone: **Email:** info@deputi.ai
City: Guildford **State:** England **PC:** **Country: United Kingdom**
Year Established: **Status 2020:** Active
Industries: Artificial Intelligence for:, IT Managed Services

Company Name: Evolve Dynamics
Description: UAV innovations company, working on computer vision, AI autopilot systems, long flight solutions and rapid ready-to-fly/deploy platforms.
Website: http://www.evolvedynamics.com
Phone: 44 (0) 1483 684814 **Email:** contact@evolvedynamics.com
City: Guildford **State:** England **PC:** **Country: United Kingdom**
Year Established: **Status 2020:** Active
Industries: ~ Aerospace and Defense (2), Artificial Intelligence for:, Computer Vision for:, ~ Transportation and Logistics (57), ~ Administrative and Support Services (1), Machine Learning

Company Name: Spend360 International
Description: Spend360 International is an analytics solution that uses deep machine learning and artificial intelligence.
Website:
Phone: **Email:** 37451@reference-encyclopedia-ai.net
City: Guildford **State:** England **PC:** **Country: United Kingdom**
Year Established: 2011 **Status 2020:** Closed
Industries:

Company Name: Synoptica
Description: Synoptica uses AI technology to automate the way sales teams research prospects
Website: http://www.synoptica.com
Phone: 44 1483 688040 **Email:** info@synoptica.com
City: Guildford **State:** England **PC:** **Country: United Kingdom**
Year Established: 2015 **Status 2020:** Active
Industries: Artificial Intelligence

Company Name: U-Linc
Description: U-Linc is a technology company spun out from the UK's 5G Innovation Centre.
Website: http://www.u-linc.com/
Phone: 44 (0) 1483 68 8403 **Email:** info@u-linc.co.uk
City: Guildford **State:** England **PC:** **Country: United Kingdom**
Year Established: 2017 **Status 2020:** Active
Industries: Artificial Intelligence for:, IT Managed Services

Company Name: Xenes
Description: Leading-Edge ML Algorithms for Biometrics, Hedge Funds and Cybersecurity
Website: http://www.xenesis.com
Phone: 44 7884422347 **Email:** tirath@xenesis.com
City: Guildford **State:** England **PC:** **Country: United Kingdom**
Year Established: **Status 2020:** Active
Industries: Artificial Intelligence

Company Name: Cardinality
Description: Cardinality's innovative new analytics platform has been designed from the ground up with the primary focus on the Telco market.
Website: http://www.cardinality.co.uk
Phone: **Email:** info@cardinality.co.uk
City: Guilford **State:** England **PC:** **Country: United Kingdom**
Year Established: 2015 **Status 2020:** Active
Industries: Analytics for:, Predictive Analytics for:, ~ Customer Relationship Management (11)

Company Name: Sensyne Heal:Thailand
Description: Sensyne Health operates as a digital healthcare company.
Website: http://www.sensynehealth.com/
Phone: 44 (0) 3300 581845 **Email:** info@sensynehealth.com
City: Headington **State:** England **PC:** **Country: United Kingdom**
Year Established: 2018 **Status 2020:** Active
Industries: Artificial Intelligence for:, ~ Healthcare (20), ~ Healthcare (20)

Company **Name:** Zoom Abroad
Description: A free AI platform which connects students to the best-fit universities globally, saving them TIME and MONEY.
Website: http://www.zoomabroad.com
Phone: 7809684143 **Email:** info@zoomabroad.com
City: Hemel Hempstead **State:** England **PC:** **Country: United Kingdom**
Year Established: 2017 **Status 2020:** Active
Industries: Artificial Intelligence for:, ~ Education (13), ~ Education (13), ~ Education (13), ~ Education (13)

Company Name: Aurora-AI
Description: Aurora-AI provides consultancy services to create bespoke AI solutions for specific business requirements.
Website: http://aurora-ai.com/
Phone: 44 (0)1933 413 800 **Email:** emailme@aurora-ai.com
City: Higham Ferrers **State:** England **PC:** **Country: United Kingdom**
Year Established: **Status 2020:** Active
Industries: Artificial Intelligence

Company Name: PolyAI
Description: Conversational AI for customer service built by team of ex-Google and Facebook AI and Apple Siri.
Website: https://poly-ai.com/
Phone: **Email:** Stefan@polyai.com
City: Holborn **State:** England **PC:** **Country: United Kingdom**
Year Established: **Status 2020:** Active
Industries:

Company Name: BrightMinded Ltd
Description: Bespoke Software Development
Website: http://brightminded.com/
Phone: 1273830331 **Email:** hello@brightminded.com
City: Hove **State:** England **PC:** **Country: United Kingdom**

Year Established: **Status 2020:** Active
Industries: Artificial Intelligence for:, Blockchain for:, E-Commerce for:, Application Services for:, ~ Professional Services (48), Cyber Security for:, Cyber Security

Company Name: Cyanap: Sweden
Description: Cyanapse delivers AI solutions to augment human perception.
Website: http://www.cyanapse.com
Phone: **Email:** contact@cyanapse.com
City: Hove **State:** England **PC:** **Country: United Kingdom**
Year Established: 2016 **Status 2020:** Active
Industries: Artificial Intelligence for:, IT Managed Services

Company Name: GoPinLeads
Description: Most extensive AI-powered local leads finder
Website: http://www.gopinleads.com/
Phone: 44 3300270912 **Email:** hello@goodmanlantern.com
City: Hove **State:** England **PC:** **Country: United Kingdom**
Year Established: **Status 2020:** Active
Industries: ~ Media-Communications (41), Artificial Intelligence

Company Name: Rittman Analytics
Description: Data Engineering, Data Strategy and Data Analytics Consultancy
Website: http://rittmananalytics.com
Phone: 44 1273 041134 **Email:** info@rittmananalytics.com
City: Hove **State:** England **PC:** **Country: United Kingdom**
Year Established: 2016 **Status 2020:** Active
Industries: Analytics for:, Big Data and Analytics for:, Data Management for:, Databases for:, Predictive Analytics for:, Predictive Analytics

Company Name: Control F1 Ltd
Description: Control F1 develops digital products and creative software solutions that make a genuine difference to your business.
Website: http://www.controlf1.co.uk
Phone: **Email:** hello@controlf1.co.uk
City: Huddersfield **State:** England **PC:** **Country: United Kingdom**
Year Established: **Status 2020:** Active
Industries: Artificial Intelligence for:, Digital Media for:, Enterprise Application Services for:, Web for:, Machine Learning for:, Application Services for:, ~ Professional Services (48), Business Process and Operations for:, ~ Professional Services (48), ~ Professional Ser

Company Name: Dark Blue Labs
Description: Learning deep representations of data to make intelligent products, including natural language understanding, a reality.
Website: http://www.darkbluelabs.com
Phone: **Email:** press@google.com
City: Hyde **State:** England **PC:** **Country: United Kingdom**
Year Established: 2014 **Status 2020:** Active
Industries:

Company Name: Flumes
Description: Flumes is a data analysis company that makes sense of large amounts of data.
Website: http://flumes.com
Phone: (203) 355-0614 **Email:** hello@flumes.com
City: Ipswich **State:** England **PC:** **Country: United Kingdom**
Year Established: 2011 **Status 2020:** Active
Industries: Analytics for:, Business Intelligence for:, Databases for:, Data Management for:, Predictive Analytics for:, Compute

Company Name: Review Display Systems Ltd.
Description:
Website: https://www.review-displays.co.uk/
Phone: 44 (0)1959 563345 **Email:** info@review-displays.co.uk
City: Kent **State:** England **Zip:** TN16 1UT **Country: United Kingdom**
Year Established: **Status 2020:** Active
Industries:

Company Name: Antix
Description: Antix automatically edits your action sports video footage into highlights. Antix makes it easy to edit and share that awesome trick.
Website: http://www.antixapp.com/
Phone: **Email:** team@antixapp.com
City: Kingston Upon Thames **State:** England **PC:** **Country: United Kingdom**
Year Established: **Status 2020:** Active
Industries: Application Services for:, Artificial Intelligence

Company Name: Relative.ai
Description: Relative.ai is a language analysis platform that enables marketers to gain insights from brand and customer language use.
Website: http://relative.ai
Phone: 44 (0) 845 094 2971 **Email:** hello@relative.ai
City: Lancaster **State:** England **PC:** **Country: United Kingdom**
Year Established: **Status 2020:** Active
Industries: Analytics for:, Artificial Intelligence for:, ~ Education (13)

Company Name: Data Language
Description: Data driven product innovation. World class data science, AI and engineering. Practical machine and deep learning engineered for scalability
Website: http://datalanguage.com
Phone: **Email:** hello@datalanguage.com
City: Leatherhead **State:** England **PC:** **Country: United Kingdom**
Year Established: 2014 **Status 2020:** Active
Industries: Artificial Intelligence for:, Big Data and Analytics for:, ~ Biotechnology (9), IT Managed Services for:, Machine Learning for:, Web for:, Web

Company Name: I-Brain
Description: i-Brain Robotics, is development of Robotic Medical Devices, Virtual Holographic Presenters and Artificial Intelligence Software.
Website: http://ibrainrobotics.com
Phone: 44 20 3318 2612 **Email:** info@ibrainrobotics.net
City: Leatherhead **State:** England **PC:** **Country: United Kingdom**
Year Established: 2016 **Status 2020:** Active
Industries: Artificial Intelligence for:, Robotics

Company Name: Cooperative Innovations Ltd
Description: Development studio (Immersive and innovative products)
Website: http://www.coopinnovations.co.uk
Phone: **Email:** simon@coopinnovations.co.uk
City: Leeds **State:** England **PC:** **Country: United Kingdom**
Year Established: **Status 2020:** Active
Industries: Artificial Intelligence for:, Augmented Reality for:, ~ Arts-Entertainment-Recreation (4), ~ Professional Services (48), ~ Arts-Entertainment-Recreation (4)

Company Name: Data Choice
Description: Programmatic Ad Technology focused on putting users back in control of their data
Website: http://www.datachoice.io
Phone: 0113 833 0565 **Email:** andrew.bruce@programmis.com
City: Leeds **State:** England **PC:** **Country: United Kingdom**
Year Established: **Status 2020:** Active
Industries:

Company Name: PinPoint Data Science
Description: PinPoint Data Science operates as an AI and machine learning firm.
Website: http://www.pinpointdatascience.com/
Phone: **Email:** info@pinpointdatascience.com
City: Leeds **State:** England **PC:** **Country: United Kingdom**
Year Established: 2016 **Status 2020:** Active
Industries: Artificial Intelligence

Company Name: RSLSteeper
Description: RSLSteeper is the leading provider of innovative prosthetic, orthotic and assistive technology products and services.
Website: http://rslsteeper.com
Phone: 113 270 4841 **Email:** enquiries@rslsteeper.com
City: Leeds **State:** England **PC:** **Country: United Kingdom**
Year Established: **Status 2020:** Active
Industries: Artificial Intelligence for:, ~ Manufacturing-Electronic (30), ~ Healthcare (20), ~ Administrative and Support Services (1)

Company Name: Solutionpath Limited
Description: Solutionpath Limited is a award winning, Learning analytics, EdTech software developer company.
Website: http://www.solutionpath.co.uk
Phone: 7890275001 **Email:** hello@solutionpath.co.uk
City: Leeds **State:** England **PC:** **Country: United Kingdom**
Year Established: 2012 **Status 2020:** Active
Industries: Analytics for:, Big Data and Analytics for:, Predictive Analytics

Company Name: Synap
Description: Online education platform using AI to revolutionise learning
Website: http://synap.ac
Phone: 0113 328 0533 **Email:** charlotte@synap.ac
City: Leeds **State:** England **PC:** **Country: United Kingdom**
Year Established: **Status 2020:** Active
Industries: Application Services for:, Artificial Intelligence for:, ~ Education (13), ~ Education (13)

Company Name: Vet-AI
Description: Using groundbreaking technologies, we are developing innovative products and services that will reshape the animal health industries.
Website: www.vet-ai.com
Phone: **Email:** ph@vet-ai.com
City: Leeds **State:** England **PC:** **Country: United Kingdom**
Year Established: **Status 2020:** Active
Industries: Artificial Intelligence for:, Machine Learning for:, Application Services for:, ~ Life Sciences (27)

Company Name: Well Good
Description: Well Good is a personalised mental health care product that prevents crisis by using data and artificial intelligence at work
Website: http://www.wellgood.io/
Phone: **Email:** dan.willis@wellgood.io
City: Leeds **State:** England **PC:** **Country: United Kingdom**
Year Established: 2019 **Status 2020:** Active
Industries:

Company Name: WIFIPLUG
Description: myma.io - the IoT cloud that powers WIFIPL: UGANDA
Website: http://www.wifiplug.co.uk/
Phone: **Email:** support@wifiplug.zendesk.co.uk
City: Leeds **State:** England **PC:** **Country: United Kingdom**
Year Established: 2013 **Status 2020:** Active
Industries: Artificial Intelligence for:, Internet of Things (IoT) for:, Machine Learning

Company Name: Harold
Description: Harold offers a disruptive Classified Ads assistant that allows users to optimize the time, price, and platform.
Website: http://www.helloharold.io
Phone: **Email:** contact@helloharold.me
City: Leicester **State:** England **PC:** **Country: United Kingdom**
Year Established: 2017 **Status 2020:** Active
Industries: Analytics for:, Artificial Intelligence for:, Machine Learning for:, Internet of Things (IoT)

Company Name: Hello Harold
Description: Harold offers a disruptive Classified Ads assistant that allows users to optimize the time, price, and platform.
Website: http://www.helloharold.io
Phone: **Email:** contact@helloharold.me
City: Leicester **State:** England **PC:** **Country: United Kingdom**
Year Established: **Status 2020:** Active
Industries: Analytics for:, Artificial Intelligence for:, ~ Media-Communications (41), Machine Learning

Company Name: Citi Logik
Description: Citi Logik provides insight into the way people move on foot, in a vehicle or by train.
Website: http://www.citilogik.com/
Phone: 44 7831 678 679 **Email:** enquiries@citilogik.com
City: Leighton Buzzard **State:** England **PC:** **Country: United Kingdom**
Year Established: 2011 **Status 2020:** Active
Industries: Analytics for:, IT Managed Services for:, IT Managed Services for:, Predictive Analytics

Company Name: Paparico
Description: Marketing Consultancy
Website: http://www.paparico.co.uk
Phone: 44 7919566338 **Email:** hello@paparico.co.uk
City: Lewes **State:** England **PC:** **Country: United Kingdom**
Year Established: 2019 **Status 2020:** Active
Industries: Artificial Intelligence for:, Machine Learning

Company Name: Tended
Description: Tended creates intelligent personal safety systems and accident detection wearables for both consumers and businesses.
Website: http://www.tended.co
Phone: 44 330 133 1195 **Email:** hello@tended.co
City: Lincoln **State:** England **PC:** **Country: United Kingdom**
Year Established: 2017 **Status 2020:** Active
Industries: Business Applications for:, Machine Learning for:, Application Services for:, ~ Government (19), Internet of Things (IoT)

Company Name: Frontier Labs
Description: Frontier Labs design and build intelligent augmented systems that help people and businesses realise their potential.
Website: http://frontierlabs.co.uk/
Phone: **Email:** info@frontierlabs.co.uk
City: Liverpool **State:** England **PC:** **Country: United Kingdom**
Year Established: 2017 **Status 2020:** Active
Industries: Artificial Intelligence for:, IT Managed Services for:, IT Managed Services

Company Name: HallHang
Description: Next door, floor and hall. The GPS for flat parties, movie and games nights inside of student halls.
Website: http://www.hallhang.com
Phone: **Email:** hello@hallhang.com
City: Liverpool **State:** England **PC:** **Country: United Kingdom**
Year Established: **Status 2020:** Active
Industries: Artificial Intelligence for:, Augmented Reality for:, Application Services

Company Name: Horsefly
Description: Horsefly is an exclusive talent mapping & talent planning software tool.
Website: http://www.horseflyanalytics.com
Phone: **Email:** enquiries@horseflyanalytics.com
City: Liverpool **State:** England **PC:** **Country: United Kingdom**
Year Established: 2011 **Status 2020:** Active
Industries: Big Data and Analytics for:, Web for:, Predictive Analytics

Company Name: Housemat: Spain
Description: Onboarding international students into accommodation and neighbourhoods.
Website: http://housemates.io
Phone: **Email:** hello@housemates.io
City: Liverpool **State:** England **PC:** **Country: United Kingdom**
Year Established: **Status 2020:** Active
Industries: Artificial Intelligence

Company Name: 3co
Description: Accelerating 3D Intelligence Through Simulation
Website: http://3co.ai
Phone: **Email:** founders@3co.ai
City: London **State:** England **PC:** **Country: United Kingdom**
Year Established: **Status 2020:** Active
Industries: Artificial Intelligence for:, Computer Vision

Company Name: 3D Industri: Spain
Description: 3D Industri.es offers three-dimensional technology-based products and solutions for enterprises and businesses.
Website: http://www.3dindustri.: Spain
Phone: **Email:** info@3dindustri.: Spain
City: London **State:** England **PC:** **Country: United Kingdom**
Year Established: **Status 2020:** Active
Industries: Artificial Intelligence for:, Data Management for:, ~ Manufacturing-Miscellaneous (34), Cyber Security for:, Supply Chain Management

Company Name: 4dface
Description: 3D face models & personal 3D face avatars for professional applications
Website: http://www.4dface.io
Phone: **Email:** info@4dface.io
City: London **State:** England **PC:** **Country: United Kingdom**
Year Established: **Status 2020:** Active
Industries: Artificial Intelligence for:, Computer Vision for:, Machine Learning

Company Name: 9f: India
Description: AI powered financial data for fixed income
Website: https://9fin.com/
Phone: **Email:** team@9fin.com
City: London **State:** England **PC:** **Country: United Kingdom**
Year Established: 2016 **Status 2020:** Active
Industries:

Company Name: 9omi.com
Description: Digital revolution in the UK retail industry through, the application of Artificial Intelligence(AI) & Internet of Things (IoT)
Website: https://9omi.com/
Phone: **Email:** info@9omi.com
City: London **State:** England **PC:** **Country: United Kingdom**
Year Established: 2017 **Status 2020:** Active
Industries: Artificial Intelligence for:, Machine Learning

Company Name: ABAKA Holdings
Description: ABAKA is an Employee Financial Wellbeing platform powered by Artificial Intelligence
Website: http://www.abaka.me/
Phone: **Email:** fahd@abaka.me
City: London **State:** England **PC:** **Country: United Kingdom**
Year Established: **Status 2020:** Active
Industries: Artificial Intelligence for:, ~ Banking and Financial Markets-Services (7), ~ Banking and Financial Markets-Services (7), ~ Banking and Financial Markets-Services (7)

Company Name: Abtrace
Description: Building artificial intelligence tools to transform antibiotic prescription and tackle antimicrobial resistance
Website: http://www.abtrace.co
Phone: **Email:** team@abtrace.co
City: London **State:** England **PC:** **Country: United Kingdom**
Year Established: **Status 2020:** Active
Industries: Artificial Intelligence for:, ~ Healthcare (20), ~ Manufacturing-Medical Equipment-Supplies (33), Natural Language Processing

Company Name: Academy of Robotics
Description: The Academy of Robotics is a technology institute with an extraordinary technical team of engineers, scientists, and researchers.
Website: http://www.academyofrobotics.co.uk/
Phone: **Email:** IamAlive@academyofrobotics.co.uk
City: London **State:** England **PC:** **Country: United Kingdom**
Year Established: 2015 **Status 2020:** Active
Industries: Artificial Intelligence for:, IT Managed Services for:, Machine Learning

Company Name: Accelerated Dynamics
Description: Accelerated Dynamics builds AI for robot mission control and fleet management.
Website: http://accelerateddynamics.co/
Phone: **Email:** 35938@reference-encyclopedia-ai.net
City: London **State:** England **PC:** **Country: United Kingdom**
Year Established: 2015 **Status 2020:** Active
Industries: Artificial Intelligence for:, ~ Telecommunications (56), ~ Telecommunications (56), Application Services for:, Internet of Things (IoT) for:, Robotics

Company Name: Acorn Machine
Description: A fintech platform that is unlocking the complex SME lending market globally by leveraging AI and machine learning
Website: http://www.acornmachine.io
Phone: **Email:** firstname.surname@acornmachine.io
City: London **State:** England **PC:** **Country: United Kingdom**
Year Established: **Status 2020:** Active
Industries: Artificial Intelligence for:, ~ Banking and Financial Markets-Services (7), Machine Learning

Company Name: ACORN OakNorth Holdings
Description: OakNorth provides debt finance (loans of £0.5m-£30m) to businesses.
Website: http://www.oaknorth.com/
Phone: **Email:** bizdevelopment@oaknorth.com
City: London **State:** England **PC:** **Country: United Kingdom**
Year Established: **Status 2020:** Active
Industries: Artificial Intelligence for:, ~ Banking and Financial Markets-Services (7), Big Data and Analytics for:, ~ Banking and Financial Markets-Services (7), ~ Banking and Financial Markets-Services (7), ~ Banking and Financial Markets-Services (7), ~ Banking and Fina

Company Name: action.ai
Description: action.ai powers sophisticated Conversational Interfaces via its Language as a Service platform.
Website: http://action.ai/
Phone: **Email:** info@action.ai
City: London **State:** England **PC:** **Country: United Kingdom**
Year Established: **Status 2020:** Active
Industries: Artificial Intelligence for:, ~ Education (13), ~ Professional Services (48)

Company Name: Acuity Trading Ltd
Description: News analytics company specialising in the visualisation of financial market sentiment for retail traders.
Website: http://www.acuitytrading.com
Phone: **Email:** info@acuitytrading.com
City: London **State:** England **PC:** **Country: United Kingdom**
Year Established: **Status 2020:** Active
Industries: Analytics for:, Artificial Intelligence for:, Big Data and Analytics for:, ~ Banking and Financial Markets-Services (7), ~ Media-Communications (41)

Company Name: Adarga
Description: Provides enterprise SaaS products enabling customers to analyse vast amounts of unstructured data faster, more accurately and effectively
Website: http://www.adarga.ai
Phone: 44 (0)203 907 4153 **Email:** hello@adarga.ai
City: London **State:** England **PC:** **Country: United Kingdom**
Year Established: **Status 2020:** Active
Industries: Analytics for:, Artificial Intelligence for:, Business Intelligence for:, Machine Learning for:, Natural Language Processing for:, ~ Professional Services (48), Data Management

Company Name: Adla
Description: Adla is a clothing company that provides an artificially intelligent styling service.
Website: https://adla.site/
Phone: **Email:** 35954@reference-encyclopedia-ai.net
City: London **State:** England **PC:** **Country: United Kingdom**
Year Established: 2018 **Status 2020:** Active
Industries: Artificial Intelligence for:, E-Commerce for:, ~ Fashion (16)

Company Name: Ad-Lib Digital
Description: Ad-Lib is a creative technology that uses artificial intelligence models to make digital advertising better and cheaper.
Website: http://www.ad-lib.io/
Phone: **Email:** contact@ad-lib.io
City: London **State:** England **PC:** **Country: United Kingdom**
Year Established: 2017 **Status 2020:** Active
Industries: Artificial Intelligence for:, ~ Customer Relationship Management (11), IT Managed Services for:, Internet of Things (IoT)

Company Name: Adlocate.io
Description: Adlocate is a Customer Engagement platform connecting brands and audiences through WiFi and digital displays
Website: https://adlocate.io/
Phone: **Email:** nicolai@adlocate.io
City: London **State:** England **PC:** **Country: United Kingdom**
Year Established: 2019 **Status 2020:** Active
Industries: Digital Media for:, Predictive Analytics for:, Internet of Things (IoT)

Company Name: Adqura
Description: Adqura Decisioning solutions use AI to seamlessly connect disparate experiences into a single, cohesive picture to drive results.
Website: http://www.adqura.com/
Phone: (415) 510-2310 **Email:** sinan.cilesiz@adqura.com
City: London **State:** England **PC:** **Country: United Kingdom**
Year Established: 2011 **Status 2020:** Active
Industries:

Company Name: Adsebook
Description: Adsebook is the innovative platform with AI for free-ebooks and pdf file, the users can upload, transform and integrated pdf with Ads, metrics
Website: http://www.adsebook.com/
Phone: 39 3939682343 **Email:** info@adsebook.com
City: London **State:** England **PC:** **Country: United Kingdom**
Year Established: 2018 **Status 2020:** Active
Industries: Artificial Intelligence for:, ~ Media-Communications (41), IT Managed Services

Company Name: ADTYPE
Description: Adtype's Science-led Marketing Tech and Methodologies harness the power of Data and AI to help your business grow at unprecedented rat: Spain
Website: http://www.adtype.com
Phone: 44 203 858 9788 **Email:** hello@adtype.com
City: London **State:** England **PC:** **Country: United Kingdom**
Year Established: **Status 2020:** Active
Industries: Artificial Intelligence for:, Digital Marketing for:, ~ Media-Communications (41), Predictive Analytics

Company Name: adverttu
Description: AI-Backed Car-Advertising Platform.
Website: http://www.adverttu.com
Phone: 44 (0) 20 7884 1393 **Email:** myteam@adverttu.com
City: London **State:** England **PC:** **Country: United Kingdom**
Year Established: **Status 2020:** Active
Industries: ~ Media-Communications (41), Artificial Intelligence for:, Machine Learning

Company Name: AdviceGam: Spain
Description: AdviceGames provides virtual financial assisting and gamification for consumers and small businesses.
Website: http://www.advicegames.com/
Phone: 0031 652 636 131 **Email:** info@advicegames.com
City: London **State:** England **PC:** **Country: United Kingdom**
Year Established: 2013 **Status 2020:** Active
Industries: ~ Banking and Financial Markets-Services (7), ~ Banking and Financial Markets-Services (7), Machine Learning for:, Robotics

Company Name: AdviceRobo
Description: AdviceRobo prevents credit risk from actually happening by delivering Innovative credit scoring and Advanced risk analytics.
Website: http://www.advicerobo.com
Phone: **Email:** info@advicerobo.com
City: London **State:** England **PC:** **Country: United Kingdom**
Year Established: **Status 2020:** Active
Industries: Artificial Intelligence for:, ~ Professional Services (48)

Company **Name:** AdWisdom
Description: Essential intelligence for advertising sales teams.
Website: http://www.adwisdom.com/
Phone: **Email:** 35962@reference-encyclopedia-ai.net
City: London **State:** England **PC:** **Country: United Kingdom**
Year Established: 2010 **Status 2020:** Active
Industries: Artificial Intelligence for:, Predictive Analytics

Company Name: Aesthetic Integration Ltd
Description: We create groundbreaking AI for making algorithms safe, explainable and fair.
Website: http://www.imandra.ai
Phone: 44 20 3773 6225 **Email:** contact@aestheticintegration.com
City: London **State:** England **PC:** **Country: United Kingdom**
Year Established: **Status 2020:** Active
Industries: Artificial Intelligence for:, IT Managed Services for:, IT Managed Services for:, IT Infrastructure

Company Name: after the flood
Description: Design consulting for the age of artificial intelligence.
Website: https://aftertheflood.com/
Phone: **Email:** info@aftertheflood.com
City: London **State:** England **PC:** **Country: United Kingdom**
Year Established: 2011 **Status 2020:** Active
Industries: Machine Learning

Company Name: Agrolabs
Description: Connected devices and AI for agriculture
Website: http://www.agrolabs.io/
Phone: **Email:** info@agrolabs.io
City: London **State:** England **PC:** **Country: United Kingdom**

Year Established: 2017 **Status 2020:** Active
Industries: ~ Agriculture (3), Artificial Intelligence for:, Internet of Things (IoT) for:, Robotics

Company Name: Ai Build
Description: Developing Artificial Intelligence to make Manufacturing easy, smart, sustainable and affordable.
Website: http://ai-build.com/
Phone: **Email:** team@ai-build.com
City: London **State:** England **PC:** **Country: United Kingdom**
Year Established: **Status 2020:** Active
Industries: Artificial Intelligence for:, ~ Manufacturing-Miscellaneous (34), Robotics

Company Name: ai nutrition
Description: ai nutrition offers a deep learning solution for online grocery automation and targeted personalized nutrition.
Website: https://www.ainutrition.co.uk/
Phone: **Email:** info@ainutrition.co.uk
City: London **State:** England **PC:** **Country: United Kingdom**
Year Established: 2018 **Status 2020:** Active
Industries: Artificial Intelligence for:, E-Commerce for:, ~ Education (13)

Company Name: AI Prescience
Description: Improving Business Performance Using Artificial Intelligence, Machine Learning & Data
Website: https://www.aiprescience.com/
Phone: **Email:** hello@aiprescience.com
City: London **State:** England **PC:** **Country: United Kingdom**
Year Established: 2018 **Status 2020:** Active
Industries: Artificial Intelligence

Company Name: AI4THINGS
Description: AI4THINGS develops embedded solutions using reinforcement deep learning Technologies
Website: http://www.ai4things.com
Phone: 32493797279 **Email:** info@ai4things.com
City: London **State:** England **PC:** **Country: United Kingdom**
Year Established: **Status 2020:** Active
Industries: Artificial Intelligence for:, Big Data and Analytics for:, ~ Education (13), IT Managed Services for:, Machine Learning for:, ~ Professional Services (48)

Company Name: Aiden
Description: Aiden provides an AI analytics platform intended to assist marketers how to spend their budget efficiently.
Website:
Phone: **Email:** 36004@reference-encyclopedia-ai.net
City: London **State:** England **PC:** **Country: United Kingdom**
Year Established: **Status 2020:** Closed
Industries:

Company Name: Aigenpulse
Description: Scientific Data Management and Analytics Platform
Website: http://www.aigenpulse.com/
Phone: 44 (0) 20 3773 5431 **Email:** contact@aigenpulse.com
City: London **State:** England **PC:** **Country: United Kingdom**
Year Established: **Status 2020:** Active
Industries: Artificial Intelligence for:, Big Data and Analytics for:, ~ Biotechnology (9), Data Management for:, ~ Healthcare (20)

Company Name: AimBrain
Description: AimBrain is a BIDaaS (biometric identity as-a-service) platform providing Cloud-based biometric authentication (voice, facial & behavioural).
Website: aimbrain.com/
Phone: **Email:** sales@aimbrain.com
City: London **State:** England **PC:** **Country: United Kingdom**
Year Established: **Status 2020:** Active
Industries: Artificial Intelligence for:, ~ Biotechnology (9), ~ Biotechnology (9), Cyber Security for:, ~ Banking and Financial Markets-Services (7)

Company Name: AINews
Description: AINews is an artificial intelligence group that focuses on business intelligence, machine learning, and chatbots.
Website: https://artificialintelligence-news.com/
Phone: **Email:** enquiries@techforge.pub
City: London **State:** England **PC:** **Country: United Kingdom**
Year Established: 2015 **Status 2020:** Active
Industries: Artificial Intelligence for:, Machine Learning for:, ~ Social Media (54)

Company Name: Airfinity
Description: Airfinity is a data driven event intelligence platform
Website: https://www.airfinity.com/
Phone: **Email:** press@airfinity.com
City: London **State:** England **PC:** **Country: United Kingdom**
Year Established: 2015 **Status 2020:** Active
Industries: Artificial Intelligence for:, Business Applications for:, Big Data and Analytics for:, ~ Event Management (15), Machine Learning

Company Name: AITrading
Description: Unique AI-powered Trading Ecosystem
Website: http://aitrading.com
Phone: **Email:** info@aitrading.com
City: London **State:** England **PC:** **Country: United Kingdom**
Year Established: **Status 2020:** Active
Industries: Artificial Intelligence for:, ~ Banking and Financial Markets-Services (7), ~ Banking and Financial Markets-Services (7), Machine Learning

Company Name: Aitrak
Description: AI solutions for brands, retailers, and advertise: Serbia
Website: https://www.aitrak.co/
Phone: **Email:** hello@aitrak.co
City: London **State:** England **PC:** **Country: United Kingdom**
Year Established: 2018 **Status 2020:** Active
Industries: Artificial Intelligence

Company Name: AiX
Description: Financial Service
Website: https://aixtrade.com/
Phone: 44 (0) 203 475 0085 **Email:** help@aixtrade.com
City: London **State:** England **PC:** **Country: United Kingdom**
Year Established: 2017 **Status 2020:** Active
Industries: Artificial Intelligence for:, ~ Banking and Financial Markets-Services (7), ~ Banking and Financial Markets-Services (7), ~ Banking and Financial Markets-Services (7), ~ Banking and Financial Markets-Services (7), ~ Banking and Financial Markets-Services (7), ~

Company Name: Akkiba
Description: Akkiba is a London based start-up specialized in Artificial intelligence (AI), Data Analytics & Machine learning
Website: https://www.akkiba.co/
Phone: 44 (0) 7495 568 442 **Email:** info@akkiba.co
City: London **State:** England **PC:** **Country: United Kingdom**
Year Established: 2018 **Status 2020:** Active
Industries: Artificial Intelligence for:, ~ Banking and Financial Markets-Services (7), IT Managed Services for:, Machine Learning

Company Name: Alana
Description: Conversational AI
Website: http://www.alanaai.com/
Phone: **Email:** info@alanaai.com
City: London **State:** England **PC:** **Country: United Kingdom**
Year Established: 2019 **Status 2020:** Active
Industries: Artificial Intelligence

Company Name: Alana AI
Description: Alana AI is a proprietary artificial intelligence for advertising.
Website: https://alana.ai/
Phone: **Email:** 36028@reference-encyclopedia-ai.net
City: London **State:** England **PC:** **Country: United Kingdom**

Year Established: 2015 **Status 2020:** Active
Industries: Artificial Intelligence

Company Name: Alchera Technologies
Description: Alchera Technologies has a strong and rich pedigree of world-leading machine learning and computer vision sensing Technologies
Website: https://www.alcheratechnologies.com/
Phone: **Email:** hello@alcheratechnologies.com
City: London **State:** England **PC:** **Country: United Kingdom**
Year Established: 2016 **Status 2020:** Active
Industries: Computer Vision for:, Machine Learning

Company Name: AlgoDynamix Ltd.
Description: Deep data risk analytics platform used by investment banks and asset managers including hedge funds and family offices.
Website: http://www.algodynamix.com/
Phone: **Email:** 36034@reference-encyclopedia-ai.net
City: London **State:** England **PC:** **Country: United Kingdom**
Year Established: 2014 **Status 2020:** Active
Industries: Artificial Intelligence for:, ~ Banking and Financial Markets-Services (7), ~ Banking and Financial Markets-Services (7), ~ Banking and Financial Markets-Services (7)

Company Name: Algorithm X Lab
Description: Algorithm X Lab is to provides artificial intelligence & machine learning news, insights, market research and events for business leaders.
Website: https://algorithmxlab.com/
Phone: **Email:** 36036@reference-encyclopedia-ai.net
City: London **State:** England **PC:** **Country: United Kingdom**
Year Established: 2017 **Status 2020:** Active
Industries: Artificial Intelligence for:, Digital Media for:, ~ Event Management (15), IT Managed Services for:, Machine Learning for:, ~ Arts-Entertainment-Recreation (4)

Company Name: Aliens by Daria Ltd
Description: A more humane approach to our everyday interactions with technology
Website: http://woogie.ai/
Phone: 40723200868 **Email:** hello@aliens.ai
City: London **State:** England **PC:** **Country: United Kingdom**
Year Established: **Status 2020:** Active
Industries:

Company Name: Allshortcode
Description: SMS shortcode directory lookup
Website: http://www.allshortcode.com
Phone: **Email:** info@allshortcode.com
City: London **State:** England **PC:** **Country: United Kingdom**
Year Established: **Status 2020:** Active
Industries:

Company Name: Ally Chatbot
Description: Ally Chatbot is a civic and social organization that features a software platform that utilizes artificial intelligence.
Website: https://allychatbot.com/
Phone: **Email:** info@allychatbot.com
City: London **State:** England **PC:** **Country: United Kingdom**
Year Established: 2017 **Status 2020:** Active
Industries: Application Services for:, Enterprise Application Services for:, Application Services for:, ~ Retail and Consumer Products (52)

Company Name: Alpha Deal Group
Description: Alpha Deal Group is a buy-side platform technology company
Website: http://www.alphadealgroup.com/
Phone: 44(0)20 7406 7657 **Email:** info@alphadealgroup.com
City: London **State:** England **PC:** **Country: United Kingdom**
Year Established: 2012 **Status 2020:** Active
Industries: Application Services

Company Name: ALPHA ENGINEER
Description: Energy Tech Start Up distruping energy through the application of novel designs, internet of things (IoT) and artificial intelligence (AI)
Website: http://www.alphaengineer.nl/
Phone: **Email:** info@alphaengineer.: Netherlands
City: London **State:** England **PC:** **Country: United Kingdom**
Year Established: 2014 **Status 2020:** Active
Industries: Application Services for:, Artificial Intelligence for:, ~ Energy and Utilities (14), IT Managed Services for:, Mobile for:, ~ Energy and Utilities (14)

Company Name: Alpha Quants
Description: Alpha Quants is a quantitative consultancy providing innovative technological solution for the financial sector.
Website: https://www.alphaquants.co/
Phone: 44 (0) 20 7262 5690 **Email:** info@alphaquants.co
City: London **State:** England **PC:** **Country: United Kingdom**
Year Established: 2015 **Status 2020:** Active
Industries: Artificial Intelligence for:, ~ Banking and Financial Markets-Services (7)

Company **Name:** Alpha Tech Capital
Description: Technology focused Private Equity firm
Website:
Phone: **Email:** 36048@reference-encyclopedia-ai.net
City: London **State:** England **PC:** **Country: United Kingdom**
Year Established: 2013 **Status 2020:** Active
Industries: Artificial Intelligence for:, Big Data and Analytics for:, ~ Biotechnology (9), ~ Healthcare (20), IT Managed Services for:, IT Managed Services for:, Machine Learning

Company Name: Alpha-i
Description: Predictive maintenance for wind energy and aeronautics
Website: http://alpha-i.co/
Phone: **Email:** info@alpha-i.co
City: London **State:** England **PC:** **Country: United Kingdom**
Year Established: **Status 2020:** Active
Industries: Artificial Intelligence for:, Machine Learning for:, Predictive Analytics

Company Name: Altviz
Description: Intelligent Automation Simplified
Website: http://www.altviz.co/
Phone: **Email:** info@altviz.co
City: London **State:** England **PC:** **Country: United Kingdom**
Year Established: 2012 **Status 2020:** Active
Industries: Enterprise Application Services for:, IT Managed Services for:, Application Services

Company Name: alva
Description: Connected Intelligence
Website: http://www.alva-group.com/en/
Phone: **Email:** info@alva-group.com
City: London **State:** England **PC:** **Country: United Kingdom**
Year Established: 2010 **Status 2020:** Active
Industries: Analytics for:, Artificial Intelligence for:, Business Intelligence for:, Web

Company Name: Amiko
Description: Upgrading care with digital medicines through proprietary sensor technologies and award-winning Artificial Intelligence
Website: http://amiko.io
Phone: 39 347 139 5942 **Email:** martijn.grinovero@amiko.io
City: London **State:** England **PC:** **Country: United Kingdom**
Year Established: 2015 **Status 2020:** Active
Industries: Artificial Intelligence for:, ~ Healthcare (20), ~ Healthcare (20), ~ Healthcare (20)

Company Name: Analytics Intelligence
Description: Analytics Intelligence offers an artificial intelligence platform that is able to automatically analyze web analytics data.
Website: http://www.analyticsintelligence.com
Phone: 44 (0)20 7754 9198 **Email:** info@analyticsintelligence.com
City: London **State:** England **PC:** **Country: United Kingdom**
Year Established: **Status 2020:** Active
Industries: Analytics for:, Artificial Intelligence for:, Business Intelligence for:, Natural Language Processing for:, ~ Professional Services (48)

Company Name: Anycareer
Description: Anycareer is an online career platform with courses, mentors, guides & automated recruitment to top employers.
Website: http://anycareer.com
Phone: 44 20 3488 1845 **Email:** hello@anycareer.com
City: London **State:** England **PC:** **Country: United Kingdom**
Year Established: 2018 **Status 2020:** Active
Industries: Machine Learning

Company Name: Anything World
Description: Anything World is a platform to create worlds powered by voice and populated with anything you can think of - with AI behaviours applied!
Website: http://anything.world/
Phone: 44 79 7740 2871 **Email:** hello@anything.world
City: London **State:** England **PC:** **Country: United Kingdom**
Year Established: 2018 **Status 2020:** Active
Industries: Artificial Intelligence for:, ~ Arts-Entertainment-Recreation (4)

Company Name: Apiary Book
Description: Our mission is to help beekeepers from around the world to make better informed decisions.
Website: http://www.apiarybook.com
Phone: 40 722 276 139 **Email:** bogdan@apiarybook.com
City: London **State:** England **PC:** **Country: United Kingdom**
Year Established: 2018 **Status 2020:** Active
Industries:

Company Name: Apomatix
Description: Stay Ahead of Risk
Website: http://www.apomatix.com
Phone: **Email:** info@apomatix.com
City: London **State:** England **PC:** **Country: United Kingdom**
Year Established: 2017 **Status 2020:** Active
Industries: Artificial Intelligence for:, Compliance for:, Cyber Security for:, IT Managed Services for:, Web for:, Risk Management for:, Business Software as a Service Apps (SaaS Apps) for:, Security for:, Security

Company Name: Applied AI
Description: Applied AI is a scaleup growth programme for applied AI companies that are focused to solve real-world problems.
Website: http://technation.io/news/artificial-intelligence-grow...
Phone: **Email:** info@technation.io
City: London **State:** England **PC:** **Country: United Kingdom**
Year Established: **Status 2020:** Active
Industries: Artificial Intelligence for:, IT Managed Services for:, Machine Learning

Company Name: Applied AI Ltd
Description: Applied AI is a data science consultancy.
Website: http://www.applied.ai
Phone: 44 (0) 20 8144 7718 **Email:** info@applied.ai
City: London **State:** England **PC:** **Country: United Kingdom**
Year Established: 2013 **Status 2020:** Active
Industries:

Company Name: Applied Data Science Partne: Serbia
Description: Applied Data Science Partners provides data science and AI solutions.
Website: http://adsp.ai/
Phone: 44-0-20-8012-7972 **Email:** hello@adsp.ai
City: London **State:** England **PC:** **Country: United Kingdom**
Year Established: 2016 **Status 2020:** Active
Industries: Artificial Intelligence for:, IT Managed Services for:, Machine Learning

Company Name: Apppli
Description: Creative Agency and R&D Practice focusing on mobile, wearables, IoT and Artificial Intelligence
Website: http://www.apppli.com
Phone: 0044 20 71127100 **Email:** contactus@apppli.com
City: London **State:** England **PC:** **Country: United Kingdom**
Year Established: **Status 2020:** Active
Industries: Artificial Intelligence for:, Mobile for:, ~ Construction (10)

Company **Name:** Archangel Imaging
Description: Archangel Imaging enables AI and human machine teaming in remote areas to save lives, animals and fight crimes.
Website: http://www.archangel.: Isle of Man
Phone: (44) 01865 600 415 **Email:** info@Archangel.: Isle of Man
City: London **State:** England **PC:** **Country: United Kingdom**
Year Established: 2016 **Status 2020:** Active
Industries: Artificial Intelligence for:, ~ Banking and Financial Markets-Services (7), Internet of Things (IoT) for:, Security

Company Name: Arctic Shor: Spain
Description: Arctic Shores pioneer behavioural assessments combining neuroscience, AI and game technology to generate data-driven people insights.
Website: http://www.arcticshores.com
Phone: 44 (0)844 848 0424 **Email:** info@arcticshores.com
City: London **State:** England **PC:** **Country: United Kingdom**
Year Established: 2013 **Status 2020:** Active
Industries: Artificial Intelligence for:, IT Managed Services for:, Web

Company Name: Arena
Description: Sports Analytics through Global Industry-Leading A.I. for Sports Right's Holde: Serbia
Website: http://www.arena.ai
Phone: **Email:** info@arena.ai
City: London **State:** England **PC:** **Country: United Kingdom**
Year Established: **Status 2020:** Active
Industries: Analytics for:, Artificial Intelligence for:, ~ Arts-Entertainment-Recreation (4)

Company Name: Ariel AI
Description: Accurate, real-time 3D Human Perception and Reconstruction on mobile devices.
Website: http://www.arielai.com
Phone: **Email:** contact@arielai.com
City: London **State:** England **PC:** **Country: United Kingdom**
Year Established: 2018 **Status 2020:** Active
Industries: Artificial Intelligence for:, IT Managed Services

Company Name: Arkera
Description: Artificial Intelligence
Website: http://www.arkera.ai
Phone: **Email:** info@arkera.ai
City: London **State:** England **PC:** **Country: United Kingdom**
Year Established: **Status 2020:** Active
Industries: Artificial Intelligence for:, ~ Banking and Financial Markets-Services (7), ~ Banking and Financial Markets-Services (7), ~ Banking and Financial Markets-Services (7), Machine Learning for:, Finance and Accounting for:, ~ Professional Services (48), ~ Banking an

Company Name: Arria NLG
Description: Arria NLG specializes in extracting information from complex data sources and communicating that information in natural language.
Website: http://arria.com
Phone: 44 207 100 4540 **Email:** hello.emea@arria.com
City: London **State:** England **PC:** **Country: United Kingdom**
Year Established: 2013 **Status 2020:** Active
Industries: Analytics for:, Artificial Intelligence for:, Big Data and Analytics for:, Business Intelligence for:, Natural Language Processing for:, Business Software as a Service Apps (SaaS Apps)

Company Name: ARROE
Description: ARROE's platform manages the batteries of electronic devices, extends their lifespan and ensures you never worry about your battery again.
Website: http://www.arroe.com
Phone: **Email:** support@arroe.com
City: London **State:** England **PC:** **Country: United Kingdom**
Year Established: 2016 **Status 2020:** Active
Industries: ~ Energy and Utilities (14), Internet of Things (IoT) for:, Machine Learning

Company Name: Art World Insights
Description: Using big data to value art works
Website: http://www.artworldinsights.com/
Phone: **Email:** info@artworldinsights.com
City: London **State:** England **PC:** **Country: United Kingdom**
Year Established: **Status 2020:** Active
Industries: Artificial Intelligence for:, IT Managed Services for:, Machine Learning

Company Name: ArtGu: Russia
Description: ArtGuru consists of a small team of art and technology enthusiasts.
Website: http://artguru.me/
Phone: **Email:** info@artguru.me
City: London **State:** England **PC:** **Country: United Kingdom**
Year Established: **Status 2020:** Active
Industries:

Company Name: Arthronica
Description: Arthronica provides Artificial Intelligence for Patient Monitoring and Rehabilitation
Website: http://arthronica.com/
Phone: 44 20 7403 4920 **Email:** info@arthronica.com
City: London **State:** England **PC:** **Country: United Kingdom**
Year Established: 2018 **Status 2020:** Active
Industries: Artificial Intelligence

Company Name: Artificial Labs
Description: We collaborate with leading insurers, using technology to save time, money and increase sales.
Website: http://artificial.io
Phone: 44(0) 7885 428 809 **Email:** ollie.fox@artificial.io
City: London **State:** England **PC:** **Country: United Kingdom**
Year Established: **Status 2020:** Active
Industries: Artificial Intelligence for:, ~ Insurance (25), ~ Insurance (25), Cyber Security

Company Name: ArtuData
Description: ArtuData helps b2c online brands grow by using Artificial-Intelligence to find, convert and monetize their high value clients.
Website: http://www.artudata.com
Phone: **Email:** ir@artudata.com
City: London **State:** England **PC:** **Country: United Kingdom**
Year Established: 2014 **Status 2020:** Active
Industries: Artificial Intelligence for:, Big Data and Analytics for:, Business Software as a Service Apps (SaaS Apps)

Company Name: ARWAY
Description: ARWAY is an indoor navigation platform that uses AR, enabled by AI to connect, inform, guide users and ensure building safety.
Website: http://arway.app
Phone: **Email:** baran@arway.app
City: London **State:** England **PC:** **Country: United Kingdom**
Year Established: 2018 **Status 2020:** Active
Industries: Artificial Intelligence for:, Augmented Reality for:, Internet of Things (IoT)

Company Name: Ascalia
Description: Ascalia helps industry and cities easily implement Industry 4.0 concepts with its AI and edge-computing based solution
Website: http://ascalia.io
Phone: **Email:** info@ascalia.io
City: London **State:** England **PC:** **Country: United Kingdom**
Year Established: 2018 **Status 2020:** Active
Industries: Artificial Intelligence for:, Enterprise Application Services for:, Industrial Solutions for:, Automation for:, Internet of Things (IoT) for:, Machine Learning for:, Predictive Analytics for:, Business Software as a Service Apps (SaaS Apps) for:, Business Software

Company Name: ASI Data Science
Description: ASI is the EMEA-based leader in data innovation that specializes in data exploration, predictive analytics & data engineering.
Website: http://www.asidatascience.com/
Phone: 44 20 3637 9415 **Email:** info@faculty.ai
City: London **State:** England **PC:** **Country: United Kingdom**
Year Established: 2014 **Status 2020:** Active
Industries: Artificial Intelligence for:, ~ Education (13)

Company Name: askporter
Description: AskPorter is an AI machine learning messaging platform that optimises property and facilities.
Website: http://www.askporter.com
Phone: **Email:** 36099@reference-encyclopedia-ai.net
City: London **State:** England **PC:** **Country: United Kingdom**
Year Established: 2017 **Status 2020:** Active
Industries: Artificial Intelligence

Company Name: Assist AI
Description: Assist makes AI powered solutions that helps Customer Service teams be more efficient
Website: http://assist.ai
Phone: **Email:** 36101@reference-encyclopedia-ai.net
City: London **State:** England **PC:** **Country: United Kingdom**
Year Established: 2015 **Status 2020:** Active
Industries: Artificial Intelligence for:, ~ Customer Relationship Management (11), Internet of Things (IoT) for:, Web

Company Name: AtHashtags
Description: Only marketplace to personalise online and in-store product recommendations from the smallest to largest brands locally and globally
Website: http://spaceandtime.biz
Phone: **Email:** berne@athashtags.com
City: London **State:** England **PC:** **Country: United Kingdom**
Year Established: **Status 2020:** Active
Industries: Artificial Intelligence for:, E-Commerce for:, ~ Fashion (16), ~ Banking and Financial Markets-Services (7)

Company Name: Atheros Intelligence
Description: Engineering & design company specializing in building AI products
Website:
Phone: **Email:** 36103@reference-encyclopedia-ai.net
City: London **State:** England **PC:** **Country: United Kingdom**
Year Established: 2019 **Status 2020:** Active
Industries: Artificial Intelligence

Company Name: Atlas ML
Description: Deep Learning software
Website: http://www.atlasml.io
Phone: **Email:** 4549@reference-encyclopedia-ai.net
City: London **State:** England **PC:** **Country: United Kingdom**
Year Established: **Status 2020:** Active
Industries: Artificial Intelligence for:, ~ Education (13), Machine Learning for:, ~ Professional Services (48)

Company Name: Attest
Description:
Website: askattest.com
Phone: **Email:** hello@askattest.com
City: London **State:** England **PC:** **Country: United Kingdom**
Year Established: **Status 2020:** Active
Industries: Artificial Intelligence for:, ~ Retail and Consumer Products (52)

Company Name: AuditXprt
Description: AuditXprt is provides artificial intelligence solution to automate regulatory compliance assurance and financial audit.
Website: http://auditxprt.com/
Phone: **Email:** Info@auditxprt.com
City: London **State:** England **PC:** **Country: United Kingdom**
Year Established: 2015 **Status 2020:** Active
Industries: Artificial Intelligence for:, Machine Learning

Company Name: Aura Vision
Description: Aura Vision enables brick-and-mortar retailers to positively influence shopper journeys with cutting-edge computer vision.
Website: http://auravisionlabs.com/
Phone: **Email:** hello@auravisionlabs.com
City: London **State:** England **PC:** **Country: United Kingdom**
Year Established: **Status 2020:** Active
Industries:

Company Name: Automorph
Description: AI for software development
Website: http://www.automorph.com
Phone: **Email:** hello@automorph.com
City: London **State:** England **PC:** **Country: United Kingdom**
Year Established: 2017 **Status 2020:** Active
Industries: Artificial Intelligence for:, Application Program Interfaces (APIs) for:, Application Services for:, Application Services for:, Automation

Company Name: Autto Limited
Description: Autto is a workflow automation based in London, England.
Website: www.autto.io/
Phone: **Email:** info@autto.io
City: London **State:** England **PC:** **Country: United Kingdom**
Year Established: **Status 2020:** Active
Industries: Artificial Intelligence for:, IT Managed Services for:, ~ Law-Legal Services (26)

Company Name: Auxuman
Description: Auxuman is a synthetic media company building the next generation of virtual entertainers and online story worlds.
Website: http://www.auxuman.space
Phone: **Email:** hello@auxuman.space
City: London **State:** England **PC:** **Country: United Kingdom**
Year Established: 2019 **Status 2020:** Active
Industries: Artificial Intelligence for:, Web for:, ~ Arts-Entertainment-Recreation (4)

Company Name: Avalon AI
Description: Stratifying Dementia using Machine Learning.
Website: http://avalonai.strikingly.com
Phone: **Email:** 36121@reference-encyclopedia-ai.net
City: London **State:** England **PC:** **Country: United Kingdom**
Year Established: 2015 **Status 2020:** Active
Industries: Artificial Intelligence for:, ~ Healthcare (20), ~ Healthcare (20)

Company Name: Avasa AI
Description: AI-driven platform for property search and finalisation for residential tenants.
Website: http://avasa.ai
Phone: **Email:** mathur.mayank@gmail.com
City: London **State:** England **PC:** **Country: United Kingdom**
Year Established: 2016 **Status 2020:** Active
Industries: Artificial Intelligence for:, Web for:, ~ Real Estate (49)

Company **Name:** Avora
Description: Avora provides a complete augmented analytics solution powered by AI that makes in-depth data analysis as easy as a web search.
Website: http://avora.com
Phone: 44 (0) 203 633 2010 **Email:** info@avora.com
City: London **State:** England **PC:** **Country: United Kingdom**
Year Established: 2014 **Status 2020:** Active
Industries: Analytics for:, Business Intelligence for:, Cloud for:, Data Management for:, Machine Learning for:, Business Software as a Service Apps (SaaS Apps)

Company Name: Axio: Morocco
Description: Automated insurance claims handling and insurance claims marketplace.
Website: http://www.axioma.co.uk/
Phone: **Email:** info@axioma.co.uk
City: London **State:** England **PC:** **Country: United Kingdom**
Year Established: 2018 **Status 2020:** Active
Industries: Machine Learning

Company Name: Babelver: Sweden
Description: Babelverse is the first and only human powered "universal translator."
Website: http://babelverse.com/
Phone: **Email:** 36132@reference-encyclopedia-ai.net
City: London **State:** England **PC:** **Country: United Kingdom**
Year Established: 2010 **Status 2020:** Active
Industries: Collaboration Solutions for:, ~ Personal-Religious-Civic (45), Databases for:, ~ Education (13), Natural Language Processing for:, Compute

Company Name: Babylon
Description:
Website: http://www.babylonhealth.com
Phone: 44-020-7100-0762 **Email:** press@babylonhealth.com
City: London **State:** England **Zip:** SW3 3DD **Country: United Kingdom**
Year Established: **Status 2020:** Active
Industries: Artificial Intelligence for:, ~ Healthcare (20), ~ Healthcare (20), ~ Healthcare (20)

Company Name: Babylon Heal:Thailand
Description: Putting an accessible and affordable health service into the hands of every person on earth.
Website: http://www.babylonhealth.com/
Phone: **Email:** support@babylonhealth.com
City: London **State:** England **PC:** **Country: United Kingdom**
Year Established: **Status 2020:** Active
Industries: Artificial Intelligence for:, ~ Healthcare (20), ~ Healthcare (20), ~ Healthcare (20)

Company Name: Banq Systems
Description: AI-empowered Omni-channel Digital Banking Platform. MultiBanQ - one online front office to your 10 different banks.
Website: http://banqsystems.com/
Phone: 1(917)378-6311 **Email:** sales@banqsystems.com
City: London **State:** England **PC:** **Country: United Kingdom**
Year Established: 2012 **Status 2020:** Active
Industries: Artificial Intelligence for:, ~ Banking and Financial Markets-Services (7), Big Data and Analytics for:, ~ Banking and

Financial Markets-Services (7), ~ Banking and Financial Markets-Services (7), IT Managed Services for:, Machine Learning

Company Name: Beamly
Description: Beamly: The social discovery and engagement platform
Website: http://beamly.com
Phone: **Email:** hello@thebeamlyagency.com
City: London **State:** England **PC:** **Country: United Kingdom**
Year Established: **Status 2020:** Active
Industries: ~ Media-Communications (41), Artificial Intelligence for:, Content for:, ~ Social Media (54), ~ Social Media (54)

Company Name: Beauty Matching Engine
Description: AI Award-winning Beauty Prediction & Personalisation Platform, helping beauty companies predict, personalise & enhance the customer journey
Website: http://www.beautymatchingengine.com
Phone: **Email:** info@beautymatchingengine.com
City: London **State:** England **PC:** **Country: United Kingdom**
Year Established: 2019 **Status 2020:** Active
Industries: ~ Beauty (8), ~ Beauty (8), Digital Marketing for:, E-Commerce for:, Machine Learning

Company Name: Behavox
Description: Holistic employee surveillance system
Website: http://www.behavox.com
Phone: **Email:** info@behavox.com
City: London **State:** England **PC:** **Country: United Kingdom**
Year Established: **Status 2020:** Active
Industries:

Company Name: Bekudo
Description: Bekudo is an intelligent way to match businesses with teams of freelancers and independent professionals around the world.
Website: http://bekudo.com
Phone: **Email:** connect@bekudo.com
City: London **State:** England **PC:** **Country: United Kingdom**
Year Established: **Status 2020:** Active
Industries: Artificial Intelligence for:, Machine Learning for:, Collaboration Solutions

Company Name: Beneficiary.io
Description: Beneficiary.io is a data collection tool powered by machine learning and behavioral science, engineered for charitable sector.
Website: http://www.beneficiary.io/
Phone: **Email:** 36144@reference-encyclopedia-ai.net
City: London **State:** England **PC:** **Country: United Kingdom**
Year Established: 2017 **Status 2020:** Active
Industries: ~ Retail and Consumer Products (52), Application Services for:, ~ Social Assistance-Non-Profits (53), Machine Learning for:, ~ Healthcare (20)

Company Name: BenevolentAI
Description:
Website: www.benevolent.ai
Phone: **Email:** hello@benevolent.ai
City: London **State:** England **Zip:** NW1 1LW **Country: United Kingdom**
Year Established: **Status 2020:** Active
Industries: Artificial Intelligence for:, Big Data and Analytics for:, Machine Learning for:, ~ Life Sciences (27)

Company Name: Best Commands
Description: Building the ultimate resource for pro commands and integrations for smart home AI devices like Google Home and Amazon Alexa
Website: http://bestcommands.com/
Phone: **Email:** team@bestcommands.com
City: London **State:** England **PC:** **Country: United Kingdom**
Year Established: **Status 2020:** Active
Industries: Artificial Intelligence for:, ~ Media-Communications (41), ~ Construction (10)

Company Name: Bibblio
Description: Content recommendation toolkit helping publishers and content businesses deliver more relevant and engaging discovery experiences.
Website: http://bibblio.org
Phone: **Email:** mads@bibblio.org
City: London **State:** England **PC:** **Country: United Kingdom**
Year Established: **Status 2020:** Active
Industries: Artificial Intelligence for:, Digital Media for:, ~ Education (13), Machine Learning

Company Name: Big Data for Humans
Description: Big Data for Humans provides a data science-as-a-service platform for customer marketing in retail and travel sectors.
Website: http://www.bigdataforhumans.com
Phone: **Email:** K.Peacock-Hardie@FrenchDuncan.co.uk
City: London **State:** England **PC:** **Country: United Kingdom**
Year Established: **Status 2020:** Active
Industries: Artificial Intelligence for:, Big Data and Analytics for:, E-Commerce for:, Predictive Analytics for:, ~ Professional Services (48), ~ Travel and Transportation (58)

Company Name: Big Data Partnership
Description: Big Data Partnership provides solutions that enable clients to extract insights from big data.
Website: http://www.bigdatapartnership.com
Phone: 44 20 7205 2550 **Email:** info@bigdatapartnership.com
City: London **State:** England **PC:** **Country: United Kingdom**
Year Established: 2012 **Status 2020:** Active
Industries: Analytics

Company Name: BigData4Analytics
Description: Management Consultants in Big Data
Website: http://www.bigdata4analytics.com
Phone: 0207 164 6260 **Email:** mike.fish@bigdata4analytics.com
City: London **State:** England **PC:** **Country: United Kingdom**
Year Established: 2012 **Status 2020:** Active
Industries: Analytics for:, Big Data and Analytics for:, Predictive Analytics for:, ~ Social Assistance-Non-Profits (53)

Company Name: BigS:
Description: Sustainable Insect Control Solutions
Website: http://bigsis.tech
Phone: **Email:** info@bigsis.tech
City: London **State:** England **PC:** **Country: United Kingdom**
Year Established: 2017 **Status 2020:** Active
Industries: ~ Agriculture (3), ~ Agriculture (3), Artificial Intelligence for:, Automation

Company Name: BioBeats
Description: Artificial Intelligence for Human Wellbeing
Website: http://biobeats.com
Phone: **Email:** help@biobeats.com
City: London **State:** England **PC:** **Country: United Kingdom**
Year Established: **Status 2020:** Active
Industries: Artificial Intelligence for:, ~ Healthcare (20), ~ Human Resources (24), IT Managed Services for:, Machine Learning

Company Name: Black Square Media
Description: AdTech Accelerator
Website: http://blacksquaremedia.com/
Phone: **Email:** info@blacksquaremedia.com
City: London **State:** England **PC:** **Country: United Kingdom**
Year Established: **Status 2020:** Active
Industries: ~ Media-Communications (41), Artificial Intelligence for:, Big Data and Analytics for:, Machine Learning for:, Compute for:, ~ Professional Services (48), ~ Media-Communications (41)

Company Name: Black Swan Data
Description: UK's Leading Smart Data, Digital and Predictive Analytics Agency
Website: http://www.blackswan.com
Phone: 0203 457 8539 **Email:** hello@blackswan.com
City: London **State:** England **PC:** **Country: United Kingdom**
Year Established: **Status 2020:** Active
Industries: ~ Media-Communications (41), Analytics for:, Artificial Intelligence for:, Big Data and Analytics for:, Business Intelligence

Company Name: BlackSwan Technologies
Description: BlackSwan Technologies is a digital transformation, cognitive computing, AI software company that revolutionizes data acquisition.
Website: http://blackswantechnologies.ai
Phone: **Email:** info@blackswan-technologies.com
City: London **State:** England **PC:** **Country: United Kingdom**
Year Established: 2014 **Status 2020:** Active
Industries: Analytics for:, Artificial Intelligence for:, Big Data and Analytics for:, Cloud for:, Cyber Security for:, Risk Management

Company Name: Bled Tech
Description: Bled Tech is a UK based company with international presence.
Website: http://www.bledtech.uk/
Phone: **Email:** bled.tech@yahoo.com
City: London **State:** England **PC:** **Country: United Kingdom**
Year Established: **Status 2020:** Active
Industries:

Company Name: Blippar
Description: Blippar is a technology company specializing in augmented reality, artificial intelligence, and computer vision.
Website: http://www.blippar.com
Phone: **Email:** info@blippar.com
City: London **State:** England **PC:** **Country: United Kingdom**
Year Established: **Status 2020:** Active
Industries: ~ Media-Communications (41), Artificial Intelligence for:, Augmented Reality for:, Computer Vision for:, ~ Education (13), Image Recognition for:, ~ Media-Communications (41), Mobile for:, ~ Professional Services (48)

Company Name: BlockClaim
Description: Lemonade style claims for every insurer
Website: http://www.blockclaim.ai
Phone: **Email:** n.thone@blockclaim.ai
City: London **State:** England **PC:** **Country: United Kingdom**
Year Established: **Status 2020:** Active
Industries: Artificial Intelligence for:, Blockchain for:, Image Recognition for:, ~ Insurance (25), ~ Insurance (25), Natural Language Processing for:, ~ Professional Services (48)

Company Name: Bloomsbury AI
Description: Bloomsbury AI enables everyone to easily create their own question-answering system.
Website: http://bloomsbury.ai/
Phone: **Email:** contact@bloomsbury.ai
City: London **State:** England **PC:** **Country: United Kingdom**
Year Established: **Status 2020:** Active
Industries: Artificial Intelligence for:, IT Managed Services for:, Enterprise Application Services for:, ~ Manufacturing-Electronic (30), Natural Language Processing

Company Name: Blue Lion Research:
Description: Blue Lion Research is an artificial Intelligence for alternative investments.
Website: http://www.bluelionresearch.com/
Phone: **Email:** info@bluelionresearch.com
City: London **State:** England **PC:** **Country: United Kingdom**
Year Established: **Status 2020:** Active
Industries: Artificial Intelligence for:, Machine Learning for:, Risk Management

Company Name: Blyng
Description: Blyng is a powerful AI driven chatbot virtual assistant serving primarily the Real Estate industry.
Website: http://blyng.io/
Phone: **Email:** contact@blyng.co.uk
City: London **State:** England **PC:** **Country: United Kingdom**
Year Established: **Status 2020:** Active
Industries: Artificial Intelligence for:, Machine Learning

Company Name: BODYSWAPS
Description: VRSaaS
Website: http://bodyswaps.co
Phone: 44(0)7827649737 **Email:** hello@bodyswaps.co
City: London **State:** England **PC:** **Country: United Kingdom**
Year Established: 2018 **Status 2020:** Active
Industries: Artificial Intelligence for:, Machine Learning for:, ~ Education (13), Virtual Reality (VR)

Company Name: Book Abacus
Description: Book Abacus is an Artificial intelligence driven Book Recommendations and price comparison.
Website: http://www.bookabacus.com/
Phone: **Email:** 36186@reference-encyclopedia-ai.net
City: London **State:** England **PC:** **Country: United Kingdom**
Year Established: 2015 **Status 2020:** Active
Industries: Artificial Intelligence

Company Name: boomApp
Description: boomApp is a mobile App with video and image recognition.
Website: http://boomapp.co
Phone: **Email:** feedback@boomapp.co
City: London **State:** England **PC:** **Country: United Kingdom**
Year Established: **Status 2020:** Active
Industries: Artificial Intelligence for:, Augmented Reality for:, Image Recognition for:, Machine Learning for:, ~ Media-Communications (41), Computer Vision

Company Name: BotsAndUs
Description: BotsAndUs develops state of the art robotics and AI products.
Website: http://botsandus.com
Phone: 44 7856 934 039 **Email:** bo@botsandus.com
City: London **State:** England **PC:** **Country: United Kingdom**
Year Established: 2015 **Status 2020:** Active
Industries: Artificial Intelligence for:, ~ Event Management (15), Machine Learning for:, Robotics

Company Name: Botskill
Description: Simplifying experiences through data-driven dialogue.
Website: http://www.botskill.co.uk/
Phone: 44 02071937172 **Email:** info@botskill.co.uk
City: London **State:** England **PC:** **Country: United Kingdom**
Year Established: 2017 **Status 2020:** Active
Industries: Artificial Intelligence for:, IT Managed Services for:, IT Managed Services for:, Machine Learning

Company Name: Bottr.co Chatbot Agency
Description: Bottr.co Chatbot Agency builds and integrates chatbots into Messenger, Slack, Twilio, Twitter, and many more.
Website: http://bottr.co/
Phone: **Email:** james@bottr.co
City: London **State:** England **PC:** **Country: United Kingdom**
Year Established: **Status 2020:** Active
Industries: Artificial Intelligence for:, Human Computer Interaction for:, Machine Learning

Company Name: Bounce
Description: Positive psychology chatbot for employee mental wellbeing
Website: http://bouncebot.io
Phone: **Email:** hello@bouncebot.io
City: London **State:** England **PC:** **Country: United Kingdom**

Year Established: **Status 2020:** Active
Industries: Artificial Intelligence for:, Business Applications for:, ~ Healthcare (20), ~ Healthcare (20), ~ Healthcare (20)

Company Name: Brainpool
Description: Brainpool AI is a worldwide network of AI and Machine Learning experts. 300 data scientists - academics and professionals
Website: http://brainpool.ai/
Phone: 44 (0) 203-393-2630 **Email:** contact@brainpool.ai
City: London **State:** England **PC:** **Country: United Kingdom**
Year Established: 2016 **Status 2020:** Active
Industries: Artificial Intelligence for:, IT Managed Services for:, Machine Learning

Company Name: Braintree Ltd
Description: Braintree is a research company specialising in providing data analysis and machine learning for large organisations.
Website: http://www.braintree.com/
Phone: **Email:** info@braintree.com
City: London **State:** England **PC:** **Country: United Kingdom**
Year Established: **Status 2020:** Active
Industries:

Company Name: BridgeU
Description: Data-driven university and careers guidance to empower your school
Website: http://www.bridge-u.com
Phone: 19175875373 **Email:** Info@bridge-u.com
City: London **State:** England **PC:** **Country: United Kingdom**
Year Established: **Status 2020:** Active
Industries: Analytics for:, Artificial Intelligence for:, Big Data and Analytics for:, ~ Education (13), ~ Education (13), Enterprise Application Services for:, Machine Learning

Company Name: Brolly
Description: Brolly is an AI-driven insurance advisory services app.
Website: http://www.heybrolly.com
Phone: **Email:** team@heybrolly.com
City: London **State:** England **PC:** **Country: United Kingdom**
Year Established: **Status 2020:** Active
Industries: Artificial Intelligence for:, ~ Banking and Financial Markets-Services (7), ~ Insurance (25), ~ Insurance (25)

Company Name: Bronze
Description: BRONZE is a technology that allows music creators to utilise AI and machine learning as tools for composition and release.
Website: http://www.bronze.ai
Phone: **Email:** info@bronze.ai
City: London **State:** England **PC:** **Country: United Kingdom**
Year Established: 2015 **Status 2020:** Active
Industries: Artificial Intelligence for:, ~ Arts-Entertainment-Recreation (4)

Company Name: brytlyt
Description: Brytlyt is a young and dynamic company with a clear mission - to empower organisations through transformation data analytics.
Website: www.brytlyt.co.uk
Phone: **Email:** Contact@Brytlyt.com
City: London **State:** England **PC:** **Country: United Kingdom**
Year Established: **Status 2020:** Active
Industries: Analytics for:, Artificial Intelligence for:, Machine Learning

Company Name: Bubblo (BubbleScene Ltd.)
Description: Bubblo is an artificial Intelligence based virtual reality discovery app and marketing platform.
Website: http://bubbloapp.com/
Phone: **Email:** 36214@reference-encyclopedia-ai.net
City: London **State:** England **PC:** **Country: United Kingdom**
Year Established: 2014 **Status 2020:** Active
Industries: Artificial Intelligence for:, Virtual Reality (VR)

Company Name: Bunny AI
Description: Local solutions globally
Website: http://bunny.ear:Thailand
Phone: **Email:** info@bunny.ear:Thailand
City: London **State:** England **PC:** **Country: United Kingdom**
Year Established: **Status 2020:** Active
Industries: Artificial Intelligence for:, E-Commerce

Company Name: Butterwire
Description: Butterwire uses machine learning to distil professional stock, portfolio, and market insights.
Website: http://www.butterwire.com/
Phone: **Email:** info@butterwire.com
City: London **State:** England **PC:** **Country: United Kingdom**
Year Established: 2018 **Status 2020:** Active
Industries: ~ Banking and Financial Markets-Services (7), Machine Learning

Company Name: Buzz Radar
Description: Buzz Radar is an industry leader in making data, insightful, accessible and actionable
Website: http://www.buzzradar.com
Phone: **Email:** info@buzzradar.com
City: London **State:** England **PC:** **Country: United Kingdom**
Year Established: **Status 2020:** Active
Industries: Analytics for:, Artificial Intelligence for:, ~ Media-Communications (41), Business Intelligence for:, Data Management for:, Data Management for:, Digital Marketing for:, ~ Social Media (54)

Company Name: ByteSumo
Description: ByteSumo are experts at data. We run Data Science and Engineering in Big Data environments to deliver analytics solutions
Website: http://bytesumo.com
Phone: 44 7970 130 767 **Email:** info@bytesumo.com
City: London **State:** England **PC:** **Country: United Kingdom**
Year Established: **Status 2020:** Active
Industries: Analytics for:, Artificial Intelligence for:, Big Data and Analytics for:, Business Intelligence for:, Data Management for:, Data Management for:, IT Managed Services for:, Machine Learning for:, Predictive Analytics

Company Name: Calip: Saudi Arabia
Description: Deep Learning powered video monitoring
Website: http://calipsa.io/
Phone: **Email:** info@calipsa.io
City: London **State:** England **PC:** **Country: United Kingdom**
Year Established: **Status 2020:** Active
Industries: Artificial Intelligence for:, Computer Vision for:, Machine Learning

Company Name: Callsign
Description: Identity fraud, authentication and authorization company using AI & machine learning to determine that user really is who they say they are.
Website: https://www.callsign.com/
Phone: **Email:** info@callsign.com
City: London **State:** England **PC:** **Country: United Kingdom**
Year Established: **Status 2020:** Active
Industries: Artificial Intelligence for:, Compliance for:, ~ Banking and Financial Markets-Services (1288), ~ E-Commerce (1293), Cyber Security for:, ~ Aerospace and Defense (1588), ~ Automotive (1591), ~ Autonomous Vehicles (1592), ~ Banking and Financial Markets-Services (

Company Name: Cambrian Intelligence
Description: Cambrian Intelligence is building a teleoperation interface to intuitively control robots at a distance with hand.
Website: http://www.caint.io
Phone: **Email:** info@caint.io
City: London **State:** England **PC:** **Country: United Kingdom**

Year Established: 2015 **Status 2020:** Active
Industries: Artificial Intelligence for:, Robotics

Company Name: Cambridge Human: United Arab Emirates
Description: Cambridge Humanae combines psychological tests and artificial intelligence to understand psychological reliability of high risk individuals.
Website: http://www.humanae.xyz/
Phone: **Email:** kirk@humanae.xyz
City: London **State:** England **PC:** **Country: United Kingdom**
Year Established: **Status 2020:** Active
Industries: Artificial Intelligence for:, ~ Healthcare (20)

Company Name: Cambridge Spark
Description: Cambridge Spark is a leader in personalised Data Science training.
Website: http://cambridgespark.com/
Phone: (781) 641-9378 **Email:** contact@cambridgespark.com
City: London **State:** England **PC:** **Country: United Kingdom**
Year Established: 2016 **Status 2020:** Active
Industries:

Company Name: Capexmove
Description: Capexmove decentralises debt capital markets by leveraging blockchain technology.
Website: http://www.capexmove.io/
Phone: **Email:** hello@capexmove.io
City: London **State:** England **PC:** **Country: United Kingdom**
Year Established: **Status 2020:** Active
Industries: Artificial Intelligence for:, Blockchain for:, ~ Banking and Financial Markets-Services (7)

Company Name: CaptionHub
Description: The enterprise platform for collaborative & automated video subtitling.
Website: http://www.captionhub.com
Phone: 020 7100 4600 **Email:** james@captionhub.com
City: London **State:** England **PC:** **Country: United Kingdom**
Year Established: 2015 **Status 2020:** Active
Industries: Artificial Intelligence

Company Name: Cardioly: Sweden
Description: Cloud ECG & HRV analytics platform for real-time remote heart health monitoring, detection and prognosis on dangerous heart events
Website: http://cardiolyse.com/
Phone: **Email:** info@cardiolyse.com
City: London **State:** England **PC:** **Country: United Kingdom**
Year Established: 2016 **Status 2020:** Active
Industries: ~ Healthcare (20), ~ Healthcare (20), ~ Healthcare (20), IT Managed Services for:, Machine Learning for:, ~ Healthcare (20), ~ Healthcare (20)

Company Name: CartMe
Description: App that buys products according to your preferences and nutritional needs automatically.
Website: http://www.cartme.io
Phone: **Email:** info@cartme.io
City: London **State:** England **PC:** **Country: United Kingdom**
Year Established: **Status 2020:** Active
Industries:

Company Name: causaLens
Description: Automated machine learning for time-series data.
Website: http://www.causalens.com/
Phone: **Email:** info@causalens.com
City: London **State:** England **PC:** **Country: United Kingdom**
Year Established: **Status 2020:** Active
Industries: Artificial Intelligence for:, Big Data and Analytics for:, Machine Learning

Company Name: Causaly
Description: On a mission to create a causal model of the world and all its generating processes.
Website: http://www.causaly.com
Phone: **Email:** info@causaly.com
City: London **State:** England **PC:** **Country: United Kingdom**
Year Established: **Status 2020:** Active
Industries: Artificial Intelligence for:, ~ Education (13), ~ Life Sciences (27), ~ Pharmaceuticals (46), ~ Media-Communications (41), Content

Company Name: Cazana
Description: Valuation and risk data to power the next generation of vehicle ownership. Used by car manufacturers, finance companies & insurers globally.
Website: http://cazana.com/uk
Phone: 0203 475 1492 **Email:** tom@cazana.com
City: London **State:** England **PC:** **Country: United Kingdom**
Year Established: **Status 2020:** Active
Industries: Artificial Intelligence for:, ~ Automotive (5), Big Data and Analytics for:, ~ Banking and Financial Markets-Services (7), ~ Insurance (25), Machine Learning for:, Predictive Analytics

Company Name: CENTURY Tech
Description: CENTURY is a personalised learning platform combining A.I., big data and behavioural science to provide real-time insights to educators.
Website: http://www.century.tech
Phone: **Email:** rebecca@century.tech
City: London **State:** England **PC:** **Country: United Kingdom**
Year Established: **Status 2020:** Active
Industries: Artificial Intelligence for:, Big Data and Analytics for:, ~ Education (13), ~ Education (13), ~ Education (13), ~ Media-Communications (41), Compute

Company Name: Cervest
Description: Cervest is building an AI-first platform to help businesses, governments and growers adapt to climate volatility, and protect our planet.
Website: http://cervest.ear:Thailand
Phone: 44 (0)20 3751 0380 **Email:** hello@cervest.ear:Thailand
City: London **State:** England **PC:** **Country: United Kingdom**
Year Established: 2016 **Status 2020:** Active
Industries: ~ Agriculture (3), Artificial Intelligence for:, Machine Learning for:, ~ Social-Environmental-Physical-Engineering Sciences (55)

Company Name: ChAI
Description: Predicting commodity prices with AI on Alternative Data to mitigate price volatility for manufacturers.
Website: http://Website www.chai-uk.com/
Phone: **Email:** info@chai-uk.com
City: London **State:** England **PC:** **Country: United Kingdom**
Year Established: **Status 2020:** Active
Industries: Artificial Intelligence for:, ~ Banking and Financial Markets-Services (7), IT Managed Services for:, Machine Learning for:, ~ Manufacturing-Miscellaneous (34), ~ Professional Services (48)

Company Name: Chainvine
Description: Next Generation Enterprise Systems / Identity Access Management (IAM) / Technology Providers Blockcha: India
Website: http://www.chainvine.com
Phone: (4673) 422-2313 **Email:** oliver@chainvine.com
City: London **State:** England **PC:** **Country: United Kingdom**
Year Established: 2015 **Status 2020:** Active
Industries: ~ Banking and Financial Markets-Services (7), Blockchain for:, Compliance for:, Cyber Security for:, Databases for:, Enterprise Application Services for:, Application Services for:, Internet of Things (IoT) for:, Internet of Things (IoT) for:, Supply Chain Managem

Company Name: Chaser
Description: Striving to build Earth's best products to help businesses get their invoices paid on time, automatically
Website: http://www.chaserhq.com
Phone: **Email:** david@chaserhq.com
City: London **State:** England **PC:** **Country: United Kingdom**

Year Established: **Status 2020:** Active
Industries: Finance and Accounting for:, Artificial Intelligence for:, ~ Banking and Financial Markets-Services (7)

Company Name: Chatterbox Labs
Description: Cognitive computing, Machine Learning, AI, Deep Learning & Reinforcement Learning
Website: http://www.chatterbox.co
Phone: 44 (0)20 3755 3675 **Email:** info@chatterbox.co
City: London **State:** England **PC:** **Country: United Kingdom**
Year Established: **Status 2020:** Active
Industries: Analytics for:, Artificial Intelligence for:, Big Data and Analytics for:, Enterprise Application Services for:, IT Managed Services for:, Web for:, Machine Learning for:, Natural Language Processing for:, Predictive Analytics

Company Name: Chattermill
Description: Chattermill applies cutting edge deep learning to help organizations make sense of their customer experience.
Website: http://chattermill.io/
Phone: **Email:** founders@chattermill.io
City: London **State:** England **PC:** **Country: United Kingdom**
Year Established: **Status 2020:** Active
Industries:

Company Name: Cheerfy
Description: Personalising Real Life Experienc: Spain
Website: http://cheerfy.com
Phone: 650 575 8660 **Email:** info@cheerfy.com
City: London **State:** England **PC:** **Country: United Kingdom**
Year Established: **Status 2020:** Active
Industries: Analytics for:, Artificial Intelligence for:, ~ Hospitality (23), ~ Food and Beverage (17), ~ Retail and Consumer Products (52)

Company Name: Chirp
Description: The world's most trusted and proven data-over-audio technology, used by the leading brands in over 90 countries.
Website: http://chirp.io
Phone: **Email:** contact@chirp.io
City: London **State:** England **PC:** **Country: United Kingdom**
Year Established: **Status 2020:** Active
Industries: Artificial Intelligence for:, Voice Recognition for:, Enterprise Application Services for:, ~ Professional Services (48)

Company Name: CHOPCHOP
Description: Dynamic learning and task management app for cooking backed by artificial intelligence
Website: http://www.mychopchop.com/
Phone: **Email:** team@mychopchop.com
City: London **State:** England **PC:** **Country: United Kingdom**
Year Established: **Status 2020:** Active
Industries: Application Services for:, Artificial Intelligence

Company Name: Chosen AI
Description: Chosen AI aggregates HR data to generate skills and capability insights that allow businesses to be predictive in their workforce planning.
Website: http://chosen.ai/
Phone: **Email:** hello@chosen.ai
City: London **State:** England **PC:** **Country: United Kingdom**
Year Established: 2018 **Status 2020:** Active
Industries: Artificial Intelligence for:, Big Data and Analytics for:, Predictive Analytics

Company Name: churnly
Description: churnly artificial intelligence gathers customer data and predicts which customers are likely to churn at each stage of the journey.
Website:
Phone: **Email:** 36275@reference-encyclopedia-ai.net
City: London **State:** England **PC:** **Country: United Kingdom**
Year Established: 2018 **Status 2020:** Active
Industries: **Company Name:** Circadia Health
Description: is an artificial intelligence company on a mission to prevent respiratory failure using contactless sensing and proprietary algorithms
Website: http://circadia.heal:Thailand
Phone: **Email:** hello@circadia.heal:Thailand
City: London **State:** England **PC:** **Country: United Kingdom**
Year Established: 2016 **Status 2020:** Active
Industries: Artificial Intelligence for:, Predictive Analytics

Company Name: Circadian
Description: Using behaviour to detect fraudsters and recognise customers.
Website: http://www.circadian-capital.co.uk/
Phone: **Email:** 36279@reference-encyclopedia-ai.net
City: London **State:** England **PC:** **Country: United Kingdom**
Year Established: 2016 **Status 2020:** Active
Industries: Artificial Intelligence for:, ~ Customer Relationship Management (11), Web

Company Name: Circuit Mind
Description: Circuit Mind develop artificial intelligence solutions.
Website: http://circuitmind.io/
Phone: **Email:** tomide@circuitmind.io
City: London **State:** England **PC:** **Country: United Kingdom**
Year Established: 2018 **Status 2020:** Active
Industries: Artificial Intelligence for:, Application Services for:, Predictive Analytics

Company Name: Circulor
Description: Using traceability to empower better business in raw materials and recycling
Website: http://circulor.com
Phone: **Email:** info@circulor.com
City: London **State:** England **PC:** **Country: United Kingdom**
Year Established: 2017 **Status 2020:** Active
Industries: Artificial Intelligence for:, Big Data and Analytics for:, Blockchain for:, ~ Telecommunications (56), Machine Learning for:, Risk Management for:, Supply Chain Management

Company Name: City Sa: Israel
Description: City Sail is a Artificial intelligence tech company.
Website: http://training.citysail.co.uk/
Phone: 44(0)2032395188 **Email:** info@citysail.co.uk
City: London **State:** England **PC:** **Country: United Kingdom**
Year Established: 2016 **Status 2020:** Active
Industries: Artificial Intelligence for:, IT Managed Services

Company Name: Clariti AI
Description: SaaS pricing software for retail banking
Website: http://www.clariti.ai
Phone: 44 207 7684 3635 **Email:** info@clariti.ai
City: London **State:** England **PC:** **Country: United Kingdom**
Year Established: 2019 **Status 2020:** Active
Industries: Business Software as a Service Apps (SaaS Apps)

Company Name: Cleo
Description: Cleo is an intelligent assistant that helps users manage their finances.
Website: http://www.meetcleo.com
Phone: 1223750869 **Email:** team@meetcleo.com
City: London **State:** England **PC:** **Country: United Kingdom**
Year Established: **Status 2020:** Active
Industries: Artificial Intelligence for:, ~ Banking and Financial Markets-Services (7), ~ Banking and Financial Markets-Services (7)

Company Name: Clever People
Description: Powerful BI tools for marketers and everyone to use.
Website: http://cleverpeople.io/
Phone: **Email:** team@cleverpeople.io
City: London **State:** England **PC:** **Country: United Kingdom**
Year Established: 2016 **Status 2020:** Active
Industries: Predictive Analytics

Company Name: Cloquo
Description: Cloquo is a tool and a social network for iPhones that allows its users to get alarms and notifications on online events.
Website: http://cloquo.com
Phone: **Email:** hello@cloquo.com
City: London **State:** England **PC:** **Country: United Kingdom**
Year Established: 2012 **Status 2020:** Active
Industries:

Company Name: Clothes Network
Description: Fashion Technology Platform for Brands, Retailers and Influence: Serbia
Website: http://www.clothesnetwork.com
Phone: 44 207 821 1182 **Email:** 36291@reference-encyclopedia-ai.net
City: London **State:** England **PC:** **Country: United Kingdom**
Year Established: 2011 **Status 2020:** Active
Industries: Big Data and Analytics for:, Application Program Interfaces (APIs) for:, ~ Fashion (16), Natural Language Processing for:, Business Software as a Service Apps (SaaS Apps) for:, Web

Company Name: Clothie A.I. Machine Vision
Description: The fastest way to find clothes that fit.
Website: http://clothie.cloud/
Phone: **Email:** daniel@clothie.co.uk
City: London **State:** England **PC:** **Country: United Kingdom**
Year Established: 2016 **Status 2020:** Active
Industries: Artificial Intelligence for:, E-Commerce for:, ~ Fashion (16), Web for:, Web

Company Name: cloud.IQ
Description: cloud.IQ is an AI and machine learning based automated conversion rate optimisation platform for e-commerce businesses.
Website: http://www.cloud-iq.com
Phone: **Email:** uk@cloud-iq.com
City: London **State:** England **PC:** **Country: United Kingdom**
Year Established: 2012 **Status 2020:** Active
Industries: Artificial Intelligence for:, E-Commerce for:, Business Software as a Service Apps (SaaS Apps)

Company Name: CloudNC
Description: CloudNC uses AI and cloud supercomputing to control CNC machines more efficiently than humans can.
Website: http://cloudnc.co.uk/
Phone: **Email:** theo@cloudnc.com
City: London **State:** England **PC:** **Country: United Kingdom**
Year Established: **Status 2020:** Active
Industries: Artificial Intelligence for:, Industrial Solutions for:, Machine Learning for:, ~ Manufacturing-Miscellaneous (34), ~ Social-Environmental-Physical-Engineering Sciences (55)

Company Name: CoControl
Description: CoControl provides the UK's first heating control and social metrics system, which is tailored.
Website: http://www.cocontrol.co.uk/
Phone: **Email:** contact@cocontrol.co.uk
City: London **State:** England **PC:** **Country: United Kingdom**
Year Established: 2014 **Status 2020:** Active
Industries: Application Services for:, ~ Energy and Utilities (14)

Company **Name:** Codec
Description: Codec provides artificial intelligence for Content Marketing.
Website: http://www.codec.ai
Phone: **Email:** info@codec.ai
City: London **State:** England **PC:** **Country: United Kingdom**
Year Established: **Status 2020:** Active
Industries: Analytics for:, Artificial Intelligence for:, Big Data and Analytics for:, ~ Social Media (54)

Company Name: Cognetivity Neuroscienc: Spain
Description: This company is a Platform technology for early, rapid and easy detection of dementia.
Website: http://www.cognetivity.com
Phone: 44 020 3002 3628 **Email:** info@cognetivity.com
City: London **State:** England **PC:** **Country: United Kingdom**
Year Established: 2013 **Status 2020:** Active
Industries: Artificial Intelligence for:, ~ Healthcare (20), ~ Healthcare (20)

Company Name: Cognio Digital
Description: A thoughtful web technology company. Web sites, web apps, A.I. and anything else that lives on your devices.
Website: http://www.cogniodigital.com
Phone: **Email:** hello@cogniodigital.com
City: London **State:** England **PC:** **Country: United Kingdom**
Year Established: **Status 2020:** Active
Industries: Artificial Intelligence for:, Application Services for:, Cyber Security

Company Name: Cognism
Description: Cognism combines company, people and event data in real-time, so B2B organizations can get lists of leads when they are most likely to buy.
Website: http://cognism.com
Phone: **Email:** joe.barron@cognism.com
City: London **State:** England **PC:** **Country: United Kingdom**
Year Established: **Status 2020:** Active
Industries: Analytics for:, Artificial Intelligence for:, ~ E-Commerce (12), ~ E-Commerce (12), ~ Media-Communications (41), Automation

Company Name: CognitionX
Description: CognitionX provides data experts, software developers, platform vendors, researchers and hardware.
Website: http://cognitionx.com/
Phone: **Email:** jobs@cognitionx.io
City: London **State:** England **PC:** **Country: United Kingdom**
Year Established: **Status 2020:** Active
Industries: Artificial Intelligence for:, Enterprise Application Services for:, ~ Manufacturing-Electronic (30), ~ Professional Services (48)

Company Name: Cognitiv
Description: Cognitiv is an artificial intelligence platform that automates knowledge extraction from legal data.
Website: http://www.cognitivplus.com
Phone: **Email:** info@cognitivplus.com
City: London **State:** England **PC:** **Country: United Kingdom**
Year Established: **Status 2020:** Active
Industries: Analytics for:, Artificial Intelligence for:, ~ Law-Legal Services (26)

Company Name: Cognitive Business
Description: Cognitive builds artificial intelligence solutions to help the world learn from its data
Website: http://cognitive.business
Phone: **Email:** hello@cognitive.business
City: London **State:** England **PC:** **Country: United Kingdom**
Year Established: 2018 **Status 2020:** Active
Industries: Artificial Intelligence for:, Machine Learning for:, ~ Energy and Utilities (14), ~ Energy and Utilities (14)

Company Name: Cognitive Finance Group
Description: An advisory and investment company specialised in Artificial Intelligence solutions for financial services.
Website: http://www.cognitivefinance.ai
Phone: **Email:** 36305@reference-encyclopedia-ai.net
City: London **State:** England **PC:** **Country: United Kingdom**
Year Established: 2016 **Status 2020:** Active
Industries: Artificial Intelligence for:, ~ Banking and Financial Markets-Services (7)

Company Name: Cognitive.Business
Description: Cognitive builds artificial intelligence solutions to help the world learn from its data
Website:
Phone: **Email:** 4936@reference-encyclopedia-ai.net
City: London **State:** England **PC:** **Country: United Kingdom**
Year Established: **Status 2020:** Active
Industries:

Company Name: Cognitochain
Description: Blockchain based digital lending SaaS
Website: http://cognitochain.io
Phone: **Email:** contact@cognitochain.io
City: London **State:** England **PC:** **Country: United Kingdom**
Year Established: **Status 2020:** Active
Industries: Artificial Intelligence for:, IT Managed Services for:, ~ Banking and Financial Markets-Services (7)

Company Name: CoMind
Description: Noninvasive neural technology
Website: http://www.comind.io
Phone: **Email:** hello@comind.io
City: London **State:** England **PC:** **Country: United Kingdom**
Year Established: 2017 **Status 2020:** Active
Industries: Artificial Intelligence for:, Machine Learning

Company Name: Comparesoft
Description: Your go-to place to shortlist & compare enterprise software. Driven by human & machine learning. Used by PwC, Honda & 8736 business: Spain
Website: http://comparesoft.com
Phone: **Email:** info@merciafund.co.uk
City: London **State:** England **PC:** **Country: United Kingdom**
Year Established: 2016 **Status 2020:** Active
Industries: Enterprise Application Services for:, Machine Learning for:, Web

Company Name: Compass News
Description: Compass News is a subscription-based journalism platform powered by an AI editor that makes you smarter, quicker.
Website: http://compassnews.co.uk/
Phone: **Email:** hello@compassnews.co.uk
City: London **State:** England **PC:** **Country: United Kingdom**
Year Established: 2016 **Status 2020:** Active
Industries: Artificial Intelligence for:, ~ Media-Communications (41), ~ Arts-Entertainment-Recreation (4), ~ Social Assistance-Non-Profits (53)

Company Name: CONCURED
Description: CONCURED uses Artificial Intelligence to show marketers exactly what topics drive engagement, and what to write about next.
Website: http://www.concured.com
Phone: 44 (0) 207 867 3773 **Email:** hello@concured.com
City: London **State:** England **PC:** **Country: United Kingdom**
Year Established: 2015 **Status 2020:** Active
Industries: Artificial Intelligence for:, ~ Media-Communications (41), Content

Company Name: Constellation AI
Description: Human-Centered AI
Website: http://constellation.ai/
Phone: **Email:** info@constellation.ai
City: London **State:** England **PC:** **Country: United Kingdom**
Year Established: **Status 2020:** Active
Industries: Artificial Intelligence for:, Machine Learning

Company Name: Context Scout
Description: A Content-Aware Web Browser for Next Generation Web Sear: Switzerland
Website: http://contextscout.com
Phone: **Email:** marc@contextscout.com
City: London **State:** England **PC:** **Country: United Kingdom**
Year Established: **Status 2020:** Active
Industries: Artificial Intelligence for:, Machine Learning for:, Natural Language Processing for:, Cyber Security for:, Content for:, Cyber Security for:, Cyber Security

Company Name: Contilio
Description: Contilio is an AI analytics platform empowering the construction industry to improve project performance and enable real-time payments.
Website: http://www.contilio.com
Phone: **Email:** contilio.official@contilio.com
City: London **State:** England **PC:** **Country: United Kingdom**
Year Established: 2018 **Status 2020:** Active
Industries: Analytics for:, Computer Vision for:, ~ Construction (10), Machine Learning for:, Business Software as a Service Apps (SaaS Apps)

Company Name: ContractPodAi
Description: ContractPodAi is one of the world's fastest growing AI based contract management solution providers.
Website: http://contractpod.com/
Phone: 44 (0) 203 735 5623 **Email:** sales@contractpod.com
City: London **State:** England **PC:** **Country: United Kingdom**
Year Established: 2012 **Status 2020:** Active
Industries: Analytics for:, Artificial Intelligence for:, IT Managed Services for:, Machine Learning

Company Name: Corax
Description: Cyber risk intelligence platform providing data and modelling on the cyber exposure of millions of companies worldwide.
Website: http://coraxcyber.com
Phone: (415)233-8402 **Email:** info@coraxcyber.com
City: London **State:** England **PC:** **Country: United Kingdom**
Year Established: 2013 **Status 2020:** Active
Industries: Artificial Intelligence for:, Cyber Security for:, IT Managed Services for:, Predictive Analytics

Company Name: CourtQuant
Description: CourtQuant is an AI platform that provides quantitative litigation risk assessment solutions for litigation funders.
Website: http://www.courtquant.com/
Phone: 44 (0) 7402 408871 **Email:** jm@courtquant.com
City: London **State:** England **PC:** **Country: United Kingdom**
Year Established: **Status 2020:** Active
Industries: Analytics for:, Artificial Intelligence for:, IT Managed Services for:, ~ Law-Legal Services (26), Predictive Analytics for:, Risk Management

Company Name: CPEC.ai
Description: Capital Project Effective Control powered by Artificial Intelligence
Website: http://www.cpec.ai
Phone: 44 20 3807 1662 **Email:** info@cpec.ai
City: London **State:** England **PC:** **Country: United Kingdom**
Year Established: **Status 2020:** Active
Industries: Artificial Intelligence for:, IT Infrastructure for:, Machine Learning for:, ~ Oil and Gas (43)

Company Name: Craft
Description: Data and analytics platform for professionals
Website: http://www.craft.co
Phone: **Email:** ilya@craft.co
City: London **State:** England **PC:** **Country: United Kingdom**
Year Established: **Status 2020:** Active
Industries: Analytics for:, Artificial Intelligence for:, IT Managed Services

Company Name: Creative AI
Description: Creative AI gives every business, big or small, the power of a dedicated marketing team.
Website: http://creativeai.co.uk
Phone: **Email:** hello@creativeai.co.uk
City: London **State:** England **PC:** **Country: United Kingdom**

Year Established: 2016 **Status 2020:** Active
Industries:

Company Name: CREID
Description: Central Real Estate Intelligence Database.
Website: http://www.creid.ai
Phone: 7507500000 **Email:** muller@capitalgrey.co.uk
City: London **State:** England **PC:** **Country: United Kingdom**
Year Established: **Status 2020:** Active
Industries: Artificial Intelligence for:, ~ Real Estate (49), Machine Learning

Company Name: Cricviz
Description: Cricviz helps to understand cricket in greater detail than ever before with depth analysis.
Website: http://cricviz.com
Phone: **Email:** marketing@cricviz.com
City: London **State:** England **PC:** **Country: United Kingdom**
Year Established: 2015 **Status 2020:** Active
Industries: Predictive Analytics for:, ~ Arts-Entertainment-Recreation (4)

Company Name: CrowdEmotion
Description: Artificial Intelligence with HEART.
Website: http://www.crowdemotion.co.uk/
Phone: **Email:** info@crowdemotion.co.uk
City: London **State:** England **PC:** **Country: United Kingdom**
Year Established: **Status 2020:** Active
Industries: Artificial Intelligence for:, ~ Automotive (5), Human Computer Interaction for:, Development and Test

Company Name: Crux AI
Description: Crux AI summarises visual content like images and videos
Website: http://cruxai.co
Phone: **Email:** ss@cruxai.co
City: London **State:** England **PC:** **Country: United Kingdom**
Year Established: 2019 **Status 2020:** Active
Industries: Artificial Intelligence for:, Computer Vision for:, ~ Arts-Entertainment-Recreation (4), ~ Social Assistance-Non-Profits (53)

Company Name: Crystal Apps Ltd.
Description: crystal is an AI assistant that allows users to interact with data as a team member.
Website: http://crystal.ai
Phone: **Email:** hello@crystal.io
City: London **State:** England **PC:** **Country: United Kingdom**
Year Established: 2015 **Status 2020:** Active
Industries: Artificial Intelligence for:, Computer Vision for:, Machine Learning for:, Natural Language Processing

Company Name: CUBE
Description: CUBE's AI-driven RegTech platform monitors regulatory change in real time, highlights areas of non-compliance, and enables remediation.
Website: http://www.cube.global
Phone: 44 7899 788116 **Email:** nicola.cowburn@cube.global
City: London **State:** England **PC:** **Country: United Kingdom**
Year Established: **Status 2020:** Active
Industries: Artificial Intelligence for:, Compliance for:, ~ Banking and Financial Markets-Services (7), IT Managed Services for:, Machine Learning for:, Risk Management

Company Name: Cube Intelligence
Description: Security and Investigations
Website: http://cubeint.io/
Phone: **Email:** 36357@reference-encyclopedia-ai.net
City: London **State:** England **PC:** **Country: United Kingdom**
Year Established: 2017 **Status 2020:** Active
Industries: Artificial Intelligence for:, ~ Automotive (5)

Company Name: Cumulus1
Description: IaaS
Website: http://www.cumulus.network
Phone: **Email:** contact@cumulus1.network
City: London **State:** England **PC:** **Country: United Kingdom**
Year Established: 2018 **Status 2020:** Active
Industries: Artificial Intelligence for:, Cloud for:, Machine Learning

Company Name: Currikula
Description: Currikula helps students get better grad: Spain
Website: http://currikula.com
Phone: **Email:** team@currikula.com
City: London **State:** England **PC:** **Country: United Kingdom**
Year Established: 2017 **Status 2020:** Active
Industries: Analytics for:, ~ Education (13), ~ Education (13), ~ Education (13), Natural Language Processing for:, Data Management

Company Name: Cursor Insight
Description: Cursor Insight is a software development company with many years of experience in human movement analysis.
Website: http://cursorinsight.com
Phone: **Email:** info@cursorinsight.com
City: London **State:** England **PC:** **Country: United Kingdom**
Year Established: 2013 **Status 2020:** Active
Industries: ~ Biotechnology (9), Cyber Security for:, Identity for:, Machine Learning

Company Name: CustomSell
Description: CustomSell Is A Fully-Automated Marketing Machine.
Website: http://meetcustomsell.com/
Phone: **Email:** support@meetcustomsell.com
City: London **State:** England **PC:** **Country: United Kingdom**
Year Established: 2015 **Status 2020:** Active
Industries: Artificial Intelligence

Company Name: Cvmat: Switzerland
Description: A revolutionary job platform that harnesses Artificial intelligence and complex Matching algorithms
Website: http://www.cvmatch.com
Phone: **Email:** admin@cvmatch.com
City: London **State:** England **PC:** **Country: United Kingdom**
Year Established: 2015 **Status 2020:** Active
Industries:

Company Name: Cyberlytic
Description: Cyberlytic's web application security software uses AI to deliver advanced threat detection and prioritisation of web-injection attacks.
Website: http://www.cyberlytic.com/
Phone: **Email:** info@cyberlytic.com
City: London **State:** England **PC:** **Country: United Kingdom**
Year Established: **Status 2020:** Active
Industries: Artificial Intelligence for:, Cyber Security for:, Machine Learning for:, Security

Company Name: CyberSparta
Description: CyberSparta provides IT network solutions.
Website: http://www.cybersparta.com/
Phone: **Email:** theteam@cybersparta.com
City: London **State:** England **PC:** **Country: United Kingdom**
Year Established: **Status 2020:** Active
Industries:

Company Name: Cybertonica
Description: Cybertonica uses Machine Learning and AI to manage risk and fraud, increasing trust and growing frictionless banking and m/e-payments.
Website: http://www.cybertonica.com/
Phone: **Email:** info@cybertonica.com
City: London **State:** England **PC:** **Country: United Kingdom**

Year Established: 2015 **Status 2020:** Active
Industries: Artificial Intelligence for:, ~ Banking and Financial Markets-Services (7), Security for:, Machine Learning for:, ~ Banking and Financial Markets-Services (7), Risk Management

Company Name: Cybertonica Ltd.
Description: Cybertonica provides a cloud risk intelligence hub to reduce basket drop-off and increase conversion for banks, PSPs and e-merchants.
Website: http://www.cybertonica.com/
Phone: **Email:** hlokhandwala@cybertonica.com
City: London **State:** England **Zip:** EC2A2BB **Country: United Kingdom**
Year Established: **Status 2020:** Active
Industries: Artificial Intelligence for:, ~ Banking and Financial Markets-Services (7), Business Intelligence for:, ~ Banking and Financial Markets-Services (678), ~ Gaming (689), ~ Hospitality (694), Compliance for:, ~ Banking and Financial Markets-Services (1288), ~ Gaming

Company Name: CYKEEP Ltd.
Description: CYKEEP Is Cyber Security Startup
Website: http://www.cykeep.com
Phone: **Email:** 4513@reference-encyclopedia-ai.net
City: London **State:** England **PC:** **Country: United Kingdom**
Year Established: **Status 2020:** Active
Industries: Artificial Intelligence for:, Cyber Security

Company Name: Cyra
Description: Cyra aiming to make the hiring process cost effective for the employers of small to medium businesses, by providing AI recruiting assistant.
Website: http://www.cyra.ai/
Phone: **Email:** hello@cyra.ai
City: London **State:** England **PC:** **Country: United Kingdom**
Year Established: 2016 **Status 2020:** Active
Industries: Artificial Intelligence for:, Machine Learning

Company Name: CyStellar
Description: CyStellar is a geospatial intelligence company on a mission to deliver real-time insights for the insurance sector.
Website: http://www.cystellar.com
Phone: 46 720 430314 **Email:** info@cystellar.com
City: London **State:** England **PC:** **Country: United Kingdom**
Year Established: 2017 **Status 2020:** Active
Industries: ~ Agriculture (3), ~ Agriculture (3), Big Data and Analytics for:, Blockchain for:, IT Managed Services for:, Machine Learning for:, Machine Learning for:, Business Software as a Service Apps (SaaS Apps)

Company Name: Cytora
Description: Cytora is an artificial intelligence company powering a new way for commercial insurers to target, select and price risk.
Website: http://www.cytora.com/
Phone: **Email:** contact@cytora.com
City: London **State:** England **PC:** **Country: United Kingdom**
Year Established: **Status 2020:** Active
Industries: Analytics for:, Artificial Intelligence for:, Big Data and Analytics for:, ~ Insurance (25), ~ Insurance (25), Risk Management

Company Name: Data Quarks Limited
Description: Online platform for democratising facts and information neutrality
Website: http://www.dataquarks.com
Phone: **Email:** info@dataquarks.com
City: London **State:** England **PC:** **Country: United Kingdom**
Year Established: **Status 2020:** Active
Industries: Artificial Intelligence for:, Machine Learning for:, Cyber Security

Company Name: Datasine
Description: Datasine's SaaS platform offers insights and scoring of ad content using AI and Psychology.
Website: http://datasine.com/
Phone: 44 79404 72935 **Email:** business@datasine.com
City: London **State:** England **PC:** **Country: United Kingdom**
Year Established: 2015 **Status 2020:** Active
Industries: IT Managed Services for:, Machine Learning for:, Business Software as a Service Apps (SaaS Apps)

Company Name: Decibel
Description: Decibel reveals exactly how users behave on websites & apps, making it easy for enterprise businesses to quantify and improve CX.
Website: www.decibelinsight.com/
Phone: **Email:** hello@decibelinsight.com
City: London **State:** England **PC:** **Country: United Kingdom**
Year Established: **Status 2020:** Active
Industries: Analytics for:, Artificial Intelligence for:, Enterprise Application Services for:, ~ Professional Services (48)

Company Name: DecisionForest
Description: AI Powered Financial Alternative Data Provider
Website: http://www.decisionforest.com/
Phone: **Email:** contact@decisionforest.com
City: London **State:** England **PC:** **Country: United Kingdom**
Year Established: **Status 2020:** Active
Industries: Artificial Intelligence for:, ~ Banking and Financial Markets-Services (7)

Company Name: Deep Index
Description: Data analytics, big data, and psychographics company that works with brands and governments to influence opinion.
Website: http://www.deepindex.co
Phone: **Email:** contact@deepindex.co
City: London **State:** England **PC:** **Country: United Kingdom**
Year Established: 2016 **Status 2020:** Active
Industries: Analytics for:, Big Data and Analytics for:, Databases for:, Predictive Analytics

Company Name: Deep Innovations
Description: Developing innovative home & commercial solutions based on advanced vision analytics, deep learning and artificial intelligence.
Website: http://www.deepinnovations.co.uk/
Phone: **Email:** info@deepinnovations.co.uk
City: London **State:** England **PC:** **Country: United Kingdom**
Year Established: **Status 2020:** Active
Industries: Artificial Intelligence for:, Machine Learning

Company Name: Deep Zen
Description: AI company focusing on audiobook production and voiceovers with an audiobook marketplace (audiowhale.com)
Website: http://deepzen.io
Phone: 44 796 2010996 **Email:** hello@deepzen.io
City: London **State:** England **PC:** **Country: United Kingdom**
Year Established: **Status 2020:** Active
Industries: Artificial Intelligence for:, IT Managed Services for:, Natural Language Processing

Company Name: DeepAR
Description: AR as a Service: Add 3D Face Masks, Lenses FX to any app with one simple SDK
Website: http://www.deepar.ai
Phone: **Email:** 36414@reference-encyclopedia-ai.net
City: London **State:** England **PC:** **Country: United Kingdom**
Year Established: 2014 **Status 2020:** Active
Industries:

Company Name: Deeper Insights
Description: Deeper Insights lead to bolder business decisions through applied data science using more of your data.
Website: http://www.deeperinsights.com
Phone: 44 207 129 7497 **Email:** sales@deeperinsights.com
City: London **State:** England **PC:** **Country: United Kingdom**
Year Established: 2014 **Status 2020:** Active
Industries: Analytics for:, Artificial Intelligence for:, Big Data and Analytics for:, Machine Learning for:, Natural Language Processing

Company Name: Deepfinity
Description: Deepfinity is an industry leader AI and automation for Prop-tech. Our Flagship product is the internal Parcel Tracker.
Website: http://www.parceltracker.com/internal-parcel-tracking
Phone: **Email:** info@deefinity.io
City: London **State:** England **PC:** **Country: United Kingdom**
Year Established: 2016 **Status 2020:** Active
Industries: Artificial Intelligence for:, IT Managed Services

Company Name: Deepmind
Description:
Website: https://deepmind.com/
Phone: **Email:** 27317@reference-encyclopedia-ai.net
City: London **State:** England **PC:** **Country: United Kingdom**
Year Established: **Status 2020:** Active
Industries:

Company Name: DeepMind
Description: Google DeepMind develops learning algorithms that use data or raw experience to better themselves.
Website: http://deepmind.com
Phone: **Email:** contact@deepmind.com
City: London **State:** England **PC:** **Country: United Kingdom**
Year Established: **Status 2020:** Active
Industries: Artificial Intelligence for:, Machine Learning for:, ~ Professional Services (48)

Company Name: Desig
Description: Fashion, Lifestyle
Website: http://www.designo.io
Phone: **Email:** connect@designo.io
City: London **State:** England **PC:** **Country: United Kingdom**
Year Established: **Status 2020:** Active
Industries: **Company Name:** Desktop Genetics
Description: Building an AI to re-engineer the human genome
Website: http://www.desktopgenetics.com
Phone: **Email:** info@desktopgenetics.com
City: London **State:** England **PC:** **Country: United Kingdom**
Year Established: **Status 2020:** Active
Industries: Artificial Intelligence for:, ~ Biotechnology (9), ~ Healthcare (20), ~ Professional Services (48)

Company Name: Devtech
Description: Devtech is a Professional Services company focused on cloud enablement solutions for Telcos, CSPs, ISVs and MSPs.
Website: http://devtechgroup.com
Phone: 44 (0)203 642 2163 **Email:** sales@devtechgroup.com
City: London **State:** England **PC:** **Country: United Kingdom**
Year Established: 2012 **Status 2020:** Active
Industries: Artificial Intelligence for:, Cloud for:, Cloud for:, Data Management for:, IT Managed Services

Company Name: DF2020 Limited
Description: Simplifying and streamlining the use of complex knowledge, across all digital touchpoints and devices.
Website: http://df2020.com
Phone: **Email:** info@df2020.com
City: London **State:** England **PC:** **Country: United Kingdom**
Year Established: 2014 **Status 2020:** Active
Industries: Artificial Intelligence for:, IT Managed Services for:, IT Managed Services

Company Name: Dhi
Description: Web applications built by AI (SIRI for building Web Applications)
Website: http://www.dhi.io/
Phone: **Email:** 36432@reference-encyclopedia-ai.net
City: London **State:** England **PC:** **Country: United Kingdom**
Year Established: 2015 **Status 2020:** Active
Industries: Artificial Intelligence for:, IT Managed Services for:, Web for:, Business Software as a Service Apps (SaaS Apps)

Company Name: Dialogue: Serbia
Description: Dialoguers is augmenting mental health therapists performance in the therapy room by using advanced digital tools and behavioural psychology
Website: http://dialoguers.com/
Phone: **Email:** info@dialoguers.com
City: London **State:** England **PC:** **Country: United Kingdom**
Year Established: 2018 **Status 2020:** Active
Industries: ~ Healthcare (20), Natural Language Processing

Company Name: Digital Catapult
Description: Digital Catapult drives early adoption of advanced digital technologies to grow the country's economy.
Website: http://digicatapult.org.uk/
Phone: **Email:** info@digicatapult.org.uk
City: London **State:** England **PC:** **Country: United Kingdom**
Year Established: 2013 **Status 2020:** Active
Industries: Artificial Intelligence for:, Augmented Reality for:, Blockchain for:, Cyber Security for:, IT Managed Services for:, Web for:, Internet of Things (IoT) for:, ~ Retail and Consumer Products (52), ~ Retail and Consumer Products (52), Virtual Reality (VR)

Company Name: Digital Insight
Description: Digital Insight provides a fully automated research solution that produces a report on an individual in five minutes.
Website: http://www.digital-insight.com/
Phone: **Email:** info@digital-insight.com
City: London **State:** England **PC:** **Country: United Kingdom**
Year Established: **Status 2020:** Active
Industries: Artificial Intelligence for:, Big Data and Analytics for:, IT Managed Services

Company Name: Digital Mycelium
Description: New Media | Digital Agency | Sustainability | Smart Cities | Blockchain | Artificial Intelligence
Website: http://digitalmycelium.com
Phone: (415) 914-5875 **Email:** connect@digitalmycelium.com
City: London **State:** England **PC:** **Country: United Kingdom**
Year Established: 2019 **Status 2020:** Active
Industries: Artificial Intelligence for:, IT Infrastructure for:, Machine Learning for:, ~ Construction (10), ~ Social-Environmental-Physical-Engineering Sciences (55), ~ Social-Environmental-Physical-Engineering Sciences (55), Web for:, Web

Company Name: Digital Startu: Palestine
Description: Digital Startups is dedicated to the 4 key Stakeholders in a successful Digital StartUp.
Website: http://www.digital-startup.com/
Phone: **Email:** andy@digital-startup.com
City: London **State:** England **PC:** **Country: United Kingdom**
Year Established: **Status 2020:** Active
Industries:

Company Name: Digital Surgery
Description: Digital Surgery is a privately-held pioneer in surgical artificial intelligence (AI), data and analytics, and digital education and training
Website: http://digitalsurgery.com/
Phone: **Email:** info@touchsurgery.com
City: London **State:** England **PC:** **Country: United Kingdom**
Year Established: 2013 **Status 2020:** Active
Industries: Artificial Intelligence for:, ~ Healthcare (20), ~ Healthcare (20)

Company Name: DigitalMR
Description: DigitalMR is a tech company that uses A.I. for customer insights
Website: http://www.digital-mr.com
Phone: **Email:** info@digital-mr.com
City: London **State:** England **PC:** **Country: United Kingdom**
Year Established: 2010 **Status 2020:** Active
Industries: Analytics for:, Artificial Intelligence for:, Big Data and Analytics for:, Machine Learning for:, Predictive Analytics for:, Business Software as a Service Apps (SaaS Apps)

Company Name: Dinabite
Description: Dinabite is a unique marketing tool for restaurant managers and a restaurant discovery tool for users.
Website: http://www.dinabite.ai
Phone: **Email:** investor@dinabite.ai
City: London **State:** England **PC:** **Country: United Kingdom**
Year Established: 2015 **Status 2020:** Active
Industries: Artificial Intelligence for:, ~ Food and Beverage (17), ~ Food and Beverage (17)

Company Name: Dinabite Limited
Description: Dinabite is a geolocation mobile app for restaurants and bars that works to attract, retain and interact with customers.
Website: http://www.dinabite.ai
Phone: **Email:** giuseppe@dinabite.ai
City: London **State:** England **PC:** **Country: United Kingdom**
Year Established: **Status 2020:** Active
Industries: Artificial Intelligence for:, ~ Food and Beverage (17), ~ Hospitality (23), ~ Media-Communications (41), ~ Food and Beverage (17)

Company Name: Disperse.io
Description: Computer vision to transform construction project delivery and on-site progress analys
Website: http://disperse.io
Phone: **Email:** amar@disperse.io
City: London **State:** England **PC:** **Country: United Kingdom**
Year Established: **Status 2020:** Active
Industries: Artificial Intelligence for:, Computer Vision for:, ~ Construction (10), IT Managed Services

Company Name: Dome
Description: Dome building the home intelligence that connects all your smart devices to make your life easier, improve your health, and much more.
Website: http://dome.ai
Phone: **Email:** team@vie.live
City: London **State:** England **PC:** **Country: United Kingdom**
Year Established: 2016 **Status 2020:** Active
Industries: Artificial Intelligence for:, ~ Healthcare (20), Internet of Things (IoT)

Company Name: Donaco
Description: In-browser web tool designed to revolutionise the donation industry, connecting charities and donors in new ways
Website: http://donaco.org.uk
Phone: **Email:** info@donaco.co
City: London **State:** England **PC:** **Country: United Kingdom**
Year Established: **Status 2020:** Active
Industries: ~ Media-Communications (41), Artificial Intelligence for:, ~ Social Assistance-Non-Profits (53)

Company Name: Doordeck
Description: SaaS smartphone-based access control, installed in under 15 minut: Spain
Website: http://doordeck.com/
Phone: **Email:** info@doordeck.com
City: London **State:** England **PC:** **Country: United Kingdom**
Year Established: **Status 2020:** Active
Industries: Artificial Intelligence for:, Cloud for:, ~ Telecommunications (56), Mobile for:, Security

Company Name: Dotspot
Description: Location based proximity meta-search engine and app powered by AI, VR/AR & Blockchain tech. for finding people, places services and products
Website: http://dotspot.online
Phone: **Email:** info@dotspot.online
City: London **State:** England **PC:** **Country: United Kingdom**
Year Established: **Status 2020:** Active
Industries: Artificial Intelligence for:, Big Data and Analytics for:, Data Management for:, E-Commerce for:, Predictive Analytics for:, ~ Media-Communications (41)

Company Name: DPI Partne: Serbia
Description: DPI Partners is a blockchain & IT consultancy that advice on aspects of IT, blockchain strategy, AI, smart contracts and distributed apps.
Website: http://dpipartners.com/
Phone: 44 (0)20 7871 5022 **Email:** info@dpipartners.co.uk
City: London **State:** England **PC:** **Country: United Kingdom**
Year Established: 2015 **Status 2020:** Active
Industries: Artificial Intelligence for:, Blockchain for:, IT Managed Services

Company Name: Drafter
Description: Drafter is an inbox assistant for sales people.
Website: http://drafterhq.com/
Phone: **Email:** foster@drafter.ema: Israel
City: London **State:** England **PC:** **Country: United Kingdom**
Year Established: 2015 **Status 2020:** Active
Industries: Artificial Intelligence for:, ~ Customer Relationship Management (11)

Company Name: Draper and Dash
Description: Draper & Dash is a provider of healthcare ML and AI driven patient flow, predictive analytics and insights platform in the UK, US and AUZ.
Website: http://www.draperanddash.com/
Phone: (845) 094-1962 **Email:** info@draperanddash.com
City: London **State:** England **PC:** **Country: United Kingdom**
Year Established: 2015 **Status 2020:** Active
Industries: Analytics for:, Artificial Intelligence for:, Data Management for:, ~ Healthcare (20)

Company Name: Drayson Technologies Group
Description: An IoT platform company using innovative wireless charging technology & machine learning software to create smart sensor networks
Website: http://www.draysontechnologies.com/
Phone: **Email:** info@draysontechnologies.com
City: London **State:** England **PC:** **Country: United Kingdom**
Year Established: **Status 2020:** Active
Industries: Artificial Intelligence for:, ~ Energy and Utilities (14), ~ Manufacturing-Electronic (30), ~ Manufacturing-Electronic (30), ~ Professional Services (48)

Company Name: Dressipi
Description: The world's only Fashion Prediction Platform, accelerating fashion retailers to be predictive & give customers the best possible experience.
Website: http://dressipi.com/
Phone: **Email:** info@dressipi.com
City: London **State:** England **PC:** **Country: United Kingdom**
Year Established: 2011 **Status 2020:** Active
Industries:

Company Name: Drone Space AI.
Description: Platform based AI for unmanned aerial and ground vehicles.
Website: http://dronespaceai.com
Phone: **Email:** arshia@dronespaceai.com
City: London **State:** England **PC:** **Country: United Kingdom**
Year Established: **Status 2020:** Active
Industries: Artificial Intelligence for:, ~ Transportation and Logistics (57), Machine Learning

Company Name: DueDil
Description: DueDil is the largest source of private company information in the UK & Ireland. It helps companies find new opportunities & mitigate risk.
Website: www.duedil.com
Phone: **Email:** enterprise@duedil.com
City: London **State:** England **PC:** **Country: United Kingdom**
Year Established: **Status 2020:** Active
Industries: Analytics for:, Artificial Intelligence for:, Compliance for:, Data Management for:, IT Managed Services for:, ~ Media-Communications (41), IT Managed Services

Company Name: DVELP Ltd
Description: DVELP is a cloud software product and consultancy company that leads change in the contact centre industry.
Website: http://www.dvelp.co.uk
Phone: 44 20 31 37 63 39 **Email:** engage@dvelp.co.uk
City: London **State:** England **PC:** **Country: United Kingdom**
Year Established: 2015 **Status 2020:** Active
Industries: Robotics

Company Name: Dynamify
Description: All-in-one platform using technology, data, and AI to enhance service delivery and marg: India
Website: http://dynamify.com
Phone: **Email:** 36464@reference-encyclopedia-ai.net
City: London **State:** England **PC:** **Country: United Kingdom**
Year Established: 2015 **Status 2020:** Active
Industries: Application Services for:, Artificial Intelligence for:, Computer Vision for:, Enterprise Application Services for:, Web for:, Machine Learning for:, Mobile for:, Business Software as a Service Apps (SaaS Apps)

Company Name: Eblur
Description: Eblur provides access to an online AI coaching companion.
Website: http://www.eblur.co.uk/
Phone: **Email:** 36467@reference-encyclopedia-ai.net
City: London **State:** England **PC:** **Country: United Kingdom**
Year Established: 2016 **Status 2020:** Active
Industries: Artificial Intelligence for:, Robotics for:, ~ Education (13)

Company **Name:** Echobox
Description: We are building the world's first artificial intelligence that understands the meaning of content.
Website: http://www.echobox.com/
Phone: **Email:** hello@echobox.com
City: London **State:** England **PC:** **Country: United Kingdom**
Year Established: **Status 2020:** Active
Industries: Artificial Intelligence for:, Big Data and Analytics for:, Digital Media for:, Machine Learning for:, ~ Media-Communications (41), ~ Media-Communications (41), ~ Social Media (54)

Company Name: eCUORE
Description: Next Generation ECG real-time monitoring and alerting solution using Artificial Intelligence""
Website: http://www.ecuore.org
Phone: 40724354594 **Email:** contact@ecuore.org
City: London **State:** England **PC:** **Country: United Kingdom**
Year Established: **Status 2020:** Active
Industries: Artificial Intelligence for:, ~ Biotechnology (9), ~ Healthcare (20)

Company Name: EDGE AI Technologies
Description: AI Software Development
Website: http://www.edge-ai.net
Phone: **Email:** s@edge-ai.net
City: London **State:** England **PC:** **Country: United Kingdom**
Year Established: 2019 **Status 2020:** Active
Industries: Analytics for:, Artificial Intelligence for:, Big Data and Analytics for:, ~ Banking and Financial Markets-Services (7), IT Managed Services for:, Predictive Analytics

Company Name: Edgify
Description: Edgify has been developing its self training AI capabilities.
Website: http://www.edgify.ai/
Phone: **Email:** 28465@reference-encyclopedia-ai.net
City: London **State:** England **PC:** **Country: United Kingdom**
Year Established: 2015 **Status 2020:** Active
Industries: Artificial Intelligence for:, ~ Education (13), ~ Healthcare (20)

Company Name: EditorEye
Description: EditorEye is an executive intelligence company.
Website: http://www.editoreye.com
Phone: (208) 080-9146 **Email:** info@editoreye.com
City: London **State:** England **PC:** **Country: United Kingdom**
Year Established: 2014 **Status 2020:** Active
Industries: Business Intelligence for:, Cloud for:, Application Services

Company Name: Eduvee
Description: Eduvee is the brainchild of engineering graduates who want to bring education into the digital age.
Website: http://www.eduvee.com
Phone: **Email:** contact@eduvee.com
City: London **State:** England **PC:** **Country: United Kingdom**
Year Established: **Status 2020:** Active
Industries: Artificial Intelligence for:, ~ Education (13), ~ Education (13)

Company Name: Eigen Technologies
Description: Eigen is a research-driven AI company specialising in NLP for businesses in finance, law and professional services.
Website: http://www.eigentech.com/
Phone: 44 (0)74 9619 6888 **Email:** contact@eigentech.com
City: London **State:** England **PC:** **Country: United Kingdom**
Year Established: **Status 2020:** Active
Industries: Artificial Intelligence for:, Business Applications for:, Data Management for:, Machine Learning for:, Natural Language Processing

Company Name: Elastacloud
Description: Elastacloud are a Cloud Architecture and Data Science Consultancy who specialise in bringing intelligence to your data.
Website: http://www.elastacloud.com
Phone: (44) 020 7859 4852 **Email:** london@elastacloud.com
City: London **State:** England **PC:** **Country: United Kingdom**
Year Established: 2011 **Status 2020:** Active
Industries: Artificial Intelligence for:, Big Data and Analytics for:, IT Managed Services for:, IT Managed Services

Company Name: Elegans.io
Description: Artificial Intelligence Data Products
Website: http://elegans.io
Phone: **Email:** info@elegans.io
City: London **State:** England **PC:** **Country: United Kingdom**
Year Established: **Status 2020:** Active
Industries:

Company Name: Eligible
Description: Eligible is a digital mortgage platform that helping mortgage brokers and lenders catapult themselves into the digital age.
Website: http://eligible.ai/
Phone: **Email:** hello@eligible.ai
City: London **State:** England **PC:** **Country: United Kingdom**
Year Established: **Status 2020:** Active
Industries: Artificial Intelligence for:, ~ Banking and Financial Markets-Services (7), ~ Banking and Financial Markets-Services (7)

Company Name: Elixivity
Description: SaaS, AI, B2B, B2C
Website: http://elixivity.com
Phone: **Email:** hello@elixivity.com
City: London **State:** England **PC:** **Country: United Kingdom**
Year Established: 2020 **Status 2020:** Active
Industries: Artificial Intelligence for:, Business Applications for:, Business Applications for:, Machine Learning for:, Business Software as a Service Apps (SaaS Apps) for:, Speech Recognition

Company Name: Elliptic
Description: Preventing, Detecting, And Pursuing Criminal Activity In Cryptocurrencies.
Website: http://www.elliptic.co
Phone: 44 20 7193 4752 **Email:** hello@elliptic.co
City: London **State:** England **PC:** **Country: United Kingdom**
Year Established: **Status 2020:** Active
Industries: Artificial Intelligence for:, ~ Banking and Financial Markets-Services (7), Blockchain for:, ~ Banking and Financial Markets-Services (7)

Company Name: Elpis Investments
Description: The first AI crypto-assets Investment Fund, that combines traditional Hedge Funds with latest innovative technologies & new business model
Website: http://elpisinvestments.com/
Phone: **Email:** 36494@reference-encyclopedia-ai.net
City: London **State:** England **PC:** **Country: United Kingdom**
Year Established: 2017 **Status 2020:** Active
Industries: Artificial Intelligence for:, ~ Banking and Financial Markets-Services (7)

Company Name: Ember
Description: Ember is a software platform to automate the accounting process for SMEs.
Website: http://ember.co/
Phone: **Email:** aaron@ember.co
City: London **State:** England **PC:** **Country: United Kingdom**
Year Established: 2019 **Status 2020:** Active
Industries: Finance and Accounting for:, ~ Banking and Financial Markets-Services (7), ~ Banking and Financial Markets-Services (7), Machine Learning for:, Business Software as a Service Apps (SaaS Apps)

Company Name: Emerge
Description: Emerge helps insurance companies to make money from insurance operations.
Website: http://www.emergeml.com/
Phone: **Email:** 36498@reference-encyclopedia-ai.net
City: London **State:** England **PC:** **Country: United Kingdom**
Year Established: 2012 **Status 2020:** Active
Industries: Machine Learning

Company Name: em: Italy
Description: Time Management AI and Smartwatch Company
Website: http://ownemit.com/
Phone: 44 7472508476 **Email:** team@ownemit.com
City: London **State:** England **PC:** **Country: United Kingdom**
Year Established: **Status 2020:** Active
Industries: Artificial Intelligence for:, ~ Manufacturing-Electronic (30), Predictive Analytics for:, Application Services for:, ~ Healthcare (20)

Company Name: Emotech LTD
Description: Emotech is a London-based AI startup aiming to redefine the relationship between humans and technology.
Website: http://heyolly.com/
Phone: **Email:** info@emotech.co
City: London **State:** England **PC:** **Country: United Kingdom**
Year Established: **Status 2020:** Active
Industries: Artificial Intelligence for:, ~ Manufacturing-Electronic (30), Robotics

Company Name: Enabling Tech Capital
Description: Where Smart Money Meets Intelligent Innovation
Website: http://www.enablingtechcapital.com
Phone: **Email:** info@enablingtechcapital.com
City: London **State:** England **PC:** **Country: United Kingdom**
Year Established: 2016 **Status 2020:** Active
Industries: Artificial Intelligence for:, ~ Banking and Financial Markets-Services (7), IT Managed Services

Company Name: Enforcd
Description: Enforcd is a global regulatory intelligence platform that helps banks and others stay up to date with regulatory change and identify risks.
Website: http://www.enforcd.com
Phone: **Email:** info@enforcd.com
City: London **State:** England **PC:** **Country: United Kingdom**
Year Established: **Status 2020:** Active
Industries: Artificial Intelligence for:, Compliance for:, ~ Education (13), ~ Education (13), ~ Banking and Financial Markets-Services (7), IT Managed Services for:, Machine Learning for:, Risk Management

Company Name: ENIAN
Description: Deal acceleration platform for energy professionals.
Website: http://www.enian.co/
Phone: 44 (0) 7742 434924 **Email:** support@enian.co
City: London **State:** England **PC:** **Country: United Kingdom**
Year Established: 2015 **Status 2020:** Active
Industries: Analytics for:, Machine Learning for:, ~ Energy and Utilities (14), Business Software as a Service Apps (SaaS Apps)

Company Name: EnigmaMS
Description: Intelligent deep science platform for the storage and analysis of data providing technology and knowledge to create science autonomously
Website: http://enigma-ms.tech
Phone: **Email:** djb@enigma-ms.tech
City: London **State:** England **PC:** **Country: United Kingdom**
Year Established: **Status 2020:** Active
Industries: Analytics for:, Artificial Intelligence for:, Big Data and Analytics for:, ~ Manufacturing-Petroleum-Coal-Chemicals-Plastics-Rubber (37), Automation

Company Name: Enterprise Bot
Description: Enterprise Bot provide banks with a powerful AI-powered customer relationship tool to enhance customer experience.
Website: http://www.enterprisebot.org/
Phone: 41-779815453 **Email:** hr@enterprisebot.org
City: London **State:** England **PC:** **Country: United Kingdom**
Year Established: **Status 2020:** Active
Industries: Artificial Intelligence for:, Enterprise Application Services for:, ~ Media-Communications (41)

Company Name: EnVsion
Description: AI Platform
Website: http://envsion.io
Phone: **Email:** hello@envsion.io
City: London **State:** England **PC:** **Country: United Kingdom**
Year Established: 2020 **Status 2020:** Active
Industries:

Company Name: EQL
Description: HealthTech
Website: http://eql.ai
Phone: **Email:** info@eql.ai
City: London **State:** England **PC:** **Country: United Kingdom**
Year Established: 2018 **Status 2020:** Active
Industries: Artificial Intelligence for:, ~ Healthcare (20), ~ Healthcare (20), ~ Healthcare (20)

Company Name: Ernest
Description: Ernest a personal Banker for All powered by Artificial Intelligence: a chatbot that answers questions, gives insights & forecasts issues.
Website: http://ernest.ai
Phone: **Email:** hello@ernest.ai
City: London **State:** England **PC:** **Country: United Kingdom**
Year Established: **Status 2020:** Active
Industries: Artificial Intelligence for:, ~ Banking and Financial Markets-Services (7), Machine Learning for:, Finance and Accounting

Company Name: Esplorio
Description: Esplorio uses social data and our iOS app to create a digital travel journal that you can use to re-live and share your adventures.
Website: http://esplorio.com
Phone: **Email:** hello@esplor.io
City: London **State:** England **PC:** **Country: United Kingdom**
Year Established: **Status 2020:** Active
Industries: Analytics for:, Artificial Intelligence for:, ~ Travel and Transportation (58)

Company Name: Essencient
Description: Essencient provides application of natural language processing technology to text analysis.
Website: http://www.essencient.com
Phone: **Email:** 36519@reference-encyclopedia-ai.net
City: London **State:** England **PC:** **Country: United Kingdom**
Year Established: 2015 **Status 2020:** Active
Industries: Natural Language Processing for:, Data Management

Company Name: EVA.AI
Description: Where Recruitment Where Recruitment Happens
Website: http://www.eva.ai
Phone: **Email:** charlie@eva.ai
City: London **State:** England **PC:** **Country: United Kingdom**
Year Established: **Status 2020:** Active
Industries: Artificial Intelligence for:, ~ Human Resources (24), Machine Learning for:, ~ Human Resources (24)

Company **Name:** Evolution AI
Description: Evolution AI works with enterprises to uncover value in data and develop a natural language processing application.
Website: http://evolution.ai
Phone: **Email:** hello@evolution.ai
City: London **State:** England **PC:** **Country: United Kingdom**
Year Established: 2015 **Status 2020:** Active
Industries: Artificial Intelligence for:, Big Data and Analytics for:, IT Managed Services for:, Machine Learning for:, Natural Language Processing

Company Name: EY
Description:
Website: http://www.ey.com
Phone: 801 805-0300 **Email:** 12642@reference-encyclopedia-ai.net
City: London **State:** England **Zip:** SE1 2DA **Country: United Kingdom**
Year Established: **Status 2020:** Active
Industries:

Company Name: EyeQuant
Description: EyeQuant is a neuromarketing SaaS that predicts within seconds how users are going to look at web & mobile designs.
Website: http://eyequant.com
Phone: 49 30 609899795 **Email:** contact@eyequant.com
City: London **State:** NDS **PC:** **Country:**
Year Established: **Status 2020:** Active
Industries: ~ Media-Communications (41), Analytics for:, Artificial Intelligence

Company Name: Fabula AI Limited
Description: Solving fake news, for good
Website: http://www.fabula.ai/
Phone: **Email:** info@fabula.ai
City: London **State:** England **PC:** **Country: United Kingdom**
Year Established: **Status 2020:** Active
Industries: Artificial Intelligence

Company Name: FaceSoft
Description: Real faces for all realiti: Spain
Website: http://facesoft.org/
Phone: **Email:** info@facesoft.co.uk
City: London **State:** England **PC:** **Country: United Kingdom**
Year Established: **Status 2020:** Active
Industries: Artificial Intelligence for:, Machine Learning

Company Name: Factmata
Description: Factmata is an artificial intelligence for automated content scoring and verification.
Website: http://www.factmata.com
Phone: **Email:** info@factmata.com
City: London **State:** England **PC:** **Country: United Kingdom**
Year Established: **Status 2020:** Active
Industries: Analytics for:, ~ Banking and Financial Markets-Services (129), ~ E-Commerce (134), ~ Government (141), ~ Healthcare (142), ~ High Tech (143), ~ Human Resources (146), ~ Peer to Peer (166), ~ Politics (169), ~ Social Media (176), Application Program Interfaces for

Company Name: Faculty Science
Description: Faculty Science provides data science and engineering training services.
Website: http://faculty.ai/
Phone: 44 20 3637 9415 **Email:** info@faculty.ai
City: London **State:** England **PC:** **Country: United Kingdom**
Year Established: 2014 **Status 2020:** Active
Industries: Artificial Intelligence for:, IT Managed Services for:, Machine Learning

Company Name: Falanx Group Ltd
Description: Falanx Group Ltd is a provider of various security and intelligence services to blue chip and government clients worldwide.
Website: http://www.falanxgroup.com/contact-us/
Phone: **Email:** info@falanxgroup.com
City: London **State:** England **PC:** **Country: United Kingdom**
Year Established: 2012 **Status 2020:** Active
Industries: Application Services for:, Security

Company Name: Fantoo
Description: Fantoo is a software company offering a personal intelligence engine for email and messaging platforms.
Website: http://www.fantoo.net
Phone: **Email:** SayHi@fantoo.net
City: London **State:** England **PC:** **Country: United Kingdom**
Year Established: **Status 2020:** Active
Industries:

Company Name: FeedbackRig
Description: FeedbackRig is a one-stop solution for gathering actionable feedback from your customers to increase customer satisfaction and retention.
Website: http://feedbackrig.com
Phone: **Email:** info@feedbackrig.com
City: London **State:** England **PC:** **Country: United Kingdom**
Year Established: 2017 **Status 2020:** Active
Industries: ~ Customer Relationship Management (11), Natural Language Processing for:, Business Software as a Service Apps (SaaS Apps)

Company Name: FeedForward
Description: FeedForward is an artificial intelligence company.
Website: http://www.feedforwardai.com/
Phone: **Email:** hello@feedforwardai.com
City: London **State:** England **PC:** **Country: United Kingdom**

Year Established: 2017 **Status 2020:** Active
Industries: Artificial Intelligence

Company Name: Felcana
Description: Felcana is a Digital Pet Health Platform of intelligent pet care products. Helping you track, monitor & understand your dog or cat's needs.
Website: http://felcana.com/
Phone: 44 (0) 20 3621 5555 **Email:** info@felcana.com
City: London **State:** England **PC:** **Country: United Kingdom**
Year Established: 2016 **Status 2020:** Active
Industries: Application Services for:, ~ Retail and Consumer Products (52), ~ Life Sciences (27)

Company Name: Felix Ma:Thailand
Description: Felix Math is an online tutoring app powered by Artificial Intelligence.
Website: http://felixmath.com/
Phone: **Email:** hi@usefelix.com
City: London **State:** England **PC:** **Country: United Kingdom**
Year Established: 2016 **Status 2020:** Active
Industries: Application Services for:, Artificial Intelligence for:, ~ Education (13), Web for:, Application Services

Company Name: Filament AI
Description: Filament helps clients to build proprietary AI capability within their organisation, through consultancy, solutions and tooling
Website: http://www.filament.ai
Phone: 0203 176 1267 **Email:** hello@filament.ai
City: London **State:** England **PC:** **Country: United Kingdom**
Year Established: 2016 **Status 2020:** Active
Industries: Artificial Intelligence for:, Machine Learning

Company Name: Filtered
Description: Filtered is the world's leading learning recommendation platform
Website: http://filtered.com/
Phone: **Email:** vinit@filtered.com
City: London **State:** England **PC:** **Country: United Kingdom**
Year Established: **Status 2020:** Active
Industries: Artificial Intelligence for:, ~ Education (13), ~ Education (13), Enterprise Application Services for:, ~ Human Resources (24), Web for:, Machine Learning for:, ~ Professional Services (48), ~ Social-Environmental-Physical-Engineering Sciences (55), ~ Education (1

Company Name: Financial Network Analytics
Description: The Standard for Graph Analytics in Finance
Website: http://www.fna.fi
Phone: (917) 907-2182 **Email:** info@fna.fi
City: London **State:** England **PC:** **Country: United Kingdom**
Year Established: **Status 2020:** Active
Industries: Analytics for:, Artificial Intelligence for:, Data Management for:, Enterprise Application Services for:, Security for:, ~ Banking and Financial Markets-Services (7), Risk Management

Company Name: Fincloud
Description: Enterprise integration in the cloud
Website: http://fincloud.io/
Phone: 44 207 099 8520 **Email:** sales@fincloud.io
City: London **State:** England **PC:** **Country: United Kingdom**
Year Established: 2017 **Status 2020:** Active
Industries: Artificial Intelligence for:, Automation for:, Enterprise Application Services for:, ~ Banking and Financial Markets-Services (7), ~ Banking and Financial Markets-Services (7), Automation for:, Natural Language Processing for:, Enterprise Application Services fo

Company Name: FindTheRipple
Description: FindTheRipple is a real-time platform supporting brands, agencies, and editors to react at a timely moment.
Website: http://www.findtheripple.com
Phone: 44 7765517931 **Email:** info@findtheripple.com
City: London **State:** England **PC:** **Country: United Kingdom**
Year Established: 2014 **Status 2020:** Active
Industries: Analytics for:, Artificial Intelligence for:, Predictive Analytics for:, Compute for:, Web for:, ~ Social Assistance-Non-Profits (53), ~ Social Assistance-Non-Profits (53), ~ Social Assistance-Non-Profits (53)

Company Name: FinGenius
Description: FinGenius is a technology company that develops artificial intelligence and natural language processing solutions for financial institutes.
Website: http://www.fingenius.com
Phone: **Email:** start@fingenius.com
City: London **State:** England **PC:** **Country: United Kingdom**
Year Established: **Status 2020:** Active
Industries: Artificial Intelligence for:, Big Data and Analytics for:, Enterprise Application Services for:, ~ Banking and Financial Markets-Services (7), Natural Language Processing for:, ~ Life Sciences (27)

Company Name: Finlight.com
Description: AI-based asset management SaaS platform
Website: http://www.finlight.com
Phone: **Email:** contact@finlight.com
City: London **State:** England **PC:** **Country: United Kingdom**
Year Established: 2016 **Status 2020:** Active
Industries: Artificial Intelligence for:, ~ Banking and Financial Markets-Services (7), ~ Banking and Financial Markets-Services (7), Compute for:, Business Software as a Service Apps (SaaS Apps)

Company Name: FintechOS
Description: Innovation acceleration technology designed for financial sector
Website: http://www.fintechos.com
Phone: 40 748042554 **Email:** marketing@fintechos.com
City: London **State:** England **PC:** **Country: United Kingdom**
Year Established: **Status 2020:** Active
Industries: Artificial Intelligence for:, ~ Banking and Financial Markets-Services (7), IT Managed Services for:, ~ Banking and Financial Markets-Services (7)

Company Name: Firedrop
Description: The world's most advanced artificial intelligence website builder - uniquely designed sites in 60 seconds
Website: http://firedrop.ai
Phone: **Email:** directors@firedrop.ai
City: London **State:** England **PC:** **Country: United Kingdom**
Year Established: **Status 2020:** Active
Industries: Artificial Intelligence for:, ~ Professional Services (48), Cyber Security

Company Name: Fleksy Keyboard
Description: Fleksy Keyboard is one of world's top 5 input method technologies company
Website: http://www.fleksy.com/
Phone: **Email:** 36579@reference-encyclopedia-ai.net
City: London **State:** England **PC:** **Country: United Kingdom**
Year Established: 2015 **Status 2020:** Active
Industries:

Company Name: Flexciton
Description: Flexciton is building powerful cloud-based production planning and scheduling technology for the manufacturing industry using A.I.
Website: http://www.flexciton.com/
Phone: **Email:** info@flexciton.com
City: London **State:** England **PC:** **Country: United Kingdom**

Year Established: 2016 **Status 2020:** Active
Industries: Artificial Intelligence for:, Industrial Solutions for:, Automation for:, Business Software as a Service Apps (SaaS Apps)

Company Name: Flock Ltd.
Description: Flock is a London-based, VC- and government-backed insurtech company building a Big Data driven risk intelligence platform for drones.
Website: http://www.flockcover.com/
Phone: 44 (0) 1234 480260 **Email:** hello@flockcover.com
City: London **State:** England **PC:** **Country: United Kingdom**
Year Established: 2015 **Status 2020:** Active
Industries: Analytics for:, Artificial Intelligence for:, Big Data and Analytics

Company Name: fluently
Description: Translation Infrastructure On Demand
Website: http://www.fluently.io
Phone: **Email:** hello@fluently.io
City: London **State:** England **PC:** **Country: United Kingdom**
Year Established: **Status 2020:** Active
Industries: Artificial Intelligence for:, Enterprise Application Services

Company Name: Fluidly
Description: Fluidly is fundamentally rethinking the way businesses plan and manage cashflow, using data science, accounting domain expertise.
Website: http://fluidly.com
Phone: (44)2076111001 **Email:** info@fluidly.com
City: London **State:** England **PC:** **Country: United Kingdom**
Year Established: 2016 **Status 2020:** Active
Industries: Finance and Accounting for:, Business Applications for:, ~ Banking and Financial Markets-Services (7), Machine Learning

Company Name: Fluxifi
Description: Easy to use social search & analysis platform, with Twitter firehose and own NLP for language detection & accurate sentiment scoring.
Website: http://www.fluxifi.com
Phone: 44 7825123266 **Email:** chris@fluxifi.com
City: London **State:** England **PC:** **Country: United Kingdom**
Year Established: 2013 **Status 2020:** Active
Industries: Analytics for:, Artificial Intelligence for:, Big Data and Analytics for:, ~ Social Assistance-Non-Profits (53)

Company **Name:** FNA
Description: FNA is a deep technology analytics company that offers financial system services.
Website: http://www.fna.fi
Phone: 44 203 538 6505 **Email:** info@fna.fi
City: London **State:** England **PC:** **Country: United Kingdom**
Year Established: 2013 **Status 2020:** Active
Industries: Analytics for:, Artificial Intelligence for:, Data Management for:, Enterprise Application Services for:, Security for:, ~ Banking and Financial Markets-Services (7), Risk Management

Company Name: Focaldata
Description: Marketing Intelligence 2.0
Website: http://www.focaldata.com/
Phone: **Email:** hello@focaldata.com
City: London **State:** England **PC:** **Country: United Kingdom**
Year Established: 2016 **Status 2020:** Active
Industries: Learning and Marketing Communications Services (MarComm) for:, Predictive Analytics

Company Name: Foorme AI
Description: The app that combines nutritional science with AI to recommend your next meal, exactly when you need it.
Website: http://www.foorme.com/
Phone: **Email:** ben@foorme.com
City: London **State:** England **PC:** **Country: United Kingdom**
Year Established: 2018 **Status 2020:** Active
Industries: Application Services for:, Artificial Intelligence for:, ~ Healthcare (20)

Company Name: Forcive
Description: Forcive is a big data platform designed to capture and operationalize any live data at extreme scale.
Website: http://www.forcive.com
Phone: 44 (0) 207 6085067 **Email:** gabriel.dedominicis@forcive.com
City: London **State:** England **PC:** **Country: United Kingdom**
Year Established: **Status 2020:** Active
Industries: Analytics for:, Artificial Intelligence for:, Big Data and Analytics for:, Cloud for:, Cloud for:, Machine Learning for:, Predictive Analytics for:, Compute for:, Data Management

Company Name: Fortuitap: Palestine
Description: Extensive use of Artificial Intelligence in order to produce truly innovative software products that solve real-world problems.
Website: http://www.fortuitapps.com
Phone: **Email:** support@fortuitapps.com
City: London **State:** England **PC:** **Country: United Kingdom**
Year Established: **Status 2020:** Active
Industries: Artificial Intelligence for:, ~ Banking and Financial Markets-Services (7), ~ Education (13), ~ Professional Services (48), Machine Learning for:, Natural Language Processing

Company Name: FOSHO
Description: A machine learning based price personalisation product for online retaile: Serbia
Website: http://fosho.co.in/demo/product-details.php
Phone: **Email:** contact@ffosho.com
City: London **State:** England **PC:** **Country: United Kingdom**
Year Established: 2015 **Status 2020:** Active
Industries: E-Commerce for:, Enterprise Application Services for:, Machine Learning

Company Name: Fractal Labs
Description: Fractal powers smart SME banking.
Website: http://www.askfractal.com
Phone: **Email:** info@fractal-labs.com
City: London **State:** England **PC:** **Country: United Kingdom**
Year Established: **Status 2020:** Active
Industries: Analytics for:, Artificial Intelligence for:, Machine Learning for:, ~ Professional Services (48)

Company Name: Fractal Logistics
Description: Fractal Logistics is an ocean freight analytics company, reinventing age old industries with big data and machine learning.
Website: http://fraclog.co/
Phone: **Email:** contact@fraclog.co
City: London **State:** England **PC:** **Country: United Kingdom**
Year Established: 2017 **Status 2020:** Active
Industries: Analytics for:, Artificial Intelligence for:, ~ Automotive (5), IT Managed Services

Company Name: Fraugster
Description: Fraugster is a German-Israeli anti-fraud company that uses artificial intelligence to eliminate fraud and increase customers' profits.
Website: http://fraugster.com/
Phone: **Email:** 36594@reference-encyclopedia-ai.net
City: London **State:** England **PC:** **Country: United Kingdom**
Year Established: 2014 **Status 2020:** Active
Industries:

Company Name: Fresh Relevance
Description: The Personalization Platform to Boost ROI. Built to Help Marketers Get Their Jobs Done..
Website: http://www.freshrelevance.com
Phone: 44 23 8011 9750 **Email:** hello@freshrelevance.com
City: London **State:** England **PC:** **Country: United Kingdom**

Year Established: **Status 2020:** Active
Industries: Analytics for:, Artificial Intelligence for:, Big Data and Analytics for:, E-Commerce for:, ~ Media-Communications (41), ~ Media-Communications (41), ~ Media-Communications (41), Compute

Company Name: FriendlyScore
Description: Open Banking Solutions for fair and responsible lending
Website: http://www.friendlyscore.com/
Phone: **Email:** info@friendlyscore.com
City: London **State:** England **PC:** **Country: United Kingdom**
Year Established: 2014 **Status 2020:** Active
Industries: Artificial Intelligence for:, Big Data and Analytics for:, ~ Banking and Financial Markets-Services (7), IT Managed Services

Company Name: Funding Options
Description: Funding Options uses modern web technology to help SMEs to find the right finance.
Website: http://www.fundingoptions.com
Phone: 0333 344 1015 **Email:** info@fundingoptions.com
City: London **State:** England **PC:** **Country: United Kingdom**
Year Established: **Status 2020:** Active
Industries: Artificial Intelligence for:, Business Applications for:, Enterprise Application Services for:, ~ Banking and Financial Markets-Services (7), ~ Banking and Financial Markets-Services (7)

Company Name: Funding Souq
Description: Funding Souq is a peer to peer platform that aims to addresss the $230bn SME funding gap in the Middle East.
Website: http://fundingsouq.com/
Phone: **Email:** admin@fundingsouq.com
City: London **State:** England **PC:** **Country: United Kingdom**
Year Established: **Status 2020:** Active
Industries: Artificial Intelligence for:, Finance and Accounting for:, Web for:, ~ Professional Services (48)

Company Name: Fusion Global Capital
Description: Fusion Global Capital is a growth-equity firm investing in b2b technology.
Website: http://www.fusionglobalcapital.com
Phone: **Email:** Info@fusioncap.com
City: London **State:** England **PC:** **Country: United Kingdom**
Year Established: 2011 **Status 2020:** Active
Industries: Big Data and Analytics for:, Business Intelligence for:, Cloud for:, Cloud for:, Cloud for:, Cloud for:, Cloud for:, Cloud for:, Cloud for:, ~ Media-Communications (41), Cyber Security for:, Databases for:, Databases for:, Data Management for:, Databases for:, Enterpris**Company Name:** Futr.
Description: Futr. is a British tech company using machine learning to provide access to data with natural language.
Website: http://futr.ai/
Phone: **Email:** hello@futr.ai
City: London **State:** England **PC:** **Country: United Kingdom**
Year Established: 2017 **Status 2020:** Active
Industries: Artificial Intelligence for:, IT Managed Services for:, Machine Learning

Company Name: FUTURE16
Description: FUTURE16 creates audiovisual content that hopes to create awareness of the future of the society and future of the arts.
Website: http://www.future16.xyz/
Phone: **Email:** oniqur@gmail.com
City: London **State:** England **PC:** **Country: United Kingdom**
Year Established: 2016 **Status 2020:** Active
Industries: Artificial Intelligence

Company Name: Gamatech
Description: Transforming ideas into reality with AI
Website: http://www.gamatechgroup.com
Phone: **Email:** info@gamatechgroup.com
City: London **State:** England **PC:** **Country: United Kingdom**
Year Established: 2015 **Status 2020:** Active
Industries: Artificial Intelligence for:, IT Managed Services for:, Application Services for:, Robotics

Company Name: Gameway
Description: Gameway is the mobile gaming experience of the future.
Website: http://www.gameway.io
Phone: **Email:** contact@gameway.io
City: London **State:** England **PC:** **Country: United Kingdom**
Year Established: **Status 2020:** Active
Industries: Artificial Intelligence for:, Augmented Reality for:, Big Data and Analytics for:, ~ Gaming (18), Machine Learning for:, Application Services for:, ~ Gaming (18), ~ Arts-Entertainment-Recreation (4)

Company Name: Gardenia Technologies
Description: Gardenia Technologies is a UHNWI / Family Office-backed FinTech company.
Website: http://www.gardeniatech.com/
Phone: **Email:** contact@gardeniatech.com
City: London **State:** England **PC:** **Country: United Kingdom**
Year Established: 2016 **Status 2020:** Active
Industries: Analytics for:, ~ Banking and Financial Markets-Services (7), ~ Banking and Financial Markets-Services (7), IT Managed Services for:, ~ Banking and Financial Markets-Services (7), Predictive Analytics for:, Supply Chain Management

Company Name: Genie AI
Description: Automatic legal contract drafting platform for anyone.
Website: http://genieai.co/
Phone: **Email:** info@genieai.co
City: London **State:** England **PC:** **Country: United Kingdom**
Year Established: 2017 **Status 2020:** Active
Industries: Artificial Intelligence for:, IT Managed Services for:, Application Program Interfaces (APIs) for:, Machine Learning

Company Name: gigl
Description: Powering the future of work.
Website: http://www.getgigl.com
Phone: **Email:** hello@getgigl.com
City: London **State:** England **PC:** **Country: United Kingdom**
Year Established: 2017 **Status 2020:** Active
Industries: Application Services

Company Name: Ginie.ai
Description: Automatic legal contract drafting platform for anyone.
Website: http://ginger.io
Phone: 1(855)446-4347 **Email:** founders@ginger.io
City: London **State:** England **PC:** **Country: United Kingdom**
Year Established: **Status 2020:** Active
Industries: Artificial Intelligence for:, IT Managed Services for:, ~ Law-Legal Services (26), Machine Learning for:, ~ Professional Services (48)

Company Name: GIUP
Description: GIUP is a system that evaluates players via the analysis of his/her behavior during playing.
Website: http://giupstudents.com
Phone: **Email:** info@giupstudents.com
City: London **State:** England **PC:** **Country: United Kingdom**
Year Established: **Status 2020:** Active
Industries:

Company Name: GiveVision
Description: GiveVision is a high tech low vision aids enhancing the remaining sight of partially sighted people.
Website: http://www.givevision.net/
Phone: **Email:** 36624@reference-encyclopedia-ai.net
City: London **State:** England **PC:** **Country: United Kingdom**
Year Established: 2014 **Status 2020:** Active
Industries: Artificial Intelligence for:, Computer Vision for:, Internet of Things (IoT)

Company Name: Globr messenger
Description: Chat freely with friends and family in any language.
Website: http://globr.launchrock.com
Phone: **Email:** 36630@reference-encyclopedia-ai.net
City: London **State:** England **PC:** **Country: United Kingdom**
Year Established: 2012 **Status 2020:** Active
Industries: Application Services for:, IT Managed Services for:, Natural Language Processing for:, ~ Social Assistance-Non-Profits (53)

Company Name: Glu: Russia
Description: Gluru is an advanced analytical & predictive user data software company, making unstructured user data smart.
Website: http://gluru.co/
Phone: **Email:** info@gluru.co
City: London **State:** England **PC:** **Country: United Kingdom**
Year Established: **Status 2020:** Active
Industries: Artificial Intelligence for:, Machine Learning for:, ~ Professional Services (48)

Company Name: goEvo
Description: goEvo helps users lose excess weight and keep it off without dieting, by changing the way we think and feel about food and our bodies.
Website: http://goevoapp.com/
Phone: **Email:** amin@bighouseventures.co
City: London **State:** England **PC:** **Country: United Kingdom**
Year Established: **Status 2020:** Active
Industries: Artificial Intelligence for:, Application Services for:, ~ Healthcare (20), ~ Healthcare (20), ~ Healthcare (20)

Company Name: Goldex
Description: Goldex is a trading technology platform that allows users to invest in physical gold through its mobile phone application Goldexapp.
Website: http://www.goldexapp.com/
Phone: 44 7920851111 **Email:** scarrasco@goldexapp.com
City: London **State:** England **PC:** **Country: United Kingdom**
Year Established: **Status 2020:** Active
Industries: **Company Name:** GoSay
Description: GoSay creates personalised e-learning chatbots to help businesses train their employees in English language
Website: http://gosay.co
Phone: **Email:** hello@gosay.co
City: London **State:** England **PC:** **Country: United Kingdom**
Year Established: **Status 2020:** Active
Industries: Artificial Intelligence for:, Business Applications for:, ~ Education (13), ~ Education (13), ~ Education (13), ~ Education (13), ~ Media-Communications (41)

Company Name: Gospel
Description:
Website: https://gospel.tech/
Phone: 44 20 7969 1459 **Email:** steve.collins@gospel.tech
City: London **State:** England **Zip:** W1W 8HS **Country: United Kingdom**
Year Established: **Status 2020:** Active
Industries:

Company Name: Grad DNA
Description: Grad DNA matches students and recent college grads with the right employers through app based psychometric assessments.
Website: http://www.grad-dna.com
Phone: (310)795-8731 **Email:** katie.weber@grad-dna.com
City: London **State:** England **PC:** **Country: United Kingdom**
Year Established: 2015 **Status 2020:** Active
Industries: Big Data and Analytics for:, ~ Education (13), Application Services for:, Predictive Analytics

Company Name: GRAKN.AI
Description: Grakn is a hyper-relational database for knowledge engineering. It is the knowledge base platform for intelligent/cognitive systems.
Website: http://www.grakn.ai
Phone: **Email:** info@grakn.ai
City: London **State:** England **PC:** **Country: United Kingdom**
Year Established: **Status 2020:** Active
Industries: Analytics for:, Artificial Intelligence for:, Big Data and Analytics for:, Application Services for:, IT Infrastructure for:, Content

Company Name: Graphaware
Description: GraphAware - consulting, training, open-source and bespoke software development for Neo4j.
Website: http://graphaware.com/
Phone: 44 (0) 333 444 7274 **Email:** info@graphaware.com
City: London **State:** England **PC:** **Country: United Kingdom**
Year Established: 2013 **Status 2020:** Active
Industries: IT Managed Services for:, Machine Learning

Company Name: Greengame
Description: Greengame works with businesses and cities to incentivise sustainable behaviour using technology, gamification and behavioural economics.
Website: http://www.greenga.me
Phone: **Email:** info@greenga.me
City: London **State:** England **PC:** **Country: United Kingdom**
Year Established: 2015 **Status 2020:** Active
Industries: ~ Energy and Utilities (14), ~ Energy and Utilities (14), IT Managed Services for:, IT Managed Services for:, Natural Language Processing for:, ~ Construction (10), ~ Social-Environmental-Physical-Engineering Sciences (55)

Company Name: GreenShoot Labs
Description: We're an applied AI and conversational interface agency.
Website: http://www.greenshootlabs.com/
Phone: **Email:** hello@greenshootlabs.com
City: London **State:** England **PC:** **Country: United Kingdom**
Year Established: 2017 **Status 2020:** Active
Industries: Artificial Intelligence for:, Machine Learning

Company Name: Greyparrot AI
Description: We provide cutting edge computer vision products & services to enterprises looking for AI partne: Serbia
Website: http://greyparrot.ai
Phone: **Email:** contact@greyparrot.ai
City: London **State:** England **PC:** **Country: United Kingdom**
Year Established: **Status 2020:** Active
Industries: Artificial Intelligence for:, IT Managed Services for:, IT Managed Services for:, ~ Telecommunications (56), ~ Media-Communications (41)

Company Name: Growth Intelligence
Description: Growth Intelligence is a UK technology company offering a software-as-a-service product to B2B corporations.
Website: http://growthintelligence.com
Phone: 44 (0) 20 3873 2731 **Email:** info@growthintelligence.com
City: London **State:** England **PC:** **Country: United Kingdom**
Year Established: 2011 **Status 2020:** Active
Industries:

Company Name: Growth Squared
Description: SaaS, AI, Machine Learning, Data Analytics, Automation
Website: http://www.growthsquared.io
Phone: 44(0)203 853 3810 **Email:** info@growthsquared.io
City: London **State:** England **PC:** **Country: United Kingdom**
Year Established: **Status 2020:** Active
Industries: Analytics for:, Artificial Intelligence for:, E-Commerce for:, Machine Learning

Company Name: GrowthEnabler
Description: GrowthEnabler delivers data, insights & intelligence on disruptive technologies and digital innovations
Website: http://www.growthenabler.com
Phone: **Email:** info@growthenabler.com
City: London **State:** England **PC:** **Country: United Kingdom**
Year Established: **Status 2020:** Active
Industries: Artificial Intelligence for:, Business Intelligence for:, IT Managed Services

Company Name: GrowthIntel
Description: Growth Intelligence is a UK technology company offering a software-as-a-service product to B2B corporations.
Website: http://growthintel.com
Phone: 44 (0) 20 3873 2731 **Email:** info@growthintel.com
City: London **State:** England **PC:** **Country: United Kingdom**
Year Established: **Status 2020:** Active
Industries: Artificial Intelligence for:, Big Data and Analytics for:, Business Intelligence for:, Enterprise Application Services for:, Compute for:, Risk Management

Company Name: Grumgo
Description: Grumgo is the ultimate travel companion for smart city breaks, powered by AI. Plan less, explore more with your personalised itinerary.
Website: http://www.grumgo.com
Phone: **Email:** hello@grumgo.com
City: London **State:** England **PC:** **Country: United Kingdom**
Year Established: **Status 2020:** Active
Industries: Artificial Intelligence for:, Mobile for:, ~ Travel and Transportation (58)

Company Name: G: TUNISIA
Description: GTN innovates a quantum machine learning technology to transform drug discovery.
Website: http://gtn.ai/
Phone: **Email:** contact@gtn.ai
City: London **State:** England **PC:** **Country: United Kingdom**
Year Established: 2017 **Status 2020:** Active
Industries: ~ Biotechnology (9), ~ Manufacturing-Petroleum-Coal-Chemicals-Plastics-Rubber (37), Machine Learning for:, ~ Education (13)

Company **Name:** gweek
Description: gweek is the category leader of Speech Intelligence. We help job candidates speak and communicate with natural agility.
Website: http://www.gweekspeech.com
Phone: 020 7118 7800 **Email:** hello@gweekspeech.com
City: London **State:** England **PC:** **Country: United Kingdom**
Year Established: 2016 **Status 2020:** Active
Industries: Computer Vision for:, ~ Education (13), ~ Education (13), Human Computer Interaction for:, Machine Learning for:, Natural Language Processing for:, ~ Education (13), ~ Education (13), Speech Recognition

Company Name: GYANA
Description: Gyana is a self-service data science platform that enables insights around locations and places, using Big data and AI
Website: www.gyana.co.uk
Phone: **Email:** info@gyana.co.uk
City: London **State:** England **PC:** **Country: United Kingdom**
Year Established: **Status 2020:** Active
Industries: Analytics for:, Artificial Intelligence for:, Big Data and Analytics for:, ~ Media-Communications (41)

Company Name: Hadean
Description: Hadean is a distributed operating system that lets a developer write, ship and run simulations at any scale, with zero ops, and zero tuning.
Website: http://hadean.com
Phone: **Email:** info@hadean.com
City: London **State:** England **PC:** **Country: United Kingdom**
Year Established: **Status 2020:** Active
Industries: Artificial Intelligence for:, Cloud for:, Application Services for:, Compute

Company Name: Happiness Works
Description: HW provides science-based, responsive analytics with instant reporting that unlocks new ways to happiness and productivity for workplaces.
Website: http://www.happinessworks.com/
Phone: 44 20 3322 4949 **Email:** hello@happinessworks.com
City: London **State:** England **PC:** **Country: United Kingdom**
Year Established: 2012 **Status 2020:** Active
Industries: Machine Learning

Company Name: Harley Therapy
Description: Psychotherapy & Counselling
Website: http://www.harleytherapy.com
Phone: **Email:** info@harleytherapy.com
City: London **State:** England **PC:** **Country: United Kingdom**
Year Established: 2017 **Status 2020:** Active
Industries: ~ Healthcare (20), Machine Learning

Company Name: Hashblu Limited
Description: An Enteprise Grade Chatbot Lifecycle Management platform to design, build & manage bots for core business processes like Sales, CRM etc.
Website: http://www.hashblu.com
Phone: **Email:** contactus@hashblu.com
City: London **State:** England **PC:** **Country: United Kingdom**
Year Established: 2015 **Status 2020:** Active
Industries: Analytics for:, Application Services for:, Artificial Intelligence for:, IT Managed Services for:, Machine Learning for:, Mobile for:, Application Services for:, Application Services for:, Business Software as a Service Apps (SaaS Apps)

Company Name: Haveyouseen
Description: Haveyouseen was born from the belief that whenever someone talks about or buys a product online, they should get rewarded for doing so.
Website: http://www.haveyouseen.com
Phone: **Email:** feedback@haveyouseen.com
City: London **State:** England **PC:** **Country: United Kingdom**
Year Established: **Status 2020:** Active
Industries: Artificial Intelligence for:, ~ Retail and Consumer Products (52)

Company Name: HayBeeSee
Description: HayBeeSee creating a novel robotics platform allowing large daily coverage as well as close proximity sensing and interaction for farmers.
Website: http://www.HayBeeSee.com
Phone: **Email:** 36673@reference-encyclopedia-ai.net
City: London **State:** England **PC:** **Country: United Kingdom**
Year Established: 2016 **Status 2020:** Active
Industries: ~ Agriculture (3), ~ Agriculture (3), Artificial Intelligence for:, Robotics

Company Name: Hazy
Description: Data anonymisation platform
Website: http://hazy.com
Phone: **Email:** alice@hazy.com
City: London **State:** England **PC:** **Country: United Kingdom**
Year Established: **Status 2020:** Active
Industries:

Company Name: Headlight AI
Description: Headlight AI provides intelligent sensing and mapping software for harsh environments.
Website: http://www.headlight.ai/
Phone: **Email:** hello@headlight.ai
City: London **State:** England **PC:** **Country: United Kingdom**
Year Established: **Status 2020:** Active
Industries: Artificial Intelligence for:, ~ Automotive (5), Machine Learning for:, ~ Professional Services (48)

Company Name: Headstart
Description: Headstart is diversity recruiting software focused on breaking the cycle of exclusion.
Website: http://www.headstart.io
Phone: **Email:** info@headstartapp.com
City: London **State:** England **PC:** **Country: United Kingdom**
Year Established: **Status 2020:** Active
Industries: Artificial Intelligence for:, ~ Education (13), ~ Human Resources (24), Machine Learning for:, ~ Human Resources (24)

Company Name: HealthUnlocked
Description: HealthUnlocked is a social platform for health.
Website: http://www.healthunlocked.com
Phone: **Email:** communications@healthunlocked.com
City: London **State:** England **PC:** **Country: United Kingdom**
Year Established: **Status 2020:** Active
Industries: Artificial Intelligence for:, ~ Personal-Religious-Civic (45), ~ Healthcare (20), Web

Company Name: HeapX
Description: FinTech Startup building the most reliable and secure Crypto Asset Platform
Website: http://heapx.io
Phone: **Email:** hello@heapx.io
City: London **State:** England **PC:** **Country: United Kingdom**
Year Established: **Status 2020:** Active
Industries: Artificial Intelligence for:, ~ Banking and Financial Markets-Services (7), Blockchain for:, ~ Banking and Financial Markets-Services (7), ~ Banking and Financial Markets-Services (7), ~ Banking and Financial Markets-Services (7)

Company Name: Heliocor
Description: Heliocor is a regulatory technology company.We are building a global anti fraud ecosystem based on our Robolitics and Dokstor SaaS products.
Website: http://heliocor.com/
Phone: 44 203 006 6405 **Email:** info@heliocor.com
City: London **State:** England **PC:** **Country: United Kingdom**
Year Established: 2014 **Status 2020:** Active
Industries: Application Services for:, Artificial Intelligence for:, Blockchain for:, Cyber Security for:, Security for:, Identity for:, IT Managed Services for:, Web for:, Web for:, Machine Learning for:, Business Software as a Service Apps (SaaS Apps)

Company Name: Helixtap
Description: Where physical commodity trading meets technology. Areas of Focus: Commodities trading, Supply Chain Management, Commoditech
Website: http://helixtap.com/
Phone: **Email:** farah@helixtap.com
City: London **State:** England **PC:** **Country: United Kingdom**
Year Established: 2020 **Status 2020:** Active
Industries: ~ Automotive (5), Business Applications for:, Enterprise Application Services for:, IT Managed Services for:, ~ Manufacturing-Petroleum-Coal-Chemicals-Plastics-Rubber (37), Predictive Analytics for:, Business Software as a Service Apps (SaaS Apps) for:, Business

Company Name: HelloDone
Description: HelloDone automates conversations across messaging apps for the Transportation, Home Delivery and Utility sectors.
Website: http://www.hellodone.ai
Phone: **Email:** ed@hellodone.ai
City: London **State:** England **PC:** **Country: United Kingdom**
Year Established: 2016 **Status 2020:** Active
Industries: Artificial Intelligence for:, ~ Transportation and Logistics (57), ~ Telecommunications (56), Natural Language Processing for:, ~ Transportation and Logistics (57), Business Software as a Service Apps (SaaS Apps) for:, ~ Construction (10), ~ Construction (10), : India

Company Name: HELPFUL
Description: Recycle plastic and break the hab: Italy
Website: http://www.helpful.world/
Phone: 2032904100 **Email:** info@helpful.world
City: London **State:** England **PC:** **Country: United Kingdom**
Year Established: **Status 2020:** Active
Industries: Application Services for:, Artificial Intelligence for:, Machine Learning for:, ~ Social-Environmental-Physical-Engineering Sciences (55), ~ Professional Services (48), ~ Social-Environmental-Physical-Engineering Sciences (55)

Company Name: HeraSpace
Description: Heraspace is helping to do better management for the fishing industry.
Website: http://heraspace.com/
Phone: **Email:** hello@heraspace.com
City: London **State:** England **PC:** **Country: United Kingdom**
Year Established: **Status 2020:** Active
Industries: Artificial Intelligence for:, ~ Biotechnology (9), Blockchain for:, ~ Food and Beverage (17), ~ Government (19)

Company Name: Hero Labs
Description: Hero Labs develops technologies that help prevent water leaks.
Website: http://www.hero-labs.com/
Phone: 44 7810 878289 **Email:** hi@hero-labs.com
City: London **State:** England **PC:** **Country: United Kingdom**
Year Established: 2018 **Status 2020:** Active
Industries: Artificial Intelligence for:, IT Managed Services for:, Business Intelligence

Company Name: Hestia International
Description: Hestia is an AI / ML powered real estate marketplace helping property buyers/sellers to complete transactions end-to-end.
Website: http://angel.co/hestia-1
Phone: 44 7787 332932 **Email:** budhahere@gmail.com
City: London **State:** England **PC:** **Country: United Kingdom**
Year Established: 2015 **Status 2020:** Active
Industries: Artificial Intelligence for:, Blockchain

Company Name: HireXtra
Description: AI Driven Crowd Staffing Platform for Employers & Hiring Agenci: Spain
Website: http://www.hirextra.com/
Phone: 44 20 3330 0319 **Email:** hirextralimited@gmail.com
City: London **State:** England **PC:** **Country: United Kingdom**
Year Established: **Status 2020:** Active
Industries: Artificial Intelligence for:, ~ Human Resources (24)

Company Name: Hivemind
Description: Data science and technology company specialising in the application of human and machine intelligence to complex unstructured data problems
Website: http://www.hvmd.io
Phone: **Email:** info@hvmd.io
City: London **State:** England **PC:** **Country: United Kingdom**
Year Established: 2017 **Status 2020:** Active
Industries: Artificial Intelligence for:, Enterprise Application Services for:, IT Managed Services for:, Natural Language Processing

Company Name: Hotelmize
Description: Hotelmize is a platform designed to improve the pricing and booking process of hotel rooms using big data analysis.
Website: http://hotelmize.com/
Phone: **Email:** hello@hotelmize.com
City: London **State:** England **PC:** **Country: United Kingdom**
Year Established: 2016 **Status 2020:** Active
Industries:

Company Name: Houseprice.AI
Description: We use our ground breaking AI Machine Valuation Model to swiftly obtain the most astonishingly accurate property valuations for our clients.
Website: http://www.houseprice.ai
Phone: 44 0203 856 8545 **Email:** vivienne.brooks@houseprice.ai
City: London **State:** England **PC:** **Country: United Kingdom**
Year Established: **Status 2020:** Active
Industries: Artificial Intelligence for:, ~ Banking and Financial Markets-Services (7), IT Managed Services for:, Machine Learning for:, ~ Real Estate (49)

Company Name: Houzen
Description: Matching property with its ideal tenants in 3-5 days
Website: http://houzen.co/
Phone: **Email:** houzen.co@gmail.com
City: London **State:** England **PC:** **Country: United Kingdom**
Year Established: **Status 2020:** Active
Industries: Artificial Intelligence for:, ~ Banking and Financial Markets-Services (7), Web for:, Machine Learning for:, ~ Real Estate (49), ~ Real Estate (49)

Company Name: HoverP: India
Description: HoverPin develops intelligent hyperlocal search and discovery technologies including web, mobile and bots apps.
Website: http://hoverpin.com
Phone: **Email:** 36710@reference-encyclopedia-ai.net
City: London **State:** England **PC:** **Country: United Kingdom**
Year Established: 2016 **Status 2020:** Active
Industries: Application Services for:, Artificial Intelligence for:, IT Managed Services

Company Name: How.to
Description: How.to is an early-stage discovery platform and managed Marketplace
Website: http://www.how.to
Phone: **Email:** contact@how.to
City: London **State:** England **PC:** **Country: United Kingdom**
Year Established: **Status 2020:** Active
Industries: Artificial Intelligence for:, Content for:, ~ Education (13), ~ Media-Communications (41), ~ Media-Communications (41)

Company Name: Hoxton Analytics
Description: IoT edge sensor which counts and profiles customers anonymously and accurately, based on their footwear.
Website: http://www.hoxtonanalytics.com
Phone: **Email:** info@hoxtonanalytics.com
City: London **State:** England **PC:** **Country: United Kingdom**
Year Established: **Status 2020:** Active
Industries: Analytics for:, Artificial Intelligence for:, Computer Vision for:, Machine Learning for:, Predictive Analytics for:, Data Management

Company Name: Hubble
Description: Hubble is an online marketplace that makes renting office space easy.
Website: http://hubblehq.com
Phone: 2036080215 **Email:** team@hubblehq.com
City: London **State:** England **PC:** **Country: United Kingdom**
Year Established: **Status 2020:** Active
Industries: Artificial Intelligence for:, Business Applications for:, Collaboration Solutions for:, ~ Real Estate (49)

Company Name: Human
Description: Human humanises technology to decipher subliminal facial expressions into emotion and characteristics, predicting human behaviour.
Website: http://wearehuman.io/
Phone: **Email:** info@wearehuman.io
City: London **State:** England **PC:** **Country: United Kingdom**
Year Established: **Status 2020:** Active
Industries: Artificial Intelligence for:, IT Managed Services for:, IT Managed Services

Company Name: Humanising Autono: Malaysia
Description: Understanding human behavior and body language to develop solutions for two-way communication between pedestrians and autonomous vehicl: Spain
Website: http://www.humanisingautonomy.com/
Phone: **Email:** hello@humanisingautonomy.com
City: London **State:** England **PC:** **Country: United Kingdom**
Year Established: **Status 2020:** Active
Industries: Artificial Intelligence for:, ~ Automotive (5), Human Computer Interaction

Company Name: Hummingbird Technologies
Description: Data analytics and machine learning business for the precision agriculture
Website: http://hummingbirdtech.com/
Phone: 44 (0) 20 8123 2389 **Email:** hello@hummingbirdtech.com
City: London **State:** England **PC:** **Country: United Kingdom**
Year Established: **Status 2020:** Active
Industries: ~ Agriculture (3), Artificial Intelligence for:, Big Data and Analytics for:, ~ Agriculture (3), IT Managed Services for:, Machine Learning

Company Name: humn.ai
Description: At Humn.ai, we are working with the insurance industry, helping the world prepare for the next big leaps in mobility and automation.
Website: http://www.humn.ai
Phone: **Email:** hello@humn.ai
City: London **State:** England **PC:** **Country: United Kingdom**
Year Established: **Status 2020:** Active
Industries: Artificial Intelligence for:, ~ Insurance (25), ~ Insurance (25), Machine Learning

Company Name: Hutoma
Description: Hutoma is a building emotionally evolved AI interfaces for connected devices, app and web powered by Deep Learning.
Website:
Phone: **Email:** 36724@reference-encyclopedia-ai.net
City: London **State:** England **PC:** **Country: United Kingdom**
Year Established: 2015 **Status 2020:** Closed
Industries: Artificial Intelligence for:, Application Program Interfaces (APIs) for:, Enterprise Application Services for:, IT Managed Services for:, Machine Learning

Company Name: HyBird Technologies
Description: HyBird Technologies develops robotic solutions to digitise and inspect industrial assets for safer, faster, and cheaper maintenance.
Website: http://www.hybirdtech.com
Phone: **Email:** contact@hybirdtech.com
City: London **State:** England **PC:** **Country: United Kingdom**
Year Established: 2015 **Status 2020:** Active
Industries: Artificial Intelligence for:, ~ Banking and Financial Markets-Services (7), Robotics

Company Name: Idio
Description: Idio.ai learns from each buyer interaction to improve omni-channel engagement and accelerate demand at B2B enterprises.
Website: http://idio.ai/
Phone: 44 (0)203 540 1920 **Email:** marketingoperations@idioplatform.com
City: London **State:** England **PC:** **Country: United Kingdom**
Year Established: **Status 2020:** Active
Industries: Artificial Intelligence for:, Business Applications for:, ~ Media-Communications (41), ~ Media-Communications (41), Predictive Analytics for:, Cyber Security for:, ~ Professional Services (48), ~ Media-Communications (41)

Company Name: Ignition Ai
Description: Delivering accountability, cost savings and step changes in marketing performance.
Website: http://www.ignition.ai
Phone: 44 (0) 203 740 6654 **Email:** hello@ignition.ai
City: London **State:** England **PC:** **Country: United Kingdom**
Year Established: **Status 2020:** Active
Industries:

Company Name: I-LAPS
Description: An Intelligent Telemetry System designed around smartphones for every sport on wheels.
Website: http://i-laps.com/
Phone: 0781 721 4236 **Email:** info@i-laps.com
City: London **State:** England **PC:** **Country: United Kingdom**
Year Established: 2016 **Status 2020:** Active
Industries: Artificial Intelligence for:, ~ Automotive (5), Cloud for:, ~ Arts-Entertainment-Recreation (4), ~ Healthcare (20), Machine Learning for:, Predictive Analytics for:, Predictive Analytics for:, ~ Arts-Entertainment-Recreation (4)

Company Name: illumr
Description: illumr helps organizations to better understand and predict patterns of behavior that affect them.
Website: http://illumr.com/
Phone: 44 1978 225116 **Email:** enquiries@illumr.com
City: London **State:** England **PC:** **Country: United Kingdom**
Year Established: **Status 2020:** Active
Industries: Analytics for:, Artificial Intelligence for:, Big Data and Analytics for:, Databases for:, Enterprise Application Services for:, IT Managed Services

Company Name: Improbable
Description: Improbable is a software company that has developed a platform for third parties to build vast virtual and simulated worlds.
Website: http://www.improbable.io
Phone: **Email:** contact@improbable.io
City: London **State:** England **PC:** **Country: United Kingdom**
Year Established: **Status 2020:** Active
Industries: Artificial Intelligence for:, Cloud for:, ~ Gaming (18), ~ Professional Services (48)

Company Name: Increasingly
Description: Increasingly uses machine learning to automate product bundling on retail websites.
Website: http://www.increasingly.com/
Phone: **Email:** hello@increasingly.com
City: London **State:** England **PC:** **Country: United Kingdom**
Year Established: 2016 **Status 2020:** Active
Industries: Artificial Intelligence for:, Machine Learning

Company Name: infloAi
Description: infloAi is a London-based software company building proprietary AI technology to make content creation simple, fast and affordable
Website: http://www.inflo.ai
Phone: **Email:** adam.b@inflo.ai
City: London **State:** England **PC:** **Country: United Kingdom**
Year Established: 2013 **Status 2020:** Active
Industries: Artificial Intelligence for:, Digital Media for:, Machine Learning for:, Business Software as a Service Apps (SaaS Apps)

Company Name: InsideDNA
Description: InsideDNA makes drug discovery faster and cheaper with artificial intelligence and genomics
Website:
Phone: **Email:** 36772@reference-encyclopedia-ai.net
City: London **State:** England **PC:** **Country: United Kingdom**
Year Established: 2013 **Status 2020:** Closed
Industries: Artificial Intelligence for:, ~ Biotechnology (9), ~ Biotechnology (9), ~ Healthcare (20), Machine Learning

Company Name: Inspection2
Description: Automate industrial asset management & inspection with Expanse, an AI-powered asset management, data analytics and reporting software
Website: http://inspection2.ai
Phone: **Email:** hello@inspection2.ai
City: London **State:** England **PC:** **Country: United Kingdom**
Year Established: 2019 **Status 2020:** Active
Industries: Artificial Intelligence for:, Business Intelligence for:, Automation for:, Predictive Analytics for:, Business Software as a Service Apps (SaaS Apps)

Company Name: InstaDeep
Description: InstaDeep host of AI solutions, ranging from optimized pattern-recognition, GPU-accelerated insights, self-learning decision making systems.
Website: http://www.instadeep.com/
Phone: 44 207 193 6553 **Email:** hello@instadeep.com
City: London **State:** England **PC:** **Country: United Kingdom**
Year Established: 2015 **Status 2020:** Active
Industries: Artificial Intelligence

Company Name: Instrumental
Description: Our TalentAI platform uses machine learning to discover emerging talent, predominantly for the music and entertainment industry.
Website: http://www.weareinstrumental.com
Phone: 44 (0)20 3176 7645 **Email:** hello@weareinstrumental.com
City: London **State:** England **PC:** **Country: United Kingdom**
Year Established: **Status 2020:** Active
Industries: Artificial Intelligence for:, Business Applications for:, ~ Arts-Entertainment-Recreation (4), ~ Arts-Entertainment-Recreation (4), ~ Arts-Entertainment-Recreation (4), ~ Arts-Entertainment-Recreation (4), ~ Arts-Entertainment-Recreation (4)

Company Name: Intelistyle
Description: Intelistyle provides A.I. styling solutions to fashion retailers, helping them address the needs of customers looking for styling advice.
Website: http://www.intelistyle.com/
Phone: **Email:** hello@intelistyle.co.uk
City: London **State:** England **PC:** **Country: United Kingdom**
Year Established: 2017 **Status 2020:** Active
Industries: Artificial Intelligence for:, ~ Fashion (16)

Company Name: Intellectual Investments
Description: Intellectual Investments will produce high-tech intellectual robots and artificial intelligence for stock market forecasting and the.
Website: http://finance-forecast.com/
Phone: 44 20 3239 3984 **Email:** victor@finance-forecast.com
City: London **State:** England **PC:** **Country: United Kingdom**
Year Established: **Status 2020:** Active
Industries: Artificial Intelligence for:, Finance and Accounting for:, Robotics

Company Name: Intelliagg.com
Description: Intelliagg is a threat intelligence platform that monitors data loss, reputational damage, and targeted physical and cyber crime .
Website:
Phone: (4470) 389-4949 **Email:** 36785@reference-encyclopedia-ai.net
City: London **State:** England **PC:** **Country: United Kingdom**
Year Established: 2011 **Status 2020:** Closed
Industries: Analytics for:, Artificial Intelligence for:, Big Data and Analytics for:, Cyber Security for:, IT Managed Services

Company Name: IntelligentX
Description: IntelligentX produces the world's first beer brewed by artificial intelligence.
Website: http://intelligentx.ai
Phone: **Email:** info@intelligentx.ai
City: London **State:** England **PC:** **Country: United Kingdom**

Year Established: **Status 2020:** Active
Industries: Artificial Intelligence for:, ~ Customer Relationship Management (11), ~ Professional Services (48)

Company Name: InteriMarket
Description: InteriMarket is an employers platform for skilled contractors.
Website: http://interimarket.com
Phone: **Email:** team@interimarket.com
City: London **State:** England **PC:** **Country: United Kingdom**
Year Established: **Status 2020:** Active
Industries:

Company Name: Interpretive
Description: Making sense of data is one of the great challenges of the information age we live in.
Website: http://www.interpretive.io
Phone: **Email:** 36800@reference-encyclopedia-ai.net
City: London **State:** England **PC:** **Country: United Kingdom**
Year Established: 2014 **Status 2020:** Active
Industries: Artificial Intelligence for:, Business Applications for:, IT Managed Services for:, Machine Learning for:, Business Software as a Service Apps (SaaS Apps) for:, Automation

Company Name: Intrinsic Semiconductor Technologies
Description: Intrinsic Semiconductor Technologies is established to developed silicon-oxide based RRAM technologies.
Website: http://www.intrinsicst.com/
Phone: 44 (0)20 7679 9000 **Email:** info@intrinsicst.com
City: London **State:** England **PC:** **Country: United Kingdom**
Year Established: 2017 **Status 2020:** Active
Industries: Artificial Intelligence for:, IT Managed Services

Company Name: Invacio
Description: Invacio is a multitude of products or solutions built to scale around multiple avenues with a vision of transforming industries through AI.
Website: www.invacio.com
Phone: **Email:** roger@invacio.com
City: London **State:** England **PC:** **Country: United Kingdom**
Year Established: **Status 2020:** Active
Industries: Artificial Intelligence for:, Blockchain for:, ~ Banking and Financial Markets-Services (7), ~ Banking and Financial Markets-Services (7), ~ Social-Environmental-Physical-Engineering Sciences (55)

Company Name: inventtory Ltd
Description: inventtory is a trading platform that creates liquidity in the asset class Intellectual Property by employing Artificial Intelligence.
Website: http://www.inventtory.com/
Phone: 44-0207-1127040 **Email:** speakto@inventtory.com
City: London **State:** England **PC:** **Country: United Kingdom**
Year Established: **Status 2020:** Active
Industries: Artificial Intelligence for:, ~ Automotive (5), ~ Media-Communications (41), Finance and Accounting

Company Name: iotec
Description: iotec are the leading, independent, ethical digital media consultants and practitioners.
Website: http://www.iotecglobal.com
Phone: **Email:** hello@iotecglobal.com
City: London **State:** England **PC:** **Country: United Kingdom**
Year Established: **Status 2020:** Active
Industries: ~ Media-Communications (41), ~ Media-Communications (41), ~ Media-Communications (41), Artificial Intelligence for:, Web for:, Machine Learning for:, ~ Professional Services (48)

Company **Name:** iSize Technologies
Description: UK company specialising in deep learning for video delivery. Precoding technology to optimize for video quality and offer significant bitrate savings on top of codec.
Website: http://www.isize.co/
Phone: 7881932090 **Email:** info@isize.co
City: London **State:** England **Zip:** E1W 3NX **Country: United Kingdom**
Year Established: **Status 2020:** Active
Industries: Artificial Intelligence for:, ~ Media-Communications (41), Computer Vision for:, ~ Education (1416), ~ Gaming (1421), ~ High Tech (1424), ~ Media-Communications (1444), ~ Social Media (1457)

Company Name: Ixy
Description: AI-mediated messaging app for conversations with better outcomes - identify, prevent or resolve conflicts in your personal relationshi: Palestine
Website: http://www.getixy.com
Phone: **Email:** team@getixy.com
City: London **State:** England **PC:** **Country: United Kingdom**
Year Established: 2017 **Status 2020:** Active
Industries: Application Services for:, Artificial Intelligence for:, Big Data and Analytics for:, IT Managed Services for:, Application Services

Company Name: JamieAi
Description: JamieAi connects graduates within Data Science, Technology and Finance to amazing companies across the UK.
Website: http://jamieai.com/
Phone: 020 7201 9292 **Email:** hello@jamieai.com
City: London **State:** England **PC:** **Country: United Kingdom**
Year Established: 2017 **Status 2020:** Active
Industries: Machine Learning

Company Name: Jiminny
Description: On a mission to help sales & success. Using Automation & AI to help your team grow and develop
Website: http://www.jiminny.com
Phone: 1 646-760-6555 **Email:** hello@jiminny.com
City: London **State:** England **PC:** **Country: United Kingdom**
Year Established: 2016 **Status 2020:** Active
Industries: Enterprise Application Services for:, Machine Learning for:, Business Software as a Service Apps (SaaS Apps) for:, Automation

Company Name: Jiva
Description: An AI Marketing Assistant For Small Business: Spain
Website:
Phone: **Email:** 36829@reference-encyclopedia-ai.net
City: London **State:** England **PC:** **Country: United Kingdom**
Year Established: 2016 **Status 2020:** Closed
Industries: Artificial Intelligence for:, Digital Marketing for:, Business Software as a Service Apps (SaaS Apps) for:, Internet of Things (IoT)

Company Name: Jobily
Description: AI-Powered JobSearch Engine
Website: http://www.Jobily.co.uk
Phone: **Email:** info@jobily.co.uk
City: London **State:** England **PC:** **Country: United Kingdom**
Year Established: **Status 2020:** Active
Industries: Artificial Intelligence for:, ~ Human Resources (24), ~ Human Resources (24), Cyber Security

Company Name: JollyDeck
Description: JollyDeck is an online training provider to increase employee understanding such as on-boarding, sales training and compliance training.
Website: http://www.jollydeck.com/
Phone: **Email:** sales@jollydeck.com
City: London **State:** England **PC:** **Country: United Kingdom**
Year Established: **Status 2020:** Active
Industries: Artificial Intelligence for:, ~ Education (13), ~ Education (13), ~ Education (13)

Company Name: Jukedeck
Description: Jukedeck is developing an artificially intelligent music composer.
Website: http://jukedeck.com/
Phone: **Email:** hello@jukedeck.com
City: London **State:** England **PC:** **Country: United Kingdom**
Year Established: **Status 2020:** Active
Industries: Artificial Intelligence for:, ~ Arts-Entertainment-Recreation (4), ~ Media-Communications (41)

Company Name: Ju: Romania
Description: The contract collaboration platform
Website: http://www.juro.com
Phone: **Email:** hello@juro.com
City: London **State:** England **PC:** **Country: United Kingdom**
Year Established: 2016 **Status 2020:** Active
Industries:

Company Name: Just AI
Description: Conversational AI technologies empowering dialogue between a human and a machine: chatbots, voice skills, smart toys.
Website: http://just-ai.com/en/
Phone: **Email:** OfficeUK@just-ai.com
City: London **State:** England **PC:** **Country: United Kingdom**
Year Established: 2011 **Status 2020:** Active
Industries: Artificial Intelligence for:, IT Managed Services

Company Name: JusTailors
Description: JusTailors is a sustainable apparel e-commerce platform with on-demand supply chain and smart tailoring
Website: http://www.justailors.com/
Phone: 44 7453 765143 **Email:** support@justailors.com
City: London **State:** England **PC:** **Country: United Kingdom**
Year Established: **Status 2020:** Active
Industries: Artificial Intelligence for:, E-Commerce for:, ~ Fashion (16), ~ Manufacturing-Miscellaneous (34), Cyber Security

Company Name: Kami.ai
Description: Kami is an AI conversational platform which powers businesses with smart robot advisory service
Website: http://kami.ai
Phone: 85261855575 **Email:** Alex.cheung@kami.ai
City: London **State:** England **PC:** **Country: United Kingdom**
Year Established: **Status 2020:** Active
Industries: Artificial Intelligence for:, Human Computer Interaction for:, Machine Learning

Company Name: KAMS
Description: Technology, Transactions, Network Research:
Website:
Phone: **Email:** 36839@reference-encyclopedia-ai.net
City: London **State:** England **PC:** **Country: United Kingdom**
Year Established: 2019 **Status 2020:** Active
Industries: Predictive Analytics for:, Business Intelligence

Company Name: Kam: Ukraine
Description: SaaS Video Editing Automation Tools
Website: http://kamua.com
Phone: 44 020 8133 7211 **Email:** hello@kamua.com
City: London **State:** England **PC:** **Country: United Kingdom**
Year Established: 2019 **Status 2020:** Active
Industries: Artificial Intelligence for:, Business Software as a Service Apps (SaaS Apps)

Company Name: Keakie
Description: Keakie is an audio platform that uses a bespoke AI engine and analytics to tailor quality content to its users.
Website: http://keakie.com
Phone: **Email:** eloka@keakie.co.uk
City: London **State:** England **PC:** **Country: United Kingdom**
Year Established: 2016 **Status 2020:** Active
Industries: Analytics for:, Artificial Intelligence for:, ~ Arts-Entertainment-Recreation (4), ~ Arts-Entertainment-Recreation (4)

Company Name: Keen Software Hou: Sweden
Description: Keen Software House is an independent game development studio known for its popular PC games Space Engineers and Medieval Engineers.
Website: http://www.keenswh.com
Phone: **Email:** info@keenswh.com
City: London **State:** England **PC:** **Country: United Kingdom**
Year Established: **Status 2020:** Active
Industries: Artificial Intelligence for:, Application Services for:, ~ Gaming (18)

Company Name: Keypla
Description: Keypla is automating human valuations using Computer Vision and Machine Learning
Website: http://www.keypla.com
Phone: **Email:** kingsley@keypla.com
City: London **State:** England **PC:** **Country: United Kingdom**
Year Established: 2016 **Status 2020:** Active
Industries: Artificial Intelligence for:, IT Managed Services

Company Name: Kheiron
Description: Kheiron is developing and building tools to help radiologists with their various everyday professional workflows.
Website: http://www.kheironmed.com/
Phone: **Email:** info@kheironmed.com
City: London **State:** England **PC:** **Country: United Kingdom**
Year Established: **Status 2020:** Active
Industries: Artificial Intelligence for:, Application Services for:, ~ Healthcare (20), ~ Healthcare (20)

Company Name: Kluster Intelligence
Description: Predictive Sales Analytics - Utilise big data and machine learning to sell smarter
Website: http://www.klusterintelligence.com
Phone: 2030950401 **Email:** info@klusterintelligence.com
City: London **State:** England **PC:** **Country: United Kingdom**
Year Established: **Status 2020:** Active
Industries: Artificial Intelligence for:, Machine Learning for:, Predictive Analytics for:, ~ Media-Communications (41), Automation

Company Name: Klydo
Description: Klydo applies next-generation machine learning to deliver moments of insight in our complex and changing world.
Website: http://klydo.ai/
Phone: **Email:** info@klydo.ai
City: London **State:** England **PC:** **Country: United Kingdom**
Year Established: **Status 2020:** Active
Industries: Artificial Intelligence for:, Business Intelligence for:, Databases for:, Data Management for:, Machine Learning for:, Natural Language Processing

Company Name: Knexus
Description: Hyper Relevant Content Delivery, Growing Sal: Spain
Website: http://www.knexusgroup.com/
Phone: 44 (0) 20 7097 5159 **Email:** sales@knexusgroup.com
City: London **State:** England **PC:** **Country: United Kingdom**
Year Established: 2017 **Status 2020:** Active
Industries: Artificial Intelligence for:, Machine Learning for:, Business Software as a Service Apps (SaaS Apps)

Company Name: Knows
Description: Knowsis is a London-based web intelligence company developing financial markets data for financial institutions.
Website: http://www.knowsis.com
Phone: 44 20 3286 6950 **Email:** hello@knows.
City: London **State:** England **PC:** **Country: United Kingdom**
Year Established: **Status 2020:** Active
Industries: Analytics for:, Artificial Intelligence for:, Big Data and Analytics for:, ~ Banking and Financial Markets-Services (7), Machine Learning

Company Name: Knox EA
Description: Knox EA is a leading software provider company that have brought together high end experts in the financial arena.
Website: http://www.knoxforexea.com
Phone: 44 20 3002 1207 **Email:** info@knoxforexea.com
City: London **State:** England **PC:** **Country: United Kingdom**
Year Established: **Status 2020:** Active
Industries:

Company Name: KOMPAS
Description: We're creating a real-time personalised city exploration experience connecting independent, and unique locations to custome: Serbia
Website: http://www.kompasapp.com
Phone: **Email:** team@kompasapp.com
City: London **State:** England **PC:** **Country: United Kingdom**
Year Established: **Status 2020:** Active
Industries: Application Services for:, Artificial Intelligence for:, Machine Learning for:, ~ Travel and Transportation (58)

Company Name: Kompli Global
Description: Kompli Global is develops networks, multi-jurisdictional, multi-lingual due diligence, search platform.
Website: http://www.kompli-global.com/
Phone: 44 20 3199 7115 **Email:** hello@kompli-global.com
City: London **State:** England **PC:** **Country: United Kingdom**
Year Established: 2016 **Status 2020:** Active
Industries: Artificial Intelligence

Company Name: Kortical
Description: Kortical is an artificial intelligence platform.
Website: http://kortical.com/
Phone: **Email:** contact@kortical.com
City: London **State:** England **PC:** **Country: United Kingdom**
Year Established: 2016 **Status 2020:** Active
Industries: Artificial Intelligence for:, Machine Learning

Company Name: Kreo
Description: Kreo is a suite of AI-powered design and construction software solutions for project owners, contractors and consultants.
Website: http://www.kreo.net/
Phone: 44 2074157031 **Email:** info@kreo.net
City: London **State:** England **PC:** **Country: United Kingdom**
Year Established: 2017 **Status 2020:** Active
Industries: Artificial Intelligence for:, IT Managed Services for:, IT Managed Services

Company Name: Krzana
Description: Krzana is a digital newsgathering engine for journalists.
Website: http://www.krzana.com
Phone: **Email:** info@krzana.com
City: London **State:** England **PC:** **Country: United Kingdom**
Year Established: **Status 2020:** Active
Industries: Artificial Intelligence for:, Digital Media for:, ~ Banking and Financial Markets-Services (7), ~ Media-Communications (41)

Company **Name:** Ksubaka
Description: We provide powerful immersive brand experience & data platform which allows brands & retailers to link offline customers to online profil: Spain
Website: http://www.ksubaka.com
Phone: **Email:** info@ksubaka.com
City: London **State:** England **PC:** **Country: United Kingdom**
Year Established: 2013 **Status 2020:** Active
Industries: Digital Media for:, IT Managed Services for:, Machine Learning for:, Web for:, Enterprise Application Services for:, Business Software as a Service Apps (SaaS Apps)

Company Name: Kubik Records
Description: The first music label that uses Blockchain Technology and AI in recording, production, remixing, promotion, sales and distribution of Music
Website: http://kubikrecords.com
Phone: **Email:** info@kubikrecords.com
City: London **State:** England **PC:** **Country: United Kingdom**
Year Established: **Status 2020:** Active
Industries: Artificial Intelligence for:, Voice Recognition for:, Blockchain for:, ~ Arts-Entertainment-Recreation (4), ~ Arts-Entertainment-Recreation (4), ~ Arts-Entertainment-Recreation (4), ~ Arts-Entertainment-Recreation (4), ~ Arts-Entertainment-Recreation (4), Predict

Company Name: Kwiziq
Description: Kwiziq is an A.I. language coach that helps people learn a second language. Currently available in French and Spanish.
Website: http://www.kwiziq.com/
Phone: **Email:** info@kwiziq.com
City: London **State:** England **PC:** **Country: United Kingdom**
Year Established: **Status 2020:** Active
Industries: Artificial Intelligence for:, ~ Education (13), ~ Education (13), ~ Education (13)

Company Name: L3C Cloud
Description: L3C Cloud is a cloud platform that provides ideal environment or analytics workloads.
Website: http://l3c.cloud/
Phone: 44 203 542 0870 **Email:** office@l3c.cloud
City: London **State:** England **PC:** **Country: United Kingdom**
Year Established: 2013 **Status 2020:** Active
Industries: Analytics for:, Artificial Intelligence

Company Name: LabGenius
Description: Harnessing evolution with AI to develop radically new protein materials and components.
Website: http://www.labgeni.us
Phone: **Email:** hi@labgeni.us
City: London **State:** England **PC:** **Country: United Kingdom**
Year Established: **Status 2020:** Active
Industries: Artificial Intelligence for:, ~ Biotechnology (9), Machine Learning for:, Robotics for:, ~ Healthcare (20)

Company Name: Leap Three
Description: Leap Three is a digital analytics consultancy specialising in end to end digital analytics.
Website: http://www.leapthree.com/
Phone: 44 20 3865 1589 **Email:** info@leapthree.com
City: London **State:** England **PC:** **Country: United Kingdom**
Year Established: 2016 **Status 2020:** Active
Industries: Predictive Analytics

Company Name: LeftBra: India
Description: LeftBrain is a marketing automation company specialized in providing 100% automation with machine learning
Website: http://leftbraintechnology.com
Phone: **Email:** info@leftbraintechnology.com
City: London **State:** England **PC:** **Country: United Kingdom**
Year Established: 2015 **Status 2020:** Active
Industries: E-Commerce for:, Machine Learning

Company Name: Let's Enhance
Description: Let's Enhance is an Estonia-based company that uses neural network to power a freemium photo upscaling service.
Website: http://letsenhance.io/
Phone: 372 602 7439 **Email:** sofi@letsenhance.io
City: London **State:** England **PC:** **Country: United Kingdom**
Year Established: **Status 2020:** Active
Industries: Artificial Intelligence for:, Machine Learning for:, ~ Media-Communications (41), ~ Media-Communications (41)

Company Name: lewis.ai
Description: Meet Lewis, your virtual travel concierge
Website: http://www.lewis.ai
Phone: **Email:** lex@lewis.ai
City: London **State:** England **PC:** **Country: United Kingdom**
Year Established: **Status 2020:** Active
Industries:

Company Name: Lexico
Description: Lexico applies AI techniques to automatically listens to what your customers are saying and uncovers actionable insights.
Website: http://www.lexicom.io
Phone: **Email:** 4686@reference-encyclopedia-ai.net
City: London **State:** England **PC:** **Country: United Kingdom**
Year Established: **Status 2020:** Active
Industries: Analytics for:, Artificial Intelligence for:, Business Intelligence for:, IT Managed Services for:, Machine Learning for:, Data Management

Company Name: LGN
Description: LGN helps to build next generational AI's solving the worlds most complex problems.
Website: http://lgn.ai/
Phone: **Email:** info@lgn.ai
City: London **State:** England **PC:** **Country: United Kingdom**
Year Established: 2019 **Status 2020:** Active
Industries: Artificial Intelligence for:, IT Managed Services

Company Name: Lifeb: Italy
Description: Lifebit is an intelligent genomics platform that understands DNA data and generates meaningful insights like humans do.
Website: http://lifebit.ai
Phone: **Email:** pr@lifebit.ai
City: London **State:** England **PC:** **Country: United Kingdom**
Year Established: 2017 **Status 2020:** Active
Industries: Artificial Intelligence for:, ~ Biotechnology (9), Machine Learning

Company Name: LifeTracker
Description: AI based context aware mobile app that reminds to do right things at the right time
Website: http://lifetracker.io/
Phone: **Email:** info@lifetracker.io
City: London **State:** England **PC:** **Country: United Kingdom**
Year Established: **Status 2020:** Active
Industries: Application Services

Company Name: Ligabis Ltd
Description: Ligabis LTD // Lawtech // AI // Blockcha: India
Website: http://www.ligabis.co
Phone: **Email:** rees@ligabis.co
City: London **State:** England **PC:** **Country: United Kingdom**
Year Established: 2017 **Status 2020:** Active
Industries: Artificial Intelligence for:, IT Managed Services for:, Web for:, ~ Education (13), Natural Language Processing

Company Name: Limbic
Description: Limbic creates neuroscience of emotion packaged for developers.
Website: http://limbic.ai/
Phone: **Email:** hello@limbic.ai
City: London **State:** England **PC:** **Country: United Kingdom**
Year Established: 2017 **Status 2020:** Active
Industries: Artificial Intelligence for:, IT Managed Services

Company Name: Limejump
Description: Limejump is a Technology-Driven Utility: harnessing the power of big data to positively disrupt and transform today's energy market.
Website: http://www.limejump.com
Phone: **Email:** info@limejump.co.uk
City: London **State:** England **PC:** **Country: United Kingdom**
Year Established: **Status 2020:** Active
Industries: Artificial Intelligence for:, Big Data and Analytics for:, ~ Energy and Utilities (14), ~ Energy and Utilities (14)

Company Name: Limitless
Description: The Limitless GigCX platform enables businesses to connect customers with qualified experts to solve customer service enquiries on-demand.
Website: http://www.limitlesstech.com
Phone: **Email:** info@belimitless.io
City: London **State:** England **PC:** **Country: United Kingdom**
Year Established: 2016 **Status 2020:** Active
Industries: Application Services for:, Artificial Intelligence for:, ~ Customer Relationship Management (11), Web

Company Name: Limitless Technology
Description: Crowd Powered Customer Service & AI
Website: http://www.belimitless.io
Phone: **Email:** info@belimitless.io
City: London **State:** England **PC:** **Country: United Kingdom**
Year Established: **Status 2020:** Active
Industries: ~ Media-Communications (41), Application Services for:, Artificial Intelligence for:, Web for:, Mobile

Company Name: Lingos
Description: Lingos is an online platform that helps language learners meet and connect with the right local language teacher.
Website: http://lingos.co/
Phone: **Email:** info@lingos.co
City: London **State:** England **PC:** **Country: United Kingdom**
Year Established: 2013 **Status 2020:** Active
Industries: Web for:, ~ Education (13), Natural Language Processing

Company Name: Linkproved
Description: Find the right product for you at the right price using AI to analyze all available information on internet and real people's opinions.
Website: http://linkproved.com
Phone: **Email:** linkproved@gmail.com
City: London **State:** England **PC:** **Country: United Kingdom**
Year Established: 2016 **Status 2020:** Active
Industries: Artificial Intelligence for:, E-Commerce for:, Natural Language Processing for:, ~ Retail and Consumer Products (52)

Company Name: Littledata
Description: Littledata automates ecommerce analytics so managers can make data-driven decisions to accelerate growth.
Website: http://www.littledata.io/
Phone: **Email:** contact@littledata.io
City: London **State:** England **PC:** **Country: United Kingdom**
Year Established: 2015 **Status 2020:** Active
Industries: Analytics for:, Business Intelligence for:, E-Commerce for:, Predictive Analytics

Company Name: LiveMetrics.io
Description: Amplifying financial forecasting with machine learning
Website: http://livemetrics.io
Phone: 44 (0) 7899 000789 **Email:** christan@livemetrics.io
City: London **State:** England **PC:** **Country: United Kingdom**
Year Established: **Status 2020:** Active
Industries: Artificial Intelligence for:, ~ Banking and Financial Markets-Services (7), ~ Banking and Financial Markets-Services (7)

Company Name: Lobster
Description: Lobster is a platform which enables brands, agencies and the media to licence visual content directly from social media users.
Website: lobster.media
Phone: **Email:** info@lobster.media
City: London **State:** England **PC:** **Country: United Kingdom**

Year Established: **Status 2020:** Active
Industries:

Company Name: Locomizer
Description: Biological Intelligence (BI) applied to branding
Website: http://locomizer.com
Phone: **Email:** info@locomizer.com
City: London **State:** England **PC:** **Country: United Kingdom**
Year Established: **Status 2020:** Active
Industries: ~ Media-Communications (41), Analytics for:, Artificial Intelligence for:, Big Data and Analytics

Company Name: Logical Glue
Description: Logical Glue is a software company that creates products to analyze data for a business to predict profitable outcomes for a business.
Website: http://www.logicalglue.com
Phone: 44 20 8720 7246 **Email:** insights@logicalglue.com
City: London **State:** England **PC:** **Country: United Kingdom**
Year Established: **Status 2020:** Active
Industries: Artificial Intelligence for:, ~ Professional Services (48)

Company Name: Logically
Description: At Logically we use Natural Language Processing, machine learning and human oversight to identify bias and misinformation on any given topic
Website: logically.co.uk
Phone: **Email:** contact@thelogically.co.uk
City: London **State:** England **PC:** **Country: United Kingdom**
Year Established: **Status 2020:** Active
Industries: Application Services for:, Artificial Intelligence for:, Natural Language Processing for:, ~ Media-Communications (41), ~ Social-Environmental-Physical-Engineering Sciences (55)

Company Name: Logikk
Description: Global data & analytics talent solutions. Logikk engage exceptional individuals for companies looking to unlock the potential of their data.
Website: http://www.logikk.com/
Phone: 0203 005 4968 **Email:** info@logikk.com
City: London **State:** England **PC:** **Country: United Kingdom**
Year Established: **Status 2020:** Active
Industries: Analytics for:, Artificial Intelligence for:, Big Data and Analytics for:, Blockchain for:, Cloud for:, Data Management for:, Databases for:, Data Management for:, Data Management for:, Predictive Analytics for:, ~ Human Resources (24)

Company Name: London Cognition
Description: research, cognition, neuroscience, artificial intelligence
Website: http://www.londoncognition.com/
Phone: **Email:** info@londoncognition.com
City: London **State:** England **PC:** **Country: United Kingdom**
Year Established: 2016 **Status 2020:** Active
Industries: Artificial Intelligence for:, Machine Learning

Company Name: loomi.ai
Description: Loomi is an Intelligent Assistant platform for organising and prioritising user's connected world.
Website: http://www.loomi.ai
Phone: **Email:** al.ramich@loomi.ai
City: London **State:** England **PC:** **Country: United Kingdom**
Year Established: **Status 2020:** Active
Industries: Artificial Intelligence for:, Web for:, Machine Learning for:, Natural Language Processing for:, ~ Media-Communications (41), Application Services for:, ~ Social Media (54)

Company Name: LoopMe
Description: LoopMe, the first company to close the loop on brand advertising attribution for offline sales using AI and mobile data.
Website: http://loopme.com
Phone: **Email:** contact@loopme.com
City: London **State:** England **PC:** **Country: United Kingdom**
Year Established: **Status 2020:** Active
Industries: ~ Media-Communications (41), Artificial Intelligence for:, Big Data and Analytics for:, Machine Learning for:, Mobile for:, ~ Media-Communications (41), ~ Media-Communications (41)

Company Name: LuckyTrip
Description: LuckyTrip is a travel inspiration app that lets you find a trip in one tap.
Website: http://www.luckytrip.co.uk/
Phone: **Email:** team@luckytrip.co.uk
City: London **State:** England **PC:** **Country: United Kingdom**
Year Established: 2015 **Status 2020:** Active
Industries: Artificial Intelligence for:, Application Services

Company Name: Lumen
Description: App
Website: http://www.lumenapp.com
Phone: **Email:** hello@lumenapp.com
City: London **State:** England **PC:** **Country: United Kingdom**
Year Established: **Status 2020:** Active
Industries:

Company Name: Lumi Social News
Description: Personalized mobile news and stories, built around an efficient recommendations engine and a powerful social layer
Website: http://lumi.do
Phone: **Email:** hello@lumi.do
City: London **State:** England **PC:** **Country: United Kingdom**
Year Established: **Status 2020:** Active
Industries: Artificial Intelligence for:, ~ Social Media (54)

Company Name: Lumilinks
Description: A marketing platform to maximise data value while preserving peoples right to privacy
Website: http://www.lumilinks.com
Phone: **Email:** hello@lumilinks.com
City: London **State:** England **PC:** **Country: United Kingdom**
Year Established: 2019 **Status 2020:** Active
Industries: Artificial Intelligence

Company Name: Lutebox
Description: Lutebox is the award winning company behind Dispatch, an on-command service that gets you food, drinks and essentials by instant message.
Website: http://www.lutebox.com
Phone: **Email:** contact@lutebox.com
City: London **State:** England **PC:** **Country: United Kingdom**
Year Established: **Status 2020:** Active
Industries: Artificial Intelligence for:, ~ Telecommunications (56)

Company Name: Maan: Switzerland
Description: Platform
Website: http://www.maanch.com
Phone: **Email:** darshita@maanch.com
City: London **State:** England **PC:** **Country: United Kingdom**
Year Established: 2018 **Status 2020:** Active
Industries: Artificial Intelligence for:, IT Managed Services

Company Name: Machine Medicine Technologies
Description: Our mission is to augment clinicians with AI. We are starting with hypervision for motor assessment in Parkinson's disea: Sweden
Website: http://machinemedicine.com/
Phone: **Email:** info@machinemedicine.com
City: London **State:** England **PC:** **Country: United Kingdom**
Year Established: 2017 **Status 2020:** Active
Industries:

Company Name: Magic Pony Technology
Description: Magic Pony Technology is a technology company that develops machine-learning based approach for visual processing on web and mobile.
Website: http://www.magicpony.technology/
Phone: **Email:** contact@magicpony.technology
City: London **State:** England **PC:** **Country: United Kingdom**

Year Established: **Status 2020:** Active
Industries: Artificial Intelligence for:, Computer Vision for:, Machine Learning for:, ~ Professional Services (48), ~ Media-Communications (41)

Company Name: Makerble
Description: Makerble enables charities to track, review and share their impact
Website: http://www.makerble.com
Phone: **Email:** matt@makerble.com
City: London **State:** England **PC:** **Country: United Kingdom**
Year Established: **Status 2020:** Active
Industries: Analytics for:, Artificial Intelligence for:, ~ Professional Services (48)

Company Name: Manas AI
Description: AI startup in NLP/ language modelling and predictions of customer and market behaviour. Retail & Finance secto: Serbia
Website: http://manas.ai/
Phone: **Email:** admin@manas.ai
City: London **State:** England **PC:** **Country: United Kingdom**
Year Established: 2018 **Status 2020:** Active
Industries: Artificial Intelligence for:, IT Managed Services

Company Name: Manifold
Description: Manifold building artificial intelligence for data science.
Website: http://manifoldx.com/
Phone: **Email:** contact@manifoldx.com
City: London **State:** England **PC:** **Country: United Kingdom**
Year Established: **Status 2020:** Active
Industries: Artificial Intelligence for:, Big Data and Analytics for:, Predictive Analytics

Company Name: Massive Analytic
Description: Massive Analytic is a London-based analytics innovator, with patented world leading technologies and global big data heritage.
Website: http://www.massiveanalytic.com
Phone: 44(0)207 100 1140 **Email:** contact@massiveanalytic.com
City: London **State:** England **PC:** **Country: United Kingdom**
Year Established: **Status 2020:** Active
Industries: Artificial Intelligence for:, Big Data and Analytics for:, Data Management for:, Machine Learning for:, Predictive Analytics for:, ~ Professional Services (48)

Company **Name:** Matchdeck Ltd
Description: Global corporate Knowledge Graph with over 16 million company profil: Spain
Website: http://www.matchdeck.com
Phone: 44 (0) 7974573170 **Email:** cp@matchdeck.com
City: London **State:** England **PC:** **Country: United Kingdom**
Year Established: **Status 2020:** Active
Industries: Artificial Intelligence for:, Big Data and Analytics for:, Databases for:, Cyber Security for:, Finance and Accounting

Company Name: Materialize.X
Description: Materialize.X combines the power of material science and machine learning to optimise new materials. First product; BioGlue (non toxic).
Website: http://www.materializex.com/
Phone: **Email:** haidin.rashid@materializex.com
City: London **State:** England **PC:** **Country: United Kingdom**
Year Established: 2016 **Status 2020:** Active
Industries: Artificial Intelligence for:, Machine Learning

Company Name: Matrix Mill
Description: Matrix Mill is a tech company that works on machine learning and computer vision to create realistic 3D occlusion effects.
Website: http://www.matrixmill.com
Phone: **Email:** 36945@reference-encyclopedia-ai.net
City: London **State:** England **PC:** **Country: United Kingdom**
Year Established: 2017 **Status 2020:** Active
Industries: Artificial Intelligence for:, Augmented Reality for:, Computer Vision for:, Machine Learning

Company Name: Maxatta Limited
Description: Maxatta is a leader in Robotic Process Automation and the delivery of AI through automation for Front Office Financial Markets.
Website: http://www.maxatta.com
Phone: 2088866354 **Email:** info@maxatta.com
City: London **State:** England **PC:** **Country: United Kingdom**
Year Established: **Status 2020:** Active
Industries: Artificial Intelligence for:, ~ Banking and Financial Markets-Services (7), IT Managed Services for:, Robotics

Company Name: Measmerize
Description: SaaS providers of a solution aimed at reducing returns and increasing sales in fashion e-commerce
Website: http://www.measmerize.com
Phone: **Email:** hello@measmerize.com
City: London **State:** England **PC:** **Country: United Kingdom**
Year Established: **Status 2020:** Active
Industries: Big Data and Analytics for:, E-Commerce for:, E-Commerce for:, ~ Fashion (16), ~ Retail and Consumer Products (52)

Company Name: MediaGam: Morocco
Description: MediaGamma is an AI technology company that uses machine learning and data science to help digital clients understand digital user behaviour
Website: www.mediagamma.com
Phone: **Email:** info@mediagamma.com
City: London **State:** England **PC:** **Country: United Kingdom**
Year Established: **Status 2020:** Active
Industries: ~ Media-Communications (41), ~ Media-Communications (41), Artificial Intelligence for:, Big Data and Analytics for:, Application Services for:, Machine Learning for:, Predictive Analytics

Company Name: MedicBank
Description: MedicBank a web & mobile platform where hospitals can hire permanent & temp workers directly using AI technology.
Website: http://medicbankapp.com
Phone: **Email:** Info@medicbankapp.com
City: London **State:** England **PC:** **Country: United Kingdom**
Year Established: 2017 **Status 2020:** Active
Industries:

Company Name: MediLiV: Spain
Description: Uberization of Healthcare & Telemedicine. Join the innovative AI based telemedicine system.
Website: http://www.medilives.io/en
Phone: **Email:** info@medilives.io
City: London **State:** England **PC:** **Country: United Kingdom**
Year Established: 2018 **Status 2020:** Active
Industries: Artificial Intelligence for:, ~ Healthcare (20)

Company Name: Medimsight
Description: Medical image triage and biomarkers analysis for precision medicine.
Website: http://www.medimsight.com
Phone: 44 (0) 7840343969 **Email:** contact@medimsight.com
City: London **State:** England **PC:** **Country: United Kingdom**
Year Established: 2013 **Status 2020:** Active
Industries:

Company Name: Medopad
Description: Medopad is a British health tech company named a $1 billion unicorn in the making by KPMG.
Website: http://www.medopad.com
Phone: **Email:** contact@medopad.com
City: London **State:** England **PC:** **Country: United Kingdom**

Year Established: **Status 2020:** Active
Industries: Application Services for:, Artificial Intelligence for:, Big Data and Analytics for:, Enterprise Application Services for:, ~ Healthcare (20), Mobile

Company Name: MeetCute
Description: Enriching conversations and relationships using AI
Website: http://meetcute.ai
Phone: **Email:** enquire@meetcute.ai
City: London **State:** England **PC:** **Country: United Kingdom**
Year Established: 2019 **Status 2020:** Active
Industries: Application Services for:, Artificial Intelligence for:, IT Managed Services

Company Name: Memgra: Philippin: Spain
Description: Memgraph offers a real-time graph database.
Website: http://www.memgraph.io/
Phone: **Email:** contact@memgraph.io
City: London **State:** England **PC:** **Country: United Kingdom**
Year Established: **Status 2020:** Active
Industries: Artificial Intelligence for:, Cloud for:, Databases

Company Name: Meniga
Description: Leader in digital banking solutions helping financial institutions worldwide utilise data to improve digital channels & customer engagement.
Website: http://www.meniga.com
Phone: 44 (0) 203 865 2663 **Email:** meniga@meniga.com
City: London **State:** England **PC:** **Country: United Kingdom**
Year Established: **Status 2020:** Active
Industries: ~ Media-Communications (41), Artificial Intelligence for:, ~ Banking and Financial Markets-Services (7), Data Management for:, ~ Banking and Financial Markets-Services (7), Machine Learning for:, Finance and Accounting for:, ~ Media-Communications (41), ~ Profess

Company Name: Mentat Innovations
Description: Mentat Innovations is creates smart data driven insights, statistically sound, in real time.
Website: http://www.ment.at
Phone: 44 203 6373330 **Email:** info@ment.at
City: London **State:** England **PC:** **Country: United Kingdom**
Year Established: **Status 2020:** Active
Industries: Analytics for:, Artificial Intelligence for:, Business Intelligence for:, Machine Learning for:, Compute

Company Name: Mentorite
Description: AI powered platform that aims to reduce the attrition rate in large companies.
Website: http://www.mentorite.co.uk
Phone: **Email:** info@mentorite.co.uk
City: London **State:** England **PC:** **Country: United Kingdom**
Year Established: 2018 **Status 2020:** Active
Industries: Artificial Intelligence for:, Enterprise Application Services

Company Name: Mercanto
Description: Mercanto is an AI-as-a-service company powering CRM experiences for B2C enterprises.
Website: http://mercanto.app
Phone: 020 8088 2222 **Email:** peter@mercanto.app
City: London **State:** England **PC:** **Country: United Kingdom**
Year Established: **Status 2020:** Active
Industries: Artificial Intelligence for:, Big Data and Analytics for:, ~ Media-Communications (41), ~ Media-Communications (41), Machine Learning for:, ~ Media-Communications (41), ~ Media-Communications (41)

Company Name: Metafused
Description: Metafused use aritificial intelligence based time series predictions to increase banking efficiency by 20%
Website: http://www.metafused.com
Phone: **Email:** mk@metafused.com
City: London **State:** England **PC:** **Country: United Kingdom**
Year Established: **Status 2020:** Active
Industries: Analytics for:, Artificial Intelligence for:, Big Data and Analytics for:, ~ Banking and Financial Markets-Services (7), ~ Insurance (25), Machine Learning

Company Name: Metage: Nigeria
Description: Metageni creates predictive models for customer journey optimisation and grow:Thailand
Website: http://www.metageni.com
Phone: 44 (0)20 8242 1734 **Email:** hello@metageni.com
City: London **State:** England **PC:** **Country: United Kingdom**
Year Established: **Status 2020:** Active
Industries: Artificial Intelligence for:, Business Intelligence for:, Machine Learning

Company Name: Metis Labs
Description: Intelligent software, improving the performance of manufacturing processes.
Website: http://www.metislabs.tech
Phone: **Email:** hello@metislabs.tech
City: London **State:** England **PC:** **Country: United Kingdom**
Year Established: **Status 2020:** Active
Industries: Artificial Intelligence for:, ~ Energy and Utilities (14), Industrial Solutions for:, Machine Learning for:, ~ Manufacturing-Miscellaneous (34)

Company Name: Mettrr
Description: Build your business, not your website. Automated DIFM at scale.
Website: http://www.mettrr.com
Phone: **Email:** hello@mettrr.com
City: London **State:** England **PC:** **Country: United Kingdom**
Year Established: **Status 2020:** Active
Industries: Artificial Intelligence for:, Cyber Security

Company Name: MICROBLINK
Description: Microblink is a research and development company focused on machine vision technology for mobile devices.
Website: http://microblink.com
Phone: **Email:** info@microblink.com
City: London **State:** England **PC:** **Country: United Kingdom**
Year Established: **Status 2020:** Active
Industries: Artificial Intelligence for:, Computer Vision for:, Application Services for:, Identity for:, Image Recognition for:, Machine Learning

Company Name: Migacore Technologies
Description: Migacore Technologies is an early stage data science startup that focuses on bringing predictive demand forecasting for airlines.
Website: http://migacore.com/
Phone: **Email:** contact@migacore.com
City: London **State:** England **PC:** **Country: United Kingdom**
Year Established: 2017 **Status 2020:** Active
Industries: ~ Aerospace and Defense (2), Application Services for:, Machine Learning for:, Natural Language Processing for:, Predictive Analytics

Company Name: Mimica Automation
Description: Mimica watches you work and learns to automate your most repetitive tasks.
Website: http://mimica.ai/
Phone: **Email:** tuhin@mimica.ai
City: London **State:** England **PC:** **Country: United Kingdom**
Year Established: **Status 2020:** Active
Industries:

Company Name: Mind Senses Global
Description: Artificial Intelligence Management Consultancy
Website: http://mindsenses.co.uk/
Phone: 44(0)7555775619 **Email:** info@mindsenses.co.uk
City: London **State:** England **PC:** **Country: United Kingdom**

Year Established: 2018 **Status 2020:** Active
Industries: Artificial Intelligence for:, Machine Learning for:, Predictive Analytics

Company Name: MindX
Description: MindX is a next generation predictive hiring & talent analytics platform powered by machine learning / AI and integrating game technology.
Website: http://mindx.co/
Phone: **Email:** hi@mindx.co
City: London **State:** England **PC:** **Country: United Kingdom**
Year Established: 2014 **Status 2020:** Active
Industries: Analytics for:, Artificial Intelligence for:, Big Data and Analytics

Company Name: Mindzilla
Description: Redefining Knowledge Discovery for Users and Enterprises Powered by Science, Blockchain and Artificial Intelligence
Website: http://mindzilla.com
Phone: **Email:** hello@mindzilla.com
City: London **State:** England **PC:** **Country: United Kingdom**
Year Established: **Status 2020:** Active
Industries: Artificial Intelligence for:, Big Data and Analytics for:, Blockchain for:, Business Intelligence for:, Databases

Company Name: Modularity Grid
Description: Intelligent sensors and software for managing electrical systems for electric utilities and aerospace markets
Website: http://www.modularitygrid.com
Phone: **Email:** hello@modularitygrid.com
City: London **State:** England **PC:** **Country: United Kingdom**
Year Established: 2017 **Status 2020:** Active
Industries: ~ Aerospace and Defense (2), ~ Energy and Utilities (14), Internet of Things (IoT) for:, Predictive Analytics

Company Name: Mokartzi
Description: soon
Website: http://www.mokartzi.com
Phone: **Email:** 37005@reference-encyclopedia-ai.net
City: London **State:** England **PC:** **Country: United Kingdom**
Year Established: 2016 **Status 2020:** Active
Industries: ~ Arts-Entertainment-Recreation (4), Artificial Intelligence

Company Name: Momentum Data
Description: AI-driven sales development & sales intelligence for the European market. Real-time enriched company data for your sales outreach.
Website: http://momentumdata.com/
Phone: **Email:** hello@momentumdata.com
City: London **State:** England **PC:** **Country: United Kingdom**
Year Established: 2017 **Status 2020:** Active
Industries: Analytics for:, Artificial Intelligence for:, Digital Marketing for:, IT Managed Services

Company Name: MoneyDrome Ltd
Description: MoneyDrome is a hybrid investment & trading platform enhanced by analytics, machine-learning and artificial intelligence
Website: http://www.moneydrome.com
Phone: **Email:** 37009@reference-encyclopedia-ai.net
City: London **State:** England **PC:** **Country: United Kingdom**
Year Established: 2015 **Status 2020:** Active
Industries: Artificial Intelligence for:, Databases for:, ~ Banking and Financial Markets-Services (7), ~ Banking and Financial Markets-Services (7)

Company Name: Monolith AI
Description: Monolith AI has built the world's first AI assistant for Engineee: Serbia
Website: http://www.monolithai.com/
Phone: **Email:** contact@monolithai.com
City: London **State:** England **PC:** **Country: United Kingdom**
Year Established: 2016 **Status 2020:** Active
Industries:

Company Name: Moogi Films
Description: Moogi is a movie discovery engine that lets you search for the movies that you want, in the way that you want.
Website: http://moogi.co
Phone: **Email:** info@moogi.co
City: London **State:** England **PC:** **Country: United Kingdom**
Year Established: **Status 2020:** Active
Industries: Artificial Intelligence

Company Name: Motuslab
Description: Motuslab provides crop analytics through the use of autonomous drones and AI, allowing farmers to increase crop yield and performance
Website: http://www.motuslab.co.uk
Phone: **Email:** press@motuslab.co.uk
City: London **State:** England **PC:** **Country: United Kingdom**
Year Established: 2018 **Status 2020:** Active
Industries: ~ Agriculture (3), Analytics for:, Artificial Intelligence for:, Machine Learning

Company Name: MOV.AI
Description: MOV.AI is an industry-grade operating system for autonomous robots.
Website: http://mov.ai
Phone: 351 21 485 2548 **Email:** opportunities@mov.ai
City: London **State:** England **PC:** **Country: United Kingdom**
Year Established: **Status 2020:** Active
Industries: Artificial Intelligence for:, ~ Automotive (5), ~ Transportation and Logistics (57), Robotics

Company Name: MOXI AI
Description: MOXI is an AI butler for your social life. The fastest way to achieve group consensus.
Website: http://www.moxibot.com
Phone: **Email:** hello@moxibot.com
City: London **State:** England **PC:** **Country: United Kingdom**
Year Established: 2019 **Status 2020:** Active
Industries: Artificial Intelligence for:, ~ Arts-Entertainment-Recreation (4)

Company Name: Muda
Description: Mudano, part of Accenture Applied Intelligence, is a data and machine learning company focused on financial services.
Website: http://mudano.com
Phone: **Email:** info@mudano.com
City: London **State:** England **PC:** **Country: United Kingdom**
Year Established: 2014 **Status 2020:** Active
Industries: Artificial Intelligence for:, Data Management for:, IT Managed Services for:, Machine Learning

Company Name: Mujo Mechanics
Description: Mujo Mechanics provides smart devices and intelligent cloud platform for a data-driven approach to musculoskeletal health.
Website: http://www.mujofitness.com/
Phone: 34961410675 **Email:** info@mujofitness.com
City: London **State:** England **PC:** **Country: United Kingdom**
Year Established: **Status 2020:** Active
Industries:

Company Name: MXX
Description: MXX is a creative AI technology company. We have built the world's first AI engine that atomises and edits any music to video, instantly.
Website: http://www.mxxmusic.com
Phone: 44 7454004165 **Email:** ken@mxxmusic.com
City: London **State:** England **PC:** **Country: United Kingdom**
Year Established: 2015 **Status 2020:** Active
Industries: ~ Arts-Entertainment-Recreation (4)

Company Name: MYCHOPCHOP
Description: Dynamic learning and task management app for cooking backed by artificial intelligence
Website: http://www.mychopchop.com/
Phone: **Email:** team@mychopchop.com
City: London **State:** England **PC:** **Country: United Kingdom**
Year Established: 2014 **Status 2020:** Closed
Industries: Application Services for:, Artificial Intelligence for:, ~ Food and Beverage (17)

Company Name: myTamar: India
Description: myTamarin is an AI-powered childcare matchmaker.
Website: http://mytamarin.com/
Phone: 44-203-432-02-34 **Email:** hello@mytamarin.com
City: London **State:** England **PC:** **Country: United Kingdom**
Year Established: 2017 **Status 2020:** Active
Industries: Artificial Intelligence for:, ~ Social Assistance-Non-Profits (53)

Company Name: Near Future Labs Ltd.
Description: Human centric design focused company creating content, simulations and platforms in Immersive technology (AR, VR, MR)
Website: http://www.nearfuturelabs.com
Phone: **Email:** hello@nearfuturelabs.com
City: London **State:** England **PC:** **Country: United Kingdom**
Year Established: 2017 **Status 2020:** Active
Industries: Artificial Intelligence for:, IT Managed Services for:, Virtual Reality (VR)

Company Name: Nebuli
Description: Cloud-based sophisticated augmented intelligence and blockchain services out of the box, making your existing systems work smarter for you.
Website: http://nebuli.com
Phone: **Email:** hi@nebuli.com
City: London **State:** England **PC:** **Country: United Kingdom**
Year Established: **Status 2020:** Active
Industries: Artificial Intelligence for:, Big Data and Analytics for:, IT Managed Services for:, Web for:, Machine Learning for:, ~ Professional Services (48)

Company **Name:** Neo AI
Description: Neo AI develops a technology that makes using machine learning cheaper and faster, enabling new applications around different industries.
Website: http://neo-ai.com/
Phone: **Email:** contact@neo-ai.com
City: London **State:** England **PC:** **Country: United Kingdom**
Year Established: **Status 2020:** Active
Industries: Artificial Intelligence for:, Application Services for:, ~ Education (13), Machine Learning

Company Name: Neon Century Intelligence
Description: Open Source Intelligence - Cyber Security - Corporate Investigations
Website: http://www.neoncentury.io
Phone: 13103827394 **Email:** enquiries@neoncentury.io
City: London **State:** England **PC:** **Country: United Kingdom**
Year Established: **Status 2020:** Active
Industries: Analytics for:, Artificial Intelligence for:, Cyber Security for:, Data Management for:, ~ Banking and Financial Markets-Services (7), Cyber Security for:, ~ Law-Legal Services (26), Machine Learning for:, Cyber Security

Company Name: NetOP Technology
Description: IoT As A Service
Website: http://netop.io
Phone: 31615582211 **Email:** connect@netop.io
City: London **State:** England **PC:** **Country: United Kingdom**
Year Established: **Status 2020:** Active
Industries: Artificial Intelligence for:, ~ Manufacturing-Electronic (30), ~ Real Estate (49)

Company Name: Neurobotx
Description: NeurobotX is a combine state-of-the-art neuroscience, AI and robotics in order to create spatial intelligence for autonomous drones & cars.
Website: http://neurobotx.org
Phone: **Email:** diana@neurobotx.org
City: London **State:** England **PC:** **Country: United Kingdom**
Year Established: 2019 **Status 2020:** Active
Industries: ~ Aerospace and Defense (2), Artificial Intelligence for:, ~ Automotive (5), ~ Automotive (5), Business Applications for:, Computer Vision for:, Internet of Things (IoT) for:, Machine Learning for:, Machine Learning

Company Name: Neurocreate
Description: NeuroCreate enable you to reach Flow mental states at will through their AI-powered digital platform.
Website: http://www.neurocreate.co.uk
Phone: **Email:** shama@neurocreate.co.uk
City: London **State:** England **PC:** **Country: United Kingdom**
Year Established: 2017 **Status 2020:** Active
Industries:

Company Name: Neurolabs
Description: Neurolabs builds a Computer Vision platform allowing users to build custom image recognition algorithms using 3D models.
Website: http://www.neurolabs.eu/
Phone: **Email:** hello@neurolabs.eu
City: London **State:** England **PC:** **Country: United Kingdom**
Year Established: 2018 **Status 2020:** Active
Industries:

Company Name: Neurons Lab
Description: Neurons Lab specializes in designing AI-based solutions for SMBs and startups.
Website: http://www.neurons-lab.com
Phone: **Email:** 37053@reference-encyclopedia-ai.net
City: London **State:** England **PC:** **Country: United Kingdom**
Year Established: 2018 **Status 2020:** Active
Industries: Artificial Intelligence for:, IT Managed Services

Company Name: newsflo
Description: Media monitoring shouldn't be a chore. With newsflo, it's easy to keep track of coverage at all levels of your institution.
Website: http://newsflo.net
Phone: 2036863371 **Email:** info@newsflo.net
City: London **State:** England **PC:** **Country: United Kingdom**
Year Established: **Status 2020:** Active
Industries: Analytics for:, Artificial Intelligence for:, Digital Media for:, ~ Social Media (54)

Company Name: NextQuestion
Description: NextQuestion builds AI models for retailers and transport companies, which improve client asset utilization and reduce excess inventory.
Website: http://nextquestion.io/
Phone: **Email:** info@nextquestion.io
City: London **State:** England **PC:** **Country: United Kingdom**
Year Established: 2017 **Status 2020:** Active
Industries:

Company Name: Nexus Frontier Tech
Description: Integration of AI solutions into existing systems, helping save time & money by employing solutions tackling inefficiency & data waste.
Website: http://nexusfrontier.tech
Phone: **Email:** info@nexusfrontier.tech
City: London **State:** England **PC:** **Country: United Kingdom**
Year Established: **Status 2020:** Active
Industries: Artificial Intelligence for:, Machine Learning for:, Natural Language Processing

Company Name: Nexus FrontierTech
Description: We integrate AI solutions into existing systems, helping save time & money by employing solutions tackling inefficiency & data waste.
Website: http://nexusfrontier.tech
Phone: **Email:** info@nexusfrontier.tech
City: London **State:** England **PC:** **Country: United Kingdom**
Year Established: 2015 **Status 2020:** Active
Industries: Artificial Intelligence for:, Application Services for:, Application Services for:, Machine Learning for:, Natural Language Processing for:, Enterprise Application Services

Company Name: Nimbletank
Description: Nimbletank is a digital product, commerce and service accelerator creating services, tools and products with a purpose.
Website: http://www.nimbletank.com/
Phone: 020 3828 6440 **Email:** paul.vallois@nimbletank.com
City: London **State:** England **PC:** **Country: United Kingdom**
Year Established: 2011 **Status 2020:** Active
Industries:

Company Name: NLSQL
Description: NLSQL is cognitive BI technology, which helps company employees to get information quickly and easily using only Natural Language
Website: https://www.nlsql.com/
Phone: **Email:** denis@nlsql.com
City: LONDON **State:** England **Zip:** En **Country: United Kingdom**
Year Established: **Status 2020:** Active
Industries: Analytics for:, ~ Healthcare (142), ~ Life Sciences (149), ~ Retail and Consumer Products (174), Application Program Interfaces (APIs) for:, Artificial Intelligence for:, Big Data and Analytics for:, Business Intelligence for:, ~ Healthcare (691), ~ Life Scienc: Spain

Company Name: Noble
Description: Noble develops innovative network cyber security applications using advanced AI-based technology.
Website: http://www.noblecss.io
Phone: 44 203 917 3918 **Email:** info@noblecss.io
City: London **State:** England **PC:** **Country: United Kingdom**
Year Established: 2016 **Status 2020:** Active
Industries: Cyber Security for:, Enterprise Application Services for:, Machine Learning for:, Security for:, Predictive Analytics

Company Name: Nome
Description: Nome is an AI-powered digital assistant for foodies.
Website: http://getnomeapp.com
Phone: **Email:** support@nomenome.com
City: London **State:** England **PC:** **Country: United Kingdom**
Year Established: 2018 **Status 2020:** Active
Industries: Application Services for:, Artificial Intelligence for:, ~ Food and Beverage (17), Web

Company Name: Novum Insights
Description: Big data, software, market mapping, AI, cybersecurity, reports, IOT, fintech, blockchain, venture capital
Website: http://www.novuminsights.com
Phone: **Email:** info@novuminsights.com
City: London **State:** England **PC:** **Country: United Kingdom**
Year Established: 2016 **Status 2020:** Active
Industries: Analytics for:, Artificial Intelligence for:, ~ Banking and Financial Markets-Services (7), Cyber Security for:, IT Managed Services for:, Web

Company Name: nPlan
Description: Artificial Intelligence to provide schedule certainty for projects, by highlighting risk and suggesting optimal execution paths.
Website: http://www.nplan.io
Phone: **Email:** hello@nplan.io
City: London **State:** England **PC:** **Country: United Kingdom**
Year Established: **Status 2020:** Active
Industries: Artificial Intelligence for:, ~ Construction (10), Application Services

Company Name: Ntropy
Description: Ntropy is a family of client-side data, algorithms and applications.
Website: http://ntropy.network
Phone: **Email:** hello@ntropy.network
City: London **State:** England **PC:** **Country: United Kingdom**
Year Established: **Status 2020:** Active
Industries: Artificial Intelligence for:, Cyber Security

Company Name: NumberEight
Description: NumberEight predicts user intent on mobile devices through artificial intelligence and sensors.
Website: http://www.numbereight.me
Phone: **Email:** hi@numbereight.me
City: London **State:** England **PC:** **Country: United Kingdom**
Year Established: **Status 2020:** Active
Industries: Artificial Intelligence for:, Machine Learning for:, ~ Manufacturing-Electronic (30), ~ Professional Services (48)

Company Name: Nurturey
Description: Nurturey is the smartest Personal Assistant for parents
Website: http://www.nurturey.com/
Phone: **Email:** tushar@nurturey.com
City: London **State:** England **PC:** **Country: United Kingdom**
Year Established: 2014 **Status 2020:** Active
Industries: Application Services

Company Name: Observe Technologies
Description: Observe applies computer vision and machine learning to optimise aquaculture farms.
Website: http://www.observanow.com
Phone: (206)900-9833 **Email:** investor-relations@observanow.com
City: London **State:** England **PC:** **Country: United Kingdom**
Year Established: 2015 **Status 2020:** Active
Industries: ~ Agriculture (3), Artificial Intelligence

Company Name: Obvious Engineering
Description: Obvious Engineering is a research & development-driven software company with a focus on consumer products.
Website: http://obviousengine.com
Phone: **Email:** info@obviousengine.com
City: London **State:** England **PC:** **Country: United Kingdom**
Year Established: 2013 **Status 2020:** Active
Industries: Computer Vision for:, Machine Learning for:, Mobile

Company Name: OilX
Description: The world's first digital oil analyst
Website: http://oilx.co/
Phone: 44 203 950 0647 **Email:** info@oilx.co
City: London **State:** England **PC:** **Country: United Kingdom**
Year Established: **Status 2020:** Active
Industries:

Company Name: Olvin
Description: Olvin is an analytics platform that serves premium quality intelligence to the drinks trade.
Website: http://www.olvin.com
Phone: **Email:** hello@olvin.com
City: London **State:** England **PC:** **Country: United Kingdom**
Year Established: **Status 2020:** Active
Industries: Artificial Intelligence for:, Business Applications for:, Big Data and Analytics for:, Business Intelligence for:, Machine Learning

Company Name: Omenics
Description: We help crypto traders and investors do their due diligence and get indicators based on news and social sentiment.
Website: http://omenics.com/
Phone: **Email:** contact@omenics.com
City: London **State:** England **PC:** **Country: United Kingdom**
Year Established: **Status 2020:** Active
Industries: Artificial Intelligence for:, ~ Banking and Financial Markets-Services (7), Blockchain for:, ~ Banking and Financial Markets-Services (7), Databases for:, ~ Banking and Financial Markets-Services (7), Machine Learning for:, ~ Social Media (54)

Company Name: Ometria
Description: Ometria is a customer insight and marketing automation platform which lets retailers communicate with their customers in a personalised way.
Website: http://www.ometria.com
Phone: 44 20 7016 8383 **Email:** info@ometria.com
City: London **State:** England **PC:** **Country: United Kingdom**
Year Established: **Status 2020:** Active
Industries: Analytics for:, Artificial Intelligence for:, E-Commerce for:, ~ Media-Communications (41)

Company Name: Onaria Technologies
Description: Onaria empower people with the digital tools they need to take control and optimise their health everyday.
Website: http://onariatech.com
Phone: **Email:** gina@onariatech.com
City: London **State:** England **PC:** **Country: United Kingdom**
Year Established: 2015 **Status 2020:** Active
Industries:

Company Name: Opalcrest
Description: Opalcrest is an AI focused investment holding company.
Website: http://www.opalcrest.com/
Phone: **Email:** info@opalcrest.com
City: London **State:** England **PC:** **Country: United Kingdom**
Year Established: 2013 **Status 2020:** Active
Industries: Artificial Intelligence

Company Name: Open Risk Exchange
Description: Open Risk Exchange (ORX) is the first online portal offering free credit scores for businesses in the United Kingdom.
Website: http://www.openriskexchange.com/
Phone: **Email:** team@openriskexchange.com
City: London **State:** England **PC:** **Country: United Kingdom**
Year Established: **Status 2020:** Active
Industries: Artificial Intelligence for:, Business Applications for:, ~ Banking and Financial Markets-Services (7), ~ Banking and Financial Markets-Services (7), ~ Insurance (25), Machine Learning for:, Risk Management for:, Supply Chain Management

Company Name: OpenSenso: Serbia
Description: OpenSensors.io are an internet of things company building a connected world that puts people first.
Website: http://opensensors.com/
Phone: **Email:** hello@opensensors.com
City: London **State:** England **PC:** **Country: United Kingdom**
Year Established: **Status 2020:** Active
Industries: Artificial Intelligence for:, ~ Automotive (5), ~ Retail and Consumer Products (52), ~ Construction (10)

Company Name: OpenSignal
Description: OpenSignal provides a mobile application that crowd-sources data on the performance and coverage of wireless networks around the world.
Website: http://opensignal.com
Phone: 44 845 834 0987 **Email:** hello@opensignal.com
City: London **State:** England **PC:** **Country: United Kingdom**
Year Established: **Status 2020:** Active
Industries: Application Services for:, Artificial Intelligence for:, Mobile

Company Name: OpenWeather
Description: OpenWeather is a tech company with strong expertise in Big Data technologies, Environmental data science and Remote sensing.
Website: http://openweather.co.uk/
Phone: **Email:** info@openweathermap.org
City: London **State:** England **PC:** **Country: United Kingdom**
Year Established: **Status 2020:** Active
Industries: ~ Agriculture (3), Analytics for:, Artificial Intelligence for:, Big Data and Analytics for:, Cloud for:, Databases for:, ~ Agriculture (3), ~ Professional Services (48), Cyber Security

Company Name: Optalitix
Description: Applied machine learning for insurance and banking
Website: http://www.optalitix.com
Phone: **Email:** info@optalitix.com
City: London **State:** England **PC:** **Country: United Kingdom**
Year Established: 2013 **Status 2020:** Active
Industries: Artificial Intelligence for:, ~ Education (13), ~ Banking and Financial Markets-Services (7)

Company Name: Optia Systems
Description: Optia's mission is to build safe AGI, and ensure AGI's benefits are as widely and evenly distributed as possible.
Website: http://optia.weebly.com/
Phone: **Email:** 37115@reference-encyclopedia-ai.net
City: London **State:** England **PC:** **Country: United Kingdom**
Year Established: 2016 **Status 2020:** Closed
Industries: Artificial Intelligence

Company Name: OptiStructure
Description: SaaS
Website: http://www.optistructure.com
Phone: **Email:** nikolas@optistructure.com
City: London **State:** England **PC:** **Country: United Kingdom**
Year Established: 2020 **Status 2020:** Active
Industries: Artificial Intelligence for:, ~ Construction (10), Machine Learning for:, Business Software as a Service Apps (SaaS Apps)

Company Name: Oreeva
Description: Oreeva is an innovative Proptech start-up that uses AI and Big Data to provide instant and accurate Property Valuations
Website: http://www.oreeva.com/
Phone: **Email:** 37123@reference-encyclopedia-ai.net
City: London **State:** England **PC:** **Country: United Kingdom**
Year Established: 2015 **Status 2020:** Active
Industries: Artificial Intelligence for:, Machine Learning

Company Name: Orpiva
Description: ORPIVA is an omni-channel Machine Intelligence Platform empowering brands to monetise their audiences more effectively.
Website: http://www.orpiva.com
Phone: 44 2038702929 **Email:** hello@orpiva.com
City: London **State:** England **PC:** **Country: United Kingdom**
Year Established: **Status 2020:** Active
Industries:

Company Name: OrxaGrid
Description: OrxaGrid develops IoT sensors and AI to predict grid losses and improve efficiency
Website: http://www.orxagrid.com
Phone: 44 7842 745460 **Email:** info@orxagrid.com
City: London **State:** England **PC:** **Country: United Kingdom**
Year Established: 2017 **Status 2020:** Active
Industries: Artificial Intelligence for:, ~ Energy and Utilities (14), ~ Energy and Utilities (14), ~ Energy and Utilities (14)

Company Name: Oseven Telematics
Description: Insurance telematics and driving behavioural analytics
Website: http://www.oseven.io/
Phone: 30 2121023146 **Email:** info@oseven.io
City: London **State:** England **PC:** **Country: United Kingdom**

Year Established: **Status 2020:** Active
Industries: Artificial Intelligence for:, ~ Insurance (25), Machine Learning for:, ~ Transportation and Logistics (57)

Company Name: OTP London Ltd
Description: Startup tech company and software publishers of OTP.AR WORLD App.
Website: http://www.otplondon.com
Phone: **Email:** Info@otplondon.com
City: London **State:** England **PC:** **Country: United Kingdom**
Year Established: **Status 2020:** Active
Industries: Artificial Intelligence for:, Augmented Reality for:, Big Data and Analytics for:, IT Managed Services for:, Machine Learning for:, Application Services for:, ~ Media-Communications (41), ~ Social Media (54), ~ Professional Services (48)

Company Name: Outra
Description: Outra is a customer data science business.
Website: http://outra.co.uk/
Phone: 020 3880 8485 **Email:** info@outra.co.uk
City: London **State:** England **PC:** **Country: United Kingdom**
Year Established: 2016 **Status 2020:** Active
Industries: Artificial Intelligence for:, Big Data and Analytics for:, IT Managed Services

Company Name: Oyler
Description: Oyler is an AI Assistant that helps discretionary trading teams make better decisions
Website: http://oyler.co
Phone: **Email:** info@oyler.co
City: London **State:** England **PC:** **Country: United Kingdom**
Year Established: 2019 **Status 2020:** Active
Industries: Artificial Intelligence for:, IT Managed Services

Company Name: Pace
Description: Intelligent Pricing for the hospitality industry. We use machine learning to help you find the right price. London, England, United Kingdom
Website: http://www.paceup.com
Phone: 44(0)20 8242 4044 **Email:** contact@paceup.com
City: London **State:** England **PC:** **Country: United Kingdom**
Year Established: **Status 2020:** Active
Industries: Artificial Intelligence for:, ~ Hospitality (23), ~ Hospitality (23), Web for:, Machine Learning

Company Name: Parallel AI
Description: If a human can conceive of a use case using AI to make a decision in real time, our platform will automatically materialise : Italy
Website: http://www.parallelai.com
Phone: 44 20 3290 1275 **Email:** info@parallelai.com
City: London **State:** England **PC:** **Country: United Kingdom**
Year Established: **Status 2020:** Active
Industries: Artificial Intelligence for:, Machine Learning for:, ~ Media-Communications (41)

Company Name: Paremus
Description: The Paremus Service Fabric: the only federated, adaptive, modular platfrom for Enterprise, Smart City, Indust 4.0 & the Mobile Compute Edge
Website: http://www.paremus.com
Phone: **Email:** info@paremus.com
City: London **State:** England **PC:** **Country: United Kingdom**
Year Established: **Status 2020:** Active
Industries: Artificial Intelligence for:, Cloud for:, Enterprise Application Services for:, Machine Learning

Company Name: Pathwise Robotics
Description: Pathwise Robotics develops autonomous robot assistants for public spaces.
Website: http://pathwise.tech
Phone: **Email:** 37144@reference-encyclopedia-ai.net
City: London **State:** England **PC:** **Country: United Kingdom**
Year Established: 2016 **Status 2020:** Active
Industries: Artificial Intelligence for:, Web for:, Web

Company Name: Paved
Description: Paved is a dedicated marketplace that matches fast growing companies with business development talent based on skills.
Website: http://mypaved.com/
Phone: **Email:** hi@mypaved.com
City: London **State:** England **PC:** **Country: United Kingdom**
Year Established: **Status 2020:** Active
Industries: Artificial Intelligence for:, ~ Human Resources (24)

Company Name: Payhawk
Description: Payhawk is the smartest Visa card that can do your expense reports, read receipts with OCR and get invoices from your email.
Website: http://payhawk.io/
Phone: 44 20 3962 1957 **Email:** friends@payhawk.io
City: London **State:** England **PC:** **Country: United Kingdom**
Year Established: **Status 2020:** Active
Industries: Artificial Intelligence for:, ~ Banking and Financial Markets-Services (7), ~ Banking and Financial Markets-Services (7)

Company Name: PayScanner
Description: Helping legacy payment ecosystems to adopt emerging payment ecosystems.
Website: http://www.payscanner.com
Phone: **Email:** 4484@reference-encyclopedia-ai.net
City: London **State:** England **PC:** **Country: United Kingdom**
Year Established: **Status 2020:** Active
Industries: Artificial Intelligence for:, Finance and Accounting for:, ~ Banking and Financial Markets-Services (7), ~ Banking and Financial Markets-Services (7), Machine Learning for:, ~ Banking and Financial Markets-Services (7)

Company Name: Pedal Global Holdings
Description: Pedal Global is a leading company within the Connected Car and Telematics industry.
Website: http://www.pedalapp.com
Phone: 7879292563 **Email:** richard@pedalglobal.com
City: London **State:** England **PC:** **Country: United Kingdom**
Year Established: **Status 2020:** Active
Industries: Artificial Intelligence for:, ~ Automotive (5), Blockchain for:, Web for:, ~ Manufacturing-Miscellaneous (34)

Company Name: Peptone
Description: AI - driven protein design and optimization.
Website: http://peptone.io C2
Phone: **Email:** hello@peptone.io
City: London **State:** England **PC:** **Country: United Kingdom**
Year Established: 2016 **Status 2020:** Active
Industries:

Company Name: Peptone - The Protein Intelligence Company
Description: Protein lead design, optimization and repurposing using AI.
Website: http://peptone.io
Phone: 39-338-592-0947 **Email:** hello@peptone.io
City: London **State:** England **PC:** **Country: United Kingdom**
Year Established: **Status 2020:** Active
Industries: Artificial Intelligence for:, Big Data and Analytics for:, ~ Biotechnology (9), ~ Life Sciences (27)

Company Name: PerchPeek
Description: AI powered Property Rental Platform
Website: http://www.perchpeek.com/
Phone: 020 8064 0974 **Email:** info@perchpeek.com
City: London **State:** England **PC:** **Country: United Kingdom**
Year Established: **Status 2020:** Active
Industries: ~ Real Estate (49)

Company Name: Perfect Channel
Description: B2B Martketplace technology and Marketplace design / engineering
Website: http://www.perfectchannel.com
Phone: 44 8000 337 815 **Email:** 37156@reference-encyclopedia-ai.net
City: London **State:** England **PC:** **Country: United Kingdom**
Year Established: 2011 **Status 2020:** Active
Industries: Analytics for:, Artificial Intelligence for:, ~ Retail and Consumer Products (52), Finance and Accounting for:, Finance and Accounting

Company Name: Permutive
Description: Permutive is a technology company focused on helping businesses use their behavioral data to make realtime decisions in their product.
Website: http://www.permutive.com/
Phone: 16502721736 **Email:** team@permutive.com
City: London **State:** England **PC:** **Country: United Kingdom**
Year Established: **Status 2020:** Active
Industries: ~ Media-Communications (41), Artificial Intelligence for:, Machine Learning for:, Compute for:, ~ Professional Services (48)

Company Name: Personify XP
Description: Personify XP automates digital experiences for anonymous digital shoppers driving an average increase of 10% in revenue.
Website: http://www.personifyxp.com
Phone: 44 (0) 203 879 1744 **Email:** ben@personifyxp.com
City: London **State:** England **PC:** **Country: United Kingdom**
Year Established: **Status 2020:** Active
Industries: Artificial Intelligence for:, ~ Media-Communications (41), ~ Professional Services (48), Machine Learning for:, ~ E-Commerce (3367), ~ Fashion (3371), ~ Gaming (3373), ~ Healthcare (3375), ~ Home (3377), ~ Hospitality (3378), Web

Company Name: PetaCrunch
Description: AI-powered media company
Website: http://petacrunch.com/
Phone: **Email:** 37158@reference-encyclopedia-ai.net
City: London **State:** England **PC:** **Country: United Kingdom**
Year Established: 2019 **Status 2020:** Active
Industries: Artificial Intelligence for:, Databases for:, Machine Learning for:, ~ Arts-Entertainment-Recreation (4)

Company Name: Photolemur
Description: Photolemur is world's first automated photo enhancement solution for Mac and Windows using image recognition.
Website: http://photolemur.com
Phone: **Email:** support@photolemur.com
City: London **State:** England **PC:** **Country: United Kingdom**
Year Established: 2016 **Status 2020:** Active
Industries: Artificial Intelligence for:, IT Managed Services for:, IT Managed Services

Company Name: Phrasee
Description: Phrasee is AI that specializes in language generation for email marketing, push, and Facebook copy.
Website: http://phrasee.co
Phone: **Email:** awesome@phrasee.co
City: London **State:** England **PC:** **Country: United Kingdom**
Year Established: **Status 2020:** Active
Industries: Artificial Intelligence for:, Digital Marketing for:, ~ Media-Communications (41), Machine Learning for:, Natural Language Processing

Company Name: Pia
Description: Pia is your smart, friendly and supportive AI companion.
Website: http://yourpia.com
Phone: 7812972829 **Email:** lily@yourpia.com
City: London **State:** England **PC:** **Country: United Kingdom**
Year Established: 2017 **Status 2020:** Active
Industries: Artificial Intelligence for:, ~ Banking and Financial Markets-Services (7)

Company Name: Pie People Ltd
Description: Fintech SaaS
Website:
Phone: **Email:** abdul@piepeople.io
City: London **State:** England **PC:** **Country: United Kingdom**
Year Established: **Status 2020:** Active
Industries: Artificial Intelligence for:, ~ Banking and Financial Markets-Services (7), Blockchain for:, ~ Banking and Financial Markets-Services (7), ~ Banking and Financial Markets-Services (7), ~ Banking and Financial Markets-Services (7), Machine Learning for:, Applicat

Company Name: Pillar Education
Description: Pillar Education offers a cloud-based feedback platform
Website:
Phone: **Email:** 37169@reference-encyclopedia-ai.net
City: London **State:** England **PC:** **Country: United Kingdom**
Year Established: 2016 **Status 2020:** Active
Industries: Artificial Intelligence for:, Big Data and Analytics

Company Name: Pimloc
Description: Pimloc's deep learning tools allow enterprises to extract value from images and video whilst maintaining control over their assets and IP.
Website: http://www.pimloc.com
Phone: **Email:** info@pimloc.com
City: London **State:** England **PC:** **Country: United Kingdom**
Year Established: 2016 **Status 2020:** Active
Industries: Artificial Intelligence for:, Big Data and Analytics for:, Enterprise Application Services

Company Name: Pimloc Ltd
Description: Pimloc is a machine learning company focussed on developing and enabling private and personalised image management solutions.
Website: http://View on Twitter
Phone: **Email:** info@pimloc.com
City: London **State:** England **PC:** **Country: United Kingdom**
Year Established: **Status 2020:** Active
Industries: Artificial Intelligence

Company Name: Pivigo
Description: Data is and will continue to change our lives. It is generated by us, for us and around us.
Website: http://www.pivigo.com/
Phone: **Email:** info@pivigo.com
City: London **State:** England **PC:** **Country: United Kingdom**
Year Established: **Status 2020:** Active
Industries:

Company Name: Pixoneye
Description: Pixoneye is a data analytics SaaS company.
Website: http://www.pixoneye.com/
Phone: 44 20 3488 3937 **Email:** office@pixoneye.com
City: London **State:** England **PC:** **Country: United Kingdom**
Year Established: 2015 **Status 2020:** Active
Industries: Artificial Intelligence for:, Machine Learning for:, Business Software as a Service Apps (SaaS Apps)

Company Name: Planet N Group of Companies
Description: Planet N Group is an emerging markets focused high-tech and social impact investment firm dedicated to development through digitization
Website: http://www.planetngroup.com
Phone: 44 (0) 207 698 4449 **Email:** info@planetngroup.com
City: London **State:** England **PC:** **Country: United Kingdom**
Year Established: 2016 **Status 2020:** Active
Industries: Artificial Intelligence for:, Digital Media for:, ~ Banking and Financial Markets-Services (7), ~ Banking and Financial

Markets-Services (7), IT Managed Services for:, ~ Arts-Entertainment-Recreation (4)

Company Name: Platform360
Description: Platform360 is the global leader in Native advertising solutions
Website: http://www.platform360.co
Phone: **Email:** sales@platform360.com
City: London **State:** England **PC:** **Country: United Kingdom**
Year Established: 2013 **Status 2020:** Active
Industries: Digital Marketing for:, Machine Learning

Company Name: PLATO Intelligence
Description: PLATO uses Artificial Intelligence and Machine Learning to help you recruit the best candidates and track them through their careers.
Website: http://simplyplato.com/
Phone: **Email:** 37178@reference-encyclopedia-ai.net
City: London **State:** England **PC:** **Country: United Kingdom**
Year Established: 2016 **Status 2020:** Active
Industries: Artificial Intelligence for:, ~ Education (13), Machine Learning

Company Name: Plum
Description: Plum is a personal savings assistant that links, monitors users current accounts, and send notifications about balances and savings.
Website: http://withplum.com
Phone: **Email:** hello@withplum.com
City: London **State:** England **PC:** **Country: United Kingdom**
Year Established: **Status 2020:** Active
Industries: Artificial Intelligence for:, ~ Banking and Financial Markets-Services (7), ~ Banking and Financial Markets-Services (7), Finance and Accounting

Company Name: Plum Fintech
Description: Plum Fintech develops personal savings assistant solutions for customers in the United Kingdom.
Website: http://withplum.com/
Phone: 020 3393 1340 **Email:** hello@withplum.com
City: London **State:** England **PC:** **Country: United Kingdom**
Year Established: 2016 **Status 2020:** Active
Industries: Artificial Intelligence for:, ~ Banking and Financial Markets-Services (7), ~ Banking and Financial Markets-Services (7), ~ Banking and Financial Markets-Services (7), Finance and Accounting

Company Name: Plumerai
Description: Plumerai is making small machines intelligent.
Website: http://plumerai.co.uk/
Phone: **Email:** 37181@reference-encyclopedia-ai.net
City: London **State:** England **PC:** **Country: United Kingdom**
Year Established: 2017 **Status 2020:** Active
Industries: Artificial Intelligence for:, Machine Learning

Company Name: Plural AI
Description: Plural AI builds knowledge engine for the finance industry.
Website: http://www.plural.ai/
Phone: **Email:** info@plural.ai
City: London **State:** England **PC:** **Country: United Kingdom**
Year Established: 2017 **Status 2020:** Active
Industries: Artificial Intelligence for:, ~ Banking and Financial Markets-Services (7), ~ Banking and Financial Markets-Services (7)

Company Name: Pobuca
Description: Pobuca is a CRM software house that offers turn-key solutions to brands and retailers.
Website: http://pobuca.com
Phone: **Email:** hello@pobu.ca
City: London **State:** England **PC:** **Country: United Kingdom**
Year Established: **Status 2020:** Active
Industries: Artificial Intelligence for:, Business Intelligence for:, ~ Retail and Consumer Products (52), Machine Learning for:, ~ Media-Communications (41), Automation for:, ~ Professional Services (48)

Company Name: Poin: Turkey
Description:
Website: https://www.pointr.tech/company
Phone: **Email:** contact@pointrlabs.com
City: London **State:** England **Zip:** W1F 9HT **Country: United Kingdom**
Year Established: **Status 2020:** Active
Industries:

Company Name: Policy Radar
Description: Discover & analyse the opinions of UK members of parliament across News, Social Media & Hansard
Website: http://policyradar.com
Phone: **Email:** 37187@reference-encyclopedia-ai.net
City: London **State:** England **PC:** **Country: United Kingdom**
Year Established: 2016 **Status 2020:** Active
Industries: Analytics for:, Artificial Intelligence for:, Machine Learning for:, ~ Social Assistance-Non-Profits (53)

Company Name: Poly AI
Description: Poly AI develops a machine learning platform for conversational artificial intelligence.
Website: http://www.poly-ai.com/
Phone: **Email:** contact@poly-ai.com
City: London **State:** England **PC:** **Country: United Kingdom**
Year Established: **Status 2020:** Active
Industries: Artificial Intelligence for:, Enterprise Application Services for:, Machine Learning for:, ~ Professional Services (48)

Company Name: Polymatica
Description: Polymatica is a data science company that pioneers new and accessible ways for global businesses to understand and use their data.
Website: http://www.polymatica.com
Phone: **Email:** info@polymatica.com
City: London **State:** England **PC:** **Country: United Kingdom**
Year Established: **Status 2020:** Active
Industries: Analytics for:, Artificial Intelligence for:, Business Intelligence

Company Name: Popcorn Metrics
Description: Popcorn Metrics is a visual integration solution to setup events and track customer actions on websites, without writing custom code.
Website: http://www.popcornmetrics.com
Phone: **Email:** info@popcornmetrics.com
City: London **State:** England **PC:** **Country: United Kingdom**
Year Established: 2013 **Status 2020:** Active
Industries:

Company Name: Popsa
Description: Popsa is a machine learning startup that automatically designs, makes, and delivers personalized physical products.
Website: http://www.ucare.ai/
Phone: **Email:** info@ucare.ai
City: London **State:** England **PC:** **Country: United Kingdom**
Year Established: **Status 2020:** Active
Industries: Artificial Intelligence for:, E-Commerce for:, Machine Learning for:, ~ Media-Communications (41), ~ Retail and Consumer Products (52)

Company Name: Potential.ly
Description: The smart lifelong learning platform
Website: http://www.potential.ly
Phone: **Email:** team@potential.ly
City: London **State:** England **PC:** **Country: United Kingdom**
Year Established: 2016 **Status 2020:** Active
Industries: Content for:, ~ Education (13), ~ Education (13), ~ Education (13), ~ Education (13), Machine Learning

Company Name: Powr of You
Description: Changing the personal data econo: Malaysia
Website: http://www.powrofyou.com
Phone: 1(925) 478-5670 **Email:** keshav@powrofyou.com
City: London **State:** England **PC:** **Country: United Kingdom**
Year Established: **Status 2020:** Active
Industries: Analytics for:, Artificial Intelligence for:, Big Data and Analytics for:, Web

Company Name: Precise TV
Description: AI driven data, insights, media and optimization platform for smarter YouTube buys
Website: http://www.precise.tv
Phone: 44 (0) 203 608 2605 **Email:** contact@precise.tv
City: London **State:** England **PC:** **Country: United Kingdom**
Year Established: 2015 **Status 2020:** Active
Industries: Analytics for:, Artificial Intelligence

Company Name: Predictive People
Description: Predictive People is a cognitive computing software which predicts employees' disengagement and stress, and provides customised action plans
Website: http://www.predictive-people.com
Phone: **Email:** stefanies@predictive-people.com
City: London **State:** England **PC:** **Country: United Kingdom**
Year Established: **Status 2020:** Active
Industries: Artificial Intelligence for:, ~ Human Resources (24), Machine Learning for:, Natural Language Processing

Company Name: Predina Tech
Description: Predina Technologies is an AI platform for predicting and mitigating risk in autonomous vehicles.
Website: http://www.predina.com
Phone: 7852403674 **Email:** info@predina.com
City: London **State:** England **PC:** **Country: United Kingdom**
Year Established: **Status 2020:** Active
Industries: Artificial Intelligence for:, IT Managed Services for:, ~ Professional Services (48)

Company Name: Previ: Sweden
Description: Previse has pioneered algorithm-driven invoice payment decisions.
Website: http://www.previ.se/
Phone: 44 191 580 4097 **Email:** help@previ.: Sweden
City: London **State:** England **PC:** **Country: United Kingdom**
Year Established: 2016 **Status 2020:** Active
Industries: Artificial Intelligence for:, Finance and Accounting for:, IT Managed Services for:, ~ Banking and Financial Markets-Services (7)

Company Name: Primafelicitas Ltd
Description: PrimaFelicitas is a full service Web & Mobile Solutions Design and Development, Blockchain Development and Digital Marketing Company.
Website: http://www.primafelicitas.com
Phone: 9999359083 **Email:** primafelicitas.llc@gmail.com
City: London **State:** England **PC:** **Country: United Kingdom**
Year Established: **Status 2020:** Active
Industries: Artificial Intelligence for:, Blockchain for:, Digital Marketing for:, Application Services for:, Cyber Security

Company Name: Priset
Description: AI and biometric data-driven online marketplace for women to find fashion recommendations according to their body shape and lifestyle.
Website: http://priset.co/
Phone: **Email:** austina@priset.co
City: London **State:** England **PC:** **Country: United Kingdom**
Year Established: **Status 2020:** Active
Industries: Artificial Intelligence for:, E-Commerce for:, E-Commerce for:, ~ Fashion (16)

Company Name: PRODA
Description: PRODA is focuses on solving core data processing pain points in real estate.
Website: http://proda.ai/
Phone: 44 (0) 203 813 0475 **Email:** info@proda.ai
City: London **State:** England **PC:** **Country: United Kingdom**
Year Established: 2017 **Status 2020:** Active
Industries: Artificial Intelligence for:, Big Data and Analytics for:, Business Software as a Service Apps (SaaS Apps)

Company Name: Prodo.ai
Description: Prodo.ai uses machine learning, data science, and human guidance to provide coding software services.
Website: http://prodo.ai/
Phone: **Email:** 37212@reference-encyclopedia-ai.net
City: London **State:** England **PC:** **Country: United Kingdom**
Year Established: 2016 **Status 2020:** Active
Industries: Artificial Intelligence for:, Enterprise Application Services for:, IT Managed Services for:, Machine Learning

Company Name: ProFinda
Description: ProFinda is a digital platform that intelligently organizes people around work by matching skills to relevant projects and bids.
Website: http://www.profinda.com
Phone: 44 (0)20 3397 8622 **Email:** enquiries@profinda.com
City: London **State:** England **PC:** **Country: United Kingdom**
Year Established: 2011 **Status 2020:** Active
Industries: Artificial Intelligence for:, Cloud for:, Collaboration Solutions for:, ~ Education (13), Enterprise Application Services for:, IT Managed Services

Company Name: Projected AI
Description: Projected AI is a London based start-up leveraging machine learning and natural language processing to assist in business decisions.
Website: http://www.projected-ai.com
Phone: **Email:** 37216@reference-encyclopedia-ai.net
City: London **State:** England **PC:** **Country: United Kingdom**
Year Established: 2017 **Status 2020:** Active
Industries: Artificial Intelligence for:, Big Data and Analytics for:, Machine Learning

Company Name: PromoMii
Description: AI driven video editing Saas platform creating multiple trailers from movies and series in minutes.
Website: http://www.promomii.com
Phone: 44 7931 503796 **Email:** michael@promomii.com
City: London **State:** England **PC:** **Country: United Kingdom**
Year Established: 2016 **Status 2020:** Active
Industries:

Company Name: Proportunity
Description: Proportunity is a financial services organisation made possible by technology.
Website: http://proportunity.co
Phone: 44 (0) 20 3962 2201 **Email:** contact@proportunity.co
City: London **State:** England **PC:** **Country: United Kingdom**
Year Established: 2016 **Status 2020:** Active
Industries: Artificial Intelligence for:, ~ Banking and Financial Markets-Services (7), ~ Banking and Financial Markets-Services (7), ~ Banking and Financial Markets-Services (7), Machine Learning

Company Name: proSapient
Description: A machine learning expert network and research platform. Helping investors and consultants conduct primary research.
Website: http://prosapient.com
Phone: **Email:** hello@prosapient.com
City: London **State:** England **PC:** **Country: United Kingdom**
Year Established: 2017 **Status 2020:** Active
Industries: Machine Learning

Company Name: Prospex
Description: AI-driven sales lead generation. SaaS start-up launching May 2018.
Website: http://www.prospex.ai/
Phone: 44(0)7940119870 **Email:** salv@prospex.ai
City: London **State:** England **PC:** **Country: United Kingdom**
Year Established: 2015 **Status 2020:** Active
Industries: Analytics for:, Artificial Intelligence for:, IT Managed Services

Company Name: ProvidensAI
Description: ProvidensAI provides artificial intelligence and machine learning solutions to real estate and asset management industry.
Website: http://providens.ai/
Phone: 44 0203 868 9211 **Email:** hello@providens.ai
City: London **State:** England **PC:** **Country: United Kingdom**
Year Established: **Status 2020:** Active
Industries: Artificial Intelligence for:, ~ Banking and Financial Markets-Services (7), Machine Learning for:, Predictive Analytics for:, ~ Real Estate (49), ~ Real Estate (49), ~ Real Estate (49)

Company Name: PSYKHE
Description: A fashion e-commerce platform powered by deep learning and personality science.
Website: http://www.psykhethestore.com/
Phone: 7722152005 **Email:** anabel@tpof.team
City: London **State:** England **PC:** **Country: United Kingdom**
Year Established: **Status 2020:** Active
Industries: Artificial Intelligence for:, ~ Fashion (16), Machine Learning for:, ~ Media-Communications (41), ~ Healthcare (20)

Company **Name:** PublishCheck
Description: PublishCheck is an editorial analytics platform tailored for editorial and audience development teams.
Website: http://www.publishcheck.com/
Phone: 020 3664 7296 **Email:** hello@publishcheck.com
City: London **State:** England **PC:** **Country: United Kingdom**
Year Established: **Status 2020:** Active
Industries: Analytics for:, Artificial Intelligence for:, Machine Learning

Company Name: Pynk
Description: Pynk is where everyday people invest better together.
Website: http://www.pynk.io
Phone: **Email:** hello@pynk.io
City: London **State:** England **PC:** **Country: United Kingdom**
Year Established: 2018 **Status 2020:** Active
Industries: Artificial Intelligence for:, Databases for:, ~ Banking and Financial Markets-Services (7), Machine Learning for:, ~ Banking and Financial Markets-Services (7), ~ Banking and Financial Markets-Services (7)

Company Name: QGS Technologies
Description: QGS Technologies is an InsurTech startup that is leveraging virtual reality and artificial intelligence.
Website:
Phone: **Email:** 37231@reference-encyclopedia-ai.net
City: London **State:** England **PC:** **Country: United Kingdom**
Year Established: 2016 **Status 2020:** Active
Industries: Artificial Intelligence for:, ~ Banking and Financial Markets-Services (7)

Company Name: Qlik (RoxAI)
Description: RoxAI's Data Engagement Platform, brings AI driven intelligent alerting to Business Intelligence. Utilizing SaaS, AI, ML, RPA.
Website: http://www.roxai.com/
Phone: **Email:** 37316@reference-encyclopedia-ai.net
City: London **State:** England **PC:** **Country: United Kingdom**
Year Established: 2017 **Status 2020:** Active
Industries: Analytics for:, Artificial Intelligence for:, Machine Learning for:, Natural Language Processing for:, Predictive Analytics for:, Business Software as a Service Apps (SaaS Apps)

Company Name: Quadrature Capital
Description: Quadrature Capital is a small tech business run by programmers.
Website: http://www.quadraturecapital.com
Phone: 44-20-3743-0400 **Email:** info@quadraturecapital.com
City: London **State:** England **PC:** **Country: United Kingdom**
Year Established: 2010 **Status 2020:** Active
Industries: Analytics for:, Artificial Intelligence

Company Name: Quantemplate
Description: Insurance data integration, automation & analytics
Website: http://www.quantemplate.com
Phone: **Email:** enquiries@quantemplate.com
City: London **State:** England **PC:** **Country: United Kingdom**
Year Established: 2013 **Status 2020:** Active
Industries: Analytics for:, Artificial Intelligence for:, Data Management for:, Enterprise Application Services for:, Machine Learning

Company Name: Quantexa
Description: Quantexa is a big data analytics company, driving actionable intelligence in the fight against financial crime and customer insight.
Website: http://www.quantexa.com/
Phone: 44 203 808 8299 **Email:** info@quantexa.com
City: London **State:** England **PC:** **Country: United Kingdom**
Year Established: **Status 2020:** Active
Industries: Analytics for:, Artificial Intelligence for:, Big Data and Analytics for:, Compliance for:, ~ Banking and Financial Markets-Services (7), ~ Banking and Financial Markets-Services (7)

Company Name: Qub: Italy
Description: Qubit gives marketers the tools to understand their visitors, and personalize their online presence to drive conversions in real time.
Website: http://www.qubit.com
Phone: **Email:** info@qubit.com
City: London **State:** England **PC:** **Country: United Kingdom**
Year Established: **Status 2020:** Active
Industries: ~ Media-Communications (41), Analytics for:, Artificial Intelligence for:, Big Data and Analytics for:, Databases for:, E-Commerce for:, Web for:, ~ Media-Communications (41)

Company Name: Quikkly Ltd.
Description:
Website: http://www.quikklycodes.com
Phone: **Email:** sales@quikklymobile.com
City: London **State:** England **PC:** **Country: United Kingdom**
Year Established: **Status 2020:** Active
Industries:

Company Name: Quorso
Description: Quorso's one-of-a-kind SaaS platform analyzes complex data and empowers the world's largest companies to improve the way they operate.
Website: http://www.quorso.com
Phone: 44 0207 031 0834 **Email:** contact@quorso.com
City: London **State:** England **PC:** **Country: United Kingdom**
Year Established: **Status 2020:** Active
Industries: Application Services for:, Artificial Intelligence for:, Big Data and Analytics for:, Business Intelligence for:, IT Managed Services for:, Machine Learning for:, Management Information Systems for:, ~ Retail and Consumer Products (52), ~ Professional Services (4

Company Name: Qutee.com
Description: Intelligent comments & data platform
Website: http://qutee.com
Phone: **Email:** twilson@sentiment360.com
City: London **State:** England **PC:** **Country: United Kingdom**

Year Established: 2013 **Status 2020:** Active
Industries: Natural Language Processing for:, ~ Social Assistance-Non-Profits (53)

Company Name: QwertyB: Italy
Description: QwertyBit is a bespoke software development company based in London, UK.
Website: http://qwertybit.com
Phone: **Email:** office@qwertybit.com
City: London **State:** England **PC:** **Country: United Kingdom**
Year Established: **Status 2020:** Active
Industries: Artificial Intelligence for:, Blockchain for:, Application Services for:, ~ Professional Services (48), ~ Professional Services (48), Cyber Security for:, Cyber Security

Company Name: Rafiqi
Description: Rafiqi leverages AI for providing a customized real-time matching of refugees to opportunities.
Website: http://www.rafiqi.net/
Phone: **Email:** 37256@reference-encyclopedia-ai.net
City: London **State:** England **PC:** **Country: United Kingdom**
Year Established: 2016 **Status 2020:** Active
Industries: Machine Learning

Company Name: Rahko
Description: Rahko is one of the world's most advanced teams in quantum machine learning
Website: http://rahko.ai/
Phone: **Email:** 37257@reference-encyclopedia-ai.net
City: London **State:** England **PC:** **Country: United Kingdom**
Year Established: **Status 2020:** Active
Industries: Machine Learning

Company Name: Rais
Description: RAIS is a customer data business with a suite of products that manage and analyse customer data for Direct-to-consumer brands, to grow Customer Lifetime Value.
Website: https://rais.io
Phone: **Email:** hello@rais.io
City: London **State:** England **PC:** **Country: United Kingdom**
Year Established: **Status 2020:** Active
Industries: Artificial Intelligence for:, Big Data and Analytics for:, ~ Customer Relationship Management (499), ~ E-Commerce (500), Business Intelligence for:, Data Management for:, ~ Customer Relationship Management (1719), ~ E-Commerce (1720), Databases for:, ~ Customer Re

Company Name: RAMM Science
Description: RAMM Science is an Artificial Intelligence (AI) and Blockchain enterprise software solutions company.
Website: http://ramm.science/x/home/
Phone: 44 (0)870 385 0425 **Email:** social@ramm.science
City: London **State:** England **PC:** **Country: United Kingdom**
Year Established: **Status 2020:** Active
Industries: Artificial Intelligence for:, Blockchain for:, Machine Learning

Company Name: Raphos
Description: Technology, services, analytics
Website: http://www.raphos.com
Phone: **Email:** contact@raphos.com
City: London **State:** England **PC:** **Country: United Kingdom**
Year Established: **Status 2020:** Active
Industries: Artificial Intelligence for:, ~ Social-Environmental-Physical-Engineering Sciences (55), Machine Learning for:, ~ Social-Environmental-Physical-Engineering Sciences (55), ~ Professional Services (48)

Company Name: RAV: India
Description: Ravin inspects vehicles using everyday mobile or stationary cameras, creating trust in car rental, sharing, sales and insurance.
Website: http://ravin.ai
Phone: **Email:** info@ravin.ai
City: London **State:** England **PC:** **Country: United Kingdom**
Year Established: 2018 **Status 2020:** Active
Industries: ~ Automotive (5), Machine Learning

Company Name: RAVN Systems
Description: RAVN Systems is experts in Artificial Intelligence.
Website: http://www.ravn.co.uk
Phone: 44 20 7566 0000 **Email:** rebecca.hawkes@ravn.co.uk
City: London **State:** England **PC:** **Country: United Kingdom**
Year Established: **Status 2020:** Active
Industries: Artificial Intelligence for:, Cyber Security for:, ~ Professional Services (48)

Company Name: re:infer
Description: Re:infer is an enterprise intelligence system that makes communications data understood and actionable.
Website: http://reinfer.io
Phone: **Email:** info@reinfer.io
City: London **State:** England **PC:** **Country: United Kingdom**
Year Established: 2015 **Status 2020:** Active
Industries: Analytics for:, Artificial Intelligence for:, Natural Language Processing

Company Name: RE•WORK
Description: A female-led company creating summits, workshops & dinners, bringing together global leaders in AI. Save 20% on all summits code: CRUNCHBA: SWEDEN
Website: http://www.re-work.co
Phone: 1 415 800 3262 **Email:** hello@re-work.co
City: London **State:** England **PC:** **Country: United Kingdom**
Year Established: **Status 2020:** Active
Industries: Artificial Intelligence for:, ~ Event Management (15), IT Managed Services for:, Machine Learning

Company Name: Reach7
Description: Reach7 is a powerful platform that allows you to use social media to discover and engage any audience in the world in their local language.
Website: http://www.reach7.com
Phone: 44 20 3086 7172 **Email:** hello@reach7.com
City: London **State:** England **PC:** **Country: United Kingdom**
Year Established: 2014 **Status 2020:** Active
Industries: Natural Language Processing for:, ~ Social Assistance-Non-Profits (53), ~ Social Assistance-Non-Profits (53)

Company Name: reachAI
Description: reachAI applies the latest advances in artificial intelligence to resolve practical consumer and business challenges.
Website: http://reachai.com/
Phone: **Email:** info@reachAI.com
City: London **State:** England **PC:** **Country: United Kingdom**
Year Established: 2016 **Status 2020:** Active
Industries:

Company Name: React
Description: Modernising market research through NLP and machine learning.
Website: http://www.reactpolls.com
Phone: **Email:** info@reactpolls.com
City: London **State:** England **PC:** **Country: United Kingdom**
Year Established: 2017 **Status 2020:** Active
Industries: Machine Learning

Company Name: Real Life Analytics
Description: Real Life Analytics enables targeted advertising on any digital screen.
Website:
Phone: **Email:** 37267@reference-encyclopedia-ai.net
City: London **State:** England **PC:** **Country: United Kingdom**
Year Established: 2014 **Status 2020:** Closed
Industries: Machine Learning

Company Name: Recruitment Smart Technologies
Description: Recruitment Smart creates disruptive technology products for the HR and Recruitment Industry, using Artificial Intelligence.
Website: http://www.recruitmentsmart.com
Phone: **Email:** info@recruitmentsmart.com
City: London **State:** England **PC:** **Country: United Kingdom**
Year Established: 2015 **Status 2020:** Active
Industries: Artificial Intelligence for:, IT Managed Services for:, Machine Learning

Company Name: Red Sift
Description: Red Sift exists to democratise the technology essential for cybersecurity.
Website: http://redsift.com/
Phone: **Email:** team@redsift.com
City: London **State:** England **PC:** **Country: United Kingdom**
Year Established: 2015 **Status 2020:** Active
Industries: Artificial Intelligence for:, Big Data and Analytics for:, Cyber Security for:, Enterprise Application Services for:, Business Software as a Service Apps (SaaS Apps)

Company Name: ReGal 38I83
Description: Regtech, Regulatory, Technology, Regulation,
Website: http://www.regal38i83.com
Phone: **Email:** talent@regal38i83.com
City: London **State:** England **PC:** **Country: United Kingdom**
Year Established: **Status 2020:** Active
Industries: **Company Name:** Relative Insight
Description: Relative Insight help brands sharpen strategy and communications by comparing and analyzing language.
Website: http://relativeinsight.com/
Phone: 44 20 3794 5476 **Email:** hello@relativeinsight.com
City: London **State:** England **PC:** **Country: United Kingdom**
Year Established: 2012 **Status 2020:** Active
Industries: Analytics for:, Big Data and Analytics for:, Predictive Analytics for:, Data Management

Company Name: RemitRadar
Description: RemitRadar services the needs of an emerging global community of 2.5bn people dependant on remittance services.
Website: http://remitradar.com
Phone: (732) 734-1995 **Email:** info@remitradar.com
City: London **State:** England **PC:** **Country: United Kingdom**
Year Established: **Status 2020:** Active
Industries: Artificial Intelligence for:, ~ Banking and Financial Markets-Services (7), ~ Banking and Financial Markets-Services (7), ~ Insurance (25), ~ Banking and Financial Markets-Services (7)

Company Name: RentersUnion
Description: RentersUnion is an AI chatbot that provides property and housing advice.
Website: http://www.rentersunion.co.uk
Phone: **Email:** hello@rentersunion.co.uk
City: London **State:** England **PC:** **Country: United Kingdom**
Year Established: **Status 2020:** Active
Industries: Artificial Intelligence for:, ~ Real Estate (49)

Company Name: reportbra: India
Description: reportbrain is a news research engine platform.
Website: http://www.reportbrain.com
Phone: 44 (203) 7691120 **Email:** info@reportbrain.com
City: London **State:** England **PC:** **Country: United Kingdom**
Year Established: **Status 2020:** Active
Industries: Artificial Intelligence for:, IT Managed Services for:, ~ Media-Communications (41), ~ Professional Services (48)

Company Name: Resolver
Description: Resolver provides an end-to-end complaint-resolution service.
Website: http://www.resolver.co.uk
Phone: **Email:** press@resolver.co.uk
City: London **State:** England **PC:** **Country: United Kingdom**
Year Established: **Status 2020:** Active
Industries: Artificial Intelligence

Company Name: Resume Worded
Description: Resume Worded equips you with AI-powered tools to help you write your most successful resume and get hired quicker.
Website: http://resumeworded.com
Phone: **Email:** contact@resumeworded.com
City: London **State:** England **PC:** **Country: United Kingdom**
Year Established: 2017 **Status 2020:** Active
Industries: Artificial Intelligence for:, ~ Education (13), ~ Education (13)

Company Name: Retechnica
Description: What it is Ingenia is a text analytics API web app that tags your content automatically.
Website: http://www.retechnica.com/
Phone: **Email:** marco@retechnica.com
City: London **State:** England **PC:** **Country: United Kingdom**
Year Established: 2012 **Status 2020:** Active
Industries: Application Program Interfaces (APIs) for:, Machine Learning for:, Business Software as a Service Apps (SaaS Apps) for:, Data Management

Company Name: RevLifter
Description: An AI powered technology provider helping brands increase revenue through real-time personalised offers.
Website: http://www.revlifter.com/
Phone: **Email:** hello@revlifter.com
City: London **State:** England **PC:** **Country: United Kingdom**
Year Established: 2017 **Status 2020:** Active
Industries: ~ E-Commerce (12), Artificial Intelligence for:, E-Commerce for:, Enterprise Application Services for:, Machine Learning

Company Name: RevTap.ai
Description: E-commerce Intelligence & AI-powered omni-channel marketer for Shopify
Website: http://revtap.ai
Phone: **Email:** hello@revtap.ai
City: London **State:** England **PC:** **Country: United Kingdom**
Year Established: 2018 **Status 2020:** Active
Industries:

Company Name: Rhythm.Ai
Description: Rhythm.AI is an artificial intelligence and deep learning startup using public domain and royalty free music to create digital revenues.
Website: http://rhythm.ai
Phone: **Email:** peterwipp@gmail.com
City: London **State:** England **PC:** **Country: United Kingdom**
Year Established: 2016 **Status 2020:** Active
Industries: Artificial Intelligence for:, ~ Arts-Entertainment-Recreation (4), ~ Arts-Entertainment-Recreation (4)

Company Name: RLC Ventures
Description: Venture Capital
Website: http://rlc.ventures/
Phone: **Email:** info@rlc.ventur: Spain
City: London **State:** England **PC:** **Country: United Kingdom**
Year Established: **Status 2020:** Active
Industries: Artificial Intelligence for:, ~ Banking and Financial Markets-Services (7), ~ Banking and Financial Markets-Services (7)

Company Name: Rocky.ai Guided journaling and coaching app
Description: The world's first A.I. coach available with curated tips for leadership development and and daily self reflection coaching question
Website: http://www.rocky.ai/
Phone: **Email:** info@rockyrobots.com
City: London **State:** England **PC:** **Country: United Kingdom**

Year Established: 2017 **Status 2020:** Active
Industries: Artificial Intelligence for:, ~ Education (13), ~ Education (13), ~ Education (13)

Company Name: Roirobot
Description: RoiRobot gives intense, rapid, and immersive education aimed at accelerating the life cycle and ROI of young innovative companies,
Website: http://roirobot.net
Phone: **Email:** info@roirobot.online
City: London **State:** England **PC:** **Country: United Kingdom**
Year Established: 2019 **Status 2020:** Active
Industries: ~ Education (13), IT Managed Services for:, ~ Administrative and Support Services (1), Predictive Analytics

Company Name: Roomor PropTech
Description: The Smart Home as a Service Platform. Transform your Landlords service with IoT and Artificial Intelligence.
Website: http://roomorapp.com/
Phone: **Email:** jose.mora@roomorapp.com
City: London **State:** England **PC:** **Country: United Kingdom**
Year Established: 2016 **Status 2020:** Active
Industries: Artificial Intelligence for:, IT Managed Services for:, Machine Learning

Company Name: Rooster
Description: Car insurance reinvented for good drivers. Powered by smartphone technology & AI.
Website: http://www.joinrooster.co.uk
Phone: **Email:** hello@joinrooster.co.uk
City: London **State:** England **PC:** **Country: United Kingdom**
Year Established: 2019 **Status 2020:** Active
Industries: Artificial Intelligence for:, Application Services

Company Name: Rossum
Description: Rossum creates a world without manual data entry.
Website: http://rossum.ai/
Phone: **Email:** dita.eckhardtova@rossum.ai
City: London **State:** England **PC:** **Country: United Kingdom**
Year Established: **Status 2020:** Active
Industries: Artificial Intelligence for:, ~ Banking and Financial Markets-Services (7), Data Management

Company Name: Rotageek
Description: Predictive data-driven technologies to effectively and fairly schedule staff
Website: http://www.rotageek.com
Phone: **Email:** office@rotageek.com
City: London **State:** England **PC:** **Country: United Kingdom**
Year Established: **Status 2020:** Active
Industries: Artificial Intelligence for:, Data Management for:, ~ Banking and Financial Markets-Services (7), ~ Healthcare (20), ~ Human Resources (24), ~ Retail and Consumer Products (52)

Company Name: Ruffle Money
Description: Serving the unbanked.
Website:
Phone: **Email:** 37319@reference-encyclopedia-ai.net
City: London **State:** England **PC:** **Country: United Kingdom**
Year Established: 2020 **Status 2020:** Active
Industries: Artificial Intelligence for:, ~ Banking and Financial Markets-Services (7)

Company Name: Saberr
Description: Saberr Saberr is helping companies in creating team design and developments.
Website: http://saberr.com
Phone: **Email:** alistair@saberr.com
City: London **State:** England **PC:** **Country: United Kingdom**
Year Established: **Status 2020:** Active
Industries: Artificial Intelligence for:, ~ Human Resources (24), Predictive Analytics for:, ~ Human Resources (24)

Company Name: SafeToNet
Description: SafeToNet makes the digital world safer for children to explore and enjoy.
Website: http://safetonet.com/
Phone: 020 3950 3047 **Email:** info@safetonet.com
City: London **State:** England **PC:** **Country: United Kingdom**
Year Established: 2013 **Status 2020:** Active
Industries: Application Services for:, Artificial Intelligence for:, ~ Social Assistance-Non-Profits (53), Cyber Security for:, IT Managed Services for:, Application Services

Company Name: Saffe
Description: Face recognition for payments and financial services.
Website: http://saffe.co/
Phone: 11985391188 **Email:** isabella@saffe.co
City: London **State:** England **Zip:** 01227-200 **Country: United Kingdom**
Year Established: **Status 2020:** Active
Industries: Application Services for:, Artificial Intelligence for:, ~ Banking and Financial Markets-Services (7), ~ E-Commerce (12), Machine Learning for:, Mobile

Company Name: Samim.ai
Description: Samim.ai helps increase the effectiveness of Sales and Customer Service. We do this with AI virtual sales and customer service assistants.
Website: http://samimai.com/
Phone: 44.78348457 **Email:** contact@samimai.com
City: London **State:** England **PC:** **Country: United Kingdom**
Year Established: **Status 2020:** Active
Industries: Artificial Intelligence for:, Machine Learning for:, ~ Media-Communications (41)

Company Name: Satago
Description: Satago is software that helps small businesses improve cashflow by getting paid faster.
Website: http://www.satago.com
Phone: 44 20 8133 3539 **Email:** hello@satago.co.uk
City: London **State:** England **PC:** **Country: United Kingdom**
Year Established: **Status 2020:** Active
Industries:

Company Name: Satalia
Description: Algorithms | Intelligence | Optimization
Website: http://www.satalia.com
Phone: 44 7773 765097 **Email:** daniel@satalia.com
City: London **State:** England **PC:** **Country: United Kingdom**
Year Established: **Status 2020:** Active
Industries: Analytics for:, Artificial Intelligence for:, Machine Learning for:, ~ Professional Services (48)

Company Name: Satoshi Systems Limited
Description: Satoshi Systems provides state of the art software solutions for the trading space, currently focusing on the commodity.
Website: http://www.satoshi.ltd/
Phone: **Email:** info@satoshi.ltd
City: London **State:** England **PC:** **Country: United Kingdom**
Year Established: 2016 **Status 2020:** Active
Industries: IT Managed Services for:, Machine Learning for:, Finance and Accounting for:, Finance and Accounting

Company Name: Save your wardrobe
Description: FashionTech startup mixing AI & IoT to help people manage their wardrobe and buy better
Website: http://www.saveyourwardrobe.com
Phone: **Email:** contact@saveyourwardrobe.com
City: London **State:** England **PC:** **Country: United Kingdom**
Year Established: **Status 2020:** Active
Industries: Artificial Intelligence for:, E-Commerce for:, ~ Fashion (16)

Company Name: Scicasts
Description: Scicasts is a dynamic, cross-sector knowledge base that brings together the best of science, engineering and business from around the world.
Website: http://scicasts.com
Phone: **Email:** info@scicasts.com
City: London **State:** England **PC:** **Country: United Kingdom**
Year Established: **Status 2020:** Active
Industries: Artificial Intelligence for:, Big Data and Analytics for:, Business Intelligence for:, Databases

Company Name: Scisse: Romania
Description: Scissero is a cloud-based legal AI platform that can draft, mark, analyze, review contracts from human lawyers.
Website: http://www.scissero.com/
Phone: 44 20 3865 1787 **Email:** info@scissero.com
City: London **State:** England **PC:** **Country: United Kingdom**
Year Established: 2018 **Status 2020:** Active
Industries: Artificial Intelligence

Company Name: Score Genius
Description: Score Genius is to improve the quality of life by providing free tools that increase monthly disposable income
Website: http://www.scoregenius.co.uk
Phone: **Email:** info@scoregenius.co.uk
City: London **State:** England **PC:** **Country: United Kingdom**
Year Established: **Status 2020:** Active
Industries: Artificial Intelligence for:, ~ Banking and Financial Markets-Services (7), ~ Banking and Financial Markets-Services (7)

Company Name: Scout
Description: The world's first web browser chatbot
Website: http://meetscout.co.uk
Phone: **Email:** marc@contextscout.com
City: London **State:** England **PC:** **Country: United Kingdom**
Year Established: 2015 **Status 2020:** Active
Industries: Artificial Intelligence for:, E-Commerce for:, Application Program Interfaces (APIs) for:, Machine Learning for:, Natural Language Processing for:, Web for:, Content for:, Web for:, Web for:, Web

Company Name: SearchSmartly
Description: Property Search, AI, Real Estate, Mobile App
Website: http://www.searchsmartly.co
Phone: **Email:** sales@searchsmartly.co
City: London **State:** England **PC:** **Country: United Kingdom**
Year Established: **Status 2020:** Active
Industries: Artificial Intelligence for:, Business Applications for:, Business Applications for:, ~ Real Estate (49)

Company Name: See Fashion
Description: AI-powered personalisation and business intelligence platform for fashion ecommerce
Website: http://see.fashion
Phone: **Email:** aaron@seefashion.co.uk
City: London **State:** England **PC:** **Country: United Kingdom**
Year Established: **Status 2020:** Active
Industries: Artificial Intelligence for:, Business Applications for:, Big Data and Analytics for:, E-Commerce for:, ~ Fashion (16), Predictive Analytics

Company Name: Seersco
Description: GDPR, SaaS, Privacy, Cyber Security, Data Protection,
Website: http://seersco.com
Phone: 2034322114 **Email:** adnan.zaheer@seersco.com
City: London **State:** England **PC:** **Country: United Kingdom**
Year Established: 2018 **Status 2020:** Active
Industries: Artificial Intelligence for:, Cyber Security for:, IT Managed Services for:, Cyber Security for:, Business Software as a Service Apps (SaaS Apps) for:, Security

Company Name: Seldon
Description: Machine Learning Deployment for Kubernet: Spain
Website: http://www.seldon.io/
Phone: 44 20 7193 6752 **Email:** hello@seldon.io
City: London **State:** England **PC:** **Country: United Kingdom**
Year Established: **Status 2020:** Active
Industries: Artificial Intelligence for:, Machine Learning for:, Application Services

Company Name: Selfhood Studios Inc
Description: A Digital age disruptive, internet - breaking influencer marketing company, started in heart of London.
Website: http://www.selfhood-studios.com
Phone: **Email:** info@selfhood-studios.co.uk
City: London **State:** England **PC:** **Country: United Kingdom**
Year Established: 2016 **Status 2020:** Active
Industries: Big Data and Analytics for:, Predictive Analytics for:, ~ Social Assistance-Non-Profits (53), ~ Social Assistance-Non-Profits (53), Development and Test for:, Web

Company Name: Semantic Evolution
Description: Semantic Evolution helps firms address all parsing needs and transforms data into actionable information.
Website: http://www.semantic-evolution.com/
Phone: **Email:** contact@semantic-evolution.com
City: London **State:** England **PC:** **Country: United Kingdom**
Year Established: 2011 **Status 2020:** Active
Industries: Artificial Intelligence for:, IT Managed Services

Company Name: Sematic Evolution
Description: Semantic Evolution helps firms address all parsing needs and transforms data into actionable information.
Website: http://www.semantic-evolution.com/
Phone: **Email:** contact@semantic-evolution.com
City: London **State:** England **PC:** **Country: United Kingdom**
Year Established: **Status 2020:** Active
Industries:

Company Name: SenSat
Description: SenSat simulates reality in real time, which helps computers solve real world problems.
Website: http://www.sensat.co.uk/
Phone: **Email:** contact@sensat.co.uk
City: London **State:** England **PC:** **Country: United Kingdom**
Year Established: **Status 2020:** Active
Industries: Artificial Intelligence for:, Machine Learning

Company Name: Sensing Feeling
Description: Advanced Human Emotion Sensing Products for Business.
Website: http://sensingfeeling.com
Phone: 44 20 3432 2004 **Email:** team@sensingfeeling.com
City: London **State:** England **PC:** **Country: United Kingdom**
Year Established: **Status 2020:** Active
Industries: Artificial Intelligence for:, Computer Vision for:, Machine Learning for:, ~ Manufacturing-Electronic (30)

Company Name: Sensio A: Iran
Description: Sensio Air is a healthcare analytics company that helps people with asthma and allergy predict prevent and manage their symptoms.
Website: http://www.wlab.io
Phone: **Email:** 37367@reference-encyclopedia-ai.net
City: London **State:** England **PC:** **Country: United Kingdom**
Year Established: 2016 **Status 2020:** Active
Industries: ~ Healthcare (20), Internet of Things (IoT) for:, ~ Healthcare (20), Predictive Analytics

Company Name: Sensitrust
Description: Decentralized job marketplace
Website: http://www.sensitrust.io/
Phone: **Email:** info@sensitrust.io
City: London **State:** England **PC:** **Country: United Kingdom**

Year Established: 2019 **Status 2020:** Active
Industries: Artificial Intelligence for:, Blockchain for:, ~ Banking and Financial Markets-Services (7)

Company Name: Sentient Machin: Spain
Description: Sentient Machines is a deep tech company analysing speech and sentiment in order to empower smarter human communication.
Website: http://sentientmachines.tech/
Phone: **Email:** hello@sentientmachines.tech
City: London **State:** England **PC:** **Country: United Kingdom**
Year Established: 2016 **Status 2020:** Active
Industries: Artificial Intelligence for:, IT Managed Services

Company Name: Sentiment Search
Description: Sentiment Search specialises in social media insights for hospitality and F&B.
Website: http://sentimentsearch.com
Phone: 44 (0) 207 867 3980 **Email:** contact@sentimentsearch.com
City: London **State:** England **PC:** **Country: United Kingdom**
Year Established: 2015 **Status 2020:** Active
Industries: Analytics for:, Artificial Intelligence for:, ~ Social Assistance-Non-Profits (53)

Company Name: Sentview
Description: The breakthrough way of gaining customer insight through analysing and identifying trends from social media platforms and more.
Website: http://www.sentview.com
Phone: **Email:** michael@sentview.com
City: London **State:** England **PC:** **Country: United Kingdom**
Year Established: 2015 **Status 2020:** Active
Industries: Artificial Intelligence for:, Big Data and Analytics for:, ~ Social Assistance-Non-Profits (53)

Company Name: Shapes AI
Description: The Shape Intelligence Company
Website: http://shapes.ai
Phone: **Email:** info@shapes.ai
City: London **State:** England **PC:** **Country: United Kingdom**
Year Established: **Status 2020:** Active
Industries: Artificial Intelligence for:, Computer Vision for:, Machine Learning

Company Name: Sharpe Capital
Description: Sharpe Capital is a machine learning and linguistic analysis company.
Website: http://sharpe.capital/
Phone: **Email:** hello@sharpe.capital
City: London **State:** England **PC:** **Country: United Kingdom**
Year Established: 2015 **Status 2020:** Closed
Industries: ~ Banking and Financial Markets-Services (7), ~ Banking and Financial Markets-Services (7), Machine Learning

Company Name: Shivom
Description: Optimising the way DNA & other biodata is shared, secured & analysed.
Website: http://shivom.io
Phone: 44 485938471 **Email:** info@shivom.io
City: London **State:** England **PC:** **Country: United Kingdom**
Year Established: 2018 **Status 2020:** Active
Industries: Artificial Intelligence for:, ~ Biotechnology (9), Blockchain for:, ~ Healthcare (20), ~ Healthcare (20), Business Software as a Service Apps (SaaS Apps)

Company Name: Shoppar Ltd
Description: Platform developed to measure, connect and engage audiences in the real world via smart sensors to enable better customer experienc: Spain
Website: http://shoppar.ai
Phone: 44 (0) 2039660012 **Email:** info@shopparapp.com
City: London **State:** England **PC:** **Country: United Kingdom**
Year Established: 2016 **Status 2020:** Active
Industries: Analytics for:, Artificial Intelligence for:, Big Data and Analytics for:, Computer Vision for:, Internet of Things (IoT) for:, Machine Learning

Company Name: Signal Media
Description: Signal Media is an Artificial Intelligence company that transforms the world's information into accessible, actionable business knowledge.
Website: http://www.signalmedia.co
Phone: 2038288200 **Email:** hello@signalmedia.co
City: London **State:** England **PC:** **Country: United Kingdom**
Year Established: **Status 2020:** Active
Industries: Analytics for:, Artificial Intelligence for:, Business Intelligence for:, Enterprise Application Services for:, Machine Learning for:, ~ Media-Communications (41), ~ Professional Services (48)

Company Name: Signalbox
Description: Signalbox provides matching location to transport service.
Website: http://www.signalbox.io/
Phone: **Email:** hello@signalbox.io
City: London **State:** England **PC:** **Country: United Kingdom**
Year Established: 2013 **Status 2020:** Active
Industries: Artificial Intelligence for:, Machine Learning

Company Name: Silicon Investing
Description: Silicon Investing develops and provides artificial intelligence and machine learning software to retail traders.
Website: http://siliconinvesting.com/
Phone: **Email:** contact@siliconmarkets.com
City: London **State:** England **PC:** **Country: United Kingdom**
Year Established: 2015 **Status 2020:** Active
Industries:

Company Name: Silobreaker
Description: Silobreaker builds intelligence technology that makes sense of unstructured data on the web.
Website: http://www.silobreaker.com
Phone: **Email:** sales@silobreaker.com
City: London **State:** England **PC:** **Country: United Kingdom**
Year Established: **Status 2020:** Active
Industries: Artificial Intelligence for:, Big Data and Analytics for:, Cyber Security for:, Databases for:, ~ Banking and Financial Markets-Services (7), Machine Learning for:, Cyber Security for:, Security for:, Data Management

Company Name: SIME CLINICAL AI
Description: Clinical AI platform company, providing data-driven and precise insights to doctors in decisive moments.
Website: http://www.simedx.com
Phone: **Email:** 37393@reference-encyclopedia-ai.net
City: London **State:** England **PC:** **Country: United Kingdom**
Year Established: 2014 **Status 2020:** Active
Industries: Artificial Intelligence for:, Data Management for:, ~ Healthcare (20), Machine Learning for:, ~ Healthcare (20)

Company Name: Simudyne
Description: Simudyne powers computer simulations to augment human intelligence and enable radically better decisions.
Website: http://www.simudyne.com
Phone: **Email:** hello@simudyne.com
City: London **State:** England **PC:** **Country: United Kingdom**
Year Established: **Status 2020:** Active
Industries: Analytics for:, Artificial Intelligence for:, Big Data and Analytics for:, Enterprise Application Services for:, ~ Professional Services (48)

Company Name: Singify
Description: AI based Karaoke app
Website:
Phone: **Email:** 37400@reference-encyclopedia-ai.net
City: London **State:** England **PC:** **Country: United Kingdom**

Year Established: 2010 **Status 2020:** Closed
Industries: Analytics for:, Machine Learning

Company Name: Singular Intelligence
Description: An AI Platform for brands and retailers that automates and augments commercial decisions leveraging all market factors.
Website: http://www.singularintelligence.com/
Phone: **Email:** sarvesh@singularintelligence.com
City: London **State:** England **PC:** **Country: United Kingdom**
Year Established: **Status 2020:** Active
Industries: Analytics for:, Artificial Intelligence for:, Big Data and Analytics for:, Data Management for:, ~ Banking and Financial Markets-Services (7), Machine Learning for:, Predictive Analytics for:, ~ Retail and Consumer Products (52)

Company **Name:** SiriusInsight.AI
Description: Real-Time Intelligence: Sea, Land, Cyber
Website: http://www.siriusinsight.ai
Phone: **Email:** malcolm.glaister@siriusinsight.ai
City: London **State:** England **PC:** **Country: United Kingdom**
Year Established: 2016 **Status 2020:** Active
Industries: Artificial Intelligence for:, Business Intelligence for:, Computer Vision for:, Data Management for:, IT Managed Services for:, Machine Learning for:, Predictive Analytics for:, Predictive Analytics

Company Name: Skarvi Systems Limited
Description: AI backed Physical Oil Trading & Risk Management solutions
Website: http://www.skarvisystems.co.uk
Phone: **Email:** contact@skarvisystems.co.uk
City: London **State:** England **PC:** **Country: United Kingdom**
Year Established: 2019 **Status 2020:** Active
Industries: Artificial Intelligence for:, IT Managed Services

Company Name: Skillennials
Description: Skillennials is a modern training academy which blends personal and professional skills development.
Website: http://www.skillennials.com/
Phone: **Email:** info@skillennials.com
City: London **State:** England **PC:** **Country: United Kingdom**
Year Established: **Status 2020:** Active
Industries: Artificial Intelligence for:, Machine Learning

Company Name: Skin Analytics
Description: Skin Analytics uses artificial intelligence to screen for melanoma skin cancer.
Website: http://www.skin-analytics.com
Phone: 44122336512 **Email:** info@skinanalytics.co.uk
City: London **State:** England **PC:** **Country: United Kingdom**
Year Established: 2012 **Status 2020:** Active
Industries: Artificial Intelligence for:, ~ Healthcare (20), ~ Healthcare (20), ~ Healthcare (20)

Company Name: SKIPJAQ
Description: SKIPJAQ provides machine learning engine which can tune server settings to give websites an improvement in speed.
Website: http://www.skipjaq.com/
Phone: **Email:** office.london@skipjaq.com
City: London **State:** England **PC:** **Country: United Kingdom**
Year Established: 2014 **Status 2020:** Active
Industries: Machine Learning

Company Name: SKY ENGINE
Description: Evolutionary AI platform for computer vision applications. SaaS/PaaS.
Website: http://www.skyengine.ai
Phone: **Email:** contact@skyengine.ai
City: London **State:** England **PC:** **Country: United Kingdom**
Year Established: 2018 **Status 2020:** Active
Industries: ~ Agriculture (3), Artificial Intelligence for:, Machine Learning for:, Robotics for:, ~ Arts-Entertainment-Recreation (4)

Company Name: Sky-Futur: Spain
Description: Sky-Futures offer end-to-end drone-based inspection services (incl. software and drone training) to the global industrial markets since 2009
Website: http://www.sky-futures.com
Phone: 44 (0) 207 148 7002 **Email:** info@sky-futures.com
City: London **State:** England **PC:** **Country: United Kingdom**
Year Established: **Status 2020:** Active
Industries: Artificial Intelligence for:, ~ Banking and Financial Markets-Services (7), ~ Manufacturing-Electronic (30), ~ Energy and Utilities (14), Enterprise Application Services for:, Enterprise Application Services for:, ~ Oil and Gas (43), Robotics

Company Name: Skyline Partne: Serbia
Description: Closing the global protection gap through innovative parametric insurance solutions.
Website: http://www.skyline.partne: Serbia
Phone: **Email:** enquiries@skyline.partne: Serbia
City: London **State:** England **PC:** **Country: United Kingdom**
Year Established: 2017 **Status 2020:** Active
Industries: Blockchain for:, Predictive Analytics for:, Risk Management

Company Name: Skysca:
Description: Skyscape is the first analytics and online marketplace platform for underutilised rooftop spac: Spain
Website: http://www.skyscape.global
Phone: **Email:** hello@skyscape.global
City: London **State:** England **PC:** **Country: United Kingdom**
Year Established: **Status 2020:** Active
Industries:

Company Name: SLAMcore
Description: SLAMcore is a developing SLAM algorithms that allow robots and drones to truly understand the space around them.
Website: http://www.slamcore.com
Phone: **Email:** 37411@reference-encyclopedia-ai.net
City: London **State:** England **PC:** **Country: United Kingdom**
Year Established: 2016 **Status 2020:** Active
Industries: Artificial Intelligence for:, Computer Vision for:, Robotics

Company Name: Smarter Human
Description: Smarter Human provides solutions to help businesses make their use of AI and machine learning ethical and compliant to regulation.
Website: http://www.smarter-human.com
Phone: **Email:** hello@smarter-human.com
City: London **State:** England **PC:** **Country: United Kingdom**
Year Established: 2017 **Status 2020:** Active
Industries:

Company Name: Snap Tech
Description: Snap Tech's mission is to make product discovery magical both online and in the real world through cutting edge AI and machine learning.
Website: http://www.snaptech.ai
Phone: 44 (0) 207 183 8878 **Email:** info@snapfashion.co.uk
City: London **State:** England **PC:** **Country: United Kingdom**
Year Established: **Status 2020:** Active
Industries: Artificial Intelligence for:, Computer Vision for:, E-Commerce for:, Machine Learning for:, Cyber Security for:, Computer Vision

Company Name: Snaptivity
Description: Snaptivity is a stadium tech that drives fan engagement by capturing key moments of events using AI, IoT sensors, and robotic cams.
Website: http://www.snaptivityapp.com
Phone: **Email:** amit@snaptivityapp.com
City: London **State:** England **PC:** **Country: United Kingdom**
Year Established: **Status 2020:** Active
Industries: Artificial Intelligence for:, Big Data and Analytics for:, ~ Personal-Religious-Civic (45), ~ Arts-Entertainment-Recreation (4),

~ Event Management (15), Mobile for:, ~ Social Media (54), ~ Media-Communications (41), ~ Arts-Entertainment-Recreation (4)

Company Name: Sns Analytics
Description: Algorithmic Trading, Machine Learning, Cryptocurrency
Website: http://snsanalytics.co.uk/
Phone: **Email:** info@snsanalytics.co.uk
City: London **State:** England **PC:** **Country: United Kingdom**
Year Established: **Status 2020:** Active
Industries: Artificial Intelligence for:, ~ Banking and Financial Markets-Services (7), Machine Learning for:, ~ Media-Communications (41), Finance and Accounting

Company Name: SoAmpli
Description: SoAmpli enables sales teams to sell more.
Website: http://www.soampli.com
Phone: **Email:** contactus@soampli.com
City: London **State:** England **PC:** **Country: United Kingdom**
Year Established: 2014 **Status 2020:** Active
Industries: Artificial Intelligence for:, IT Managed Services for:, Business Software as a Service Apps (SaaS Apps) for:, ~ Social Assistance-Non-Profits (53), ~ Social Assistance-Non-Profits (53)

Company Name: Socital
Description: Socital is trusted by online fashion, sports, cosmetics, home retail and pharmacy stores to boost their sales with personalization.
Website: http://www.socital.com
Phone: **Email:** theo.vasiliadis@socital.com
City: London **State:** England **PC:** **Country: United Kingdom**
Year Established: 2016 **Status 2020:** Active
Industries: Analytics for:, Artificial Intelligence for:, E-Commerce for:, Business Software as a Service Apps (SaaS Apps)

Company Name: Sonalytic
Description: Sonalytic develops a content identification approach that enables us to connect creators and rights-holders to monetization opportunities.
Website: http://www.sonalytic.com/
Phone: **Email:** jobs@sonalytic.com
City: London **State:** England **PC:** **Country: United Kingdom**
Year Established: **Status 2020:** Active
Industries: Artificial Intelligence for:, Voice Recognition for:, Content for:, Identity

Company Name: Sonantic
Description: Sonantic provides world's most expressive and realistic artificial voices.
Website: http://sonantic.io/
Phone: **Email:** 37434@reference-encyclopedia-ai.net
City: London **State:** England **PC:** **Country: United Kingdom**
Year Established: 2018 **Status 2020:** Active
Industries: Artificial Intelligence

Company Name: Soply
Description: Soply is make video, photo, animation, illustration, design for customers or clients and hire creative design professionals.
Website: http://soply.com/
Phone: 44 (0) 7800 722708 **Email:** support@soply.com
City: London **State:** England **PC:** **Country: United Kingdom**
Year Established: **Status 2020:** Active
Industries: Artificial Intelligence for:, Content for:, ~ Media-Communications (41), Digital Media for:, ~ Social Media (54)

Company Name: Soter Analytics
Description: Solving the $140B workplace musculoskeletal injury problem with wearable sensors and powerful analytics.
Website: http://www.soteranalytics.com
Phone: **Email:** info@soteranalytics.com
City: London **State:** England **PC:** **Country: United Kingdom**
Year Established: 2015 **Status 2020:** Active
Industries: Artificial Intelligence for:, ~ Healthcare (20)

Company Name: Sparrho
Description: Sparrho is a personalised science research discovery platform allowing users to discover, curate and share over 60m research articles.
Website: http://www.sparrho.com
Phone: **Email:** hello@sparrho.com
City: London **State:** England **PC:** **Country: United Kingdom**
Year Established: **Status 2020:** Active
Industries: Artificial Intelligence for:, Digital Media for:, ~ Law-Legal Services (26), ~ Education (13)

Company Name: Spinview
Description: Provides a visual, digital representation of real environments to be fused with data, analytics and visual info for business intelligence
Website: http://spinview.io/
Phone: **Email:** linda@spinview.io
City: London **State:** England **PC:** **Country: United Kingdom**
Year Established: 2016 **Status 2020:** Active
Industries: Augmented Reality for:, IT Managed Services for:, Internet of Things (IoT) for:, Predictive Analytics for:, Business Software as a Service Apps (SaaS Apps) for:, Virtual Reality (VR)

Company Name: Spirit AI
Description: Spirit AI breathe life into digital interactions using the transformative power of artificial intelligence.
Website: http://www.spiritai.com
Phone: **Email:** hello@spiritai.com
City: London **State:** England **PC:** **Country: United Kingdom**
Year Established: 2015 **Status 2020:** Active
Industries:

Company Name: Spixii
Description: Spixii helps insurers design and implement white-label chatbot solutions.
Website: spixii.com
Phone: **Email:** team@spixii.ai
City: London **State:** England **PC:** **Country: United Kingdom**
Year Established: **Status 2020:** Active
Industries: Analytics for:, Artificial Intelligence

Company Name: Spoon Guru
Description: tailored food search & discovery
Website: http://www.spoon.gu: Russia
Phone: **Email:** hello@spoon.gu: Russia
City: London **State:** England **PC:** **Country: United Kingdom**
Year Established: **Status 2020:** Active
Industries: Artificial Intelligence for:, Big Data and Analytics for:, ~ Food and Beverage (17), Machine Learning for:, ~ Healthcare (20), ~ Retail and Consumer Products (52)

Company Name: SpoonGu: Russia
Description: Spoon Guru is the world's leading food search and discovery solution. Using the latest advances in AI and machine learning, Spoon Guru's award winning technology enables food businesses to refine their product offering based on individual consumer profile
Website: https://spoonguru.wpengine.com
Phone: **Email:** markus@spoon.gu: Russia
City: London **State:** England **PC:** **Country: United Kingdom**
Year Established: **Status 2020:** Active
Industries: Artificial Intelligence for:, Big Data and Analytics for:, ~ Food and Beverage (17), Machine Learning for:, ~ Healthcare (20), ~ Retail and Consumer Products (52)

Company Name: SportingPortal
Description: applied analytics
Website:
Phone: **Email:** 37455@reference-encyclopedia-ai.net
City: London **State:** England **PC:** **Country: United Kingdom**
Year Established: 2013 **Status 2020:** Closed
Industries: Analytics for:, Big Data and Analytics for:, ~ Fashion (16), Predictive Analytics for:, ~ Arts-Entertainment-Recreation (4), ~ Arts-Entertainment-Recreation (4)

Company Name: SportsFinder **Description**: Sports events website
Website:
Phone: **Email:** 37456@reference-encyclopedia-ai.net
City: London **State:** England **PC:** **Country: United Kingdom**
Year Established: 2013 **Status 2020:** Closed
Industries: Artificial Intelligence for:, ~ Arts-Entertainment-Recreation (4)

Company **Name:** Spot Intelligence
Description: Artificial Intelligence for Document Processing.
Website: http://www.spotintelligence.com/
Phone: **Email:** contact@spotintelligence.com
City: London **State:** England **PC:** **Country: United Kingdom**
Year Established: **Status 2020:** Active
Industries: Artificial Intelligence for:, Knowledge Management for:, Machine Learning for:, Natural Language Processing for:, Data Management

Company Name: Spring Financial Group
Description: Spring Financial Group is set to transform the way people in the UK get a mortgage.
Website: http://www.spring-fg.com/
Phone: **Email:** info@spring-fg.com
City: London **State:** England **PC:** **Country: United Kingdom**
Year Established: 2016 **Status 2020:** Active
Industries: Artificial Intelligence for:, Finance and Accounting for:, ~ Banking and Financial Markets-Services (7), ~ Banking and Financial Markets-Services (7), ~ Banking and Financial Markets-Services (7)

Company Name: Squareify
Description: Squareify is an analytics platform which uses artificial intelligence to helps businesses unlock hidden value in their data.
Website:
Phone: **Email:** 37464@reference-encyclopedia-ai.net
City: London **State:** England **PC:** **Country: United Kingdom**
Year Established: 2013 **Status 2020:** Closed
Industries: Analytics for:, Artificial Intelligence for:, Predictive Analytics

Company Name: Squelo
Description: Squelo leverages the power of artificial intelligence to match talent with companies based on personality and organizational culture.
Website: http://squelo.com
Phone: **Email:** hello@squelo, .com
City: London **State:** England **PC:** **Country: United Kingdom**
Year Established: 2015 **Status 2020:** Active
Industries: Artificial Intelligence for:, ~ Peer to Peer (44), ~ Social Assistance-Non-Profits (53)

Company Name: Stage Intelligence
Description: SAAS Micromobility solutions that delivers real-time intelligence.
Website: http://stageintelligence.co.uk/
Phone: 44 (0)20 3752 6603 **Email:** info@stageintelligence.co.uk
City: London **State:** England **PC:** **Country: United Kingdom**
Year Established: 2015 **Status 2020:** Active
Industries: Artificial Intelligence for:, IT Managed Services for:, Business Software as a Service Apps (SaaS Apps)

Company Name: Starcount
Description: Starcount is the definitive measure of social media popularity.
Website: http://www.starcount.com/
Phone: 44 20 3770 7554 **Email:** team@starcount.com
City: London **State:** England **PC:** **Country: United Kingdom**
Year Established: 2010 **Status 2020:** Active
Industries: Predictive Analytics

Company Name: Startup Wharf Ltd
Description: Digita Maritime Startup Accelerator
Website: http://startupwharf.com
Phone: **Email:** info@startupwharf.com
City: London **State:** England **PC:** **Country: United Kingdom**
Year Established: 2017 **Status 2020:** Active
Industries: Artificial Intelligence for:, Blockchain for:, IT Managed Services

Company Name: Statmetrix
Description: Helping sports teams identify and develop talent using data
Website: http://statmetrix.co
Phone: **Email:** info@statmetrix.co
City: London **State:** England **PC:** **Country: United Kingdom**
Year Established: 2016 **Status 2020:** Active
Industries: Analytics for:, IT Managed Services for:, Machine Learning for:, ~ Arts-Entertainment-Recreation (4)

Company Name: StatusToday
Description: The world's first employee insights platform that helps companies boost employee wellness and transform workplace productivity.
Website: http://www.statustoday.com/
Phone: **Email:** info@statustoday.com
City: London **State:** England **PC:** **Country: United Kingdom**
Year Established: **Status 2020:** Active
Industries:

Company Name: Stepsize
Description: We build devtools for teams to develop better software faster
Website: http://stepsize.com/
Phone: **Email:** hello@stepsize.com
City: London **State:** England **PC:** **Country: United Kingdom**
Year Established: **Status 2020:** Active
Industries: Artificial Intelligence

Company Name: Sterling AI Solutions
Description: Legal tech company involved in developing AI and ML products for the UK legal sector in many legal areas.
Website: http://www.sterling-ai-solutions.com/
Phone: **Email:** info@sterling-ai-solutions.co.uk
City: London **State:** England **PC:** **Country: United Kingdom**
Year Established: 2018 **Status 2020:** Active
Industries: Artificial Intelligence

Company Name: Stitched
Description: The new standard in talent analytics
Website: http://stitched.ai
Phone: 44 7887 677 175 **Email:** nic@stitched.io
City: London **State:** England **PC:** **Country: United Kingdom**
Year Established: **Status 2020:** Active
Industries: Analytics for:, Artificial Intelligence for:, Enterprise Application Services for:, ~ Human Resources (24), Machine Learning for:, Management Information Systems for:, Natural Language Processing for:, ~ Professional Services (48)

Company Name: StorkCard
Description: StorkCard is the world's first family finance app to help new parents navigate the costly adventure of raising a family.
Website: http://www.storkcard.com
Phone: **Email:** info@storkcard.com
City: London **State:** England **PC:** **Country: United Kingdom**
Year Established: 2018 **Status 2020:** Active
Industries: Application Services for:, Artificial Intelligence for:, ~ Banking and Financial Markets-Services (7), ~ Banking and Financial Markets-Services (7), ~ Education (13), ~ Retail and Consumer Products (52)

Company Name: Story Terrace
Description: Story Terrace helps people to capture their life story using professional writers and software.
Website: http://www.storyterrace.com
Phone: **Email:** info@storyterrace.com
City: London **State:** England **PC:** **Country: United Kingdom**
Year Established: **Status 2020:** Active
Industries: **Company Name:** Streetbees
Description: Streetbees connects you with real people on the ground to gather real time insights.
Website: http://www.streetbees.com
Phone: 020 3488 0670 **Email:** hello@streetbees.com
City: London **State:** England **PC:** **Country: United Kingdom**
Year Established: 2015 **Status 2020:** Active
Industries: Analytics for:, Predictive Analytics

Company Name: Students for AI
Description: S4AI is a NPO that links students with charity projects in advanced analytics and Machine Learning for social good.
Website: http://studentsfor.ai
Phone: **Email:** info@s4ai.org
City: London **State:** England **PC:** **Country: United Kingdom**
Year Established: 2018 **Status 2020:** Active
Industries: ~ Education (13), Machine Learning for:, ~ Retail and Consumer Products (52)

Company Name: SuccessData
Description: SuccessData is an AI data extraction start-up
Website: http://www.successdata.ai/
Phone: **Email:** 37474@reference-encyclopedia-ai.net
City: London **State:** England **PC:** **Country: United Kingdom**
Year Established: 2017 **Status 2020:** Active
Industries: Artificial Intelligence for:, IT Managed Services for:, IT Managed Services

Company Name: Suggestv
Description: Video Recommendation For Publishe: Serbia
Website: http://suggestv.io
Phone: **Email:** hello@suggestv.io
City: London **State:** England **PC:** **Country: United Kingdom**
Year Established: **Status 2020:** Active
Industries: Artificial Intelligence

Company Name: Suits Me
Description: The mission is to develop the most personalised lifestyle assistant in the world; starting with fashion.
Website: http://www.trysuitsme.com/
Phone: **Email:** 37477@reference-encyclopedia-ai.net
City: London **State:** England **PC:** **Country: United Kingdom**
Year Established: 2015 **Status 2020:** Active
Industries: Artificial Intelligence

Company Name: Sum&Substance
Description: Sum&Substance is an identity verification platform for KYC/KYB/AML.
Website: http://sumsub.com
Phone: **Email:** hello@sumsub.com
City: London **State:** England **PC:** **Country: United Kingdom**
Year Established: **Status 2020:** Active
Industries: Artificial Intelligence for:, ~ Banking and Financial Markets-Services (7), ~ Gaming (18), ~ Telecommunications (56), ~ Transportation and Logistics (57), Computer Vision for:, Cyber Security for:, ~ Banking and Financial Markets-Services (1593), ~ E-Commerce (15

Company Name: Summly
Description: Summly is a web platform and smartphone app that provides algorithmically-generated summaries from thousands of sources.
Website: http://www.summly.com
Phone: **Email:** hello@summly.com
City: London **State:** England **PC:** **Country: United Kingdom**
Year Established: **Status 2020:** Active
Industries: Application Services for:, Artificial Intelligence for:, Mobile for:, ~ Media-Communications (41)

Company Name: Sumsub
Description: One answer to all onboarding and compliance challenges. Identity verification, KYC, KYB, KYT, AML screening, antifraud.
Website: http://sumsub.com
Phone: 44 12 44 94 07 03 **Email:** info@sumsub.com
City: London **State:** England **PC:** **Country: United Kingdom**
Year Established: 2015 **Status 2020:** Active
Industries: Artificial Intelligence for:, Computer Vision for:, ~ Banking and Financial Markets-Services (7)

Company Name: Suntri
Description: Blockchain Operating System
Website: http://www.suntriplatform.com/
Phone: **Email:** office@suntriplatform.com
City: London **State:** England **PC:** **Country: United Kingdom**
Year Established: **Status 2020:** Active
Industries:

Company Name: SUPERPERSONAL
Description: AI, Visual Personalisation, Virtual Dressing Room
Website: http://www.superpersonal.com
Phone: **Email:** hello@superpersonal.com
City: London **State:** England **PC:** **Country: United Kingdom**
Year Established: 2018 **Status 2020:** Closed
Industries: ~ Fashion (16), IT Managed Services

Company Name: Sure
Description: Sure curates the most "Instagrammed" food and drink spots.
Website: http://surebot.io
Phone: **Email:** founders@surebot.io
City: London **State:** England **PC:** **Country: United Kingdom**
Year Established: **Status 2020:** Active
Industries: Artificial Intelligence for:, ~ Food and Beverage (17), IT Managed Services for:, ~ Arts-Entertainment-Recreation (4), ~ Telecommunications (56), ~ Travel and Transportation (58), ~ Travel and Transportation (58)

Company Name: Suzu
Description: Artificial Intelligence to understand, predict & influence customer behaviour in real-time
Website:
Phone: **Email:** 37489@reference-encyclopedia-ai.net
City: London **State:** England **PC:** **Country: United Kingdom**
Year Established: 2015 **Status 2020:** Closed
Industries: Artificial Intelligence for:, Digital Marketing

Company Name: Swace Ltd
Description: Swace is a blockchain-based social gaming platform where users gain rewards for engaging with brands.
Website: http://swaceapp.com
Phone: **Email:** hello@swaceapp.com
City: London **State:** England **PC:** **Country: United Kingdom**
Year Established: **Status 2020:** Active
Industries: ~ Media-Communications (41), ~ Media-Communications (41), Application Services for:, Artificial Intelligence for:, Augmented Reality for:, ~ Arts-Entertainment-Recreation (4), ~ Education (13), ~ Event Management (15), ~ Arts-Entertainment-Recreation (4), Applicat

Company Name: SweepTEQ
Description: SweepTEQ autonomously detects and collects debris at and around airport airfields via smart rovers with AI-enabled cameras.
Website:
Phone: **Email:** 37494@reference-encyclopedia-ai.net
City: London **State:** England **PC:** **Country: United Kingdom**
Year Established: 2017 **Status 2020:** Closed
Industries: ~ Aerospace and Defense (2), Artificial Intelligence

Company Name: Sweet Pricing
Description: Sweet Pricing is a company that provides tools that boost revenue for in app purchases.
Website: http://sweetpricing.com/en/
Phone: **Email:** support@sweetpricing.com
City: London **State:** England **PC:** **Country: United Kingdom**
Year Established: **Status 2020:** Active
Industries: Analytics for:, Application Services for:, Artificial Intelligence for:, Big Data and Analytics for:, Machine Learning for:, Mobile for:, Predictive Analytics

Company Name: SwiftERM
Description: Automatic additional email software for ecommerce, predicts imminent consumer purchas: Spain
Website: http://www.swifterm.com
Phone: 44-207-998-3901 **Email:** info@swifterm.com
City: London **State:** England **PC:** **Country: United Kingdom**
Year Established: 2014 **Status 2020:** Active
Industries: Analytics for:, E-Commerce for:, Predictive Analytics

Company Name: SwiftKey
Description: SwiftKey is a technology company that aims to enhance interaction between keyboards and people.
Website: http://swiftkey.com/
Phone: **Email:** press@swiftkey.com
City: London **State:** England **PC:** **Country: United Kingdom**
Year Established: **Status 2020:** Active
Industries: Artificial Intelligence for:, Mobile for:, ~ Professional Services (48)

Company Name: Swogo
Description: Swogo provides bundle solutions for e-commerce retails and helps them increase their average order value.
Website: http://www.swogo.com
Phone: **Email:** contact@swogo.com
City: London **State:** England **PC:** **Country: United Kingdom**
Year Established: **Status 2020:** Active
Industries: Artificial Intelligence for:, E-Commerce for:, Machine Learning for:, ~ Retail and Consumer Products (52), ~ Professional Services (48)

Company Name: Symilarity
Description: Unsupervised Deep Learning Platform, Unsupervised Artificial Intelligence AI, Unsupervised Cognitive Computing Platform.
Website: http://www.symilarity.com
Phone: 61450890034 **Email:** ian.haynes@symilarity.com
City: London **State:** England **PC:** **Country: United Kingdom**
Year Established: 2014 **Status 2020:** Active
Industries: Artificial Intelligence for:, ~ Education (13), IT Managed Services for:, Web for:, Internet of Things (IoT) for:, Machine Learning

Company Name: Symmitree Ltd
Description: Symmitree aims to give every refugee a smartphone by 2020.
Website: http://www.symmitree.com
Phone: **Email:** info@symmitree.com
City: London **State:** England **PC:** **Country: United Kingdom**
Year Established: **Status 2020:** Active
Industries: Artificial Intelligence for:, ~ Manufacturing-Electronic (30), ~ Professional Services (48)

Company Name: Symphony Ventur: Spain
Description: Symphony is a professional services firm passionate about creating value for the world's leading organizations
Website: http://www.symphonyhq.com/
Phone: 44 203 6082072 **Email:** enquiries@symphonyhq.com
City: London **State:** England **PC:** **Country: United Kingdom**
Year Established: **Status 2020:** Active
Industries: Artificial Intelligence for:, ~ Professional Services (48), Robotics

Company Name: Synthace
Description: Synthace uses open source technology to make process in biotechnology move faster.
Website: http://synthace.com
Phone: 44 (0) 20 7554 5877 **Email:** info@synthace.com
City: London **State:** England **PC:** **Country: United Kingdom**
Year Established: **Status 2020:** Active
Industries: Artificial Intelligence for:, ~ Biotechnology (9)

Company Name: Synthesia
Description: Synthesia provides next-gen visual content creation.
Website: http://www.synthesia.io
Phone: **Email:** hello@synthesia.io
City: London **State:** England **PC:** **Country: United Kingdom**
Year Established: 2017 **Status 2020:** Active
Industries:

Company Name: Synthesized
Description: Privacy-preserved artificial intelligence
Website: http://synthesized.io
Phone: **Email:** team@synthesized.io
City: London **State:** England **PC:** **Country: United Kingdom**
Year Established: **Status 2020:** Active
Industries: Artificial Intelligence for:, Machine Learning for:, ~ Professional Services (48)

Company Name: SyntheticGestalt
Description: SyntheticGestalt develops machine learning models for drug discovery and software for facilitating and automating research.
Website: http://www.syntheticgestalt.com/
Phone: **Email:** 37499@reference-encyclopedia-ai.net
City: London **State:** England **PC:** **Country: United Kingdom**
Year Established: 2018 **Status 2020:** Active
Industries: IT Managed Services for:, Machine Learning

Company Name: Talent Rank
Description: Talent Rank Arena. Real-world work experience from your browser.
Website: http://talentrank.co
Phone: **Email:** 37507@reference-encyclopedia-ai.net
City: London **State:** England **PC:** **Country: United Kingdom**
Year Established: 2013 **Status 2020:** Active
Industries: ~ Education (13), Predictive Analytics for:, Web

Company Name: Talent Ticker
Description: Talent Ticker is an AI and predictive technology company making the Recruitment Industry faster, more efficient and more profitable
Website: http://www.talentticker.ai/
Phone: **Email:** hello@talentticker.ai
City: London **State:** England **PC:** **Country: United Kingdom**
Year Established: 2018 **Status 2020:** Active
Industries: Artificial Intelligence

Company Name: TalentHunter.AI
Description: TalentHunter.AI is an anonymous careers marketplace for IT sales talent.
Website: http://www.talenthunter.ai
Phone: 44 (0) 20 8133 5914 **Email:** hello@talenthunter.ai
City: London **State:** England **PC:** **Country: United Kingdom**
Year Established: **Status 2020:** Active
Industries: Artificial Intelligence for:, Machine Learning for:, ~ Human Resources (24)

Company **Name:** Tallysticks
Description: Tallysticks is an international trade solution for SMEs.
Website: http://www.tallysticks.io
Phone: **Email:** info@tallysticks.io
City: London **State:** England **PC:** **Country: United Kingdom**
Year Established: **Status 2020:** Active
Industries: Finance and Accounting for:, Artificial Intelligence for:, ~ Banking and Financial Markets-Services (7), ~ Banking and

Financial Markets-Services (7), ~ Banking and Financial Markets-Services (7), Automation for:, Supply Chain Management

Company Name: Teamflow
Description: Teamflow unlocks the power of human intelligence in organizations to improve productivity.
Website: http://www.jointeamflow.com/
Phone: **Email:** 37510@reference-encyclopedia-ai.net
City: London **State:** England **PC:** **Country: United Kingdom**
Year Established: 2018 **Status 2020:** Active
Industries: Artificial Intelligence for:, Web for:, Machine Learning

Company Name: techUK
Description: techUK offers information technology services to small and medium businesses.
Website: http://www.techuk.org/
Phone: **Email:** info@techuk.org
City: London **State:** England **PC:** **Country: United Kingdom**
Year Established: 2015 **Status 2020:** Active
Industries: IT Managed Services for:, Application Services

Company Name: Techwisely Ltd
Description: Available on mobile and smartwatch platform, we offer world's first hands-free counterless checkout solution eliminating the need of queuing
Website: http://www.planckly.com
Phone: 44(0)7449768696 **Email:** uzair.siddiqui@techwisely.co.uk
City: London **State:** England **PC:** **Country: United Kingdom**
Year Established: **Status 2020:** Active
Industries: ~ Media-Communications (41), Artificial Intelligence for:, Big Data and Analytics for:, ~ Banking and Financial Markets-Services (7), ~ Retail and Consumer Products (52), Machine Learning for:, ~ Banking and Financial Markets-Services (7), ~ Retail and Consumer

Company Name: Teebly
Description: The new way high-trust companies interact with their clients.
Website: http://www.teebly.co
Phone: **Email:** contact@teebly.co
City: London **State:** England **PC:** **Country: United Kingdom**
Year Established: **Status 2020:** Active
Industries: Artificial Intelligence for:, Enterprise Application Services for:, Natural Language Processing for:, Business Strategy and Design

Company Name: Teens in AI
Description: Teens in AI empowers young people to change the world through artificial intelligence for social good.
Website: http://teensinai.com
Phone: **Email:** elena.sinel@teensinai.com
City: London **State:** England **PC:** **Country: United Kingdom**
Year Established: 2014 **Status 2020:** Active
Industries: Artificial Intelligence for:, Web for:, ~ Retail and Consumer Products (52)

Company Name: Telectic
Description: Telectic applies artificial intelligence (AI) to interpret the Web and discover insights about the professional world.
Website: http://www.telectic.io
Phone: **Email:** hello@telectic.io
City: London **State:** England **PC:** **Country: United Kingdom**
Year Established: **Status 2020:** Active
Industries: Analytics for:, Artificial Intelligence for:, Big Data and Analytics for:, Enterprise Application Services for:, Machine Learning for:, ~ Media-Communications (41), ~ Peer to Peer (44), Content

Company Name: Tenderla: Kenya
Description: Tenderlake is the easy and intelligent gateway to the $3 Trillion European public sector procurement market.
Website: http://www.tenderlake.com
Phone: 44(0)2080501947 **Email:** hello@tenderlake.com
City: London **State:** England **PC:** **Country: United Kingdom**
Year Established: 2016 **Status 2020:** Active
Industries: Artificial Intelligence for:, Business Applications for:, Big Data and Analytics for:, Machine Learning for:, ~ Administrative and Support Services (1)

Company Name: Tessian
Description: Tessian (formerly CheckRecipient) prevents highly sensitive information being sent to the wrong people over email.
Website: http://www.tessian.com
Phone: 0044 208 068 5223 **Email:** contact@tessian.com
City: London **State:** England **PC:** **Country: United Kingdom**
Year Established: **Status 2020:** Active
Industries:

Company Name: TextAwesome
Description: Awesome | Your Own Personal Assistant and Concierge by SMS
Website: http://textawesome.co.uk/
Phone: **Email:** done@textaweso.me
City: London **State:** England **PC:** **Country: United Kingdom**
Year Established: **Status 2020:** Active
Industries: Application Services for:, Artificial Intelligence for:, ~ Transportation and Logistics (57)

Company Name: The AI Core
Description: The AI Core is an intercollegiate community of top student AI Talent.
Website: http://theaicore.com/
Phone: **Email:** team@theaicore.com
City: London **State:** England **PC:** **Country: United Kingdom**
Year Established: 2019 **Status 2020:** Active
Industries: Artificial Intelligence for:, ~ Education (13), IT Managed Services for:, Machine Learning

Company Name: The Institute for Ethical AI & Machine Learning
Description: The IEML is a UK-based think-do-tank that builds frameworks and standards that ensure the ethical development of machine learning systems.
Website: http://ethical.institute
Phone: **Email:** a@ethical.institute
City: London **State:** England **PC:** **Country: United Kingdom**
Year Established: 2018 **Status 2020:** Active
Industries: Artificial Intelligence

Company Name: The Quarry
Description: Data > Insights > Impact
Website: http://thequarry.io
Phone: **Email:** info@thequarry.io
City: London **State:** England **PC:** **Country: United Kingdom**
Year Established: **Status 2020:** Active
Industries: Analytics for:, Artificial Intelligence for:, Business Intelligence for:, Data Management for:, Predictive Analytics

Company Name: The Square Tech Group
Description: The Square is an award winning network & automated hiring marketplace for specialist skilled industries.
Website: http://www.thesquareapp.com/
Phone: **Email:** hello@thesquareapp.com
City: London **State:** England **PC:** **Country: United Kingdom**
Year Established: **Status 2020:** Active
Industries: Artificial Intelligence for:, ~ Banking and Financial Markets-Services (7), Business Intelligence for:, ~ Human Resources (24), ~ Social Media (54)

Company **Name:** thesocialCV.com
Description: TheSocialCV.com is a natural language search platform serving social CRM, reputation indexing, and recruitment platforms.
Website: http://thesocialcv.com
Phone: 7939325585 **Email:** bill@thesocialcv.com
City: London **State:** England **PC:** **Country: United Kingdom**
Year Established: 2010 **Status 2020:** Closed
Industries: Natural Language Processing for:, Web for:, Content for:, ~ Social Assistance-Non-Profits (53)

Company Name: TheySay
Description: TheySay is a sentiment analysis firm developing a platform that uses a linguistic approach interpreting sentiments computationally.
Website: http://www.theysayanalytics.com
Phone: **Email:** contact@theysay.io
City: London **State:** England **PC:** **Country: United Kingdom**
Year Established: **Status 2020:** Active
Industries: Analytics for:, Artificial Intelligence

Company Name: ThingCo
Description: Telematics, Cars, IoT, SaaS, Insurance, ADAS, Intelligent voice, Automotive
Website: http://www.thingco.com
Phone: **Email:** interested@thingco.com
City: London **State:** England **PC:** **Country: United Kingdom**
Year Established: 2018 **Status 2020:** Active
Industries: Artificial Intelligence for:, ~ Automotive (5), Internet of Things (IoT)

Company Name: ThinkSense.ai
Description: Cognitive Robotic Process Automation (RPA) and AI /ML Process Mining
Website: http://thinksense.ai
Phone: **Email:** hello@thinksense.ai
City: London **State:** England **PC:** **Country: United Kingdom**
Year Established: 2017 **Status 2020:** Active
Industries: Artificial Intelligence for:, Robotics

Company Name: Third Space Auto
Description: Head-quartered in London, UK with development teams in Finland and India.
Website: http://www.thirdspaceauto.com/
Phone: **Email:** emmithirdspace@gmail.com
City: London **State:** England **PC:** **Country: United Kingdom**
Year Established: **Status 2020:** Active
Industries: Artificial Intelligence for:, ~ Automotive (5), Machine Learning for:, Natural Language Processing

Company Name: ThoughtRiver
Description: ThoughtRiver reviews and rates contracts via a contract Intelligence engine.
Website: http://thoughtriver.com
Phone: 44 207 382 8000 **Email:** info@thoughtriver.com
City: London **State:** England **PC:** **Country: United Kingdom**
Year Established: **Status 2020:** Active
Industries: Artificial Intelligence for:, Blockchain for:, ~ Law-Legal Services (26)

Company Name: Ticklr
Description: The worlds first social market rewarding its users like no other platform when they discover, share and enjoy exclusive perks.
Website: http://www.ticklr.co.uk
Phone: **Email:** hello@ticklr.co.uk
City: London **State:** England **PC:** **Country: United Kingdom**
Year Established: **Status 2020:** Active
Industries: Artificial Intelligence for:, Big Data and Analytics for:, ~ Banking and Financial Markets-Services (7), ~ Retail and Consumer Products (52), ~ Social Media (54)

Company Name: Tictrac
Description: Tictrac is a connected health platform that engages people in their health through their data
Website: http://www.tictrac.com
Phone: **Email:** mail@tictrac.com
City: London **State:** England **PC:** **Country: United Kingdom**
Year Established: **Status 2020:** Active
Industries: Artificial Intelligence for:, Data Management for:, ~ Healthcare (20), Predictive Analytics

Company Name: TIFY
Description: At tify our vision is to provide businesses with simple yet effective tools to perform consumer analytics.
Website: http://www.tifyapp.com/
Phone: **Email:** bhildebrand@tifyapp.com
City: London **State:** England **PC:** **Country: United Kingdom**
Year Established: 2017 **Status 2020:** Active
Industries:

Company Name: Timista
Description: TIMISTA LIMITED is a Computer Software company located in 19 Thurlow Rd, London, United Kingdom.
Website: http://www.timista.com
Phone: **Email:** feedback@timista.com
City: London **State:** England **PC:** **Country: United Kingdom**
Year Established: **Status 2020:** Active
Industries: Artificial Intelligence for:, ~ Professional Services (48), Business Process and Operations for:, ~ Travel and Transportation (58)

Company Name: Titan Alpha Systems
Description: Artificial Intelligence Systems
Website: http://www.titanalpha.ai
Phone: **Email:** partner@titanalphacap.com
City: London **State:** England **PC:** **Country: United Kingdom**
Year Established: 2018 **Status 2020:** Active
Industries: Artificial Intelligence for:, IT Managed Services

Company Name: Tonguesten
Description: We turn your favourite music videos into the easiest English teaching tool on the planet, powered by real time artificial intelligence.
Website: http://www.tonguesten.com/
Phone: 44 20 7734 5558 **Email:** info@tonguesten.com
City: London **State:** England **PC:** **Country: United Kingdom**
Year Established: 2013 **Status 2020:** Active
Industries: Artificial Intelligence for:, ~ Education (13), ~ Arts-Entertainment-Recreation (4), ~ Education (13)

Company Name: TopiHub
Description: TopiHub is a create a new search experience.
Website: http://searchguide.level3.com/
Phone: **Email:** 37546@reference-encyclopedia-ai.net
City: London **State:** England **PC:** **Country: United Kingdom**
Year Established: 2017 **Status 2020:** Active
Industries: Artificial Intelligence

Company Name: Trackener
Description: Trackener is revolutionising the equine care with data and technology.
Website: http://www.trackener.com
Phone: **Email:** contact@trackener.com
City: London **State:** England **PC:** **Country: United Kingdom**
Year Established: 2015 **Status 2020:** Active
Industries: Analytics for:, ~ Healthcare (20), Internet of Things (IoT) for:, Machine Learning for:, Internet of Things (IoT)

Company Name: Tractable
Description: Tractable develops artificial intelligence for accident and disaster recovery.
Website: http://tractable.ai/
Phone: **Email:** information@tractable.ai
City: London **State:** England **PC:** **Country: United Kingdom**
Year Established: **Status 2020:** Active
Industries: Artificial Intelligence for:, ~ Insurance (25), Machine Learning for:, ~ Professional Services (48)

Company Name: TradeRiser
Description: TradeRiser is an AI Research Assistant that enables users to query data using natural language questioning
Website:
Phone: 44(0)800 689 3063 **Email:** 37551@reference-encyclopedia-ai.net
City: London **State:** England **PC:** **Country: United Kingdom**

Year Established: 2014 **Status 2020:** Closed
Industries: Analytics for:, Artificial Intelligence for:, Machine Learning for:, Robotics

Company Name: Transformative AI
Description: Transforming Healthcare Through Deep Learning
Website: http://transformative.ai/
Phone: **Email:** 37557@reference-encyclopedia-ai.net
City: London **State:** England **PC:** **Country: United Kingdom**
Year Established: 2017 **Status 2020:** Active
Industries: Artificial Intelligence for:, ~ Healthcare (20), ~ Healthcare (20)

Company Name: TravelAi
Description: We help tell the story of how your customers use transport systems via licensing our SDK and DaaS subscription to the highly granular data
Website: http://www.travelai.info
Phone: **Email:** info@travelai.co.uk
City: London **State:** England **PC:** **Country: United Kingdom**
Year Established: **Status 2020:** Active
Industries: Artificial Intelligence for:, ~ Automotive (5), Big Data and Analytics for:, Machine Learning for:, ~ Transportation and Logistics (57), ~ Professional Services (48), ~ Transportation and Logistics (57)

Company Name: Travtus
Description: Travtus is a London based Artificial Intelligence Research & Development company with an aim to automate property management by 2021.
Website: http://www.travtus.com
Phone: **Email:** 37560@reference-encyclopedia-ai.net
City: London **State:** England **PC:** **Country: United Kingdom**
Year Established: 2013 **Status 2020:** Active
Industries: Artificial Intelligence for:, Machine Learning for:, Application Services

Company Name: Traydstream Limited
Description: Traydstream automates the most critical aspects of converting, checking and managing trade finance documents
Website: http://traydstream.com/
Phone: **Email:** info@traydstream.com
City: London **State:** England **PC:** **Country: United Kingdom**
Year Established: **Status 2020:** Active
Industries: Artificial Intelligence for:, ~ Banking and Financial Markets-Services (7), ~ Banking and Financial Markets-Services (7), IT Managed Services

Company Name: Trudera
Description: We're On A Mission To Bring Intelligent AI To The Enterprise.
Website: http://trudera.com
Phone: 44 (0)20 8798 3271 **Email:** info@trudera.com
City: London **State:** England **PC:** **Country: United Kingdom**
Year Established: **Status 2020:** Active
Industries: Artificial Intelligence for:, Big Data and Analytics for:, Business Intelligence for:, Cyber Security

Company Name: True AI
Description: True AI is a London-based artificial intelligence company that aims to improve customer experience and save service agent time.
Website: http://trueai.io
Phone: **Email:** info@trueai.io
City: London **State:** England **PC:** **Country: United Kingdom**
Year Established: **Status 2020:** Active
Industries: Artificial Intelligence for:, Business Intelligence

Company Name: Truerent
Description: Bringing Real Estate Appraisal to the Next Level through AI decision making that enhance real estate investment
Website: http://truerent.fr/
Phone: 33668838957 **Email:** contact@truerent.fr
City: London **State:** England **PC:** **Country: United Kingdom**
Year Established: 2017 **Status 2020:** Active
Industries:

Company Name: Turbo AI
Description: AI Technology PHV Platform
Website: http://www.turbocabs.com
Phone: 44 203 93 646 93 **Email:** info@turbocabs.com
City: London **State:** England **PC:** **Country: United Kingdom**
Year Established: **Status 2020:** Active
Industries: Artificial Intelligence for:, ~ Education (13), IT Managed Services for:, ~ Transportation and Logistics (57)

Company Name: Turing Intelligence Technology Limited
Description: TurinTech.AI is a research-driven Artificial Intelligence company.
Website: http://turintech.ai/
Phone: **Email:** 37580@reference-encyclopedia-ai.net
City: London **State:** England **PC:** **Country: United Kingdom**
Year Established: 2018 **Status 2020:** Active
Industries: Artificial Intelligence for:, Machine Learning

Company Name: tweedle
Description: Eradicating recruitment bias using AI
Website: http://tweedle.io
Phone: **Email:** founders@tweedle.io
City: London **State:** England **PC:** **Country: United Kingdom**
Year Established: **Status 2020:** Active
Industries: Artificial Intelligence for:, ~ Human Resources (24), ~ Human Resources (24)

Company Name: Twizoo
Description: Twizoo is a non-stop source of user-generated content from social media.
Website: http://www.twizoo.com
Phone: **Email:** 37582@reference-encyclopedia-ai.net
City: London **State:** England **PC:** **Country: United Kingdom**
Year Established: 2013 **Status 2020:** Active
Industries: Artificial Intelligence for:, Machine Learning for:, ~ Social Assistance-Non-Profits (53), ~ Social Media (54)

Company Name: Ubisend
Description: Ubisend provides custom chatbot solution that meets your KPIs and business goals.
Website: http://www.ubisend.com
Phone: **Email:** 37587@reference-encyclopedia-ai.net
City: London **State:** England **PC:** **Country: United Kingdom**
Year Established: 2016 **Status 2020:** Active
Industries: Artificial Intelligence for:, Machine Learning

Company Name: UCROWDME
Description: Global ideas marketplace leveraging blockchain, AI and best-of-breed technology.
Website: http://ucrowdme.com
Phone: 44 (0) 0203 866 1185 **Email:** Info@ucrowdme.com
City: London **State:** England **PC:** **Country: United Kingdom**
Year Established: 2014 **Status 2020:** Active
Industries: Business Applications for:, Business Applications for:, Machine Learning for:, Machine Learning for:, ~ Retail and Consumer Products (52)

Company Name: UCW Industries Ltd.
Description: Services in the IoT prototyping, embedded systems programming, custom hardware design, IoT integration, and custom software development.
Website: http://ucwindustries.com
Phone: **Email:** info@unitycloudware.com
City: London **State:** England **PC:** **Country: United Kingdom**
Year Established: **Status 2020:** Active
Industries: Analytics for:, Artificial Intelligence for:, Big Data and Analytics for:, Cloud for:, Cloud for:, Cloud for:, Cloud for:, Application Services for:, Embedded for:, Embedded for:, Enterprise Application Services for:, Machine Learning

Company Name: Uhura Solutions
Description: An AI platform that reads and understands contracts and agreements just as humans do.
Website: http://uhurasolutions.com/
Phone: **Email:** info@uhurasolutions.com
City: London **State:** England **PC:** **Country: United Kingdom**
Year Established: 2017 **Status 2020:** Active
Industries: Artificial Intelligence for:, ~ Banking and Financial Markets-Services (7), ~ Banking and Financial Markets-Services (7), IT Managed Services

Company Name: Umano AI
Description: Umano is a human analytics AI platform for mental health autism & ADHD. This is world's first behavioural study based on image analysis.
Website:
Phone: **Email:** 1askumano@gmail.com
City: London **State:** England **PC:** **Country: United Kingdom**
Year Established: 2019 **Status 2020:** Active
Industries: Artificial Intelligence for:, ~ Healthcare (20), ~ Healthcare (20)

Company Name: Uncloak
Description: Computer & Network Security
Website: http://summary.uncloak.io/
Phone: **Email:** 37590@reference-encyclopedia-ai.net
City: London **State:** England **PC:** **Country: United Kingdom**
Year Established: 2016 **Status 2020:** Active
Industries: Artificial Intelligence for:, Blockchain for:, IT Managed Services for:, Web for:, Security

Company Name: United Visual Artists
Description: UVA is a London based art practice that combines a wide range of disciplines: sculpture, installation, live performance, and architecture.
Website: http://uva.co.uk/
Phone: 44 20 7378 0303 **Email:** mail@uva.co.uk
City: London **State:** England **PC:** **Country: United Kingdom**
Year Established: **Status 2020:** Active
Industries: Artificial Intelligence

Company Name: Untrite
Description: We help companies make sense of their dark data.
Website: http://www.untrite.com
Phone: **Email:** info@untrite.com
City: London **State:** England **PC:** **Country: United Kingdom**
Year Established: 2015 **Status 2020:** Active
Industries: Big Data and Analytics for:, Databases for:, Enterprise Application Services for:, IT Managed Services for:, Application Program Interfaces (APIs) for:, Machine Learning

Company Name: Upside
Description: investment idea marketplace utilizing Artifical Intelligence and Machine Learning
Website: http://www.upsidetechnology.co
Phone: **Email:** info@upsidetechnology.co
City: London **State:** England **PC:** **Country: United Kingdom**
Year Established: 2018 **Status 2020:** Active
Industries: Artificial Intelligence for:, IT Managed Services for:, Web

Company Name: US Ai Ltd
Description: US provides Ai focused services to organisations across the UK
Website: http://www.talktous.ai
Phone: **Email:** 37605@reference-encyclopedia-ai.net
City: London **State:** England **PC:** **Country: United Kingdom**
Year Established: 2017 **Status 2020:** Active
Industries:

Company Name: USIO Energy
Description: USIO Energy are building the energy company of the future, using AI to deliver electricity and gas to perfectly match people's lifestyles.
Website: http://usioenergy.com
Phone: **Email:** help@usioenergy.com
City: London **State:** England **PC:** **Country: United Kingdom**
Year Established: **Status 2020:** Active
Industries: Artificial Intelligence for:, ~ Energy and Utilities (14)

Company Name: V2X Network
Description: V2X Network is a decentralized In-Vehicle data access platform powered by blockchain.
Website: http://www.v2x.network/
Phone: **Email:** hello@v2x.network
City: London **State:** England **PC:** **Country: United Kingdom**
Year Established: **Status 2020:** Active
Industries: Artificial Intelligence for:, ~ Automotive (5), Blockchain for:, ~ Banking and Financial Markets-Services (7), ~ Banking and Financial Markets-Services (7), IT Managed Services for:, Web for:, Machine Learning

Company Name: V7
Description: V7 creates deep learning models to learn to perform life sciences experiments and double the pace of critical scientific research.
Website: http://www.v7labs.com
Phone: **Email:** 37608@reference-encyclopedia-ai.net
City: London **State:** England **PC:** **Country: United Kingdom**
Year Established: 2018 **Status 2020:** Active
Industries: Analytics for:, Artificial Intelligence for:, Big Data and Analytics for:, ~ Biotechnology (9), ~ Education (13)

Company Name: Vamstar
Description: AI powered platform for predicting and matching public contracts in healthcare
Website: http://www.vamstar.io/
Phone: 44 330 133 1383 **Email:** info@vamstar.io
City: London **State:** England **PC:** **Country: United Kingdom**
Year Established: 2019 **Status 2020:** Active
Industries: Artificial Intelligence for:, Big Data and Analytics for:, ~ Healthcare (20), ~ Healthcare (20), Machine Learning for:, ~ Healthcare (20), Natural Language Processing for:, Natural Language Processing for:, ~ Administrative and Support Services (1)

Company Name: Vapu
Description: Vapu is a vaping site dedicated to saving you more money.
Website: http://vapu.io
Phone: **Email:** hello@davvc.com
City: London **State:** England **PC:** **Country: United Kingdom**
Year Established: **Status 2020:** Active
Industries: Artificial Intelligence for:, ~ Agriculture (3), ~ Healthcare (20)

Company **Name:** VCfund.me
Description: Artificial intelligence powered matching engine enabling startups and fund managers to connect with the right investors.
Website: http://vcfund.me
Phone: **Email:** max@pioneerventures.io
City: London **State:** England **PC:** **Country: United Kingdom**
Year Established: 2019 **Status 2020:** Active
Industries: Artificial Intelligence for:, ~ Customer Relationship Management (11), IT Managed Services for:, Machine Learning for:, ~ Banking and Financial Markets-Services (7)

Company Name: vendi
Description: vendi is an AI-assisted marketplace to buy and sell verified products, starting with phones.
Website: http://vendiapp.com/
Phone: 44 (0)7591 082207 **Email:** contact@vendiapp.com
City: London **State:** England **PC:** **Country: United Kingdom**

Year Established: **Status 2020:** Active
Industries: Artificial Intelligence for:, E-Commerce for:, Network

Company Name: Verbo AI
Description: AI Conversational Commerce Platform
Website: http://verbo.ai
Phone: **Email:** saul@verbo.ai
City: London **State:** England **PC:** **Country: United Kingdom**
Year Established: 2019 **Status 2020:** Active
Industries: Artificial Intelligence for:, E-Commerce for:, Natural Language Processing

Company Name: Verchable
Description: Artificial Intelligence for Contextual Video Understanding
Website: http://www.verchable.com/
Phone: **Email:** verchableai@gmail.com
City: London **State:** England **PC:** **Country: United Kingdom**
Year Established: 2019 **Status 2020:** Active
Industries: Artificial Intelligence for:, Computer Vision

Company Name: Verv
Description: Verv is a clever home energy assistant that gives you intelligent information about home applianc: Spain
Website: http://verv.energy/
Phone: 44 800 907 0006 **Email:** info@verv.energy
City: London **State:** England **PC:** **Country: United Kingdom**
Year Established: **Status 2020:** Active
Industries: Artificial Intelligence for:, ~ Manufacturing-Electronic (30), ~ Energy and Utilities (14), ~ Energy and Utilities (14), ~ Energy and Utilities (14), IT Managed Services for:, Machine Learning for:, Network

Company Name: vHealth Lab
Description: vHealth Lab is a smart telemedicine platform supporting a multitude of portable, FDA-approved ECG devices.
Website: http://www.vhealthlab.london
Phone: **Email:** 37622@reference-encyclopedia-ai.net
City: London **State:** England **PC:** **Country: United Kingdom**
Year Established: 2017 **Status 2020:** Active
Industries: Artificial Intelligence for:, ~ Healthcare (20), IT Managed Services

Company Name: Video Agnostic
Description: Artificial Intelligence TV and video optimization
Website:
Phone: 44 (0) 207 099 4651 **Email:** 37627@reference-encyclopedia-ai.net
City: London **State:** England **PC:** **Country: United Kingdom**
Year Established: 2015 **Status 2020:** Closed
Industries: Artificial Intelligence for:, Machine Learning for:, ~ Arts-Entertainment-Recreation (4)

Company Name: VIEBEG TECHNOLOGIES
Description: We transform the way medical products are bought and sold, advancing the 4th industrial revolution in the developing world.
Website: http://viebeg.com
Phone: **Email:** tobias@viebeg.com
City: London **State:** England **PC:** **Country: United Kingdom**
Year Established: 2018 **Status 2020:** Active
Industries: Artificial Intelligence for:, ~ Healthcare (20), IT Managed Services

Company Name: Viewsy
Description: Viewsy creates unique datasets to help businesses thrive in an insight driven age.
Website: http://www.viewsy.com
Phone: **Email:** hello@viewsy.com
City: London **State:** England **PC:** **Country: United Kingdom**
Year Established: **Status 2020:** Active
Industries:

Company Name: Visii
Description: Visii is helping people discover images or products they love without using words.
Website: http://www.visii.com
Phone: 7340581926 **Email:** beng@visii.com
City: London **State:** England **PC:** **Country: United Kingdom**
Year Established: **Status 2020:** Active
Industries: Artificial Intelligence for:, E-Commerce for:, Application Services for:, Machine Learning for:, Computer Vision

Company Name: Vision in Motion
Description: Vision in Motion is a startup that is developing an innovative software-based platform.
Website: http://www.vimotion.tech
Phone: 961 03 149222 **Email:** amer@vimotion.tech
City: London **State:** England **PC:** **Country: United Kingdom**
Year Established: 2016 **Status 2020:** Active
Industries: Artificial Intelligence for:, IT Managed Services for:, Robotics

Company Name: Visionalia ltd
Description: A NEW KIND OF A.I. TO START A MUSIC REVOLUTION
Website: http://www.visionalia.it/
Phone: **Email:** 37634@reference-encyclopedia-ai.net
City: London **State:** England **PC:** **Country: United Kingdom**
Year Established: 2018 **Status 2020:** Active
Industries: Analytics for:, Artificial Intelligence for:, ~ Education (13), ~ Arts-Entertainment-Recreation (4)

Company Name: Vivacity Labs
Description: Vivacity Labs makes intelligent cameras to gather transport data, using the latest machine learning & computer vision techniques.
Website: http://vivacitylabs.com/
Phone: **Email:** contact@vivacitylabs.com
City: London **State:** England **PC:** **Country: United Kingdom**
Year Established: 2015 **Status 2020:** Active
Industries: Artificial Intelligence for:, Internet of Things (IoT) for:, Machine Learning

Company Name: VIVE
Description: Vive is a technology healthcare company focused on providing honest, expertly researched and personalised nutritional products.
Website: http://www.vivewellness.com
Phone: **Email:** hello@vivewellness.com
City: London **State:** England **PC:** **Country: United Kingdom**
Year Established: **Status 2020:** Active
Industries: Company Name: Vize.ai
Description: Vize AI is the most accurate custom vision API.
Website: http://vize.ai
Phone: **Email:** support@vize.: Italy
City: London **State:** England **PC:** **Country: United Kingdom**
Year Established: **Status 2020:** Active
Industries: Artificial Intelligence for:, Computer Vision for:, Digital Media for:, Image Recognition for:, Machine Learning for:, Computer Vision

Company Name: Vizibl
Description: Vizibl is a global cloud platform that enables enterprise companies to manage their innovation lifecycle.
Website: http://vizibl.co
Phone: 44 (0) 203 540 7341 **Email:** sayhello@vizibl.co
City: London **State:** England **PC:** **Country: United Kingdom**
Year Established: 2013 **Status 2020:** Active
Industries: Collaboration Solutions for:, ~ Administrative and Support Services (1), Predictive Analytics for:, ~ Administrative and Support Services (1), Business Software as a Service Apps (SaaS Apps) for:, Supply Chain Management

Company Name: Volatile
Description: Volatile AI builds hardware AI systems to enables a digital sense of smell.
Website: http://volatile.ai
Phone: **Email:** 37642@reference-encyclopedia-ai.net
City: London **State:** England **PC:** **Country: United Kingdom**
Year Established: 2019 **Status 2020:** Active
Industries: Artificial Intelligence for:, Machine Learning

Company Name: Vortexa
Description: Intelligent energy markets - Real time information analytics with the most complete set of oil cargo data available
Website: http://www.vortexa.com/
Phone: **Email:** 37644@reference-encyclopedia-ai.net
City: London **State:** England **PC:** **Country: United Kingdom**
Year Established: 2016 **Status 2020:** Active
Industries: Analytics for:, Artificial Intelligence for:, Finance and Accounting

Company Name: VUNU
Description: VUNU is changing the way they interact with music content
Website: http://vunu.tv/
Phone: **Email:** 37648@reference-encyclopedia-ai.net
City: London **State:** England **PC:** **Country: United Kingdom**
Year Established: 2017 **Status 2020:** Active
Industries: Artificial Intelligence for:, ~ Arts-Entertainment-Recreation (4), ~ Arts-Entertainment-Recreation (4)

Company Name: Vyking
Description: Vyking creates AR try-on technology for footwear brands
Website: http://www.vyking.io
Phone: **Email:** matthew.klimpke@vyking.io
City: London **State:** England **PC:** **Country: United Kingdom**
Year Established: 2015 **Status 2020:** Active
Industries: Artificial Intelligence for:, Augmented Reality for:, Computer Vision for:, Facial Recognition for:, Machine Learning

Company Name: Vyking - The Mobile AR Marketing Platform (3D Face Tracking & Graphics Engine SDK)
Description: Computer vision solutions for brands, e-commerce and mobile ad platforms.
Website: http://www.vyking.io
Phone: **Email:** matthew.klimpke@vyking.io
City: London **State:** England **PC:** **Country: United Kingdom**
Year Established: **Status 2020:** Active
Industries: ~ Media-Communications (41), Analytics for:, Artificial Intelligence for:, Augmented Reality for:, Computer Vision for:, Facial Recognition for:, Machine Learning

Company Name: Waive
Description: Waive's Consumer Intelligence Platform uses AI to connect businesses with their future consumer putting them at the centre of every decision
Website: http://www.letswaive.com
Phone: **Email:** hi@letswaive.com
City: London **State:** England **PC:** **Country: United Kingdom**
Year Established: 2017 **Status 2020:** Active
Industries: Artificial Intelligence for:, Business Intelligence for:, Predictive Analytics for:, Predictive Analytics

Company Name: Wandera
Description: Mobile Data
Website: http://www.wandera.com
Phone: 91 (80) 28440011 **Email:** 12783@reference-encyclopedia-ai.net
City: London **State:** England **Zip:** W1W 8HJ **Country: United Kingdom**
Year Established: **Status 2020:** Active
Industries:

Company Name: Warblr
Description: Warblr is an app which uses audio recognition technology to identify birdsong.
Website: http://warblr.net/
Phone: **Email:** hello@warblr.co.uk
City: London **State:** England **PC:** **Country: United Kingdom**
Year Established: **Status 2020:** Active
Industries: Application Services for:, Artificial Intelligence

Company Name: Waymark Tech
Description: Waymark provides time savings, peace of mind, and transparency to regulated industries by providing services that accelerate regulatory change management.
Website: https://www.waymark.tech
Phone: **Email:** support@waymark.tech
City: London **State:** England **PC:** **Country: United Kingdom**
Year Established: **Status 2020:** Active
Industries: Artificial Intelligence for:, ~ Banking and Financial Markets-Services (7), ~ Law-Legal Services (26), Business Intelligence for:, ~ Banking and Financial Markets-Services (678), ~ Government (690), ~ Insurance (696), ~ Law-Legal Services (697), ~ Professional : Sweden

Company Name: We Love Work
Description: We Love Work™ People analytics platform that provides the fastest and simplest way to audit and improve your company culture.
Website: http://www.welovework.com
Phone: 44 07955 825 119 **Email:** paris.p@welovework.com
City: London **State:** England **PC:** **Country: United Kingdom**
Year Established: 2015 **Status 2020:** Active
Industries: Predictive Analytics

Company Name: Weave.ai
Description: Weave.ai is a new computing layer between the OS and the apps that reinvents what search means.
Website: http://www.weave.ai/
Phone: **Email:** inbox@weave.ai
City: London **State:** England **PC:** **Country: United Kingdom**
Year Established: **Status 2020:** Active
Industries: Application Services for:, Artificial Intelligence for:, Compute for:, ~ Professional Services (48)

Company Name: webRun: Spain
Description: We are the team of freelancers specializing in various IT fields and other areas of expertise that are developing WRIO Internet OS platform
Website: http://wr.io
Phone: **Email:** info@webrunes.com
City: London **State:** England **PC:** **Country: United Kingdom**
Year Established: 2010 **Status 2020:** Active
Industries: Artificial Intelligence for:, Big Data and Analytics for:, Blockchain for:, ~ Banking and Financial Markets-Services (7), IT Managed Services for:, Web for:, Web for:, Web for:, Web for:, Web

Company Name: WebzSuite
Description: AI neural-networked powered B2B SaaS platform with fully integrated analytics, marketing management, web audits, social/competition/metrics
Website: http://webzsuite.com
Phone: **Email:** invest@webzsuite.com
City: London **State:** England **PC:** **Country: United Kingdom**
Year Established: **Status 2020:** Active
Industries: Analytics for:, Artificial Intelligence for:, Cloud for:, Cloud for:, Cloud

Company Name: Wefarm
Description: Wefarm is the world's largest farmer-to-farmer digital network that enables farmers to share information via SMS, without the internet.
Website: http://wefarm.co/
Phone: **Email:** 37659@reference-encyclopedia-ai.net
City: London **State:** England **PC:** **Country: United Kingdom**

Year Established: 2015 **Status 2020:** Active
Industries: ~ Agriculture (3), ~ Personal-Religious-Civic (45), ~ Banking and Financial Markets-Services (7), ~ Agriculture (3), Web for:, Machine Learning for:, Network

Company Name: WeSee
Description: WeSee delivers safety, security and integrity across society and business using the latest computer vision technology.
Website: http://www.wesee.com
Phone: **Email:** info@wesee.com
City: London **State:** England **PC:** **Country: United Kingdom**
Year Established: **Status 2020:** Active
Industries: Artificial Intelligence for:, Computer Vision for:, Content for:, Image Recognition for:, ~ Insurance (25), ~ Insurance (25), ~ Life Sciences (27), ~ Media-Communications (41)

Company Name: Wevolve
Description: Wevolve gets work to work by giving employees personalised, interactive app coaching and leaders real-time x-ray vision into change.
Website: http://wevolve.work/
Phone: **Email:** letstalk@wevolve.work
City: London **State:** England **PC:** **Country: United Kingdom**
Year Established: 2016 **Status 2020:** Active
Industries: Application Services for:, Machine Learning

Company Name: Whitehat Analytics
Description: Whitehat is a boutique technology research & development company
Website: http://whitehatanalytics.co.uk/
Phone: **Email:** contact@whitehatanalytics.com
City: London **State:** England **PC:** **Country: United Kingdom**
Year Established: 2015 **Status 2020:** Active
Industries: Analytics for:, Business Intelligence for:, Cloud for:, IT Managed Services for:, Machine Learning for:, Predictive Analytics

Company Name: Wholi
Description: Wholi is a collection of lists of people for the startup community in London.
Website: http://wholi.com
Phone: **Email:** 37671@reference-encyclopedia-ai.net
City: London **State:** England **PC:** **Country: United Kingdom**
Year Established: 2014 **Status 2020:** Active
Industries: ~ Personal-Religious-Civic (45), Machine Learning for:, Web

Company Name: Win FX
Description: Artificial Intelligence for Automated Trading
Website: http://www.winfx.co
Phone: **Email:** info@winfx.co
City: London **State:** England **PC:** **Country: United Kingdom**
Year Established: **Status 2020:** Active
Industries: Artificial Intelligence for:, ~ Banking and Financial Markets-Services (7), ~ Banking and Financial Markets-Services (7), Machine Learning

Company Name: Winning Minds
Description: Winning Minds is a conversational analysis tool that generates insights on interaction dynamics and productivity patterns within your teams.
Website: http://winningminds.ai/
Phone: 44 203 384 0325 **Email:** info@winningminds.ai
City: London **State:** England **PC:** **Country: United Kingdom**
Year Established: 2017 **Status 2020:** Active
Industries: Application Services for:, Artificial Intelligence for:, Business Process and Operations

Company Name: Winnow
Description: Winnow produces digital tools to help chefs measure, monitor, and reduce food waste.
Website: http://winnowsolutions.com
Phone: **Email:** info@winnowsolutions.com
City: London **State:** England **PC:** **Country: United Kingdom**
Year Established: 2013 **Status 2020:** Active
Industries:

Company Name: WIREWAX
Description: WIREWAX is the interactive video tool for creating engaging video experiences. Connect anything in video to everything online.
Website: http://www.wirewax.com
Phone: (646)455-0123 **Email:** hello@wirewax.com
City: London **State:** England **PC:** **Country: United Kingdom**
Year Established: **Status 2020:** Active
Industries: Artificial Intelligence for:, ~ Arts-Entertainment-Recreation (4), Digital Media for:, Web for:, ~ Media-Communications (41), ~ Media-Communications (41)

Company Name: Wisestate
Description: Building Automation and Intelligence Solutions
Website: http://www.wisestate.io
Phone: 44 2070487456 **Email:** info@wisestate.io
City: London **State:** England **PC:** **Country: United Kingdom**
Year Established: **Status 2020:** Active
Industries: Artificial Intelligence for:, ~ Energy and Utilities (14), ~ Energy and Utilities (14), Machine Learning for:, ~ Construction (10)

Company Name: Wluper
Description: Wluper builds dialogue and knowledgebase technology for creating conversational AI.
Website: http://wluper.com
Phone: **Email:** contact@wluper.com
City: London **State:** England **PC:** **Country: United Kingdom**
Year Established: 2017 **Status 2020:** Active
Industries: Artificial Intelligence for:, Machine Learning for:, Natural Language Processing

Company Name: Woodseer Global
Description: Woodseer Global is an advanced algorithmic system that gives huge coverage matched with high levels of accuracy.
Website: http://www.woodseer.global/
Phone: **Email:** contact@woodseer.global
City: London **State:** England **PC:** **Country: United Kingdom**
Year Established: 2011 **Status 2020:** Active
Industries: Data Management for:, Databases for:, Application Program Interfaces (APIs) for:, ~ Banking and Financial Markets-Services (7), ~ Banking and Financial Markets-Services (7), Natural Language Processing

Company Name: Wrapidity
Description: Wrapidity is a web data extraction company.
Website: http://wrapidity.com/
Phone: **Email:** info@wrapidity.com
City: London **State:** England **PC:** **Country: United Kingdom**
Year Established: **Status 2020:** Active
Industries: Artificial Intelligence for:, Big Data and Analytics for:, Data Management for:, IT Managed Services for:, Machine Learning for:, Cyber Security

Company Name: Xihelm
Description: Xihelm is automating robotic, laborious handwork.
Website: http://www.xihelm.com/
Phone: **Email:** 37698@reference-encyclopedia-ai.net
City: London **State:** England **PC:** **Country: United Kingdom**
Year Established: 2016 **Status 2020:** Active
Industries: ~ Agriculture (3), Robotics

Company Name: YIPO Technologies Ltd
Description: AI Technology company based on machine language learning.
Website:
Phone: **Email:** 37714@reference-encyclopedia-ai.net
City: London **State:** England **PC:** **Country: United Kingdom**
Year Established: 2015 **Status 2020:** Active
Industries: Artificial Intelligence for:, ~ Education (13), IT Managed Services

Company Name: Yossarian
Description: Metaphorical Search & Lateral Discovery
Website: http://yossarian.co
Phone: **Email:** hello@yossarianlives.com
City: London **State:** England **PC:** **Country: United Kingdom**
Year Established: **Status 2020:** Active
Industries: Analytics for:, Artificial Intelligence for:, Big Data and Analytics for:, Content for:, Cyber Security

Company Name: Your.: Moldova
Description: Your.MD is an AI-based health information service platform and a marketplace of health service providers and products.
Website: http://www.your.: Moldova
Phone: **Email:** pr@your.: Moldova
City: London **State:** England **PC:** **Country: United Kingdom**
Year Established: **Status 2020:** Active
Industries: Artificial Intelligence for:, ~ Healthcare (20), ~ Healthcare (20), ~ Healthcare (20)

Company Name: ZappyAI
Description: Cognitive Robotic Process Automation (RPA) with AI/ML Process Mining
Website: http://zappy.ai/
Phone: 44 7448 378204 **Email:** team@zappy.ai
City: London **State:** England **PC:** **Country: United Kingdom**
Year Established: 2019 **Status 2020:** Active
Industries: Robotics

Company Name: ZEE9
Description: Biometric, AI & ML solutions
Website: http://www.zeered.com
Phone: **Email:** investment@izee9.com
City: London **State:** England **PC:** **Country: United Kingdom**
Year Established: 2017 **Status 2020:** Active
Industries: Analytics for:, Artificial Intelligence for:, ~ Biotechnology (9), Machine Learning for:, Predictive Analytics

Company Name: ZEG.ai
Description: On-demand photos for e-commerce using just 1-2 smartphone photos
Website: http://www.zeg.ai
Phone: **Email:** contact@zeg.ai
City: London **State:** England **PC:** **Country: United Kingdom**
Year Established: 2018 **Status 2020:** Active
Industries: Artificial Intelligence for:, E-Commerce for:, ~ Fashion (16)

Company Name: Zego
Description: Zego is flexible commercial insurance for businesses and professionals headquartered in London, England.
Website: http://www.zego.com/
Phone: **Email:** support@zego.com
City: London **State:** England **PC:** **Country: United Kingdom**
Year Established: **Status 2020:** Active
Industries: Artificial Intelligence for:, ~ Insurance (25), ~ Banking and Financial Markets-Services (7), ~ Banking and Financial Markets-Services (7), ~ Insurance (25), ~ Insurance (25), ~ Professional Services (48), ~ Insurance (25)

Company Name: Zeus Group
Description: Mobile Apps and Enterprise Solutions (Back-end, Web Services, ERP/CRM, UX/UI Design), Big Data&Machine Learining, Artificial Intelligence
Website: http://www.ze-us.xyz
Phone: **Email:** alex@ze-us.xyz
City: London **State:** England **PC:** **Country: United Kingdom**
Year Established: **Status 2020:** Active
Industries:

Company Name: Ziligence
Description: Ziligence is an AI driven platform that helps businesses connect with emerging companies.
Website: http://www.ziligence.com
Phone: **Email:** manoj.madhusudanan@ziligence.com
City: London **State:** England **PC:** **Country: United Kingdom**
Year Established: **Status 2020:** Active
Industries: Artificial Intelligence for:, ~ Administrative and Support Services (1)

Company Name: Zoral
Description: Zoral develops software that adapts to customer behavior by implementing intelligence into digital products.
Website: http://zorallabs.com
Phone: 44 (0) 203 897 4278 **Email:** sales@zorallabs.com
City: London **State:** England **PC:** **Country: United Kingdom**
Year Established: **Status 2020:** Active
Industries: Artificial Intelligence for:, Big Data and Analytics for:, Cloud for:, Machine Learning for:, Natural Language Processing for:, Predictive Analytics for:, ~ Professional Services (48)

Company Name: Ztudium
Description: ztudium is maker of the industry 4.0 technologies for the future present: blockchain, AI and digital transformation solutions
Website: http://www.ztudium.com/
Phone: **Email:** info@ztudium.com
City: London **State:** England **PC:** **Country: United Kingdom**
Year Established: 2011 **Status 2020:** Active
Industries: Artificial Intelligence for:, Big Data and Analytics for:, Blockchain for:, ~ Banking and Financial Markets-Services (7), ~ Social Assistance-Non-Profits (53)

Company Name: TermSet
Description: TermSet provides solutions that unlock the information inside documents.
Website: http://www.termset.com/
Phone: **Email:** 37519@reference-encyclopedia-ai.net
City: Malvern **State:** England **PC:** **Country: United Kingdom**
Year Established: 2014 **Status 2020:** Active
Industries: Artificial Intelligence for:, IT Managed Services for:, Security

Company Name: Altavox
Description: Voice-first design studio and consultancy
Website: https://www.altavox.co/
Phone: 44 (0) 161 531 4943 **Email:** hello@altavox.co
City: Manchester **State:** England **PC:** **Country: United Kingdom**
Year Established: 2019 **Status 2020:** Active
Industries: Development and Test for:, Internet of Things (IoT)

Company Name: Big Cloud
Description: Global recruiters specialising in Data Science, Machine Learning and AI.
Website: http://www.bigcloud.io
Phone: (161) 647-7222 **Email:** hi@bigcloud.io
City: Manchester **State:** England **PC:** **Country: United Kingdom**
Year Established: 2013 **Status 2020:** Active
Industries: Artificial Intelligence for:, Big Data and Analytics for:, ~ Customer Relationship Management (11), IT Managed Services

Company Name: BlackDice
Description: BlackDice is a machine learning software for device management and cybersecurity.
Website: http://www.blackdice.io/
Phone: **Email:** info@blackdice.io
City: Manchester **State:** England **PC:** **Country: United Kingdom**
Year Established: 2019 **Status 2020:** Active
Industries: Artificial Intelligence for:, Cyber Security for:, Machine Learning

Company Name: Chief.AI
Description: Chief.AI is a global AI resourc: Spain
Website: http://chief.ai/
Phone: **Email:** 36267@reference-encyclopedia-ai.net
City: Manchester **State:** England **PC:** **Country:** United Kingdom
Year Established: 2018 **Status 2020:** Active
Industries: Artificial Intelligence

Company Name: Deep Med IO
Description: DeepMed IO is a MedTech company based in the UK.
Website: http://www.deepmed.io/
Phone: 30 697 7631 030 **Email:** 36412@reference-encyclopedia-ai.net
City: Manchester **State:** England **PC:** **Country:** United Kingdom
Year Established: 2017 **Status 2020:** Active
Industries: Artificial Intelligence for:, ~ Biotechnology (9), ~ Healthcare (20)

Company Name: Desap
Description: Software and app development company
Website: http://desap.co.uk
Phone: 44 161 457 2390 **Email:** info@desap.co.uk
City: Manchester **State:** England **PC:** **Country:** United Kingdom
Year Established: **Status 2020:** Active
Industries: Artificial Intelligence for:, Augmented Reality for:, Blockchain for:, Data Management for:, Enterprise Application Services for:, Enterprise Application Services for:, Development and Test for:, Cyber Security

Company Name: DigitalBridge
Description: DigitalBridge is a computer vision and machine learning platform that allows customers to visualise home decor/furniture in their own room
Website:
Phone: **Email:** info@digitalbridge.com
City: Manchester **State:** England **PC:** **Country:** United Kingdom
Year Established: **Status 2020:** Active
Industries: Artificial Intelligence for:, Computer Vision for:, IT Managed Services for:, IT Managed Services for:, ~ Professional Services (48), Machine Learning for:, ~ Retail and Consumer Products (52), Security

Company Name: Dreamsgate
Description: Creating products and services to advance the use of Ai in business.
Website: http://www.dreamsgate.com
Phone: 44 (0)161 413 6030 **Email:** info@dreamsgate.com
City: Manchester **State:** England **PC:** **Country:** United Kingdom
Year Established: 2012 **Status 2020:** Active
Industries: Artificial Intelligence

Company Name: Dutytaker
Description: Customer Experience & Operational Support for Compani: Spain
Website: http://dutytaker.com
Phone: **Email:** admin@dutytaker.com
City: Manchester **State:** England **PC:** **Country:** United Kingdom
Year Established: 2018 **Status 2020:** Active
Industries: IT Managed Services for:, Application Services for:, Business Process and Operations

Company Name: Duuzra
Description: Easily create and transfer material, engage audiences, and track analytics in a variety of business areas.
Website: http://www.duuzra.com
Phone: (888) 795-0046 **Email:** info@duuzra.com
City: Manchester **State:** England **PC:** **Country:** United Kingdom
Year Established: 2010 **Status 2020:** Active
Industries:

Company Name: EnergiMine
Description: Using AI & Blockchain in the energy markets.
Website: http://energimine.com/
Phone: 44 (0)161 804 2034 **Email:** contact@energimine.com
City: Manchester **State:** England **PC:** **Country:** United Kingdom
Year Established: 2016 **Status 2020:** Active
Industries: Artificial Intelligence for:, Blockchain for:, ~ Energy and Utilities (14), Business Software as a Service Apps (SaaS Apps)

Company Name: MedCircuit
Description: MedCircuit is a groundbreaking AI triage software assisting doctors and nurses in the clinical setting
Website: http://www.medcircuit.com/
Phone: **Email:** info@medcircuit.com
City: Manchester **State:** England **PC:** **Country:** United Kingdom
Year Established: 2016 **Status 2020:** Active
Industries: Artificial Intelligence for:, ~ Healthcare (20), ~ Healthcare (20), ~ Healthcare (20)

Company Name: Mindtrace
Description: Mindtrace builds intelligent systems which exploit the synergy of brain-inspired algorithms and neuromorphic hardware.
Website: http://www.mindtrace.ai/
Phone: 44 (0)333 358 3708 **Email:** info@mindtrace.ai
City: Manchester **State:** England **PC:** **Country:** United Kingdom
Year Established: 2017 **Status 2020:** Active
Industries: Artificial Intelligence for:, Machine Learning

Company Name: Nud: Greece
Description: Rescue cart abandonment before it happens
Website: http://nudgr.io
Phone: 44 (0)800 772 0982 **Email:** support@nudgr.io
City: Manchester **State:** England **PC:** **Country:** United Kingdom
Year Established: **Status 2020:** Active
Industries: Artificial Intelligence for:, ~ Education (13), ~ Education (13), Machine Learning

Company Name: Peak
Description: Peak's Artificial Intelligence System sits at core of your business and drives sustainable business growth using AI and Machine Learning.
Website: http://peak.ai
Phone: **Email:** info@peak.ai
City: Manchester **State:** England **PC:** **Country:** United Kingdom
Year Established: **Status 2020:** Active
Industries: Artificial Intelligence for:, Business Intelligence for:, Cloud for:, Data Management for:, IT Managed Services for:, Machine Learning

Company Name: Pre-PIM AI
Description: Most advanced Visual AI for converting images to feature rich attributes and descriptions for the Retail Industry.
Website: http://www.prepimai.com/
Phone: 0161 641 8587 **Email:** elizabeth@prepimai.com
City: Manchester **State:** England **PC:** **Country:** United Kingdom
Year Established: 2019 **Status 2020:** Active
Industries: Artificial Intelligence for:, Computer Vision for:, E-Commerce for:, Machine Learning

Company Name: Pubrica Healthcare
Description: Pubrica's services span all phases of Scientific Medical and Academic Writing, Editing, and Publishing.
Website: http://pubrica.com/
Phone: 91 9884350006 **Email:** sales@pubrica.com
City: Manchester **State:** England **PC:** **Country:** United Kingdom

Year Established: 2017 **Status 2020:** Active
Industries: ~ Healthcare (20), Predictive Analytics for:, ~ Education (13)

Company Name: Summize
Description: Legal Tech
Website: http://www.summize.it/
Phone: **Email:** hello@summize.: Italy
City: Manchester **State:** England **PC:** **Country: United Kingdom**
Year Established: 2018 **Status 2020:** Active
Industries: IT Managed Services for:, Natural Language Processing for:, Predictive Analytics

Company Name: talentpuddle.
Description: HR Tech that utilises ai and machine learning that makes a live match of candidates to resume/cv across corporate ATS's and HR platforms.
Website: http://www.martindangerfield.com/talentpuddle
Phone: 44161 408 4005 **Email:** me@martindangerfield.com
City: Manchester **State:** England **PC:** **Country: United Kingdom**
Year Established: 2017 **Status 2020:** Active
Industries: Artificial Intelligence for:, IT Managed Services

Company Name: Wondrwall
Description: Wondrwall has pioneered the first intelligent living system that will transform how people interact with their homes.
Website: http://wondrwall.co.uk
Phone: 1615330150 **Email:** hello@wondrwall.co.uk
City: Manchester **State:** England **PC:** **Country: United Kingdom**
Year Established: 2013 **Status 2020:** Active
Industries: ~ Home (22), Application Services

Company Name: Deep Learning Partnership
Description: Deep Learning Partnership is an AI consulting company that offers consulting and training services for enterprise customers.
Website: http://www.deeplp.com/
Phone: **Email:** info@deeplp.com
City: Mayfair **State:** England **PC:** **Country: United Kingdom**
Year Established: 2012 **Status 2020:** Active
Industries: Machine Learning for:, ~ Education (13)

Company Name: Mindway AI
Description: Mindway AI is a company that provides software solutions for the identification of at-risk gambling and problem gambling behaviour.
Website: http://mindway-ai.com/
Phone: **Email:** sak@mindway-ai.com
City: Middle **State:** England **PC:** **Country: United Kingdom**
Year Established: 2018 **Status 2020:** Active
Industries: Artificial Intelligence

Company Name: Carbon by Clicksco
Description: Carbon is an AMP that uses data & AI to understand customer behaviour and intent for personalised UX and better data monetisation.
Website: http://www.clicksco.com/technology/
Phone: **Email:** 36230@reference-encyclopedia-ai.net
City: Middlesbrough **State:** England **PC:** **Country: United Kingdom**
Year Established: 2017 **Status 2020:** Active
Industries: Analytics for:, Artificial Intelligence for:, Big Data and Analytics for:, Digital Marketing for:, Machine Learning

Company Name: Immense Simulations
Description: Immense Simulations specialize in solutions in autonomous vehicles via artificial intelligence.
Website: http://www.immense.ai
Phone: **Email:** collaborate@immense.ai
City: Milton Keynes **State:** England **PC:** **Country: United Kingdom**
Year Established: 2016 **Status 2020:** Active
Industries:

Company Name: Visio Ingenii Ltd
Description: Next generation technology in Machine vision and Learning.
Website: http://www.visioingenii.com
Phone: 44(0) 1908 933 765 **Email:** contactus@visioingenii.com
City: Milton Keynes **State:** England **PC:** **Country: United Kingdom**
Year Established: 2012 **Status 2020:** Active
Industries: Computer Vision for:, Facial Recognition for:, Image Recognition for:, Machine Learning for:, Robotics

Company Name: Medicto
Description: Transforming Healthcare Delivery
Website: http://medicto.com
Phone: **Email:** info@medicto.com
City: New Malden **State:** England **PC:** **Country: United Kingdom**
Year Established: 2016 **Status 2020:** Active
Industries: Artificial Intelligence for:, ~ Healthcare (20), IT Managed Services

Company Name: Exonar Ltd
Description: Exonar is a software company that enables enterprise data to be better organised, de-risked & more productive.
Website: http://www.exonar.com
Phone: (016)358-8858 **Email:** tellmemore@exonar.com
City: Newbury **State:** England **PC:** **Country: United Kingdom**
Year Established: **Status 2020:** Active
Industries: Artificial Intelligence for:, IT Managed Services for:, Enterprise Application Services for:, ~ Professional Services (48)

Company Name: Colourtext
Description: Natural language processing software
Website: http://www.colourtext.com
Phone: 0191 244 4944 **Email:** jason.brownlee@colourtext.com
City: Newcastle Upon Tyne **State:** England **PC:** **Country: United Kingdom**
Year Established: 2013 **Status 2020:** Active
Industries: Natural Language Processing for:, Business Software as a Service Apps (SaaS Apps)

Company Name: Equiwatt
Description: A digital platform enabling households to get paid for saving energy at peak times.
Website: http://www.equiwatt.com
Phone: **Email:** hello@equiwatt.com
City: Newcastle Upon Tyne **State:** England **PC:** **Country: United Kingdom**
Year Established: **Status 2020:** Active
Industries: Artificial Intelligence for:, ~ Energy and Utilities (14), ~ Professional Services (48)

Company **Name:** Refract
Description: Coachable insight on every rep on every call, using AI to highlight what aligns with success & your top performers, & coach decisive moments
Website: http://www.refract.ai
Phone: **Email:** info@refract.ai
City: Newcastle Upon Tyne **State:** England **PC:** **Country: United Kingdom**
Year Established: 2015 **Status 2020:** Active
Industries: Artificial Intelligence for:, ~ Education (13), Business Software as a Service Apps (SaaS Apps)

Company Name: Ricochet.ai
Description: Automated lead development for busy sales teams
Website: http://ricochet.ai
Phone: **Email:** paul@ricochet.ai
City: Newcastle Upon Tyne **State:** England **PC:** **Country: United Kingdom**

Year Established: 2018 **Status 2020:** Active
Industries: ~ E-Commerce (12), Natural Language Processing for:, Automation

Company Name: Spark EV Technology
Description: Spark develops and supplies personalised journey prediction and map display software products for electric vehicles.
Website: http://www.sparkevtechnology.com
Phone: 44 1223 781 200 **Email:** sales@sparkevtechnology.com
City: Newmarket **State:** England **PC:** **Country: United Kingdom**
Year Established: 2017 **Status 2020:** Active
Industries: Machine Learning

Company Name: Vemotion
Description:
Website: https://www.vemotion.com/
Phone: 1 800 342 5774 **Email:** iain.janes@vemotion.com
City: North Yorkshire **State:** England **Zip:** Y07 3BX **Country: United Kingdom**
Year Established: **Status 2020:** Active
Industries:

Company Name: Humley
Description: Humley uses AI and machine learning techniques to power digital assistant services for brands and organisations.
Website: http://humley.com
Phone: **Email:** info@humley.com
City: Northampton **State:** England **PC:** **Country: United Kingdom**
Year Established: 2014 **Status 2020:** Active
Industries: Artificial Intelligence for:, Machine Learning for:, ~ Customer Relationship Management (11)

Company Name: Cascade.bi
Description: Cascade.bi platform provides deep graphic analysis of company data in cloud based dashboards.
Website: http://cascade.bi/
Phone: **Email:** info@cascade.bi
City: Norwich **State:** England **PC:** **Country: United Kingdom**
Year Established: 2014 **Status 2020:** Active
Industries: Analytics for:, Big Data and Analytics for:, Predictive Analytics

Company Name: Rainbird Technologies Ltd
Description: Truly intelligent automation for complex decisions and scenarios
Website: https://rainbird.ai/
Phone: 0800 612 2666 **Email:** follow@rainbird.ai
City: Norwich **State:** England **Zip:** NR3 1DJ **Country: United Kingdom**
Year Established: **Status 2020:** Active
Industries: Artificial Intelligence for:, Automation for:, ~ Banking and Financial Markets-Services (373), ~ Healthcare (386), ~ Insurance (391), ~ Professional Services (414), Enterprise Application Services

Company Name: TrainAsONE
Description: The award-winning AI running coach for runners of all abilities and goals.
Website: http://www.trainasone.com/
Phone: **Email:** info@trainasone.com
City: Norwich **State:** England **PC:** **Country: United Kingdom**
Year Established: 2014 **Status 2020:** Active
Industries: Artificial Intelligence for:, ~ Healthcare (20), ~ Healthcare (20), ~ Healthcare (20)

Company Name: Spotlight Data
Description: Spotlight Data - Strategic KM Ltd. Is an artificial intelligence data company working the UK Government and multi nationals
Website: http://www.spotlightdata.co.uk
Phone: **Email:** 37459@reference-encyclopedia-ai.net
City: Nottingham **State:** England **PC:** **Country: United Kingdom**
Year Established: 2015 **Status 2020:** Active
Industries:

Company Name: ZASTI
Description: ZASTI AI platform provides a scientific and proven way of predicting component or mechanical failure using a transparent SaaS model.
Website: http://www.zasti.ai
Phone: **Email:** ram@zasti.ai
City: Nottingham **State:** England **PC:** **Country: United Kingdom**
Year Established: **Status 2020:** Active
Industries: Artificial Intelligence for:, IT Managed Services for:, ~ Healthcare (20), ~ Insurance (25), Machine Learning for:, ~ Social-Environmental-Physical-Engineering Sciences (55), ~ Professional Services (48)

Company Name: Biorelate
Description: Biorelate is a venture-backed AI start-up with a mission to curate truths in biomedicine.
Website: http://biorelate.com/
Phone: **Email:** info@biorelate.com
City: Oldham **State:** England **PC:** **Country: United Kingdom**
Year Established: **Status 2020:** Active
Industries: Artificial Intelligence for:, Big Data and Analytics for:, ~ Biotechnology (9), ~ Life Sciences (27), ~ Healthcare (20)

Company Name: Energi Mine
Description: Using AI & Blockchain in the energy markets.
Website: http://energimine.com/
Phone: 44 (0)161 791 0640 **Email:** support@energimine.com
City: Oldham **State:** England **PC:** **Country: United Kingdom**
Year Established: **Status 2020:** Active
Industries: Artificial Intelligence for:, Blockchain for:, ~ Energy and Utilities (14), ~ Oil and Gas (43)

Company Name: Anumerics
Description: Advanced numerical computation for the future of engineering and business.
Website: http://anumerics.com
Phone: **Email:** contact@anumerics.com
City: Oxford **State:** England **PC:** **Country: United Kingdom**
Year Established: **Status 2020:** Active
Industries: Artificial Intelligence for:, Business Intelligence for:, Databases for:, Automation for:, ~ Manufacturing-General (31), Machine Learning for:, ~ Social-Environmental-Physical-Engineering Sciences (55), ~ Professional Services (48)

Company Name: Brainomix
Description: Using Artificial Intelligence (AI) algorithms we are bringing our complete stroke imaging decision support solution to hospitals worldwide.
Website: http://www.brainomix.com
Phone: 44 (0) 1865 582730 **Email:** info@brainomix.com
City: Oxford **State:** England **PC:** **Country: United Kingdom**
Year Established: 2010 **Status 2020:** Active
Industries: Artificial Intelligence for:, ~ Healthcare (20)

Company **Name:** DiffBlue
Description: An Oxford spin-out using AI to write code, starting with Java unit test suites that catch errors earlier and faster in a DevOps pipeline
Website: http://www.diffblue.com/
Phone: 44 1865 689304 **Email:** info@diffblue.com
City: Oxford **State:** England **PC:** **Country: United Kingdom**
Year Established: 2016 **Status 2020:** Active
Industries: Artificial Intelligence for:, Application Services

Company Name: Dynium Robot
Description: The World's Smartest Tracto: Serbia
Website: http://www.dyniumrobot.com/
Phone: **Email:** team@dyniumrobot.com
City: Oxford **State:** England **PC:** **Country: United Kingdom**
Year Established: 2017 **Status 2020:** Active
Industries: ~ Agriculture (3), Artificial Intelligence for:, IT Managed Services

Company Name: Edtopia
Description: Edtopia develops an AI-based learning support applications.
Website: http://www.edtopia.io/
Phone: **Email:** 36477@reference-encyclopedia-ai.net
City: Oxford **State:** England **PC:** **Country: United Kingdom**
Year Established: 2017 **Status 2020:** Active
Industries: Artificial Intelligence for:, Machine Learning

Company Name: Exscientia
Description: Exscientia is applying AI and big data processing to accelerate drug discovery and development
Website: http://www.exscientia.co.uk/
Phone: 44 (0)1382 202136 **Email:** contact@exscientia.co.uk
City: Oxford **State:** England **PC:** **Country: United Kingdom**
Year Established: **Status 2020:** Active
Industries: Artificial Intelligence for:, ~ Pharmaceuticals (46)

Company Name: Green Sea Guard
Description: Green Sea Guard provides a unique toolset that measures and tracks ship emissions from a computer on land or at sea.
Website: http://greenseaguard.com/
Phone: **Email:** 36646@reference-encyclopedia-ai.net
City: Oxford **State:** England **PC:** **Country: United Kingdom**
Year Established: 2014 **Status 2020:** Active
Industries: Big Data and Analytics for:, Data Management for:, Application Services

Company Name: iLoF - Intelligent Lab on Fiber
Description: iLoF - Intelligent Lab on Fiber is enabling a new era of personalized, precision medicine.
Website: http://ilof.tech/
Phone: 351 220 426 664 **Email:** info@ilof.tech
City: Oxford **State:** England **PC:** **Country: United Kingdom**
Year Established: 2019 **Status 2020:** Active
Industries: Artificial Intelligence for:, ~ Biotechnology (9), ~ Healthcare (20), ~ Healthcare (20)

Company Name: impact RI Ltd
Description: Software that delivers Amplified Intelligence
Website: http://www.impactri.com
Phone: **Email:** mark@impactri.com
City: Oxford **State:** England **PC:** **Country: United Kingdom**
Year Established: **Status 2020:** Active
Industries: Analytics for:, Artificial Intelligence for:, Enterprise Application Services

Company Name: Latent Logic
Description: Deep learning technology for autonomous ca: Serbia
Website: http://www.latentlogic.com
Phone: **Email:** info@latentlogic.com
City: Oxford **State:** England **PC:** **Country: United Kingdom**
Year Established: **Status 2020:** Active
Industries: Artificial Intelligence for:, ~ Automotive (5), Machine Learning

Company Name: MeVit: United Arab Emirates
Description: MeVitae is a data-driven cognitive recruitment system that makes intelligent and personalized hiring decisions.
Website: http://mevitae.com/
Phone: **Email:** admin@mevitae.com
City: Oxford **State:** England **PC:** **Country: United Kingdom**
Year Established: **Status 2020:** Active
Industries:

Company Name: Mind Foundry
Description: Mind Foundry is a spin out from the University of Oxford combining leading edge machine learning research with advanced software engineering
Website: http://mindfoundry.ai/
Phone: **Email:** info@mindfoundry.ai
City: Oxford **State:** England **PC:** **Country: United Kingdom**
Year Established: **Status 2020:** Active
Industries: Artificial Intelligence for:, ~ Banking and Financial Markets-Services (7), Industrial Solutions for:, Machine Learning for:, Enterprise Application Services

Company Name: OpenMined
Description: OpenMined is a community focused on building open-source technology for the decentralized ownership of data and intelligence.
Website: http://www.openmined.org/
Phone: **Email:** 37112@reference-encyclopedia-ai.net
City: Oxford **State:** England **PC:** **Country: United Kingdom**
Year Established: 2017 **Status 2020:** Active
Industries: Analytics for:, Artificial Intelligence for:, Blockchain for:, IT Managed Services

Company Name: Optellum
Description: Optellum develops an imaging biomarker for smart lung cancer detection.
Website: http://www.optellum.com
Phone: **Email:** 37114@reference-encyclopedia-ai.net
City: Oxford **State:** England **PC:** **Country: United Kingdom**
Year Established: 2016 **Status 2020:** Active
Industries: ~ Healthcare (20), Machine Learning

Company Name: Oxademy Technologies
Description: Adaptive learning technologies, powered by knowledge-based artificial intelligence.
Website: http://oxademy.com
Phone: **Email:** contact@oxademy.com
City: Oxford **State:** England **PC:** **Country: United Kingdom**
Year Established: **Status 2020:** Active
Industries: Artificial Intelligence for:, ~ Education (13), ~ Education (13), Machine Learning

Company Name: Oxbotica
Description: Oxbotica is developing the next generation of autonomous vehicles, creating the software that makes them go.
Website: http://www.oxbotica.com/
Phone: **Email:** info@oxbotica.com
City: Oxford **State:** England **PC:** **Country: United Kingdom**
Year Established: 2014 **Status 2020:** Active
Industries: Artificial Intelligence for:, ~ Automotive (5), ~ Automotive (5)

Company **Name:** Oxbotica Ltd
Description: Oxbotica is developing the next generation of autonomous vehicles, creating the software that makes them go.
Website: http://www.oxbotica.com/
Phone: **Email:** info@oxbotica.com
City: Oxford **State:** England **PC:** **Country: United Kingdom**
Year Established: **Status 2020:** Active
Industries: Artificial Intelligence for:, ~ Automotive (5), ~ Automotive (5), ~ Transportation and Logistics (57), Robotics for:, ~ Transportation and Logistics (57)

Company Name: Oxtractor
Description: Oxtractor extracts actionable insights from social data using natural language processing.
Website: http://www.oxtractor.com
Phone: 44 (0) 7818 830 817 **Email:** info@oxtractor.com
City: Oxford **State:** England **PC:** **Country: United Kingdom**

Year Established: **Status 2020:** Active
Industries: Artificial Intelligence for:, Big Data and Analytics for:, Natural Language Processing

Company Name: Plyable
Description: Building the definitive global marketplace for composite tooling
Website: http://www.plyable.com
Phone: 01865 686164 **Email:** Info@plyable.com
City: Oxford **State:** England **PC:** **Country: United Kingdom**
Year Established: 2018 **Status 2020:** Active
Industries: Automation for:, Machine Learning

Company Name: RowAnalytics Ltd
Description: RowAnalytics is a complex data analytics company specialising in digital health, precision medicine, genomics and semantic sear: Switzerland
Website: http://www.rowanalytics.com
Phone: **Email:** info@rowanalytics.com
City: Oxford **State:** England **PC:** **Country: United Kingdom**
Year Established: 2013 **Status 2020:** Active
Industries: Analytics for:, Artificial Intelligence for:, ~ Healthcare (20), IT Managed Services

Company Name: Training Mule
Description: Training Mule is a tool that allows the quick, easy and collaborative creation of large data sets for Machine Learning and other areas.
Website: http://trainingmule.com/
Phone: **Email:** 37554@reference-encyclopedia-ai.net
City: Oxford **State:** England **PC:** **Country: United Kingdom**
Year Established: 2017 **Status 2020:** Active
Industries: Artificial Intelligence for:, ~ Education (13), IT Managed Services

Company Name: Ultromics
Description: Ultromics clinicians and engineers working together to set new standards for world-class cardiovascular diagnostic tools.
Website: http://www.ultromics.com/
Phone: **Email:** info@ultromics.com
City: Oxford **State:** England **PC:** **Country: United Kingdom**
Year Established: 2017 **Status 2020:** Active
Industries: Artificial Intelligence for:, Computer Vision for:, ~ Healthcare (20), ~ Healthcare (20), ~ Healthcare (20)

Company Name: Vision Factory
Description: Vision Factory is creating the future of visual search and recognition products.
Website: http://www.visionfactory.co
Phone: 1 (650) 262-0100 **Email:** contact@visionfactory.co
City: Oxford **State:** England **PC:** **Country: United Kingdom**
Year Established: **Status 2020:** Active
Industries: Artificial Intelligence for:, Computer Vision for:, Machine Learning for:, Cyber Security for:, ~ Professional Services (48)

Company Name: Zegami
Description: Data Visualisation Made Easy
Website: http://zegami.com/
Phone: 00441865 306635 **Email:** info@zegami.com
City: Oxford **State:** England **PC:** **Country: United Kingdom**
Year Established: 2016 **Status 2020:** Active
Industries: Artificial Intelligence for:, Data Management for:, Machine Learning

Company Name: TouchByte
Description: TouchByte provides real-time customer insight, recognition and validation of "PEOPLE in PLACES" using face recognition technology.
Website: http://www.touchbyte.co.uk/
Phone: **Email:** 37548@reference-encyclopedia-ai.net
City: Penryn **State:** England **PC:** **Country: United Kingdom**
Year Established: 2012 **Status 2020:** Active
Industries:

Company Name: Witsy
Description: Witsy is a cloud-based, full-stack, AI enablement platform that builts to simplify and accelerate Deep Learning.
Website: http://witsy.ai/
Phone: **Email:** 37679@reference-encyclopedia-ai.net
City: Pinner **State:** England **PC:** **Country: United Kingdom**
Year Established: 2019 **Status 2020:** Active
Industries: Artificial Intelligence for:, Cloud for:, Natural Language Processing

Company Name: The Small Robot Company
Description: The Small Robot Company is an agri-tech start up that commercializes a deceptively simple idea.
Website: http://www.smallrobotcompany.com/
Phone: **Email:** 37527@reference-encyclopedia-ai.net
City: Portsmouth **State:** England **PC:** **Country: United Kingdom**
Year Established: 2017 **Status 2020:** Active
Industries: ~ Agriculture (3), ~ Agriculture (3), Artificial Intelligence for:, ~ Agriculture (3), ~ Food and Beverage (17), Robotics

Company Name: Missum
Description: Missum is a mobile news app that allows users to obtain a spherical view on topics that matter to them.
Website: http://www.missum.com/
Phone: 44 20 8819 6910 **Email:** contactus@missum.com
City: Potton **State:** England **PC:** **Country: United Kingdom**
Year Established: **Status 2020:** Active
Industries: Artificial Intelligence for:, ~ Media-Communications (41), ~ Media-Communications (41), ~ Media-Communications (41)

Company Name: Neuron soundware
Description:
Website: https://www.neuronsw.com/
Phone: **Email:** martina.wallkova@neuronsw.com
City: Prague **State:** England **Zip:** 140 00 **Country: United Kingdom**
Year Established: **Status 2020:** Active
Industries: Artificial Intelligence for:, ~ Manufacturing-Electronic (30), ~ Manufacturing-General (31), ~ Manufacturing-Machinery (32), ~ Manufacturing-Medical Equipment-Supplies (33), ~ Manufacturing-Nonmetallic Mineral (35), ~ Manufacturing-Petroleum-Coal-Chemicals-Plas

Company Name: Dream AI Ltd T/A Dream Agility
Description: Multi-award winning, AI company with proprietary Visual AI and Machine Learning, specialising in Reta: Israel
Website: http://dreamagility.com
Phone: 44 (0)161 641 8585 **Email:** sales@dreamagility.com
City: Ramsbottom **State:** England **PC:** **Country: United Kingdom**
Year Established: 2015 **Status 2020:** Active
Industries: Artificial Intelligence for:, Machine Learning for:, Business Process and Operations

Company Name: CloudFactory
Description: CloudFactory, a distributed workforce company, automates business processes involving large volumes of data entry, collection or processing.
Website: http://cloudfactory.com
Phone: 1(203)701-6275 **Email:** mark@cloudfactory.com
City: Reading **State:** England **PC:** **Country: United Kingdom**
Year Established: **Status 2020:** Active
Industries: Artificial Intelligence for:, Computer Vision for:, Databases for:, Enterprise Application Services for:, Image Recognition for:, Machine Learning for:, Natural Language Processing for:, Business Process and Operations

Company Name: Orb Data
Description:
Website: www.orb-data.com
Phone: 44 (0) 7973-858-099 **Email:** jason.taylor@orb-data.com
City: Reading **State:** **Zip:** RG2 6GP **Country: United Kingdom**
Year Established: **Status 2020:** Active
Industries:

Company Name: SharemyInsight
Description: SharemyInsight is an IoT platform that provides retail IoT solutions, revenue generating insights, and actions across operations.
Website: http://www.sharemyinsight.com/contact form only
Phone: 44 (203) 239 8676 **Email:** 37374@reference-encyclopedia-ai.net
City: Reading **State:** England **PC:** **Country: United Kingdom**
Year Established: 2012 **Status 2020:** Active
Industries: Artificial Intelligence for:, ~ Customer Relationship Management (11), Internet of Things (IoT)

Company Name: Digital Contact
Description: Digital Contact provides digital media analytics and enriched metrics for the financial industry, public sector and media.
Website: http://digitalcontact.co.uk/
Phone: **Email:** hello@digitalcontact.co.uk
City: Rochester **State:** England **PC:** **Country: United Kingdom**
Year Established: **Status 2020:** Active
Industries: Artificial Intelligence for:, ~ Banking and Financial Markets-Services (7), ~ Professional Services (48)

Company Name: Aitekz plc
Description: Aitekz technology enables finance professionals to harness the power of AI to grow business and drive continuous improvement.
Website: http://www.aitekzfinance.com/
Phone: **Email:** 36022@reference-encyclopedia-ai.net
City: Romsey **State:** England **PC:** **Country: United Kingdom**
Year Established: 2016 **Status 2020:** Active
Industries: Artificial Intelligence for:, IT Managed Services

Company Name: Feebr
Description: AI-enabled platform bridging the gap between community and health system.
Website: http://feebris.com/
Phone: **Email:** info@feebris.com
City: Saffron Walden **State:** England **PC:** **Country: United Kingdom**
Year Established: 2017 **Status 2020:** Active
Industries: Artificial Intelligence for:, ~ Healthcare (20)

Company Name: WOW Intelligence
Description: WOW Intelligence is an intelligent machine learning for cash flow forecasting and credit control.
Website: http://wowintelligence.com
Phone: 44 (0) 161 413 8405 **Email:** info@wowintelligence.com
City: Sale **State:** England **PC:** **Country: United Kingdom**
Year Established: 2017 **Status 2020:** Active
Industries: ~ Banking and Financial Markets-Services (7), Machine Learning

Company Name: Delver Ltd
Description: Delver is a platform for natural language Interfaces
Website: http://delver.io
Phone: **Email:** thom@delver.io
City: Sheffield **State:** England **PC:** **Country: United Kingdom**
Year Established: 2013 **Status 2020:** Active
Industries: Business Intelligence for:, Natural Language Processing for:, Business Software as a Service Apps (SaaS Apps)

Company Name: Otus Labs
Description: The intelligence behind industry leading service
Website: http://otuslabs.com
Phone: **Email:** hello@otuslabs.com
City: Sheffield **State:** England **PC:** **Country: United Kingdom**
Year Established: **Status 2020:** Active
Industries:

Company Name: We are beep
Description: beep (Business Enterprise Engagement Platform), a world changing enterprise platform, that unlocks the wisdom of employe: Spain
Website: http://www.kielyand.co/
Phone: **Email:** Katz@kielyand.co
City: Sheffield **State:** England **PC:** **Country: United Kingdom**
Year Established: 2016 **Status 2020:** Active
Industries: Artificial Intelligence for:, Enterprise Application Services for:, Machine Learning for:, Application Services

Company Name: Symbiotica AI
Description: Symbiotica is a real-time Liquidity Optimisation platform for capital market participants, trading venue and exchang: Spain
Website:
Phone: **Email:** info@symbiotica.ai
City: Shipley **State:** England **PC:** **Country: United Kingdom**
Year Established: 2019 **Status 2020:** Active
Industries: Artificial Intelligence for:, Big Data and Analytics for:, ~ Banking and Financial Markets-Services (7)

Company Name: pillar
Description: A digital support group, connecting mums 1 step ahead in the parenting journey to seek advice from & 1 step behind to offer expertise to.
Website: http://ourpillar.com
Phone: **Email:** leila@ourpillar.com
City: Shoreditch **State:** England **PC:** **Country: United Kingdom**
Year Established: **Status 2020:** Active
Industries: Application Services for:, Artificial Intelligence for:, ~ Personal-Religious-Civic (45), Databases for:, ~ Healthcare (20), Application Services

Company Name: Third Republic
Description: Next Generation Sourcing Provider delivering the advanced tech skills needed to drive digital transformation
Website: http://www.ThirdRepublic.com
Phone: **Email:** info@thirdrepublic.com
City: Shoreditch **State:** England **PC:** **Country: United Kingdom**
Year Established: 2015 **Status 2020:** Active
Industries: Web for:, Predictive Analytics

Company Name: IMGeospatial
Description: Automated Business Intelligence
Website: http://www.imgeospatial.com
Phone: **Email:** hello@imgeospatial.com
City: Slough **State:** England **PC:** **Country: United Kingdom**
Year Established: 2015 **Status 2020:** Active
Industries: Artificial Intelligence for:, Big Data and Analytics for:, IT Managed Services for:, Machine Learning

Company Name: Faultless AI
Description: Faultless AI is a psychology startup with deep-tech roots in the manufacturing industry.
Website: http://enquiries@faultless.ai
Phone: **Email:** 36555@reference-encyclopedia-ai.net
City: Snodland **State:** England **PC:** **Country: United Kingdom**
Year Established: 2018 **Status 2020:** Active
Industries:

Company Name: BOON
Description: Creating a personalised internet.
Website: http://www.yourboon.co
Phone: **Email:** hello@yourboon.co
City: Southampton **State:** England **PC:** **Country: United Kingdom**
Year Established: 2017 **Status 2020:** Active
Industries: Artificial Intelligence for:, ~ Retail and Consumer Products (52), Web for:, Machine Learning for:, ~ Healthcare (20)

Company Name: Incisively Limited
Description: Incisively Limited increase eCommerce margins by optimizing products, pricing, promotions and placement using machine learning algorithms.
Website: http://info@occamzrazor.com
Phone: **Email:** info@incisive.ly
City: Southampton **State:** England **PC:** **Country: United Kingdom**
Year Established: 2014 **Status 2020:** Active
Industries: Analytics for:, E-Commerce for:, Machine Learning

Company Name: NquiringMinds
Description: NquiringMinds provides a secure IoT platform designed to run cities intelligently.
Website: http://nquiringminds.com/
Phone: 44(0) 2380 000 021 **Email:** info@nquiringminds.com
City: Southampton **State:** England **PC:** **Country: United Kingdom**
Year Established: 2010 **Status 2020:** Active
Industries: Artificial Intelligence for:, Internet of Things (IoT) for:, Security

Company Name: Senseye
Description: Scalable Predictive Maintenance
Website: www.senseye.io/
Phone: **Email:** hello@senseye.io
City: Southampton **State:** England **PC:** **Country: United Kingdom**
Year Established: **Status 2020:** Active
Industries: Artificial Intelligence for:, ~ Manufacturing-Miscellaneous (34), Predictive Analytics

Company Name: Pintrack Ltd
Description: Pintrack Ltd is a tech company focused on software development.
Website: http://www.pintrack.com
Phone: **Email:** freddeer@pintrack.com
City: Southend-on-sea **State:** England **PC:** **Country: United Kingdom**
Year Established: **Status 2020:** Active
Industries: Artificial Intelligence for:, Compute

Company Name: Spherical Systems
Description: Spherical Systems is a company focused on developing natural language processing systems.
Website:
Phone: **Email:** 37453@reference-encyclopedia-ai.net
City: Southend-on-sea **State:** England **PC:** **Country: United Kingdom**
Year Established: 2013 **Status 2020:** Closed
Industries: Application Services for:, Natural Language Processing

Company Name: aiH: Italy
Description: aiHit provides company data for business information, market research, and lead generation enterprises.
Website: http://aihit.com
Phone: 44 20 3598 1002 **Email:** contact@aihit.com
City: Staines-upon-thames **State:** England **PC:** **Country: United Kingdom**
Year Established: **Status 2020:** Active
Industries: Analytics for:, Artificial Intelligence for:, Business Intelligence for:, Machine Learning

Company Name: Elemendar
Description: Elemendar is building Artificial Intelligence that reads cyber threat reports by humans and turns.
Website: http://www.elemendar.com/
Phone: 44 2039849841 **Email:** sales@elemendar.com
City: Stourbridge **State:** England **PC:** **Country: United Kingdom**
Year Established: 2017 **Status 2020:** Active
Industries:

Company Name: BrightTarget
Description: BrightTarget is specialist in Artificial Intelligence solutions for B2B Sales & Marketing.
Website: http://www.brighttarget.com/
Phone: **Email:** 36208@reference-encyclopedia-ai.net
City: Sutton Coldfield **State:** England **PC:** **Country: United Kingdom**
Year Established: 2014 **Status 2020:** Active
Industries: Artificial Intelligence

Company Name: Synthetix
Description: A complete platform for automated, self-service digital Customer Experience
Website: http://synthetix.com/
Phone: **Email:** neldi@synthetix.com
City: Takeley **State:** England **PC:** **Country: United Kingdom**
Year Established: **Status 2020:** Active
Industries: Artificial Intelligence for:, ~ Professional Services (48)

Company Name: Hertzian
Description: Specialists in understanding user generated content through the use of Natural Language Processing & Machine Learning.
Website: http://www.hertzian.co.uk
Phone: **Email:** hello@hertzian.co.uk
City: Truro **State:** England **PC:** **Country: United Kingdom**
Year Established: **Status 2020:** Active
Industries: Artificial Intelligence for:, Big Data and Analytics for:, Machine Learning for:, Natural Language Processing

Company Name: Lumiere Property
Description: Lumiere Property uses software to automatically identify suitable development sites.
Website: http://www.lumiereproperty.co.uk
Phone: 0208 434 7044 **Email:** enquiries@lumiereproperty.co.uk
City: Tunbridge Wells **State:** England **PC:** **Country: United Kingdom**
Year Established: 2010 **Status 2020:** Active
Industries: Artificial Intelligence for:, ~ Banking and Financial Markets-Services (7), Big Data and Analytics for:, Internet of Things (IoT) for:, ~ Telecommunications (56), ~ E-Commerce (12)

Company Name: Information Builde: Serbia
Description:
Website: http://www.informationbuilders.co.uk/
Phone: 44 (0) 207 107 4000 **Email:** info_uk@ibi.com
City: Uxbridge **State:** England **Zip:** UB8 1QG **Country: United Kingdom**
Year Established: **Status 2020:** Active
Industries: Company Name: TBSCG
Description:
Website: http://www.tbscg.com
Phone: 321-418-6490 **Email:** Info@techrev.com
City: Uxbridge **State:** England **Zip:** UB8 1JN **Country: United Kingdom**
Year Established: **Status 2020:** Active
Industries: Data Management

Company Name: Aktivebot
Description: Aktivebot is an AI-powered chatbot.
Website: http://www.aktivebot.com/
Phone: **Email:** info@aktivebot.com
City: Waddesdon **State:** England **PC:** **Country: United Kingdom**

Year Established: **Status 2020:** Active
Industries: Artificial Intelligence

Company Name: Q-Bot
Description: Q-Bot is a robotics company that develops intelligent tools for a wide range of industries and applications.
Website: http://q-bot.co
Phone: **Email:** info@q-bot.co
City: Wandsworth **State:** England **PC:** **Country: United Kingdom**
Year Established: 2012 **Status 2020:** Active
Industries:

Company Name: Eatron Technologies
Description: Eatron provides intelligent software solutions like Battery Management Systems (BMS), L1/L2 ADAS for electric and autonomous vehicles.
Website: http://eatron.com/
Phone: **Email:** 4640@reference-encyclopedia-ai.net
City: Warwick **State:** England **PC:** **Country: United Kingdom**
Year Established: **Status 2020:** Active
Industries: Artificial Intelligence for:, ~ Automotive (5), ~ Automotive (5), ~ Automotive (5), IT Managed Services for:, Machine Learning for:, ~ Manufacturing-Electronic (30)

Company Name: Affective Systems Plc
Description: Next Generation Marketing Management System designed to maximise your greatest asset
Website:
Phone: **Email:** 35969@reference-encyclopedia-ai.net
City: Watford **State:** England **PC:** **Country: United Kingdom**
Year Established: 2014 **Status 2020:** Active
Industries: Application Services

Company Name: SentiSum
Description: SentiSum is a technology startup which is leveraging AI and big data to help enterprises gain competitive advantage.
Website: http://www.sentisum.com/
Phone: **Email:** contact@sentisum.com
City: Westminster **State:** England **PC:** **Country: United Kingdom**
Year Established: **Status 2020:** Active
Industries: Analytics for:, Artificial Intelligence for:, Big Data and Analytics

Company Name: Artesian Solutions
Description:
Website: www.artesian.co/
Phone: **Email:** info@artesian.co
City: Winnersh **State:** England **PC:** **Country: United Kingdom**
Year Established: **Status 2020:** Active
Industries: Artificial Intelligence for:, ~ Banking and Financial Markets-Services (7)

Company Name: Panintelligence
Description: Panintelligence provides white-labelled, embedded business intelligence and analytics solutions for SaaS vendors.
Website: http://www.panintelligence.com/
Phone: 44 113 818 7040 **Email:** info@panintelligence.com
City: Yeadon **State:** England **PC:** **Country: United Kingdom**
Year Established: 2014 **Status 2020:** Active
Industries: Analytics for:, Business Intelligence for:, Data Management for:, Predictive Analytics for:, Business Software as a Service Apps (SaaS Apps)

Company Name: Cawamo
Description: Cawamo is a security company that provides an infrastructure for advanced video applications.
Website: http://www.cawamo.com
Phone: 44 20 37695000 **Email:** info@cawamo.com
City: York **State:** England **PC:** **Country: United Kingdom**
Year Established: 2016 **Status 2020:** Active
Industries:

Company Name: Adoreboard
Description: Adoreboard helps brands to understand online customer emotion.
Website: http://www.adoreboard.com
Phone: 44 28 9097 3887 **Email:** office@adoreboard.com
City: Belfast **State:** Northern Ireland **PC:** **Country: United Kingdom**
Year Established: **Status 2020:** Active
Industries: Analytics for:, Artificial Intelligence for:, Big Data and Analytics

Company Name: Ampliphae Ltd
Description: Ampliphae uses analytics and machine learning to understand and automate wide-area networks
Website: http://www.ampliphae.net
Phone: **Email:** info@ampliphae.com
City: Belfast **State:** Northern Ireland **PC:** **Country: United Kingdom**
Year Established: **Status 2020:** Active
Industries: Artificial Intelligence for:, ~ Telecommunications (56)

Company Name: Limitless Insight
Description: Limitless combines location store & social data in a light to no touch cloud platform. Providing Google & Amazon for Physical place
Website: http://www.limitlessinsight.com/
Phone: **Email:** gary@limitlessinsight.com
City: Belfast **State:** Northern Ireland **PC:** **Country: United Kingdom**
Year Established: 2017 **Status 2020:** Active
Industries: Business Intelligence for:, Predictive Analytics

Company Name: Sentireal
Description: At Sentireal, we create software and media platforms that turn mobile devices and headsets into smart assistants.
Website: www.sentireal.com/
Phone: **Email:** info@sentireal.com
City: Belfast **State:** Northern Ireland **PC:** **Country: United Kingdom**
Year Established: **Status 2020:** Active
Industries: Artificial Intelligence for:, Augmented Reality for:, ~ Education (13), ~ Healthcare (20), Machine Learning for:, ~ Healthcare (20)

Company Name: Woog: Ireland
Description: Woogie are business consultants & innovative advisors.
Website: http://www.woogie.io
Phone: **Email:** hello@woogie.io
City: Belfast **State:** Northern Ireland **PC:** **Country: United Kingdom**
Year Established: 2014 **Status 2020:** Active
Industries: Artificial Intelligence for:, Big Data and Analytics for:, ~ Education (13)

Company **Name:** Yedup Limited
Description: Yedup develops real-time, continually adaptive AI technology for high value, ultra-low latency capital markets applications.
Website: http://yedup.com
Phone: **Email:** martin.spollen@yedup.com
City: Belfast **State:** Northern Ireland **PC:** **Country: United Kingdom**
Year Established: **Status 2020:** Active
Industries: Artificial Intelligence for:, Big Data and Analytics for:, ~ Banking and Financial Markets-Services (7), ~ Banking and Financial Markets-Services (7), Machine Learning for:, Natural Language Processing for:, Compute

Company Name: Pearlai
Description: Péarlaí has the best of Google analytics & Adwords for physical spaces with greater detail, insights and greater benefits.
Website: http://business.pearlai.com/
Phone: 2830256246 **Email:** peter@pearlai.com
City: Newry **State:** Northern Ireland **PC:** **Country: United Kingdom**
Year Established: 2016 **Status 2020:** Active
Industries: Analytics for:, Predictive Analytics

Company Name: The Data Lab
Description: The Data Lab is a new innovation centre
Website: http://www.thedatalab.com/
Phone: 44 (0) 1316514905 **Email:** info@thedatalab.com
City: Aberdeen **State:** Scotland **PC:** **Country: United Kingdom**
Year Established: 2014 **Status 2020:** Active
Industries: Artificial Intelligence for:, IT Managed Services

Company Name: Ed: Jordan
Description: Platform to track & handle of plagiarism of digital creative content in real-time using blockchain & AI.
Website: http://edjo.io
Phone: **Email:** harjyot@edjo.io
City: Edinburgh **State:** **PC:** **Country: United Kingdom**
Year Established: **Status 2020:** Active
Industries: Artificial Intelligence for:, Blockchain for:, IT Managed Services

Company Name: Machines With Vision
Description: Downward sensing for autonomous systems.
Website: www.machineswithvision.com
Phone: **Email:** info@machineswithvision.com
City: Edinburgh **State:** Scotland **PC:** **Country: United Kingdom**
Year Established: **Status 2020:** Active
Industries: Artificial Intelligence for:, ~ Automotive (5), ~ Transportation and Logistics (57), Robotics for:, ~ Manufacturing-Electronic (30)

Company Name: Winterwell
Description: Winterwell is an artificial intelligence (AI), statistics, mathematics and computer science consultancy.
Website: http://www.winterwell.com
Phone: 00 44 772 5172 612 **Email:** info@winterwell.com
City: Edinburgh **State:** **PC:** **Country: United Kingdom**
Year Established: **Status 2020:** Active
Industries: Analytics for:, Artificial Intelligence for:, Big Data and Analytics for:, ~ Life Sciences (27), ~ Social Media (54), ~ Professional Services (48)

Company Name: Wootza
Description: Wootzano allows robots and autonomous systems to sense and feel like humans do with their own skin through our e-skin called Wootzkin.
Website: http://www.wootzano.com
Phone: **Email:** info@wootzano.com
City: Edinburgh **State:** **PC:** **Country: United Kingdom**
Year Established: **Status 2020:** Active
Industries: Artificial Intelligence for:, IT Managed Services for:, Machine Learning for:, ~ Manufacturing-Miscellaneous (34), ~ Professional Services (48), ~ Manufacturing-Electronic (30), ~ Professional Services (48)

Company Name: Bellrock Technology Ltd.
Description: Bellrock Technology Ltd. is a high-tech software company.
Website: http://www.bellrock.tech
Phone: 44 (0) 141 548 2655 **Email:** info@bellrock.tech
City: Glasgow **State:** Scotland **PC:** **Country: United Kingdom**
Year Established: 2012 **Status 2020:** Active
Industries: Artificial Intelligence for:, IT Managed Services for:, Predictive Analytics

Company Name: Bird.i
Description: Big data from Space, SaaS, Artificial Intelligence
Website: http://www.hibirdi.com
Phone: 44 (0) 141 582 1256 **Email:** info@hibirdi.com
City: Glasgow **State:** Scotland **PC:** **Country: United Kingdom**
Year Established: **Status 2020:** Active
Industries:

Company Name: Clear Returns
Description: Predictive analytics technology helping enterprise retailers protect profits by tackling returns
Website: http://www.clearreturns.com
Phone: 44 141 554 4175 **Email:** info@clearreturns.com
City: Glasgow **State:** Scotland **PC:** **Country: United Kingdom**
Year Established: **Status 2020:** Active
Industries: Analytics for:, Artificial Intelligence for:, Enterprise Application Services

Company Name: KeyPoint Technologies
Description: Redefining mobile search and discovery. Innovating mobile text input technology.
Website: http://www.keypoint-tech.com
Phone: 7795111101 **Email:** pnarayan@keypoint-tech.com
City: Glasgow **State:** Scotland **PC:** **Country: United Kingdom**
Year Established: **Status 2020:** Active
Industries: Application Services for:, Artificial Intelligence for:, Content for:, ~ Education (13), Mobile for:, Natural Language Processing

Company Name: Unlisted Ltd
Description: Real-time AI-powered company valuations
Website: http://unlistedvaluations.com/
Phone: **Email:** info@unlistedvaluations.com
City: Glasgow **State:** Scotland **PC:** **Country: United Kingdom**
Year Established: 2018 **Status 2020:** Active
Industries: Artificial Intelligence for:, ~ Banking and Financial Markets-Services (7)

Company Name: Renalytix AI
Description: RenalytixAI is a developer of artificial intelligence (AI) enabled clinical diagnostic solutions for kidney disease.
Website: http://renalytixai.com/
Phone: 44 (0)20 7933 8780 **Email:** renalytix@walbrookpr.com
City: Penarth **State:** Vale of Glamorgan **PC:** **Country: United Kingdom**
Year Established: 2018 **Status 2020:** Active
Industries: Artificial Intelligence for:, ~ Healthcare (20), ~ Healthcare (20)

Company Name: Emote Robotics
Description: Artificial intelligence with Humanistic Qualiti: Spain
Website: http://www.emoterobotics.com
Phone: **Email:** info@emoterobotics.com
City: Abergavenny **State:** Wales **PC:** **Country: United Kingdom**
Year Established: 2014 **Status 2020:** Active
Industries: ~ Arts-Entertainment-Recreation (4), Artificial Intelligence for:, Mobile

Company Name: Tendertec
Description: Stay safe & worry-free knowing that if emergencies happen at home, family & caregivers will be automatically alerted.
Website: http://tendertec.co.uk/
Phone: **Email:** contact@tendertec.co.uk
City: Caerphilly **State:** Wales **PC:** **Country: United Kingdom**
Year Established: **Status 2020:** Active
Industries: Artificial Intelligence for:, ~ Healthcare (20), ~ Healthcare (20), ~ Healthcare (20), Embedded for:, ~ Healthcare (20), Machine Learning for:, ~ Healthcare (20), ~ Manufacturing-Electronic (30)

Company Name: AMPLYFI
Description: AMPLYFI is a privately held company that provides software platform capable of intelligently harvesting open source data from the internet.
Website: http://www.amplyfi.com/
Phone: **Email:** info@amplyfigroup.com
City: Cardiff **State:** Wales **PC:** **Country: United Kingdom**
Year Established: 2015 **Status 2020:** Active
Industries: Analytics for:, Artificial Intelligence for:, Big Data and Analytics for:, IT Managed Services for:, Machine Learning for:, Predictive Analytics

Company Name: Antiver: Sweden
Description: Antibody drug discovery in 1 day
Website: http://antiverse.io
Phone: **Email:** info@antiverse.io
City: Cardiff **State:** Wales **PC:** **Country: United Kingdom**
Year Established: 2017 **Status 2020:** Active
Industries: Artificial Intelligence for:, ~ Biotechnology (9), ~ Healthcare (20)

Company Name: Artimus
Description: Artimus is an IT consulting company that provides the best Artificial Intelligence and Machine Learning solutions on the market.
Website: http://www.artimus-uk.com/
Phone: 44.7826.852610 **Email:** info@artimus-uk.com
City: Cardiff **State:** Wales **PC:** **Country: United Kingdom**
Year Established: 2016 **Status 2020:** Active
Industries: Artificial Intelligence for:, IT Managed Services

Company Name: dataly: Sweden
Description: Small and medium enterprises accelerate Scalable Growth through a digital transformation platform that adapts to them.
Website: https://www.datalyse.io
Phone: 44 29 2168 0133 **Email:** mcastro@datalyse.io
City: Cardiff **State:** Wales **Zip:** CF10 5EQ **Country: United Kingdom**
Year Established: **Status 2020:** Active
Industries: Application Program Interfaces (APIs) for:, Big Data and Analytics for:, ~ Administrative and Support Services (489), Business Software as a Service Apps for:, ~ Administrative and Support Services (916), ~ Insurance (940), Digital Marketing for:, ~ Insurance (

Company Name: Resilio
Description: Data Integration and Real-time Analytics to Amplify Humans and Make Time!
Website: http://resil.io
Phone: 44 (0)2920448138 **Email:** info@resil.io
City: Cardiff **State:** Wales **PC:** **Country: United Kingdom**
Year Established: 2014 **Status 2020:** Active
Industries: Analytics for:, Big Data and Analytics for:, Business Intelligence for:, Data Management for:, Predictive Analytics

Company Name: ThinJetty
Description: AI and Conversational Design
Website: http://www.ThinJetty.com
Phone: **Email:** info@ThinJetty.com
City: Cardiff **State:** Wales **PC:** **Country: United Kingdom**
Year Established: **Status 2020:** Active
Industries: Artificial Intelligence for:, Machine Learning for:, Natural Language Processing for:, ~ Education (13), Development and Test

Company Name: Tramshed Tech
Description: A space designed to promote collaboration between some of the finest creative businesses in Wales.
Website: http://www.tramshedtech.co.uk/
Phone: 44 29 2010 3090 **Email:** info@tramshedtech.co.uk
City: Cardiff **State:** Wales **PC:** **Country: United Kingdom**
Year Established: 2015 **Status 2020:** Active
Industries: Artificial Intelligence for:, ~ Personal-Religious-Civic (45), Cyber Security for:, ~ Food and Beverage (17), Web

Company Name: Twistar
Description: Mobile, IoT, Customer Experience, Hardware, Voice, AI
Website: http://www.twistar.co/
Phone: **Email:** contact@twistar.co
City: Cardiff **State:** Wales **PC:** **Country: United Kingdom**
Year Established: 2017 **Status 2020:** Active
Industries:

Company Name: Class Charts
Description: Seating Charts & Behavior Management
Website: http://www.classcharts.com
Phone: 0845 094 6427 **Email:** support@classcharts.com
City: Fishguard **State:** Wales **PC:** **Country: United Kingdom**
Year Established: 2013 **Status 2020:** Active
Industries: Artificial Intelligence for:, ~ Education (13), Web for:, ~ Education (13)

Company Name: projectbrainsaver limited
Description: Researching technology that helps.
Website: http://projectbrainsaver.com
Phone: **Email:** markdj@projectbrainsaver.com
City: Harlech **State:** Wales **PC:** **Country: United Kingdom**
Year Established: 2012 **Status 2020:** Active
Industries: Big Data and Analytics for:, Application Services for:, Identity for:, IT Managed Services for:, Web for:, ~ Healthcare (20), Predictive Analytics

Company Name: DashHound
Description: DashHound designs a data-science backed platform that locates and purchases beauty products.
Website: http://dashhound.co/
Phone: **Email:** founders@dashhound.co
City: Newport **State:** Wales **PC:** **Country: United Kingdom**
Year Established: 2016 **Status 2020:** Active
Industries: Artificial Intelligence for:, ~ Beauty (8), ~ Beauty (8), E-Commerce for:, Machine Learning

Company Name: Locke Data
Description: Locke Data helps organisations get started with data science.
Website: http://itsalocke.com
Phone: **Email:** 36909@reference-encyclopedia-ai.net
City: Wales **State:** Wales **PC:** **Country: United Kingdom**
Year Established: 2016 **Status 2020:** Active
Industries: Artificial Intelligence for:, ~ Customer Relationship Management (11), IT Managed Services

Company Name: Tryolabs
Description:
Website: http://www.tryolabs.com
Phone: **Email:** hello@tryolabs.com
City: Montevideo **State:** **PC:** **Country:**
Year Established: **Status 2020:** Active
Industries: Artificial Intelligence for:, Application Services for:, Machine Learning for:, Natural Language Processing for:, ~ Professional Services (48)

Uruguay

Company **Name:** Botsfactory
Description: Design and develop awesome conversational experiences using a modular platform that connects with multiple AI systems, saving time and effort
Website: http://botsfactory.io
Phone: 598 2601 3724 **Email:** info@botsfactory.io
City: Montevideo **State:** Montevideo Department **PC:** **Country:** Uruguay
Year Established: 2016 **Status 2020:** Active
Industries: Artificial Intelligence for:, IT Managed Services

Company Name: Inter: Iran
Description: Artificial Intelligence applied to Financial Markets. Interir simplifies every decision-making of financial market participants.
Website: http://interir.com
Phone: **Email:** info@interir.com
City: Montevideo **State:** Montevideo Department **PC:** **Country:** Uruguay
Year Established: 2019 **Status 2020:** Active
Industries: Artificial Intelligence for:, ~ Banking and Financial Markets-Services (7), ~ Banking and Financial Markets-Services (7), IT Managed Services for:, Machine Learning for:, ~ Banking and Financial Markets-Services (7)

Vietnam

Company Name: EM AND AI - GOnJOY
Description: SaaS, chatbot, NLP, AI, Mobile App, F&B, Loyalty
Website: http://www.gonjoy.com
Phone: (90) 353-3725 **Email:** contact@gonjoy.com
City: Da Nang **State:** Da Nang **PC:** **Country: Vietnam**
Year Established: 2017 **Status 2020:** Active
Industries: Artificial Intelligence for:, ~ Food and Beverage (17), IT Managed Services for:, Application Services for:, Business Software as a Service Apps (SaaS Apps)

Company Name: Hekate
Description: Artificial Intelligence and Chatbot
Website: http://hekate.ai/
Phone: (8490) 657-7379 **Email:** ducnguyen@hekate.ai
City: Da Nang **State:** Da Nang **PC:** **Country: Vietnam**
Year Established: 2016 **Status 2020:** Active
Industries: Artificial Intelligence for:, IT Managed Services for:, Machine Learning

Company Name: ABIV: India
Description: ABIVIN provides AI-powered supply chain optimization solutions for enterprises.
Website: https://www.abivin.com/
Phone: 84 2462 767 159 **Email:** info@abivin.com
City: Hanoi **State:** Hanoi **PC:** **Country: Vietnam**
Year Established: 2015 **Status 2020:** Active
Industries: Analytics for:, Artificial Intelligence for:, Big Data and Analytics for:, ~ Construction (10), ~ Telecommunications (56), Machine Learning for:, Business Software as a Service Apps (SaaS Apps) for:, Supply Chain Management

Company Name: AgileTech Viet Nam Limited Company
Description: AgileTech Vietnam is a global quality software company
Website: https://agiletech.vn/
Phone: 84 936 281 059 **Email:** contact@agiletech.: Vietnam
City: Hanoi **State:** Hanoi **PC:** **Country: Vietnam**
Year Established: 2015 **Status 2020:** Active
Industries: Artificial Intelligence for:, Blockchain for:, IT Managed Services for:, Application Services for:, Web

Company Name: AI News
Description: a Vietnamese startup focusing on improving news producing, news consuming and news distributing habits in Vietnam
Website: https://uat.bangtin.vn/
Phone: 84963520636 **Email:** dhloc@bangtin.: Vietnam
City: Hanoi **State:** Hanoi **PC:** **Country: Vietnam**
Year Established: 2019 **Status 2020:** Active
Industries: Artificial Intelligence for:, Web

Company Name: AIConverter
Description: AIConverter is a converter using artificial intelligence, online unit conversion tool will help you convert measurement units fastest
Website: http://aiconverter.com/
Phone: **Email:** tech@aiconverter.com
City: Hanoi **State:** Hanoi **PC:** **Country: Vietnam**
Year Established: **Status 2020:** Active
Industries: Artificial Intelligence for:, Web

Company Name: AiTalent.Asia
Description: Connecting Vietnamese AI Talents With Silicon Valley Tech Compani: Spain
Website: https://aitalent.asia/
Phone: 84868185362 **Email:** contact@aitalent.asia
City: Hanoi **State:** Hanoi **PC:** **Country: Vietnam**
Year Established: 2020 **Status 2020:** Active
Industries:

Company Name: DB Methods
Description: DB Methods provides affordable, tailored forecasting solutions by mining existing and newly captured data with machine learning algorithms.
Website: http://www.dbmethods.com/
Phone: **Email:** info@dbmethods.com
City: Hanoi **State:** Hanoi **PC:** **Country: Vietnam**
Year Established: 2017 **Status 2020:** Active
Industries: Analytics for:, ~ Banking and Financial Markets-Services (7), Machine Learning

Company Name: Eastgate Software
Description: Eastgate Software is a software development company that builds custom business solutions and applications.
Website: http://www.eastgate-software.com/
Phone: 49 (241) 565 29576 **Email:** info@eastgate-software.com
City: Hanoi **State:** Hanoi **PC:** **Country: Vietnam**
Year Established: 2014 **Status 2020:** Active
Industries: Artificial Intelligence for:, Machine Learning

Company Name: Lotus Quality Assurance
Description: First Vietnam based independent QA Services Company. Offering QA services; Data Annotation services for AI
Website: http://www.lotus-qa.com
Phone: **Email:** hello@lqa.com.: Vietnam
City: Hanoi **State:** Hanoi **PC:** **Country: Vietnam**
Year Established: **Status 2020:** Active
Industries: Artificial Intelligence for:, ~ Automotive (5), Computer Vision for:, Business Process and Operations for:, Business Process and Operations

Company Name: PingTaxi
Description: PingTaxi is the system services software that supports intelligent interaction between users and taxi drivers through mobile devices.
Website: http://pingtaxi.com.vn/
Phone: **Email:** 37170@reference-encyclopedia-ai.net
City: Hanoi **State:** Hanoi **PC:** **Country: Vietnam**
Year Established: 2010 **Status 2020:** Active
Industries: IT Managed Services

Company Name: Pique
Description: Pique helps turn visitors into customers, with an AI recommendation engine proven to turbocharge ecommerce growth.
Website: http://www.pique.ai
Phone: **Email:** giangt@pique.ai
City: Hanoi **State:** Hanoi **PC:** **Country: Vietnam**
Year Established: 2016 **Status 2020:** Active
Industries: Artificial Intelligence for:, E-Commerce for:, Machine Learning for:, Business Software as a Service Apps (SaaS Apps)

Company Name: Polygons Technologies
Description: Image Annotation Services for Computer Vision, AI
Website: http://www.polygons.tech
Phone: 1331-481-8888 **Email:** hello@polygons.tech
City: Hanoi **State:** Hanoi **PC:** **Country: Vietnam**
Year Established: 2018 **Status 2020:** Active
Industries: Artificial Intelligence for:, ~ Automotive (5), Blockchain for:, Computer Vision for:, Machine Learning for:, Application Services for:, Computer Vision

Company Name: Se: Romania
Description: Sero.ai is a crop intelligence company, that optimizes rice production with full-cycle data analytics.
Website: http://www.sero.ai/
Phone: **Email:** 37371@reference-encyclopedia-ai.net
City: Hanoi **State:** Hanoi **PC:** **Country: Vietnam**
Year Established: 2016 **Status 2020:** Active
Industries: ~ Agriculture (3), ~ Agriculture (3), Analytics for:, Artificial Intelligence for:, Big Data and Analytics for:, Computer Vision for:, ~ Agriculture (3), IT Managed Services for:, IT Managed Services for:, Machine Learning

Company Name: Deep Solution
Description: AI, SaaS
Website:
Phone: **Email:** 4990@reference-encyclopedia-ai.net
City: Ho Chi Minh City **State:** Ho Chi Minh City **PC:** **Country: Vietnam**
Year Established: **Status 2020:** Active
Industries: Artificial Intelligence for:, ~ Professional Services (48)

Company Name: TMA Innovation Center
Description: AI/ML, IoT, Blockchain, Big Data & Data Science, Mobile, Cloud.
Website: http://www.tmainnovation.com/
Phone: (84) 28 3995 1062 **Email:** contact@tma-innovation.center
City: Ho Chi Minh City **State:** Ho Chi Minh City **PC:** **Country: Vietnam**
Year Established: 2017 **Status 2020:** Active
Industries: Artificial Intelligence for:, IT Managed Services for:, Business Process and Operations

Company Name: AgriPredict
Description: Agricultural risk management with Artificial Intelligence
Website: http://www.agripredict.com/
Phone: **Email:** hello@agripredict.com
City: Lusaka **State:** Lusaka Province **PC:** **Country:** ZAMBIA
Year Established: 2016 **Status 2020:** Active
Industries: ~ Agriculture (3), ~ Agriculture (3), Artificial Intelligence for:, Business Intelligence for:, ~ Agriculture (3), Machine Learning

Zambia

Company Name: GreenUpp
Description: GreenUpp is a SaaS that uses sustainable technology and AI to help farmers or environmentalists to monitor and control their environment.
Website: http://greenuppweb.000webhostapp.com/
Phone: **Email:** cephaschapa@gmail.com
City: Livingstone **State:** Southern Province **PC:** **Country:** Zambia
Year Established: 2017 **Status 2020:** Active
Industries: ~ Agriculture (3), Analytics for:, Artificial Intelligence for:, IT Managed Services for:, Internet of Things (IoT) for:, Business Software as a Service Apps (SaaS Apps)

Zimbabwe

Company Name: Dr CADx
Description: Dr CADx is an AI-based health platform.
Website: http://www.drcadx.com/
Phone: 263 773 738 135 **Email:** info@drcadx.com
City: Bulawayo **State:** Bulawayo Province **PC:** **Country:** Zimbabwe
Year Established: 2016 **Status 2020:** Active
Industries: Artificial Intelligence for:, ~ Healthcare (20)

www.ingramcontent.com/pod-product-compliance
Lightning Source LLC
LaVergne TN
LVHW071343210926
848486LV00003B/218